Architects' Data

Dedicated to Ernst Neufert

Ernst and Peter Neufert

Architects' Data

Fourth Edition

Updated by Professor Johannes Kister
on behalf of the Neufert Foundation
with support from the University of Anhalt
Dessau Bauhaus (Dipl. Ing. Mathias Brockhaus,
Dipl. Ing. Matthias Lohmann and
Dipl. Ing. Patricia Merkel)

TRANSLATED BY DAVID STURGE

A John Wiley & Sons, Ltd., Publication

English language first published 2012

Blackwell Publishing was acquired by John Wiley & Sons in February 2007. Blackwell's publishing program has been merged with Wiley's global Scientific, Technical and Medical business to form Wiley-Blackwell.

Registered office:
John Wiley & Sons, Ltd, The Atrium, Southern Gate, Chichester, West Sussex, PO19 8SQ, UK

Editorial offices:
9600 Garsington Road, Oxford, OX4 2DQ, UK
The Atrium, Southern Gate, Chichester, West Sussex, PO19 8SQ, UK
2121 State Avenue, Ames, Iowa 50014-8300, USA

For details of our global editorial offices, for customer services and for information about how to apply for permission to reuse the copyright material in this book please see our website at www.wiley.com/wiley-blackwell.

First English language edition published by Crosby Lockwood Staples 1970
Reprinted 5 times
Second (International) English language edition published by Granada Publishing 1980
Reprinted 3 times
Reissued in paperback by Collins Professional and Technical Books 1985
Reprinted by Blackwell Science Ltd 12 times
Third English language edition published by Blackwell Science Ltd 2000
Fourth Edition language edition published by Blackwell Publishing Ltd 2012

Originally Published in the German Language by Vieweg + Teubner, 65189 Wiesbaden, Germany, as "Ernst Neufert: *Neufert* Bauentwurfslehre. 39. Auflage (39th Edition)"

Library of Congress Cataloging-in-Publication Data
Data available on application

A catalogue record for this book is available from the British Library.

ISBN: 978-1-4051-9253-8

Set in 8/10 Arial by Aptara
Printed and bound in Singapore by Markono Print Media Pte Ltd

1 2012

Using this book

This book provides architects and designers with a concise source of the core information needed to form a framework for the detailed planning of any building project. The objective is to save the designers of buildings time during their basic investigations. The information includes: principles of the design process, basic information on siting, constructing and servicing buildings, as well as illustrations and descriptions of a wide range of building types. Architects need to be well informed about the requirements for all the constituent parts of new projects, to ensure that their designs satisfy their clients and the buildings conform to accepted standards and regulations.

The contents list shows how the book is organised and the order of the subjects discussed.

To avoid repetition and keep the book to a manageable length, the different subjects are covered only once in full. Readers should therefore refer to several sections to glean all the information they require. For instance, an architect wanting to prepare a scheme for a college will need to refer to sections other than that on universities and colleges, such as: drafting guidelines; multi-storey buildings; various sections on services and environmental control; catering; residential buildings, hotels and flats (for student accommodation); office buildings (for working environments); libraries; car parks; accessible building; indoor and outdoor sports facilities; gardens; details on doors, windows, stairs and other building components; the section on construction, and more.

Readers should note that most of the material is from European (substantially German) contributors. This means, for example, that information on climate and daylight is from the perspective of a temperate climate in the northern hemisphere. The actual conditions at the site of a proposed building will always have to be ascertained. Similarly, in the section on roads, illustrations show traffic driving on the right-hand side.

References to standards, regulations and guidelines reflect the book's origins. For this translation, the publishers took the decision to leave the specific text references to German standards, regulations and guidelines in place, to indicate where similar standards, regulations and guidelines might exist in other jurisdictions. Users elsewhere must familiarise themselves separately with such national and local legislation and guidance. Again, local conditions must be taken into consideration for each individual case.

The terminology and style of the text is UK English, which will need to be taken into account by readers accustomed to American English. These readers will need to be aware that, for example, 'lift' has been used instead of 'elevator' and 'ground floor/first floor' instead of 'first floor/second floor'.

The data and examples included in the text are drawn from a wide range of sources; as a result a variety of conventions for dimensions is used throughout. The measurements shown are all metric but a mixture of metres, centimetres and millimetres is used (and sometimes not identified).

Readers will also find some superscript numbers associated with measurements. When these appear by dimensions in metres with centimetres, for instance, they represent the additional millimetre component of the measure (e.g. 1.26^5 denotes 1 m, 26 cm, 5 mm). Anyone familiar with the metric system will not find this troublesome. Those people less comfortable with metric units can use the conversion tables (to imperial measures) at the end of the book.

The plans and diagrams of buildings do not have scales as the purpose here is to show the general layout and express relationships between different spaces, making exact scaling unnecessary. However, all relevant dimensions are given on the detailed drawings and diagrams of installations, to assist in the design of specific spaces and constructions.

To help readers identify relevant background information, details of British Standards Institute (BSI) and German Institute of Standardisation (DIN) building-related standards are provided in two types of location. At the end of the book is a selected list of BS and DIN standards, arranged broadly by topic. Additionally, the margin of many pages of the main text contains relevant BS and DIN codes. Please note that, if a British or German code includes EN or ISO (signifying European or international), there is automatically a German or British counterpart with the same code and title.

Acknowledgements

The publishers wish to thank the translator, Mr David Sturge. The publishers also wish to acknowledge and thank the copyeditor and proofreader, Ms Kay Hyman, for the very significant contribution she has made to this publication.

Contents

Foreword

The 'Neufert' continues to be the most comprehensive, yet compact, first source of information on the design of buildings. Just as the daily office grind of the architect proceeds in many small steps and a few long strides, the sustained progress of the 'Neufert' is characterised not only by meticulous attention to standards and regulations, whose omnipresence in construction is undeniable, but also by reflection of the great issues of our time as they affect building project design. These important matters undoubtedly include concern for our environment and the absolute demand for sustainability in architecture. Sustainable building has many aspects, to be weighted differently according to the design brief.

The team working with Professor Johannes Kister has set out, right through the book, to emphasise new sustainability standards and perspectives using the criteria 'objective information' and 'topicality', which is presumably how Ernst Neufert would have approached the task. We hope that this new edition, which continues the redesign commenced in the previous one, will further consolidate the Foundation's reliable and exhaustive reference volume on building design.

Neufert Foundation, March 2009

The new German edition has once again been produced at the same location that was formative for Neufert's development as the office manager for Walter Gropius – the Bauhaus in Dessau. The decision to return to the roots here seems to have been the right one, because the previous edition was greeted positively by architects, students, lecturers and other interested parties. The concepts in this edition have been developed further by Nicole Delmes, née Neufert, and Ingo Neufert. My thanks are due to them both, for the trust and understanding they have shown, which made our collaboration straightforward and enjoyable. Also, I would especially like to thank Mathias Brockhaus, Matthias Lohmann and Patricia Merkel, a team that works in an exceptionally professional manner, the students of the Hochschule Anhalt – Fanjuan Kong, Tobias Schwarzwald and Mandy Wagenknecht – and the external consultants, whose valuable advice and reliable collaboration made an essential contribution to the success of the project.

Dessau, March 2009 Johannes Kister

External consultants:

Prof. Dr. Dirk Bohne	Building services
Karl-Heinz Breuer	Basics
Paul Corall	Fire protection
Thomas Ehrenberg	Filling stations and service areas
Olaf Gersmeier	Design and construction management
Lydia Haack, John Höpfner	Filling stations and car wash
Karl-Josef Heinrichs	Building physics
Prof. Alfred Jacoby	Synagogues
Stefan Jäckel, Tobias Micke and Andreas Kotlan	External works
Dr. Jörg Junhold	Zoos
Lür Meyer-Bassin	Theatre
Hans-Peter Mühlethaler	Restaurants
Prof. Dr. Gunther Nogge	Zoos
Marcellus Puhlemann	Design and construction management
Hermann Schnell	Facility management
Finn Stoll	Administration
Wolfgang Thiede	Health
Carsten Thiemann	Railways
Heiko Uelze	Catering
Prof. Susanne Weber	Lighting
Carola Wunderlich	Air transport

Preface

This handbook developed from the notes made for my lectures at the Bauhochschule in Weimar. They derive from measurements, experience and understanding gained from practice and research in the human sphere, necessary for the design of buildings, but also keeping an eye open for new opportunities and demands.

On the one hand we stand on the shoulders of our forebears but, on the other, everything is fluid and we are children of our time with our gaze towards the future, though the outlook of each individual is often different. This results from differences in education and training, the influence of the environment, personal predisposition and the relevant degree of internally driven self-development.

Whether the 'fixed opinion' of today is absolutely correct remains to be seen, however, because it is only valid at the time of formation. Experience shows that fairer judgement develops with time than is possible immediately, since we do not have the necessary detachment for breadth of vision. This makes clear what reservations need to be imposed on teaching to prevent heresy. All teaching remains subjective and determined by its time and environment, despite all efforts to achieve truth and objectivity and all intentions to critically examine our favourite opinions. The danger of heresy can be avoided if the teaching also makes clear that it is not an end product but rather serves, and is subject to, all that is vital, upcoming and unfolding

This will then provide for our students the attitude meant by Nietzsche when he said, 'Only those who change themselves remain associated with me.'

The essential feature of such teaching of continuous progress, the servant of development, is that there are no ready recipes, no 'canned wisdom', but rather only building blocks, components or corners requiring the addition of combination, construction, composition and harmony.

Confucius put it like this more than 2500 years ago: 'I give my students a corner and they will have to find the other three themselves!' Born architects, or those who yearn to build, will keep their ears and eyes closed when a solution to a task is prescribed, because born architects are full of their ideas and ideals, and only need the elements in order to set to work and make something of them!

Those who have found faith in themselves, an insight into connectivity, the play of forces, materials, colours, dimensions, who can absorb the reality and the appearance of a building, study its effect, investigate it critically and rebuild it in the mind, are on the only true path to the great satisfaction offered by active creation. This view of life should help them on their way. It should liberate them from all teachings, when it comes down to it even from this one, and lead them to their own creative work. It should provide initial assistance: run – everyone must build for themselves.

The architectural forms of our time are the result of the same process, which our predecessors underwent in order to produce their splendid temples, cathedrals and palaces. They had no models other than their own imaginations and intentions, ideas and ideals, with which they neared their aspirations. The commission formulated along these lines was enough to enliven concepts, which took solid form in line with the technological possibilities of the time and local conditions, and only bore a remote similarity to what had gone before. These new buildings could be technically much better and deliver more because of improvement in the state of technology. They could, however, also be compared artistically to similar structures from the past.

If we compare an industrial building of today – light, roomy, with good dimensions and slimmer, lightweight construction – with a factory from the 18th century or a workshop of the 15th century, then the advantages of our modern buildings will be apparent even to the most blinkered conservationist. This means that, whenever construction projects serve a genuine requirement of our time, work can be expected from energetic contemporary architects that will bear comparison to, or even overshadow, the best of old buildings.

A lively-minded university should offer primarily a view of our time and a look to the future, glancing back only to the extent that this is advisable or unavoidable. This was the advice of one of the greatest of our profession, Fritz Schumacher, when he warned a young student in his architecture lectures against getting too lost in art history issues while researching the past. Being led astray by a doctorate into learned byways could be at the cost of the energy required to meet the more varied requirements of the profession.

In contrast to this, it is better just to hand students the elements of architecture, as is done in this *Architects' Data*, where I have attempted to reduce the building blocks of design to the essentials, to schematise and even to abstract in order to make imitation difficult and force students to produce form and content from within themselves. Their various design ideas will be coordinated anyway to a certain extent by current fashion, that idiosyncratic feeling of community which characterises mankind's joint efforts at a particular time and finds a durable and visible expression in contemporary style.

Ernst Neufert

ABBREVIATIONS AND SYMBOLS

Abbreviation	Meaning
AEG	General Railway Law
AFP	Agricultural Investment Support Programme
ArbStättR	Workplace Guidelines
ArbStättV	Workplace Regulations
BauGB	Building Law
BGB	German Civil Code
BGR	Association of Commercial Accident Insurance Companies
BImSchG	Federal Prevention of Emissions Law
BOStrab	Construction and Operation of Trams Regulation
BS(I)	British Standards (Institute)
CEN	Committee for European Normalisation
CHP	combined heat and power
CIE	International Lighting Commission
CPM	Critical Path Method
DB	Deutsche Bahn – German Railways
DEHOGA	German Hotel and Inn Association
DFS	German Air Traffic Control
DiBt	German Institute for Building Technology
DIN	German Institute for Standardisation
DN	normal diameter
EBO	Construction and Operation of Railways Regulation
EEG	Renewable Energy Law
EIA	Environmental Impact Assessment
EN	European (standard)
EnEV	Energy Saving Regulation
FEA	Federal Environment Agency
FEU	40-foot equivalent unit (container)
FFL	finished floor level
FIS	International Ski Federation
FGSV	Research Company for Roads and Traffic
GEFMA	German Facility Management Association
GIF	Company for Property Industry Research
GUV	Guidelines of the German Association of Accident Insurers (health and safety)
HeizAnlV	Heating Plant Regulation
HGV	heavy goods vehicle
HOAI	Fee Regulations for Architects and Engineers
HWR	auxiliary inverter
ICAO	International Civil Aviation Organisation
ICE	Inter-City Express
IndBauR	Industrial Building Guidelines
ISO	International Standards Organisation
KfW	'Reconstruction' Subsidy Bank
KFZ	vehicle
LBO	state building regulation
LC	liquid crystal
LED	llight emitting diode
LIDC	luminous intensity distribution curve
LiTG	German Technical Light Association
LPZ	lightning protection zone
LU	large animal unit (500 kg live weight)
MBO	model building regulation (basis for LBO)
MPM	Metra Potential Method
MTA	medical/technical assistant
MVZ	outpatient medical centre
ODP	operating department practitioner
ÖPNV	public transport
PKW	passenger car
RAL	German quality assurance mark
RAS-L (-EW/-Q)	Road Construction Guidelines – Road Layout (Drainage / Cross-section)
SchBauR	School Building Guidelines
StLB	Standard Book of Bill Items
StVo	Street Traffic Regulations
SUV	sports utility vehicle
TEU	20-foot equivalent unit (container)
UIC	International Union of Railways
VDE	Association of German Electrical Engineers
VDI	Association of German Engineers
VdS	Loss Prevention (fire and security testing institute)
VkVO	Retail Regulations
VOB	Contract Regulations for Building Works
VStättVO	Places of Assembly Regulations
Wh	withers height (horse)
WSG	Water Protection Law
ZH	Indicates Guidelines of BGR (Association of Commercial Accident Insurance Companies)
ZVEI	Central Association of Electrical and Electronics Industries

Unit, Abbreviation	
10^{12}	10 cm 12 mm (superscript number = mm)
″	English inch
′	English foot
H or h	height or high
W or w	width or wide
h	hour
min	minute
s	second
12°	degrees in Celsius (C)
J	joule, energy
N	newton, force
Pa	pascal, pressure
2° 3′ 4″	2 degrees, 3 min, 4 s. 360-degree division
%	per cent, hundredth
‰	per thousand, thousandth
Ø	diameter
/	per (e.g. t/m = tonne per m)

Greek Alphabet			
Α	α	(a)	Alpha
Β	β	(b)	Beta
Γ	γ	(g)	Gamma
Δ	δ	(d)	Delta
Ε	∈	(e)	Epsilon
Ζ	ζ	(z)	Zeta
Η	η	(e)	Eta
Θ	ϑ	(th)	Theta
Ι	ι	(i)	Iota
Κ	κ	(k)	Kappa
Λ	λ	(l)	Lambda
Μ	μ	(m)	Mu
Ν	ν	(n)	Nu
Ξ	χ	(x)	Xi
Ο	ο	(o)	Omicron
Π	π	(p)	Pi
Ρ	ρ	(r)	Rho
∑	σ	(s)	Sigma
Τ	τ	(t)	Tau
Υ	υ	(y)	Upsilon
Φ	ϕ	(ph)	Phi
Χ	ψ	(ch)	Chi
Ψ	ν	(ps)	Psi
Ω	φ	(o)	Omega

Mathematical Symbols	
>	greater than
≧	equal or greater than
<	less than
≦	less than or equal
Σ	sum of
<|	angle
sin	sine
cos	cosine
tan	tangent
ctg	cotangent
=	equal
≠	not equal
~	approximately
∞	infinity
||	parallel
×	times, multiplied by
/	divided by
⊥	right-angled
∨	volume
ω	solid angle
√	square root of
≅	congruent
Δ	triangle
↑↑	same direction, parallel
↑↓	opposite directions, parallel

Roman Numbers	
I =	1
II =	2
III =	3
IV =	4
V =	5
VI =	6
VII =	7
VIII =	8
IX =	9
X =	10
XV =	15
C =	100
CL =	150
CC =	200
CCC =	300
CD =	400
D =	500
DC =	600
DCC =	700
DCCC =	800
CM =	900
M =	1000
MCMLX =	1960

SI units – Système International d'Unités

The international system of units: the most commonly used system of measurement and units in science. Basic units, which are not derived from any other.

Quantity	Basic unit name	Symbol	Definition based on	SI units included in definition
1 length	metre	m	wavelength of krypton radiation	–
2 mass	kilogram	kg	international prototype	–
3 time	second	s	period of caesium radiation	–
4 electrical current	ampere	A	electrodynamic force between two conductors	kg, m, s
5 temperature (thermodynamic temperature)	kelvin	K	triple point of water	–
6 luminous intensity	candela	cd	radiation from freezing platinum	kg, s
7 amount of substance	mole	mol	molecular mass	kg

❶ Basic SI units

a) Thermal insulation		
Symbol	Unit	Description
t	(°C, K)	temperature
t	(K)	temperature difference
q	(Wh)	quantity of heat
λ	(W/mK)	thermal conductivity
λ'	(W/mK)	equivalent thermal conductivity
Λ	(W/m^{2}K)	coefficient of thermal transmittance
α	(W/m^{2}K)	coefficient of thermal transmission
U	(W/m^{2}K)	coefficient of thermal transmittance
$1/\Lambda$	(m^{2}K/W)	thermal insulation value
$1/\alpha$	(m^{2}K/W)	thermal transmission resistance
1/k	(m^{2}K/W)	thermal transmittance resistance, 1/U
D′	(m^{2}K/W × cm)	thermal resistance per cm
c	(Wh/kgK)	specific thermal capacity
S	(Wh/m^{3}K)	volumetric specific heat
β	(1/K)	coefficient of thermal expansion
a	(mK)	distance coefficient
P	(Pa)	pressure
P_o	(Pa)	(partial) vapour pressure
g_o	(g)	vapour quantity
g_k	(g)	condensed water quantity
ν	(%)	relative air humidity
μ	(–)	diffusion resistance coefficient
$\mu \times d$	(cm)	diffusion-equivalent air layer
Λ_o	(g/m^{2}hPa)	water vapour resistance factor
$1/\Lambda_o$	(m^{2}hPa/g)	diffusion resistance
$\mu\lambda$	(W/mK)	layer factor
$\mu\lambda'$	(W/mK)	layer factor of air layers
P	(€/kWh)	cost of heat
b) Sound insulation		
λ	(m)	wavelength
f	(Hz)	frequency
f_{gr}	(Hz)	limit frequency
f_η	(Hz)	resonance frequency
E_{dva}	(N/cm^2)	dynamic elasticity modulus
S′	(N/cm^3)	dynamic stiffness
R	(dB)	sound reduction CONTENTS (airborne sound) in laboratory
R_m	(dB)	median airborne sound reduction
R′	(dB)	sound reduction CONTENTS with flanking transmission (airborne sound)
LSM	(dB)	airborne sound insulation margin
L_n	(dB)	impact sound pressure level
V/M	(dB)	sound improvement due to one floor or ceiling layer
TSM	(dB)	impact sound reduction
a	(–)	degree of sound absorption
A	(m^2)	equivalent sound-absorbing area
r	(m)	resonance radius
L	(dB)	sound level reduction

❷ Physical symbols in the SI system

Prefixes and their Abbreviations are:

T (tera-)	= 10^{12}	(million million)	c (centi-)	= 1/100	hundredth
G (giga-)	= 10^9	(thousand million)	m (milli-)	= 10^{-3}	thousandth
M (mega-)	= 10^6	(million)	μ (micro-)	= 10^{-6}	millionth
k (kilo-)	= 10^3	(thousand)	n (nano-)	= 10^{-12}	
h (hekto-)	= 100	(hundred)	p (pico-)	= 10^{-12}	
da (deca-)	= 10	(ten)	f (femto-)	= 10^{-15}	
d (deci-)	= 1/10	(tenth)	a (atto-)	= 10^{-18}	

only one prefix may be used to describe a decimal multiple

❸ Decimal multipliers and dividers of units

Quantity to be measured		Unit in the SI system, compulsory from 1978	Conversion factor
length	m	metre	
area	m^2	square metre	
volume	m^3	cubic metre	
mass	kg	kilogram	
force	N	newton = 1 kg m/s^2	9.8
pressure	Pa	pascal = 1 N/m^2	133.3
	bar	bar = 100,000 Pa Pa = 100,000 N/m	0.98
temperature	°C K	degree Centigrade kelvin*	1 10
work (energy, heat quantity)	Ws, J, Nm	watt second = joule = newton metre	4186
	Wh	watt hour = 3.6 KJ	1.163
	kWh	kilowatt hour = 10^3 Wh = 3.6 MJ	1.163
power (energy transfer, heat transfer)	W W	watt watt	736 1.163

*compulsory from 1975

❹ Conversion of basic units

1 m × m = 1 m^2 1 m × 1 s^{-1} = 1 m s^{-1} (= 1 m/s)
1 m × 1 s^{-2} = 1 ms^{-2} (= 1 m/s^2)
1 kg × 1 m × 1 s^{-2} = 1 kg m s^{-2} (= 1 kg m/s^{-2})
1 kg × 1 m^{-3} = 1 kg m^{-3} (= 1 kg/m^3)
1 m × 1 m × 1 s^{-1} = 1 m^{2}s^{-1} (= 1 m^2/s)

❺ Examples of 'derived SI units' through combining basic units

coulomb	1 C	= 1 As	ohm	1 Ω	= 1 V/A
farad	1 F	= 1 As/V	pascal	1 Pa	= N/m^2
henry	1 H	= 1 Vs/A	siemens	1 S	= 1/Ω
hertz	1 Hz	= 1 s^{-1} = (1/s)	tesla	1 T	= 1 Wb/m^2
joule	1 J	= 1 Nm = 1 Ws	volt	1 V	= 1 W/A
lumen	1 lm	= 1 cd sr	watt	1 W	= 1 J/s
lux	1 lx	= 1 lm/m^2	weber	1 Wb	= 1 Vs
newton	1 N	= 1 kg m/s^2			

For apparent electrical power, the watt may be described as volt ampere (VA), idle electrical power as Var (ver).

❻ Names and symbols for derived SI units

1 N 2 1 s 2 1 m^2 = 1 Nsm^2 1 A2 1 s = 1 As = 1 C
1 rad 2 1 s^2 = 1 rad s^t (= 1 rad/s) 1 As/V = 1 C/V = 1 F

❼ Examples of SI units derived through combining basic units with named derived units

thermal resistance	$1/\Lambda$ = 1 m^{2}h K/kcal	= 0.8598 m^{2}K/W
thermal conductivity	λ = 1 kcal/m h K	= 1.163 W/m K
coefficient of thermal transmittance	U = 1 kcal/m^2 h K	= 1.163 W/m^{2}K
coefficient of thermal transmission	α = 1 kcal/m^{2}h K	= 1.163 W/m^{2}K
bulk density	= 1 kg/m^3	= 1 kg/m^3
calculation weight	= 1 kp/m^3	= 0.01 kN/m^3
compressive strength	= 1 kp/cm^2	= 0.1 N/mm^2

❽ Conversion of table values to new units

Units of measurement in building

The international system of measurement with SI units has been valid since 1 January 1978.

Measurement	Symbol	SI unit		Statutory unit		Old unit		Description
		Name	Symbol	Name	Symbol	Name	Symbol	
normal angle	α β γ	radian	rad					1 rad = 1 m/m = 57.296° = 63.662 gon
				round angle	pla			1 pla = 2 π rad
						right angle	L	1^L = ¼ pla = (π/2) rad
				degree	°			1° = 1^L/90 = 1 pla/360 = π/180 rad
				minute	8			18 = 1°/60
				second	(			1(= 18/60 = 1°/3600
				gon or grad	gon	new degree	9	1 gon = 1 g = 1^L/100 = 1 pla/400 = π/200 rad
						new minute	a	1 c = 10^{-2} gon
						new second	cc	1 cc = (10^{-2}) c = 10^{-4} gon
length	l	metre	m	micrometre	μm	inch	in	1 in = 25.4 mm
				millimetre	mm	foot	ft	1 ft = 30.48 cm
				centimetre	cm	fathom	fathom	1 fathom = 1.8288 m
				decimetre	dm	mile	mil	1 mile = 1609.344 m
				kilometre	km	sea mile	sm	1 sm = 1.852 km
area, cross-sectional area, area of plot of land	A, q	square metre	m^2					
				are	a			1 a = 10^2 m^2
				hectare	ha			1 ha = 10^4 m^2
volume	V	cubic metre	m^3					
				litre	l			1 l = 1 dm^3 = 10^{-3} m^3
normal volume	V_η					normal cubic metre	Nm^3	1 Nm^3 = 1 m^3 in normal condition
						cubic metre	cbm	
time, period, duration	t	second	s					
				minute	min			1 min = 60 s
				hour	h			1 h = 60 min = 3600 s
				day	d			1 d = 24 h = 86 400 s
				year	a			1 a = 8765.8 h = 31.557 × 10^6 s
frequency	f	hertz	Hz					1 Hz = 1/s for the expression of frequencies in
duration of a cycle								dimensional equations
angular frequency	φ	reciprocal second	1/s					$\varphi = 2 \times f$
angular velocity	φ	radians per s	rad/s					$\varphi = 2 \times n$
speed of revolutions	n	reciprocal second	1/s	revolutions per sec/min	r/s	revs per sec/min	r.p.s.	1/s = t/s = U/s
					r/m		r.p.m	
velocity	v	metre per second	m/s	kilometres per hour	km/h			1 m/s = 3.6 km/h
						knot	kn	1kn = 1sm/h = 1.852 mph
acceleration due to gravity	g	metre per second squared	m/s^2			gal	gal	1 gal = 1 cm/s^2 = 10^{-2} m/s^2
mass:	m	kilogram	kg					
weight (on scales)				gram	g			1 g = 10^{-3} kg
				tonne	t			1 t = 1 Mg = 10^3 kg
						pound	lb	1 lb = 0.45359237 kg
						metric hundredweight	cwt (metric)	1 cwt (metric) = 50 kg
force	F	newton	N					1 N = 1 $kg/m/s^2$ = 1 Ws/m = 1 J/m
thrust	G					dyne	dyn	1 dyn = 1 g cm/s^2 = 10^{-s} N
						pond	p	1 p = 9.80665 × 10^{-3} N
						kilopond	kp	1 kp = 9.80665 N
						megapond	Mp	1 Mp = 9806.65 N
						kilogram force	kg	1 kg = 9.80665 N
						tonne force	t	1 t = 9806.65 N
mech. stress, strength	σ	newton per square metre	N/m^2	newton per square millimetre	N/mm^2			
							kp/cm^2	1 kp/cm^2 = 0.0980665 N/mm^2
							kp/mm	1 kp/mm^2 = 9.80665 N/mm^2
work, energy	W,E	joule	J					1 J = 1 Nm = 1 Ws = 10^7 erg
				kilowatt hour	kWh			1 kWh = 3.6 × 10^6 J = 3.6 MJ
						horsepower per hour	h.p./h	1 h.p. = 2.64780 × 10^6 J
						erg	erg	1 erg = 10^{-7} J
heat quantity	Q	joule	J			calorie	cal	1 cal = 4.1888 J = 1.163 × 10^{-3} Wh
torque	M	newton metre	Nm			kilopond metre	kpm	1 kpm = 9.80665 J
bending moment	M_b	or joule	J					
power,	P	watt	W					1 W = 1 J/s = 1 N m/s = 1 kg m^2/s^3
energy current						horsepower	h.p.	1 h.p. = 0.73549675 kW
thermodynamic temperature	T	kelvin	K			degree Kelvin	°K	1°K = 1 K
						degree Rankine		1°R = 5/9 K
Centigrade temperature	ϑ		K	degree Centigrade	°C		°R, °RK	$\vartheta = T - T_0$ T_0 = 273.15 K
								$\Delta\vartheta = \Delta T$, where:
temperature interval and differential	$\Delta\vartheta$ or ΔT				°C	degree	deg	1 K = 1°C = 1 degree to be used in equations
Fahrenheit temperature	ϑ_F					degree Fahrenheit	°F	ϑ_F = 9/5 ϑ + 32 = 9/5 T − 459.67
Reaumur temperature	ϑ_R					degree Reaumur	°R	ϑ_R = 4/5 ϑ, 1°R = 5/4 °C

❶ SI units and statutory units (excerpt applicable to building)

DRAWINGS

Paper Formats

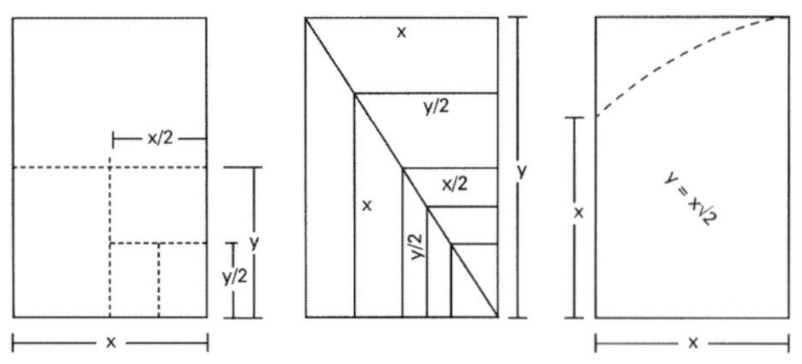

❶–❸ Basis of paper formats

Standardised formats provide a foundation for office furniture design, which then determines the development of the floor plan. Good knowledge of paper formats is therefore important for the designer.

Paper formats have generally been standardised (apart from in the USA) to conform to the internationally accepted (ISO) series of paper sheet sizes (A,B,C,D). These were developed on the basis of an area of 1 m^2, divided according to the ratio of the sides:

$x : y = \sqrt{2}$ → ❸ length of side x = 0.841 m

$x \times y = 1$ length of side y = 1.189 m

The basic format (a rectangle with an area of 1 m^2 and side lengths as above) forms the basis for all the smaller sizes. The A format series is produced by halving or doubling the basic format → ❶ + ❷. The additional series B and C are intended for items in dependent paper sizes, e.g. envelopes, binders and files → ❹.

The formats in the B series are the geometric mean dimensions of the A series. The formats in the C series are the geometric mean dimensions of the A and B series → ❹.

Format	Series A	Series B	Series C
0	841 × 1189	1000 × 1414	917 × 1297
1	594 × 841	707 × 1000	648 × 917
2	420 × 594	500 × 707	485 × 648
3	297 × 420	353 × 500	324 × 458
4	210 × 297	250 × 353	229 × 324
5	148 × 210	176 × 250	162 × 229
6	105 × 148	125 × 176	114 × 162
7	74 × 105	88 × 125	81 × 114
8	52 × 74	62 × 88	57 × 81
9	37 × 52	44 × 62	
10	26 × 37	31 × 44	
11	18 × 26	22 × 31	
12	13 × 18	15 × 22	

❹ Sheet sizes

Strip (or side margin) formats are made by dividing the main formats lengthwise into halves, quarters and eighths (for envelopes, signs, drawings etc.) → ❺ + ❻.

Format	Abbreviation	mm
half length A4	½ A4	105 × 297
quarter length A4	¼ A4	52 × 297
eighth length A7	¼ A7	9 × 105
half length C4	½ C4	114 × 324
etc.		

❺ Strip formats

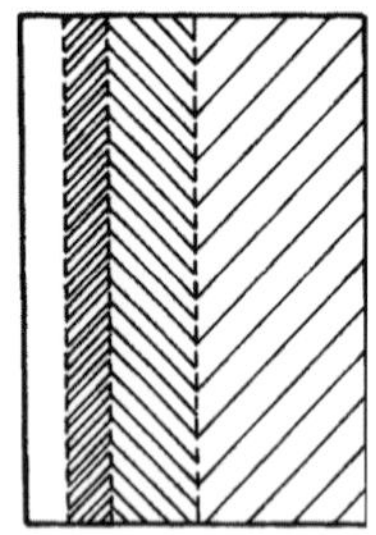

❻ Strip formats in A4

File cards without tabs correspond exactly to the standard formats. Tab cards are larger to allow for the tab, i.e. they have a projection at the upper edge for classification.

Binders, files and folders are wider than the standard format to provide space for the fixing mechanism. Widths should if possible be selected from the possible dimensions from series A, B, C → ❼.

❼ Loose-leaf binder

Pads and carbonless duplicate books have precisely the standard formats; if there is a standing perforated edge, then here the sheets are smaller than the standard format → ❽.

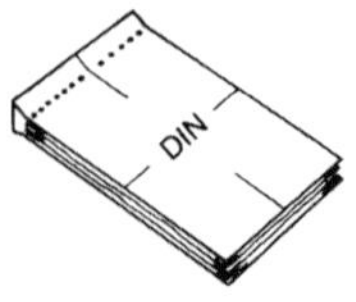

❽ Pads, carbonless duplicate books

Bound and trimmed books have precisely the standard format. If a further trim is necessary during binding, then the pages will be slightly smaller than the standard format, and the cover will project accordingly. The cover size must be at least the standard format → ❾. The cover width is determined by the binding process.

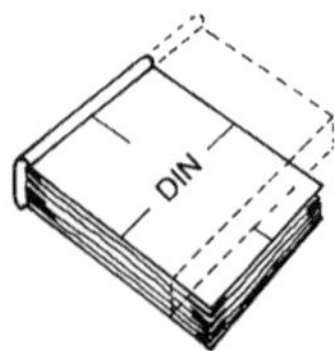

❾ Bound and trimmed books

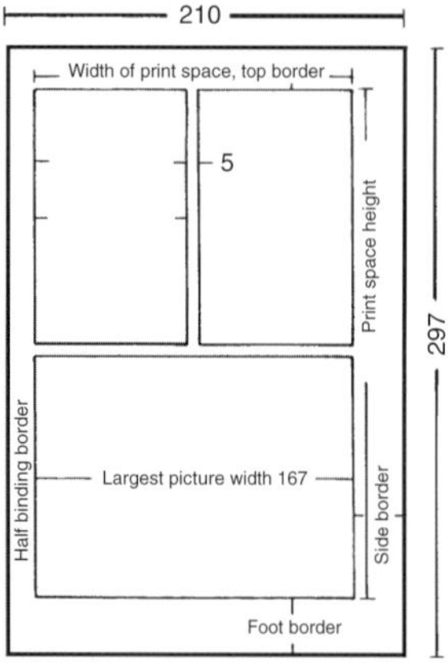

❿ → ⓫

	picas		mm	
type area width	39.5	40.5	167	171
type area height (without header/footer)	58.5	59	247	250
space between columns	1		5	
max. width, double columns	39.5		167	
max. width, single column	19		81	
inside (gutter) margin, nominal			16	14
outer (side) margin, nominal			27	25
top (head) margin, nominal			20	19
bottom (foot) margin, nominal			30	28

⓫ Layouts and type area of the A4 standard format → ❿

BS EN ISO 128
BS 1192
BS EN ISO 4157
DIN 824

The use of **standard drawing formats** makes it easier for architects to lay out drawings for discussion in the design office or on the building site, and also facilitates posting and filing. The trimmed, original drawing or print must therefore conform to the formats of the ISO A series → ❶, ❸–❻.

The **title block** should be the following distance from the edge of the drawing:

for formats A0–A3 10 mm
for formats A4–A6 5 mm

For small drawings, a filing margin of up to 25 mm can be used, which reduces the usable area of the finished format. As an exception, **narrow formats** can be made by adding together a row of identical or adjacent shapes from the format range.

From normal roll widths, the following sizes can be used to provide formats in the A series:

for drawing paper, tracing paper 1500, 1560 mm
(derived from these: 250, 1250, 660, 900 mm)
for print paper: 650, 900, 1200 mm.

If all the drawing formats up to A0 are to be cut from a paper web, a roll width of at least 900 mm will be necessary.

Drawings which are to be stored in A4 box files should be folded as follows → ❽:

1. The title block must always be at the front, in the correct position and clearly visible.
2. At the start of folding, a width of 21 cm must always be folded first (fold 1), ideally with the use of a 21 × 29.7 cm template.
3. A triangle is folded into the drawing starting from **c** (fold 2) so that on the completely folded drawing only the below left field marked with a cross is punched or clamped.
4. The drawing is then folded parallel to side **a** to a width of 18.5 cm, for which a template of 18.5 × 29.8 cm is useful. The last section is folded in half to adjust the sheet size, bringing the title block to the front. Long narrow formats can be correspondingly folded.
5. The resulting strip is folded from side **b**.

A piece of card of size A5 = 14.8 × 21 cm can be glued to the back of the punched side to reinforce the edge. Any sheet size can be folded by following the instructions above. If the drawing length remaining after the folding of the first 21 cm cannot be divided by 18.5 cm into an even number 2, 4, 6, etc., then the remaining width should be folded in the centre.

uncut drawing sheet, depending on requirement, is 2–3 cm wider than final trimmed original drawing and print

box for written details and parts list

❶ Standardised drawing

Sheet sizes according to ISO series A	ISO A0	ISO A1	ISO A2	ISO A3	ISO A4	ISO A5
Format: untrimmed blank sheet (mm)	880 × 1230	625 × 880	450 × 625	330 × 450	240 × 330	165 × 240
Format: trimmed finished sheet (m)	841 × 1189	594 × 841	420 × 594	297 × 420	210 × 297	148 × 210

❷ Sheet sizes

❸ ISO size A2; A1; A0

cut-out ISO A2, A1, A0

❹ ISO size A3

cut-out ISO A3

❺ ISO size A4

❻ ISO size A5

cut-out ISO A4

Division for	No. identical fields by sheet size				
	A0	A1	A2	A3	A4
a	16	12	8	8	4
b	12	8	6	6	4

❼ Field divisions (grid squares)

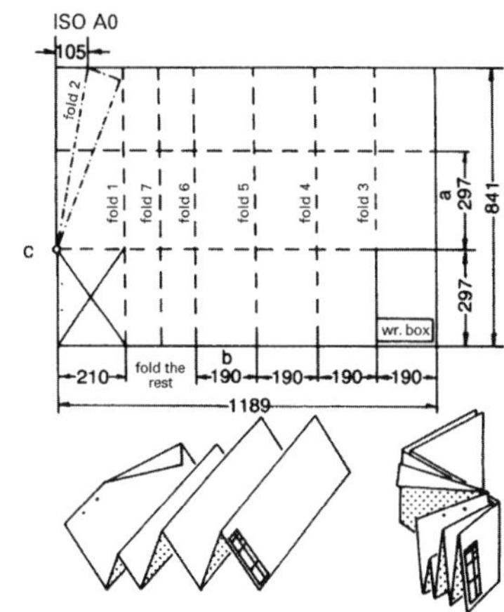

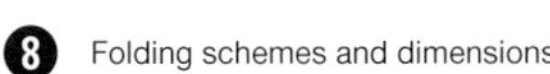
❽ Folding schemes and dimensions

BS EN ISO 9431
BS EN ISO 10209
BS EN ISO 14617
DIN 406
DIN 825
DIN 1356

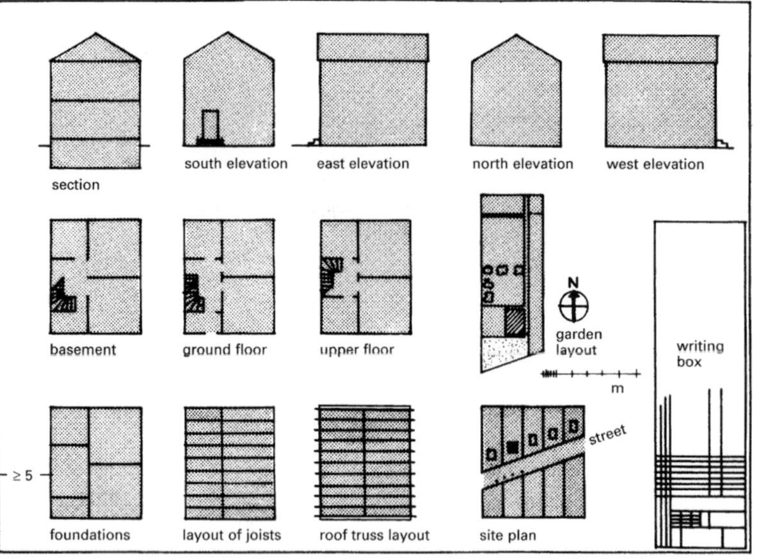

❶ Suitable layout for a construction drawing

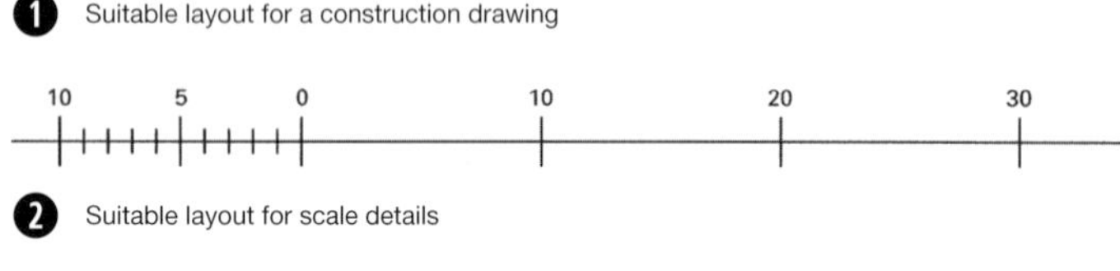

❷ Suitable layout for scale details

A strip 5 cm wide should be left blank at the left-hand edge for binding or filing. The title block on the right ❶ should include:

1. Description of the type of drawing (sketch, preliminary design, for construction etc.)
2. Category of building shown or type of drawing (layout plan, ground plan, section, elevation, diagram etc.)
3. Scale
4. If appropriate, details of dimensions.

Drawings for building permit applications (to the building regulations authorities) should also include:

1. Name (signature) of the client
2. Name (signature) of the architect
3. If required, (signature) of the site manager
4. If required, (signature) of the contractor
5. Comments by the building regulations authorities:
   a) About inspection
   b) About approval
   If necessary, on back of sheet

Layout plans, floor plans etc. should show the compass direction with a north pointer.

❸ Example of a standard dimensioned drawing of an angled floor plan. The dimensions given are structural dimensions without finishings

Scales → ❷
The main scale of the drawing should be shown in large letters in the title block and in smaller letters for other scales; the latter should be repeated next to their respective diagrams. All objects should be drawn to scale; dimensions of parts which are not drawn to scale should be underlined. Scales should be restricted to the following if at all possible:
for construction drawings 1:1, 1:5, 1:10, 1:20, 1:25, 1:50, 1:100, 1:200
for site layouts 1:500, 1:1000, 1:2000, 1:2500, 1:5000, 1:10000, 1:25000.

Dimensioning
Dimensioning is indicating dimensions on a drawing.
Levels should be given on sections and plans or elevations. The signs + or – before the number refer to the difference from level ± 0.00 (generally the planned finished floor level, on the ground floor in the entrance area, related to sea level). For parapets, the structural height above the structural slab level may also be given.
If the height of wall openings, particularly for doors and windows, is to be given on drawings in addition to their width, then the width measurement is given above the dimension line and the height measurement is given below it. Rectangular cross-sections can, as a simplification, be dimensioned by stating their side lengths as a fraction, e.g. 12/16 (in section: width/height).
Round cross-sections have the diameter sign ∅ before the measure: e.g. ∅ 12. Radii have the capital letter *R* before the measure.

Dimensions and other markings → ❸
All dimensions are given in the unfinished structural condition (wall thicknesses). In continental Europe, dimensions of less than 1 m on building drawings are generally given in cm, dimensions over 1 m are given in m or mm. (However, recently the trend has been to give all dimensions in mm, which is standard practice in the **UK**.)

Sections on plans
On plans, vertical planes of one or more sections are shown as lines with short and long dashes → p. 9 ❶, and the direction of viewing is also given. The entire line of the section does not have to be shown, but if the plane of a section breaks, this does → ❸. If there is more than one section, then each should be clearly labelled.
Room numbers are given in a circle.
Room areas, in m^2, are shown in a square or rectangle → ❸.

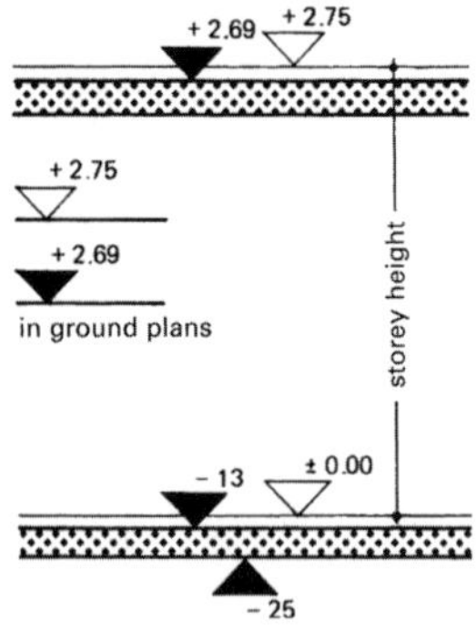

❹ Marking of heights on sections and elevations

❺ ← 6250 → ←

❻ 6250

❼ 6250
5250

BS EN ISO 4157
DIN 1356

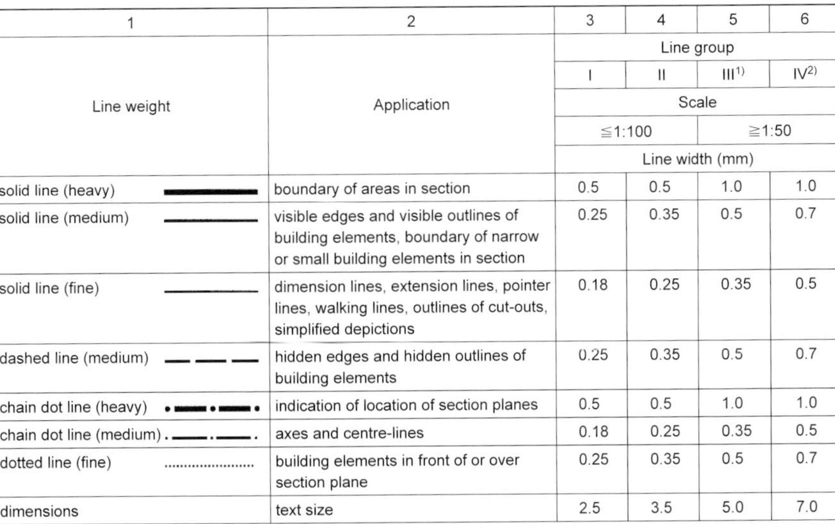

1	2	3	4	5	6
Line weight	Application	Line group			
		I	II	III[1]	IV[2]
		Scale			
		≦1:100		≧1:50	
		Line width (mm)			
solid line (heavy)	boundary of areas in section	0.5	0.5	1.0	1.0
solid line (medium)	visible edges and visible outlines of building elements, boundary of narrow or small building elements in section	0.25	0.35	0.5	0.7
solid line (fine)	dimension lines, extension lines, pointer lines, walking lines, outlines of cut-outs, simplified depictions	0.18	0.25	0.35	0.5
dashed line (medium)	hidden edges and hidden outlines of building elements	0.25	0.35	0.5	0.7
chain dot line (heavy)	indication of location of section planes	0.5	0.5	1.0	1.0
chain dot line (medium)	axes and centre-lines	0.18	0.25	0.35	0.5
dotted line (fine)	building elements in front of or over section plane	0.25	0.35	0.5	0.7
dimensions	text size	2.5	3.5	5.0	7.0

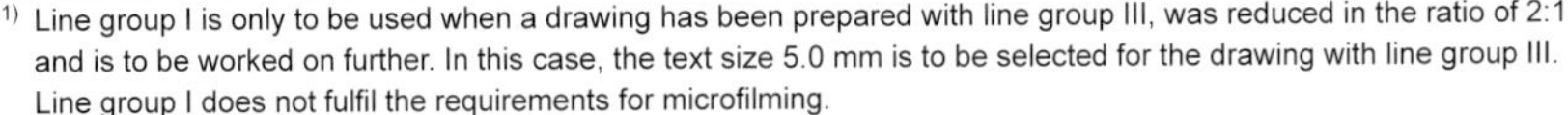

[1] Line group I is only to be used when a drawing has been prepared with line group III, was reduced in the ratio of 2:1 and is to be worked on further. In this case, the text size 5.0 mm is to be selected for the drawing with line group III. Line group I does not fulfil the requirements for microfilming.

[2] Line group IV is to be used for construction drawings if a reduction from scale 1:50 to scale 1:100 is intended and the reduction has to meet the requirements for microfilming. The reduction can then be further worked on using widths in line group II.

If building drawings are manually or mechanically drawn with ink and standardised drawing equipment, then the line widths according to the above should preferably be used. These widths are suitable for the usual application of common reproduction methods.

❶ Line types and thicknesses to be used in construction drawings

Dimensioning consists of: dimension figure, dimension line, extension line, dimension arrow → ❻.

Dimension figures are normally located above the relevant continuous dimension line so that they can be read from below or from the right when the drawing is used → ❷ + ❹.

Dimension lines are shown as solid lines → ❶. They are located parallel to the length being dimensioned.

Extension lines: dimensions which cannot be shown directly on the arrow at the edge of an area, are relocated outside with the aid of extension lines. These are generally at right angles to the dimension line and extend a little past it.

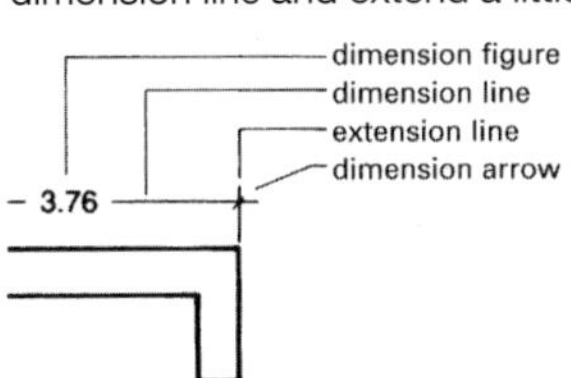

❻ Dimensioning terms

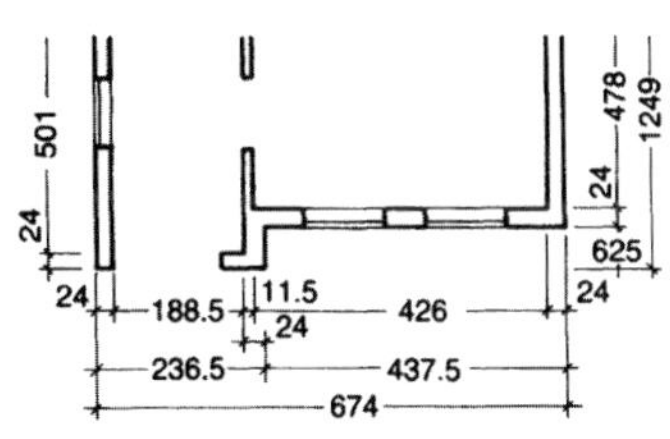

❷ Dimensioning outside the drawing (scale 1:100, units = cm)

	1	2	3	4
	unit for dimensions	dimensions <1 m, e.g.	dimensions >1 m, e.g.	
1	cm	24	88.5	388.5
2	m and cm	24	88^5	3.88^5
3	mm	240	885	3885

NB Recent trend is to give all dimensions in mm, standard practice in UK → p. 6.

❸ Units for dimensions

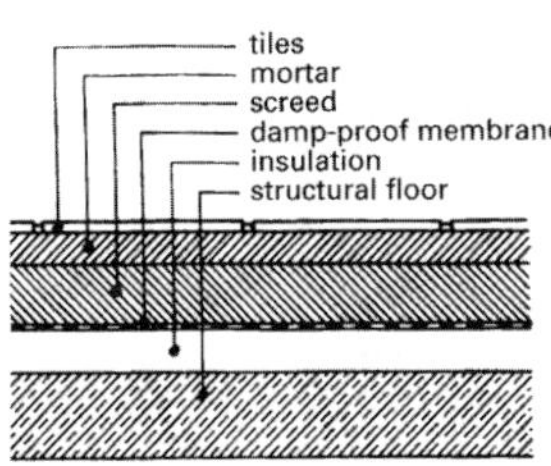

❼ Pointer lines to notes

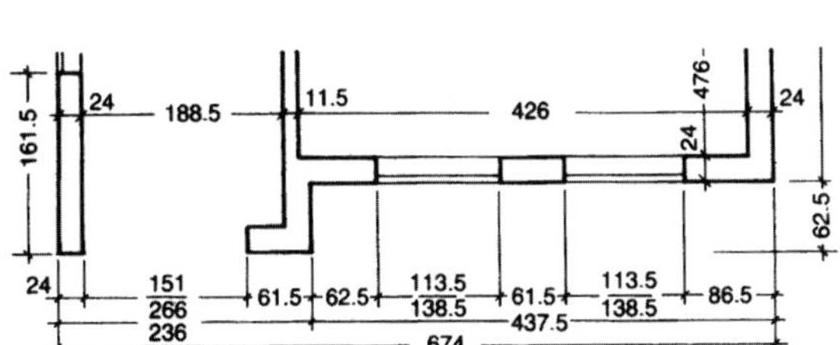

❹ Dimensioning of pillars and openings, e.g. scale 1:50 cm, units = cm

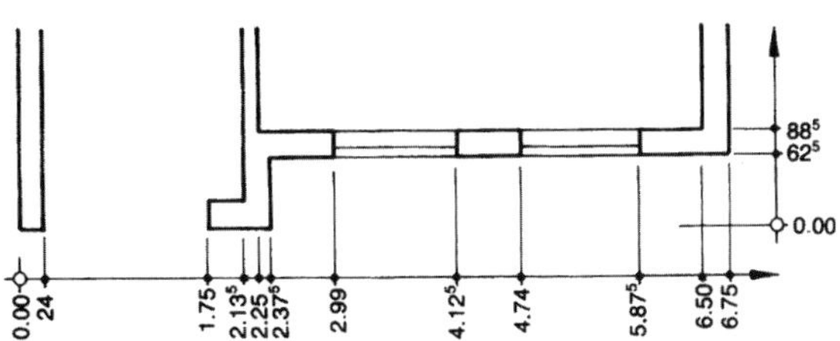

❺ Dimensioning with coordinates, e.g. scale 1:50 m, cm, units cm and mm

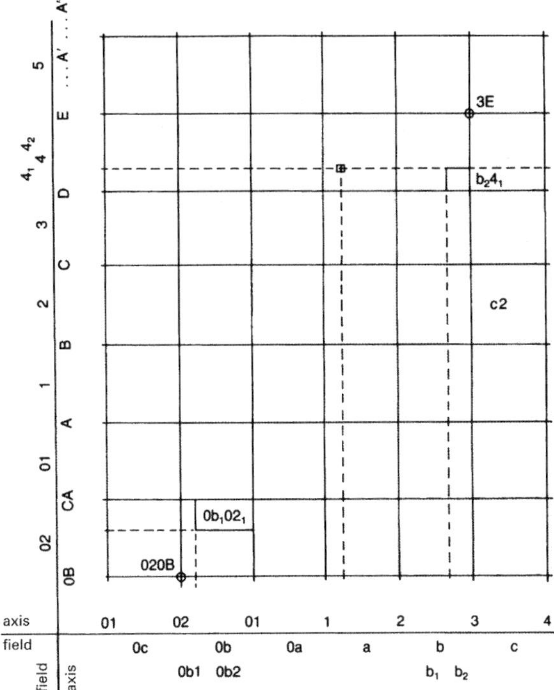

❽ Axis-field grid

BS EN ISO 4157
DIN 1356

Monochrome	Colour	To be used for
	light green	grass
	sepia	peat dust and similar
	burnt sienna	ground
	black/ white	infilled earth
	brown-red	brick masonry in lime mortar
	brown-red	brick masonry in cement mortar
	brown-red	brick masonry in cement-lime mortar
	brown-red	porous brick masonry in cement mortar
	brown-red	hollow pot brick masonry in cement lime mortar
	brown-red	clinker block masonry in cement mortar
	brown-red	sand lime block masonry in lime mortar
	brown-red	alluvial stone masonry in lime mortar
	brown-red	stone masonry in mortar
	brown-red	natural stone masonry in cement mortar
	sepia	gravel
	grey black	slag
	zinc yellow	sand
	ochre	screed (gypsum)
	white	plaster
	violet	pre-cast concrete elements
	blue green	reinforced concrete
	olive green	unreinforced concrete
T	black	metal
	brown	timber in section
	blue grey	insulation materials
	black and white	sealants
	grey	existing building elements

❶ Symbols and colours used on plans and sections

❷ Symbols for building permit applications

Building element	Opening	Dimensions	Location	Related to
C ceiling W wall F floor FO foundation	BR break-through G groove D duct	width × depth × height	u under o over	T top B bottom UF unfinished floor FF finished floor

❸ Labelling of openings: examples

	Description	Label	Dimensions W	D	H	Depiction Plan	Elevation, (section, view)
Slab	slab breakthrough	SBR	A × B				
Slab	groove in slab (top)	GS	A × B × C				
Slab	groove in slab (underneath)	GS	A × B × C				
Lowest storey: floors, foundations	floor slab breakthrough (foundation = FO)	FSBR	A × B				
Lowest storey: floors, foundations	floor slab duct floor slab groove	FSD FSG	A × B × C				
Walls	wall breakthrough (foundation = FO dashed on basement plan)	WBR	A × C				
Walls	wall groove(horizontal) foundation = FO → ❸	WG	A × B × C				
Walls	wall groove (vertical) foundation = FO → ❸	WG	A × B × C				

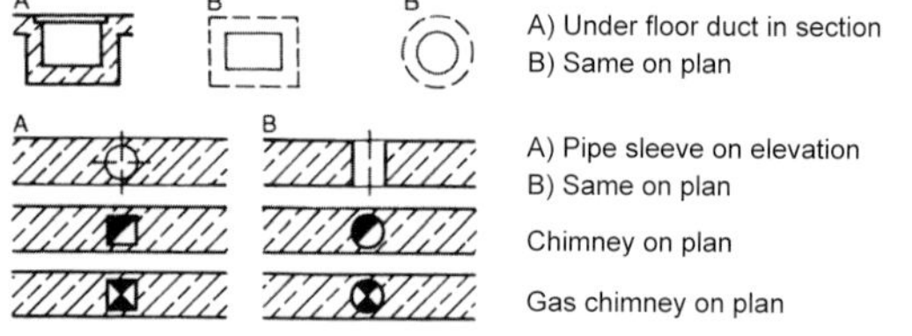

A) Under floor duct in section
B) Same on plan

A) Pipe sleeve on elevation
B) Same on plan

Chimney on plan

Gas chimney on plan

❹ Presentation of openings, grooves and channels: examples

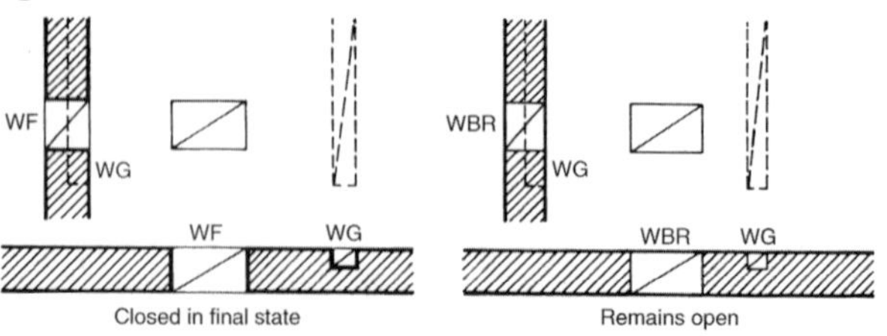

Closed in final state

Remains open

❺ Grooves , apertures and breakthroughs in walls

Natural monument (border with points) according to:
NSG = conservation area
LSG = landscape conservation area
GLB = Protected landscape element
§23 = under §23 HENatG protected habitat
GA = Population of particularly protected or threatened species

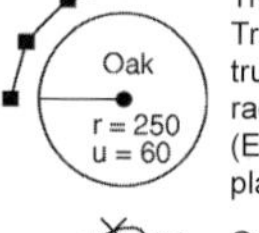

Tree protection
Tree with species, trunk centre, crown radius & trunk dia.
(Existing: full line, planned: dot-dash line

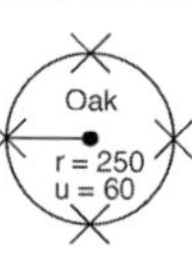

Tree to be removed with species, trunk centre, crown radius & trunk dia.

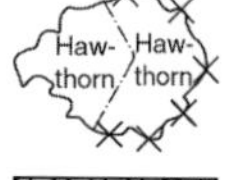

Group of bushes to be partly removed
Existing: full line
Planned: dot-dash line
To be removed: crossed-out full line

Border of area to be built on, whose soil is considerably contaminated with harmful substances.
Border of areas, whose soil is considerably contaminated with harmful substances.

❻ Symbols used in open spaces planning

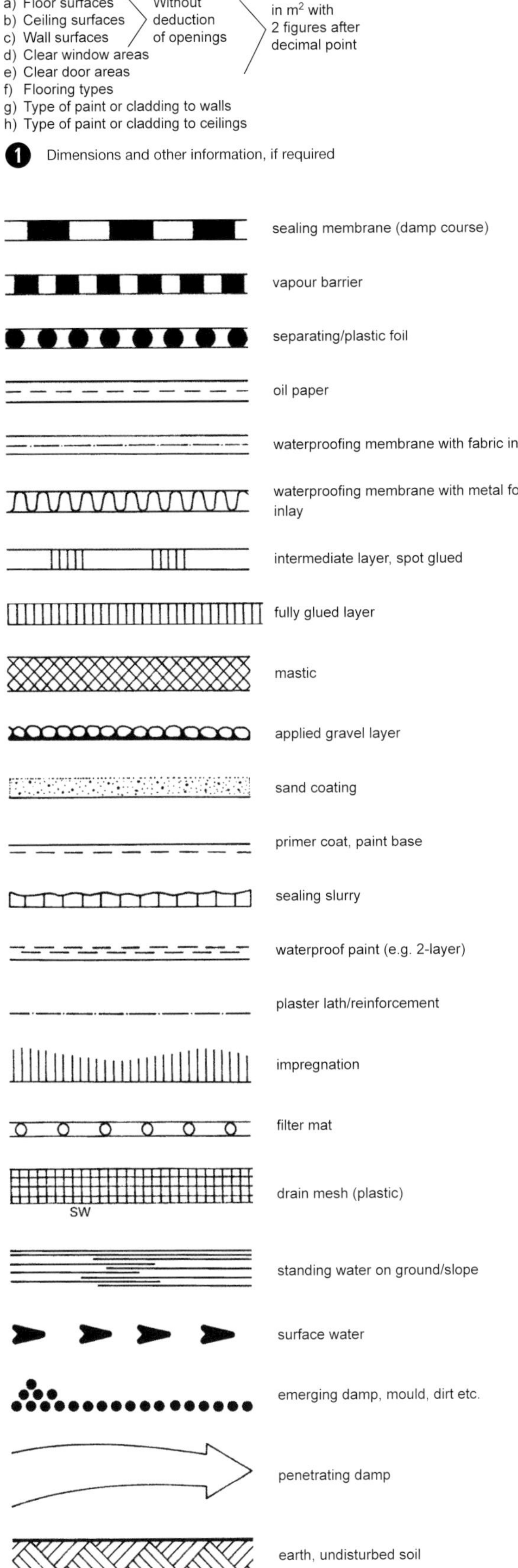

1 Dimensions and other information, if required

2 Symbols for waterproofing, drainage, insulation, non-pressurised water etc.

general insulation layer against heat loss and noise

mineral wool insulation

glass fibre insulation

wood fibre insulation

peat fibre insulation

synthetic foam

cork

magnesite-bonded wood wool board

cement-bonded wood wool board

gypsum building boards

plasterboards

3 Symbols for insulation

BS EN ISO 4157
DIN 1356

Windows set in reveals, scale 1:100

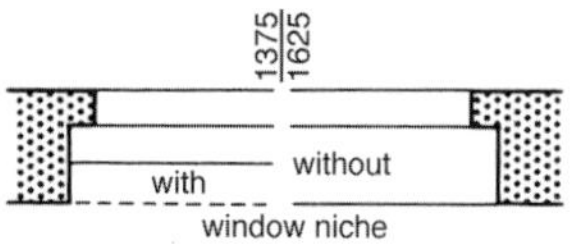

1375 1625

with | without

window niche

❶ Single window opening inward gains space and offers a place for the radiator

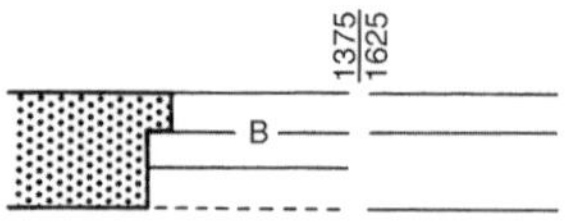

1375 1625

B

❷ Box window (B) opening inward, double window, combined window

1375 1625

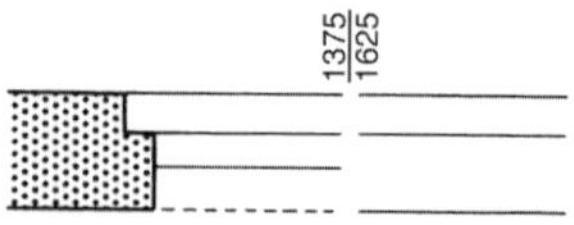

❸ Single window opening outward

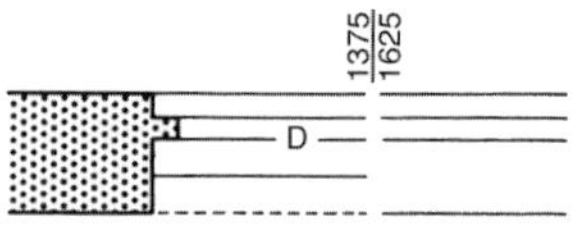

1375 1625

D

❹ Double window (D) opening outward

Sash window, scale 1:100

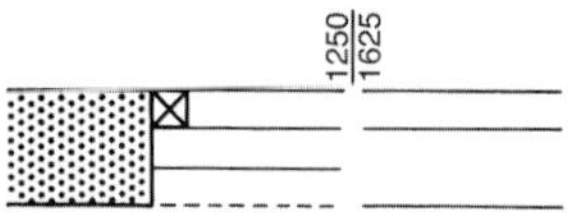

1250 1625

❺ Single window

Sliding window, scale 1:100

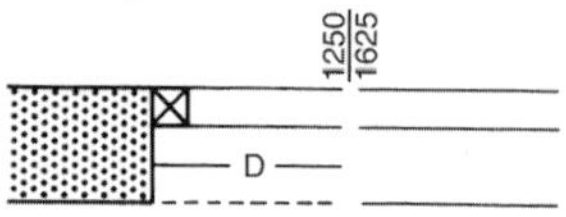

1250 1625

D

❻ Double window (D), box window, combined window

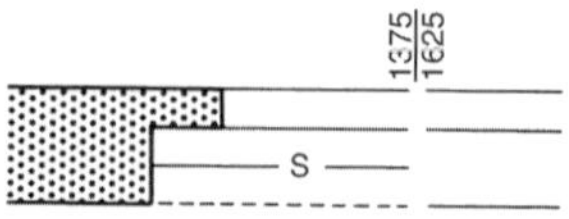

1375 1625

S

❼ Single window (S)

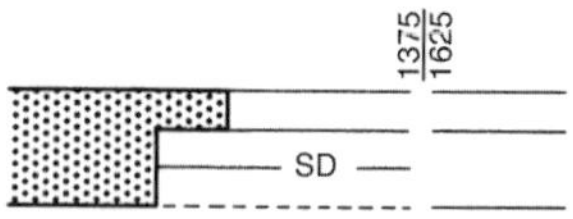

1375 1625

SD

❽ Double window (SD)

Doors, scale 1:100

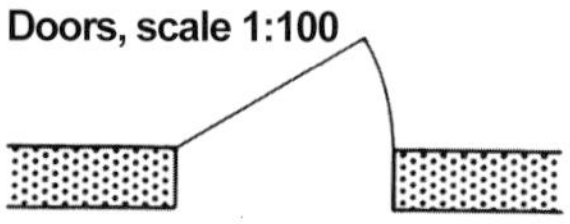

❾ Single-leaf door without lintel

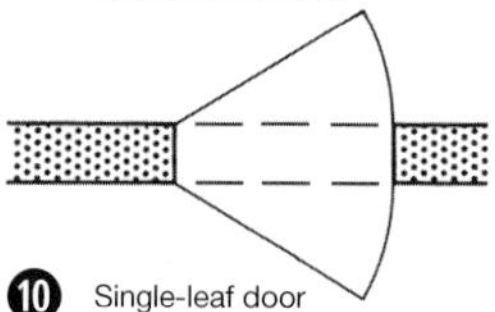

❿ Single-leaf door pair, with lintel

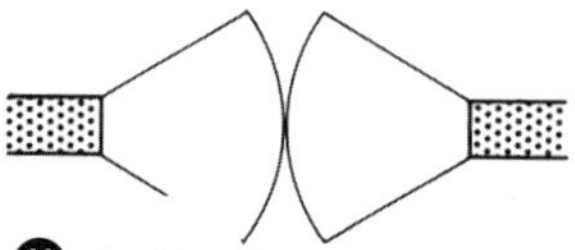

⓫ Double-leaf swing door

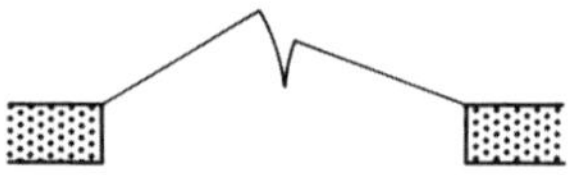

⓬ Double-leaf door

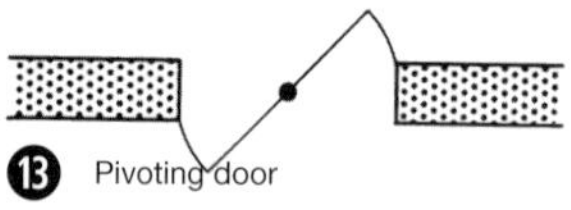

⓭ Pivoting door

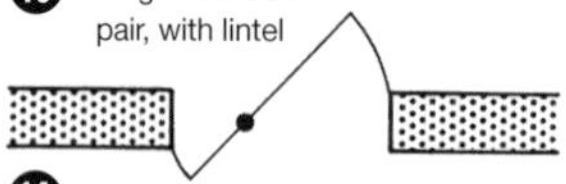

⓮ Pivoting door

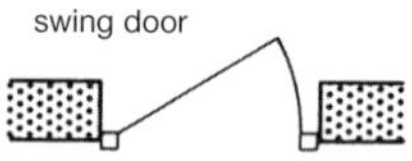

⓯ Without threshold

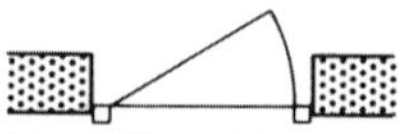

⓰ Threshold one side

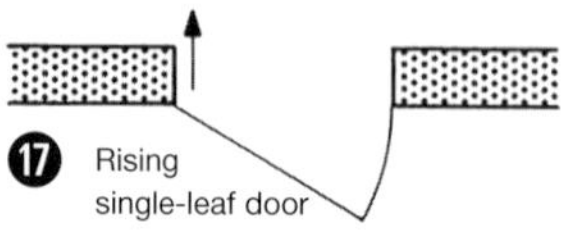

⓱ Rising single-leaf door

⓲ Sliding door

⓳ Double sliding door

⓴ Sliding door with lifting mechanism

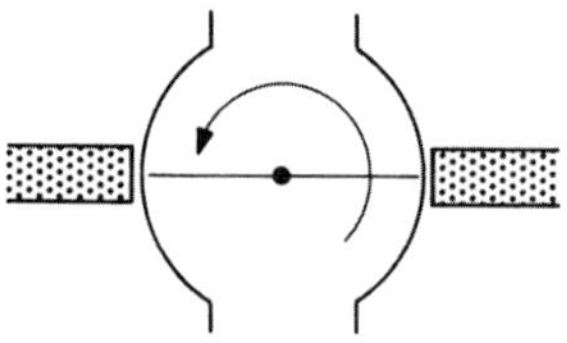

㉑ Two-leaf revolving door

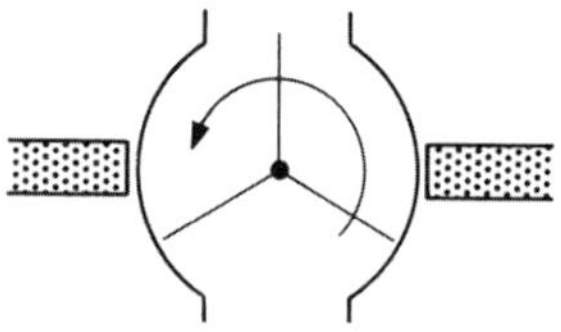

㉒ Three-leaf revolving door

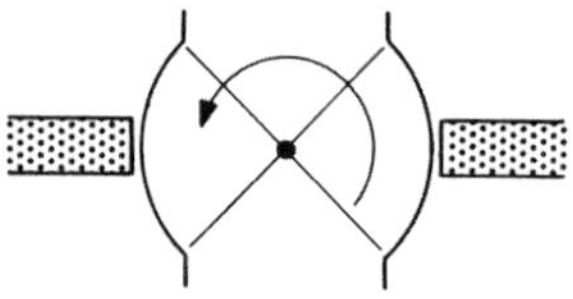

㉓ Four-leaf revolving door

㉔ Folding partition

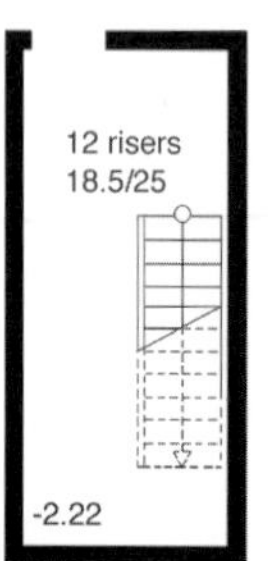

Cellar

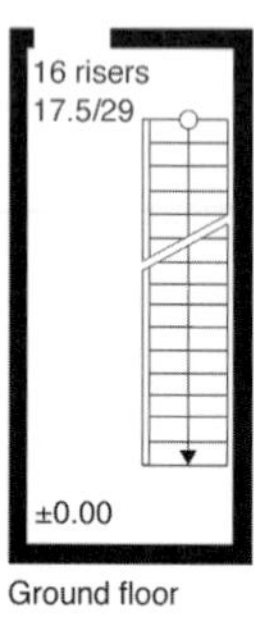

Ground floor

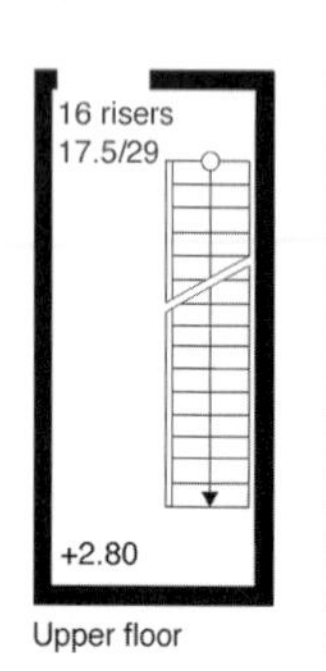

Upper floor

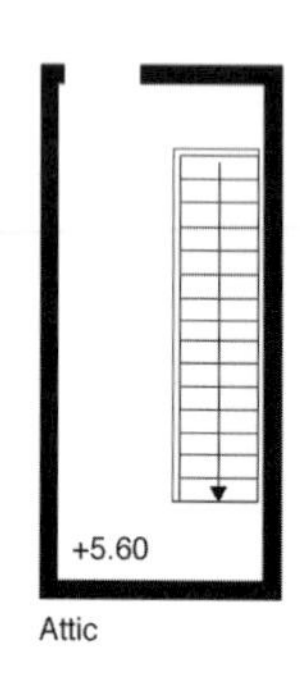

Attic

㉕ Stairs with one flight

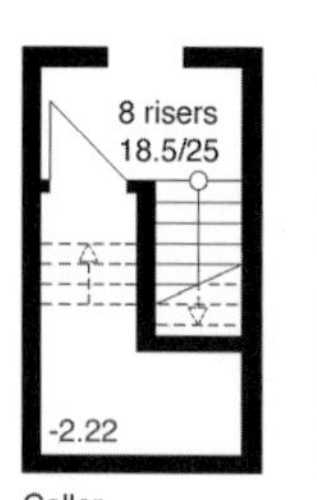

Cellar

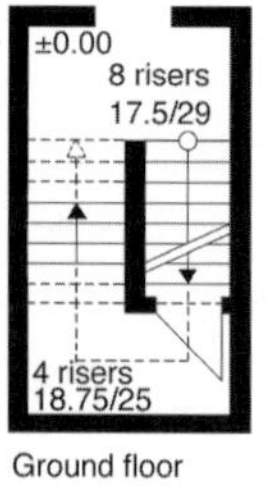

Ground floor

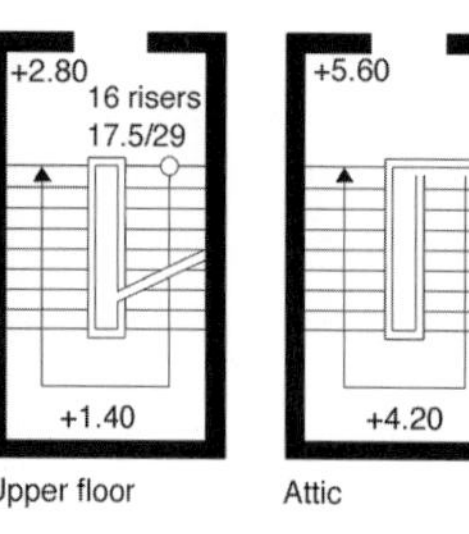

Upper floor

Attic

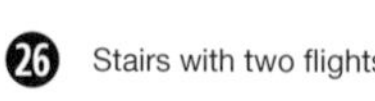

㉖ Stairs with two flights

When drawing **windows,** the left side is always shown with wall niche and the right side without → ❶ – ❽.

Revolving doors replace wind lobbies → ㉑ – ㉓ and offer an opening without draughts. Because revolving doors can cope with relatively little through traffic, the door leaves can be folded at peak times and pushed to the side.

The horizontal section through the stairwell on each floor's plan is shown at about ⅓ storey height or 1 m above floor level. The steps should be continuously numbered upwards and downwards starting from ± 0.000. The number of steps below ± are preceded by a minus sign –. The numbers begin on the first step and exit on the landing. The centre-line starts at the first step with a circle and ends on arriving with an arrow (also in the cellar).

Living room

table
85 × 85 × 78 = 4 places
130 × 80 × 78 = 6 places

round table
∅ 90 = 6 places

shaped table 70 – 100

pull-out table 120 × 180

stool ∅ 45 × 50

armchair 70 × 85

couch 95 × 195

sofa 80 × 175

upright piano
60 × 140 – 160

grand pianos:
baby grand 155 × 114
salon grand 200 × 150
concert grand 275 × 160

television

sewing table 50 × 50–70
sewing machine 50 × 90

BCU — nappy changing table 80 × 90

LB — washing basket 40 × 60

Ch — chest 40 × 100–150

cupboard 60 × 120

Clothes storage

hook spacing
15–20 cm

hanging rail

clothes and linen cupboard 50 × 100–180

desk
70 × 130 × 78
80 × 150 × 78

Bedroom

bed
100 × 200

side table
50 × 70, 60 × 70

double bed
100 × 200

twin bed (French bed)
145 × 200

children's bed
70 × 140 – 170

clothes cupboard
60 × 120

Bathroom

bath
75 × 170,
85 × 185

small bath
70 × 105,
70 × 125

shower 80 × 80,
90 × 90, 75 × 90

symbol scale 1:100 | symbol scale 1:50

washbasin 50 × 60,
60 × 70

2 washbasins

double washbasin
60 × 120, 60 × 140

vanity unit 45 × 30

WC 38 × 70

urinal 35 × 30

bidet 38 × 60

urinal stand

Kitchen

sink 60 × 100

double sink 60 × 150

stepped sink

kitchen bucket sink

floor cupboard

wall cupboard

ironing board

electric oven

DW — dishwasher

Fr — refrigerator

DF — chest freezer

Stoves with fuel type

solid fuel

oil

gas

electric

radiator

heating boiler with grate

gas-fired

oil-fired

waste disposal unit

waste chute

air supply and extraction shaft

PTL = patient lift
GL = goods lift
PL = passenger lift
FL = food lift (paternoster)
HL = hydraulic lift

BS EN 12056
DIN 1451
DIN 1986

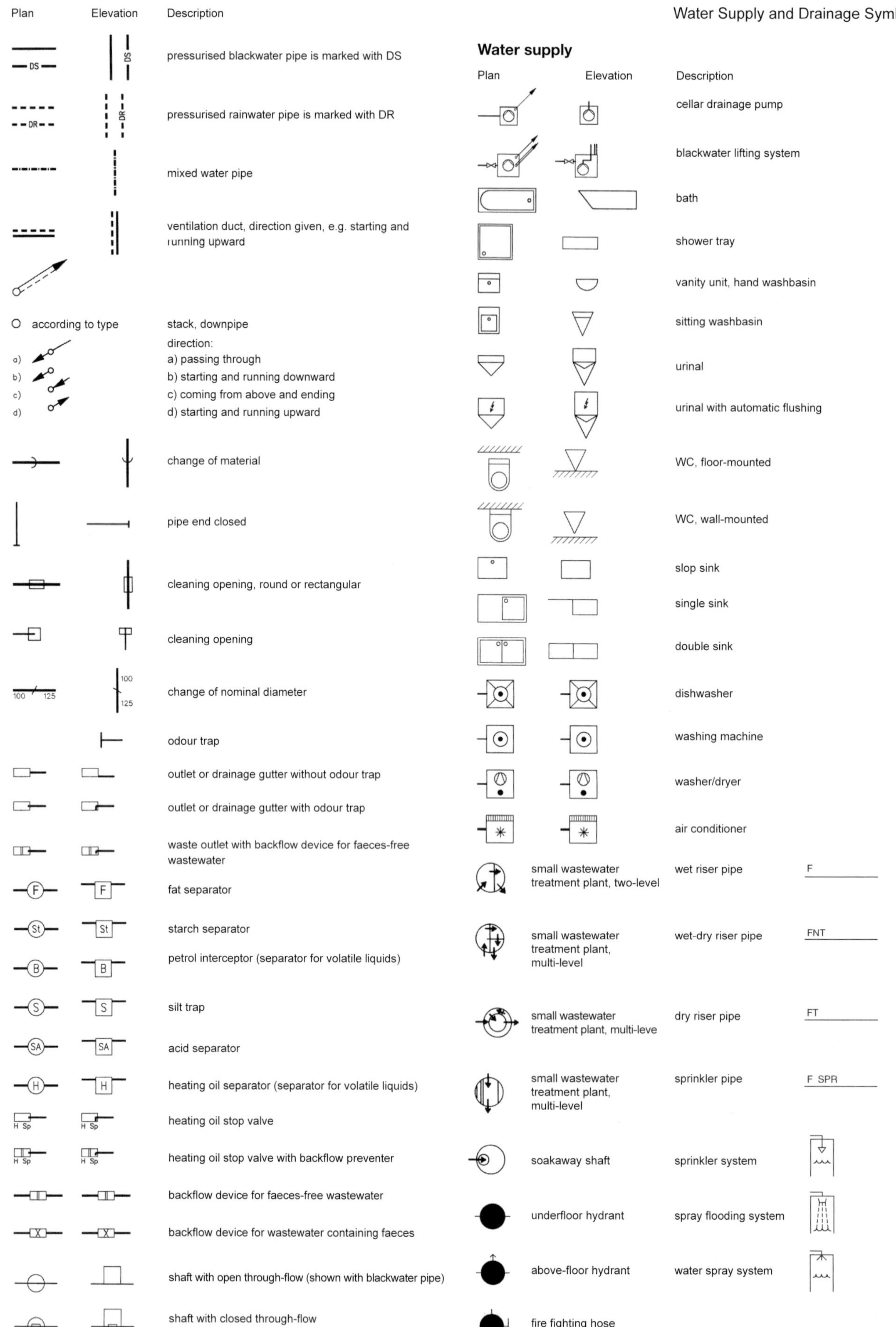

Drainage pipes and appliances

Plan	Elevation	Description
DS	DS	pressurised blackwater pipe is marked with DS
DR	DR	pressurised rainwater pipe is marked with DR
		mixed water pipe
		ventilation duct, direction given, e.g. starting and running upward
according to type		stack, downpipe
a) b) c) d)		direction: a) passing through b) starting and running downward c) coming from above and ending d) starting and running upward
		change of material
		pipe end closed
		cleaning opening, round or rectangular
		cleaning opening
100 125	100 125	change of nominal diameter
		odour trap
		outlet or drainage gutter without odour trap
		outlet or drainage gutter with odour trap
		waste outlet with backflow device for faeces-free wastewater
F	F	fat separator
St	St	starch separator
B	B	petrol interceptor (separator for volatile liquids)
S	S	silt trap
SA	SA	acid separator
H	H	heating oil separator (separator for volatile liquids)
H Sp	H Sp	heating oil stop valve
H Sp	H Sp	heating oil stop valve with backflow preventer
		backflow device for faeces-free wastewater
X	X	backflow device for wastewater containing faeces
		shaft with open through-flow (shown with blackwater pipe)
		shaft with closed through-flow

Water supply

Plan	Elevation	Description
		cellar drainage pump
		blackwater lifting system
		bath
		shower tray
		vanity unit, hand washbasin
		sitting washbasin
		urinal
		urinal with automatic flushing
		WC, floor-mounted
		WC, wall-mounted
		slop sink
		single sink
		double sink
		dishwasher
		washing machine
		washer/dryer
		air conditioner

Symbol	Description	Description	Symbol
	small wastewater treatment plant, two-level	wet riser pipe	F
	small wastewater treatment plant, multi-level	wet-dry riser pipe	FNT
	small wastewater treatment plant, multi-leve	dry riser pipe	FT
	small wastewater treatment plant, multi-level	sprinkler pipe	F SPR
	soakaway shaft	sprinkler system	
	underfloor hydrant	spray flooding system	
	above-floor hydrant	water spray system	
	fire fighting hose connection pipe		

Water supply *(continued)*

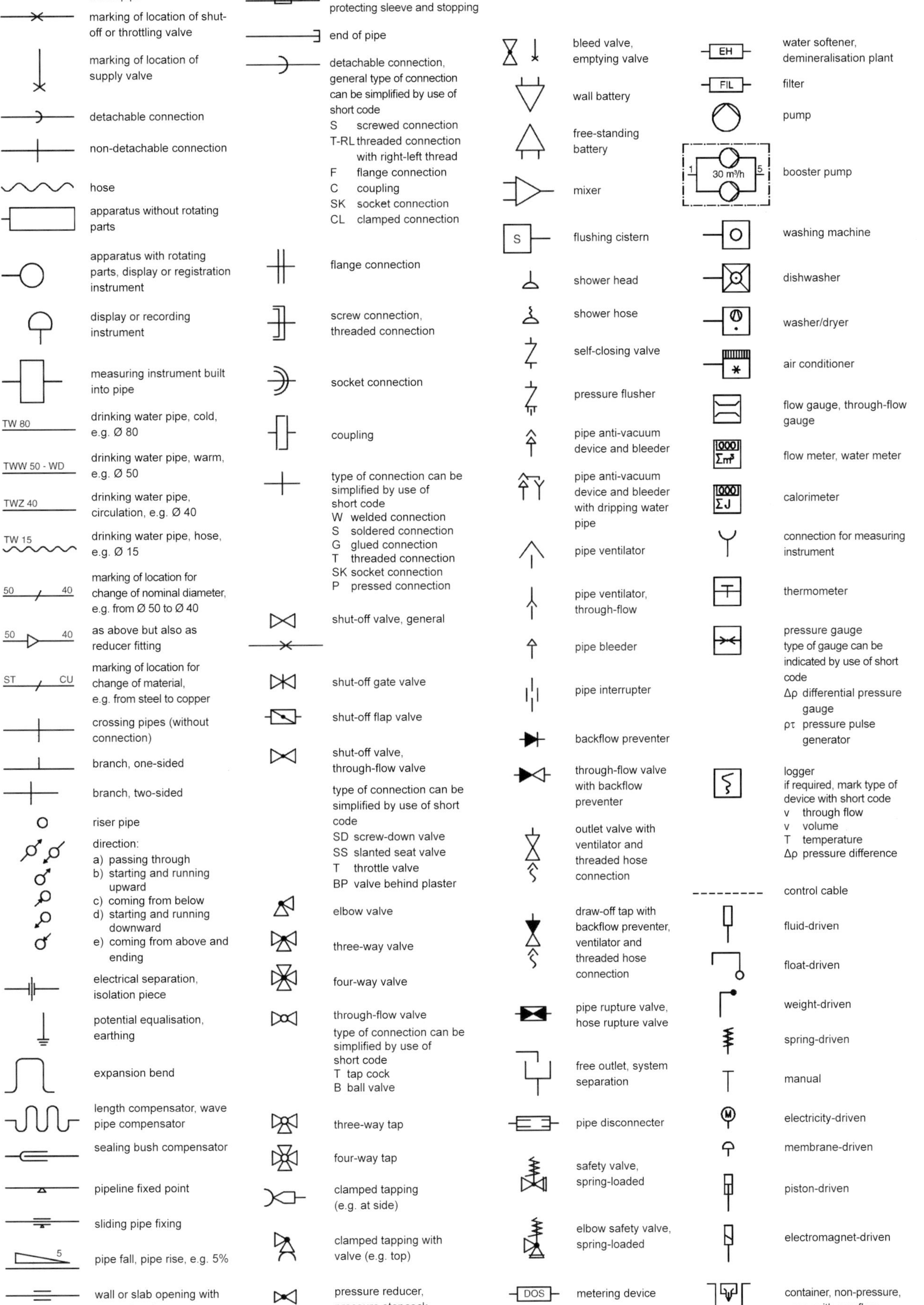
water pipe
marking of location of shut-off or throttling valve
marking of location of supply valve
detachable connection
non-detachable connection
hose
apparatus without rotating parts
apparatus with rotating parts, display or registration instrument
display or recording instrument
measuring instrument built into pipe
TW 80
drinking water pipe, cold, e.g. Ø 80
TWW 50 - WD
drinking water pipe, warm, e.g. Ø 50
TWZ 40
drinking water pipe, circulation, e.g. Ø 40
TW 15
drinking water pipe, hose, e.g. Ø 15
50
40
marking of location for change of nominal diameter, e.g. from Ø 50 to Ø 40
50
40
as above but also as reducer fitting
ST
CU
marking of location for change of material, e.g. from steel to copper
crossing pipes (without connection)
branch, one-sided
branch, two-sided
riser pipe
direction:
a) passing through
b) starting and running upward
c) coming from below
d) starting and running downward
e) coming from above and ending
electrical separation, isolation piece
potential equalisation, earthing
expansion bend
length compensator, wave pipe compensator
sealing bush compensator
pipeline fixed point
sliding pipe fixing
5
pipe fall, pipe rise, e.g. 5%
wall or slab opening with protecting sleeve
wall or slab opening with protecting sleeve and stopping
end of pipe
detachable connection, general type of connection can be simplified by use of short code
S screwed connection
T-RL threaded connection with right-left thread
F flange connection
C coupling
SK socket connection
CL clamped connection
flange connection
screw connection, threaded connection
socket connection
coupling
type of connection can be simplified by use of short code
W welded connection
S soldered connection
G glued connection
T threaded connection
SK socket connection
P pressed connection
shut-off valve, general
shut-off gate valve
shut-off flap valve
shut-off valve, through-flow valve
type of connection can be simplified by use of short code
SD screw-down valve
SS slanted seat valve
T throttle valve
BP valve behind plaster
elbow valve
three-way valve
four-way valve
through-flow valve
type of connection can be simplified by use of short code
T tap cock
B ball valve
three-way tap
four-way tap
clamped tapping (e.g. at side)
clamped tapping with valve (e.g. top)
pressure reducer, pressure stopcock
bleed valve, emptying valve
wall battery
free-standing battery
mixer
S
flushing cistern
shower head
shower hose
self-closing valve
pressure flusher
pipe anti-vacuum device and bleeder
pipe anti-vacuum device and bleeder with dripping water pipe
pipe ventilator
pipe ventilator, through-flow
pipe bleeder
pipe interrupter
backflow preventer
through-flow valve with backflow preventer
outlet valve with ventilator and threaded hose connection
draw-off tap with backflow preventer, ventilator and threaded hose connection
pipe rupture valve, hose rupture valve
free outlet, system separation
pipe disconnecter
safety valve, spring-loaded
elbow safety valve, spring-loaded
DOS
metering device
EH
water softener, demineralisation plant
FIL
filter
pump
1
30 m³/h
5
booster pump
washing machine
dishwasher
washer/dryer
air conditioner
flow gauge, through-flow gauge
flow meter, water meter
calorimeter
connection for measuring instrument
thermometer
pressure gauge
type of gauge can be indicated by use of short code
Δp differential pressure gauge
pτ pressure pulse generator
logger
if required, mark type of device with short code
v through flow
v volume
T temperature
Δp pressure difference
control cable
fluid-driven
float-driven
weight-driven
spring-driven
manual
M
electricity-driven
membrane-driven
piston-driven
electromagnet-driven
container, non-pressure, open, with overflow

BS EN 12056
DIN 1451
DIN 1986

Electrical consumer appliances

electrical appliance, general

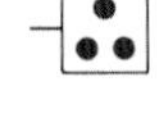
electric stove with three rings

electric stove with built-in coal oven

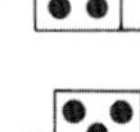
electric stove with oven for baking

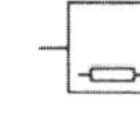
oven for roasting and baking

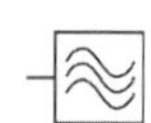
microwave cooker

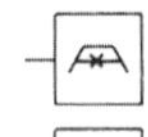
infra red grill

warming plate

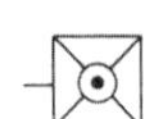
dishwasher

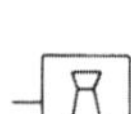
food processor

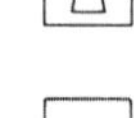
refrigerator, e.g. freezer compartment, no. stars

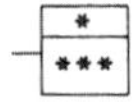
freezer, no. stars

air conditioner

water heater, general

hot water storage cylinder

continuous-flow water heater

fryer

fan

generator, general

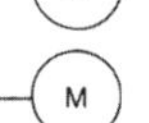
motor, general

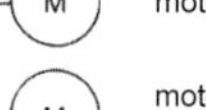
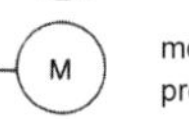
motor with statement of protection type

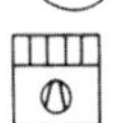
hand dryer, hair dryer

washing machine

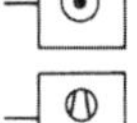
washer/dryer

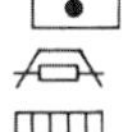
infra red lamp

room heating, general

storage heater

electrically heated clear-view screen

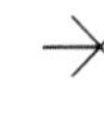
light fitting, general

multiple light fitting stating no. lamps and power, e.g. five lamps at 60 W

adjustable light fitting

light fitting with switch

light fitting with current bridge for lamp chains

light fitting, dimmable

panic light

emergency light

searchlight

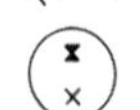
light fitting with additional emergency light

light fitting with two separate filaments

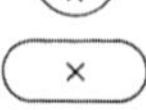
light fitting for discharge lamps with accessories

light fitting for discharge lamps with details

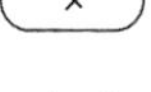
light fitting for fluorescent lamp, general

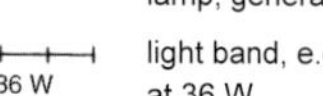
light band, e.g. three lamps at 36 W

light band, e.g. two lamps at 2 × 58 W

Signal and radio devices

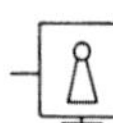
motion detector, e.g. with safety circuit

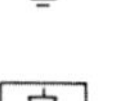
vibration detector (safe pendulum)

light beam detector, light barrier

press-knob fire alarm

automatic fire alarm

police alarm

fire alarm with drive

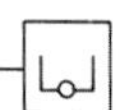
fusible link alarm, automatic

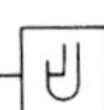
automatic temperature alarm

automatic extension fire alarm

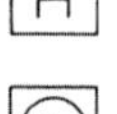
pass lock security systems

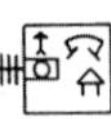
centre of fire alarm system

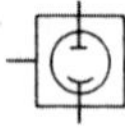
light beam alarm system, automatic, e.g. photo cell

secondary clock

main clock

main clock with signal

amplifier, cable peak denotes amplification direction

telephone, general

multiple telephone

telephone, long-distance

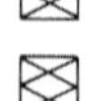
telephone, semi-internal

telephone, internal

loudspeaker

radio

television

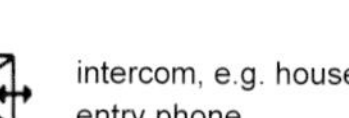
intercom, e.g. house or door entry phone

two-way intercom, e.g. house or door entry phone

telephone exchange, general

door opener

alarm lamp, signal lamp, light signal

bell button

call buttons with name labels

microphone

earpiece

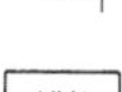
main distributor (communications)

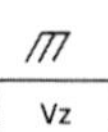
splitter, flush

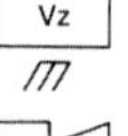
splitter, surface-mounted

beeper or horn, general

beeper or horn stating current type

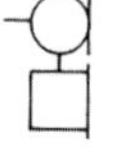
house intercom

entry phone

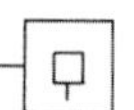
sound recorder

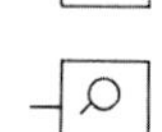
sound pick-up

magnetic tape recorder

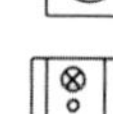
call and switch off panel

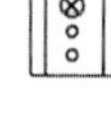
meter

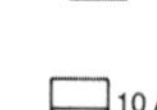
meter panel, e.g with a fuse

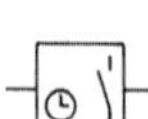
time clock, e.g. for switching tariff

temperature detector

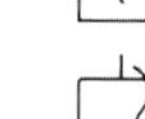
time relay, e.g. for stair lighting

blink relay, blink switch

current impulse switch

sound frequency ripple control relay

sound frequency cut-off

alarm clock, general

alarm clock, stating current type

gong alarm clock

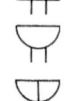

alarm clock for safety circuit

alarm clock with run-down drive

motor alarm clock

alarm clock without automatic cancel, continuously ringing alarm clock

alarm clock with visual alarm

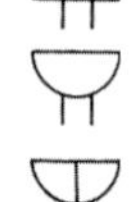
buzzer

buzzer

siren, general

siren stating current type

siren stating frequency, e.g. 140 Hz

siren with wailing tone, e.g. varying between 150 and 270 Hz

DRAWINGS

Electrical Installation Symbols

Electricity

- direct current
- A — alternating current, general
- 2 kHz — stating the frequency
- T — technical alternating current
- direct current or alternating current (universal current)
- mixed current
- sound frequency alternating current
- high frequency alternating current
- very high frequency alternating current

Supporting points in mast cables

- cable, general
- underground cable
- support point, mast, general
- guyed mast
- timber mast
- roof stands, brackets, tubular mast, general
- guyed mast
- lattice mast, general
- guyed mast
- reinforced concrete mast, general
- guyed mast
- mast with foot
- double mast
- transverse H-mast or portal mast
- portal mast of lattice masts
- lengthwise A-mast
- support point with tension anchor
- support point with brace
- mast with lamp

Cables and cable connections

- existing
- under construction
- planned
- mobile cable
- underground cable
- overground cable, e.g. mast-mounted
- cable on porcelain isolators (isolation bells)
- cable on surface of plaster
- cable plastered in
- cable beneath plaster
- isolated cable in installation duct
- (t) — isolated cable for dry rooms, e.g. sheathed wire
- (f) — isolated cable for wet rooms, e.g. wet room cable
- (k) — cable for outdoor or underground laying

Cables, marking, application

- protection cable, e.g. for earthing, neutralisation or protection circuit (old)
- signal cable
- telephone cable
- radio cable
- cable with marking
- 3 — simplified depiction
- protective earth cable (PE)
- PEN cable
- neutral cable
- Cu 20 × 4 — conductor rail
- foreign cable
- further markings, e.g. telephone, night circuit, blinking light cable, emergency lighting cable
- twisted cable, e.g. two-wire
- coaxial cable
- rectangular hollow cable, e.g. for very high frequency
- cable running upward
- cable running downward
- cable running upward and downward
- cable connection
- branch connection box, depiction if necessary
- socket
- sealing end, end branch
- high-voltage house connection box, general
- IP 54 — as above, stating protection type
- distribution
- framing for devices, e.g. housing, switching cabinet, switching panel
- earthing, general
- connection point for earth wire
- mass, body
- element, accumulator or battery
- 230/8V — transformer, e.g. doorbell transformer

- converter, general
- rectifier, e.g. alternating current mains connection
- rectifier, e.g. pole changer, chopper
- fuse, general
- screw-in fuse, e.g. 10A and type DII, three-pole
- low-voltage high-performance fuse, e.g. 50A size 00
- 3 — trip, e.g. 63A, three-pole
- switch, make contact
- 4 — earth leakage circuit breaker, four-pole
- B 16A, 3 — cable protection switch, e.g. 16A, three-pole
- 3 — motor protection switch, three-pole
- excess current switch, e.g. ballast switch
- emergency off switch
- star-delta switch
- 5 — starter, rheostat, e.g. with five starting steps
- button switch
- light switch
- switch with indicator light
- switch 1/1 (off switch, single-pole)
- switch 1/2 (off switch, two-pole)
- switch 1/3 (off switch, three-pole)
- switch 4/1 (group switch, single-pole)
- switch 5/1 (series switch, single-pole)
- switch 6/1 (two-way switch, single-pole)
- Z — two-way switch as pull switch
- switch 7/1 (cross-switch, single-pole)
- t — time switch
- dimmer
- approach switch
- contact switch

- approach effect, general
- contact effect, general
- passive infra red motion detector
- t — time relay, e.g. for stair lighting
- current impulse switch
- empty connection box
- 3 — multiple socket
- single earthed socket
- 3/N/PE — as above but for three-phase current
- double earthed socket
- socket with off switch
- socket, lockable
- depiction of vertical if required
- socket for isolating transformer
- E — electrical connection, general
- E 3/N/PE — three-phase connection
- smoke extraction ventilator switch
- RWA — smoke extraction press-button alarm
- fire alarm (press-button alarm)
- EDV — IT connection socket
- BK — broadband communications system
- Vt — telephone distributor
- telephone socket
- aerial socket
- aerial splitter, e.g. twice
- aerial distributor ,e.g. twice
- aerial amplifier
- aerial socket (through sockets)
- aerial socket with end resistance

DRAWINGS

Electrical Installation Symbols

Visual indicators

- indicator light, general
- blinking indicator light with direction pointer
- indicator light with darkening switch
- indicator light with glimmer light
- pointer indicator with automatic return
- pointer Indicator with automatic return, lit
- pointer indicator with automatic return, lit or swinging
- pointer indicator without automatic return
- pointer indicator without automatic return, lit
- indicator with filling device
- recording indicator
- meter
- meter with indicator lamp
- multiple detector
- acknowledgement detector

Batteries

- elemental battery
- accumulator battery (four cells)
- element, accumulator

Lightning protection installations

- building outline
- gutter and downpipe
- reinforced concrete with connection
- steel construction, metal rails
- metal covering
- chimney
- roof stands for electric lines
- diaphragm tank, tank
- snow guards
- aerial
- metal pipe
- lightning conductor, open
- lightning conductor, underground
- lightning conductor, under roof and under plaster
- terminal pole, flagpole
- connection point to pipes
- separation point
- pipe and rod earth terminal
- earthing
- sparking distance
- closed sparking distance
- excess voltage discharge conductor
- roof fixing
- lift
- water meter, gas meter

No.	Type of appliance	No. (min.) of Sockets[1)]	No. (min.) of Outlets	Connections for appliances of ≧2 kW	Connected load (kW) AC	Connected load (kW) 3-phase
	Living room and bedroom					
	sockets[2)], lighting					
1	for living area up to 8 m²	2	1			
2	8–12 m²	3	1			
3	12–20 m²	4	1			
4	>20 m"	5	2			
	Kitchen, kitchenette					
	sockets, lighting					
5	for kitchenette	3	2[3)]			
6	for kitchen	5	2[3)]			
7	ventilator/extractor hood		1[4)]			
8	stove			1		8.0–14.0
9	refrigerator/freezer	1			0.2	
10	dishwasher			1	3.5	4.5
11	water heater			1[5)]	2.0	4.0–6.0
	Bathroom					
12	sockets, lighting	2[6)]	2[7)]			
13	extractor fan		1[4), 8)]			
14	washing machine[9)]			1[10)]	3.3	7.5
15	heater					
16	water heater			1[5)]	2.0	4.0–6.0
	WC					
17	sockets, lighting	1[11)]	1			
18	extractor fan		1[4), 8)]			
	Utility room					
19	sockets, lighting	3	1[3)]			
20	extractor fan		1[4)]			
21	washing machine			1[12)]	3.3	7.5
22	washer/dryer			1[12)]	3.3	
23	ironing machine			1	2.1–3.3	
	Hall, corridor					
	Sockets, lighting					
24	for length up to 2.5 m	1	1[13)]			
25	over 2.5 m	1	1[14)]			
	Outdoor sitting area					
26	sockets, lighting	1	1[15)]			
	Storeroom >3 m²					
27	lighting		1			
	Hobby room					
28	sockets, lighting	3	1			
	Residential cellar and basement [16)]					
29	sockets, lighting	1	1			
	Commercial cellar and basement					
	Sockets, lighting					
30	for usable area up to 20 m²	1[17)]	1			
31	over 20 m²	1[17)]	2			
	Cellar and basement passage					
32	lighting		1[18)]			

1) Or junction boxes for consumer devices <2 kW.
2) Sockets next to beds are double sockets, which, arranged next to aerial sockets, are triple sockets. These multiple sockets, are counted in the table as single sockets.
3) The worktops should be lit with as little shadow and glare as possible.
4) If a single extract fan is to be provided.
5) Unless hot water is provided by other means.
6) Of which one may be combined with the vanity unit light.
7) For bathrooms with 4 m² usable area, one connection above the vanity unit is sufficient.
8) For bathrooms and WCs without windows, the switch is via the general lighting, with a time lag.
9) In residential property necessary only once.
10) Unless a utility room is provided or the appliances can be accommodated in another suitable room.
11) For WCs with a vanity unit.
12) Unless accommodated in the bathroom or another suitable room.
13) Switchable from one location.
14) Switchable from two locations.
15) From 8 m² usable space.
16) Does not apply to cellar and basement rooms with grating-like partitions, e.g. wire mesh.
17) For signal amplifiers, only required once per system.
18) For passages >6 m long, one outlet every 6 m of length begun.

❶ Power supply to electrical appliances

Living area (m²)	No. circuits for lighting and sockets
up to 50	2
50–75	3
75–100	4
100–125	5
over 125	6

❷ No. circuits by size of living area

Living area (m²)	No. circuits for lighting and sockets
up to 45	3
45–55	4
55–75	6
75–100	7
over 100	8

❸ High level of equipment

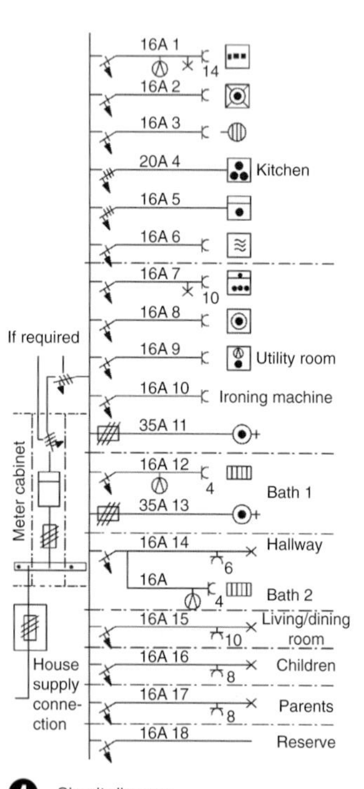

❹ Circuit diagram

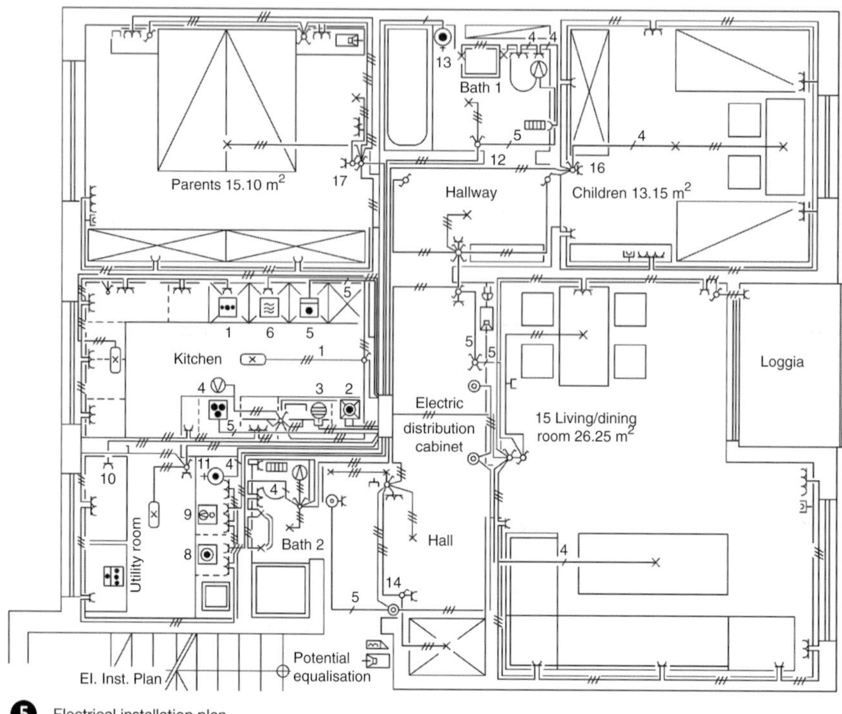

❺ Electrical installation plan

Burglar alarm systems

strike plate contact
opening contact
magnetic contact
vibration sensor
oscillation contact
thread tension switch
foil
breakthrough sensor
pressure sensor/step mat
glass breakage sensor
structure-borne sound sensor
passive infrared sensor
light barrier
light sensor
image detector
microwave doppler motion detector
microwave barrier
HF field alteration sensor
LF field alteration sensor
capacitive field alteration sensor
HF barrier
ultrasound doppler motion detector
ultrasound barrier
banknote contact
attack detector
electromechanical switchgear
mental switchgear
time clock switchgear
light switch device
acoustic signal generator
optical signal generator
connection relay
remote switching device
alarm searchlight

Fire alarm systems

maximum heat detector
differential heat detector
optical smoke detector
ionisation smoke detector
infra red flame sensor
ultra violet flame sensor
pressure sensor (sprinkler activation)
manual alarm
connection relay
fire brigade key depot

Control centres/accessories

ÜEM attack and break-in alarm control centre
BM fire alarm control centre
ZK access control centre
FÜ CCTV surveillance control centre
LD shop theft alarm control centre
WS intercom control centre
TÖ door opener control centre
converter
transmission system
analog-digital converter
mains rectifier
accumulator battery
automatic dialling and announcement device
recording system handle
connection relay
digital line coupler
analog-digital converter with line coupler signal flow device
display tableau
operating panel
housing
monitored housing
monitored distributor

CCTV surveillance systems

TV camera
TV camera with varifocal lens
TV camera protective housing
protective housing with pan and tilt head
TV camera with pan and tilt head
TV camera with motion detector
monitor
operating panel view selection device
monitor with video signal-dependent picture switching

Access control systems

pass reader
stand-alone reader with additional code entry
online reader
pass reader with additional code entry
stand-alone reader with additional code entry
data terminal with operating panel

man lock
turnstile
revolving door
electrically unlocked door
electrically opened door
overlight
protective grille
security escutcheon
long security handle plate
tilt and turn window casement lock
lock for four-sided key
falling bolt lock
deadbolt lock
hinge bolts (dog bolts)
roller shutter locking
folding shutter locking
two-key lock system
lockable window handle
security strike plate
cross-bolt lock, double bolt lock
cellar grating security
cylinder lock
vertically sliding door lock
fence
barbed wire fence
solid fence, mesh
R roller shutter with closing security
SR steel roller shutters
GR roller or concertina shutter
G safe
VSG laminated safety glass

DRAWINGS

Gas Installation Symbols

Gas installations

- 25 — exposed horizontal pipe (stating nominal diameter)
- concealed horizontal pipe (stating nominal diameter)
- change of cross-section (stating nominal diameter)
- gas pipe house entry
- isolating piece
- riser pipe
- continuously rising pipe
- downpipe
- crossing of two pipes without connection
- crossing connection
- branch location
- RT — cleaning T-piece
- RK — cleaning K-piece
- long-threaded connection
- screwed connection
- flanged connection
- welded connection
- shut-off tap
- shut-off gate valve
- shut-off valve
- thermally activated shut-off device
- elbow valve
- pressure regulator
- gas meter
- gas stove (four rings)
- gas oven (four rings)
- gas refrigerator
- gas heat pump
- 80 ⌀ — exhaust gas/flue pipe (stating diameter)
- CM — exhaust gas systems (stating dimensions), also for exhaust gas flue/chimney
- filter
- gas room heater
- continuous flow gas water heater
- combi gas water heater

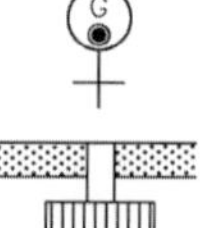

- gas storage water heater
- gas room heater for external wall connection (stating connection capacity)
- gas heating boiler
- flexible hose

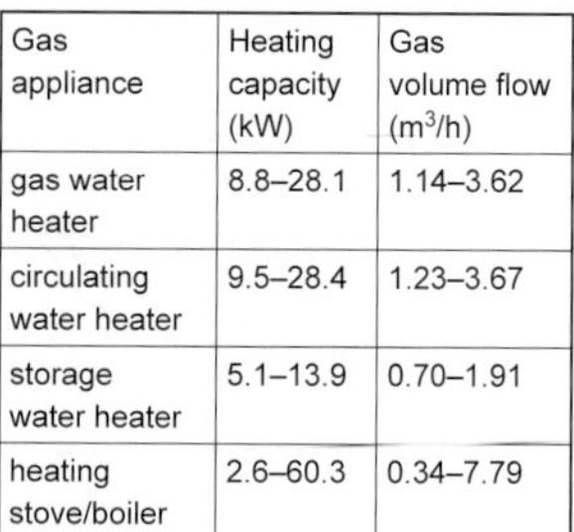

Gas appliance	Heating capacity (kW)	Gas volume flow (m^3/h)
gas water heater	8.8–28.1	1.14–3.62
circulating water heater	9.5–28.4	1.23–3.67
storage water heater	5.1–13.9	0.70–1.91
heating stove/boiler	2.6–60.3	0.34–7.79

❶ Connection specifications for gas appliances

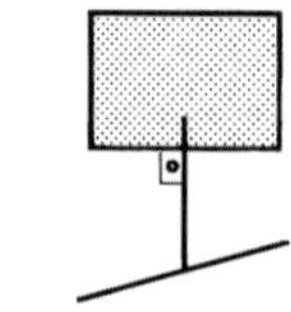

❷ House supply connection at right angles to front of building

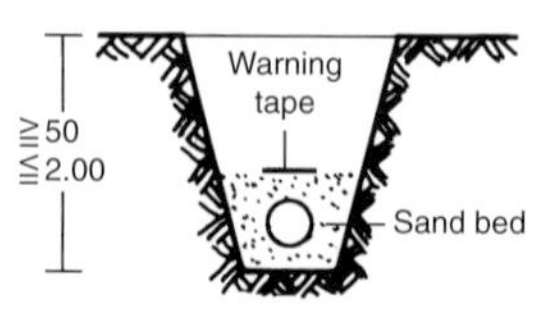

❸ Gas pipe laid on undisturbed soil; does not have to be frost-free

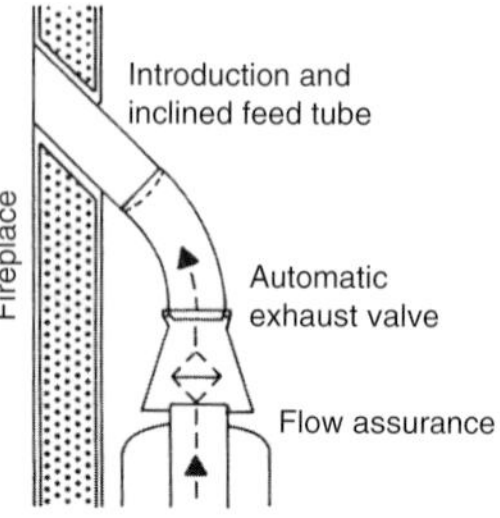

❹ Flow-operated safety device and flue gas flap valve

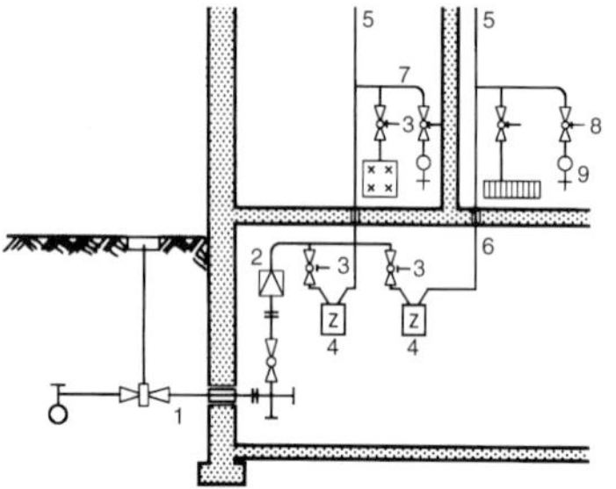

1 house introduction combination
2 pressure regulator
3 shut-off
4 gas meter
5 riser
6 gas supply line
7 branch line
8 devices connecting fitting thermally activated device
9 gas equipment: stove, water heater

❺ Gas meter in cellar

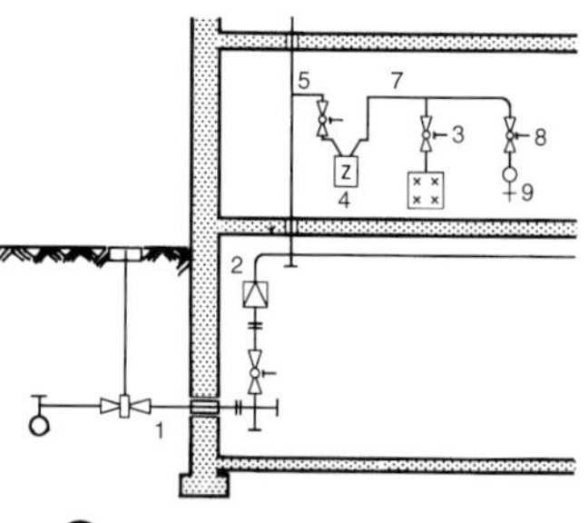

❻ Gas meters on each storey

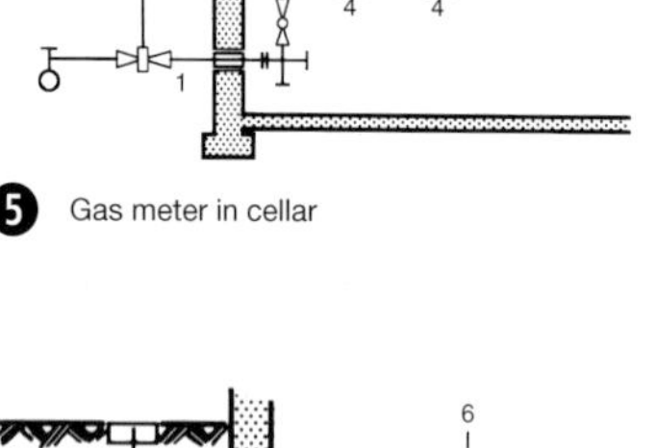

1 power cable, local area network management
2 steel service pipe
3 casing
4 pull out
5 shut off the main with integrated insulating joints
6 boundary between gas valve unit (GVU) and installer
7 pressure regulator

❼ Gas supply

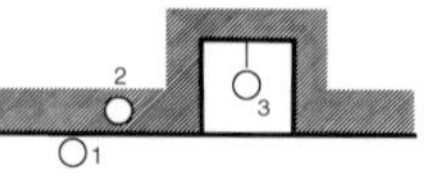

1 A gas line installed free, gas lines can also be laid outside the building, such as a gas heater on the roof. A gas line needs to be frost-free.
2 Gas pipe laid under plaster.
3 Gas pipelines in shafts or channels have to be loaded and ventilated. Openings approximately 10 cm^2. For suspended ceilings, these openings are placed diagonally.

❽ Laying gas pipes

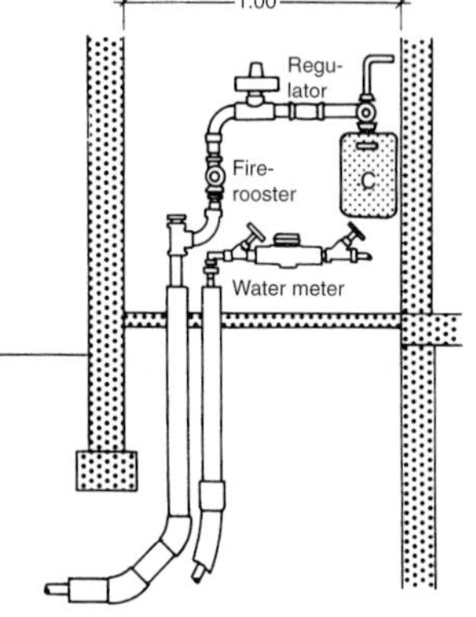

❾ House supply connection for water and gas in one compartment 1 m wide and 0.30 m deep

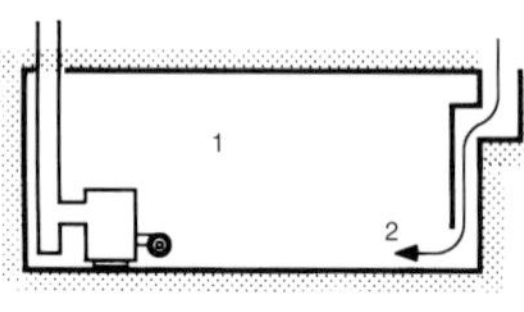

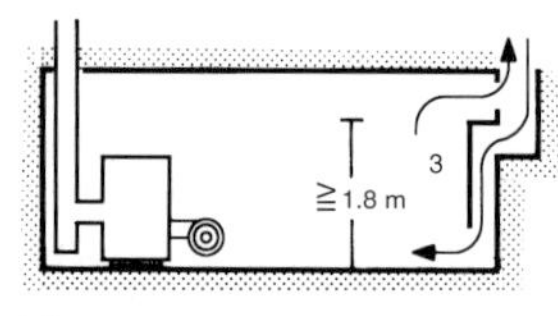

1 Minimum size 1 m^3/kW
2 Combustion air opening in boiler output to ≧50 kW cm^2 at ground level
3 Combustion air opening at about 50 kW boiler capacities. Cross-section of the opening of 150 cm^2 per kW + 2cm^2, the over 50 kW goes out. Example: boiler output 65 kW 50 kW + 15 kW 150 cm^2 + (15 × 2 = 30) cm^2 = 180 cm^2

❿ **Heating room ≧35 kW**

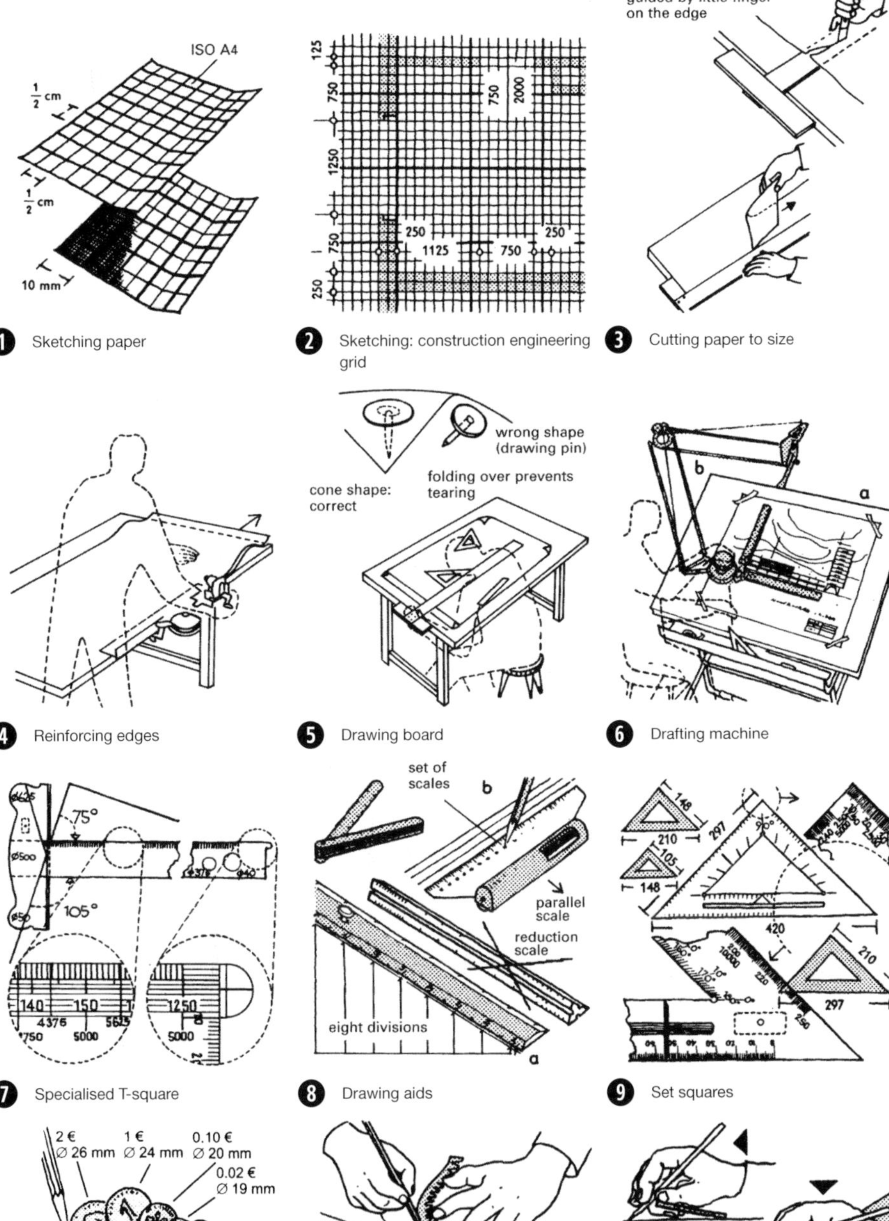

❶ Sketching paper

❷ Sketching: construction engineering grid

❸ Cutting paper to size

❹ Reinforcing edges

❺ Drawing board

❻ Drafting machine

❼ Specialised T-square

❽ Drawing aids

❾ Set squares

❿ Drawing aids

⓫ French curves

⓬ Good drawing practice

⓭ Drawing aid

⓮ Aid for hatching

⓯ a) Clutch pencil (lead holder);
b) Correct way of holding pencil

Designers use drawings and diagrams to communicate information in a factual, unambiguous and geometric form that can be understood anywhere in the world. Unlike painting, construction drawing is a means to an end, and this differentiates diagrams/working drawings and illustrations from artistic works. A4 sketch pads with 0.5 cm squared graph paper are ideal for freehand sketches to scale. For more accurate sketches, millimetre graph paper with thick centimetre, faint 0.5 cm and even finer millimetre divisions should be used → ❶. Different paper is used for drawing and sketching according to standard modular coordinated construction and engineering grids → ❷. Use tracing paper for sketching with a soft lead pencil. Suitable sheet sizes for drawings can be cut straight from a roll, single pages being torn off using a T-square → ❸ or cut on its underside → ❸. Construction drawings are done in hard pencil or ink on clear, tear-resistant tracing paper, bordered with protected edges → ❹ and stored in drawers. Ink drawings are made on transparent paper and water-resistant paper is used for paintings or diagrams. Fix the paper on a simple drawing board (designed for standard formats) made of limewood or poplar, using drawing pins with conical points → ❺. First turn over 2 cm of the paper's edge (later to be used as a filing edge – see p. 4): this lifts the T-square a little during drawing and prevents the T-square from smudging the work. (For the same reason, draw from top to bottom!) The drawing can be fixed with drafting tape rather than drawing pins → ❻ (which means that the drawing underlay can be made of plastic – Cellon or a similar smooth material). Drafting machines are common in engineering disciplines → ❻. In addition to simple parallel rules, there are also special versions with built-in protractors for setting angles; these are ruled with centimetre and octametre divisions → ❼. Other drawing aids feature pocket scale sets, parallel scale for hatching, division of lengths → ❽.

BS EN ISO 8560
BS 6750
DIN 4172

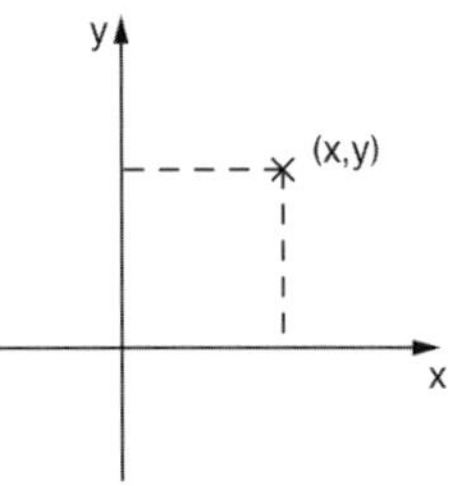

❶ Cartesian coordinate system. All points are defined through their x and y coordinates. The zero point can be set for each drawing or related to world coordinates.

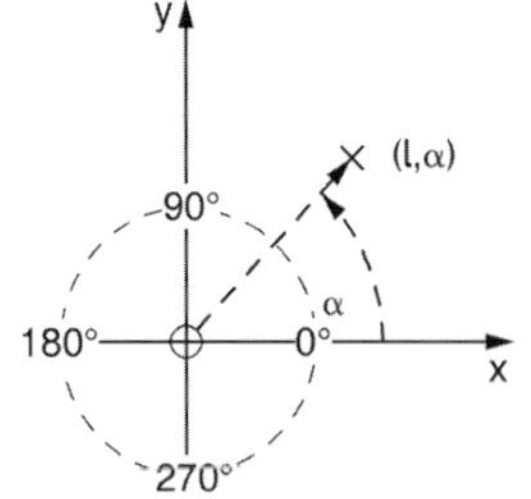

❷ Polar coordinate system. All points are defined through their distance l from the zero point and the angle α related to the x-axis.

Measurement system	Abbr.	1 mm =	1 unit
point	pt	2.8346 pt	0.3528 mm
inch	in″	0.0394″	25.4 mm

Conversion factors for common computer units

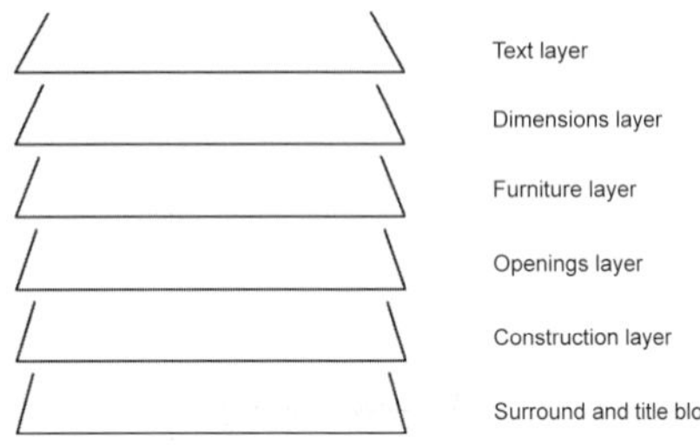

❹ Structuring of a CAD drawing by arranging groups of similar objects on their own layers

Obligatory					–	Facultative					–	Obligatory							
W	h	o			W	h	e	r	e			W	h	a	t				
1	2	3	4	5	6	7	8	9	10	11	12	13	14	15	16	17	18	19	20

Who-where-what naming of layers with variable field sizes (according to CadForum). The layer names have suitable abbreviations containing 2 or 3 pieces of information, each separated by an underscore. The content should be clear from the first 20 characters, because some CAD systems restrict the layer names to this length. Special characters should be avoided in order to prevent exchange problems.

Who (1–5) = author

possible abbreviations for authors
Arch = Architect
IArch = Interior architect
LArch = Landscape architect
Blng = Building engineer
Ei = Electrical engineer
St = Structural engineer
HLS = Heating/ventilation/sanitary
Geom = Surveyor

Where (7–11) = categorisation

possible categories
BS = basement
GR = ground floor
FL1 = 1st floor
EL_N = north elevation
SEC_A = section A-A

What (13–20) = description

possible descriptions
axes
structure
openings
finishings
furniture
hatching

dimensioning
labelling
drawing outline

examples of layer names

Arch_GR_axes
Arch_GR_structure
Arch_GR_finishes
Arch_GR_hatching

on smaller projects, the 2nd category (facultative) can be left out:
Geom_level curves
Arch_structure
Blng_openings

❺ Example of naming layers with variable, understandable labels

Drawings

Drawings are always an abstraction of reality because they are in two dimensions. The degree of abstraction depends on the content and, above all, on the intended purpose of the drawing. The lowest degree of abstraction is represented by perspectives, collages and renderings, which attempt to come quite close to reality. In order to produce the desired impression, it is particularly important to leave some free rein for the fantasy of the viewer. Diagrams can be used to explain functional interactions. Working drawings contain all the required information about dimensions, materials and arrangement of the object to be produced. In this case, all details must be unambiguous and comprehensible for the producer, and therefore have a high degree of abstraction.

In the age of computer-generated images, it still remains important to have a command of the rules and regulations of traditional drawing → pp. 39–40.

Computer-aided drawings

Drawing with a computer is very different from the classic methods of drawing on paper. There are two basic principles: raster graphics, in which every pixel of a drawing is saved (image processing), and vector graphics, where the start, end and the properties of a drawing element are saved (CAD). Because the output appears on a monitor screen or plot, there are also problems representing bodies and rooms in two dimensions. Only very simple CAD programs work with two-dimensional data models. More common are three-dimensional data models (object-oriented programs), which produce the desired type of illustration on output (monitor, plotting). The information required for this is stored in a database in the computer. This enables the elements of a drawing (line type, line thickness and colour) to be linked to further information, which is not visible, e.g. which layer they belong to, dependence on other objects, material properties, manufacturing information, order numbers etc. These properties can be exploited for the structuring of content or for further use (e.g. tenders or cost estimation).

Volume modules permit further simulations. Structural, acoustic, climatic or lighting investigations can make precise statements about a building through the use of the appropriate software. 3D scanners, CNC machines and 3D plotters also enable the input and output of three-dimensional objects.

Data exchange

Because data is normally processed by a number of operators (various specialist technicians and engineers), a unified, understandable and clear system of organisation is important. When selecting a CAD system or deciding the working methods, it is important to know that all future processors of the data will work with the same software, or which interfaces can be used to exchange data. Exchange formats usually have a limited range of structuring possibilities and therefore organisation categories, which are not supported, will be lost or have to be recreated, with the associated waste of time. The naming of layers is governed by ISO 13567, which, however, uses cryptic abbreviations. It seems more practical to use the more flexible and easily understood naming system published by the specialist magazine CadForum → ❺.

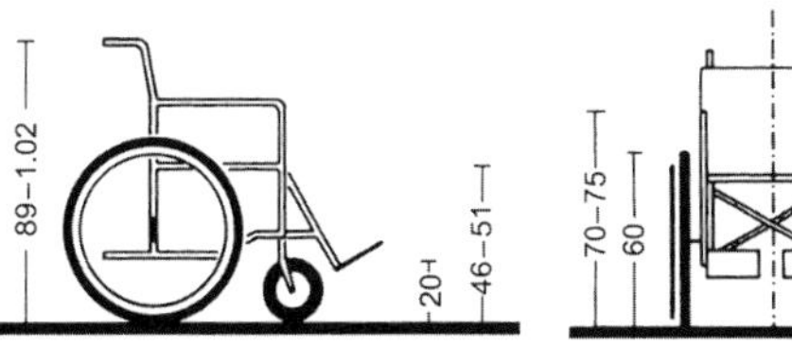

❶ Standard wheelchair, side elevation

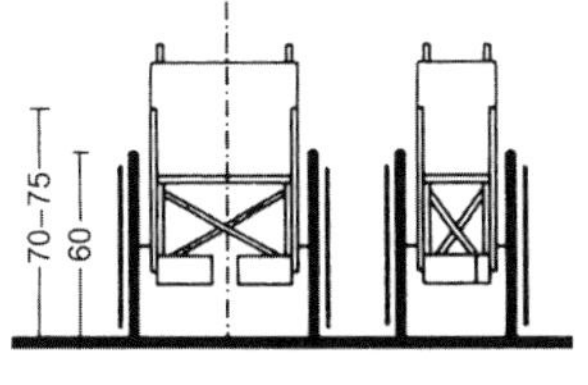

❷ Front elevation, folded

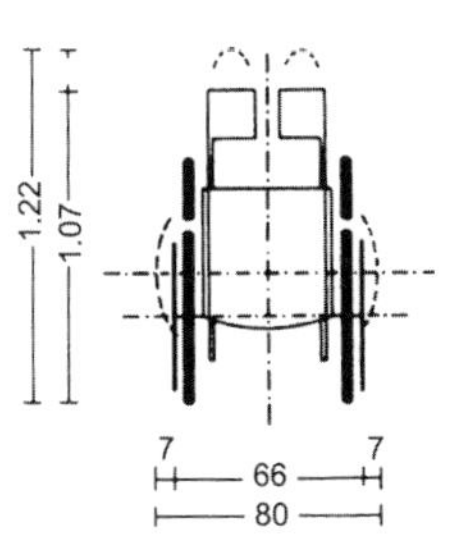

❸ Plan

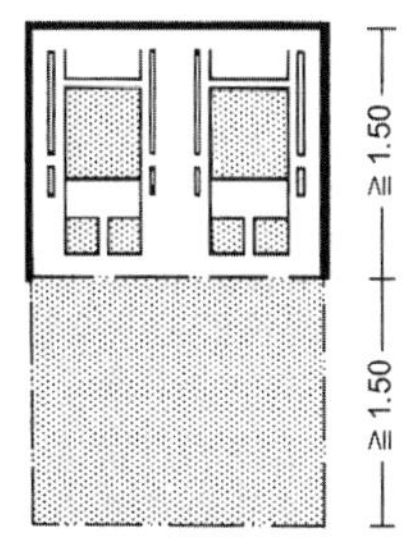

❹ Space requirement for wheelchair parking space and movement area

General design basics

Building regulations cover the design, construction and furnishing of housing, of accessible public buildings or parts of buildings, of workplaces and their external spaces. These buildings must be accessible for all people free of barriers. The users must be in a position to be almost completely independent of outside help. This applies notably to wheelchair users, the blind and visually impaired, those with other disabilities, old people, children and those of exceptionally short or tall stature.

Movement areas

Are those necessary for moving a wheelchair and are to be designed according to the minimum space requirement of a wheelchair user. The wheelchair → ❶ – ❹ and the movement area for the person → ❾ – ⓬ provide the modules for this. The dimensions of the movement area are 0.90–1.80 m and may overlap – except in front of lift doors. A depth and width of at least 1.50 m should be provided in every room for turning. (More information on movement areas is found on the following pages.)

ACCESSIBLE BUILDING

Dimensions for wheelchair users

Accessible public buildings

Accessible housing

BS 8300

DD 266

DIN 18024

DIN 18025

MBO

see also: Lifts pp. 128–134

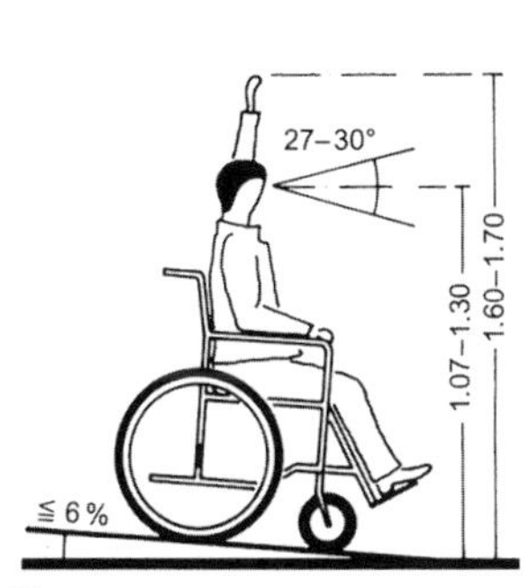

❺ Wheelchair on slope

❻ On stairs

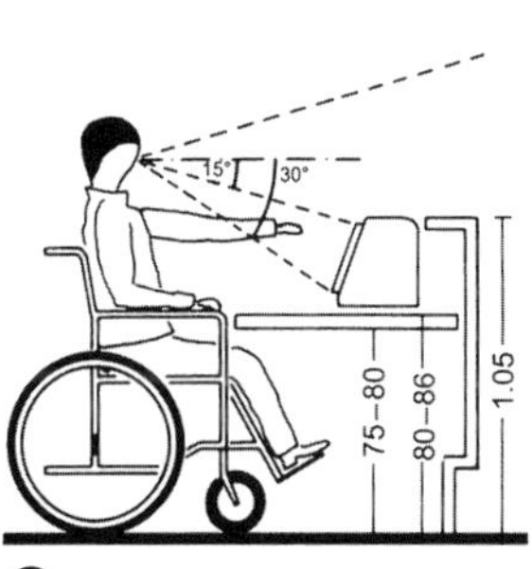

❼ Computer workplace

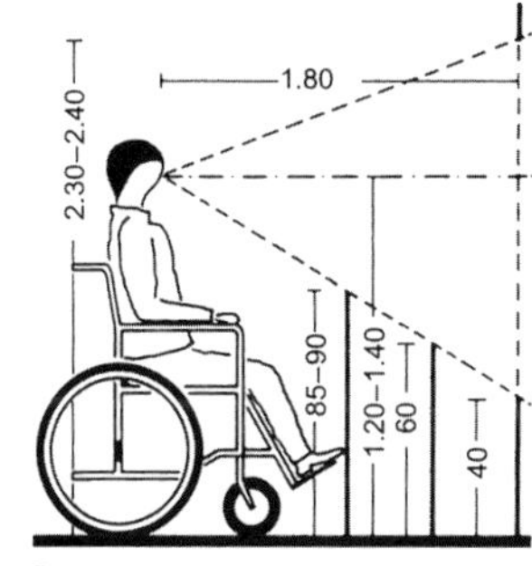

❽ At a window

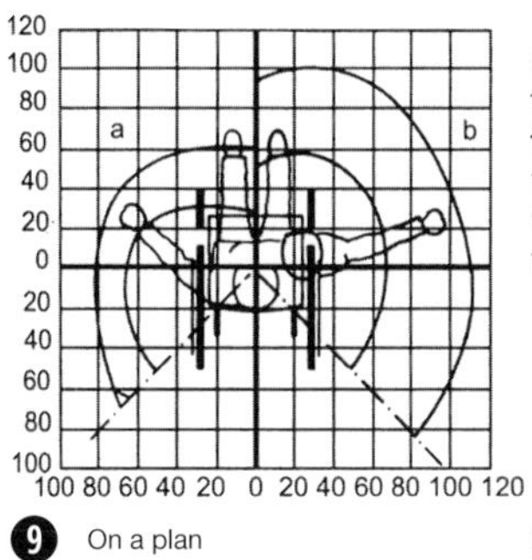

❾ On a plan

❿ From the side

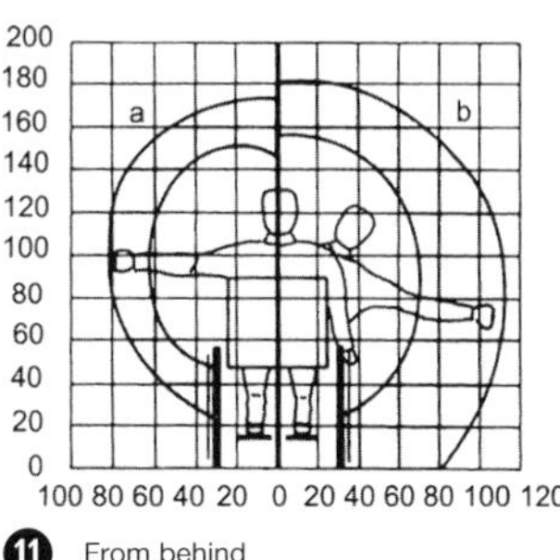

⓫ From behind

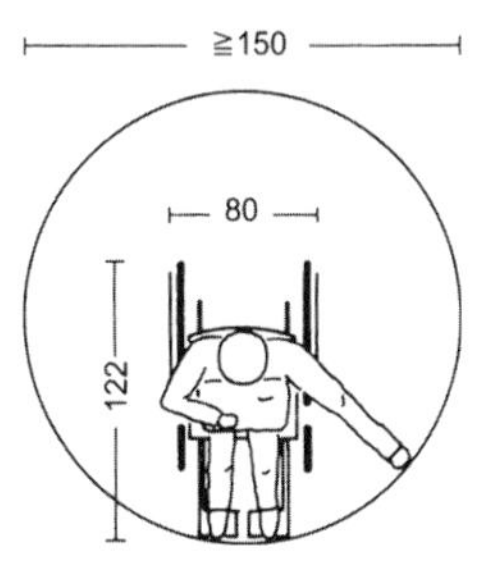

⓬ Minimum turning space

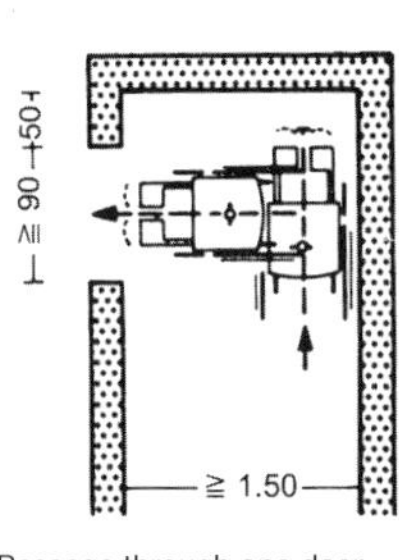

⓭ Passage through one door

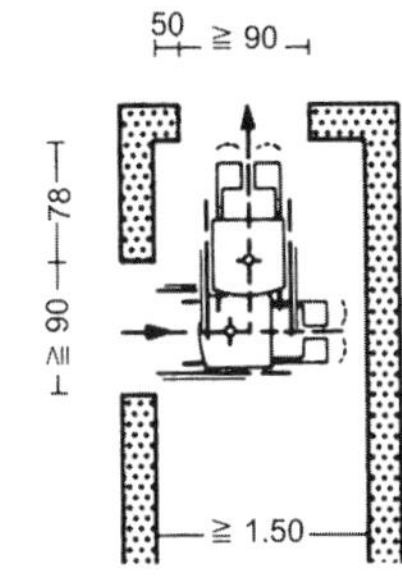

⓮ Through two doors

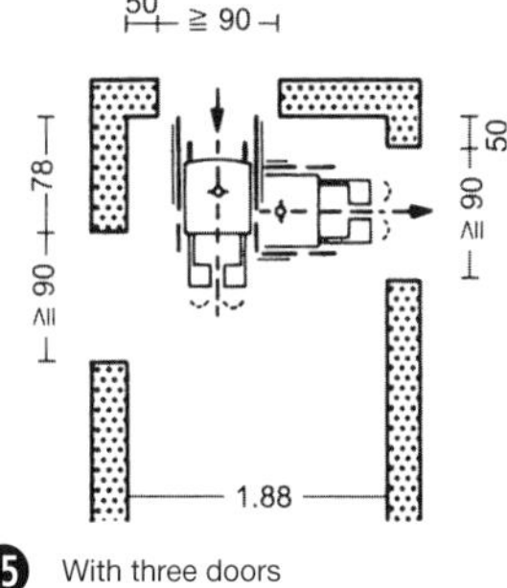

⓯ With three doors

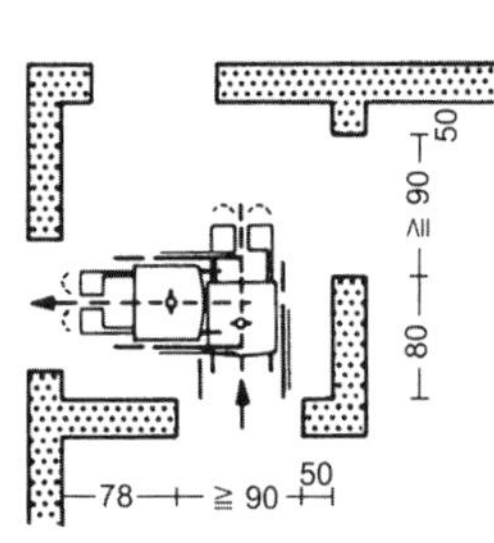

⓰ With four doors

see also: Lifts 128–134

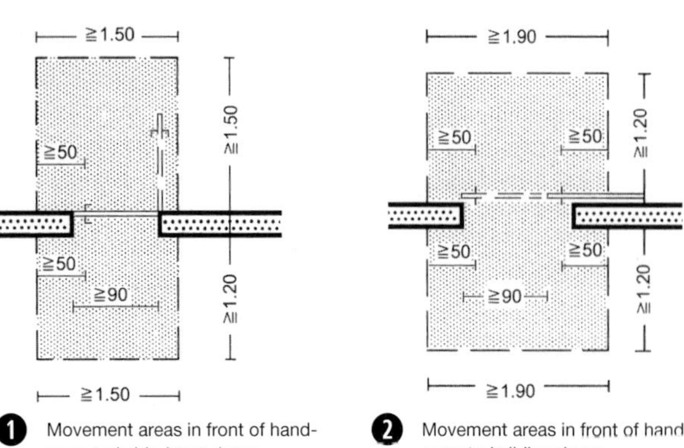

❶ Movement areas in front of hand-operated side-hung doors

❷ Movement areas in front of hand-operated sliding doors

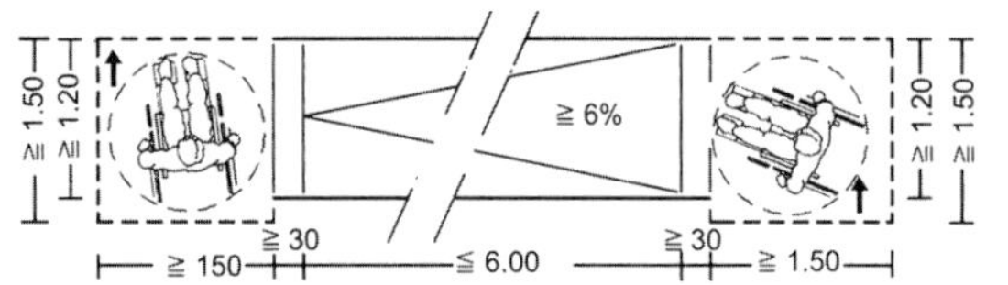

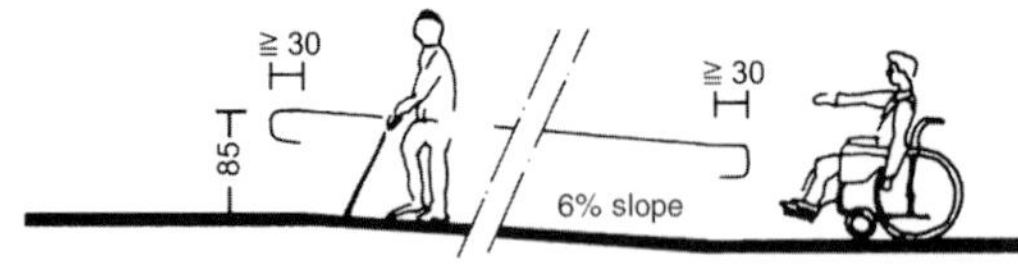

❸ Ramp

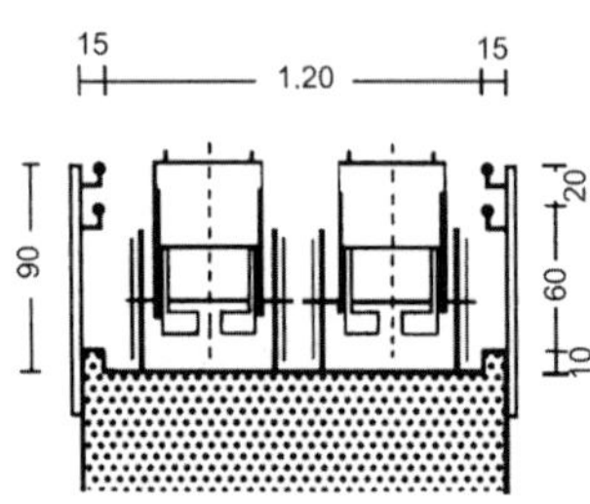

❹ Ramp in section

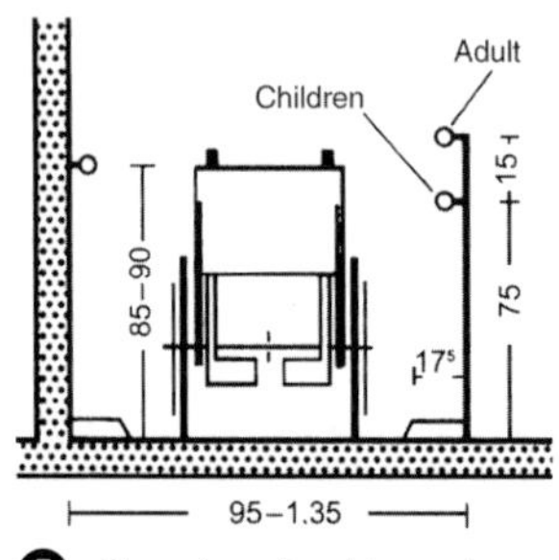

❺ Dimensions of corridors and passages

❻ Plan, with clear dimensions of the lift car and movement area in front of the doors

❼ Movement area in front of stairs going up and down

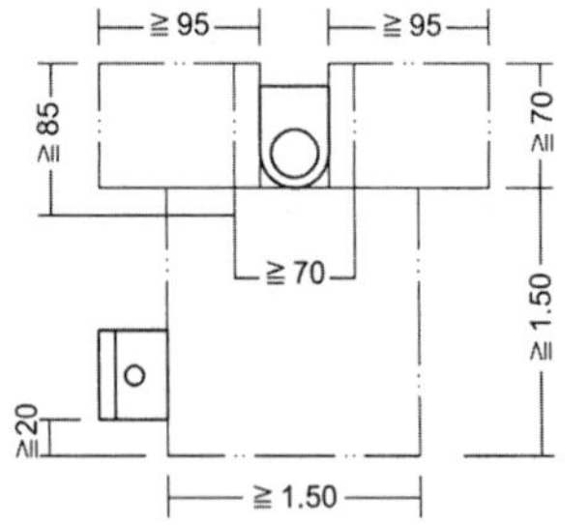

❽ Overlapping of movement areas in sanitary facilities

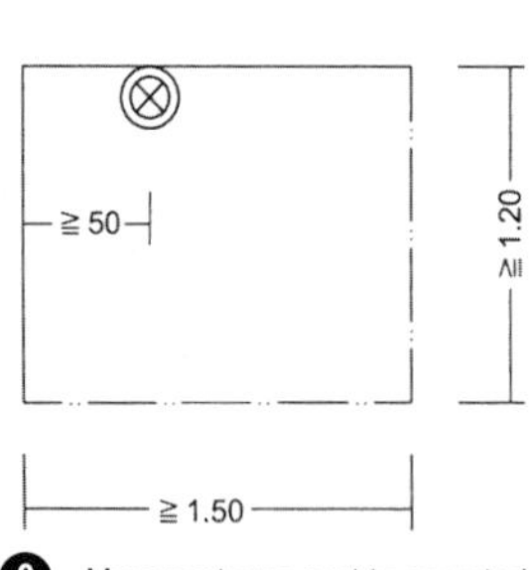

❾ Movement area next to operated facility

Movement areas must be:

min. 1.50 m wide and min. 1.50 m deep…
in every room as a place to turn, at the start and end of ramps, in front of telephone boxes, public telephones, service counters, passages, pay desks, checkpoints, post boxes, automatic service machines, calling/speaking equipment.

min. 1.50 m wide …
in corridors, main routes and next to stairs up and down.

min. 1.50 m deep …
in front of therapy facilities (e.g. bath, couch), in front of wheelchair parking places, next to the long side of the vehicle of a wheelchair user in car parks → p. 23 ❿.

min. 1.20 m wide …
alongside facilities which a wheelchair user has to approach from the side, between the wheel kerbs of a ramp and next to operated equipment.

min. 0.90 m wide …
in access ways next to cash desks and checkpoints and on side routes.

Accessibility without steps
All levels of buildings designed in accordance with the principles of accessibility must be accessible without steps, i.e. using a lift or a ramp.

Lifts
Cars of lifts must have a min. clear width of 1.10 m and a clear depth of 1.40 m. The movement area in front of the doors must be as large as the floor area of the car, but min. 1.50 m wide and 1.50 m deep → ❻. This area must not overlap with other traffic routes and movement areas.

Ramps
May have a maximum slope of 6% → ❸. If ramps are longer than 6 m, an intermediate landing of min. 1.50 m length is required. The ramp and the intermediate landing are both to be provided with 10 cm high wheel kerbs and handrails (diameter 3–4.5 cm) at a height of 85 cm. The clear ramp width must be min. 1.20 m. Wheel kerbs and handrails must project 30 cm horizontally into the platform area. There must be no stairs down in the extension of the ramp.

Stairs. The movement area next to the stairs going up and down must be min. 1.50 m wide; the tread of the first step is not to be included in the calculation of the movement area → ❼.

Doors
Clear passage width of doors ≧0.90 m → ❶ + ❷. Doors to toilets, showers and changing rooms must open outward.

Sanitary facilities
At least one toilet must be provided for wheelchair users in all sanitary facilities. The seat height should be 48 cm → ❽.

Corridors and meeting areas
Corridors and routes longer than 15 m must have a passing place for two wheelchair users of at least 1.80 m width and depth.

Wheelchair parking place
A wheelchair parking place for each wheelchair user is to be included in the design, preferably in the entrance area. Space requirement and movement area → p. 21 ❹.

ACCESSIBLE BUILDING
Dimensions for wheelchair users
Accessible public buildings
Accessible housing

BS 8300
DD 266
DIN 18024
DIN 18025

MBO

❶ Movement area by shower; alternative – bath

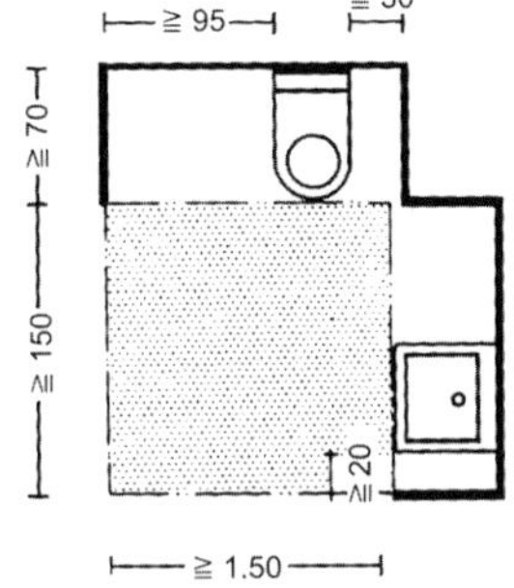

❷ Movement area in front of and next to WC and washbasin

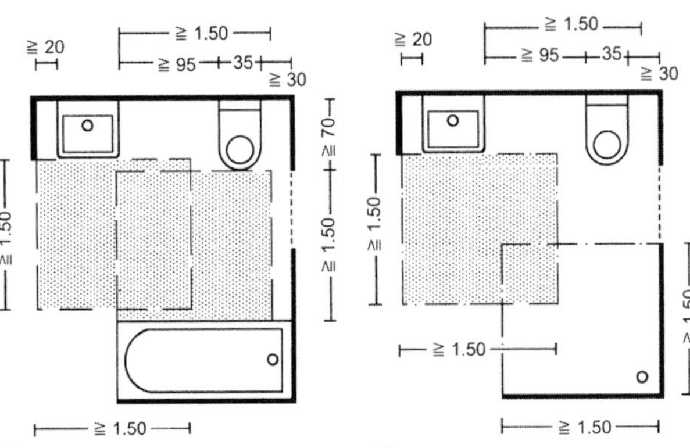

❸ Overlapping of movement areas in bathroom (with bath)

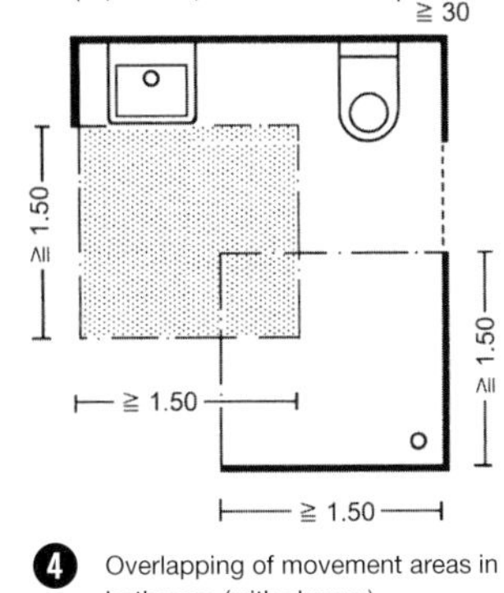

❹ Overlapping of movement areas in bathroom (with shower)

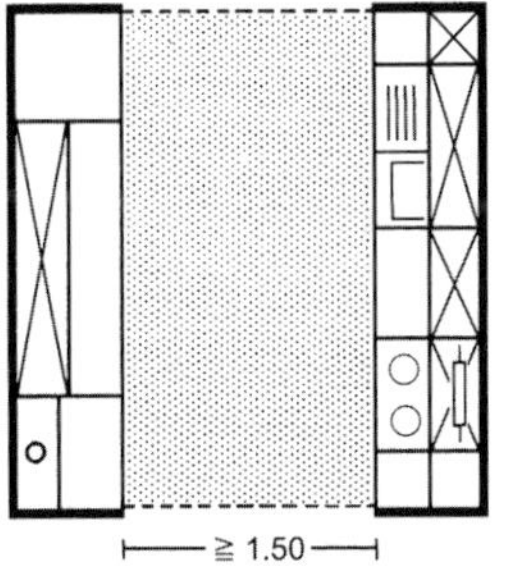

❺ Movement area in a double-space kitchen

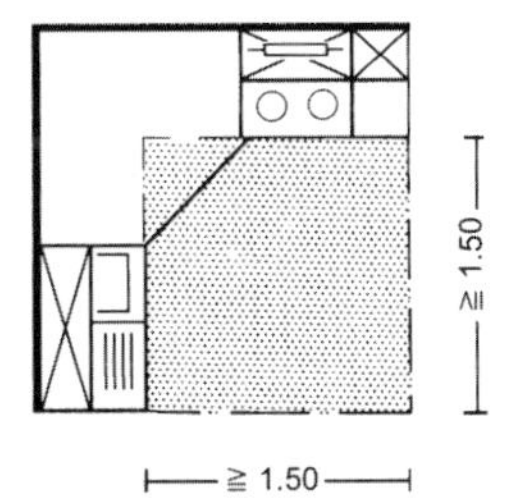

❻ Movement area in an L-layout kitchen

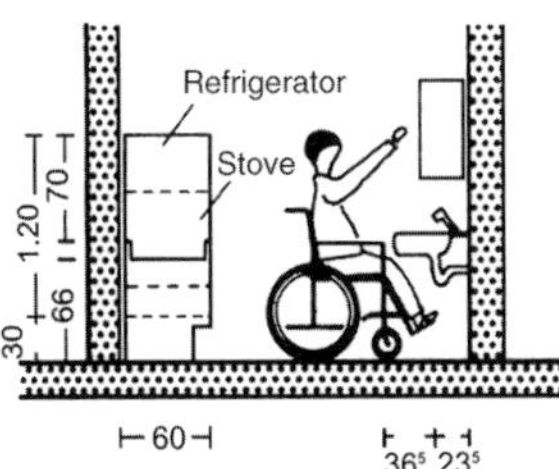

❼ Dimensions at the sink, stove and refrigerator

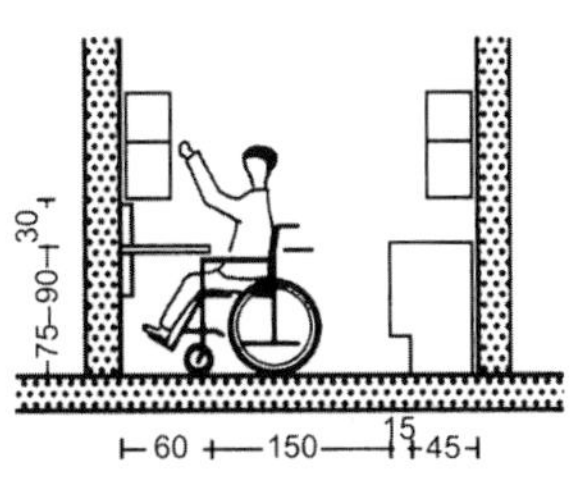

❽ Dimensions in the kitchen

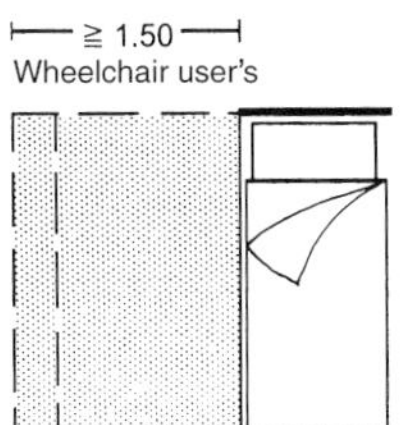

❾ Space requirement at the long side of a wheelchair user's and non-wheelchair user's bed

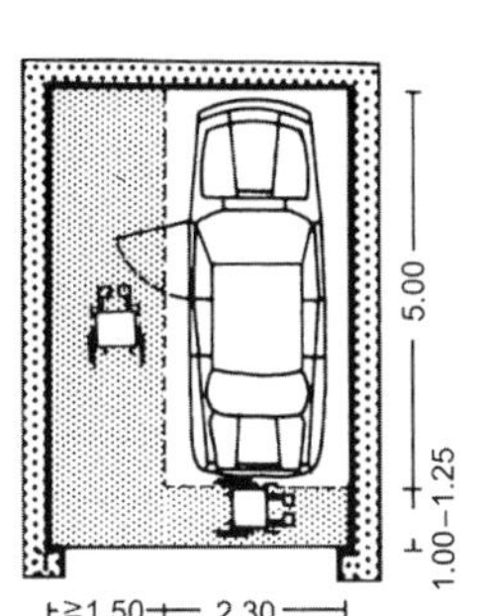

❿ Space requirement in a garage

Movement areas which must be:

min. 1.50 m wide and min. 1.50 m deep…
a turning place in every room (excepting small rooms, which the wheelchair user can use by moving backwards and forwards), the shower → ❶ + ❹, in front of the WC and vanity unit → ❷ – ❹, in an outside seating area, in front of lift shaft doors, at the start and end of a ramp and in front of the intake of a rubbish chute.

min. 1.50 m deep…
in front of the long side of a wheelchair user's bed → ❾, in front of cupboards, in front of kitchen installations → ❺ – ❽, in front of the access side of a bath → ❶ + ❸, in front of a wheelchair parking place and in front of the long side of a vehicle → ❿.

min. 1.50 m wide…
between walls outside the house, next to steps going up and down, where the tread of the uppermost step is not to be included in the movement area.

min. 1.20 m wide…
along furniture which the wheelchair user approaches from the side, along the access side of a non-wheelchair user's bed → ❾, between walls within the dwelling, next to operated equipment → p. 22 ❾, between wheel kerbs of a ramp → p. 22 ❸ and on routes within a house.

Accessibility without steps
All rooms belonging to a dwelling and the communal facilities of a house must either be without steps, or have a lift → p. 22 ❻, or be accessible with a ramp → p. 22 ❸. Door stops and thresholds at the bottom of doors should be avoided, but if absolutely necessary may not be higher than 2 cm.

Wheelchair parking place
A wheelchair parking place is to be included in the design for each wheelchair user, preferably located in the entrance area, for transferring from street to indoor wheelchair. Space requirement and movement area → p. 22 ❾.

Bathroom
The bathroom is to be provided with a wheelchair-accessible shower. The later installation of a bath should be possible near the shower. The movement area to the right or left of the WC must be at least 95 cm wide and 70 cm deep. From one side of the WC towards the wall, or furniture, there must be a distance of min. 30 cm → ❷ – ❹. No bathroom doors may open inwards.

Kitchen
The main items of equipment items like the refrigerator, stove and sink, plus the worktop, are to be arranged as close as possible to each other. It must be possible for a wheelchair to pass under the sink and worktop without limitation. For the sink, this means that either a waste fitting behind the plaster or a flat fitting on the surface is necessary. Shelf space must be accessible for the wheelchair user and no tall units should be included in the design. The horizontal reach area is about 60 cm, and the vertical activity range is 40–140 cm. The optimum height of the worktop (approx. 75–90 cm) should be discussed with the disabled person and fixed at a height to suit the user → ❼ + ❽.

Car parking place
A weather-protected car parking place or garage is to be provided for each dwelling. A movement area of 1.50 m depth should be provided next to the long side of the car → ❿.

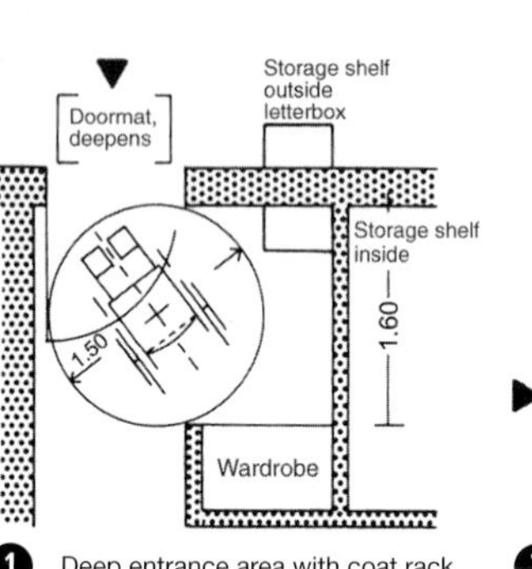

❶ Deep entrance area with coat rack

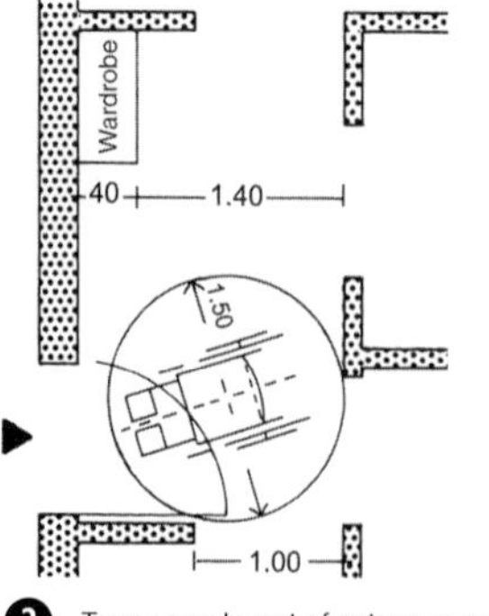

❷ Transverse layout of entrance area

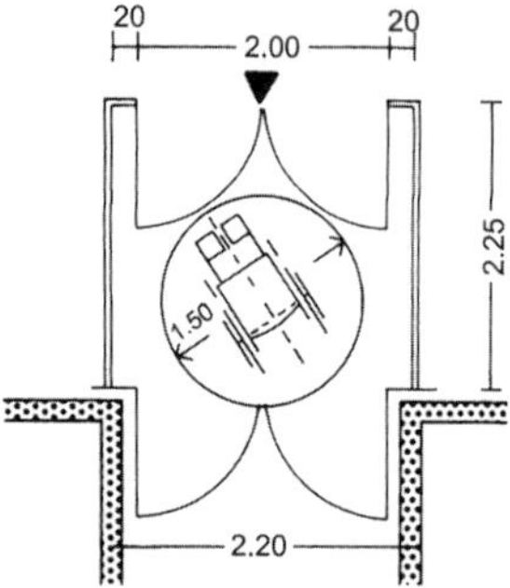

❸ Entrance lobby with double-leaf door

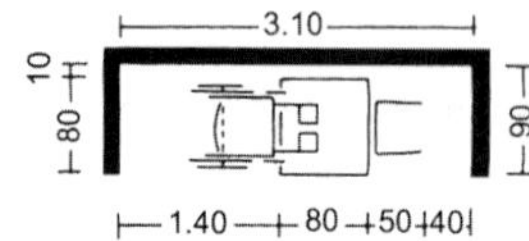

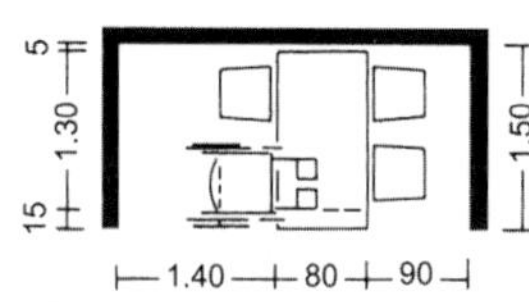

❹ Dining area layout for two or four people

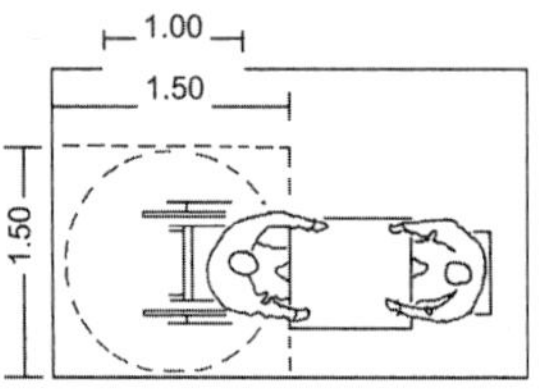

❺ Plan of open-air seating area

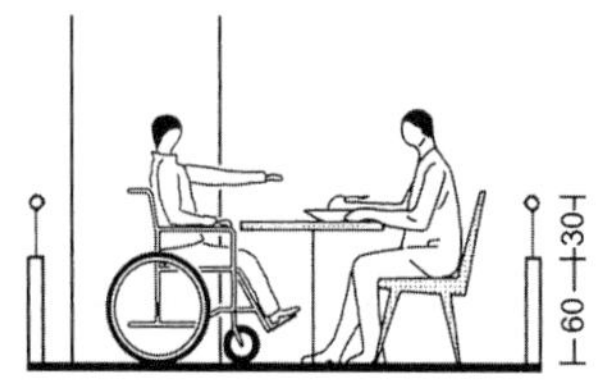

❻ Elevation of open-air seating area

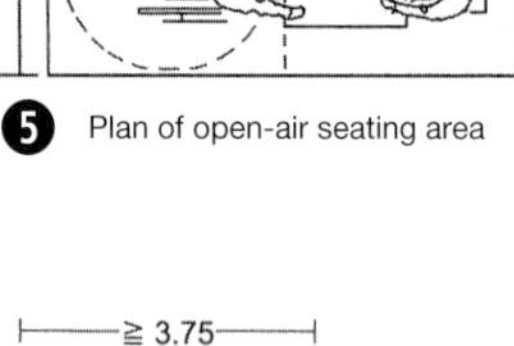

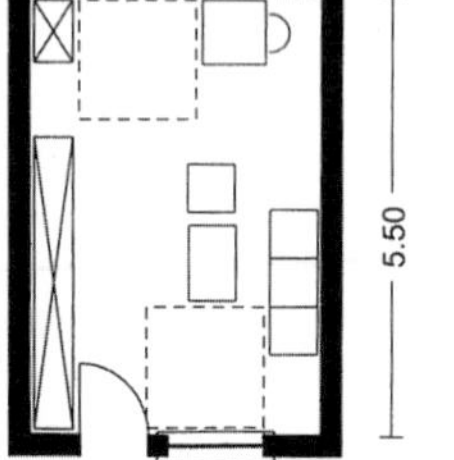

❼ Living room for 1–2 people

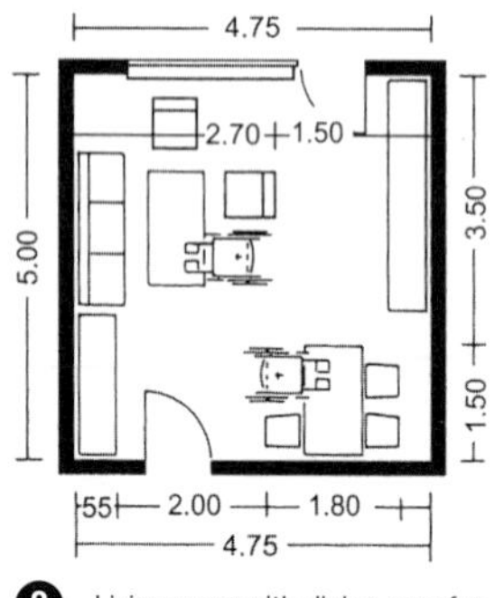

❽ Living room with dining area for 4–5 people (23.75 m²)

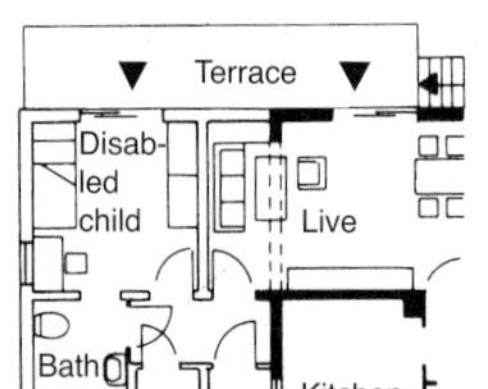

⓫ Accessible extension to two-family house; ramp to overcome level difference

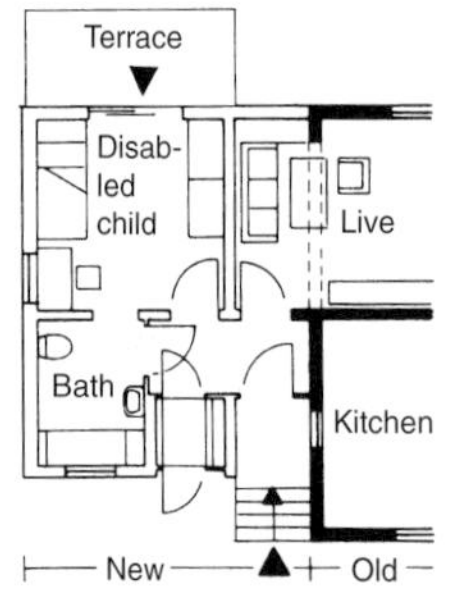

⓬ Installation of an accessible vertical lift

Housing suitable for wheelchairs

Wheelchair users must be able to travel into all the rooms of a dwelling, and into all rooms available to the residents of a house in common, and to use all facilities. The wheelchair user must be in a position to be mostly independent of outside help. This applies notably to the blind and visually impaired, the deaf and hearing-impaired, the physically disabled, old people, children and people of exceptionally short or tall stature.

In order to turn 180°, a wheelchair user requires at least 1.50 m² → ❶ + ❷. This space requirement determines the size of, and movement area in, corridors, rooms, garages etc. In residential apartment blocks, access through corridors or hallways is the most frequent arrangement. In this case, angles and corners are to be avoided as far as possible; a straight access corridor is suitable. The minimum area of an entrance hall should be 1.50 × 1.50 m, and an entrance lobby with a single-leaf door 1.70 × 1.60 m. A window with a clear view from a parapet height of 60 cm should be provided in at least one living room of a dwelling. An entry phone at the flat or house door is an important item of equipment for a blind resident.

Living area

Adequate freedom of movement for wheelchair users is important in living rooms. There should also be room for at least two further wheelchair users as visitors. For a living room with an eating area, the minimum floor area should be: in a flat for one person 22 m², for 2–4 people 24 m², for five people 26 m² and for six people 28 m²; minimum room width 3.75 m (1–2 person household).

Open-air seating area

Every dwelling should be provided with an open-air seating area such as a terrace, loggia or balcony with a min. size 4.5 m². The movement area must be min. 1.50 m wide and 1.50 m deep → ❺.

Additional living space

Additional living space should be provided for every wheelchair user if required. The floor area of a flat is normally increased by about 15 m² by this requirement.

❾ Single-room flat for wheelchair user (40–45 m²)

❿ Two-room flat (50–55 m²)

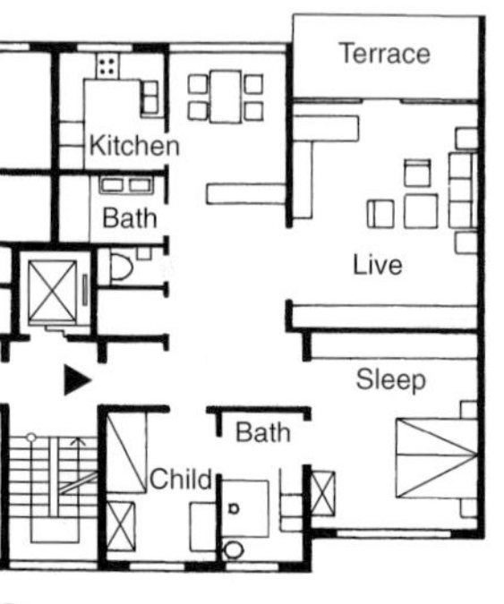

⓭ Accessible flat for three people in a block with two flats per floor

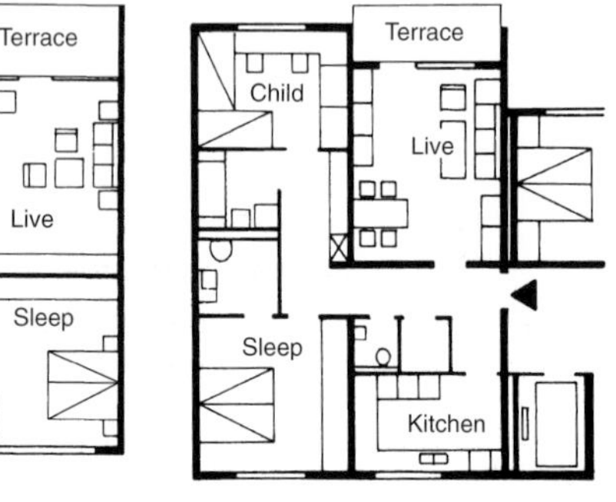

⓮ Accessible flat for four people in a block with three flats per floor

BS 8300
DD266
DIN 18024
DIN 18025

MBO

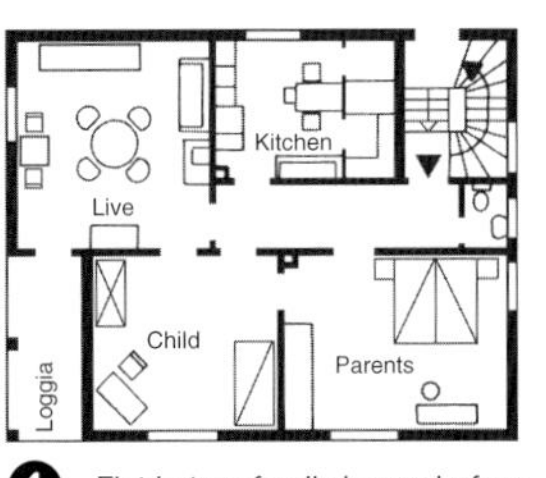

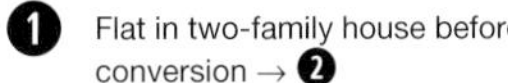
❶ Flat in two-family house before conversion → ❷

❷ Flat in two-family house after conversion for serious disability

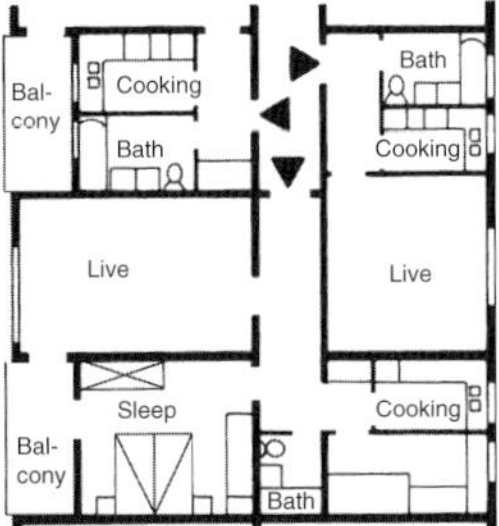

❸ 2½ living room and 1 bedroom flat before conversion → ❹

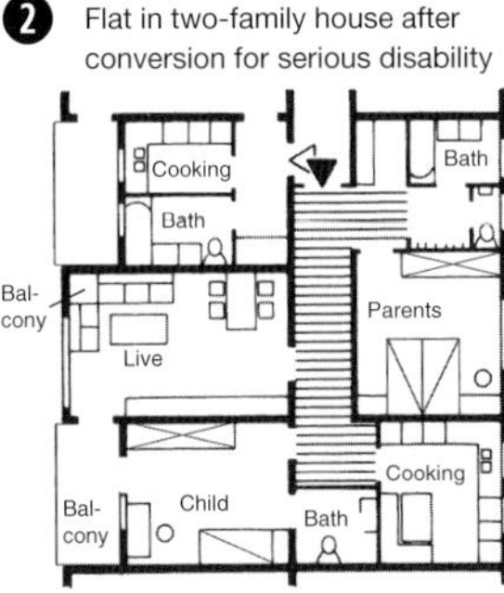

❹ One living room and two bedroom flat after conversion (for a visually impaired child)

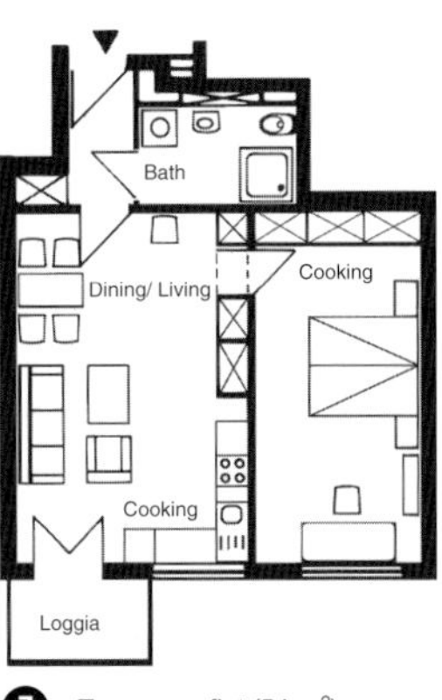

❺ One-room flat (40 m²)

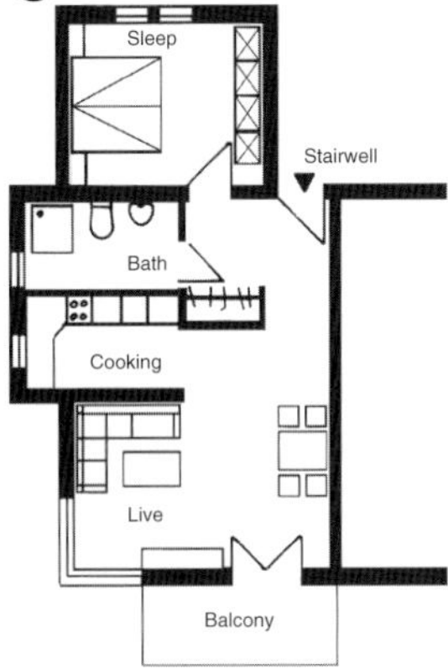

❻ One-room flat (45 m²)

❼ Two-room flat (54 m²)

❽ Flat (60 m²)

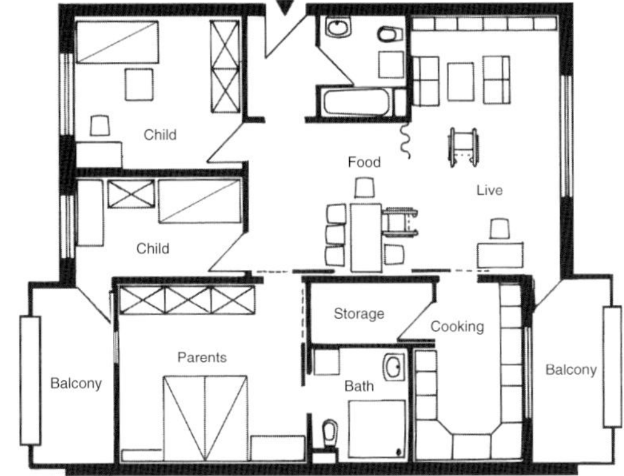

❿ Four-room flat (110 m²)

ACCESSIBLE BUILDING

Accessible Housing

Accessible building
(§ 50 of MBO – Model Building Regulations – applied at state level)

(1) In buildings with more than two flats, the flats on one floor must be accessible. In these flats, the living rooms and bedrooms, one toilet, one bathroom and the kitchen or kitchenette must be accessible with a wheelchair.

(2) Buildings which are publicly accessible, must in their parts serving the general public be capable of being accessed and used, according to their purpose, by disabled people, old people and people with small children, without outside help. This requirement applies notably to cultural, educational, sport, leisure and health facilities, offices, administration buildings and courts, sales and catering establishments, parking, garages and toilets.

(3) Buildings, according to (2), must be accessible through an entrance with a clear opening width of at least 0.90 m without steps. An adequate movement area must be available in front of doors. Ramps may not have a slope of more than 6%, must be at least 1.20 m wide and have a fixed handrail with a safe grip on both sides. A landing is to be provided at the start and end of the ramp and also an intermediate landing every 6 m. The landings must have a length of at least 1.50 m. Stairs must have handrails on both sides, which are to be continued past landings and window openings and past the last steps. The stairs must have solid risers. Corridors and entrance halls must be at least 1.50 m wide. One toilet must also be suitable and accessible for wheelchair users; this is to be indicated by a sign.

(4) Sections 1–3 do not apply if the installations can only be fulfilled with unreasonable expense on account of difficult terrain conditions, the installation of an otherwise unnecessary lift, unsuitable existing buildings or the safety of disabled or old people.

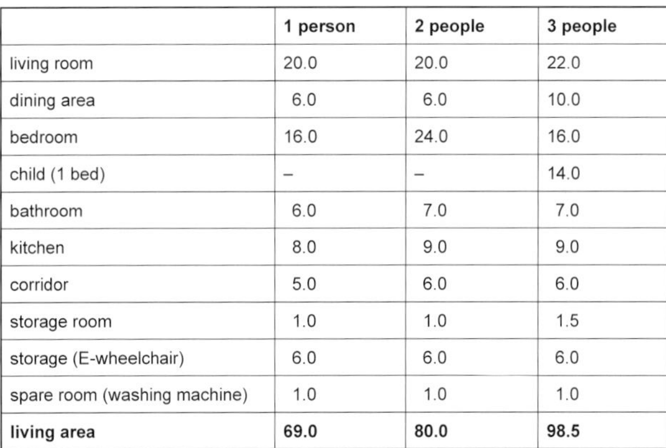

	1 person	2 people	3 people
living room	20.0	20.0	22.0
dining area	6.0	6.0	10.0
bedroom	16.0	24.0	16.0
child (1 bed)	–	–	14.0
bathroom	6.0	7.0	7.0
kitchen	8.0	9.0	9.0
corridor	5.0	6.0	6.0
storage room	1.0	1.0	1.5
storage (E-wheelchair)	6.0	6.0	6.0
spare room (washing machine)	1.0	1.0	1.0
living area	**69.0**	**80.0**	**98.5**

❾ Guideline sizes for flats with one wheelchair user – living area in m² [determination of requirements www.nullbarriere.de]

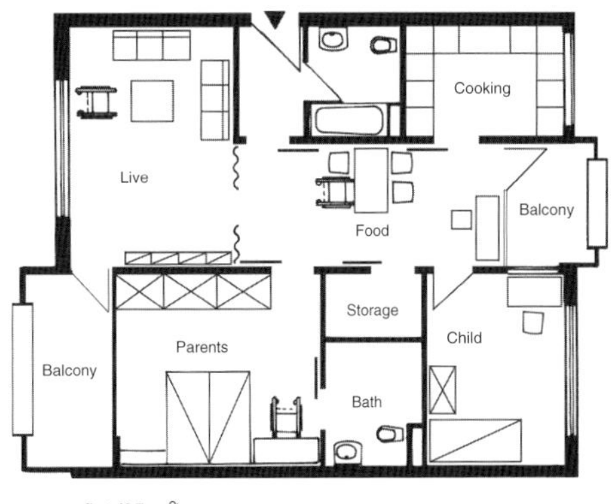

⓫ Three-room flat (95 m²)

Throughout history human beings have created things to be of service to them, using measurements relating to their bodies. Until relatively recent times people's limbs were the basis for all the **units of measurement**. Even today we can still have a better idea of the size of an object if it is compared to humans or their limbs: it was so many men high, so many ells (arm lengths) long, so many feet wider or so many heads bigger. These are expressions that we are born with: it could be said that their sizes are in our nature. But the introduction of the **metre** brought all that to an end.

We should therefore attempt to achieve the most precise and vivid possible idea of this unit. Building clients do the same when they measure out the rooms of their properties in order to envisage the dimensions shown on the drawings. Anyone who intends to learn how to build should start by visualising the size of rooms and objects as clearly as possible, and constantly practise, so that every line they draw and every stated dimension of yet to be designed furniture, rooms or buildings can appear as an image before their eyes.

We do, however, immediately have an accurate idea of the scale of an object when we see a **person** beside it, whether in the flesh or as an illustration. It is a poor reflection on our times that our trade and professional journals only too often depict rooms or buildings without any people in them. Such pictures can often create a false impression of the scale of a building and it is often astonishing how different they look in reality – mostly much smaller. This contributes to the frequent lack of cohesive relationships between buildings, because their designers have worked to various arbitrary scales and not to the only proper scale, human beings.

If this is to be changed, then **architects and designers** must be shown where these haphazard dimensions, mostly accepted without thought, originated. They must understand the relationships of the size of the limbs of a healthy human being and how much space a person occupies in various postures and in movement. They must also be familiar with the dimensions of the **appliances**, clothing etc. which people encounter every day, in order to be able to determine the appropriate sizes for containers and furniture. They must know how much **space** a person needs between furniture in the kitchen, dining room, libraries etc. in order to undertake the necessary reaching and working among these fittings in comfort without squandering space. They must know how **furniture** should be placed so that people can fulfil their tasks or relax in the home, office or workshop. And, finally, the architect and designer need to know the minimum practical dimensions of spaces in which people move around on a daily basis, like trains, trams, vehicles etc. These typically very restricted minimum spaces give the designer fixed impressions, which are then used, even if unintentionally, to derive dimensions of other spaces.

The human being, however, is not just a living creature that needs space. The **emotional response** is no less important. The way a room is dimensioned, divided, painted, lit, entered and furnished has great significance for the impression it makes. Starting from all these considerations and insights, I set out in 1926 to collect, in an organised way, the experience gained from a wide variety of professional practice and teaching.

The present data book was developed from this work, starting from the human being and providing the framework for assessing the dimensions of buildings and their constituent parts. This involved, for the first time, the investigation, development and comparison of many fundamental questions.

Current technical options have been included here to the greatest possible extent. Account is taken of common **standards**. Description is often reduced to the absolute minimum and supplemented or even replaced with illustrations wherever feasible. This should provide the creative architect or designer, in methodically ordered, brief and coherent form, the necessary information which would otherwise have to be laboriously extracted from countless books or researched circuitously by surveying existing buildings. Great value has been placed on the restriction of the content to a digest of the fundamental data and experience, with the inclusion of completed buildings only where they seemed necessary as general examples.

By and large, of course, each building commission is different and (apart, of course, from adherence to relevant standards) should be studied, approached and designed anew by the architect. Completed projects can much too easily tempt us to imitate, or at least establish conventions, which the architect entrusted with a similar task can often escape only with difficulty. If, however, as is intended here, creative architects are given only the tools, then this compels independent thinking so that they weave all the components of the current commission into their own imaginative and unified construction.

Finally, the tools presented here have not been collected more or less randomly from some journal or other, but systematically sought out in the literature as the data required for each building task. They have been checked against well-known examples of similar buildings and, where necessary, data has also been acquired through models and experiments. This was always with the intention of saving the practising architect or designer the effort of these basic investigations, so that sufficient time and leisure can be devoted to the important creative aspects of the commission.

Ernst Neufert

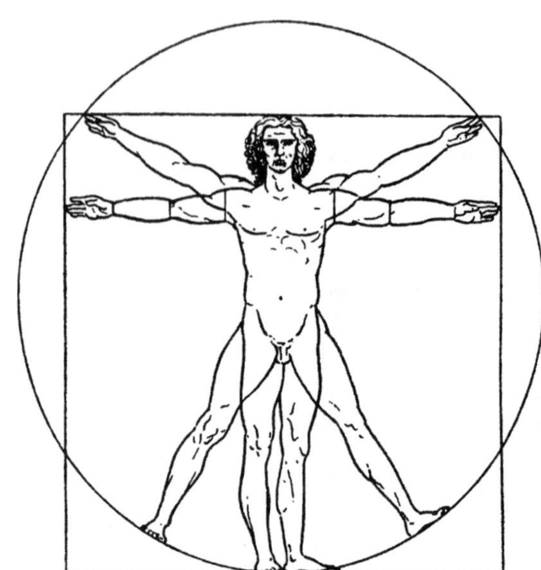

1 Leonardo da Vinci: Rules of Proportion

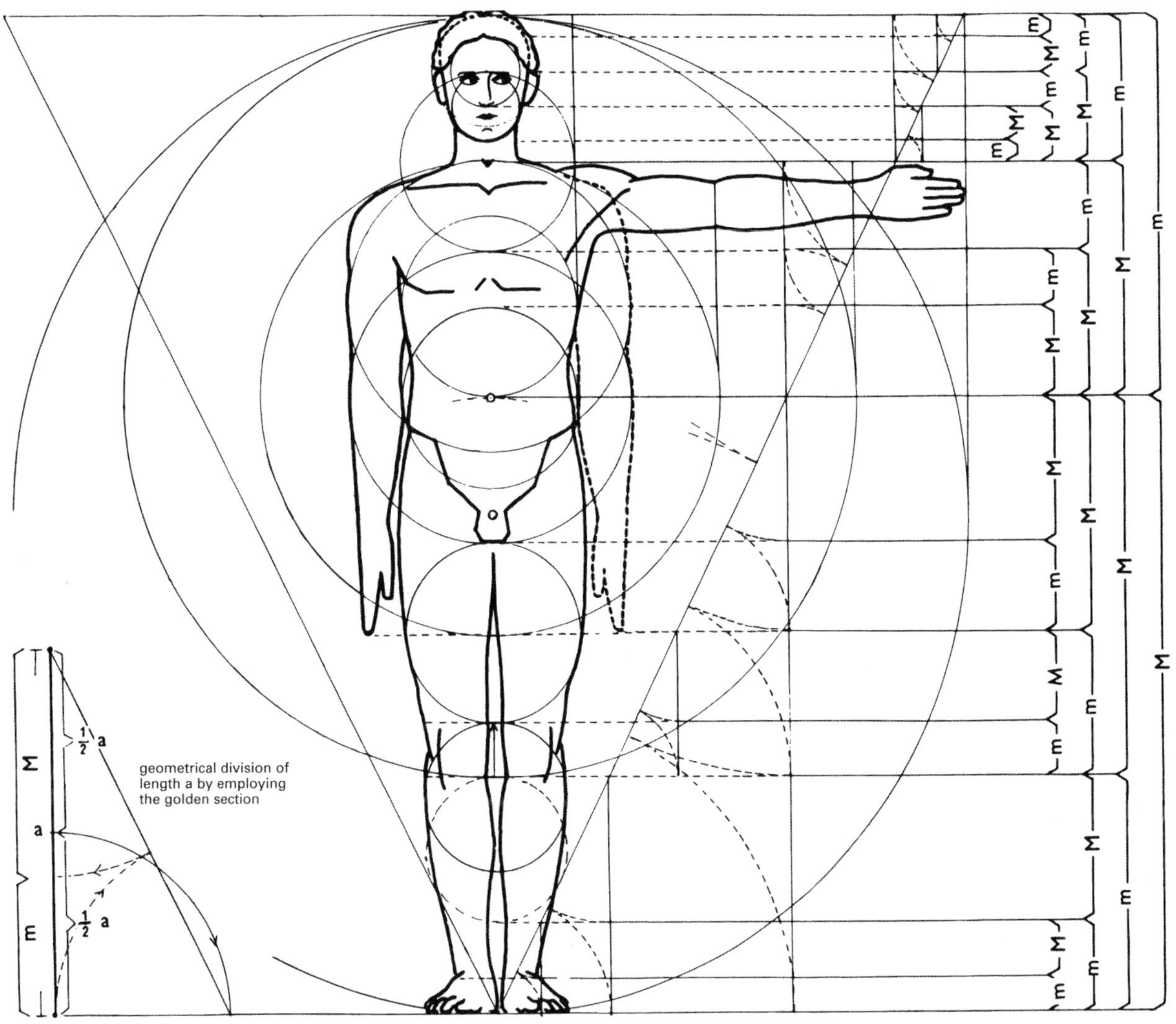

Man's dimensional relationships

The oldest known canon describing the dimensional relationships of the human being was discovered in a burial chamber among the pyramids near Memphis (about 3000 BCE). Certainly, since then, scientists and artists have been engaged in trying to decipher human proportional relationships. We know about the proportional systems of the Egyptian pharaohs, of the time of Ptolemy, of the ancient Greeks and Romans, and the Canon of Polykleitos, which was long considered the standard, plus the work of the Middle Ages and of Alberti, Leonardo da Vinci, Michelangelo and, above all, Dürer's world-famous advances.

In all these systems, the human body was measured according to lengths of head, face or foot, which were than later sub-divided and related to each other so that they were applicable in everyday life. Even into our own times, the foot and the ell (arm's length) have remained common measures. In particular, the details worked out by Dürer became a common standard. He started from the height (h) of a human being and expressed the sub-divisions as fractions:

$1/2$ h = the entire torso from the crotch upwards
$1/4$ h = leg length from ankle to knee, length from chin to navel
$1/6$ h = foot length
$1/8$ h = head length from hair parting to underside of chin, spacing of nipples
$1/10$ h = face height and width (including ears), hand length to the wrist,
$1/12$ h = face width at level of underside of nose, leg width (above the ankle) etc.

The sub-divisions extend to $1/40$ h.

In the last century, A. Zeising achieved greater clarity than anyone on this subject with his investigations of the dimensional relationships of man's proportions. He made exact measurements and comparisons based on the golden section → p. 33. Unfortunately, this work did not earn appropriate recognition until recently, when E. Moessel, an important researcher in this area, endorsed Zeising's work with detailed examinations using his methods.

From 1945, Le Corbusier also used, for all his projects, the sectional relationships of the golden ratio, which he called 'Le Modulor'. His measures were human height = 1.829 m; navel height = 1.130 m etc. → p. 33.

DIMENSIONAL BASICS AND RELATIONSHIPS

Body Measurements and Space Requirements

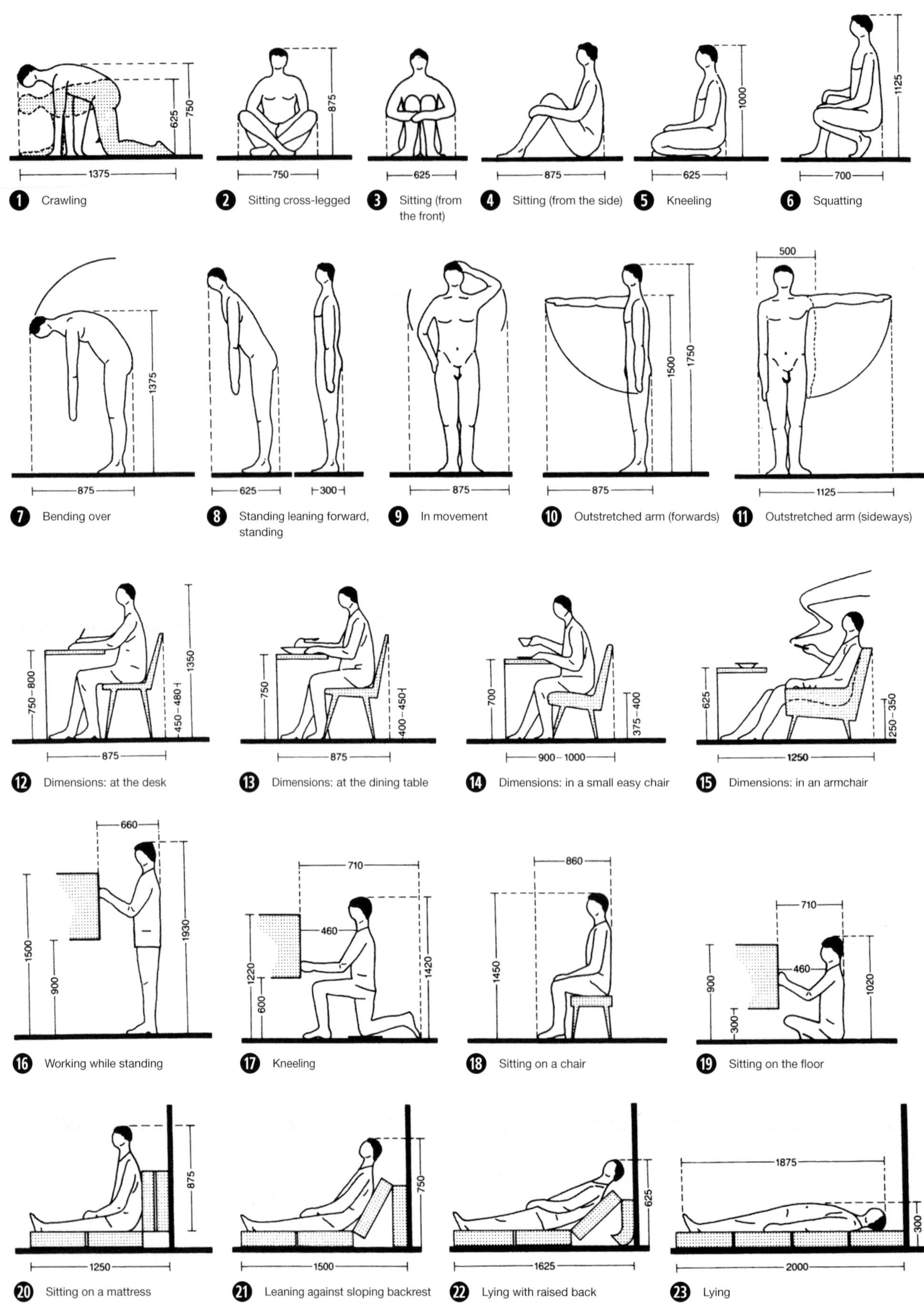

1 Crawling
2 Sitting cross-legged
3 Sitting (from the front)
4 Sitting (from the side)
5 Kneeling
6 Squatting
7 Bending over
8 Standing leaning forward, standing
9 In movement
10 Outstretched arm (forwards)
11 Outstretched arm (sideways)
12 Dimensions: at the desk
13 Dimensions: at the dining table
14 Dimensions: in a small easy chair
15 Dimensions: in an armchair
16 Working while standing
17 Kneeling
18 Sitting on a chair
19 Sitting on the floor
20 Sitting on a mattress
21 Leaning against sloping backrest
22 Lying with raised back
23 Lying

DIMENSIONAL BASICS AND RELATIONSHIPS

Man as measure and purpose
The universal standard
Body measurements and space requirements
Geometrical relationships
Dimensions in building

SPACE REQUIRED BETWEEN WALLS

In accordance with normal measurements and energy consumption

1 Between walls (≧10% supplement for people moving)

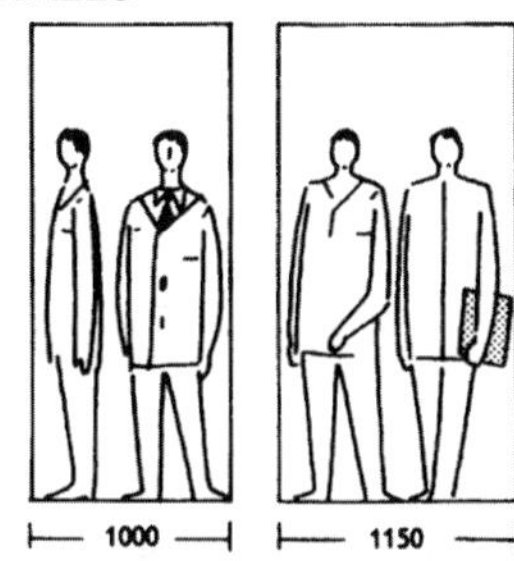

2 Two people next to each other

3 Three people next to each other

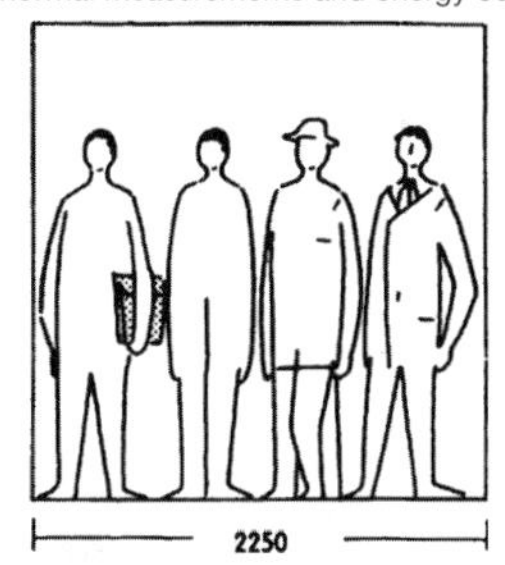

4 Four people next to each other

SPACE REQUIRED BY GROUPS

5 Closely packed

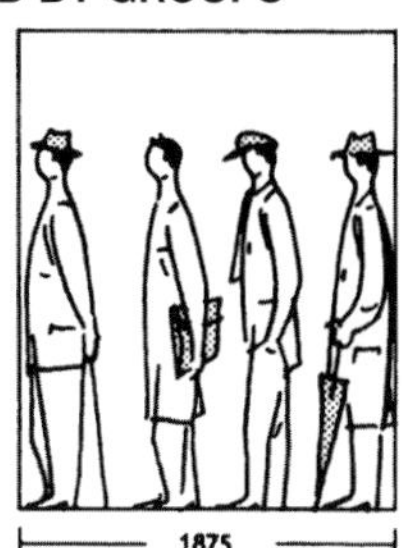

6 Normal spacing

7 Choir group

8 Longer periods of standing

9 With back packs

STEP LENGTHS

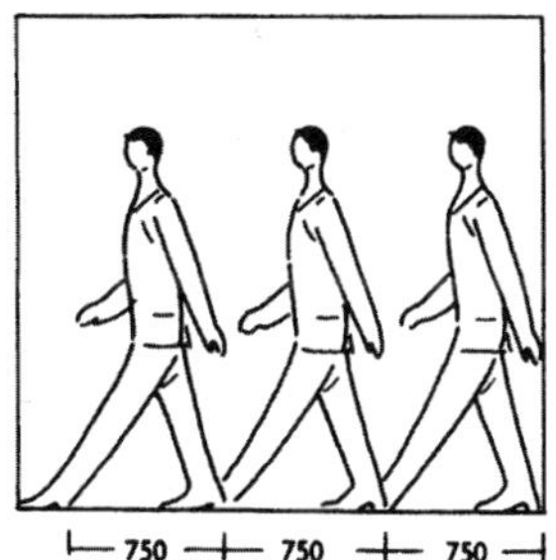

10 Walking in step

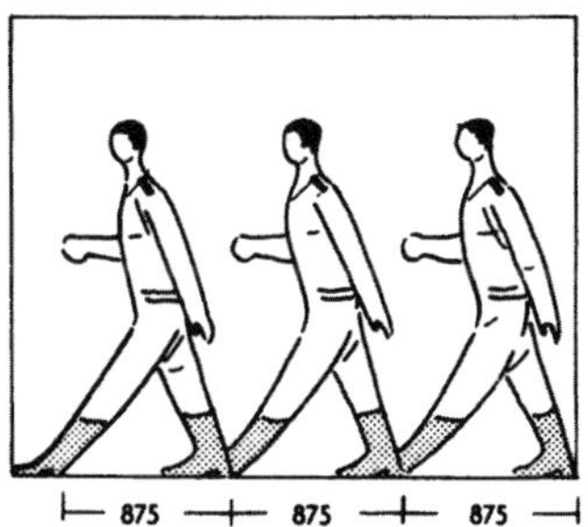

11 Marching

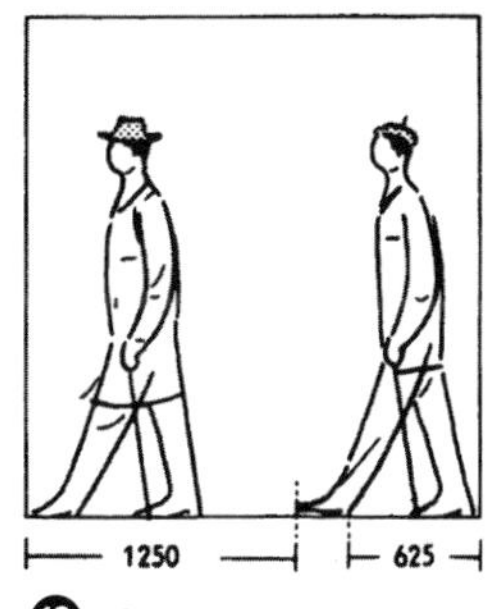

12 Strolling

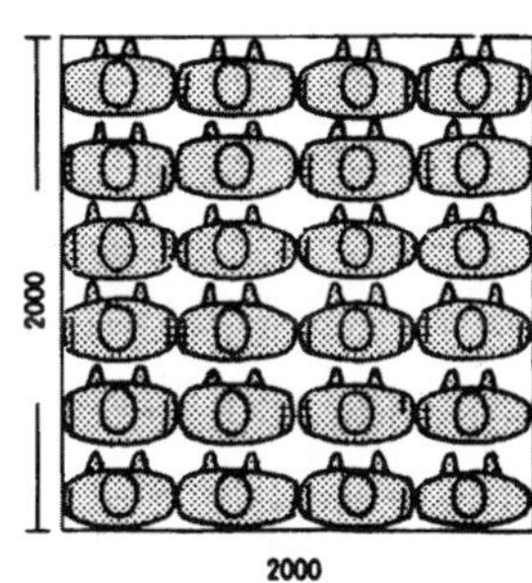

13 Max. no. people per m^2: 6 (e.g. cable car)

SPACE REQUIRED FOR VARIOUS BODY POSTURES

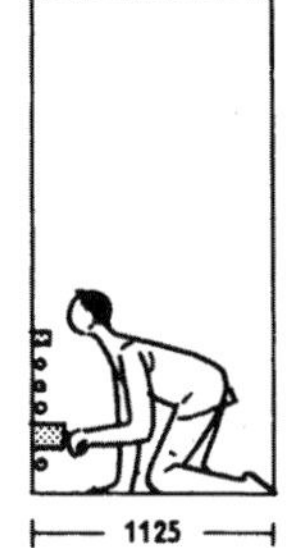

14 Kneeling

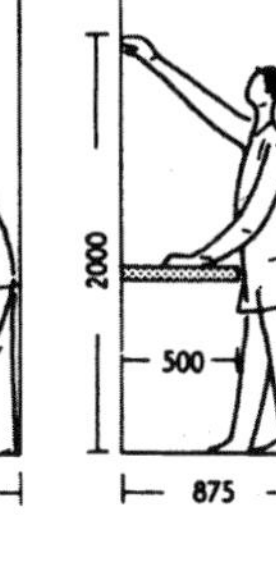

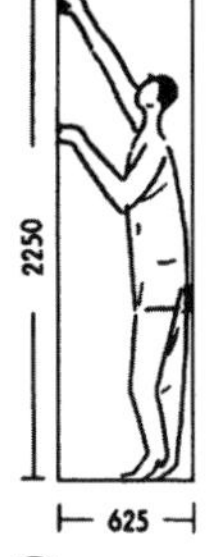

15 At the desk

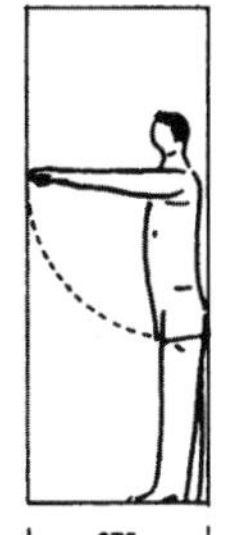

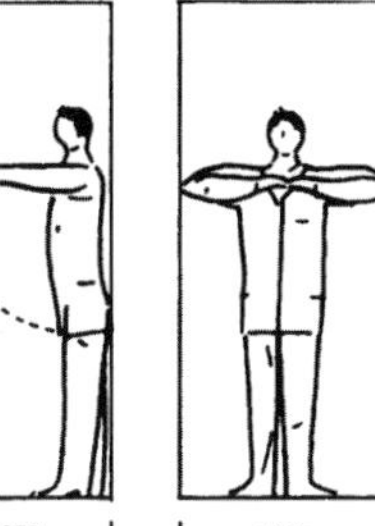

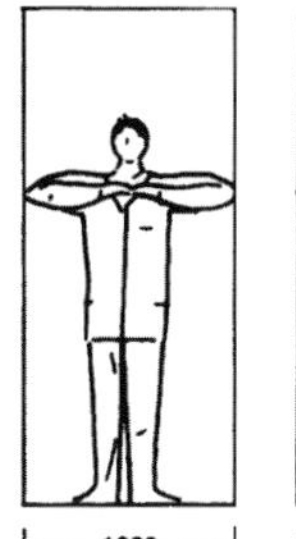

16 Stretching

SPACE REQUIRED WITH HAND LUGGAGE

17 One suitcase

18 Two suitcases

19 Two people with two suitcases each

SPACE REQUIRED WITH WALKING STICK AND UMBRELLA

20 Handbag

21 With walking stick

22 With umbrella

23 Two people with umbrellas

DIMENSIONAL BASICS AND RELATIONSHIPS

Geometrical Relationships

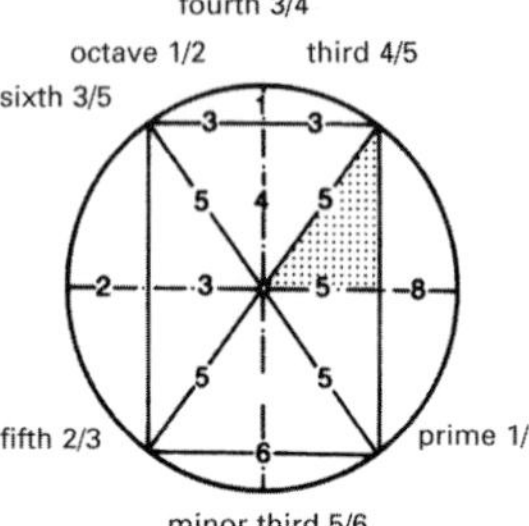

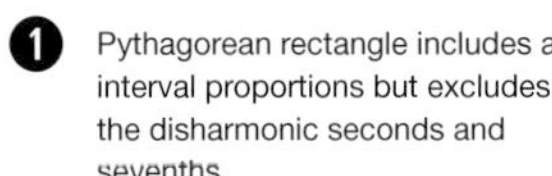

❶ Pythagorean rectangle includes all interval proportions but excludes the disharmonic seconds and sevenths

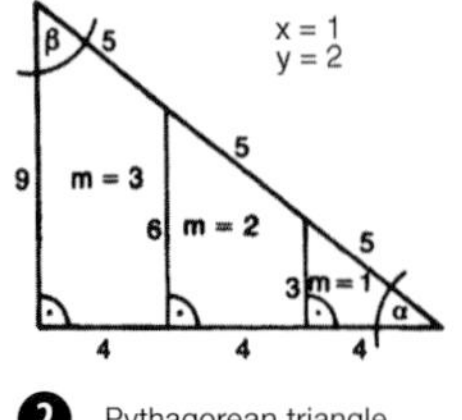

❷ Pythagorean triangle

α	a	b	c	β	m	x	y
36°87'	3	4	5	53°13'	1	1	2
22°62'	5	12	13	67°38'	1	2	3
16°26'	7	24	25	73°74'	1	3	4
28°07'	8	15	17	61°93'	0.5	3	5
12°68'	9	40	41	77°32'	1	4	5
18°92'	12	35	37	71°08'	0.5	5	7
43°60'	20	21	29	46°40'	0.5	3	7
31°89'	28	45	53	58°11'	0.5	5	9

❸ Number relationships from Pythagorean equations (selection)

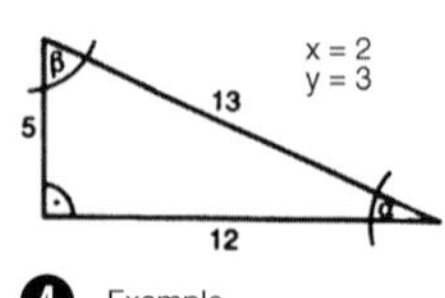

❹ Example

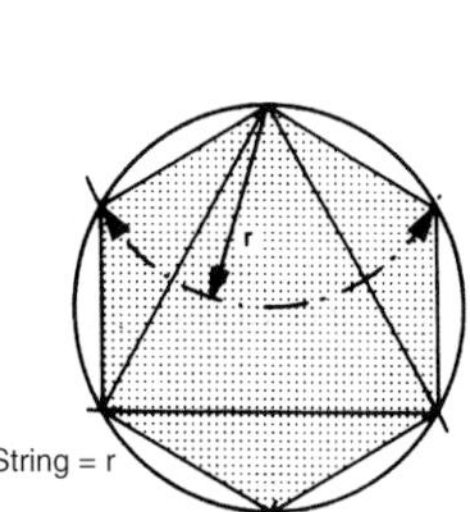

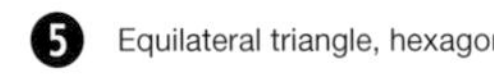

❺ Equilateral triangle, hexagon

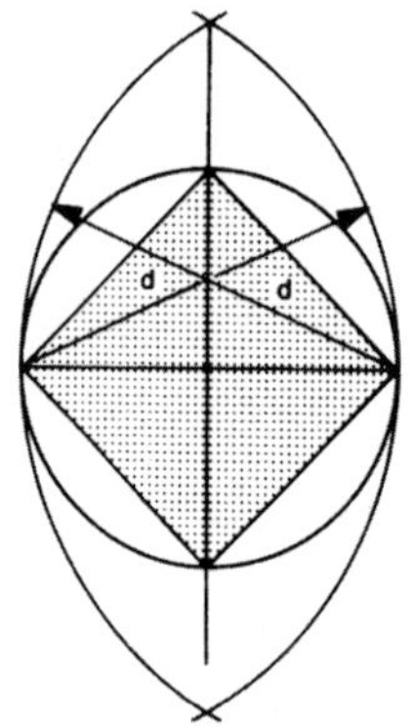

❻ Square

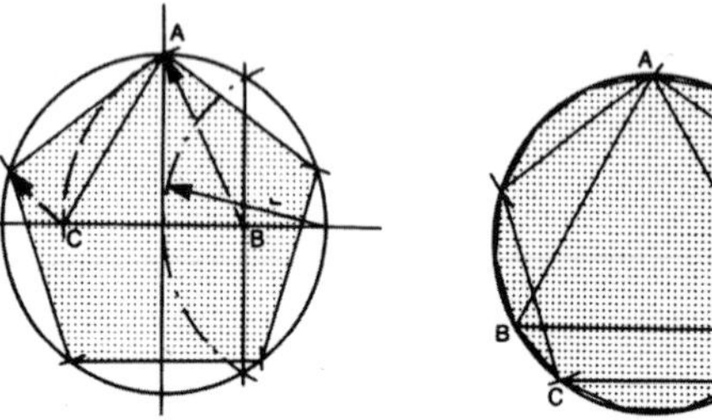

❼ Pentagon: bisection of the radius gives point B; an arc with centre B and radius AB gives point C; distance AC equals the side of a pentagon

❽ 15-sided polygon

$$AC = \frac{2}{5} - \frac{1}{3} = \frac{1}{16}$$

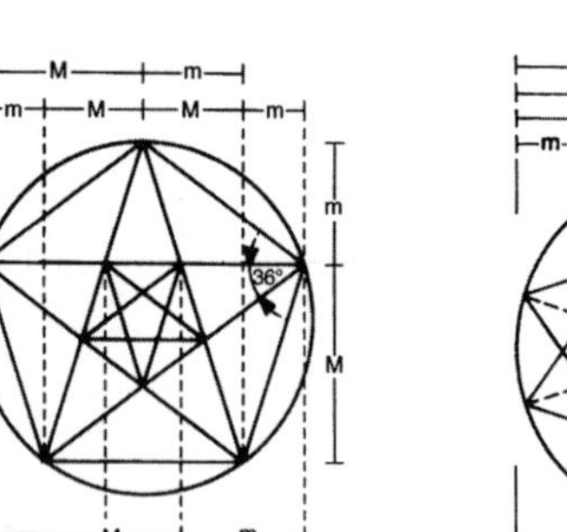

❾ Pentagon and golden section

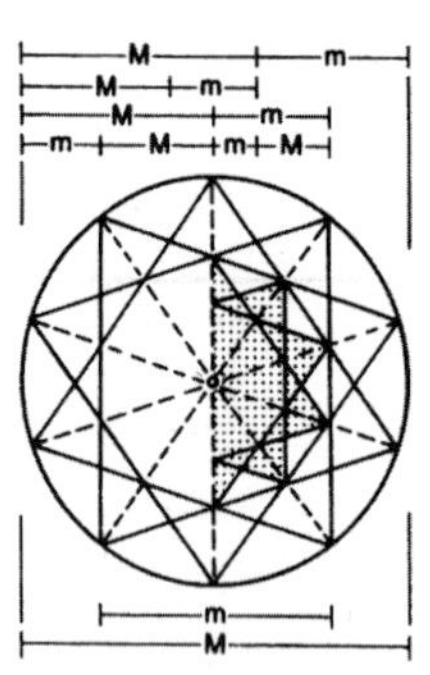

⓬ Decagon and golden section

There have been agreements about the dimensioning of buildings since early times. The first specific statements date from the time of Pythagoras, who started from the basis that the numerical proportions found in acoustics must also be optically harmonic. This led to the development of the **Pythagorean rectangle** → ❶, which contains all the harmonic interval proportions but not the two disharmonic intervals – the second and seventh.

Spatial measurements can be derived from these number relationships. Pythagorean or diophantic equations produce number groups ❷ – ❹, which should be used for the width, height and length of rooms:

$$a^2 + b^2 = c^2$$
$$a = m\,(y^2 - x^2)$$
$$b = m \times 2 \times x \times y$$
$$c = m\,(y^2 + x^2)$$

Where **x**, **y** are whole numbers, **x** is less than **y**, **m** is the magnification or reduction factor.

The geometric shapes named by Plato and Vitruvius are also of critical importance: **circle**, **triangle** → ❺ and **square** → ❻, from which **polygonal traverses** can be constructed. Each halving then gives further polygonal traverses. Other polygonal traverses (e.g. heptagon → ❾, nonagon → ❿) can be formed only by approximation or by superimposition. For example, a 15-sided polygon → ❽ can be constructed by superimposing an equilateral triangle onto a pentagon.

The pentagon → ❼ or **pentagram** has a natural relationship to the golden section, as does the derived decagon, but in earlier times its particular dimensional relationships were hardly ever used → p. 32 ❶ – ❸.

Polygonal traverses are necessary for the design and construction of so-called 'round' buildings.

The determination of the most important measurements – radius r, chord c and height of a triangle h – is shown in → ⓭ – ⓮ → p. 32.

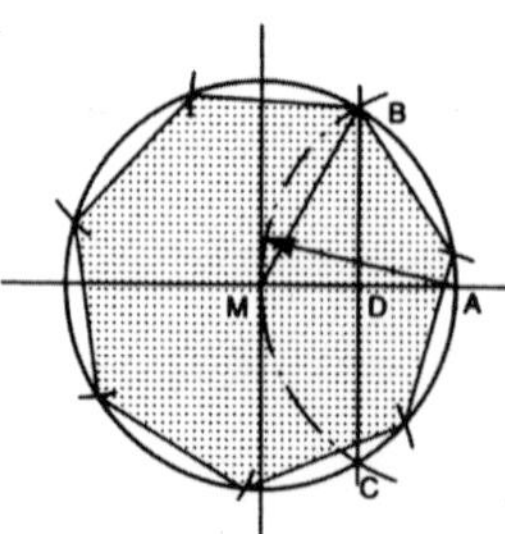

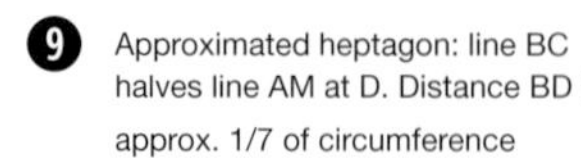

❾ Approximated heptagon: line BC halves line AM at D. Distance BD is approx. 1/7 of circumference

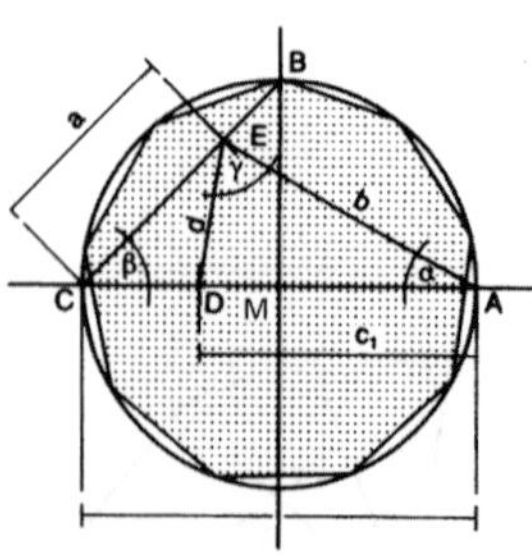

❿ Approximated nonagon: arc centred on A with radius AB gives point D on line AC. Arc centred on C with radius CM gives point E on arc BD. Distance DE is approx. 1/9 of circumference

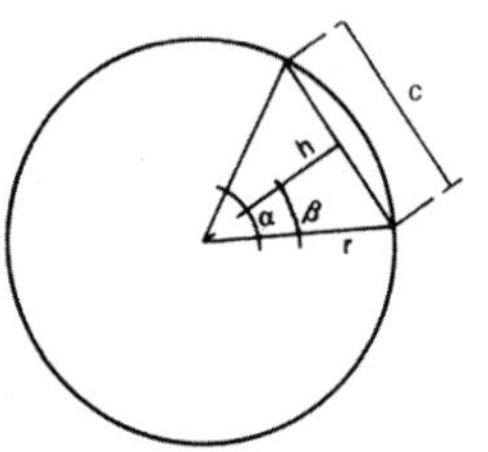

⓭ Calculation of dimensions in a polygonal traverse → p. 34

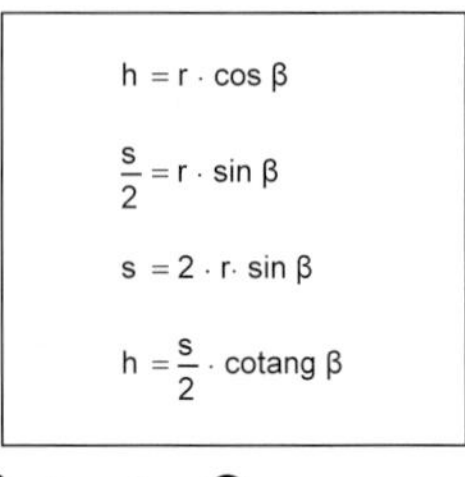

$$h = r \cdot \cos\beta$$
$$\frac{s}{2} = r \cdot \sin\beta$$
$$s = 2 \cdot r \cdot \sin\beta$$
$$h = \frac{s}{2} \cdot \text{cotang}\,\beta$$

⓮ Formula → ⓭

DIMENSIONAL BASICS AND RELATIONSHIPS

Geometrical Relationships

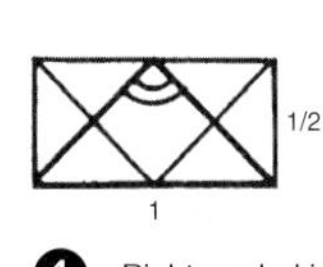

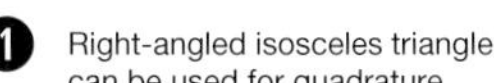
❶ Right-angled isosceles triangle: can be used for quadrature

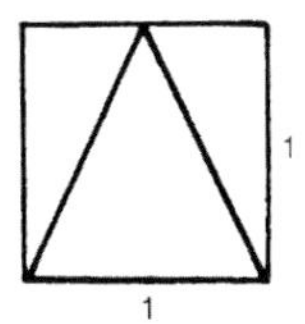

❷ Triangle (base = height)

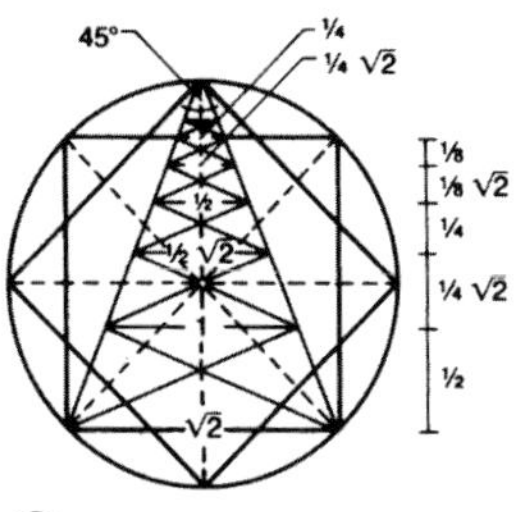

❸ π/4 triangle (A. v. Drach)

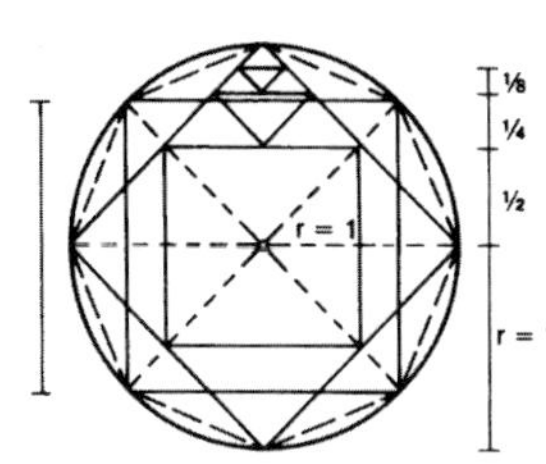

❹ Squares developed from the octagon → ❹ – ❻

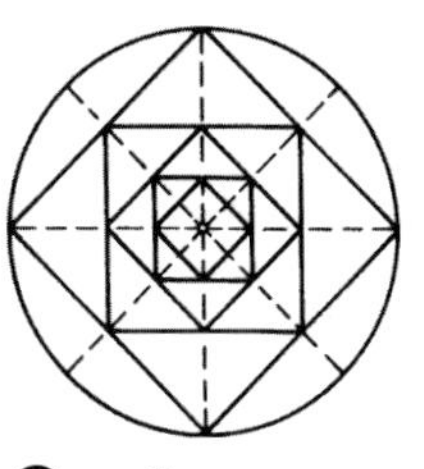
❺ → ❹

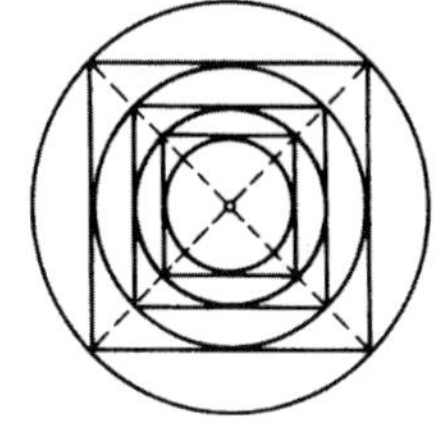
❻ → ❹

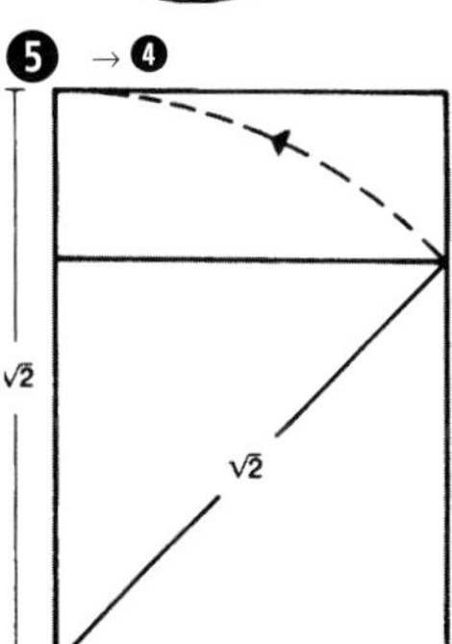

❼ 1:√2 rectangle

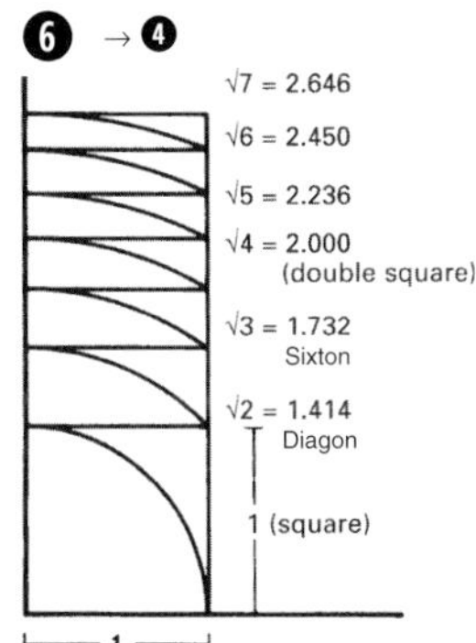

❽ Hierarchy of square roots

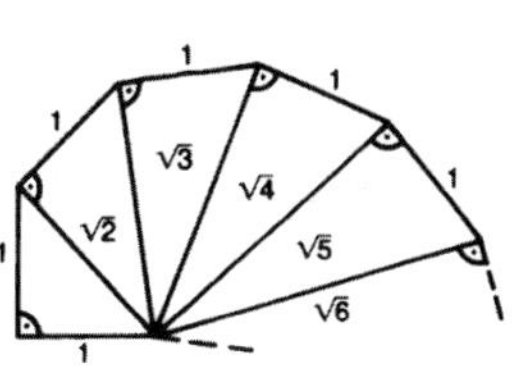

❾ Relationship between square roots

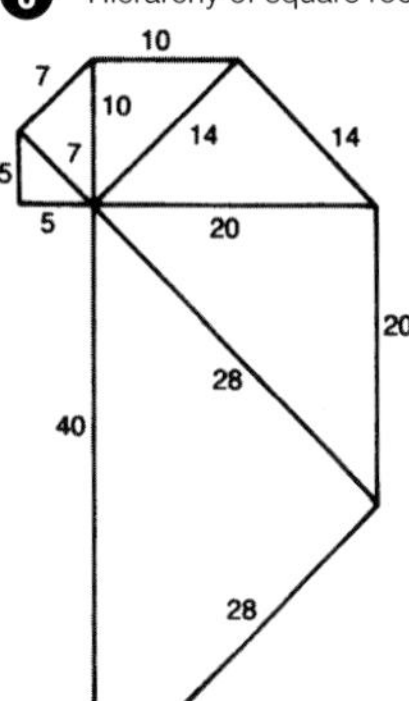

❿ Related numbers as approximation of √2 ('snail')

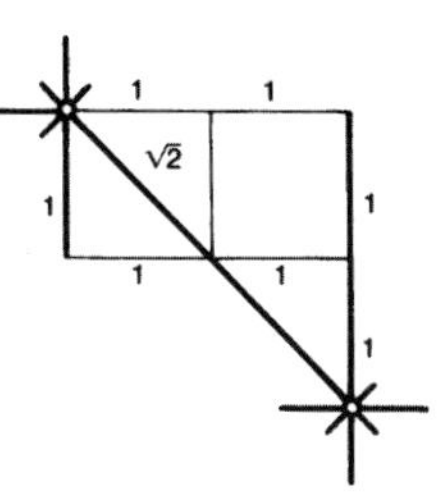

⓫ Examples of non-rectangular coordination → p. 34 MERO space frames: based on √2 and√3

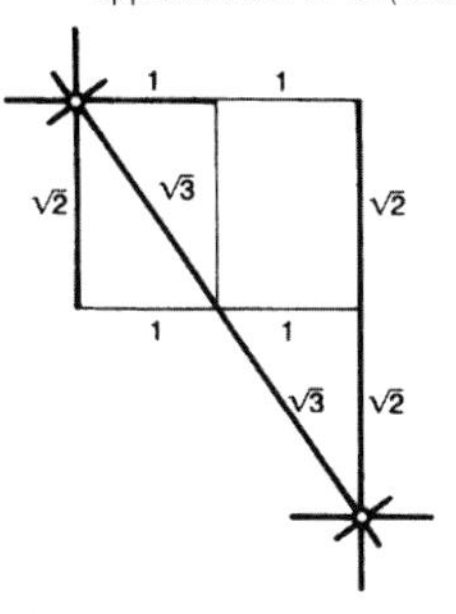

⓬ √3

A right-angled isosceles **triangle** (two sides of equal length), with a relationship of baseline to height of 2:1, can be used for **quadrature** (the process of constructing a square of equal area to a given shape) → ❶. An isosceles triangle with the base and height forming two sides of a square was used successfully by the master cathedral builder Knauth to determine the dimensional relationships of the cathedral in Strasbourg → ❷.

The π/4 triangle of A. v. Drach → ❸ is rather more pointed than that described above because its height is determined by the point of the slewed square. It was used successfully by its inventor for details and devices.

The investigations of L. R. Spitzenpfeil into a number of old buildings have discovered octagonal relationships. These are based on the so-called **diagonal triangle**, where the height of the triangle is the diagonal of the square constructed over half of the base → ❹ – ❻. The sides of the rectangle formed from the diagonal triangle → ❼ have a ratio of 1:√2, so all halving or doubling of the rectangle produces the same ratio of 1:√2. This was used as the basis for the **ISO A series paper formats** → p. 4. Geometrical progressions in this relationship are produced by the hierarchies inside an octagon → ❹ – ❻ and the hierarchy of the square roots of numbers 1–7 → ❽.

The relationship between the square roots of whole numbers is shown in → ❾. The factorisation procedure permits the application of square roots for the installation of non-rectangular building elements. Building from approximated values for square numbers, Mengeringhausen developed the **MERO space frame**. The principle is the so-called 'snail' → ❿ – ⓬. The imprecision of the right angle is compensated by the screw connections of the rods at the nodes. A different approximate calculation of the square roots of whole numbers √n for non-rectangular building elements is offered by continued fractions (→ p. 33) according to the formula:

$$G = \sqrt{n} = 1 + \frac{n-1}{1+G} \rightarrow ⓭.$$

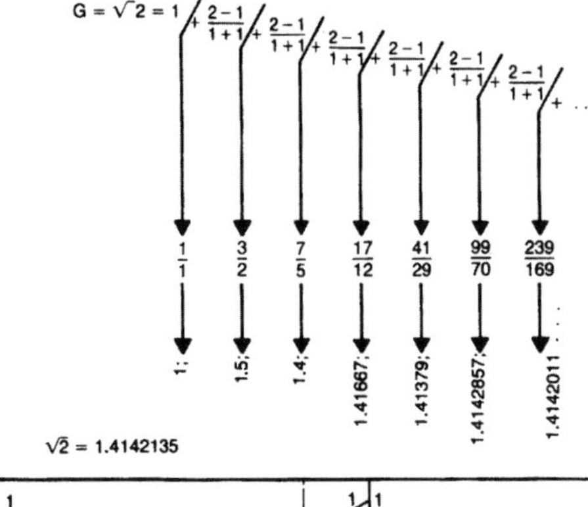

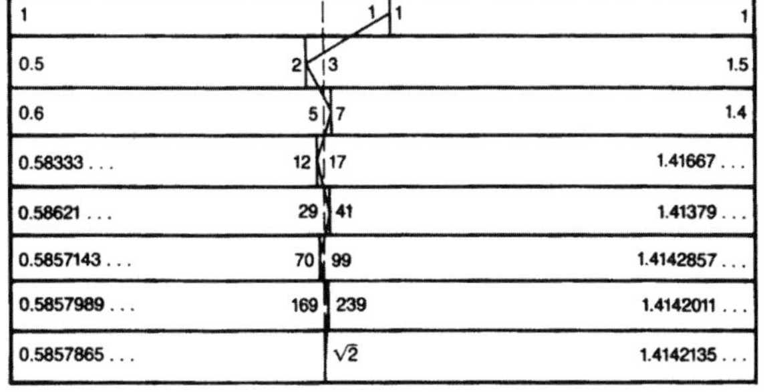

1	1	1	1
0.5	2	3	1.5
0.6	5	7	1.4
0.58333 . . .	12	17	1.41667 . . .
0.58621 . . .	29	41	1.41379 . . .
0.5857143 . . .	70	99	1.4142857 . . .
0.5857989 . . .	169	239	1.4142011 . . .
0.5857865 . . .		√2	1.4142135 . . .

⓭ Continued fractions of √2

DIMENSIONAL BASICS AND RELATIONSHIPS
Man as measure and purpose
The universal standard
Body measurements and space requirements
Geometrical relationships
Dimensions in building

DIMENSIONAL BASICS AND RELATIONSHIPS

Geometrical Relationships

The use of geometrical and dimensional relationships based on the previous information was described by Vitruvius: according to his investigations, the Roman theatre, for example, is based on a triangle rotated four times → ❶, and the Greek theatre on a square rotated three times → ❷. Both constructions result in a dodecagon, which is recognisable on the stairs.

Moessel claims to have verified dimensional relationships according to the golden ratio, although this is unlikely → ❹. The only Greek theatre based on a pentagon is in Epidaurus → ❸. The design principle of the **golden** (holy, divine) **section** (ratio, mean) was applied in a Roman residential quarter excavated in Ostia Antica, the ancient harbour of Rome → ❺ – ❽. This principle is based on the bisection of the diagonals of a square. If the points at which the arcs (radius $\sqrt{2}/2$) intersect the sides of the square are joined up, this produces a nine-part grid. Its centre is the square of the golden section. The arc **AB** is with up to 0.65% deviation the same length as the diagonal **CD** of the original halved square. The golden section therefore represents an approximate method for squaring the circle. The entire complex at Ostia, from layout to fitting out details, was based on this ratio.

Palladio, in his four books on architecture, provides a geometrical key based on the work of Pythagoras. He used the same spatial relationships (circle, triangle, square etc.) and harmonies for his buildings → ❾ – ❿.

Similar laws of proportion are also expressed in clear rules by the ancient cultures of the East. The Indians with their 'Manasara', the Chinese with their modulation according to the 'Toukou', and above all the Japanese with their 'Kiwariho' methods created building systems which ensure traditional development and offer immense economic advantages → ⓫.

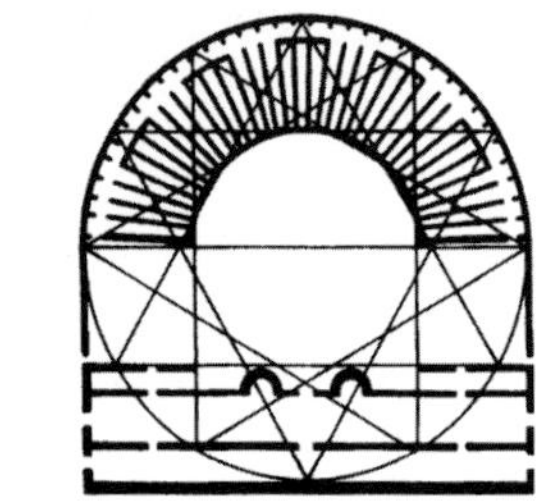
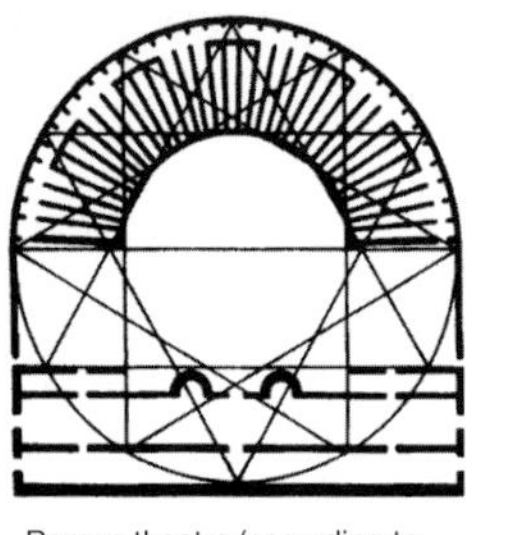

❶ Roman theatre (according to Vitruvius)

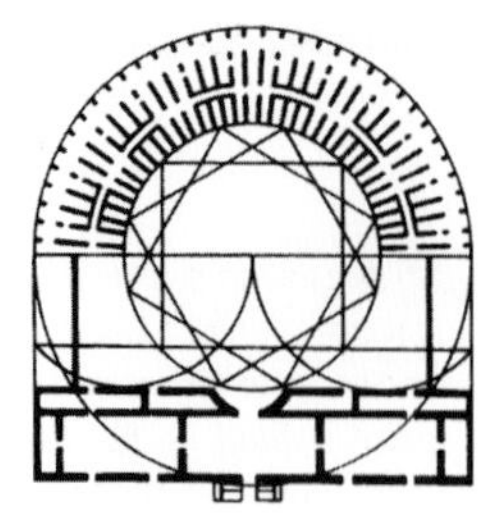

❷ Greek theatre (according to Vitruvius)

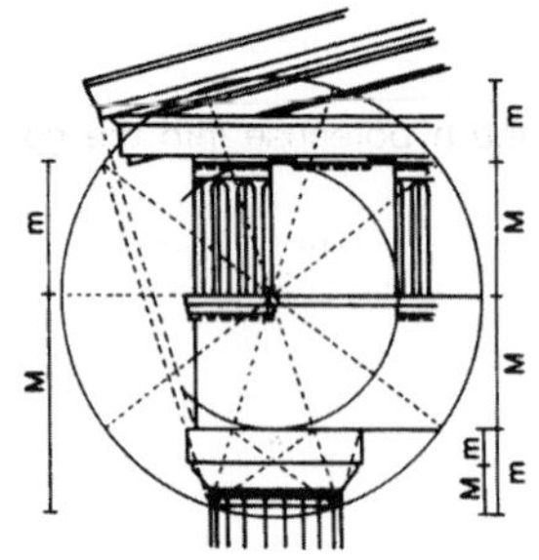
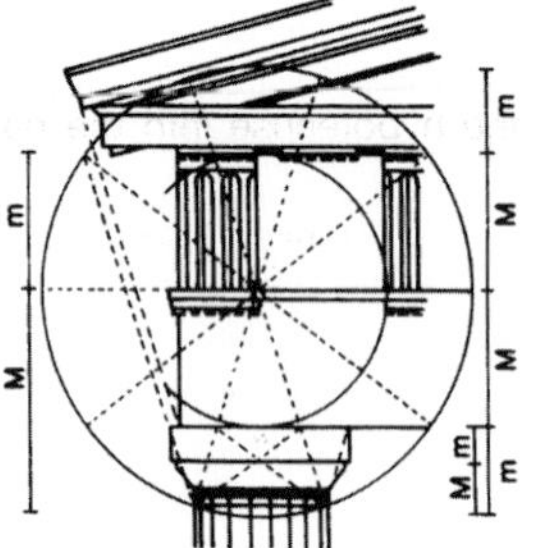

❸ Gable corner of a Doric temple: dimensional relationships based on the golden section

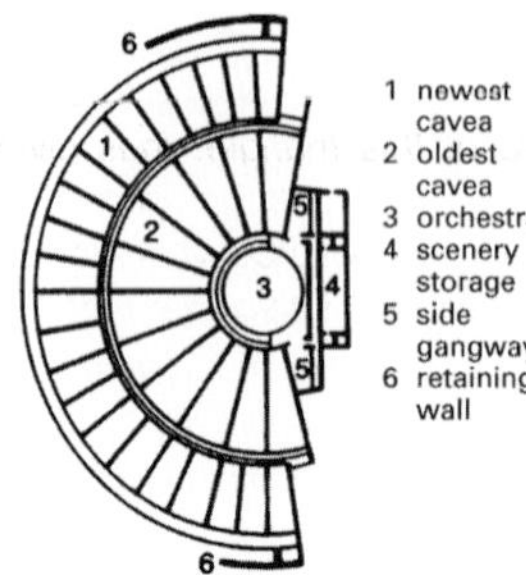

❹ Theatre in Epidaurus

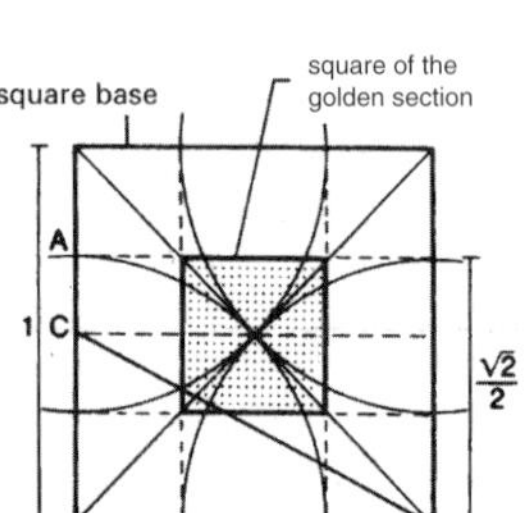

❺ Golden section, buildings in Ostia Antica

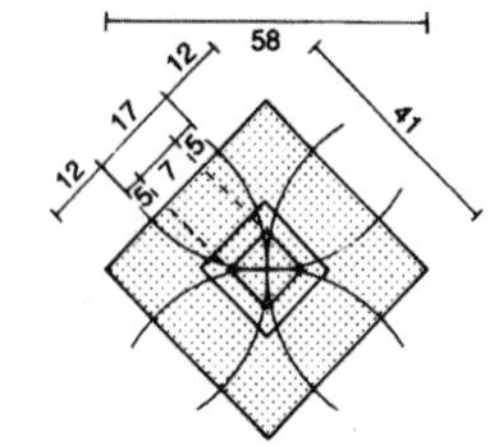
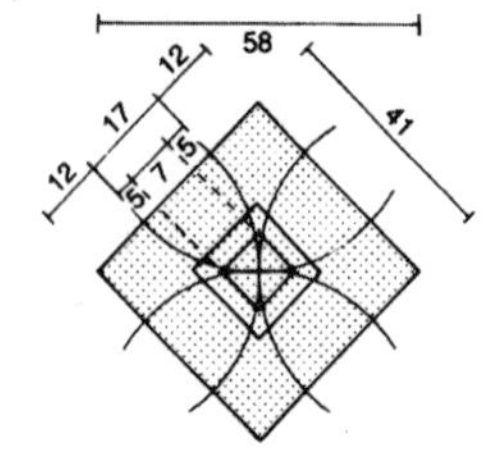

y	x	y/x ($\sqrt{2}$ = 1.4142...)
1	1	1
3	2	1.5
7	5	1.4
17	12	1.4166...
41	29	1.4137...

❻ Dimensional relationships of the golden section

❼ Plan of the entire quarter

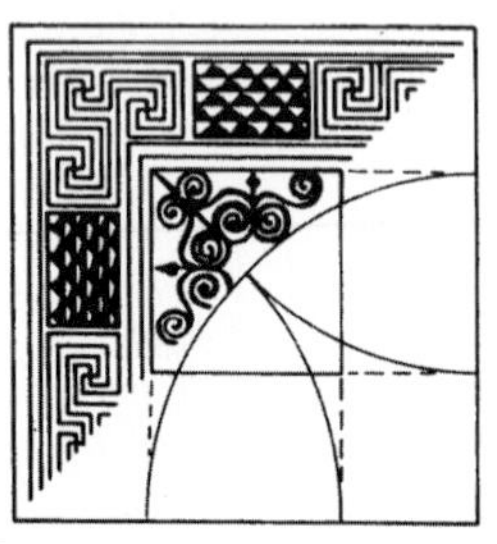

❽ Floor mosaic in a house in Ostia Antica

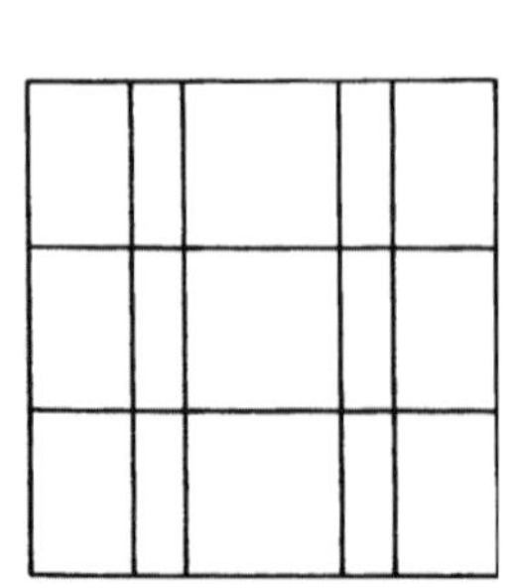

❾ Geometrical key to Palladio's villas

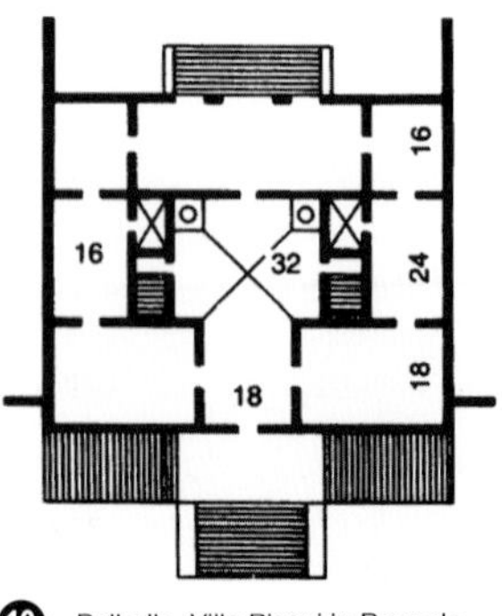

❿ Palladio, Villa Pisani in Bagnolo

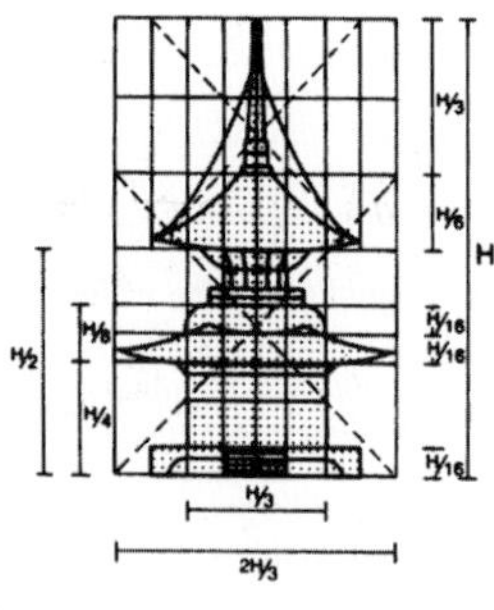

⓫ Japanese treasury

⓬ Rügen guildhall in Zürich

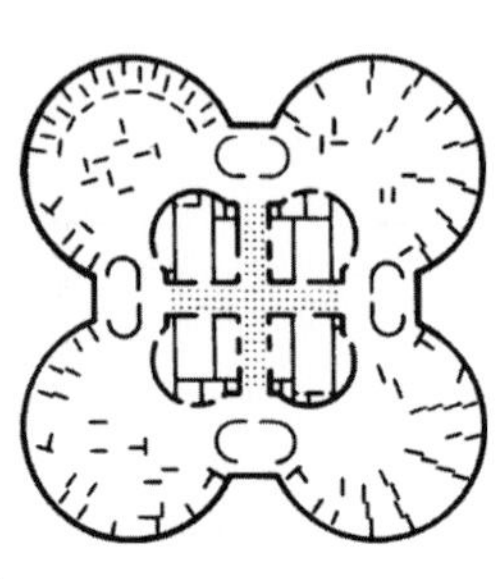

⓭ Plan of the BMW Administration Building in Munich

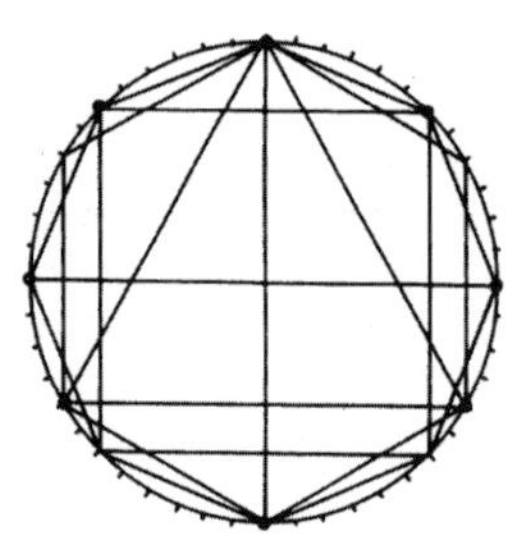

⓮ 48-sided polygon developed from a triangle → ⓭

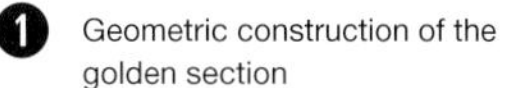

❶ Geometric construction of the golden section

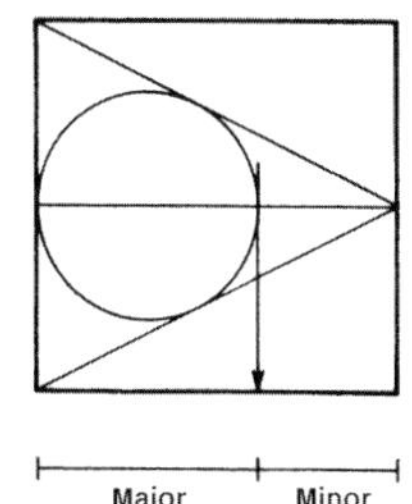

❷ Relationship between square, circle and triangle

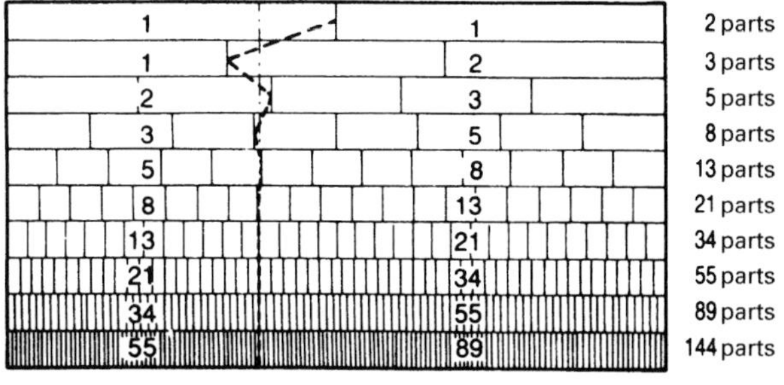

❸ Continued fraction: golden section

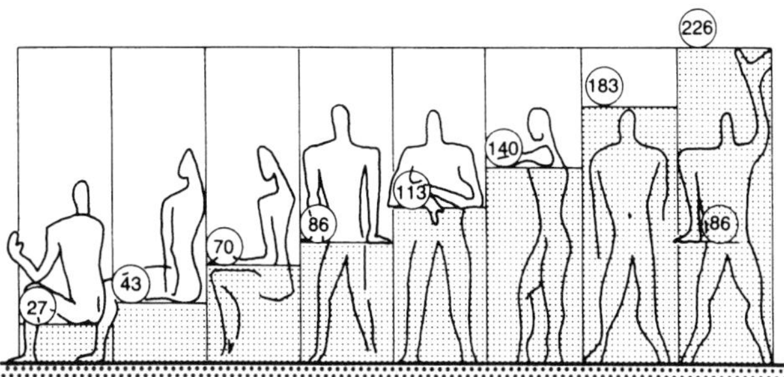

❹ Unlimited values

Values expressed in the metric system			
Red series		Blue series	
Centimetre	Metre	Centimetre	Metre
95280.7	952.80		
58886.7	588.86	117773.5	1177.73
36394.0	363.94	72788.0	727.88
22492.7	224.92	44985.5	449.85
13901.3	139.01	27802.5	278.02
8591.4	85.91	17182.9	171.83
5309.8	53.10	10619.6	106.19
3281.6	32.81	6563.3	65.63
2028.2	20.28	4056.3	40.56
1253.5	12.53	2506.9	25.07
774.7	7.74	1549.4	15.49
478.8	4.79	957.6	9.57
295.9	2.96	591.8	5.92
182.9	1.83	365.8	3.66
113.0	1.13	226.0	2.26
69.8	0.70	139.7	1.40
43.2	0.43	86.3	0.86
26.7	0.26	53.4	0.53
16.5	0.16	33.0	0.33
10.2	0.10	20.4	0.20
6.8	0.06	7.8	0.08
2.4	0.02	4.8	0.04
1.5	0.01	3.0	0.03
0.9		1.8	0.01
0.6		1.1	
etc.		etc.	

❺ Illustration of the values and sets of the Modulor, according to Le Corbusier

The golden section

The 'golden section' means that a length l is divided so that the ratio of the entire length to the larger part is the same as the ratio of the larger part to the smaller part. The golden section of a length can be determined either geometrically or by using a formula:

For the geometrical construction, the distance l (to be divided) is drawn as a vertical **AB** and the horizontal line **AC** (= AB/2) as the baseline of a right-angled triangle. The length of the baseline **AC** is transferred using a compass with centre **C** onto the hypotenuse **BC** of this triangle, thus dividing the hypotenuse into the parts **BD** and **DC**. The distance **BD** is the major part **M** of the vertical **AB**. This distance **M** is then transferred onto the vertical **AB**, thus dividing **AB** into a major part (M) and a minor part (m) → ❶.

Therefore: $$\frac{\textbf{l}}{\textbf{major}} = \frac{\textbf{major}}{\textbf{minor}}$$

The connection between the golden section and the proportions of square, circle and triangle is shown in → ❷. The golden sectioning of the distance can also be determined with the continued fraction

$$G = 1 + \frac{1}{G}$$

This is the simplest infinite regular continued fraction → ❸.

The Modulor

The architect Le Corbusier developed a theory of proportion based on the golden section and the dimensions of the human body. He marked out three intervals in the human body, which formed what Fibonacci named a golden section series: between **the foot, the solar plexus, the head, the fingers of the raised hand**. Le Corbusier first assumed 1.75 m to be the average height of a European, and divided this, according to the golden section, into the dimensions 108.2 – 66.8 – 41.45 – 25.4 cm → ❽.

Because this last dimension is almost exactly 10 in, Le Corbusier found a connection with the English inch, but this did not apply to the larger dimensions. Consequently he later altered his average body height to 6 English feet (= 1.828 m) and from there developed, according to the golden section, the so-called **red series** upwards and downwards → ❺. Because the steps in this series were too large for practical use, he then developed an additional **blue series**, starting from 2.26 m (fingertips of the raised hand), with double the values in the red series → ❺. The values in the red and blue series were then implemented by Le Corbusier as practical measurements → ❹.

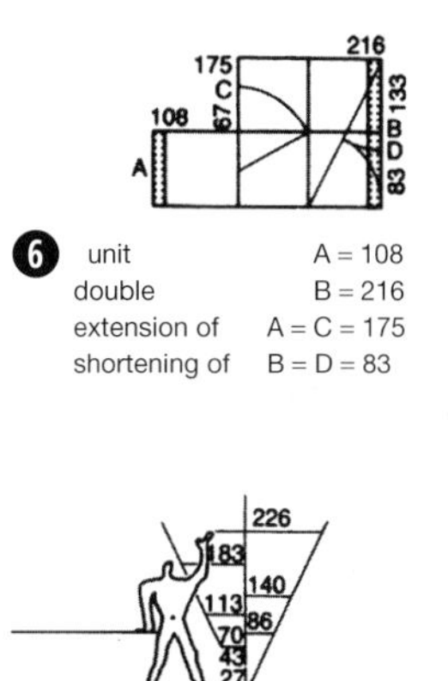

❻ unit A = 108
double B = 216
extension of A = C = 175
shortening of B = D = 83

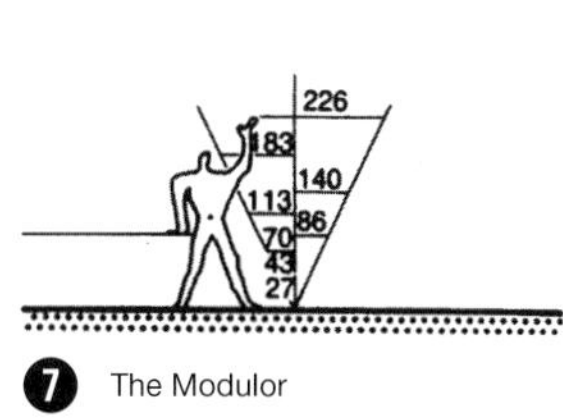

❼ The Modulor

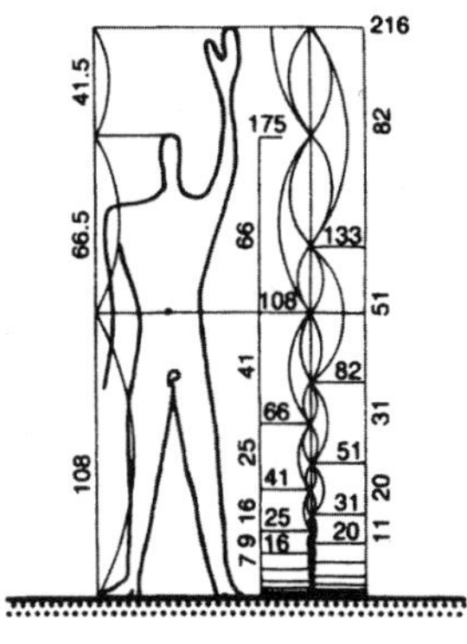

❽ Proportional figure

BS 6750
BS EN ISO 8560
BS 2045
DIN 323
DIN 4172

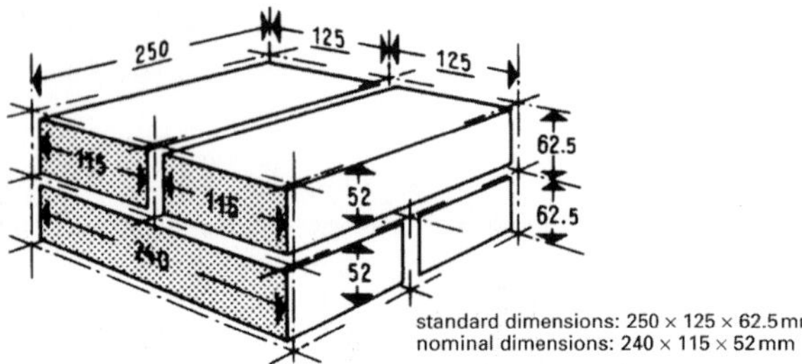

❶ Nominal and standard size of continental European wall bricks

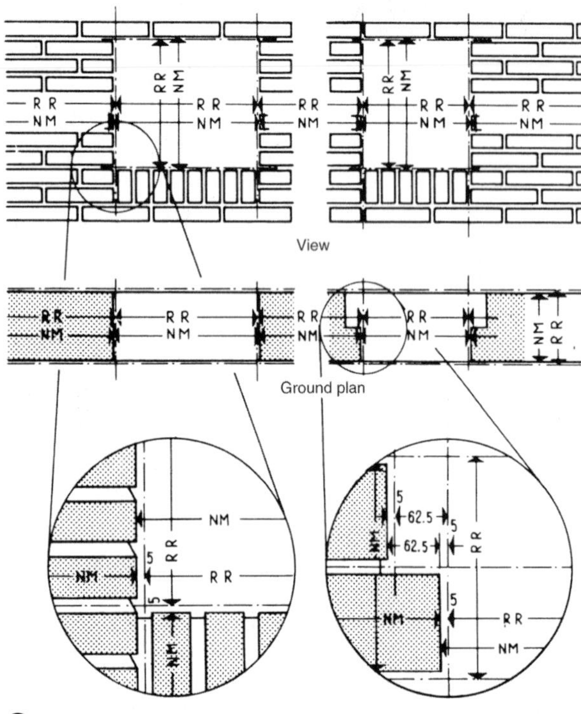

❷ Modular structural dimensions (RR) and nominal dimensions (NM) for brickwork

Terms

Building preferred numbers are those for modular construction dimensions and the individual, structural and finished dimensions derived from them.

Modular dimensions are only theoretical dimensions, but are the basis for the individual, structural and finished dimensions used in practice. Structural dimensions or nominal dimensions (for construction types with joints and wall finishes) are derived from modular dimensions by deducting or adding the component for the joint or the finish thickness. (Example: modular dimension for the length of a brick = 25 cm; thickness of the vertical joint = 1 cm; nominal dimension for the length of the brick = 24 cm; modular dimension for the thickness of poured concrete walls = nominal dimension = 25 cm).

Individual dimensions are dimensions (mostly small) for units of structure or finishing such as joint thicknesses, plaster thicknesses, door rebate sizes, wall projection sizes, tolerances.

Structural dimensions are of the unfinished structure, such as masonry dimensions (without plaster thicknesses), structural slab thicknesses, sizes of unplastered door and window openings.

Finished dimensions are for the finished building, such as clear sizes of plastered rooms and openings, storage space dimensions, floor-to-floor heights.

Nominal dimensions are the same as modular dimensions for building types without joints. For building types with joints, the nominal dimension is the modular dimension less the joint thicknesses.

Small dimensions are 2.5 cm and less. They can be selected from the sizes: 2.5 cm; 2 cm; 1.6 cm; 1.25 cm; 1 cm; 8 mm; 6.3 mm; 5 mm; 3.2 mm; 2.5 mm; 2 mm; 1.6 mm; 1.25 mm; 1 mm.

Preferred numbers

Preferred numbers have been introduced for the standardised sizing of machinery and technical devices. The starting point is the continental unit of length the metre (→ 40 in). The engineering requirement for geometrical graduation made the purely decimal division of the metre impractical. The geometrical 10-part preferred number series is therefore: **1; 2; 4; 8; 16; 31.5; 63; 125; 250; 500; 1000**. These are formed from the **halving series** (1000, 500, 250, 125) and the **doubling series** (1, 2, 4, 8, 16); the doubling number 32 was rounded down to 31.5 towards the exact value of the halving number (31.25), and the halving number 62.5 was rounded up to 63. The larger 5-part and the finer 20- and 40-part series fit in accordingly with their intermediate numbers.

Preferred numbers offer many advantages for calculation: products and quotients of any number of preferred numbers are themselves preferred numbers, whole-number percentages of preferred numbers are again preferred numbers, and doubled and halved preferred numbers also remain preferred numbers.

Although there is scarcely a need for geometrical graduation in building (considering the predominantly arithmetical addition of similar elements like: blocks, joists, rafters, trusses, columns, windows and similar) the so-called **building preferred numbers** have been defined and laid down.

Brickwork dimensions in the UK differ: in the past large variations in the size of fired clay products often led to critical problems with bonding clay bricks. Now, BS 3921 provides one standard for dimensioning → ❶: coordinating size (225 × 112.5 × 75 mm, including 10 mm in each direction for joints and tolerances), and the relating work size (215 [2 headers plus 1 joint] × 102.5 × 65 mm).

Series preferred for the structure				Series preferred for individual dimensions	Series preferred for finishings			
a	b	c	d	e	f	g	h	i
25	$\frac{25}{2}$	$\frac{25}{3}$	$\frac{25}{4}$	$\frac{25}{10}$	5	2 × 5	4 × 5	5 × 5
				2.5				
				5	5			
			6¼	7.5				
		8⅓		10	10	10		
	12½			12.5				
			12½	15	15			
		16⅔		17.5				
			18¾	20	20	20	20	
				22.5				
	25	25	25	25	25			25
				27.5				
			31¼	30	30	30		
		33⅓		32.5⅔				
				35	35			
	37½		37½	37.5				
		41⅔		40	40	40	40	
			43¾	42.5				
				45	45			
50	50	50	50	50	50	50		50
				52.5				
			56¼	55	55			
		58⅓		57.5				
				60	60	60	60	
	62½		62½	62.5				
				65	65			
		66	68¾	67.5				
				70	70	70		
				72.5				
75	75	75	75	75	75			75
			81¼	80	80	80	80	
		83⅓		82.5				
				85	85			
	87½		87½	87.5				
		91⅔		90	90	90		
			93¾	92.5				
				95	95			
				97.5				
100	100	100	100	100	100	100	100	100

❸ Building preferred numbers

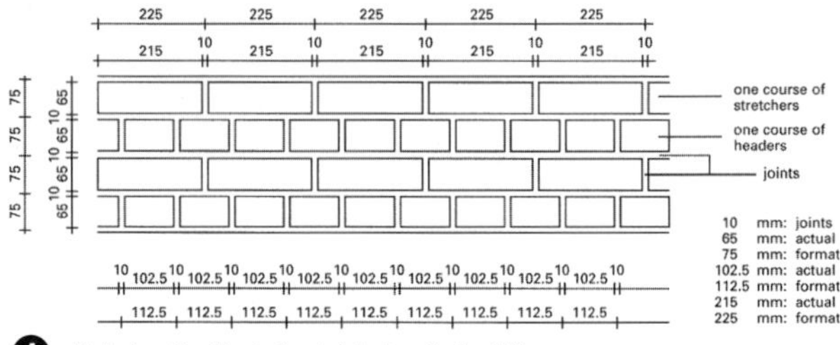

❹ Wall elevation illustrating brick sizes in the UK

DIMENSIONAL BASICS AND RELATIONSHIPS

Dimensions in Building

BS EN ISO 8560
BS 6750
DIN 18000

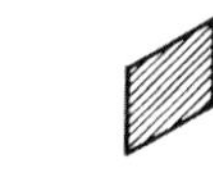

❶ Coordinate plane

❷ Coordinate system

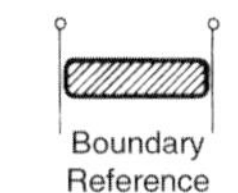

❸ Boundary reference, centre-line reference

❹ Coordinate line (intersection of two planes)

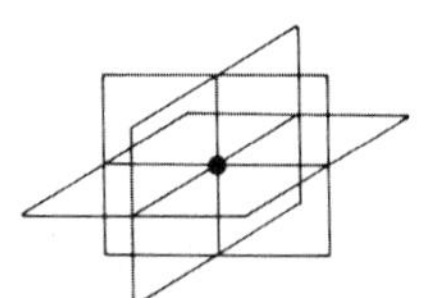

❺ Coordinate point (intersection of three planes)

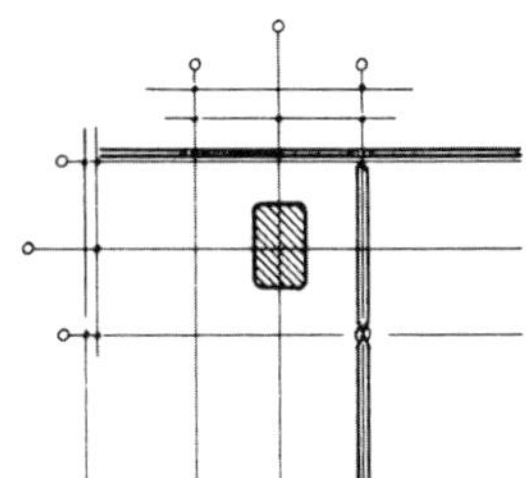

❻ Superimposed partial coordinate systems

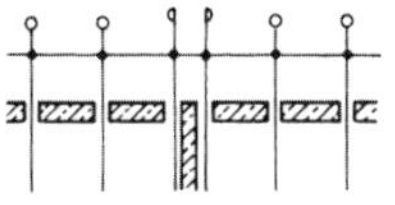

❼ Non-modular zone

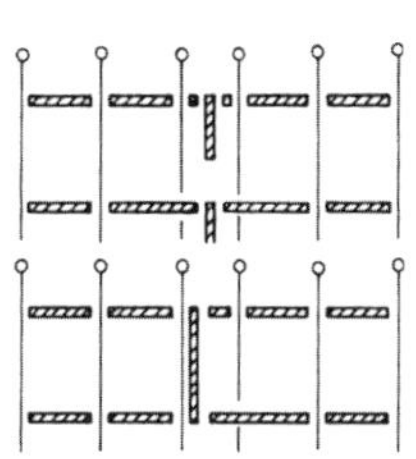

❽ Modular zone with laterally connected, non-modular building components

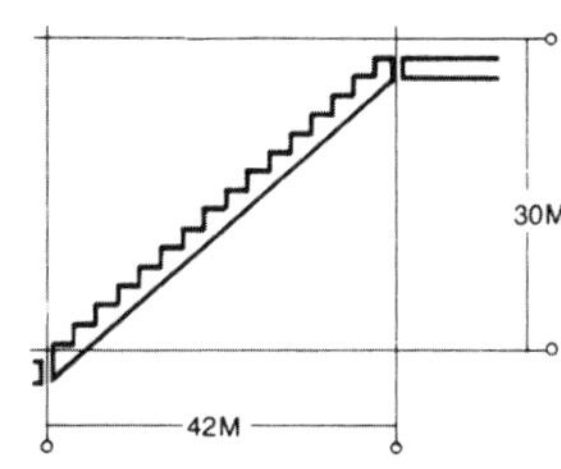

Storey height = 30 m
Flight length on plan 42 m
Selected:
16 risers 18.75/26.2 cm
(assuming/cm joints)

❾ Pre-cast reinforced concrete stair element

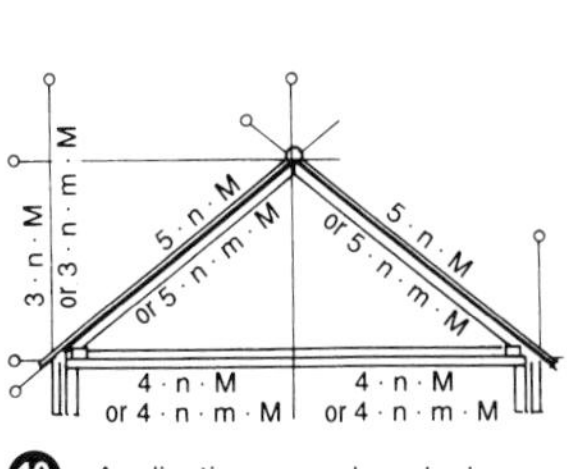

❿ Application example – sloping roof

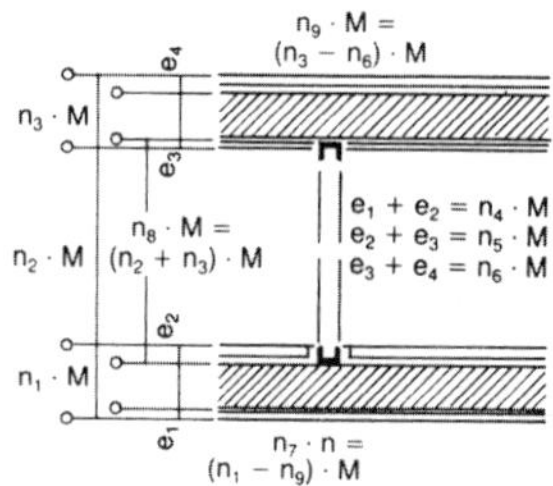

⓫ Compensating measure on the verticals

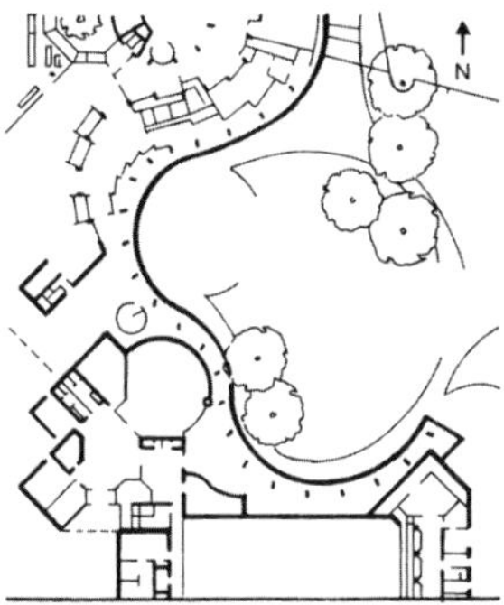

⓬ Construction of a curving roof edge from regular polygon traverses (site plan)

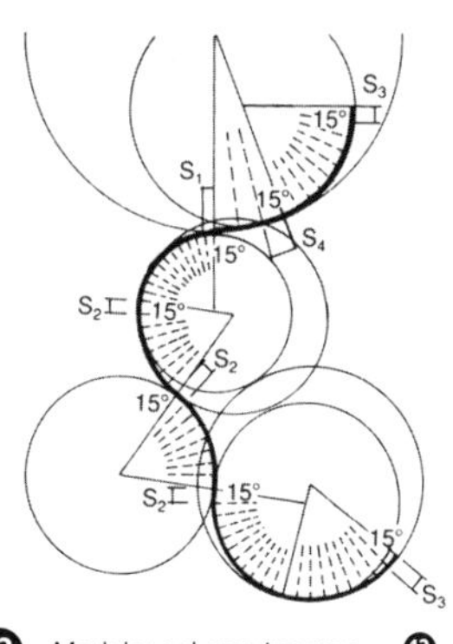

⓭ Modular polygon traverse → ⓬

Modular coordination in building

The modular system is a means of coordinating the dimensions applicable to building work. The term 'coordination' is the key: a modular building standard contains details of a design and detailing system based on coordination as an aid in the design and construction of buildings. It gives geometrical and dimensional definitions for the spatial coordination of building components. It also enables technical areas, which depend on each other with regard to geometry and dimensions (e.g. building, electrical engineering, transport) to be connected.

Geometrical considerations

A coordinate system is always object-specific. It is used to coordinate building structures and components, and determine their position and size. From these are derived nominal dimensions of building components, plus joint and connection thicknesses → ❶ – ❺. A coordinate system consists of planes arranged at right angles to each other, spaced according to the coordinate measurements. Depending on the system, these can be of different sizes and in all three dimensions.

Building components are normally arranged in one dimension between two parallel coordinate planes so that they fill the coordinate dimension, including the joint component and also taking tolerances into account. A building component is therefore defined in its extent, i.e. its size and position, in one dimension. This is called **boundary reference** → ❸. In other cases, it can be advantageous not to position a building component between two planes but rather to have its centre-line coincide with a coordinate plane. The component is thus specified in one dimension, but only in terms of position. This is called **centre-line reference** → ❸. A coordinate system can be sub-divided into various sub-systems for different groups of building elements (e.g. load-bearing structures, space-demarcating components etc.) → ❻.

It has become apparent that not all individual components have to be modular (e.g. each step in a staircase, windows, doors, etc.), but only the building elements they are combined into (e.g. staircases, façade or partition elements etc.) → ❾. For non-modular building components which continue along or across the whole building, a **non-modular zone** can be introduced, which completely divides the coordinate system into two sub-systems. The precondition is that the size of the building component in the non-modular zone is already known at the time when the coordinate system is set out, because the non-modular zone can only have completely specified dimensions → ❼. Further ways of arranging non-modular building components are the so-called central position and edge position in modular zones → ❽.

The units of the modular system are the **basic module M** = 100 mm and the **multi-modules** 3 M = 300 mm, 6 M = 600 mm and 12 M = 1200 mm. There are also standardised non-modular supplementary dimensions I = 25 mm, 50 mm and 75 mm for fitting elements or overlapping connections → ⓫. Combination rules can be used to fit building components of various sizes into a modular coordinate system.

Number groups (e.g. Pythagoras') or factorisation (e.g. continued fractions) can be utilised to fit non-rectangular building components into a modular coordinate → ❿. The construction of polygon traverses (e.g. triangle, square, pentagon and their halves) can be used to design so-called 'round' building structures → ⓬ – ⓭.

BUILDING BIOLOGY

Basics

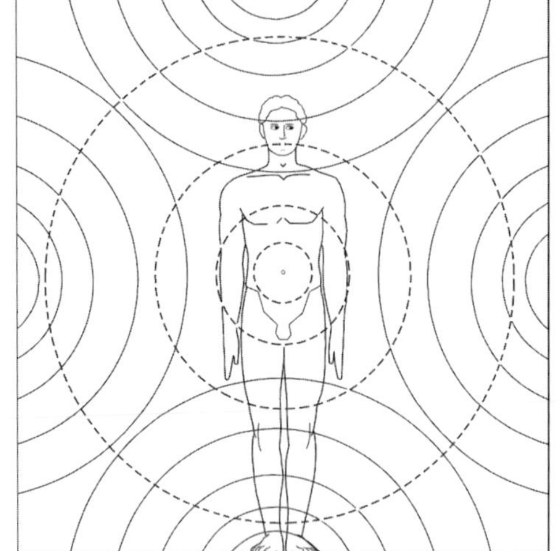

❶ Building biology as the study of the holistic interaction between building and resident

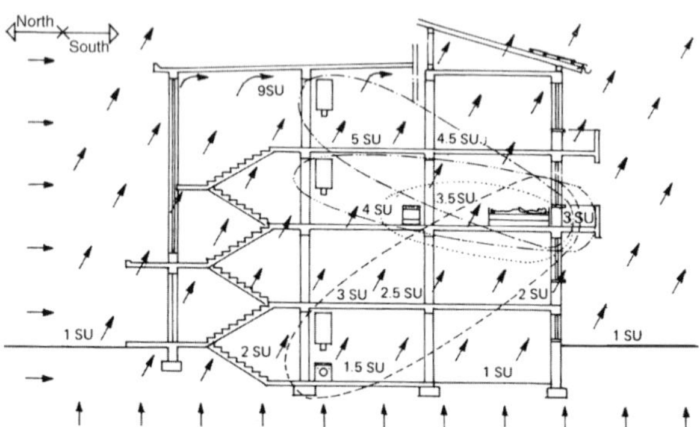

❷ Electromagnetic fields in and around a building

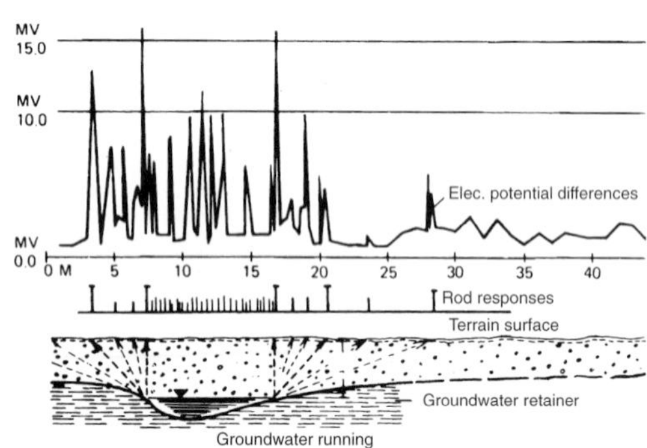

❸ Differences in electrical potential above a groundwater aquifer

electrical and magnetic fields ('electro-smog')	low-frequency alternating electrical fields through connected power cables, electrical devices etc. low-frequency alternating magnetic fields through switched-on electrical devices etc. high-frequency fields from mobile phone transmitters, telephone etc. static electricity from synthetic materials, wools etc. static magnetic fields
building material measurements	heavy metals, toxins, radiation
air pollutants	air pollution, toxins, gases, fine dust, allergens
noise/vibration	
earth radiation and earth magnetic field	geopathogenic disturbance zones (e.g. underground watercourses and 'earth rays')

❹ The extent of building biology measurements of the built environment (example)

Building biology is a collective term for the study of the **holistic interaction between building and resident** → ❶ – ❷. Its aim is to determine any **deleterious effects** for the human organism through the consideration of physical, chemical and microbiological conditions in interiors and, if appropriate, take measures to relieve the causes (via 'healthy living'). The themes of building biology partially overlap with other disciplines: building ecology**,** whose main focus is the protection of nature and environment in the construction and operation of buildings and in the manufacture, processing and final disposal of building materials, building physics and electrical engineering as well as biology, chemistry and medicine.

The principles of building biology are especially suitable for application in residential building but also in the construction of schools, hospitals, kindergartens and offices.

The fact that the people today spend 90% of their lives inside buildings and are surrounded to an increasing degree by electromagnetic fields has increased public interest in building biology in recent years. Meanwhile, 2–5% of the German population now suffer complaints (e.g. headaches, insomnia, tiredness and concentration problems) due to the presence of building biological pollution of their homes and offices.

The investigation of a building therefore normally includes the following areas:

- measurement of **electric, magnetic and electromagnetic** fields from technical devices in the low- and high-frequency ranges
- testing of **building materials** for toxins, heavy metals and radiation
- testing of **rooms' air quality** for pollutants (toxins and gases, fibres, fine dust and allergens)
- microbiological investigations of **bacteria and mould formation,** and measurements of **noise, vibration and light** → ❹.

Measurements related to **radiaesthesia** ('radiation sensitivity') can also be carried out, in attempts to demonstrate geopathogenic disturbance zones (e.g. underground watercourses and 'earth rays') can be discovered using dowsing, pendulums and other alternative scientific methods → ❸.

The term '**building biology**' is not yet officially regulated in Germany. This means that anyone can call themselves a building biologist independent of their level of education and practical experience. It is possible to discern two basic directions in the field of building biology. **Scientific-oriented** building biology attempts to use scientific methods to create healthy living and working conditions. Measurements must be carried out using scientifically recognised and reproducible methods, in order that harmful effects in buildings can be reliably detected and remedied. **Alternative-oriented** building biology assumes that the influences affecting people have so far been recognised scientifically only to a limited extent. The resulting measurements, and the theories and threshold values they are based on are therefore disputed, as there are sometimes no reliable methods for measuring such threshold values.

BUILDING BIOLOGY
Basics
Room climate
Electromagnetic fields

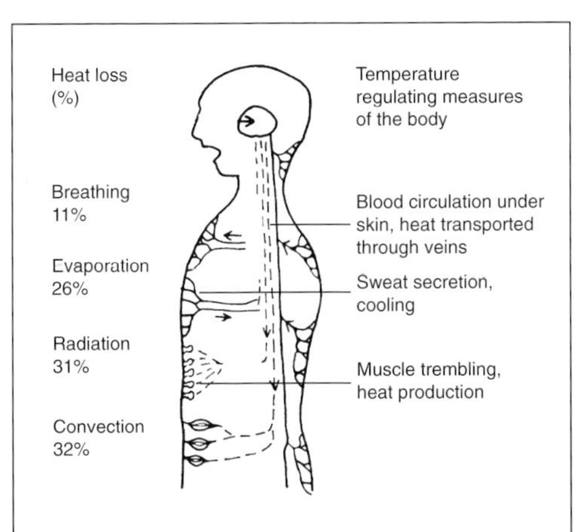

❶ Heat output and temperature-regulating measures of the human body

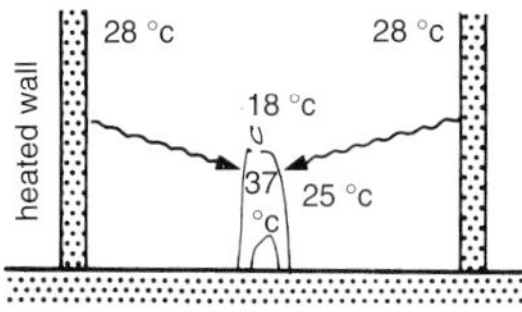

❷ Thermal comfort

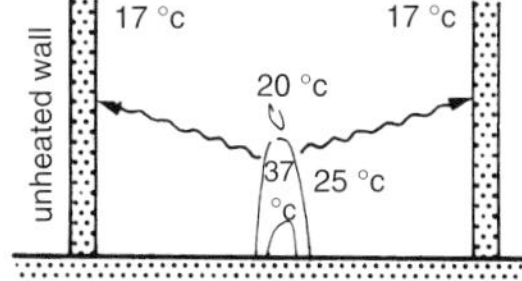

❸ Thermal discomfort

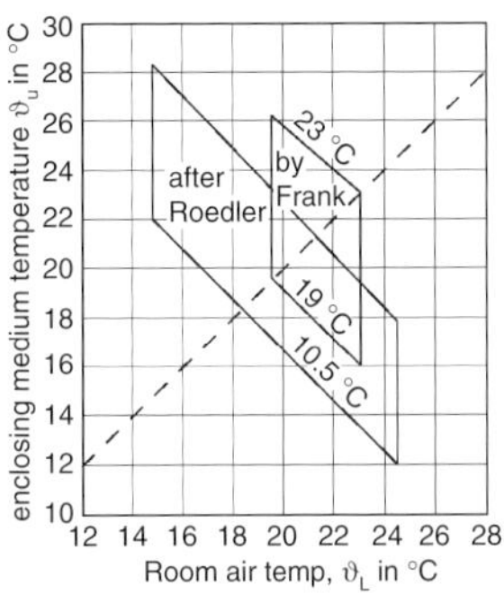

❹ Thermal comfort zone (temperature of surrounding surfaces and of air)

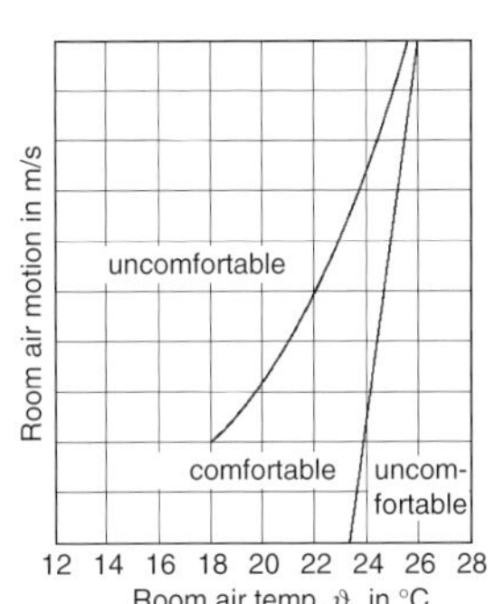

❺ Thermal comfort zone (room air movement and room air temperature)

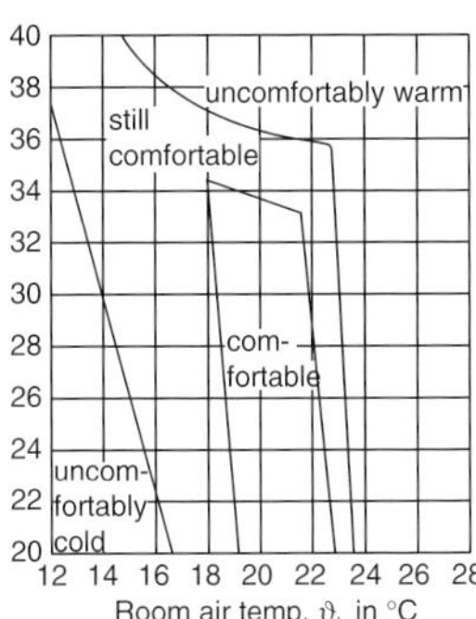

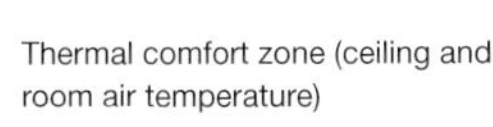

❻ Thermal comfort zone (ceiling and room air temperature)

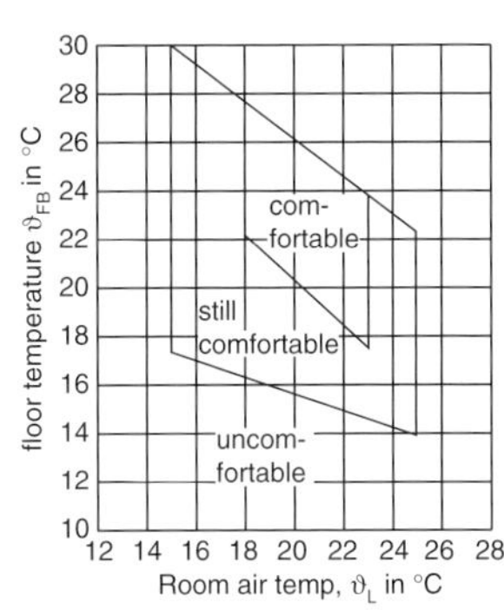

❼ Thermal comfort zone (floor and room air temperature)

Thermal comfort is experienced when the thermal circulation regulated by the body is in balance, i.e. the body can regulate warmth with as little effort as possible. This type of comfort is experienced when the heat produced by the body corresponds to the actual heat loss to the surroundings.

Temperature-regulating measures in the body
Warming: flow of blood through the skin, increase of blood flow rate, vascular enlargement and muscle shivering. Cooling: sweating.

Heat exchange between the body and the surroundings
Inner heat flow: heat flow from the inside of the body to the skin depending on blood circulation. Outer heat flow: heat conduction through the feet; convection (air speed, room air and temperature difference between clothed and unclothed areas of the body); radiation (temperature difference between the external area of the body and the surroundings); evaporation, breathing (body surface, vapour pressure difference between skin and surroundings) → ❶.

Water content of the air (g/kg)	Suitability for breathing	Sensation of breathing
0–5	very good	light, fresh
5–8	good	normal
8–10	satisfactory	still bearable
10–20	increasingly bad	heavy, muggy
20–25	already dangerous	damp heat
over 25	unsuitable	unbearable
41	water content of exhaled air 37°C (100 %)	
over 41	water condenses pulmonary alveoli	

❽ Air humidity values for breathing air

Low radiation temperature. Recommendations for room climatic conditions and temperature of air and surrounding surfaces
In summer, 20–24°C is comfortable, in winter about 21°C (± 1°C). The temperature of the surrounding surfaces should not differ from the air temperature by more than 2–3°C. Alterations of the air temperature can be compensated for to a certain extent by alteration of the temperature of the surrounding surfaces (sinking air temperature – rising surface temperature). If these temperatures are too different, this causes excessive air movement. The critical locations are above all the windows. Large heat transfers to the floor through the feet should be avoided (floor temperature should be greater than 17°C). Hot feet and cold feet are experienced by the sufferers and are not properties of the floor. The bare foot feels heat/cold through the floor covering and its thickness, the clothed foot through the floor covering and the temperature of the floor. The surface temperature of the ceiling depends on the room height. The temperatures perceived by people correspond to approximately the average of the temperature of the air and that of the surrounding surfaces.
Air and air movement. Air movement is experienced as draughts, which in this case result in a local cooling of the body.
Air temperature and relative humidity. Relative humidity of 40–50% is thermally comfortable. If the humidity is less than 30%, dust particles can fly.
Fresh air and air exchange: The ideal is controlled ventilation rather than incidental or permanent ventilation. The CO_2 content of the air must be replaced by oxygen. A CO_2 content of 0.10% by volume should not be exceeded, which requires 2–3 air changes per hour in living rooms and bedrooms. The fresh air required by a person is about 32.0 m^3/h. Air changes in living rooms: 0.4–0.8 × room volume per person/h.

BUILDING BIOLOGY

Electromagnetic Fields

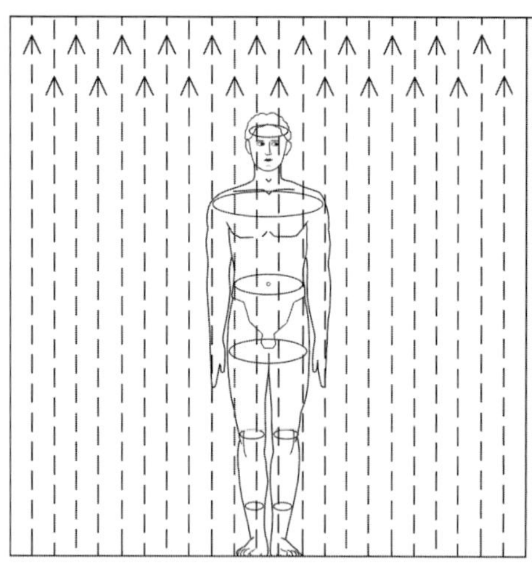

❶ Induction of body currents as the main effect on the body of alternating magnetic and electromagnetic fields

The 26th German Federal Emissions Protection Regulations (BimSchV) lay down **threshold values for electrical field strength and magnetic flux density**. These are, for the mains supply frequency (50 Hz), 5 KV/m or 100 μT, and for railway power supply (16 2/3 Hz) 10 KV/m or 300 μT.

Because of the state of **scientific uncertainty** about the possible effects on health of low-frequency fields, the Federal Office for Radiation Protection (BfS) recommends the following precautionary measures:

Optimise cable runs and isolation of electrical installations to keep the exposure of people as low as possible. Possible field sources and devices should be completely switched off after use and not left in 'standby' mode (this applies particularly to televisions and hi-fi systems). Field sources in sleeping areas (e.g. mains radio-alarm clocks) should be placed as far as possible from beds.

body current density (mA/ m ≈)

body current density	
above 1000	damage clearly possible additional heart contractions ventricular fibrillation
100–1000	danger to health possible clear changes in excitability of central nervous system
10–100	confirmed effects: optical sensations reports of accelerated bone healing
1–10	no confirmed effects no verified reports of individual discomfort
below 1	no confirmed biological effects

❷ Biological effects of body current densities (BfS → refs)

Device/appliance	3 cm	30 cm	100 cm
telephone	6–2000	0.01–7	0.01–3
electric razor	15–1500	0.08–9	0.01–3
fluorescent lamp	40–400	0.5–2	0.02–0.25
microwave	73–200	4–8	0.25–0.6
television	2.5–50	0.04–2	0.01–0.04
computer	0.5–30	<0.01	
refrigerator	0.5–1.7	0.01–0.25	0.01

❸ Values of magnetic flux densities of household appliances, measured in μT, at various distances (SSK → refs)

The use of technologies like power supply networks and mobile telephones creates various **electrical, magnetic and electromagnetic fields** in the human environment. These can be described through their field strength, given in volt/metre (V/m), their magnetic flux density, in tesla (T), their wavelength, measured in metres (m) and their frequency, in hertz (Hz). This last unit describes the number of cycles per second of the change of polarity of the electrical current. There is a difference between high- and low-frequency fields.

In contrast to ionising radiation (e.g. X-rays), the energy of these fields is not sufficient to electrically charge – to ionise – atoms and molecules. Nonetheless, these fields, above a certain strength, have certain effects on health, and are sometimes described as '**electrosmog**'. The nature and extent of the harmfulness of electrical, magnetic and electromagnetic stimulation for people and environment implied by this term has been the central theme of many building biology investigations.

Building biology effects

In everyday life, exposure is mostly from low-frequency electrical and magnetic fields **between 1 Hz and 100 kilohertz (kHz)**, which are emitted from the power supply (50 Hz) and electrified transport systems like railways (16 2/3 Hz). In the course of the rapid development of mobile telephones, the population is also increasingly subjected to high-frequency electromagnetic fields of up to **300 gigahertz (gHz)**.

If an external **electrical field** acts on a person, then forces act on charges in the body and result in '**body currents**'. This process is called **influence**. In the case of alternating fields, the charge redistribution is constantly repeated at the frequency. Above a certain threshold value, which varies from person to person, electrical fields are perceived. In addition to direct effect, there are also indirect effects of electrical fields, like **discharge currents and electrification**. The causes of this are charge differences between variously charged objects and the affected person. These charge differences reach equilibrium as soon as an electrically conducting contact is created by touching ('shock').

In contrast to an alternating electrical field, an **alternating magnetic field** directly causes currents inside the body as a result of **induction currents**. The decisive parameter for the evaluation of health effects is the density of these body currents, measured in milliampere/square metre (mA/m^2).

Electrical currents also occur inside the body without external fields. Nerves carry their signals by transporting electrical impulses, the heart is electrically active (→ electrocardiogram) and almost all metabolic processes include the movement of charged particles (ions). These natural body currents have densities in the range of 1–10 mA/m^2. **A threshold value of 2 mA/m^2 has been established for the body current density caused by fields.**

Low-frequency electrical and magnetic fields are produced by household appliances and electrical installations. In this case, as with railway traction power and high-voltage cables, the electrical and magnetic field strength reduces rapidly with distance → ❸. Electrical fields present outdoors are mostly shielded by the external walls of buildings, but the shielding of magnetic fields is not possible without great expense. (Drawings and text from: www.bfs.de/elektro, abbreviated – BfS → refs).

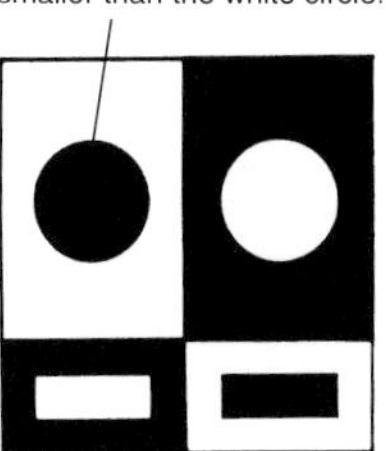

The black circle looks from a distance about 1/3 smaller than the white circle.

❶ Black areas and objects appear smaller than those of the same size that are white; people wearing black clothes seem slimmer, and those wearing white fatter, than they really are. This also applies correspondingly to building elements

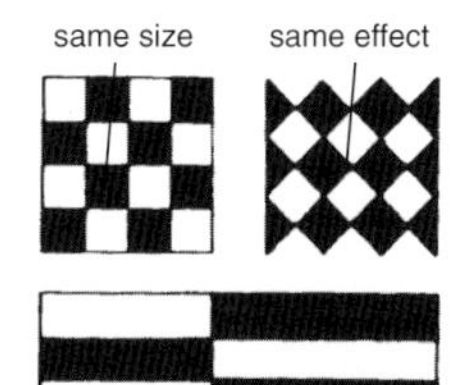

❷ If black and white areas are to appear equally large, then the latter have to be correspondingly smaller. A light colour next to a dark colour makes the latter seem darker.

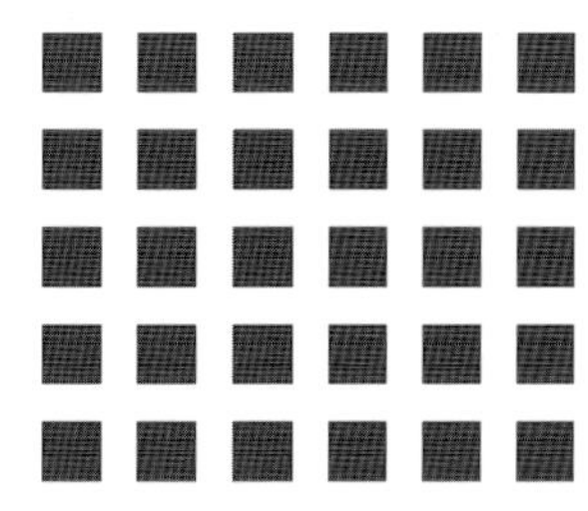

❸ Do you see grey circles between the squares? Our brain 'thinks up' these circles.

❹ Deception of the senses: we think we see a white square. In fact, the outer lines are not there.

❺ Spirals? The picture consists of circles.

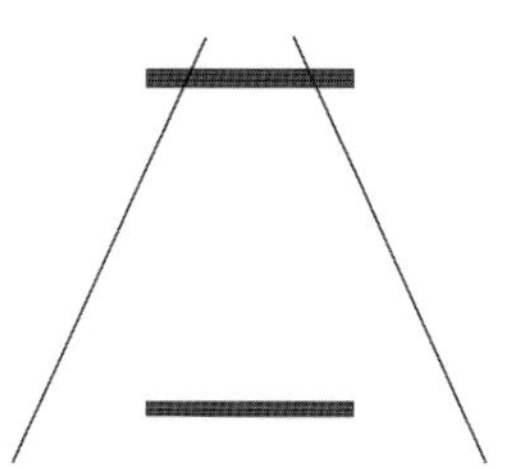

❻ The lower line is not shorter than the upper – just an optical illusion.

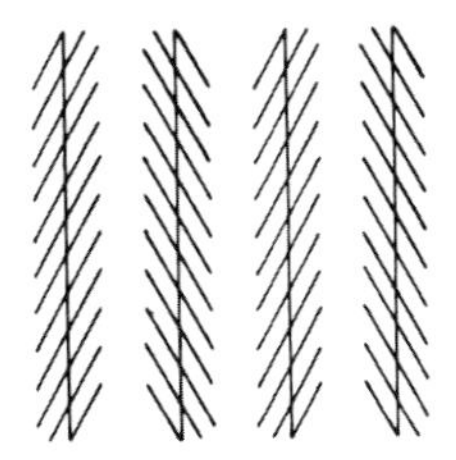

❼ The vertical lines are actually parallel in this 'Zöllner figure' but seem to converge due to the hatching.

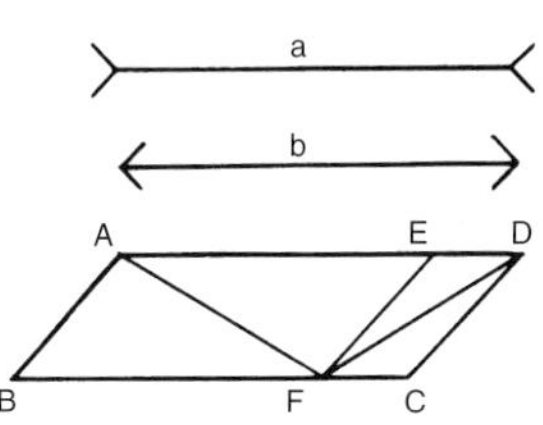

❽ The lines a and b appear to be of different lengths due to minor attributes, and A–F and F–D also appear to be different due to inclusion in various figures. They are all the same length.

❾ How many trees? Not one! There is no connection between roots and crowns.

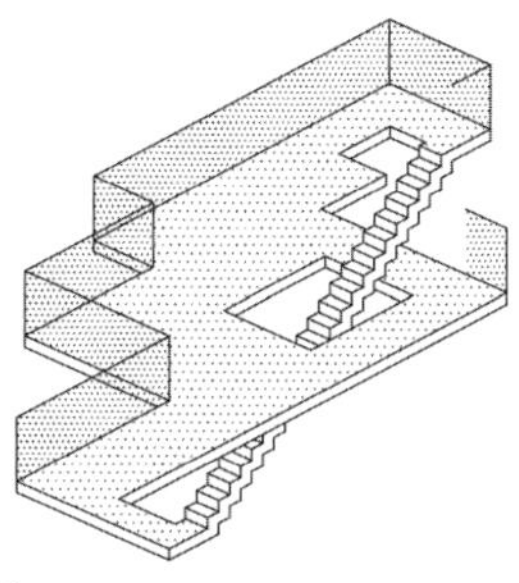

❿ Deceptive illustration infringing the conventional rules of perspective.

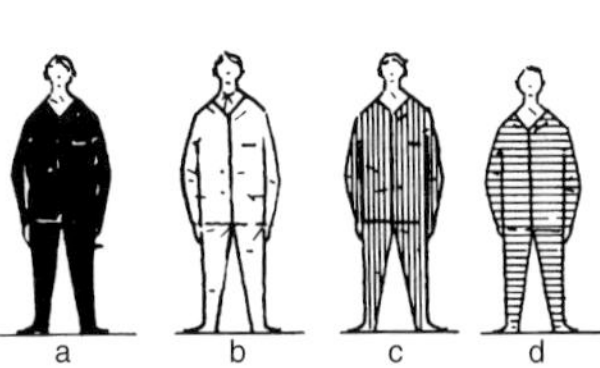

⓫ The colour and patterning of clothing changes people's appearance. Black makes people look thin → a, because black absorbs light. People appear fatter if wearing white → b, because white scatters light. Vertical stripes increase height → c, horizontal stripes increase width → d.

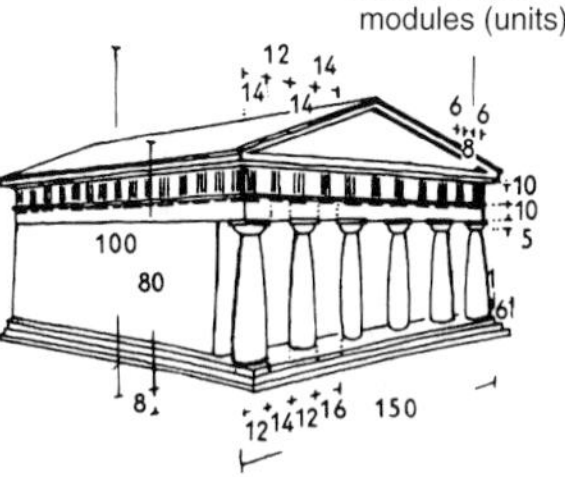

⓬ Walls which slant inward with increasing height appear vertical, and steps, cornices and friezes when bowed correctly upwards look horizontal (horizontal curvature)

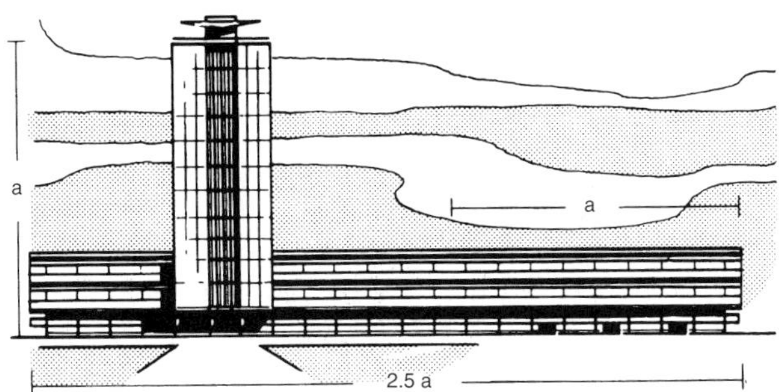

⓭ Dimensions in the vertical appear much more impressive than those in the horizontal.

⓮ Quite apart from the architectural articulation (vertical, horizontal or mixed) → ⓭, the perception of scale can be altered just by the ratio of window openings to the remaining area of wall, despite the building and storey heights being the same (window bar layout can have a significant effect).

VISUAL PERCEPTION

The Eye

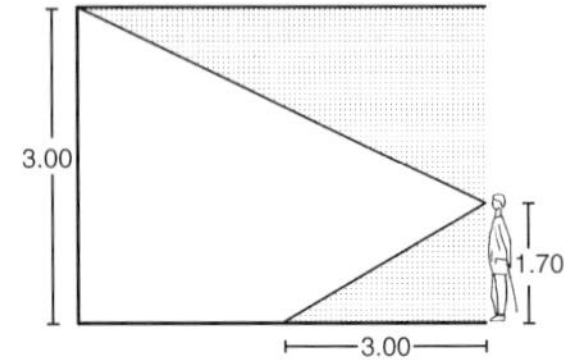

❶ A room with a low ceiling is perceived 'at a glance' (still image)

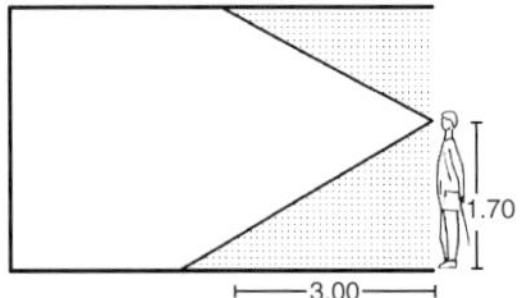

❷ A room with a high ceiling is perceived through the eye scanning upwards (scanned image)

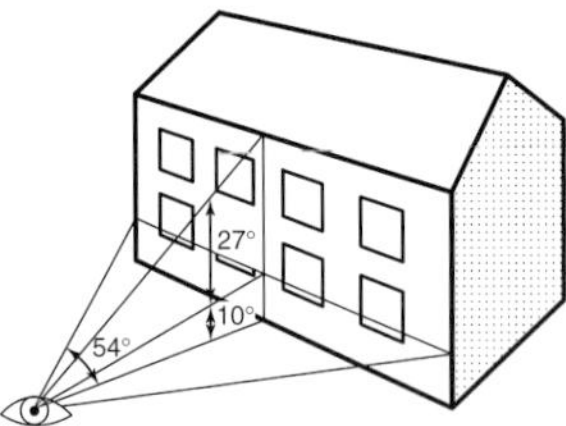

❸ The human field of view, with steady head and moving eye, is 54° horizontally, 27° upwards, 10° downwards.

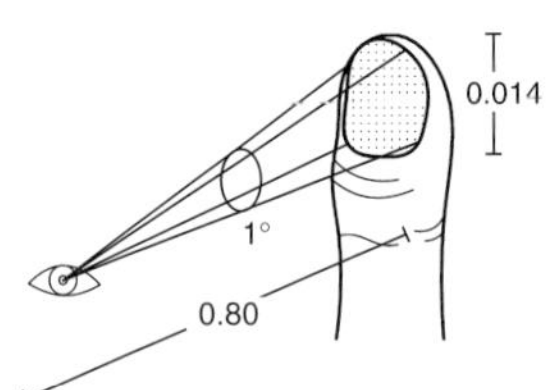

❹ The field of vision of the fixed normal eye covers 1° of the perimeter, i.e. about the area of the thumbnail of an outstretched hand

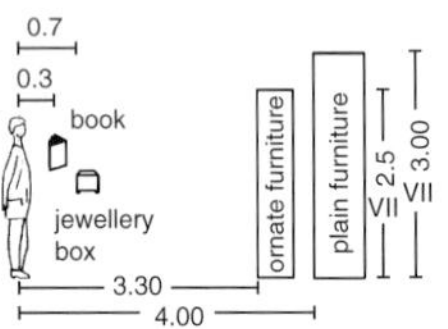

❺ Borderline distances

The eye makes precise distinctions in only 0°1′ of the perimeter = field of detailed vision (readability). The borderline distance **E** of the details to be distinguished can therefore be calculated according to the formula:

$$\mathbf{E} = \frac{\text{size of detail } \mathbf{d}}{\tan 0°1'}$$

Minimum size d of the detail:

$$\mathbf{d} = \mathbf{E} \times \tan 0°1'$$

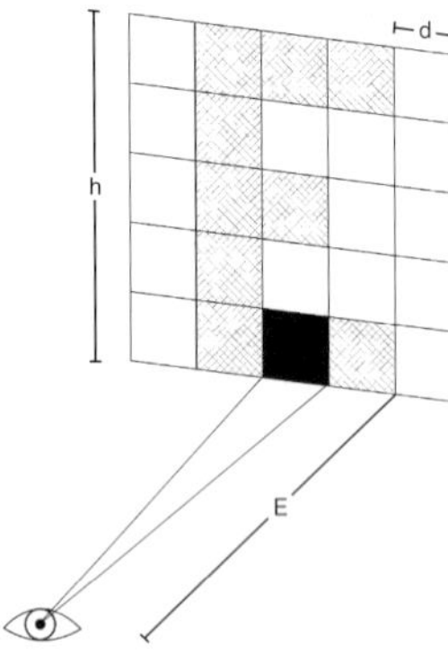

❻ Should, for example, text still be legible at a distance E = 700 m, the width d of the letters must be ≧700 m × tan 0°1′ = 0.204 m (→ ❺); the normal height h for many fonts is 5 × d = 5 × 0.204 = 1.02 m

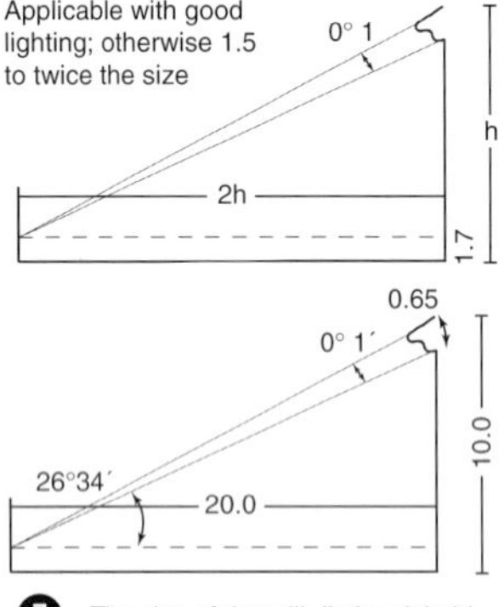

❼ The size of the still distinguishable building elements can be calculated easily using the normal viewing distance and trigonometry (→ ❺)

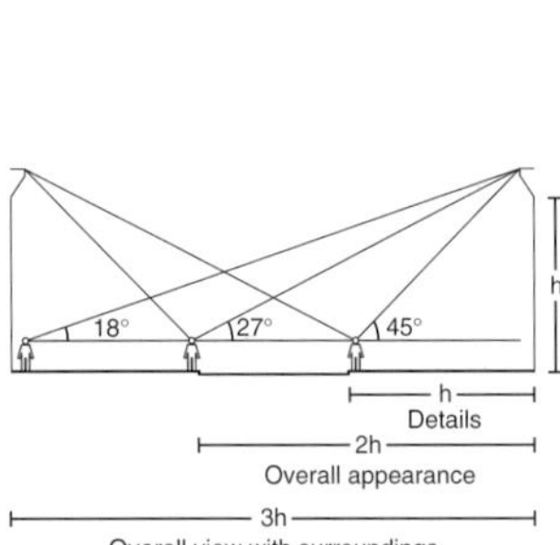

❽ The above distances are appropriate for street widths, if the intention is to permit an overview and the observation of details.

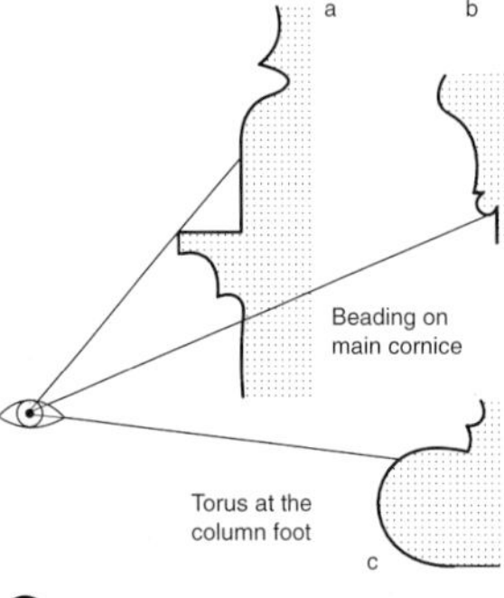

❾ Building elements intended to be seen but located above projections must be high enough (a); single elements can present larger surfaces to the eye through slight deformations (b, c)

The activities of the eye can be divided into seeing and observing. Seeing is primarily for our physical safety, but observation starts where seeing stops, leading to the enjoyment of the 'pictures' registered through seeing.

Images perceived by the eye differ according to whether the eye remains still on an object or scans around it. The **still image** is displayed in what approximates to a segment of a circle, whose diameter is the same as the distance of the eye from the object → ❸. Inside this 'field of view', the objects appear to the eye 'at a glance'. The ideal still image appears balanced. Balance is the first characteristic of architectural beauty. (Physiologists are working on a theory of the sixth sense, the balance or static sense, which is also supposed to explain the beauty we see in symmetrical, harmonious objects and proportions → pp. 30–33 or in elements which are in balance.)

Outside this framework, the eye receives its impressions from the **scanned image.** The scanning eye progresses along lines of resistance, which it discovers going away from us in width or depth.

If these lines of resistance are found at even or repeating distances, the eye perceives this as beat or rhythm, which results in a stimulus similar to the ear receiving music ('Architecture, frozen music', Neufert → refs).

This effect also occurs in a closed room, via the still or scanned image → ❶ – ❷. A room whose upper boundary (the ceiling) is perceived by us in our still image provides a sense of security, but on the other hand in long rooms also a depressed feeling. If the ceiling is higher and the eye only sees it while scanning upwards, then the room is perceived as free, exalted even, always supposing that the wall spacing, and thus the overall proportions, are in harmony.

It should not be forgotten here that the eye is subject to optical illusions. It estimates the width more accurately than depths or heights, which always seem larger. As is well known, a tower seen from above seems much higher than from below → p. 39 ⓭. Vertical edges appear to overhang upwards and horizontal edges appear curved in the middle; see also → p. 39 ❶ – ⓮.

When considering these matters, one should not fall into the opposite way of thinking (exemplified by the Baroque) and, for example, emphasise the perspective effect via inclined windows and cornices (e.g. St Peter's, Rome) or even through cornices, vaulting or similar painted in perspective.

The decisive factors for the measurement of dimensions are the size of the field of view → ❸, or the field of vision → ❹ and, for the exact distinction of details, the size of the field of detailed vision (readability) → ❺ – ❻. The distance of the latter determines the size of the details to be distinguished. The Greeks worked to precisely these principles and determined the size of the smallest bead moulding under the cornice's corona, a different dimension in each temple, so that, at an angular distance of 27°, it always filled the field of detailed vision of 0°1′ → ❼.

From this also arise the reading distances for books (which vary according to the size of the letters), of audience seats from the performance etc. (Maertens → refs; see here the illustrations developed from his writing → ❸ – ❾).

red
red and blue (violet)
yellow and red (orange)
blue
yellow
green

❶ Goethe's colour circle: basic colours – red-blue-yellow; mixed colours: green-orange-violet (= mixed colours of the first rank, obtained by mixing the basic colours)

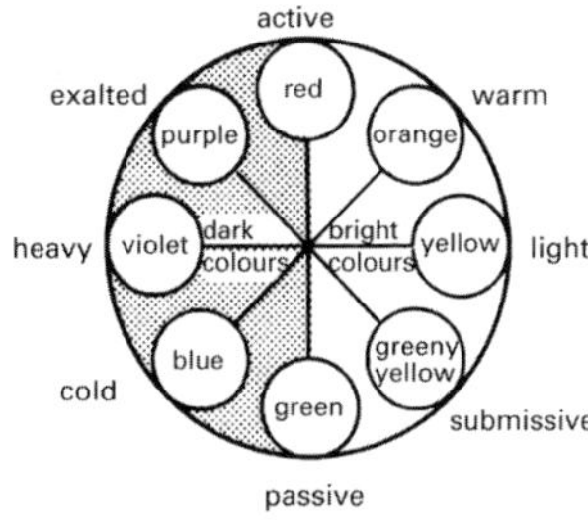

❷ Dark and bright colours and their effect on people

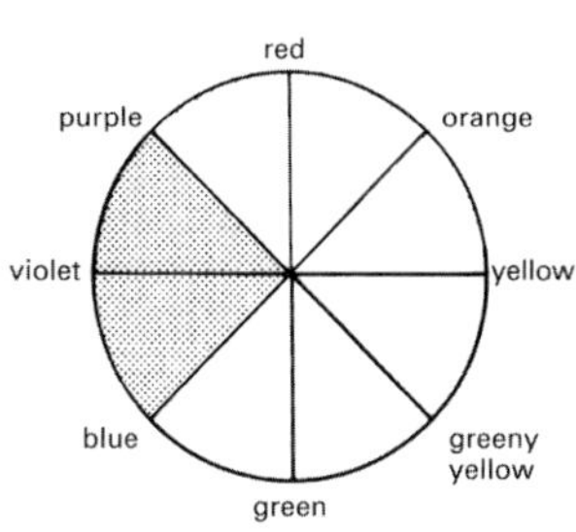

❸ Heavy and light colours (not the same as dark and light colours) → ❷.
(In addition to the darkness, the natural red component is also decisive for the impression of heaviness)

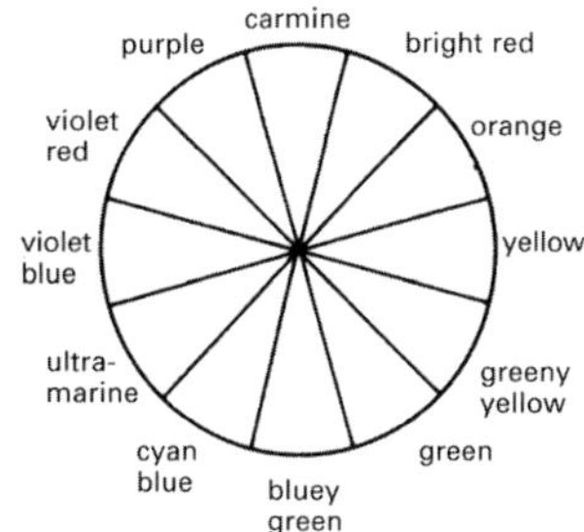

❹ The 12-segment colour circle

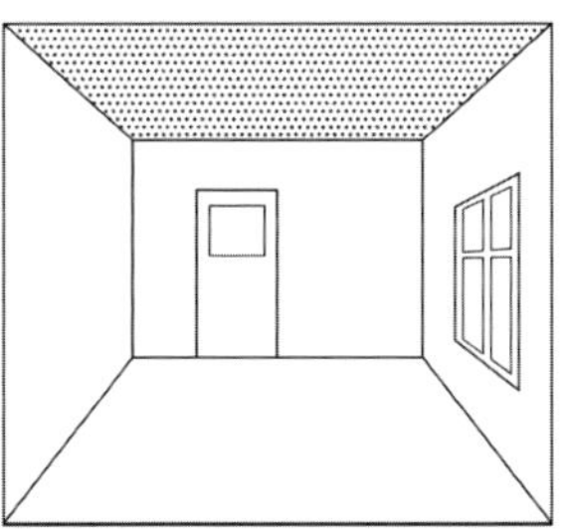

❺ Rooms seem lower when the ceiling is heavily coloured

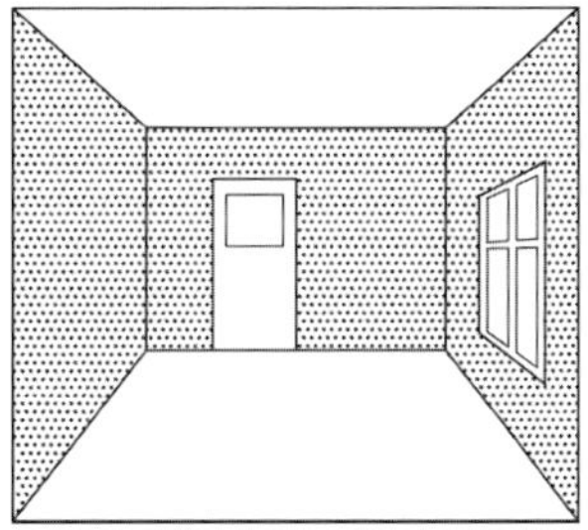

❻ Colourful side walls seem to extend the room upwards and downwards

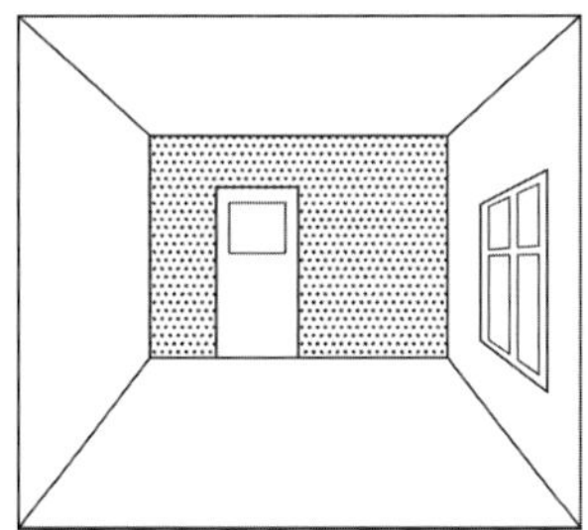

❼ Colourful end walls make long rooms seem shorter

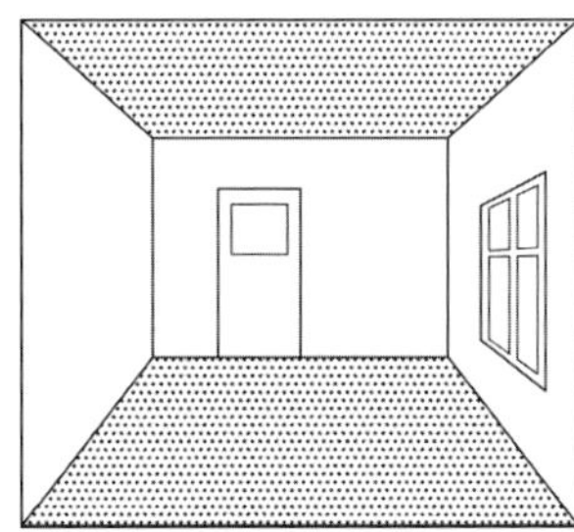

❽ Colourful floors and ceilings make rooms seem lower and wider

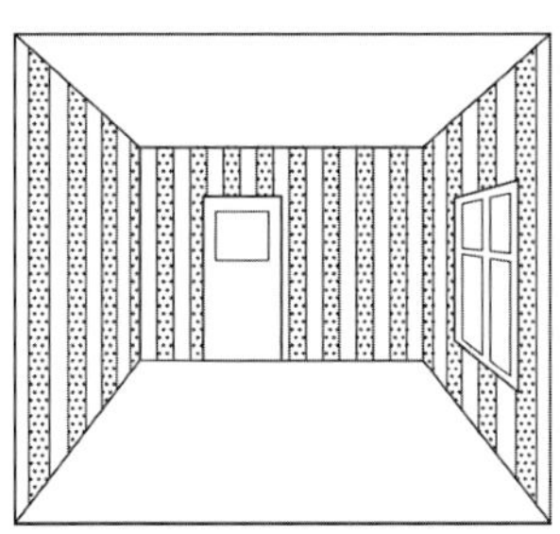

❾ Vertical stripes make walls seem higher

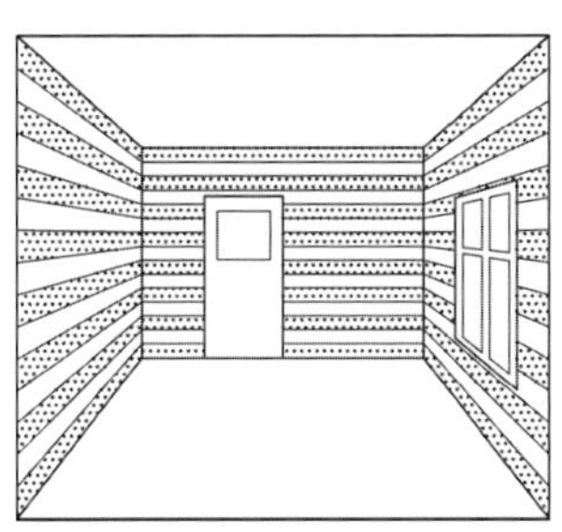

❿ Horizontal stripes widen the wall and the room seems lower

Colours have a power over people. They can create feelings of well-being, unease, activity or passivity. Paint schemes in factories, offices or schools can improve or dull performance, in hospitals can improve the health of the patients. The influence of colour on people can take place indirectly through physiological effect, for example making rooms appear wider or narrower, leading to an oppressive or liberating feeling → ❺ – ❿. Colour's influence is also exercised directly through impulses produced by each colour → ❷ – ❸. Orange has the strongest impulse power, followed by yellow, red, green and purple. Blue, turquoise and violet (cold and passive colours) have the lowest power.
Strongly impulsive colours are suitable only for small areas within rooms, but non-impulsive colours can be used across extensive stretches. Warm colours have an active effect, stimulating or even exciting. Cold colours are passive, calming or spiritual. Green is relaxing for the nerves.
The effect produced by colours also depends on their brightness and location. Warm and light shades viewed overhead have a mentally stimulating effect; at the side, warming and coming close; below, relaxing and lifting. Warm and dark colours overhead exert an enclosing and dignified influence; at the side, surrounding; below, they offer secure grip and footing.
Cold and light colours viewed overhead are brightening and, relaxing; at the side, they seem to lead away; below, they are smooth and encourage walking. Cold and dark colours viewed overhead are threatening; at the side, cold and sad; below, burdensome and dragging down.
White is the colour of absolute purity, cleanliness and order. White plays a major role in interior design, to separate and neutralise other colour groups, then to structure them with light and vitality. As the colour of order, white is used to denote areas in warehouses and car parks, and for road markings.

Surface	Value	Surface	Value
white paper	84	pure turquoise blue	15
lime white	80	grass green	≈ 20
lemon yellow	70	pastel green	≈ 50
ivory	≈ 70	silver grey	≈ 35
cream	≈ 70	lime plaster grey	≈ 42
pure gold yellow	60	dry concrete grey	≈ 32
straw yellow	60	plywood	≈ 38
light ochre	≈ 60	yellow brick	≈ 32
pure chrome yellow	50	red brick	≈ 18
pure orange	25–30	dark brick	≈ 10
light brown	≈ 25	Solnhofen slab	≈ 50
pure beige	≈ 25	medium stone	35
medium brown	≈ 15	dry asphalt	≈ 20
salmon pink	≈ 40	wet asphalt	≈ 5
full scarlet red	16	dark oak	≈ 18
vermilion red	20	light oak	≈ 33
carmine red	10	walnut	≈ 18
deep violet	≈ 5	light spruce	≈ 50
light blue	40–50	aluminium foil	83
deep sky blue	30	zinc plated steel	16

⓫ Brightness of surfaces. Values between theoretical white (100%) and absolute black (0%)

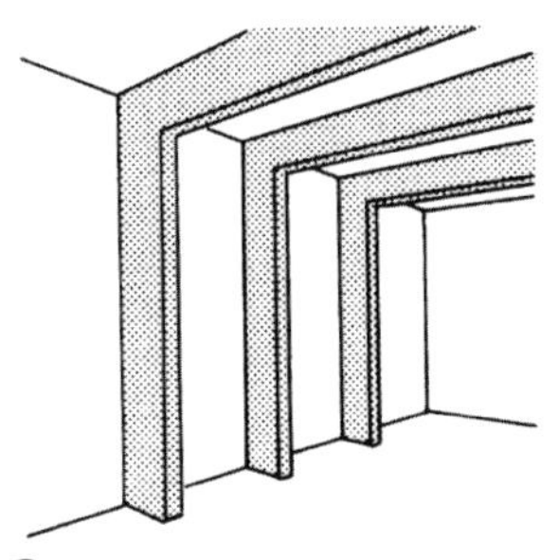

⓬ Dark single elements in front of light walls are powerfully emphasised

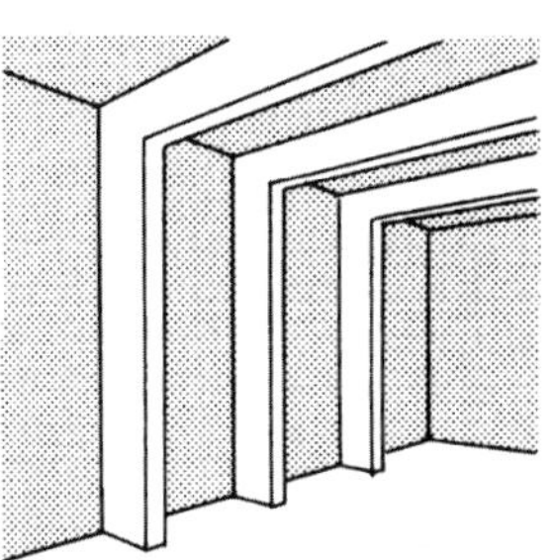

⓭ Light elements in front of dark walls seem even lighter

"(...)
The work starts with the production of a detailed building programme by an experienced architect on the basis of the questionnaire → pp. 44 and 45.(...)

The sketch scheme is begun by drawing individual rooms of the required areas as simple rectangles, to scale, grouped in the desired relationships to each other (...) and to the compass directions. During this stage, the building commission becomes increasingly clear and a picture forms in the architect's eye. Instead of starting on the drawings, however, on the basis of the previous work establishing the building area, the final position of the structure on the site should be determined. This is often decided by exploring the compass direction, the wind direction, possible access routes, the lie of the land, existing trees and the neighbourhood. Unless the one correct location of the building is obvious in advance, this will require many attempts to exhaust the possibilities (...) and detailed discussions about the pros and cons. These investigations will normally render decision-making fairly quick, and the image of the future building gradually into focus (...).

And now come the birth pains of the actual design stage, first in the architect's imagination out of their deep immersion in the organic and organisational issues raised by the commission and the thoughts behind them. This creates a schematic idea in the mind of the architect of the overall configuration of the building and its spatial atmosphere, from which can be developed the outline of its appearance in plan and elevation.

On the other hand, according to the architect's temperament, for some a rapid sketch or an intricate scribble is the first product of this birth process. The impetus of the first sketch can often be squandered by unskilled helpers, however. The clarity of this image in the mind normally increases with the experience and character of the designer. Older, mature architects are often capable of drawing the final design layout freehand to the precise scale and in full detail. Some refined, mature works are produced in this way, although they mostly lose the verve of earlier designs.

Once the preliminary design is completed (...) a rest period of 3–14 days is advisable, as this allows detachment from it and permits defects to become more obvious, but also offers suggestions for their remedy, because such a waiting time removes many preconceived notions, not least through discussions with employees or the client.

Now the detailed processing of the design starts, the meetings with the structural and services engineers, in short the determination of the construction and the installations. After this (but mostly in advance), the drawings are sent off to the building approval authority, whose examination normally takes 3–6 months.

During this time, the costs are estimated and the works put out to tender using ready-made forms, so that the tenders are available when the building approval is granted, the contracts can be awarded promptly and work can start. All the tasks described here can keep the architect busy for 2–3 months (for a large detached house) or 3–12 months (for a larger project such as a hospital), depending on the circumstances.

It is not advisable to try to save money on design work, as more time spent on careful preparation at this stage can quickly be recouped during the building phase. In addition, the client saves costs and interest."

Quoted from: Ernst Neufert, Architects' Data, 1st ed., p. 34

What is design?
How does design work and what differentiates 'building' from 'architecture'?

Reading the text by Ernst Neufert from the first edition of 'Architect's Data', opposite, it is still clear that he is talking about the essential stages of the design process and describing for the reader the human experience of the working method, which we can understand via his encouraging but pretention-free words.

Ernst Neufert's views of the influences driving the creative process in architecture would certainly be different if he wrote them today. In what way and to what purpose, we cannot know, considering the developments in architectural theory in the last 20–30 years. So the current generation is faced with the question, what should be the fundamentals of design, in order to encourage an authentic architectural form?

Design seems to be very easy, and at the same time very difficult, with many influences. But it is always about **space** and its construction through architectural elements: if a single space is formed by its function, then a number of spaces require overall organisation, a **spatial theme**. The architectural elements are in accordance with the theme and mould the specific form and the authenticity of style in its time. History shows that a building commission is only fixed to a certain extent in its spatial style. A building type often changes for reasons which do not always have to do with function. A building can offer many uses, because it more than just a 'glove' for the function – which is demonstrated by the long lives of old buildings.

The essential drivers of change in typological characteristics are more often pictorial ideas about the cultural significance of a building, which result in alterations to the spatial and architectural elements. Buildings with a great influence on architectural history mostly have a very precisely emphasised spatial theme, which determines the overall layout. Excellent and masterful can have two different meanings in this case: **Reduction in the complexity of a commission to a single simple concept or a combination of themes with great variety.**

Design is never academic; works are the result of intuitive processes, in which the entire sensual perception of their creator plays a role. Nonetheless, they make use of an architectural grammar, which is organised thematically rather than stylistically.

The architectural considerations determining a building form a complex system of themes, which arise as knowingly staged or work coincidentally to different extents, but at any rate are inseparably intertwined. The basic elements of an architectural language are to be displayed and implemented according to an architectural grammar. The reference planes are **typology**, **topography** and the **architectural elements**. Each building relates to a location and a topographical situation. These create and offer a topos. It is selected for a function and a spatial typology, and architectural elements provide the stylistic form.

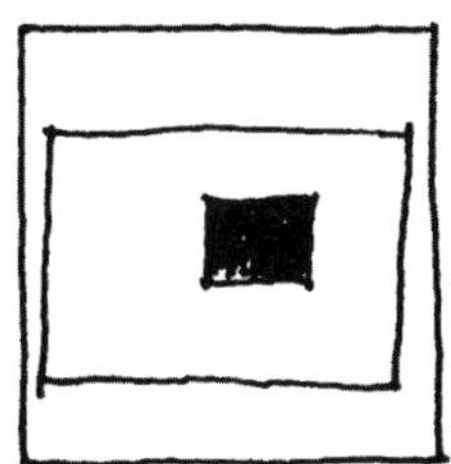

1 Volumes in the structure

Bodily composed building elements, which take plastic shape inside a structure

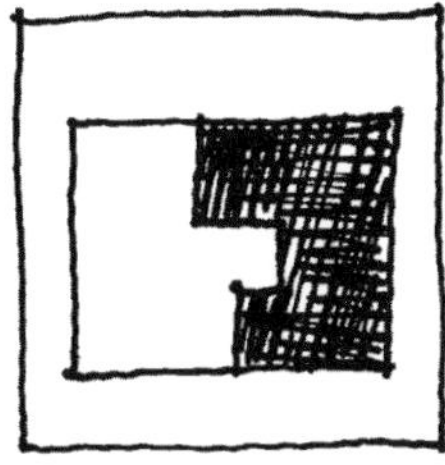

2 Open and enclosed bodies

Free spaces and volumes are inseparably connected to each other. The spatial theme extends from courtyard concepts to solitary buildings

3 Room plan/cavities in volumes

Single or a composed sequence of interior rooms organise themselves in their specific form within the volume

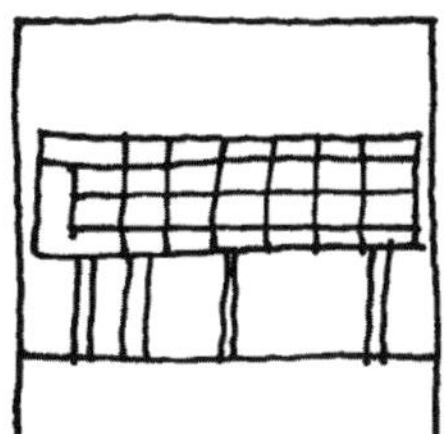

4 On columns

The volume of the structure frees itself from underground to create an especially impressive space in-between.

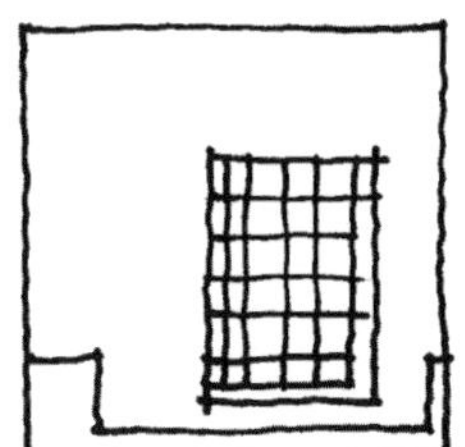

5 Hollow

The structure creates a place related to itself; the weight of the volume sinks in.

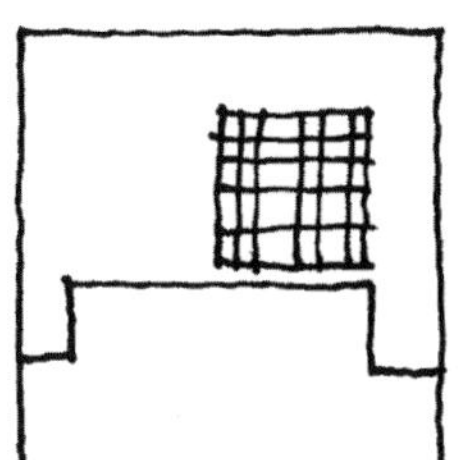
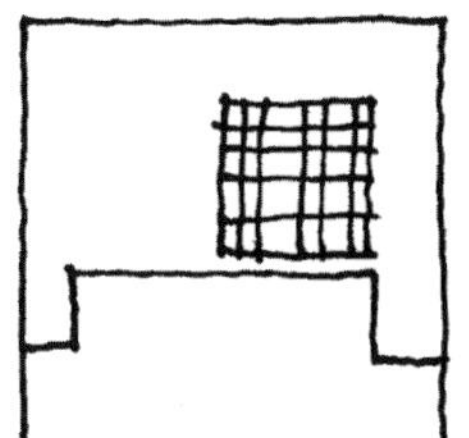

6 Plateau

The plinth zone separates the rising façade from the street; the topographical elevation liberates the structure and creates a special place.

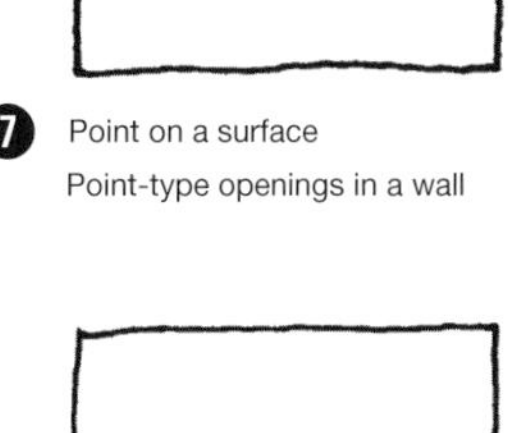

7 Point on a surface

Point-type openings in a wall

8 Line on a surface

Horizontal or vertical ribbon windows

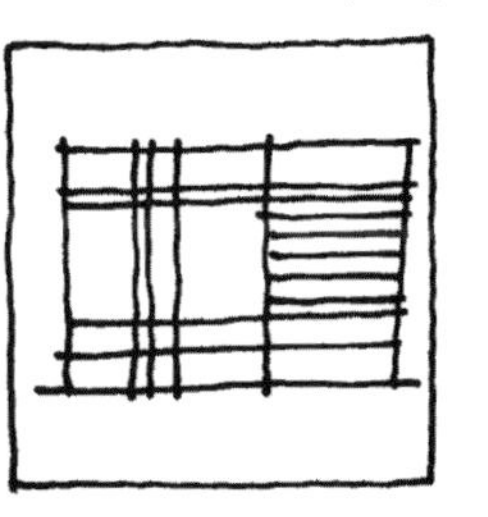

9 Structuring on a surface

Glass division and construction form a network of lines, an independent design element.

10 Wall panel and columns

Punctiform – striped – flat wall element

11 Cut-outs

Cut-outs and deepened cavities in the volume

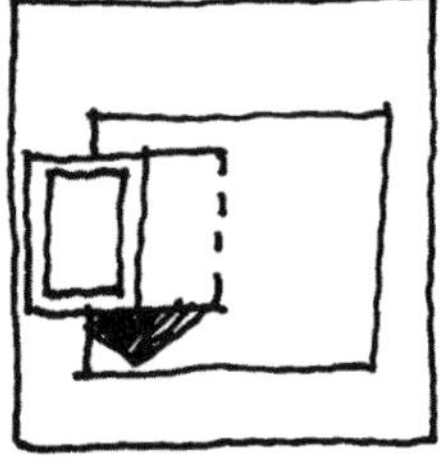

12 Projections

Plastic elements projecting from the volume

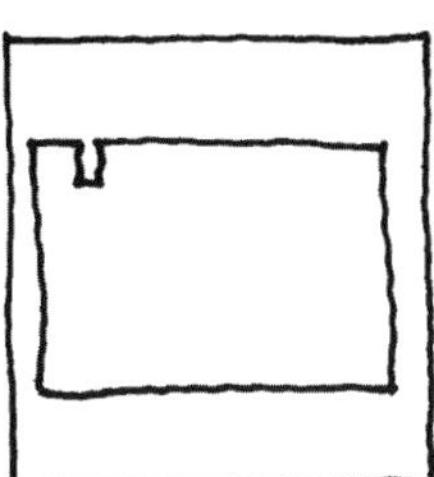

13 Flat roof

Horizontal upper edge emphasises the body of the building

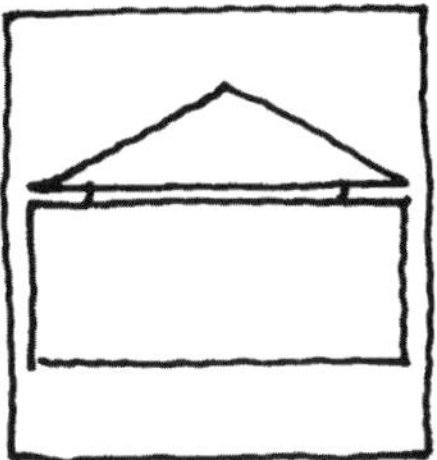

14 Roof as body

Pitched roof surfaces form a geometrical body

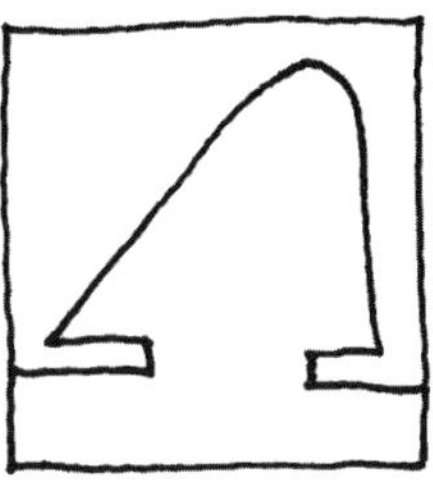

15 All over

Equal treatment of roof and wall

Typology
The typological structure of a building grows out of the function and also from the construction and town planning situation. It is three-dimensional and therefore to be understood as a spatial theme.

Topography
The theme of topography refers to the unique location of the building and develops from this a town planning or landscape-related statement. This statement has a major influence on the quality of the public space.

Architectural elements
The structural elements composing a building are always to be designed in keeping with the overall appearance and follow design principles just as much as technical requirements and utility criteria.

Façades/openings → **7** – **9**
All opening elements form a graphical structure on the surface of the wall. A mixture and combination of various structural principles can lead to an over-loaded façade.

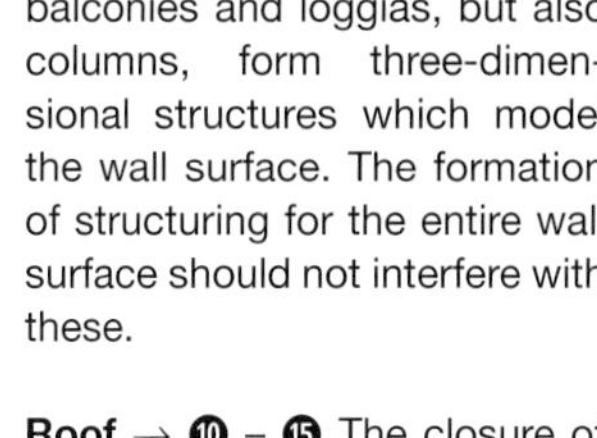

Plastic elements → **10** – **12**
Functional components like balconies and loggias, but also columns, form three-dimensional structures which model the wall surface. The formation of structuring for the entire wall surface should not interfere with these.

Roof → **10** – **15** The closure of the roof makes the building a complete sculpture. Town planning context and architectural concepts are decisive for the selection of a type of roof.

DESIGN
What is design?
Planes of reference
Questionnaire

The design process is often rushed; projects are tendered and started with insufficient documents. So it has to be understood that the 'final' drawings and costs are available only when the building is almost complete. Explanations to clients will not help this situation; the only answer is faster and better organised work by the architect, with adequate preparation in the office and on the site.

Every project demands similar information; detailed questionnaires and forms, which should already be to hand when the project is commissioned, can help speed up progress. Variations will of course always be necessary but a long list of decisions is so generally applicable that questionnaires can assist every building professional, even if only as an encouragement.

The following questionnaire forms just a part of the work-saving forms which an efficient architect's office should have available, along with forms for cost estimates etc.

Briefing questionnaire

Commission no.:
Client:
Project:
Information collected by:
Copies to:

I. Information about the client

1. Company's outlook? Financial situation? Level of employment? Total capital? Where was this information obtained? Confidential!
2. How does the business seem to be conducted?
3. Who is our main contact? Who is their deputy? Who has the final authority?
4. Has the client any special wishes regarding design?
5. What attitude do they have to art? Particularly with regard to our way of working?
6. Which personal views/characteristics of the client should be taken into account?
7. Who is likely to cause us difficulties? Why? With what potential effects?
8. Is the client interested in later publication of their building?
9. Do the drawings have to be understandable by non-experts?
10. Who was the client's previous architect?
11. For what reason did the former architect not receive this commission?
12. Is the client planning further buildings? Which? How large? When? Have designs already been produced for these? Is there a chance that we could obtain the commission? What steps have been taken in this direction? With what success?

II. Agreements on fees

1. On what agreement is the calculation of the fees based?
2. What approximate degree of finishing is to be assumed?
3. Should the project cost be estimated, is this the basis for the fee calculation?
4. What is the estimated project cost?
5. Will we also be responsible for the finishing works?
6. Has a contract been signed or a written confirmation of agreement?

III. People and firms involved in the project

1. With whom do we conduct preliminary discussions?
2. Who is responsible for what special areas of activity?
3. Who is responsible for checking the invoices?
4. What ordering and checking procedure will be used?
5. Will we have authority to award contracts directly in the name of the client? Up to what value? Has the authorisation been issued to us in writing?
6. Which contractors are recommended by the client? (Trade, address, telephone, etc.)
7. Is a site manager required? Desired? Experienced or junior? When? Permanent or temporary? For how long?
8. Is the client in agreement with our decisions about the legal situation of the site manager?
9. Will the client make space available for the site office? Equipment (telephone, computer, etc.)?

IV. General

1. If there is no enclosure, must a fence or hoarding be installed? Can this be let for advertising? Should a signboard be erected? What lettering should be on it?
2. Precise address of the project? Its later name?
3. Address of nearest railway station?
4. Address of nearest post office?
5. Is there a telephone connection at the site?
6. Working time on the site?

V. Construction

1. Who has drawn up the building schedule? Is it sufficiently detailed? Will it have to be added to by us or others? Does it have to be approved by the client before the start of design work?
2. To which existing or future buildings does the building have to relate? → VIII, 9.
3. Which local or statutory regulations are applicable? Local planning responsibility?
4. What has been written about this building in the specialist press? What is in our collection of cuttings?
5. Where has a similar commission been carried out, with excellent results?
6. Via whom is it possible to view it? Already notified?

VI. Basic design factors

1. What do the surroundings look like? Landscape? Existing trees? Climate? Compass direction? Wind direction?
2. What is the form of the existing buildings? Of what building materials are they? → *VIII*, 9.
3. Are photographs available of the surroundings of the new project (stating where taken from)? Ordered?
4. What must the design also take into consideration?
5. Existing storey and building heights? Street frontages? Building lines? Later streets? Trees (type, size)?
6. What later construction has to be taken into account now?
7. Is a general development plan desirable?
8. Are there local rules for the external appearance of new buildings on this site?
9. Who will check the building application with regard to aesthetic matters? What is their attitude? Is it advisable to present a preliminary design for discussion?
10. What office is responsible for complaints at a higher level? What is the procedure? The duration of a complaint? What is the attitude of this office?

Questionnaire *(continued)*

VII. Technical basics

1. What type of subsoil is found in the area?
2. Have site investigations been undertaken at the site? At what locations? With what results?
3. What ground pressure can be assumed?
4. Normal groundwater level? High groundwater level? Exceptionally high groundwater level?
5. Has the plot been built on previously? With what? How many storeys? How deep was the cellar?
6. What type of foundations seem sensible?
7. What method of construction should be used for the building? Cellar floor: Construction? Loading? From what? Coverings? Protective coating? Measures to resist groundwater? Slab over cellar: Construction? Loading? From what? Protective coating? Ground floor slab: Material? Loading? From what? Coverings? Roof slab: Construction? Loading? From what? Coverings? Protective coating? What roof covering? Gutters? Downpipes inside or outside?
8. What insulation types should be provided? Against noise? Horizontal? Vertical? Against vibration? Against heat? Horizontal? Vertical?
9. How should the columns be detailed? External walls? Internal walls?
10. What type of stairs? Loading?
11. What windows? Steel? Timber? Aluminium? Type of glass? Sound insulation or sun protection glass? Opening inward or outward? Single-glazed, combined, double-glazed windows? Sound insulation windows?
12. What doors? Steel linings? Plywood? Steel? With rubber seals? Fire-resisting or fireproof? With door closers?
13. What type of heating? Fuel? Storage for what duration? Oil heating? Electric heating?
14. What domestic water heating? What quantities are required? When? At which locations? What is the chemical composition of the drinking water? Provide water softener?
15. What type of ventilation? Air changes? In which rooms? Smoke extraction?
16. What cooling? Ice supply?
17. What water supply? Diameter of the supply pipe? Diameter of the hoses of the local fire brigade? Water supply pressure? Does this vary widely? Details? Water price per m^3? Outside taps?
18. What drainage? Connection to sewers? Where? What diameter does the main sewer have? Depth? Where does drain water go to? Is percolation possible? Sensible? Allowed? Own treatment plant? Will mechanical cleaning suffice or is biological cleaning required? Rainwater collection?
19. What diameter gas supply? Efficiency? Price per m^3? Discount for large consumers? Are there special regulations about laying pipes? Venting?
20. What lighting? Electricity supply? Voltage? Possible connections? Consumer limit? Price per kW for lighting? Power? Off-peak price from, to? Discount for large consumers? Transformer? High-voltage station? Own power generation? Diesel, steam turbine, wind generator?
21. What telephone system?
22. What intercom? Entry phone? Light? Command system?
23. What type of lift? Special loadings? Floor or parapet access? Speed? Machine room at top or bottom?
24. What other transport systems? Extent? Route? Performance? Pneumatic tube?
25. Waste chutes and waste disposal units? Where? How large? For what waste? Waste incineration? Paper press?
26. Other.

VIII. Design documents

1. Has the land registry been viewed? Copy obtained? What significance for the design?
2. Is there a plan of the town? Ordered? With details of transport systems?
3. Is there a layout plan? Ordered? Officially approved?
4. Is there a level plan? Ordered?
5. Has the water supply plan been clarified?
6. Has the drainage plan been clarified?
7. Has the gas supply connection been determined on plan?
8. Has the electrical supply connection been determined on plan? Confirmed by the utility supplier? Cable or masts?
9. Has the front of the neighbouring houses been surveyed? Has the type of building been determined (general development plan).
10. Has a benchmark been determined without problems and fixed?
11. Is a building site set-up plan required?
12. Where does the building application have to be handed in? How many copies? In what form? Paper size? Prints? Blue? Red? On linen? How do the drawings have to be coloured (plan regulations)?
13. What are the requirements for handing in structural calculations? Who is accredited as a checking engineer? Who could be considered? (Who is named by the building authority?)

IX. Tender documents

1. What is the distance of the site from a goods station?
2. Is there a siding to the building site? Normal gauge, narrow gauge? What are the unloading possibilities?
3. How are the access routes? Site roads required?
4. What storage space is available for building materials? Flat open spaces? Flat-roofed spaces? What height relationship to the building? Can a number of contractors work next to each other without problems?
5. Will any deliveries or works be undertaken by the client? What? Building cleaning? Security? Gardening?
6. Is there a prospect of advance payment, cash payment? Or what payment terms and financial distribution are to be observed?
7. What building materials are usual locally? Particularly cheap? Particularly expensive?

X. Production deadlines for

1. Sketches for meetings with the employees?
2. Sketches for meetings with the client?
3. Preliminary design (scale) with estimate?
4. Design (scale)?
5. Cost estimate?
6. Handing in the building approval drawings with structural calculations and any other verifications?
7. Forecast duration of the building approval procedure? Appeal route? Possibilities of acceleration?
8. Construction drawings?
9. Start of tender period?
10. Tender deadline?
11. Contract award procedure? Construction schedule?
12. Start of construction?
13. Completion of structure?
14. Final completion (ready for moving in)?
15. Final invoice?

investigation of the need for the planned building	is a new building necessary or could an existing building be suitable?
optimisation of the space allocation programme	layout of the space allocation programme for actual needs optimisation of route relationships
checking and optimisation of the plot situation	plot suitable for the building project? supply situation, vehicle flows etc.
optimisation of the building design	optimum usability and possible conversion (building depths, structural system, access cores etc.) design: typology, relationship of plan to façade, contemporary and original appearance etc. thermal comfort for the users
long, useful service life	durability, conversion possibilities, simple to renew
use of durable building materials	longer life cycle, reduction of maintenance and renewal cost suitability and ageing characteristics of the materials used
optimisation of building element geometries	to increase the usefulness, greater scope of use, better continued use and reuse
avoidance of composite materials and parts, which can only be separated with difficulty	better suitability for recycling and reuse, continued use or reuse of used materials and parts
low content of damaging substances in building components and materials	simpler continued use or reuse, simple disposal of waste, protection of soil and groundwater
controlled demolition when no further use is possible	separation of materials and mostly continued use or reuse of building materials and parts

1 Cascade of design principles (Federal Office for Building and Planning → refs)

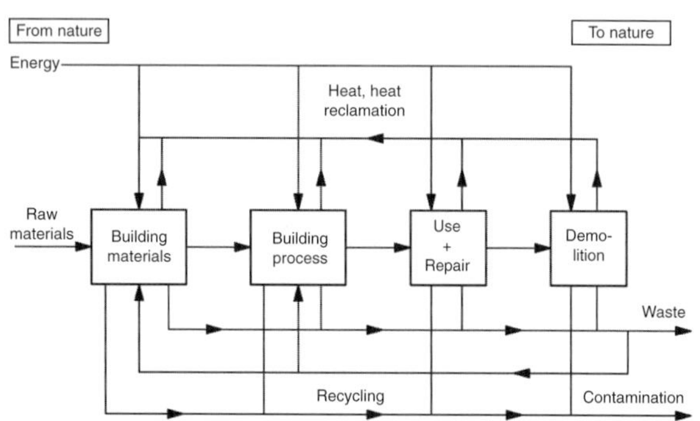

2 Energy and raw material circulation in buildings' phases of existence

ecological dimension	use on area use, scattering and mixing of mineral and energy raw materials emissions in the form of undesirable release of solid, liquid or gaseous substances, which could damage the biosphere or environment waste products, which release pollutants and remove valuable resources from the natural cycles noise, dust and vibration
economic dimension	lifecycle costs of buildings rebuilding and maintenance costs in relation to initial investment
social dimension	creation and maintenance of jobs preservation of living space in accordance with needs, by age and size of household creation of a suitable residential environment creation of cheap residential space, increasing the owner-occupier percentage networking of work, living and leisure in residential areas, 'healthy living' inside and outside the home

3 Evaluation of aspects of sustainability

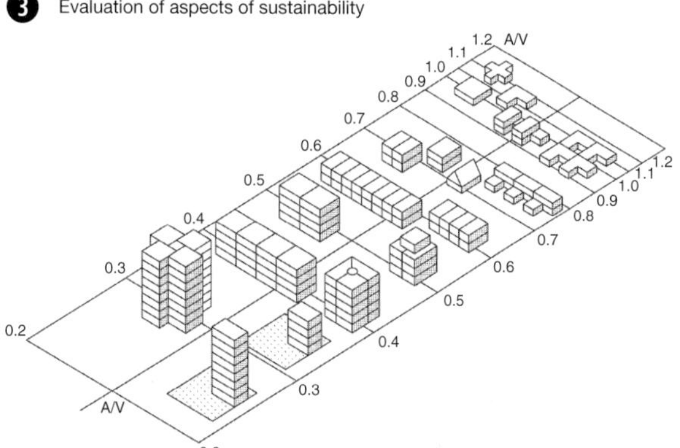

4 Comparison of the relationship of area of building envelope to usable building area per m^2 (Schema Solarbüro, Dr. Peter Goretzki)

SUSTAINABLE BUILDING

General, Design, Construction

Sustainability

Since the agreement of Agenda 21 at the Rio de Janeiro Conference for Environment and Development in 1992, sustainability has been a central theme of national and international environmental policy. Sustainable development has for years been considered the best model for mankind to meet the challenges of the future. 'Sustainable development describes development in accord with the needs of the current generation without endangering opportunities for future generations to satisfy their own needs and choose their own lifestyle . . .' (Brundtland Report, 1987). The Federal Ministry of the Environment introduced management rules for sustainable development in 1998 – Regeneration: renewable natural resources may only be exploited in the long term within their capability of regeneration; Substitution: non-renewable resources may only be used to the extent that their use cannot be replaced by other materials or energy sources; Adaptability: the release of substances or energy may not be greater than the adaptability of ecological systems.

Sustainable building

Building and the built environment can play a key role in our future development. The construction and operation of buildings is a basic strain on the environment which should be reduced as far as possible. The construction and use of buildings consume a considerable share of natural resources, energy and water but construction according to sustainable principles works within an economic, ecological and social context.

Sustainable building consists of a multitude of concepts and measures, which have to be appropriate to the particular project. The social and cultural effects of the project (function, design and aesthetics, listed status etc.) are to be considered with equal weighting.

Buildings are normally operated over a long time period, i.e. savings or extra costs can be effective in the long term. The intention is a minimisation of the use of resources and energy and the least possible impairment of the natural ecological system for all phases of the life cycle of a building (design, construction, use, refurbishment, demolition). Instruments have been developed with which the various materials, construction methods etc. can be compared with each other and balanced according to differentiated criteria.

Sustainable architecture

The quality of architecture, design and the planning of buildings play a decisive role in the sustainability of a building. The cost of constructing a building is always to be related to the (forecast) duration of its use, and a longer service life often justifies more expensive design and construction.

The average service life of a building is 50–100 years (2–3 generations), although many buildings which are still in use today are much older. The cycles of renewal and modernisation are therefore much longer term than for the building services. As a result, a typologically flexibly usable structure is worth much more for sustainability than ever could be the case with the building services installation. The attention of the architect should therefore concentrate on the design of the building as a composition of structure and design.

BS EN ISO 13370
BS ISO 15686-5
DIN EN 15232
ASTM E917-05
DIN 276
DIN 4108-2
DIN EN ISO 13791
DIN EN ISO 13792
DIN EN 15232
DIN 18386

Heating	Domestic hot water
– optimum design of control and regulation – consideration of incoming solar radiation through façade-related zoning of the heating system in the control process. – different regulation circuits for parts of the building with different requirements – extended regulation concepts for flexible room layouts – setting of the temperature per room and prescription of time programme	– checking if hot water is necessary – for the remaining hot water supply: observation of the requirements for the maintenance of hygiene regulations concerning drinking water, rational energy and water consumption, optimisation of the system and operating costs – investigate the possibilities of solar-assisted domestic water heating

❶ Potential savings of heating energy

Lighting	Heating, cooling	Air conditioning	Electrical devices
fullest exploitation of daylight efficient lamps electronic ballast for fluorescent lights lighting controls economical lighting outlay for external areas	energy-saving, independently regulating circulation pumps constructional measures for summer thermal protection cooling load calculation for necessary air-conditioning systems	reduction of air flows to the absolute minimum low pressure loss ductwork fans and motors of high efficiency	energy-saving devices (normal operation and stand-by) devices with off-switch at the mains (if operationally possible)

❷ Potential savings of electrical energy

ecological criteria	environmental impact through treatment of building waste transport impact emission of health-impairing substances emissions with global effects (ozone hole, acid rain, greenhouse effect) noise, dust emissions use of land use of new material energy required for waste disposal recognition and separation of polluted batches waste materials and their disposal
saving of environmental impact through substitution of new production processes	transport required for new production emissions of hazardous substances use of land area use of regenerative and non-regenerative resources minimisation of energy consumption for building material production waste materials from building materials production and their disposal
effects of thermal exploitation	calorific value of the building waste
economic criteria	regulations, their application and tightening acceptance of products from the recycling of building waste materials necessary capacities costs
technical criteria	high-quality recycling technical feasibility

❸ Evaluation of the waste disposal process

1.	avoidance reuse (e.g. steel joists, bricks etc.) further use (e.g. pre-cast elements with new function)
2.	exploitation recycling e.g. crushing of concrete for aggregate downcycling, e.g. calcium silicate blocks as fill material thermal exploitation, e.g. timber
3.	disposal composting landfill

❹ Disposal routes (basics of recycling)

Many factors are decisive for the sustainability of architecture:
- relationship of the design to the location and the building purpose
- contemporary and original appearance of the design
- easily usable and effective structures
- durability of construction and materials
- suitability and ageing characteristics of the materials used
- flexibility for changes of use
- possibility of conversion if required

The intensive use of raw materials and energy in the erection of buildings is normally connected with a long period of usefulness. This phase of the life cycle of a building is therefore very significant.

A significant part of the use of energy and raw materials takes place during the use of the building through the operation of technical devices and installations. New buildings should always be designed in accordance with the current state of technology and existing buildings should be regularly checked to investigate whether any updating (thermal insulation, building services etc.) is possible or necessary in order to ensure energy-saving operation. In addition to the durability and long life of the services installation, mechanisms and methods of saving resources should be the highest priority. Ideally, cycles should be set up to enable the reuse of water and energy.

The aims are:
- health and thermal comfort in the use phase
- minimisation of the energy, operating and maintenance costs, reduction of cleaning costs (partially self-cleaning: e.g. façades, roofs etc.)
- minimisation of the servicing and maintenance cost

Rules and regulations:
- Energy Saving Regulations (EnEV)
- SIA 380/4 Electrical Energy in Building: Swiss Engineers and Architects Association, Recommendations
- 'Verification of sufficient summer thermal protection' standards
- 'Building automation' standards
- Heating systems regulations (HeizAnlV)

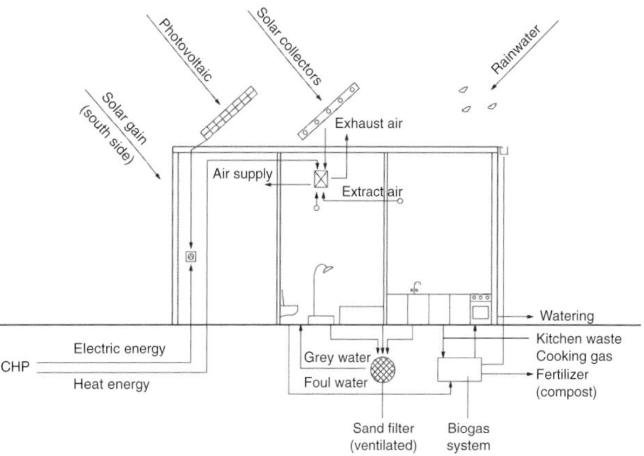

❺ The application of cycles through the example of a residential building in Freiburg-Vauban

Arch.: Common & Gies

BS ISO 15686-5
PD 6079-4
DIN 276
DIN 277
DIN 18205

see also → Office buildings pp. 231 ff.

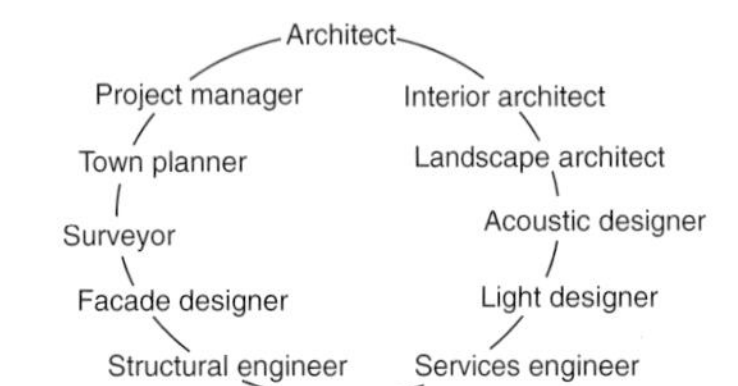

professional client – CREM (corporate real estate management) – technical project manager – facility management		**trade and industry** 50–100 trades
Client	**Architect** renaissance	**Tradesmen** 10 trades
Client	**Master builder** middle ages	**Site hut** 3 trades
User	**Man builds** early times	**Self-build**

❶ Product and producers – development since the beginning of culture

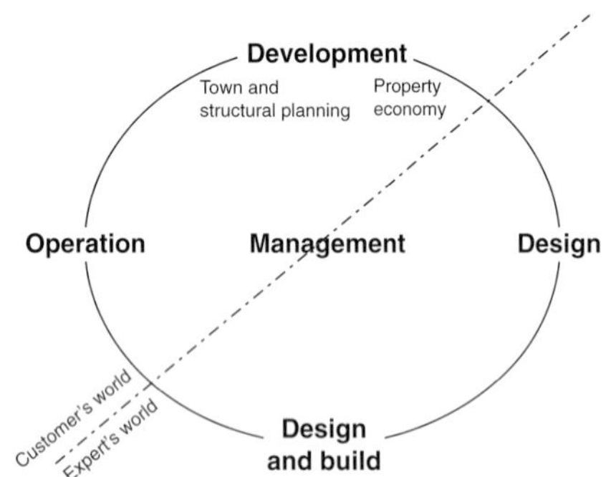

❷ The life-cycle assessment of a building

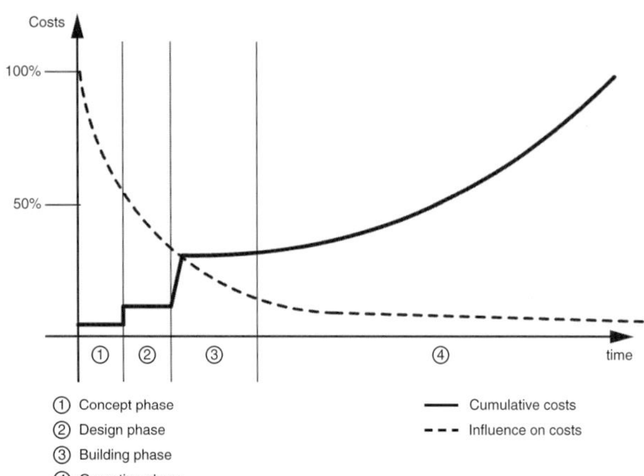

❸ Possibilities for project development to influence building costs

Client – responsibility and duties

The client, or commissioner, as the actual decision-maker about its characteristics, bears an essential part of the responsibility for the quality and sustainability of a planned building.

The architect has a central role as the consulting expert, who directs and coordinates all the specialists involved in the design and construction process in a single-minded intention to meet the formulated project aims. In relation to the client, the architect has a role which combines typical expert duties, like exercising their power of persuasion regarding innovative design and construction solutions, with the disciplines of a modern service provider, for example transparency and ensuring the reliability of completion dates and cost estimate.

Considering the oversupply of property since the start of the 21st century and the resulting aggressive competition for building purchasers and tenants, it seems advisable to look in detail into the economic requirements of the typical client.

Clients may be owner-occupiers or investors:

- The owner-occupier or owner-operator is mainly concerned with a reasonable relationship between function and an appropriate image for their company, on the one hand, and cost, on the other.
- The investor is, in contrast, interested in letting or selling with the greatest possible success under current market conditions.

These demand different development, design and construction processes, which, especially in the US and UK, have achieved a high degree of professionalism and success that has motivated investment.

Complex requirements for buildings

The expression 'added value' comes from the field of production and has increasingly been adopted in the property management field. It includes a complex combination of quantitative and qualitative parameters:

- actually achievable rents, disregarding tax or political effects
- complete and comprehensible costs over the entire life cycle of the building
- practical conversion possibilities laid out in use scenarios planned long term, with all relevant consequences, particularly disturbance-free operation.

Life-cycle assessment

The modern approach in architectural design is typified by the holistic consideration of all phases of the lifetime of a building, called the life-cycle or whole life assessment → ❷. This means that all relevant functional, aesthetic, cost, scheduling and organisational features are systematically categorised for each phase. Of particular importance is the transfer of experience gained during the operation phase to the start of the life cycle of later projects. The result is to transform the planned building into an asset supported by comprehensive responsibility, which can normally continue to be used and maintained after its original purpose has expired.

Project development and programme production

The initial work phase, in which the room and function programmes are developed for an owner-operator, is of course of great significance in the architectural life cycle. When the client is an investor, typical tenant scenarios will be developed → ❸. Careful programming of rooms and functions can result in a considerable increase in the value of a building project:

- functional improvement of typical working and communication processes (the primary or core processes) in the building
- reduction of the space consumed to fulfil functions through appropriate compression of use

BS 8536
BS EN 15221
DIN 18960
DIN 32736

GEFMA 100
GEFMA 130

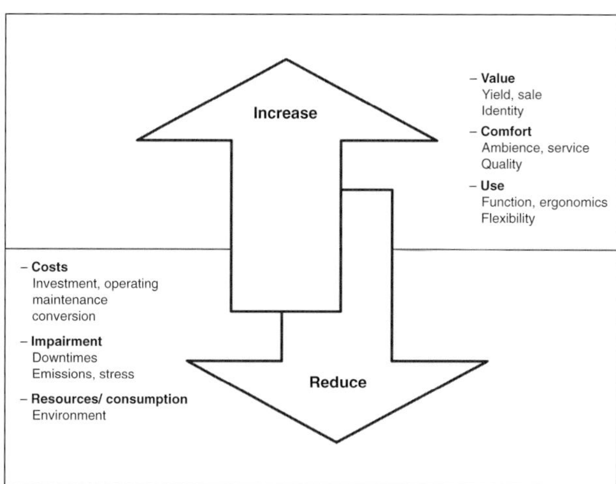

❶ Factors which can be influenced and controlled by facility management

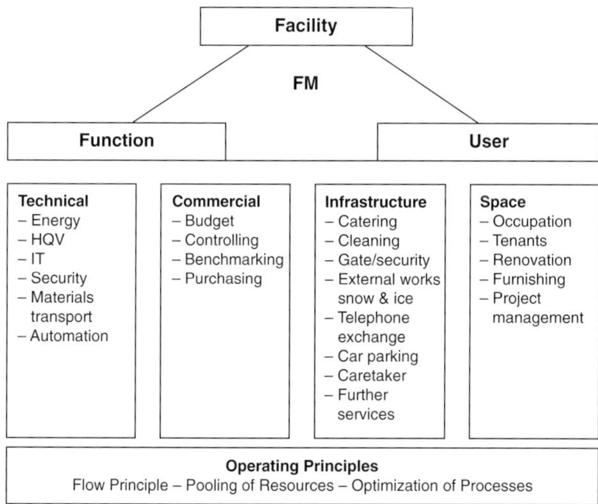

❷ The four columns of facility management

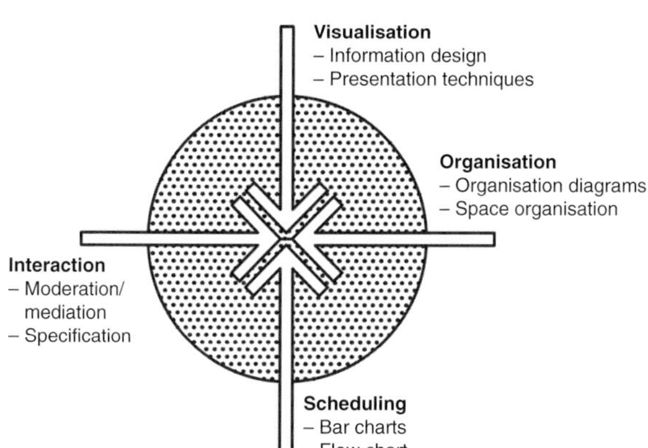

❸ Methods of facility management

A new professional discipline

A facility manager is the description for the professional manager of an entire building operation. They undertake all the tasks of the client which can be delegated to specialists. This profession arrived from the USA at the end of the 20th century and has developed very positively in recent years, against the trend for most property-related professions. Its origins were in the planning of the occupation of space (property management). Facility management (FM) developed from related professions like those of architects, building services engineers or infrastructure service providers.

The consistent implementation of FM can save up to 30% in comparison with traditional forms of building management for the same user requirements. Because the operating costs amount to about 80% of the total costs for the entire life-cycle, FM is quickly becoming established as the key profession for the sustainable implementation of architecture → ❶. A range of national and international facility management associations, such as GEFMA, IFMA and BIFM, produce guidelines for facility managers.

The main principle of FM is the combination and optimisation of the many services concerned with a building and its users, which normally already exist but are scattered in their organisation. The architect provides the essential roots for successful FM, is thus the most important partner of a facility manager and also has the best qualifications to take over the tasks of this discipline.

Structural and service aspects

FM is based on a four-column model → ❷. These columns list the technical fields involved, ordered according to their qualification background. These are very heterogeneous, which means that the facility manager has to be a generalist, who typically comes from one specialisation and controls the others. Utilising the wide range of thinking skills included in FM, the facility manager has to be able to provide the users and owners of property with an all-round consulting interface, covering complex specialist issues in an understandable fashion and managing decisions under pressure.

A further special feature of the job description is, similar to the architect, the varied extent of functions, from strategic and intellectual to operative and practical, and thus the requirement to be qualified to work with very diverse partners. This places above-average moderating, management and personal capabilities at the top of the requirement list. Ethical and philosophical qualities like authenticity and integrity are also important qualifications for the sustainable control of complex buildings.

Management methods

The working methods relevant in FM do not normally come from the building industry, but from technical sectors such as the car industry and aviation. Only the building databases that form the foundation of all planning and operational processes and the as-built building drawings, which can be activated to illustrate various aspects (CAFM = computer-assisted facility management) are closely derived from modern architectural, drawing, tendering and room schedule tools → ❸.

For the purposes of facility management planning and decision-making, various management methods from the industries named above are used:

– examination of alternatives and scenarios with total-cost assessment
– complex quality and risk management
– psychology-based moderation/mediation
– 'information design', the graphically descriptive illustration of abstract, multi-faceted and complex information.

Average life expectancy of building elements

Up to 10 years
lime-washed façade
window paint, external
wallpaper
textile flooring
surface treatment of floors
pumps

Up to 20 years
felt roof covering
mineral paints
awnings
plastic external elements
plastic-based emulsion paint
double glazing
silicon seals and joints
linoleum and PVC floor coverings
taps and valves
measurement and control equipment
electrical devices
heating boilers
air-conditioning plant

Up to 40 years
external render
pointing to facing brickwork
plastic windows
window ironmongery
fibre cement roof covering
zinc gutters
external wall insulation system
floating screed
heating pipes and radiators
water installations
electrical installations
lifts

Up to 80 years
external render
fair-faced concrete
roof construction of:
– nailed trusses
– laminated timber trusses
roof tiles
stairs, indoor, softwood
doors
timber, aluminium windows
external windowsills:
– concrete
– natural stone
unbonded screed
bonded screed
stone/ceramic floor coverings
sanitary appliances, porcelain
drainpipes

Over 80 years
massive construction of:
– brick
– calcium silicate blocks
– concrete
steel construction
façade cladding of:
– glass
– stone
timber with constructional weather protection
external stainless steel elements
roof construction of:
– solid timber
– steel
slate roofing
internal windowsills:
– stone
– hardwood
external windowsills, hard brick

The life expectancy of building elements can be affected by the quality of construction and maintenance. Maintenance costs can be reduced if elements liable to wear out are easily accessible.

Measure	definition	costs tax deductibility grant eligibility	treatment under HOAI	approval requirement
Maintenance	inspection service maintenance improvement	operating costs	increase of fee for phase 8 up to 50%	no
Modernisation	improvement of serviceability	investment, measures perhaps grant-aided	increase of fee by up to 20–30 %	possibly
Rebuilding	change of use	investment	increase of fee by up to 20–30 %	yes
Extension	new building work connected to existing	investment	increase of fee by up to 20–30 %	yes

Classification of works to existing buildings according to HOAI, and effects

Conservation
– simple preservation and maintenance of the existing material of a historic monument or listed building with its historic defects and traces.

Restoration
– purposeful recreation and making visible of aesthetic and historic assets. The priority is the production of a historic condition; deleterious and concealing additions may be removed. Layers from other periods can be covered or destroyed in favour of a uniform appearance.

Reconstruction
– recreation of a destroyed building. If no existing structure is present, then this is not the care of an old building but new building.
Anastylose = rebuilding of a building from available original elements
Translocation = relocation of an existing building.

Classification of works to existing buildings, in light of listed building issues

Once buildings have been built, they continue to require care and maintenance. Building and finishing elements have differing lifetime expectations according to their function, use and maintenance. The scale of operations from maintenance, repair, replacement or conversion is blurred → ❶.
Projects involving work on existing buildings should be split into measures under the categories listed below. In addition to advice about the need for approvals, this enables the client to clearly divide the required investment into items which can be grant-aided and those which can be forwarded to tenants. It also enables the architect to correctly assign fee supplements → ❷.
Many of the measures for which the term **renovation** is used stem from construction law but are relevant only in the context of municipal building. As the term is not differentiated regarding building costs and contracts, it should not be applied.

The following measures are differentiated in **HOAI**, which governs the fees of German architects:

Maintenance:
– measures for the preservation of the required condition of a building.

Repair:
– measures to recreate the required condition of a building for its intended use, but not including rebuilding or modernisation. The definition in the standard is the "preservation or recreation of the functional condition".

Modernisation:
– building measures which lead to the sustainable improvement of the serviceability of a building without altering the function, such as the improvement of lighting, sound insulation, access (lifts, disability access) and the energy exploitation.

Rebuilding:
– rebuilding works are changes of the design of an existing property with considerable intervention in construction or existing structure.

Extensions:
– additions to an existing building, extending it upwards or sideways.

Recreation:
– new construction of destroyed buildings on existing building or site elements. This counts as a new building if a new design is required.

Conversion:
– describes changes to the type of use of a building. Because this normally leads to different requirements under building regulations, conversion works require building permission like a new building! Conversion includes a change of trade (e.g. from a shop to a restaurant) and also the fitting out of an existing unoccupied attic for residential purposes.

Project preparation
It should be noted for all work on existing buildings that the HOAI is primarily intended for new building and rebuilding, where the requirements are clear in advance. The framework for the determination of fees according to the HOAI is not adequate for the production of a resilient design with varied uses and their effects on cost and listed building protection. The appropriate preliminary investigations (measurement and the surveying of defects), and the ensuing use concepts and variants with cost breakdown, should therefore always be agreed as 'special services' or, better, as the production of an expert report before starting design work, in order to give the client 'design security' before the start of the project. The absence of such design foundations is one of the main reasons for exploding costs in refurbishment work.

Florence cathedral

Artistic significance
Building as
– individual work of art
– typical example of a style

Mine

Technical/scientific significance
Building as example
– of special construction, or first use
– particular craftsmanship
– unaltered original condition of typical construction

Goethe's garden house

Historic significance
Building as site of
– important historic event
– the career of important personalities (birth, residence, death)

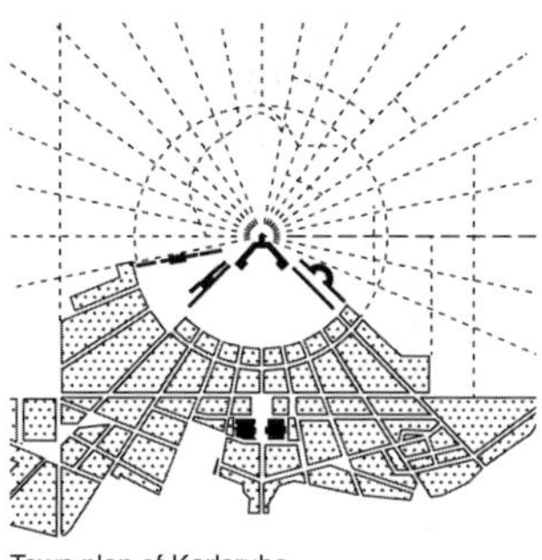
Town plan of Karlsruhe

Urban planning significance
Building as part of:
– a planned layout
– a historically developed town plan
– a typical village structure

❶ Criteria for the evaluation of historic building substance

	Conservation	Restoration
Point of view	historical, documentation, structure-related	artistic, aesthetic, related to form and function
What to be protected	**structure** – original structure with all historic alterations as a medium of the historic and building quality	**impression** – visual impression / artistic idea as a medium of the building quality
Aim of historic monument protection	preservation of the structure in the condition in which it has survived. History remains visible.	making the original condition clear and visible, including its recreation
Types of measures	**preservation through conservation** – continual building checks. Immediate repair of any damage by the original methods	**recreation** – repair and if necessary demolition to recreate the original condition
Recreation of destroyed buildings	not allowed, or at most in the form of anastylose (rebuilding using original material)	rebuilding as a recreation of the original condition according to archive sources
Contemporary extensions and alterations	... problematic, because the continuation of history is included in the conservation approach, but is scarcely possible without the destruction of historic building structure.	... problematic, because this would make statements in competition with the original structure.
Criticism	only understandable by experts. Disfigured buildings will be preserved. Changes of use, rebuilding and modernisation are permissible as part of the historical development, under stringent conditions (no destruction of historic building structure) but scarcely practical.	obscuration of the historical development. Destruction of later historically valuable additions. If the sources are insufficient, there is a danger of historical invention. Frequent conflict: which historical state should be chosen for preservation and made visible?

❷ Restoration and conservation principles: various positions and consequences

The care of historic monuments encompasses all measures to preserve such cultural assets in their original substance. The purpose is the preservation, for the benefit of present and future generations, of historic structure that is considered valuable, in order to preserve cultural memory, which can bestow identity and also sustainability in the form of a cultural resource. An important principle was formulated in the Venice Charter of 1964. Listed historic buildings can normally be preserved only in connection with a practical use. This makes it necessary to find a compromise between conservation and alteration.

Statutory protection of historic monuments

The purposes of the statutory protection of historic monuments include their recognition, recording (drawing up inventories), preservation and publicising. Scientific background research, the preservation and furthering of traditional craft skills, expert consulting for clients and contractors, and public relations work in the form of publications, exhibitions and conferences are further tasks of authorities responsible for the care of historic monuments. All historic buildings and monuments which are placed under protection are entered in the official lists. An individual justification for the listed status must be produced for every building. The evaluation criteria are based on the cultural, historical, town planning, scientific, technical or ethnological significance of a historic building → ❶. According to locally applicable law, lists of historic monuments can be constitutive or declarative → p. 52 ❸ The determination as to which aspects of the value as a monument are most important leads to the contrasting approaches of the preservation of the current state or the recreation of the original state of a historic monument. → ❷

The **restoration approach** has the aim of the recreation of a certain historical condition of the building (e.g. the Bauhausmeisterhäuser in Dessau). This can, however, remove the traces of history. When building elements are reconstructed, there is a danger that, if the documentation is insufficient, the original is falsely interpreted. The preservation of the current state (**conservation approach**) leaves the course of history visible, but takes into account that this may obscure the original appearance (e.g. the Rathaus, Esslingen).

Both approaches have their justification but tend to be put forward dogmatically. They should, however, always be discussed and decided for each individual case, because they have important consequences for the treatment of the historic building. It can be argued that the conservation approach will permit modern additions and rebuilding as the continuation of historical development, but this produces the dilemma that any work involves the destruction of historic building structure.

Historic monuments in the ground

Archaeological monuments serve to protect the signs of human history in the ground (archaeological sites). In contrast to historic buildings, not only known but also unknown sites are placed under protection. They should if possible remain in the ground as an 'archive', because any investigation or excavation would mean their destruction and they would be denied improved methods of investigation in the future. If preservation is not possible, then the responsible party has to pay for recovery and documentation (archaeological excavation). This duty also covers remains discovered in the course of building work.

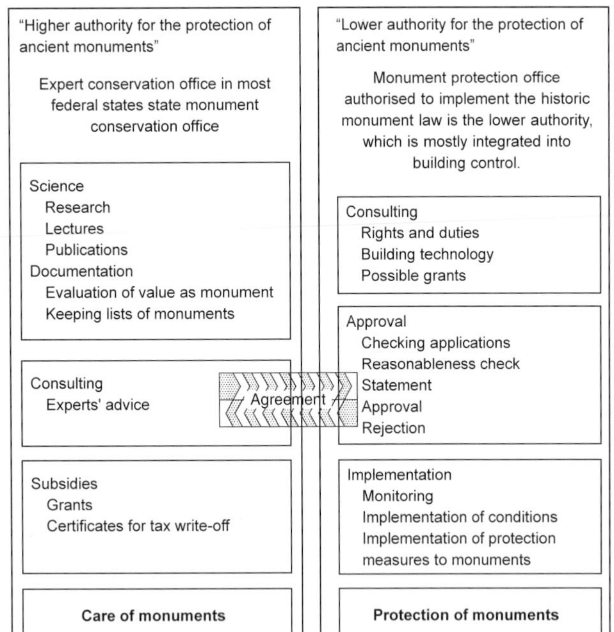

❶ Principles of the division of responsibilities regarding listed building protection and the care of historic buildings. The individual tasks can vary according to state.

	Basis of protection	Effects
Single listed building	historic buildings protection law	structure and appearance are protected and a permit is required for any alterations or interventions.
Conservation area Protection of an ensemble	situation directly next to a listed building, or location in a conservation area laid down in a by-law (based on the historic buildings protection law)	only the external appearance is protected, not the structure. Alterations to the appearance may have to be discussed and approved.
Preservation by-law	location in an area defined in a by-law (based on planning law)	protection is based on planning concerns, but not the character or appearance.

❷ Difference and effects of various legal protection measures

	Constitutive Hamburg, Nordrhein-Westfalen, Rheinland-Pfalz, Schleswig-Holstein	**Declarative** all other German states
Historic building property	entered in an official document, which leads to listing.	dwells in the building as property and is dependent on an entry in a list.
Incorporation into historic buildings list	formal process, which serves as the basis for the application of the historic buildings law. Owner must be informed of entry.	has no legal consequences and only serves for scientific information. Owner does not have to be informed.
Result	legal security for the owner but higher expense for authorities and citizens	listing status can be obtained on enquiry to the responsible authority.

 Legal consequences of the types of statutory lists of historic buildings

The listing of buildings is the legal basis for the state to influence the treatment of historic structures. In Germany, the listing of buildings is part of the cultural sovereignty of the states and is regulated by state laws for the protection of historic buildings. These laws have equal status alongside the other laws governing building. If a conflict arises, then each individual case is balanced against the other(s). Conflicts often derive from fire safety requirements and between the free market exploitation of property and the duty of the owner to preserve a building. Because legally all interests have equal weight, the state requires decisions in accordance with the aims of historic building preservation through information, advice and financial support (grants, depreciation schemes and tax reductions).

Types of listed building protection

For a single building, the material condition and the direct surroundings are protected. Any alterations to the structure, appearance or use require approval. Because the surroundings are also protected, alterations to neighbouring buildings which impair the impression of the historic building can also require an approval.

The protection of historic buildings in Germany does not differentiate value or categories. There is only an indirect grading of the character of protection through the protection applied to the surroundings of historic buildings and the intention of preserving entire areas or parts of a town in their particular character. The protection of buildings in this case applies only to the external appearance. Conservation areas, the protection of ensembles or local preservation orders are decided by towns and councils as by-laws. The procedure can be very different according to the origin, whether from historic building protection or planning laws. When work is to be undertaken in such areas, this should be discussed and a permit may have to be obtained before starting any alteration to the external appearance of a building or also to the landscape, even if the intended work itself does not require a building permit. → ❷

Because of the scope of discretion and the different attitudes of the various authorities, discussions should be opened with the people responsible as soon as possible before undertaking work to listed buildings, in order to work out a reasonable and tolerable solution.

Protection of existing use

The principle of existing use is intended to prevent new regulations or laws making existing uses impermissible. This applies to buildings, or their use, which would not obtain approval under current regulations, but formerly would have been approved or suitable for approval. Buildings which were never in need of approval are not protected under this principle! The age of a building in this case is immaterial. Buildings with protected existing use may be maintained and also modernised, but the work must preserve their identity. In the case of a change of use, replacement of building structure or other alterations in need of approval, this protection no longer applies, in which case the building must be adapted to modern standards. If this is not done, the authorities can order its demolition. It is important to open discussions at the earliest feasible stage with the responsible authority for historic buildings or the building controller in order to clarify whether and to what extent the protection of existing use applies. Exemptions can be applied for as part of the approval process under listed building legislation, but in order to provide certainty for design work this should be applied for and agreed in advance.

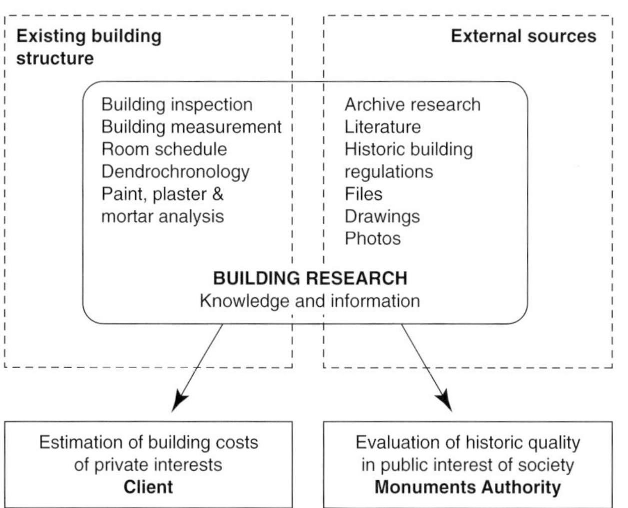

❶ Building research and documentation give the client a sound basis for design and costs and the evaluation criteria for protection and grant aid under historic building legislation

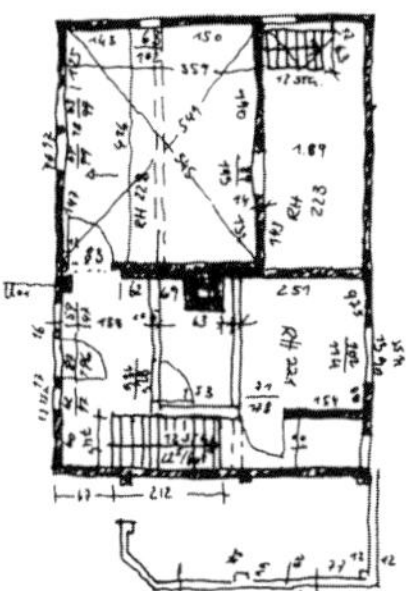

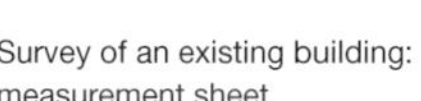

❷ Survey of an existing building: measurement sheet

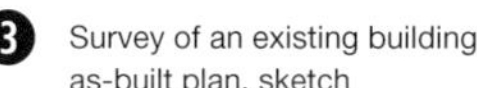

❸ Survey of an existing building: as-built plan, sketch

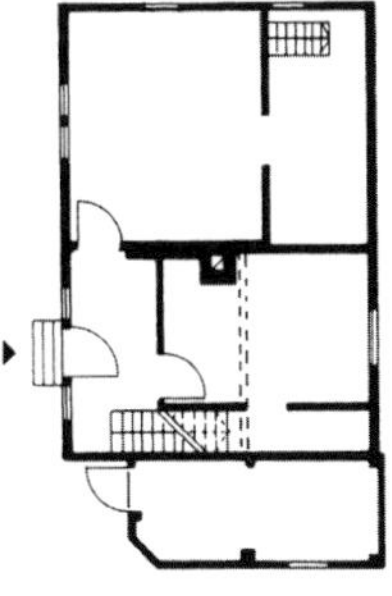

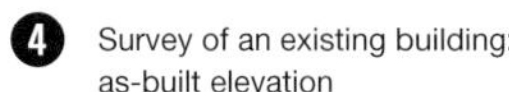

❹ Survey of an existing building: as-built elevation

❺ Survey of an existing building: as-built floor plan, structure

	Scale	
I	**1:100**	schematic recording of the building type and the plan structure for layout plans, approximate calculation of floor areas, analysis of use – sufficient for works which do not alter the structure
II	**1:50** precision ± 10 cm	almost precise survey of the geometry, relation of the vertical position of the floors, illustration of the load-bearing structure
III	**1:50** precision ± 2.5 cm	exact measurement, including historical deformation, as basis for restoration, construction drawings and scientific investigations
IV	**1:25–1:10** precision ± 2–0.5 cm	exact measurement, including historical deformation, for building with stringent scientific and technical construction requirements
V	**1:25–1:1** precision ± 2–0.1 cm	exact measurement, including historical deformation, for archaeology and building research for particularly demanding buildings

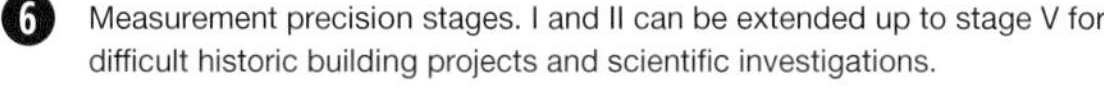

❻ Measurement precision stages. I and II can be extended up to stage V for difficult historic building projects and scientific investigations.

Surveying an existing building

With the implementation of rebuilding works, documentation of the existing building in the form of drawings and text is an important base for planning. The surveying and investigation of an existing building should ideally be undertaken before decisions are made about construction measures and future use, because only substantiated knowledge about the building structure and potential costs can lead to a sensible solution.

Drawings of the existing building and a room schedule should be produced by the architect on site even if old drawings are available, because this enables an understanding of the defects and the condition of the building at an early stage. The investigations should be carried out with as little damage as possible, but if intrusions into the structure are required, they should be agreed with the client and the historic buildings authority and be performed by experts (restorers, building research consultants).

Drawings of the existing building

The depiction and the precision of the drawings showing the existing building and its condition depend on the aims of the intended work. → ❻ There is a difference between the precision of measurement and the precision of the drawings. The precision of measurement does not depend only on the measuring instruments used but on the system of measurement and any resulting imprecision (out-of-parallel, adding errors). In precision stages I and II → ❻, the measured dimensions are normally more precise than can be shown on the drawing.

The drawings produced in this way serve as the basis for defect mapping, plans of building age and documentation of finds and are then processed further for design, listing of works and construction drawings.

Text description of the existing building

A general building description should contain all the significant information about the building. This includes details about the plot, property relationships, planning conditions, building use, data for financing, tenants and rent income, age of the building, historical building phases, historical design elements, building materials, standards of equipment, building services, structure, constructional properties and other features.

A room schedule should record each room in text and graphics (sketches, drawings and photos), describing necessary measures and work that has already been carried out. The rooms should be numbered on each floor, starting from the entrance hall and proceeding clockwise. The floor number should be legible from the key (e.g. G05 for a room on the ground floor or 1.08 for a room on the first floor).

Building research

Information about each phase of building development, the methods used and later interference with the structure are not only useful for the evaluation of historic quality → p. 51 ❶, but also for sound preliminary design and cost estimation. Some investigations can be undertaken by the architect, e.g. research in the appropriate archives (building authority, town archive etc.), but other tasks will require the appointment of specialists (restorers, conservators, scientific investigations of building materials, colour research, dendrochronology, C14 method, analyses of paint, plaster and mortar). The results can not only give pointers to the age and possible problems arising from earlier rebuilding, but also enable the selection of compatible building materials and enable a precise description of items in the bill of quantities and specification. → ❶

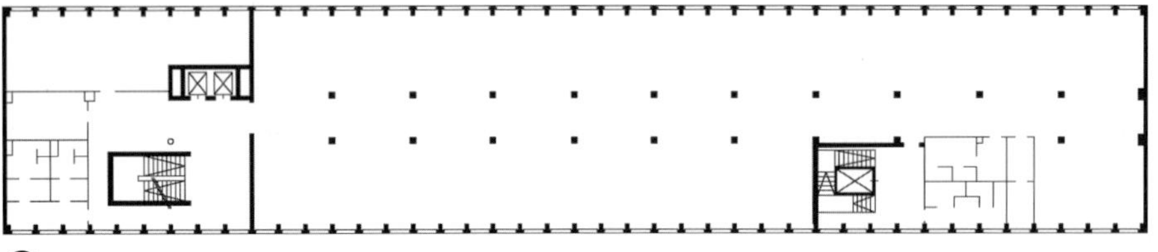

1 As-built plan of an office block from 1965

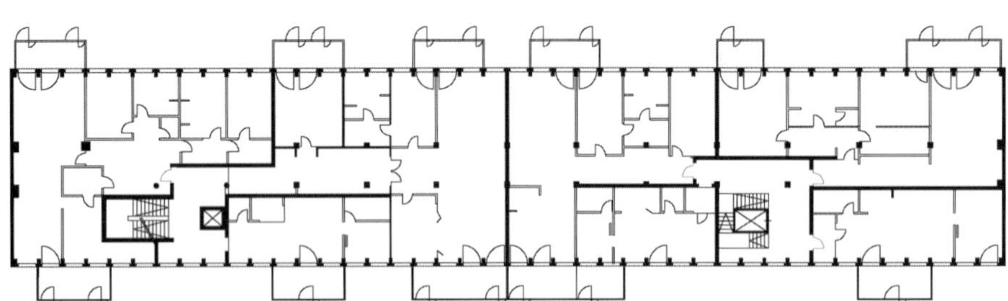

2 Conversion of the office block into flats with a floor area of 60–200 m^2 each

3 Conversion of a former warehouse into a residential and office building. New façade design

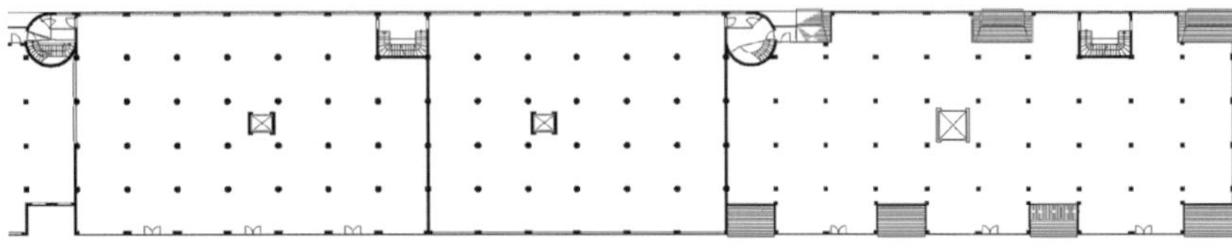

4 As-built floor plan

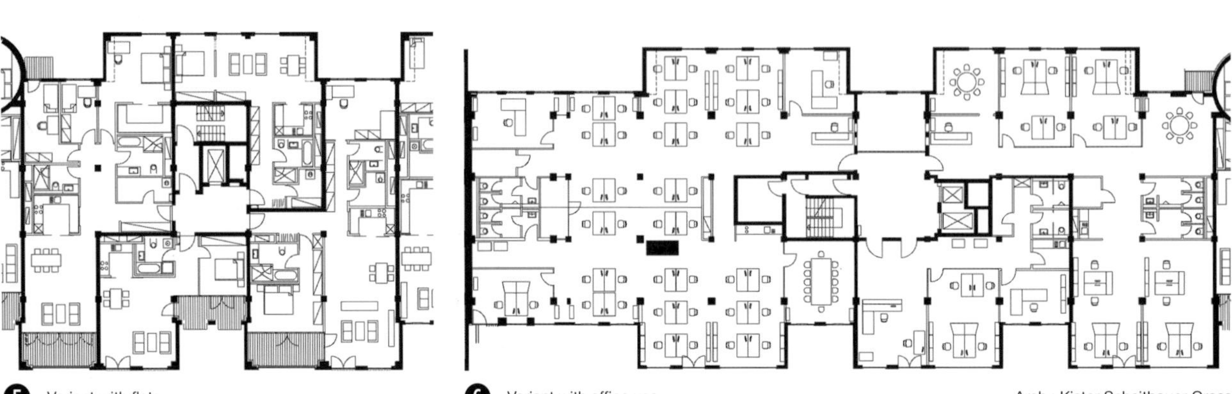

5 Variant with flats

6 Variant with office use

Arch.: Kister Scheithauer Gross

Concrete construction

The preservation of historically valuable building structure is only one aspect of work with old buildings. The conversion and further use of existing buildings is also a contribution to sustainability. A large proportion of the office and industrial buildings of the last hundred years no longer meet current requirements. The most important foundation for the decision as to whether these buildings, mostly constructed in reinforced concrete, are suitable for use is the analysis and checking of the structural system. This should ideally be undertaken by an experienced engineer before the design work starts, because it is an important factor in determining whether the building structure is appropriate for further use.

Building archives and knowledge of historic building regulations are helpful in addition to investigation on site, because non-destructive testing of concrete construction is hardly possible.

Together with the structural requirements, building physics stipulations also have to be complied with. Updating work is made necessary by the increased concrete covering required for fire protection and the more stringent regulations about thermal insulation (EnEV). The necessary cost of this can be more easily estimated.

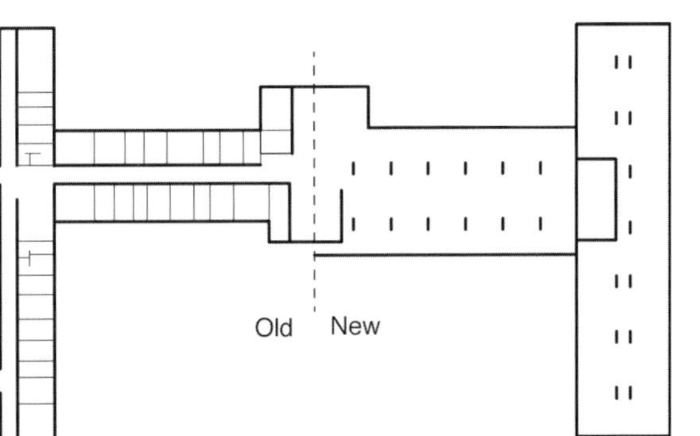

❶ The existing structural system with slabs as continuous beams on the internal and external walls.

❷ Conversion of an office building to flats. The main wing was extended to the garden side, and new slabs and a new load-bearing structure enable varied floor layouts.

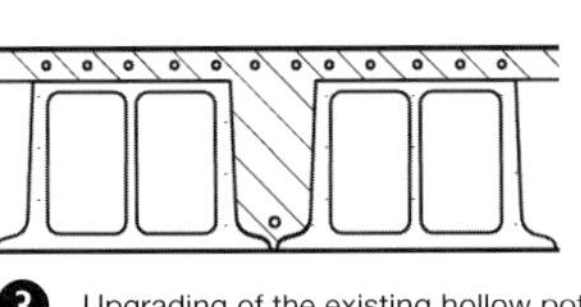

❸ Upgrading of the existing hollow pot floor would have been possible only at great expense.

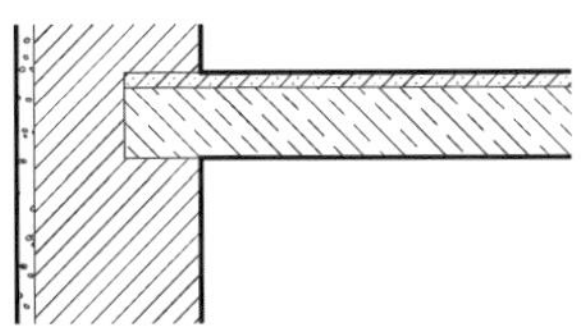

❹ The original hollow pot floor was replaced with a reinforced concrete slab, supported on thermally insulating bearings on the external wall to avoid cold bridging.

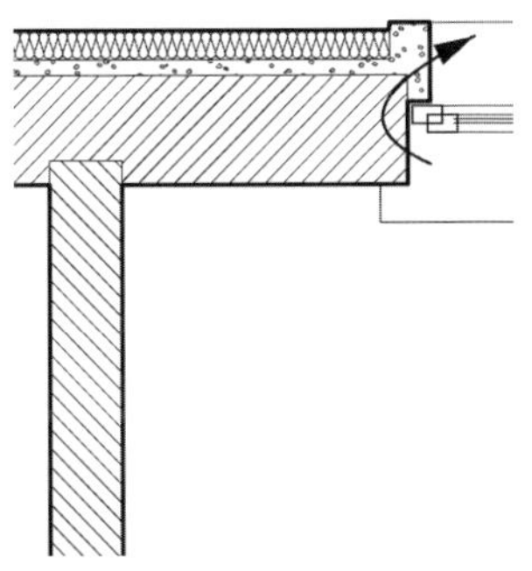

❺ External façade insulation system: façade structuring is lost and cold bridging is hard to avoid.

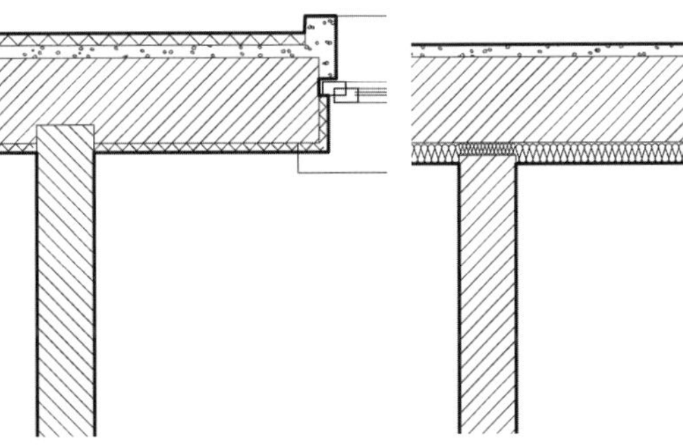

❻ Thermal insulation: external render, calcium silicate boards inside. The optical effect of the structuring elements is weakened.

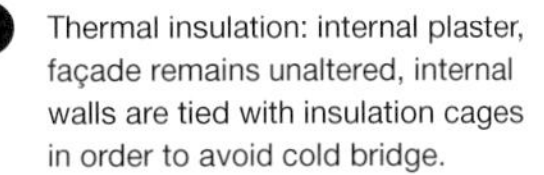

❼ Thermal insulation: internal plaster, façade remains unaltered, internal walls are tied with insulation cages in order to avoid cold bridge.

Upgrading of masonry buildings

Conversions count as new building and require building permission. The floor slabs cannot normally comply with the requirements for sound, thermal and fire insulation and thus have to be upgraded. Impact sound insulation, fire protection construction and the structural strengthening required for additional loading reduce the clear ceiling height considerably. In an example of the conversion of an office building to high-quality apartments, the slabs were designed as continuous beams over the internal walls. The only solution in this case was the complete exchange of the internal slabs. The use of thermally separated bearings enables internal thermal insulation without cold bridges and does not impair the external elevation → ❶ – ❼.

Conversions require compromise. For a listed factory hall with a large building depth and a 5 m ceiling height, the insertion of an internal courtyard and reduction of the height of the less important rooms of the maisonettes was approved → ❽.

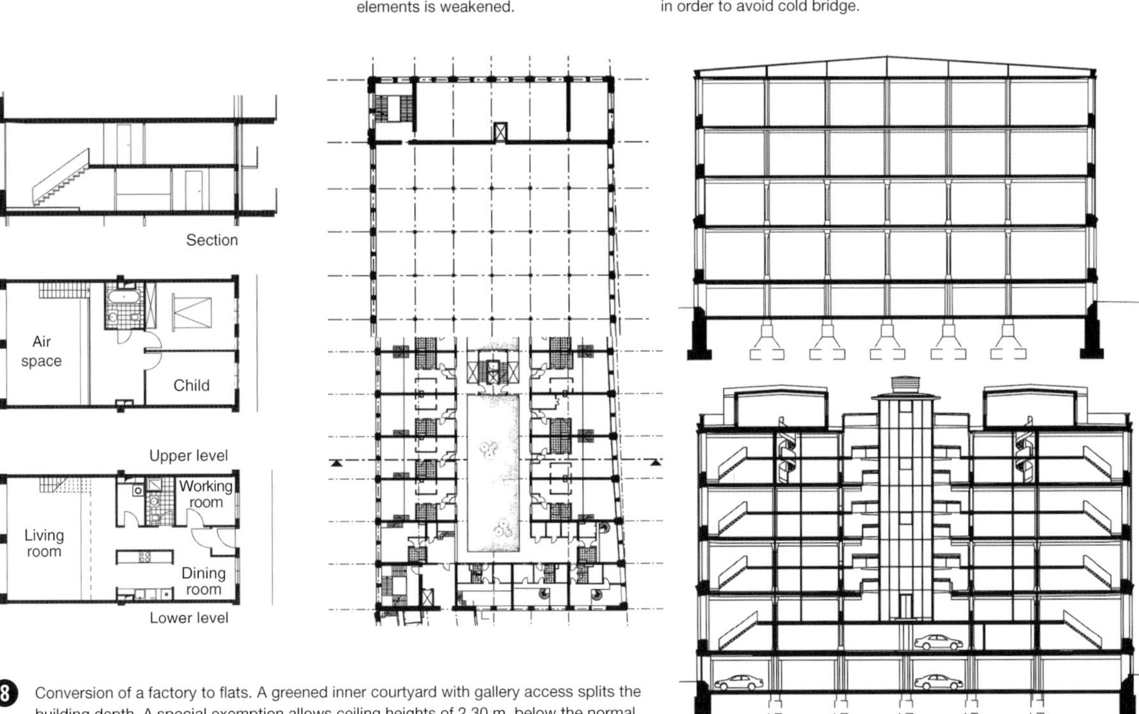

❽ Conversion of a factory to flats. A greened inner courtyard with gallery access splits the building depth. A special exemption allows ceiling heights of 2.30 m, below the normal minimum. Buntgarnwerke Leipzig Arch: Fuchshuber and Partner

General provisions	scope of application, terms, general requirements	§ 1–3
The plot and its building development	building on plots	§ 4
	access and exit routes	§ 5
	setback areas, spacings	§ 6
	division of plots	§ 7
	non-built areas, play areas	§ 8
Buildings	design	§ 9
	advertising, vending machines	§ 10
	general requirements for construction	§ 11–16
	building products, types	§ 17–25
	walls, floor slabs, roofs	§ 26–32
	escape routes, openings, fencing	§ 33–38
	building services	§ 39–46
	use-related requirements	§ 47–51
Parties involved in building	basic duties	§ 52
	client	§ 53
	designer	§ 54
	contractor	§ 55
	site manager	§ 56
Building control authorities, administrative procedures	structure, responsibilities, tasks	§ 57–58
	approval requirement, exemption	§ 59–62
	approval procedure	§ 63–77
	building supervision measures	§ 78–80
	official supervision	§ 81–82
	easements	§ 83
Summary offences	summary offences, legal regulations, transitional and final provisions	§ 84–87

❶ Structure of the MBO (model building regulations, at state level), general provisions (overview)

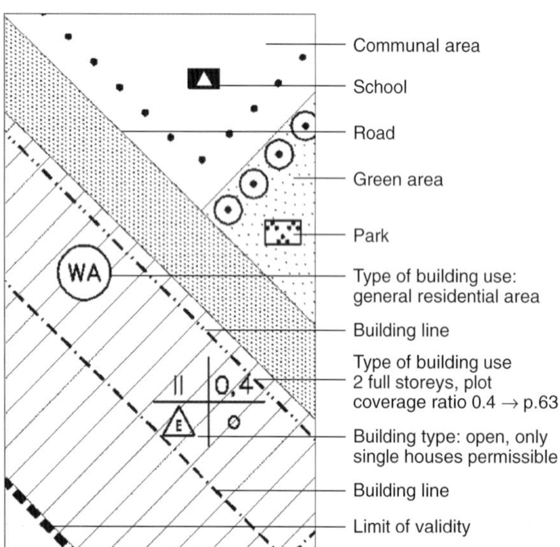

❷ Decisions in development plans according to the building law code and the land use regulation (example)

Building law code

This federal law contains the most important regulations about **public building law** and **planning law**. It provides local councils in particular with the instruments and procedure for controlling land use in their areas by applying their statutory planning authority. The most important instrument is **town planning**. It regulates the permissibility of new building in unzoned urban areas and outside built-up areas and the organisation of land use (reallocation). The 'special town planning law' includes mainly provisions concerning refurbishment and development projects and town remodelling.

Land use regulation

This controls the land use to be laid down in **zoning plans**. It is divided into the sections **nature** of building use (e.g. general residential area, industrial area), **measures** of building use (e.g. floor area ratio, plot coverage ratio, full storeys → p. 63), **type** of building (e.g. open, closed) and **buildable plot area** (e.g. boundaries, building lines).

Planning drawings regulation

This lays down the uniform illustration of decisions on zoning plans.

Regional planning law

This federal law contains provisions about the basics and problems of regional planning and the regional planning responsibilities of the federal states. The basics of the law are put into practice through the state development plans, development programmes and regional plans. Aims laid down at this level have to be complied with at all lower levels. The law prescribes regional planning procedures.

State building regulations

This legislation, passed by the states, controls building regulations. These cover requirements for building and properties, and serve to reduce risk. They include, for example, provisions about setback areas, fire protection, rescue routes and building approval procedures.

Land-use planning

The building law code differentiates between preparatory land-use planning (**land use plan**) and binding zoning plans (**development plan** and **project development plan**). All zoning plans are produced under a fixed procedure, including the participation of the public, and public agencies and authorities. With the **land use plan,** the intended land use is displayed for an entire council area. The plan is binding on authorities, which means that it has to be complied with at lower levels. The **development plan** is then produced from the land use plan and regulates as an ordinance the control of building for an entire council area, with a catalogue of possible provisions. The **project development plan** is a special form for a defined project. The promoter of the project undertakes in an implementation contract to complete the building commission within a certain time frame and, partially or completely, to bear the design and development costs.

BS 1600
BS 6079
BS 7000-4
ISO 22263
DIN 1960/1
DIN 18299–18386
DIN 18421
DIN 18451

BGB
HOAI
VOB

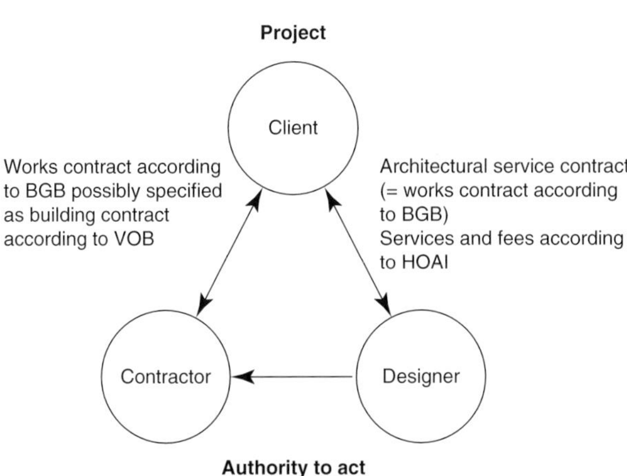

❶ Principal legal relationships between the parties involved in a building contract

	% fee	Work phase	No.
Design	3	collection basic information	1
	7	preliminary design	2
	11	design	3
	6	building permit application	4
Construction	25	detailed design	5
	10	preparation for tendering	6
	4	collaboration in tendering	7
	31	supervision of works	8
	3	supervision of snagging and documentation	9

❷ Services performed in each work phase, HOAI (→ refs)

BGB works contract		VOB/B	
§ 632	payment	§ 2	payment
		§ 14	invoicing
		§ 15	day works
§ 632a	stage payments	§ 16	payment (No. 1)
§ 633	defects	§ 4	construction (No. 7)
		§ 13	defect claims (No. 3, 5, 6)
		§ 17	security
§ 634	rights of the employer in case of defect	§ 13	defect claims
§ 634a	limitation of defect claims	§ 13	defect claims (No. 4, 5)
§ 635	supplementary performance (with § 634 No. 1)	§ 13	defect claims (No. 5 section 1)
§ 636	particular provisions for damages (with § § 634 No. 4, 280, 281, 283, 311a) particular provisions for termination (with § § 634 No. 3, 323, 326 Section 5)	§ 4	construction (No. 7)
		§ 8	termination by the employer (No. 5)
		§ 13	defect rights (No. 7)
			– not included
§ 637	self-remedy of defects (with § 634 No. 2)	§ 13	defect rights (No. 5 section 2)
§ 638	price reduction (with § 634 No. 3)	§ 13	defect rights (No. 6)
§ 639	exclusion of liability	§ 13	defect rights (No. 3)
§ 640	acceptance	§ 12	acceptance
§ 641	payment due date	§ 16	payment
§ 641a	certificate of completion		– not included
§ 642	duties of the employer	§ 4	construction
§ 643	termination by contractor	§ 9	termination by contractor
§ 644	transfer of risk	§	– note § 12 No. 6
§ 645	responsibilities of the employer	§ 7	sharing of risk
§ 646	completion instead of acceptance	§ 12	acceptance
§ 647	contractor's lien rights		– not included
§ 648	building works security mortgage		– not included
§ 648a	collateral of the employer (tradesman collateral)		– not included
§ 649	right of termination by employer	§ 8	termination by the employer
§ 650	cost estimate		– note in § 2
§ 651	application of commercial law		– not part of VOB

❸ Comparison of BGB works contract law and the corresponding provisions in the VOB (according to: Boisserée, Mantscheff, Baubetriebslehre 1, p. 53 → refs)

Legal relationships

The legal relationships between parties involved in a building project are normally classified as **works contracts** under the German civil code (BGB), or as **building contracts** under the contract award procedure and contract regulations for building works (VOB) → ❶.

The essence of a building contract is to produce a contractually determined result, in this case the construction of a building. In contrast to this, the subject of a service contract (BGB) is the work as such or working.

HOAI

HOAI (Fee Regulations for Architects and Engineers – Germany) controls the invoicing of fees for the services of architects and engineers. The fee is based on the **fee zone** to which a building project has been assigned, the **chargeable costs** (according to the fee table) and the **work phases** undertaken by the architect or engineer, to each of which a percentage of the total fee is assigned (services performed in each phase → ❷). In each of the work phases, there is a differentiation between **basic services**, which are always performed as part of the proper performance of the service, and **special services**, which are separately ordered and invoiced to fulfil particular requirements (e.g. building remeasurement) → p. 58 ff.

HOAI is undergoing revision at the moment. Its scope of application is to be restricted to smaller projects through the lowering of the final values in the fee table, and the removal of work phases 6–9 and the consulting services. Furthermore, the fees should in the future be determined on the basis of building costs agreed in advance.

VOB

The VOB (contract award procedure and contract regulations for building works) is neither law nor legal regulation but represents **freely agreed contract rights**, which amend or add to the provisions of the BGB, from whose provisions it varies in essential areas (practical completion, defect claims, payment) → ❸. Federal authorities and many public clients are obliged to apply the VOB in the tendering and contract award procedure of building works.

The VOB is laid out as follows:
Part A contains guidelines for the layout and composition of tender documents, contract award procedures and building contracts.
Part B contains the general conditions of contract for the construction of building works, as laid out → ❸.
Part C contains, categorised according to trades, general technical contract conditions**,** according to the following uniform system:
0. Notes for the production of bills of quantities and specifications
(an aid for clear and exhaustive tendering)
1. Scope of application (terms, definition of trades, differentiation from other trades)
2. Materials / building elements (definition of the quality conditions for the materials and building elements to be used according to DIN standards
3. Construction (definition of the standards for construction with reference to current DIN standards)
4. Ancillary work / extra work (differentiation of ancillary work (without extra payment) and extra work)
5. Invoicing (invoicing regulations, units, remeasurement, deductions etc.)

Design process

DESIGN AND CONSTRUCTION MANAGEMENT

Legal basis

Work phases

Measures of building use

Setback areas

Construction costs

BS ISO 15686-5
ASTM E917-05
DIN 276

see also: HOAI p. 57

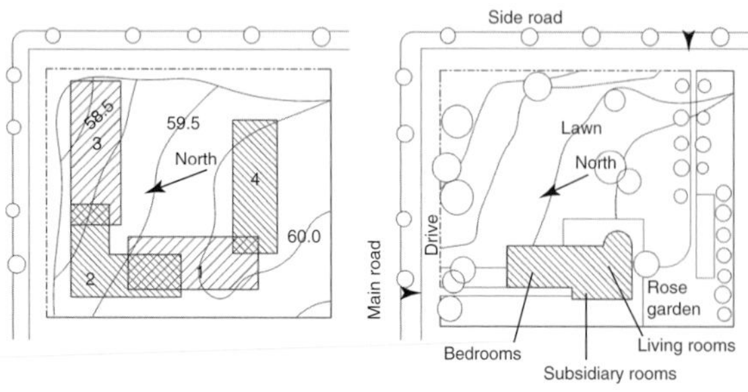

❶ Consideration of the location of the house on the plot: building development proposal

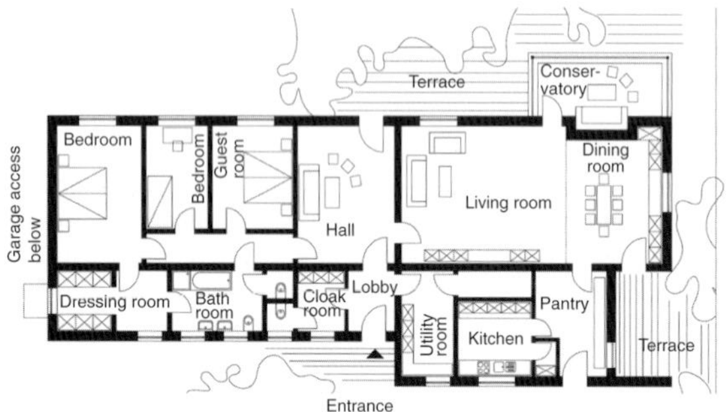

❷ Development of the design from the building development proposal

Architectural services and fees are contained in the respective guidelines for each country / professional body, e.g. in Germany **HOAI** (Fee Regulations for Architects and Engineers), which has broadly the same structure as the Royal Institute of British Architects (**RIBA**) Architects' Plan of Work.

Collection of basic information
(HOAI, work phase 1 → refs)

Basic services:
1. Clarification of the task
2. Consulting concerning extent of services required
3. Assistance with decisions in the selection of specialist engineers
4. Summary of the results

Special services:
- *Recording of the existing condition*
- *Analysis of the location*
- *Production of a room or function schedule*
- *Investigation of the environmental impact or relevance*

Preliminary design
(HOAI, work phase 2 → refs)

Basic services:
1. Basic analysis
2. Discussion of the aims (constraints, conflicts)
3. Production of a design-related catalogue of aims
4. Production of a design concept with alternatives (for the same requirements) in the form of drawings and descriptions
5. Integration of the services of other involved experts
6. Clarification and explanation of the essential interactions and conditions (e.g. town planning, construction, building services)
7. Preliminary negotiations with authorities and other technical experts about the suitability for approval
8. Cost estimate according to DIN 276 or the local calculation regulation
9. Summary of all results

Special services:
- *Collaboration in obtaining credit*
- *Preliminary inquiry about building permission*
- *Preparation of diagrams on special techniques*
- *Preparation of a time and organisation schedule*
- *Additional design work for building optimisation (e.g. reduction of energy consumption) to a greater extent than the requirements of legal regulations and standards*

Design
(HOAI, work phase 3 → refs)

Basic services:
1. Working through the design concept from work phase 2, using the contributions of the other specialist parties
2. Description of the building work
3. Drawings showing the overall design in the form of fully worked-through design drawings
4. Negotiation with authorities and other specialist parties about the suitability for approval
5. Cost calculation according to DIN 276 or the local calculation regulation
6. Cost control through the comparison of cost estimate and cost calculation
7. Summary of all results

Special services:
- *Investigation of concept variants and their (cost-related) evaluation*
- *Calculation of cost-effectiveness*
- *Cost calculation with quantity framework or building element catalogue*
- *Processing particular measures for the optimisation of the building from work phase 2*

see also: HOAI p. 57

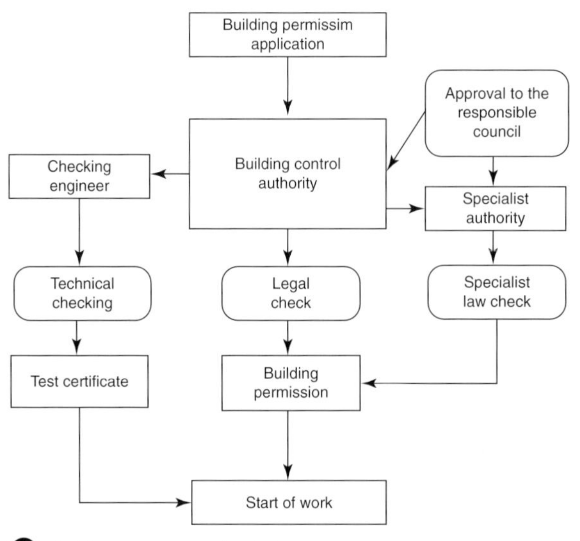

❶ Building permit process (outline)

Building permission (MBO)
The construction, alteration or change of use of buildings always requires approval from the building supervision authorities.

There are, however, **exemptions** for certain buildings. These are essentially:

Approval-free building projects (e.g. single-storey building with a gross floor area up to 10 m^2 and garages up to 30 m^2 with average wall heights of up to 3 m (except outside built-up areas → p. 55); **retaining walls and fencing** up to 2 m high, the alteration of load-bearing and bracing building elements in buildings of classes 1 and 2; **cladding of external walls** (except to high-rise buildings); pergolas, entrance porches and **facilities which require approval under other regulations**, such as power stations and traffic-related buildings, in which case the authority responsible for the appropriate legal regulations undertakes the role of building control.

In connection with a **building notification procedure**, approval is also not required for the construction and alteration of buildings of low height which fully correspond to the decisions of a legally binding building development plan, whose utility supply and access is ensured. This applies unless the council demands an application under the simplified building permission procedure within a certain deadline or applies for an interim prohibition.

The **simplified building approval process** is applicable for the construction and alteration of buildings of classes 1–3 within the scope of validity of a legally binding building development plan, if the proposed building corresponds to the decisions in the building development plan to the full extent and the utility supply and access are ensured. In this case, the building control authority only checks the compliance with the regulations of the German building law code concerning general permissibility.

Outline building permission
In advance of the building approval application, a preliminary decision can be obtained from the building control authority about individual (critical) questions concerning the building approval application by making a preliminary enquiry, in order to simplify further processing of the building approval application. Outline building permission is legally binding and valid for one year; the period can be prolonged on application.

Building permit application
(HOAI, work phase 4 → refs)

Basic services:
1. Production of the application documents required for permission or approval in accordance with official regulations, including any application for exceptions and exemptions, making use of the contributions of other specialists involved in the design and including any negotiations necessary with the authorities.
2. Handing in these documents.
3. Completion and adaptation of design documents, descriptions and calculations making use of the contributions of other specialists involved in the design.
4. (For external works and extensions forming rooms) checking whether permits are necessary, obtaining of permissions and approvals.

Special services:
- *Collaboration in the obtaining of approval from neighbours, production of documents for special testing procedures, expert and organisational support of the client in protest procedures, legal actions etc.*
- *Alteration of the application documents resulting from circumstances for which the appointed party is not responsible.*

Building permit application and application documents
The building approval application contains the following details:
1. Name and address of the client
2. Name and address of the architect
3. Description of the proposed building measure
4. Description of the plot (street, house number, plot number etc.)
5. Utility supply and access
6. Details of already granted permits
7. All documents required for evaluation

(layout plan, building drawings, building description, verification of structural safety and other technical verifications)
All appended documents must be signed by the client, the architect and other specialist parties.
The building approval application is to be handed in to the responsible council in writing, which will then forward it with their comments to the responsible building control authority. This authority will request comments from all further responsible authorities (fire service, care of historic buildings, etc.) and the owners of neighbouring properties.

Building permit issue
After the completion of checking, the applicant receives the written building permit together with copies of the approved documents (possibly with conditions).
A partial building permit can be issued for single building elements or stages (e.g. excavation) before the issue of the final building permit.
The building permit and partial building permit lapse if building work is not started within one year of their issue or the works are interrupted for more than one year. This period can be prolonged on application.

Building supervision by the authorities
The MBO provides for supervision during the building phase. This can be limited to spot checks and essentially consists of the acceptance of the structure (testing of the construction for structural safety, sound and thermal insulation, fire safety) and final acceptance. After the final acceptance certificate has been issued, the building can be used.

see also: HOAI p. 57

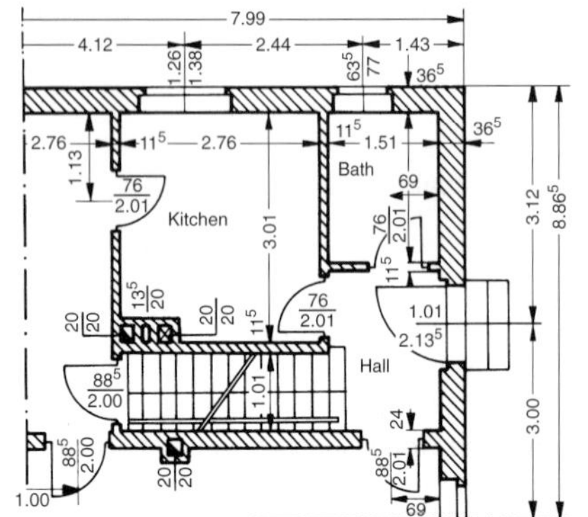

❶ Dimensioned drawing for construction, scale 1:50 (reduced excerpt)

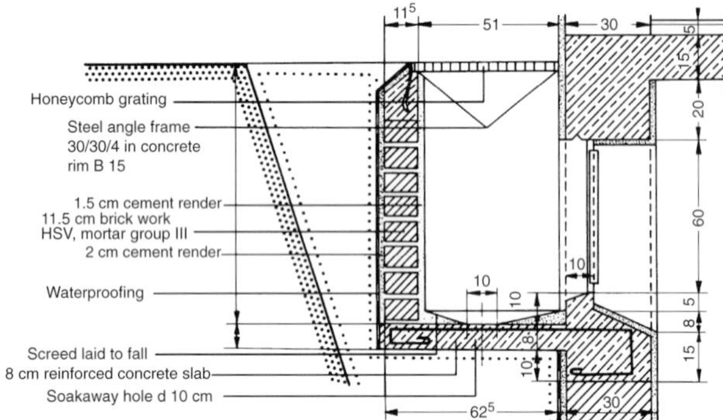

❷ Detail drawing of cellar light shaft, scale 1:20 (reduced)

Means / instruments for construction design
Construction drawings → ❶, with all the details and dimensions required for construction (scale 1:50).
Detailed drawings → ❷ supplement construction drawings for certain sections of the building works (scale 1:20/10/5/1).
Special drawings are intended for the requirements of particular specialist areas (e.g. reinforced concrete, steel or timber construction etc.) and only if necessary show building elements not directly relevant to this specialist area (scale 1:50, depending on subject).
Room schedules → ❸ contain complete details about dimensions (length, height, floor area, volume) of the room or part of the building, materials (e.g. wall finishes, floor finishes etc.), equipment (e.g. heating, sanitary, ventilation, electrical installations etc.) in the form of tables. These are in some cases the basis for a performance specification. **Room schedules and construction drawings can be linked with appropriate software for tendering, contract award procedure and invoicing.**

Detailed design

(HOAI, work phase 5 → refs)

Basic services:

1. Working through the results of work phases 3 and 4 (staged processing of information and presenting solutions) – taking into account town planning, design, functional, technical, building physics, economical, energy-related (e.g. rational consumption of energy), biological and ecological requirements – and making use of the contributions of other specialist parties, until the design is ready for construction.
2. Drawings showing the building with all details required for construction, i.e. the final, complete working drawings, details and construction drawings.
3. For extensions which form rooms: detailed drawings of the rooms and sequence of rooms at scale 1:25 to 1:1, with the required textual details and material descriptions.
4. Development of the basis for the other specialist parties involved in the design and integration of their contributions until the design is ready for construction.
5. Continuation of the detailed design during the construction of the building.

Special services:

- *Setting up a detailed description of the proposed works as a building schedule, to be the basis of a works specification with a performance specification.*[*)]
- *Setting up a detailed description of the proposed works as a room schedule, to be the basis of a works specification with a performance specification.*[*)]
- *Checking the working drawings produced by contracting companies on the basis of the works specification with performance specification for compliance with the design.*[*)]
- *Setting up detailed models. Checking and approving the drawings of third parties who are not specialists in the design team for compliance with the construction drawings (for example workshop drawings from companies, location and foundation drawings from machine suppliers), as long as the services apply to facilities which are not included in the chargeable costs.*

[*)] This special service becomes wholly or partly a basic service if the works are specified through a performance specification. In this case, the corresponding basic services in this work phase are omitted.

A2 room description					B2 room dimensions						B4 service connections for						B5 values			
1			2	3		1		2		3	1	2	3	4	5	6	1	3	6	
Prov. room no.			Use	User	Type	Area	Type	Height	Type	Volume	Heating	Ventilation	Sanitary	Elec.	Comms.	Transport	Temp.	Vent.	Light	Remarks
A	B	C		(dept)		m²		m		m³							°C	/h	lx	(addresses)
	W	104	hall		N	6.92	L	2.47	N	14.87	–	–	–	SW	TS		20	1		AS aerial connection socket
														CL	SI					CL ceiling light
														WVT						SSO power socket
	W	204	bathroom/ WC		N	3.47	L	2.475	N	8.588	CH	ZWE	BA	WB	–		24	7		TF potential equalisation
																				SW switch
													WB	SO						SI sink
													WC	TF						IC entry phone
																				SO socket
	W	304	kitchen		N	6.09	L	2.47	N	15.04	CH	MV	SI	SW	–			20	4	TS telephone socket
														SO						BA bathtub
														SWL						WB washbasin
														SSO						WL wall light without SO
														CL						SWL ditto with switch
	W	404	loggia		N	1.69	L	2.363	N	4.000	CH	MV		–	–		–	–		WC WC
	W	504	liv./din.		N	19.77	L	2.47	N	48.63				SW	AS		21	1		FB fuseboard
														SO						CH central heating
														CL						MV mechanical ventilation
	W	604	serv. rm.		F	0.36	L	2.475	N	0.891				–	–		–	–		

❸ Room schedule (short form): A2 room description

Tender documents			
	contents of tender		
covering letter (request to tender) + application conditions	technical content	legal content	+ award
	(1) bill of quantities	(2) special contract conditions	
	(4) additional technical regulations	(3) additional contract conditions	
	(5) general technical regulations	(6) general contract terms	
	Building contract		

 Tender documents required and their collection to form a building contract (VOB)

Tender and contract

The **contract award procedure** aims to create a contract structure which will guarantee that the plans of a project are carried out within the framework of civil law with its accompanying regulations (→ p. 57). The contract can be awarded when tenders have been received for defined tender documents (specifications, contract conditions and letter stating the possibilities of seeing the tender documents, location and date of the opening deadline, additional costs deadline, binding deadline etc.).

The priced tender documents and signature of the bidder or their authorised representative constitute an **offer**, and if these are accepted and the contract awarded, they become, unaltered, the building contract → ❶.

Building contracts (and thus also tender documents) should comprehensively and completely remove any differences of opinion between the contract parties in advance and clearly regulate the duties on each side.

The specification of the works is therefore the basis for the later building contract. This consists either of bill of quantities or performance specification and building specification:

Bills of quantities → ❷ are listings of the individual items (description of a part of the works according to type, quality, quantity, dimensions with an item number) and can be structured by batch (building stage, building phase/production phase) or title (trade-related).

Performance specifications are functional descriptions of the essential design, technical and economic requirements of the completed work. In contrast to bills of quantities, they do not have a detailed listing of individual items.

The bills of quantities are normally supplemented by **preliminaries** in the form of **general and general technical contract conditions** (= VOB/B or VOB/C), **additional and additional technical contract conditions** from clients who regularly award building works (e.g. German Railways, State of Berlin) and **special contract conditions**, which regulate conditions for special cases.

Software is almost always used for the production of bills of quantities today, because this field is ideal for computerisation due to the linking of tender data with detailed design. The **Standard Book of Bill Items (StLB)** for the building industry helps with the production of bills of quantities with standard text building blocks for individual items, which are assigned to the appropriate areas of work (these approximate to trades according to VOB/C). **Model bills of quantities** for the production of bills are similar to standard books. They include possible text blocks (texts are created by deleting) and are generally very extensive. **Manufacturer's model bills of quantities** for the production of bills offer additional information and are useful for particular constructional solutions.

Preparation of / collaboration in tendering

HOAI 15, work phases 6 + 7 → refs)

Basic services:

1. Determination and listing of quantities as a basis for production of the works specification, making use of the contributions of other design specialists.
2. Production of the works specification and bills of quantities, by areas of work.
3. Approval and coordination of the works specifications produced by other design specialists.
4. Collection of tender documents for all areas of work.
5. Obtaining of tenders.
6. Checking and assessment of tenders, including the production of a price comparison list, by work sections.
7. Checking and collation of the services of specialists collaborating in the tendering process.
8. Negotiations with bidders.
9. Cost forecast according to DIN 276 from the unit or lump sum prices of the tenders.
10. Collaboration in the awarding of the contract.

Special services:

- *Production of work specifications with performance specification, making use of building schedules / room schedules.*[*)]
- *Production of alternative work specifications for distinct areas of work.*
- *Production of comparative cost outlines, with evaluation of the contributions of other specialists.*
- *Checking and assessing the tenders from the works specification with performance specification, including price comparison list.*[*)]
- *Production, checking and assessment of price comparison lists for special requirements.*

*) see note p. 60

Item	Quantity	Description	Unit price	Total price
Example 1 – quantities and unit prices outside the text				
2.02	105.0	m^2 construct ground slab of in-situ concrete B 25, d = 15 cm incl. formwork. The surfaces are to be formed with falls to gullies. for 1 m^2	35.70	3748.50
disadvantages:		a) extensive space required for text b) no details about unit price components c) unit price not in words		
Example 2 – unit price inside the text				
2.02	105.0	m^2 construct ground slab of in-situ concrete B 25, d = 15 cm incl. formwork. The surfaces are to be formed with falls to gullies. wages: € 24.60 material: € 11.10 other: € –.– for 1 m^2 unit price in words: thirty five 70/100	35.70	3748.50
disadvantages:		quantity and unit price not on one line		
Example 3 – unit price and quantity inside the text and on one line				
2.02		construct ground slab of in-situ concrete B 25, d = 15 cm incl. formwork. The surfaces are to be formed with falls to gullies. 105 m^2 W/M/O: € 24.60/€ 11.10/€ –.– unit price in words: thirty five 70/100	35.70	3748.50
advantages:		a) extensive space saving b) quantity × unit price = total price in one line		

 Bill of quantities (example)

BS ISO 15686-5
ASTM E917-05
DIN 276

see also: HOAI p. 57
VOB p. 57

BS ISO 15686-5
ASTM E917-05
DIN 276

see also: HOAI p. 57

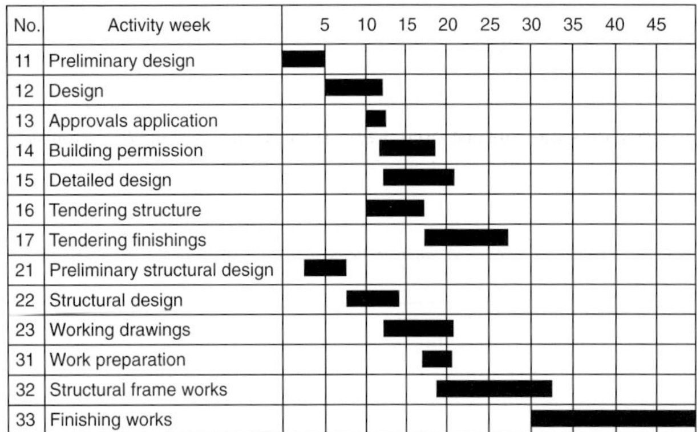

No.	Activity week	5	10	15	20	25	30	35	40	45
11	Preliminary design									
12	Design									
13	Approvals application									
14	Building permission									
15	Detailed design									
16	Tendering structure									
17	Tendering finishings									
21	Preliminary structural design									
22	Structural design									
23	Working drawings									
31	Work preparation									
32	Structural frame works									
33	Finishing works									

❶ Building schedule as bar chart

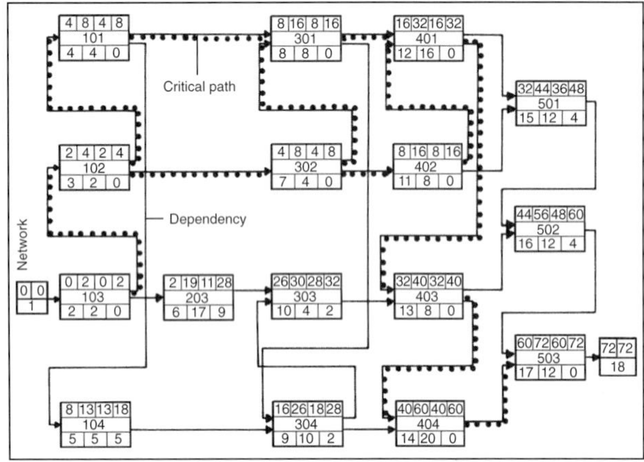

❷ Network diagram; example: forward arrow method / Critical Path Method (CPM)

Techniques of work scheduling

Bar charts → ❶ show the work activities vertically and the relevant construction time horizontally in a coordinate system. The duration of each activity is shown by the length of the relevant bar. Following activities are shown below each other. Bar charts are widely used in construction because they are simple and easy to understand. However, the interdependencies of activities (critical paths) and working directions can scarcely be shown.

Line diagrams (time–distance diagrams) show a linear graph of the relationship between work time and distance (or work quantity) in a coordinate system. The speed of work (the slope of the line) and the critical spacings of individual work activities (mutual hindrance) can be made clear. Line diagrams are mainly used for construction processes with a pronounced direction of work (roads, tunnels etc.).

Network diagrams → ❷ are used for the analysis, planning and control of complex construction sequences with consideration of as many parameters as possible. The sequence of work is divided into part activities or events, which are shown as **nodes** (Metra Potential Method (MPM), event node method/ Program Evaluation and Review Technique (PERT)) or **arrows** (Critical Path Method (CPM)), with nodes shown as starting and finishing events. Nodes thus indicates important process or event parameters.

Supervision and support of construction
(HOAI, work phases 8 + 9 → refs)

Basic services:

1. Supervision of the construction of the works for compliance with the building permit, the construction drawings and the specifications, as well as the generally recognised qualities of workmanship and applicable regulations.
2. Monitoring of the construction of load-bearing structures with a low degree of difficulty for compliance with the structural safety certificate.
3. Coordination of the parties involved in supervision of the works.
4. Supervision and correction of the details of prefabricated elements.
5. Production and monitoring of a construction time plan (bar chart).
6. Keeping a building site diary.
7. Joint measuring up of work with the contracting firms.
8. Acceptance of building works in collaboration with other design and supervision specialists and identification of defects.
9. Checking invoices.
10. Final cost statement according to DIN 276 or the local calculation regulation.
11. Application to authorities for grants, with follow-up.
12. Handing over the building, including collection and issue of required documents.
13. Listing of guarantee periods.
14. Monitoring of the remediation of defects identified at acceptance.
15. Cost control through the checking of works invoices from contracting firms and comparison with the contract prices and cost estimate.
16. Inspection of the works to identify defects before the expiry of the guarantee periods applicable to the relevant contractors.
17. Monitoring of the remediation of defects occurring within the guarantee period, but at the latest before five years since the acceptance of the building works.
18. Collaboration in the release of securities.
19. Systematic collection of the drawings and calculation results for the building.

Special services:

- *Set up, monitor and update a payment plan.*
- *Set up, monitor and update comparative progress, cost or capacity schedules.*
- *Activity as responsible construction manager, to the extent that this exceeds the basic services of work phase 8 according to the relevant state regulation.*
- *Production of as-built drawings.*
- *Production of equipment and materials lists.*
- *Production of maintenance and care instructions.*
- *Building security.*
- *Building administration.*
- *Building visits after handover.*
- *Supervision of maintenance and care.*
- *Preparation of payment material for a project file.*
- *Enquiries and cost calculations for standard cost evaluations.*
- *Checking the building and operating cost-use analysis*

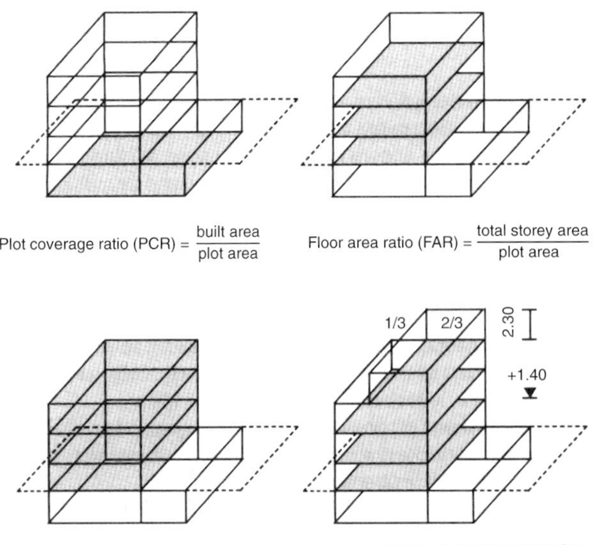

Plot coverage ratio (PCR) = $\frac{\text{built area}}{\text{plot area}}$ Floor area ratio (FAR) = $\frac{\text{total storey area}}{\text{plot area}}$

Building mass number (BMN) = $\frac{\text{built volume}}{\text{plot area}}$

Full storey (according to MBO): Ceiling height over 2/3 of the floor area min 2.30 m, slab level min. +1.40 m.

❶ Measures of building use

Housing area regulations → p. 136

Housing area regulations apply to calculations of residential area according to the law to promote living space (includes housing subsidies): the living area of a dwelling covers all rooms which belong exclusively to the relevant dwelling, including conservatories, swimming pools (if enclosed on all sides), balconies, loggias, terraces, but not subsidiary rooms (cellars, garages etc:), offices and rooms which do not comply with the building regulations.

The floor area of a room is determined from the clear dimensions between the building elements, from the outer face of the element's cladding (which includes window and door claddings, skirting boards, stoves, ovens, baths, built-in furniture, free-standing installations, movable partitions). The floor area is measured in completed rooms or from a suitable building drawing.

Floor areas are included in the calculation either completely (for rooms and parts of rooms with a clear ceiling height of at least 2 m), or a half (for rooms and parts of rooms with a clear ceiling height of at least 1 m and less than 2 m) or a quarter (balconies, loggias, terraces etc.).

Calculation of commercial letting areas

The guidelines for the calculation of commercial letting areas, issued by the Property Industry Research Company (GIF) creates a uniform standard for the determination of leased commercial and office space. The leased space is calculated from two types of area:

1. Areas with exclusive right of use, individually listed in types of area according to DIN 277: basement garage with number of places (see above), indirectly usable areas (loggias, balconies, atriums, areas with room heights between 1.50 m and 2.30 m.

2. Areas with communal right of use, individually listed as: rooms for communal use (WCs/bathrooms, staff rooms, etc.) and communal traffic areas (entrance halls, corridors, etc.).

The following do not belong to the letting area: stairs, lifts, emergency exits, escape balconies, services rooms, shafts, protection rooms, areas of columns, pillars and separate walls, areas with a clear ceiling height of 1.50 m or less.

The relevant areas are measured at floor level between solid walls (including skirtings and fittings built in on site (radiators etc.), and room heights are measured between top of finished floor level and underside of the (suspended) ceiling.

Measures of building use → ❶

The land use regulation specifies parameters for the measurement of building use in planning law: the **plot coverage ratio** determines the permissible ratio of built area on the plot (*plan area of building including garages, parking places and their access, subsidiary areas... and underground facilities beneath the plot*) and the **floor-area ratio** (determines the permissible ratio of storey area (*external dimensions of all full floors, without subsidiary areas..., balconies, loggias, terraces and structures which are permissible inside setback areas*) to the plot area.

The **building mass number** represents how many cubic metres of building mass (external dimensions of the building facilities from floor level of the lowest to the ceiling of the highest **full storey**, including occupied rooms in the intermediate floors with their stairwells, surrounding walls and slabs but without subsidiary rooms..., balconies, loggias, terraces and structures which are permissible inside the setback area under state law) are permissible per square metre of plot area.

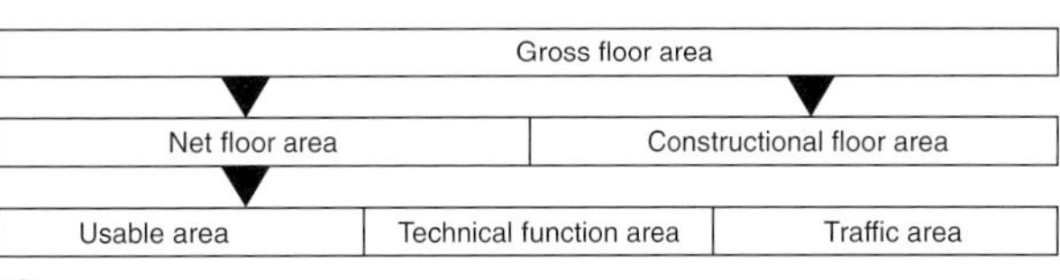

 Breakdown of floor areas (according to DIN 277-1)

Floor areas and volumes

DIN 277 contains parameters for the calculation of floor areas and room volumes of buildings → ❷. All parameters are calculated separately according to whether they belong to the following categories:

a) roofed over and enclosed on all sides
b) roofed over but not enclosed on all sides
c) not roofed over

The **gross floor area** is the sum of the plan area of all levels (without usable roof areas), measured between the external dimensions of the surrounding building elements at floor height.

The **constructional floor area** is the sum of the plan area of all surrounding building elements (walls, columns, pillars, chimneys, non-accessible shafts, door openings, niches, apertures) measured between the external dimensions at floor height. The **net floor area** is the usable floor area between the building elements (without door and window openings, cut-outs and niches) measured at floor level. The net floor area is the sum of the **usable area** (area which serves the building's intended purpose), the **technical function area** (rooms for building services, such as utility connection room, accessible shafts, etc.) and the **traffic area** (e.g. stairwells, corridors, lift shafts, escape balconies etc.).

The **gross built volume** is the sum of the floor areas of all levels multiplied by the relevant height (measured between top of floor covering and top of floor covering of the next level, in the basement from the underside of the constructional structural invert in the roof to the top of the roof covering, without external stairs, light wells, roof overhangs, dormer windows, chimneys, etc.). The **net built volume** is the net floor area multiplied by the relevant clear ceiling height.

DESIGN AND CONSTRUC-TION MANAGE-MENT
Legal basis
Work phases
Measures of building use
Setback areas
Construction costs

BS7641
ISO 9836
ASTM C1407-98
DIN 277

see also: Land use regulation p. 56

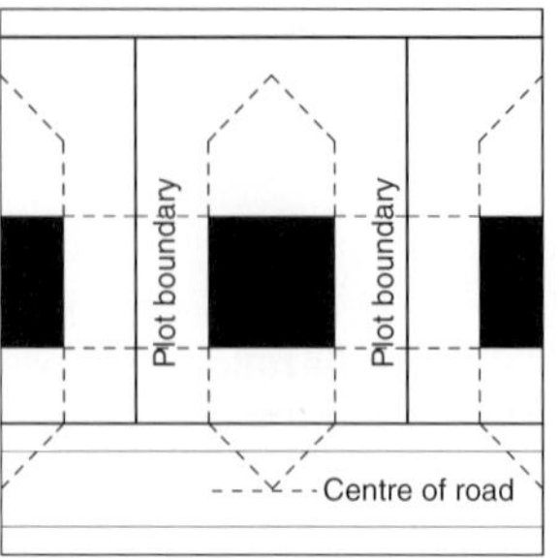

❶ Setback areas

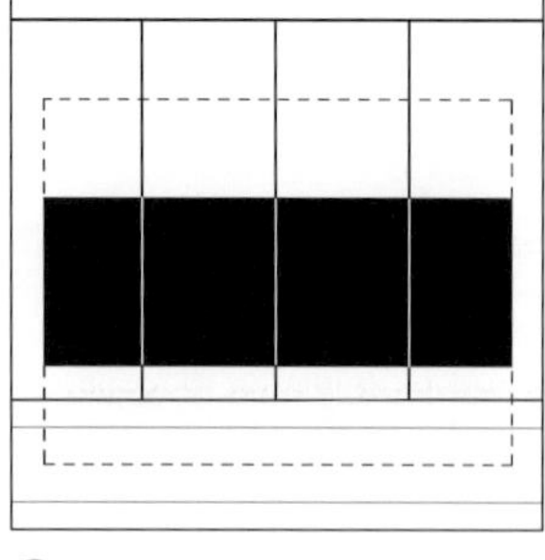

❷ Building on the boundary

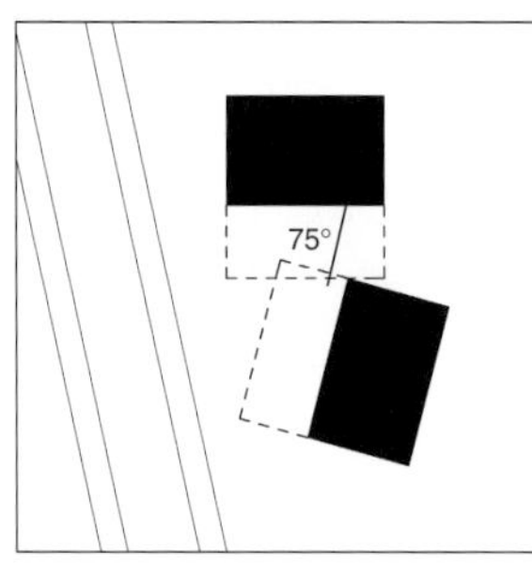

❸ Overlapping of setback areas at more than 75°

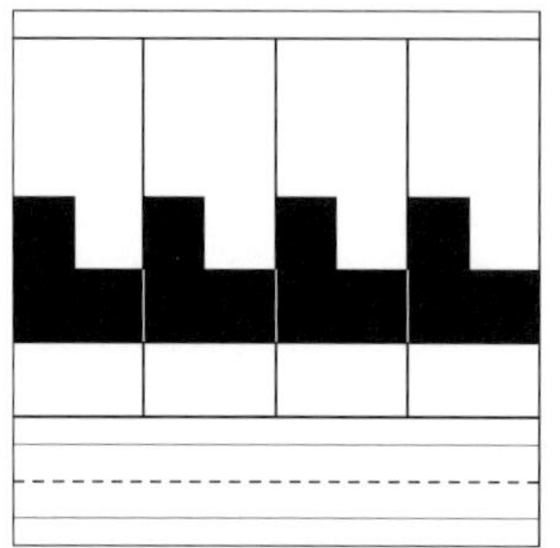

❹ Overlapping of setback areas with a garden courtyard

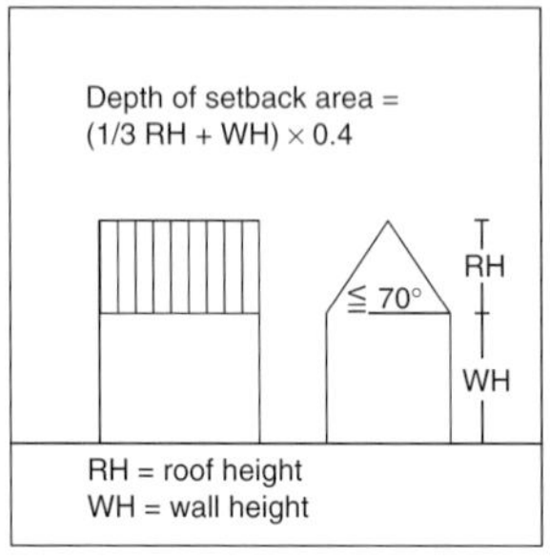

❺ Depth of the setback area

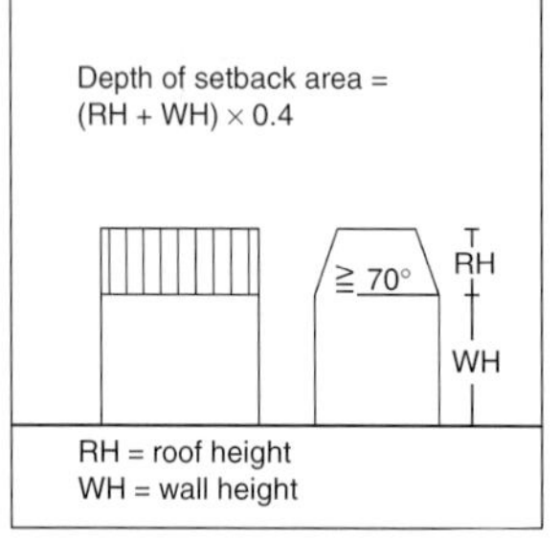

❻ Depth of the setback area with a roof pitch of more than 70°

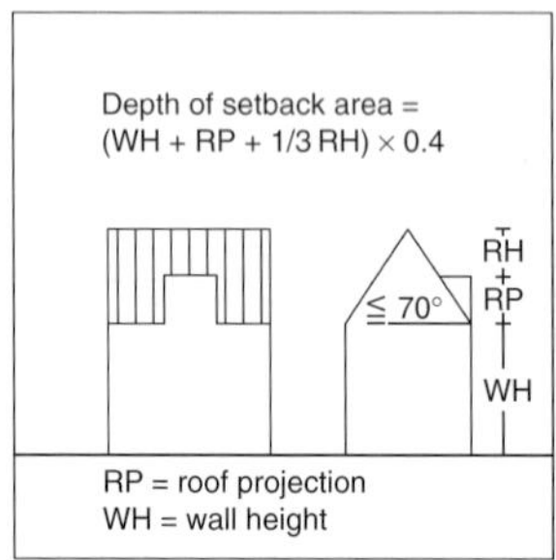

❼ Depth of the setback area with roof projections (roof window)

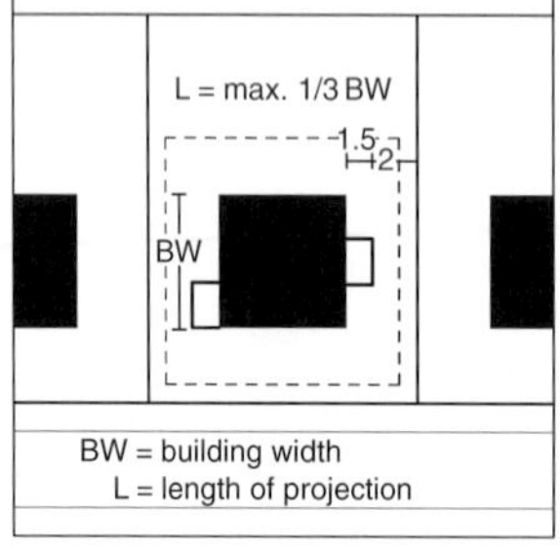

❽ Projecting building elements

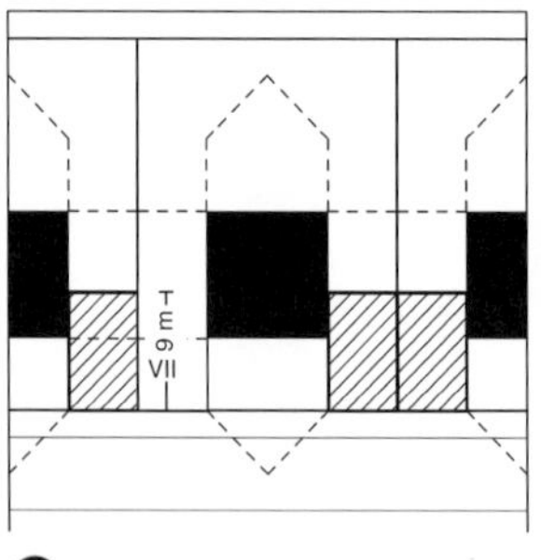

❾ Garages

❿ Walls, fencing

Setback areas are the spaces between buildings and their plot boundaries.

1. Setback areas next to above-ground buildings have to be kept free in front of the external walls of buildings → ❶ – ❷. This also applies to other facilities with effects similar to buildings, which are opposite buildings and plot boundaries. Setback areas are not required in front of external walls which are built on plot boundaries, if they may be or must be built on the boundary according to planning regulations → ❷.
2. Setback areas must be on the plot itself → ❶ – ❷. They may also lie on public traffic, green and water areas, but only to their centre. Setback areas and spaces may wholly or partly extend onto other plots, if it is certain according to public law that they cannot be built on, though they may not be deducted from the other plot's setback areas.
3. Setback areas may not overlap unless:
   – the external walls are at an angle of more than 75° to each other → ❸
   – they are external walls facing a garden courtyard in dwellings of building classes 1 and 2 → ❹
   – buildings and other built facilities are permissible in the setback areas.
4. The depth of the setback area is measured according to wall height → ❹ – ❻.This is measured at right angles to the wall. Wall height means the dimension from ground level to upper extent of the wall or to the intersection of the wall with the roof covering → ❹. The height of roofs with a pitch of ≦70° is included to one third, ≧70° fully with the wall height → ❺.The same applies to roof projections → ❼.
5. The depth of setback areas differs in the various state building regulations (LBO)). According to the model building regulations (MBO), it is 0.4 × H, but at least 3 m (0.2 × H, min. 3 m for commercial and industrial areas). In front of the outside walls of building classes 1 and 2 with not more than three overground storeys, 3 m depth is also sufficient. In some LBOs, there are further exceptions (e.g. narrow side privilege).
6. Building elements projecting from the outside wall (cornices, roof overhang) are not considered in the measurement of setback areas → ❽. Projections remain unconsidered if they:
   – take up altogether less than one third of the width of the outside wall
   – project by a max. 1.50 m in front of the outside wall
   – stay at least 2 m distant from the opposing plot boundary
7. The following are permissible inside the setback area of a building and do not have their own setback areas (even if they are built on the plot boundary or on the building) → ❾ – ❿:
   – garages and buildings without occupied rooms or fireplaces with an average wall height of up to 3 m and a total length per plot boundary of 9 m → ❾
   – solar energy systems independent of the building with a height of up to 3 m and a total length per plot boundary of 9 m
   – retaining walls and closed fencing in commercial and industrial areas, outside these areas with a height of up to 2 m → ❿. The depth of setback areas opposite plot boundaries but not stopping building may not altogether exceed 15 m on the plot.

❶ Influence on the construction costs in the course of design and construction

Cost group			
1st level	2nd level	3rd level	Description
100			plot
200			site preparation and utility connections
300			construction
→	012...		– masonry
	→	012.111	– cored block internal wall block type 12/1.6 mortar group: II wall thickness: 11.5 cm
400			building services
500			external works
600			finishing and artworks
700			ancillary costs, professional fees

Breakdown of costs, DIN 276

Cost estimate

The cost estimate is for the approximate determination of construction costs. It is included in work phase 2 (preliminary design). It is based on:

1. results of the preliminary design (if necessary as a sketch),
2. calculation of the quantities of reference units in the cost groups
3. explanations and building description
4. details of plot, utility supply and access.

The cost estimate should contain the total costs according to cost groups at the 1st level of cost breakdown and thus has at least seven items of cost data. The required description should correspond to the state of information of the preliminary design

Cost calculation

The cost calculation is defined as 'approximate determination' of the construction costs. It is part of work phase 3 (preliminary design). The basis for the cost calculation are:

1. complete design drawings and, if appropriate, details
2. calculation of the quantities of reference units in the cost groups
3. descriptions relevant for the calculation.

The cost calculation should determine the total costs according to cost groups down to the 2nd level of cost breakdown and contain 40 individual items of cost data.

The building description should correspond to the differentiated state of information of the preliminary design.

(Drawings and text from: Neddermann, slightly abbreviated → refs)

Influence over the building costs reduces very rapidly during the course of design and construction. The parties involved in the preparation of the project have the greatest influence over the building costs, because decisions are made at this time about the size, volume etc. of the project. In the further course of construction, costs can be influenced only to a decreasing degree. The flow of money behaves the other way around; it is still very small in the preparation phase and increases in steps → ❶. Efficient cost control should therefore always attempt to apply the brakes during the work phases of a project; control as part of works planning (material selection, etc.) normally has, by way of contrast, no noticeable success.

HOAI requirements

HOAI obliges the architect to produce four determinations of cost during the course of design and construction: **cost estimate, cost calculation, cost forecast, final cost statement)**. These cost determinations are basic services → pp. 58–62. They are regarded as basic services with a special weighting, i.e. neglecting a cost determination can have dire legal consequences in the case of a dispute.

Basic rules of cost determination

The basic rules of cost determination are laid down in DIN 276. This classifies the building costs into seven **cost groups** and three **(cost) levels** → ❷. Each cost determination must be structured in the same way and consist of defined building blocks:

1. Statements about the cost in all cost groups
2. Building description
3. Cost situation at the time of the determination
4. Details of VAT
5. Date of the cost determination
6. Reference to the relevant design work

Cost forecast

The cost forecast is the most precise determination of the building costs, taking place in work phase 7 (collaboration in tendering). The cost forecast is based on:

1. complete construction drawings, details, etc.
2. structural verifications, thermal insulation calculations etc.
3. calculations of quantities of reference units in the cost groups or bill items
4. building description with explanations of construction
5. listing of tenders, awards and already accrued costs

As the last cost determination before the start of construction, this has particular significance. The cost forecast should include the total cost according to cost groups down to the 3rd level of cost breakdown and contain 218 individual cost data. The building description belonging to the cost forecast corresponds to the state of design and has the highest degree of detail in the course of the design work. The purpose of the cost forecast is to produce a document before the start of construction based on tenders, awards, already accrued costs and, if necessary, extra calculations, because this is the only possibility of cost control and correction.

Final cost statement

The final cost statement serves to record the actual costs accrued for purposes of comparison and documentation. The final cost is based on: 1. checked invoices, 2. remeasurement quantities, 3. explanations. In the final cost statement, the total costs should be classified down to the 2nd level of cost breakdown.

BS ISO 15686-5
ASTM E917-05
DIN 276
see also: HOAI p. 57

Setting out

Before the start of groundworks, the planned building is set out on the plot by a publicly appointed surveyor working from the official site plan in the building permit documents. The intended excavation for the building (basement) is marked out with pegs → ❶ – ❹. To secure the points that have been set out, **profile boards** → ❽ are set up, set back from the planned top of the excavation's batter (sloped bank). After the excavation, **string lines** are stretched between the profiles to mark the corners of the building again. The intersections of the string lines are then plumbed down to mark the external corners of the building.

The levels also have to be set out. These are based on benchmarks in the surroundings. **Geometric surveying** measures the difference in height of a horizontally set up **level** from a benchmark with a **levelling staff** held vertically → ❾. Intermediate levels can be obtained with a **long spirit level**, normally a 3 m long light metal rail with built-in bubble, and a **measuring stick** → ❻. **Hydrostatic levelling** uses a **water level**, a flexible hose filled with water. This has glass cylinders at each end calibrated in mm, and can be used to transfer levels between points without visual contact because the water in the tube finds the same level at each end.

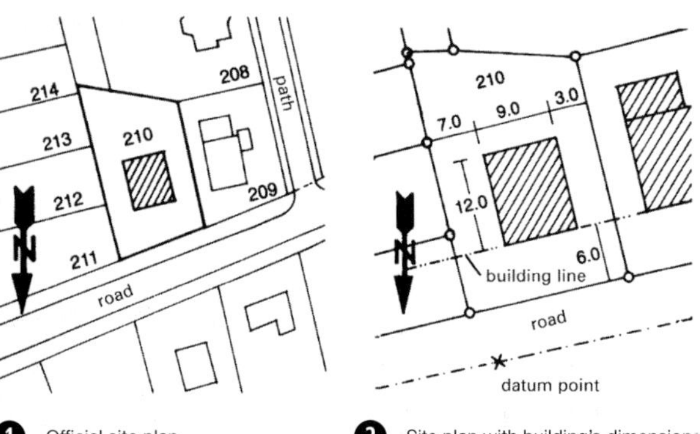

❶ Official site plan

❷ Site plan with building's dimensions

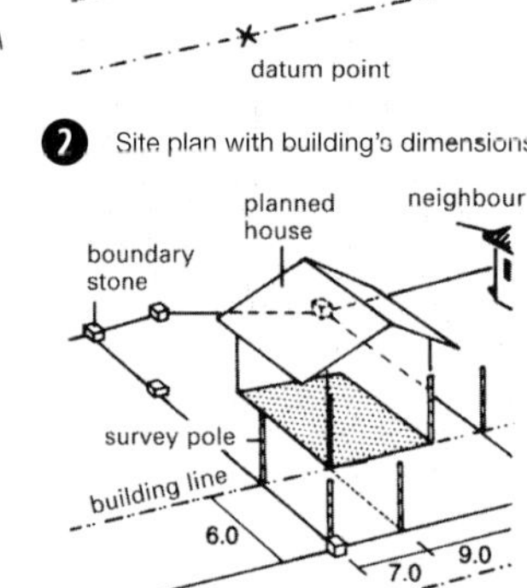
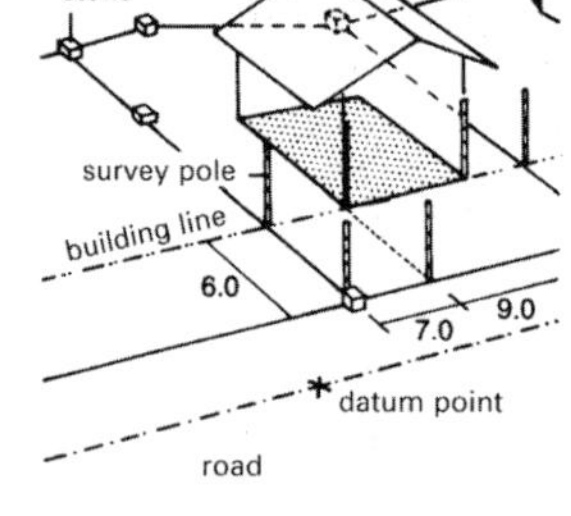

❸ Building (basement) excavation

❹ Planned house set out on the lot

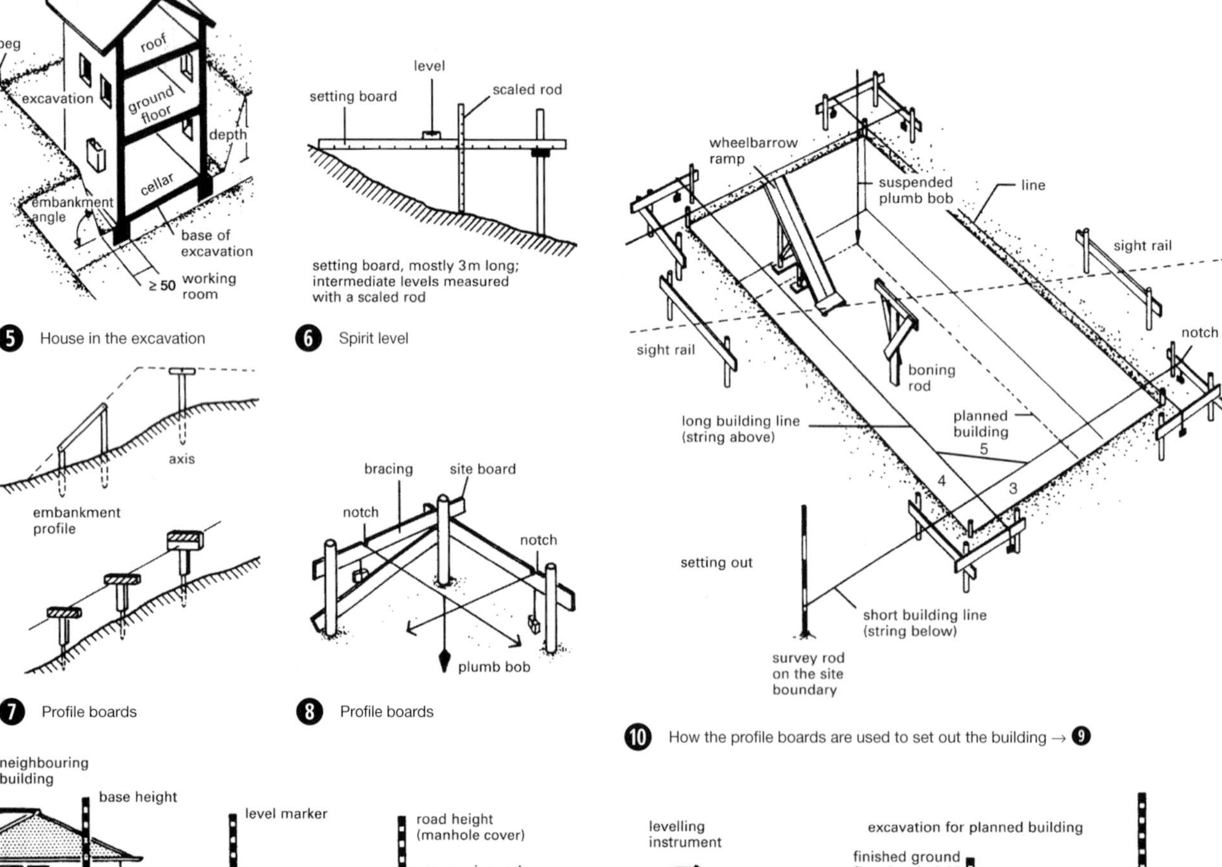

❺ House in the excavation

❻ Spirit level

❼ Profile boards

❽ Profile boards

❿ How the profile boards are used to set out the building → ❾

neighbouring building
base height
level marker
road height (manhole cover)
measuring rod
road
pavement
levelling instrument
excavation for planned building
finished ground floor level ±0.00
excavation floor −4.05
sight rail
sight rail
possible datum points

❾ Surveying the building site

Incorrect interpretation of the subsoil and groundwater conditions, and the behaviour of the planned foundations, often lead to technically and economically irreparable damage. This applies particularly to lateral displacement of the soil under foundation loading (**load-bearing failure of the ground, slope failure**), where the foundations sink into the soil or are laterally displaced, or **settlement**, through compression of the subsoil under the foundations due to ground pressure and/or loads applied next to the foundations. The results can be deformation or cracking in masonry.

BS 6031
BS EN 14199
BS 22475
DIN 1054
DIN 4123/4

Soil investigation

If there is insufficient local experience about the properties, extent, bedding and thickness of the soil strata on the site, a **soil investigation** performed as early as possible by a geotechnical specialist is essential. The specialist can obtain information through **trial pits** (excavator or hand excavation), drilling **boreholes** (auger/rotary/core drilling), with extraction of samples, and **probing** (number and depth depending on the topography, structure and particular investigation). The **groundwater table** is measured with gauges in boreholes and regular measurement of variations in level.

Soil investigations should provide data for the design and construction of the building without technical or economic problems:

– Soil samples are tested for grading, water content, consistency, density, compressibility, shear strength and permeability. – Probing provides continuous information about strength and density for the investigated depth. – **Groundwater samples** can be investigated for aggressiveness towards concrete.– The results of the investigations are provided to the client as a **site investigation report**.

Building excavations

Basement excavations are normally battered (with sloped banks) → ❶. The following **slope angle** β can normally be assumed without verification of the structural safety by calculation:

a) non-cohesive or soft, cohesive soils	β ≦45°
b) stiff or semi-hard, cohesive soils	β ≦60°
c) rock	β ≦80°.

In order to provide protection against surface water, frost and drying out, it is recommended to cover batter slopes with **protective foil, shotcrete or similar** and also possibly to keep water away from the top of the batter → ❹. If the excavation is deep, it must be expected that parts of the slope will slide, even if the angle is correct. **Banks** should therefore be provided to break up the slope → ❸. If the ground will not stand up or the space is limited, then the sides must be **supported**. This can be done with thick, vertical planks tied with ground anchors or braced → ❾, steel profiles with a filling of round or squared timber → ❼ or **sheet steel piles** → ❻. Difficult cases, where the support can be integrated as a part of the later foundations, are constructed with **bored piles** or **diaphragm walls** supported with bentonite. A **working space** of ≧50 cm should be provided between the foot of the batter or support construction → ❶ - ❷.

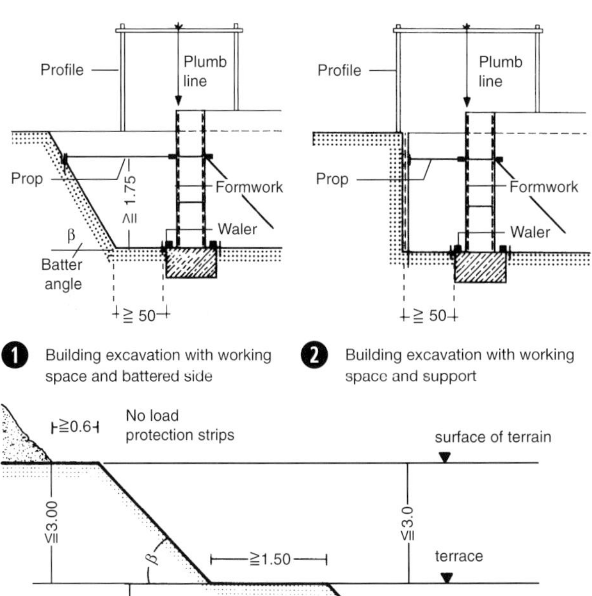

❶ Building excavation with working space and battered side

❷ Building excavation with working space and support

❸ Battered side to building excavation with banks to catch slipping material

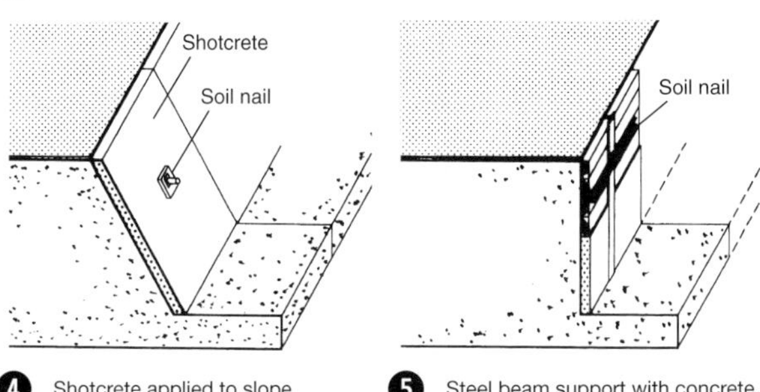

❹ Shotcrete applied to slope

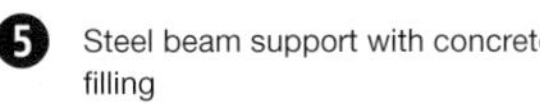

❺ Steel beam support with concrete filling

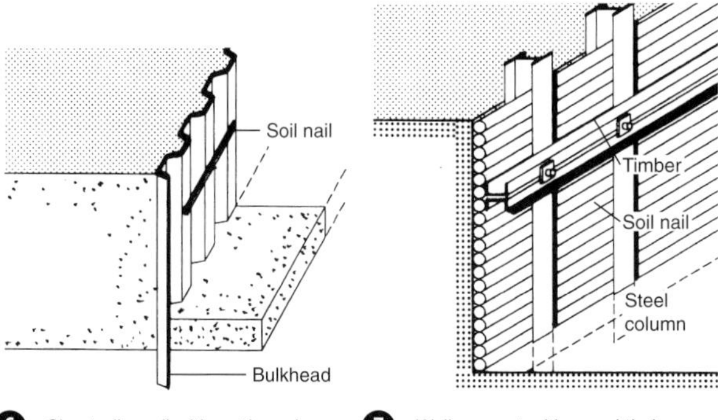

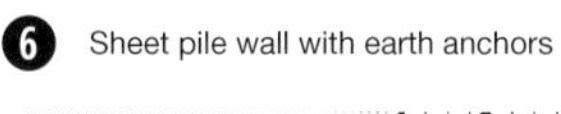

❻ Sheet pile wall with earth anchors

❼ Wall support with round timbers

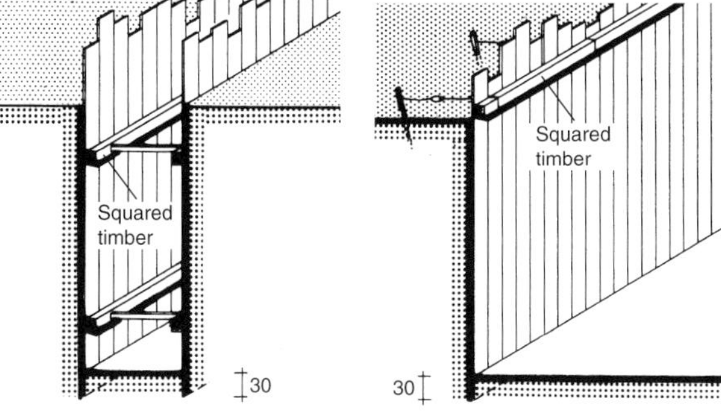

❽ Vertical support with trench planks

❾ Wall support with thick vertical boards

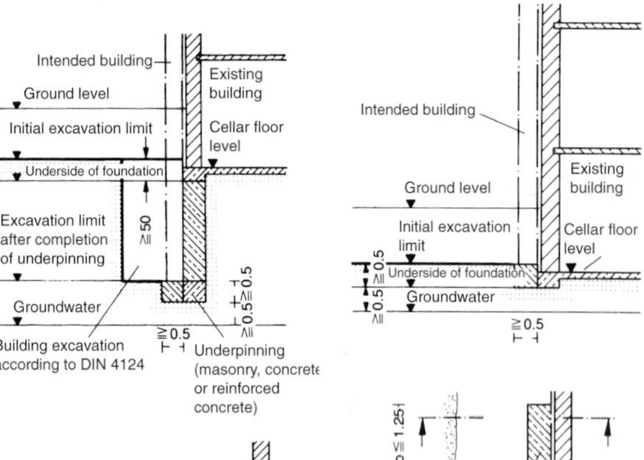

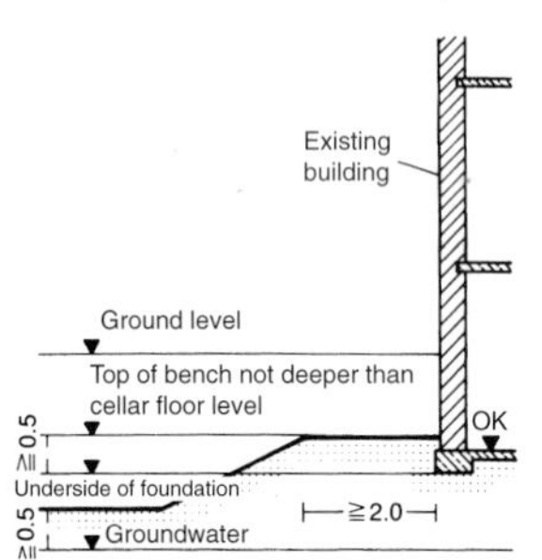

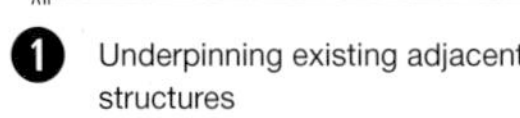

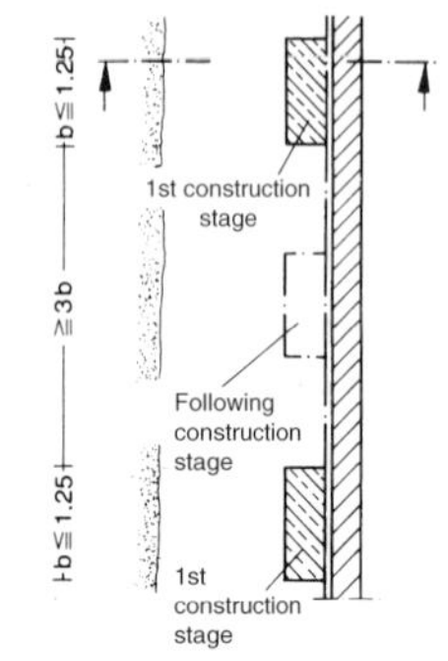

❶ Underpinning existing adjacent structures

❷ Foundations

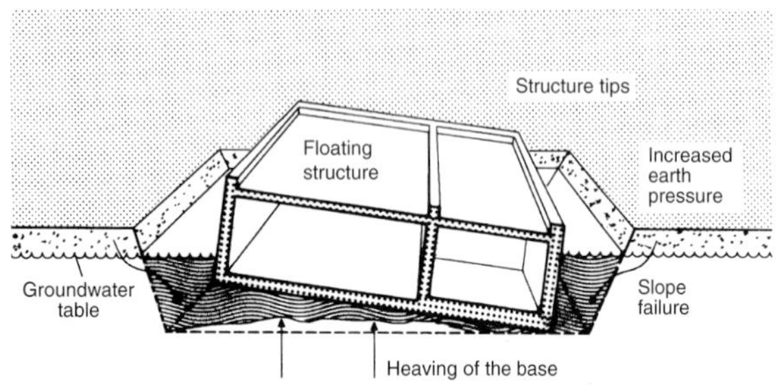

❸ Excavation below the water table – buoyancy of the structure

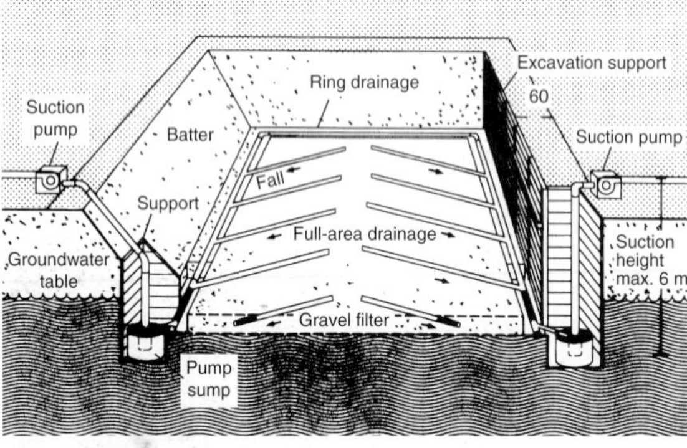

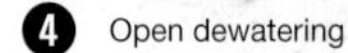
❹ Open dewatering

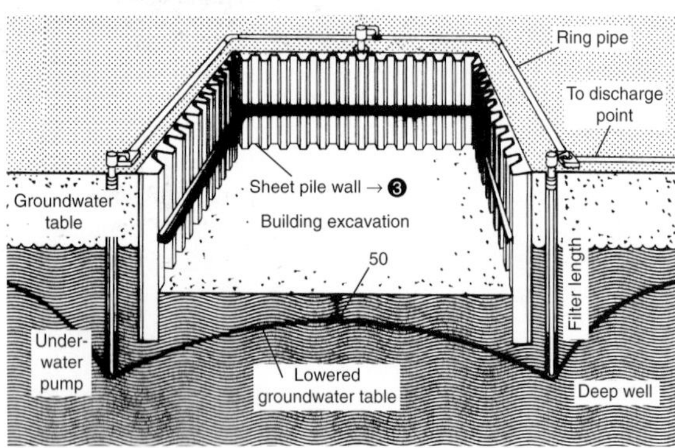

❺ Groundwater control and lowering

Underpinning

If a new building is to be erected directly next to an existing building with the underside of its foundations at a higher level, then the existing foundations have to be underpinned to prevent damage to the existing building through settlement or ground failure.

Excavations, foundations and underpinning work next to existing buildings should therefore be thoroughly and carefully designed, prepared, planned and constructed in accordance with DIN 4123 → ❶ – ❷.

A competent site manager must be present on the site during the underpinning work.

Even work undertaken with careful planning and construction in accordance with this standard cannot rule out **slight deformation** of the existing building, according to condition and type of construction.

Fine cracking and settlement of the underpinned building by up to 5 mm is generally considered unavoidable. It is therefore recommended to perform a survey of the existing building before starting work, with the participation of all involved parties, to determine its condition and survey reference levels and possibly also deflection points.

Groundwater

If the bottom of the excavation is below the water table, then special measures will be required:

This can be **open dewatering**, with the water being continuously pumped out of sumps in the bottom, trenches and drains → ❹.

If the quantity of water is higher, then **closed dewatering** is necessary → ❺: the groundwater is lowered using underwater pumps (with a safety distance of about 50 cm) under the base of the excavation.

If the excavation is larger or deeper, however, there is a risk that this lowering of the water table could impair the soil conditions near the site (settlement of neighbouring buildings!) or the use of public surface water drains could be forbidden. In this case, the entire area of the bottom of the excavation will have to be **waterproofed**.

To achieve this, the excavation is normally supported with a continuous back-anchored sheet pile or diaphragm wall. Then the excavation is dug down to floor level 'under water' and an **underwater concrete base** designed to be safe from floating is laid (if necessary, from a pontoon). After the concrete has hardened, the water can be pumped out and any leaks grouted. Alternatively, a **soft gel base** can be constructed by grouting the subsoil with sodium silicate plus a chemical hardener additive to produce a nearly waterproof layer.

The actual structure with external walls of **watertight concrete** can be built in the basin produced in this way.

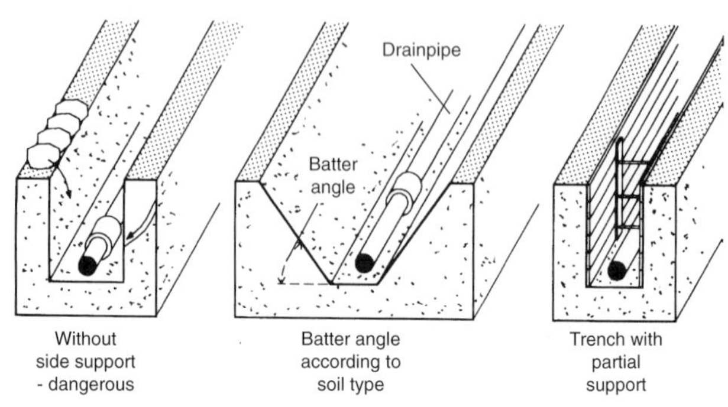

❻ Trenches for drainage

❶ Pad foundations for a lightweight building without cellar

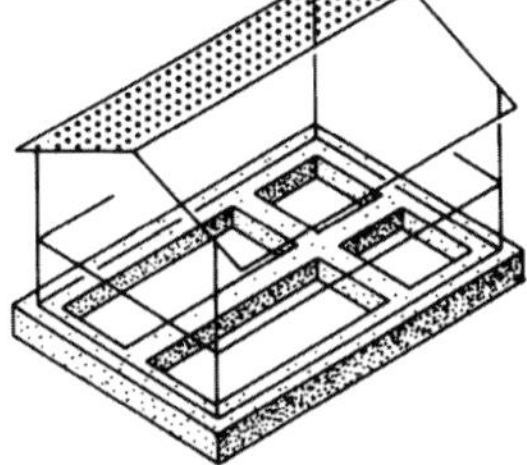

❷ Strip footings are the most commonly used

❸ Raft foundation with steel reinforcement

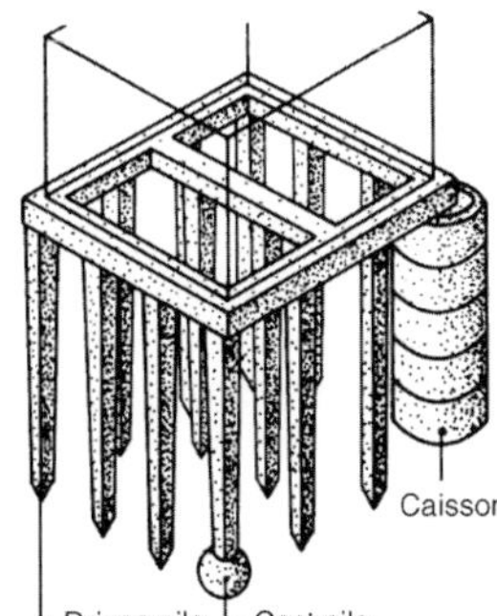

❹ Pile grillage and caisson deep foundations

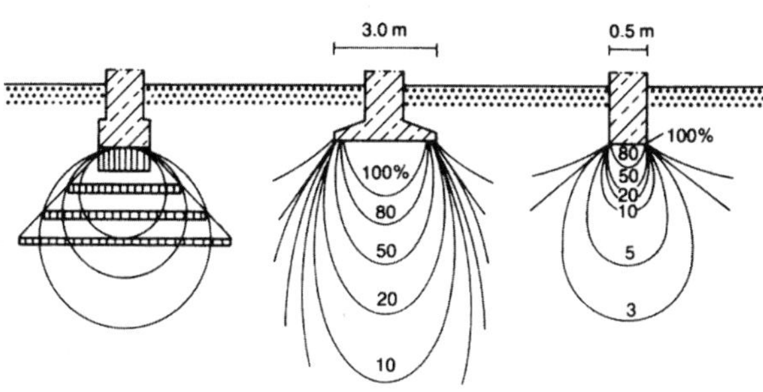

❺ Wide foundations result in greater permissible stresses than narrow foundations for the same ground pressure.

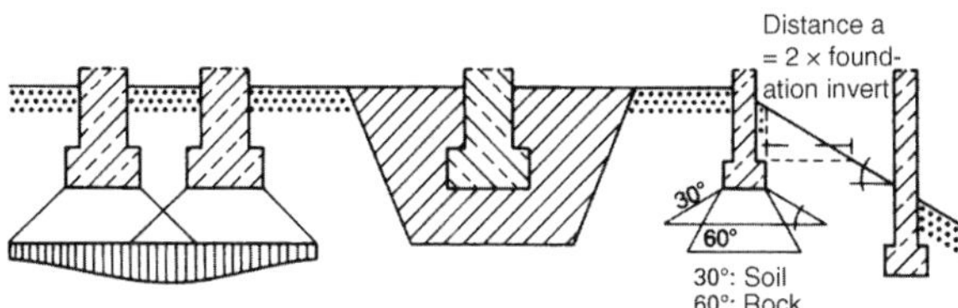

❻ The overlapping of areas loaded by adjacent foundations brings the danger of settlement or cracking, an important fact to remember for new buildings next to existing buildings. Foundations on sandfill of 0.80 to 1.20 m thickness, compacted in layers of 15 cm and soaked, can distribute loading onto a wider area. Foundations next to a slope. Pressure distribution lines – angle of slope of the subsoil.

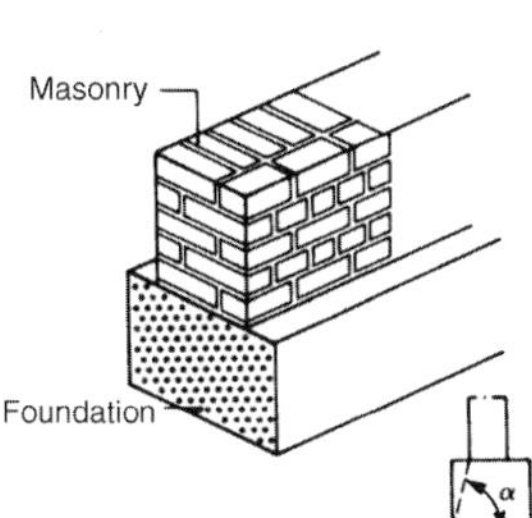

❼ Simple strip footing of lean concrete

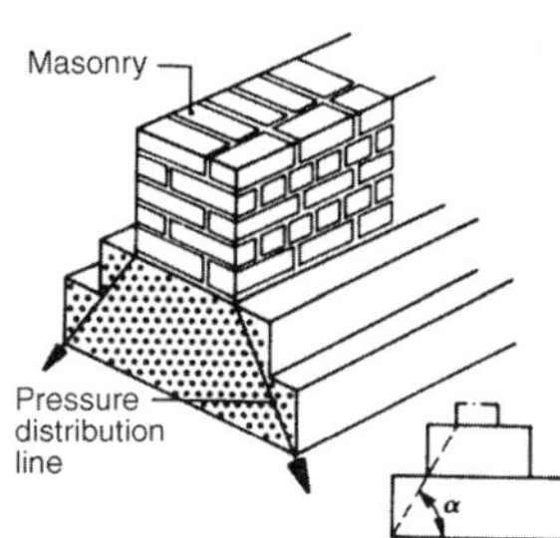

❽ Widened, stepped foundations of unreinforced concrete

Foundations can be constructed as spread or shallow foundations (**pad foundations** → ❶, **strip footing** → ❷, **ground-bearing slab or raft** → ❸) or deep foundations (**piled foundations** → ❹ → p. 70).

Spread foundations

Masonry foundations are technically feasible but seldom used today on account of the high cost.

Unreinforced concrete foundations are used for smaller widths and relatively small buildings.

Reinforced concrete foundations are used where the ground pressure is higher or the projection outside the wall is wider → ❼ – ❽ (reinforcement to resist the tension forces → ⓬). Reinforced concrete requires less thickness, weight and excavation depth than unreinforced concrete. The detailing of foundations at expansion joints and next to existing buildings or boundaries is shown in → ❾.

Raft foundations → ❿ are used where the load-bearing capacity of the subsoil is low or where pad foundations or strip footings are insufficient to bear the load.

The foundation level must be at a frost-free depth, so that the subsoil under it cannot move due to freezing and thawing. According to DIN 1054, a depth of 0.80 m (for engineered structures 1.0–1.5 m) counts as frost-free.

Improvement in the load-bearing capacity of the subsoil

a) **Vibroflotation compaction**: uses vibration to compact a radius of 2.3–3 m; spacing of the vibration cores approx. 1.5 m. Settlement is topped up. The improvement depends on the grading of the soil and its original bedding density.

b) **Vibro stone columns**: columns are formed by vibration of aggregate of various grading without binder.

c) **Stabilisation and compaction of the soil:** Cement grouting cannot be used for soils which are cohesive or aggressive to cement. Grouting with chemicals (silica solution, potassium chloride) produces immediate and permanent petrifaction, but can be used only with soils containing quartz (gravel, loose rock).

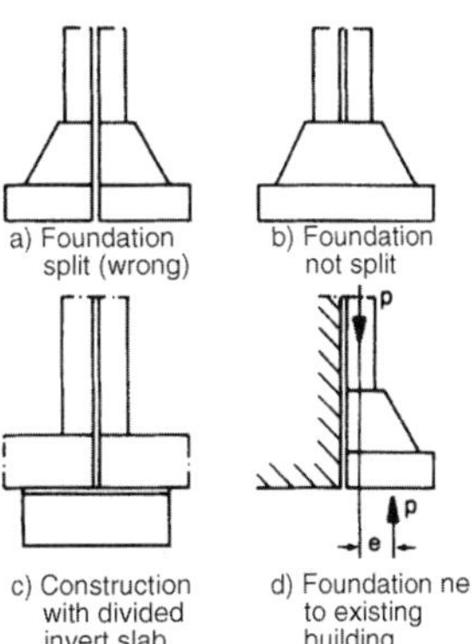

❾ Foundation details at separation and expansion joints

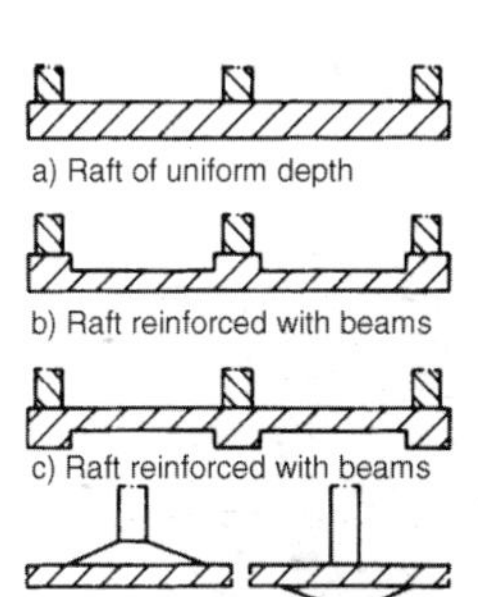

❿ Sections through raft foundations

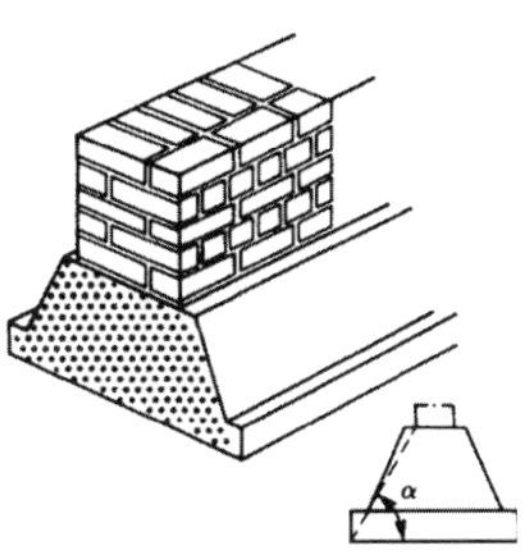

⓫ Widening foundations of unreinforced concrete

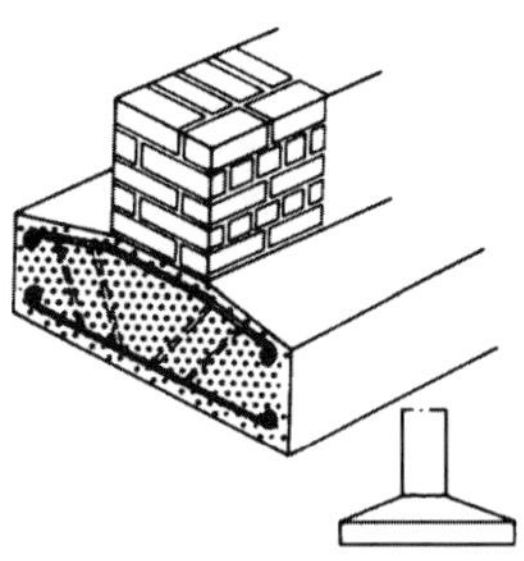

⓬ Still wider strip foundations of reinforced concrete

BS EN 12794
DIN EN 1536

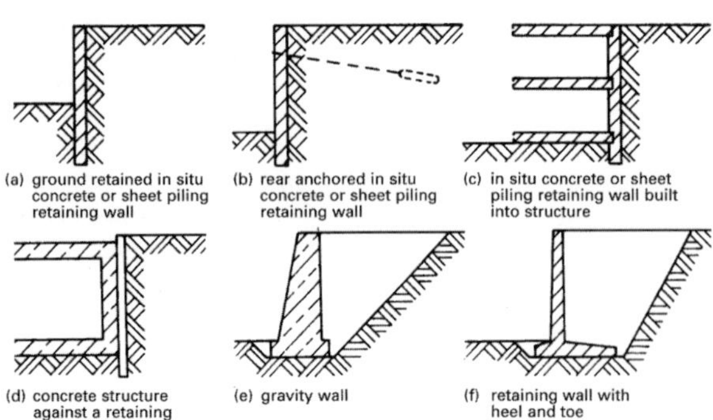

1 Building elements designed to resist active ground pressure

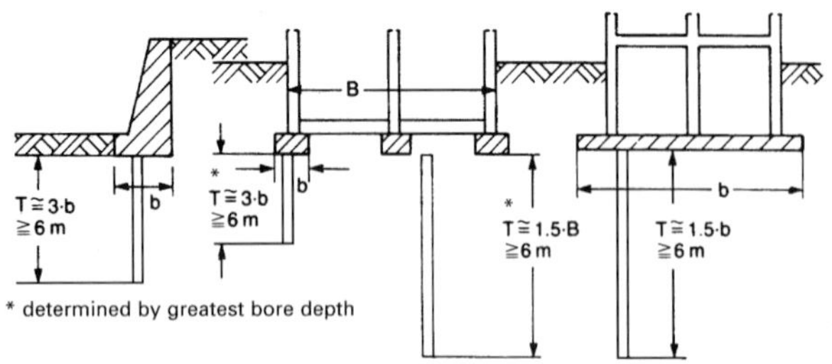

2 Minimum depths for structural boring

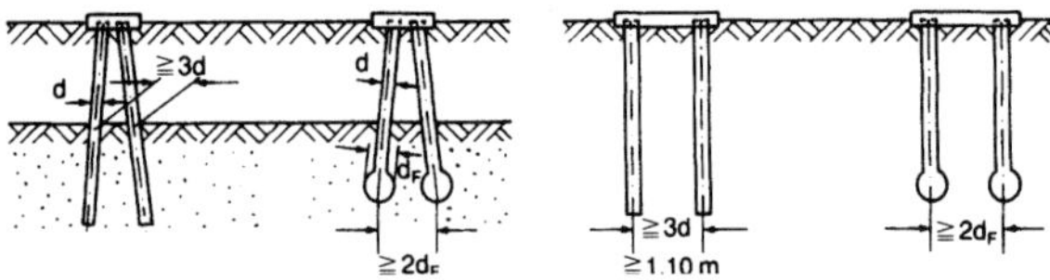

3 Bored piles (principle)

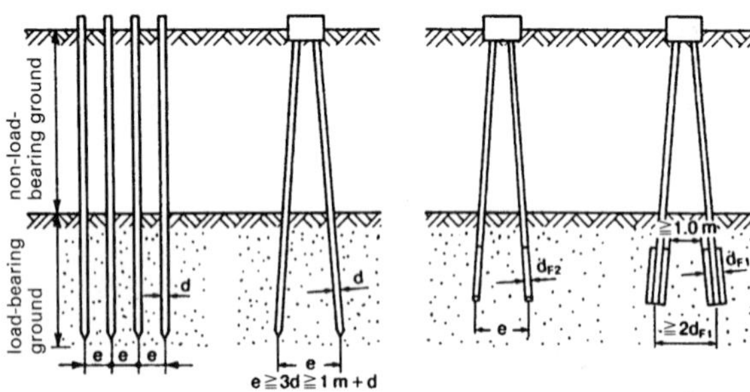

4 Driven piles (principle)

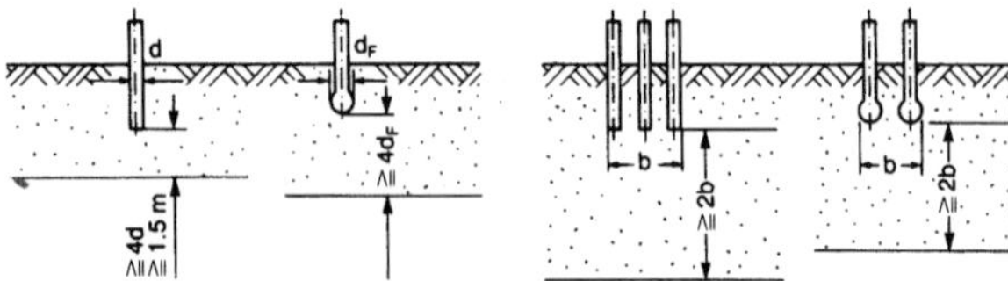

5 Required depth of load-bearing subsoil under bored piles (guideline values)

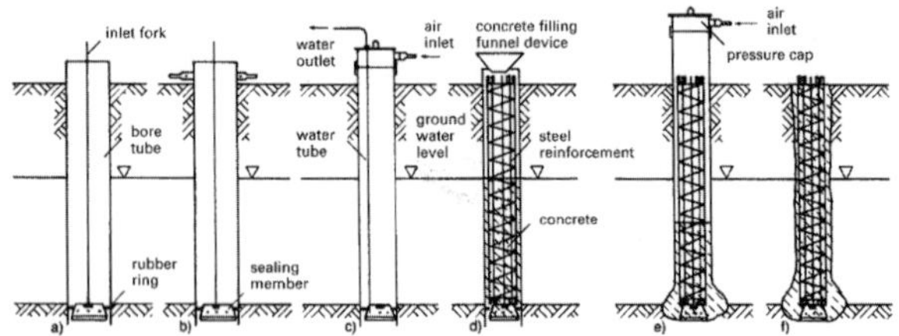

6 Pressed concrete bored pile (Brechtel system)

Deep foundations

Deep foundations are used where sufficiently load-bearing strata only occur at a great depth under the planned building and thus cannot be reached by shallow foundations.

They are normally constructed of reinforced concrete piles, which transfer the loading from the building through the weak ground to the load-bearing ground below. The design of piled foundations is based on the permissible loading on the ground and the type, properties, extent, density and thickness of the subsoil layers, which have to be established by investigation boreholes and probing if local experience cannot deliver sufficient certainty.

Basic terms

The force in the pile can be transferred to the stable ground by **skin friction**, **end-bearing** or a combination of both (the type of load transfer depends on the ground conditions and type of pile).

Standing pile foundations: load transfer is through the end of the pile into load-bearing ground, additionally through skin friction.

Hanging pile foundations: the pile ends do not reach load-bearing ground. Weakly load-bearing layers are compacted by the driving of the pile.

Piles are categorised according to the method of load transfer into: **friction piles**, which essentially transfer load into load-bearing layers by skin friction between the pile surface and the ground. **End-bearing piles** mainly transfer load into the ground through pressure under the end, with skin friction being irrelevant. The permissible force on the can be increased considerably by making the end larger (under-reaming).

According to the location of the piles in the ground, they can be **ground piles**, which are underground for their entire length, while **long piles** (free-standing piles) are in the ground only for part of their length and the upper part is free-standing, and therefore at risk of buckling.

According to the method of installation, there are piles which compact, displace or loosen the ground. **Driven piles** (driven with a pile hammer), **pressed piles** (pressed in), **bored piles** (installed in a bored hole), **screwed piles** (turned into the ground) and **jetted piles** (jetted into the ground).

According to the type of loading, they can be: axially loaded piles, **tension piles** (which are loaded in tension and transfer the force in the pile into the ground through skin friction), **compression piles** (which are loaded in compression and transfer load through end pressure and skin friction) and **piles subject to bending** (for example horizontally loaded large-diameter bored piles).

According to the method of production and installation, piles can be:

- **precast piles**, in prefabricated lengths or complete, which are delivered to the site and driven into the ground, jetted, vibrated, pressed, screwed or inserted into prepared holes.
- **in-situ piles**, which are concreted in a hole prepared in the ground by boring, driving, pressing or vibrating.
- **mixed foundation piles**, which consist of a combination of locally produced and prefabricated components.

In-situ piles have the advantage that their length can be determined during construction, from the data recorded during driving or from the inspection of the spoil from boring.

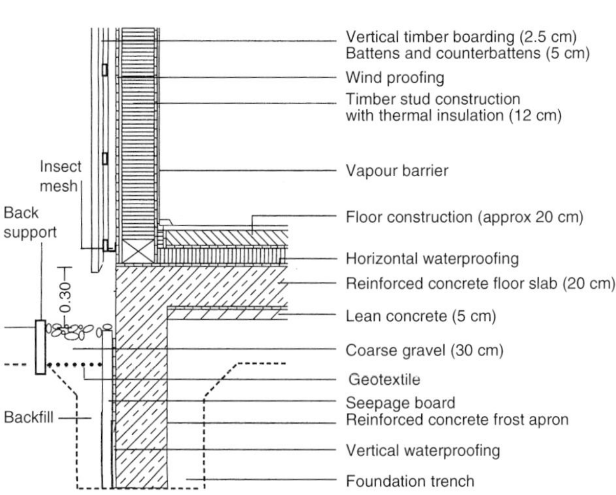

❶ Plinth detail of a timber-framed building without cellar with open ground transition in strongly permeable soil

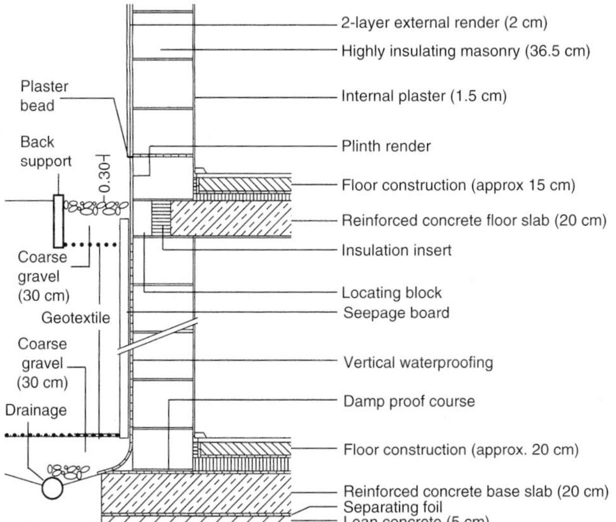

❷ Plinth detail of a building with masonry cellar walls in weakly permeable or cohesive soil

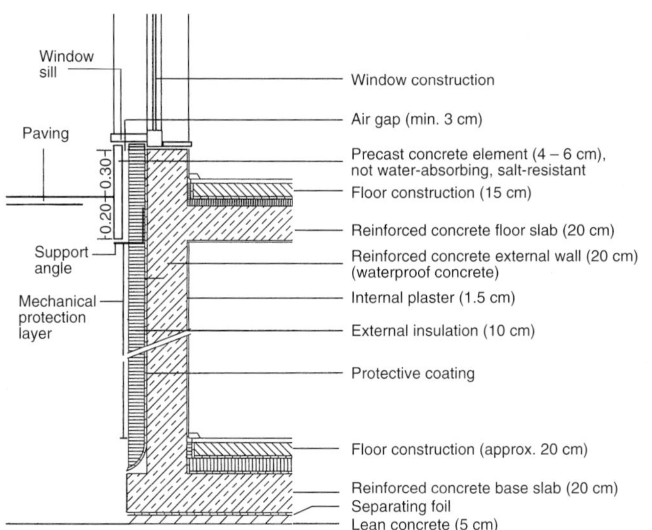

❸ Plinth detail of a building with cellar, ground floor at street level, construction as a waterproof basin

Waterproofing

External walls and slabs in contact with the ground must be waterproofed against **damp under external pressure**. External and internal walls in cellars and ground floors without cellars also have to be protected with horizontal waterproofing against **rising damp**.

This occurs as **ground moisture** (capillary, suction and residual water in the ground, which can be carried against gravity by capillary action) or **seepage water**, from precipitation and non-standing, which is not under pressure (e.g. earth-covered cellar roofs under courtyards), as well as **water under pressure** from the outside or occasionally **standing water** (groundwater and floodwater).

Waterproofing **materials** can be sheet material from the roll based on bitumen, plastic or elastomer, metal bands, mastic asphalt or thick plastic-modified bitumen coatings.

Vertical and horizontal waterproofing layers are to be brought together and sealed so that no moisture bridges remain. They must generally be continued 30 cm above ground level. Protective layers should also be provided in order to protect the waterproofing until the assignment of the various types of waterproofing to the various actions of water is shown in → ❹.

Type of building element	Nature of water	Installation situation	Type of water action
walls and slabs in contact with the ground **above** the estimated water table	capillary water residual water seepage water	very permeable soil $>10^{-4}$ m/s	**ground dampness** and non-standing seepage water
		low permeability soil $\leqq 10^{-4}$ m/s **with drainage**	
		low permeability soil $\leqq 10^{-4}$ m/s **without drainage** (up to foundation depth of 3 m below ground level)	**standing seepage water**
horizontal and sloping surfaces in the ground	precipitation water seepage water	used roof areas (e.g. covered cellar roof)	**water without pressure**, high loading
walls and slabs in contact with the ground **below** the estimated water table	groundwater flood water	any type of soil, building and construction	**water under pressure** from outside

❹ Building elements in contact with the ground: water action, installation situation and type of waterproofing

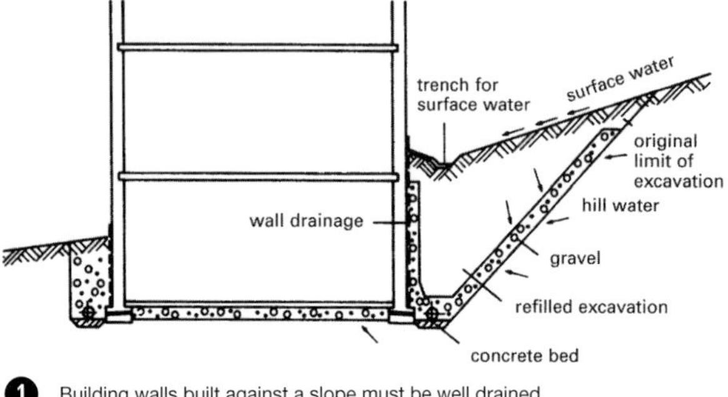

❶ Building walls built against a slope must be well drained

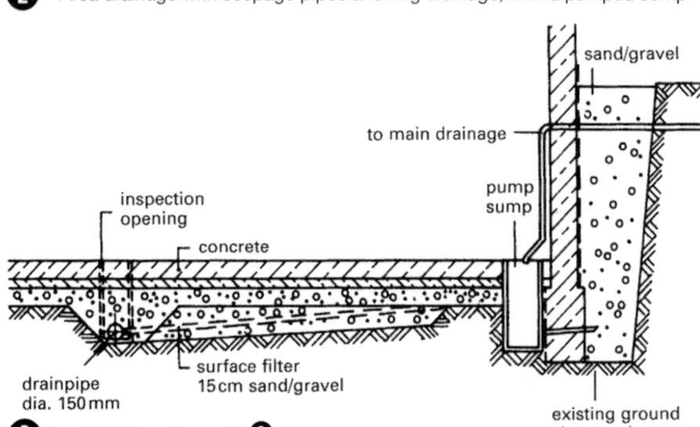

❷ Area drainage with seepage pipes and ring drainage, with a pumped sump

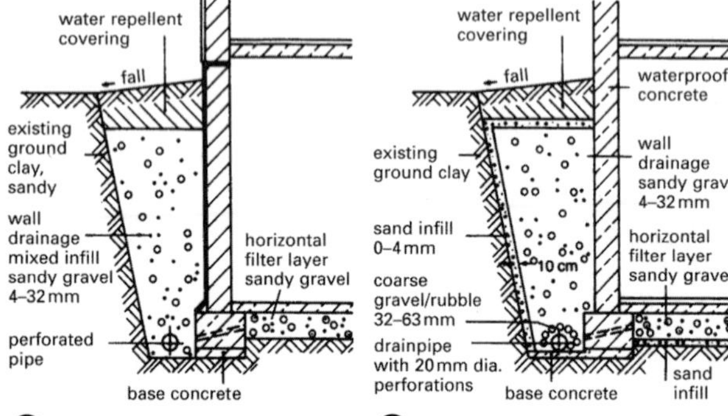

❸ Cross-section A–B → ❷

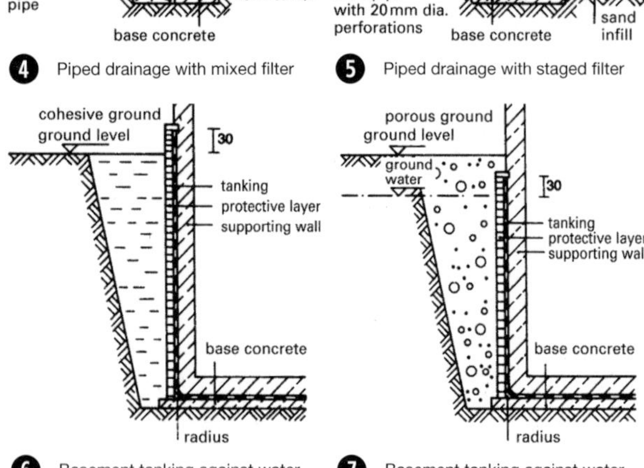

❹ Piped drainage with mixed filter

❺ Piped drainage with staged filter

❻ Basement tanking against water pressure

❼ Basement tanking against water pressure

FOUNDATIONS

Basement drainage

The ground can be drained through a **drainage layer** and **drainage pipes** in order to prevent the occurrence of water under pressure against an external wall. The entire procedure consists of drainage, inspection and flushing shaft and drainage pipes → ❽.

Drainage pipe, DN 100, fall 0.5. Flushing and control pipe, DN 300. Flushing, control and collector shaft, DN 1000. The required nominal diameter for round drainage pipes and operating roughness k_b = 2 mm can be determined from → ❽. The flow speed in the drainage pipe when full should not be less than v = 0.25 m/s. For areas over 2000 m^2, full-area drainage should be provided, through drainage pipes. The spacing of the individual drainage pipes should be calculated, and if necessary inspection shafts should also be provided → ❷.

The precondition for effective drainage is that the water runs away into a sewer or stream even at the highest water level in the main drainage channel. The best arrangement is a connection with free fall into an open stream or rainwater sewer, to avoid the need for pumping. If a pump is necessary, it must be protected against water coming back from the sewer or stream by a suitable device like a backflow preventer valve. This device must be accessible and must be maintained. Water from drainage can also be percolated into permeable subsoil, for example in a soakaway.

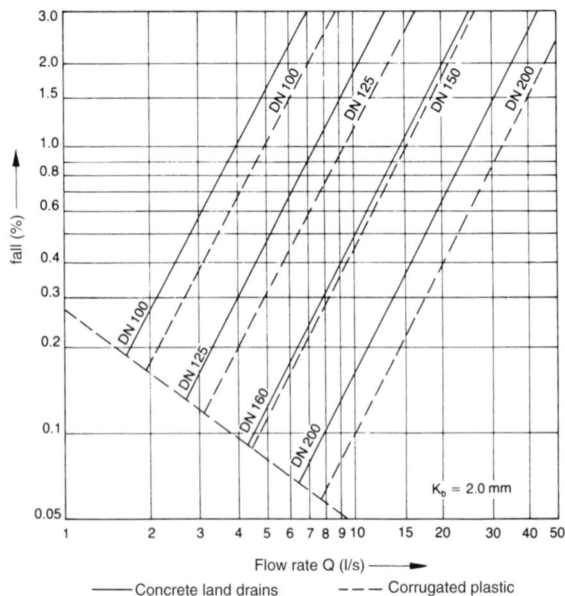

❽ Design example for circular drainage pipes

Tanking

If there is water under pressure or it is not possible to divert standing water through the provision of drainage, then the building elements must be constructed of **watertight concrete**, or a **continuous waterproofing layer** capable of resisting water pressure must be applied to the invert and side walls. This can consist of bituminous sheeting, metal waterproofing or plastic foil. It must be resistant to aggressive water and must maintain its effectiveness despite shrinkage, settlement and temperature-related deformation → p. 71. Bentonite waterproofing is also possible.

Watertight concrete is today the generally preferred method of resisting water under pressure. If the cellar floor and walls are separated by a construction joint, this must be waterproofed with a suitable waterstop or raised edge. The external surface of the walls is also provided with a protective coating based on bitumen or artificial resin as additional protection → ❻ – ❼.

FOUNDATIONS

Repair

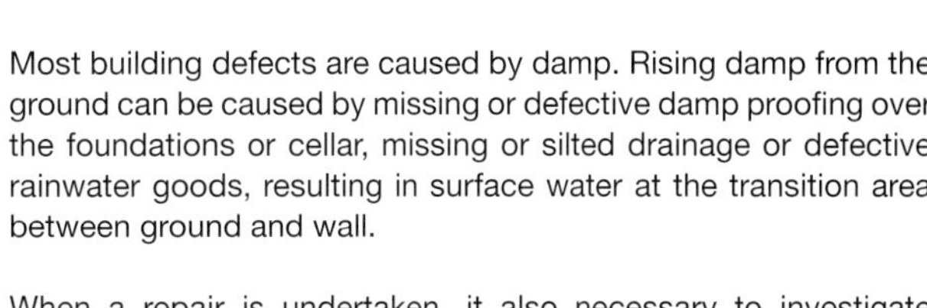

Most building defects are caused by damp. Rising damp from the ground can be caused by missing or defective damp proofing over the foundations or cellar, missing or silted drainage or defective rainwater goods, resulting in surface water at the transition area between ground and wall.

When a repair is undertaken, it also necessary to investigate and remedy the cause of the moisture penetration. Missing or damaged horizontal damp courses are laborious to replace, and the work needs to be carried out very carefully because the capillary transport of moisture must be interrupted. Building elements, which are impossible to waterproof, or only at excessive expense, can be coated using special plaster systems, which enable the damp to evaporate. The efflorescence of mineral salts resulting from evaporation can be absorbed for a long time, but the durability of such remedial plasters is still considerably shorter than plaster on a dry substrate.

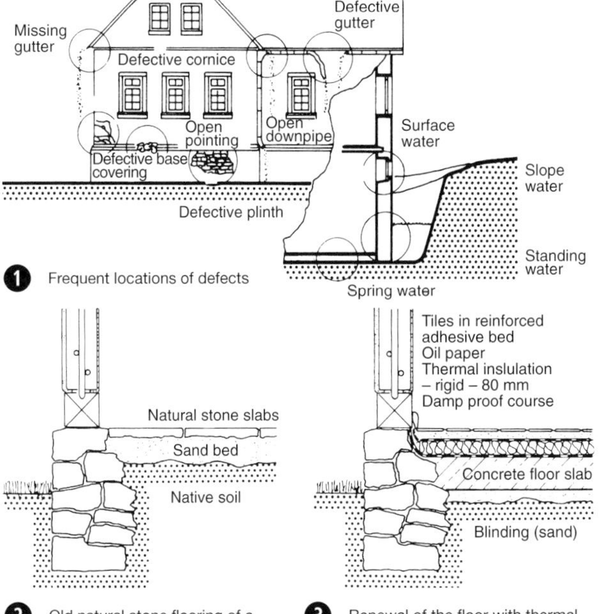

1 Frequent locations of defects

2 Old natural stone flooring of a ground floor without cellar

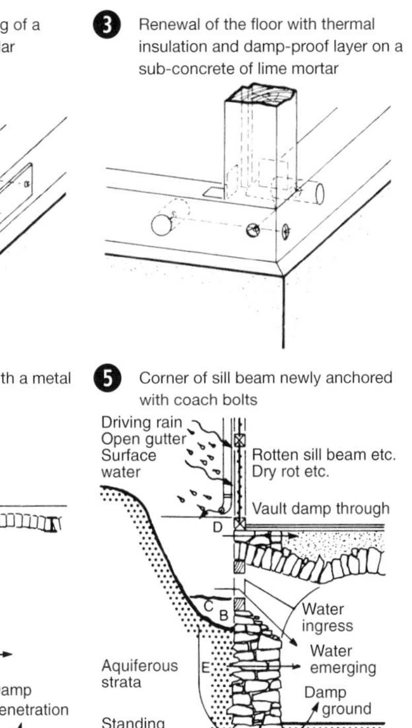

3 Renewal of the floor with thermal insulation and damp-proof layer on a sub-concrete of lime mortar

4 Corner reinforcement with a metal angle

5 Corner of sill beam newly anchored with coach bolts

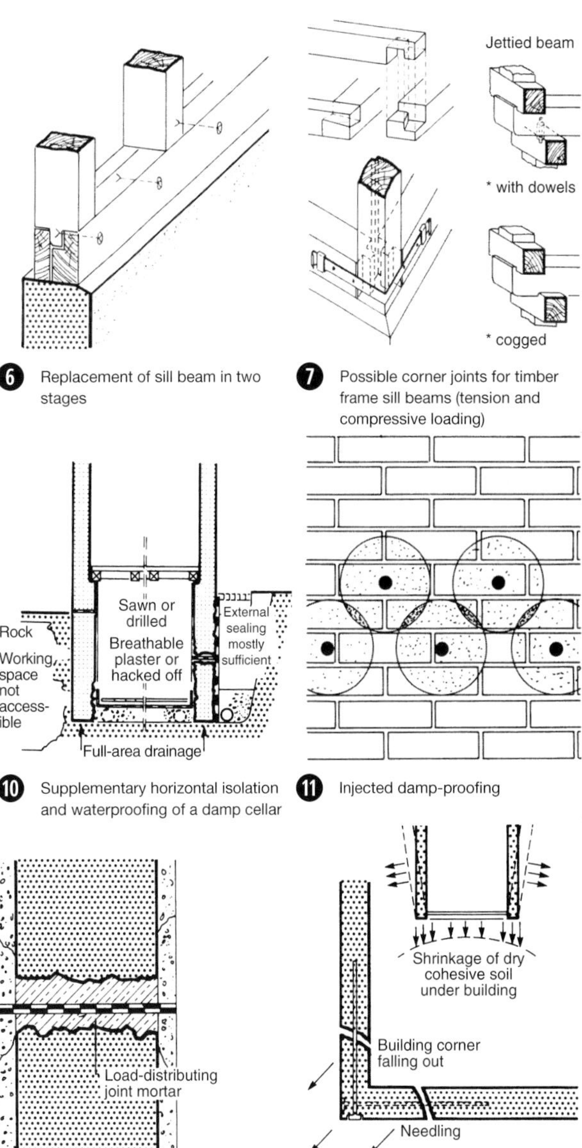

6 Replacement of sill beam in two stages

7 Possible corner joints for timber frame sill beams (tension and compressive loading)

8 Main sources of damage from water without pressure

9 Main sources of damage from water under pressure

10 Supplementary horizontal isolation and waterproofing of a damp cellar

11 Injected damp-proofing

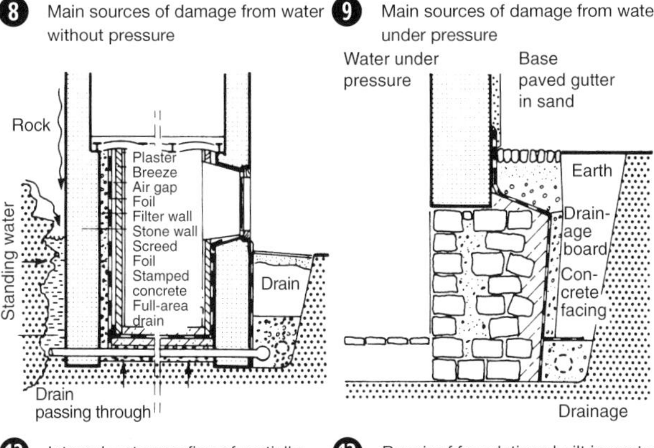

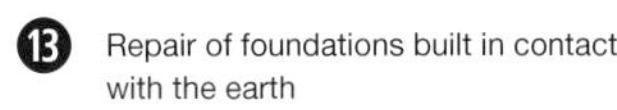

12 Internal waterproofing of partially inaccessible external walls

13 Repair of foundations built in contact with the earth

14 Supplementary insertion of horizontal waterproofing (wall separation)

15 Needling of a subsiding house corner

Natural stone walling can be categorised into **rubble, cyclopean, coursed, ashlar and composite.**
Stone, which has a natural plane of cleavage, should be split and laid according to the cleavage, e.g. → ❶, ❸, ❹, which looks better and is also structurally sounder because the loading is then mostly at right angles to the natural bedding.
The size of the individual blocks is of great importance. The block length should not be more than four to five times the block height and should not be less than the height (the stones should be bonded well on all sides). Pure natural stone masonry must be bonded in the entire cross-section in accordance with good trade practice.
There should never be more than three joints meeting at the front or rear surfaces of a block and no vertical joint should pass through more than two courses. For structural reasons, a course should be brought flat and level every ≦1.5 m (spacing of scaffold platforms).
Header and stretcher courses must alternate, or there must be at least one header for every two stretchers in each course. The depth (into the wall) of the headers must be at least 1½ times the course height but at least 30 cm.
The depth (into the wall) of the stretchers must be about equal to the course height. The vertical joints must be covered by ≧10 cm in coursed masonry and ≧15 cm in ashlar masonry → ❺ + ❼, and the largest blocks should be laid at the **corners** → ❶ – ❻. **Face surfaces** should subsequently be fully pointed, first scratching out a depth equal to the joint width. The joints should be about 3 cm thick according to roughness and method of working. Lime or lime-cement mortar should be used, as cement can discolour certain types of stone. In **composite masonry**, the worked stone facing can be integrated into the load-bearing cross-section → ❾. Non-load-bearing **stone cladding** of 2.5–5 cm thickness is fixed to the backing wall with anchors → ❿.

❶ Dry stone walling / section

❷ Cyclopean masonry of volcanic stone

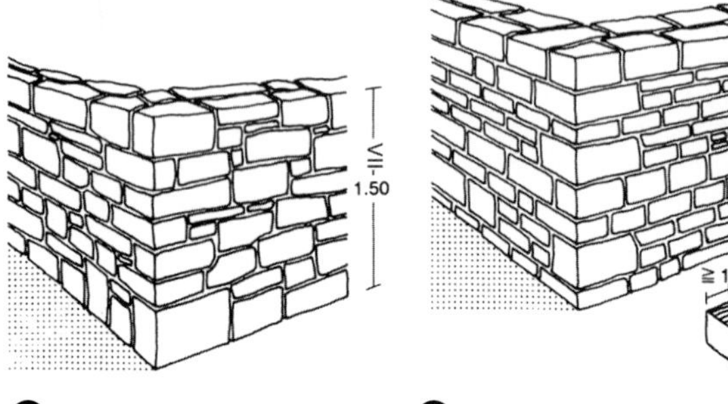

❸ Rubble masonry

❹ Rubble masonry squared with a hammer into courses

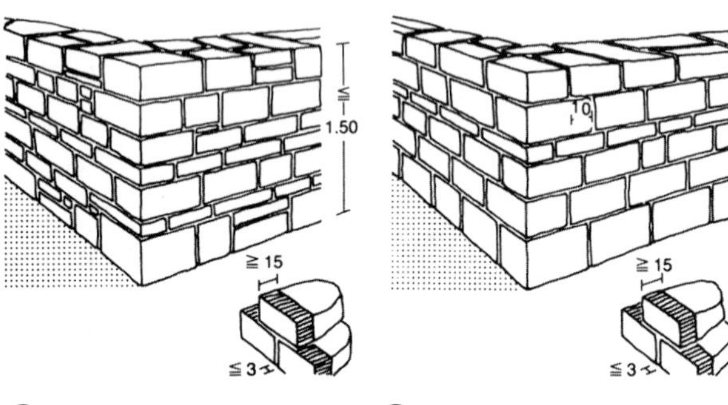

❺ Irregularly coursed masonry

❻ Regularly coursed masonry

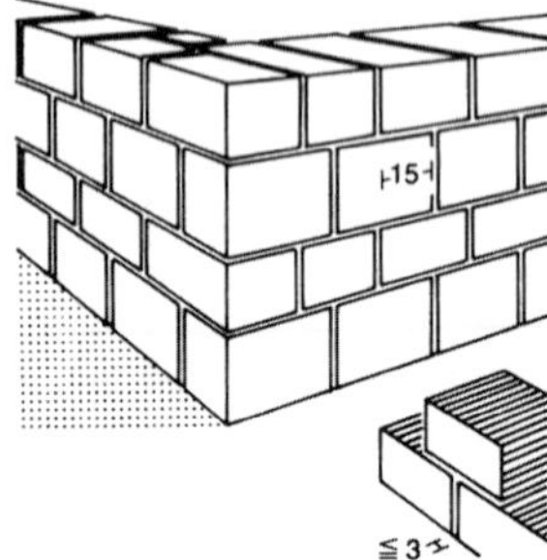

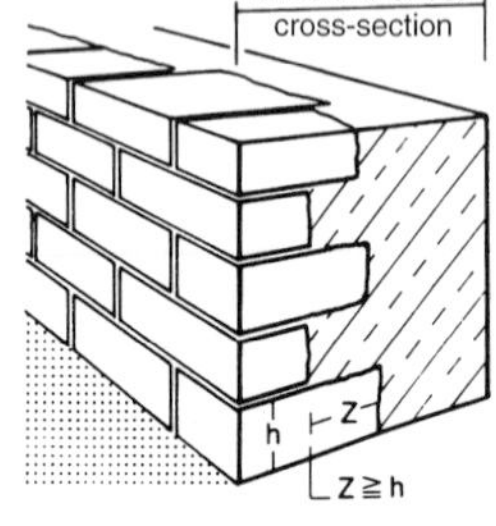

❼ Ashlar masonry

❽ Composite masonry

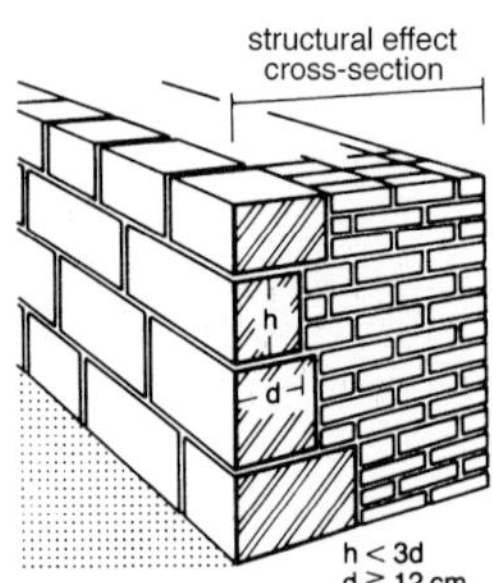
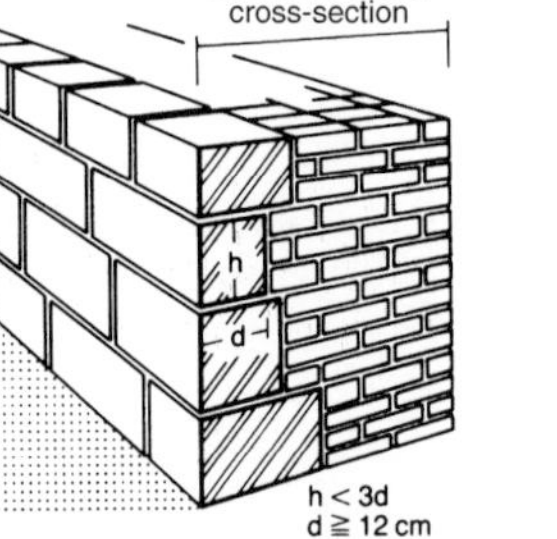

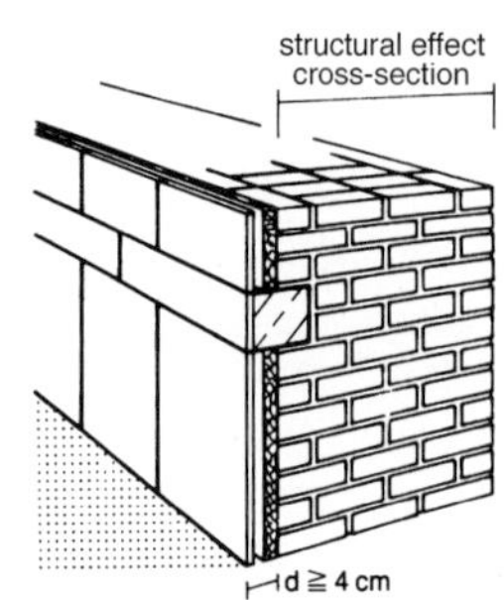

❾ Composite masonry showing the structurally effective section

❿ Stone cladding without structural contribution

Stone type	Compressive strength (N/mm²)
limestone, travertine, volcanic tuff	20
weak sandstone (with clay binder) and similar	30
dense (strong) limestone and dolomite (incl. marble), basalt lava and similar	50
quartzitic sandstone (with siliceous binder), greywacke and similar	80
granite, syenite, diorite, quartz porphyry, black porphyry, diabase and similar	120

⓫ Minimum compressive strengths of building stone

Grade	Stone strength βst (N/mm²)	Basic values σ_O [1] for mortar group			
		I (MN/m²)	II (MN/m²)	IIa (MN/m²)	III (MN/m²)
N1	≧20	0.2	0.5	0.8	1.2
	≧50	0.3	0.6	0.9	1.4
N2	≧20	0.4	0.9	1.4	1.8
	≧50	0.6	1.1	1.6	2.0
N3	≧20	0.5	1.5	2.0	2.5
	≧50	0.7	2.0	2.5	3.5
	≧100	1.0	2.5	3.0	4.0
N4	≧20	1.2	2.0	2.5	3.0
	≧50	2.0	3.5	4.0	5.0
	≧100	3.0	4.5	5.5	7.0

[1] If joints are more than 40 mm thick, then the basic values σ_O are to be reduced by 20%.

⓬ Basic values σ_o of the permissible compressive stresses for natural stone masonry with normal mortar

Grade	Basic category	Joint height / block length	Slope of bed joint – tan α	Transfer factor η
N1	rubble masonry	≦0.25	≦0.30	≧0.50
N3	masonry hammered into courses	≦0.20	≦0.15	≧0.65
N3	coursed masonry	≦0.13	≦0.10	≧0.75
N4	ashlar masonry	≦0.07	≦0.05	≧0.85

⓭ Guideline values for the grading of natural stone masonry

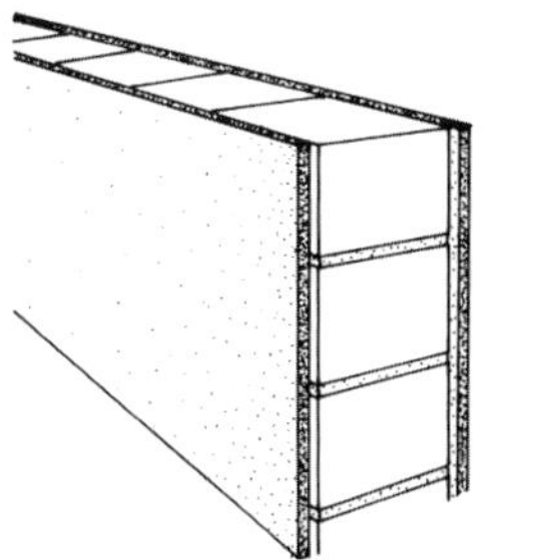
❶ Single-leaf plastered

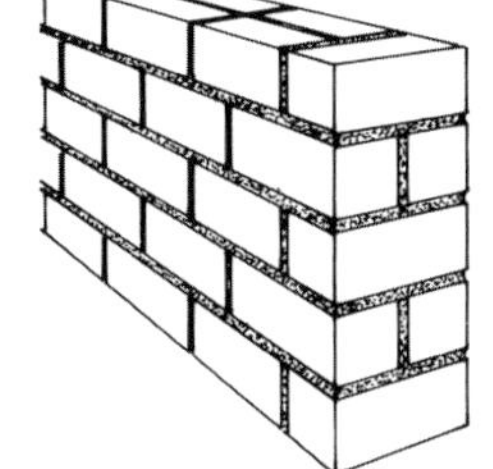
❷ Single-leaf faced

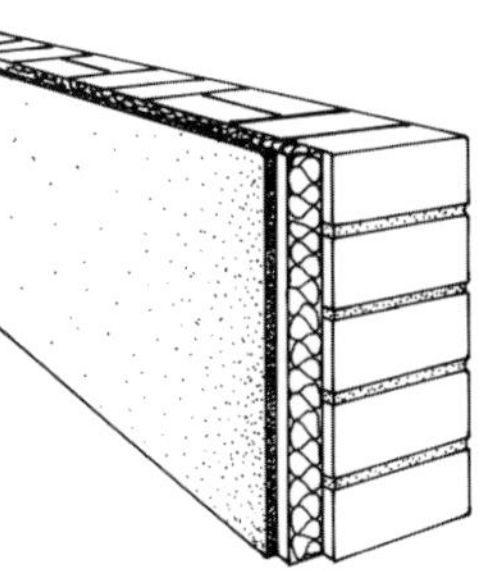
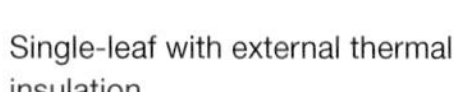
❸ Single-leaf with external thermal insulation

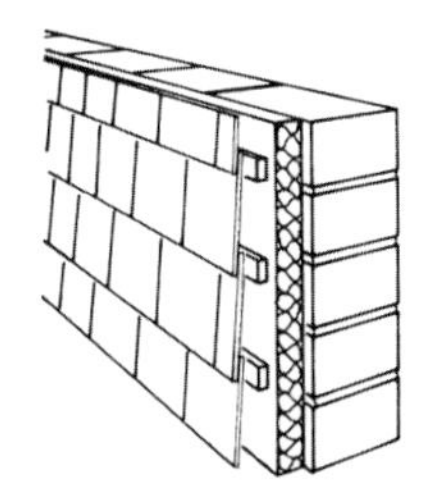
❹ Single-leaf with thermal insulation and weather protection

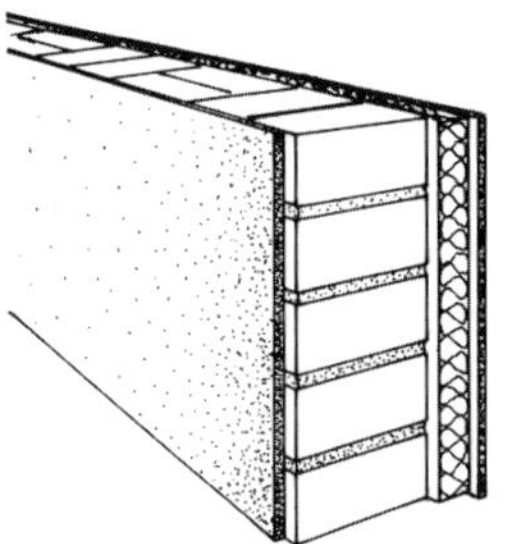
❺ Single-leaf with internal insulation

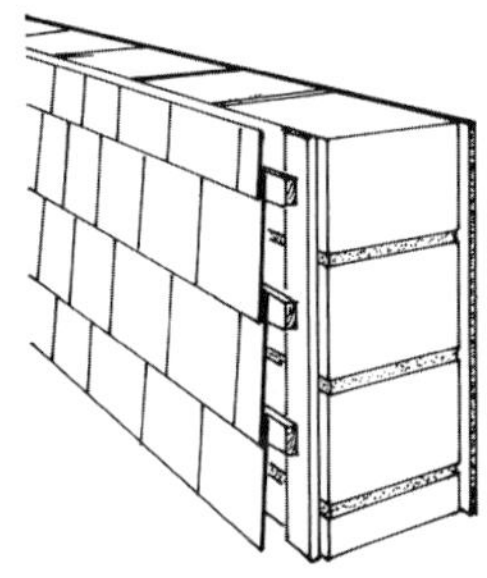
❻ Tiled cladding on masonry with a high thermal insulation value

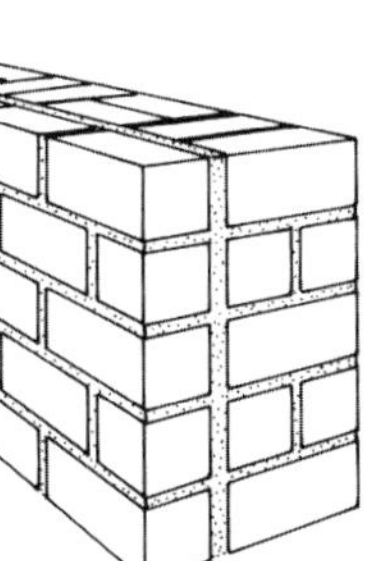
❼ Two-leaf composite masonry with internal plaster layer

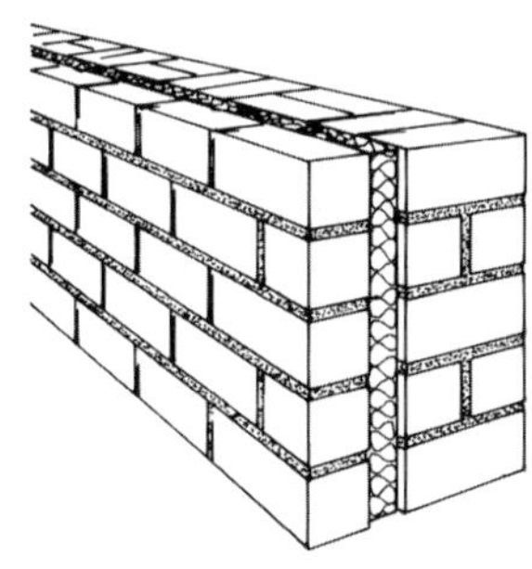
❽ Faced cavity wall without air gap

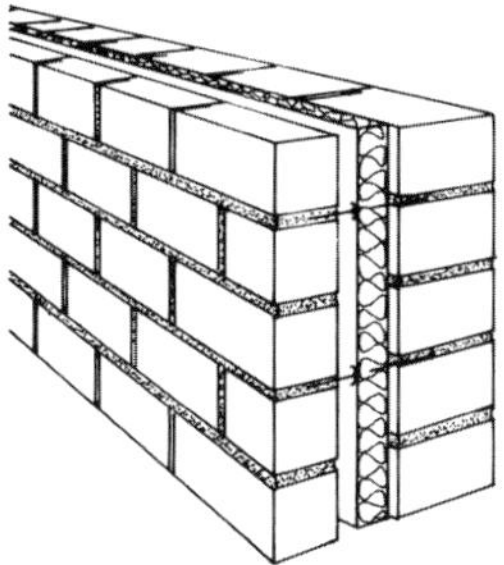
❾ Faced cavity wall with air gap

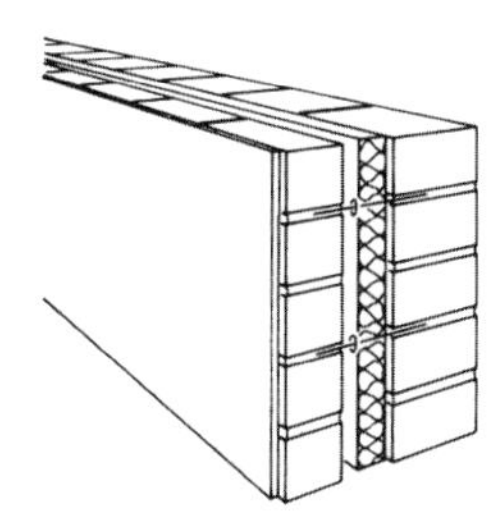
❿ With/without air gap plastered

Building materials

Countless bricks and blocks are available for the production of masonry walls in various forms, sizes and qualities → ⓫.
The dimensions (formats) are normally multiples of the standard format and thin format → ⓬.

Clay bricks and blocks	Sand-lime blocks
solid brick	solid and holed blocks
facing solid brick	facing blocks
hard-burnt solid brick	facing blocks
vertically cored block	cored and hollow blocks
facing vertically cored block	plan blocks (for thin mortar laying)
vertically cored hard-burnt block	
ceramic solid hard-burnt block	**granulated slag aggregate concrete blocks**
ceramic vertically cored hard-burnt block	
aerated concrete blocks	**solid aerated concrete blocks**
lightweight hollow concrete blocks	**concrete masonry units**

⓫ Brick and block types

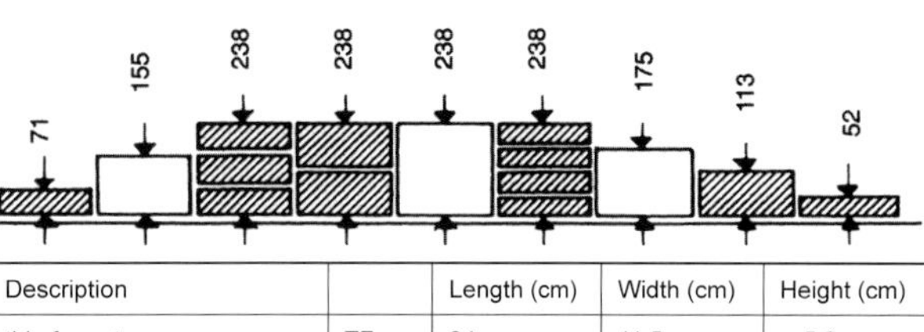

Description		Length (cm)	Width (cm)	Height (cm)
thin format	TF	24	11.5	5.2
normal format	NF	24	11.5	7.1
2 thin format	2 TF	24	11.5	11.3
3 thin format	3 TF	24	17.5	11.3

⓬ DIN brick formats (excerpt)

External wall construction

Single-leaf external walls → ❶ – ❷ are unproblematic regarding building physics, but on account of the high thermal insulation requirements can only be built with materials with high thermal insulation value (e.g. aerated blocks) and special thermally insulated mortars and plasters. If the blocks used are susceptible to frost damage, they have to be rendered or protected in other ways. If the masonry is externally visible, then each course must consist of at least two rows of blocks of the same height with a continuous 20 mm thick longitudinal joint between them, and each course staggered and mortared without voids.

Single-leaf walls with additional insulation layers → ❸ – ❻ (external, internal insulation → Building physics, p. 471 ff.) are therefore a common alternative.

Cavity walls consist of an inner load-bearing wall and an outer non-load-bearing weather protection facing (**minimum thickness 90 mm**). They can be built with an air gap, with air gap and thermal insulation, with cavity-filling insulation and with intermediate plaster layer → ❼ – ❿. The masonry leaves are connected with **ties** of non-rusting steel. The width of the air gap should be min. 40 mm (max. 150 mm). Vertical expansion joints should be provided in the external leaf and there should also be ventilation openings (e.g. open vertical joints) at the top and bottom, with the openings at the bottom also serving to drain water p. 77 → ❸.

see also:
Building physics
pp. 471 ff.

BS 8103-2
DIN 1053

❶ English bond

❷ Cross bond

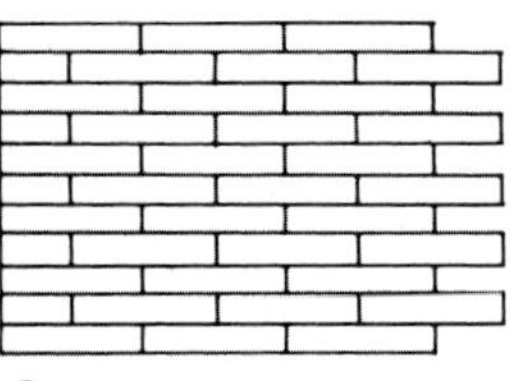

❸ Stretcher bond with ½ brick displacement

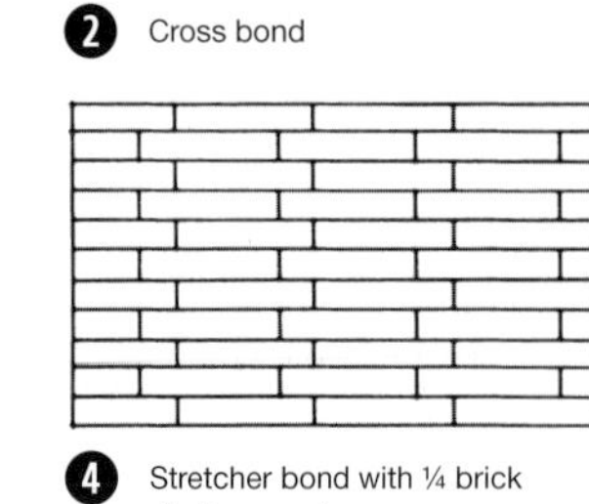

❹ Stretcher bond with ¼ brick displacement

❺ Flemish bond; one header, one stretcher, alternate courses

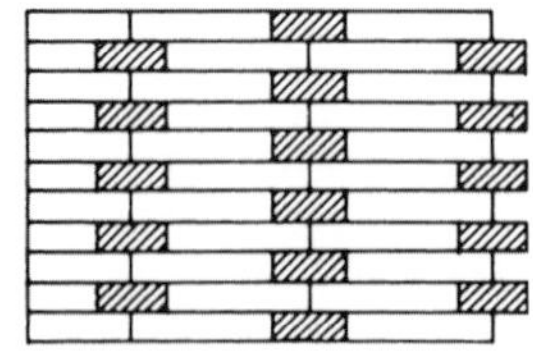

❻ One header, two stretchers, alternate courses

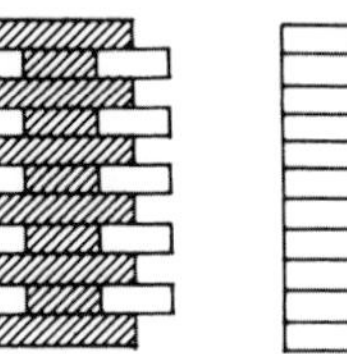

❼ One stretcher and one header course, alternating with header course

❽ Two stretcher and one header course, alternating with header course

❾ Stretcher bond with ¼ brick displacement, joints rising to the right

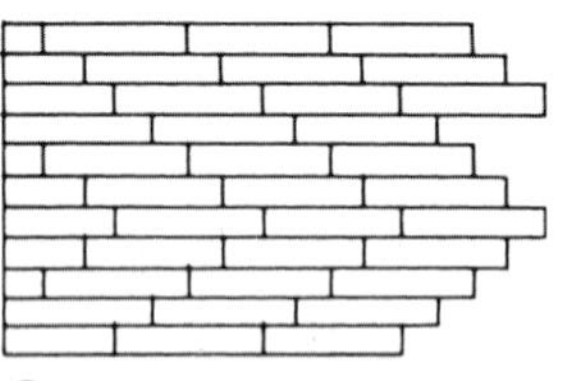

❿ Stretcher bond with ¼ brick displacement, joints rising to the right and left

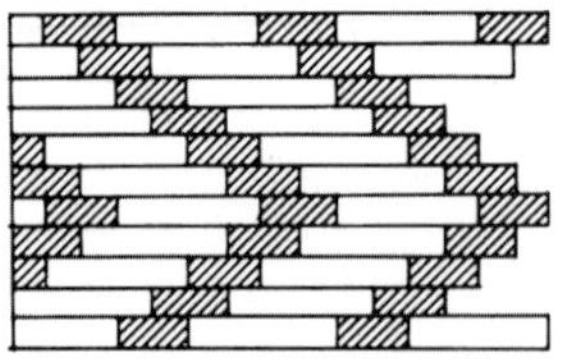

⓫ One header and one stretcher alternating in courses with ¼ brick displacement, joints rising to the right and left

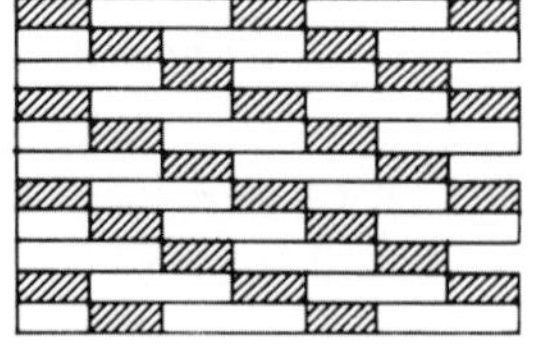

⓬ One header and one stretcher alternating in courses, with ½ brick displacement, joints rising to the left

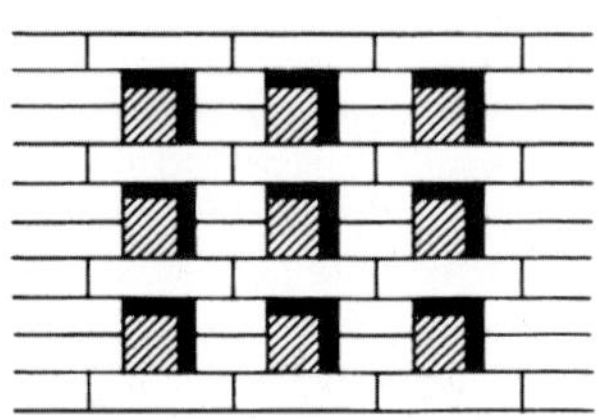

⓭ Hole coursed into the masonry for light or ventilation (hole ½ × ½ brick)

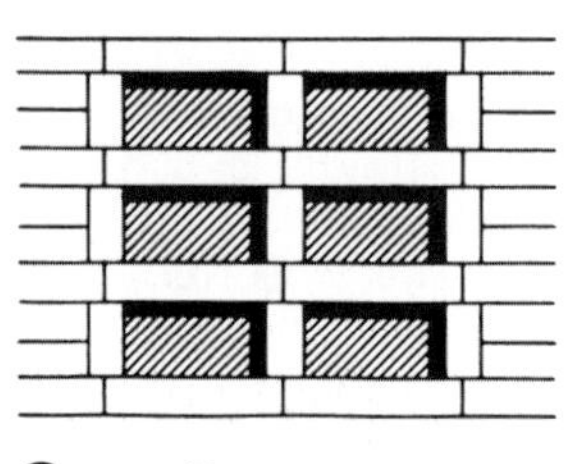

⓮ as → ⓭ (hole ½ × ¾ brick)

Bonding of masonry

In order to evenly transfer the loads acting on masonry and ensure crack-free wall surfaces, bricks and blocks are normally laid in regular courses and bonded. Masonry courses are named, according to their method of integration into the bond, **stretcher, header or soldier courses**:

Stretcher courses lie with their length along the face of the wall. Header courses lie with their end in the face of the wall and are bonded into the masonry by their length.

Masonry courses should continue horizontally through all walls in a building. **Vertical joints** in adjacent courses must always be overlapped, i.e. displaced relative to the adjacent course by a certain dimension (at least ¼ brick). In order to reduce the proportion of joints, as many whole bricks as possible should be used (in the currently prevalent single-leaf wall made of large-format blocks, the joints are the thermal weak point and have to be carried out in lightweight or thin mortar, or with the vertical joints toothed → ⓯). The type and dimension of the displacement of the vertical joints in adjacent courses leads to the basic pattern of the various masonry bonds, in addition to the sequence of stretchers and headers.

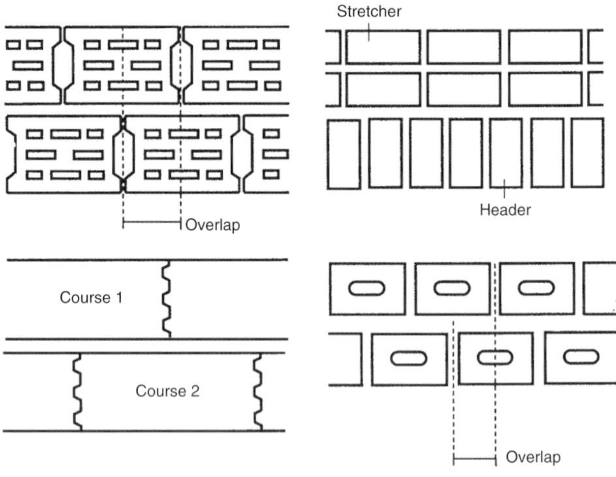

⓯ Modern masonry bonds

Modern masonry bonds are normally laid in **stretcher bond** → ❸ as 'middle bond' with displacement of the vertical joint by ½ brick in the next course or, alternatively, as 'English bond' with displacement of the vertical joint by ⅓ brick in the next course → ❶, or with 'cross bond', alternating stretcher and header courses → ❷.

There are many other bonds in classical bricklaying such as 'Flemish bond' → ❺, or one header and three stretchers in each course → ❻ and other decorative bonds.

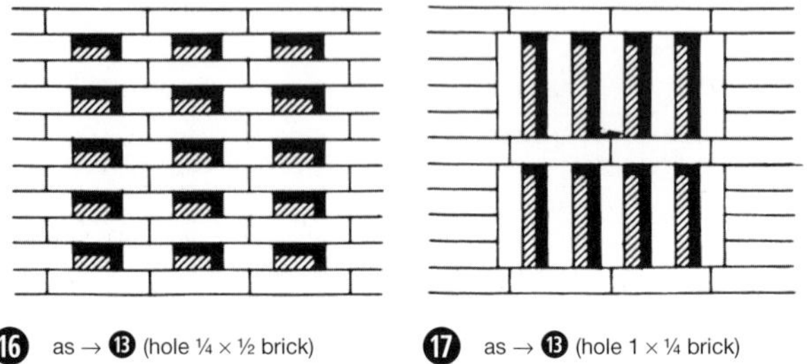

⓰ as → ⓭ (hole ¼ × ½ brick)

⓱ as → ⓭ (hole 1 × ¼ brick)

WALLS
Natural stone masonry
Brick and block masonry
Composite construction
Repair

BS 8103-2
DIN 1053

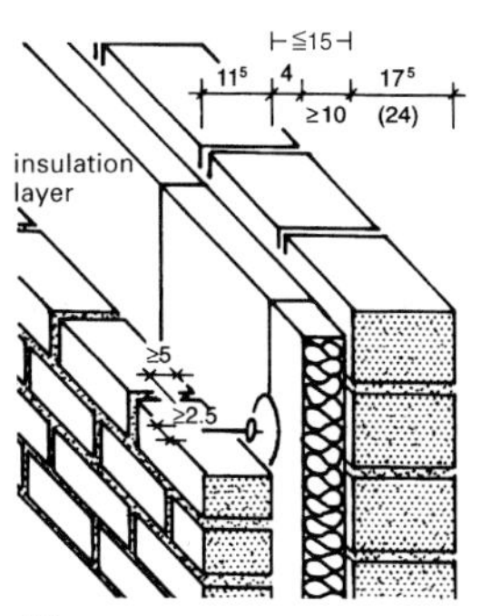

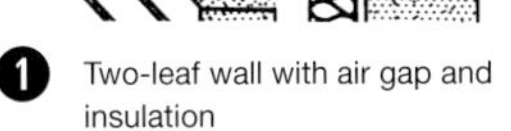
❶ Two-leaf wall with air gap and insulation

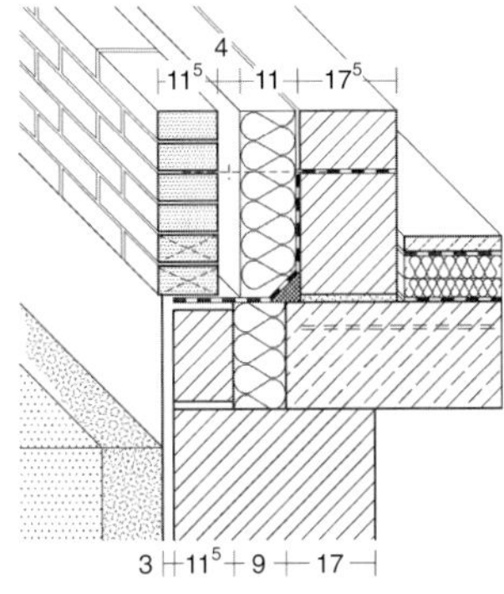

❷ Plinth connection

Building element	Conditions		
	Wall thickness (τ in cm)	Clear wall height (η in cm)	Imposed load (π in kN/m^2)
internal wall	$\geqq 11^5$ $\leqq 24$	$\leqq 275$	$\leqq 5$
	$\geqq 24$	–	
solid external wall	$\geqq 17^5$ $\leqq 24$	$\leqq 275$	
	$\geqq 24$	$\leqq 12$ t	
load-bearing leaf of a cavity external wall and cavity party wall	$\geqq 11^5$ $\leqq 17^5$	$\leqq 275$	$\leqq 3$
	$\geqq 17^5$ $\leqq 24$		$\leqq 5$
	$\geqq 24$	$\leqq 12$ t	

❸ Conditions for the application of the simplified calculation procedure for building heights $\leqq$20 m (DIN 1053-1 → refs)

Load-bearing walls

Walls which have to bear more than their self-weight on one storey are called load-bearing walls.

Bracing walls

Masonry can be secured by bracing walls and slabs below and above (three-dimensional cell principle). Bracing walls are building elements which work as deep beams to transfer horizontal loads (e.g. wind loads).

Non-load-bearing walls

Walls which are only loaded by their self-weight and are not used for bracing against buckling are called non-load-bearing.

Cut-outs and chases

Cut-outs and chases can either be chased out mechanically or formed in bond by the bricklayer. Their details can require structural verification under certain circumstances → ❹.

Perimeter tie

Perimeter ties are required for the **transfer of horizontal forces** over all external and transverse walls in buildings with more than two full storeys or more than 18 m length and walls with many or large openings under the floor slab. These are normally made of reinforced concrete and constructed together with columns and massive floor slabs. A simplified verification procedure can be used under certain circumstances for the design of masonry construction → ❸.

Wall thickness (cm)	Horizontal and inclined chases carried out later (cm)		Vertical chases and cut-outs, carried out later (cm)			Vertical chases and cut-outs in bonded masonry (cm)			
	Chase length		Chase depth	Chase width	Distance of chase or cut-out from openings	Chase width	Residual wall thickness	Minimum distance of chases and cut-outs	
	Unlimited	$\leqq$1.25 m						From openings	To each other
	Chase depth	Chase depth							
$\geqq 11^5$	–	–	$\leqq 1$	$\leqq 10$	$\geqq 11^5$	–	–	$\geqq 2 \times$ chase width or $\geqq 24$	$\geqq$chase width
$\geqq 17^5$	–	$\leqq 2^5$	$\leqq 3$	$\leqq 10$		$\leqq 26$	$\geqq 11^5$		
$\geqq 24$	$\leqq 1^5$	$\leqq 2^5$	$\leqq 3$	$\leqq 15$		$\leqq 38^5$	$\geqq 11^5$		
$\geqq 30$	$\leqq 2$	$\leqq 3$	$\leqq 3$	$\leqq 20$		$\leqq 38^5$	$\geqq 17^5$		
$\geqq 36^5$	$\leqq 2$	$\leqq 3$	$\leqq 3$	$\leqq 20$		$\leqq 38^5$	$\geqq 24$		

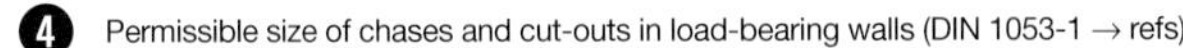
❹ Permissible size of chases and cut-outs in load-bearing walls (DIN 1053-1 → refs)

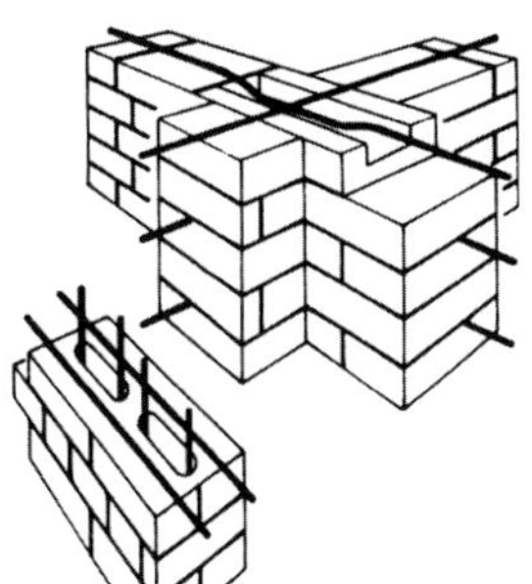
❺ Crossing of reinforced aerated concrete blockwork

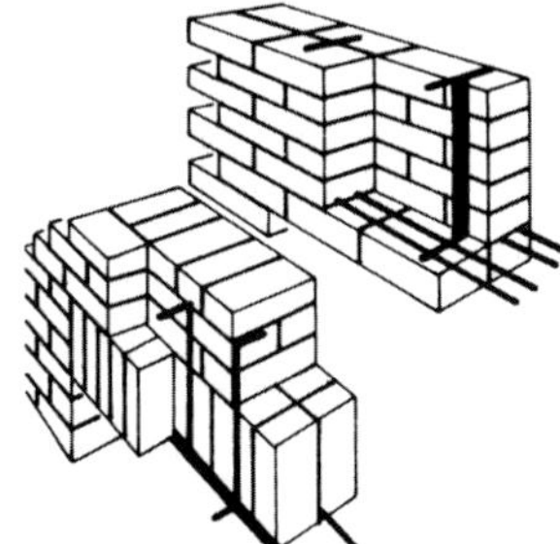
❻ Reinforced masonry door and window lintels

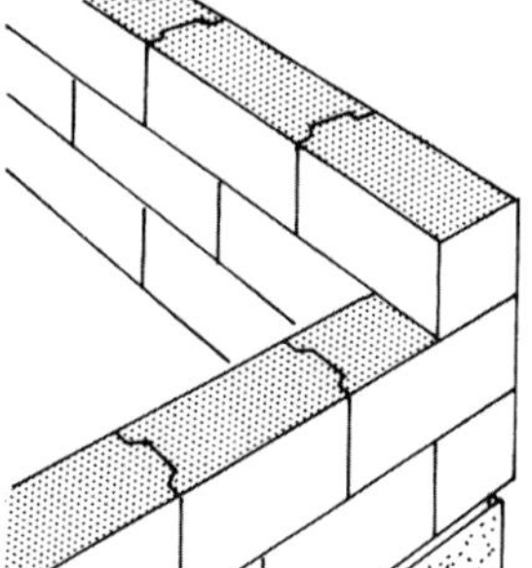
❼ Glued aerated concrete blockwork, 1 mm joints

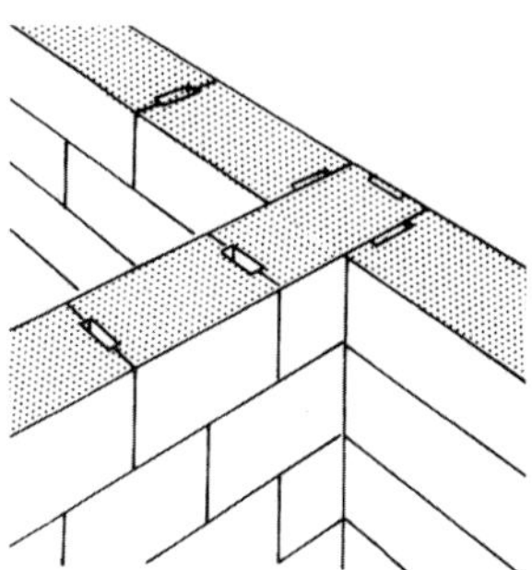
❽ Vertically cored clay bricks and blocks laid or with poured mortar

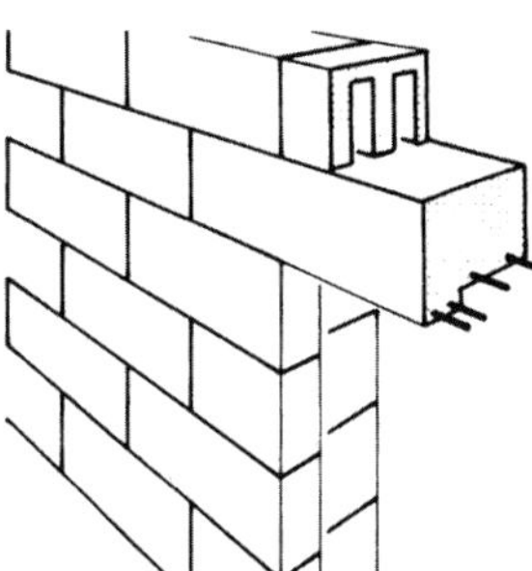
❾ Masonry of aerated concrete (hollow blocks) with reinforced pumice concrete lintel

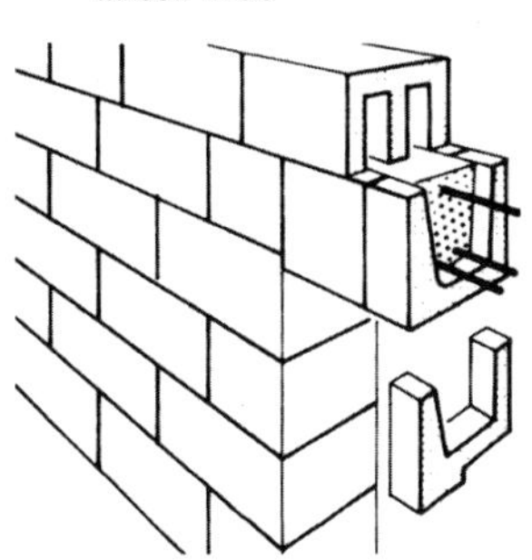
❿ Masonry of hollow blocks with cast trough lintel

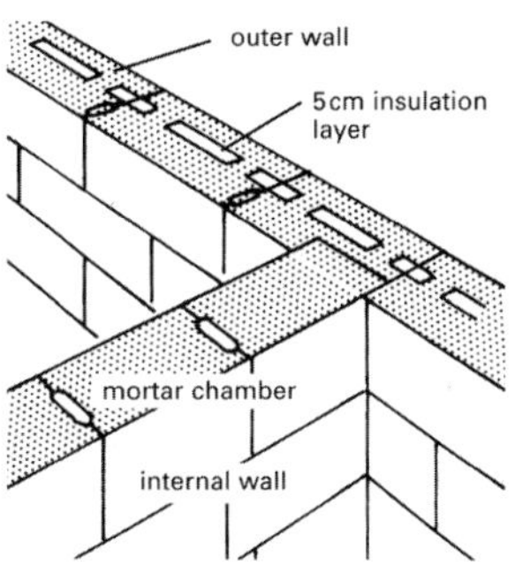

⓫ Blocks with 5 cm insulation layer and mortar pockets

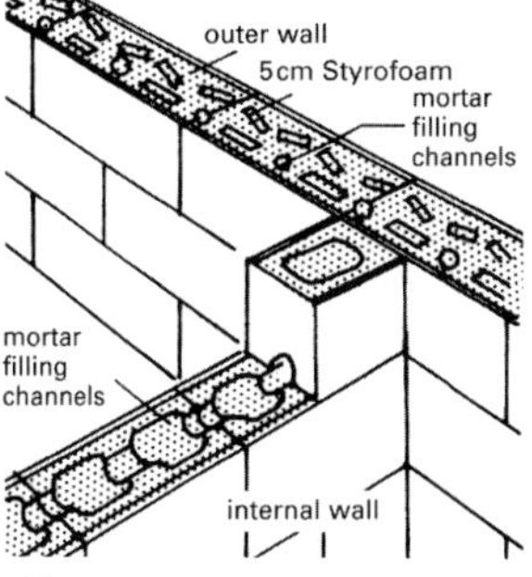

⓬ Assembly blocks with insulation and cavities for mortar filling

Building components

WALLS
Natural stone masonry
Brick and block masonry
Composite construction
Repair

see also: Glass pp. 104 ff.
Building physics pp. 471 ff.

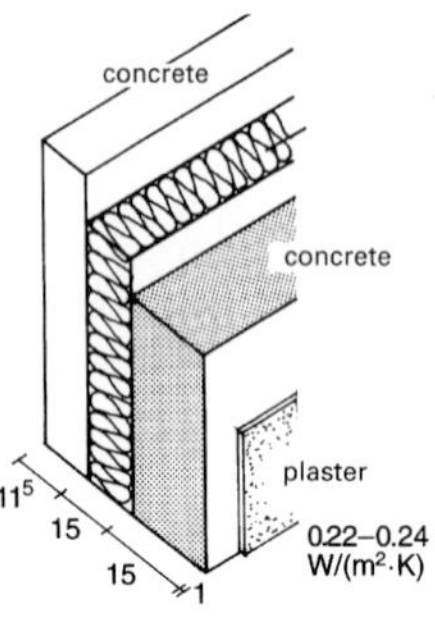

❶ Two-layer concrete

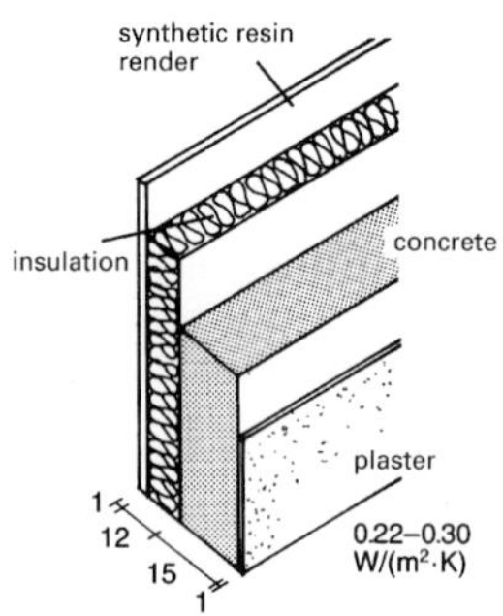

❷ Concrete with external thermal insulation system

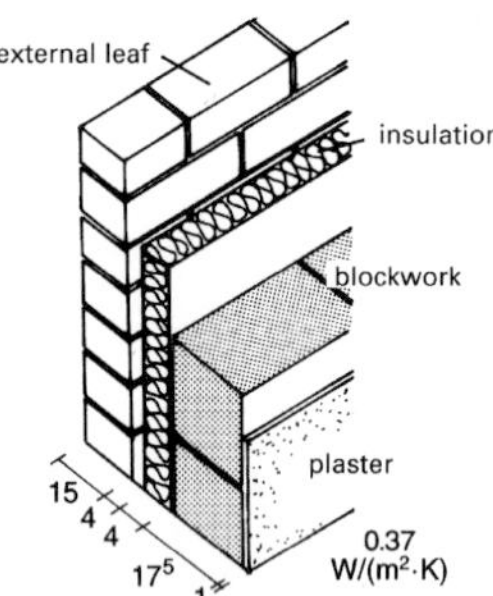

❸ Two leaves of aerated concrete

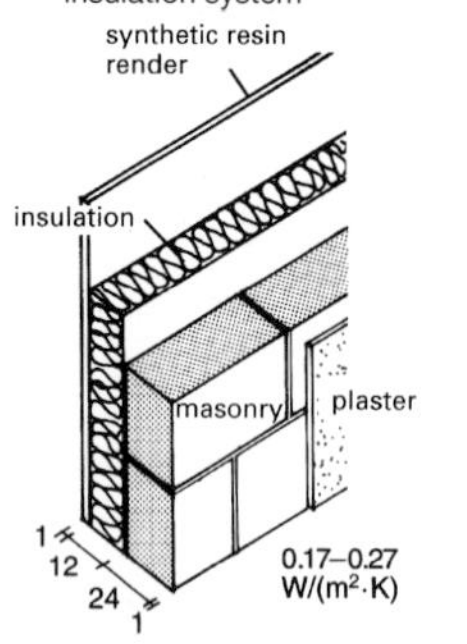

❹ Masonry with external thermal insulation system

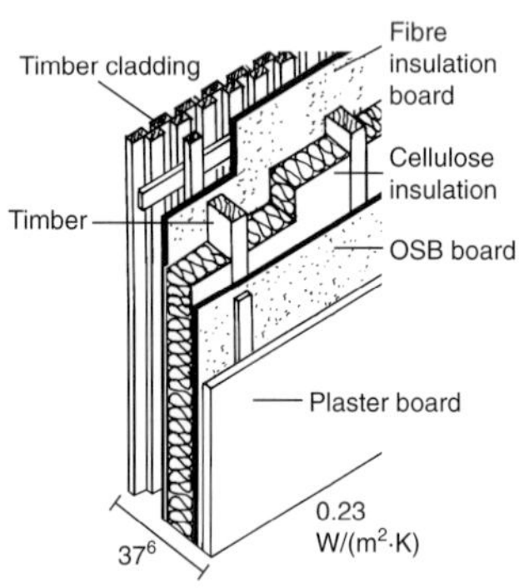

❺ Low-energy wall (Heckmann Ökohaus)

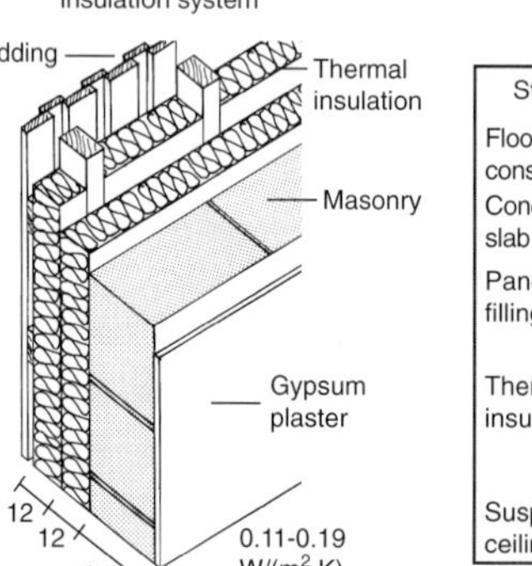

❻ Masonry with external cladding

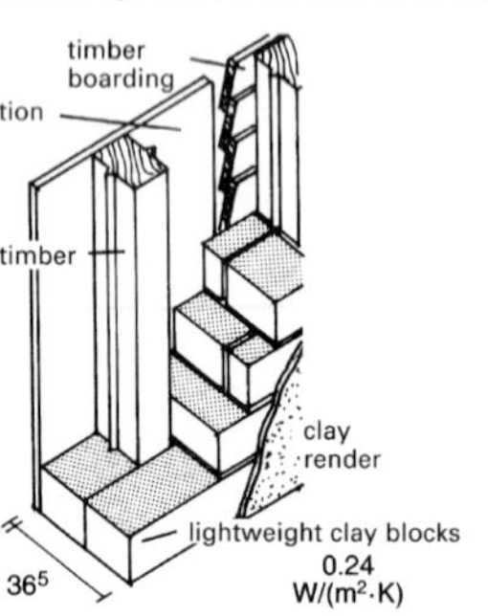

❼ Stud framing with lightweight clay elements

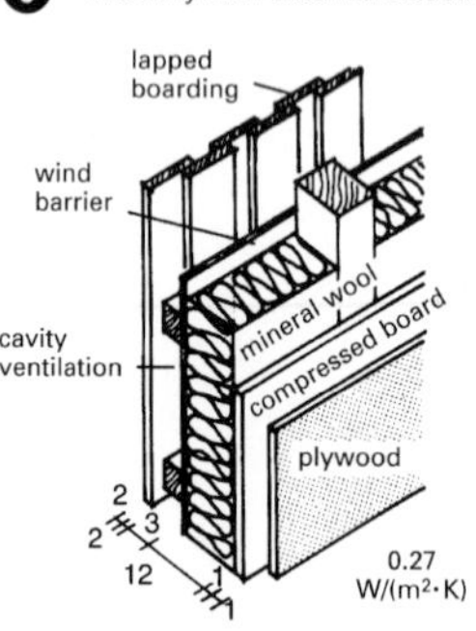

❽ Timber framing (insulation between the posts)

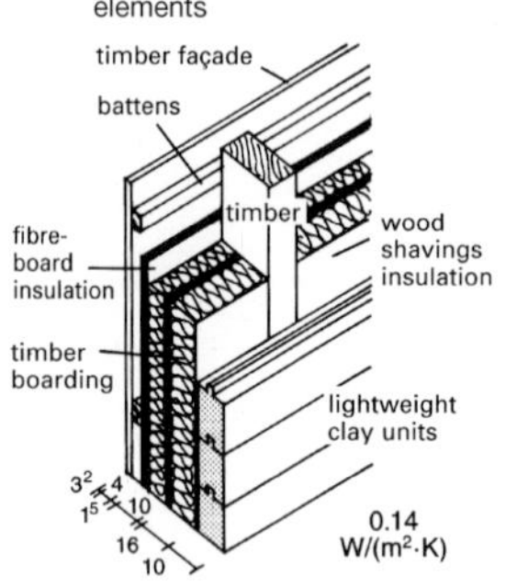

❾ Timber framing with lightweight clay blocks

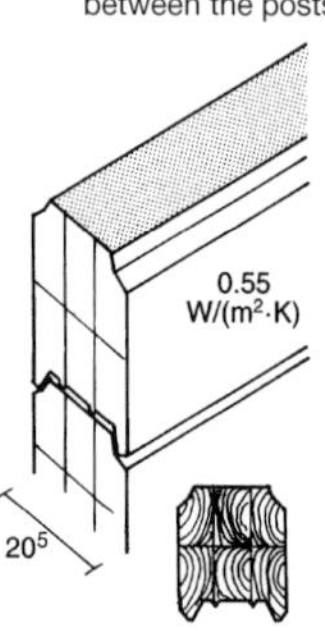

❿ Laminated timber sections for log house construction

Reinforced concrete walls → ❶ – ❷
Reinforced concrete walls can be concreted on site or pre-cast. **Solid concrete walls** can be used as external walls only with an additional thermal insulation layer. This can be as an external thermal insulation system → ❶ or as a multi-leaf construction (analogous to p. 75) with core insulation and possibly back-ventilation. **Two-layer reinforced concrete walls** → ❶ with core insulation are used particularly as large-format external wall elements.

Timber-framed walls → ❺ – ❿
The oldest form of timber walling is **log cabin construction** with the round logs or beams laid on top of one another and cogged at the corners → ❿. Timber-framed walling (with the panels filled in with various materials) is economical and the most common method, with vertical loads being transferred through the studs. A variant of timber framing is the erection of framed panels, which are prefabricated with thermal insulation. When timber-framed walls are to be used, provide sufficient roof overhang and design cladding in the splash area to be easily replaced.

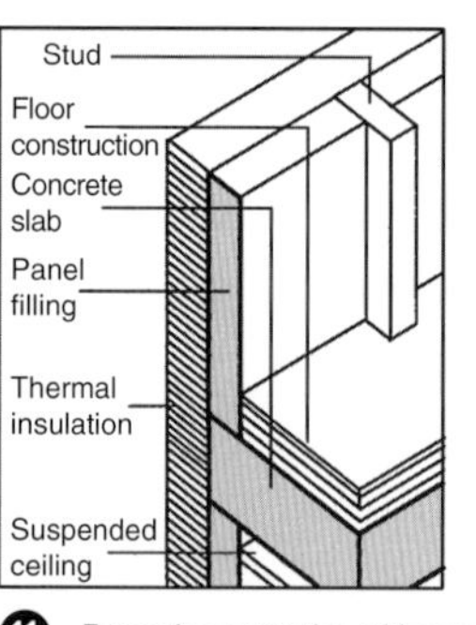

⓫ Framed construction with non-load-bearing masonry panels

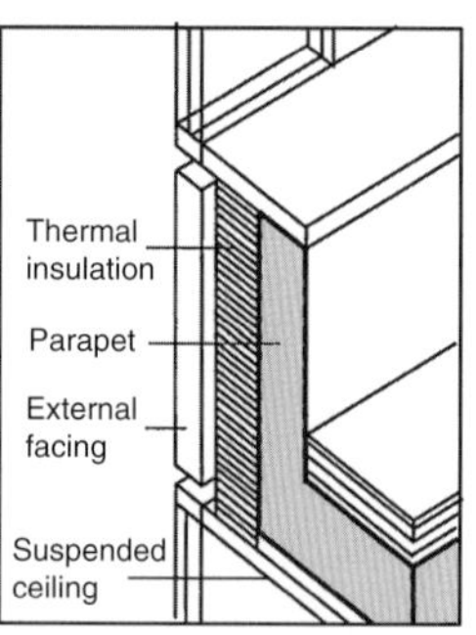

⓬ Curtain wall with back-ventilated façade

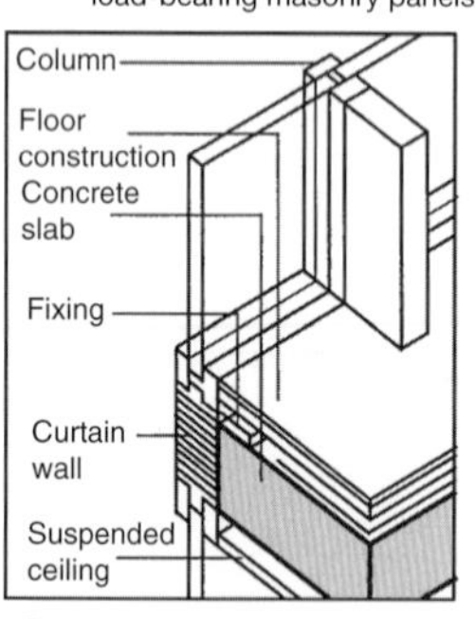

⓭ Curtain wall of multi-layer façade elements

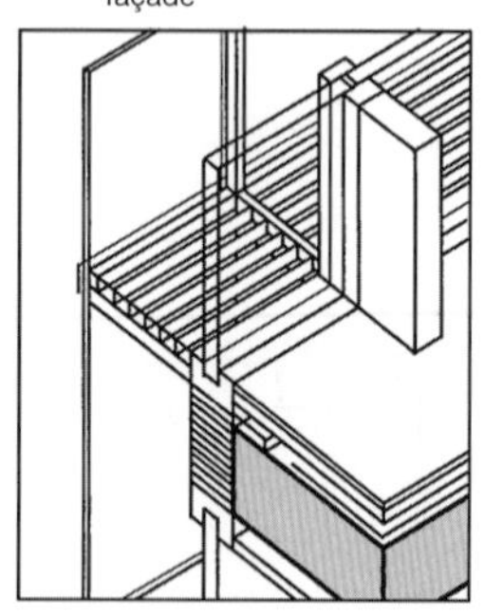

⓮ Curtain wall as double façade

Non-load-bearing external walls
Light and often prefabricated panels are frequently used for non-load-bearing external walls (e.g. for framed buildings) → ⓫. The advantage is the low loading on the edges of the slabs, rapid assembly and simpler replacement later.

Curtain walls → ⓬ – ⓮ can be made of light, prefabricated metal-glass construction in the form of **façade panels** of metal or plastic, **multi-layer façade elements** complete with windows and parapets or **pre-cast concrete elements**. The most common elements are fixed to the slabs (or framed columns) with fixing brackets or anchors and can be combined to form any size of wall.

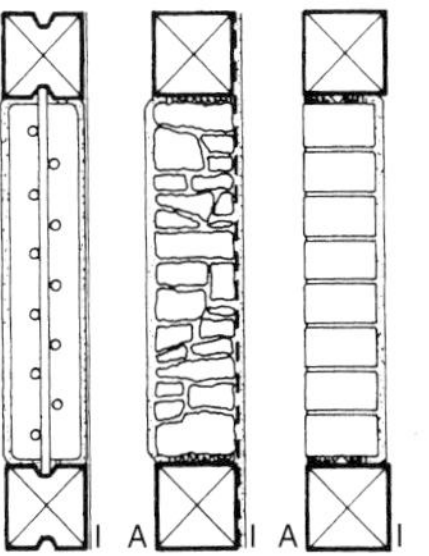

❶ Panel infilling (left to right) of loam on stakes (wattle and daub), with rubble masonry and with hard-burnt bricks

bad well H≧15

❷ Avoidance of dragged transitions when repairing loam infilling

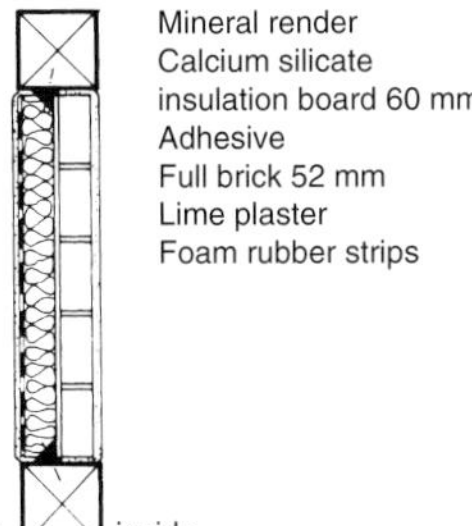

❸ New infilling of mineral insulation panels and brick: timber framing visible on both sides

Silicate render 15 mm
Mesh
Wood-wool board 20 mr
Mineral fibre insulation batt 80 mm
Wood-wool board 25 mr
Mesh (not metallic)
Lime plaster
A inside

❹ Lightweight infilling (no thermal storage possible!): timber framing visible on both sides

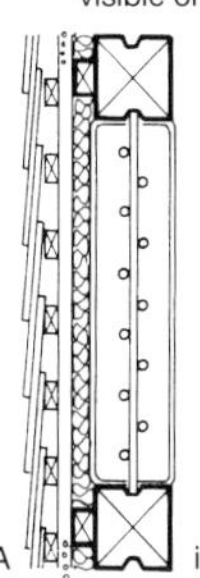

❺ External insulation with highly diffusible material behind ventilated cladding = constructional timber protection: timber framing visible on the inside

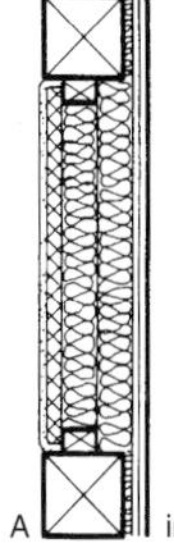

❻ New infilling with good thermal insulation: timber framing clad on the inside without damp barrier!

A inside

The original structure of natural stone tiles on a concrete base and masonry parapet was solid. To preserve the external view and insert large-scale French windows affecting the inside view, the windows and parapet were replaced with casement windows with natural stone parapet elements.

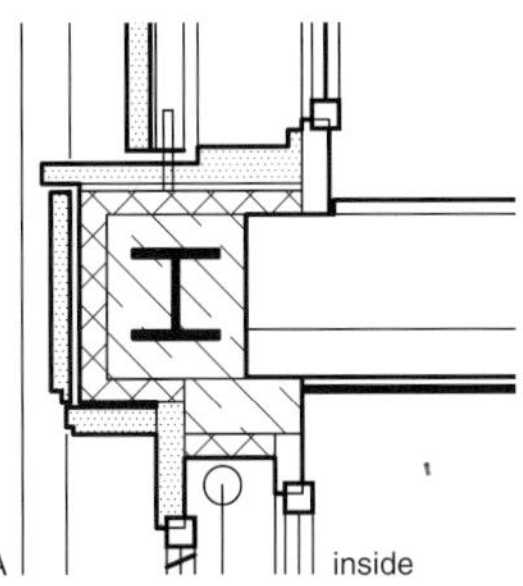

The design used natural stone slabs on self-supporting sub-structure and upgraded with interjacent thermal insulation, without changing much the proportions of the profile.

Arch.: Kister Scheithauer Gross, Cologne

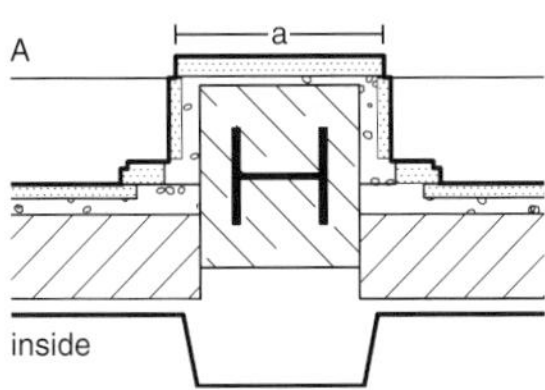

❼ Existing situation: natural stone cladding to concrete structure

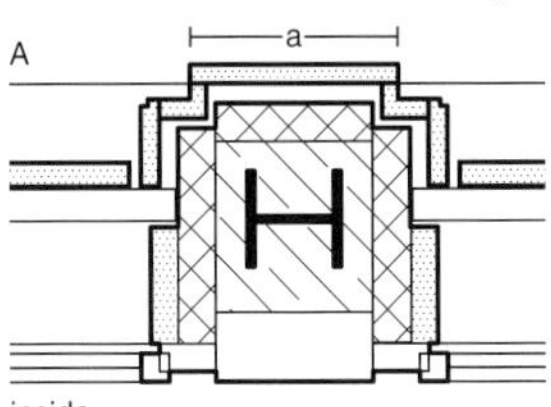

❽ Improvement in thermal insulation while mostly preserving the outline and proportions which determine the façade

External walls

Defects to external walls are caused by natural weathering, poor maintenance and often also incorrectly carried out repairs and modernisation attempts. When modernisation or conversion work is undertaken, walls have to be upgraded to meet current energy and structural requirements.

Timber framing

A main characteristic of timber-framed houses is the separation of the load-bearing timber construction from the non-load-bearing panels between (the panels should always be fitted so they receive no loading). Timber construction was originally carried out without metal fixings and can normally be repaired without the use of steel or iron parts (water condensation on metal parts can damage the timber, which in Germany is often softwood). The original infilling of the panels is usually facing brick or a clay daub → ❶ – ❷. The timber functions and the appearance of joints at the contact between timber and panel is unavoidable. Triangular strips or grooves in the timber are used to fix the panel infilling and prevent draughts. Constructional timber protection (wide roof overhang, full-surface render or ventilated cladding) can avoid damage due to water penetrating from outside. Waterproof paints and permanently elastic mastic also stop water from infiltrating but are one of the main causes of damage to timber framing!

Loam panels should always be preserved and damaged ones repaired. There is still no other panel infilling material available that is as good as loam → ❶ + ❺ in terms of good trade practice, building physics and building biology. It also counters fungal and insect attack. Brick infilling has a stiffening effect, which acts against the structural principles of timber framing, and lightweight infilling has no thermal storage capacity.

Natural stone and stucco façades

The energy performance of solid walls with structured façades of natural stone or stucco is often improved by internal insulation → p. 55 ❼. When natural stone cladding is replaced, insulation can be installed behind the stone façade. The stone facing panels must be fixed to an independent support structure while maintaining the outline and proportions of the façade. If the expense of insulation to EnEV standards is too high (i.e. economically unreasonable), an exemption from certain requirements can be agreed with the responsible authority. When installing external insulation, attention should be paid to whether the extra projection infringes any boundary or building line → ❼ + ❽.

Aim	Element	Measure according to	Residential buildings and zones in other buildings with temperatures >19 °C	Zones of non-residential buildings with indoor temperatures from 12 to <19 °C
			max. of heat transmission coefficients U_{max} (W/m^2 × K)	
1	external walls	No. 1 a to d	0.24	0.35
4a	ceilings, roofs and roof pitches	No. 4.1	0.24	0.35
4b	flat roofs	No. 4.2	0.20	0.35
5a	roofs and walls next to unheated rooms or earth	No. 5 a, b, d and e	0.30	no requirement
5b	floor construction	No. 5 c	0.50	no requirement
5c	slabs with outside air below	No. 5 a to e	0.24	0.35

❾ Maximum heat transmission coefficients with new installation, replacement or conversion of building elements, in existing buildings, EnEV 2009 (windows and doors → p. 99)

FLOOR SLABS
Slab construction
Refurbishment
Concrete repair
Floors

BS EN 1168
BS EN 12058
DIN 1045
DIN 1055

see also: Building physics pp. 471 ff.
Fire protection pp. 511 ff.

FLOOR SLABS

Slab Construction

Floor slabs separate storeys and have to fulfil sound insulation and fire protection requirements in addition to their structural function. In addition to the main building materials (natural/artificial stone, concrete, steel, timber and lightweight concrete), slabs can be divided by their structural system into **vaulted** (subject to compression) and **flat** (subject to bending).

They can be built as **slab** or **joist/beam** constructions:

Slabs are flat structures loaded at right angles to their plane and spanning in one or two directions with linear or point loading.

Common forms are solid reinforced concrete slabs → ❾ – ⓫, as in-situ, pre-cast or partially prefabricated elements; hollow pot slabs → ❺ with structurally connected clay pots forming cavities; pre-stressed concrete cored planks → ❻, made out of welded single elements; and composite slabs → ⓮.

Joist constructions consist of single beams, mostly loaded in bending.

In addition to timber joist floors → ❶ – ❹, solid beam slabs → ❼ – ❽, ⓭, and steel joist slabs → ⓯ can also be used.

For large spans and loads, there are double-T slabs → ⓬ and ribbed slabs, structurally optimised mixed constructions.

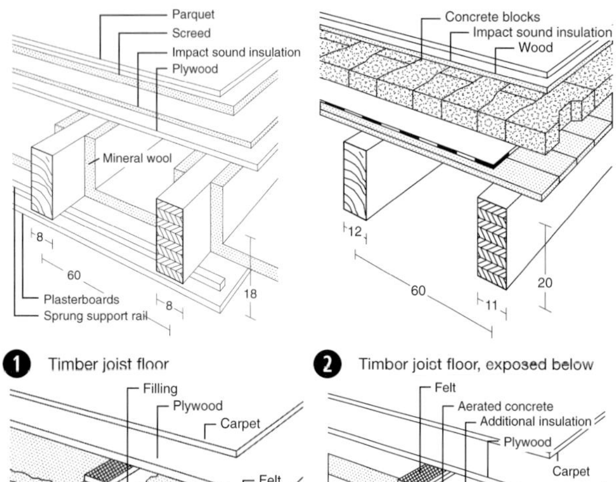

❶ Timber joist floor

❷ Timber joist floor, exposed below

❸ Timber joist floor with filling

❹ Timber joist floor with aerated concrete and additional insulation (refurbishment)

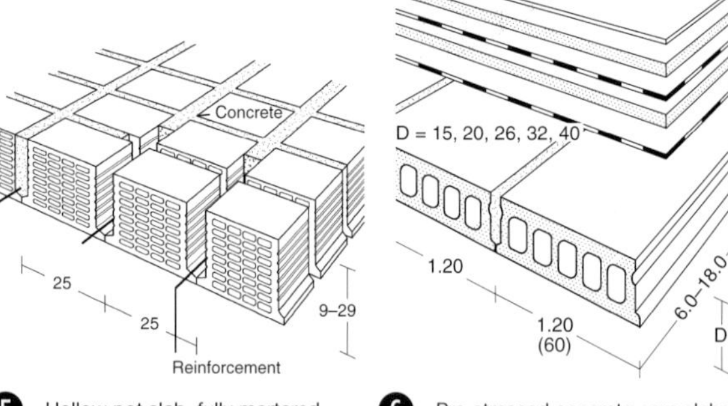

❺ Hollow pot slab, fully mortared

❻ Pre-stressed concrete core slabs

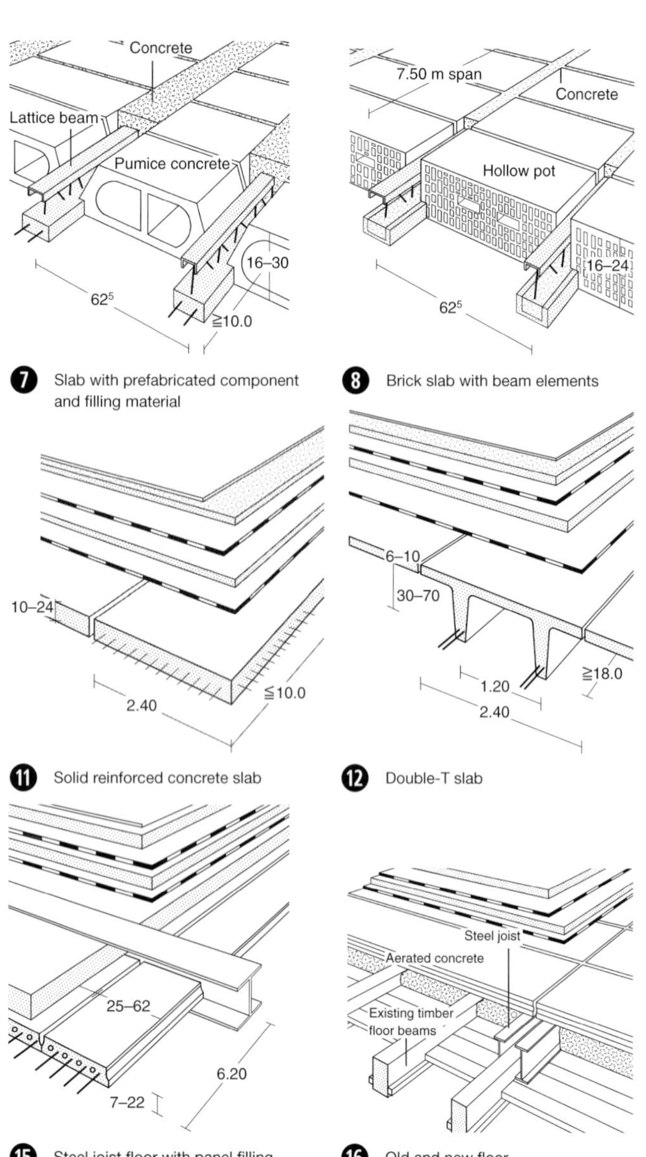

❼ Slab with prefabricated component and filling material

❽ Brick slab with beam elements

❾ Reinforced concrete composite floor slab

❿ Aerated concrete floor slab

⓫ Solid reinforced concrete slab

⓬ Double-T slab

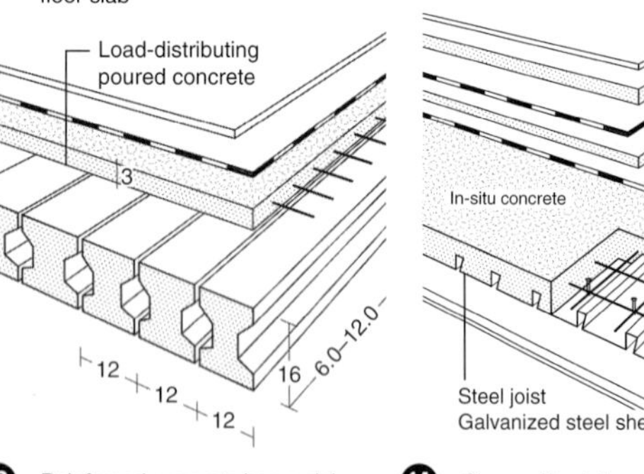

⓭ Reinforced concrete beam slab

⓮ Composite slab

⓯ Steel joist floor with panel filling

⓰ Old and new floor

Floor slabs

Load-bearing floor joists in old buildings used to be designed empirically by the carpenter. The loads were mostly carried on transverse joists spanning one or more longitudinal support beams. In an old building book from 1900, a ratio of joist height to width of 5:7 is given as a guideline for the determination of joist size. The rule: half the room depth in decimetres = the joist height in cm. Because of this sizing, old timber joist floors often sag considerably, though this does not compromise structural safety as long as the permissible stresses are not exceeded.

Refurbishment possibilities → ❶. Strengthen the timber joist by adding a second. Improve the load distribution by inserting additional floor joists or a steel beam → ❶. Shorten the span by inserting one or more additional support beams or a load-bearing cross wall. Alterations to the load-bearing structure should always be preceded by a precise survey of load-transferring and bracing functions. In order to guarantee the load transfers, all connections must be in firm contact.

Improvement in sound insulation can normally be achieved only through an increase in the weight of the floor, so the floor will probably have to be strengthened as well. Impact sound can be reduced by separating the walking surface from the structure and by using soft floor coverings → ❶.

If new building standards are to be achieved, it will normally be necessary to change the entire floor structure → p. 55. The installation of wet rooms above timber joist floors requires particular attention because it will scarcely be possible to check for penetration of water and damp damaging the structure → ❹ – ❾.

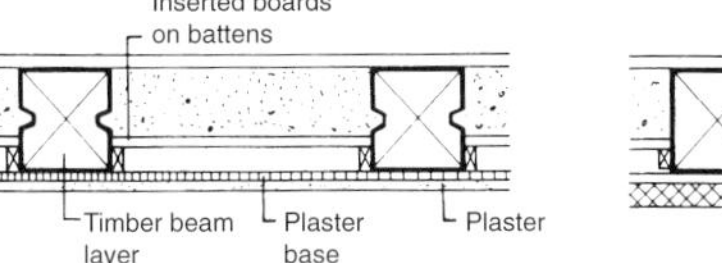

Floor construction with new inserted boards on battens

Sand fill
Battens
Wood-wool board

Insulation ot a timber floor on cellar side

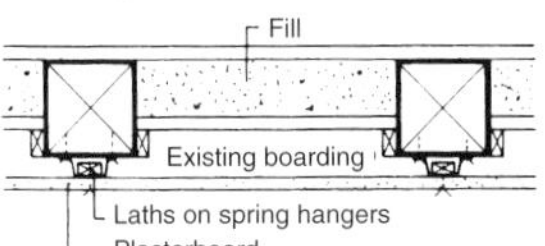

Improvement of sound and thermal insulation with suspended ceiling

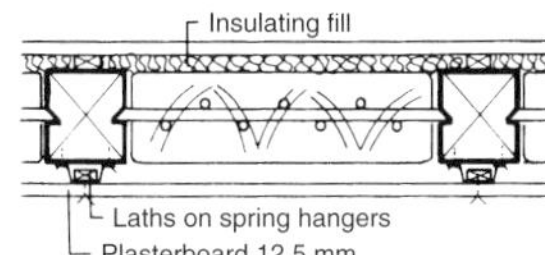

Sound insulation improvement of a loam floor

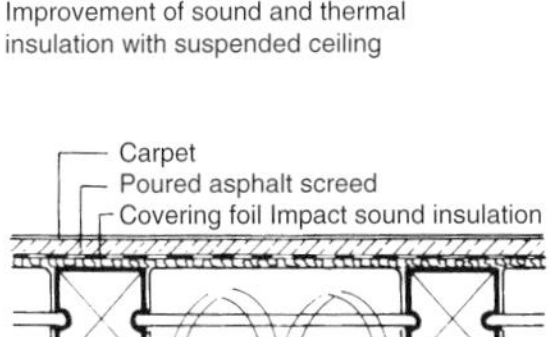

Sound-insulating floor construction with poured asphalt screed

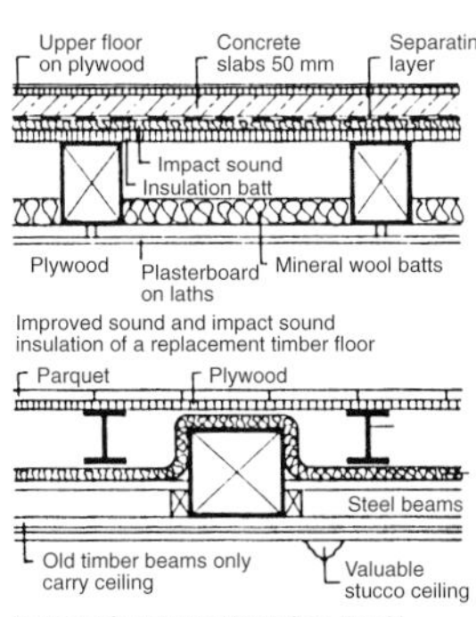

Improved sound and impact sound insulation of a replacement timber floor

Insertion of a new steel beam floor, the old timber beams are retained with valuable stucco ceiling

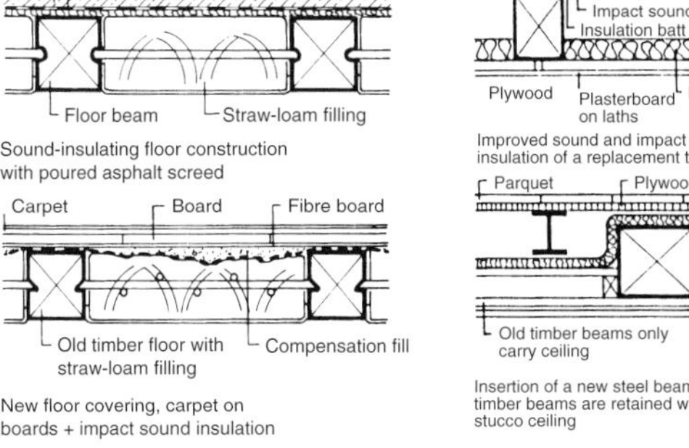

New floor covering, carpet on boards + impact sound insulation

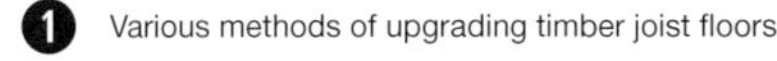

❶ Various methods of upgrading timber joist floors

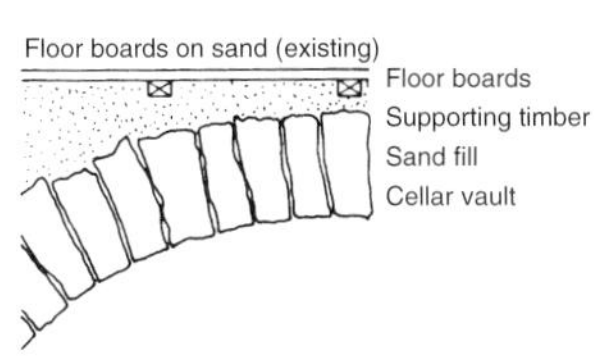

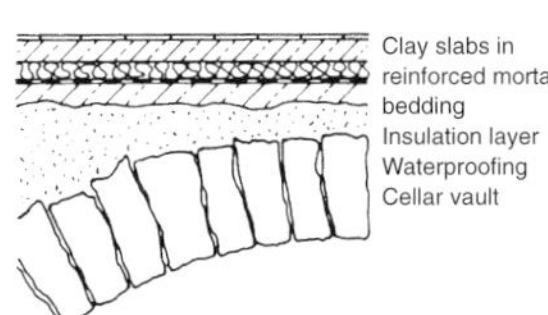

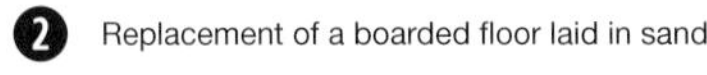

❷ Replacement of a boarded floor laid in sand

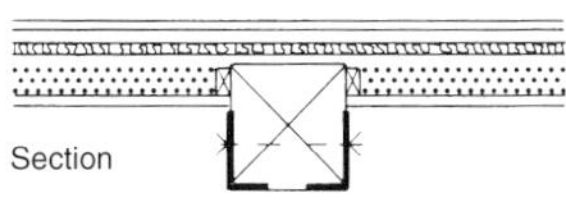

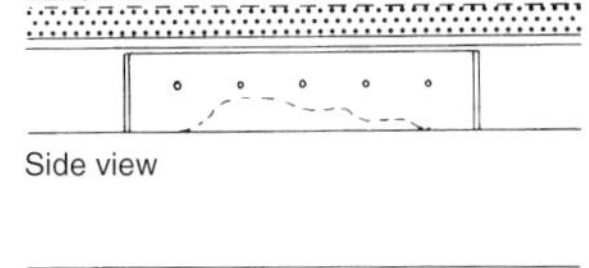

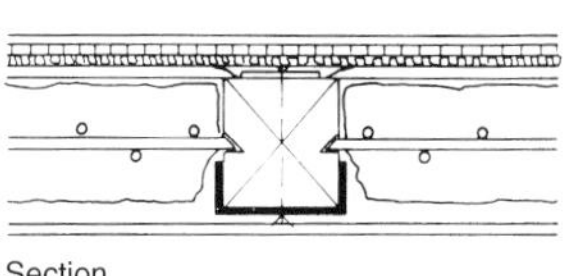

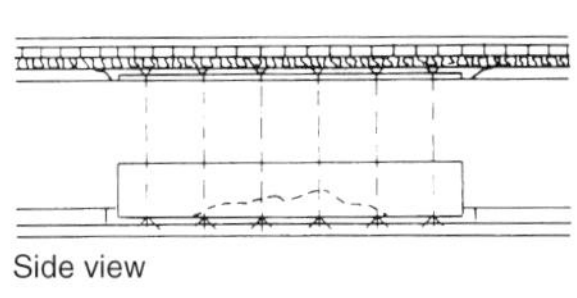

❸ Strengthening weak parts of joists in the span

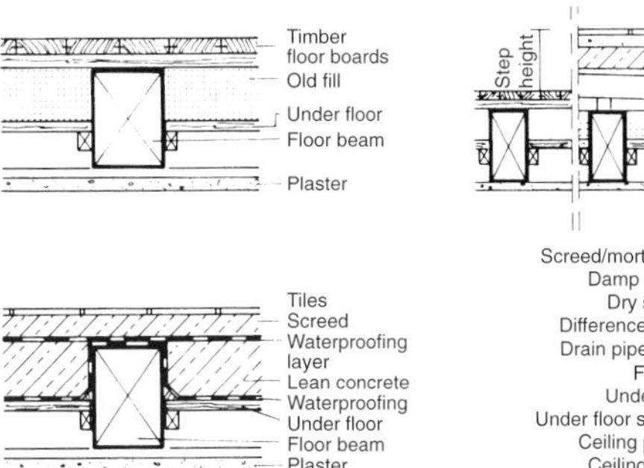

❹ Conventional ways of waterproofing timber joist floors in old buildings

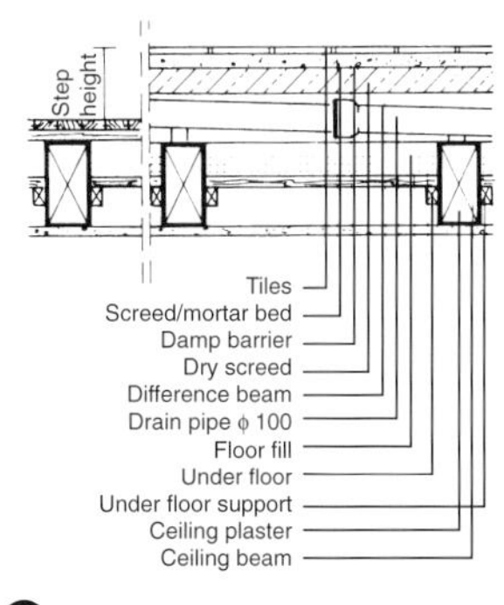

❺ Distortion of drain pipe under a new floor

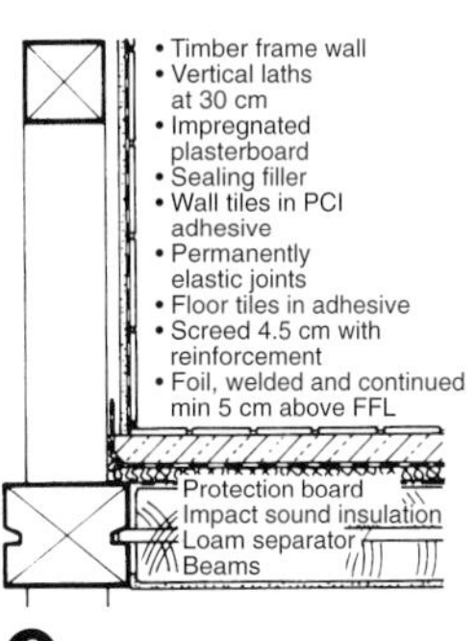

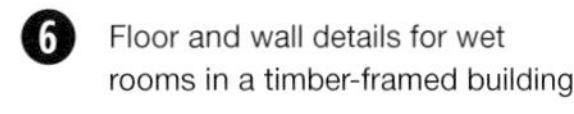

❻ Floor and wall details for wet rooms in a timber-framed building

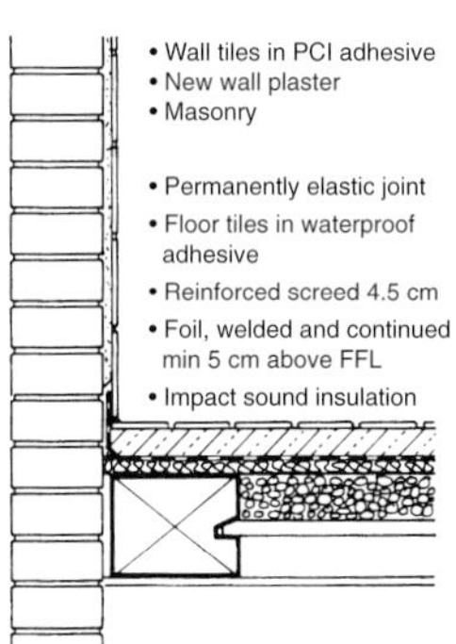

❼ Floor and wall details for wet rooms in a masonry building with timber joist floors

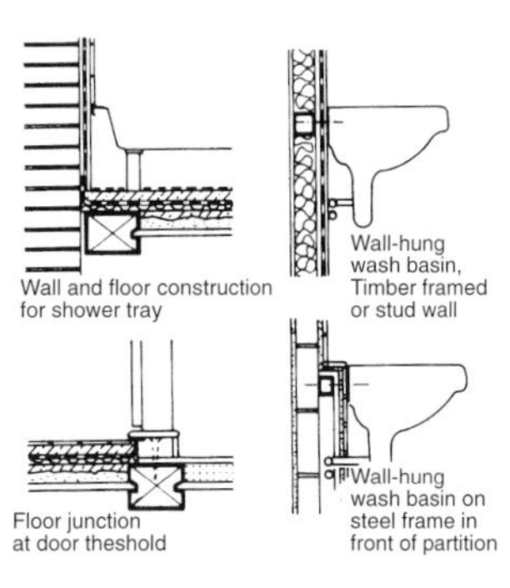

❽ Important details in wet rooms

Pipe installation in two-layer partition

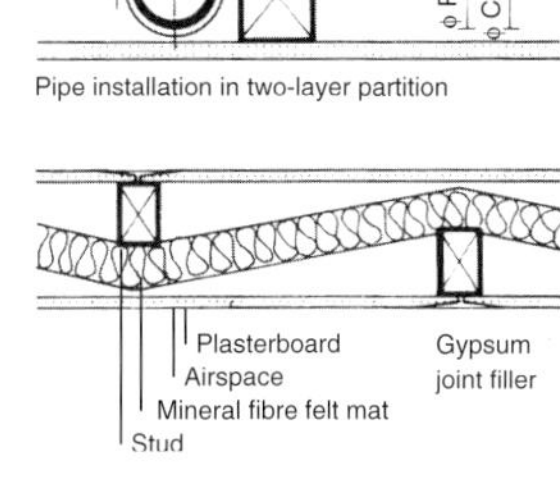

❾ Sound-insulating double-leaf wall construction

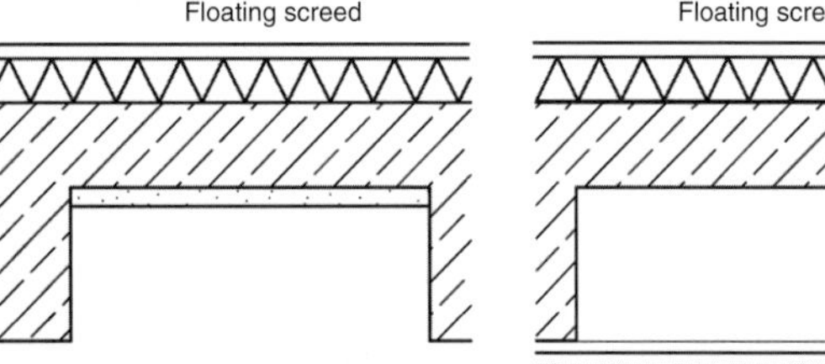

Shotcrete (approx. 3 cm) increases the cover to the reinforcement and thus improves fire and airborne sound insulation

Suspended ceilings must either provide the entire fire rating (here F90) or they may not be considered. Advantage: the impact sound insulation is also improved

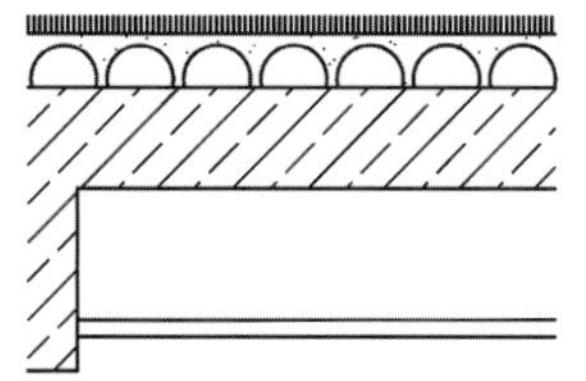

Suspended F90 ceiling between the ribsin low rooms. If bonded screed is used, impact sound insulation can be improved by carpeting

1 Upgrading of concrete slabs in refurbishment or conversion of buildings

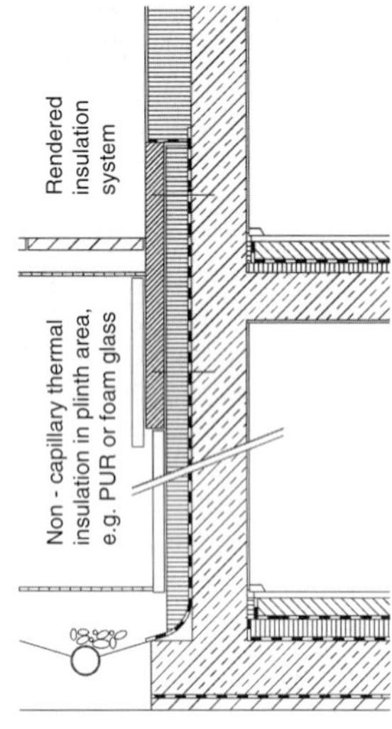

2 Improvement of an external wall with composite insulation system

Evaluation criterion	Testing method/equipment
presence of voids	hammering with hammer or steel rod, drag chain method
surface tension strength	Herlon device, Schenk-Trebel device etc.
compressive strength (non-destructive)	Schmidt hammer
crack widths	measuring magnifying glass, crack width ruler
alteration of crack widths	crack marks, dial gauge, inductive transducer
carbonisation	phenolphthalein test on freshly exposed substrate
presence of chlorides	spraying of silver nitrate (qualitative), Quantab process (semi-quantitative)
concrete cover of reinforcement	electromagnetic meters
corrosion activity	potential field measurement
degree of rusting of reinforcement	calliper

3 Methods of testing concrete quality (Kind-Barkansas → refs)

Environmental class	Example of environmental conditions	Concrete reinforcement (mm)			Pre-tensioning reinforcement (mm)		
		General	Slabs	C40/50	General	Slabs	C40/50
1	interior of residential and office buildings (only applies if no worse conditions were present for a significant time during construction)	15	15	15	25	25	25
2 2a	– rooms with high humidity (e.g. laundries) – external building elements – building elements in non-aggressive ground or water	20	15	15	30	25	25
2b	– external building elements exposed to frost – building elements in non-aggressive ground or water with frost – interior building elements with high humidity and frost risk	25	20	20	35	30	30
3	– external building elements exposed to frost and defrosting agents	40	35	35	50	45	45
4 also with frost	– building elements in splash zone or dipping into seawater, a part exposed to air – building elements in salty air (directly on coast)	40	35	35	50	45	45
5 5a	weakly chemically aggressive environment (gaseous, liquid, solid), aggressive industrial atmosphere	25	20	20	35	30	30
5b	moderately chemically aggressive environment (gaseous, liquid, solid)	30	25	25	40	35	35
5c	strongly chemically aggressive environment (gaseous, liquid, solid)	40	35	35	50	45	50

4 Minimum cover to reinforcement (Association of German Cement Industry → refs)

Old	B 15	B 20	B 25	B 30	–	B 40	–	B 50	–	B 60
New	C12/15	C16/20	C20/25	C25/30	C30/37	–	C35/45	C40/50	C45/55	C50/60

5 New descriptions of concrete strength (Association of German Cement Industry → refs)

Requirements

The existing condition must be surveyed and damage analysed before starting the repair of concrete buildings. The following points are particularly important:

Surfaces: damage through insufficient cover to the reinforcement. The cause may be the low requirements of earlier guidelines and, often, inappropriate construction. Carbonisation (conversion of alkaline concrete into acid through environmental effects) can lead to corrosion of the reinforcement, which results in spalling of the concrete surface.

Joints: elastic joints should be replaced after max. 10 years. If this is not done, damage can be caused to the structure by penetrating water (e.g. frost damage).

Building elements: if the walls or slabs are too thin for the fire protection and sound insulation requirements, then additional measures are necessary.

Building materials for concrete replacement:

- cement concrete and cement mortar (CC)
- plastic-modified cement concrete and cement mortar (PCC)
- reaction resin concrete and reaction resin mortar (PC). Mortar and concrete with artificial resin additives are not suitable for the improvement of fire protection requirements!

The surfaces must be cleaned and have the surface strength specified for the relevant treatment. Large areas of concrete surface can be removed and the reinforcement derusted by using high-pressure water jetting. If it is possible to provide sufficient thickness of concrete cover, then no further rust protection is necessary for the reinforcement. If only a thinner cover is possible, then the reinforcement must be protected against rust. In this case, the requirements for derusting are higher.

BS 8204
BS EN 13813
DIN 18560

see also: Building physics pp. 471 ff.
Fire protection pp. 511 ff.
Heating pp. 532 ff.

Floor construction

Floors are normally built up in many layers, consisting of covering, screed (if necessary, with substructure), separation, waterproofing and insulation layers. The nature, arrangement and thickness of these layers is determined by the requirements for thermal insulation, sound insulation and waterproofing (against water penetrating from above). Screeds can be constructed as **bonded screed** → ❶, **unbonded screed** → ❷ or **floating screed** → ❼. Screed can be based on cement, anhydrite or flowing anhydrite, or poured asphalt. The load-bearing capacity of screed depends on the thickness and quality of the material as well as the load-bearing capacity of other layers (e.g. insulation). The requirements for expansion joints also have to be observed.

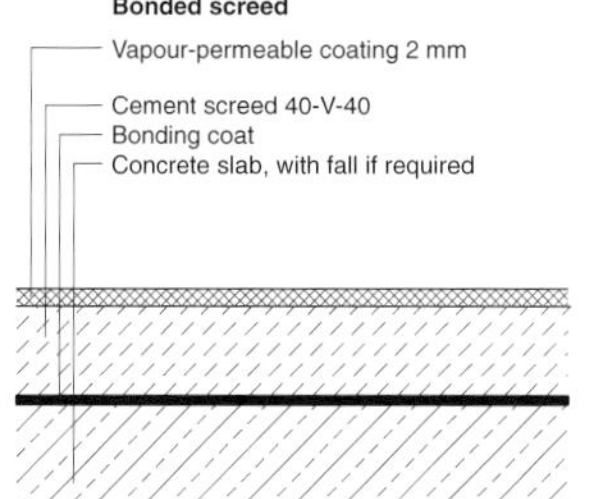

❶ Bonded screed (for industrial flooring), construction height approx. 4 cm, traffic load 10 KN/m²

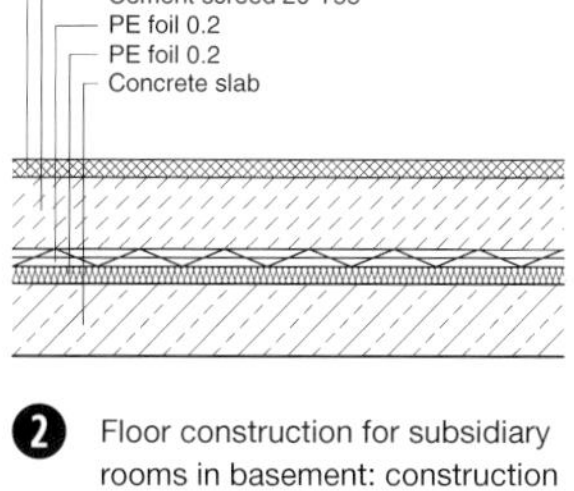

❷ Floor construction for subsidiary rooms in basement: construction height approx. 6 cm, traffic load 2 KN/m²

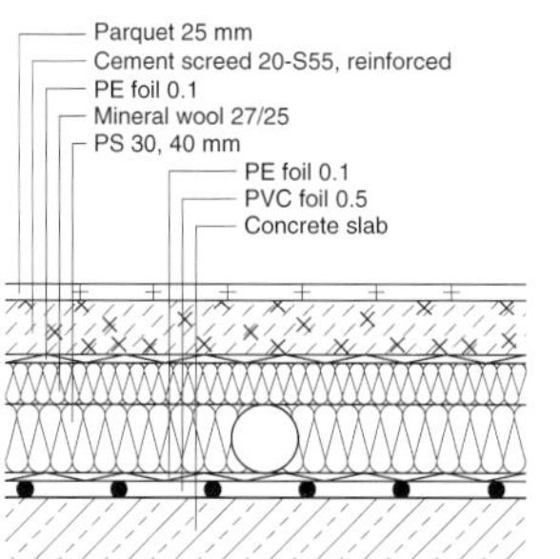

❸ Floor construction for slabs between living rooms: construction height approx. 14.5 cm, traffic load 2 KN/m²

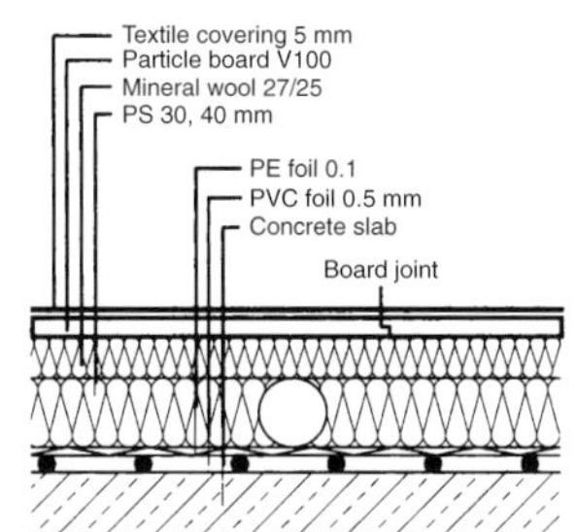

❹ as → ❺ but as dry screed: construction height approx. 10.5 cm, traffic load 2 KN/m²

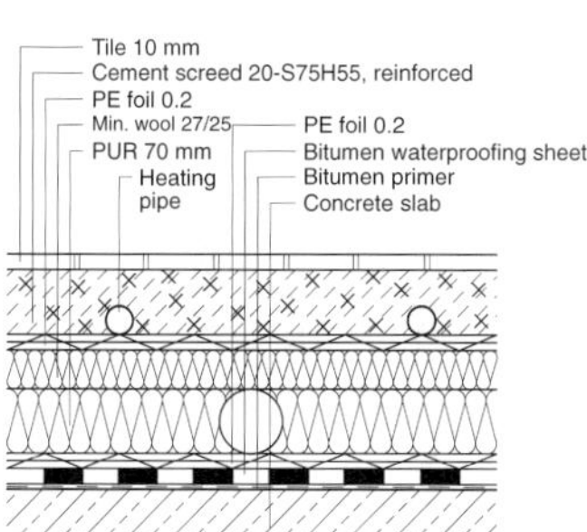

❺ Floor construction (underfloor heating) for living rooms above cold areas: construction height approx. 19 cm, traffic load 2 KN/m²

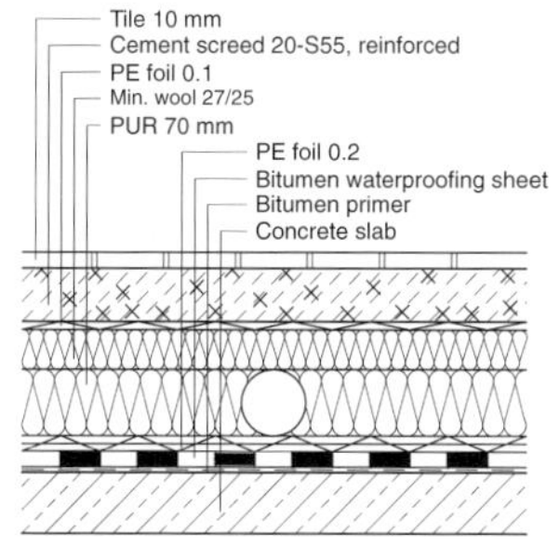

❻ as → ❺ but without underfloor heating: construction height approx. 17 cm, traffic load 2 KN/m²

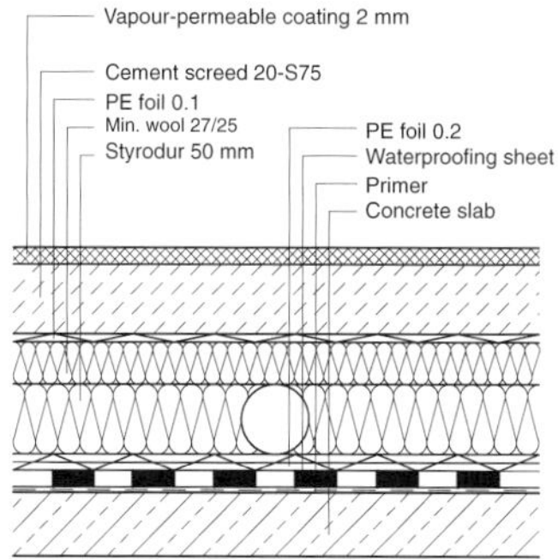

❼ Floor construction for above–ground office space: construction height approx. 16 cm, traffic load 5 KN/m²

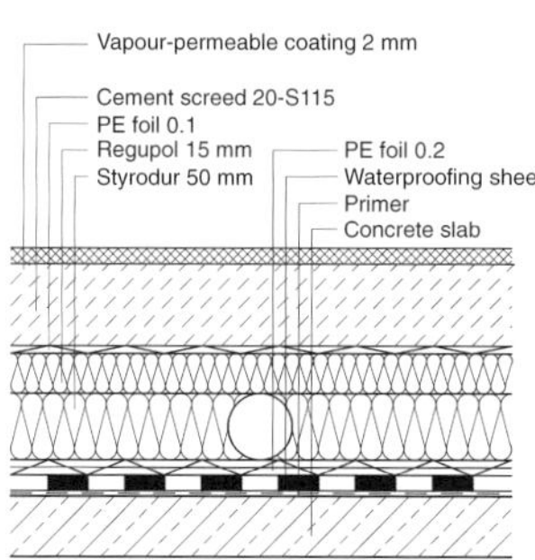

❽ as → ❼ but for higher loading: construction height approx. 19 cm, traffic load 10 KN/m²

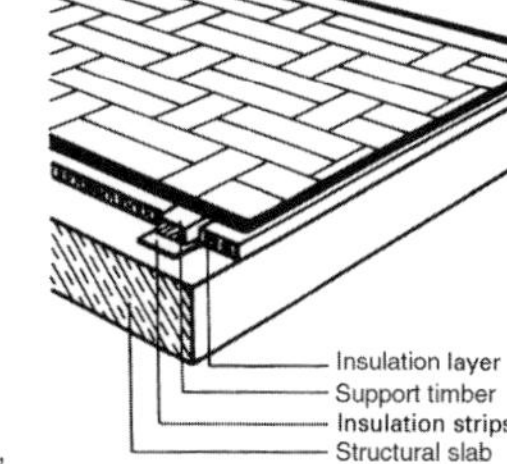

❾ Prefabricated parquet blocks on support timbers

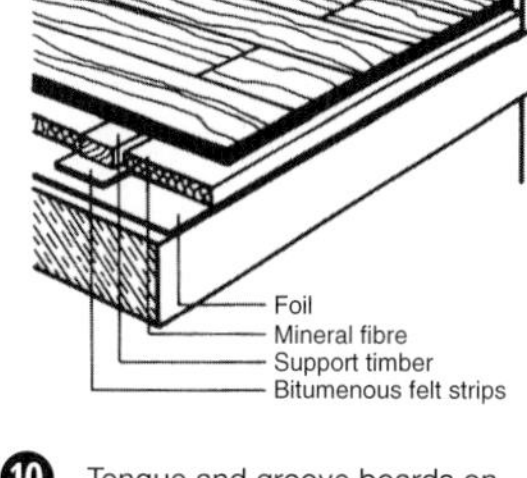

❿ Tongue and groove boards on support timbers

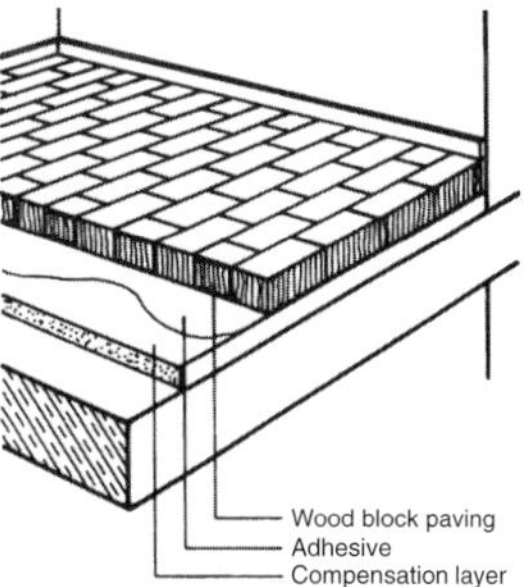

⓫ Wood-block paving (rustic type) laid tight with surface treatment (living areas)

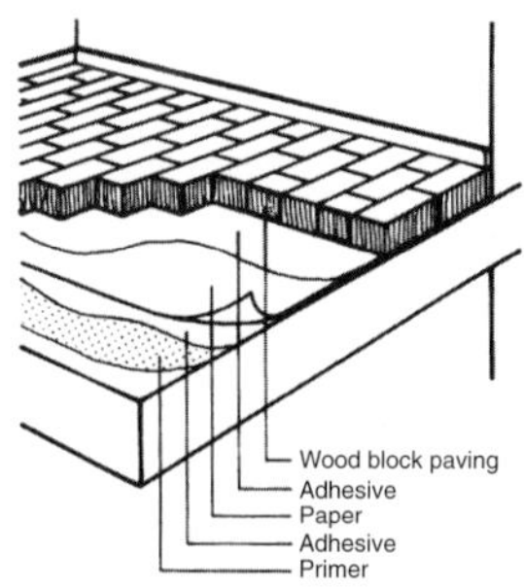

⓬ Wood-block paving (heavy duty) laid tight on flat-floated base concrete (industrial building)

Prefabricated screed (dry screed) is becoming more common as construction schedules become shorter. This can be made of mechanically fixed, engineered wood boards (e.g. resin-bonded boards), gypsum fibre board or gypsum plasterboard. It is laid floating on insulation or dry leveller fill → ❹ or on flooring sleepers.

Parquet and wood-block paving

Parquet is available in the form of parquet blocks, mosaic parquet blocks, made-up panels and parquet strip → ❾ – ❿. The surface layer consists of oak, or another parquet timber, in various grades.

Timber species for floorboards: softwood spruce/fir; for tongued and grooved floorboards: Nordic spruce/fir, American red pine and pitch pine.

Wood-block paving is also available as end-on paving (square or round and laid on a sub-floor) → ⓫ – ⓬.

Floor coverings

Natural stone slabs: Limestone, slate and sandstone slabs can be laid either with the natural roughness from splitting, or half or fully sanded → 1 – 2. Sawn slabs such as limestone (marble), sandstone and all volcanic stone types can have any surface treatment specified. The slabs are laid in a mortar bed or glued to screed.

Mosaic flooring consists of various materials such as glass, ceramic or natural stone and is laid in a mortar bed or glued → 3 – 8.

Ceramic floor tiles: stoneware and mosaic floor tiles are made of clay; they are sintered during the firing process so that they absorb almost no water.
They are therefore frost-resistant, acid-resistant to a certain degree and suffer little mechanical wear; but they are not resistant to oil → 5 – 12.

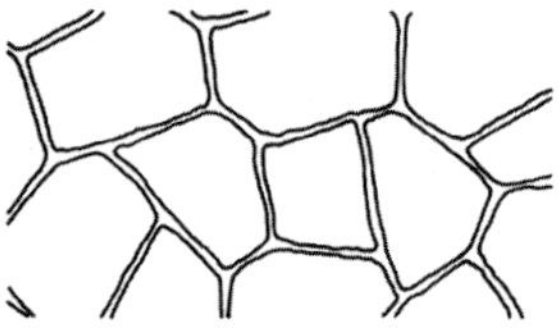

1 Irregular laying of natural stone (crazy paving)

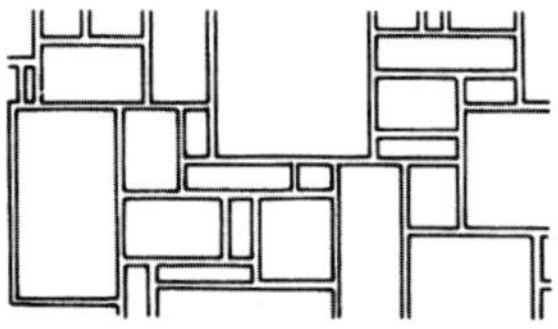

2 Natural stone slabs in Roman bonding

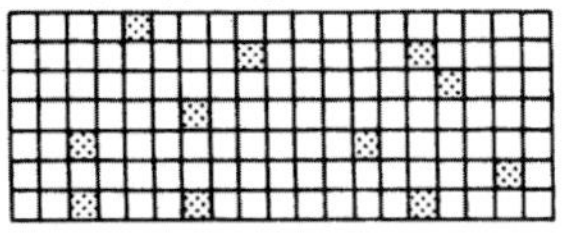

3 Small mosaic squares 20/20, 33/33 mm

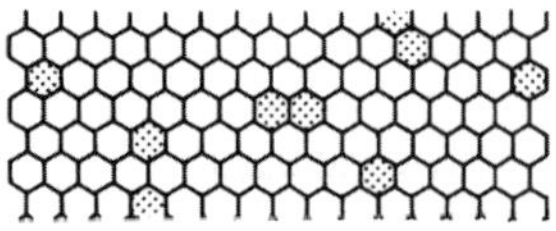

4 Small mosaic hexagons 25/39, 50/60 mm

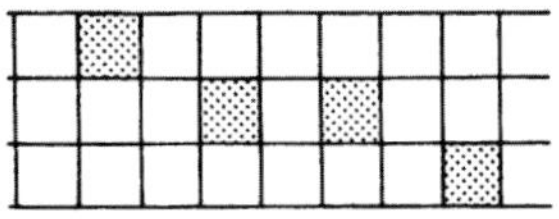

5 Mosaic squares 50/50, 69/69, 75/75 mm

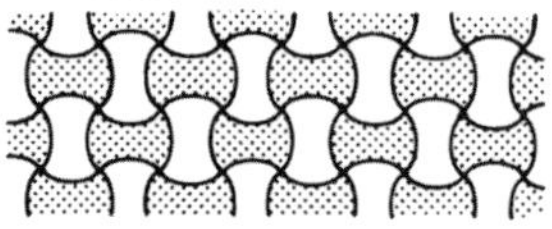

6 Small mosaic, circular cut-out 35/35, 48/48 mm

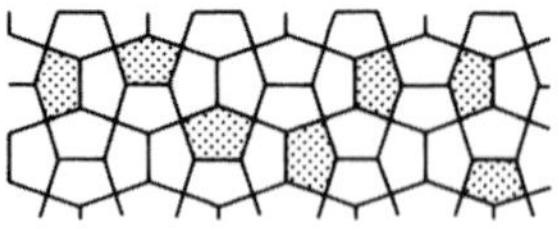

7 Small mosaic, five-sided 45/32 mm

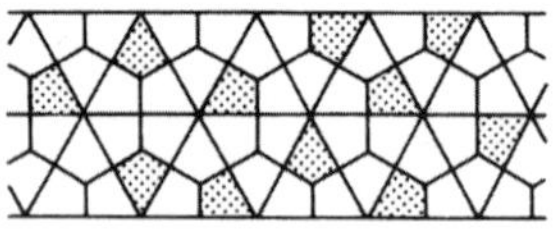

8 Small mosaic in Essen pattern 57/80 mm

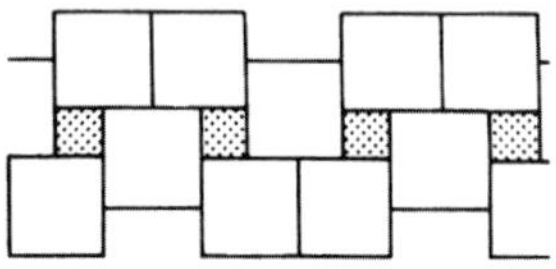

9 Squares with smaller inserts, weave pattern

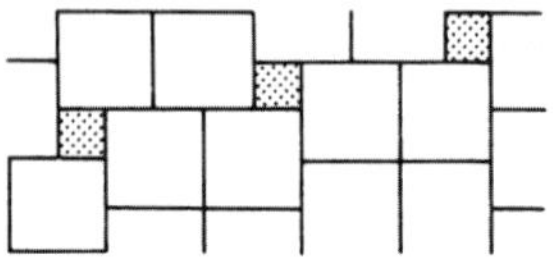

10 Squares with smaller inserts 100/100, 50/50 mm

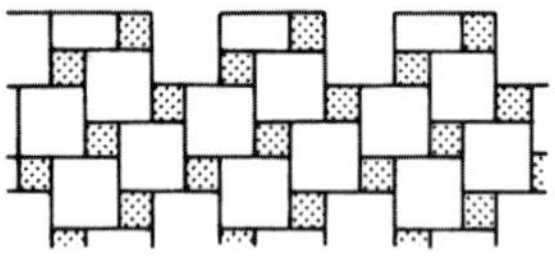

11 Squares with smaller inserts, displaced pattern

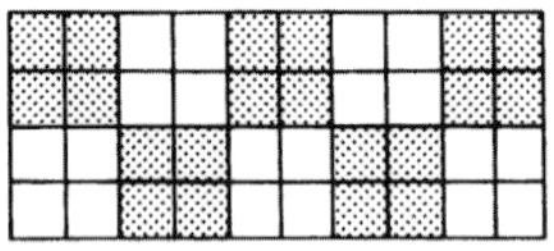

12 Squares with double chessboard pattern

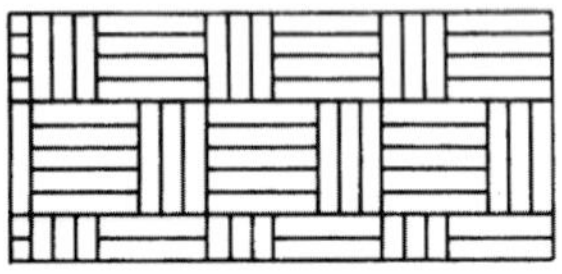

13 Open basket

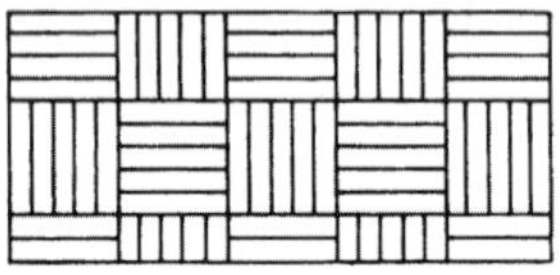

14 Square basket

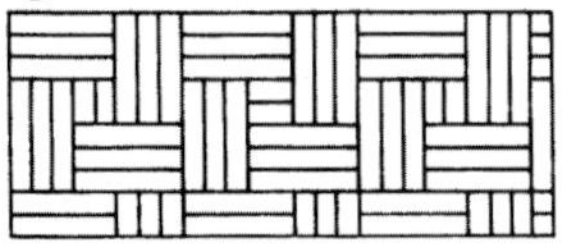

15 Open basket

16 Herringbone pattern

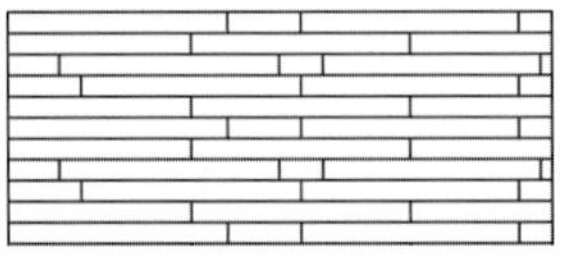

17 Ship deck

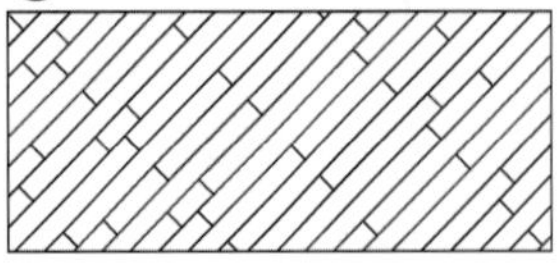

18 Ship deck, diagonal

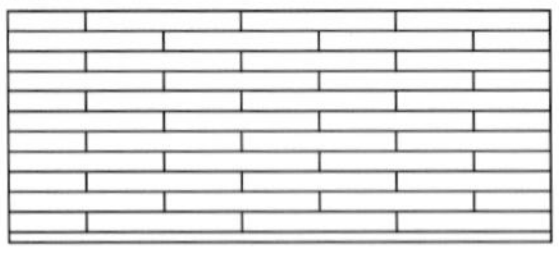

19 English

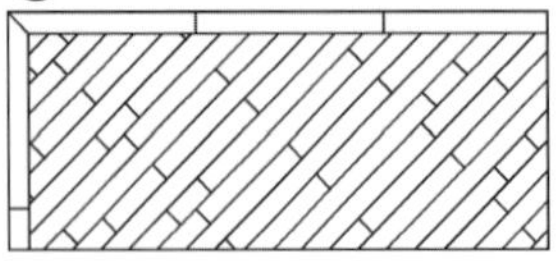

20 Ship deck with frieze

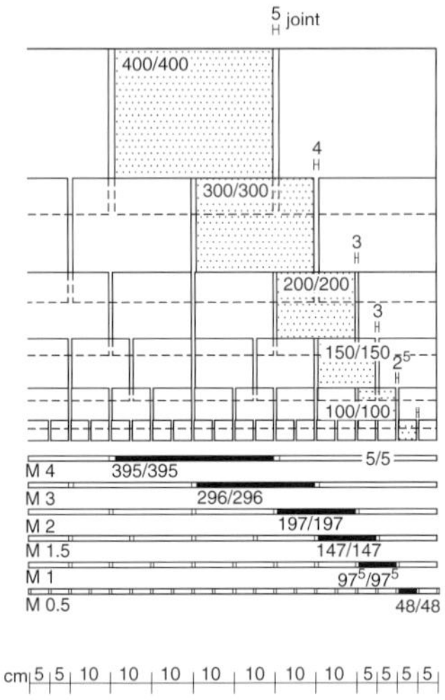

21 Modular system for stoneware

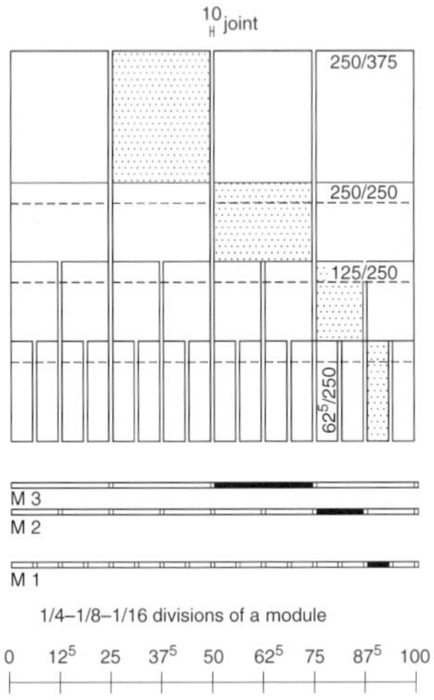

22 Modular system for split tiles

23 Herringbone

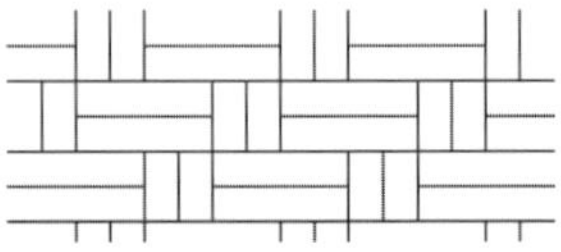

24 Weave pattern

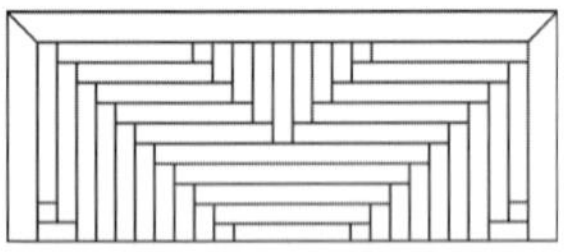

25 Herringbone with frieze

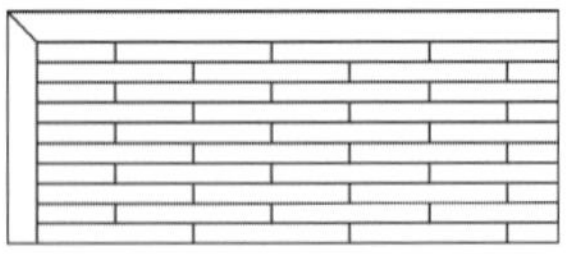

26 English with frieze

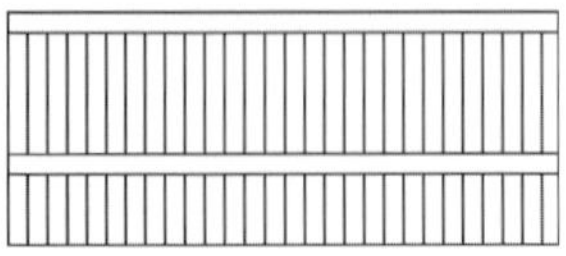

27 Ladder pattern

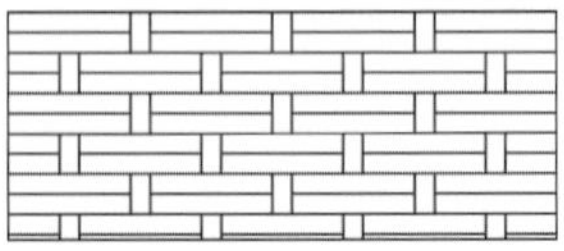

28 Burgundy pattern

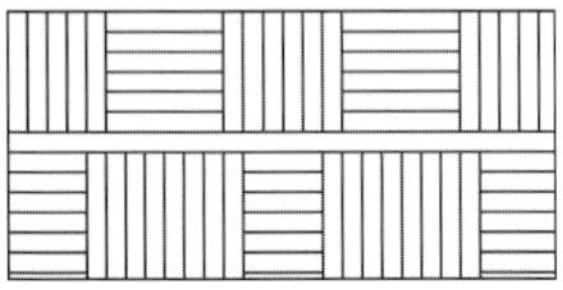

29 Cube with strip pattern

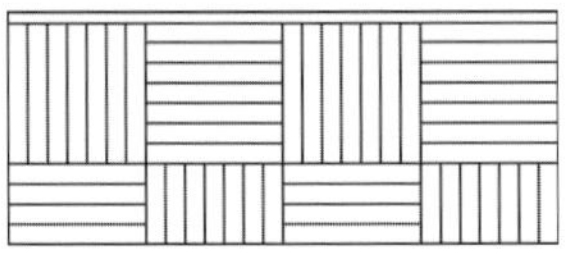

30 Cube pattern

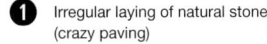

Roof shape and **roof pitch**: the selection of roofing material and the detailing of the **roof edges** at the verge and eaves have a decisive influence on the appearance of buildings. ❶ – ⓰ show the basic forms of roofs and roof projections.

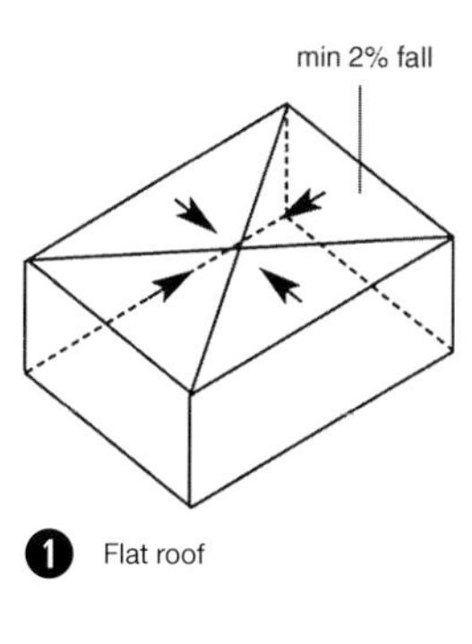

❶ Flat roof

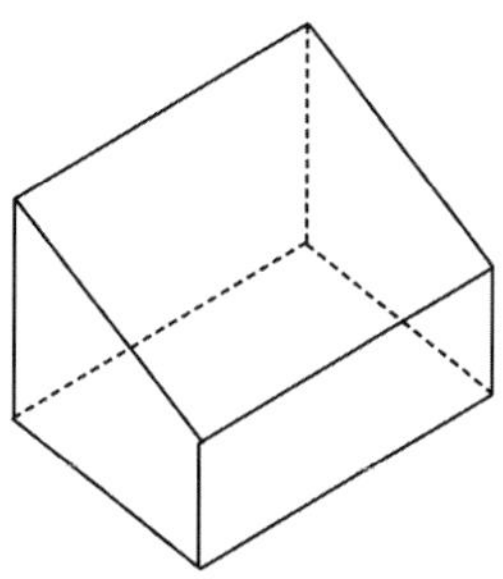
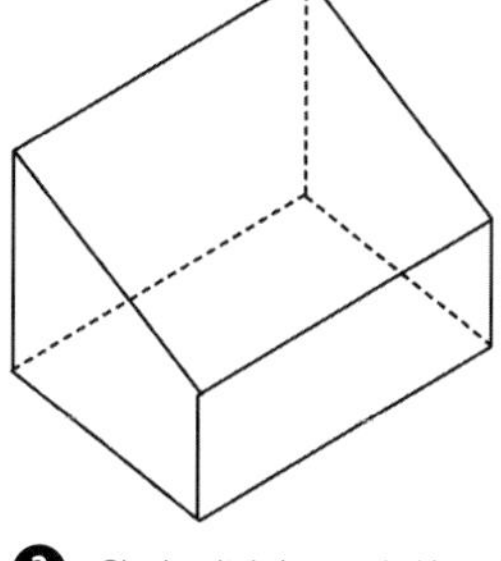
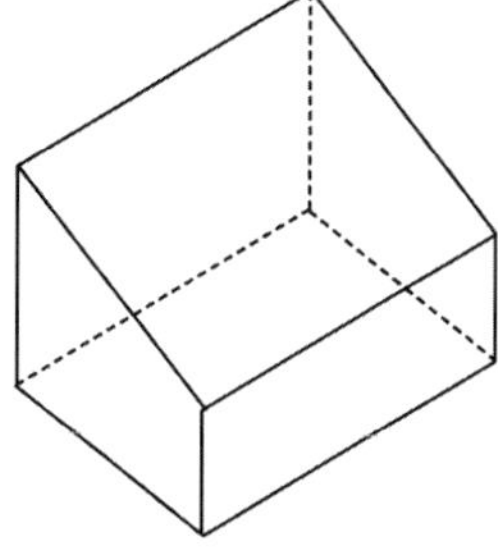

❷ Single-pitch (monopitch) roof

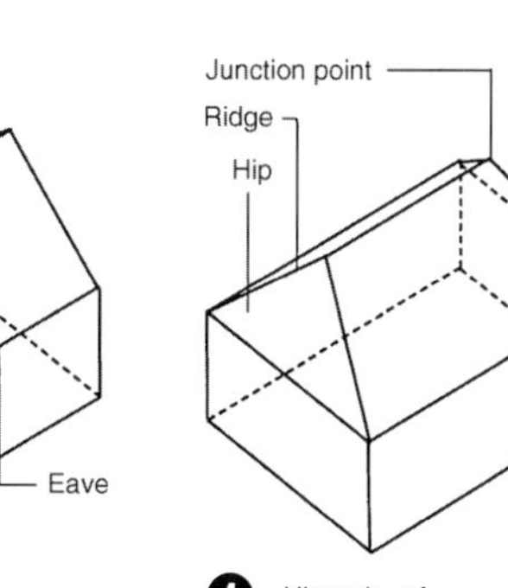

❸ Gabled roof

❹ Hipped roof

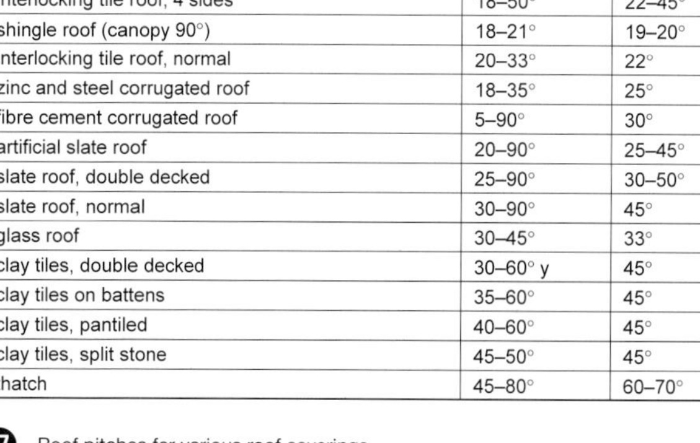

Roof covering	Pitch range	Usually
accessible paved roof	2–4°	3–4°
wood cement roof	2.5–4°	3–4°
felt roof, gravel covered	3–30°	4–10°
felt roof, double	4–50°	6–12°
zinc roof, double standing seams	3–90°	5–30°
felt roof, single	8–15°	10–12°
steel sheeting roof	12–18°	15°
interlocking tile roof, 4 sides	18–50°	22–45°
shingle roof (canopy 90°)	18–21°	19–20°
interlocking tile roof, normal	20–33°	22°
zinc and steel corrugated roof	18–35°	25°
fibre cement corrugated roof	5–90°	30°
artificial slate roof	20–90°	25–45°
slate roof, double decked	25–90°	30–50°
slate roof, normal	30–90°	45°
glass roof	30–45°	33°
clay tiles, double decked	30–60° y	45°
clay tiles on battens	35–60°	45°
clay tiles, pantiled	40–60°	45°
clay tiles, split stone	45–50°	45°
thatch	45–80°	60–70°

⓱ Roof pitches for various roof coverings

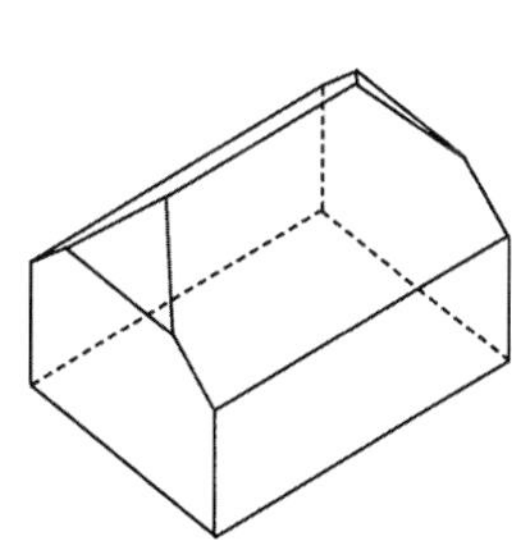

❺ Half-hipped roof

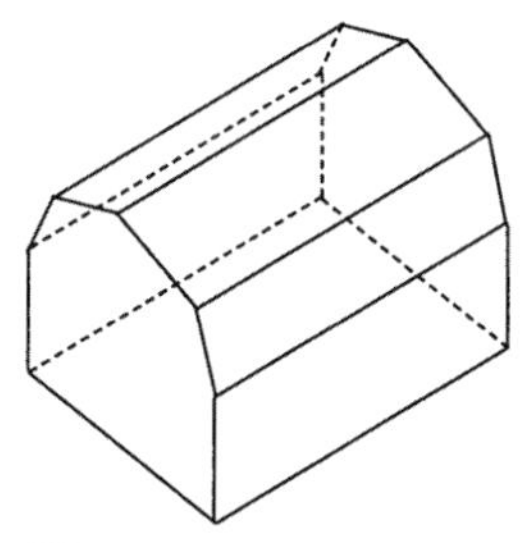

❻ Mansard roof

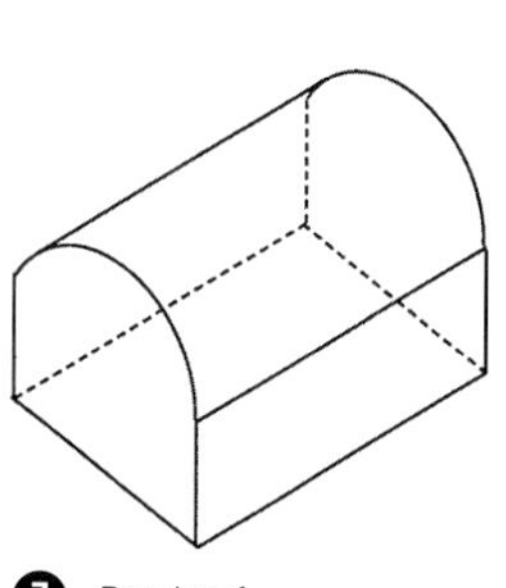

❼ Barrel roof

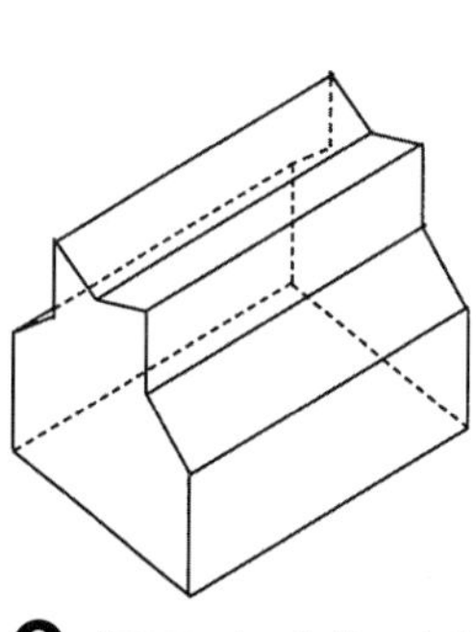

❽ Compound roof with central gutter

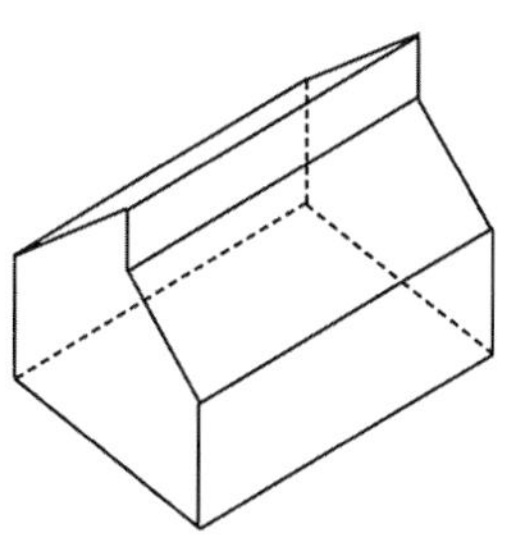

❾ Two single pitches

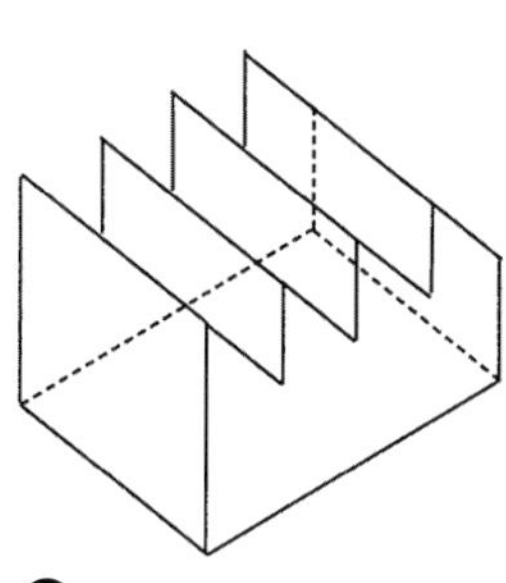

❿ Northlight or saw-tooth roof

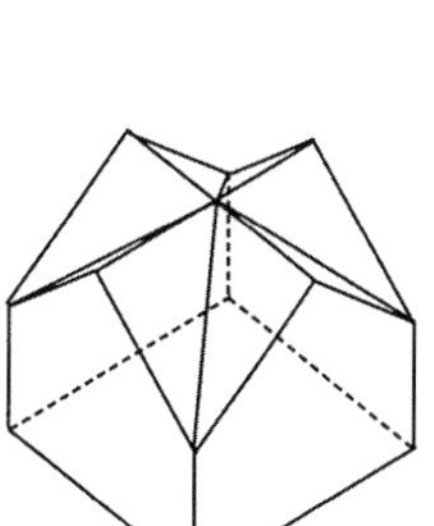

⓫ Four gables

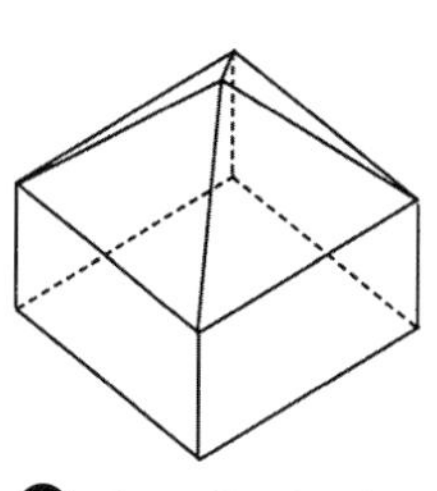

⓬ Square hipped roof

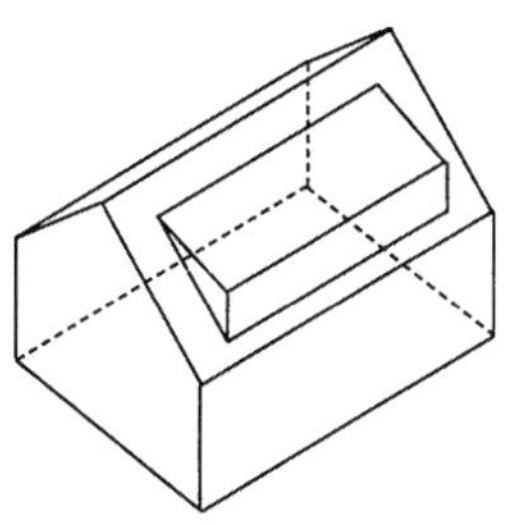

⓭ Wide dormer with sloping roof

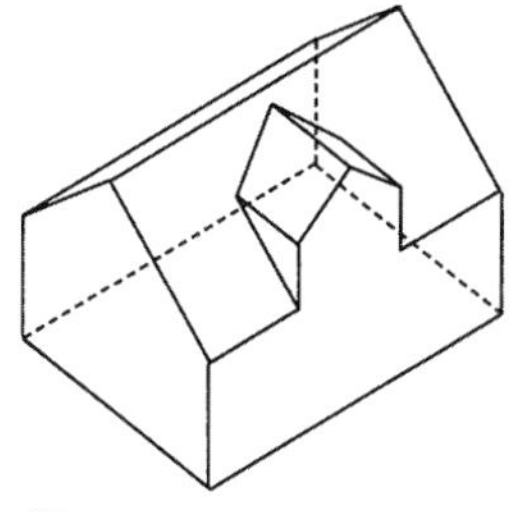

⓮ Gabled dormer window

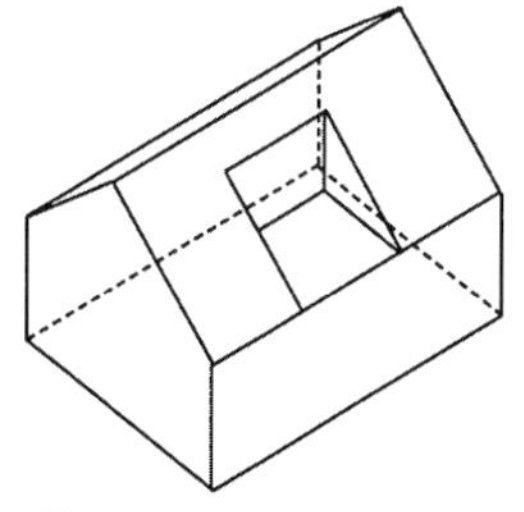

⓯ Roof cut-out

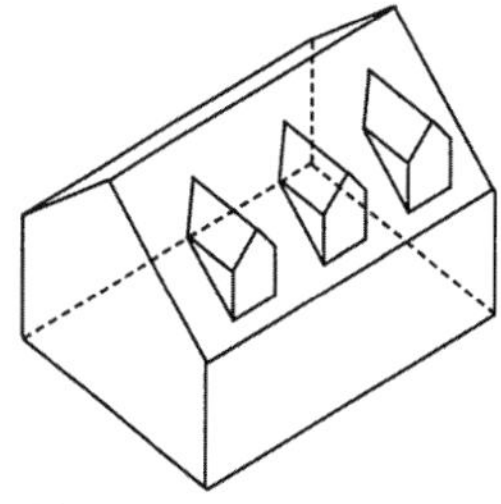

⓰ Single pitched-roof dormers

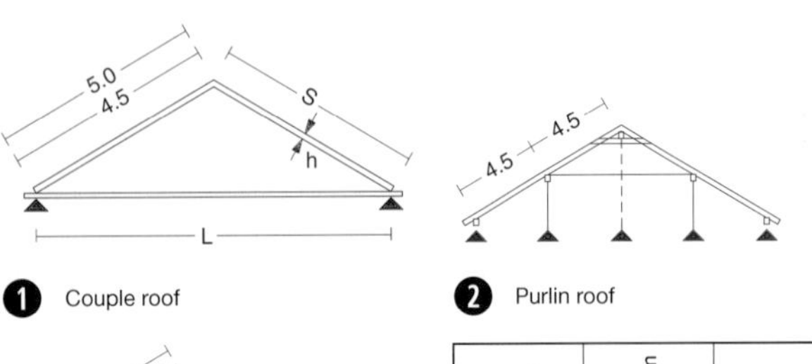

❶ Couple roof

❷ Purlin roof

❸ Collar roof

Roof pitch in degrees	Span L in m	Height of building element h
15–40	10–20	$h^2 \frac{1}{25} \times S$
30–60	10–20	$h^2 \frac{1}{30} \times S$

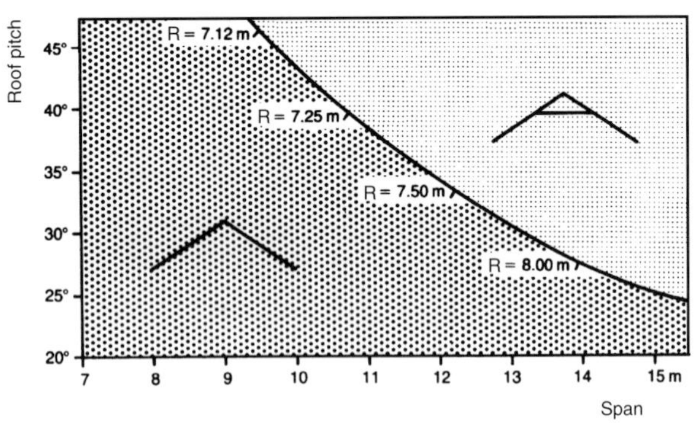

❹ Couple or collar roof: economic limits, slope vs span. R = rafter length

The roof forms the upper edge of a building and protects it from rain and atmospheric influences (wind, cold, heat). A roof consists of a supporting structure (**roof frame, roof truss**) and **roof covering**. The design of the roof truss depends on material (timber, steel, reinforced concrete), roof pitch, loading (self-weight, traffic load, wind and snow load), etc. Roof trusses for pitched roofs are traditionally divided into **purlin roofs** and **couple roofs**. These vary according to the structural function of the members → ❶ – ❸.

Purlin roof

The purlin roof is the simplest form of roof construction. The rafters are supported by cross-beams called **purlins**, which are either mounted directly onto the masonry (monopitch principle) or form load-bundling support beams as part of a roof truss, supported by various arrangements of **posts**. Purlin trusses in relatively narrow houses mostly have a single row of posts in the centre of the roof, but wider roofs have two rows of posts or more → ❷.

There are various further forms of construction for wider span roofs, like 'strutted purlin' → ❽ and 'centre hanger' → ❺.

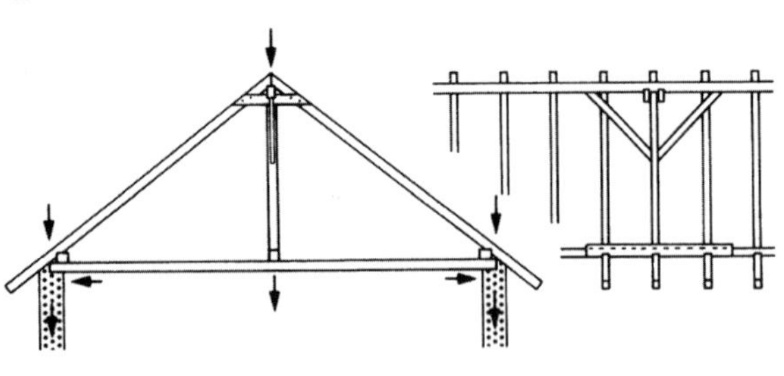

❺ Strutless purlin roof with centre hanger

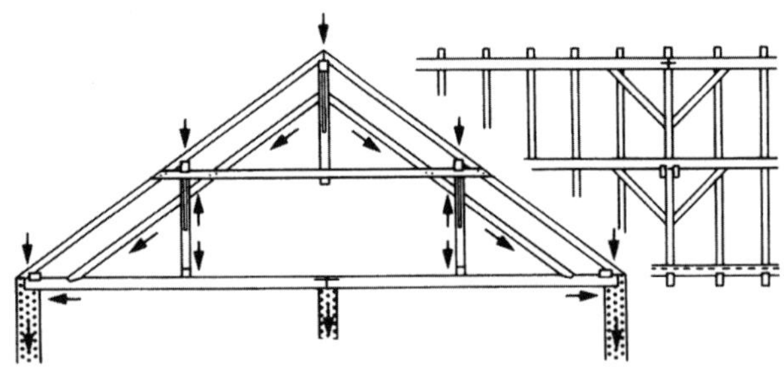

❽ Strutted purlin roof

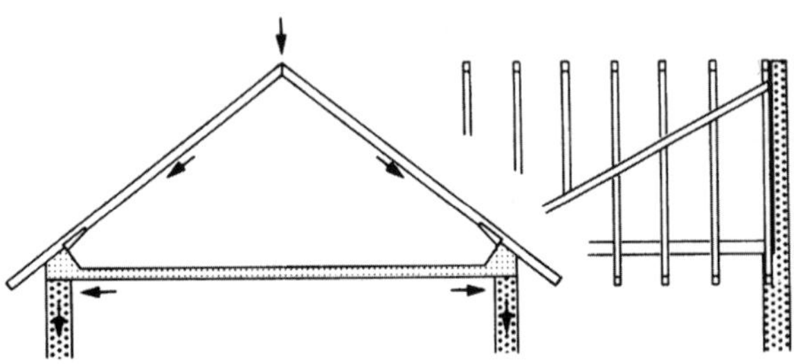

❻ Couple roof

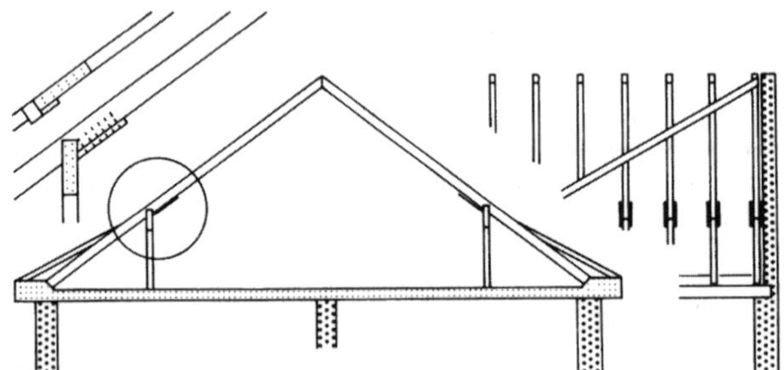

❾ Couple roof with hangers

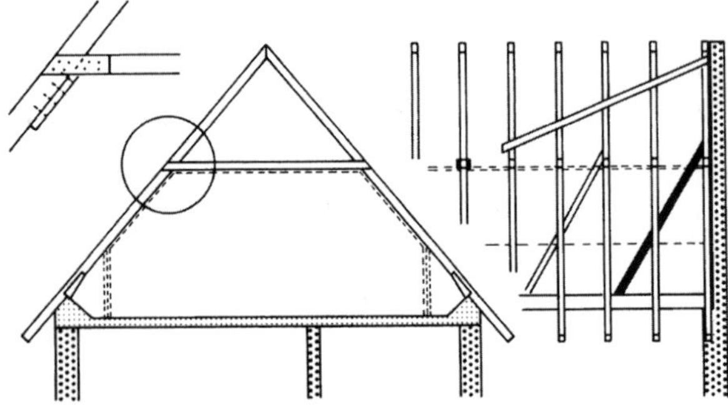

❼ Collar roof with loft conversion

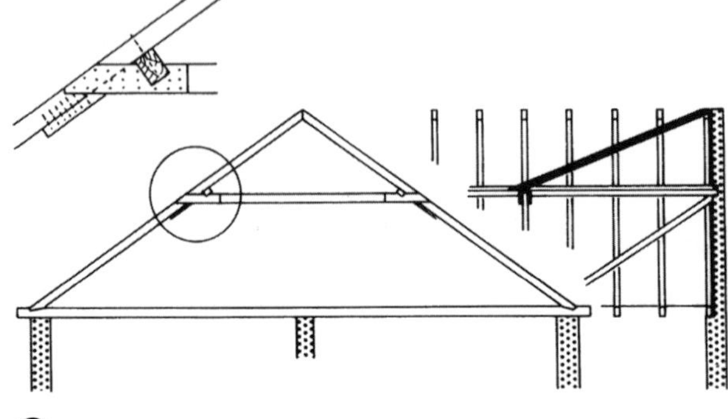

❿ Collar roof with purlins

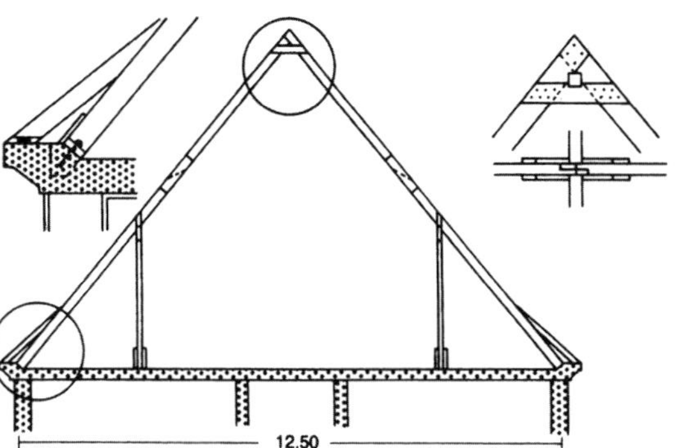

❶ Couple roof with hangers and jointed rafters

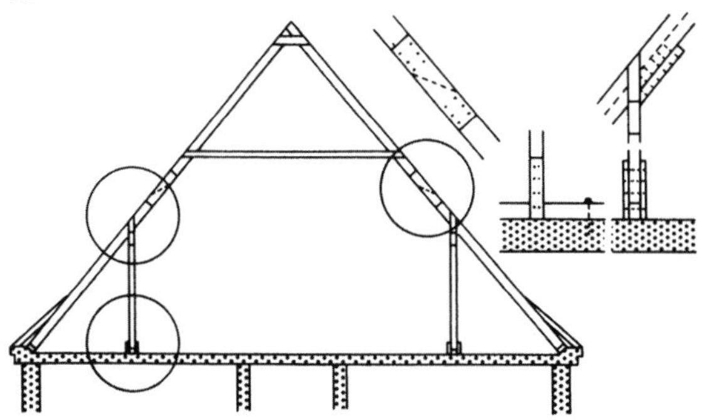

❷ Couple roof with jointed rafters, stiffened at three points

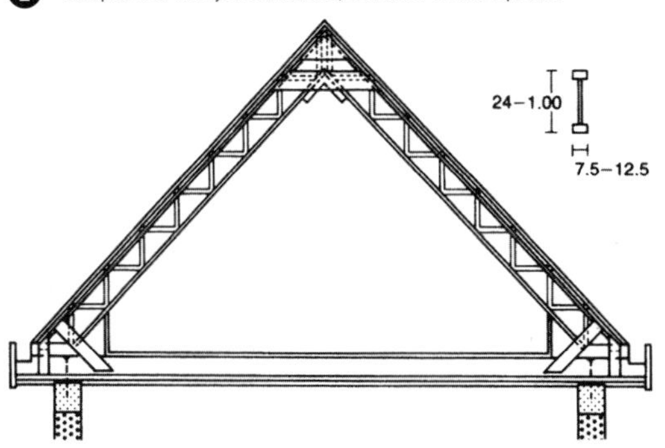

❸ Couple roof in timber framing with lifetime-guaranteed glued joints and 45° inclined struts as twin supports; span ≦25 m

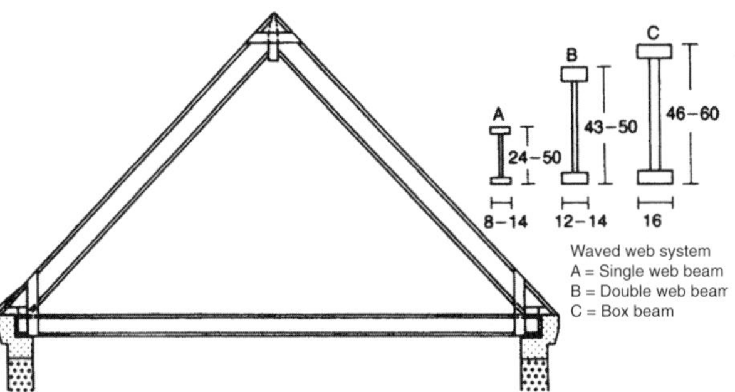

❹ Couple roof with composite, corrugated web beams (waved web system); ratio of profile height to span 1:15–1:20

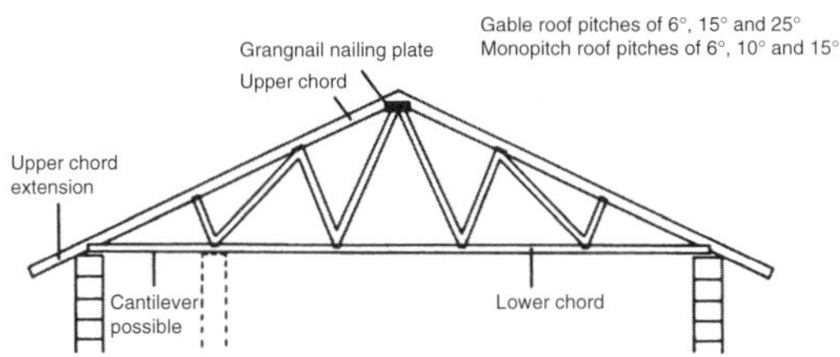

❺ Euro prefabricated truss and gang-nail system: depending on octametre sizes, for flat roof, single-pitch and two-pitch roofs

Couple roof

The couple roof is a structural system in which **two rafters and a ceiling joist** (or the corresponding strips of a solid ceiling slab) form a **rigid triangle** → p. 86 ❶.

The weight of the roof is transferred to the external walls without loading the ceiling. This makes possible large roof spaces without posts. The necessary joint to transfer tension at the junction of rafter and ceiling joist traditionally leads to the characteristic change of roof pitch in couple roofs, which is constructed with a sprocket fixed at the top to the rafter and at the bottom to the projecting end of the ceiling joist → p. 86 ❾ (modern couple roofs with upstands at the edge of the solid ceiling slab 'rafter shoes') can be constructed without this change of pitch → p. 86 ❻). Very wide buildings (with rafter lengths of more than 4.5 m) lead to uneconomical rafter sections; and in these cases they are braced with a collar → p. 86 ❼. **Collar roofs** are suitable for buildings up to 12 m wide (rafter length up to 8 m, collar up to 4 m). Much larger widths are possible with modern structures (e.g. latticed beam → ❸, composite, corrugated web beam – waved web system → ❹) or with gang-nail trusses → ❺.

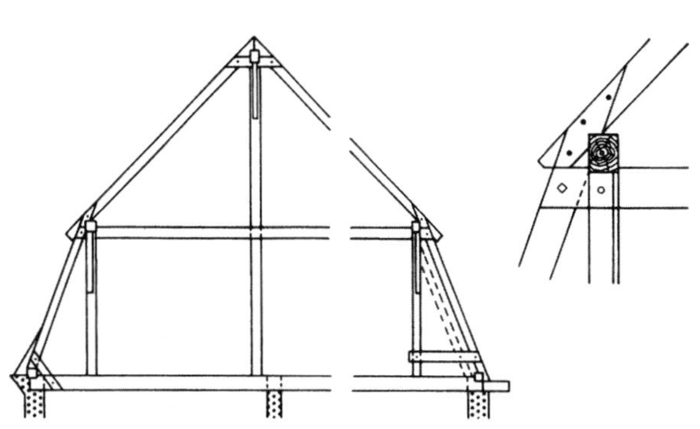

❻ Mansard roof

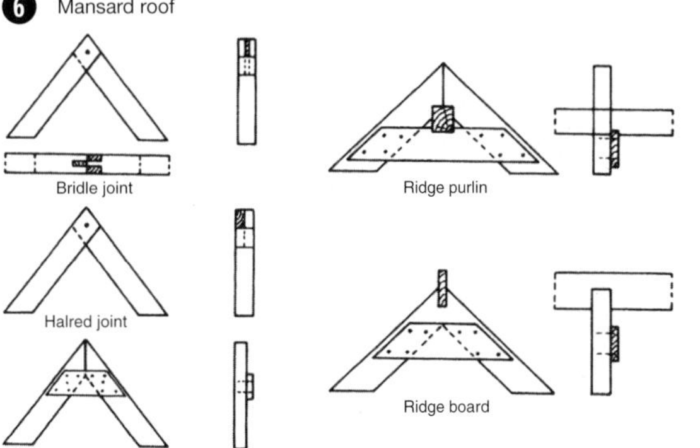

❼ Butt joint with fishplate

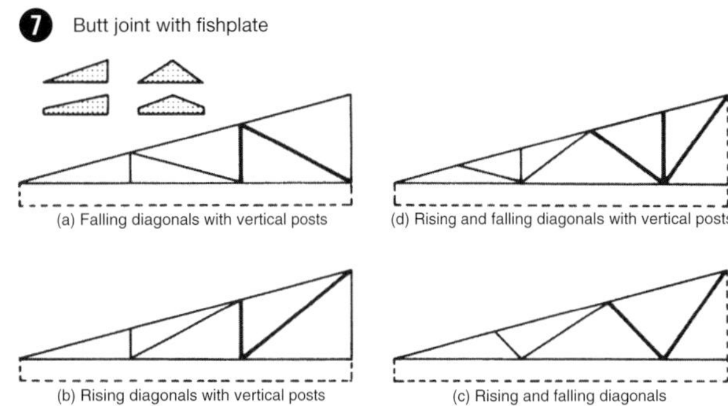

❽ Timber truss forms and bracing

Roof coverings

Reed thatching → ❶: 1.2–1.4 m long, on battens, spacing 20–30 cm, fixed with ends upwards in a thickness of ≧28 cm (better 35–40 cm). Lifetime in sunny districts 60–70 years, half that in wet districts.

Wood shingle roof → ❷: of oak, beech, larch, pine or, unusually, spruce. The lifetime of wooden shingles depends on the quality and treatment of the material, the intensity of precipitation and the pitch of the roof. Rule of thumb: degrees of roof slope = years of lifetime. Wooden shingles are suitable for covering all sorts of roof.

Slate → ❸ – ❽ (at pitches of 15–90°) on ≧24 mm thick boarding made of 12 cm wide planks. Sanded roofing felt (200 gauge) protects against dust and wind. Lap ≧8 cm (better 10 cm). Various types of slating are used for roof and wall covering in Germany: 'exclusive', 'Old German' and 'wild', as well as 'decorative slating' (mostly template slates such as shingle, sharp angle, fish scale, octagonal etc.)

Reasonably priced slating types: rectangular and curved-cut template. Template slating is also suitable for artificial slate.

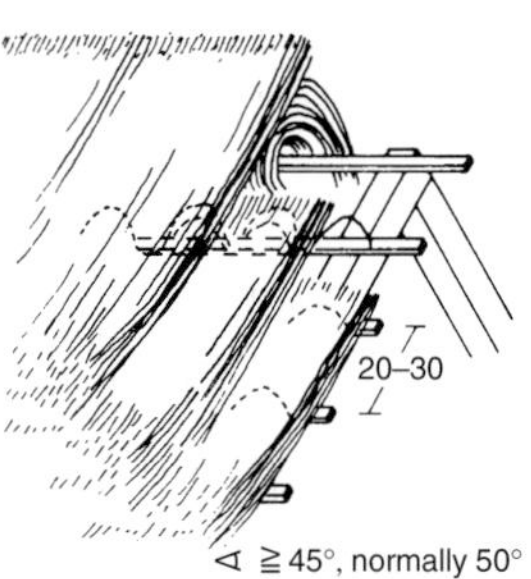

❶ Reed thatch, load 0.70 KN/m²

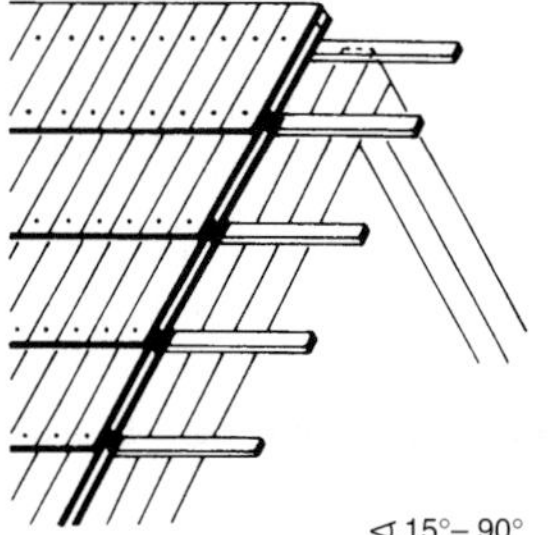

❷ Wood shingle roof, load 0.25 KN/m²

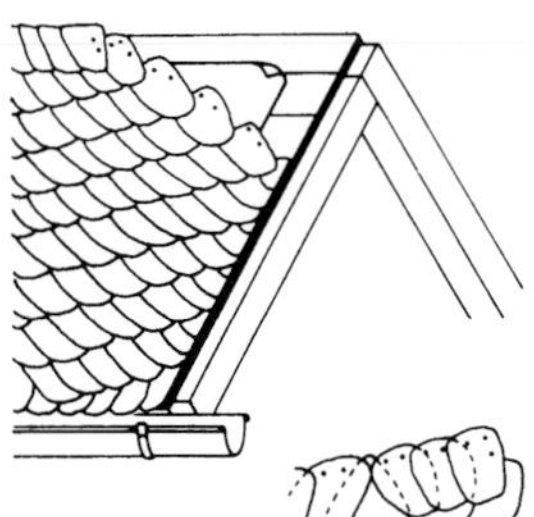
❸ 'Old German' slate roof, load 0.45–0.50 KN/m² → ❺ - ❽

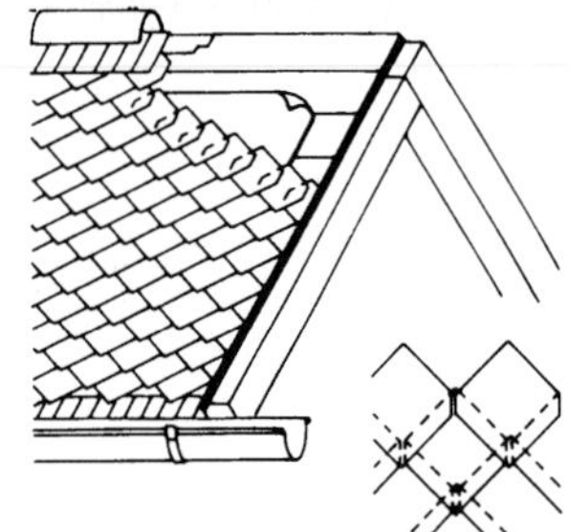
❹ English slating with fibre cement slates, load 0.45–0.50 KN/m²

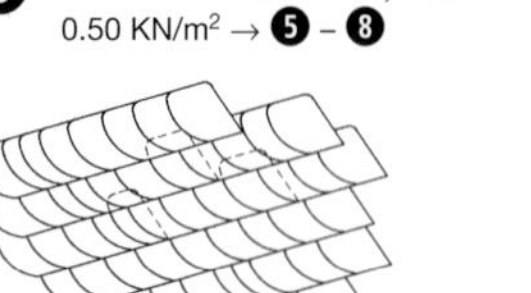
Old German slating, roof pitch ≧25°

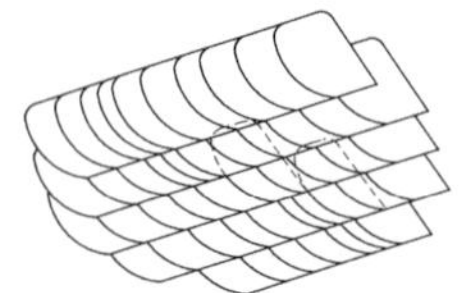
Old German double slating, roof pitch ≧22°

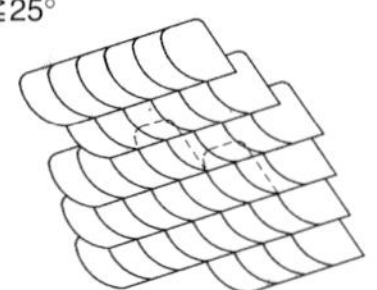
❺ ≧25° fish scale slating

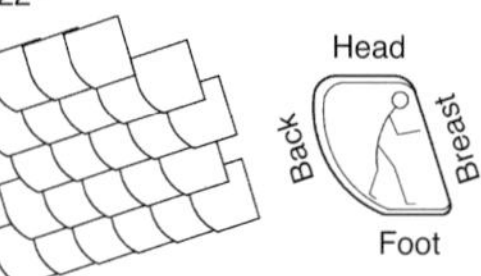

❻ ≧25° curved-cut slating

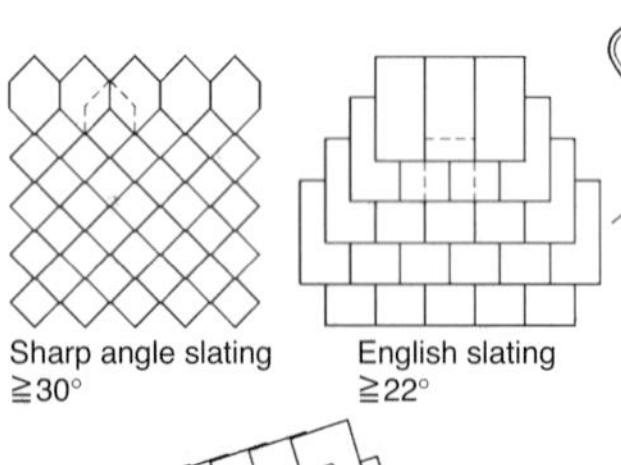
Sharp angle slating ≧30°

English slating ≧22°

❼ Curved-cut slating with solar elements

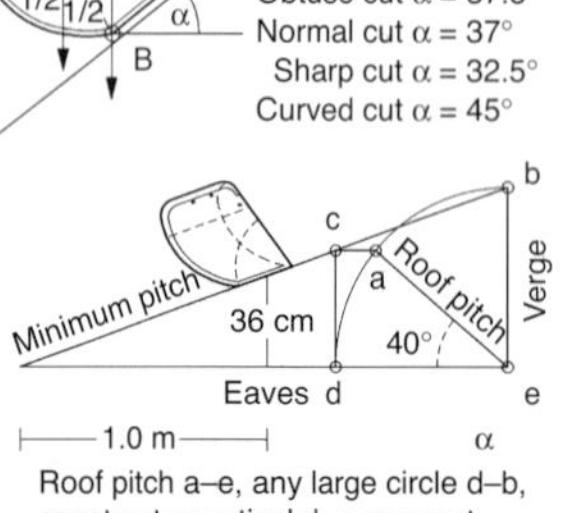

Roof pitch a–e, any large circle d–b, construct a vertical d–c; connect point a–c parallel to the eaves: c–b gives the minimum pitch of the slating courses.

❽ Minimum angle of truss, e.g. 40°

1 mono-pitch: edge tile, corner tile right
2 eaves tile
3 mono-pitch roof tile
4 wall connecting tile
5 eaves: wall connecting, corner tile right
6 wall connecting tile right
7 wall connecting tile left
8 lean-to roof: wall connecting, corner tile left
9 ridge end tile left
10 ridge and hip tile
11 edge tile left
12 eaves edge tile left
13 ridge connecting edge tile, corner tile left
14 ridge starting tile right
15 ridge edge connecting tile corner tile right
16 ridge connecting tile
17 edge tile right
18 eaves edge corner tile right

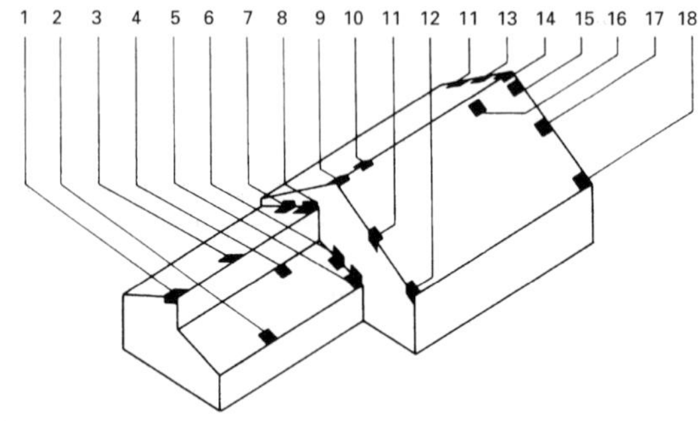

⓫ Special tiles

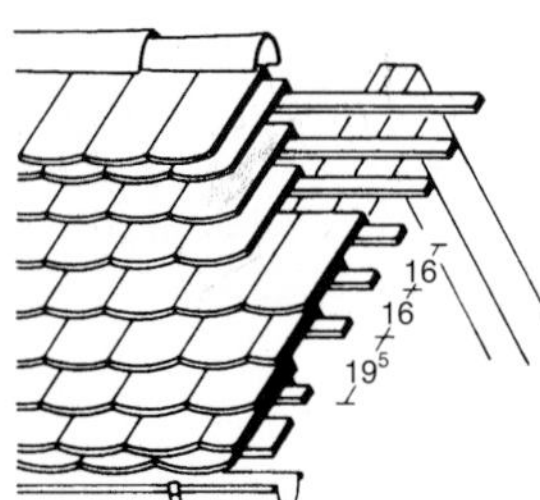

❾ Double-lap tiling ('beaver tail'), heavy roof covering, load 0.60 KN/m², 34–44 tiles/m²

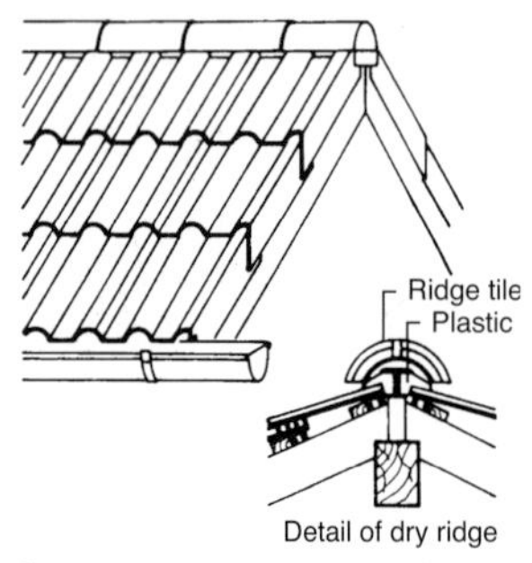

❿ Concrete tiles, 0.60–0.80 KN/m², pitch 18°

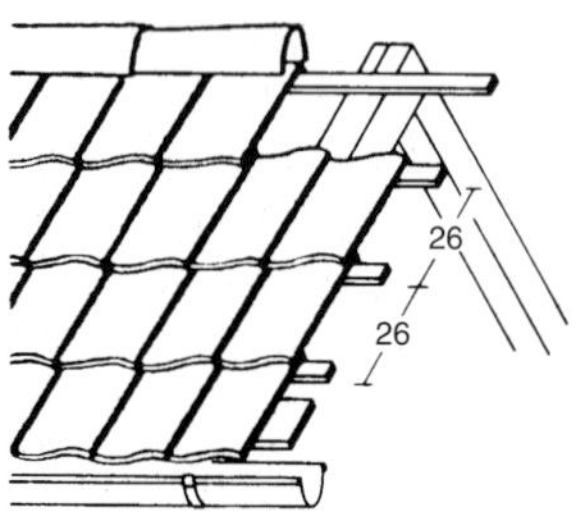

⓬ Pantile roof, lightweight, load 0.50 KN/m²

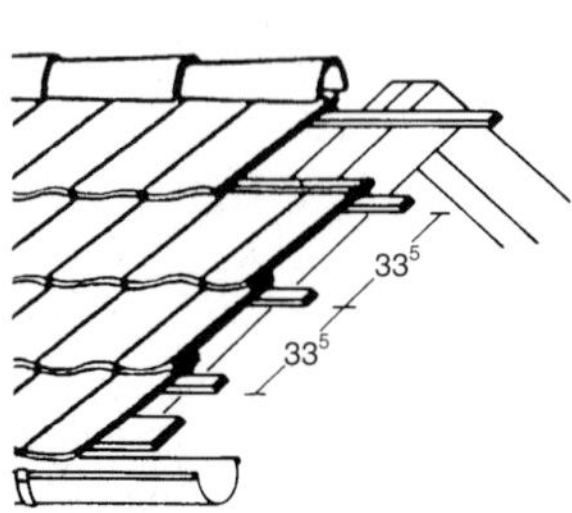

⓭ Interlocking clay tile roof, load 0.55 KN/m²

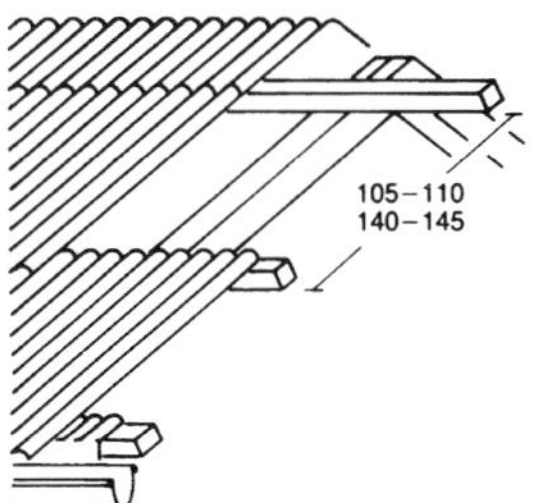

❶ Corrugated cement fibre roofing with shaped pieces for eaves and ridge, load 0.20 kN/m²

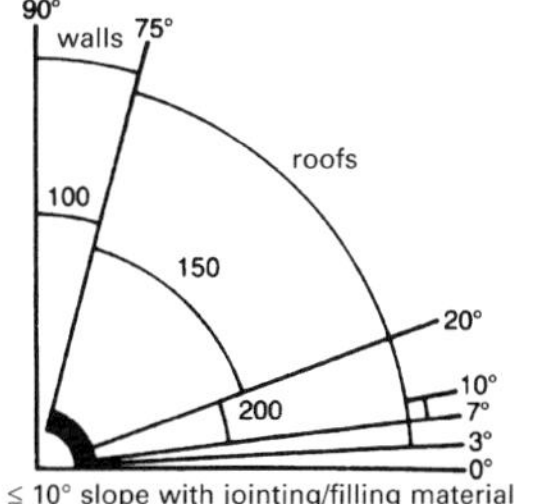

❷ Minimum roof pitches → ❶ and lap lengths

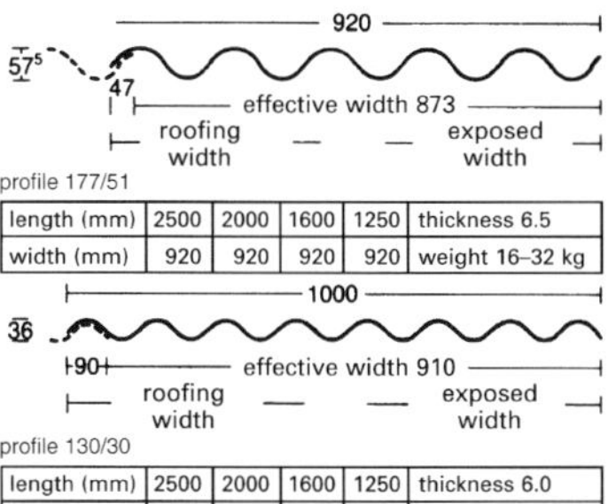

length (mm)	2500	2000	1600	1250	thickness 6.5
width (mm)	920	920	920	920	weight 16–32 kg

length (mm)	2500	2000	1600	1250	thickness 6.0
width (mm)	1000	1000	1000	1000	weight 15.8–31.5

❸ Corrugated cement fibre roofing sheets

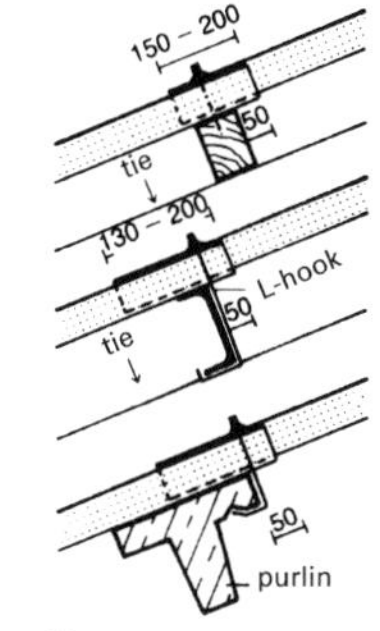

❹ Methods of fixing

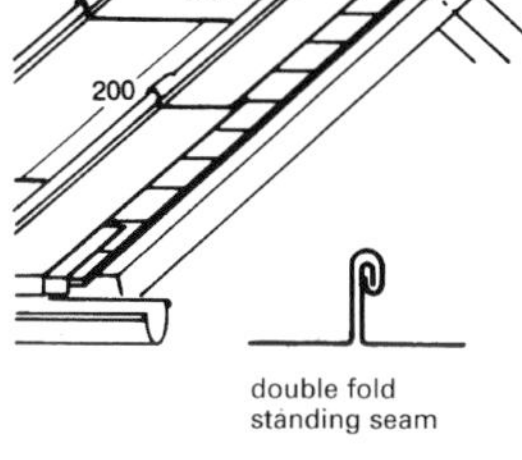

❺ Metal sheet roof with welted joint construction, load 0.25 KN/m²

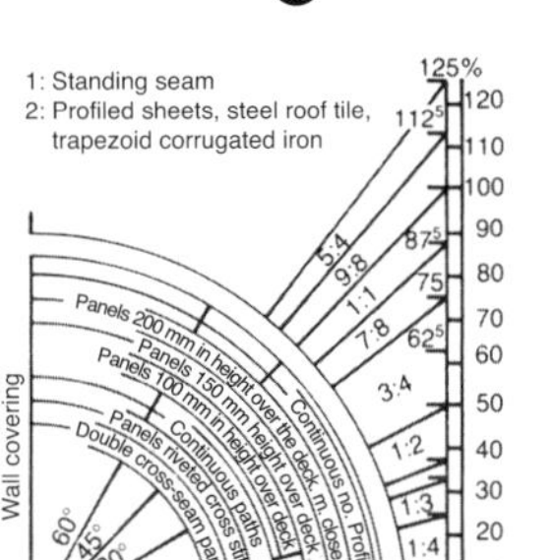

❻ Minimum roof pitch for roof covering of galvanised steel sheet

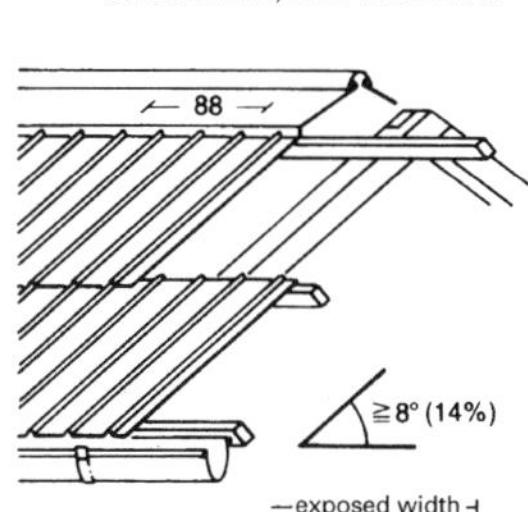

❼ Steel pantile roofing, load 0.15 KN/m²

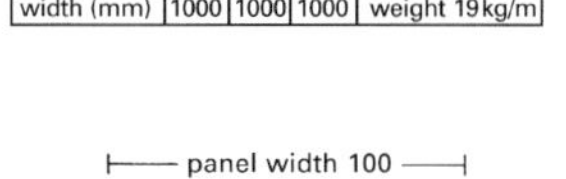

length (mm)	9000	7500	4000	thickness 8.0
width (mm)	1000	1000	1000	weight 19 kg/m

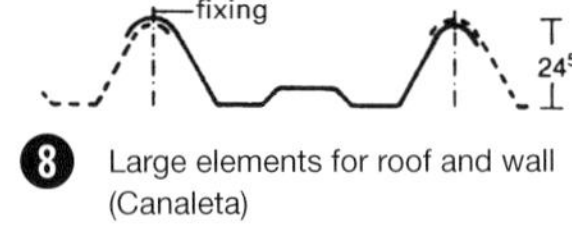

❽ Large elements for roof and wall (Canaleta)

roof drainage

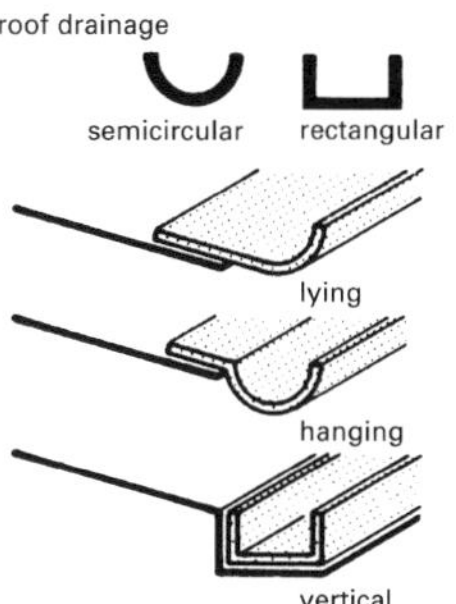

❾ Possible shapes and locations of gutter

Zinc sheet DIN 9721 at least 0.7 mm	(Zn)
Gutter brackets: zinc-coated strip steel	(St 2)
Galvanised strip steel DIN 1541 leaded	(St 2)
Gutter bracket: galvanised strip steel	(St 2)
Semi-hard copper sheet DIN 1787	(Cu)
Gutter brackets: flat copper	(Cu)
Aluminum sheet cut in half DIN 1725	(Al)
Gutter brackets: galvanised strip steel	(St 2)

Specification:
(example: semi-circular gutter 333 Zn 0.75 mm; with gutter bracket 333 St Zn)

❿ Materials

Roof coverings (continued)

Cement fibre roof → ❶ – ❷ composed of corrugated sheets with purlin spacing of 70–145 cm for 1.6 m sheets, of 1.15 and 1.175 m for 2.50 m sheets; lapped 150 or 200 mm.

Sheet metal roof → ❺ – ❼ of zinc, titanium-zinc, copper, aluminium, galvanised steel sheet etc. Many special shapes available for ridge, eaves, edge etc. Copper sheeting is in commercially produced sizes → ⓬. Copper has the highest elongation at break of any metal sheeting and is therefore suitable for embossing, pressing, stretching and compressing. The typical patina of copper roofing is very popular. Combination with aluminium, titanium-zinc and galvanised steel should be avoided, but with lead and high-grade steel there is no problem. Copper roofs are impermeable to water vapour and thus particularly suitable for cold roofs → p. 90.

	kN/m²
'beaver-tail' tiles and 'beaver-tail' concrete tiles	
with underlay incl. underlay parts	0.60
clay tiles, single or double lap	0.80
extruded interlocking clay tiles	0.60
interlocking tiles, reform pantiles, interlocking pantiles, flat tiles	0.55
interlocking tiles	0.55
Spanish tiles, concave tiles	0.50
pantiles	0.50
large-format pantiles (up to 10 per m²)	0.50
Spanish tiles without mortaring, 0.70 with mortaring	0.90
metal sheeting, aluminium roof (aluminium 0.7 mm thick) incl. boarding	0.25
copper roof with double seams (copper sheet 0.6 mm thick) incl. boarding	0.30
double standing seam roof of galvanised seamed sheeting (0.63 mm thick)	
including underlay and boarding	0.30
German slate roof on boarding incl. felt underlay and boarding	
large format (360 mm × 280 mm)	0.50
small format (about 200 mm × 150 mm)	0.45
English slate roof incl. battens	
on battens with double lap	0.45
on boarding and underlay incl. boarding	0.55
Old German slate roof on underlay and boarding	0.50
with double lap	0.60
steel pantile roof (galvanised steel sheets)	
on battens incl. battens	0.15
on boarding incl. underlay and boarding	0.30
corrugated steel roof (galvanised steel sheets) incl. fixings	0.25
zinc roof with cover strips of zinc sheet incl. boarding	0.30

⓫ Loads per 1 m² pitched roof surface (without rafters, purlins or trusses, but including battens). If mortar-pointed, add 0.1 kN/m².

supplied form	rolls	panels
length (m)	30–40	2.0
max. width (m)	0.6 (0.66)	1.0
thickness (mm)	0.1–2.0	0.2–2.0
specific wt (kg/dm³)	8.93	8.93

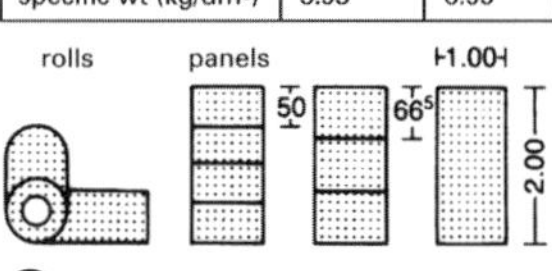

⓬ Form and dimensions of rolled copper material for strip and sheet roofing

½ corrugation standard
1 corrugation
1½ corrugations

roof depth eaves/ridge	profile ht 18–25 mm	26–50 mm
up to 6 m	10° (17.4%)	5° (8.7%)
6–10 m	13° (22.5%)	8° (13.9%)
10–15 m	15° (25.9%)	10° (17.4%)
over 15 m	17° (29.2%)	12° (20.8%)

8–10°	200 mm with sealing of overlap
10–15°	150 mm without sealing of overlap
over 15°	100 mm without sealing of overlap

⓭ Corrugated sheet metal roofing, minimum roof pitch, side laps

Roof area to be drained with semi-circular gutters (m²)	Guideline size of gutters (mm ∅)	Cut lengths for metal gutters (mm)
up to 25	70	200
25–40	80	200 (10-part)
40–60	90	250 (8-part)
60–90	125	285 (7-part)
90–125	150	333 (6-part)
125–175	400 (5-part)	400 (5-part)
175–275	200	500 (4-part)

Gutters should generally be installed on a slope as greater flow speed helps prevent blocking, corrosion and freezing. Guttering supports normally consist of galvanised steel strips, width 20–50 mm and thickness 4–6 mm.

⓮ Guideline sizes for gutters

Roof area to be drained with round downpipes (m²)	Guideline size of downpipe (mm ∅)	Cut lengths for metal pipes (mm)
up to 20	50	167 (12-part)
20–50	60	200 (10-part)
50–90	70	250 (8-part)
60–100	80	285 (7-part)
90–120	100	333 (6-part)
100–180	125	400 (5-part)
180–250	150	500 (4-part)
250–375	175	
325–500	200	

Fixing with pipe clips (corrosion-protected), whose inner diameter is that of the downpipe. Minimum distance of downpipe from the wall 20 mm. Pipe clip spacing 2 m.

⓯ Guideline sizes for downpipes

Building components

ROOFS
Roof shapes
Pitched roofs
Flat roofs

see also: Building physics pp. 465 ff.

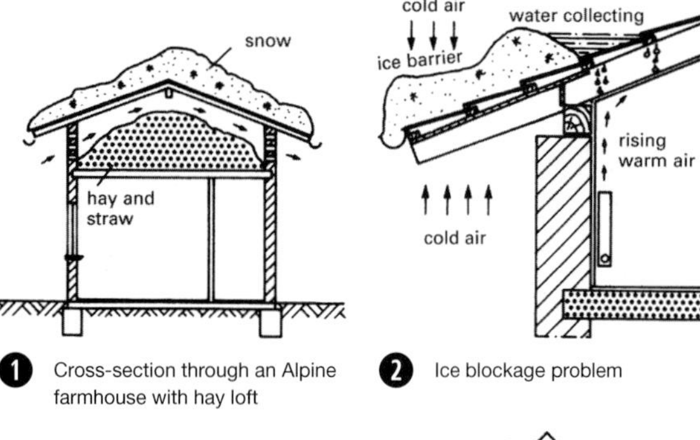

❶ Cross-section through an Alpine farmhouse with hay loft

❷ Ice blockage problem

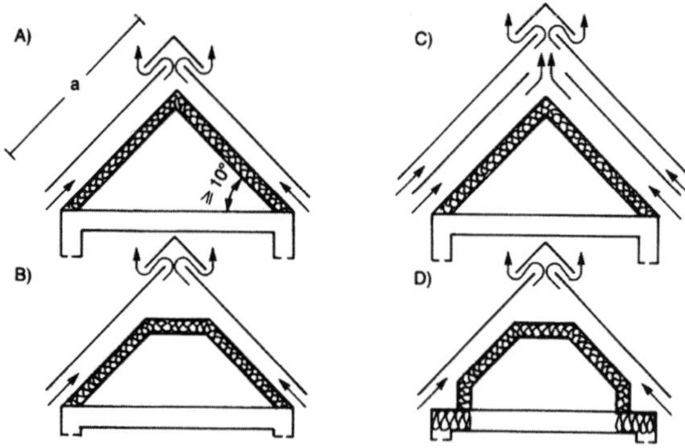

❸ Arrangement of thermal insulation in roof spaces (cold roofs)

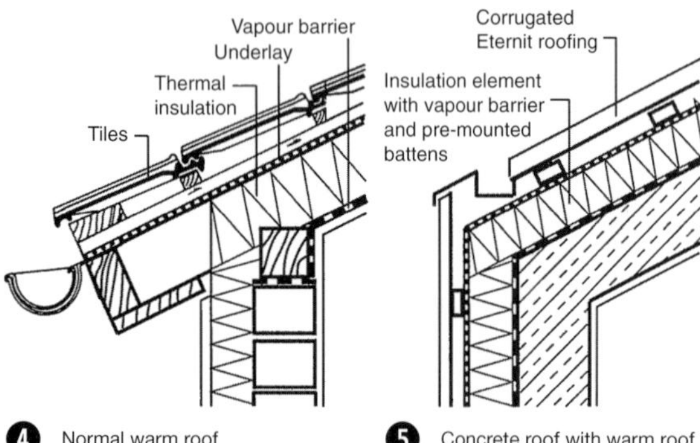

❹ Normal warm roof

❺ Concrete roof with warm roof construction

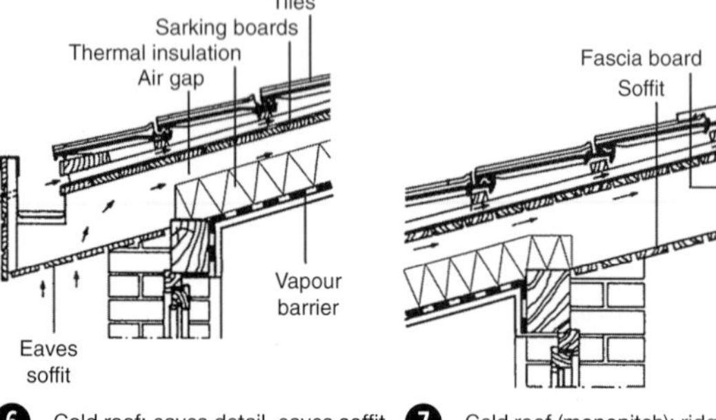

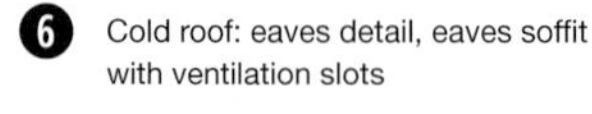

❻ Cold roof: eaves detail, eaves soffit with ventilation slots

❼ Cold roof (monopitch): ridge detail, fascia board with ventilation slots

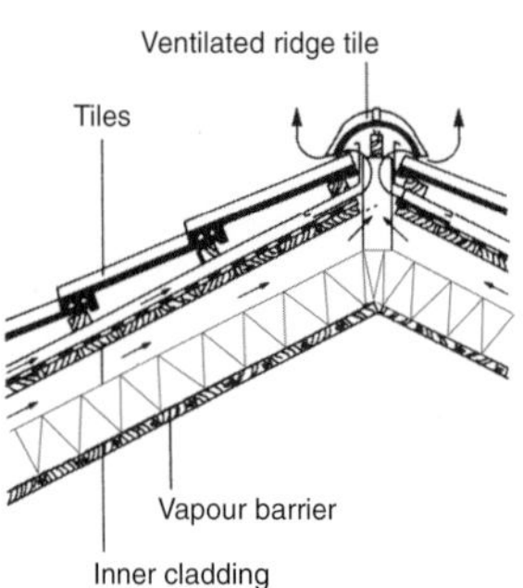
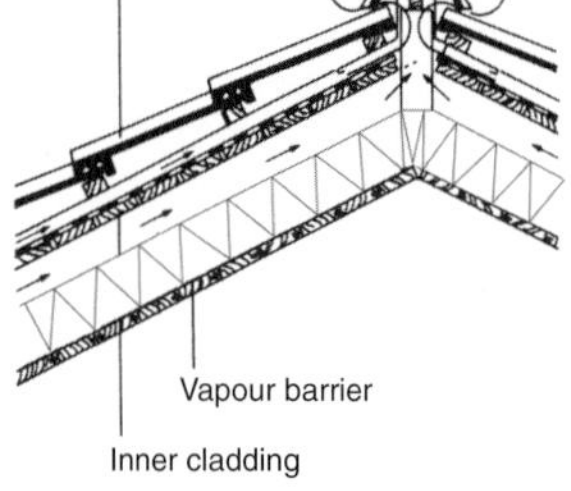

❽ Cold roof: eaves detail with exposed rafters

❾ Cold roof: ridge detail

Roof spaces

Spaces under pitched roofs were formerly used as naturally ventilated 'hay lofts' for the storage of the harvest. The rooms below were protected from cold by the stored produce → ❶. Today, roof spaces are converted into habitable rooms. The roof construction must comply with additional building physics requirements.

Building methods

Thermally insulated roofs can be divided into **ventilated** and **non-ventilated** construction. In addition to the ventilation space between roof covering and underlay (or lower layer of roof), which is required in both cases, ventilated roof construction has an additional ventilation gap between underlay and thermal insulation, to remove spray and condensate.

Ventilated roofs require additional rafter depth and work properly only with a correctly installed vapour barrier and functioning roof ventilation. Therefore the building industry commonly prefers **unventilated roof construction.**

Standard build-up of layers

Roof coverings, battens → pp. 88–89

Underlay of plastic mesh-reinforced foil or vapour-permeable plastic sheeting serves to carry away any spray water or snow penetrating under the roof covering.

Roof boarding of tongue and groove boards with applied waterproofing (e.g. welded bitumen sheeting) is installed instead of underlay in conditions of severe exposure.

The **air gap** in ventilated roof construction serves as an additional ventilation layer (e.g. to remove condensation). The necessary ventilation cross-sections depend on the roof pitch.

Thermal insulation is generally in the form of mineral wool roll material and is installed between and under the rafters or as prefabricated insulation elements, sometimes with interlocking, vapour barrier on the room side and battens fixed to the rafters → ❿.

The **vapour barrier** is under the thermal insulation to prevent condensation inside the roof construction. When the vapour barrier is installed, it is important that all air flow between interior and roof construction is prevented. Any penetration points, laps and junctions with building elements must be carefully sealed.

Inner cladding is normally plasterboard on support construction (pay attention to the possibility of cracks!).

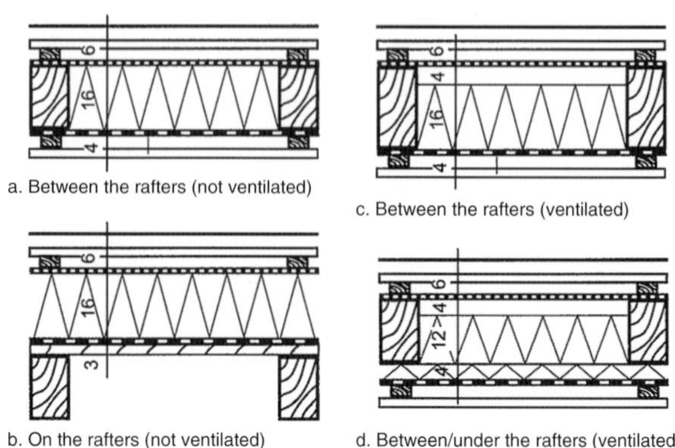

❿ Location of thermal insulation for pitched roofs converted for storage

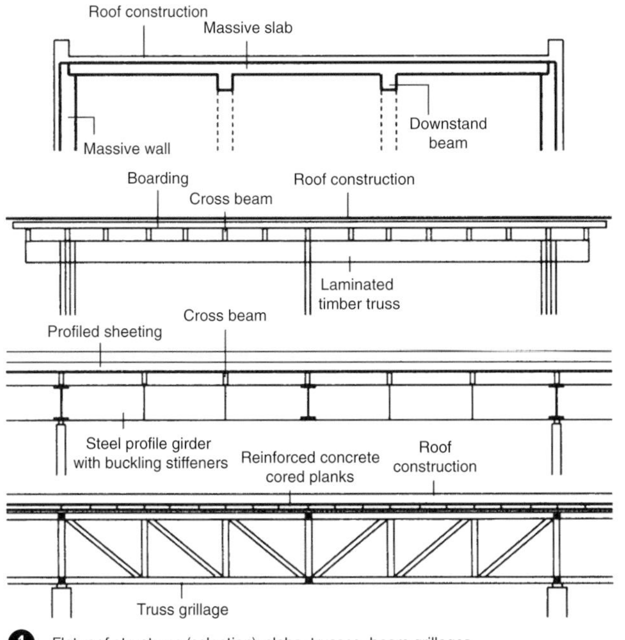

1 Flat roof structures (selection): slabs, trusses, beam grillages

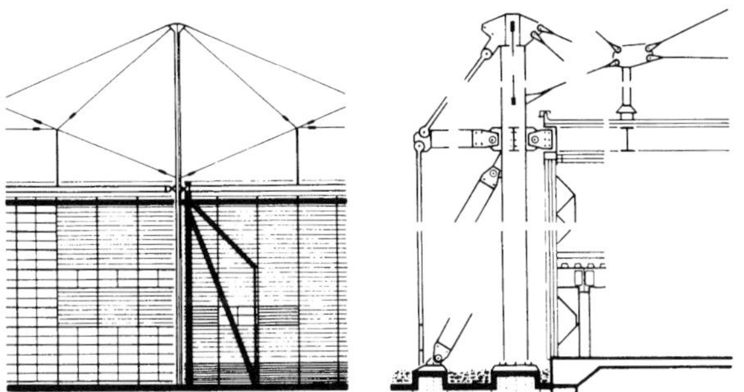

2 Guyed structure: Fleetguard factory, Quimper Arch.: Rogers & Partner

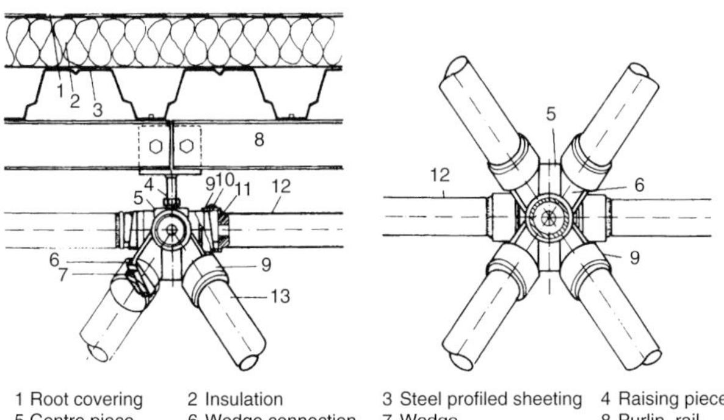

1 Root covering 2 Insulation 3 Steel profiled sheeting 4 Raising piece
5 Centre piece 6 Wedge connection 7 Wedge 8 Purlin, rail
9 Cage ring 10 Grooved dowel pin 11 Wedge cheek 12 Horizontal tube
13 Diagonal tube

3 Upper and middle nodes of space frames (KEBA tube nodes)

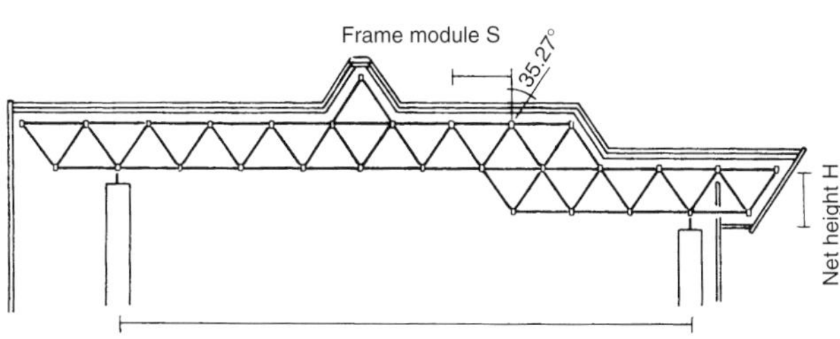

4 Space frame with KEBA tube node connections (example), details → 3

Flat roofs are defined as roofs with a slope of up to 5%. Flat roofs without slope are possible as a special construction in exceptional cases. Flat roofs should generally have a minimum slope of 2%. On account of unavoidable flatness tolerances and deflection of the construction, however, it is recommended to construct flat roofs with a minimum slope of 5% (3°).

Construction

There are many different structural types for flat roofs. The basic difference is between **planar** and **linear** structural systems:

Planar structures are based on flat elements spanning one or two axes, with point or linear supports and loaded at right angles to their plane (e.g. floor slabs, roof slabs, beam grillages, space frames).

Linear structures are systems comprising parallel-laid beam elements (e.g. full-web steel beams, trussed beams, cable-trussed beams) and intermediate components not laid in the direction of the beam (e.g. cross-beams with boarding) to transfer the roof loading.

Both structural types are differentiated into various degrees of resolution of the structural elements, in addition to the material:

Slabs → 1

Flat roofs are mostly constructed as flat solid reinforced concrete slabs. These are fire-resistant, not susceptible to damp and form a stable structural system in combination with solid walls.Their disadvantage lies in their high dead weight, wet installation and poor thermal and sound insulation. Movement resulting from thermal expansion, creep or shrinkage must be compensated with additional insulation layers and appropriately detailed bearings and joints.

Truss structures → 1 – 2

Trusses are linear structures. Commercially available truss beams can be made of timber, steel or pre-cast reinforced concrete with intermediate elements of various materials. Longer spans may involve: truss beams of squared timber or with steel struts, laminated timber beams, box beams of plywood or laminated timber, specially produced full-web girders with high web plates and bracing against buckling, and castellated or lattice beams. Additional guying and cable trussing can reduce the cross-section of the beams, effecting light and delicate structures.

Beam grillages → 1 – 2

Beam grillages are planar structures made of wide-span beams laid in both directions and crossing in a plane. They are normally composed of prefabricated components (e.g. of laminated timber beams with node plates or steel trusses) and are particularly suitable for roofing over industrial sheds etc. If there are fire protection requirements, then additional measures must be undertaken to protect the structure.

Space frames→ 3 – 4

The space frame is a further development of the beam grillage. Steel rods are connected with spherical nodes to form stiff three-dimensional structures which require no additional stiffening.

ROOFS

Roof shapes
Pitched roofs
Flat roofs

BS 8298
BS EN 12730
DIN 18531

Flat Roof Guidelines, Central Association of German Roofers

see also: Building physics pp. 471 ff.

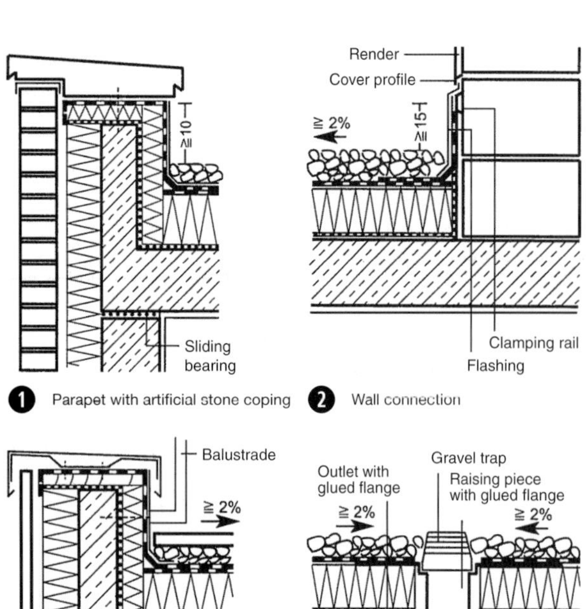

❶ Parapet with artificial stone coping

❷ Wall connection

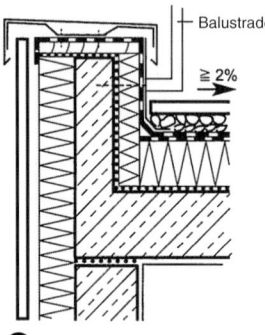

❸ Roof edge detail (terrace)

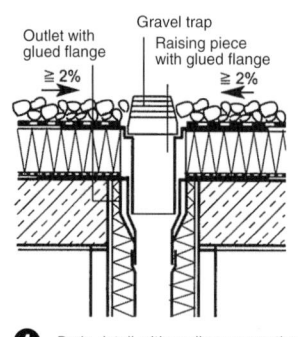

❹ Drain detail with sealing connection

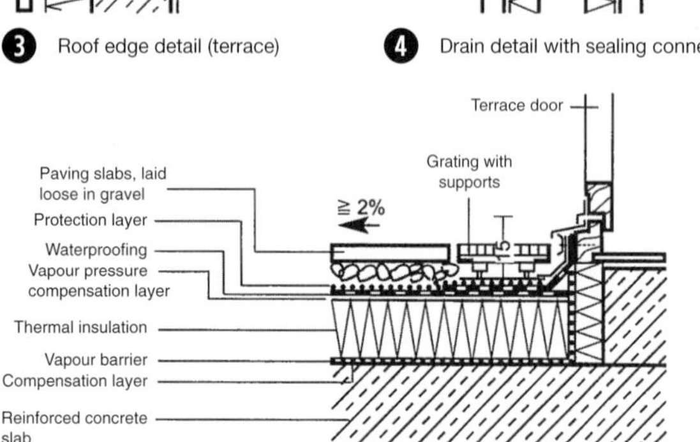

❺ Terrace connection with extended grating

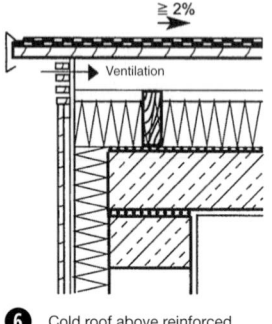

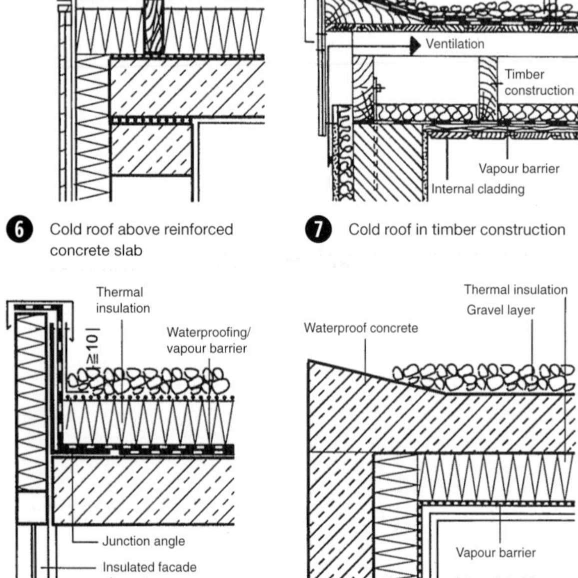

❻ Cold roof above reinforced concrete slab

❼ Cold roof in timber construction

❽ Upside-down roof

❾ Watertight concrete roof with internal insulation

ROOFS

Flat Roofs

There are two methods of building a flat roof from the building physics perspective:

Non-ventilated, single-layer construction ('warm roof'), in which the load-bearing structure, vapour barrier, thermal insulation and waterproofing (including intermediate layers) form a composite element.

This can either be the conventional construction → ❿, or an '**upside-down roof**' → ❽ (waterproofing and vapour barrier are applied as one layer directly onto the load-bearing construction and the closed-cell insulation is loosely laid on top and secured with a gravel layer), or a combination of both construction types (e.g. a '**plus roof**'), or with **internal insulation** → ❾.

Ventilated two-layer construction ('cold roof'), where there is a ventilation layer between the waterproofing (and its sub-structure) and the thermal insulation → ❻ – ❼. The advantage of this arrangement (evaporation of condensation) is, however, effective only if the through-ventilation is fully functional and a defect-free vapour barrier is installed on the inner side of the construction. Otherwise, the waterproofing acts as a **wrongly positioned vapour barrier,** which can cause the roof construction to become damp!

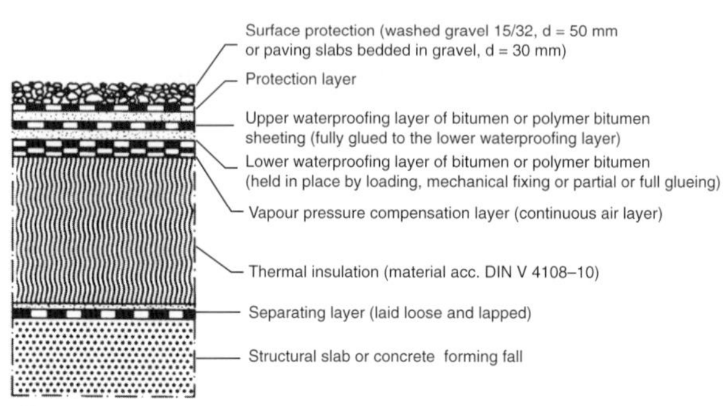

❿ Standard construction of a warm roof with heavy surface protection and multi-layer waterproofing

Standard construction (warm roof) → ❿

Surface protection can either be heavy (gravel layer – depth ≧5 cm, slabs laid in a bed of stone chips, or an extensive green roof) or lightweight (pre-applied gravel covering of bitumen sheeting) to prevent the formation of bubbles, temperature shocks, mechanical stress to the waterproofing or UV damage.

Protection layers (e.g. PVC protective sheeting, synthetic fleece, rubber granulate protection mats, protection against penetrating roots), waterproofing with many layers of bitumen sheeting and polymer-bitumen sheeting (fully glued to each other) or a single layer of plastic or elastomer waterproofing membrane. The waterproofing can be held in place by a superimposed load, mechanical fixing, or full or partial gluing.

Vapour pressure compensation layer: ribbed felt or holed bitumen sheeting, to prevent bubble formation resulting from evaporated residual dampness or the construction layers above.
Insulation is provided by thermal insulation boards (cork, rigid foam, fibre insulation or foam glass), laid without joints or with all-round interlock edges.

Separation/compensation layer: mostly loosely laid.
Load-bearing construction on a slope → p. 91, with sliding bearings on account of thermal expansion (consequent formation of a sliding joint over the load-bearing walls and separation of internal wall and slab. Glue Styrofoam strips to the underside of the slab in advance)

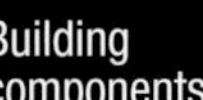

Roof planting

The Babylonians were constructing roof gardens and green roofs as long ago as the 6th century BC. In Berlin around 1890, farmhouses were covered with a layer of soil for fire protection purposes, causing plants to grow. In the 20th century, during the classic modernist period and with the introduction of flat roofs, the almost forgotten green roof was rediscovered.

Properties of planted roofs

1. Insulation, due to the air layer within the plants and the growing layer (corresponding to soil) with its roots, and also through warmth from microbial processes
2. Sound insulation and thermal storage capacity
3. Improvement of the air in built-up areas
4. Improvement of the microclimate
5. Positive effect on urban rainwater drainage and landscape water cycle
6. Building physics advantages: UV radiation and severe temperature variations are prevented by the protective growing and plant layer.
7. Dust retention
8. Design element/improved quality of life
9. Reclamation of green areas

❶ Roof gardens on rented housing: 'Pointer towards a new architecture'

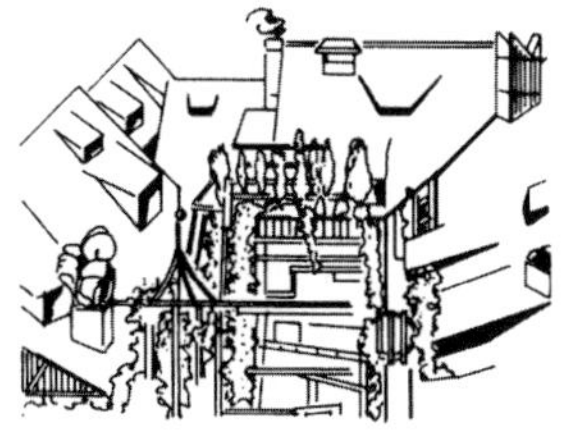

❷ Roof garden in the form of a collection of plant containers on balconies and roof terraces

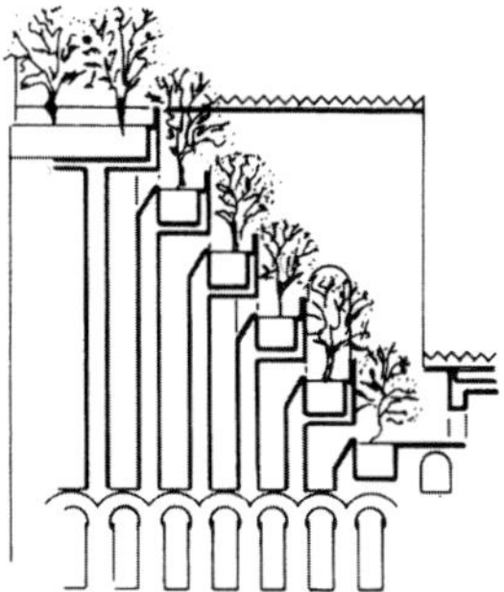

❸ The Hanging Gardens of Semiramis in Babylon (6th century BC)

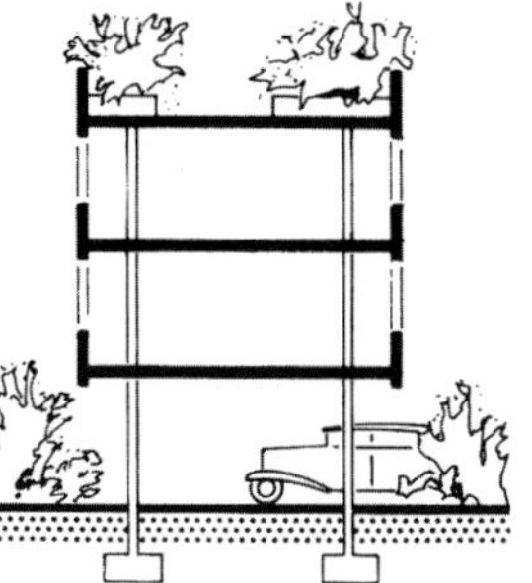

❹ Lost green areas can be regained by planting roofs

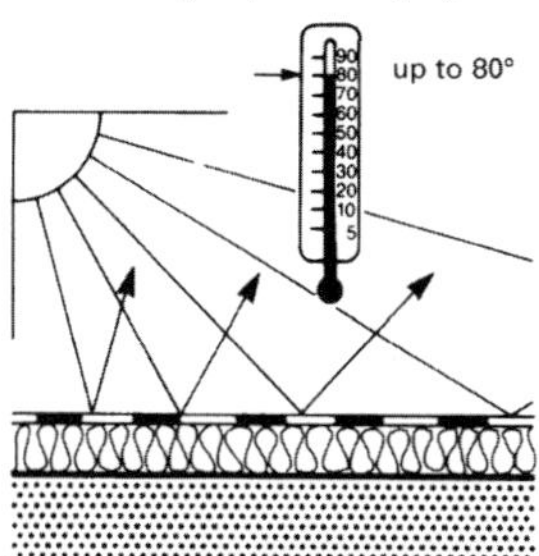

❺ Overheated, dry urban air → ❻

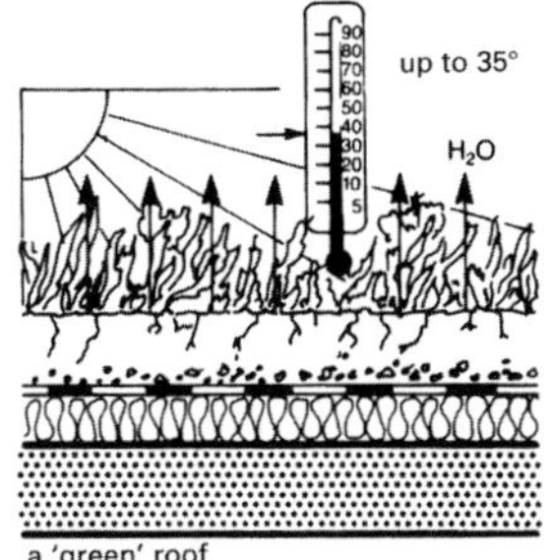

❻ Cooler and moister air through the energy consumption of plant transpiration

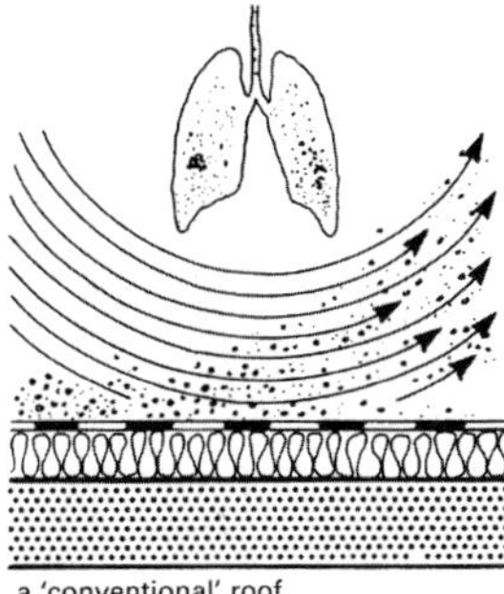

❼ Dust production and circulation → ❽

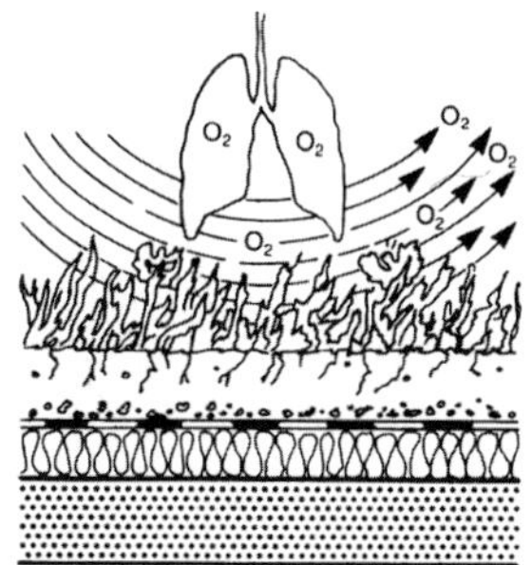

❽ Improvement of urban air through the filtering and binding of dust and the oxygen production of the plants

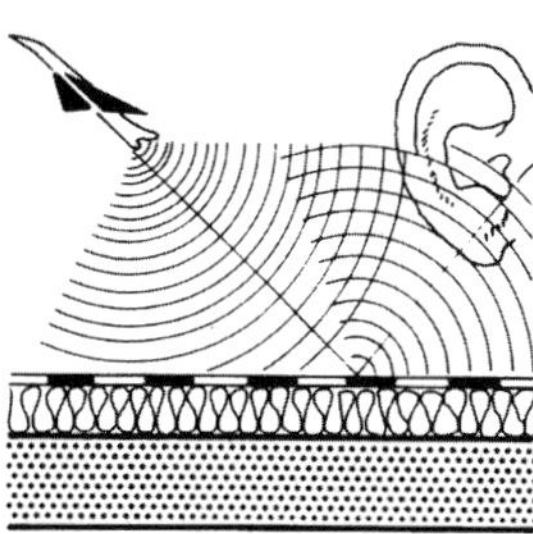

❾ Sound reflections from 'hard surfaces' → ❿

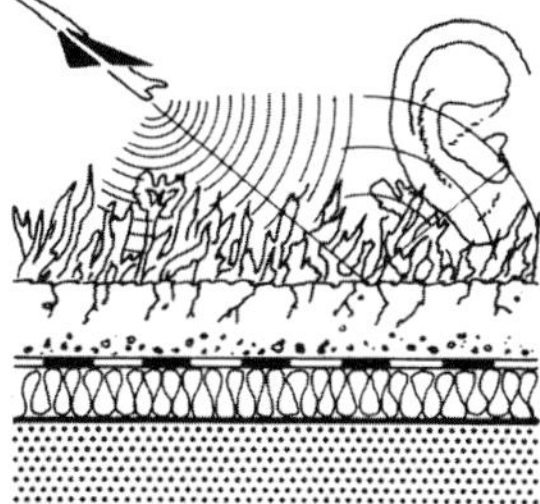

❿ Sound absorption by soft plant surfaces

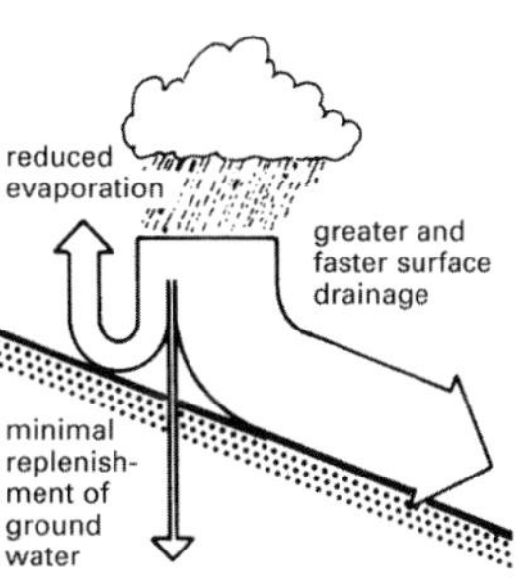

⓫ Distribution of rainwater run-off – paving → ⓬

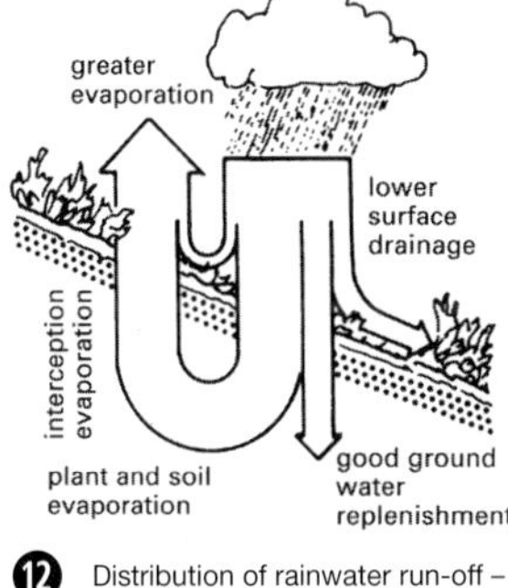

⓬ Distribution of rainwater run-off – unbuilt areas

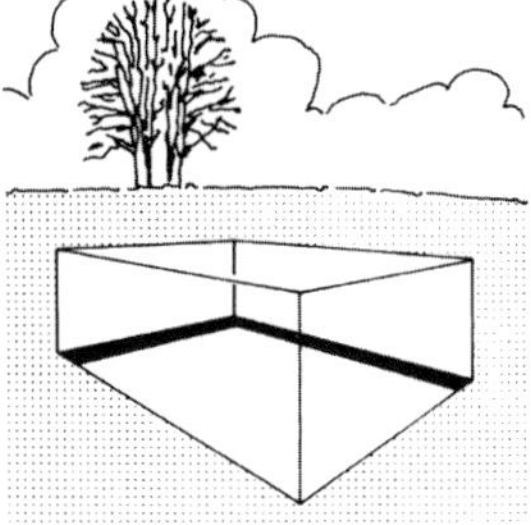

⓭ The building of every house causes the loss of open landscape → ⓮

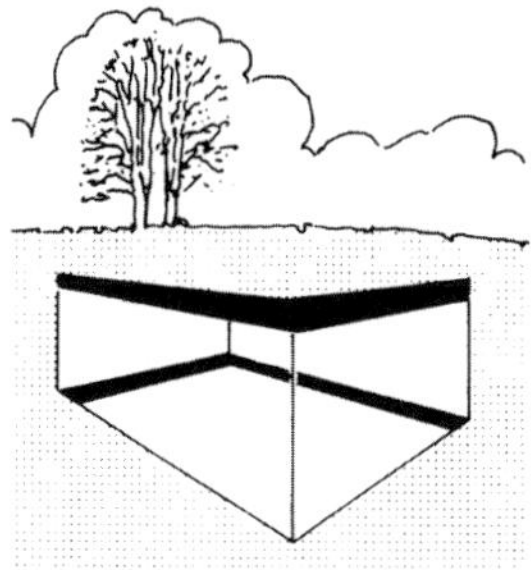

⓮ A large part of the lost green areas could be reclaimed by planting roofs

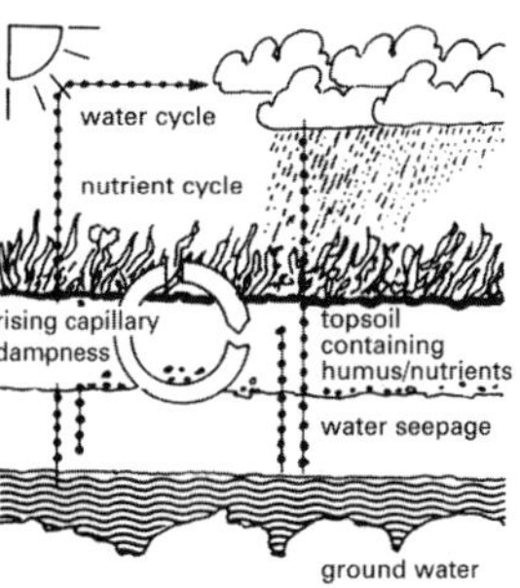

⓯ Natural water and nutrient cycle

⓰ Mental and physical value of green areas

Building components

ROOFS
Roof shapes
Pitched roofs
Flat roofs

Slopes for roof planting

The pitch of gabled roofs should not exceed 25° and flat roofs should have a maximum slope of 2–3%.

Types of roof planting

Intensive: The roof becomes a residential garden with features like pergolas and loggias. Constant care and maintenance are required. Plants: lawn, shrubs, bushes, trees

Extensive: The planting is onto thin soil and requires the minimum of care. Plants: moss, grass, herbs, shrubs, bushes

Mobile greening: Plants in containers can be used for the greening of roof terraces, parapets and balconies.

Watering

Natural watering with rainwater: Water is backed up in the drainage and growing layers.

Dammed watering: Rainwater is backed up in the drainage layer and mechanically refilled when required.

Drip irrigation: Drip irrigation hoses in the drainage or growing layers keep the plants watered through dry periods.

Sprinkler: Sprinkler equipment above the growing layer.

Plant feeding

Fertiliser can be applied to the growing layer or as an additive to artificial watering.

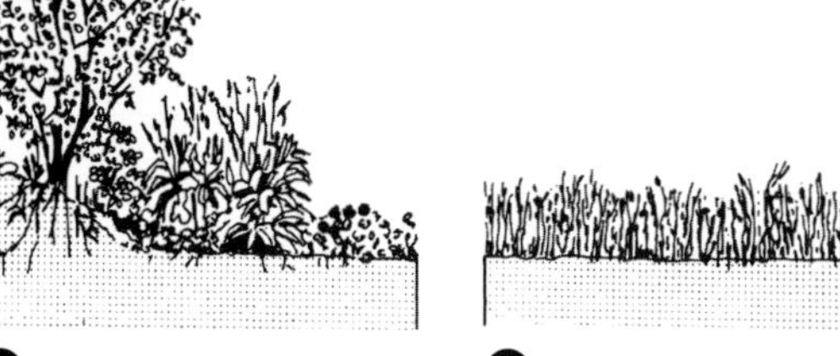

❶ Intensive planting

❷ Extensive planting

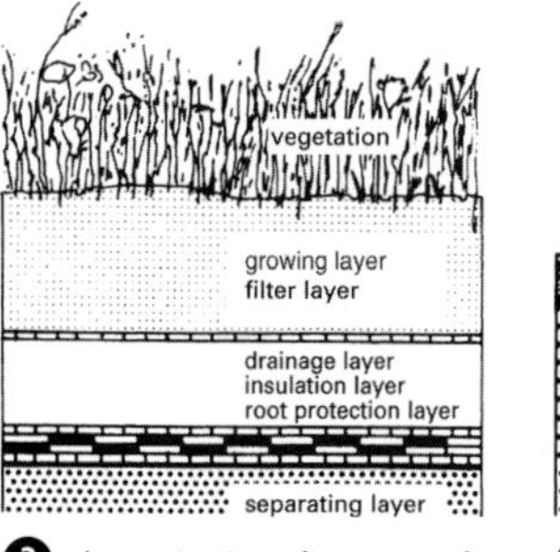

❸ Layer structure of a green roof

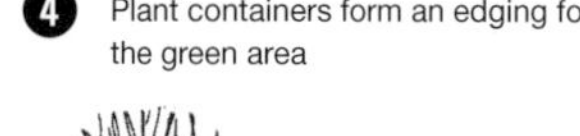

❹ Plant containers form an edging for the green area

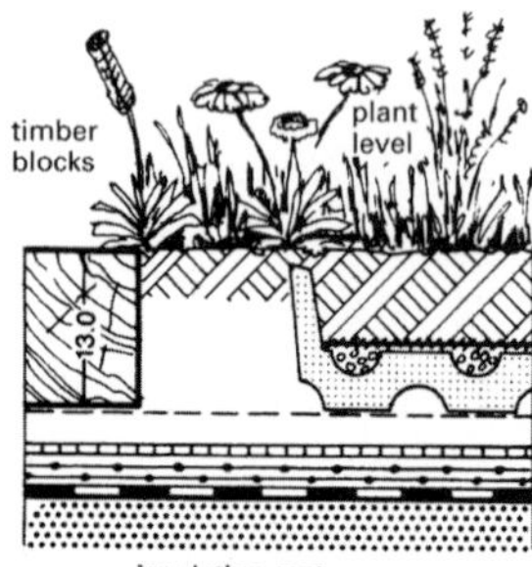

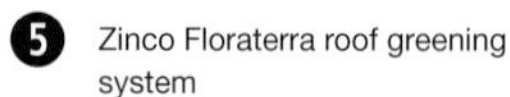

❺ Zinco Floraterra roof greening system

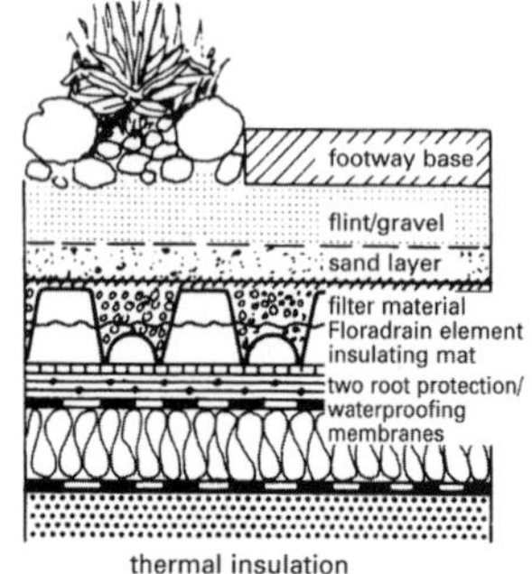

❻ Zinco Floradrain roof greening system

Botanical name	English name (colour of flowers)	Height	Month of flowering
Saxifrage aizoon	encrusted saxifrage (white-pink)	5 cm	VI
Sedum acre	biting stonecrop (yellow)	8 cm	VI–VII
Sedum album	white stonecrop (white)	5 cm	VI–VII
Sedum album 'Coral Carpet'	white variety	5 cm	VI
Sedum album 'Laconicum'	white variety	10 cm	VI
Sedum album 'Micranthum'	white variety	5 cm	VI–VII
Sedum album 'Murale'	white variety	8 cm	VI–VII
Sedum album 'Cloroticum'	(light green)	5 cm	VI–VII
Sedum hybr.	autumn delight (yellow)	8 cm	VI–VII
Sedum floriferum	Bailey's gold (gold)	10 cm	VIII–IX
Sedum reflexum, 'Elegant'	rock stonecrop (yellow)	12 cm	VI–VII
Sedum sexangulare	tasteless stonecrop (yellow)	5 cm	VI
Sedum 'White Tatra'	bright yellow variety	5 cm	VI
Sedum spur. 'Superbum'	sedum	5 cm	VI–VII
Sempervivum arachnoideum	cobweb houseleek (pink)	6 cm	VI–VII

❽ Proven plant species and varieties for extensive roof greening (selection)

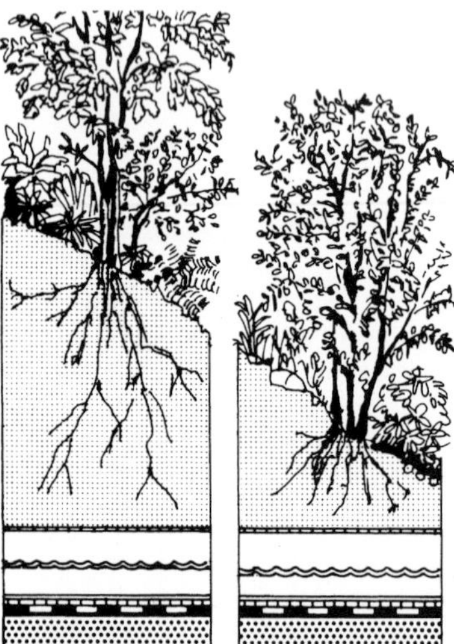

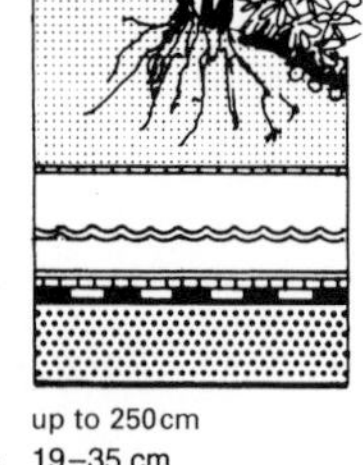

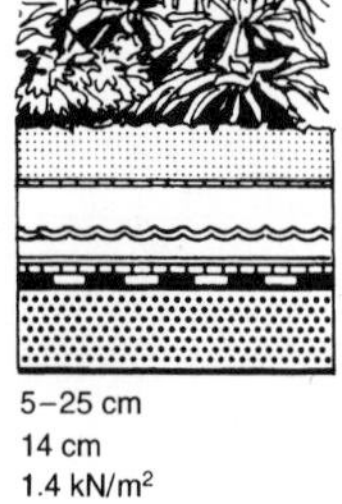

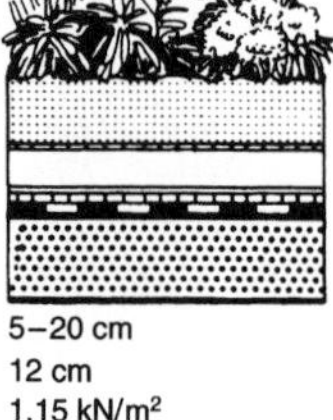

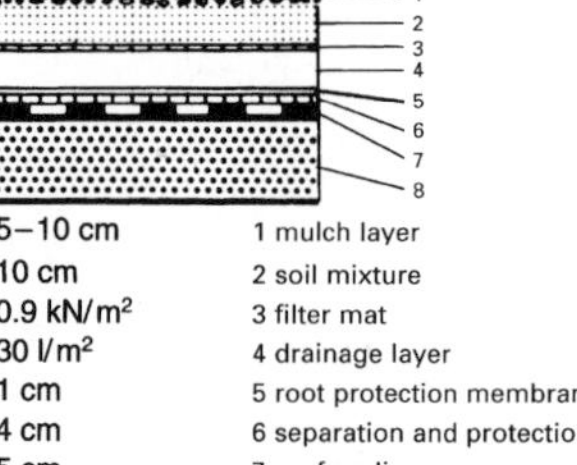

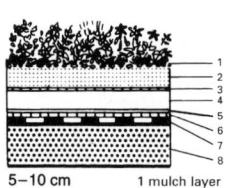

growth height > 250 cm	up to 250 cm	5–25 cm	5–20 cm	5–20 cm	5–10 cm
build-up height fm 35 cm	19–35 cm	14 cm	12 cm	12 cm	10 cm
surface loading 3.7 kN/m²	1.9–3.7 kN/m²	1.4 kN/m²	1.1 kN/m²	1.15 kN/m²	0.9 kN/m²
water supply 170 l/m²	80–170 l/m²	60 l/m²	45 l/m²	40 l/m²	30 l/m²
mulch layer – cm	– cm	– cm	1 cm	– cm	1 cm
soil mixture 23 cm	7–23 cm	5 cm	4 cm	7 cm	4 cm
drainage layer 12 cm	12 cm	9 cm	7 cm	5 cm	5 cm
watering, by hand or automatic	by hand or automatic	by hand or automatic	by hand	by hand	by hand

1 mulch layer
2 soil mixture
3 filter mat
4 drainage layer
5 root protection membrane
6 separation and protection layers
7 roof sealing
8 supporting construction

❼ Various types of roof greening

Planted roof: construction layers

Growing layer: expanded clay and expanded slate are used. These offer structural stability, soil ventilation, water storage and soil modelling. Functions: nutrient storage, soil reaction (pH value), ventilation, water storage.

Filter layer: consisting of filter material, it hinders silting in the drainage layer.

Drainage layer: prevents the plants from becoming waterlogged. Material: woven mats, plastic boards, protective building materials.

Protection layer: protects during the building phase and against point loading.

Root protection layer: the roots are retained in PVC/ECB and EPDM sheeting.

Separation layer: separates the load-bearing construction from the roof greening.

Examples →❶ – ❽ show common layer structures for roof greening. Before planting, check that the roof is in perfect condition and that each layer can fulfil its function. Carefully inspect the technical condition of the roof surface. Pitched roofs can also be greened → ❾ – ⓬, but this demands yet more extensive constructional preparations to prevent slippage and soil drying out.

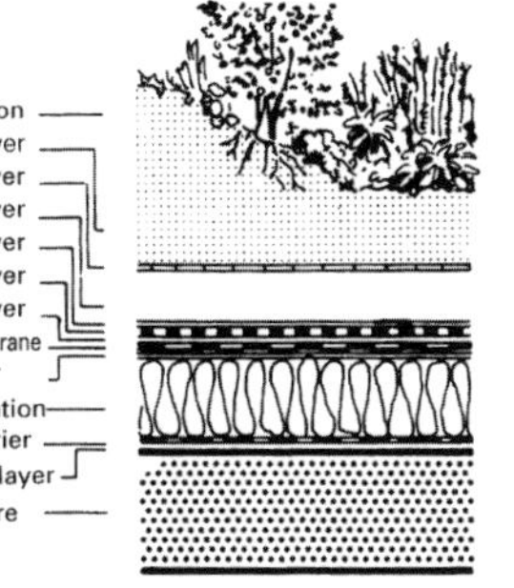

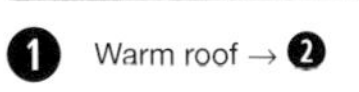
❶ Warm roof → ❷

❷ Warm roof with greening

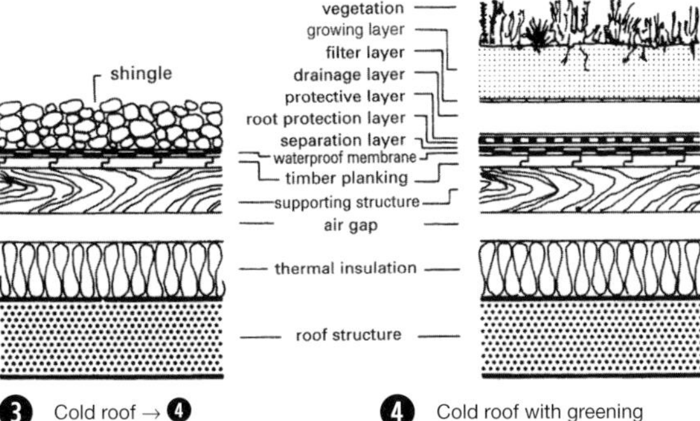

❸ Cold roof → ❹

❹ Cold roof with greening

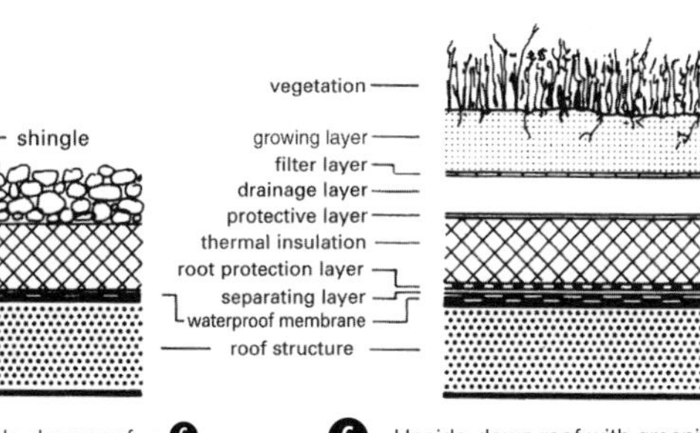

❺ Upside-down roof → ❻

❻ Upside-down roof with greening

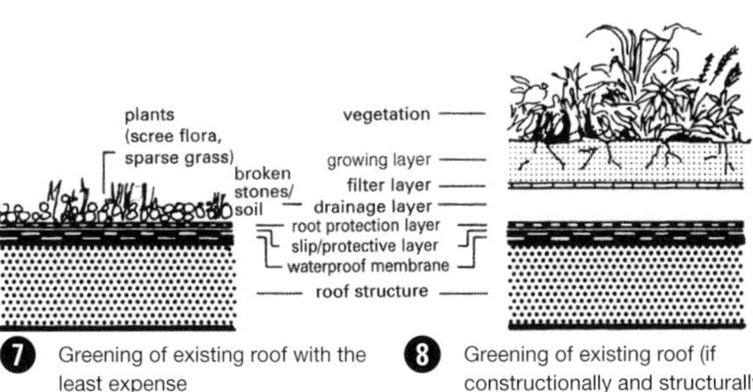

❼ Greening of existing roof with the least expense

❽ Greening of existing roof (if constructionally and structurally possible)

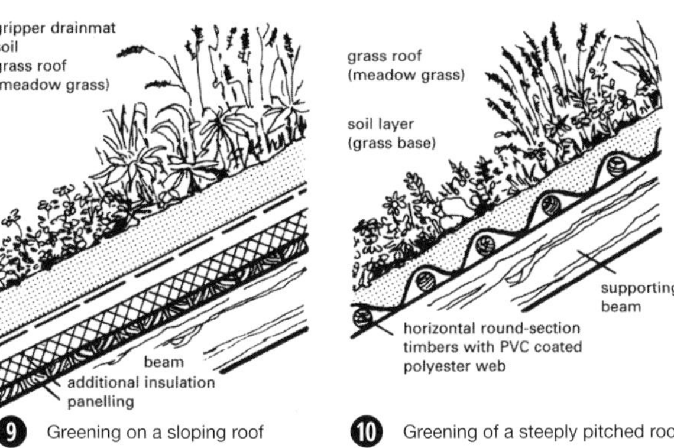

❾ Greening on a sloping roof

❿ Greening of a steeply pitched roof

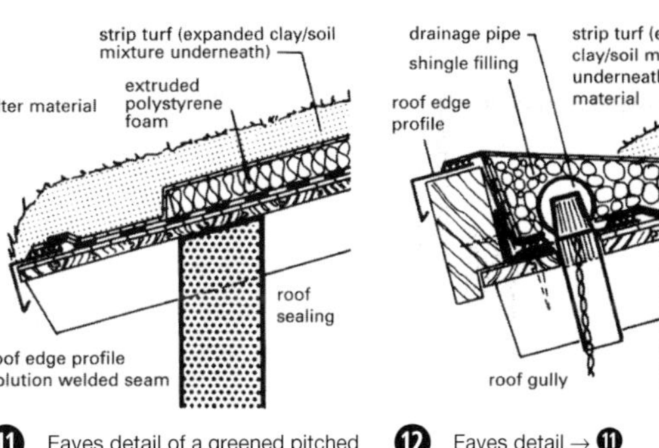

⓫ Eaves detail of a greened pitched roof

⓬ Eaves detail → ⓫

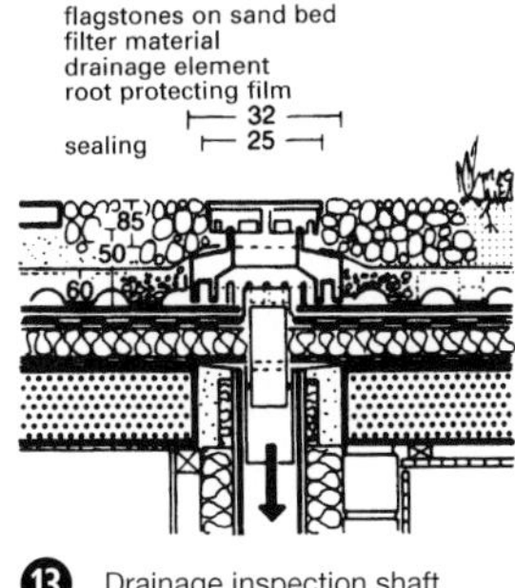

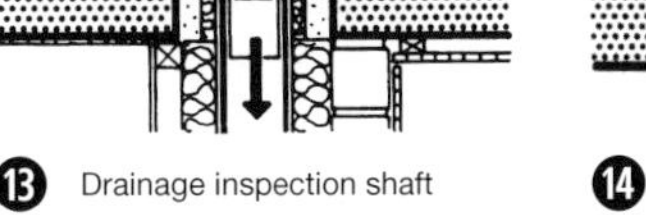
⓭ Drainage inspection shaft

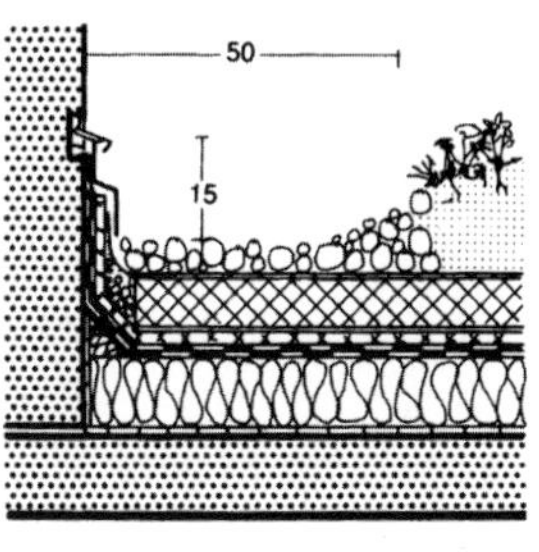

⓮ Wall connection with shingle safety strip

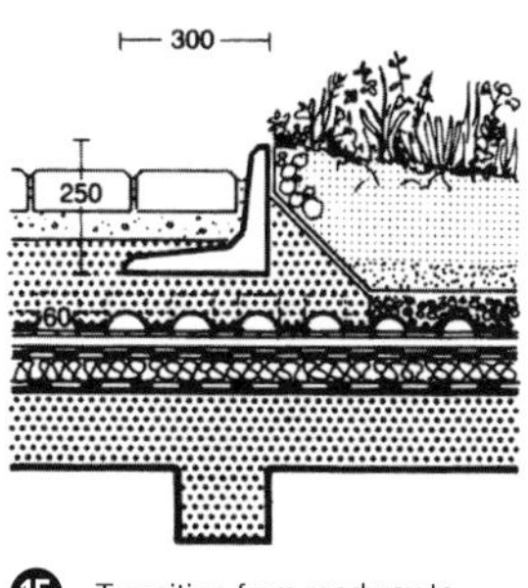

⓯ Transition from roadway to intensive roof greening

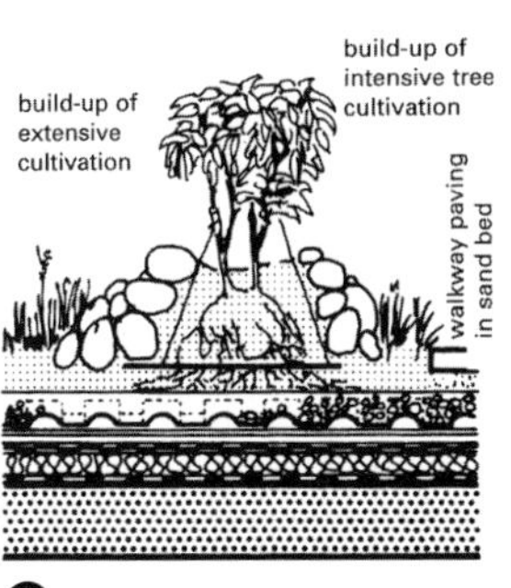

⓰ Transition from pathway to intensive or extensive roof greening

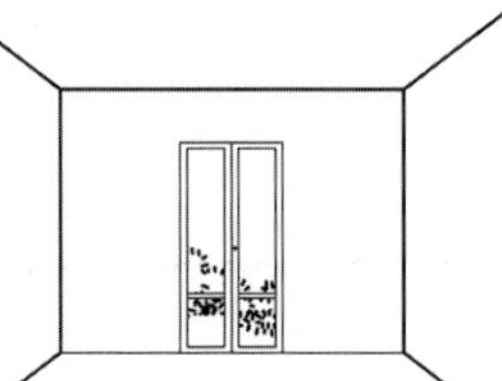

1 Vertical window, floor-level underfloor heating or radiators at the side

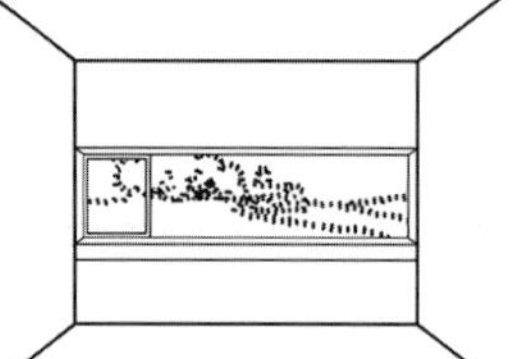

2 Horizontal window with single opening light at the side, enclosed window sill for heating/media duct

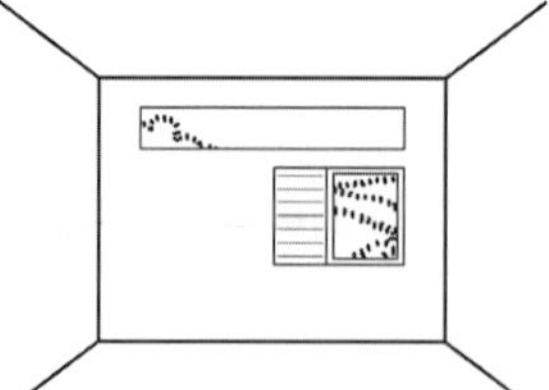

3 Window composition: upper window brings light deep into the room, small window provides view out and ventilation

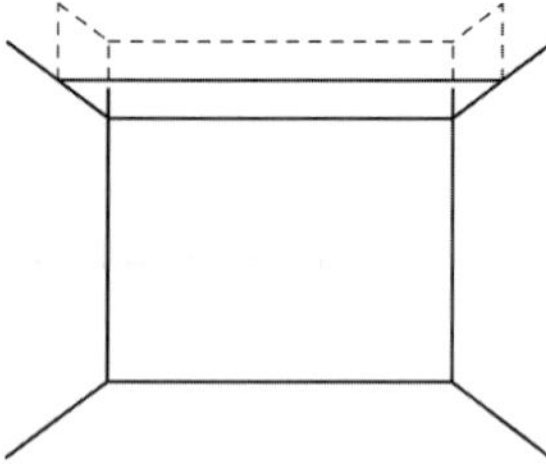

4 Rooflight for scattered light on a wall

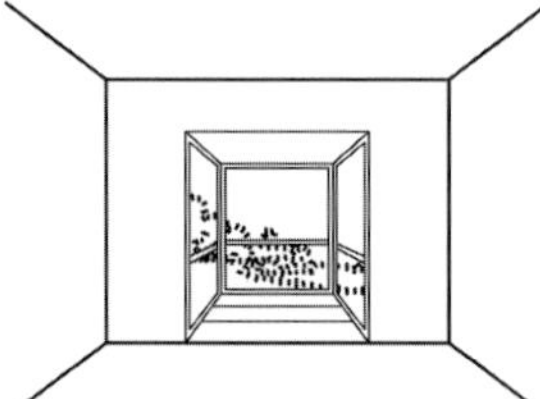

5 Bay window, plastic projection

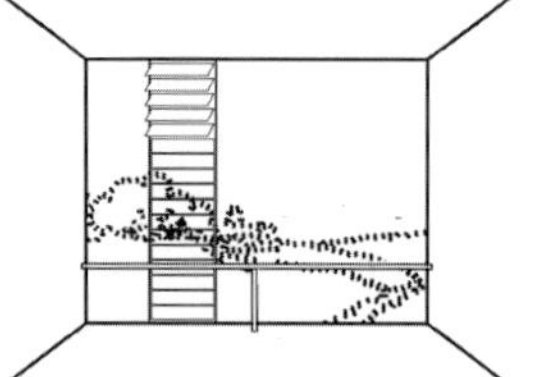

6 Full-length fixed glazing with parapet handrail and ventilation flaps with sound insulation boxes

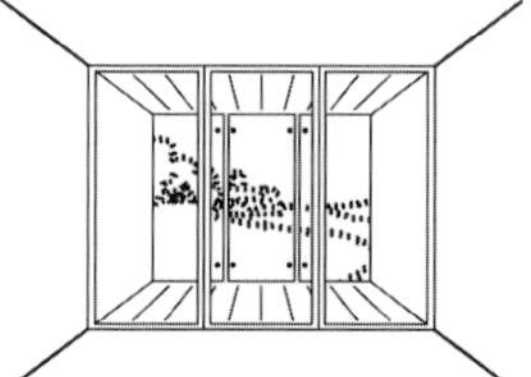

7 Double glazing with accessible space between (façade as second skin; conservatory glazing)

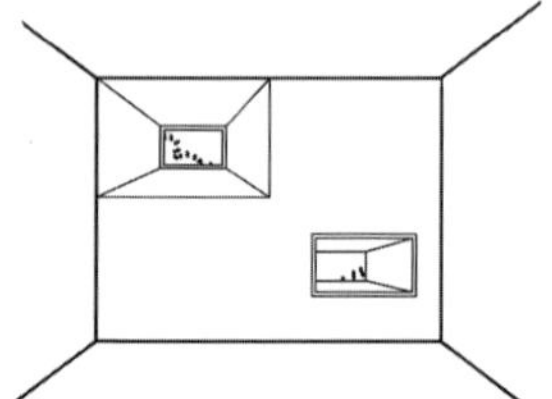

8 Plastically modulated wall with window flush with outer or inner face

ELEVATION

9 A scenic view and projecting building elements

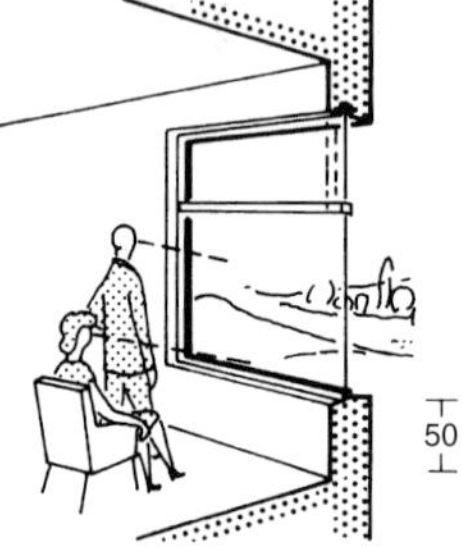

10 Room with a view

11 Normal window height (table height)

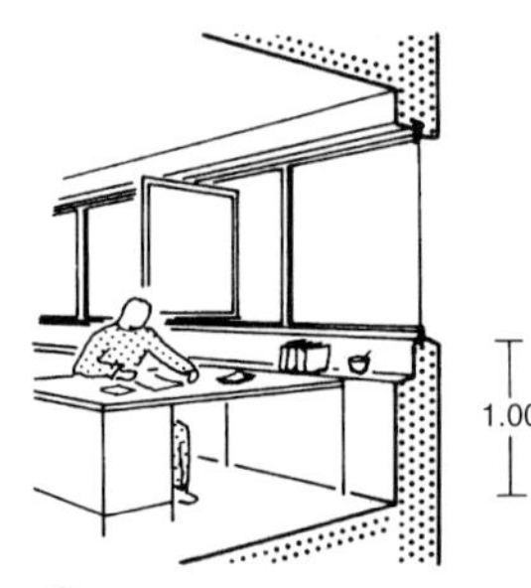

12 Office

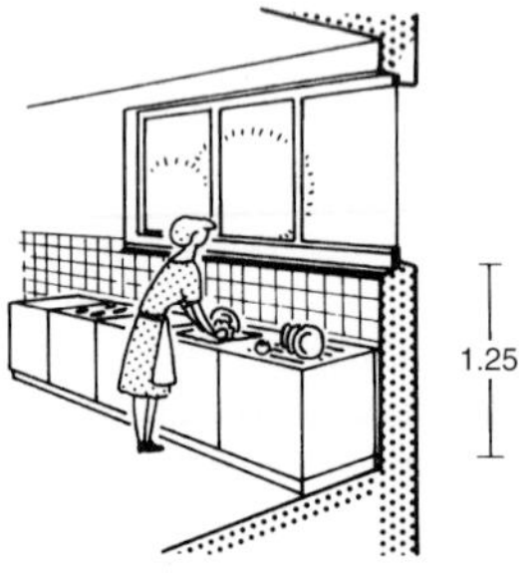

13 Kitchen

14 Office (filing cabinet)

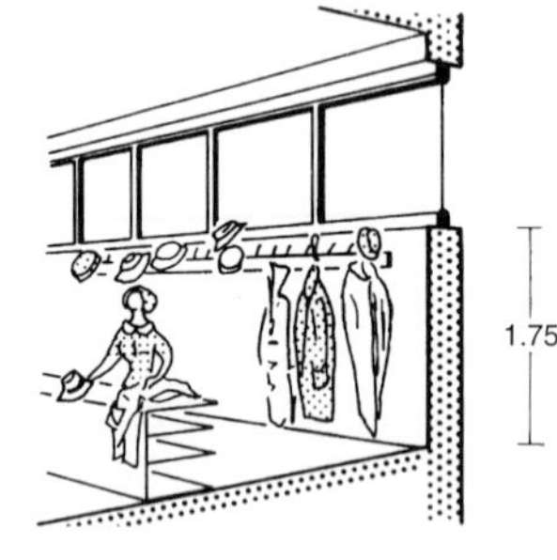

15 Coat rack

16 Rooflight, e.g. drawing office

VISUAL PROTECTION

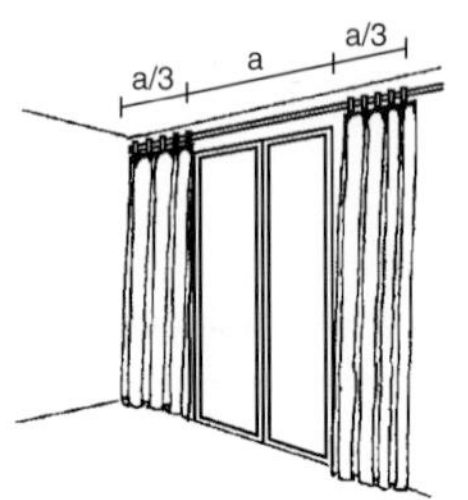

17 Sufficient space in the corners for curtains

18 Vertically hung panel blinds

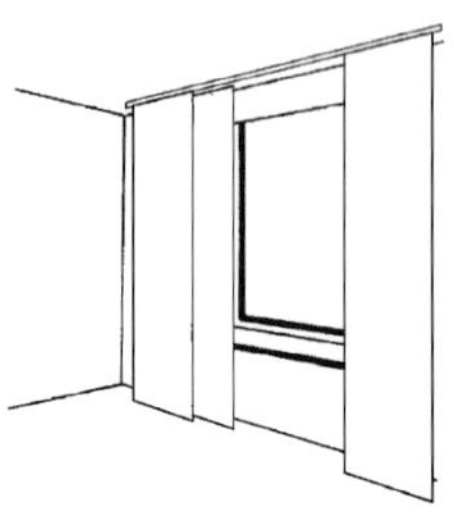

19 Sliding cloth panels

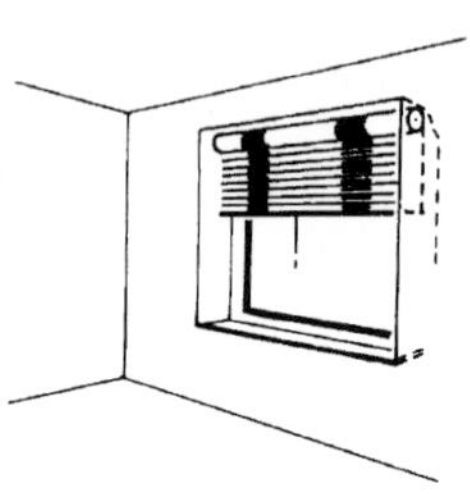

20 Venetian blinds of cloth or plastic (darken the interior)

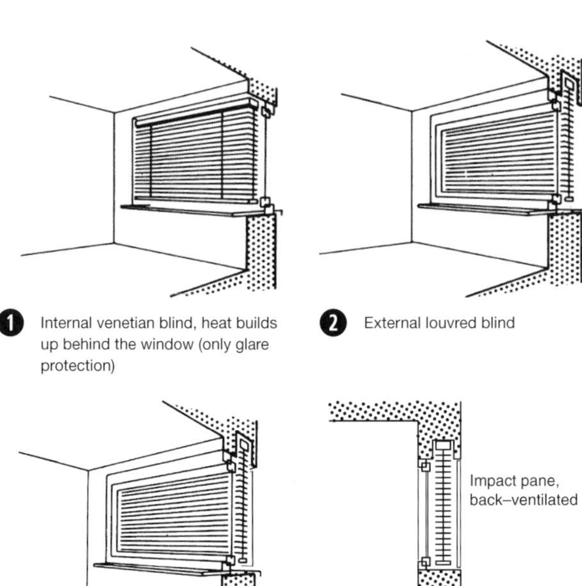

❶ Internal venetian blind, heat builds up behind the window (only glare protection)

❷ External louvred blind

❸ External louvred blind with impact pane (shields external sun protection)

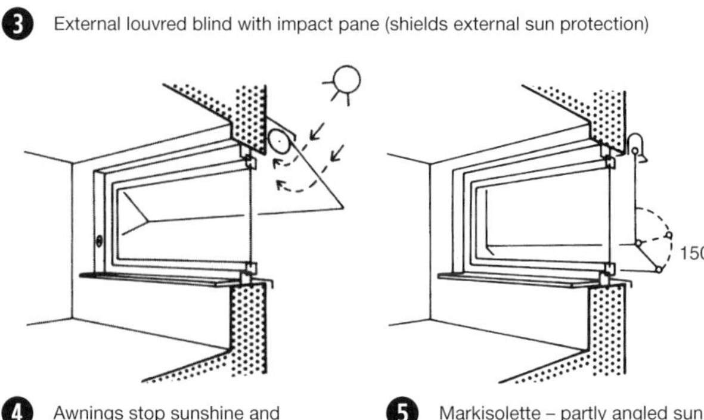

❹ Awnings stop sunshine and warmth. Distance from wall prevents heat build-up

❺ Markisolette – partly angled sun blind

WINDOW SIZES

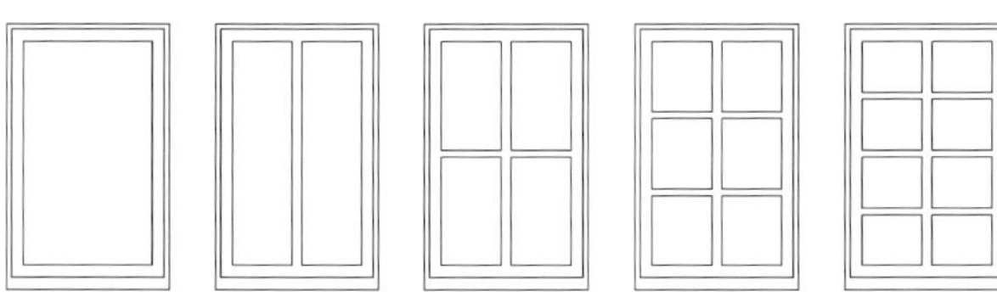

For a 1.5 m wall opening, 1 m² glass area remains = 66%	For a 1.5 m wall opening, 0.92 m² glass area remains = 61%	For a 1.5 m wall opening, 0.89 m² glass opening remains = 59%	For a 1.5 m wall opening, 0.87 m² glass area remains = 58%	For a 1.5 m wall opening, 0.84 m² glass area remains = 56%

❻ Example of reduction in glass area with glazing bars

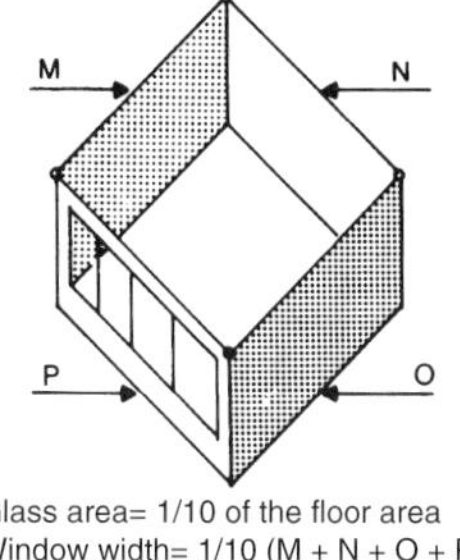

❼ Window sizes in industrial building

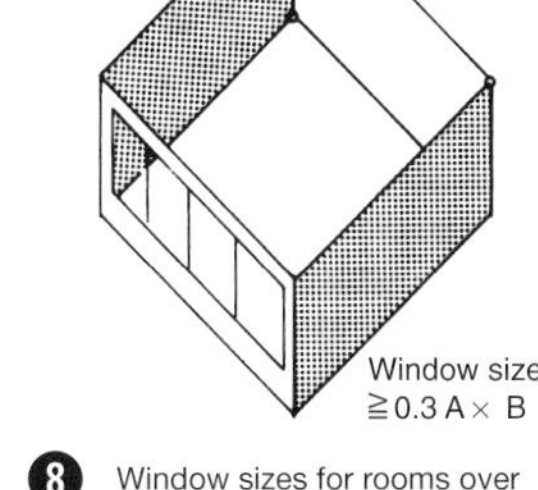

❽ Window sizes for rooms over 3.5 m high

The window, as an element built into the wall, has essential functions apart from just closing the opening. It controls the level of natural lighting, the supply and extraction of air to and from the room, and the view out for connection with the world. These functions can also be fulfilled by separate elements: overhead lights, ventilation flaps and shop windows, respectively.

The size and location of windows in rooms, in addition to the requirements under building regulations and the rules for daylight in interiors (see Daylight → pp. 488 ff.), are determined above all by architectural considerations. Their external impact has a decisive influence on the appearance of the façade. Important factors are: the location in the wall, with internal windows emphasising the wall depth and external windows allowing the wall to present as a surface; the proportions of width to height; the ratio of construction thickness to glass area (visible frame, casements and possibly glazing bar widths); and the relationship to other façade elements (which is often neglected when replacing windows).

In the interior, windows are responsible for light direction, which is essential for the architectural effect of a room. Most decisive is the location on plan, which may have to be supplemented by sun shading equipment or light directing glass. The type of opening determines the functional quality as a ventilation element. How far do the casements open into the room? Is the window sill still usable when the window is open? (Tilted windows are not sufficient for through ventilation! They ensure only the slow cooling of a room.) There may also be specific requirements for fire protection or for resistance against break-in or damage. Resistance classes → pp. 107, 118. If the window serves as an escape route, it must have a clear opening of at least 0.9 × 1.2 m and a sill height of max. 1.2 m above floor level.

In the Netherlands, regulations stipulate the sizes of windows in relation to the angle of incidence of the light.

Refurbishment

If windows are replaced by those with better thermal insulation, then the installation demands particular attention. There is a danger with improved windows that condensation may occur at other less well-insulated locations (window reveals, outside corners of rooms), which can lead to mould formation! In order not to impair the appearance of the façade and the entrance of light, the dimensions of the panes should not be altered (pay attention to frames, casements and glazing bar width → ❻).

Residential construction

The minimum requirement for structural window apertures in occupied rooms is specified in the state building regulations and is 1/8 or 1/10 of the plan area of the room. Further design constraints are the distance from buildings opposite (shadow formation) and the requirements of the energy saving regulation EnEV. In order to optimise the energy balance, the criteria for workrooms can be applied.

Workrooms

The required window area can be roughly worked out using the following rules. The total width of all visual connections to the outside must be at least 1/10 of the total width of all walls, according to workplace guidelines → ❼. Possible visual connection to the outside should be at eye level (window sill heights of 0.85 –1.25 m) → p. 96 ❾ – ⓰. For workrooms more than 3.5 m high, the glass area of the window must be at least 30% of the outside wall area → ❽. For rooms with dimensions corresponding to those of residential rooms, the minimum height of the glass area is 1.3 m.

With the increasing use of existing sources of energy, the optimisation of thermal losses and gains and the control of light through windows merit a separate design prepared by experts.

Building components

WINDOWS
Arrangement
Requirements
Design types
Thermal insulation
Sound insulation
Cleaning buildings
Roof windows
Rooflights

see also: Daylight pp. 488 ff. (Directing sunlight p. 499, Sun shading p. 500)

OPENING TYPES

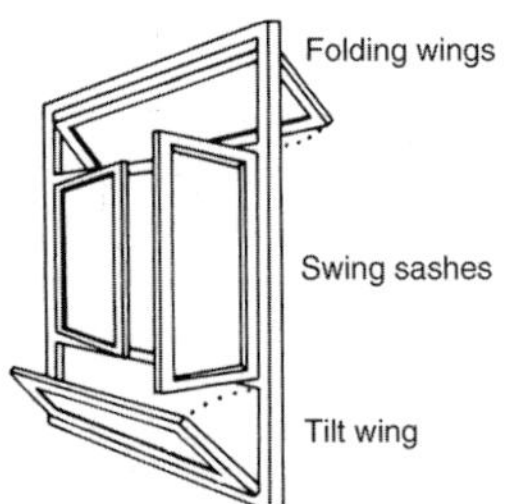

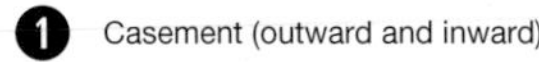

1 Casement (outward and inward)

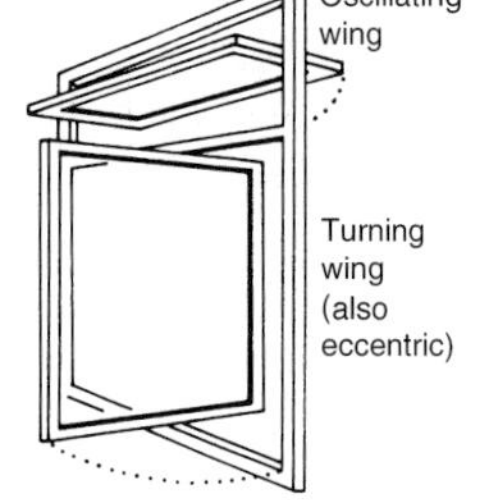

2 Centre pivot-hung casement

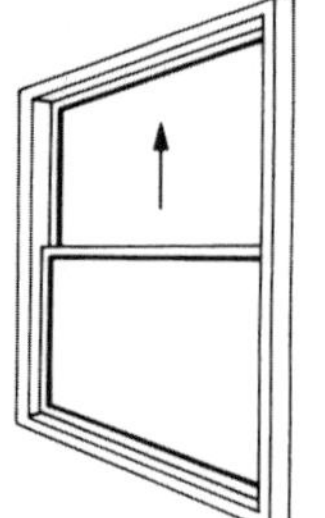

3 Vertically sliding window

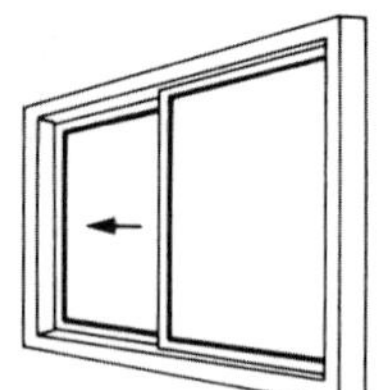

4 Sliding window

REBATE TYPES

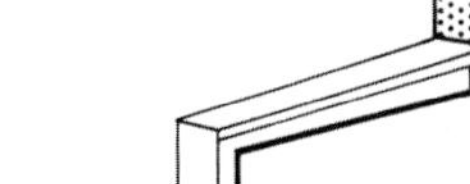

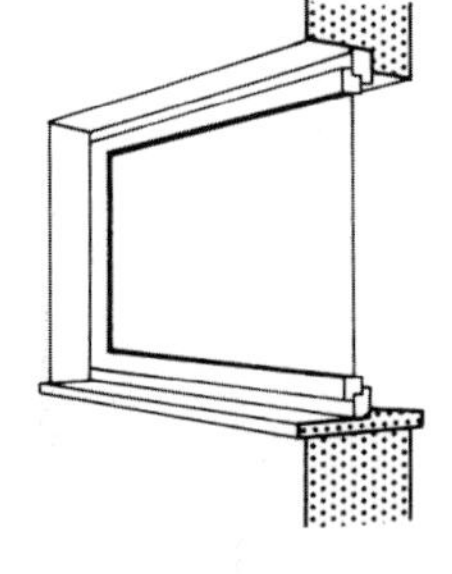

5 Opening inward with frame behind recessed jamb

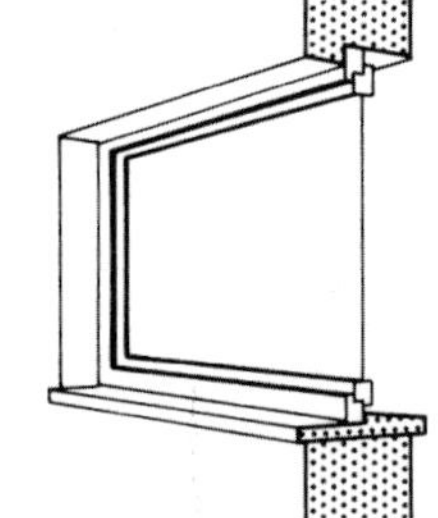

6 Opening outward with frame behind recessed jamb

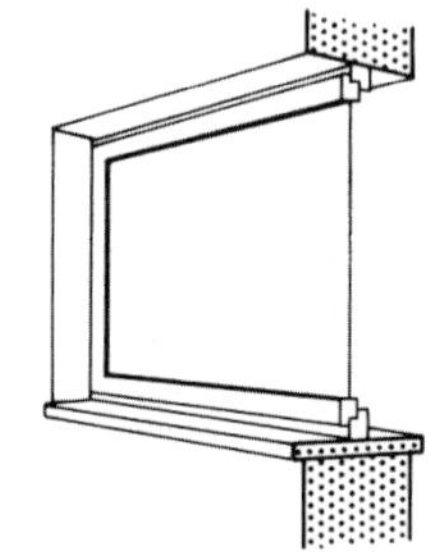

7 Plain jamb with rebated frame

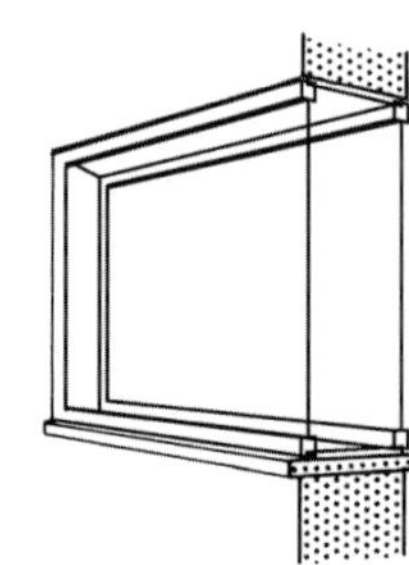

8 Plain jamb with wrap-around window frame

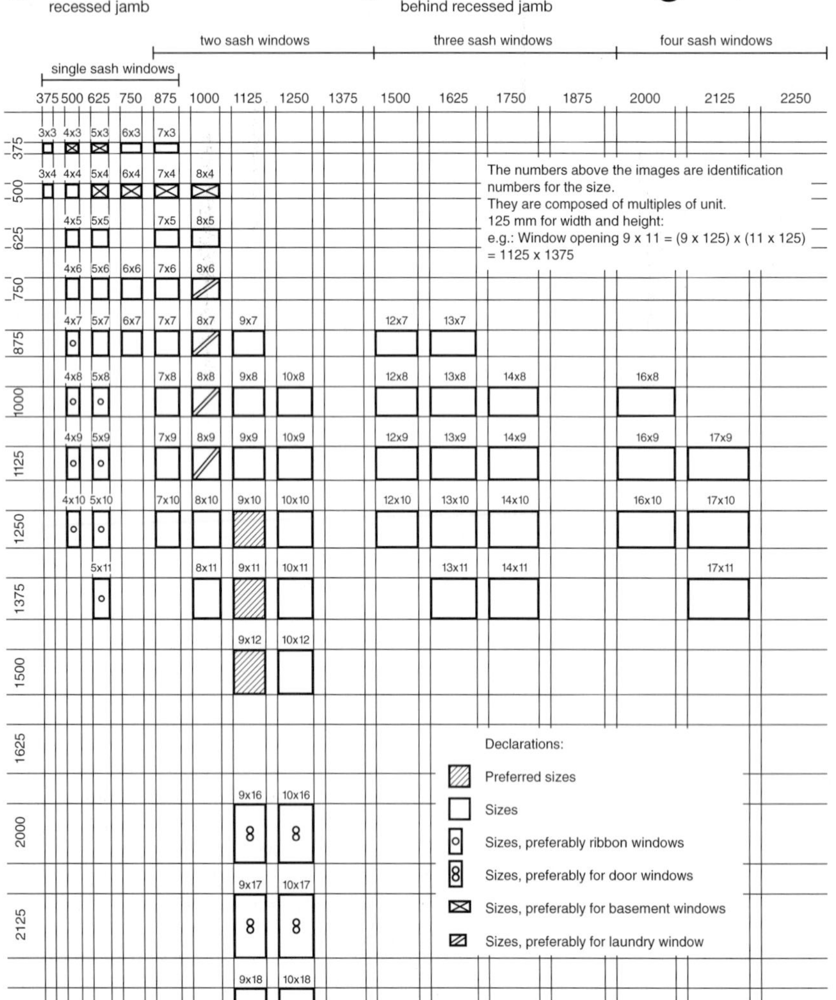

9 Guideline sizes for structural window openings

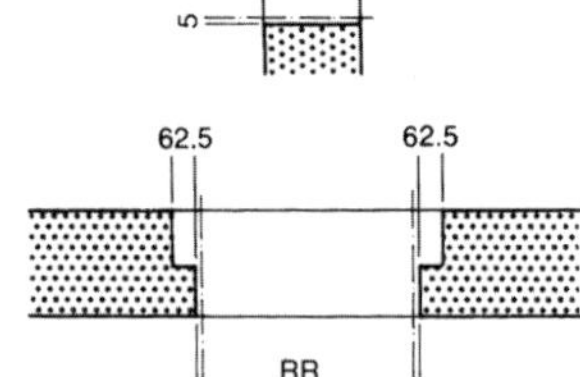

10 Meeting type 1 (rebated inward opening). RR = structure

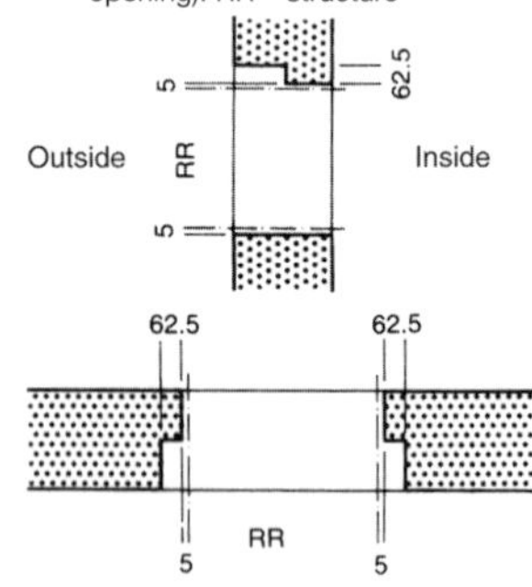

11 Meeting type 2 (rebated outward opening)

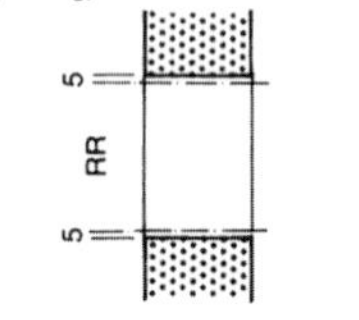

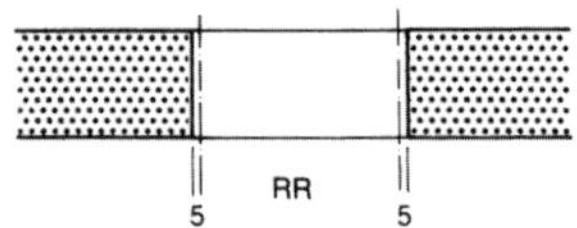

12 Meeting type 3 (no rebate)

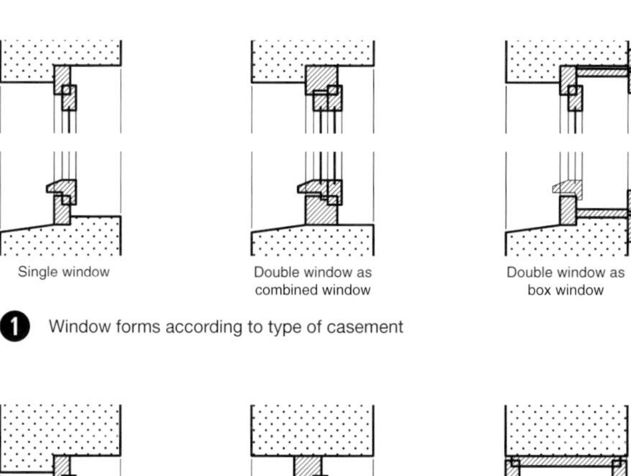
Single window — Double window as combined window — Double window as box window

❶ Window forms according to type of casement

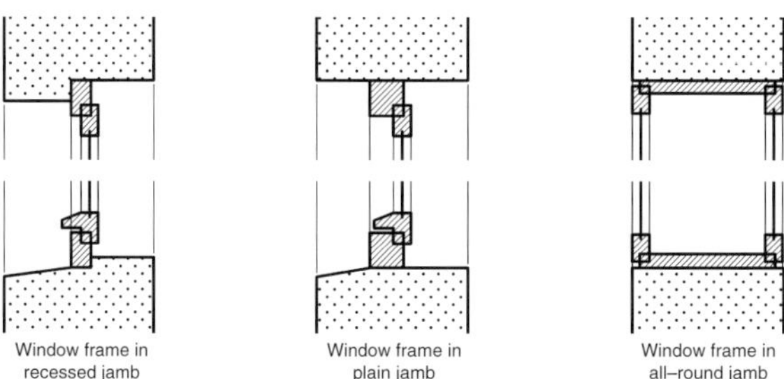
Window frame in recessed jamb — Window frame in plain jamb — Window frame in all–round jamb

❷ Window forms according to type of frame (left: outside, right: inside)

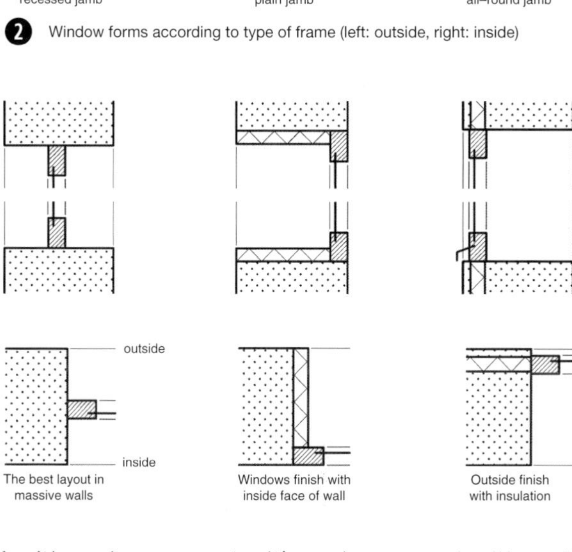

The best layout in massive walls — Windows finish with inside face of wall — Outside finish with insulation

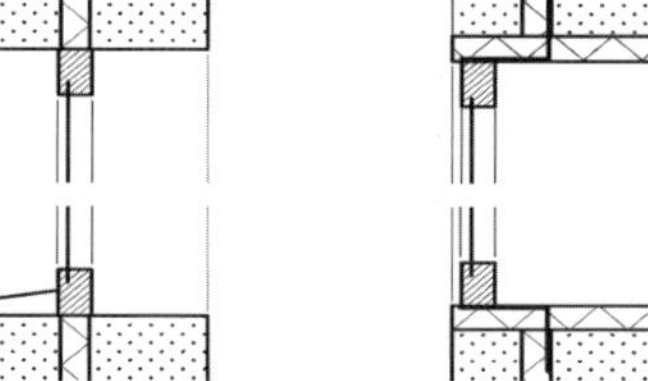
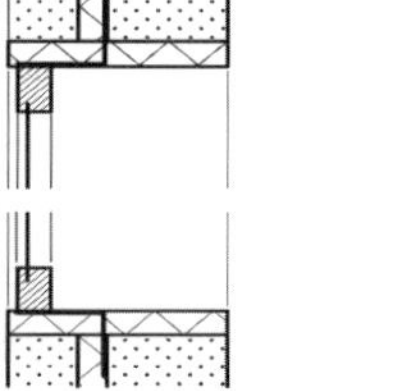
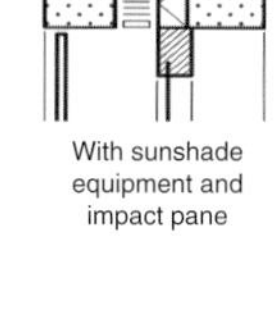
With sunshade equipment and impact pane

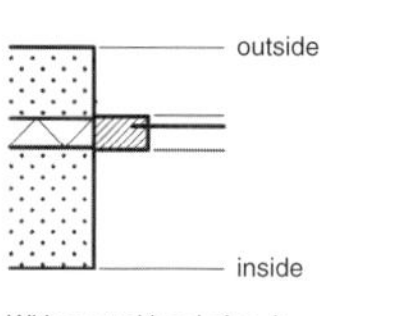

With central insulation, in the plane of the insulation

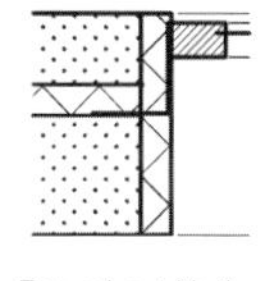
External, outside the plane of insulation with surrounding frame fixed to load–bearing wall

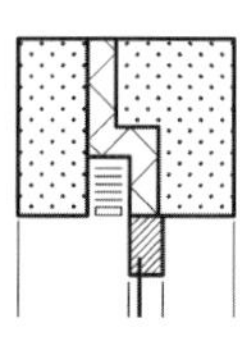
With sun protection equipment in the outer leaf

❸ Location of window in the wall (left: outside, right: inside)

Row	No. full storeys in building	Joint permeability class
1	up to 2	2
2	more than 2	3

❹ Joint permeability classes in external windows, French windows and roof windows

Various forms of window according to type of casement → ❶ and type of frame → ❷ are shown opposite. The stringent requirements for windows (thermal and sound insulation) result in a multitude of window types and constructions. The location of the window in the wall is a significant design feature of the façade. The arrangement of the insulation and any sun protection are also important → ❸. An impact pane (external, no closing function) serves, like double façade systems, as wind protection for the sun protection system and enables natural ventilation in strong wind and rain. A staggered layout of window and insulation planes should be avoided if possible, because it leads to expensive and defect-prone insulation and weatherproofing construction. The permissible dimensional tolerances for window and door openings up to 3 m long are max. 12 mm and, for elements up to 6 m, max. 16 mm.

External windows and French windows of heated rooms must be constructed with at least insulating or double glazing. The thermal transmittance (U-value) of windows in new buildings must, according to EnEV 2009, be determined together with a survey of the whole building. Solar gains are included in the calculation → p. 474 ff. For new installations, replacement and renewal in existing buildings, the values according to → ❺ are to be observed. In addition, windows, French windows and roof windows have to comply with requirements for airtightness and minimum air change → ❹.

Row	Building element	Residential buildings and zones of non-residential buildings with interior temperatures >19°C	Zones of non-residential buildings with interior temperatures 12–19°C
		Highest value of thermal transmittance U_{max}[1] in $W/(m^2 \times K)$	
2a	external windows, French windows	1.30 [2]	1.90 [2]
2b	roof windows	1.40 [2]	1.90 [2]
2c	glazing	1.10 [3]	no req'ment
2d	curtain walls	1.40 [4]	1.90 [4]
2e	curtain walls	1.90 [4]	no req'ment
2f	glass roofs	2.00 [3]	2.70 [3]
3a	external windows, French windows, roof windows with special glazing	2.00 [2]	2.80 [2]
3b	special glazing	1.60 [3]	no req'ment
3c	curtain walls with special glazing	2.3 [4]	3.0 [4]

[1] Thermal transmittance of the building element, taking into account the new and existing building layers.
[2] Design value of the thermal transmittance of the window; this is to be taken from the technical product specification or according to the known energy characteristics of the product according to building regulations. This applies particularly to energy characteristics from European technical approvals and from the regulations according to the building rules and based on decisions contained in general approvals under the building regulations.
[3] As [2] but regarding the glazing.
[4] Thermal transmittance of the curtain walling; this is to be determined in accordance with the generally recognised data relating to the technology.

❺ The maximum values approach for single building elements is applicable only to new buildings, and replacement or renewal in existing buildings, EnEV 2009

EnEV 2009

see also: Glass pp. 107 ff., Building physics pp. 471 ff., Daylight pp. 488 ff.

BS EN ISO 140
BS 8233
BS EN ISO 15186
DIN 4109

see also: Glass p. 107

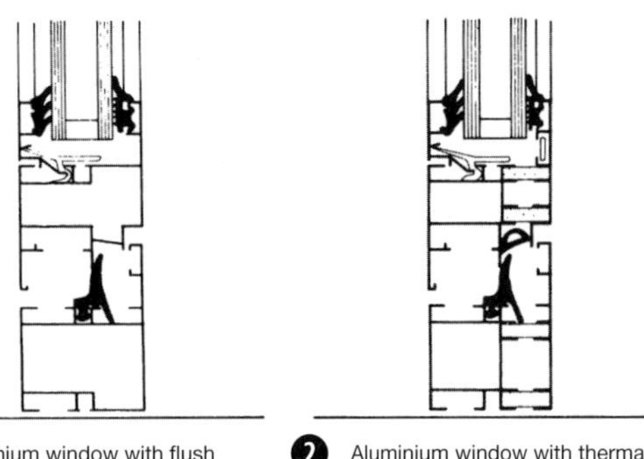

❶ Aluminium window with flush casements

❷ Aluminium window with thermally separated profiles, up to 37 dB

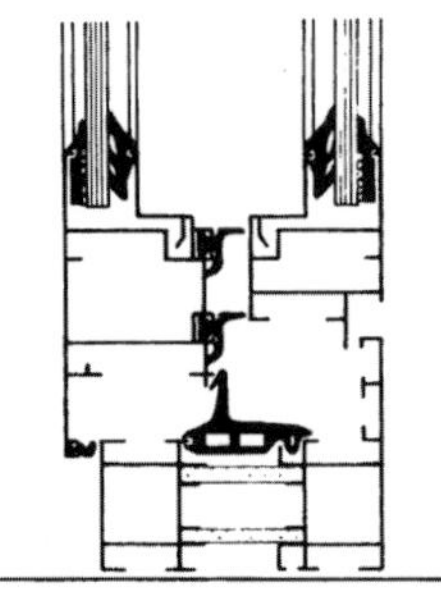

❸ Universal aluminium window, sun protection possible between panes, up to 47 dB

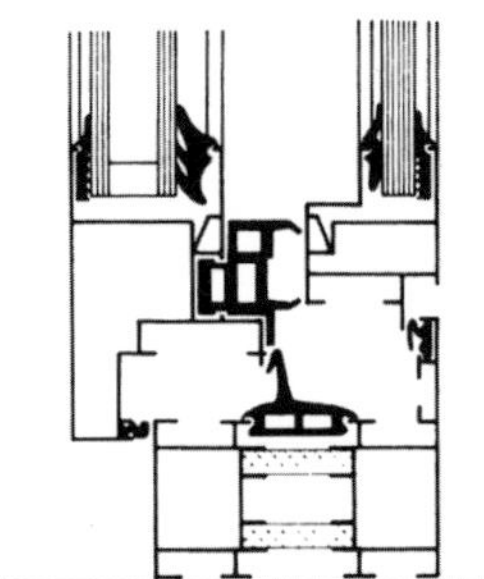

❹ Aluminium combined window, thermally insulated, up to 47 dB

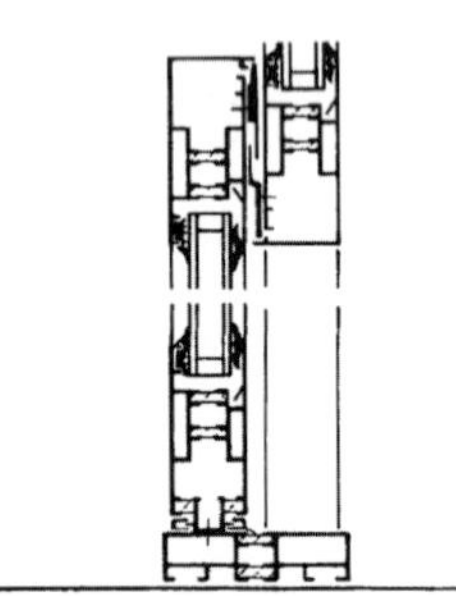

❺ Aluminium sliding window, thermally insulated, up to 35 dB

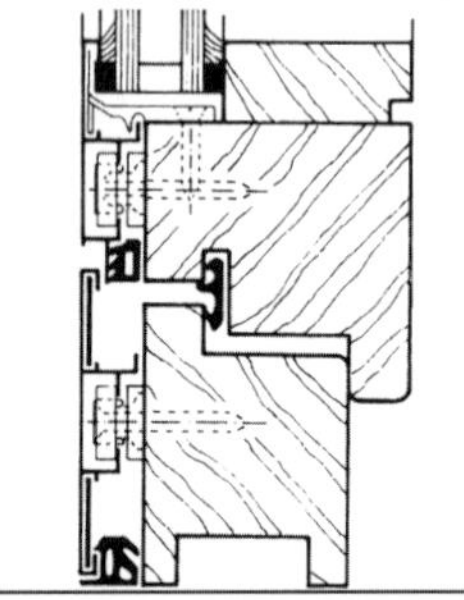

❻ Aluminium/wood window with composite construction, up to 40 dB

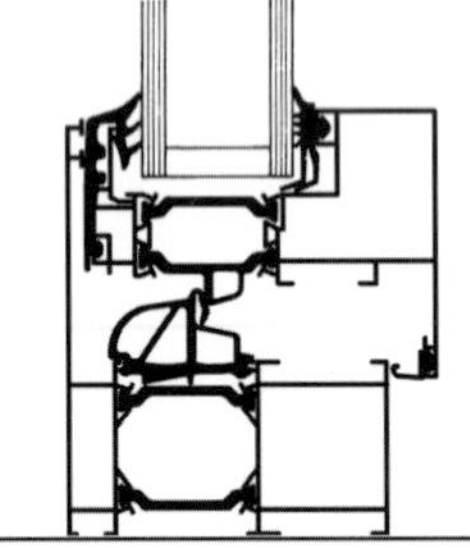

❼ Aluminium window with thermally separated profiles; narrow casement is covered by frame, up to 40 dB

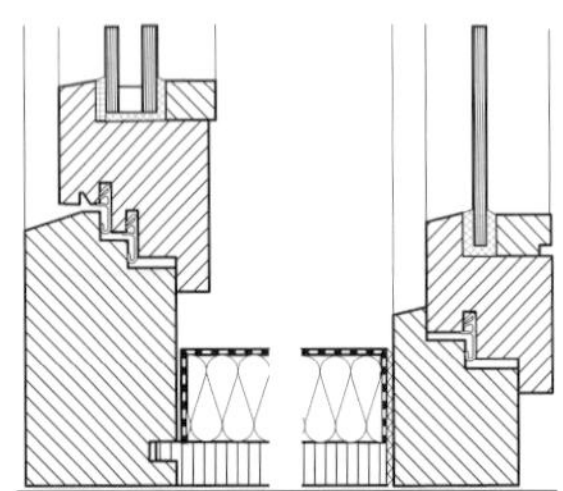

❽ Wooden box-type window with sound-absorbing surround, up to 45 dB

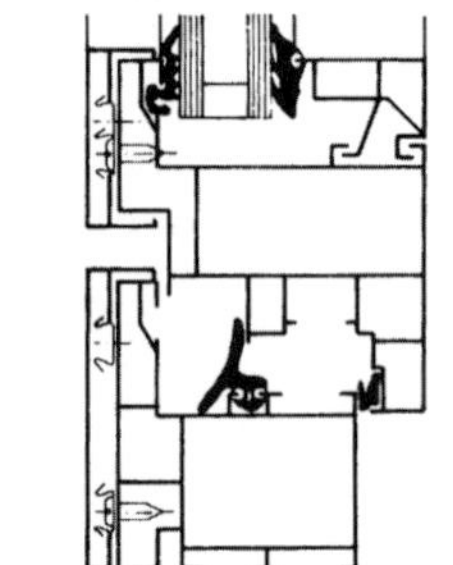

❾ Plastic window with aluminium frame facing, up to 42 dB

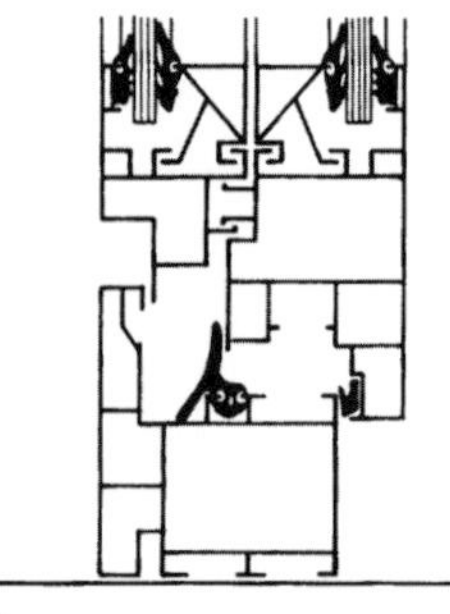

❿ Plastic combined window, sun protection possible between panes, up to 45 dB

In order to improve the sound insulation of windows, a number of glass layers are installed behind each other. To reduce the reciprocal effect of resonance, different glass thicknesses are combined (e.g. 4/8 mm; 6/12 mm). The greater the distance between the panes, the better is the sound insulation. Further improvements can be gained from the separation of the frame and the sound-absorbing construction of the resulting wrap-around window surround. Box-type windows, even with only single glazing, have better sound insulation values than double-glazed windows.

If the requirements for sound insulation are very high, then suitably sound-insulated ventilation equipment must also be provided, because the sound insulation is only effective with the windows closed.

Road type	Distance from window to centre of road (m)	Traffic load in daytime, both directions (vehicles/h)	Noise level range
residential road		<10	0
residential road	<35		0
(2-lane)	26–35	10–50	I
	≦10		III
residential feeder road	>100		0
	36–100		I
(2-lane)	26–35	50–200	II
	11–25		III
	≦10		IV
rural road	101–300		
in village[1)]	101–300		I
(2-lane)	36–100		II
residential feeder road	11–35	200–1000	III
	≦10		IV
(2-lane)			
urban road	101–300		III
main road	36–100	1000–3000	IV
industrial areas	>35		V
4- to 6-lane main roads	101–300		IV
motorway slip roads and motorways	≦100	3000–5000	V

[1)] Outside built-up areas and for roads in industrial and commercial areas, the next noise level range applies

⓫ How loud is it?

relevant noise level range	average outdoor noise level (dB)	necessary window sound insulation value R_W (dB) in occupied rooms of dwellings [1)]
0	≦50	25 (30)
I	51–55	25 (30)
II	56–60	30 (35)
III	61–65	35 (40)
IV	66–70	40 (45)
V	>70	45 (50)

[1)] Values in brackets apply for external walls and must also be used for windows if they comprise more than 60% of external wall area.

⓬ Selection of the correct sound insulation

Sound insulation class	Sound insulation value (dB)	Orientation notes on construction features of windows and ventilation systems
6	50	box-type window with separated frames in reveals and special sealing, wide spacing of panes and thick glazing
5	45–49	box-type window with special sealing, wide spacing of panes and thick glazing; combined window with decoupled casement frames, special sealing, spacing of panes over about 100 mm and thick glazing
4	40–44	box-type windows with additional sealing and centre-seal glazing; combined window with special sealing, spacing of panes over about 60 mm and thick glazing
3	35–39	box-type window without additional sealing and with centre-seal glass; combined window with additional sealing, normal spacing of panes and thick glazing; double-glazed unit in heavy multi-pane construction; 12 mm glass, non-opening or in sealed window.
2	30–34	combined window with additional sealing and centre-seal glazing; thick double-glazed unit, non-opening or in sealed window; 6 mm glass, non-opening or in sealed window
1	25–29	combined window with additional sealing and centre-seal glazing; thin double-glazed unit in window with additional sealing
0	20–24	unsealed single- or double-glazed window

⓭ Sound insulation classes of windows (excerpt from VDI guideline 2719)

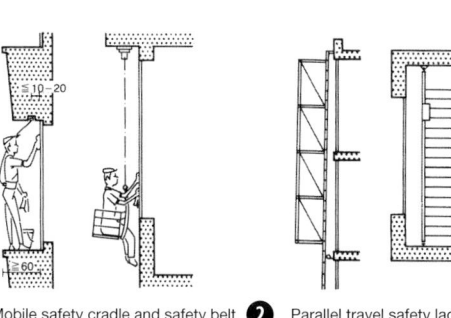

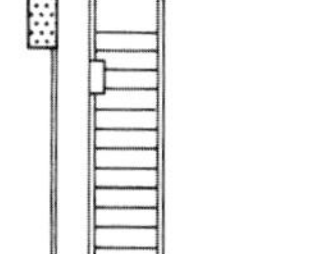

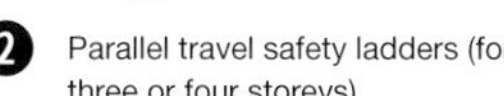

❶ Mobile safety cradle and safety belt

❷ Parallel travel safety ladders (for three or four storeys)

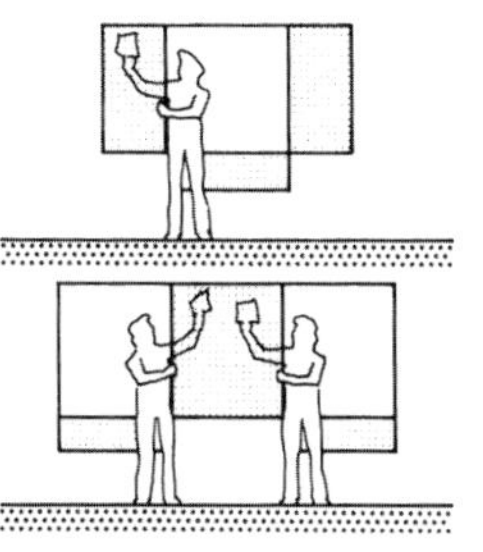

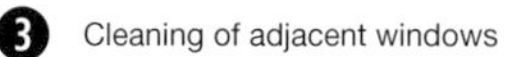

❸ Cleaning of adjacent windows

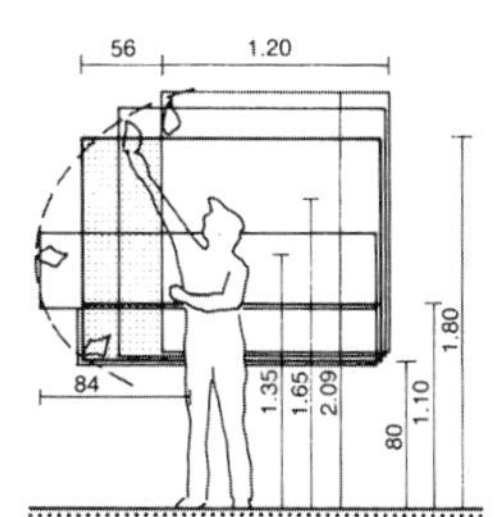

❹ Shading shows acceptable cleaning surface area

Façade hoists and mobile equipment

Safety belts with straps, safety cables or safety equipment for working at height should be used as a protection against falls → ❶

Façade hoists and mobile equipment (allowing access to fixed glazing) for cleaning windows and façades → ❽ – ⓫ are available to carry out maintenance and repair work (thus saving the cost of scaffolding). If fitted at the right time, they can also be used to carry out minor building work (such as fixing blinds, installing windows etc.). With slight modifications, façade hoists and access equipment can be used as rescue apparatus in the event of a fire. The options available include mobile suspended ladders mounted on rails, trackless roof gantry equipment with a cradle, and a rail-mounted roof gantry with a cradle and attached to the roof deck or the balustrade, with curves and points.

Suspended light metal ladder equipment (for façade access) → ❷ consists of a suspended mobile ladder on rails. The width of the ladder is 724 mm or 840 mm, and the total overall length is 25 m maximum, depending on the shape of the building. The maximum safe working load (S.W.L.) is 200 kg (i.e. two men and the apparatus itself). Alternatives are available, such as maintenance gangways → ❺ and cleaning balconies → ❻.

Building components

WINDOWS
Arrangement
Requirements
Opening types
Thermal protection
Noise protection
Cleaning buildings
Loft windows
Rooflights

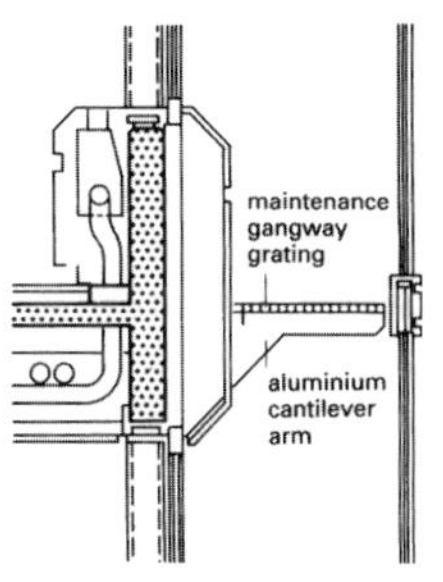

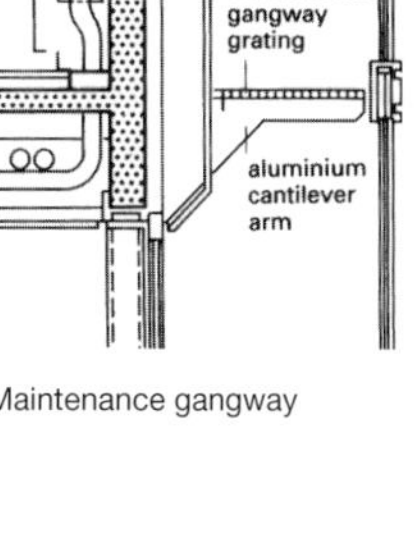

❺ Maintenance gangway

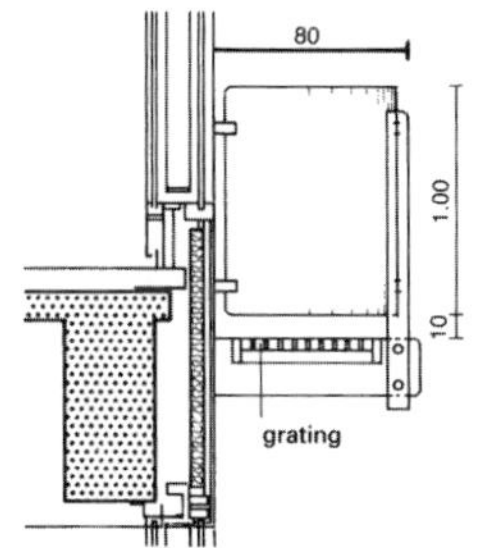

❻ Cleaning platform

Type of building	External windows	Roof windows
offices	every 3 months*	every 12 months
public offices	2 weeks	3 months
shops	outside, weekly inside, every 2 weeks	6 months
shops (high street)	outside, daily inside, every week	3 months
hospitals	3 months	6 months
schools	3–4 months	12 months
hotels (first class)	2 weeks	3 months
factories (precision work)	4 weeks	3 months
factories (heavy industry)	2 months	6 months
private houses	4–6 weeks	–

* ground floor windows must be cleaned more frequently

❼ Intervals of time for window cleaning

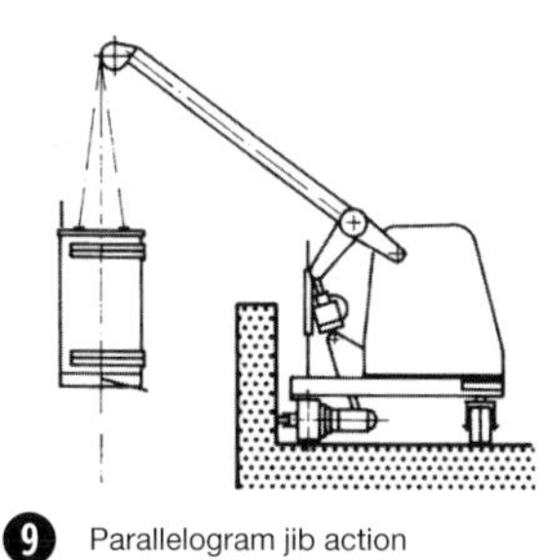

❽ One-person façade cable lift

❾ Parallelogram jib action

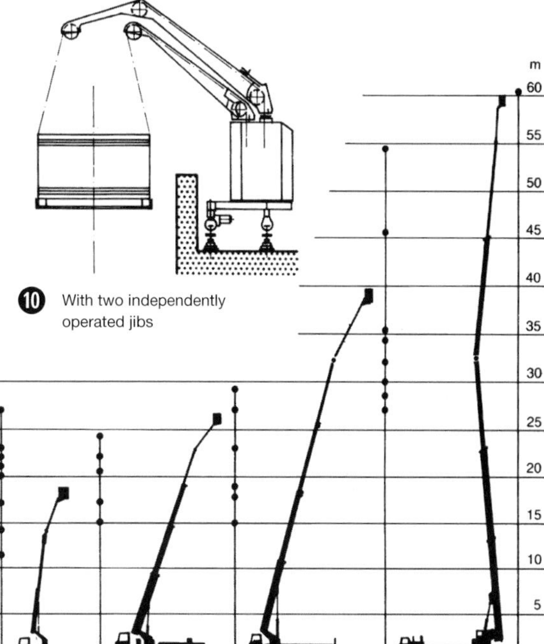

❿ With two independently operated jibs

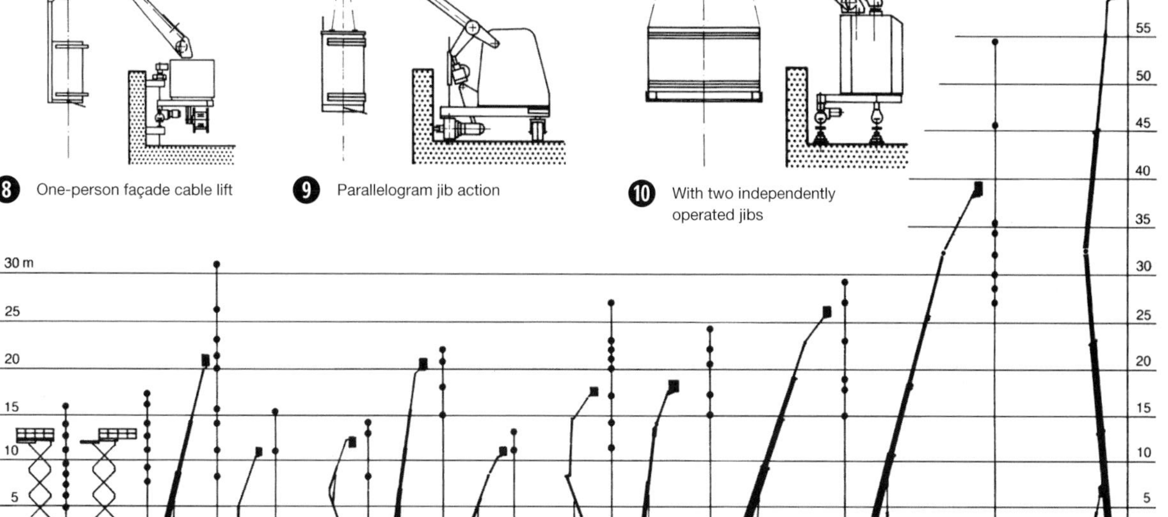

⓫ Work platform hoists

Gardemann system

see also: Dormer windows p. 85

WINDOWS

Loft Windows

The required quality of living is decisive for the determination of window size in inhabited loft spaces. Building regulations require a minimum window area of ⅛ of the floor area for living rooms → ⓫. Large windows make these rooms more comfortable. The window widths in secondary rooms can be chosen according to the distance between the rafters.

Generously wide windows in living rooms can be achieved through the installation of rafter trimmers and additional rafters. Steeper roofs need shorter windows, while flatter roofs require longer windows.

Loft windows can be joined using flashing → ❹ and can be arranged horizontally or vertically in rows or window groups.

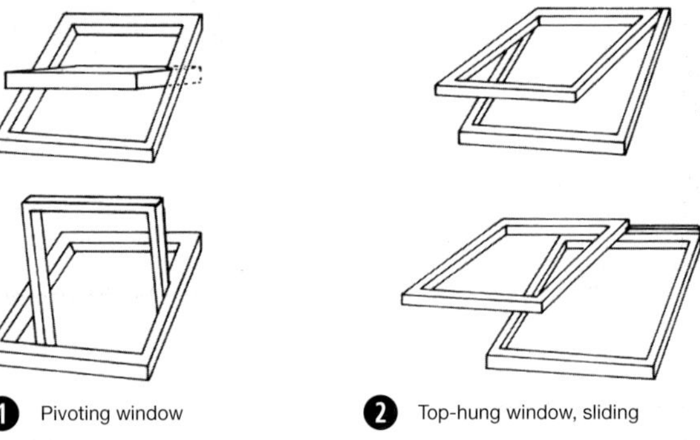

❶ Pivoting window

❷ Top-hung window, sliding

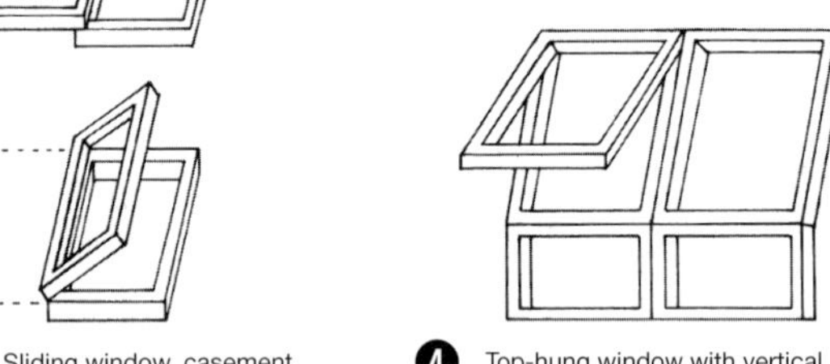

❸ Sliding window, casement door

❹ Top-hung window with vertical unit

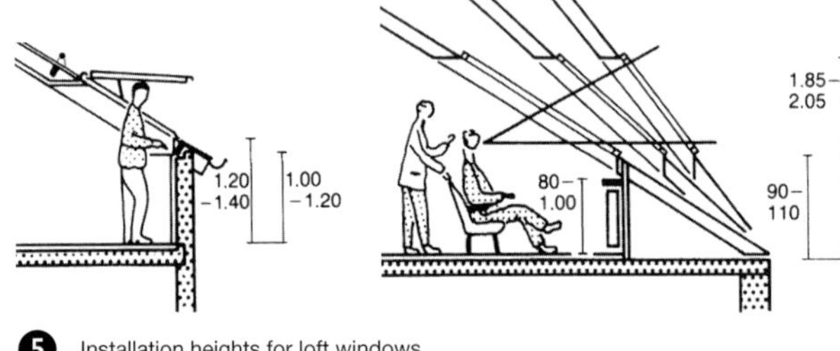

❺ Installation heights for loft windows

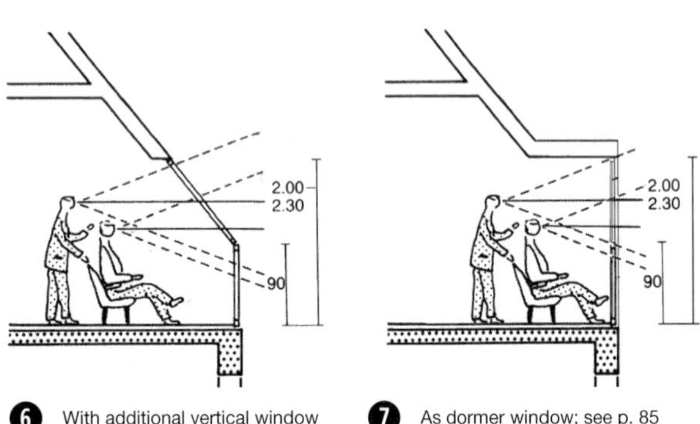

❻ With additional vertical window

❼ As dormer window; see p. 85

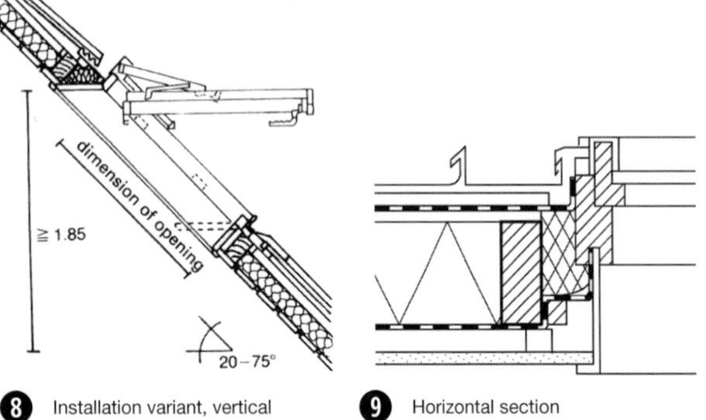

❽ Installation variant, vertical section

❾ Horizontal section

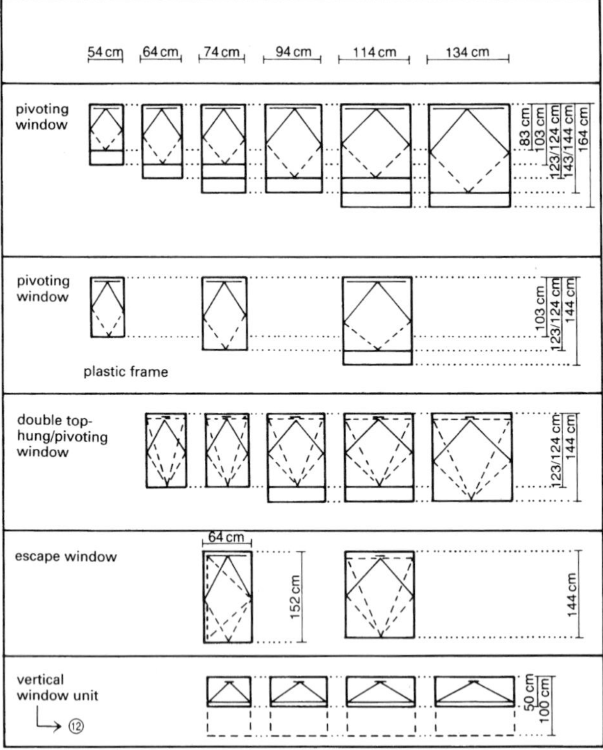

❿ Window sizes

window size	54/83	54/103	64/103	74/103	74/123	74/144	144/123	114/144	134/144
surface area of light admitted (m^2)	0.21	0.28	0.36	0.44	0.55	0.66	0.93	1.12	1.36
floor area (m^2)	2	2–3	3–4	4–5	6–7	9	11	13 m^2	

⓫ Calculation of window size, in relation to floor area

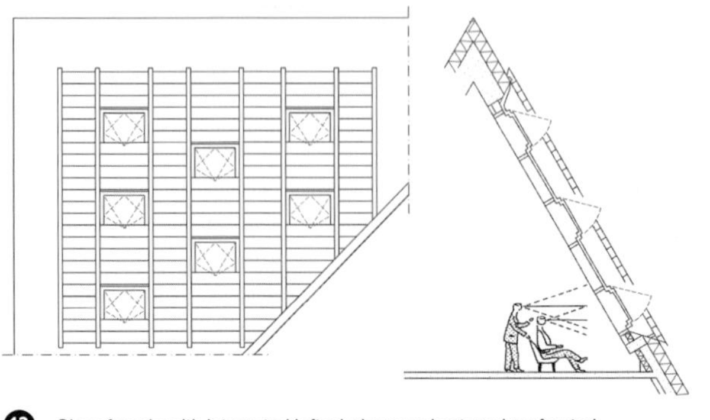

⓬ Glass façade with integrated loft windows and external perforated metal screen Arch.: Kister Scheithauer Gross

Domes, skylights, coffers, smoke vents and louvres, as fixed or movable units, can be used for lighting and ventilation, and for clearing smoke from rooms, halls, stair wells etc.

By positioning dome rooflights facing north sunshine and glare are avoided → ❹. Glare from low sun can be avoided by the use of a high curb → ❶ Dome rooflights used for ventilation should face into the prevailing wind in order to utilise the extraction capacity of the wind. The inlet aperture should be 20% smaller than the outlet aperture. Forced ventilation, with an air flow of 150–1000 m^3/h, can be achieved by fitting a fan into the curb of a skylight → ❷. Dome rooflights can also be used for access to the roof.

Attention should be given to the aerodynamic extraction surfaces of smoke exhaust systems. Orientating each extraction unit at an angle of 90° from the adjacent one will allow for wind coming from all directions. Position to leeward/windward if pairs of extraction fans are to be mounted in line with or against the direction of the prevailing wind.

Smoke extraction vents are required for stairwells more than four complete storeys high. Variable skylight aperture widths up to 5.50 m are available, as is a special version up to 7.50 m wide which does not need extra support.

Skylight systems offer diffused room lighting which is free from glare → ⓮. North-facing saw-tooth skylights with spun glass fibre inlays guarantee all the climatically important advantages of a full workshop space → ⓭.

Building components

WINDOWS

Arrangement
Requirements
Opening types
Thermal protection
Noise protection
Cleaning buildings
Loft windows
Rooflights
see also: Daylight pp. 488 ff.

15 – 30

with solid or ventilated curb

60 × 60 80 × 80 90 × 90 1.00 × 1.00 1.00 × 2.00 1.20 × 1.20 1.20 × 1.80	1.20 × 2.40 1.25 × 2.50 1.50 × 1.50 1.50 × 1.80 1.50 × 2.40 1.80 × 1.80	1.80 × 2.40 1.80 × 2.70 1.80 × 3.00 2.20 × 2.20 2.50 × 2.50
round domes: 60, 90, 100, 120, 150, 180, 220, 250cm dia.		

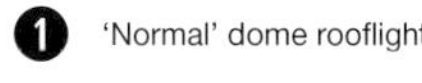

❶ 'Normal' dome rooflight

fan 50

50 × 1.00	1.00 × 1.00	1.20 × 1.50
50 × 1.50	1.00 × 1.50	1,20 × 2.40
60 × 60	1.00 × 2.00	1.50 × 1.50
60 × 90	1.00 × 2.50	1.50 × 3.00
90 × 90	1.00 × 3.00	1.80 × 2.70

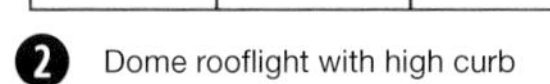

❷ Dome rooflight with high curb

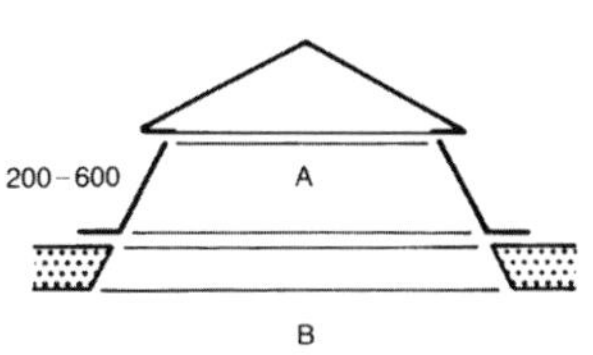

A	B	A	B
40 70 80 1.00 1.30	60 × 60 90 × 90 1.00 × 1.00 1.20 × 1.20 1.50 × 1.50	1.6 1.7 2.20 2.30 2.40	1.80 × 1.80 2.00 × 2.00 2.00 × 2.20 2.50 × 2.50 2.70 × 2.70

❸ Pyramid rooflight

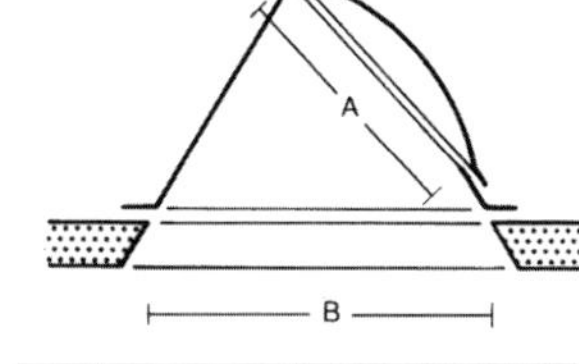

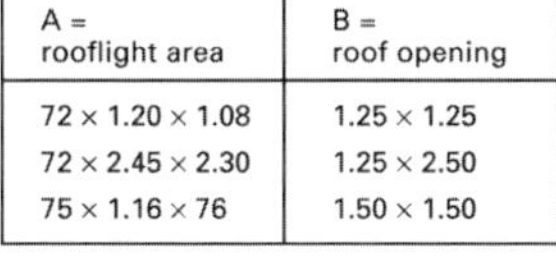

A = rooflight area	B = roof opening
72 × 1.20 × 1.08	1.25 × 1.25
72 × 2.45 × 2.30	1.25 × 2.50
75 × 1.16 × 76	1.50 × 1.50

❹ North light dome

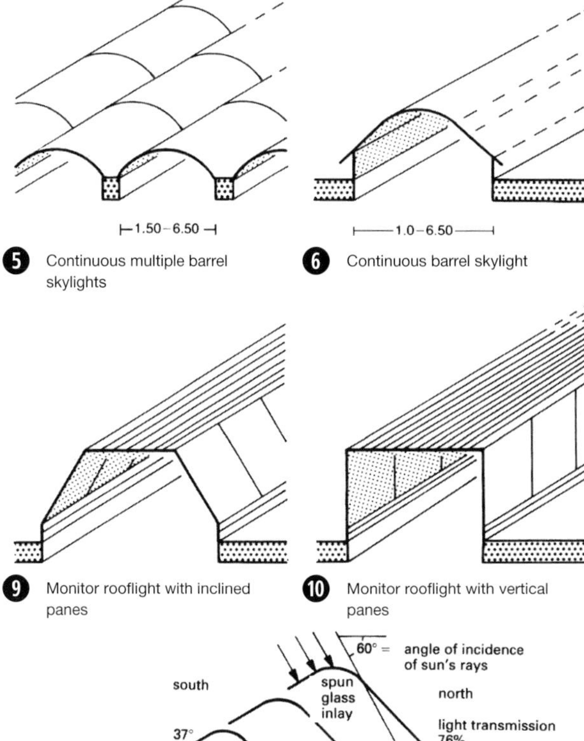

❺ Continuous multiple barrel skylights

❻ Continuous barrel skylight

❾ Monitor rooflight with inclined panes

❿ Monitor rooflight with vertical panes

5.0

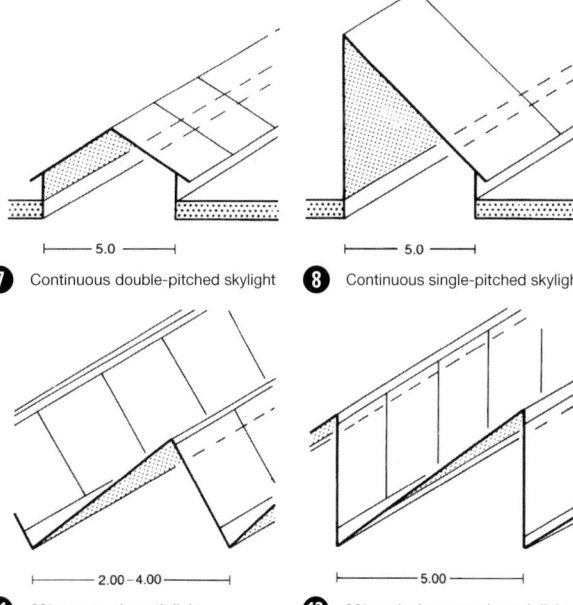

❼ Continuous double-pitched skylight

5.0

❽ Continuous single-pitched skylight

2.00–4.00

⓫ 60° saw-tooth north light

5.00

⓬ 90° vertical saw-tooth north light

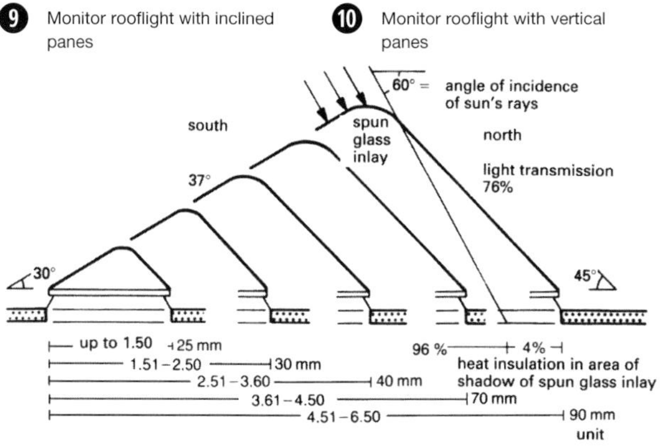

⓭ Saw-tooth glass fibre-reinforced polyester skylight

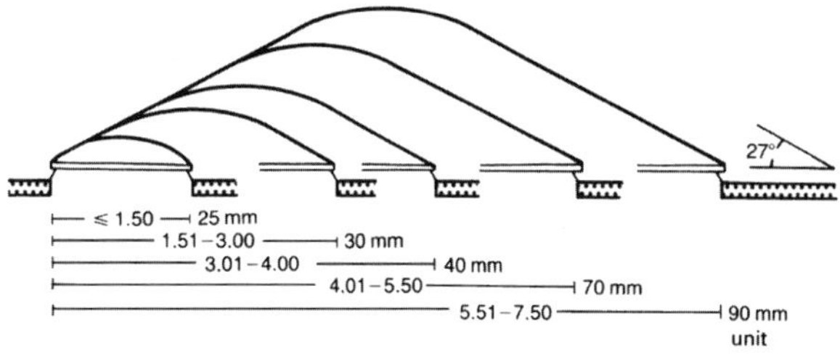

⓮ Double-skinned rooflight units

Building components

GLASS
Basics
Insulated glazing
Security and noise control glass
Optically variable glass
Cast glass
Profiled glass
Glass blocks
Fire protection glass
Curtain walling

BS EN 410
BS 6262
DIN EN 410

Plate coplanar

❶ Directional transmittance of clear glasses with the refraction of slanting rays

❷ Dispersed transmittance of opal milk glasses, alabaster etc.

❸ Mixed transmittance of ornamental glasses, silk, light opal glasses etc.

Material	Dispersion	Thick-ness (mm)	Reflec-tion (%)	Transmit-tance (%)	Absorb-ance (%)
clear glass	none	2–4	6–8	90–92	2–4
mirror glass	none	6–8	8	88	4
wire glass	none	6–8	9	74	17
raw glass	none	4–6	8	88	4
ornamental glass	slight	3.2–5.9	7–24	57–90	3–21
clear glass, externally opaque	slight	1.75–3.1	7–20	63–87	4–17
clear glass, internally opaque	slight	1.75–3.1	6–16	77–89	3–11
porcelain	good	3.0	72–77	2–8	20–21
marble, polished	good	7.3–10	30–71	3–8	24–65
marble, soaked	good	3–5	27–54	12–40	11–49
alabaster	good	11.2–	49–67	17–30	14–21
cardboard, lightly soaked	good	13.4	69	8	23
parchment, undyed	good		48	42	10
parchment, light yellow soaked	good		37	41	22
parchment, dark yellow	good		36	14	50
silk, white	nearly good		28–38	61–71	1
silk, coloured	nearly good	1.1–2.8	5–24	13–54	27–80
laminate, tinted	good		32–39	20–36	26–48

❹ Light properties of transparent materials
Reflectivities → p. 498 ❷, p. 507 ❼

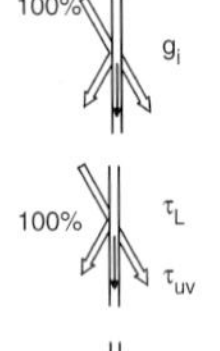

g The overall energy transmittance g refers to the wave length range from 300 mm to 2500 mm. It is the sum of the radiation allowed to pass directly through and the inward secondary heat output (radiation and convection).

τ_L The statement of the light transmittance τ_L refers to the wavelength range of visible light from 380 mm to 780 mm and is weighted with the brightness sensitivity of the human eye.

τ_{UV} The UV transmittance τ_{UV} for ultraviolet radiation is given for the wavelength range from 280 mm to 380 mm.

U_g The thermal transmittance U_g (DIN EN 673) of glazing is a measure of how much energy is lost per second and per m² with a temperature difference of 1 kelvin. The lower this value is, the less heat is lost. Coatings, gas filling and the width of the space between the panes decisively influence the thermal transmittance of glazing.

R_a The colour rendering index R_a describes the colour rendering of glazing. An Ra value of more than 90 denotes very good colour rendering.

❺ Technical data relating to light and energy

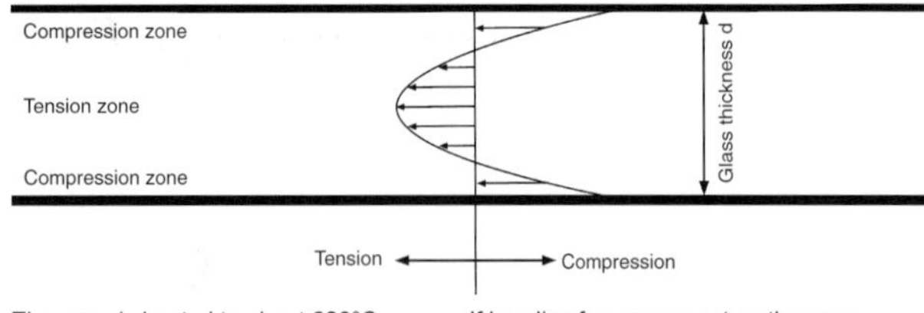

The pane is heated to about 680°C. Blowing with cold air cools the outer layers more quickly so they harden. Under further cooling, the hardened edge zones prevent the core zone from contracting. The outer zones are compressed while a tension stress is caused in the middle.

If bending forces now act on the pane, this first has to relieve the existing compression stresses before the material has to accept tension stresses. This measure can increase the bending strength from about 24 N/mm² of normal float glass to 120 N/mm².

❻ Properties of pre-stressed panes of toughened or partially toughened glass

Transparent, translucent building materials

For the determination of size, colour, window dimensions and lighting of rooms, knowledge of the visual transmittance, dispersion and reflection characteristics of glass materials are important for their artistic and economic effect.

Light-reflecting materials are able to demonstrate directional, completely dispersed or incompletely dispersed reflection and transparent materials directional → ❶, dispersed → ❷ and mixed transmittance → ❸.

Note that frosted glasses, which are internally opaque (which is preferable because they become less dirty), absorb less light than externally opaque glasses.

Manufacture

Glass is drawn in a mechanical process and leaves the drawing machine in a condition ready for use without further processing. The glass is clear and translucent, colourless and of uniform thickness. The surface is flat on both sides and fire-polished. The basic composition of float glasses varies slightly due to the origin of the raw materials used. This has practically no effect on the physical properties. Colour values and visual and energy (heat) transmittance can be exceptions. Tinted glasses are made with the addition of various metallic oxides. The possible spectrum of colours is very limited. A greater variety of colours and patterns can be produced by enamel, which is applied to the surface using a screen-printing process. These can only be applied to toughened safety glass.

Glass panes which are inclined at more than 10° from the vertical are considered as roofing glass on account of the additional loadings (self-weight, snow, wind and climatic loads) and are subject to the 'Technical regulations for the use of glazing with linear support' (TRLV) of the DIBt (German Institute for Construction Technology).

Properties

Glass is physically a super-cooled liquid. It is a brittle material, which can bear high compression stresses, but the tension strength is only about 1/10 of the compressive strength. If the limits of elasticity are exceeded by mechanical or thermal stresses, it breaks. Normal glass then breaks into jagged pieces of various sizes, which can be dangerous.

Different processes can be used to adapt the properties of glass for the most varied requirements.

Tempering of the sheets produces a basic stress in the glass, which increases its tension and bending strength → ❻. If the glass breaks, this pre-stress causes it to shatter into blunt fragments (**toughened safety glass**). Coatings can be applied to change the transmittance or the reflection of defined wavelengths (e.g. thermally insulated glazing).

Two or more panes can be combined with an intermediate layer to fulfil the most varied functions. Tear-resistant foils can prevent glass splinters falling out (**laminated glass** → p. 106 ❹), and many layers make glazing resistant to breaking. Printed intermediate layers offer a range of colourful and graphic design possibilities. Special fillings can hinder the transmittance of unwanted thermal radiation (fire protection glazing → p. 111).

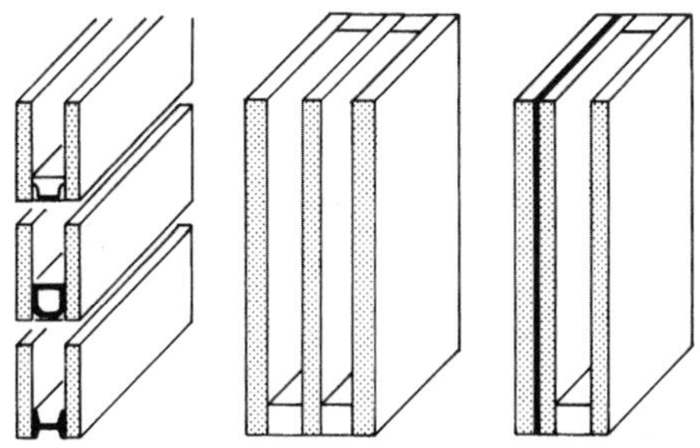

1 Insulated glazing can consist of two or three panes. The specific properties can be influenced by a multitude of combinations of coatings and composite glasses.

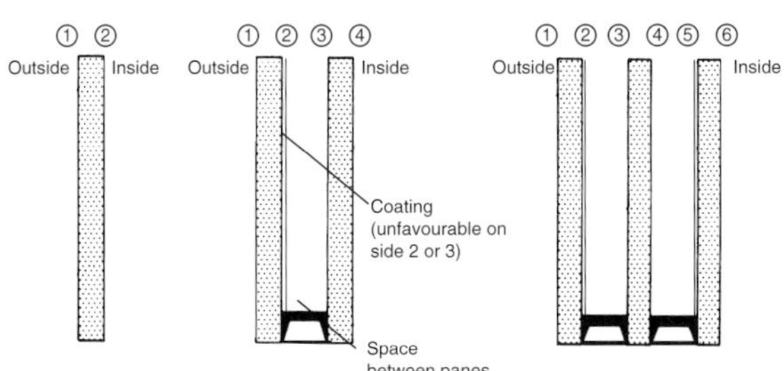

2 Description of the pane surfaces for the numbering of the position of coatings

Type of glass	Glass thickness, outer (mm)	Visual transmittance T_L (%)	Light reflection to the outside R_{LA} (%)	Overall energy (heat) transmittance (%)
float glass	4	80	13	61
outer	6	79	13	59
THERMOPLUS→S3	8	78	12	57
at pos. 3	10	77	12	56

3 Light and energy values of insulated glazing with various thicknesses of the external pane and coating of the inner pane (position 3)
Inner pane: clear float glass pane with a thickness of 4 mm. (EnEV → refs)

Type of glass	Glass thickness, outer (mm)	Visual transmittance T_L (%)	Light reflection to the outside R_{LA} (%)	Overall energy (heat) transmittance (%)
float glass®	4	80	14	59
outer	6	79	14	57
THERMOPLUS® S3	8	78	14	56
at pos. 2	10	78	14	55

4 Light and energy values of insulated glazing with various thicknesses of the coated outer pane (pos. 2)
Inner pane – clear float glass pane with a thickness of 4 mm. (EnEV → refs)

Glass type	Visible transmittance	Overall energy transmittance	U_g-value (W/m²K) acc. DIN EN 673 Space between panes			Light reflection		UV transmittance	Absorption	General colour rendition
	T_L(%)	g (%)	12 mm	14 mm	16 mm	outside	inside	T_{UV} (%)	A_{Ea} (%)	R_A
blue 50/27	50	28	1.2	1.1	1.1	19	19	6	39	95
70/35	70	37	1.2	1.1	1.1	16	17	11	29	97
66/33	66	36	1.2	1.1	1.1	16	18	11	32	94
brilliant 50/25	50	27	1.2	1.1	1.1	19	20	7	42	92
40/22	40	23	1.2	1.1	1.1	20	22	7	44	91
30/17	30	19	1.2	1.1	1.1	26	17	6	47	88
neutral 70/40	71	43	1.3	1.2	1.1	10	11	18	31	95
silver 50/30	50	32	1.2	1.1	1.1	39	33	17	28	94

5 Infrastop® – solar control insulating glass with argon filling. Construction layers 6 (16) 4 mm. Technical and physical data under vertical radiation. (EnEV → refs)

Simple double glazing

Double-glazed units normally consist of two panes. These are connected at the edge with an air-tight and gas-tight spacer.

A considerable improvement in the coefficient of thermal conductivity (U-value) has been achieved through special coating of the panes. Such thermally insulating and solar control glazing has, since the introduction in Germany of the Insulation Regulations in 1995 and the Energy Saving Regulations (EnEV) in 2002, replaced uncoated glazing on account of its improved coefficients of thermal conductivity. Only in isolated cases does the calculation according to EnEV permit the use of normal double-glazed units.

Current types of glass with their optical features and the current construction physics properties and maximum sizes can be taken from the information provided by the glass industry. The combination with any kind of wire glass or tinted cast glass causes stress in the glass in direct sunshine and can lead to breakages, and so should be avoided. In addition, the glass dimensions and the selection of the construction of the double glazing should take into account all current standards, the technical regulations for the use of glazing with linear support and secured against falling out, glazing guidelines and workplace regulations. Only products with general technical approval should be used.

Thermally insulating double-glazed units

Thermally insulating double-glazed units are neutral in appearance and transparency, so that they look similar to simple double-glazed units. The low coefficients of thermal conductivity (U_g-value) are achieved through a coating of precious metal in position 3. Because the coatings applied to thermal insulation glass show low emissivity, this is often described as low-E glazing. Filling with inert gas can produce a further improvement of the coefficient of thermal conductivity. These units have high visual and overall energy (heat) transmittance in order to make the greatest possible part of the solar radiation available for passive energy gain. If the thermal insulation coating is applied to position 2, then the overall energy passing through is reduced. The visual impression can show slight differences, particularly if units are directly next to each other.

Solar control glass

Solar control glass is characterised by high visual transmittance at the same time as low overall energy transmittance. The passive energy gain from incoming solar radiation is low. This is made possible by a wafer-thin coating based on precious metal, which is applied in the protection of the space between the panes. In addition to its good solar control properties, solar control glass fulfils all current requirements for high-quality insulated glazing. Solar control units are normally labelled with a pair of values, which show firstly the visual transmittance and secondly the overall energy transmittance as percentages. Solar control units can be delivered with various grades of colour and reflection as seen from outside.

In order to select the optimal coloration of glass, sample panes should be requested from the manufacturer of the solar control glass. Absolute conformity of colour in the external elevation is not practically possible to produce, particularly when replacements are ordered. The mirror image of highly reflecting glazing can be distorted by imperfections in flatness.

The view of colour from inside to outside is insignificantly falsified. If the view is compared directly with the view through an open window, a slight toning will be recognised. This toning can be more apparent for some types of solar control glass.

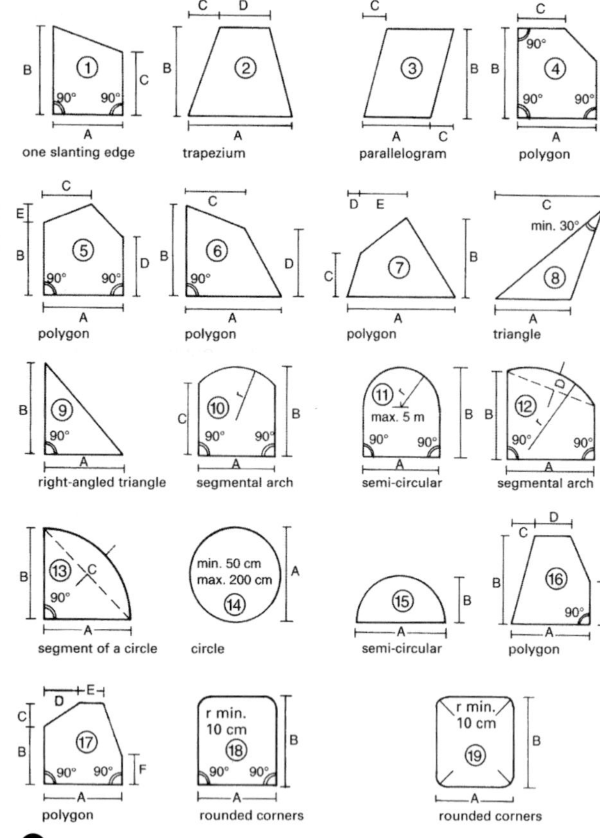

❶ Delivery shapes of model panes (examples)

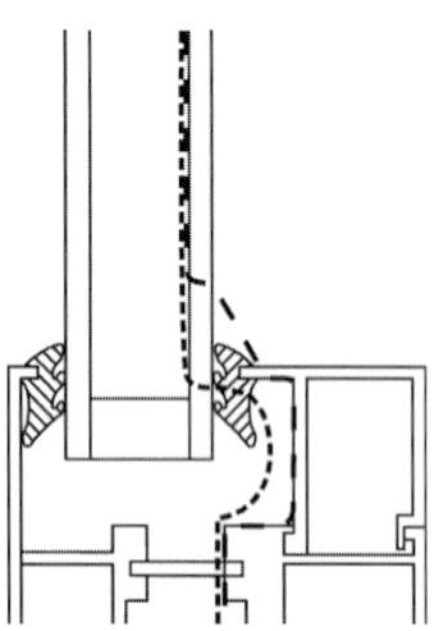

The illustration shows schematically the isotherms, that is lines of equal temperature, for thermal insulation glass with thermally optimised edge bonding in comparison to a conventional spacer of aluminium or steel.

It can be clearly seen that the isotherms with the improved spacers lie closer to the bottom of the glass, which shows that the glass is warmer on the room side so that less condensation will be created at the edge of the double-glazed unit, or none at all.

❷ Heat flow at the glass–frame transition for highly insulated windows (EnEV → refs)

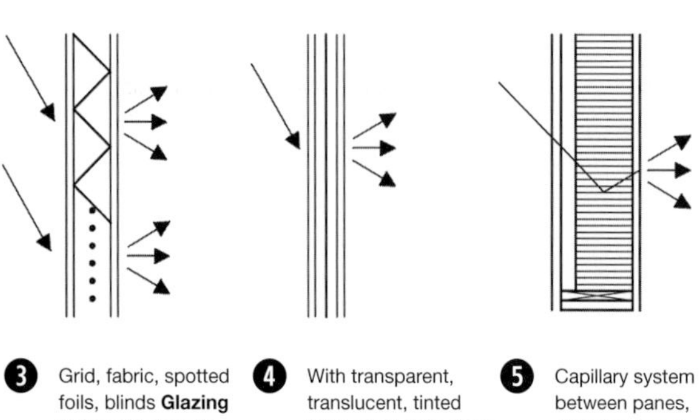

❸ Grid, fabric, spotted foils, blinds **Glazing units with inserts**

❹ With transparent, translucent, tinted foils; stuck onto glass **Laminated safety glass**

❺ Capillary system between panes, diffusing, low U_g-values **Transparent thermal insulation**

Model panes are described with sketches and dimensioned according to the system in → ❶. For acute angles of less than 30°, at the top a blunt edge of at least 10 mm is required. Smaller panes (≦60 cm edge length) should be avoided because these have a higher risk of breakage and the edge seal can tend to leak due to the reduced elasticity of the panes.

Thermally improved spacers

The Energy Saving Regulations (EnEV) and more stringent standards and guidelines have resulted in the increased significance of thermally improved spacers. The thermal properties of the spacers may be taken into account in the new verification process under EnEV. This improvement is, however, not reflected in the U_g-value, but ψ is additionally applied as lengthwise heat transmittance and is thus reflected in the official verification.

This improved thermal insulation in the critical transition from glass to window frame results in higher surface temperatures on the room side than with the use of conventional aluminium spacers. This results in less or even no condensation, which always forms at the coldest point under unfavourable conditions, like for example high air humidity → ❷. For windows with wooden frames, the harmful effects of damp and the danger of mould are reduced.

Light deflection and solar control in the space between the panes

Various light deflection systems can be installed in the space between the panes of insulated glazing → ❸. Rigid light control elements use reflection and dispersion to allow diffused light into the room and shield direct sunlight according to the position of the sun, or direct it deep into the room. Sunshading blinds, which can either be rotated or completely raised, are protected from dirt by the location between the panes. They can be operated manually or electrically. The panes of glass at each side must be of toughened glass, because increased stresses could be caused by the heat. The width of the space between the panes varies from 20 to 27 mm according to construction.

Thermal insulation between the panes

Transparent thermal insulation → ❺ enables high thermal insulation values at the same time as high heat transmission (heat trap). These systems diffuse the light passing through to varying extents. Glass or plastic tubes can be used, installed at right angles to the glass surface. They reflect the light further into the inside of the room and hinder air movement when the gap between the panes is large. Units with more panes, or filled with foam particles, reflect more light externally. Transparent thermal insulation elements need effective shading in summer. They are mostly used for heat-storage walls.

Self-cleaning coating on the weather side

Various glass manufacturers offer self-cleaning coatings in position 1 (→ p. 105) of insulated glazing. This coating results in a slight alteration of the colour and also a slight influence on the visual and energy values compared to standard. The coatings can be applied to thermal insulation and solar control glazing and also on façade panels; it will be necessary to request further information from the manufacturer. The manufacturer's cleaning instructions are to be observed absolutely.

BS EN 356
BS EN 1063
BS EN 1279
BS EN 12758
DIN EN 356
DIN EN ISO 717
DIN EN 1063
DIN EN 13123

1. Weight of glass: the heavier the glass pane, normally the higher the acoustic insulation
2. The more elastic the pane (e.g. resin-filled cast-in-place), normally the higher the acoustic insulation
3. The thicknesses of the inner and outer panes must be different; the greater the difference, normally the higher the acoustic insulation

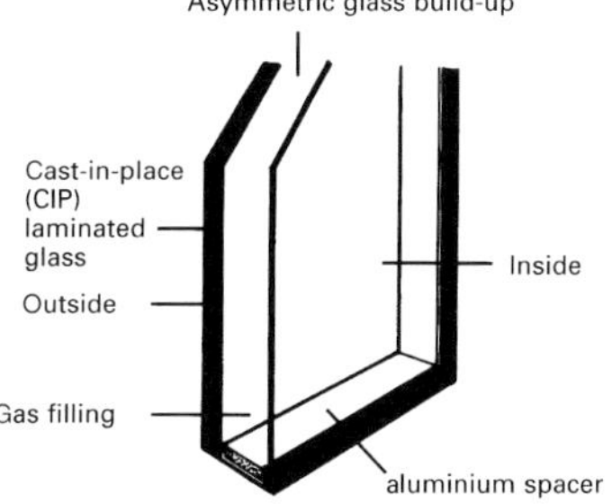

1 Improvement of the sound reduction properties of insulated glazing

C	– motorway traffic – rail traffic with medium or high speed – jet aircraft, short distance away – factories emitting mostly medium or high frequency noise
C_{tr}	– urban road traffic – rail traffic at low speed – propeller aircraft – jet aircraft, far away – disco music – factories emitting mostly low and medium frequency noise

2 Adaptation terms C and C_{tr} for the sound reduction value R_w for particular noise types. C 100–5000 or C_{tr} 100–5000 describe an extended frequency spectrum.

Type	R_w (dB)	C	C_{tr}	C 100–5000	C_{tr} 100–5000	Configuration (mm)	Thickness (mm)	Weight (kg/m2)
28/37	37	-2	-5	-1	-5	8(16)4	28	30
30/38	38	-2	-6	-1	-6	10(16)4	30	35
28/38 V	38	-2	-6	-1	-6	4(16)8 VSG	28	30
30/38 X	38	-2	-6	-1	-6	4(16)10 VSG	30	35
30/38 V	38	-3	-7	-2	-7	6(16)8 VSG	30	35
29/39 L	39	-1	-5	0	-5	4(16)8,8 L	29	30
32/40 V	40	-2	-6	-1	-6	6(16)10 VSG	32	40
31/41 L	41	-3	-7	-2	-7	6(16)8,8 L	31	35
33/42 L	42	-3	-7	-2	-1	6(16)8,8 L	33	40
33/43 L	43	-3	-7	-2	-7	8(16)9,1 L	33	40

3 Sound reduction and adaptation terms for Phonstop® glasses. U_g-values of Phonstop® TH-SN 1.2 W/m²K and Phonstop® TH S3 1.1 W/m²k (EnEV→ refs)

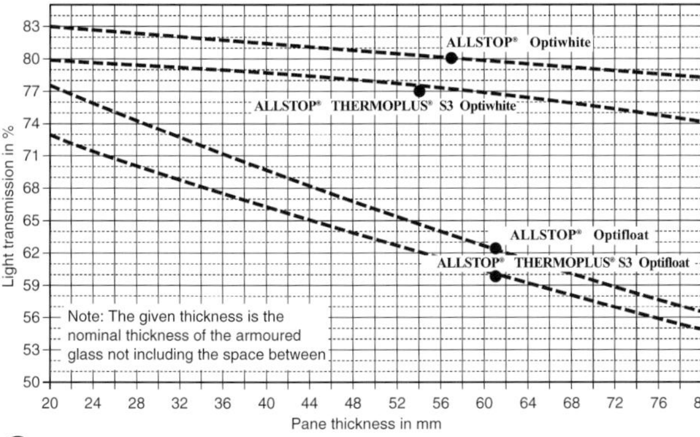

4 Comparison of light transmittance values of armoured glass with and without white glass → (EnEV→ refs)

Attack-resistant glazing, DIN 52290-3, DIN 52290-4	DIN EN 356	Break-in-resistant windows, doors, DIN V ENV 1627	According to the security guidelines of VdS Loss Prevention	Health and safety regulations
A1	P2A	–	–	–
A2	P3A	–	–	P3A
A3	P4A	WK 2	EH01	–
–	P5A	WK 3	EH02	–
B1	P6B	WK 3–4	EH1*	–
B2	P7B	WK 5	EH2*	P7B
B3	P8B	WK 6	EH3*	–

*Certification by VdS is required.

5 Comparison table of security classes according to insurance regulations. This table is only an overview: it must be possible to fulfil and verify the required values.

Noise reduction

All thermal insulation and solar control units can also fulfil noise control functions, but need additional measures. These additional measures can influence the visual transmittance, the g-value and the U_g-value. These altered values have to be taken into account in the verification under EnEV.

As examples, these additional measures are possible, according to the required level of noise reduction: poured resin or heavy glass fillings, composite glass with noise reduction foil etc. The noise reduction values or sound transmission class for all glass combinations are listed in the individual manufacturers' handbooks and should be taken into account in the design. Only products with the required test certificates should be used. For sound reduction classes of windows → p. 100 **13** and p. 386. In addition to the evaluated sound reduction value R_w, spectrum adaptation terms can be given, which are used to modify the R_w-value to the subjective response of the ear to certain noise types → **2**.

Security glazing

These requirements on glazing units lead to thick glass, which causes a green coloration. This can be reduced by white glass. Combination with thermal insulation and solar control glazing is also possible.

Break-in resistance (private areas)

This is security glass for private clients, intended to dissuade an opportunist criminal, through to high-quality break-in resistant glazing according to the security guidelines of VdS Loss Prevention. These requirements can be met by a composite secure glazing unit consisting of at least two panes with a high-strength plastic foil.

Resistance against manual attack (commercial use)

In these cases, the security effect can be provided only by a multi-layer configuration with the use of various glass thicknesses and plastic foil inserts.

If the security glazing is to be used and recognised by insurance companies, VdS Loss Prevention's guidelines are to be complied with, the break-in resistance classes being categorised as EH1, EH2 or EH3.

Bullet-proof glass

The following 'BR' resistance classes are defined according to European standards:

Class BR 1:	.22 rifle
Class BR 2 (C1):	9 mm pistol
Class BR 3 (C2):	.357 Magnum pistol
Class BR 4 (C3):	.44 Magnum pistol
Class BR 5:	5.56 × 45 rifle
Class BR 6 (C4):	7.62 rifle × 51 standard ammunition
Class BR 7 (C5):	7.62 rifle × 51 hard-core ammunition
Class SG 1:	shotgun calibre 12/70 (1 hit)
Class SG 2:	shotgun calibre 12/70 (3 hits)

These glasses can be produced with the grading 'splinter-free' (on the inside).

Glazing for counters in banks etc. should comply with the regulations of Accident Insurance for Administration. The technical solutions from Accident Insurance Information (BGI) do not exclude other solutions, which are just as safe.

Explosion resistance

Glazing was tested with maximum dimensions of 900 × 1100 mm and fixed all round in a retaining construction. This must be installed in accordance with the test certificate or the window unit should be tested.

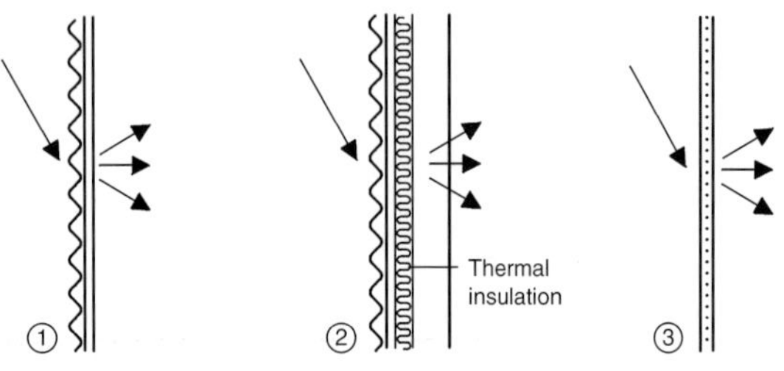

① Cast glass ornamental surface etc.
② Cast glass profile
③ Cast glass with amorphous structures, rough surface, transparent, translucent

❶ Light dispersion and light modifying effects of cast glasses

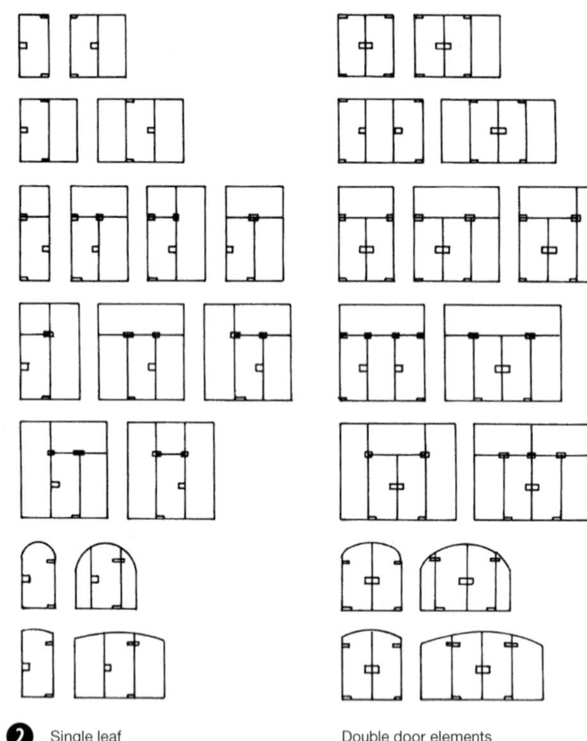

❷ Single leaf — Double door elements

DELODUR®	Glass thickness (mm)	Maximum size (cm × cm)	Thickness tolerance (mm)
blank, grey, bronze, optiwhite	10 12	244 × 510 244 × 510	0.3 0.3
green	8 10	244 × 510 244 × 510	0.3 0.3
structure 200 master glasses	8 10	194 × 425 194 × 425	0.5 0.5
bamboo, chinchilla blank/bronze	8	175 × 425	0.5

❸ Whole glass door elements (fanlights and side elements) – maximum sizes of toughened panes that can be produced (EnEV → refs)

	Size in 1/1 G (mm × mm)	Size in 2/2 G (mm × mm)	Size in 3/3 G (mm × mm)
outside door size standard	709 × 1972 709 × 2097	834 × 1972 834 × 2097	959 × 1972 959 × 2097
lining rebate size	716 × 1983 716 × 2108	841 × 1983 841 × 2108	966 × 1983 966 × 2108
structural size	750 × 2000 750 × 2125	875 × 2000 875 × 2125	1000 × 2000 1000 × 2125

❹ Glass doors: dimensions (EnEV → refs)

OPTICALLY VARIABLE GLASS

Double-glazed units whose transmission properties can be altered are differentiated into switching and switchable units. Switching units are conditioned during production so that they react automatically to certain influences (e.g. thermotropic units). The visual transmittance of switchable layers can be altered at any time by changing the gas layer in between the panes or by applying a voltage.

Thermotropic units
These composite units react with alterations of temperature by changing from clear (transparent) to opaque (diffuse). This is achieved with a mixture of two components with different refraction properties, which align their structures differently according to temperature, altering the refraction of the layer. The alteration is reversible.

Electrochromatic units
The transmittance of these units can be altered by applying a voltage to the reactive layer. For internal use, this can be achieved with the use of liquid crystals in the space between the panes (LC foils function reliably only between –40°C and +40°C). Other systems make use of the property of some materials to alter their visual transmittance and coloration with the absorption or release of ions (by applying a voltage). These units are suitable for external glazing.

CAST GLASS

Properties
Cast glass is produced mechanically by rolling certain surface structures. It is not clear to look through. Cast glass is used for applications where obscure glass is required (bathroom, WC) and as a design element. Ornamental glass is available as white and tinted, raw white glass, and white and tinted ornamental wired glass. Wired glasses are no longer classified as safety glass, with exceptions when used in overhead glazing.

Most cast glasses can be further processed to make toughened glass, laminated safety glass and thermally insulated glazing units. The structure is normally faced to the outside in order to ensure a proper edge joint. If the glass is only lightly structured, the structured side can be faced inwards in order to simplify cleaning. Tinted cast glass cannot be used in combination with tinted classes like float glass, toughened glass or laminated safety glass, nor with coated glass with thermal insulation or solar control functions.

GLASS DOORS

Whole glass doors
The dimensions of doors correspond to the dimensions of metal door linings → ❹. They can be installed in all the metal door linings produced to DIN 18111 standard. The doors are made of toughened glass panes. If violently smashed, the glass crumbles into a network of small fragments, which more or less stay loosely together. The normal glass thicknesses of 10 or 12 mm comply with the structural requirements. Structured cast glass and printable toughened float glass panes are available. Printable laminated safety glass panes can also be supplied (the composite glass foil is printed).

Whole glass door elements consist of one or more glass doors, the side elements and the fanlight. Further possibilities are sliding, folding, segmented arch, and round arch door elements. Various tints and glass structures are available, and standard or special sizes.

Profiled glass is a cast glass produced with a U-shaped profile. It is translucent with an ornamentation on the outside surface of the profile, and conforms to the properties of cast glass. It has low maintenance requirements. It is suitable for lift shafts and roof glazing. Rooms using this glass for fenestration are rendered glare free. Heat-absorbing glasses Reglit and Profilit 'Plus 1.7' are coated with metallic oxides and attain a U_g-value of 1.8 W/m²K.

Solar control glass (Type R, "Bernstein'; Type P, 'Antisol'), which reflects and/or absorbs ultra-violet and infra-red radiation, can be used to protect delicate goods from UV radiation. The transmission of radiant energy into the room is reduced, as is the convection from the glazing, whilst the light transmission is maintained.

For glazing subject to impacts, e.g. in of sports halls (ball throwing safety), Reglit SP2 or Profilit K22/60/7 without wire reinforcement should be used.

Regulit and Profilit are allowed as fire-glass with a fire resistance class of G30. Normal and special profiles are also available with longitudinal wires.

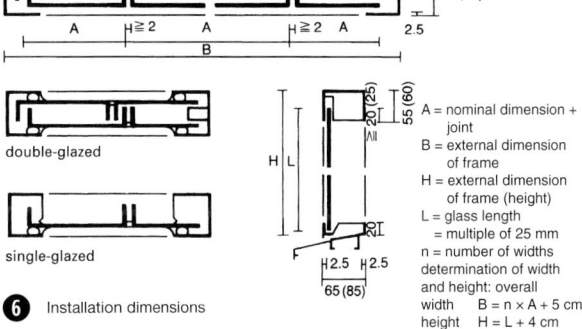

NP 2: 220 (6 | 6), 232, 41 — K 22/41/6
NP 26: 250 (6 | 6), 262, 41 — K 25/41/6
NP 3: 319 (6 | 6), 331, 41 — K 32/41/6
NP 5: 486 (6 | 6), 498, 41 — K 50/416
SP 2: 218 (7 | 7), 232, 60 — K 22/60/7
SP 26: 248 (7 | 7), 262, 60 — K 25/60/7
317 (7 | 7), 331, 60 — K 32/60/7

NP/SP = Reglit
K = Profilit

❶ Profiled glass – cross–sections

Height above ground level clear opening	I up to 8 m	I up to 20 m	I up to 100 m	II up to 8 m	II up to 20 m	II up to 100 m	III up to 8 m	III up to 20 m	III up to 100 m
glass type → ❶	L*	L*	L*	L*	L*	L*	L*	L*	L*
NP 2 K 22/41/6	2.67	2.11	1.80	3.19	2.52	2.15	3.77	2.98	2.55
NP 26 K 25/41/6	2.53	2.00	1.70	3.02	2.39	2.03	3.57	2.82	2.41
NP 3 K 32/41/6	2.27	1.80	1.53	2.72	2.15	1.83	3.21	2.54	2.17
NP 5 K 50/41/6	1.88	1.49	1.27	2.25	1.78	1.52	2.66	2.11	1.80
SP 2 K 22/60/7	4.22	3.33	2.84	5.04	3.98	3.40	5.96	4.71	4.02
SP 26 K 25/60/7	3.99	3.16	2.69	4.77	3.77	3.22	5.65	4.46	3.81
K 32/60/7	3.59	2.84	2.42	4.29	3.39	2.89	5.08	4.02	3.43

❷ Sheltered buildings (0.8–1.25 × g)

	h/a = 0.25; – (1.5 × q)						H/a = 0.5; – (1.7 × q)					
Height above ground level clear opening	up to 8 m	up to 20 m	up to 100 m	up to 8 m	up to 20 m	up to 100 m	up to 8 m	up to 20 m	up to 100 m	up to 8 m	up to 20 m	up to 100 m
glass type → ❶	L*	L*	L*	L*	L*	L*	L*	L*	L*	L*	L*	L*
NP 2 K 22/41/6	2.18	1.72	1.47	3.08	2.44	2.08	2.05	1.62	1.38	2.90	2.29	1.95
NP 26 K 25/41/6	2.06	1.63	1.39	2.92	2.31	1.97	1.94	1.53	1.31	2.74	2.17	1.85
NP 3 K 32/41/6	1.85	1.47	1.25	2.62	2.07	1.77	1.74	1.38	1.17	2.46	1.95	1.66
NP 5 K 50/41/6	1.54	1.22	1.04	2.17	1.72	1.47	1.44	1.14	0.97	2.04	1.61	1.38
SP 2 K 22/60/7	3.44	2.72	2.32	4.87	3.85	3.28	3.23	2.56	2.18	4.57	3.62	3.08
SP 26 K 25/60/7	3.26	2.58	2.20	4.61	3.64	3.11	3.06	2.42	2.06	4.33	3.42	2.92
K 32/60/7	2.93	2.32	1.98	4.15	3.28	2.80	2.76	2.18	1.86	3.90	3.08	2.63

L* = length of glass sheets in metres

❸ Exposed buildings

light transmittance:	single skin	up to 86%
	double skin	up to 75%
noise reduction	single skin²	up to 29 dB
	double skin	up to 41 dB
	triple skin	up to 55 dB
thermal insulation	single skin	k = 5.6 W/m²K
	double skin	NP U_g = 2.8 W/m²K
		SP U_g = 2.7 W/m²K

❹ Physical data

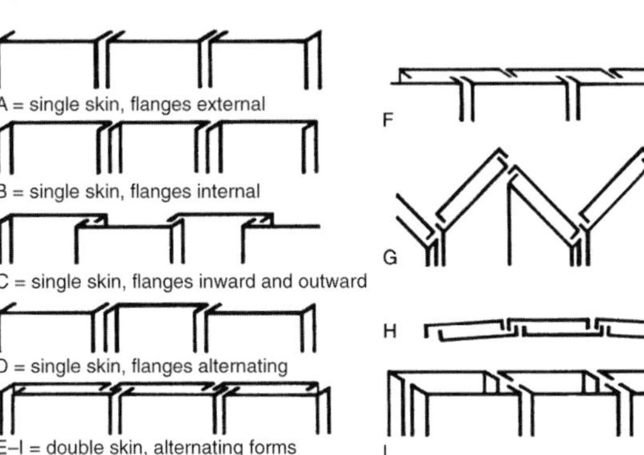

❺ Installation possibilities

55 (60) — nominal size — 55 (60)
25
65 (85)
A ≧2 A ≧2 A 2.5
B
double-glazed
single-glazed
H L 20 (25) 55 (60) ≧ 20
2.5 2.5
65 (85)

A = nominal dimension + joint
B = external dimension of frame
H = external dimension of frame (height)
L = glass length = multiple of 25 mm
n = number of widths
determination of width and height: overall
width B = n x A + 5 cm
height H = L + 4 cm

❻ Installation dimensions

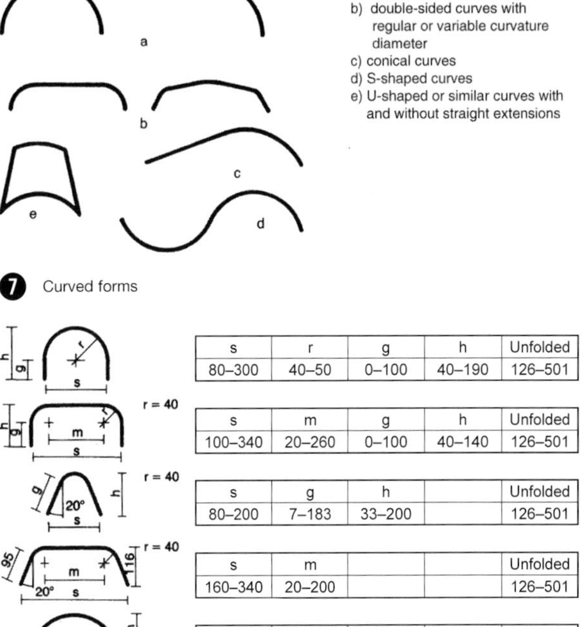

a) circular curves with and without straight extensions
b) double-sided curves with regular or variable curvature diameter
c) conical curves
d) S-shaped curves
e) U-shaped or similar curves with and without straight extensions

❼ Curved forms

s	r	g	h	Unfolded
80–300	40–50	0–100	40–190	126–501

r = 40

s	m	g	h	Unfolded
100–340	20–260	0–100	40–140	126–501

r = 40

s	g	h		Unfolded
80–200	7–183	33–200		126–501

r = 40

s	m			Unfolded
160–340	20–200			126–501

s	h	R		Unfolded
140–300	60–100	71–163		126–501

❽ Sample configurations of the possibilities of bending ornamental glass (dimensions in mm)

BS EN 1051
ISO 21690
DIN EN 1051
DIN 4102-3,
DIN 4242

$A = n_1 \cdot b + n_2 \cdot a$ n_1 = number of blocks (b)
$B = A + 2 \cdot c$ n_2 = number of joints (a)
$H = A + c + d$ c = 8.5cm
d = 6.5cm

formula to calculate the minimum structural opening

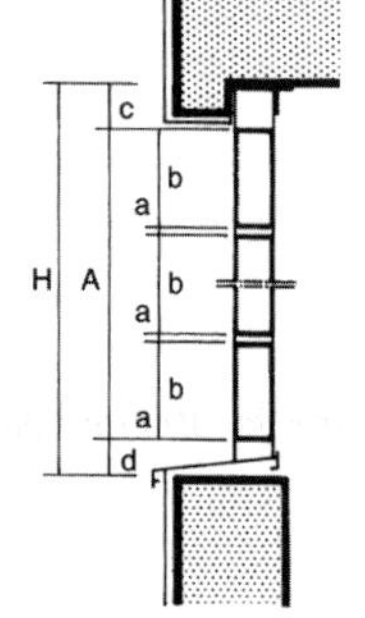

❶ Standard dimensions for glass block walls

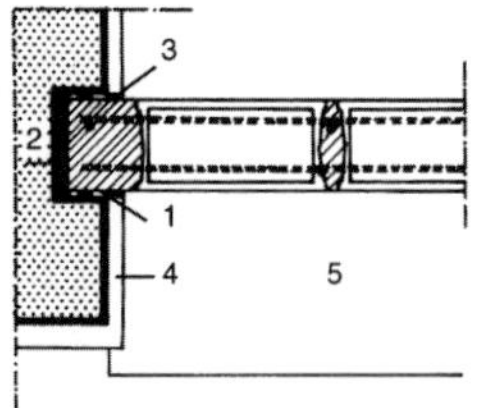
built into a recessed groove

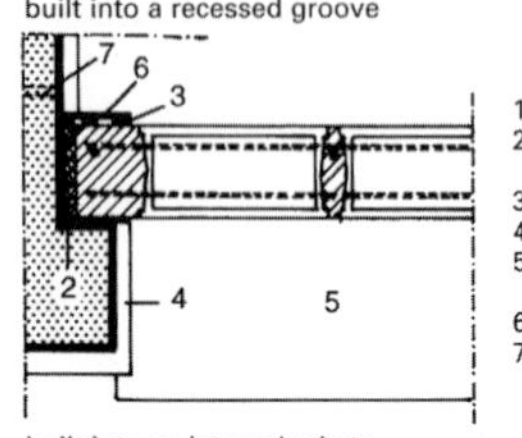
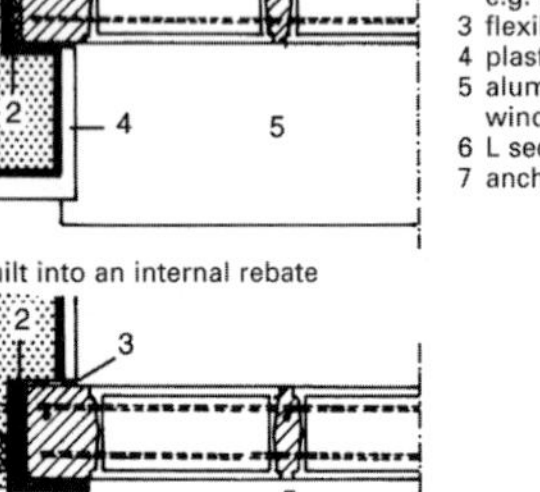
built into an internal rebate

1 slip joint
2 expansion joint, e.g. rigid foam
3 flexible sealing
4 plaster
5 aluminium window sill
6 L section
7 anchor or peg

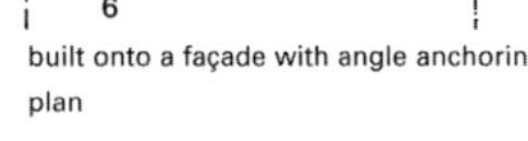
built onto a façade with angle anchoring
plan

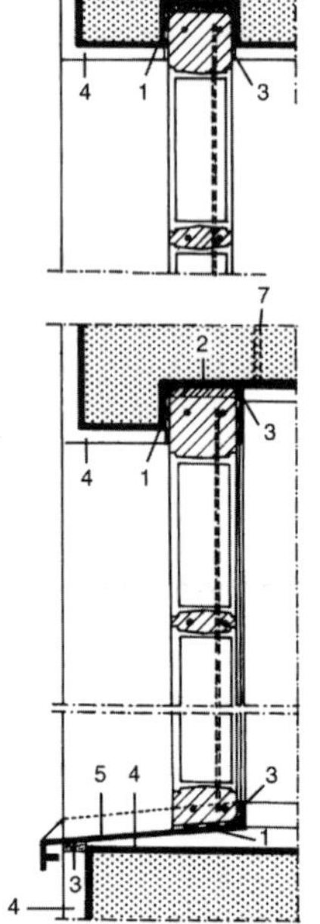
section

❷ Examples of glass block wall construction

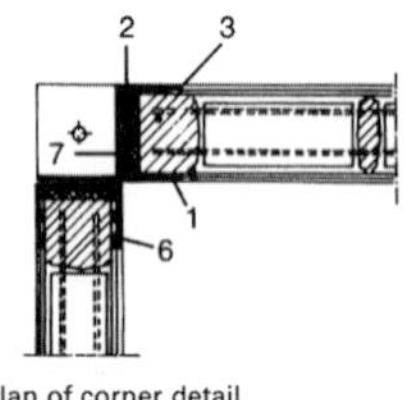
plan of corner detail

1 slip joint
2 expansion joint, e.g. rigid foam
3 flexible sealing
4 plaster
5 aluminium window sill
6 U section
7 L section
8 anchor or peg

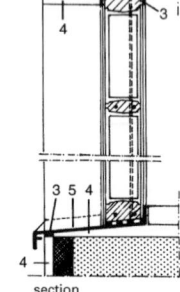

section

❸ Installation with U-profiles and external thermal insulation

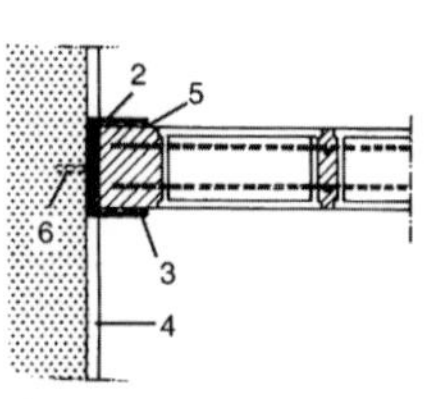
plan

1 slip joint
2 expansion joint, e.g. rigid foam
3 flexible sealing
4 plaster
5 U section
6 anchor or peg

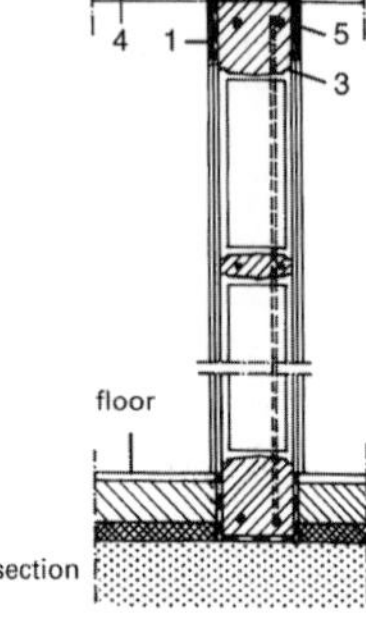

section

❹ Interior wall junction using U-profiles

Glass blocks are hollow units which consist of two sections melted and pressed together, thereby creating a sealed air cavity. Both surfaces can be made smooth and transparent, or very ornamental and almost opaque. Glass blocks can be obtained in different sizes, coated on the inside or outside, uncoated, or made of coloured glass. They can be used internally and externally, e.g. transparent screen walls and room dividers (also in gymnastic or sports halls), windows, lighting strips, balcony parapets and terrace walls. Glass blocks are fire-resistant up to G60, G120 or F60 when used as a cavity wall with a maximum uninterrupted area of 3.5 m^2, and can be built either vertically or horizontally. They are used as building elements, but cannot be load-bearing. Their properties: good sound and thermal insulation; high light transmittance (up to 82%); transparent, translucent, diffusing and low-glare according to decor; increased impact resistance. The thermal insulation of a glass block wall: with cement mortar U_g-value = 3.2 W/m^2K, with lightweight mortar U_g = 2.9 W/m^2 K, with special bricks up to U_g = 1.5 W/m^2 K.

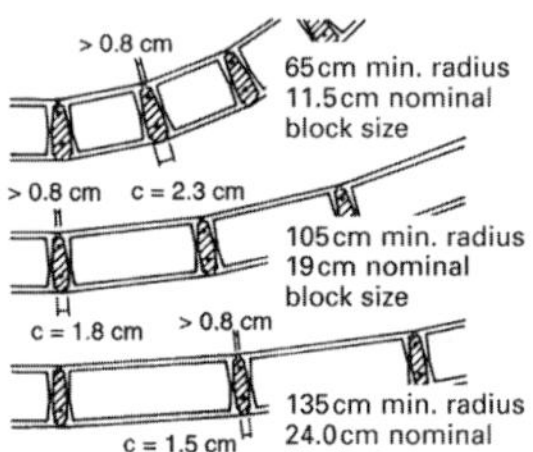

smallest radius R with glass thickness 8cm joints must be < 1.0cm wide			
glass block nominal size	11.5cm	19.0cm	24.0cm
joint width c = 1.5cm	200.0cm	295.0cm	370.0cm
joint width c = 1.8cm	95.0cm	180.0cm	215.0cm
joint width c = 2.3cm	65.0cm	105.0cm	135.0cm

❺ Minimum radii of glass block walls

	Dimensions mm	Weight kg	Stock m²	Stock carton	Stock range
	115 × 115 × 60	1.0	64	10	1.000
	146 × 146 × 98 6″ × 6″ × 8″	1.8	42	8	512
	190 × 190 × 50	2.0	25	14	504
	190 × 190 × 80	2.3	25	10	360
	190 × 190 × 100	2.8	25	8	288
	197 × 197 × 98 8″ × 8″ × 4″	3.0	25	8	288
	240 × 115 × 80	2.1	32	10	500
	240 × 240 × 80	3.9	16	5	250
	300 × 300 × 100	7.0	10	4	128

❻ Dimensions of glass blocks

Unreinforced glass block walls

Glass block walls that meet the requirements of → ❼ may be built without reinforcement and without specific structural verification. Take note of DIN 4242 with regard to the structural reinforcement of the edge strip.

Arrangement of joints	Thickness (mm)	Wall dimensions		
		Shorter side (m)	Longer side (m)	Wind load (kN/m²)
Continuous	≧80	≦1.5	≧1.5	≦0.8
Overlapped (bonded)		≦6.0		

❼ Permissible limits for unreinforced glass block walls

Glass brick format (mm)	Airborne sound insulation margin	Weighted sound reduction R'$_w$
190 × 190 × 80	−12 dB	40 dB
240 × 240 × 80	−10 dB	42 dB
240 × 115 × 80	−7 dB	45 dB
300 × 300 × 100	−11 dB	41 dB
double-glazed wall, 240 × 240 × 80	−2 dB	50 dB

❶ Sound insulation of glass block walls

Sound insulation class	R_w	Achievable with glass brick windows with wall structure:
6	50 dB	double skin
5	45–49 dB	single skin
4	40–44 dB	single skin
3	35–39 dB	single skin
2	30–34 dB	single skin
1	25–29 dB	single skin
0	25 dB	single skin

Sound insulation classes, VDI guideline 2719 for windows

Room type	Guideline values for permissible external noise level	
	Average noise level*	Average maximum level
1. domestic living rooms, guest rooms in hotels, wards in hospitals and sanatoria	daytime 30–40 dB (A) night time 20–30 dB (A)	daytime 40–50 dB (A) night time 30–40 dB (A)
2. school rooms, single private offices, scientific work rooms, libraries, conference and lecture rooms, doctors' surgeries and operating theatres, churches, auditoriums	30–40 dB (A)	40–50 dB (A)
3. multiple-use offices	35–45 dB (A)	45–55 dB (A)
4. open-plan offices, inns and restaurants, shops, halls	40–50 dB (A)	50–60 dB (A)
5. entrance, waiting and departure halls	45–55 dB (A)	55–55 dB (A)
6. opera houses, theatres, cinemas	25 dB (A)	35 dB (A)
7. recording studios	observe special requirements	

*equivalent maximum permitted constant level

❸ Permitted maximum sound levels for different categories of room, VDI guideline 2719

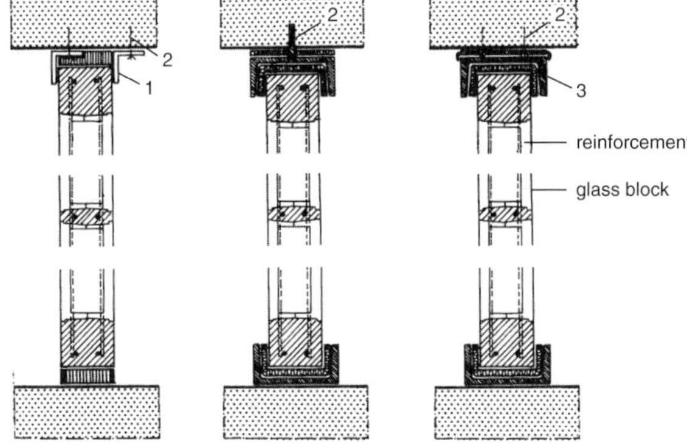

1 angle steel, 50 × 55 mm length >100 mm, at least four per glazed area
2 allowable fire-resistant pegs and steel screws M 10
3 flat steel strips to fix the glass block wall (welded)

❹ Installation details: fire-resistant glazing with glass blocks

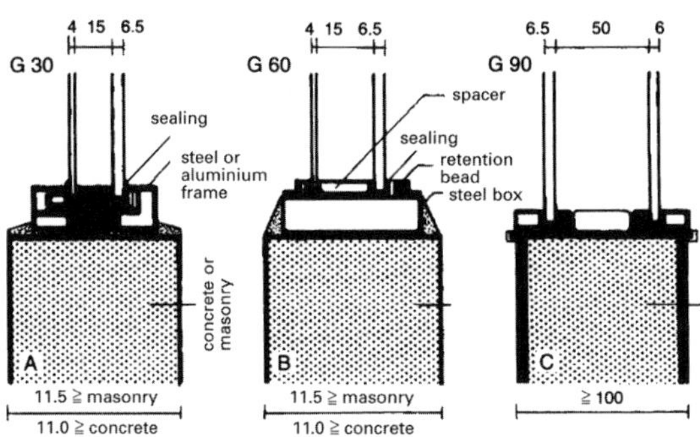

❺ Glazing with fire resistance class 'G'

GLASS

GLASS BLOCKS

Sound reduction

Because of its weight, a glass block wall has particularly good sound insulation properties:
1.00 kN/m^2 for 80 mm glass blocks
1.25 kN/m^2 for 100 mm glass blocks
1.42 kN/m^2 for special BSH glass blocks.
To be effective, the surrounding building elements must have at least the same sound reduction characteristics. Glass block construction is the ideal solution in all cases where good reduction is required. In areas where a high level of sound reduction is necessary, economical solutions can be achieved by using glass block walls to provide the daylight, while keeping ventilation openings and windows. These can serve as secondary escape routes if they conform to the minimum allowable size.

DIN 4109 should be complied with. The weighted sound reduction measurement R'$_w$ is determined according to DIN 52210 → ❶:
R_w = airborne sound insulation margin + 52 dB
Single-skin glass block construction fulfils the requirements of sound insulation class 5 → ❷.

Glass blocks with steel reinforcement

The fire-resistant glazing of glass blocks can, like all other glass block walls, be built with and without U-profiles, and all the possible connections are in principle identical. Because of the strong linear expansion in case of fire and the release of smoke, glass block walls are bedded all round with mineral fibre. → ❹. Fire resistance classes up to G 120 or F 60 can be achieved, depending on the construction and the manufacturer.

FIRE PROTECTION GLASS

Normal glass is of limited suitability for fire protection. In case of fire, the action of heat on one side can cause float glass panes to burst very quickly and large broken pieces to fall out, which can result in the fire spreading. The required fire resistance classes for exposed glazing will be laid down in the building permission. The following fire resistance classes are defined:
G30, G60, G90, G120, G180
F30, F60, F90, F120, F180
T30, T60, T90, T120, T180

Fire resistance classes 'G' and 'F'

'G glasses' must prevent flames or combustion gases passing through for a certain duration of fire (e.g. G30 = 30 minutes). There must be an official technical approval for all 'G glazing', including the installation details. Heat radiation may, however, be transmitted by this glazing, which restricts the possible applications. Such glazing is not permissible for emergency exits.

There are three possibilities for construction of G glazing:
Wired glass with spot-welded mesh
Elaborate special toughened glass combinations in composite isolated glazing
Pre-stressed borosilicate glass, like Pyran.

F glazing has to prevent the transmission of heat radiation, in addition to stopping smoke and fire. This is achieved by using special composite glass panes with a gel layer, which foam or can absorb energy through evaporation effects and can thus prevent radiated heat passing through the pane. The pane and also its connection to the framed construction and adjacent construction elements all have to possess technical approval valid under building regulations.

Construction fire protection can be evaluated only in combination with the adjacent building elements (Fire Protection chapter → p. 511 ff.)

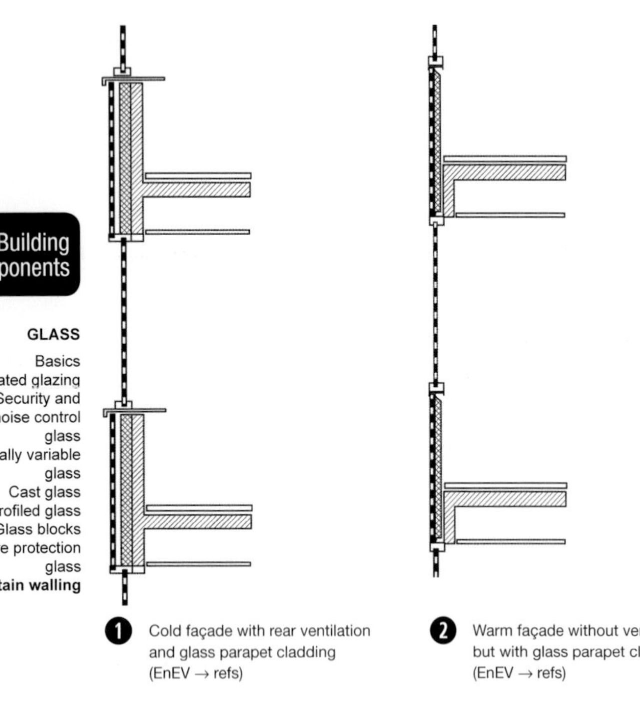

1 Cold façade with rear ventilation and glass parapet cladding (EnEV → refs)

2 Warm façade without ventilation but with glass parapet cladding (EnEV → refs)

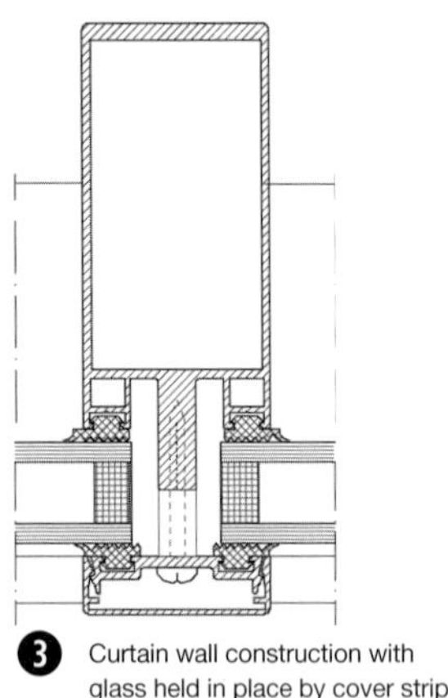

3 Curtain wall construction with glass held in place by cover strip

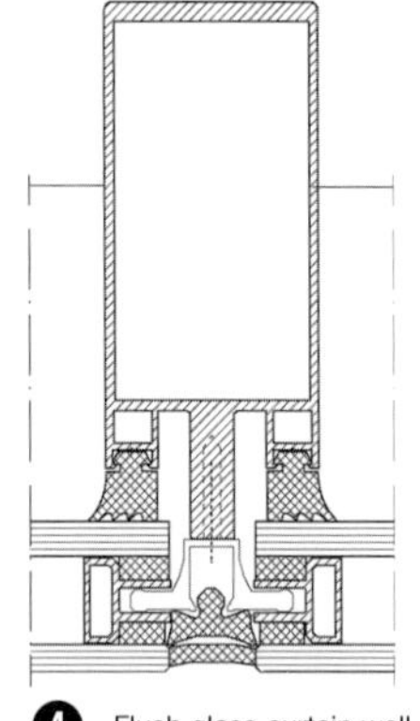

4 Flush glass curtain wall

Radar damping

Radar reflection damping is a requirement of German Air Traffic Control (DFS), applying to the façades of all larger buildings in the vicinity of airports. The purpose is to suppress the reflection of radar signals, which can occur from large façade surfaces, because these reflected signals can lead to false information on the radar screens of air traffic controllers and thus endanger air traffic.

Special coatings can be used to achieve high damping through absorption and phase-delayed overlaying (interference) of the radar signal hitting and being reflected from the insulated glazing. Because of the particular requirements for insulated glazing, the glass structure must be specifically calculated for every application. Light and energy values are determined in each case by the glass structure. The level of radar damping required depends on many factors, including the size of the building and its distance from and orientation to the radar equipment.

A radar report is generally to be commissioned for each building from an accredited institute in order to determine the required radar damping. The glass manufacturers develop a glass structure and this is then discussed with the institute. All other façade surfaces have to be investigated for this report as well, in order to take the necessary measures into account for construction.

Cold façades

A cold façade is a single skin curtain walling construction with a ventilated cavity at the rear, width approx. 40 cm, and single- or double-glazed external cladding panels. Sufficient and controlled heat dissipation must be guaranteed. The façade panels can be fixed all round, on two sides or at points according to official standards and guidelines. Technical approval is required for panels fixed at points, or a special-case approval has to be applied for.

The façade panels can be fully colour-coated on the back or partially printed by the screen-printing process. Special coatings are available from the various manufacturers in order to achieve colour matching with solar control glass. Samples are necessary to ensure a correct colour match. All visible edges must be finely ground and polished and non-visible edges must be ground.

Warm façade without ventilation at rear

The warm façade can consist of post and rail curtain walling or storey-height curtain walling elements. In both cases, the non-transparent parts or parapets have a glass panel. The construction of the external panel can be, for example, an external façade panel with the necessary thermal insulation behind it, thickness in accordance with EnEV, and an internal layer, which is sealed against diffusion of water vapour, e.g. aluminium sheet.

Mixed forms can be constructed, if an additional glass layer is set in front of the warm curtain wall in order to create a two-dimensional appearance (see below). If the panel remains the layer that drains water, then this is still a warm façade.

Flush glass curtain wall

This structural glazing façade is characterised by a uniform flat appearance. A full-surface glass appearance is possible only if the panes are glued to metal frames. The system used must possess technical approval or special case approval. The structural sealing must be carried out with a material (e.g. Dow Corning GmbH Technical Approval No. Z-70. 1–75) that possesses general technical approval valid under building regulations.

In Germany, all façades over 8 m in height must have an additional mechanical fixing of the panes. All insulated glazing must have a UV-resistant edge seal.

Curtain walling with fire-resistant glass

F fire-resistant glazing has only limited practicality for external use, because the foaming fire-protection layer cannot be heated over 50–60 °C. This is only possible to guarantee for façades subject to direct sunshine if effective sun shading is provided and guaranteed.

Sun screens

Sun screens are normally used as additional external transparent sun shading layers. They consist of metallic oxide-coated toughened glass panes. When installing sun screens, the coating should always be on the weather side. Sun screens can, according to official standards and guidelines, be fixed all round, on two sides or at points. Technical approval is required for panels fixed at points, or a special-case approval must be applied for.

Building components

DOORS

Arrangement
Construction details
Special doors
Garage/industrial doors
Locking systems
Security of buildings and grounds

BS 6375
DIN 107

see also: Construction drawing symbols p. 10

Doors must be sensibly arranged inside a building, because unfavourably distributed or unnecessary doors impair the use of rooms, or cause difficulties, and can lead to the loss of storage places → ❶ + ❷.

Categories: Inward-opening doors, which open into the room; outward-opening doors, which open out of the room; doors normally open into the room. Description of types of door according to location and purpose: opening direction, style detail, door lining, construction of door, type of rotation and opening.

Internal doors: Room doors, entry doors of flats, cellar doors, doors for bathroom, WC and subsidiary rooms.

External doors: House front door, back door or yard door, balcony and patio doors.

Special types like centre-hung doors and balanced doors → ❼ require very little strength to open, but the ironmongery is elaborate and the danger of accident at the hinge side has to be taken into account. These are suitable for through-doors in corridors, entrance lobbies, etc.

The width of a door depends on the intended use and the type of room to be accessed. **Minimum clear width for walking through** is 55 cm. In residential buildings, the clear opening width of doors is:

single-leaf doors

room doors	approx. 80 cm
bath, WC	approx. 70 cm
entrance doors to flats	min. 90 cm
front doors	up to 115 cm

double doors

room doors	approx 170 cm
front doors	140–225 cm

clear opening height of internal doors

minimum	210 cm
better	210-225 cm

Sliding doors and revolving doors are not permissible at emergency exits, which they can block in circumstances of danger.

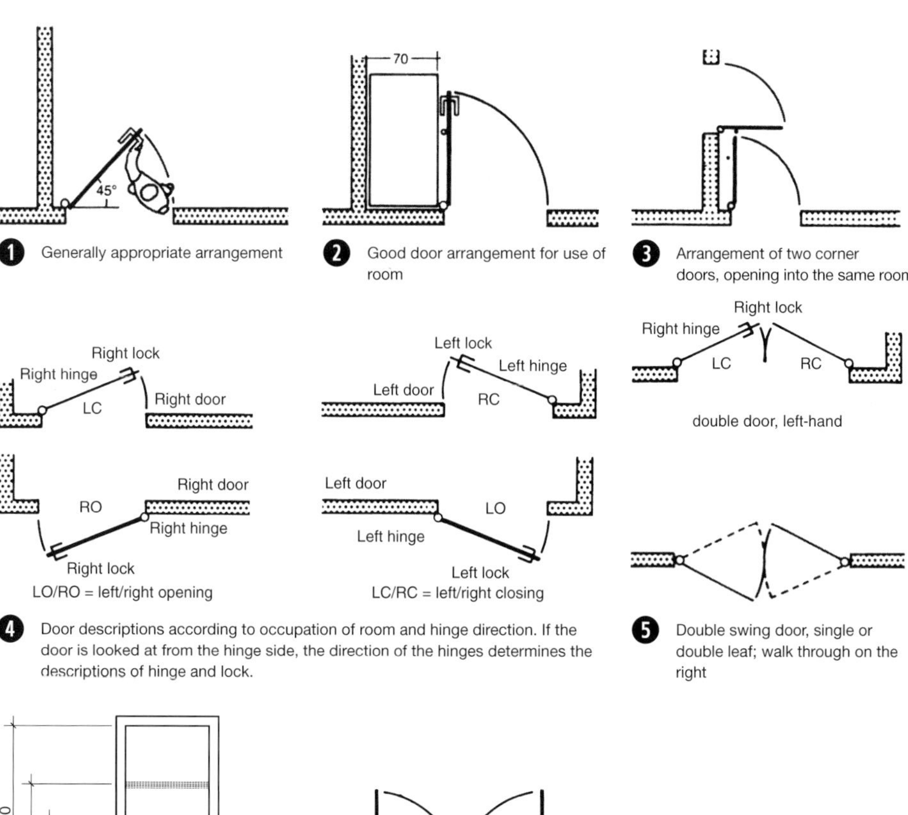

❶ Generally appropriate arrangement

❷ Good door arrangement for use of room

❸ Arrangement of two corner doors, opening into the same room

❹ Door descriptions according to occupation of room and hinge direction. If the door is looked at from the hinge side, the direction of the hinges determines the descriptions of hinge and lock.

❺ Double swing door, single or double leaf; walk through on the right

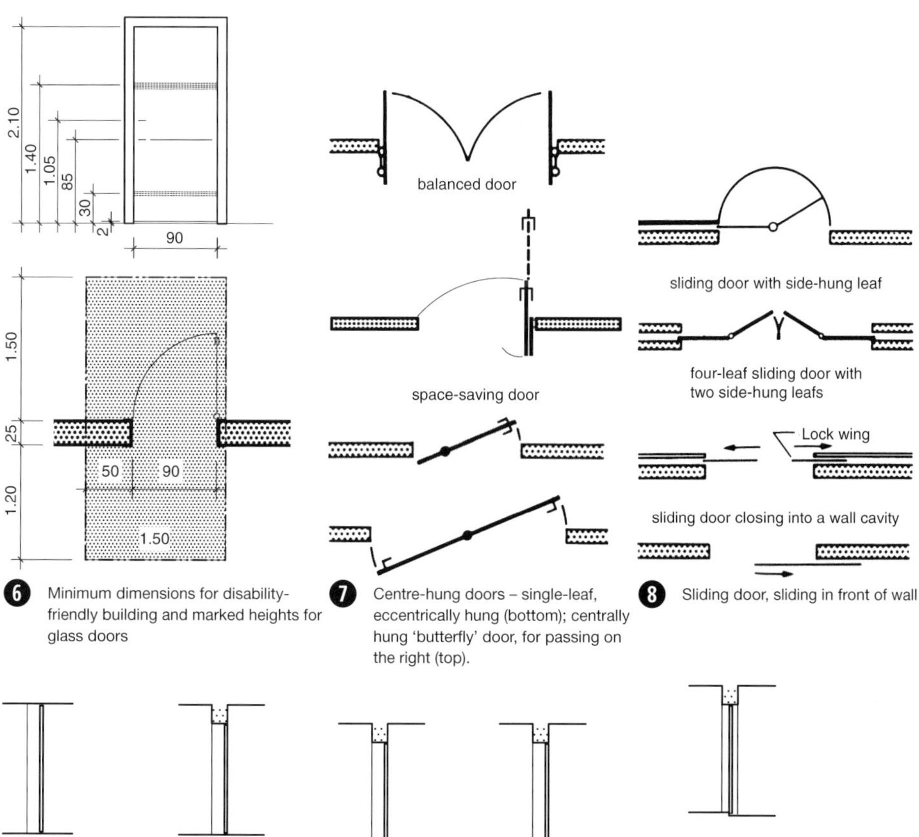

❻ Minimum dimensions for disability-friendly building and marked heights for glass doors

❼ Centre-hung doors – single-leaf, eccentrically hung (bottom); centrally hung 'butterfly' door, for passing on the right (top).

❽ Sliding door, sliding in front of wall

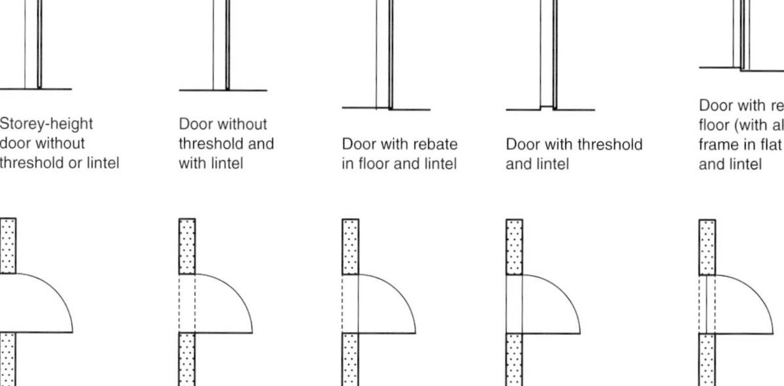

❾ Depiction of lintel and threshold on plan (in this case at 1:100). Height differences in the floor are shown by a continuous line and lintels with a dashed line.

BS 4787
BS 6375
BS 8213
BS EN 14220/1
BS EN 14351
DIN 4172
DIN 18100
DIN 18111

Preferred sizes shown in thick outline

Structural openings for these preferred sizes are, as a rule, for double doors

The standards give the exact measurements concerning frames and door panels for those sizes which are indicated with a number → ⑧

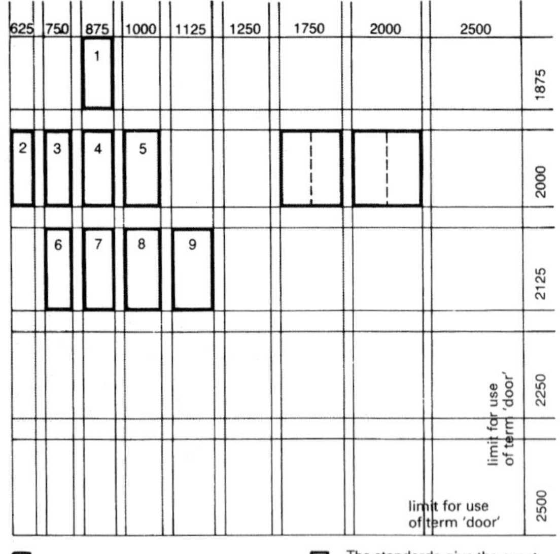

❶ Modular wall openings → ❷

Var.	Standard modular building dimensions		Door dimensions				Lining dimensions	
	Wall openings for door		Outside door panel width		Door panel rebate width, tolerance		Clear opening width, tolerance	Clear opening height, tolerance
					±1	+2 0	±1	0 −2
1	875	1875	860	1860	834	1847	841	1858
2	625	2000	610	1985	584	1972	591	1983
3	750	2000	735	1985	709	1972	716	1983
4	875	2000	860	1985	834	1972	841	1983
5	1000	2000	985	1985	959	1972	966	1983
6	750	2125	735	2110	709	2097	716	2108
7	875	2125	860	2110	834	2097	841	2108
8	1000	2125	985	2110	959	2097	966	2108
9	1125	2125	1110	2110	1084	2097	1091	2108

❷ Rebated doors and rebated linings

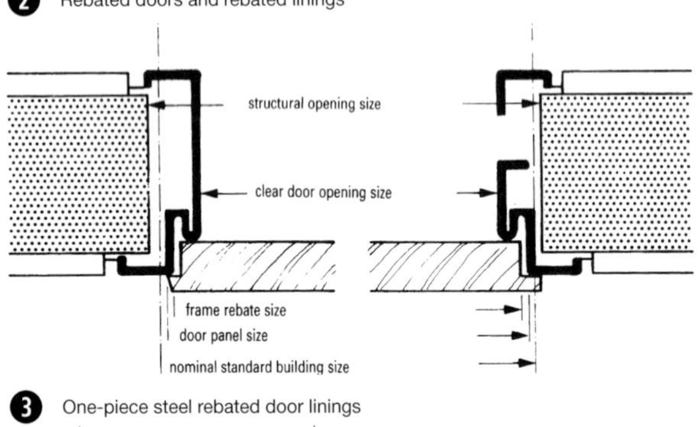

❸ One-piece steel rebated door linings

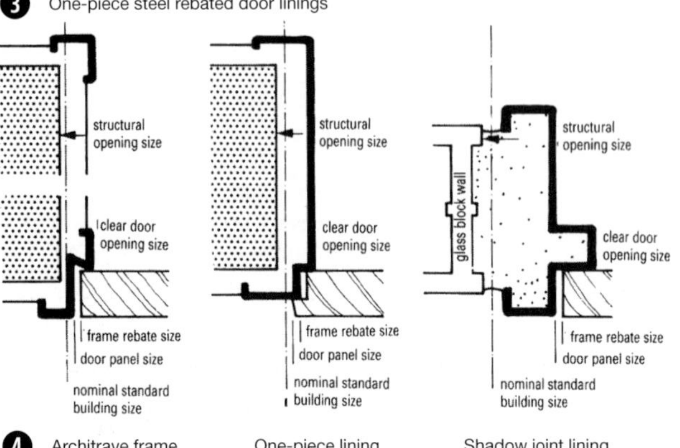

❹ Architrave frame One-piece lining Shadow joint lining

Standard dimensions

Dimensions of wall openings for doors → ❶ are **standard modular dimensions**. If, in exceptional cases, different dimensions are required then their modular dimensions should be whole multiples of 125 mm (100 mm according to British Standards). A wall opening with 875 mm width and 2000 mm height (modular dimensions) can be described as: wall opening DIN 18100 – 875 × 2000. In order to determine the door width, the frame detail has to be taken into account in the calculation of the structural opening, because some variants offer interesting creative possibilities of reducing the clear opening width by more than standard cased doors on account of the thickness of their construction → ❻ – ⓫.

Frame construction

In the specification of a classic frame construction, in addition to the consideration of the differing constructional thicknesses (difference between structural opening and clear pass-through dimension), the different variants of **rebated frame (UK) or rebated door and frame (German)** have to be taken into account, together with the location of the door in the wall. For plain doors in rebated frames → ❿, the quality of construction is important, because inaccuracies in the frame or in hanging the door will immediately be clearly visible. The joint between frame and wall surface can only remain in order in the long term if a shadow joint is specified, because otherwise the transition from wall to door frame will become disarranged with the first redecoration at the latest. Architraves can only solve this problem until the first redecoration.

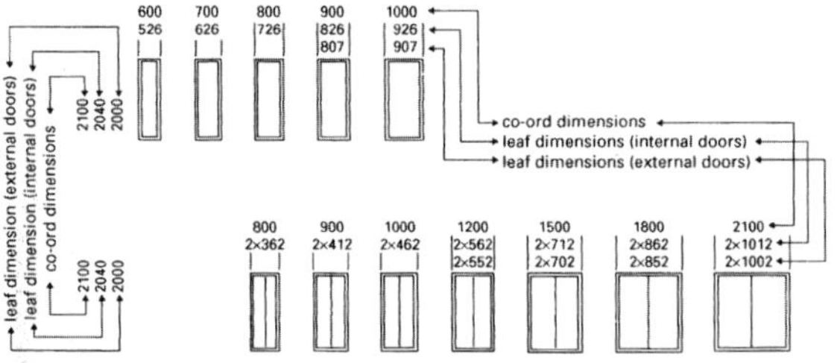

❺ Sizes of internal and external doors, UK, BS 4787-1

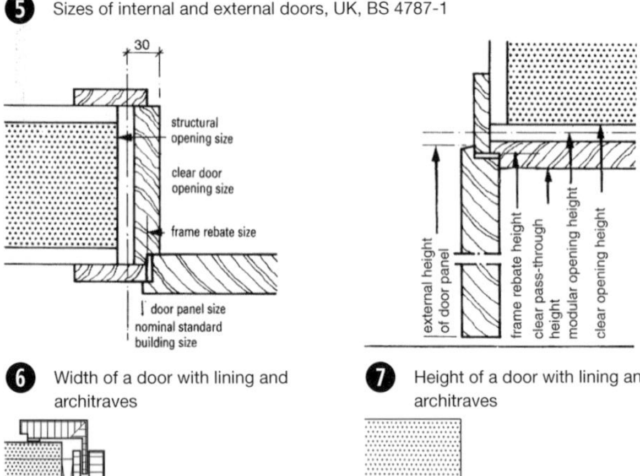

❻ Width of a door with lining and architraves

❼ Height of a door with lining and architraves

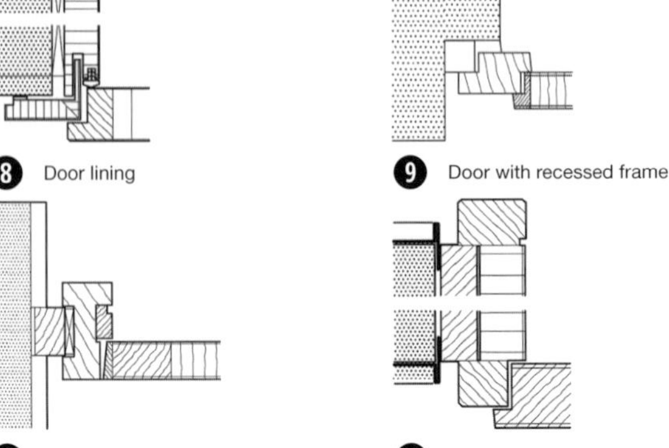

❽ Door lining

❾ Door with recessed frame

❿ Jamb-mounted frame with plain door panel

⓫ Steel door lining with integrated plaster beads

DOORS

Special Doors

min 1.80
normal 2.40
max 2.60

2.00

❶ Two-panel revolving door

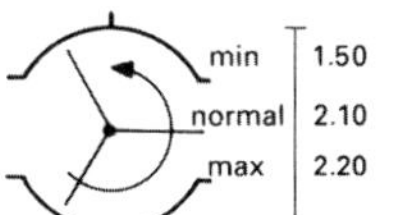

❷ Three panels

❸ Four panels

min 1.80
normal 2.40
max 2.60

❹ Four panels, folded flat

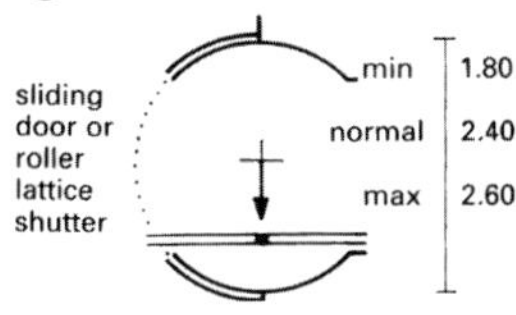

❺ Door assembly pushed to side

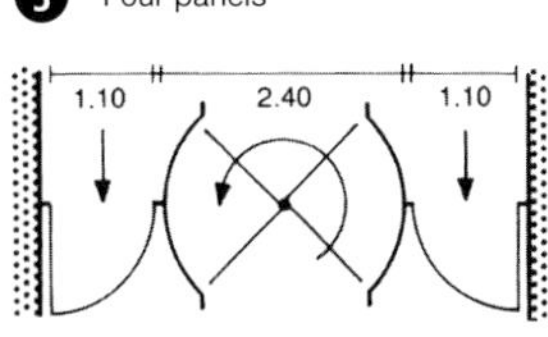

❻ Revolving door with additional emergency exits

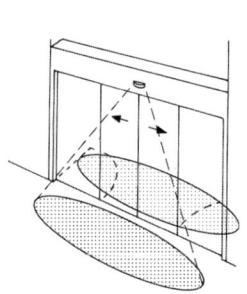

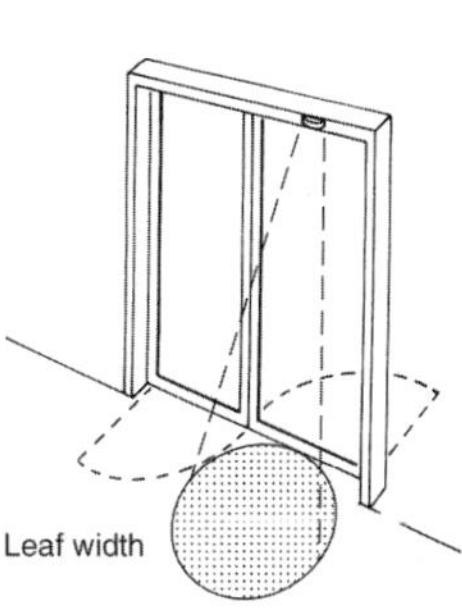

❼ Automatic hinged doors

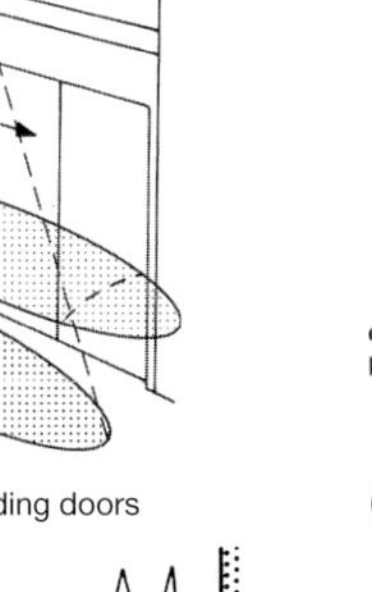

❽ Automatic sliding doors

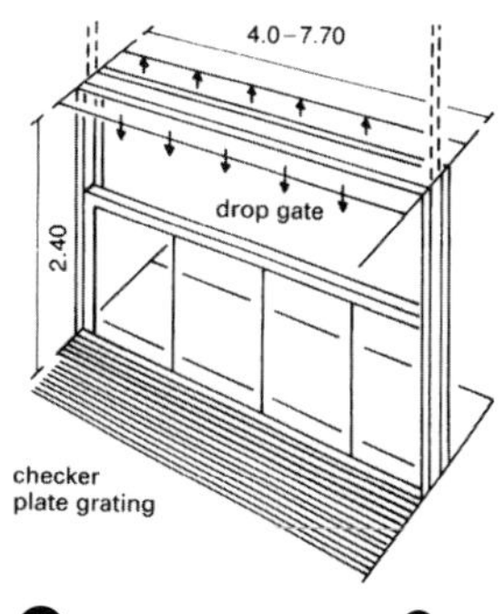

❾ Drop gate installation → ⓳

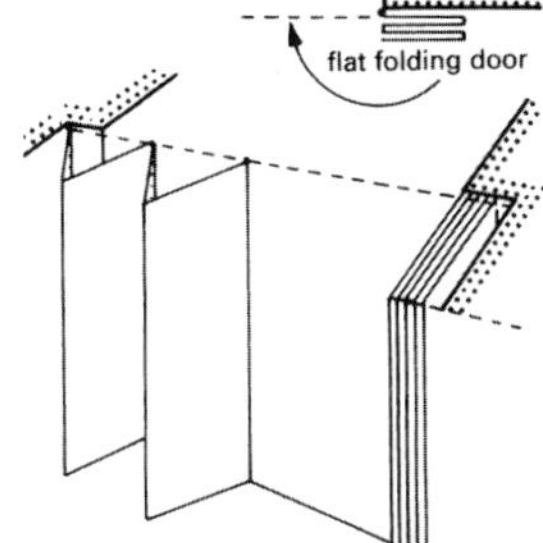

❿ Folding door with side guides

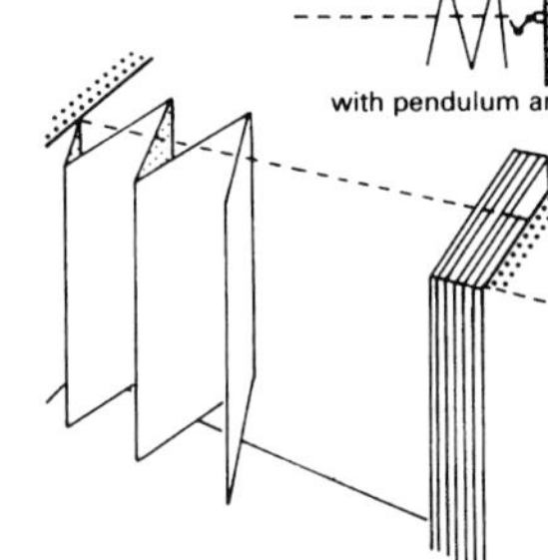

⓫ Folding door with central guides (harmonica door)

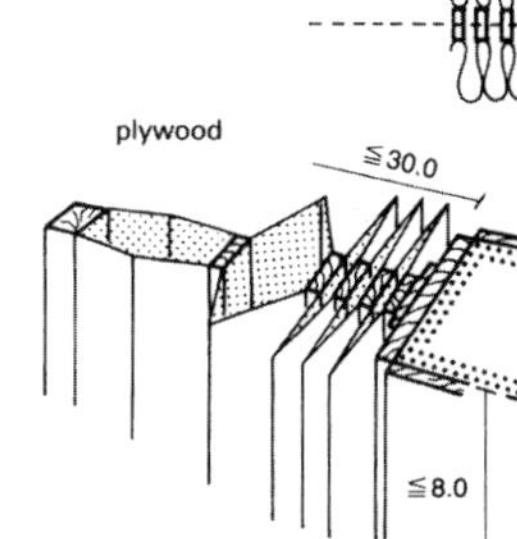

⓬ Accordion door made of wooden panels or flexible material

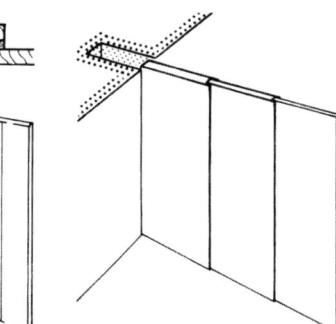

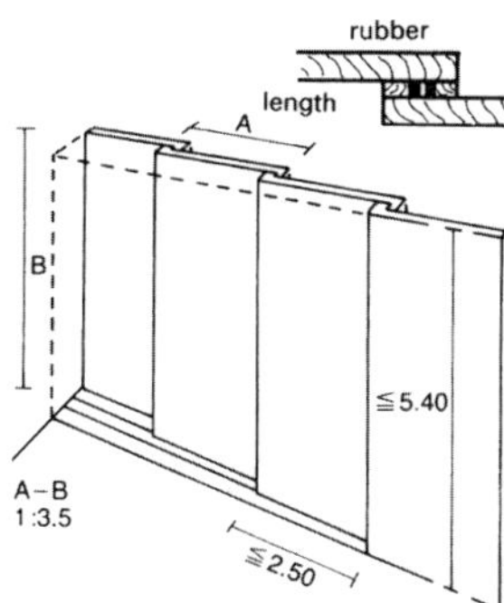

⓭ Telescopic door

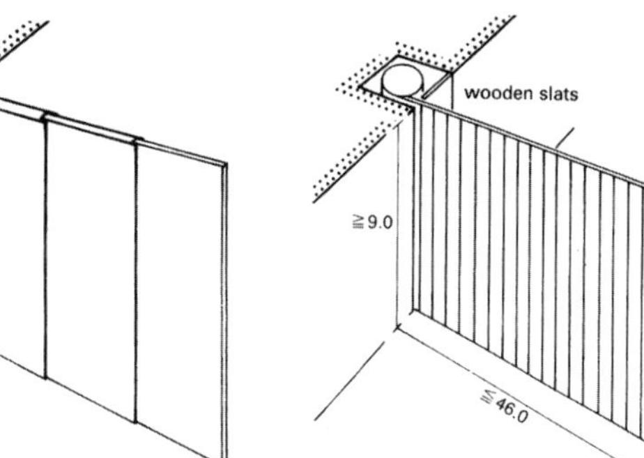

⓮ Telescopic door

⓯ Roller partition

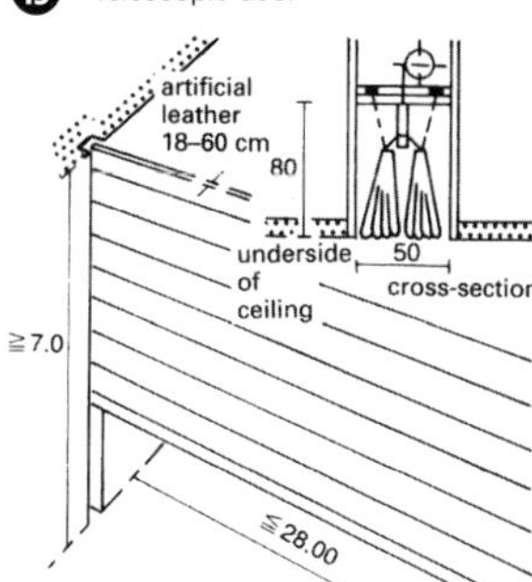

⓰ Partition curtain → p. 341 ❺ – ❽

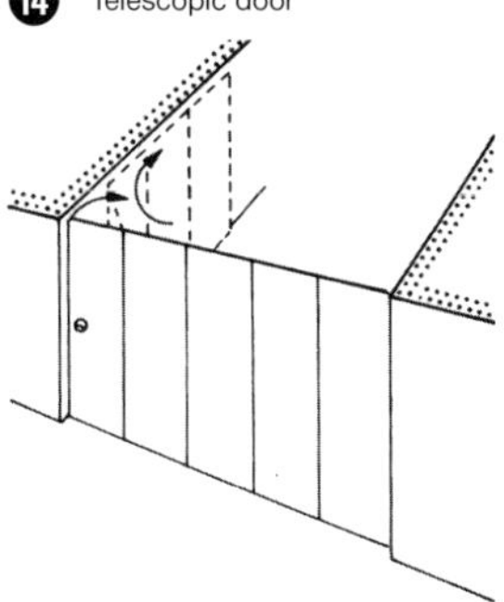

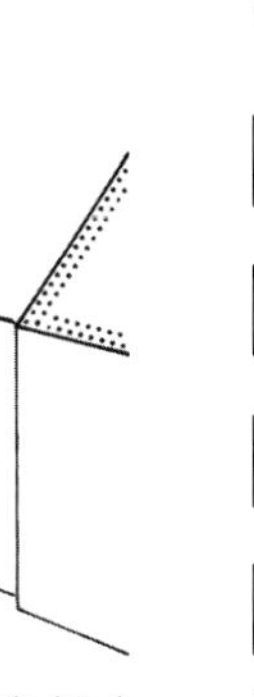

⓱ Corner sliding door, articulated sliding gate

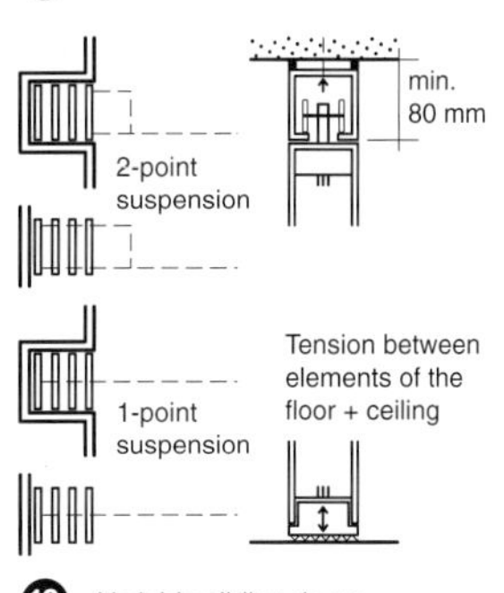

⓲ Variable sliding doors

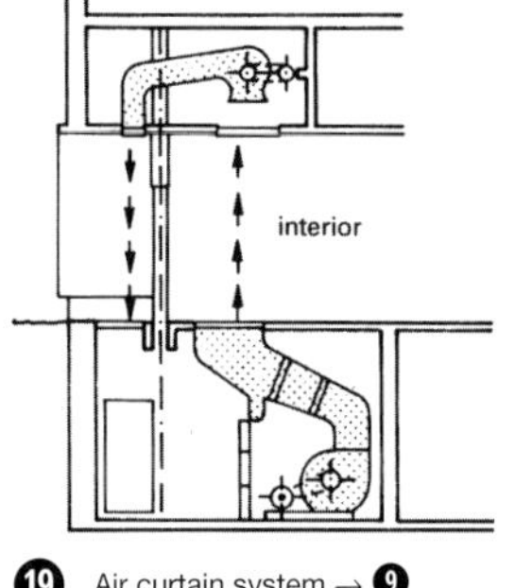

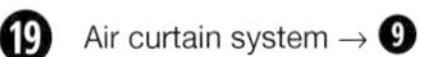

⓳ Air curtain system → ❾

Revolving doors are made in several different designs → ❶ – ❻. Some are adjustable, e.g. when the number of users is large, particularly in the summer, the panels can be folded into the middle to allow people to go in on one side and out on the other simultaneously. Some designs have panels which can be pushed to the side if traffic is only in one direction (e.g. when business closes for the day) → ❹ – ❺. Actuating devices for **automatic doors** can be controlled by radar control, electric contact mats → ❼ – ❽ or pneumatic floor contacts. Unidirectional or reflecting light barriers controlling automatic sliding doors, with six panels up to 8 m wide, are ideal for installation on emergency exits in office blocks, public buildings, and supermarkets. Air curtain doors → ⓳ can be shut off at night by a raised door → ❾.

Folding doors can act as room dividers, guided from the side → ❿. Concertina doors are centrally hung → ⓫ for closing off wide openings. A revolving movement can be combined with a sliding movement. Harmonica doors can be made of plywood, artificial leather or fabric → ⓬. **Telescopic doors** have several panels joined by engagers. Externally guided telescopic doors with external guides are single-skinned→ ⓭; those with internal guides are double-skinned → ⓮.

Sliding partitions → ⓯ + ⓲ make good room dividers (sound insulation) but cannot be installed without tools. Provide room for the relatively bulky partition package in the design!

Folding partitions folded from above → ⓱ or horizontally upwards → ⓰ enable large rooms to be partitioned.

see also:
Fire protection
pp. 511 ff.

DOORS

Garage/Industrial Doors

Up and over doors → ❶ can be used for garages and similar: sliding and/or folding doors, with a spring counterbalance or a counterbalance weight. They may be single skin, double skin, solid, partially glazed, fully glazed, constructed of wood, plastic, aluminium, or galvanised steel. The largest drive-though dimensions are 4.82 × 1.96 m. Max. panel size is approx. 10 m². Installation is possible under a round or segmental arch. Operation is by door gear with radio control. Also available are doors folding upwards → ❸, sectional doors → ❹, telescopic lifting doors → ❺ and roller doors → ❻ made of aluminium, plus large single and multi-skin doors for use in industrial buildings, transport and workshops: max. 18 m wide and 6 m high.

Doors can be operated by: pull switches, light beams, induction or wireless remote control contact pads. There are rapid-opening drive-through doors, flexible PVC doors → ⓭, with single layer, wear- and impact-resistant clear PVC; PVC is also used as strip curtain → ⓮. Single and double panel T30–T90 fire doors → ⓯ and sliding fire-protection doors → ⓰ can be fitted. Movable fire-resistant wall closures such as sliding, lifting or hinged doors must function independently of the electricity network and close automatically in the case of fire (Fischer-Riegel mechanism).

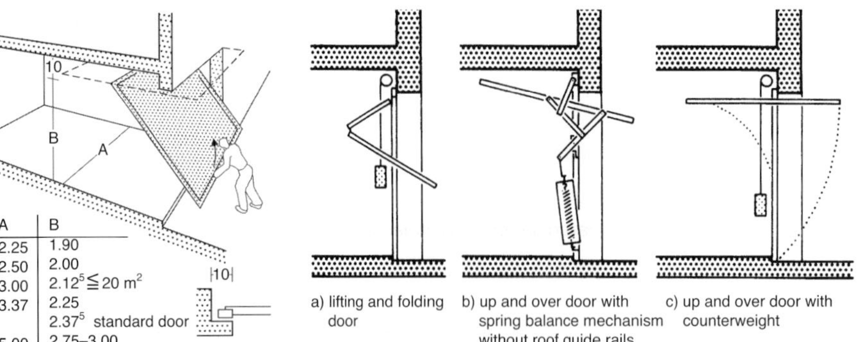

10
B
A
A | B
2.25 | 1.90
2.50 | 2.00
3.00 | 2.12⁵ ≦ 20 m²
3.37 | 2.25
2.37⁵ standard door
5.00 | 2.75–3.00
10

❶ Up and over door

a) lifting and folding door
b) up and over door with spring balance mechanism without roof guide rails
c) up and over door with counterweight

❷ Variants → ❶

20 – 35
B
A
A | B
2.25 | 2.00
5.00 | 3.00

❸ Upward-folding door

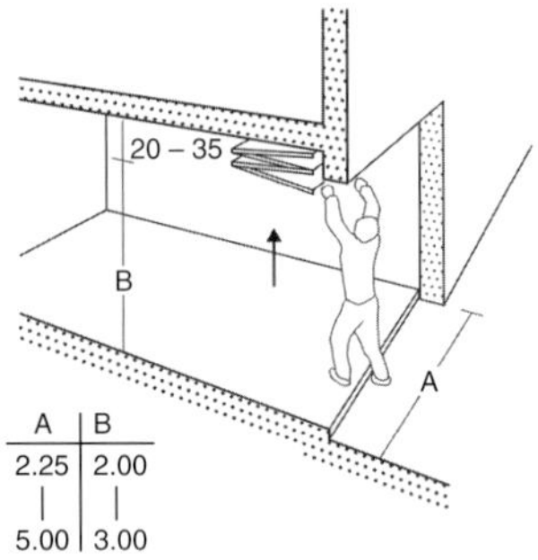

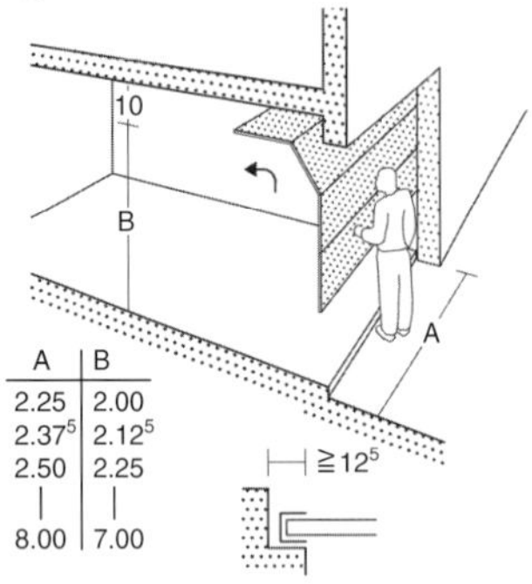

10
B
A
A | B
2.25 | 2.00
2.37⁵ | 2.12⁵
2.50 | 2.25
8.00 | 7.00
≧12⁵

❹ Sectional door

24

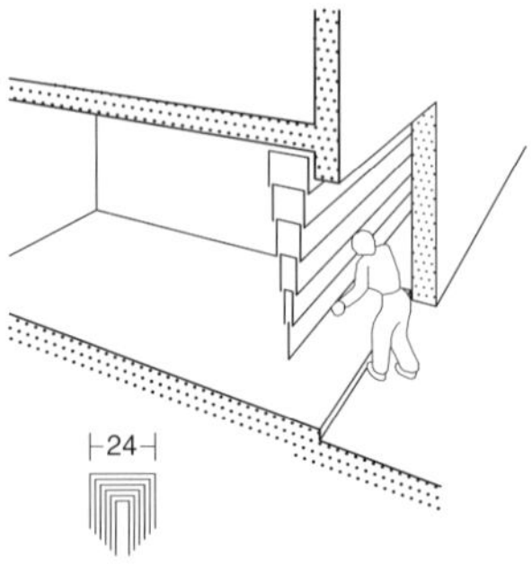

❺ Telescopic lifting door

30 – 40
B
A
A | B
2.00 | 2.00
5.40 | 5.00
8.00 | 8.00
8⁵

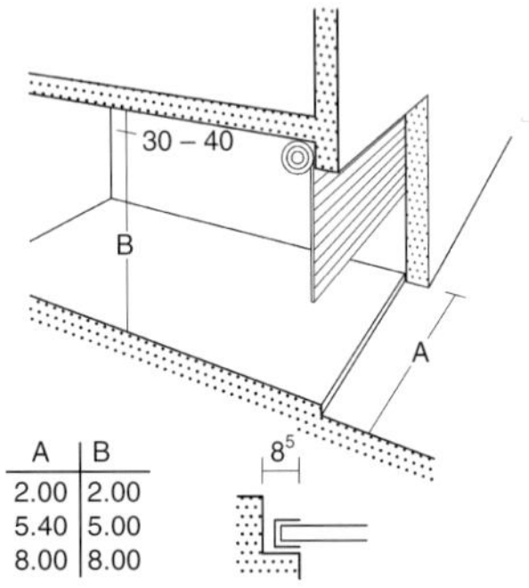

❻ Roller door, shutter (steel and aluminium)

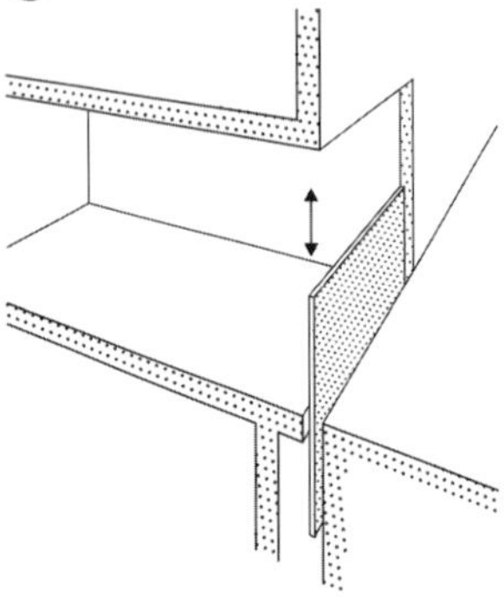

❼ Drop door

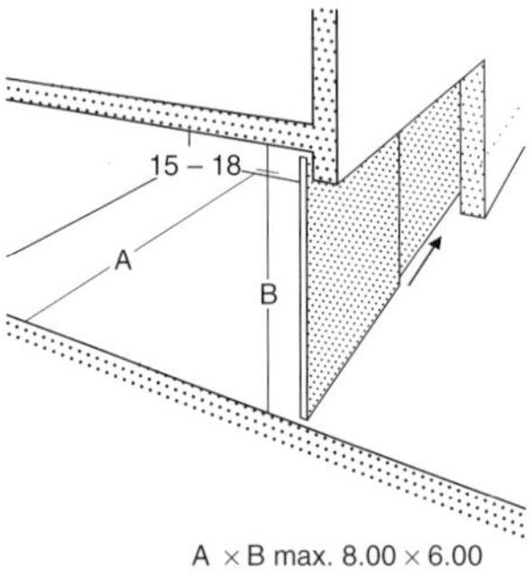

15 – 18
A
B
A × B max. 8.00 × 6.00

❽ Sliding door
steel sliding door T30–T90
T30: 5.00 × 4.00; T90: 8.50 × 3.50

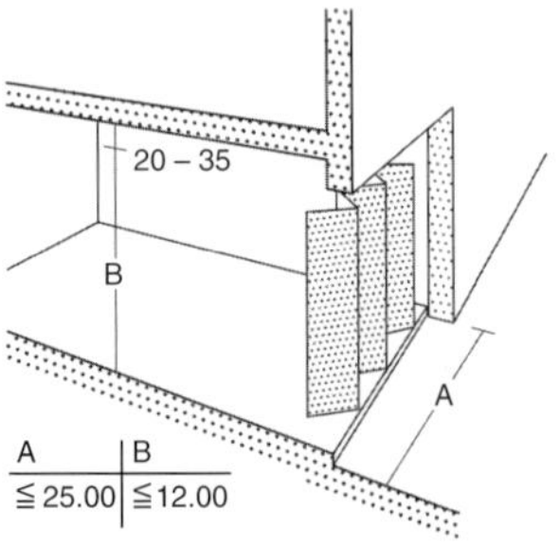

20 – 35
B
A
A | B
≦25.00 | ≦12.00

❾ Folding door → ❿

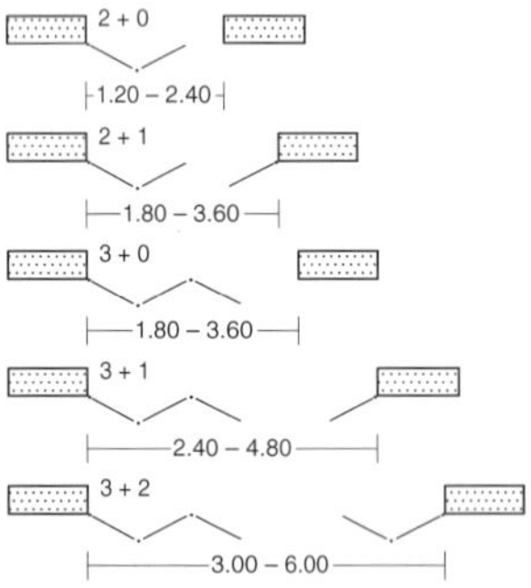

2 + 0
1.20 – 2.40
2 + 1
1.80 – 3.60
3 + 0
1.80 – 3.60
3 + 1
2.40 – 4.80
3 + 2
3.00 – 6.00

❿ Folding doors → ❾

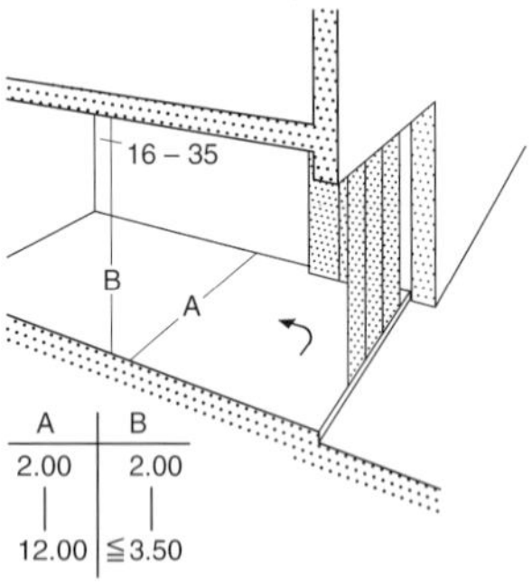

16 – 35
B
A
A | B
2.00 | 2.00
12.00 | ≦3.50

⓫ Sideways-opening sectional door

≦12.00
35 – 40
6.00

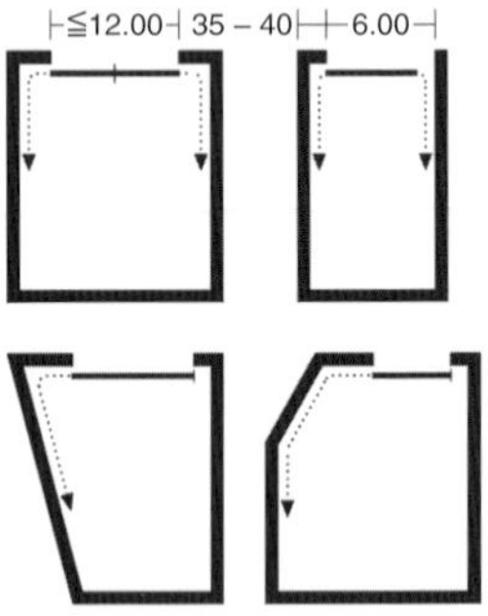

⓬ Possible building layout → ⓫

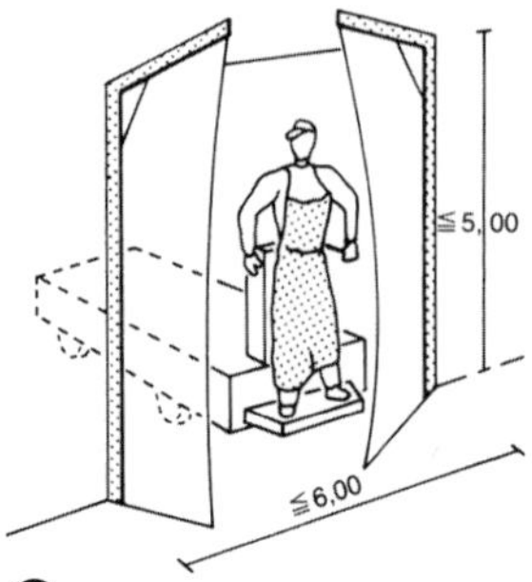

≦5,00
≦6,00

⓭ Flexible rubber door

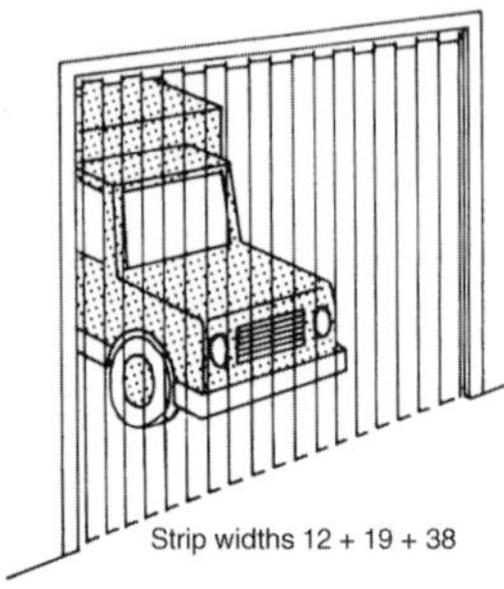

Strip widths 12 + 19 + 38

⓮ Strip curtain

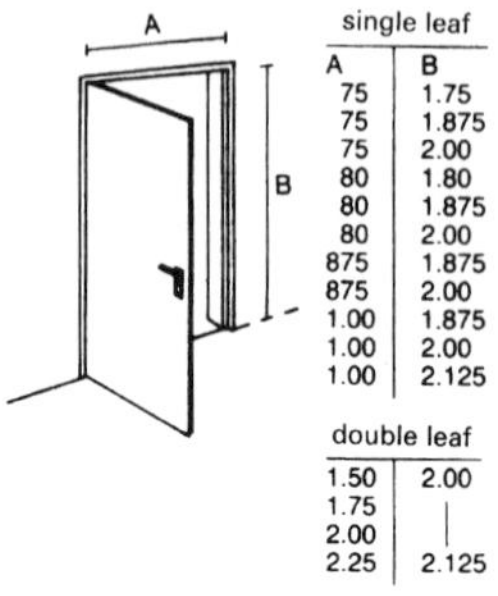

A
B
single leaf
A | B
75 | 1.75
75 | 1.875
75 | 2.00
80 | 1.80
80 | 1.875
80 | 2.00
875 | 1.875
875 | 2.00
1.00 | 1.875
1.00 | 2.00
1.00 | 2.125
double leaf
1.50 | 2.00
1.75
2.00
2.25 | 2.125

⓯ Fire doors T30–T90

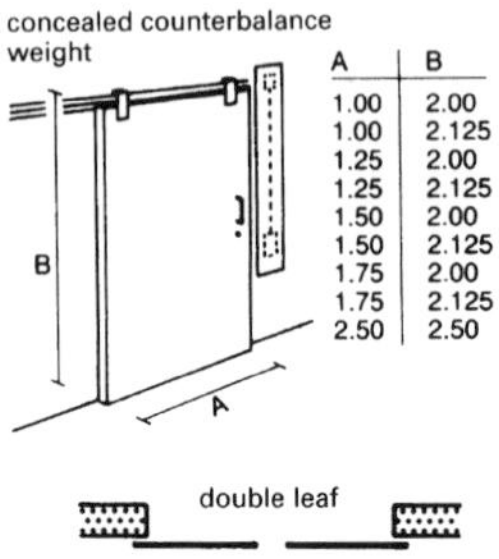

concealed counterbalance weight
B
A
A | B
1.00 | 2.00
1.00 | 2.125
1.25 | 2.00
1.25 | 2.125
1.50 | 2.00
1.50 | 2.125
1.75 | 2.00
1.75 | 2.125
2.50 | 2.50
double leaf

⓰ Sliding fire doors T30–T90

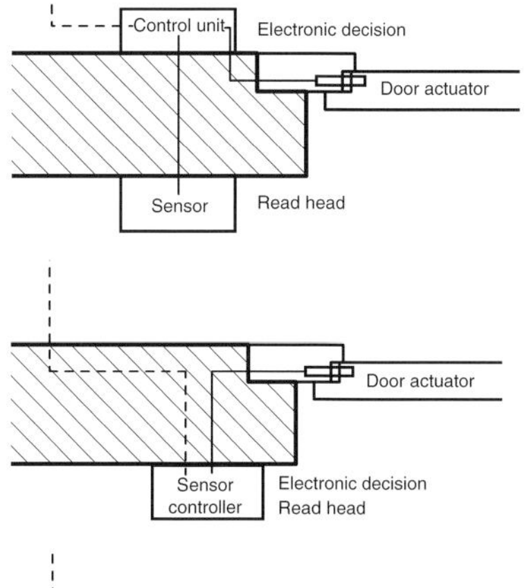

for high security requirements, sensor and control must be separated (control unit in secure area). It must not be possible to operate the control by manipulating the sensor (e.g. short circuit).

when the access control is situated in a supervised area, sensor and control can be located in one building element.

Electronic control unit decision
Door actuator
Sensor read head

mechatronic lock cylinders contain sensor and control unit, with the task of the actuator being undertaken by the mechanical key or a turning knob.

----- possible connection to central monitoring system

❶ Arrangement of the components of electronic locking systems, depending on the security requirements. The systems can be operated either independently (offline) or in connection with a central monitoring system (online).

means of identification

electronic identification

Identification information is read by a sensor from the memory of the identification medium and evaluated by a control system. The following systems vary according to the type of transfer:

with contact	
Passive	magnetic strips – cheap, but can be copied easily (small storage capacity, unencrypted data) chip cards + encryption of the data is possible larger storage capacity than with magnetic cards
Active	chip with battery in the key. Data are transmitted on contact + mechatronic cylinder locks can operate without their own battery

without contact	
Passive	identification medium uses the transmission energy of the querying transmitter for the answer (e.g. RFID chips) + no independent power supply necessary – results in a small range of max. 1 m
Active	infra-red and radio transmitters – independent power supply necessary + range >1 m

biometric identification

Individual characteristics of each person are recorded by a sensor for identification and compared with a database. On account of the complexity of the recognition system, real identification and verification are differentiated.

Identification	the user is recognised through stored biometric data – high computing time, because all reference data have to be compared

Verification	user identifies themselves through a password or an identification medium. The identity of the person is checked against biometric data stored in a database + double system offers high security rapid access to comparative biometric data

❷ Keys are increasingly being supplemented or replaced by electronic and biometric identification methods

Mechanical locking systems

Cylinder locks offer great security, because unlocking using tools is almost impossible. Cylinders can be supplied as required with extensions by multiples of 5 mm on either side to match the particular door thickness.

Locking systems

When a locking system is designed and ordered, a diagram is produced with the associated security certificate. Replacement keys can be delivered only on production of this certificate.

Central locking systems

One key locks the entrance door to a flat and all general and also central doors, e.g. yard, cellar, or front door. Suitable for blocks of flats or houses on estates.

Hierarchical master key locking system

Master keys can lock many cylinders across the entire system. The system can reflect the structure of access rights in a company. Each cylinder has its own key pattern and can be locked only by its own key and by any master keys also intended to open it. For sensitive locations which should be considered in the building design see → ❸

Electronic access control systems

The main disadvantages of mechanical locking systems are the impossibility of altering the lock hierarchy and the inconvenience which results if a master key is lost (replacement of cylinders is expensive). With electronic access systems, right of access can be assigned or deleted at short notice without having to replace building components. Mechatronic cylinders also permit the upgrading of an existing locking systems without wiring it. Elaborate electronic access control systems can make possible the networking of personal identification, access rights according to area and time, and also the recording of working time → ❶ + ❷.

Code locks are also used in private buildings to permit access to anyone who knows the number combination. Entitled people like postmen, tradesmen, suppliers etc. can obtain access without problems.

Emergency exits and panic doors

Since 2004, there have been various requirements for the construction of ironmongery for emergency exits and panic doors. These doors must be tested, approved and labelled as a complete system.

Emergency exits are provided in buildings and areas which are not open to the public and where people familiar with the location understand the function of the escape doors.

Panic doors are used in buildings and areas which are open to the public and in which people familiar with the location do not understand the function of the escape doors.

filing cabinets, bath cubicles, letter boxes, access doors, emergency exits, wardrobes, cool rooms, furniture doors, tube frame doors, roller doors, cupboard doors, desks, drawers, changing cubicles	at risk
lift machinery rooms, lift switches, electrical rooms, garage access doors, up and over garage doors, lattice grille gates, heating room doors, fire-resistant cellar doors, fire-retarding cellar doors, oil filling connections, distribution cabinets	at great risk
office access doors, roof windows, turn and tilt windows, IT rooms, entrance doors, shutters, front doors, lifting doors, cellar windows, fanlights, counters, entrance doors to flats	at very great risk

❸ Risk of break-in according to use

Building components

DOORS
Arrangement
Construction details
Special doors
Garage/industrial doors
Locking systems
Security of buildings and grounds

PAS 3621
PAS 10621
BS EN 12209
DIN 18252

DOORS
Arrangement
Construction details
Special doors
Garage/industrial doors
Locking systems
Security of buildings and grounds

PAS 24
BS 8220
DIN 57100
DIN 57800
DIN 57804

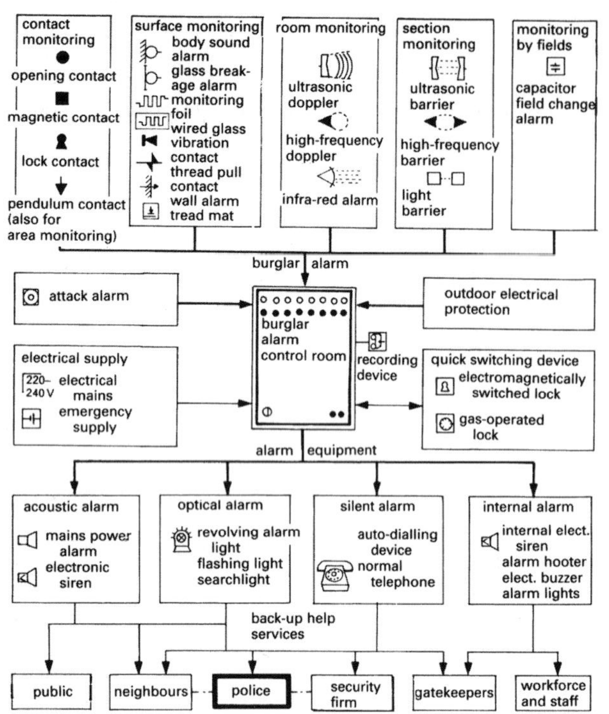

❶ Burglar alarm systems – components and function

RC 1	offers basic protection against casual offenders, who only attempt to break in with physical strength – walking in, causing damage etc.
RC 2	resists attempts to break in with simple tools (screwdriver, pliers, wedges etc.). Doors of this class defeat 80% of all attempts to break in.
RC 3	also resists criminals, who use crowbar or professional-quality screwdriver.
RC 4	also resists attempts even if the criminal uses hammer, axe, nail bar and cordless drill.
RC 5–6	security doors of classes RC 5 and 6 resist attack using heavy drills, angle grinders and jig saws for a long period.

❷ Resistance classes (RC) of building components,

Resistance class	Windows	External doors	Roller shutters
RC 1	–	–	ER 1
RC 2	EF 0/1	ET 1	ER 2
RC 3	EF 2	ET 2	ER 3
RC 4	EF 3	ET 3	ER 4
RC 5	–	–	ER 5
RC 6	–	–	ER 6

❸ Correlation table for the old and new security classes. The assignment of building components, which were evaluated according to old resistance classes, to new resistance classes is not permissible.

The term 'security technology' covers all devices used for defence against criminal danger to the body, life, or valuables. In reality, all parts of a building can be penetrated, even those made of steel and reinforced concrete. The need for security should be identified by an in-depth study of vulnerable areas, with an estimate of costs and benefits.

The police will advise on on the choice of security and monitoring system equipment.

Mechanical protection devices are construction measures which provide mechanical resistance to an intruder. These can only be overcome by the use of force, which will leave physical traces behind.

An important consideration is the effectiveness of this resistance. Such measurements are necessary in blocks of flats at the entrance doors, windows and cellar entrances; and in business premises the display windows, entrances, other windows and skylights. Mechanical protection devices include steel grilles, either fixed or as roller grilles over the building's apertures and ventilation openings, secure roller shutters, secure locks, chains and light shafts. Wire and steel thread inserts in glass can retard breaking in and acrylic and polycarbonate window panes offer enhanced protection.

Electrical security devices will automatically set off an alarm if any unauthorised entry to the protected premises or access to monitored rooms is attempted. An important consideration is the time taken from when the alarm is triggered until the arrival of security staff or the police.

1. Burglar and attack alarm systems help to monitor and protect people and property.

They cannot prevent intruders entering premises, but should give the earliest possible warning of such an attempt. Optimum security can therefore only be achieved by mechanical protection and the sensible installation of burglar alarm systems. Surveillance measures include surveillance of external envelope, of each room, and of individual objects, plus case by case security and emergency calls.

Fire alarm systems give an early warning of danger, and enable direct calls for help in case of fire and/or recognise and report fire at an early stage. Fire alarms serve to protect life and property.

2. Open-air surveillance systems monitor areas outside enclosed rooms. They serve to protect a building against events in the vicinity or in the surrounding open area, which normally extends to cover the property boundary. They consist of mechanical and construction, electronic detection and/or organisational/personnel measures. Their purpose is legal definition, deterrence, prevention, delay, early warning, detection of persons, vehicles, observation, identification, sabotage attempts, spying.

Construction measures may feature building work, fences, ditches, walls, barriers, gates, access control, lighting. Electrical work may includes control centre, detectors, sensors, video/television, access control systems, alarming of next level PO/telemetry exchange/telephone dialler/radio. Organisational measures may concern personnel, observation, supervision, security, security guards, technical personnel, guard dogs, emergency call action plan.

Parts of building and equipment to be protected	Lock contact	Magnetic contact	Surveillance contact	Transitional contact	Glass breakage alarm	Monitoring foil	Glass wired for alarm	Body noise alarm	Vibration contact	Wallpaper alarm and wiring	Tread mat	Trip wire contact	Pendulum alarm	Special types
front doors, external doors	●2)	●	○											
internal security doors	●2)	●	●							○				●4)
room doors[12]	●3)	●	●							○	○5)			
internal sliding doors[12]	○3)	○	●	●						○	○5)			
up and over garage doors		●	○											●8)
windows with casements		●	○		●	○	●		○7)					
glass doors, lifting doors		●	○	○	●	○	●		○7)		○5)			
external glass sliding doors		○		●	●	○	●		○7)		○5)			
rooflight dome		○										●	○	●8)
loft windows		●			●		○9)		○7)					
glass block walls								○	●					
display windows, large fixed glazing					●	●	●		○7)					
heavy walls and ceilings								●	●	○				
light walls and ceilings										●				
loft ladder – retractable		○	○							●	○5)	●	○	
individual objects[12] – sculptures paintings		●												●10)
internal floor surfaces[12]											●			
safes[12]								●			○5)			●11)
cupboards for apparatus[12]		●	●								○5)			
conduits, ventilation shafts, service installations												●	●	

burglar alarm ● very suitable ○ still suitable

1) various alarms to be used only with reservations (e.g. not on wired, laminated or toughened glass)
2) principally as a security device
3) if there is rapid switching on this door
4) if only the internal security door is to be protected (see also door interlock with alarm)
5) designed for security traps
6) magnetic contact – special type for floor mounting
7) not to be used where it can be touched by hand, if panels are unstable or there are vibration sources nearby
8) there are rooflight domes with built-in alarm protection
9) note reservations concerning the weight of glass
10) individual protection is recommended for very valuable furnishings or those with very valuable contents
11) capacitative field alarms are the recommended protection
12) and/or included in the room surveillance

1 Contact and area surveillance – appropriate use of burglar alarms

Feature		Ultrasound room protection	Ultrasound doppler	High-frequency doppler	Infra-red detector
surveillance characteristics preferred, direction of movement covered					
surveillance range per unit – guidelines for range		ceiling mounted 90–110 m², wall mounted approx. 40 m² up to 9 m	according to device 30–50 m² up to 14 m	according to device 150–200 m² up to 25 m	according to device 60– 80 m² rooms up to 12 m corridors up to 60 m
surveillance of entire room (over 80% of the room monitored)		guaranteed	not guaranteed	not guaranteed	guaranteed
typical application		– small to large rooms – corridors – surveillance of whole and parts of rooms	– small to large rooms – parts of rooms – motion detection	– long, large rooms – parts of rooms – motion detection in large rooms	– small to large rooms – surveillance of whole rooms or parts of rooms – motion detectors – also fire alarm
permissible ambient temperature	under 0°C	permissible in some cases	permissible in some cases	permissible	permissible
	from 0° to 50°C	permissible	permissible	permissible	permissible
	over 50°C	not permissible	not permissible	permissible	not permissible
are many sensors in one room possible?		no problem	with care	with care	no problem
effects from neighbouring rooms or adjacent road traffic		no problem	no problem	not recommended	no problem
possible causes of false alarms		– loud noises at ultrasound frequency – air heating near sensor – strong air turbulence – unstable walls – moving objects, e.g. small animals	– loud noises at ultrasound frequency – air heating – air turbulence – unstable walls – moving objects, e.g. small animals – disturbing influences near sensor (increased sensitivity)	– ray deflection through reflection from metallic objects – ray passes through walls and windows – unstable walls – moving objects, e.g. small animals, fans – electromagnetic effects	– heat sources with rapid temperature alterations, e.g. light bulbs, electric heating, open fires in working area – direct, strong and changeable or actions on the sensor – moving objects, e.g. small animals

2 Room surveillance – the most important comparative features

Security systems *(continued)*

Symbols → p. 17

3. Goods security systems, also called shoplifting prevention systems, are electronic systems that serve to prevent theft and the unauthorised and illegal removal of goods from a controlled room or area in normal daily use.

4. Access control systems: electronic access control works together with mechanical elements to permit or refuse access to a building, room or zone through an identity check. This is done by electronically testing the personal identity or by checking the authorisation on site. Combination of an access control with a time recording system is technically possible. → p. 117

5. Remote control systems enable data transmission/exchange between two remote locations over public telephone, mobile phone or Internet. They are used for remote monitoring, measurement, control, diagnosis, regulation and remote querying of information, data and condition of one object in relation to another.

6. Surveillance systems: observation, control, recording of occurrences and events using camera and monitor, manually and/or automatically, inside and outside buildings, any time of day or night and 365 days of the year.

7. Lift emergency system can be used in passenger lifts and goods lifts. Lift emergency systems ensure the safety of the users of lifts and are mainly intended to enable the rescue of trapped people, who have direct voice communication with a constantly manned emergency centre, responsible for rescue.

PAS 24
BS 8220
DIN 57100
DIN 57800
DIN 57804

STAIRS

Principles
Regulations
Construction
Ramps
Spiral stairs
Access and escape ladders
Escalators
Moving walkways

BS 5395
BS 5578
DIN 18065

STAIRS

Principles

Various calculations and dimensional requirements for the construction of stairs appear in national building regulations and standards. In the UK, British Standards and the building regulations should be consulted (see Approved Document K). For workplaces, the regulations of the relevant health and safety body are to be observed. According to German standards, residential buildings with no more than two flats must have a usable stair width min. 0.80 m, 17/28 riser to tread ratio, stairs not deemed by building regulations to be legally essential (as fire escape routes) 0.50 m, 21/21 but legally essential stairs 1.00 m, 17/28, high-rise flats 1.25 m width. Stair width in public buildings is calculated according to the required evacuation time → p. 318 (Stadiums).

Length of runs on legally essential stairs is ≧3 steps up to ≦18 steps → ❺, landing length = *n* times length of stride + 1 depth of tread (e.g. riser to tread 17/29 = 1 × 63 + 29 = 92 cm or 2 × 63 + 29 = 1.55 m). Doors opening into the stairwell must not obstruct the stair width. The 18-step rule is a 'should' regulation. For stairs intended to be prestigious the requirement to provide landings is mitigated.

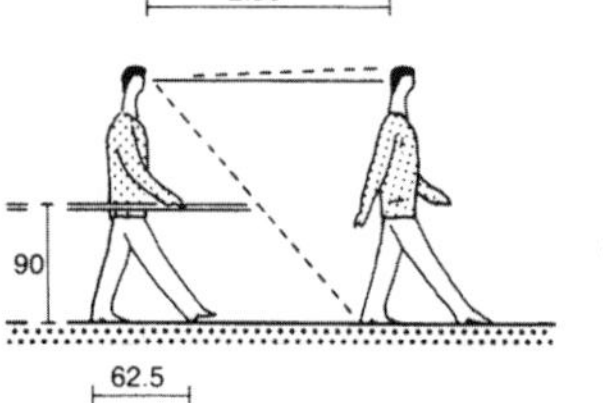

❶ Standard stride of an adult on a horizontal surface

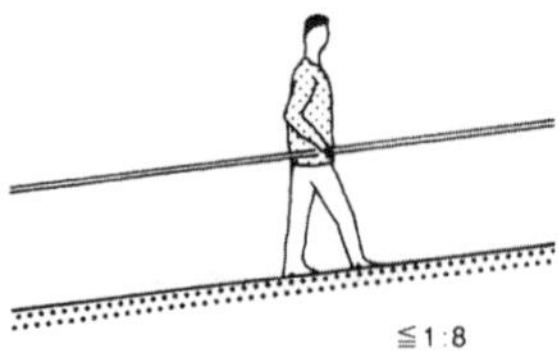

❷ On a slope the stride is reduced: a comfortable slope is 1:10–1:8

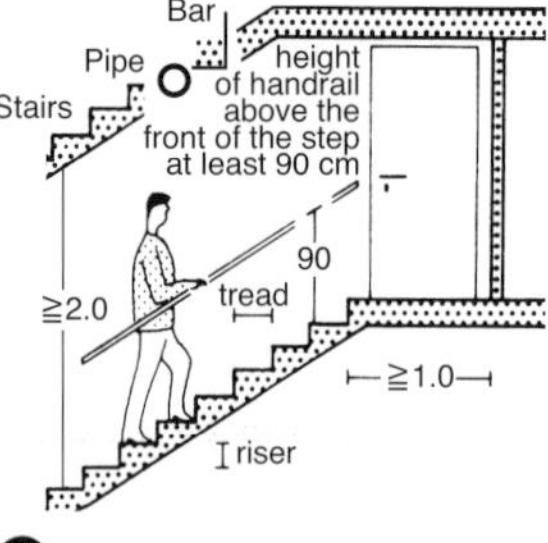

❸ Good standard riser to tread ratio 17/29, stride 2 risers + 1 tread = approx. 62.5 cm

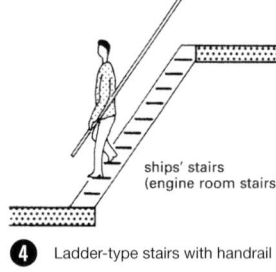

ships' stairs (engine room stairs)

❹ Ladder-type stairs with handrail

landing

max. of 18 steps

❺ Normal stairs 17/29, landing after max. 18 steps for legally essential stairs. Prestigious-style stairs can climb up to a 4 m storey height without a landing.

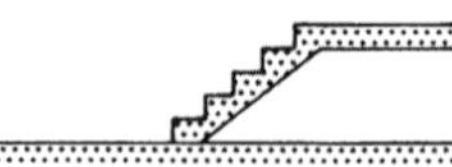

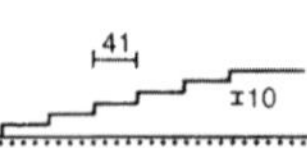

stairs with a rise of less than 1:4 do not require handrail

❻ Stairs without a handrail

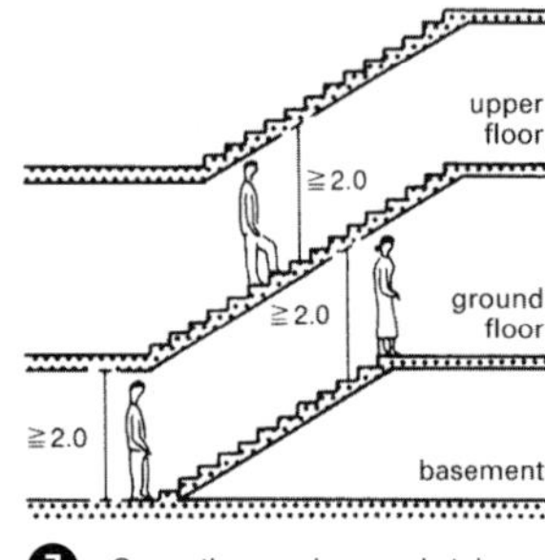

❼ Correctly superimposed stairs save space

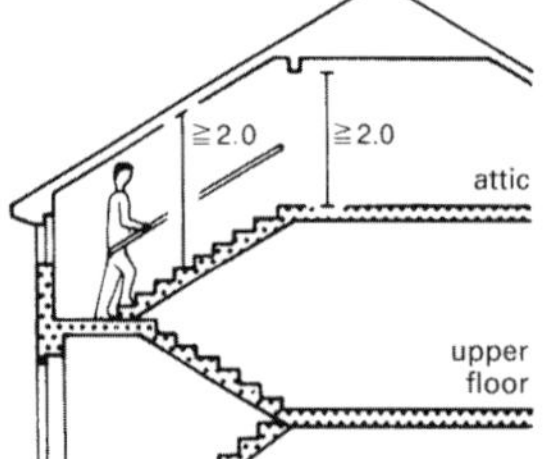

❽ If rafters and beams are arranged in the direction of the stairs, this saves space and expensive trimmers

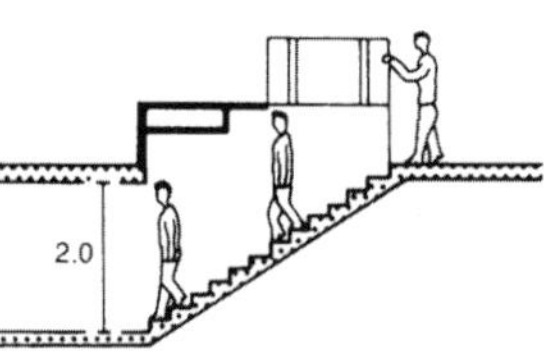

❾ Covered entrances to cellars necks and trapdoors are to be avoided; but the arrangement shown here has advantages and is safe

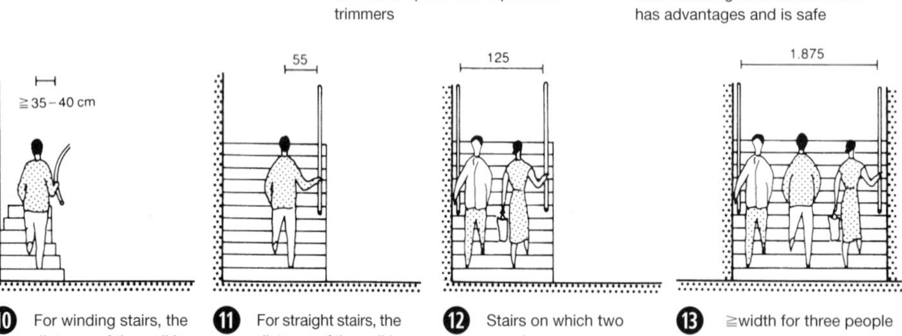

❿ For winding stairs, the distance of the walking line to the inner cheek is 35–40 cm

⓫ For straight stairs, the distance of the walking line to the handrail is 55 cm

⓬ Stairs on which two people can pass

⓭ ≧width for three people

Storey height	Two flight stairs Flat (good) pitch		One, two and three flight plus building stairs Flat (good) pitch	
	No. steps	Riser	No. steps	Riser
a	b	c	f	g
2250	–	–	13	173.0
2500	14	178.5	15	166.6
2625	–	–	15	175.0
2750	16	171.8	–	–
3000	18	166.6	17	176.4

⓮ Storey height and stair risers

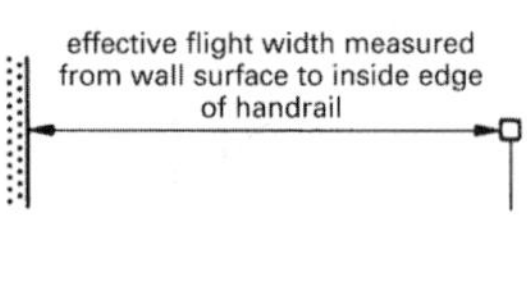

. . . or between the handrails

stairs must have a fixed handrail; if stair width is greater than 4 m, there must also be a central handrail; spiral staircases must have a handrail on the outside

⓯ Stairs: minimum width

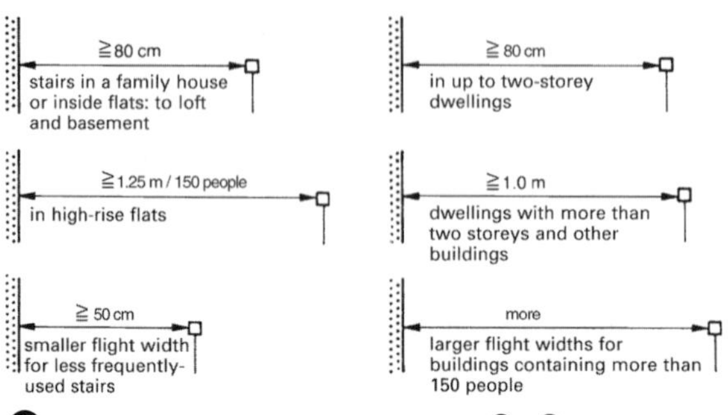

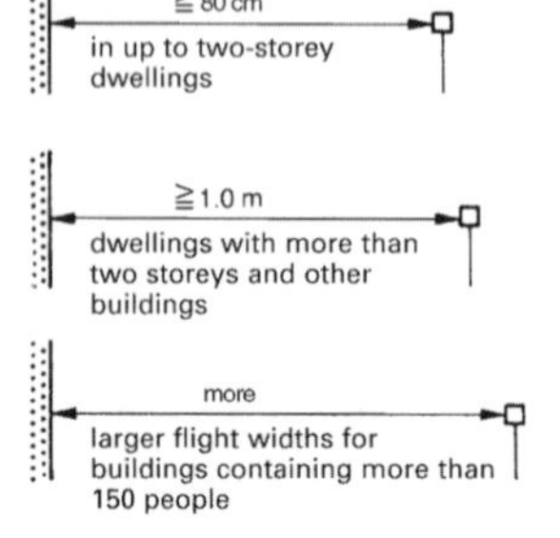

⓰ Measurement of usable passing width → p. 121 ❷ – ❸

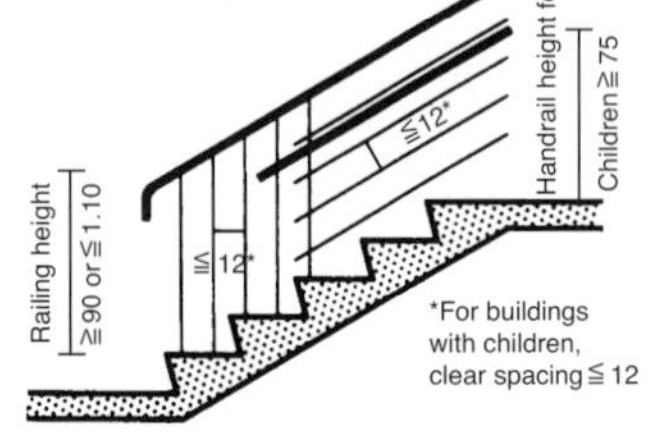

⓱ Handrail heights, hand heights, avoid ladder effect

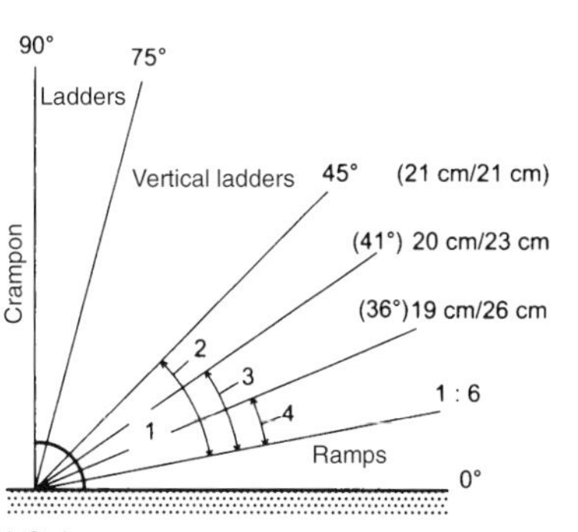

1 Stairs
2 Cellar and attic stairs, which do not lead to occupied rooms, and stairs which are not required under building regulations (additional stairs) according to Table 3, lines 2, 3 and 5.
3 Stairs required under building regulations, which lead to occupied rooms, for residential buildings with not more than two flats, according to Table 3, line 1.
4 Stairs required under building regulations in other buildings according to Table 3, line 4.

1 Incline for ramps, stairs and ladders

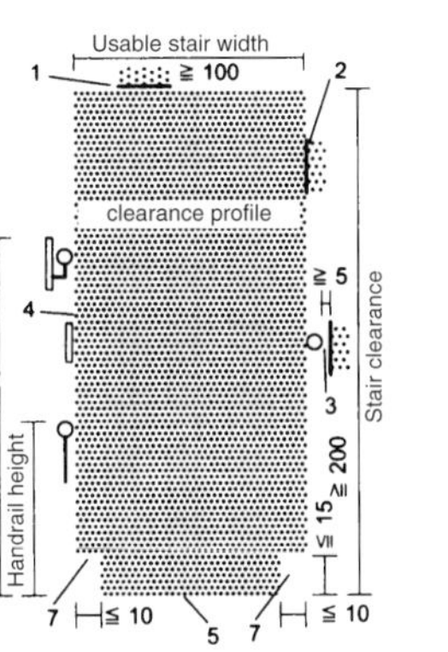

1 Without limitation of the clear opening section, e.g. the underside of the stair flight above
2 Limitation of the clear opening section at the side, e.g. through the surface of the finished wall (cladding)
3 .... e.g. to the inner edge of a handrail on the wall side; side mounted handrail spaced min. 5 cm from the wall
4 e.g. through the inner edge of a balustrade or handrail on the balustrade side
5 lower edge of the clear opening section
6 Upper edge of the clear opening section, e.g. to a ceiling slope
7 Lower edge (limitation) of the clear opening section e.g. through stair string or continuous skirting at stair pitch

2 Stairs: clearance profile

Row	Type of building	Type of stairs	Usable stair width (min)	Stair riser (R)[2]	Stair tread (T)[3]
1	residential	stairs leading to habitable rooms	80	20	23
2	buildings with not more than	cellar stairs, which do not lead to habitable rooms	80	21	21
3	two storeys[1]	loft stairs, which do not lead to habitable rooms	50	21	21
4	other buildings	legally essential stairs	100	19	26
5	all buildings	non-essential (additional) stairs	50	21	21

1. also excludes maisonette flats in buildings with more than two storeys
2. but not <14 cm
3. but not >37 cm = stipulation of the pitch riser/tread
4. for stairs with a tread <26 cm, the overhang (*o*) must be at least so large that a total tread of 26 cm ($t + o$) is given
5. for stairs with a tread <24 cm, the overhang must be at least so large that a total tread of 24 cm ($t + o$) is given

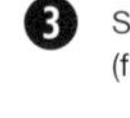

3 Stairs in buildings – limits of dimensions (finished dimensions)

Type of building	Max. distance
– high-rise buildings – schools – shops	25 m
– enclosed and underground garages – buildings where people congregate (from exit to stairwell) – hospitals	30 m
– buildings without special status, according to LBO – restaurants and hotels	35 m

4 Maximum distance of any location in an inhabitable room from a stairwell deemed legally essential by MBO (and observe LBO!)

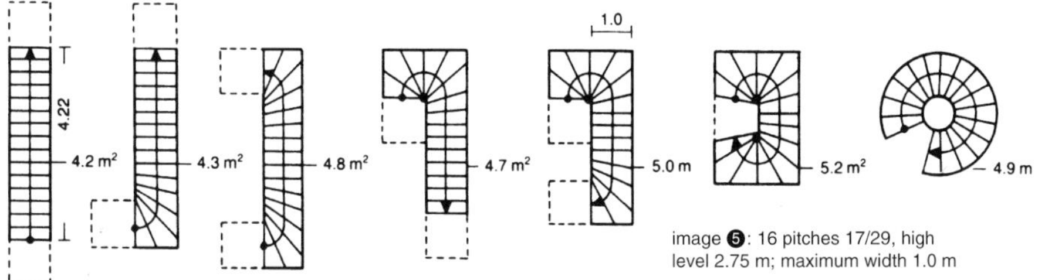

image **5**: 16 pitches 17/29, high level 2.75 m; maximum width 1.0 m

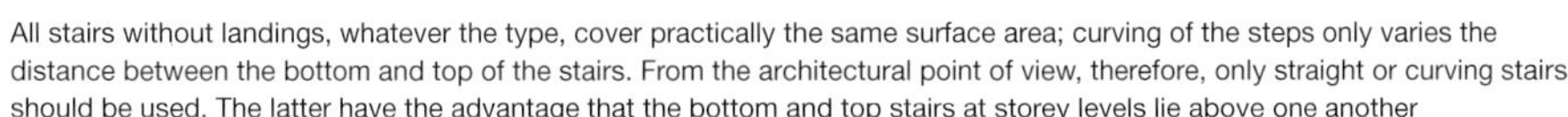

5 All stairs without landings, whatever the type, cover practically the same surface area; curving of the steps only varies the distance between the bottom and top of the stairs. From the architectural point of view, therefore, only straight or curving stairs should be used. The latter have the advantage that the bottom and top stairs at storey levels lie above one another

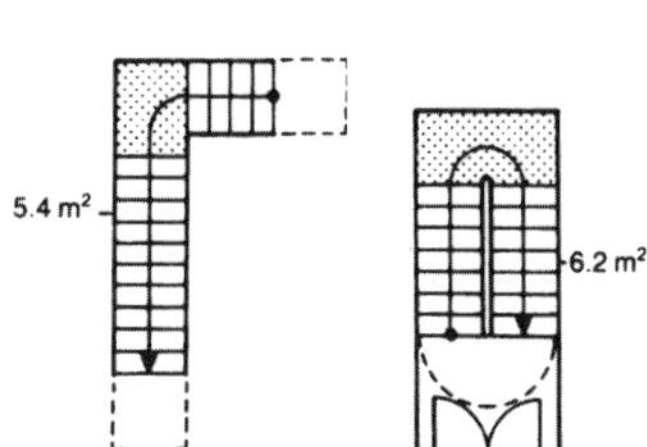

6 Stairs with landings cover the surface area of single flight stairs + the landing. Stairs with landings are required in legally essential stairways with a storey height of ≧2.75 m. Landing width ≧ stair width.

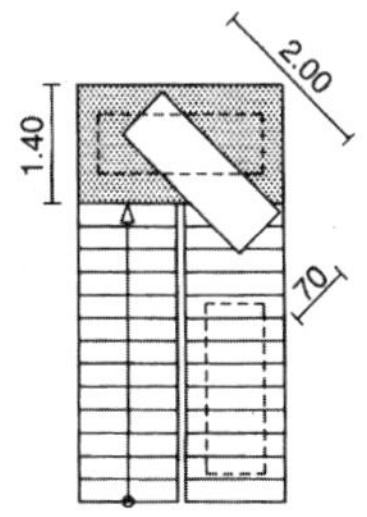

7 Minimum space required for furniture transport

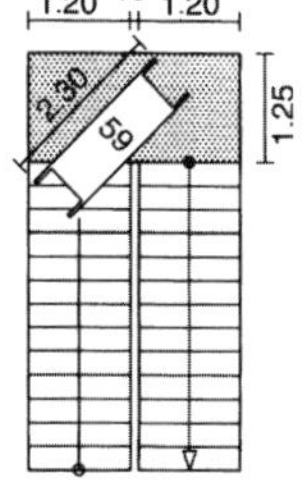

8 For the carrying of stretchers

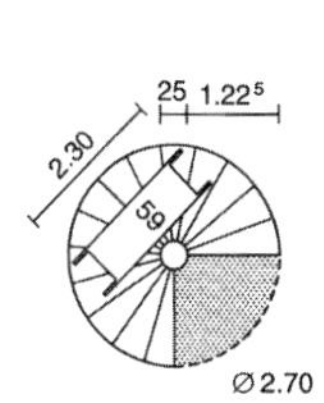

9 For a spiral staircase

The experience of using stairs and access routes is very varied: from the creative possibilities of the most diverse residential stairs to an elaborate outside staircase, which one can stride up and down. Climbing stairs takes on average seven times the energy input as walking on the flat. From the physiological point of view, the best use of 'climbing effort' is at a stair pitch of 30° and a ratio of riser (*r*) to tread (*t*) of 17/29. The pitch is determined by the stride length of an adult (approx. 59–65 cm). In order to determine a suitable pitch with the lowest energy requirement, this formula applies: $2\,r + t = 59–65$ cm.

For determining the dimensions and form of stairs, their overall functional and design purpose is just as important as the relationships described above. Not just changing level is important, but how the level is changed. For outside stairs, low steps are preferable, with dimensions of 12 × 41 to 16 × 30 cm. Stairs in offices or emergency stairs should, in contrast, make it possible to change level quickly. All main staircases must be enclosed in a continuous stairwell, which is designed and arranged so that, including its access routes and exit to the open air, it can safely be used for escape. Exit width should be ≦ stair width.

Every location in inhabited rooms and basements must be ≦35 m from the stairwell of at least one legally essential stairway or exit. If a number of stairways are necessary, then they should be arranged so that the escape route is as short as possible. Any openings from stairwells into cellars, uninhabited roof spaces, workshops, shops, storerooms, and similar must be fitted with self-closing doors with a fire resistance rating of 30 minutes.

Building components

STAIRS

Principles
Regulations
Construction
Ramps
Spiral stairs
Access and escape ladders
Escalators
Moving walkways

BS 5395
BS 5578
DIN 18065

Building components

STAIRS
Principles
Regulations
Construction
Ramps
Spiral stairs
Access and escape ladders
Escalators
Moving walkways

BS 5395
BS 5578
DIN 18065

see also: Fire protection pp. 511 ff.

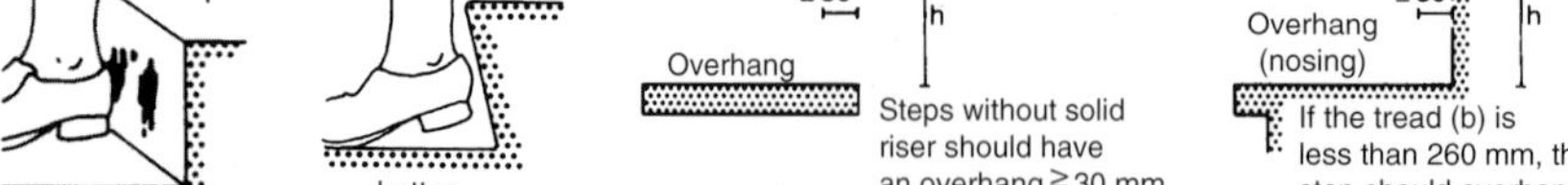

❶ Step profile of a steep flight of stairs. Nosings are not allowed in publicly accessible buildings

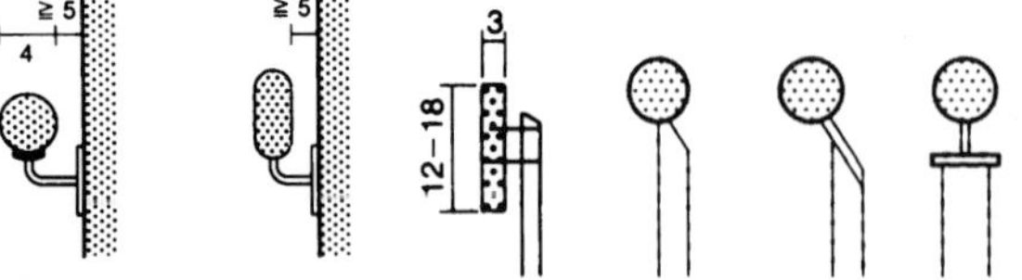

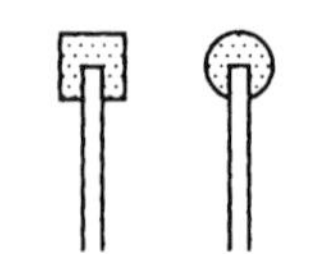

❷ Handrail profiles

Timber or steel profiles for steel balustrades

Timber or steel profiles for glass balustrades with sections of clamps

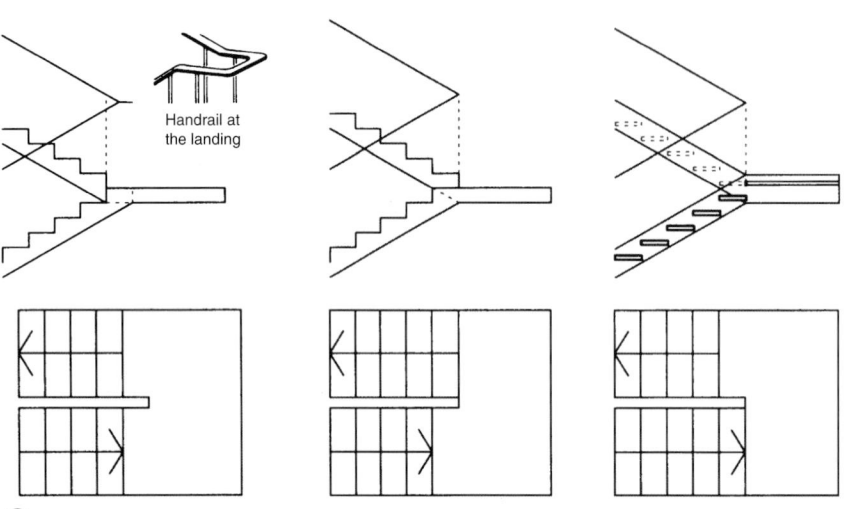

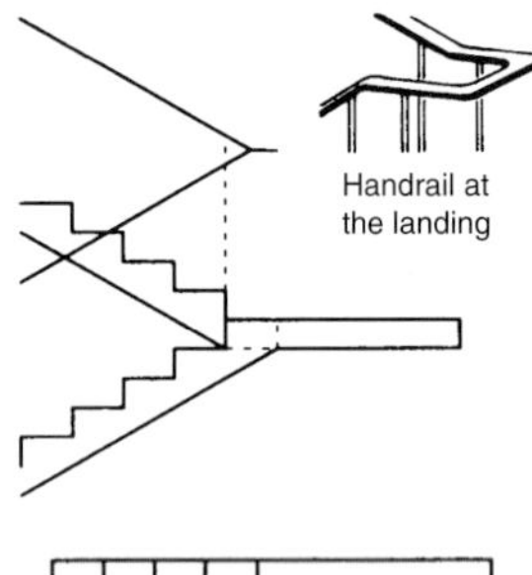

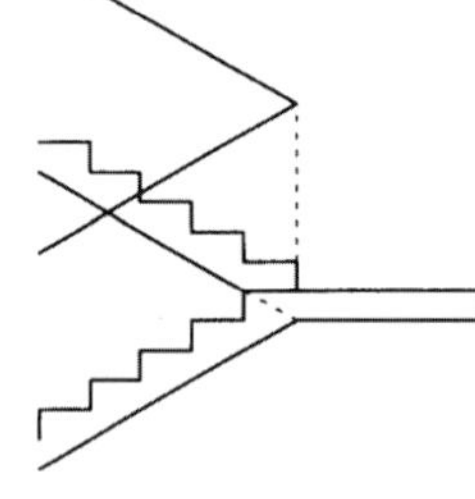

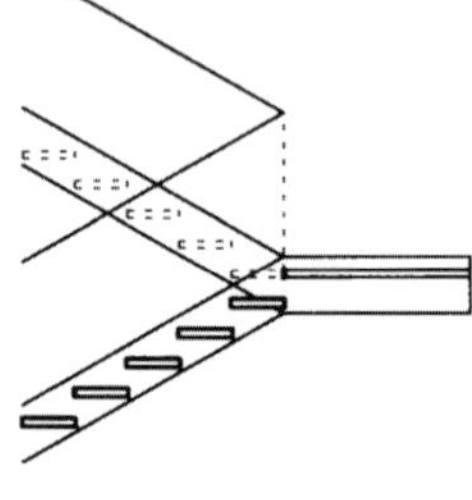

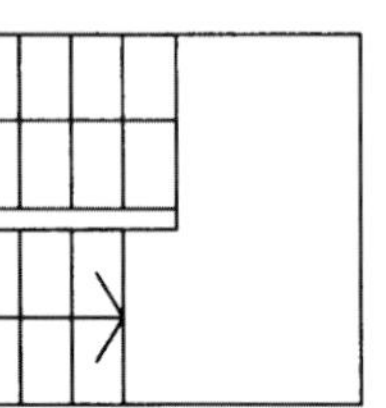

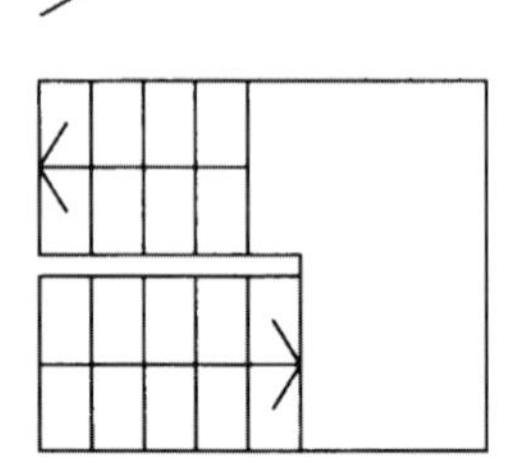

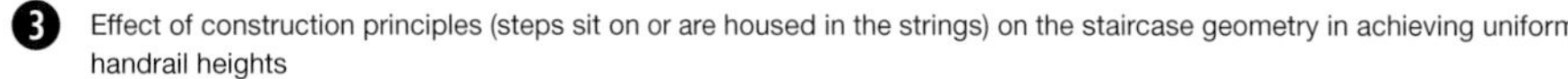

❸ Effect of construction principles (steps sit on or are housed in the strings) on the staircase geometry in achieving uniform handrail heights

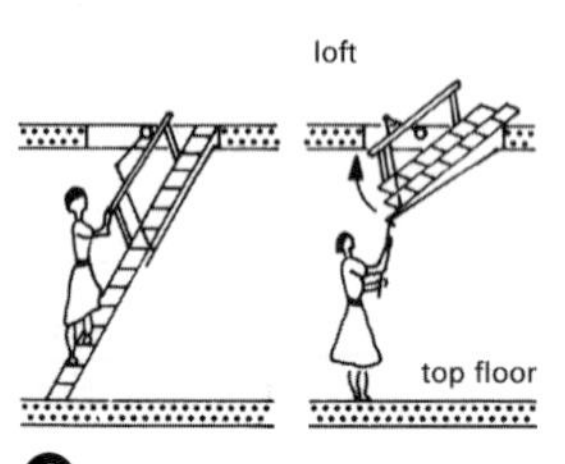

❹ If there is too little space, an aluminium or timber folding loft ladder may suffice

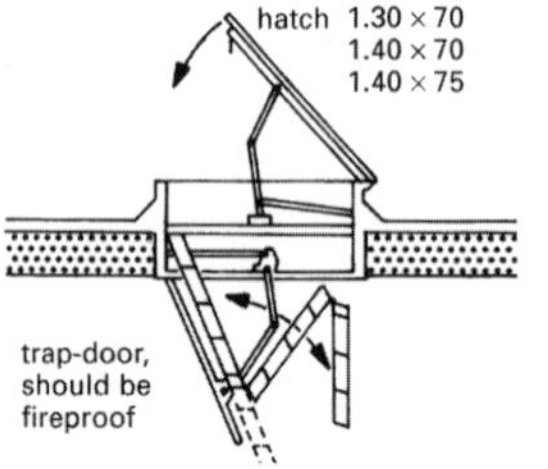

❺ Flat roof access with folding steps

Clear room height	Loft ladder size (cm)
220–280	100 × 60 (70)
220–300	120 × 60 (70)
220–300	130 × 60 (70 + 80)
240–300	140 × 60 (70 + 80)
width of frame: W = 59; 69; 79 cm	
length of frame: L = 120; 130; 140 cm	
height of frame: H = 25 cm	

❻ Telescopic loft ladders

❾ Normal stairs (tread too short)

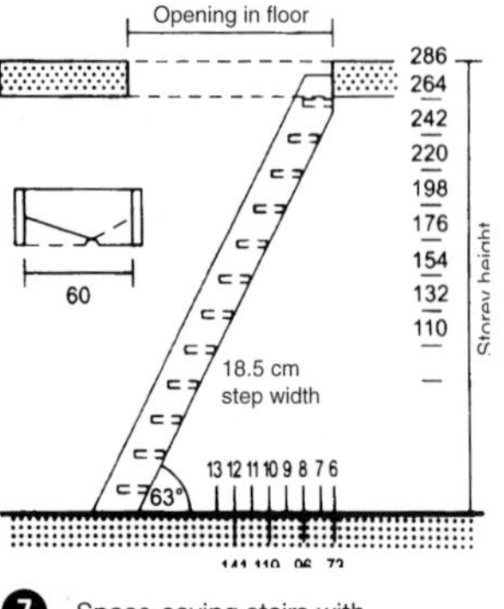

❼ Space-saving stairs with strings

❽ Alternating tread, staggered or samba stairs of wood: section through centre

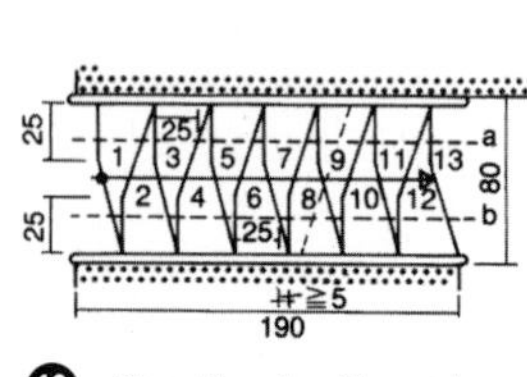

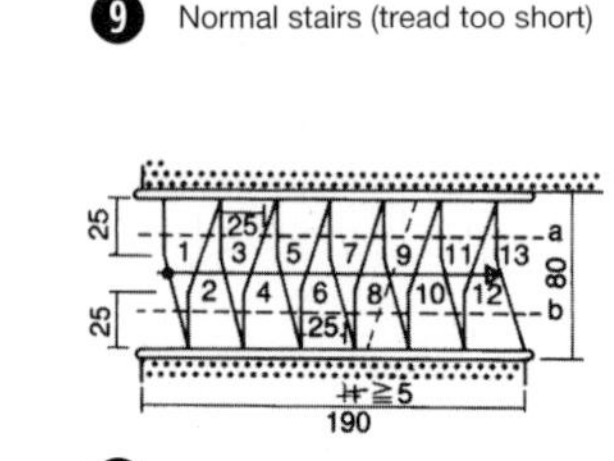

❿ Plan of treads with a and b ≧20 cm

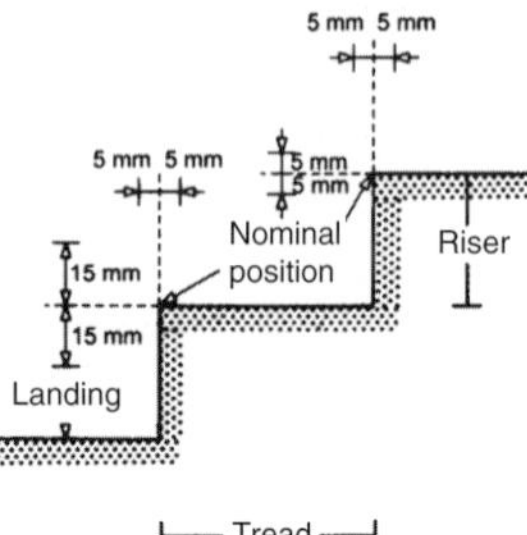

⓫ Tolerances in the positions of the steps' leading edges. Tolerances must, however, still comply with the required dimension limits

Step profile

For stairs in buildings subject to disability-friendly building rules, steps may have no nosing! In order to avoid ugly streaks of rubbed-off shoe polish on the risers of vertical stairs → ❶, profiles with an undercut riser are better, and this produces more tread surface. For a tread width <260 mm → ❶ (b), the step is to be undercut ≧30 mm; this also applies to open stairs without risers. A human being requires the most space at handrail height, and considerably less at foot height. The stair width here can be made narrower in favour of a larger stairwell.

Galleries, mezzanines, balconies and circle seating in theatres must have a protective guard rail (height *h*), compulsory from 1 m height difference:

drop <12 m, *h* = 0.90 m
drop <12 m, *h* = 1.00 m for workplaces and if the stairwell is at least 20 cm wide, also for over 12 m *h*.

drop >12 m, *h* = 1.10 m

Loft ladders have a pitch of 45–75°. If, however, stairs of such a pitch are required for operational purposes, for example because there is not enough space for a normal flight, then alternating tread (staggered or samba) stairs may be chosen → ❽ + ❿. The risers in an alternating tread staircase should be a few as possible, the riser height anyway ≦20 cm. The treads in this case are measured (staggered) for the tread axes a + b → ❿ of the left and right feet.

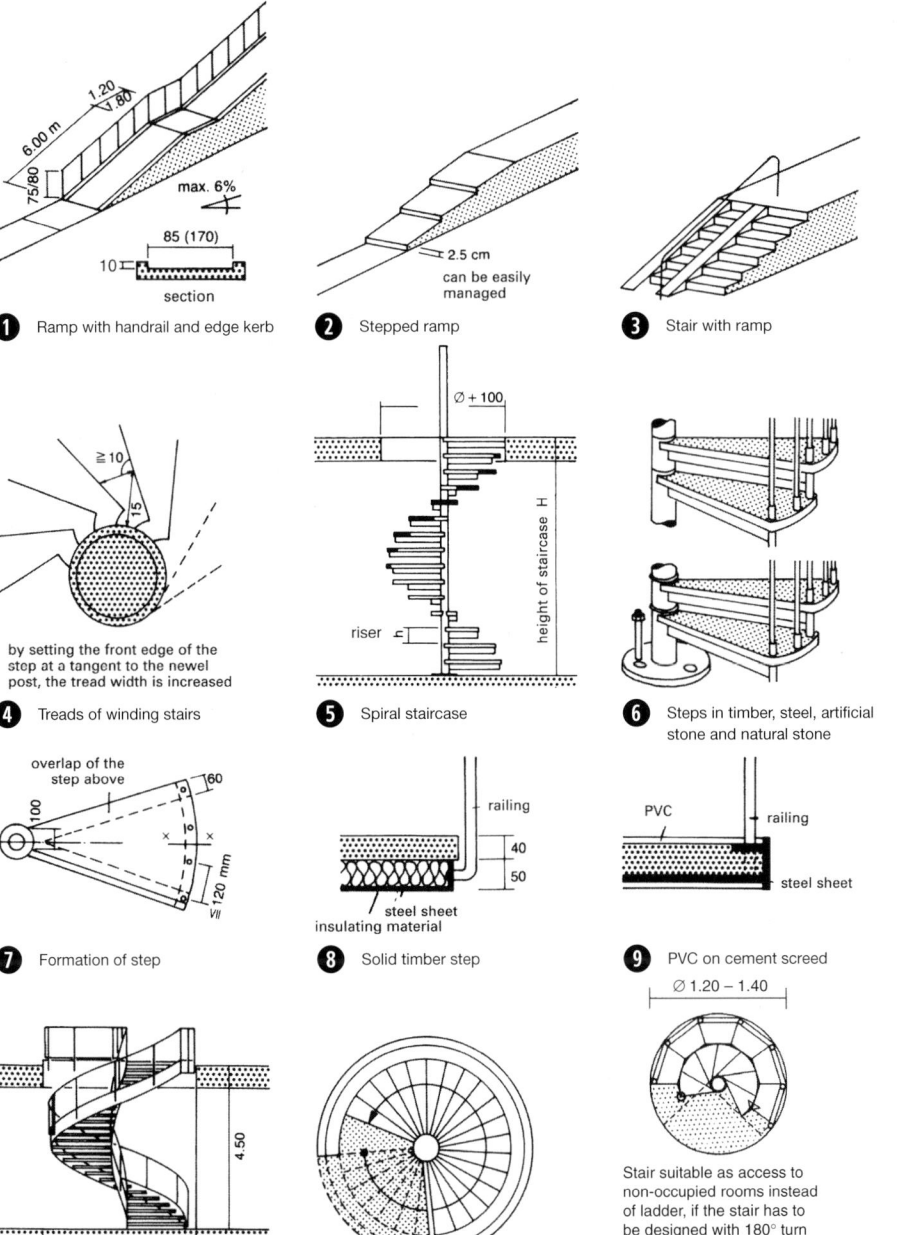

1 Ramp with handrail and edge kerb

2 Stepped ramp

3 Stair with ramp

4 Treads of winding stairs

5 Spiral staircase

6 Steps in timber, steel, artificial stone and natural stone

7 Formation of step

8 Solid timber step

9 PVC on cement screed

10 Elevation of winding staircase

11 Plan of 10

12 Space-saving spiral staircase with staggered steps

Pedestrians, wheelchair users and people with prams or push-chairs should be able to move easily from one level to another.

Ramps → 1 stepped ramp → 2 stair with ramp → 3 gradient → 1.

Winding and spiral staircases

These are permissible for a few family houses as the 'staircase required by building regulations DIN 18065' when there is an approx. 210 cm diameter aperture in the floor (min. 80 cm flight width); for other buildings from approx. 260 cm (min. 1.00 m flight width). Spiral staircases with less then 80 cm of usable flight width are permitted only as 'legally non-essential stairs'. They are suitable for cellars, lofts, subsidiary rooms or if a primary escape route is already provided. Spiral staircases save space and can be constructed with adequate strength with a newel post in the central axis → 5 – 6.

The central axis can also be cleared, which leads to an open spiral staircase with a stairwell → 10 – 11. For spiral staircases, the curve can be chosen freely within the range laid down by regulations. The tread is measured at the walking line. In the curved part of the walking line, the tread is equal to the chord resulting from the intersection of the curved walking line with the leading edge of the step.

Building components

STAIRS

Principles
Regulations
Construction
Ramps
Spiral stairs
Access and escape ladders
Escalators
Moving walkways

BS 5395-2
DIN 18065

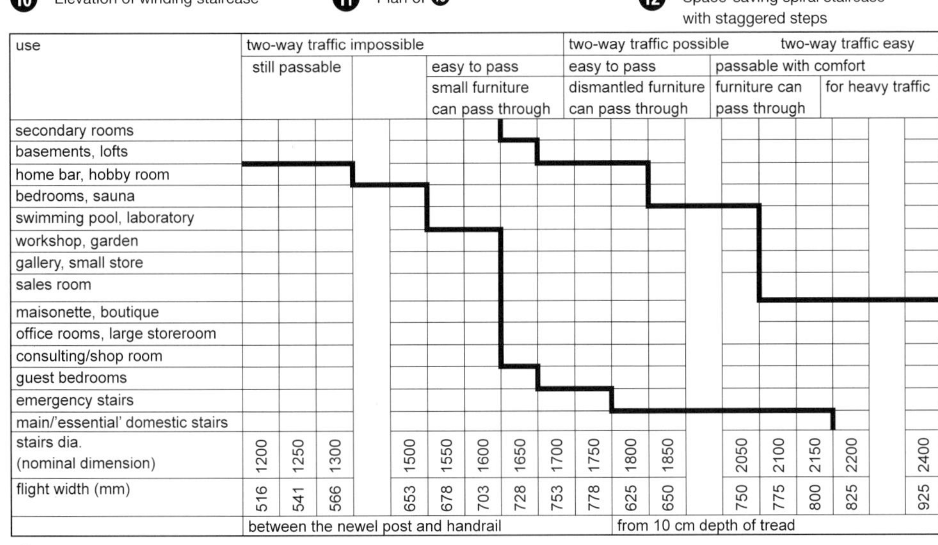

use	two-way traffic impossible								two-way traffic possible					two-way traffic easy					
	still passable					easy to pass				easy to pass			passable with comfort						
						small furniture can pass through				dismantled furniture can pass through			furniture can pass through			for heavy traffic			
secondary rooms																			
basements, lofts																			
home bar, hobby room																			
bedrooms, sauna																			
swimming pool, laboratory																			
workshop, garden																			
gallery, small store																			
sales room																			
maisonette, boutique																			
office rooms, large storeroom																			
consulting/shop room																			
guest bedrooms																			
emergency stairs																			
main/'essential' domestic stairs																			
stairs dia. (nominal dimension)	1200	1250	1300		1500	1550	1600	1650	1700	1750	1800	1850		2050	2100	2150	2200		2400
flight width (mm)	516	541	566		653	678	703	728	753	778	625	650		750	775	800	825		925
	between the newel post and handrail										from 10 cm depth of tread								

13 Determination of the minimum dimensions of spiral staircases of all types according to application

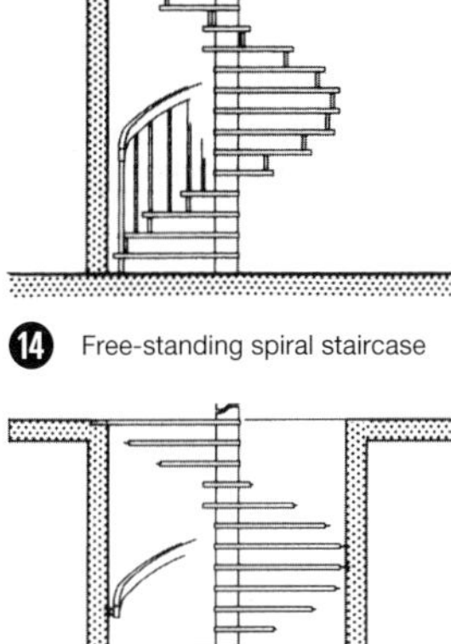

14 Free-standing spiral staircase

15 Wall-supported spiral staircase

STAIRS

Spiral Stairs

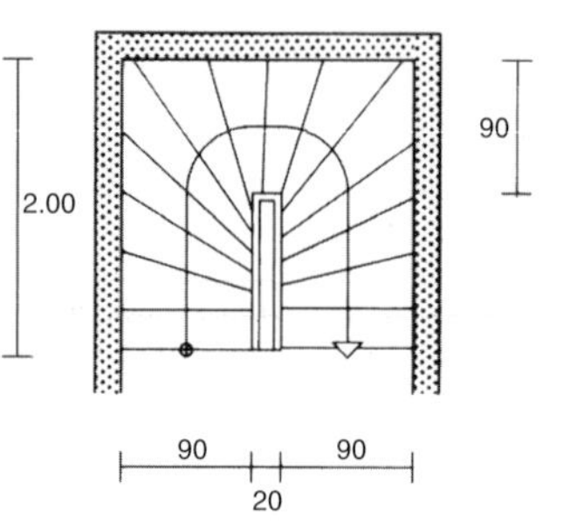

❶ Semi-winding staircase. Usable width 90 cm/tread 26.5 cm

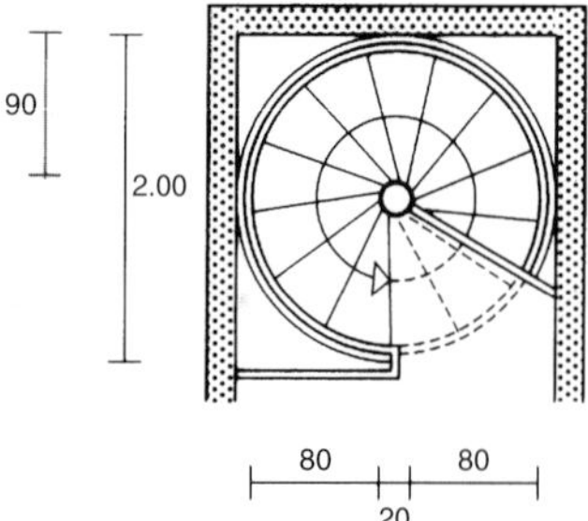

❷ Round spiral staircase. Usable width 80 cm/tread 24 cm

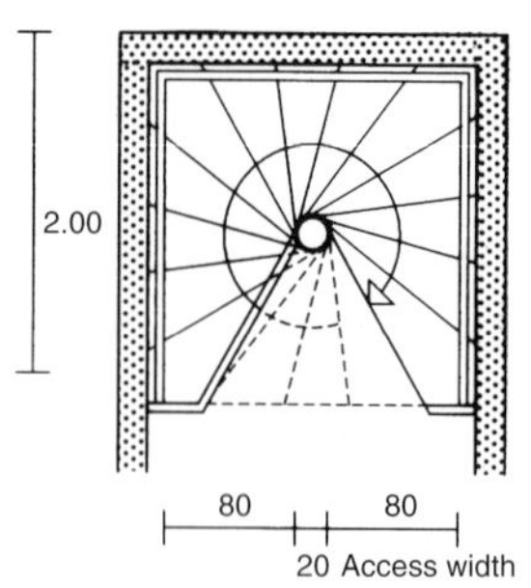

❸ Square shaped spiral staircase

❹ Spiral staircase landing types. Landing access as wide as the steps. Min. landing angle 60–72°

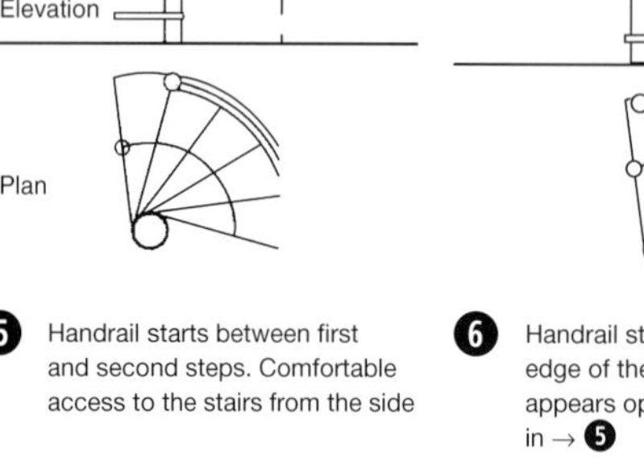

❺ Handrail starts between first and second steps. Comfortable access to the stairs from the side

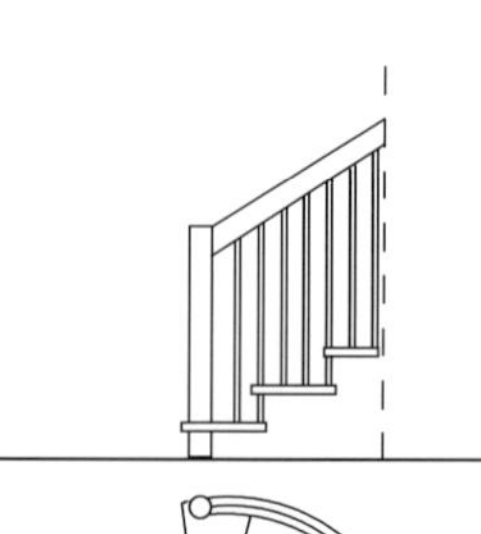

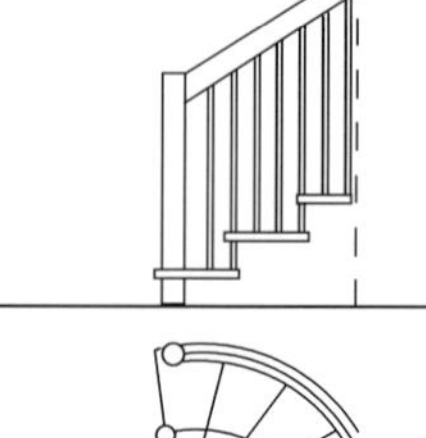

❻ Handrail starts at the leading edge of the first step. Handrail appears optically lower than in → ❺

❼ Spiral staircase with ≧60° landing

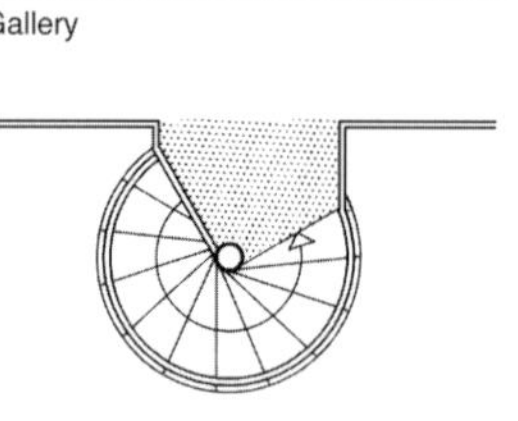

❽ Spiral staircase with obliquely angled landing

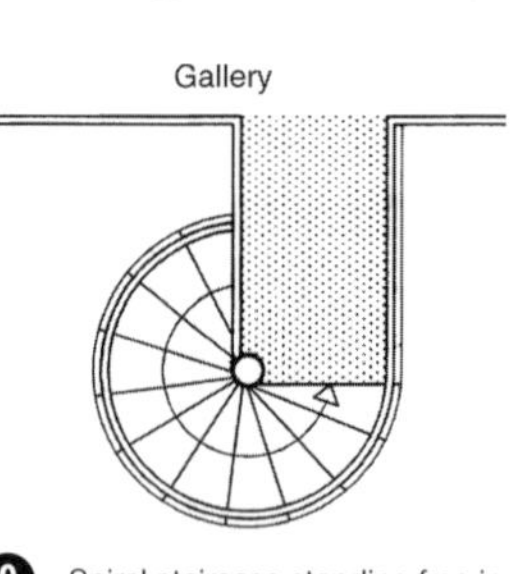

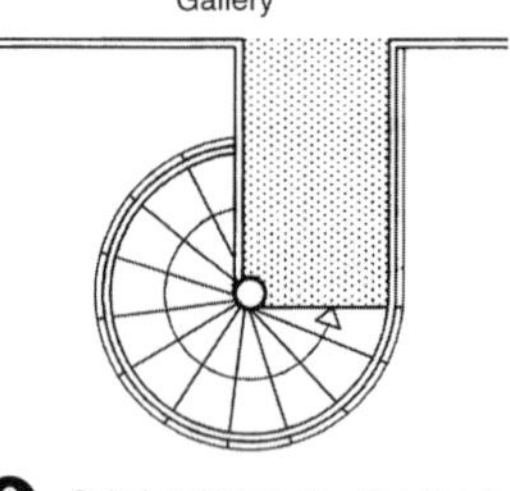

❾ Spiral staircase standing free in the room with extended landing

❿ Arc division method for the construction of angled steps, in this case for a 90° turning staircase. Also applicable for a 180° turning staircase

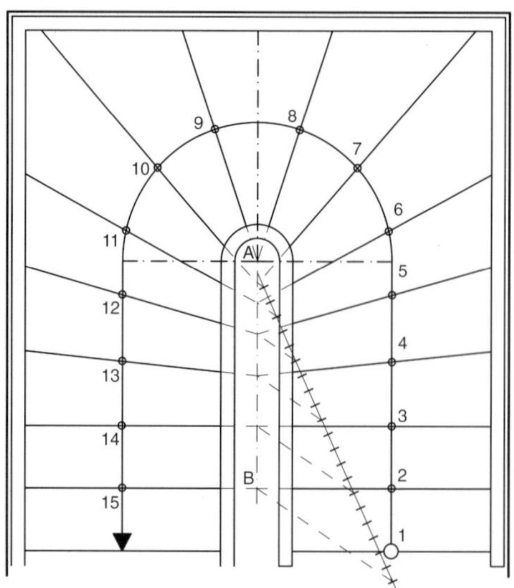

⓫ Proportional division method for the construction of angled steps, in this case for a 180° turning staircase. Also applicable for a 90° turning staircase.

Although spiral staircases appear generous, they should not be installed where every last centimetre of tread is important. Compare → ❶ + ❷, staircases in a 2 × 2 m niche. Spiral staircases work best if they lead to galleries or parapets → ❼ – ❾. The construction is really shown to its full advantage in an open space.

Entrance landings have an angle of at least 60° → ❹. Starting the handrail between the first and second steps works more generously → ❺ – ❻. Spiral staircases are permissible from 190 cm in diameter as the sole connecting stairs inside houses with 80 cm usable walking width → ❷ – ❸. Uniform curving of winding steps can be produced by geometrical construction. In order to achieve a regular curve of the steps, the tolerances can be larger here.

Arc division method → ❿

1. Decide the walking line
2. Plot the steps onto the walking line, starting with the corner tread
3. Plot the smallest width of the corner tread and the edges of the tread
4. Intersection B of the last straight step with the staircase's axis is the middle point of a circle tangential to the convexity at A
5. Determine intersection 0' on the circle and point 0
6. Divide the arc between 0 and the last straight step into as many equal lengths as there are steps between these points
7. The division points on the inner cheek provide the connection points of the steps

Proportional division method → ⓫

1. Decide the walking line
2. Plot the steps onto the walking line
3. With an even number of steps and the upper and lower flights of equal lengths: first plot the middle tread symmetrically on the axis of the staircase (in the diagram, treads 8–9). If there is an odd number of steps: first place the middle step on the axis of the stairs
4. Mark the narrowest width of the narrowest step on the inner cheek. Plot from the resulting points from the steps' edge through the walking line point.
5. Extend the edges of the steps to their intersection A
6. Extend the last even step to the axis of the staircase (point B)
7. Divide the line AB in the ratio 1:2:3:4... (as many divisions as curved steps). This line division can be applied to any axis
8. Leading edges of the curved steps go through the points on the walking line and the division points on the axis of the staircase

BS 4211
BS 5395
ASTM F21755
DIN 14094
DIN 18065
DIN 18799
DIN 24532

Ladder access points must be located so that those in danger can attract the attention of people on public roads. Emergency ladders are items of building equipment which can be used for the rescue of occupants → ❶ – ❹ + ⓭. Access ladders, also described as vertical fixed ladders, are required for climbing onto roofs, chimneys, silos, containers, tanks, machines, plant etc. For buildings over 5 m high, access ladders are required to have back protection. Each ladder run has a maximum climbing height of 10 m → ⓬ – ⓭. Hoop diameter 0.70 m.

≦1.20
All windows necessary for escape min. 0.90 × 1.20 clear opening
Legally essential stairs
≦1.20
≦8.0
Portable ladder
If ≧8.0 m, turn table ladder is required
Railing

❶ Escape routes

Sliding window, fully opening
Occupied room
Clear opening 0.90 × 1.20
Access steps
≦8.0

❷ Roof window as escape route

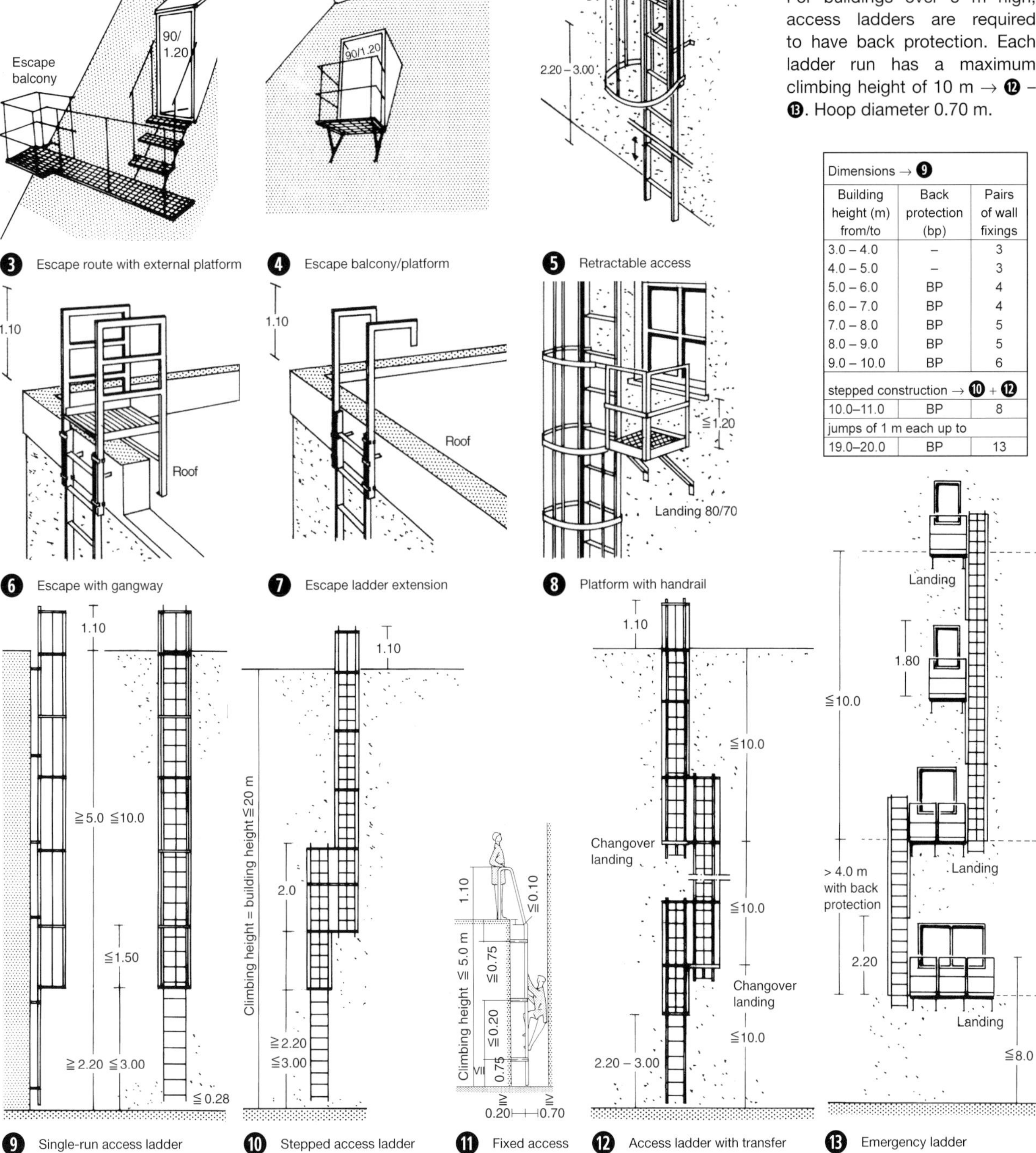

❸ Escape route with external platform

❹ Escape balcony/platform

❺ Retractable access

❻ Escape with gangway

❼ Escape ladder extension

❽ Platform with handrail

❾ Single-run access ladder

❿ Stepped access ladder

⓫ Fixed access ladder

⓬ Access ladder with transfer platforms

⓭ Emergency ladder

Dimensions → ❾		
Building height (m) from/to	Back protection (bp)	Pairs of wall fixings
3.0 – 4.0	–	3
4.0 – 5.0	–	3
5.0 – 6.0	BP	4
6.0 – 7.0	BP	4
7.0 – 8.0	BP	5
8.0 – 9.0	BP	5
9.0 – 10.0	BP	6
stepped construction → ❿ + ⓬		
10.0–11.0	BP	8
jumps of 1 m each up to		
19.0–20.0	BP	13

ESCALATORS

For Shops and Offices

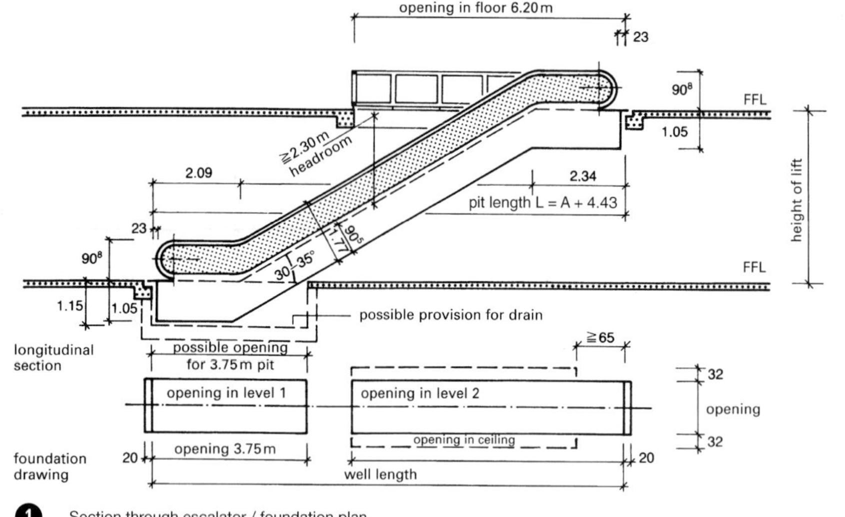

❶ Section through escalator / foundation plan

opening
step width
C
A
level 2
emergency stop button
height of lift
level 1
emergency stop button
30
B
30

❷ Width of steps

transportation capacity

$$Q = 3600 \times \frac{G_p \times v}{t} \times f \text{ (people/h)}$$

where

G_p = people per step (1, 1.5, 2)
v = conveyor speed (m/s)
t = tread (m)
f = 0.5–0.8 escalator utilisation factor

❸ General calculation formula for transport capacity

step width	800	1000
A	80–820	1005–1020
B	1320–1420	1570–1620
C	1480	1680
capacity/h	7000–8000 people	8000–10000 people

❹ Dimensions and capacities of escalators with 30° and 35° (27°; 18°) pitch. Step width → ❷

speed	travel time for one person	with a width sufficient for	
		1 person	2 people next to each other
0.5 m/sec	~18 sec	4000	8000
0.65 m/sec	~14 sec	5000	1000
		people/h transported	

❺ Capacity data

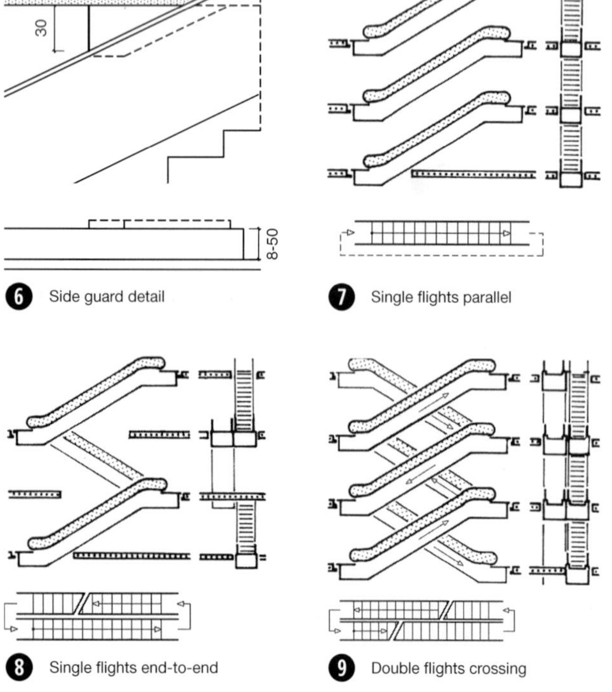

❻ Side guard detail

❼ Single flights parallel

❽ Single flights end-to-end

❾ Double flights crossing

In the UK, construction and operation of escalators is regulated by BS EN 115: 'Safety rules for the construction and installation of escalators and passenger conveyors'. In Germany, construction and operation of escalators follow the 'Guidelines for escalators and moving walkways', ZH1/484, issued by the Association of Commercial Accident Insurers. (The German situation is described below.)

Escalators are utilised for the continuous transport of large numbers of people (they do not count as stairs for the purposes of building regulations) and, for example in department stores, have a pitch of 30 or 35°. The 35° escalator is more economical because it requires less space. For travel heights ≧6 m, the 30° escalator is required . The transportation capacity is about the same for both pitches. When installed as part of transport facilities, a pitch of 27–28° should be used if possible. The pitch is derived from a gradient relationship of 16 × 30 cm, a comfortable size for a step.

For the width of steps, there is a worldwide standard of 60 cm (1 person without hand luggage, no longer permissible in Europe), 80 cm (1–2 people) and 100 cm (2 people) → ❸ – ❺. With a 100 cm step width, people carrying loads have sufficient room for movement. Provide sufficient queuing room at the bottom and top of the escalator, ≧2.50 m deep.

In department stores, offices and administration buildings, trade fair halls and airports, escalator speed is normally no higher than 0.5 m/s. In underground railway stations and public transport facilities, 0.65 m/s is preferred.

The average distribution of upward traffic in department stores is: fixed stairs 2%, passenger lifts 8%, escalators 90%. Approx. three quarters of downward traffic uses the escalators. Although the average shopping area for each escalator is 1500 m^2 at present, this should be lowered to an optimum of 500–700 m^2.

Escalators in transport facilities. According to Bostrab ('Regulations on the construction and operation of trams'), there are stringent requirements (function, construction, safety) for pitches 27, 18 and 30°. Dimensions and capacities → ❶ – ❷, ❹

Length on plan → ❶

For 30° pitch = 1.732 × storey height
For 35° pitch = 1.428 × storey height

Example: storey height 4.50 m and 30° pitch (35° is sometimes not permissible abroad), length on plan: 1.732 × 4.5 = 7.794. With the level access and exit areas, this gives a length of approx. 9 m, therefore about 20 people can stand on the escalator at the same time.

BS EN 115
BS 7801
DIN EN 115

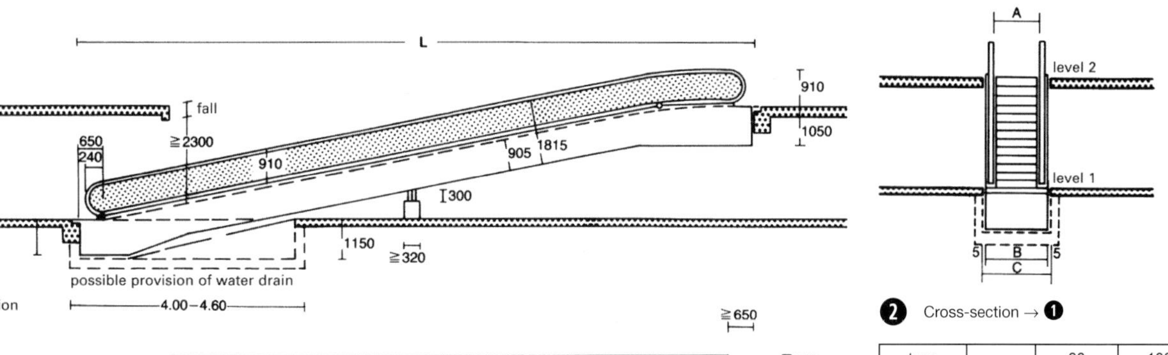

❶ Section through moving walkway with foundation plan

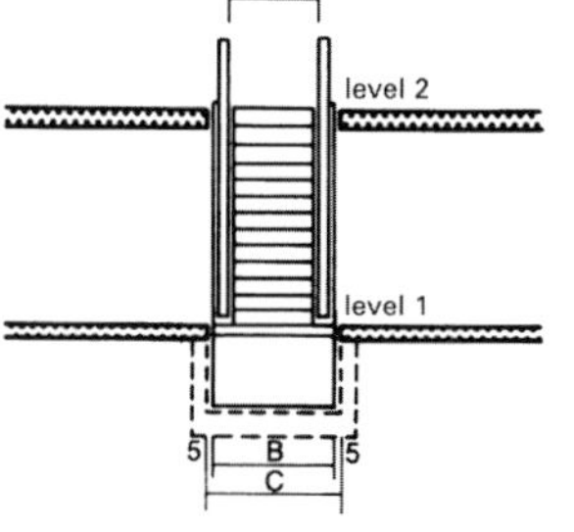

❷ Cross-section → ❶

type		80	100
A		800	1000
B		1420	1620
C		1500	1700

❸ Dimensions → ❶ – ❷

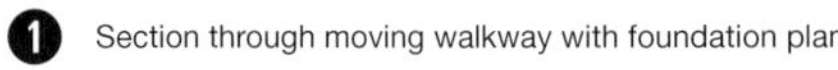

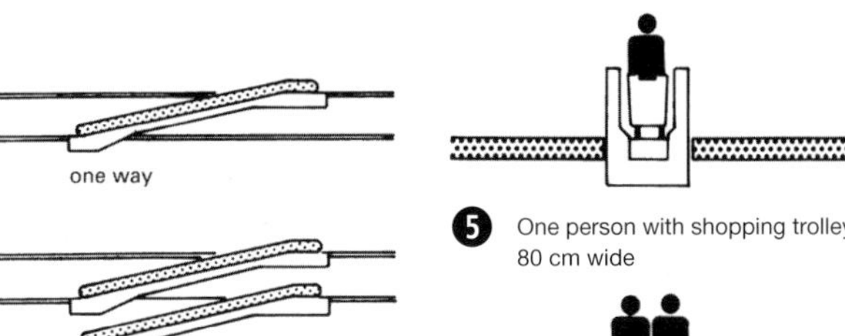

❺ One person with shopping trolley 80 cm wide

❻ Two people, 1 m wide

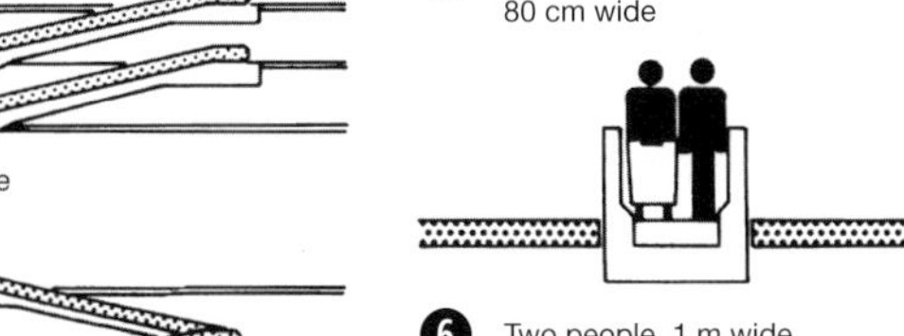

❹ Arrangement 'of moving walkways

The hourly capacity of a moving walkway is calculated according to the formula:

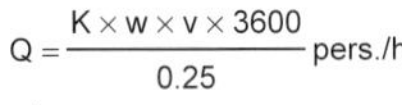

$$Q = \frac{K \times w \times v \times 3600}{0.25} \text{ pers./h}$$

where
w = transportation width (m)
v = velocity (m/s)
K = load factor
the load factor varies between 0.5 and 0.9 (average 0.7) according to the use. The 0.25 in the denominator represents a step area of 0.25 m²/person.

MOVING WALKWAYS FOR SHOPS AND OFFICES (ACCORDING TO THE GUIDELINES FOR ESCALATORS AND MOVING WALKWAYS)

Bostrab guidelines, DIN EN 115

Moving walkways, also called conveyors or travelators, are a means of transporting pedestrians on the level or at a slight gradient. The advantage of a moving walkway is that it can also carry prams, wheelchairs, shopping trolleys, bicycles and bulky luggage with little danger. At the design stage, the expected traffic must be established carefully, so that the equipment can provide optimal capacity. The transport capacity depends on the clear width, travel speed and occupation density.

Capacities of 6000–12000 pers/h are possible. Maximum gradient of moving walkways is 12° = 21%. Normal travel speeds are 0.5–0.6 m/s horizontal; installations with gradients up to 4° are slightly faster at 0.75 m/s. Short moving walkways are about 30 m long. Long moving walkways can be built up to a length of 250 m. To enable entry and access at the right time, it is good to design a number of short moving walkways.

The advantage of two-directional moving walkways is that the horizontal return route of the walking surface, → ❾ – ❿, requires a lower construction height of 180 mm, in contrast to → ❼ – ❽. This makes two-way walkways more suitable for installation in existing buildings.

Values for the cotangent of the moving walkway gradient:
formula = cot × B × transport height

gradient in °	10°	11°	12°
cot B	5.6713	5.1446	4.7046

e.g. transport height 5 m, gradient 12°
average length = 4.7046 × 5 m = (rounded) 23.52 m

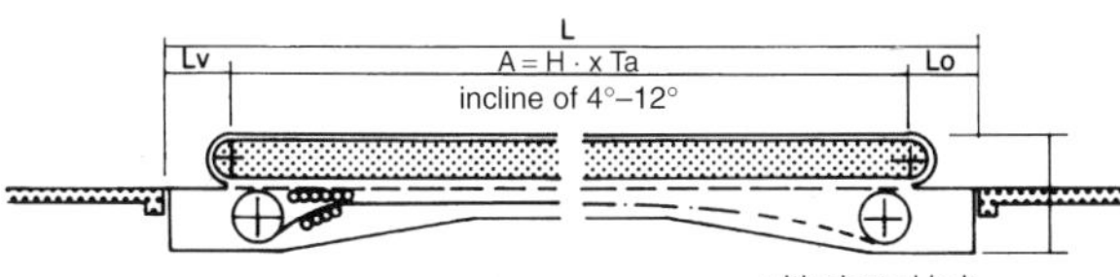

❼ Section through moving walkway with rubber conveyor belt with cleated belt

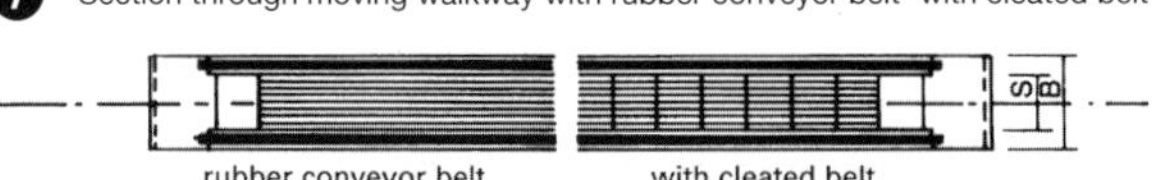

❽ Plan → ❼

gradient	10°	11°	12°
d	S × 5.6713 + 15480	S × 5.1446 + 14100	S × 4.7046 + 12950
g	6400	5900	5450
i	H × 5.6713 + 3340	H × 5.1145 + 3150	H × 4.7046 + 2990

⓫ Moving walkway with transition curve at top → ❶

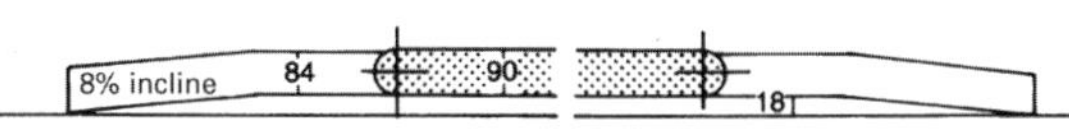

❾ Diagrammatical section of a two-way moving walkway → ❿

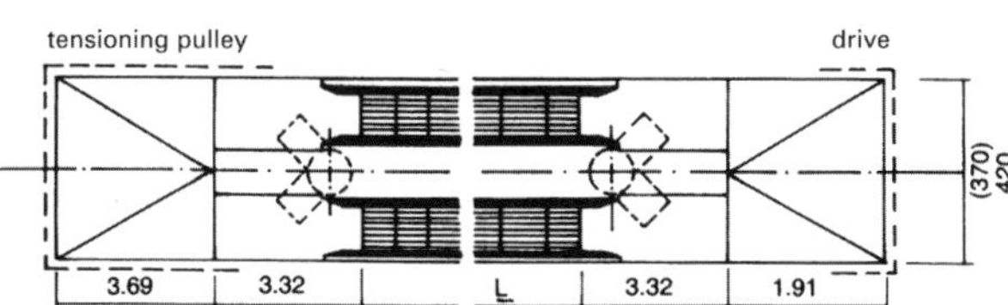

❿ Plan of a two-way moving walkway with horizontal turnaround → ❾

horizontal moving walkway	with cleated belt	with conveyor belt (rubber belt)	two-way moving walkway
usable width SW	800 + 1000	750 + 950	2 × 800 + 2 × 1000
external width B	1370 + 1570	1370 + 1570	3700 + 4200
construction	flat construction ≧4° gradient		
length of a section	12–16 m	~10 m	
support spacing	according to structural requirements		
possible practical length L	225 m ≧300 m		
transport capacity	40 m/min	11000 people/h	

⓬ Dimensions and capacities of horizontal moving walkways → ❼ – ❽

BS EN 81
BS ISO 4190
DD CEN/TS 81
DIN EN 81
DIN 15306
DIN 15309

(In the US lifts are called elevators.)

LIFTS

Principles

For all buildings, lifts should normally be positioned at the source of traffic flow. Provide sufficient space for waiting and queuing → p. 130 which must not infringe on stairs. Carefully plan the connection to the traffic routes. There are two different drive systems for lifts:

1. Traction sheave drive (for cable lifts) → ❶
2. Hydraulic lifts → ❷ – ❸

Traction lifts: ideally have their drives above the shaft. The empty weight of the car and half the live load are balanced by the counterweight. Placing the drive at the top or at the bottom next to the shaft makes necessary additional pulleys, resulting in higher operating costs. The machinery and control system can be accommodated in a separate machine room or, in the case of lifts without a machine room, placed in the shaft → p. 134.

With **hydraulic lifts**, a push cylinder is mostly used → ❷ – ❸. The lifting cylinder can be arranged directly or indirectly. The arrangement of a direct cylinder inside a protective tube under the ground is no longer suitable because of the requirements for the protection of groundwater. The use of a pull cylinder → ❸ B–D can be appropriate in some cases. A pull cylinder in its basic form balances a part of the weight of the car. This has even more effect with additional weights → ❸ D, because the pump motor runs only when the load is lifted by the cylinder, while downward travel is enabled simply by opening the valve, which requires no energy and almost halves the consumption.

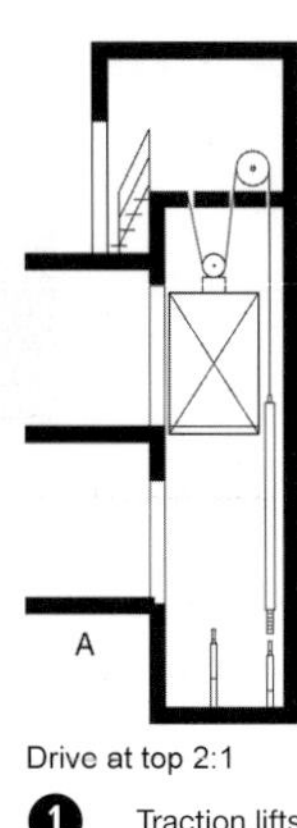
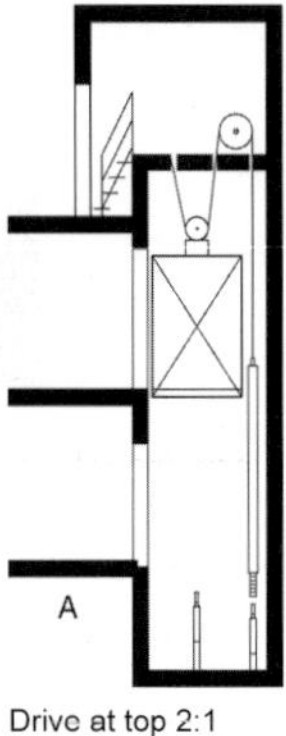

Drive at top 2:1

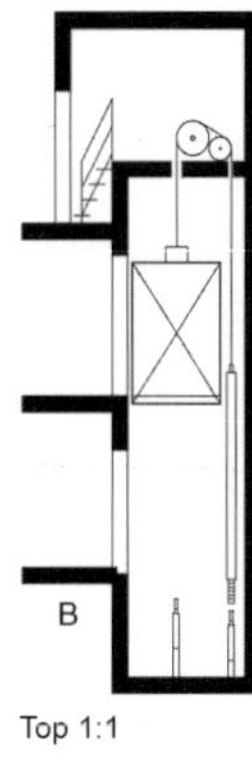

Top 1:1

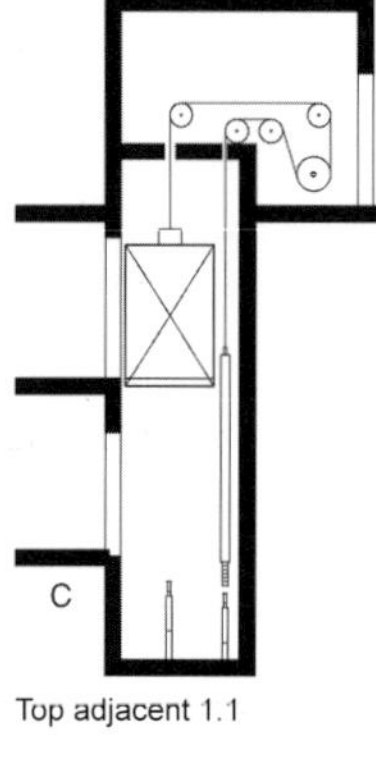

Top adjacent 1:1

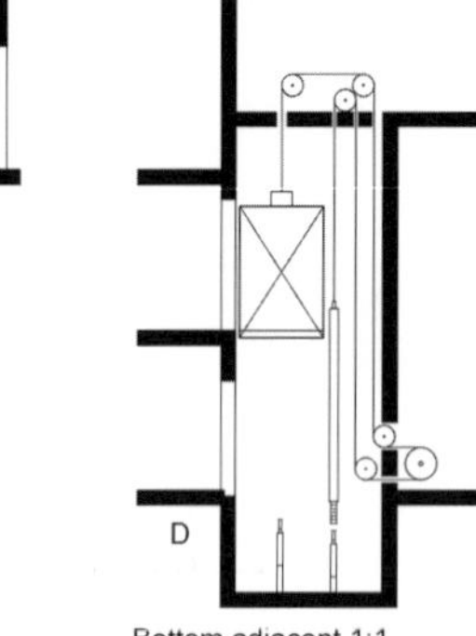

Bottom adjacent 1:1

❶ Traction lifts

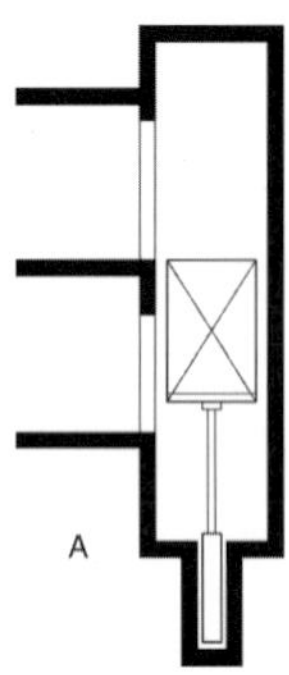

Direct drive central 1-stage

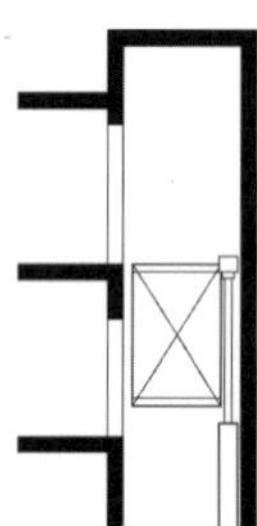

Direct central 1-stage telescopic

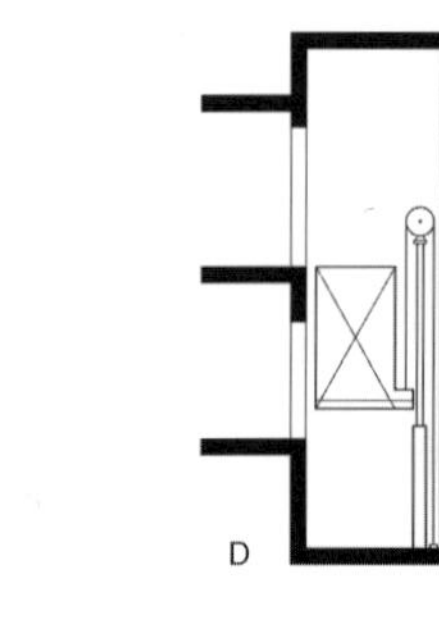

Direct adjacent 1-stage

D

Indirect adjacent 2:1

❷ Hydraulic lifts

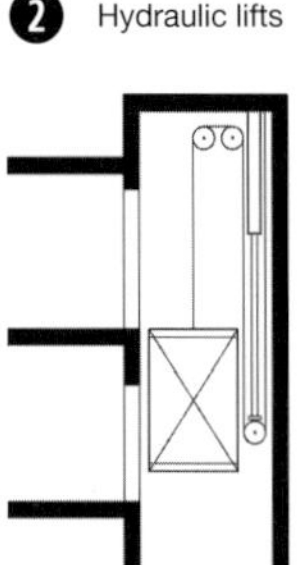
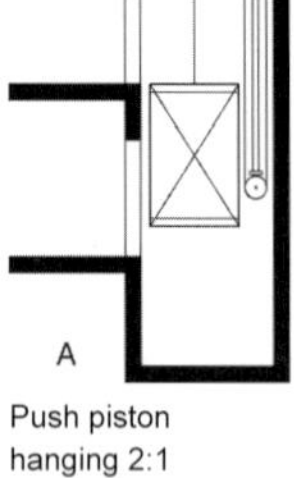

Push piston hanging 2:1

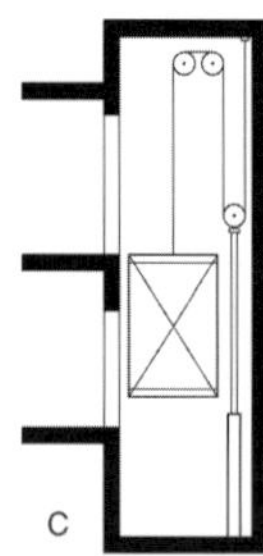

Pull piston hanging 1:1

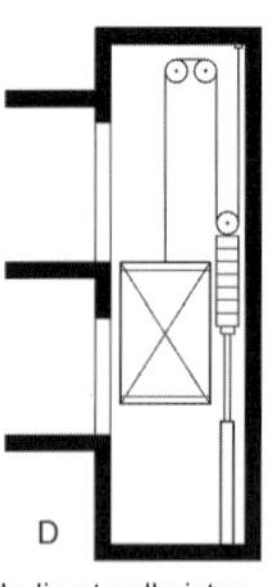

Pull piston indirect 2:1

D

Indirect pull piston with additional weight

❸ Hydraulic lifts, special versions →❶ – ❷

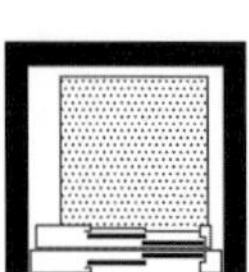

telescopic sliding door opening to one side: shaft width = 1.5 × clear passage width + 27 cm ≧1.60 m

centrally opening sliding door: shaft width = 2 × clear passage width + 20 cm ≧1.80 m suitable for cars, which should be emptied quickly

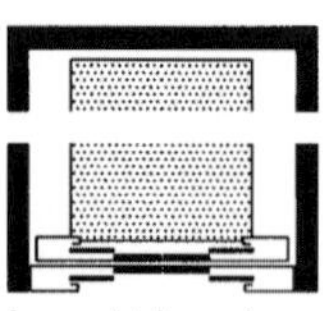

four-part telescopic sliding door: shaft width depends on the type of drive

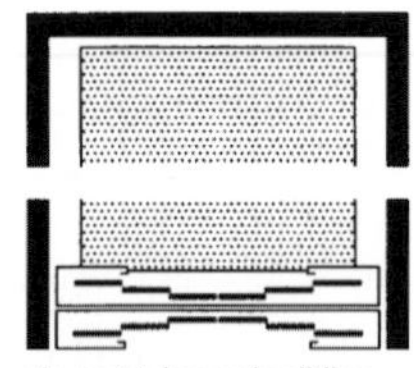

six-part telescopic sliding door: suitable for cars with wide openings e.g. in hospitals and commercial buildings

❹ Relationship of door-opening type to shaft width

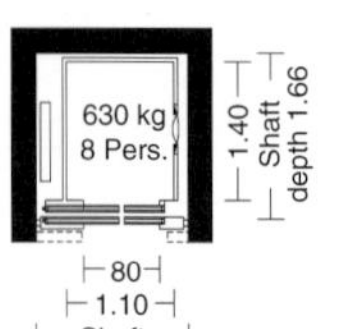

❺ Plans of lifts → p. 130 ff.

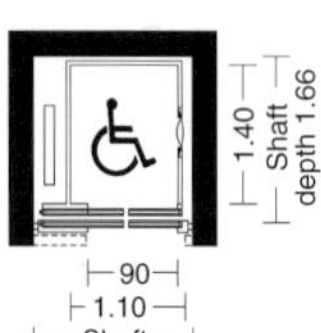

Wheelchair-suitable

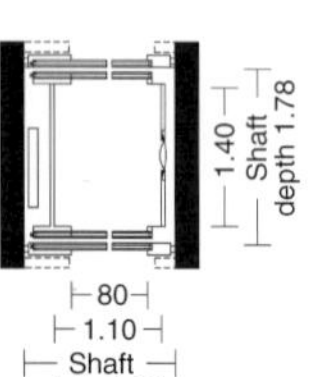

Through-loading

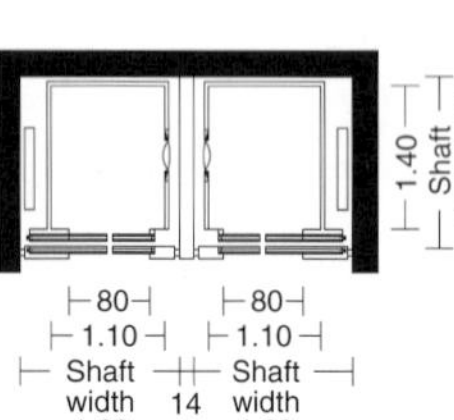

Double

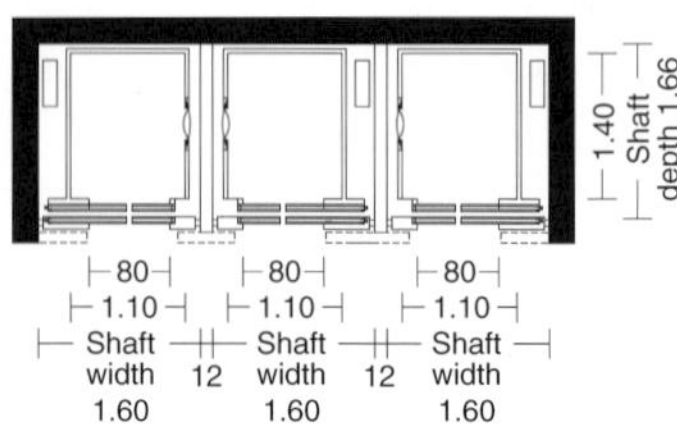

Triple

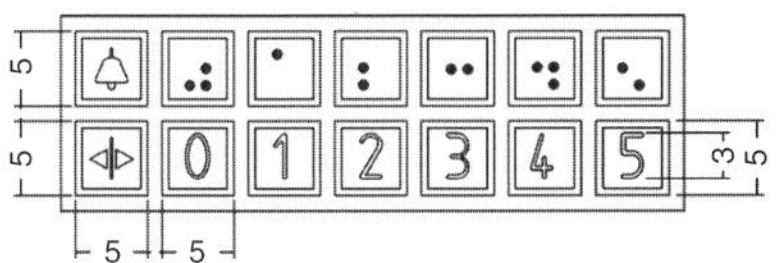

❶ Disability-friendly control panel at a height of 85–100 cm above floor level or car floor level in the central area of the lift car → ❷. Ideally horizontal panels with buttons about 3 × 3 cm, with contrasting and raised labelling and acoustic signals

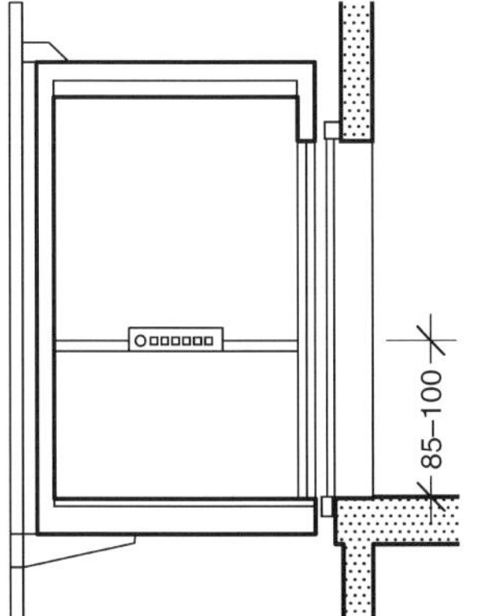

❷ Disability-friendly control panel

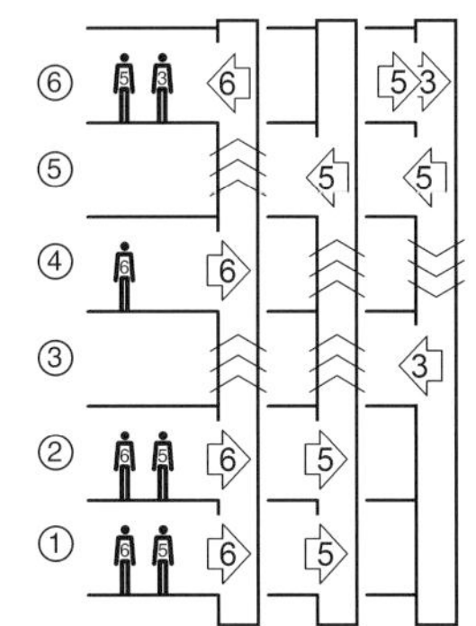

❸ Sensible transport of passengers with a group of three lifts with destination selection control

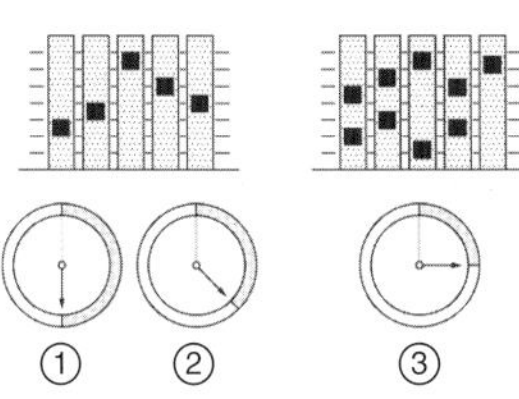

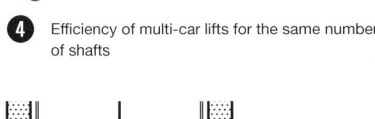

Time to reach the destination
① 5 shafts with conventional control
② 5 shafts with destination selection control
③ 4 shafts with twin lifts

❹ Efficiency of multi-car lifts for the same number of shafts

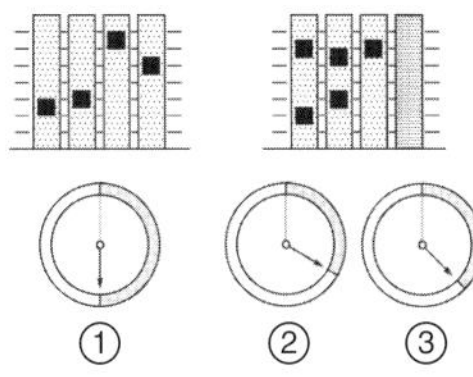

Time to reach the destination
① 4 shafts with conventional control
② 2 shafts with twin lifts
③ 2 shafts with double-decker cars

❺ Efficiency of multi-car lifts with a reduced number of shafts

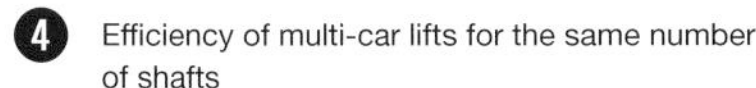

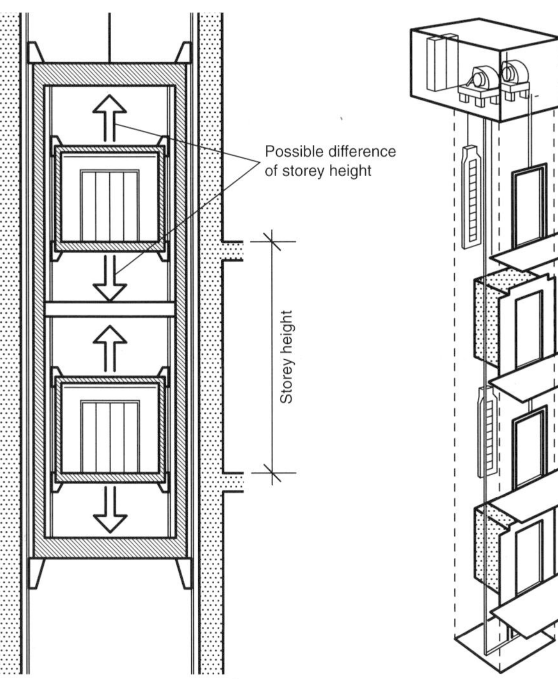

❻ Double-decker cars with a mechanism to compensate for different storey heights

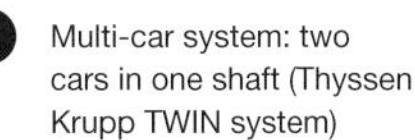

❼ Multi-car system: two cars in one shaft (Thyssen Krupp TWIN system)

Single-button collective control

This control system saves calls and destination instructions, but travels according to a car call to the highest or lowest destination. Landing calls, however, are taken into account only during downward travel, in order to transport users to the main stop. This simple form of control is mainly suitable for buildings with low lift frequency and one main stop, like residential buildings or multi-storey car parks.

Two-button collective control

This control system, dependent on direction and landing calls, can also give the intended direction. The lift primarily serves car calls, but stops in order to collect further passengers in the travel direction. Two-button collective control systems are particularly suitable where there is frequent traffic at intermediate storeys, as in department stores and office buildings. When there is a group of lifts, the calls and destination instructions of all lifts can be taken into account.

Destination floor control system

With a destination floor control system, the user has to indicate the intended destination at a terminal, and is then allotted a lift by the control system. The car will normally have no selection buttons. For groups of lifts, a destination floor control system enables significant optimisation of the transport capacity. The user does not have to differentiate between express and local lifts, and not all lift access points have to be visible from the waiting area. Special lifts, like double-decker and multi-car lifts, can be integrated into groups of lifts. This control system is suitable above all for high-rise buildings and those where there are different security levels and passenger selection is required, because the control system can also provide access control through identification (card reader, PIN code, etc.), for example among hotel guests, personal areas and areas let to third parties → ❸.

Double-decker lifts

Two cars are fixed one above the other and thus always serve different floors. This increases the transport capacity, particularly of express lifts, for the same shaft size. The access level and the sky lobby have to be constructed at two levels. If individual floors are to be visited, then escalators can be provided at the access level to separate the flow of users into odd and even numbered storey destinations. Double-decker lifts are suitable for transport to panorama and restaurant levels, or as express lifts to a sky lobby in very high buildings → ❻.

Multi-car lifts

Two or more lifts travel – each equipped with their own traction sheave drive and counterweight – above and below each other in the same guide rails → ❼. A destination selection control system records the intended direction and destination of the user before they enter the lift, and it then assigns the call to one of the cars and ensures that the two cars do not obstruct each other → ❸. This system can achieve 30% more transport capacity for the same number of shafts. Because the cars cannot overtake in one shaft, travel from the lowest to the highest stop is not possible without changing cars. Therefore, multi-car systems should have at least one conventional express lift → ❹ – ❺.

BS EN 81
DD CEN/TS 81
BS ISO 4190
DIN 15306
DIN 15309

see also: Lifts in high-rise buildings p. 246

LIFTS
Principles
Control
Residential buildings
Public buildings
Small goods lifts
Hydraulic lifts
Special lifts

BS EN 81
BS 5655
DIN EN 81
DIN 15306
DIN 15309

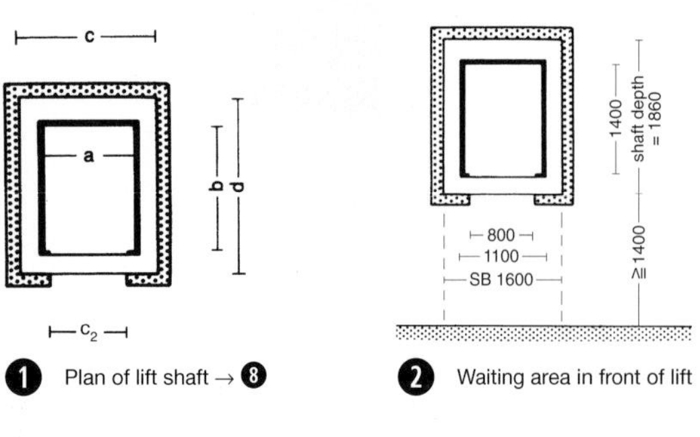

❶ Plan of lift shaft → ❽

❷ Waiting area in front of lift

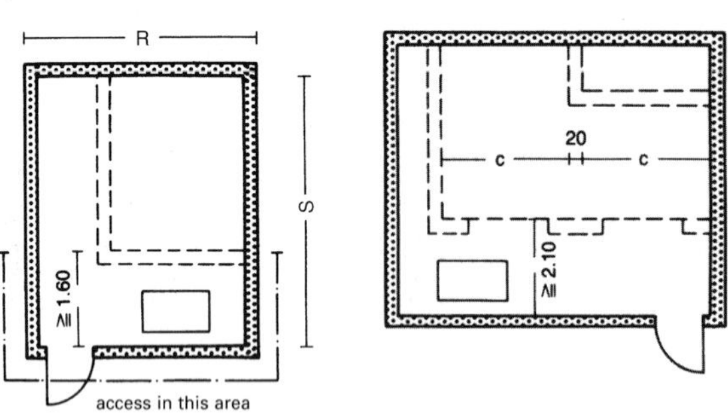

❸ Machine room

❹ Machine room: set of lifts

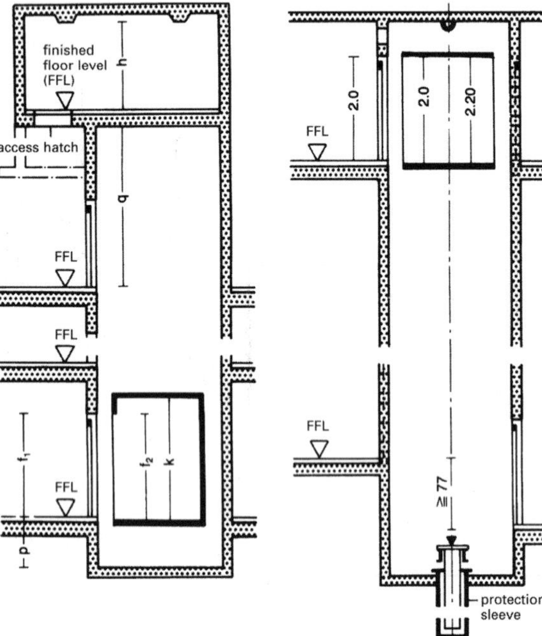

❺ Shaft and machine room

❻ Shaft for hydraulic lift

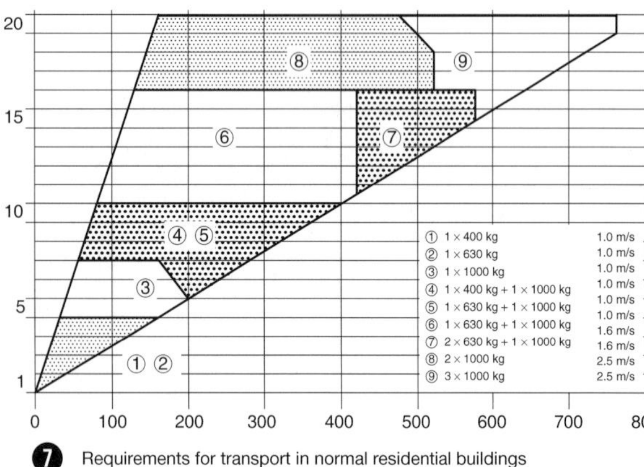

❼ Requirements for transport in normal residential buildings

LIFTS

Passenger Lifts for Residential Buildings

Vertical transport in newbuild multi-storey buildings is mostly provided by lifts. The guidelines given here are based on German standards. In the UK, lift installation is covered by BS 5655, which includes recommendations from CEN and ISO.

The architect normally appoints a specialist engineer for the design of lifts. In larger multi-storey buildings, it is usual to locate the lifts at a central pedestrian circulation point. Goods lifts should be arranged with visible separation from passenger lifts, though their design should take into account that they can also be used by passengers at peak times.

The following load capacities are laid down for passenger lifts in residential buildings:

400 kg (small lift)	for passengers, who may be carrying loads
630 kg (medium lift)	for passengers with prams or wheelchairs
1000 kg (large lift)	suitable for the transport of stretchers, coffins, furniture and wheelchairs → ❽

The waiting area (lobby) in front of the lift shaft must be laid out and designed so that:

- lift users entering and leaving the lift do not obstruct each other more than necessary, even if carrying luggage
- the largest items to be transported by the lift (e.g. prams, wheelchairs, stretchers, coffins, furniture) can be loaded and unloaded without risk of injury to people or damage to the building or the lift, and causing the least possible obstruction to other users.

Waiting area in front of a single lift:

- minimum usable depth between shaft door wall and opposing wall, measured in the direction of the depth of the car, should equal the car depth → ❷.
- minimum usable area should equal the product of lift car depth and shaft width.

Waiting area in front of adjacent lifts:

- minimum usable depth between shaft door wall and opposing wall, measured in the direction of the depth of the car, should equal the depth of the deepest car.

load capacity	Kg		400			630				1000			
nominal speed	≦m/s		0.63	1.00	1.60	0.63	1.00	1.60	2.50	0.63	1.00	1.60	2.50
shaft	min. shaft width c	mm	1600 + 1800 → ❶										
	min. shaft depth d	mm	1600			2100				2600			
	min. pit depth p	mm	1400	1500	1700	1400	1500	1700	2800	1400	1500	1700	2800
	min. shaft head height q	mm	3700	3800	4000	3700	3800	4000	5000	3700	3800	4000	5000
door	clear shaft door width c_2	mm	800; min. 900										
	clear shaft door height s_2	mm	2000										
machine room	min. area of machinery	m^2	8		10		10	12	14	12	14		15
	min. width of machinery r	mm	2400		2400		2700	2700	3000	2700	2700		3000
	min. depth of machinery s	s mm	3200		3200		3700	3700	3700	4208	4200		4200
	min. height of machinery h	mm	2000		2200		2000	2200	2600	2000	2200		2600
car	clear car width a	mm	1100										
	clear car depth b	mm	950		1400			2100					
	clear car height k	mm	2200										
	clear car access width c_2	mm	800; min. 900										
	clear car access height f_2	mm	2000										
	permissible no. passengers		5		8			13					

❽ Structural, car and door dimensions → ❶ – ❻

LIFTS
Principles
Control
Residential buildings
Public buildings
Small goods lifts
Hydraulic lifts
Special lifts

BS EN 81
DIN EN 81
DIN 15306
DIN 15309

LIFTS

Passenger Lifts for Offices, Banks, Hotels, Hospitals

The building and its function dictate the basic type of lifts which need to be provided. They serve as a means of vertical transport for passengers and patients. Lifts are mechanical installations which are required to have a long service life (anything from 25 to 40 years). They should therefore be planned in such a way that even after 10 years they are still capable of meeting increased demand. Alterations to installations that have been badly or too cheaply planned can be expensive or even completely impossible. During the planning stage the likely usage should be closely examined. Lift sets normally form part of the main stairwell.

Analysis of use: types and definitions

Turnaround time is a calculated value indicating the time which a lift requires to complete a cycle with a given type of traffic.

Average waiting time is the time between the button being pressed and the arrival of the lift car:

$$= \frac{\text{cycle time (s)}}{\text{number of lifts/set}}$$

Transportation capacity is the maximum achievable carrying capacity (in passengers) within a five minute (300 s) period:

$$= \frac{300\,\text{(s)} \times \text{car load (passengers)}}{\text{cycle time (s)} \times \text{no. of lifts}}$$

Transportation capacity expressed as per cent:

$$= \frac{100 \times \text{transportation capacity}}{\text{no. occupants in building}}$$

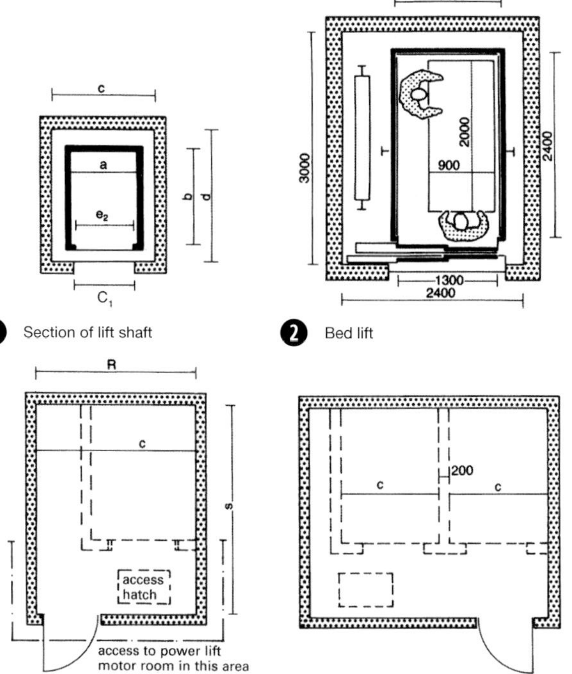

❶ Section of lift shaft

❷ Bed lift

❸ Machine room

❹ Common machine room for set of lifts

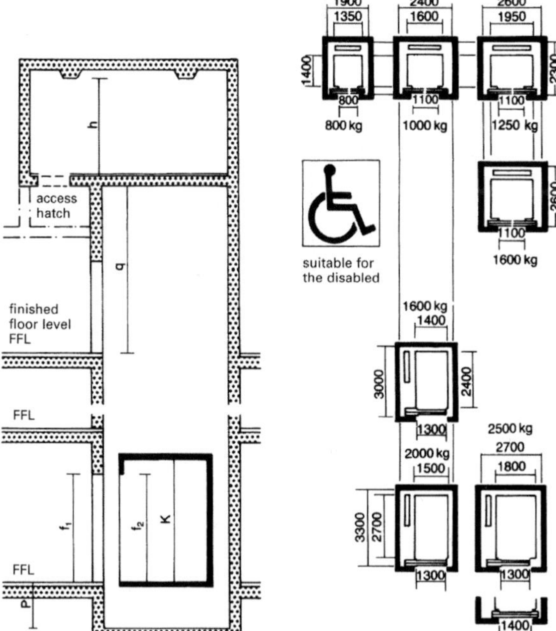

❺ Shaft for single lift

❻ Overview of lifts → ❽ – ❾

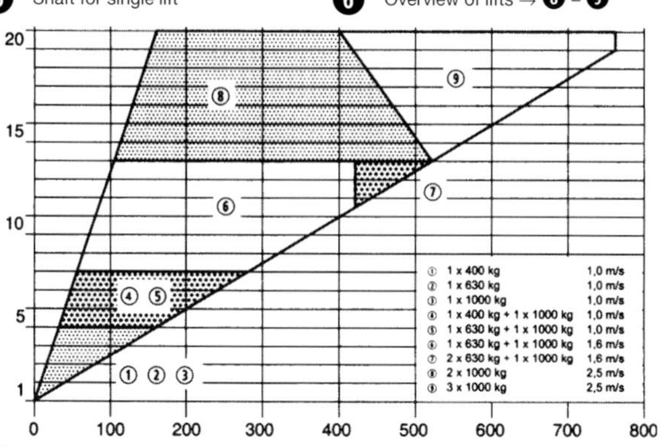

❼ Transport capacity requirements for comfortable residential buildings with and without office floors

load capacity	kg	800				1000 (1250)				1600			
nominal speed	m/s	0.63	1.0	1.6	2.5	0.63	1.0	1.6	2.5	0.63	1.0	1.6	2.5
min. shaft width	c	1900				2400 (2600)				2600			
min. shaft depth	d	2300				2300 (2600)				2600			
min. shaft pit depth	p	1400	1500	1700	2800	1400	1700		2800	1400	1900	2800	
min. shaft head height	q	3800		4000	5000	4200			5200	4400			5400
shaft door width	c_1	800; min. 900				1100				1100			
shaft door height	f_1	2000				2100				2100			
min. area of machine room	m^2	15			18	20				25			
min. width of machine room	r	2500			2800	3200				3200			
min. depth of machine room	s	3700			4900	4900				5500			
min. height of machine room	h	2200			2800	2400			2800	2800			
car width	a	1350				1500				1950			
car depth	b	1400				1400				1750			
car height	k	2200				2300				2300			
car door width	e_2	800; min. 900				1100				1100			
car door height	f_2	2000				2100				2100			
permissible no. passengers		10				13 (16)				21			

❽ Passenger lifts are preferable for more than residential buildings (offices, banks, hotels); lifts enable use with wheelchair

load capacity	kg	1600				2000				2500			
nominal speed	m/s	0.63	1.0	1.6	2.5	0.63	1.0	1.6	2.5	0.63	1.0	1.6	2.5
min. shaft width	c	2400								2700			
min. shaft depth	d	3000				3300							
min. shaft pit depth	p	1800	1700	1900	2800	1600	1700	1900	2800	1800	1900	2100	3000
min. shaft head height	q	4400			5400	4400			5400	4800			5600
shaft door width	c_1	1300								1300 (1400)			
shaft door height	f_1	2100											
min. area of machine room	m^2	26				27				29			
min. width of machine room	r	3200								3500			
min. depth of machine room	s	5500				5800							
min. height of machine room	h	2800											
car width	a	1400				1500				1800			
car depth	b	2400				2700							
car height	k	2300											
car door width	$e_2{}^7$	1300								1300 (1400)			
car door height	f_2	2100											
permissible no.passengers		21				26				33			

Dimensions in mm → ❶ – ❻

❾ Structural dimensions for bed lifts → ❶ – ❻

LIFTS
Principles
Control
Residential buildings
Public buildings
Small goods lifts
Hydraulic lifts
Special lifts

BS EN 81
DIN EN 81
DIN 15306
DIN 15309

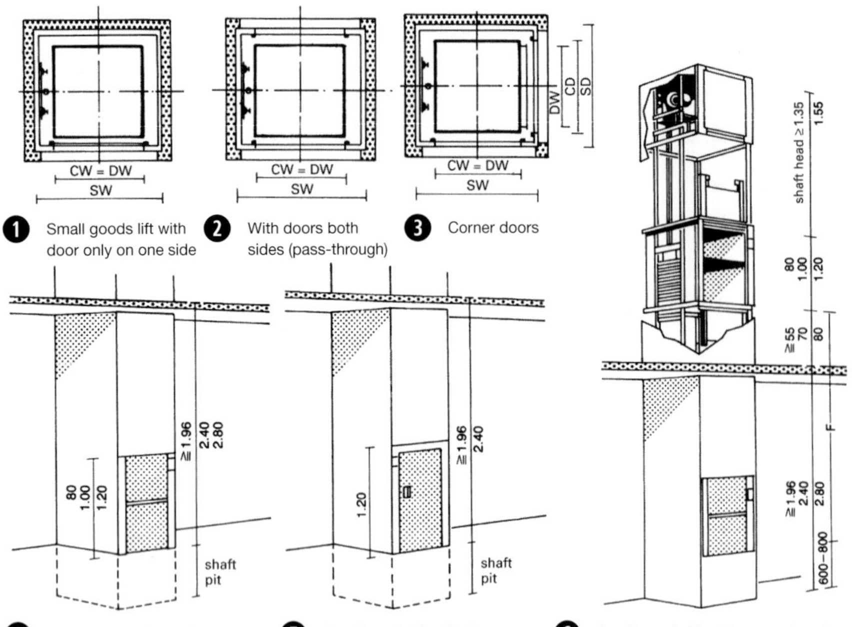

❶ Small goods lift with door only on one side ❷ With doors both sides (pass-through) ❸ Corner doors

❹ Small goods lift with floor-level sliding doors ❺ Small goods lift with floor-level hinged door ❻ Small goods lift with parapet and vertical sliding door

Loading arrangement		One side access and loading from both sides							Corner access and corner access with loading from both sides				
payload	Q kg	100					300		100				
speed	v m/s	0.45					0.3		0.45				
car width = door width	W = DW	400	500	600	700	800	800	800	500	600	700	800	800
car depth	CD	400	500	600	700	800	1000	1000	500	600	700	800	1000
car height = door height	CH = DH	800					1200	1200	800				1200
door width of the corner doors	DW	–	–	–	–	–	–	–	350	450	550	650	850
shaft width	SW	720	820	920	1020	1120		1120	820	920	1020	1120	1120
shaft depth	SD	580	680	780	880	980	1180	1180	680	780	880	980	1180
shaft head height min.	SHH	1990					2590	2590	2145				2745
machine room door width		500	500	600	700	800	800	800	500	600	700	800	800
machine room door height		600							600				
min. distance between loading points	1.)	1930					2730	2730	1930				2730
min. distance between loading points	2.)	700						450	700				
parapet height min., lowest stop only	B	600					800	800	600				800

❼ Structural dimensions of small goods lifts → ❶ – ❻

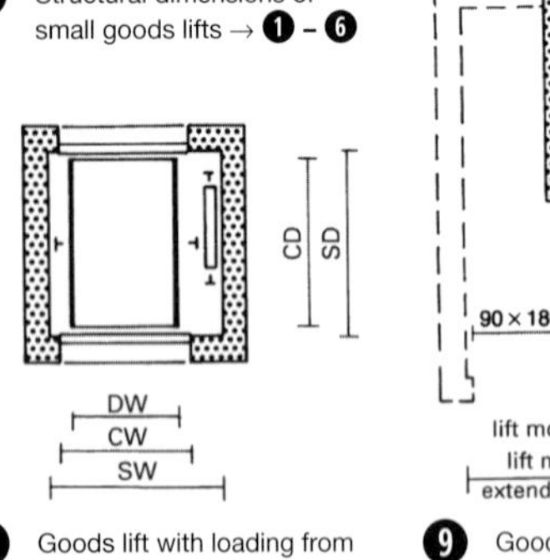

❽ Goods lift with loading from both sides (pass-through doors)

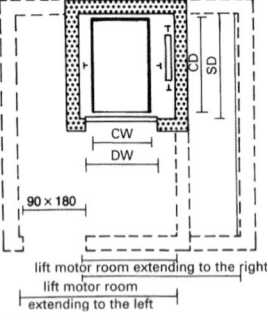

CW
DW
CD
SD
90 × 180
lift motor room extending to the right
lift motor room extending to the left

❾ Goods lift with loading only one side, and machine room

load capacity	kg	630	1000	1600	2000	2500	3200
nominal speed	m/s	← 0.40 --- 0.63 --- 1.00 →					
car dimensions	mm						
CW		1100	1300	1500	1500	1800	2000
CD		1570	1870	2470	2870	2870	3070
CH		2200	2200	2200	2200	2200	2200
door dimensions	mm						
DW		1100	1300	1500	1500	1800	2000
DH		2200	2200	2200	2200	2200	2200
shaft dimensions	mm						
SW		1800	2000	2200	2300	2600	2900
SD		1700	2000	2600	3000	3000	3200
SPH 0.4 and. 0.63	m/s	1200	1300	1300	1300	1300	1400
1.0	m/s	1300	1300	1600	1600	1800	1900
SHH 0.4 and 0.63	m/s	3700	3800	3900	4000	4100	4200
1.0	m/s	3800	3900	4200	4200	4400	4400
PHH		1900	1900	1900	2100	1900	1900

❿ Structural dimensions of traction sheave goods lifts → ❽ – ❾

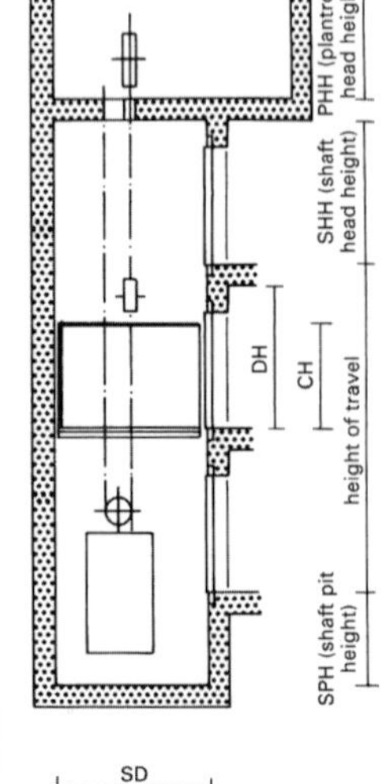

⓫ Cross-section → ❽ – ❾

Small goods lifts (also called dumb waiters): payload ≦300 kg; car floor area ≦1.0 m^2; intended for transporting light goods, documents, food etc.; not for use by passengers. The shaft framework is normally made of steel sections set in the shaft pit or on the floor, and clad on all sides by non-flammable building materials. → ❶ – ❻. Calculation of the transport capacity of goods lifts → ❼. The following formula is used to estimate the time, in seconds, of one transport cycle:

$$T = 2\frac{h}{v} + L_T + H\,(t_1 + t_2) = \ldots s$$

2 = constant factor for round trip
h = height of the lift, v = operating speed (m/s), L_T = loading and unloading time (s), H = number of stops
t_1 = time for acceleration and deceleration (s)
t_2 = time for closing and opening the shaft doors: single doors 6 s, double doors 10 s, vertical sliding doors in small goods lifts about 3 s.

The transportation capacity C can be calculated from the time for one transport cycle, T, according to the formula:

$$C = \frac{60}{\text{time for a cycle (s)}}$$

$$= \frac{60}{T} = \ldots \text{ journeys/min.}$$

Structural requirements: The machine room must be lockable, have sufficient illumination and be of a size to prevent accidents. Area for the machinery must be ≧1.8 m high. Food lifts in hospitals: lift shafts must have washable smooth internal walls. External press-button control must be provided for calling and despatching the lift to/from each stopping point.

Goods lifts
Goods lifts are those intended
a) to transport goods or
b) passengers who are employed by the operator of the lift.

Stopping precision
Goods lifts without travel delay ± 20–40 mm
Passenger and goods lifts with travel delay ± 10–30 mm
Speed: 0.25–0.4 up to 0.63–1.0 m/s.

BS EN 81
BS 5655-10
BS 8486-2
PAS 32-2
DIN EN 81
DIN 15306
DIN 15309

❶ Shaft plan

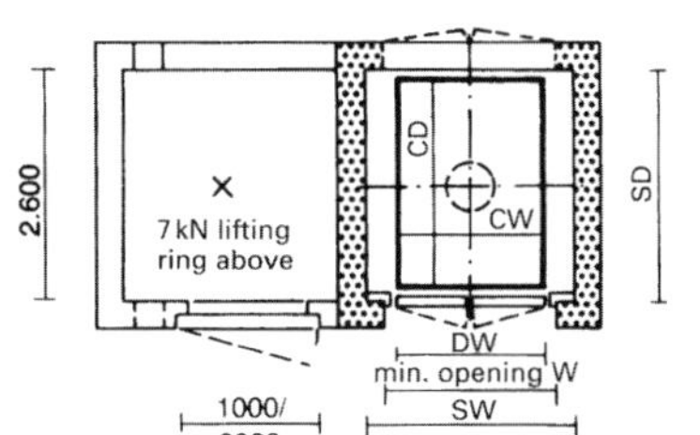

❷ Shaft plan with machine room for hydraulic lift

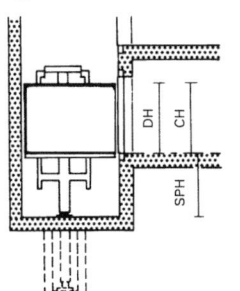

Hydraulic lifts meet the demand for transporting heavy loads economically up and down shorter lift heights and are best used for up to 12 m lift height. The machine room can be located remotely from the shaft itself.

Standardised direct-acting push piston lifts can be used to lift payloads of as much as 20 t up to a max. height of 17 m → ❶ – ❸, while indirect-acting push piston lifts in standard operation can lift max. 7 t to a max. 34 m. The operating speed of hydraulic lifts is between 0.2 and 0.8 m/s (considerably slower than traction sheave lifts!). A roof-mounted machine room is not required.

Several variations in hydraulics can be found → ❻ – ❾. The most commonly used is the centrally mounted ram → ❶ – ❸. This requires a bored hole. The ram retraction control, regardless of load, must be kept within ± 3 mm.

Height clearance of the lift doors is min. 50–100 mm greater than for other doors, so that a completely level entry into the lift car is obtained. Double swing doors, or hinged sliding doors, can be fitted – either hand-operated or fully automatic, with a central or side opening.

❸ Vertical section of shaft

❹ Diagram to determine the shaft head height SHH; shaft pit depth SPD; cylinder shaft depth CSD; cylinders shaft diameter D

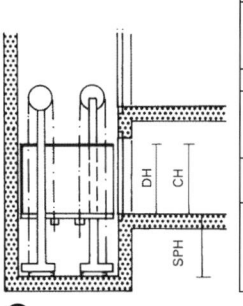

Payload			Q ≠ 5000 kg	Q ≠ 10000 kg
shaft width	SW	=	CW + 500	CW + 550
shaft depth	SD	=	CD + 150 loading from one side CD + 100 loading from both sides	
machine room dimensions approx.	width	=	2000	2200
(other locations of the machine room at up to max. 5 m distance from the shaft are possible, greater distance on request)	depth	=	2600	2800
	height	=	2200	2700

❺ Technical data → ❶ – ❸

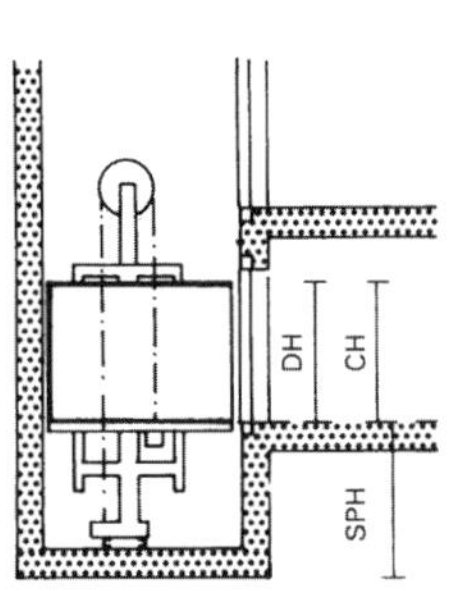

❻ Rucksack arrangement 1:1

load capacity kg		630	1000	1600
speed m/s		0.30	0.18	0.23
		0.47	0.28	0.39
lift height max. m		6.0	7.0	7.0
car dimensions mm	W	1100	1300	1500
	D	1500	1700	2200
	H	2200	2200	2200
door dimensions mm	W	1100	1300	1500
	H	2200	2200	2200
shaft dimensions mm	W	1650	1900	2150
	D	1600	1800	2300
	SPH min.	1200	1400	1600
	SHH min.	3200	3200	3200

dimensions → ❻

❼ Tandem arrangement 1:1

load capacity kg		1600	2000	2500	3200
speed m/s		0.15	0.18	0.24	0.20
		0.24	0.30	0.38	0.30
lift height max. m		6.0	7.0	7.0	7.0
car dimensions mm	W	1500	1500	1800	2000
	D	2200	2700	2700	3500
	H	2200	2200	2200	2200
door dimensions mm	W	1500	1500	1800	2000
	H	2200	2200	2200	2200
shaft dimensions mm	W	2200	2200	2600	2800
	D	2300	2800	2800	3600
	SPH min.	1300	1300	1300	1300
	SHH min.	3450	3450	3450	3450

dimensions → ❼

❽ Rucksack arrangement 2:1

load capacity kg		630	1000	1600
speed m/s		0.28	0.30	0.24
		0.46	0.50	0.42
		0.78	0.80	0.62
lift height max. m		13.0	16.0	18.0
car dimensions mm	W	1100	1300	1500
	D	1500	1900	2200
	H	2200	2200	2200
door dimensions mm	W	1100	1300	1500
	H	2200	2200	2200
shaft dimensions mm	W	1650	1900	2150
	D	1600	2000	2300
	SPH min.	1200	1400	1600
	SHH	3200	3200	3200

dimensions → ❽

❾ Tandem arrangement 2:1

load capacity kg		1600	2000	2500	3000
speed m/s		0.23	0.19	0.25	0.21
		0.39	0.32	0.39	0.31
		0.61	0.50	0.64	0.51
lift height max. m		13.0	14.0	16.0	18.0
car dimensions mm	W	1500	1500	1800	2000
	D	2200	2700	2700	3500
	H	2200	2200	2200	2200
door dimensions mm	W	1500	1500	1800	2000
	H	2200	2200	2200	2200
shaft dimensions mm	W	2300	2300	2600	2900
	D	2300	2800	2800	3600
	SPH min.	1300	1300	1300	1300
	SPP	3400	3550	3650	3650

dimensions → ❾

Building components

LIFTS
Principles
Control
Residential buildings
Public buildings
Small goods lifts
Hydraulic lifts
Special lifts

BS EN 81
DIN EN 81
DIN 15306
DIN 15309

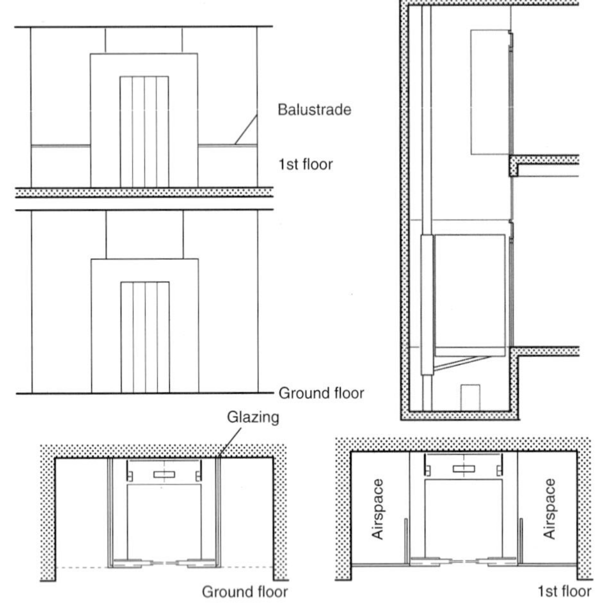

❶ Contact with moving parts must be prevented in glazed lifts: safety barrier around shaft doors min. up to 3.5 m high and on the other sides min. 2.5 m, with the distance to moving parts at least 0.5 m; with greater distances, the height can be reduced.

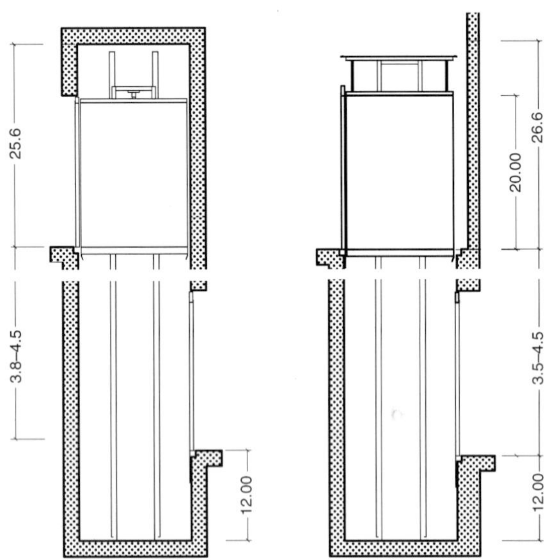

❷ Load and goods lifts. Because passengers are not allowed to travel, the car does not require doors. This results in a good relationship between shaft cross-section and usable car area.

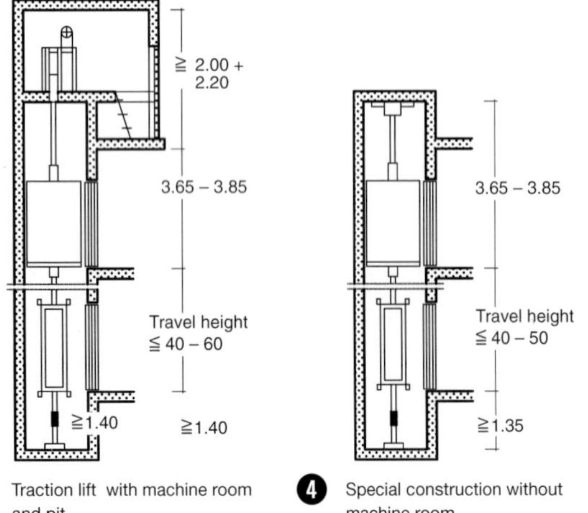

❸ Traction lift with machine room and pit

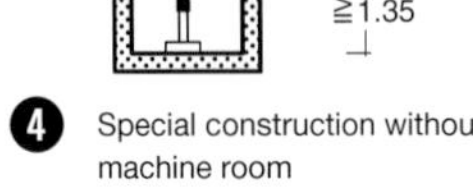

❹ Special construction without machine room

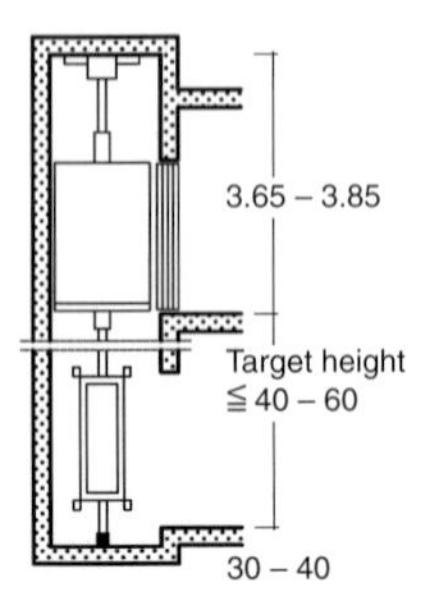

❺ Special construction without machine room and with reduced pit depth

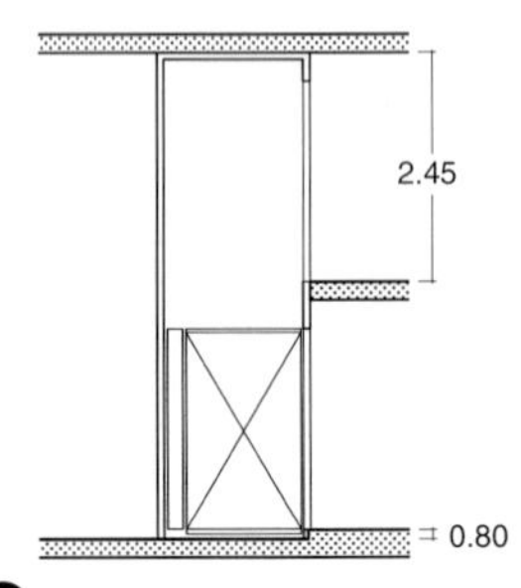

❻ Lift for disabled people
These lifts are approved solely for use by those with impaired mobility.

Glazed lifts

Glazed lifts offer a view and improve the users' feeling of safety. They can be constructed either with glazed shafts (observing fire resistance requirements) or as shaftless lifts (panoramic lifts) → ❶. These can only be installed near buildings in which, to prevent the spread of fire, no lift shafts are permitted. This makes the inclusion of panoramic lifts into traffic calculations difficult. The glazing must prevent the users touching moving parts with the hand or with objects held in the hand. Glazed lifts are non-standard constructions and require a special prototype approval.

Goods and underfloor lifts (without passenger transport)

Lifts only intended for loads like rubbish bins or goods deliveries can be installed inside a building or in front of it → ❷. Passenger transport is not permissible with this type of lift. A machine room is not normally necessary.

Underfloor lifts are controlled from the uppermost station. The cover of the lift must be in the field of view of the operator.

Lifts with reduced shaft dimensions

In refurbishment projects, it is often a major inconvenience to construct the parts of the shaft above and below the working range. For such projects, there are special lifts, which require less pit depth (min. approx. 80 mm) and shaft head heights (min. approx. 2500 mm above the highest stop) → ❸ – ❺. When lifts are installed without machine rooms, special requirements have to be considered for the shaft (ventilation, possible condensation on the ceiling and fire protection measures). These requirements can be taken from the information provided by the particular manufacturer, because such lifts have to undergo a special prototype approval.

Such special constructions also include **lifts for disabled people** → ❻, which may be used only by the specified group. Dead man's controls and similar measures make simple, space-saving installations without pit and car doors permissible. Home stairlifts enable those with impaired mobility to move easily between floors (on straight or curved stairways) and across landings. The requirements for such installations are provided in BS 5776.

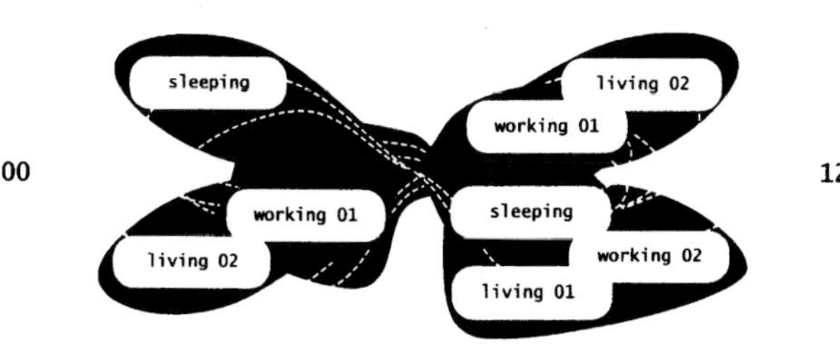

❶ Functional diagram dependent on daily routines (UN Studio → refs)

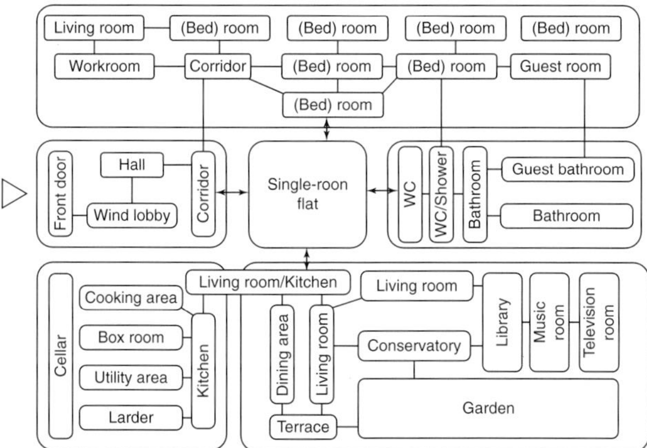

❷ Traditional spatial layout of room division 'from the single-room flat to the palace'. Read backwards, a programme for the spatial expression of uses and flexible uses of living space

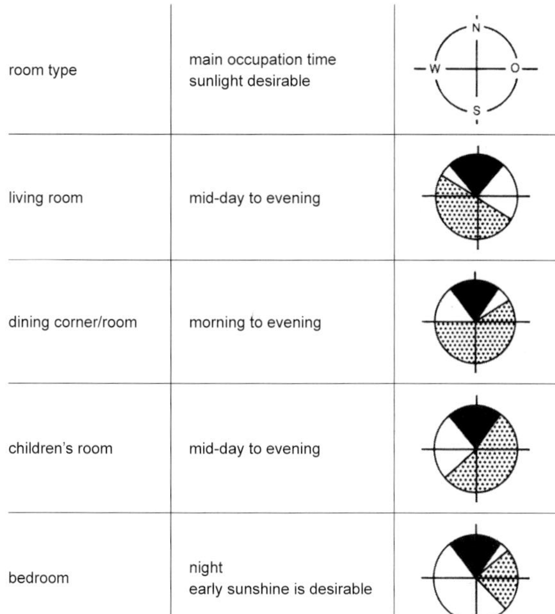

room type	main occupation time sunlight desirable	N / W / O / S
living room	mid-day to evening	
dining corner/room	morning to evening	
children's room	mid-day to evening	
bedroom	night early sunshine is desirable	

❸ Periods of occupation and desirable sunlight in residential rooms

Living in houses, originally the spatial realisation of basic human needs, has developed in modern society into a complex interaction of a multitude of influences subject to the most varied requirements and individual quality standards.

The lifestyle, principles and pretensions of the (potential) inhabitants come up against building regulations, political subsidy ideas and their consequences for town planning and also (underlying ideological) architectural predispositions about location, type of building, development and ground plan.

Historical development

In the course of industrialisation and the movement of population to urban areas, residential building developed into a central task of the construction industry in the 19th century, and on account of the world wars this was still the case during the last century.

The planning preoccupations with privacy and prestige, which originated in the feudal system and still apply as models and clichés, have entered the awareness of a wide public. Prosperous urban society expressed this by building villas and impressive mansions. In parallel, much Victorian accommodation was built as dense blocks in rental districts as a result of the massive (working class) housing shortage and with the aim of maximising land use and profit.

The architects of the modernist movement (and their successors) developed opposing concepts to those of the 'stone' city. They investigated the individual home, its **lighting** and **orientation** → ❸, the optimal (minimum) **room size** and **functional layout** → ❷ and also rational and standardised methods of construction. The results ranged from ambitious private houses to new 'fresh from the drawing board' housing developments.

The present day: community and individual

Modern housing requires the separation in space and time of individual and community interests within the house as well as meeting the demand for privacy and publicity (or anonymity) in the urban context → ❶.

The increasing relaxation of traditional family lifestyles and, as a result of the information age, the approaching end of the separation of housing and workplace mean that the classic functional and utilitarian procedures inside houses → ❷ have to be re-examined. The established terms like living room or children's room often have little validity.

The place of residence is understood to be a private space with controlled and graduated access from the outside world. The classic common and individual areas within a house are becoming less significant in terms of area, and the 'multi-purpose room' (living-working room, shared living space as in a flat etc.), which occurs in both private and public housing, is developing into a significant room type.

Room division and functional neutrality

The consequence of the individualisation of lifestyles could be customised layouts with differentiated and often luxurious room division, but it could also be a functionally neutral division of space with qualitatively similar rooms suitable for flexible use by families, flat sharers, 'multi-generation living' groups or living-and-working models.

These considerations result in increased significance for the neutrality of the developing decor.

The task of a century

Among the changes in society caused by industrialisation, since the middle of the 19th century house building has developed into a central activity of the construction industry. Housing shortage and mass poverty became a decisive political dimension, which still continued into the 20th century due to the World Wars.

The regulation and encouragement of house building is therefore an essential aspect of national construction policy. Political instruments have been developed in the form of planning laws and building regulations → p. 56, intended to set **minimum standards** to protect privacy, avoid danger and protect health.

Laws to subsidise housing construction and a repeatedly modified system of financial grants and tax exemptions have been set up to support private investment in rented and owner-occupied housing (**property incentives**). In consideration of the current over-supply of housing and increasing demands in the market regarding area and quality, the subsidy laws have been amended in recent years.

The essential subsidy instruments in Germany are: the **Law to Subsidise House Building**; the **state subsidy for house building**, laid down in the Law to Subsidise Social Housing of 13/09/2001. The subsidising of house building includes the new construction of flats with subsidised rents, the new construction of owner-occupied housing, the purchase and refurbishment of existing houses and the purchase of rights of occupancy.

Housing subsidy is carried out at the **state level**: the extent of grants, the size details of subsidised houses and application conditions can therefore differ from state to state and are laid down in the relevant **housing subsidy regulations** → ❶. The target housing subsidy group are households whose income does not exceed the level stipulated in the laws and regulations, and also households with two or more children and households with disabled members. The subsidy is in the form of loans at preferential rates, grants, guarantees, housing entitlement certificates and the provision of cheap building land.

Household size	Maximum living area	
1 person	50 m²	for each further person belonging to the household, the living area can be exceeded by max. 10 m².
2 persons	60 m²	
3 persons	75 m²	
4 persons	85 m²	

Limits on the living area in subsidised housing (example)

Owner-occupied House Allowance Law

This legislation provides for a limited period a subsidy from taxation via a fixed annual allowance for the purchase of owner-occupied flats and houses. The target group for this allowance is households whose income does not exceed the limits laid down in the law. On account of the current over-supply of housing, the political justification for this law is often questioned.

Housing area regulation

The 'Regulation for the calculation of the housing area' of 25/11/2003 is used to work out the area of houses and flats for the purpose of the Law to Subsidise House Building. The area of a house or flat includes the floor area of all rooms which belong exclusively to the house or, in the case of a residential home the areas intended for the sole use of the owner → ❷.

The floor area of a room is determined from the clearance space between building components and starts from the face of the cladding of the building component → ❸. The floor area is measured in the completed room, or can be calculated from a suitable construction drawing. Floor areas are calculated according to → ❹.

Living area includes:	Living area does not include:
all rooms which belong solely to the house, or are intended for the sole use of the occupants, including **conservatories, swimming pools**, etc. (if enclosed on all sides), **balconies, loggias and terraces**	**subsidiary rooms** (cellars, store rooms, cellar replacement rooms, wash houses, attic rooms, drying rooms, heating rooms, garages), rooms which do not correspond to the requirements of planning law for the relevant use, **offices**

Rooms included in living area (housing area regulation, excerpt)

floor area of a room includes:	floor area of a room does not include:
clear area (from face of cladding) between building components, including the area of **door and window frames, skirtings, permanently installed objects, free-standing installations, built-in furniture**, movable room dividers	**chimneys, masonry cladding, claddings, pillars** (from 1.5 m height and 0.1 m² floor area), **stairs and landings** (from 3 steps), **door niches, window and wall niches** (which do not reach to the floor or are at least 0.13 cm deep),

Floor area of a room included in living area (housing area regulation, excerpt)

complete	rooms and parts of rooms with a clear height of at least 2 m
half	rooms and parts of rooms with a clear height of at least 1 m and less than 2 m, unheated and fully enclosed conservatories, swimming pools etc.
normally a quarter, at the highest a half	balconies, loggias, roof gardens and terraces

Inclusion of floor areas in the calculation

KfW Subsidy Bank

The KfW Subsidy Bank is a public body with its capital provided by the Federal Republic of Germany and the states. The main emphasis of its activity is the provision of favourable loans for the encouragement of house building. The subsidies are in the form of a subsidy programme with fixed aims. Currently (autumn 2008) the following programmes are active:

KfW property programme
for the building or purchase of owner-occupied houses and flats.

Ecological building
for the construction of passive houses, KfW energy-saving houses and the installation of renewable energy heating systems

Housing modernisation
for the modernisation and repair of residential buildings with emphasis on the reduction of energy consumption

CO_2 building refurbishment plan
for single measures intended to reduce the energy consumption of old buildings

Solar electricity production
to finance photovoltaic systems on residential buildings

HOUSING DENSITY

Parameters

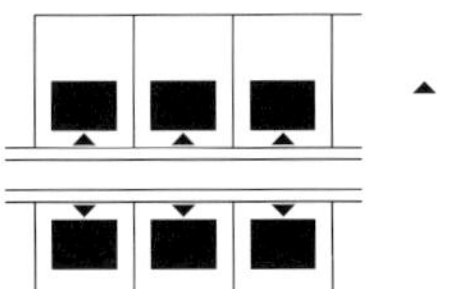

DETACHED HOUSE (ESTATE)

plot	350 – 450 m²
storeys	1–2 (+ attic)
gross floor area	150–160
floor-area ratio	0.3–0.5
inhabitants/ha	70–90

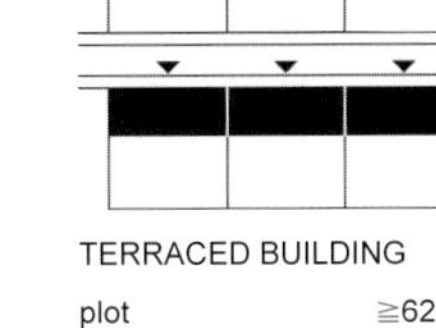

TERRACED BUILDING

plot	≧625 m²
storeys	2–4 (+ attic)
gross floor area	≧500
floor-area ratio	≧0.8
inhabitants/ha	≦400

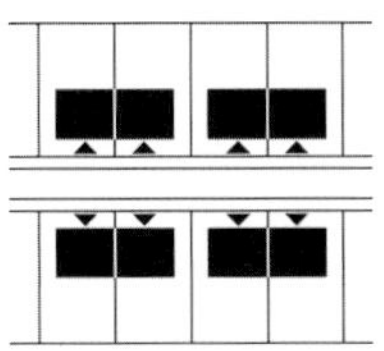

SEMI-DETACHED HOUSE

plot	250–300 m²
storeys	1–2 (+ attic)
gross floor area	150–160
floor-area ratio	0.5–0.6
inhabitants/ha	115–135

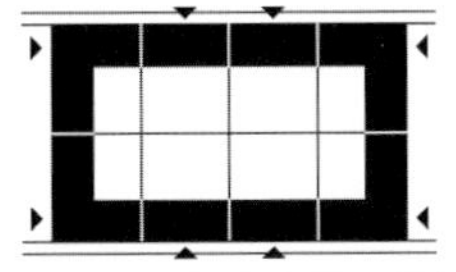

BLOCK DEVELOPMENT

plot	≦1550 m²
storeys	5 (+ attic)
gross floor area	1250
floor-area ratio	≧0.8
inhabitants/ha	400–450

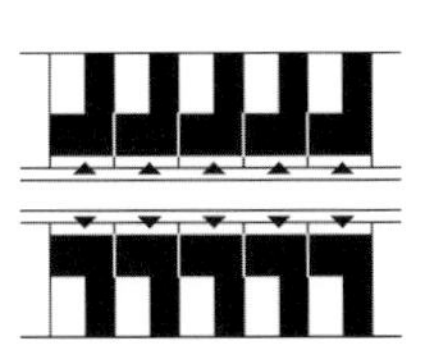

LINKED/COURTYARD-GARDEN HOUSE

plot	200 – 250 m²
storeys	1 – 2 (+ attic)
gross floor area	150 – 160
floor-area ratio	0.6 – 0.8
inhabitants/ha	150 – 180

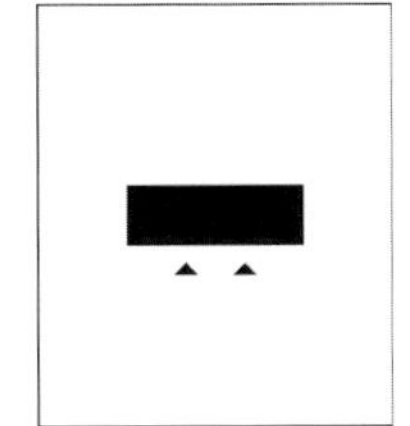

NARROW HIGH-RISE

plot	≧5000 m²
storeys	10
gross floor area	600/storey
floor-area ratio	1.2
inhabitants/ha	approx. 450

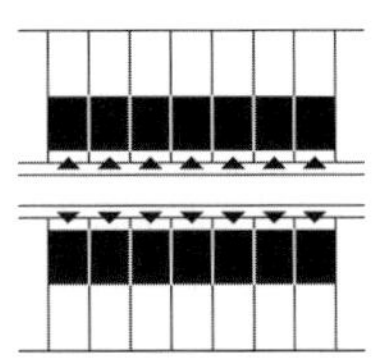

TERRACED HOUSE

plot	150 – 200 m²
storeys	2 – 3 (+ attic)
gross floor area	130 – 150
floor-area ratio	0.6 – 0.9
inhabitants/ha	200 –250

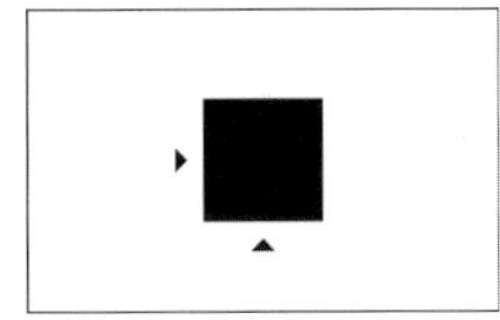

SQUARE HIGH-RISE

plot	≧1875 m²
storeys	10
gross floor area	225/storey
floor-area ratio	1.2
inhabitants/ha	approx. 450

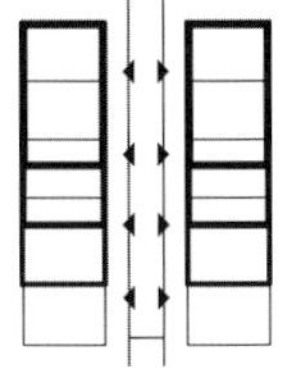

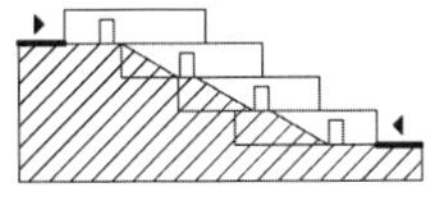

STEPPED HOUSE

storeys	1
gross floor area	130 – 150/terrace
floor-area ratio	1.5 – 2.0
inhabitants/ha	300 – 350

❶ Town planning parameters of various house types (indicative)

The extent of residential development (urban housing density) is an important measure in public land-use planning. The urban housing density is laid down in the development (zoning) plans of cities and councils and is the indirect result of the provisions of planning law regarding the permissibility of building projects in unplanned inner areas and in outer areas → p. 56. The essential statutory parameters describing urban housing density are the plot coverage ratio (the built area related to the plot area), and the floor-area ratio (the total area of all floors related to the plot area), as well as provisions regarding the number of full storeys and the height of buildings → p. 63.

Urban housing density and house type

The urban housing density has a considerable influence on the selection of house type, determines the type and extent of development and specifies the land use of a housing development. The urban housing densities of various types of housing (housing density) are shown in → ❶, as described by the statutory parameters. The average population density (inhabitants/m²) is also shown for clarification. The density increases in a range from free-standing detached houses, semi-detached houses, linked and terraced houses to multi-storey residential buildings, block developments and stand-alone blocks. Based on the required plot area, dense terraced and block development achieves similar densities to multi-storey stand-alone blocks.

Housing density and housing quality

The qualitative evaluation of housing density is complex and depends on a multitude of factors. It cannot be estimated solely from a plot or group of houses, but is also influenced by the larger scale urban development conditions. The term quarter has become established to describe an urban planning unit with its own infrastructure (shopping, recreational provision, schools, kindergartens and connections to local transport).

Further points of interest are the number of inhabitants for whom the infrastructure is adequate and the accessibility (transport provision and times). These parameters interact with the requirement for housing space per inhabitant and other spatial aspects concerning privacy and individuality as well as the long-distance connections, distance from and relation to city centres, plot prices, accessibility of workplaces etc.

Model calculations demonstrate that with a floor-area ratio of 0.8 (related to net building land) and development with, for example, multi-storey blocks in rows, the result is quarters where 6500 inhabitants can live on a gross area of 75 ha (900 × 900 m). This results in distances from supply facilities of not more than 500 m, which can be reached on foot or by bicycle.

In contrast, with a floor-area ratio of 0.4 and development of detached houses, 6500 inhabitants will live in a quarter with an area of 235 ha (1500 × 1500 m), which is too far on foot (particularly for elderly people) and too small for public transport, so that a car has to be used for daily shopping. In terms of the supply of energy in pipes or cables, it can be stated as a simplification that the cost for a floor-area ratio of 0.4 is nearly double that for 0.8.

These considerations should make clear that the apparent advantages of living in a green belt mean that large parts of our country are scarcely habitable without using a car, which offers no perspective for a sustainable use of land and energy (Bott, Haas → refs)

ORIENTATION

Layout of Buildings

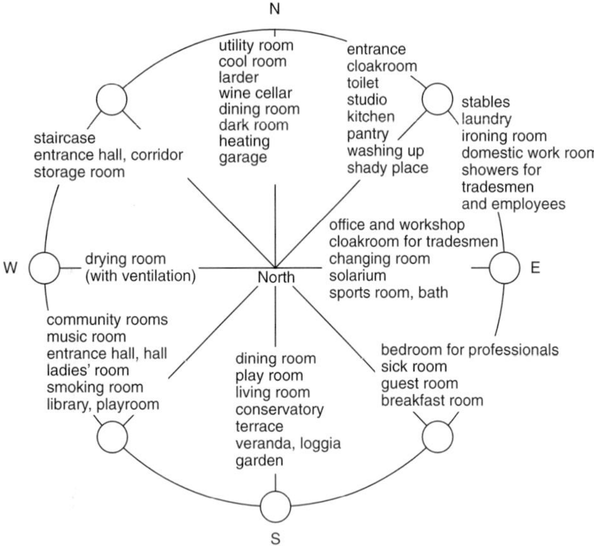

❶ Optimal orientation of rooms

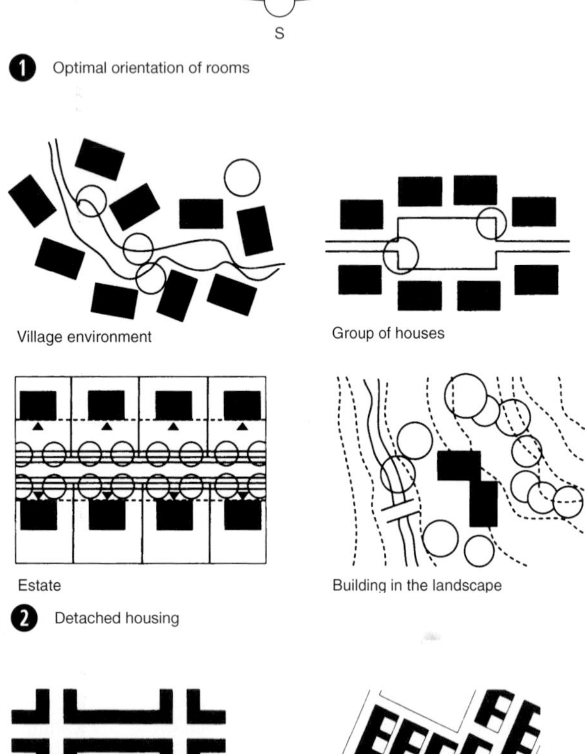

❷ Detached housing

Block

Courtyard

Cells

Rows

Naturally developed town

Planned town

❸ Housing in blocks

Detached housing → ❷ (detached and semi-detached houses with boundary walls) offers the opportunity to orientate a building in four (three) directions of the compass → ❶ (although at the expense of high development costs and low urban planning density → p. 137).

The plots are mostly narrow and long, in order to reduce the road frontage as much as possible. In this case, plots to the **south** of the road are more favourable. This enables a north-facing arrangement of the rooms next to the entrance to the road and the arrangement of the living rooms and bedrooms away from the road, with tranquillity and sunshine (east – south – west) and an exit to and view of the garden.

If the plot is **north** of the road, then the house should be sited at the back of the plot, despite the extra expense of a driveway, in order to exploit the sunny front garden. Plots to the west and east of a (north–south) road should place garden and living rooms on the wind-protected east side (arrangement of the house to the north of the plot), so that no neighbouring buildings shadow the low east sun, as with an east–west road.

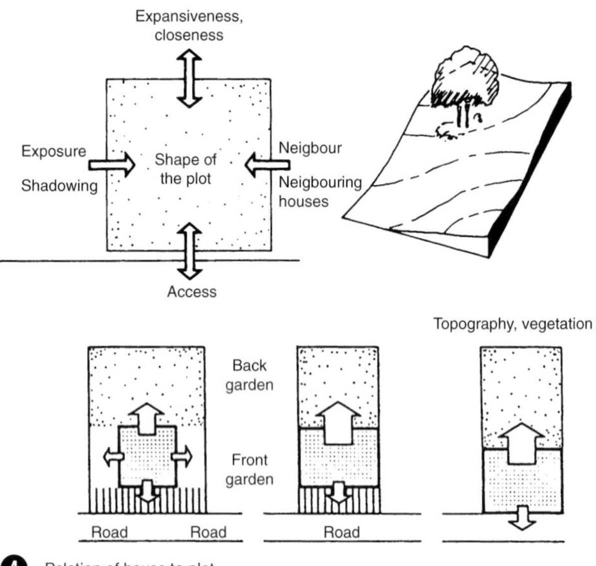

❹ Relation of house to plot

For **housing in blocks** → ❸ (built in blocks and rows), most of the houses or flats will be orientated in two opposing directions with different qualities (view, lighting, noise).

Traditional block development, with varied layouts and orientations of the flats, the planning of the layout of each flat should attempt to compensate for unfavourable lighting conditions. In addition to the traditional functionally neutral corridor floor plans, open, flowing and flexible floor plans can also be used for such situations. The quality of life in block structures results from the multitude of views out and through the street and the inner courtyard, which can be emphasised in the design.

Compass direction is a central consideration of modern town planning. An **east–west orientated arrangement of rows** with green areas in between can achieve (at the cost of public space and the risk of a certain monotony of appearance) uniform lighting and orientation of as many flats as possible → ❸.

see also: Fire protection p. 511

ACCESS

Detached and Terraced Development

The selection of a house type includes decisions about development, access and utilities. This has an important effect on the proportions and organisation of the plan and is also an important cost factor.

Access is also the subject of a multitude of building regulations because of its function as **escape route** → p. 511. The route to the house or flat and the connection of the houses to each other represent an important **location for social interaction** as an immediate part of the surroundings of the inhabitants.

Access principles

The following forms of access can be differentiated according to the principle of adding houses:

– detached house
– (horizontal) **row**: terraced house, passage access
– (vertical) **stacking**: access with lifts and stairs

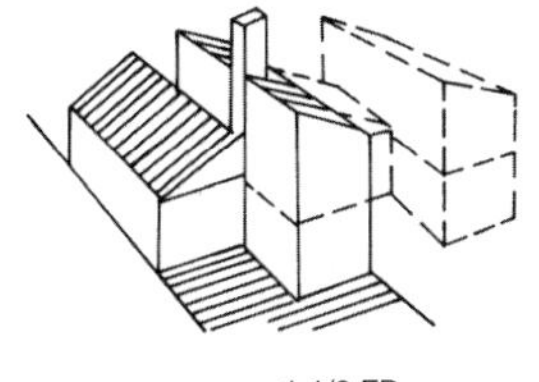
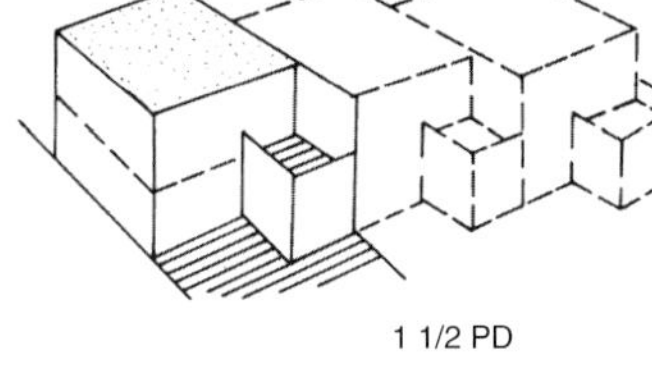
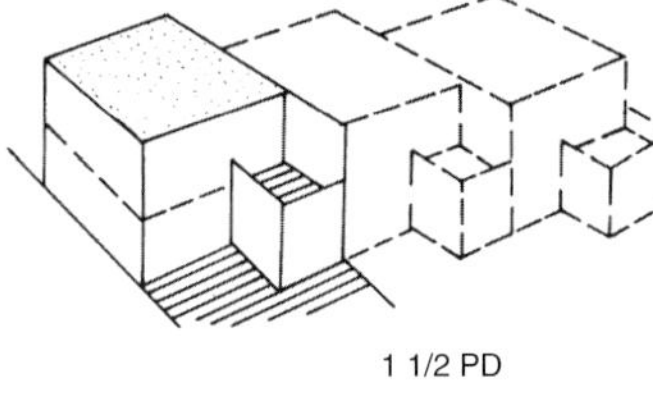
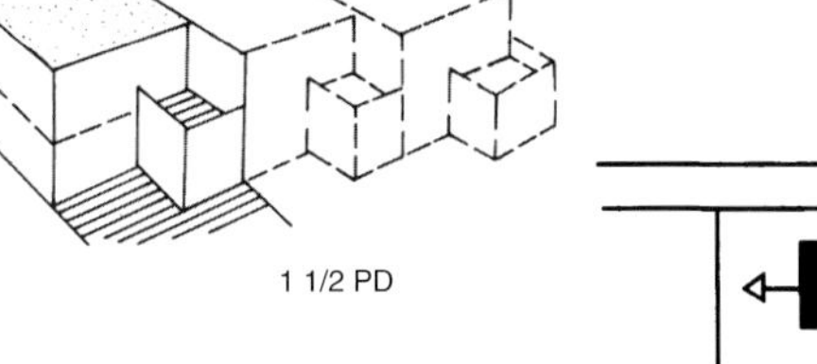

❶ Detached/semi-detached houses

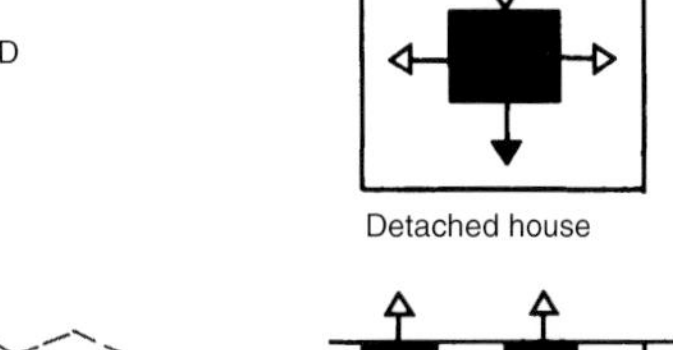

❷ Linked houses

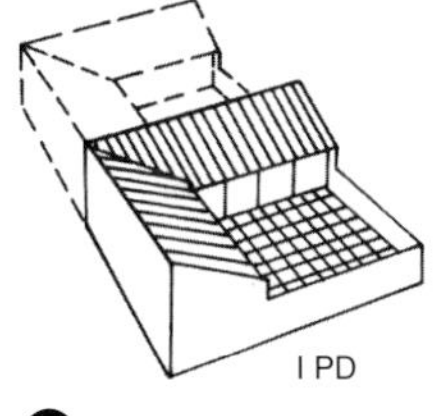

❸ Houses with courtyard garden

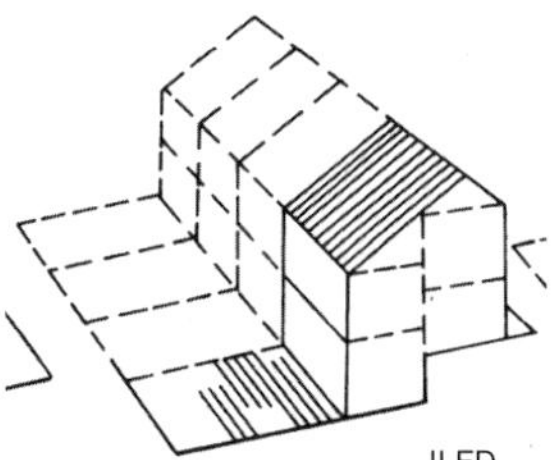
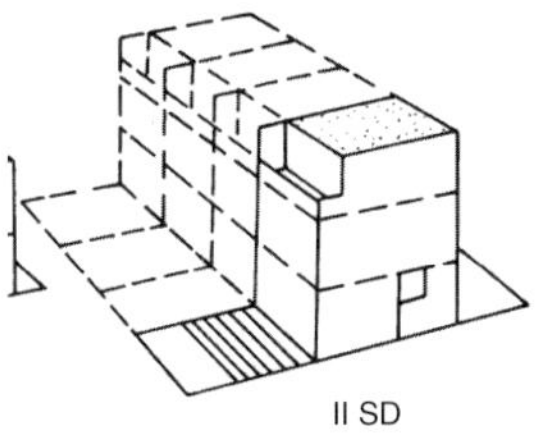
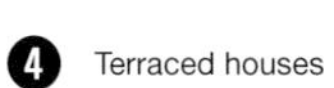

❹ Terraced houses

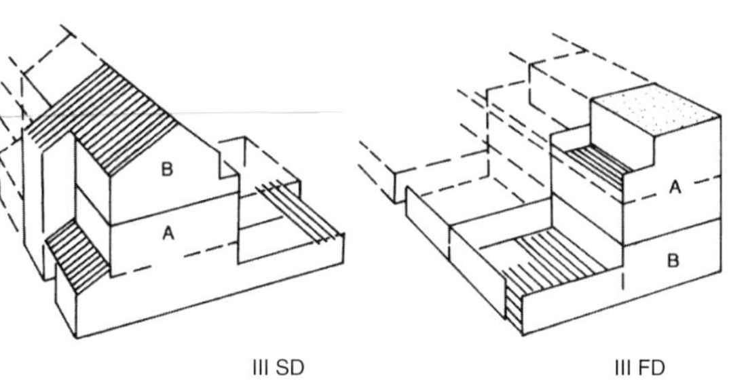

❺ Town houses

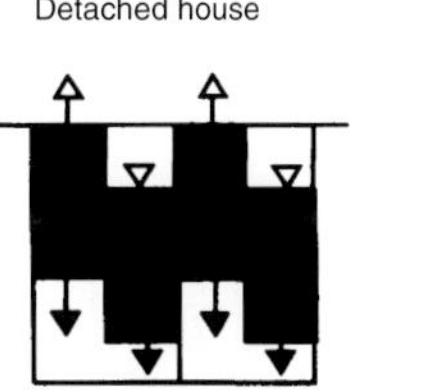
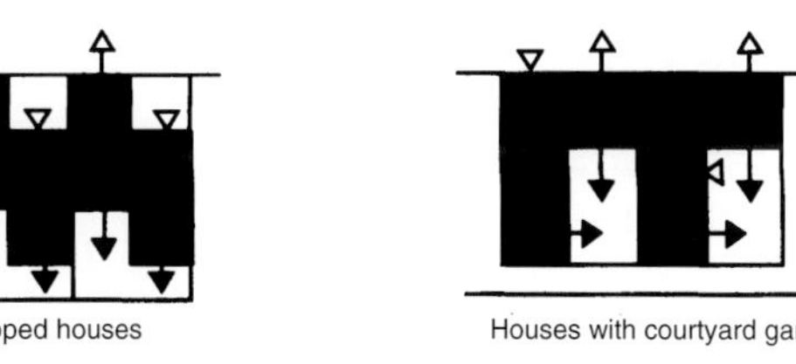
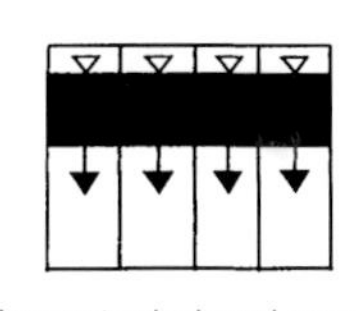

❻ Access to single and rows of houses

Detached house and row access

The individually accessed, detached house standing on its own plot is the prototype for the 'owner-occupied' house. It has a prestigious level access from the road, which is reached through an area at the front ('front garden'). It has direct access from each storey to further private or semi-public open spaces (e.g. garden. terrace, inner courtyard or roof garden) → ❷.

With row access, as with individual access, each residential unit, as its 'own' **terraced, linked** or **courtyard-garden house,** is accessed on the level from the road and has a direct exit into the open air → ❷ – ❹. There is a direct relation between private and public space. A sensible height is 2–3 storeys.

Town houses → ❺ also use this access principle for an upper floor flat, which in this case has its own front door and stairs. Terraced houses with good residential value offer the most economic form of house with garden → p. 144.

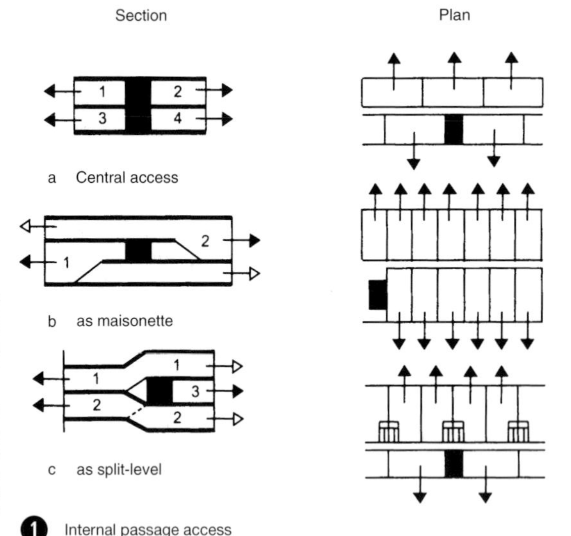

❶ Internal passage access

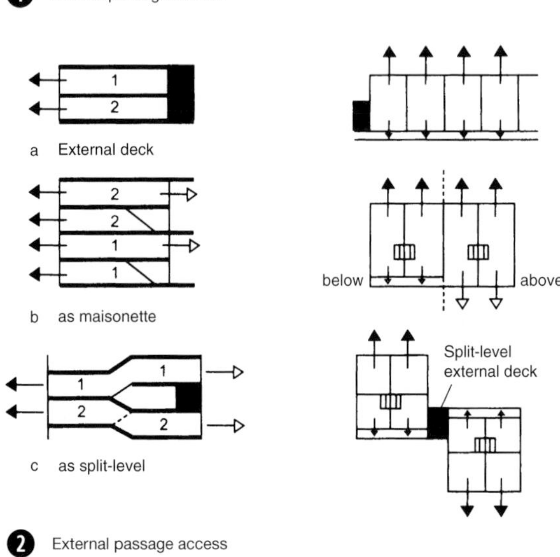

❷ External passage access

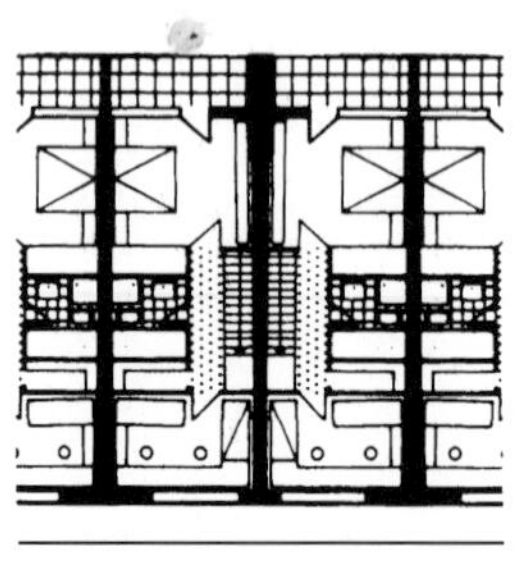

❸ Maisonette with external passage access

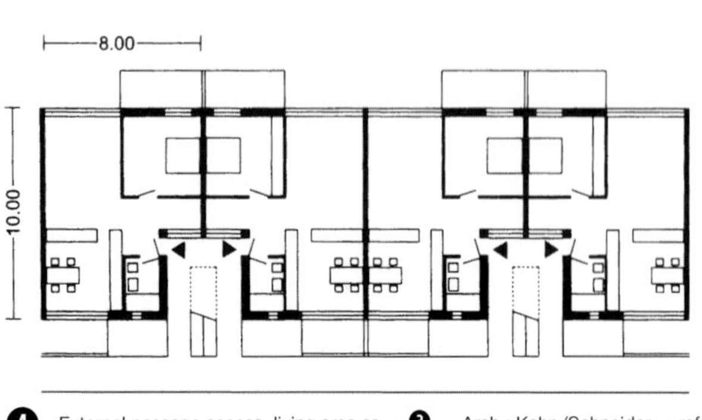

❹ External passage access, living area as → ❸ Arch.: Kohn (Schneider → refs)

Deck access means that the individual storeys of a block of flats are accessed along horizontal **passages**, which are connected to each other and to the entrance by one or more internal, projecting or free-standing **fixed vertical structures** (stair shafts, lifts). The flats are organised along the passages singly, on two sides or on three sides (with an internal function zone). The passages can be arranged internally (**internal passage** → ❶) or along an external surface (**external deck** → ❷).

They have (with corresponding detailing) the appearance of a **semi-public street** → p. 139. The route of this 'street' directly in front of a (for internal passages unlit) wall of the flat produces a tendency to a one-sided orientation of the flat.

The variety of possibilities with this access type therefore results from the **layering** of multi-storey and mezzanine residential units, which offer the possibility, by building over the access passages, of double-aspect living on two sides of the flat.

❺ Gallery access house, split-level flats Arch.: Hirsch

Internal passage

If the access passage is inside the building, this is called an internal passage block → ❶. With this solution, living on one level leads to single-sided orientation. It is therefore better to divide residential units over two or more storeys → ❶ (b+c)

External passage

In an external passage building, the horizontal access is along one long side of the structure → ❷. The open passage is not without problems under the climatic conditions in Central Europe, and in addition it is normally practical to place only subsidiary rooms next to the external passage → ❷ (a).

Living spaces on only one level are therefore particularly suitable for flats and studios → ❹. It is better if the residential unit extends over two or more storeys → ❸. If the floor levels are staggered by just **half a storey in height**, this produces favourable preconditions for the overlapping of functionality and stratification → ❷ (c). The range of possible variations is therefore considerably extended if the residential units are not the same width for the entire depth of the building, but rather overlapped with the neighbouring unit.

Horizontal access **to every second storey** → ❷ (b) permits desirable arrangements of larger residential units on different levels, combined with small units at the entrance level. Good solutions also result from the alternating arrangement of the external passage zones. Symmetrical stacking of maisonettes or a corresponding arrangement of split-level flats makes it possible to limit the number of horizontal access points.

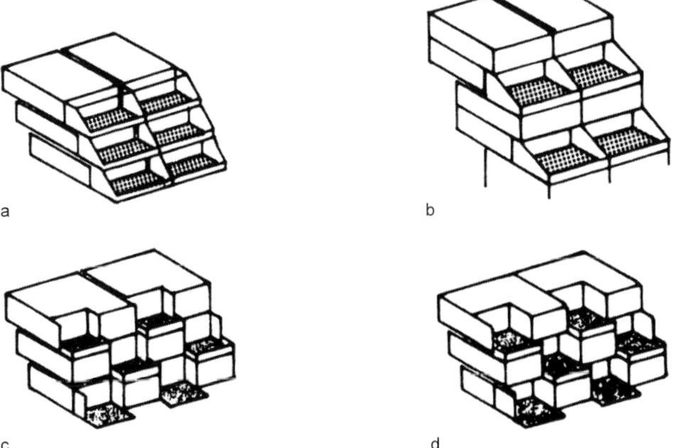

❶ Possible one- and two-storey arrangements of stepped flats with the open-air terraces wholly or partially recessed into the body of the building

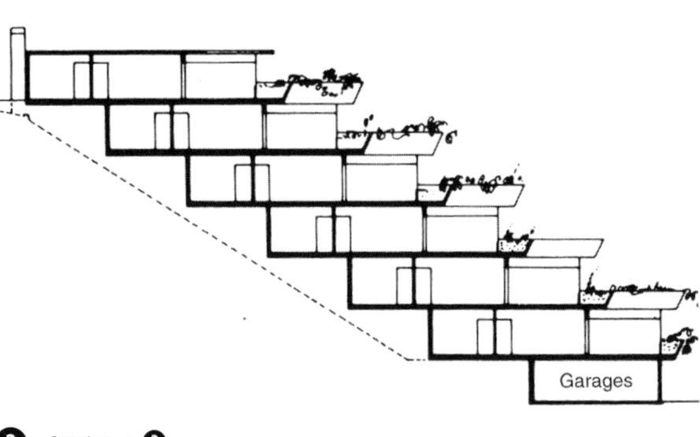

❷ Section → ❸

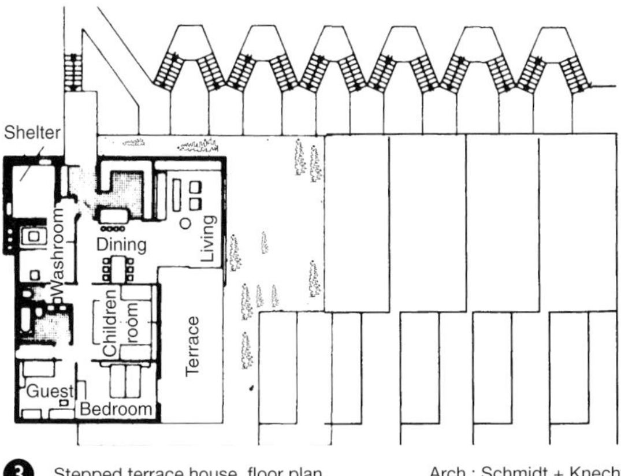

❸ Stepped terrace house, floor plan Arch.: Schmidt + Knecht

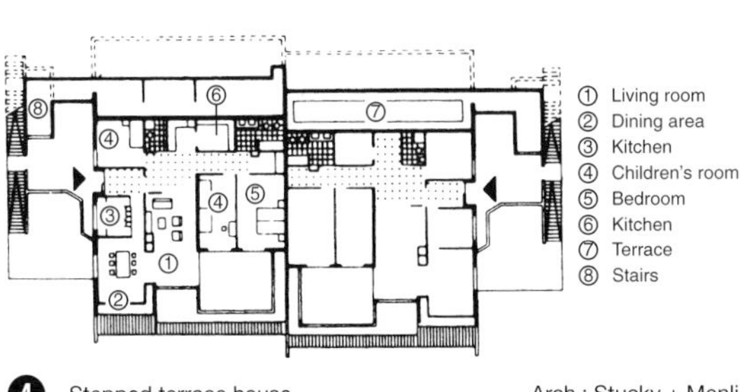

❹ Stepped terrace house Arch.: Stucky + Menli

Steeply sloping sites encourage the construction of stepped buildings. These can be **stepped on one or two sides** → ❷ + ❻. The terracing can be produced by setting back residential units of similar depth or through the arrangement of varying depths of unit, decreasing towards the top. The stacking angle (storey height to terrace depth) mostly corresponds to an average slope of 8–40°. This results in **generous terraces** as space for relaxing, working or for children to play, like a ground-floor flat with garden, usually facing south, protected from the inward look of strangers but with an unobstructed view out. **Planting the parapets** enhances the residential quality.

The advantages of large open-air terraces has and does also lead to the construction of stepped houses on level sites, sometimes built over large spaces. The resulting unlit rooms on the lower floors are not, however, without problems.

Trough depths

If an open view of the downhill terrace is to be prevented, then the necessary trough depth depends on the storey height and the horizontal repeating dimension → ❺. More favourable conditions regarding the possible view are produced if the terrace is recessed into the body of the building → ❶.

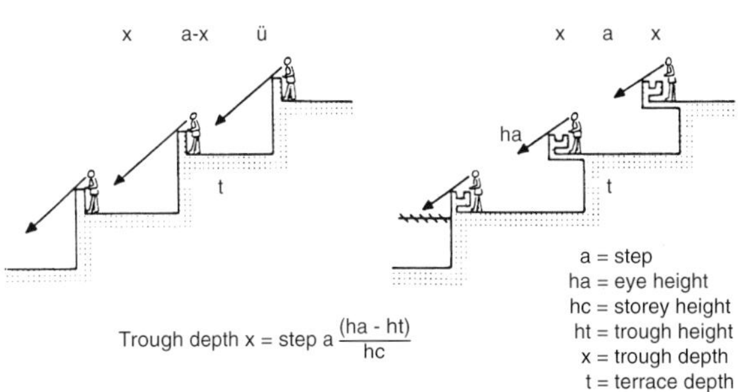

Trough depth $x = \text{step } a \frac{(ha - ht)}{hc}$

❺ Relationship of the horizontal repeating dimension a and trough depth x

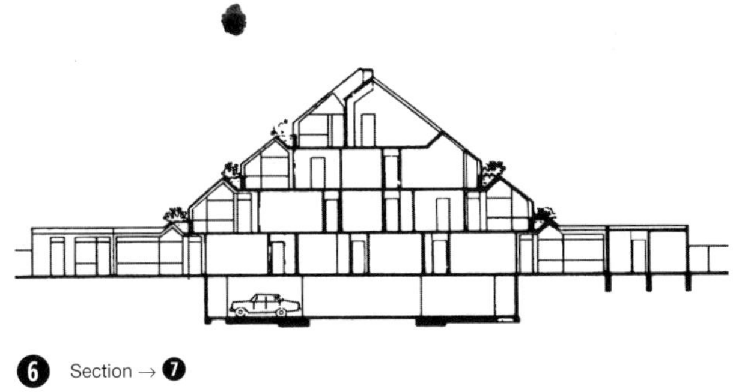

❻ Section → ❼

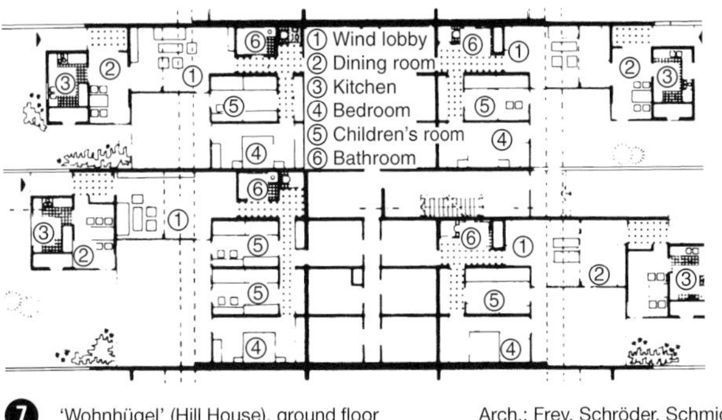

❼ 'Wohnhügel' (Hill House), ground floor Arch.: Frey, Schröder, Schmidt

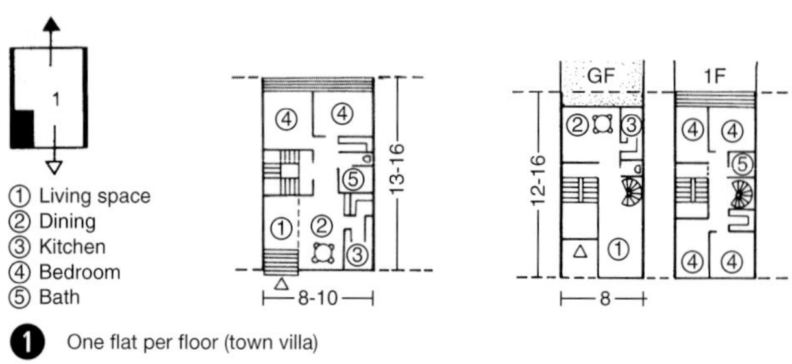

❶ One flat per floor (town villa)

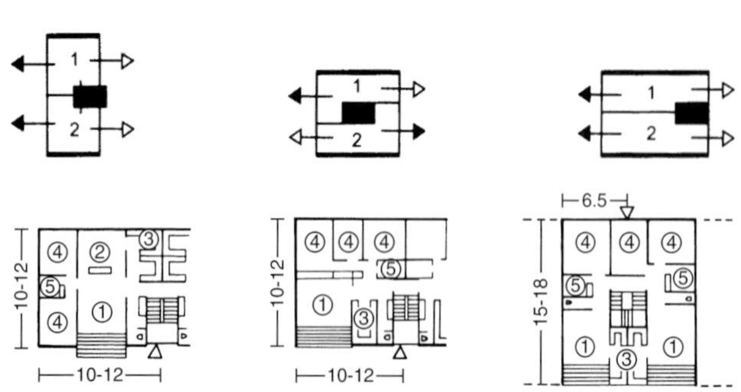

❷ Two flats per floor with plan variants (key → ❶)

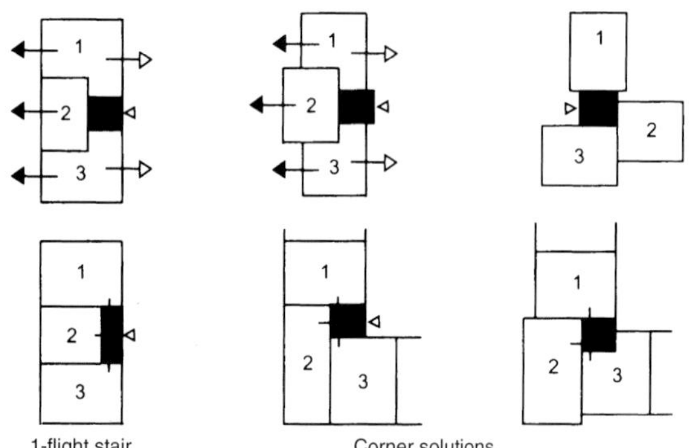

❸ Three flats per floor

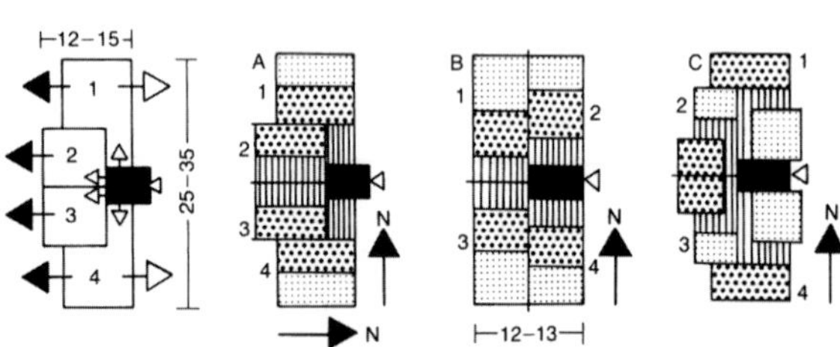

❹ Four flats per floor

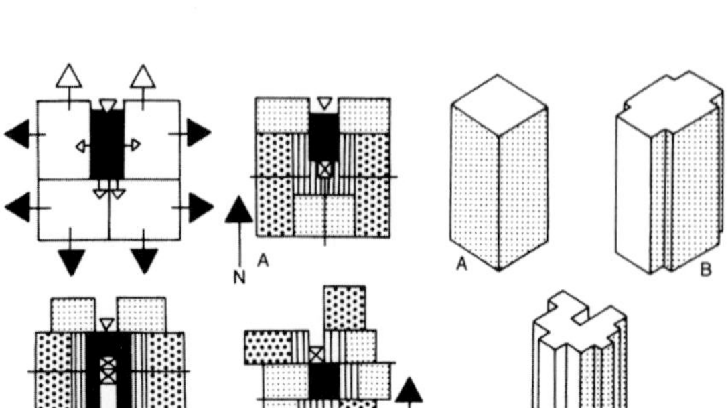

❺ Multiple flats per floor (point houses)

Identical and similar flats are 'stacked' one above the other over a number of storeys and accessed via a common stairway. One or more flats can be connected at each floor. According to the number of flats, this is called **one**, **two**, **up to four (or multiple) flats per floor** access. The stairway in this case becomes a semi-public part of the building → p. 139.

One flat per floor → ❶
There is access to only one flat on each floor. This is relatively uneconomic due to the high proportion of the total floor area taken up for access, but can often give the feeling of living in a 'stacked terrace'. The flats are also marketed as town villas. There is a general limitation to four floors without a lift.

Two to four flats per floor → ❷ – ❹
Two flats per floor is the most common access method, with balanced advantages of residential quality and value for money. The arrangement allows various (and flexible) floor plan solutions → ❻ and offers good possibilities for adaptation in every compass direction.

Three flats per floor offers a favourable combination of residential quality and value for money. This layout is also suitable for corner buildings → ❸. Flats with differing numbers of rooms can be arranged on each floor (e.g. 2-, 3- and 4-room flats). **Four flats per floor** offers an adequate combination of residential quality and value for money if the floor plans are designed appropriately. In particular the so-called **point houses** → ❺ + ❼ enable differentiated orientation of flats on each floor.

Lifts are required for residential buildings of more than five full floors → p. 128. If a residential building is more than **22 m** above ground level, then the provisions for **high-rise buildings** apply → p. 244.

❻ Plan variants for vertical access

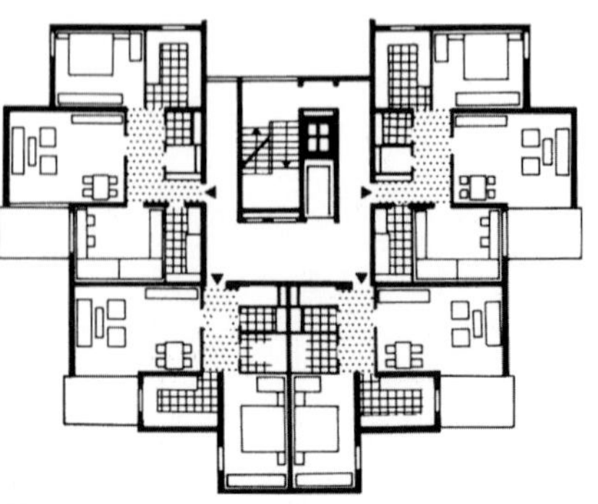

❼ Free-standing building with four flats per floor (point house)

The plan of a house is the result of a multitude of influential factors. In addition to the local conditions like plot layout and orientation, the current building regulations and decisions made about access, the design of many plans is determined by spatial ideas (in their combined effects):

– the prestigious, extroverted idea of publicity → ❺
– and the introverted idea of privacy → ❻

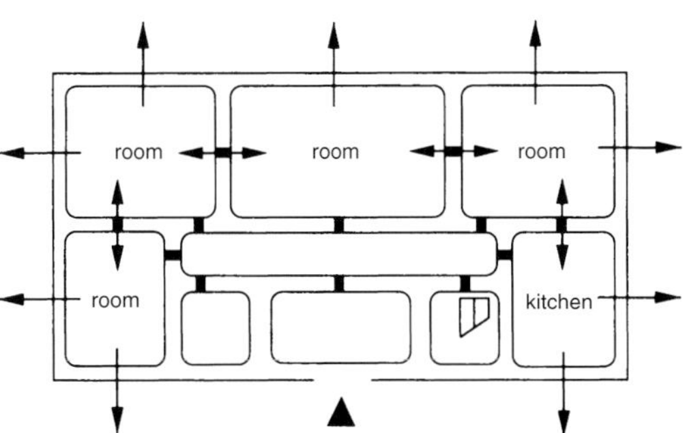

❶ The 18th-century house

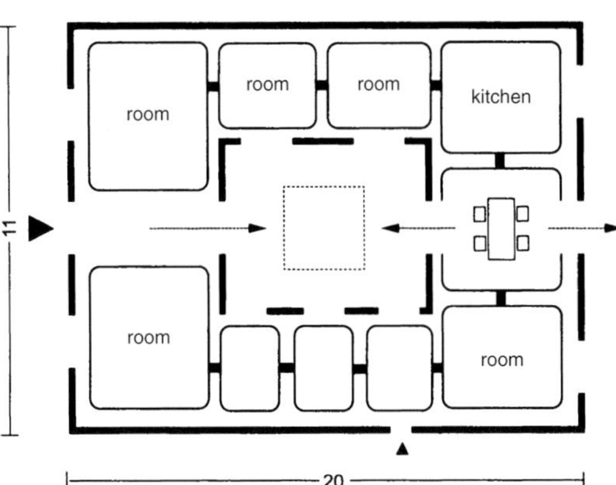

❷ The atrium house

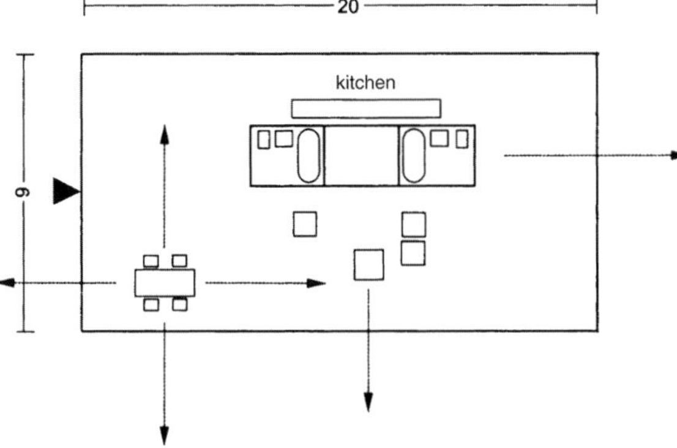

❸ The open plan

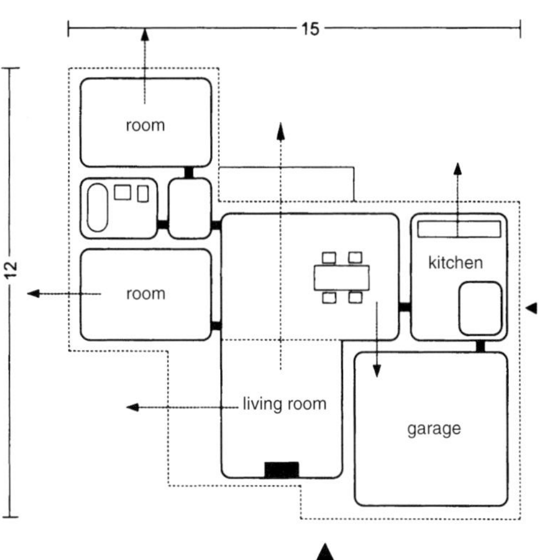

❹ The flowing floor plan

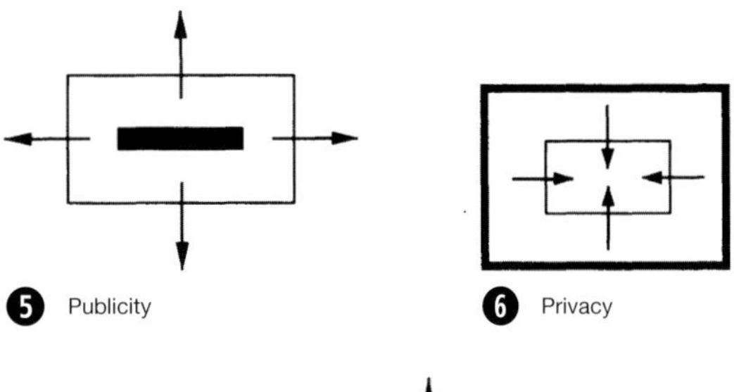

❺ Publicity ❻ Privacy

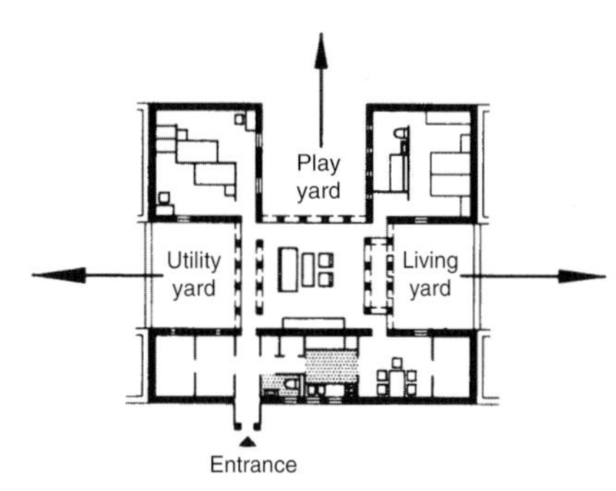

❼ Overlapping Arch.: Ungers

The '18th-century house' → ❶
The house was formerly developed as an axially laid out one- or two-storey plan based on feudal precedents. The free-standing building is lit on all sides and has an architecturally prestigious entrance and garden side; the living rooms and bedrooms (and to some extent service areas) have mostly similar floor areas and are distributed around and connected to a hallway arranged along the building axis.

The atrium house → ❷
The atrium house is one of the classic urban house types. All the rooms of the one- or partially two-storey building are arranged round a private atrium, which also provides access and light. Contact with the outside world is entirely on the street side. The atrium plan is not fully practical for houses in Northern Europe (access from the open air or many entrances) but is an extremely popular model concept → ❼.

The open plan → ❸
The open plan attempts to meld together the inside and outside spaces as far as possible through an almost complete lack of solid (unglazed) external walls. The aspects of privacy and publicity are (supposedly) neutralised. Minimalist and often subtly adapted fittings increase the contrast to a total view.

The flowing floor plan → ❹
The flowing (also: organic) floor plan is developed from an analysis of the functional relationships between the individual areas of the plan and is often customised for a particular user group. This leads to differentiated zones running into each other, with interesting views without obstruction by neutral intermediate zones.

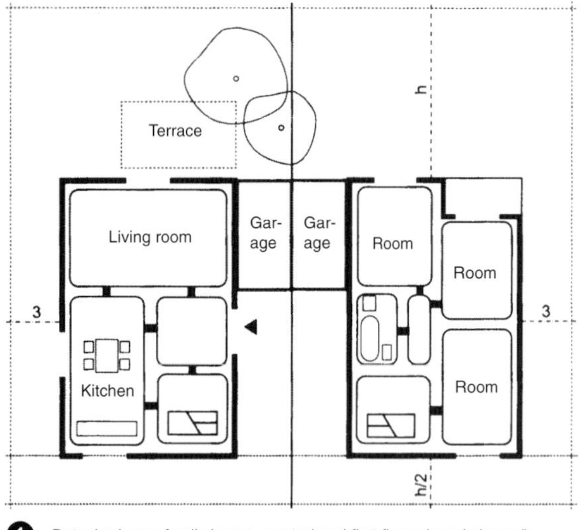

❶ Detached, one-family house, ground and first floor plans (mirrored)

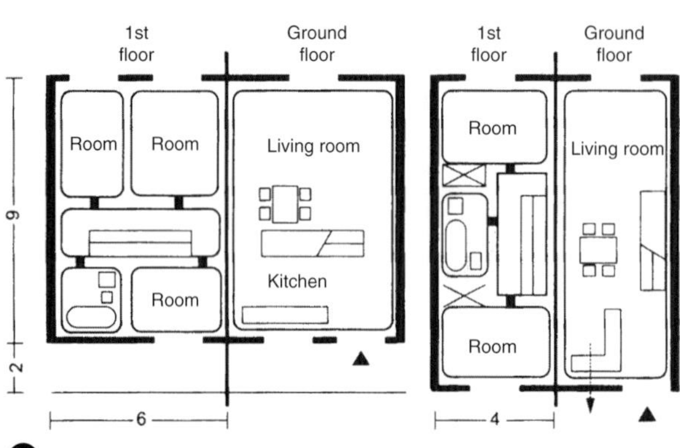

❷ Gallery access house, terraced house (minimum dimensions)

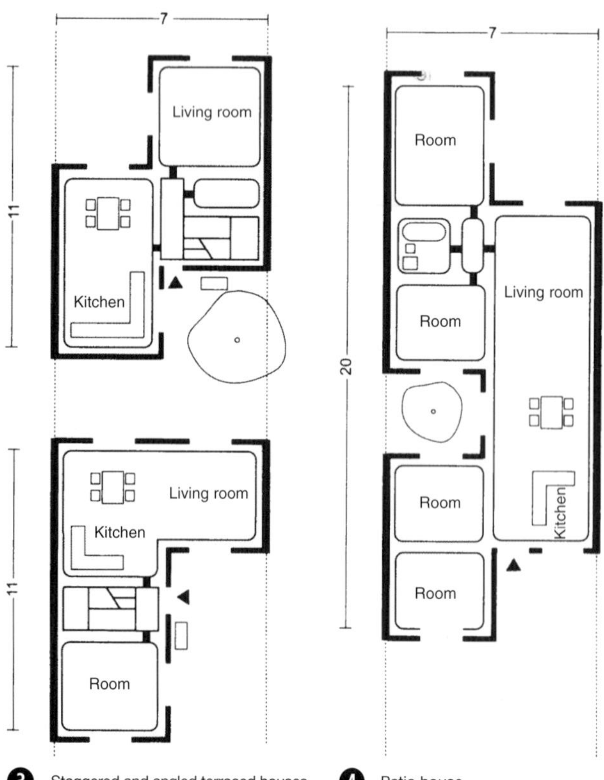

❸ Staggered and angled terraced houses ❹ Patio house

Detached, one-family house → ❶
The detached, one-family house is the adaptation of the 'middle class house' → p. 143 for private house building on new estates. Plot sizes, infrastructure and setback rules are often intended for this type.

Because of the limited road frontage of the plot, the original plan is mostly rotated so that the entrance is at the side. The driveway becomes a (garage) access. The building has light on all sides, and the architectural pretensions of the original are often preserved only as clichés. The division of the floor plan is simple and rational. The common area with kitchen can extend over the entire depth of the building and receive light on three sides. The central hallway arrangement leads to an economic division of the first floor with little area wasted for access.

The lack of semi-public external areas due to the proximity of neighbouring houses is often seen as a fault with this house type and is remedied by the users with improvised offsetting measures (fences, pergolas, awnings, carports etc.).

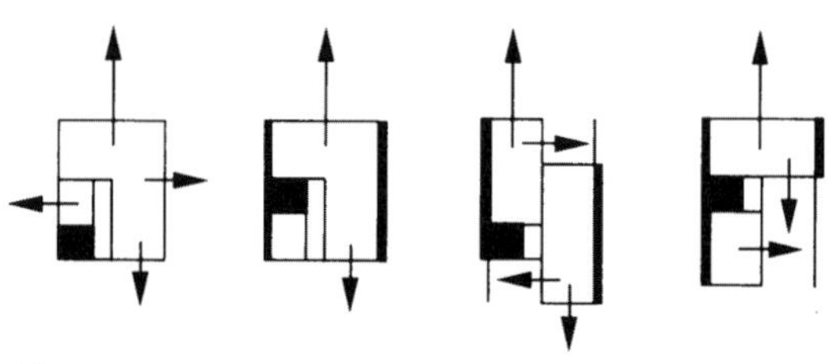

❺ Detached and non-detached house types

Terraced house and gallery access → ❷
Terraced houses often give the feeling of living in one's own house. Attempts are therefore often made to produce the spatial repertoire of a detached house → ❶.

Building in a row restricts the possibilities for direct lighting to two façades so that, with economic building depths of up to 12 m and widths between 4 and 8 m, the existence of a badly lit or dark middle zone containing the stairs, subsidiary rooms and often also the dining area becomes unavoidable. This can be countered with intruding communal areas receiving daylight from both façades, which enables the different qualities of the two sides of the house (environment, compass point etc.) to be experienced together.

The access gallery, if it is appropriately generous, produces a transfer of the terraced house idea into blocks of flats. The passage projecting on one side results in reduced lighting there and makes less depth possible for the flats. It is therefore common to provide transverse stairs when two-storey plans are used.

Half-open external area → ❸ – ❹
When angled and staggered terraces are built on rather more generous plots, simple alterations of the floor plan geometry can result in various protected private and semi-public external areas for the same or similar plan area (and room layout).

This is often achieved by moving floor plan areas together → ❸ or by moving them apart and creating external areas → ❹. Internal rooms can be oriented toward these external patio areas.

Residential buildings

FLOOR PLANS
Houses
Flats

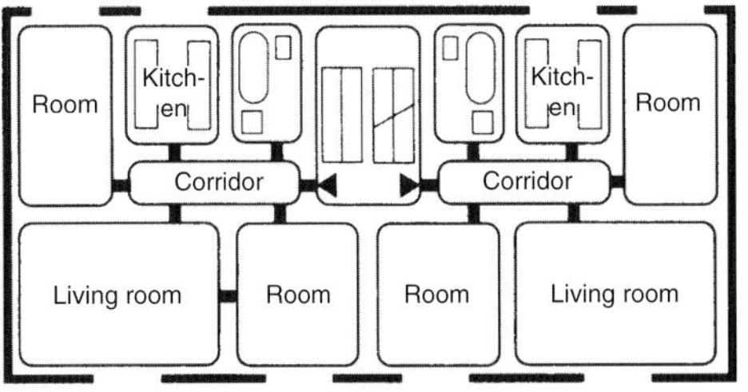

❶ Classic plan with two flats per floor and central corridor

Central corridor plan → ❶

The central corridor plan is the classic floor plan of late 19th-century urban apartment blocks. The rooms are arranged along the two façades and are separated by the (load-bearing) middle wall and the central corridor parallel to it. All rooms can be accessed and used separately. Common and individual areas can be arranged on opposing sides of the façade and related to the particular qualities of the specific side of the building.

There is natural lighting to all living areas and, when the building is deeper, the unlit central corridor can be widened into a central hall. The central corridor style flat is accessed either axially or sideways through a front zone. In the age of functionally neutral flats, the central corridor plan is still a popular and functional type.

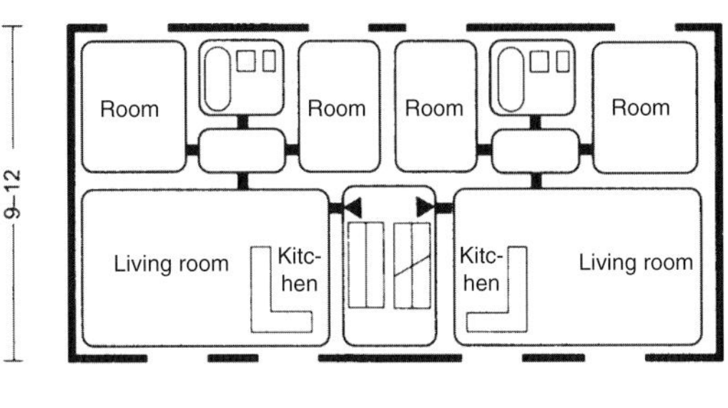

❷ Grouped room floor plan

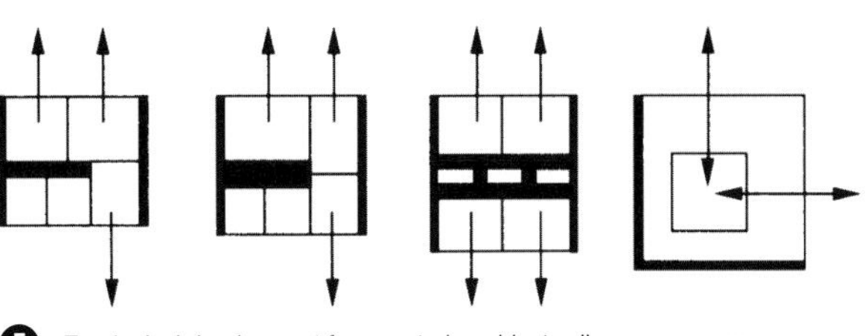

❺ Typological development from central corridor to all-purpose room

Grouped room floor plan → ❷

The idea of the grouped room floor plan developed at the start of the 20th century and is based on the separation of areas inside the apartment into two 'room groups': the living areas (living room, kitchen and dining area) and the sleeping area (bedrooms and bathrooms).

The characteristic feature of this type of grouped room layout is the so-called 'slipper corridor', a minimised corridor which combines the two bedrooms and the bathroom into one spatial unit and is separated from the living areas by a door. The spatial separation of the two room groups is intended to produce less disturbance within the flat with its small floor area and minimal use of space for access.

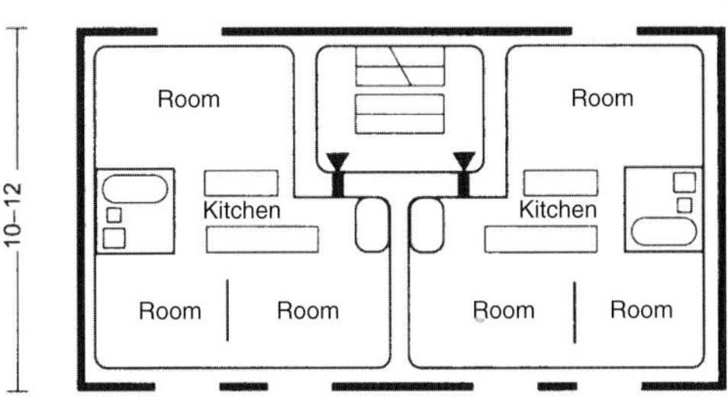

❸ Central function zone

Central function zone → ❸

In buildings of greater depth, the central area of the flat can be widened to form a zone of subsidiary space and the façades can be completely used for living areas. Bathrooms with artificial lighting (or lit indirectly from other areas of the flat), kitchens, cupboard and storage areas can be placed here, and appropriate passages and spaces provide the connection to the outside rooms.

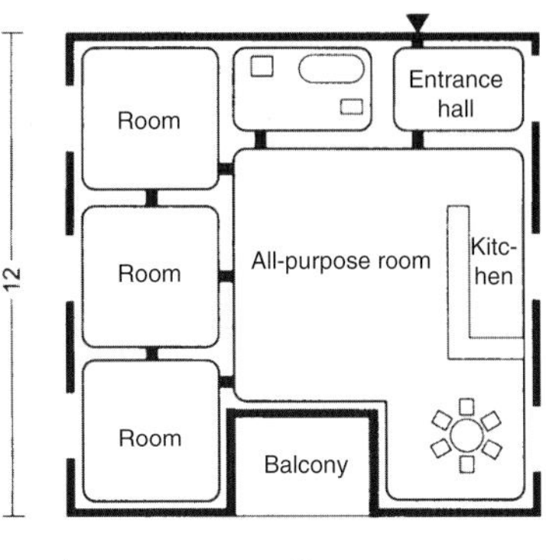

❹ Centre as all-purpose room

Widened central corridor → ❹

As an alternative to → ❸ in free-standing point houses → p. 142 ❹, the central area of the flat can be usefully widened to form an (all-purpose) living room as the centre of the flat. The resulting space serves both as living room and access and is lit indirectly through the other rooms or directly through appropriate recesses in the façade (e.g. recessed balconies).

The all-purpose room is typologically comparable to the atrium, and ideally forms a functionally neutral communication (and play) area. A definite functional (use) description is, however, often difficult.

BS EN 81
BS EN 15644
DIN 4109
DIN 18025
MBO

see also: Sound insulation p. 475
Doors p. 114
Lifts p. 128

Entrance

The entrance is the face of a house, where visitors gain their first impression. A multitude of functions have to be practically arranged and appropriately designed → 1. If the entrance is into the open air, it should be protected from the prevailing wind direction if possible. If weather conditions are unfavourable, a lobby is also recommended to prevent wind blowing through → p. 136 (if the entrance is into a stair shaft, then this can provide wind protection).

According to the MBO, front doors of flats which are accessed by lifts must have a clear opening width of **90 cm** (for wheelchair access). The door height in this case should be at least 2.10 m. Door thresholds are to be avoided. The entrance door must also comply with acoustic and fire protection requirements.

Entrance recesses should be at least **1.25 m** (better 1.50 m) wide and approx. **1.00 m** deep, so that two people can wait comfortably and protected in front of the door → 4.

For typical entrance arrangements for single- and multi-family houses and flat entrances see → 5 – 8.

An important element of the entrance to a block of flats is the stair shaft with staircase and lift → p. 128. The layout and size of the lifts determine the dimensions of the waiting area, which should offer enough space for a number of people, wheelchair users or stretcher bearers → 9 – 12.

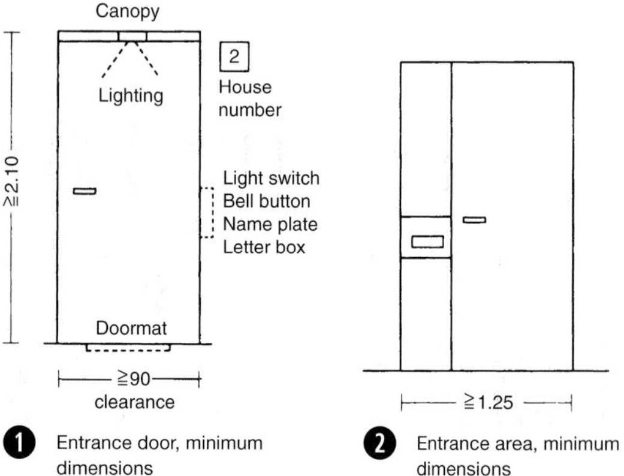

1 Entrance door, minimum dimensions

2 Entrance area, minimum dimensions

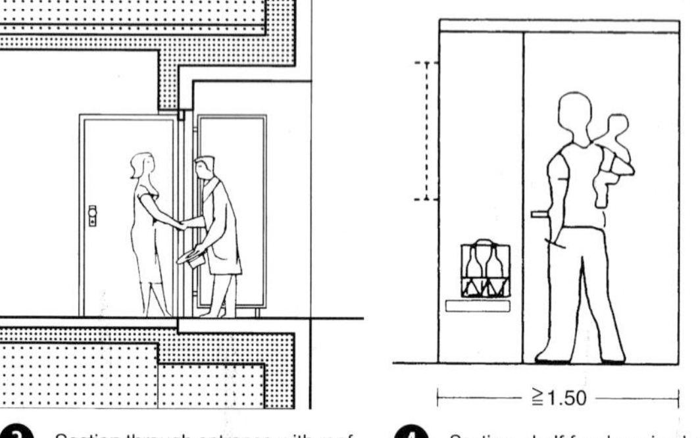

3 Section through entrance with roof

4 Seating, shelf for shopping bags etc.

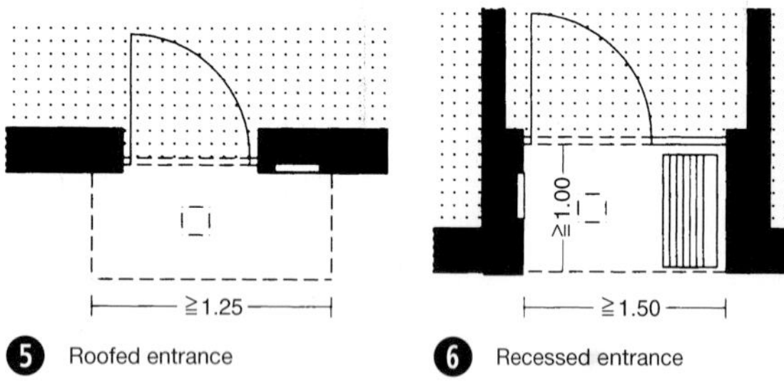

5 Roofed entrance

6 Recessed entrance

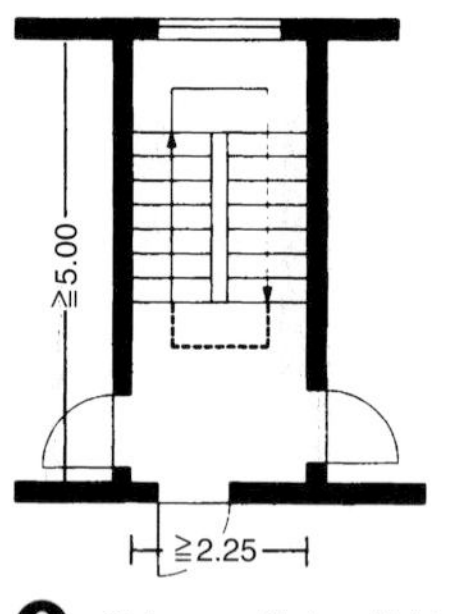

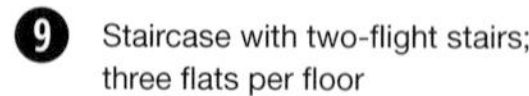

9 Staircase with two-flight stairs; three flats per floor

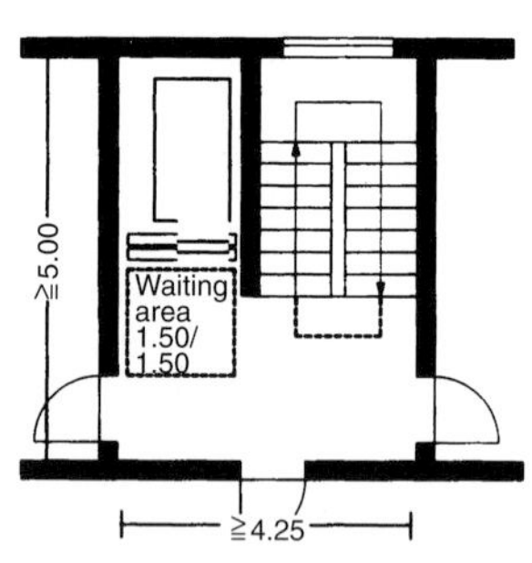

10 Parallel arrangement of stairs and lift; three flats per floor

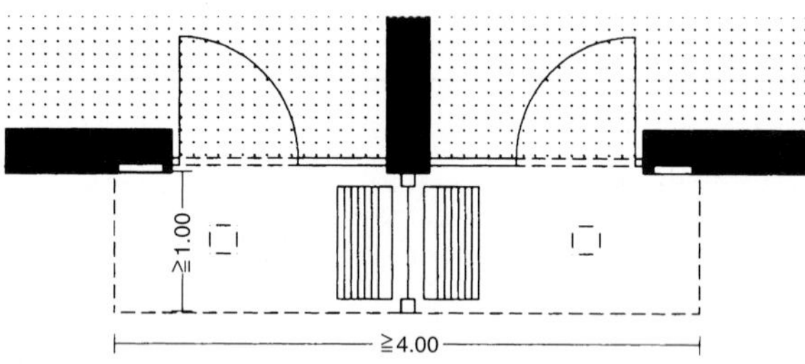

7 Two entrances under a common projecting roof

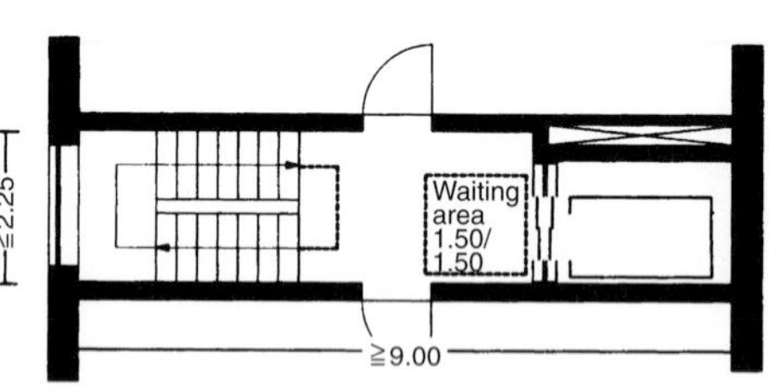

11 Opposed arrangement of stairs and lift; two flats per floor

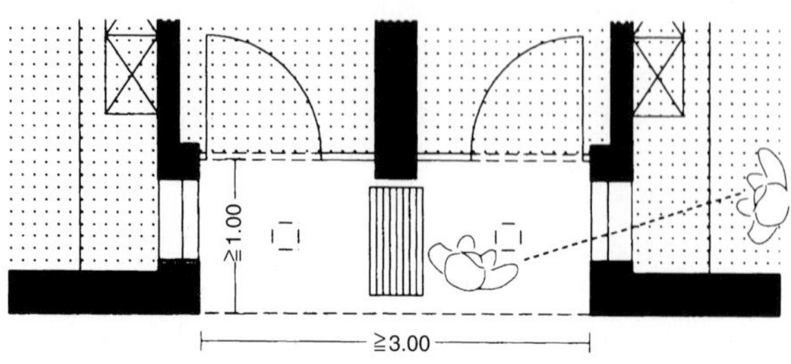

8 Semi-detached houses with common entrance area

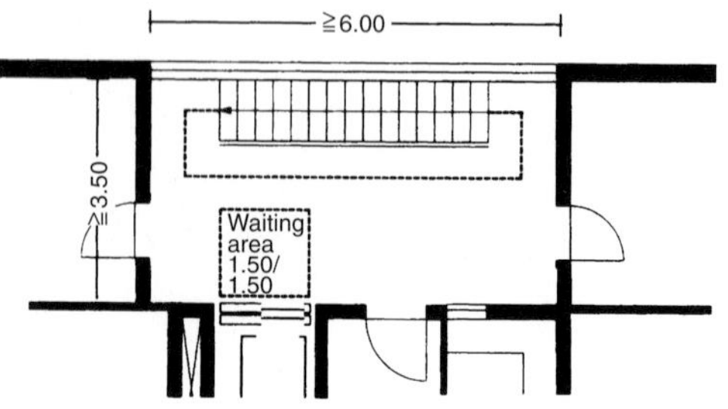

12 Single-flight stairs, displaced arrangement of stairs and lift

❶ Space requirement in the entrance hall for comfortable greeting

❷ For easy removal of coats

Entrance hall

The entrance hall should be enclosed where the entrance leads directly to the open air with an inner door (wind lobby function). It should also offer sufficient room for a lot of moving around → ❹. This is where **reception, greeting, taking off and putting on coats, and taking leave** all take place, but also offers the first **orientation** for the visitor → ❶ – ❸. Countless objects therefore have to be arranged practically yet tidily in this limited space → ❺, ❻. The most important communal areas like the kitchen, WC and staircase should be directly accessible from the entrance hall.

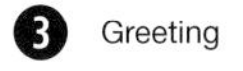

❸ Greeting

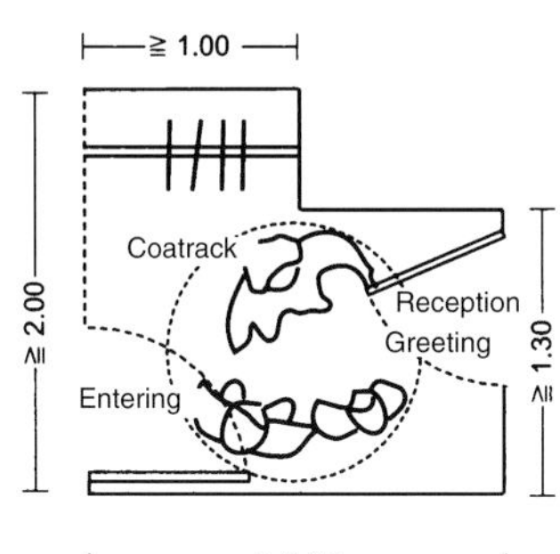

❹ Floor plan with movements

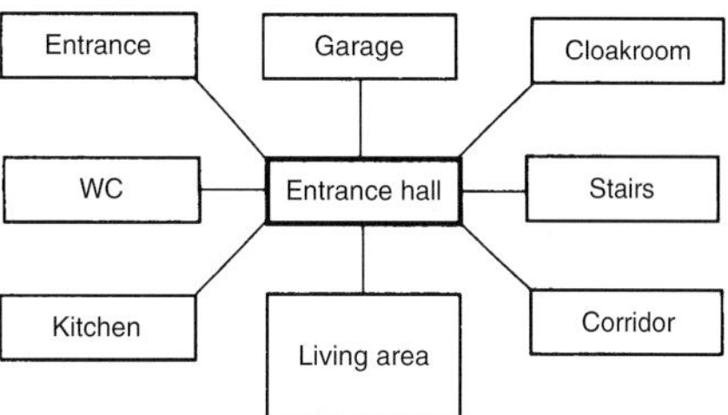

❼ Relationship between entrance hall and other areas of the house

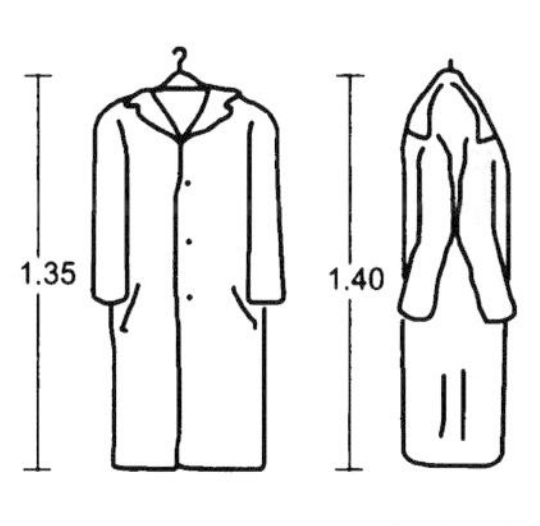

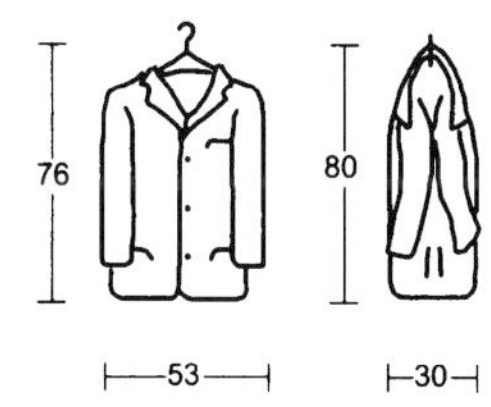

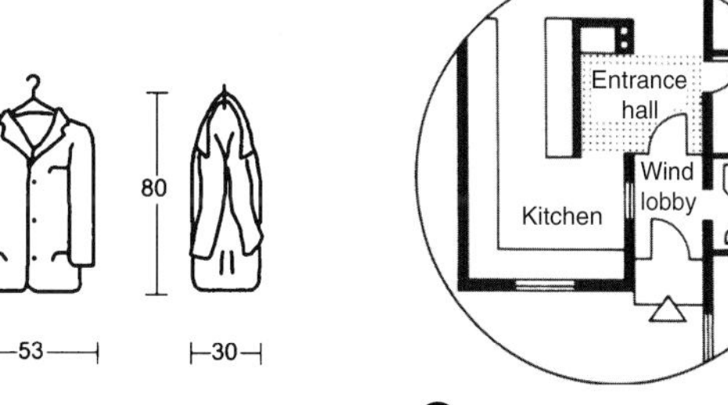

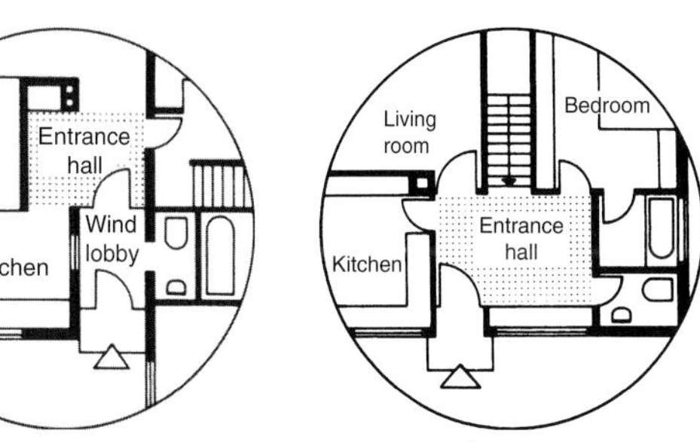

❽ In relation to wind lobby

❾ In relation to kitchen, WC, cellar stairs and bedroom

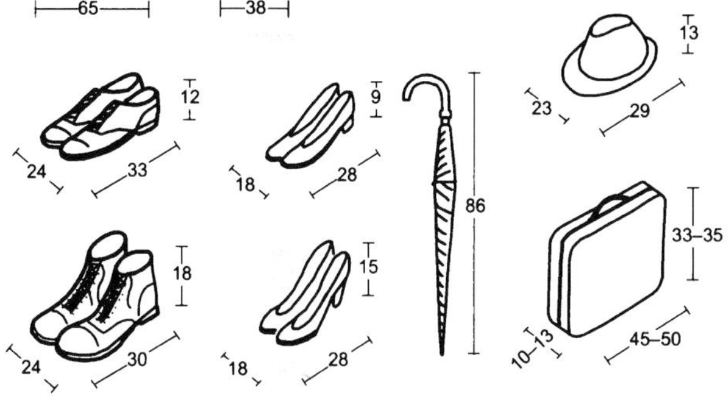

❺ Dimensions of coats and jackets, umbrellas, hats, briefcases and shoes

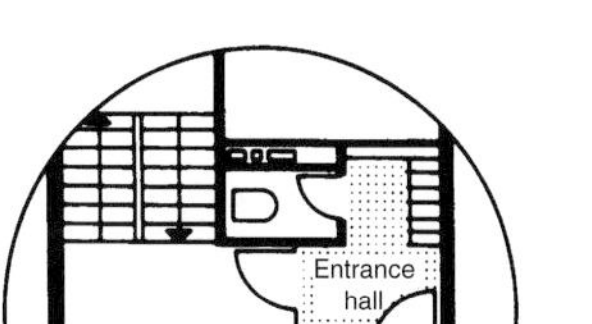

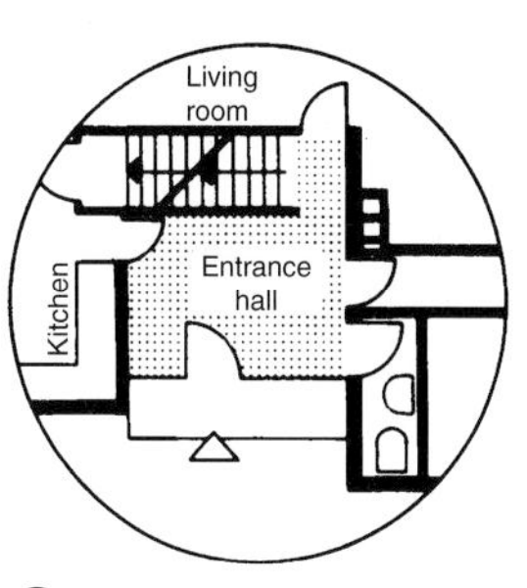

❿ Side entrance

⓫ In relation to cellar stairs

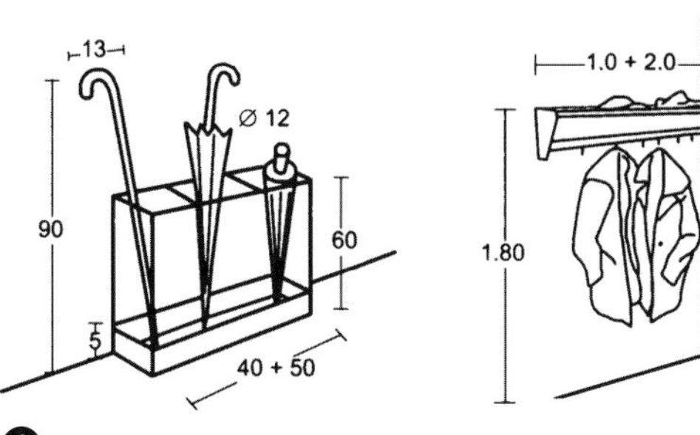

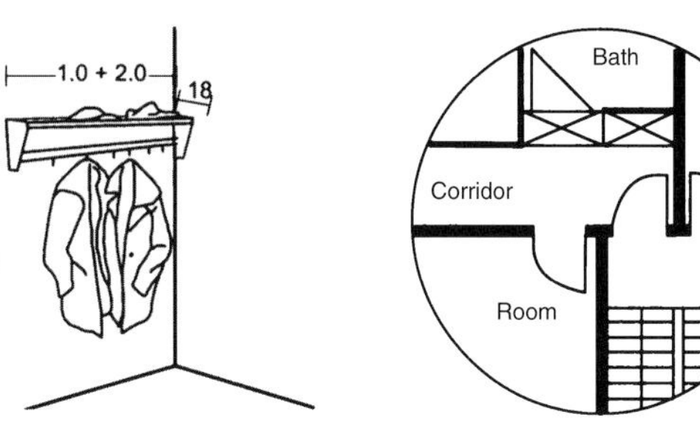

❻ Umbrella stand with watertight base, coat rack (six hooks across 1 m)

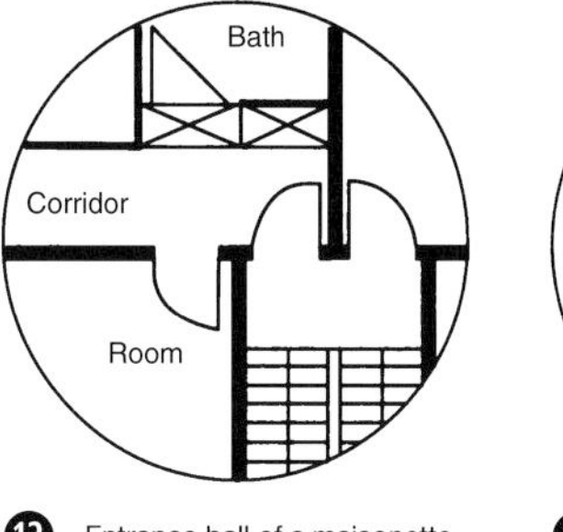

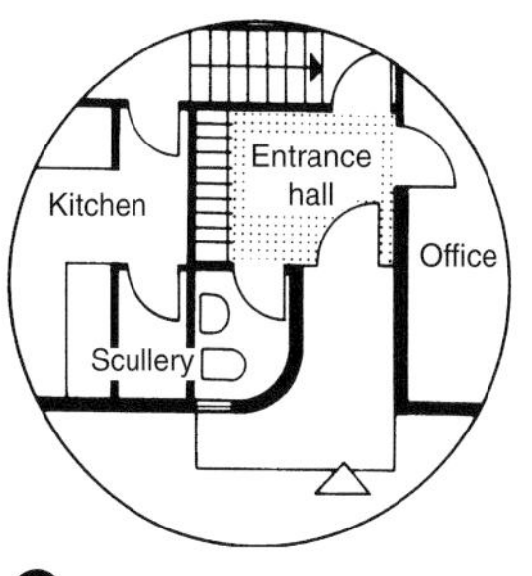

⓬ Entrance hall of a maisonette

⓭ Lobby in relation to office

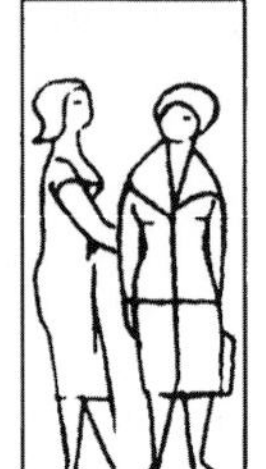

❶ Corridor widths

Corridor type	Little traffic	Heavy traffic
doors one side, opening into the rooms	0.90 m	1.30 m
doors both sides, opening into the rooms	1.60 m	
doors one side, opening into the corridor	1.40 m	1.80 m
doors both sides, opening into the corridor		2.20 m
doors both sides and opposite each other, opening into the corridor	2.40 m	2.60 m

❷ Minimum corridor widths depending on door arrangement (separate, opposing), opening direction and traffic volume

Corridors

Corridors form the neutral connection between the rooms in a house. Although they do not actually belong to the living area, they should be laid out generously and be as spatially varied as possible. Partial opening to living areas and natural lighting is desirable. Adjacent rooms often seem roomier next to a more generous corridor, because of the better arrangement of doors to bedrooms and cupboards → ❺.

Corridor widths

The width of a corridor depends on its location, the number and arrangement of the doors opening off it (doors one side, both sides) and the number of people using it → ❷. The greatest accessibility offered by various sizes and layouts of corridors to rooms more than 2 m wide is shown in → ❸ – ⓮. The examples assume a minimum corridor width of 1 m, which allows two people to pass. This width does not, however, permit the siting of cupboards, which would be better built-in → ❻ + ❾. When arranging the doors, the location of beds and built-in cupboards needs to be taken into account (see above).

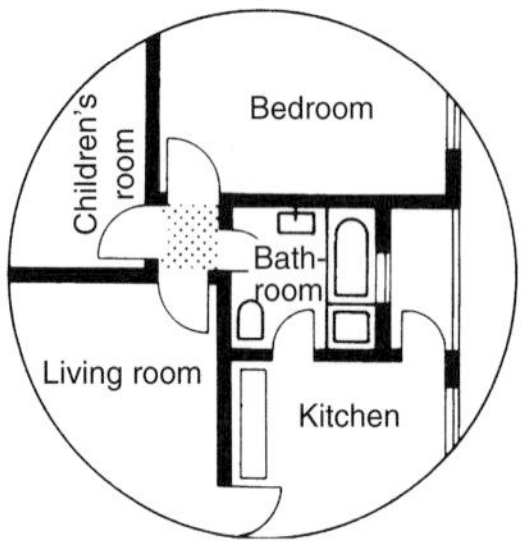

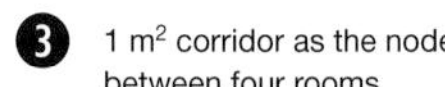

❸ 1 m² corridor as the node between four rooms

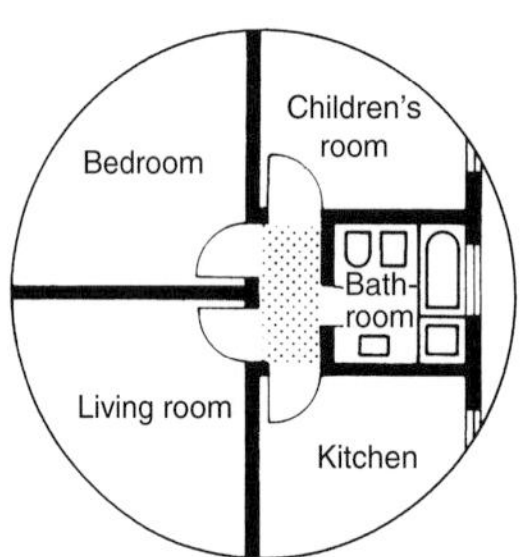

❹ 2 m² corridor: four rooms, otherwise as ❸

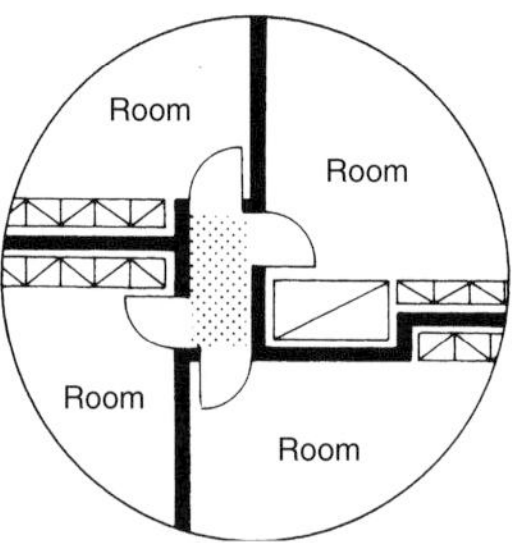

❾ 2 m² corridor: four rooms with built-in cupboards and beds

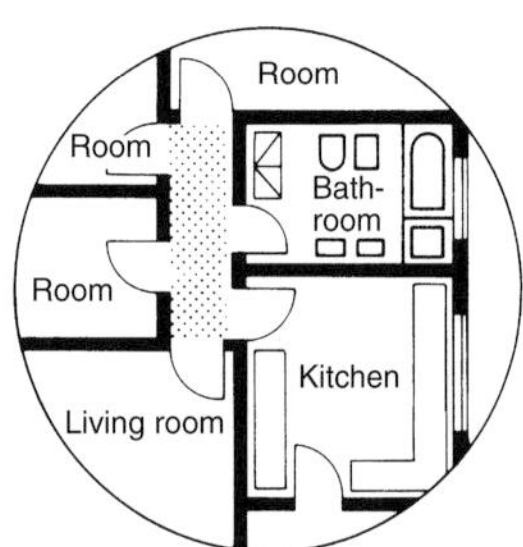

❿ 3 m² corridor: six rooms

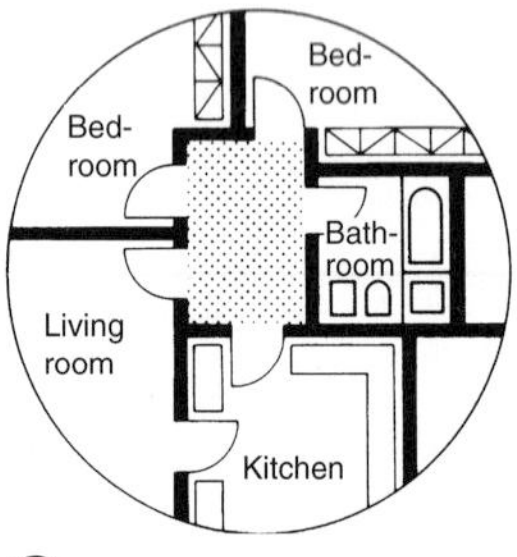

❺ 4 m² corridor: five rooms and built-in cupboards

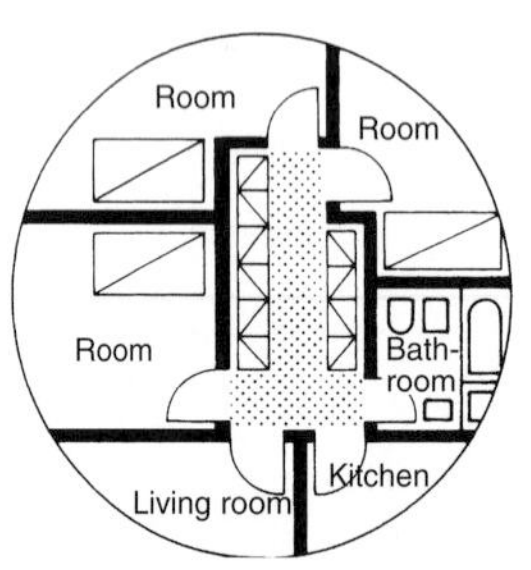

❻ 5.2 m² corridor: six rooms with some built-in cupboards and beds

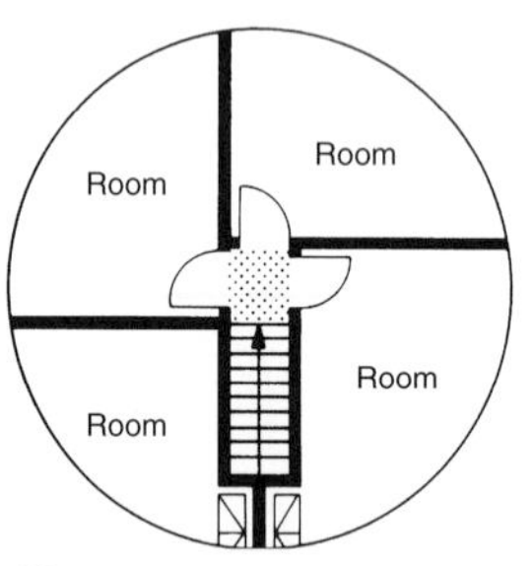

⓫ 1 m² corridor: three large rooms at the end of a flight of stairs

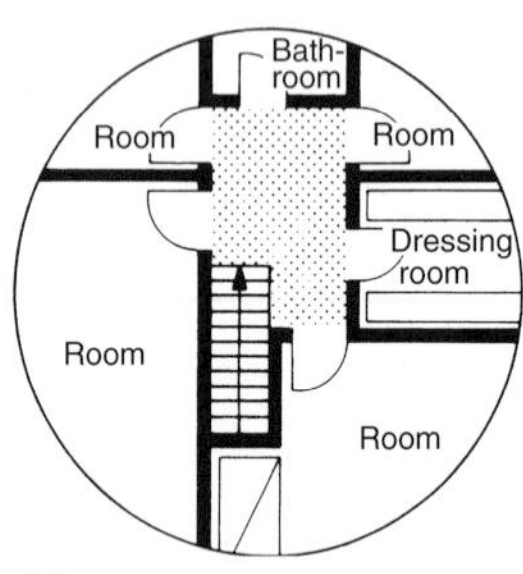

⓬ 5 m² corridor: four large and two small rooms (bathroom, changing room)

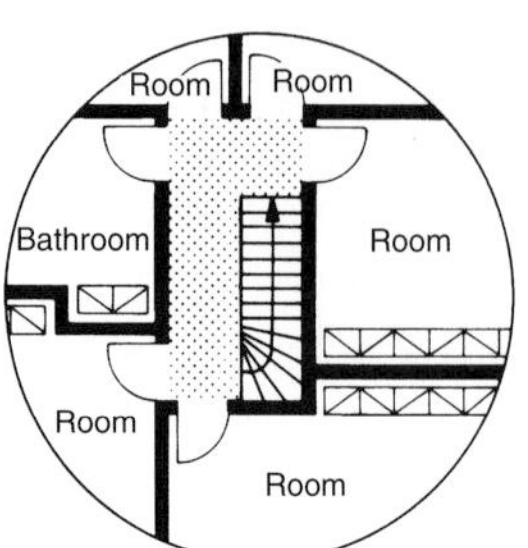

❼ 5 m² corridor: five rooms and one bathroom

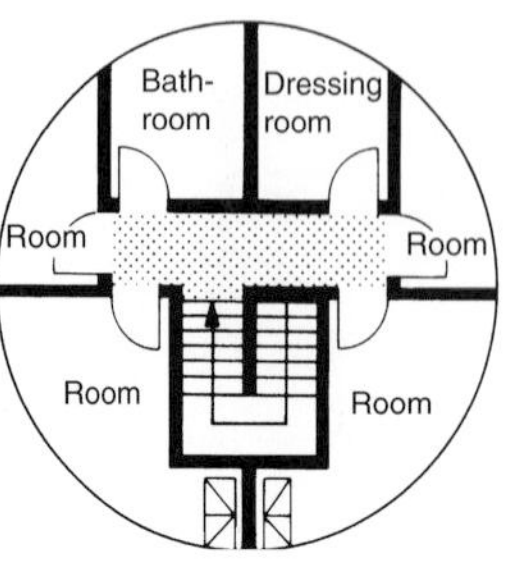

❽ 4 m² corridor: four rooms, one bathroom and one dressing room

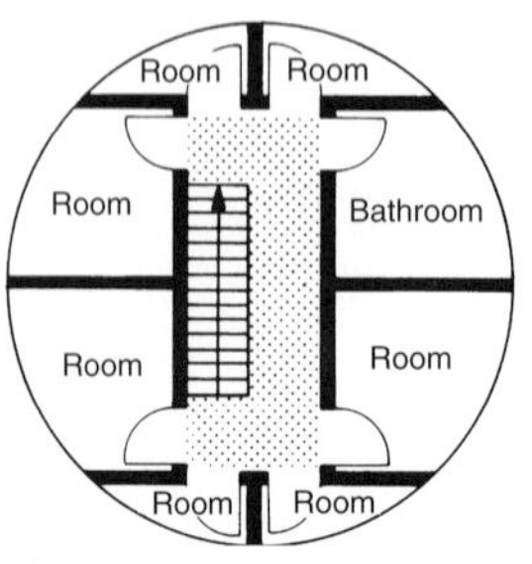

⓭ 7 m² corridor: eight rooms with single-flight stairs

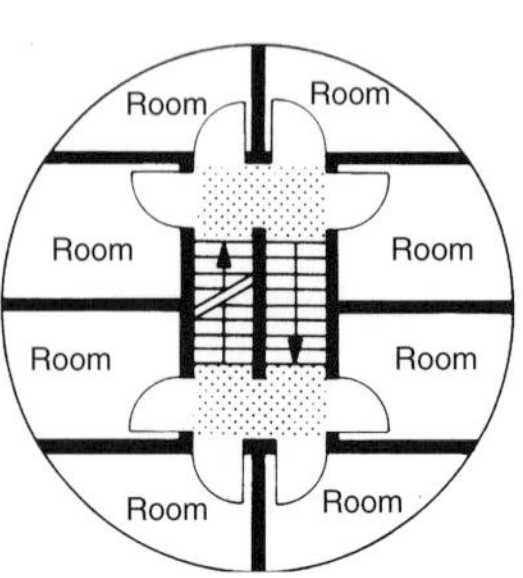

⓮ 4 m² corridor: eight rooms with floors on different levels

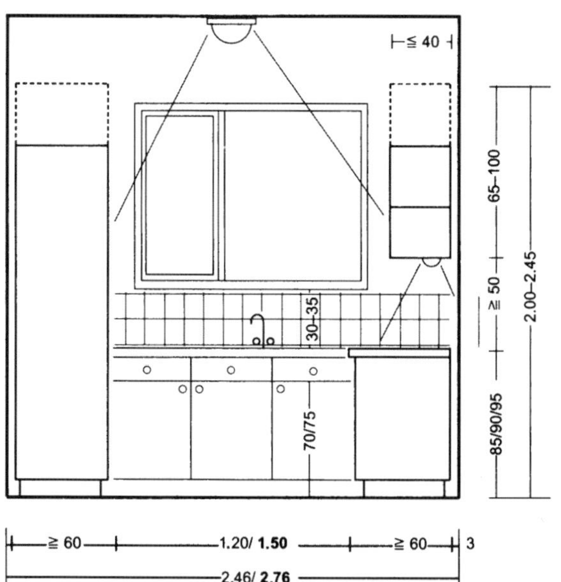

❶ Dimensional requirements for kitchens

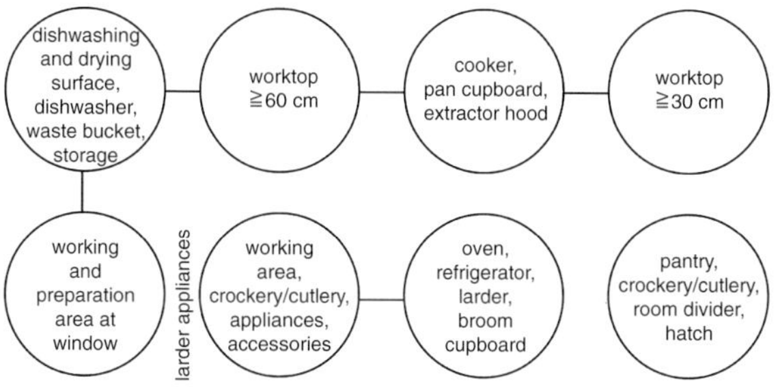

❷ Practical arrangement of working areas in the kitchen

Unit or appliance	Space required	
	Width (cm)	Depth (cm)
Cupboards for crockery/cutlery, foodstuffs etc.		
1 base unit cupboard	30–150	60
2 broom cupboard	60	60
3 wall cupboard	30–150	≦40
Cooling and freezing appliances		
4 refrigerator	60	60
5 freezer	60	60
6 chest freezer	≧90	acc. to maker
Worktops		
7 small worktop between cooker and sink	≧60	60
8 large worktop	≧120	60
9 surface to set down appliances	≧60	60
10 worktop next to cooker	≧30	60
11 worktop next to sink	≧60	60
Cooking appliances		
12 cooker with oven and extractor hood	60	60
13 built-in cooker with base unit	60–90	60
14 built-in oven with base unit	60	60
15 microwave oven	60	60
Washing-up equipment		
16 single-basin sink with draining board	≧90	60
17 double-basin sink with draining board	≧120	60
18 dishwasher	60	60
19 washing-up unit (single-basin sink with draining board, base unit and dishwasher	≧90	60

❸ Dimensions of kitchen units and appliances

The **kitchen** is a workplace inside the home and at the same time an important living room and meeting point for the occupants and their guests, with various relationships to other areas of the house. According to the building regulations, **every house or flat must have at least one kitchen or kitchenette for cooking.**

Kitchens and kitchenettes without windows are generally undesirable and only permissible if effective ventilation is guaranteed. As a habitable room, the kitchen must have a clear ceiling height of at least 2.40 m and a window area (structural dimensions) of at least 1/8 of the net floor area.

Location

The location of the kitchen is ideally on the northeast or northwest, in the immediate vicinity of the entrance area (short distances for shopping, rubbish etc.), to the (vegetable) garden and the cellar. There should be sensible **internal room relationships** with the dining room, utility room and larder. It should ideally be possible to see the front door, children's play area and terrace from the kitchen → ❹.

entrance
entrance hall
utility room
back door
garden door
kitchen
larder
cellar stairs
children's play area
larder
pantry
vegetable garden
lobby

–·–·–·– visible from the kitchen
——— routes
----------- usual only in larger houses

❹ Room relationships of a larger kitchen

Coordinated dimensions for kitchen furniture are provided in → ❸. The dimensions given here do not take into account the movement areas of the elderly or disabled so are to be considered absolute minimum values. In general, the design of kitchens should be based on **movement areas for accessible housing** → p. 21 ff.

The planning of a kitchen should make possible a **flowing work sequence** with sufficient space for movement, while avoiding unnecessarily long distances. A movement area of **1.50 m** (min. 1.20 m) is therefore required between the stretches of worktop. With most kitchen units having a depth of 60 cm on each side of the movement area, this results in a minimum kitchen width of **2.70 m** (min 2.40 m) (plus approx. 6 cm spacing up to the wall).

The **height of the worktops** should if possible be adapted to suit the height of the user and can vary between 85 and 95 cm → ❶. Working while standing should be minimised through the provision of (slide-out) worktops.

Good posture while working in the kitchen and good lighting in the work area are general requirements → p. 154. In order to make the work in the kitchen easier, a **practical arrangement of work areas** is desirable → ❷.

BS EN 1116
BS 6222
BS EN 60335
BS EN 14749
DIN EN 1116

MBO

see also:
Accessible building p. 21

BS EN 1116
BS 6222
BS EN 60335
BS EN 14749
DIN EN 1116

MBO

see also: Accessible building p. 21

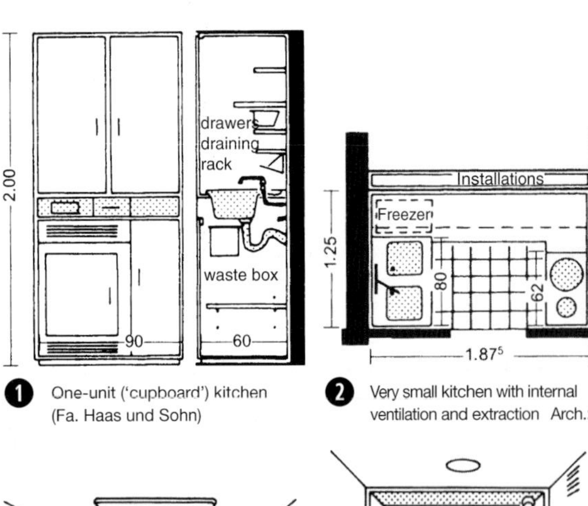

❶ One-unit ('cupboard') kitchen (Fa. Haas und Sohn)

❷ Very small kitchen with internal ventilation and extraction Arch.: Neufert

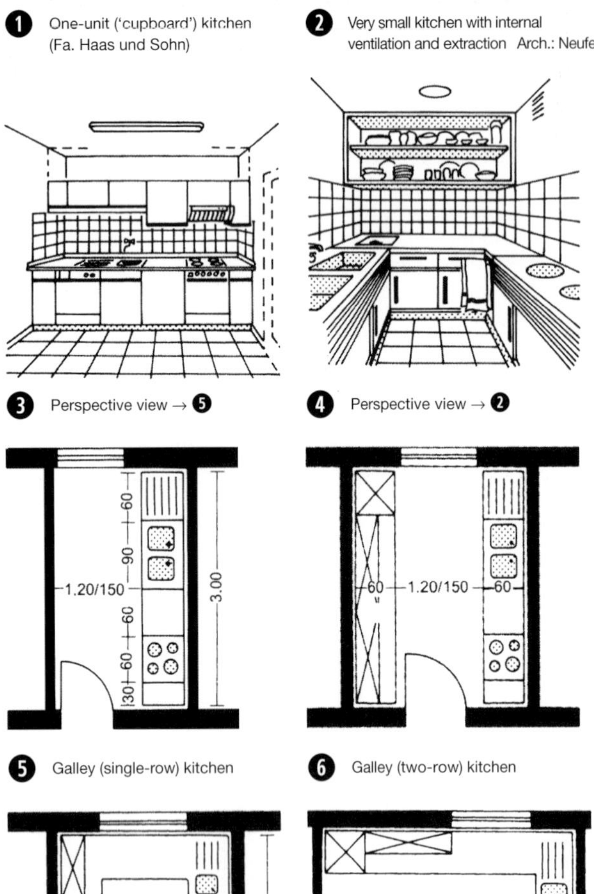

❸ Perspective view → ❺

❹ Perspective view → ❷

❺ Galley (single-row) kitchen

❻ Galley (two-row) kitchen

❼ U-shaped kitchen

❽ L-shaped kitchen with dining area

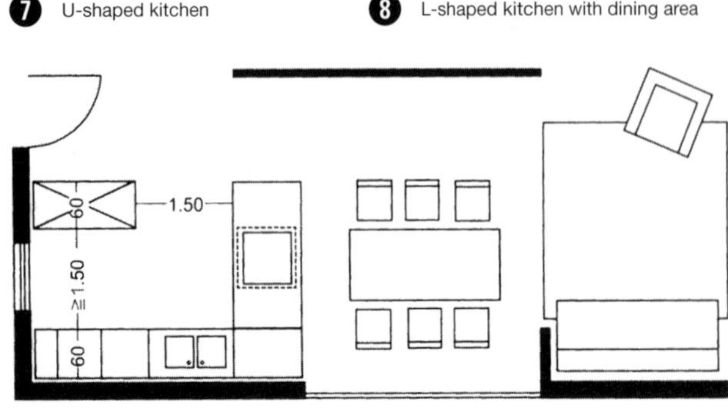

❾ Open kitchen continuous with the room

Kitchen types

The kitchen types shown here are produced from the requisite kitchen arrangements and their floor areas. The basic types are:

Compact kitchens or **kitchenettes**: These are only adequate for housekeeping requirements to a limited extent (scarcely any shelf or cupboard space) and are really only suitable for holiday flats and (student) apartments. Kitchenettes do not normally require their own room and can be sited in passages or corridors → ❶ – ❷.

Kitchen as working room: The kitchen equipment is functionally arranged in the smallest possible area as a **one-row, two-row** or **U-shaped** configuration, normally as a fitted kitchen. The location of the appliances and worktops are optimised for rational working → ❾. This results in practical working spaces on a floor area of between 5.5 m² and 9.5 m² (though not suitable for purposes other than kitchen work) → ❺ – ❼. The connection to the dining area is via the corridor or hall and can be supported with hatches etc.

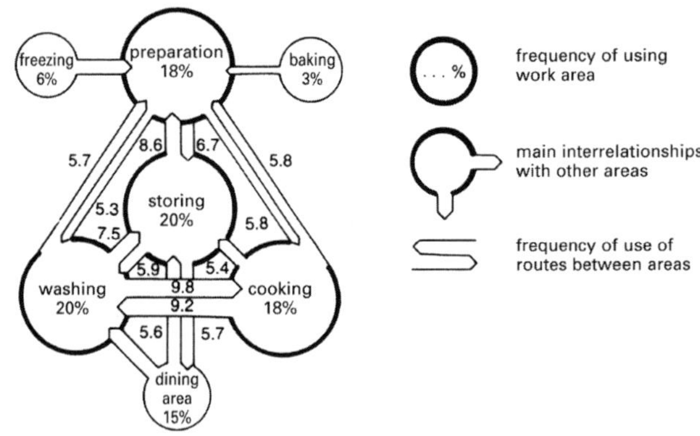

❿ Practical arrangement of working space in the kitchen

Kitchen with dining area

The kitchen with dining area offers, in addition to the actual kitchen fittings, space for a table with chairs or benches, to be used as an additional dining area (breakfast area). The kitchen thus becomes a lived-in room, providing improved opportunities for conversation. Kitchens with dining areas can be planned from approx. 10 m². A good arrangement is an L shape with doors connecting to the living room and corridor: area approx. 14 m² → ❽.

A parallel development to the kitchen with dining area is the **'open' kitchen**, where the kitchen area is open to the living room and dining area. This can be designed as an 'American fitted kitchen', a functional area connected to the living room, with for example a kitchen breakfast/snack bar as divider → p. 154 ❸.

Modem kitchen designs are moving away from the fitted kitchen. The kitchen area is seen as an ensemble of independent objects developed in each case from formal and functional conditions, which are grouped like pieces of furniture in an (ideally generous) residential room. Open kitchens require good ventilation and extraction in order not to impair the living and dining room areas with cooking smalls. In many cases, a mobile divider is to be recommended, for example using a curtain → ❾.

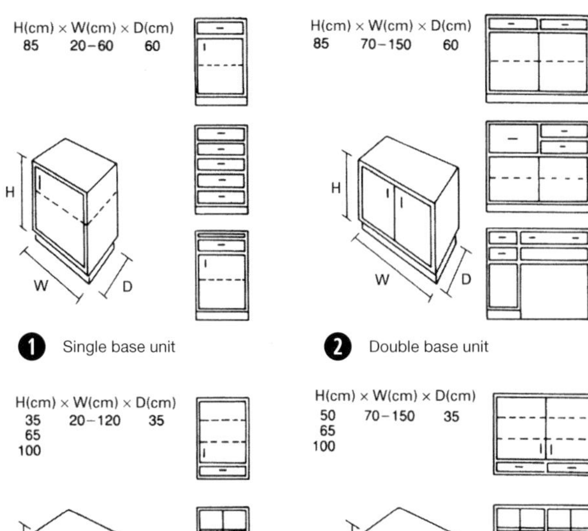

❶ Single base unit

❷ Double base unit

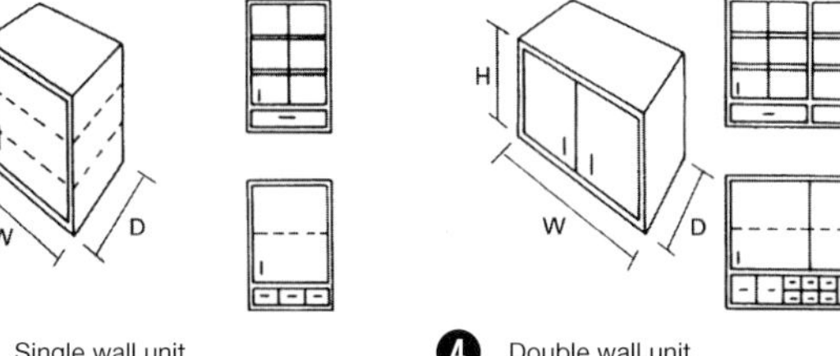

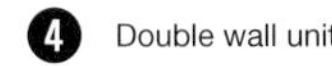

❸ Single wall unit

❹ Double wall unit

Kitchen fittings

Numerous modular systems with fixed functions and dimensions are available for fitting kitchens, mostly arranged along continuous worktops. Types of kitchen unit and appliances:

- **base unit** with large drawers or cupboards for provisions, large pots and pans and as shell for built-in appliances → ❶ – ❷.
- **wall cupboards** for provisions and equipment or for lightweight appliances (e.g. microwave) → ❸ – ❹.
- **tall cupboards** with a height of approx. 2 m, to store provisions, as a broom cupboard or as a shell for the installation of fridge, oven etc.
- **cooker with extractor hood** with 2–4 rings, electric or gas, often split into an oven built into a tall unit and a hob built into the worktop → ❺ – ❼.
- **sinks**, normally built into the worktop with 1–2 sinks and an integrated draining board → ⓫ – ⓬
- the base unit under the sink generally houses a **dishwasher** → ❾ and also a waste bin
- the **refrigerator** is housed under the worktop (in smaller kitchens) or integrated into a tall cupboard at standing height, with **freezer compartment**, separate **freezer** or in combination with a **chest freezer** → ⓯ – ⓰.

Residential buildings

ROOMS
Access
Kitchens
Living areas
Bathrooms
Subsidiary rooms
Garages

BS EN 1116
BS 6222
BS EN 60335
BS EN 14749
DIN EN 1116

❺ Built-in oven

❻ Hobs

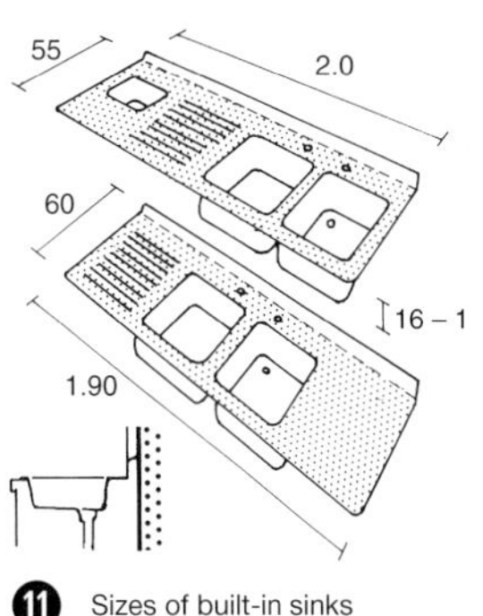

⓫ Sizes of built-in sinks

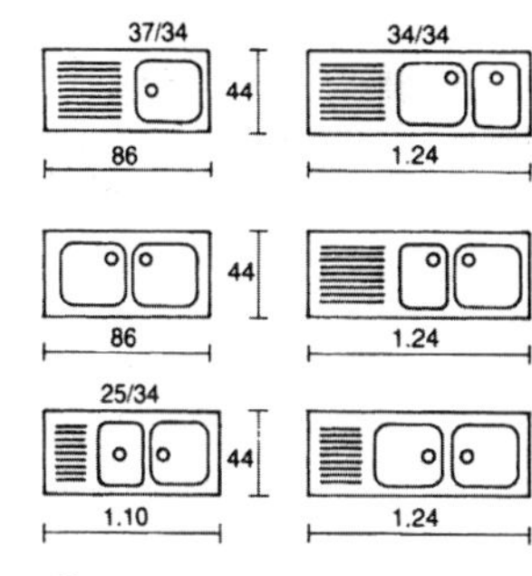

⓬ Built-in sinks

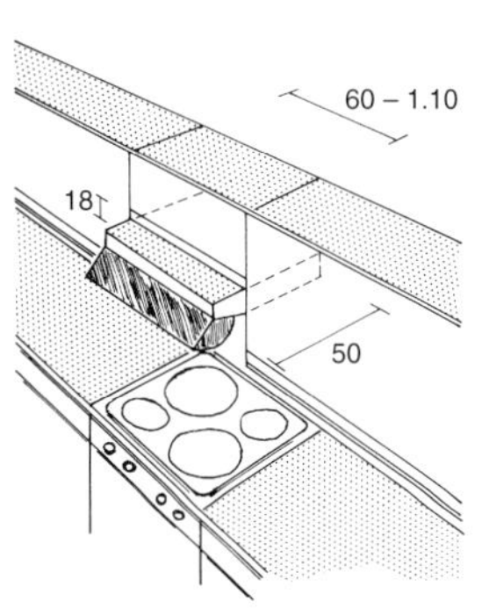

❼ Extractor hood

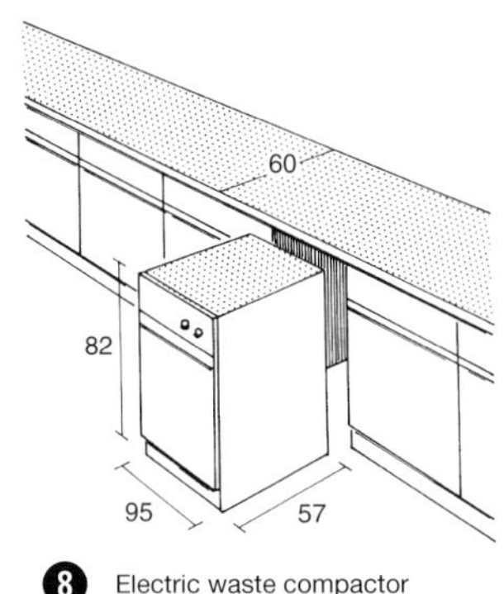

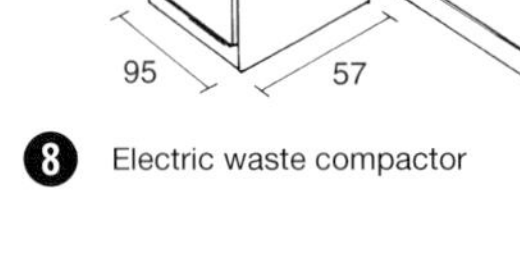

❽ Electric waste compactor

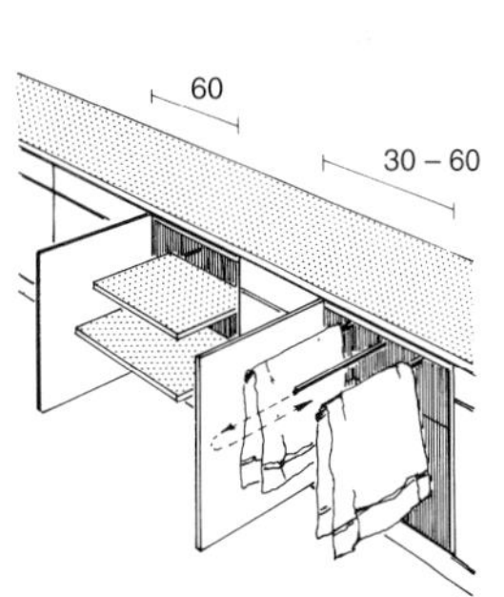

⓭ Small appliance and drying cupboard

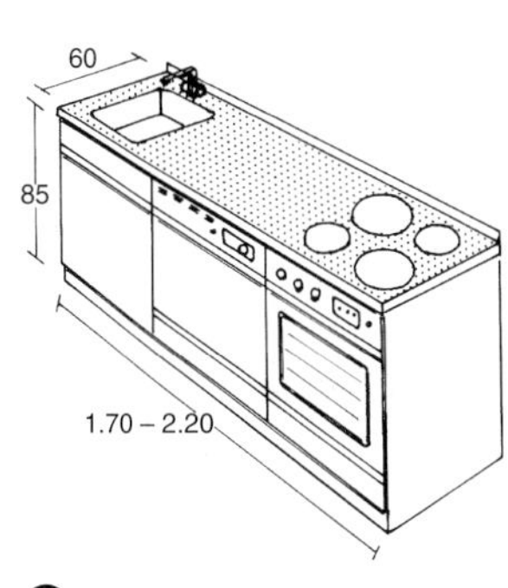

⓮ Kitchen: central elements

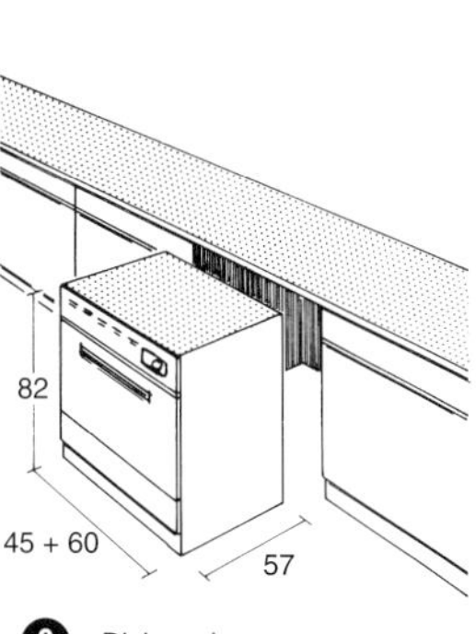

❾ Dishwasher

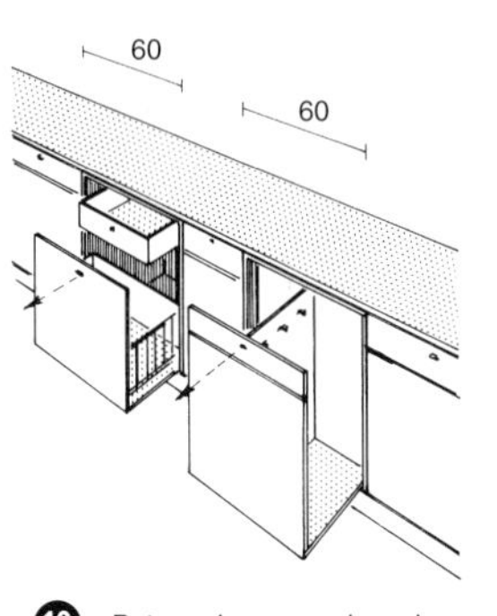

❿ Pots and pans cupboard

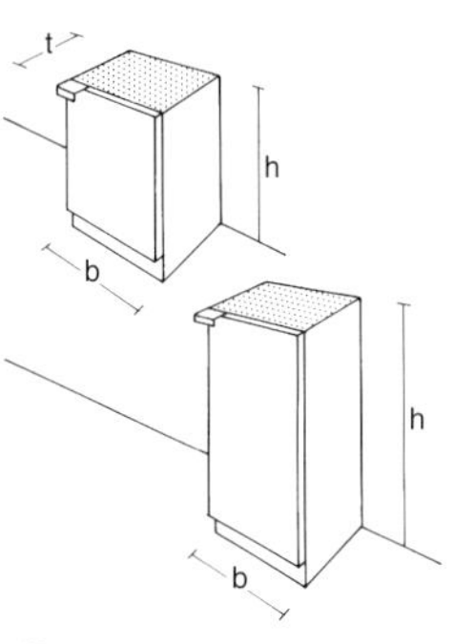

⓯ Refrigerators

Refrigerators

vol. (l)	w (cm)	d (cm)	h (cm)
50	55	55–60	80–85
75	55	60–65	85
100	55–60	60–65	85
125	55–60	65–70	90–100
150	60–65	65–70	120–130
200	65–75	70–75	130–140
250	70–80	70–75	140–150

Built-in refrigerators

vol. (l)	w (cm)	d (cm)	h (cm)
50	55	50–55	80–85
75	55	55–60	85–90
100	55	60–65	90

⓰ Dimensions → ⓯

1 Place setting for meal: soup, meat dish, dessert, drink

2 Place setting for meal: soup, fish and meat dishes, dessert, white and red wine

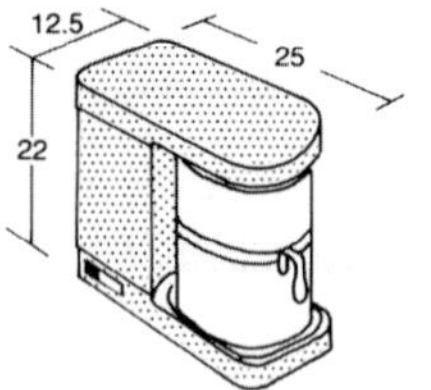

7 Coffee machine

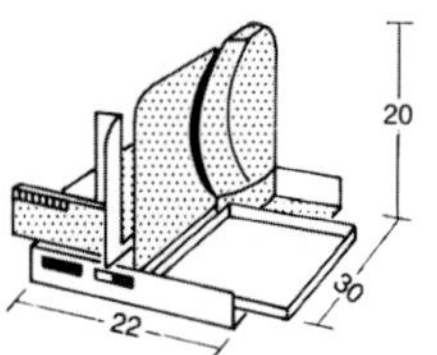

3 Place setting for meal: soup, fish and meat dishes, ice cream, sparkling, white and red wine

4 Place setting for meal: starter, fish and meat dishes, dessert, sparkling, white and red wine

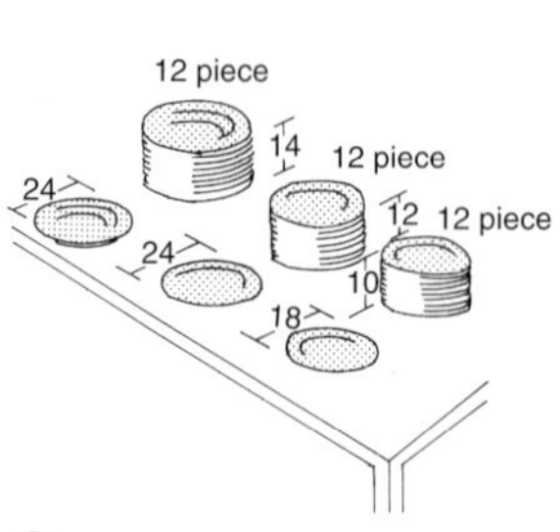

8 Plates

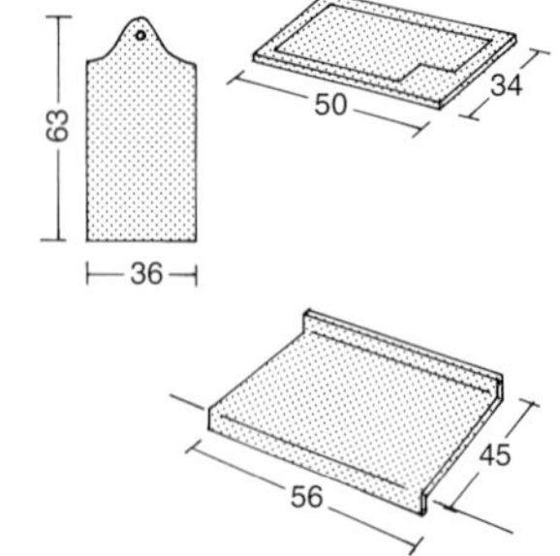

9 Multipurpose slicer; kneading, rolling and slicing boards

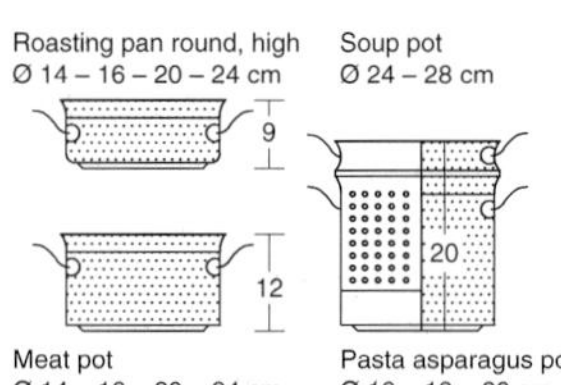

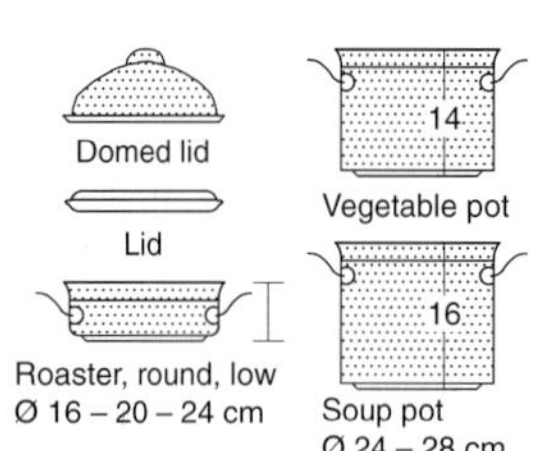

5 Stackable pans

10 Tea and coffee set

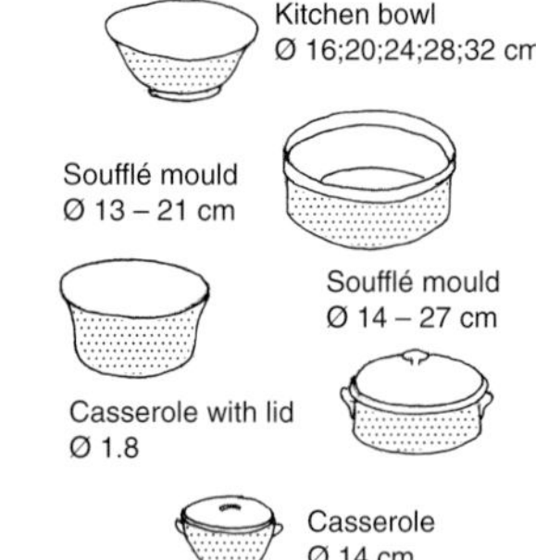

11 Dishes

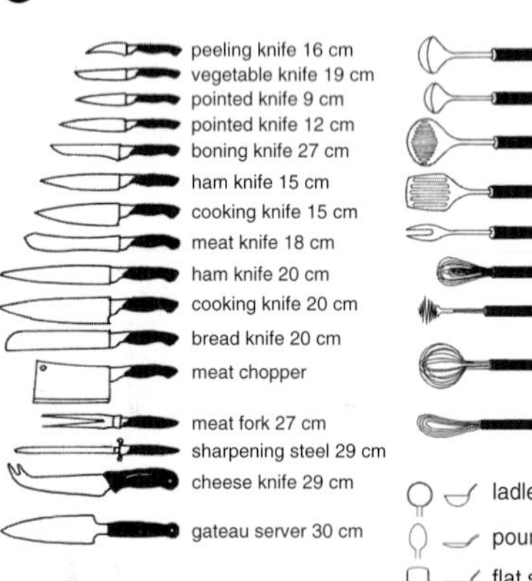

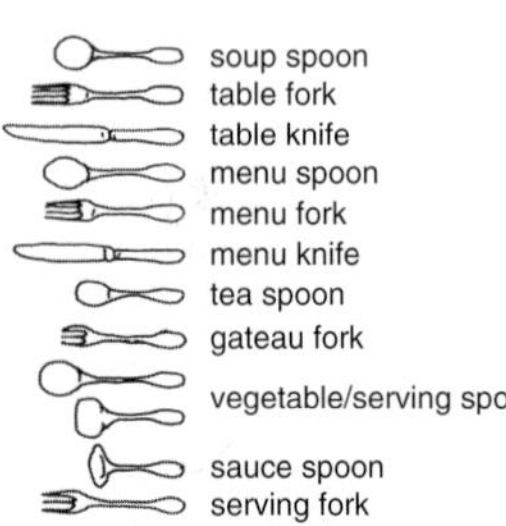

6 Kitchen utensils

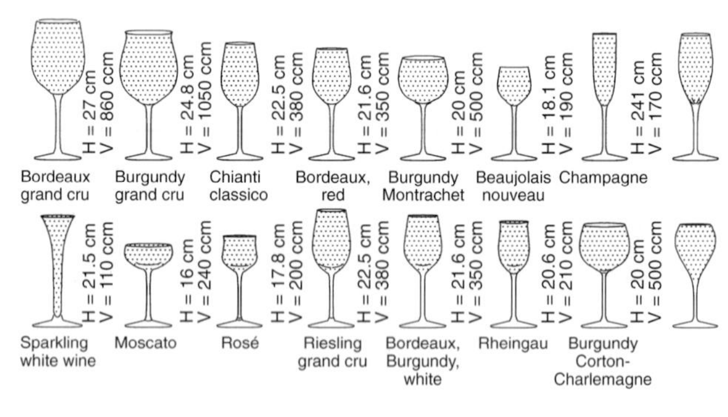

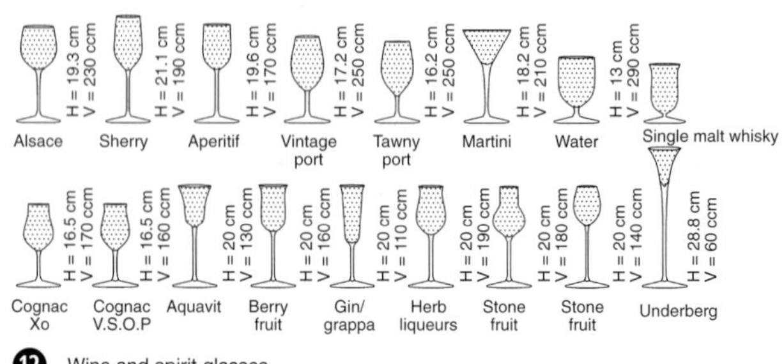

12 Wine and spirit glasses

Working processes

The layout of a kitchen should enable rational and time-saving working. In addition to a suitable arrangement of appliances, shelves and worktops → p. 149, working processes can also be optimised and accelerated with opposing worktops → ❶. The kitchen can also be used by two people at the same time in the same area if the worktops and appliances are appropriately arranged → ❷.

High cupboards and shelves should be suitably positioned relative to the working areas and should be comfortable to reach → ❸ – ❹. Worktops placed at the correct height for the relevant activity can make kitchen work considerably easier → ❽.

Kitchens are frequently used areas of the house and should be comfortable and easy to clean → ⓮. It is a good idea to set window sills at a suitable height above the worktop so that windows can be opened without having to clear the worktop → ❸.

The lighting should include lights fixed under the wall cupboards → ❼. The arrangement of switches and sockets and the additional space required for installations built into cladding, radiators and their pipework should be taken into account in the planning and spacing of the worktops.

BS EN 1116
BS 6222
BS EN 60335
BS EN 14749
DIN EN 1116

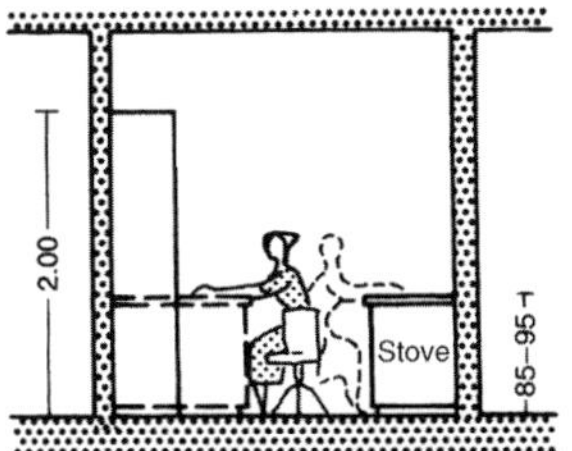

❶ Section through kitchen with two workplaces

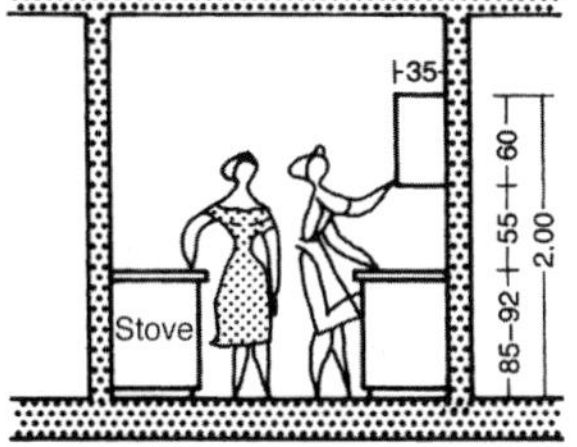
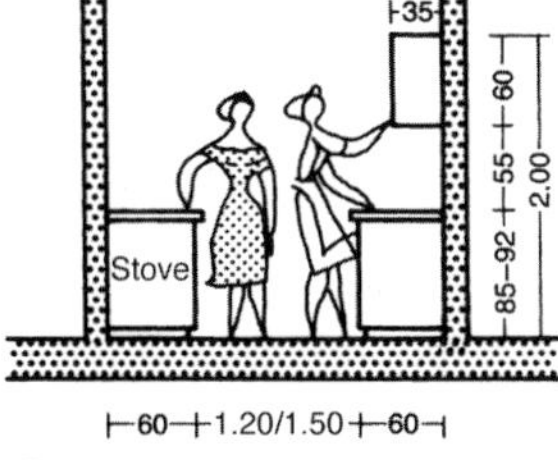

❷ Section through kitchen with room for two people

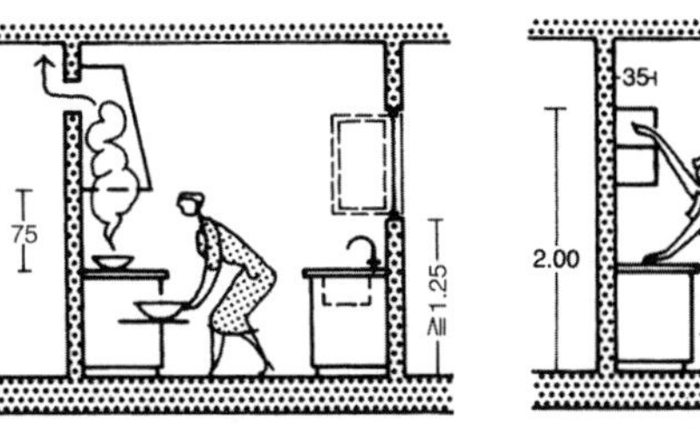

❸ Low-level ovens require appropriate room for movement; provide an extractor fan above the cooker

❹ Worktops 60 cm deep

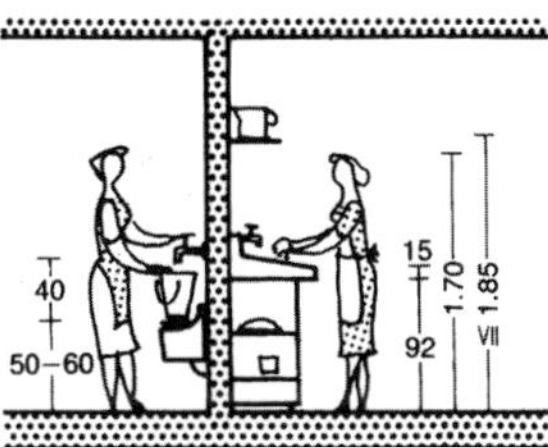

❺ Normal height for bucket sinks and the maximum height for sinks with usable high-level shelf

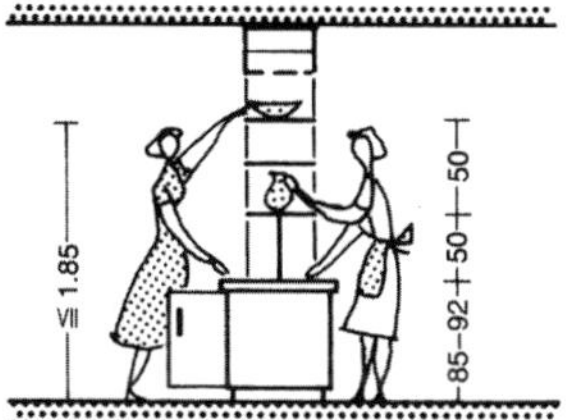

❻ Reach-through hatch between kitchen and dining area with shelves for crockery at higher level; can be opened from either side

⓫ Adjacent working

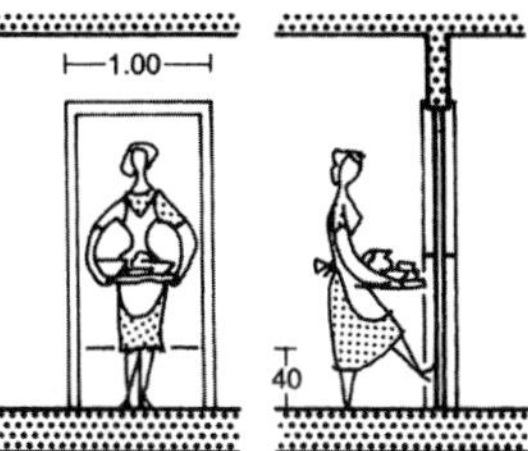

⓬ The best height for a metal plate to enable a door to be kicked open between pantry and dining room

❼ Correct and incorrect kitchen lighting

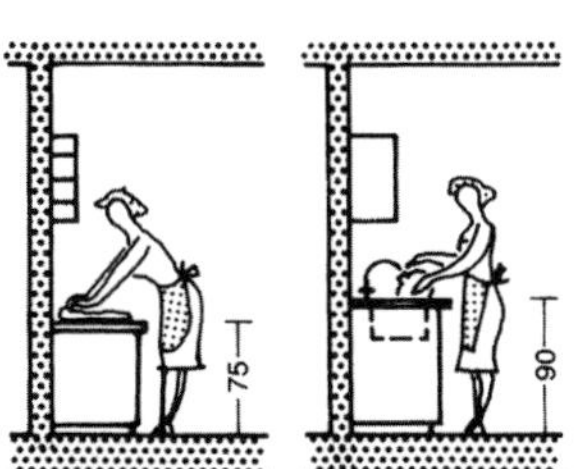

❽ Normal table height of 85 cm lies between the best height for breadmaking and the sink

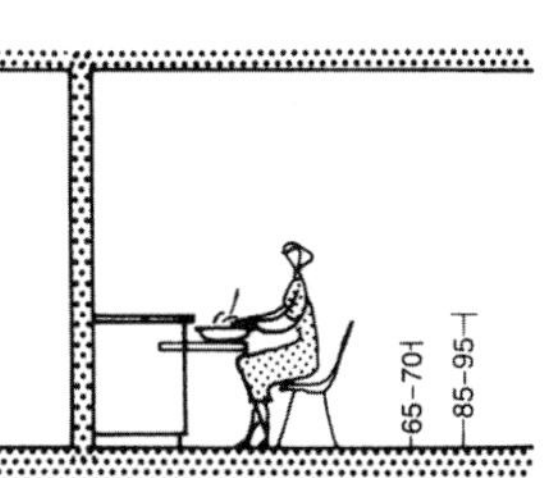

⓭ Pull-out worktop intended for seated working

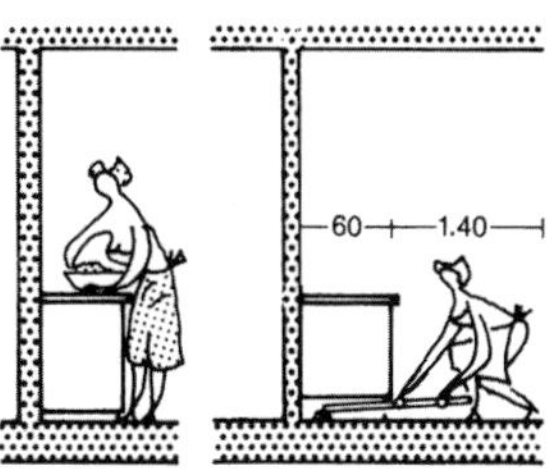

⓮ Correct installation of cupboard base for comfortable cleaning and working ≧10 cm

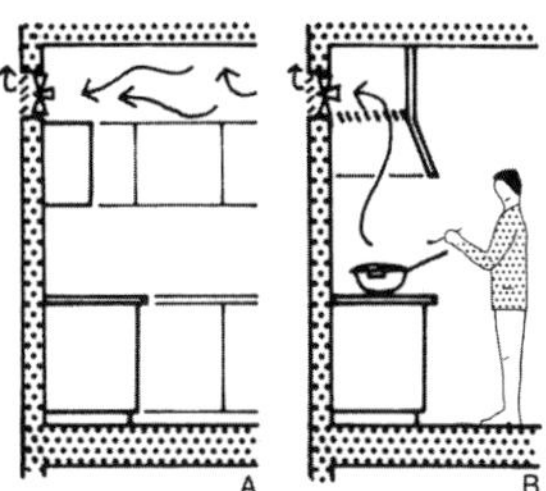

❾ Artificial ventilation with a fan (A) or extractor hood (B)

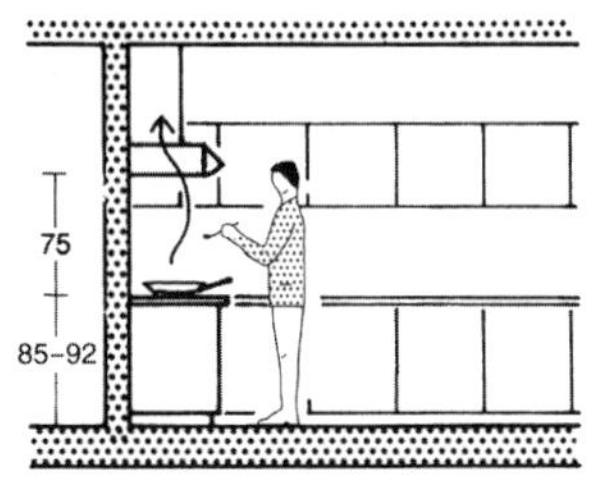

❿ Extractor fan above cooker

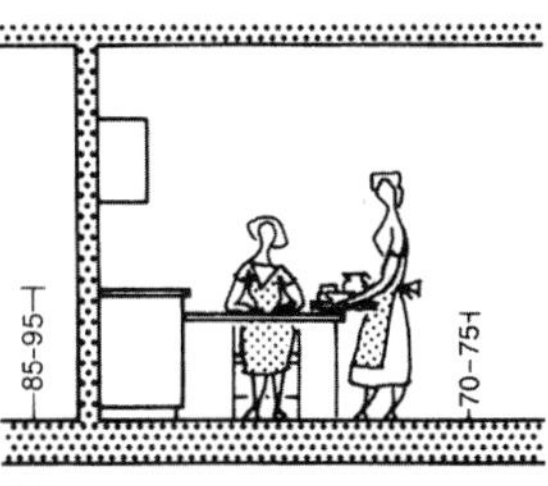

⓯ Slide-out, swivelling table

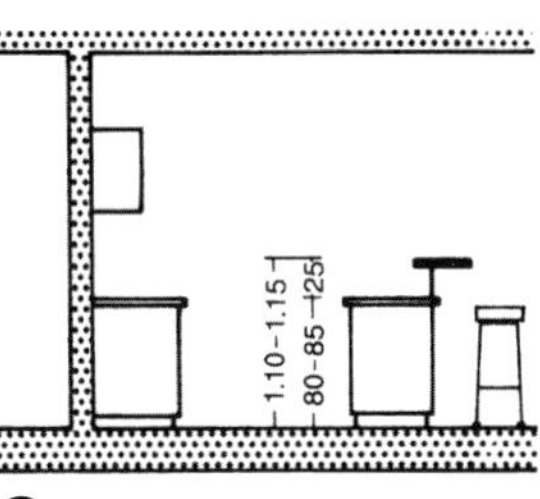

⓰ At the breakfast/snack bar

❶ Place setting for: soup, fish dish, dessert, drink

❷ Place setting for: soup, fish and meat dish, ice cream, sparkling, white and red wine

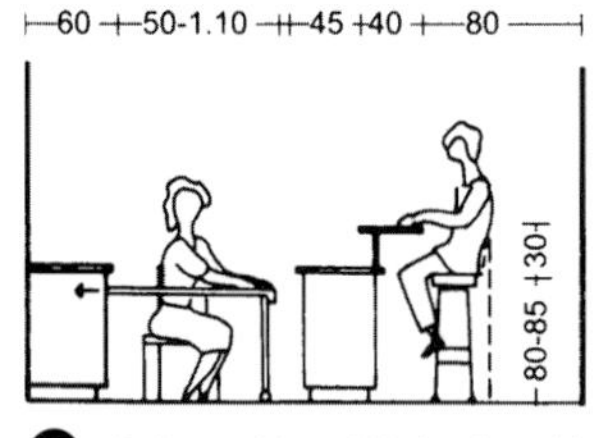

❸ Pull-out table and kitchen bar with bar stools

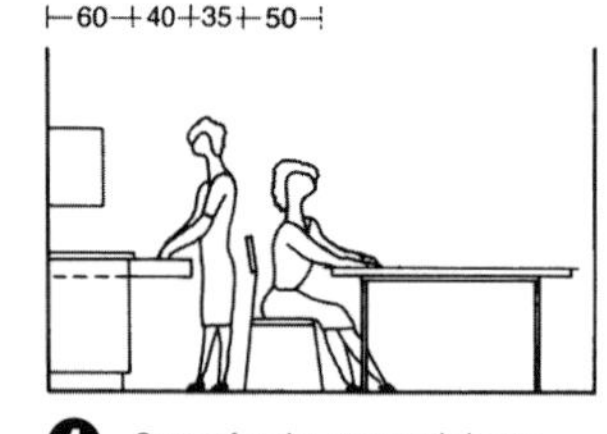

❹ Space for drawers and doors

❺ Space between sideboards and tables

❻ Minimum distance of table from wall

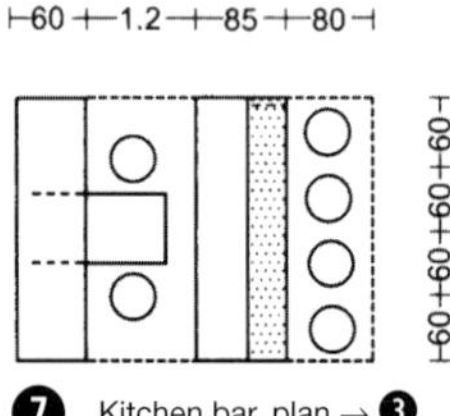

❼ Kitchen bar, plan → ❸

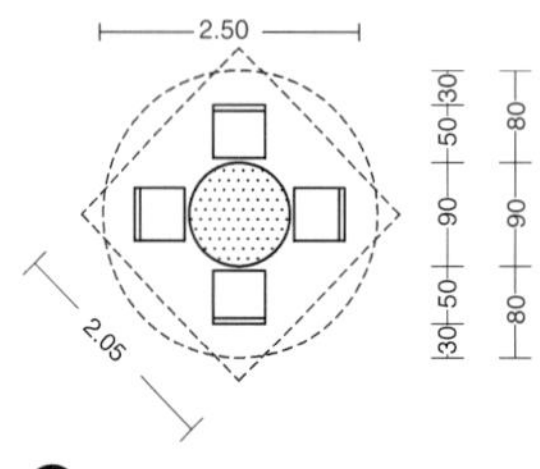

❽ Round table, 4–6 people

❾ Minimum space required for snack and dining areas (five people)

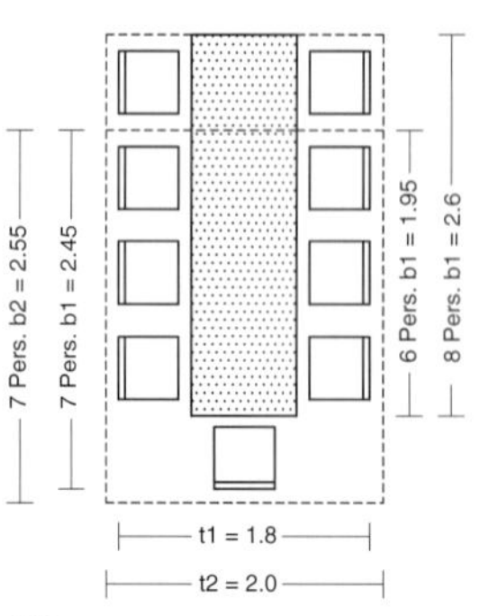

❿ Minimum space required for snack and dining areas (nine people)

Dining rooms

Dining rooms fulfil communication, social and prestige functions. They form a central part of the (communal) life within a home. The spectrum ranges from a breakfast/snack bar in the kitchen to the occupants of the house taking meals together to dining with guests (in a separate dining room). The requirements for the design and spatial layout of the dining areas are correspondingly varied. The dining table may well be considered the central point of organisation in the home → p. 150 ❾.

Minimum requirements

The dining area should be laid out to accommodate the anticipated size of the household. It should always offer space for at least 4 people.

Spatial layout

Dining areas are normally oriented to the south or west. A direct connection to the kitchen (or pantry) is practical. It is good to provide for extension (with sliding partitions etc.) for special events. Dining areas should have access to the balcony or terrace if possible.

If a separate breakfast area is desired, this is best placed to the south or east of the house. If it is sited in the kitchen, it will require additional storage and movement areas.

Equipment and space requirements

In order to be able to eat comfortably, a person needs a table area of approx. 60 × 40 cm → ❶. This results in sufficient distance from a neighbour and room for a complete place setting. The centre of the table should have a 20 cm strip for plates, pots and bowls.

A snack area can be formed from a pull-out table with a height of 70–75 cm → ❸. If there is room, a folding table fixed to a free-standing cupboard is a good solution. A movement area of 80 cm is required to the left and right of the table.

A space-saving kitchen bar also has a depth of 40 cm, but needs less space because of the projection of 15 cm. Special bar stools or chairs are needed in this case → ❸ + ❼. A dining area in the kitchen needs an amount of space according to the layout, but can often replace a dining room.

A comfortable round dining table has a diameter of min. 0.90 m, though 1.10–1.25 m would be preferable.

A corner bench with table takes up less space than any other dining area layout. If more than three people are to be accommodated, the movement area increases by 80 cm per seating place. Dining table lighting should avoid glare.

large dining room for	6–24 people
width of table	55–110 cm
width of places	55–70 cm
additional for head of table places	10–20 cm

$\geqq$ round table $= \frac{\text{place width} \times \text{no. people}}{3.14}$

e.g. for 60 cm place width and 6 people

$= \frac{60 \times 6}{3.14} = 1.04$ m

⓫ Minimum space required for snack and dining areas (4–8 people)

Tables and chairs for	Width (cm) w1	Width (cm) w2	Depth (cm) d1	Depth (cm) d2	Area (m²) A1	Area (m²) A2
4 people	130	–	180	200	2.34	2.6
5 people	180	190	180	200	3.24	3.8
6 people	195	–	180	200	3.51	3.9
7 people	245	255	180	200	4.41	5.1
8 people	260	–	180	200	4.68	5.2

w1, d1, A1 without space for pulling out chair
w2, d2, A2 with space for pulling out chair

⓬ Minimum table sizes according to number of people

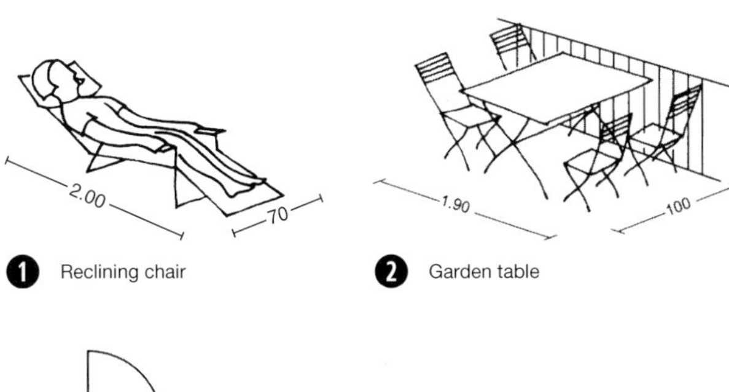

❶ Reclining chair

❷ Garden table

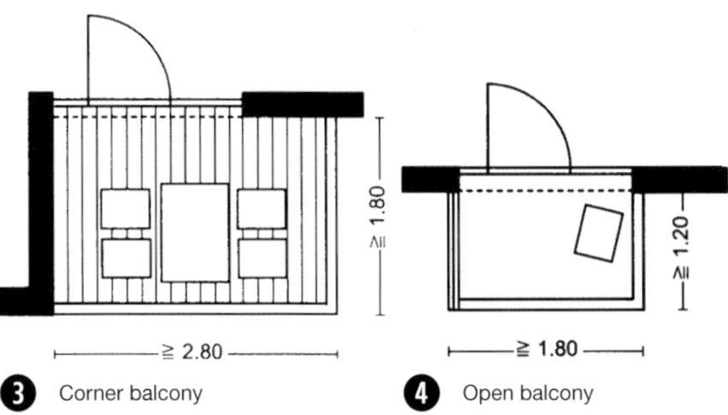

❸ Corner balcony

❹ Open balcony

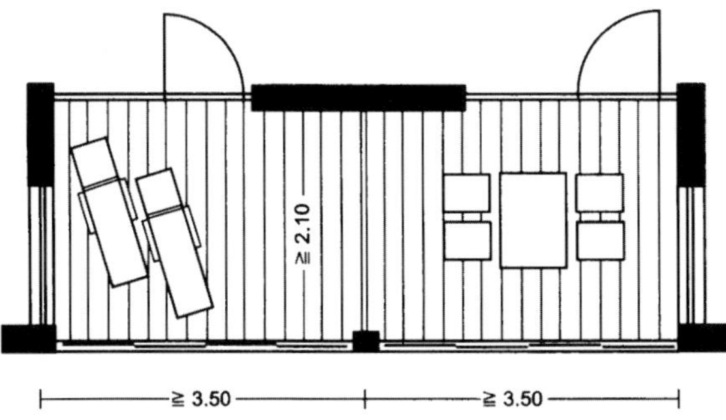

❺ Recessed balcony (loggia)

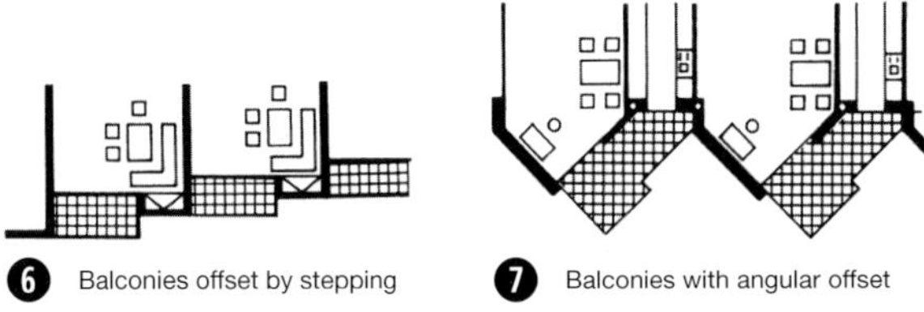

❻ Balconies offset by stepping

❼ Balconies with angular offset

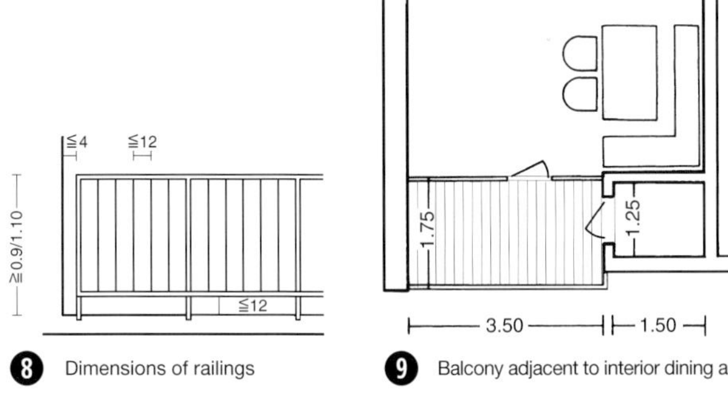

❽ Dimensions of railings

❾ Balcony adjacent to interior dining area

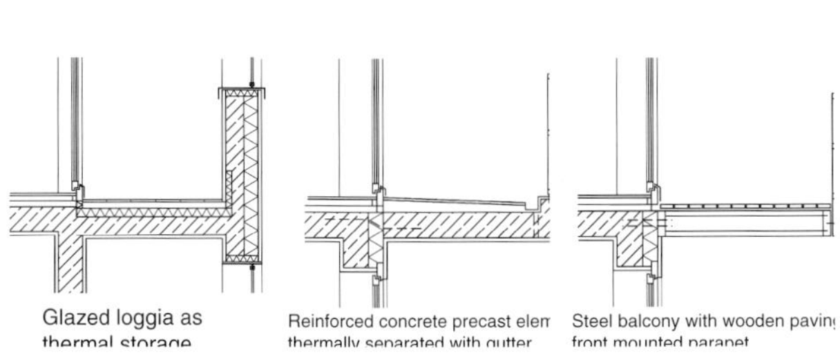

❿ Possible structural details for balconies

Open-air areas

The attractiveness of housing can be considerably enhanced through open-air areas (balconies, loggias and terraces) adjoining the rooms. In the summer these offer a desirable extension of living space for relaxing, lounging, sleeping, reading and eating, and can also offer an extended working area or an easily supervised open-air play area for children. Balconies, loggias and terraces are a part of the living areas, for which they are normally calculated as 25–50% → housing area regulation, p. 136.

They generally have a spatial relationship to living and working areas and dining rooms (with more than one open area, this can also include bedrooms, kitchens etc.). Good orientation (compass direction, view), sufficient size and protection from overlooking, noise and weather (wind, rain, strong sunshine) are decisive for the quality of open areas.

The space required for the parapet (and its planting) has to be included in the functionally required depth.

Corner balconies → ❸ offer privacy and wind protection, and are more comfortable than open balconies → ❹. Open balconies should therefore be protected on the weather side. Recessed balconies (loggias) → ❺ enlarge the external wall area of the adjoining rooms (causing heat loss) but offer the nearest to an 'open-air room'. From plan stage, offset balconies provide excellent protection against overlooking and wind → ❻ – ❼.

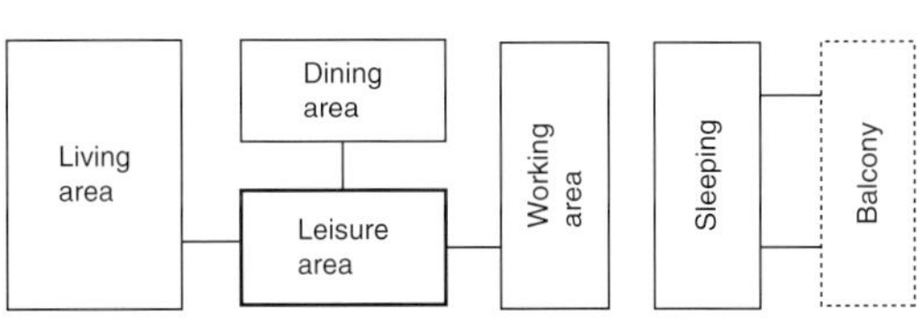

⓫ Possible relationships of rooms to open areas

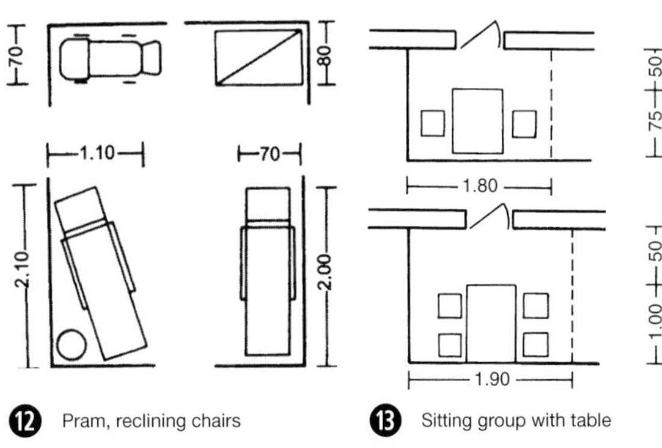

⓬ Pram, reclining chairs

⓭ Sitting group with table

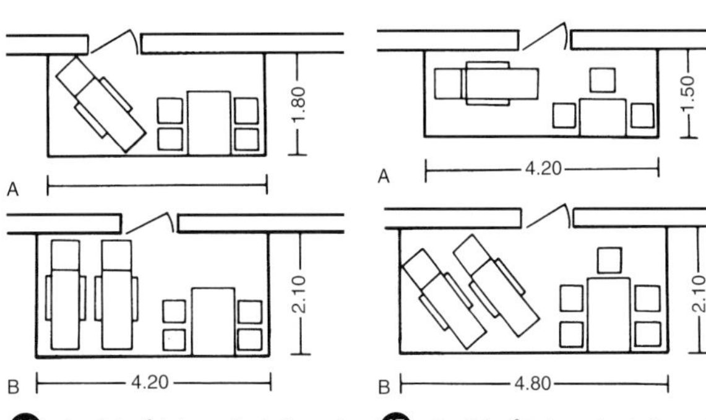

⓮ A = 7.0 m^2 balcony for 3–4 people
B = 9.0 m^2 balcony for 5–6 people

⓯ A = 6.0 m^2 balcony for 1–2 people
B = 10 m^2 balcony for 3–4 people

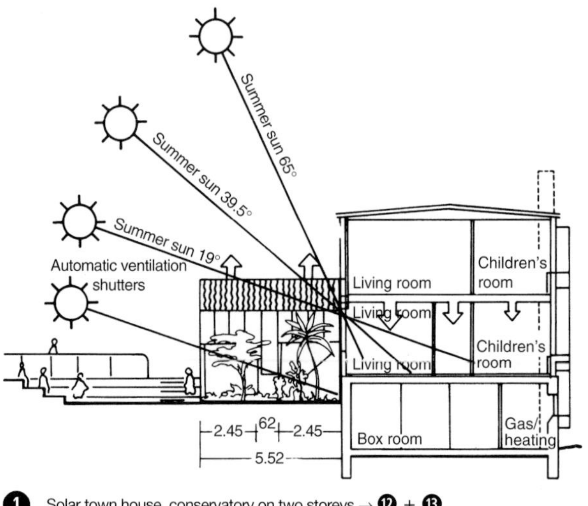

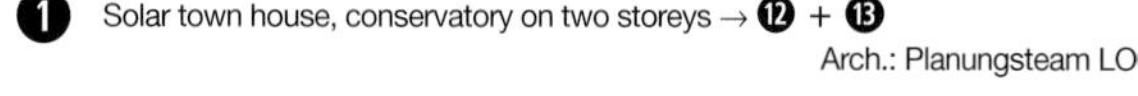
❶ Solar town house, conservatory on two storeys → ⓬ + ⓭
Arch.: Planungsteam LOG

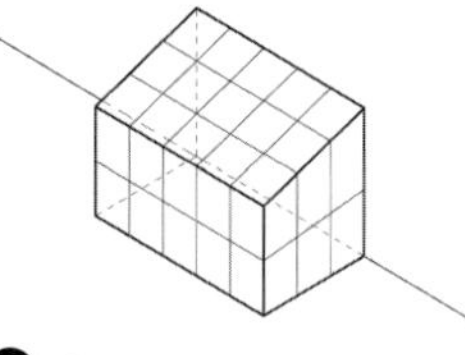
❷ Projecting conservatory

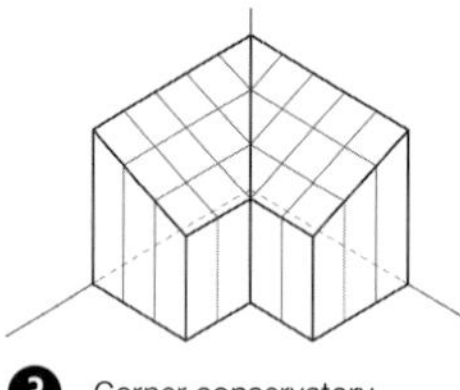
❸ Corner conservatory

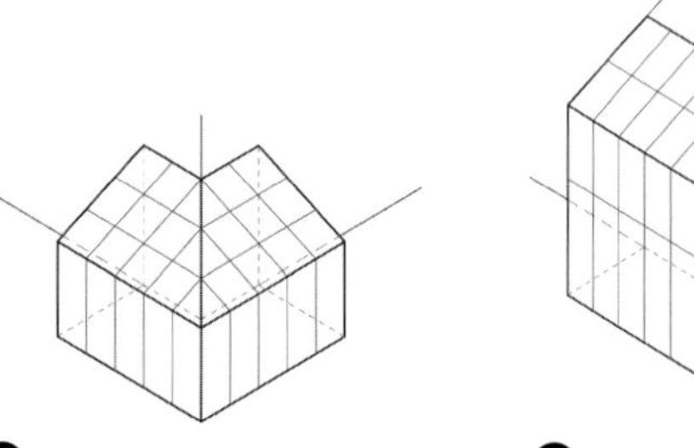
❹ External corner conservatory

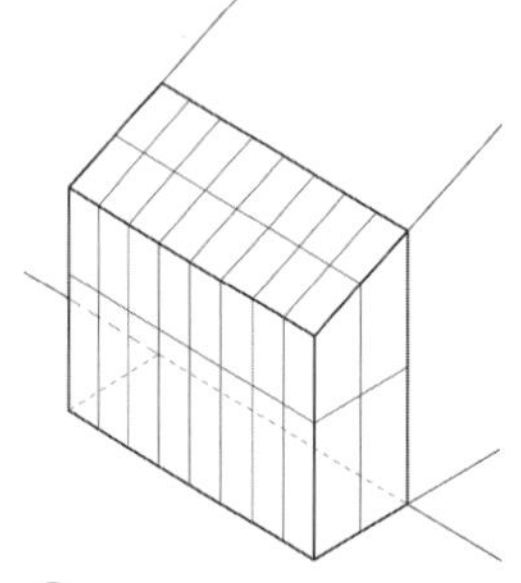

❺ Conservatory covering entire building width

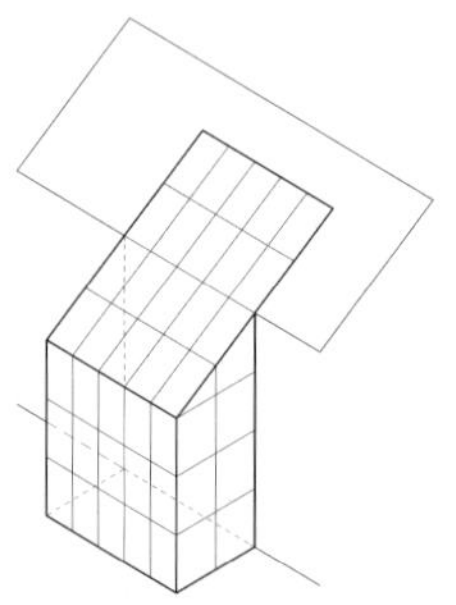
❻ Recessed conservatory

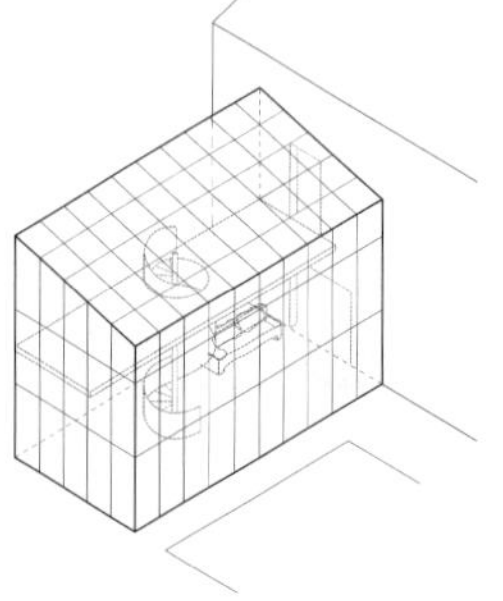
❼ Transverse projecting conservatory

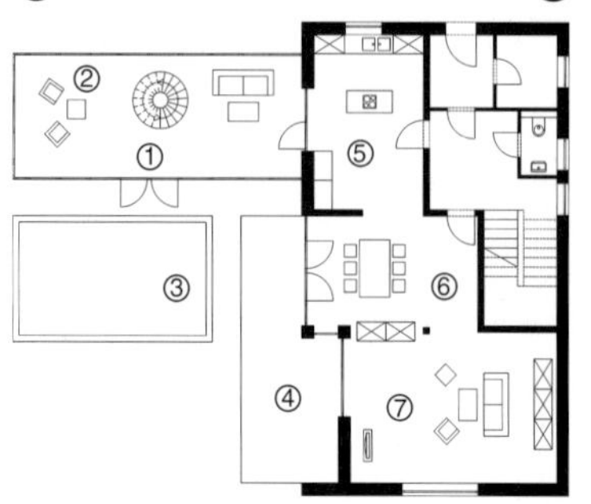

Plan

① Conservatory
② Gallery
③ Swimming pool
④ Terrace
⑤ Kitchen
⑥ Dining room
⑦ Living room

❽ Plan → ❼ Arch.: Heim + Müller Architektur GmbH

Conservatories

Conservatories project from living rooms with their large glazing areas. Originally they were heated by sunshine, naturally ventilated → ❿ – ⓫ and served as climatic buffer zones and to preserve plants in the cold part of the year.

Nowadays conservatories are mostly seen as an extension of living space, and used particularly in the spring and autumn. If equipped with appropriate additional heating and automatic ventilation, they can accommodate sub-tropical plants. In many cases they are part of the heated building volume with corresponding requirements for their outer envelope.

❾ Natural shade

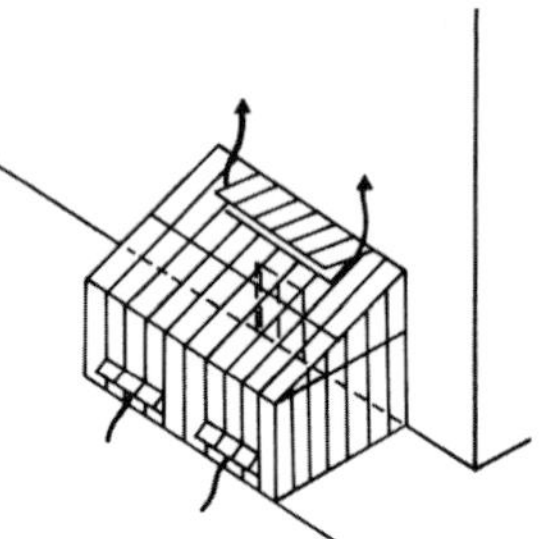
❿ Ventilation and extraction

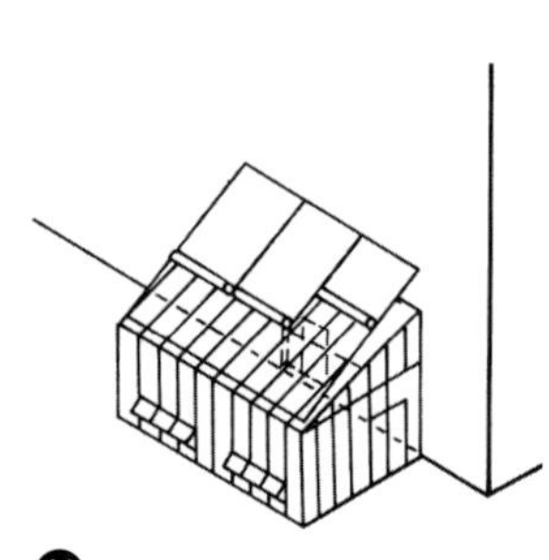
⓫ External sun shades

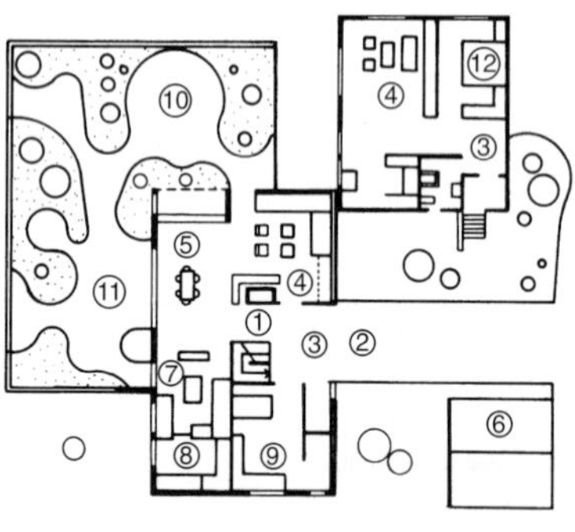

Plans

① Corridor
② Wind lobby
③ Hall
④ Living room
⑤ Dining room
⑥ Double garage
⑦ Kitchen
⑧ Utility room
⑨ Children's room
⑩ Energy greenhouse
⑪ Storage surface
⑫ Bedroom
⑬ Balcony

⓬ Ground floor of solar town house → ❶ + ⓭

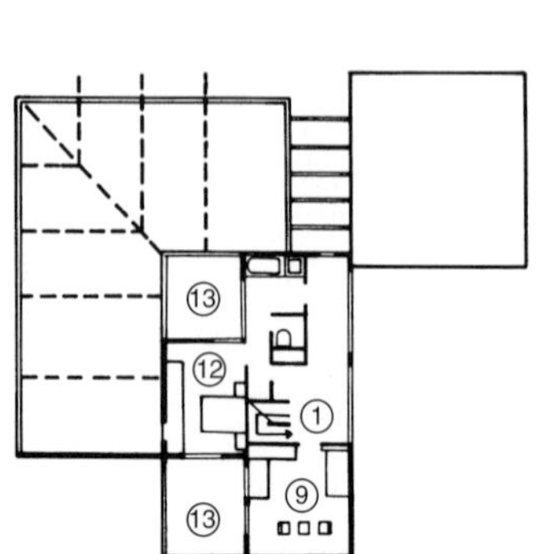
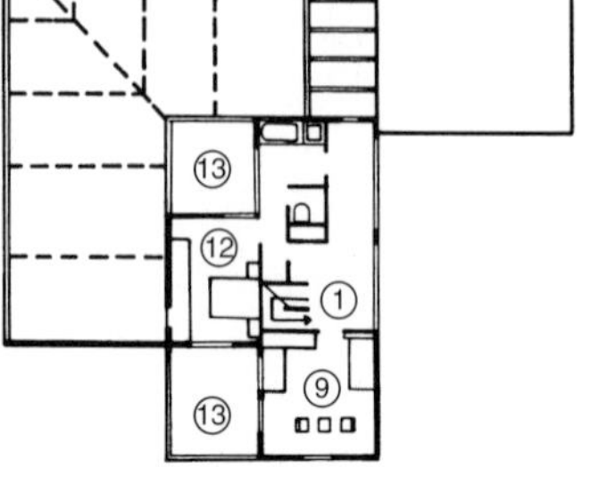
⓭ First floor → ❶ + ⓬ Arch.: Planungsteam LOG

≧3.50
1.50 × 1.50
≧3.60

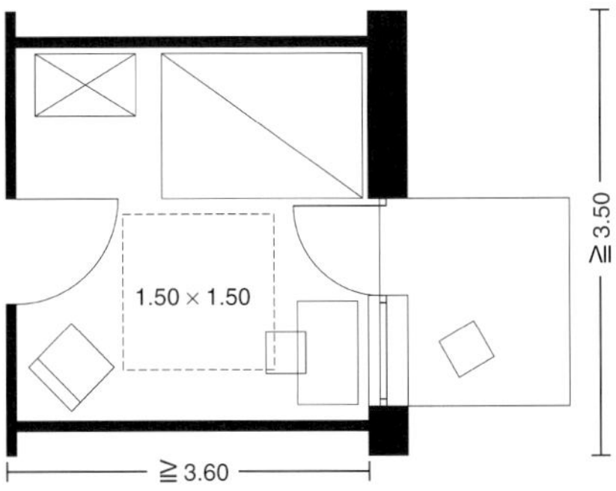

❶ Flexibly functional individual room (movement area suitable for a wheelchair)

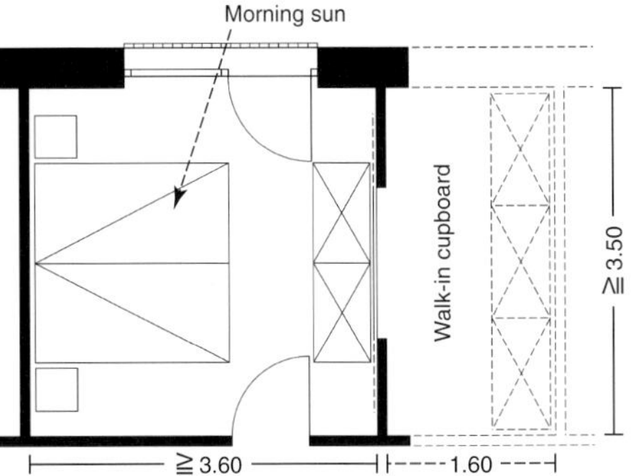

❷ (Parents') bedroom with walk-in cupboard extension

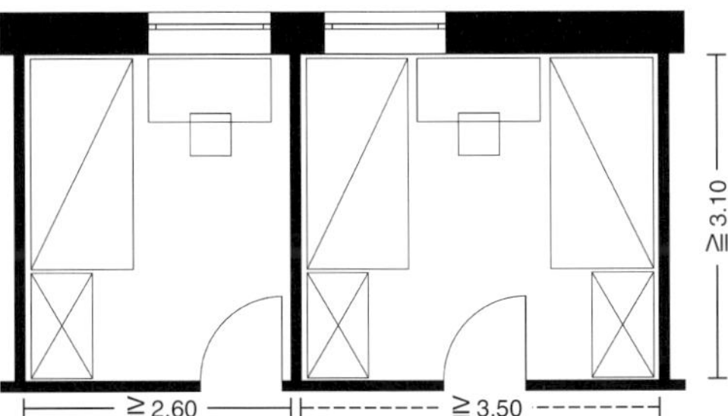

❸ Small bedroom and small twin bedroom

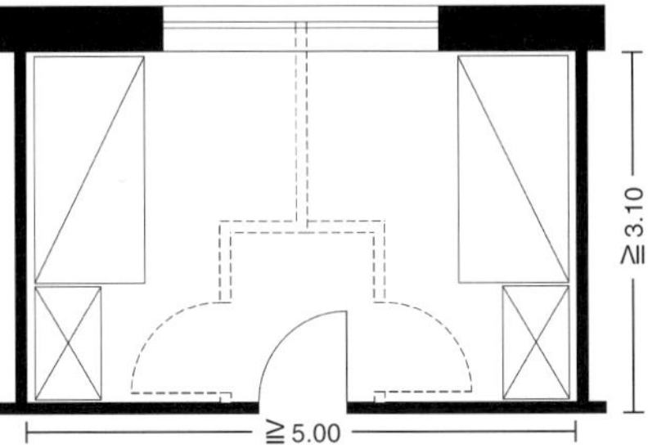

❹ Twin bedroom (can be partitioned)

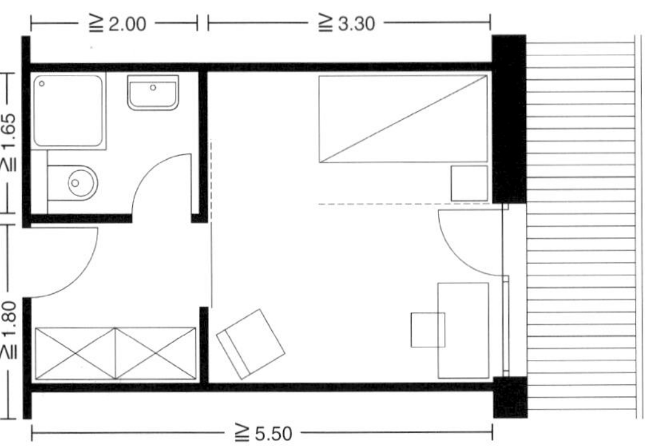

❺ Small individual area with shower room and cupboard zone

Living areas are categorised into those with shared rooms (living and dining rooms, kitchens) and individual (private) rooms for one or two people (parents' (bed)room, children's room, guest room). This differentiation leads to the conventional room layouts, particularly in commercial house building.

But the way living areas are actually used is much more complex and varied. Bedrooms today are often used for **work**, **play and relaxation** and thus have some of the functions of shared rooms. This makes the fitting out of an individual room within a house as a small **apartment** worth considering.

→ ❶: an individual room which can be used for a flexible range of functions. It has an area of approx. 13 m^2, including movement areas suitable for a wheelchair and possible extension onto an open balcony.

→ ❷ – ❸: bedrooms with **minimal** space of approx. 13 m^2 (as parents' room or twin bedroom) and approx. 8 m^2 (single room). These would normally be aligned to east or southeast (parents) or south to west (children) and separated from the living room in another part of the home.

→ ❹: the options for a generous twin bedroom of 16.5 m^2, which could be partitioned (for example, for children as they grow up).

→ ❺: a small, independent individual area with shower room and separate cupboard zone.

The conventional **living room** as a shared residential room and prestigious face of the house for visitors is increasingly developing into a multi-functional **communications zone**, which has to serve the needs of residents, but also guests and visitors → ❻ – ❼.

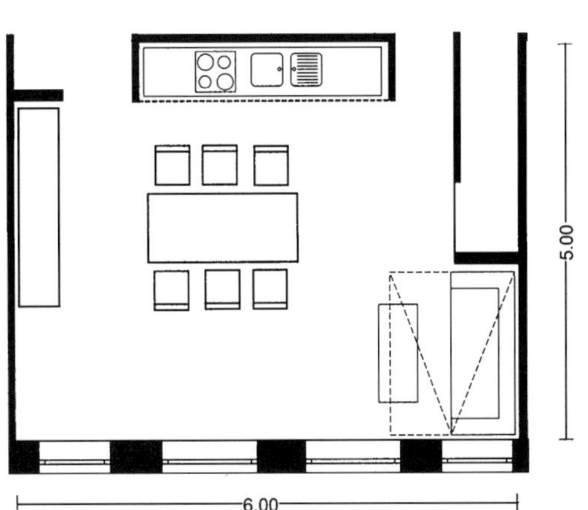

❻ All-purpose room with cloakroom, kitchen, and eating and living areas

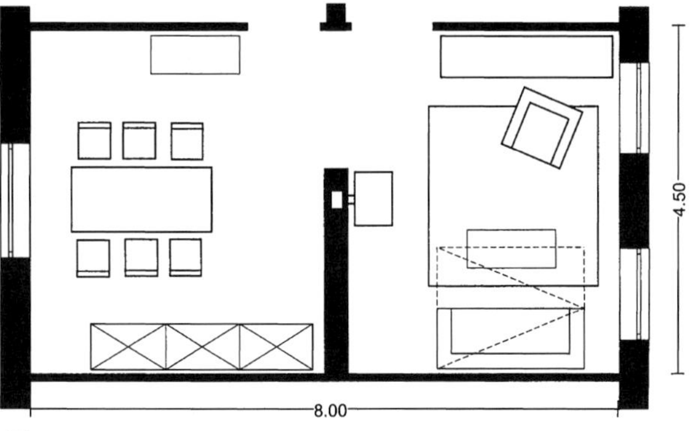

❼ Classic living room with dining area

BS 8300
DD 266
DIN 18025

MBO

see also: Design basics p.135

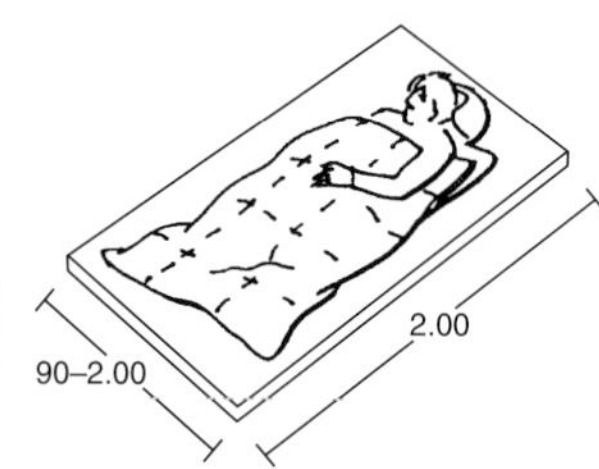

1 Sheepskin roll-up futon, the Japanese form of bed

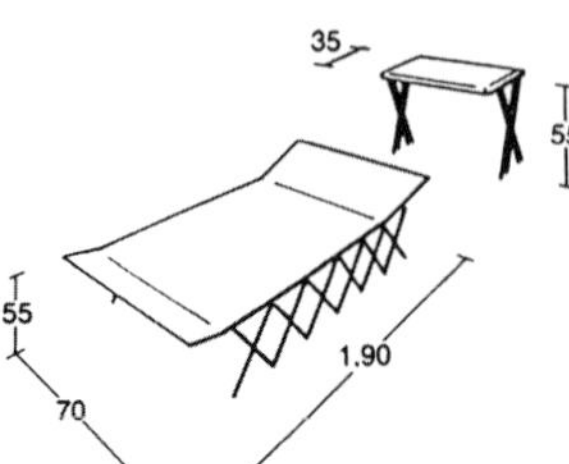

2 Camp bed with canvas cover, can be folded up and used as a bench

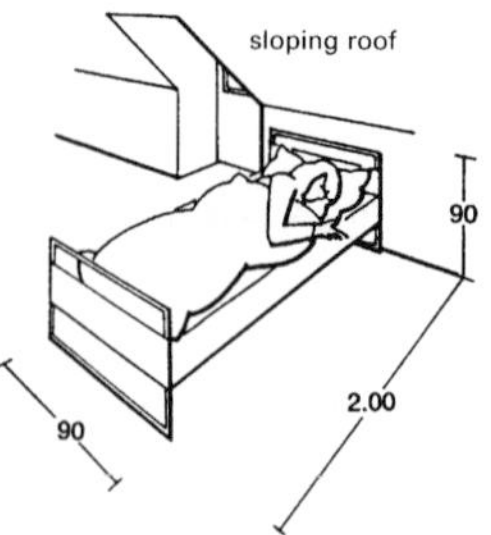

3 Low-level steel tubular bed with quilt or woollen blankets

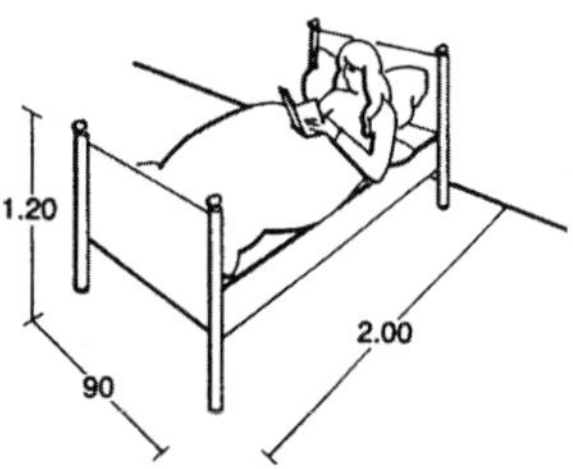

4 Classic wooden bed with footboard and headboard

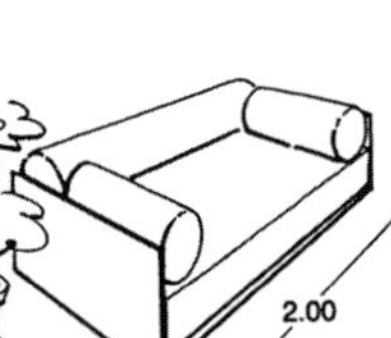

5 Sofa bed: duvet and pillows can be rolled up during the daytime and zipped into the covers

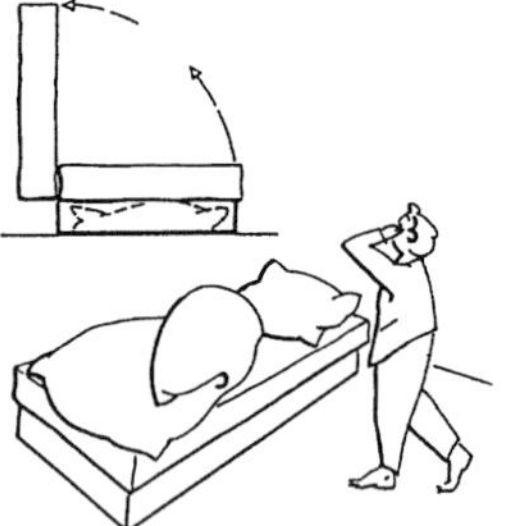

6 As before, but with compartment under the mattress to store the bedding during the day

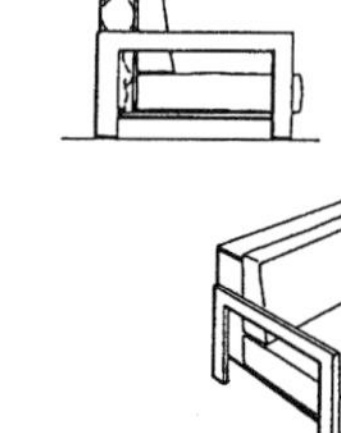

7 Sofa with divan behind the inclined backrests

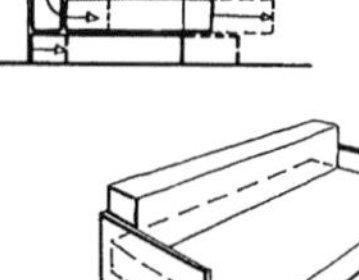

8 Sofa bed with pull-out mattress unit

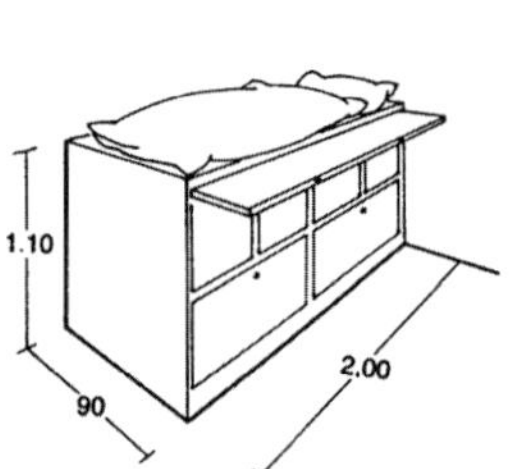

9 High bed with deep drawers and slide-out board on top, with covers

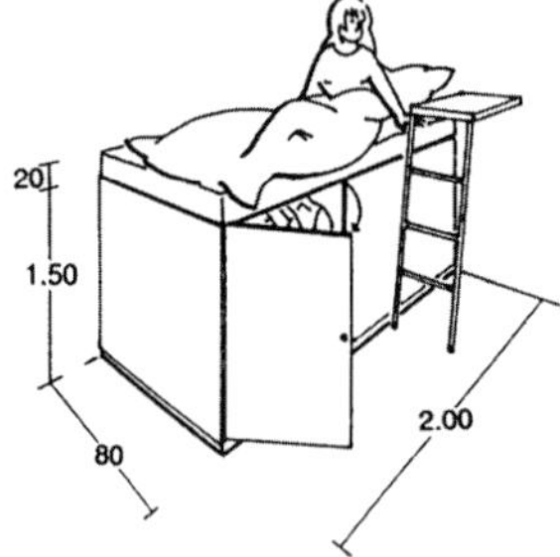

10 Cupboard-bed with low cupboard for clothes, suitable for very small rooms, ship's cabins, studio rooms etc.

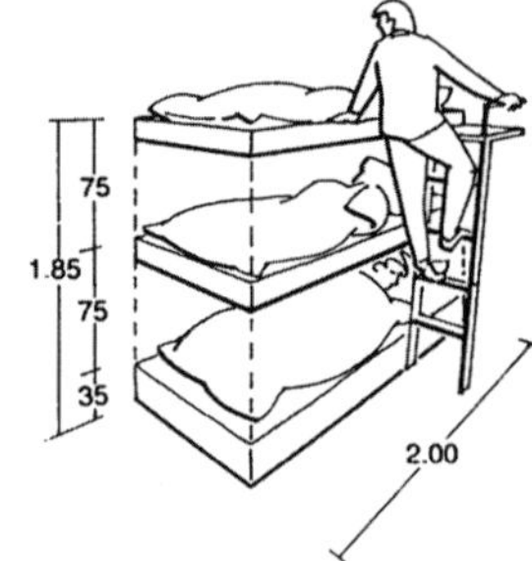

11 Three-level bunks for dormobiles, weekend houses and children's rooms, space required 0.338 m^2 per bed

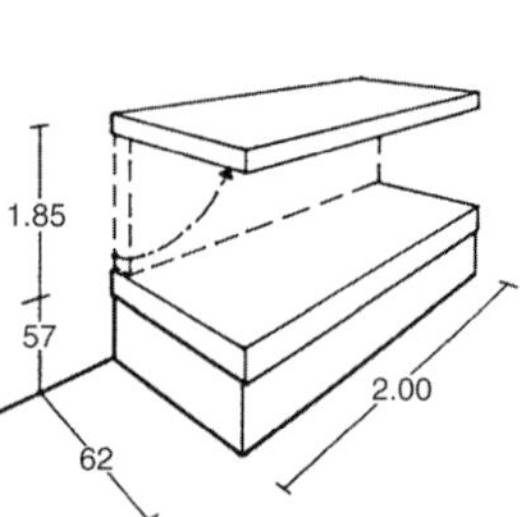

12 Pullman bed for sitting and sleeping in vehicle; backrest folds up to form second bed

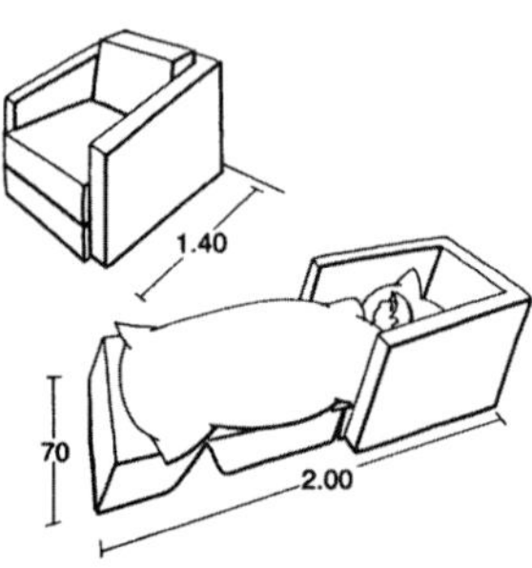

13 Armchair bed (fold-out); separate container required for bedding

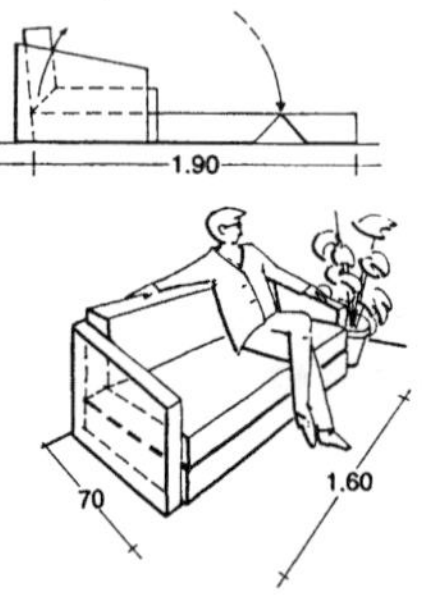

14 Sofa bed (fold-out)

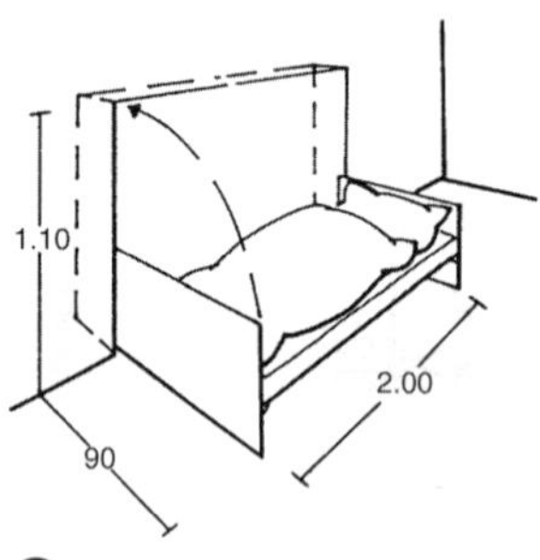

15 Frankfurt bed (folds away sideways)

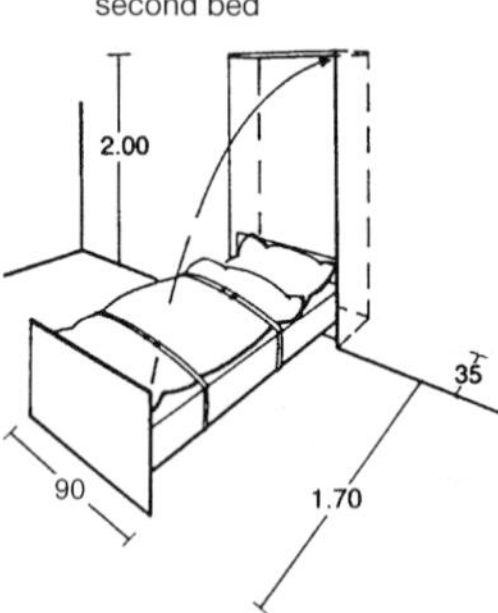

16 Frankfurt bed (folds away vertically), two adjacent or as double bed

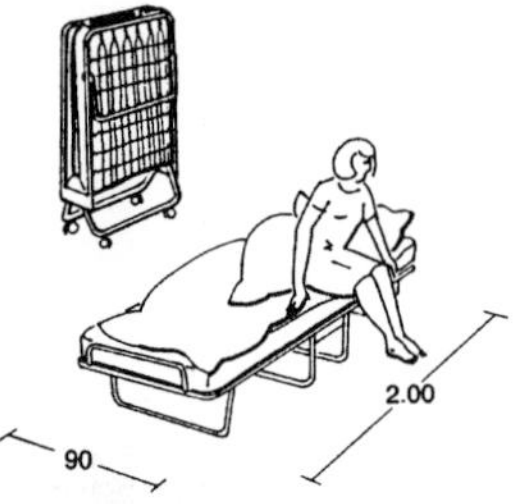

17 Fold-up bed on rollers for one or two people, can be rolled into a cupboard during the daytime

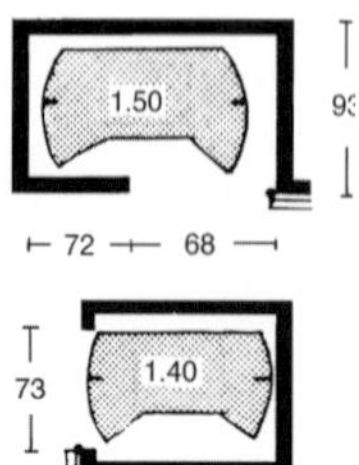

18 Wall cupboard for roller bed with narrow door opening

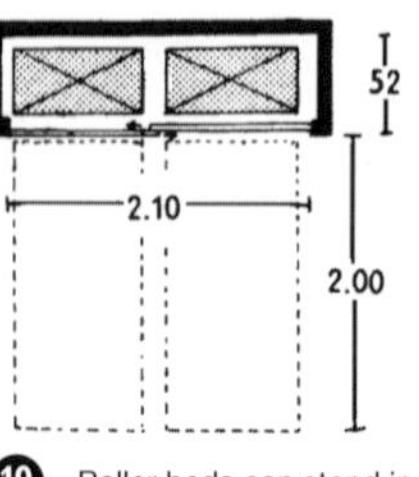

19 Roller beds can stand in front of closed cupboard door

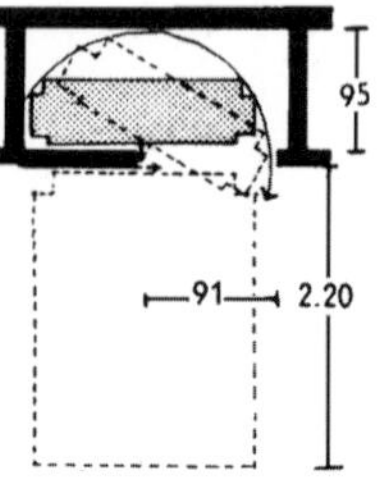

20 With swivelling and folding beds, the wall cupboard stays open at night

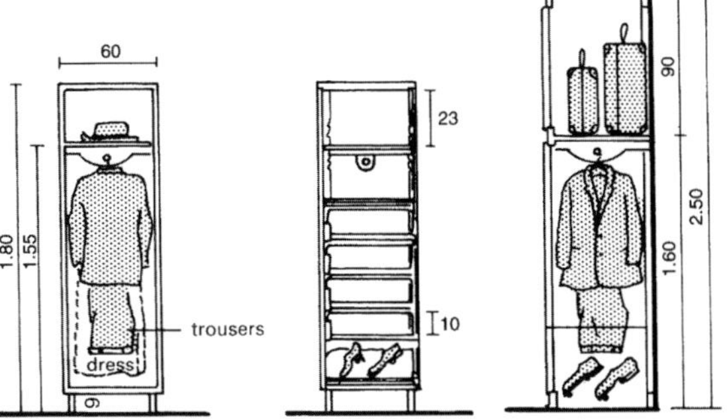

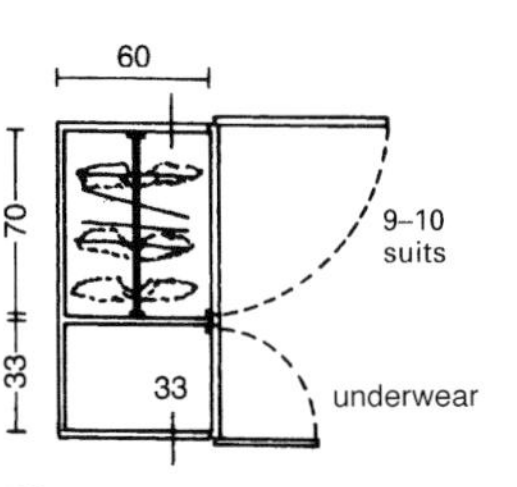

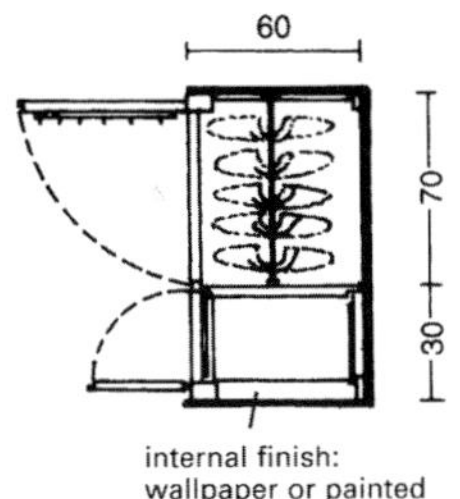

❶ Free-standing wardrobe and linen cupboard: plan, sections

❷ Built-in wardrobe and linen cupboard with upper compartment

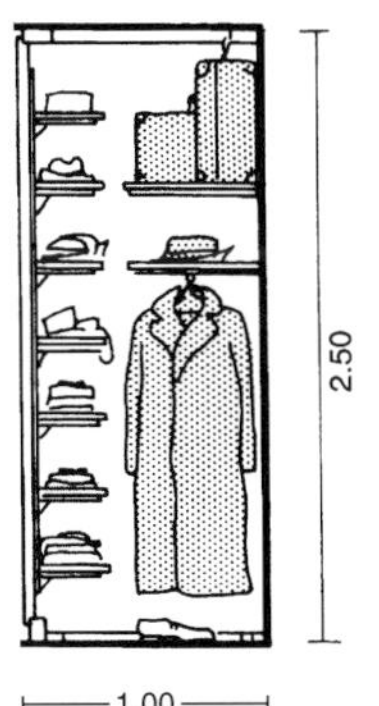

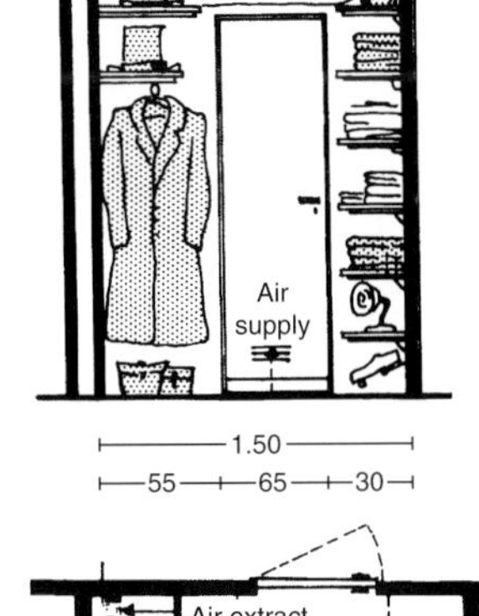

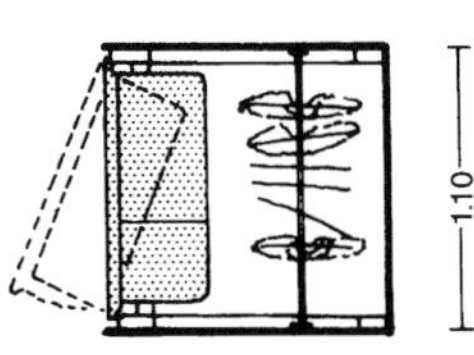

❸ Built-in double wardrobe, saving cost and space

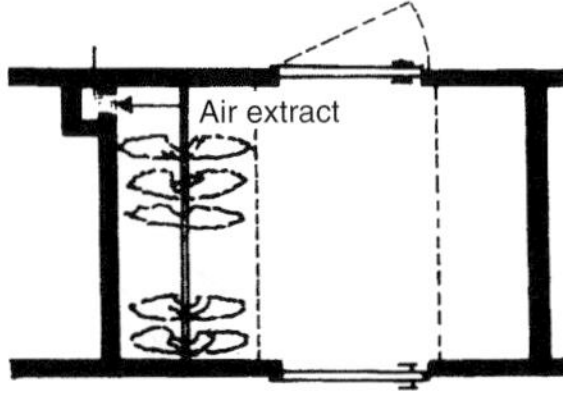

❹ Movable wardrobe between two rooms

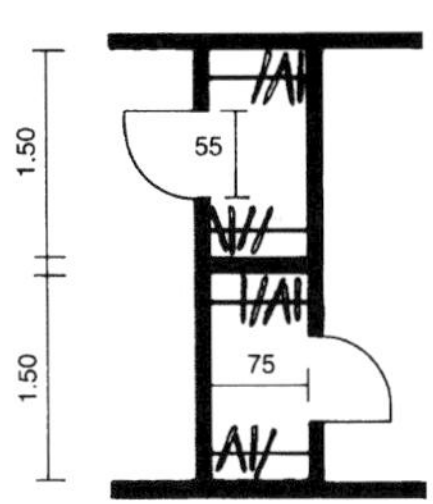

❺ Built-in wall units, with wardrobes both sides

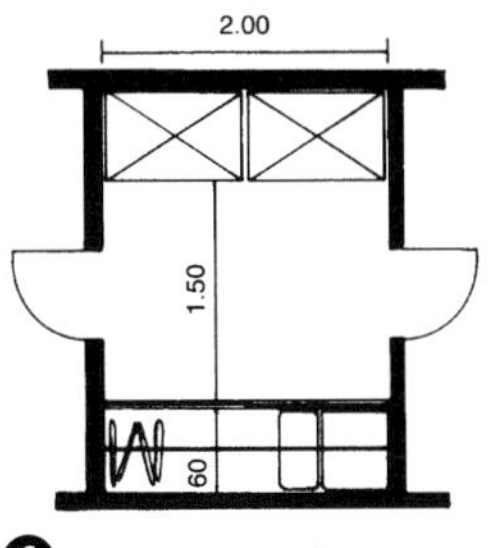

❻ Wardrobe/dressing room

Wardrobes and linen cupboards

Contents (example):

For men	For women
8 suits	6 suits
6 coats	10 coats
8 jackets	5 jackets
12 pairs trousers	20 dresses
20 shirts	15 skirts
15 T-shirts	15 blouses
12 jumpers	20 tops
4 pairs pyjamas	15 jumpers
8 pairs shoes	15 pairs trousers/leggings
2 hats	6 pyjamas/nightdresses
	10 pairs shoes
	4 hats

Sundry items

6 sheets
6 duvet covers
12 pillows and cases
8 bath towels
8 hand towels

Details and fitting out

Wardrobes and linen cupboards are an essential part of fitting out a home. They serve to store (larger) items of clothing, linen, shoes and suitcases, and are normally situated in the bedroom.

The essential elements of a wardrobe are a **drawer unit**, a **hanging rail** and additional **shelves**. It can be a **free-standing wardrobe** → ❶, a **built-in wardrobe** (wall cupboard, single or double wardrobe constructions) → ❷ – ❸ or in the form of a walk-in wardrobe or dressing room → ❹ – ❻.

Built-in wardrobe wall units → ❺ are useful as partitions between bedrooms. In small rooms space can be optimally used with cupboards built into wall niches → ❼ with continuous flooring (and sliding doors).

When determining a house's layout, appropriate space should be planned for. Free-standing (movable) wardrobes are suitable for fitting out rented flats, and built-in wardrobes are often desired in owner-occupied houses and flats.

When wardrobes are sited along external walls, care should be taken that the thermal insulation is adequate and that ventilation is provided. Walk-in wardrobes also require appropriate ventilation → ❹.

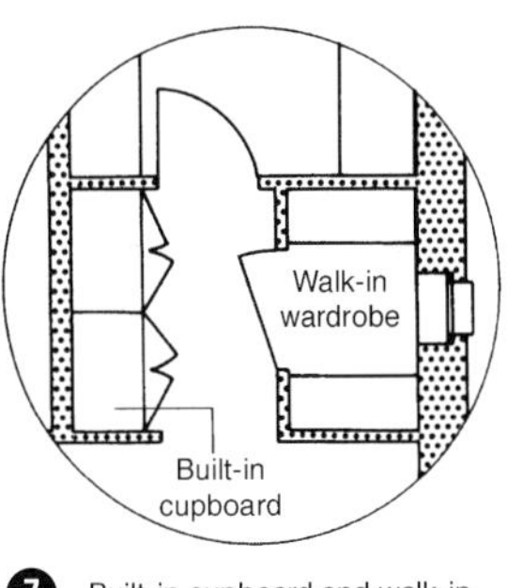

❼ Built-in cupboard and walk-in wardrobe

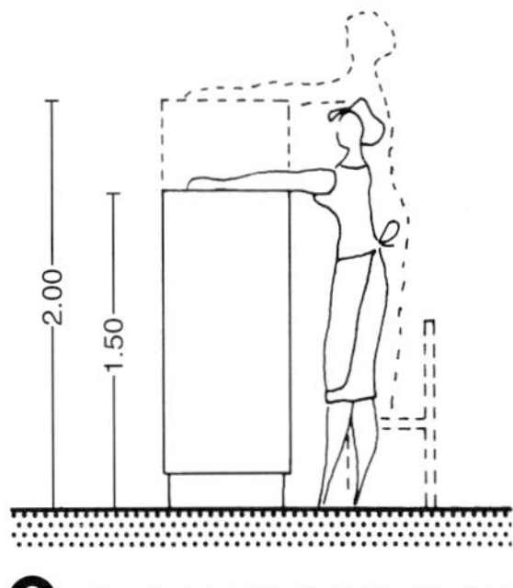

❽ Practical heights for free-standing cupboards

Residential buildings

ROOMS
Access
Kitchens
Living areas
Bathrooms
Subsidiary rooms
Garages

see also: Store rooms p. 162

see also: Sound insulation p. 477

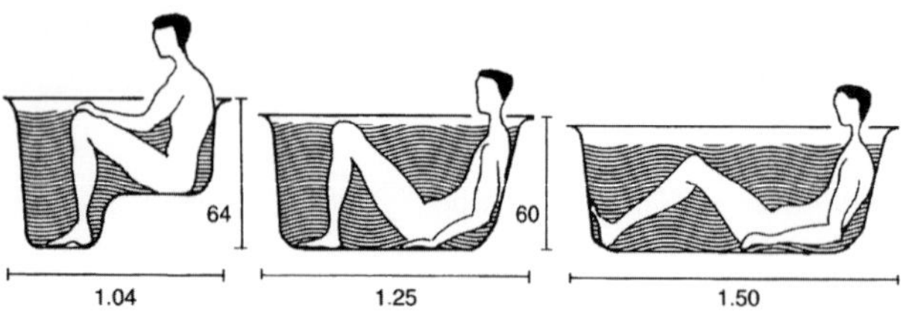

Warm water required for:	Warm water quantity (l)	Warm water temperature (°C)	Duration of use (approx. min)
full bath	140–160	40	15
sitting bath	40	40	5
footbath	25	40	5
shower	40–75	40	6

1 Bathtubs and warm water requirement. Shorter tubs reduce the quantities (guideline values)

Equipment	Area required	
	Width (cm)	Depth (cm)
Washbasins, hand basins and bidets		
1. single washbasin	≧60	≧55
2. double washbasin	≧120	≧55
3. built-in vanity unit with one washbasin and cupboard underneath	≧70	≧60
4. built-in vanity unit with two washbasins and cupboard underneath	≧140	≧60
5. hand basin	≧45	≧35
6. bidet, floor-standing or wall-hanging	40	60
Tubs		
7. bathtub	≧170	≧75
8. shower tray*	≧80	≧80*
WCs and urinals		
9. WC with wall installation or pressure flush	40	75
10. WC without cistern (with cistern installed in wall)	40	60
11. urinal	40	40
Laundry equipment		
12. washing machine	40–60	60
13. washer/dryer	60	60
Bathroom furniture		
14. low cupboards, wall cupboards, high cupboards	according to manufacturer	≧40
* for shower trays, width = 90 also 75 cm		

2 Space required for items in bathroom and WC

Arrangement	Measurements	MD*	Mi**
M₁ M₂ M₃	M_1	1200	1050
	M_2	2100	1900
	M_3	1350	1200
M MM MM₁ MM₂	M	450	400
	MM	675	600
	MM_1	750	575
	MM_2	675	500
M MM M₁ MM₁	M	450	400
	MM	675	600
	M_1	450	400
	MM_1	600	525
M MM M₃ M₁ M₂	M	450	400
	MM	675	600
	M_1	450	400
	M_2	550	500
	M_3	1100	1000
*MD = Average, recommended dimension	M_2	750	700
**Mi = Absolute minimum dimension	M_3	950	900

3 Centre-line and wall spacing for sanitary fittings

A bathroom is defined as an independent room with **bath/shower** and **toilet** and, according to building regulations, belongs to the **minimum equipment** of a flat or house. In larger houses, bath and WC should be in separate rooms, or an additional WC (guest WC) should be provided. The bathroom should be oriented to the **north**, and if possible have natural ventilation and lighting (otherwise provide effective mechanical ventilation according to DIN 18017-3). The bathroom is normally next to the bedroom → **5** – **6**, **8** – **10**, although it is also often convenient for technical reasons to place bath and kitchen (or WC and kitchen) on a common installation shaft → **8** – **9**.

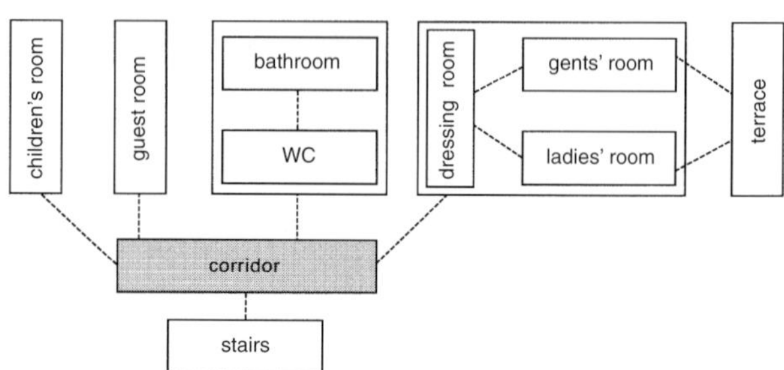

4 Relationships of rooms to the bathroom

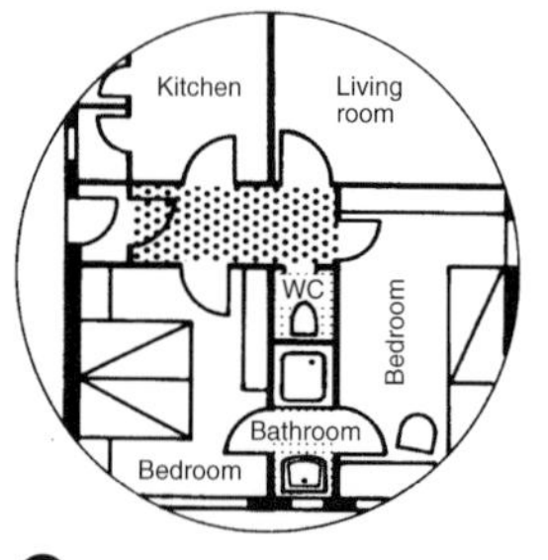

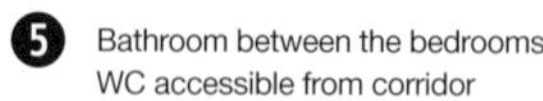

5 Bathroom between the bedrooms, WC accessible from corridor

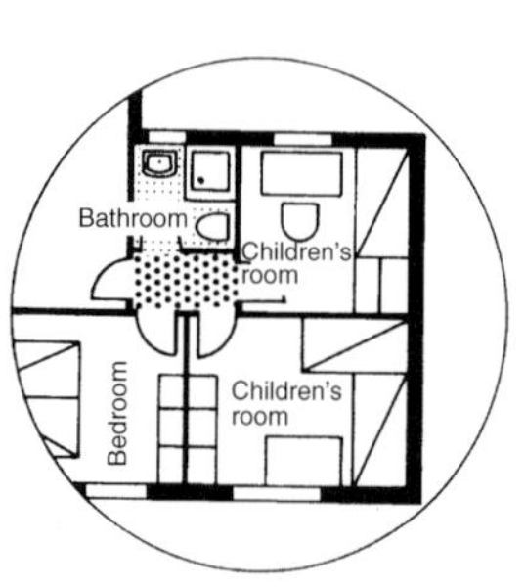

6 Bathroom on corridor between living room and the three bedrooms

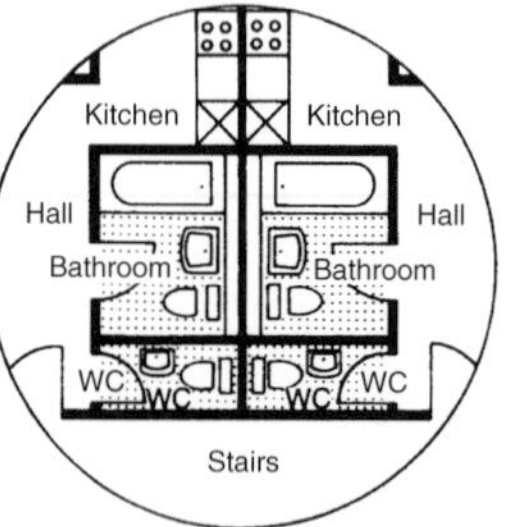

7 Kitchen, bathroom and WC on one installation wall

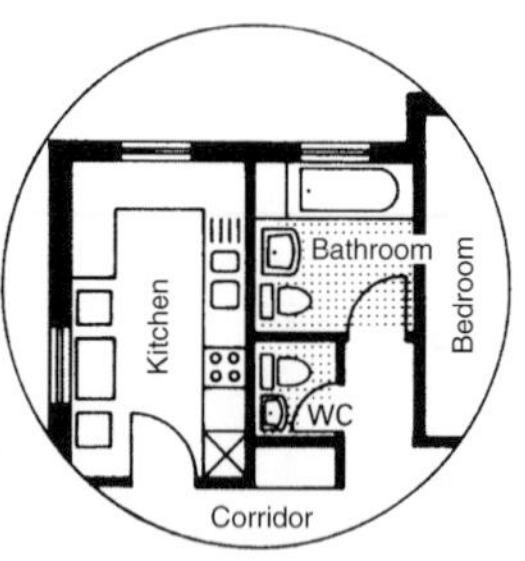

8 Kitchen, bathroom and WC on one installation wall

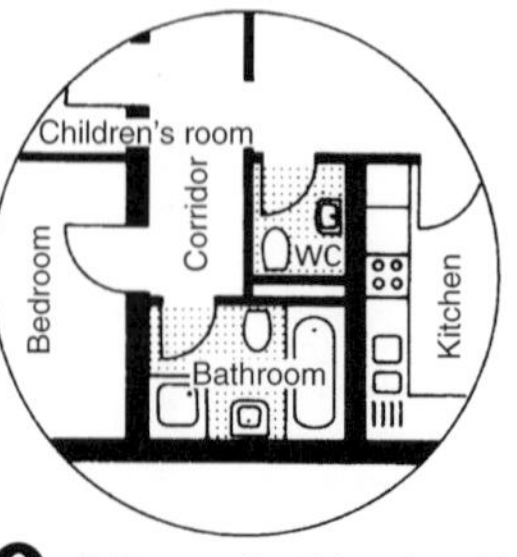

9 Bathroom off an internal corridor

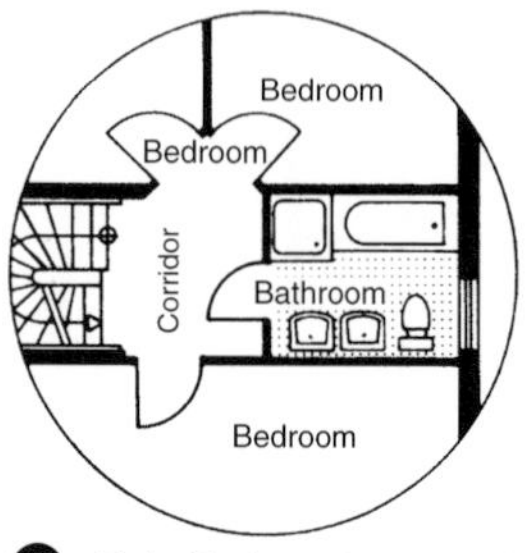

10 Typical bathroom in terraced house

Residential buildings

ROOMS
Access
Kitchens
Living areas
Bathrooms
Subsidiary rooms
Garages

see also:
Accessible building p. 21
Sound insulation p. 477

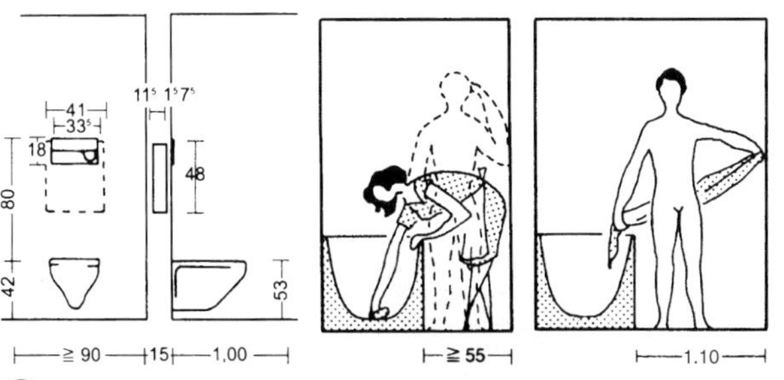

❶ Space requirements in bathroom (guideline values). Room between bath and wall

38
45
17
51
65
53
30
105
50
1,70
30

❷ In the shower At the washbasin Bathing and sitting

Details and fitting out

The former standard valid for movement areas in bathrooms was withdrawn without replacement in 2007, because it inadequately considered the requirements of disabled people. The dimensions given here should therefore be considered as absolute minimums. **The movement areas in bathrooms should generally be based on the 'Accessible building' standard → ⓫ → p. 21 ff.**

The basic bathroom categories are: (guest) **WCs** with WC and washbasin → ❸ – ❹, **shower rooms** with shower and basin → ❺ – ❻, **bathrooms** with bath, washbasin and WC → ❼ – ❽, **full bathrooms** with bath, shower, washbasin and WC → ❿.

Because of the high humidity and resulting **condensation**, the surfaces must be **easy to clean**. Wall and ceiling plaster should be able to absorb and release enough moisture. Floor coverings should be sufficiently **slip-resistant**. If there is no laundry room, the bathroom must be designed with space and connections for a **washing machine**, washer/dryer and laundry basket.

One **earthed socket** is to be provided (next to the mirror). In addition, the following should be included in the design of bathrooms and WCs: cupboards for towels and cleaning materials, lockable medicine cabinet, towel rail (perhaps with additional heating), hand grips above the bath.

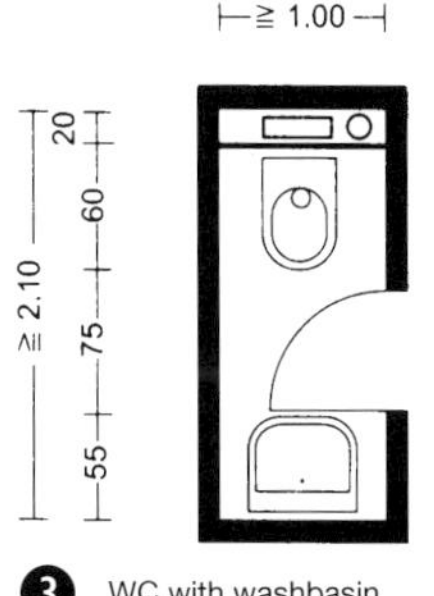
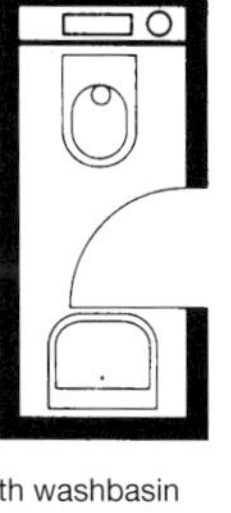

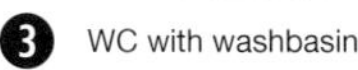

❸ WC with washbasin

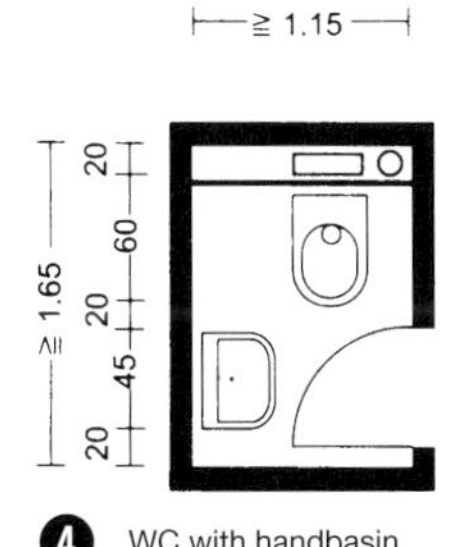

❹ WC with handbasin

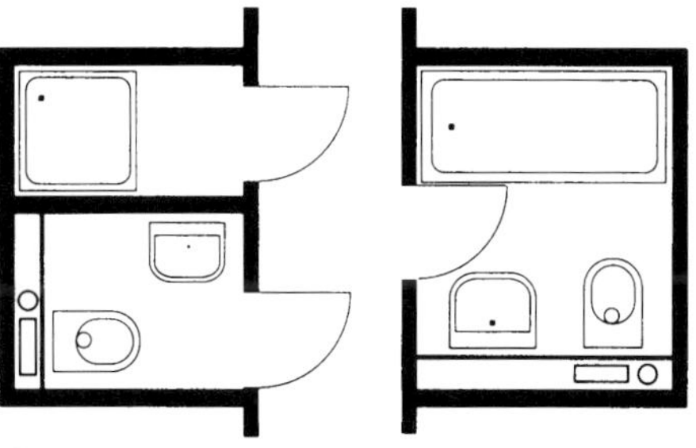

❾ Functional split of the bathroom into separate rooms

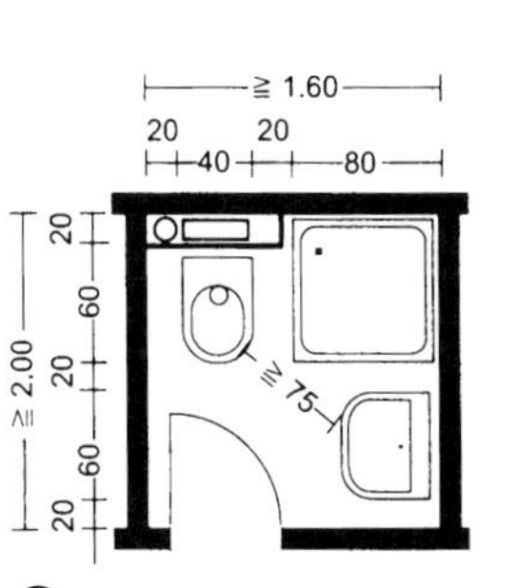

❺ Space required for shower

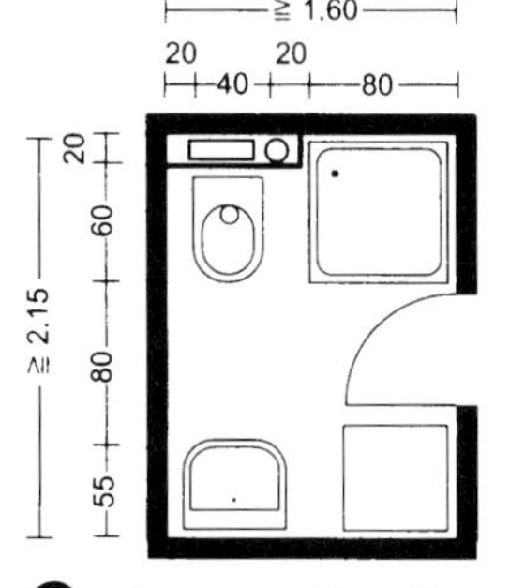

❻ Shower room with washing machine

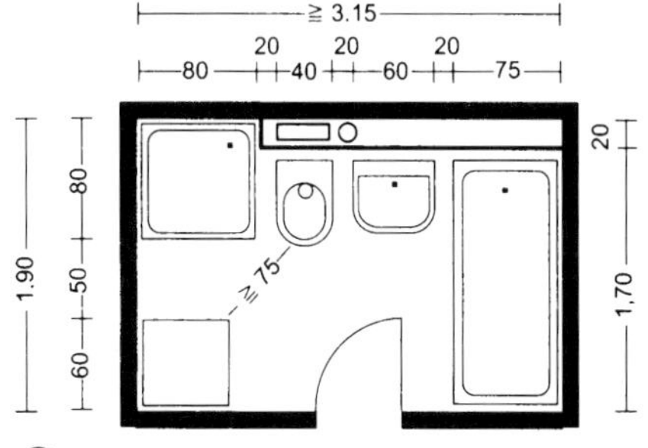

❿ Full bathroom with space for washing machine

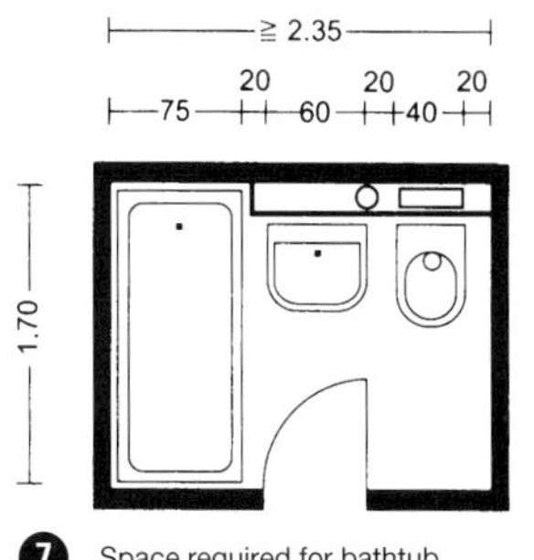

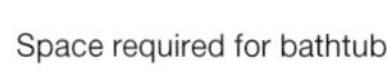

❼ Space required for bathtub

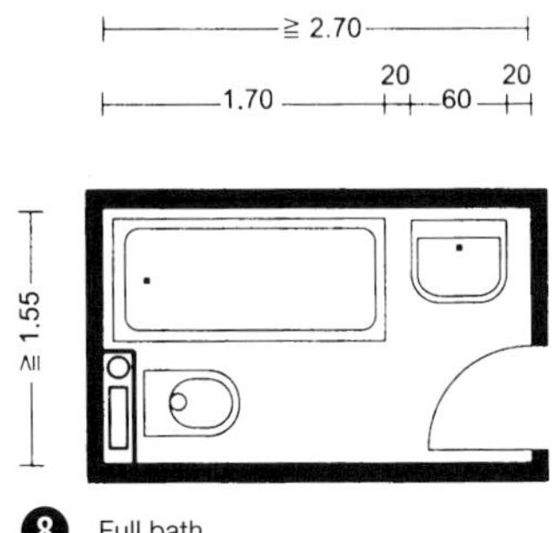

❽ Full bath

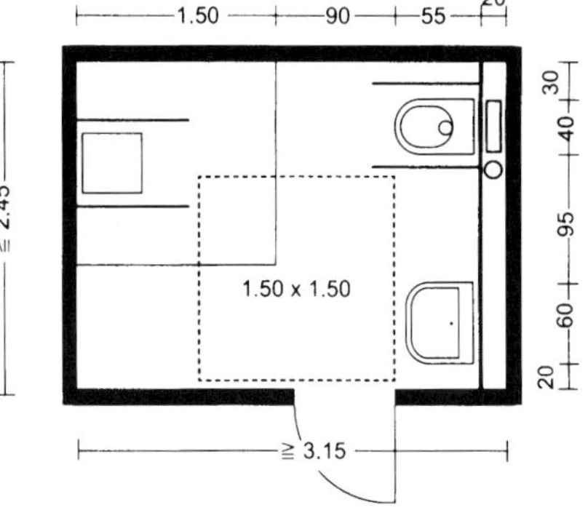

⓫ Accessible bathroom with showering space

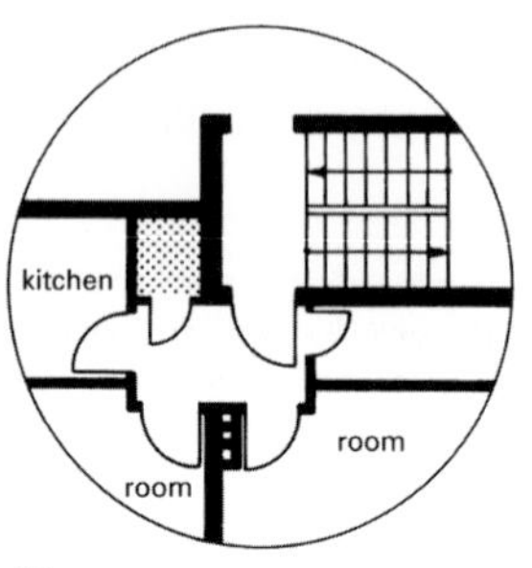

❶ Storeroom on internal corridor

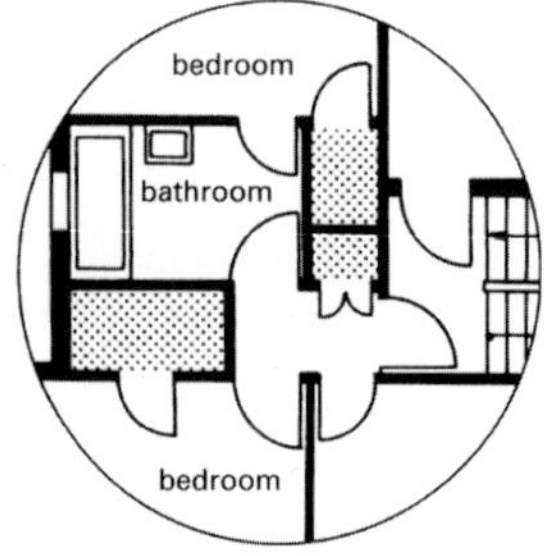

❷ Storage spaces in the corridor and bedrooms

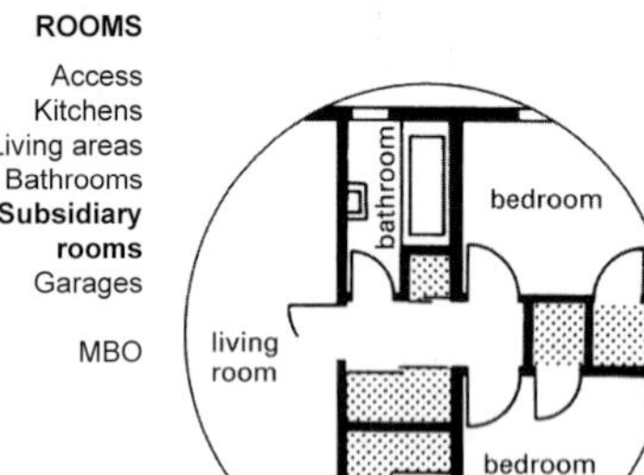

❸ Storage and cupboard spaces

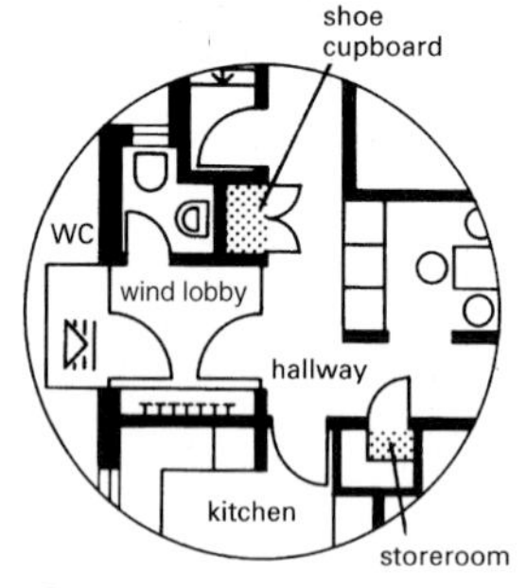

❹ Storeroom and shoe cupboard in the entrance area

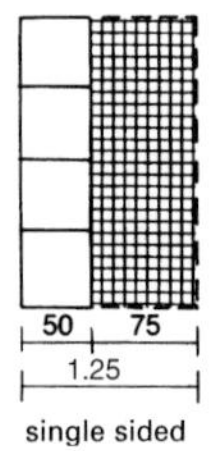

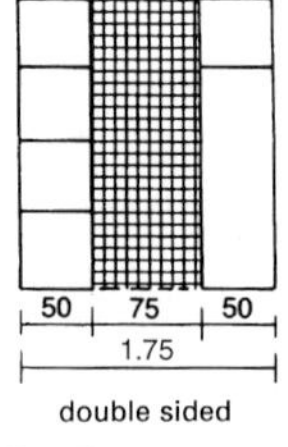

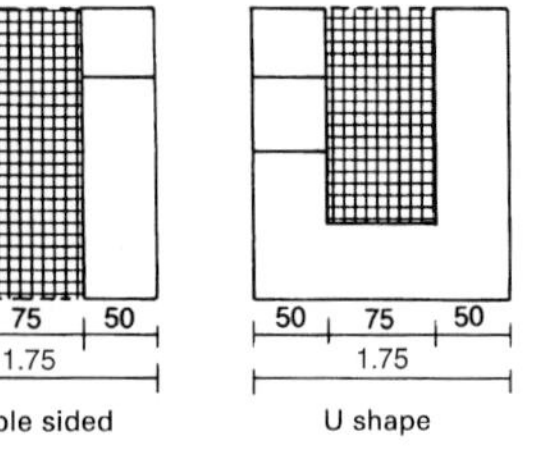

❺ Larders → ❻ – ⓭

Storerooms

Storerooms are used for keeping and storing cleaning equipment, tools, cleaning agents, shopping baskets, and bulky items like bags, suitcases, washing baskets and stepladders. Sufficiently large storerooms, particularly in flats, make a considerable contribution to comfort. **The building regulations require that every flat or house be provided with a sufficiently large storeroom.**

In addition to cellar and attic areas in a property, storage space should therefore be provided within a flat of ≧**1 m²** with a clear width of 75 cm. In larger flats, **2% of the floor area** should be provided as storage space (split into many small areas is also acceptable). It is practical to locate a part of this storage area near the kitchen.

Storage rooms can be in the form of niches (for built-in cupboards) or box rooms → ❶ – ❹. Doors to storerooms should open outward for reasons of space. The light inside the room should be operated by a contact switch by the door. Good ventilation should be provided.

Larder, pantry

When designing a flat or house, a larder (or pantry) should be installed in addition to the general provision of storage space, despite the additional space required, with shelves to the ceiling. This is for the storage of supplies of food and drink, as well as fresh foodstuffs which keep relatively well; space can thus be saved space in the refrigerator. Basic layouts of larders → ❺. It is most practical when the larder is next to the kitchen. It should be cool, ventilated and protected from direct sunlight → ❻ – ⓭. If required, a socket for a freezer should be provided, and possibly also a wine cooler.

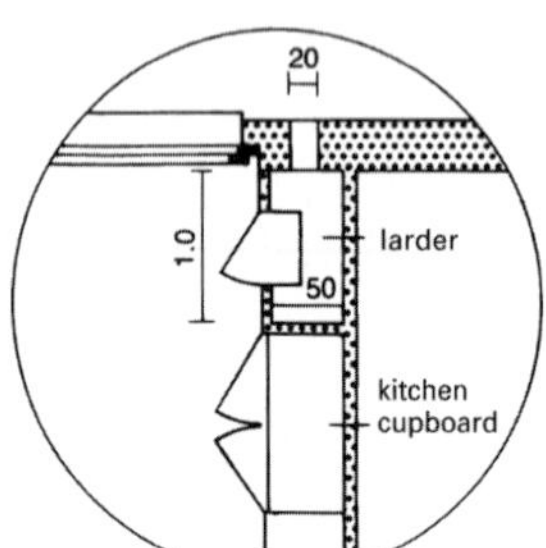

❻ Larder next to cupboard

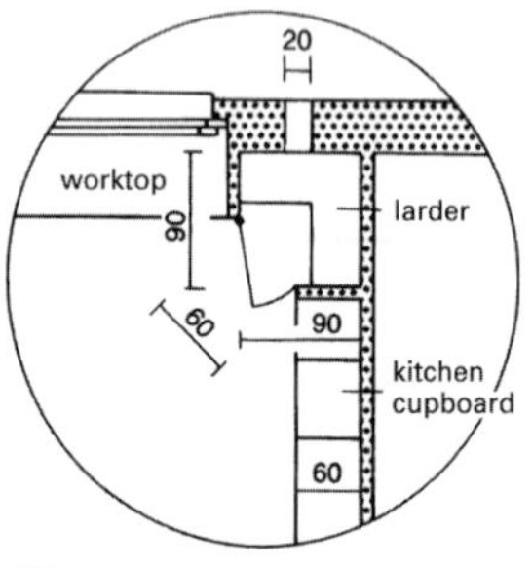

❼ Corner larder

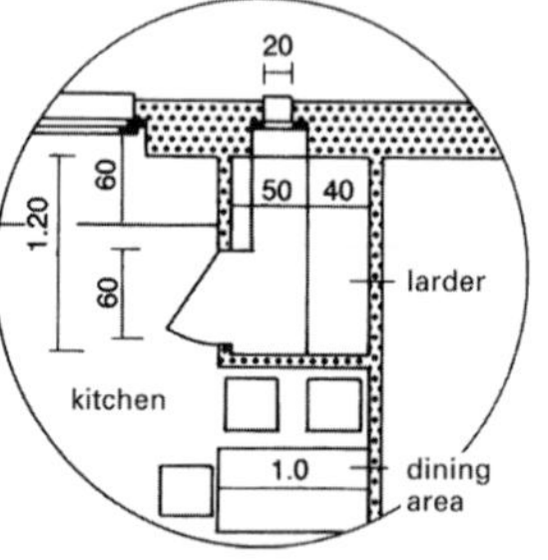

❿ Larder next to eating area

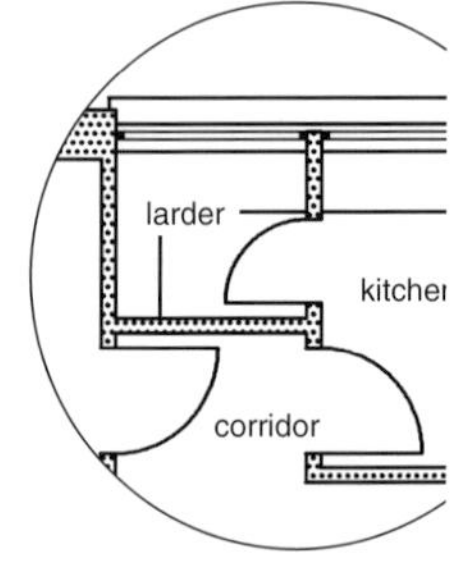

⓫ Larder with high-level window

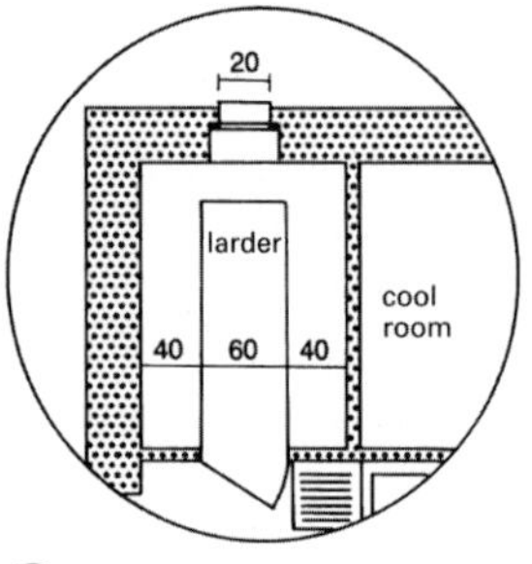

❽ Spacious larder

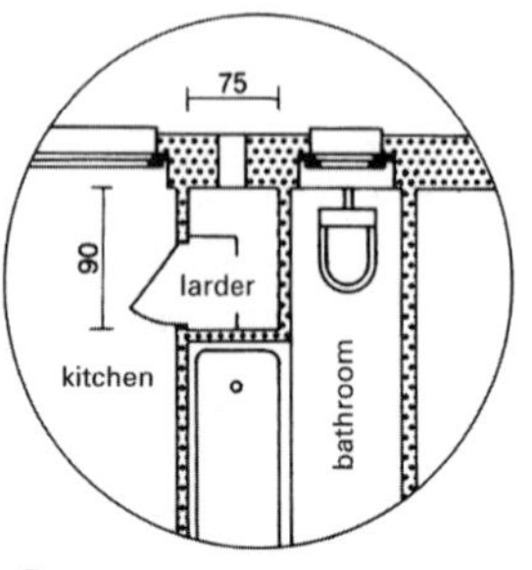

❾ Larder using space next to bath

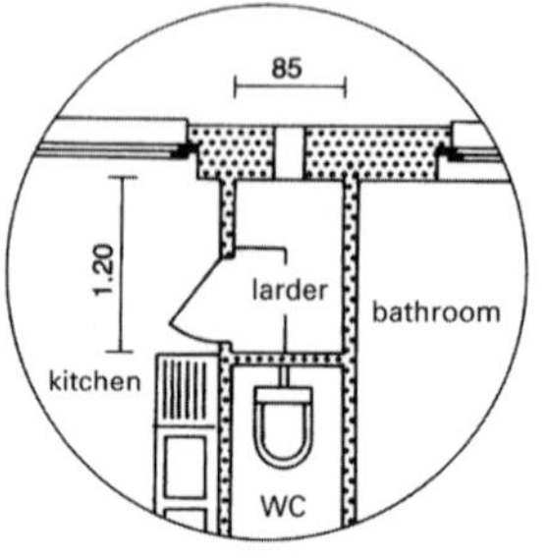

⓬ As before, next to WC

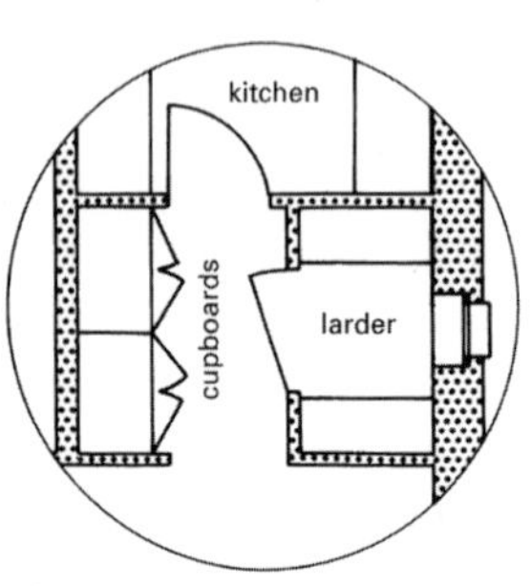

⓭ Larder in lobby to kitchen

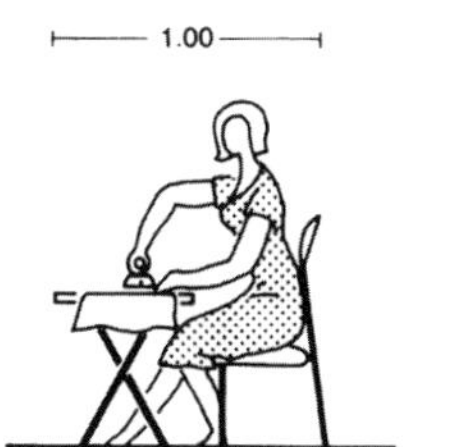

Space required for ironing while seated

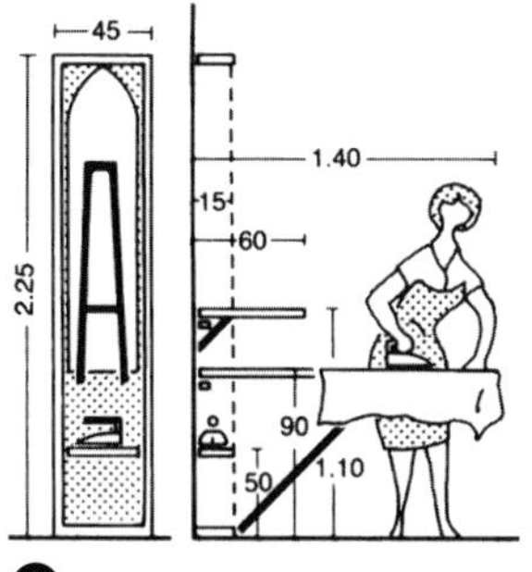
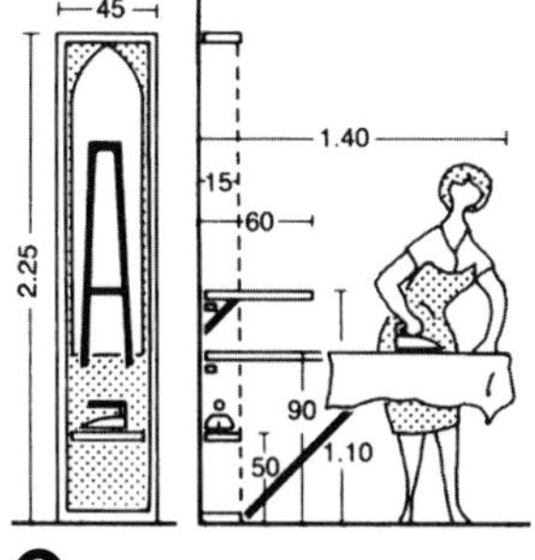
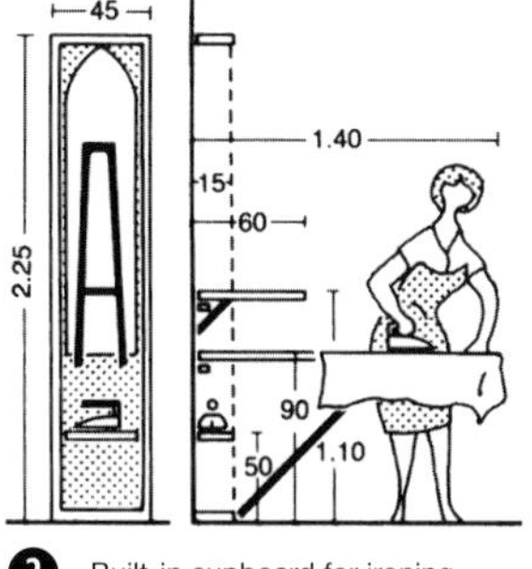

Built-in cupboard for ironing board

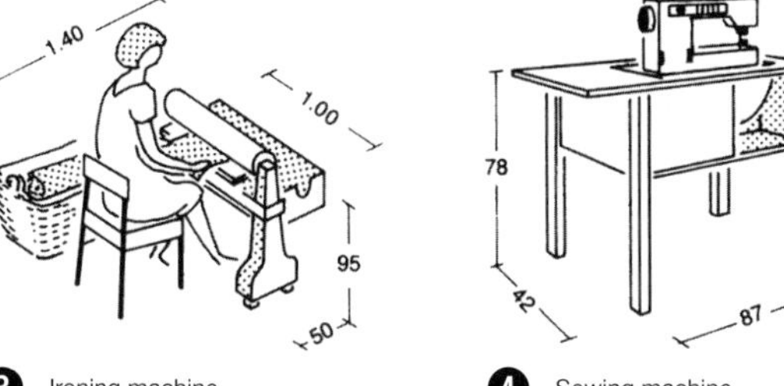

Ironing machine

Sewing machine

Laundry/utility rooms

Laundry/utility rooms are used to carry out domestic work like washing and drying clothes, ironing and sewing. They can also be storage rooms for small items of equipment, detergents, cleaning agents and polishes, buckets and vacuum cleaners, tools and ladders. The provision of a laundry/utility room is particularly useful in flats, despite the additional space required.

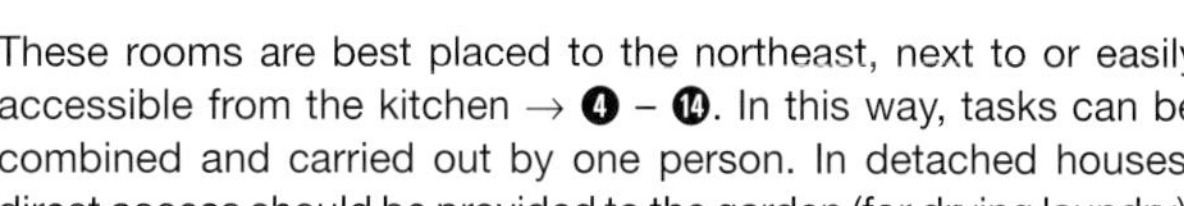

These rooms are best placed to the northeast, next to or easily accessible from the kitchen → ❹ – ⓮. In this way, tasks can be combined and carried out by one person. In detached houses, direct access should be provided to the garden (for drying laundry).

In the design of utility rooms, a comfortable and healthy arrangement of appliances is important: An ironing board used in the standing position requires a different height to one that is used seated → ❶ – ❸. A fully adjustable ironing board is ideal. A worktop of 1.20 m width should be provided to deal with the washing. Good uniform lighting is required in the working area of the laundry/utility room (average light intensity ≈ 350 lx).

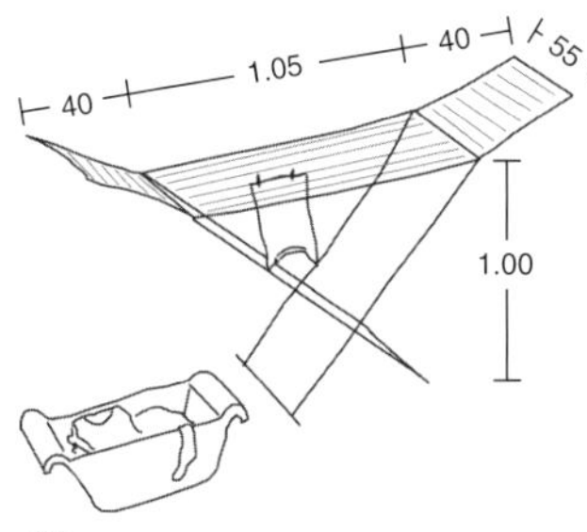

Space required for clothes horse

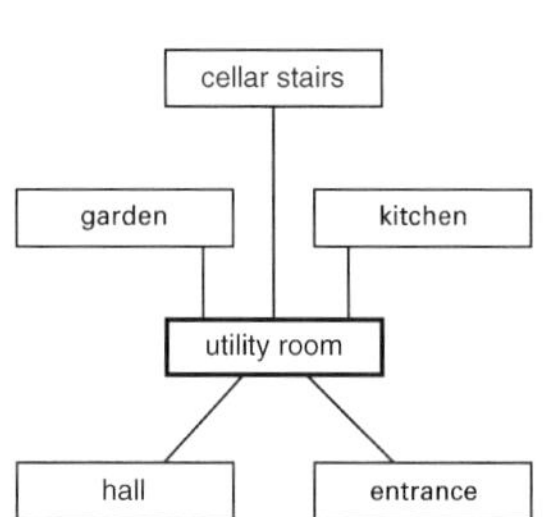

Scheme of relationships of rooms to the laundry/utility room

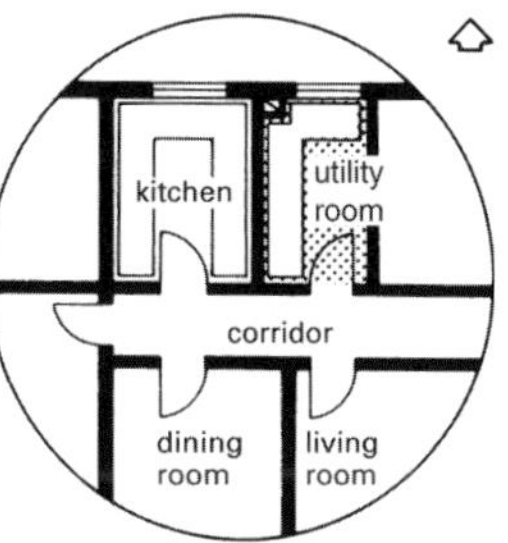

Next to the kitchen, accessible from the corridor

Accessible from the kitchen

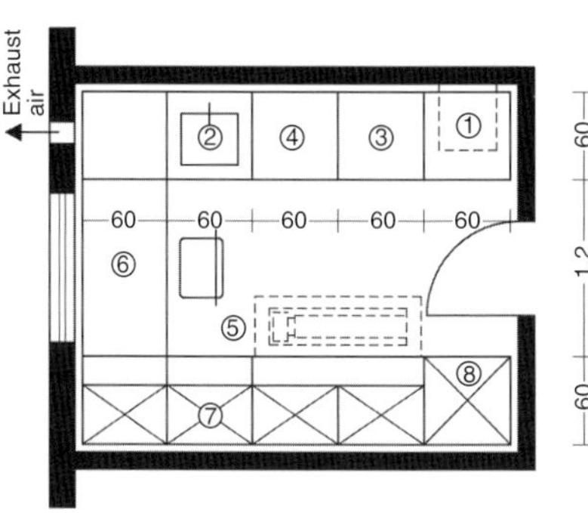

U-shaped laundry/utility room

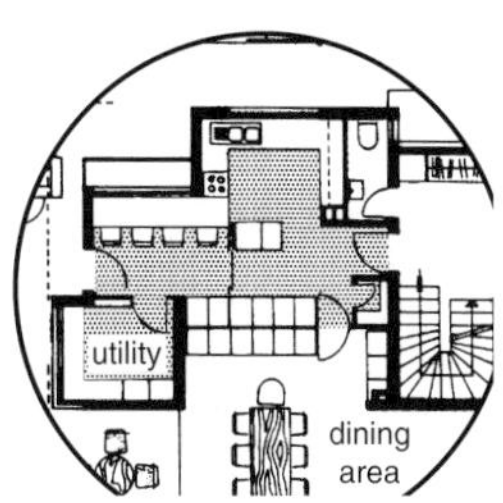

Kitchen–eating area–laundry/utility room

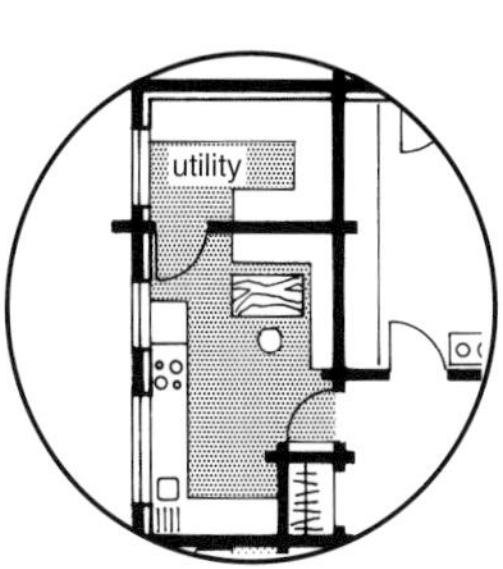

Next to eating area

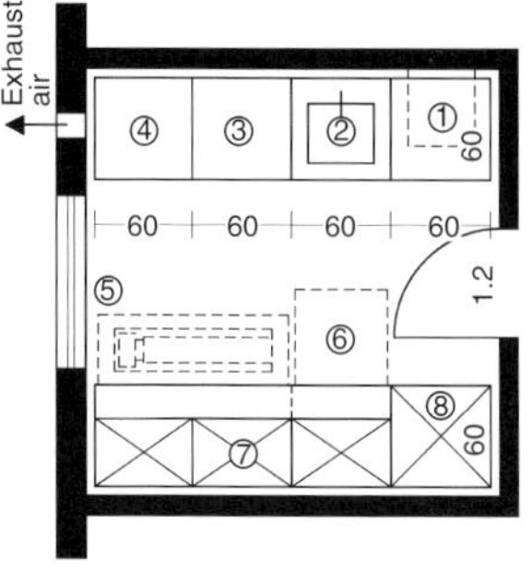

Two-lane laundry/utility room

Equipment and appliances	Width (cm)	Better
automatic washing machine and washer/ dryer above each other	60	60
washbasin with water heater	60	60
laundry basket	50	60
washing worktop	60	120
ironing machine	approx. 100	100
cupboard space for minor equipment	50	60
total	approx. 380	460

Equipment and space required

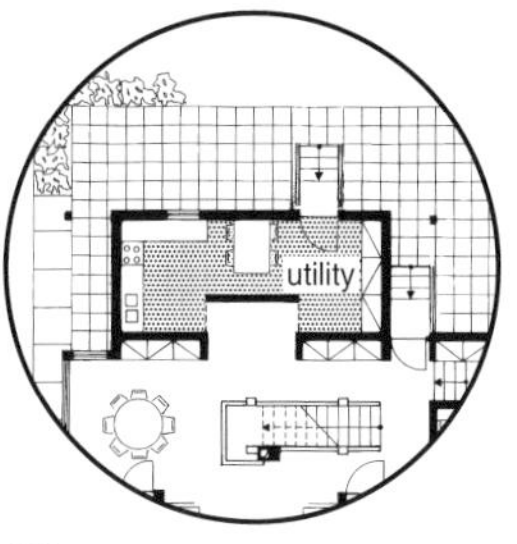

Kitchen–eating area–laundry/utility room

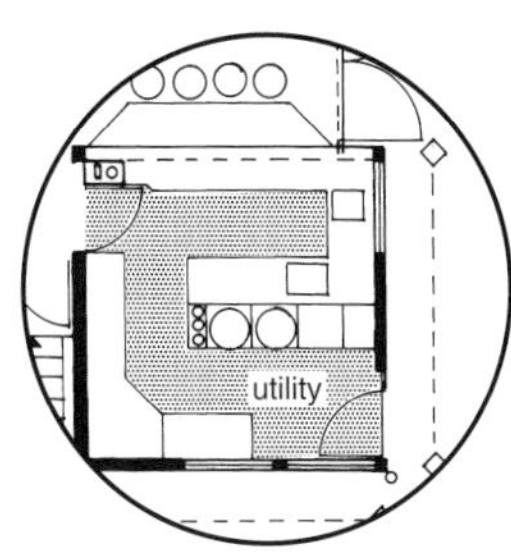

One-room kitchen and laundry/ utility room

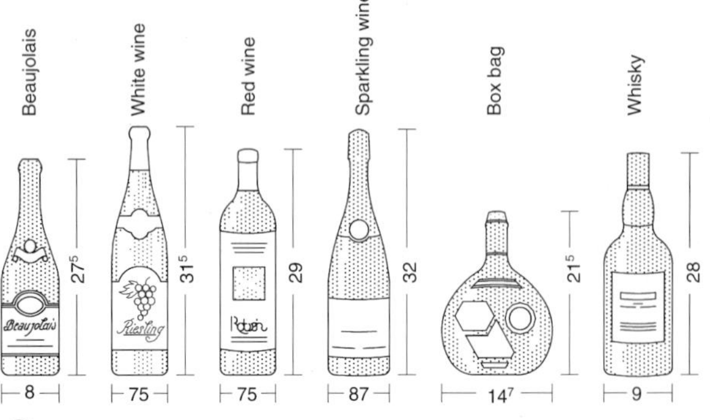

❶ Bottles

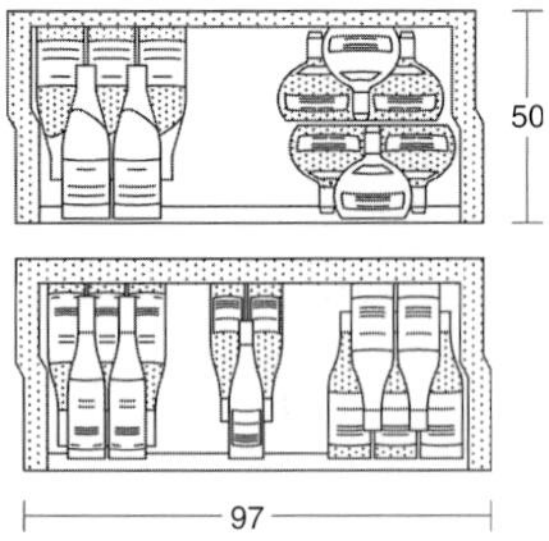

❷ Example of stacking in storage units → ❸

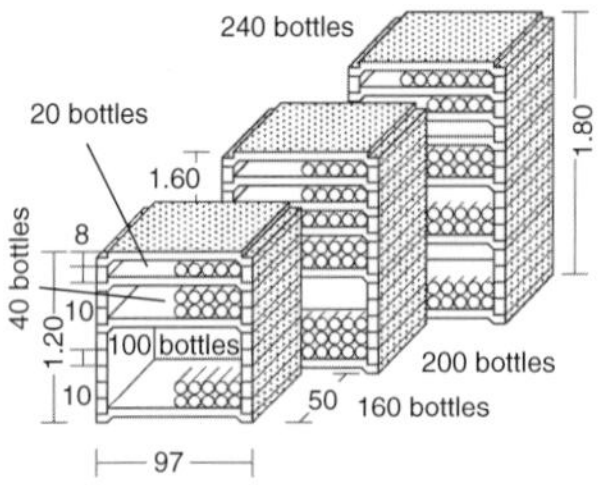

❸ Wine rack/breeze block

Wine cellars

Wine cellars should if possible be below ground on all sides. The location should be next to the house; the north side is recommended. Ideal conditions are 70% humidity, 10–12 °C. Wines age quicker with every degree above 12 °C. (Temperatures of 1–10 °C do not damage wine.) Such requirements can be met through the use of air conditioning, or an air-conditioned cupboard or door → ❿. When air conditioning is used, the ceiling and walls should be insulated. A sealed door (2.01 × 0.63 m) of coated and insulated steel plate should be installed. A porous, breathing floor, like sand or unglazed bricks, and brick walls provide natural humidity.

The room ventilation has to be regulated flexibly according to climate and time of year.

Lighting in a wine cellar should be as low as possible and only switched on when required. Storage shelves should be of porous, breathing materials, e.g. breeze block, quarried natural stone, sand-lime blocks or Hydroton expanded clay elements. This regulates the humidity and stabilises the temperature. A natural microclimate is created in the room → ❷ – ❼.

On account of the temperature graduation, sparkling wines should be stored near the floor, white wines in the middle and red wines as high as possible → ❾ + ⓫.

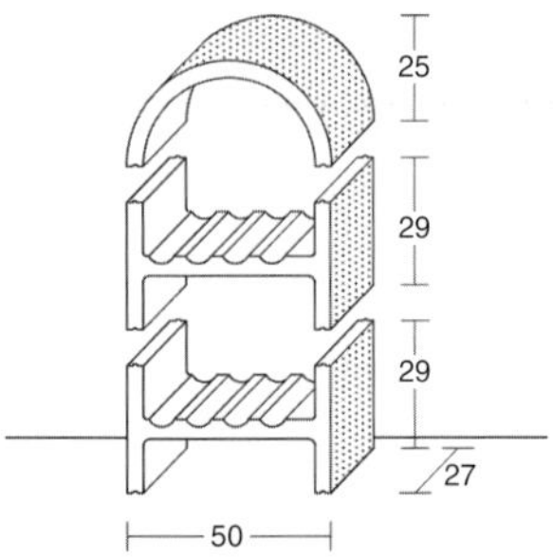

❹ Wine rack of quarried natural stone

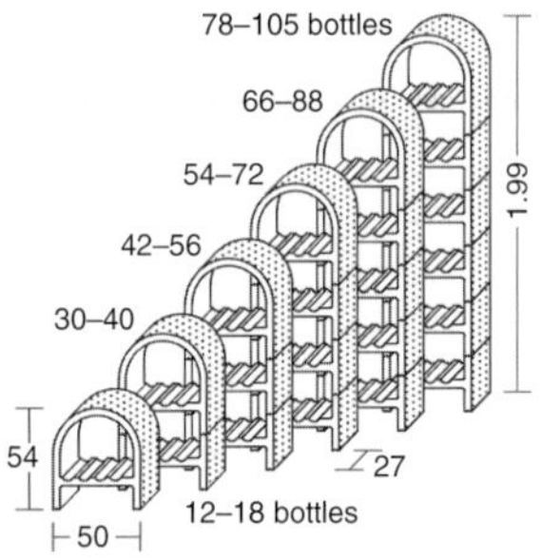

❺ Rack heights → ❹

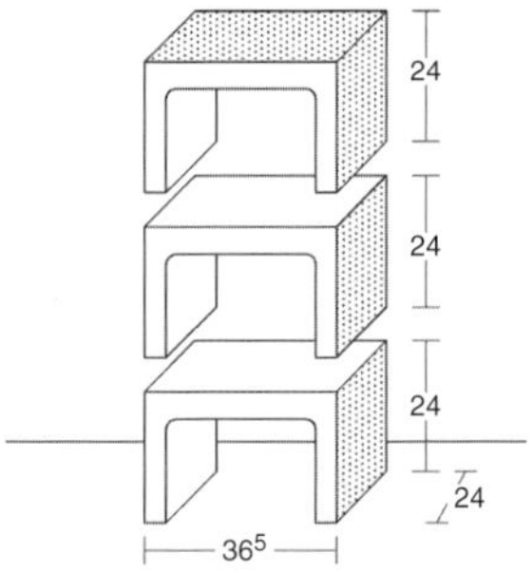

❻ Sand-lime rack blocks

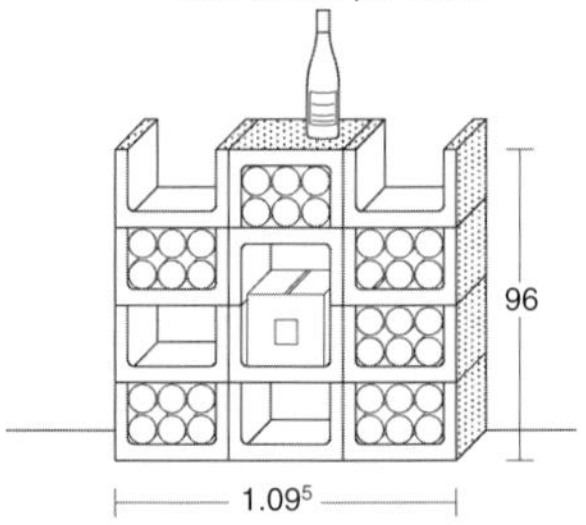

❼ Inspection rack → ❻

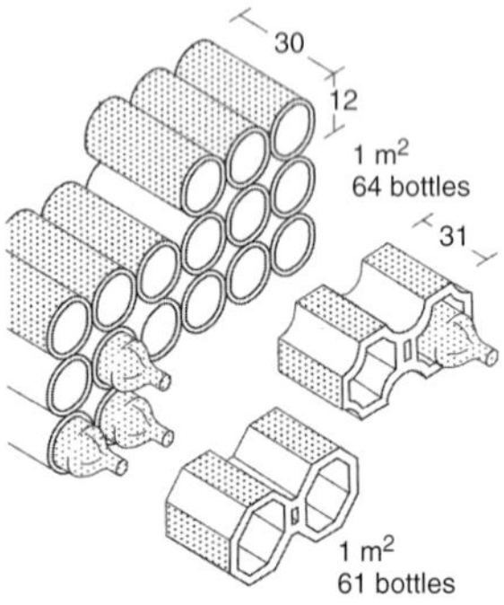

❽ Clay tubes and ornamental blocks

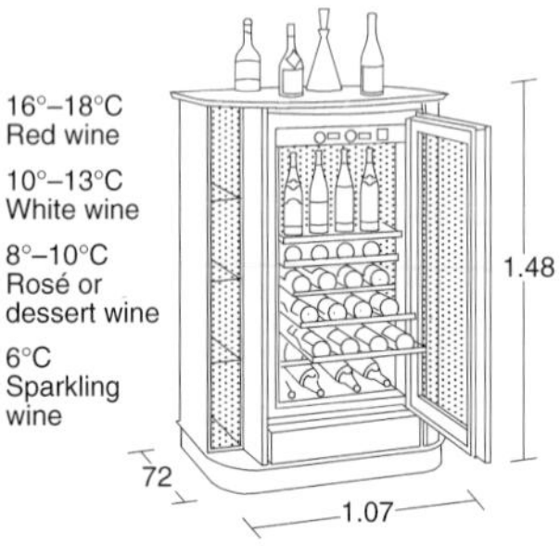

❾ Air-conditioned cupboard for wine

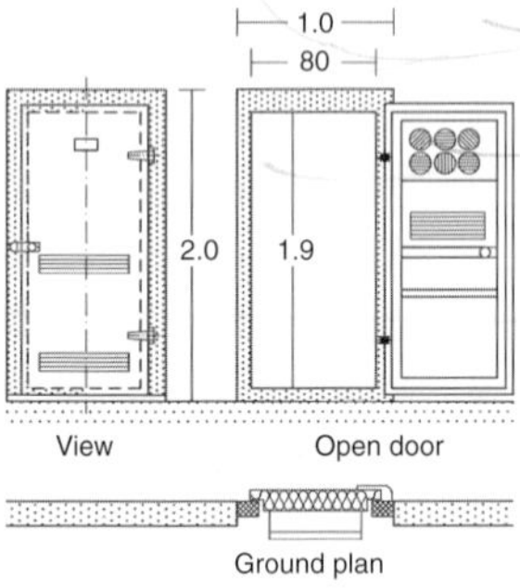

❿ Air-conditioned door for wine

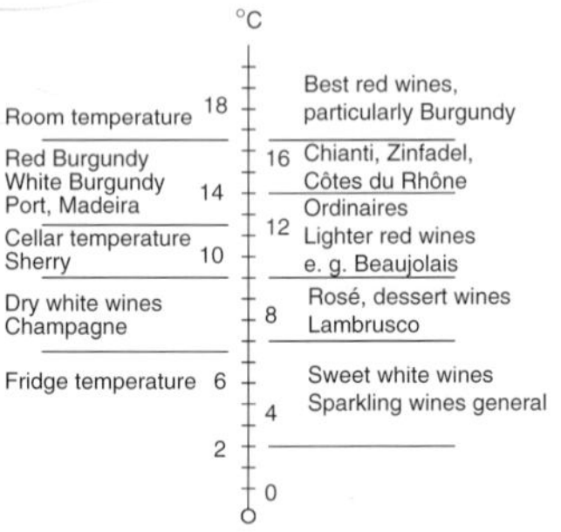

⓫ Storage temperatures for wines

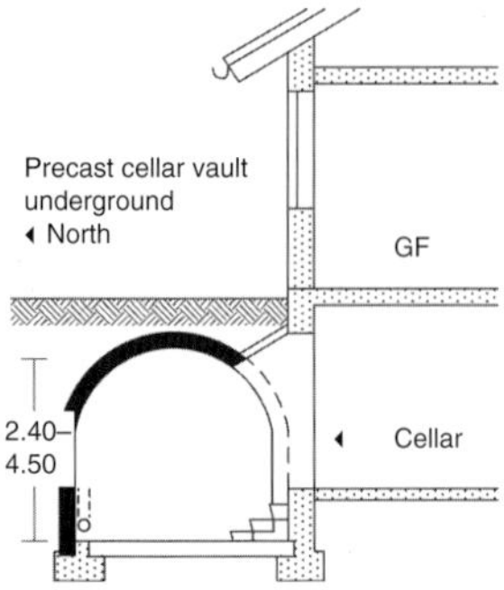

⓬ Vaulted cellar

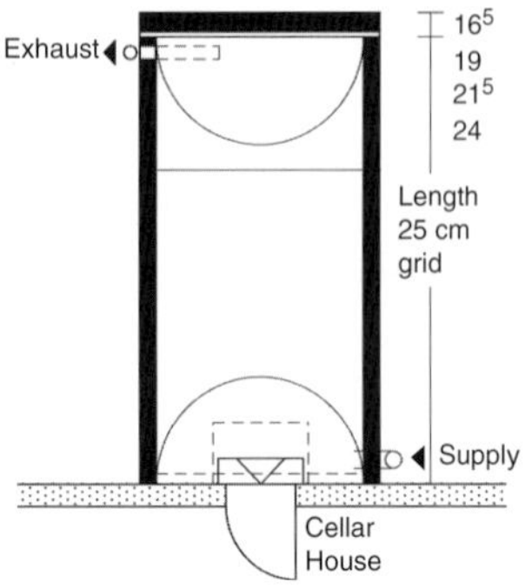

⓭ Plan → ⓬

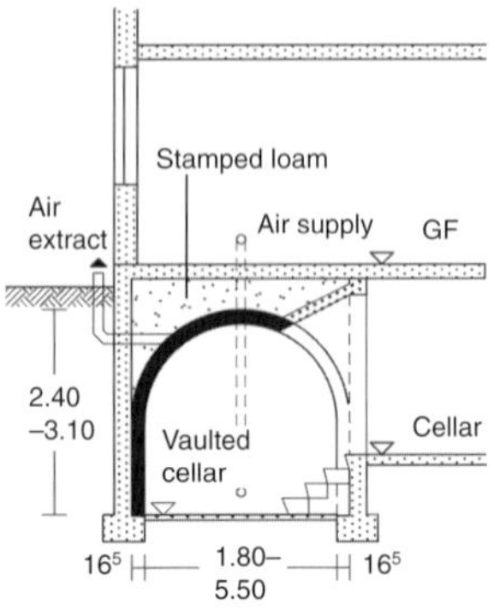

⓮ Installed in a cellar

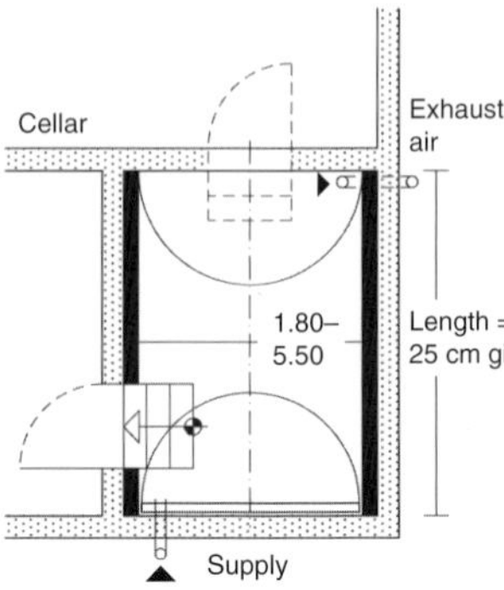

⓯ Plan → ⓮

Residential buildings

ROOMS
Access
Kitchens
Living areas
Bathrooms
Subsidiary rooms
Garages

MBO

see also:
Storerooms
p. 162

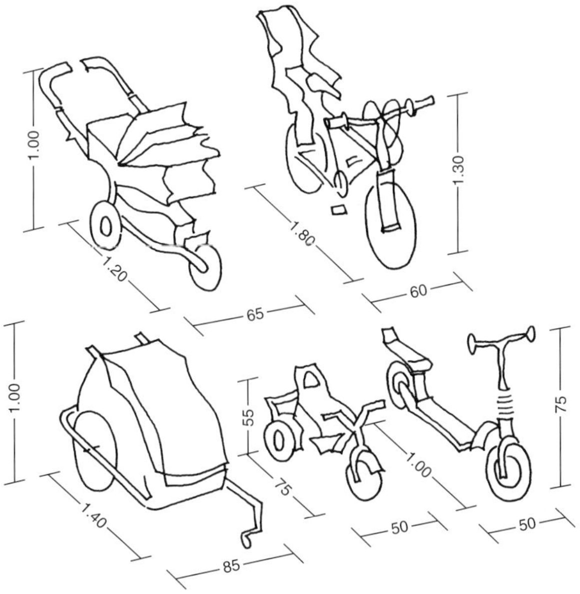

❶ Space required for bicycles, prams, pushchairs, bicycle trailers, tricycles, mopeds etc.

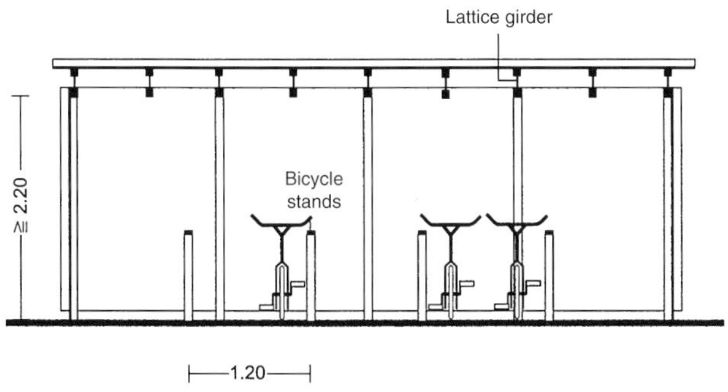

❷ Section → ❸

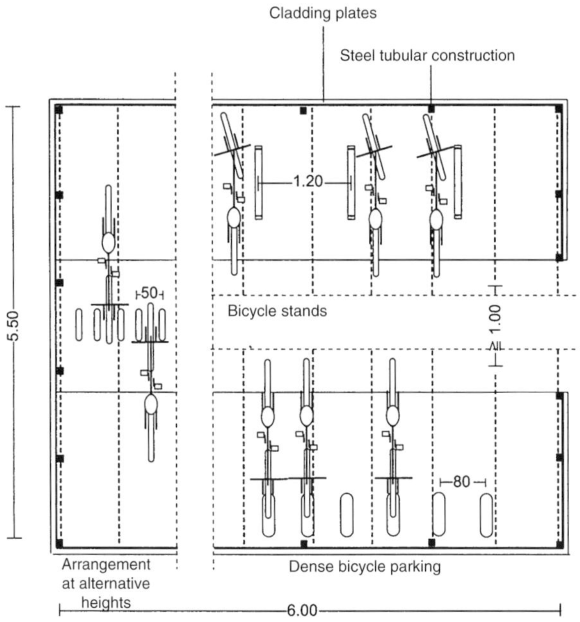

❸ Bicycle/pram room for about 20 vehicles (example)

Communal storerooms

In addition to the storerooms or storage spaces in each flat, for residential buildings in building classes 3–5, the building regulations require an easily accessible (communal) storeroom for prams, pushchairs and bicycles. Corresponding areas should also be provided in other residential buildings and detached houses.

For the design of these rooms, it can be assumed that at least one vehicle per occupant (including children) has to be accommodated. In addition to bicycles, prams and pushchairs, it is also necessary to consider mopeds, tricycles, trailers etc. → ❶.

The rooms should if possible be located at street level, be lockable and equipped with hooks and bicycle stands to secure the stored vehicles. They can be laid out as storerooms inside the building (with access to the entrance) or as separate bicycle sheds → ❷ – ❸. A sufficient number of additional bicycle stands should be provided in the open air, particularly if the storeroom has been situated in the cellar.

Cellar

The storage space provided for each flat normally consists of a storeroom inside the flat → p. 162, and an additional space outside the flat. This is normally provided as a cellar compartment → ❹ – ❺, but can also be provided inexpensively as a parking shed in the grounds. Cellar storerooms should be dry and well ventilated. Natural lighting is to be recommended. Appropriate detailing of the window opening can optimise the light entering → ❹.

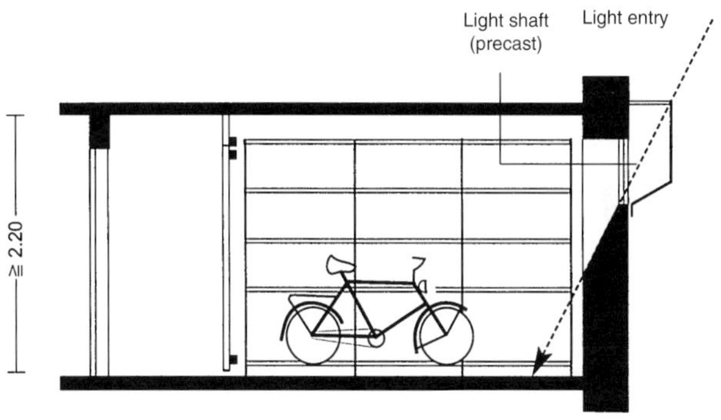

❹ Section → ❺

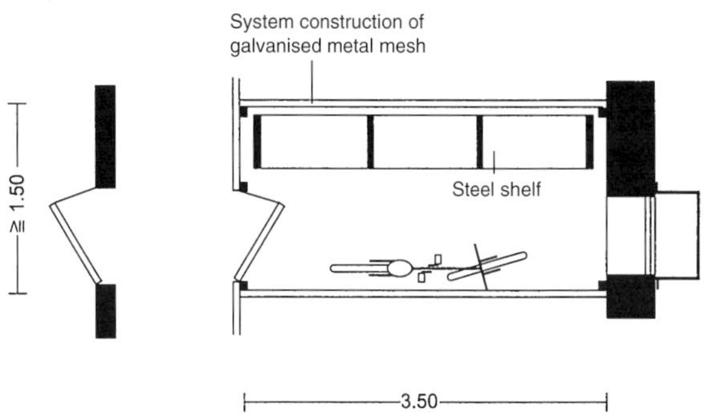

❺ Cellar compartment in a residential building (example)

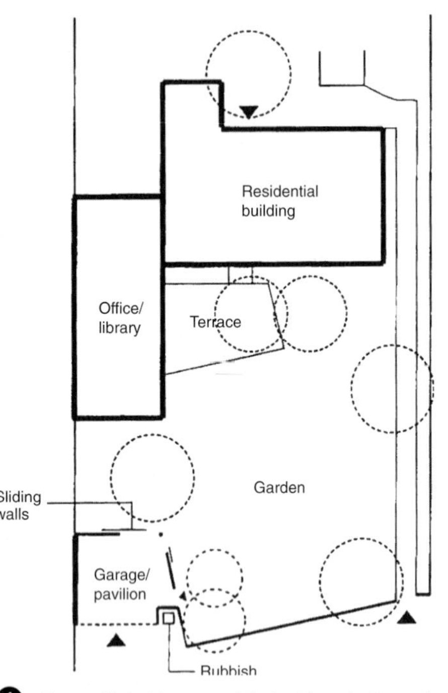

❶ House with double garage at the front (can also be used as a garden pavilion)
Arch.: Studio Paretaia

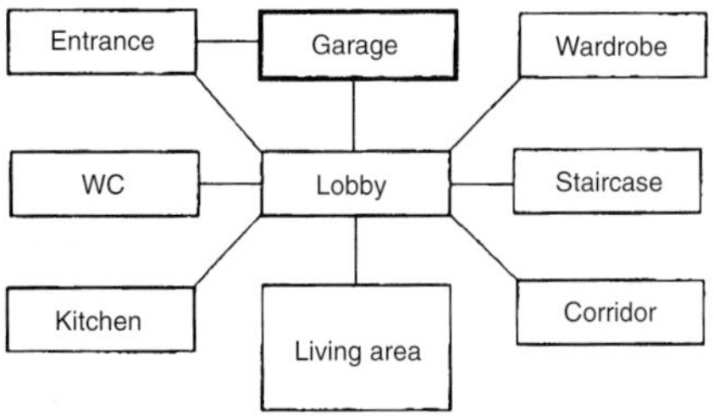

According to the building regulations, the necessary parking spaces must be provided **in the grounds** of the residential building itself or in other suitable grounds at a reasonable distance where it is legal to park. The parking spaces are often provided as **single** or **double garages** or **car parks**, free-standing or attached to the building.

Space requirement → ❼ – ⓬. A reduction in the parking area is possible for private houses. The tendency of modern cars to get larger (including in height) should be taken into account.

In addition to garages, roofed-over parking places (**carports**) represent a cheaper, more beneficial in terms of building physics (no condensation in cold cars in the winter!) and space-saving possibility for protecting cars adequately from the weather (a close wall on the weather side is a good idea). A combination with enclosed storerooms (for bicycles etc.) is to be recommended → ⓫. Carports are particularly suitable for communal parking places → ⓬.

Examples of the layout and design of parking places for cars in connection with residential buildings → ❸ – ❼.

❷ Relationship between the garage and other areas of the house

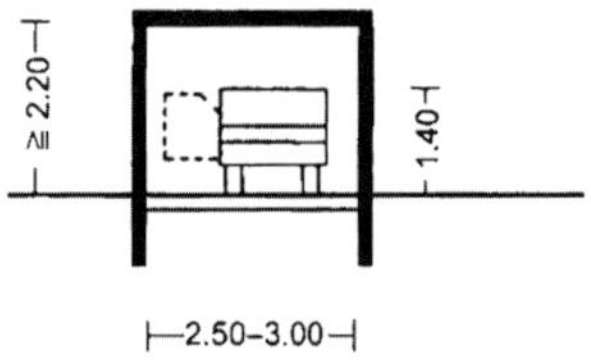

❼ Section → ❾

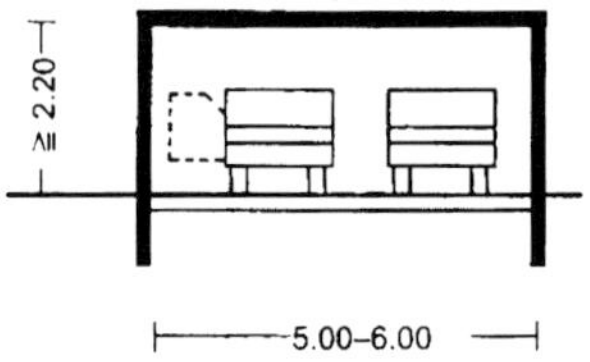

❽ Section → ❿

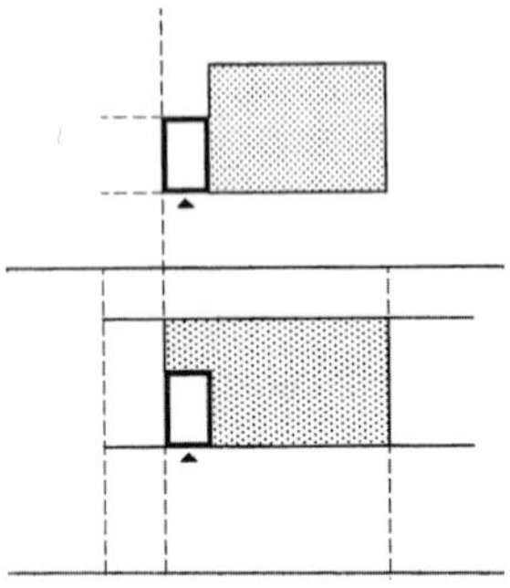

❸ Garage next to or in a detached house

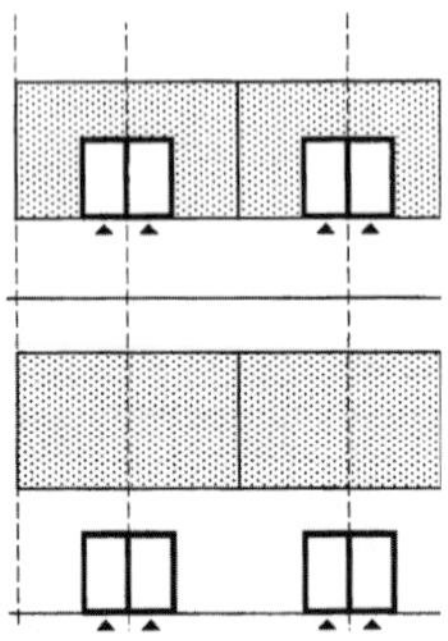

❹ Garages next to or in terraced houses

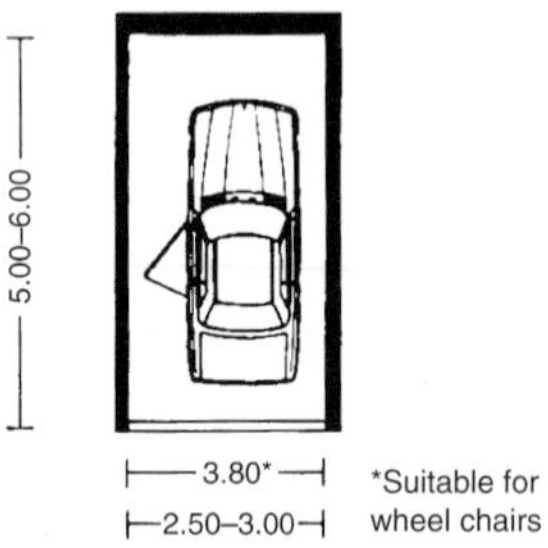

❾ Single garage

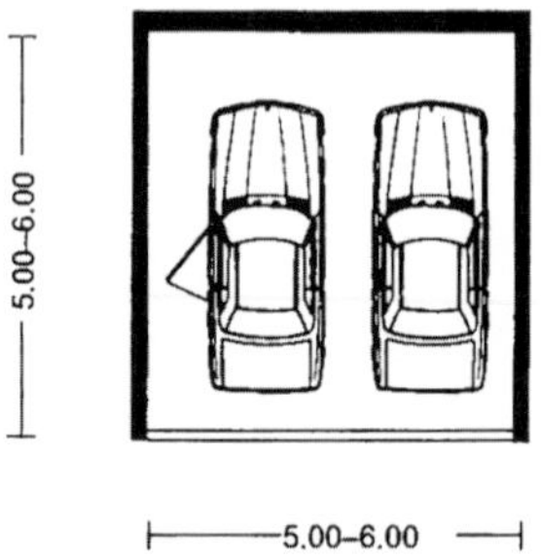

❿ Double garage

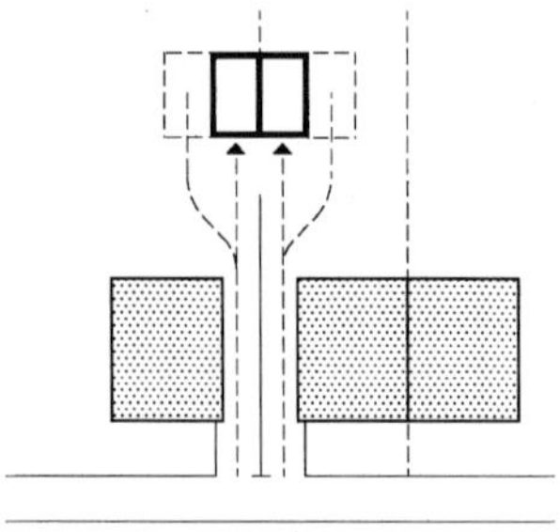

❺ Garage at the back of the plot

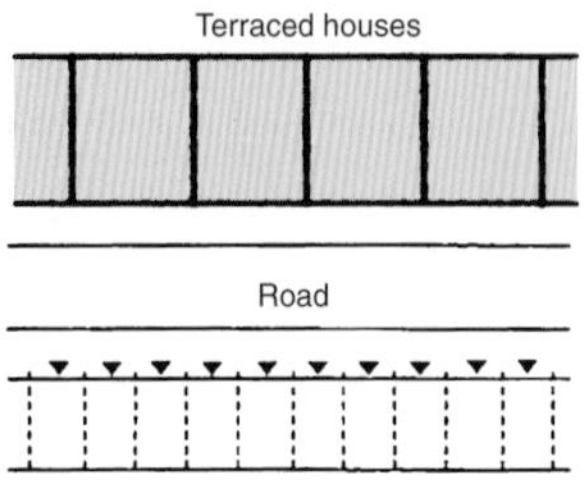

❻ Communal parking spaces

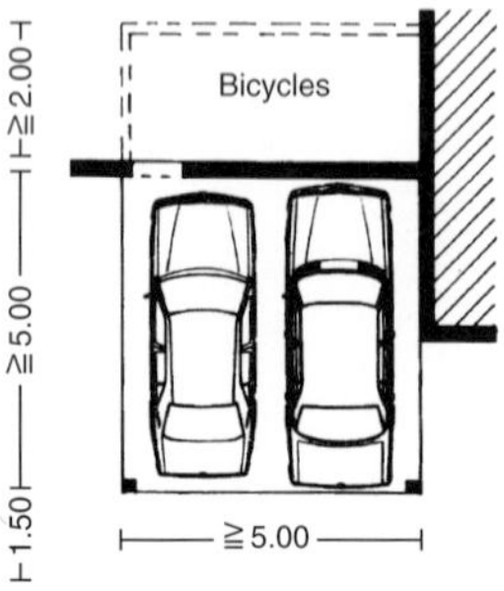

⓫ Carport for two cars and possibly bicycles

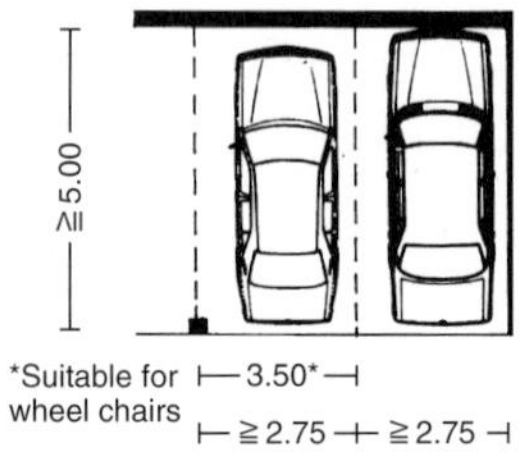

⓬ Carport as communal parking place

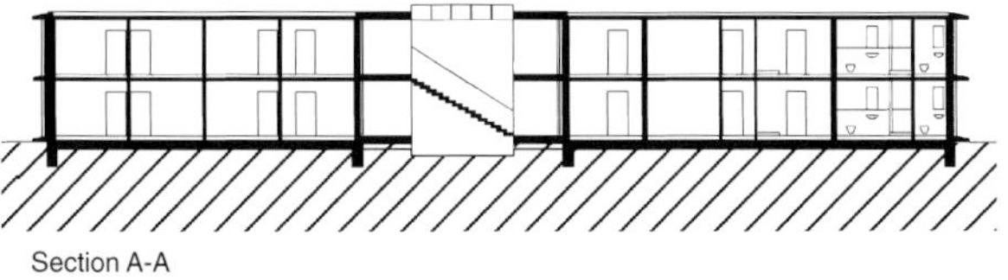

❶ Student residence in Halle/Saale — Arch.: Gemot Schulz in: Hillebrandt + Schulz, Cologne

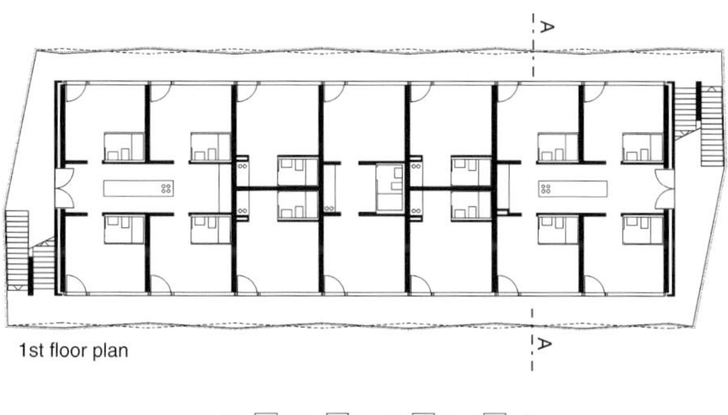

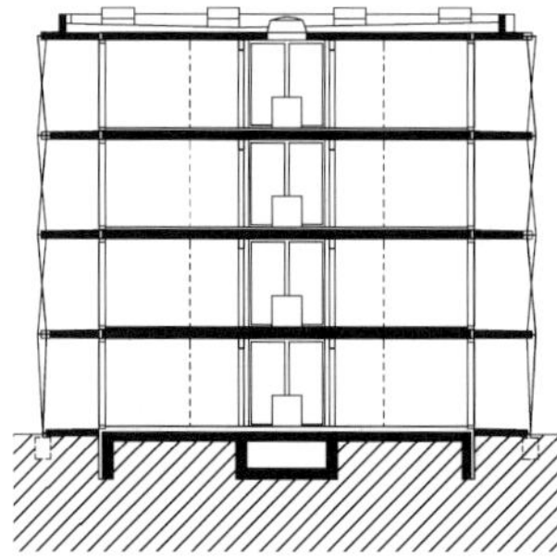

❷ Student residence in Garching — Arch.: Fink und Jocher, Munich

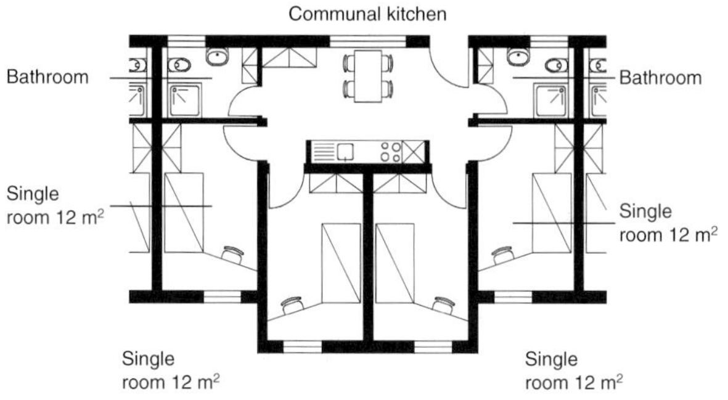

❸ Shared flat with single rooms, communal bathrooms and central communal kitchen

Halls of residence are normally provided near colleges and universities for students and are normally built and operated in various architectural forms (20–30 units in courtyard layout or groups of open structures, large buildings with 80 or more units). They are used for the accommodation of students for the duration of their course. The size and equipping of the rooms is often very limited. Options such as single rooms, (double) flats and flat sharing groups have proved successful. The arrangement and design of the communal areas within and around the residences are decisive for their acceptance.

STUDENT RESIDENCES

MBO

State guidelines for student residences

Requirements
Student flats are '**living places**' and not considered as residential homes in the sense of the building regulations. The general requirements of the building regulations essentially concern residential rooms with minimum requirements for floor area (8 m^2), ceiling height (2.40 m), orientation, ventilation and lighting (window area $\frac{1}{8}$ of the room area), accessibility requirements (i.e. for disabled people) and escape routes (two independent escape routes from each floor, one of which is a legally essential stairway). The **state guidelines for student residences** set recommended dimensions for living places (approx. 12 m^2 for single rooms and approx. 16 m^2 for flats). In addition to this, a certain area will be required for communal use.

Forms of living
These can be categorised into **flat sharing** → ❷ – ❸ and **individual rooms** → ❹ – ❻.

When flats are shared, the communal area is of more importance, similar to a home. A group of rooms (4–8) with some functions transferred to the communal area (kitchen, bathroom) has a **linear** → ❷ or **central** → ❸ type of layout. Single rooms located along a corridor with communal bathroom and kitchen form the classic (but anonymous) form of student residence. What has proved successful is the further development of the single room as flat → ❹ (room with shower room and perhaps kitchenette) and the double flat → ❺ – ❻ (two rooms with communal kitchen and bath). This latter form of residence can be used very flexibly by singles and also by couples (with child).

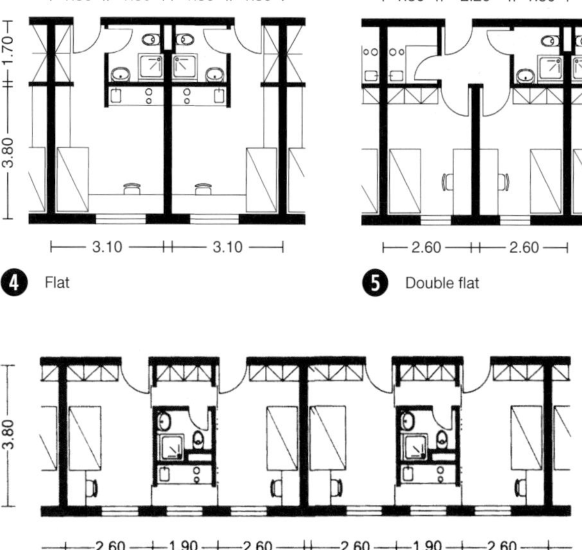

❹ Flat

❺ Double flat

❻ Double flat with communal bathroom, kitchen and cupboard zone

ELDERLY PEOPLE'S ACCOMMODATION

Retirement Flats

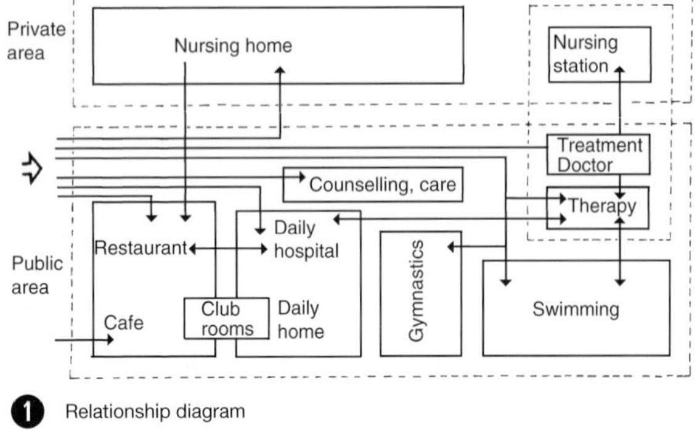

❶ Relationship diagram

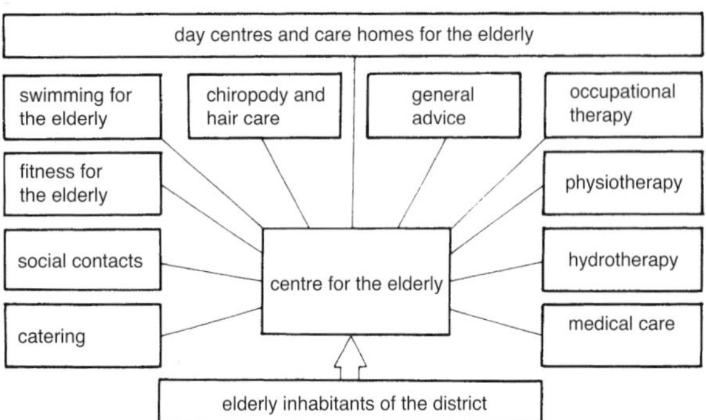

❷ Functions of a centre for the elderly

❸ One-person retirement flat, 40 m²

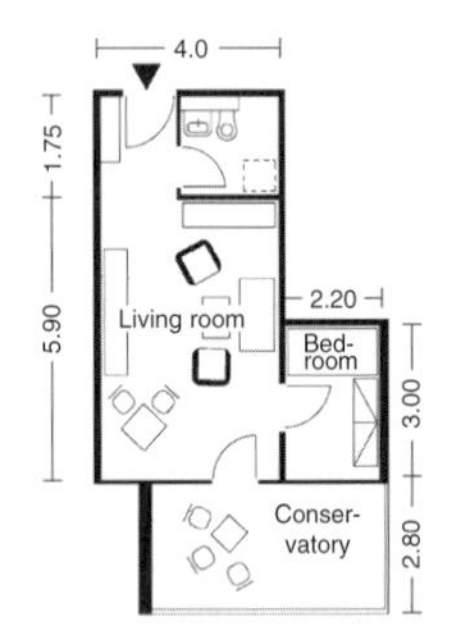

❹ One-person retirement flat, 37 m²

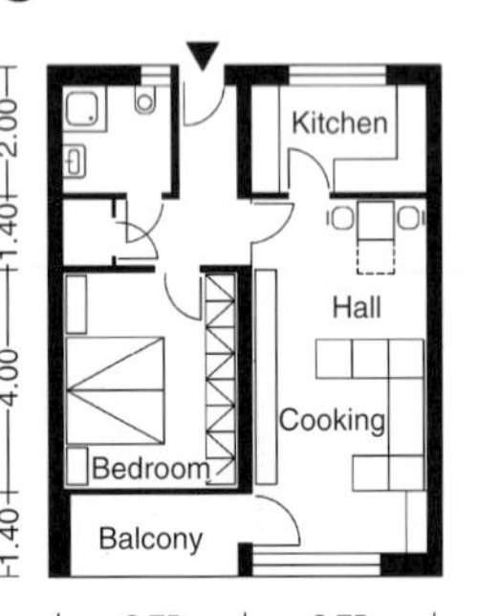

❺ Two person retirement flat, 58 m²

❻ Two-person retirement flat, 55.5 m²

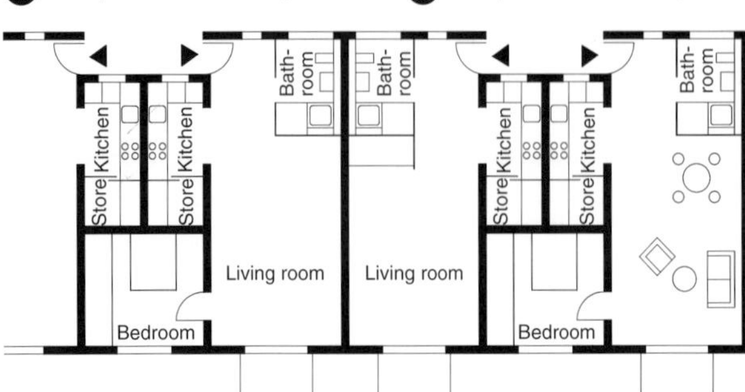

❼ Retirement flats

Accommodation for elderly people

A **retirement flat** → ❸ – ❽ is a self-contained flat which takes the needs of elderly people into account, so that they can live as independently as possible and not in an old people's home. Such housing is usually scattered around residential areas, with a density of 2–10%. One-person flat 25–35 m², two-person flat 45–55 m² with weather-protected balconies ≧3 m², min. depth 1.40 m, balcony door without threshold.

Assisted flats for the elderly (≧20 m² per flat) are in a building, supplemented by communal rooms with tea kitchen. Convenient if sited in the vicinity of a care home for the elderly with facilities for dining, recreation, relaxation and therapy. Features a nursing support point with ward bath, therapeutic work room, central washing-up kitchen and cleaning room. One car parking space per 5–8 occupants. Heating 2% above normal. Support of outpatient services for the elderly.

Home for the elderly with residential living and care facilities. According to the law concerning such homes, there are stringent regulations on planning, licensing and operation. The large ancillary areas mean that an economic size is about 120 places with the provision of care, function and therapy rooms. There is an integrated care department for short-term care. General fitting out: stair steps 16/30 cm without underlay, colour-highlighted step edges and handrails on both sides, also in the corridors. Lifts for moving patients on stretchers or in folding chairs. Accessible building standard applies. Location: as near as possible to town or village infrastructure and public transport.

Day centres for the elderly: function as meeting points and for outpatient care for independently living elderly people. Approx. 1600 elderly citizens per day centre. With meeting room (can be divided) up to 120 m², service and consulting room 20 m², rooms for movement and occupational therapies, changing rooms, group rooms, WCs, tea kitchen, bowling alley.

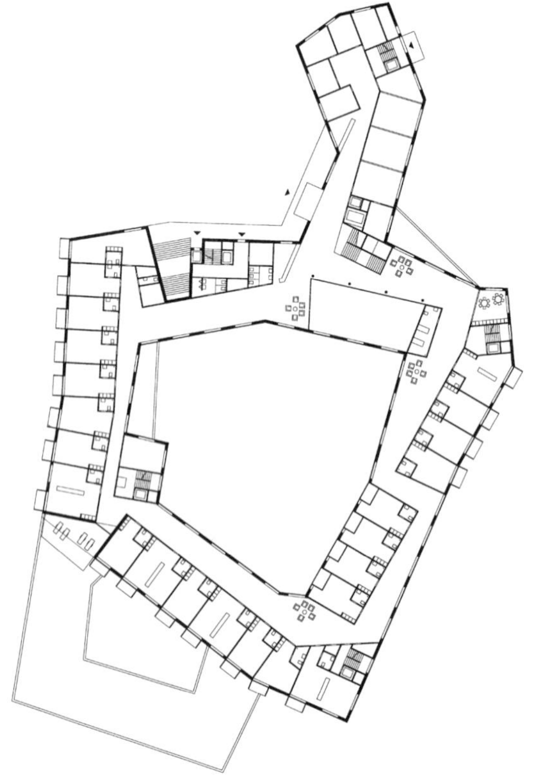

❽ Centre for the elderly in Frauensteinmatte, Zug — Arch.: Graber Pulver

❶ One-bed care room

❷ Two-bed care room

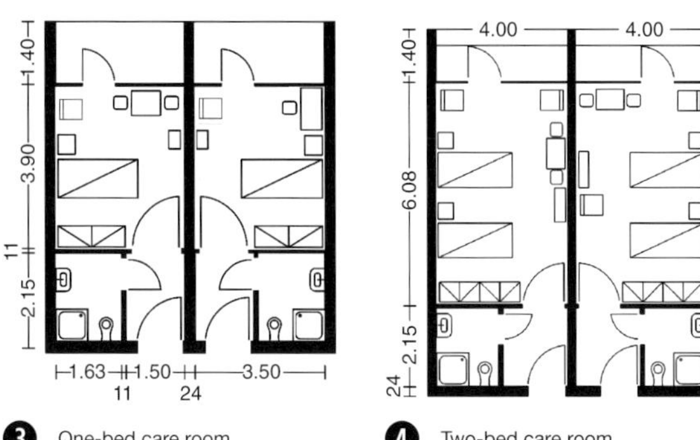

❸ One-bed care room

❹ Two-bed care room

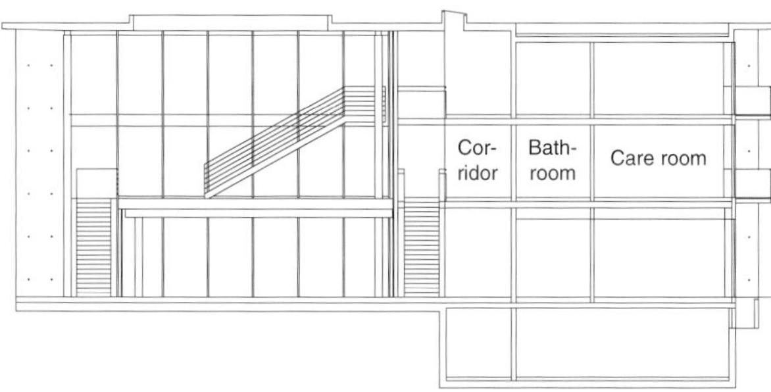

❺ Section → ❻

❻ 'Haus Gisingen' care home for the elderly, Feldkirch/Vorarlberg, first floor

Arch.: Noldin & Noldin

Nursing and care homes for the elderly
These provide nursing, support and care for chronically ill and other vulnerable elderly people. Activating therapy is intended to exercise, maintain and rehabilitate failing powers via medical and care-related assistance. There is a clear separation of residential and operational areas → ❻.

Guideline dimensions: residential = 50% individual rooms = 18 m^2 single rooms, 20 m^2 double rooms → ❶ – ❹. If the bedroom is separate = 7 m^2 single, 12 m^2 double room. The entrance should if possible have a minimum size of 1.25 m × 1.25 m (suitable for wheelchairs) and the wet cell should be fitted with WC, washbasin and shower.

A residential group consists of approx. 8–10 elderly people with communal living room and tea kitchen, in which meals are also taken. One adapted bath is required for every two residential groups. Corridor zones and niches can be used for communication and group building.

Room requirements:
- nurses' sitting and handover rooms (support points)
- WC and cloakroom
- care department incl. bathroom with acid-resistant bath (also suitable for medical baths), washbasins, WC, bidet and shower
- cleaning room with bucket sink and sluice for human waste
- washroom
- subsidiary room for equipment and wheelchairs
- centralised facilities can be situated in the ground floor and basement or distributed in the individual departments.

The short-term care department takes in those temporarily in need of care while their relatives are on holiday, and also provides hospital aftercare, rehabilitation etc.

Space should be provided for administration, consulting rooms, function and common rooms, cafeteria, occupational therapy, gymnastics, chiropody and hairdresser.

Laundry
Kitchen
Chapel
Restaurant or café
Foyer
Occup. therapy
Secretary
Office, house manager
Office, care manager
Rest room
Garden house
Care staff break room
Mobile assistance service
Nurse asso-ciation
Physio-therapy
Caretaker
Daycare
Post
Bath-room
Bath-room
Living room
Balcony
Salon
Nurses' room
Nurses' room

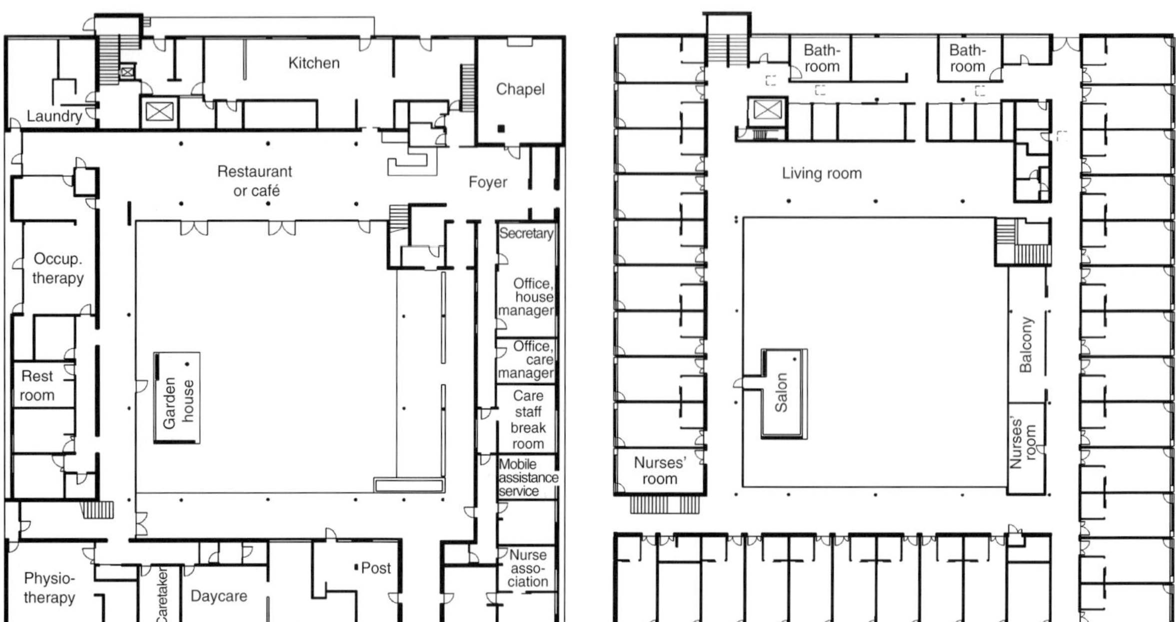

1 'Haus Nofels' care home for the elderly, Feldkirch/Vorarlberg, ground and first floors — Arch.: Rainer Köberl

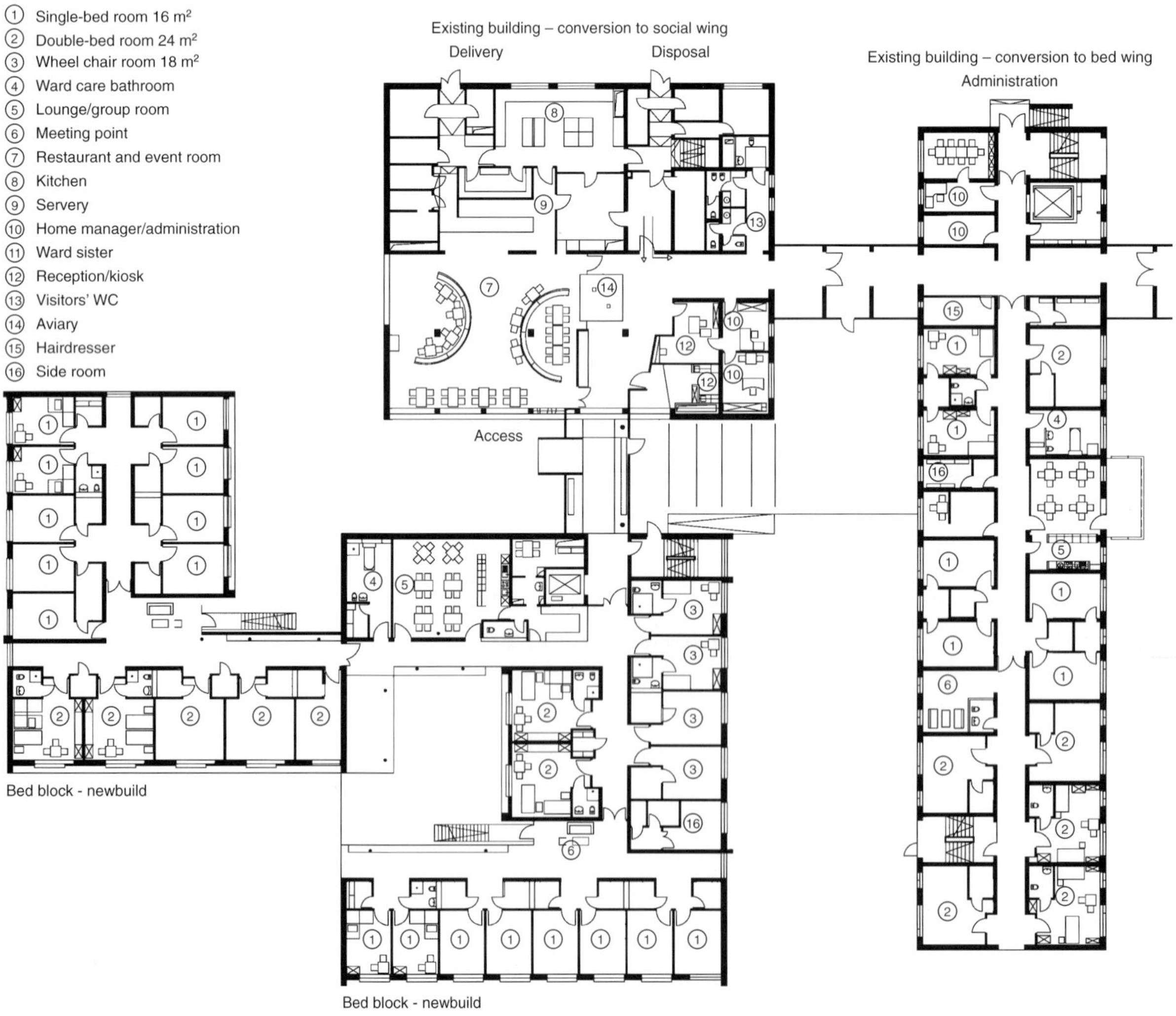

1 Single-bed room 16 m²
2 Double-bed room 24 m²
3 Wheel chair room 18 m²
4 Ward care bathroom
5 Lounge/group room
6 Meeting point
7 Restaurant and event room
8 Kitchen
9 Servery
10 Home manager/administration
11 Ward sister
12 Reception/kiosk
13 Visitors' WC
14 Aviary
15 Hairdresser
16 Side room
Existing building – conversion to social wing
Delivery
Disposal
Existing building – conversion to bed wing
Administration
Access
Bed block - newbuild
Bed block - newbuild

2 'Elbe Fläming' care home for the elderly, Dessau-Rosslau, ground floor — Arch.: Kister Scheithauer Gross

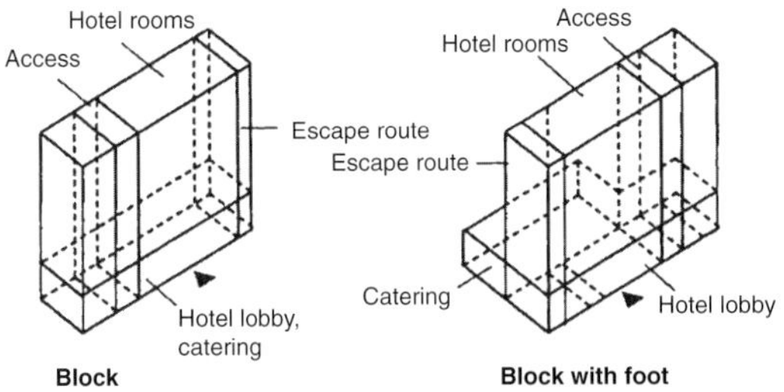

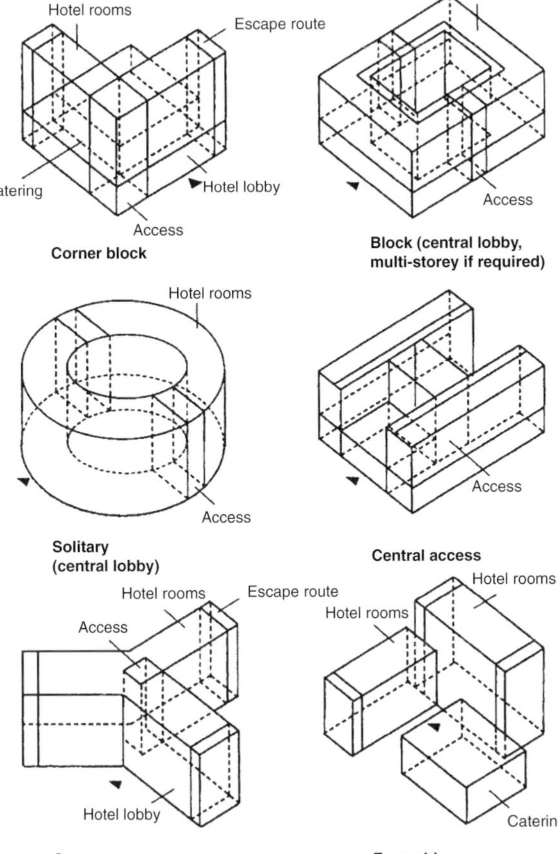

❶ Basic forms of hotels

Stores
Laundry
Deliveries
Stores
Cool room
Services
Staffrooms
Kitchen
Washing up
Administration
Room
Room
Room
Room
Room
Reception
Lobby
Bar
Lounge
Restaurant
Breakfast
Ballroom
Seminar rooms
Relaxation, Sport, Sauna, Swimming pool
Access road (parking, garage)
Shops

❷ Room and access scheme of a hotel

The hotel, formerly a business offering accommodation and catering, often with exclusive flair, has today become a complex and efficient (mass) service provider business with a wide spectrum of possibilities (conferences, wellness, holidays).

There are hotels in various price and comfort classes, which are classified according to five categories → p. 172. A scheme of the basic room and route relationships within a hotel is shown in → ❷.

The essential areas are: **hotel lobby and reception** as the central, well-arranged and prestigious nerve centre between the various parts of the operation, **catering area** in connection with the hotel lobby (extent of the services depend on the hotel category), **administration**, a staff area, which is separately accessed and partly in direct connection with other areas of the hotel, **guest room area** with differentiated rooms and individual access areas arranged under the aspects of category, orientation and noise screening, **service area** with kitchens, store and associated rooms. The percentages of hotels' surface areas required for the various functions are shown in → ❹.

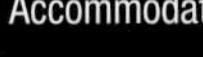

HOTELS
Basics
Rooms
Examples

Accommodation Regulations (BeVO)

see also: Catering pp. 174 ff.

Building regulations, building law code, zoning plans, etc.	general preconditions for the permissibility of a project; type and extent of the building use etc. → p. 56
MBO	general construction requirements for buildings and building elements, general fire protection requirements
DIN 4107	noise protection requirements, see → p. 480
Accommodation regulations	additional construction requirements for buildings and elements for the accommodation of large numbers of people (constructional requirements on walls, columns, floors, doors, escape routes, legally essential corridors, alarm systems, safety equipment etc.)
Catering guidelines	additional construction requirements for catering establishments (mostly related to fire protection)
Public assembly places regulations	additional construction requirements for buildings and elements in relation to the presence of crowds (escape routes, exits, corridors, windows, doors etc.)
Workplace regulations and guidelines	additional construction requirements for buildings and elements concerning health and safety at the workplace
Other requirements	e.g. requirements of the accident insurers, accident prevention regulations, health inspectors, trade supervisors

❸ Laws, guidelines, provisions and regulations for the design of businesses offering accommodation and catering (excerpt)

1.	guest rooms, bathrooms, corridors, room service	50–60%
2.	public areas, lobby, reception etc.	4–7%
3.	catering	4–8%
4.	events, ballroom, seminar rooms	4–12%
5.	wellness/ fitness area	5–10%
6.	other areas, cosmetics, hairdresser	1–2%
7.	management, administration	1–2%
8.	service area, kitchen, staff rooms, stores	9–14%
9.	building services	5–10%

Parking and garage areas and special areas (e.g. wellness and bathing area) are also to be taken into account (and can vary widely according to the range of services)

	Hotel type	m^2/room
1.	luxury	90–110
2.	first class	60–70
3.	comfort	50–60
4.	standard (holiday hotel, motel)	40–60
5.	tourist (low-budget)	15–20

❹ Guideline values for (above) shares of hotel surface area taken by each function and (below) gross areas per room in various categories of hotel

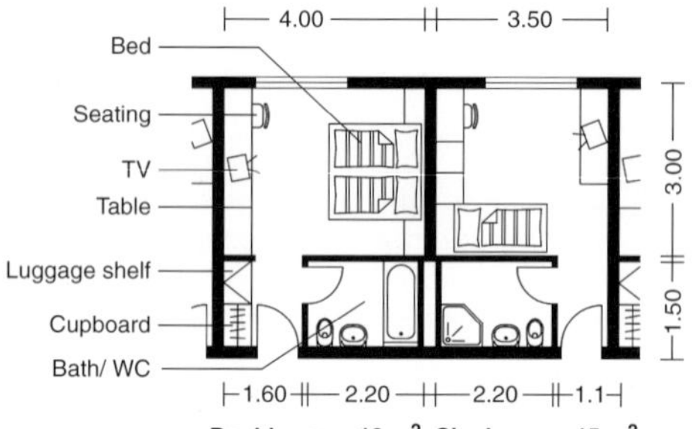

❶ 3-star hotel rooms showing features and main dimensions (according to DEHOGA classification, single room slightly enlarged)

Hotel rooms account for the largest share of a hotel by area. The quality of hotel rooms is an essential criterion for the evaluation of a hotel by a guest. Traditionally, the trend has been to standardise and schematise floor plans and arrangements → ❶.

In light of the extended significance of the hotel room (living, relaxation,work and sleeping room), architects normally attempt to answer the economic and technical requirements by reflecting the demand for comfort through spatial division, while still meeting concerns for individuality and identity ❷ – ⓫.

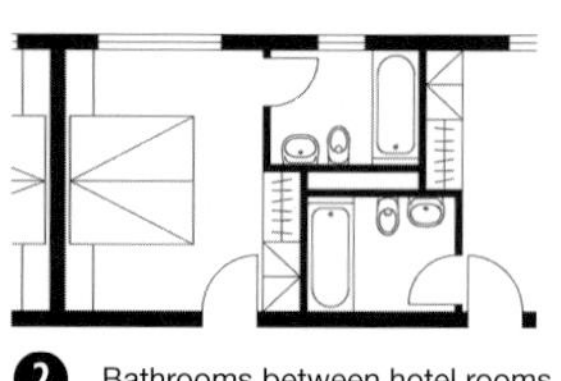

❷ Bathrooms between hotel rooms

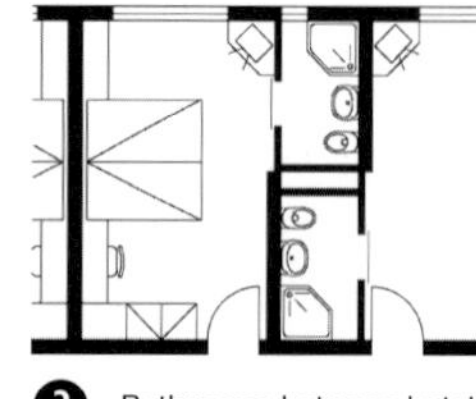

❸ Bathrooms between hotel rooms

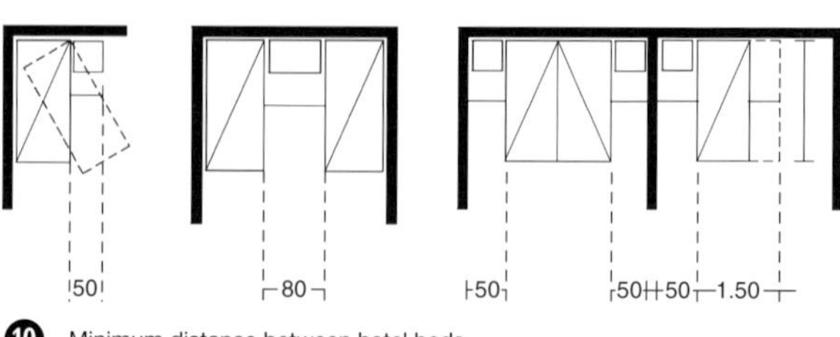

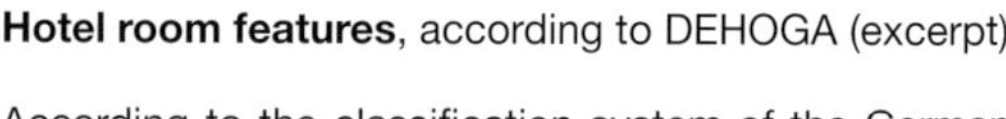

❿ Minimum distance between hotel beds

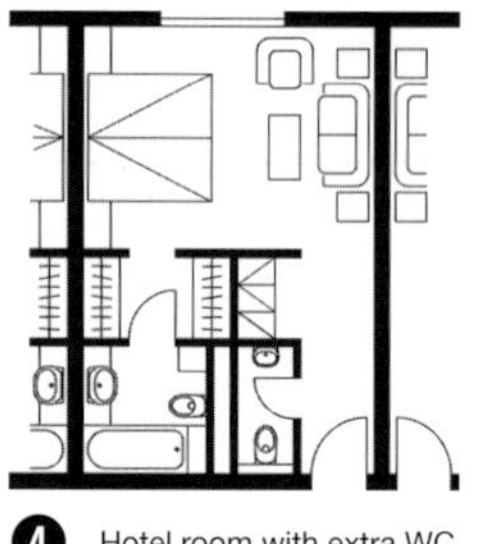

❹ Hotel room with extra WC

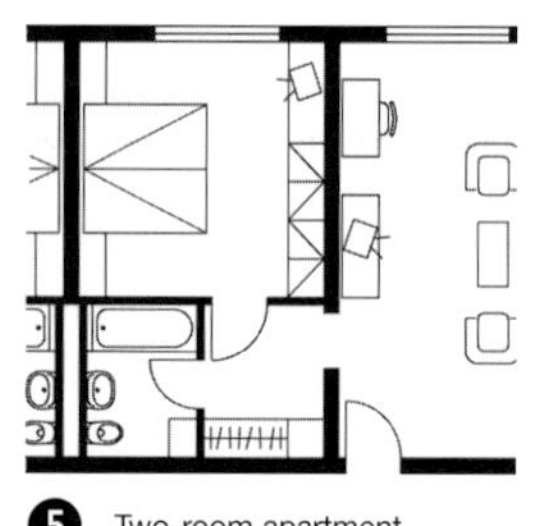

❺ Two-room apartment

Hotel room features, according to DEHOGA (excerpt)

According to the classification system of the German Hotel and Inn Association (DEHOGA), there are five categories, essentially determined by the room's size and features:

1 Star (Tourist): single room 8 m², double room 12 m² (minimum area for 75% of the hotel rooms, without bathroom), bed, wardrobe, seat, washbasin in the room, reception as a separate area

2 Stars (Standard): as before, but single room 12 m², double room 16 m² (minimum area for 75% of the hotel rooms, including bathroom and corridor), bathroom in room (for 70% of hotel rooms), seat per bed, colour television (in 70% of the hotel rooms)

3 Stars (Comfort): as before, but single room 14 m², double room 18 m² (minimum area, see above), bathroom in room (for all rooms in the hotel), telephone, reception area with seating for group, independent reception

4 Stars (First Class): as before, but single room 16 m², double room 22 m² (minimum area, see above), minibar, armchair/couch with coffee table, lobby with seating and drinks service

5 Stars (Luxury): as before, but single room 18 m², double room 26 m², (minimum size, see above), 2% of the hotel rooms as suites (at least two), each with an armchair/sofa per bed, additional washbasin in double rooms and suites, additional colour television in suites, reception lobby.

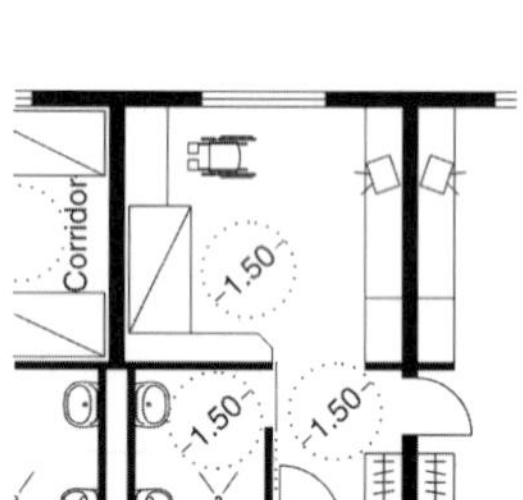

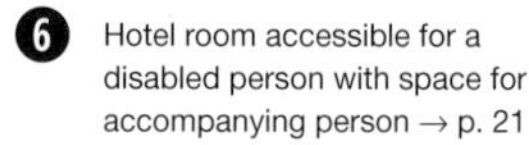

❻ Hotel room accessible for a disabled person with space for accompanying person → p. 21

❼ Two-room apartment with small kitchen

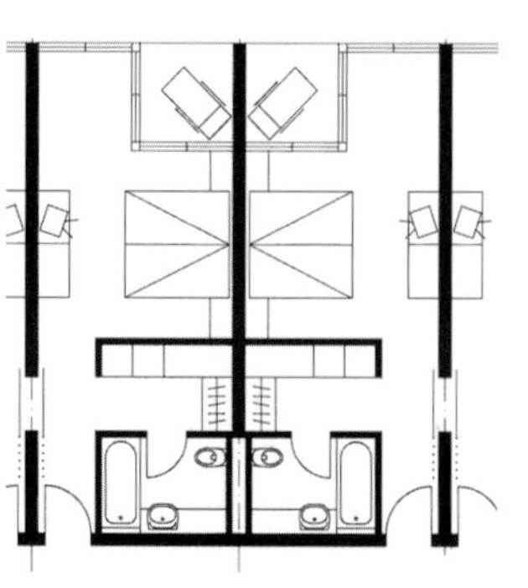

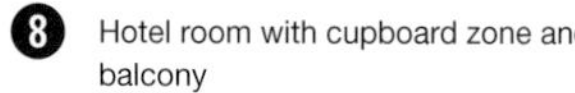

❽ Hotel room with cupboard zone and balcony

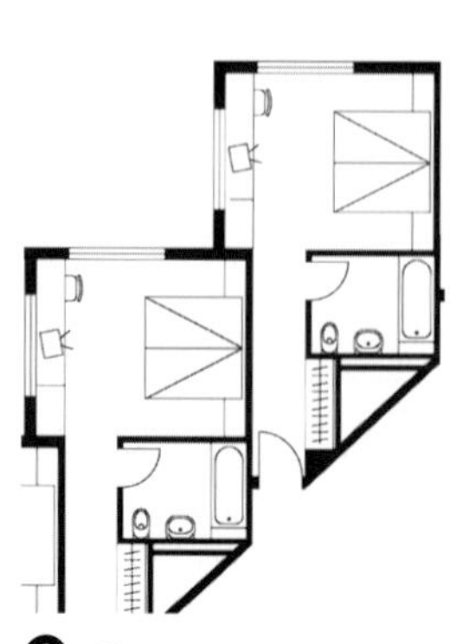

❾ Diagonal room arrangement

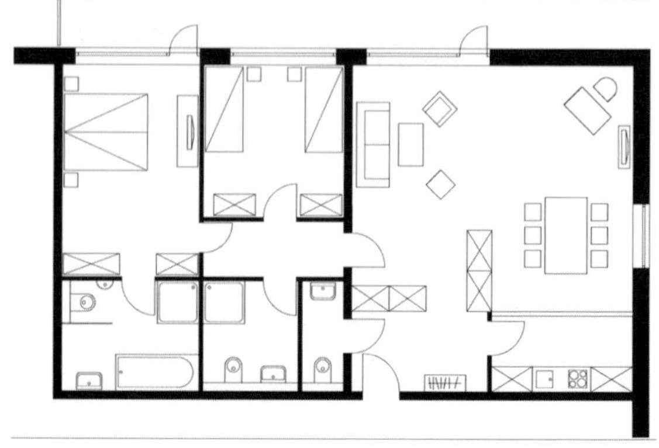

⓫ Three-room apartment (suite) with cooking niche, two bathrooms and guest WC

❶ Guest house, Havelland, ground floor Arch.: Subsolar

Guest house in a village environment
The 'Hof der Stille' guest house → ❶ is located in the buildings of a converted courtyard in an agricultural village in the Havelland near Berlin.

The individual buildings of the former farm are arranged around an internal yard, which, in the place's new identity, serves the role of central access and orientation in the conversion. This also forms a spatial and visual focus point with the ambience of a cloister. The simple guest rooms fitted out in the former stables, the main house with dining room, lounge and seminar rooms, the flat belonging to the owner and the former barn containing sauna, fitness and relaxation area are all directed toward this centre.

The individual guest rooms have the character of apartments. They are equipped within the least possible area with a wet cell and mini-kitchen arranged in the back of the apartment as an 'installation rail' along the boundary wall to the neighbouring property.

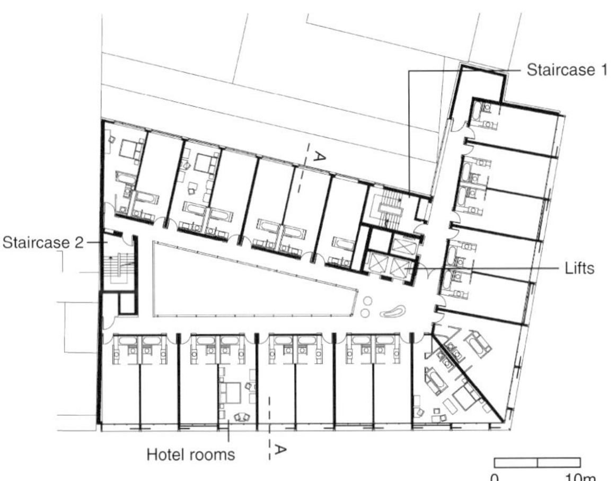

❷ SIDE Hotel, Hamburg, standard floor Arch.: Jan Störmer Architekten

Luxury hotel in an urban context
The SIDE Hotel in Hamburg → ❷ – ❹ is part of an urban block and has an (obtuse) corner → p. 171. Its shape results from an external angle (which fits the block structure) and a rearward block, which is four storeys higher than the angle and surmounts it. Between these, a 'Sky Lounge' on the eighth floor, a naturally lit 30 m high hotel lobby, forms the central architectural element. This mediates between the angles of the street alignments and is also the integrating and orienting core of the ensemble.

On the standard floors → ❷, the hotel rooms (all of 5-star grade) are mostly arranged around the open space of the lobby, with bathrooms parallel to the corridor as a one-sided access gallery system, In the corners and also on the first and twelfth floors are the suites (partially built over the lobby). Restaurant and conference rooms are situated in the corner on the ground and first floors. The kitchens and administration are in the rear part of the ground floor and the large conference rooms (with daylight entering through a light well), spa, swimming pool and underground car park and services areas are in the four basements.

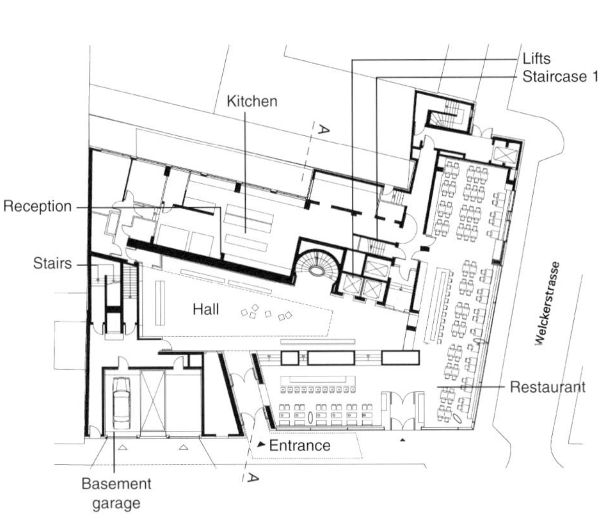

❸ SIDE Hotel, Hamburg, ground floor

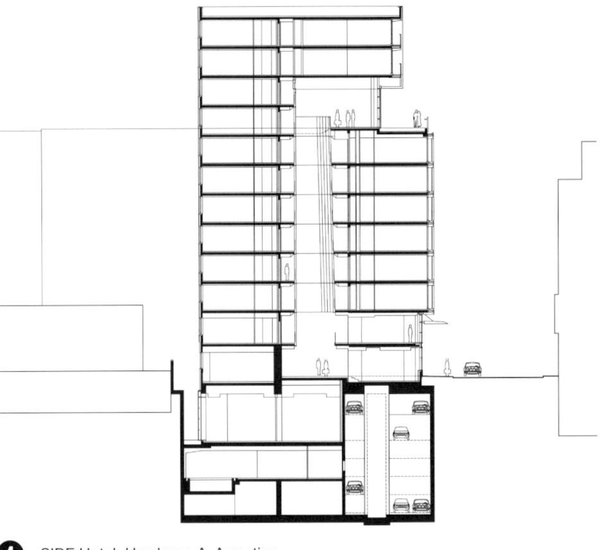

❹ SIDE Hotel, Hamburg, A–A section

see also: Dining rooms p. 152

To be able to eat in comfort, one person requires a table area around 60 cm wide and 30–40 cm deep → ❷ – ❹. This provides sufficient distance between adjacent diners. Although an additional 20 cm space in the centre for dishes and large bowls is sometimes desirable, an overall width of 80–85 cm is suitable for a dining table. If the food is served on plates, then 70 cm is sufficient, and for fast food 60 cm table depth.

Distance between table and wall ≧75 cm → ❶, because the chair alone requires a space of 50 cm. If the space between table and wall is also used for access, the distance should be ≧100 cm. Round tables need a little more space, a difference of up to 50 cm.

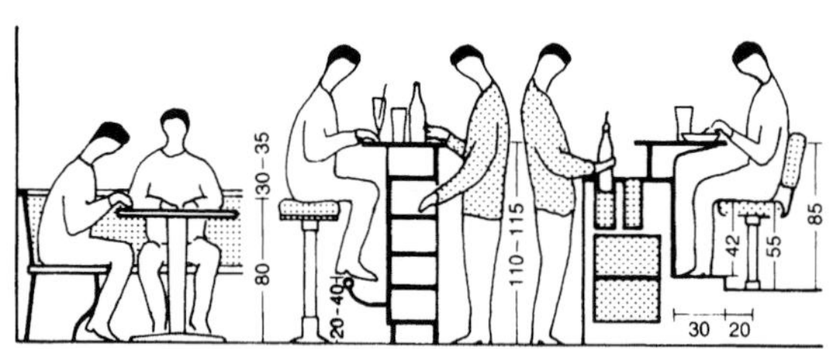

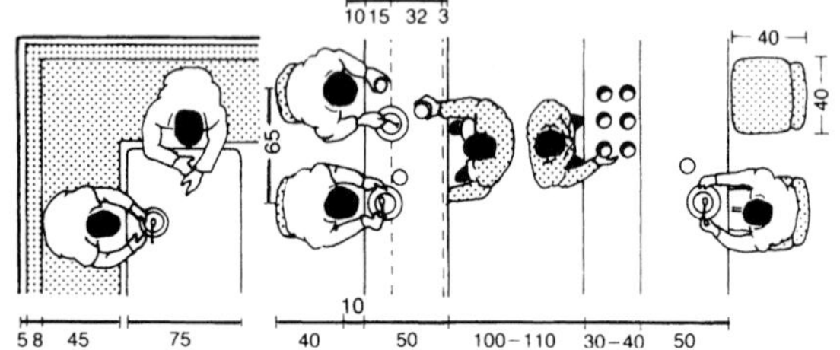

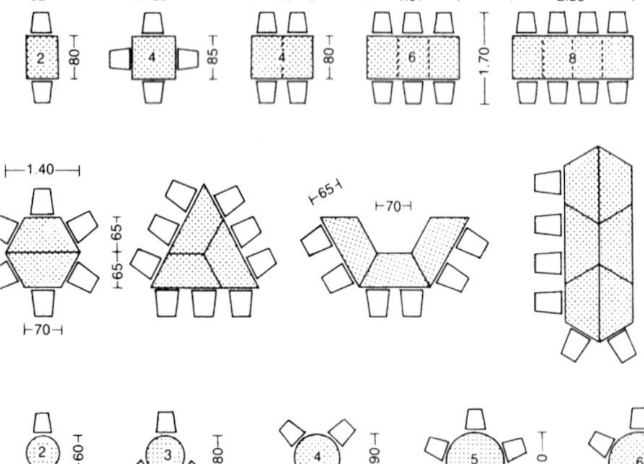

❶ Space required for waiter and diner

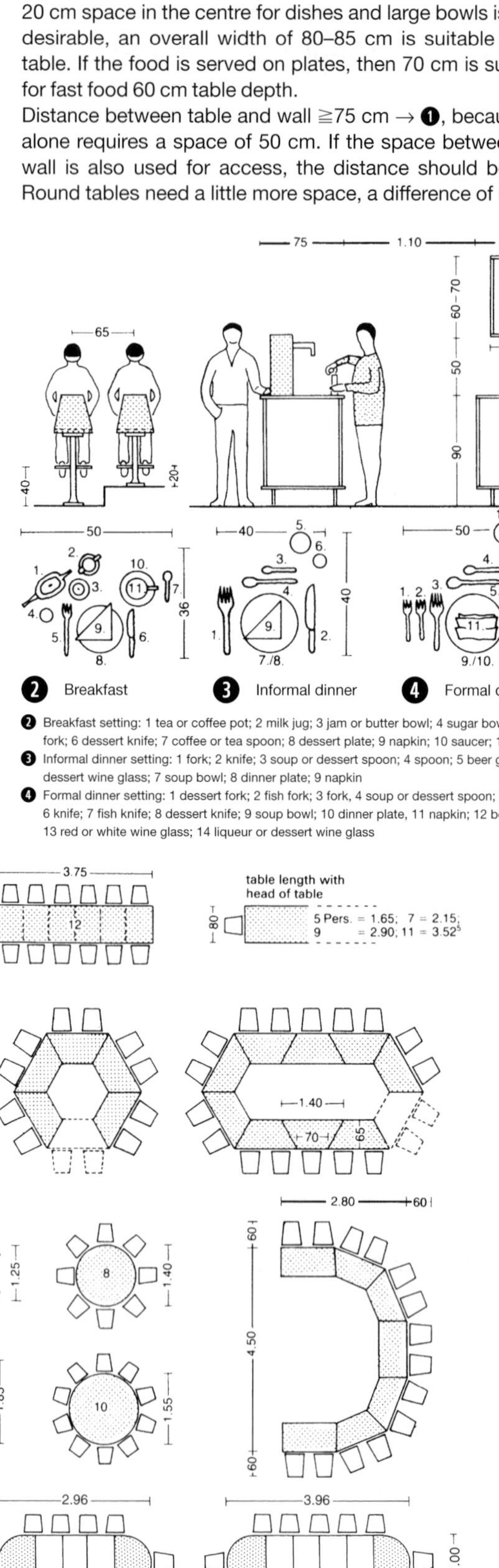

❷ Breakfast ❸ Informal dinner ❹ Formal dinner

❷ Breakfast setting: 1 tea or coffee pot; 2 milk jug; 3 jam or butter bowl; 4 sugar bowl; 5 dessert fork; 6 dessert knife; 7 coffee or tea spoon; 8 dessert plate; 9 napkin; 10 saucer; 11 coffee cup

❸ Informal dinner setting: 1 fork; 2 knife; 3 soup or dessert spoon; 4 spoon; 5 beer glass, 6 wine or dessert wine glass; 7 soup bowl; 8 dinner plate; 9 napkin

❹ Formal dinner setting: 1 dessert fork; 2 fish fork; 3 fork, 4 soup or dessert spoon; 5 spoon; 6 knife; 7 fish knife; 8 dessert knife; 9 soup bowl; 10 dinner plate, 11 napkin; 12 beer glass; 13 red or white wine glass; 14 liqueur or dessert wine glass

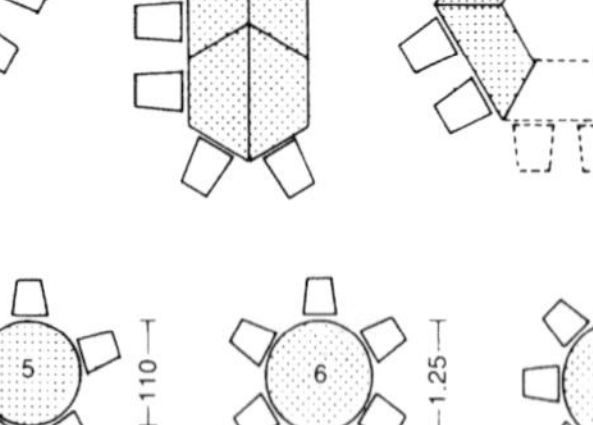

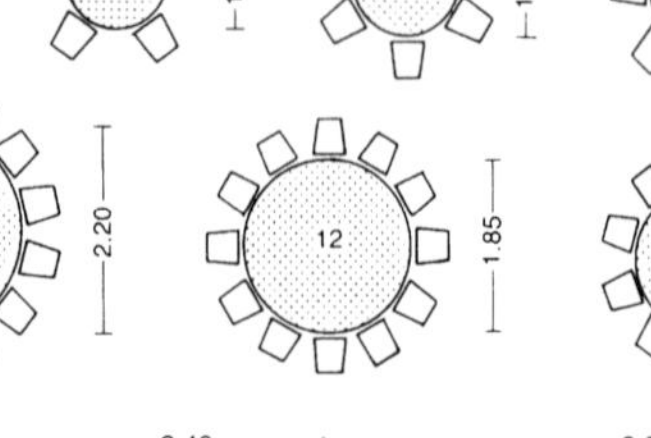

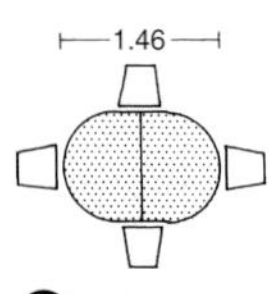

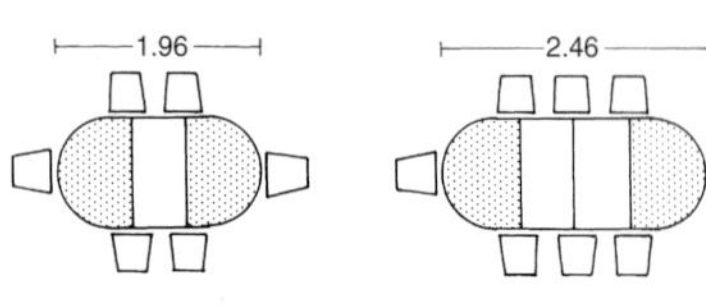

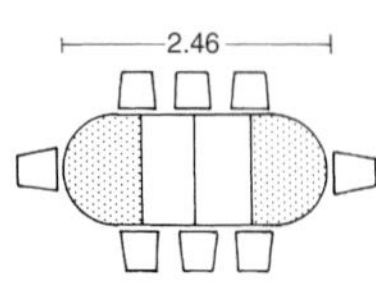

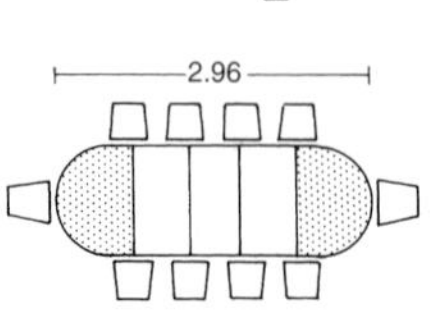

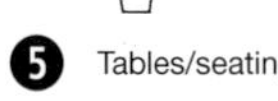

❺ Tables/seating

Closest seating layout (1)

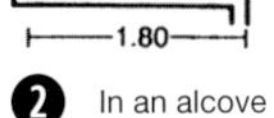
In an alcove (2)

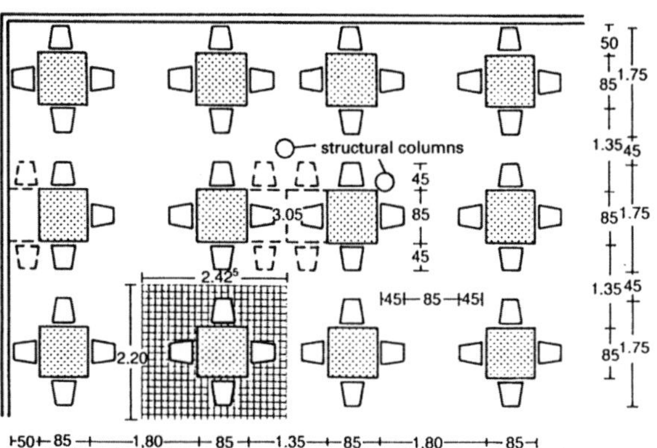

Parallel arrangement of tables (3)

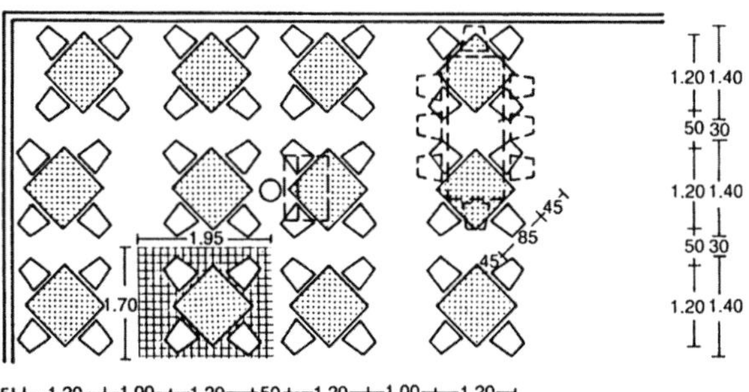
Diagonal arrangement of tables (4)

Closest table spacing (5)

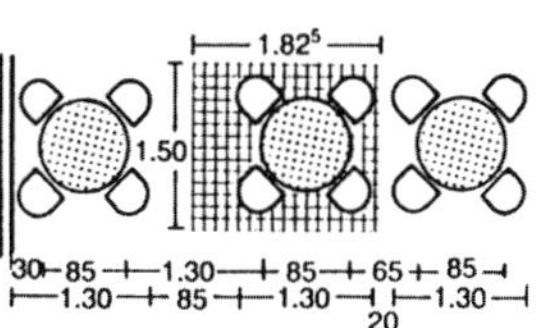

Tables in a café (6)

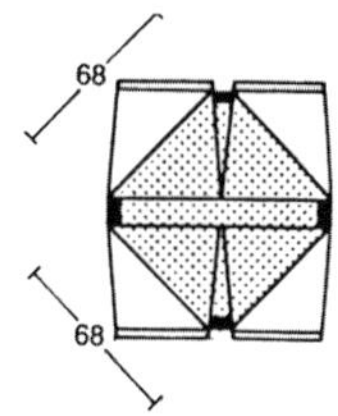
Zuntz table (7)

Before any restaurant or other catering establishment is built, the organisational processes must be determined with the operator. The following have to be decided: what food will be on the menu, what quality and quantity will be on offer? Which service system will be used, whether à la carte with fixed or changing daily menus, plate or table service, self-service or mixed? For design purposes, it is important to know which target clientele is aimed for. The site itself will help to determine the most suitable type of restaurant. Appoint specialists in: kitchen equipment, electrical, heating, ventilation and sanitary design.

The main room in a restaurant is the dining room. Its furniture and fittings should be appropriate for the business. A number of additional tables or chairs should be available, so that table groupings are flexible. Provide special tables for regulars. Side rooms and conference rooms should always be flexibly furnished in order to permit variations. A food bar with fixed stools can be arranged for customers in a hurry. Larger dining rooms should be split into zones. Kitchen, side rooms, toilets and sanitary installations should be grouped around the dining room, also in the basement → (8).

Columns in a dining room are best located in the centre of a group of tables or at the corners of the tables → (3). The ceiling heights of dining areas with a floor area ≦50 m² = 2.50 m, > 50 m² = 2.75 m and >100 m² ≧3.00 m; above or below galleries ≧2.50 m.

Emergency exits 1.0 m wide per 150 people using them. Minimum clear width of aisles in restaurants 0.80 m, doors 0.90 m → (9).

Toilets in public houses, bars or restaurants: Stairs to toilets, wash, staff and storage rooms, usable width ≦1.10 m. Clear walk-through height ≦2.10 m measured vertically. Window area ≦1/10 of the floor area of a restaurant.

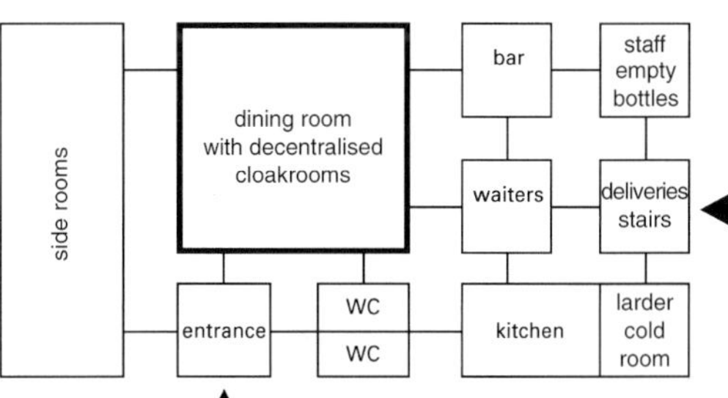

(8) Functional scheme of a small restaurant

Floor area of dining room	Usable walking width
≦100 m²	≧1.10 m
≦250 m²	≧1.30 m
≦500 m²	≧1.65 m
≦1000 m²	≧1.80 m
>1000 m²	≧2.10 m

(9) Usable width of stairs

Dining places	WCs, gents	WCs, ladies	Urinals, no.	Channel (m)
≦50	1	1	2	2
≦50–200	2	2	4	3
= 200–400	3	4	6	4
≦400	– decision for each case –			

(10) Toilet facilities

Type	Seat occupancy per meal	Kitchen floor area (m²/cover)	Dining room floor area (m²/seat)
exclusive restaurant	1	0.7	1.8–2.0
restaurant with rapid turnover, e.g. department store	23	0.5–0.6	1.4–1.6
standard restaurant	1.5	0.4–0.5	1.6–1.8
inn, guest house	1	0.3–0.4	1.6–1.8
for storerooms, personnel rooms etc., add approx. 80%			
cover = seat × seat turnover.			

(11) Space requirements

Furnishing (tables)	No. places	Waiter (m²/place)	Self-service (m²/place)
square	4	1.25	1.25
rectangular.	4	1.10	1.25
rectangular	6	1.00	1.05
rectangular	8	1.10	1.10

(12) Total space required for dining room: 1.4–1.6 m²/place

main aisles	min. 2.00 m wide
intermediate aisles	min. 0.90 m wide
side aisles	min. 1.20 m wide

(13) Aisle widths

CATERING

Dining Rooms, Service

The space required varies very widely according to the character of a restaurant. Apart from fast food outlets, the least space required is in cafés. The most is needed in restaurants and diners. Diagonal arrangement of the tables generally takes up less space than an aligned pattern, with a space saving of up to 35%. Alcoves are beneficial for use of space because the distance between seats and wall is no longer required. In larger restaurants, many groups of tables (a waiter's 'territory') are collected together to form units.

Basically, the design of dining rooms based on 'number of heads = m^2, formulas is to be avoided, as they are not applicable to rooms under 100 m^2 and can lead to false results. Fixing the dimensions of rooms should in any case be done from concrete furniture layout plans. The functional design of dining rooms involves determining the following:

1. Entrances and traffic axes, which limit the usable area, according to number and required width.
2. Service points (with the exception of variable forms of furniture): stations for 40 places each with at least one service point as centrally placed as possible.
3. Table sizes and shapes according to the character of the business and the expected guest structure. A good procedure is to design a percentage structure of desirable table sizes with various combinations, starting from the intended total capacity. Table sizes and shapes result from the intended use. Areas of about 20 (12–24) places are designed according to the character, type of business and intended visual organisation, to avoid the impression of a waiting room.

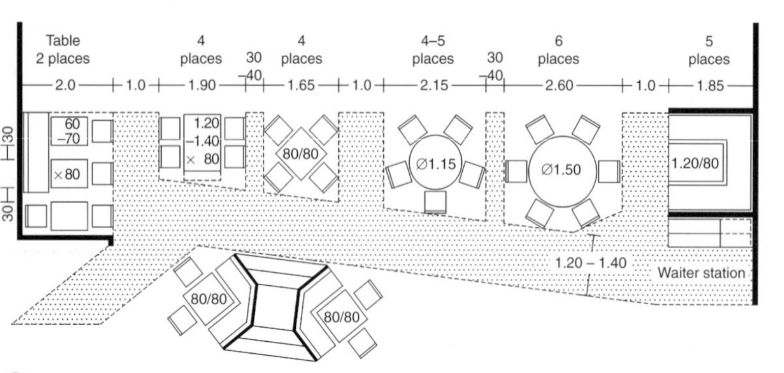

❶ Table sizes in a restaurant: with predominantly plate service the table depth can be reduced to 70 cm

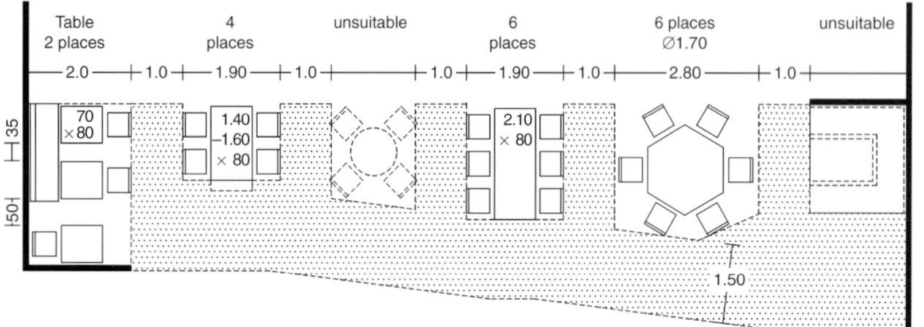

❷ In a self-service restaurant

❸ Bistro–café–bar

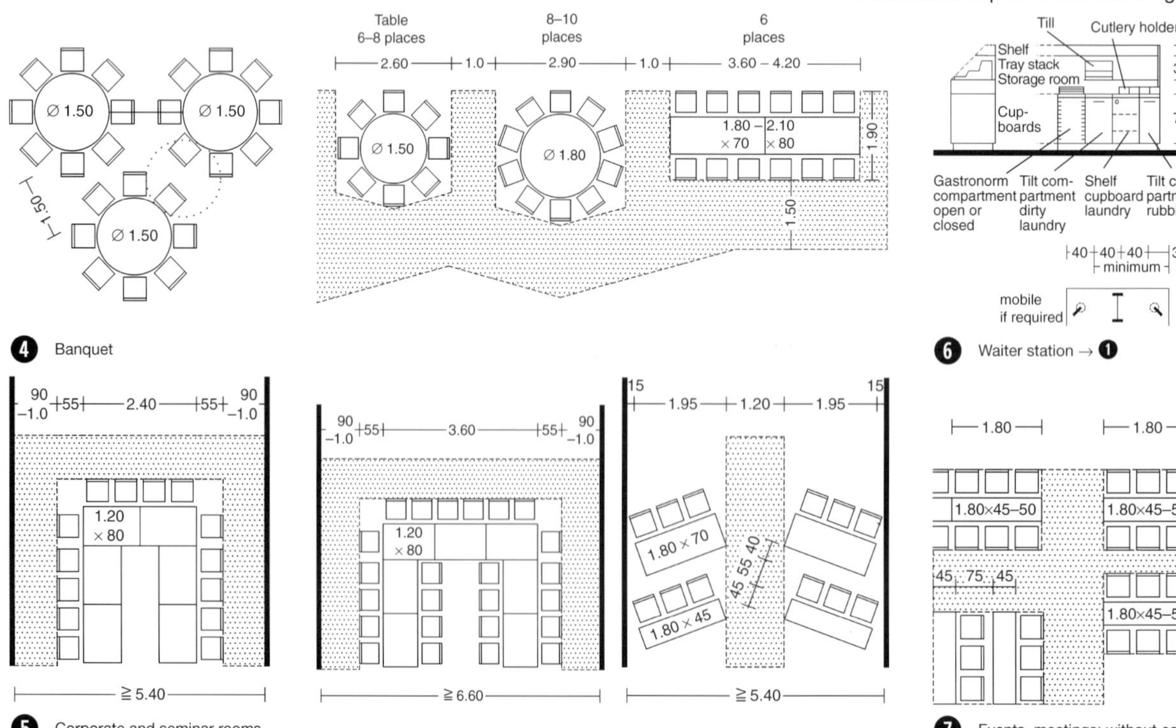

❹ Banquet

❺ Corporate and seminar rooms

❻ Waiter station → ❶

❼ Events, meetings: without eating

CATERING

Fast Food Outlets

The heavy traffic of people resulting from fast turnover demands larger sales areas to ensure smooth operation. Tables and chairs are kept as small as possible and tightly grouped → ❶ – ❹. The customer space, 1.50–2.15 m^2 per person, features groups of seats and the longest possible bar at which to eat → ❺ – ❻.

If the business is favourably placed to catch street traffic, a built-in kiosk will be able to serve food on the pavement as well as indoors → ❼ – ❽.

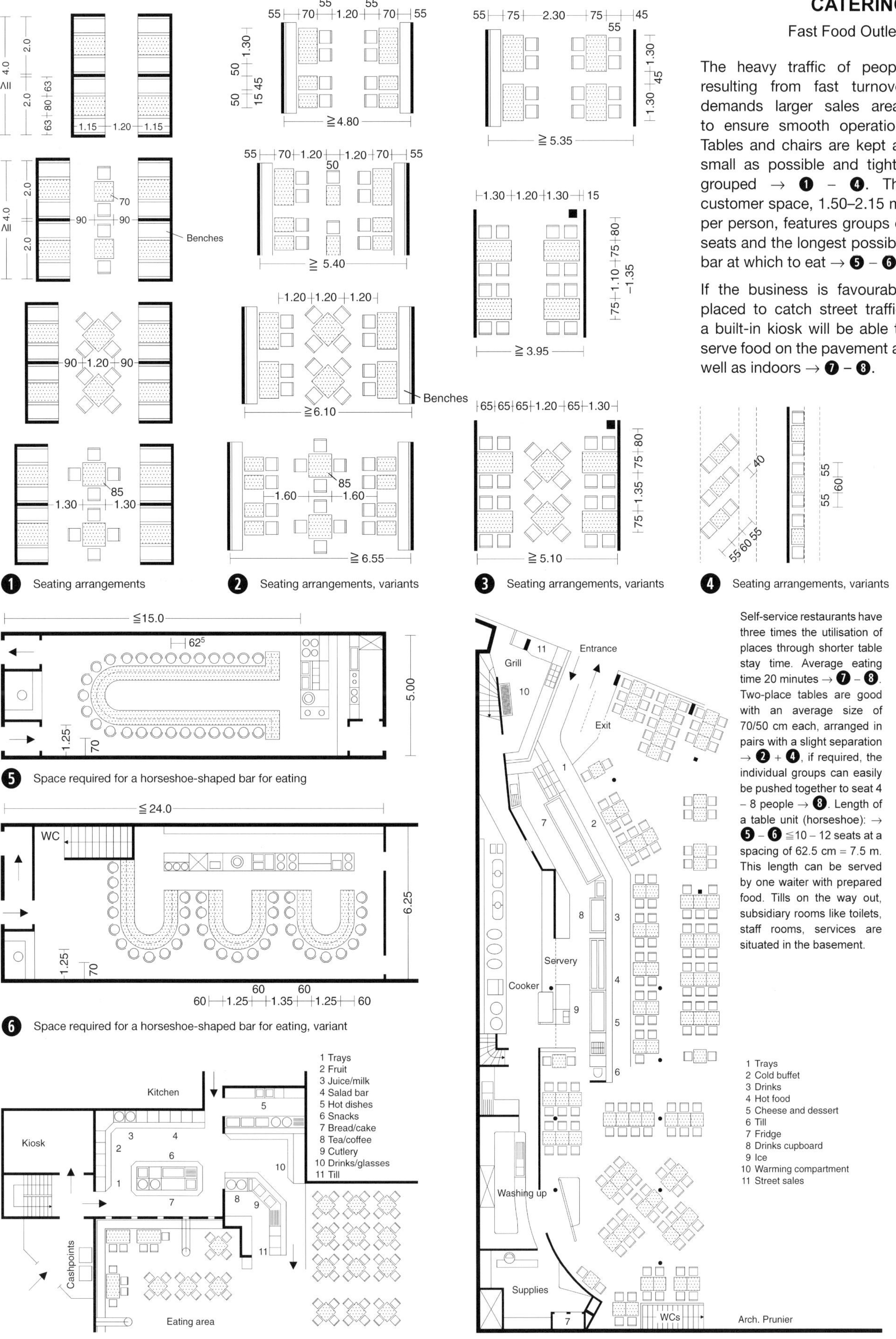

❶ Seating arrangements

❷ Seating arrangements, variants

❸ Seating arrangements, variants

❹ Seating arrangements, variants

❺ Space required for a horseshoe-shaped bar for eating

❻ Space required for a horseshoe-shaped bar for eating, variant

Self-service restaurants have three times the utilisation of places through shorter table stay time. Average eating time 20 minutes → ❼ – ❽. Two-place tables are good with an average size of 70/50 cm each, arranged in pairs with a slight separation → ❷ + ❹, if required, the individual groups can easily be pushed together to seat 4 – 8 people → ❽. Length of a table unit (horseshoe): → ❺ – ❻ ≦10 – 12 seats at a spacing of 62.5 cm = 7.5 m. This length can be served by one waiter with prepared food. Tills on the way out, subsidiary rooms like toilets, staff rooms, services are situated in the basement.

❼ Example of a fast food restaurant, self-service

❽ Fast food restaurant in Paris

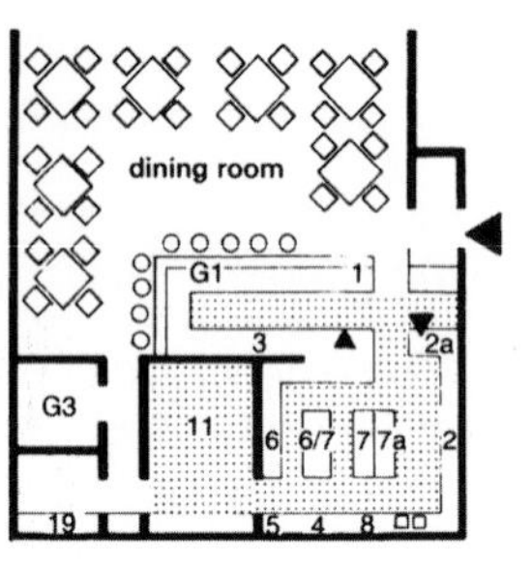

❶ Snack bar

1 meals and drinks servery
2 dishwasher
2a crockery returns
3 drinks bar with mixer, toaster, food containers etc.
4 oven for small pastry items
5 food storage
6 rotisserie
6/7 cooker rings
7a water boiler and steam machine
8 pot and pan washer
11 stores/office; catering size refrigerators and freezers instead of cold store
19 staff toilets
G1 bar counter
G3 customer toilets

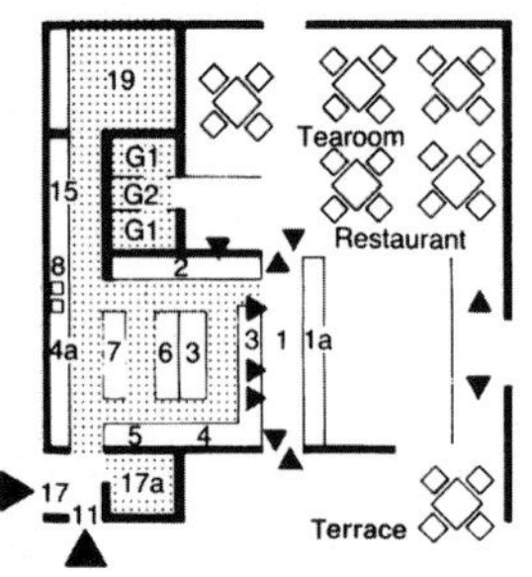

❷ Café-restaurant

1 waiters' walkway
1a service counter and cash tills
2 dishwasher
3 drinks bar with mixer, toaster, ice cream freezer etc.
4 pastry preparation
4a pastry oven
5 sandwich preparation
6 reheating equipment (e.g. soup)
7 cooker rings
8 pot and pan washer
11 empties
15 linen store
17 deliveries and (a) store
19 staff toilets and cloakroom
G1 toilets
G2 telephone cubicle

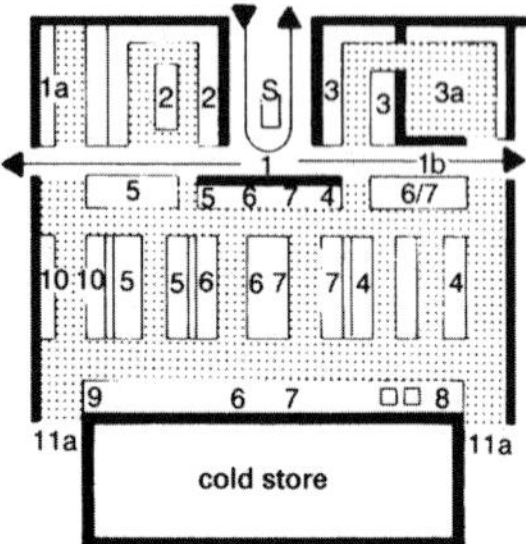

❸ Large hotel restaurant kitchen

1 waiters' walkway
1a garden service counter
2 dish-washing area
3 drinks counter
3a drinks cellar
4 pastry counter
5 cold dishes
6 hot dishes and sauces
6/7 table with hot store
8 pot and pan washer
9 vegetable preparation
10 meat preparation
11a deliveries, and access to stores, offices, staff cloakrooms and toilets
S service accessories and tills

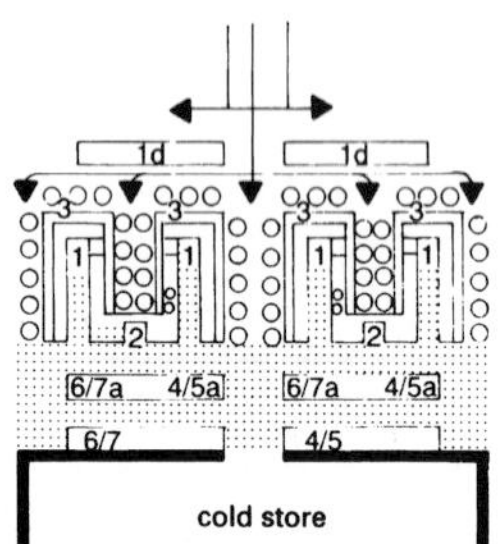

❹ Restaurant with buffet and vending machines

1 serving aisles in U-shaped counters
1d vending machines
2 link between two counters with covered dishwashers, operated from both sides, each with two rinsing basins
4/5 cold meal preparation
4/5a cold servery (salads, ices, desserts)
6/7 griddle, soup heater, water boiler etc.
6/7a hot servery (bain-marie, hotplates)

entrance

cold room

deliveries

❺ Self-service restaurant

1d self-service buffet with grill and chip fryer
1e sauces, condiments, cutlery
1f cash till
2 dishwasher
2a crockery returns
3/4 food and drinks servery (service to street possible)
5a cold meal preparation table
6/7 heating units, used from both sides
6/7a hot meal preparation table
11a refrigerators, used from both sides
12 sales kiosk (serving inside and to street)
E entrance

Snack bar → ❶, corner pub, bistro, café, restaurant: capacity 55–60 seats (2–4 place turnover at lunchtime, 2 in evenings). Between lunch and evening meals: serving coffee, cakes and snacks. Kitchen: supplied predominantly with pre-prepared items. Storeroom need not be particularly large if deliveries are daily.

Café-restaurant → ❷ with tea room. Urban business in heavy traffic location.

Café: alcohol-free drinks, except bottled premium beer, liqueurs etc., patisserie and light food – cold and hot.

Tea room: alcohol-free drinks, patisserie, sandwiches. Capacity approx. 150 seats, continuous operation 6.30 – 24.00. Kitchen: predominantly pre-prepared items, little storage.

Large hotel restaurant kitchen → ❸ also for large catering establishments with side rooms, external deliveries or production for outside companies. Capacity 800–1000 people. Waiters' walkway: in the centre with special service in the garden or also bowling alley and direct access to the side rooms. Kitchen: cell system fronted by the backs of the large appliances.

Restaurant with buffet and vending machines → ❹ for fast midday meals in canteens, department stores and motorway services. Capacity 500 people/h. Kitchen: only warming of pre-prepared foodstuffs, except for salads and soups.

Self-service restaurant → ❺ suitable for department stores or attached to offices. Kitchen: no in-house production. Outside delivery and preparation using deep frozen process.

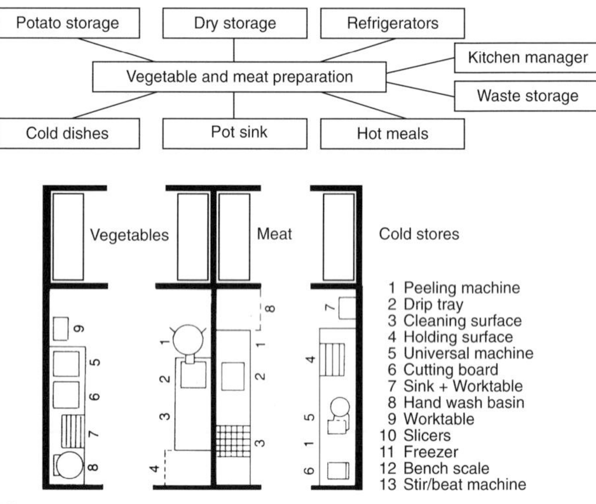

❻ Separate preparation of vegetables and meat

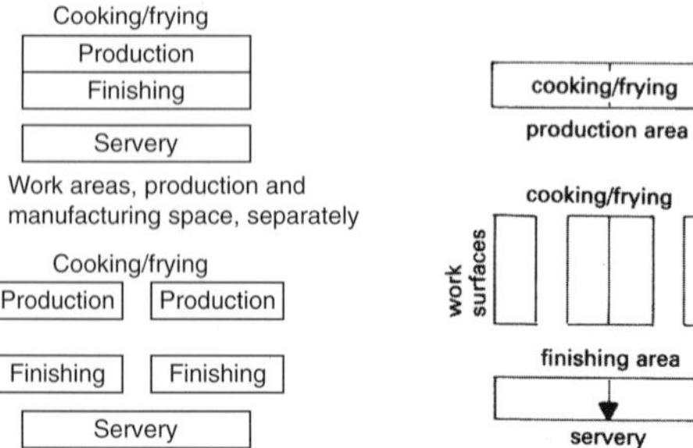

❼ American hotel kitchen system: boiling and roasting areas arranged parallel to the servery

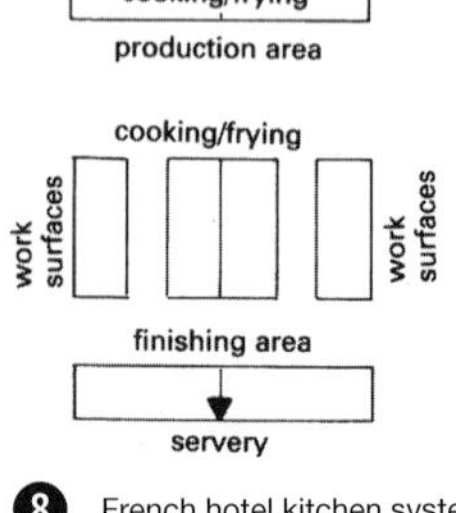

❽ French hotel kitchen system: boiling and roasting area arranged perpendicular to the servery, separation of production and finishing zones

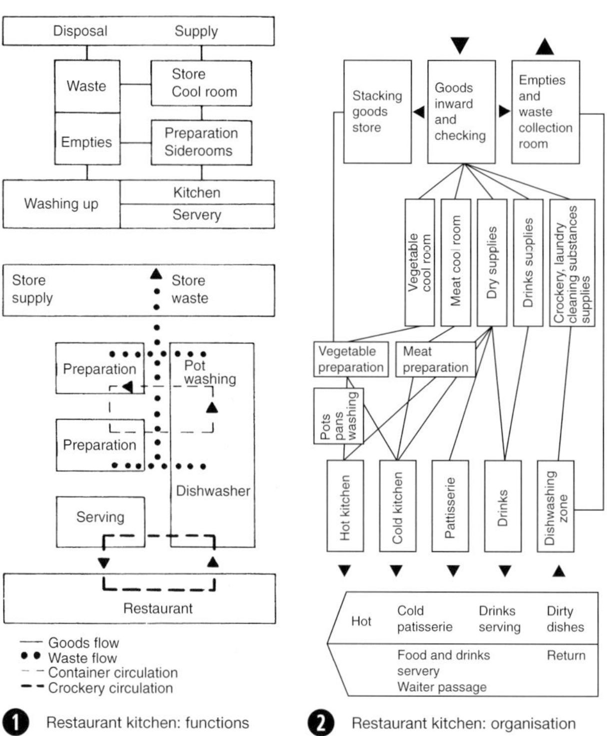

❶ Restaurant kitchen: functions

❷ Restaurant kitchen: organisation

Bistros, snack bars, small cafés – or speciality restaurants with 40–60 seats – are classified as small operations. Small to medium units (70–100 places) require on the other hand carefully zoned and fully equipped kitchen facilities. Large businesses (service areas, fast food restaurants, large hotel kitchens) achieve considerably higher place numbers, often with an integrated eating bar or self-service areas.

Seats	80	120	200
goods inward	0.05–0.075	0.05–0.067	0.05–0.06
empties	0.05–0.075	0.05–0.067	0.05–0.06
waste/rubbish	0.05–0.075	0.03–0.050	0.03–0.04
delivery/disposal	0.15–0.225	0.13–0.183	0.13–0.16
cold room meat	0.05–0.075	0.05–0.067	0.04–0.05
cold room fruit and vegetables	0.05–0.075	0.05–0.067	0.04–0.05
cold room dairy products	fridge	0.03–0.05	0.03–0.05
cold room cold service	fridge	fridge	0.02–0.03
cool room drinks	fridge	fridge	0.05–0.07
freezer room	0.05–0.075	0.05–0.067	0.06–0.08
cooled goods delivery	0.15–0.225	0.183–0.25	0.24–0.32
store dry goods	0.15–0.175	0.117–0.13	0.09–0.1
store drinks	0.075–0.1	0.1–0.117	0.08–0.1
store non-food	0.075–0.1	0.067–0.083	0.07–0.08
cooled goods storage	0.3–0.375	0.283–0.33	0.24–0.28
vegetable preparation	0.075–0.1	0.067–0.083	0.04–0.05
meat preparation	0.075–0.1	0.05–0.067	0.04–0.05
fish/poultry preparation	0	0.03–0.05	0.03–0.04
hot kitchen	0.325–0.35	0.217–0.23	0.16–0.18
cold kitchen	0	0.05–0.067	0.04–0.05
patisserie	0	0	0.04–0.05
pot washing	0.05–0.075	0.05–0.067	0.03–0.04
office kitchen manager	0	0	0.03–0.04
kitchen facilities	0.525–0.625	0.47–0.567	0.41–0.5
dishwasher	0.1–0.125	0.1–0.117	0.09–0.1
service/waiter office	0.075–0.1	0.083–0.1	0.07–0.08
dishwasher/office	0.175–0.225	0.183–0.217	0.16–0.18
= Total	1.3–1.675	1.25–1.55	1.18–1.44

❸ Kitchen areas: space required (m^2/seat)

The trend away from conventional restaurants to those offering a wide range of food not only affects the planning and design of dining rooms, but also of kitchens. Small and medium-sized restaurant kitchens play a particular role here, and the following details are primarily based on this type of business.

Gastronorm system

The dimensions of containers, tables, shelves, devices, crockery and built-in units are all based on a 530 × 325 mm module → p. 181 ❹.

Function and organisation of the restaurant kitchen → ❶ – ❷

The capacity of the kitchen is primarily dependent on the number of customer seats, customer expectations (type, extent and quality of the meals offered), the proportion of products freshly prepared from raw (in contrast to ready-prepared food) and the rate of customer turnover all day or at mealtimes (consumer frequency).

In fast food restaurants the rule of thumb for seat changes is about 1–3 times per hour, in conventional restaurants about 2. In speciality and evening-based restaurants, the guests stay on average for 1.3–2 hours.

Percentage of total kitchen space requirement → ❹

Differentiated according to small, medium and large kitchens, floor area values for individual functions are be based on → ❸.

Aisle widths in storage, preparation and production areas differ according to whether they are purely traffic routes or also overlap the service area. Working aisle widths should be 0.90–1.20 m, side traffic routes with (temporary) overlapping use 1.50–1.80 m and main traffic routes (transport and two-way through traffic) 2.10–3.30 m wide. For kitchen areas in small to medium restaurants, aisle widths of 1.00–1.50 m should be sufficient.

Area	Proportion (%)
goods delivery including inspection and waste storage	10
storage in freezer, cold and dry rooms	20
daily store	
vegetable and salad preparation area	2
cold dishes, desserts	8
patisseries/cakes	8
meat preparation	2
cooking area	8
washing area	10
traffic area	17
staff rooms and office	15
Total	100

❹ Basis for dimensions and space requirements

empties
lift
deliveries
waste
staff changing room
dry goods store
cold room
vegetables
office
washroom
toilets
daily store
meat prep.
veg prep.
potato prep.
restroom
pure zone
pot washer
hot dishes
cold dishes
cake shop
dishwasher
servery, waiter's walkway
coffee room
pure zone
buffet
bar servery

❺ Kitchen areas: classification and relationships of functional areas in clean and unclean zones (if earth-covered vegetables are prepared, this must take place in a separate part of the unclean area!)

BS EN 203
BS EN 631
BS 6173
BS EN 12851
BSEN ISO 22000
BIP 2130/2078
DIN EN 631
DIN 66075

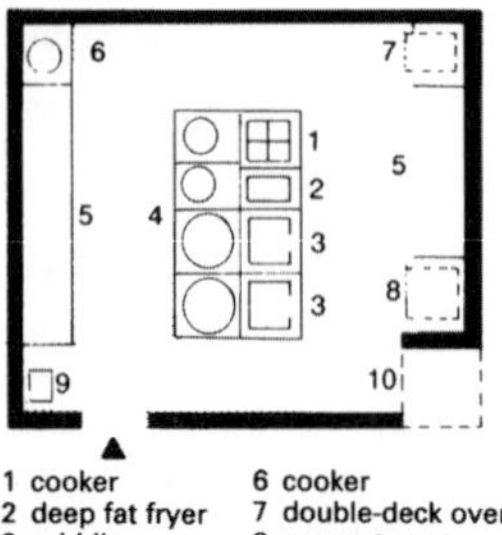

❶ Basic organisation of the hot kitchen → ❷–❸

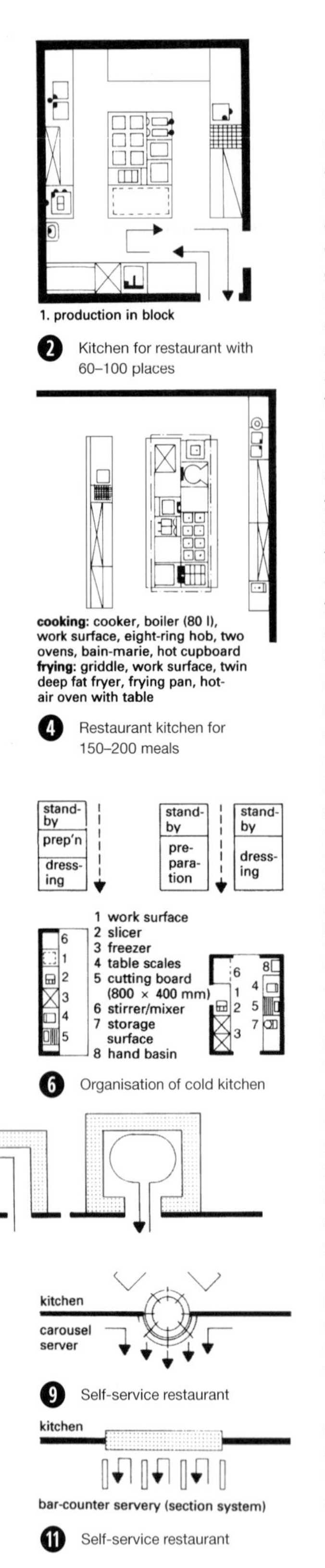

❷ Kitchen for restaurant with 60–100 places

BS EN 203
BS EN 631
BS 6173
BS EN 12851
BSEN ISO 22000
BIP 2130/2078
DIN EN 631
DIN 66075

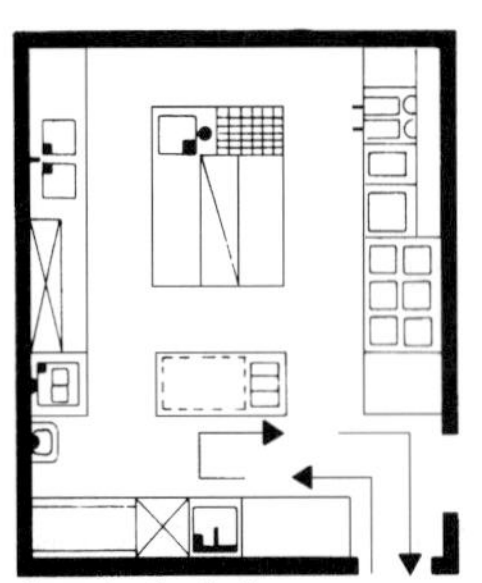

❸ Kitchen for restaurant with 60–100 places

❹ Restaurant kitchen for 150–200 meals

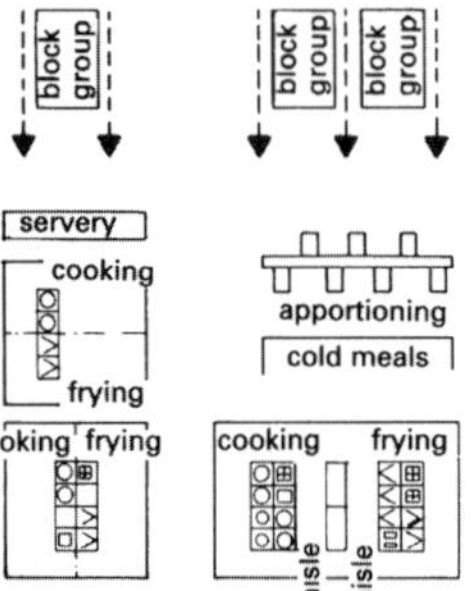

❺ Functions and organisation of hot kitchen

❻ Organisation of cold kitchen

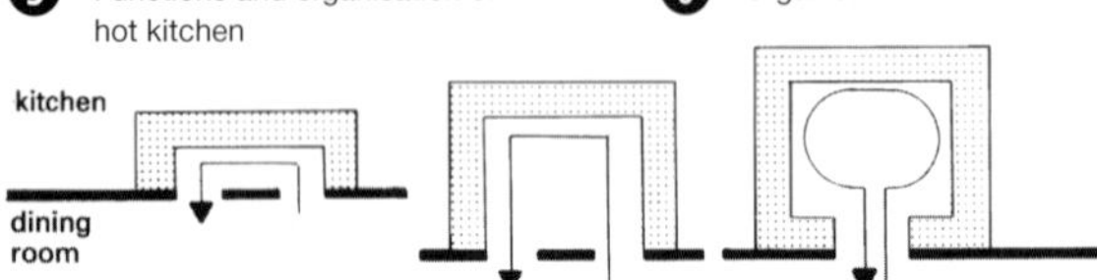

❼ Servery, waiter walkway

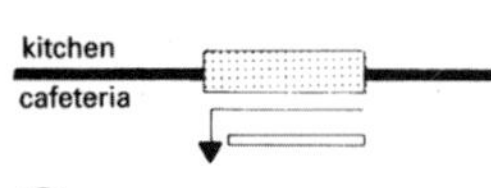

❽ Self-service restaurant

❾ Self-service restaurant

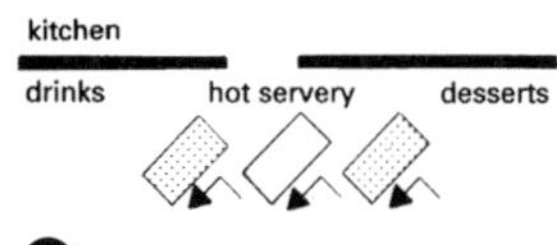

❿ Free-flow restaurant

⓫ Self-service restaurant

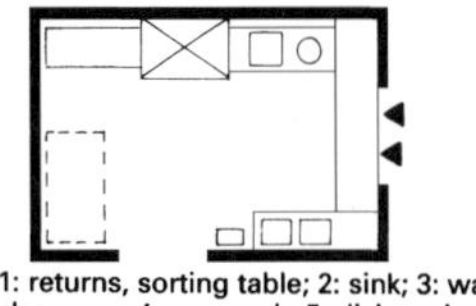

1: returns, sorting table; 2: sink; 3: waste clearance; 4: pre-wash; 5: dishwasher; 6: discharge table; 7: crockery area

⓬ Basic solution: dishwashing area

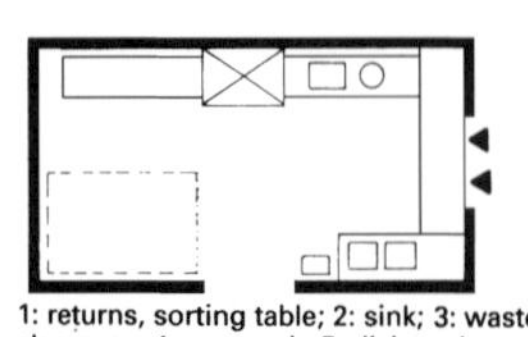

1: returns, sorting table; 2: sink; 3: waste clearance; 4: pre-wash; 5: dishwasher 6: discharge table; 7: crockery area

⓭ Basic solution: dishwashing area

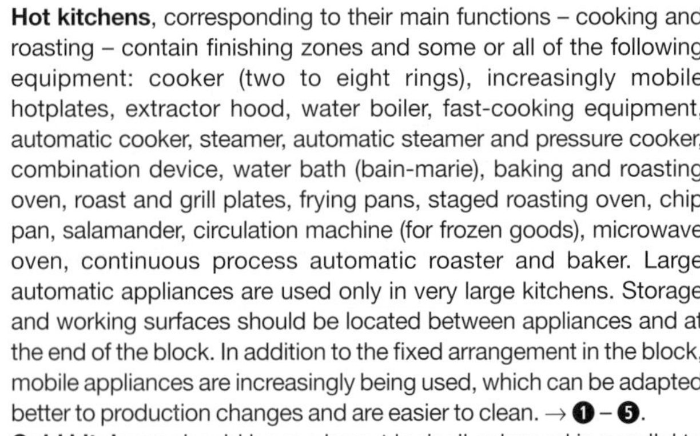

Hot kitchens, corresponding to their main functions – cooking and roasting – contain finishing zones and some or all of the following equipment: cooker (two to eight rings), increasingly mobile hotplates, extractor hood, water boiler, fast-cooking equipment, automatic cooker, steamer, automatic steamer and pressure cooker, combination device, water bath (bain-marie), baking and roasting oven, roast and grill plates, frying pans, staged roasting oven, chip pan, salamander, circulation machine (for frozen goods), microwave oven, continuous process automatic roaster and baker. Large automatic appliances are used only in very large kitchens. Storage and working surfaces should be located between appliances and at the end of the block. In addition to the fixed arrangement in the block, mobile appliances are increasingly being used, which can be adapted better to production changes and are easier to clean. → ❶ – ❺.

Cold kitchens should have a layout logically planned in parallel to the hot kitchen and be convenient for the (common) servery and bread area. The regular equipment is a day refrigerator under/over the cold table, various cutting and slicing machines (bread, cold cuts, meat, cheese), mixing machine, scales, cutting boards, salad table with lower cold cabinet, toaster or salamander, microwave oven and sufficient working and storage space → ❻.

Servery for restaurant kitchens with counter or self-service, ideally situated between the preparation area and the dining room. There should be sufficient shelf space, a hot cabinet with heated plates and a cool zone for cold foods. Crockery shelves or upper fixings, cutlery container. In large businesses, also basket, plate and soup bowl dispensers.

Crockery return: the difference between washing crockery and pots is considerable. With waiter service, the plates are brought back to their own area of the servery → ⓬ – ⓯. In addition to one or two sinks with drainers, storage space and shelves for pot washing, small kitchens naturally also require dishwashers in various sizes, feed types and operational types. Dishwashers under the worktop are usual, but also tunnel and rotary batch washers. Provide surfaces for the return (temporary storage, worktops, sorting, soaking) and space for the crockery → ⓬ – ⓮.

Staff area: about 10–15% of the total space required in a kitchen facility should be allocated for offices and staff rooms. The kitchen staff will need changing rooms, washing facilities and toilets. For more than 10 employees, a rest/break room is necessary (workplace regulations). It is important that changing and social rooms are near the kitchen, to avoid staff having to cross unclean room areas or corridors. For changing rooms, > 6 m^2 floor area, 4–6 air changes per hour and privacy. Provide each employee with a well-ventilated, lockable cupboard. In large operations, even differentiate street and working clothes. Guidelines for the toilets: per unit (WC and washbasin) 5–6 m^2 and for the shower areas (for more than five male or female employees) a washbasin and shower, approx. 5.5 m^2 per unit.

Ventilation and extraction: according to VDI guideline 2052, large kitchens should be equipped with mechanical air supply and extraction. Extract the air at each cooker and run it through ductwork into the open air. Supply fresh air (no recirculation). Take the heat production from the appliances into account (e.g. induction ovens can reduce the unused heating of the surroundings).

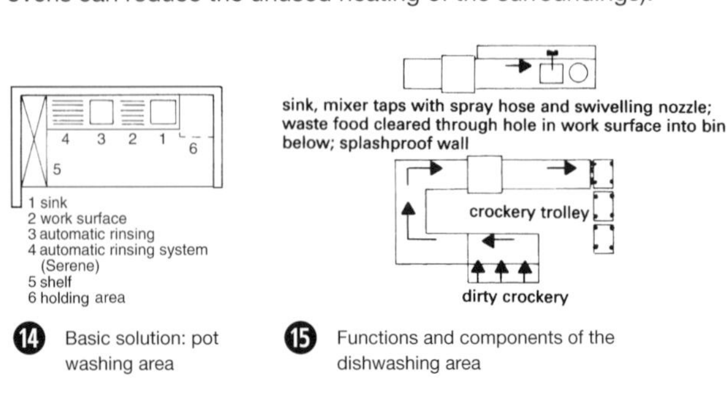

⓮ Basic solution: pot washing area

⓯ Functions and components of the dishwashing area

m²/Person

a Main kitchen
b Cold kitchen
c Cake shop
d Wash cabinet
e Vegetable preparation
f Adjoining rooms
g Meat and fish processing
h Salad kitchen
i Refrigerator
j Stocks

0.50, 0.45, 0.40, 0.35, 0.30, 0.25, 0.20, 0.15, 0.10, 0.05, 0
0, 100, 200, 300, 400, 500, 600, 700, 800, 900, 1000, 1100, 1200 Pers.

1 Space required for kitchen and utility rooms in restaurants and hotels. a–k = m² required per person in each room group

Food preparation and cooking (core temp. min 70°C)

Portioning

Shock cooling to + 3°C in max 90 min.

Storage and distribution in max 5 days at + 3°C

Cold portioning at max + 10°C

Reheating (core temp. min 70°C)

In hot steamer on pallet trolley | In transport trolley to station | In hot steamer

Portioning

Serving

Banquet | Hospitals, Old people's homes, Care homes | Student refectories, Cafeterias, Canteens

2 Cook chill portioning variants for various service requests

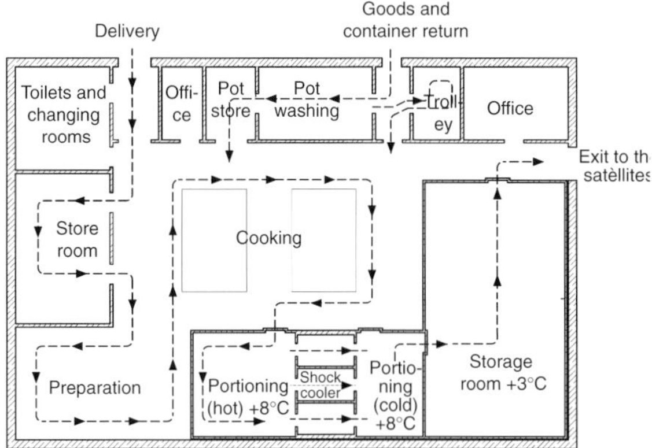

3 Schematic plan of cook chill kitchen with the product routes
Drawing: FDS Consulting H. Uelze

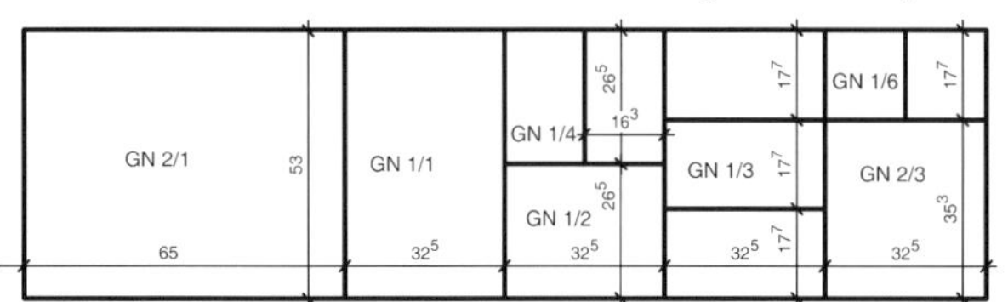

4 Container sizes in the Gastronorm system (GN)

With communal catering for many people in offices, hospitals and factories, a large number of meals have to be supplied in a short period of time. Under the conventional system, 'cook and serve', the kitchen has to be designed to cope with this peak demand, and the working times of the staff are also directly linked to the serving cycle. In order to employ staff and kitchens more regularly and effectively, **'cook and chill'** has been developed → **2** – **3**.

Under this system, the meals are prepared conventionally or purchased as convenience products, cooked in advance, quickly cooled and stored cool. The dishes are then completely cooked (finished) just before serving. This results in a separation of the production time and the serving time. The possibility of storing the prepared dishes enables the capacity of the kitchen to be increased considerably, with up to three times as many meals being produced as in a conventional large kitchen. The extra work involved in the production phase in cooking, cooling and rewarming has to be balanced against the advantages of better utilisation of the kitchen and service.

The meals are prepared in a kitchen, which has a shock cooler in addition to the conventional cooking equipment. One of the most important factors involved with this system is the hygienic requirements in production (similar to industrial food production). The design must therefore implement an absolute separation of clean and unclean areas → p. 179 **5**.

Unclean areas

These are the goods reception, storerooms, preparation rooms, washing up area, waste disposal and cleaning agent store.

Clean areas

These are those for storage and preparation of pre-prepared products, food production, shock cooling, portioning and packaging, plus finishing cold rooms for ready-to-serve meals and the service counters.

When preparing the food, it is important to make sure that the core temperature is at least 70°C during cooking and that the subsequent cooling to +3°C takes place within 90 minutes.

The food is also to be stored at +3°C. The **cold portioning** should take place at a temperature of +12°C and the transport to the consumer locations at max. +3°C. The cool chain from goods delivery to eating must never be interrupted. The statutory hygiene regulations are to be observed absolutely.

A recent innovation is the introduction of cook chill assembly kitchens. These are only portioning kitchens, which put together individual parts of meals. All food is produced by an external supplier as cook chill products. This results in the saving of a large part of the storage rooms and the whole of the cooking and roasting kitchens.

The planning should always be left to experienced designers, because additional details are important concerning hygiene for the kitchen employees.

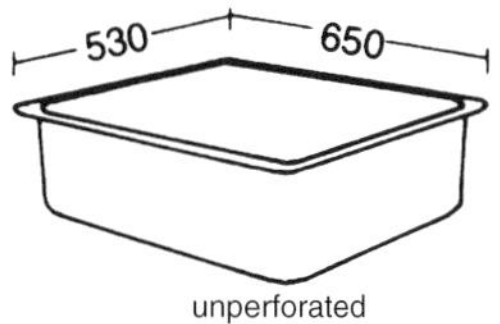

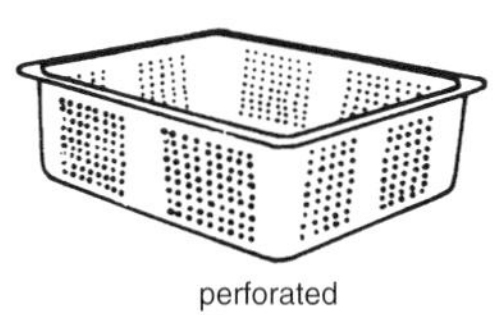

5 Transport and heating containers in Gastronorm sizes (GN)

BS EN 203
BS EN 631
BS 6173
BS EN 12851
BSEN ISO 22000
BIP 2130/2078
DIN EN 631
DIN 66075

BS EN 203
BS EN 631
BS 6173
BS EN 12851
BSEN ISO 22000
BIP 2130/2078
DIN EN 631
DIN 66075

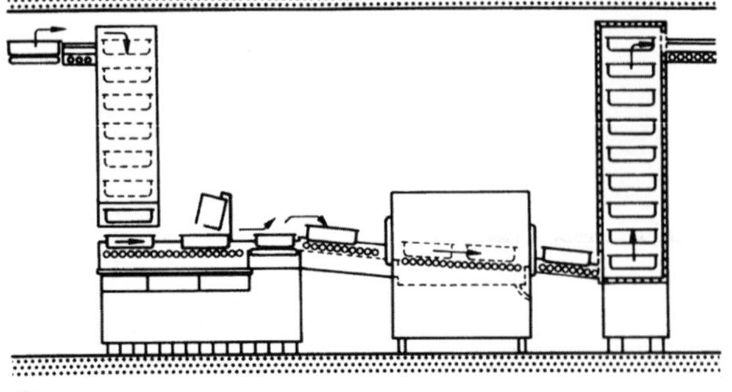

❶ Container transport in the Contiport system

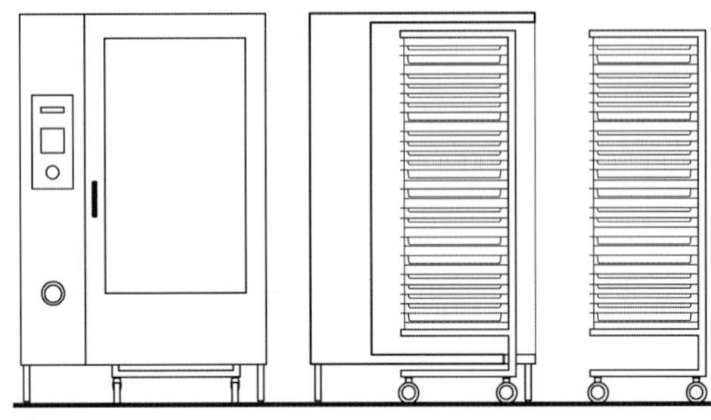

❷ Combi steamer oven: foods are cooked or finished on trays

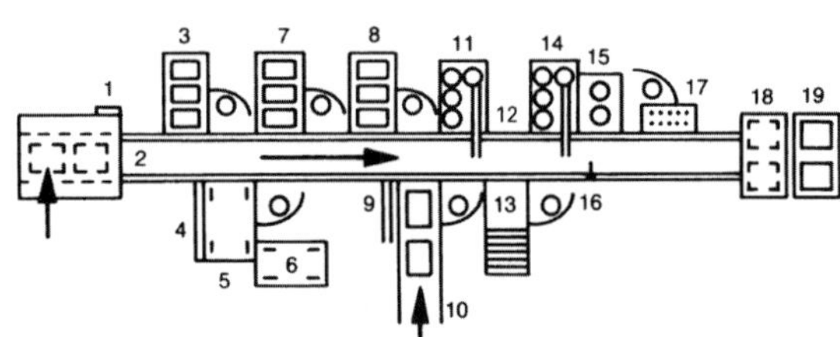

1 automatic crockery dispenser and tray unloader; dispensing from heated cabinet below; punched card reading device
2 meal distribution conveyor
3 electronically controlled serving trolley for potatoes
4 illuminated display for desserts and salads
5 rack trolley for desserts
6 rack trolley for salads
7 electronically controlled serving trolley for vegetables
8 electronically controlled serving trolley for meat
9 illuminated display for special diets
10 supplementary conveyor for special diets
11 automatic sauce dispenser
12 cutlery dispenser
13 soup plate dispenser
14 automatic soup dispenser
15 dispenser for heat-retaining container lids
16 automatic closing device for soup plate covers
17 control desk for diet assistant
18 automatic tray stacker
19 tray distribution trolley

❸ Food serving system

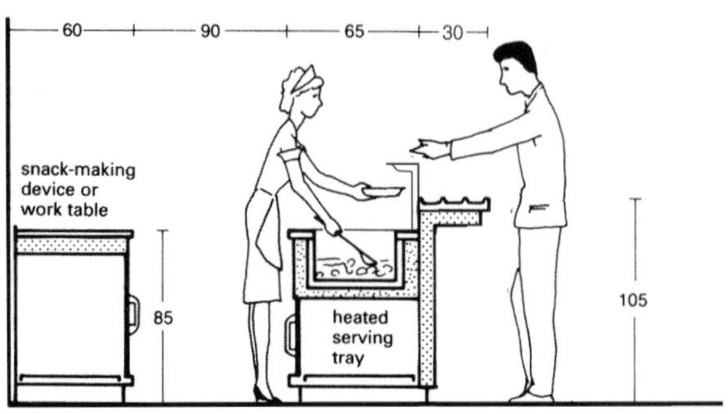

❻ Food service, cafeteria

Container transport → ❶ of unit containers in Gastronorm sizes → p. 181 ❹. Automatic through-flow roasters and cookers → ❹ – ❺. Mainly used in industrial food production.

Combi steamer ovens enable the most varied modes of cooking in one appliance (hot air steaming, roasting and reheating. The core temperature of the food can be used for computer control of the cooking process). Heated by electricity or gas. Water supply needed. When cook and chill production takes place in the immediate vicinity of the cold portioning room or shock cooler, the cooler motor for the shock cooler should if possible be located in a side room (to prevent noise nuisance and heat production). The cold portioning is arranged between the shock cooling room and the cook chill storeroom. This is useful for the checking, portioning and assembly of the cooled foods.

In addition to the serving system with hot and cold counters → ❸, ❻ – ❼, cook and chill production is also well suited for serving in front cooking systems.

In hospitals and residential/nursing homes, the serving is done on a portioning conveyor. The finishing of cook chill foods can then be carried out on special tray trolleys by induction, conduction or convection. According to the system used, special crockery may be required and/or space for the docking station in the ward. With all systems, it is possible to equip the trolley with cooling to ensure the unbroken cool chain for the cook chill system and also to keep cold foods like salads and desserts cool. Especially in large kitchens with long traffic routes, these systems can keep the food warm for a long time and avoid the core temperature dropping under the specified value.

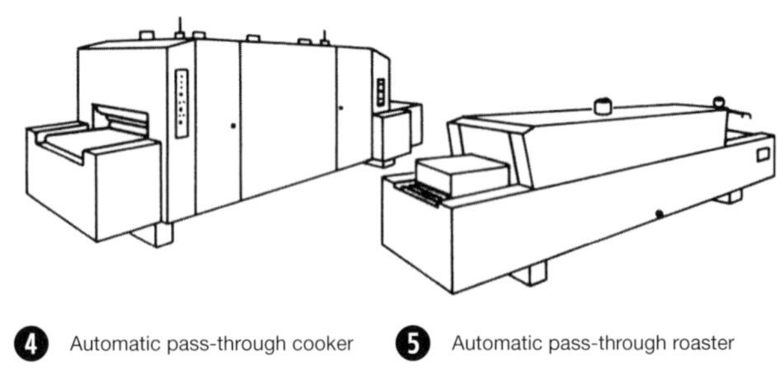

❹ Automatic pass-through cooker ❺ Automatic pass-through roaster

① Ventilation ceiling
② Shelves for casseroles and salamanders
③ Work surface/cooker
④ Floor unit with fridge/freezer, oven or cupboard

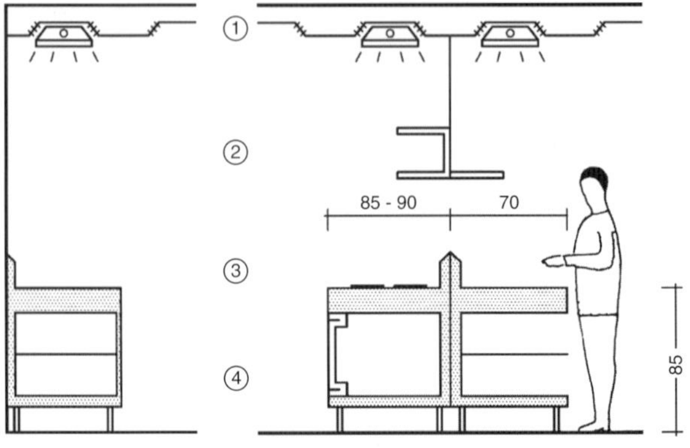

❼ Section through working area

CATERING

Examples of Large Kitchens

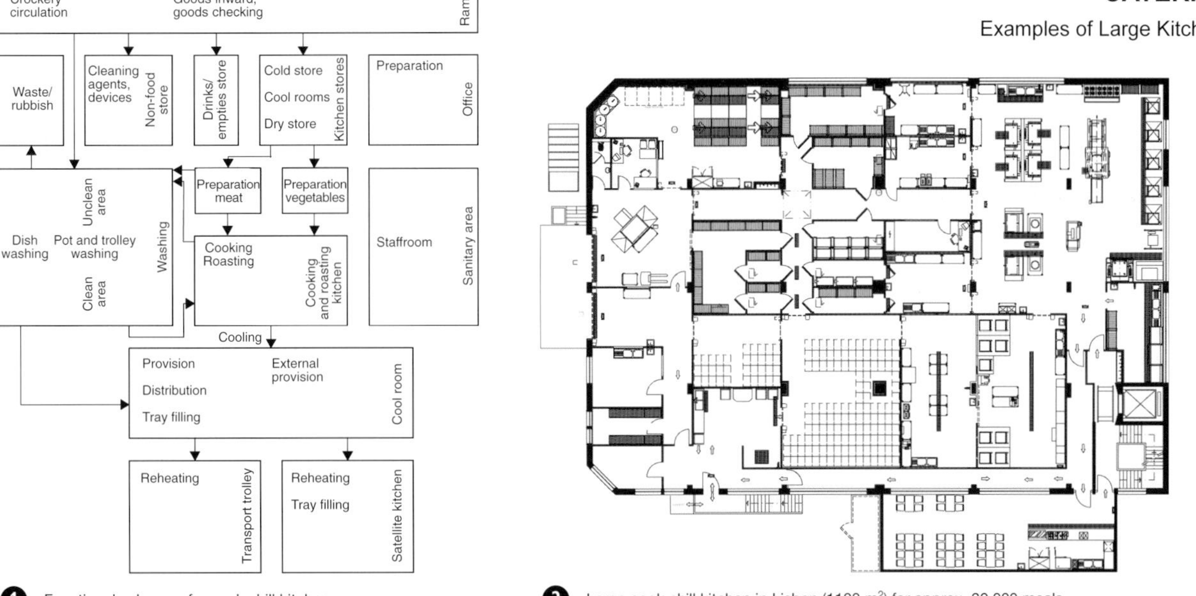

1 Functional scheme of a cook chill kitchen

2 Large cook chill kitchen in Lisbon (1100 m²) for approx. 30 000 meals

Designer: FDS Consulting H. Uelze

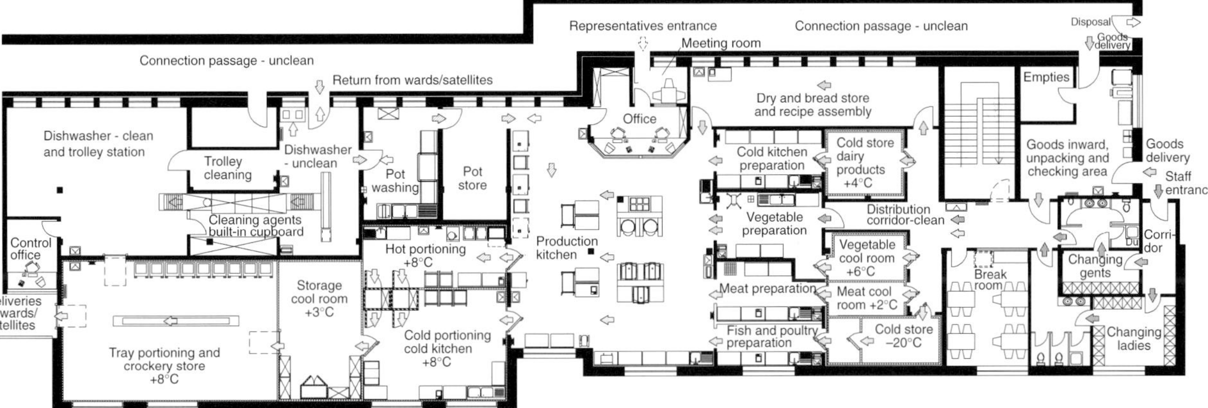

3 Cook chill kitchen in a hospital

Designer: FDS Consulting H. Uelze

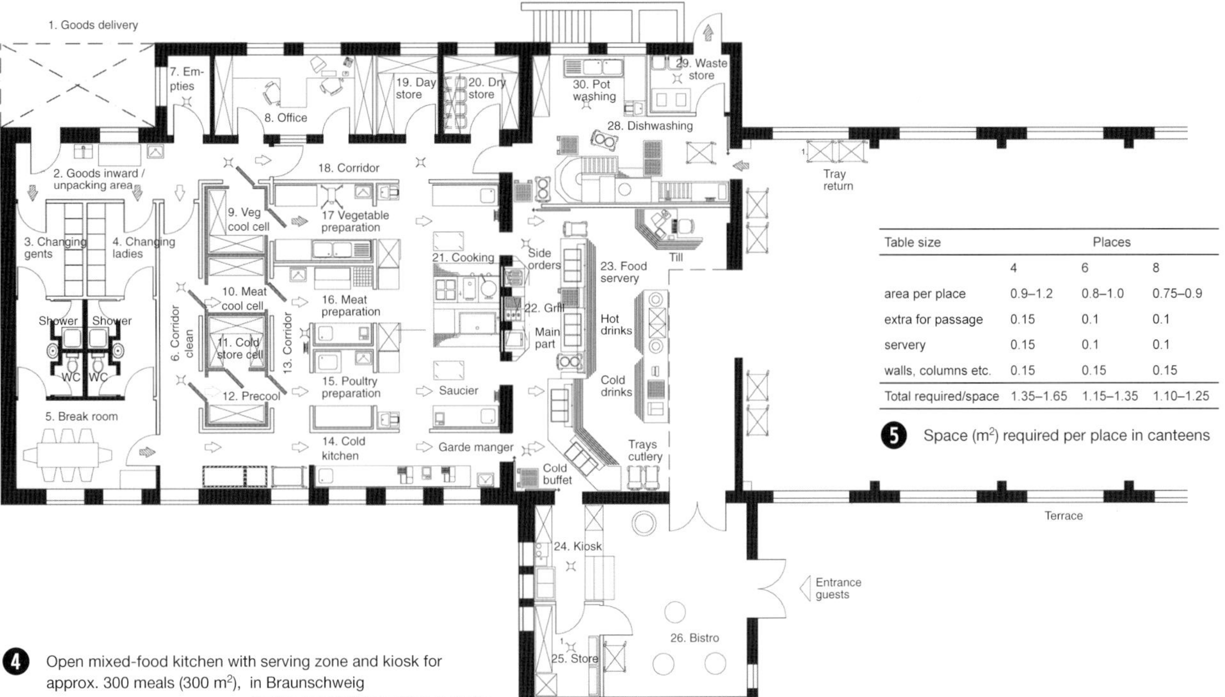

4 Open mixed-food kitchen with serving zone and kiosk for approx. 300 meals (300 m²), in Braunschweig

Designer: FDS Consulting H. Uelze

Table size	Places		
	4	6	8
area per place	0.9–1.2	0.8–1.0	0.75–0.9
extra for passage	0.15	0.1	0.1
servery	0.15	0.1	0.1
walls, columns etc.	0.15	0.15	0.15
Total required/space	1.35–1.65	1.15–1.35	1.10–1.25

5 Space (m²) required per place in canteens

BS EN 203
BS EN 631
BS 6173
BS EN 12851
BSEN ISO 22000
BIP 2130/2078
DIN EN 631
DIN 66075

YOUTH HOSTELS

General design notes

YOUTH HOSTELS
MBO Guidelines
German Youth Hostel Association

Mattress with duvet
Camp bed and palliasse
(Bunk) bed

① (Traditional) bedding in youth hostels

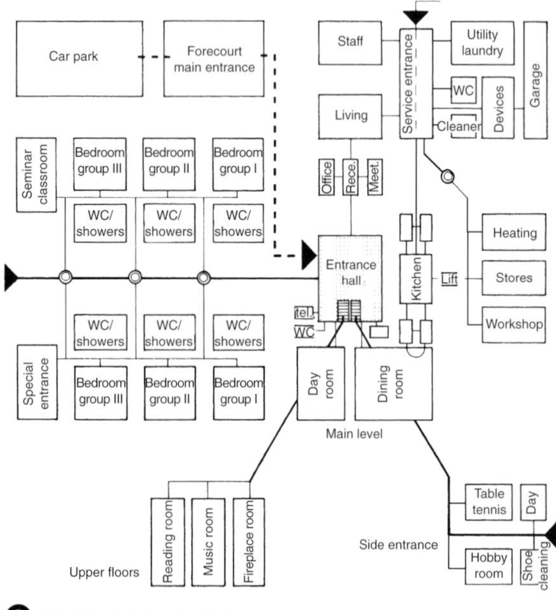

② Youth hostel: functional scheme

Traditionally, youth hostels have offered reasonably priced accommodation for young people, youth groups and school classes, but the range of services of a modern youth hostel also includes meetings, courses, seminars, education of young people and adults, leisure facilities, school trips, and walking for singles and families. In rural areas, there are children's hostels (up to age 13) and youth hostels (13–17), and in towns there are youth guest houses offering tourist and cultural services. The tendency among youth hostels is towards the 3-star hotel standard → p. 172, with sizes of 120–160 beds.

Functional areas

Bedrooms in hostels consist of 4–6 (maximum 8) rooms in groups with a leader room (one bed, one folding bed as day couch), and in guest houses 2–4 bedrooms, leader/teacher accommodation 1–2 rooms with work area, family rooms with 4–6 beds; the trend is to separate rooms for parents and children. Boys and girls are separated, mostly allocated rooms starting from the head of a corridor with a number of dividing doors, which can be locked if required (for flexibility). Showers and washbasins connected to the rooms, separate WC (accessible for disabled people), lockable luggage store. Cleaning rooms on each floor and shoe store/ cleaning room.

Lounge and meeting rooms: One room per 20–25 beds. Multiple dining rooms, multi-purpose areas with individual corners, cafeteria, lecture room, dining room also suitable for events, same number of places as beds, entrance hall/reception and office for the warden. Outdoor camping area (door to sanitary facilities), sports and games, parking for buses and cars, garden for the warden. Inside, separated noise zones for table tennis, hobbies and workrooms.

Utility area: kitchen serving individual portions or group meals, serving trolleys, no self-service counter, utility room, staff lounge.

Living areas: flat for the warden, bedrooms for staff, 12–15 m^2.

UK issues: Youth hostels, for financial reasons and because they are frequently located in sensitive surroundings, are often conversions of existing buildings. Consequently the UK Youth Hostels Association (YHA) is reluctant to impose definitive architectural guidelines. However, some are applied, especially regarding fire safety and space per bed.

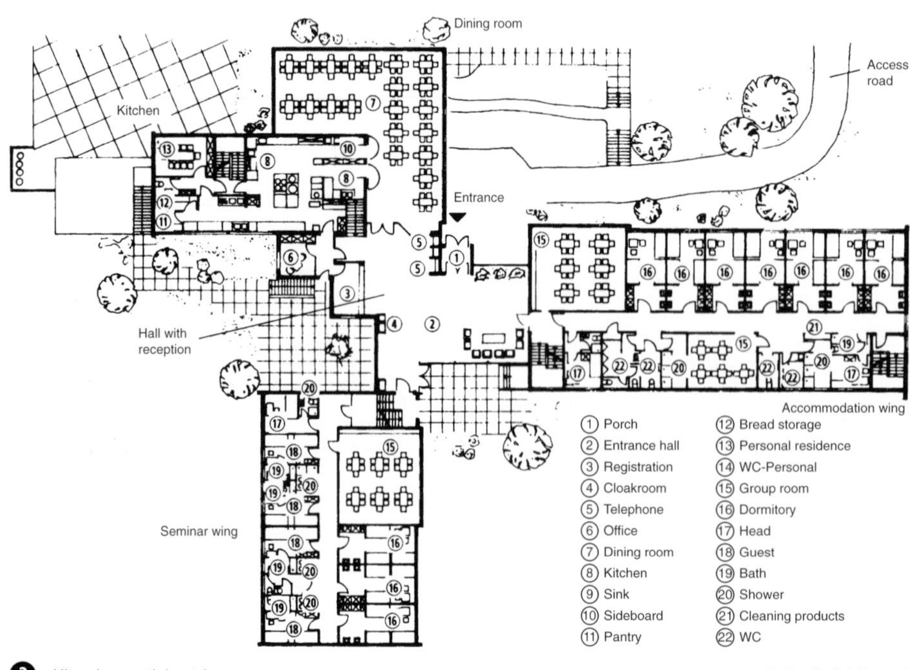

③ Hitzacker youth hostel

Arch.: C. Schönwald

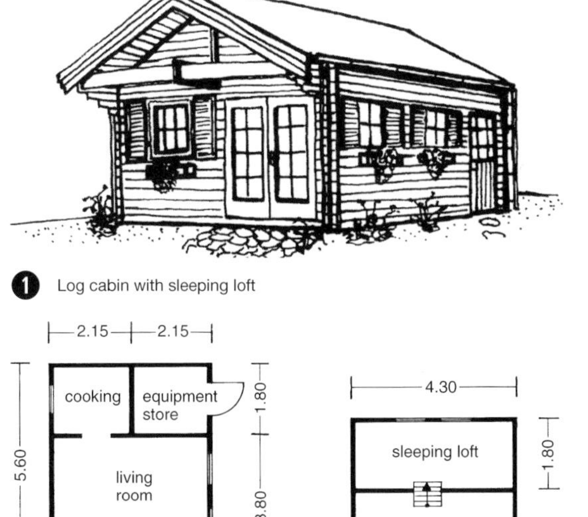

❶ Log cabin with sleeping loft

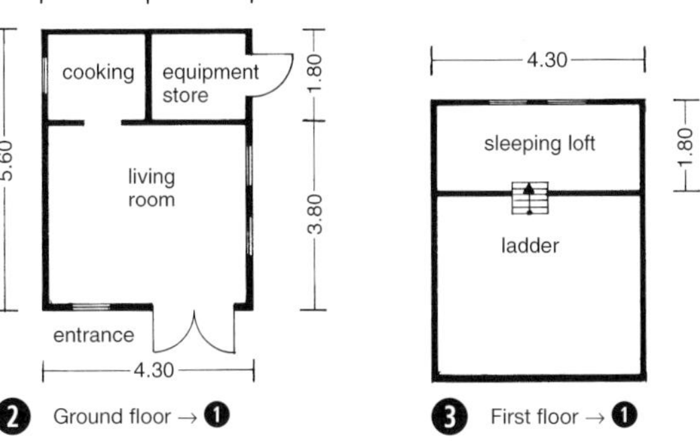

❷ Ground floor → ❶

❸ First floor → ❶

Holiday homes are for temporary holiday accommodation, either for the user or for (paying) guests. They can be single buildings on their own plot or grouped in a holiday park and are subject to the LBO.

Weekend homes, which make use of appropriate waivers under the LBO concerning the quality of residential rooms, thermal insulation, sound insulation and fire protection, may be erected only on suitable sites and are restricted to certain sizes laid down in the States' Camping and Weekend Home Regulations (e.g. floor area max. 40 m² (+ 10 m² veranda), height max. 3.50 m). The features of rented holiday homes are often controlled by the **German Tourism Association**, which issues classifications. In general, weekend homes should have a living area, a proper kitchen (partitioned), an enclosed shower, with WC and washbasin, and at least one enclosed sleeping area.

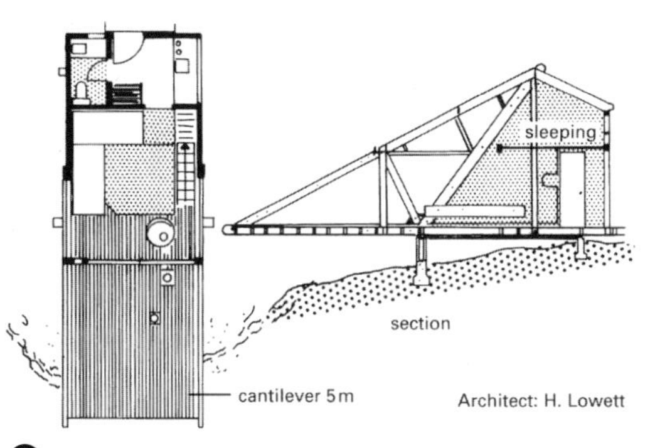

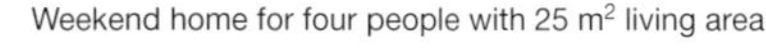

❹ Weekend home for four people with 25 m² living area Arch. H. Lowett

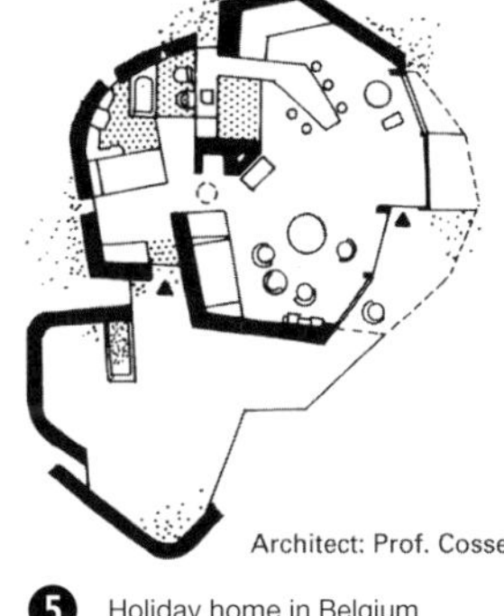

❺ Holiday home in Belgium

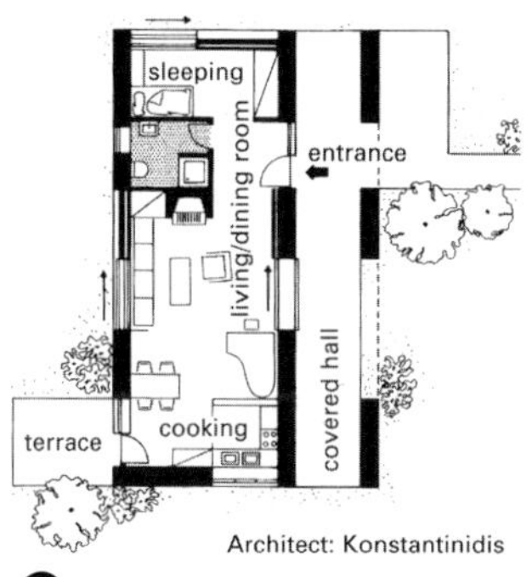

❻ Holiday cabin in Greece

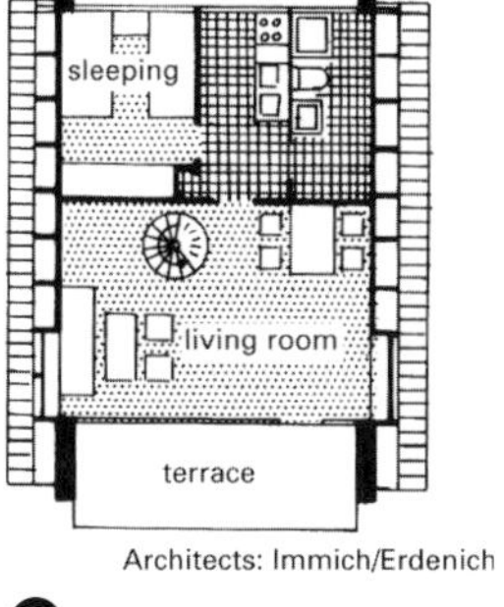

❼ Weekend home

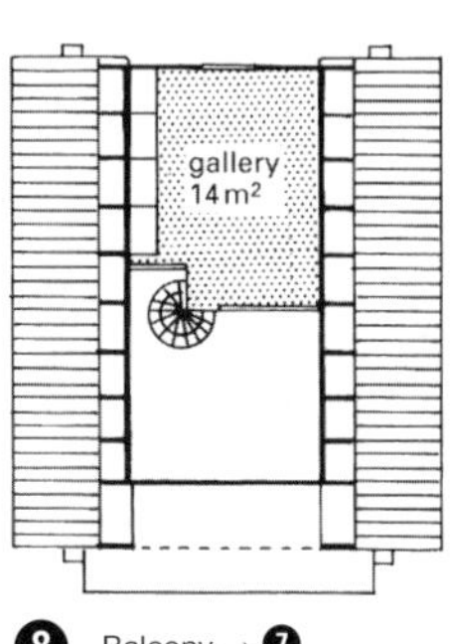

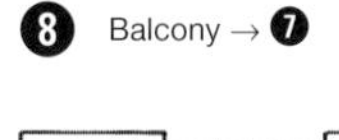

❽ Balcony → ❼

❾ Section → ❼

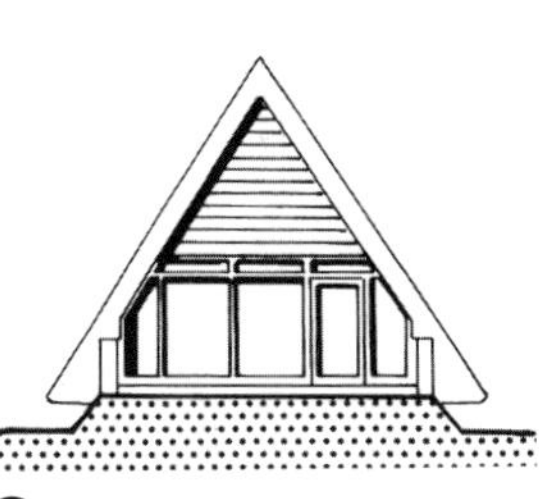

❿ Elevation → ❼

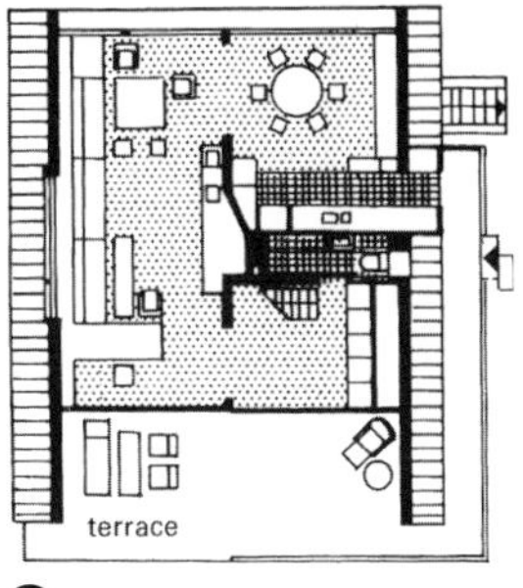

⓫ Ground floor of a holiday home in Nordseeland

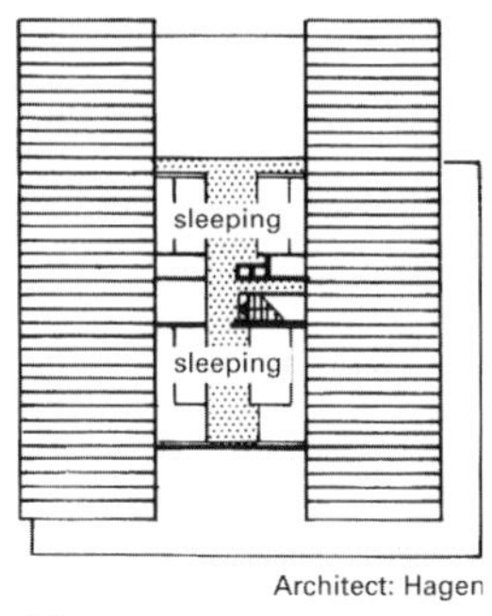

⓬ First floor → ⓫

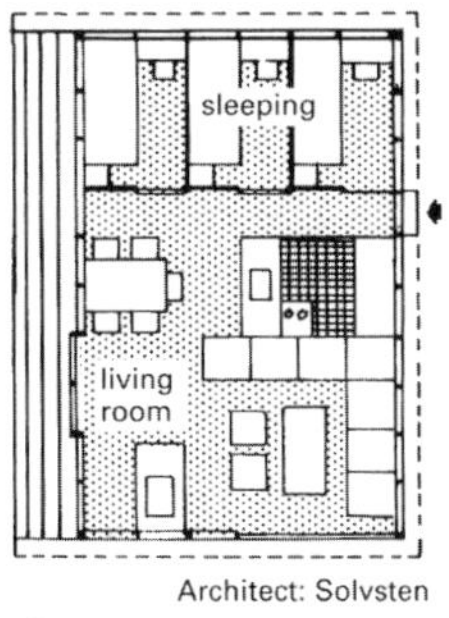

⓭ Weekend home

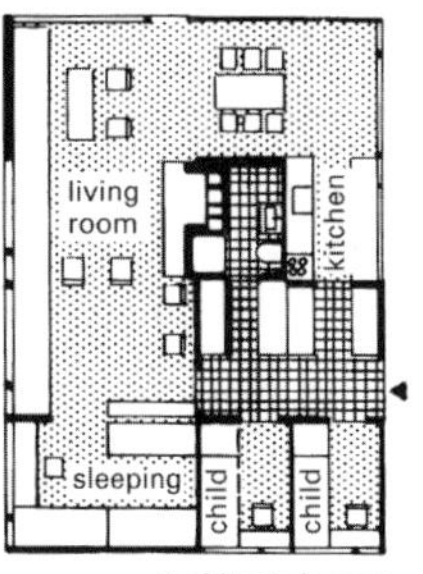

⓮ Holiday home on Bornholm

MOTELS

General Design Notes

Motels offer reasonably priced accommodation for travellers. They are located at the edge of towns in places easily reachable by motorway or arterial roads, near tourist attractions and holiday regions. It is beneficial to have restaurants, petrol stations and services for motorists in the immediate vicinity. In contrast to city hotels, motels are mostly single-storey, widely spread facilities → 7. The access road normally leads to the registration (short-term parking), then to a car park or carport as near to the room as possible. (Departure also via registration with check-out and return of key.)

Room sizes 4 × 4 m – 5 × 5 m, with bathroom and sometimes kitchenette → 1 – 6. Furnishing is cost-saving and simple (most of the guests stay only one night). Community rooms for guests, with desks and reading tables, radio, television; play area should be situated away from the guest rooms so as not to disturb sleepers.

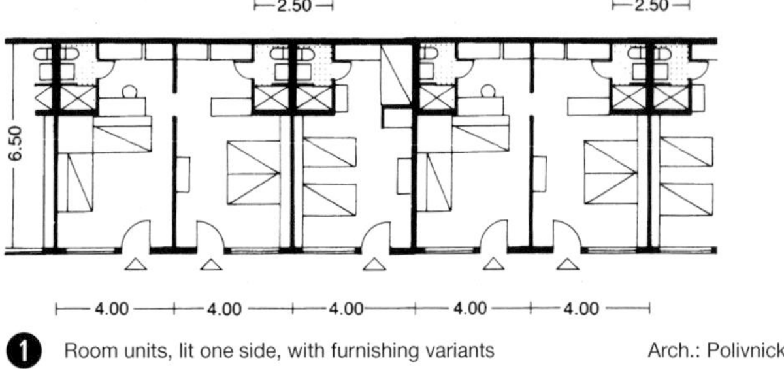

1 Room units, lit one side, with furnishing variants Arch.: Polivnick

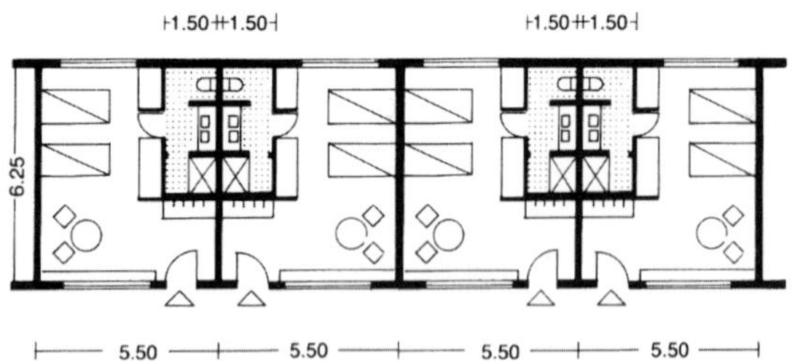

2 Room units, exposed two sides Arch.: Roberto

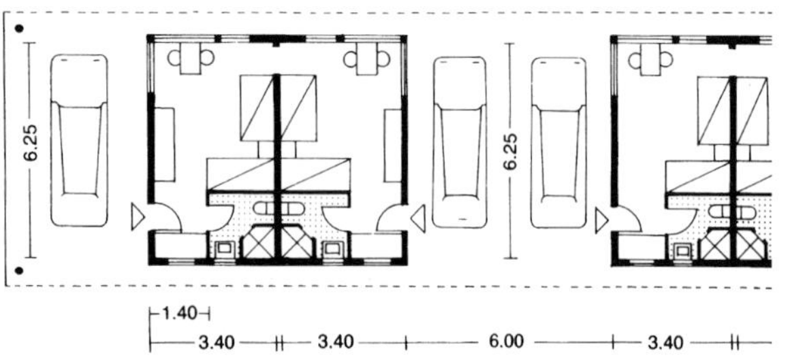

3 Group of six room units with covered parking places Arch.: Duncan

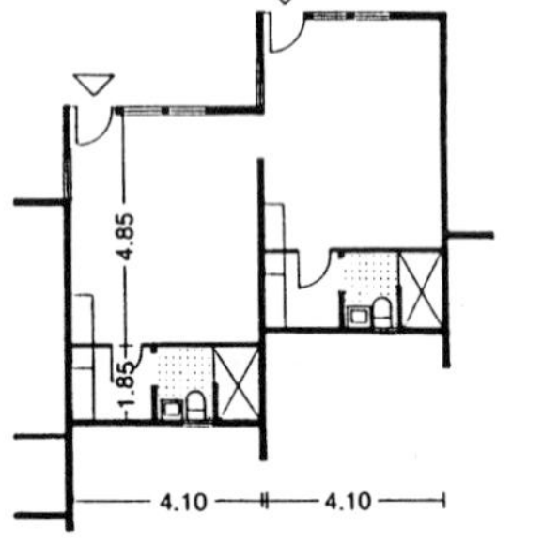

4 Stepped arrangement Arch.: Thompson

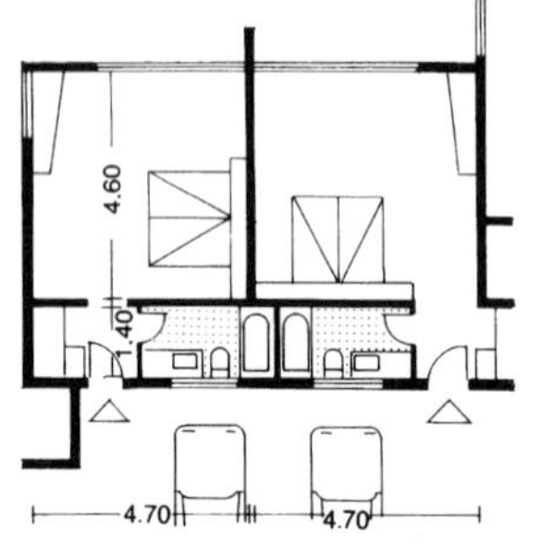

6 Stepped arrangement Arch.: Hornbostel

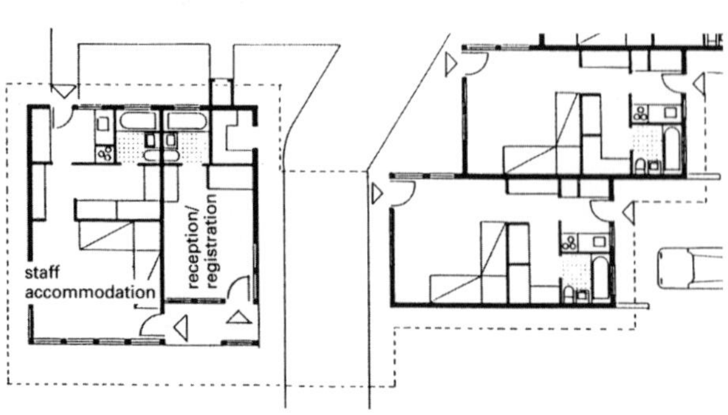

5 Stepped arrangement of room units with registration and manager's flat Arch.: Williams

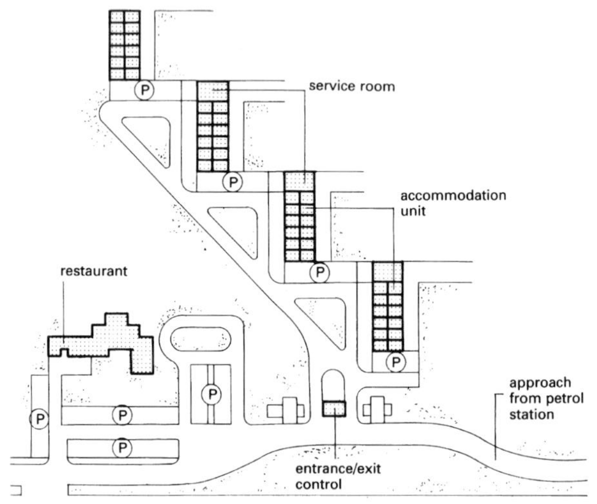

7 Motel facility with joint car park for each building and restaurant as separate business Arch.: Fried

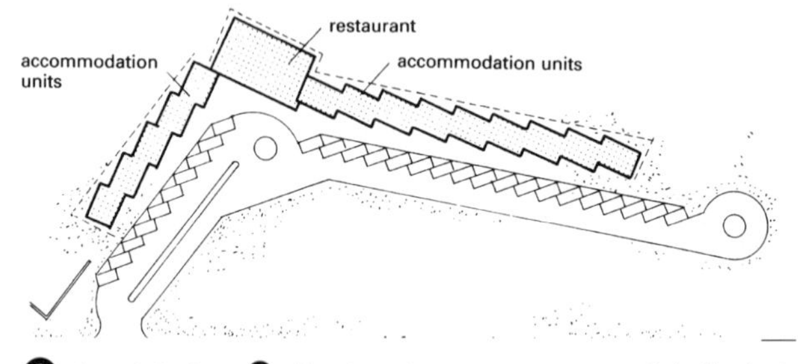

8 Layout plan for → 5 with restaurant Arch.: Hornbostel

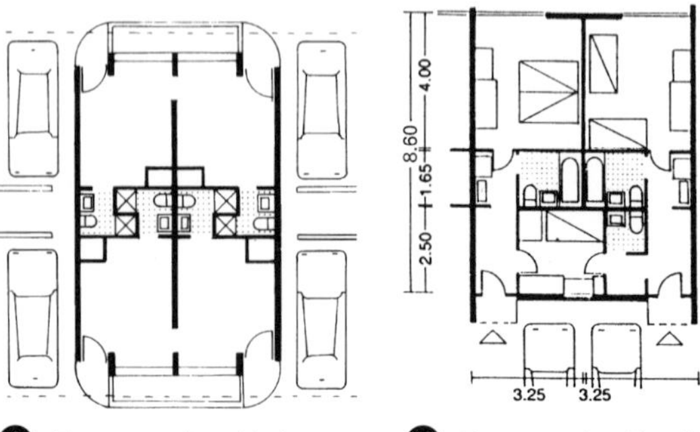

9 Four room units as block Arch.: Tibbals, Crumley, Musson

10 Two room units with optional additional room

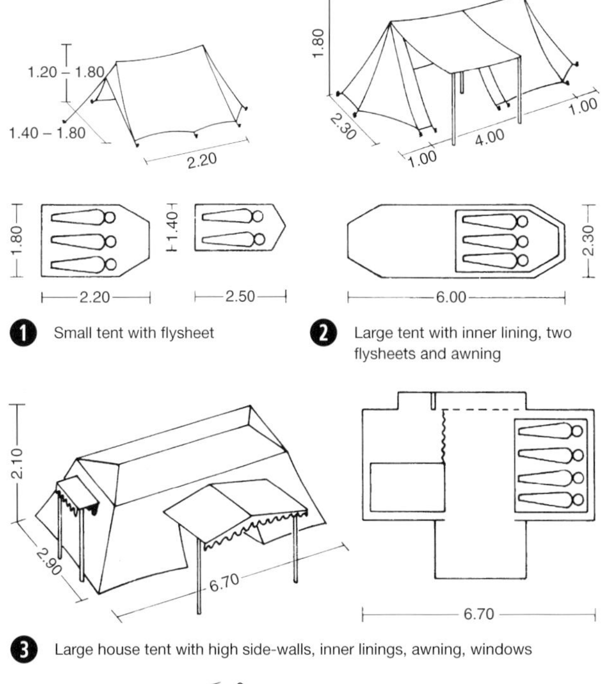

❶ Small tent with flysheet

❷ Large tent with inner lining, two flysheets and awning

❸ Large house tent with high side-walls, inner linings, awning, windows

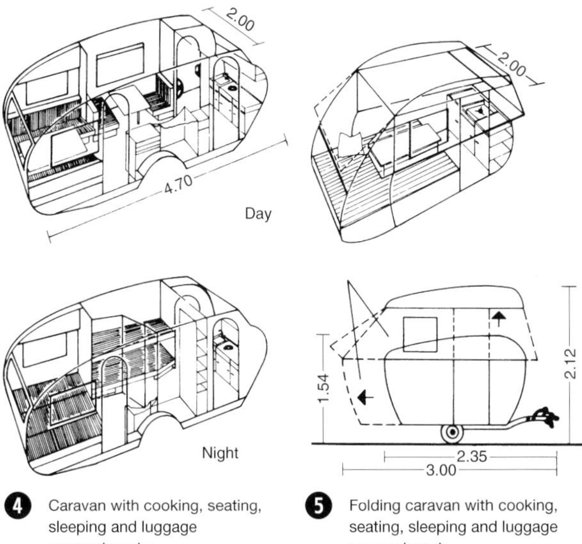

❹ Caravan with cooking, seating, sleeping and luggage compartments

❺ Folding caravan with cooking, seating, sleeping and luggage compartments

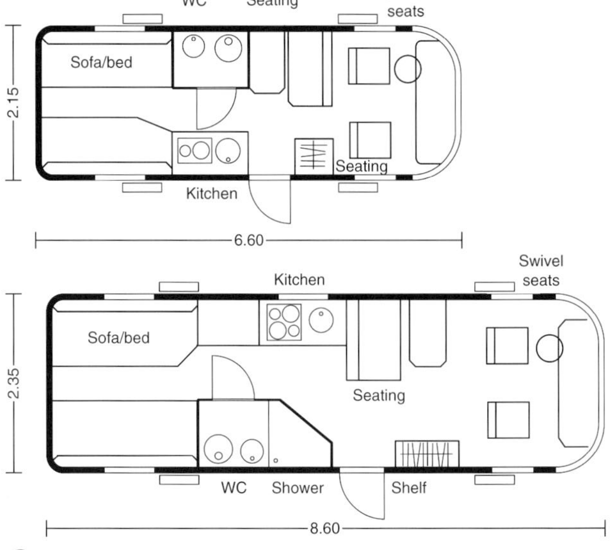

❻ Motorhome with seating, swivelling chairs, sofa/bed and WC

CAMPING

Camping sites → ❼ offer the cheapest legal accommodation – in tents → ❶ – ❸, or caravans → ❹ – ❺ or motorhomes → ❻. The spectrum ranges from **natural camping sites** in holiday areas, mostly in attractive countryside (e.g. on the coast) to **motorhome parks**, as a cheap alternative to hotels and motels, in reachable locations near towns (they are mainly for motorhomes).

The requirements for camping sites are laid down in the states' **Camping and Weekend Parks Regulations**. Camping sites generally need to have an access road from a public road, with access control (barrier), reception and assignment of places, an area for waiting vehicles, visitor's car parks and internal access with roads adequate for fire service vehicles (width min. 3.0 m).

Camping sites and motorhome parks should be separated. A place should be provided for each caravan or motorhome. These places are min. 75 m^2 (65 m^2 if car parking spaces are provided separately) and are grouped into sections of 20 places by fire roads (5 m wide). It may be necessary to provide firebreak strips next to the boundaries.

Accommodation

CAMPING

MBO
States' Camping and Weekend Parks Regulations

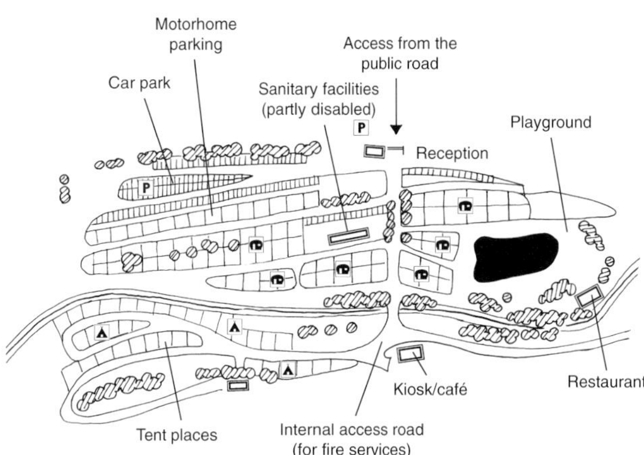

❼ Example of a camping site with tent area and places for caravans

Communal facilities

Camping sites have the following communal facilities:

- **drinking water taps** (one tap for every 20 places supplied from the public water main), **electricity sockets** (parking places for motorhomes and larger caravans should ideally have water supply, drains and electricity supply), **fire hydrants** and **fire extinguishers** (one fire extinguisher per 40 places)
- sanitary facilities with: **toilet blocks** (guideline: 1 block per 100 places with: 4 WCs/2 urinals/1 washbasin (gents'), 6 WC/1 washbasin (ladies'), 1 WC for the disabled), **washing facilities** (guideline for each 100 places: 3 showers, 5 washbasins for gents and ladies, 1 shower and washroom for the disabled), sink for washing crockery and clothes, **emptying facility for waste water and toilets**, sufficient and appropriately distributed waste **bins**
- **telephone** line with emergency call function, **kiosk**, **supermarket**, **snack bar** or **restaurant**, **leisure facilities** (play area, sports grounds, barbecue site, open area).

CHILDREN'S DAYCARE

Access and Building Forms

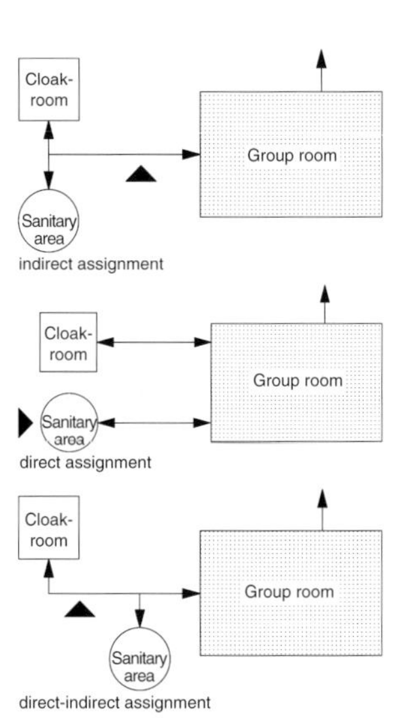
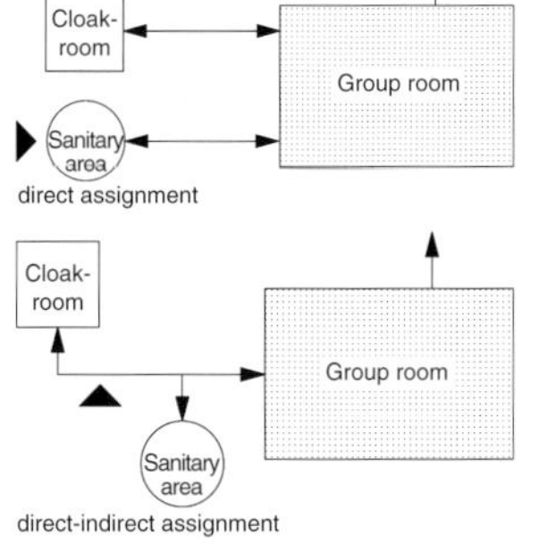

❶ Functional arrangement of group room, cloakroom and sanitary facilities

① terrace
② common room 45–48 m²
③ dining
④ kitchen
⑤ role-play 4 m²
⑥ building 4 m²
⑦ bonding 4 m²
⑧ group room 18 m²
⑨ washroom/WC

❷ Typical plan of a kindergarten group Arch.: Franken/Kreft

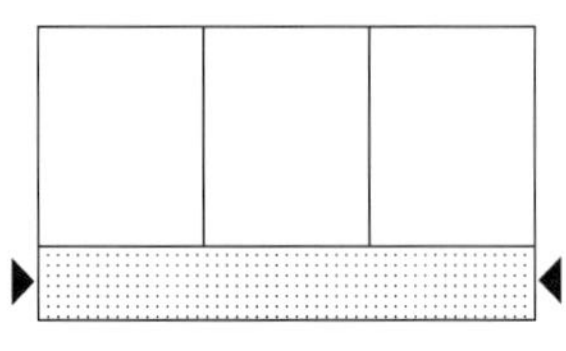

❸ Children's daycare centres access types: in a single block

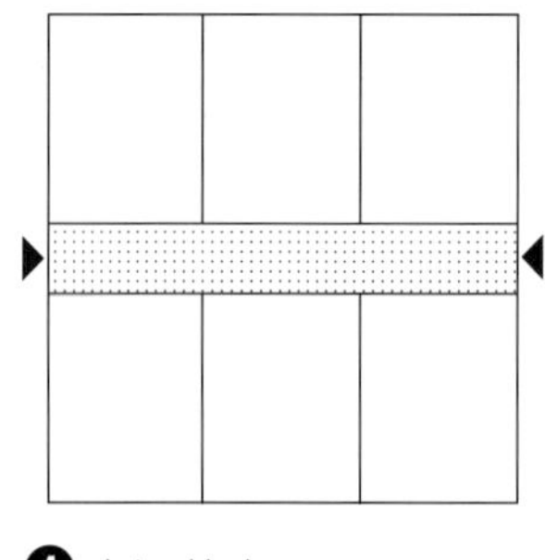

❹ In two blocks

The design of facilities for children should consider their needs and size. There are no regulations or guidelines for the construction of children's daycare buildings. The regulations of the relevant state and the LBO are used as guidelines. Accessibility building design standards are recommended.

Children's daycare centre

This term includes crèches, kindergartens, after-school care etc. The daycare centre is organised so that a mixture of children with all-day and part-time arrangements can be looked after.

Crèche, nursery

Cares for small children from babies to three years old. The group size is generally approx. 10 children.

Kindergarten

Looks after children from min. three years old until they go to school. It may be possible for them to eat lunch and sleep. The group size is generally 20 children.

Children's after-school care

For the care of school-age children until 14 years old. Lunch after school and assistance with homework are offered. These establishments are often combined with kindergartens and the group size is generally 20 children.

Age	1	2	3	4	5	6	7	8	9	10	11	12
Height (cm)	75	85	94	101	108.5	115	121.5	127	131.5	137	143	148
Eye level (cm)	64	74	83	91	96	103	108	113	117	122	127	131
Reach (cm)	30	36	42	48	52	57	61	64	66	69	72	75

❺ Guideline sizes of children (Gralle, Port → refs)

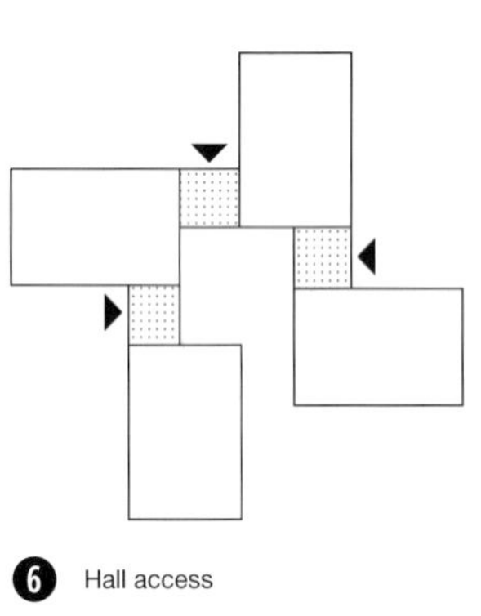

❻ Hall access

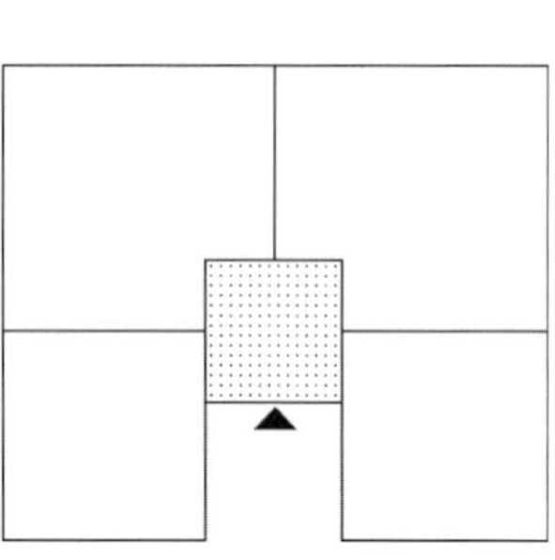

❼ Courtyard access

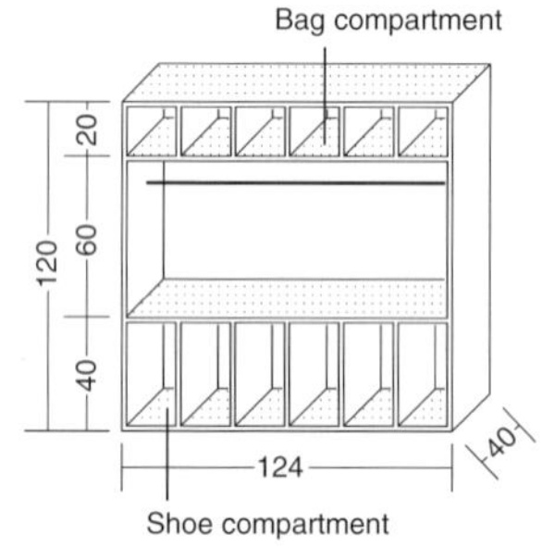

❽ Cloakroom cupboard for six children

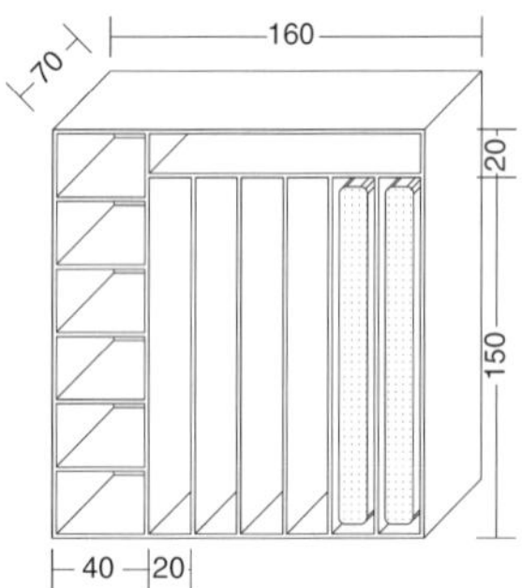

❾ Cupboard for storing children's mattresses (size: 140/70 and 120/60 cm)

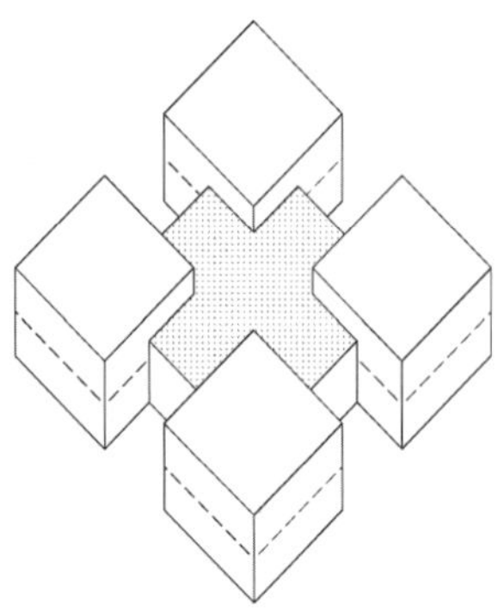

❿ Building form: grouped pavilions

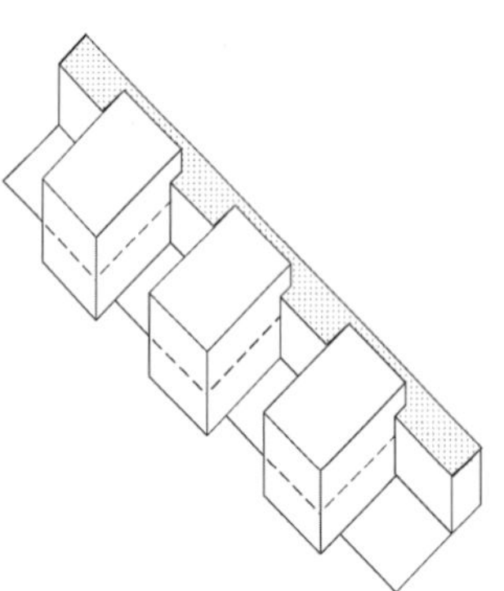

⓫ Building form: rows of pavilions

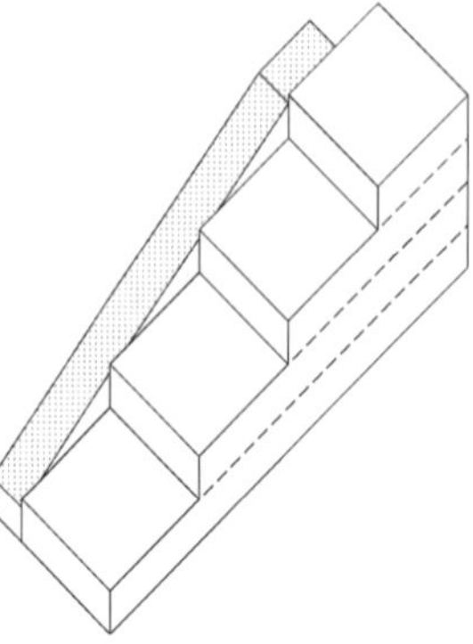

⓬ Building form: stepped

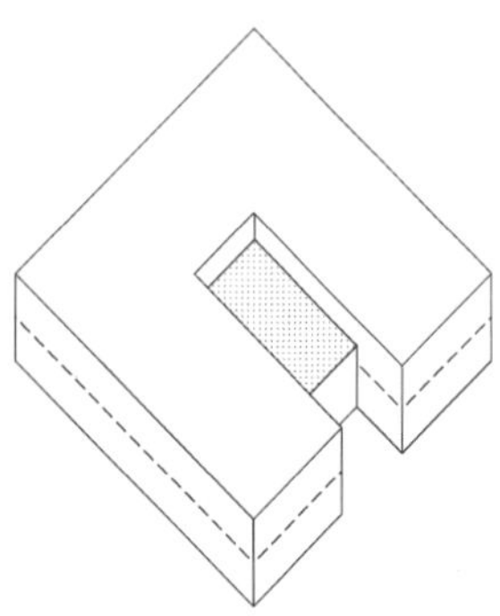

⓭ Building form: compact

Group room

Most time in the children's daycare centre is spent here. Required floor area approx. 2.5 m^2 per child. Create zones as varied as possible and design a second floor level and a stage (play-stage half-open, with a snug cave). Play decks up to a height of 1.50 m must have a handrail at least 70 cm high; play decks more than 1.50 m high must have handrails min. 1.00 m high. The group room should have as short a distance as possible to the WC area. Ideally, provide direct access to the open air and align to the south.

Rest or sleeping rooms

These are not always considered necessary, as mattresses are often laid out in the group room for the midday sleep (cupboard to store the mattresses → p. 188 ❾).

Kitchen

The status of the kitchen in the children's centre can vary according to the paedagogical concept, for example a central kitchen for all groups or as a series of kitchens, one in each group room. Different floor heights are recommended so that adults and children can cook together.

Dining room

The group room is normally used for eating. An extended corridor or the entrance hall are also suitable as communicative places to eat.

Stairs

The risers of stairs in children's centres should not be more than 16 cm, and the treads between 30 and 32 cm.

Height recommendation	Washing facilities	WC, seat height
nursery	for every 10 children	
potty room	1, 45–60 cm	1, 20–25 cm
kindergarten	approx. for every 5 children	
potty room	1, 45–60 cm	1, 25–30 cm
after-school	approx. for every 10 children	
girls boys	1–2. 1–2 65–70 cm	1 1 30–35 cm

Height guidelines for washbasins and WCs

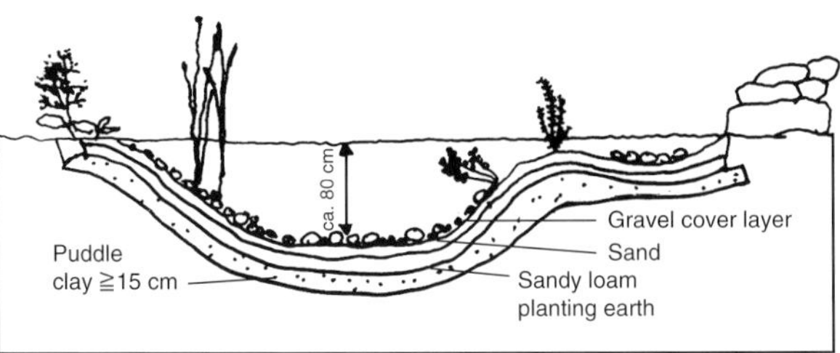

❷ Pond with clay lining for outside area in children's daycare centre

Outdoor areas

Outside playgrounds should be designed to be as varied as possible. The design of external works for children's centres is regulated by several standards. The stipulated minimum area outside per child is variable between the German states.

Hilly landscape Modelling the terrain by heaping and excavating the ground surface. The coarse shape is produced by a hydraulic excavator, and the fine modelling by hand. The hills can incorporate plants, shrubs, hedges, flowers and clover of various heights.

Compost heap as the core of an organic garden. Semi-shaded location for organic waste from the centre.

Trees for climbing, to provide shade, deliver fruit and be educational. Also worth considering are vegetable/herb gardens, sandpits, bird tables, dry stone walls, meadows etc.

Pond should have min. 6 m^2 water surface and a depth of 80 cm to avoid oxygen deficiency. For safety reasons, either a coarse net should be spread over the water or builder's steel mesh installed 10 cm under the water surface.

BS EN 1176
ASTM F1487
DIN EN 1176
DIN EN 1177
DIN 18034

LBO

PLAYGROUNDS

Playground Equipment

Playgrounds must be varied in design, changing and changeable. They must meet the needs of children. Some of the requirements for children's playgrounds are: traffic safety, no pollution by emissions, sufficient sunshine, groundwater level not too high,

Play equipment in playgrounds is often made of timber (e.g. larch, robinia) and the surface of the wood can be additionally protected with beeswax treatment. Standing water and damp should be avoided on all wooden surfaces, so galvanised steel is often set into the ground at the base of verticals.

Playgrounds should be orientation points within residential districts and connected to housing with simple networks of paths. Do not banish playgrounds to the periphery, but design in combination with other communication systems.

Guideline values for the design of playgrounds are built up from individual data: age group, usable area per resident, play area size, distance from home:

Age (years)	m^2/resident	Accessibility, max. distance from home (m)	(min.)
0–6	0.6	up to 200 and in sight	2
6–12	0.5	up to 400	5
12–18	0.9	up to 1000	15

Playgrounds for children are to be provided, as private facilities within the building plot, with the construction of houses or flats: for small children up to 6, for children from 6 to 12, plus leisure areas for adults. This is a requirement for three flats or more. The uniform basis for the provision of all public playgrounds is: 5 m^2 playing area per residential unit, minimum area of playground: 40 m^2. Outdoor play areas must be fenced at least 1 m high (thick hedges, fence or similar) to prevent access to roads, car parking, railway lines, deep watercourses, cliffs and similar dangers.

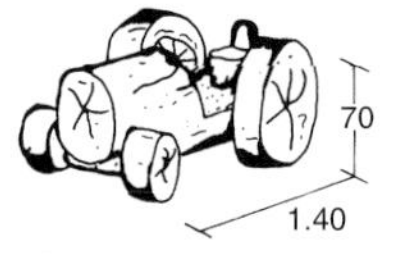

1 Tractor

2 Trailer → 1

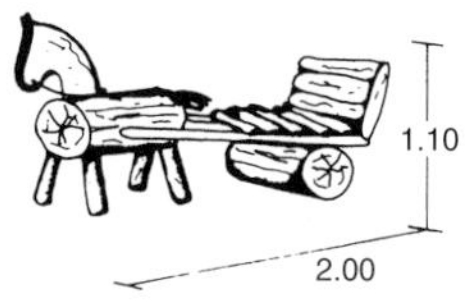

3 Horse and cart

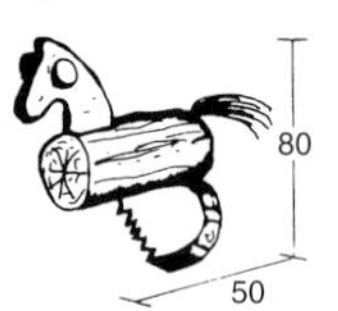

4 Rocking horse

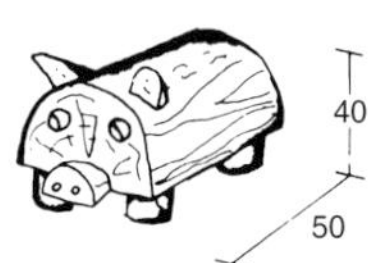

5 Pig

6 Snail

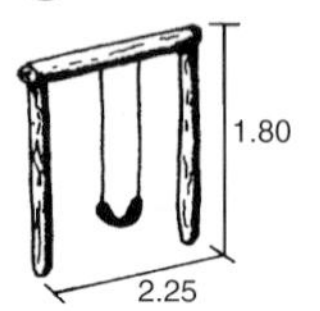

7 Swing for small child

8 Snack table

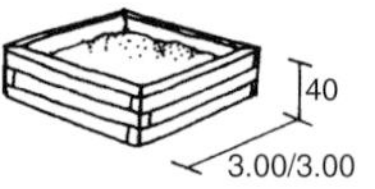

9 Sandpit (squared timber)

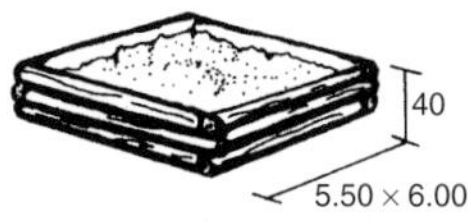

10 Sandpit (round timber)

11 Playhouse

12 House group

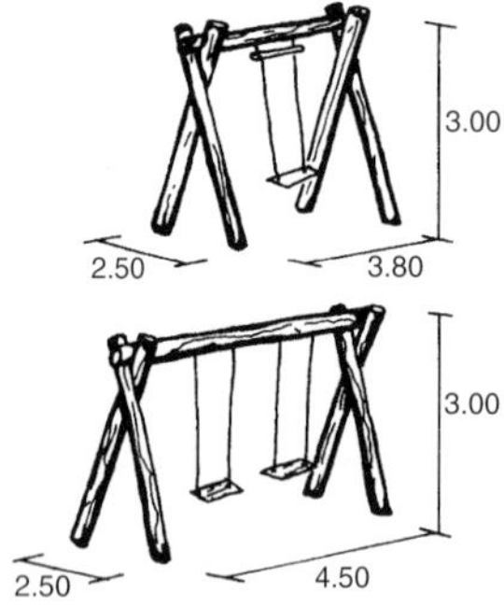

13 Swings

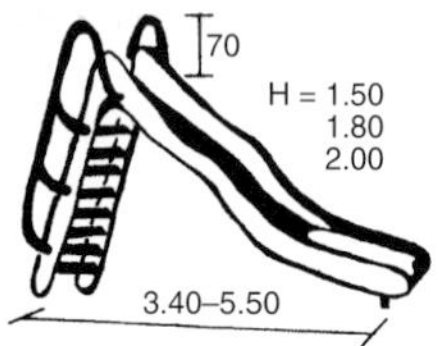

14 Slide

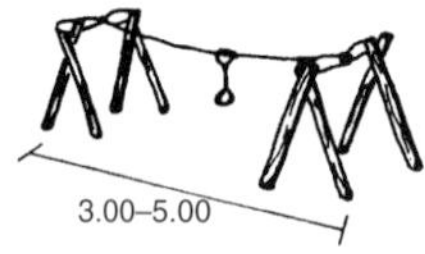

15 Cable run

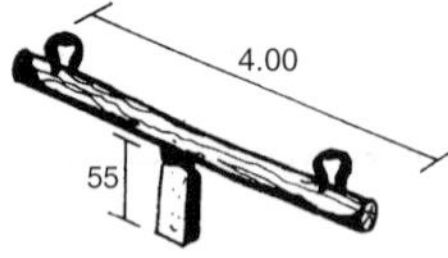

16 Vertical bars

17 Seesaw

D/W/H 7.30/3.80/3.40

18 Slide and climbing house

19 'Karnacksweg' playground

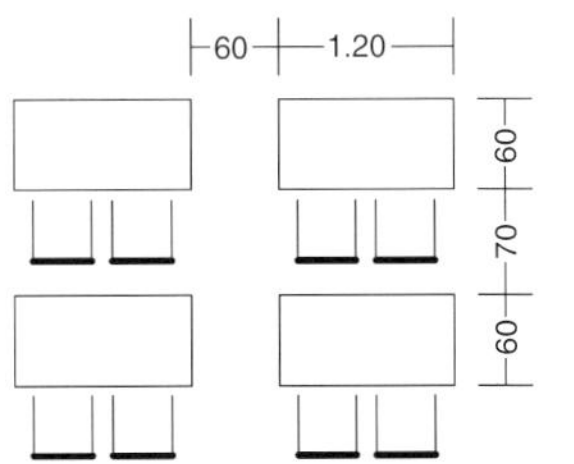

❶ Minimum dimensions for table arrangement in regular classrooms (Saxony → refs)

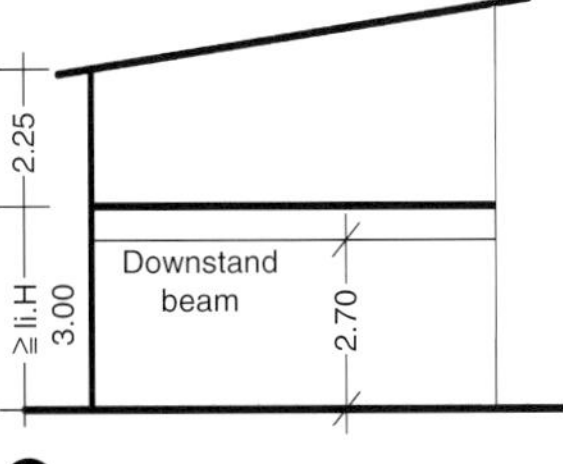

❷ Room heights of classrooms

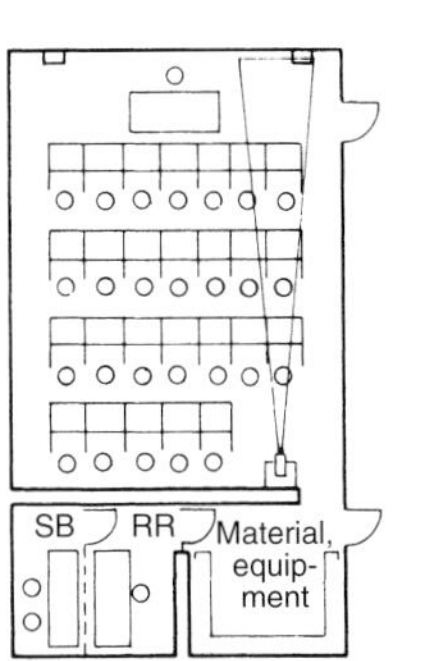

❸ LTR (= listen, talk, record) laboratory, SB = speaker's booth, RR = recording room

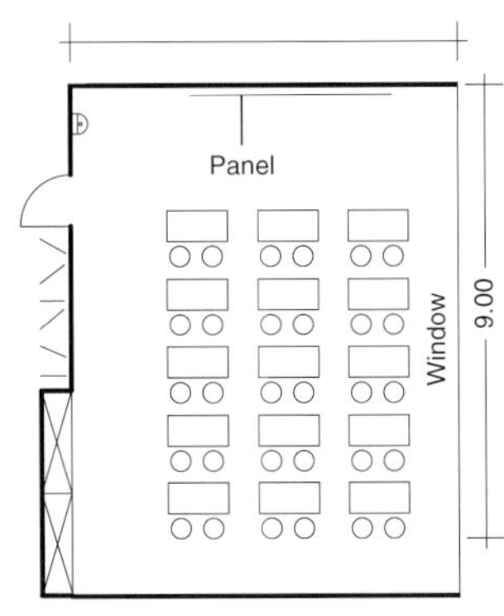

❹ Max. depth of classrooms with one-sided daylight

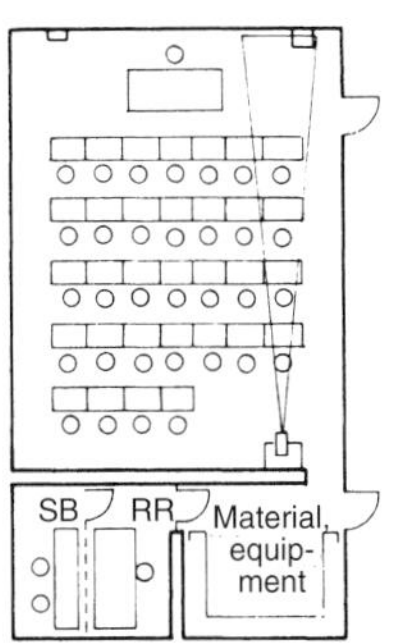

❺ LT (= listen and talk) laboratory

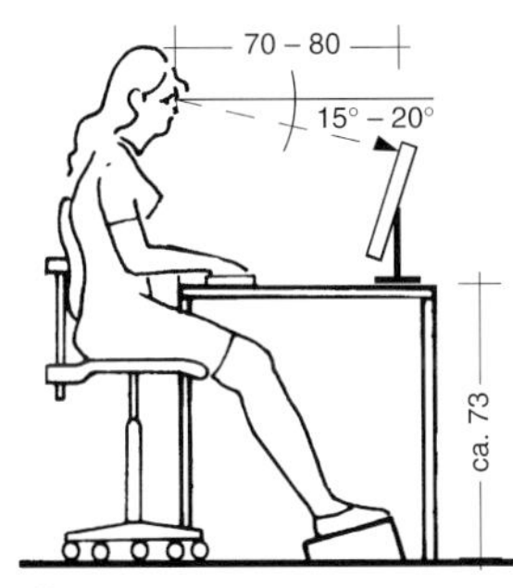

❻ Workplace with monitor

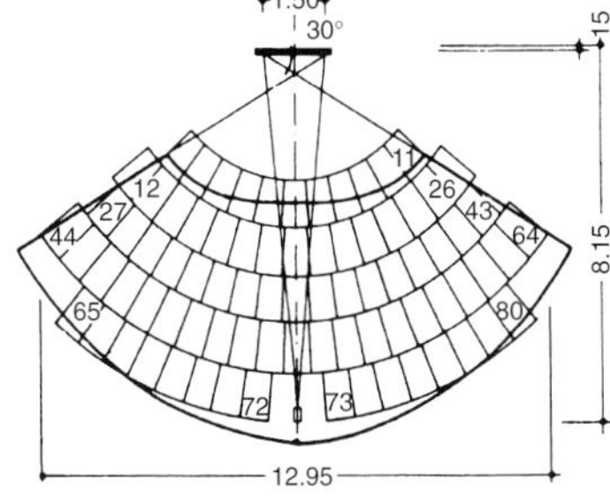

❼ Seating arrangement for 80 pupils ≧10 years old, for film, slides and overhead projection

Design parameters

The basis for the planned development of schools are the school building guidelines of each German state (including model room layouts), in conjunction with relevant national building standards and health and safety regulations.

General classroom area

This includes standard and replacement classrooms, course rooms, rooms for languages and social studies, language laboratories, teaching equipment and map rooms, and other subsidiary rooms. The subjects taught in the general classroom area are: languages, general studies, mathematics, religion, social studies and politics, as well as optional subjects and remedial teaching.

Group rooms

In primary and special schools it should be arranged that these are each accessible from two classrooms. Multi-purpose rooms can be assigned to other areas.

Number of floors

This should lie between three and four. Schools for pupils who are physically disabled or have learning difficulties should have 1–2 storeys.

Room dimensions

The maximum number of pupils in a class is 32.
According to the school building guidelines, the design of classrooms should normally be based on tables with two workplaces → ❶. If the windows are all on one side, the max. room depth is 7.20 m. If possible, have windows on both sides to permit furniture to be freely positioned. The distance between the blackboard and the pupil workplaces at the back should not exceed 9.00 m → ❹. Guideline values: area: ≦1.80–2.00 m^2/pupil. Air volume: ≦5.00–6.00 m^3/pupil. The ceiling height of classrooms (min. 3 m) may not be reduced by more than 0.30 m by individual construction elements → ❷.

Language laboratory → ❸ – ❺

Located within the general classroom area or near the media centre/library. Guideline: approx. 30 language laboratory places per 1000 pupils. Size: LT (listen and talk) and LTR (listen, talk, record) laboratory size, total approx. 80 m^2, language laboratory cabins approx. 1 × 2 m, number of places per laboratory 24–30 m^2, i.e. 40–60 m^2 plus subsidiary areas. LTR laboratory → ❸: 23 workplaces as cabins, approx. 65 m^2 (approx. 2.8 m^2/place) including subsidiary rooms approx. 95 m^2.
LT laboratory → ❺: 33 workplaces as desks, approx. 65 m^2 (approx. 2.0 m^2/place) including subsidiary rooms approx. 95 m^2. Side rooms: studio, recording room, archive for teacher and pupil tapes. Language laboratories are also possible in inner areas of the building with artificial light and air conditioning.

Computer room

Should if possible face north and not be on the ground floor (Saxony → refs). The IT workplaces are designed according to the guidelines for computer workplaces. The upper edge of the monitor should be below eye level so that the pupil's head is tilted at 15–20° → ❻.

BS 4163
BS EN 14434
DIN 18024
DIN 58125
GUV 16.3

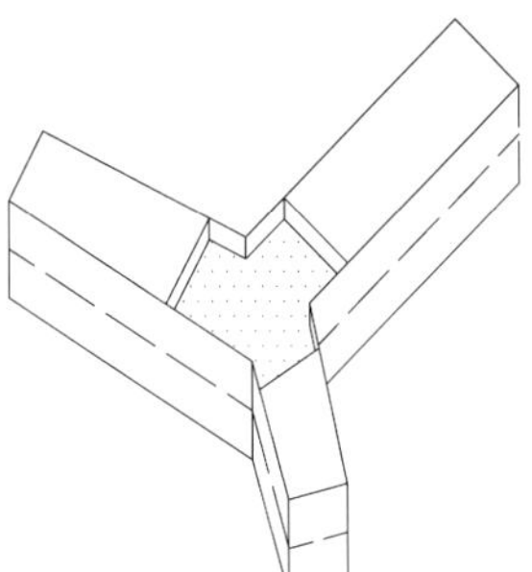

❽ Building form: grouping with central access

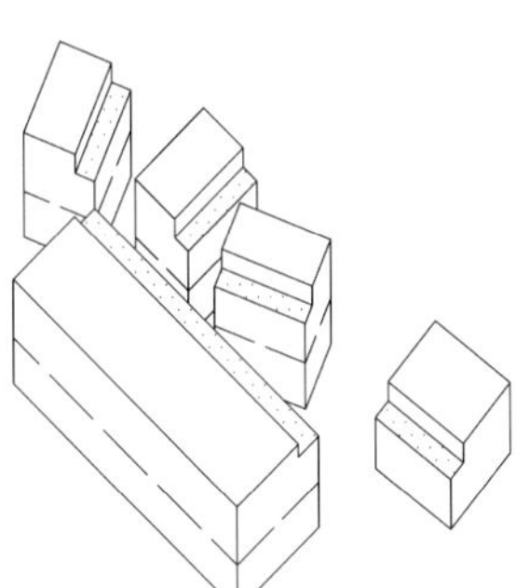

❾ Building form: grouped pavilions

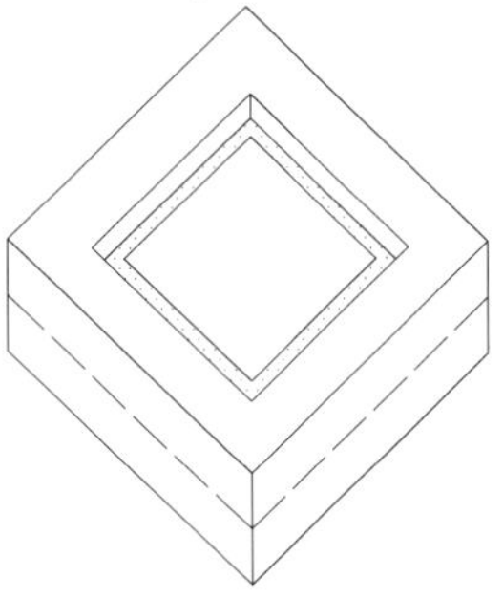

❿ Compact building form: with central courtyard access

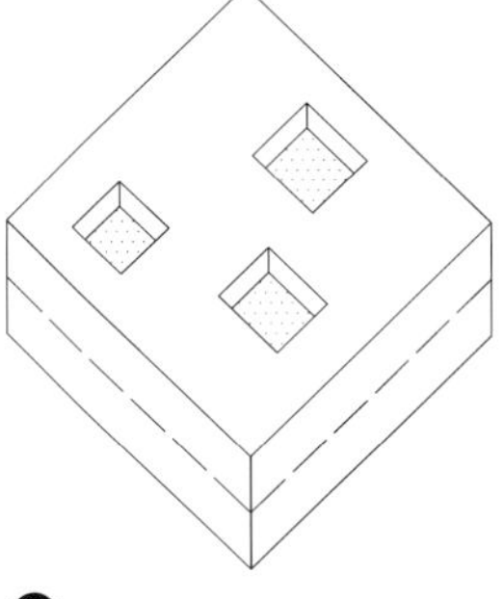

⓫ Compact building form: with light wells

1.00 1.60 80 85 80

❶ Minimum dimensions for table layouts in practical rooms, in rows

1.00 1.60 80 1,50

❷ Minimum dimensions for table layouts in practical rooms, back-to-back

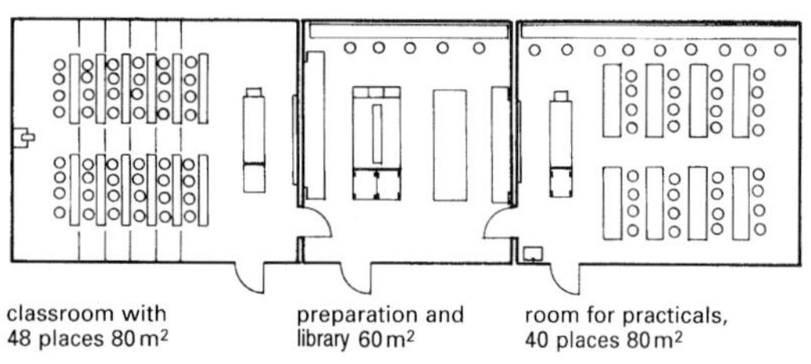

❸ Rooms and areas for science teaching

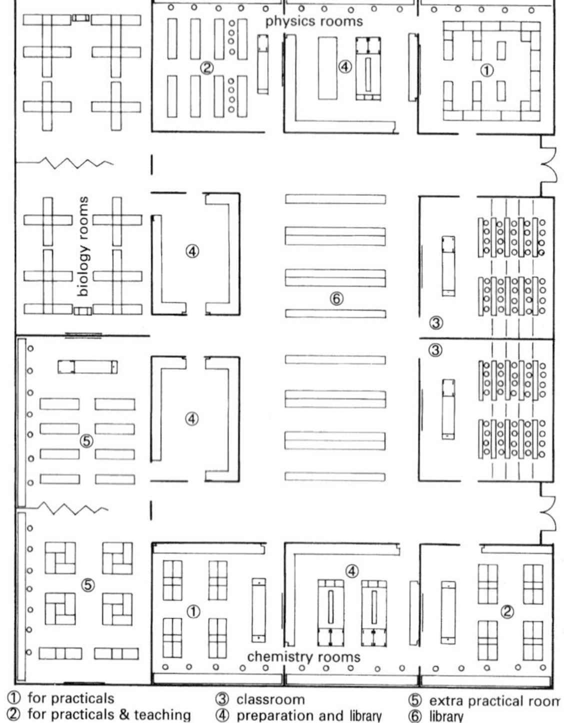

❹ Science area, approx. 400 places, approx. 1400 m²

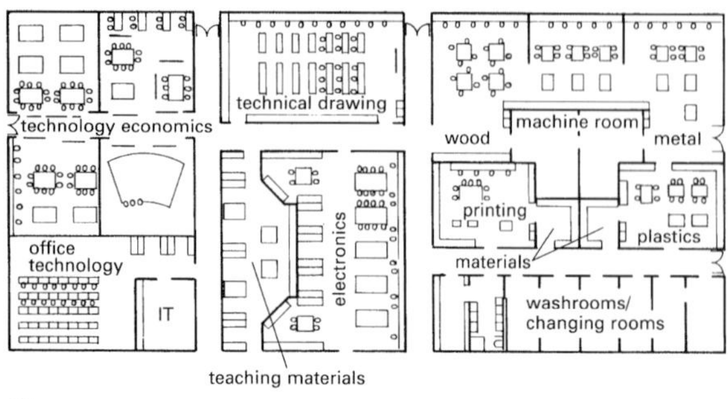

❺ Areas for technology/business studies, office technology, technical drawing, subjects altogether approx. 350 places, approx. 1600 m²

Science teaching area

This includes teaching, teaching/practical, practical, preparation and meeting rooms, photo work and photo lab rooms. Teaching rooms for biology, physics and chemistry approx. 2.50 m²/place. For lectures and demonstrations approx. 4.50 m²/place.

Demonstration and practical room for natural sciences, chemistry and biology, and physics, chemistry and biology approx. 70–80 m² → ❸. Teaching room for lecturing and demonstrations in the subjects physics, biology and perhaps chemistry approx. 60 m², with permanently installed, ascending auditorium seating. A second entrance and exit may be necessary. This room may be in an internal location with artificial lighting. Practical room for pupils, collaborating groups etc. in biology and physics or also interdisciplinary practical area, space sub-divided by means of partitioning, area per room or section approx. 80 m².

Preparation, meeting and materials room for subject combinations or single subjects: together approx. 30–40 m² or approx. 70 m², according to the size of the science area. This room may be in an internal location with artificial lighting.

Music and art teaching

Rooms for drawing should have uniform natural light, if possible from the north. Music rooms should have an appropriate layout and sound insulation to avoid disturbing other facilities.

Technical teaching

Workrooms should be arranged so that teaching in other rooms is not disturbed by the noise. The working area should be subdivided into the various media (wood, paper, metal, plastic) and ideally be located on the ground floor.

Photo laboratory

The photo laboratory is a dark room for positive work (one enlargement table for 2–3 pupils, combined with wet working areas), for negative work (film development) and a film storage room. If possible it should be north-facing with constant room temperature. Space requirement: 6–14 pupils per work group, min. 3–4 m² per work place.

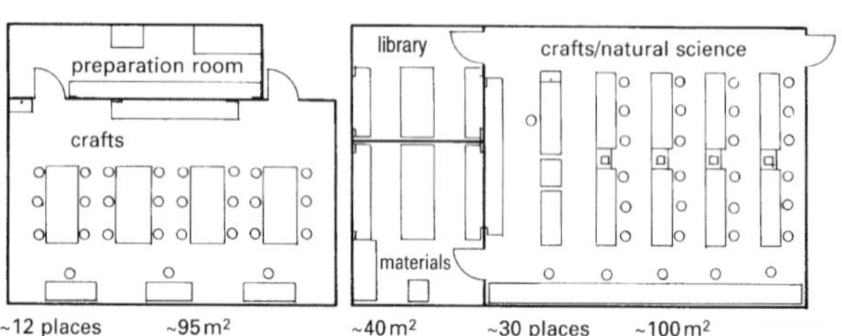

❻ Rooms and areas for technology

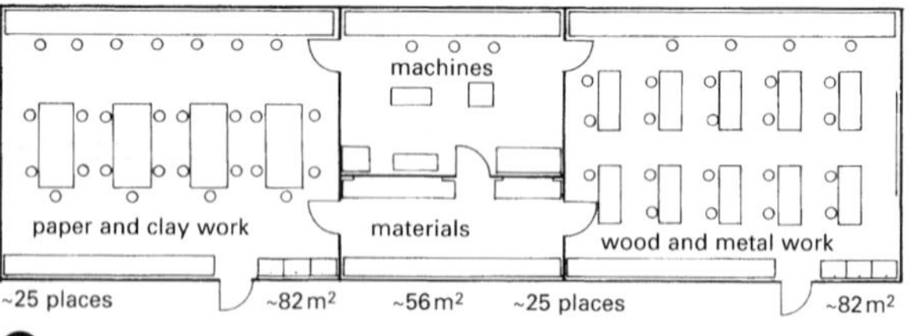

❼ Areas for technology

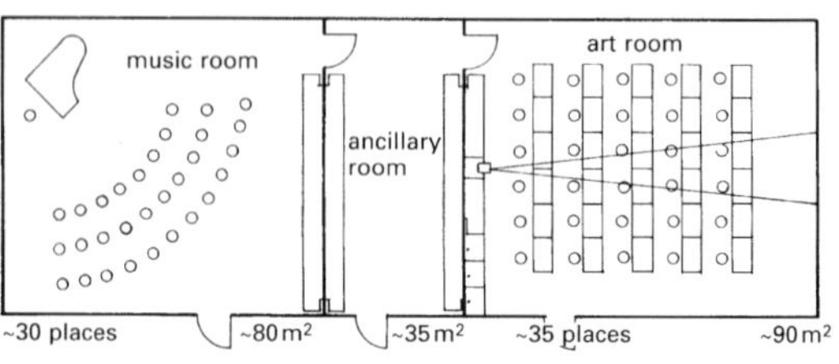

❽ Areas for music and art

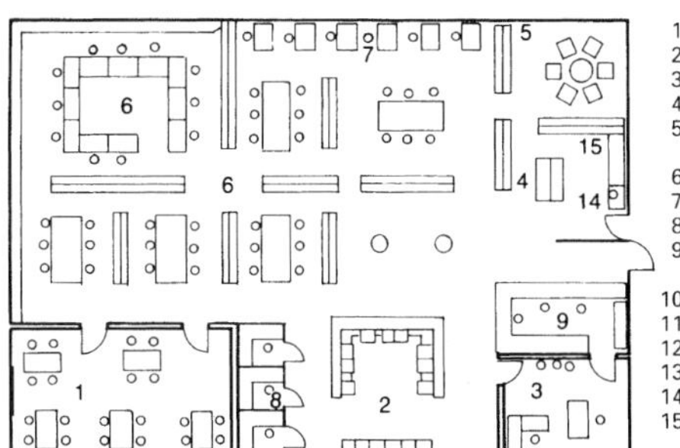

1 multi-purpose room
2 audio booths
3 office
4 central catalogue
5 newspapers, magazines
6 group area
7 individual places
8 typing booths
9 information, lending desk
10 lecture room
11 audiovis. studio
12 racks
13 free access
14 photocopier
15 cloakroom, lockers

❶ Example of school library/media centre

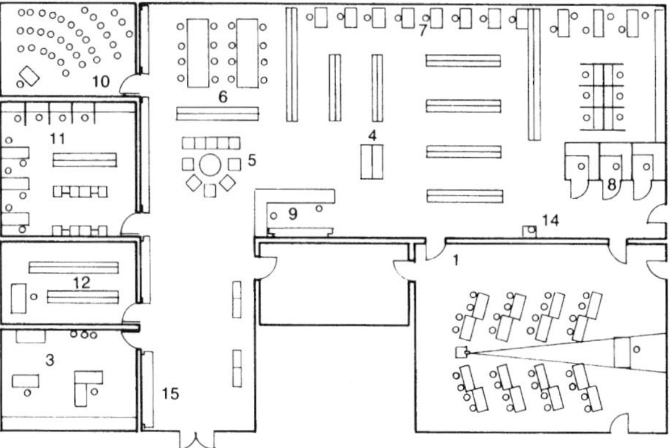

❷ Example of school library/media centre

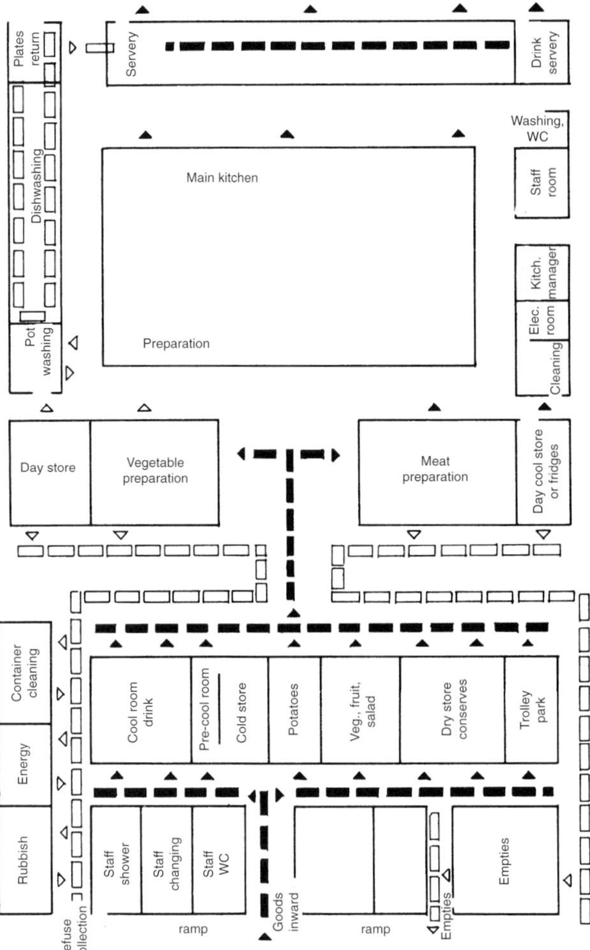

❸ Organisation of space and functions in a school kitchen

Library, media centre and central facilities

Information centre for teaching, further education and leisure. The users are pupils, teachers and external participants. **Library** denotes a conventional school and lending library including lending, reading and work spaces and the appropriate shelves for books and magazines. **Media centre** describes the extension of the library to cover recording and reproduction technology (hardware) for radio, film, television, cassettes, tapes, CD, DVD, i.e. so-called audio-visual material and a corresponding stock of software.

Guideline space requirement

Total for library and media centre 0.35–0.55 m^2/pupil.

Details: Book issue and return, per work space approx. 5 m^2 including catalogue areas approx. 20–40 m^2.
Advisors (librarian, media teacher, media technician etc.), per employee approx. 10–20 m^2. Compact book storage per 1000 volumes at approx. 20–30 volumes per running m of shelf, approx. 4 m^2 self-service shelves incl. movement areas; reading places and catalogue per 1000 volumes of non-fiction and reference works approx. 20–40 m^2; general working zone per 1000 reference volumes approx. 25 m^2 for approx. 5% of pupils/teachers but min. 30 work spaces each 2 m^2, approx. 60 m^2, per carrel approx. 2.5–3.0 m^2. Group work room, 8–10 people, approx. 20 m^2 → ❶ – ❷.

Kitchen and dining room

For a dining room with more than 400 places, the places of assembly regulations should be complied with.

The size and equipment depends on the catering system, food service and return of plates. For young pupils meals may be served at table (portions possibly served by the teacher) otherwise self-service (from conveyor, counter, cafeteria line, free-flow cafeteria, turntable etc.). Serving capacity: from 5–15 meals/minute or 250–1000 meals/hour with varied personnel requirement.

Space required for serving system approx. 40–60 m^2. Dining room size depends on number of pupils and sittings, per seat min. 1.20–1.40 m^2. Larger areas should be partitioned into smaller rooms. At entrance, provide one washbasin per 40 seats → ❸ – ❹.

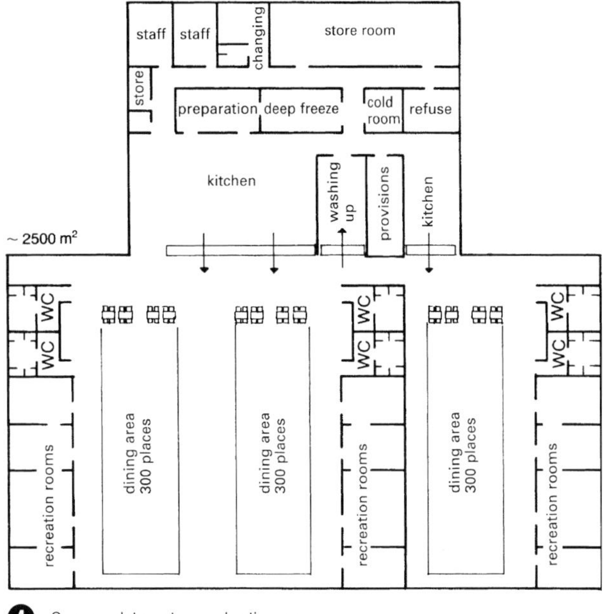

❹ Servery, plates return and eating area

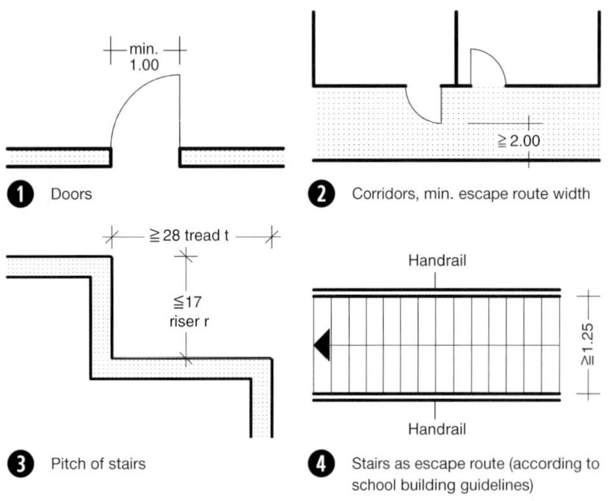

❶ Doors

❷ Corridors, min. escape route width

❸ Pitch of stairs

❹ Stairs as escape route (according to school building guidelines)

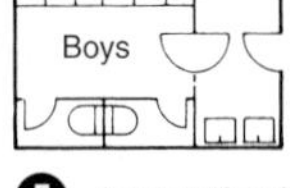

❺ Lesson-time WC facilities, e.g. for approx. 100 boys, approx. 15 m^2

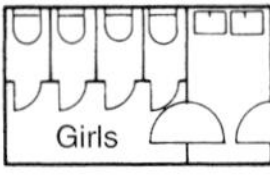

❻ e.g. for approx. 100 girls, approx. 15 m^2

❼ Break-time WC facilities, e.g. single-row facilities for approx. 250 girls, approx. 40 m^2; for approx. 250 boys, approx. 40 m^2

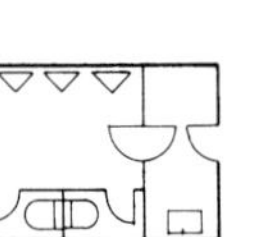

❽ Teacher WC facilities, e.g. for approx. 30 teachers, approx. 15 m^2

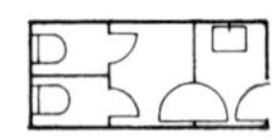

❾ e.g. for approx. 20 women teachers, approx. 10 m^2

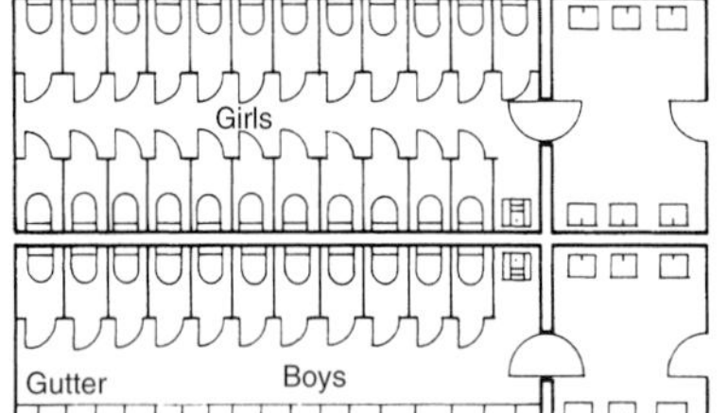

❿ Break-time WC facilities e.g. two-row facilities for approx. 500 girls, approx. 65 m^2; for approx. 500 boys, approx. 40 m^2

No. users	WC	Urinals
40 boys	1	2
20 girls	1	–
15 teachers	1	1
10 women teachers	1	–

⓫ Guideline for number of sanitary facilities (Saxony → refs)

Circulation and escape routes

Horizontal and vertical access routes are normally also emergency escape routes. Escape routes must have a clear width of min. 1.00 m/150 people but min. width of corridors in classroom areas is 2.00 m, or 1.25 m with up to 180 people. Stairs in classroom areas must be 1.25 m wide, other escape routes 1.00 m wide. Max. length of escape routes: 25 m measured in a straight line from the stairwell door to the farthest work place, or 30 m in an indirect line to the centre of the room. Capacity of stairs dependent on number of users and average occupancy, e.g. stair width: 0.80 m for each 100 people (min. 1.25 m, but not wider than 2.50 m).

Doors → ❶

These may open inward or outward. Outward opening doors should not endanger pupils and project max. 20 cm into the escape route. → ❷.

Doors from rooms with more than 40 pupils or increased fire risk (chemistry, work rooms) must open in the direction of the escape route.

Stairs, ramps → ❸ – ❹

The pitch of stairs is to be based on length of pace: 2 riser + tread = 59–65 cm. Ramps ≦6% gradient.

Cloakrooms

Cloakrooms are to be provided outside classrooms.

Break areas

The space guideline for enclosed break areas is 0.4–0.5 m^2/pupil. They are to be designed so that they can be used for school events. Dining and multi-purpose rooms may be used as break areas. If the connection between school building and sports hall is roofed over, this can be designed as a break area or covered sports area (Saxony → refs).

Communal area

A communal area should be provided in each larger school for events and celebrations. This can be achieved through the temporary connection of several rooms and circulation areas. Whether the building of a school hall is necessary is regulated by the relevant state school building guidelines.

Sanitary facilities → ❺ – ⓬

The necessary WCs, urinals and washbasins are provided according to the total number of pupils (divided between boys and girls) according to the school building guidelines → ⓫. One washbasin is provided for every boys' WC or for every two girls' WCs. Toilets should be as directly lit and ventilated as possible. The accesses for girls and boys are to be separate.

Context	Form	Separation boys/girls	Location	Use	Notes
class WC	toilets with lobby	no	near a classroom	during lesson	possibly for preschool and school kindergarten, poss. 2 WCs and lobby
lesson WC	toilets	yes	accessible from corridor or hall	several classes during lesson	each classroom without WC should be max. 40 m distance (incl. stairs) from lesson WC
break WC	toilets	yes	accessible from schoolyard or hall	for classes during the break	WCs at ground level, not in centre of building, accessible from break areas
teacher WC	toilets	ladies/gents	for teachers or administration	during the break	possibly linked to staff cloakroom

⓬ Recommended WC facilities

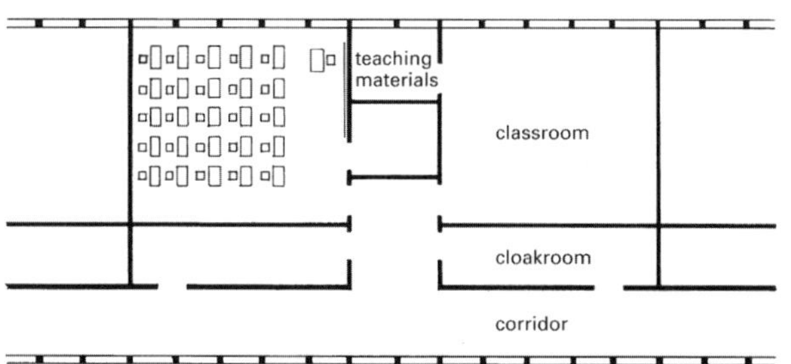

❶ Classroom lit and ventilated on both sides through cloakroom and corridor, corridor opening up every two classrooms into teaching equipment room
Arch.: Yorke, Rosenberg, Mardall

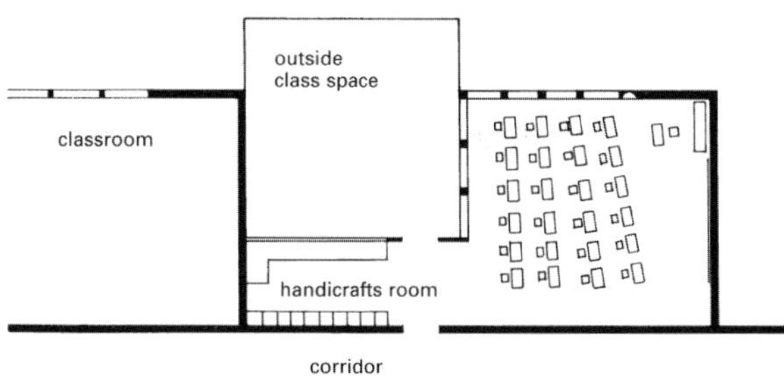

❷ Design proposal: combination of classroom, open-air classroom and hobby room
Arch.: Neutra

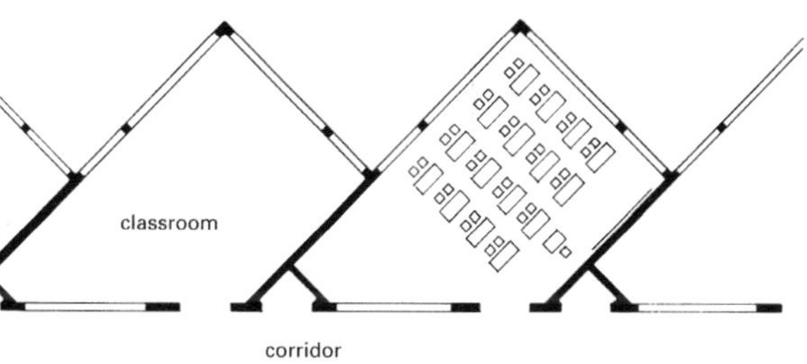

❸ Saw-tooth plan
Arch.: Carbonara

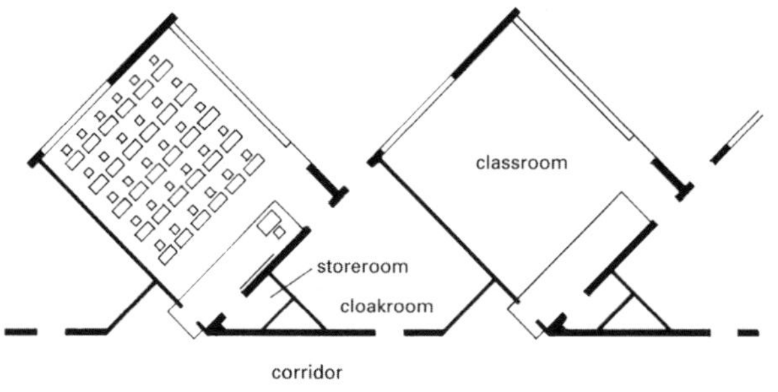

❹ Classrooms with additional daylight through high-level window, without view in from the back. Corridor opens up at each classroom into cloakroom and storeroom
Arch.: Carbonara

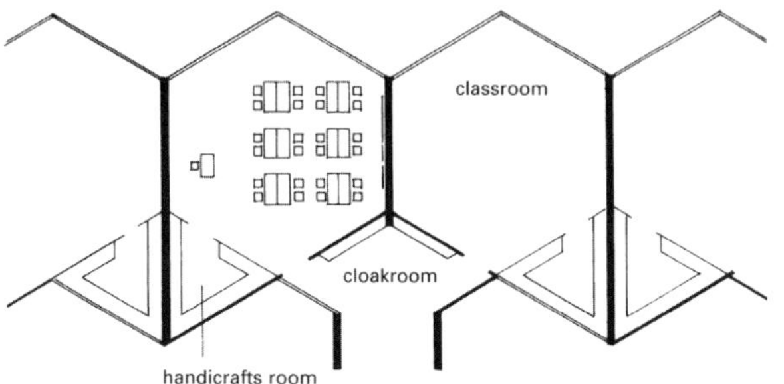

❺ Hexagonal classrooms with enclosed triangular hobby rooms
Arch.: Brechbühlen

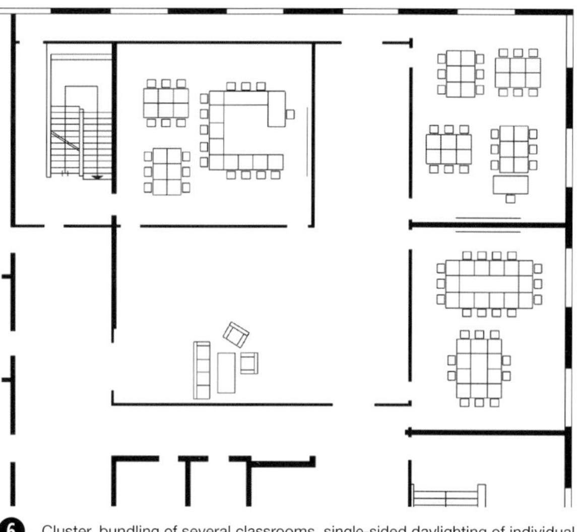

❻ Cluster, bundling of several classrooms, single-sided daylighting of individual rooms

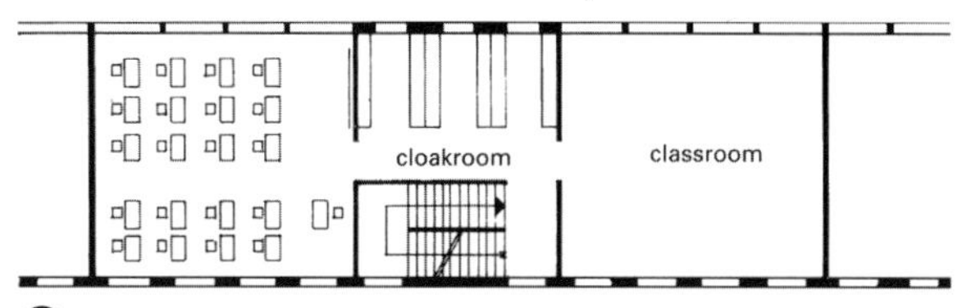

❼ Multi-storey building: two classrooms to each staircase, daylight from two sides
Arch.: Schuster

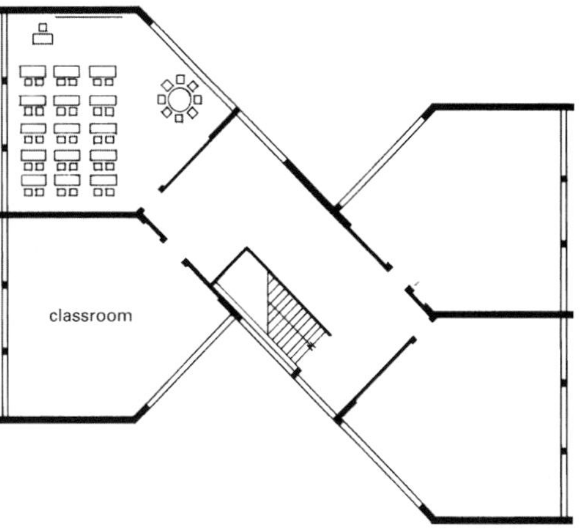

❽ Four classrooms per storey with daylight from both sides, side extension for group teaching
Arch.: Haefeli, Moser, Steiger

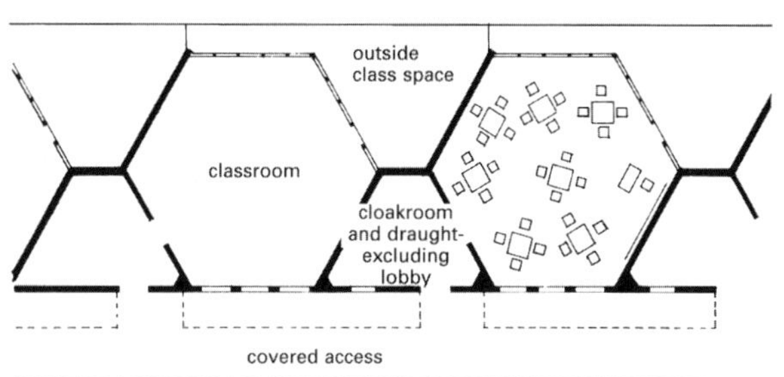

❾ Hexagonal classroom without corridor, accessed through cloakroom and lobby
Arch.: Gottwald, Weber

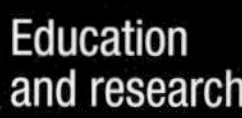

			1 cohort 4 classes 120 pupils		2 cohorts 8 classes 240 pupils	
	Places	**m^2/room**	**No.**	**m^2**	**No.**	**m^2**
General teaching rooms				**326–490**		**592–748**
classrooms	24 – 32	50–66	4	200–264	8	400–528
group rooms	12–18	36–50			2	72–100
multi-purpose rooms	32	72	1	90	1	72
side rooms		18–36	1	18	1	24
teaching equipment room		18–36	1	18	1	24
Specialist classrooms						**96**
work room	16	72			1	72
side room		24			1	24
music room	32	72				
School library/media centre				**60**		**72**
Administration				**36**		**102**
head teacher's room		12–18				60
secretariat		18—24		36		
teachers' room		24–50		12		
sick room		18			1	18
parents' meeting room		12			1	1
caretaker's room		12			1	12
Communal areas				**92**		**92**
kitchen servery		24	1	24	1	24
dining/multi-purpose room			1	50	1	50
side room		18–24	1	18	1	18
Utility areas				**24**		**66**
caretaker's workshop		18			1	18
room for cleaning materials		12			1	12
storeroom			1	24	1	36
Caretaker's flat					**1**	**80**
Sports hall					**1**	**600**
Open-air sports facilities						
break areas with gymnastic and play equipment				600		1200
school garden				150		300
playing field			1 pitch		1 pitch	
100 m track	4 tracks					
long jump facility	3 tracks					
gymnastics lawn				400		400
Subtotals						
general classrooms				326–390		592–748
specialist classrooms						96
school library/media centre				60		72
administration				36		102
utility areas				24		66
Total				**446–510**		**928–1084**
m^2/pupil				**4.0**		**4.2**

❶ Model room programme, primary school, school building regulations (Saxony → refs)

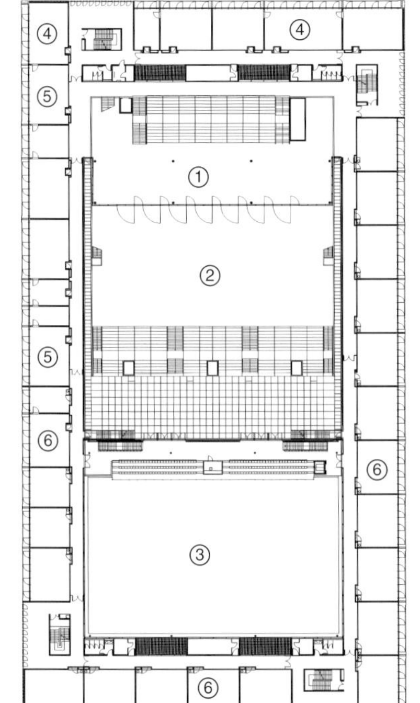

① Break hall
② Break yard
③ Sports hall
④ Physics classroom
⑤ Drawing/crafts
⑥ Class/course rooms

❶ Markt Indersdorf grammar school, first floor
Arch.: Allmann Sattler Wappner Architekten

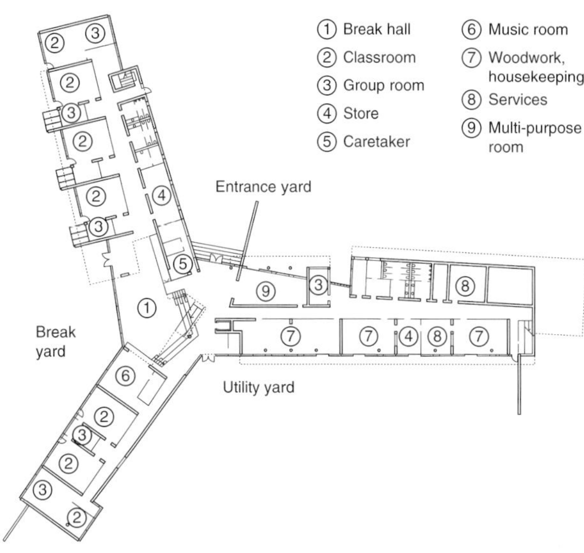

① Break hall
② Classroom
③ Group room
④ Store
⑤ Caretaker
⑥ Music room
⑦ Woodwork, housekeeping
⑧ Services
⑨ Multi-purpose room

❸ School for individual promotion of learning, Alzenau, primary and secondary school, ground floor Arch.: (se) arch Stefanie Eberding und Stephan Eberding

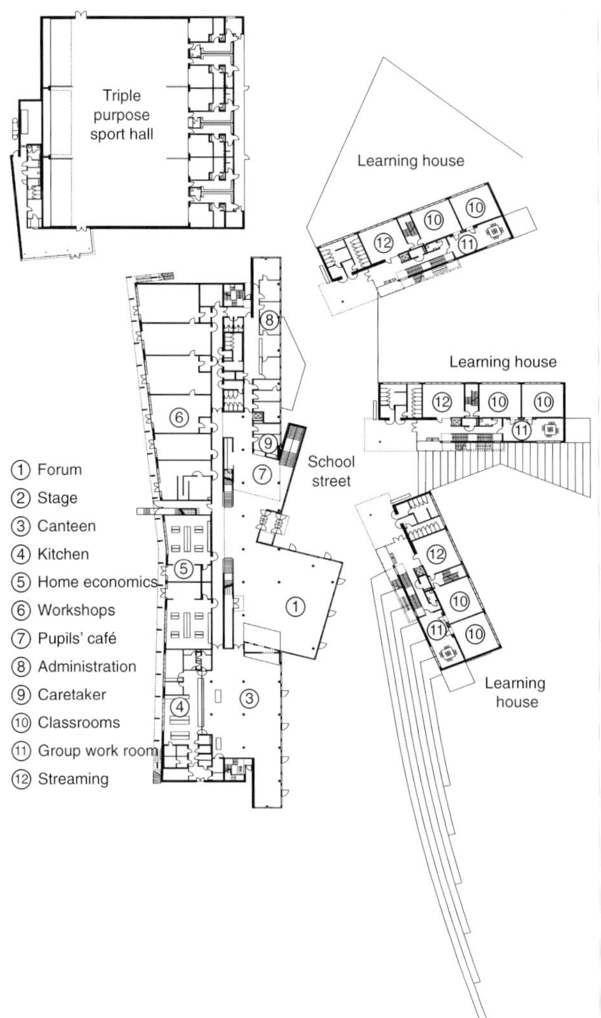

① Forum
② Stage
③ Canteen
④ Kitchen
⑤ Home economics
⑥ Workshops
⑦ Pupils' café
⑧ Administration
⑨ Caretaker
⑩ Classrooms
⑪ Group work room
⑫ Streaming

❷ Montessori school, Aachen, one-stage school, ground floor
Arch.: Prof. Ernst Kasper, Prof. Klaus Klever

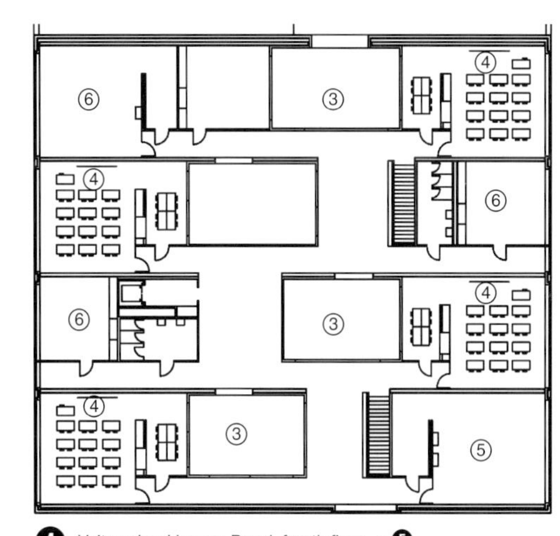

❹ Volta school house, Basel, fourth floor → ❺

→ ❹ – ❺

① Entrance hall
② Sport hall
③ Yard light well
④ Classroom with group
⑤ Crafts
⑥ Religion/remedial teaching/ languages

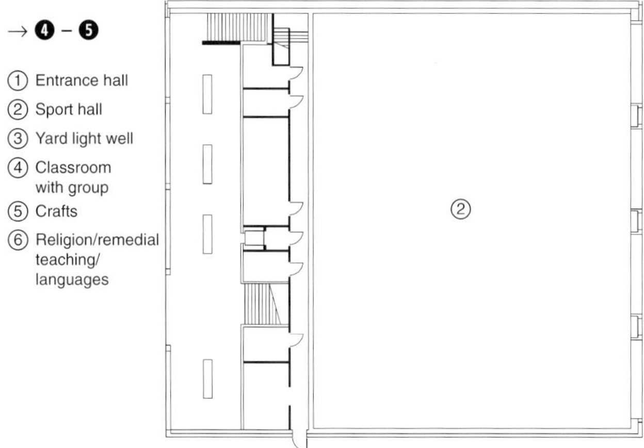

❺ Volta school house, Basel, ground floor Arch.: Miller & Maranta

Education and research

UNIVERSITIES AND COLLEGES
Lecture theatres
Examples of lecture theatres
Seating
Projection
Seminar and service rooms
Laboratories

see also: Student residences, p. 167

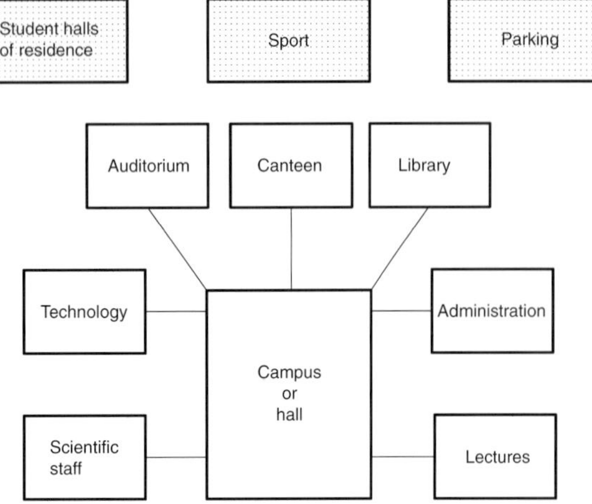

❶ Scheme of university facilities

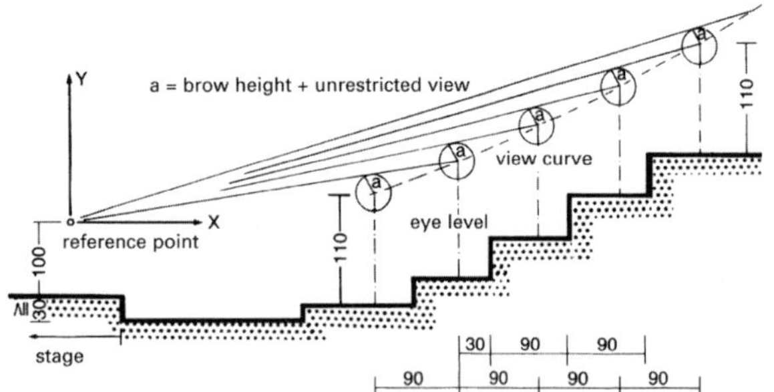

❷ Geometrical determination of the listener curve

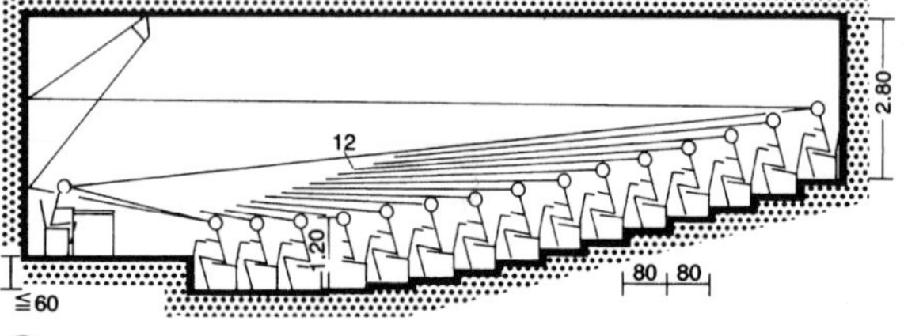

❸ Normal lecture theatre design (humanities)

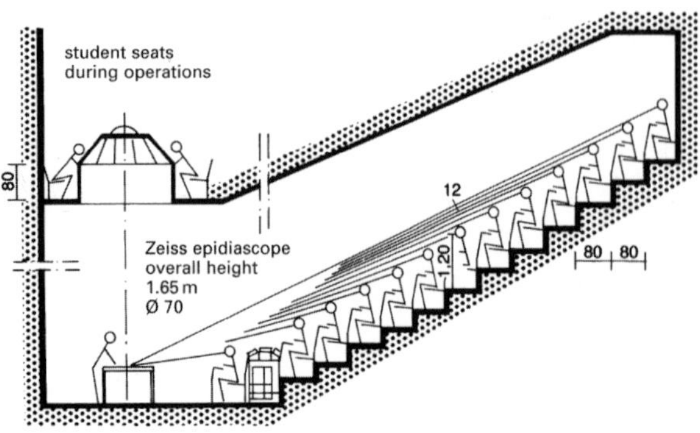

❹ Lecture theatre for demonstrations on a bench (medicine)

Central university facilities include: great hall, event hall, administration, deanery and student union. Also prominent are libraries, canteens, sports facilities, car parks and student residences (→ p. 167).

Basic space requirements for all subjects
Lecture theatre for basic and special lectures, seminar and tutorial rooms (partially with PC workplaces) for detailed instruction of the course material, specialised libraries, rooms for scientific assistants, conference and examination rooms.

Space requirements for specific subjects:
Humanities: lecture theatre with seating raked (rising) at a low pitch → ❸. No particular requirements for blackboards or projection.
Technical and artistic subjects: e.g. architecture, art, music: drawing, studio, workshop, practice and meeting rooms of all types.
Technical and natural science subjects: e.g. physics, mechanical engineering, electrical engineering: drawing rooms, laboratories, workshops.
Natural science and medical theory subjects: e.g. chemistry, biology, anatomy, physiology, health care, pathology: laboratories with associated practical rooms, scientific workshops, animal keeping and experiment rooms. Medical demonstration ('anatomy') theatres with steeply raked seating → ❹. Natural science lecture theatres with experiment benches and steeply raked seating → ❻.

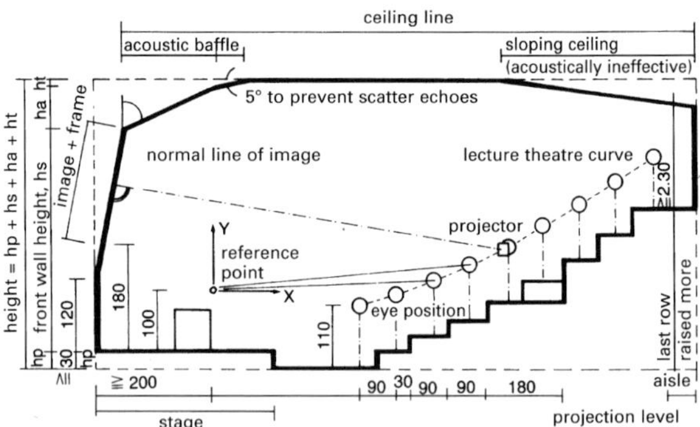

❺ Longitudinal section through a lecture theatre

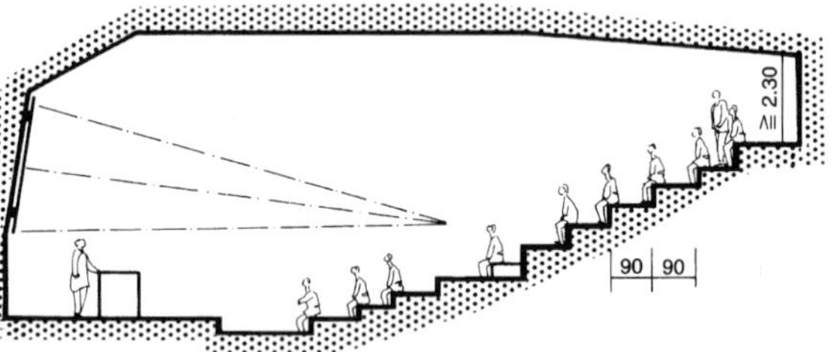

❻ Steeply raked lecture theatre (natural sciences)

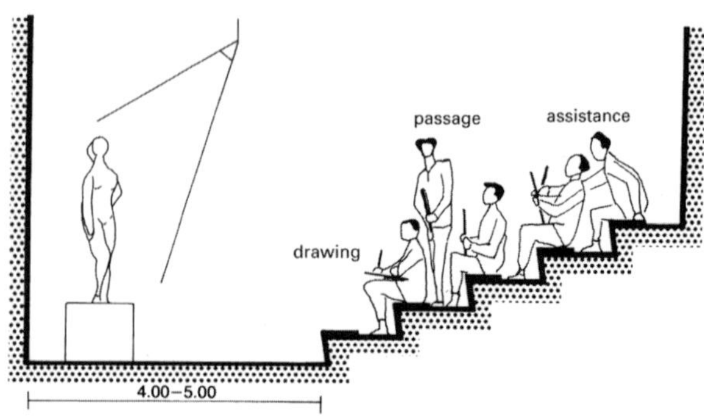

❼ Steps in life drawing class with seated area of 0.65 m^2 per student (technical artistic subjects)

1 Rectangular lecture theatre with 200 seats

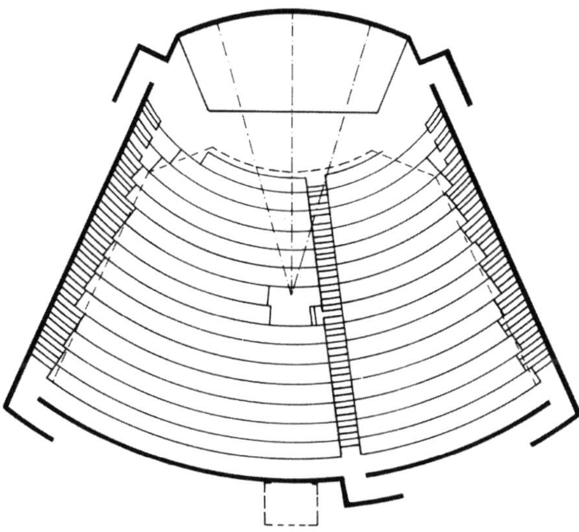

2 Trapezoidal lecture theatre with 400 seats

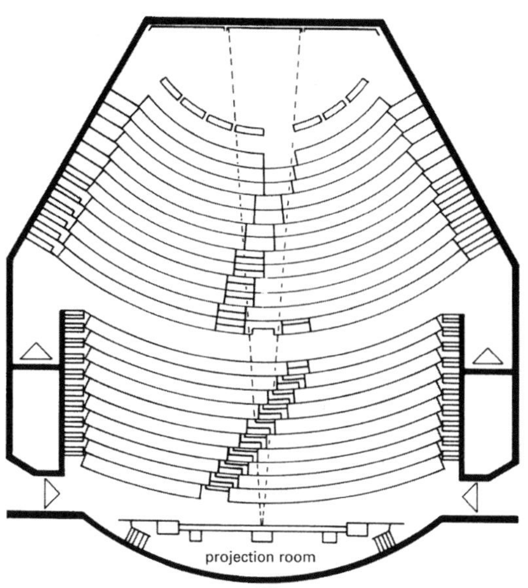

3 Lecture theatre with 800 seats

Larger lecture theatres for central lectures are preferably accommodated in auditorium buildings, and smaller lecture theatres for specialist lectures in institute or seminar buildings. Access to the lecture theatre is best separated from the research facilities, with the shortest possible route from outside to the back of the lecture theatre (in the case of raked seating, entrances behind the uppermost row, or in larger lecture theatres also at the side at middle height → **3**). Lecturers enter the lecture theatre at the front, from the preparation room, and experimental apparatus can be rolled into the theatre. Common lecture theatre sizes are 100, 150, 200, 300, 400, 600, 800 seats. Lecture theatres with up to 200 seats, ceiling height approx. 3.5 m can be integrated into an institute building; larger theatres should ideally have their own building.

Experiment benches should be easily changeable, on wheels and suitable for laboratory work. Media connections are required.

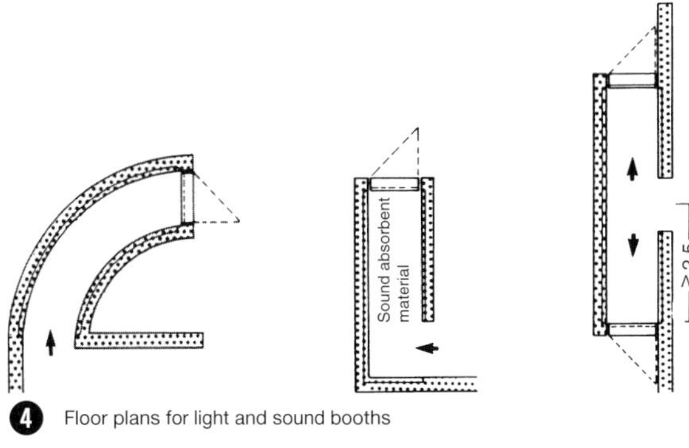

4 Floor plans for light and sound booths

① movable blackboard
② service duct in floor
③ experiment bench
④ point of reference

5 Longitudinal section → **6**

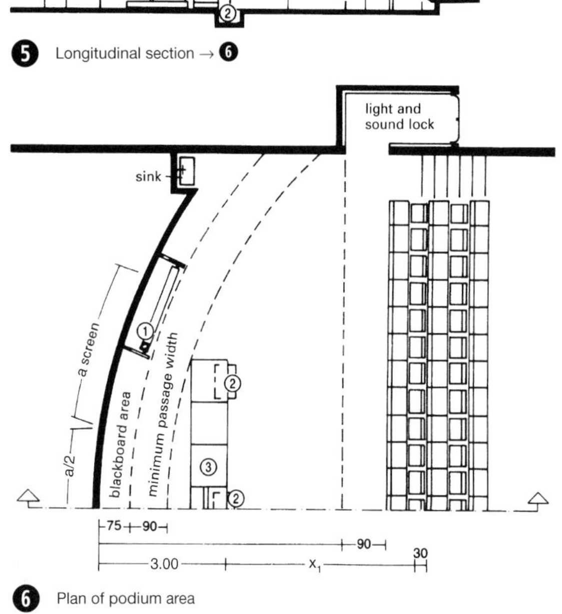

6 Plan of podium area

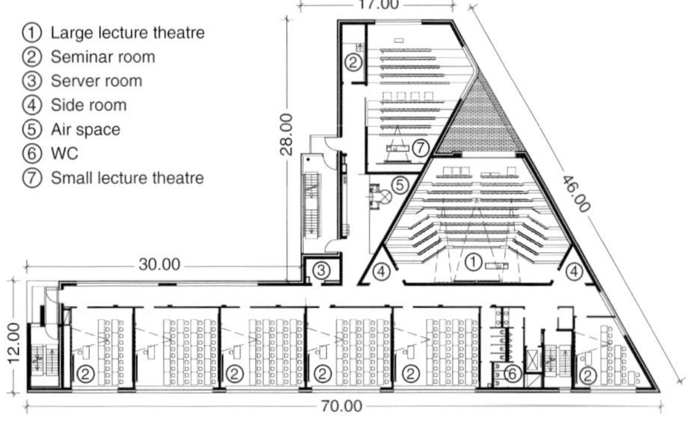

❶ Bremerhaven University, third floor Arch.: Kister Scheithauer Gross

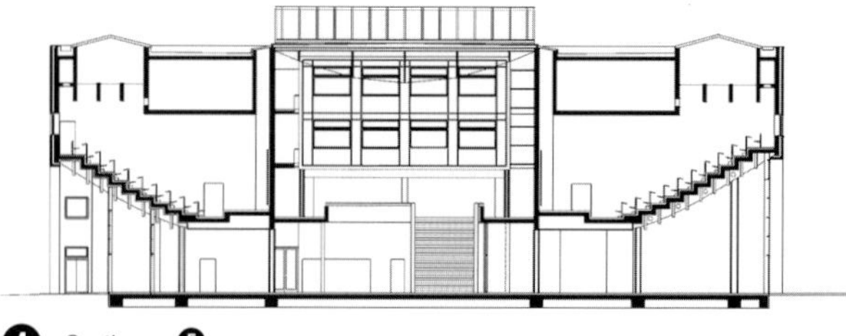

❹ Section → ❺

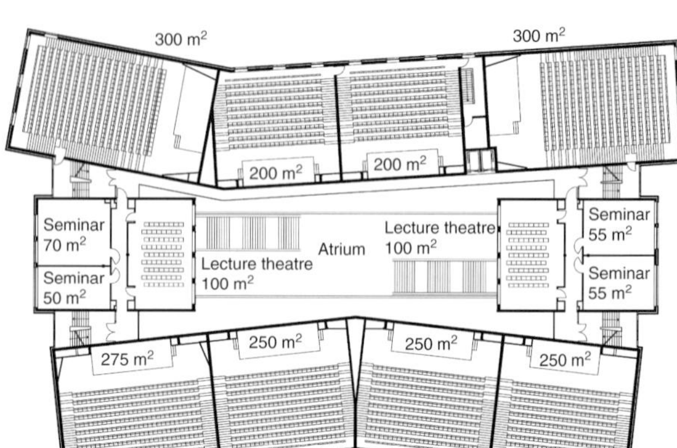

❺ Lecture theatres, Gräfin Dönhoff Building, first floor, Frankfurt an der Oder University Arch.: Yamaguchi und Essig Architekten BDA

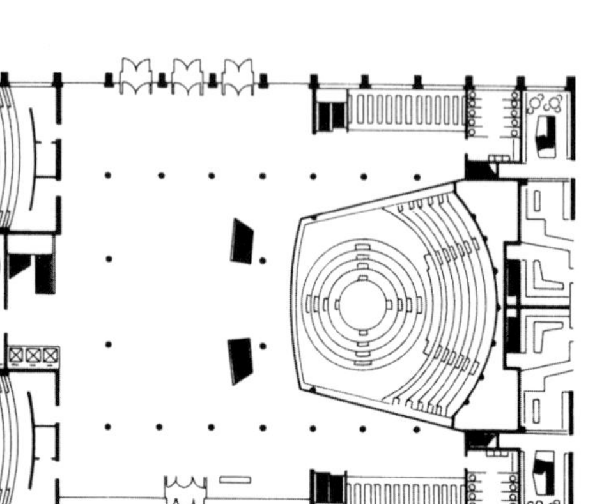

❷ Council building, Freiburg University, ground floor entrance hall and two-storey Auditorium Maximum Arch.: O.E. Schweizer

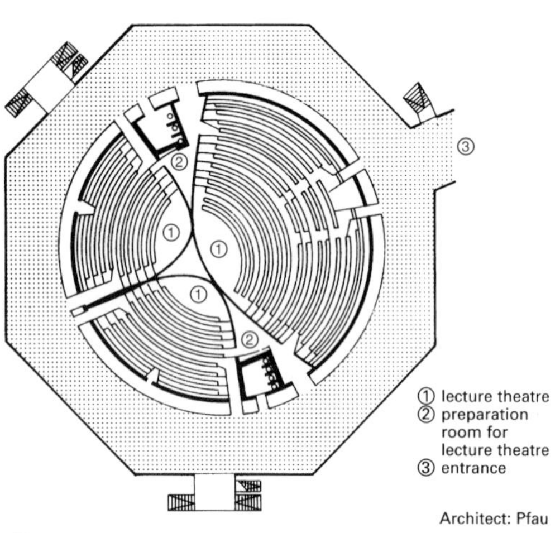

❻ Student building in Düsseldorf

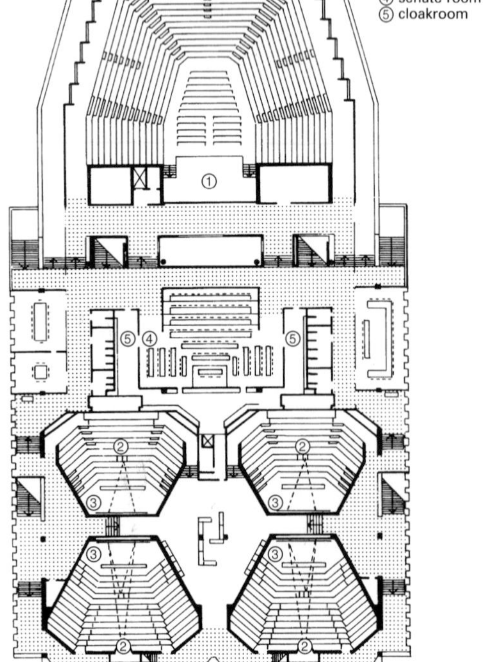

❸ Auditorium of the Technical University of Delft Arch.: Broek + Bakema

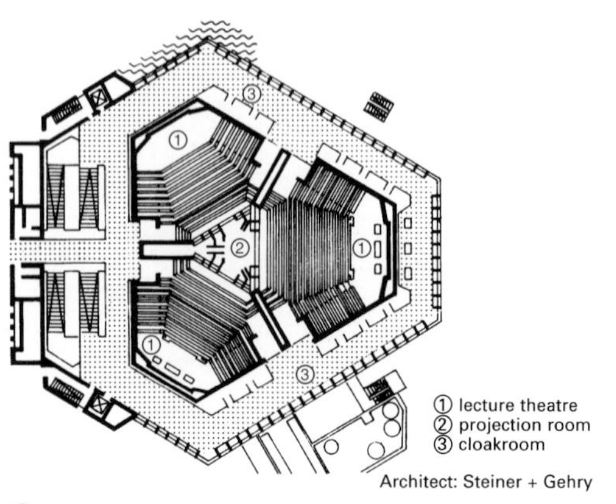

❼ Lecture theatre of the ETH Hönggerberg, Zurich

Education and research

UNIVERSITIES AND COLLEGES
Lecture theatres
Examples of lecture theatres
Seating
Projection
Seminar and service rooms
Laboratories

Level

On 15 cm steps

Sloping floor up to 12% incline

❶ Lecture theatre seating

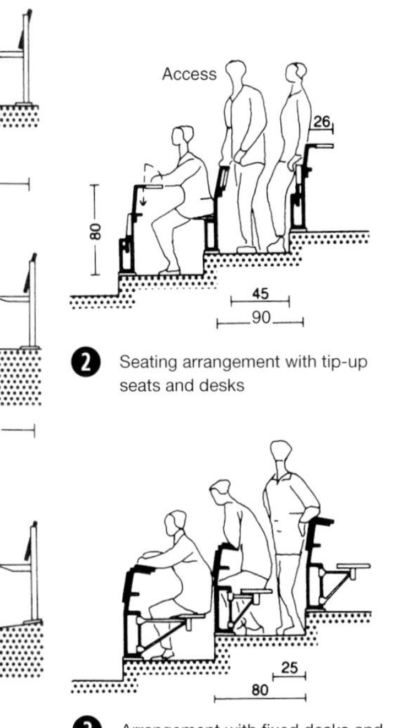

❷ Seating arrangement with tip-up seats and desks

❸ Arrangement with fixed desks and rotating seats (required space)

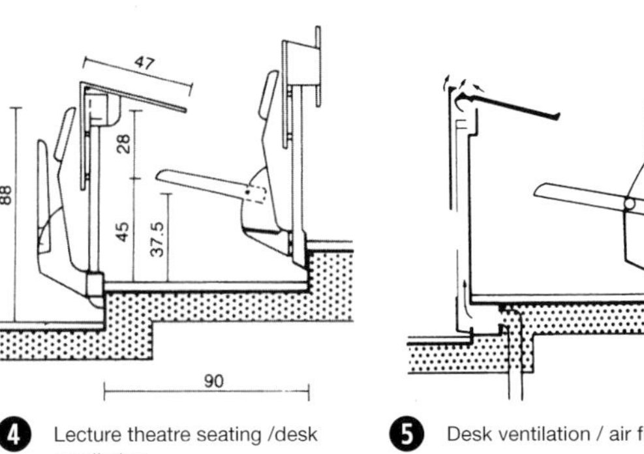

❹ Lecture theatre seating /desk ventilation

❺ Desk ventilation / air flow

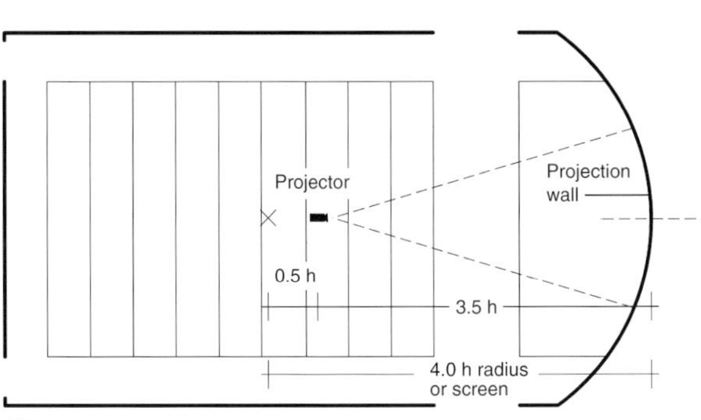

❻ Layout of projectors, plan

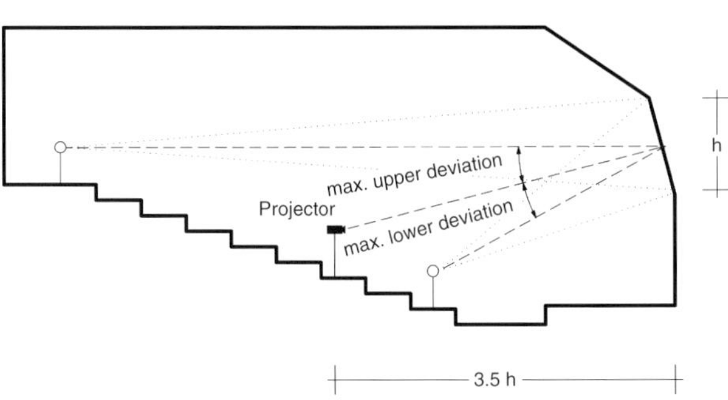

❼ Layout of projectors, section, showing distribution of the angle of inclined view to places above and below the projectors

Lecture theatre seating

Combined units with tip-up or slewing seat, backrest and desk (with shelf or hook for case or bag), mostly fixed mounting → ❶ – ❸. Arrangement is according to subject, number of students and type of tuition: from light (slide shows, electro-acoustic facilities) to heavy. Some lecture theatres (surgery, internal medicine, physics) have raked (rising) rows of seating → ❶. The space requirement per student depends on type of seating, desk depth and floor pitch. Per student (including all walking areas in larger lecture theatres in a cramped situation), the space requirement is 1.10 m^2, in smaller lecture theatres and in a normal situation 0.80–0.95 m^2.

Projection, boards, acoustics, lighting:

Projection screens and black-/whiteboards can be designed as segmented surfaces, or fixed to a straight back wall. Wall boards in many sections, mostly vertically sliding, manual or mechanical, can be dropped down below the projection area. Wheeled boards or screens are also possible.

Speech should reach the listener as uniformly as possible, with no disturbing echo. Suspended ceilings will aid reflection and absorption. Rear walls should be clad with sound-absorbing material, other walls flat. Light intensity in windowless lecture theatres: 600 lx.

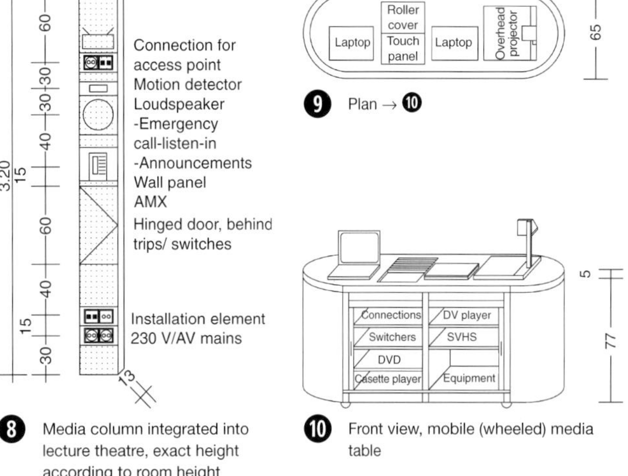

❽ Media column integrated into lecture theatre, exact height according to room height

❾ Plan → ❿

❿ Front view, mobile (wheeled) media table

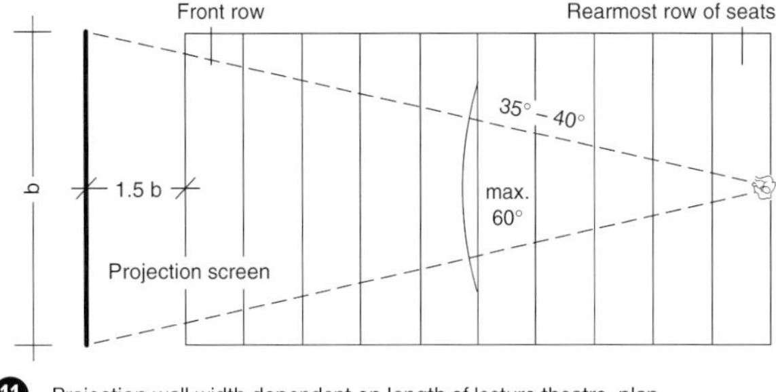

⓫ Projection wall width dependent on length of lecture theatre, plan

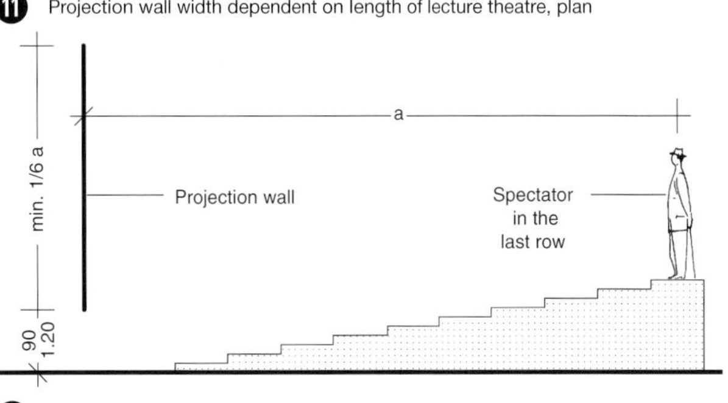

⓬ Projection wall width dependent on length of lecture theatre, section

UNIVERSITIES AND COLLEGES
Lecture theatres
Examples of lecture theatres
Seating
Projection
Seminar and service rooms
Laboratories

Places of Assembly Regulations

see also:
Libraries, pp. 247 ff.

The design of lecture theatres and seminar rooms has to comply with the places of assembly regulations. It should also be ensured that wheelchair users have sufficient space in lecture theatres in line with standards.

Service rooms for lecture theatres
Every lecture theatre should have a directly accessible side room. This has no fixed function and can be used as a storage room. Sufficient preparation area should be provided next to all lecture theatres featuring experiments, positioned at the same level and with a short route to the podium. Guideline for the min. size: for rectangular plan lecture theatre, approx. 0.2–0.25 m^2/seat; trapezoidal plan 0.15–0.18 m^2/seat; natural science and pre-clinical subjects 0.2–0.3 m^2/seat.
Areas for storage and staff rooms are necessary for the proper operation of a lecture theatre building: a room for technical staff to maintain the facilities; for cleaning staff; storeroom for replacement parts, light bulbs, fluorescent tubes, black-/whiteboard, clothing etc. Min. size per room 15 m^2; space required for all side rooms min. 50–60 m^2.

Computer room
The size of the computer room is related to the number and size of the computer desks, which depends on the size of the displays.

General tuition rooms
Seminar rooms, usual sizes: 20, 40, 50, 60 seats; mobile double tables, width 1.20 m, depth 0.60 m, space required per student 1.90–2.00 m.
Variable arrangement of the tables for tutorial and group work. If there is free ventilation from only one external wall, the depth of the room should not exceed 2.5 × clear ceiling height.

Offices for scientific personnel → ❺
professor 20–24 m^2
scientific assistant 15 m^2
assistant 20 m^2
secretary 15 m^2 (double occupation 20 m^2)

Cloakroom and WC facilities
Rough estimate for both together: 0.15–0.16 m^2/seat
Faculty and open-access libraries (→ Libraries pp. 247 ff.)
Storage for 30 000–200 000 vols on open-access shelves.

Book storage space → ❻
Bookcases with 6–7 shelves, 2 m high (reaching height)
Distance between bookcases 1.50–1.60 m
Space required 1.0–1.2 m^2/200 vols

Reading places → ❼
Width 0.9–1.0 m/depth 0.8 m
Space required 2.4–2.5 m^2 per place
Entrance control, with storage for cases/bags; catalogue, copier room

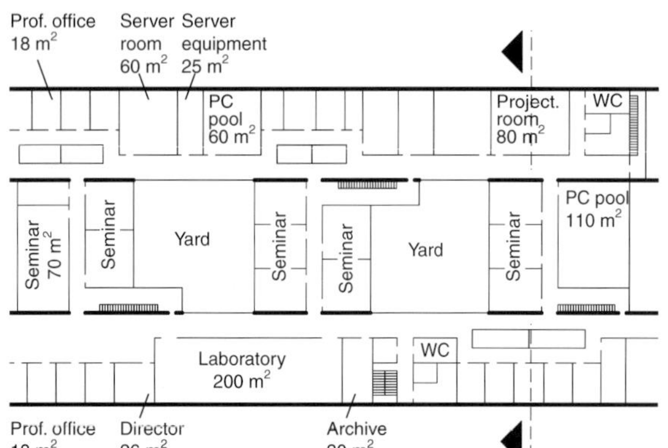

❶ Plan of a university building; seminar rooms are used by many departments

Corridor Corridor Seminar rooms
Office Corri-dor Project rooms
1.80 2.00
5.00 16.00 3.00 8.00
2.20
38.00

❷ Section → ❶: column-free pre-stressed concrete floor boards supported on the external walls

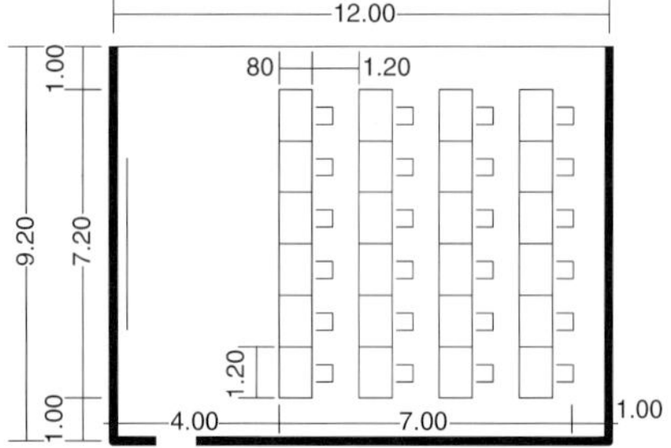

❸ Dimensions of a computer room

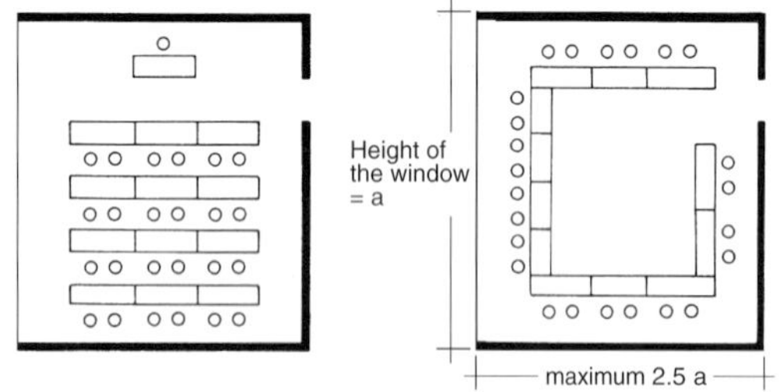

❹ Dimensions of seminar rooms with natural ventilation

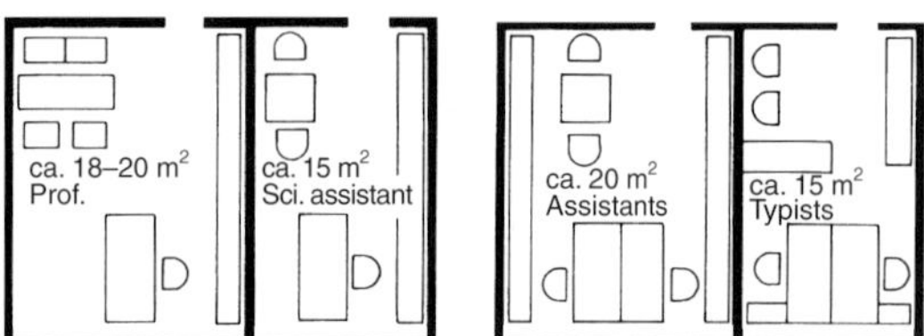

❺ Basic equipment for service rooms

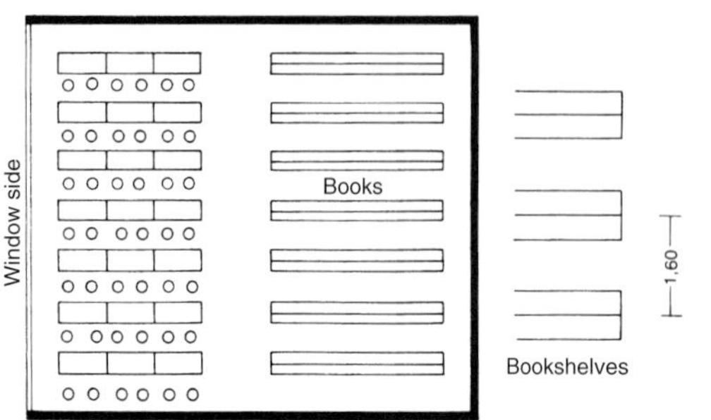

❻ Arrangement of reading places and bookshelves

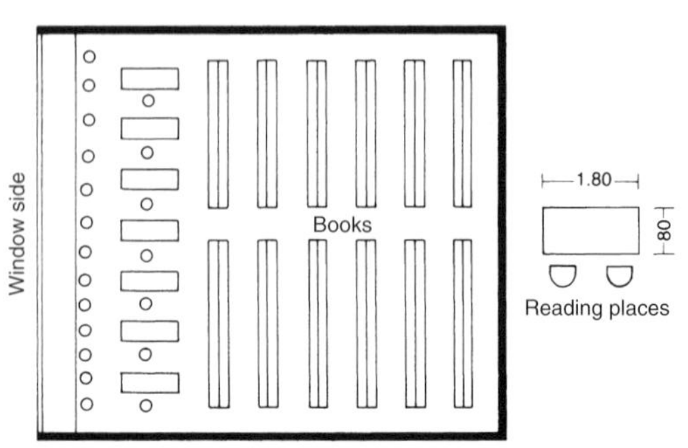

❼ Arrangement of reading places and bookshelves

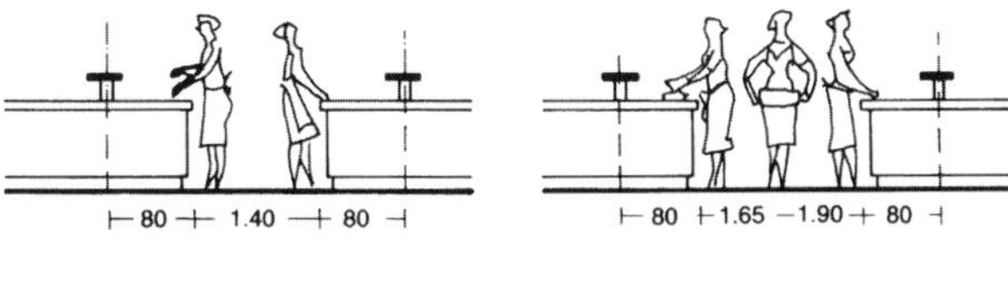

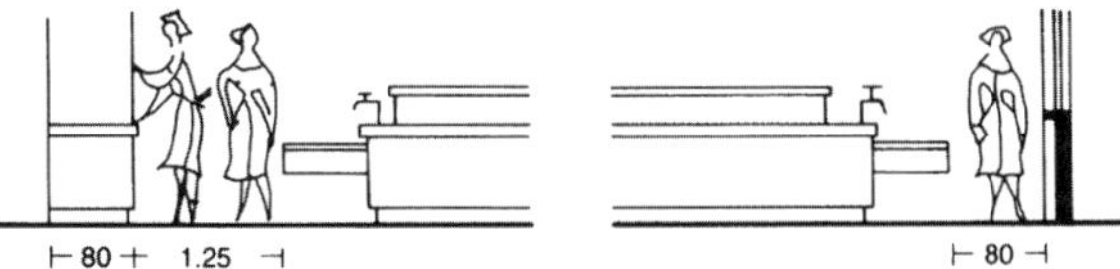

❶ Minimum passage width at workstations

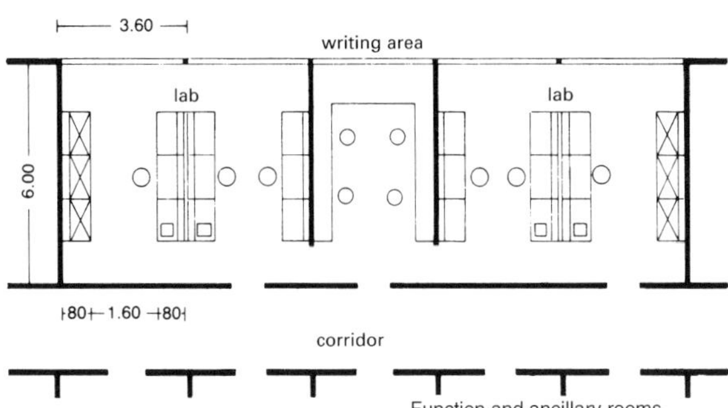

❷ Research laboratory

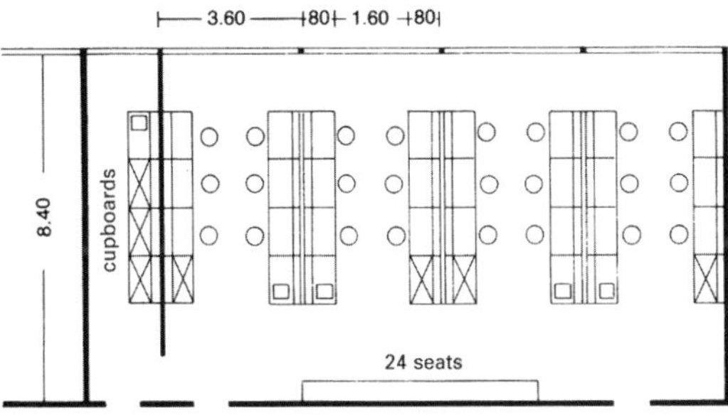

❸ Teaching and practical laboratory

Lab safety level 3
1. warning sign
2. double-door safety lobby, self-closing doors
3. outdoor clothing
4. protective clothing
5. floor trough (pos. disinfectant mat) in front of shower
6. hand wash basin with disinfectant dispenser
7. workbench (clean bench) with separate special filter
8. extractor
9. autoclave (in lab or building)
10. flat panel radiator (7.5 cm from wall)
11. control and monitoring cupboard: electricity box, emergency mains off-switch, error board
12. pressure difference display readable from inside and out with acoustic alarm
13. emergency telephone, telephone
14. two-way intercom, electric door-opener
15. windows: gas-tight, non-combustible, leaded
16. pass-door: fireproof

Lab safety level 4
2. three-chamber safety lobby. Doors self-closing and gas-tight
5. personal shower (L-3 system can be upgraded*). Collect and disinfect waste water
7. gas-tight, enclosed workbench, separate air supply and extraction, additional special filter
9. autoclave with lockable doors on both sides, disinfect condensation
10. flood lock
18. autoclavable container for used protective clothing

*) Only required if upgrading to L-4 lab.

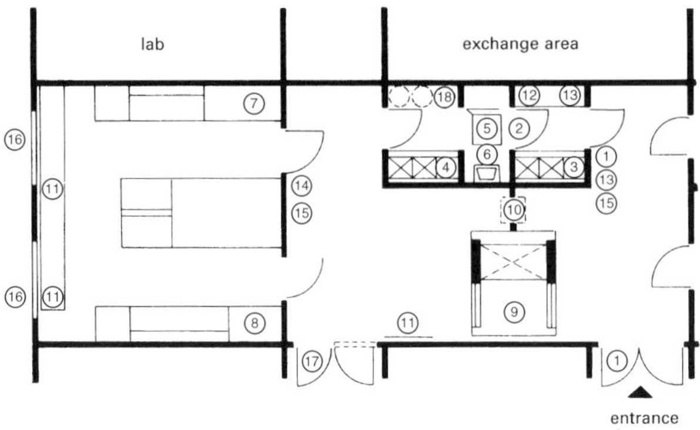

❹ Clean room laboratory, example

Laboratories differ according to use and subject. According to use:

Tuition-related practical laboratories with a large number of workstations collected together and mostly with simple basic equipment → ❸.

Research-related laboratories, mostly in smaller rooms with special equipment and additional practical spaces like weighing and measurement rooms, centrifuge and autoclave rooms, rinsing kitchens, air-conditioned and cold storage rooms with constant temperature, photographic/dark rooms etc. → ❷.

According to subject:
Chemistry and biology laboratories have permanently installed laboratory benches. Rooms have a high rate of air exchange and frequently additional fume cupboards with air extraction → p. 204 → ❼ for work producing gas and smoke. Fume cupboards are often installed in their own rooms ('stink rooms').

Physics laboratories mostly have mobile benches and sophisticated electrical equipment in cable ducts in the wall or suspended from the ceiling. Low rate of air exchange → p. 204. There are special laboratories for specific requirements, e.g. isotope laboratories for work on radioactive substances in various safety classes.

Clean room laboratories are used for work requiring especially dust-free filtered air, e.g. in microelectronics or for particularly dangerous substances, whose release into the surrounding rooms should be prevented by special air circulation and filtering (microbiology, gene technology) → ❹.

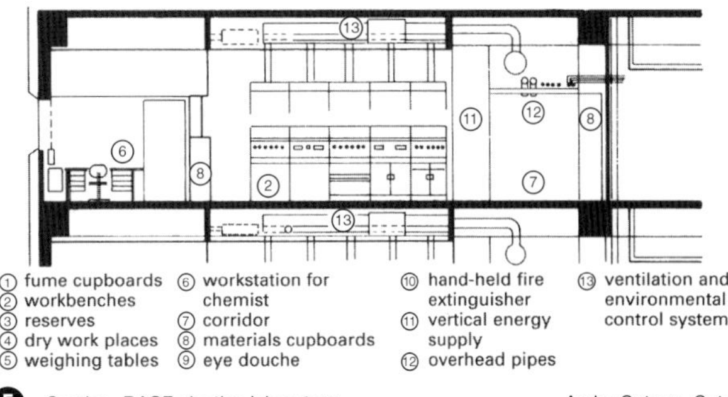

1. fume cupboards
2. workbenches
3. reserves
4. dry work places
5. weighing tables
6. workstation for chemist
7. corridor
8. materials cupboards
9. eye douche
10. hand-held fire extinguisher
11. vertical energy supply
12. overhead pipes
13. ventilation and environmental control system

❺ Section, BASF plastics laboratory — Arch.: Suter u. Suter

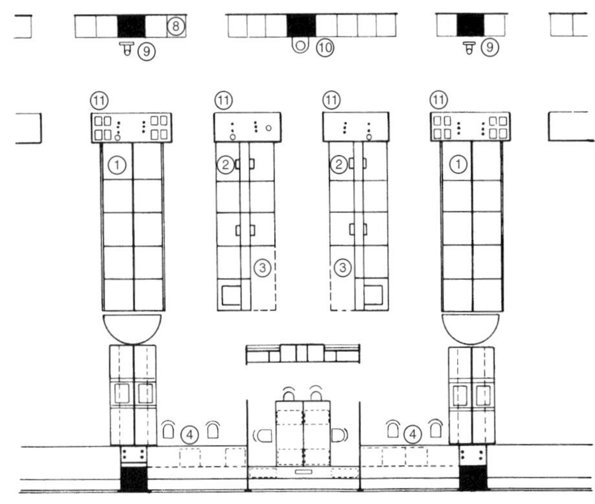

❻ Plan → ❺

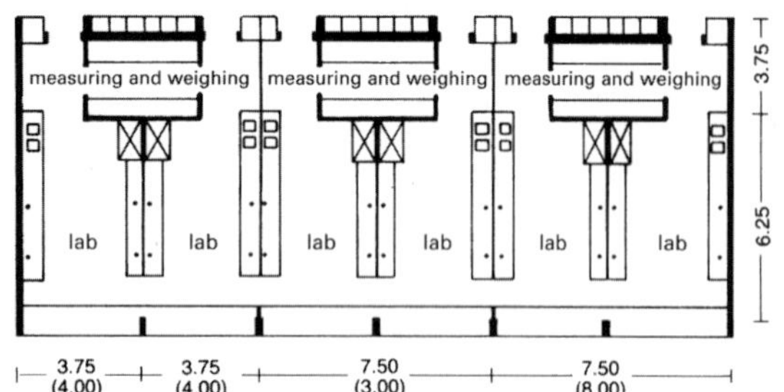

❶ Room dimensions derive from size of bench (workstation). Services and cupboards are in the corridor wall. Weighing room is separate.

measuring and weighing | measuring and weighing | measuring and weighing
lab lab lab lab lab lab
3.75 (4.00) 3.75 (4.00) 7.50 (3.00) 7.50 (8.00)
3.75 6.25

❷ Uniform laboratories with measurement and weighing rooms in front, University Clinic, Frankfurt am Main Arch.: Schlempp + Schwethelm

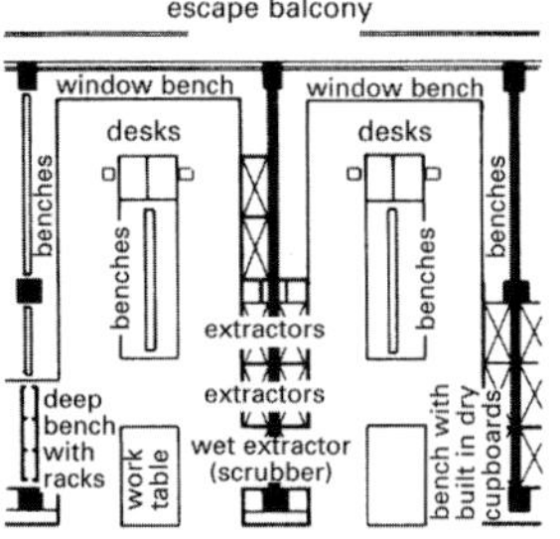

❸ Laboratory equipment in main scientific laboratory (Bayer AG dye plant)

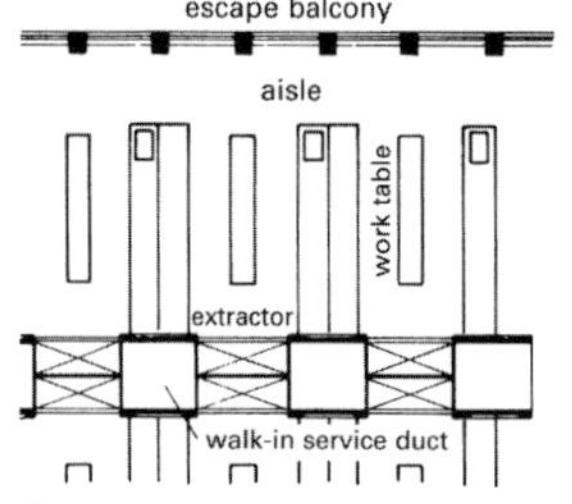

❹ Arrangement of equipment in accessible service ducts (BASF)

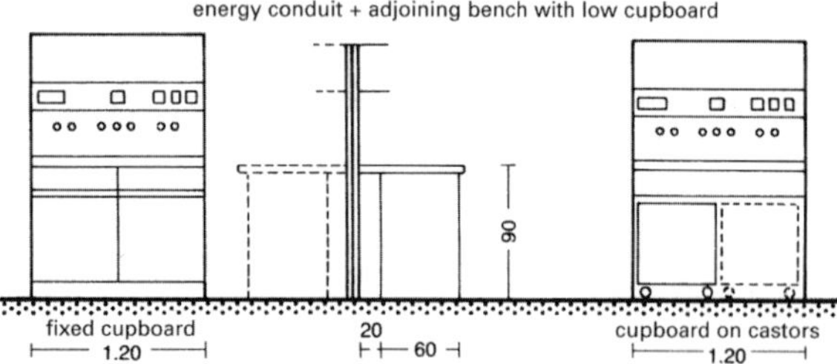

❺ Chemistry laboratory bench

energy conduit + adjoining workbench
72–75
1.20 20 60

❻ Physics laboratory bench

Cold laboratories are used for tasks requiring extreme temperature conditions, photographic work and as darkrooms. Workrooms without equipment installed also belong in the close laboratory area:
Study cubicles; social/rest rooms for laboratory staff; central rooms for general storage, chemical stores and issue, with particular safety measures; isotope stores with decay containers etc.
Animal laboratories are a special case, with rooms for keeping the animals, which have special equipment appropriate to the species and require their own air circulation.

Laboratory workstations

The determining design unit for the laboratory workstation is the laboratory bench, permanently installed or mobile, whose dimensions together with the associated work and passage areas define the laboratory axis, which forms the basic spatial unit → ❶ – ❸.
Standard dimensions for the normal working bench:
120 cm width in practical laboratories, several times that in research laboratories, 80 cm depth work surface including socket strip → ❺ – ❻.
Benches and fume cupboards are mostly in the form of a building block system: element widths 120 cm, fume cupboards 120 and 180 cm → ❼.
The socket strip is an independent element with all electricity supply systems. Benches and low-level cupboards are placed in front of it → ❺ – ❼.
Steel tubing supports the construction of laboratory benches, whose work surfaces are of artificial stone panels without joints, seldom tiled, and chemically resistant plastic panels. Low-level cupboards are of wood or plastic-coated chipboard. Supply services are fed from above out of the ceiling cavity or from below through the floor structure.

Ventilation

Of low- or high-pressure systems, the latter are particularly recommended for multi-storied institute buildings with large-scale air requirements, in order to reduce the ducts' cross-section. Cooling and humidification as required. Ventilation equipment has the highest demand for space of all services installations.
All laboratories in which work with chemicals takes place must have artificial ventilation and extraction.

Air changes per hour: chemistry laboratories 8 times
biology laboratories 4 times
physics laboratories 3–4 times
(in the extraction area)

Electrical installation

Each building will need its own transformer station if the numbers of connections are high or if special electricity supplies are specified. Electrical service rooms must be enclosed in fire-resistant walls and may not be crossed by other pipework or cables.

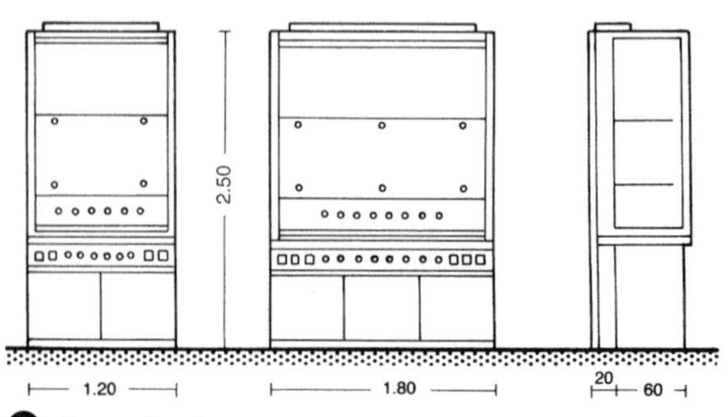

❼ Fume cupboards

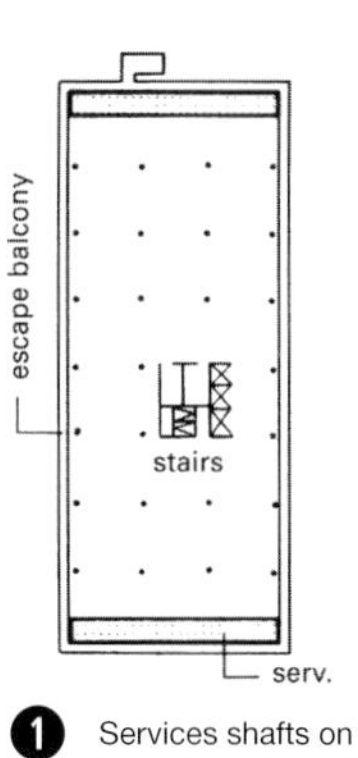

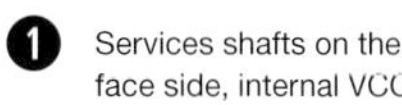
❶ Services shafts on the face side, internal VCC

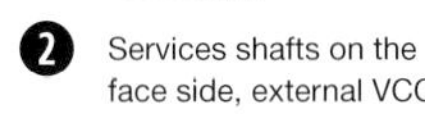

❷ Services shafts on the face side, external VCC

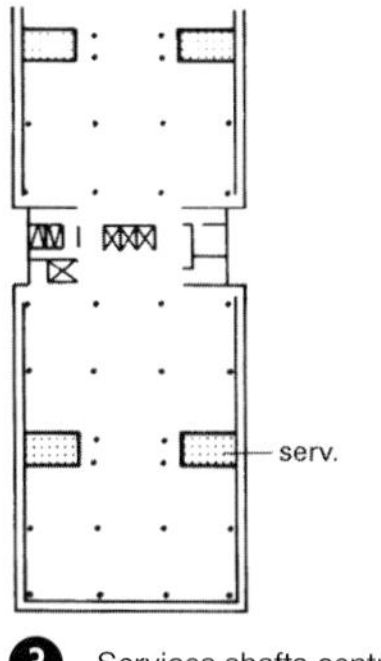

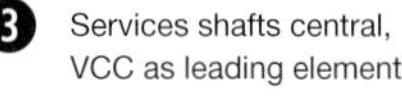
❸ Services shafts central, VCC as leading element

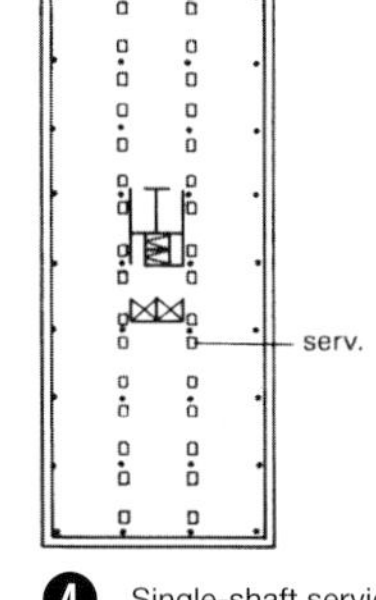

❹ Single-shaft services, internal VCC

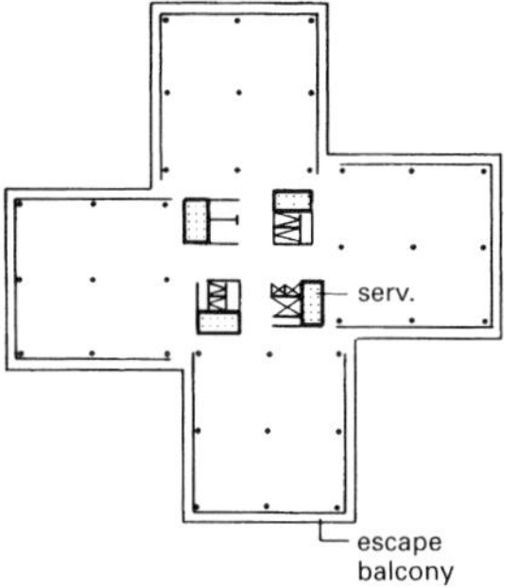

❺ Internal installation, coupled with VCC

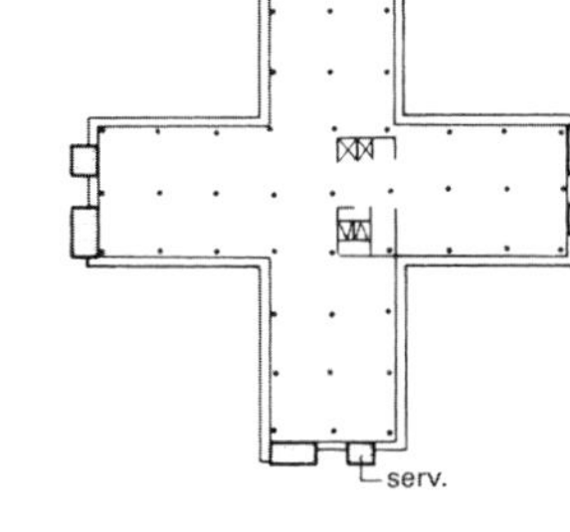

❻ External services shafts, central VCC

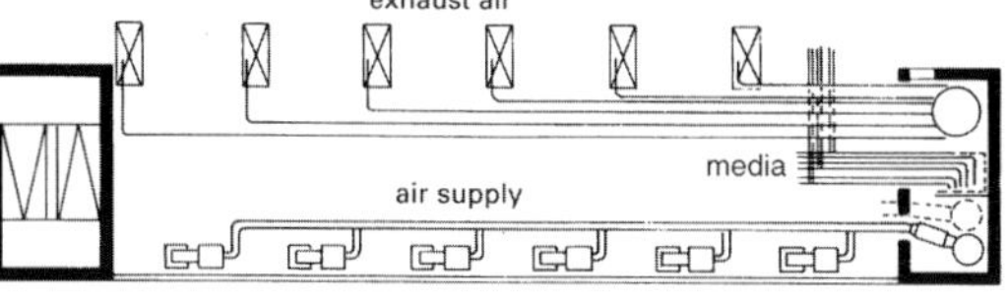

❼ Horizontal conduits and ducts: laboratory floor. Plan → ❽

CW	cold water	St	steam	E	emptying
HW	hot water	Co	condensate	RE	reserve
C	circulation	A	air	LW	lab water
DW	distilled water	G	gas	SAE	secondary air extraction
CWS	cooling water supply	SM	special medium		
CWR	cooling water return			SWW	sanitary waste water
I	1st pressure level			RWP	rainwater pipe
II	2nd pressure level				

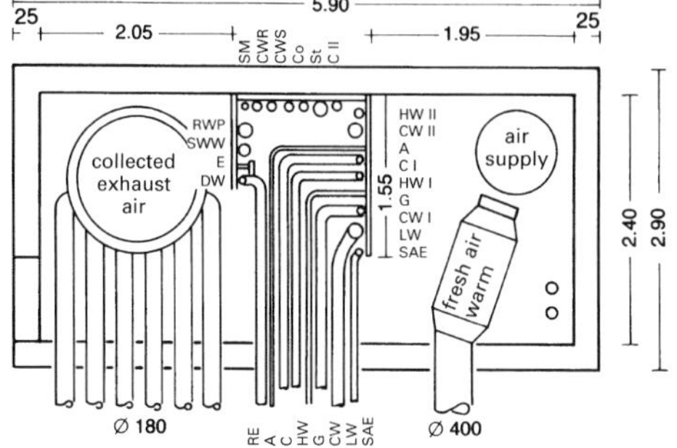

❽ Plan of joint shaft → ❼

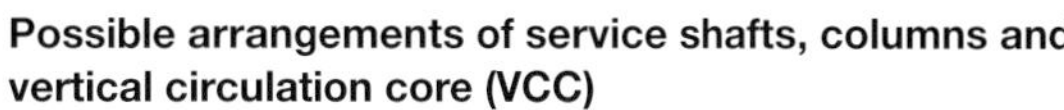

Possible arrangements of service shafts, columns and vertical circulation core (VCC)

Services concentrated in:

- joint shafts on face side of building, internal VCC → ❶
- external joint shafts, external VCC → ❷ – central joint shafts, VCC as leading element → ❸
- services distributed among single-shaft installations, internal VCC → ❹
- internal installation, coupled with VCC → ❺
- external shafts, central VCC, cruciform plan → ❻

Vertical services system → ❾

Many vertical supply lines, internally or on the façade, run the media in individual shafts to the laboratories. Decentrally routed air supply and extraction ducts to the fume cupboards, separate ventilators on the roof.

Advantage: maximum individual supply; short horizontal connections to laboratory bench.

Disadvantage: limited floor layout flexibility; greater space requirement on working and services floors.

Horizontal services system → ❿:

Vertical main services for all media concentrated in joint shafts and distributed horizontally from there into the services floors with upper or lower connection to laboratory benches.

Advantages: less space required in the services shafts, greater flexibility of floor layout, simpler maintenance, central ventilation equipment, better adaptability. High density of installation requires large amount of space. Vertical joint shafts are simpler, more accessible and allow revisions.

Conduits should be insulated against condensation, heat, cold and noise transmission → ❼ – ❽.

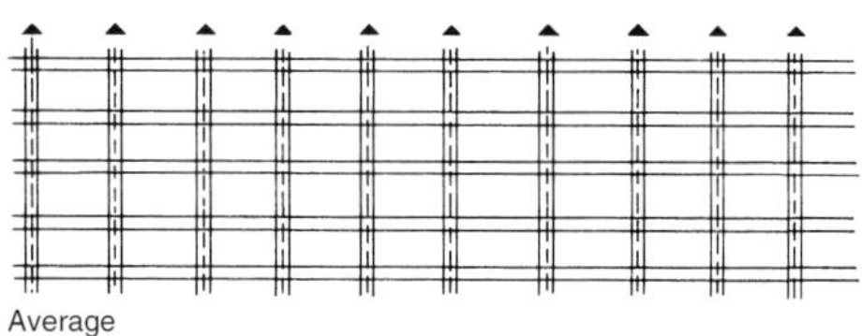

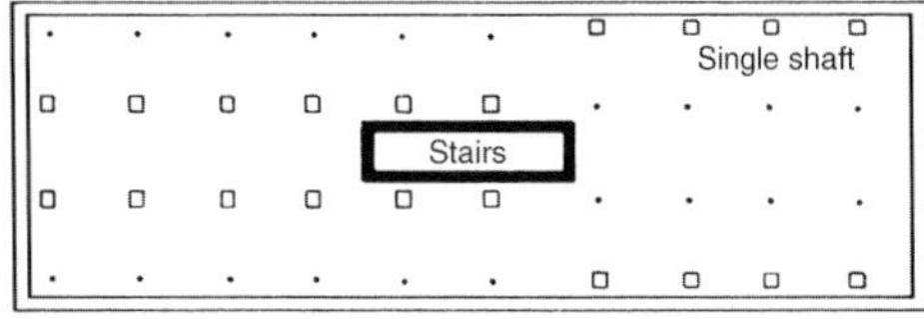

❾ Vertical services system: single shafts for installation of building, horizontal direct connection to laboratory benches, fume cupboards etc.; limited flexibility of floor layout

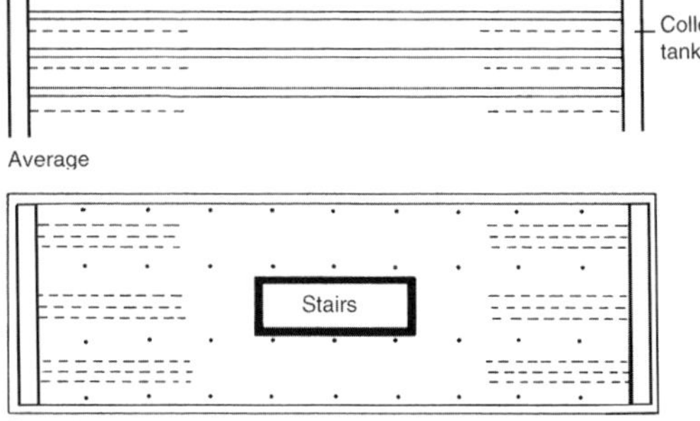

❿ Horizontal services system: horizontal conduits and ducts in ceiling space, good flexibility of floor layout

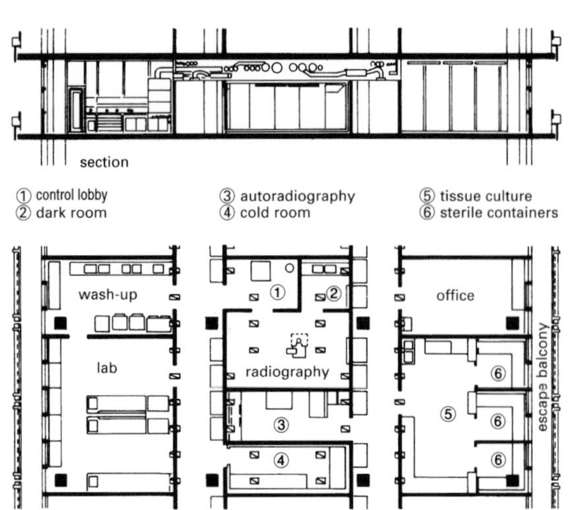

❶ Part of the floor plan of cancer research centre, Heidelberg
Arch.: Heinle, Wischer u. Partner

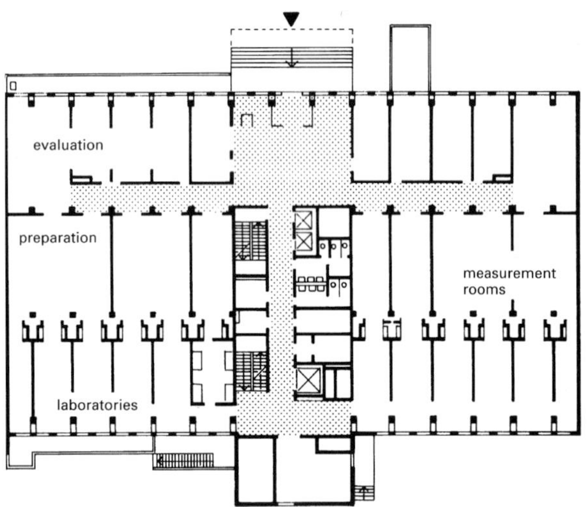

❷ Analytical physics laboratory building (BASF Ludwigshafen)

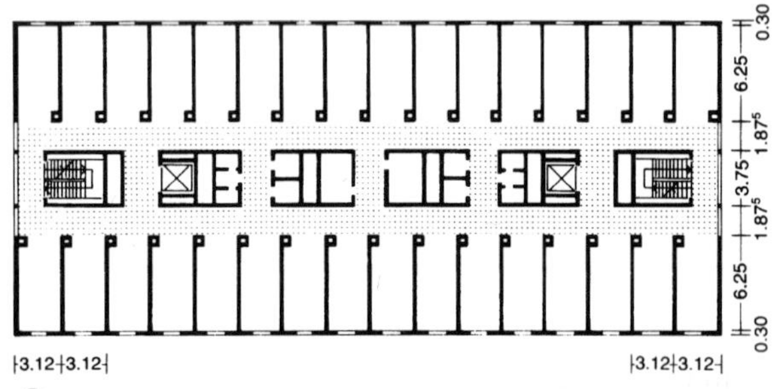

❸ Typical floor plan of an adaptable multi-purpose institute
Arch.: W. Haake

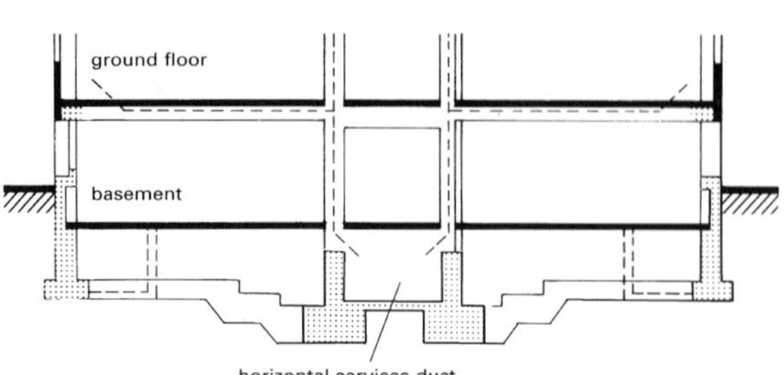

❹ Cross-section of laboratory with well-placed central corridor

Structure and fittings grid

Good structural grids to achieve mostly column-free rooms have the following dimensions:

7.20 × 7.20 m, 7.20 × 8.40 m, 8.40 × 8.40 m, normal storey height 4.0 m, clear room height ≧3.0 m.

The structural grid is a multiple of the typical planning grid of 120 × 120 cm (decimetric system). Reinforced concrete frame construction, as pre-cast elements or cast in situ, is preferred on account of the flexibility of plan.

Following programme and layout requirements, with installation at high and low level, plus natural and artificial lighting and ventilation rooms, results in areas with different potential uses and technical qualities. Laboratories therefore have large internal zones and are arranged as three-block facilities → ❶ – ❸. The length of the building is influenced by the maximum reasonable length of the horizontal runs of wet services.

Columns are placed on a grid offset from the structural grid to increase the flexibility of servicing. Separation of areas is via a room-enclosing system consisting of partitions and suspended ceilings. Movable partitions should be easily operated and have chemical-resistant surfaces. Ceilings should permit disassembly and have sound insulation. Floor coverings should be resistant to water and chemicals, without joints and with low electrical conductivity. Normally, plastic roll flooring material or tiles with welded joints should be used.

Windows in the doors or next to them are important to provide a view into laboratories.

Isotope laboratories should have flat, non-porous ceiling and wall surfaces, rounded corners, be surrounded by lead and concrete, monitored waste water, and shower cubicles between laboratory and exit. Concrete containers for active residues or waste and concrete safes with lead doors etc. must be provided.

Weighing tables are part of every laboratory, and are normally installed in their own weighing room. The tables should be at the wall side of vibration-free walls.

Services floors for plant are normally placed in the basement or on the top storey.

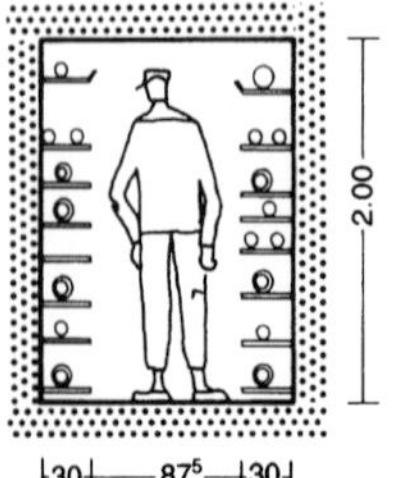

❺ Main pipe duct (accessible): cross-section varies according to number of pipes

A museum is a public collection of objects testifying to human cultural development. It collects, documents, receives, researches, interprets and communicates these through display.

The following museum types can be categorised according to the origin and nature of the items in the collection:

Art gallery: Collection of works of fine art (including craftworks and graphics).

Cultural history museum: Collection of devices, weapons, clothing, written documents etc. which show the cultural development of a geographically restricted area (ethnological museum, open-air museum, local history museum).

Ethnology museum: Works from the cultural heritage of traditional peoples and lost cultures.

Science museum: Collection of educational and display material connected with scientific and technical themes.

Lighting

There should be no direct daylight falling on museum objects as this could cause damage. Therefore display rooms should be provided with flexible lighting systems: no permanently built-in lights, no fixed wall and ceiling lights.

Guidelines for lighting:

Very sensitive display objects	50–80 lx
Sensitive display objects:	100–150 lx
Less sensitive display objects:	150–300 lx

UV radiation must not be exceed 25 W/m^2.

It must be possible to completely darken all display rooms. In public rooms where no items are displayed, e.g. entrance area, café, library, a greater amount of daylight is desirable.

The lighting calculations for museums are highly theoretical: the quality of lighting is decisive. American tests can be more informative.

Room climate in the store and the display areas

The ideal temperatures in the store and the display areas are 15–18°C in the winter and 20–22°C in the summer. Except as short peaks, in the summer 26°C should not be exceeded. Stores should not therefore be located in uninsulated attics, for example.

Because the reproduction of insects is very limited under 15°C, above all for science and ethnography collections a temperature of 12–13°C is optimal.

Photo and film material is relatively chemically unstable and the material should therefore be stored cool and dry at temperatures under 16°C (ideally at approx. 5°C).

The relative humidity in the store and the display areas depends on the displayed and stored materials: the optimal values are for wood 55–60%, canvas 50–55%, paper 45–50% and metals, max. 40%. It is important to avoid short-term variations in relative humidity: the variation within one hour should not exceed 2.5%, or not more than 5% in one day. Seasonal variations should not be more than +5% in summer or –5% in winter. The changing flow of visitors in museums leads to continuous variation in the climatic parameters.

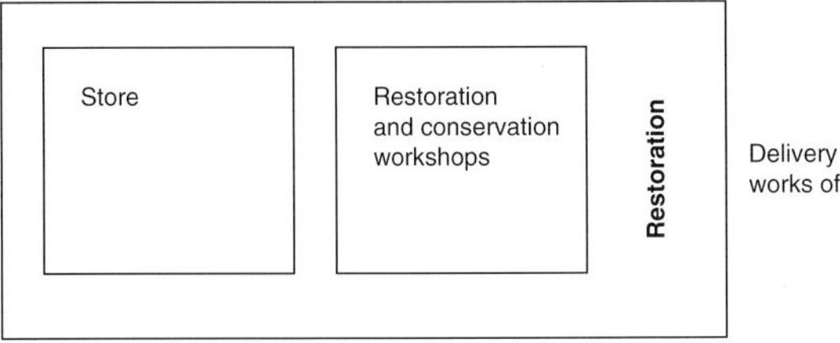

1 Functional scheme

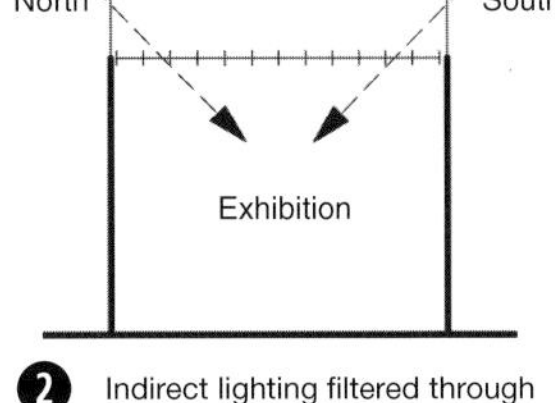

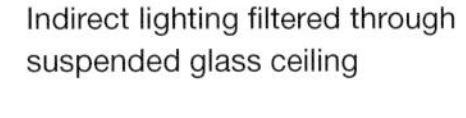

2 Indirect lighting filtered through suspended glass ceiling

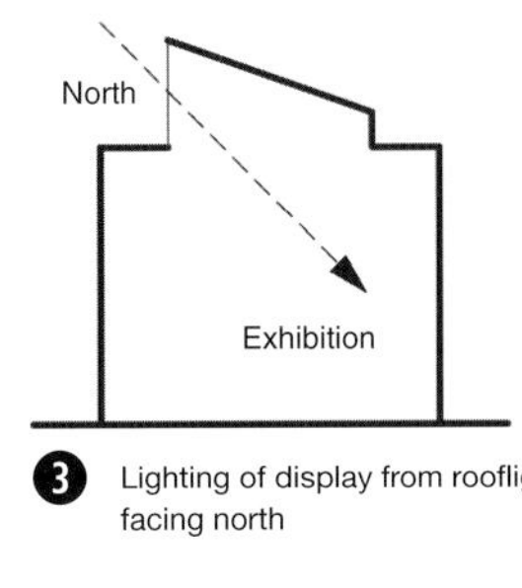

3 Lighting of display from rooflight facing north

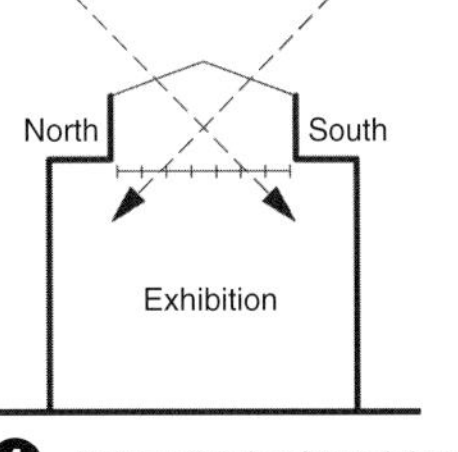

4 Indirect lighting filtered through suspended glass ceiling

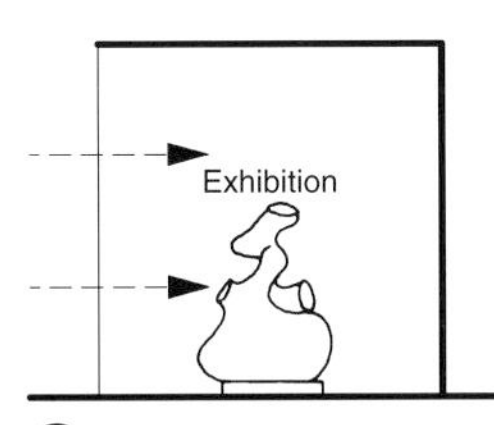

5 Side lighting from north

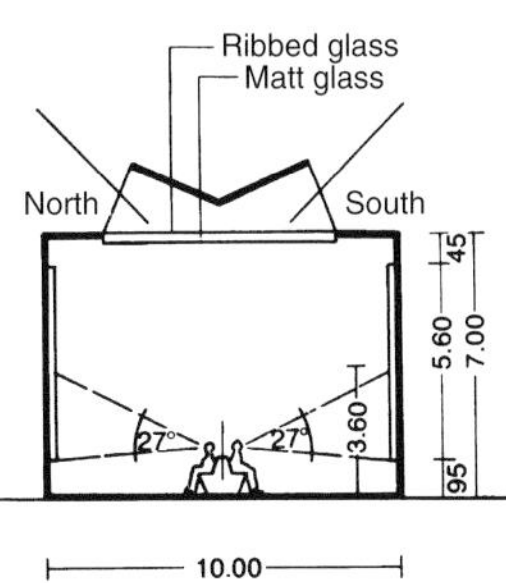

6 Well-lit display room according to Boston tests

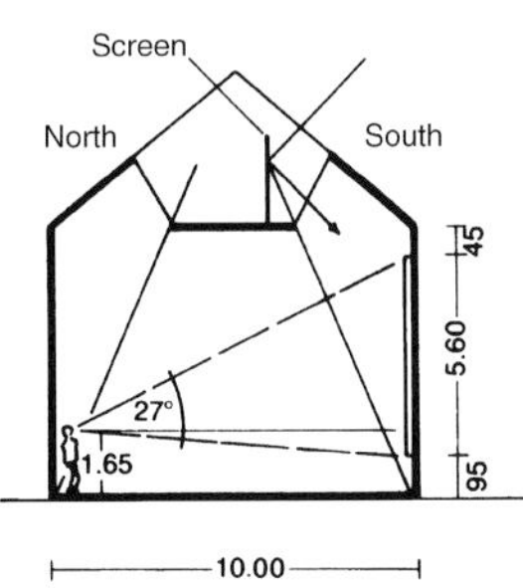

7 Uniformly lit gallery with light according to S. Hurst Seager

see also: Lighting, pp. 501 ff.

The decisive factor in the layout of display rooms is the relationship between the collection and the way it is to be displayed (display concept). There are the following basic types of layout → ❶ – ❻:

Open plan → ❶: large and visually autonomous items on display, free circulation, function rooms in basement.

Core and satellite rooms → ❷: main room for orientation in the museum or the exhibition, side rooms for autonomous displays (themes/collections)

Linear chaining → ❸: linear sequences of rooms, controlled circulation, clear orientation, separate entrance and exit.

Labyrinth → ❹: free circulation, guided route and direction are variable, entrance and exit can be separate.

Complex → ❺: combined groups of rooms with typical features of → ❶ – ❹, complex organisation of collection and display concept.

Round tour (loop) → ❻: similar to linear chaining → ❸, controlled circulation leads back to entrance.

Display concept	Spatial arrangement
oriented on display items	open plan → ❶
systematically oriented	main and side rooms (core and satellites) → ❷
thematically oriented	linear chaining → ❸, round tour → ❻
complex oriented	labyrinth → ❹, complex → ❺

The size and height of the display and store rooms depend on the dimensions of the works and the extent of the collection, but the minimum height is 4 m clear.

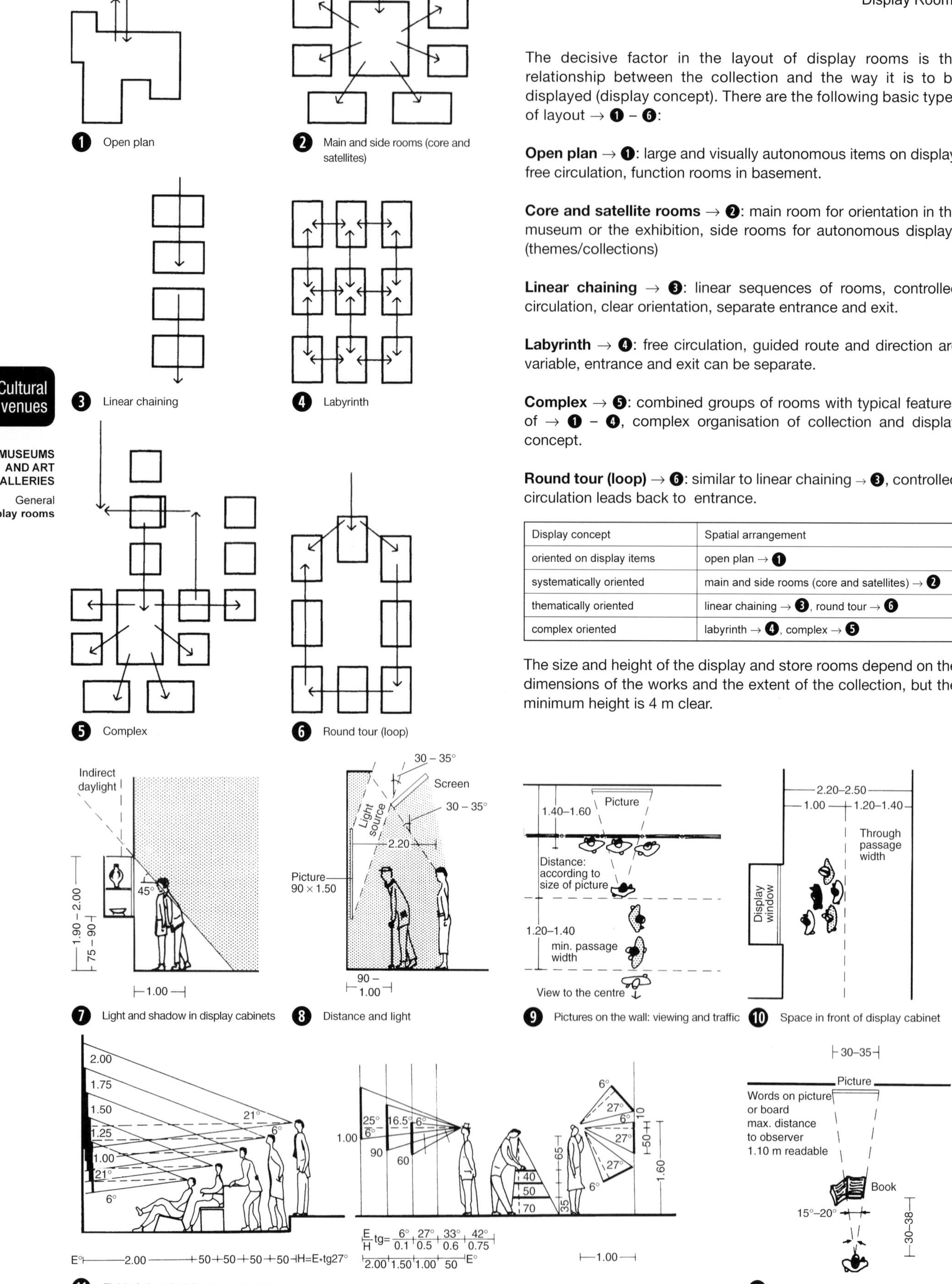

❶ Open plan

❷ Main and side rooms (core and satellites)

❸ Linear chaining

❹ Labyrinth

❺ Complex

❻ Round tour (loop)

❼ Light and shadow in display cabinets

❽ Distance and light

❾ Pictures on the wall: viewing and traffic

❿ Space in front of display cabinet

⓫ Field of view: height, size and distance

⓬ Ensure labels/commentaries readable

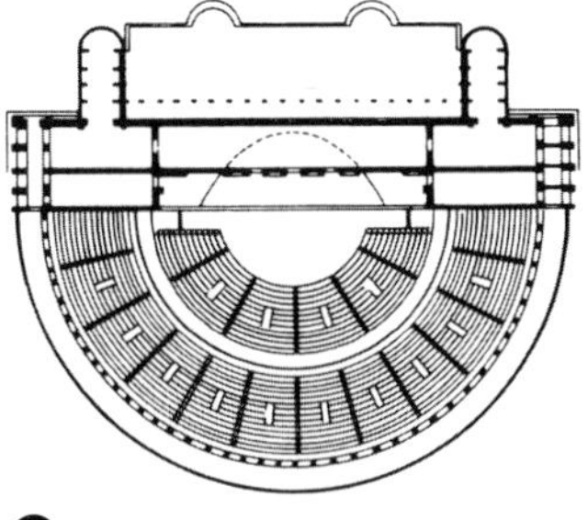

❶ Theatre of Dionysos, Athens, 452–330 BCE: plan

❷ Theatre of Marcellus, Rome, 11,500 seats, 11 BCE: plan

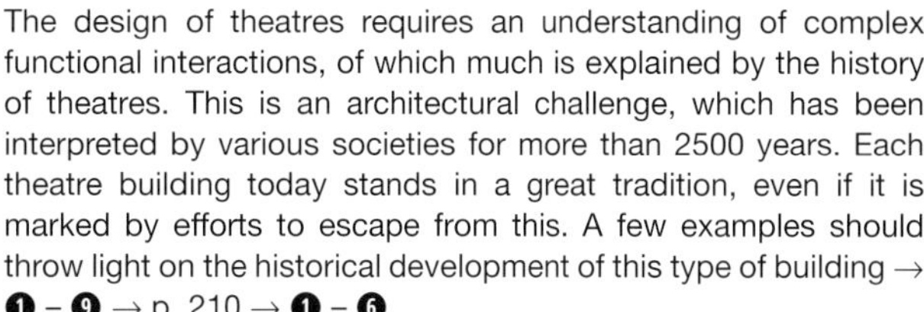

The design of theatres requires an understanding of complex functional interactions, of which much is explained by the history of theatres. This is an architectural challenge, which has been interpreted by various societies for more than 2500 years. Each theatre building today stands in a great tradition, even if it is marked by efforts to escape from this. A few examples should throw light on the historical development of this type of building → ❶ – ❾ → p. 210 → ❶ – ❻.

Ancient theatres

Theatre of Dionysos, the start of European theatre building → ❶. Greek theatres were located next to towns and embedded in the landscape. Theatre of Marcellus, Rome. The first theatre in Rome built completely of stone → ❷. Rows of seating and the back wall of the stage were connected and of the same height.

Middle ages

Medieval stage theatre. Temporary stage and buildings → ❸. Interior space of the Swan Theatre, according to a drawing by van de Witt 1596. Only a curtain separated the front and back stages and the upper stage served for balcony or siege scenes → ❹.

Renaissance

The early Italian Renaissance theatres were temporary wooden installations in existing halls → ❺. Vasari, for example, developed a wooden, reusable system for the theatre installation in the Salone dei Cinquecento in the Palazzo Vecchio, Florence. Teatro Olimpico, Vicenza → ❻. The first permanent theatre of the Renaissance, which resumed the ancient tradition of theatre building. Semi-circular and rising rows of seating for the audience and a stage house with façade. Next to this were the loggia courtyards with spectator boxes arranged in a horseshoe. The Teatro Farnese, Parma → ❽ + ❾ was the first building with movable scenery system in a deep stage space.

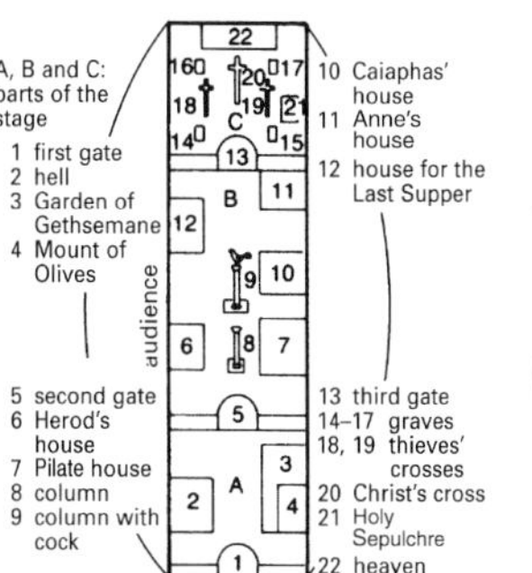

❸ Plan of medieval stage facilities

❹ Swan Theatre, London

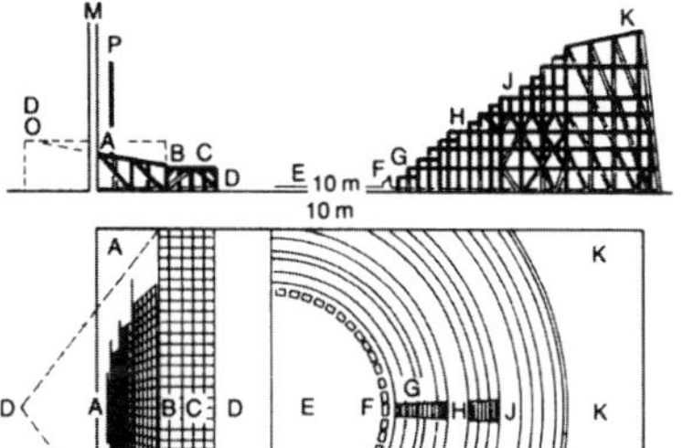

❺ Theatre layout, Sebastiano Serlio, 1545

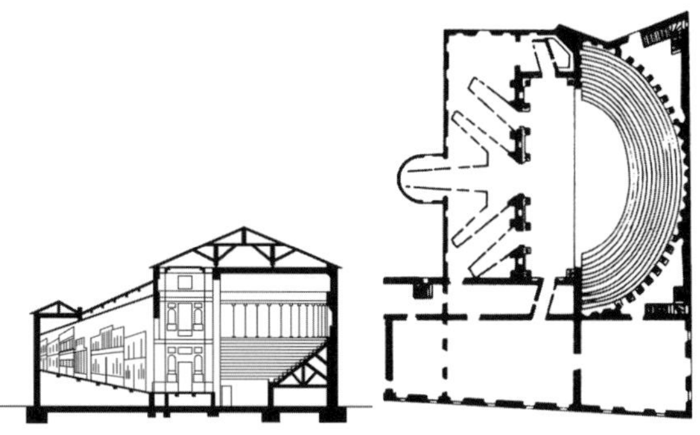

❻ Teatro Olimpico, Vicenza, 1585, section and plan — Arch.: Andrea Palladio and Vicenzo Scamozzi

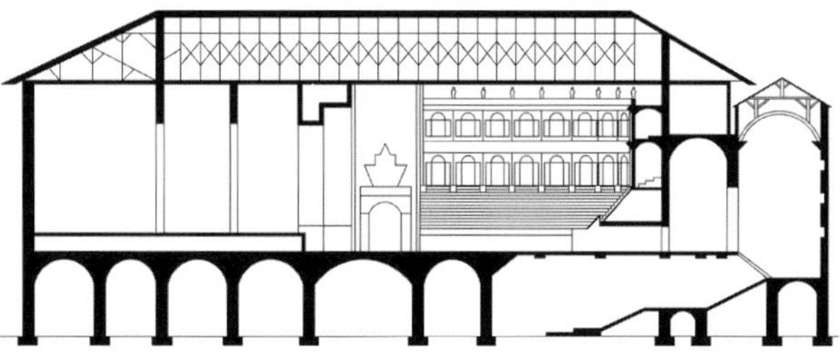

❽ Section of Teatro Farnese, Parma, 1618–1628 — Arch.: Giovanni Battista Aleotti

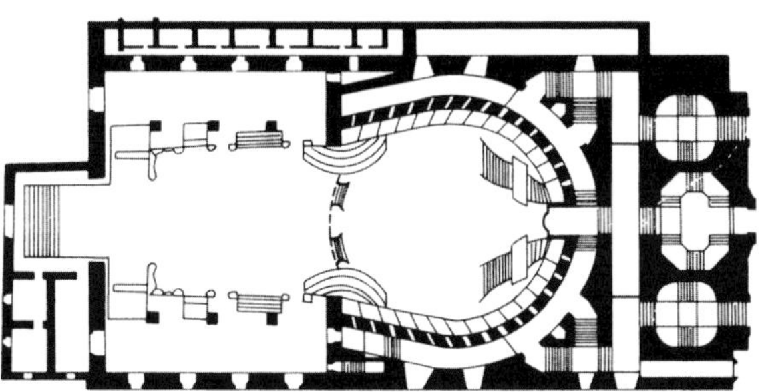

❼ Teatro 'San Carlo', Naples, 1737 — Arch.: Antonio Medrano and Angelos Carasale

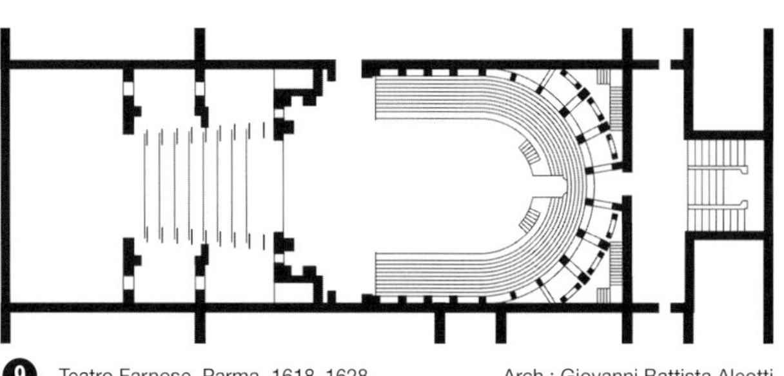

❾ Teatro Farnese, Parma, 1618–1628 — Arch.: Giovanni Battista Aleotti

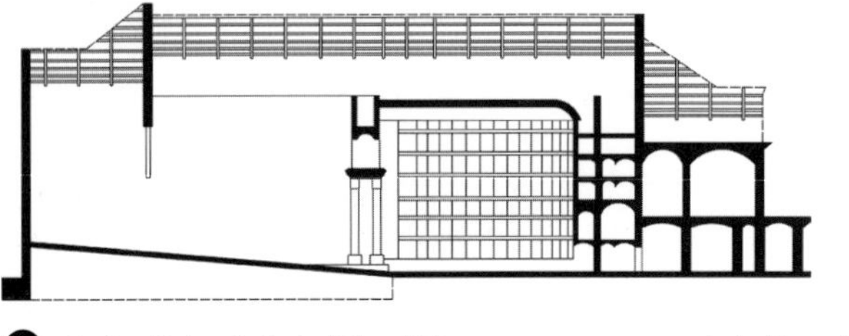

❶ Section, Teatro alla Scala, Milan, 1779 Arch.: Piermarini

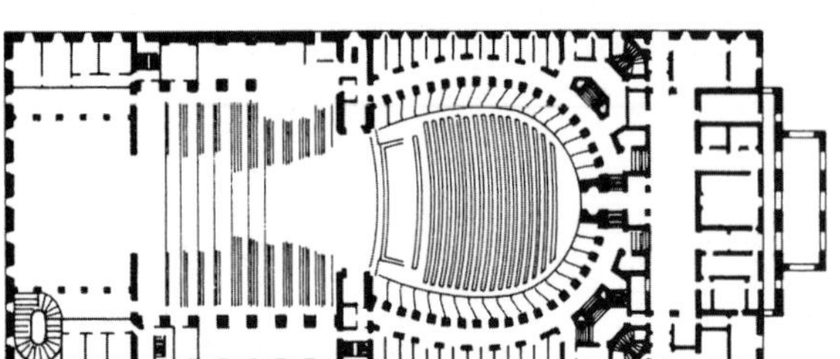

❷ Teatro alla Scala, Milan, 1779 Arch.: Piermarini

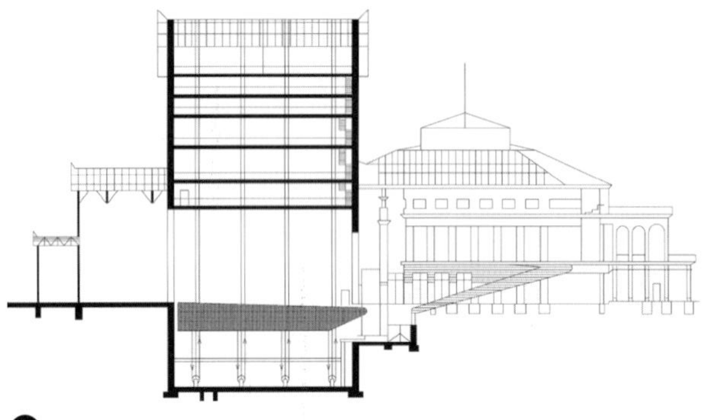

❸ Section, Festival Opera House, Bayreuth, 1876 R. Wagner and Arch. O. Bruckwald

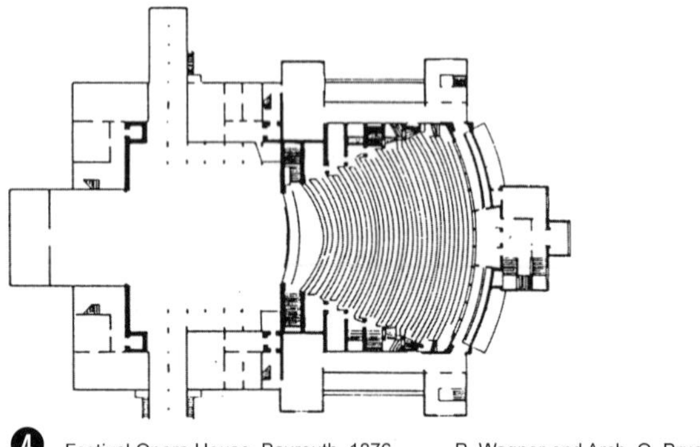

❹ Festival Opera House, Bayreuth, 1876 R. Wagner and Arch. O. Bruckwald

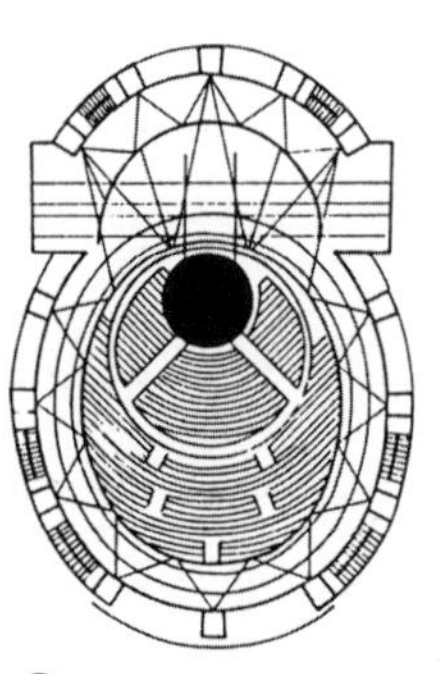

❺ Walter Gropius: Design for the 'Totaltheater', 1927

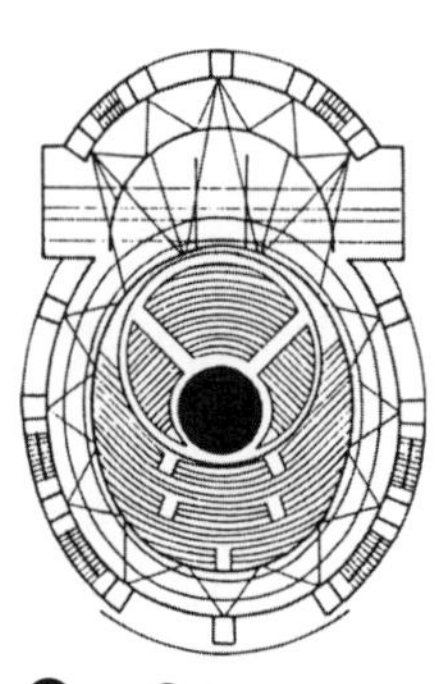

❻ → ❺ Stage rotated

Baroque
The theatre with boxes and a 'peephole' single-room stage steadily became more prevalent. Teatro 'San Carlo', Naples, p. 209 → ❼, and Teatro alla Scala, Milan → ❶ + ❷ are considered the models for the building of opera theatres in the 18th and 19th centuries, but also the new 'Met', in New York 1966.

19th and 20th centuries
Festival Opera House, Bayreuth → ❸ – ❹. Richard Wagner introduced this form of theatre (auditorium in a classical semicircle and rising) and set a counterpoint to the Grand Opéra in Paris. Totaltheater Project (Gropius/Piscator), cf. 'The Stage in the Bauhaus', Dessau 1924. Note: audience space can be rotated, stage with paternoster system, surrounding projection on walls and ceilings → ❺ – ❻. Playhouse on Lehniner Platz, Berlin, first large new building of a flexible theatre space (rebuilding of the Mendelsohn building, 'Universum', of 1928) → p. 213 → ❽ – ❾. Opéra Bastille, Paris, the largest theatre yet, with 10 side stages on two levels.

Tendencies in current theatre building
There are two tendencies today:

1. Preservation, restoration and modernisation of existing theatres from the 19th to mid-20th century → p. 218
2. New buildings with 'experimental' open-space character, e.g. Playhouse on Lehniner Platz → p. 213. A similar direction is demonstrated by the many projects to rebuild existing spaces into workshop theatres with a size of 80–160 seats.

Different types of theatre building
1. Opera house:
This belongs to the tradition of 18–19th century Italian opera buildings → ❶ – ❷. It is characterised by a clear spatial and architectural separation between auditorium and stage, by high numbers of seats (1000 to nearly 4000) and the corresponding system of boxes or tiers, which is necessary for so many theatre-goers, e.g. Scala, Milan, 3600 seats; Deutsche Oper, Berlin, 1986 seats; Metropolitan Opera, New York, 3788 seats; Opéra Bastille, Paris, 2700 seats. The counterpoint to the form of opera house as tiered/box theatre is the Festival Opera House, Bayreuth → ❸ – ❹. This is designed as a theatre with stalls according to the Greek and Roman pattern, but has only 1645 seats.

2. Playhouse:
This is in the tradition of the German reform theatre of the 19th century. It is characterised by the stalls layout (that is, the audience sit on a large, rising and curved floor) and by a pronounced apron stage (area in front of the proscenium), which can be used for the play as well. The playhouse also, however, follows the tradition of the English theatre → p. 209 ❹, i.e. theatre in the round. The open and variable layout became more intensive with the spatial experimentation of theatres in the 1970s. Variations in layout are shown, for example, by the Playhouse on Lehniner Platz, Berlin → p. 213.

3. Multi-purpose theatre:
This mixed form of opera, theatre and ballet is a speciality in German-speaking regions. The space is mostly characterised by the predominant influence of the opera. The frequent changes of scenery are enabled by the appropriate subsidiary rooms (store, scenery store, workshops). Example: Heilbronn City Theatre, Arch.: Biste u. Gerling 1982 → p. 217 ❹.

4. Musical theatre:
Actually no separate type of building, but rather a theatre built, usually, for a particular musical by an impresario. A specific challenge for the designer is the adaptation of the building to the concept of the musical without neglecting the needs of later uses for other productions.

In addition to the local building regulations, decisive for the design of theatres are the Places of Assembly Regulations of the relevant state. This is based on the Model Places of Assembly Regulations, which can vary in detail from those of a particular state! This legislation applies from 200 spectators. It should be noted that it is not the actual number of seating or standing places that counts: it is assumed that there are two spectators per m^2 in the place of assembly (for rows of seats; two spectators per running m for standing places).

Auditorium and stage/acting area

Size of auditorium: the number of people in the audience gives the required floor area. For seated spectators, assume ≧0.5 m^2/ spectator. This number results from:

seat width × row spacing	≧0.45 m^2	/seat
add ≧0.5 × ≧0.9	= 0.05	/seat
	≧0.50 → ❶	

Length of the rows of seats per aisle: 10 places → ❸ + ❺, 25 places per aisle if an exit door of 1.2 m width is available at the side per 3 or 4 rows → ❹

Exits, escape routes 1.2 m wide per 200 people → ❸ – ❺.

1% of the seats (at least two) must be accessible for wheelchair users, if possible in connection with a seat for an accompanying person.

Auditorium volume

This is determined by acoustic requirements (reverberation) → p. 221 as follows: playhouse approx. 4–5 m^3/spectator; opera house approx. 6–8 m^3/spectator. Air volumes must not be less for technical ventilation reasons, in order to avoid too rapid air changes (draughts).

Proportions of the auditorium

These are derived from the psychological awareness and angle of view of the spectator, or the requirement for a good view from all seats. Options are:

1. Good view, without moving head, but light eye movements of approx. 30°.
2. Good view with slight head movements and light eye movements of approx. 60° ❼.
3. Max. awareness angle without head movement approx. 110°, i.e. all actions in the field are 'in view'. Outside this field, there is uncertainty, because 'something' is out of view.
4. Full head and shoulder movement allows an angle of view of 360°.

Proportions of the classic auditorium

Opera, multi-purpose theatre, and traditional playhouse → ❼: distance of the furthest row from the start of the stage should not exceed: – playhouse, max. 24 m (max. distance for the recognition of facial expressions); opera, 32 m (large movements are still recognisable). **Auditorium width** is determined by the spectators at the side being able to see the stage adequately → ❽. The comfortable proportions and sometimes good acoustics of the classic theatres of the 18th and 19th centuries are based on particular rules of proportion → ❾ – ❿.

Cultural venues

THEATRES
Historical review
Typology
Auditorium
Stage
Subsidiary rooms
Workshops and staff rooms
Rehearsal and public rooms
Modernisation

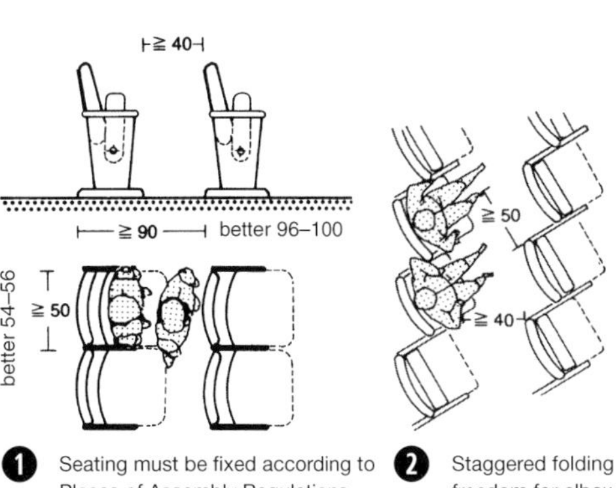

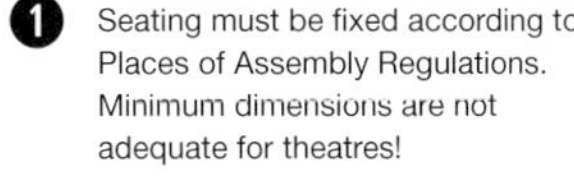
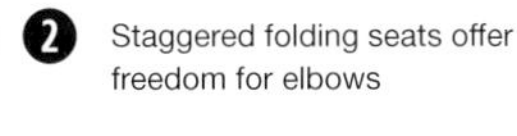

❶ Seating must be fixed according to Places of Assembly Regulations. Minimum dimensions are not adequate for theatres!

❷ Staggered folding seats offer freedom for elbows

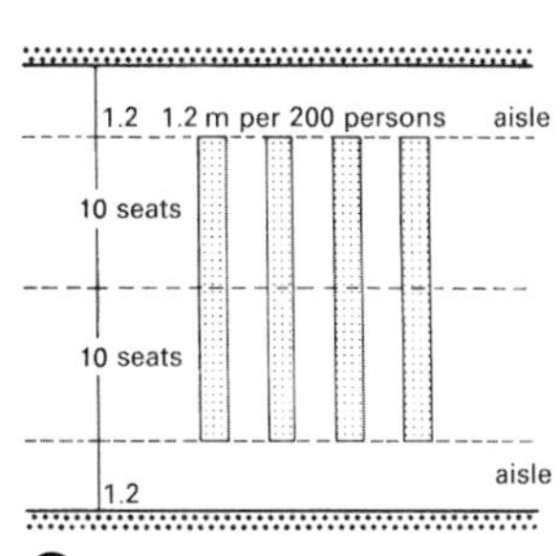

❸ Row width 20 places

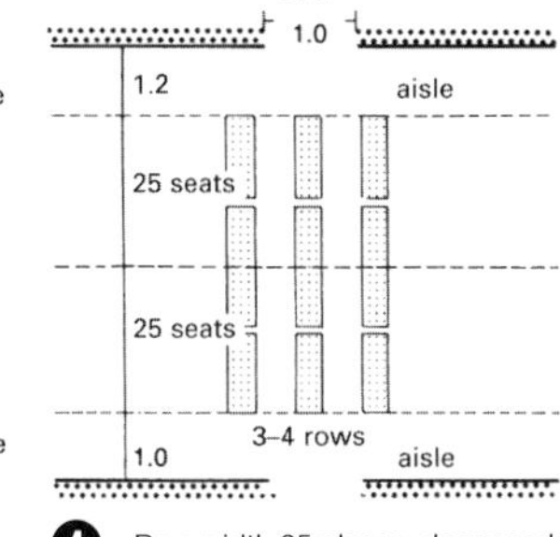

❹ Row width 25 places, door needed

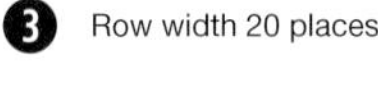

❺ Row width max. 10 places, side aisle at left and right

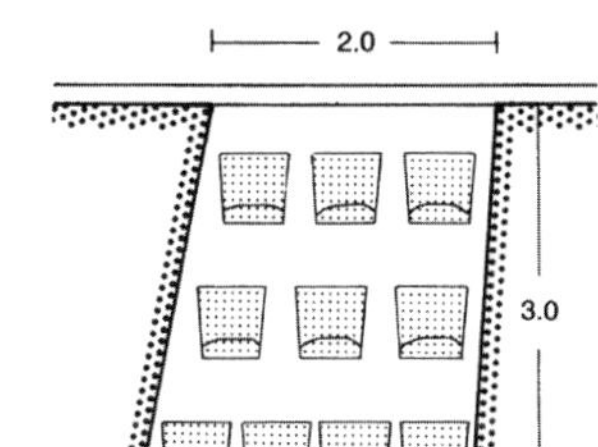

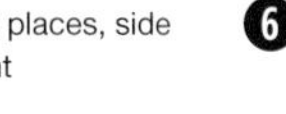

❻ Boxes may have ≦20 loose chairs, or fixed seating if necessary; per person ≧0.65 m^2 floor area

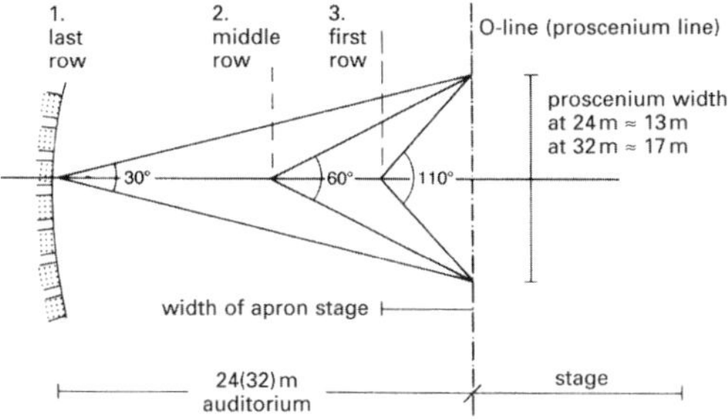

❼ Proportions of traditional auditorium plan

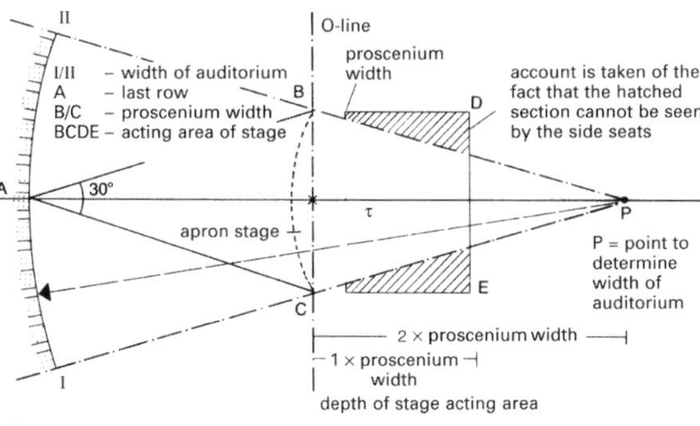

❽ Auditorium width

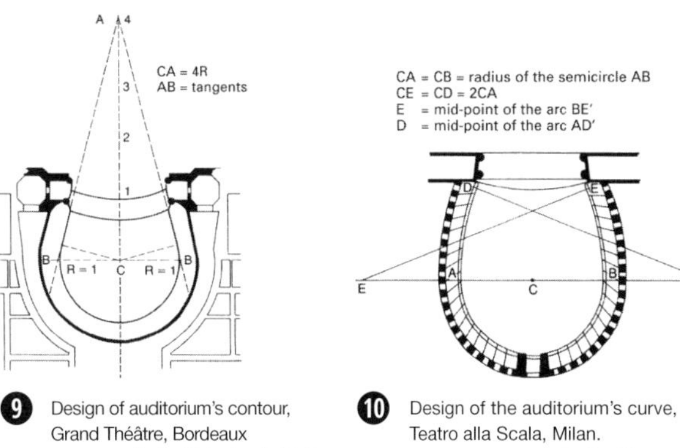

❾ Design of auditorium's contour, Grand Théâtre, Bordeaux
Arch.: Victor Louis 1778

❿ Design of the auditorium's curve, Teatro alla Scala, Milan.
Arch.: Piermarini

The elevation (gradient) of the seating in the auditorium is derived from the sight lines. The sight line construction applies for all places in the auditorium (stalls, but also tiers) → ❶. It can be assumed that the spectators sit sensibly and so only every second row requires full sight super-elevation (12 cm). Specialised mathematical literature addresses problems of view in the theatre, including, for example, the distribution of people's heights.

Rows of spectators should be positioned in arcs, not only for better alignment toward the stage, but also to achieve a better perception of each other (security effect) → ❹. The stepped side aisle must rise 10–19 cm and the tread must not be less than 26 cm. The floor between the seats must be on the same level as the adjacent aisle at the side.

Overall layout of the auditorium

Firstly, determine the height of the proscenium. In stalls theatres, the relationship should be:

$$\frac{\text{proscenium height } 1}{\text{proscenium width } 1.6}$$

This derives from the golden section and the physiological field of awareness, respectively → ❺. After determining the proscenium height, the ramp height, the pitch of the stalls and the volume of the room, this gives the room height. The ceiling is to be adapted for acoustic requirements. It should be the case that the noise reflected from the stage and apron is distributed evenly over the room → ❼.

For tiers, it is important that there is also a sufficiently deep view of the stage from the uppermost level → ❻. This may render it necessary to make the proscenium higher.

Proportions of an experimental space → p. 213

These are neutral or open theatre spaces, which permit different arrangements of spectators and stage areas. This variable arrangement is achieved through:

A. Mobile stage platforms and mobile stands for the audience on a fixed floor.
B. Mobile sections of floor, which consist of moveable podiums. This solution is technically more elaborate and is therefore used only in larger spaces for min. 150–450 or more people.

The simpler option A is particularly suitable for smaller theatres and for unused spaces, which normally do not have extensive space underneath. Size: up to max. 199 places, because the regulations apply from 200.

199 seats × 0.5 m^2 = 100 m^2 (2/3) + 30 m^2 (1/3) stage area = 130 m^2.

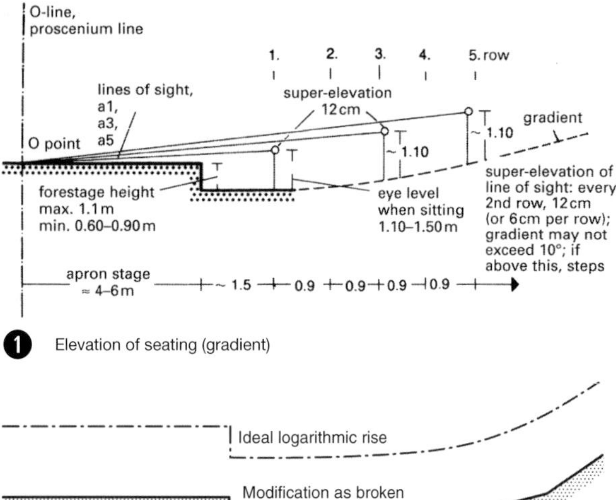

❶ Elevation of seating (gradient)

❷ Gradient curve and its modification

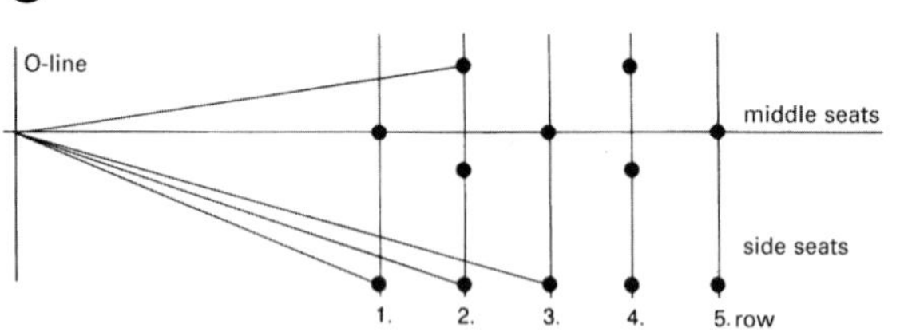

❸ Offsetting of the seats in a row is achieved through variable seat widths (0.50–0.53–0.56)

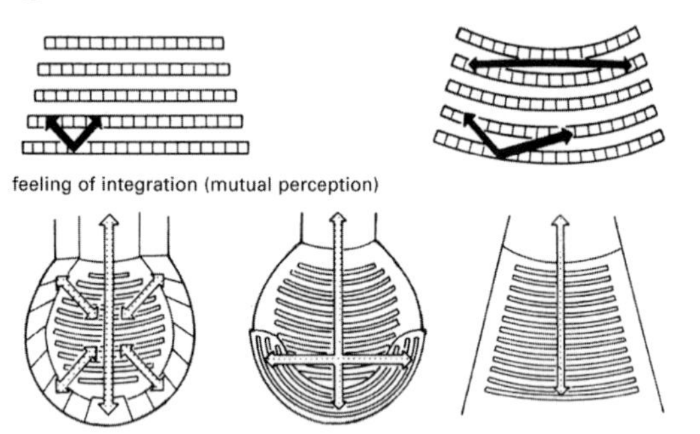

❹ Contact relationship between the audience and the stage and with each other

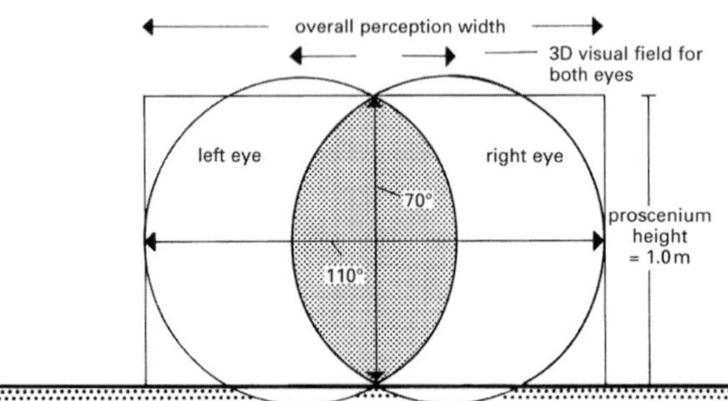

❺ Field of perception and proportions of the proscenium arch

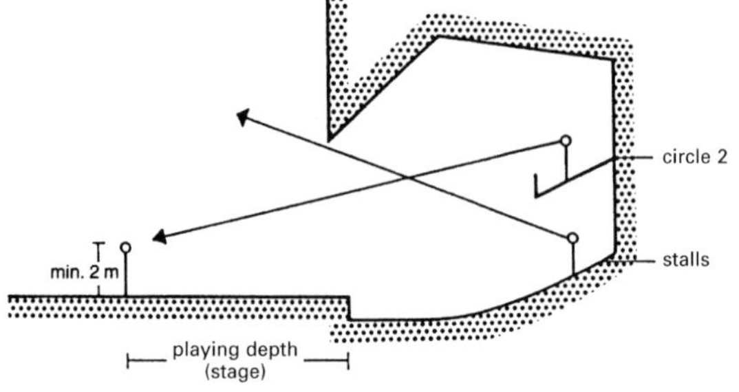

❻ Tiered theatre and view of stage

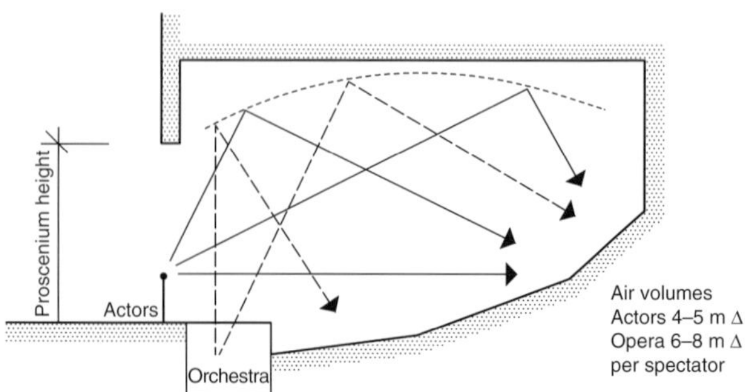

❼ Acoustics must be adapted through appropriate measures like ceiling shape or acoustic 'sails' → p. 220

Size of stage

The Places of Assembly Regulations, which apply to all venues with audiences of more than 200, differentiate two types of stage: large stage and open stage (single-room theatre).

Large stage

Large stages are defined as having a stage area of more than 200 m^2 behind the stage opening and with an upper stage of 2.5 m height above the stage opening or an apron. The essential requirement is the fire-resistant separation of stage and auditorium. This necessitates an iron protection curtain between the stage and the auditorium in case of danger.

Open stage

Open stages are divided into those with more or less than 200 m^2 and those with or without sprinkler systems. The special feature of open stages is the regulations about curtains and scenery. These affect above all the operation and not the design of the open stage.

Spaces for experimental forms of theatre (black box theatres) can abolish the separation of stage and audience in various ways through differentiated design of the floor topography (mobile sections of floor or podiums) and the free distribution of audience area and stage. Example: Playhouse on the Lehniner Platz, Berlin → ❽ – ❾.

Section of the room for single-room (black box) theatres

Single rooms can make do without the technical ceiling → ❶, but manual lifting devices can be provided (battens, which are lifted into the ceiling with manual hoists). In large theatres, a smaller, more variable space is often included for experimental theatre. Examples: Podium Ulm, Arch:. Schäfer, approx. 150–200 places, 1969 → ❻ + ❼; Kleines Haus Münster, Arch:. v. Hansen, Rane, Ruhnau, 1971, 180–380 places, central field of the floor can be varied with mobile podiums → ❷ – ❺.

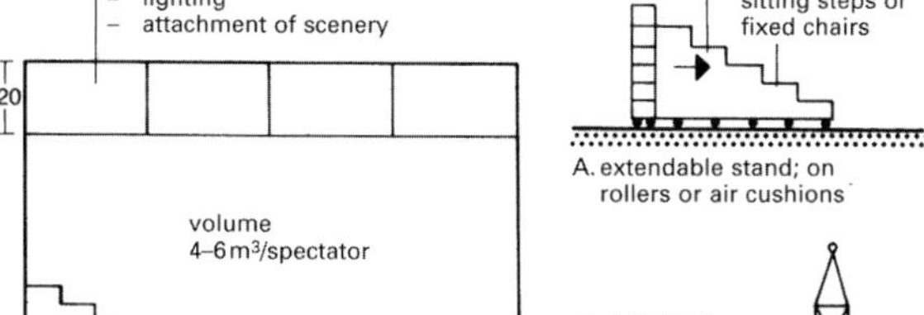

❶ Experimental theatre space

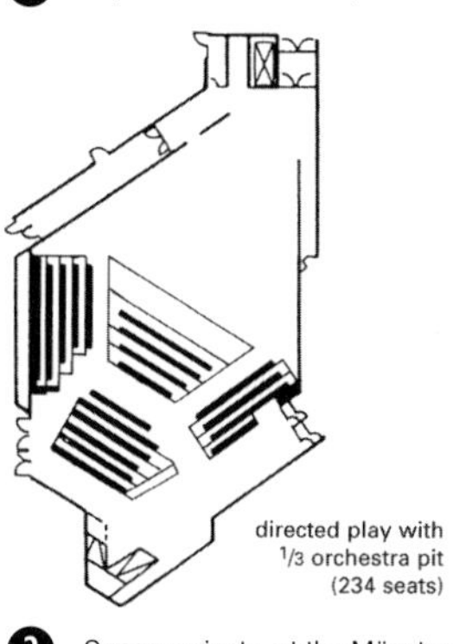
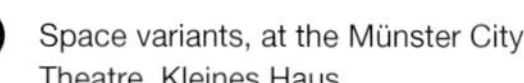

❷ Space variants, at the Münster City Theatre, Kleines Haus

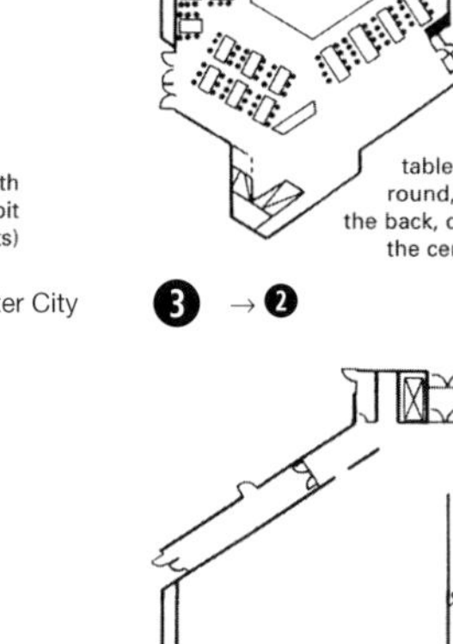

❸ → ❷

❹ → ❷

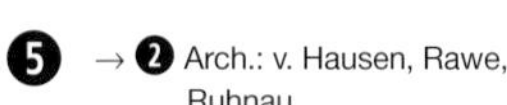

❺ → ❷ Arch.: v. Hausen, Rawe, Ruhnau

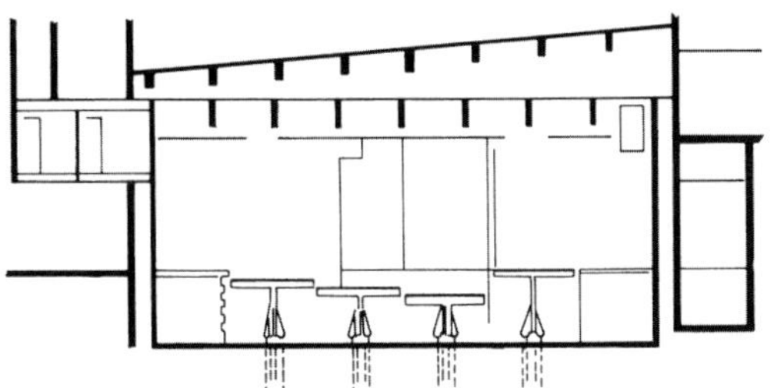

❻ Ulm Theatre, section through podium Arch.: Fr. Schäfer

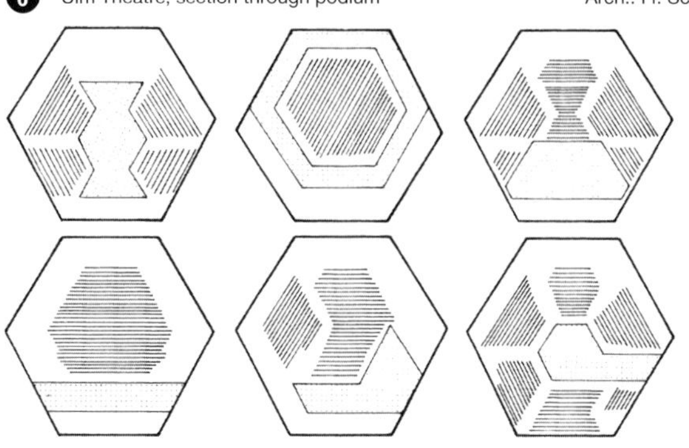

❼ Podium Ulm, six variants for arrangement of performance areas

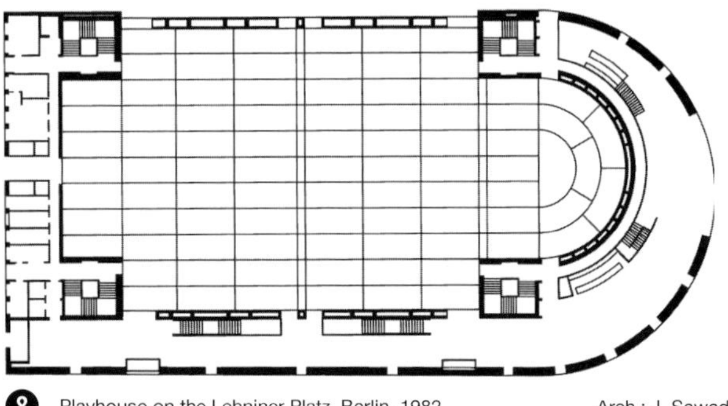

❽ Playhouse on the Lehniner Platz, Berlin, 1982 Arch.: J. Sawade

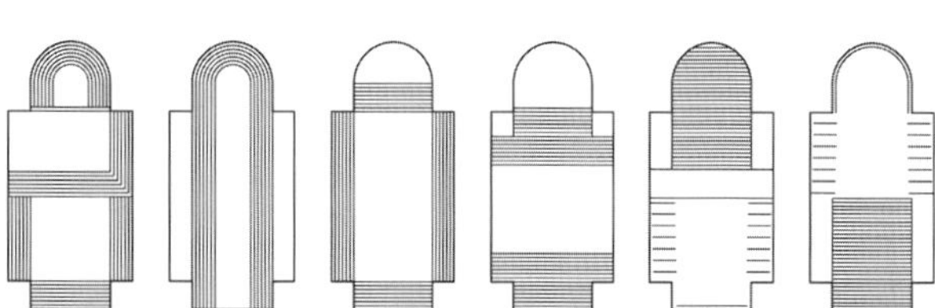

❾ Playhouse on the Lehniner Platz, six variants for arrangement of possible open stages

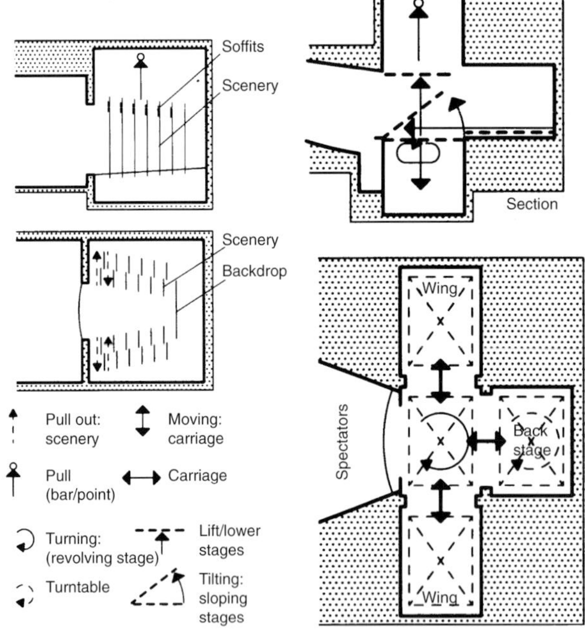

❶ Backdrop theatre: change of scene by pushing the painted scenery

❷ 'Peephole' single-room stage. Large wing and rear stage areas enable the quick changing of scenery structures

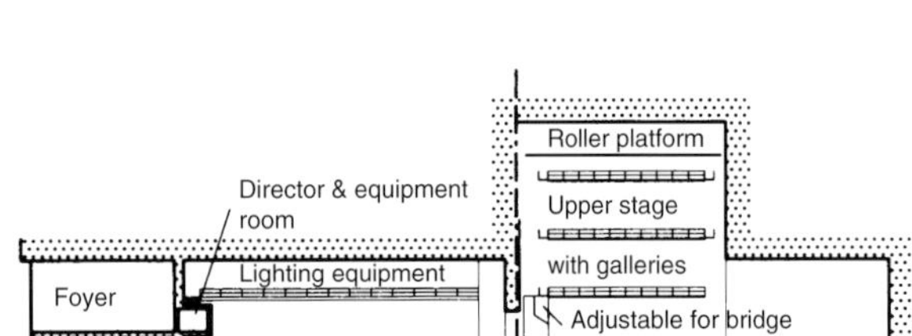

❸ System section of theatre

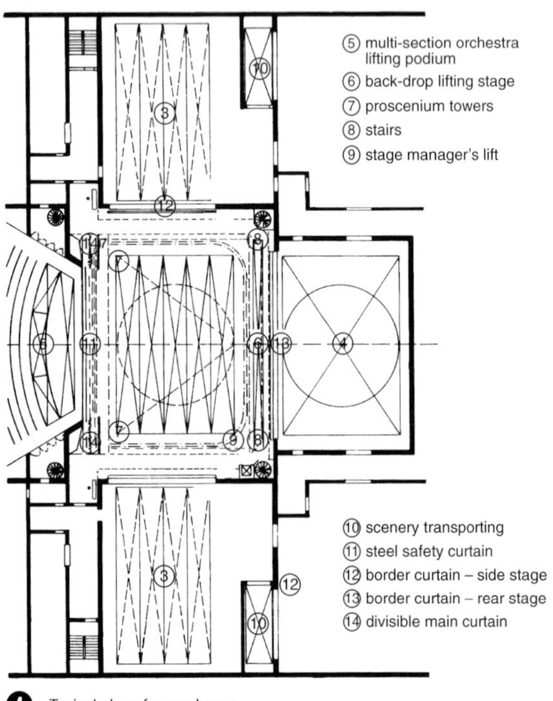

❹ Typical plan of opera house

Scenery stage

The classical stage system of the 18th and 19th centuries had only the main stage; the scenes were changed, in little space and with uncanny speed, using sliding painted scenery. A small rear stage had the function of providing room for deeper stage perspectives → ❶.

Full stage

In order to be able to quickly change more elaborate and sculptural scenery structures, stages were supplemented by wings and under-stages of about the same size. Complete sets of scenery were mounted on wagons, lifting platforms or turntables and could be prepared with little effort during the performance → ❷.

For design purposes, the technical constraints must be established early, e.g. whether a turntable on a wagon is sufficient or whether a turntable with single lifting elements or even a two-level turntable should be used.

Proportions of the stage

The proportions of the stage are developed from the sight lines in the auditorium. The stage is the area for acting and also a handling and working area. The conventional layout of a traditional full stage → ❸ – ❹.

The mobile scenery surface is formed by platforms of adjustable height or through lifting platforms. The variability of form is achieved by splitting the surface into separate flats. Basic module 1 × 2 m.

Section of stage

The size of the stage space is determined by the number of scenery sets to be kept ready, which can be moved into the stage quickly by lifting or pushing. At least one rear space and one wing are usual. The height of the stage space is determined by the (iron) safety curtain, which must be able to close the fire compartment between auditorium and stage within 30 s in case of fire. It is a complete closure joined at the ends to a fire wall (F90) and no cables or scenery are permitted in the space for the safety curtain.

Stage direction room

Control of lighting and sound on stage, with sound mixing desk, light controls, computer connections and projection equipment → ❸.

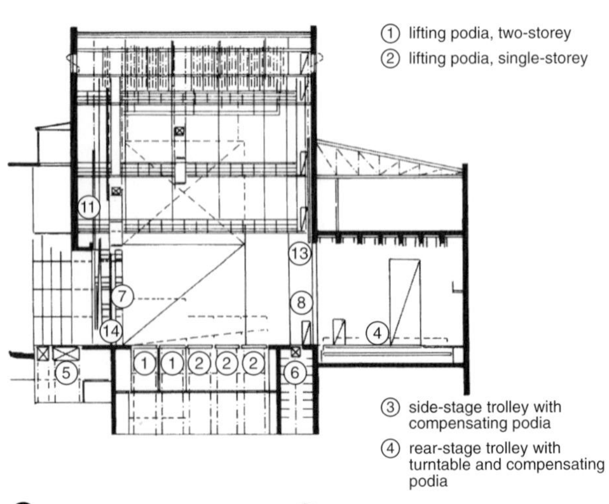

❺ Typical section of opera house → ❹

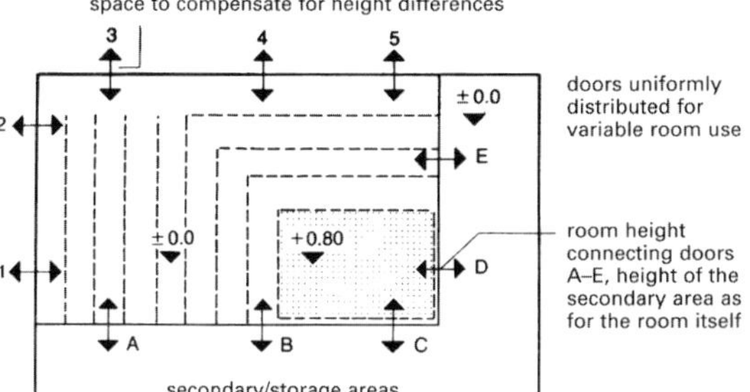

❶ Subsidiary areas/storage space for open stages

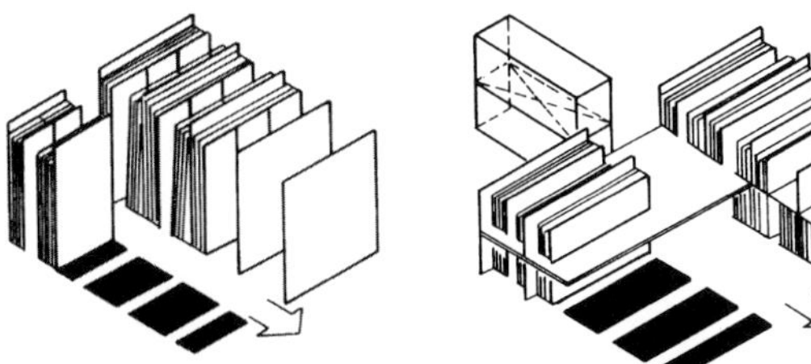

traditional storage of back-drops
- on edge in boxes, manual transport, large proportion of area required, height: 9–12 m
- in boxes, manual transport, large proportion of area required for moving

❷ Storage near the stage

modern back-drop storage
- loading of containers by hand from secondary stage, or specific storage areas
- transport of container to external store
- computer-controlled storage of containers in multi-storey shelving

❸ Storage in containers

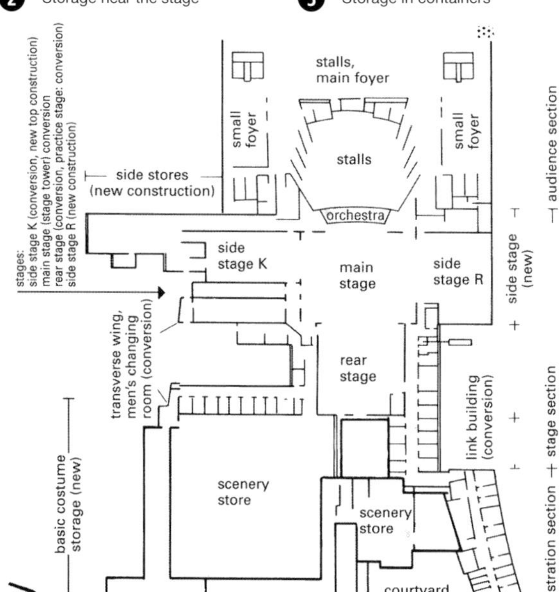

❹ Deutsche Oper Berlin, plan

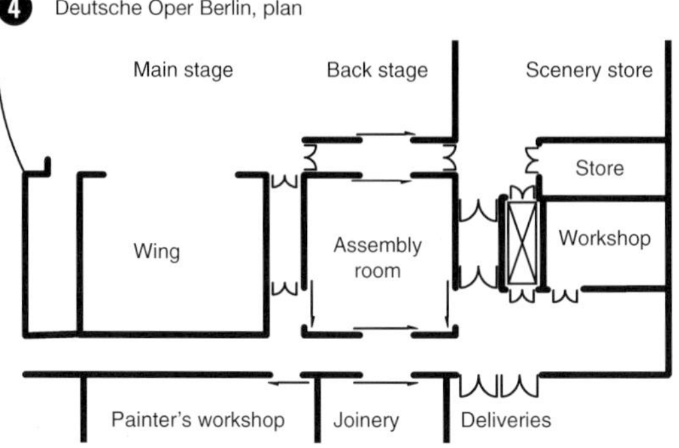

❺ Access points from the subsidiary areas to the stage. Height and location of doors and lift must be determined from max. backdrop height and fire protection measures

Experimental (black box) theatre

Open stages require subsidiary areas for scenery and storage places for platforms and stands. The subsidiary areas should be of the same size as the stage. The space required for storage can be calculated from the folded platforms and stands. Subsidiary areas plus storage area amount to about 30% of the total area → ❶.

Considerably less scenery is used with open stages than with normal stages, the reasons for which are:

- the stage is viewed from many sides.
- regulations limit the use of scenery for safety reasons.

Large stages

Storage areas are required for:

Scenery, backdrops, furniture, props, costumes, hats, shoes, make-up, wigs, lighting, etc. Scenery and costume stores require a great amount of space.

Scenery store:

Specially for heavy items. Location: at stage level and immediately next to the stage. At access points and on traffic routes (particularly at fire exits and lifts), the height of the scenery, normally proscenium height + 2 m, must be taken into account.

A rough estimate for the size of the scenery and costume store can be made from the number of productions in the repertoire and the frequency with which they are played. For theatres the number of productions might be 15–20 and for multi-purpose theatres and opera up to 50 per season. About 20–25% of the stage area is required for storage per production, i.e. for theatres about 3 times the stage area, for the opera at least 10 times. Practice shows that, as time passes, the store always turns out to be too small, and theatres, and particularly operas, have to make arrangements outside the building.

The high cost of transport has forced the introduction of the most modern transportation and storage technology: container systems with computer-controlled warehouse technology (per performance about 2–4 containers – in special cases for operas about 12 containers).

Examples:

- Deutsche Oper Berlin: the stores are in direct connection with the stage → ❹
- Nationaltheater Mannheim: storage outside the building in containers.

The storage area required for costumes is determined by the number of productions in the repertoire and the size of the ensemble, e.g. for opera: the chorus and ballet in addition to the singers. Space required for costumes: 1–12 cm/costume or 1–15 costumes per running m of rail → ❻ – ❼.

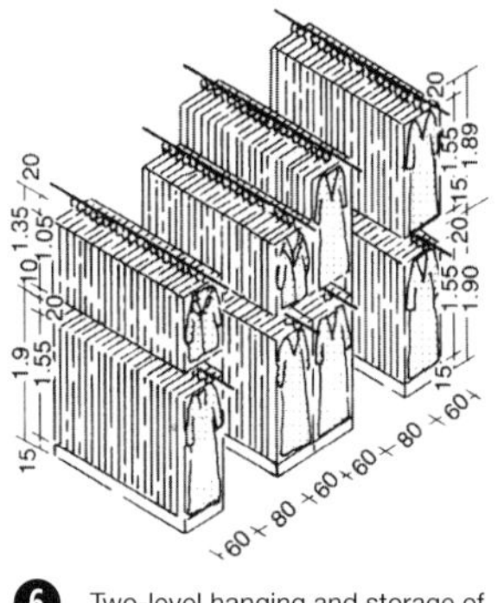

❻ Two-level hanging and storage of costumes in fixed clothing storage

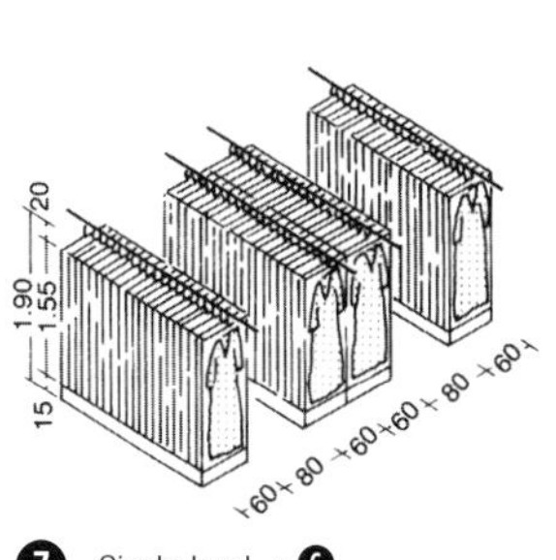

❼ Single-level → ❻

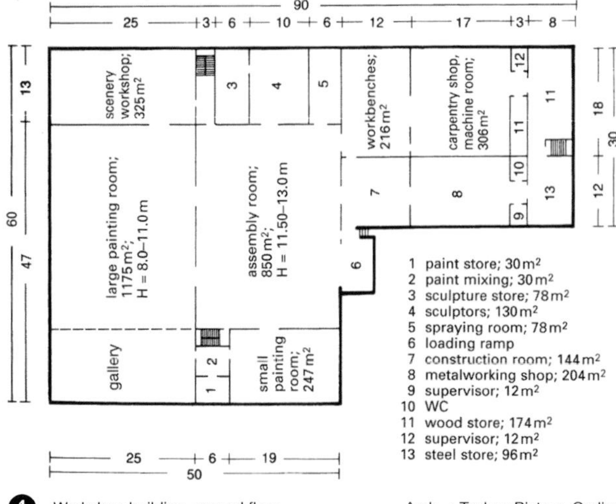

❶ Workshop building, ground floor — Arch. + Techn.: Biste u. Gerling

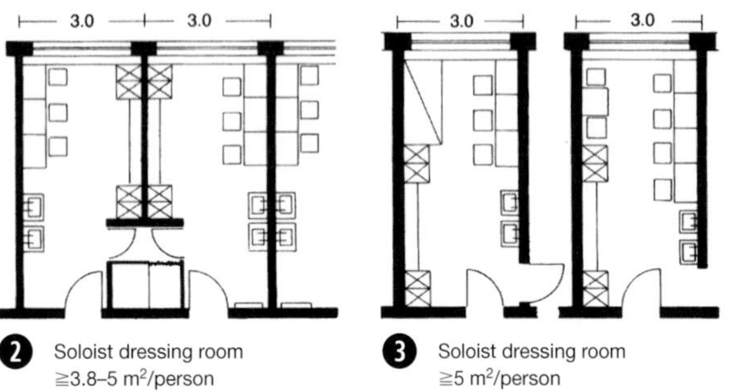

❷ Soloist dressing room ≧3.8–5 m²/person

❸ Soloist dressing room ≧5 m²/person

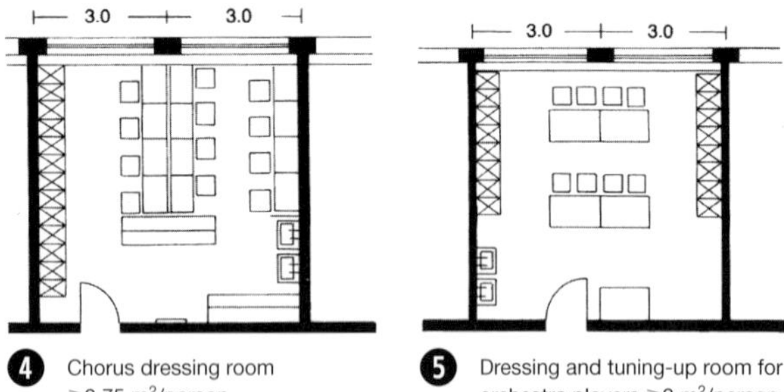

❹ Chorus dressing room ≧2.75 m²/person

❺ Dressing and tuning-up room for orchestra players ≧2 m²/person

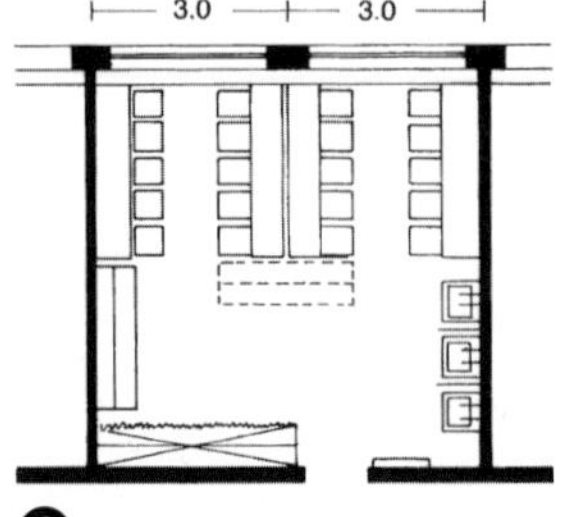
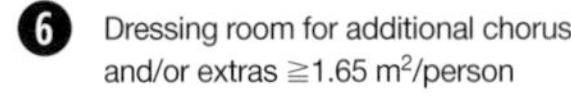
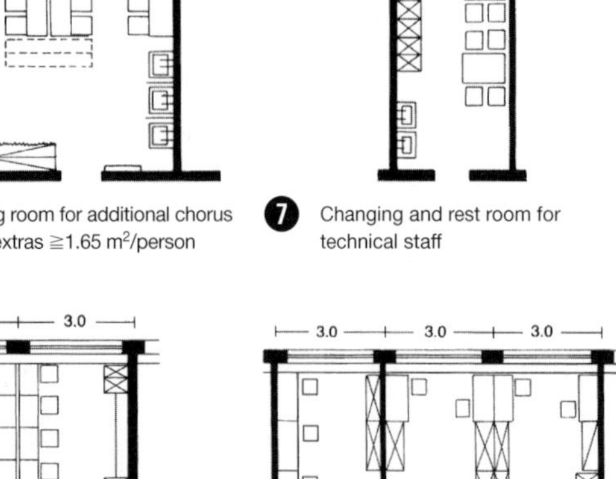

❻ Dressing room for additional chorus and/or extras ≧1.65 m²/person

❼ Changing and rest room for technical staff

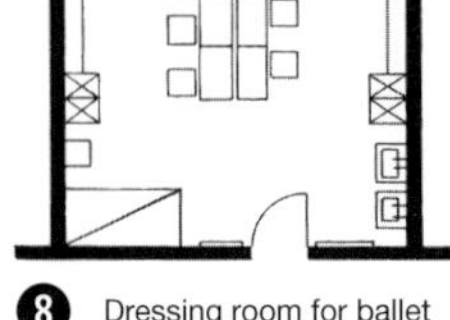
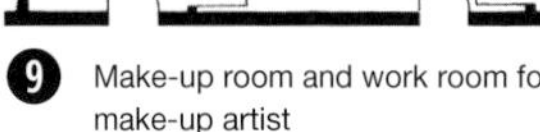

❽ Dressing room for ballet group ≧4 m²/person

❾ Make-up room and work room for make-up artist

Cultural venues

THEATRES
Historical review
Typology
Auditorium
Stage
Subsidiary rooms
Workshops and staff rooms
Rehearsal and public rooms
Modernisation

Workshops for production of scenery

The area required for scenery workshops is 4–5 times the main stage area for medium-sized theatres (theatres and multi-purpose theatres); in large opera houses or double theatres (opera and theatre), 10 times. Workshops, in or outside the building, should always be accommodated on one level. The Workplace Regulations and their technical rules and the work protection and accident prevention rules of insurers have to be taken into account in the design. In some cases, the company and collective agreements with the employees can also have an effect.

Scenery workshops are categorised as follows:

a) Painting room:

The floor area must be designed to accommodate two large backdrops or 'cycloramas' (Rundhorizonte – curved backdrops) rolled out on the floor for painting. The average size of a cyclorama is 10 × 36 m. It must be possible to sub-divide the room with a thick curtain for spraying work. Also required are underfloor heating to dry the painted backdrops; wooden floors for spreading out the canvases; a gallery from which to check the work lying on the floor. The painting room is located next to the sewing room (with a size about ¼ of the painting room) joining the pieces of material.

b) Carpenter's shop:

Divided into bench and machine rooms, it has wooden floors and an adjoining timber store for 3–10 productions.

c) Upholstery: approx. 1/10 area of painting room.

d) Metalwork: as carpenter's shop, screeded floor.

e) Sculpture workshop.

f) Workshops should be grouped round an assembly room, which serves to test-assemble the scenery and has the same floor area as the stage. The height should be proscenium plus 2 m, diameter 9–10 m.

g) Changing, washing, and rest (canteen) rooms are to be provided for technical staff, and offices for the technical management. Further workshops for sound, lighting, props and costumes, size as required (production intensity, personal equipment).

Personnel rooms

Artistic staff, stage manager, administration. Historically, personnel rooms were situated on both sides of the stage: left, ladies, right, gentlemen, although this was operationally impractical. Today, these rooms are located on one side, opposite the technical side on several floors. This includes make-up, frequently also the costume workshop, administration and stage manager.

Dressing rooms: → ❷ – ❾ typical floor plans.

Visitors	Sanitary facilities
for 30–40 female visitors	1 WC, 1 washbasin
for 40–50 male visitors	1 WC, 2 urinals, 1 washbasin
for 1000 visitors	1 wheelchair WC, accessible
Theatre and opera performers incl. chorus, ballet and extras	
for 10 female performers	1 WC
for 15 male performers	1 WC, 2 urinals
for room for 1 soloist	1 washbasin
for dressing rooms for 2 soloists	1 washbasin, 1 shower
for the soloist dressing rooms[1] together	2 baths
for every 4 ballet, chorus member or extra[1]	2 washbasins, 1 shower
for the ballet[1]	2–4 foot washbasins
Staff of workshops etc.	
for 15 women	1 WC
for 20 men	1 WC, 2 urinals
for 4 people[1]	1 washbasin
for 5 people[1]	1 shower
for 10 people[1]	1 bath

The composition of the visitors is assumed to be 3/5 women and 2/5 men.
[1] The facilities are to be provided separately for women and men.

❿ Guidelines for sanitary facilities in theatres

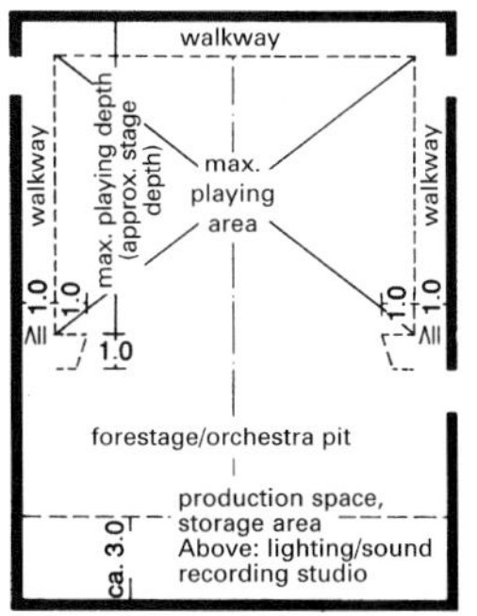

❶ Large rehearsal stage, typical plan

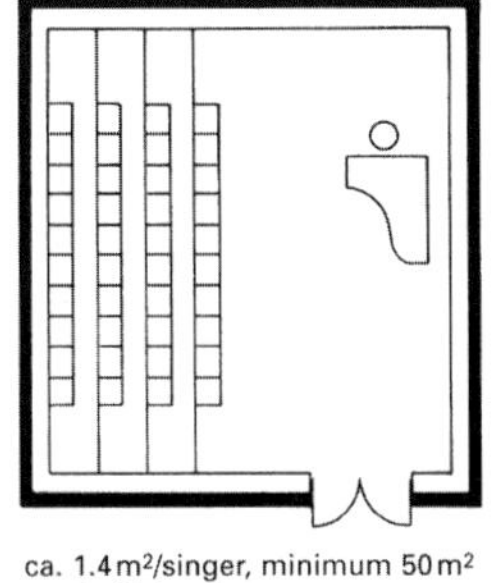

❷ Chorus rehearsal room, typical plan

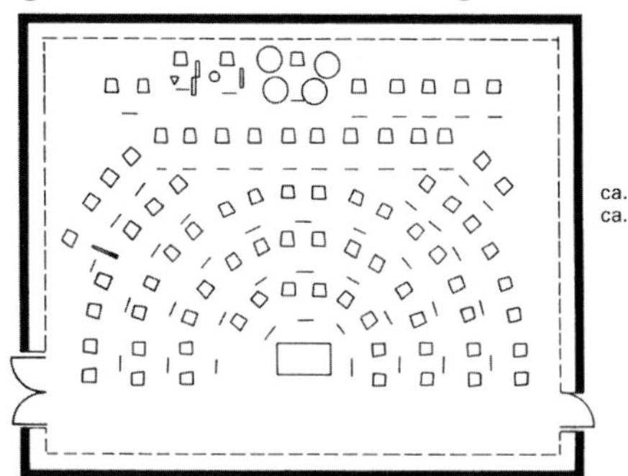

❸ Orchestra rehearsal room, typical plan

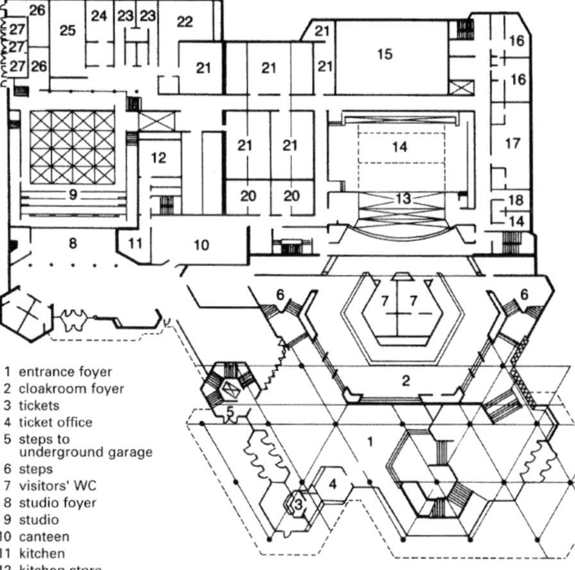

❹ Entrance floor of Heilbronn City Theatre Arch.: Biste u. Gerling

Rehearsal rooms

Every theatre needs at least one rehearsal stage to back up the main stage. For example, a small theatre: the main stage has the scenery of the current play and the rehearsals take place on the rehearsal stage. The dimensions should correspond to the main stage. Typical floor plan of the rehearsal stage of a traditional theatre → ❶. Multi-purpose theatres and opera houses also require: orchestra rehearsal room → ❸, chorus rehearsal room → ❷, soloist rehearsal room and ballet room.

Experimental theatres

These also require, in reduced form, staff and rehearsal rooms, workshops and stores, if in continual operation.

Technical rooms

Rooms for transformer, medium- and low-voltage switchgear, emergency power supply batteries, air conditioning and ventilation plant, water supply (rainwater system), according to local conditions and specialist design work.

Public rooms

The classical Italian opera had only narrow entrances and stairs, with no actual foyer. This makes the generous public rooms at the Grand Opéra in Paris particularly impressive. The Vienna theatre fire in 1881 led to extensive changes: the audience is now required to have enclosed emergency stairs for each tier. This requirement continues in principle today (Public Assembly Regulations).

In the traditional theatre, the foyers are split into: actual foyer (lobby), restaurant (buffet), smoker's foyer. Area of the foyers 0.8–2.0 m^2/spectator (more realistic is 0.6–0.8 m^2/spectator). The function of the foyer has changed today: it must include provision for exhibitions, performances and regular plays there.

Cloakrooms

Per 100 visitors: 4 running m of rail. Sometimes lockers are also provided: one locker for every four visitors. The foyer is also a waiting and queuing room, and has the usual extent of associated WCs: one WC/100 people. 1/3 gents, 2/3 ladies; min. one gents' and one ladies' WC. Total number of sanitary facilities: → p. 216 ❿.
Entrance hall (lobby) with day and evening cash desks, which should be opposite each other.

External access, emergency exits

According to local conditions → p. 211 ❸ – ❺ and Public Assembly Regulations.

see also:
Location of building → p. 223 ❹ – ❺

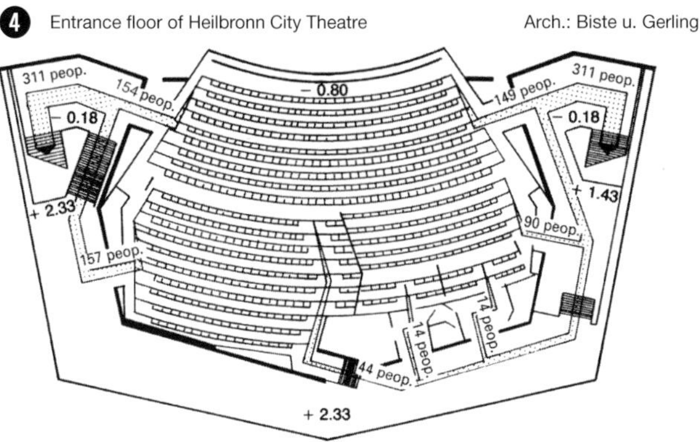

❺ Evacuation plan, Trier City Theatre (626 seata) Arch.: G. Graubner and H. Schneider; stage technician: A. Zotzmann 1964

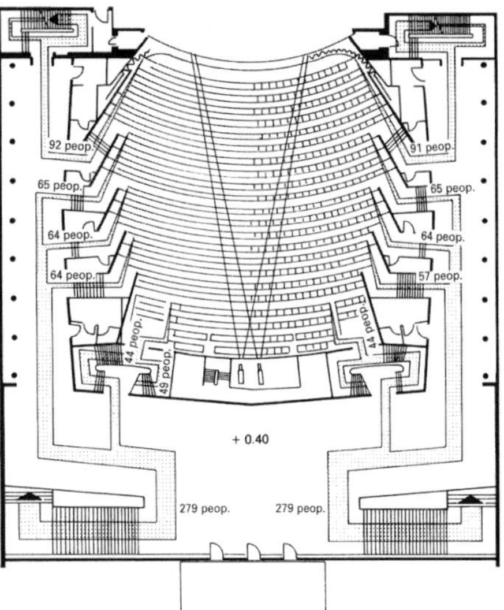

❻ Evacuation plan, Lünen City Theatre (765 seats) Arch.: G. Graubner; stage technician: W. Ehle 1958

Saxony State Theatre, Radebeul

The home base of a renowned travelling theatre that covers the entire spectrum of a multi-purpose stage company (music, dance, theatre) consisted before rebuilding of a conglomeration of extensions and reconstructions at various times of a former hotel hall. The intention was to relieve the resulting functional and organisational problems and improve the external appearance.

The entrance for the audience was extended with a new two-storey foyer area of steel and glass, in which the cloakrooms, lobby and a snack bar could be integrated.

An extension of the storeroom and wings was possible only on one side because of the plot boundaries and the topographical situation, but the most functional possible connection of workshops, rehearsal rooms and props was still the intention. Another feature was the improvement of fire protection and workplace safety.

The existing stage equipment was only renewed and slightly extended. No elaborate solutions like lifting platforms or turntables were planned, in order that plays developed here can also be presented on simple stages on tour.

The extension of the existing building with new elements will still be possible after completion.

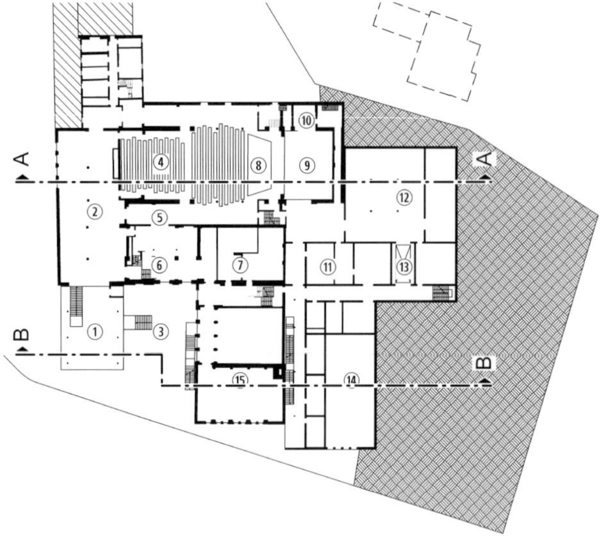

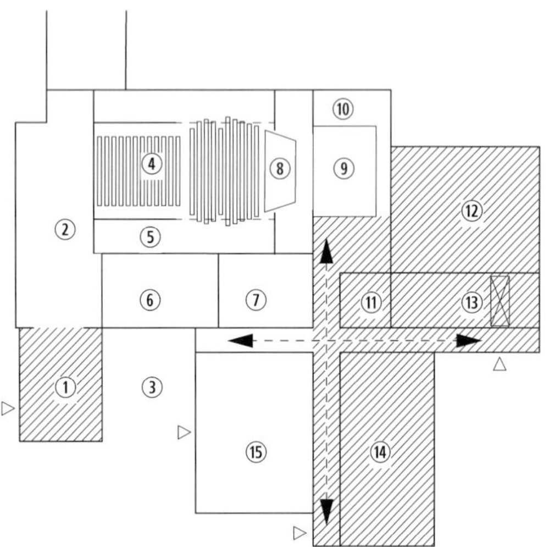

❶ Saxony State Theatre Radebeul, ground floor with new building hatched

(1) New foyer
(2) Main foyer
(3) Theatre courtyard
(4) Cloakrooms, WCs
(5) Auditorium
(6) Canteen
(7) Changing rooms
(8) Orchestra pit
(9) Stage
(10) Wing
(11) Stage make-up
(12) Scenery store
(13) Store
(14) Changing/orchestra practice
(15) Small rehearsal room, ballet hall
(16) External restaurant

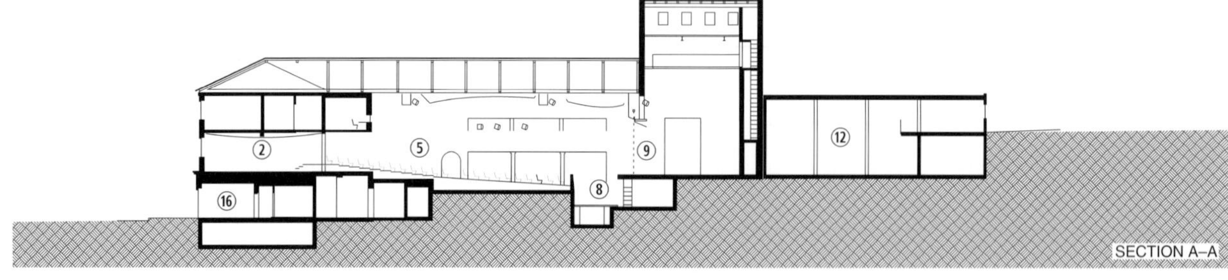

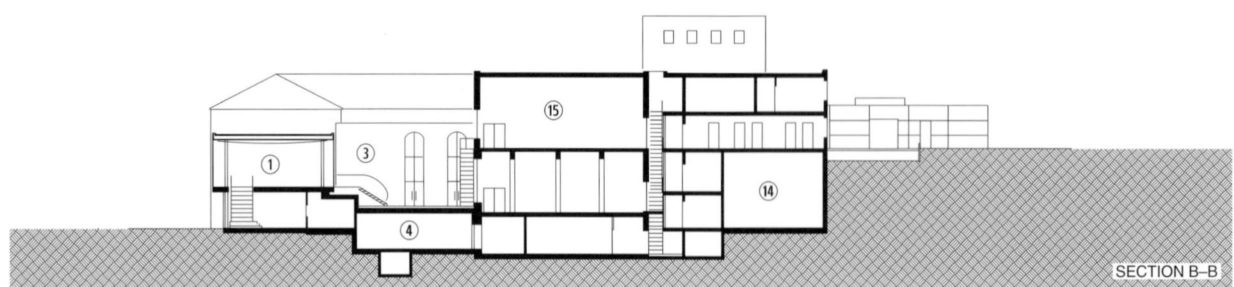

❷ Saxony State Theatre Radebeul, sections

Arch.: meyer + bassin, Dresden

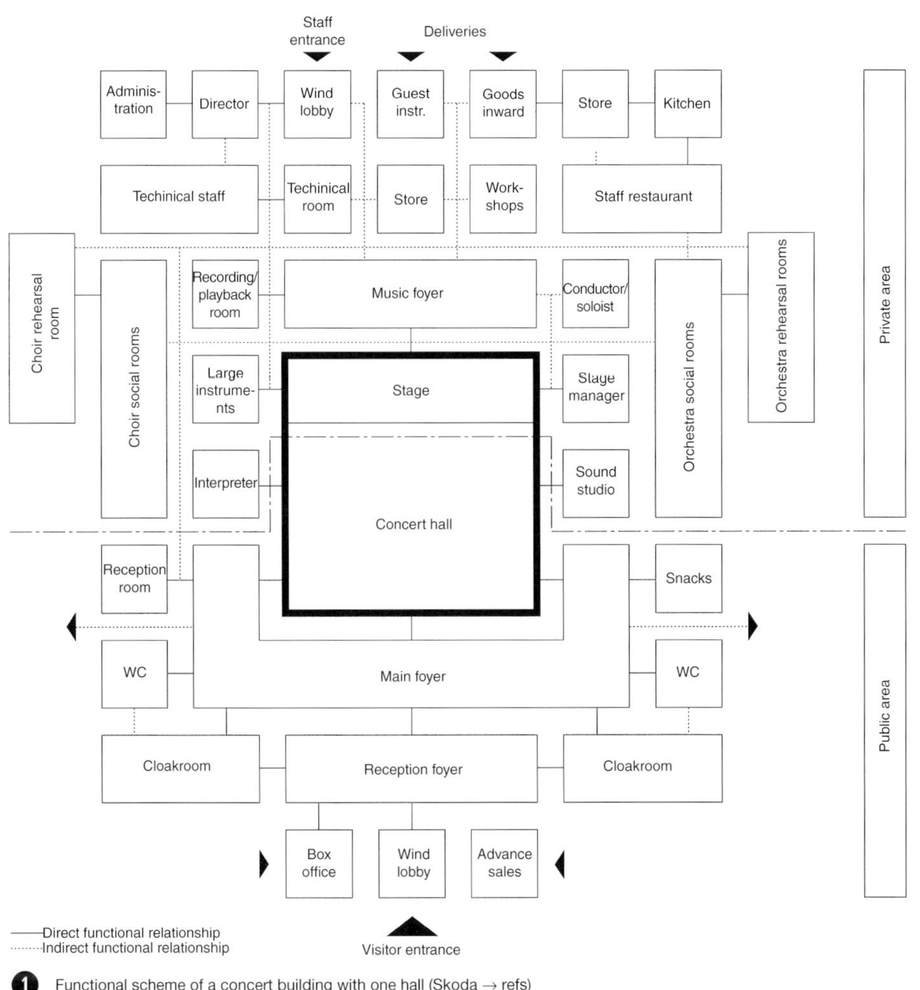

❶ Functional scheme of a concert building with one hall (Skoda → refs)

Concert houses

Intended for musical performances, but other uses are also possible (congresses, lectures etc.), can also if required be supplemented by chamber music hall, rehearsal hall, tuning and warming up rooms and stores. Hall sizes of 1500 and 2000 (in isolated cases 2800) seats in the audience have become usual, for chamber music 400 to 700 seats.

Acoustic multi-purpose rooms

Churches were the first form of concert hall, with strong reverberation. The echo increases the holiness of the place, but domes and vaults are problematic for sermons and orchestral music.

The first theatres and opera houses were stages and auditoriums installed into existing halls. There was good understanding of speech due to the open view and short distance to the stage, but insufficient reverberation due to decoration with soft materials and surfaces with little reflection of sound.

In a tiered theatre, the stalls are surrounded on three sides by tiers, generally leading to short reverberation times, as empty wall surfaces are obstructed by boxes and galleries and are full of people. This is advantageous for the understanding of speech but music sounds rather dull and toneless.

Concert halls

Today four types of concert hall are common (possibly modified): block, arena, fan and horseshoe → ❷ – ❺. The selection of hall type depends on the urban planning situation, intended space and acoustic requirements.

Block form
Rectangular plan
Pattern: redoubt, ballroom and dance hall
View is not optimal due to flat stalls
Polyfunctionally usable with level seating
Primary structure according to conditions, similar to the golden section enables a very good sound

Arena
Polygonal ground plan
Pattern: amphitheatre
Orchestra area is completely surrounded by audience
Optimal viewing conditions, communicative effect
Good direct sound transfer
Optimal acoustics are possible, but expensive to create

Horseshoe form
Horseshoe-shaped plan
Pattern: box theatre
Good view, good direct sound transfer
Sufficient short reflections, few complex reflections
Little space and good sound transparency

Circle/arc form
Fan-shaped plan
Good view, good direct sound transfer
Acoustic disadvantages due to fan-shaped opening of hall
Optimal acoustics are possible, but expensive to create

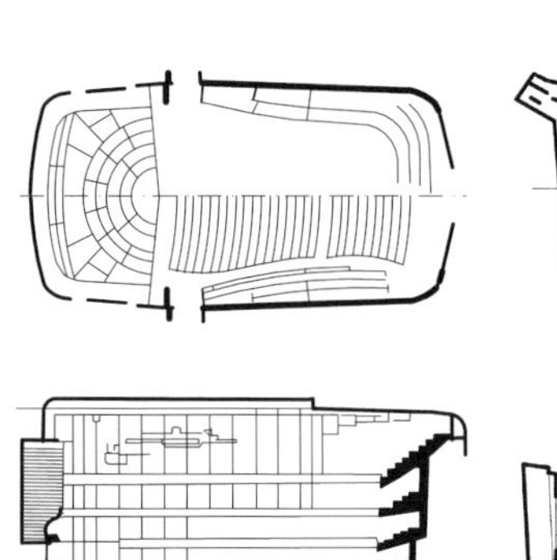

❷ Block form: Lucerne Concert Hall, 1995–98 Arch.: Jean Nouvel

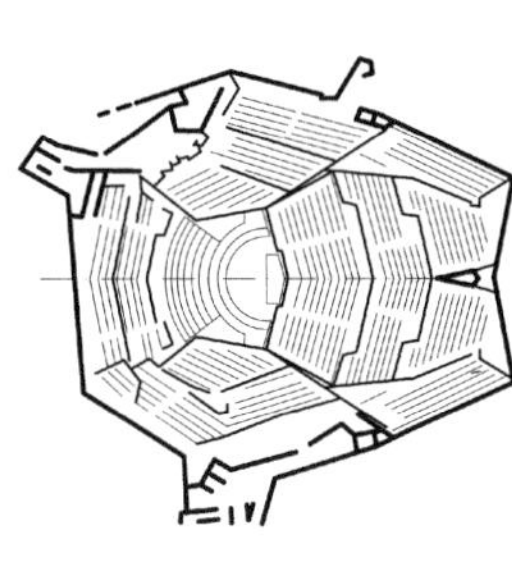

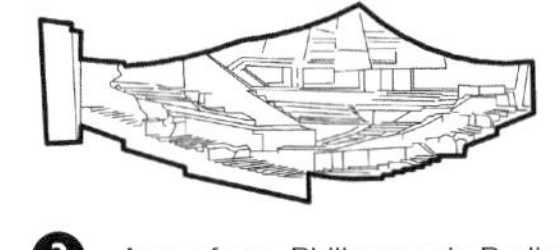

❸ Arena form: Philharmonie Berlin, 1960–63 Arch.: Hans Scharoun

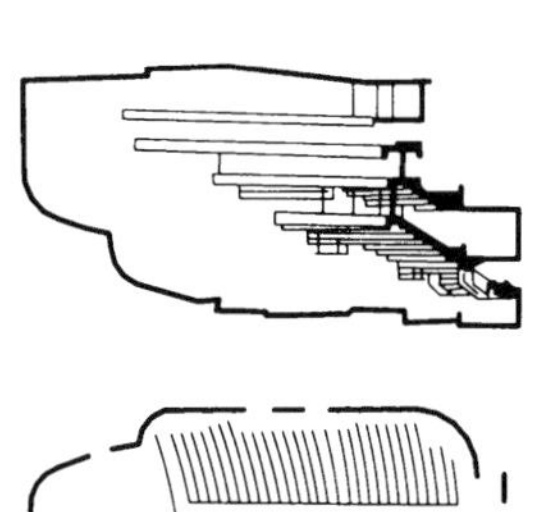

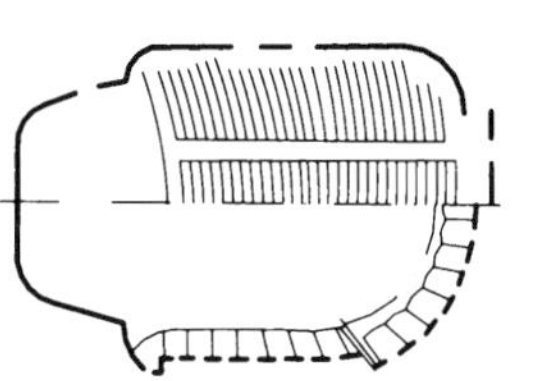

❹ Horseshoe form: Carnegie Hall, New York, 1888–91 Arch.: W.B. Tuthill

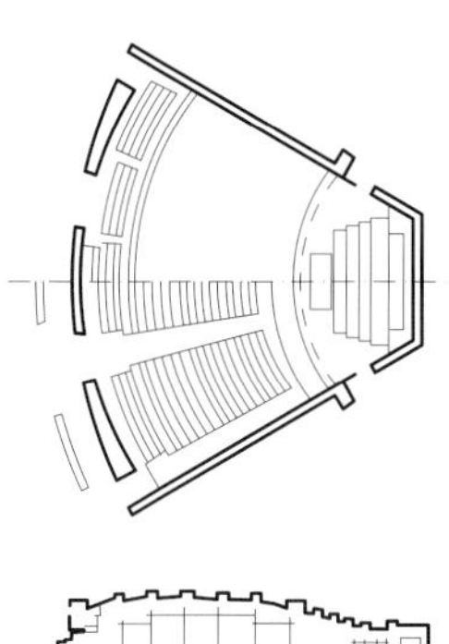

❺ Fan shape: Brucknerhaus Linz, 1969–73 Arch.: Heikki Siren

Cultural venues

CONCERT HALLS
Origins
Variants
Requirements
Organs
Orchestra
Acoustics

see also:
Religious buildings
pp. 285 ff.

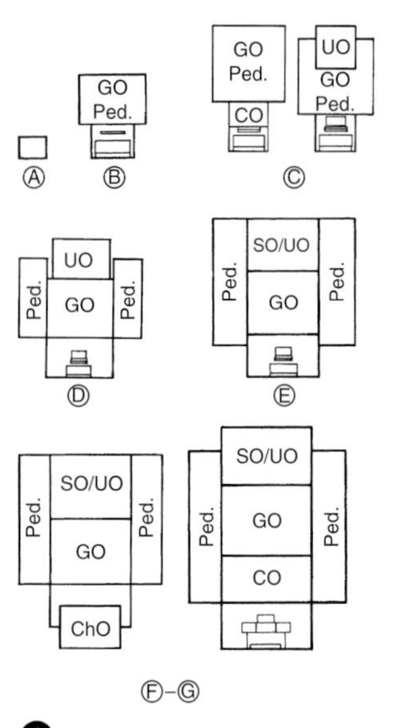

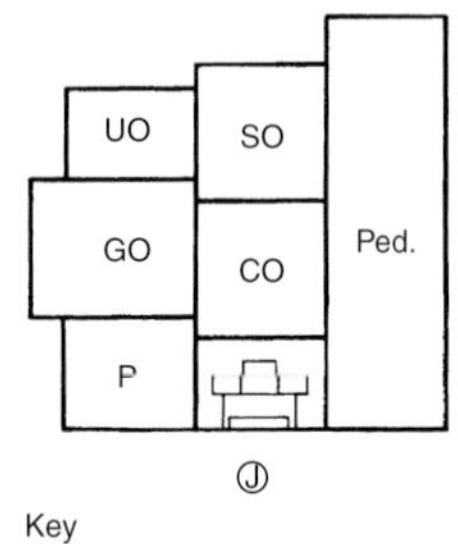

Key
GO great organ
SO swell organ
CO choir organ
ChO chair organ
UO upper organ
P positive
Ped pedal organ

❶ Sizes and forms of organs

Type	Size	Registers	Height (m)	Width (m)	Depth (m)
A	chest	3–7	0.6–0.8	1.0–1.2	0.7–1.2
B	positive	8–12	2.5–3	1.6–2.5	0.8–1.6
C	small organ	12.20	4–6	3–3.5	1.2–1.8
D	II manuals	20–30	6–7	5.5–6.5	1.2–2
E	II manuals	25–35	6.5–9	4.5–7	1.5–2.5
F–G	III manuals	30–60	7.5–10	7–9	2–3
H–I	IV–V manuals	60–100	9–13	8–12	2–4

❷ Organ types and sizes (housing)

Register number = room volume in m²/300 + number seats/50

❸ Formula to determine the number of registers (according to Walcker)

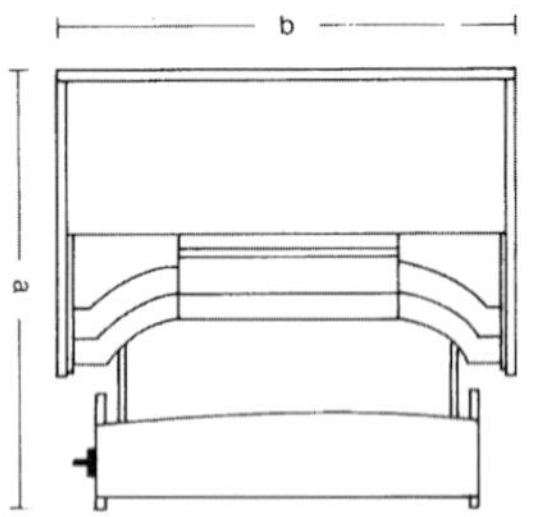

a = Width including filing
b = Deep including bank
c = Height without music stand

	2 Manuals	3 Manuals	4 Manuals
a	180	200	220
b	150	160	170
c	110	120	130

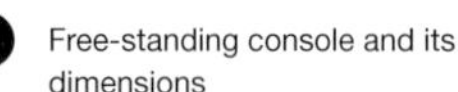

❹ Free-standing console and its dimensions

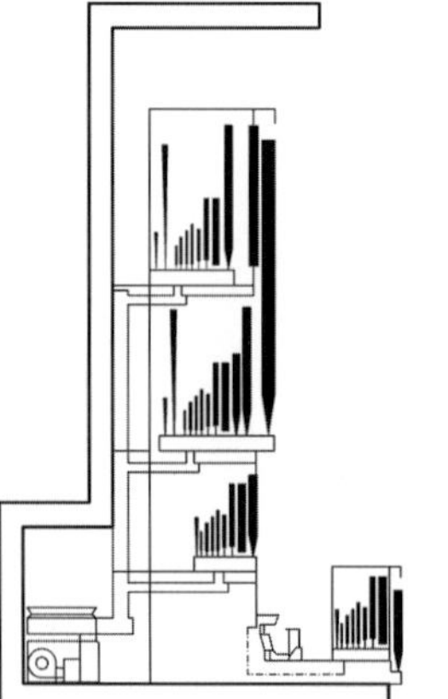

❺ Organ with IV manuals (section)

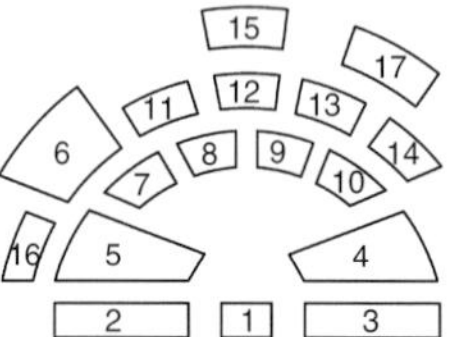

❻ German seating arrangement

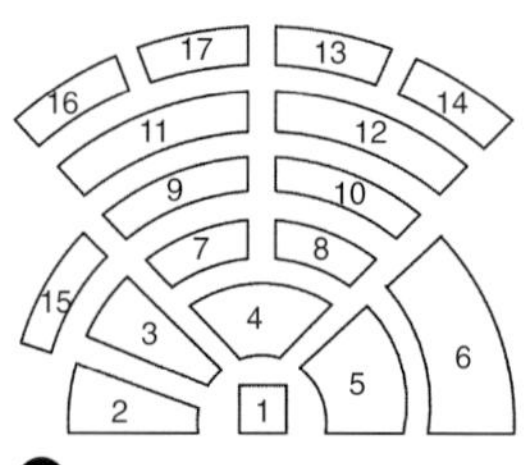

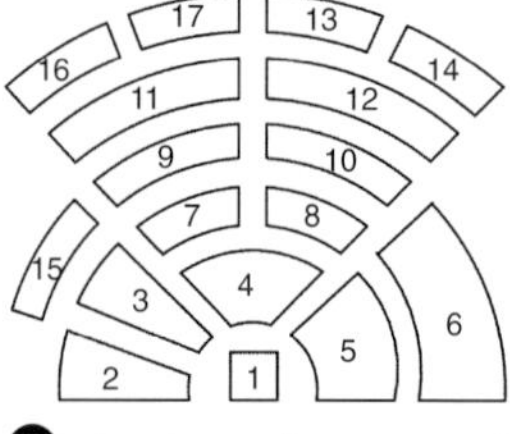

❼ American seating arrangement

1. Conductor
2. 1st violins
3. 2nd violins
4. Violas
5. Cellos
6. Basses
7. Flutes
8. Oboes
9. Clarinets
10. Bassoon
11. Trumpets
12. Horns
13. Trombones
14. Tubas
15. Harps
16. Percussion
17. Kettle-drums

CONCERT HALLS

There is little stage equipment: elements of floor structure in the area for the orchestra, adjustable wall and ceiling fixtures, transport aids, loudspeakers and lighting equipment.

Lifts to extend/reduce the stage

Large concert halls have special compartmentalised systems in the orchestra area to make various orchestra configurations possible, enlarge the stage area or maximise the number of seats in the hall by placing seating units on lifts. There is also transport of items between basement and stage, electrical spindle drive with limited lift and low raising speed.

Mobile seating units

The lifting platforms can be lowered to allow a smaller stage and the positioning of additional seating, which can be in the form of mobile units.

Orchestra stage

Modular system with flexible stage options for music groups. Transport and storage is on storage wagons in the store room. The floor covering matches the concert platform.

Choir platforms

Additional to the choir seats, when extra space is required, large seating platforms are rolled onto the stage and mounted in front of the fixed choir seating; the seating in both types is identical. Access is via detachable balcony elements in the choir seating area or up temporary stairs on the choir platform.

Mixing desk

Area consisting of three rows in the auditorium stalls; can be quickly adapted for the most varied performance and conference conditions.

A motorised platform under the stalls can be occupied in various ways: mobile seating unit, mobile mixing desk, or empty (e.g. if guest musicians bring their own mixing desk).

Cyclorama scaffold

Motorised tubular scaffold, used to fix curtains and banners, portable stage lighting and other production elements at the rear of the stage, and can if required be partially or completely dismantled.

Organ built into the concert hall

There is no fixed standard for the layout, with organs being designed musically and architecturally for each individual space; it is an important visual eye-catcher. The location of the organ should be at the back of the stage, with a location in front of the back wall being ideal, free-standing and not in a niche.

The size depends on the volume of the hall, acoustics, position in the room, number of seats, musical requirements (solo or accompanist instrument). The better the acoustics and the location of the organ, the smaller can it be → ❶ – ❸.

To the depth of the organ housing should be added: 1–2 m for the organist and min. 0.5 m for tuning access behind the organ, min. 1.5 m free space necessary above the organ → ❸ – ❹.

In concert halls, a second organ platform is necessary (electric, mobile); this is placed near the orchestra, so the organist becomes part of the orchestra. The dimensions depend on the size of the organ → ❹ + ❺. Necessary cable connections should be provided.

Orchestra sizes and layouts

The various orchestra seating layouts, formerly German and today mostly American, are important for the sound in the hall → ❻ – ❼. The following sizes of orchestra are usual today in Europe and North America: large symphony orchestra with 60–150 musicians and chamber orchestra with 25–40 musicians; this determines the additional space requirement on the stage (e.g. Gewandhaus Leipzig, approx. 180 m²).

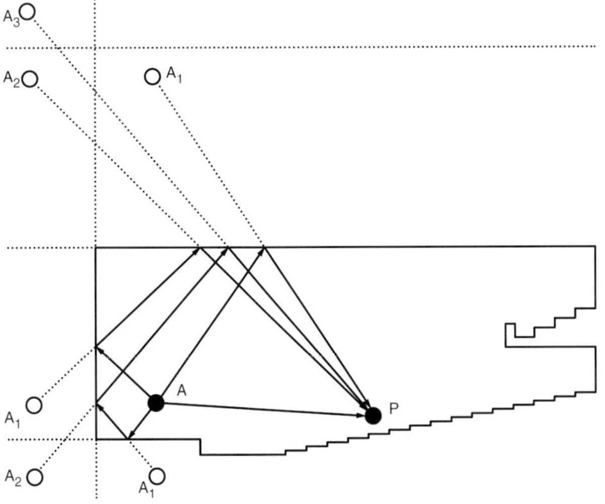

❶ Sound waves and sources of reflected sound in an auditorium. A = sound source A1 = source of first order reflected sound etc. (Kuttruff → refs)

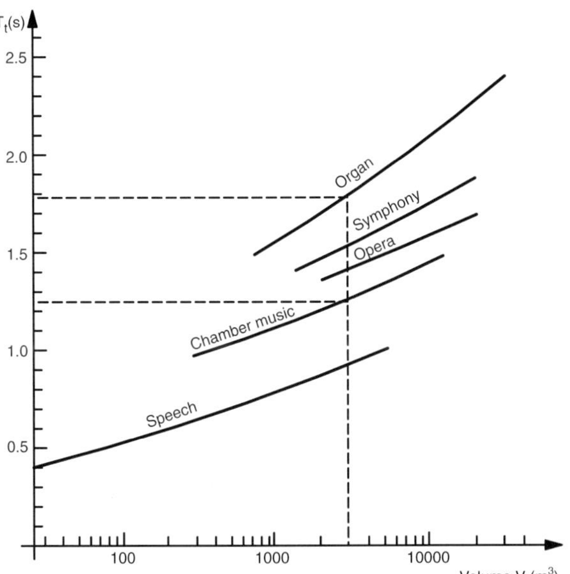

❷ Relationship of reverberation, hall volume and music type (Hall → refs)

The most important objective in designing a concert hall is a superb sound. Acoustics result from the interaction of various elements: size, volume and proportions of the concert space, number and arrangement of the seats, materials used, surfaces and finishes.

The sound properties of various instruments and the human (singing) voice have to be taken into account, alone and together, and also differences in pitch range and character (volume, frequency distribution and time structure of a sound). The various layouts of the orchestra are of significance for the sound in the hall: the positioning of various groups of instruments (particularly the string section).

For the effect of the instruments in the hall, the relationship of the sound travelling directly to the listener to the early reflection from the sides plays a decisive role → ❶.

Optimal reverberation is important for the quality of hearing: excessive reverberation reduces clarity, and too little reverberation makes music sound dull. It is dependent on air changes/person (older concert halls 4–5 m^3/seat, newer over 6–15 m^3/seat).

The acoustics are influenced by hall size, shape and (surface) material used; these can be adapted for different acoustic requirements through the selection of various materials. The following variants are possible and usual:

Acoustic reflector

Installed over the stage, this is an adjustable, wide, heavy, sound-reflecting surface consisting of two or three independent sections; each section must be 2–3 m above the stage and adjustable up to 2 m under the ceiling. The height and position of reflectors is determined by the type of concert: smaller concerts, light chamber music and concerts with string instruments require a lower height for the reflectors.

Sound-absorbing curtains and banners

These influence the length and strength of the reverberation (lowered by widening the curtains). If not required, the curtains are retracted into curtain niches (and must then be without effect).

Acoustic regulation spaces (promenades)

Additional volume can be gained for works with long reverberation (those for organ, large orchestras and large choirs, as well as with acoustic amplification) through the extension of the auditorium. Access passages and foyer areas can be used for this. They can be opened into the hall with movable panels using central control.

Cultural venues

CONCERT HALLS
Origins
Variants
Requirements
Organs
Orchestra
Acoustics

The reflection characteristics of various materials are of great importance for the acoustic design. Hard surfaces are preferable to achieve long reverberation. The seats should also be provided with surfaces of hard material. Upholstering of seats can achieve uniformity of reverberation, even with different numbers in the audience.

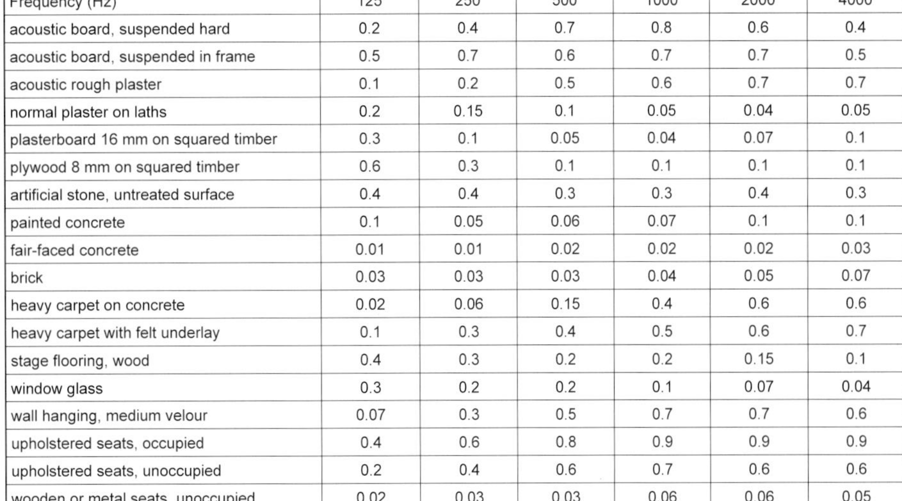

Frequency (Hz)	125	250	500	1000	2000	4000
acoustic board, suspended hard	0.2	0.4	0.7	0.8	0.6	0.4
acoustic board, suspended in frame	0.5	0.7	0.6	0.7	0.7	0.5
acoustic rough plaster	0.1	0.2	0.5	0.6	0.7	0.7
normal plaster on laths	0.2	0.15	0.1	0.05	0.04	0.05
plasterboard 16 mm on squared timber	0.3	0.1	0.05	0.04	0.07	0.1
plywood 8 mm on squared timber	0.6	0.3	0.1	0.1	0.1	0.1
artificial stone, untreated surface	0.4	0.4	0.3	0.3	0.4	0.3
painted concrete	0.1	0.05	0.06	0.07	0.1	0.1
fair-faced concrete	0.01	0.01	0.02	0.02	0.02	0.03
brick	0.03	0.03	0.03	0.04	0.05	0.07
heavy carpet on concrete	0.02	0.06	0.15	0.4	0.6	0.6
heavy carpet with felt underlay	0.1	0.3	0.4	0.5	0.6	0.7
stage flooring, wood	0.4	0.3	0.2	0.2	0.15	0.1
window glass	0.3	0.2	0.2	0.1	0.07	0.04
wall hanging, medium velour	0.07	0.3	0.5	0.7	0.7	0.6
upholstered seats, occupied	0.4	0.6	0.8	0.9	0.9	0.9
upholstered seats, unoccupied	0.2	0.4	0.6	0.7	0.6	0.6
wooden or metal seats, unoccupied	0.02	0.03	0.03	0.06	0.06	0.05

❸ Degree of sound absorption (alpha) of various surfaces (Hall → refs)

Before embarking on the design of a cinema, ask the advice of a cinema equipment company.

Picture projection: Fire-separation materials are no longer required in the projection room due to the use of safety film. One projectionist operates a number of projectors, so the projection room is no longer considered as continuously occupied by staff. It has 1 m spacing from the projector at the back and on the operator side, 2.80 m height, ventilation and extraction, and sound insulation to the auditorium. The projection rooms of several auditoriums can be combined together.

Film widths are 16 mm, 35 mm and 70 mm. The centre of the projection beam should not deviate more than 5° horizontally and vertically from the centre of the screen or it should be redirected by a deflection mirror → ❶.

Conventionally, two projectors are operated with cross-blending. Automated operation with one projector plus horizontal film tray showing 4000 m reels without pause has become established worldwide, in many projection rooms remotely run from projection and control points. The film gives automatic signals for all projection functions like lens changing, hall lighting, stage lighting, curtain and picture covering.

Picture sizes: These depend on the distance of the projector from the screen and having a height-side relationship of 1:2.34 (Cinemascope) or 1:1.66 (wide screen) with a narrow auditorium width. The angle from the centre of the back row of seating to the outer edge of the picture should not exceed, for Cinemascope, 38° = distance of the back row : screen = 3:2 → ❷ – ❸.

Screen: Distance of the screen from the wall with BTX (→ p. 223) is min. 120 cm; according to cinema size and system this can be reduced to 50 cm on the setting up of the sound system.

The screen is perforated (sound-permeable). Retracting blinds or curtains restrict the screen at the sides with the same picture height. Large screens are curved in a radius centred on the back row of seats. The lower edge of the screen should be min. 1.20 m above the floor → ❶.

Auditorium: This should receive no incoming light except for emergency lighting. The walls and ceilings should be of non-reflecting material in relatively dark colours. The audience should sit within the outer edge of the screen. The viewing angle from the first row of seats to the centre of the picture should not exceed 30°.

longitudinal section
1.20
280
120
max. 5°
2.00
7.26
1.20
30
max. 30°
1.20
first row of seats

rear wall
max. outer edge of seating block
= outside edge of picture
last row of seats
projection screen
120
38°
A
25.00
17.00
+ = A
plan view

❶ Optimal auditorium

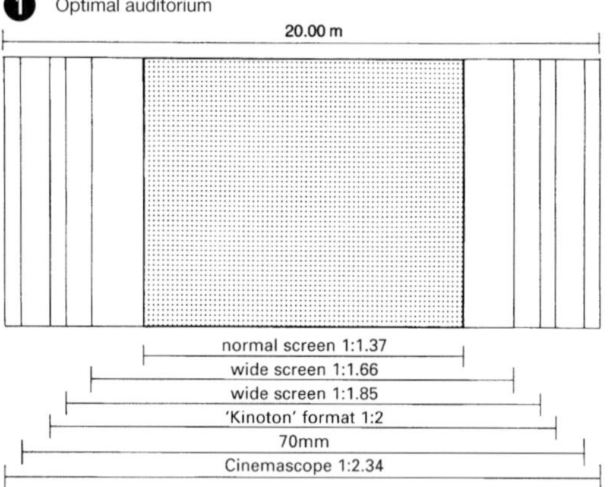

❷ Picture formats with same picture height

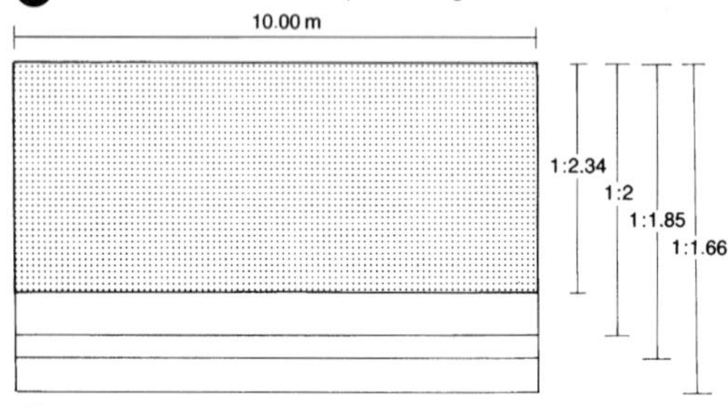

❸ Picture formats with same picture width

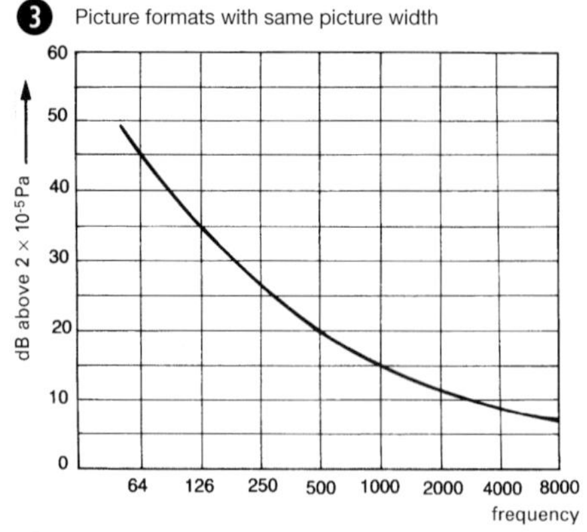

❹ Permissible disturbance level

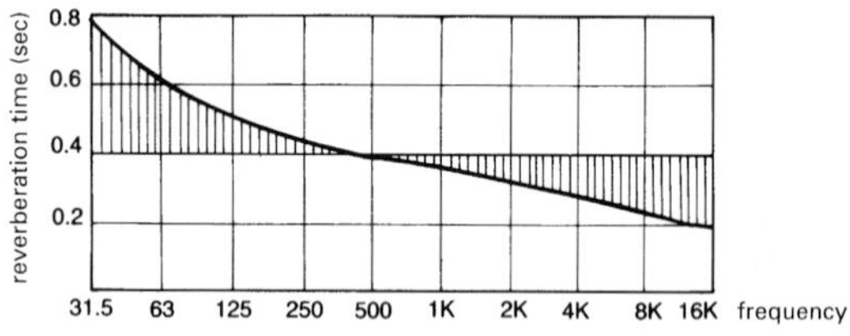

❺ Permissible reverberation time depending on frequency

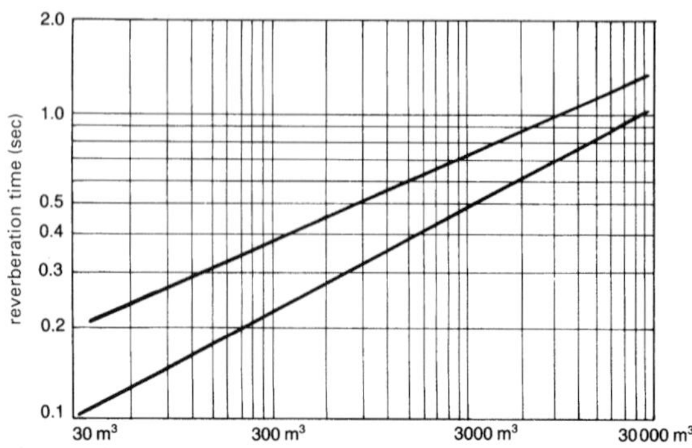

❻ Reverberation time relative to auditorium volume

≦56–60
≦56–60
≦40 ≦40
1–1.2 m row spacing

❶ Spacing and rows of seats. Cinema seats are normally larger than the minimum dimensions stipulated by the Public Assembly Regulations.

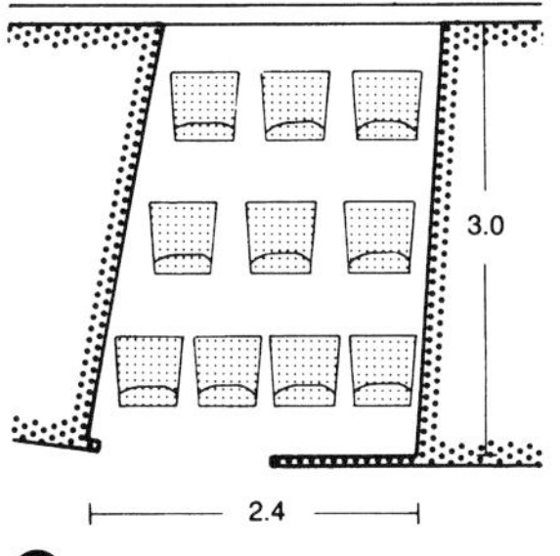

❷ Boxes may have ≧20 loose chairs; ≧0.65 m² floor area for each person

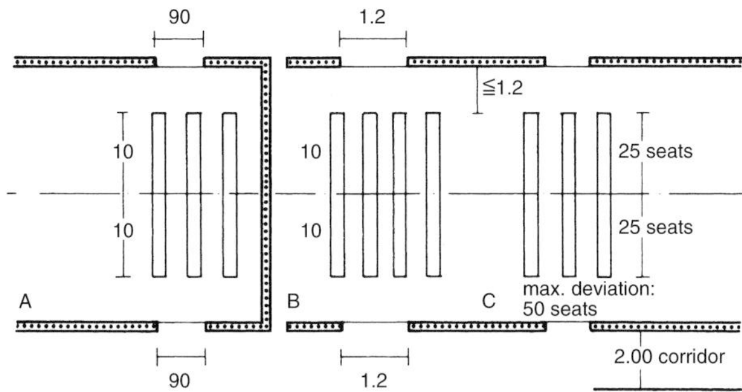

❸ Seating – A: for auditorium ≦200 people; B: ≧200 people; C: 50 seats, if there is a door at the side for every four rows

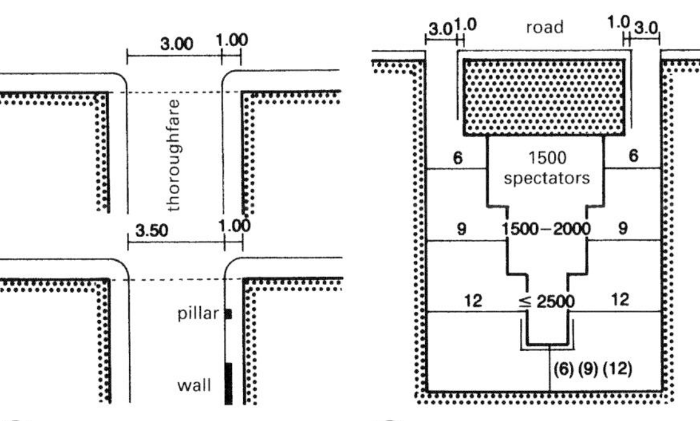

❹ Access roads and through roads

❺ Distance of the building from the plot boundaries depending on number of visitors

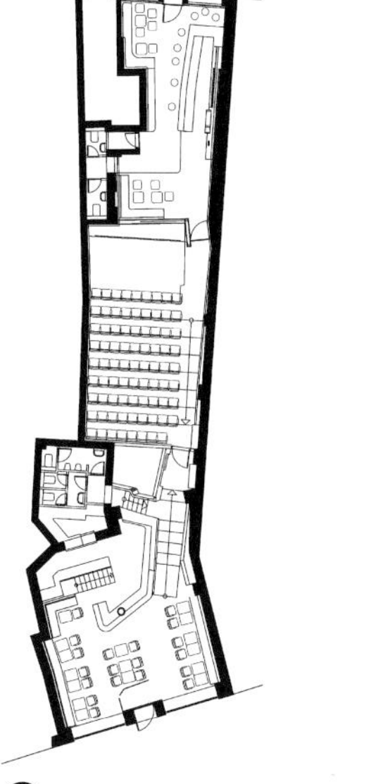

❻ Zazie 'programme cinema' with café and bar, Halle (Saale)
Arch.: Complizen.com

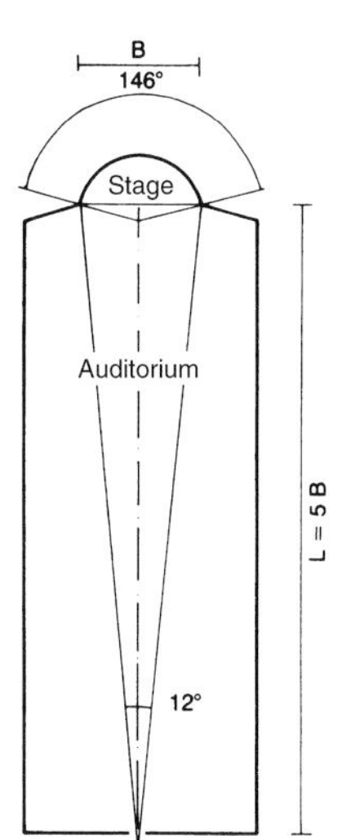

❼ Auditorium for flat films

Up to a 10% floor gradient is permissible, or else steps with max. 16 cm risers and aisles of 1.20 m width → ❶. Up to 10 seats may be arranged on each side of each aisle → ❸.

Acoustics

Adjacent auditoriums should be separated by walls of approx. 85 dB 18–20 000 Hz → p. 222 ❹. The ceiling should feature sound-directing surfaces with low acoustic delay difference time.

The reverberation time can increase with growing auditorium volume and reduces from 0.8 to 0.2 s from low to high frequencies. → p. 222. The rear wall behind the last row of seats should have an insulated surface to prevent echo.

Loudspeakers are distributed in the auditorium so that the difference in volume between the front and back rows does not exceed 4 dB.

Sound reproduction

In addition to mono optical sound reproduction, the Dolby stereo optical system with four channels will be required in the future, using three loudspeaker combinations behind the screen and additional speakers at the sides and back. For 70 mm film, 6 channel magnetic sound, there are additional speaker combinations behind the screen. With BTX, behind the screen there is a sound-absorbing wall (following the Lucas film system), in which the loudspeaker combinations are installed.

Cash desks

Predominantly electronic booking and reservation systems: 1 cash desk per 300–400 seats, requiring approx. 5 m².

Types of cinema

'Programme cinemas': As a counter-trend to multiplex cinemas → p. 224, city centres have seen the establishment of 'programme cinemas', which mostly show specialist films. Sizes of 50–200 seats are usual, normally in combination with eating/drinking facilities → ❻.

Circarama/Panorama cinemas: Round or spherical screens increase the impression of being directly involved in the action. Because special film techniques are required for these (a number of cameras have to film the same view simultaneously), there are only a few films available, and this type of cinema is therefore restricted to adventure parks and planetariums → ❽ – ❾.

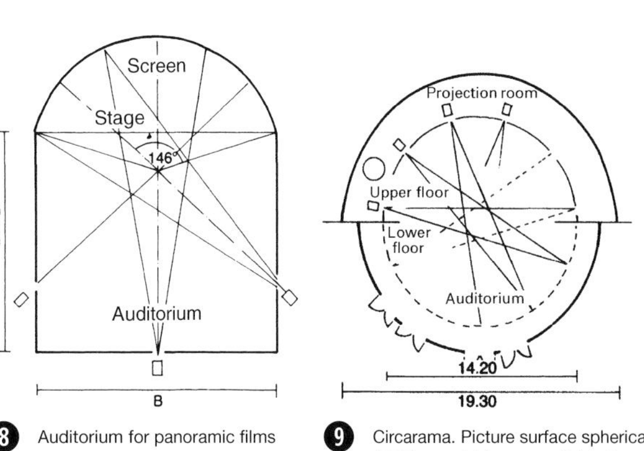

❽ Auditorium for panoramic films

❾ Circarama. Picture surface spherical (360°), on which a consolidated picture from 11 simultaneously running projectors can be shown. Example: Brussels Expo

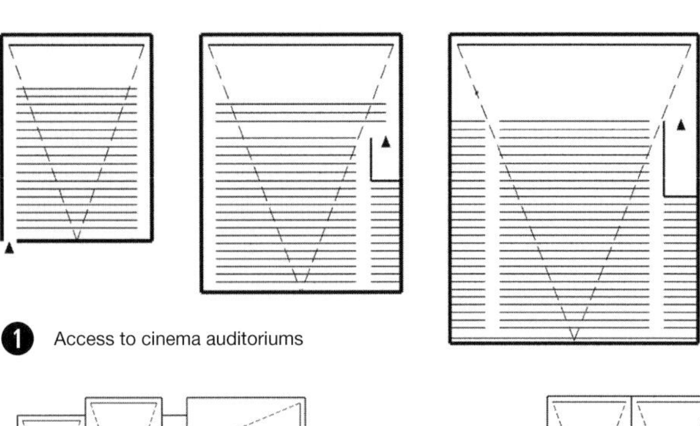

❶ Access to cinema auditoriums

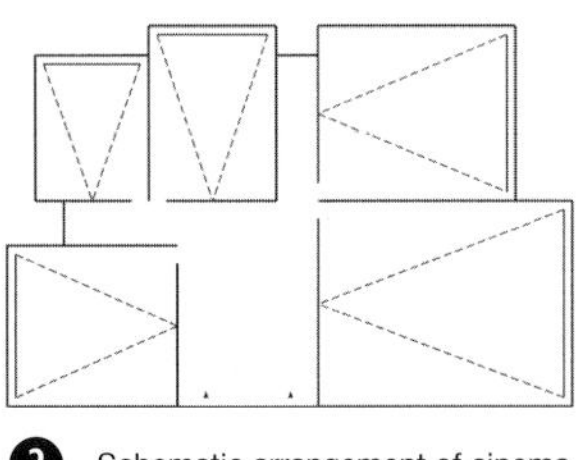

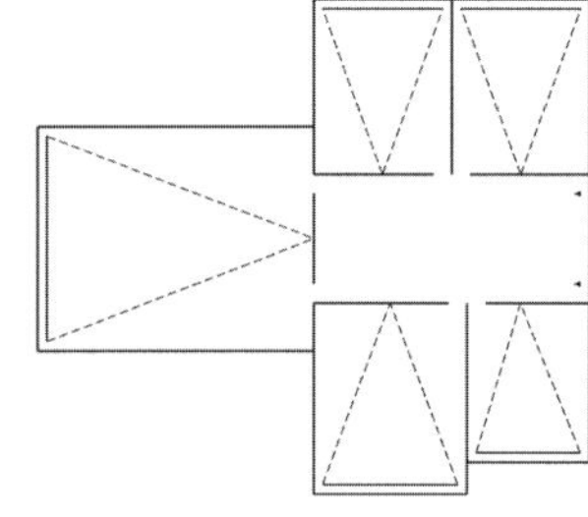

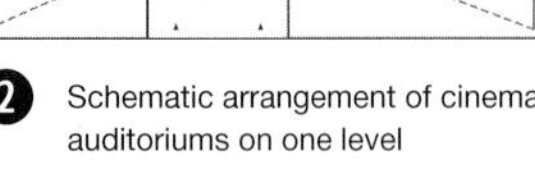

❷ Schematic arrangement of cinema auditoriums on one level

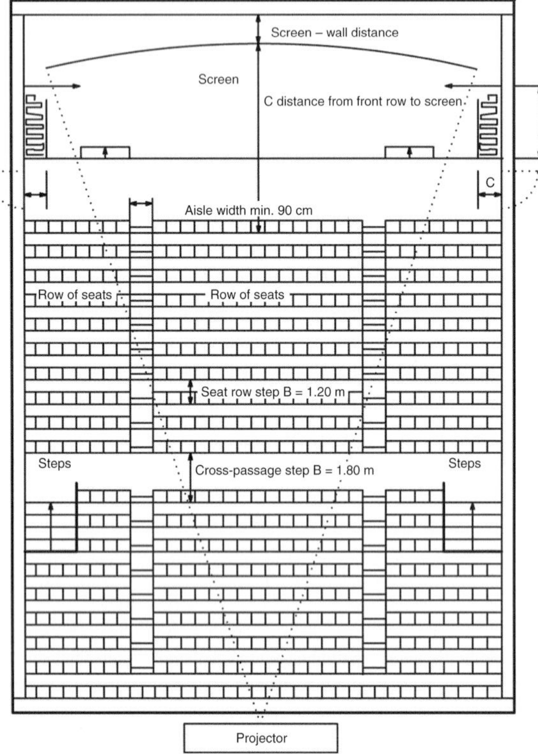

Hall proportions: 1.1.3 – 1.4:0.5 (W × D × H) Screen distance A = 1.20 – 1.50 m
Curtain storage space B: each side approx. 10% of the screen width
Distance C (head front row – screen): approx. 75% of the clear room height
Width of curtain pocket: approx. 40 cm
Screen curvature: circular arc (centre projector), from about 500 seats
Top of screen: about 0.30 m below ceiling, bottom of screen: about 0.80 m above FFL
Height of screen: results from the values given above
Width of screen: screen height × 2.35 (largest format: Cinemascope)
Clear ceiling height above the back row: min. 2.30 m

❸ Generalised ground floor plan of a larger auditorium with technical dimensions

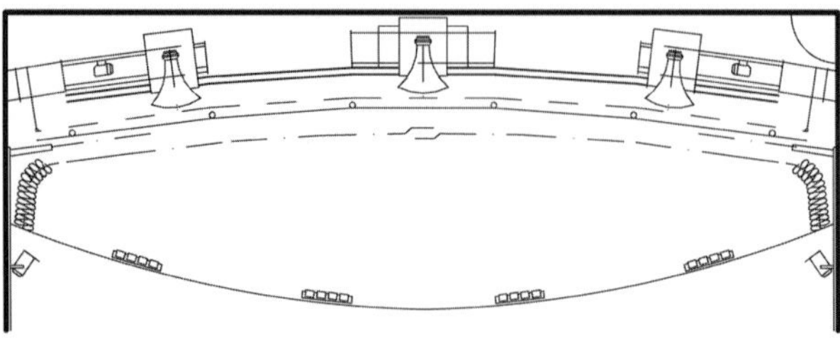

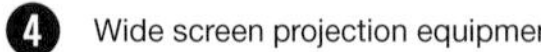

❹ Wide screen projection equipment

With a number of screens of various sizes in one building, multiplex cinemas are often combined with shopping centres, car parks etc, which require extensive parking space → p. 225. The auditoriums are reached via a common entrance and sometimes stacked. On account of the large numbers of visitors, good orientation and clear signing to the individual screens is important. The location of the screens in relation to the entrance foyer should be according to their size (large screens nearest to the foyer), or the largest screen in a central location/on the direct route from the foyer. The sizes of the single auditoriums depend on the requirements of the operator, as also the spacing of the rows, foyer design etc.

The cash desk zone should be near the entrance, the number of desks dependent on the number of seats: approx. 5 m^2 floor area/ cash desk; for 2500 seats, approx. 6–8 cash desks.

The entrance foyer should be of generous proportions, clearly laid out and at a prominent location in the building; it includes the main entrance, food/drink counters and access to the screens. Before the access points to the individual screens on different floors, there are normally additional foyers with bar counters, WCs etc. The main foyer should be of adequate size for events (premières, presentations etc.).

Because eating and drinking are normally a significant part of the cinema concept, counters should be provided in central locations with the necessary storage and service facilities.

Cinema auditorium

The screen should fill the entire wall; there should be no exits in this wall or the side walls near to it. Cross-passages should be provided as a connection between the doors or at a side entrance to reach the side aisles → p. 235.

Projection room

Minimum room size: 6.50 × 2.80 × 2.80 m (W × D × H). Projection window size approx. 150/250 × 50 cm (one or two projectors) Film can be supplemented by video projectors, and space should also be provided for horizontal film tray equipment and control desk.

The platform under the projectors should be vibration-free. A noise level of approx. 75 dB must be damped to 30 dB by the projection window. The working temperature should not exceed 22°C in order to protect film copies and equipment.

Subsidiary rooms

These are to be provided as required: offices for the manager, secretary and employees, archive, IT room, staff rooms (changing rooms, ladies' and gents' WCs, staff rest room).

For the foyer and food/drink area: catering stores, counter stores, cool room, room for empties, rubbish room, cleaning equipment room, stores for cleaning firm and decoration.

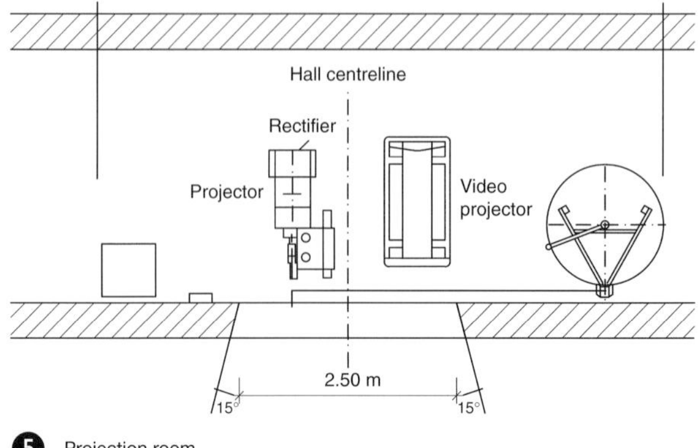

❺ Projection room

The town-planning situation plays a significant role in the number of cinema screens that can be combined into a unit. Possible forms are layered stacking (screens stacked as a cube, access and service functions connected in free form at the side) → ❸ – ❹, or a horizontal row of screens (larger cinemas from the 1960s were extended with further screens, sunk into the ground for conservation reasons) → ❶ – ❷ or combination forms. A common form is the combination with other functions like shopping centres and car parks, with sales areas on the ground floor, cinema screens and parking on the first floor: a prominent urban landmark in conjunction with two high-rise point buildings → ❺ – ❼.

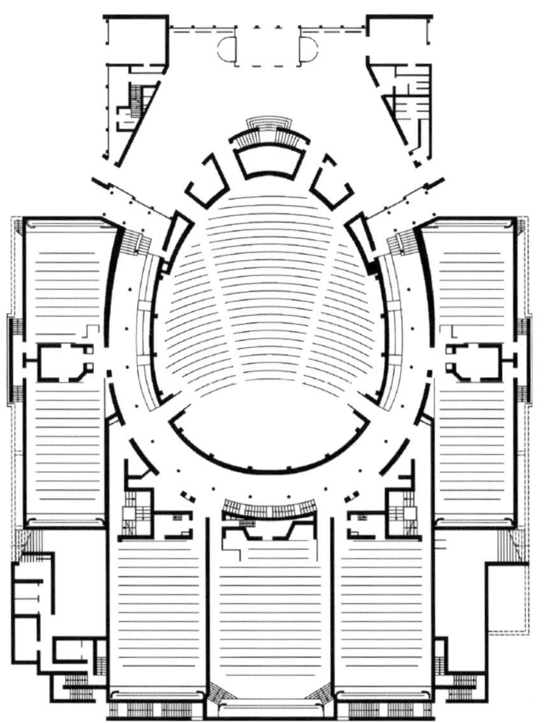

❶ Kosmos cinema, Berlin, plan Arch.: Rohde Kellermann Wawrowsky

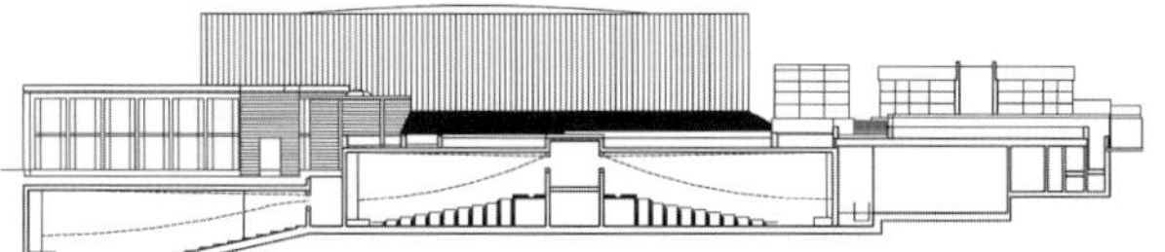

❷ Kosmos cinema, Berlin, elevation/section Arch.: Rohde Kellermann Wawrowsky

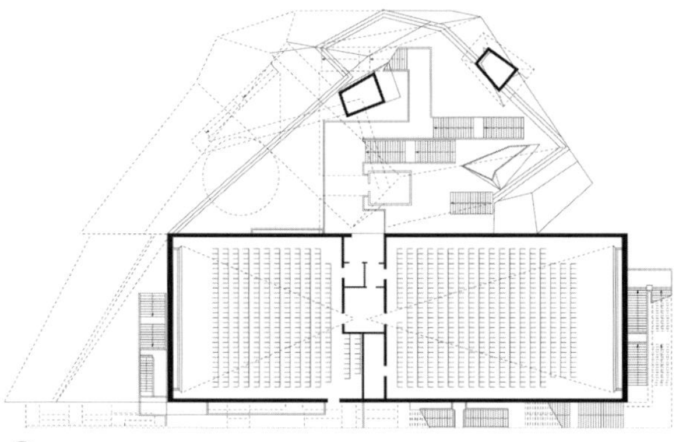

❸ Filmpalast Dresden, plan Arch.: Coop Himmelb(l)au

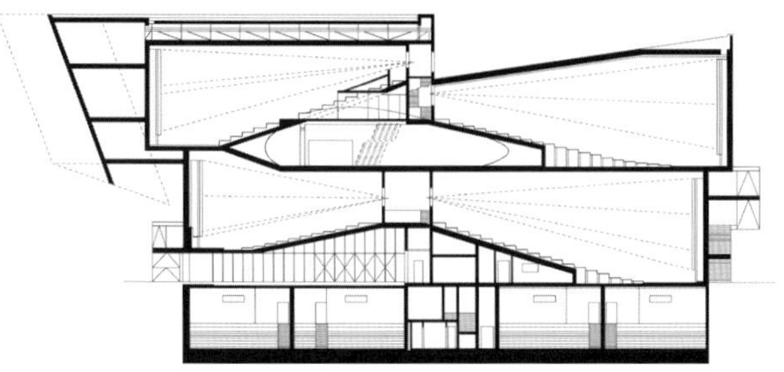

❹ Filmpalast Dresden, view/section Arch.: Coop Himmelb(l)au

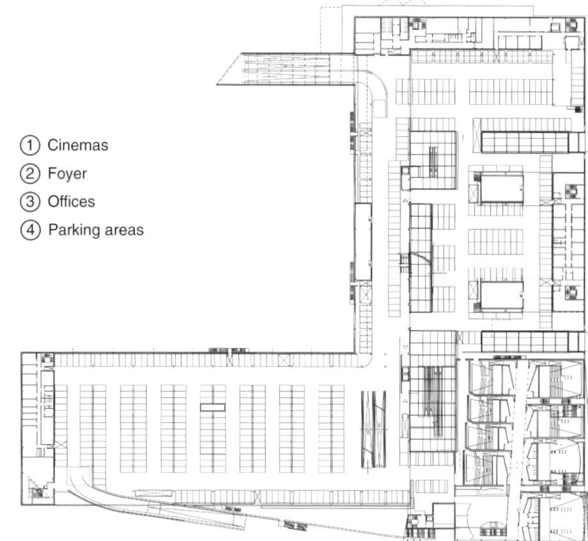

❺ Neustadt Centrum Halle, first floor plan (cinema level 1)
Arch.: Hermann & Valentiny with Noack und Partner

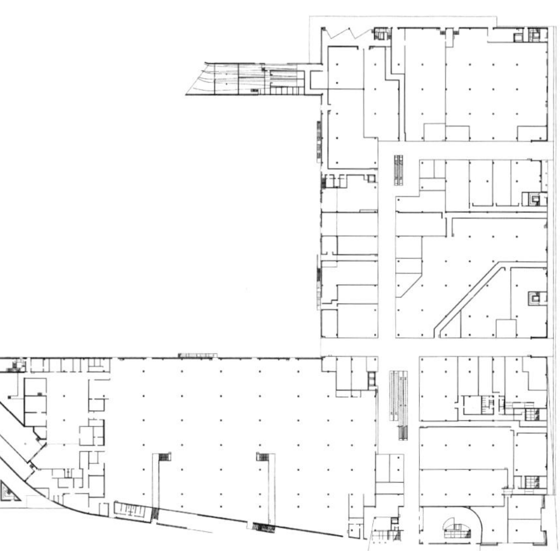

❻ Neustadt Centrum Halle, ground floor plan (shopping level)
Arch.: Hermann & Valentiny with Noack und Partner

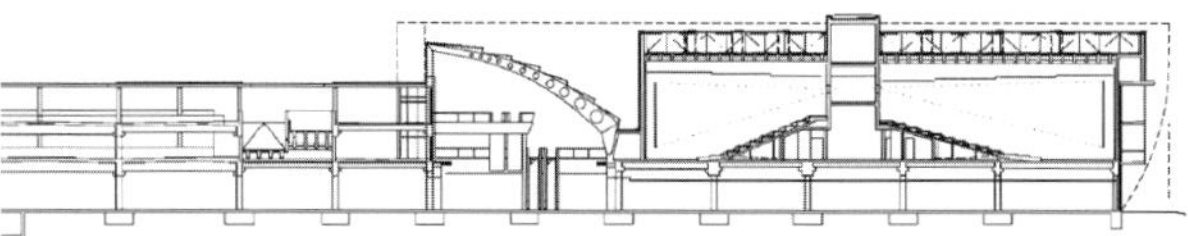

❼ Neustadt Centrum Halle, section
Arch.: Hermann & Valentiny with Noack und Partner

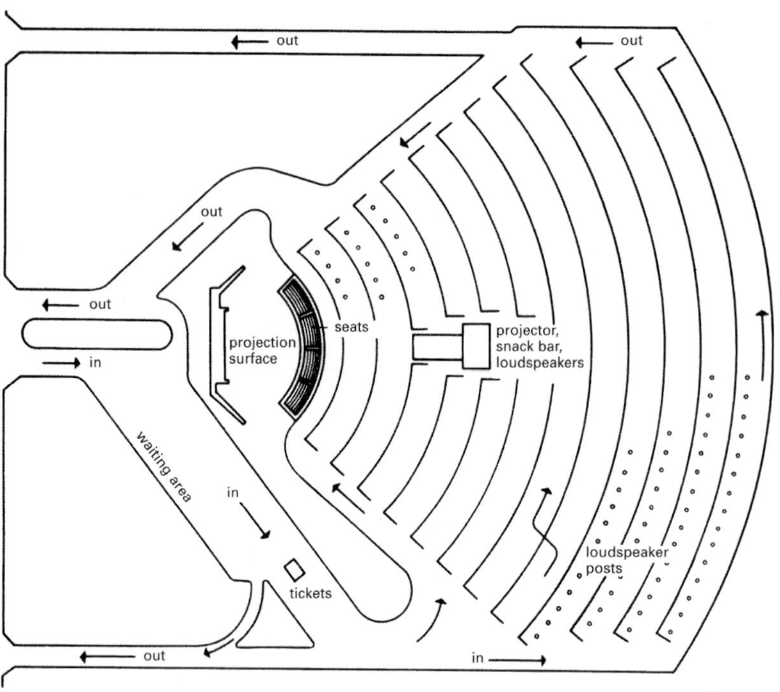

❶ Drive-in cinema in a fan shape with inclined ramps and low projection cabin, which only takes up two rows

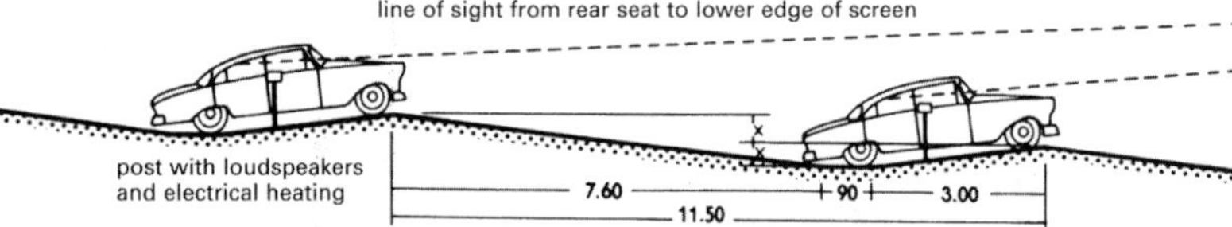

❷ Ramp arrangement and dimensions: elevations can be different according to screen picture height

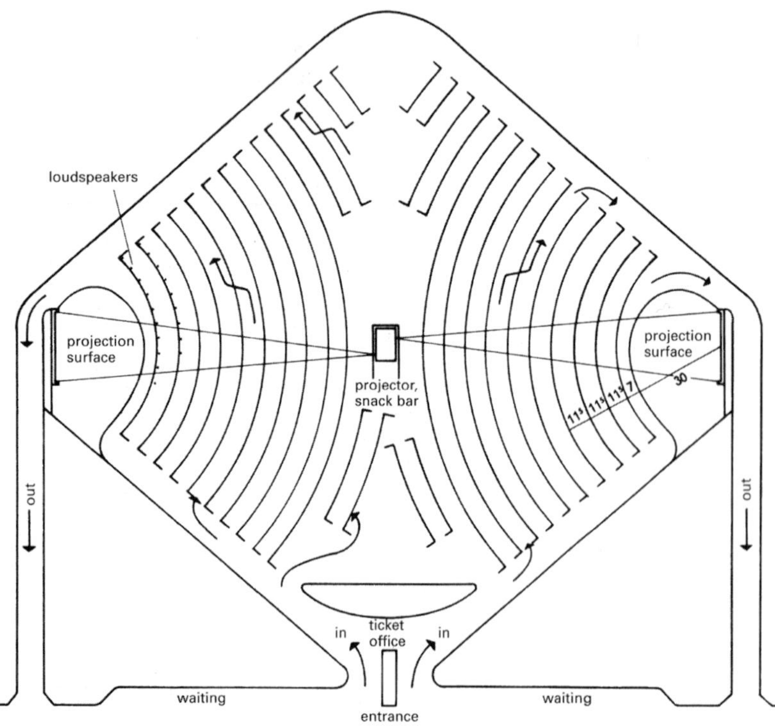

❸ Double cinema. One projection room for both screens, with the possibility of staggered starting times. All other areas (cash desks, bar, toilets etc.) are common

CINEMAS

Drive-in Cinemas

Drive-in cinemas, where the audience do not have to leave their cars.

The size is limited by ramps, number of cars ≦1000–1300, while still ensuring a good view. Normal is 450–500 cars → ❶.

Cars	No. ramps	Screen to back edge of ramp (m)
500	10	155
586	11	170
670	12	180
778	13	195
886	14	210
1000	15	225

Location: on the motorway, near petrol stations and services, with screening so that light and sound do not distract passing traffic.

Ramps are curved and sloping in order to lift the front of the cars, so back seat passengers also have a good view of the screen → ❷.

Entrance road: with waiting area, in order to avoid backing up of traffic on the road. Drive-past ticket counter, so that tickets from the cars can be checked → ❹.

Exit: ideally after leaving the ramp forwards.

Detailing of the entire area to avoid dust and skidding in wet weather.

Ticket counter: one counter for 300 cars; two for 600; three for 800; four for 1000.

Screen: depends on the number of cars: for 650 cars 14.50 × 11.30 m; for 950 cars 17.0 × 13.0 m. Ideally facing east or north, which enables earlier performances. For the Central European latitude, the screen is better installed in a solid, permanent structure.

Cinema screen in the Billbrook drive-in cinema near Hamburg: 36 m high × 15.5 m wide. Height above ground level depends on ramp gradient and sight angle. Screen tilted upward avoids distortion. Scaffolding and screen must be able to bear wind loading.

Rows of seats should be provided, and a play area for children is also a good idea.

Projection building: mostly central, at a distance of 100 m from the screen.

Projection room contains projectors, generators, sound amplification system.

Sound reproduction ideally has loudspeakers inside the cars; the loudspeakers are attached to a post for every two cars at 5.0 m separation and are attached inside the cars by the visitors.

Heating: on loudspeaker posts, possibly also a connection for heating in the cars.

CIRCUS

Stationary

Show theatre, permanent venue

Amphitheatre-type hall, laid out as three quarters of a circle, offering seats for an audience of 1600. The last quarter is intended for the stage, which consists of five stacked lifting platforms. This enables the stage sets to be changed very quickly → ❸.

Access to the hall on the third floor + 13.00 m above road level. A 27 m high reinforced concrete dome spans the circus arena.

Project: Berlin Leipziger Platz
Arch.: Aldo Rossi Milan
Planungs AG Neufert/Mittmann/Graf, Berlin
Sceno-Plus Experts-Conseils, Montreal

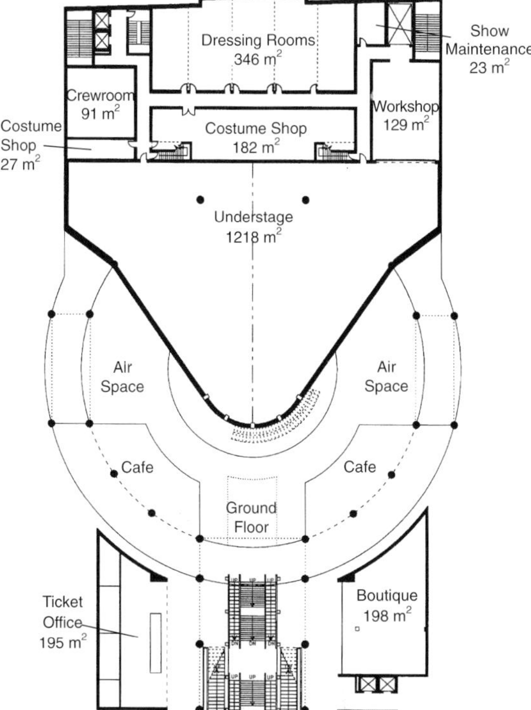

❶ Second floor + 9.00 m (underfloor theatre)

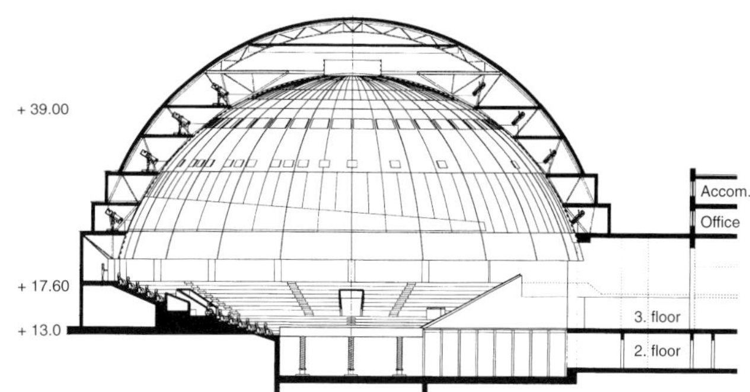

❸ Section

❷ Third floor (stage area) + 13.00 m

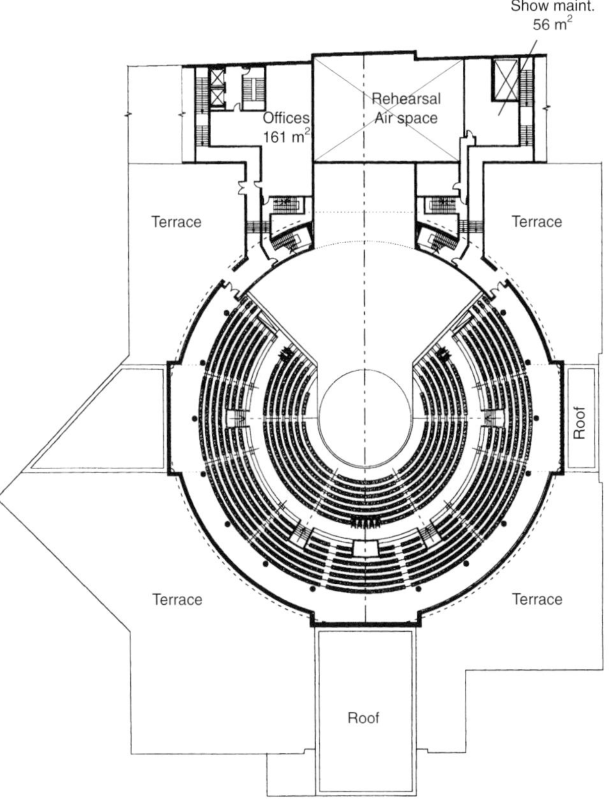

❹ Fourth floor (audience seating level) + 16.50 m

Directive 1999/22/EC Animal Protection Law Report, Minimum Requirements for Animal Husbandry, Federal Ministry for Consumer Protection, Agriculture and Forests

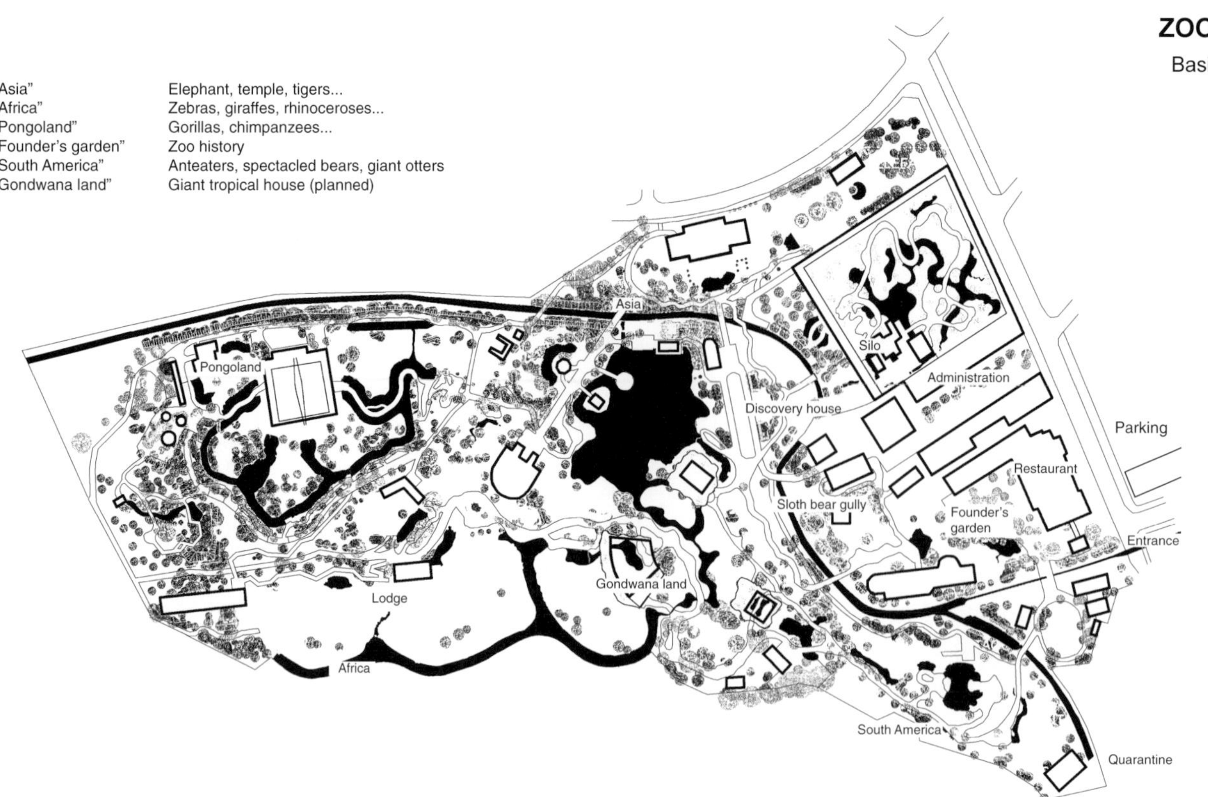

❶ Master plan of a modern zoo with adventure world (animal geography), from the example of Leipzig Zoo Arch.: Rasbachr Architekten

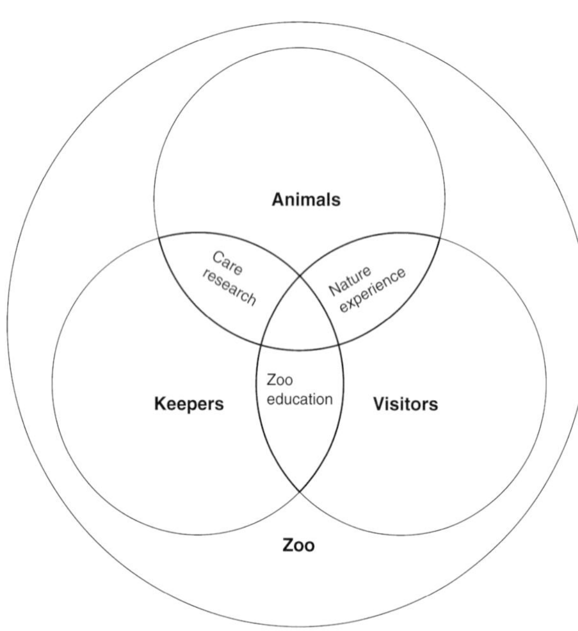

The modern zoo attempts to balance the interests of research, animal protection and the experience of nature.
On one side stand the requirements for keeping the animals, feeding, cage design and veterinary care in line with the needs of the species, research activities for the conservation of species, participation in international breeding programmes and zoo educational publicity work.
On the other hand, the zoo is also a business, whose success mainly depends on visitor numbers and is in competition with other leisure providers.
The basis of any zoo design is therefore the orientation on the state of research into the keeping of animals in a way suitable for the species, and also the consideration of the demands of the potential visitors. The staging of exotic ("near to nature") animal worlds and spectacular visitor facilities should therefore be evaluated against this background.

❷ Tasks of the modern zoo, combining the interests of research, animal conservation and providing exciting experiences

Objectives of zoos
Starting with Directive 1999/22/EC, zoos are subject to the following requirements → ❷:

1. Involvement in research activities for species conservation
2. Zoo educational publicity work
3. Keeping and feeding the animals correctly for the species
4. Protection against animals escaping or pests and vermin infiltrating
5. Keeping a register of the zoo collection

Infrastructure of a modern zoo → ❶
Access: good accessibility, clear signposting, sufficient number of parking spaces, stops for public transport

Main entrance: distinctive entrance area, pay booths/counters, kiosks, administration, tidy paths, welcoming seating

Further infrastructure: event and lecture room, high-class restaurant with view of zoo facilities and separate entrance from outside (for evening business), further restaurants according to zoo size, self-service cafeteria, kiosks, toilets, picnic sites, zoo shops, zoo school

Operations and staff building: separate access (out of public view) with adequate external areas for the storage of feed and litter, building materials, etc., staff department with washing and changing facilities, cafeteria, training and rest rooms (security staff), breeding of feed animals, central/dispersed feed preparation, water distribution, storage and cool rooms, rubbish removal, sheds for parking and maintenance of cleaning machines, transport vehicles and cages, workshops, gardening, heating, air conditioning, ventilation

Medical care of animals: animal clinic, quarantine station, laboratories, research facilities, acclimatisation and breeding areas, cadaver storage

Access roads and paths: wheelchair-accessible main paths (5–6 m wide), with weather protection, laid out as round route, side paths (3–4 m wide) to each group of animals, independent operational roads (3–4 m wide) for supply, waste disposal, animal transport and as emergency access (fire service, ambulance).

ZOOS

Keeping Animals

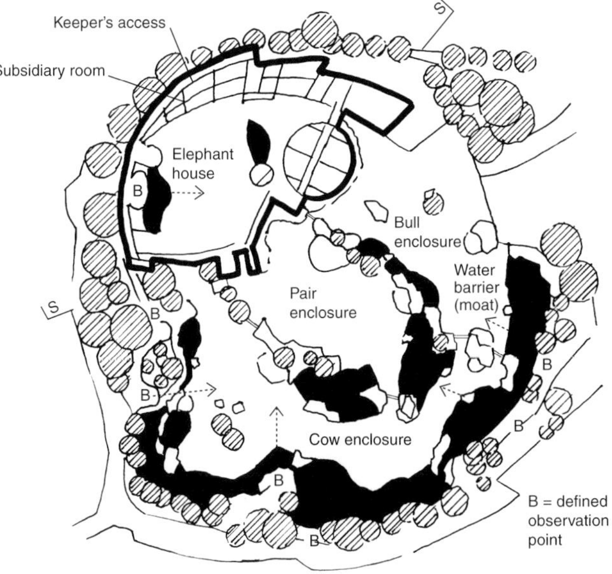

❶ Elephant park, Cologne Zoo — Arch.: Oxen und Römer, external works: Fenner, Steinhauser, Weisser

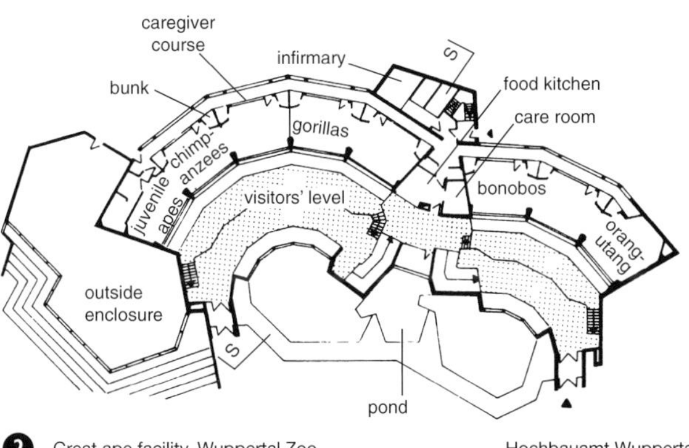

❷ Great ape facility, Wuppertal Zoo — Hochbauamt Wuppertal

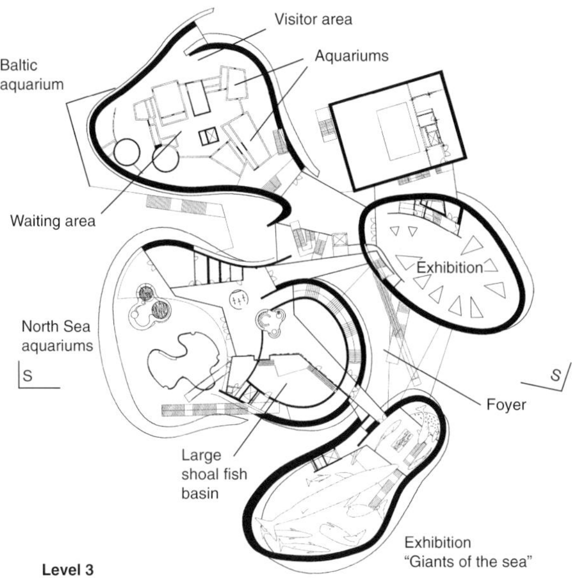

❸ Ozeaneum, Stralsund — Arch.: Behnisch, Behnisch und Partner

'**Hands-on**', the traditional principle of keeping zoo animals: it denotes direct contact between the (tame) animals, the keepers (feeding, care) and the zoo visitors (petting zoo) → ❷.

Functional aspects include separation into public and private or invisible areas, assignment of visitor areas, enclosures, keeper access and subsidiary rooms. The most important aspects are hygienic considerations and the presentation of the animals.

Hands-off' (protected contact) was originally developed as a safe method of handling dangerous animals (indirect, technically supported contact between animal and keeper), and today often corresponds to the expectations of zoo visitors for species-appropriate keeping of animals in zoos → ❶: The large area and natural character of the reproduced original habitat, with appropriate fixed points (drinking trough, climbing rocks, etc.) and the possibility of observing from selected and protected (secretive) positions are also seen as desirable regarding lack of disturbance and encouraging reproduction in human care. "Hands-off" facilities have excellent potential for research and breeding.

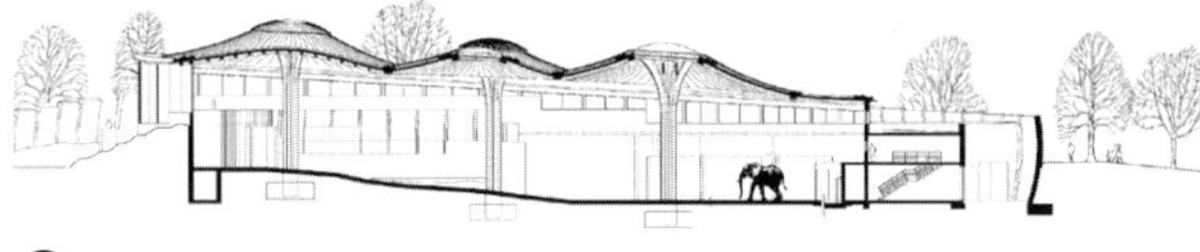

❹ Section → ❶

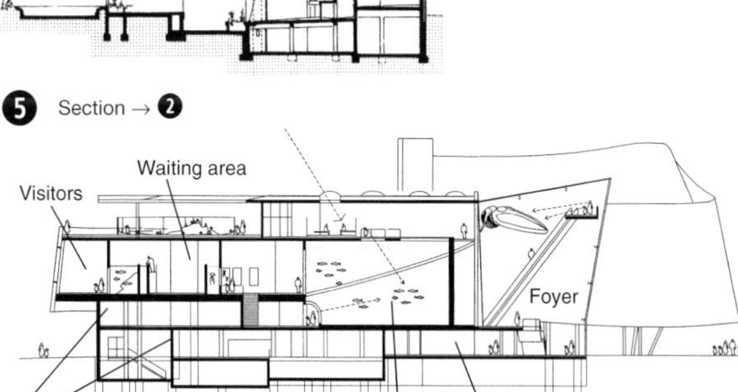

❺ Section → ❷

❻ Section → ❸

Examples

Animal houses and open-air enclosures are differentiated. Combinations are possible, with and without water:

The elephant park at Cologne Zoo → ❶ is an example of an integrated '**hands-off' facility** (animal house and open-air enclosure). The partially roofed area can be divided into various sections from a control centre by means of mechanical gates. The visitor areas are separated from the enclosures by water-filled ditches or differences in level

The great ape house at Wuppertal Zoo → ❷ is an **animal house** (with outside enclosure built subsequently), consisting of the internal enclosure lit from above with protected sleeping bunks, glass partition to the visitor area, keeper access from behind, feed kitchen and special cages (sick bay, baby apes).

The Ozeaneum, Stralsund → ❸, as an example of a **multifunctional animal house/aquarium** with an extensive round tour for visitors, thematically divided aquariums (Baltic, North Sea) and central area for keepers. The facility serves the purposes of **exhibition and research** and is elaborately conceived with spectacular views into the tanks (shoal fish tank with 15 × 5 m glass pane, tunnel aquarium, overhead aquarium, touch pools, simulation tanks).

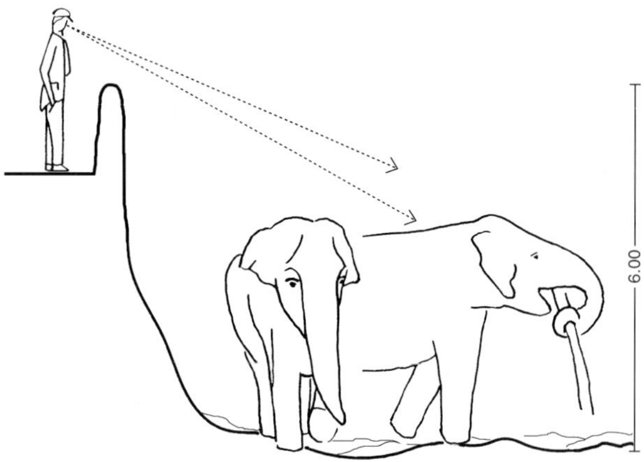

1 Concealed visitor position

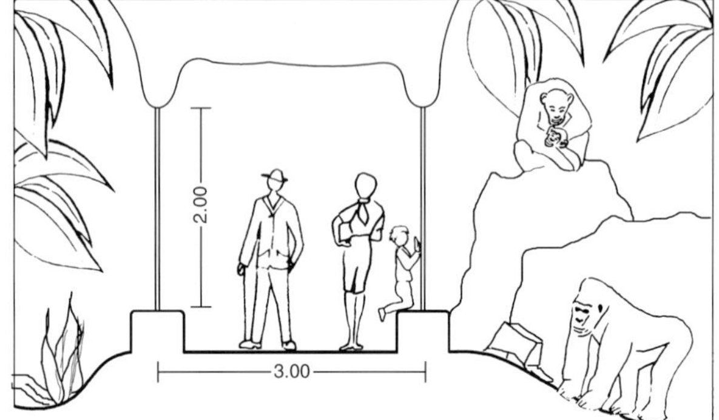

2 Indoor enclosure with glass corridor: view from dark into light

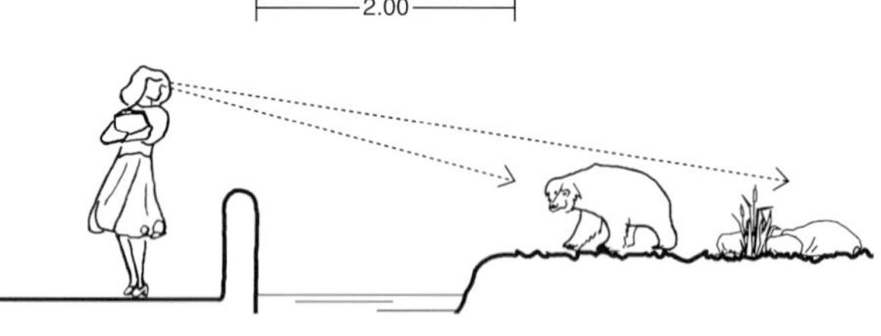

3 Water barrier: visitor and animal outdoors

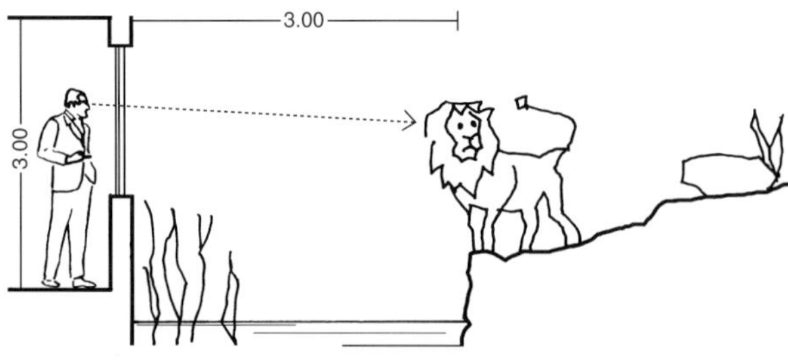

4 Water barrier: visitor behind protective glass screen and animal outdoors

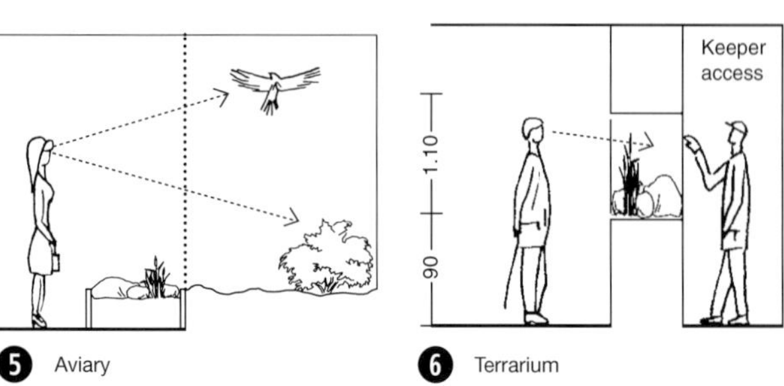

5 Aviary

6 Terrarium

Design aspects

Near to nature: The enclosure should correspond to the ideas of the visitors regarding the appropriate habitat for the animals, be aesthetically pleasing and give a generous impression.

Physical nearness: The nearer people can come to the animals, the greater the interest and the longer they stay.

Emotional nearness: Enclosure boundaries should scarcely be noticed.

Observation: Animal enclosures should work secretively and be an invitation to exploration (e.g. view into the enclosure through a cave or a waterfall). Routes should invite lingering, not passing an enclosure but rather leading to it. It should be possible to see only one enclosure from each location; distracting views, and also masses of people in front of the enclosure, should be avoided.

Enable comfortable observation in a relaxed position, not into the sun or through a reflecting pane of glass; the visitor should look into a bright, lit enclosure from shadow (this also has the advantage that the animals do not immediately notice the visitors). Areas where the animals like to pass the time and are active should be clearly visible.

Withdrawal: It is, however, also important that the animal can withdraw from view and be unobserved.

Information: Signage; sufficient information should be available

Accessibility: Access to the enclosures (only for the zoo keepers) is provided by dedicated roads and care areas; the appropriate animal catching and transport facilities are here.

Barriers

Ditches were originally developed as dry ditches, but are today generally constructed as **water barriers (moats)** → 3. A natural appearance is advantageous, but the water becomes dirty quickly and the animals can leave the enclosure over the ice if it freezes over, so the water level therefore has to be lowered in winter. There are normally fences or walls to provide additional protection.

Glass is becoming accepted by most zoos → 2 + 4, because it gives the impression of direct contact with the animals and also prevents the infection of animals by humans.

Iron bars disturb the visitor and the animal. The classic method of keeping animals in cages is therefore avoided in modern zoos.

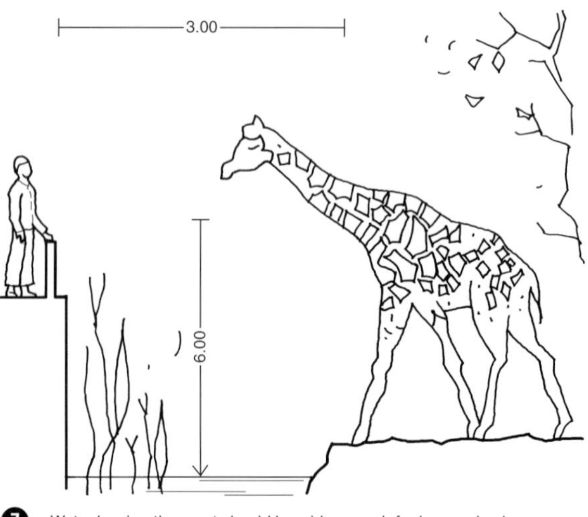

7 Water barrier: the moat should be wide enough for large animals

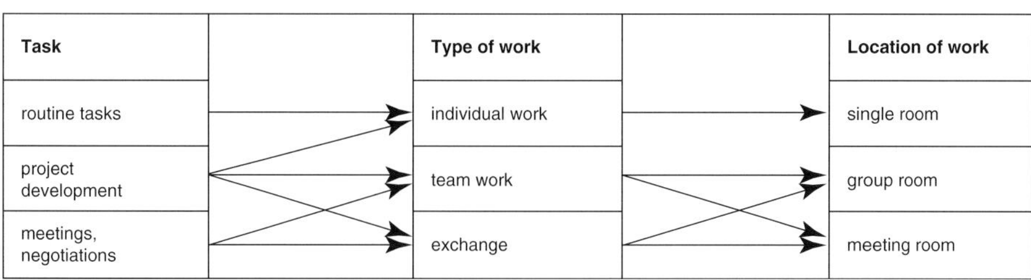

1 Relationship between duties and room type

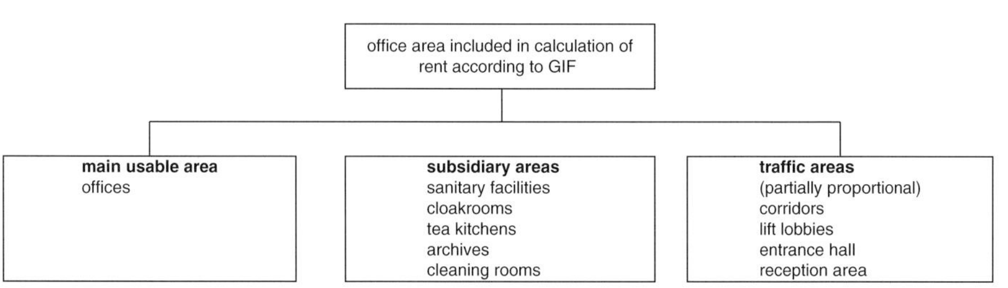

2 The GIF (Association for Property Economics Research), in collaboration with the DIN standards committee, has developed definitions of working areas in offices ('MF-B') and commercial rooms ('MF-H'), for the purpose of comparing commercial rents. Based on the concepts of DIN 277 1973/87 ('Areas and volumes of buildings'), certain areas have been categorised into 'rented areas for office space' and 'rented areas for commercial space'. Areas with shared use are only considered proportionally. Application is not binding.

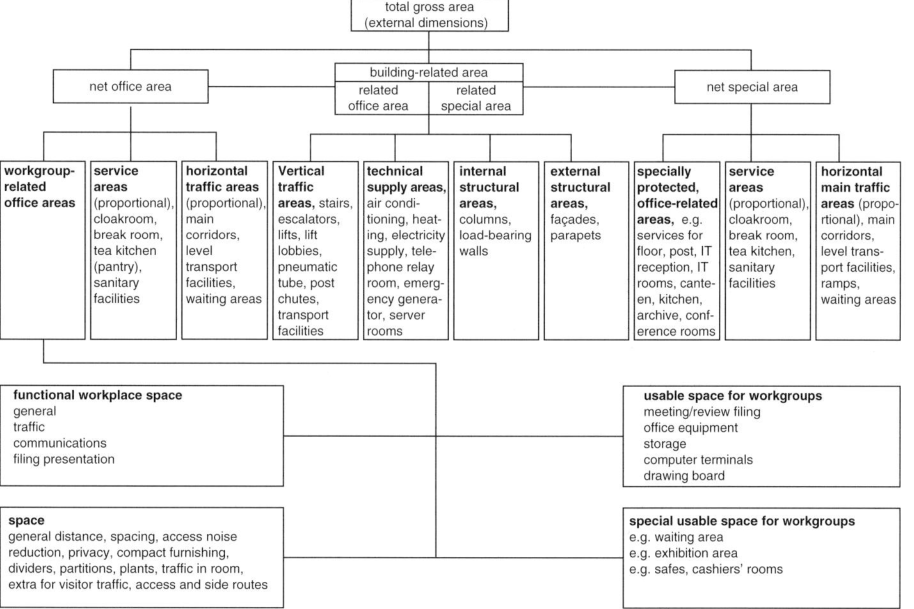

3 Organisational structure of office space (Lappat)

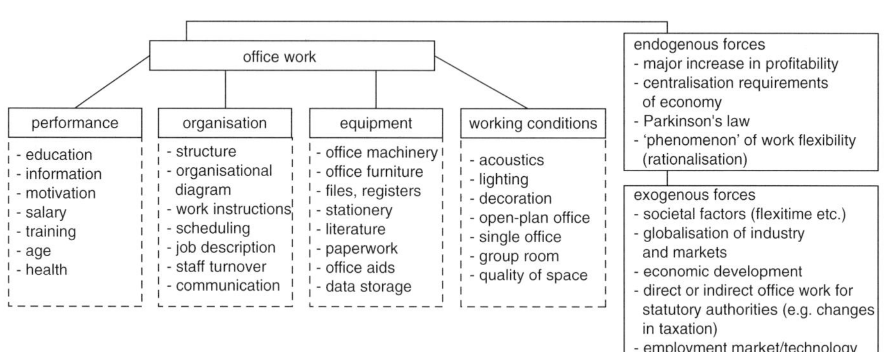

4 The factors determining office work (Henkel → refs)

Office work

Administrative work is the processing of information. The emphasis of office work is changing from routine processing of data (traditional card systems) to more creative information processing and evaluation on account of changes in storage and improved ways of accessing information.

Employees are becoming ever more important in the organisation of office work. Factors like the image of the company (corporate identity), design of areas for breaks and relaxation and the individual configuration of workplaces are all intended to increase employees' performance. Global networking means that routine work can be carried out on a decentralised basis (home working, neighbourhood and rented offices).

The company headquarters is becoming an information market place, which is made use of by many employees either temporarily or in changing groups to achieve their tasks. These changes result in the very variable demands made on the workplace in an office building.

The range of options runs from the single workplace in a cubicle office through group rooms to workstations which are only used at specific times ('hot desking'). The more flexible the rooms in a building are, the easier it is for the company to adapt to ever-changing requirements.

Design

Detailed recording of the business and organisational structure, and thus the specific functions and working relationships in the company, enable the determination of a schedule of requirements (needs assessment).

In rented buildings, flexible room layout is of great importance, to achieve the most variable sizes of office unit possible.

Administration and offices

OFFICE BUILDINGS
Structures
Tendencies
Typology
Until 1980
Since 1980
Space requirement
Computer workstations
Archives
Additional areas
Room typology
Grid
Access
Building services
Construction

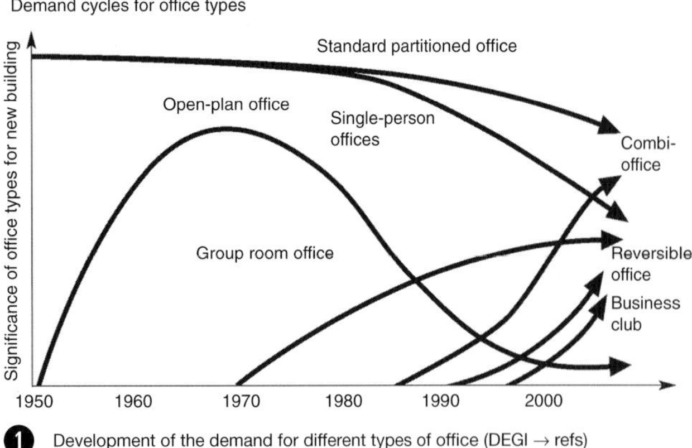

❶ Development of the demand for different types of office (DEGI → refs)

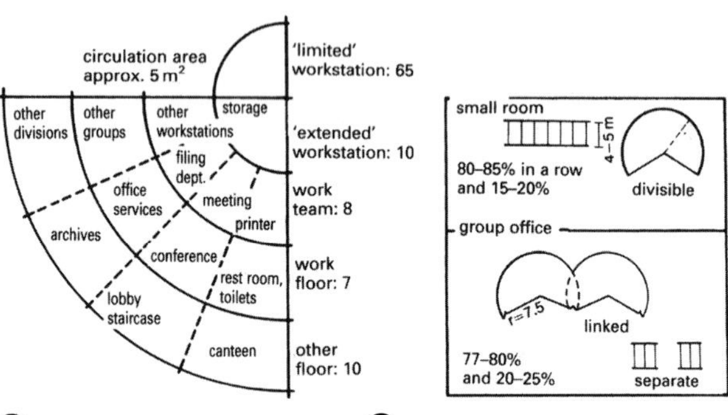

❷ Analysis of daily use in an office, area %

❸ Recommendation for relationship of permanent and flexible room structures in small and group room offices, area %

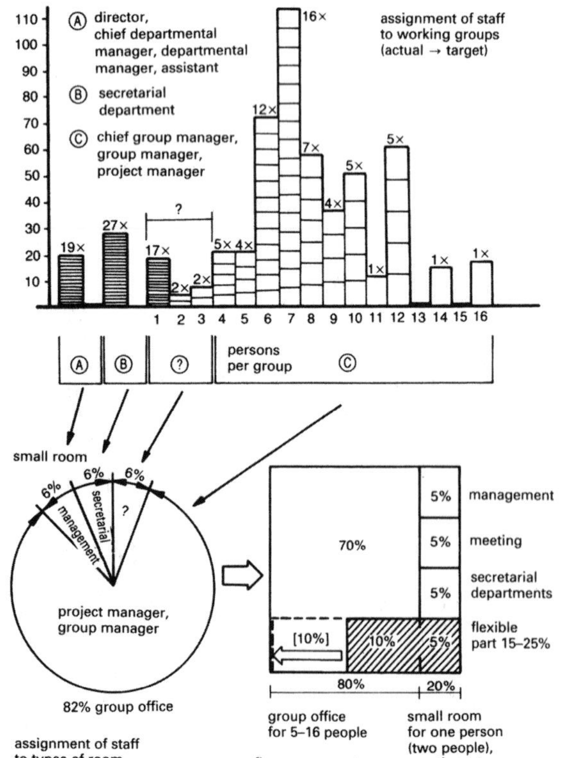

❹ Usage basics for division of rooms (all figs, Gottschalk → refs)

Influence of information technology and office automation

The developments in information and communication technologies are leading to changed working conditions in offices.

Multifunctional terminals are replacing single components in data, text and image processing. Individual systems are being networked into integrated office communication systems. The ever-improving public data networks (ISDN, DSL, 3G) make it possible to exchange great quantities of data over long distances. Flat screens, laptops and mobile telephones reduce the amount of space required at each workstation. The effect of office technology on the office layout and workstations is creating evaluation criteria like: more emphasis on immediate workplace quality; ensuring company-wide flexibility; ecologically sound working environment, to whose spatial configuration older office buildings no longer measure up. New Workplace Regulations stipulate working areas according to demand (no more minimum areas).

The rationalisation potential of administrative activities (filing, sorting, copying, searching, acquisition of material) and communication activities (conferences, meetings) is about 25% of weekly working time. Routine tasks acting as active relaxation breaks would be reduced by about 50%. Increasing telecommuting leads to a reduction in office space, because only some activities (meetings etc.) then take place in the office building at specific workstations, which are no longer personalised and can be used by various employees as required ('hot-desking'). Personal areas are reduced to office containers, which contain a post box and files. Mobile telephone and computer WLAN networks make a change of location simple. The potential independence of location (decentralisation) is countered by other possible losses (concentration of staff at central locations, headquarters in prestigious situation, urban location as sign of continuity, ambience, work and leisure activities in one place), which can play important roles.

Changes at the workplace

The rationalisation effect of information technology and altering workplace requirements (procedures and organisational pattern) are changing the structure of offices. Staff levels are falling and work groups are getting smaller. The former hierarchical division of labour among staff, like manager, secretary, specialist employee etc., is changing to integrated work groups and thus altering the assignment of office space.

A more sensitive relationship to the direct working environment is closely linked to the predominant value orientation in the company. This is reflected in the attitude to the quality of the workplace (daylight, environmental context, energy consumption), and the activity (ecological viewpoints, material use, waste disposal). The workplace is an important place for social interaction among the users, which is increasing in relevance due to formalised work structures (IT, work organisation etc.). Increased mental and physical stress leads to a greater awareness of the working environment (sufficient space, some personal choice in furnishings, ventilation, lighting, sufficient protection from disruptions). 75% of daily work takes place at the 'close and extended workplace' → ❷. Necessary work contacts and collectively used facilities are significant, thus the requirement for a mixed provision of single and group rooms, 'personal' and 'collective' workplaces → ❸ – ❹. In addition to the refurbishment of existing office space, new spatial concepts involving single and group rooms are starting to appear (Fuchs, Gottschalk, Henkel → refs).

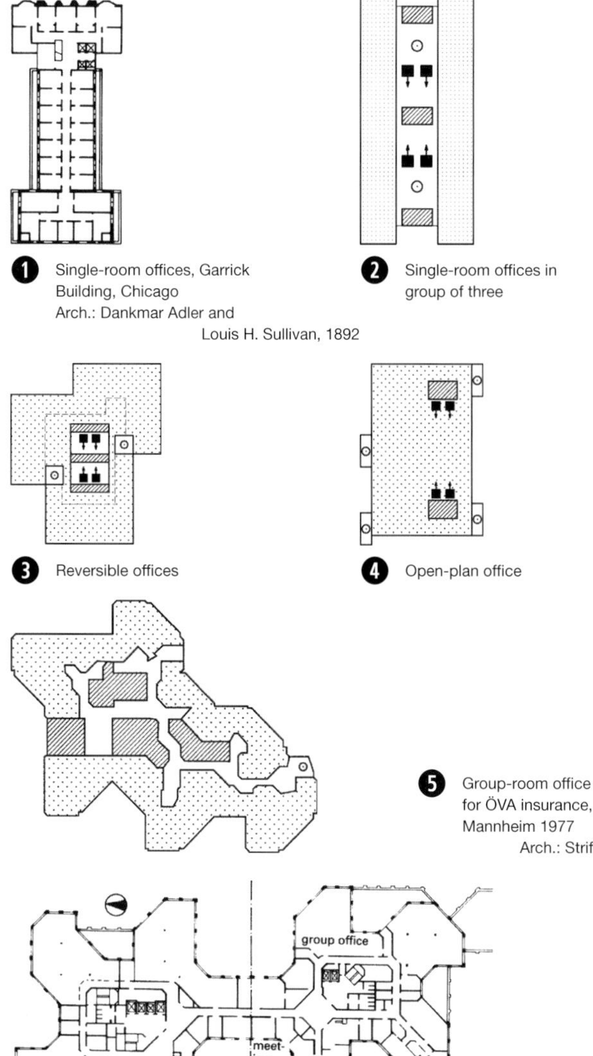

❶ Single-room offices, Garrick Building, Chicago
Arch.: Dankmar Adler and Louis H. Sullivan, 1892

❷ Single-room offices in group of three

❸ Reversible offices

❹ Open-plan office

❺ Group-room office for ÖVA insurance, Mannheim 1977
Arch.: Striffler

group offices
core with access
small rooms, fixed;
small rooms, flexible;
secretarial area
zoned group offices

❽ Application of linked and partially zoned group rooms; these are connected by reversible small-room zones and can be partially zoned when required for common areas.

Key
Elevator
Main staircase
Side stairs
Core areas
Group rooms
Small spaces

❾ State Central Bank of Hesse, Frankfurt am Main, 1988
Arch.: Jourdan, Müller et al.

Forms of office organisation

Open-plan offices (Mies van der Rohe: '... clearly laid-out, undivided, only structured...' → refs) are suitable for large groups of employees who are predominantly engaged in shared work and for routine activities with a low concentration threshold. This is increasingly the exception rather than the rule today. The concept appeared in the 1960s with arguments like transparency and manageability of work processes, development of community feeling, and a rationally organised multifunctional area. IT machines were in separate rooms and not available in offices. The extensive room depths of 20–30 m resulted in high costs for building services, which is of limited suitability for the conversion of buildings, and the potential flexibility has its limits in the light of today's demands (opening windows, control of lighting, air conditioning and electricity supply) (Henkel → refs). The open-plan office is attested by sociologists to be afflicted with a character of compulsion (social controls, dependence on technical equipment, optical and acoustic disturbance), and therefore led to a negative reaction among its occupants.

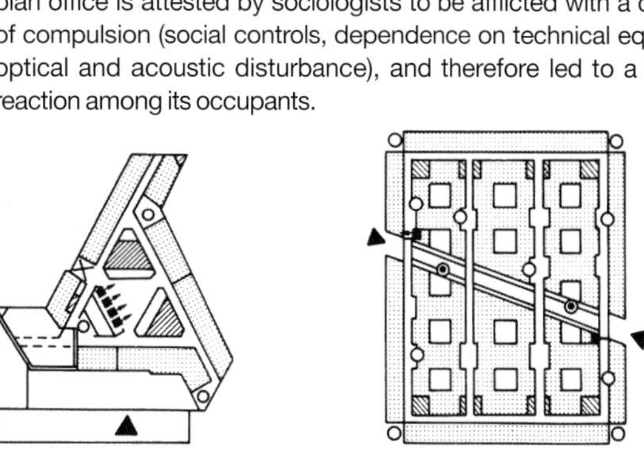

❻ BfG Frankfurt
Arch.: Nowotny-Mähner, HPP, Speer und Partner

❼ Cantonal building, Berne
Arch.: Matti, Bürgi, Ragaz, Liebefeld

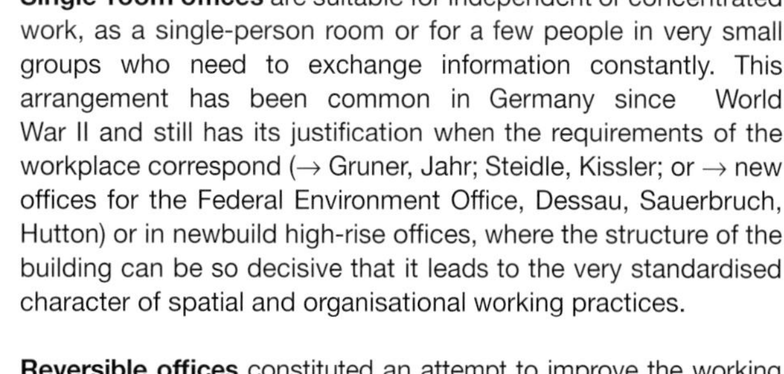

Single-room offices are suitable for independent or concentrated work, as a single-person room or for a few people in very small groups who need to exchange information constantly. This arrangement has been common in Germany since World War II and still has its justification when the requirements of the workplace correspond (→ Gruner, Jahr; Steidle, Kissler; or → new offices for the Federal Environment Office, Dessau, Sauerbruch, Hutton) or in newbuild high-rise offices, where the structure of the building can be so decisive that it leads to the very standardised character of spatial and organisational working practices.

Reversible offices constituted an attempt to improve the working conditions in open-plan offices, which are often found to be inadequate on many grounds (no differentiated air conditioning, daylight, optical and acoustic disturbance). The possibility of partitioning producing a more effective single-room office structure (i.e. cubicles) when required for more concentrated work considerably increased technical input to enable flexibility. However, not only the dissatisfaction of the users but also the increasing lack of cost-effectiveness with increasing energy prices led to this form of office being questioned. The working structure as changed by new technologies (e.g. the use of PCs) enabled organisation into small groups. First example: the building of the ÖVA, Mannheim.

Group rooms (smaller open-plan) are suitable for work groups with constant information exchange. This form of office was an attempt to install room layouts with more scope for individual decisions (→ **Changes at the workplace**, p. 232), via the size of the workplace surroundings (max. 7.5 m to a window), and thus improve the working conditions of an open-plan arrangement (light, air, individuality), which were found to be inadequate with the increasing demands on office work. It is possible to do without full air conditioning in favour of back-up ventilation services, in addition to opening windows and using radiators.

❶ Office in an existing building with workplaces laid out to meet needs, which can be occupied by employees for specific tasks. This form of organisation with non-territorial workstations is called a 'hot desk office'.
Arch.: Schnell und Partner, Munich

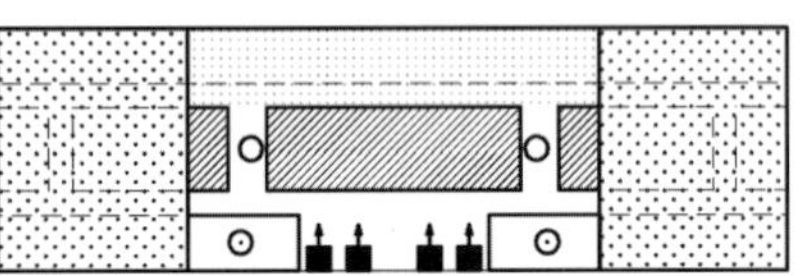

❷ Scheme of a small group of three rooms (high-rise plan) with flexibly usable zones at the ends and areas for cubicles in the core

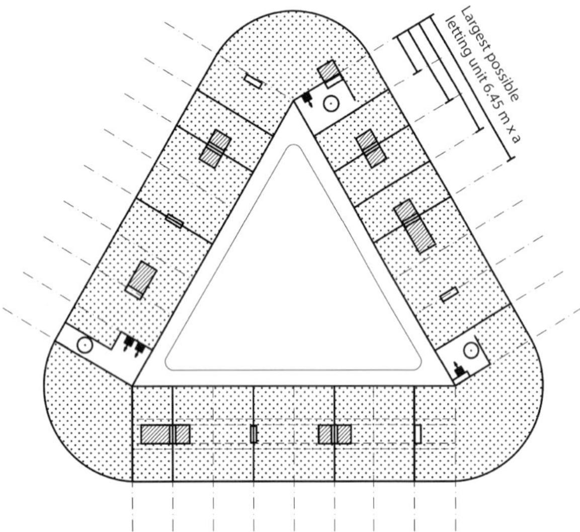

❸ Scheme of a building with variable areas for rent. The external access to the rented units along the gallery leaves the internal access to be decided by the tenant. The smallest possible unit is a half grid between two supply cores. Building depth approx. 15 m and spacing of the supply shafts 12.90 m, the smallest letting unit approx. 90 m². UFO, Frankfurt am Main Arch.: Dietz Joppien Architekten AG

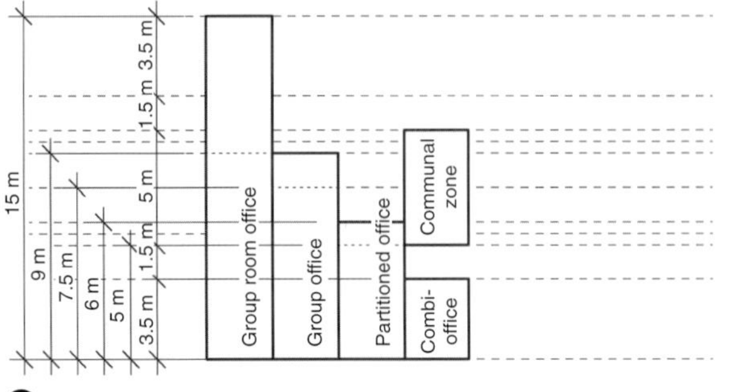

❺ Room depths for various types of office

The continuing progress of information technology is resulting in new job descriptions for employees. The requirements for office space are also changing and often require the **refurbishment** of existing office buildings. An additional factor of equal importance is that the open-plan configuration has been found to be inadequate (→ **Changes at the workplace**, p. 232).

The means used for this reorganisation are rebuilding, provision of daylight from inner courtyards, straightforward plan layouts, creation of workplaces of equal rank with regard to light, air and sound reduction, or the use of office furnishing systems, which can increasingly undertake the function of building services like cabling, sockets etc., and also of partitions.

The **combi-office** principle attempts to provide a suitable room concept for the specific requirements of an office organisation. This entails a room arrangement that is flexible where required, enables group work, provides individual rooms for concentrated work and a temporarily usable collective layout for particular communal activities. It is particularly suitable for independent, highly qualified work where the workplace can change with the daily programme.

'**Hot desk offices**' or '**business clubs**' are not spatial layouts but denote a particularly flexible organisation of work without fixed personal workplaces. Particular value is placed on variable room use possibilities and differentiated room qualities. For combi-groups and open-plan offices, efficiency is not achieved through rebuilding of rooms but via the business organisation and a flexible 'club' atmosphere conducive to wellbeing.

In new buildings, this experience leads to more value being placed on reversibility, in order to be able to react better to the ever-shorter innovation cycles of office technology. This leads to buildings which can be divided into user units of varying sizes without great inconvenience (**rented offices**) →❸ – ❹, or even permit a combination of production and administration (**start-up centres**) → ❸. The changed values regarding the workplace, plus high energy prices, are leading to new architectural forms with building elements intended to provide temperature regulation and natural ventilation (conservatories, halls, double façades).

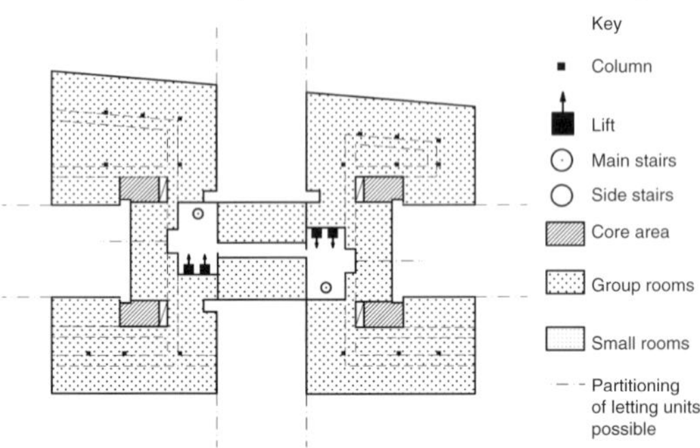

❹ Scheme of a building with variable areas for rent. The central building zone can be opened to the various rental units as required. Kennedyhaus, Düsseldorf
Arch.: Kister Scheithauer Gross, Prof. U. Coersmeier, Cologne

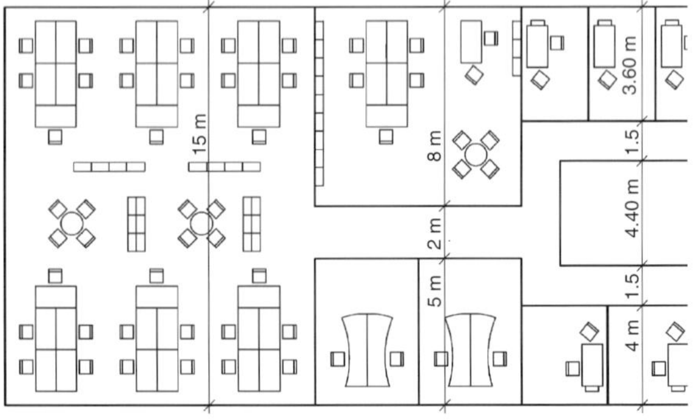

❻ Possible arrangements of various office depths in a 15 m wide plan

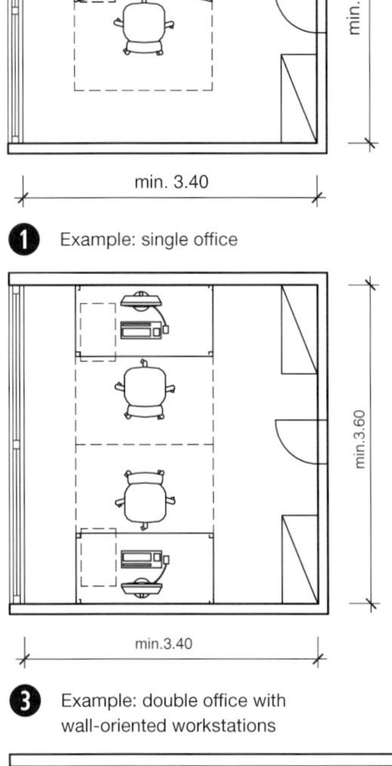

1 Example: single office

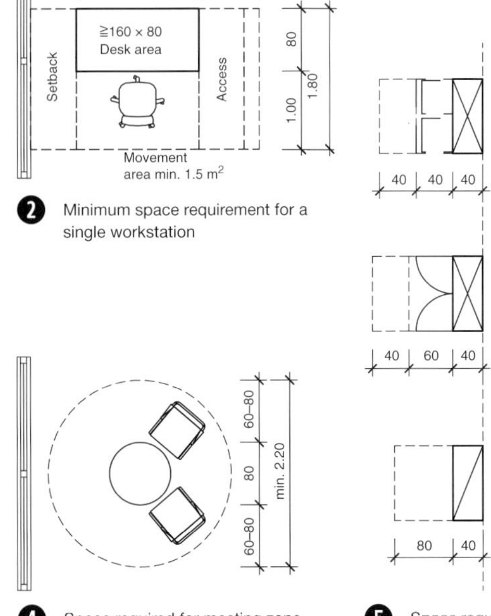

2 Minimum space requirement for a single workstation

3 Example: double office with wall-oriented workstations

4 Space required for meeting zone

5 Space required for files

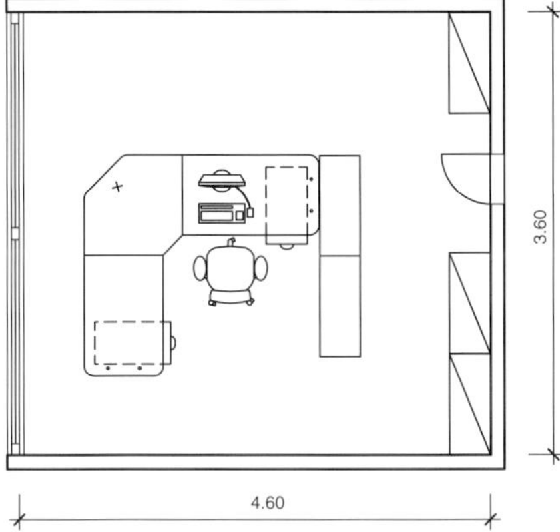

6 Example: office management

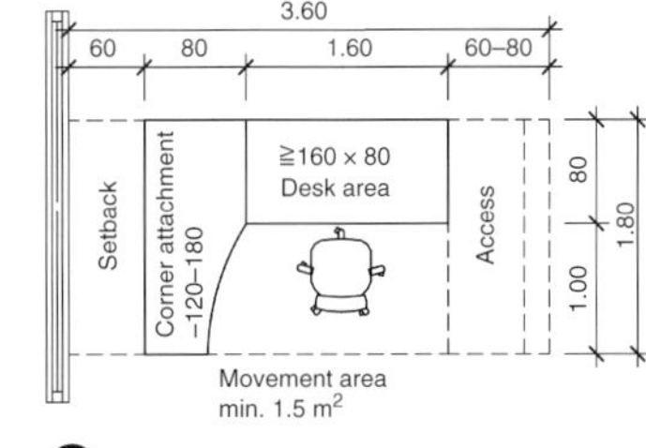
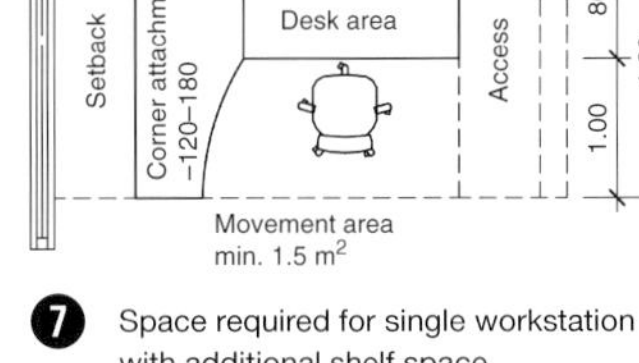

7 Space required for single workstation with additional shelf space

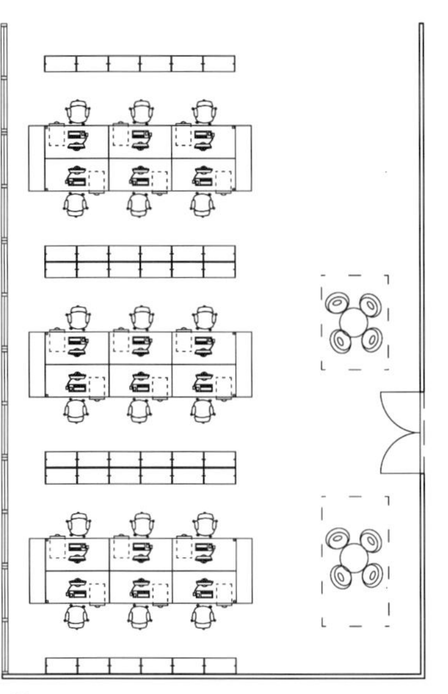

8 Example: workstation layout in a large group office

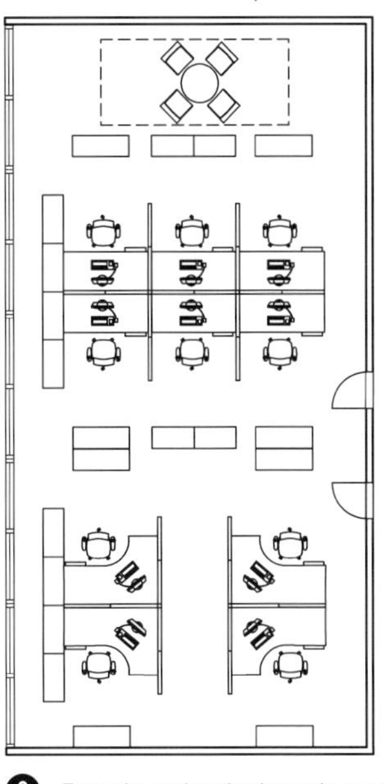

9 Example: workstation layout in a small group office

OFFICE BUILDINGS

Space Requirement

Workplace

According to the new Workplace Regulations, there are no longer any fixed minimum dimensions for workplaces. But the requirements of the accident insurers and the fact that all workplaces today have computer screens means that the minimum dimensions in the relevant DIN EN standards and regulations apply.

Furniture areas

The standard no longer prescribes fixed dimensions for workplaces, but requires sufficient working and movement areas for changing positions at work and for the individually adaptable placing of work equipment.

The assignments of various areas are differentiated by the standard; however, they can overlap if this results in no limitation of the function.

The areas are:
- work area: table
- shelf area: plan area of the furniture
- furniture function area: space required for doors and drawers
- movement area at the workstation
- traffic and through-passages

Forms of office and work

The office's form and thus its room layout are part of a system influenced by activity, procedural organisation, IT technology and company culture. The building structure and design of rooms can have a significant influence on the use. Efficiency gains can result from factors like reduction of the area per workstation, rooms designed to support procedures and improve motivation, for which emotional factors above all are decisive, like material and colour ideas, but also the provision of quiet and communication areas for formal and informal meetings. The analysis of requirements can produce valuable pointers to possible forms of office.

DIN 4543-1

BS EN ISO 9241
DIN EN ISO 9241
ZH 1/618, 1/535

see also: Daylight pp. 488 ff.

❶ Vertical field of view

❷ Horizontal field of view

❸ Preferred and permissible reach areas

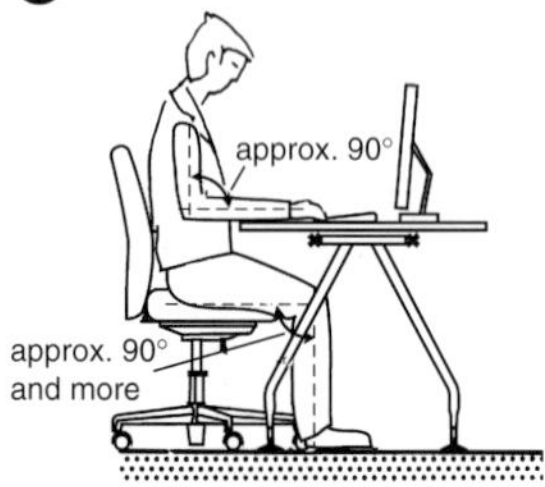

❹ Ergonomically correct basic posture at computer workstation

❺ Ergonomically designed computer workstation with fixed desk

values in brackets are target values

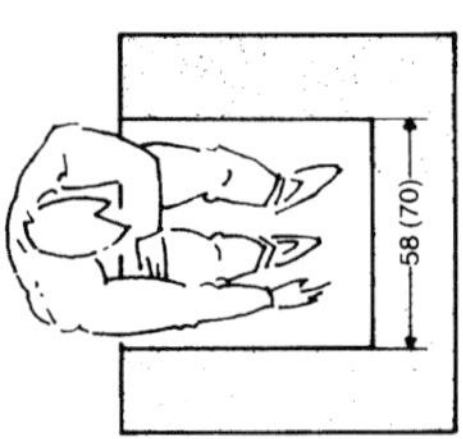

❻ Legroom

Job type 1 table adjustable in height chair adjustable in height		
	Women	Women and Men
T (Table height)*	(630-t) – (730-t)	(630-t) – (780-t)
S (Chair height)	420-460	420-500

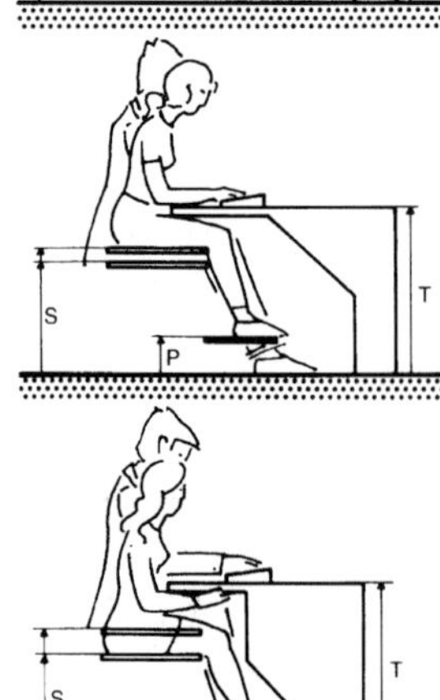

Job type 2 not height-adjustable table not height-adjustable chair not height-adjustable footrest		
	Women	Women and Men
T (Table height)*	(700-t) – (730-t)	(750-t) – (780-t)
S (Chair height)	420-460	500-550
P (Height footrests)	0-100	0-150

Job type 2 not height-adjustable table not height-adjustable chair		
	Women	Women and Men
T (Table height)*	(630-t) – (730-t)	(630-t) – (780-t)
S (Chair height)	420-460	420-500

* t means keyboard height above the table top

❼ Dimensions for workstation furniture

Workstations are where elements such as computer screen, alphanumeric keyboard and document or sound recording device are decisive for dealing with the work. Computer workstations are not based on one standard solution but according to the specific work procedure (e.g. information point, data entry point etc.).

The regulations are laid down in ZH 1/618, 'Safety rules for visual display workstations in office areas', issued by the Association of Commercial Accident Insurance Companies. They include:

- Workplace Guidelines and Workplace Regulations
- more than 40 DIN regulations, particularly:
- DIN EN ISO 9241 T1–T7, 'Ergonomic requirements for office work with visual display terminals'
- ZH 1/535 'Safety rules for office workstations'
- VDI and VDE (German engineering and electrical associations) standards for technical services (heating, ventilation, electricity). Computer workstations should be designed to comply with these regulations and the generally recognised rules of the technology or in accordance with the relevant state of occupational health and ergonomic knowledge.

Workplace layout

Items which are frequently used during the working day should be put in the preferred places where they are visible and reachable → ❶ – ❸. There should be a free movement area of at least 1.5 m^2 at the workstation.

Furniture: This should enable the correctly defined working posture – upper arm and elbow vertical at an angle of approx. 90° and thigh and lower leg vertical at an angle of 90° → ❹. To achieve the correct posture for people of different heights, table and chair sizes must be adjustable. Two ergonomically equally valuable possibilities are:

A: workstation type 1, desk at variable height	60–78 cm
chair at variable height	42–54 cm
B: workstation type 2, type 3, desk of fixed height	72 cm
chair of variable height	42–50 cm
footstool of variable height	00–15 cm

There should be sufficient legroom → ❻.

The desktop working area should be at least 120 × 80 cm (few documents, predominantly screen work; for specialist employees, at least 200 × 80 cm)

Environment: All furniture in the immediate vicinity (desktop etc.) should have a coefficient of reflection of 20–50%.

Lighting intensity should be 300–500 lx, and lamps have limited glare, e.g. through recessed ceiling grid luminaires or 2-K lighting → p. 501–510. Light bands should be arranged parallel to the window. Matt surfaces in the room with recommended coefficients of reflection (approx: ceiling 70%, walls 50%, partitions 20–50%).

The view to the screen should be parallel to the window façade and to light bands, with the screen if possible in-between. Install computer workstations in windowless zones.

Recommendations for climatic conditions and sound reduction should be complied with. The increased use of equipment in offices will more probably result in a cooling load rather than a heating load (→ p. 466).

Psychology of the computer workstation

Negative effects can arise for the management that determines computer work if a strategy of rationalisation is pursued which excludes the employees from the working process as much as possible and attempts to restrict them to residual activities. Prof. Walter Volpert (→ refs) formulated nine criteria for the design of workstations, which define contrasting (machine–person) work tasks with the following features:

- wide scope for action and decision
- reasonable amount of time allowed
- possibility of personal structuring of demands
- performing tasks free of hindrance
- sufficient physical activity
- stimulation of varied senses
- concrete handling with real objects (or direct social relations)
- possibility of variations
- encouragement and enabling of social cooperation and immediate contact between people

(→ **Changes at the workplace**, p. 232)

1 Cupboard system, series A

2 Series B → 3 – 10

3 Shelves, usable depth 42 cm; 1.37 m wide

4 Slide-out shelf with telescopic runners

5 Hanging rail for magnetic tapes, 49 single positions

6 Slide-out shelf for microfilm cassettes, holds up to 164

7 Slide-out unit for suspended files

8 Rails with suspended files parallel to the front

9 Pull-out shelf for diskettes, holding up to 190

10 Rail for centre-mounted suspended files

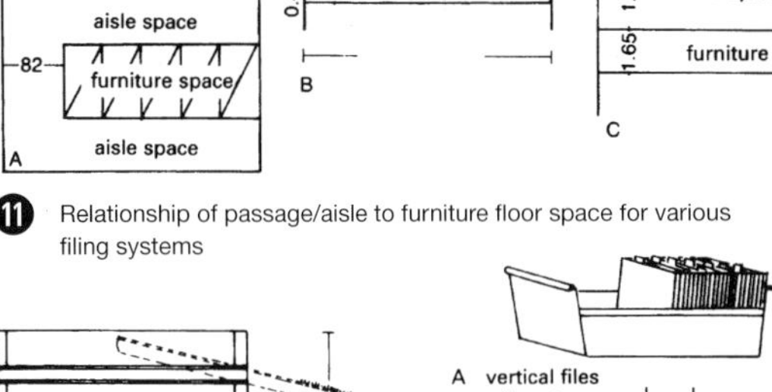

11 Relationship of passage/aisle to furniture floor space for various filing systems

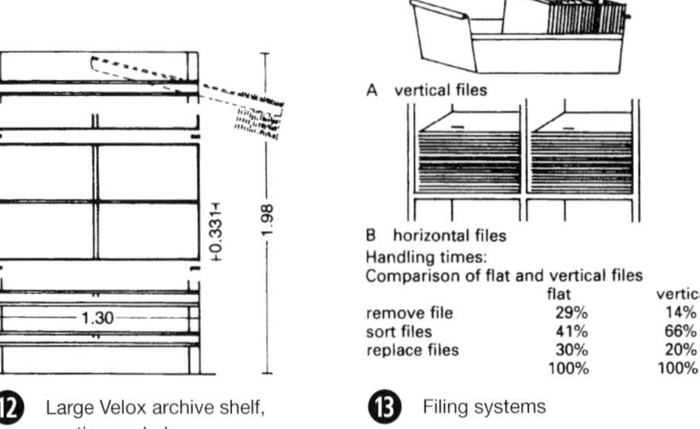

1.30
1.98
A vertical files
B horizontal files
Handling times:
Comparison of flat and vertical files
flat vertical
remove file 29% 14%
sort files 41% 66%
replace files 30% 20%
100% 100%

12 Large Velox archive shelf, section and plan

13 Filing systems

Filing

Despite the application of new office technologies, the use of paper as the main information storage medium has increased. Until 1980, paper consumption doubled every four years. Computer-aided storage is increasingly used as information depository in office communication systems. Letters, texts and newspapers, which are described as uncoded information, will continue to be part of the paper volume.

Purpose: Clearly arranged ordering and storage of files within short walking distance and efficient exploitation of the space. Space requirements for filing systems (according to Ladner → 1). Increasing depth of shelves also increases the distance to walk between them.

L × W (filing furniture) = space for furniture
+ ½ L × W + 0.5 m = passage space
total space required = space for furniture + passage space

Deep filing cabinets are more economical. The relationship between furniture floor space and passage space for a vertical filing system using large archive shelves (Velox system) and for a horizontal filing system is made clear in → 11. Furniture floor space needed with vertical storage is 5.2 m^2, passage space 4.6 m^2 (100:90). With horizontal storage, furniture floor space 3.2 m^2, passage space 3.6 m^2 (90:100, ratio inverted). A horizontal filing system offers less storage space and the high shelves are hard to organise. **Vertical storage** offers a personnel saving of over 40%. Suspended files make about 87% better use of wall area than files on shelves → 15. Files can be transported with a paternoster lift. Workstations should include sorting shelves, small desk, chairs on castors.

The filing system should be centrally located. A favourable window centre-line is 2.25–2.50 m, ceiling clearance height 2.10 m (2 storeys of normal office space = 3 storeys of filing). The rooms must be dry, so attic and cellar are inadvisable. Continuous table → 16 + 17 with suspended files and writing surfaces combines workstations effectively. Trolleys can be used as writing surfaces, or for card index boxes. Mobile filing systems (Soenneken Compaktus system) enable a space saving of 100–120%) by eliminating intermediate passages → 18B Systems are not standardised and are adapted to the relevant requirements of filing systems, archives, libraries, stores. Take note of the higher loading per m^2 of floor area (→ Libraries, pp. 247 ff.). Movement of the filing system is manual or by a drive. The entire filing system or just parts of it can be closed with one hand.

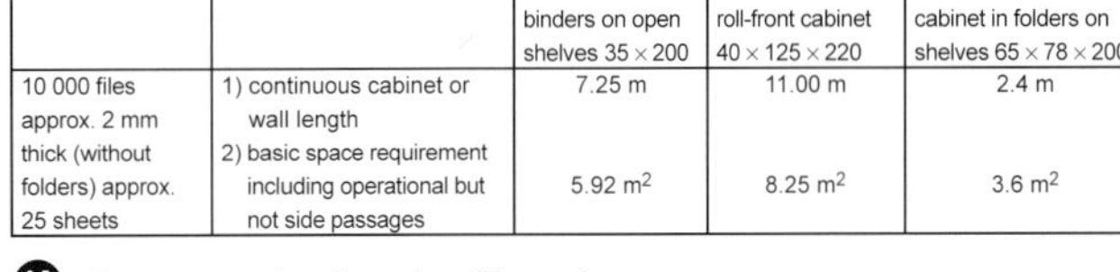

		horizontal storage in loose-leaf binders on open shelves 35 × 200	library storage in letter organisers in roll-front cabinet 40 × 125 × 220	combined vertical and suspended filing cabinet in folders on shelves 65 × 78 × 200
10 000 files approx. 2 mm thick (without folders) approx. 25 sheets	1) continuous cabinet or wall length	7.25 m	11.00 m	2.4 m
	2) basic space requirement including operational but not side passages	5.92 m^2	8.25 m^2	3.6 m^2

14 Space comparison for various filing systems

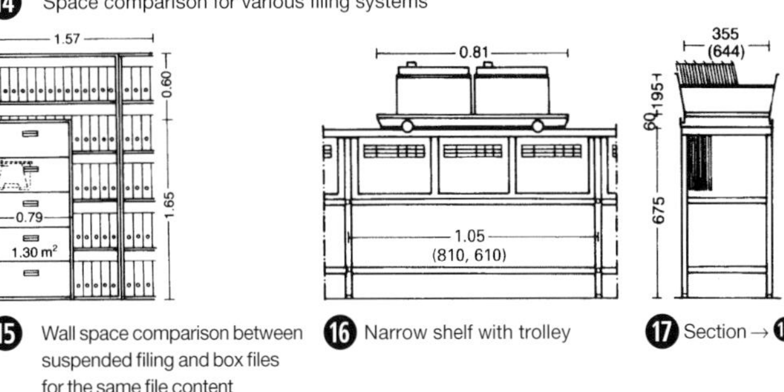

15 Wall space comparison between suspended filing and box files for the same file content

16 Narrow shelf with trolley

17 Section → 16

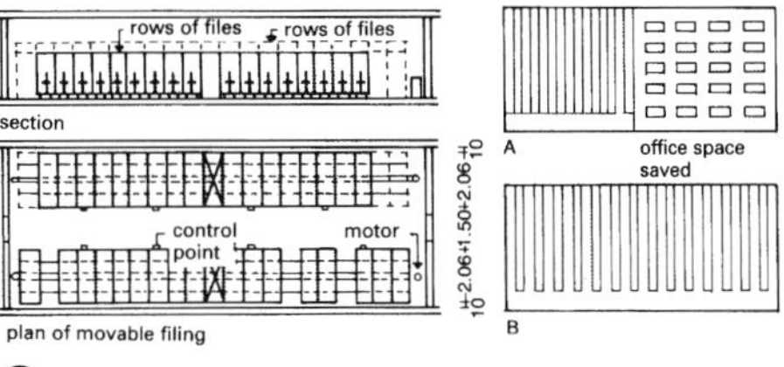

18 A = mobile filing system B = space comparison with normal filing cabinet

Administration and offices
OFFICE BUILDINGS
Structures
Tendencies
Typology
Until 1980
Since 1980
Space requirement
Computer workstations
Archives
Additional areas
Room typology
Grid
Access
Building services
Construction
see also: Libraries/Archives pp. 247 ff.

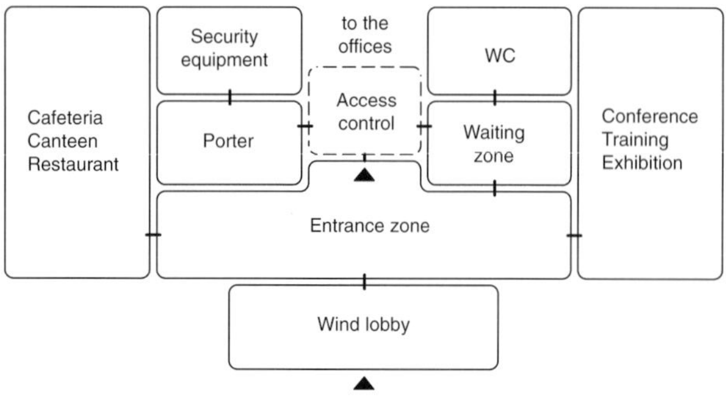

❶ Relationships of publicly accessible rooms to the entrance area and access control

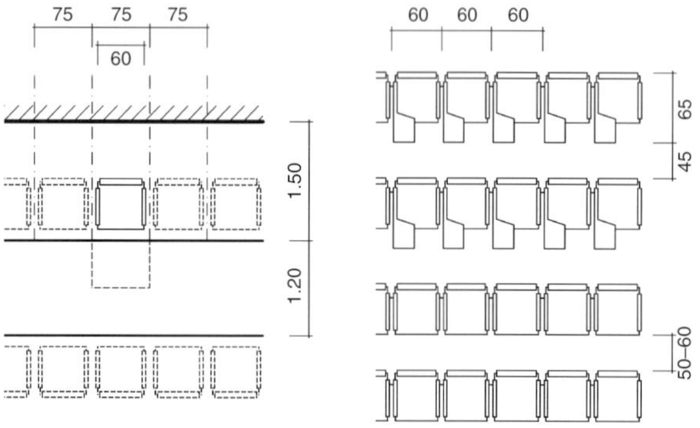

❷ Space requirement for seating in conference and training rooms

Area (m^2)		Range	Average	Total
Workstation	Immediate workstation	11–15	13	15.5
	Additional area (consulting, storage)	1.5–4.2	2.5	
Subsidiary areas	Sanitary facilities	0.6–0.8	0.7	9.0
	Conference/training	0.3–1.0	0.6	
	Archive	0.4–1.0	0.6	
	Stores	0.4–1.5	0.6	
	Canteen, cafeteria, tea kitchen	0.6–1.6	1.1	
	Entrance area	0.2–0.7	0.4	
	Supply and disposal	0.5–1.5	1.0	
	Post room	0.3–0.5	0.4	
	Server room	0.5–1.5	1.0	
	Garage parking	0–13	2.6	
Building	Construction area	1.9–3.8	3.0	10.5
	Building services	2.4–4.6	3.0	
	Traffic area	2.2–6.0	4.5	

❸ Average gross space requirement for a workstation

see also: Daylight pp. 485 ff.

Subsidiary and additional areas

The total space requirement per workstation varies between 23 and 45 m^2, depending on organisational and status requirements. This includes 2.6 m^2 car parking area in the basement, which is not included in the floor to space ratio. The tendency has been increasing since the 1970s.

Entrance area

Connection between public and working areas. The important functions are lobby, access control, information, visitor registration and waiting zone. Important area for the company's corporate identity – the first impression is decisive!

Conferences, training

Conference areas should be directly accessible from the entrance area. Provide sliding partitions (which can divide large rooms), tables, seating, presentation media, and also store rooms and a pantry for catering (these subsidiary rooms require about ⅓ of the conference area). Good noise reduction is important. A conference area requires about 2.5 m^2 per seat (without subsidiary areas). Space requirement ~ 0.3–1.0 m^2 per workstation.

Post room

Undertakes the distribution of all incoming and outgoing post and goods. Work positions (packing and sorting tables) should be sufficiently large so that distribution can be rapid at peak times. Space requirement ~ 0.3-0.5 m^2 per work position.

Archive rooms

Files and written documents, which are seldom needed but have to be kept (statutory storage requirements), are stored here to take up as little space as possible (purely paper archives rapidly take up 10–20 m per workstation). For this reason, microfilming and some electronic archiving are worth looking into at an early stage. Archive rooms should be designed for an increased floor loading of 7.5–12.5 kN/m^2 (for mobile units) → Archives, p. 252.

IT technology

Early planning of network technology is important. This will determine whether data centres or server rooms with or without constantly manned workstations are necessary and whether these should be placed centrally or decentralised in the building. These rooms should have a 70 cm raised floor on account of the large amount of installation, and should be air-conditioned. Access control is particularly important. Back-up systems should if possible be separated from the data centre in fire-protected areas.

Social areas

Canteens or cafeterias (→ Catering, p. 174 ff.) are mostly operated as units by outside companies. Location near the reception and outside the access control allows outside visitors in.

Tea kitchens should be as near to the workstations as possible and connected with communication zones. For every approx. 50–100 workplaces, one ~10 m^2 kitchen.

Toilets

Sanitary facilities are to be provided in accordance with the Workplace Regulations (→ p. 270) and separation between the anteroom with washbasins and the actual toilets is important. A good ratio is one toilet unit per 50–80 workstations. Space requirement ~0.6–0.8 m^2 per workstation.

Cleaning services

A cleaner's room should be provided on every floor, as a store for cleaning equipment and ideally with water supply and bucket sink. A central waste room, possibly enclosed waste collection rooms with separate collection containers and shredders. The caretaker should have a rest room, store and workshop in a central location.

Further special areas

Garage areas with maintenance and parking facilities for company vehicles; company sports facilities, swimming pool, sauna and kindergarten should be considered as required.

❶ Single-room office

❷ Group office

❸ Open-plan office

❹ Combi-office

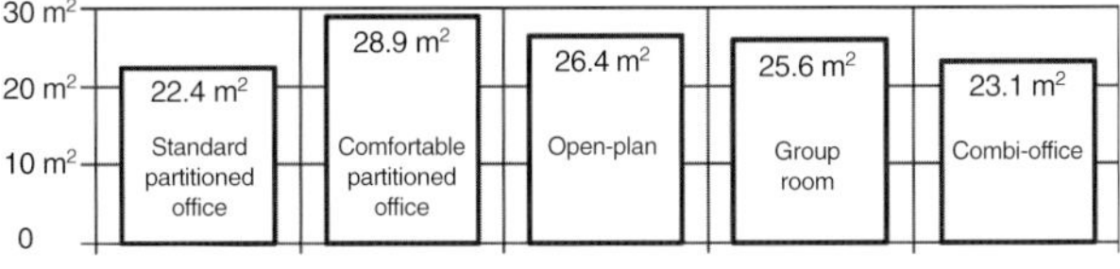

❺ In an investigation on cost-saving (by Prof. H. Sommer), five alternative room arrangements were set up, in order to obtain quantitative data about space requirements.

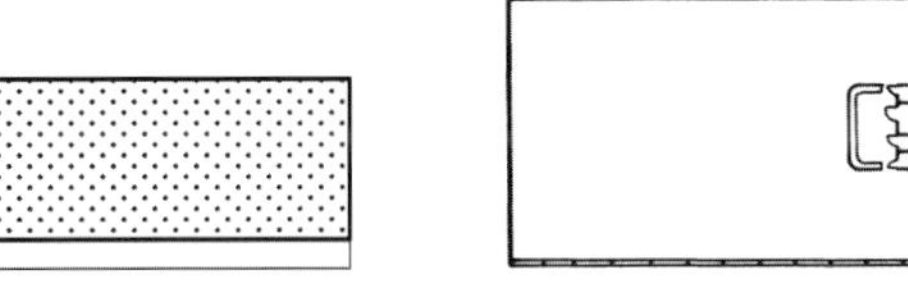

❻ Single-row layout, economical as very deep offices

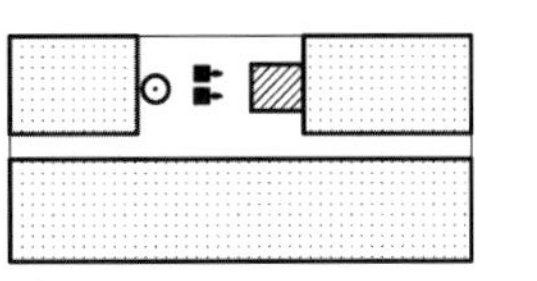

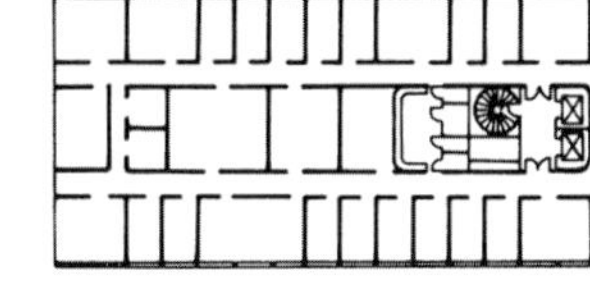

❼ Two-row layout

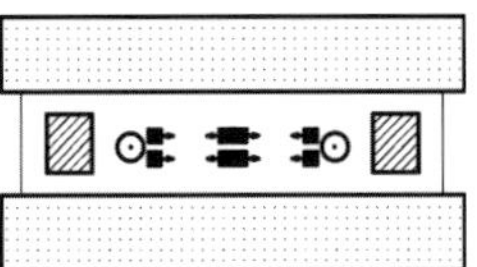

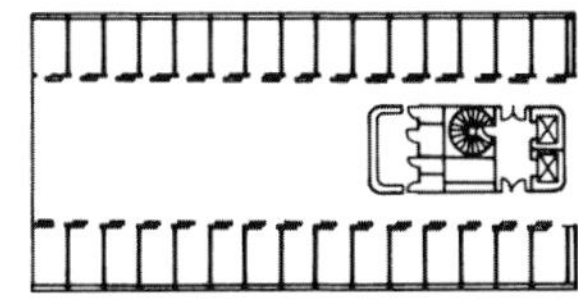

❽ Three-row layout

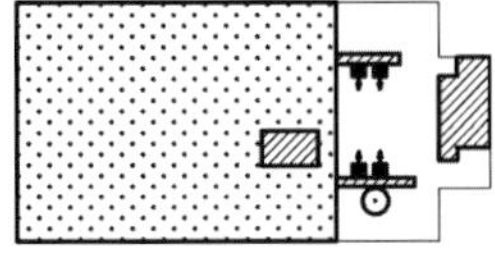

❾ Layout without corridor

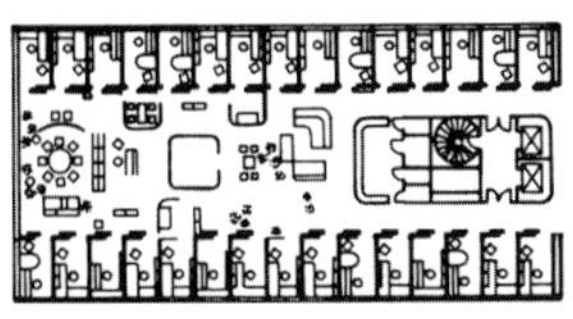

❿ First design for a combi-office: ESAB Head Office., Stockholm, 1976. Layout variants: open-plan, group room, single rooms, combi-office Tenbom Architektur AB

Legend:

 Lift  Main stairs 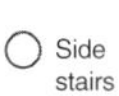 Side stairs  Core area  Group room  Small room

Types of offices

Offices can be categorised according to size and occupation into two types: single rooms and open-plan offices. All further types are variations and different arrangements of these basic types.

Room types

Single-room offices: Single and double rooms are arranged in rows along a mostly artificially lit corridor. Jointly used infrastructure occupies expensive window space in occupied rooms, because no furniture is allowed in escape routes. The most economical occupation, by two or three people, disturbs concentrated work. Single rooms hinder internal communication. This is still the most common form of office layout → ❶.

Open-plan office: A form of office developed in the 1960s and 1970s of the last century. Large-scale office landscapes with 100 or more workstations are made possible by artificial lighting and ventilation; they stand for free communication and openness. Economical cubic structures, however, have the disadvantage of high maintenance costs. This form is not very popular among users → ❸.

Group office: The experience with the open-plan layout led to the development of group offices with approx. 4–16 workstations; each office is used by a single team or department. This arrangement is preferred above all for creative, design or coordination and development activities with high internal communication needs. → ❷

Room systems

Combi-office: Very small single offices are separated by glass walls from the deep connection zone, in which communally used infrastructure is located. The combi-office was developed in the 1980s as an attempt to combine the advantages of single-room and open-plan offices. Each employee is provided with an individual workstation for concentrated work and a jointly used room in the central zone, with its glass partitions, encourage communication → ❿.

'Hot desk' office, 'business club': Certain functions are assigned to workstations. The users choose the suitable working location for the current activity (non-territorial offices). The personal area of the employee is limited to a mobile desk/cupboard unit. This type of office is only made possible by new forms of business organisation and technical equipment like mobile phones and laptops. Combined with teleworking or with a high proportion of travelling representatives, savings of 20–50% are possible compared with personalised offices → p. 234 → ❶.

Satellite office: Office space is located in decentralised locations, for example in residential areas near the employee. In the form of rented office space, satellite offices provide 'service stations', not only as branch offices of large companies but also varied sizes of office and infrastructure for small firms or self-employed people. The intention is to relieve rush-hour traffic and offer seldom-used office space like meeting, conference or training rooms when required.

Reversible office (Revibüro): This is actually not a type of office but rather a form of building which hosts functions of different office companies at more or less expense. The cost of equipment rises with increasing adaptability and compromises have to be accepted concerning office sizes and organisation. This type of building is mainly suitable for offices for renting to tenants who are not yet known → pp. 234, 235.

OFFICE BUILDINGS

Grid

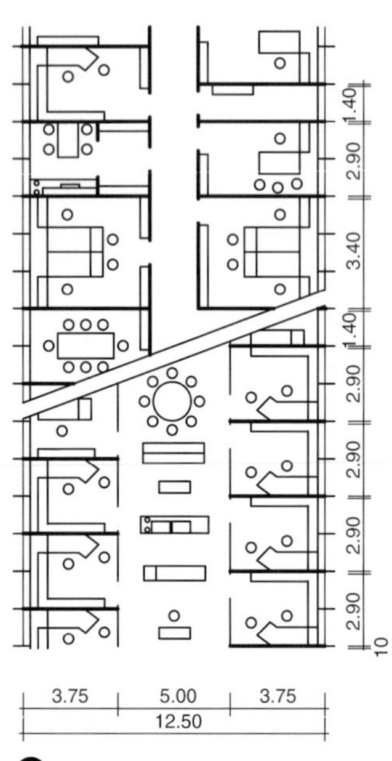

❶ Grid module 1.50 m, building depth 12.50 m, an economical form of building for single offices or for combi-offices; this provides a narrow communal zone and 10% fewer workstations at the window than with ❷.

4.30 | 5.00 | 4.30 | 13.40

❷ Grid module 1.35 m, building depth 13.40 m, an economical form of building for combi-offices, but for single offices this produces deep and badly proportioned rooms.

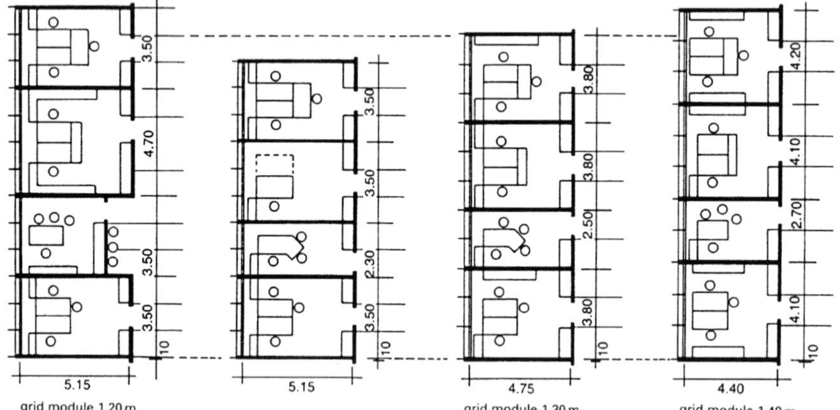

❸ Possible uses for various window axis dimensions

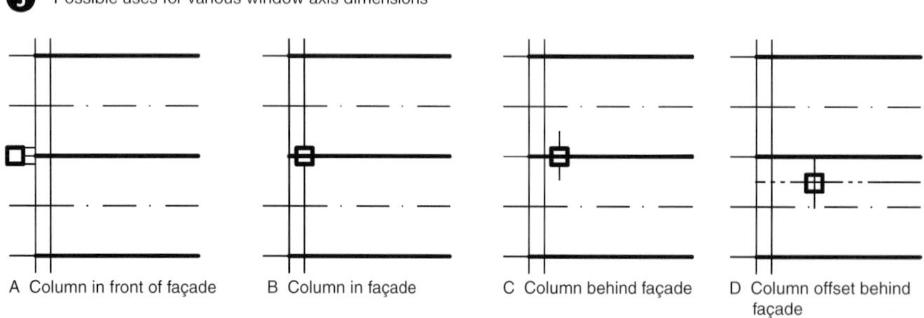

A Column in front of façade
B Column in façade
C Column behind façade
D Column offset behind façade

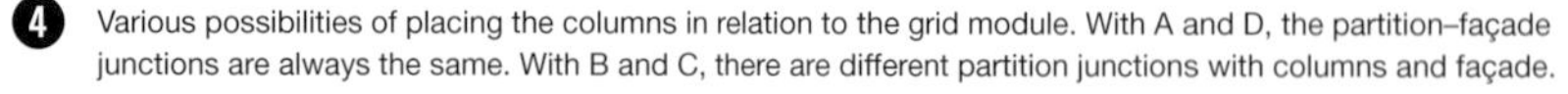

❹ Various possibilities of placing the columns in relation to the grid module. With A and D, the partition–façade junctions are always the same. With B and C, there are different partition junctions with columns and façade.

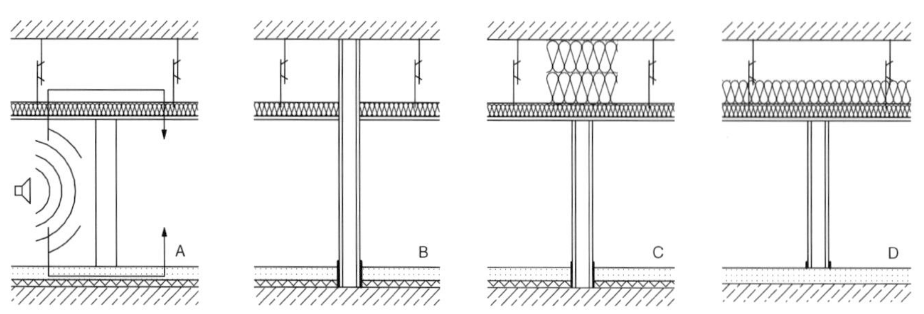

❺ Avoidance of sound transfer through junction elements above and below light partitions (Schulz → refs)

Grid module spacings define possible room sizes through the resulting spacing of columns and façades. The fitting out and façade grids must be the same in order to enable the partitions to connect to the windows. The structural grid can be offset against the fitting out grid. This reduces the problem of connecting the partitions to columns, but loses space in the rooms, which contain columns. Because of the different lifecycles of the building elements, an adaptable module dimension should be chosen. The modular dimensions, which have proved successful in recent years, are 1.50 m for single-room offices and 1.35 m for office types based on the combi principle.

Modular dimension 1.50 m

This is the economical module dimension for single-room offices consisting mainly of double workstations. Workstation depth 2.20 m (80 cm desk, 1 m movement area, 40 cm shelf behind). With 10 cm wall thickness, this gives 4.40 m clear room space.

The usual depth of buildings with central corridors is 12–13 m. This dimension is only of limited practicality for combi-offices.

Modular dimension 1.35 m

Room widths of 3.80 m (~18 m^2 usable area) enable:

- additional filing storage; two computer workstations with a depth of 0.90 m, as recommended by accident insurance companies; one drawing board or drawing machine and one desk; one desk and meeting table for four people. All usual office workstations are possible, offering high flexibility of use without moving the partitions.

Partitions

The junctions of light partitions demand particular attention to noise reduction. When glass partitions are specified, the required degree of sound proofing should be discussed with the user!

Façade

Vertical profiles in the façade, which lie on the modular grid, should be wide enough to connect a partition. A better solution is with sound-insulated profiles running along the façade. Take care with the opening lights of the windows.

Ceiling and floor

Screed bonded to the slab is good for sound insulation →❺, D with integrated cable ducts, because airborne sound is transmitted only to a slight degree.

With raised access floors and suspended ceilings, either vertical continuation of any possible partitions is to be provided or these elements are to be sound-insulating in themselves → ❺ B + C

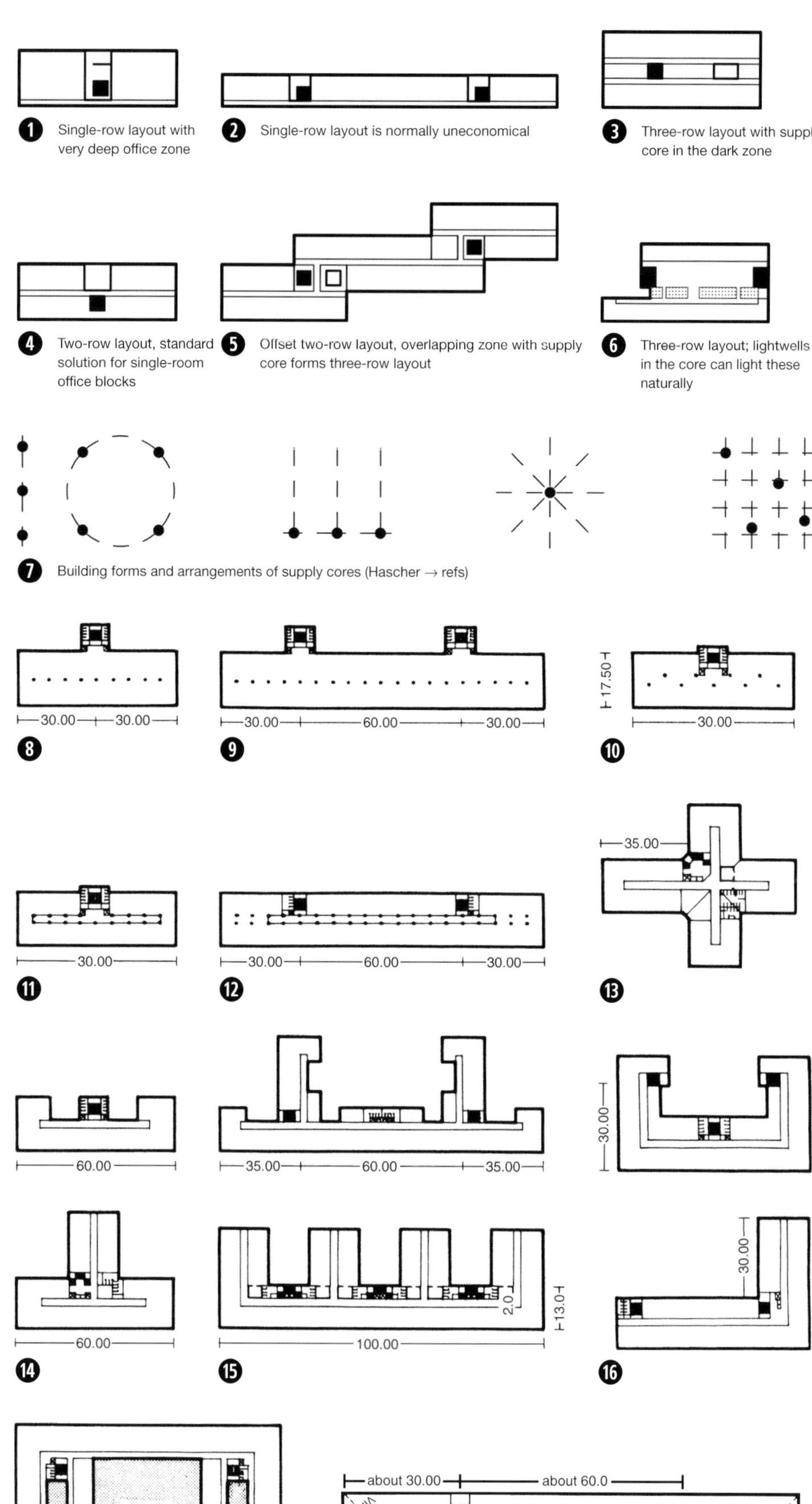

❶ Single-row layout with very deep office zone

❷ Single-row layout is normally uneconomical

❸ Three-row layout with supply core in the dark zone

❹ Two-row layout, standard solution for single-room office blocks

❺ Offset two-row layout, overlapping zone with supply core forms three-row layout

❻ Three-row layout; lightwells in the core can light these naturally

❼ Building forms and arrangements of supply cores (Hascher → refs)

❽ ❾ ❿ ⓫ ⓬ ⓭ ⓮ ⓯ ⓰

⓱ Building with lightwell

⓲ According to MBO 2002, every point in an occupied room must be ≦35 m from a staircase. This in practice leads to a spacing of the staircases from the end of the building of 30 m and from each other of 60 m → ❶ – ⓲. Take note of deviating stipulations in the current LBO!

Building concepts

Single-row layouts are uneconomical, and only acceptable with deep office rooms (daylight?) → ❶ – ❷.

Two-row layouts have mostly been used for administration buildings until now; single rooms and small offices are possible with daylight → ❹. The supply cores are situated in well-lit zones. The transitional form, three-row, is produced by offsetting the two-row layout in the supply area → ❺.

Three-row layouts (typical of office high-rise) → ❸ + ❻
A large supply zone at the centre of the building is normally practical only for high-rise buildings (greater proportion of vertical transport). Daylight can mostly be exploited into a room depth of about 7.00 m. New daylight systems for the deflection and transport of light (prisms, reflectors → p. 499), exploit the available daylight still better. Lightwells can illuminate the centre of three-row buildings naturally → ❻.

Building alignment

Compass orientation is variously estimated. According to Rosenauer, 90% of all office buildings in the USA have a main axis E/W, because the deeply penetrating morning and evening sun is a disturbance. Sun from the south can be shaded more easily with sun blinds. According to Joedicke (→ refs), the main axis in the N/S alignment is to ensure sunlight through all rooms. North-facing rooms are acceptable only for layouts without a corridor.

Access systems

Fixed points are sanitary facilities, stairwells, lift shafts etc., situated at maximum spacings defined in the building regulations → ❽ – ⓬. The arrangement of these determines urban development's building structure → ❼ – ⓰. For combined use units of less than 400 m^2, the corridors are not subject to the requirements for escape routes.

Administration and offices

OFFICE BUILDINGS
Structures
Tendencies
Typology
Until 1980
Since 1980
Space requirement
Computer workstations
Archives
Additional areas
Room typology
Grid
Access
Building services
Construction

see also: Daylight pp. 485 ff.

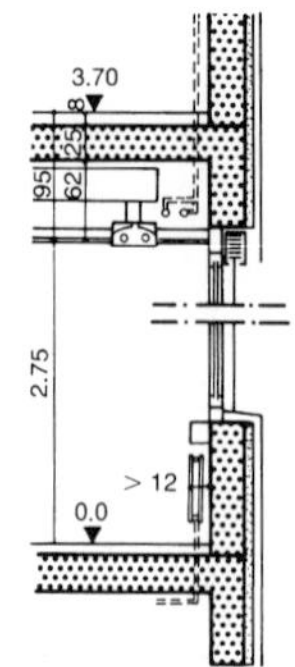

Storey height 3.00/3.10 m
Building with a low degree of installation. No suspended ceilings. Heating pipes in external wall. Electrical supply through windowsill or floor duct. Ceiling lighting supplied through ducts or standing partitions. Corridor areas for installation.

Storey height 3.40 m
Building with installation requirements, without ventilation system. In the ceiling void (h = 32 cm): electric cables and heating and water pipework. Installation ducts in the corridor.

Storey height 3.70 m
Building with air-conditioning system. A ceiling void of min. 50 cm is recommended for air-conditioned offices. Ducts along the corridor.

Storey height 4.20 m
Office with 3.00 m ceiling height. Crossing ventilation ducts require a storey height of approx. 4.20 m. All height-dependent building elements influence the ratio of building costs to usable office space.

❶ Storey heights according to the degree of installation (installed zone can either be in the ceiling void or above the bare floor slab)

Bare ceiling slab serves as heat buffer. Transverse ventilation through tilted windows and ventilation ducts over the corridor zone enable night-time cooling of the storage mass. If building elements are additionally temperature-regulated through heating or cooling pipework, then it is called building element activation. The system saves energy but reacts sluggishly and is not individually controllable.

Bare ceiling slab serves as heat buffer. Underfloor convector with air supply from outside serves to heat or cool (for which a fan is required). The system is individually controllable only to a limited degree because the heating and cooling medium flows in the same circuit.

Bare ceiling slab serves as heat buffer. Underfloor convector serves for heating. Cooling convectors in the cupboards cool warm air under the ceiling and lead it back to the floor area of the room (without fans). The system can be well controlled individually but requires a double system of pipework.

❷ Alternatives to air conditioning of offices: saving of storey height through reduction of the supply cross-sections (water instead of air)

Air conditioning

Two fifths of the operating costs of an administrative building are energy costs. The energy required for cooling in the summer is considerably higher than for heating in the winter.

The room temperature should be min. 19°C and max. 26°C (legal interpretation of the Workplace Regulations). The construction and alignment of the building are decisive for the energy consumption to provide air conditioning and light. Building elements which store heat, double façades and light deflection systems reduce energy consumption.

Fully air-conditioned rooms

The gross built volume and the total construction costs for air-conditioned buildings are 1.3–1.5 times higher than for buildings without air conditioning → ❶.

Gentle cooling → ❷ – ❸

In order to reduce peaks of energy consumption, large areas of solid building elements should be in direct contact with rooms as heat buffers. Ceilings are particularly suitable for this purpose because the partitions should normally be easy to relocate. A further development is building element cooling, e.g. capillary tube mats with refrigerant flowing through. Radiant ceilings work without the buffer effect of heavy building elements. Further savings of energy can be achieved with geothermal heat exchangers, which can pre-warm or cool the air supply to ventilation plant or passively heated halls by making use of the constant temperature underground. In order to achieve better regulation capability, there are suitable systems which regulate the temperature of the air supply with convectors. The radiant heating capacity of a building element in connection with temperature-regulated air supply can provide sufficient heating (usable area can be gained through less floor or ceiling construction). The cost of air-conditioning systems with building element cooling are not more than conventional air-conditioning systems. Advantages: no draughts, no noise, reduction of the investment and operating costs (water has 1000 × less pumped volume than air for the same performance, closed circuit, heat reclamation), reduction of the supply cross-sections (water instead of air) and size of the building's energy control room.

Floor construction	Floor construction thickness above slab (mm)	Duct type
bonded screed	30	open duct with distribution above floor
	55	duct under the screed with distribution above floor
	70	open duct with underfloor distribution
		duct under screed with underfloor distribution
	70	raised floor with underfloor distribution
	70–1000	cavity floor with underfloor distribution

❸ Floor installation dependent on floor construction

Fresh air m^3/h per person	According to VDI ventilation rule	According to US ASRE guideline
10	non-smoker with air heating, under 0°C outside temperature	
10–27		office
20–30	non-smoker	
26–34		
30–40	smoker	
34–51		
51–68		directors' room (smokers)

❹ Ventilation requirement for office rooms

element	lifetime
structure	50 years
building envelope	20 years
building services	7–15 years
finishings	5–7 years
technical devices, furniture and communications technology	Constant

❺ Lifetime of building elements

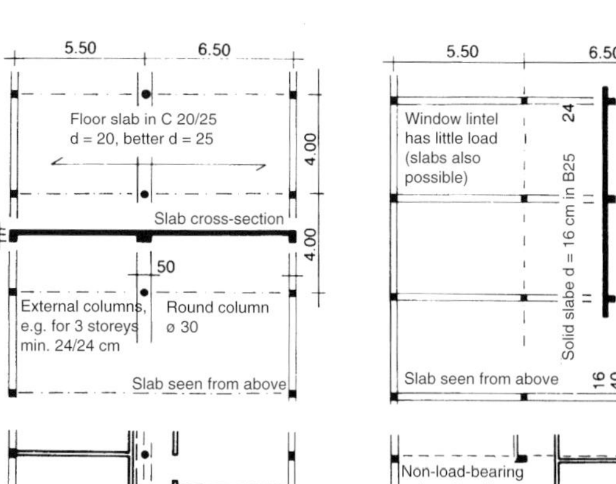

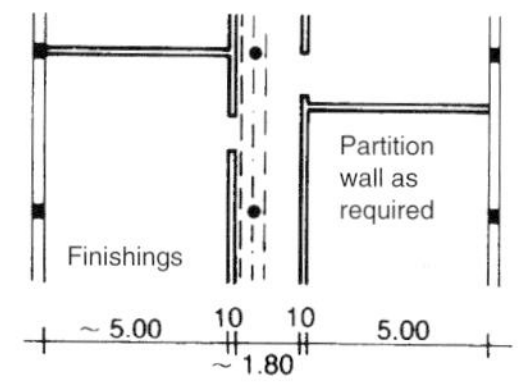

Floor spanning across building. Supporting beams running along the building. Central support beam and columns at the side of the corridor separate from corridor wall.

- flexibility and reversibility unlimited
- sufficient corridor width for clear passage between column and wall
- highly suitable if no suspended ceiling or for enclosed car parking with access route along the building

❶ Structural system, asymmetrical two-span beam

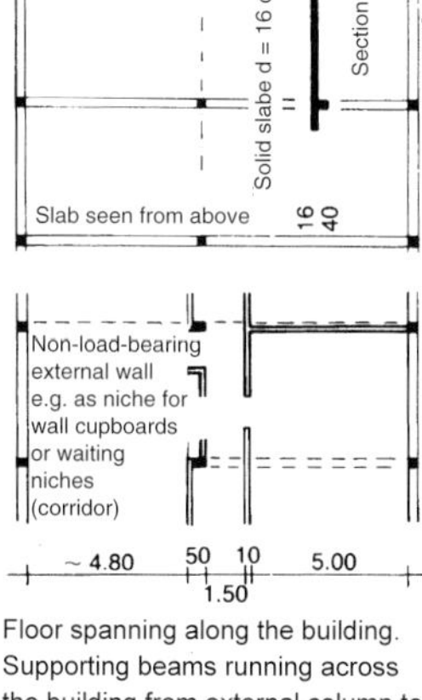

Floor spanning along the building. Supporting beams running across the building from external column to centre column to external column.

- flexibility and reversibility unlimited
- additional sound insulation measures required on account of insufficient density of floor (suspended ceiling, floating screed
- highly suitable for enclosed car parking with access route along the building.

❷ Structural system, multi-span beam

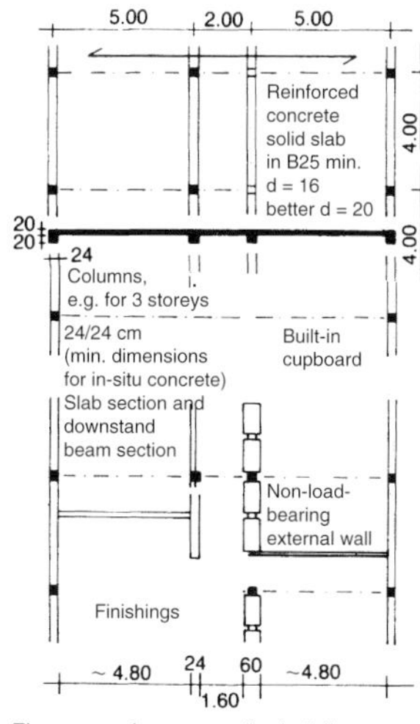

Floor spanning across the building. Supporting beams running along the building on both sides of the corridor in the middle span. The corridor wall can also be constructed as a load-bearing/ bracing wall to increase longitudinal rigidity.

- masonry corridor wall cannot be altered, so limited flexibility in room depth
- floor thickness min. 20 cm (impact sound insulation) if no suspended ceiling or floating screed
- not suitable above enclosed car parking
- construction of corridor wall as load-bearing is cost-effective
- construction increasingly cost-effective with greater building depth and longer spacing of columns along building

❸ Structural system, three-span beam

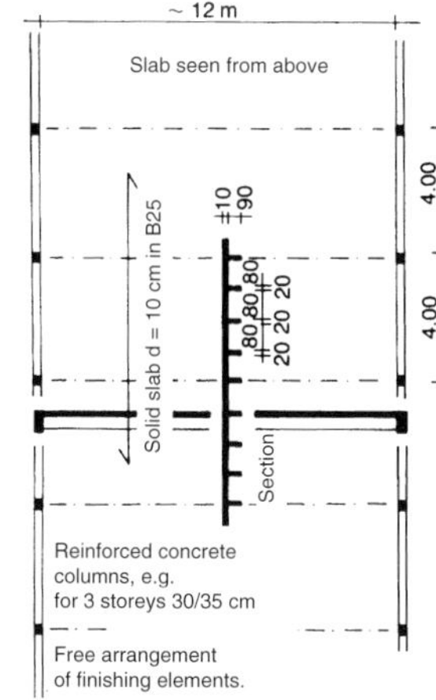

Supporting beams spanning across building freely from external column to external column.

- flexibility and reversibility unlimited
- suspended ceiling is required – services run across the building between webs, longitudinal arrangement in holes in beams (cut-outs) is not practical
- construction uneconomical overall, high supporting beams (also in steel), large building volume, only for column-free superstructures.

Reduced supporting beam height of 60 cm, structure susceptible to vibration and high degree of deflection.

❹ Structural system, slab acting as beam

Structure – influence of construction on the layout of offices → ❶ – ❹. Construction proposals for the cross-sections of two-row office buildings with the following loading assumptions: normal 5 KN/m^2, additional 2 KN/m^2 for screed (8 cm for floor duct and supply connections).

Ceiling height 2.75 m according to Vst regulation (enables the later installation of raised floor and deeper suspended ceilings). For predominantly sedentary activities, the reduction of the ceiling height by 25 cm is possible, but min. 2.50 m clear. Corridors and sanitary facilities are permitted to be 2.30 m high (this can be exploited for installation runs). According to Kahl (→ refs), the cost-effectiveness of a structure is less dependent on the optimisation of the individual components (e.g. pre-cast elements), and much more on their integration into a functional building. Differentiation between longitudinal and transverse spanning systems → ❶ – ❹. Constructive scope for decision-making via the example of a reinforced concrete slab with 6.50 m span. Criteria: almost identical costs; higher weight has influence on costs for load transfer and foundations; thicker slab has advantages through greater stiffness under differing loading (box-outs, spreader beams, point loads, various spans, various floor constructions).

Ribbed slabs: Only economical over longer spans (less self-weight, higher labour costs for formwork). Cutting through the ribs is not possible, due to lack of space. Supporting beams have the same soffit level.

Slab beams (double T or Pi-slabs): These are structurally advantageous for long spans. Installation should run parallel to the web; crossing runs should be carried out in the corridor → ❶ – ❹. The façade plane can lie behind, between or in front of the structural plane. Greatest variability with separation of construction and external envelope. Layout of columns, front face of façade, back face of façade, in front or behind, have no influence on the compartmentalisation of the façade or the division arrangement (grid, corner detail).

Internal columns → p. 240 ❹ A–D: If the slab cantilevers with a cantilever of c = 1/5 L–1/3 L, the span is economical. Bracing through walls acting as deep beams, storey frames and the provision of solid access cores and end-fixed side zones.

Building the walls: Solid partition walls can replace columns and supporting beams, or can be considered as deep beams to provide rigidity → ❺ – ❼. Not reversible, openings should be specified in advance. The use of lightweight (non-load-bearing) partitions has the advantage of potential relocation, but also delays decisions about room layout, even during construction (construction, studding – both sides 2 × 12.5 mm plasterboards approximately correspond to the sound reduction value of a 24 cm block wall of density 1.2 kg/dm^3, plastered both sides).

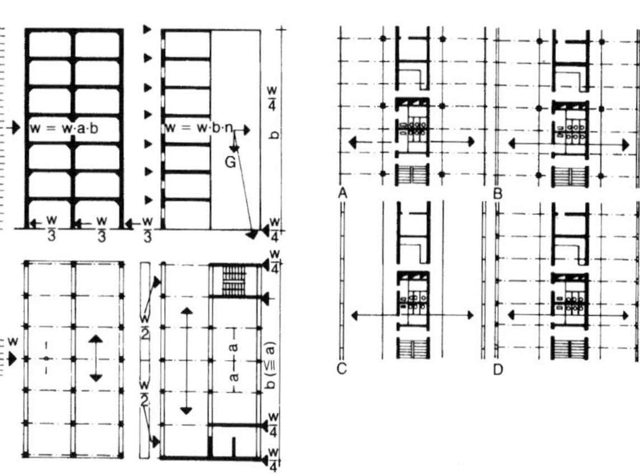

❺ Frame bracing, which transfers wind load into the foundations

❻ Bracing using wall panels

❼ Four ways of distributing the floor loading onto columns and core zone in three-row layouts

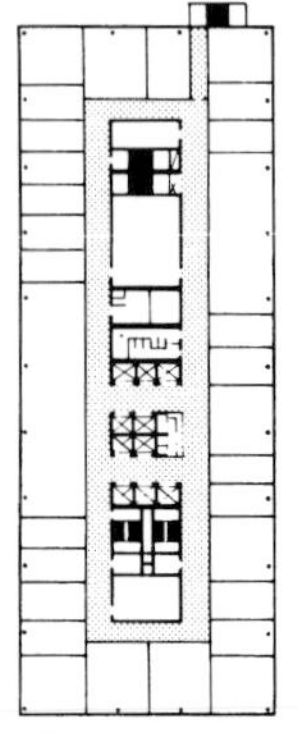

❶ Internal traffic areas and subsidiary rooms are purely artificially lit and ventilated
Arch.: Rosskotten

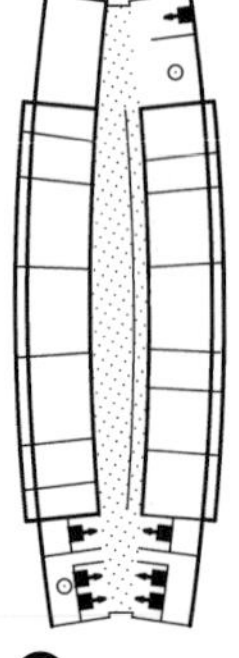

❷ Two-row floor plan with access at the external façade

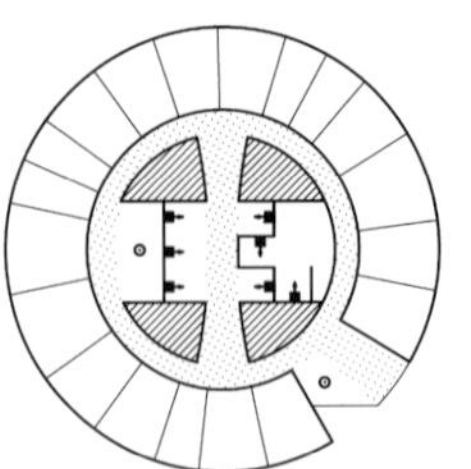

❸ Cruciform floor plan with bracing core and external emergency stairs

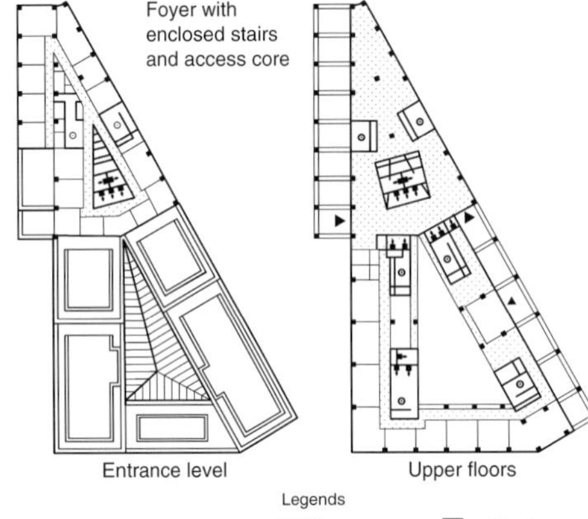

❹ High-rise building developed from the ground plan of the block, Daimler Chrysler Building, Berlin
Arch.: Kollhoff

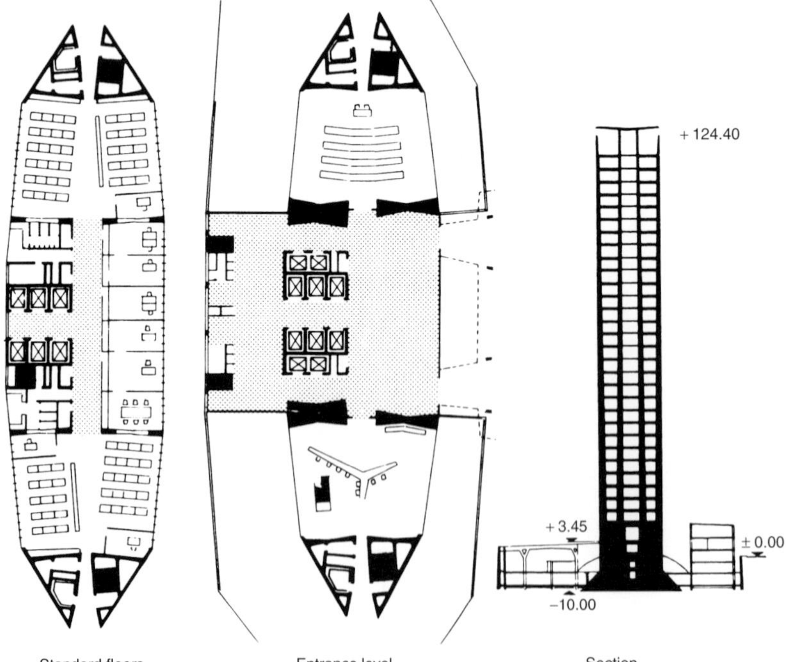

❺ The load-bearing construction forms the towers, between which pre-stressed floors are ≦24 m wide, but only 0.75 m deep
Arch.: Ponti-Nervi

Definition of high-rise buildings

High-rise buildings are those intended for long-term human occupation whose uppermost floor on one side of the building is more than 22 m above ground level.

Typology

There are two basic types of high-rise building:

1. The **block**, which has been designed as a high-rise building for economic reasons, and whose form has been developed from urban structure and planning, and from building regulations. Predominantly found in densely built cities, e.g. New York → ❹.
2. The **tower**, erected as a solitary building and mainly intended to provide a symbolic and prestige effect to keep the client and the city at the forefront of attention → ❺.

Use

High-rise buildings are a sign of extreme urban density and can also be seen as a town within the town. Use is therefore correspondingly varied: on the lower floors, public establishments (plaza, hall); and, above, offices, hotels and apartments.

Because high-rise buildings in Europe are mainly built as prestige projects, these are often company headquarters / office buildings with additional uses like hotels or apartments. In Germany, use as schools, hospitals or homes for elderly people is ruled out by the applicable regulations.

Location

In Europe, the construction of high-rise buildings is mainly determined by political decisions. Because their effect is decisive for a city's character, the city normally decides where and what type of high-rises. The integration of a high-rise building into the urban landscape poses many questions for urban development planning. The preservation of street spaces, extension of public access areas, connection to public transport, pedestrian circulation, the needs of neighbouring buildings to receive natural light and alteration of the urban microclimate all have to be considered.

Approval

In addition to the normal authorities, further specialised bodies are also involved in the approval of high-rise buildings according to location and federal state, e.g. the requirements of air-traffic control (Radar damping → p. 112), broadcasting authorities, state criminal offices and water protection boards have to be considered and their approval gained.

Frame construction in steel or reinforced concrete is the standard solution. Spans vary according to material and type of construction. Solid reinforced concrete slabs span 2.5–5.5 m, ribbed slabs 5.0–7.5 m, both with a maximum 12.5 m between main beams. Pre-stressed concrete can span up to 25 m with only 0.75 m structural depth → p. 244 ❺. The exterior wall should be a curtain wall in front of set-back external columns (take note of fire protection → p. 246 ❼). There are a multitude of mixed forms of construction such as steel frame with concrete floors. In areas at risk of earthquakes, special construction is necessary to prevent oscillation of the building.

The design of high-rise buildings is determined by the construction system and the vertical access elements. The ratio of usable floor area to building cost becomes ever less favourable with the increasing height of the building. Construction and access areas take up a large part of the plan area. The division of high-rise buildings into sections with transport to 'sky lobbies' by express lift, where the passengers can transfer to normal lifts, reduces the space required for lifts and the travel time → p. 246 ❻.

Cost-effectiveness depends on the 'sway factor', the ratio of maximum permissible horizontal deformation at the top to the total height of a building (max. 1:600).

The decisive factor for the design of very high buildings is the horizontal forces (wind) and not the vertical loads. 90% of horizontal deformation comes from the shifting of the frame, or 'shear sway', and 10% comes from the slant of the entire building. Frame structures without special wind bracing are economic only up to about 10 storeys. Conventional frame systems lead to uneconomic dimensions for more than 20 floors. Reinforced concrete frames are practical up to 10 storeys without, and for 20–30 storeys with, bracing walls, and higher than that for concrete tube and double tube structures. The cost-effectiveness of a building is determined by material used, suitable type of construction and application of rational construction technology → ❷.

An example of a structurally economical solution is the John Hancock Center, Chicago, 1965, by Skidmore, Owings & Merrill. The visible structural elements form the design concept. The tube principle considerably reduced the amount of steel required and the operational economics are improved by layered usage:

Floors 1–5 shops, 6–12 parking, 13–41 offices with flexible use, 42–45 services and 'sky lobby', 46–93 apartments, 94–96 visitors and restaurants, 97–98 TV transmitter → ❼ – ❽.

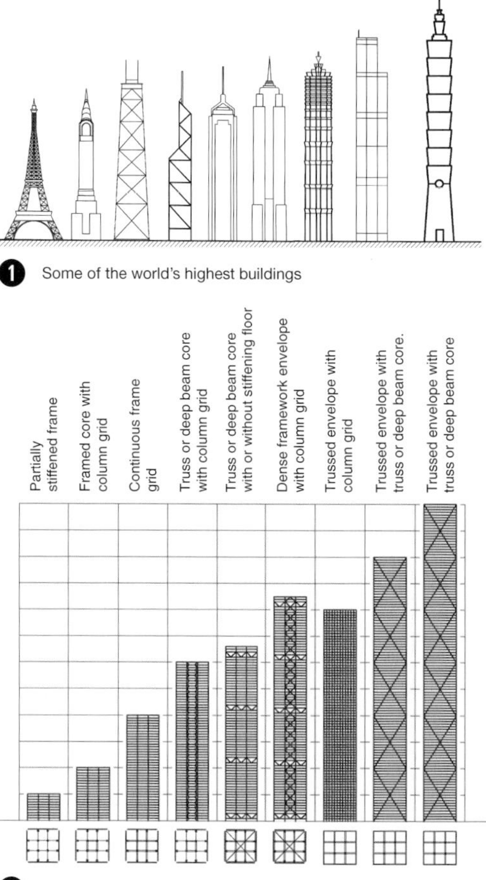

❶ Some of the world's highest buildings

❷ Range of cost-effectiveness for structural systems

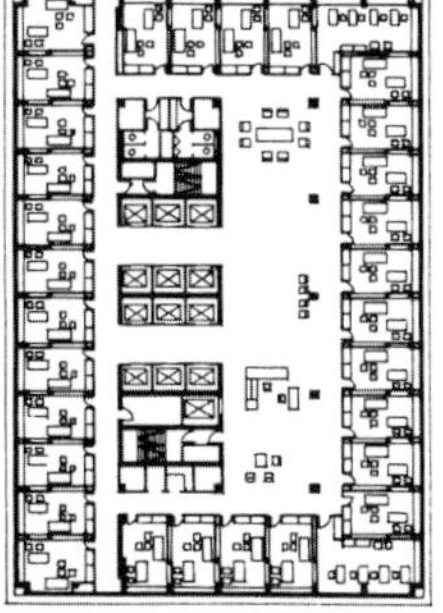

❸ House of Representatives, Bonn, 1969
Arch.: E. Eiermann with BBD

❹ Eccentric placement of the core zone enables different room configurations

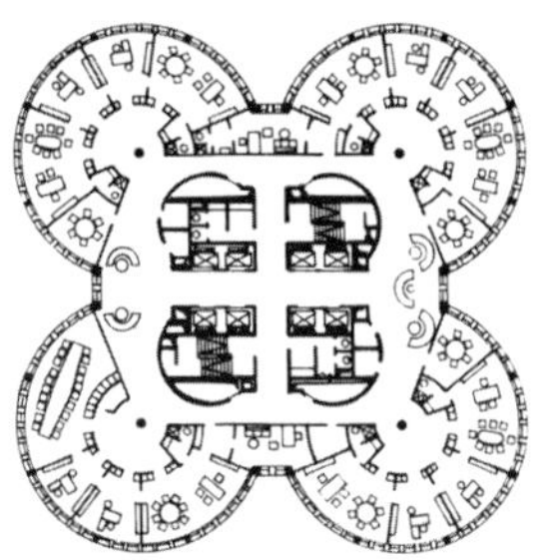

❺ BMW headquarters, Munich, 1972, standard open-plan floor
Arch. Karl Schwanzer

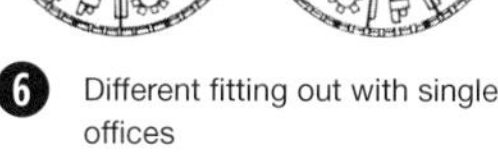

❻ Different fitting out with single offices

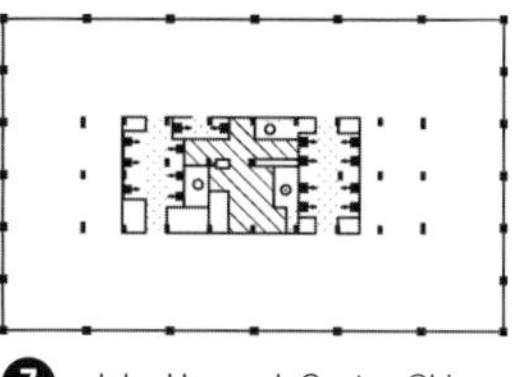

❼ John Hancock Center, Chicago, floors 13–14, offices with flexible use

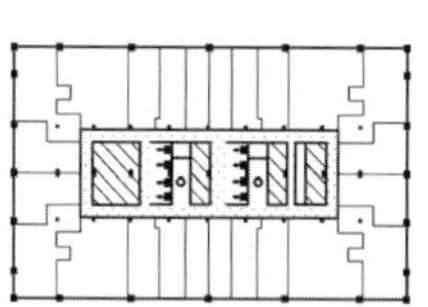

❽ John Hancock Center, Chicago, floors 46–93, apartments
Arch. Skidmore, Owings & Merrill

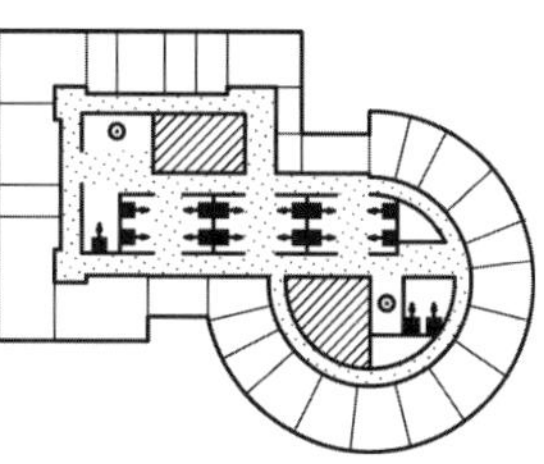

❾ Additive basic form

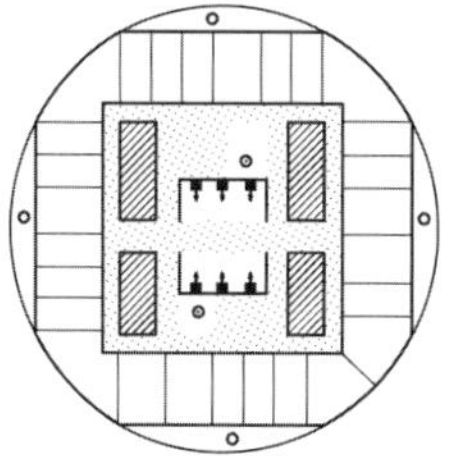

❿ Compact basic form

see also: Fire protection pp. 511 ff.
Lifts pp. 128 ff.

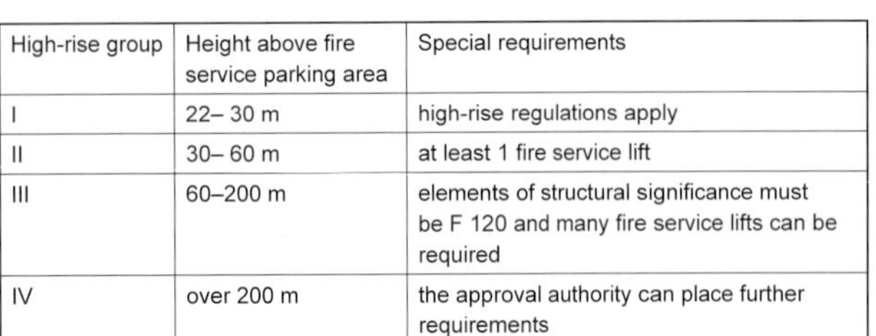

High-rise group	Height above fire service parking area	Special requirements
I	22– 30 m	high-rise regulations apply
II	30– 60 m	at least 1 fire service lift
III	60–200 m	elements of structural significance must be F 120 and many fire service lifts can be required
IV	over 200 m	the approval authority can place further requirements

❶ Approval requirements for high-rise building groups

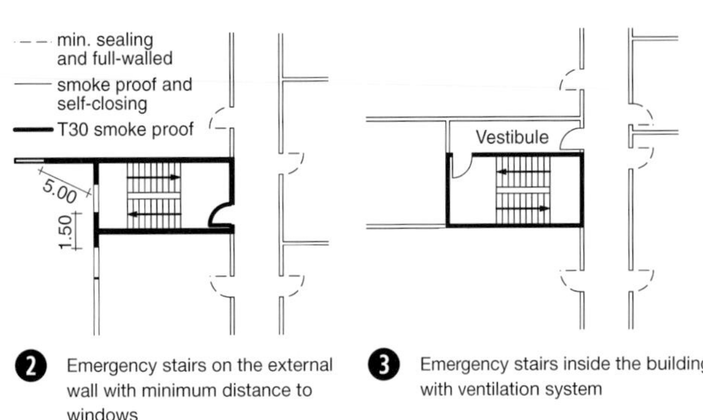

❷ Emergency stairs on the external wall with minimum distance to windows

❸ Emergency stairs inside the building with ventilation system

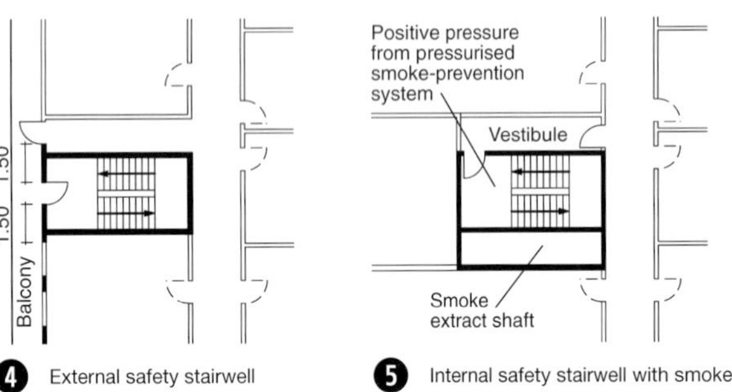

❹ External safety stairwell

❺ Internal safety stairwell with smoke protection pressure system

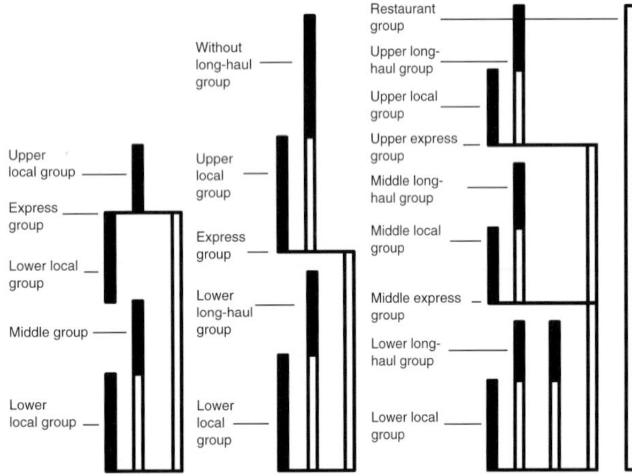

❻ Running a number of lift groups in the same shaft by arranging express groups ('sky lobbies')

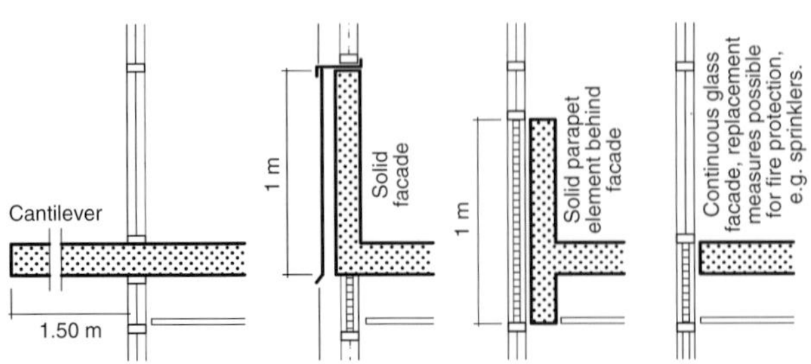

❼ Requirements for the parapet area in high-rise buildings to prevent fire spreading from one storey to the next

The requirements of the high-rise building guideline are mostly derived from the need for fire protection. Described here are mostly those relevant to the structural layout of a design. The exact requirements for particular building elements should be taken from the relevant state building regulations and the high-rise building guideline. Specific local regulations should be clarified at an early stage.

Escape routes

Escape routes are min. 1.25 m wide and should if possible lead in two directions, to each staircase. The maximum walking distance from each point of an occupied room may not exceed 25 m. Corridors with two escape directions may be max. 40 m long. After 20 m, a smoke-proof self-closing door must be installed. Branch corridors with only one escape direction may be max. 10 m long. If a second escape route (e.g. an escape balcony) is available, max. 20 m.

Stairs

High-rise buildings up to 60 m high: at least two emergency stairs must be available, which must be located opposite in two separate fire compartments. Their walking width must be at least 1.25 m. The wellhole must be min. 0.80 m wide in order to avoid having to lay hoses on the stairs. Smoke outlets must be provided at their highest point (5% of the floor area but min. 1 m^2). The exit must be directly into the open air or through a lobby without any fire load. In exceptional cases, one staircase can be approved for high-rise buildings up to 60 m in height, if it is a safety staircase. Requirements for the location of stairs → ❷ – ❺.

Lifts

Up to about 25 storeys, it is usual to provide one group of lifts with all lifts serving all floors. If more than 6 lifts are necessary, they should be divided into two groups.

In higher buildings, the lifts are split into groups. A group of lifts serves a certain number of floors with priority. When there are more than three groups, this system becomes uneconomic because of the high number of lifts in the lower area. High-rise buildings above about 200 m therefore have 'sky lobbies' reached by an express group (mostly 2–3) and further distribution continues from there. This enables a number of lifts in one shaft to provide the fine distribution → ❻.

Fire service lift

In high-rise buildings more than 30 m high, there must be at least one fire service lift in its own shaft, from where every point of an occupied room can be reached within a radius of 50 m. It must have an anteroom with a hydrant, which is large enough to enable the transport of stretchers to the lift. Access routes must be at least T 30 fire-retarding.

Façade

In order to avoid fire spreading from one storey to the one above, there must be W 90 A fire-resistant parapets at least 1 m high (fire spreading height). Alternatively, a W 90 A horizontal building element projecting at least 1.5 m from the façade can be provided. All-glass façades (also double façades) are permitted only with special approvals if particular protection measures (area sprinklers, mist extinguishing systems) can prevent the spread of fire to the next storey → ❼.

Window areas which cannot be cleaned safely from inside, must be cleaned from the outside by trained personnel using suitable apparatus → p. 101.

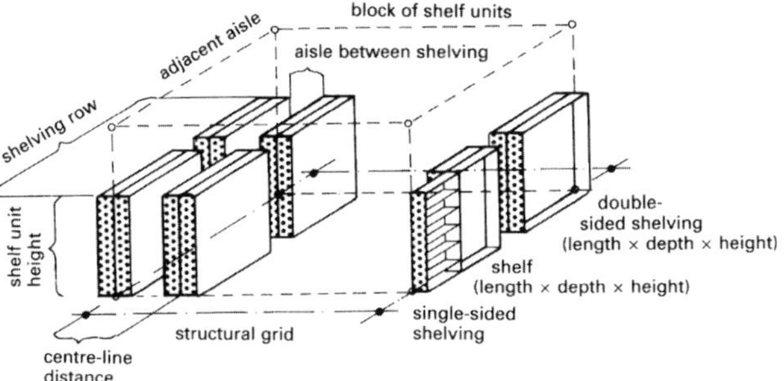

❶ Unscaled sketch to clarify the terms used in the calculation of areas for stock

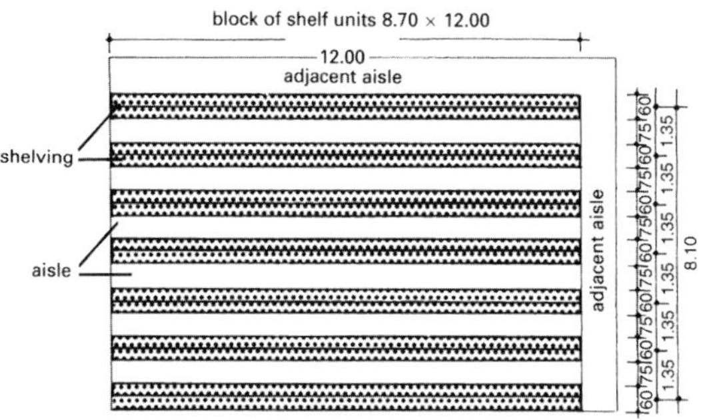

❷ Floor area for bookshelves in stacks (stores), which are closed to the public

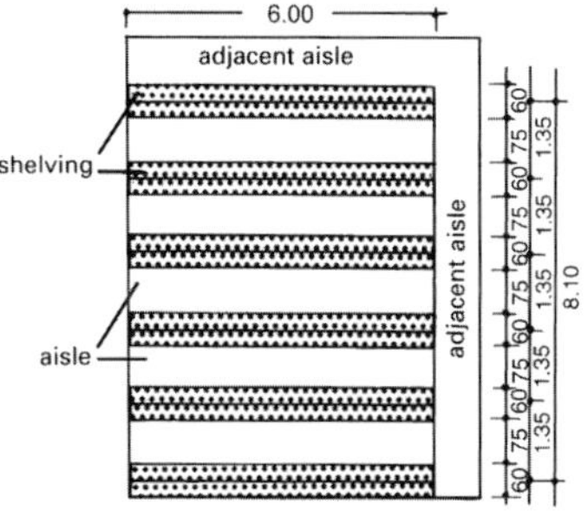

Area	Centreline distance (m)
store	1.35 (1.20) 1.44
self-service area	1.40 1.70
information area and reading room	1.60 2.00

❸ Floor area for bookshelves in self-service area, standard block 8.70 × 6.00 m

Library area/floor type	Stacks and self-service store	Compact systems	Reading room and self-service area	Administration
on floors arranged transversely	7.5	12.5	5.0	5.0
on floors not arranged transversely	8.5	15.0	5.0	5.0

❹ Load assumptions for floors (kN/m²)

	Structural grid							
	3.60	4.20	4.80	5.40	6.00	6.60	7.20	8.40
Stacks (St)		1.05	1.08		1.10		1.05	
Self-service areas (S1)	1.20	1.20	1.20	1.10	1.20	1.20	1.20	1.12/1.2 1.29
Self-service areas (S2)		1.40	1.37	1.35	1.33	1.32	1.31	1.40
	1.44				1.50	1.47	1.44	
			1.60	1.54			1.60	1.53
		1.68				1.65		1.68
Reading room areas (R)	1.80			1.80	1.71		1.80	
			1.92		2.00			
Workplaces (2.25) (W)	2.40	2.10					2.07	2.10
	2.40	2.10	2.40	2.10	2.40	2.20	2.40	2.10
Group workplaces (G)	3.60	4.20	4.80	3.60	4.00	4.40	3.60	4.20

❺ Suitability of common structural grids for essential functions of a library

Types of library

Public lending libraries → p. 250: offer a wide range of literature and other information, preferably on open shelves. The supply of literature covers all population and age groups. In larger cities, the functions of scientific and public libraries are sometimes combined.

Scientific libraries → p. 251: collection, acquisition and provision of literature on specific subjects for education and research, mostly publicly accessible without limitation.

State libraries: federal state and national libraries; collections, for example, of literature produced in the state or a region (legal deposit copies); publicly accessible.

Specialist libraries: scientific libraries for the collection of specialist literature and media on specific subjects, often with very limited group of users.

Components

Three areas in every library: user and reading area, store and administration. The space requirement for these areas differs according to the type of library.

User and reading area: With a good orientation system (signposting of routes, functions and shelves with easily read signs), the reading area with reading and working places should if possible be spread over as few floors as possible, also for ease of book transport; staggered floors should be avoided. Access should if possible be by stairs. All areas of the user and reading room should also be accessible by lift (book transport, disability-friendly). The floor in the user and reading area should be designed for a loading of 5.0 kN/m².

Traffic routes > 1.20 m wide, clear distance between the shelves – in public areas always fixed – up to max. 1.30–1.40 m. Entrance and reading room area separated by access control with book security system. If possible, only one entrance and exit. The access control should ideally be situated near the lending counter/central information.

Outside access-controlled area: cloakrooms or lockers for clothing and bags/cases, toilets, cafeteria, newspaper reading corner, exhibition room, lecture and conference room (which may be open outside library opening hours), central information point, possibly also card index and microfiche catalogue, online catalogue terminals, book return, collection point for ordered books.

Inside access-controlled area: reader information, bibliographies, online catalogue terminals, handing out and return of books only to be used in reading area, issuing of books in educational book collection, copiers (in separate rooms), book stock on open shelves, user workplaces, possibly access to self-service stores.

The provision of user workplaces in **university libraries** depends on the number of students and the distribution of the individual subject groups. Special workplaces for disabled people (wheelchair users, visually impaired), special work tasks (microform reading and enlargement devices, PCs, terminals, CD-ROM and similar: observe the guidelines for computer workplaces p. 236!) and single workplaces (cubicles, carrels, single work rooms). The arrangement of the reading places should be in daylight. Space requirement per single reading/working place 2.5 m², per PC or single working place ≧4.0 m². Traffic routes ≧1.20 m wide, clear distance between the shelves, which in public areas should always be fixed, up to max. 1.30–1.40 m.

Administration and offices

LIBRARIES
Basics
Fittings
Lending counter
Public libraries
Scientific libraries
Archives

DIN specialist report 13

	Distance between centreline of double shelves (m)	Volumes/ m standard shelves	Vertical shelves	Volumes/m double shelves	Space needed for 1000 books (m²)	Volumes/ m²
for stores closed to users (additional 20%)	1.20	30	6	360	3.99	250.6
		30	6.5	390	3.68	271.7
		25	6.5	325	4.43	225.7
		30	7	420	3.42	292.3
		25	6	300	4.80	208.3
	1.25	30	6	360	4.16	240.3
		30	6.5	390	3.84	260.4
		25	6.5	325	4.61	216.9
		30	7	420	3.56	280.8
		25	6	300	4.99	200.4
	1.30	30	6	360	4.33	230.9
		30	6.5	390	3.99	250.6
		25	6.5	325	4.80	208.3
		30	7	420	3.70	270.2
		25	6	300	5.19	192.6
	1.35	30	6	360	4.50	222.2
		30	6.5	390	4.15	240.9
		25	6.5	325	4.98	200.8
		30	7	420	3.85	259.7
		25	6	300	5.40	185.1
self-service area (additional 25%)	1.40	30	6	360	4.85	206.1
		30	6.5	390	4.47	223.7
		25	6.5	325	5.17	193.4
		30	7	420	4.16	240.3
		25	6	300	5.82	171.8
		20	5.5	220	7.63	131.0
	1.44	25	6	300	6.00	166.6
		25	5.5	275	6.53	153.1
		20	6	240	7.50	133.3
		20	5.5	220	8.17	122.3
	1.50	25	6	300	6.25	160.0
		25	5.5	275	6.81	146.8
		20	6	240	7.81	128.0
		20	5.5	220	8.51	117.5
reading room area (additional 25%)	1.68	25	6	300	7.00	142.8
		25	5.5	275	7.62	131.2
		20	6	240	8.75	114.2
		20	5.5	220	9.53	104.9
	1.80	20	5.5	220	10.22	97.8
		20	5	200	11.25	88.8
	1.87	20	5.5	220	10.62	94.1
		20	5	200	11.68	85.6
	2.10	20	5.5	220	11.92	83.8
		20	5	200	13.12	76.2
		20	4	160	16.40	60.9

Source: Schweigler

❶ Space calculation

Structural grid	7.20 m × 7.20 m	7.50 m × 7.50 m	7.80 m × 7.80 m	8.40 m × 8.40 m
n × distance between centre-line (m)	6 × 1.20 5 × 1.44 4 × 1.80	6 × 1.25 5 × 1.50 4 × 1.87	6 × 1.30 5 × 1.56 4 × 1.95	6 × 1.20 4 × 1.40 4 × 1.68

❷ Example of standard spacing for usual structural grids

Area	Volumes per shelf
stacks	25–30
self-service area	20–25
information area and reading room	20

❸ Volumes per shelf

No. shelves	Standard distance between centre-line (m)							
	1.10	1.20	1.30	1.40	1.50	1.60	1.70	1.80
4	3.83	3.72	3.62	3.54	3.46	3.39	3.33	3.27
5	4.38	4.24	4.11	4.00	3.90	3.81	3.73	3.65
6	4.93	4.75	4.60	4.46	4.34	4.23	4.13	4.03
7	5.48	5.27	5.09	4.93	4.78	4.65	4.53	4.42
8	6.03	5.79	5.58	5.39	5.22	5.07	4.93	4.80
9	6.58	6.31	6.07	5.85	5.66	5.49	5.33	5.18

❹ Live floor loads for various number of shelves and centre-line distances

Vertical shelves n	7	6	5	Assuming a format distribution of
Max. book height (cm)	25	30	35	25 cm 65%
Average book depth (cm)	18	20	22	25–30 cm 25%
Load per shelf (kN)	0.38	0.51	0.55	30–35 cm 10%
				results in a required load assumption of 7.5 kN/m²

❺ Floor load assumption for stacks of 7.5 kN/m²

Lighting in the user area: generally approx. 250–300 lx; reading and working places, card index, information, lending counter 500 lx. **Climate** in the user area: 20° ± 2°C, ~50 ± 5% relative humidity, air changes (flow of outside air) 20 m^3/h × no. of people; these values can sometimes be exceeded according to the weather. Avoid direct sunshine as UV and heat radiation destroy paper and bindings. Air-conditioning systems should be used sparingly because of the high energy consumption and thus high operation costs. Window ventilation is possible for low building depth.

Safety and security in the user area: **fire protection** is adequately covered in the regulations and requirements of the local building inspectors. **Burglary prevention** through motion detectors and burglary-resistant glazing and **theft protection** through book security systems, optimally **securing** unsupervised emergency doors through electronically controlled automatic locking on alarm. Mechanical securing of **emergency doors**, also with acoustic and/or optical signals, is not very effective.

The stacks (store) should ideally be situated in the basement on account of the more even climate and support of the higher loadings. 'Book towers' are inconvenient on account of the increased cost of air conditioning, transport and staff because of the limited space and flexibility. The largest possible continuous areas without steps are the most practical. Divide into fixed and mobile shelf blocks ('compact systems') depending on the structural grid of the columns (→ DIN specialist report 13). Mobile stacks can increase the capacity by up to ~100%. Floor load-bearing capacity for fixed shelves is min. 7.5 kN/m^2; for mobile stacks min. 12.5 kN/m^2 (→ DIN specialist report 13).

Climate in stacks: 18 ± 2°C, 50 ± 5% rel. humidity, air changes (flow of outside air) ≧3 m^3/h × m^2; filtering of harmful substances (dust, SO_2, NO_x etc.) is required according to location. The use of wall materials with a good capacity to retain moisture and heat can reduce the need for air conditioning. Slight air movement is useful for the avoidance of mould formation, particularly with mobile stacks (use open ends). Special collections and materials (e.g. slides, film or sound and data storage media as well as card, drawings and graphics) require a particular climate.

Floor load-bearing capacity in administration and book processing areas >5.0 kN/m^2; can be higher in the technical areas (workshops) on account of machinery (individual structural verification required).

Construction: Reinforced concrete or steel frame construction with a grid of >7.20 m × 7.20 m and room heights of ≧3.00 m have proved successful on account of the flexibility of fitting out.

Traffic routes: avoid crossings and overlapping of routes for users, staff and books.

Transport: Book transport carried out **horizontally** with trolleys (no thresholds, differences of level should have ramps for ≦6% or lifting platforms) and conveyor belts; **vertically** in lifts, conveyor belts (plan the route carefully, with sloping upward inclines; very low maintenance costs), container transport systems (mechanically programmable, combination of horizontal stretches and paternoster lifts) or automatic container transport systems (routes can be horizontal or vertical as required, automatic, mostly computer route control; high investment cost, currently very high maintenance costs).

Space requirement for bookshelves depends on the form of organisation, accessibility for users, type of shelves (fixed or mobile), systematic subject categorisation with corresponding display, format separation and construction grid (tables → DIN specialist report 13).

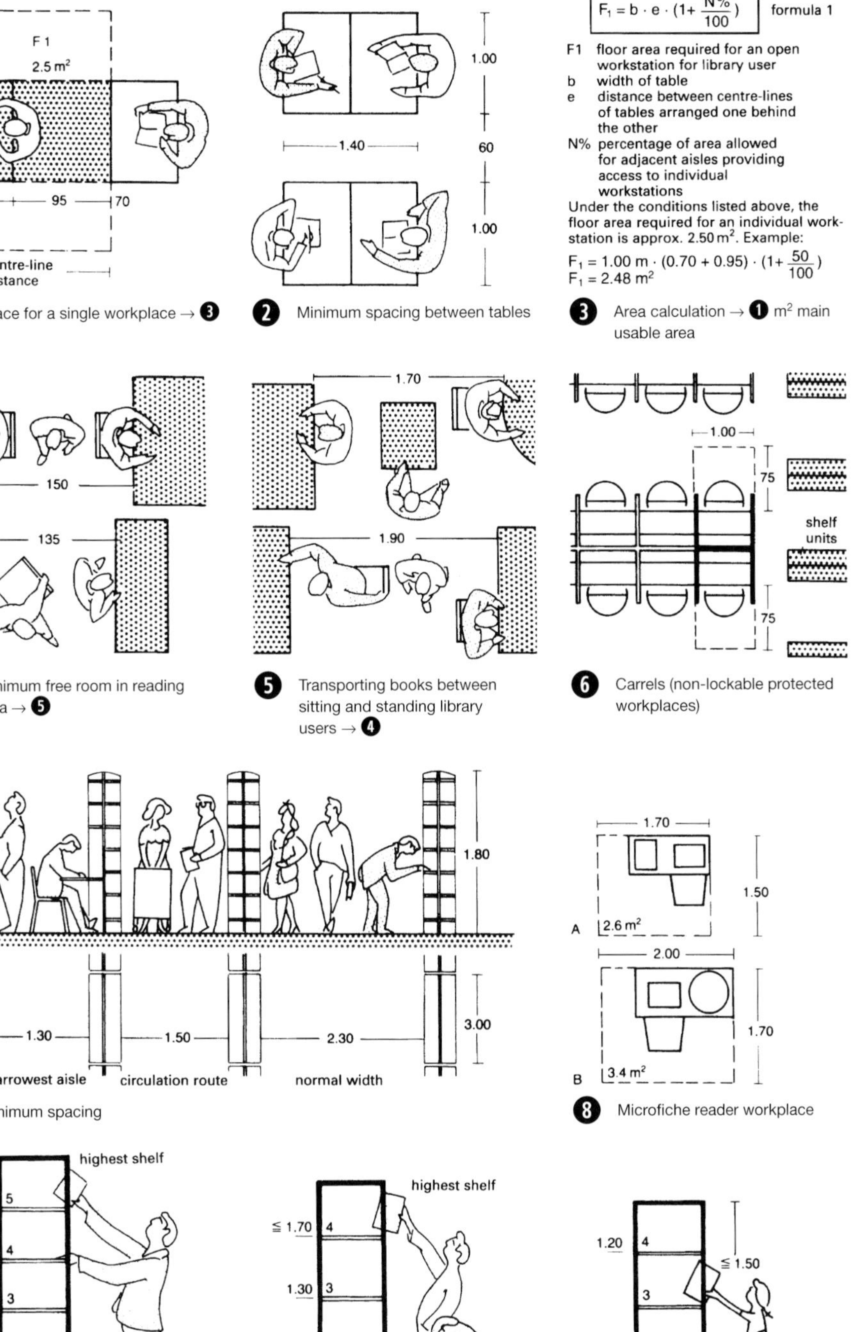

❶ Space for a single workplace → ❸

❷ Minimum spacing between tables

$$F_1 = b \cdot e \cdot \left(1 + \frac{N\%}{100}\right) \quad \text{formula 1}$$

F1 floor area required for an open workstation for library user
b width of table
e distance between centre-lines of tables arranged one behind the other
N% percentage of area allowed for adjacent aisles providing access to individual workstations

Under the conditions listed above, the floor area required for an individual workstation is approx. 2.50 m². Example:

$F_1 = 1.00\ \text{m} \cdot (0.70 + 0.95) \cdot (1 + \frac{50}{100})$
$F_1 = 2.48\ \text{m}^2$

❸ Area calculation → ❶ m² main usable area

❹ Minimum free room in reading area → ❺

❺ Transporting books between sitting and standing library users → ❹

❻ Carrels (non-lockable protected workplaces)

❼ Minimum spacing

❽ Microfiche reader workplace

❾ Shelf unit, five shelves

❿ Shelf height for schoolchildren

⓫ Shelf unit, four shelves – small children

System furniture for reference and lending libraries for all types of devices (telephone, PC, terminals, microfiche readers) and for all required cable ducts for network and communications systems.

Cupboards with special drawers for card catalogues, microfiches, slides, film, audio and videocassettes, compact discs, drawing cabinets for maps, drawings and graphics.

Shelving systems for books, magazines, media; mostly freestanding double shelf units (vertical steel profiles, shelves steel sheet or wood) h = 2.25 m, spacing of verticals = 1.00 m, depth of shelves = 0.25–0.30 m, but also extra depths, e.g. for atlases and newspaper collected editions; shelves adjustable for height min. every 15 mm. Height of the freestanding double shelves max. 5 × depth. Capacity of the shelves depends on the number of shelves per unit, calculated at 25–30 vols/running m (→ DIN specialist report 13). Shelf spacing in stacks > 0.75 m, longer in accessible areas.

Mobile shelf units (only permissible in closed stacks) can, if the column grid is favourable and the shelf blocks fit, result in a capacity increase of up to approx. 100%. Required: floor load-bearing capacity ≧12.5 kN/m² (extra costs compared to the usual 7.5 kN/m²).

Microfilm reader workplaces will be necessary in the future to make available microfilmed media (predominantly newspapers). The tendency, however, is towards digitalisation because this creates better use and access possibilities.

1,00 | 54 | 30 | 1.80 | 22,5 | 30 | double-sided | single-sided | 1,00 | 54 | 30 | 1.50 | 30 | 20

⓬ Bookshelves for adults 5–6 shelves, for children 4–5 shelves → ⓫

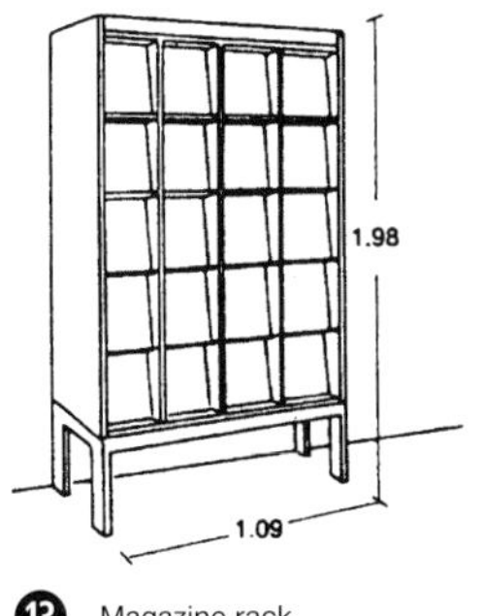

⓭ Magazine rack

Monitoring entry and exit
Permanent workplace for staff
Near to the administration
Counter
Issue/return of media. Book transport automatic and hidden it possible
Informing the users Explanation of IT catalogue
Near to computer terminals for catalogue research

❶ Demands on the lending counter/issue desk

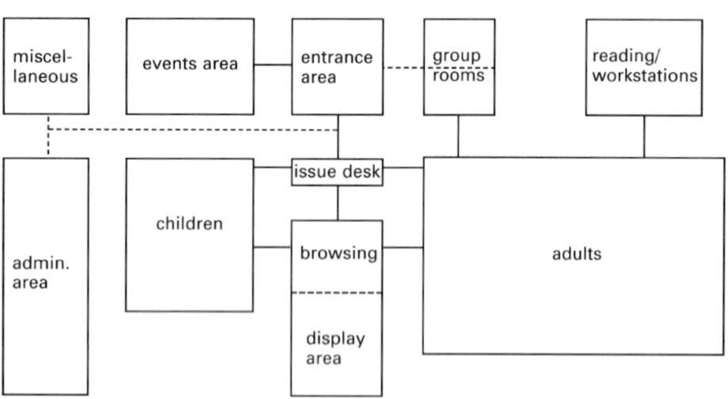

❷ Functional scheme of a medium-sized library

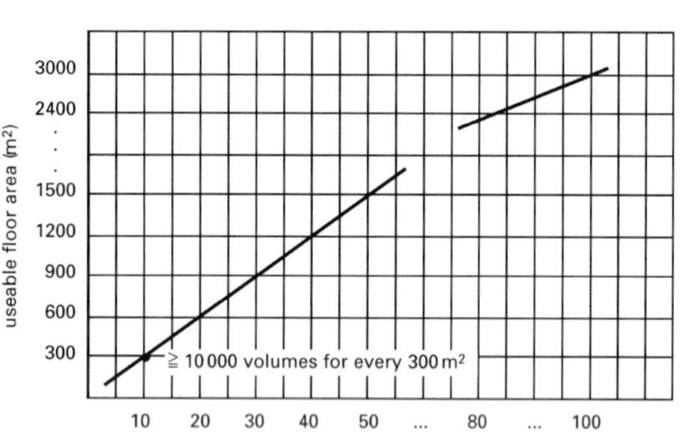

❸ Scheme: space requirement of a library depending on the amount of stock

Post room goods entrance/ ramp	Technical processing Reception booking Store, sort and distribute Packaging (remote lending)
Administration office workplace	Invoicing
Librarian Office workplace with additional shelf space for media ≦2 m² Parking for book trolley (50 cm × 100 cm)	Stock-taking Title registration Issue of signature Subject assignment Catalogue processing
Technical processing Bookbinding workshop ≦50 m² Restoration workshop ≦200 m² (for 4 employees) Material store ≦15 m²	Binding Labelling Restoration
Distribution Book sorting room ≦ 14 m²	Sorting Distribution
Stacks / self-service shelves	

❹ Route of book processing from delivery to lending

Lending counter

This is the interface between entrance areas and the normally accessible catalogue areas, the reading room with microfilm device, the stacks and the administration. Here the issuing and return of books takes place, information about the library is given and people are checked on entering or leaving the reading room. So there are many demands on the counter.

Mobile counters of combined units are mainly suitable for smaller libraries. Larger libraries, especially when the book transport systems are integrated into the counters, tend to prefer permanently installed systems. The height of the counter depends on the main activity undertaken → ❹, 95–105 cm is appropriate. It is better not to have any additional units above the counter in libraries mainly used by young people and children. The surface of the counter is subject to very heavy wear, so suitable materials should be specified, which can still look presentable after a long period of use (e.g. solid wood, linoleum or laminates coloured right through). Provide connections for computer and telephone, adequate lighting and a view into the open air (comply with the requirements of the Workplace Regulations, as the counter is normally a permanent workplace).

Public libraries

These offer general literature and other media on directly accessible self-service display. Systematic collection and cataloguing by content of printed and other media is restricted to a few large public libraries. Public libraries have no scientific collection duty or archive function, but are lending libraries, which normally have small stores or none at all. The users are children, young people and adults. Public libraries aim their range of stock and services at meeting the needs of the users. As a place of communication ('market place') for the population, they offer, in addition to the traditional lending of books, browsing zones, citizen's advice, information, cafeteria, listening to music, areas for sitting and events, art lending, and/or travelling library.

Stock ('media') can be not only books and newspapers but also magazines, brochures, games or new media (CD, DVD, video, PC games), which can be borrowed or used in the library. Rooms should encourage visitors to stay by being welcoming. Structure the areas into those for adults, children and young people with activity-oriented movement rooms, not separated but in zones with flowing transition. The space requirement is in line with the amount of stock → ❸. The target is two media units per inhabitant, but a minimum size of 300 m² usable area with 10 000 media units in stock. They should be large, connected areas, almost square and flexibly usable, and extending horizontally rather than vertically (less staff), capable of extension and with an inviting entrance area. The shelf units in the adult area will have five or six shelves (max. reach height 1.80 m → p. 249 ❿), and in the children's area four shelves (reach height ~1.20 m → p. 249 ⓫ – ⓬). Passages should not be longer than 3 m, neither niches nor compartments. Books are transported with a book trolley (L × H × W: 92 × 99 × 50 cm). Goods lift at the goods entrance, and in larger libraries also book transport systems. Floor loading in public libraries: 5.0 kN/m², in store-type self-service areas with denser stacking 7.5 kN/m², with compact storage (mobile shelving units) 12.5 or 15.0 kN/m².

Administration and offices

LIBRARIES
Basics
Fittings
Lending counter
Public libraries
Scientific libraries
Archives

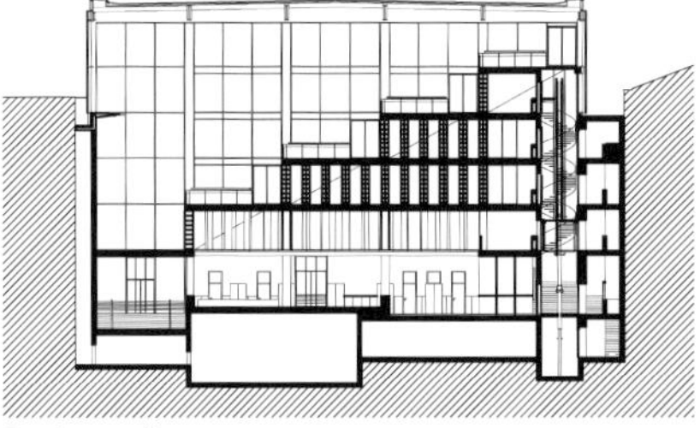
Section reading room

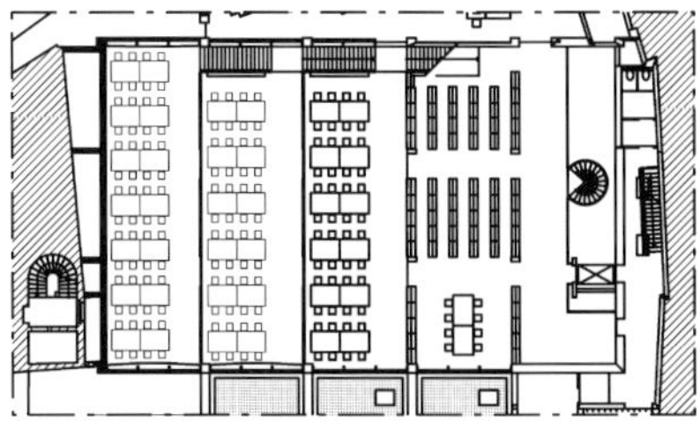
3rd floor reading room

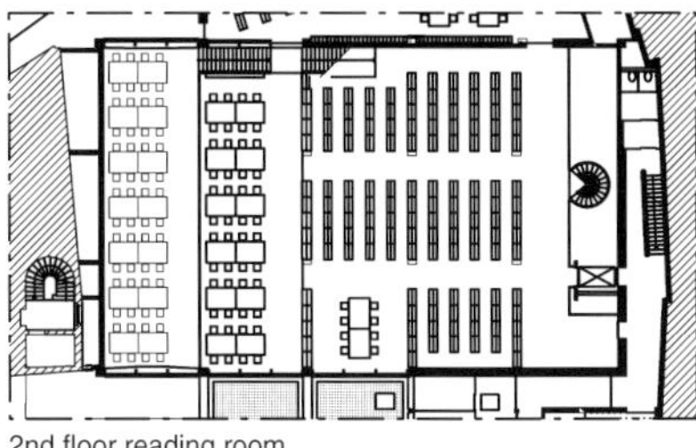
2nd floor reading room

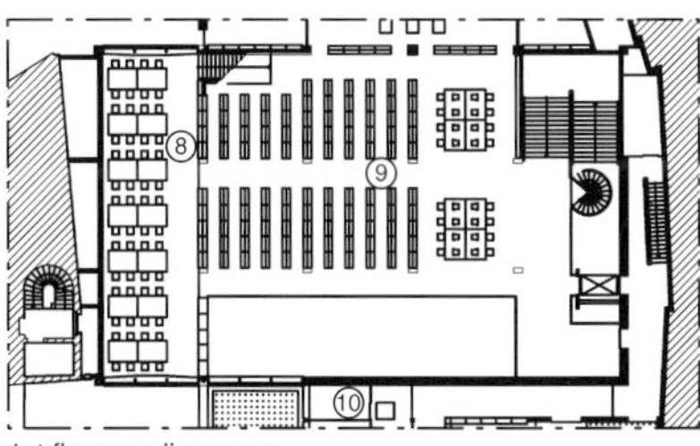

1st floor reading room

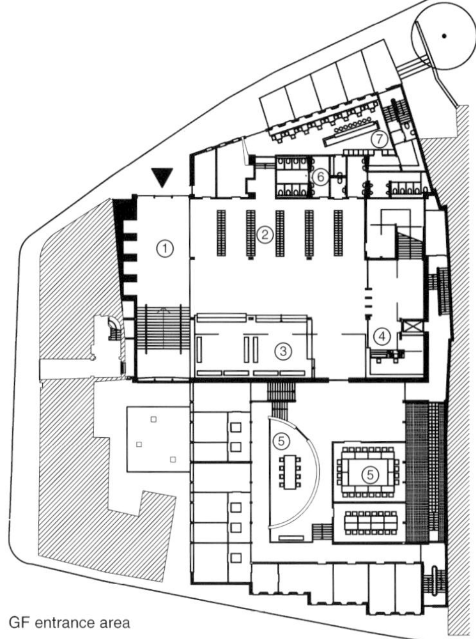

GF entrance area

❶ Juridicum Halle: specialist law library, Halle University, Wittenberg

Scientific libraries have always had a key role in the history of science and in the life of universities. They are not only a location for storing books, but places where books can be worked with. An important and decisive part of world literature has been produced in libraries. Their erection is among society's greatest building projects. Important architectural examples from the 19th century show what high prestige has been applied to the task (Biblioteca Laurentiana, Florence; Bibliothèque Nationale, Paris).

They collect and access printed publications and other information media for education and research, and offer it for use in reading rooms (stock which is not lent out) and also for lending from the closed stacks, the self-service shelves and, to select in the reading rooms, separately displayed teaching material or specially gathered collections for one term. As well as books and magazines, most other types of audiovisual media are collected, catalogued and available for use. The number of reading places is related to the number of students in the various subjects. Orientation is provided by systematic classification of stock by subject. The services offered include remote lending (obtaining literature from distant libraries), copying services and enlargement of micro-forms (microfiche and microfilm).

Example: Juridicum Halle → ❶ – ❷.

University libraries

These are single- or two-storey buildings: single-storey systems are centrally administered (book processing and services) and mostly have at least a few separate user areas in branch or specialist libraries. Two-storey libraries include a central library and an (often larger) number of libraries for faculties, specialist areas and institutes. Stock is often freely available in reading rooms, often in self-service stacks (shelving units spaced as in closed stacks) and in closed stacks, the different forms of display being mixed in most university libraries. The ratio of stored to display and lending stock is determined by the structure of the stock, and/or the organisation type or library concept, and often also the space available in existing buildings.

① Main entrance
② Lockers
③ Waiting area
④ Staff/supervision
⑤ Exam room
⑥ WC
⑦ Café, accessible from outside
⑧ Reading places
⑨ Bookshelves
⑩ Computer places

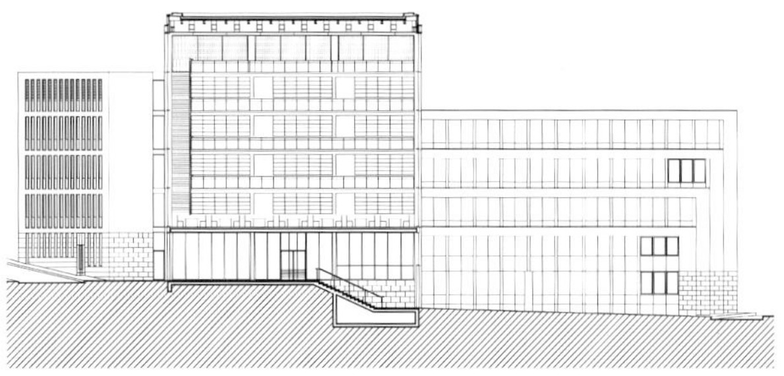

❷ Juridicum Halle, section

Arch.: Thomas van den Valentyn, Gernot Schulz

❶ Extension of the State Archive in Dresden, section through old building and new archive building
Arch.: Kister Scheithauer Gross

❷ The archive storerooms are arranged round the access and ventilation core. The room can be flexibly divided due to the three entrances. Pre-stressed concrete slabs enable thin floor structures with high loadings, so that space-saving rolling storage units can be used.

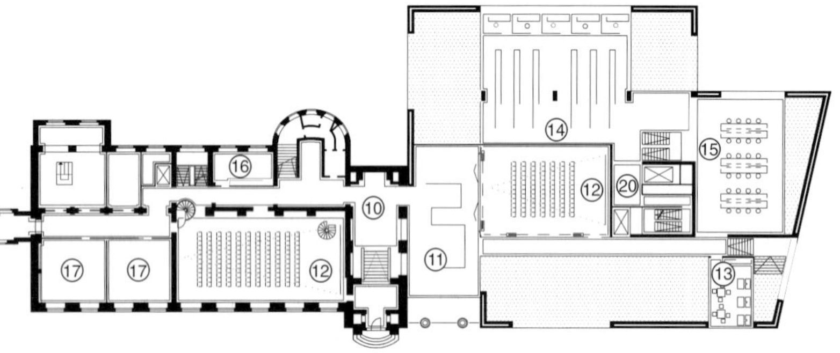

❸ First floor serves to connect to the old building and houses seminar rooms, cafeteria and reading room.

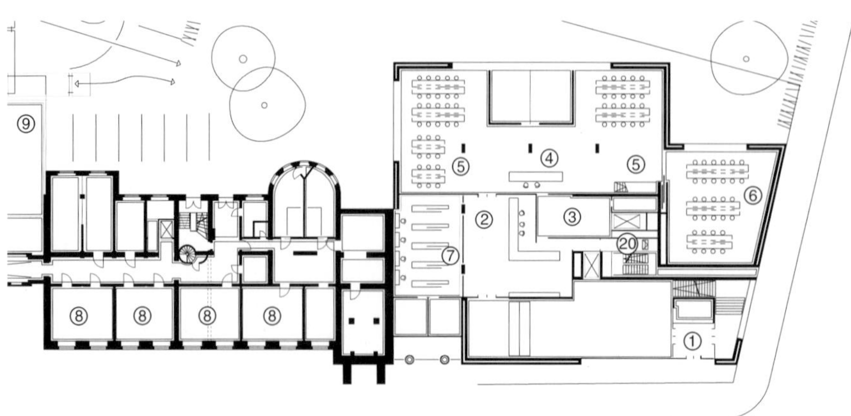

❹ Ground floor and first floor serve public functions. The foyer in the new building enables disability-friendly access and connection to the old building.

Basics

Archives do not, unlike libraries, serve mainly to make available written, graphic and audio media, but for their systematic cataloguing and long-term preservation.

In this function, they are often part of libraries, museums or universities. State archives keep all sorts of files, business records, maps, drawings and documents.

In order to be able to accept the rapidly increasing stock, suitable storage systems such as rolling shelving units or plan chests (→ pp. 237, 248) must be provided. The loading on the floor slab should be paid particular attention (→ p. 248). For the durability of the preserved media, the maintenance of a uniform climate is the most important factor, but full air conditioning has not proved acceptable on account of the high cost. Natural ventilation is the ideal, but also brings the danger of entry by air-borne pollutants. Systems without air conditioning need solid walls with the best possible diffusion values, and the temperature should be maintained by simple wall surface heating (skirting radiators).

① Controlled access for users
② Information, issue
③ Store
④ Supervision
⑤ Reading room
⑥ Map reading room
⑦ Search aids
⑧ Workshops
⑨ Delivery
⑩ Staff access
⑪ Display
⑫ Seminar/ lecture
⑬ Bistro/café
⑭ Self-service films
⑮ Film reading room
⑯ Post room
⑰ Director
⑱ Administration
⑲ Archive rooms
⑳ Stair and ventilation core

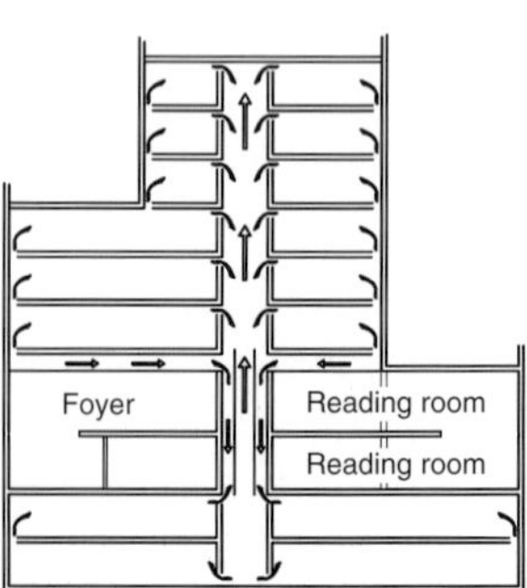

❺ Principle of source ventilation: prepared air is blown in through shafts and fed to the floors through ventilation blocks.

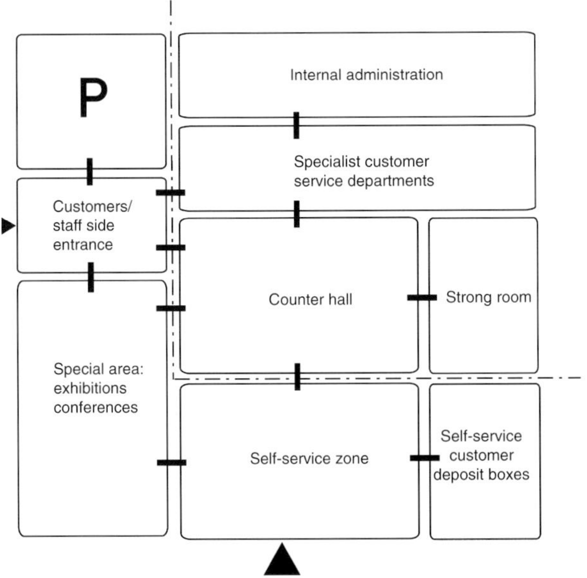

❶ Room layout for a branch of a clearing bank with customer business

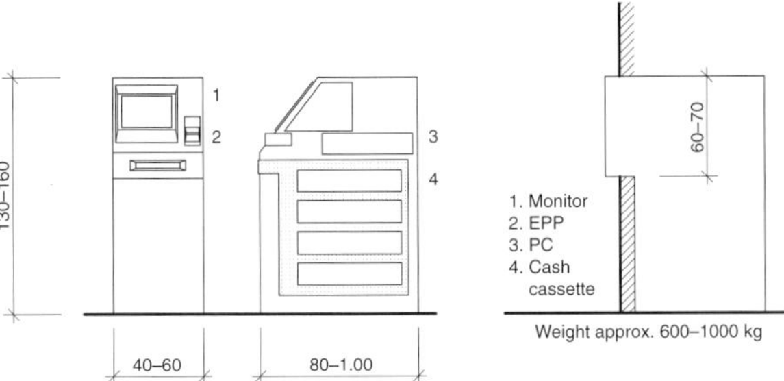

❷ Cashpoint

ATM cash dispenser:		**Statement printer:**	
height:	1.30 – 1.60 m	height:	1.10 – 1.30 m
width:	0.40 – 0.60 m	width:	0.50 – 0.80 m
depth:	0.80 – 1.00 m	depth:	~ 0.60 m
weight:	600 – 1000 kg	weight:	~ 150 kg

❸ Dimensions of cashpoint and statement printer

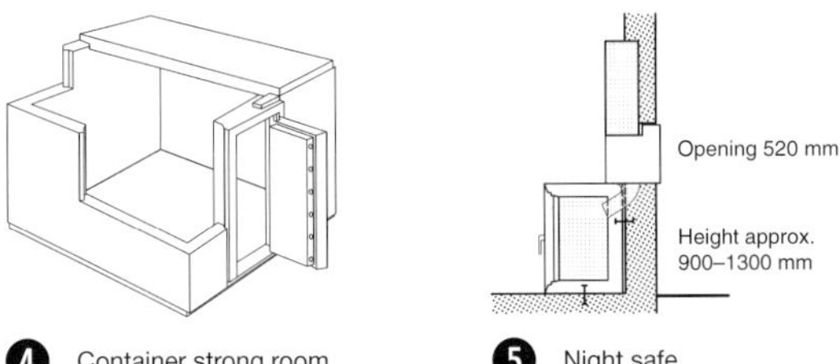

❹ Container strong room

❺ Night safe

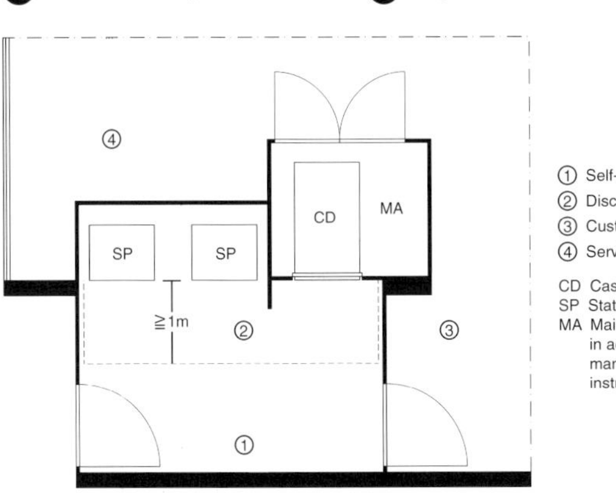

❻ Self-service zone

Bank buildings

There are two basic types of bank buildings: high street clearing bank branches with customer transactions and special or central banks without public access. The latter institutions are large-scale investment and/or corporate buildings.

High street clearing bank branches are a mixture of administration offices and customer service centres. The administrative share is larger for main offices and considerably less in smaller branches, because administration is mostly centrally organised. The main preconditions for the banking business are security, trust and reliability, which should also be visible in the design.

The UK, in addition, has long-established building societies, originally funding house purchase loans from the deposits they accepted, but now most are also functioning as banks. Their operating basis resembles that of a bank, so their building design requirements are similar.

Banks' functional areas are as follows:

Processing zone

Internal office area for administration without public access (→ p. 231 ff.).

Special zones

In addition to the social rooms for staff and the normal subsidiary rooms for administration offices (→ p. 238), there are conference and prestige-promoting areas. These serve training purposes and provide space for exhibitions.

Security area

Safes, today described as bank vaults or strong rooms, are mainly installed in larger bank branches or head offices. In new buildings there is solid and specially reinforced concrete construction and in old buildings a room-in-room structure of pre-cast elements. The ideal location is in the cellar near the entrance, because the shaft from the night safe has to be almost straight. The routes to the customer safe deposit boxes and to the bank strong room should if possible be separate. Delivery of cash and valuables by armoured vehicles also has to be considered. An access gallery with surveillance mirrors can be provided to monitor the strong room. Wall thicknesses are in accordance with the security level, from 80 cm (T10) to 100 cm (T20). For the customer safe deposit boxes, 'fully automated safe deposit systems' open at all times are available. These can be reached from the self-service area through an additional access control vestibule without staff involvement. The design should take into account the recommendations of the Research and Testing Association for safe and strong rooms and above all the requirements of the insurers.

Customer zone

The introduction of automatic teller cash dispensers (cash dispensers operated by bank staff) with restricted and time-locked cash release means that the structural protection of the counter area is no longer necessary. Cash dispensing and simple information is mostly at self-service cash points (ATMs). Cashless transactions can be carried out by home banking. This reduces the space requirement in the customer area, because the activity mostly consists of consultations and reference to specialist departments. For initial information, standing consultation counters are sufficient, but thorough consultations require a separate room for privacy. Expert departments (e.g. credit and investment) are often located on the first floor of the customer area.

The self-service zone is also accessible outside business hours. It is therefore mostly relocated into a lobby outside the customer area → ❻. This zone is equipped with cashpoints, account statement printers, deposit slot for the night safe and possibly the access to the safe deposit system.

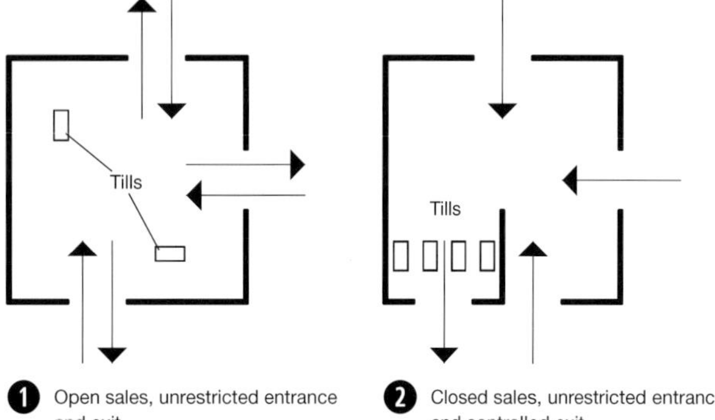

❶ Open sales, unrestricted entrance and exit

❷ Closed sales, unrestricted entrance and controlled exit

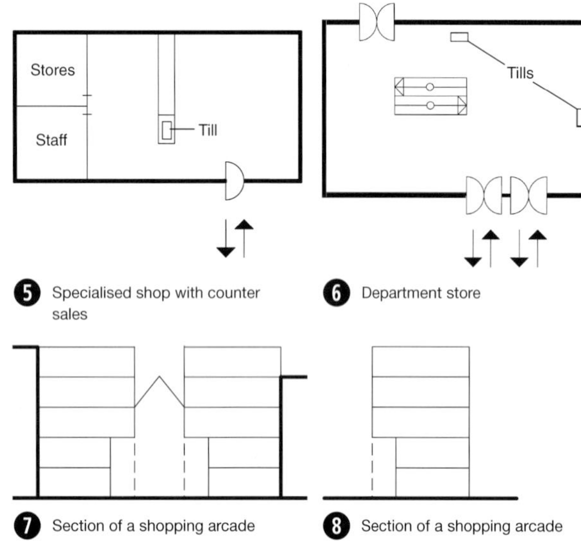

❸ Specialised shop

❹ Specialised supermarket (self-service)

❺ Specialised shop with counter sales

❻ Department store

❼ Section of a shopping arcade

❽ Section of a shopping arcade

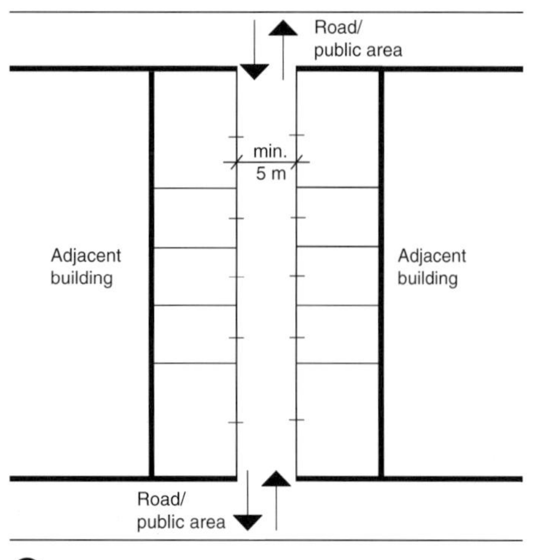

❾ Plan of a shopping arcade

Business types

Open sales → ❶: unrestricted entrance and exit (specialised shops and retail chains, department stores).

Closed sales → ❷: unrestricted entrance, exit only through staffed checkout (specialised supermarkets).

Sales types and typologies

Specialised shops → ❸: small shops (50–500m^2), mostly only one sector (pharmacy, shoe shop, flower shop), service and consultation → ❶.

Specialised retail chains → ❸: chain stores, mostly only one sector, presented like specialised shops (jeweller, fashion, shoe shop), open sales → ❶.

Specialised supermarkets → ❹: chain stores, small to very large businesses, one or more branches, self-service (pharmacy/drugstore, toys, DIY, electrical goods, groceries, supermarket), closed sales → ❷.

Department stores → ❻: often chain stores, very large shops, mostly multi-storey, various sectors, sections can be rented to other chains (shop-in-shop principle), open sales → ❶.

Shopping arcades, shopping centres/malls → ❾ **❿:** concentration and conglomeration of specialised shops, supermarkets and department stores, on one or more floors, with additional cafés, bars, restaurants.

A shopping arcade → ❾ is from 10,000 m^2 in area, usually approx. 20,000–25,000 m^2 in area, roofed, mostly a 2–3 storey street space with multi-level access, exploiting urban block zones, external access (min. two) via squares, streets or shopping areas, semi-public access routes; no fixed opening times. Smaller shops are often along the internal street, with well-known large-area chains mostly in the corners or at the end of a street as a 'magnet'. Internal streets often lead into squares or courtyards.

A shopping centre/mall → ❿ is a larger and more elaborate collection of retail outlets, eating places etc. It has fixed opening times, therefore no semi-public access routes; main external access normally from only one road, but additional side access from a car park or multi-storey car park is possible.

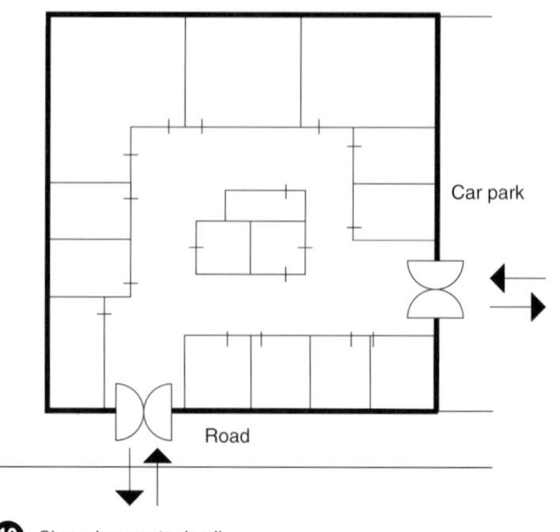

❿ Shopping centre/mall

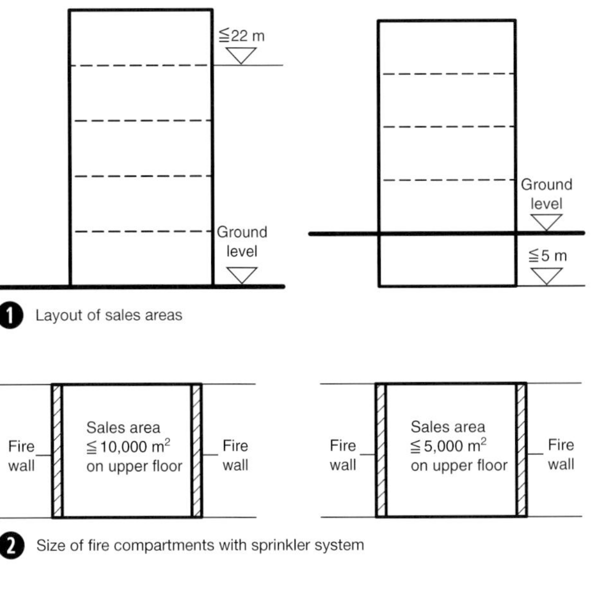

❶ Layout of sales areas

❷ Size of fire compartments with sprinkler system

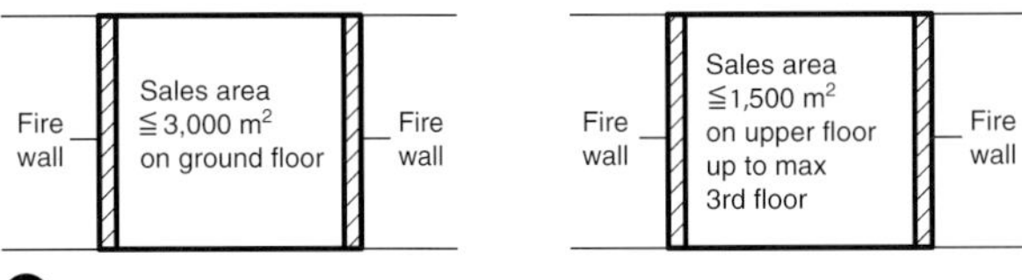

❸ Size of fire compartments without sprinkler system

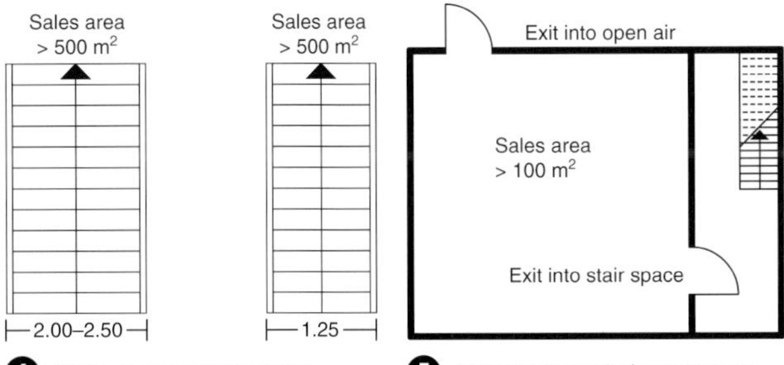

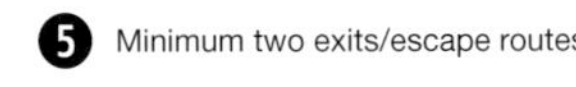

❹ Width of emergency stairways

❺ Minimum two exits/escape routes

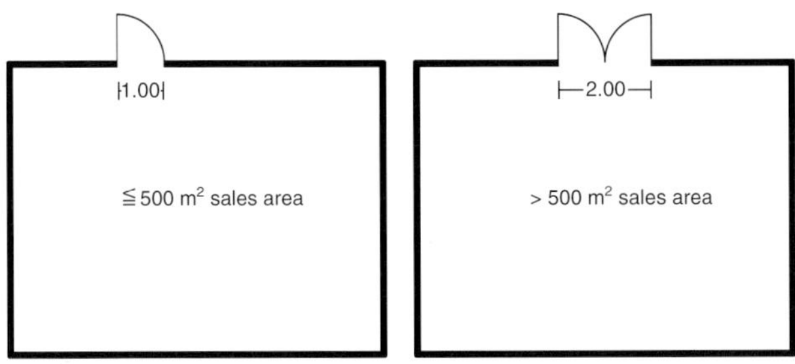

❻ Width of exits, depending on size of sales areas

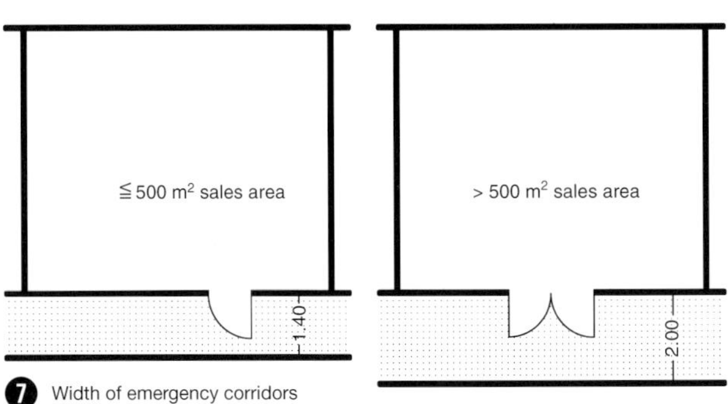

❼ Width of emergency corridors

The provisions of the retail regulations apply to retail outlets whose sales area and shop passages, including building elements, have a total area of >2,000 m².

Sales areas

Those in which goods for sale or other services are offered (except for emergency staircases, staircase extensions and garages. Shop passages do not count as sales areas.

Shop passages

These are roofed or covered routes adjacent to sales areas, which contain customer traffic. They must be at least 5 m wide.

Layout of sales areas

Sales areas, except for catering establishments, may not have a floor level >22 m above ground level, or >5 m below ground level → ❶.

Fire compartments

Sales outlets are to be divided into fire compartments with partitioning walls built like fire walls → ❷ – ❸.

The permissible areas of fire compartments on each floor are:

	with sprinkler system	without sprinkler system
ground floor sales outlets	10,000 m²	5,000 m²
other sales outlets	5,000 m²	1,500 m²*

* if the sales areas extend over more than three floors and the total area of all floors within a fire compartment is not more than 3,000 m²

Emergency stairways

Emergency stairways for customers must be at least 2.0 m wide and may not exceed a width of 2.5 m. A width of 1.25 m is adequate if the stairway is provided for sales areas <500 m² in total → ❹.

Exits

Every sales area, occupied room and shop passage must have a min. 2 exits leading to the open air or into an emergency stairway. One exit is sufficient for sales areas <100 m² in total → ❺. Exits from a floor of a sales outlet into the open air or into an emergency stairway must have a width of 30 cm per 100 m² of sales area, and be min. 2 m wide, but for exits from sales areas <500 m², a width of 1 m is sufficient → ❻. An exit leading into a corridor may not be wider than the corridor, and an exit leading into an emergency stairway may not be wider than the stairway.

Escape routes

For every sales area, occupied area and shop passage, min. two escape routes must be provided on the same floor, if possible going in opposite directions, leading to exits into the open air or to an emergency stairway. These must be accessible within a distance of 25 m from every point of a sales area (or 35 m for other areas or shop passages). The doors must open in the direction of escape and be without thresholds. A main entrance or a shop passage must be provided within 10 m (linear distance) of every point in a sales area.

Emergency corridors

For customers these must be at least 2 m wide. A width of 1.40 m is sufficient if corridors are intended for sales areas <500 m² → ❼.

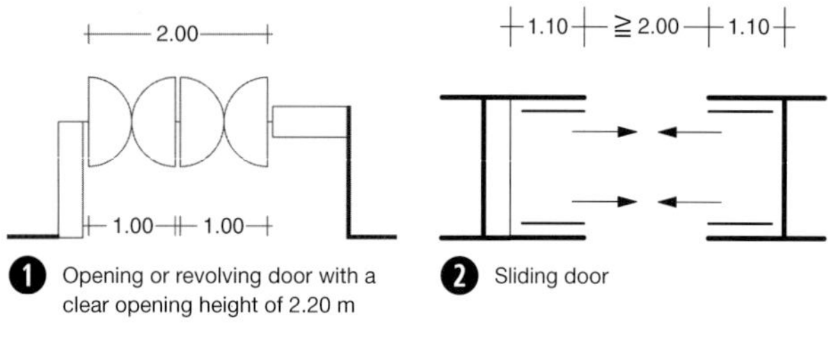

1 Opening or revolving door with a clear opening height of 2.20 m

2 Sliding door

3 Revolving doors with side doors

4 Folding door

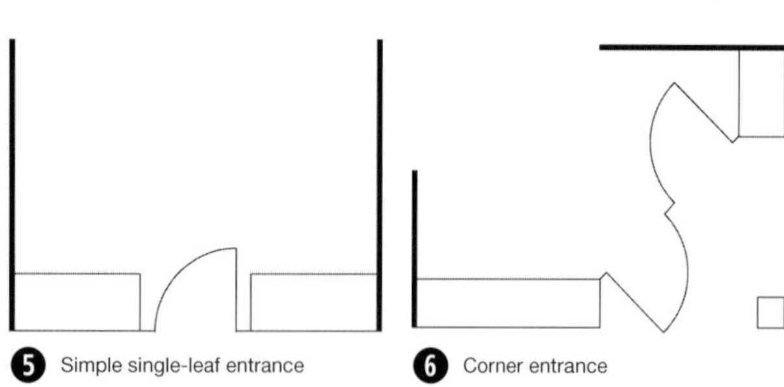

5 Simple single-leaf entrance

6 Corner entrance

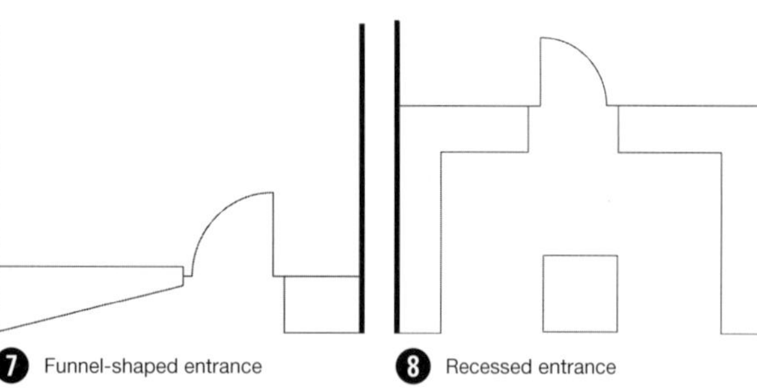

7 Funnel-shaped entrance

8 Recessed entrance

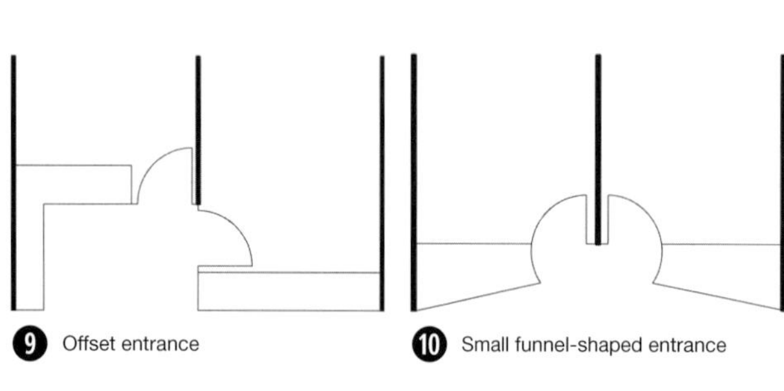

9 Offset entrance

10 Small funnel-shaped entrance

Entrances

With entrances to sales outlets <2000 m^2 the door widths can be >1.00 m; to those >2000 m^2 they must be disability-friendly and have automatic doors. According to the retail regulations, the clear opening width must be >2.00 m, and the clear height >2.20 m → 2.

Shop windows

These serve, outside the shop, to present the goods on sale, to wake the interest of customers and to present an invitation to purchase → 11 – 12, 15 – 18. The design of shop windows depends on the particular goods being sold and should complement the layout, form and size of the entrance. The two basic types are windows with display area → 11 and windows with a view of the shop → 17.

Shop windows with display area: separation of the displayed goods and the sales area, mostly in department stores and specialised retail chains.

Shop windows with a view of the shop: view through the window into the sales area, mostly for specialised shops (e.g. baker, butcher...)

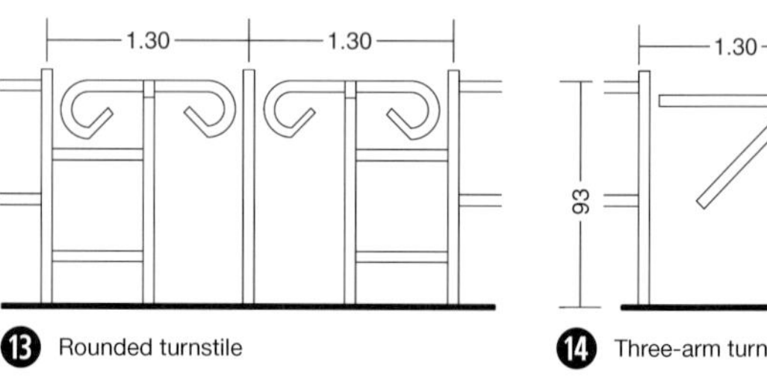

13 Rounded turnstile

14 Three-arm turnstile

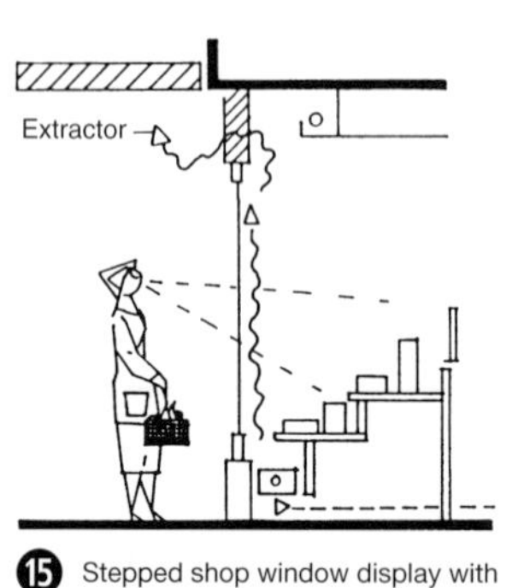

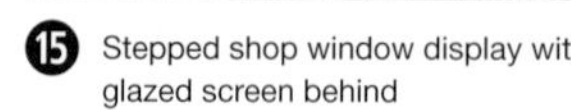

15 Stepped shop window display with glazed screen behind

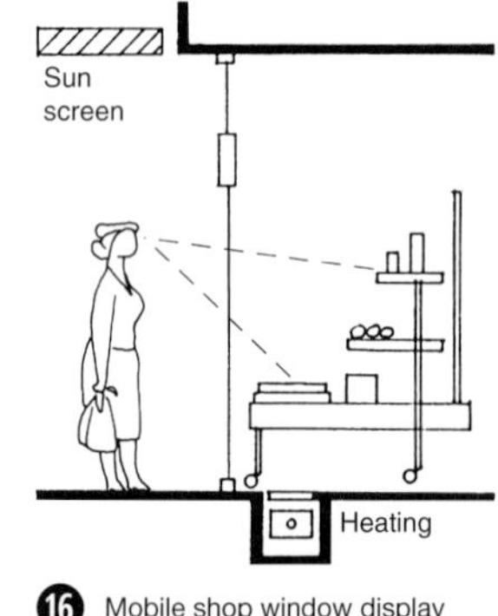

16 Mobile shop window display unit with screen behind

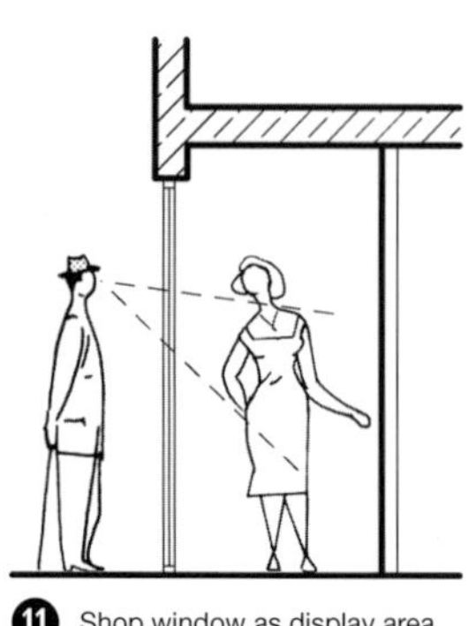

11 Shop window as display area

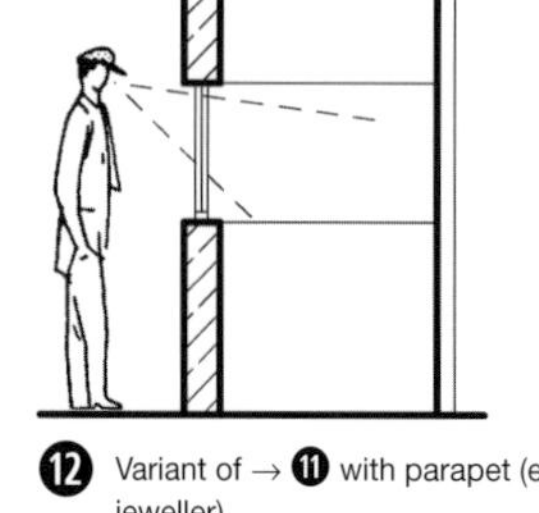

12 Variant of → 11 with parapet (e.g. jeweller)

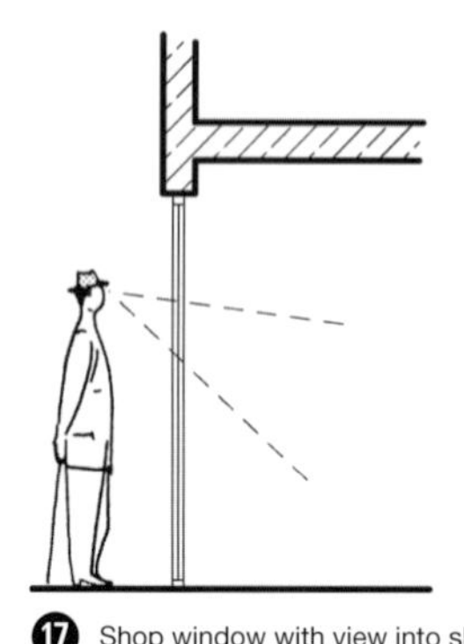

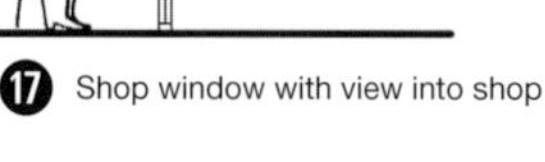

17 Shop window with view into shop

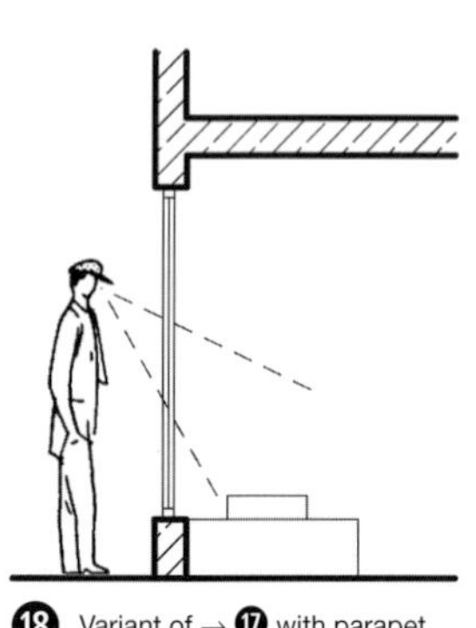

18 Variant of → 17 with parapet (e.g. book shop)

Retail

RETAIL OUTLETS
Guidelines and typologies
Retail regulations
Entrances and shop windows
Checkout and waiting zones
Waiting zones – examples
Routeing, escalators
Furnishing – dimensions
Food shops
Self-service shops

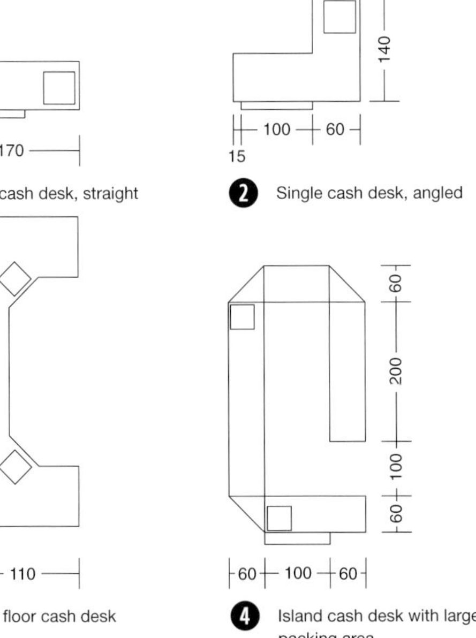

❶ Single cash desk, straight

❷ Single cash desk, angled

❸ Area or floor cash desk

❹ Island cash desk with large packing area

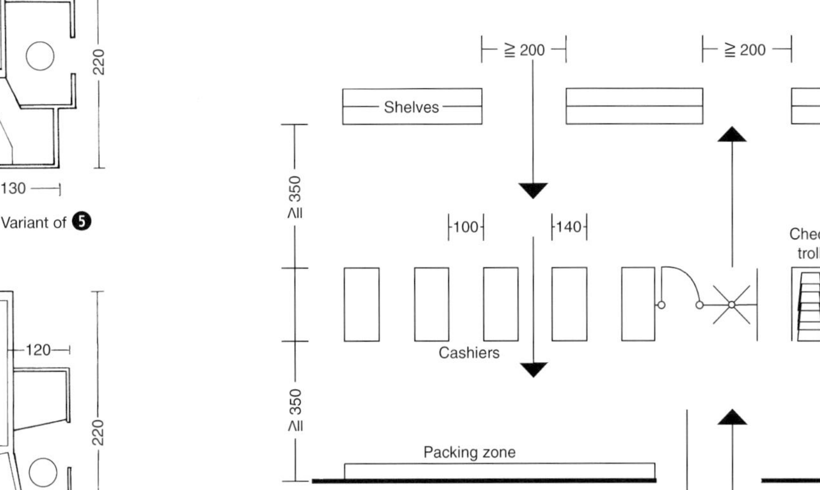

❺ Checkout desk in self-service supermarket

❻ Variant of ❺

❼ Variant of ❺

❽ Variant of ❺

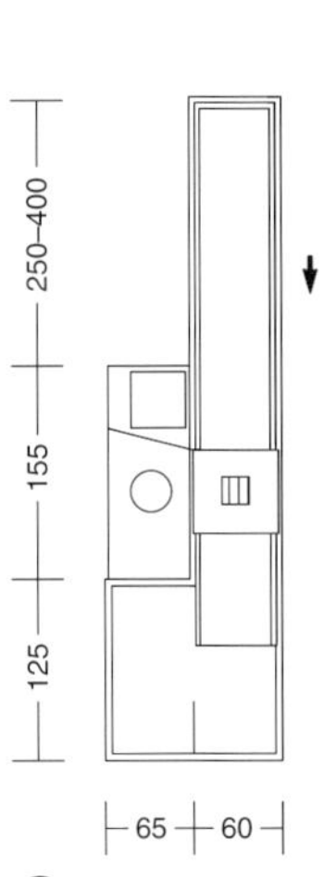

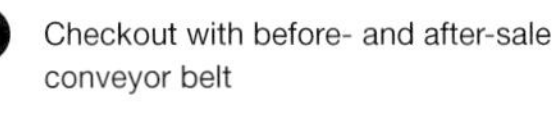

❾ Checkout with before- and after-sale conveyor belt

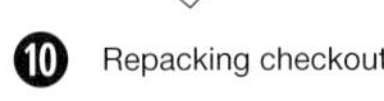

❿ Repacking checkout

Types of checkout

According to the product and shop type, there are various types of checkout: single, area and central cash desks and rows of check-outs.

Row of checkouts

In specialised supermarkets (self-service area), these form the only exit from all shops with a closed sales area. The passing width between the checkouts should be sufficiently wide that shopping trolleys, pushchairs and wheelchairs can pass through, i.e. min. 1 m. Checkouts are mostly equipped with a conveyor belt (sometimes a before- and after-sale belt) and stationary scanner. Self-checkouts are also available as complete products.

Single, area, floor and central cash desks

In specialised shops, specialised retail chains and department stores with open sales, depending on the functional organisation of the shop, cash desks can be arranged as single, by area, by floor or centrally. Department stores with different specialised sections have mostly area cash desks, specialised retail chains often have cash desks on each floor or grouped centrally, specialised small shops mostly have single cash desks.

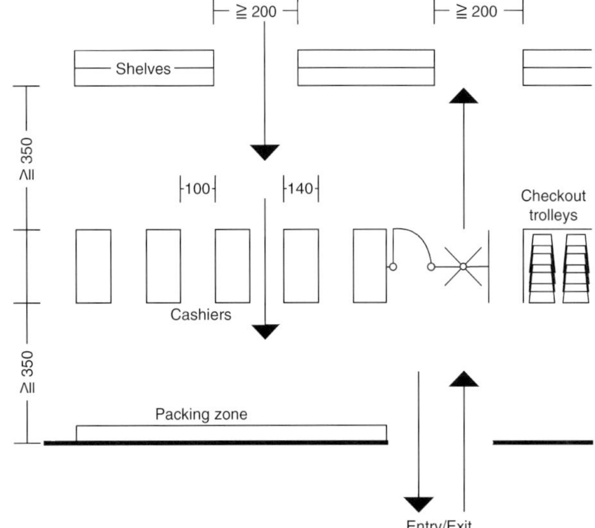

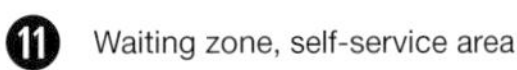

⓫ Waiting zone, self-service area

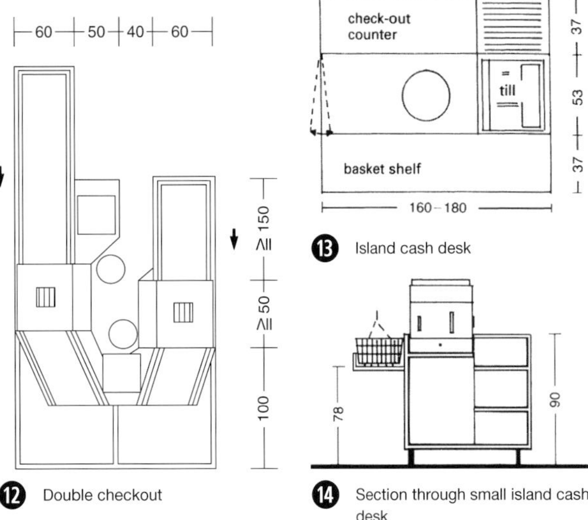

⓬ Double checkout

⓭ Island cash desk

⓮ Section through small island cash desk

(1) confectioner
(2) glazed frontage
(3) bakery
(4) ovens
(5) lockers
(6) staff area
(7) cold room
(8) store-room
(9) washing-up
(10) silo
(11) standing consumption
(12) snacks
(13) folding glass partition
(14) plants and flowers
(15) flower arrangement room
(16) flower store
(17) bar
(18) check-out area
(19) pasta specialities
(20) tobacconist, lottery
(21) cold room
(22) fish specialities
(23) preparation
(24) bar/eating area
(25) standing consumption

entrance
exit
emergency exit

1 Checkout waiting zone

While you wait: buying, with the emphasis on experience – consumption on the spot or take-away.

Impulse buying

Addressing the senses, suggestive display, lifestyle, quality of life, convenience for employed people and homemakers. Prepared products, warm or to be warmed up = fast food. No self-service = free flow. Shop-in-shop. Multitude of ideas, concentration, smaller shops, high turnover. Matching designs from one designer. Storage for one day, deliveries typically every morning, fresh stock. Minimal sanitary facilities for standing customers. One WC for staff.

Range

Bakery – sales only 40–80 m^2, + eat in shop 80–120 m^2. Butcher's – sales only 40–80 m^2, + eat in shop 80–120 m^2. Café, pastries, ice cream parlour – sales only 40–80 m^2, + eat in shop from 220 m^2. Fish – sales 40–80 m^2, + eat in shop 80–120 m^2. Fresh food market, eat in shop as extension from 600 m^2 in checkout waiting zone → **1**: seafood, fruit, flowers, drinks, wine, champagne, delicatessen, up-market snacks.

Additionally

Pizza, steaks, organic food, brewery bar etc. → **3**

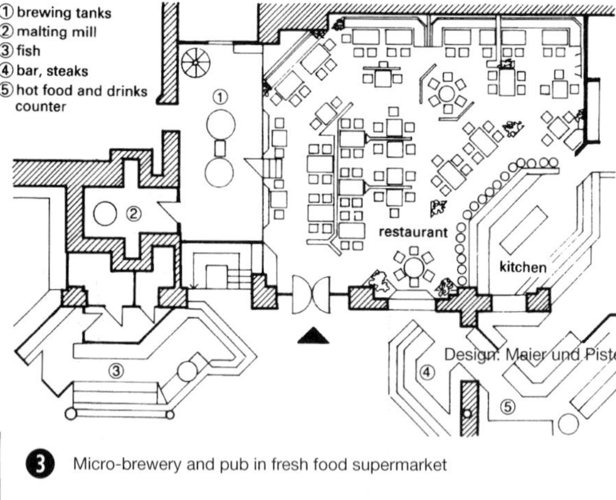

3 Micro-brewery and pub in fresh food supermarket

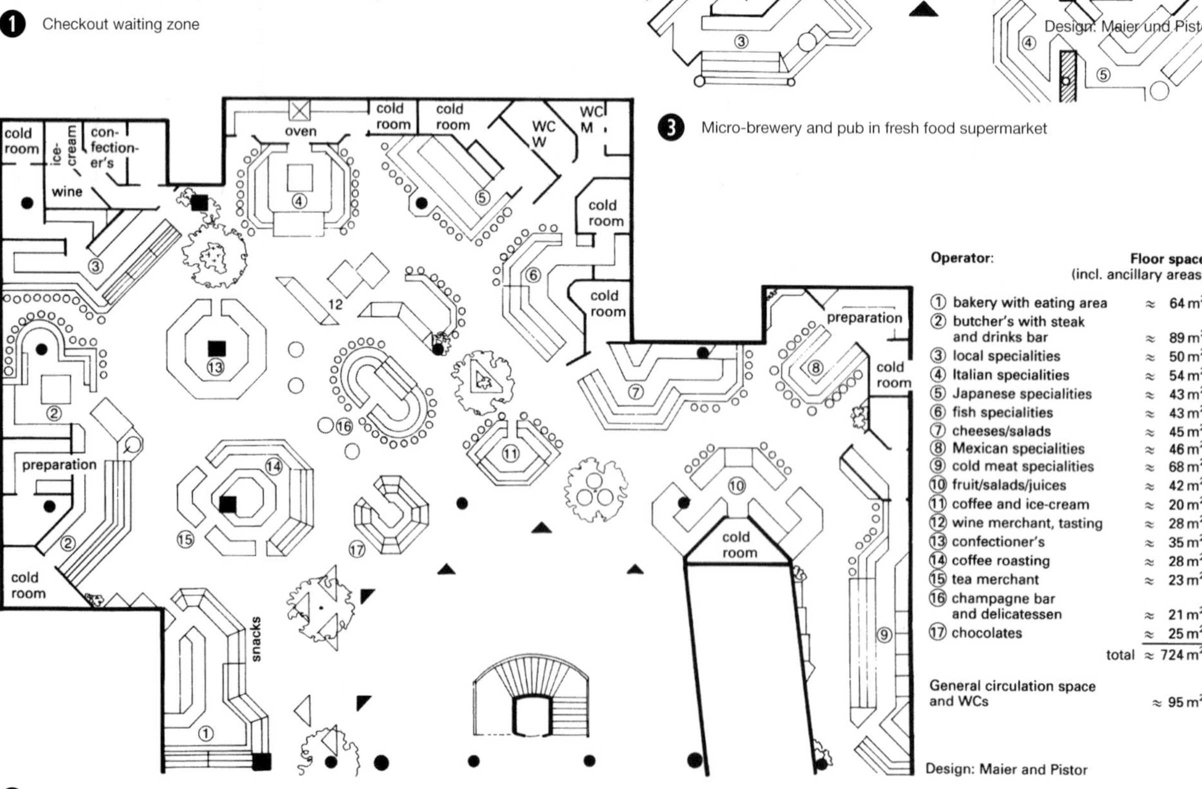

Operator:	Floor space (incl. ancillary areas)
(1) bakery with eating area	≈ 64 m^2
(2) butcher's with steak and drinks bar	≈ 89 m^2
(3) local specialities	≈ 50 m^2
(4) Italian specialities	≈ 54 m^2
(5) Japanese specialities	≈ 43 m^2
(6) fish specialities	≈ 43 m^2
(7) cheeses/salads	≈ 45 m^2
(8) Mexican specialities	≈ 46 m^2
(9) cold meat specialities	≈ 68 m^2
(10) fruit/salads/juices	≈ 42 m^2
(11) coffee and ice-cream	≈ 20 m^2
(12) wine merchant, tasting	≈ 28 m^2
(13) confectioner's	≈ 35 m^2
(14) coffee roasting	≈ 28 m^2
(15) tea merchant	≈ 23 m^2
(16) champagne bar and delicatessen	≈ 21 m^2
(17) chocolates	≈ 25 m^2
total	≈ 724 m^2
General circulation space and WCs	≈ 95 m^2

Design: Maier and Pistor

2 Fresh food supermarket at Hamburg main station

Design: Maier und Pistor

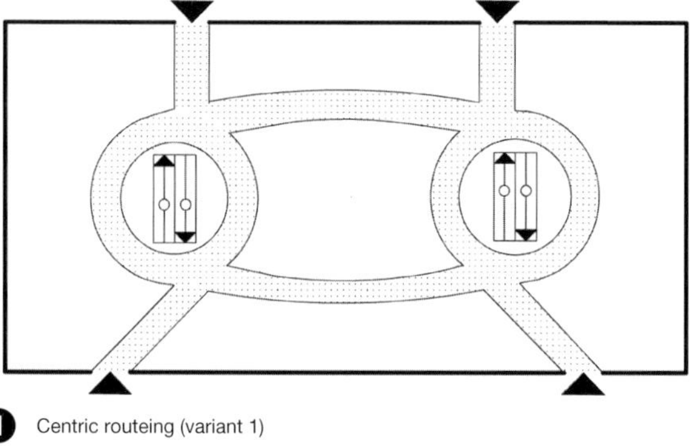

❶ Centric routeing (variant 1)

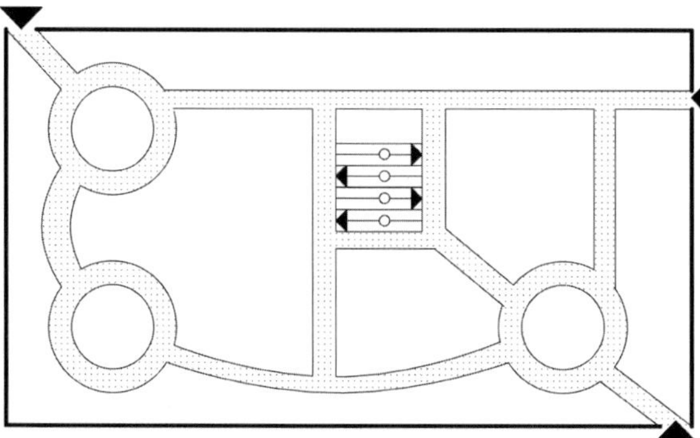

❷ Centric routeing (variant 2)

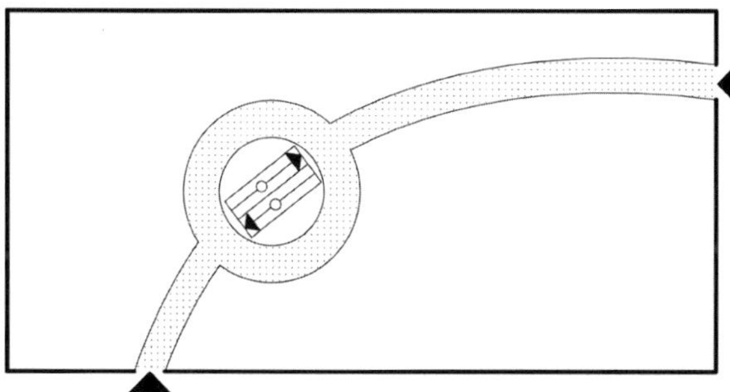

❸ Polygonal routeing

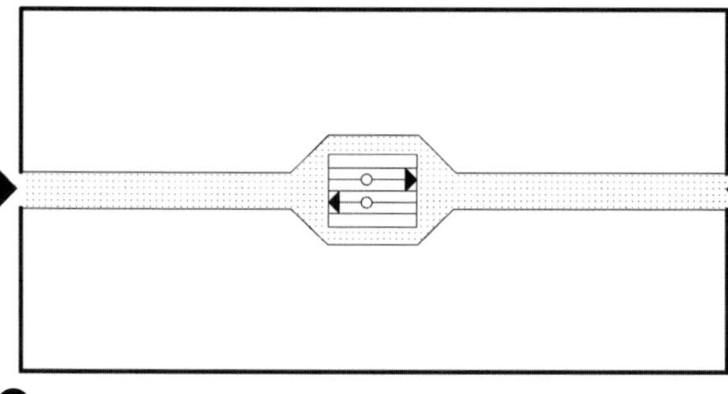

❹ Routeing in a single loop

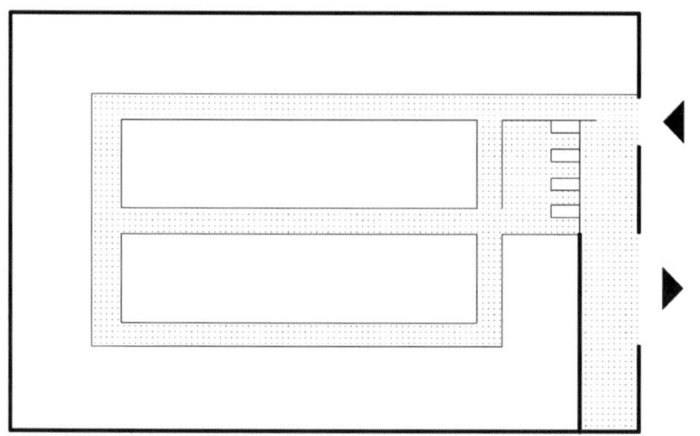

❺ Routeing in a self-service supermarket

Routes and escalators serve above all to highlight the promotion of goods and special offers. The larger the area of a retail outlet, the more important is the routeing concept. It can be put into practice through different means on the floor of the shop: lighting, fittings and positioning of the goods on offer. The location of the goods is determined by the intention to encourage customers to buy by displaying, as they pass by, shelves, stock and thus all the product ranges → ❶ – ❷.

The following variants are common for vertical escalator access in shops:

Double criss-cross: → ❼
The direction of travel of this escalator is 180°.

Parallel layout: → ❻
Escalators in the same direction lie above one another.

The rule of thumb is one escalator for every approx. 1000 m^2 of sales area.

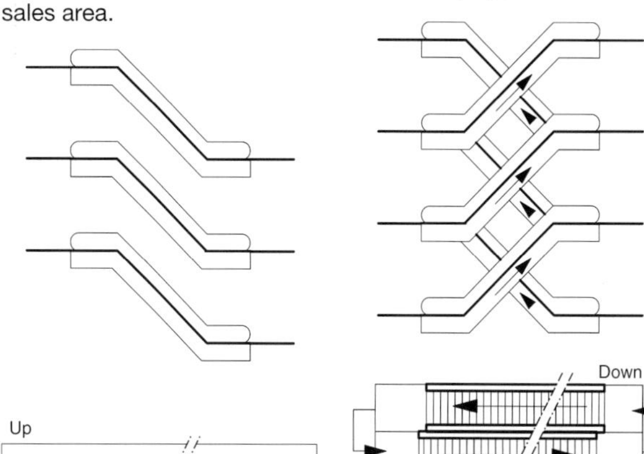

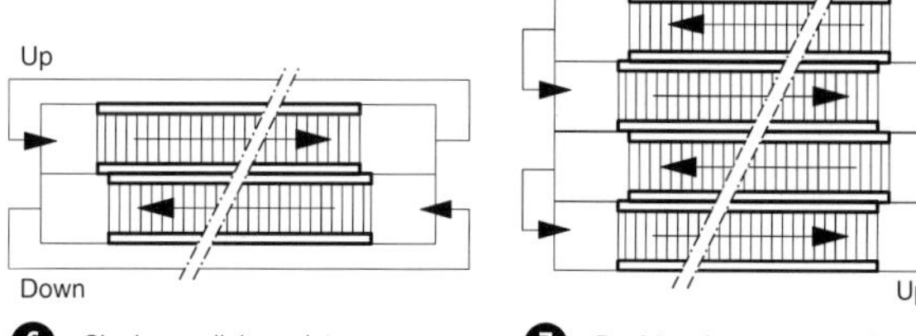

❻ Single parallel escalators

❼ Double criss-cross escalators

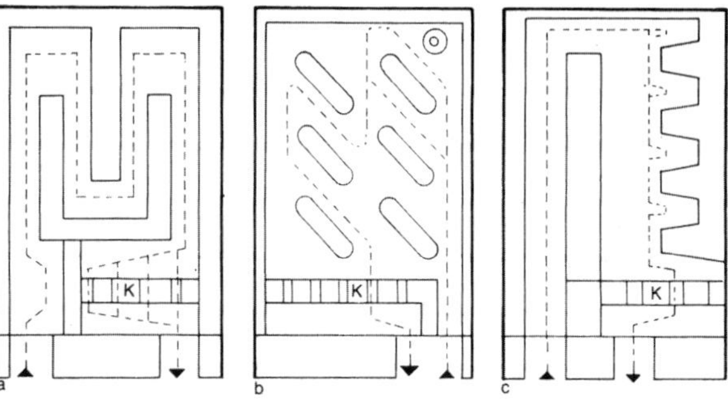

❽ Routes should include corner areas; separate entrance and exit in a and c, doubled in b. K = checkout

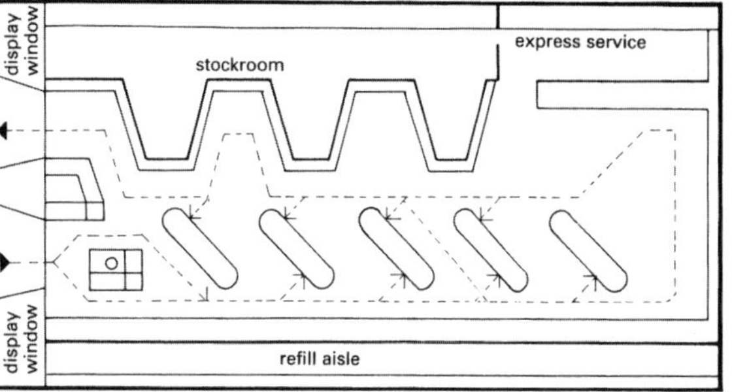

❾ The shop should be clearly laid out for customers and control (checkout), so the customer is not forced to make diversions → ❽ a

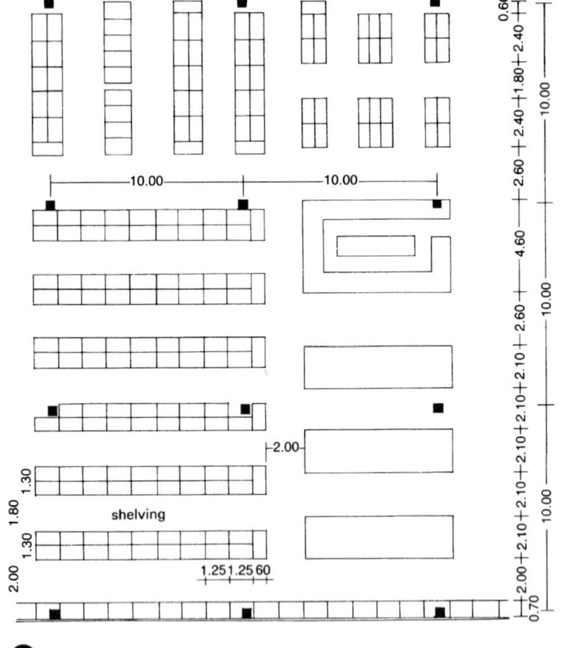

❶ Dimensions of the counters and shelves, column grid 10 × 10 m

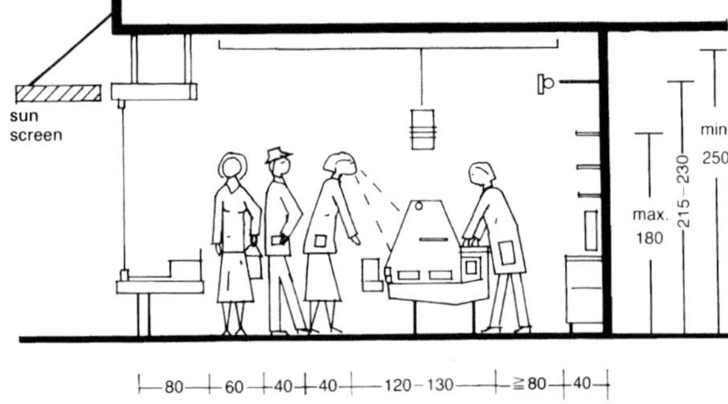

❷ Minimum width of a shop ≧4.0 m, better 5.0 m

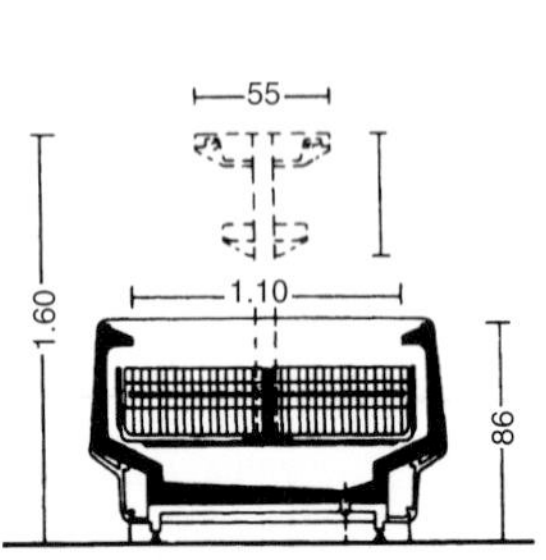

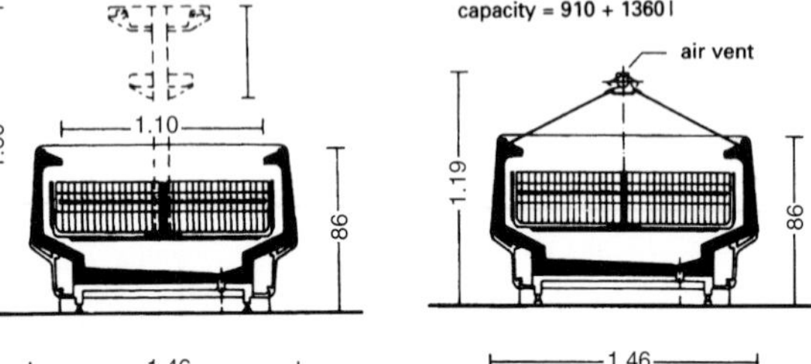

❸ Refrigerated display case with upper shelves

❹ Refrigerated display case without upper shelves

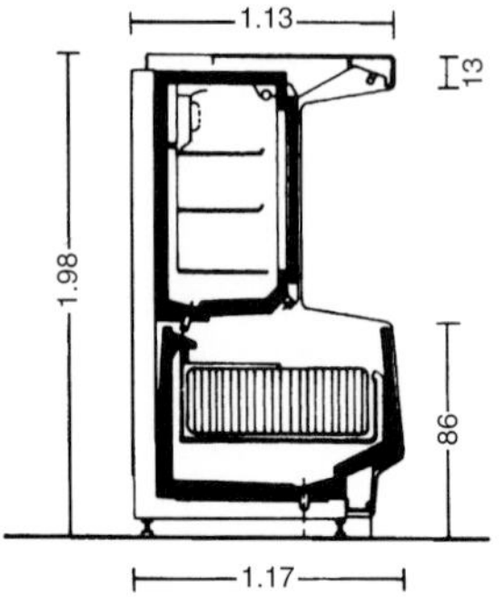

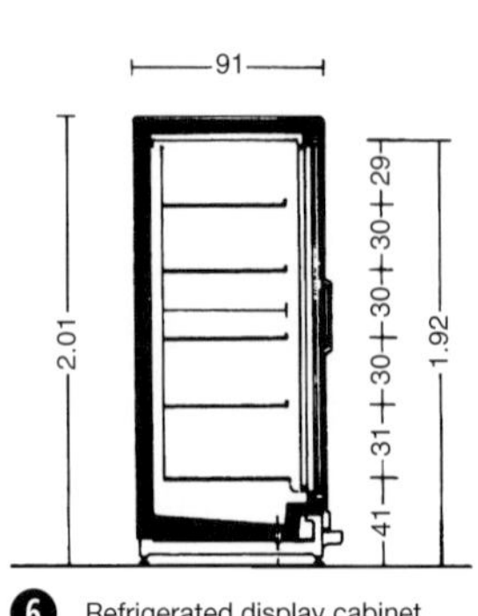

❺ Vertical refrigerated display case with upper shelves

❻ Refrigerated display cabinet

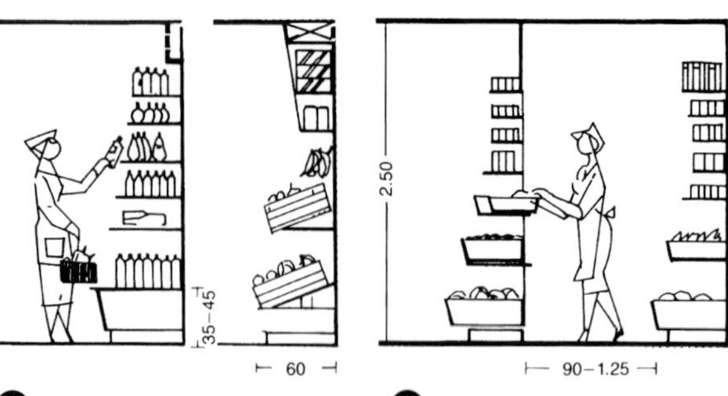

❼ Wall shelves for bottles

Wall shelves for fruit and vegetables (goods to restock)

❽ Wall with drawers, passage for restocking (sliding baskets are exchanged)

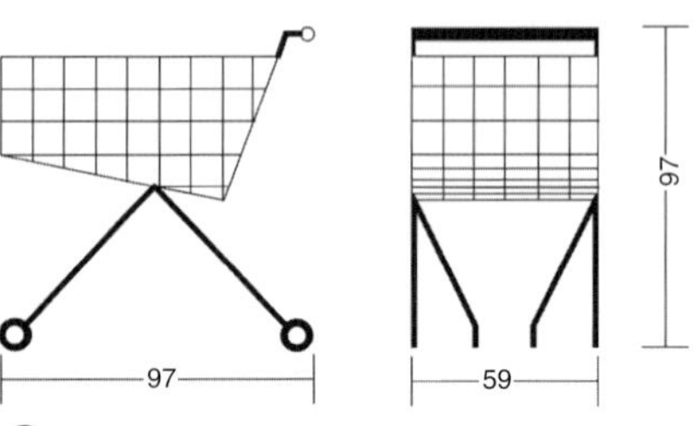

❾ Small shopping trolley (e.g. drugstore)

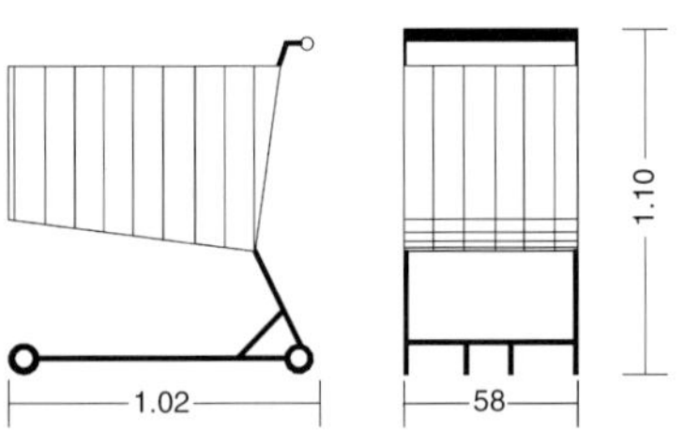

❿ Large shopping trolley (e.g. large supermarket chain)

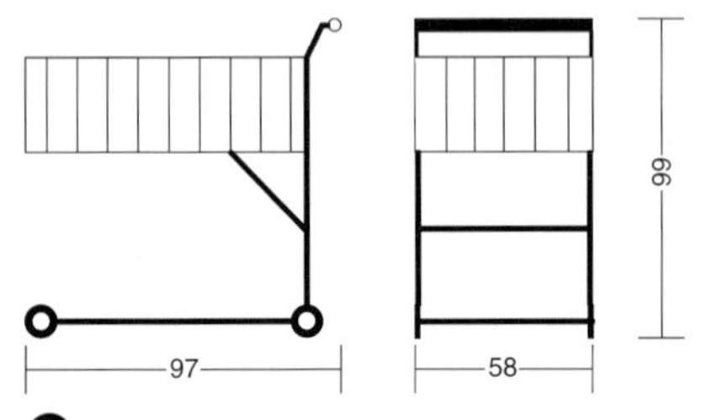

⓫ Shopping trolley (e.g. DIY store)

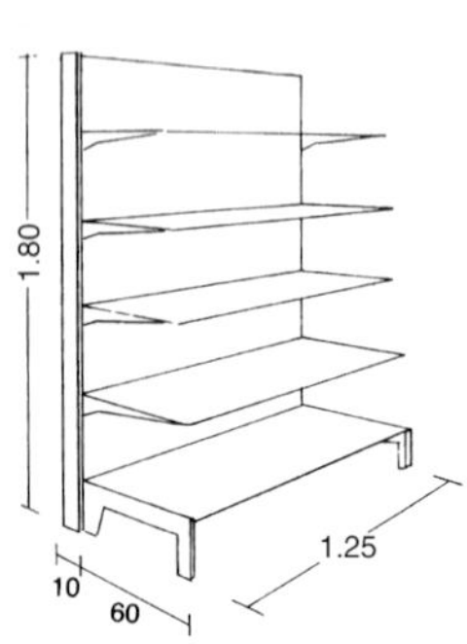

⓬ Island shelf unit

⓭ Wall shelf unit

Fishmonger

Because fresh fish do not keep very long, they are stored cool, but smoked fish have to be stored dry. The goods are odour-intensive, so the shops are accessed through control doors or protective curtains. Walls and floors must be easy to clean. Take into account bulk deliveries in the design. Consider an aquarium (display advertising). → ❶ – ❷

Game and poultry dealer

This business is often combined with a fishmonger. Storage for only a day's needs. A workroom must be provided with plucking machine and game scraper. Because poultry is susceptible to odour, it must be stored separately in the shop and the cold room.

Counter worktops and walls (marble, tiles, mosaic, plastic) must be washable. Provide plenty of refrigerated display cases or cabinets. → ❸ – ❹.

Greengrocer

Fresh vegetables, unprocessed or kitchen-ready, must be stored cool, but not chilled. Potatoes are stored in dark rooms and sold from the deposit-bearing containers they are delivered in (baskets, crates, boxes). Protective sliding inserts are provided under storage trays. Greengrocers → ❼ – ❽ can possibly be combined with flower shops. Self-service shops offer pre-packed goods in transparent packs.

Butcher

Work steps: 1. delivery of live animals, 2. slaughter, 3. butcher, 4. process, 5. cool/store, 6. sell → ❿ – ⓫. A single-storey shop is advantageous, possibly with hanging and sliding rail system, because sides of pork or quarters of beef weigh 50 kg. Processing and cold rooms must be 1.5–2 times the size of the shop. Walls: tiled, mosaic etc. and washable. Counter tops: marble, glass, ceramic.

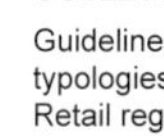

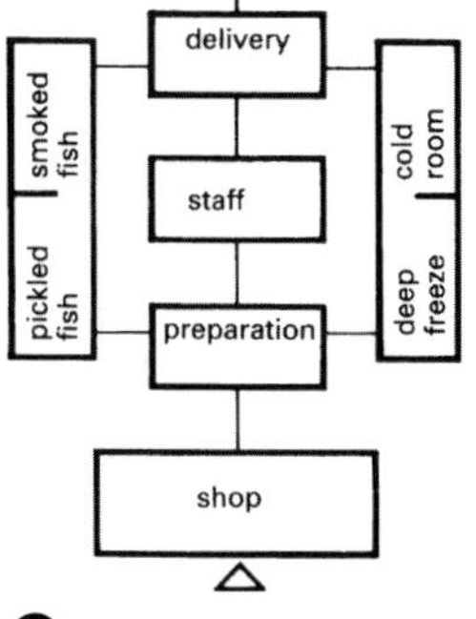

❶ Traffic scheme for fishmonger

❷ Fish display case with cooler and extraction

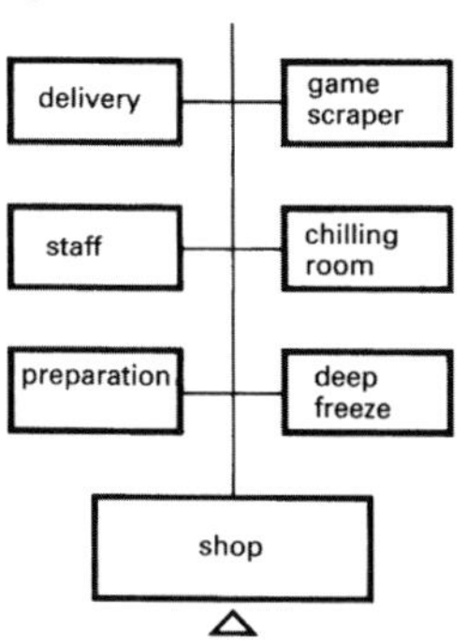

❸ Traffic scheme for game and poultry dealer

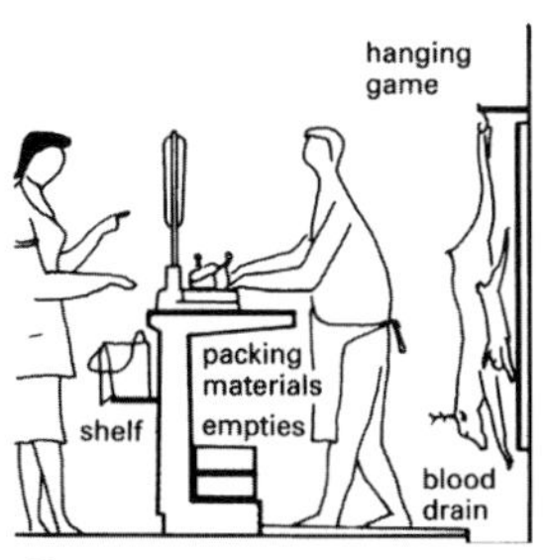

❹ Solid counter with marble and tiled worktop

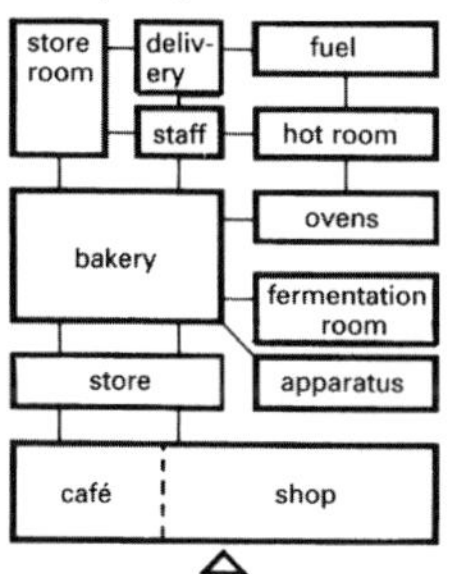

❺ Traffic scheme for bakery. Storerooms should be well ventilated, possibly with vapour extraction.

❻ Sales counter with screen

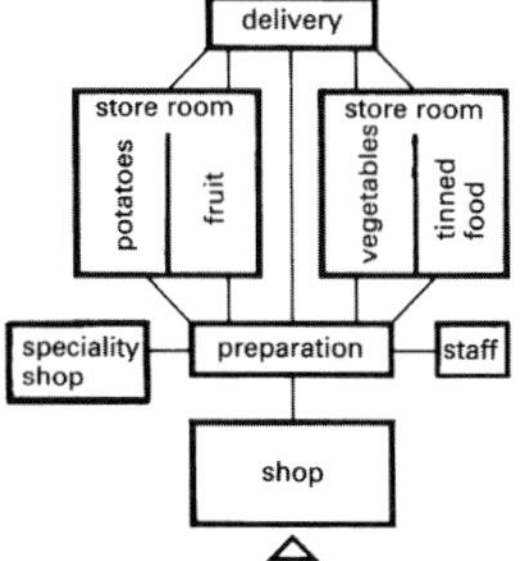

❼ Sales scheme for greengrocer; small storeroom, as mostly delivered daily

❽ Counter with mounting for boxes and wire baskets; draining shelf and dirt drawer

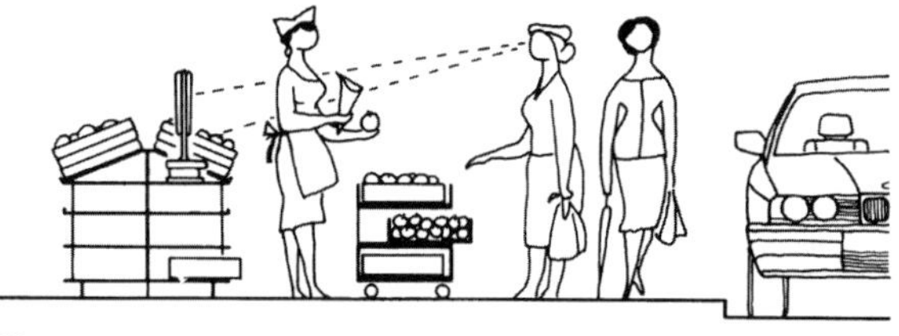

❾ Pavement sales to 'passers-by' on wheeled stand or at shop front with goods displayed for advertising purposes

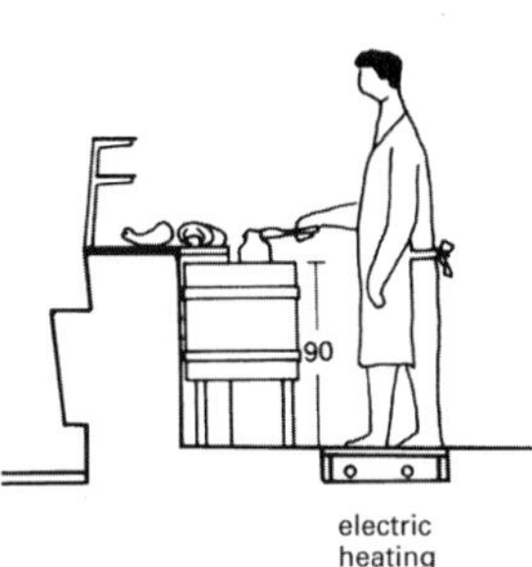

❿ Counter with chopping block for butcher

⓫ Normal counter for butcher → ❷ and for fishmonger

Self-service shops mostly sell food. The staff is responsible for advice, assistance and service. The butchery, cold meats, fruit and vegetable sections are staffed. The goods are displayed clearly in packaging according to type. It is important to design practical routeing. The round trip starts at the basket stack or trolley park and ends at the checkout or packing table. Wall shelves extend up to reach height (top shelf is 1.80 m high and lowest 0.30 m above the floor).

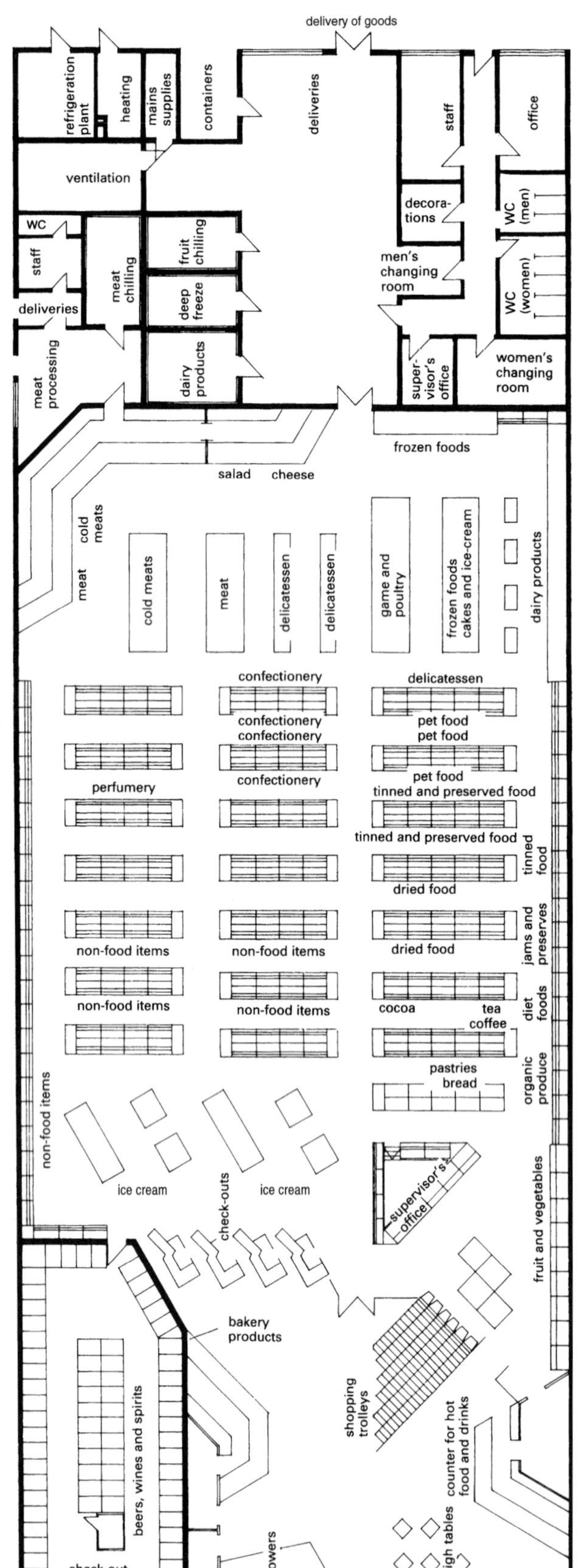

1 Supermarket

Important design parameters	up to 399 m²	400–499 m²	500–599 m²	600–799 m²	800–899 m²	1000–1499 m²
1. full-time staff needed	10.6	12.9	15.3	17.7	22.1	30.2
range	7–14	10–16	12–18	16–20	18–25	25–33
2. fresh and cold meat department						
a) turnover share (%)	22	21	20	19	18	17
	19–28	20–32	20–28	17–25	16–24	14.5–24
b) counter length (m)	6.50	7.60	8.75	9.08	9.75	11.75
	6.0–7.0	7.0–8.2	7.5–9.0	1.5–10.5	9.0–10.5	10.0–13.5
c) preparation room (m^3)	14	19	24	26	30	36
	8–20	13–25	18–30	20–32	23–38	23–50
d) cold room (m^3)	11	13.5	15	15	22	25
	7–15	9–18	10–20	10–20	14–30	16–35
3. dairy and fats department						
a) cool wall shelves (running m)	6.75	8.0	8.75	10.25	11.25	15.7
	6.3–7.3	6.5–9.5	7.5–11	9–12	10–13.5	12–18.5
b) cold room (m^2)	6.0	7.6	10.0	12.0	13.0	15.0
	4.0–8.0	5.0–10.5	8.0–12.0	8.0–15.5	8.0–18.0	10.0–20.0
4. frozen food (without ice cream)						
a) normal island (m)	5.5	6.1	7.5	8.75	10.1	13.5
	5.0–6.0	5.5–7.0	6.5–8.5	7.5–10.0	7.5–12.0	12.0–15.0
b) wide island (m)	3.85	4.1	5.5	6.75	7.75	8.75
	2.6–4.6	3.0–5.0	4.0–7.0	4.0–7.5	5.5–10.0	6.0–10.0
c) cabinets (m)	2.4	2.75	3.6	4.4	5.8	6.6
	2.3–2.5	2.3–3.2	3.2–4.0	4.0–4.8	5.0–6.5	5.5–8.0
d) freezer room (m^2)	2.4	3.25	5.0	5.75	8.25	8.5
	2.0–2.8	2.0–4.5	4.0–6.0	4.0–7.5	6.0–10.5	6.0–11.0
5. fruit and veg wall shelving (with 2 shelves) (m)	6.5	7.5	7.5	8.75	10.0	10.75
	5.0–8.0	6.5–8.5	7.0–8.0	7.0–10.5	8.0–12.0	9.0–12.5
6. no. cash desks						
– at checkout	2.5	2.9	3.4	3.9	4.9	6.3
	2–3	2–3	3–4	3–4	4–5	6–7
– in the departments	0.2	0.3	0.4	0.5	1.3	1.3
	0–1	0–1	0–1	0–1	1–2	1–2
7. no. shopping trolleys required	85	105	120	150	180	240
	70–100	85–130	100–160	100–200	150–220	200–300

Note: first line = average values; second line = range of the parameter

2 Planning data for the design and fitting out of self-service shops and supermarkets

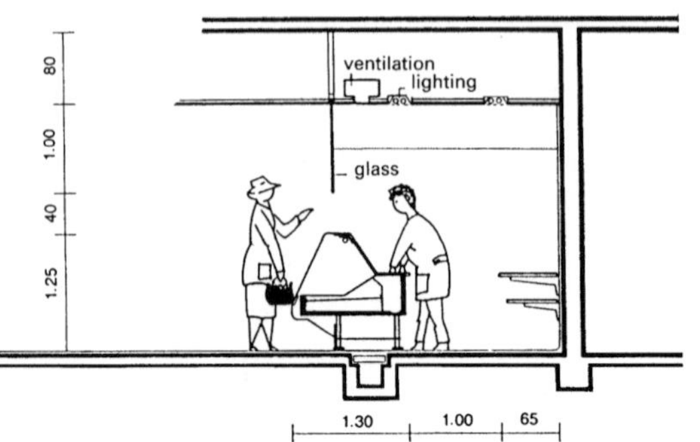

3 Service counter in self-service shop, section

factory planning
operational planning
building planning
basic planning
site planning
preliminary planning
preliminary planning
operational diagram
materials flow plan
machine arrangement
workforce plan
operating facilities
layout
flow diagram
schedule
construction
building land
building
technical construction
energy supply
transport/traffic

❶ Planning diagram of a factory

Environmental protection
federal emissions protection law with criteria for an approval process, possibly including environmental impact assessment (EIA) technical instructions for the avoidance of noise nuisance technical instructions for clean air preservation groundwater protection law
Workplace Regulations
Workplace Regulations Workplace Guidelines, **revised to 2010, newly available are A 1.3 (2007) and A 2.3 (2007)** guidelines of the federal association of commercial accident insurers accident prevention regulations of the accident insurers and the federal association of accident insurers German engineers' association (VDI) standards
Fire protection
industrial construction guideline with minimum requirements for fire protection in industrial buildings → p. 500 structural fire protection in industrial building technical rules for flammable liquids technical rules for hazardous substances

❷ Basic planning regulations for the construction of industrial and commercial buildings (selection)

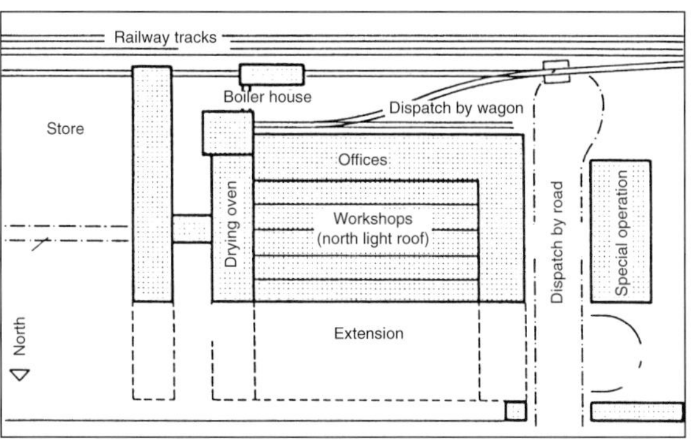

❸ Additive typology: Fagus Werk, Alfeld Architect: Walter Gropius

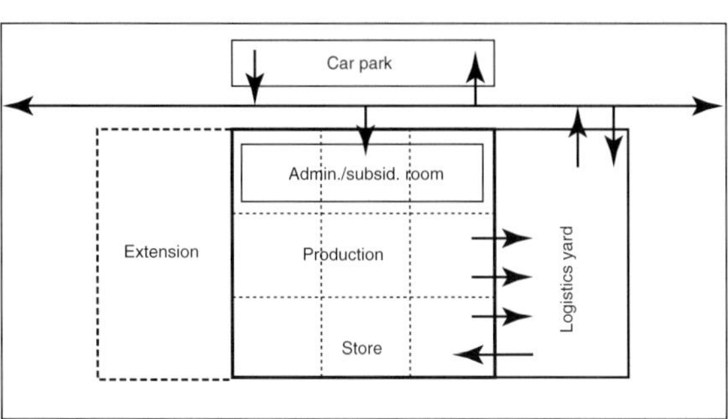

❹ Integrated typology: 'open workspace'

Industrial buildings, directly or indirectly, are designed for the production of goods. In addition to the actual **production buildings** (preparation, manufacture, consignment, packaging) these are also **warehouses** (raw materials, finished products), **technical and administration buildings** and **transport systems**. The spectrum of production ranges from labour-intensive heavy industry to 'smart' low-emission and highly automated light industry. The requirements for the design are accordingly varied: if the traditional factory hall is little more than a tool, the requirements extend to 'corporate identity', from recognition value to sympathetic and communication-oriented workplaces.

Layout planning

The layout is the classic basis of factory building. The various parameters of the planned production plant are defined and systematised in the layout → ❶. It is processed in various stages (ideal, trial, rough and precise layout). One of the results of layout planning is the room allocation plan as a scaled functional scheme of the planned plant and as the basis for the design of the building. The structure designed in line with the layout is product-specific. In the course of the various non-specific design work (e.g. start-up centres) and the simultaneous development of product and production plant, the layout becomes ever less significant as a design basis, being replaced by more flexible concepts.

Design basis

The design of industrial buildings is subject to numerous laws, guidelines, standards and regulations. In addition to the public planning law → p. 56, these are mainly environmental, health and safety, and fire protection requirements → ❷. Further, there are various state laws and product-specific regulations.

Life cycles

Analogous to the life cycles of the product, industrial building is subject to various economic phases → ❺. Ever shorter product cycles (5–7 years) are not in accord with the life of a normal building. Aspects of adaptability, suitability for letting and resale value are therefore becoming increasingly significant in the design of industrial buildings.

Product **5 years**

product development	market introduction	growth	maturity	market saturation	decline
idea	design	construction	use	rebuilding	demolition

Building **25 years**

❺ Life cycles of products (above) and buildings (below)

Typologies

The basic types of industrial building can be split into additive and integrative plants.

In additive plants, the individual functional units are shaped according to their purpose and added to planar or linear structures (often along a production line). The units can be extended, developed and exchanged separately → ❸.

In integrative plants, the functional units are assembled to form a neutral structure → ❹. The advantages here are the minimisation of access areas and reusability. Possibilities for extension have to be planned into the building structure.

Machine | Person

Control display → Decision → Operation → Production → Control display

❶ Human performance – mechanical performance

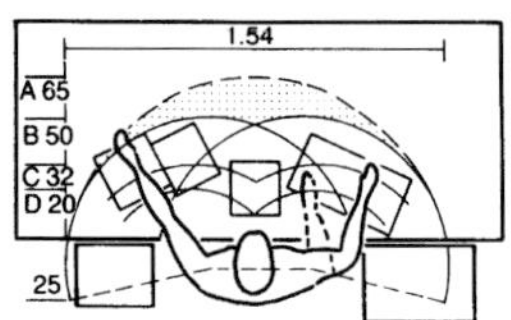

A maximum possible reach (≈65 cm)
B physiological limits of reach (≈50 cm)
C normal reach (≈32 cm)
D physiological inner limits of reach (16–20 cm)

❷ Reach zones at a workplace (according to Stier)

operation	flow diagram: product / work group (○ ⇨ D ▽ □)	time (min)	distance (m)
1			
2		4	11
3		12	
4		6	
5		33	
6		4	
7		10	23
8		18	
9		10	2
10		16	

❸ Production flow chart for an item (example)

planning symbols		AMSE	VDI
no.	action		
1	process	○	
2	store	▽	△
3	delay	D	D
4	test	□	□
5	transport	⇨	>
6	handle		○
7	finish + test	⊡	□

The VDI (Association of German Engineers) symbols apply in Germany; the ASME (American Society of Mechanical Engineers) symbols are recommended for international use.

❹ Planning symbols

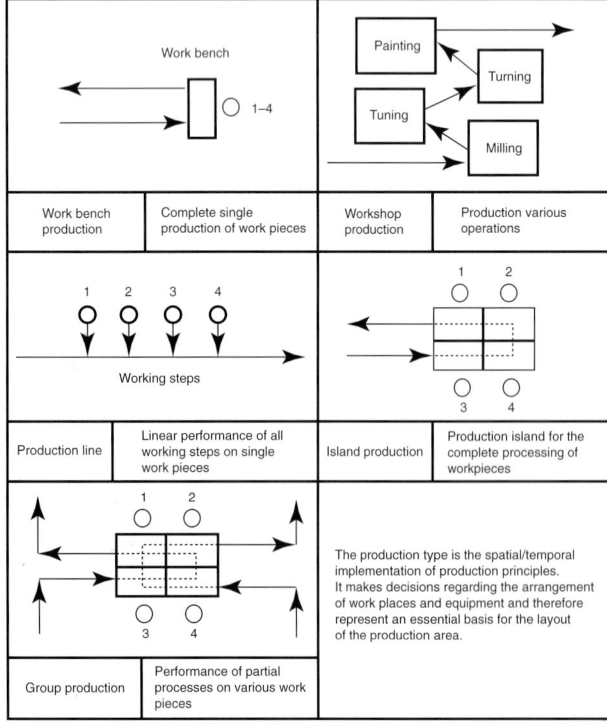

❺ Types of production (examples)

Production

Production is the assembly over space and time of work, material and tools (machines, raw material etc.) to produce products and services. The performance required for production (work/time unit) is described as relevant performance and is a combination of **human performance** (motor and exploratory skills) and **machine performance.**

Human and machine collaborate in the **production cycle** → ❶. This comprises various forms of production → ❺ and can be planned using flow charts → ❸. Human performance is not constant, but is subject to numerous individual and collaborative factors (strain – tiredness – recovery, age, sex, health).

The general requirements for workplaces are collected in the **Workplace Regulations** (2004) of the Federal Ministry for Industry and Employment → ❻, of which detailed expansion is laid down in the **Workplace Guidelines** (→ p. 263 ❷).

Buildings in general	**Construction** and **strength** according to type of use
Dimensions of workplaces, air space	sufficient **floor area** and clear **height** (depending on size of floor area) for the performance of the work without impairment of safety, health or well-being; **air space** measured depending on the number of employees and the type of physical effort.
Floors, walls, ceilings, roofs	**surfaces** must be formed according to the requirements of the business and be easy to clean, with sufficient insulation against heat, cold and damp at the workplace: **floor** without unevenness, tripping hazards, dangerous slopes; must be load-bearing, safe for walking, not slippery; **glass walls** near workplaces must be clearly marked, non-breakable or shielded, and **roofs** which are not safe must be walked on only when adequate safety equipment is provided.
Windows, fanlights	must be safe to open, close, adjust and fix, must pose no danger in the opened position, and be safe to clean.
Doors, gates	**location, number, construction** according to type and use of the rooms and areas, **transparent doors** are to be marked at eye level, non-breakable or constructed with protection against breakage; construct **hinged doors** to see through with a view window; secure doors against levering out and falling out or over; provide highly visible **doors for pedestrians** in the immediate vicinity of **gates for vehicle traffic; powered doors and gates** must be safely usable, and in emergency capable of being opened automatically or manually.
Transport routes	must be easily and safely usable (including stairs, access ladders and ramps), **sized** according to number of users and type of business; where vehicles are used on access routes, sufficient space for pedestrians; **transport routes for vehicles** must run with sufficient distance from doors, footpaths, stair exits, etc. if necessary mark **borders of transport routes**.
Escape routes and emergency exits	**number, size and arrangement** according to use, equipment and size of workplace and number of people present, shortest possible **route into the open air**/into a safe area, permanent **marking** in suitable form, if necessary safety lighting, escape doors easily operable at any time, open outward, **revolving and sliding doors** are not permissible as emergency exits.

❻ General requirements for building (elements), Workplace Regulations 2004 (excerpts)

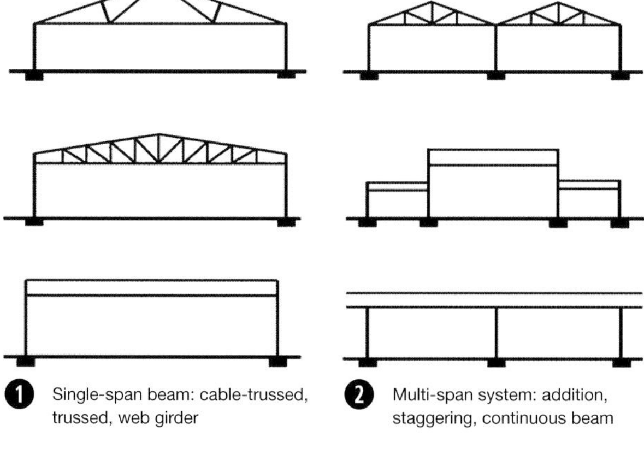

❶ Single-span beam: cable-trussed, trussed, web girder

❷ Multi-span system: addition, staggering, continuous beam

Production and warehouse buildings are often built as industrial sheds without internal floors but with large spans and room heights.

Construction, spans and heights

Timber, steel or reinforced concrete construction with spans of 5–50 m according to client requirements (arrangement of machines, access routes and turning circles of vehicles) and room heights of 3–6 m. Built as solid, trussed or cable-trussed structures with fixed-end columns → ❶, frames → ❺ – ❻ or as a framed construction stiffened with bracing, often as added or staggered buildings. Shed height and load assumptions are often dependent on the proposed overhead crane → p. 287.

Advantages of shed construction

Low construction cost due to light roof construction and omission of expensive floor slabs; uniform natural lighting with rooflights, even for very deep spaces; heavy floor loading possible; few(er) fire protection requirements; flow of materials and people on one level.

Disadvantages of shed construction

Large area of land required; unfavourable ratio of plan area to volume; unfavourable thermal behaviour (heat loss, heat build-up in summer).

Lighting, ventilation, building services

Lighting and ventilation (and smoke extraction) are provided by light bands, north lights or light domes in the roof construction → ❼ – ⓬ or also strip windows in the façade.

Heating is normally (central/decentralised) air heating or overhead radiant heating (temporary heating of single areas).

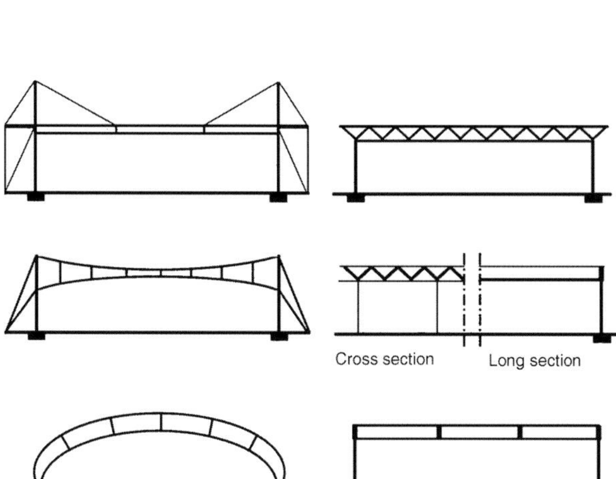

❸ Tension bracing, cable structure, pneumatic construction

❹ Space frame, folded structure, beam grillage

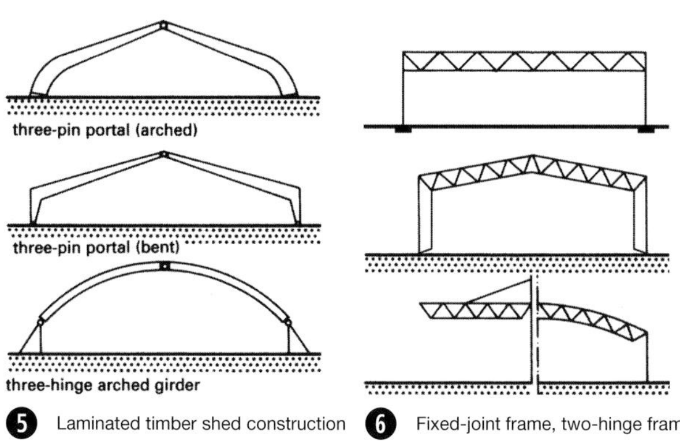

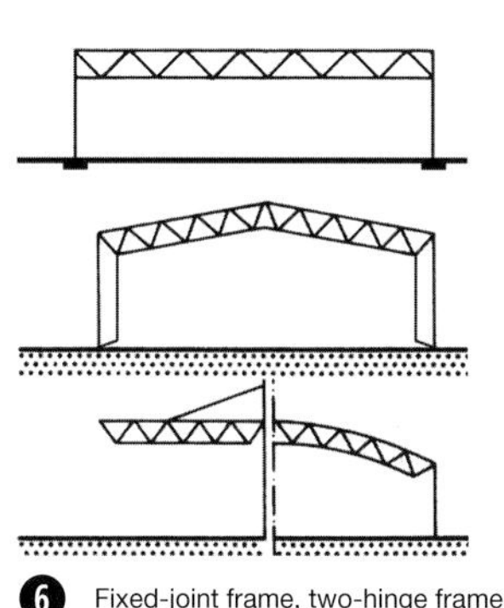

❺ Laminated timber shed construction

❻ Fixed-joint frame, two-hinge frame

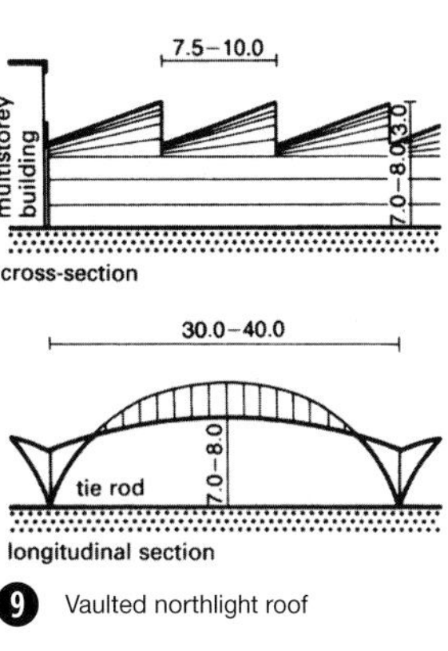

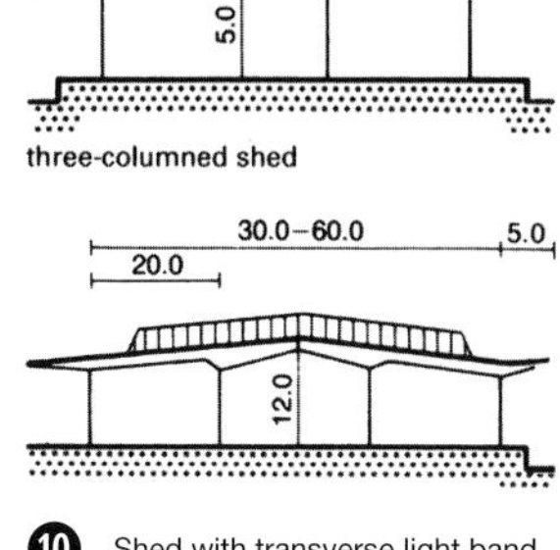

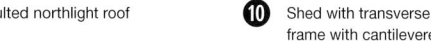

❾ Vaulted northlight roof

❿ Shed with transverse light band, frame with cantilevered beams

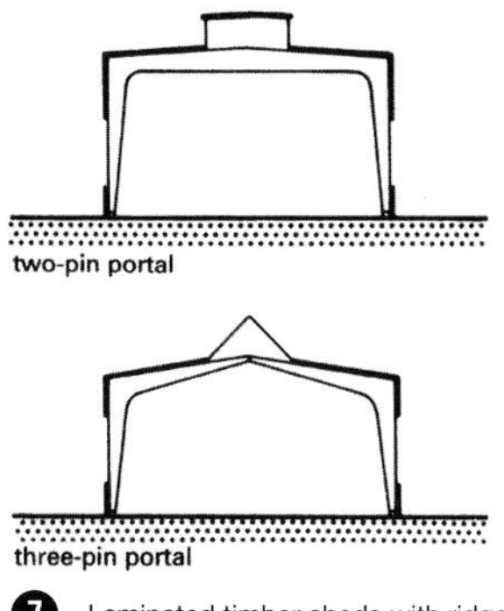

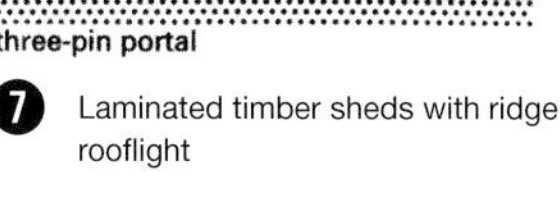

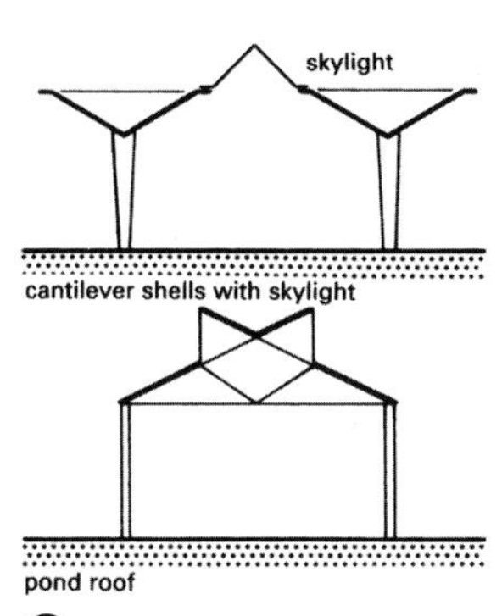

❼ Laminated timber sheds with ridge rooflight

❽ Pond roof with fixed-end columns

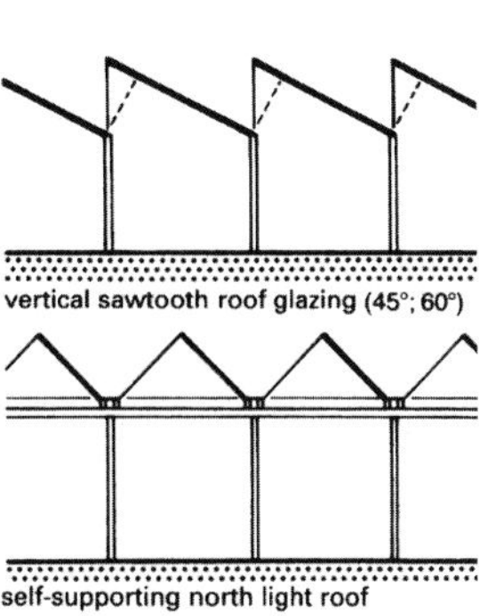

vertical sawtooth roof glazing (45°; 60°)
self-supporting north light roof

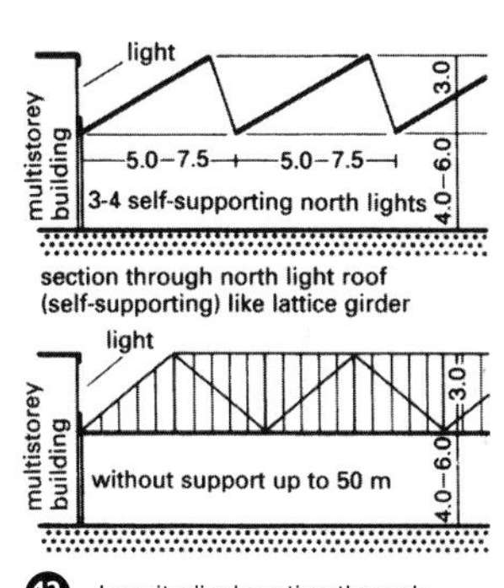

⓫ Sheds with northlight glazing

⓬ Longitudinal section through northlight roof with cross-bracing in the glazing

Production facilities can be located over a number of storeys if required for town planning, development or operational reasons: this type of structure is particularly suitable for breweries, paper mills, warehouses and other buildings, where the working material is conveyed once to the uppermost floor and then descends under gravity, and also electronic, precision mechanical and other branches of light industry.

Advantages/disadvantages of multi-storey buildings

Compact, space-saving but expensive construction method, limited floor loadings, short (installation) routes through vertical connections, good operating costs, simple ventilation, good light from side.

Construction, spans, room heights

Room heights should be determined depending on building depth and working room height (guideline 3.00 m for working rooms larger than 100 m^2).

A good ratio is 2:1 (plan depth : room height) for free-standing multi-storey factory buildings with windows without visible lintels (traffic routes in centre of building not included in calculation) → ❶.

Economic building depths are 12.0–15.0 m (3 m clear height) for rooms without columns → ❸ – ❹, 15.0 or 17.5 m (4 m clear height) with 1 or 2 columns → ❺, 20 or 22.5 m (5 m clear height) with two columns → ❻.

Lighting

Multi-storey buildings with windows on one side should face northeast, and, with windows on both sides facing north and south, they should be oriented east–west. The summer sun thus only shines into the interior to a limited extent and is easy to shade with blinds (possibly continuously motorised sun awnings), but in winter the room is pleasantly sunlit (no disturbing shadows in the working area) → ❹. The distance of the working area from the window should be twice as long as the clear window height → ❷.

Stairs and toilets (cool) can be located on the north side.

The best lighting is provided by free-standing buildings which are twice as far from each other as they are high (ground floor angle of light = 27°) → ❷; single-storey buildings with rooflights can be located between these.

Approx. figures for window areas: 1/10 of the floor area for rooms up to 600 m^2 (Workplace Guidelines 7/1 → p. 263); for fine work, provide 1/5 of the floor area.

If the room depths are large, a scattering of the light coming in is advantageous (sun shades, venetian blinds, light-scattering glass etc.), in which case the spanning direction of the main supporting beam is significant → ❶ – ❷.

❶ Joists running along the external wall; uneven, weak lighting

❷ Optimal spacing of buildings for good lighting

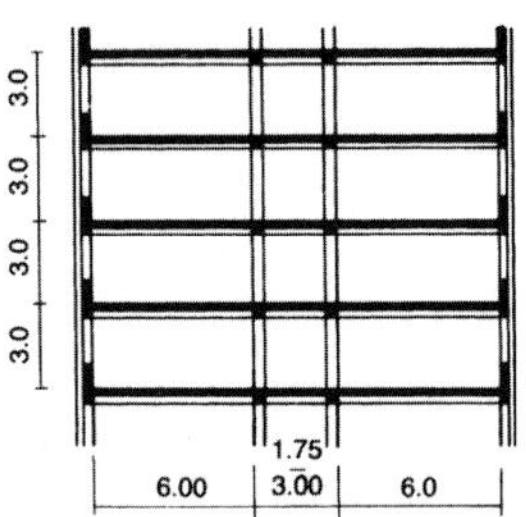

❸ Building depths for given storey heights

❹ Truss spanning room, free use of floor space

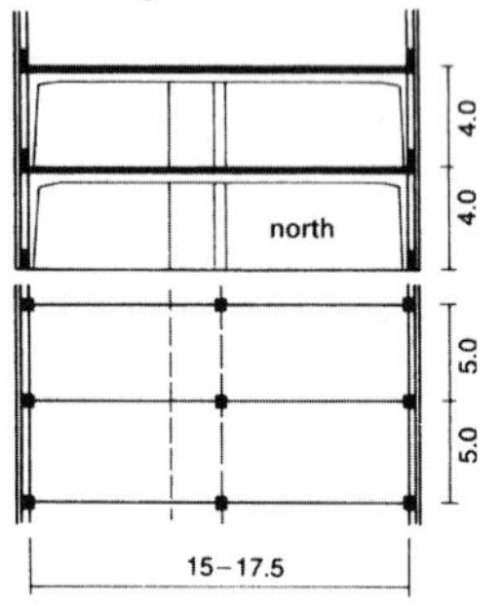

❺ Central column determines layout of middle passage with columns to right or left; larger space to the north

❻ Cantilever beams offer structural advantages, but the columns mostly obstruct the working area

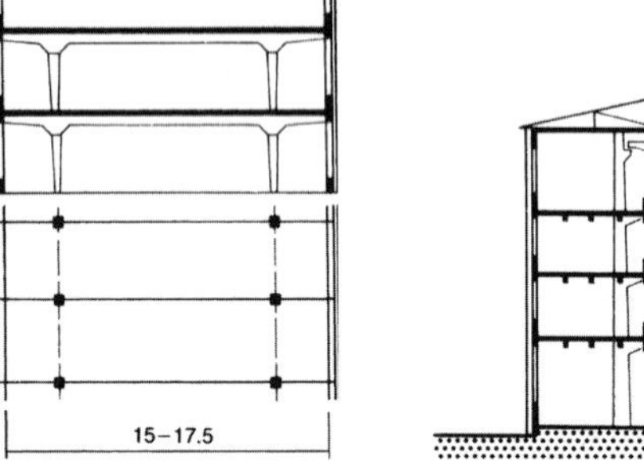

❼ Deepest space with two internal columns providing bracing. External pin-ended columns

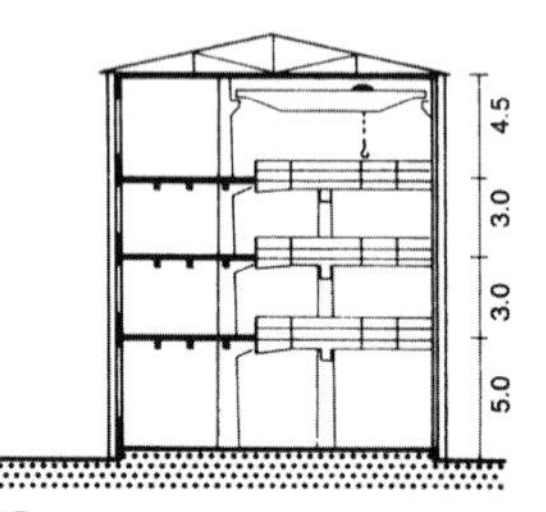

❽ Multi-storey building with crane shed, also acting as lifting shaft for transporting work items to the offset balconies projecting on the upper floors

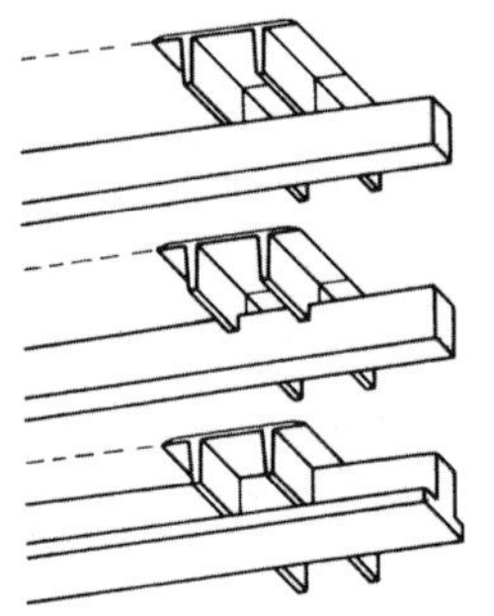

❾ Floor slab supports: TT section

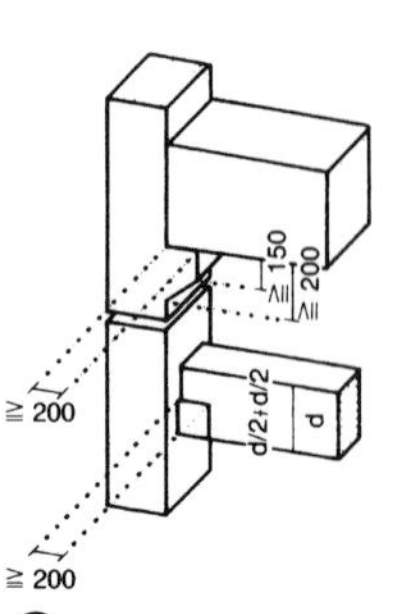

❿ Joist/cross member support, rectangular cross-section

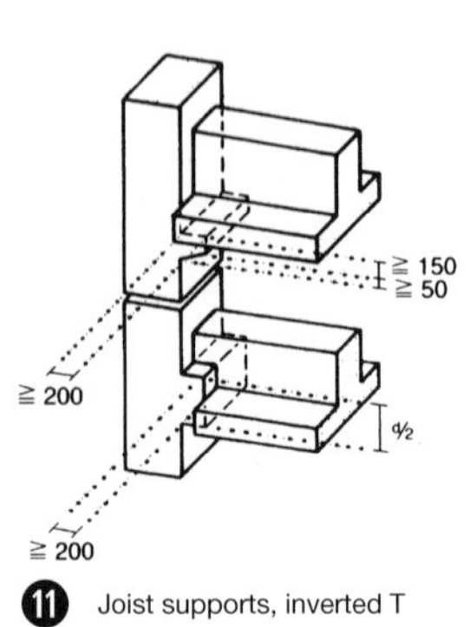

⓫ Joist supports, inverted T

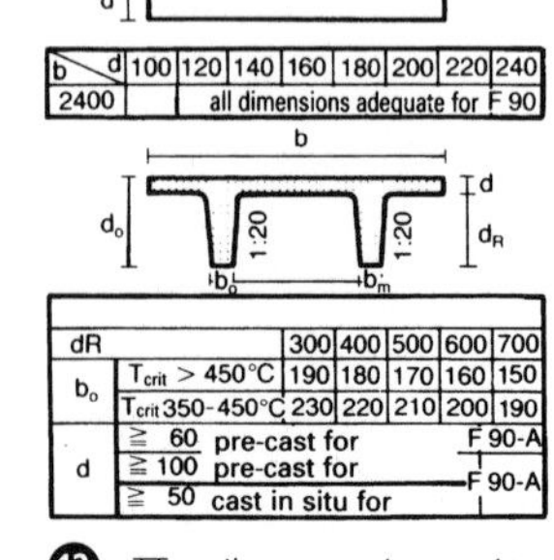

b \ d	100	120	140	160	180	200	220	240
2400		all dimensions adequate for F 90						

dR		300	400	500	600	700
b_o	T_{crit} > 450°C	190	180	170	160	150
	T_{crit} 350–450°C	230	220	210	200	190
d	≧ 60 pre-cast for					F 90-A
	≧ 100 pre-cast for					F 90-A
	≧ 50 cast in situ for					

⓬ TT-section pre-cast concrete elements, floor slabs

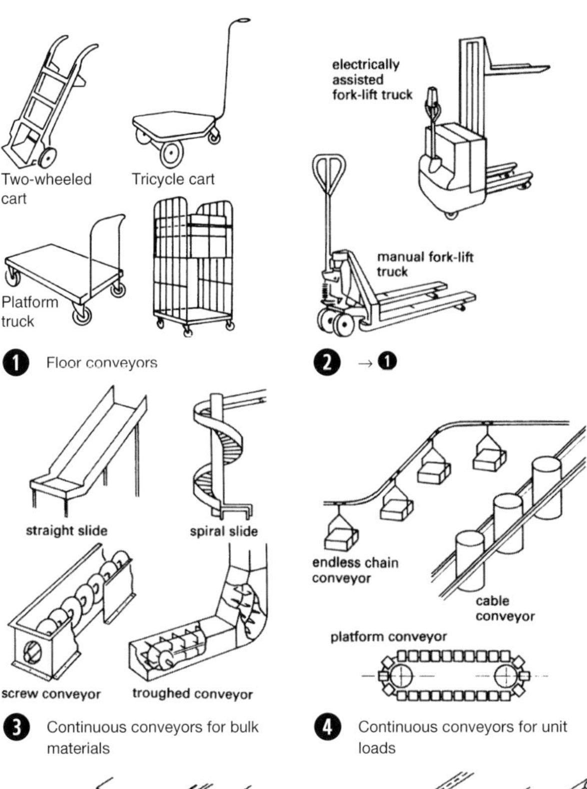

❶ Floor conveyors

❷ → ❶

❸ Continuous conveyors for bulk materials

❹ Continuous conveyors for unit loads

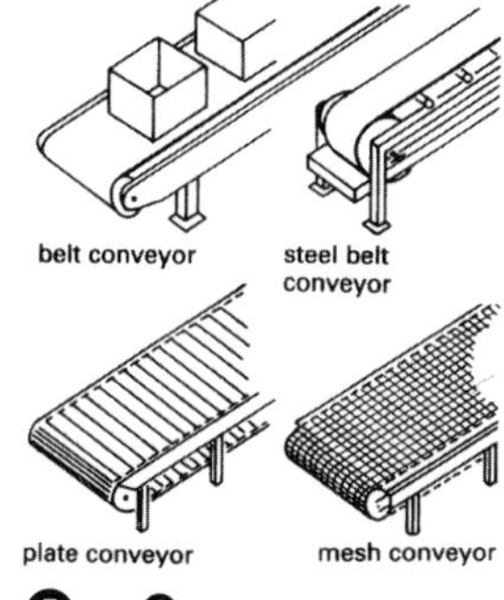
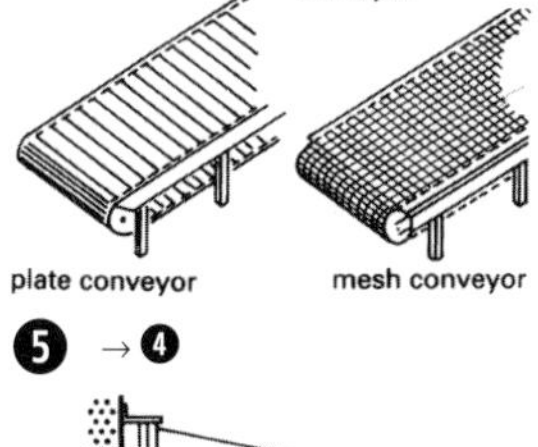

❺ → ❹

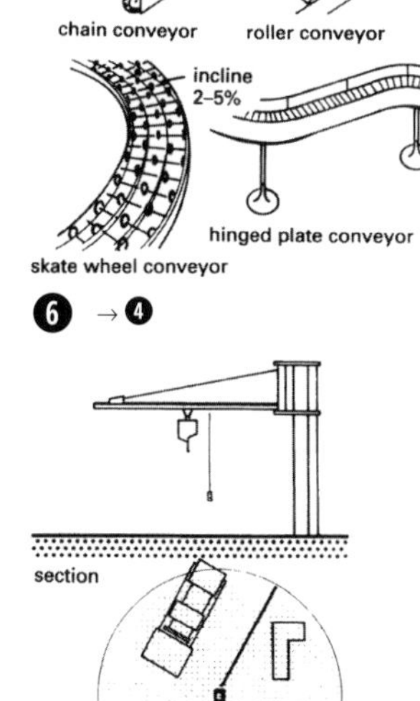

❻ → ❹

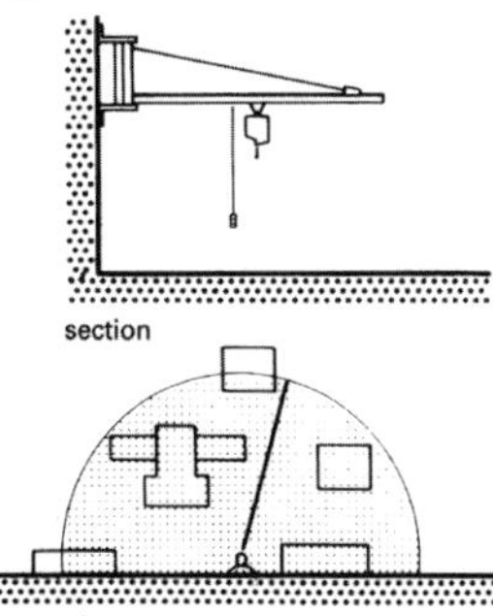

❼ Wall-mounted swivel crane

❽ Column-mounted swivel crane

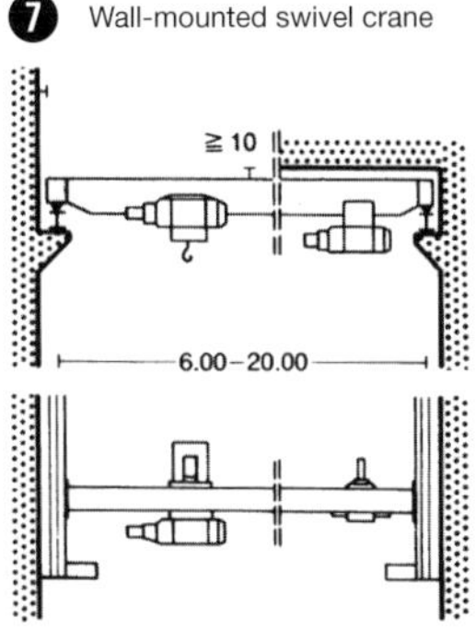
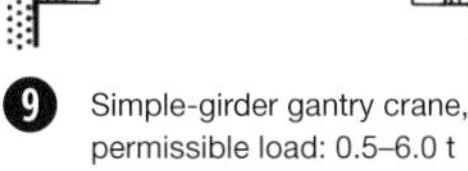

❾ Simple-girder gantry crane, permissible load: 0.5–6.0 t

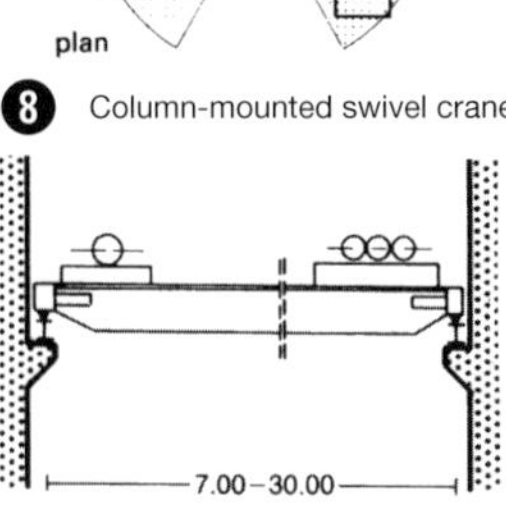
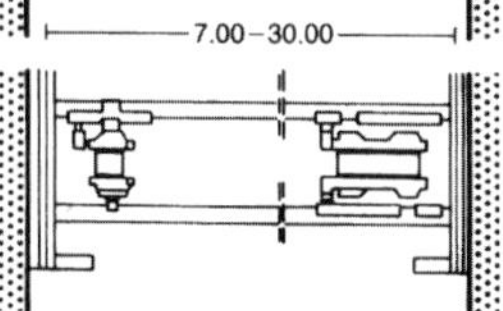

❿ Double-girder gantry crane, permissible load 2–20 t

Transport is a part of the material flow process. Transport planning is the definition of the transport relationships or tasks within the material flow and the planning of the interactions with storage → p. 268. Essential terms in transport planning are:

transported goods (material, transport unit)
transport performance (quantity, times, deadlines)
transport type (course of the transport routes) and
means of transport (or conveyance) technical equipment for the direct and indirect transport of goods.

Means of transport can be divided into continuous and discontinuous conveyors:

Continuous conveyors

Continuous conveyors are mechanical, hydraulic or pneumatic systems with a defined transport route (permanent or mobile), along which the transported goods are continuously (regularly, in cycles or with variable speed) moved between loading and unloading locations. Continuous conveyors are particularly suitable for the transport of similar goods over a fixed route, but the high automation and transport capacity comes at the cost of high investment and low adaptability.

Continuous conveyors include:

Conveyor belts → ❺, track and chain conveyors → ❻, screw conveyors, slides → ❸, endless overhead chain and rope conveyors, moving tables → ❹, pneumatic (pressure and suction) conveyors (bulk goods and liquids), centrifugal conveyors and bucket chain conveyors.

Discontinuous conveyors

Discontinuous conveyors work discontinuously. They can be differentiated into industrial trucks (running on wheels on a floor) and lifting devices (mostly cranes).

Floor conveyors

Industrial trucks are manually or mechanically driven, mostly without being on tracks, for stacking heights up to 6 m, in special cases up to 10 m. The advantages are the low plant costs and good suitability for medium distances between unloading and loading locations on a flat road or floor.

Floor conveyors include hand sack trucks, platform trolleys, pallet trucks and fork lift trucks → ❶ – ❷ → p. 269.

Cranes

Cranes are machines for the vertical lifting of large and heavy goods. Horizontal mobility can also be provided through wheeled trolleys or winch trolleys → ❾ – ⓬.

Swivel cranes → ❼ – ❽ enable the lifting of objects from any point in their radius of operation.

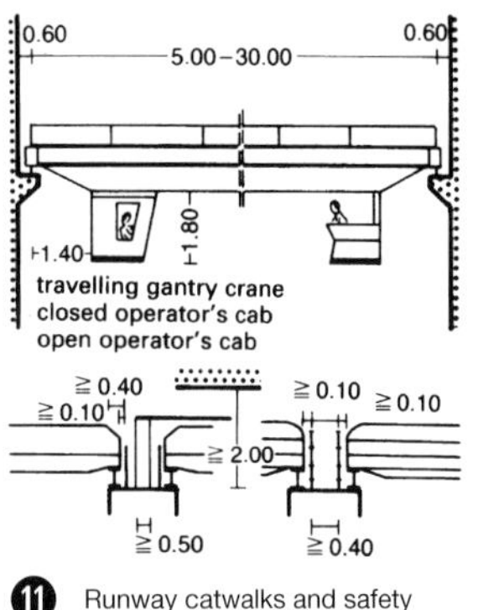
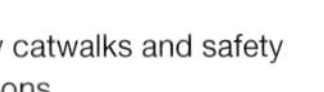

⓫ Runway catwalks and safety dimensions

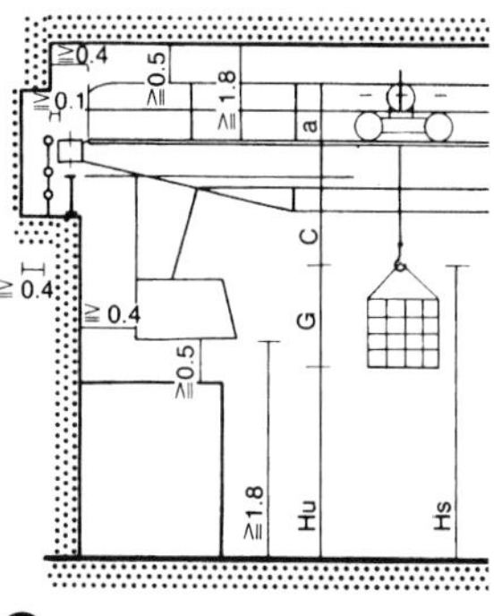

⓬ Gantry crane (with driver's cabin) and safety dimensions

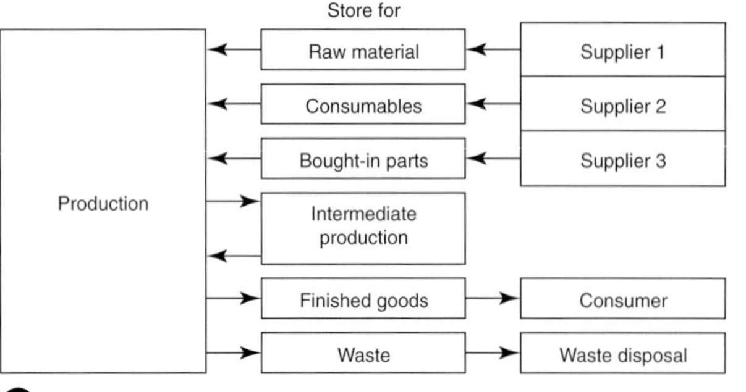

❶ Warehouse as a buffer between market and production (Führer, Störmer → refs)

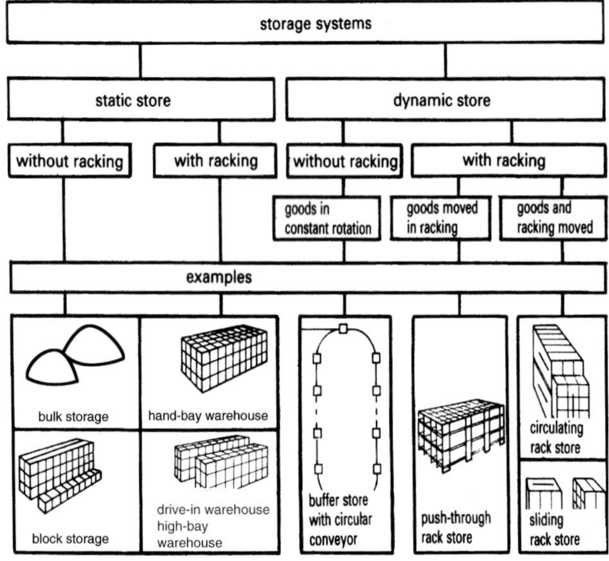

❷ Classification of warehouse systems (excerpt)

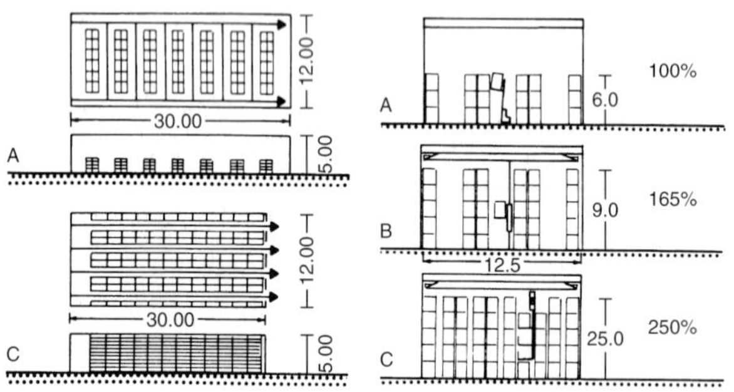

❸ Comparison of possible uses of a warehouse

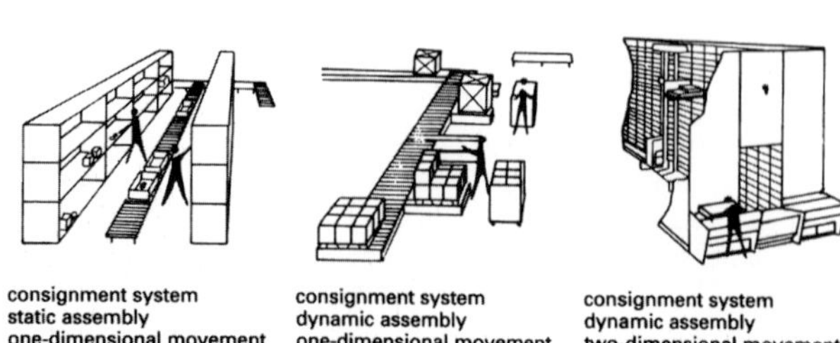

❹ Alternative systems of picking

Basics

Storage is part of the material flow process and logistically forms the connection between production and marketing → ❶. Storage is cost-intensive and does not create economic value, leading to attempts to minimise the storage quantities and times or effectively combine the storage and transport of materials and goods through flexible **'just-in-time production'**.

There is a wide range of different static and dynamic storage systems available for each storage situation and the goods needing storage → ❷. The spatial arrangement of the different warehouses in the production process can also be dealt with in various ways → ❺.

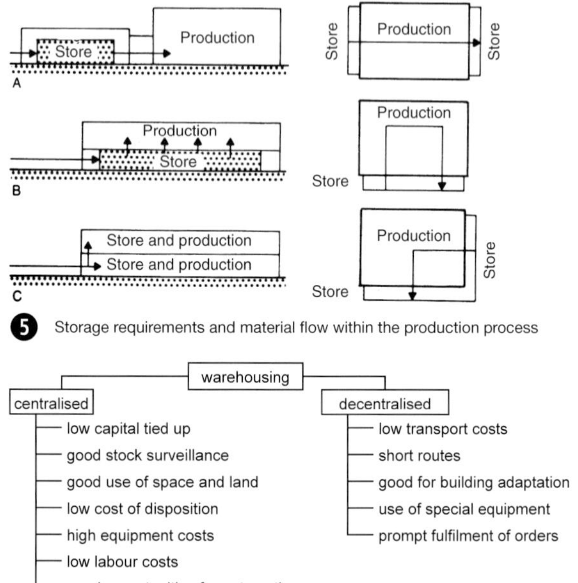

❺ Storage requirements and material flow within the production process

❻ Advantages of centralised and decentralised storage

traffic routes inside warehouses	
pedestrians pedestrians and powered stackers	min. **1.25 m** **vehicle width + 2 x 0.50 m**
passage widths between racks	
with manual operation with forklift operation (swivelling forks) with forklift operation (rigid forks)	min. **0.75 m** **forklift width + 2 × 0.50 m** **forklift + fork + 0.50 m**
rack heights (depending on equipment)	
hand shelves single-storey (two-storey) pallet warehouse with forklift operation high-bay warehouse with high-bay forklifts high-bay warehouse with stacking crane	up to **3.0 m** (up to 6.0 m) up to **6.0 m** up to **9.0 m** up to **25.0 m**

❼ Basic dimensions in warehouses (MBO, Workplace Regulations, Industrial Building Guidelines, ZH, Health and Safety Regulations)

Picking

Picking, or order assembly, denotes collecting articles out of the warehouse and making them ready for dispatch in accordance with an order. This can be single-stage picking (specific to one order) or two-stage picking, with an intermediate picking zone for temporary storage and assignment of the articles to a number of orders.

The work is performed flexibly and with no technical support, or very little, as a 'man to goods' system → ❹, left, or for more capacity with partly or fully automated transport vehicles and complex infrastructure as a 'goods to man' system → ❹, centre and right.

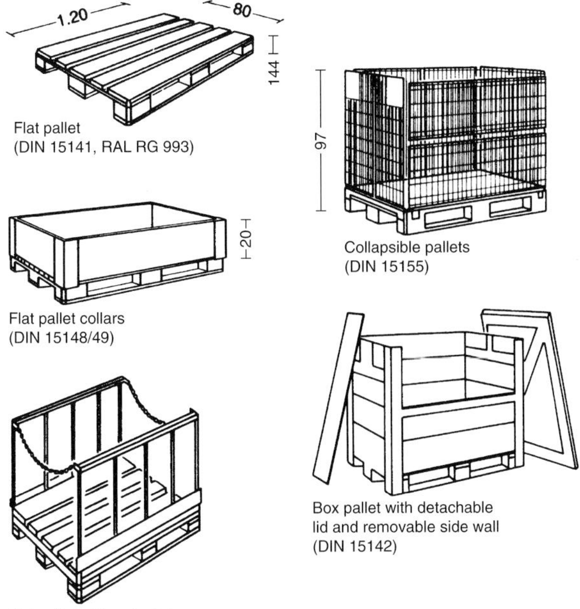

❶ Pallets and accessories

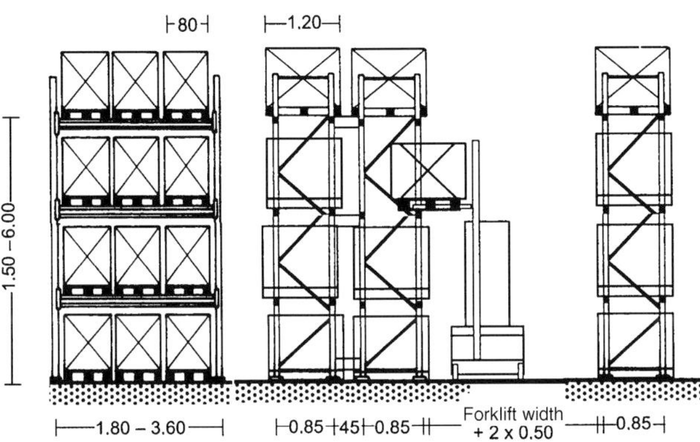

❷ Pallet rack for forklift operation (swivelling fork), elevation, section

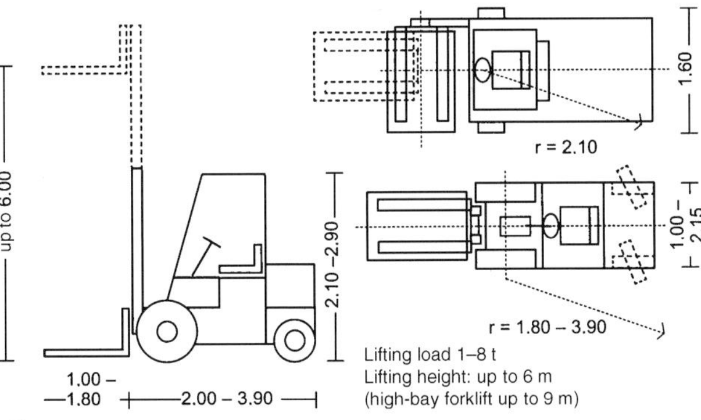

❸ Forklifts with rigid and swivelling forks (elevation, plan)

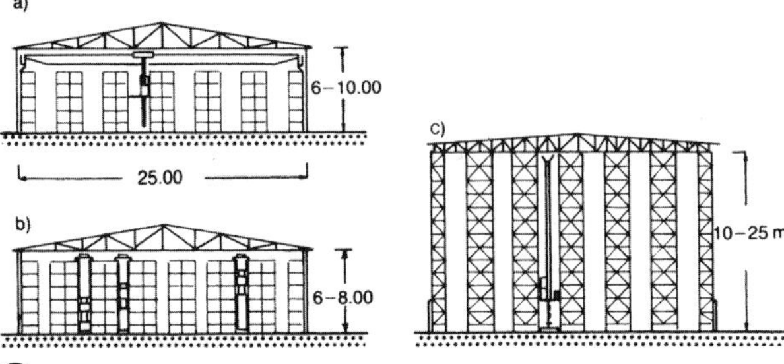

❹ a) universal warehouse with stacking crane, b) warehouse with installed pallet racking, c) high-bay system

Storage and shipping containers

Storage containers serve to combine the goods into loading units with the purpose of maximising the exploitation of space and transport capacity and the avoidance of handling. The most common storage containers for unit goods are **stackable crates** made of timber or plastic, **pallets** (flat pallets, pallets with side rails and additional equipment) and also increasingly **containers**.

On order to simplify international transport, the European pallet pool has introduced the **standardised transport pallet** (Europallet, Pool pallet, 800 × 1200 × 144 mm) with various stacking attachments → ❶.

Standardised pallets can be exchanged within the pool without reloading. Numerous standard sizes for packaging, transport and storage have been derived from the dimensions of the Europallet.

On account of the variety of uses and the rough handling and loading, storage pallets are subject to many quality standards.

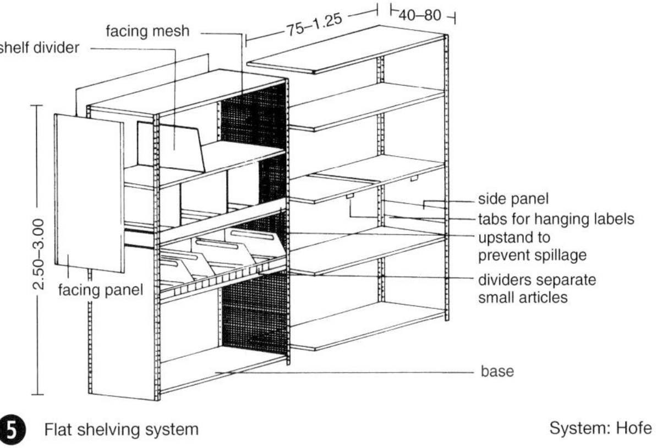

❺ Flat shelving system

System: Hofe

Warehouse equipment

The selection of warehouse equipment has a similar importance in the design of warehouses. This depends on the quality, quantity, weight and handling frequency of the stored goods and also warehouse organisation and means of transport. Warehouse equipment is subject to numerous regulations (an overview can be found, for example, in Association of Commercial Accident Insurance Companies 234 → p. 263). The traditional storage system in industrial warehouses is **flat shelves** → ❺ as manual shelving for small parts. These are constructed as bolted or slot-in systems (e.g. angle profiles with holes) with inserted steel shelves, wire mesh compartments, drawers or doors. These systems can be up to approx. 4.50 m high (with accessible hop-up level) and are suitable for loadings of 250 kg/shelf.

For larger loadings and heights, **pallet racks** are available as standardised modular systems made of channel and I-beam profiles. Bays with an axial spacing of approx. 2.80 m (for three Europallets horizontally) have become established. Using forklift trucks, heights of up to 6.00 m are practical → ❷. The passage width between the racks depends on the size and type of the forklift truck to be used (rigid forks, swivelling forks) and the requirements of Health and Safety Regulations / ZH 1 (vehicle width + 2 × 50 cm) → ❸.

In order to store items still more densely, fully automated **high-bay warehouses** are used, often independent of production location. These have special swivelling stacking cranes that stack at heights of up to 25.00 m. They are normally supplied by specialist firms as an integrated system (racking and building envelope) → ❹.

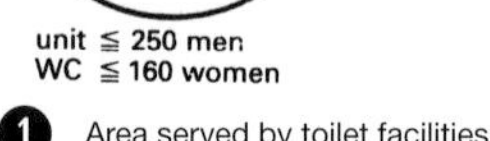

❶ Area served by toilet facilities

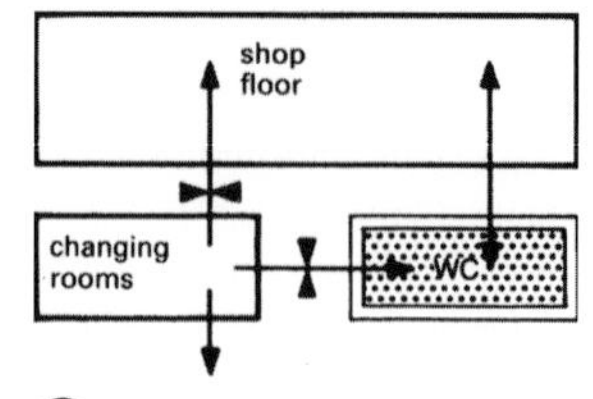

❷ Arrangement of toilet facilities

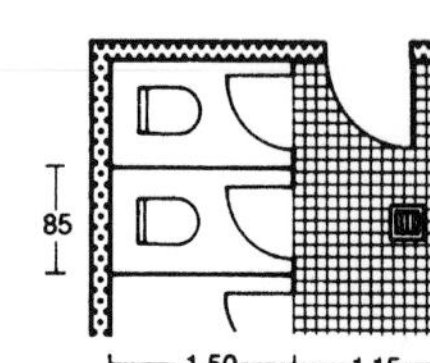

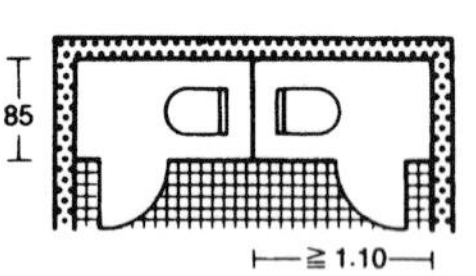

❸ Single-row WCs, doors open outward

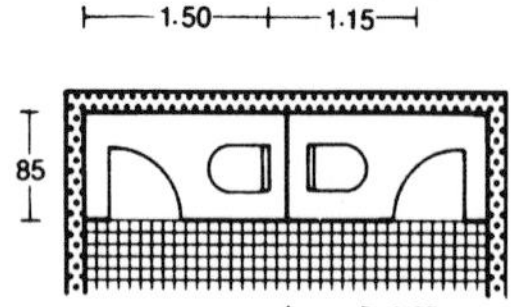

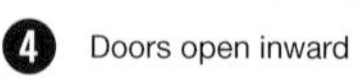

❹ Doors open inward

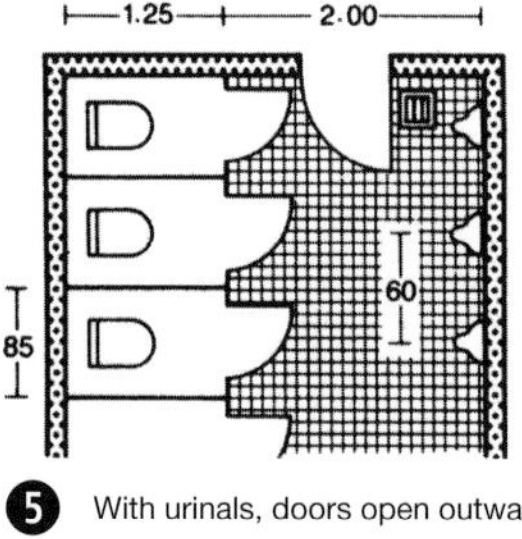

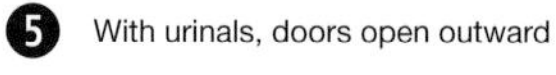

❺ With urinals, doors open outward

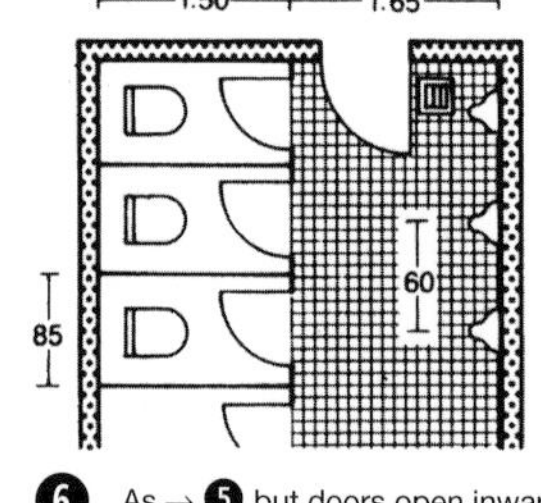

❻ As → ❺ but doors open inward

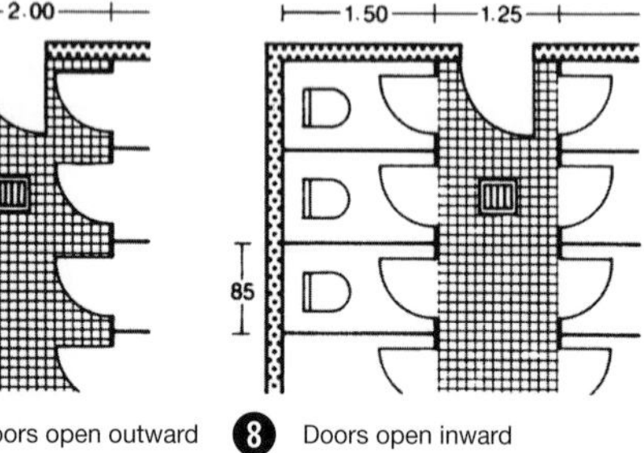

❼ Two-row WCs, doors open outward

❽ Doors open inward

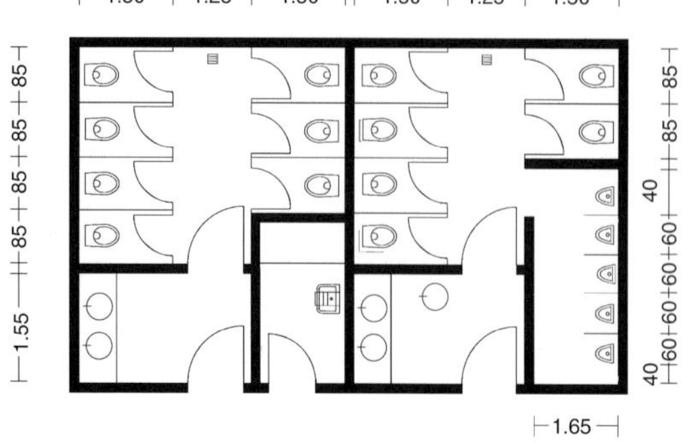

❾ Toilet facilities for 100 women and men (example)

Industry and trade

INDUSTRY
Basics
Shed construction
Multi-storey industrial buildings
Transport
Warehousing
Subsidiary rooms
Examples

Workplace Regulations
Workplace Guidelines 37/1

see also: Industry/Basics p. 263 ❷

Toilets

These are to be provided at a distance from each workstation of not more than **100 m** or, at the farthest, one storey height (if no escalator is available). Toilets should also be provided near social, readiness, washing and changing rooms → ❶. If there are more than **five employees**, separate toilets must be provided for women and men and these should be available exclusively to employees. The number of necessary toilets depends on the number of employees → ❿: the site and arrangement are shown → ❸ – ⓫. Disability-friendly toilets are to be provided in accordance with regulations → p. 21 ff.

Toilet facilities consist of a **lobby** with washbasins (at least one washbasin per five WCs) and a **completely separate room** with at least one WC (unless the facilities contain only one toilet and have no direct access to a work, social, changing, wash or sanitary room). Toilet cubicles must be lockable and, if light partitions (incompletely separated WC cubicles) are used, the partition should have a height of at least 1.90 m, and at the bottom a gap of 10–15 cm. Urinals must be placed so as not to be visible from the entrance. **Toilet facilities should not contain more than 10 WC cubicles and 10 urinals**. Further details of the requirements for toilets are contained in Workplace Guidelines 37/1. With **natural ventilation**, the minimum ventilation sections are: with window ventilation on one side 1700 cm^2/WC, 1000 cm^2/urinal; with through ventilation (ventilation shaft and opening window opposite) 1000 cm^2/WC, 600 cm^2/urinal. **Ventilation equipment** is to be designed for 30 m^3/WC and 15 m^3/urinal (altogether at least five air changes/h).

Men							Women					
number of employees	flushing WCs	urinals	gutter (m)	washbasins	additional flushing WCs	additional urinals	number of employees	flushing WCs	washbasins	additional flushing WCs	waste bins	bucket sink
10	1	1	0.6	1	1	1	10	1	1	1	1	1
25	2	2	1.2	1	1	1	20	2	1	1	1	1
50	3	3	1.8	1	1	1	35	3	1	1	1	1
75	4	4	2.4	1	1	2	50	4	2	2	1	1
100	5	5	3.0	2	1	2	65	5	2	2	1	1
130	6	6	3.6	2	2	2	80	6	2	2	1	1
160	7	7	4.2	2	2	2	100	7	2	3	1	1
190	8	8	4.8	2	2	3	120	8	3	3	1	1
220	9	9	5.4	3	3	3	140	9	3	4	1	1
250	10	10	6.0	3	3	4	160	10	3	4	1	1

❿ Required number of WC fittings (according to Workplace Guidelines 37/1, → p. 263 ❷)

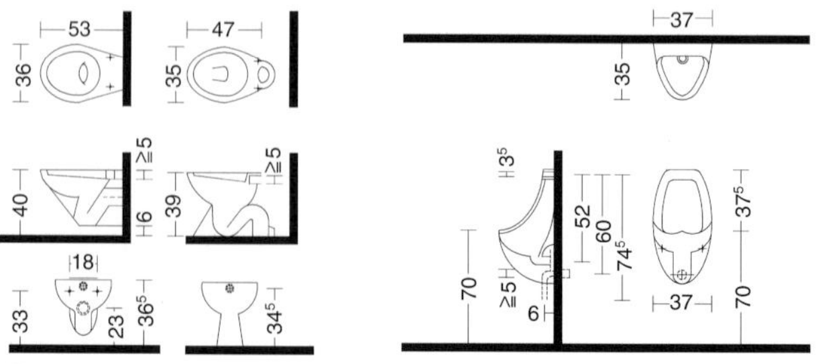

⓫ WC: wall-mounted – floor-mounted

Urinal

Washrooms

Washrooms are to be provided for employees engaged in activities dangerous to health or with strongly odorous substances, or who are subjected to the effects of heat or damp. Washing and changing rooms → p. 273 must be easily accessible from each other.

For every four employees (or in case of only moderately dirty activity every five employees), **one washroom** is to be provided, dimensions and layout → 9 – 16, designed for the largest shift. Special washrooms are to be provided for disabled people according to regulations → p. 21 ff. Permissible washing equipment: wash places (sluice, washbasin, washing fountain) and showers. Wash places: width and depth min. 70 × 55 cm, upper edge 70–80 cm above floor level, equipped with towel holder, soap dish, disposable towels (for hand drying) and waste bins. Provide at least **one shower**, and in the case of very dirty activity 30% of the washing facilities as showers; for employees engaged in activities dangerous to health or with strongly odorous substances, one shower per four employees. Provide a **foot wash** for every 10 wash places. With **natural ventilation**, minimum sections are to be observed: for ventilation from one side 400 cm^2 /m^2 floor area; or with through-ventilation from opposing windows 120 cm^2 (80 cm^2 with ventilation shafts) for supply and extract openings. **Ventilation equipment** is to be designed for at least 10 air changes/h.

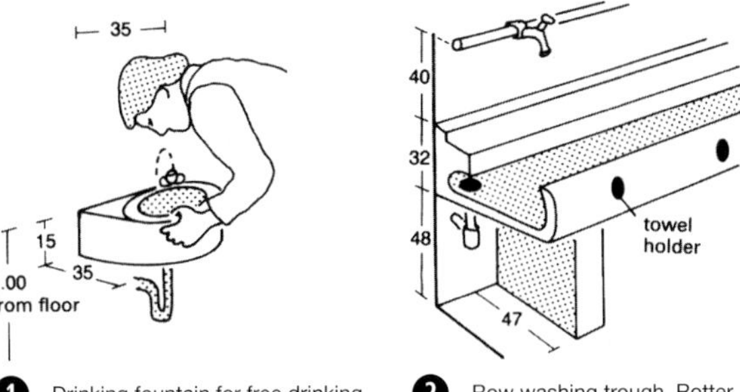

1 Drinking fountain for free drinking, activation by lever, <100 m from workstation

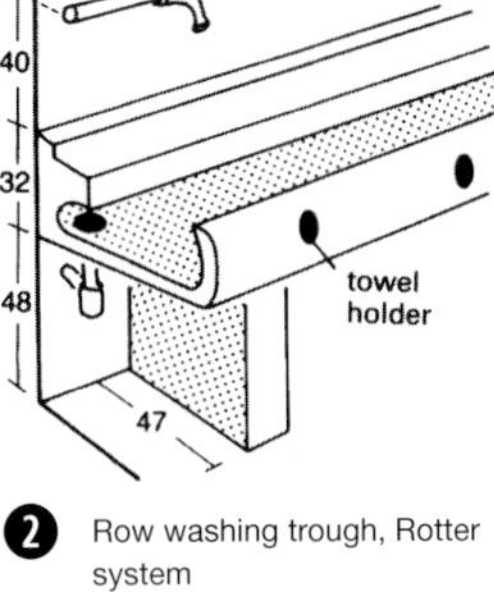

2 Row washing trough, Rotter system

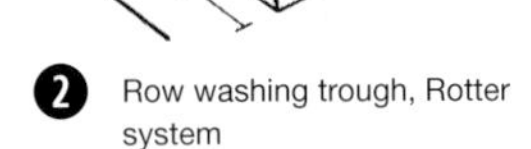

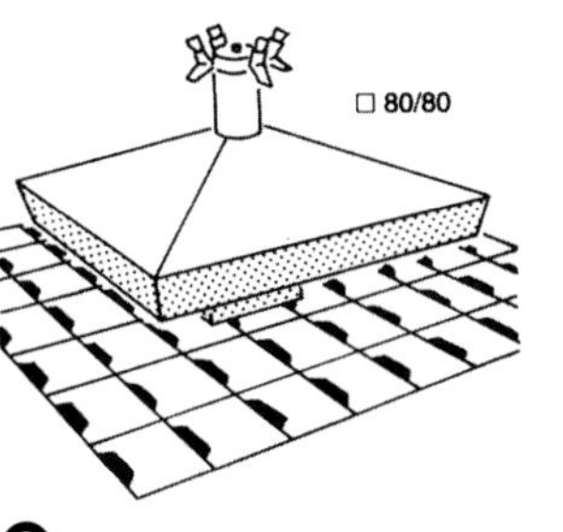

3 Foot washing system

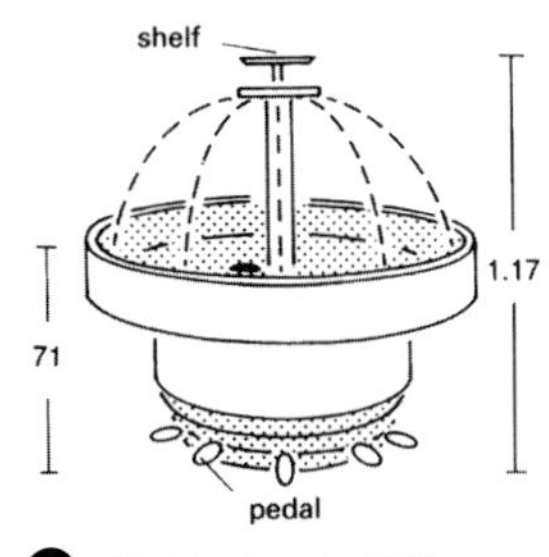

4 Washing fountain: 25% space saving compared to rows of basins → 2 – 11

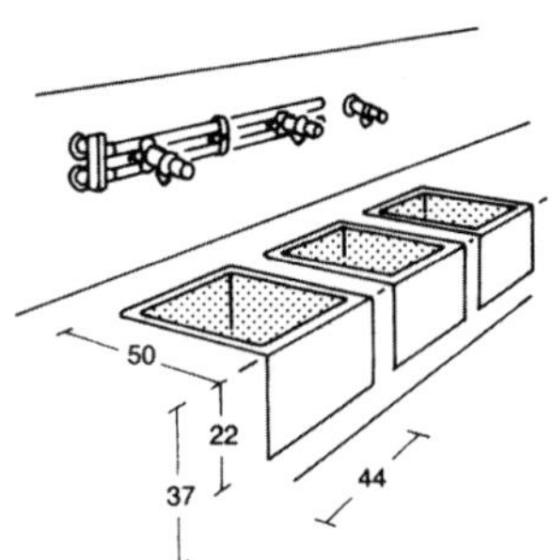

5 Foot baths

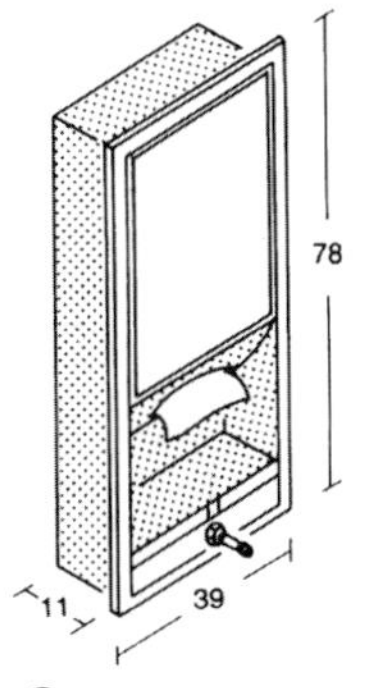

6 Paper towel dispenser, shelf and soap dispenser

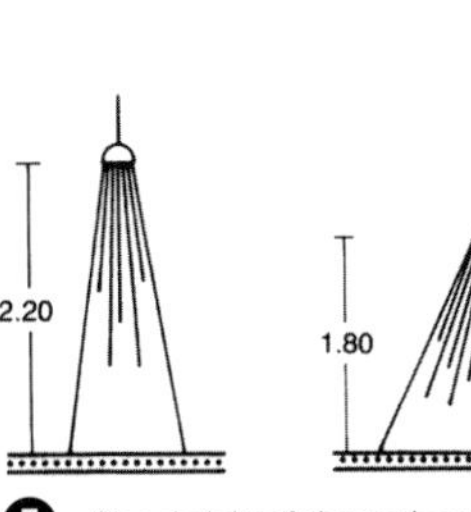

7 Clear height of shower heads

8 Space required for circular washbasins

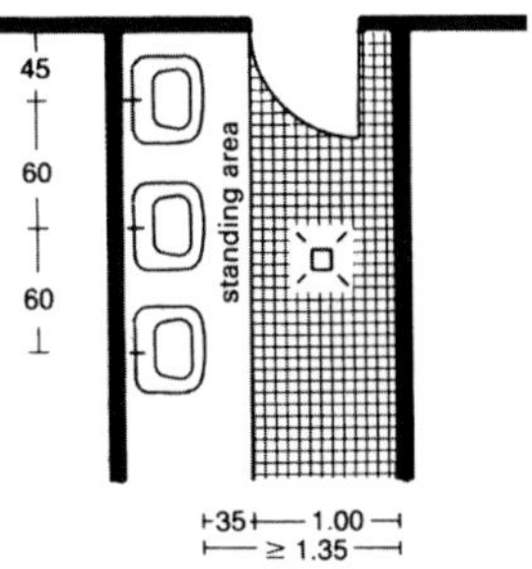

9 Washing facilities with washbasins

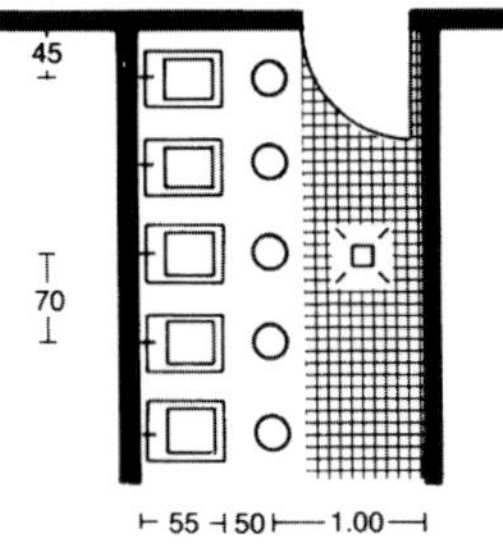

10 Washing facilities with foot baths

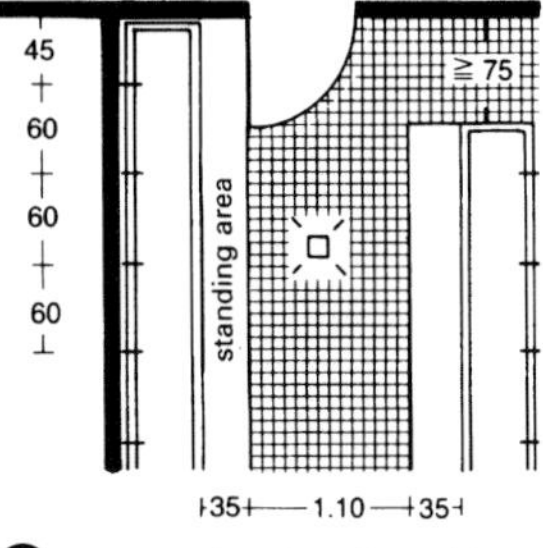

11 Washing facilities with washing trough

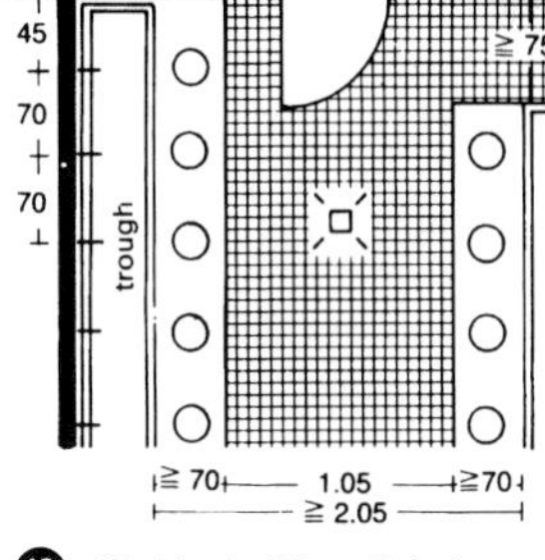

12 Washing facilities with foot washing trough

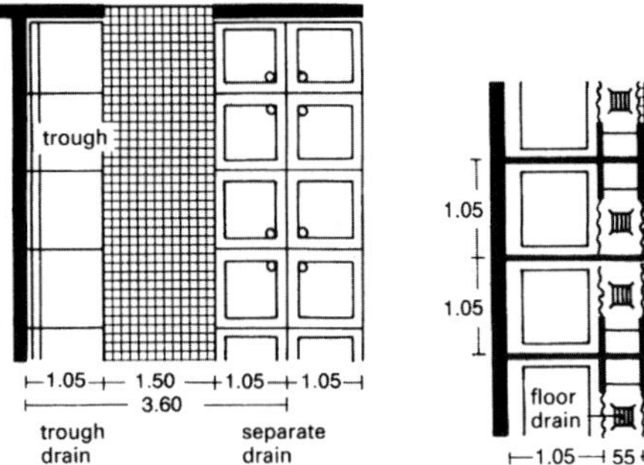

13 Semi-open showers

14 Single showers with changing booth

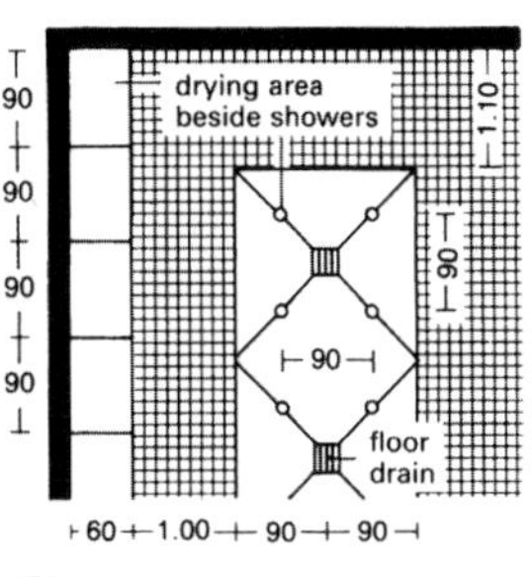

15 Open showers with drying places

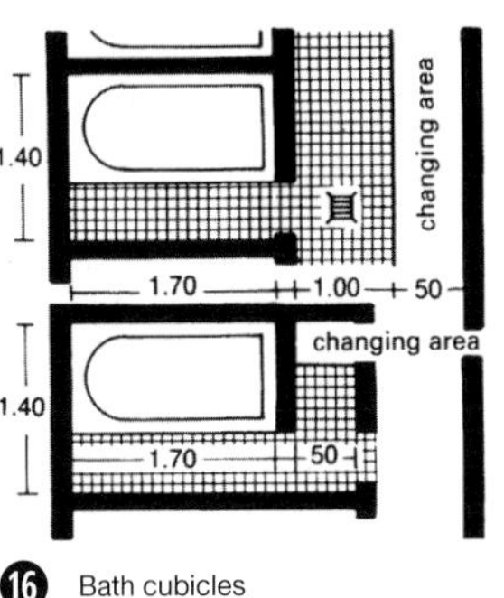

16 Bath cubicles

Industry and trade

INDUSTRY
Basics
Shed construction
Multi-storey industrial buildings
Transport
Warehousing
Subsidiary rooms
Examples

Workplace Regulations
Workplace Guidelines 35/1-4

see also:
Industry/Basics
→ p. 263 2

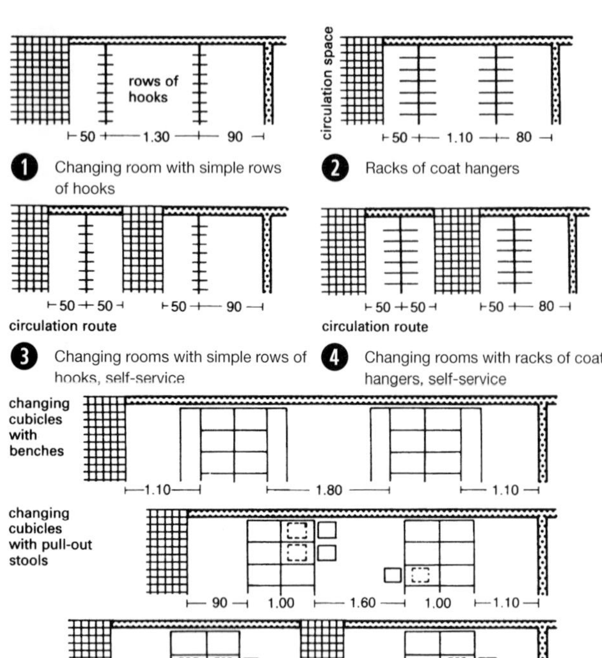

❶ Changing room with simple rows of hooks

❷ Racks of coat hangers

❸ Changing rooms with simple rows of hooks, self-service

❹ Changing rooms with racks of coat hangers, self-service

❺ Minimum dimensions for changing rooms

< 4.00 — 75 — 90 — 1.00 — counter — ≧ 0.03 m² per hook

❻ Staffed cloakroom, single rows of hooks

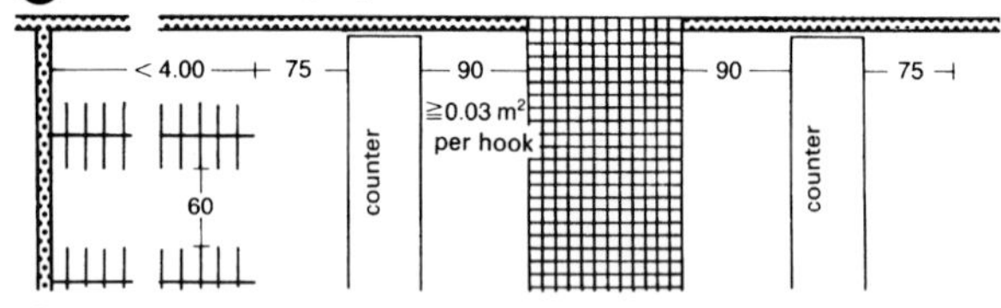

❼ Staffed cloakroom, double rows of coat hanger racks, with service

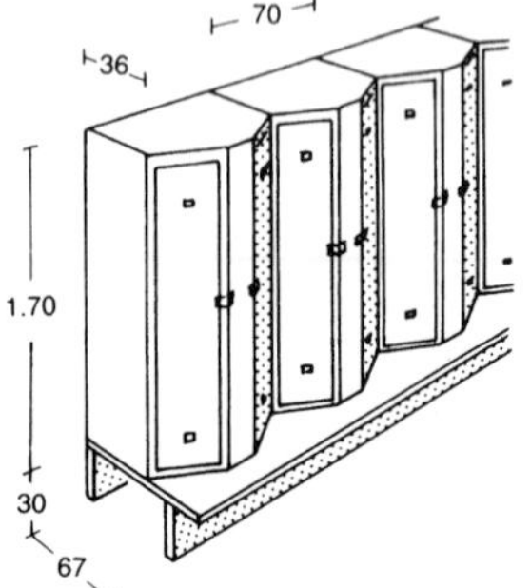

❾ Trapezoidal changing cubicles, System Rotter

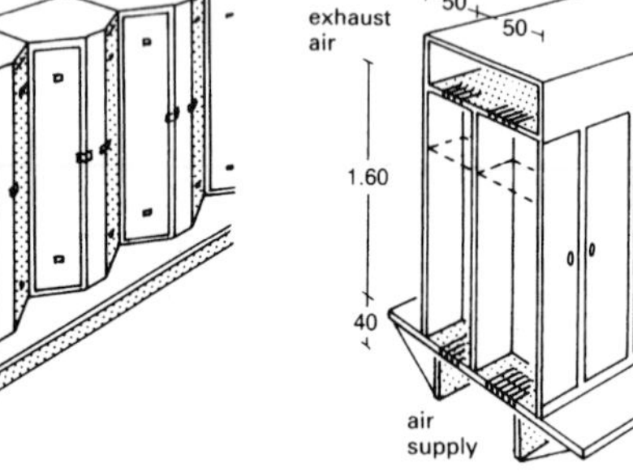

❿ Double row of ventilated clothes lockers with benches

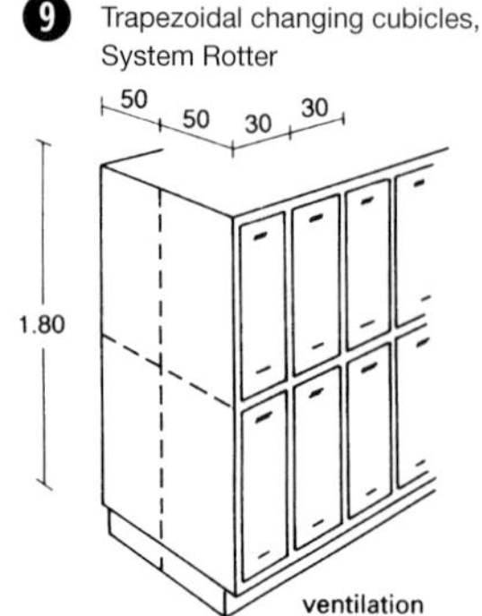

⓭ Two-level row of lockers

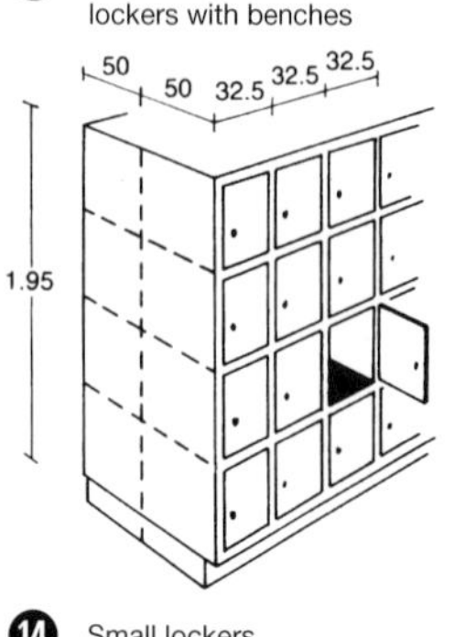

⓮ Small lockers

Changing rooms, clothes storage/lockers

Changing rooms are intended for changing clothes and the storage of house, street and working clothing, by the employees of a company. They are required when the employees wear working clothes at work and changing elsewhere is not reasonable.

Changing rooms should be on the direct route between entrance to the site and the working area. Separate washing and changing rooms should be easily accessible from each other: there must be room for unobstructed changing in light of the number of users at the same time. If changing rooms are not required, clothes storage must be provided for each employee → ⓭ – ⓮.

They must be separate for men and women and be secure against draughts and view from outside.

Changing rooms are to be equipped with seating, lockers (for storing the clothing of all employees), waste bins, mirrors and, if appropriate, a shoe cleaning machine. It is a good idea to align rows of cupboards and racks at right angles to the window wall. Window sills should if possible be at locker level.

Minimum dimensions for changing rooms → ❶ – ❻. Passage widths between changing rooms → ❽.

No.	people	Width a_P[1]
1	up to 5	0.88
2	up to 20	1.00
3	up to 100	1.25
4	up to 250	1.75
5	up to 400	2.25

[1] building guideline

❽ Width of passages

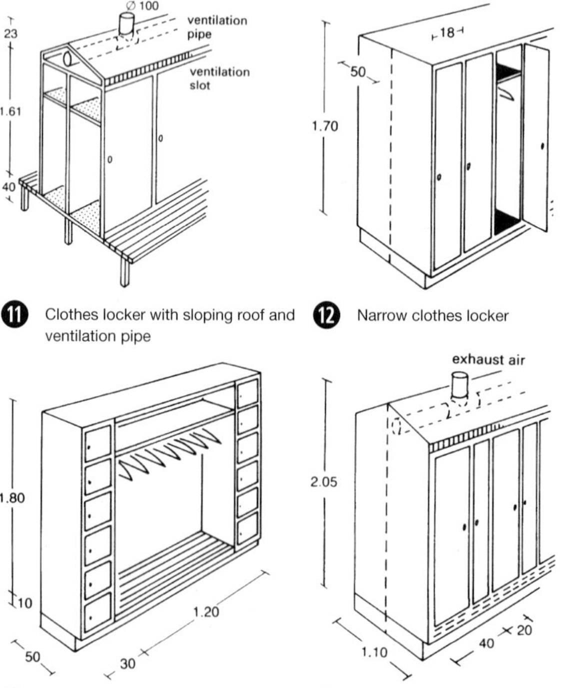

⓫ Clothes locker with sloping roof and ventilation pipe

⓬ Narrow clothes locker

⓯ Small lockers with open coat rack

⓰ Clothes locker, two compartments 20 and 40 cm wide, for street and working clothes

see also: Industry/Basics p. 263 ❷

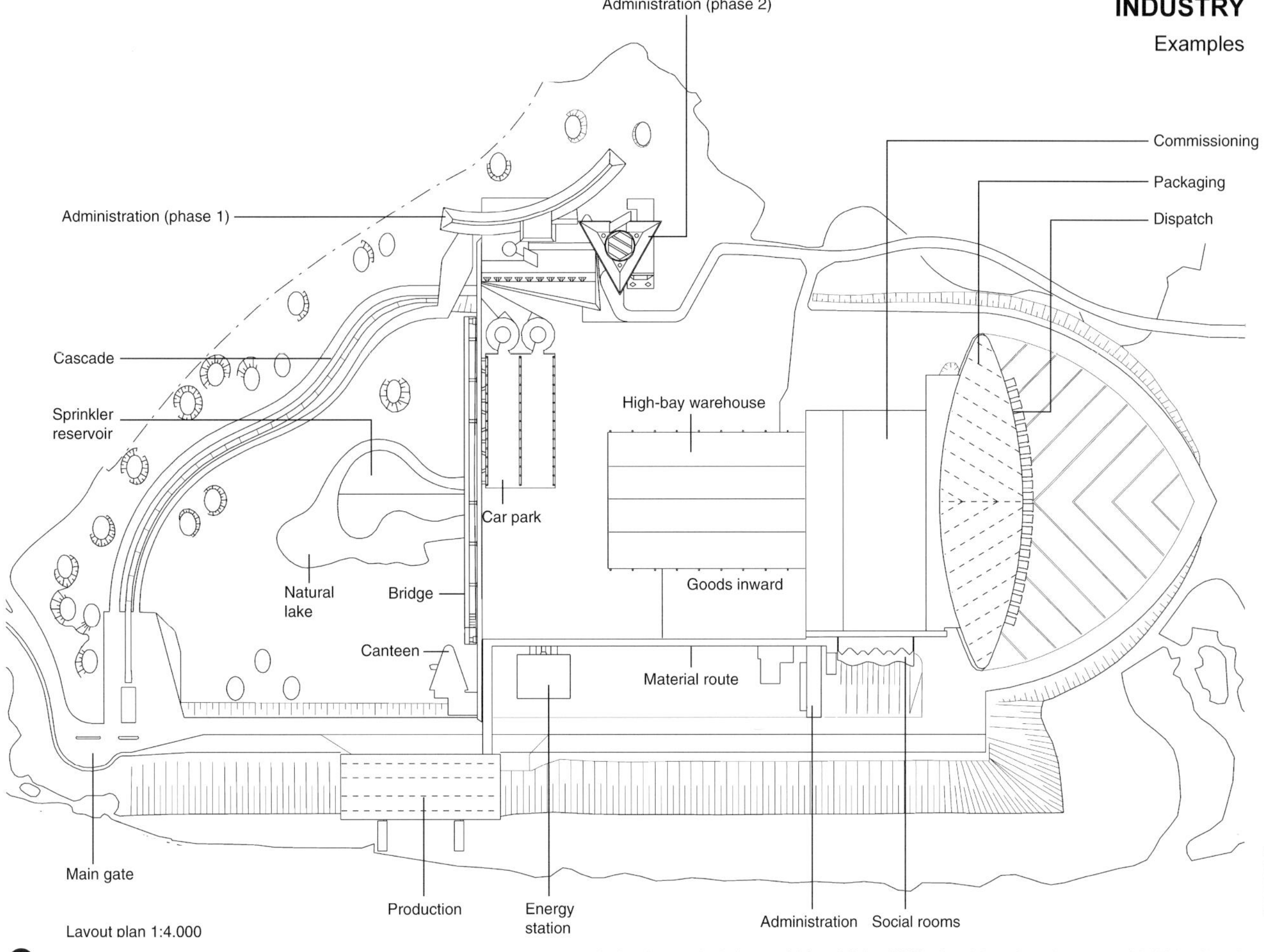

1 B. Braun Melsungen AG, Pfieffewiesen works

Arch.: (1st section): James Stirling, Michael Wilford and Associates in assoc. with Walter Nägeli
Arch.: (2nd section): Wilford Schupp Architekten GmbH

Road in
Road out
Manual sorting
Sales
Shelf warehouse
Entrance
Stairs to offices
Delivery/ dispatch
Customer car park
Ground floor plan

2 Industrial shed for Aug. Hülden GmbH in Düren

Arch.: Kister Scheithauer Gross

Offices
Store
Sales

3 Section → **2**

scale 1:1250

Additive industrial plants → 1: The functional units (administration, production, multi-storey car park, high-bay warehouse, picking, goods dispatch) are developed according to their requirements, architecturally independent and grouped in a naturally laid out landscape. The units are connected by a branching access system (material route, access bridge).

Integrated industrial plants → 2: Warehouse, status two-storey sales and administration area, and delivery at the back are combined in a cubical block. This consists of a free-standing steel structure (span length 40 m) with diamond-shaped beam grillage on fixed-end columns projecting on the entrance side and diamond-shaped grillage of secondary beams.

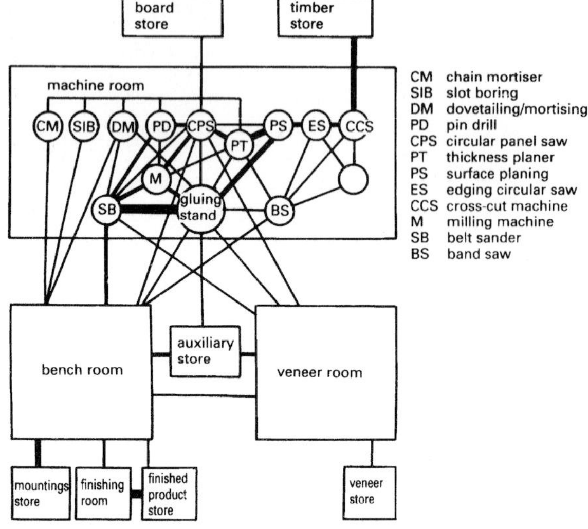

❶ Relationships of equipment and rooms in a joinery. Line thickness denotes internal traffic density

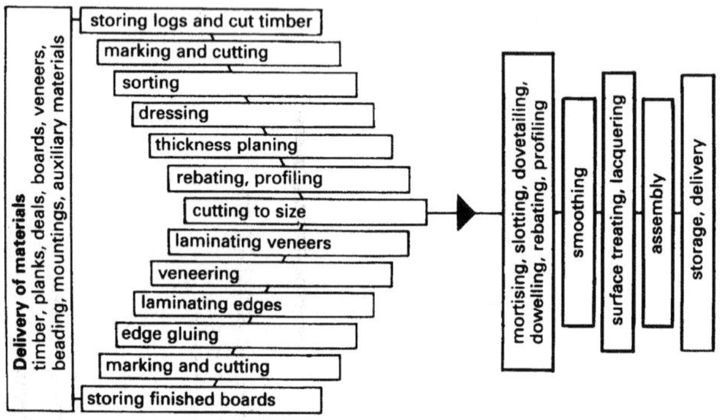

Delivery of materials
timber, planks, deals, boards, veneers, beading, mountings, auxiliary materials

- storing logs and cut timber
- marking and cutting
- sorting
- dressing
- thickness planing
- rebating, profiling
- cutting to size
- laminating veneers
- veneering
- laminating edges
- edge gluing
- marking and cutting
- storing finished boards

mortising, slotting, dovetailing, dowelling, rebating, profiling → smoothing → surface treating, lacquering → assembly → storage, delivery

❷ Production sequence, approximate

The development of plan forms from long sheds to more compact buildings → ❶ has been altogether more economical (better exploitation of the site, shorter working routes for mixed production, shorter supply pipework and cables, lighting also from above). Multi-storey buildings are not appropriate for production areas, but can be recommended for offices, subsidiary rooms, stores for small parts and valuable furniture.

Predominant construction types: framed construction of steel, reinforced concrete or timber. Walls and roof of large-format building elements,with good thermal and sound insulation. Double-glazed windows, mostly without opening lights, with a smaller proportion of opening windows according to regulations for ventilation and to see out.

The space requirement for the illustrated examples is approx. 70–80 m^2 per employee (without open storerooms).

General production flow: in small businesses with up to approx. 10 employees: linear, angled-shaped. In medium-sized businesses with over 10 employees: U-shaped or circular (square) layouts are better for workflow.

Working sequence: timber store, cutting area, drying room, machine room, bench workshop, surface treatment, storage, packing. The machines are placed according to working sequence: door, loading and unloading, ramp, supervision, testing, acceptance, delivery.

There is separation between machine and bench rooms consisting of a wall with doors. Company office and foreman's office are glazed with a view of the workshop. Workshop flooring: wood, wood-block paving or magnesite/sawdust screed. It should be possible to work against the light in all places. Continuous strip windows, high sills (1.00–1.35 m).

In order to deal with chips, sawdust and fine dust, an extraction system is required in almost all cases, even in the smallest joineries, for working in accordance with workplace regulations and for operational reasons. Reduce excessive noise from machinery with rubber-bonded metal bearings.

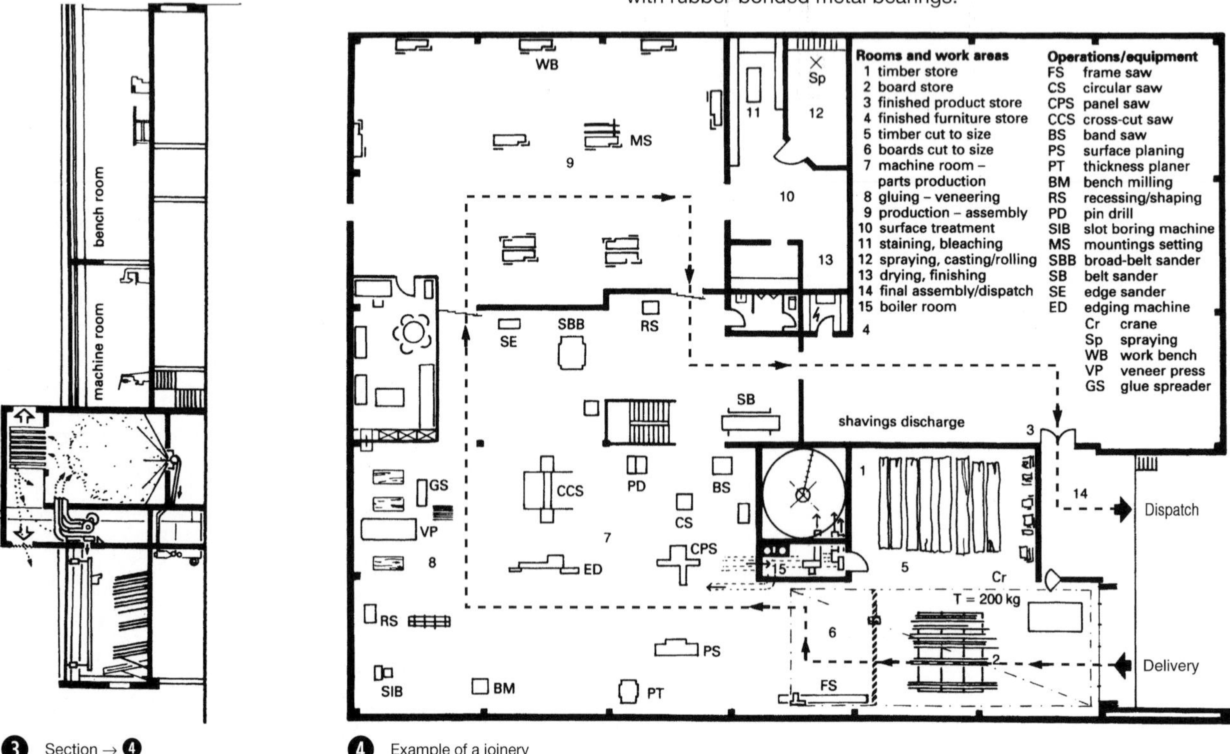

❸ Section → ❹

❹ Example of a joinery

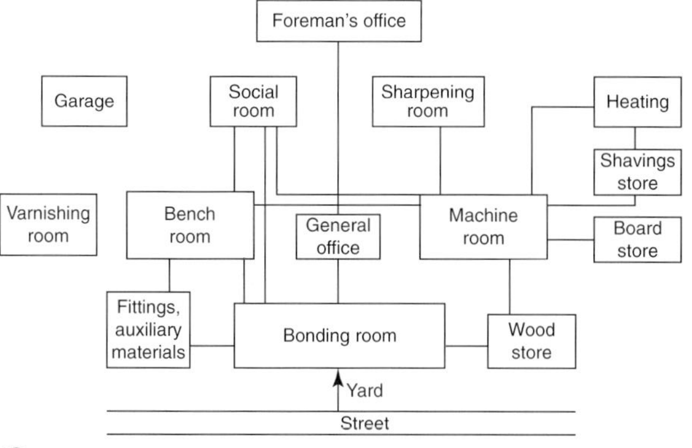

❶ Functional scheme of a carpentry and woodworking business

The layout of the carpenter's shop can be planned on the basis of the following operational data:
Equipment, utilisation, cost-effectiveness, power requirements, floor loadings, space requirement, cost, production process, production times, number of employees, technical organisation of the business, operating procedures and working sequence

Materials: types, quantities, weights, space requirement
Stores: size, space requirement
Energy supply: heat, electricity, compressed air.
Waste products: types, space requirement, waste disposal.

1–4	Lathes
5	Stave lathe
6	Autolathe
7	Round bar machine
8	Spraying stand
9	Storage bench
10	Varnish dipping apparatus
11	Varnish drying cupboard
12	Polishing drum
D	Drill
LD	Long-reach drill
CDP	Combined dressing and planing machine
BM	Bench milling machine
CS	Cut-off saw
BSR	Band sander
BS	Band saw
CRS	Circular saw
WB	Work bench
HB	Heating boiler for waste wood

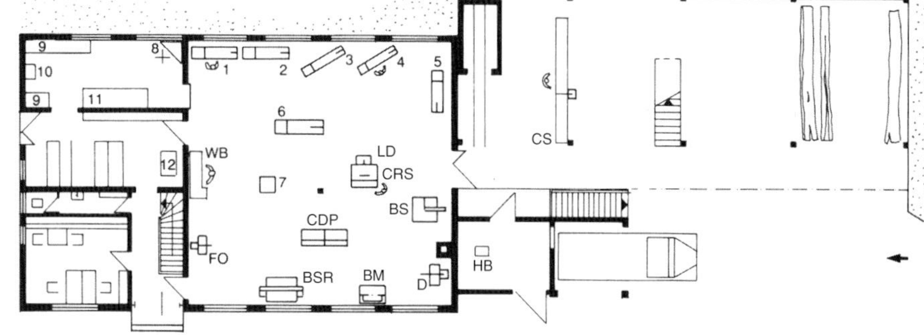

❷ Example of a turnery

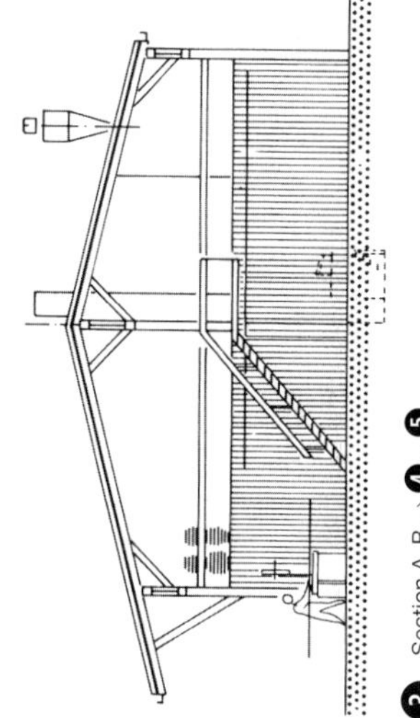

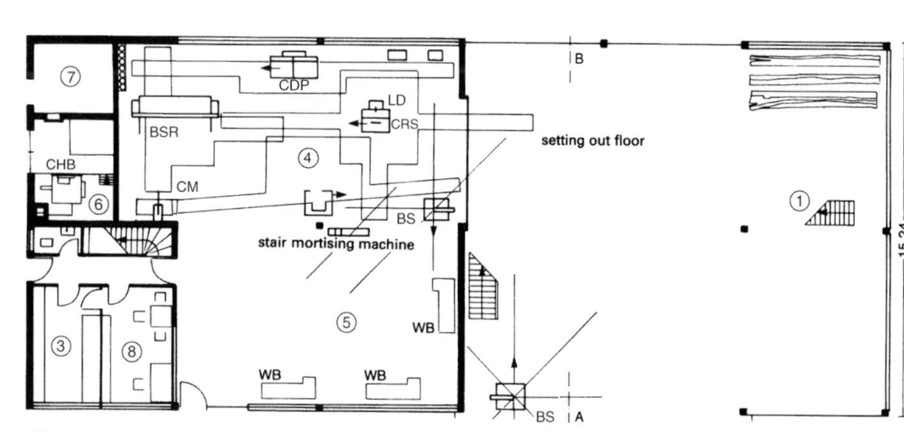

❸ ❹ Example of woodworking business, ground floor → ❸ + ❺

D	Drill
LD	Long-reach drill
CDP	Combined dressing and planing machine
BM	Bench milling machine
CM	Cut-off saw
BSR	Band sander
BS	Band saw
CRS	Circular saw
WB	Work bench
HB	Heating boiler for waste wood
CHB	Combined heating boiler for oil and waste wood
①	Solid wood store
②	Board store
③	Small machine store
④	Machine production
⑤	Bench production
⑥	Heating room
⑦	Sawdust silo
⑧	Foreman's office
⑨	Break room
⑩	Washroom

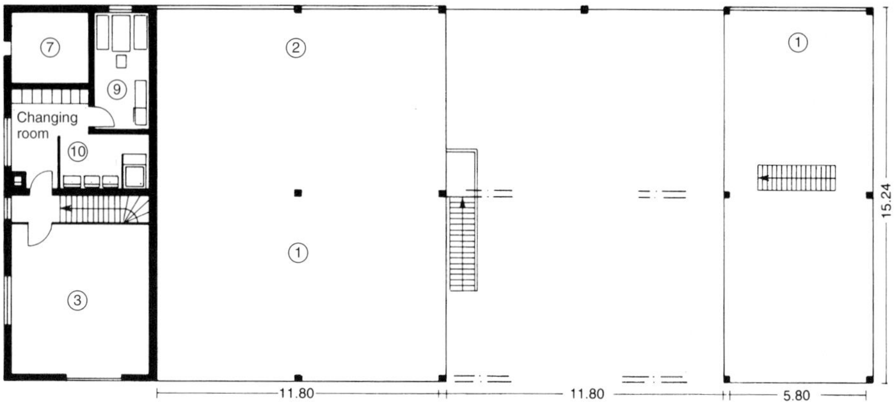

Changing room

11.80 11.80 5.80 15.24

❺ First floor → ❸ – ❹

A large business is divided into workshops for gas welding, fitting, construction and repair, a smithy for ornamental ironmongery, plus construction and mechanical metalwork areas. The room relationships correspond to the functional scheme → ❺.

The company office and foreman's office should if possible be located in the centre, with a view of all workshops if possible.

Welding and forging should take place in rooms enclosed by steel doors, even in medium-sized workshops. The workshops should be lit from above, and additional lighting is required for individual machines (provide socket boxes in the floor).

The floor should be of concrete, preferably on a concrete base slab. The welding bench is fitted with fire bricks. A charcoal pit is required for pre-warming before welding of metal and cast iron, with a small chimney above it; it is also suitable for brazing, forging and annealing. There should be water and oil containers next to this for annealing.

❶ Upright storage of rods — sheet metal stored on shelves

❷ Store for short metal pieces — loading by hoists

❸ Metalwork shop with machine location and arrangement of stores

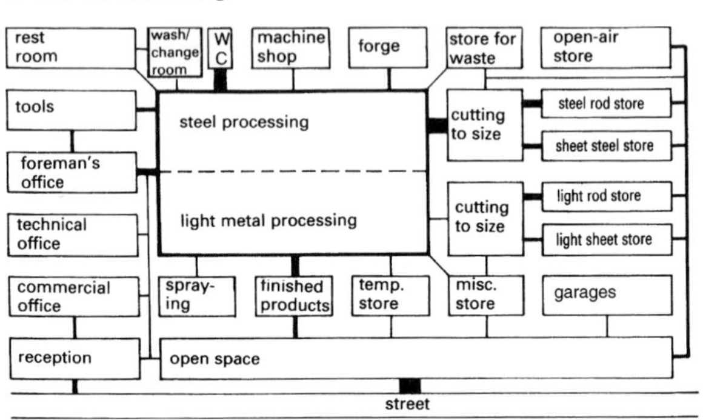

❺ Room relationship plan for large business in steel treatment and metal construction

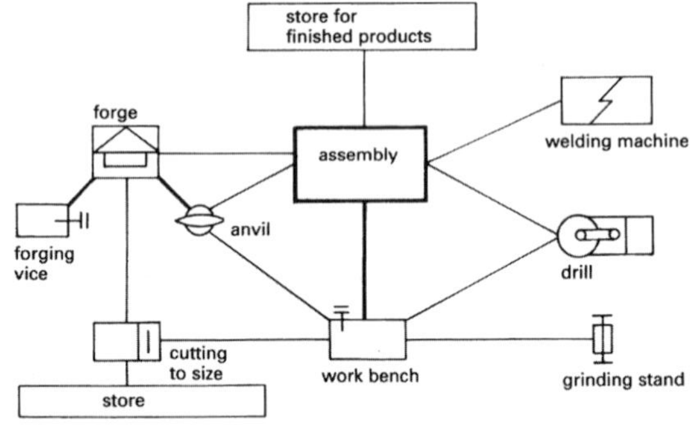

❻ Example of working sequence for architectural ironmonger's

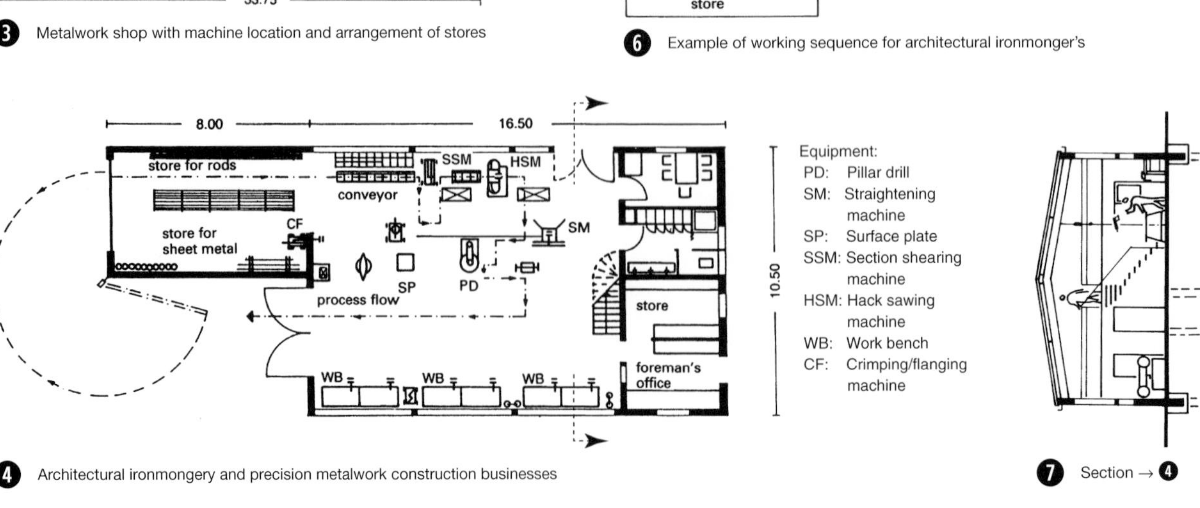

❹ Architectural ironmongery and precision metalwork construction businesses

❼ Section → ❹

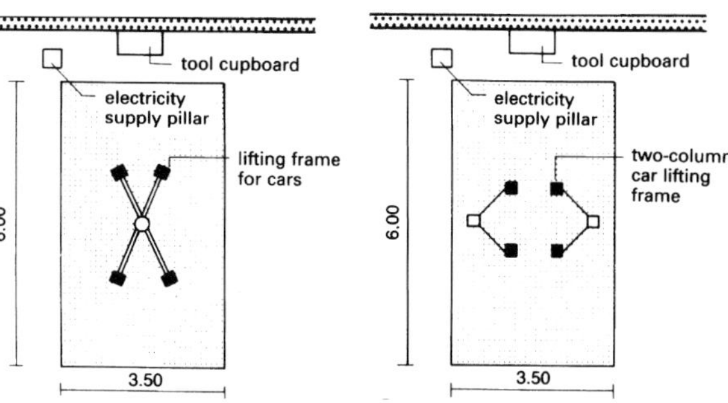

❶ One-jack car hoist, lifting height 1.0 m

❷ Two-column car hoist, lifting height 0.70–1.10 m

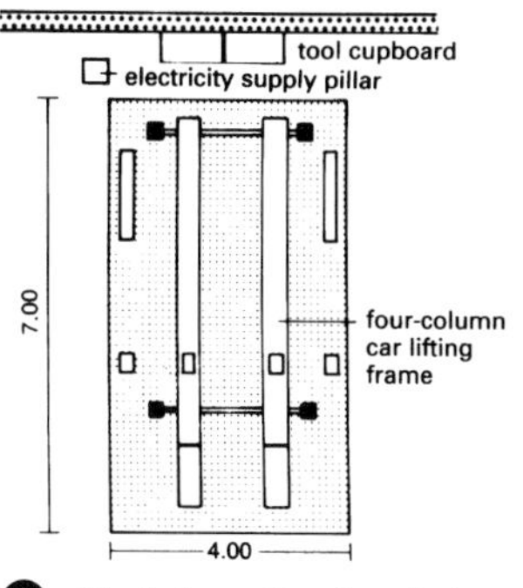

❸ Wheel alignment bay for optical wheel alignment

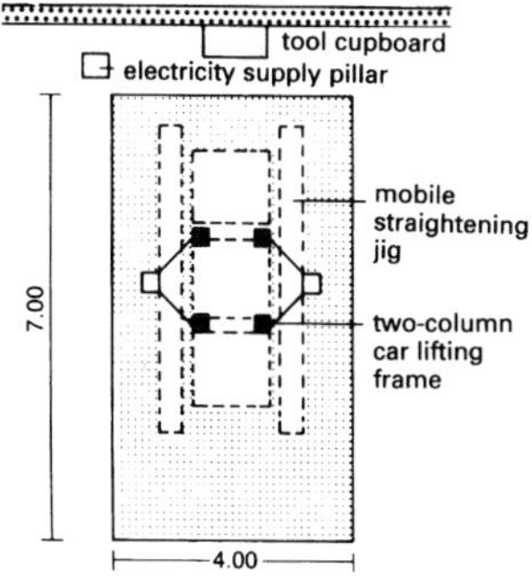

❹ Bodywork straightening bay

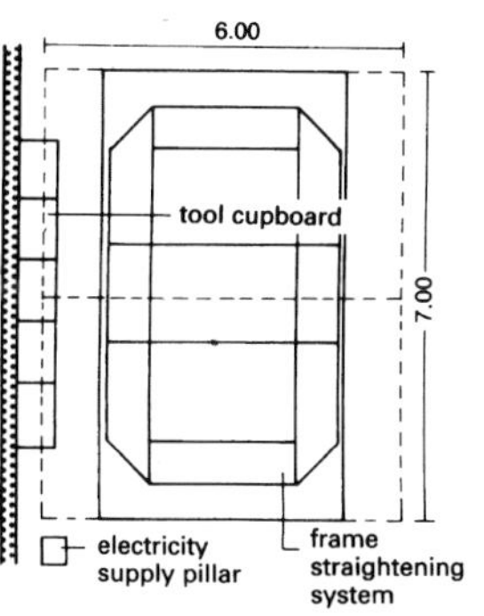

❺ Bodywork straightening stand

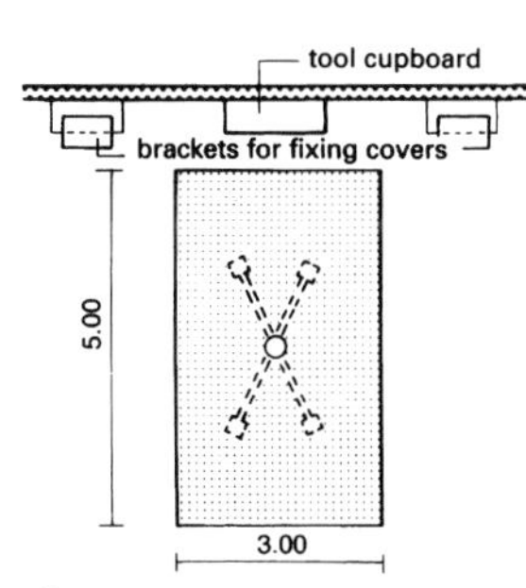
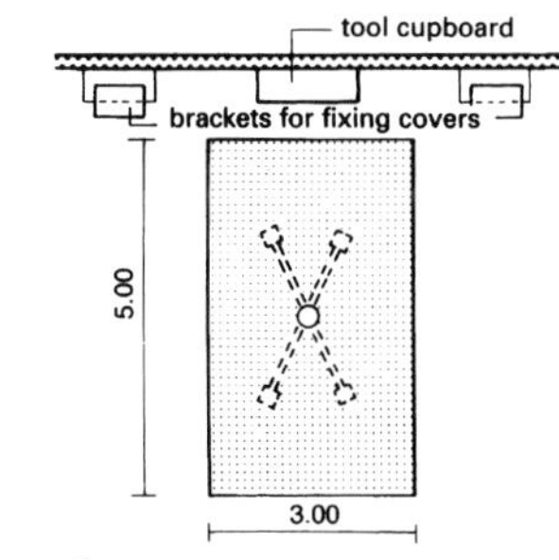

❻ Work bay for painting preparation with/without car hoist

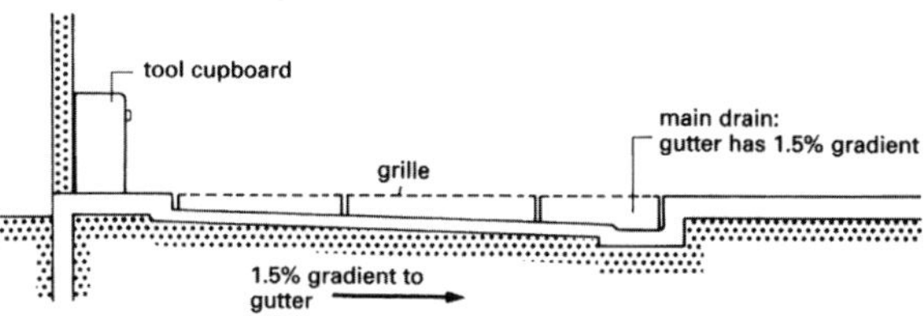

❼ Schematic diagram of a work bay with grating for painting preparation → ❻

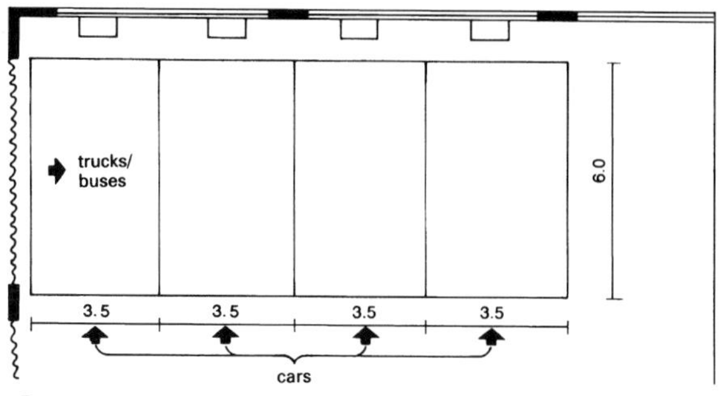

❽ Truck work area, 6.0 m × 14.0 m, consisting of 4 standard work bays, each 3.5 m × 6.0 m

A customer-service business should be located with a good road connection (even if this results in higher access and building costs). In a location on the edge of town, advertising and customer loyalty require particular attention.

Basic rule: site ⅓ built, ⅔ unbuilt. Take possible later extension into account. For larger businesses, the average is 200 m^2 per employee for workshop operation. In addition to this, rooms are required for sales, office, customer waiting room and social rooms etc.

The building will be mostly steel construction, single-storey. Free-spanning shed construction without obstructive columns is preferred. Possible future extension should be taken into account in the spacing of the bays.

The workshop floor should be sealed against penetration of oil and grease, and grease separators installed in the drainage system. Provide extract duct for exhaust gases. Design automatically opening doors with air curtain. Installation ducts for electricity, compressed air, waste oil and water are recommended. Check utility supply connections. Carwash equipment has high water consumption.

Examples of vehicle repair workshops of various sizes → ❾ – ❿.

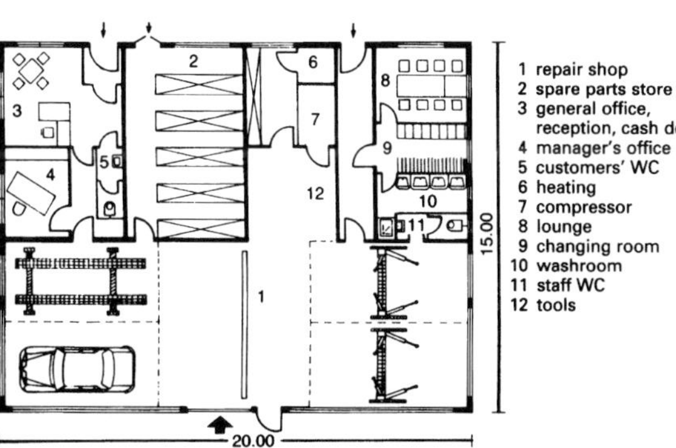

❾ Design example for a business with four employees: site with wide road frontage

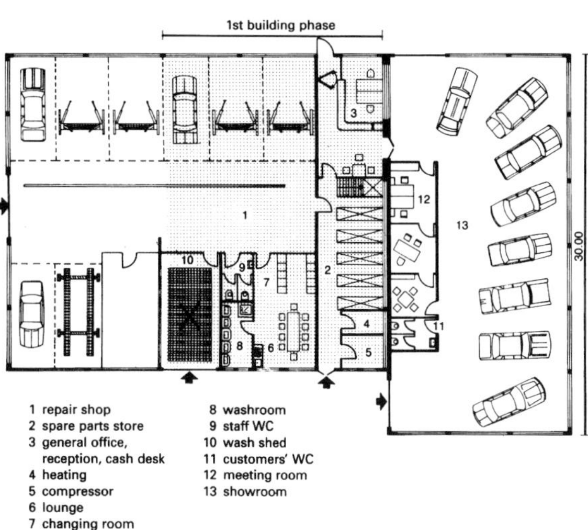

❿ Design example for a business with eight employees: carwash shed and showroom

Industry and trade

WORKSHOPS
Joinery
Carpenter's shop
Metalwork
Vehicle repairs
Bakery
Meat processing plant
Other trades
Laundry
Fire station

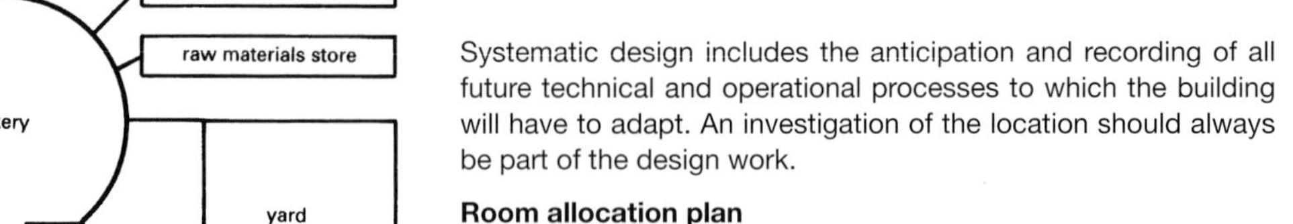

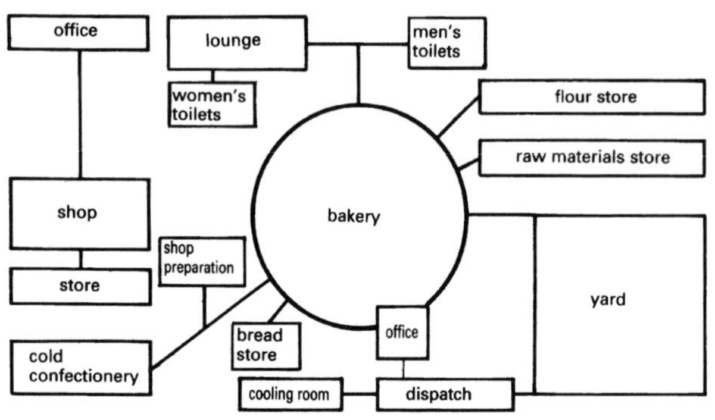

❶ Functional scheme

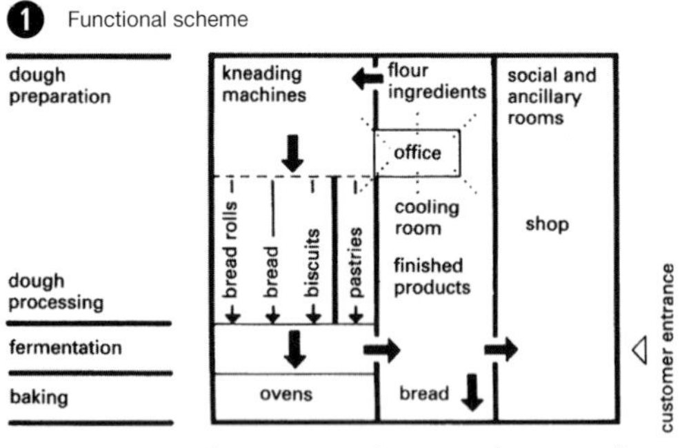

❷ Room connection plan

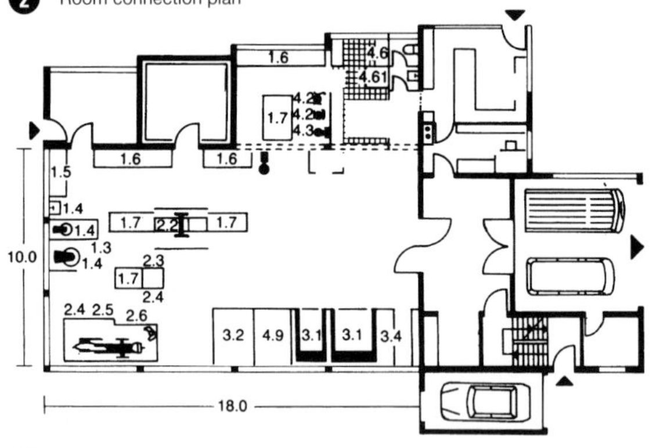

❸ Example: floor plan of a bakery

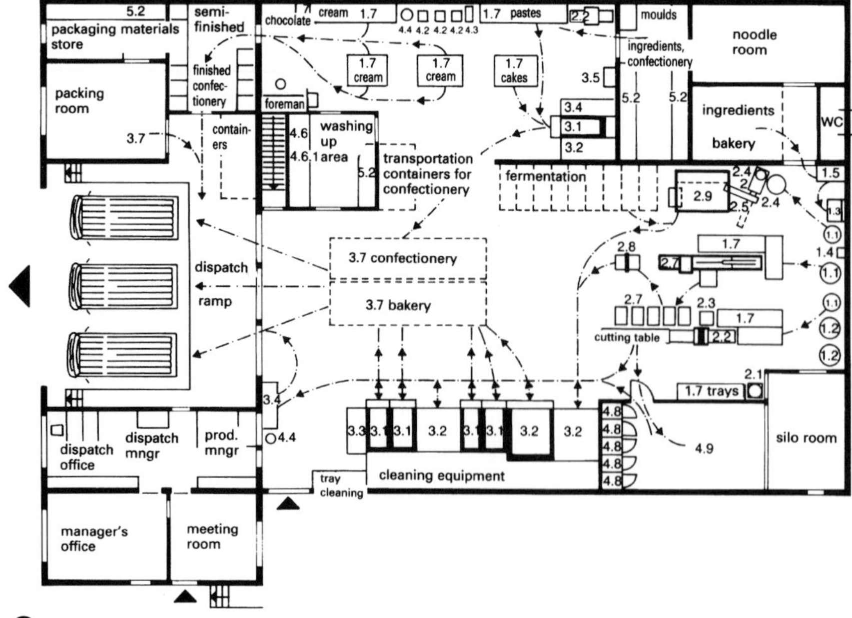

❹ Example: floor plan of a large bakery

Systematic design includes the anticipation and recording of all future technical and operational processes to which the building will have to adapt. An investigation of the location should always be part of the design work.

Room allocation plan
Basic division: storerooms, production rooms, sales rooms, building services rooms, administration and business rooms, social and subsidiary rooms → ❶. Work processes in or between the individual rooms → ❷. Storerooms for raw materials, ingredients and packaging. Daily supplies are stored in work areas.

Basic types of storage
Raw material store: grains, sugar, salt, baking agents, dry goods in sacks, flour in silos or sacks.

Ingredients room: fruit, toppings, dry fruit, fats, eggs.

Packaging store: space requirement for containers (shelving, racks, cupboards), stacking, counters. Space for traffic (passages).

Minimum area for stores 15 m^2; approx. 8–10 m^2 per employee for all stores.

Short routes between stores and work areas.

Separation of workrooms for bakery and pastries
Bakery requires warm and humid room climate; pastry room should be cooler. Bakery has following areas: dough preparation, dough processing, baking, storage of finished products. Pastry room: cold area – cream, creme, chocolate, fruit; warm area – ready mixes, kitchen, fine pastries.

Workroom area is sum of:
Space required for equipment, handling and processing, intermediate storage (trolleys) and side counters. Space for traffic (passages); lost space.

Working from the internal operational plan (layout), the necessary space requirements can be determined.

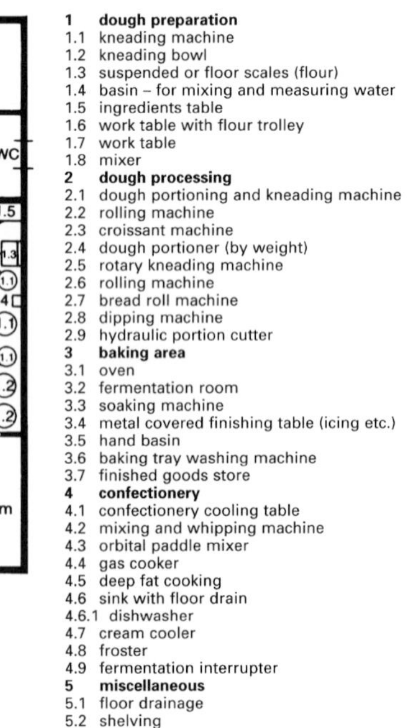

❸ – ❹ key

1 dough preparation
1.1 kneading machine
1.2 kneading bowl
1.3 suspended or floor scales (flour)
1.4 basin – for mixing and measuring water
1.5 ingredients table
1.6 work table with flour trolley
1.7 work table
1.8 mixer
2 dough processing
2.1 dough portioning and kneading machine
2.2 rolling machine
2.3 croissant machine
2.4 dough portioner (by weight)
2.5 rotary kneading machine
2.6 rolling machine
2.7 bread roll machine
2.8 dipping machine
2.9 hydraulic portion cutter
3 baking area
3.1 oven
3.2 fermentation room
3.3 soaking machine
3.4 metal covered finishing table (icing etc.)
3.5 hand basin
3.6 baking tray washing machine
3.7 finished goods store
4 confectionery
4.1 confectionery cooling table
4.2 mixing and whipping machine
4.3 orbital paddle mixer
4.4 gas cooker
4.5 deep fat cooking
4.6 sink with floor drain
4.6.1 dishwasher
4.7 cream cooler
4.8 froster
4.9 fermentation interrupter
5 miscellaneous
5.1 floor drainage
5.2 shelving

Industry and trade

WORKSHOPS
Joinery
Carpenter's shop
Metalwork
Vehicle repairs
Bakery
Meat processing plant
Other trades
Laundry
Fire station

On the ground floor → ❸, sausages, cold meat, ham and delicatessen goods are produced in an area of 4500 m². Offices, laboratories, canteen, kitchen, washing and changing rooms are located on the first floor → ❷. Daily production is about 25 t. The building requires various groups of rooms with different room temperatures: social rooms, offices, WC, 20°C; production rooms, 18°C; air-conditioned rooms, 14–18°C; cool rooms, 10–12°C; cold rooms, 0–8°C; deep-freeze, –20°C. High physical requirements for construction and materials.

Production building: raw material is delivered in form of halves of pork, quarters of beef and coarsely dismembered, wrapped pieces.

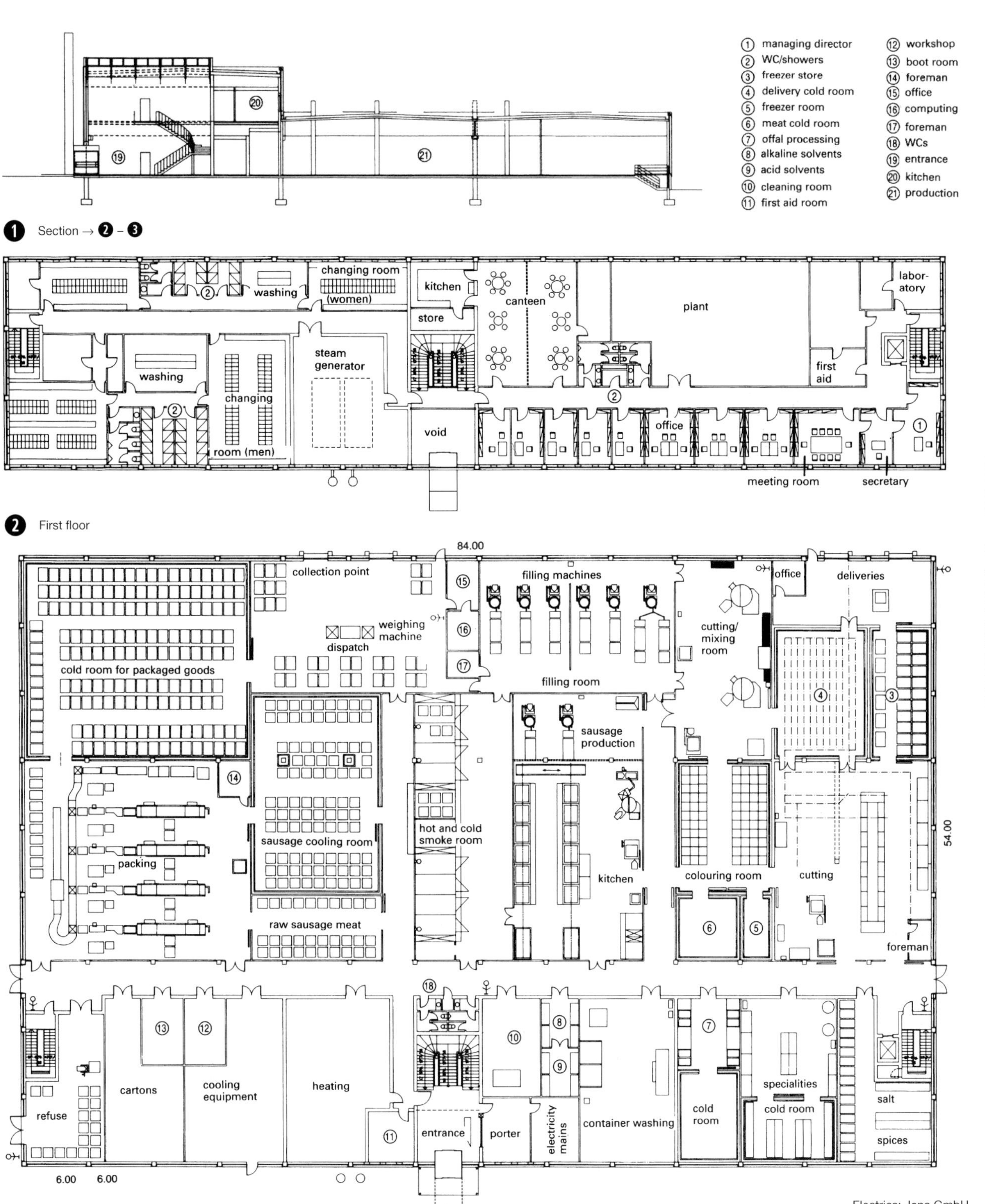

❶ Section → ❷ – ❸

❷ First floor

❸ Ground floor, Thüringer Fleischzentrum

Electrics: Jena GmbH
ZPN Rhinstr. 149 Berlin
Planning: AG Neufert, Mittmann, Gref.

Industry and trade

WORKSHOPS
Joinery
Carpenter's shop
Metalwork
Vehicle repairs
Bakery
Meat processing plant
Other trades
Laundry
Fire station

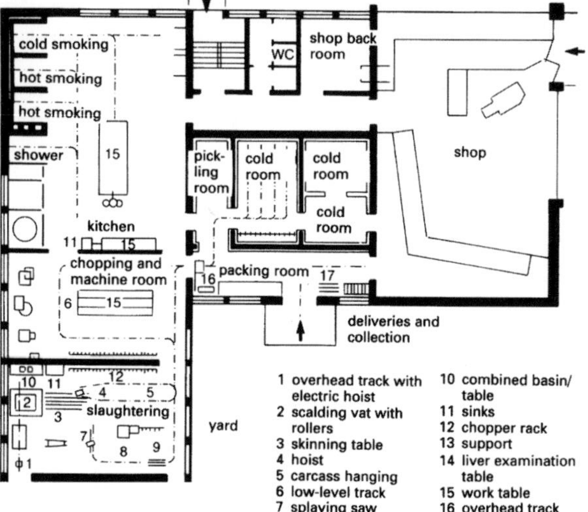

❶ Example of a butcher

1 technician's work bench
2 general work bench
3 work bench with vice
4 counter
5 record bar
6 shelving for repair work
7 shelving for parts
8 display shelves
9 sales counter
10 shop window and display shelves

❷ Example of a radio and television shop with workshop

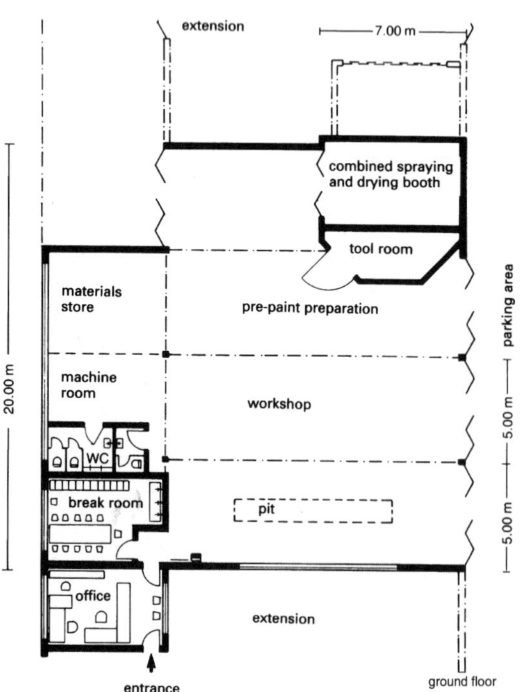

❸ Example of a paint spraying workshop

Butcher → ❶: example ground plan for 6–7 employees

Functional scheme for in-house sausage and cold meat production: meat arrives in sausage machine room (cutting/mincing), into smoke house, then boiler (sausage kitchen) and from there to the cool store or the shop.

Height of workrooms (according to size of business) ≧4.0 m, width of passages for goods transport ≧2.0 m. Work space at sausage machine, in front and every 1.0 m at side = 3.0 m^2 each. Machine spacing from walls (for repairs) 40–50 cm.

Sound insulation is required for cooling plant, which works day and night. Provide water taps with hose fittings in the sausage kitchen, machine room and salting room. Floor rough and waterproof, ideally of rough or ribbed tiles with gully. Walls tiled completely. Good general lighting of 300 lx at the work spaces. Provide social room, clothes cupboards, WC and showers for employees.

Radio and television shop with workshop → ❷

Workrooms: clear height ≧3 m and 15 m^3 minimum air volume per employee. On account of the great danger of electrocution, the workshop should have well-insulated flooring, or at least the workbenches of the employees should be insulated. Recommended light intensity: 500 lx. For the assembly of very fine electronic components, 1500 lx is required.

Workbench must have a spacious worktop, ideally 1.00 × 2.00 m. 2 shelves under desk for storage of circuit plans, appliance descriptions etc. and tools in easily accessible drawers.

Paint spraying workshop → ❸
Tailor → ❹ example plan for 10 employees

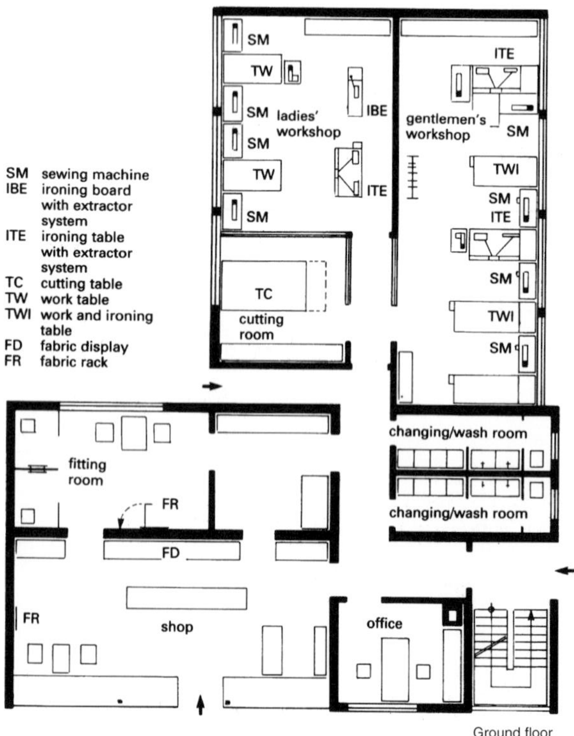

❹ Example of a tailor

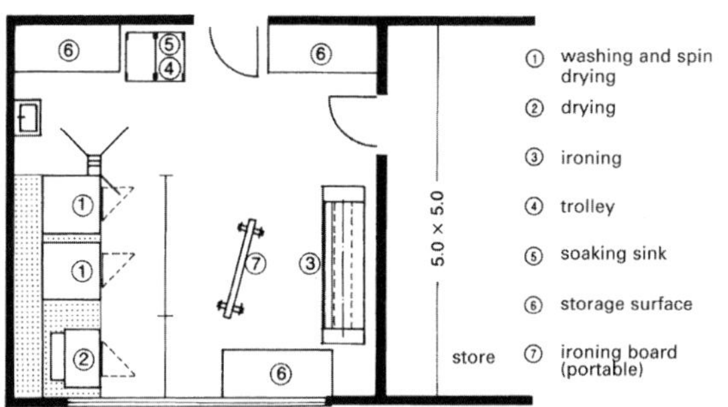

❶ Small laundry for hotel

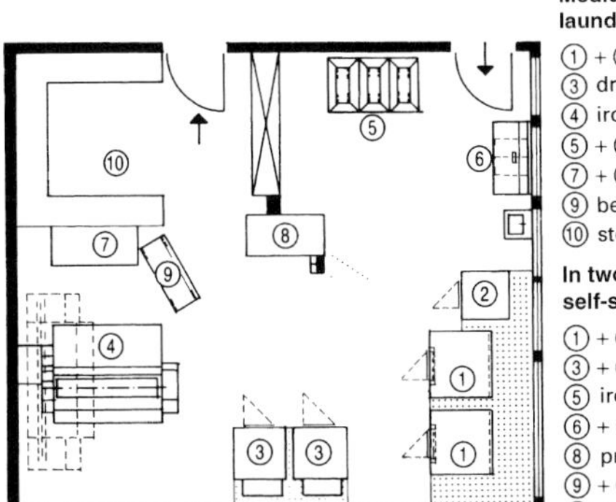

Medium-sized laundry ❷

①+② washers
③ dryers
④ ironing
⑤+⑥ sorting
⑦+⑧ pressing
⑨ bench
⑩ storage

In two rooms ❸ and self-service ❹

①+② washers
③+④ dryers
⑤ ironing
⑥+⑦ sorting
⑧ pressing
⑨+⑩ ironing, bench
⑪ repairs
⑫+⑬ storage

❷ Medium-sized laundry

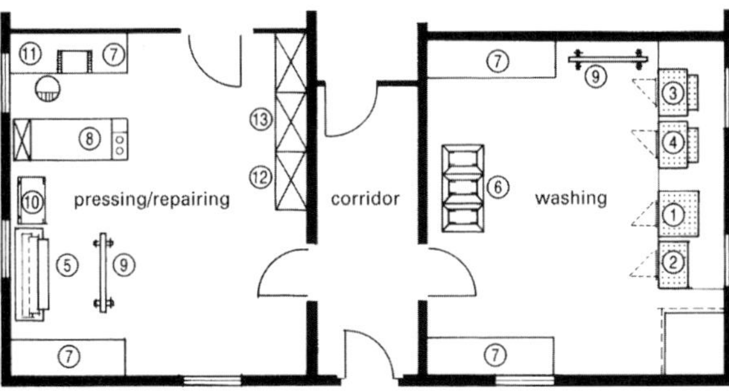

❸ in two separate rooms

❹ Self-service launderette

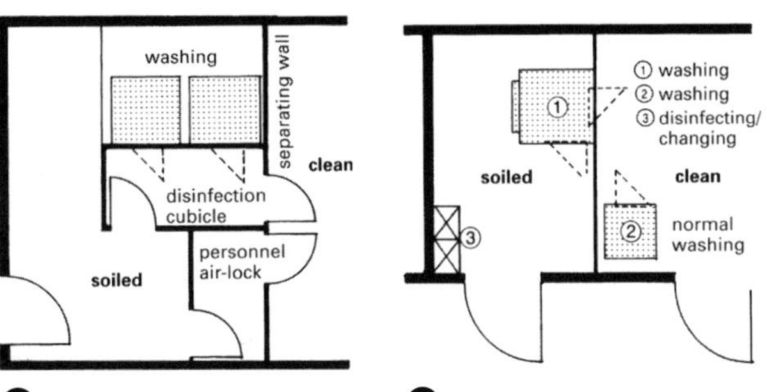

❺ Single-door washing machines in the disinfection cubicle

❻ Washing with room separation into clean and soiled

Laundries for hospital washing are to be separated into two areas for soiled and clean, each with their own entrance → ❺ – ❻, ❽. In the soiled area, it must be possible to damp-clean and disinfect the floor, walls and external surfaces of built-in equipment and machines.

Passages between the dirty and clean sides of the laundry are to be equipped with personnel control lobbies plus hand disinfection and a place for protective clothing. The doors of the staff control lobby must be fitted with devices making it impossible to open both doors at once → ❺.

gents	Weight (g)
shirt	170
light vest	100
heavy vest	150
short underpants	75
long underpants	180
pyjamas	450
handkerchief	20
pair of socks	70
ladies	
blouse	140
underclothes	140
petticoat	75
night dress	350
night shirt	170
handkerchief	10
apron	170
blouse	130
children	
small dress	110
underclothes	80
jacket, pullover	75
dungarees	25
handkerchief	15
pair of socks	70
pair of tights	100

bathing	Weight (g)
bathrobe	900
towel	800
beach towel	400
hand towel	200
bathing trunks	100
bathing costume 1-pce	260
2-pce	200
bed linen	
bed cover	850
under-sheet	670
top sheet	600
pillow cover	200
table linen	
table cloth	370
long table cloth	1000
serviette	80
hand towel	100
tea towel	100
working clothes	
protective suit	1200
dungarees	800
apron	200
man's overalls	500
lady's overall	400

❼ Average weights of clothes for washing

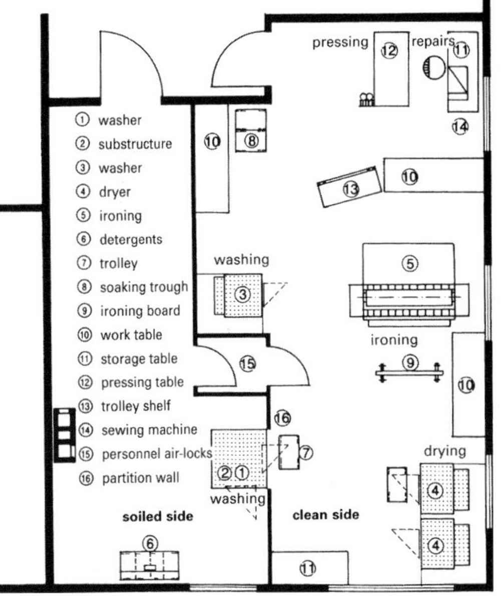

❽ Laundry in centre for the elderly

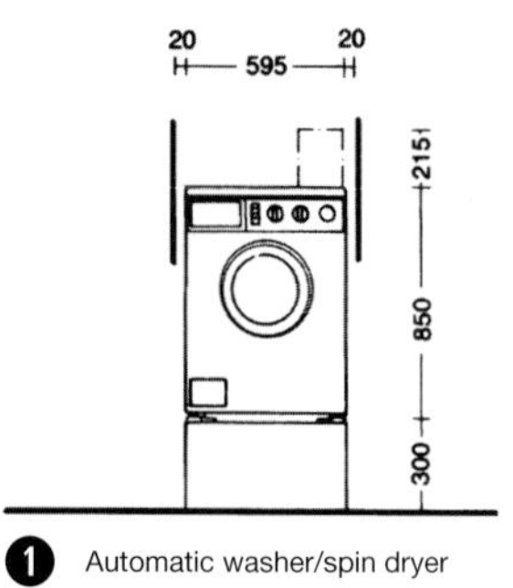

1 Automatic washer/spin dryer

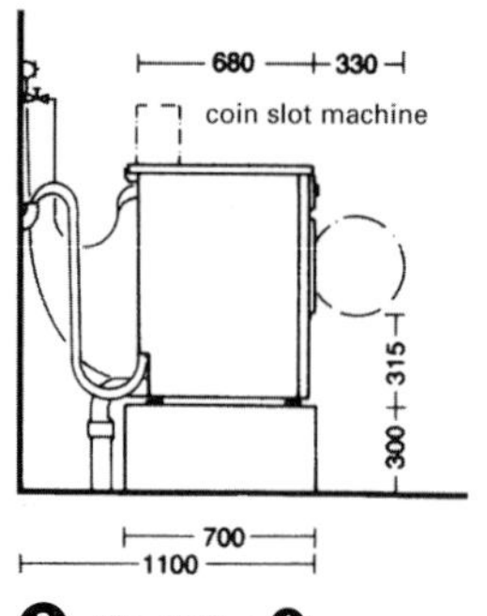

2 Side view → 1

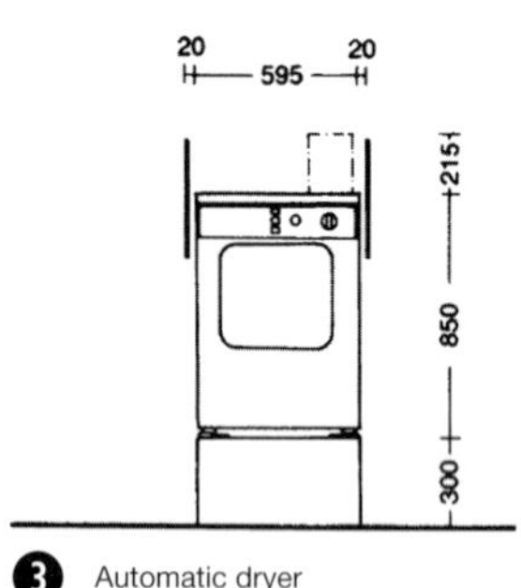

3 Automatic dryer

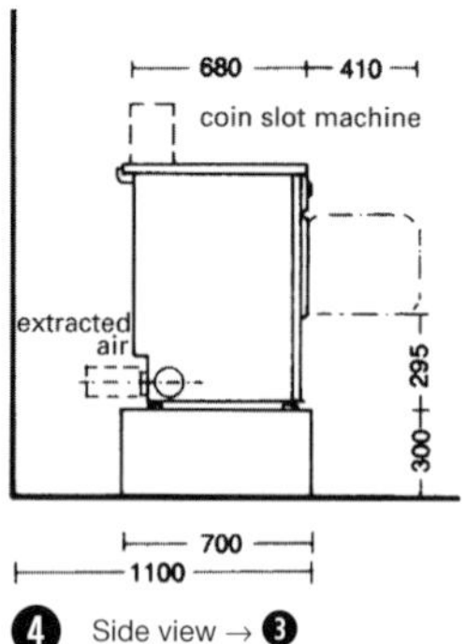

4 Side view → 3

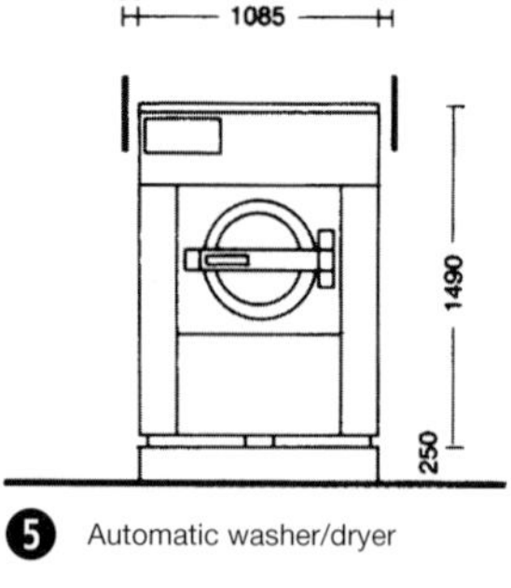

5 Automatic washer/dryer

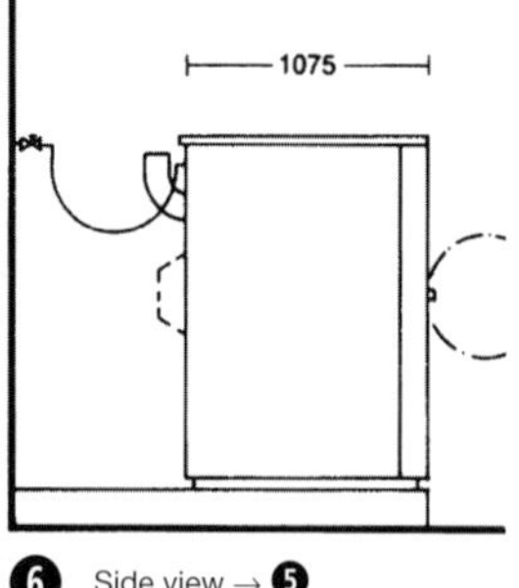

6 Side view → 5

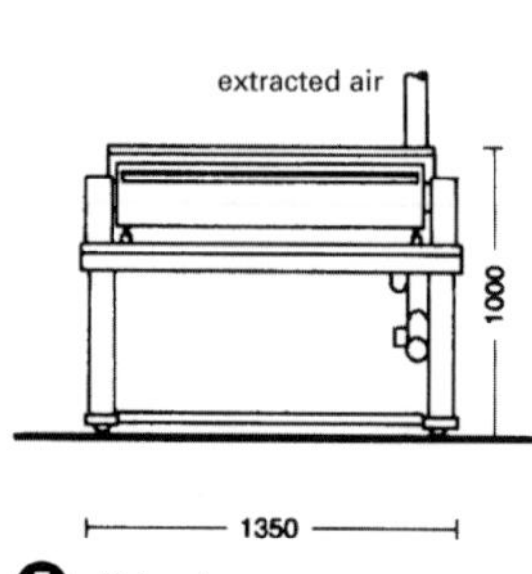

7 Rotary iron

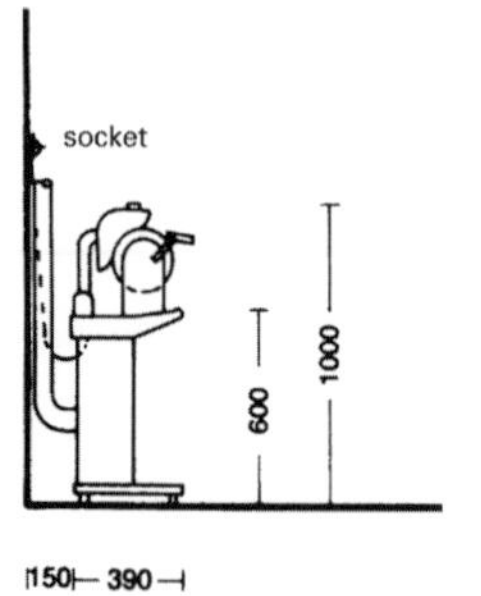

8 Side view → 7

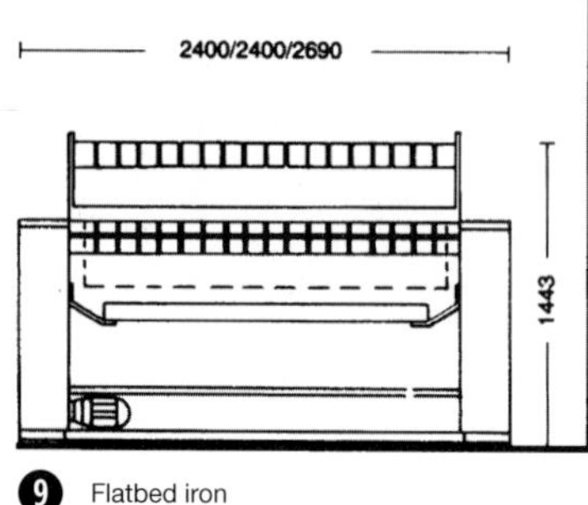

9 Flatbed iron

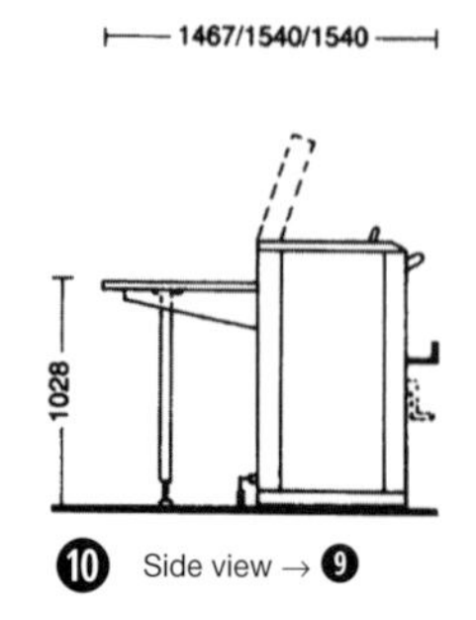

10 Side view → 9

Dry laundry produced per week:
Household: approx. 3 kg/person (ironing share approx. 40%)
Hotel: approx. 20 kg/bed (daily sheet and towel changing)
approx. 12–15 kg/bed (4 changes/week)
approx. 8–10 kg/bed (2–3 changes/week)
approx. 5 kg/bed (1 change/week)
(above values include hotel restaurant)
Guesthouse: approx. 3 kg/bed
Restaurant: approx. 1.5–3 kg/place
(for hotels, guesthouses and restaurants, ironing share approx. 75%)
Home for elderly: approx. 3 kg/bed (residential)
approx. 8 kg/bed (care home)
approx. 25 kg/bed (incontinent)
Children's home: approx. 4 kg/bed,
Baby home: approx. 10 kg/bed
Nursing and care establishments: approx. 4 kg/bed
approx. 25 kg/bed (incontinent)
(for the above homes, ironing share approx. 60%)
Hospitals, clinics (up to approx. 200 beds):
general hospital: 12–15 kg/bed
maternity clinic with births: approx. 16 kg/bed
children's clinic: approx. 18 kg/bed
(for hospitals and clinics, ironing share approx. 70%)
care staff: approx. 3.5 kg/person

$$\text{Required washing capacity} = \frac{\text{washing quantity/week}}{\text{washing days/week} \times \text{washes/day}}$$

Example calculations:

1. Hotel with 80 beds (utilisation 60% = 48 beds)
4 bedding changes/week
daily towel changes (approx. 12 kg/bed) 576 kg/wash
table and kitchen washing approx. 74 kg/week
650 kg/week

$$\text{required washing capacity} = \frac{650\text{ kg}}{3 \times 7} = 18.6\text{ kg/wash}$$

2. Hotel with 150 beds (utilisation 60% = 90 beds)
daily bed and towel changes (20 kg/bed)
90 beds @ 20 kg washing 1800 kg/week
table and kitchen washing approx. 200 kg/week
2000 kg/week

$$\text{required washing capacity} = \frac{2000\text{ kg}}{3 \times 7} = 57.1\text{ kg/wash}$$

3. Home for elderly (50 residents, 70 care patients)
70 care places @ 12 kg washing 840 kg/week

$$\text{required washing capacity} = \frac{840\text{ kg}}{5 \times 5} = 33.6\text{ kg/wash}$$

50 residential places @ 3 kg washing 150 kg/week
table and kitchen washing approx. 100 kg/week
250 kg/week

$$\text{required washing capacity} = \frac{250\text{ kg}}{3 \times 6} = 8.3\text{ kg/wash}$$

4. Block of flats with 90 residents
approx. 3 kg dry washing per person and week
90 people × 3 kg = 270 kg
(6 days × 5 washes) = 9.0 kg/wash
5 kg/washing machine = 1.8 machines

1.8 machines will be needed = 2 machines

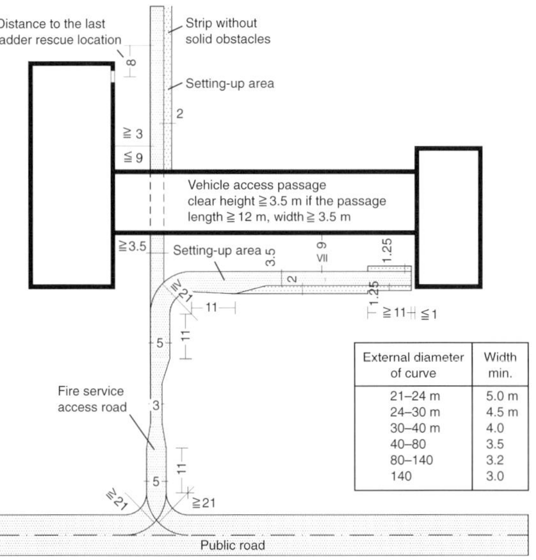

❶ Examples: areas for a fire station on a site

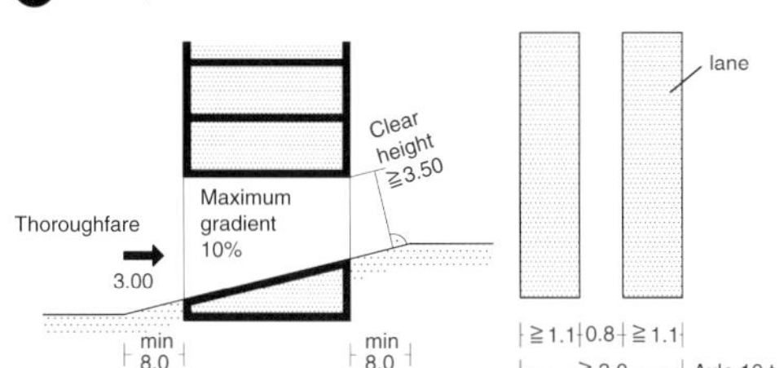

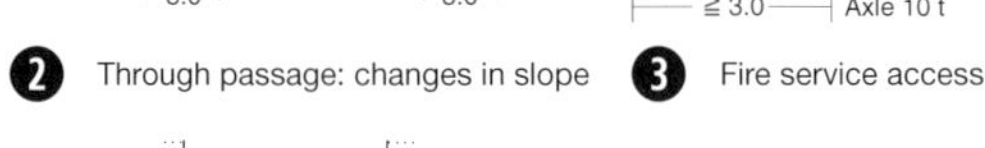

❷ Through passage: changes in slope ❸ Fire service access

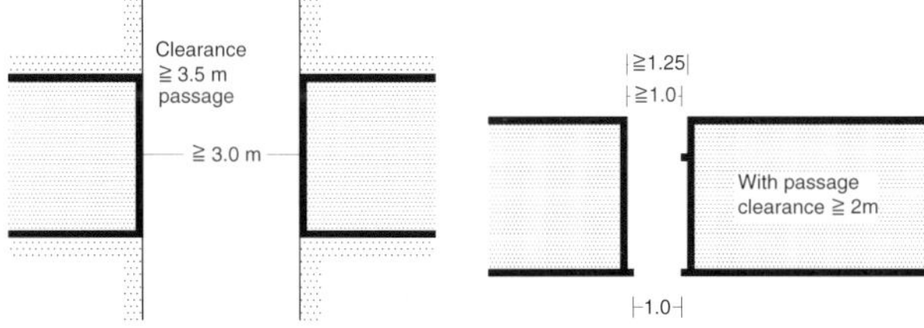

❹ Fire service access ❺ Pedestrian access

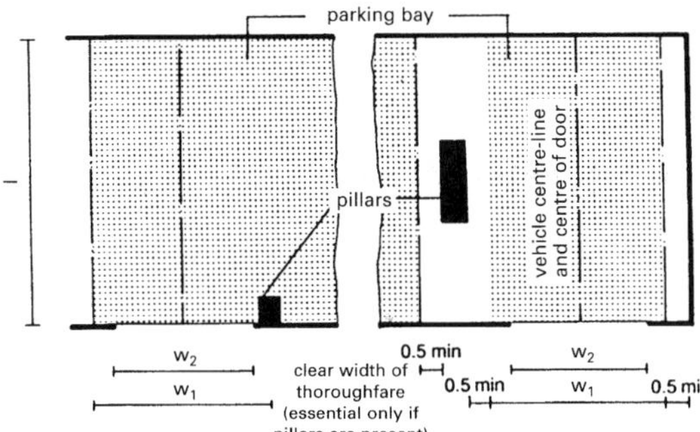

❻ Parking places and gates → ❼

Size[1]	Parking place Width b_1 min.	Length L min.	Gate (drive-through width b^2 × drive-through height)	Unit (U) Calculated acc. to → ❽[2] m^2
1 (avoid if possible)	4.5	8	3.5 × 3.5	9
2	4.5	10	3.5 × 3.5	11.25
3	4.5	12.5	3.5 × 3.5	14
4	4.5	12.5	3.5 × 4	14

[1] see also → ❶ notes; [2] corresponds to ¼ of parking place

❼ Dimensions of parking places → ❻

a) **Fire sub-station for local call-outs** can consist of: fire engine parking, equipment room, store for special equipment, training room (multi-purpose room for administration and control centre), social rooms, building services.

b) **Fire station for local and regional call-outs**, for example for preventative fire protection and technical assistance, with central workshop, repair, training and exercise rooms, can consist of: fire engine parking (with additional places if ambulances are also stationed), equipment room, store for special equipment, training room, staff rooms like washroom, showers, WC, changing room, drying room, social rooms (like on-call lounge, kitchenette), administration, chief's office, vehicle and equipment workshop, building services, room for ABC (disaster) service, central workshop (if required). Unless there are centralised hose maintenance and breathing equipment maintenance workshops, these will also be required. If the workshops are centralised, then appropriate stores will still be needed at each station.

	units[1]
equipment room	1 U
store room for special equipment	1 U
training room	4 U
associated side room	1 U
staff rooms:	
washroom, showers, WC, changing room, drying room	3 U
on-call lounge, kitchenette	3 U
administration	
room for fire service chief	1 U
control room	1 U
workshops: hose maintenance workshop, hose washing and testing room (min. 26 m long and 3 m wide)	8 U
hose store	1 U
hose drying tower with exercise wall (clear height of tower 23 m)	1 U
(If a horizontal hose drying installation is intended instead of a hose drying room, then this should be accommodated in the hose washing and testing room, whose min. area must then be 9 U and clear height min. 3 m)	
breathing equipment workshop	4 U
maintenance, repair, storage incl. radiation protection, diving[2]	
room for ABC (disaster) service	4 U
vehicle and equipment workshop including:	
battery charging station, next door to existing parking place	2 U
washing hall	4 U
building services:	
heating, fuel room	1 U

[1] units (U) according to → ❼ determine the floor area of rooms. For fire stations with parking places of various sizes, the unit is based on the largest. The floor areas determined through the units give the minimum size of the rooms.
[2] this does not include breathing equipment exercise facility.

❽ Floor areas of rooms → ❼

Fire service vehicles	Actual total weight (kg) (permissible)	Wheelbase (mm)	Turning circle B (mm)	Length (mm)	Width (mm)	Greatest height (mm) for 4WD vehicles with rooflights
fire engine with pump and crew LF 8	5450 (5800)	2600	11,700 (2WD)	5650	2170	2800
fire engine with pump and crew LF 8	7490 (7490)	3200	15,050 (4WD)	6400	2410	2950
fire engine with pump and crew LF 16	11,300 (11,500)	3750	16,100 (4WD)	8000 with hose reel trailer	2470	3090
fire engine with pump and crew LF16-TS	10,200 (11,000)	3750	16,100 (4WD)	7600	2470	3100
water tender with tank and pump TLF 8/18	7490 (7490)	3200	14,800 (4WD)	6250	2410	2850
water tender with tank and pump TLF 16/25	10,700 (11,500)	3200	14,400 (4WD)	6450	2470	2990
water tender with tank and pump TLF 24/50	15,900 (16,000)	3500	15,400 (4WD)	6700	2500	3270
foam tender with tank and pump TLF16	11,500 (12,000)	3750	16,100 (4WD)	7000	2470	2990
foam tender with tank and pump 1000	7300 (7490)	3200	14,800 (4WD)	6100	2410	3250
foam tender with tank and pump 2000	10,100 (11,600)	3200	14,400 (4WD)	6450	2410	3300
turntable ladder DL 30	12,550 (13,000)	4400	18,600 (2WD)	9800 with hose reel trailer	2430	3250
turntable ladder LB30/5 with cradle	20,200 (21,000)	3800 × 1320	19,900 (4WD)	9800	2490	3300
equipment truck RW1	7200 (7490)	3200	14,800 (4WD)	6400	2420	2850
equipment truck RW2	10,850 (11,000)	3750	16100 (4WD)	7600	2480	3070
hose truck SW2000	10,200 (11,000)	3200	14,400 (4WD)	6500	2500	2980

❾ Usual dimensions of current fire service vehicles from one of the largest German manufacturers

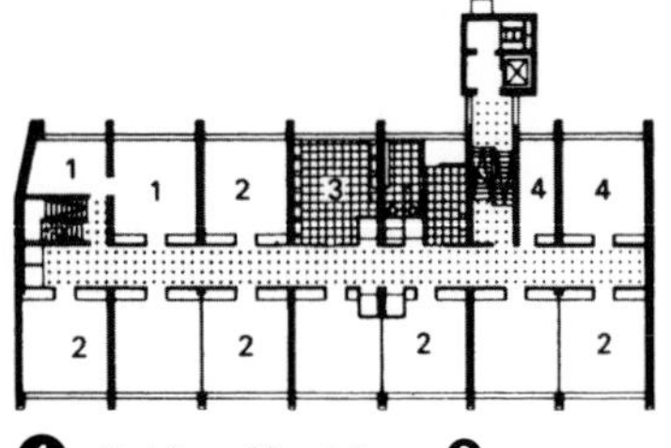

1 watch room
2 bedroom
3 washroom
4 station commander

❶ First floor of fire station → ❸

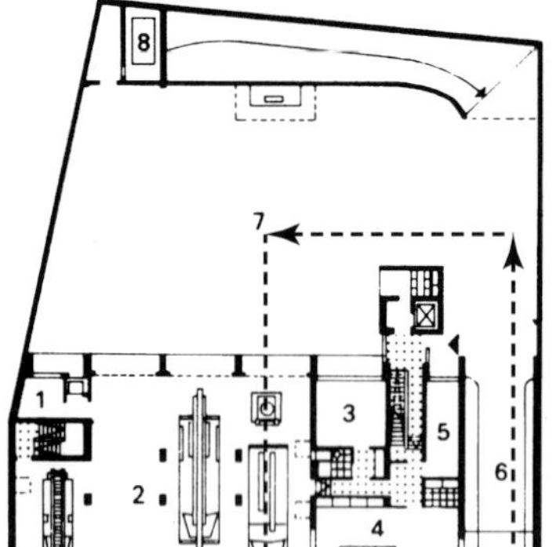

1 battery charging room
2 fire-appliance hall
3 bedroom
4 control centre
5 apparatus room
6 passage
7 yard
8 oil store

❷ Ground floor of fire station → ❸

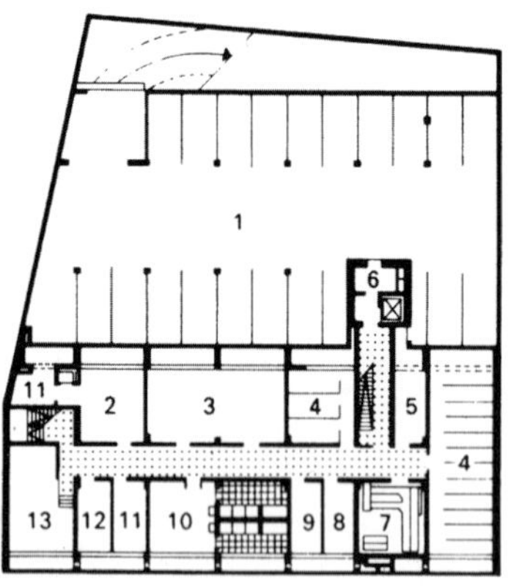

1 underground garage
2 day stores
3 hose room
4 cellar
5 ventilation
6 sluice
7 main control room
8 emergency power supply
9 pump room
10 changing room
11 store
12 gas and water supply
13 generator and central heating room

❸ Basement of fire station 4, Munich

Arch.: Ackermann + P.

Fire station: is used for the accommodation of vehicles and other equipment.

Staffed fire station: is used for the accommodation of personnel, vehicles and other equipment in readiness for emergency services and also in some cases the constantly staffed control centre for the centralised receipt of reports, alarming, coordination and control of emergency personnel. A flat should ideally be provided. The crews are either in readiness or on call for call-outs by telephone or fire alarm, either entirely or as reinforcement. Emergency call, warning and fire alarm equipment.

Functions before the call-out: Parking of private cars. Changing near the vehicle and fitting of equipment. Getting into vehicle.

After the call-out: Vehicles returning from a call-out are parked forwards into the vehicle hall via the yard. The vehicles are then re-equipped and fire-fighting water and fuel filled up. The crew change and wash. The plot should be in a position central to all parts of town or suitable for risk hotspots. Provide clear and unobstructed access and exit routes and sufficient open areas, e.g. consider the turning circles for vehicles. Vehicle washing area with sand trap and petrol separator, tanks for diesel and petrol. The yard should be suitable for heavy vehicles (about 16 t). Underground and overground hydrants. Space is required for additional vehicles, perhaps also a helipad (50 x 50 m) with an additional 15 m of free space. Sport facilities and green areas.

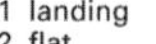

1 landing
2 flat
3 training room
4 training material
5 meeting room
6 garage
7 oil store
8 vehicle wash
9 fire-appliance hall
10 hose wash
11 hose store
12 parts store
13 workshop
14 breathing apparatus
15 courtyard
16 station commander
17 duty room
18 changing room
19 washroom
20 locker room
21 porch
22 lobby
23 recreation room
24 practice room
25 breathing apparatus training room
26 heating plant
27 ventilation plant
28 store
29 battery room
30 telephone/radio room

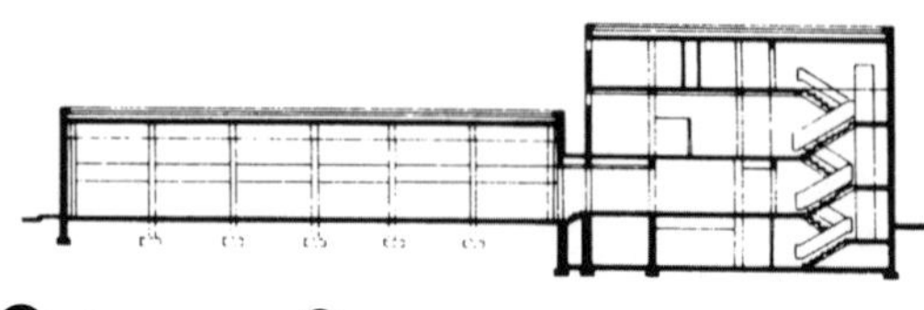

❹ Cross-section → ❼

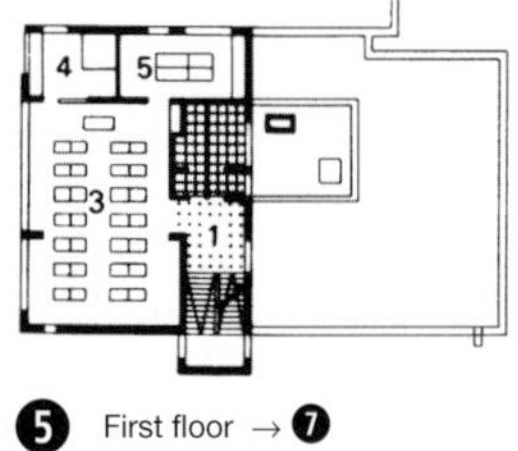

❺ First floor → ❼

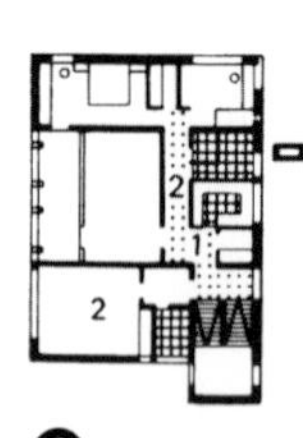

❻ Second floor → ❼

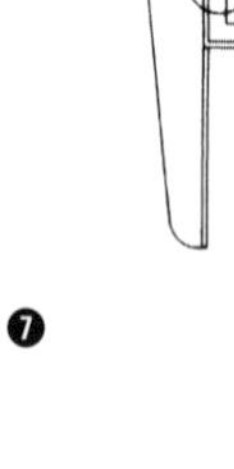

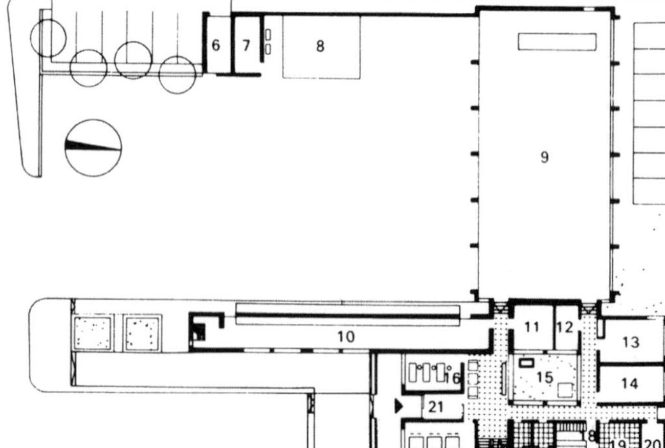

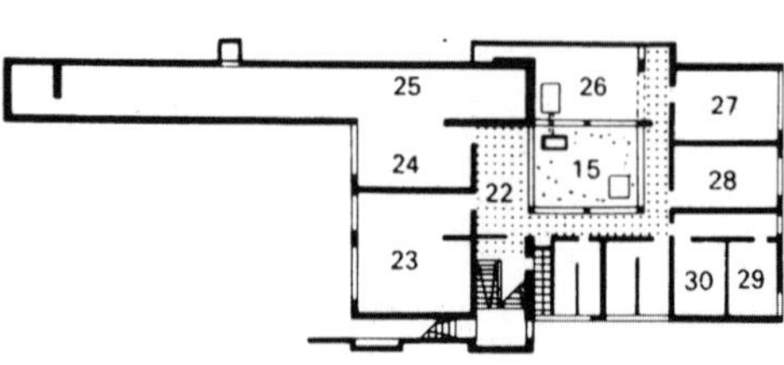

❼ Basement and (right) ground floor of fire station

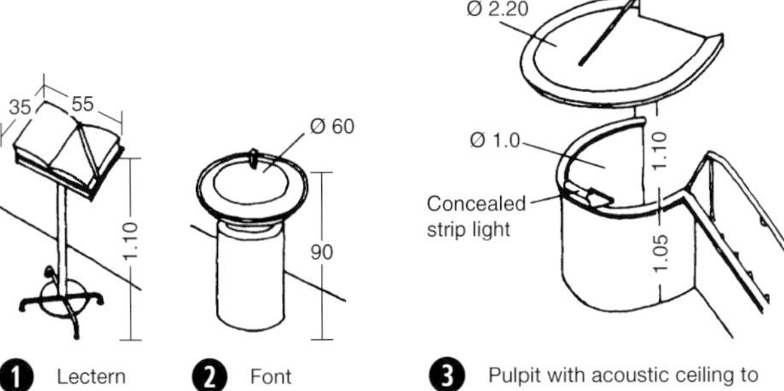

❶ Lectern ❷ Font ❸ Pulpit with acoustic ceiling to reflect the sound towards the congregation

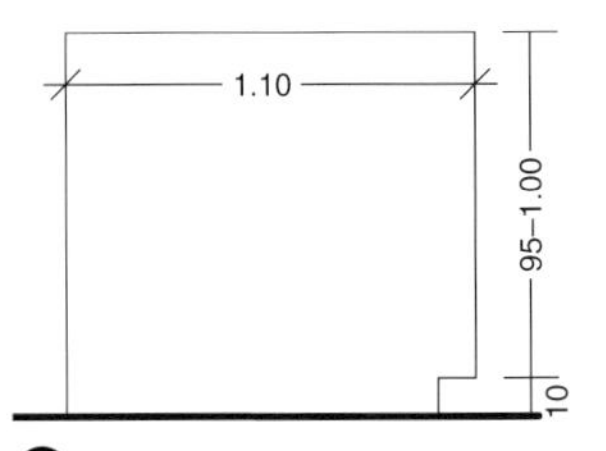

❹ Altar with toe-kick, section

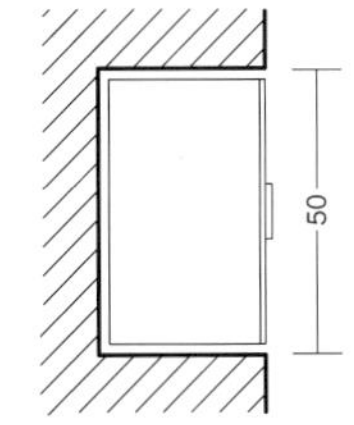

❺ Tabernacle integrated into the wall

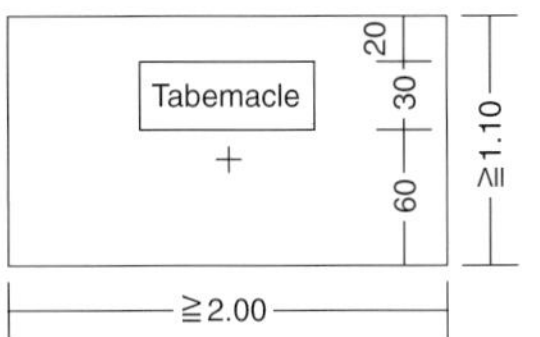

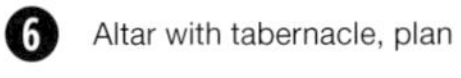

❻ Altar with tabernacle, plan

❼ Altar without tabernacle, plan

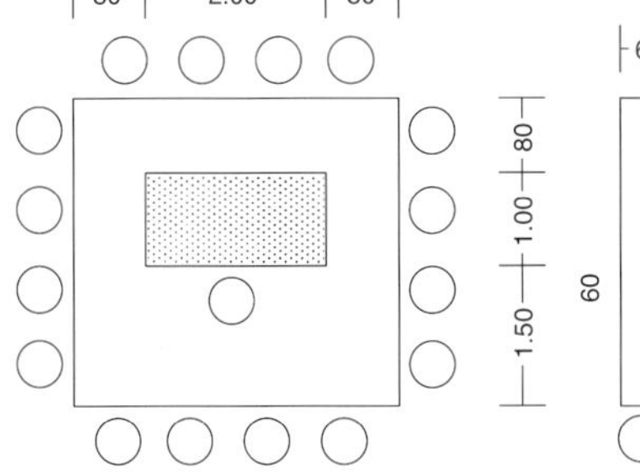

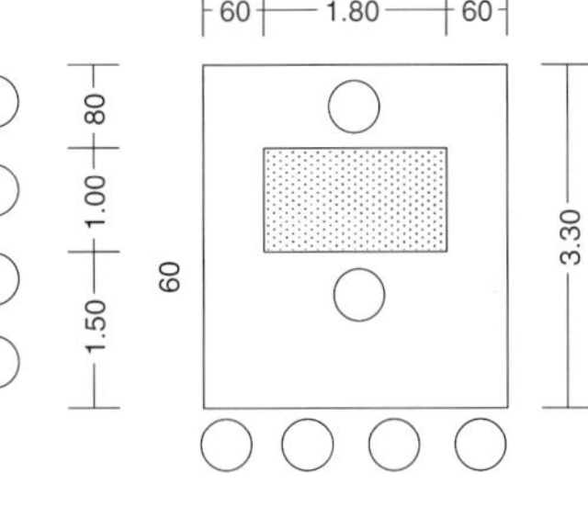

❽ Variants of area around altar

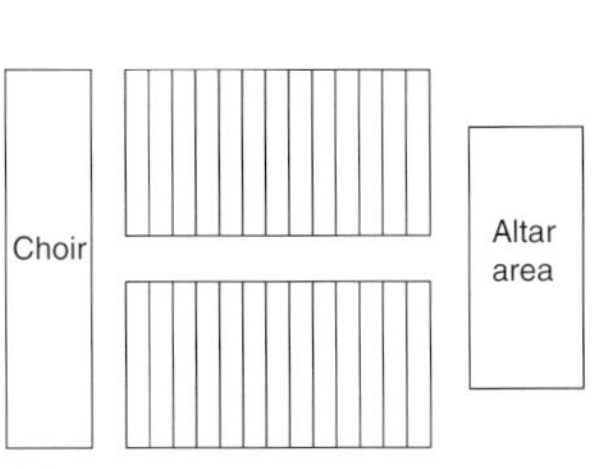

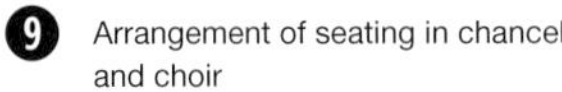

❾ Arrangement of seating in chancel and choir

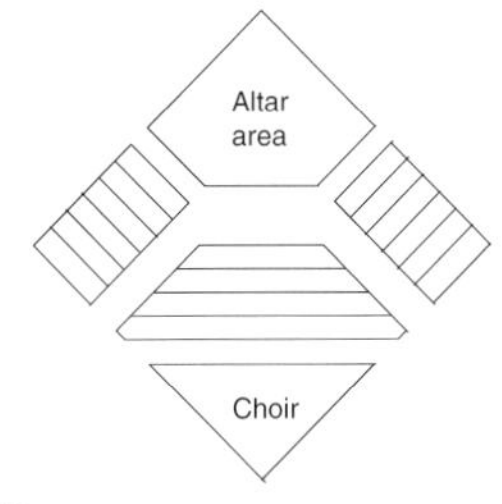

❿ Rhombus-shaped arrangement

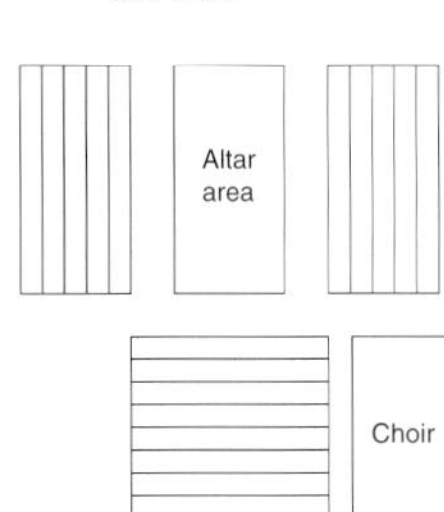

⓫ Three-sided arrangement

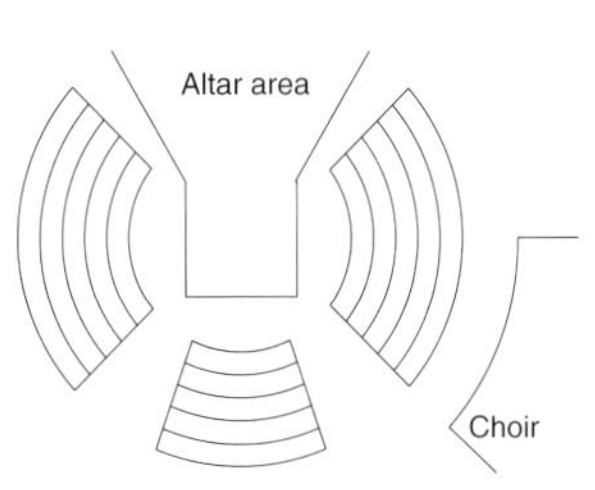

⓬ Central arrangement in ¾ circle

Guidelines for church building

The individual state Churches and bishoprics have special guidelines for the churches to be built in their areas. In addition, the Places of Assembly Regulations also apply to spaces which are not predominantly intended for church services. For new building, alteration and refurbishment, the advice of the diocesan commission should be requested. Approvals are issued by the bishop's representative.

Because churches serve religious faiths, the form of the building should be developed from the belief and the liturgy.

Liturgical elements

Religious elements required for all regular acts of worship.

Pulpit → ❸

Raised enclosed platform for preaching and the proclamation of the Word. The pulpit stands in a close liturgical relationship to the altar, but there are no precise regulations regarding its location. This is frequently to the right of the altar as seen from the nave. The height of the pulpit is 1.00–1.20 m (pulpit floor level) above the church floor .

Lectern → ❶

In early Christian churches this was a mobile reading desk called the ambo for the reading of the Gospels and Epistles. The lectern should, despite being mobile, be placed in the immediate vicinity of the altar.

Altar

'God's table', focus of the celebration of the Eucharist. Fixed and mobile altars or sacrament tables are possible. The shape and material are not regulated. The altar is mostly rectangular, 0.95–1.00 m high and free-standing, so that it is possible to walk around it without difficulty → ❽. In reformed churches, however, other shapes are possible. An altar should not be used before it is consecrated by the bishop.

Altar steps

There should be an at least 1.50 m level area in front of the altar, next to and behind the altar min. 0.80 m (if the altar can be walked around). This area is often raised by one or two steps.

Tabernacle → ❺

Shrine for the storage of the reserved sacrament. Tabernacle and altar are in a close liturgical and spatial relationship to one another.

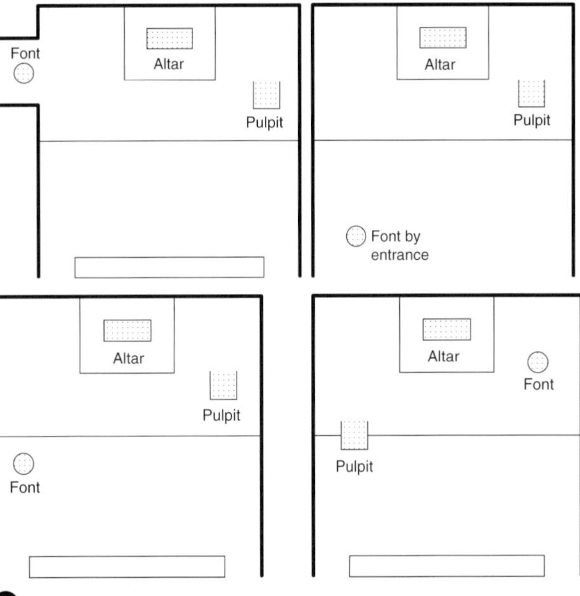

⓭ Layouts of altar, pulpit and font

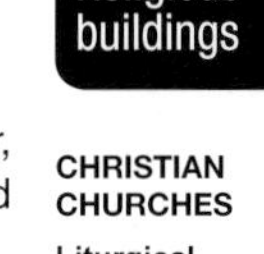

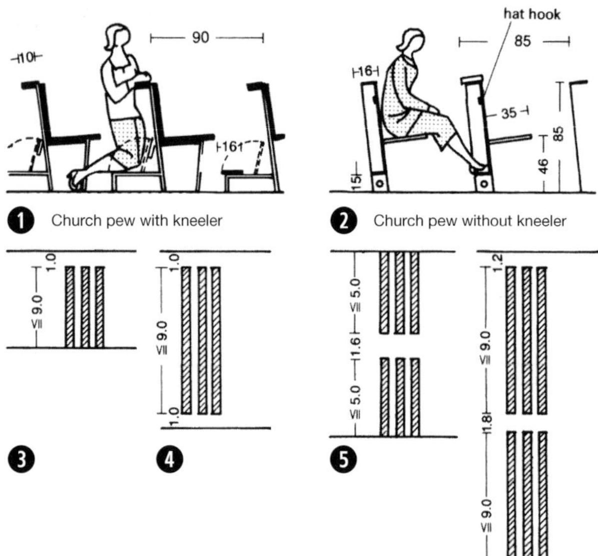
❶ Church pew with kneeler
❷ Church pew without kneeler
❸ – ❻ Arrangements of pews

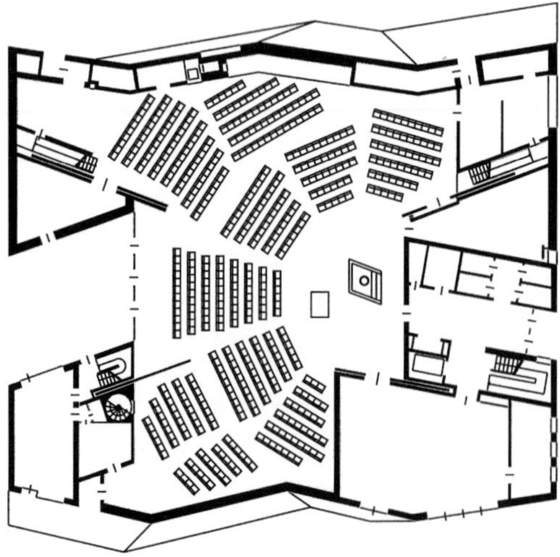

❼ Church building shared by two denominations

❽ Movable partitions create a common space in a double church for two denominations, Freiburg Arch.: Kister Scheithauer Gross

Arrangement of seating

Space requirement for pew without kneeler (Protestant) → ❷ = 0.4–0.5 m^2 (without aisles), for pew with kneeler (Catholic) → ❶ = 0.43–0.52 m^2 (without aisles).

The layout and form of seating is of great importance for the dimensions and effect of the space, quality of hearing and view. In smaller churches (chapels), an aisle of 1.00 m width is sufficient → ❸ with pews containing 6–10 seats, or a central aisle of 1.60 m width with seating both sides as → ❺.

Because of possibly noticeable cold emanating from the external walls, two side aisles with pews in between → ❻ containing 12–18 seats is normal.

Wider churches will have correspondingly more aisles. The total space requirement for each seat is therefore approx 0.63–1.0 m^2. For standing places, 0.25–0.35 m^2 each is sufficient; for these a large part of the aisles, particularly in front of the back wall, is occupied. The width of the exit doors and steps must comply with the Places of Assembly Regulations.

A central aisle on the altar axis is often desired for weddings, processions etc.

Confessional → ❿

Three-compartment enclosed booth made of wood, in the central part of which the Catholic priest sits to hear confession. The person confessing speaks to the Catholic priest through one of the two side compartments through a grille of approx. 30 × 40 cm. The lower edge of the opening should be approx. 1.00 m above floor level. The confessional should be situated inside the church at a location which is not too bright. Sufficient ventilation and extraction should be provided.

Today, a confessional room is possible as an alternative.

Vestry → ⓫

The vestry (also known as sacristy) is a side room in the church for the clergy, vestments and equipment for the service. It is best placed near and to the side of the altar.

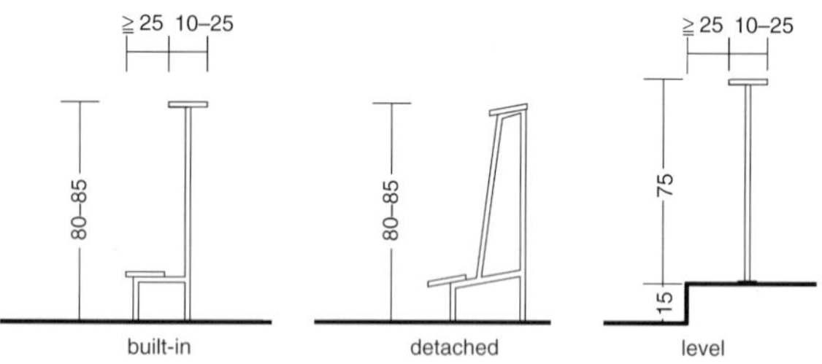

❾ Altar rail, various forms

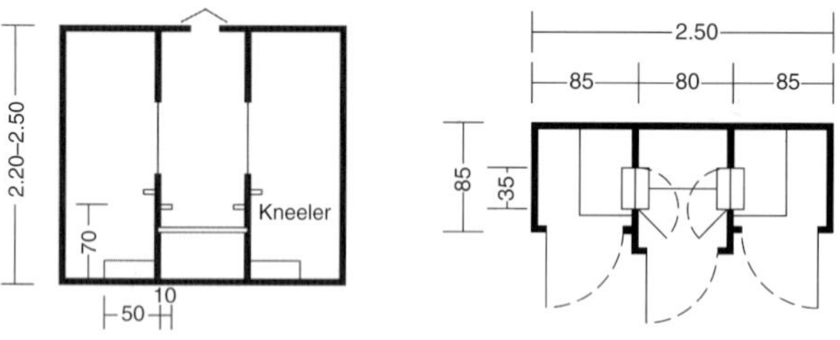

❿ Two-sided, enclosed confessional, vertical and horizontal sections

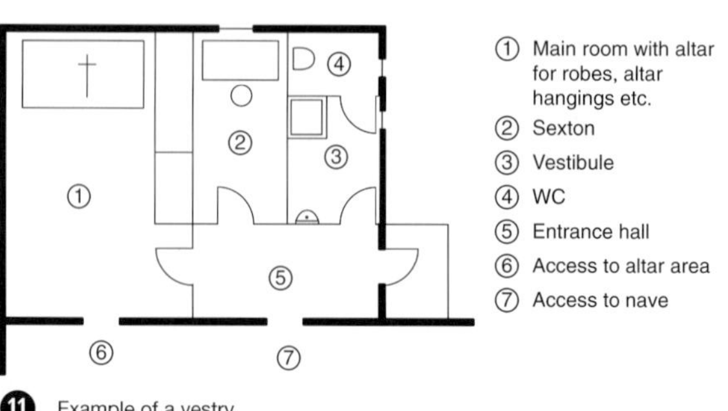

⓫ Example of a vestry

Religious buildings

CHRISTIAN CHURCHES
Liturgical elements
Furnishing
Vestry
Bell towers

Design

The standards on bell towers should be complied with.

A bell specialist can provide advice about the size and pitch of the bells, acoustics and weights. A bell founder designs the bell frame as the basis for the dimensions and layout of the belfry and sound openings, and also contributes loadings for the structural engineer, who has to consider static and dynamic loadings.

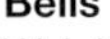

Bells

Weight, alloy and wall thickness determine the sound. Electric ringing machines are often used today.

Bell tower → 8 – 9

According to regulations, this is a 'solo musical instrument' and forms an 'orchestra' together with the neighbouring bell towers.

The desired audible range determines the height of the belfry (or bell loft) in the tower, which should be above the surrounding buildings. The quality of the bell tone depends on the tower's construction materials and the acoustic design.

The **belfry** is a resonance and mixing space which decides the musical quality of the sound transmission. The room is fully enclosed apart from the sound openings. The natural resonance frequency of the tower should not result in any resonance at the frequency of the bells.

Sound shutters → 7

A fair number of small openings at right angles to the direction of the bell swing is better than a few larger ones. The sound transmission angle should not be more than 30° from the horizontal (to protect the neighbourhood). The clapper strike should not radiate, which should also be considered in the layout of the sound shutters. The total openings should be max. 5% of the interior walls of the belfry if the wall surfaces are smooth, and max. 10% if rough. Concrete ceilings and floors can be clad with wood.

1 Dimensional relationships depending on the wall thickness

2 Terms

3 Returned steel yoke

4 Straight yoke

5 Horizontal thrust

6 Suspension near centre of gravity

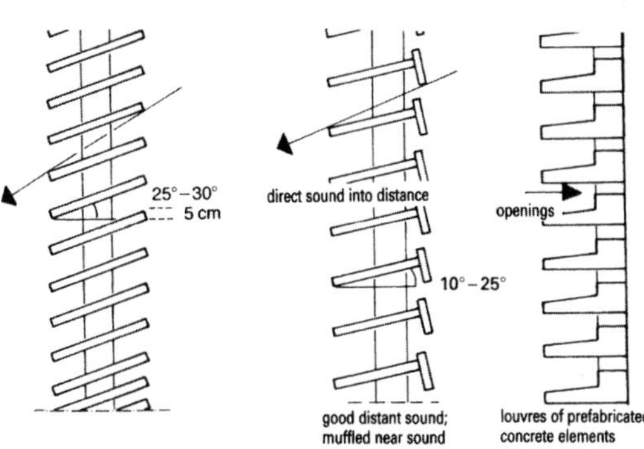

7 Sound shutters

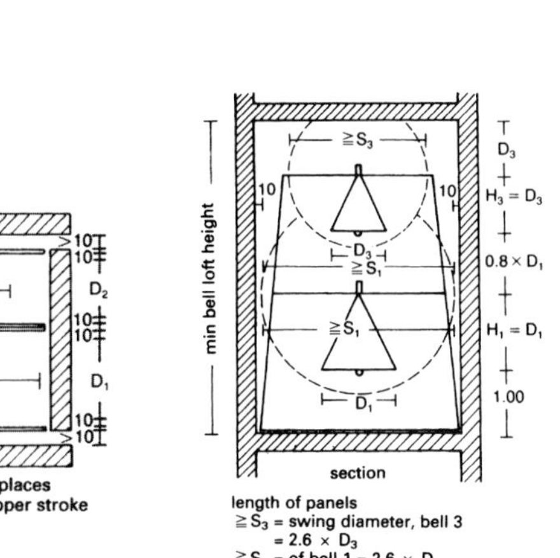

8 Belfry (plan)

9 Belfry (section)

	a	b	a	b	a	b
	Bell diameter d (mm)	Bell dead load L (kN)	Bell diameter d (mm)	Bell dead load L (kN)	Bell diameter d (mm)	Bell dead load L (kN)
	Wall thickness					
Note	Light		Medium		Heavy	
F	2250	58	2320	71		
F sharp° G flat°	2120	48	2220	59		
G°	2000	40	2100	50		
G sharp° A flat°	1880	34	2000	41		
A°	1780	28	1880	35		
A sharp° B°	1680	24	1760	29		
B°	1580	20	1660	24		
c	1400	16	1570	20	1680	31
c sharp d flat'	1400	14	1475	17	1580	25
d'	1325	11	1390	14	1500	21
d sharp' e flat'	1240	10	1310	12	1410	17
e'	1170	8.0	1240	10	1330	15
f'	1110	7.0	1170	8.0	1250	13
f sharp' g flat'	1035	5.5	1100	7.2	1175	11
g'	980	4.6	1040	6.0	1110	9.0
g sharp' a flat'	930	4.0	980	5.0	1040	7.2
a'	875	3.2	925	4.3	985	6.2
a sharp' b'	830	2.8	870	3.5	930	5.3
h'	780	2.3	820	3.0	880	4.3
c"	740	2.0	775	2.5	830	3.7
c sharp" a flat"	690	1.6	730	2.1	780	3.2
d"	650	1.4	690	1.7	735	2.6
d sharp" e flat"	600	1.1	645	1.5	690	2.1
e"	575	0.90	610	1.2	650	1.7
f"	550	0.80	580	1.0	620	1.5
f sharp" g flat"	510	0.65	545	0.80	595	1.2
g"	480	0.55	510	0.70	550	1.0
g sharp" a flat"	450	0.45	480	0.59	525	0.90
a"	425	0.38	455	0.50	495	0.75
a sharp" b"	390	0.32	430	0.40	465	0.65
b"	370	0.25	405	0.35	440	0.50
c"	350	0.20	380	0.30	415	0.43
form with value	c = 0.75		c = 0.76		c = 0.78	

10 Bell parameters

DIN 4178

SYNAGOGUES

General Design Notes

The Tabernacle, the Jews' first place of worship → 2

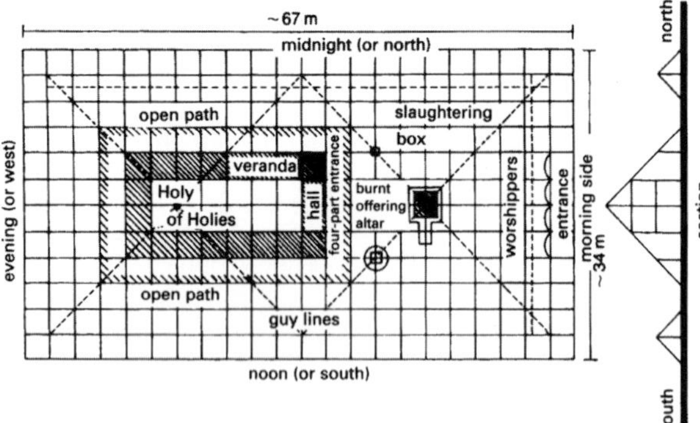

Court of the Tabernacle → 1

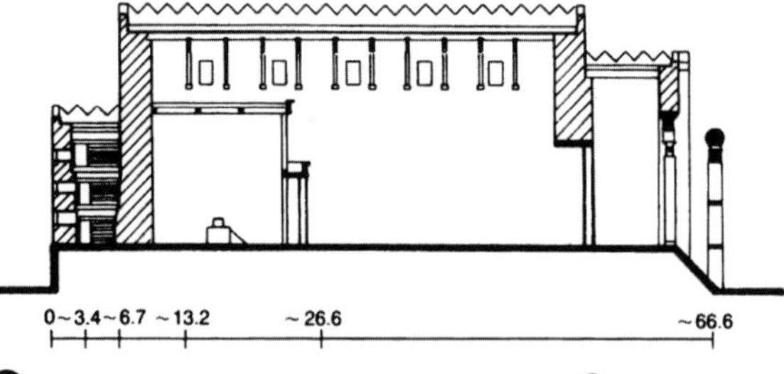

Solomon's Temple, Jerusalem, longitudinal section → 4

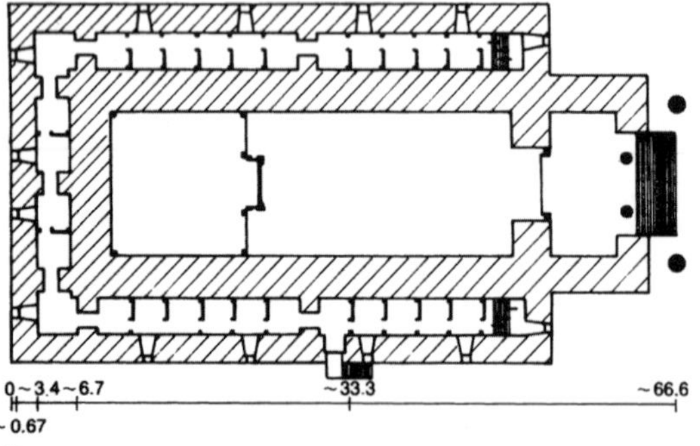

Solomon's Temple, Jerusalem, plan → 3

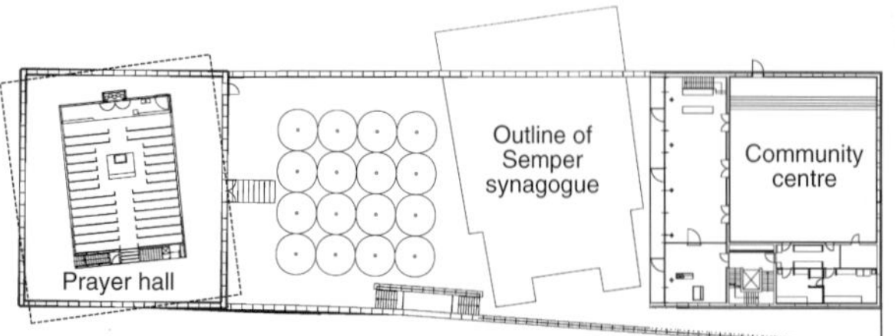

Prayer hall and community centre divided by a courtyard into separate buildings, New Dresden synagogue Arch.: Wandel-Hoefer Lorch + Hirsch

The first building commission from God, for a religious sanctuary, with exact technical and design specifications for the erection of the Tabernacle (dwelling place), can be found in the Bible (Exodus 25–27).

In a synagogue, the focal point is not an altar but the raised preaching rostrum (almemor → 6), from where Torah excerpts are read. The synagogue is aligned towards Jerusalem. In the front wall is the ark or chest (Aron Hakodesh), where the Torah scrolls are kept → 6.

Between the rostrum and the ark is an aisle for the ceremonial procession before the reading from the scrolls.

Constructing the plan of a synagogue is always an attempt to solve anew a spatial conflict defined by the positioning of two room elements of equal significance – the preaching rostrum (almemor) and the holy ark (Aron Hakodesh) – in a sacred room. In orthodox synagogues, the ark is mostly located on the east (mirach) wall and the rostrum in the middle of the room. In more liberal synagogues, the two elements are spatially combined and orientated toward the east wall.

The space for women is at least symbolically separated from, and out of the view of, the men, often in the form of a balcony. At the entrance to the synagogue, there is a fountain or washbasin for handwashing. The ritual bath (mikva) for women, with immersion pool, is normally in the cellar. It should have natural running water that has not flowed through metal pipes. A more liberal synagogue might have an organ, but it would be unobstrusive.

The symbols of the Star of David, the seven-branched candlestick (menorah) and tablets of the Mosaic law are essential elements. The decoration consists of plant, geometrical or written ornamentation: depictions of people are excluded.

① Prayer hall
② Almemor
③ Aron Hakodesh
④ Kosher kitchen
⑤ Community hall
⑥ Administration area
⑦ Social rooms

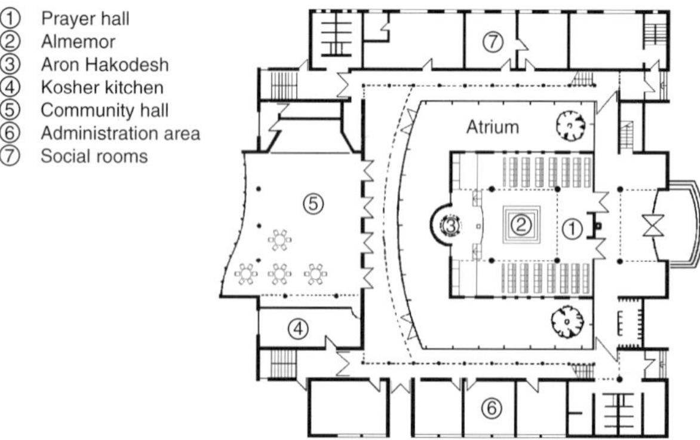

Prayer hall surrounded by inner courtyard, Darmstadt synagogue Arch.: Alfred Jacoby

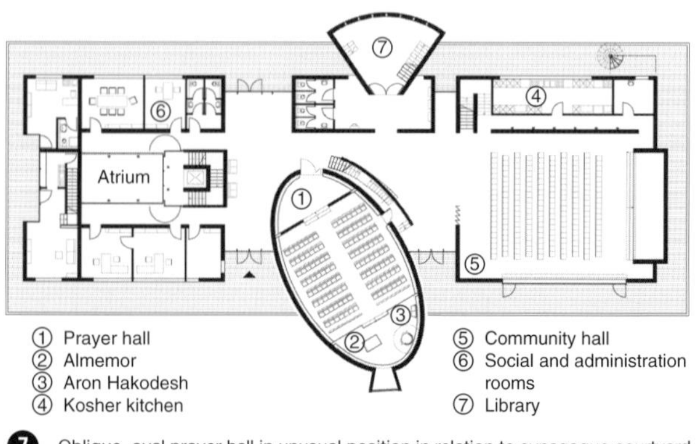

① Prayer hall
② Almemor
③ Aron Hakodesh
④ Kosher kitchen
⑤ Community hall
⑥ Social and administration rooms
⑦ Library

Oblique, oval prayer hall in unusual position in relation to synagogue courtyard

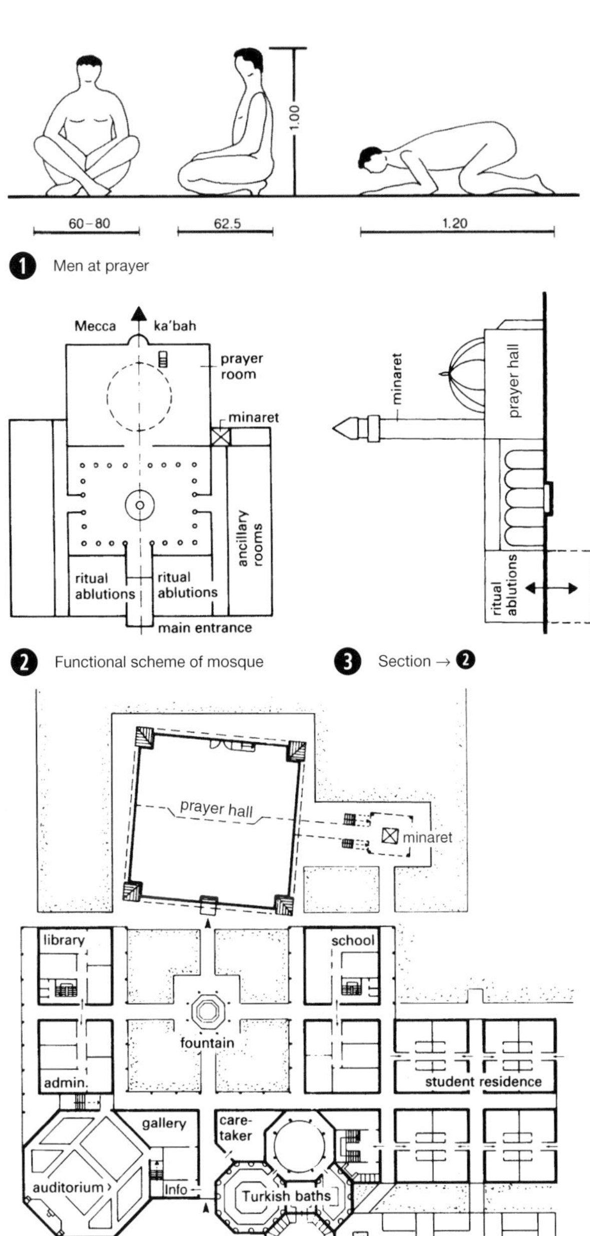

❶ Men at prayer

❷ Functional scheme of mosque

❸ Section → ❷

❹ Islamic cultural centre in Cologne

The mosque – in Arabic, masjid (smaller), jamia masjid (larger) – is a prayer house, cultural centre, community place of assembly, courthouse, school and university, with the Qur'an being the central source of life rules, teaching, law and religion for Islam.

In Islamic countries, the mosque stands in the bazaar (souk) at the centre of public life. Where bazaars are missing in other countries, they should be designed into the mosque (hairdresser, shop for halal food, café).

There are basic categories of mosque design and seven distinctive regional styles, e.g. the pillared hall and courtyard in much of the Middle East, Spain and North Africa, and the triple domes and courtyard of the Indian sub-continent. In the decoration, depictions of people or animals are not allowed. Plant and geometrical ornaments (arabesques) and verses from the Qur'an in Arabic calligraphy are popular and have developed into a high art form.

Minaret

Smaller mosques seldom have a minaret, but larger ones always do. There are neither organ nor bells in Islam. From the minaret, with stair or lift to the mostly roofed upper walkway, the muezzin calls to prayer five times daily, today often with a loudspeaker (which in some countries is not allowed).

Prayer hall

The prayer hall is laid out with a praying area of 0.85 m^2 for each person. The hall is normally rectangular to square, often with a central dome and is aligned to Mecca as prayer direction (qibla). On the interior of the front wall, there is the prayer niche (mihrab), and next to that the pulpit for the Friday prayers (minbar), always with an odd number of steps, for the mosque prayer leader (imam). An often only symbolic separation or a balcony serves to segregate the men and the women.

Entrance

At the entrance, there are shelves for the shoes of the believers and rooms for ritual washing and showers, always with flowing water. The WCs are mostly as squatting closets aligned at right angles to the direction of Mecca. Mosques often have separate entrances for men and women, or the stairs to the women's balcony can be in the entrance area.

Decorative well

Many mosques have an inner courtyard of the same size as the prayer hall, which can also be used as an extension for festivals and a decorative fountain or well (sabil) for ritual washing. In warm countries, geometrically arranged trees are planted here to give shade.

Subsidiary rooms

Office, library, lecture and tuition room, store rooms and flats for at least the imam and muezzin complete the room allocation plan.

mihrab pulpit

❺ Islamic cultural centre in Frankfurt, ground floor

Ground floor
1. entrance/men
2. draught lobby
3. shoe racks
4. office
5. prayer hall ground floor/ men
6. information/ men
7. women's entrance
8. draught lobby
9. information/ women
10. shoe racks
11. prayer hall gallery/ women
12. balcony
13. minaret with lift

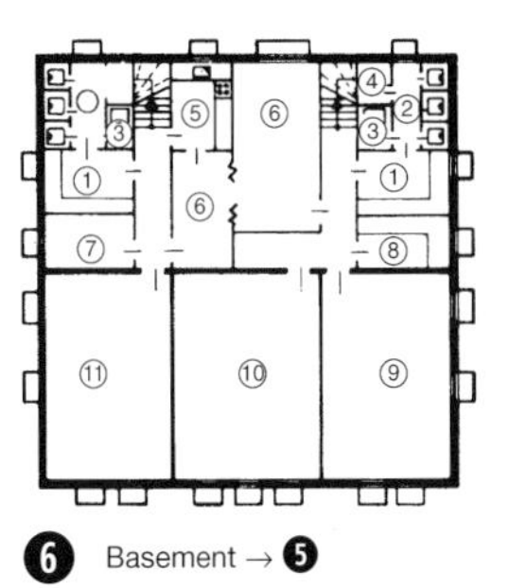

Basement
1. rows of wash basins
2. WCs
3. shower
4. hoist
5. kitchen
6. dining room
7. heating
8. hairdresser
9. classroom/ men
10. library and lecture room
11. classroom/ women

❻ Basement → ❺

DOCTORS' PRACTICES

Single and Group Practices

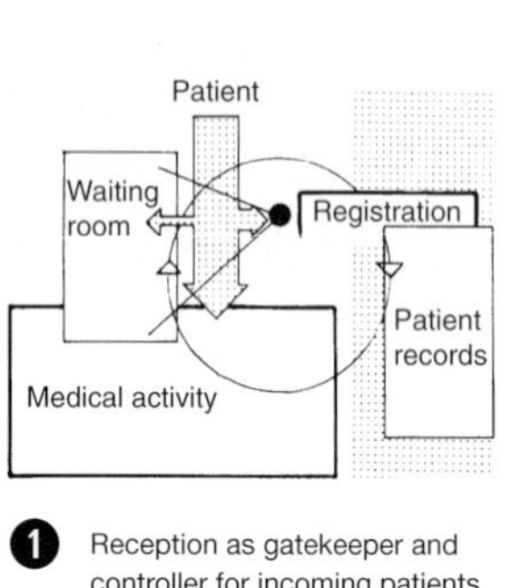

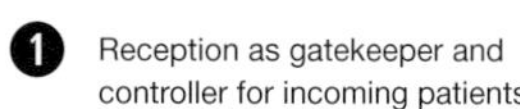

1 Reception as gatekeeper and controller for incoming patients

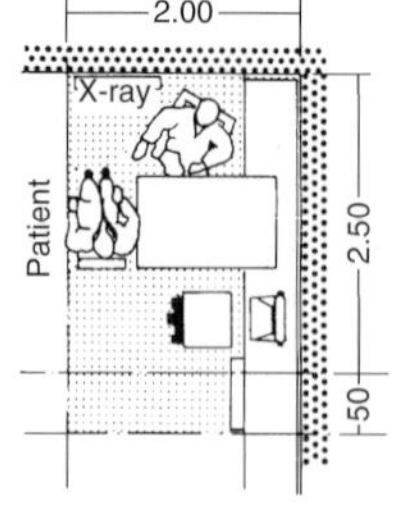

2 Minimum space required: doctor's consultation area

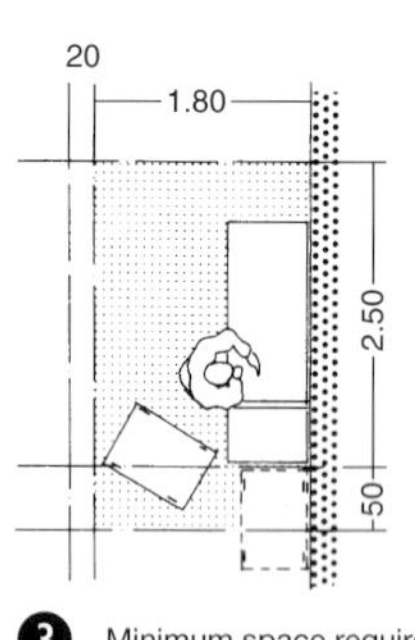

3 Minimum space required: examination of reclining patient

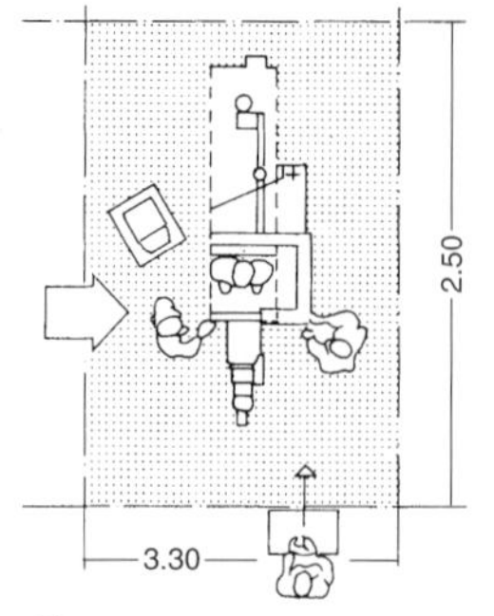

4 X-ray machine with control desk

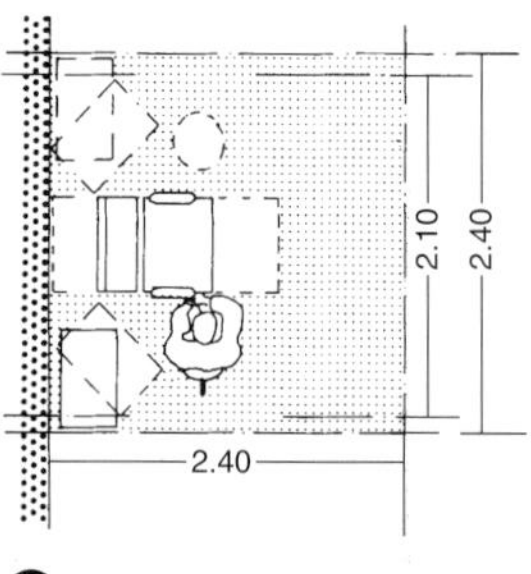

5 Minimum space required: taking a blood sample

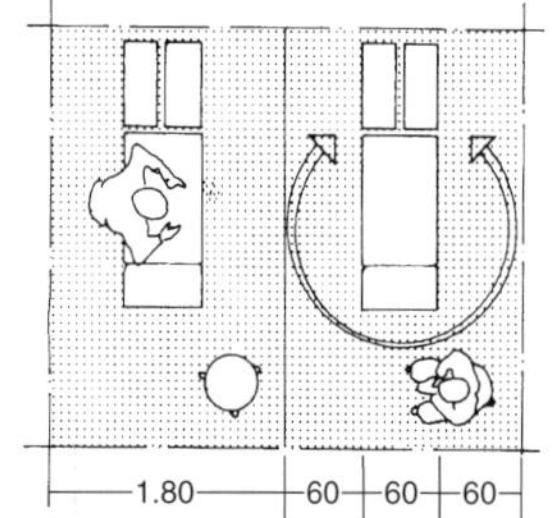

6 Physiotherapy couches

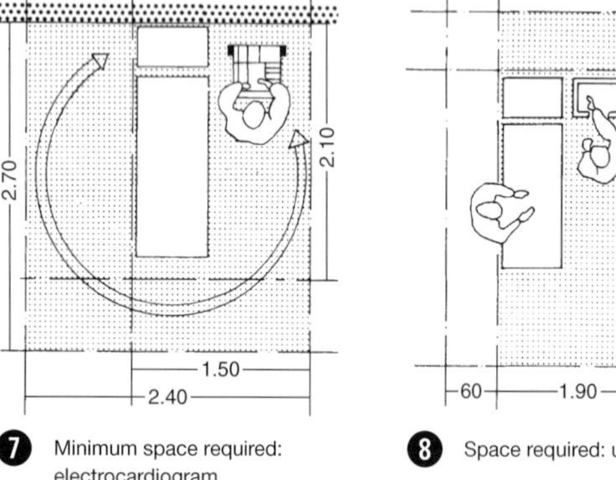

7 Minimum space required: electrocardiogram

8 Space required: ultrasound

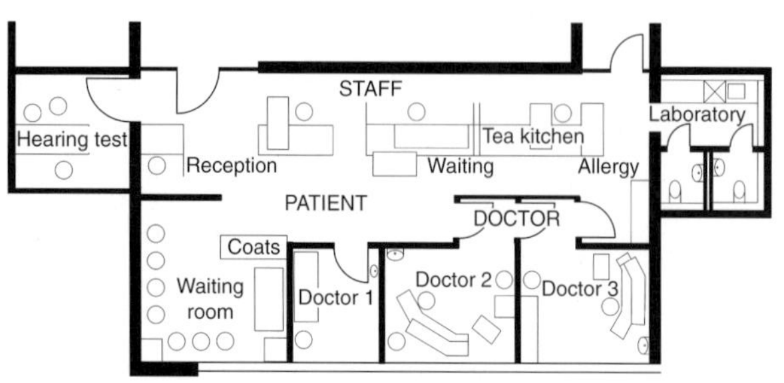

9 Ear/nose/throat practice, Stuttgart   Arch:. Prof. Ulrike Mansfeld

Single practices

A practice of a single specialist must have a minimum amount of space (approx. 150 m^2) and functions separated into rooms, which are differentiated and extended according to speciality. There is a general division between the patient and the staff areas.

At the entrance, there is a waiting area with cloakroom and WC, and the doctor's area with consultation room is placed near the waiting area. The treatment room and laboratory are next door. An extension of the consultation and examination area for repeated treatments and a separate diagnostic zone are sensible. The number and size of the rooms are based on the particular specialist qualifications of the doctor (internist and general practitioner, surgeon, orthopaedist, gynaecologist etc.). Patient WCs, staff changing rooms with WCs and staff lounge complete the programme. Separate children's play areas can be a good idea in the waiting area (e.g. gynaecology).

Waiting room

The size is in accordance with the number and frequency of visits to the treatment rooms, depending on the specialisation of the doctor. If the practice is organised to require appointments, the size of the waiting room can be reduced.

Appointment planning and recording of services take place in the **reception**. The staff here must be able to oversee the waiting room and the entrance, and the connection to the medical area should be as short as possible.

Consultation room

The doctor's consultation room (12–16 m^2) is a visually and acoustically enclosed room and primarily intended for the purposes of establishing case history, consultation, study of diagnostic findings, development of therapy plans and protocols. The furniture should include a desk with PC workstation, at least two chairs and an X-ray display.

Examination and treatment rooms

In size $\geqq 20$ m^2, these rooms differ according to the nature and form of treatment. The minimum furnishing would be a chair and couch for the patient, revolving stool, workbench with basin and instrument table. Adequate space for movement should be planned for the doctor and patient.

The size of other specific examination and treatment rooms (X-ray, taking blood samples, various therapies) depends on the required specialist instruments, apparatus and storage room plus integrated changing room (1.5 m^2). Separate office support is not necessary. Better is a generous reception with daylight and desks (equipped with PCs) with direct access to patient files. Washbasins with additional disinfectant dispensers are to be provided in all rooms with patient contact and treatment.

Medical centres/group practices

These terms denote the combination of two or more doctors practising together with shared staff and facilities. The creation of such practices can result in a clear saving of space with improved performance and convenience, for example if facilities like X-ray, laboratory tests and various therapies, as well as administration and staff rooms, can be used communally.

In the UK group practices mainly consist of general practitioners (GPs), who if necessary refer patients to specialists (usually based in hospitals). The group practice may also include practice nurses, midwives, health visitors, physiotherapists and other health professionals.

	Care dept.	Surgery	Intensive care	Sterilisation	Maternity	A & E	Pathology	Nuclear medicine	Out-patients	X-ray dept.	Dialysis
Care dept.		△	△	□	△		△	□	△	○	△
Surgery	△		○	○	○	○	△	△	△	△	
Intensive care		○		△	△	△	△		△	△	△
Sterilisation	□	○	△		△	△			△		
Maternity	△	○	△	△		△	△		□	□	
A & E		○	△	△	△		△		○	○	
Pathology	△	△	△		△	△		△	○	□	△
Nuclear medicine	□	△					△		○	○	
Out-patients	△	△	△	△	□	○	○	○		○	
X-ray dept.	○	△	△		□	○	□	○	○		□
Dialysis	△		△				△		△	□	

○ Very good connection required △ Good connection sensible □ Connection is desirable

1 Operational links

Area guideline		Usable area
For a general hospital with regular provision and approx. 300 beds		
Operational departments		Usable area per bed/m²
1.00 investigation and treatment 2.00 care 3.00 administration 4.00 social services 5.00 supply and waste disposal		12.0 18.0 2.0 3.0 7.0
Total	usable area	42.0 m²
operational area traffic area		8.0 m² 19.0 m²
Total	net floor area	69.0 m²
construction area (newbuild framed construction)		11.0 m²
Total	gross floor area	80.0 m²
	gross floor area/usable area	= 1.9

2 Space guidelines for a general hospital

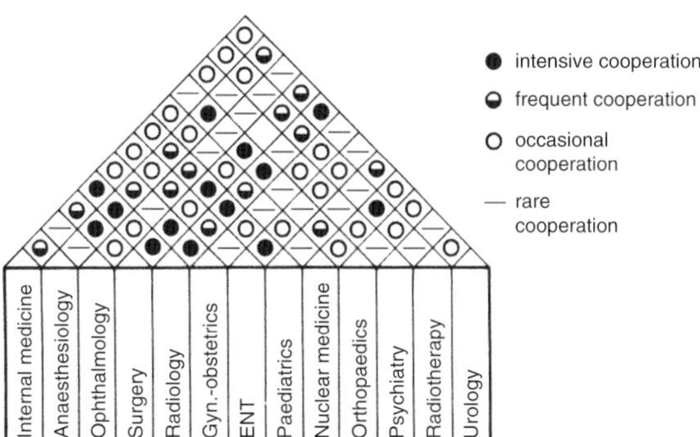

3 Diagram of cooperation between medical specialist departments

The investment and operating costs of a hospital are extremely high, so operational planning and an economical room allocation plan must be produced as a priority to reduce the operating and staffing costs. This is discussed and laid down at the preliminary design stage through collaboration by the responsible authorities, client, doctors, architects, specialist designers and the hospital administration. Based on the operational planning and the room allocation plan, the architectural design team can proceed with the construction and form of the building and the installation of systems, while planning equipment for medical requirements, fittings and furnishings.

Hospitals, clinics and health centres serve to treat and care for patients with acute and chronic illnesses. The medical and care objectives determine the size of the specialist departments and treatment facilities according to the nature and extent of the conditions. Regarding domestic requirements, modern hospitals offer something of the nature of a hotel. The atmosphere of a sanatorium with particular emphasis on hygiene, which was usual in the last century, is no longer desirable. Patients' length of stay is becoming increasingly short. In a main hospital the ratio of the areas for care to the areas for examination and treatment is approaching 1:1. Reform of health provision is making great changes in the hospital landscape and among service providers, which can be public, non-profit making or private.

Structure

The general hospital is functionally divided into areas for examination and treatment, care, administration, social services, supply and waste disposal and services. Additionally, there are residential areas and sometimes areas for tuition and research (university teaching hospital). The above operational areas are close neighbours but operationally separate. It is necessary to maintain short horizontal and vertical connections while preserving the greatest possible flexibility and a smooth flow of traffic between all departments. Hospitals are categorised according to their function into general and specialist hospitals and university teaching hospitals. The current changes in health policy are leading to different financial structures and also to new types of building like outpatient medical centres and patient hotels. Hospitals are also divided into those for basic provision (up to about 240 beds), normal provision (up to about 520 beds) and main hospitals (up to 800 beds), depending on their particular purpose.

University teaching hospital

With their maximum provision, teaching hospitals are comparable to some main hospitals in their departmental structure and service provision. They possess particularly extensive diagnostic and therapeutic equipment and at the same time are engaged in education and research. Lecture theatres and demonstration rooms should be included so that the operation of the hospital is not disturbed by students. Wards need to be larger to accommodate rounds attended by a large number of people. The specialisations and particular requirements of a teaching hospital demand special organisation, function and room allocation plans.

Specialist hospital

Specialist hospitals are intended for particular types of treatment or groups of complaints: accident and emergency, rehabilitation clinic, orthopaedic clinic, gynaecology etc. There are also hospitals specialising in tuberculosis, cancer, mental disorders, different types of surgery etc. There is a flexible overlap with health resorts and care, rehabilitation and homes for the elderly. The number of specialist hospitals is increasing greatly (e.g. dermatology, lung and allergy clinics) due to the growing specialisation of medicine.

Helicopter landing pad
Special ward 30 beds | 3rd floor | Care 42–48 beds
Care 36 beds | 2nd floor | Care 42–48 beds
1st floor | Care 42–48 beds
Staff | Out patients | Functional diagnosis/endoscopy | GF | Cafe | Administration | Accident & emergency | X-ray | Ambulance access
Possibly physiotherapy, special functions | Basement | Utility yard
Main entrance

❶ Vertical diagram of compactly structured hospital with approx. 200 beds

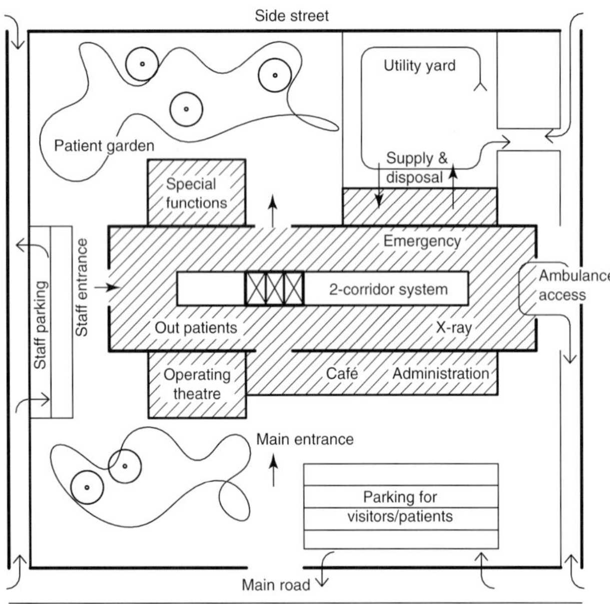

❷ Site: approx. 15,000 m² for hospital with approx. 200 beds and 3–4 storeys, Breitfuss type

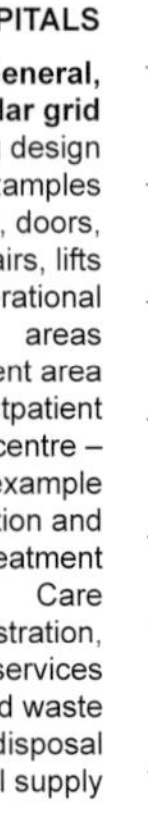

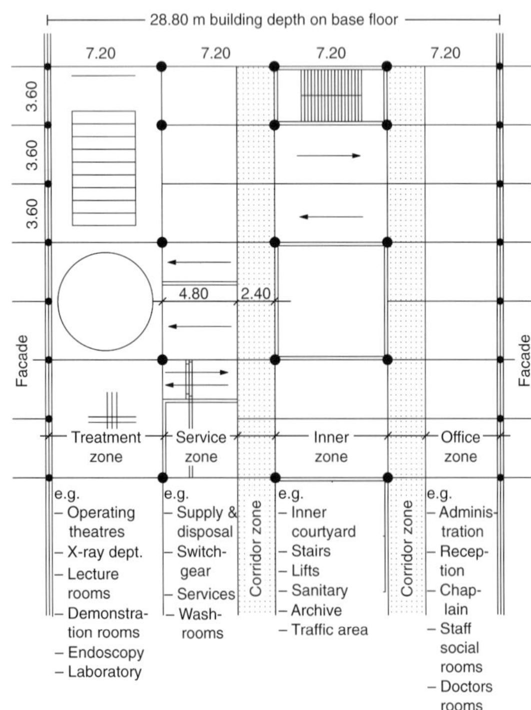

❸ Structural grid for examination and treatment area

Space allocation plan

A space allocation plan has to be produced as part of the design process, and this forms the basis of the structure and requirements of the entire hospital. Any specialist emphasis in a hospital has an effect on the nature and size of other departments. The area guideline values can give an overview of the size of the individual departments. It should be noted that these guideline values are only recommendations and depend on the specialist equipment and services of the hospital in question.

Building design

Possible alterations of use in the course of the period of operation of a hospital will have a considerable influence on the design concept, and need to be considered in addition to shortness of distances, efficient work flows and operational interactions. For the design of new hospitals intended for regular provision, approx. 42 m² usable area per bed can be assumed, and for the gross built volume approx. 200–280 m³ per bed.

Hospitals are frequently built in a number of construction phases or are extensions of existing hospitals. Therefore a comprehensive target and development plan (scale 1:500) should be produced at an early stage showing and arranging logistically the different phases. The construction and the design (routes, corridors) must be laid out so that the building can be extended in various ways. The architect should take note of the current regulations and guidelines (model hospital building regulations, operational regulations of the hospital, state building regulations etc.) at the beginning of the project.

Modular coordination

The application of modular coordination of dimensions should form the basis for the design of a hospital. This involves the adoption of a reference system, basic module and multiple modules in order to determine the purpose, location and dimensions of a building element. For hospital building, the preferred dimension of 12 M = 1.20 m is recommended. If this module is too coarse, then preferred dimensions of 6 M or 3 M can be chosen. All building elements are integrated into this modular system and matched with each other. The creation of the basic grid, horizontally and vertically, defines the load-bearing structure. The effects of using a modular system are short construction times, the simpler exchange of finishing elements and thus less disturbance to existing use.

Structural grid

The structural grid must enable good route planning and the possibility of differentiating the operational departments into zones: main function, subsidiary functions and traffic. A comparison of the individual departments and their required rooms leads to a structural grid, which is suitable for all operational departments.

Structural grids of 7.20 m or 7.80 m have proved successful in practice. Column spacings of 7.20 m or 7.80 m enable the various departments to be included in the design with the least difficulty. Smaller structural grids (e.g. 3.60 m × 7.20 m) are also possible, because the number of larger rooms such as operating theatres (approx. 40 m²) is relatively small. Reinforced concrete slabs should be designed without downstand beams in order to simplify the routeing of the service installations.

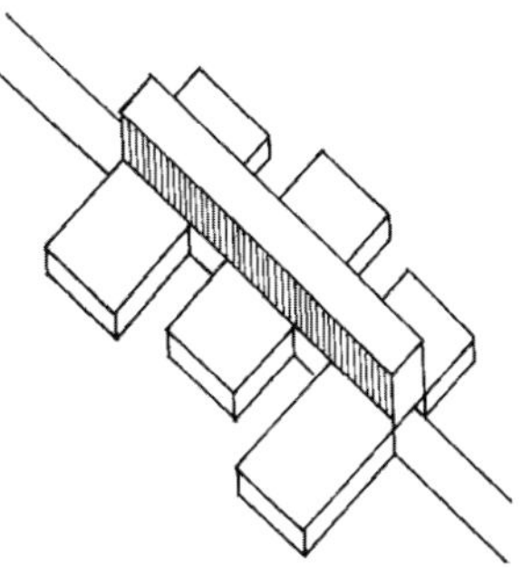

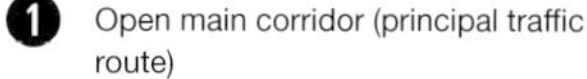

❶ Open main corridor (principal traffic route)

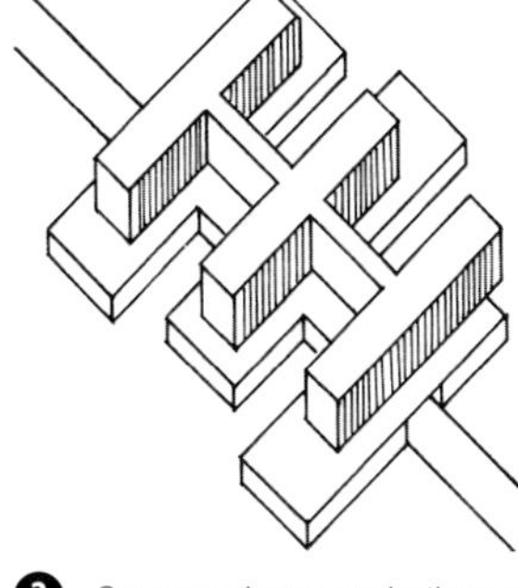

❷ Care area above examination and treatment area

❸ Open main corridor, care area next to examination and treatment area

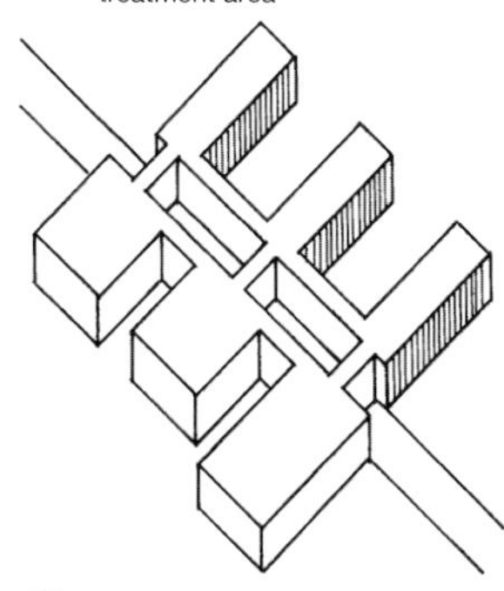

❹ → ❸

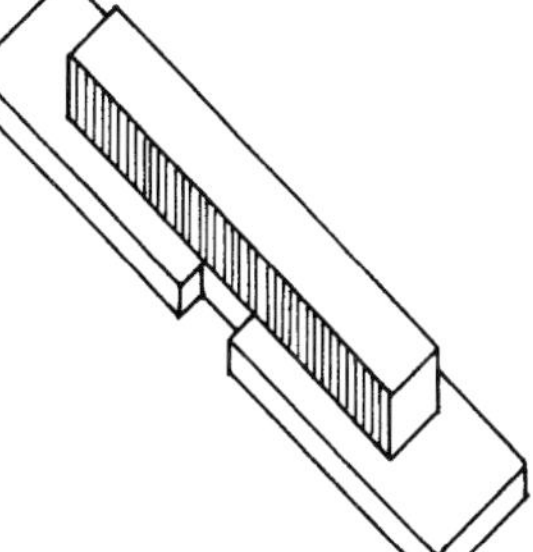

❺ Enclosed main corridor, care area above examination and treatment area

❻ → ❺

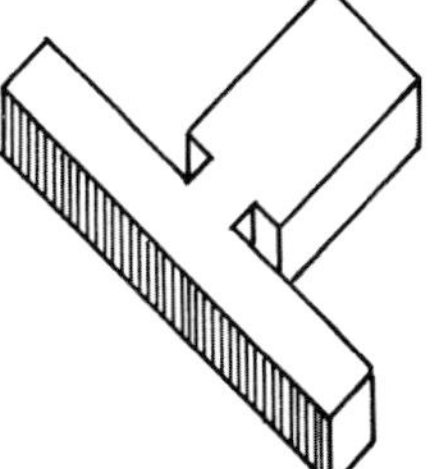

❼ Enclosed main corridor, care area next to examination and treatment area

❽ → ❼

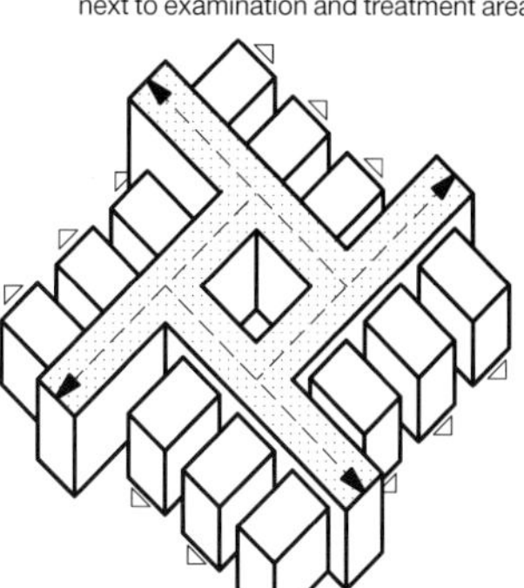

❾ Extension possibilities

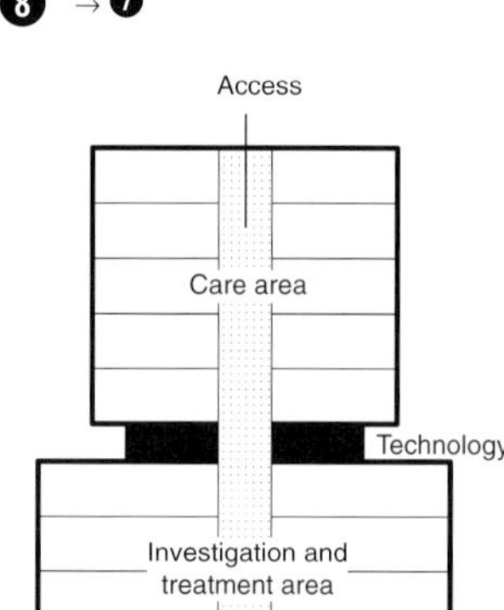

❿ Vertical structure: section through a hospital with care area above examination and treatment area

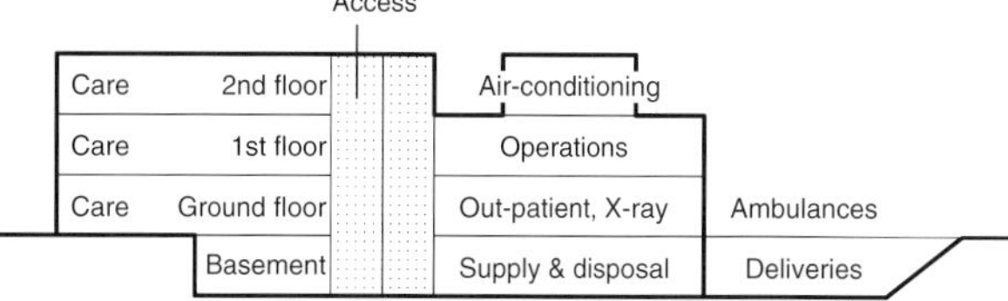

⓫ Horizontal structure: section through hospital with care area next to examination and treatment area

Useful life

Structure, walls, fittings and finishings have different lifetimes. The structure should if possible be framed in order to keep the construction of the walls and partitions flexible. Medical equipment is replaced after approx. 5–10 years according to department and depreciation, which can have significant effect on the spatial arrangements (e.g. linear accelerators, MRI scanners). The possible installation and removal of such equipment without disrupting the load-bearing structure should be taken into account in the design.

Site

The site for a hospital needs enough space for the building, its access and any possible extensions, and should be in a quiet area. Contaminated ground should be avoided. Separated access roads for visitors and patients, staff, goods and emergency vehicles, as well as a helicopter pad, all need to be taken into account in the selection of a site. The minimum land area for an acute hospital with rectangular layout is approx. 15,000 m^2.

Orientation

The best orientation for treatment and operational rooms is between north-west and north-east. For the fronts of patient rooms, south-east or south-west is favourable, with pleasant morning sun, little heat build-up, few sun protection measures necessary and temperate evenings. East–west rooms in contrast have deeper summer sun penetration but little winter sun.

Building forms

The form of the building is determined to a considerable extent by the selection of access and routeing. A decision should be reached at an early stage whether a design with a main corridor (spine) and branches (transverse corridors) is chosen or whether circulation will be radially outwards from a cruciform core. Possible extensions and construction phases should be taken into account. The vertical section of a hospital should be designed so that the functions care, examination and treatment, supply and waste disposal, delivery of patients on stretchers, service yard, storage, administration and clinical medical service can be laid out separately and reached quickly.

An example of a **vertical structure**:
- top floor: helipad, air conditioning plant
- 2nd–3rd floors: care wards
- 1st floor: operating theatre area, central sterilisation, intensive care, maternity, nursing mothers, children's ward
- ground floor: entrance and information, radiology, clinical medical service, outpatients, delivery of stretcher patients, emergency cases, administration, cafeteria
- basement: archive, physiotherapy, linear accelerator, radiation therapy, laboratory, kitchen with service yard

The different floors' height requirements should be noted: care area approx. height 3.40 m (less construction = flat slab with floor structure = 35 cm = 3.05 m clear height), examination and treatment height approx. 4.20 m, supply and waste disposal and services approx. height 4.20–5.00 m.

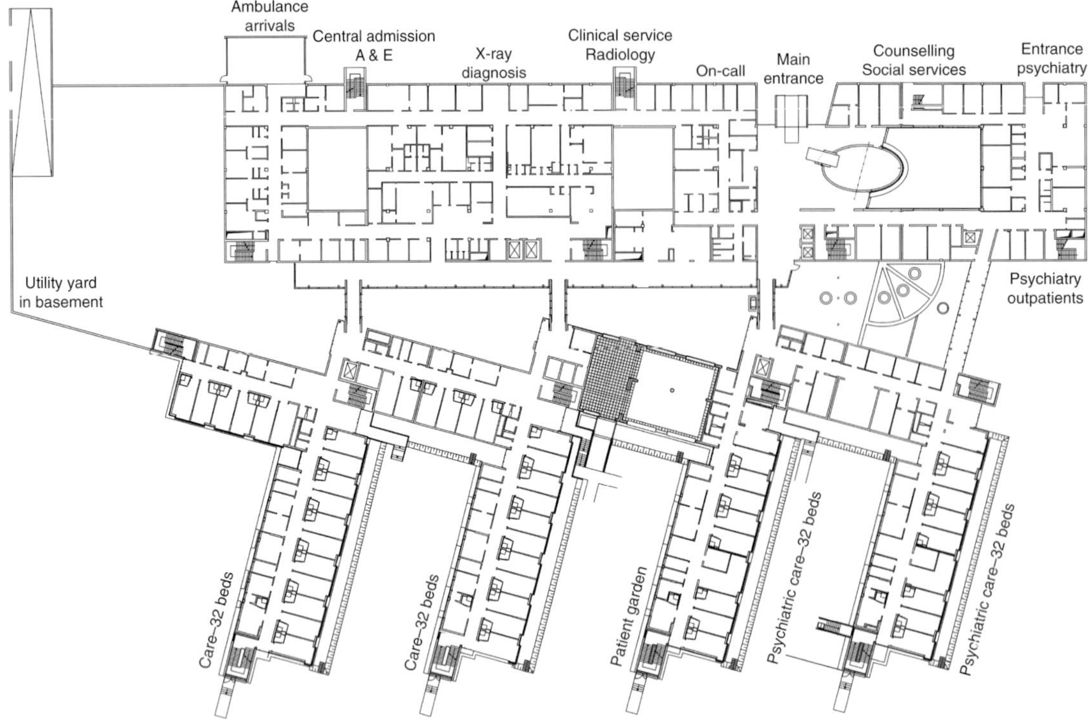

1 St Johann Nepomuk Catholic Hospital, Erfurt, ground floor — Arch.: Thiede Messthaler Klösges

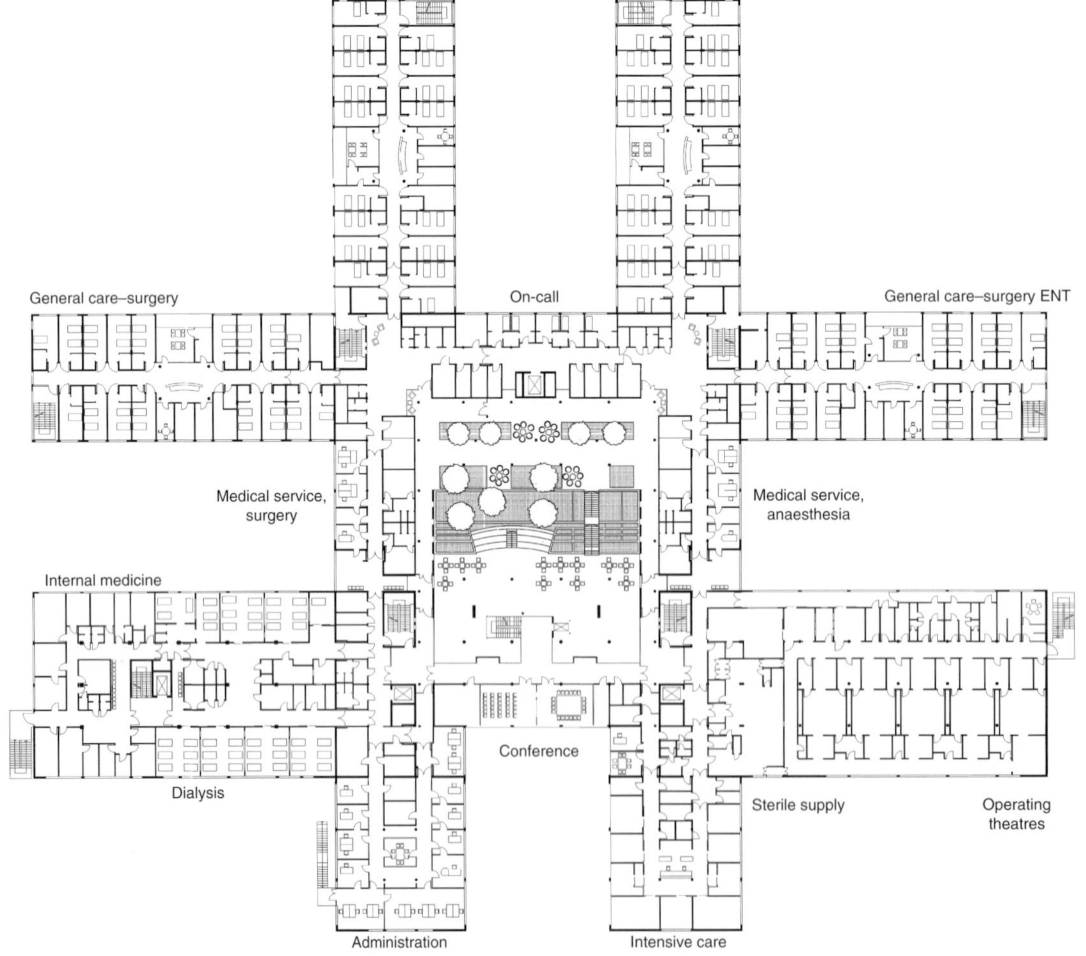

2 Helios Clinic, Gotha, first floor — Arch.: WÖRNER+PARTNER

HOSPITALS

Corridors, Doors, Stairs, Lifts

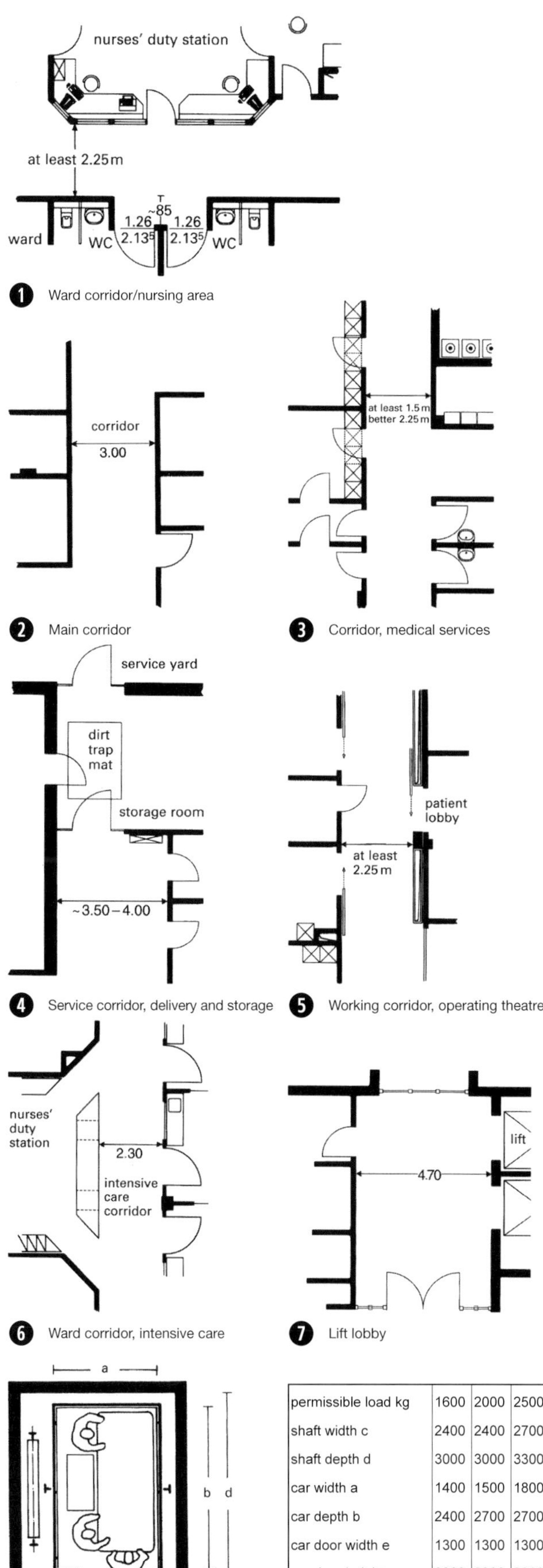

1 Ward corridor/nursing area

2 Main corridor

3 Corridor, medical services

4 Service corridor, delivery and storage

5 Working corridor, operating theatres

6 Ward corridor, intensive care

7 Lift lobby

8 Bed lift

permissible load kg	1600	2000	2500
shaft width c	2400	2400	2700
shaft depth d	3000	3000	3300
car width a	1400	1500	1800
car depth b	2400	2700	2700
car door width e	1300	1300	1300
car door height	2300	2300	2300
car door height	2100	2100	2100
permissible no. people	21	26	33

9 Dimensions of bed lifts → 8

Corridors

Corridors have to be of suitable dimensions for the expected traffic. Generally accessible corridors should be at least 1.50 m wide and those in which patients are transported on beds must have a usable width of at least 2.25 m. The suspended ceiling in corridors can be lowered down to a height of 2.40 min. in order to provide room for service runs. This does, however, lead to the use of special fire protection ceilings in order to secure escape routes. Fire protection requirements must be observed. Internal corridors should be avoided because these have to be mechanically smoke extracted. The usable width of corridors should not be narrowed by installations, columns or other building elements. Windows for lighting and ventilation should not be wider than 25 m apart.

Doors

The placing and selection of suitable doors in hospitals deserves particular attention. The construction and quality of room doors must meet the requirements of sound reduction and fire protection, and the surface cladding must resist long-term cleaning and disinfection.

The clear opening height of doors is according to type and function:

- standard door (unfinished): 885 × 2135 mm
- doors through which beds pass: 1260 –1375 × 2135 mm
- corridor doors, double: 2400 × 2400 mm

In firewalls, T90 doors (held open) should be installed in order not to obstruct traffic.

Stairs

For safety reasons, stairs must be built so that they can accept the entire vertical traffic in case of need. They must also be constructed to prevent sound and odour transfer and prevent draughts. Stairs must have handrails without free ends on both sides. Spiral stairs are not permissible as emergency stairs. The usable width of emergency stairs and their landings must be at least 1.50 m and not more than 2.50 m.

Door leaves must not restrict the usable width of the stair landings. Risers of 17 cm are permissible and treads of 30 cm are recommended. Doors to the stairwells must open in the direction of the escape route.

Lifts

Lifts transport patients, staff and also all supplies and waste. A separation of use should be established for hygienic and aesthetic reasons. The cars of bed lifts require sufficient space for a bed and two accompanying people. The internal surfaces of the lift car must be flat, capable of being washed and disinfected, and the floor must be non-slip. Lift shafts must be fire-resistant.

A multi-purpose lift for beds, ambulant patients and visitors should be provided for every 100 beds. Additionally, there should be suitably located smaller lifts to transport equipment and staff:

- car, clear dimensions: 0.90 × 1.20 m
- shaft dimensions: 1.25 × 1.50 m

Key No.	Area/dept	Key No.	Area/dept
1.00	**Examination and Treatment**	3.03	Information and Documentation
1.01	Admission and Emergency Provision	3.04	Library
1.02	Medical Service		
1.03	Functional Diagnostics	4.00	**Social Services**
1.04	Endoscopy	4.01	Service Facilities
1.05	Clinical Pathology	4.02	Pastoral Care and Social Services
1.06	Pathology	4.03	Staff Changing
1.07	Radiological Diagnosis	4.04	Staff Catering
1.08	Nuclear Medicine Diagnosis	5.00	**Supply and Waste Disposal**
		5.01	Pharmaceutical Supply
1.09	Surgery	5.02	Sterile Goods Supply
1.10	Maternity	5.03	Equipment Supply
1.11	Radiotherapy	5.04	Bed Preparation
1.12	Nuclear Medicine Therapy	5.05	Catering
1.13	Physiotherapy	5.06	Laundry
1.14	Occupational Therapy	5.07	Storage and Goods Handling
1.15	On-call Duty		
		5.08	Maintenance and Repair
		5.09	Waste Disposal
2.00	**Care**	5.10	House and Transport Services
2.01	General Care		
2.02	Nursing Mothers and Antenatal Therapy	6.00	**Education and Research**
2.03	Intensive Care	6.01	Research
2.04	Dialysis	6.02	Education
2.05	Paediatric Care	6.03	Training
2.06	Infectious Diseases		
2.07	Psychiatric Care		
2.08	Nuclear Medicine Care	7.00	**Other**
2.09	Admission Care	7.01	Ambulance Service
2.10	Geriatric Care	7.02	Limited Care Dialysis
2.11	Day Clinic	7.03	Child Care
		7.04	Outward Services
		7.05	Inward Services
3.00	**Administration**	7.06	Residential
3.01	Management and Administration		
3.02	Records		

1 Categorisation of a hospital into functional areas and departments

Hospitals are laid out according to operational areas and operational departments:

- examination and treatment
- care
- administration
- social services
- education and research
- other

The examination and treatment area is, besides care, the most important within the overall organisation of a hospital and is characterised by particular features resulting from its specialisation and equipment.

Patient–doctor contact varies according to discipline, as does the frequency of patient examinations. The precise determination of the location of the various examination and treatment areas in the building and their relation to each other can be made in general terms. The individual departments in the examination and treatment area are preferably situated in the basement, or on the ground floor and first floor, with outpatient attendance concentrated in the ground floor. The combination of all medical disciplines into a cohesive area is important in order to improve cooperation and consultation.

NB: On hospital plans, Pumi and Fango are types of therapy. OT = occupational therapy.

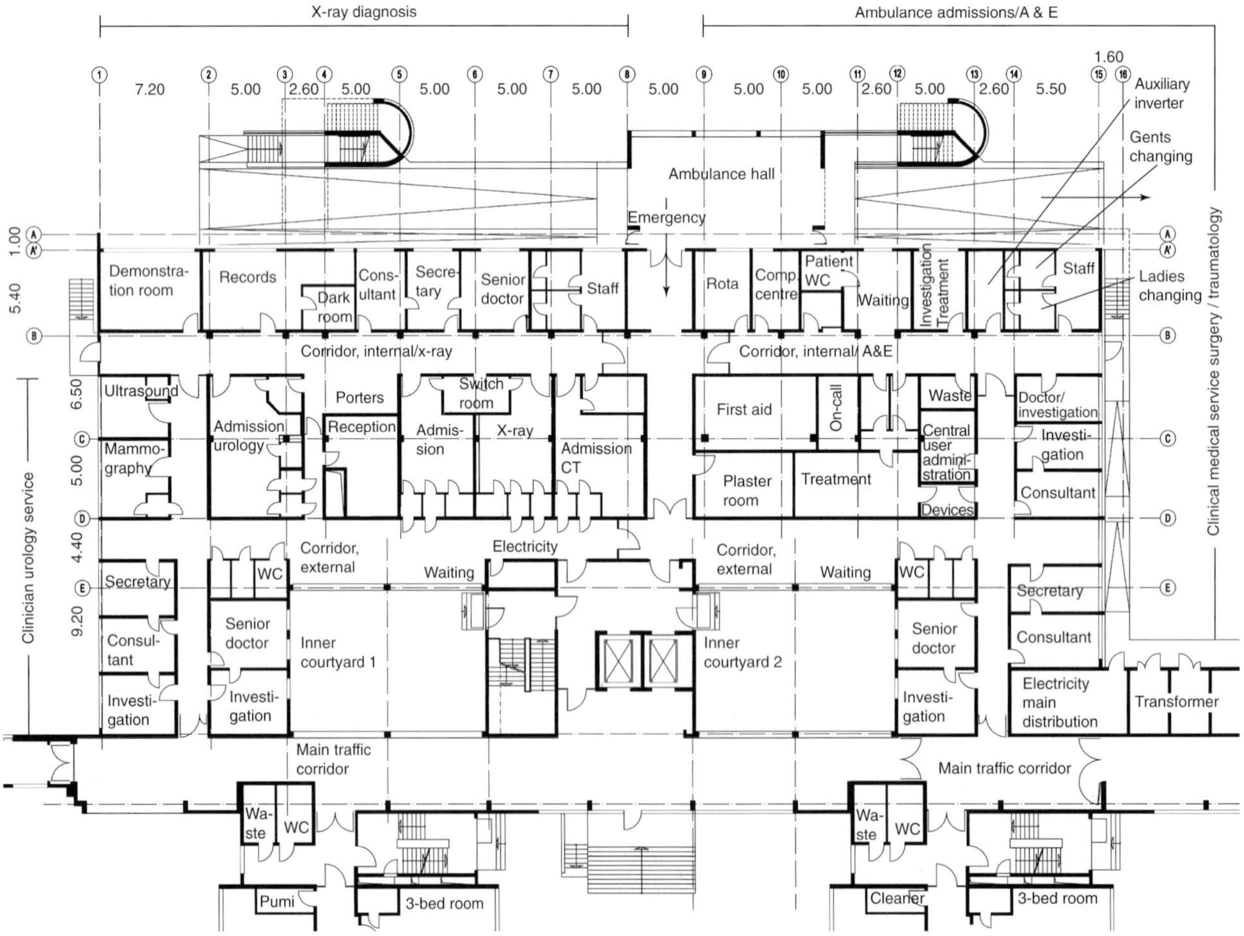

2 Partial plan of Luckenwalde Hospital, 300 beds

Arch.: Thiede Messthaler Klösges

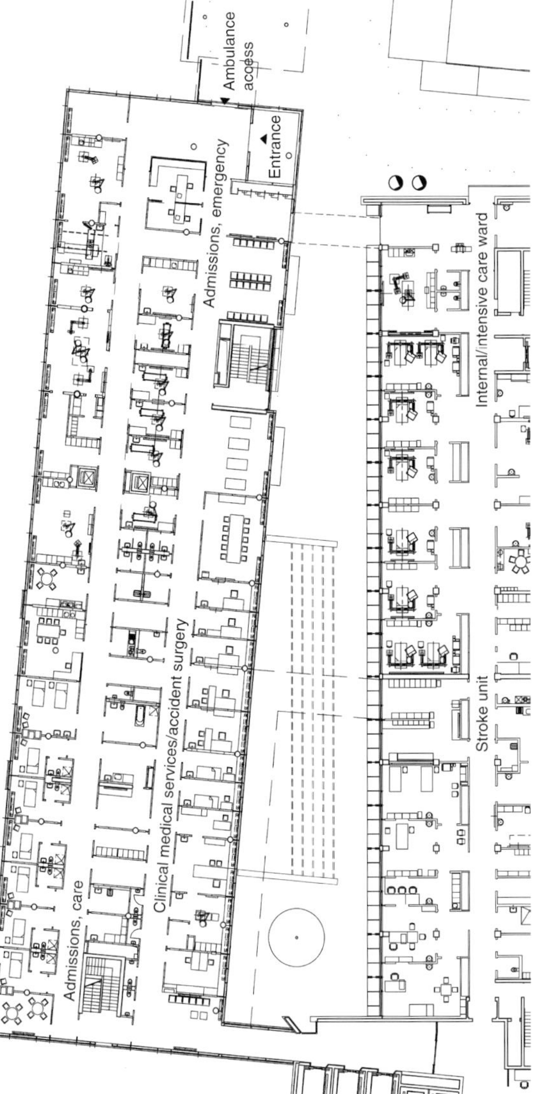

❶ Outpatients, ground floor, Berlin-Spandau Hospital; today: Vivantes Clinic Berlin-Spandau Arch.: Heinle, Wischer und Partner Freie Architekten

❷ Emergency admission, Helios Clinic, Gotha Arch.: Wörner + Partner

Outpatient facilities

Facilities for outpatient treatment are visited daily or consulted many times, according to an appointment schedule, by patients capable of walking.

Of particular importance is the allocation of outpatient rooms. A separation of the routeing of outpatients and inpatients should be included in the design work at an early stage. The number of outpatients attending depends on the size of, and the specialist departments in, a particular hospital. If there are a large number of outpatients, then a larger dedicated area can be provided, separate from the rest of the activity. There must, however, always be a rapid connection to the X-ray department. The increasing significance of outpatient (day) surgery should also be considered (larger waiting rooms, more outpatient rooms).

Outpatient surgery

The share of operations performed on outpatients will increase further. Outpatient (or day) surgery departments can be added to existing hospitals, integrated into the surgical department or set up as independent clinics. In the hospital, the department should be near the main entrance and the emergency care department.

The patients in an outpatient surgical centre (mainly undergoing elective operations as part of an outpatient, day clinic or short-stay treatment arrangement) are in a different physical and mental state from patients delivered as emergency cases. A clear guidance and signposting system and friendly, confidence-boosting ambience are particularly recommended.

One surgical department which concentrates on elective outpatient treatment, has a 'modern' room arrangement with smaller operating theatres (approx. 30 m^2), a multi-functional preparation room, smaller washrooms for two operating theatres, one recovery room with five places, and a quiet zone. There are no purely preparation and post-op rooms, storerooms or classic access control lobbies for patients.

Outpatient medical centre

This is a separate establishment associated with a hospital for the treatment of patients on an outpatient or short-stay basis; the room and organisational structure differ considerably from inpatient hospital treatment. The spectrum of complaints treated and the medical services offered have to be considered. The technical medical equipment can be reduced and the room furnishing can be designed rather more generously regarding hygiene (e.g. carpets, parquet).

Inpatient care and therapy of patients with infectious diseases, chronic illnesses, serious complications after an operation etc. are not provided here, so the stringency of the hospital building regulations can be partially relaxed or even waived for a particular project with carefully reasoned exemption applications.

The decision about the quantity and quality of ventilation equipment, anaesthetic technology, ceiling supply units, radiation protection equipment etc. should be critically examined, because there are considerable potential savings. For most operations, air-handling systems to reduce bacteria counts and particles are not necessary, so the advance determination of the planned spectrum of operations is also of economic significance.

① Operating room
② Services – ventilation 32 m²
③ Instrument preparation 6 m²
④ Internal corridor
⑤ Preparation, post-op room 19 m²
⑥ Store 8 m²
⑦ Staff vestibule 6 m²
⑧ Waste disposal 6 m²
⑨ Changing room
⑩ Doctor's room 15 m²
⑪ Reception/waiting 55 m²
⑫ Records, server 15 m²
⑬ Consulting room approx. 13 m²
⑭ Writing room 13 m²
⑮ Staff social room 14 m²
⑯ Waste disposal vestibule 8 m²
⑰ Sterile goods store 50 m²
⑱ Services – electricity 7 m²
⑲ Devices operations approx. 12 m²
⑳ Operating room, washing 15 m²
㉑ Operating room 7 m²
㉒ Operating theatre
㉓ Washing 7 m²
㉔ Waste disposal vestibule 7 m²
㉕ Patient vestibule 19 m²
㉖ Recovery room (4 places) 40 m²
㉗ Sedation 10 m²
㉘ Regional anaesthesia 19 m²
㉙ Post-op room (12 places) 110 m²
㉚ Nurse's station, monitoring 17 m²
㉛ Waiting, outpatient operations 23 m²
㉜ Disinfection room 14 m²
㉝ Staff social room 14 m²
㉞ Isolation room 8 m²
㉟ Waiting room 17 m²
㊱ Operations vestibule 14 m²
㊲ Treatment 12 m²
㊳ Pain, outpatients 16 m²
㊴ Office 15 m²
㊵ Consulting room

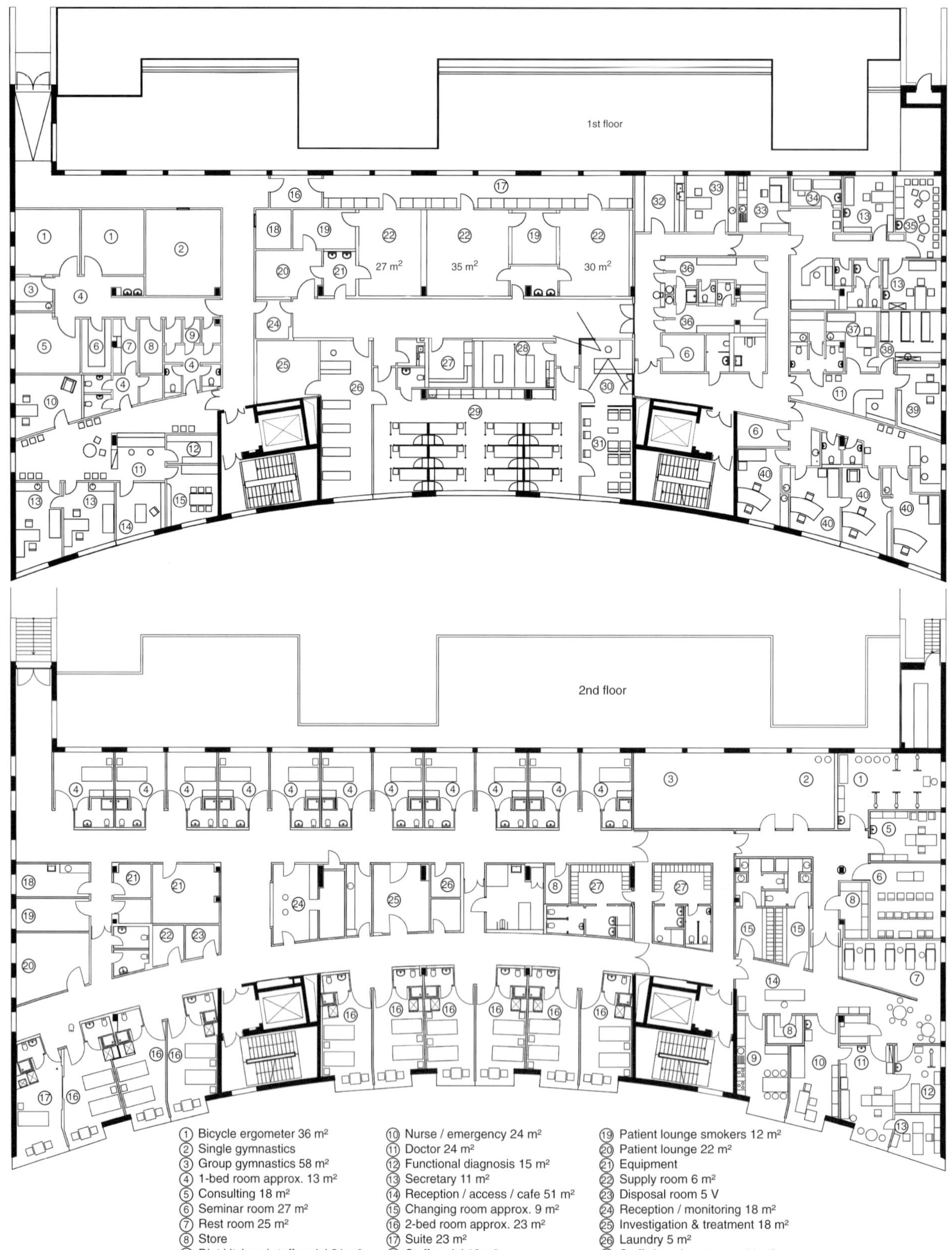

① Bicycle ergometer 36 m²
② Single gymnastics
③ Group gymnastics 58 m²
④ 1-bed room approx. 13 m²
⑤ Consulting 18 m²
⑥ Seminar room 27 m²
⑦ Rest room 25 m²
⑧ Store
⑨ Diet kitchen / staff social 21 m²
⑩ Nurse / emergency 24 m²
⑪ Doctor 24 m²
⑫ Functional diagnosis 15 m²
⑬ Secretary 11 m²
⑭ Reception / access / cafe 51 m²
⑮ Changing room approx. 9 m²
⑯ 2-bed room approx. 23 m²
⑰ Suite 23 m²
⑱ Staff social 12 m²
⑲ Patient lounge smokers 12 m²
⑳ Patient lounge 22 m²
㉑ Equipment
㉒ Supply room 6 m²
㉓ Disposal room 5 V
㉔ Reception / monitoring 18 m²
㉕ Investigation & treatment 18 m²
㉖ Laundry 5 m²
㉗ Staff changing approx. 11 m²

1 Medical centre at the Oskar-Ziethen Hospital, Berlin-Lichtenberg — Arch.: Deubzer König Architekten

Health

HOSPITALS
General, modular grid
Building design
Examples
Corridors, doors, stairs, lifts
Operational areas
Outpatient area
Outpatient medical centre – example
Examination and treatment
Care
Administration, social services
Supply and waste disposal
Technical supply

1 Clinical medical unit

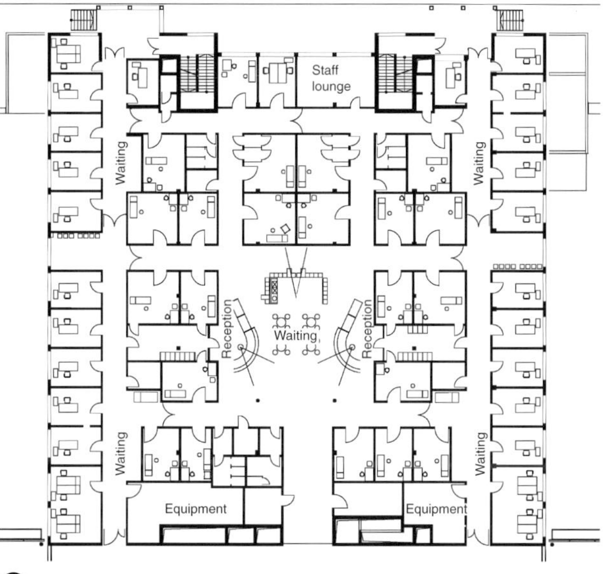

2 Interdisciplinary clinical medical service Arch.: Thiede Messthaler Klösges

3 Endoscopic and functional diagnosis department, with beds, at Beizig Hospital Arch.: Thiede Messthaler Klösges

Reception and emergency provision

The accident and emergency unit must be quickly reached by accident patients (on stretchers) via the ambulance hall (clear access road height = min. 3.50 m) and by ambulant patients from the main entrance.

A good location for this department is the opposite side to the main entrance. The department consists of a row of small examination and treatment rooms (16–21 m^2), equipped with a couch, small operating light, cupboard units with sink and possibly patient cubicles. There must also be a plaster room with plastering bench and a first-aid room for treating shock. Additionally, surgery rooms (similar to operating theatres) should be available. The X-ray department should be nearby. Storage places for at least two stretchers and for wheelchairs should be provided in the ambulance hall.

The clinical service doctors, surgeons and anaesthetists should be grouped in the vicinity.

Clinical medical service

This term describes all the management rooms of the individual specialist departments/clinics. The classic medical service facilities include a medical superintendent's room with office support, a senior doctor's room and an examination room with waiting area and toilets. These clinical medical service rooms form the core of the outpatient zone on the ground floor of the hospital.

General medicine (internal medicine)

Further rooms should be provided for the following specialisms:
Ophthalmology: Treatment room (25 m^2) with slit lamp, capable of being darkened; squint treatment room; laser room.

Ear, nose and throat: Treatment room (25–30 m^2), capable of being darkened, with treatment table or treatment chair for examinations.

Urology: Urological treatment is connected with X-ray diagnosis. The treatment room (25–30 m^2) has a table for endoscopic examinations and is equipped with suspended irrigator and floor drainage. Next door is an instrument room with sink.

Functional diagnosis

Functional diagnosis is becoming ever more important in hospitals, partly due to progress in heart/thorax examinations and also the increase in complaints relating to heart-lung and circulation functions.

All examination rooms must be accessible through patient cabins, possibly also preparation rooms (for left heart catheter measurement).

Endoscopy

An endoscope is a mirror instrument used to illuminate and observe cavities inside the body. It is inserted through natural body openings with the patient under partial anaesthesia. The categories are gastroscopy, bronchoscopy, rectoscopy, laparoscopy and cystoscopy. The device is prepared directly in the examination and treatment room. WCs should be provided for the patients before entering. This department should have a bedded waiting area and rest room (beds = no. of endoscopy rooms × 2) .

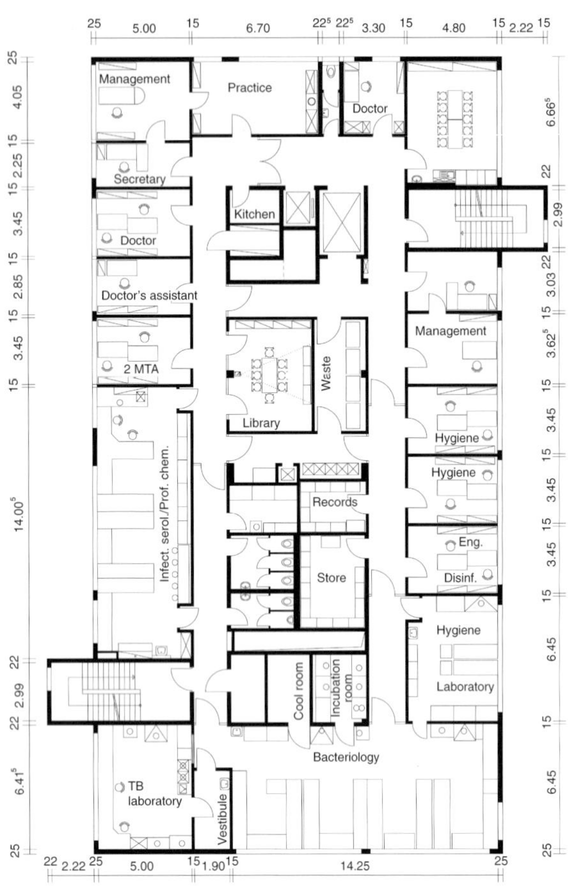

❶ Laboratory area at the Dr. Horst Schmidt Clinics, Wiesbaden
Arch.: Wörner + Partner

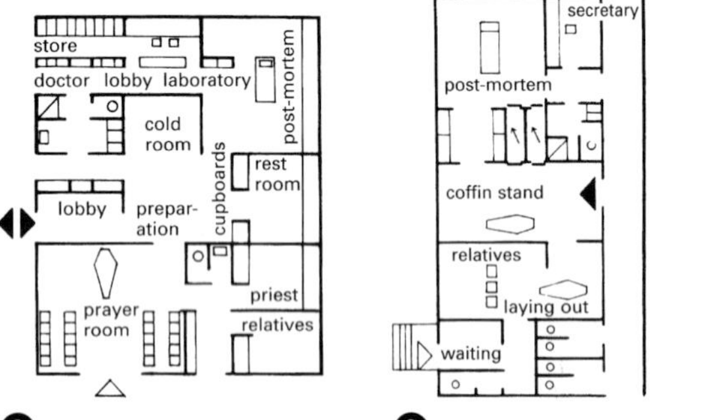

❷ Soltau District Hospital, 354 beds
Arch.: Poetzig, Biermann

❸ Pathology department at the St. Clemens Hospital, Geldern, 480 beds
Arch.: Poetzig, Biermann

Architects: Wichtendahl, Roennich

❹ Munich-Perlach Hospital, 687 beds

Laboratory medicine

The laboratory is mostly concerned with the preparation and processing of blood, urine and stool samples. The laboratory should be a large room with standing and sitting workstations. Specialist laboratories are added on as separate rooms. Subsidiary rooms include rest room for staff, rinsing room, sluice room, disinfection room, cold room. Quick connection to other departments is provided by a pneumatic delivery system. Laboratory areas can also be completely off-site and serve several hospitals.

Pathology

The pathology department of a hospital includes rooms for storage of bodies, dissection, refrigeration of bodies, laying out, placing into coffins, coffin storage and changing rooms for the pathologists. Separate access for relatives and the shortest possible road access for undertakers are important. This department should not be in the vicinity of the service yard.

Radiology

Radiology requires rooms in which ionising radiation is applied for diagnostic and therapeutic purposes. It should be near the outpatients department and the ambulance approach road. The heavy weight of the equipment (up to approx. 14 t) means that this department is better located on the ground or first basement. A connecting room for staff, which also serves as store, dictation room and possibly as switchroom, is advantageous. The size of the departments' rooms is determined by the large medical equipment and related technology. Sonography, mammography and jaw radioscopy need room sizes of approx. 15–18 m^2, radioscopy and exposure rooms approx. 20–30 m^2. The access for patients should be through two changing cubicles for each radioscopy room and a wide (1.25 m) door for beds is also necessary. WCs for gastroscopy, colonoscopy and contrast medium patients should be attached to the radioscopy rooms. Angiography rooms require a preparation room with cupboard units (sink, pharmaceutical refrigerator). The exposure room for computer tomography must have dimensions of approx. 35 m^2. Between the switchroom and the exposure room is a door and a clear window. An additional room for switching cabinets and a room for film development are also sensible. The walls and ceilings are protected with lead inserts (e.g. in plasterboard walls). The lead equivalent values in walls and ceilings depend on the X-ray equipment and its manufacturer, with whom early collaboration is essential.

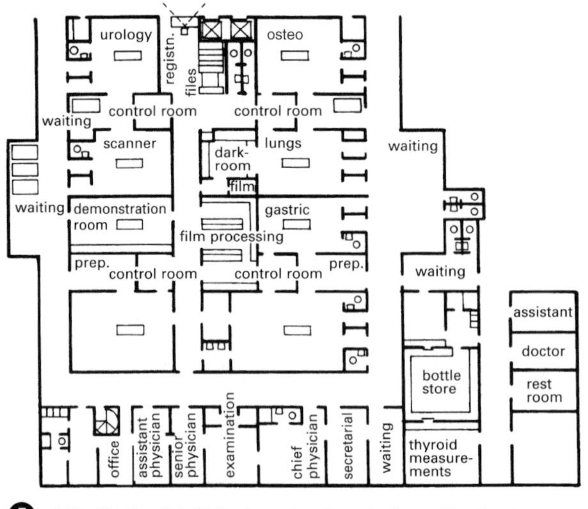

❺ Fulda City Hospital, 732 beds: centre of examination and treatment area, near the functional diagnosis and nuclear medicine diagnosis departments
Arch.: Köhler, Kässens

1. overhead operating lamp
2. operating table with fixed base
3. wall or ceiling pendulum
4. anaesthesia equipment
5. dish stand with heater
6. electric suction pump
7. X-ray display box
8. anaesthesia table
9. instrument table
10. waste bin, used instrument container
11. dish stand without heater
12. suturing materials table
13. operating steps
14. swivel stool for surgeon
15. drum stand
16. infusion stand

1 Equipment plan for operating theatre

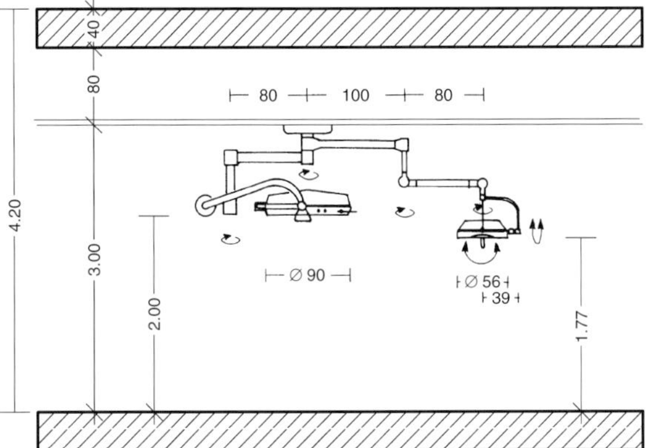

2 Suspended lamp for operating theatre with satellite

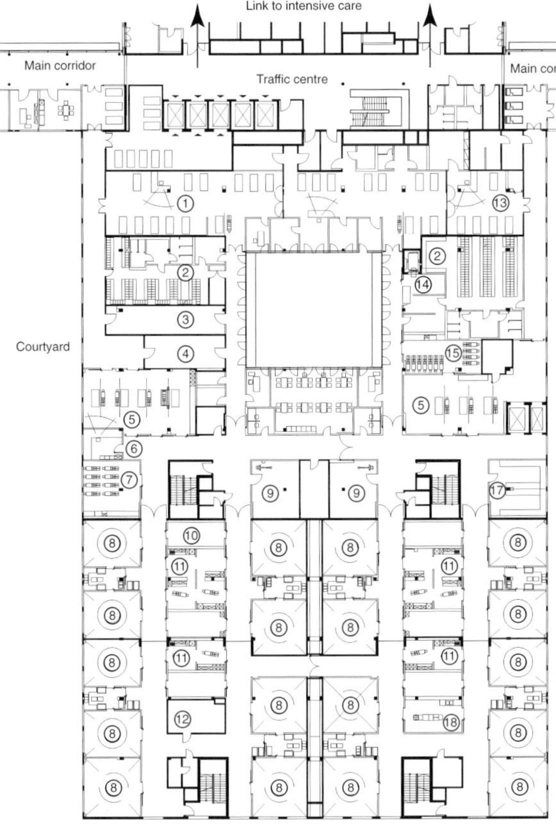

1. Recovery room
2. Staff changing room
3. Supply vestibule
4. Waste disposal vestibule
5. Patient rebedding
6. Operations control centre
7. Trolley cleaning/store
8. Operating theatre
9. Equipment
10. Wash places
11. Entrance and exit zone
12. Electricity
13. Children's recovery room
14. Disposal of sterile goods
15. Trolley cleaning
16. Staff lounge
17. Rapid section laboratory
18. Plaster room

3 Surgery zone at the Helios Clinic Berlin-Buch, 1000 beds
Arch.: Thiede Messthaler Klösges Keitel

Operating department

The location of the operating department in the overall organisation of the hospital is of great significance. The design should include a short distance to the intensive care unit, recovery room and central sterile store, because rapid access between these departments must always be ensured. Surgical departments are best placed centrally and with easy accessibility in the core of the hospital.

Organisation of the operating department

The following rooms or room zones belong in every operating department:

- operating theatre, preparation, transfer, scrub room, sterile goods store, with a total area of approx. 80 m^2.

The operating theatre should be as square as possible to enable proper working with the operating table (size approx. 6.50 × 6.50 m) turned in any direction. The clear ceiling height must be 3.00 m with a space above the ceiling of approx. 70–80 cm for air conditioning and other services. Operating theatres should be designed to be as uniform as possible to enable interdisciplinary work. The doors to the operating theatre operate automatically.
The basic equipment includes an adjustable and transportable operating table system mounted on a fixed plinth in the centre of the operating theatre.

Routeing

In order to reduce infection through contact, the various work processes should be separated.
The one-corridor system, in which pre- and post-operative patients, clean and dirty goods can all be present in one corridor leading to the theatres, is still often used today for reasons of cost and space.
Two-corridor systems are better, with the patients and staff or patients and dirty goods separated. The separation of the flow of patients from the work area of the operating theatre is important.
In exceptional cases a **preparation room** is sensible. The size is approx. 3.80 × 3.80 m. Electrical sliding doors on the side toward the operating theatre, with 1.40 m clear opening width and clear windows, which should provide a connection to the operating theatre. The fixtures should include refrigerator, sink, rinsing unit, cupboard for cannulas, sockets for anaesthetic equipment and emergency power supply.
Likewise, a **transfer room** is advisable only in exceptional cases. It is equipped like the preparation room. There is a sliding door to the working corridor with a clear width of 1.25 m. There should be a sink.
A **scrub room** with at least six places should be provided in the immediate vicinity of the operating theatre. The minimum width of the room should be 1.80 m.
One **sterile goods room** is required per operating theatre, of approx. 10–15 m^2. This must be directly accessible from the operating theatre. There are also floor layouts with a large central sterile goods store. The **equipment room** should not be too far from the operating theatre; size 20 m^2.
The **operating theatres control centre** should be centrally located and have a large area of glass from which to oversee the working corridor. In addition to a desk, there should be cupboards and a pin-board for organisational planning.
Dictation rooms can be provided as small room units of approx. 6 m^2, as the surgeons need this room only for reports after operations.
There must be a **cleaning room** of 5 m^2 in every operating department, because cleaning and disinfection is performed after each operation. Near the control lobby for patients, sufficient space should be provided for clean, prepared beds, one clean bed per operation.
Toilet facilities should not be located near the patients' control lobbies, and are to be avoided in the operating area for hygienic reasons.

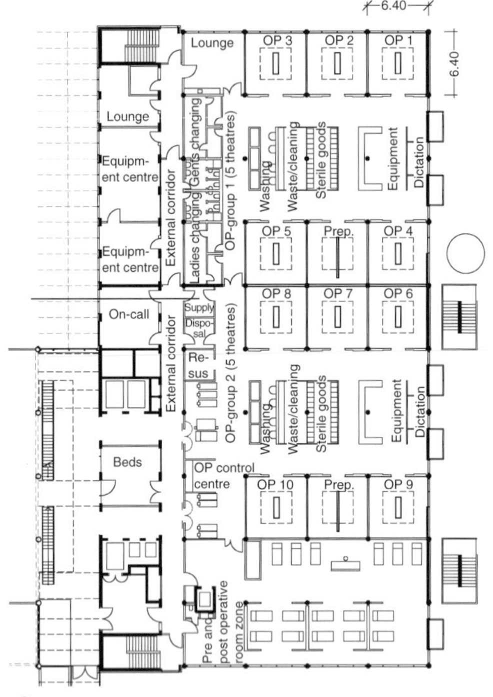

❶ Operating department (10 theatres), first floor, Brandenburg an der Havel City Clinic, Newbuild West Arch.: Heinle, Wischer und Partner Freie Architekten

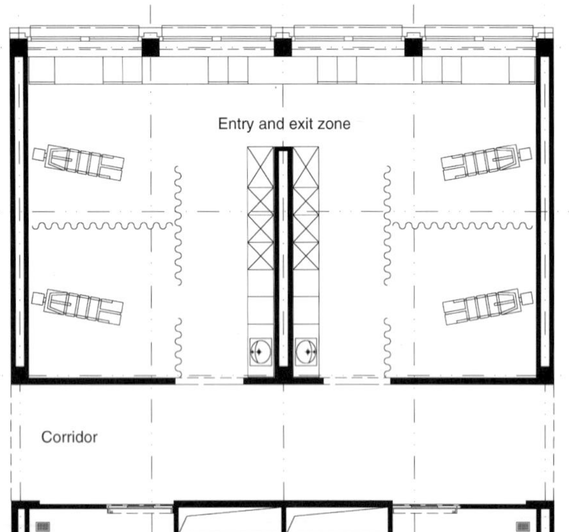

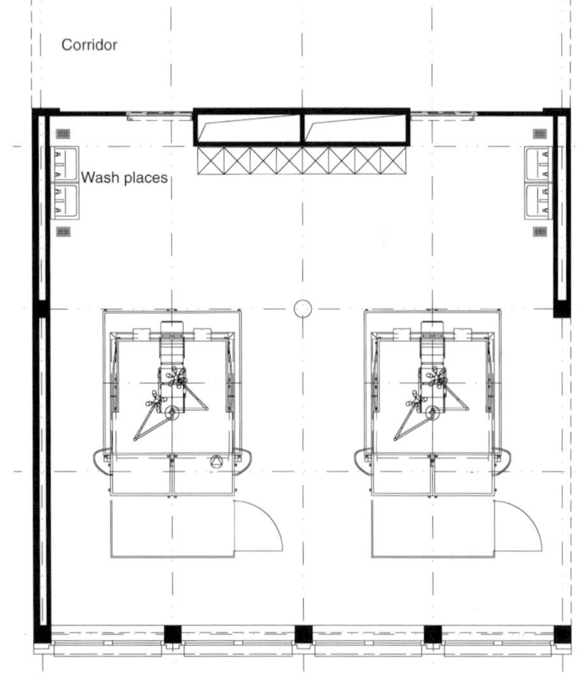

❷ Large operating theatre with associated entry and exit zones

A number of essential supply and workrooms are associated with the operating theatre. The operating department includes staff and patient control lobbies, instrument preparation, waste disposal control lobbies, supply control lobbies, storage space for operating trolleys and also, in the direct vicinity, the recovery room. Integrated into the patient control lobby are the functions bed transfer, preparation of the operating table and storage for operating tables.

A replacement power supply is necessary for operating departments to ensure the continuance and completion of operations in case of a mains failure.

Post-operative patient monitoring

The **recovery room** has to accept post-op patients from several theatres. The number of beds required is thus 1.5 times the number of theatres. There should be a nurse's observation point with a view of all beds and a dirty room next door. The recovery room should be designed as a large, suitably arranged space.

The **equipment preparation room for anaesthetic devices** has a dirty side for unsterile (infected) material and a clean side for devices prepared for use. The fittings include sink, storage and worktop space, and steam sterilisers. Operating instruments are prepared exclusively in the central sterile store, which is situated outside the operating zone.

A **plaster room** with plastering bench also belongs in the operating suite, particularly where many surgical-orthopaedic operations are carried out.

The dimensions of the **staff lounge** correspond to the size of the operating department. Each theatre team (surgeons, anaesthetists, operating department practitioners (ODPs), theatre nurses, anaesthesia nurses) should be assumed to have eight members. The lounge should have sufficient seating, cupboards and a sink.

Natural **lighting** of the operating theatre is psychologically advantageous, but is often impractical due to the layout of the rooms. The artificial **lighting** of the operating environment must be designed so that the light can fall from various directions according to the layout of incisions. The most frequently used lighting system is the mobile operating light suspended from the ceiling. This consists of a swivelling ceiling light, usually equipped with an additional light in the form of a satellite. The main light contains a number of small lights in order to avoid sharp shadows.

The division of the operating theatre into septic and aseptic zones is medically controversial, but is still sensible as a precaution. Floor and walls must be flat and easily washable throughout.

Air conditioning

Operating departments are nearly always air-conditioned. The ventilation serves to reduce micro-organisms by filtering, diluting and replacing the air. The supply of appropriately conditioned air in the required quantities is provided by the air-conditioning system. 15–20 air changes are required per hour to achieve a reasonable decontamination of the air between operations. In order to create an extensively sterile zone in the operating theatre, there should be no uncontrolled air intake from surrounding rooms. This can be achieved through an airtight envelope around the operating theatre (tightest possible joint sealing during construction) and/or by protective pressurising (i.e. pressure dropping from the room to be protected to other, less vulnerable areas). A standard lays down the air flow direction in the operating area. The operating theatre has the highest pressure in order to prevent air entering. The lowest pressure should be in the subsidiary and functional rooms. Windows in operating theatres should be lockable.

1 Maternity/birth assistance St Elisabeth Hospital, Halle

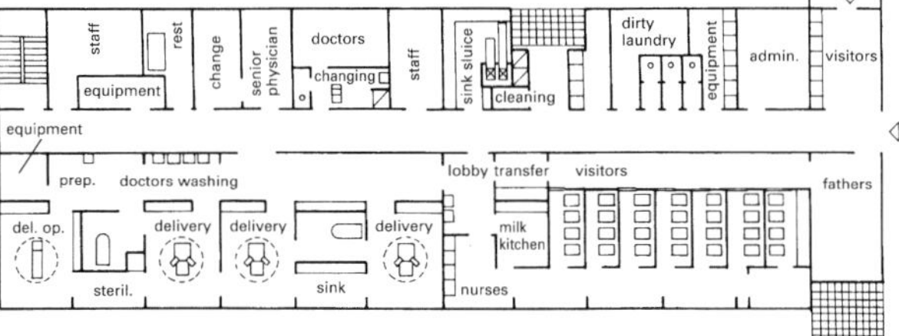

2 Waldbröl District Hospital, 448 beds; bath and sink provided next to every two maternity places Arch.: Karl Monerjan

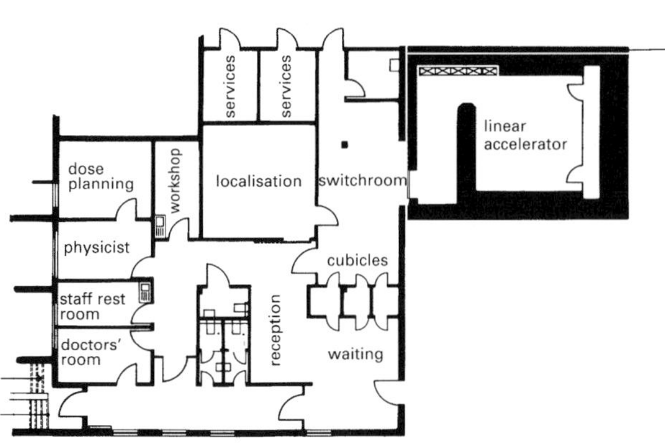

3 Linear accelerator department Arch.: U + A Weicken

Maternity unit

In addition to the task of overseeing normal births, the maternity unit also treats women with complications. A room similar to an operating theatre, for caesarean births, is therefore absolutely necessary in addition to the normal delivery rooms. In situations where a theatre-like delivery room is not possible inside the maternity unit, the unit should be next to the general operating theatre. The maternity area should be attached to the post-natal and baby care zones.

The delivery suite should include a room for midwives and for observation (large glass window) and a labour room. The delivery room should be equipped with a changing table with integrated baby bath and a radiant heater. A demand has arisen recently for further equipment for various types of birth (water birth etc.), and a bath for relaxation near the delivery room is also very popular. A specific team of staff work in the maternity unit and require the appropriate lounge, clean and dirty workrooms, reception, and toilets for staff and patients.

Radiotherapy

Conditions diagnosed as tumours are treated in the radiotherapy department. Each treatment room requires a changing cubicle for ambulant patients and a waiting area for bedbound patients, and each department requires doctor's rooms, a switchroom, possibly a localisation room, services rooms and a film development room. A workshop and at least one physics laboratory are also necessary.

The safety conditions are particularly stringent for radiation therapy: a series of laws, regulations and standards is in place. Radiation protection can be achieved by using lead inserts or thick concrete (e.g. barite concrete) walls.

The massive weight of radiation equipment and its required constructional radiation protection mean that radiation therapy will be located in the basement or ground floor. The clear ceiling height of radiation rooms must be 3.00 m and the concrete walls can, depending on the exact equipment, be up to 3.00 m thick for the treatment and examination area in the primary radiation area and up to 1.50 m thick for the secondary area.

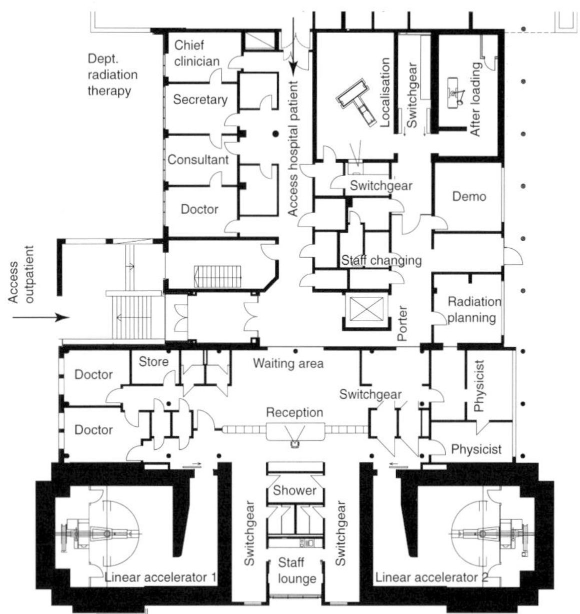

4 Radiation therapy department, Werner-Forssmann Hospital, Eberswalde, 475 beds Arch.: Thiede Messthaler Klösges

Physiotherapy

This department can be placed on the ground floor, but should have adequate natural ventilation through rooflights or light shafts. It must be accessed through a reception area.

Physiotherapy is divided into a dry and a wet area, the latter consisting of exercise bath (approx. 4 × 6 m), 'four-cell' bath, 'butterfly' bath, inhalation rooms, massage baths, hand-foot baths and the associated subsidiary rooms. The separation between wet and dry areas should be implemented completely.

The necessary subsidiary rooms are changing rooms for women and men, wheelchair-friendly toilet, staff and patient toilets, lounge, laundry store, waiting zone, cleaning room and services rooms for the exercise bath.

In the dry area, there are gymnastics rooms (approx. 40–50 m^2) for group treatment and single therapy rooms (approx. 20 m^2) for Bobath concept and exercise therapy. The clear ceiling height must be min. 3.00 m.

Decentralised therapy rooms can also be convenient near the wards (e.g. accident surgery, orthopaedics).

1 Physiotherapy, first floor, Berlin-Spandau Hospital; today: Vivantes Clinic, Berlin-Spandau Arch.: Heinle, Wischer und Partner Freie Architektenen

2 Physiotherapy, ground floor, Thüringen Clinics, Saalfeld-Rudolstadt Arch.: Thiede Messthaler Klösges Kasper

3 Physiotherapy, Helios Clinic, Gotha Arch.: Worner + Partner

← ① Special use (66 m^2)
② Personal residence
③ Office
④ Treatment
⑤ Gymnastics
⑥ Exercise pool
⑦ 4-cell bath
⑧ Occupational therapy
⑨ Massage
⑩ Elevator hall
⑪ Waiting
⑫ Cosmetics
⑬ Locker room
⑭ Rest room
⑮ Spa / Sauna
⑯ Pharmacy (132 m^2)

Health
HOSPITALS
General, modular grid
Building design
Examples
Corridors, doors, stairs, lifts
Operational areas
Outpatient area
Outpatient medical centre – example
Examination and treatment
Care
Administration, social services
Supply and waste disposal
Technical supply

❶ One-bed patient room

❷ Two-bed patient room

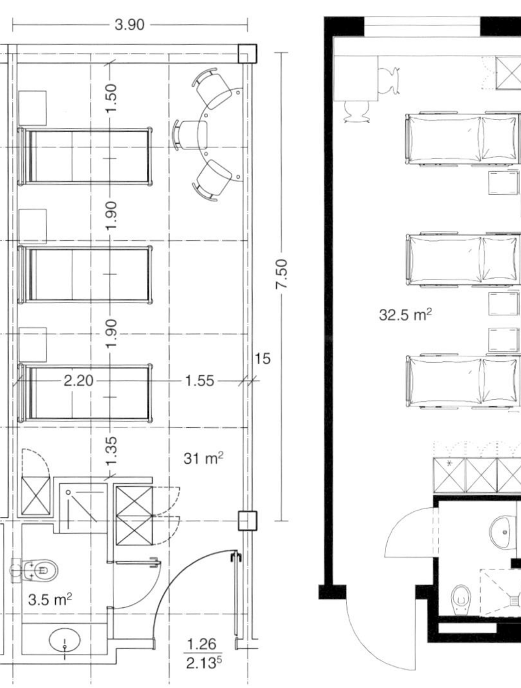

❸ Three-bed patient room with shower (column grid 7.80 m)

❹ Three-bed patient room (standard)

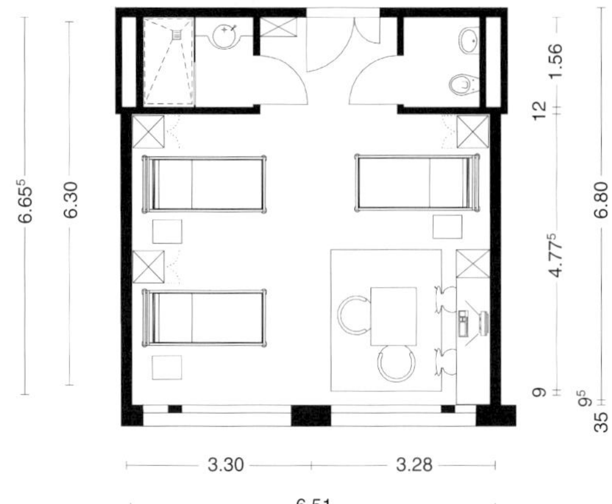

❺ Three-bed patient room (superior)

The care department is laid out as an enclosed unit and through traffic should be avoided. The wards must be naturally lit but functional rooms, like those for treatment, or the duty station with clean workrooms and pharmaceutical stores, can be located in the internal artificially lit area.

The normal size of a care ward is 30–36 beds. If the arrangement of the central functional rooms is appropriate (nurses' station, clean workroom etc.), then a number of wards can be structurally combined.

With other organisational forms of medical care, economic ward sizes of up to 48 beds can be reached. The rooms must be laid out so that there is sufficient room for movement. A sufficient number of patient cupboards, and space for care equipment (walking frame, commode) and care devices must be available.

General care

Standard care units provide general inpatient care, particularly for short-term and acute illnesses, with predominantly short stays. Units with the same space requirement should be structured above each other, in bed blocks.

The individual wards of a hospital are increasingly being run on an interdisciplinary basis and mixing the sexes, so the wards should be planned as units capable of being combined. Each ward must have at least one doctor's room where minor examinations can take place.

Room relationships

The ward entrance lobby must be clearly visible from the glazed nurses' station, and pharmaceutical stores and wash rooms should be easily accessible. The logistics of patient supply requires centrally located supply and waste disposal rooms for medication, laundry, waste and catering.

Wet cells

Each patient room should have its own wet cell with WC, washbasin and sometimes also shower, although these can also be separated as shower rooms. The wet cells should be accessible for disabled people.

The heights of vanity unit and WC are important (vanity unit min. 86 cm so that wheelchairs can fit underneath). The WC for wheelchair users should be at a height of approx. 49 cm, i.e. top level of the toilet seat. Each ward should also have staff, visitor and wheelchair WCs.

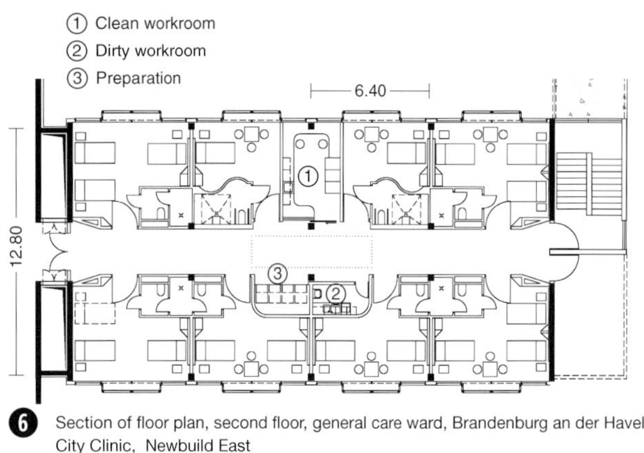

❻ Section of floor plan, second floor, general care ward, Brandenburg an der Havel City Clinic, Newbuild East

Arch.: Heinle, Wischer und Partner Freie Architekten

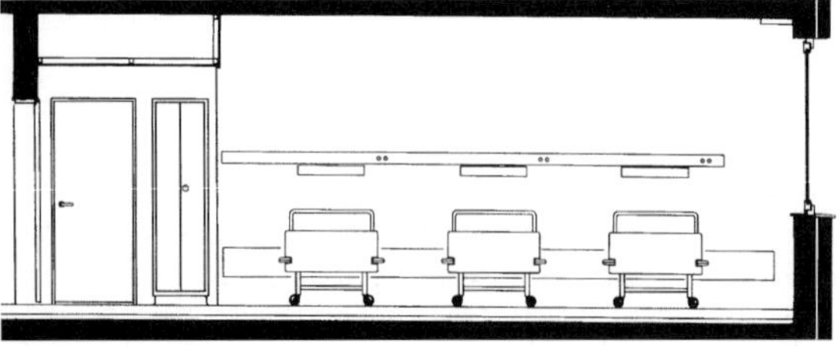

❶ Three-bed room, section

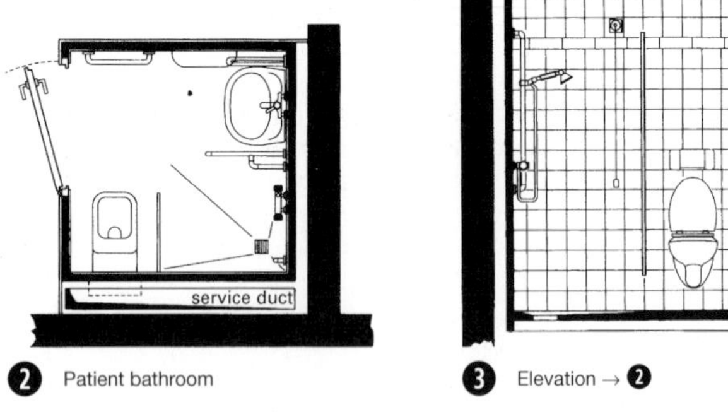

❷ Patient bathroom

❸ Elevation → ❷

Size of patient room

Patient beds should be accessible on three sides, and next to the bed there should be at least one side table. On the window side, a table (90/90 cm) with chairs (one per patient) should be provided. It must be possible to open the built-in cupboard without having to move bed or side table.

The minimum size for a single bedroom is 16 m^2, for two and three bedrooms 8 m^2 per bed (Hospital Regulations). The room widths should be chosen so that the beds at the back can be wheeled out of the room without having to move the first bed out of the room (minimum width 3.45 m with an axial width of 3.60 m).

Fitting out patient rooms

In order to protect the walls of the room from damage by beds, side tables or trolleys, a protection rail made of suitable material must be fixed to all walls (height min. 40–70 cm above floor level). This also applies to the corridors in the ward.

Patient cupboards must be sufficiently large. A suitcase compartment above the cupboard and a lockable compartment for valuables inside the cupboard are useful.

The **room doors** must be large, 1.26 × 2.13 m, on account of frequent bed transport, and sound protection to the corridor should be 32 dB. Behind the beds, there is a supply rail for air/gas and lighting. Special sockets can supply oxygen, vacuum and compressed air. Also integrated are sockets, reading lamp, telephone, nurse call button and radio.

① Patient lounge
② Care/doctors' station
③ Equipment
④ Staff lounge
⑤ Supply & disposal
⑥ Bathroom
⑦ Bed preparation
⑧ Cleaners' room

❹ Care unit (337 beds), second floor, Brandenburg an der Havel City Clinic, Newbuild East Arch.: Heinle, Wischer und Partner Freie Architekten

Health

HOSPITALS
General, modular grid
Building design
Examples
Corridors, doors, stairs, lifts
Operational areas
Outpatient area
Outpatient medical centre – example
Examination and treatment
Care
Administration, social services
Supply and waste disposal
Technical supply

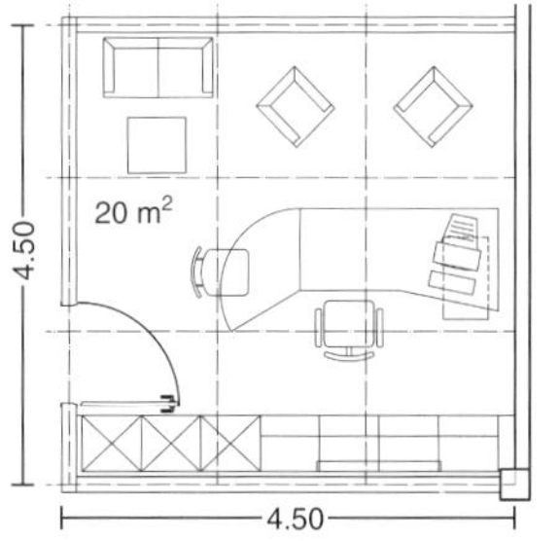

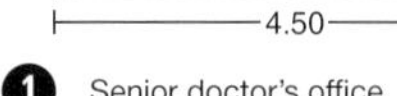
1 Senior doctor's office

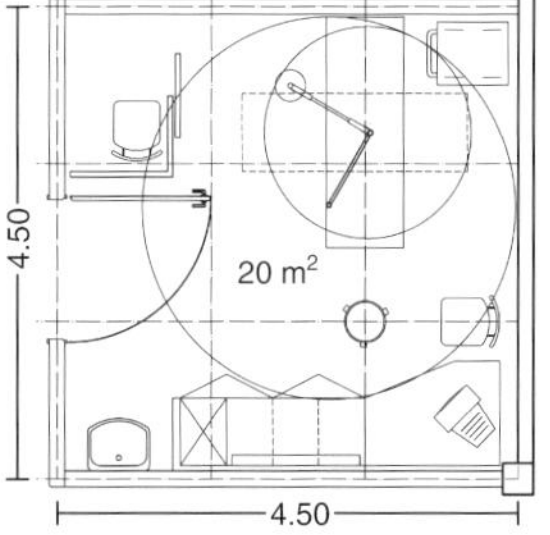

2 Examination and treatment room

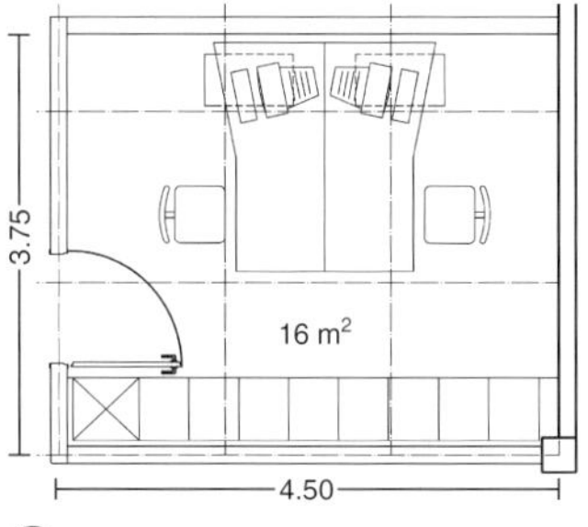

3 Ward doctor's office

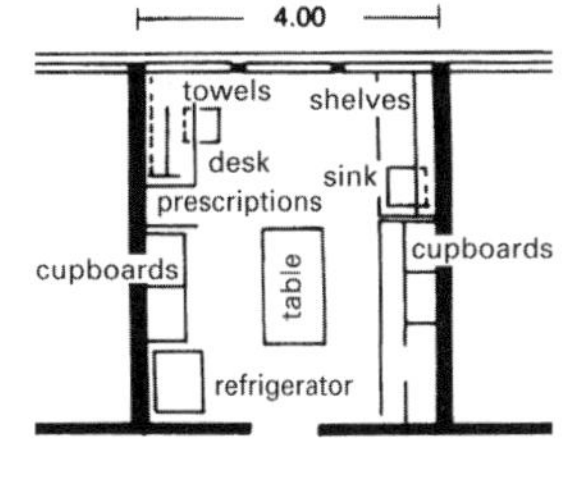

4 Clean/medication workroom

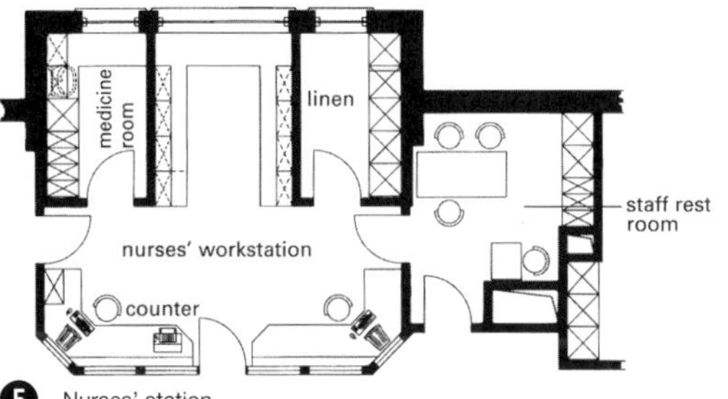

5 Nurses' station

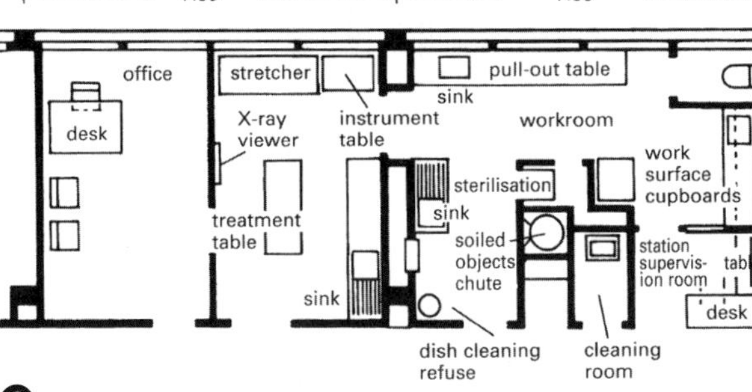

6 Combination of doctor's office, treatment room, nurses' workroom and nurses' station into one unit Arch.: Rosenfield

Workroom, clean/medication

The clean workroom should be about 20 m². The fitting out consists of fixed shelving or a flexible storage system of modular units, which are filled up in the central stores, and pharmaceutical cabinets. Special cupboards for medicines should be available and also a safe for narcotics.

Workroom, dirty

This room is for the staff in the vicinity of the patient rooms. One dirty workroom should be provided for every eight beds. There should be cleaning and disinfection sinks (emptying bed pans), wash-hand basins, worktop with lighting, cupboards or shelves for dirty washing bags, room size approx. 8–10 m².

Nurses' station

The nurses' station, size approx. 25–30 m², should be in the centre of the ward. It should have a large glazed opening to the corridor for visual and communication contact (observe fire regulations).

Staff lounge/kitchenette

The staff lounge, size approx. 16 m², with its own kitchen work area, staff refrigerator and possibly lockers for valuables. The **kitchenette** is for preparation and warming up of small amounts of food for patients. The equipment depends on the organisation of the main kitchen, e.g. catering distribution system with insulated trolley.

Ward doctor's office

The ward doctor must be able to examine patients here. In addition to the desk, there should be room for shelves and an examination couch. Room size approx. 16–20 m².

Patients' lounge

As general meeting point for patients, size approx. 22–25 m². The furnishing should be homely. A television set no longer has to be provided here, as this is normally mounted on the wall in each patient room. The question of separate lounges for smokers and non-smokers should be clarified at an early stage with the hospital management.

Patient bathroom

The equipment includes a bath with lifting device, which is accessible on three sides. An additional shower in a version designed for disabled people is also useful and an accessible WC should be integrated.

Services room

Each ward must have its own electricity distribution board for high-voltage electricity, emergency power supply and communications/IT. Room size 8 m².

Health

HOSPITALS
General, modular grid
Building design
Examples
Corridors, doors, stairs, lifts
Operational areas
Outpatient area
Outpatient medical centre – example
Examination and treatment
Care
Administration, social services
Supply and waste disposal
Technical supply

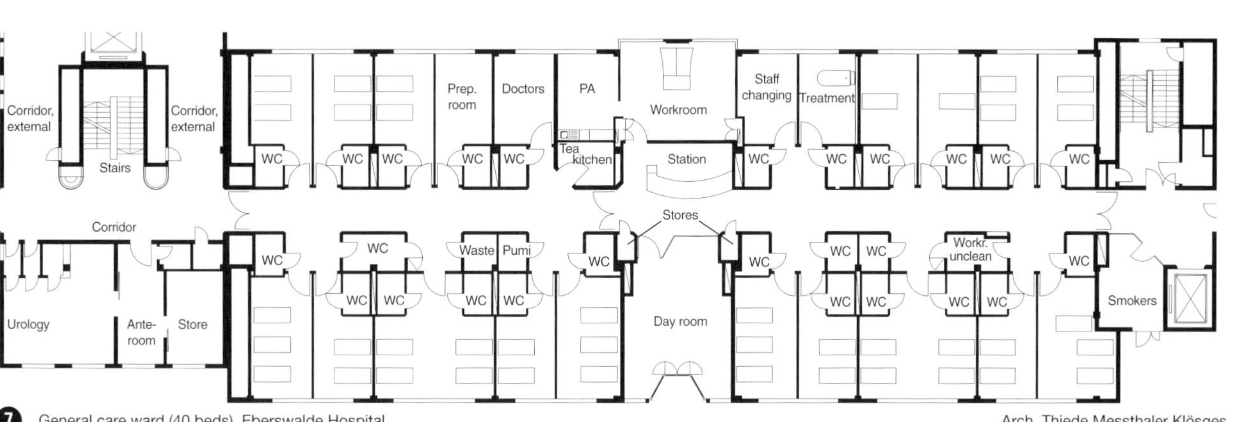

7 General care ward (40 beds), Eberswalde Hospital Arch. Thiede Messthaler Klösges

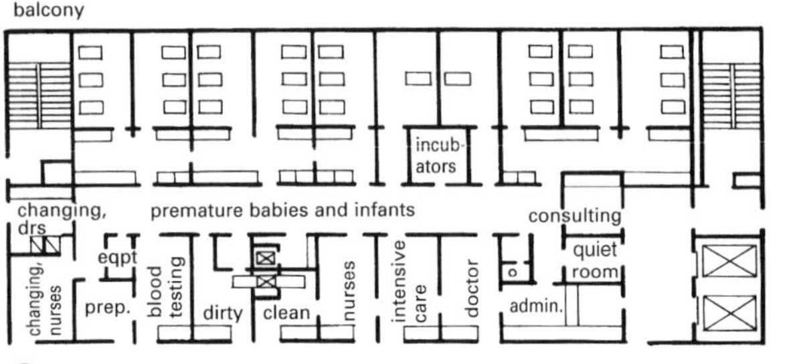

❶ Premature baby and infant ward with 27 beds, Fulda Arch.: Köhler, Kässem

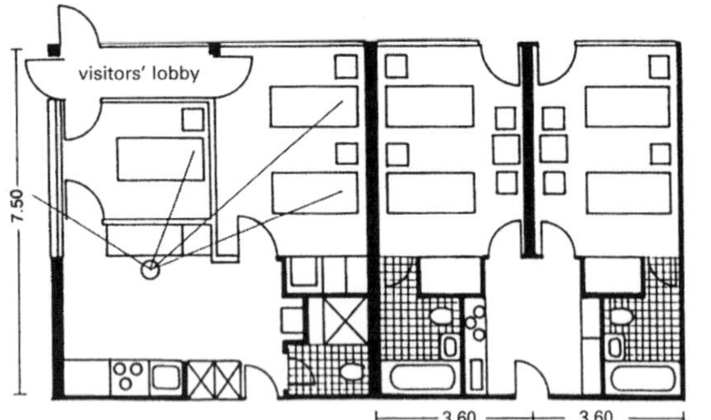

❷ Care of infectious children, room variant Arch.: Deilmann

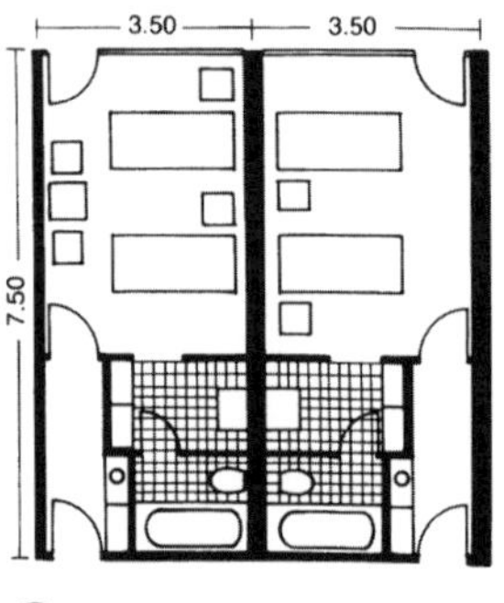

❸ Care of infectious children, room variant Arch.: Deilmann

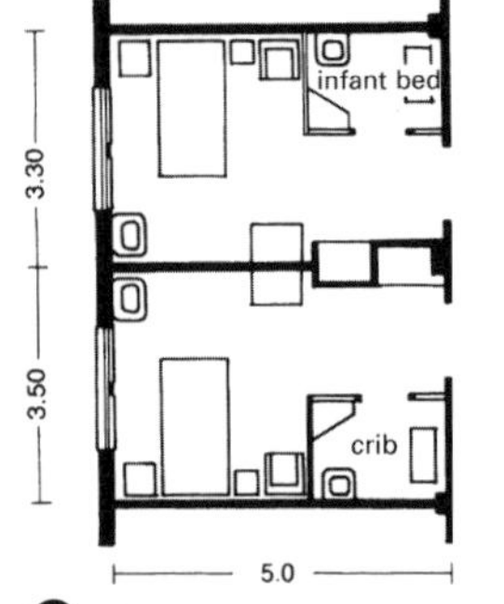

❹ Single-bed room with separate infant room Arch.: Mayhew

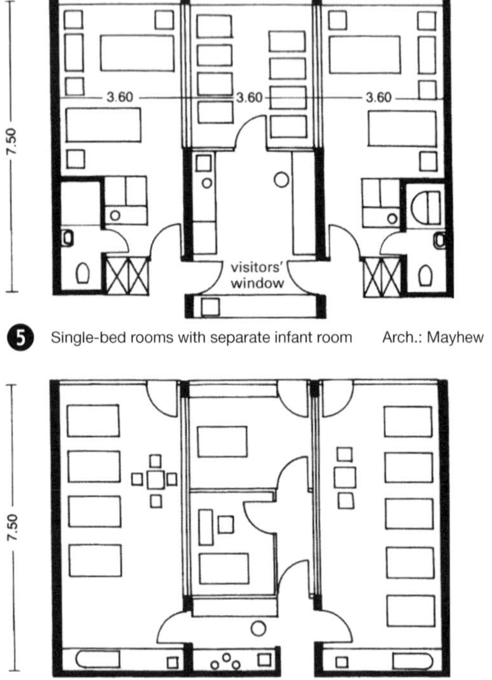

❺ Single-bed rooms with separate infant room Arch.: Mayhew

❻ Room unit for infants' and children's care Arch.: Mayhew

Nursing mother and neonatal care

The care of nursing mothers and babies includes all activities necessary after a hospital delivery for the bodily, medical, psychological and social support of nursing mothers and newborns with normal progress.

The organisation of care for nursing mothers is similar to that for general care. Where the care of newborns is centralised, their care unit is located at the edge of or within the nursing mothers' unit. In order to reduce infection, the area is divided into small rooms or compartments. The babies are carried or wheeled on trolleys into the nursing mothers' room for breastfeeding. This creates a more frequent and intensive contact between mother and child than the former arrangement with a central breastfeeding room. The accommodation of new mothers and newborns in one room ('rooming-in') avoids the transport of babies and makes less work for the staff.

Care units are mostly smaller than for normal care; limiting the size of the care group to 10–14 beds is sensible. For hygienic reasons, the requirements for the care of nursing mothers and newborns are higher than for normal care. Therefore, in addition to the normal control lobby system, a lobby plus cloakroom must be provided for visitors. The bed space can be designed as with normal care but the spacing of the beds needs to be larger to allow for the baby's cot. The sanitary facilities must include hip-bath/shower combinations and showers.

Neonatal care units comprise: cot spaces for newborns, nappy removal, baby bathing, nappy fitting, cradle space, work area for neonatal nurse, possibly parking for transport trolley, work area for the departmental sister, nurses' lounge, kitchenette, doctor's office, examination and treatment room, clean workroom, patient bath, day room for patients and visitors, store, equipment and cleaning rooms, staff and visitors' WCs, linen cupboards.

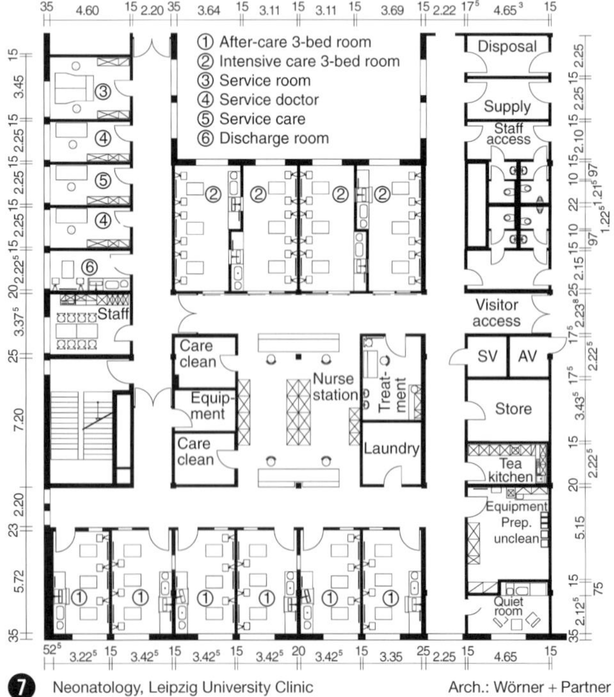

❼ Neonatology, Leipzig University Clinic Arch.: Wörner + Partner

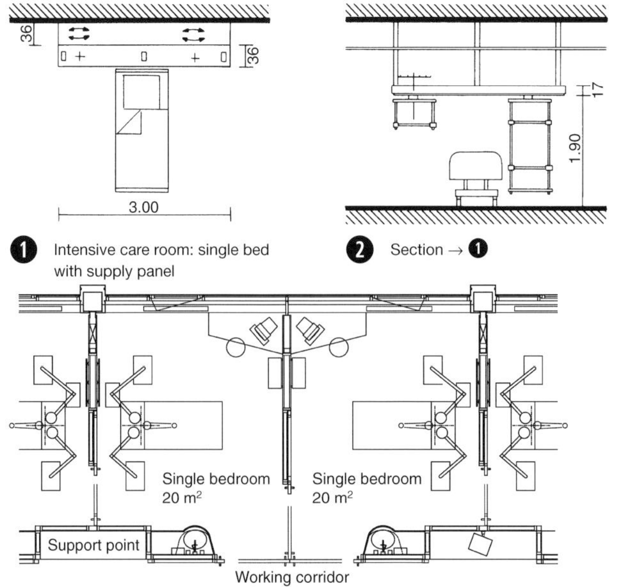

❶ Intensive care room: single bed with supply panel

❷ Section → ❶

❸ Intensive care rooms at the Heinrich Heine University, Düsseldorf
Arch.: Henie, Wishcher und Partner Freie Architekten

Link to operating area
Patients from theatres
Access inpatients
Doctor work room
Pumi
Changing
Changing
Staff tea kitchen
2-bed
1-bed
2-bed
2-bed
1-bed
2-bed

(1) Work room, clean
(2) Work room, unclean
(3) Disposal
(4) Bed vestibule/visitors/supply

❹ Intensive care ward, Luckenwalde Hospital, 10 beds
Arch.: Thiede Messthaler Klösges

Intensive care medicine

Patients with significant disturbance of vital bodily functions are treated in intensive care. A direct, short route to the surgical department and to the medical service (anaesthesia) is necessary. The patients are permanently monitored by doctors and care staff. The organisation of intensive care is similar to that of related disciplines like neurosurgery, heart/thorax surgery, transplant surgery and neurology or interdisciplinary fields like surgery or internal medicine.

For general hospitals without a particular medical specialisation, the integration of intensive care with surgery and internal medicine is usual. Intensive care must be spatially separated from the general care area and accessible only through a system of control lobbies (for hygiene reasons).

The central point of every intensive care ward is an open nurses' station with a view of every room. The number of patients (6–36) in an intensive care unit depends on the total size of the hospital. Each unit requires a duty station, a clean workroom (preparation of medication and infusions) and a materials and equipment room.

The beds can be arranged in an open, closed or combined layout. The open layout requires a spacious area. The patients are separated visually by half-height partitions with glazed window elements. In the closed arrangement, the patients are separated into different rooms.

Further facilities should be provided: anaesthesia preparation room, clean material room, dirty workroom, cleaning room, waiting room for relatives, doctors' on-call lounge, documentation room, and possibly consulting room. There should be connections for oxygen, compressed air and vacuum at every bed space.

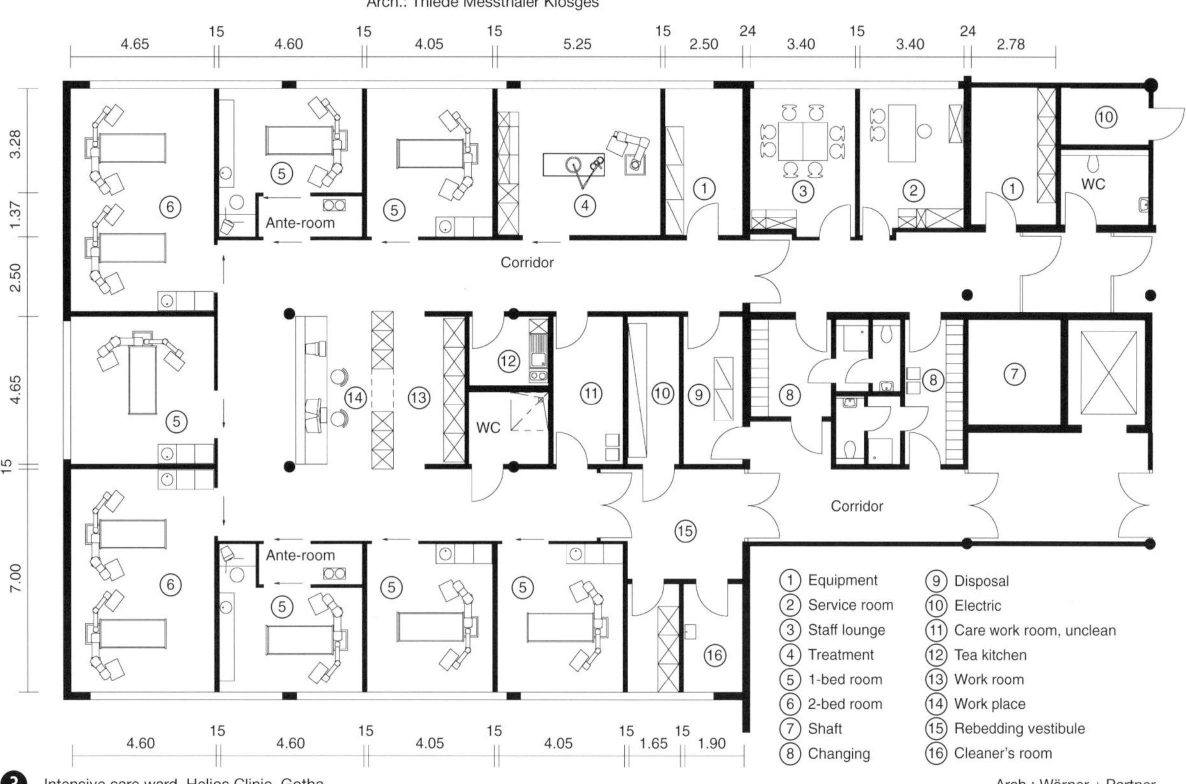

❸ Intensive care ward, Helios Clinic, Gotha

Arch.: Wörner + Partner

Health

HOSPITALS
General, modular grid
Building design
Examples
Corridors, doors, stairs, lifts
Operational areas
Outpatient area
Outpatient medical centre – example
Examination and treatment
Care
Administration, social services
Supply and waste disposal
Technical supply

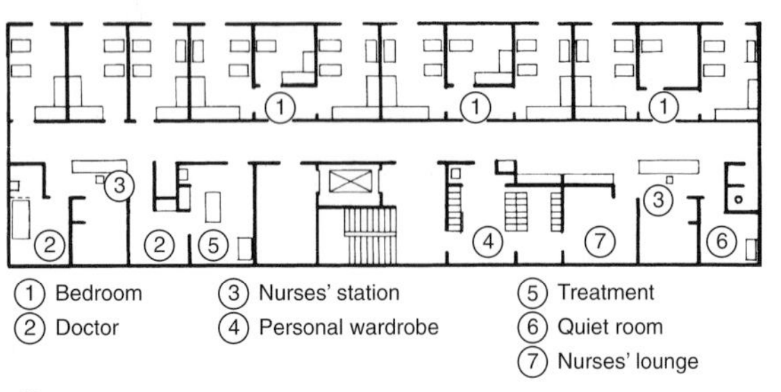

1 Children's ward with 28 beds, Velbert City Hospital Arch.: Krüger, Krüger, Rieger

7.20
3.60 3.60

2 Single- and two-bed rooms with strong radiation protection, in the controlled area of a radiology ward Arch.: Deilmann

7.20

3 Four-bed room with all equipment for basic care (for long-term psychiatric patients) Arch.: Deilmann

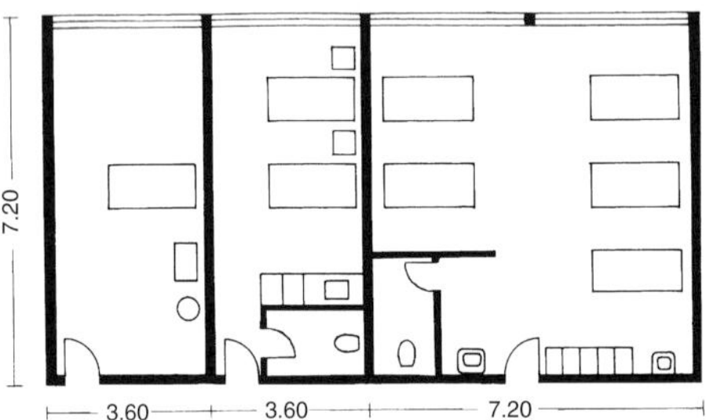

4 Room unit for patients with mild mental illness and for those needing care Arch.: Deilmann

Paediatric care

The proportions of patients in dedicated children's hospitals are babies (35%), premature babies (13%), small children and schoolchildren up to 14 years old (22%) and all ages after infectious illnesses (22%). The accommodation of this last group should aim to avoid contact between patients and other patients/staff. Isolation wards should be provided for measles, chickenpox, diphtheria, scarlet fever and TB. Rooms should also be provided for teaching, activity and play. The design of children's wards should be similar to that of a kindergarten, rather than a sterile clinical area.

Care of the mentally ill

This can be open or closed (as well as in the special forensic form under a hospital treatment order). The special nature of mental illness results in a higher space requirement for day rooms, dining rooms and rooms for occupational and group therapy. Small care units (up to 18 patients) should be created with short circulation routes and homely design in order to give the patients a feeling of security. The trend is towards the integration of psychiatric departments into general hospitals.

Care of radiotherapy patients

In the design of nuclear medicine care groups, which address the diagnosis and therapy of patients undergoing radiation treatment, compliance with the Radiation Protection Regulations is the first principle. The size of a care group should correspond to a normal care group. The operational centre is divided into a controlled area and a supervised area. In this way, patients who have received the greatest radiation doses are separated from those treated with less. Patients should therefore be accommodated in single-bed rooms.

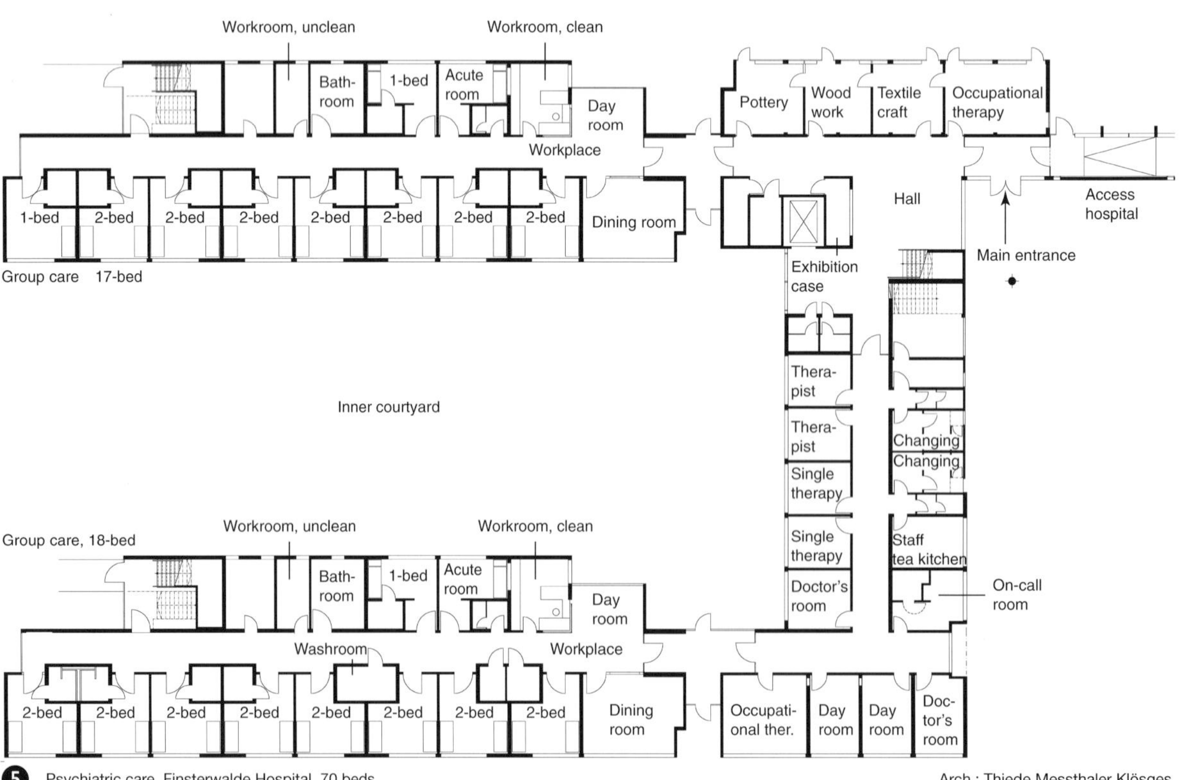

5 Psychiatric care, Finsterwalde Hospital, 70 beds Arch.: Thiede Messthaler Klösges

Music therapy
Shower
Rest room
OT
OT
Bio-therapy
Office therapy
Control centre
Chan-ging
Atrium
Patients kitchen
Store
Tea kitchen
Gymnastics
Events
Function room
Patients lounge
Self-help

1 First floor → **2**

Day clinic

In the course of the reform of health provision, many hospitals are partially outsourcing certain clinical areas, which can be operated by private doctors' collectives. These specialist clinics are for patients who are cared for only during the daytime without a bed in the hospital. Outpatient operations can also be carried out. Because these patients are separate from the usual operation of the hospital, a separate entrance is required. The reception and waiting areas are designed in a similar way to a doctor's practice and should avoid a 'hospital' atmosphere.

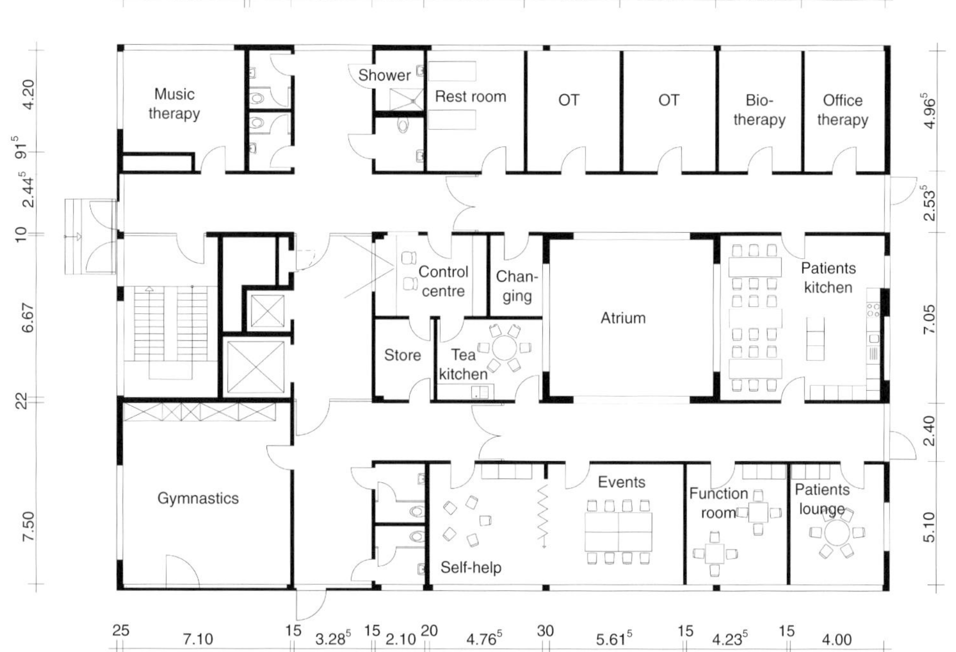

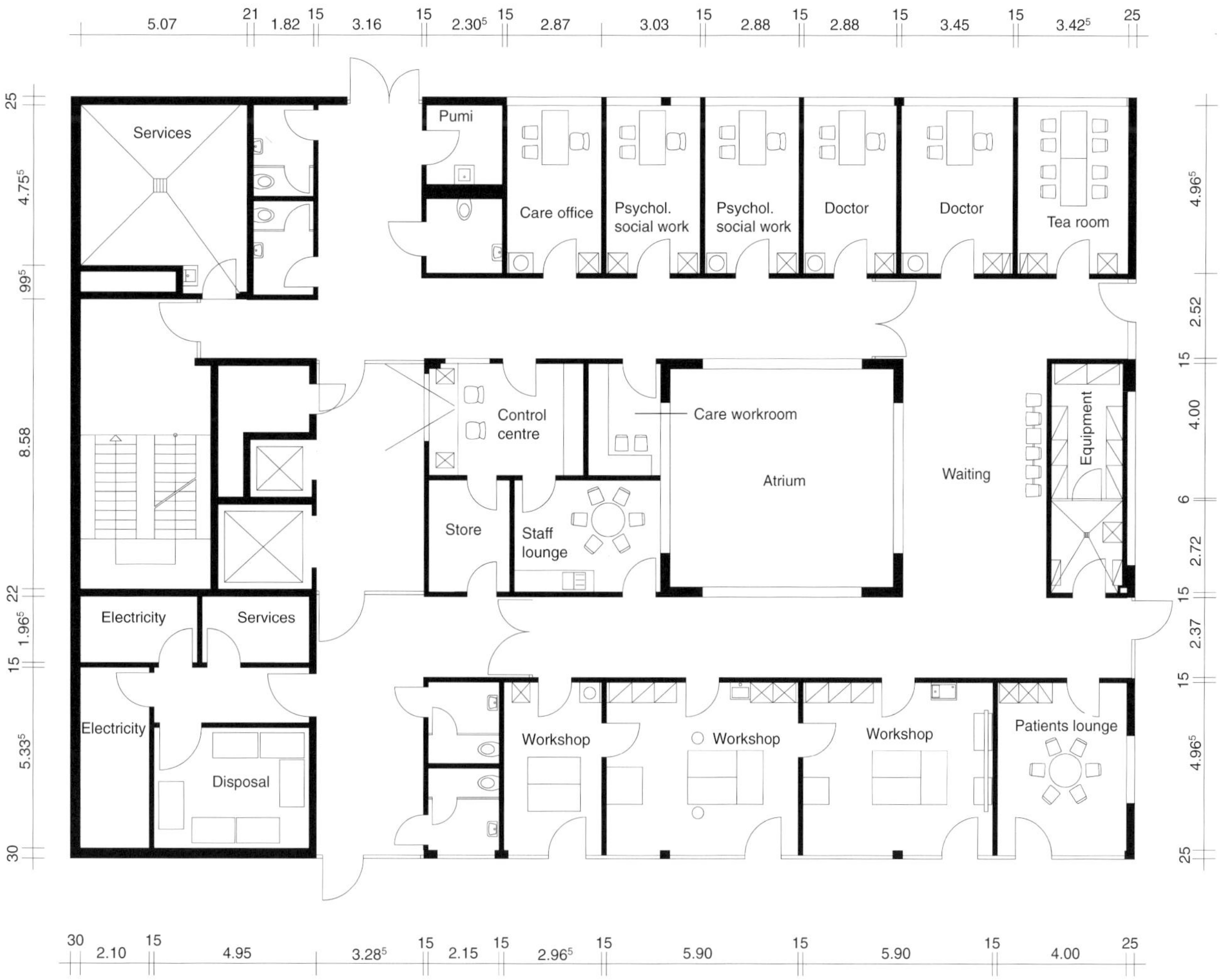

Services
Pumi
Care office
Psychol. social work
Psychol. social work
Doctor
Doctor
Tea room
Control centre
Care workroom
Atrium
Waiting
Equipment
Store
Staff lounge
Electricity
Services
Electricity
Disposal
Workshop
Workshop
Workshop
Patients lounge

2 Ground floor plan, psychiatric day clinic, Dr. Horst Schmidt Clinics, Wiesbaden

Arch.: Wörner + Partner

Health

HOSPITALS
General, modular grid
Building design
Examples
Corridors, doors, stairs, lifts
Operational areas
Outpatient area
Outpatient medical centre – example
Examination and treatment
Care
Administration, social services
Supply and waste disposal
Technical supply

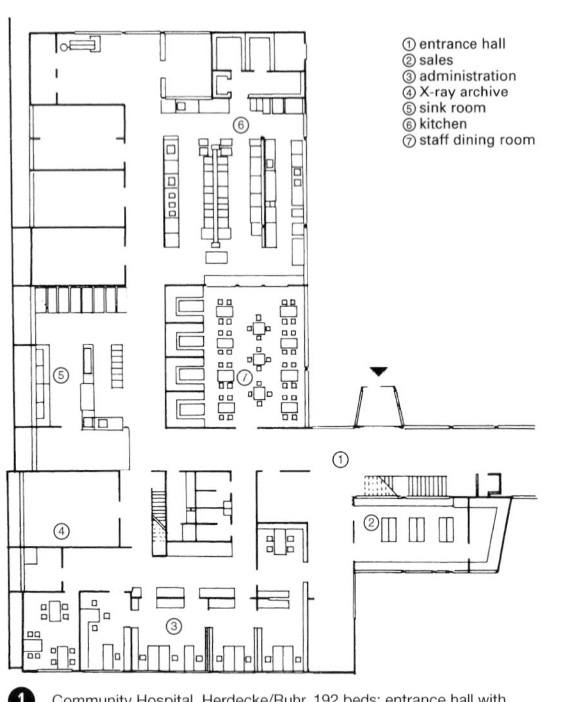

❶ Community Hospital, Herdecke/Ruhr, 192 beds; entrance hall with administration area Arch.: Bockenmühl

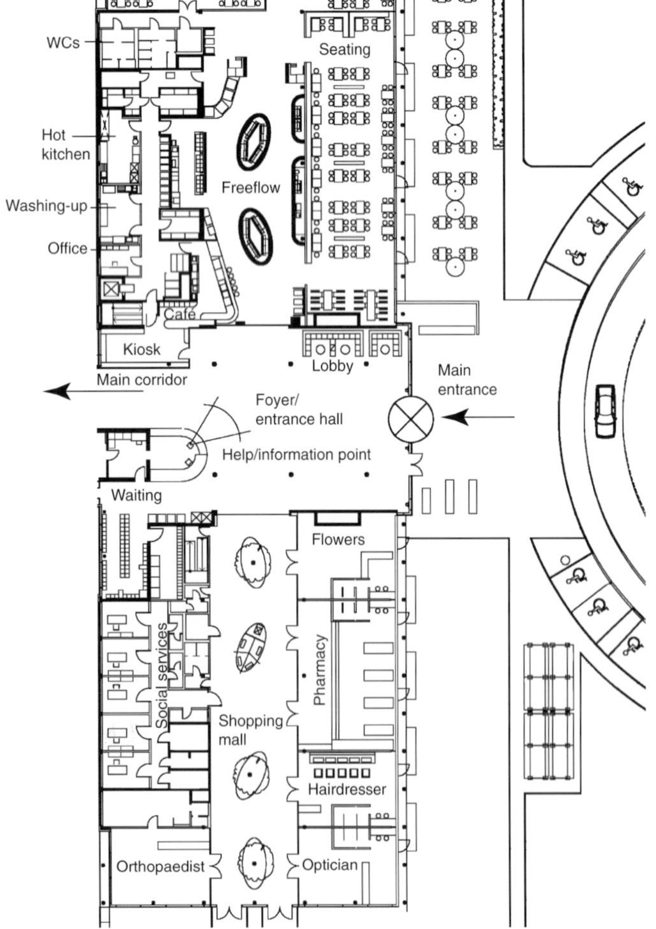

❷ Entrance and café, Helios Clinic, Berlin-Buch Arch.: Thiede Messthaler Klösges

Management and administration

Administration offices are divided into those dealing directly with patients, and other offices. Offices for patient admission and dealings with friends and relatives should be provided near the main entrance. The offices for internal hospital business are: administrative director's office with secretarial support, accounts department and personnel department. Conference and meeting rooms are also required. In larger hospitals, social workers and psychologists also work in the administration.

Increasing rationalisation in accounting and the application of IT need to be considered in the design, perhaps involving raised floors and the central accounts office with pneumatic postal delivery connections.

Records

A short distance between records and working areas is advantageous but mostly difficult to achieve. A location in the basement with access by stairs is possible.

There is a difference between stores and records rooms for files, literature, films, administration, X-ray department etc. Mobile shelving is useful to reduce the space requirement for the same storage capacity. The high loading assumptions for shelves (up to 1000 kg/m^2) have to be considered. The storage term for patient files is 30 years.

Library

Medical libraries should be provided with open shelving, without closed stores and book issue. A large part of the literature is journals. Sufficient availability of reading tables with lamps is important. Hospital libraries are divided into patient libraries and medical libraries for doctors. The significance and use of these is reducing through today's omnipresent IT and Internet resources.

Main entrance and services

A simple and easily recognisable main entrance with vehicle access and disability parking places must be created for general patient and visitor traffic and delivery by taxi. Special entrances should be avoided if possible. The entrance hall should be designed as a waiting room for visitors on the open door principle, with the layout today more like a modern hotel lobby. From here, visitors, outpatients, inpatients capable of walking and business traffic go their separate ways.

The size of the entrance hall is in accordance with the hospital's bed capacity. The reception can put telephone calls through and also act as the post room. Also in the entrance hall are coin telephones, and kiosks for sweets, flowers, stationery etc. A cafeteria for visitors and patients is situated directly next to the entrance and is open all day offering a free choice of warm and cold food and drink. Also important are storage facilities and the provision of rooms for staff in accordance with Workplace Regulations.

Pastoral care and social services

There should be a non-denominational chapel or prayer room. This has adjoining rooms for the chaplain and vestry, and side rooms. These facilities also need offices for the chaplain and the social workers.

❶ Supply centre, Cologne University Clinic: kitchen, prepared stores
Arch.: Heinle, Wischer und Partner Freie Architekten

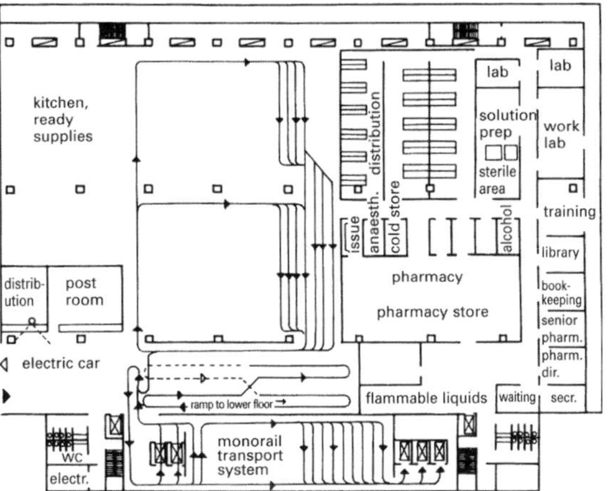

❷ Supply centre, Cologne University Clinic: kitchen and pharmacy, prepared stores
Arch.: Heinle, Wischer und Partner Freie Architekten

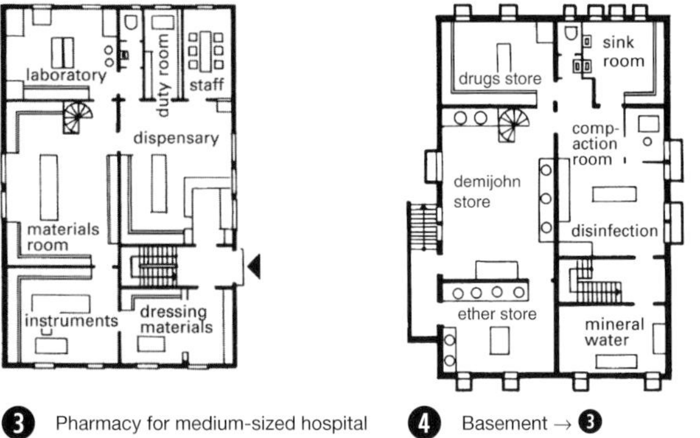

❸ Pharmacy for medium-sized hospital with 500–600 beds, ground floor

❹ Basement → ❸

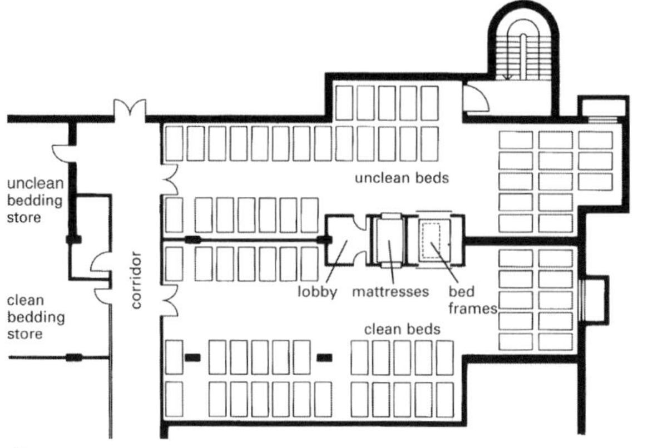

❺ Central bed unit, St. Elisabeth Hospital, Halle/Saale
Arch.: U. + A. Weicken

Supply area

Commercial and technical supply enters the hospital either via a separate service building or at a neutral supply and waste disposal level (basement) under the main building. There should be an access for deliveries into the service yard, separated from the main entrance and the arrival of patients on stretchers. The location of delivery and waste disposal areas to the north is ideal. External and internal traffic routes should be designed so that interaction with the traffic in the care and treatment areas is avoided as much as possible.

It should be taken into account in the design that this area of the hospital can potentially cause noise and odour nuisance (waste containers, kitchen waste, etc.). There is a noticeable tendency towards increasing centralisation of supply and waste disposal facilities and also the outsourcing of certain functional areas (e.g. laundry, kitchen).

Sterile goods supply

The central sterile store should be near the surgical department, the largest consumer (smaller stores of sterile goods in the theatres themselves are no longer needed). The layout is structured according to the direction of flow of materials into acceptance, pre-cleaning, washing machine, sterilisers, packing zone and sterile goods store. All the instruments for use in the hospital are prepared here. The departments with particularly heavy use are surgery with 40% and operative intensive care and internal intensive care with 15% each.

The number of sterilisers required depends on the size of the hospital and the surgical department. Size of central sterile store approx. 40–120 m^2.

Pharmaceutical supply

Pharmacy: In medium-sized and large hospitals, the pharmacy stores formulations and carries out the production of drugs under the management of a qualified pharmacist. For design purposes, the rooms required are dispensary, materials room, drug store, laboratory and possibly also issue desk. Rooms may also be required for herbs, dressings, substance storage, on-call room. The equipment of pharmacy and laboratory includes formulation table, work or packing table and a sink. The fitting out is similar to that of the dispensary. The location of the pharmacy should involve a short route to the lifts, pneumatic post etc. Since fire-hazardous substances and acids are stored here as well as various narcotics, the walls, ceilings and doors need to meet security standards.

Dispensary: In hospitals without a full pharmacy, medicines requiring approval are issued from the dispensary. This consists of work and dispensing rooms with direct access to the circulation corridor. The equipment consists of desk, washbasin, sink, scales and lockable cupboards. Adjacent rooms are the dry and proprietary medicines stores, cold store for hazardous substances, a dressings room and a damp store according to fire regulations.

Bed preparation

The processing of used beds and mattresses is normally done today with spray and wipe disinfection in the ward, or possibly even in the room.

Pushing numbers of beds through the building and the heavy mechanical wear and wetting of the beds, usual in central bed processing, is no longer necessary. It can, however, be sensible to provide for separate disinfection of mattresses in the basement, possibly combined with a bed repair room.

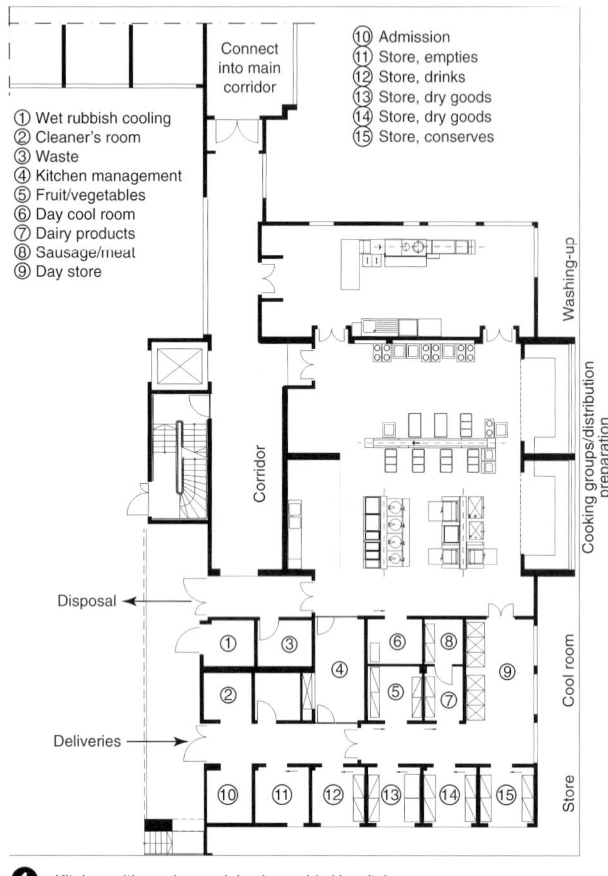

1 Kitchen with service yard, Luckenwalde Hospital
Arch.: Thiede Messthaler Klösges

Catering

Providing patients with appropriate nutrition places high demands on the preparation because there are often particular requirements regarding protein, fats, carbohydrates, vitamins, minerals, dietary fibre or flavourings. The predominant catering systems rationalise the individual phases of conventional food preparation (preparing, processing, transporting, serving). The processing of food is separated into normal and diet recipes. After preparation and cooking, the food is assembled on the portioning conveyor. The ready-portioned trays are taken to the wards on serving trolleys for distribution. The same trolleys transport the washing up back to the central washing up and trolley cleaning room. Staff catering amounts to about 40% of total catering. The cafeteria for staff should be very close to the central kitchen.

The location of the kitchen on the supply level guarantees an efficient flow of delivery, storage, preparation, processing and serving. When frozen food is used, the function and fitting out of the kitchen alters. The clear ceiling height in the kitchen is 4.00 m, and the size depends on the requirements and the number of patients in the hospital.

The design should also provide a special diet kitchen (min. 60 m^2) with a desk for the head chef, vegetable cleaning area (30 m^2) with room for waste (5 m^2), a daily supply room (8 m^2), a cold room with compartments for meat, fish and dairy products (each 8 m^2), and a pre-cool room (10 m^2) with chest freezer and cooler.

The **goods reception** should have sufficient storage space (15–20 m^2). The main store, with fruit and vegetable store (20 m^2), dry goods store (20 m^2) and store for conserves is next door. Provide sufficient changing rooms and social rooms for the kitchen staff.

The **central washing-up** unit of the central kitchen is organised around one or more large dish washing machines (approx. 30 m^2). There should be sufficient worktop space for dirty and clean racks.

New cooking methods make it possible to supply food for a number of hospitals from one central location.

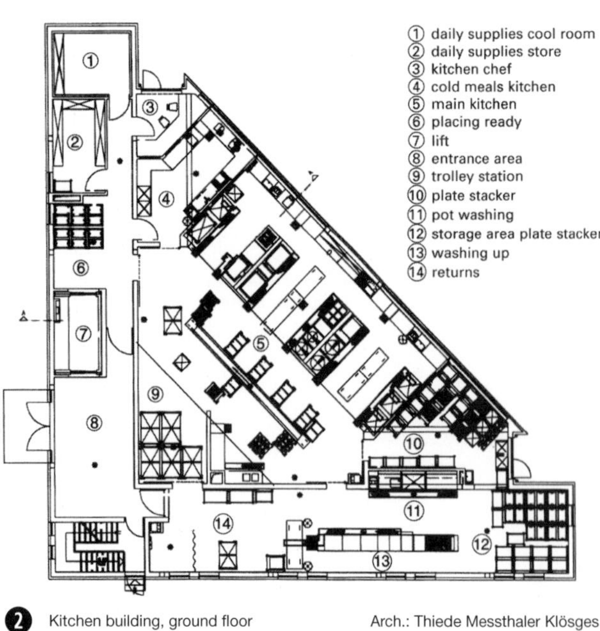

2 Kitchen building, ground floor Arch.: Thiede Messthaler Klösges

① cold meals/salads
② vegetable preparation
③ vegetable cool store
④ meat cool store
⑤ dairy
⑥ cool store
⑦ supplies (one-way goods)
⑧ delivery area
⑨ freezer room
⑩ supply store
⑪ dry goods/conserves store
⑫ detergents
⑬ office

3 Basement → **2**

Laundry provision
The collection and delivery of laundry is normally undertaken by an external organisation. In the hospital, only collecting rooms for dirty and clean washing (each 30 m^2) need to be provided, near the service yard.

Storage
This is divided into coarse pallet storage, rack storage and special storage. All storerooms should be centrally placed near the service yard and very robustly built. A logistics room is required, from where the collection and delivery services for the hospital are controlled. The distribution and storage of goods is rationally controlled from here. Important: for hygienic reasons, dirty and clean items should be separated. Automatic laundry transport systems are cost effective only for large hospitals (from 400 beds).

Workshops
Connected with the service yard, these could be metalwork, joinery and electrical workshops, and a medical technology office with materials stores, replacement parts store, general stores and parking for vehicles.

Housekeeping and transport service
Multi-purpose mobile units and trolleys are often used for the distribution of requested items to each location of use and at the same time for storage. A pneumatic delivery system should be provided for the sending of small goods (medicines, paperwork). The scope of the transport facilities depends on the size of the institution; the supply and disposal quantity is about 30–35 kg per bed and day. For large, bulky goods (beds, ventilators, heart-lung machines), normal bed lifts are available. Separate groups of lifts can be arranged for the transport of medium-sized goods (food, laundry, rubbish, consumables).

Service yard
The design should consider the parking and turning areas for delivery trucks, also the multitude of types of waste (kitchen and special rubbish, glass, waste paper, developing fluid etc.) and their storage areas. The service yard can also provide service rooms for emergency power generator, sprinklers, oxygen and compressed air, and other supply requirements. With its location in the basement, the service yard will require a ramp (gradient less than 15%!) for access. Minimum size of a service yard: 30 × 30 m.

delivery
removal
technical supply
mortuary
goods accepted
disposal
large store
kitchen
sterile area
ready store
laundry, dry cleaning
central distribution
pharmacy
central bed store
entrance
staff rooms
administration
general rooms
therapy
special care
diagnosis
normal care
inpatient treatment
intensive care

❶ Supply and disposal area – traffic relationships

(1) Glass
(2) Plastics
(3) Scrap metal
(4) Special waste
(5) Paper press
(6) Household rubbish
(7) UV treatment
(8) Mech. services
(9) Laundry container (56.2 m^2)
(10) Container washing plant, automatic goods transport storage space, clean (162.6 m^2)
(11) Automatic goods transport storage, unclean
(12) Control centre (27.1 m^2)
(13) Office (24.3 m^2)
(14) Disinfection plant
(15) Special waste
(16) Waste disposal

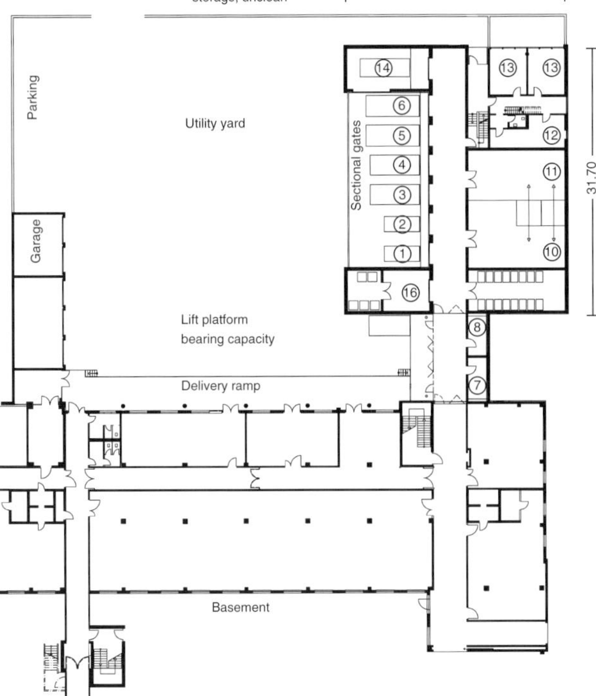

❷ Supply and disposal station, Erfurt Clinic Surgical Centre (KEC)
Rossmann + Partner Architekten

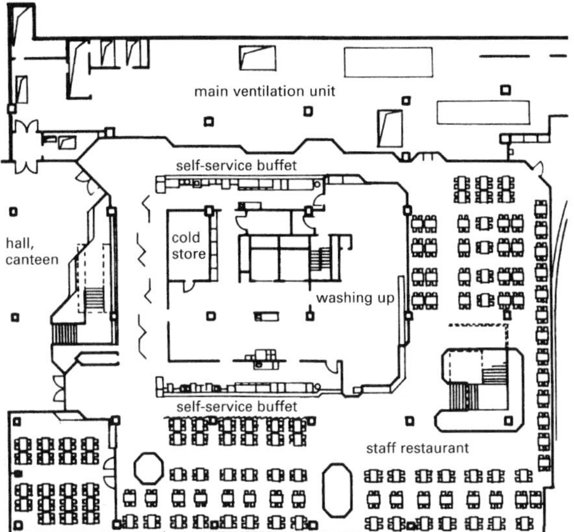

❸ Staff restaurant for 150 staff, Cantonal Hospital, Basel Arch.: Suter&Suter

Heating, ventilation, sanitary, medical gas supply
Plant and service rooms, shafts and installation areas

Early consideration of the buildings/rooms required for the installation of building services is a precondition for optimised layout and for hygienic and energy-saving operation of the facilities. The size and location of plant areas should generally be able to fulfil the following requirements:
a) optimal transport of air (short routes)
b) energy-saving specification of building elements
c) compliance with hygienic requirements and provision for cleaning
d) provision of maintenance and repair areas at central plant area

Building requirements
Space required for air-conditioning plant
The area and space requirement for air-conditioning equipment is determined by:
a) volume flow
b) number of thermodynamic conditioning stages
c) installed elements
d) connection situation for the duct network

The minimum height of a central plant room should be 3 m clear for optimal operation; 4–4.5 m following the number of functional units. The calculation of the area needed should be discussed according to the specific technical requirements, and a specialist building services engineer should be appointed. General note: the size of the air-conditioning equipment can be estimated via the volume flow with a speed of 2 m/s. The total length is the sum of the length of the individual elements required, taking the thermodynamic functions into account, and additional space for connection at each end and maintenance.

Cooling plant room
The cooling plant room has to provide space for chillers, expansion vessels, cold water and cooled water distributor and collector, main pumps and the associated control equipment. The space required depends on the nature and type of chiller and the capacity. Room heights should be more than 3 m, which may depend on the output.

Recooling plant
The area and space requirement for recooling plant is determined from the required cooling capacity, the type of cooling, the form of the air intake and outlet, the mounting and the noise insulation. The selection of the room height and the floor area must take into account the lateral proportion, operation, maintenance and repair. The installation should also take special aspects of noise emission and fumes emission into account. The recooling capacity depends on the type and capacity of cooling.

General equipment of plant rooms
Preferably, plant rooms should be located near the supply area. The location of the central plant area should ensure suitable conditions for supply and disposal and result in short distances for air/gas supply.

Plant rooms must comply with the fire protection and safety requirements of the relevant state building regulations, the conditions imposed on the particular building and the Workplace Regulations if appropriate. The operation of the technical equipment in the plant rooms should not impair the environment nor cause nuisance in the building through noise or vibration.

Technical details, temperature requirements
The temperature in plant rooms must not sink below 5 °C for technical reasons (danger of frost!) and should also not exceed 40 °C (because of electrical equipment), which should be ensured by suitable technical measures. Damp and increased humidity should be avoided. Plant rooms should be equipped with a water supply with hose connection and backflow preventer, and also at least one floor gully. The EU safety data sheets for the equipment and consumables should be at hand in case of breakdowns. The installation of electrical equipment should comply with German Association of Electrotechnicians (VDE) standards. Plant rooms should have at least one power socket (230 V, 16 A) and a three-phase connection (400 V) suitable for the particular situation. The nominal lighting intensity in plant rooms should be 100 lx; and at switching panels, and regulation and measurement equipment 200 lx.

Requirements for service shafts and horizontal ducts
Shafts are employed for vertical service runs and horizontal services use service ducts or are fixed below the floor slab, with cables in cable trays. In accordance with the applicable state building regulations, installation shafts and cable runs in buildings, with the exception of buildings of limited height and any installation shafts or cable runs which bridge fire compartments, must be detailed so that fire and smoke cannot enter staircases, other storeys or other fire compartments. Installation shafts and ducts must comply with fire resistance class L30, L60 or L90 for the relevant pipe or cable. Comb-shaped connection to functional areas is ideal. The sum of air ducts, pipe runs and cable trays should remain constant in relation to the height of the storey. Shafts and ducts should be detailed so that they cannot act as structural stiffening. Only main shafts and ducts are permissible in this case. Accessible shafts should be reachable from a corridor.

Suspended ceilings
The space between structural and suspended ceiling should not be used directly for air supply and cannot be used directly for air extraction, depending on the extracted air collection arrangements. The spacing between the bottom of the slab and the top of the suspended ceiling depends on the degree of installation (air ducts, water pipework, electric cable runs, lighting elements, air handling units, air intakes and outlets, sprinkler pipework) and should normally be min. 400 mm. A smaller ceiling space is possible in exceptional cases.

Gas supply plant room
The special oxygen pipework is supplied from operational and reserve units with automatic switchover equipment. In order to ensure short transport distances, direct access to the service yard is sensible, e.g. for delivery and collection of the cylinders. The storage of the cylinders can be combined with the air/gas pumps (vacuum, nitrogen, compressed air) in order to enable centralised control (possibly computer-controlled). The gas cylinders are being replaced nowadays with bulk tanks, which must be situated in the open air and at least 5.0 m from buildings.

Electrical installation / high voltage plant
Electricity supply is generally from a public medium-voltage mains network (10–20 kV) provided by the electricity supply organisation. The mains connection transformation to low voltage (400 V) and distribution inside the building take place in the hospital sub-station. The appropriate switchgear and transformers should each be placed in their own room, and the Regulations for Building Electrical Service Rooms and the VDE standards should be complied with. In larger hospitals, a number of specialised electrical rooms should be provided in addition to the sub-station. The installation is sized depending on the dimensions of the building and the energy requirements of the individual pieces of equipment. The hospital sub-station should be situated centrally and provided with good, ideally level, road access as well as adequate ventilation and extraction. A location in the basement is not suitable if there is any risk of flooding.

A hospital should also have an emergency power system, which continues to supply certain defined equipment in case of a mains failure. This arrangement is provided by emergency power generation sets with diesel motors and alternating current generators. This equipment should be placed in its own room with ensured air supply and extraction, and exhaust gas escaping above the roof. An additional emergency power supply must be provided for lighting in operating theatres and certain vital medical devices. Decentralised battery sets are provided for this for use in the room containing the medical device.

Starting from the sub-station, the general and emergency power supplies are distributed separately, in a star shape, through the hospital. Depending on the building structure and the distance, this may be via distribution boards on each floor or one central distribution board. The arrangement and number of distribution boards on the floors have to be in accordance with fire compartments, whose assignment to functional areas should also be taken into account. The distribution boards are separated into general and emergency power supply and placed in their own rooms.

Telecommunications / IT
The correct functioning of telephone and data networks in a hospital is essential for the care of patients and the basis for economic success. A central telecommunications room and also at least one server (IT) room should be provided to accommodate the system components, each with a size of 35–70 m^2. Uninterruptible power supplies and an extra cooling system should be provided.

In order to optimise availability, a further IT room should be planned for backup systems in another building or at least another part of the same building. Starting from the central telecommunications or server room, the star-shaped distribution cabling (copper or fibre-optic cables) runs to the distribution hubs on each floor. The telecommunications and IT devices are connected from here.

The modern 'structured cabling topology' provides unified sockets for telephone, IT and medical technology, enabling rapid reaction to the very fast progress of development in communications technology.

Speech communication in administrative areas is provided by analogue and digital telephones, which are connected directly to a central telephone system. Cordless mobile DECT phones in connection with powerful communications servers are rapidly replacing traditional pagers, and provide a second route for communication.

Each patient room is provided with a patient operating panel with call light, signal connections for wall-mounted TV and/or bedside devices and sockets for telephone and Internet access. TV signals come either from a cable operator or from a satellite reception system and are fed centrally into the signal network. When a patient presses the call button, the light signal system communicates with the locations where the care staff have logged in. The prioritisation of calls:

- patient call
- WC call
- emergency call
- resuscitation call etc.

is also supported, as is forwarding of any calls to the mobile DECT phones of the care staff, including detailed information. The fire early warning and alarm scheme includes a fire alarm system with automatic and manual alarms as a loop system, which saves cabling, and an electro-acoustic system with its own cable network to maintain function. The delivery routes and roads to the parking places are secured by barriers. These can be manually controlled by the gatekeepers or automatically controlled according to identification or invoicing.

Cameras are provided, either fixed or adjustable, to monitor the entrance areas, access roads and specific areas; the images are sent through a central cross-loop to the monitors for observation.

The operating units for the telecommunications components:

- switchboard for the telephone system
- camera control
- server for the hospital information system
- control server for the patient media system
- lift surveillance etc.

are installed in the lodge or entrance area in smaller hospitals.

In larger hospitals, these will be installed in a central control room. This is where all relevant fault reports arrive and are processed centrally. The requirement for prompt recording of and access to all relevant clinical and patient data is ensured by the use of complex software. The functionality of the user applications is based on active network components in the central server rooms and IT rooms on each floor, together with the system of servers.

Stationary PC workstations in functional and care departments and mobile data recording stations in the wards are integrated into the network and support the care staff. The internal network is secured from access by unauthorised third parties by firewall solutions, which have to be updated constantly.

Speech and data integration (VoIP – Voice over IP) and database consolidation (SAN) of all IT and medical IT systems are an important part of hospital IT.

The radiology department, in particular, with a number of systems producing and processing images, places very high demands on the quality and capacity of the network.

The appointment of specialist engineers is absolutely necessary.

Regulations for Building Electrical Service Rooms
VDE standards

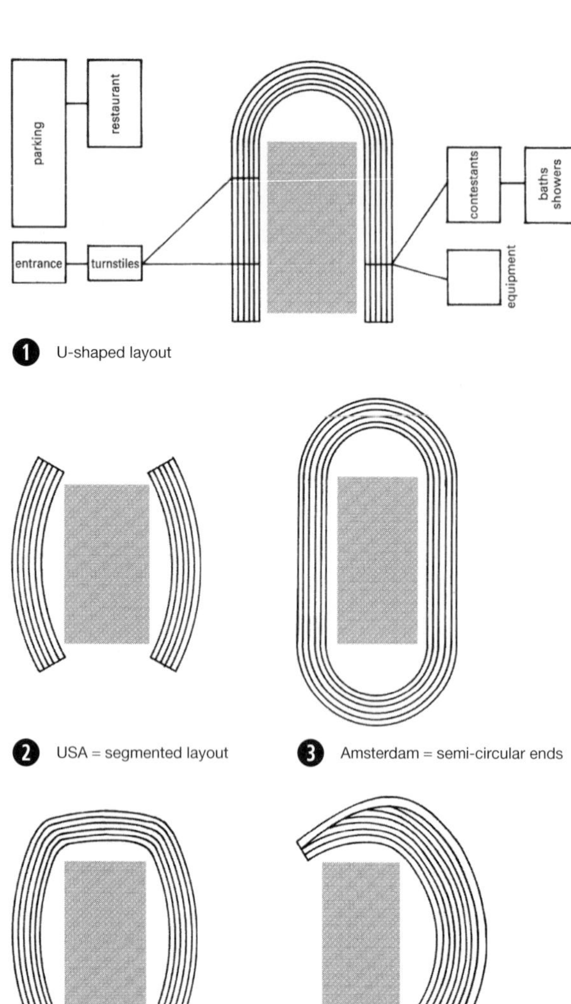

❶ U-shaped layout

❷ USA = segmented layout

❸ Amsterdam = semi-circular ends

❹ Rotterdam = curved sides and corners. Only for football

❺ Budapest = horseshoe around transverse axis

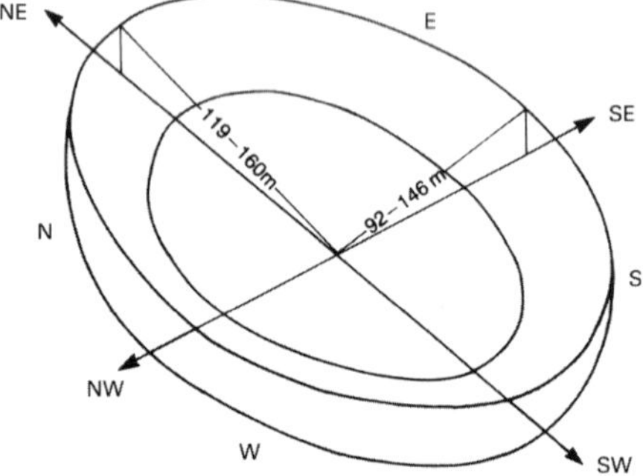

❻ Viewing distance determines size of sports ground

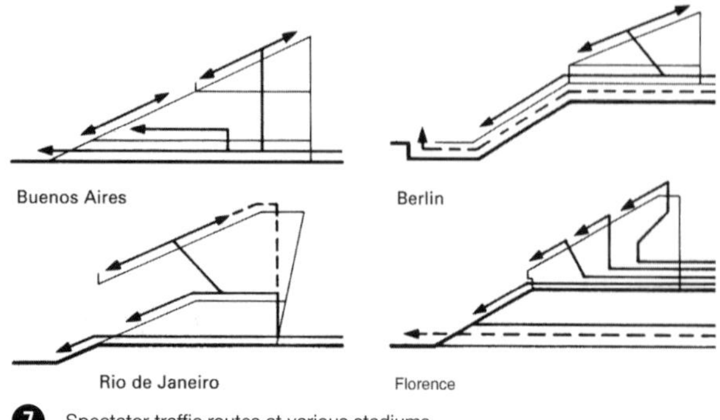

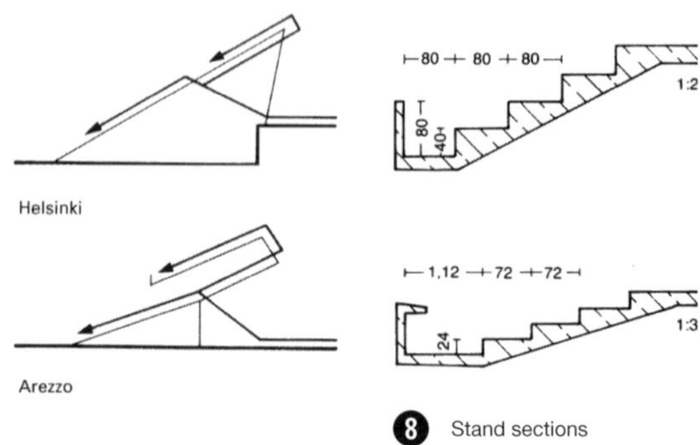

❼ Spectator traffic routes at various stadiums

❽ Stand sections

STADIUMS

Overview

Ancient stadiums, whose size has never been matched (the Circus Maximus in Rome had room for 180,000 spectators), still form the basis for today's sports venues. The dimensions are normally determined by the 70 × 109 m layout of a football pitch and the running track around it → p. 323. The basic shape of the playing area is an ellipse, which is similar to the ancient egg shape. A stadium is normally partially dug into the ground and the earth removed is heaped around it. From the town planning aspect, sports facilities must fit well into the terrain and the transport and utility supply conditions should be good: rail, bus, tram stops, large car parks etc. Industry in the immediate vicinity should be avoided because smoke, smell and noise are undesirable. Covered and open-air facilities for various types of sport can be combined and integrated into the zoning plan of the city.

The orientations of ancient arenas were usually west–east or south–north, according to the various times of competitions → ❻; in Europe, northeast–southwest so that most spectators had the sun behind them. Open entrances are therefore at the eastern end. The pay booths were placed far forward, and behind them the flow of visitors distributed itself to various points in the stadium. These provide access, mostly up the heaped areas, or up stairs, to the stand at half-height and then to the rows above and below → ❼. For acoustic reasons, the Roman architect Vitruvius recommended a fixed gradient of 1:2 for both rows of seating and standing places. Nowadays, when loudspeakers are used, the inclination only has to ensure a good view.

Accordingly, with staggered seats, the audience in each row should be able to see over the heads of those two rows in front. This results in a parabolic curve. The best viewing conditions are from the long side of an arc.

The width of the access passages and stairs must be worked out using the sudden flow of spectators leaving (in contrast to the gradual trickle of those arriving). According to the calculations of C. van Eestern, each 5000 spectators at the Amsterdam stadium → ❸ require 7 minutes (or 420 seconds) to leave using the 9.5 m wide stairs provided (in Los Angeles 12 minutes, in Turin 9 minutes).

So one spectator uses 1 m stair width in

$$\frac{9.5 \times 420}{5000} = 0.8 \text{ s}$$

or in 1 s, for each 1 m stair width,

$$\frac{5000}{9.5 \times 420} = 1.25 \text{ s}$$

spectators leave. The formula for the necessary stair width for a defined number of spectators intending to leave the stadium in a desirably short time would therefore be

$$\text{stair width (m)} = \frac{\text{no. spectators}}{\text{evacuation time (s)} \times 1.25}$$

First-aid rooms should be provided according to the number of spectators and close to the spectator area. A group of rooms is necessary for every 20,000 spectators: treatment and rest room 15 m^2, store room 2 m^2 and two toilets with lobbies to prevent odour transmission. For stadiums with room for more than 30,000 spectators, there should also be a 15 m^2 room for public safety personnel (police, fire service). The commentary boxes will be in the main stand with a good view of the sports field, each box 1.5 m^2. Behind every five media boxes, a switchroom of 4 m^2. One car parking space for every four spectators and parking places for coaches should be allocated.

viewpoint

❶ Sight line construction

standing terrace

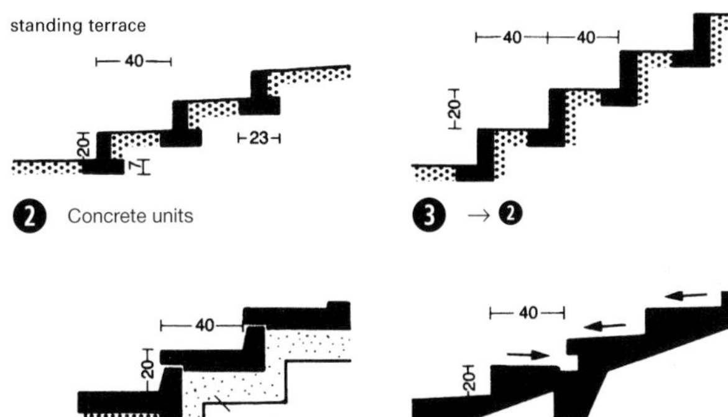

❷ Concrete units

❸ → ❷

❹ → ❷

❺ Sloping reinforced concrete with drainage

seating steps

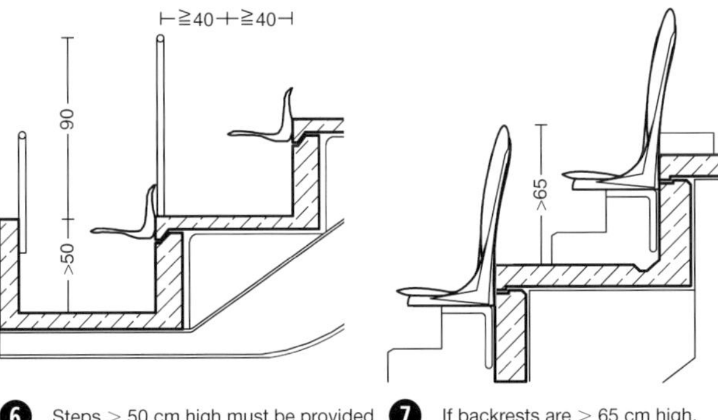

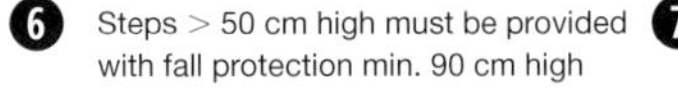

❻ Steps > 50 cm high must be provided with fall protection min. 90 cm high

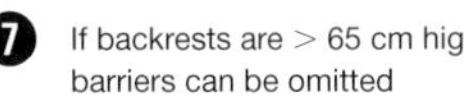

❼ If backrests are > 65 cm high, barriers can be omitted

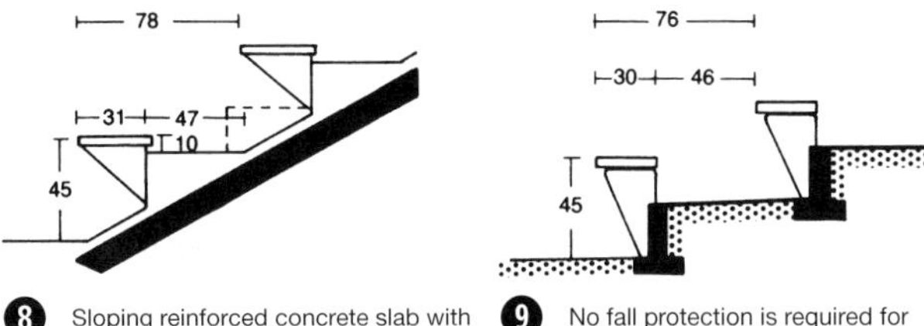

❽ Sloping reinforced concrete slab with steps

❾ No fall protection is required for steps < 50 cm high

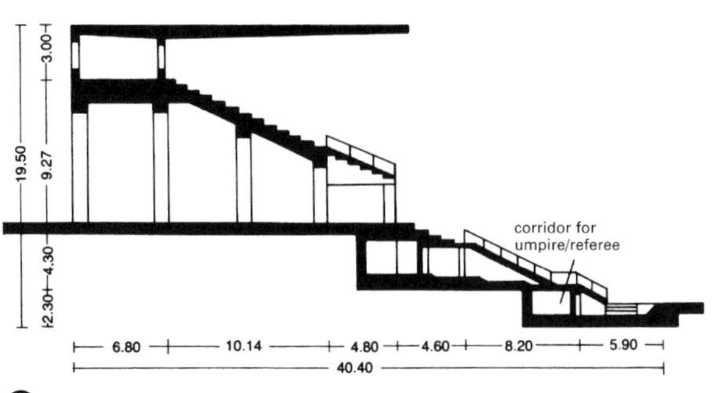

❿ Section through the Berlin Olympic stadium Arch.: Prof. Werner March

Spectator and VIP areas

The design is based on the relevant state Places of Assembly Regulations, which contain requirements for access routes, stairs, ramps and spectator places. Further regulations can be prescribed by ruling sports bodies, e.g. the FIFA guidelines for international games prohibit standing places in stadiums.

According to the number of spectator places planned, stands are either placed on the long sides of the sports field (a good view, because the distance is not too far) or, for more than approx. 10,000 places, around the entire playing area. Because sporting events mostly take place in the afternoon, the best spectator places are on the west side (no glare). If the spectator places are arranged in a multi-row layout, sufficient super-elevation should be provided to improve the viewing conditions. For smaller stands with up to 20 rows of standing places or 10 rows of seating, this can be a linear gradient of 1:2, but in all other stadiums the linear gradient should be parabolic. In this case the gradient for sitting and standing places can be determined by using spectators' sight line construction, with the super-elevation 12 cm for standing places and 15 cm for rows of seats → ❶.

Seated areas (Places of Assembly Regulations)

Seated place width 0.5 m

For design purposes, in rows of seating the required space is two visitors per m². This can be provided as row seating (benches) or as individual seats, which have to be fixed and immovable when there are more than 5000 visitor places. Seats with backrests offer more comfort (height min. 30 cm according to FIFA guidelines) and there must be a clear passage width of 40 cm between rows of seats. Seats must be arranged in blocks of max. 30 rows. Behind and between the blocks, there must be aisles with a min. width of 1.20 m. Depending on the layout of the access and exit routes, each row of seats may contain:

20 places if there is an aisle to the open air at one side, or

40 places if there is an aisle to the open air at both sides

Sitting and standing places must be separated. A 1.20 m width of escape route (stairs, ramps, level surfaces) must be provided for every 600 places, with a minimum width of 1.20 m.

Standing terraces (Places of Assembly Regulations)

Standing space width 0.5 m

For design purposes, in standing terraces the required space is two visitors per running metre of terrace. A 1.20 m width of escape route (stairs, ramps, level surfaces) must be provided for every 600 places, with a minimum width of 1.20 m. In order to ensure that standing areas fill and empty evenly and to avoid dangerous crushes, they should be divided into blocks of about 2500 places. These blocks should be fenced apart and separately accessed.

Within a block of standing terrace, 'wave breakers' (crush barriers) should be provided. It must be ensured that, seen from each standing place, there is a suitably strong parapet about 1.1 m high within 10 rows. Possible diagonal surging must be hindered by a staggered arrangement of the 'wave breakers'.

VIPs: Larger stadiums should provide a covered VIP box with movable seating.

Roofing of stands: The intention should be to provide cover for as many places as possible. Overlapping of stand structures can increase the number of covered places. The Berlin Olympic stadium has recently received a new roof → ❿ – ⓫.

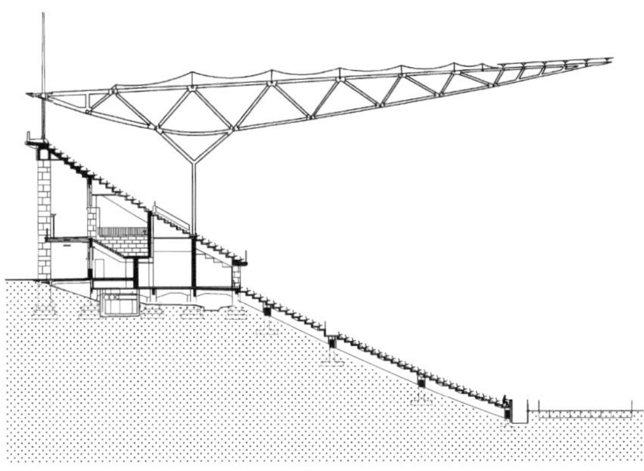

⓫ Section through the Berlin Olympic stadium after rebuilding Arch.: Gerkan Marg u. Partner

Sport	Competitive sport				Leisure sport				Net	Goal / basket (m)
	Playing area dimensions (m)	Free space around sides (m)	Free space around ends (m)	Total area (m)	Playing area dimensions (m)	Free space around sides (m)	Free space around ends (m)	Total area (m)	Height (m)	W = width H = height
Football	45–90 × 90–120	1	2	46–91 × 92–122	68 × 105	1	2	69 × 107	—	W = 7.32 H = 2.44
Football, FIFA requirements	45–90 × 90–120	2	3.5	47–92 × 93.5–123.5	68 × 105	2	3.5	70 × 108.5	—	W = 7.32 H = 2.44
Rugby	68.4 × 100	2	12–23	70.4 × 123	68.4 × 100	2	12–23	70.4 × 123	—	W = 5.60 H = 3.00
Handball	55–65 × 90–110	1	2	56–66 × 92–112	60 × 90	1	2	61 × 92	—	W = 3.00 H = 2.00
Indoor handball	18–22 × 38–44	1	2	19–23 × 40–46	20 × 40	1	2	21 × 42	—	W = 3.00 H = 2.00
Hockey (field hockey)	—	—	—	—	55 × 91.4	2	4	57 × 95.4	—	W = 3.66 H = 2.14
Netball	25 × 60	1	2	26 × 62	25 × 60	1	2	26 × 62	—	net H = 2.50
Softball/ rounders	25 × 50–70	10	10	35 × 60–80	—	—	—	—	—	pole H = 1.50
Indoor cycle polo	9–11 × 12–14	0.5	0.5–1	9.5–11.5 × 13–15	—	—	—	—	—	W = 2.00 H = 2.00
Volleyball	9 × 18	2	3	11 × 21	9 × 18	2	3	11 × 21	2.43	—
Prellball	8 × 16	2	4	10 × 20	8 × 16	2	4	10 × 20	—	—
Schleuderball	—	—	—	—	15 × 100	8	30	23 × 130	—	—
Fistball	—	—	—	—	20 × 50	6	8	26 × 58	2.00	—
Basketball	15 × 28	1	1	—	—	—	—	—	—	3.05
Streetball	13–15 × 24–28	1 2	1 2	14–16 × 26–30	—	—	—	—	—	3.05

❶ Football

❷ Rugby (German)

❸ American football, goals 5.50 × 3.05 m

❹ Handball

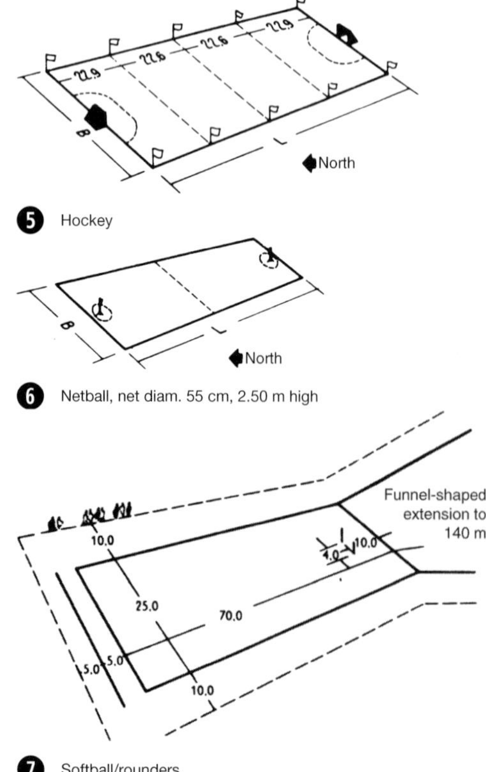

❺ Hockey

❻ Netball, net diam. 55 cm, 2.50 m high

❼ Softball/rounders

❽ Indoor cycle polo

❾ Volleyball

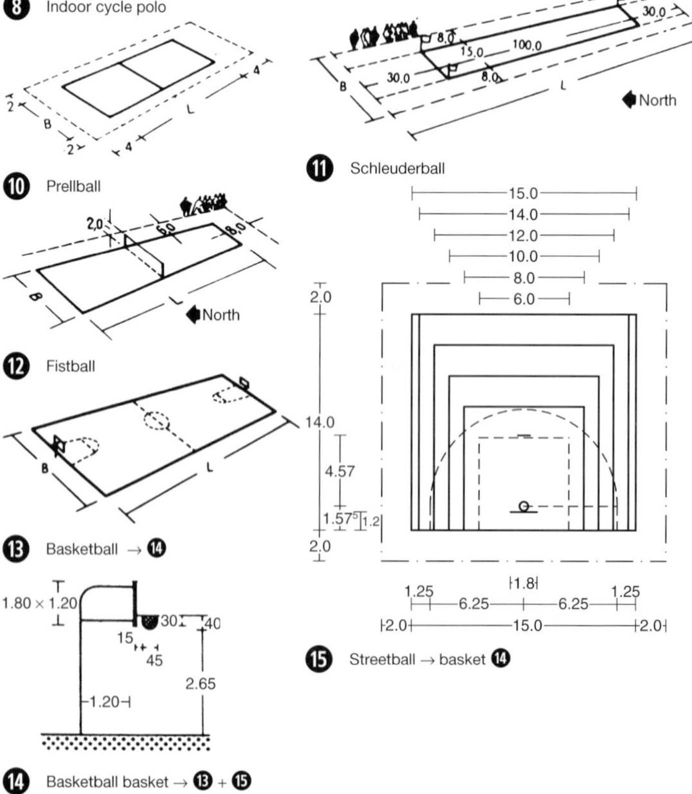

❿ Prellball

⓫ Schleuderball

⓬ Fistball

⓭ Basketball → ⓮

⓮ Basketball basket → ⓭ + ⓯

⓯ Streetball → basket ⓮

Playing area size (m)						
Game	max.		min.		Standard dimensions[1]	
	L	W	L	W	L	W
❶ School football	70	40	40	20	44	22
❷ Indoor football	50	25	40	20	44	22
❸ Indoor handball	—	—	—	—	44	22
❹ Indoor hockey	40	20	36	18	44	22
❺ Indoor netball	60	25	64	27	—	—
❻ Cycle polo on grass	—	—	—	—	60	40
❼ Horseshoe throwing	15	3	12	3	—	—
❽ Croquet	—	—	—	—	20	4
❾ Fencing piste	24	2	13	1.80	—	—
❿ Boccia	—	—	—	—	24	3
⓫ Shuffleboard	—	—	—	—	17	3
⓬ Tennikoit	12.20	5.50	—	—	18.20	11.50
⓭ Baseball	—	—	—	—	18.29	18.29

[1] including safety margin

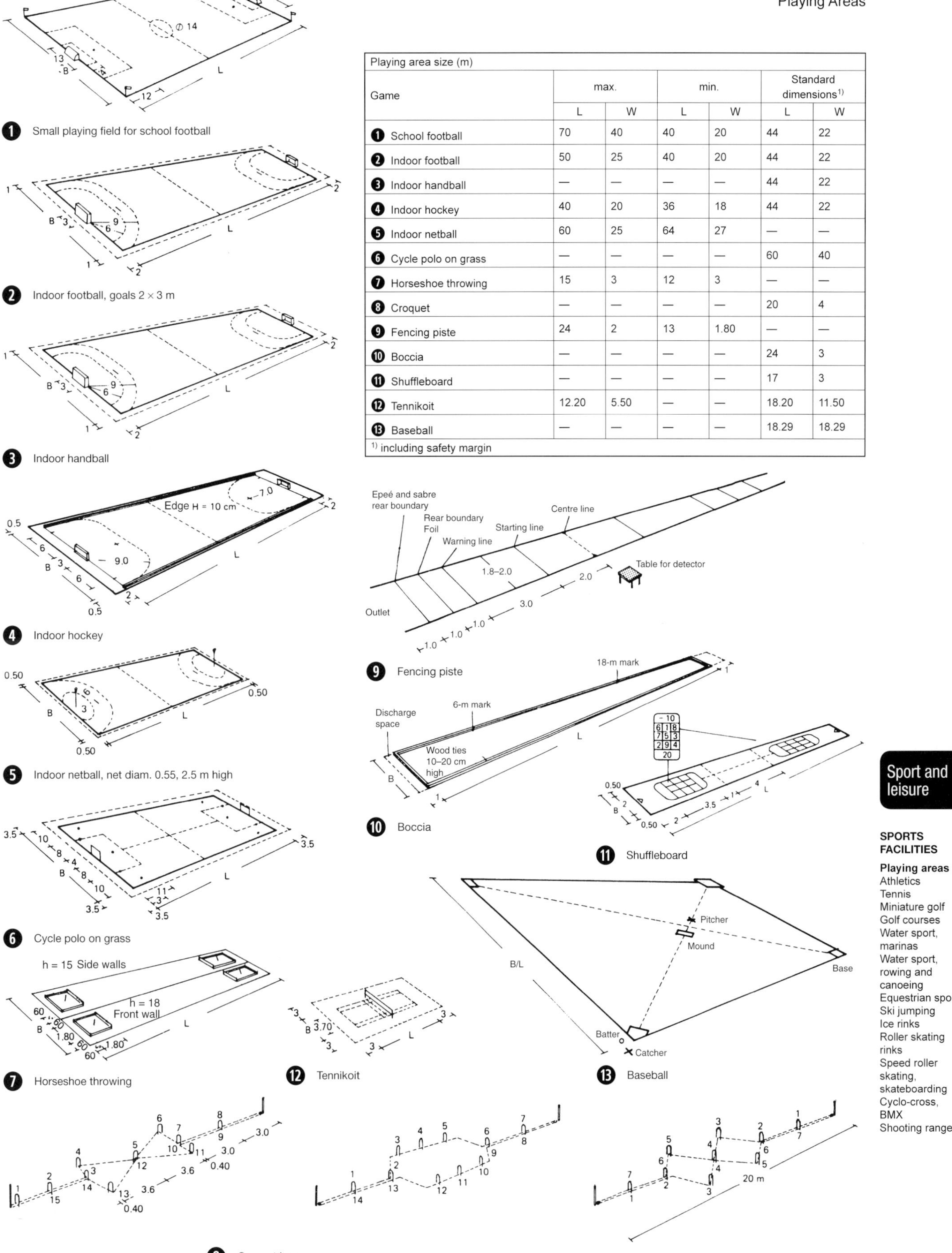

❶ Small playing field for school football

❷ Indoor football, goals 2 × 3 m

❸ Indoor handball

❹ Indoor hockey

❺ Indoor netball, net diam. 0.55, 2.5 m high

❻ Cycle polo on grass

❼ Horseshoe throwing

❾ Fencing piste

❿ Boccia

⓫ Shuffleboard

⓬ Tennikoit

⓭ Baseball

❽ Croquet lawns

Beach sport type	Competitive sport				Leisure sport				Net	Goal/basket	Sports hall
	Size of playing area (m)	Free space around sides (m)	Free space around ends (m)	Total area (m)	Size of playing area (m)	Free space around sides (m)	Free space around ends (m)	Total area (m)	Height (m)	W = width H = height (C) = competition (m)	Clear height (m)
Volleyball	18.00 × 9.00	5.00	5.00	28.00 × 19.00	18.00 × 9.00	3.00	3.50	25.00 × 1500	2.24 F 2.43 M	—	reg >5.50 nat >7.00 int >12.50
Football ('professional')	36.00 × 28.00	1.00	2.00	40.00 × 30.00	—	—	—	—	—	W=7.32 (C) H=2.44 (C)	—
('amateur')	31.00 × 25.00	1.00	2.00	35.00 × 27.00	—	—	—	—	—	W=5.00 (C) H=2.00 (C)	—
	—	—	—	—	27.00 × 12.00	1.50	1.50	30.00 × 15.00		W=3.00 H=2.00	—
Football tennis	—	—	—	—	18.00× 9.00	1.00	2.00	22.00 × 11.00	1.30	—	—
Sepak takraw	18.00 × 9.00	2.00	2.00	22.00 × 13.00	12.00 × 6.00	2.00	2.00	16.00 × 10.00	1.10	—	—
Handball	27.00 × 12.00	3.00	3.00	33.00 × 18.00	27.00 × 12.00	1.50	1.50	30.00 × 15.00	—	W=3.00 H=2.00	—
Badminton	13.40 × 6.10	2.00	2.00	17.40 × 10.10	13.40 × 6.10	1.50 exceptionally 0.30	2.00 exceptionally 1.30	16.40 × 10.10	1.55	—	reg >7.00 nat >7.00 int >9.00
Beachminton	12.30 × 3.80	0.45 0.70	1.00 1.50	14.30 × 4.70 15.30 × 5.20	12.80 × 3.80	0.30	0.35	13.00 4.40	1.28	—	reg >5.20 nat >6.50 Int >9.00
Basketball	12.00 (basket spacing)	—	—	—	15.00 × 8.00	1.00	—	15.00 × 10.00	—	12.00 (basket spacing)	—
Tennis (single court)	18.00 × 9.00 18.00 × 6.00	3.00 3.00	3.00 3.00	24.00 × 15.00 24.00 × 12.00	18.00 × 9.00 18.00 × 6.00	300 300	3.00 3.00	24.00 × 15.00 24.00 × 12.00	1.50 1.50	—	reg >7.00[1] nat >9.00 int >9.00
TAMbeach (single court)	24.00 × 11.00 24.00 × 7.50	1.00 1.00	2.00 2.00	28.00 × 13.00 28.00 × 9.50	18.00 × 9.00 18.00 × 6.00	1.00 1.00	2.00 2.00	22.00 × 11.00 22.00 × 8.00	2.10 to 2.15	—	—

[1] Regional leisure sport can take place from a hall height of 5.50 m

7 Dimensions of beach playing areas

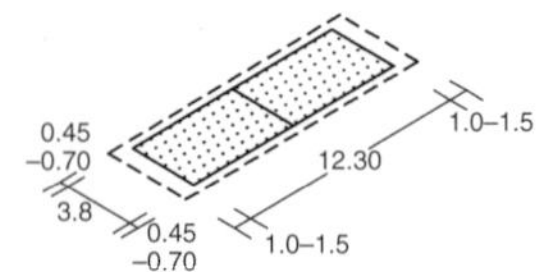

1 Beachminton

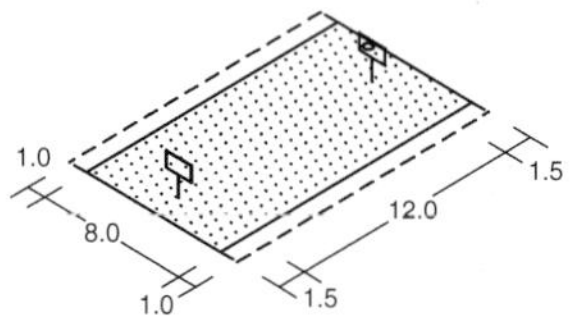

2 Beach basketball

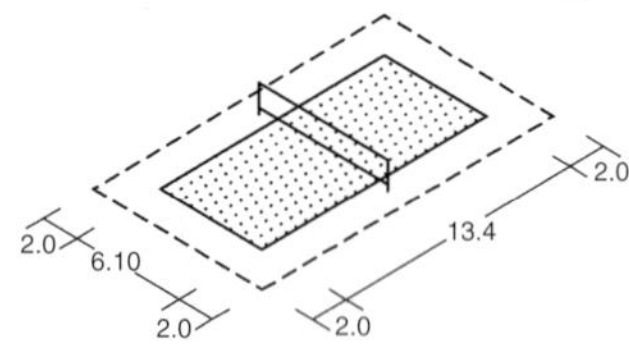

3 Beach badminton (competitive)

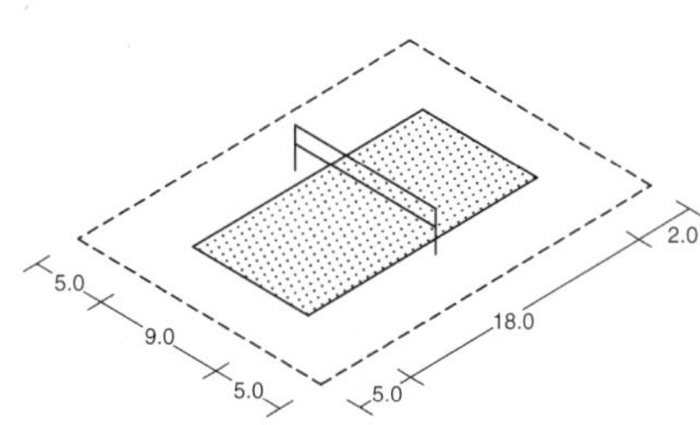

4 Beach volleyball (competitive)

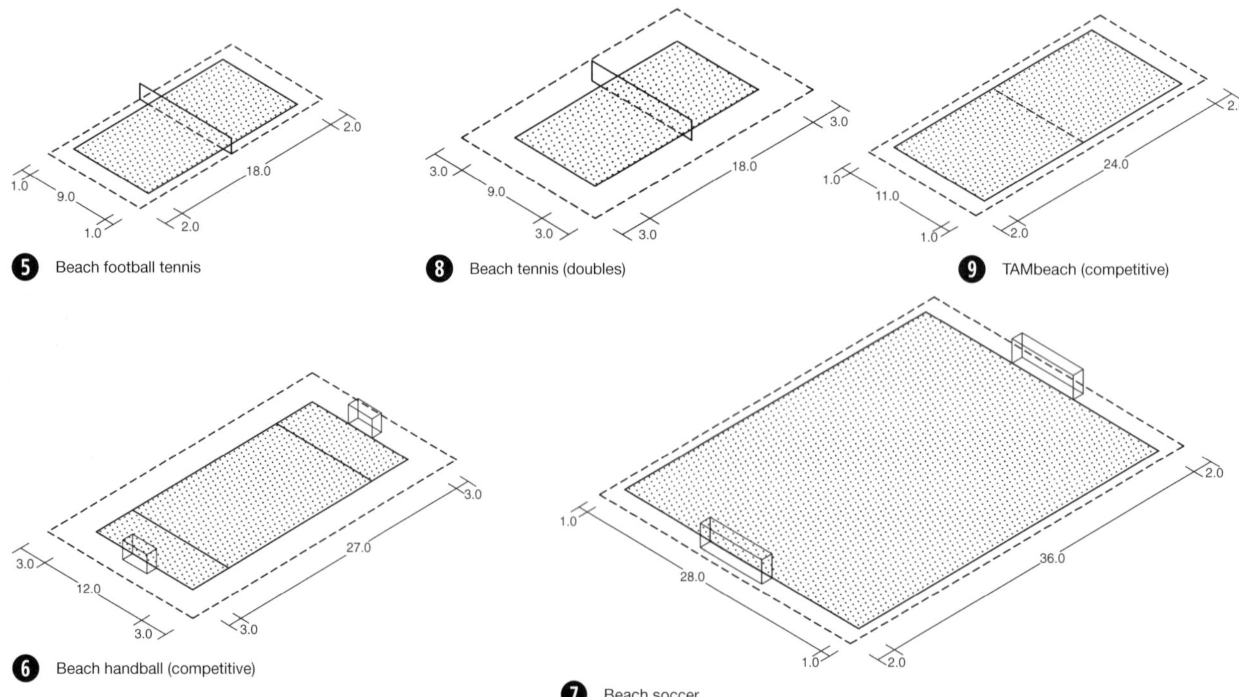

5 Beach football tennis

8 Beach tennis (doubles)

9 TAMbeach (competitive)

6 Beach handball (competitive)

7 Beach soccer

1 playing field
2 running track
3 high jump
4 pole vault
5 long and triple jump
6 shot put
7 discus and hammer
8 javelin
9 water jump

❶ Track and field, arena type A

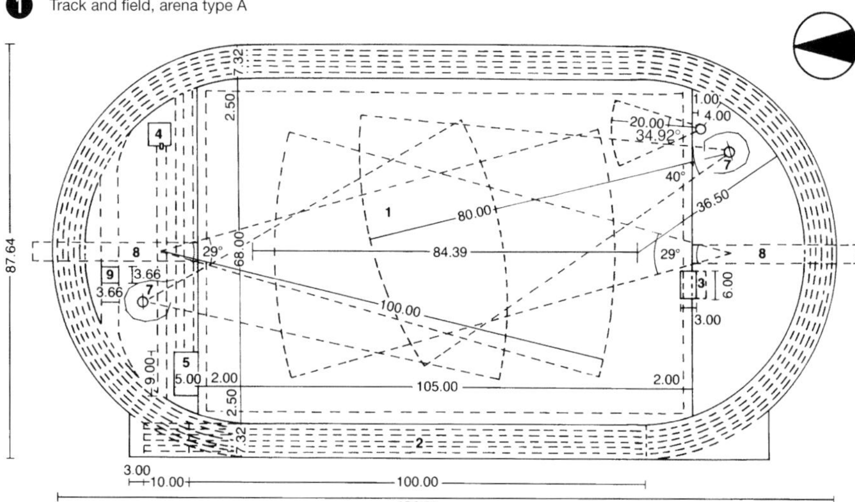

❷ Track and field, arena type B

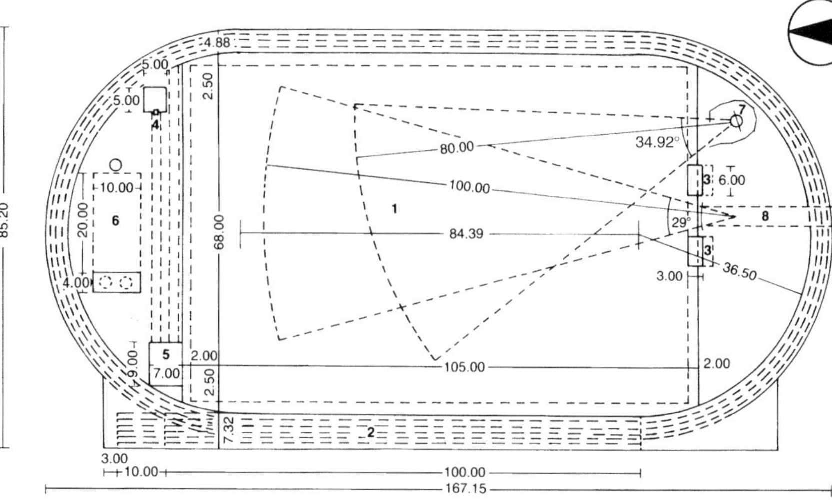

❸ Track and field, arena type C

Track and field, arena type A

This consists of an eight-lane perimeter track and large inner field; shot put, discus/hammer throwing, high jump and javelin in southern segment; shot put, discus/hammer throwing, javelin and water jump for obstacle race in northern segment; pole vault pit with run-up from both sides on eastern side outside perimeter track; long jump and triple jump pit with two run-ups on western side outside perimeter track.

Track and field, arena type B

This consists of a six-lane perimeter track and large inner field; shot put, discus/hammer throwing, high jump and javelin in southern segment; pole vault, javelin, discus/hammer throwing, long jump with three run-ups and water jump for obstacle race in northern segment; pole vault, long jump and triple jump pits can also be arranged outside perimeter track.

Track and field, arena type C

This consists of four-lane perimeter track and large inner field; discus/hammer throwing, high jump and javelin in southern segment; pole vault, discus/hammer throwing, long jump and triple jump pits with three run-ups and shot putting in northern segment.

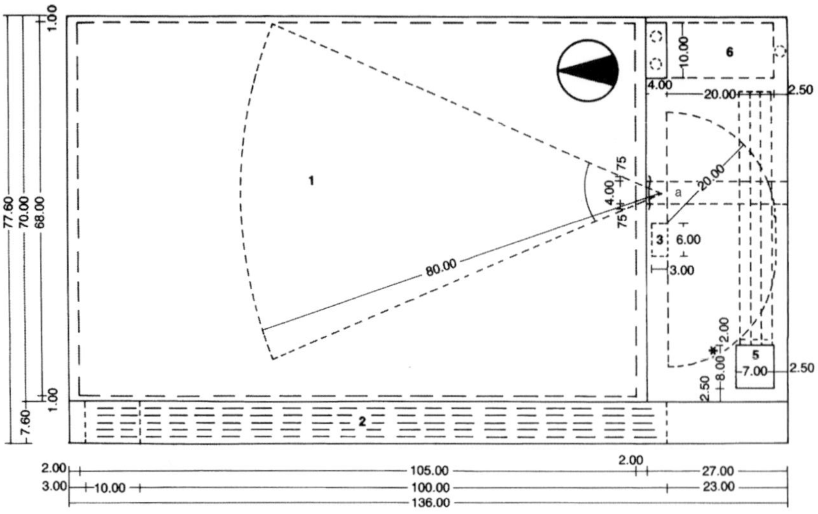

Track and field, arena type D consists of facilities for the following events → ❶:

4–6 single lanes for straight sprints and straight hurdles

1 playing field 68 × 105 m (70 × 109 m including safety zones)

1 shot put practice area, throwing southwards

1 triple facility for long jump, triple jump; run-up to the west

1 high jump area; run-up northwards

1 shot put ring; throwing direction northwards

1 softball throwing area; throwing direction northwards

1 small playing field 27 × 45 m (including safety zones)

The running track in type D is normally clay paved, but synthetic paving is recommended for very heavy use.

A **combined large field** includes a large playing field, with areas for track and field events next to and on the field. It consists of the following areas: → ❷

1 playing field 68 × 105 m (70 × 109 m with safety zones)

1 high jump area; run-up northwards over the field

1 shot put practice area; throwing direction eastwards

1 shot put ring; throwing direction westwards

For practice in throwing disciplines, the provision of a run-up or throwing field is recommended for safety reasons. This consists of a grass area for landing about the size of a large field and a run-up or throwing area for javelin, discus and hammer on the southern short side → ❸.

❶ Track and field, arena type D

* 9.00 m for competitions (take-off board offset 1.00 m)
8.00 m for training (take-off board offset 2.00 m – see also the following page)

1 playing field
2 running track
3 high jump
4 pole vault
5 long jump
6 shot put
7 discus and hammer
8 javelin and ball throwing

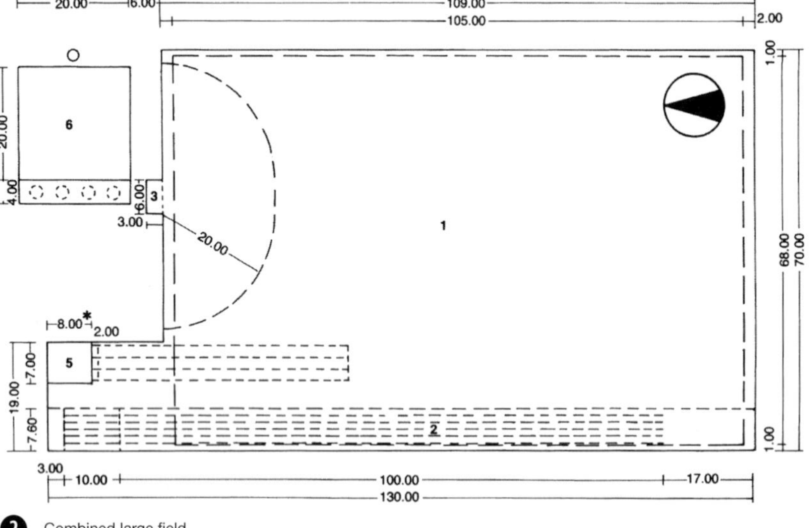

❷ Combined large field

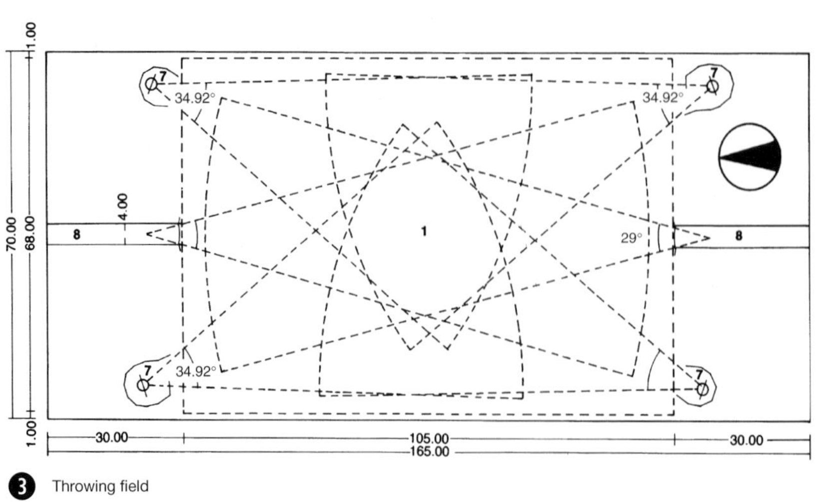

❸ Throwing field

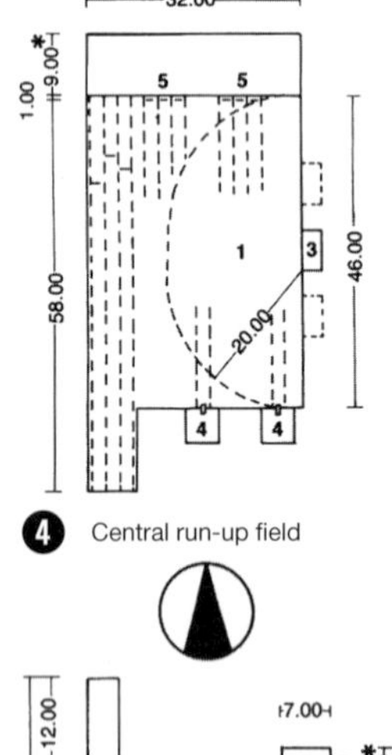

❹ Central run-up field

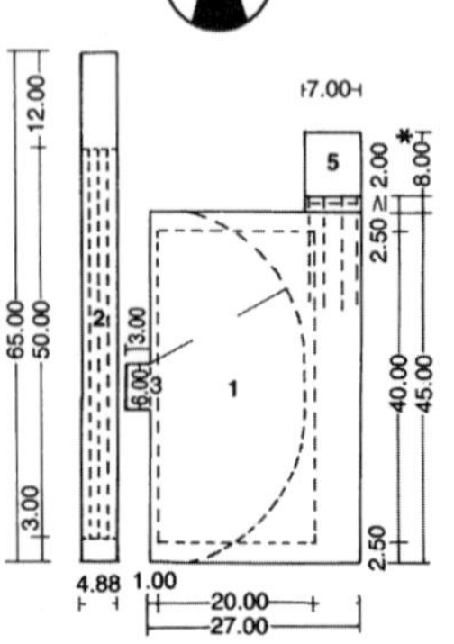

❺ Combined small field

Plan

❶ Long jump and triple jump layout

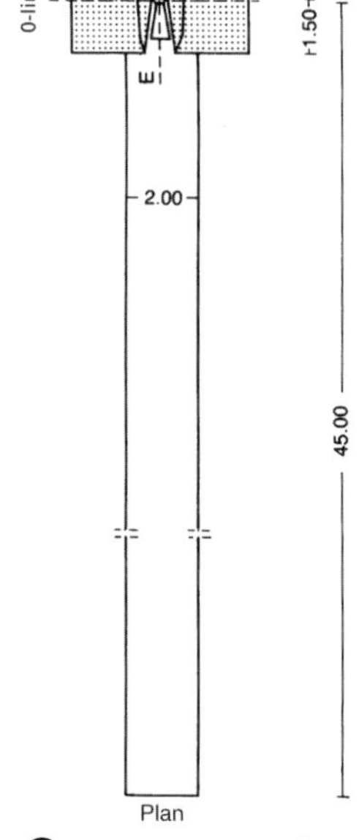

❷ Pole vault layout → ❺

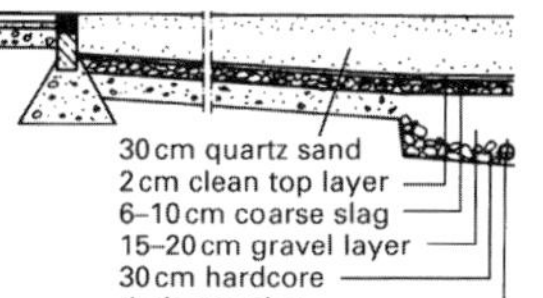

section through long jump pit

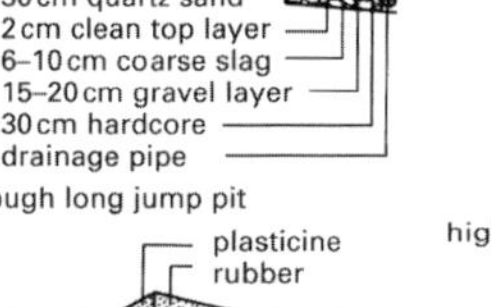

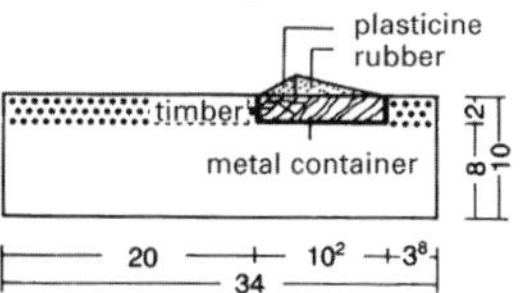

section through take-off board

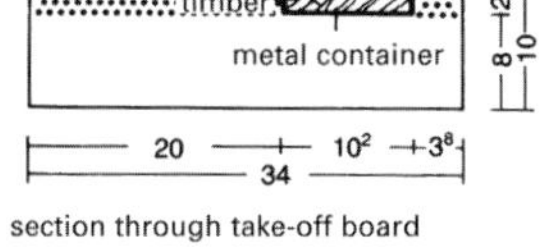

❸ Long jump and triple jump details

high jump: plan

direction of run-up

mat

timber underframe

section A–B through mat and mat-frame

❹ High jump layout and details

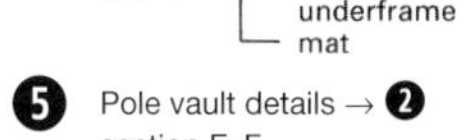

❺ Pole vault details → ❷ section E–F

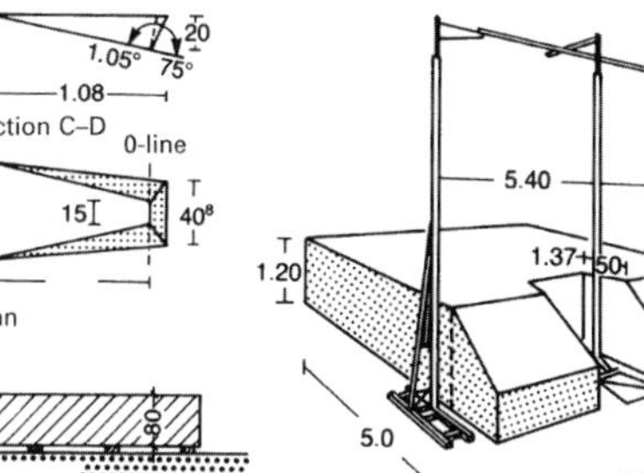

❻ Sprung stand and landing pad for pole vault → ❷

Area for:	Run-up length (m)	Width (m)	Pit (P) or landing pad (L)	Length (m)	Width (m)
long jump	≧45[1]	1.22[2]	P	≧8	2.75
triple jump	≧45[3]	1.22[2]	P	≧8	2.75
pole vault	≧45	1.22	LP	≧5	5.00
high jump	semicircle r ≧2.00		L	3	5–6

[1] the take-off board is min. 1 m in front of the pit, because the distance between the take-off line and the end of the landing area must be at least 10 m. For high-standard layouts, the landing area is 9 m long.
[2] for multiple layouts, the width of each lane is 2 m.
[3] the take-off board is 11 m in front of the landing area (for juniors 9 m, for top athletes 13 m).

❼ Dimensions for jumping sports → ❶ – ❷

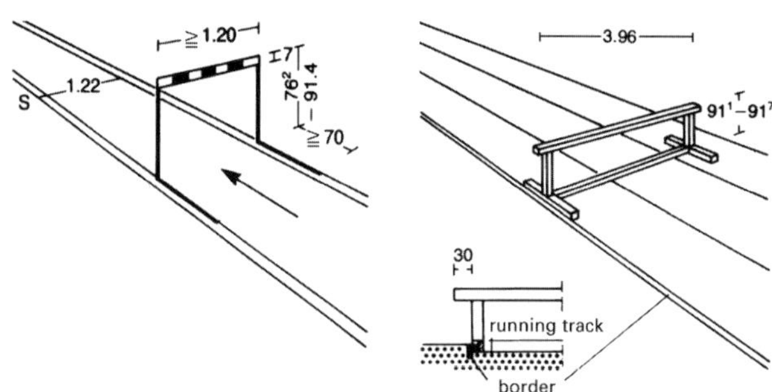

❽ Hurdle with counterweight ❾ Hurdle

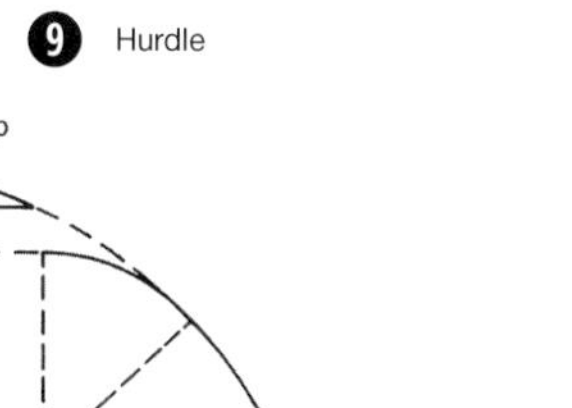

❿ Obstacle race with 16 m radius and water trough

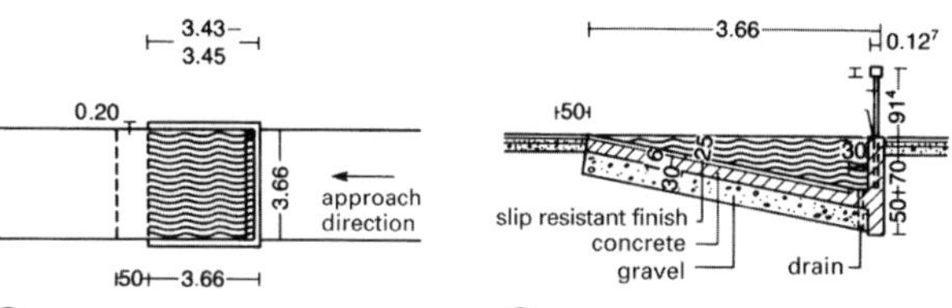

⓫ Water jump ⓬ Steeplechase water jump

Type of track	Length of start (m)	Track	Run-out	Width of each lane[1]
sprint	3	110[2]	17	1.22
circular	—[3]	400	17	1.22

[1] the circular track needs an additional 28 cm safety zone, which does not have to be constructed as a track
[2] the length of 110 m results from the 110 m hurdles; for other sprint events the distance is 100 m
[3] no additional starting space necessary

⓭ Track dimensions → ❽

Track length (m)	Class	No. hurdles	Height of hurdles (m)	Distance to first hurdle (m)	Spacing of hurdles (m)	Distance after last (m)
400	Men and men, junior A + B	10	0.914	45.00	35.00	40.00
400	Women and women, junior A	10	0.762	45.00	35.00	40.00
110	Men	10	1.067	13.72	9.14	14.02
110	Men, junior A	10	0.996	13.72	8.90	16.18
110	Men, junior B	10	0.914	13.50	8.60	19.10
100	Women and women, junior A	10	0.840	13.00	8.50	10.50
100	Women, junior B (from 1984)	10	0.762	13.00	8.50	10.50
100	Women, junior B (from 1983)	10	0.840	12.00	8.00	16.00
80	Schoolboys A	8	0.840	12.00	8.00	12.00
80	Schoolgirls A	8	0.762	12.00	8.00	12.00
60	Schoolboys and schoolgirls B	6	0.762	11.50	7.50	11.00

Note: a tolerance of ± 3 mm is allowed in the standard height

⓮ Hurdle tracks → ❽

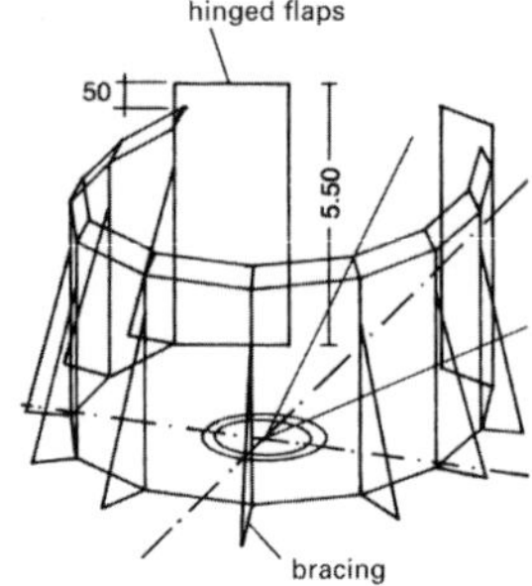

❶ Side view of combined hammer throwing circle and cage → ❷

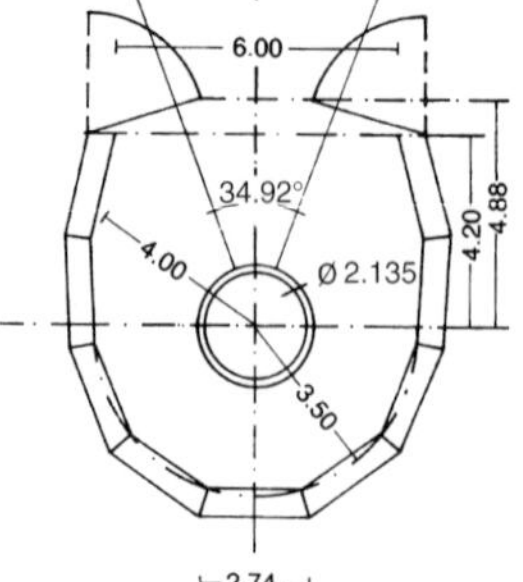

❷ Plan of hammer throwing circle and cage

❸ Plan of discus throwing circle and cage

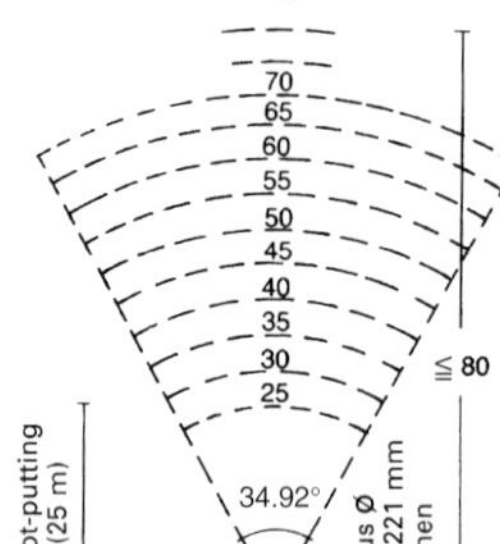

❹ Discus throwing area; discus ≧219 mm ≦221 mm (men)

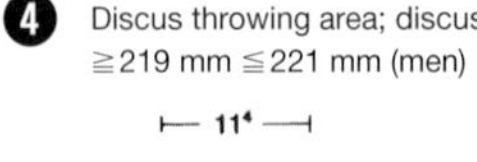

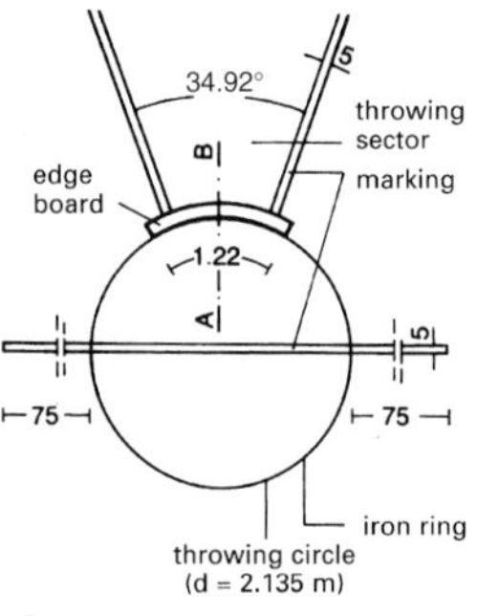

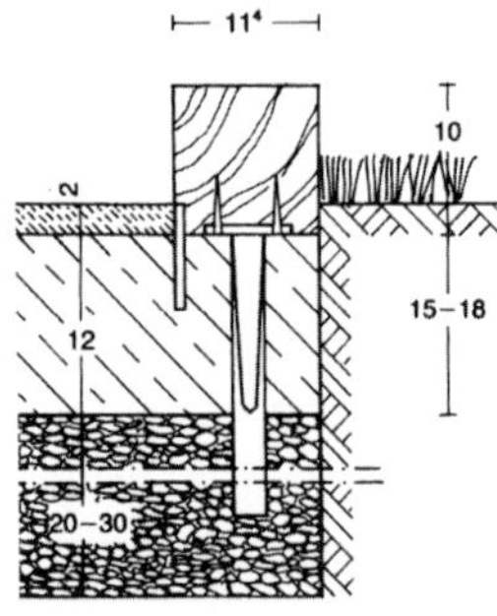

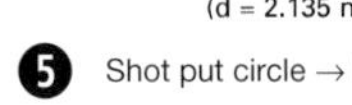

❺ Shot put circle → ❻

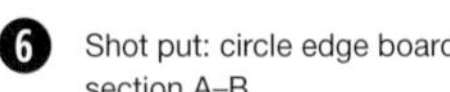

❻ Shot put: circle edge board, section A–B

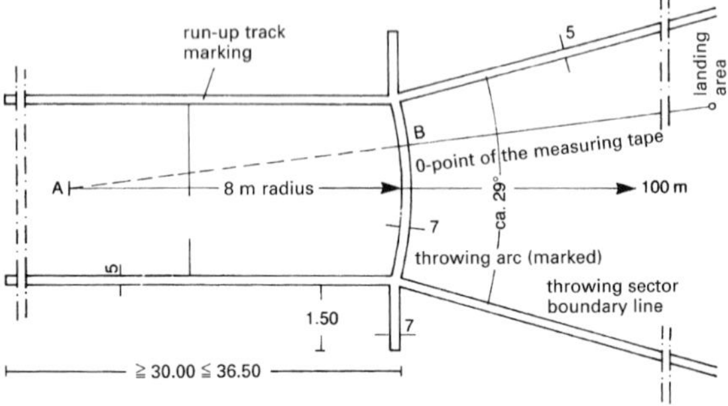

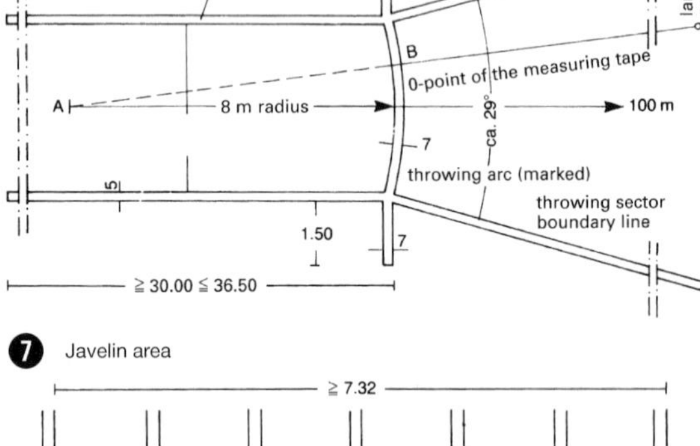

❼ Javelin area

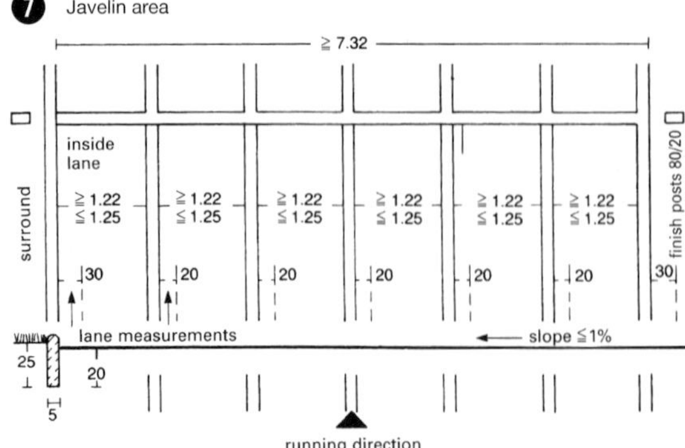

❽ Track dimensions, track and field type B

The dimensions given in → ❾ are in line with the competition rules and must be observed. Deviations are possible for school sport, training and leisure sport.

Hammer throwing equipment is laid out similarly to discus equipment → ❶ – ❹, except the throwing circle has only ≧2.135 m safety cage → ❶ – ❷ for competitive facilities; otherwise, the more simply constructed safety cage, as for the discus, can be used → ❸.

Javelin facilities consist of a run-up track and a throwing sector. The width of the run-up track is 4 m, length is normally 36.5 m, but min. 30 m. The run-up track is divided from the throwing sector by a permanently marked curved throwing line.

Shot put facilities consists of a ring and a landing sector → ❺ – ❻. The normal length of shot put facilities is 20 m, for top-level sport 25 m.

The following design examples I–V for the allocation of the usable space (4 m²/inhabitant) in various catchment areas should be seen only as an orientation aid.

Example I: Sport facilities for a catchment of approx. 5000 inhabitants

1 track and field arena, type D	10,554 m²
2 small playing fields 27 × 45 m	2430 m²
1 training playing field	4500 m²
2 leisure playing fields	250 m²
1 grass play and gymnastics area	1000 m²
1 fitness area	1400 m²
total usable area	approx. 20,000 m²

Example II: approx. 7000 inhabitants

1 track and field arena, type D	10,554 m²
1 large playing field 70 × 109 m	7630 m²
2 small playing fields 27 × 45 m	2430 m²
leisure play area	3000 m²
1 grass play and gymnastics area	1000 m²
1 fitness track	2300 m²
1 roller skating track	800 m²
total usable area	approx. 28,000 m²

Example III: 7000 inhabitants

1 track and field arena, type B	14,000 m²
1 large playing field 70 × 109 m	7630 m²
3 small playing fields 27 × 45 m	3645 m²
1 grass play and gymnastics area	1000 m²
1 fitness area	1400 m²
total usable area	approx. 28,000 m²

Example IV: approx. 15,000 inhabitants

1 track and field arena, type B	14,000 m²
3 large playing fields 70 × 109 m	22,890 m²
7 small playing fields 27 × 45 m	8505 m²
leisure play area	6000 m²
1 fitness track	3300 m²
1 fitness area	1400 m²
1 fitness playing area	1000 m²
2 grass play and gymnastics areas	2000 m²
total usable area	approx. 60,000 m²

Example V: approx. 20,000 inhabitants

1 track and field arena, type B	14,000 m²
1 combined large playing field	8400 m²
4 large playing fields 70 × 109 m	30,520 m²
10 small playing fields 27 × 45 m	12,150 m²
leisure play area	6000 m²
1 fitness track	3300 m²
1 fitness area	1400 m²
1 fitness play area	1000 m²
2 grass play and gymnastics areas	2000 m²
total usable area	approx. 80,000 m²

Area for sport	Throwing area (m)	Landing sector	
		Angle	Length (m)
Discus	Circle diam. = 2.50[1]	34.92°	80
Hammer	Circle diam. = 2.13	34.92°	80
Javelin	Run-up length = 36.50[2]		
	Run-up width = 4	approx. 29°	100
Shot put	Circle diam. = 2.13	34.92°	up to 25

[1] also suitable for hammer throwing with insertion of profiled ring

[2] ≧ 30 m

❾ Dimensions of throwing areas

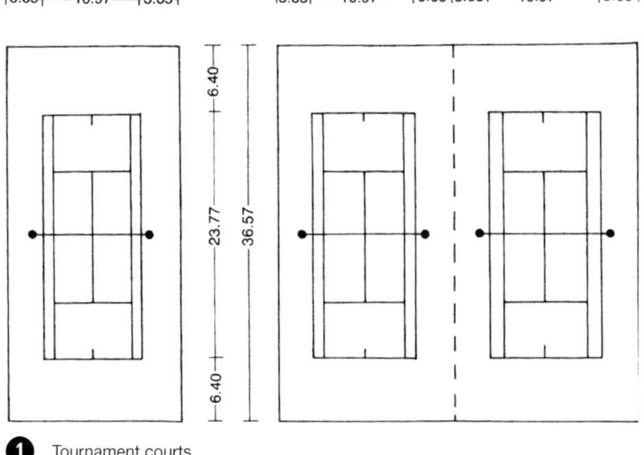

❶ Tournament courts

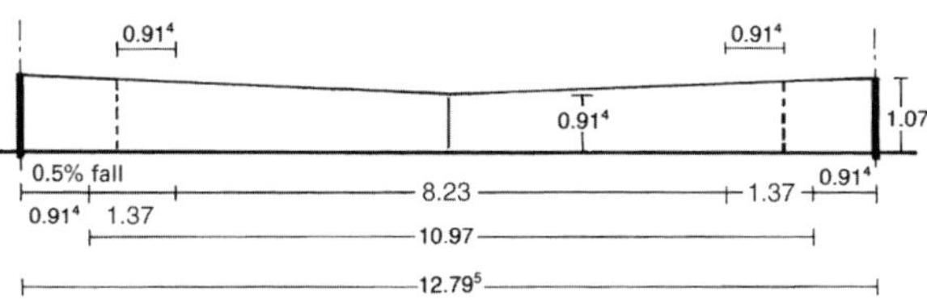

❷ The net

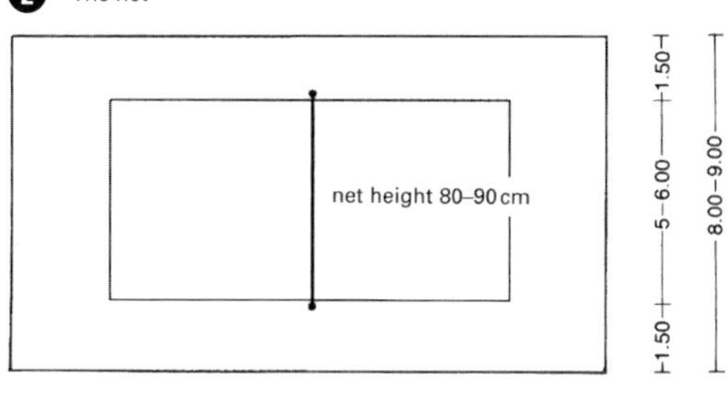

❸ Children's tennis court

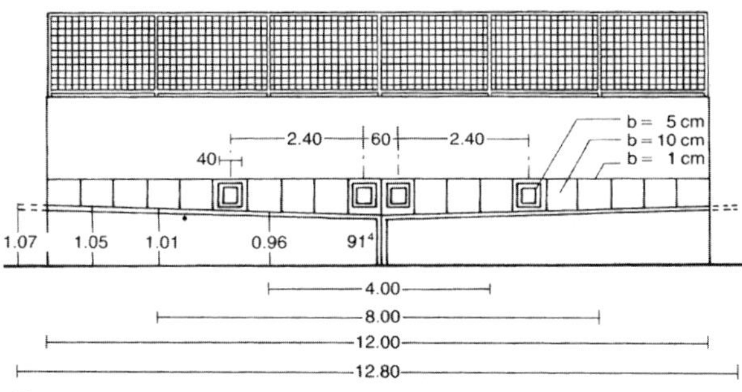

❹ Wall marking (for serves, passing shots etc.)

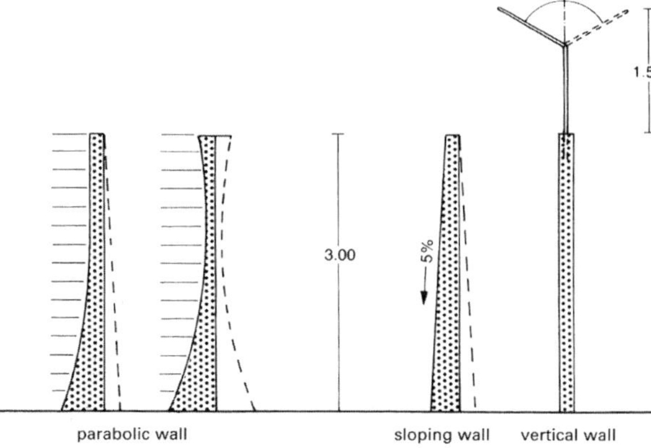

❺ Types of tennis wall

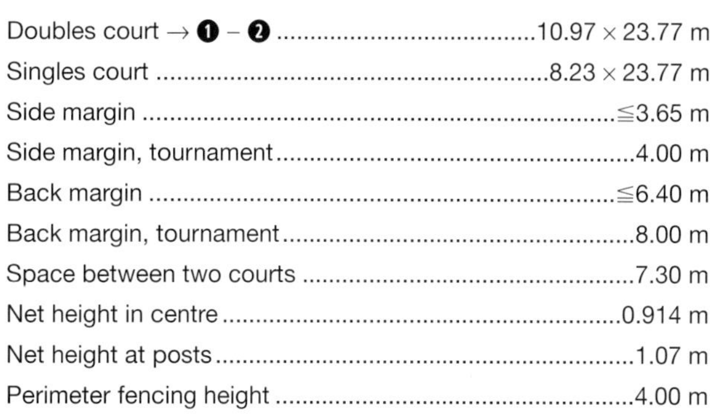

Doubles court → ❶ – ❷ ....10.97 × 23.77 m
Singles court ....8.23 × 23.77 m
Side margin ....≦3.65 m
Side margin, tournament..4.00 m
Back margin ....≦6.40 m
Back margin, tournament..8.00 m
Space between two courts ....7.30 m
Net height in centre ....0.914 m
Net height at posts ....1.07 m
Perimeter fencing height ....4.00 m
Fencing: 2.5 mm thick wire mesh with 4 cm mesh size.

Number of courts required:
Currently the number of active tennis players is 1.6–3% of the total population. Ratio of courts to players for new courts is 1:30; formula to determine the approximate number of courts required:

$$\text{no. courts required (T)} = \frac{\text{population} \times 3}{100 \times 30}$$

Area required for children's court → ❸.

Parking places: normal tennis playing (without spectators), four vehicle parking places per court.

Plot size: net area ('usable sport area') is identical to the tennis court and the areas required for the practice wall and the children's court. Experience shows a 60–80% supplement to the net area gives the plot size. The location of the courts should be in the N–S direction if possible.

Deviations are possible (W is better than E). More than two courts next to each other is not recommended, behind each other only with visual separation. Artificial lighting at 10 m height is needed at the long sides.

The production of the space allocation plan should include later requirements for flats (caretaker, trainer, tenant) and garages from the start. The project should be designed so that building can proceed in stages without disturbing the tennis.

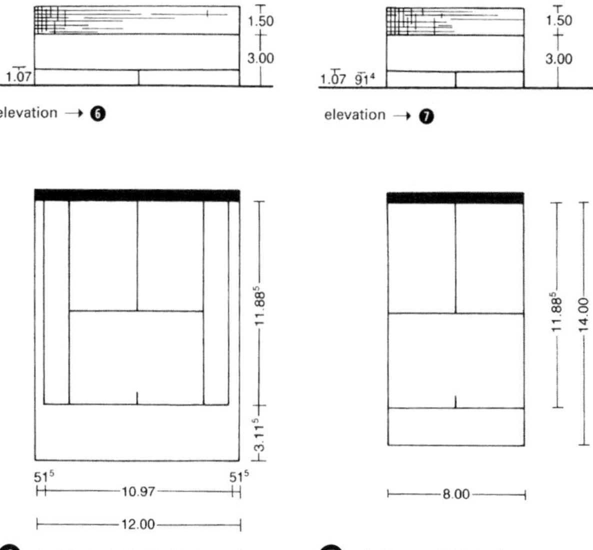

❻ Training wall (doubles): shown above are recommended dimensions for tennis walls + playing area in front of wall

❼ Training wall (singles)

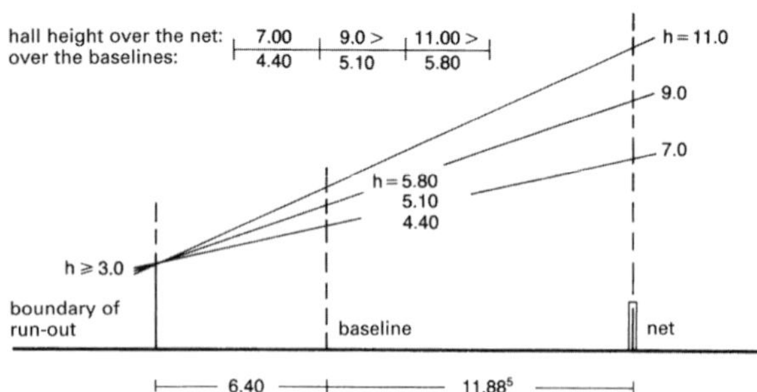

❶ Hall heights

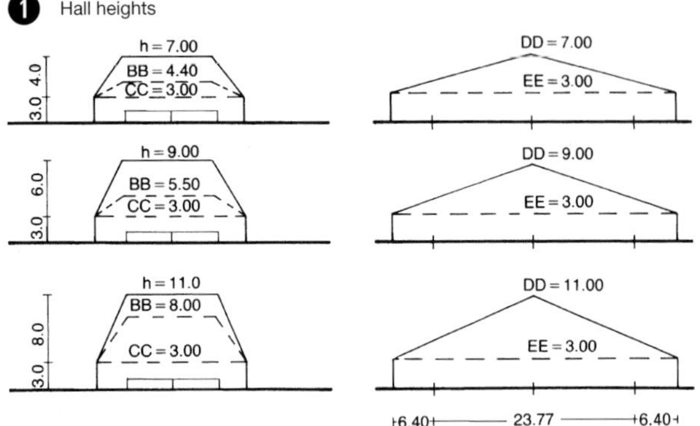

❷ Cross- and longitudinal sections of hall types hipped on the long sides → ❸

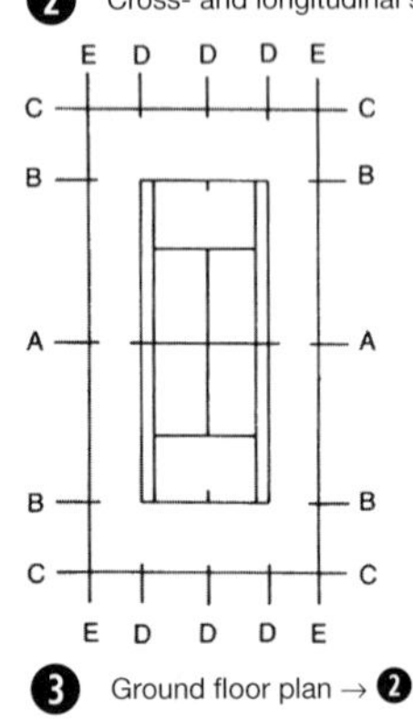

❸ Ground floor plan → ❷

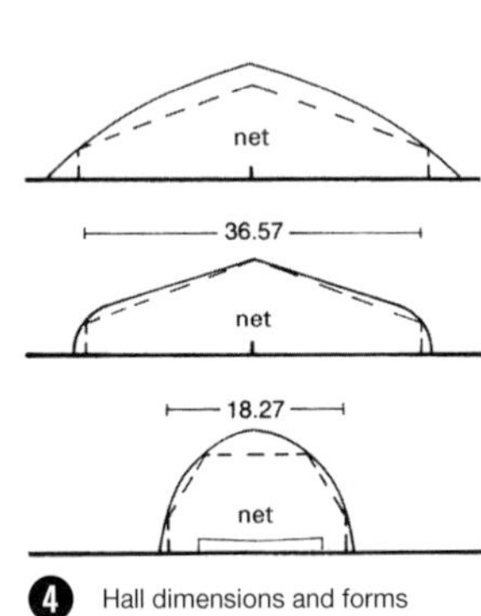

❹ Hall dimensions and forms

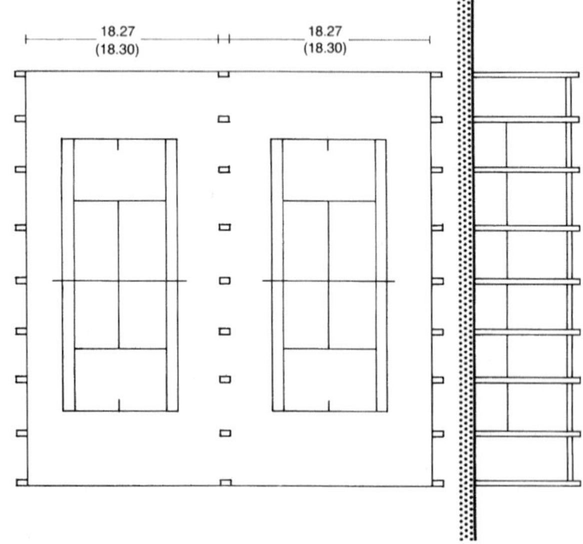

❺ Permanent hall over one or more courts

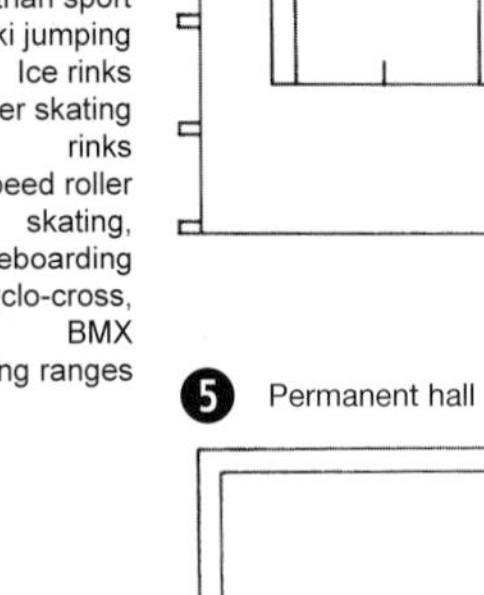

cross-section → ❺

Ceiling heights for indoor tennis halls are fixed internationally. Davis Cup rules require a height of 10.67 m; recommended height 9–11 m, although 9 m will normally suffice → ❶. Tennis is also possible in gymnastics and sports halls with 7 m height. The hall height is measured from the floor, at the net, to the underside of the roof truss, and must be the same over the entire 10.97 m width of the court. The height is min. 3 m at the outer edge of the playing area. Types of halls: demountable hall, permanent hall, convertible hall. Hall internal dimensions 18.30 × 36.60 m → ❻. Because the size of the courts and the prescribed areas of the court outside the markings are fixed internationally, this gives:

tennis hall with 2 courts $\frac{\text{Te H 2}}{\text{(S + D)}}$ singles + doubles

$(2 \times 18.30) \times (1 \times 36.60) = 36.60 \times 36.60$

with 3 courts $\frac{\text{Te H 3}}{\text{(S + D)}}$

which gives analogously a hall area of 54.90 × 36.60 m. These dimensions are the ideal for sporting flexibility. If 'economical tennis halls' are planned, this makes a reduction of the built area possible but will restrict the use.

The uses are:

1. both courts suitable for singles competition
2. one court suitable for doubles competition
3. practice or leisure play on both courts, 2 singles games or 1 singles and 1 doubles.

Considering the possible savings, this gives the following hall size:

$\frac{\text{Te H 2}}{\text{1 S + 1 D}}$ 32.40 × 36.60m

The following table shows some of the possible options:

Hall type	Courts	Singles (S)	Doubles (D)	Width	Length	Use C*	No use C*
1	1	1	1	18.30	36.60	S/D	—
2	2	2	2	36.60	36.60	2 S/2D	
2 practice	2	2	2	33.90	36.60	2 S/1 S/1 D	2 D or 2 S
3	3	3	3	54.90	36.60	3 S/3D	—
3 practice	3	3	3	49.50	36.60	3 S/2D	3 D or 3 S
2a	2	1	1	33.90	36.60	1 S/1 D	—
2a practice	2	1	1	32.40	36.60	1 S/1 D	—

* = suitable for competition

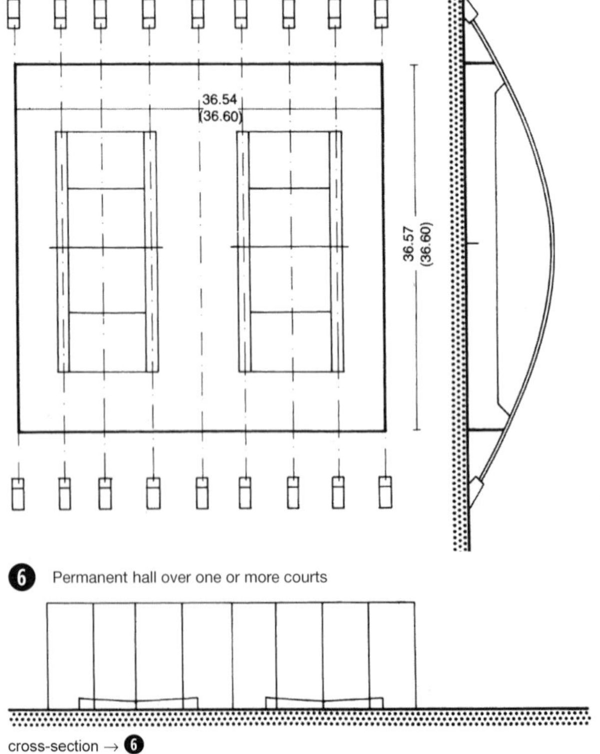

❻ Permanent hall over one or more courts

cross-section → ❻

A miniature golf course consists of 18 clearly separated lanes (exception: driving shots), which are numbered and must correspond to the standard regulations of their system. Lanes suitable for competitions have the following features:

- actual playing area
- lane demarcations (mostly strips)
- tee marking
- one or more obstacles (can be omitted)
- borderline (can be omitted)
- set-down markings (can be omitted)
- hole

and perhaps further components and/or markings specific to the system.

Playing area size: min. width 80 cm, min. length 5.50 m. Playing areas intended to be level must be completely flat (90 cm spirit level). In case the edges of the playing area are not determined by strips, then they must be marked otherwise (exception: driving shots). The edge strips must be so installed so that they enable a strategy to be implemented. Each lane must have a tee-off marking. The type of marking must be standardised within one course or for a certain lane system. The obstacles must be practical in construction and shape and installed permanently (according to the sporting purpose). The location of obstacles which are not fixed should be marked.

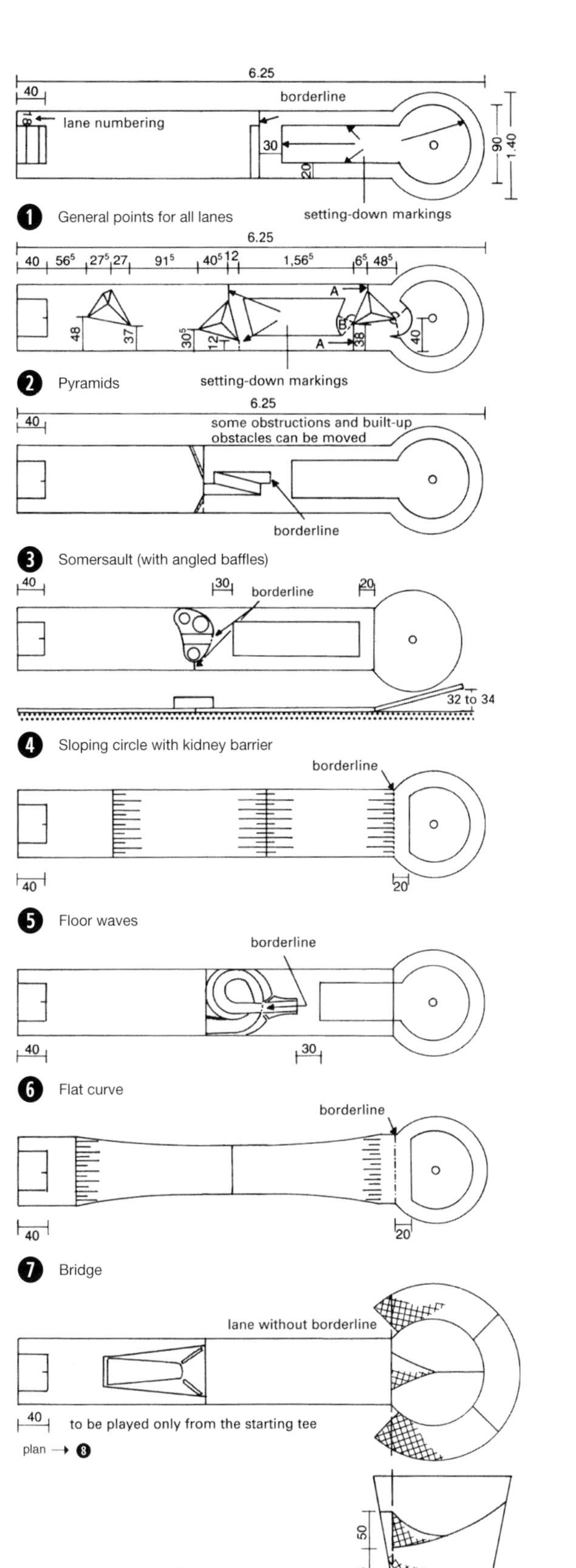

1 General points for all lanes

2 Pyramids

3 Somersault (with angled baffles)

4 Sloping circle with kidney barrier

5 Floor waves

6 Flat curve

7 Bridge

8 Ski jump

9 Rocker with hoop

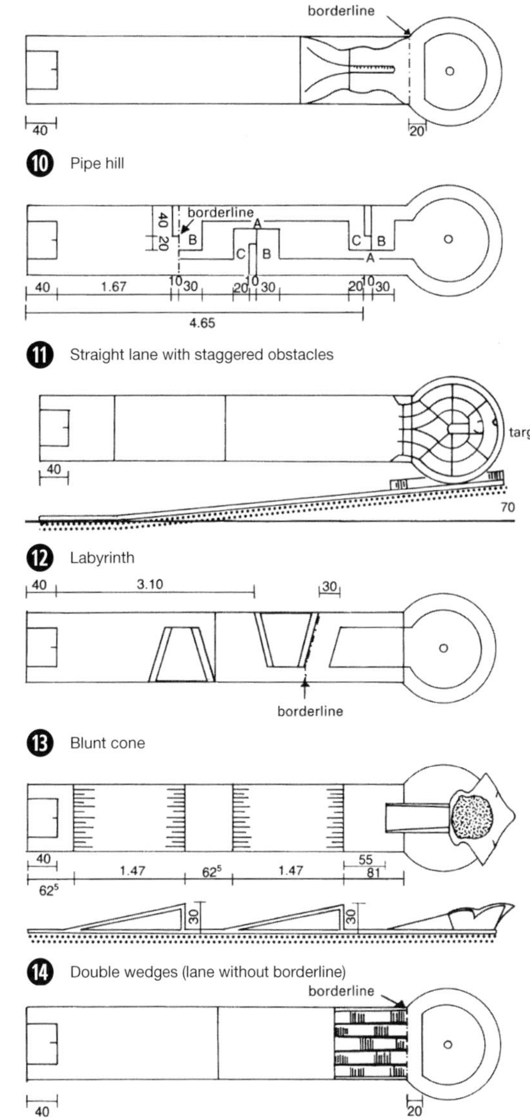

10 Pipe hill

11 Straight lane with staggered obstacles

12 Labyrinth

13 Blunt cone

14 Double wedges (lane without borderline)

15 Irregular passages

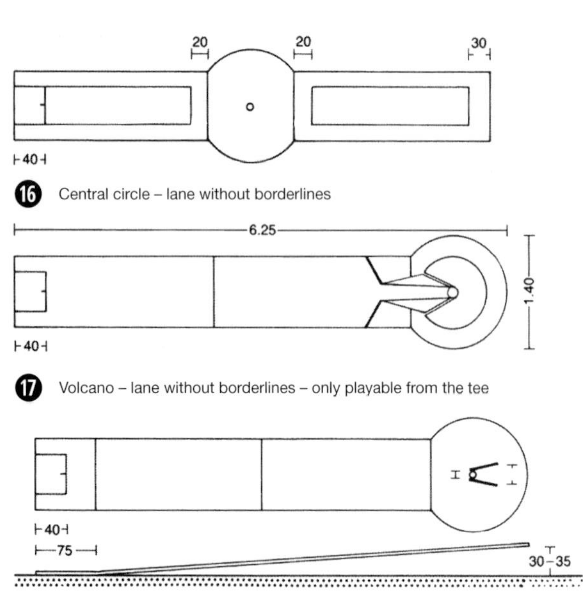

⑯ Central circle – lane without borderlines

⑰ Volcano – lane without borderlines – only playable from the tee

⑱ Steep slope with V-obstacle – lane without borderlines – only playable from the tee

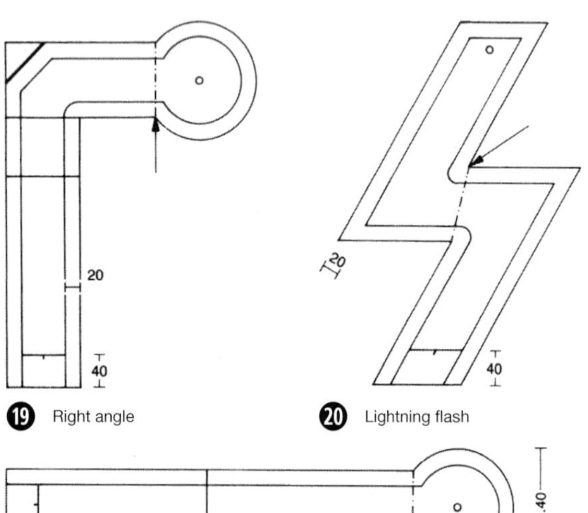

⑲ Right angle

⑳ Lightning flash

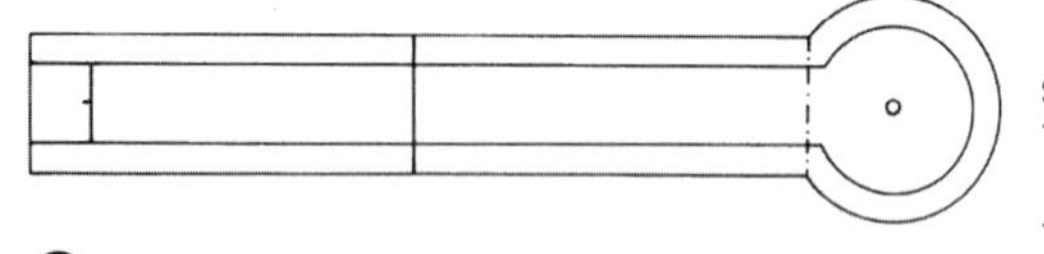

㉑ Straight lane without obstacles

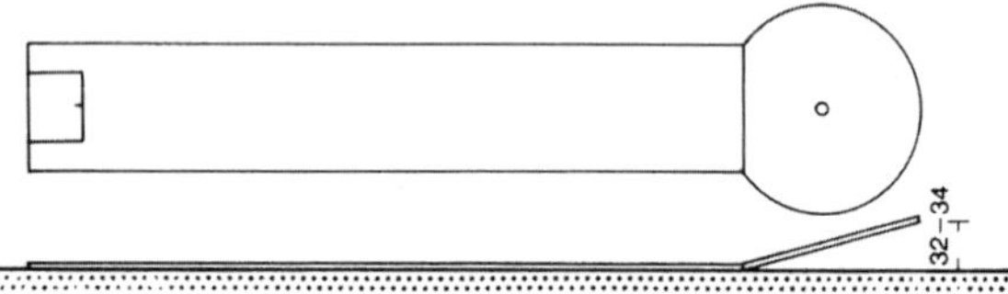

㉒ Sloping circle without obstacles – lane without borderlines – only playable from the tee

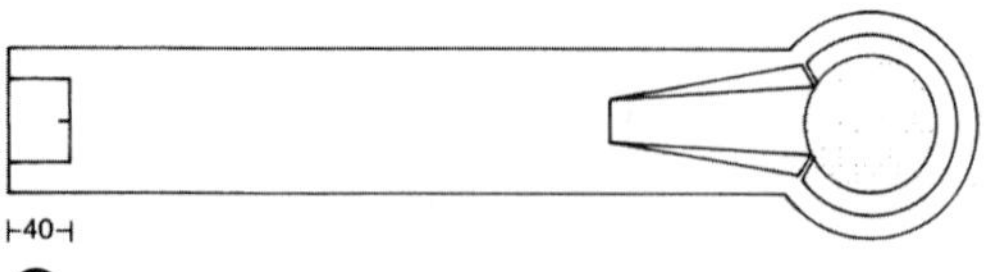

㉓ Circular plateau – lane without borderlines – only playable from the tee

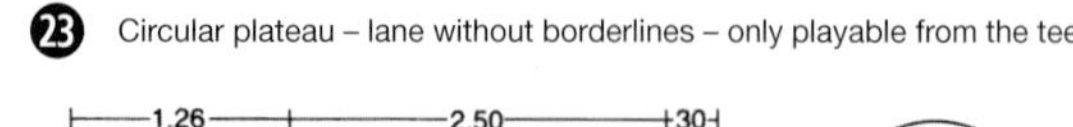

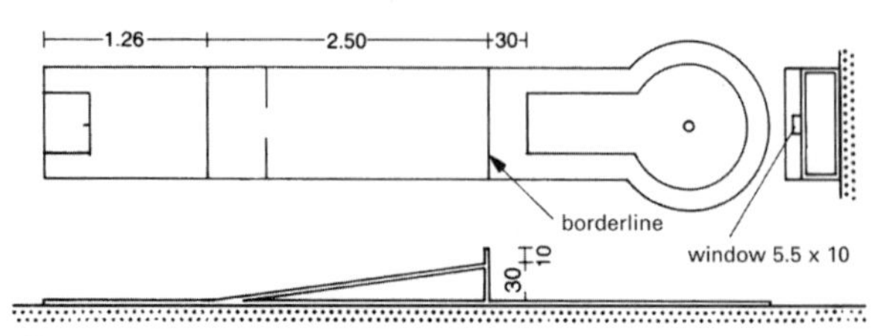

㉔ Run-up ramp with central opening (window)

Each obstacle must be different from all the others on the course, not only externally but in how they are played. A strategy must be possible.

The borderline marks the end of the first obstacles. On lanes without built-in obstacles, it shows the minimum distance the ball has to be hit from the tee in order to remain in the game. If the first obstacle takes up the entire width of the lane, then the borderline is identical with the end of the obstacle. Lanes which can only be played from the tee have no borderline. Borderline markings should be laid out so that the marking edge pointing to the tee is identical with the obstacles.

Set-down markings: when setting down or moving the ball during play is permissible, there must be markings showing where the ball may be set down.

It must be possible to reach the target from the tee marking with one stroke. If these are target holes, then the diameter may not exceed 120 mm. For the systems Minigolf, Miniaturgolf or Sterngolf, 100 mm is the limit.

Markings must be applied to all lanes. The game is played with golf clubs and golf balls. All clubs which are usual in golf, or similar objects, are permissible.

The striking area of the club head may not exceed 40 cm^2. All miniature golf and golf balls are permissible of any material. Ball diameter $\geqq 37$ mm and $\leqq 43$ mm. Balls made of wood, metal, glass, glass fibre, ivory or similar material, and also billiard balls, are not recognised as miniature golf balls.

Miniature golf lanes normally have the following standard sizes:

Lane length 6.25 m, lane width 0.90 m, target circle diameter 1.40 m → p. 329 ❶.

Minigolf:
Developed by the Swiss Bogni at the start of the 1950s; consists of 17 concrete pistes (12 m long) and one long piste (approx. 25 m long). The concrete pistes are surrounded by tubular steel frames. The obstacles are made of natural stone.

Cobigolf:
One of the most difficult lane systems, the ‘little gates’ set in front of the obstacles are a special feature. The course also consists of 18 lanes.These are in large format (12–14 m length) and also in small format (6–7 m).

Sterngolf:
A Sterngolf course consists of 18 lanes; 17 of the concrete pistes have a semi-circular target area and the last has a star as a ‘target circle’. This gives the system its name. The lane length is 8 m, lane width 1 m and end circle diameter 2 m. The lanes are bounded by pipes. The tee is marked by a circle of 30 cm diameter and the hole is 10 cm diameter.

All the obstacles are standardised for all lane golf systems, and selected and constructed according to sporting requirements. Therefore it is possible to hole every lane in one stroke, because every player of miniature golf aims to take as few strokes as possible on every lane.

A score of 18 – every lane holed in one – has often been achieved.

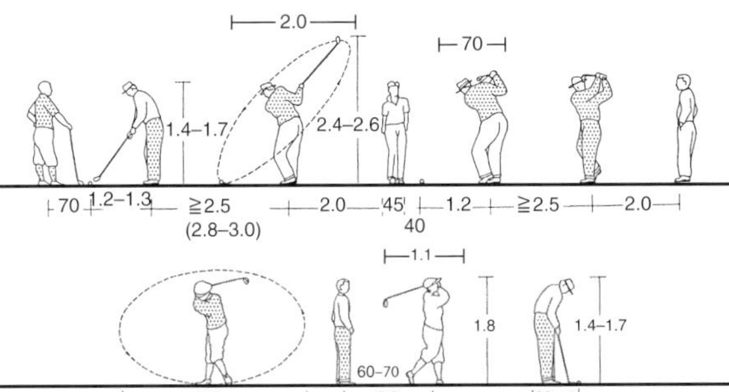

❶ Space requirements for golfers

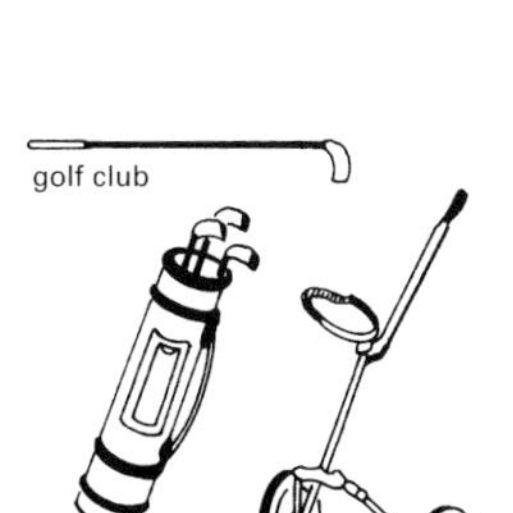

❷ Golf bag with trolley

growing layer 30 5 10 coarse sand drainage gravel/hardcore

growing layer 30–35 drainage layer 15–20 drainage

improved upper layer 35/45 watering/drainage membrane

❸ Construction details for types of green

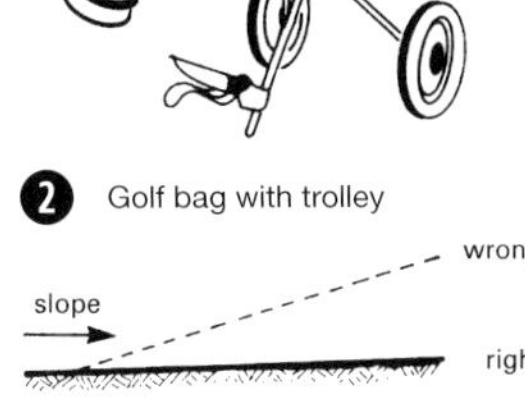

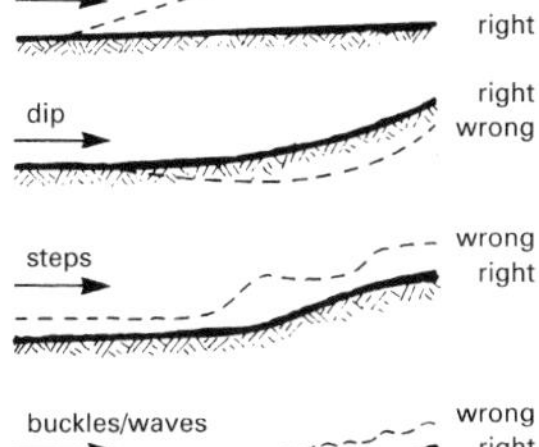

❹ Surface modelling of greens

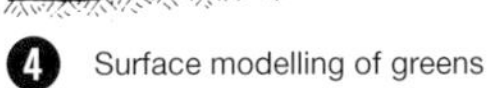

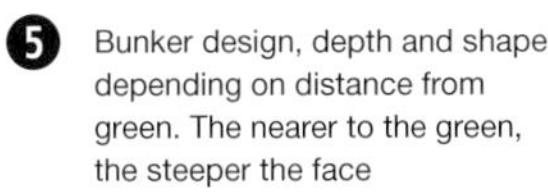

❺ Bunker design, depth and shape depending on distance from green. The nearer to the green, the steeper the face

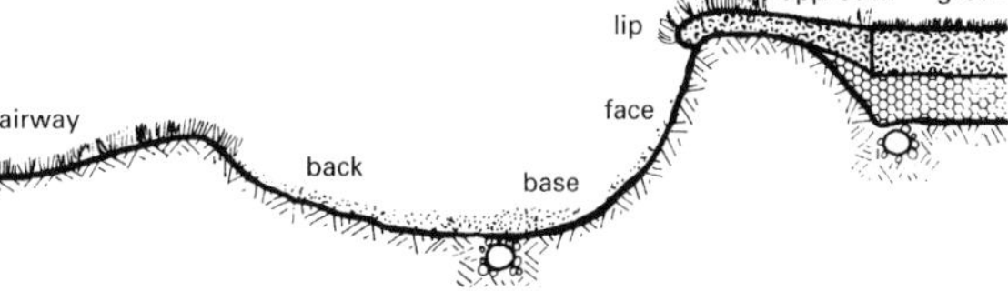

❻ Section through a bunker next to a green

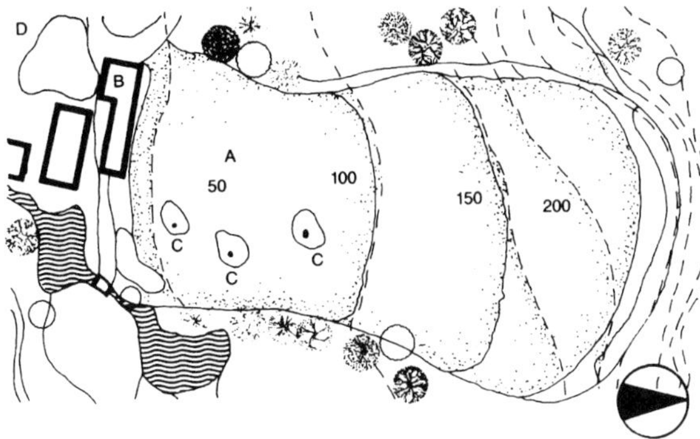

A Practice green
B Driving range hut
C Pitching greens
D Parking

❼ Basic layout of a practice area → ❾

Practice areas → ❼ are used either to practise the short game or for beginners taking up golf. A golf centre as an independent sports facility can, for example, be laid out on an area of only 10 ha. This would include a practice area, an approach green, a practice green and a 9-hole golf course (par 3) → ❾.

Recognised standard lengths of golf courses vary between the standard 60 with a normal length of 3749 m and the standard 74 with a normal length of 6492 m. These overall lengths of golf courses result in the 'par' score.

Elements of a golf course

The course starts at the tee, which has no specified size. It should be about 200 m^2 with adequate width. Fairways are 30–50 m wide and 100 to > 500 m long. At the end of the fairway is the green, min. 400 m^2, but normally 500–600 m^2. Aprons to the greens, which are not usual everywhere, min. width 2.5 m. Roughs are areas with growth of various heights at the edge of the fairways and over the remaining areas. Bunkers are the most common artificial obstacle, but have the disadvantage of working as foreign bodies in the landscape.

Golf courses are best situated in uneven terrain with flat slopes between wooded thickets, trees or tree groups without undergrowth, with natural hazards (watercourses, lakes), with cuttings and hillocks, or among dunes on the coast. The size of a course depends on the number of holes and their length (distance from tee to hole).

'Par'	Length of hole	
	Men	Ladies
3	up to 228 m	up to 201 m
4	229–434 m	202–382 m
5	above 435 m	above 383 m

❽ Golf hole lengths

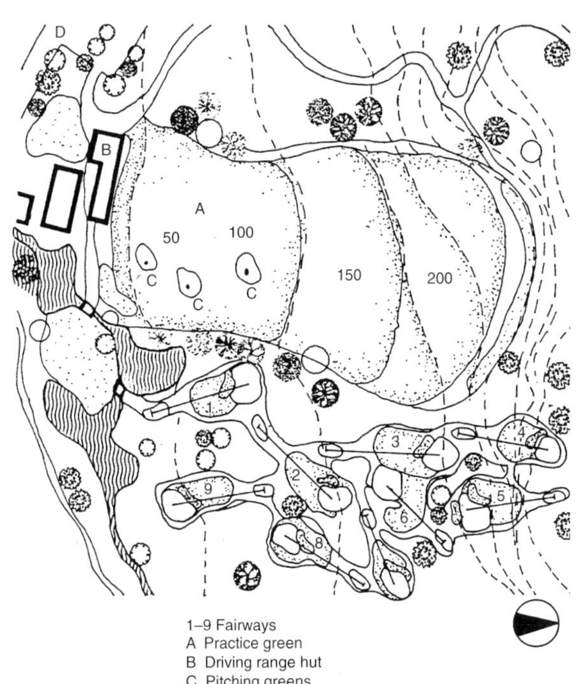

1–9 Fairways
A Practice green
B Driving range hut
C Pitching greens
D Parking

❾ Extension of practice area

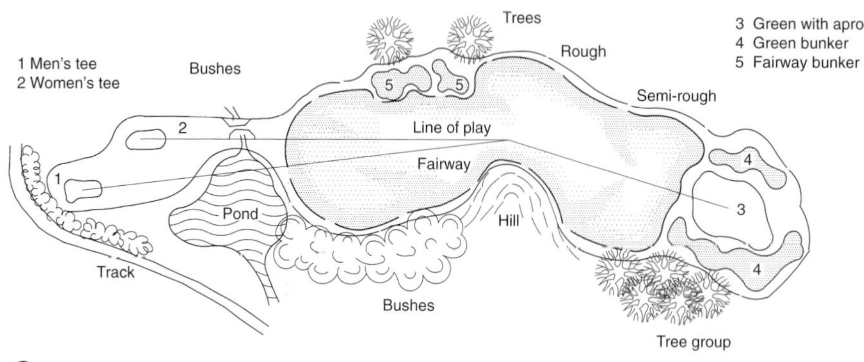

❶ Elements of a golf hole

A Practice green
B Driving range hut
C Pitching greens
D Parking
1–18 Fairways

❷ Example of an 18-hole course

Golf courses are not standardised as sports facilities and are generally unique. Nearly always today, they can be constructed only on former forest or agricultural areas. Golf course design requires the direction of a versatile expert, who needs the expertise of a landscape architect, landscape ecologist, soil scientist, cultural technician, economist etc. – and golfer. Before the actual design work can begin, background data has to be collected. Catchment area of the intended site: number of inhabitants in the area within 30 minutes by car required for a 9-hole golf course is approx. 100 000, in order to achieve a sufficient number, about 300, members of a golf club.

An important part of a golf club is the practice area, which comprises a grass area, a practice green and an approach green → p. 331 ❼. Grass practice areas should be as flat as possible with a width of min. 80 m in order to provide practice space for about 15 golfers simultaneously. The length should be min. 200 m (better 225 m) and arranged so that neighbouring holes are not disturbed. The ideal location is near the clubhouse. Approach greens should have a minimum area of 300 m^2 and be shaped. A sand trap for practice strokes should be min. 200 m^2 and have various depths.

The design of a golf course should generally assume that the completed facility will provide an 18-hole course, which means sufficient land of min. 55 ha (better 60 ha) must be available in the longer term. In order to offer the alternative of a half round (9 holes) on an 18-hole golf course, the 1st tee, 9th green, 10th tee and 18th green should all be within reasonable distance of the clubhouse if possible → ❷.

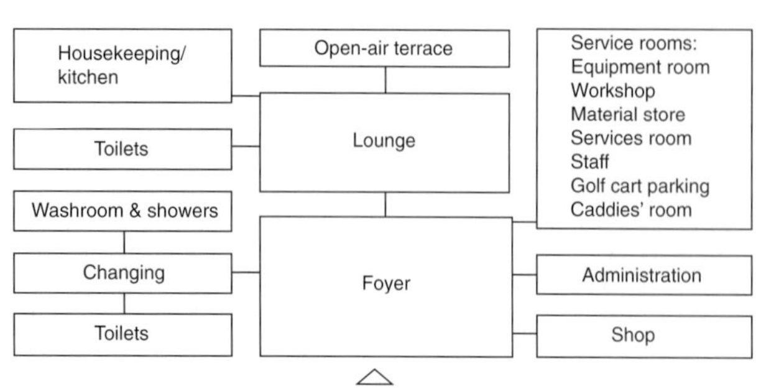

❸ Space allocation plan for a golf clubhouse

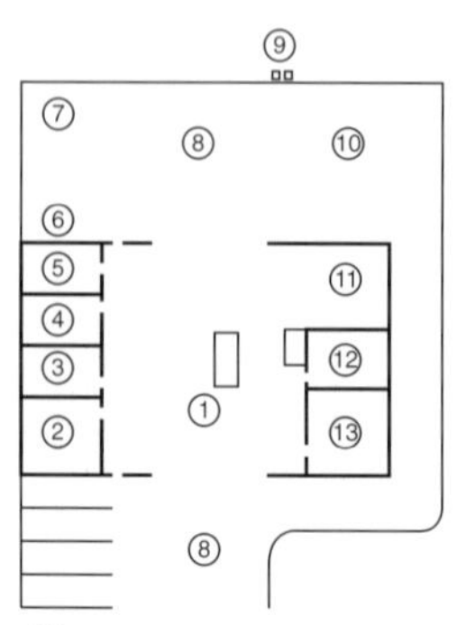

① Workshop with car lift or pit
② Office
③ Lounge
④ Sanitary area
⑤ Changing room
⑥ Machine shed
⑦ Material store
⑧ Paved yard
⑨ Fuel store
⑩ Washing area with oil separator
⑪ Storage area for small machines
⑫ Spares and tools
⑬ Fertiliser and seed store

❹ Functional example of a golf course utility building

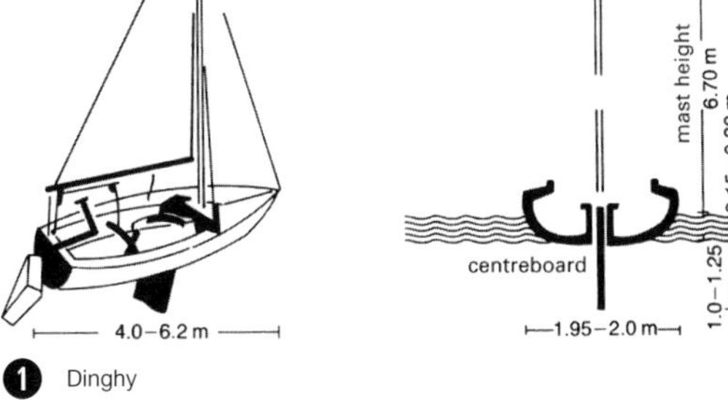

❶ Dinghy

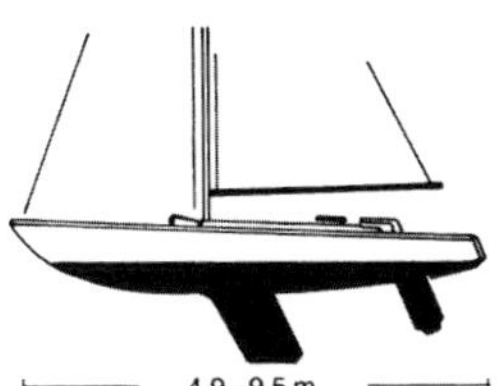
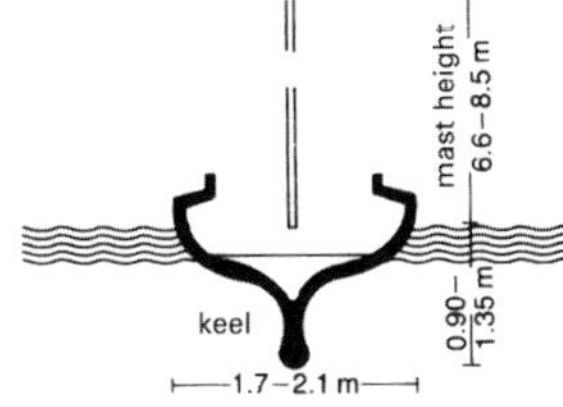

❷ Open keelboat

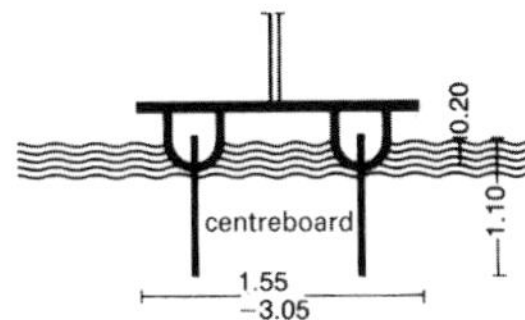

❸ Open catamaran

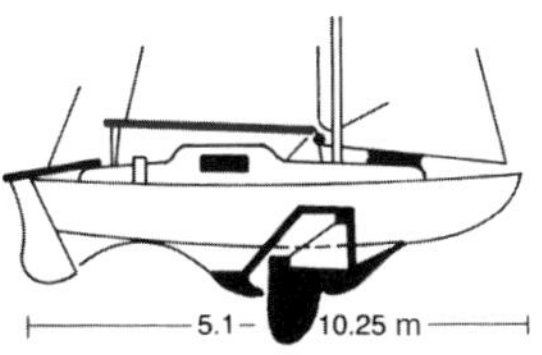
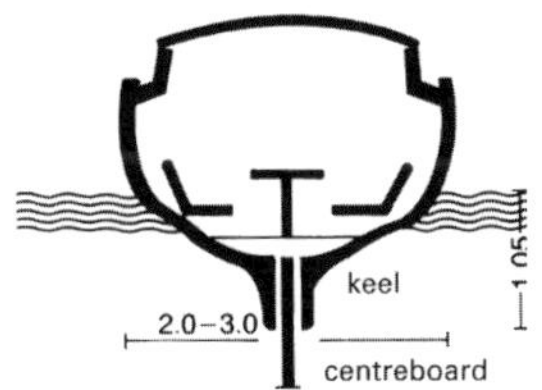

❹ Keelboat cruiser

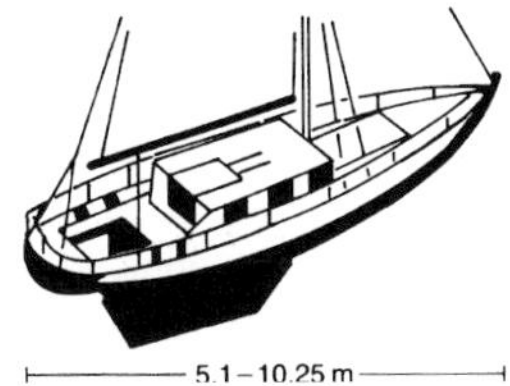
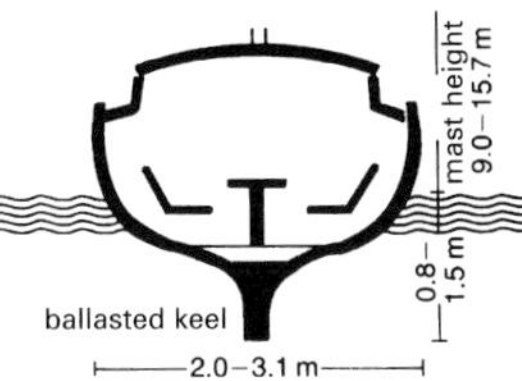

❺ Keel cruiser

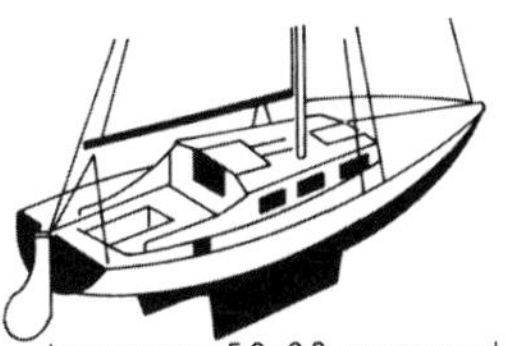
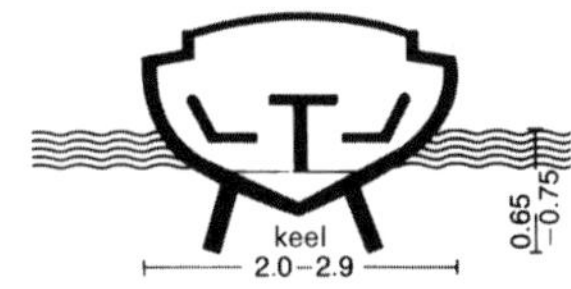

❻ Bilgeboard cruiser

❼ Inflatable boat

Boat types

Competitive races are possible only if every competitor has the same equipment. This has led to mostly standardised types of boats competing in sailing regattas. National classes are recognised by national ruling bodies and international classes by the International Sailing Federation in London. This also regulates the Olympic classes, which are newly specified after each Games (→ ❽ Examples of sailing boat classes and dimensions).

The depth of water required in harbours, marinas and watercourses depends on the type of boat. Usually specified are 1.25 m (dinghies, centreboard boats) and 4–5 m (keelboats) depth of water. Uniform water levels are favourable for the construction of harbours and safety of the boats.

Sailing boat type/class (crew) (1–3)	Unitary (U) or constructed (C) class	Size – length/width (m)	Draught (m)	Sail area 3 – S = spinnaker (m^2)	Distinguishing mark on sail
internat. classes:					
Finn dinghy[1)] (1)	U	4.50/1.51	0.85	10	two blue wavy lines above one another
Flying Dutchman (2)	U	6.05/1.80	1.10	15 (S)	black letters FD
Star[1)] (2)	U	6.90/1.70	1.00	26	five-pointed red star
Tempest	U	6.69/2.00	1.13	22.93 (S)	black letter T
Dragon (3)	U	8.90/1.90	1.20	22 (S)	black letter D
Soling (3)	U	8.15/1.90	1.30	24.3 (S)	black letter Ω (Omega)
Tornado[1)](2)	U	6.25/3.05	0.80	22.5 (S)	black letter T with two parallel underlinings
470[1)](2)	U	4.70/1.58	1.05	10.66 (S)	black number 470
5.50-m yacht	C	9.50/1.95	1.35	28.8	black number 5.5
Yngling[1)] (2)	U	6.35/1.75	1.05	14	black letter Y
49er[1)](2)	U	4.99/1.7(2.9)	1.50	21.2 (S)	black number 49er
Pirate (2)	U	5.00/1.62	0.85 +	10 (S)	red axe
Optimist (1)	U	2.30/1.13	0.77 +	3.33	black letter O
children & junior cadet (2)	U	3.32/1.27	0.74 +	5.10 (S)	black letter G
OK dinghy(1)	U	4.00/1.42	0.95	8.50	blue letter O and K
Olympia dinghy (2)	U	5.00/1.66	1.06 +	10	red ring
420 dinghy (2)	U	4.20/1.50	0.95 +	10 (S)	black number 420 sloping and staggered
some national classes:					
15 m^2 Wanderjolle or H-boat (2)	C	6.20/1.70	—	15 (S)	black letter H
15 m^2 dinghy cruiser (2)	C	6.50/1.85	—	15 (S)	black letter P
20 m^2 dinghy cruiser	C	7.75/2.15	—	20 (S)	black letter R

[1)] Olympic classes + with lowered centreboard

❽ Examples of sailing boat classes and dimensions

5–9 m
2.5 m
0.4–0.8 m

❾ Motor cruiser

5–9 m
2.5 m
0.4–0.8 m

❿ Classic boat

9–15 m
4–6 m
0.8–1.2 m

⓫ Motor yacht

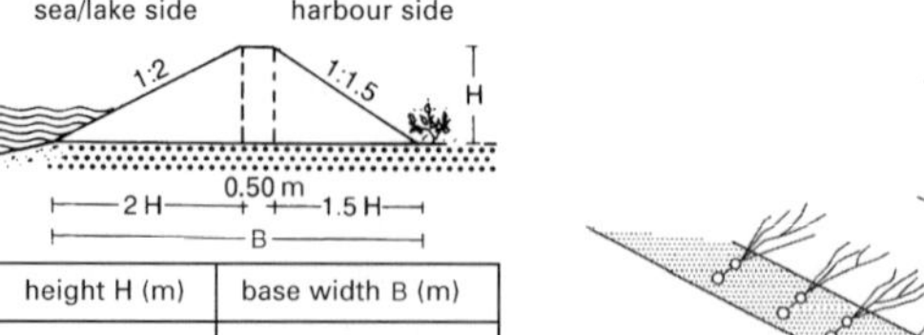

height H (m)	base width B (m)
1	4.00
2	7.50
3	11.00
4	14.50
5	18.00
6	21.50

❶ Sections of moles and seawalls

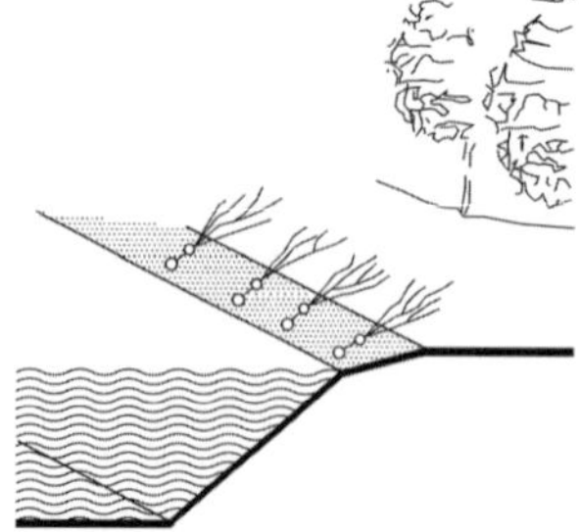

❷ Reeds with at least two layers of vegetation

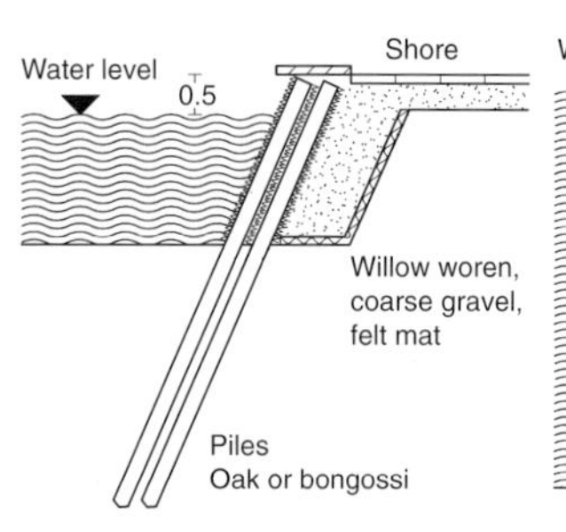

❸ Rammed timber piles

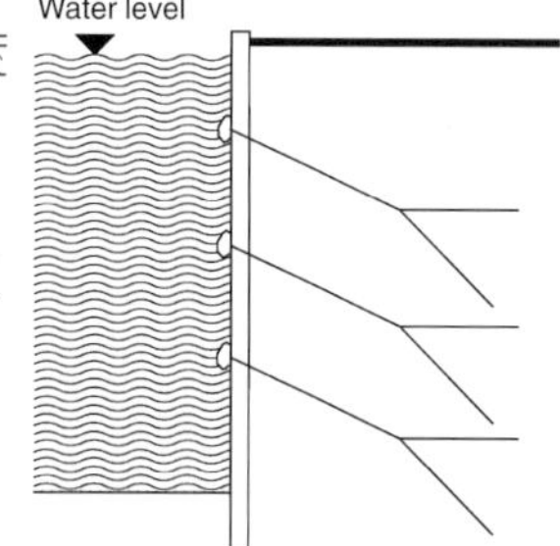

❹ Sheet steel pile wall

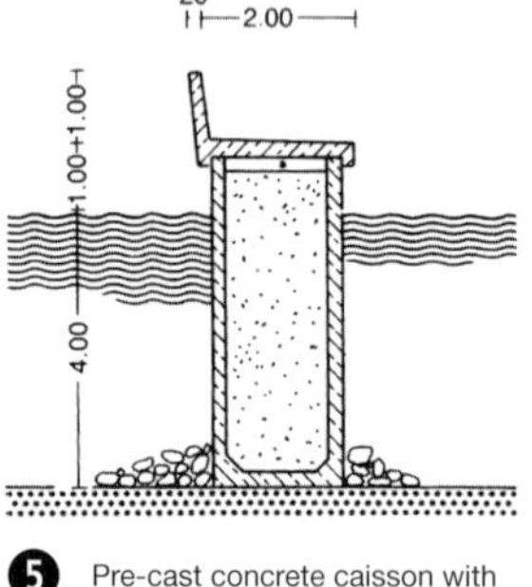

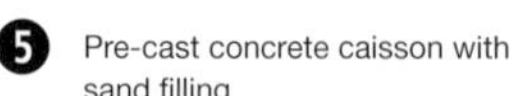

❺ Pre-cast concrete caisson with sand filling

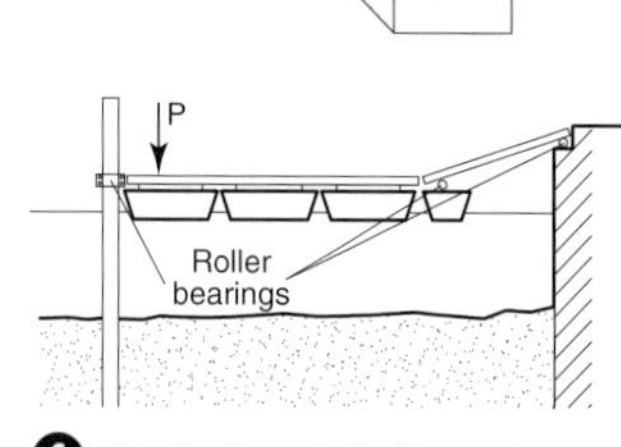

❻ Section through floating pontoon, edge loading P min. 2.5 kN

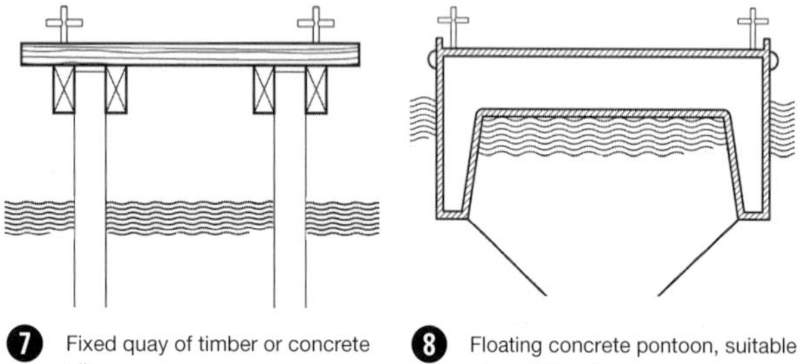

❼ Fixed quay of timber or concrete piles

❽ Floating concrete pontoon, suitable as a breakwater

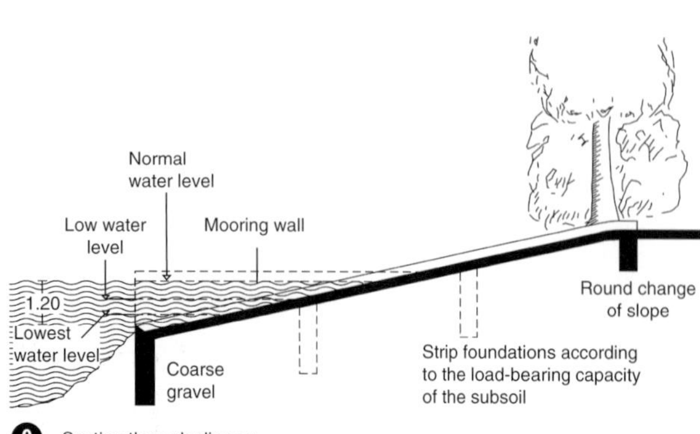

❾ Section through slipway

Marine engineering works

Structures protecting against wave impact, suction and swell are important for every marina.

Breakwaters (or **moles**) are formed of rammed sheet piles or stone boulders → ❷ – ❹. Concrete caissons can be used only in relatively shallow water. → ❺ Floating piers consisting of concrete pontoons are also possible. → ❽ Breakwaters should permit pedestrian access for sightseeing.

Sheet pile walls offer permanent coastal protection with the least use of space. They normally consist of rolled steel profiles with vertical interlocking, but can also be of timber or plastic. A sheet pile wall is nearly watertight and, because of the great resistance of heavy sheet pile in place, can bridge large spans. Sporting boats, which are tied up against a sheet pile wall, must be protected against mechanical damage with fenders. Steel pile walls can also rust, which does not look good in a marina. → ❹

Dolphins consist of steel pipes, sometimes filled with concrete or timber. Min. length 3 × water depth, depending on the seabed. Boats and quays are fixed to dolphins. The average lifetime of timber dolphins in seawater is 15 years and of steel pipes 35 years. Because this lifetime varies greatly with location, information should be sought locally.

Banks stabilise coasts and are formed by rubble, concrete or planting. Slopes depend on the height, ground conditions and detailing. → ❷ + ❸

Slipways and cranes

Boat cranes can be permanently mounted in the service wharf area or else be mobile cranes. This requires load-bearing ground and sufficient space for landside access (car with trailer + truck), according to the size of the crane and the boat. The coastal protection at this location will have to be vertical.

A **travellift** is a mobile lifting device for transporting boats in the marina. → p. 335 ❾

Slipways are ramps for launching boats. Smaller and lighter boats can be launched on a trailer, but larger ones will require the trailer to be towed. → ❾ – ❿

Construction materials and details for marine works are exposed to attack by the sea and should be made of stable, durable and lasting materials. Corrosion is considerable in water, especially seawater. Buildings should be sealed against wind and spray, and insulated for thermal protection in summer and winter.

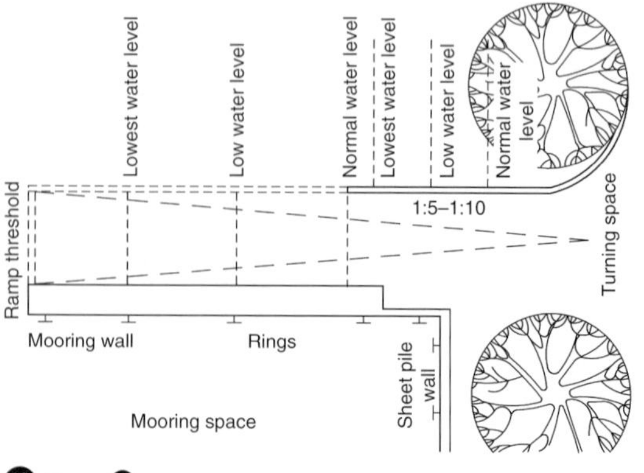

❿ Plan → ❾

0.50 1.50
Boat length
Boat width + ca. 1.00
Floating boom
1.00 Width 0.30 0.80
0.50
Stem mooring posts
Jetty
Boat length × 0.75
Boat length × 1.5 – 1.8
Approx. dimensions

❶ Manoeuvring between quays

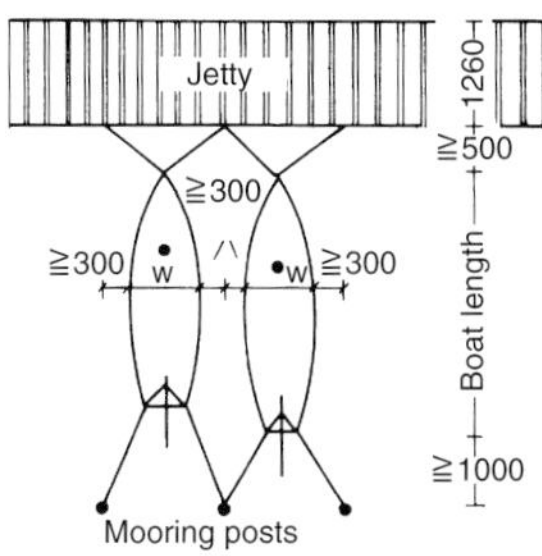

❷ Mooring a boat: mooring between quay and posts

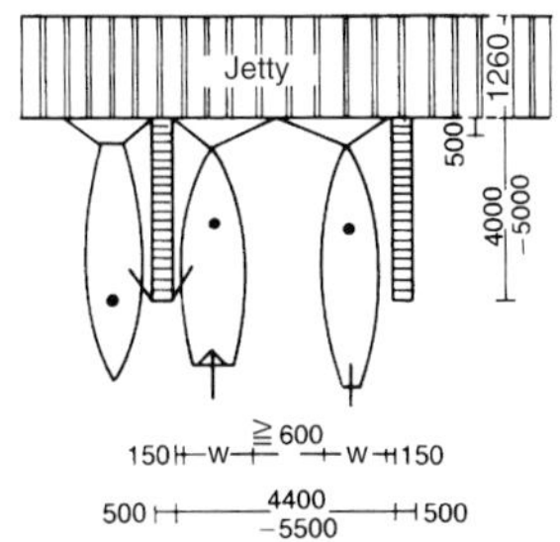

❸ Mooring a boat: diagonal boat mooring; quay and outrigger

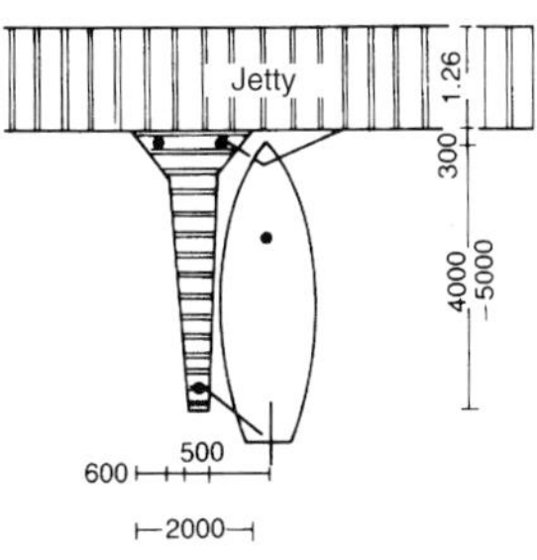

❹ Mooring a boat: mooring a boat between quay and outrigger in a Y-shape

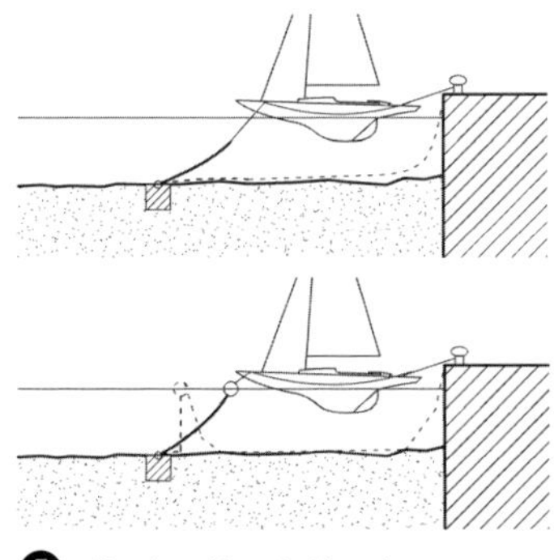

❺ Mooring with and without buoy

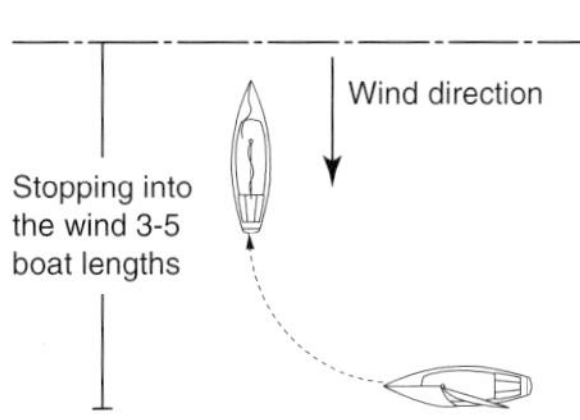

❻ Manoeuvring space for stopping under sail

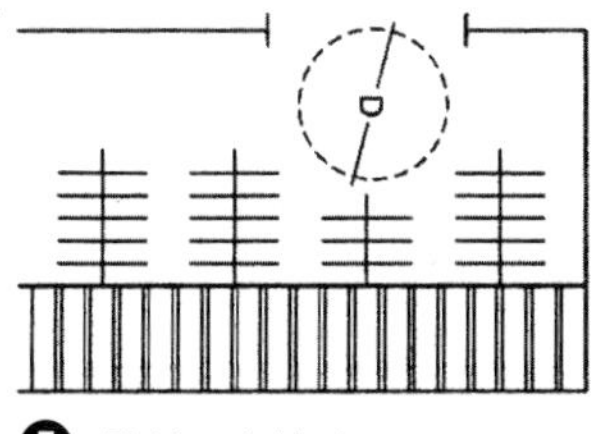

❼ Right-angled harbour

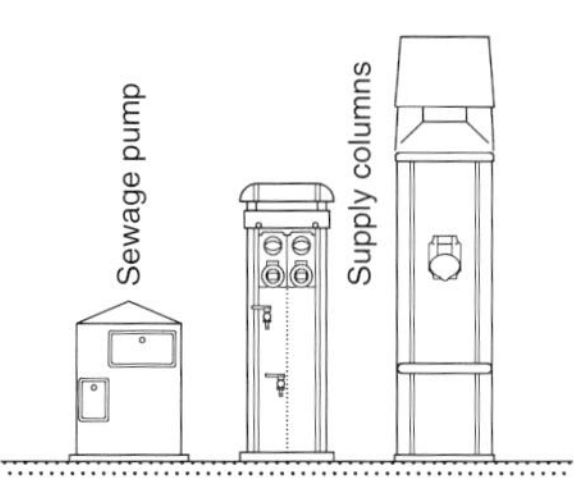

❽ Toilet, bilge and foul water, electricity and water supply, cable TV and Internet connection

❾ Travellift for land transport and rapid launching

Design of moorings

Berths should always be aligned to the wind, with the size of berths appropriate to the type of boat and how the boat is moored (bow or stern). If sailing boats without motors are to be expected (a regatta harbour), there should be sufficient space for manoeuvring to halt the boats. Sailing boats stop by running into the wind, which can take 2–5 boat lengths according to type → ❻.

Behind the harbour mouth, there should be a turning circle to allow the largest ship to turn. This turning circle, ~35–60 m diameter, is necessary to enter the harbour safely and for manoeuvring in a storm → ❼.

Quays

The choice of type of quay is determined by the strain from the load, ship impact and hawser tension.

Fixed quays on rammed piles are endangered by high tides. → p. 354 ❼

Modern **floating quays** are fixed to mooring posts or anchored, and enable safe and controllable docking at any water level. → p. 354 ❻

Berthing at a mooring is normal in southern waters → ❺

The water depth at the mooring place should be min. 1.8 times the deepest draught. The berth should be provided with electricity and water and a drainage connection. Tying-up equipment like bollards, clamps or rings of adequate size is needed. Slip-resistant surfaces and planking of quays are necessary, as are a handrail on one or both sides and lighting for the quays and berths.

Provide waste containers of sufficient number and size (rubbish separation!).

Size of berths

The size of berths depends on the boats in the marina. Berths of various sizes should be offered, ideally sorted according to size. A few berths for superyachts (length over 21 m) are also necessary. Manoeuvring and tying up at the berths should be safe.

Dry storage marina

If there is too little space available on the water, boats can be stored on shore and transported by a travellift to be launched in max. 30 min. The dry storage marina is equipped with quays and berths on land so that the use of the boat is also possible on land (water, drainage and electricity connections). The ratio of land to water in such a marina is about 80:20.

The investment costs are only about 40% of a comparable conventional marina.

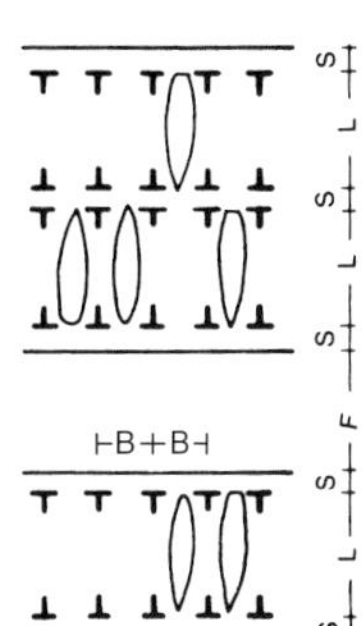

Boat class	Required berth size (m) length (L)	width (W)	Safety spacing (m) (S)	Passage width (m) (P)
Finn dinghy	4.50	3.00	3.00	5.00
Flying Dutchman	6.00	3.00	1.00	6.50
Star	7.00	3.50	1.50	7.50
Tempest	6.70	4.00	2.00	8.00
Dragon	9.00	4.00	2.00	9.50
Soling	8.50	4.00	2.00	9.50
Tornado	6.50	6.00	2.00	7.00
470	5.50	3.50	1.50	5.00
S safety spacing in front of and behind the berth length L				

❿ Sizes of berths on land for Olympic sailing boat classes

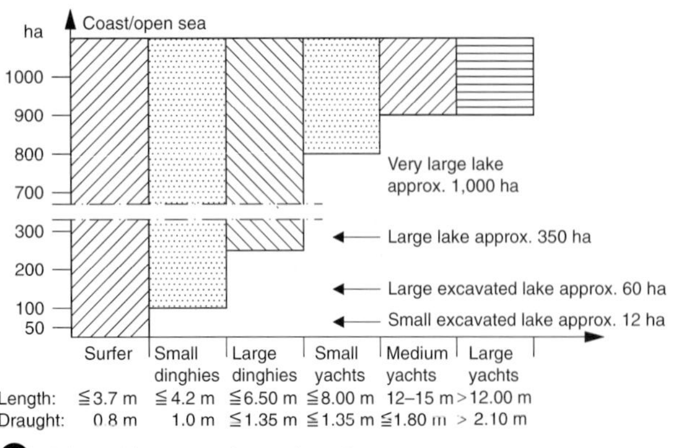

❶ Relationship – extent of water : boat size

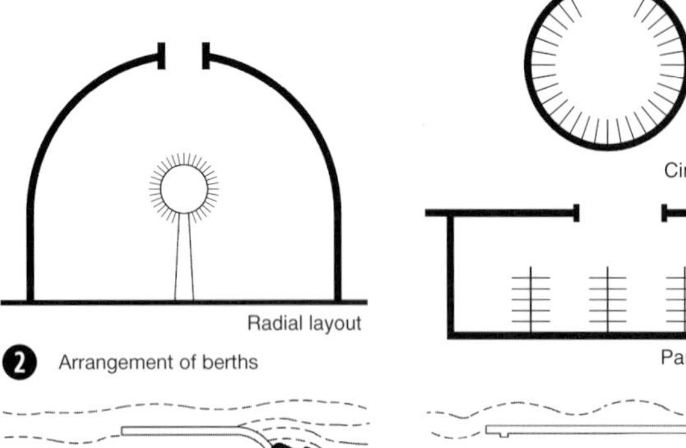

❷ Arrangement of berths

❸ Breakwater closed on one side

❹ Open breakwater parallel to the shore

❺ Funnel-shaped breakwaters

❻ Island and river mouth

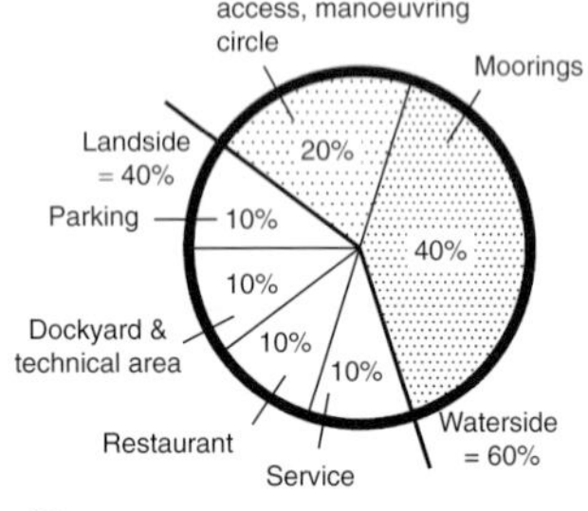

❼ Area distribution of a marina – land:water approx 1:1.5

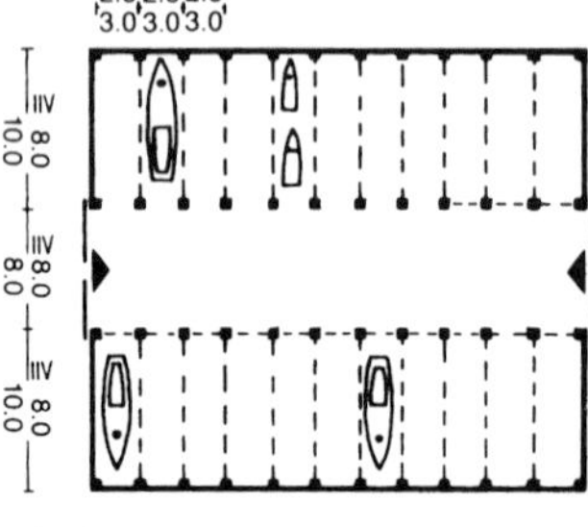

❽ Boat storage hall scheme, doors facing stern side

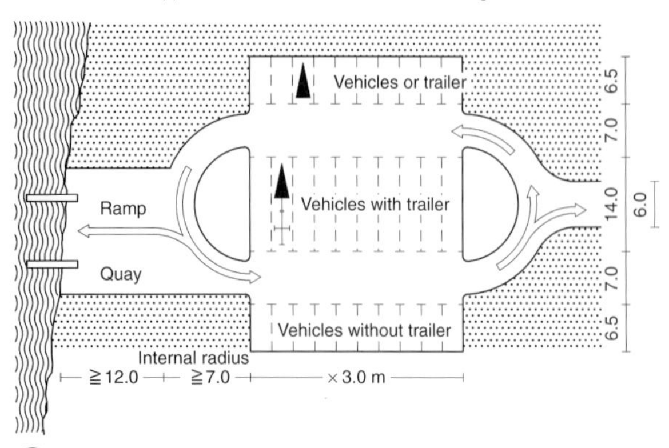

❾ Land storage places

The first stage of designing a marina is a feasibility study and various approvals on land and water. A marina is always intended for leisure and tourism. The specialisation trends for marinas are fitting-out marina, event marina, berth marina, mini-marina, dry store marina etc. → p. 337.

Selection of location

The boats must be protected. Access by water and by road on land must be guaranteed. Marinas should ideally not be built in open countryside but rather in connection with leisure, urban or tourist attractions.

Size and capacities of marinas

There should be a minimum depth of water to suit the intended sporting boats. Avoid sporting and ecological conflicts and overloading on the water. On average, only 33% of the marina's boats will be on the water at the same time. Consider the simultaneity factor (describes the ratio of the total permitted number of boats to the average number of boats underway), determination of the technical space requirements for individual types of boats, and sufficient spacing from other boats.

Organisation of areas

Mooring area: toilet pump, lifebelts, supply columns for electricity, water, waste disposal; this area should be safe, attractive and functional → p. 335. **Technical area:** slip ramp, crane, chandler, workshop, motor service, repair area (consider emissions and influence of pollution). **Restaurant area:** with terrace overlooking the water. **Service area:** harbour master, showers, toilets, information (must be easy to find). **Parking:** safe and easily accessible for cars and trailers → ❾.

Layouts

Right-angled harbour → ❸: mainly for medium-sized marinas (100–400 berths), long major breakwater running parallel to the shore, closed at one end; alignment to the main wind direction and to waves must be considered.

Open breakwater parallel to the shore → ❹: the breakwater is not accessible and offers only limited protection, as the harbour is open on two sides. It is suitable only for shores without sediment deposition, but can be used for inland waters. Disadvantage: reflection of the waves from the shore through the harbour against the inside of the breakwater.

Enclosing breakwaters → ❺: two breakwaters run from the shore and form a funnel-shaped harbour entrance. This is very expensive to construct and suitable only for locations with the best possible natural conditions – the ideal type for a protected coastal marina.

Island harbour → ❻: with sensitive shores, if water depth is insufficient or space is a problem. According to local conditions, an island marina can be piled or constructed on pontoons.

Land storage of boats

Larger boats are stored in sheds or in the open air over the winter. Storage should be safe against storms if on blocks and jack stands, with sufficient safety spacing between boats → ❽.

Open areas and roads in marinas must be adequate for boat transport and storage. The car park should have an associated lockable place for trailers.

Turning areas should be sufficiently large for vehicles with trailers and cranes and in front of slipways, diameter min. 18 m, and load-bearing (min. 6 t axle load). In large marinas, these areas should be concrete or asphalt surfaced. → ❾

Sport and leisure

SPORTS FACILITIES

Playing fields
Athletics
Tennis
Miniature golf
Golf courses
Water sport, marinas
Water sport, rowing and canoeing
Equestrian sport
Ski jumping
Ice rinks
Roller skating rinks
Speed roller skating, skateboarding
Cyclo-cross, BMX
Shooting ranges

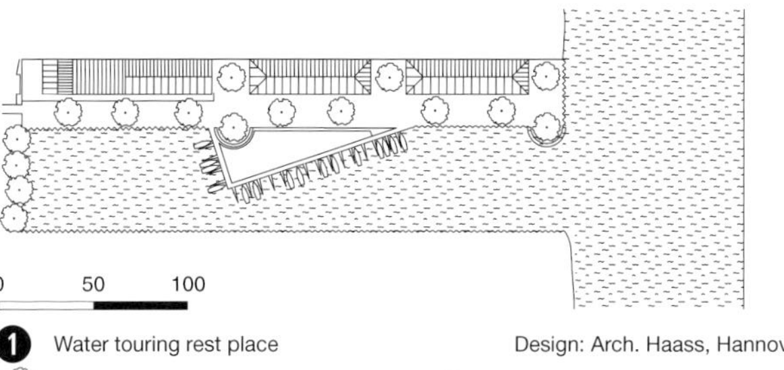

❶ Water touring rest place Design: Arch. Haass, Hannover

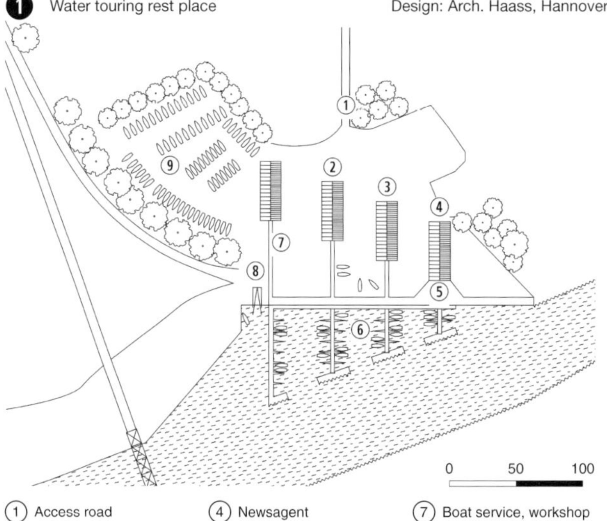

(1) Access road
(2) Reception
(3) Charter area
(4) Newsagent
(5) Catering
(6) Moorings
(7) Boat service, workshop
(8) Slip, crane, travellift
(9) Land storage

❷ Dry marina on a creek Design: Arch. Haass, Hannover

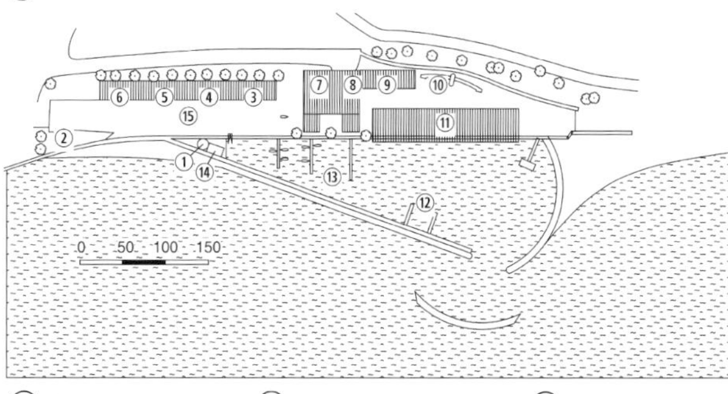

(1) Olympic fire
(2) Helipad
(3) Competition office
(4) VIP lounge
(5) Teams' sanitary facs
(6) Press
(7) Info. & communications
(8) Multi-stone car park
(9) Workshop, surveying
(10) Weather station & first aid
(11) Land storage
(12) Moorings
(13) Moorings
(14) Surfers' hall
(15) Mixed area

❸ Olympic sailing harbour at Travemünde Design: Arch. Haass, Hannover

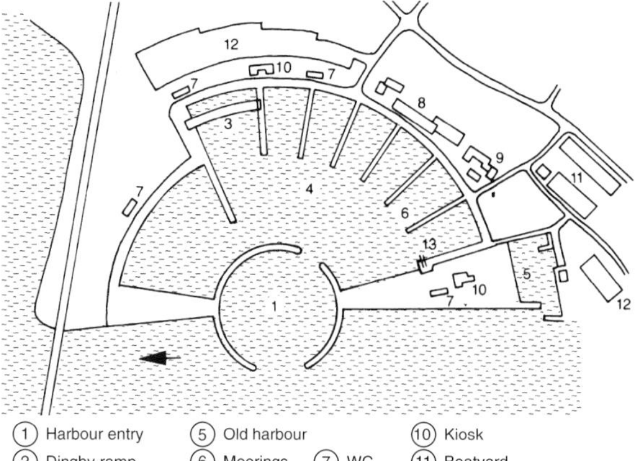

(1) Harbour entry
(2) Dinghy ramp
(3) Boats
(4) New harbour
(5) Old harbour
(6) Moorings (7) WC
(8) Hotel & restaurant
(9) Shopping centre
(10) Kiosk
(11) Boatyard
(12) Winter storage for boats
(13) Travellift

❹ Example of a yacht harbour

Marina types

Day marina: floating location; only for daily mooring of boats on the coast as a floating marina.

City marina/Mini-marina/Water touring rest place: → ❶ in attractive urban location, only for overnight stays by boating tourists, minimal service.

Event marina: urban location; only intended for boating tourists visiting events, temporary and with minimal service.

Regatta and Olympic marinas: → ❸ Olympic flame, helicopter pad, workshop/verification hall, weather station, medical care and doping testing, organisation and competition office, security, VIP lounge, press boxes, cranes, washing area. Berths: Star and Yngling. Land storage area: 49er, Tornado, 470, Laser, Finn, Europe Star and Yngling (all including container storage), surfer hall. Shuttle jetty, changing rooms/sanitary facilities/WCs for the teams, information and communications centre (for team meetings, official committee, competition transmission for participants, bistro). Parking, mooring for trainers' boats, moorings, mixed area.

Berth marina: location at the edge of town is possible, only water berths without additional service. Suitable for clubs and associations.

Tourist marina: harbour office, berths, sanitary facilities, chandler, restaurant.

Association and club marinas: club house, terrace, car parking, access, jetties, berths, land storage space, repair/workshop.

Dry marina: → ❷ location at the edge of town or industrial estate, predominantly land storage with well-functioning travellift launching of boats. Service, facilities, minimal space on water.

Technical marina: possible location on industrial estate; only technical services like crane, repair, winter service, boat building, refitting etc.

Winter marina: possible location on industrial estate; only winter storage of boats in sheds or the open air. Observe sufficient space between boats and possibly separate storage areas for equipment and working materials (fire hazard from paint and varnish).

Task/function	Requirements	Construction
1. Transport areas for trailers and towing vehicles, etc.	– sufficient width – turning space for towing vehicles – sufficiently loadbearing – surface drainage	– frostsafe construction – drainage – solid surfacing of concrete, asphalt or similar
2. Land areas for boats	– sufficient size – sufficiently loadbearing – anchorage for tarpaulins	– frostsafe construction – waterbound surfacing – founded anchorages, e.g. rings
3. Access roads for emergency services	– width according to RAST – sufficiently loadbearing – turning circles for vehicles – surface drainage	– frostsafe construction – drainage – surfacing of paving, concrete, asphalt or similar
4. Parking for vehicles	– sufficient space – sufficiently loadbearing – clear marking of places	– waterbound surfacing – paving strips to mark spaces – frostsafe construction
5. Footpaths and cycle ways	– width 1.5–2.5 m – separated from vehicles – safe and clearly laid out – surface drainage	– frostsafe construction – waterbound surfacing or paving – drainage

❺ Roads and car parks: functions and construction quality

❶ Superyacht marina, section showing separation into crew and owner areas
Arch.: Haass, Hannover

size of yachts	10–21 m	30–80 ft
small superyachts	21–30 m	80–100 ft
medium superyachts	30–60 m	100–200 ft
large superyachts	over 60 m	over 200 ft

❷ Superyacht categories according to size

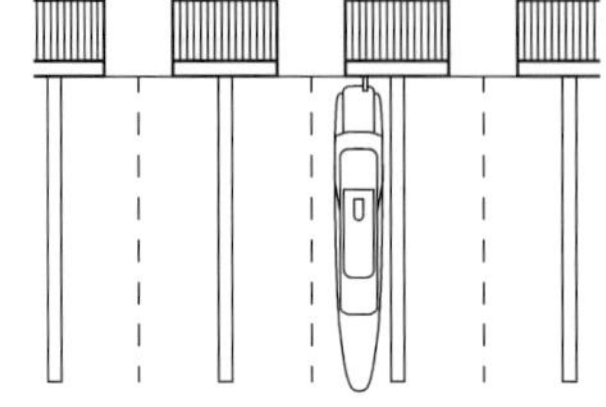

❸ Theoretical sketch of a superyacht marina with service building and lounge

Medium	Connection on board	Capacity
Electricity		Operated by crew
Fresh water		min. 50 l / min Operated by crew
Waste-water		Pump-out station Operated by crew
Fuel		Diesel / petrol operated by marina

❹ Requirements and usual location of the utility aspects of superyachts

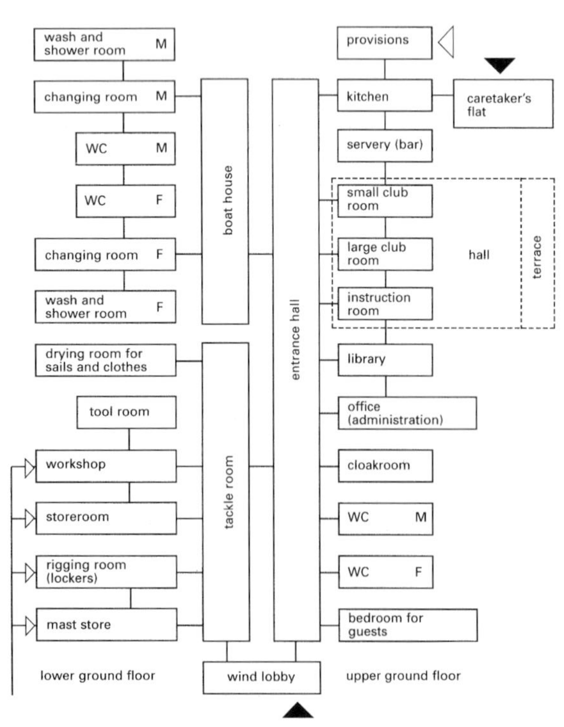

❺ Functional scheme of club house

Superyacht marinas

Yachts of more than 21 m/70 ft length are described as superyachts. From a length of more than 30 m, these yachts have professional crews. Such yachts require particular attention in the design of a marina, either as an extension of an existing marina or as an independent marina.

The location can only be exclusive with high-quality tourist attractions, and connection to an airport and a major city. The superyacht business in Europe is mostly concentrated in the Mediterranean.

Superyachts require extensive space for berths ❶ – ❸ and have heavy utility requirements ❹. Water depths of min. 8–9 m are required.

The concept of a superyacht marina corresponds to the requirements of a 5-star hotel, with 24-hour service for technical support and a personal reception service. Zoning is similar to a 5-star hotel, plus separated areas for crew and service → ❺. The security of ships and crews need to be ensured through appropriate facilities. 24-hour security service, video surveillance and electronic access control systems, as well as the lighting of the most significant areas of the marina, are important.

Security in marinas

Security facilities in marinas protect boats, equipment (electronics) and people from the forces of nature and criminality, vandalism and terror.

Active measures:
Arrangement, visibility of berth areas
Alarm systems on boats
Security for berths, jetties (gates)
Passive measures:
Video surveillance of berths
Lighting of the marina
Security service, security patrols
Emergency measures, security plan
Security management

Marinas inside waterfronts with public access require a lockable central area (harbour office) and additional 24-hour surveillance. The marina should be marked with notices and rules, which can be implemented as marina regulations and enforced by police.

Each marina requires an emergency plan, which provides the greatest possible safety in an emergency, with employee instruction and training. Training days should be carried out at least twice a year.

Sustainability

Environmental technologies can be implemented in marinas to save energy, but also for the exploitation of alternative energy: geothermal, wind power, waterpower, photovoltaic, solar heating etc. can all be employed in marinas. A good marina should function without external energy supply. An environmentally friendly marina protects water and subsoil through the use of environmentally safe materials (no water pollution).

Environmental acceptability is achieved through concentrating the marina equipment and technology into functional areas, which can be switched off in the winter – energy zones and levels of operational intensity. Public transport instead of shuttle/taxi service, energy-saving times (e.g. 24:00–6:00), price levels according to energy use etc.

1.65–1.70 8.5 20 35

1 Racing shell: single

11.0/13.5 20 50 60

2 Coxless pair / four

19.50 70

3 Racing shell: eight

7.5/12.5/17.5 20 35 60 70

4 Racing skiff: single/four/eight

6.50–7.0/8.25–8.5 30 54–60 78–90

5 Touring skiff: single/pair

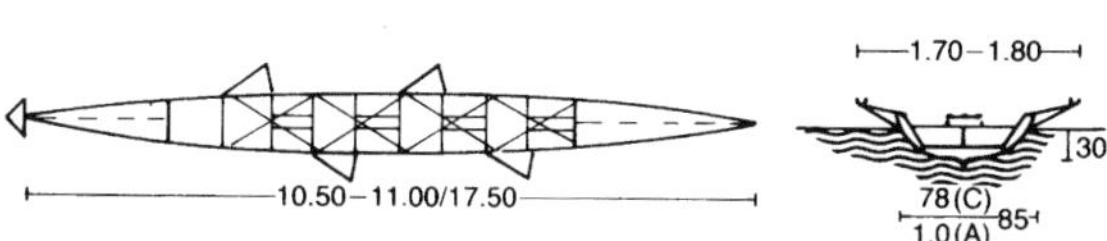

6 Touring skiff: four/eight

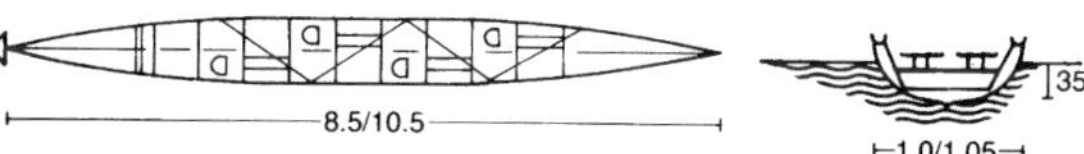

7 Seagoing gig: pair/four

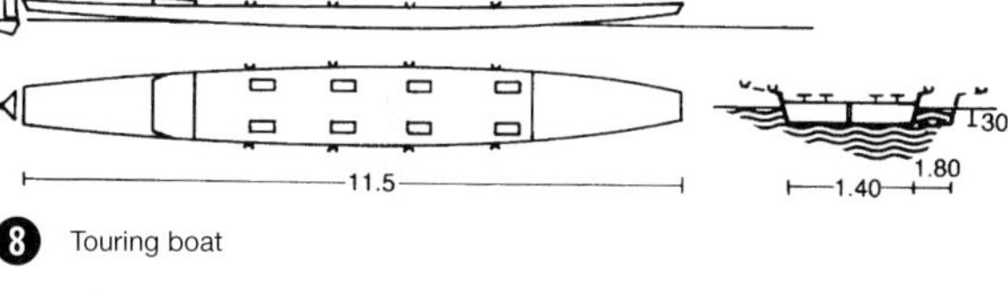

8 Touring boat

4.0–5.2/4.0–6.5 7 14/18 75–80

9 Canoe with single-bladed paddle

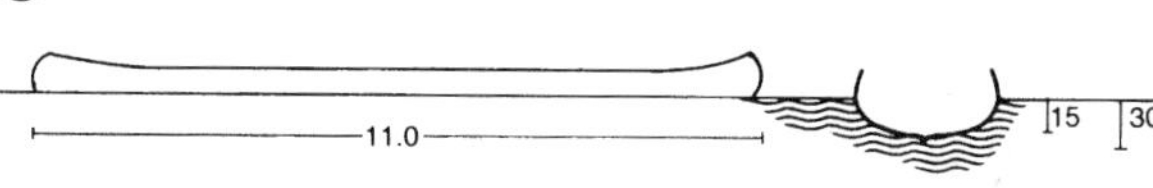

10 Racing canoe: eight with cox

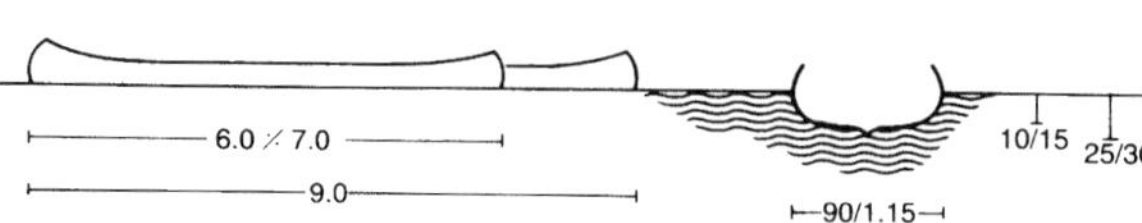

11 Touring crew canoe: eight and ten with cox

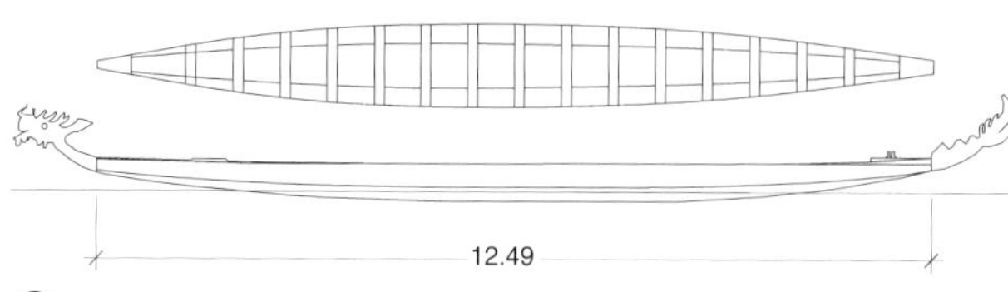

12 Dragon boat, IDBF racing standard

Rowing boats are predominantly team boats belonging to clubs. Like kayaks and canoes, they are mostly found on flowing waterways which are free of obstacles, in attractive countryside.

A boathouse has windows or skylights to the north, in order to keep sun out. Doors ≧2.50 × 2.75 m, to carry boats in above the head. Boathouse width ≧6.00 m, length ideally 30 m, height 4.0 m if possible → **15**. Oars 3.80 m long, spoons 15–18 cm. Storage near the entrance, horizontally on racks or, better, hanging from a clamping ring above a pit (depending on boathouse height).

Between boathouse and water jetty, a shore strip ≧20–30 m wide is required for cleaning and preparing the boats, with water taps and parking space for trailers. If possible, provide nearby lawn or woodland areas for camping.

Rowing basin for training with shortened oars → **17**, basin size for an eight 12.60 × 7.60 m. Single or double-sided rowing basin (also offset). Water circulation creates similar currents to open water. Ideally, this facility should be combined with a sports hall or indoor pool and their changing rooms.

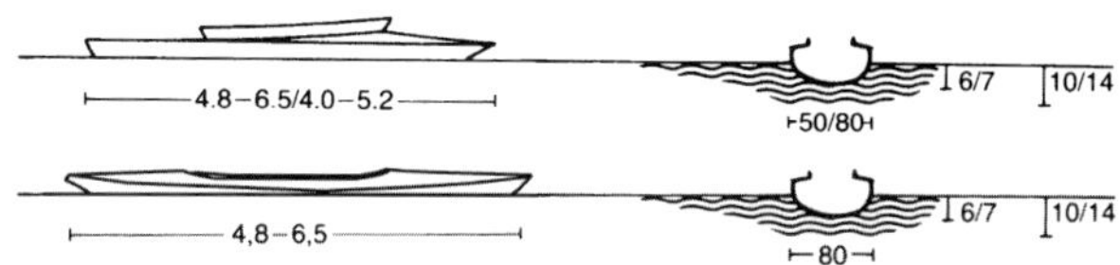

13 Kayak with double-bladed paddle: single/pair

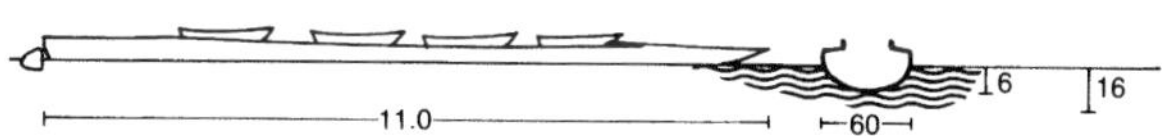

14 Kayak with double-bladed paddle: four

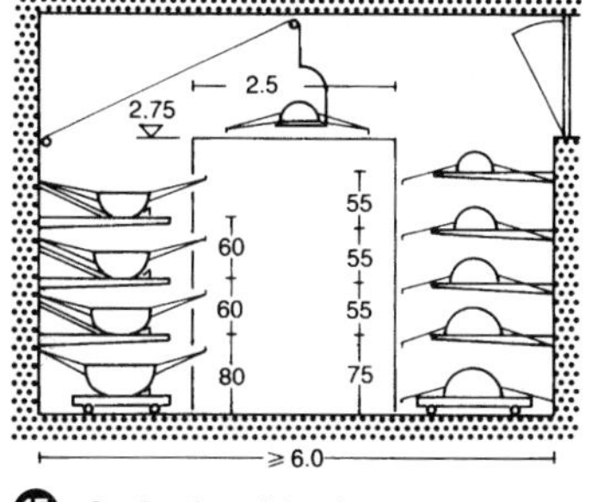

15 Section through boathouse

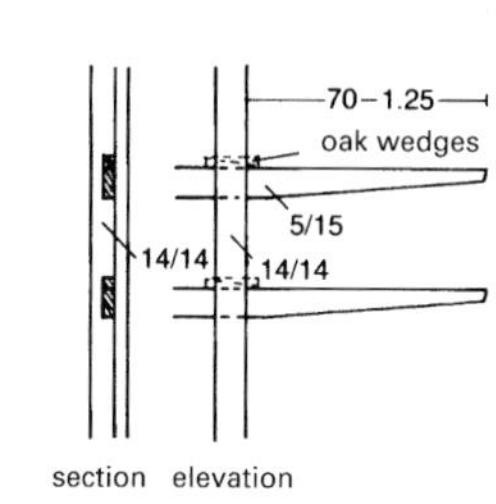

16 Boat stands every 2.00–2.50 m

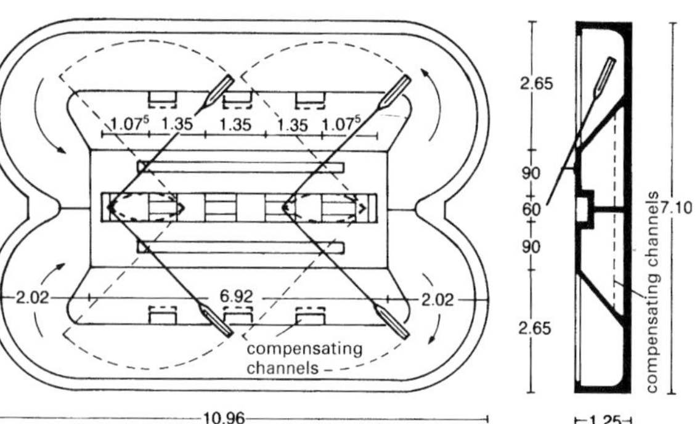

17 Double-sided sculling pool

Sport and leisure

SPORTS FACILITIES

Playing fields
Athletics
Tennis
Miniature golf
Golf courses
Water sport, marinas
Water sport, rowing and canoeing
Equestrian sport
Ski jumping
Ice rinks
Roller skating rinks
Speed roller skating, skateboarding
Cyclo-cross, BMX
Shooting ranges

Requirements for regatta and training courses for canoe and slalom:

1. Natural facilities: In steep sections (min. 1:100 gradient) of waterways not suitable for normal boating traffic or similar rivers with min. 10 m^3/s flow (at mean low water or as controlled by an upstream weir). Also in tailwater from mills and power stations, min. 8 m wide, with and without obstacles (installation of gates) → ❸

2. Artificial facilities: Olympic course in the Eiskanal/Lech near Augsburg, 550 m long. Reinforced concrete channel with concrete rock obstacles and 6 m falls, invert waterfall, up to 32 gates.

Requirements for regatta and training courses for competitive international rowing and canoeing → ❺.

Minimum requirements for water touring courses → ❼ – ❿. Criteria for water touring rest places and canoe stations are laid down by the DKV (German Canoe Association). See also p. 337.

❶ Regatta course for canoe slalom

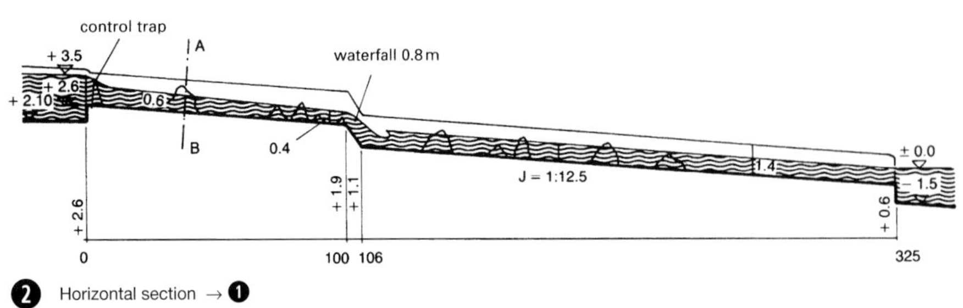

❷ Horizontal section → ❶

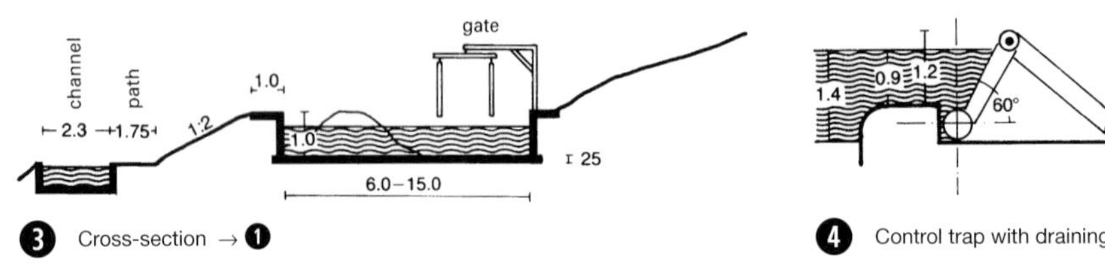

❸ Cross-section → ❶

❹ Control trap with draining base

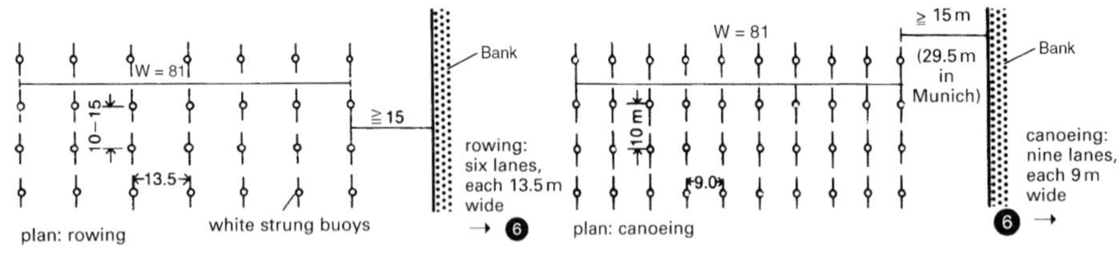

❺ Track markings (international dimensions) for competitive rowing and canoeing

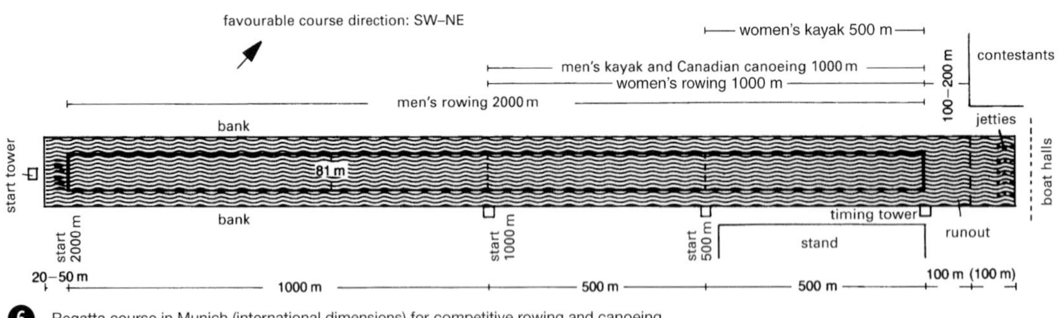

❻ Regatta course in Munich (international dimensions) for competitive rowing and canoeing

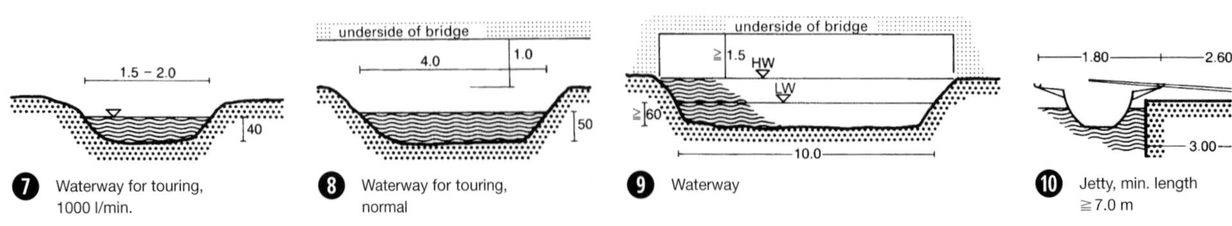

❼ Waterway for touring, 1000 l/min.

❽ Waterway for touring, normal

❾ Waterway

❿ Jetty, min. length ≧ 7.0 m

Riding facilities/stables should, if possible, be in the immediate vicinity of land suitable for riding. Areas with high ground and air humidity, as are often found in valleys, should be avoided, as should windless locations, where providing the desired ventilation may be difficult. Ideal sites are in hilly and windy areas. However, slope gradients for buildings and riding arenas should be <10%.

Saddle rooms, as far as possible, should be long and rectangular, with a large wall space and a width of 4.0–4.5 m. Saddles can be hung in three rows, staggered above each other → ❽. Saddle rooms and grooming rooms should have heating and be well ventilated.

In riding arenas the minimum headroom for show-jumping and horseback acrobatics is 4.00 m → ❺ – ❻. No universal rule can be applied to the space allocated to spectators. In general, though, spectators should not look down too steeply on the horses. An effective solution can be to use a spectators' gallery → ⓭, with the first row for seating and the second for standing. Behind this is room for two rows of circulating people. This arrangement will create 200 seated and standing places in a 20 × 40 m arena. The size of the main entrance has to be large enough to allow access for medium-sized lorries (3.00 m wide, 3.80 high). Side entrances should be 1.20 m or more wide and min. 2.80 m high. Doors have to open outwards.

The ring fence as enclosure of a riding ring has many purposes → ⓬. It simplifies dressage riding of horses and saves the riders from injury. Angle of the slope to the vertical ≧20°. Glass windows < 2 m above the floor of the riding arena should be protected by a fine mesh grille. An exercise area of approx. 1000 m^2 is sufficient for 10 horses, mostly in pairs daily and weekly.

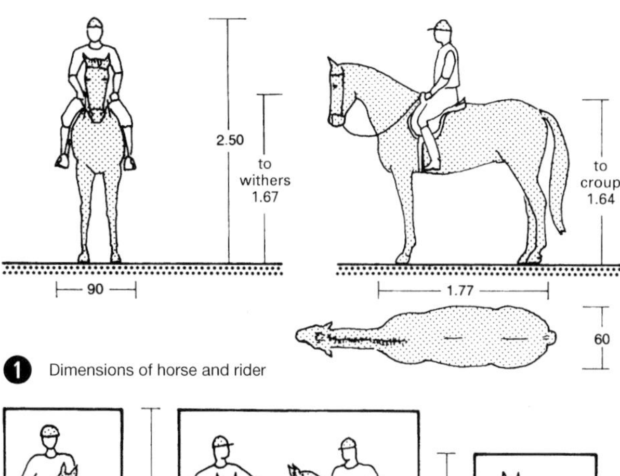

❶ Dimensions of horse and rider

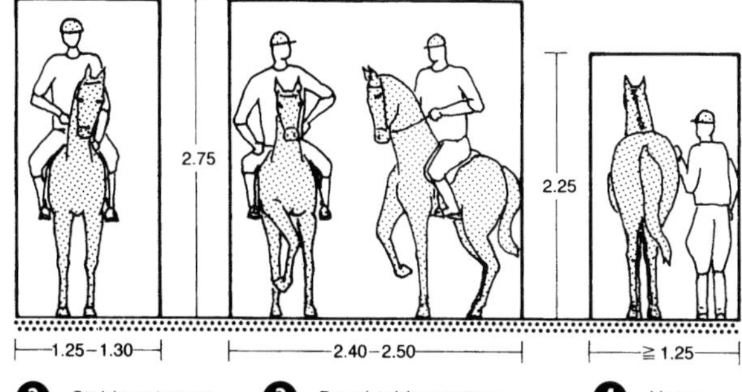

❷ Stable entrance, mounted

❸ Door/stable passage

❹ Horse and rider, dismounted

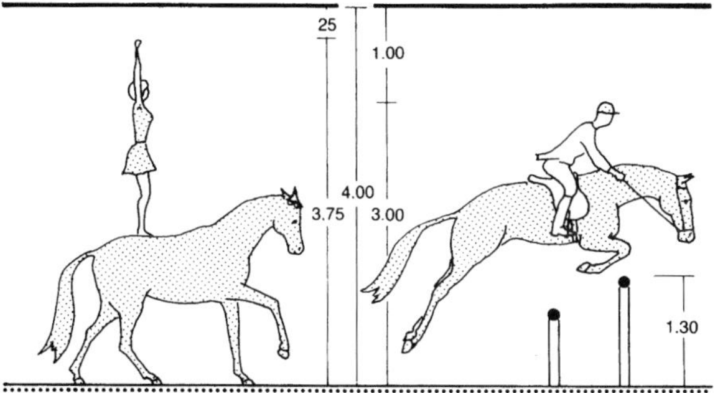

❺ Space for stunt riding

❻ Space for show-jumping

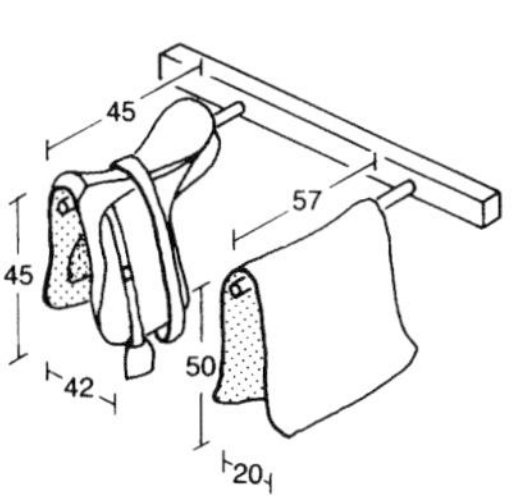

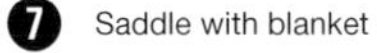

❼ Saddle with blanket

❽ Saddle rack on wall

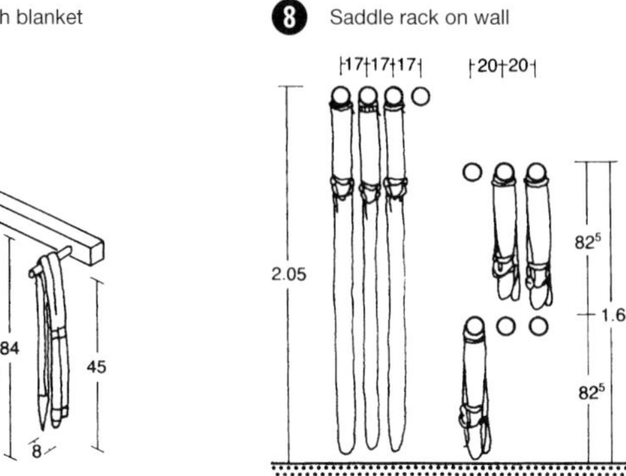

❾ Tack rack

❿ Bridle rack

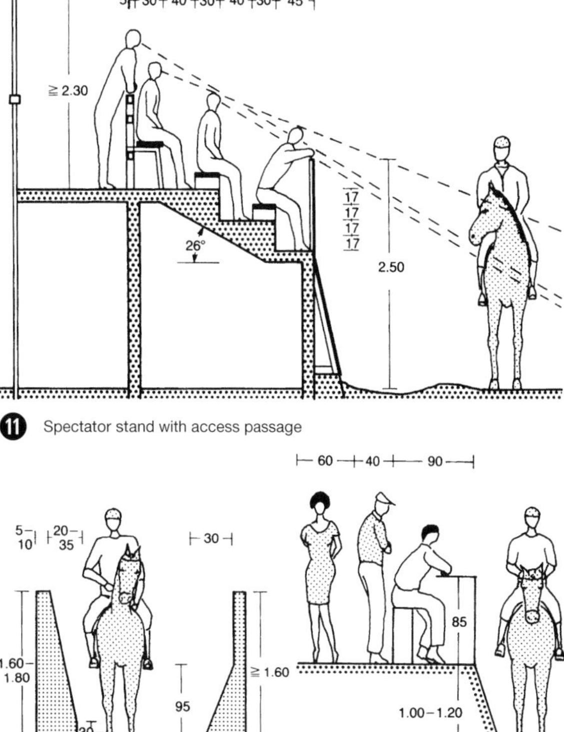

⓫ Spectator stand with access passage

⓬ Ring fence profile

⓭ Practical spectator stand

Sport and leisure

SPORTS FACILITIES

Playing fields
Athletics
Tennis
Miniature golf
Golf courses
Water sport, marinas
Water sport, rowing and canoeing
Equestrian sport
Ski jumping
Ice rinks
Roller skating rinks
Speed roller skating, skateboarding
Cyclo-cross, BMX
Shooting ranges

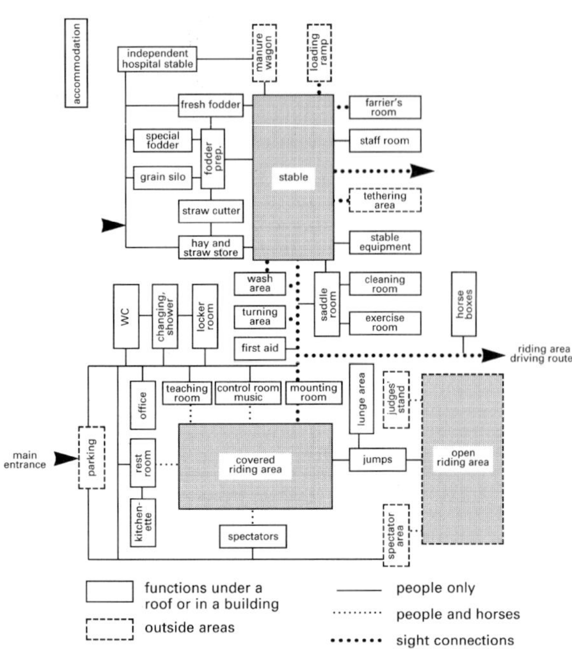

❶ Scheme of the indoor spatial relationships of a riding facility

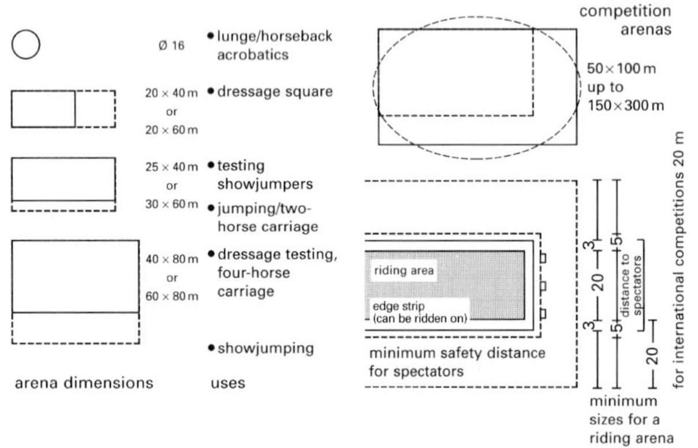

❷ Functional dimensions of open-air riding areas

format of riding halls	arena dimensions	uses
○	≧ 14.0 m	lunge/horseback acrobatics: alternative to a hall in the smallest clubs and private stables; used to relieve the main arena in larger establishments
▭	12.5 × 25.0 m	smallest arena: for private stables only and as an emergency solution for clubs; suitable as a second arena for larger establishments
▭	15.0 × 30.0 m	private stables and smaller club stables; second arena for larger establishments
▭	20.0 × 40/45 m	normal size for every type of establishment; dressage exams possible
▭	20.0 × 60.0 m	for larger establishments and institutions which specialise in dressage
▭	25.0 × 66.0 m	for large schools providing jumping and dressage training, and boarding establishments; hall dressage exams possible

❸ Clear dimensions of riding halls

Stored substance		100 kg needs m³ space	Daily requirement per horse (kg)	Stored quantity per horse		
				No. of months	kg	m³
oats (grain)		0.22	5	1	150	0.33
hay	long, stored compressed	1.00–1.18	8	12	2900	29–34
	wired bales	0.59				17
straw	long, stored compressed	1.43–2.00	approx. 20 (clean straw for box stalls)	3	1825	26–37
	strung bales	1.05–1.18				19–22
	wired bales	0.42–0.50				8–9
	chopped 100 mm long	2.22–3.33	approx. 15		1375	31–16

❹ Storage space for horse feedstuffs

Most of the operational functions of the various types of riding facilities are basically the same, apart from variations due to special operational features or local conditions. Building specifications vary primarily according to the size of the business or stable occupation number, which is decisive for the design of the individual elements and determines whether various functions can be combined → ❶. Generally, the core of the organisation is the buildings needed for the accommodation, care and feeding of the horses, always designed as a self-contained structure. A covered riding area is essential to enable activity to continue in all weathers. Flats for stable boys, grooms and instructors should be designed together with the facilities.

The long axis of the show-jumping arena should be aligned north–south out of consideration for the horse and rider → ❸ because most of the jumps are approached towards the main axis of the riding arena. Tournament arenas, which are aligned north–south, should have the stand for the judges and single-sided spectator stands on the west side, because major events take place in the afternoon. The minimum area of the riding space is 20 × 40 m net (pure riding area) → ❷. 20 × 60 m riding areas are required for dressage from class M and eventing. The riding space needs additional spaces at the sides (≧3.0 m) and at the entrance (≧5.0 m), so the arena has a gross area of 26 × 48 m → ❷. For competitions, the minimum distance of the spectators from hooves is 5 m, for indoor trials 20 m.

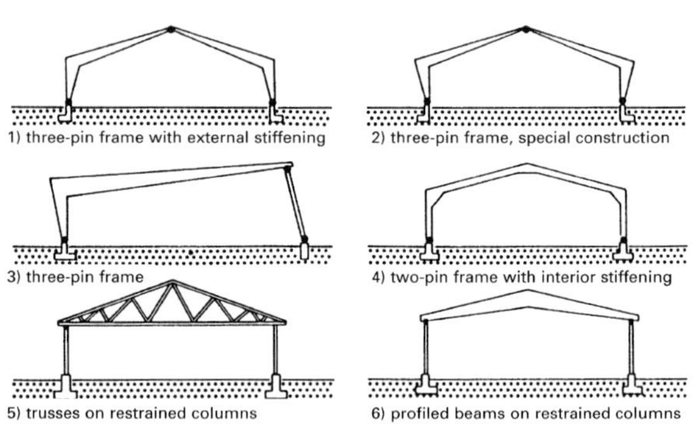

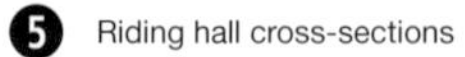

❺ Riding hall cross-sections

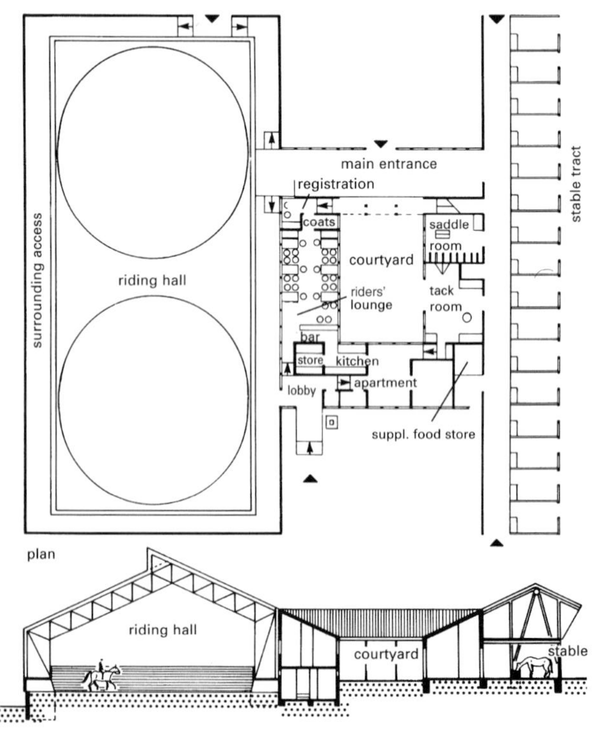

❻ Riding facility in Gerolstein/Eifel Arch.: Schnitzer

❶ Sketch of the construction of a ski jump

P = datum point
TP = table point
K = critical point (end of section where slope is parallel to the flight path)
B = end of the landing track curve
M = slow-down section (distance from P to K)
M_1 = distance from P to B
L = distance from edge of slope to P
L_1 = distance from edge of slope to K
H = vertical projection of L
N = horizontal projection of L
H:N = ratio of vertical to horizontal
a = slope of launch platform
b = slope of landing track from normal point (P) to critical point (K)
c = slope of starting ramp
R_1 = radius of curve from starting ramp to launch platform
R_2 = radius of curve from landing track to run-out
R_3 = radius of curve from launch platform to landing track
T = length of launch platform
U = part of starting ramp, in which speed no longer increases
E = part of starting ramp, in which speed increases
F = total length of starting ramp (F = U + E + T)
A = length of run-out
V_o = speed at launch platform in m/s
D = horizontal distance from launch platform to lower edge of judge's tower
Q = distance from the landing track axis to front edge of judge's tower

❷ These symbols should be used

medium and large ski jumps											
E			L								
c	c	c	9–12°						8–10°		←a
30°	35°	40°	U	T	V_o	H:N = 0.56	0.54	0.52	0.50	0.48	b ↓
62	52	44	8.8	4.6	21				53.0	51.0	35–37°
71	58	49	9.7	4.8	22	65.3	63.0	60.8	58.5	56.2	
80	65	54	10.6	5.1	23	71.5	69.0	66.5	64.0	61.5	36–38°
89	72	60	11.4	5.3	24	77.7	75.0	72.2	69.5	66.7	
99	80	67	12.5	5.5	25	84.0	81.0	78.0	75.0	72.0	37–39°
111	90	74	14.0	5.7	26	90.2	87.0	83.7	80.5	77.2	
124	100	81	15.0	5.9	27	96.3	93.0	89.5	86.0	82.5	38–40°
137	110	88	16.0	6.2	28				91.5	87.7	

❸ Dimensions of medium and large ski jumps

small ski jumps													
E						L							
c	c	c				8–10°		7–9°		6–8°		← a	
30°	35°	40°	U	T	V_o	H:N = 0.50	0.48	0.46	0.44	0.42	0.40	0.38	b↓
26	23	21	4.5	3.3	15	20.0	19.5	19.0	18.5	18.0	17.5	17.0	30–34°
32	28	25	5.1	3.5	16	25.5	24.8	24.0	23.3	22.5	21.8	21.0	30–35°
39	32	28	5.8	3.7	17	31.0	30.0	29.0	28.0	27.0	26.0	25.0	33–36°
46	37	32	6.5	4.0	18	36.5	35.3	34.0	32.8	31.5	30.3	29.0	33–36°
52	43	37	7.2	4.2	19	42.0	40.5	39.0	37.5	36.0	34.5	33.0	34–37°
59	49	42	8.0	4.4	20	47.5	45.8	44.0	42.3	40.5	38.8	37.0	34–37°

❹ Dimensions of small ski jumps

Example: according to the terrain, the following details were given for L1 and H:N, for example H:N = 0.54; c = 35°; L = 87 m.
In the table, you can find: L = 87 and in the left column V_o = 26; at the same level under c = 35°, E = 90 m, U =14 and T = 5.7; F = E + U + T = 90 + 14 + 5.7 = 109.7 m.
A ski jump which has dimensions different from the above can be approved by the FIS. In such a case, the designer of the ski jump must provide a detailed justification in writing.

The distance of the parapet of the lowest judge's cabin from the horizontal 'd' through the tip of the ski jump = D × tan 16° – tan 20°. The cabins should be arranged as steps in the sloping line passing through the ski jump table edge to the end of the point 'd'. The upper edge of the floor of the individual cabins is 1–1.20 m below the parapet. The slope of the tower to the track axis should be 7–10°, so that the judge can observe the entire flight and landing. At the top of the starting ramp, as many starting places as possible should be uniformly distributed along the length E/5, whose vertical spacing should be about 1 m. Lowest starting place = E – E/S.
Minimum width of the landing piste at K = Li/7 + 4 m.

Notes:

All slopes are to be given in old divisions (360°). If the transfers are parabolic, then R1 and R2 are the smallest curves of the parabolas. If the starting ramp is natural, the parts actually used should be marked every 2 m in order to simplify the exact determination of the starting place. The slope of the ski jump table and also a number of points on the curve between starting ramp and the tip of the ski jump table should be determined on both sides with fixed profiles, so that even non-experts can produce the exact and correct profile during the construction of the jump. It is recommended that profile markers should be placed at both sides alongside the landing profile and into the run-out to enable the creation of the exact snow profile, particularly if there is a lot of snow. Ski jumps whose L is >50 m should not normally be built with a V_o <21 m/sec. Ski jumps with L >90 m are not approved by the FIS (International Ski Federation); exception: flying ski jumps.

The standard values for the most important parts of the ski jump:
H:N = 0.48–0.56
The datum point of a ski jump is to be determined:
P = L_1–M, where the standards are for M:
M = 0.5–0.8 V_o for ski jumps up to P = 70 m
M = 0.7–1.1 V_o for ski jumps up to P = 90 m
M = 0–0.2 V_o
$R_1 = 0.12\,V_o^2 - 0.12\,V_{o2} + 8$ m
$R_2 = 0.14\,V_o^2 - 0.14\,V_o^2 + 20$ m
R_3 = profile for the front structure is selected to best suit the flight profile
T = 0.22 V_o
U = 0.02 V_o^2
A = 4–5 V_o with horizontal run-out
D = 0.5–0.7 × L_1 to lower edge of the tower
Q = 0.25–0.50 × L_1

❺ The data point of a ski jump is to be determined

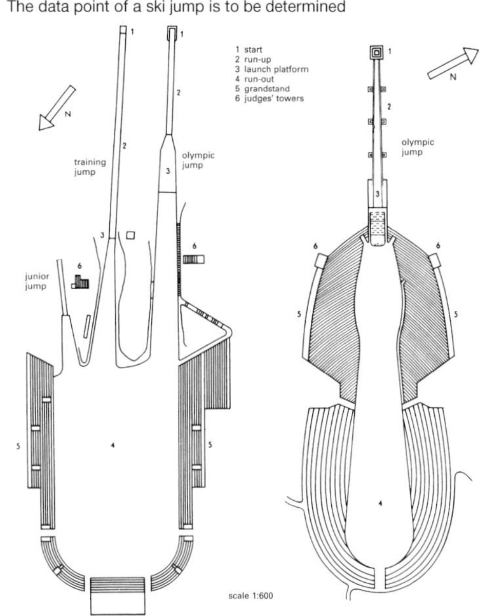

❻ Garmisch-Partenkirchen

❼ Holmenkollen

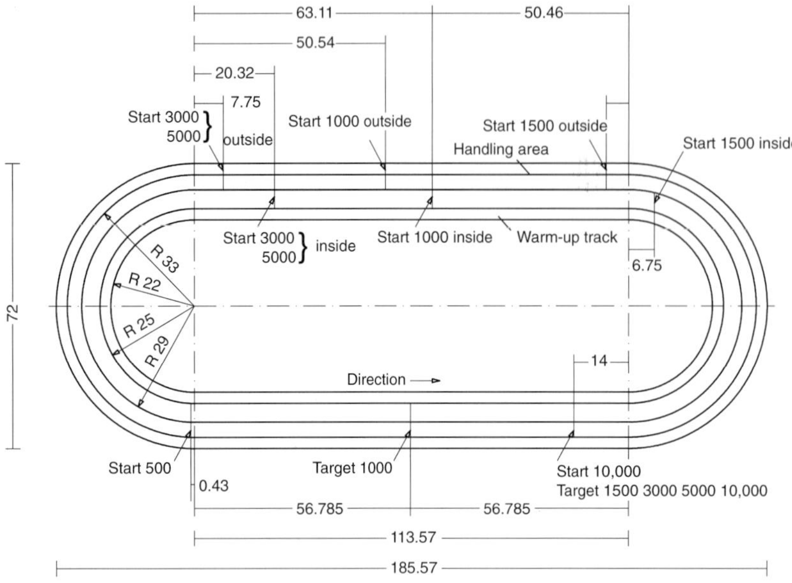

❶ Standard ice racing rink with marking

❷ Plan for short track

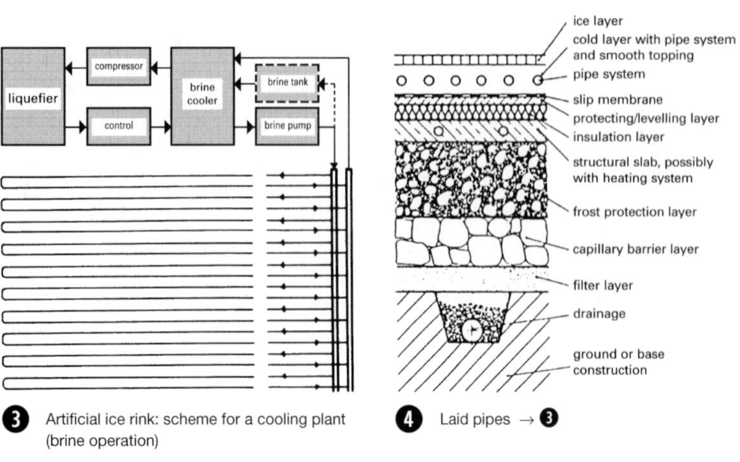

❸ Artificial ice rink: scheme for a cooling plant (brine operation)

❹ Laid pipes → ❸

Ice rinks are for skating, ice hockey and curling, which may of course also take place on naturally frozen lakes and rivers, also on frozen open-air swimming pools (the edge must be strong enough to resist ice pressure).

Sprayed ice rinks can be created on tennis courts, roller skating rinks and other large flat areas (surrounding wall about 10–15 cm). Water is sprayed 2 cm thick; drainage will be needed for water run-off.

Artificial ice rinks with cooling pipe system, 2.5 cm under screed layer. Pump system with deep-frozen salt solution or chambers with cold air (mostly ammonia compression process) → ❸ – ❹.

Standard ice racing rink. Length ≧300 m; 333½ m; normal 400 m. Measured 50 cm from the inner edge of the track. Radii of the inner curves ≧25 m crossings ≧70 m. It should be a double track → ❶.

2 × central axis = 2 × 111.94 = 223.89 m
inner curve = 25.2 × 3.1416 = 80.11 m
outer curve = 30.5 × 3.1416 = 95.82 m

crossing
√crossing length² × track width²
from 70 m
= 0.18 m
total length 400 m

Standard ice racing track

Width of a circular track: 4 m; width of the inside warming-up track: 3 m (for better training, 4 m is recommended).

Bob tracks with steeply banked curves of ice blocks. Spectator places should ideally be inside curves, otherwise with protecting walls of snow or straw bales in front of them.

Toboggan tracks lie on N-NW-NE slopes, ideally in a hollow. Length 1500–2500 m; slope 15–25%; width ≧2 m.

Flat run-out or uphill section, banking of curves and protection of obstacles with straw bales or snow walls. Climbing up not on the track but next to it.

Long curling rinks → ❺

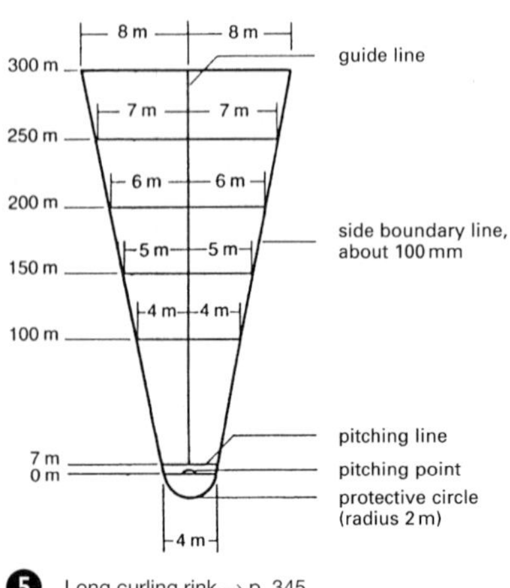

❺ Long curling rink → p. 345

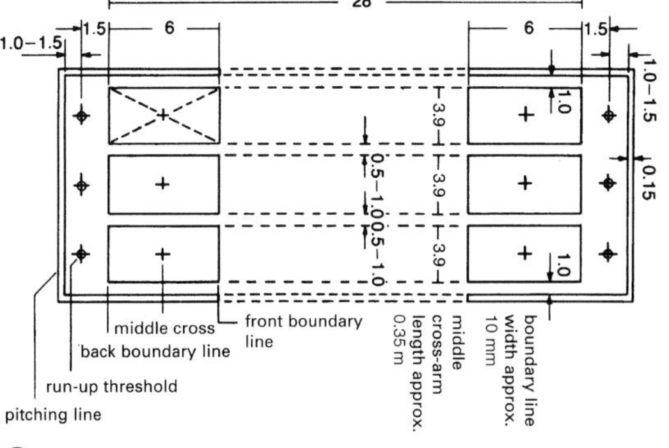

❶ Curling rink

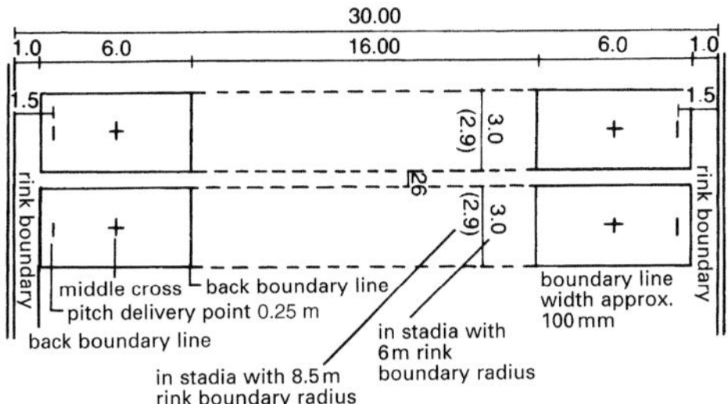

❷ Ice stock sport in an artificial ice rink

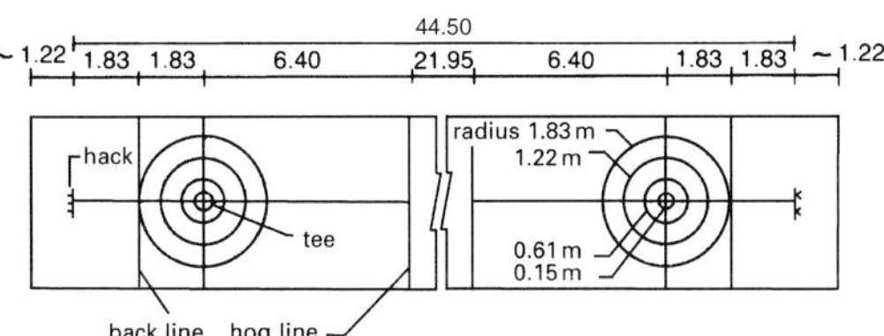

❸ Scottish curling sheet

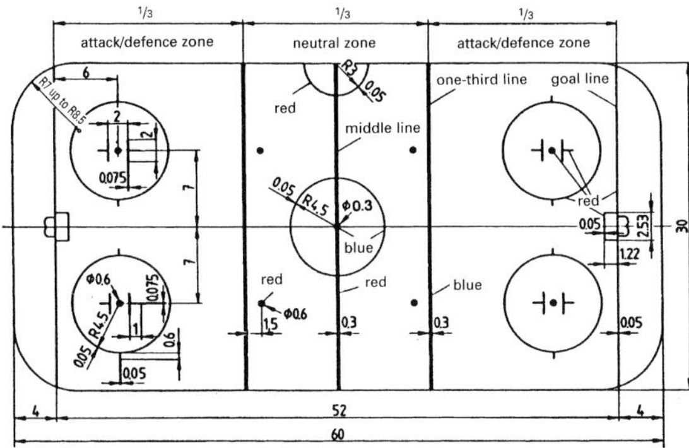

❹ Standard rink with markings for ice hockey

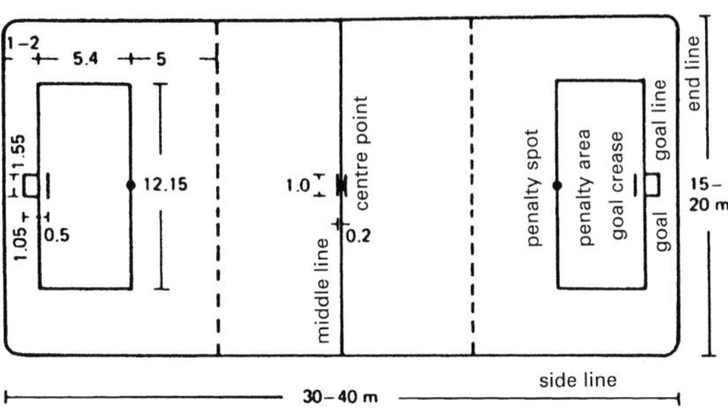

❺ Roller hockey rink

SPORTS FACILITIES

Ice Rinks

Ice stock or Bavarian curling → ❶ playing area length 28 m; width 3.9 m (30 × 3 m is also possible). Between playing areas, bands 1 m; at the ends ≧60 cm. Start and target areas are enclosed on three sides by wooden barriers, which can be stepped over.

Curling → ❸: playing area (sheet) length 44.5 m; target circle (house) ≧3.65 m. To the centre point of the target circle 34.74 m, shortened on bad ice to 29.26 m. Curling stone: weight ≧19.985 kg. Circumference ≧91.4 cm, height ≧$\frac{1}{8}$ of circumference.

Long curling rinks → p. 344 → ❺.

Ice hockey: playing field 30 × 61 m. Goal 1.83 m wide, 1.22 m high, play continues behind it. Playing field requires 1.15–1.22 m high perimeter barrier (wood or plastic) → ❹.

Figure skating: ice area rectangular ≧56 × 26 m ≧30 × 60 m. Combination of roller skating rink in summer (March to November) and ice rink in winter (December to February). Cold pipe system 2.5–5 cm under the surface of the rink (not possible with terrazzo)

ROLLER SKATING RINKS

1. Sport rinks	
roller hockey	15 × 30 to 20 × 40 m
roller figure skating	25 × 50 m
2. Recreational rinks	10 × 10 to 20 × 20 m

Crash board 25 cm high, 3 cm over rink, 80 cm parapet on all sides, 2 m wire mesh fence at the ends (to catch the ball), perimeter round playing area 1.2 m; 5–10 cm deeper, joints ≦5–6 mm, gradient ≦0.2‰. Surface water in gutters or trenches, frost protection layer ≧20 cm → ❺.

Construction types

1. Fibre cement boards, 15 mm; laid on squared timbers or on a sand bed.
2. Concrete tracks, 10–15 cm according to sub-base properties, as few joints as possible, possibly cut dummy joints 2–3 mm wide, expansion joints every 25–30 m, width ≧15 mm.
3. Hard concrete screed, ≧8 mm on fresh base concrete (if possible, with 2 cm cement mortar as stress compensation between screed and base concrete).
4. Cement screed with additives 1–10 mm.
5. Terrazzo, ground, ≧15 mm, brass, aluminium or plastic joint strips, only indoor.
6. Poured asphalt, on solid base layer,-, as usual.

Skater hockey → ❻
The playing surface consists of wood, tiles, parquet or other flat and smooth materials suitable for roller skating. The rink is surrounded by a ring barrier min. 0.20 m and max 1.22 m high. Hall walls are also allowed.

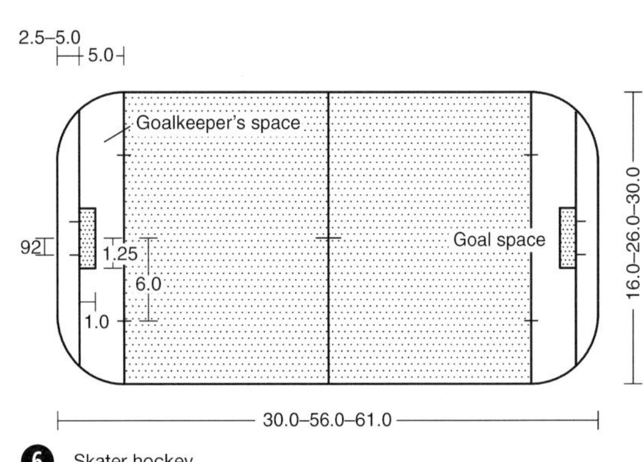

❻ Skater hockey

Sport and leisure

SPORTS FACILITIES
Playing fields
Athletics
Tennis
Miniature golf
Golf courses
Water sport, marinas
Water sport, rowing and canoeing
Equestrian sport
Ski jumping
Ice rinks
Roller skating rinks
Speed roller skating, skateboarding
Cyclo-cross, BMX
Shooting ranges

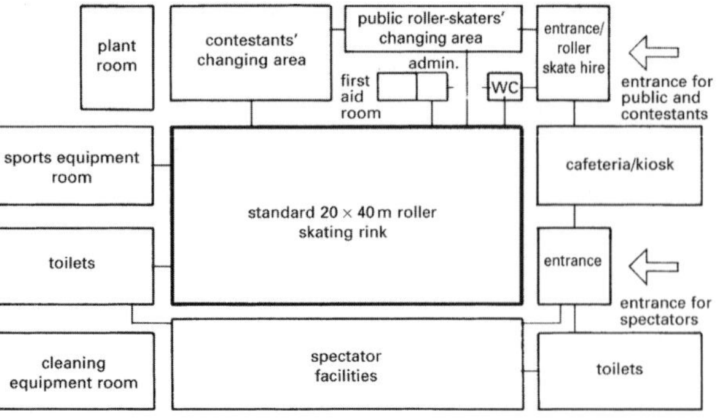

❶ Functional diagram of a speed roller skating rink

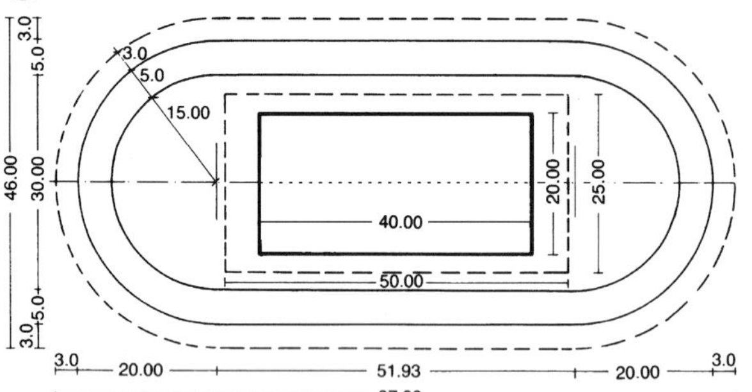

❷ Dimensions of a 200 m speed roller skating track with inner standard rink 20 × 40 m

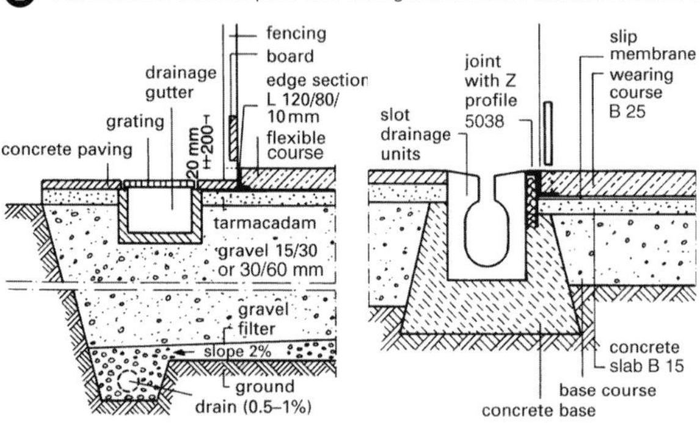

❸ Example of paving: with drainage on cohesive soil

❹ Edge detail: floating slab without fixed point or step down to perimeter

Quarter with wall ride

Height + wall: 2 m
Width: 3 m
Radius: 2 m

Funbox

Height: 1.35 m
Width: 2.5 m
Radius/jump: 2.5 m
Table length: 2.5 m
Landing: 4.2 m

Quarter with roll-in, rear or sub box, front

Quarter
Height: 2 m
Width: 4 m
Radius: 2.5 m
Table length: 1.5 m
Roll-in (top part at back)
Height: 1 m
Width: 1.25 m
Radius: 2 m
Sub-box (top part at front)
Height: 1 m
Width: 2 m
Depth: 90 cm

It should be noted for layouts for flybox jumping: The run-up must always be higher than the jumping point. Normally, twice the jump-off height.

❻ Flybox for jumping with skateboard, inline skates and BMX bikes

Space required: standard area 20 × 40 m → ❶

Rooms for athletes:

2 (4) communal changing rooms, each with 8 m bench and clothes hangers (roller hockey, 4 communal changing rooms). For roller hockey, if required additional clothes hooks every 3 m^2.

2 shower rooms with 4 showers, drying zone, 2 washbasins, 2 hairdryers and separate toilet in anteroom. 4 drying rooms (only roller hockey) per 6 m^2. 1 umpires' and trainers' room, approx. 9 m^2.

Facilities for public speed skating: entrance area with ticket machine and turnstile or staffed cash desk, approx. 40 m^2. Changing rooms for public skating, also serve for putting on skates. Use all-year-round. 30 single, 60 double lockers and bench length 20 m.

1 ladies' toilet with 2 WCs, separate anteroom and washbasins. 1 gents' toilet with 2 WCs, 3 urinals, separate anteroom and washbasin, 1 sanitary room 9 m^2, 1 skate rental room 12 m^2 (in connection with cash desk).

1 supervisor and control room (also control room for lighting and loudspeaker system) 8 m^2. Changing, shower, washbasins, toilets and cloakroom for 1–2 people, 1 workshop 4 m^2, 1 sporting equipment room (large items) 15 m^2, 1 sporting equipment room (small items) 6 m^2, cleaners' room 12 m^2, heating 10 m^2, electricity room 4 m^2, supply room 3 m^2.

Possible uses	Required skating area (m)	Remarks
public roller skating, roller figure skating, roller dancing and roller hockey	20 × 40 m	**standard area** min. area for roller hockey 17 × 34 m
public roller skating, roller figure skating, dancing and hockey	20 × 50 m	in particular cases
public roller skating, roller figure skating, dancing and hockey, inline speed skating and ice rink	30 × 60 m	in general only if combined with ice rink; 110 m short track for speed skating is possible on an area of 30 × 60 m
inline speed skating track	200 m 333⅓ m 400 m	**standard track** only in combination with cycle track and ice speed skating rink
track width	5 m	

❺ Possible uses and dimensions of sports areas

SKATEBOARDING

Skateboarding is related to inline skating and roller facilities are also suitable for skateboarding. Space required for a facility min. 200 m^2.

Suitable locations: 1. Existing road-like surfaces in schoolyards, playgrounds, ice rinks, closed roads, separated areas of car parks, houses and back yards. 2. Suitable paving newly laid in sports centres, public parks and green areas.

Type	Height (m)	Width (m)	Radius (m)	Centre part (m)	Verticals (m)
skateboard mini-ramp	1	5	1.5	2	none
BMX mini-ramp	2	6	2.5	3	none
fun pipe	3	6	2.8	3	0.3
half-pipe – standard	3.5	6	3	3	0.5
half-pipe – king-size	4.1	10	3.5	3.5	0.6

❼ Dimensions of half-pipes

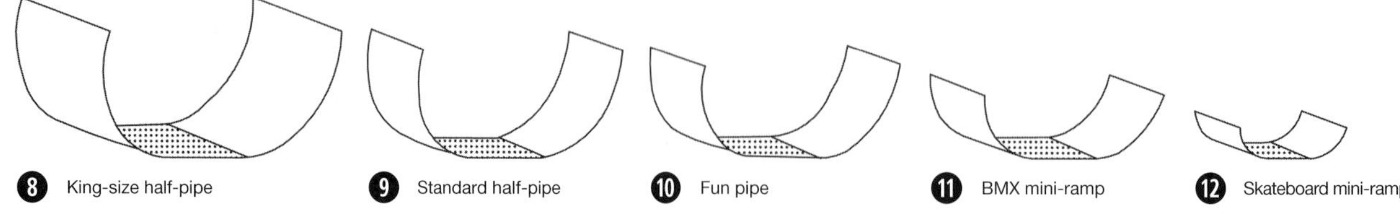

❽ King-size half-pipe ❾ Standard half-pipe ❿ Fun pipe ⓫ BMX mini-ramp ⓬ Skateboard mini-ramp

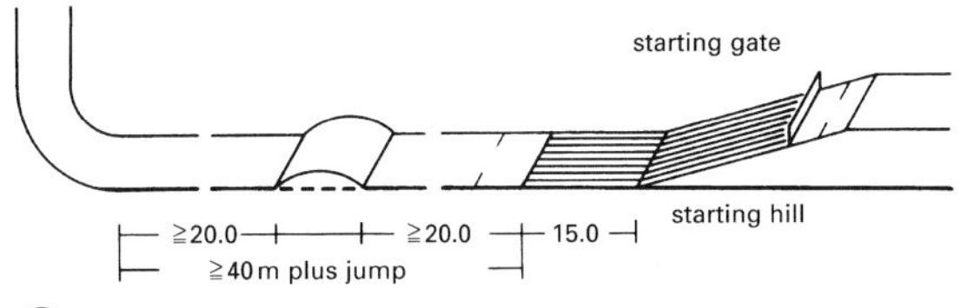

❶ Starting hill

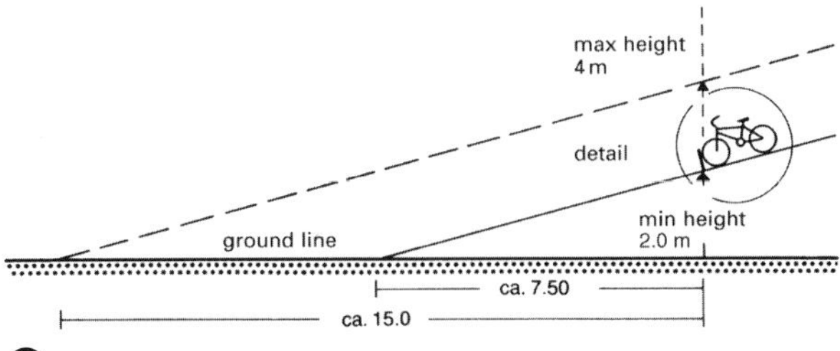

❷ Heights of the starting hill

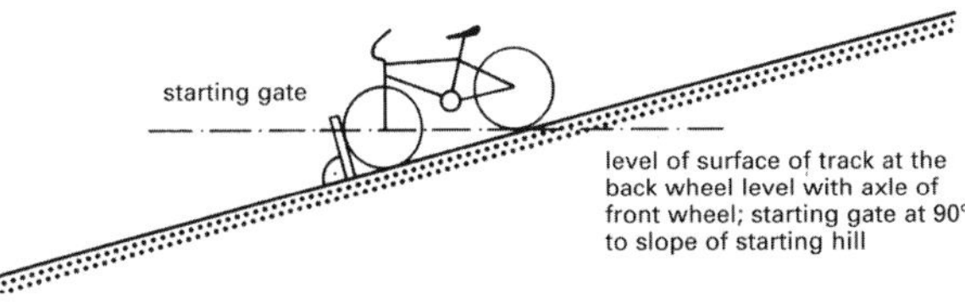

❸ Starting hill detail → ❷

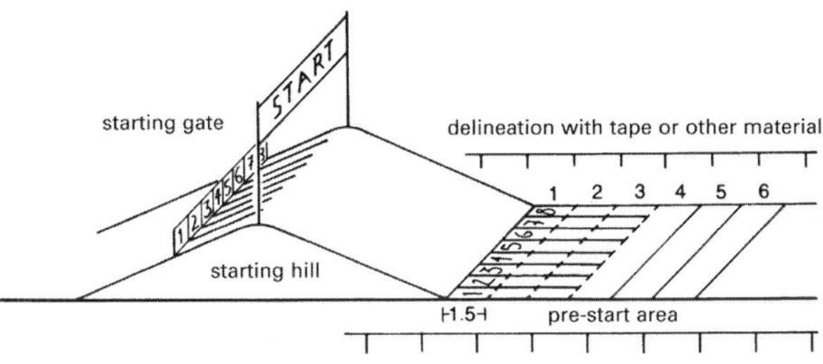

❹ Starting ramp with pre-start area

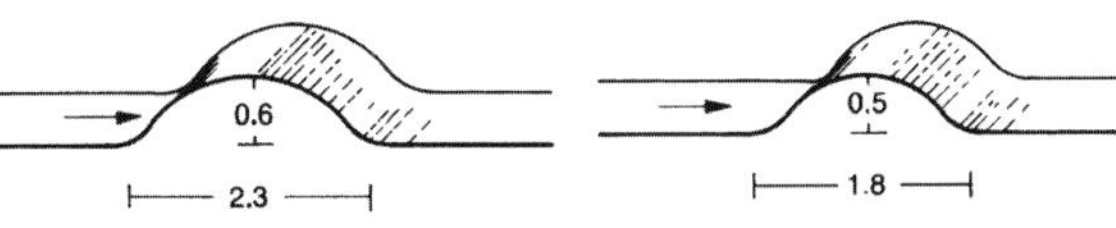

❺ Speed jump

❻ Speed jump

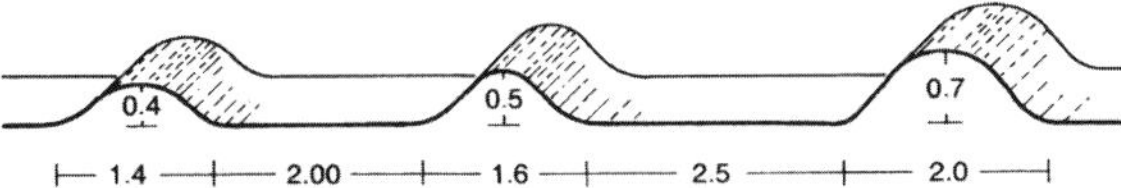

❼ Triple jump (or triple combination)

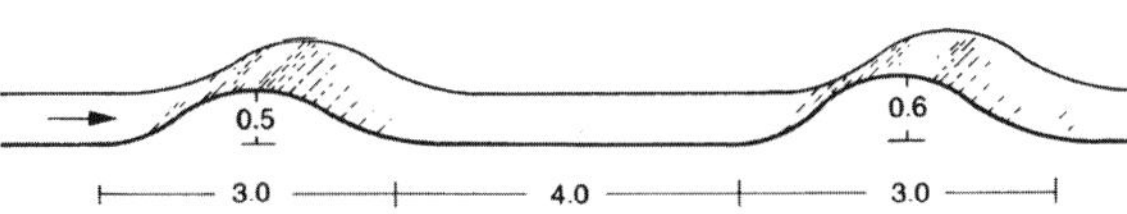

❽ Double speed jump

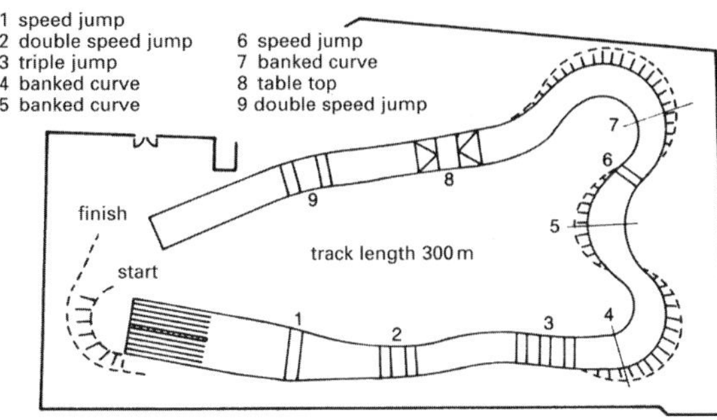

⓭ BMX track at the WM '87 in Bordeaux

Minimum plot size for BMX sport facilities 50 × 60 m. Maximum dimensions for a generous track with sufficient spectator places 100 × 200 m. Observe safety spacing of tracks in opposite directions. Four types of BMX track are possible according to local conditions.

C track, B track, A track/national, A track/international.

C track min. length 200 m. Starting hill width = 5 m = 4 starting places,

B track 250 m. Starting hill width = 7 m = 6 starting places, min. lap time 30 s.

A track/national min. length 270–320 m. Starting hill width = 9 m = 8 starting places, min. lap time 35 s.

A track/international min. length 300 m Starting hill width = 9 m = 8 starting places, min. lap time 35 s.

Paved surface on the starting straight. Lap time must be achievable by an average 15-year-old rider. Trackside markings are not of solid materials (stone, concrete, timber or similar). Safety barriers of car tyres or straw bales are sufficient. Fixed barriers must have a min. distance of 1 m. Closure to spectator space must be marked with warning tape. No spectators allowed inside the track. Max. speed on downhill sections 40 km/h. Curves and obstacles can be placed as desired along the course.

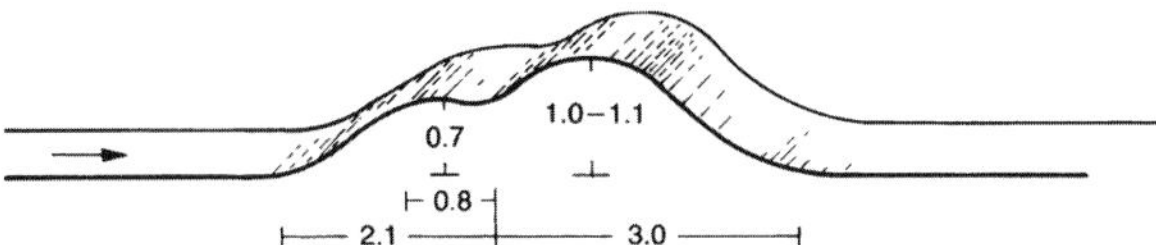

❾ Step jump

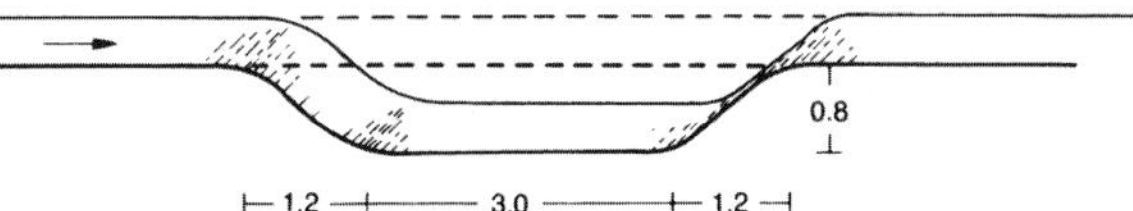

❿ Canon jump

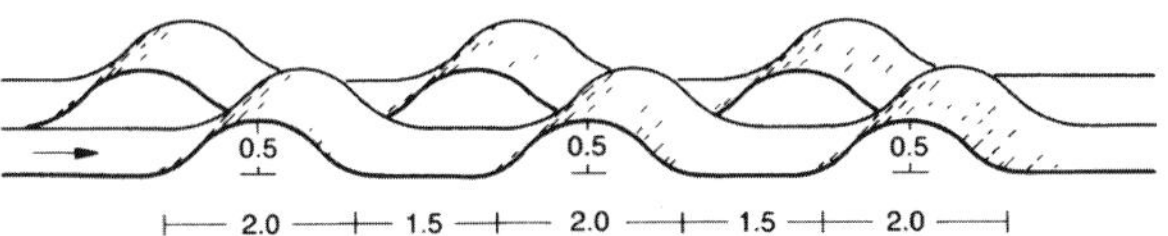

⓫ Mogul jump (moguls)

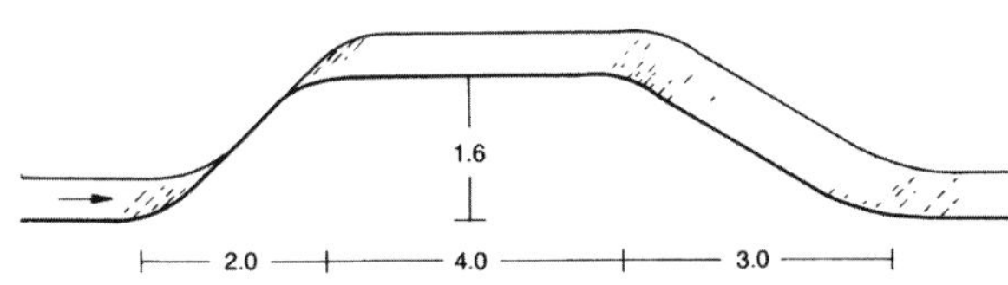

⓬ Table top

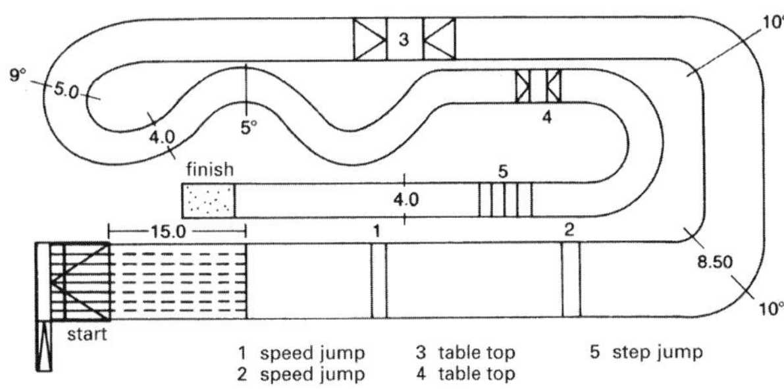

⓮ BMX track at the IFMA '84 in Cologne

Location: if possible in a gully within a wooded area, with surrounding hillside to catch bullets naturally, away from public roads and buildings. Shooting ranges are also possible in buildings, e.g. in combination with public multi-purpose sports halls. Common categories are air gun range, pistol and small calibre range → ❶ – ❺ → p. 349.

The safety requirements for Germany are laid down in the 'Guidelines for the construction and acceptance for shooting ranges for sporting and hunting shooting' from the German Shooting Association. Apart from the normal permission for the building of a shooting range, a report is also required from an accredited shooting range expert. The right of 'neighbours' to object on the grounds of noise nuisance is mostly upheld. Safety constructions like overhead baffles, side protection (walls or earth banks) and the closing off of the range must be built of approved construction materials or are tested by the expert.

In the UK, rifle and pistol (but not air gun) ranges require the approval and safety certificate of the Ministry of Defence. Early approval is also needed from the National Small-Bore Rifle Association (NSRA) or the National Rifle Association (NRA).

Shooting programme

Olympic competitions: x = for men, xx = for women and men, xxx = only for women.

Rifle shooting: air rifle 10 m xx; Zimmerstutzen rifle 15 m; small-calibre rifle 50 m x; KK standard rifle xxx; sport rifle 100 m; large-calibre rifle 300 m; GK standard rifle 300 m.

Pistol shooting: air pistol 10 m xx; Olympic quick-fire pistol 25 m x; sport pistol 25 m xxx; standard pistol 25 m, free pistol 50 m x.

Clay pigeon shooting: trap shooting x; skeet shooting x.

Running target: moving boar, 10 m and 50 m x.

Archery: hall conditions, international conditions xx, field bow.

Crossbow: national conditions, international conditions 10 and 30 m.

Muzzle loader shooting: national conditions.

❶ Section → ❷

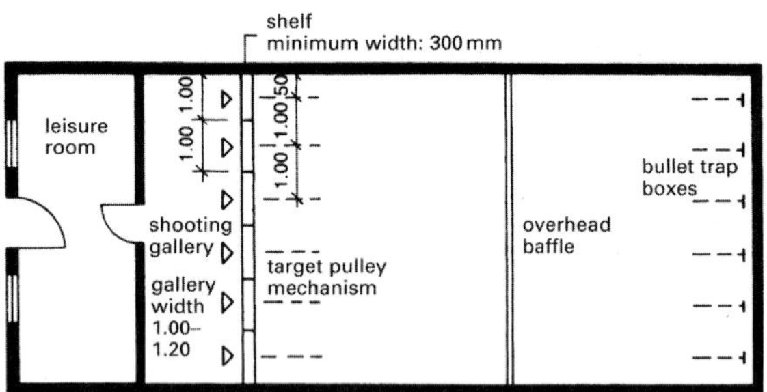

❷ Shooting range for air pressure and CO_2 guns, covered shooting gallery, open-air range

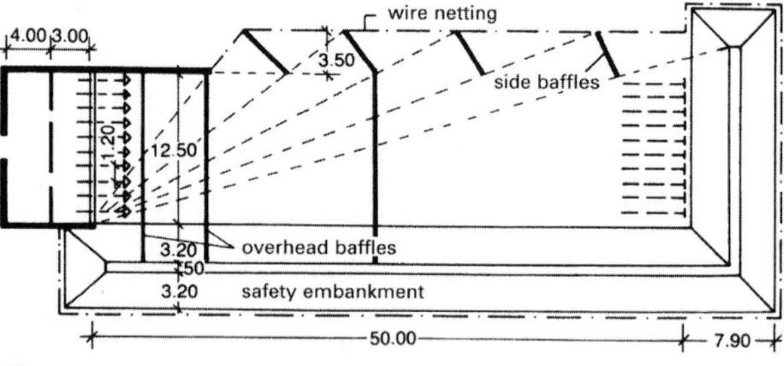

❸ Small-calibre range for target-pulling

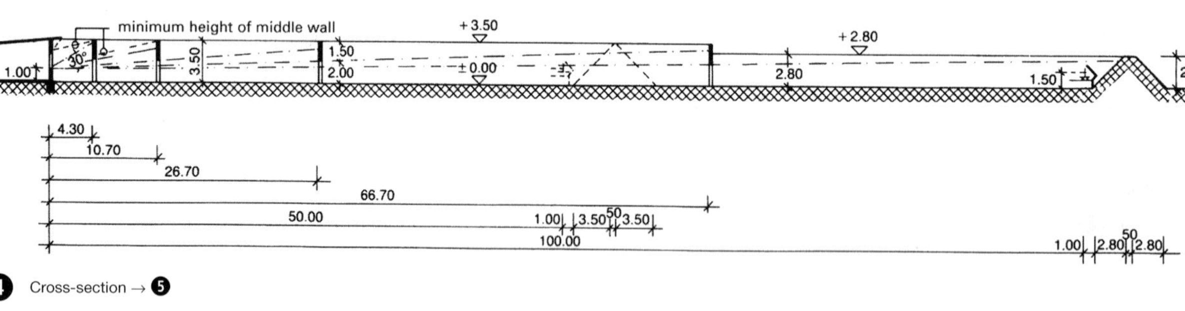

❹ Cross-section → ❺

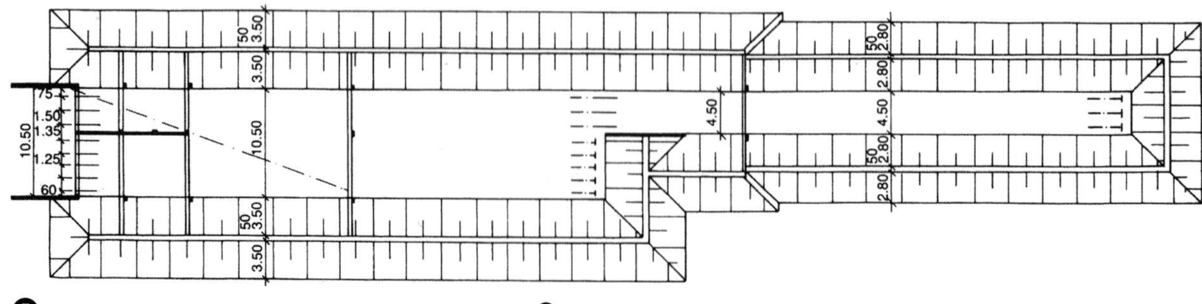

❺ Combined 100 m range for all rifles and a 50 m small-calibre range → ❹

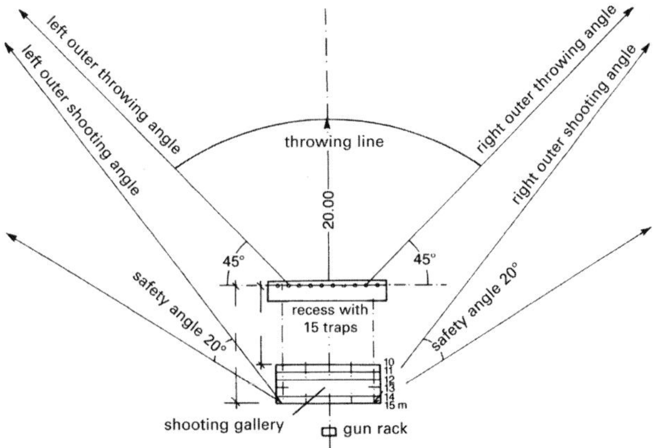

❶ Clay pigeon shooting range

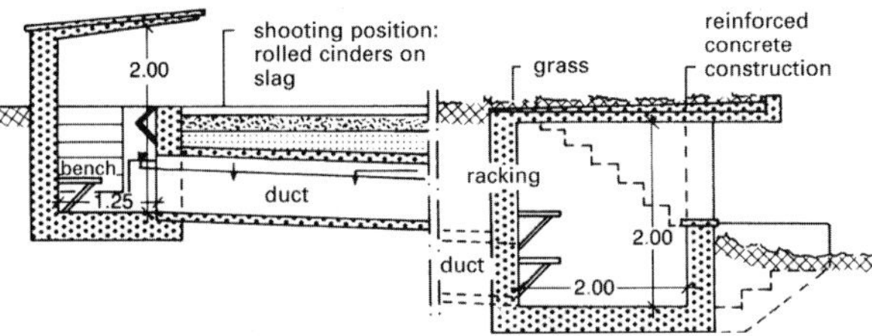

❷ Longitudinal section through clay pigeon range

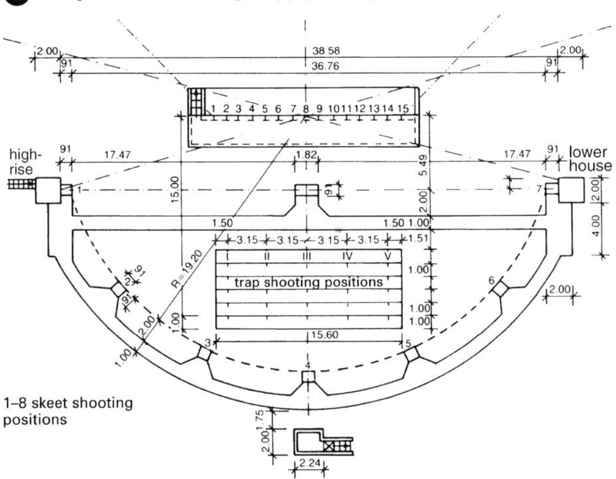

❸ Combined trap and skeet shooting range

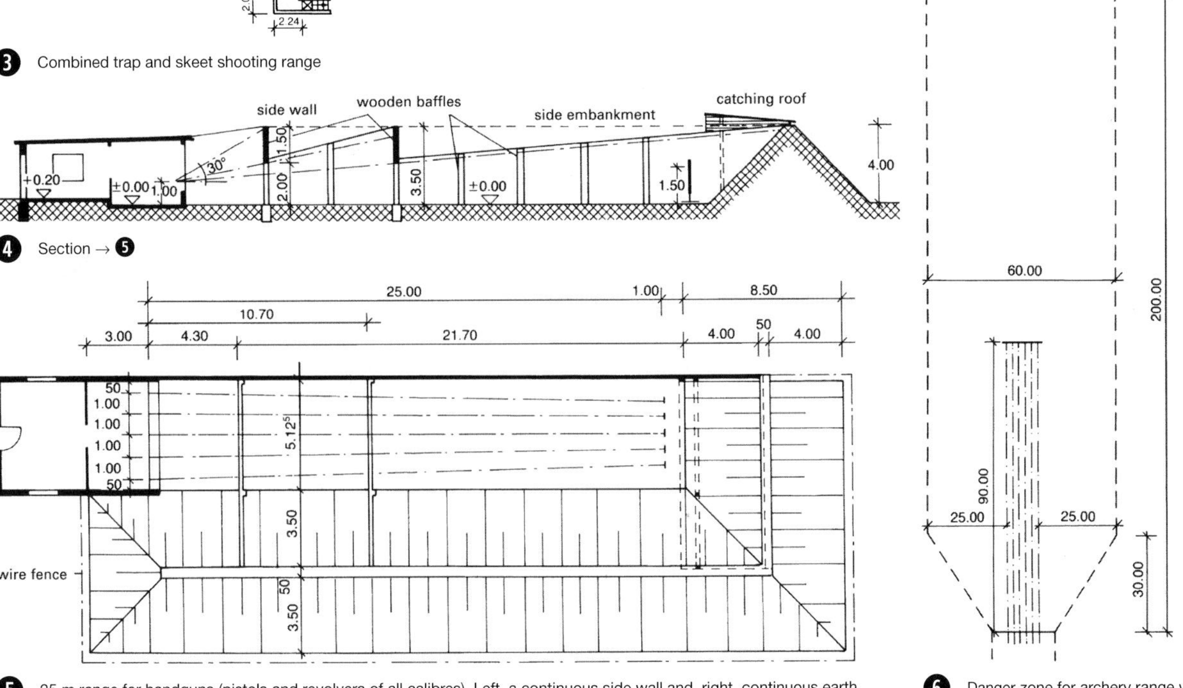

❹ Section → ❺

❺ 25 m range for handguns (pistols and revolvers of all calibres). Left, a continuous side wall and, right, continuous earth bank (wall or earth bank can be used either side).

❻ Danger zone for archery range with six targets

Elevation safety

The total range of a shot is mainly determined by the ideal angle of elevation. According to experience, the vertical elevation needing to be safely restrained is 20° for air pressure and CO_2 guns and Zimmerstutzen rifles, and 30° for rifle ranges and handguns.

For high crossbow and archery ranges, the regulations differ. Endangered areas are to be protected by dedicated safety structures. A shooting range must be constructed so that, according to experience, no danger to shooters taking part can arise internally nor externally to the surrounding neighbourhood. The requirements of the Federal Pollution Control Law must be complied with.

An assessment whether a specific site is suitable for the building of a shooting range is essential for the estimation of the cost of building. An accredited expert on shooting ranges can provide the architect with the necessary specialist information, and should always be consulted. Particular points to note are:

Distance from existing or planned built-up areas and inhabited houses, intended shooting direction (north or north-east), soil conditions and features of terrain, utility supplies, waste disposal, road connection, routeing of roads (also planned), car parking, holiday and leisure areas. Can or must there be deviations from the guidelines? Any required protection measures should be included in the design from the start. Ranges can be built in separate construction sections.

The procedures for approval and permission are determined by state regulations. The layout and extent of a shooting range should include the consideration of additions and extensions, which could become necessary in the future and can be built at reasonable cost. The design of open-air ranges should include noise protection measures.

SPORTS HALLS

Dimensions

The design basics are: multi-functional hall, sports hall and multi-purpose hall. The design has to include consideration of the competition rules of the specialist sport associations and also the best-possible integration of the individual sports → ❶.

The required site size depends on the playing area required and the administrative offices. It can normally be estimated as follows if the detailed room schedule is not yet available: required sports area × 2 + necessary open areas to the site boundary + necessary parking space for vehicles.

Dimensions of halls → ❶. Halls capable of being sub-divided are preferable, on grounds of flexibility, to a number of single halls.

Operational rooms for sporting events

Entrance hall, with cash desk, spectators' cloakroom and perhaps cleaning equipment room, based on → ❷ 0.1 m^2 per spectator. Space needed per seat for spectators and VIPs, press, radio and television (incl. immediate traffic area): 0.5 × 0.4–0.45 m; per press place 0.75 × 0.8–0.85 m; per reporting cabin 1.8 × 2.0 m; per camera platform: 2.0 × 2.0 m. 1 cloakroom place for every 3 spectators, 1 m of cloakroom service counter for every 30 cloakroom places. No. toilets per spectator: 0.01: 40% WCs, ladies; 20% WCs, gents; and 40% urinals. Per seat incl. anteroom 2.5 m^2, per urinal incl. anteroom 1.0 m^2. cash desk, cafeteria, police, fire service, administration, storeroom, press rooms as required.

Hall type	Dimensions (m)	Usable playing area (m^2)	Hall sports[1]	No. training courts/fields	No. competition courts/fields[2]
Multi-functional halls					
single hall	15 × 27 × 5.5	405	badminton	4	
			basketball	1	
			volleyball	1	
triple hall	27 × 45 × 7[3][4] divisible into 3 sections (15 × 27)[5]	1215	badminton	12	5[6]
			basketball	3	1
			indoor football		1
			indoor handball		1
			indoor hockey		1
			volleyball	3	1
quadruple hall	27 × 60 × 7[3] divisible into 4 sections (15 × 27)[5]	1620	badminton	16	7[6]
			basketball	4	2
			indoor football		1
			indoor handball		1
			indoor hockey		1
			volleyball	4	1
possibly also double hall	22 × 44 × 7[3][4] divisible into 2 sections (22 × 28 + 22 × 16 or 22 × 26 + 22 × 18)[5]	968	badminton	6	5[6]
			basketball		1
			indoor football		1
			indoor handball		1
			indoor hockey		1
			volleyball	3	1
Sports halls					
single hall	22 × 44 × 7[3][4]	968	badminton	6	5
			basketball		1
			indoor football		1
			indoor handball		1
			indoor hockey		1
			volleyball	3	1
triple hall	44 × 66 × 8[3] divisible into 3 sections (22 × 44)[5]	2904	badminton	24	15
			basketball		4[6]
			indoor football		
			20 × 40		3
			30 × 60		1
			indoor handball		3
			indoor hockey		3
			volleyball	9	3
quadruple hall	44 × 88 × 9[3] divisible into 4 sections (22 × 44)[5]	3872	badminton	32	25[6]
			basketball	5[6]	4
			indoor football		
			20 × 40		4
			40 × 80		1
			indoor handball		4
			indoor hockey		4
			volleyball	12	4

1) common indoor sports not incorporating national or regional customs
2) dimensions according to guidelines of the international sport ruling bodies; can perhaps be reduced in national use
3) height of hall can perhaps be reduced at the edges according to sporting functions
4) if there are a number of halls on one site or in the planned area, height can be reduced to 5.5 m in part of the halls according to intended use
5) less the proportional thickness of the relevant partition
6) maximum number without consideration of the partition

❶ Dimensions of halls

Room	Dimensions (m)	Usable playing area (m^2)
Conditioning/power training room	depends on equipment, min. height 3.5	35–200
Fitness room	depends on equipment, min. height 2.5	20–50
Gymnastics room	10 × 10 × 4 to 14 × 14 × 4	100–196

❸ Dimensions of rooms for additional sports

Hall type	Entrance hall (m^2)	Changing rooms (min. 20 m^2)[2]	Showers (min. 15 m^2)[3]	Toilets			Teaching room[4] (min. 12 m^2) without first aid function (min. 8 m^2)	Equipment room		Cleaning equipment room min. 5 m^2	Waiting room min. 10 m^2
				per changing room	lobby min. no.			Multi-functional hall	Sports hall		
	m^2	min. no.	no.	min. no.	F	M	min. no.	min. m^2 [5]	min.m^2 [5]	min. no.	no.
Single hall	15	2	1[6]	1	1	1	1	60[7]	20[8]	1	1[9]
Double hall	30	2	2	1	1	1	1	90[7]	—	1	1[9]
Triple hall	45	3[10]	3[10]	1	1	1	2	120[7]	60[8]	1	1
Quadruple hall	60	4[10]	4[10]	1	1	1	3	150[7]	80[8]>	1	1

1) minimum room height generally 2.5 m
2) space requirement per person is 0.7–1.0 m^2, based on allowances of 0.4 m bench length per person, 0.3 m sitting depth and min. 1.5 m between benches or between bench and wall (1.8 m recommended)
3) 1 shower per 6 persons (but a minimum of 8 showers and 4 washbasins per facility), shower space including a minimum circulation area of 10 m^2 and circulation space at least 1.2.m wide
4) training supervisors', umpire/referees' room, perhaps including first aid post (min. 8 m^2 for separate first aid room), with changing cubicle and shower; can also be used as an administration room if correctly positioned, designed and of sufficient size
5) because the range of apparatus provided varies according to location, it is likely that these minimum dimensions will have to be exceeded; no hall section in a multi-functional hall should have less than a 6 m length apparatus room
6) divided into 2 sections, each with half of the apparatus
7) room depth normally 4.5.m, max. 6.0.m
8) room depth normally 3 m, max. 5.5 m
9) according to need
10) alternatively, 2 bigger rooms with proportionally more shower and washing facilities

❷ Operational rooms for sports halls

Type of sport	Usable playing area (net)				Additional unobstructed zone at the:		Unobstructed playing area with standard dimensions (gross)		Clear hall height[1]
	Permissible dimensions:		Standard dimensions:						
	length (m)	width (m)	length (m)	width (m)	sides (m)	ends (m)	length (m)	width (m)	(m)
Badminton	13.4	6.1	13.4	6.1	1.5	2.0	17.4	9.1	9[2]
Basketball	24–28	13–15	28	15	1[3]	1[3]	30	17	7
Boxing	4.9–6.1	4.9–6.1	6.1	6.1	0.5	0.5	7.1	7.1	4
Fistball	40	20	40	20	0.5	2	44	21	(7)
Football	30–50	15–25	40	20	0.5	2	44	21	(5.5)
Weight lifting	4	4	4	4	3	3	10	10	4
Netball	40	20	40	20	1[4]	2	44	22	7[5]
Hockey	36–44	18–22	40	20	0.5	2	44	21	(5.5)
Judo	9–10	9–10	10	10	2	2	14	14	(4)
Netball	28	15	28	15	1	1	30	17	(5.5)
Sports acrobatics	12	12	12	12	1	1	14	14	(5.5)
Gymnastics	52	27	52	27	—	—	52	27	8
Cycle football/ polo/gymnastics	12–14	9–11	14	11	1	2	18	13	(4)
Rhythmic gymnastics	13[6]	13[6]	13[6]	13[6]	1	1	15	15	8[2]
Wrestling	9–12	9–12	12	12	2	2	14	14	(4)
Roller hockey	34–40	17–20	40	20	—	—	40	20	(4)
Roller acrobatics/ dancing	40	20	40	20	—	—	40	20	(4)
Sports dancing	15–16	12–14	16	14	—	—	16	14	(4)
Tennis	23.77	10.97	23.77	10.97	3.65	6.4	36.57	18.27	(7)
Table tennis	2.74	1.525	2.74	1.525	5.63	2.74	14	7	4
Trampolining	4.57	2.74	4.57	2.74	4	4	12.57	10.74	7
Volleyball	18	9	18	9	5	8	34	19	12.5[2]

1) nos in brackets: recommended; 2) for national events, 7 m is sufficient; 3) for spectator stands bordering the playing area, ideally 2 m; 4) additional space requirement for timers' table and reserves' bench (poss. in sports equipment room); 5) in a 3.3 m wide zone around the playing area (net), a uniform reduction to 5.5 m is permissible; 6) for national competitions 12 m.

Playing area dimensions for competitive sports use

Apparatus	Unobstructed total sport area[1] length × width × height (m)	Safety distance[2] (m)			
		Sides	Forwards	Backwards	To each other
Floor gymnastics	14 × 14 × 4.5	—	—	—	—
Pommel horse	4 × 4 × 4.5	—	—	—	—
Vaulting horse	36[3] × 2 × 5.5	—	—	—	—
Suspended rings[4]	8 × 6 × 5.5	—	—	—	—
Parallel bars	6 × 9.5 × 4.5	4.5[5][6]	4[5]	3[5]	4.5
Horizontal bar	12 × 6 × 7.5[7]	1.5	6	6	—
Assymmetric bars	12 × 6 × 5.5	1.5	6	6	—
Beam	12 × 6 × 4.5	—	—	—	—
Swinging rings[4]	18 × 4 × 5.5	1.5[5] (2) A	10.5[5] (7.5) A	7.5[5]	1.5[5]
Climbing rpe	—	1.5	4.5 (4) A	4.5 (4) A	1.5 (0.8) A
Header hanging ball	—	4.5[5]	4.5[5]	4.5[5]	7
Wall bars	—		4.5[5][6]	4.5	4.5

1) for competitive sport; 2) for school and leisure sport (between fixed apparatus and wall or other fixed apparatus); 3) run-up length 25 m, apparatus length 2 m, run-out length 9 m; 4) distance between centres of ropes 0.5 m; 5) measured either from centres or top of apparatus posts, or end of crossbar, or centre of rope; 6) reduction to 4 m to walls or to 3.5 m to netting walls possible; 7) for national competitions 7 m height is sufficient; A = Austria.

❷ Unobstructed areas and safety distances for fixed sports apparatus

Operational rooms for multi-purpose use (in addition to entrance hall) → p. 350 ❷. Per visitor: 0.1 m^2. Cloakroom: 1 place per visitor. Per cloakroom place: 0.05–0.1 m^2 (incl. 1 m of service counter in cloakroom for every 30 cloakroom places). Number of WCs per visitor 0.01, of which 40% WCs for ladies, 20% WCs for gents, 40% urinals.

Storeroom for tables and chairs per visitor: 0.05–0.06 m^2. Raised stage and associated equipment, per m^2 stage area: 0.12 m^2. Cash desk and sundries: as required.

Catering: standing space per vending machine 1.0 × 0.6–0.8 m, tea kitchen 12–15 m^2, store 6 m^2, kiosk with drinks 8–12 m^2, store 10–12 m^2. Cafeteria/restaurant per seat: 1.5–2.7 m^2, of which altogether for the guest area 1–1.5 m^2, for kitchen and stores 0.5–1.2 m^2. Servery for self-service: per 50 visitor places = 1 m counter. With waiter service: per 100 visitor places = 2 m counter.

Small stage <200 m^2 → p. 203. Athletes' cloakroom, multi-purpose room for meetings, training, lectures, leisure use. Playroom for board games, billiards etc., reading room and bowling alley as required.

Operations rooms for technical services are included in sports halls. Open-air facilities which do not have a dedicated building must be provided with an equipment room for sports and maintenance equipment in the room arrangements of the sports hall. Open-air sports equipment room = 0.3 m^2 per 100 m^2 usable playing area (net area) = 15 m^2. Maintenance equipment room for hand appliances = 0.04 m^2 per 100 m^2; gross open area = 8 m^2. Maintenance equipment room for machines = 0.06 m^2 per 100 m^2; gross open area = 12 m^2. (If maintenance is carried out externally, or else centrally – and the machines are delivered and taken away – the last mentioned room can be omitted.)

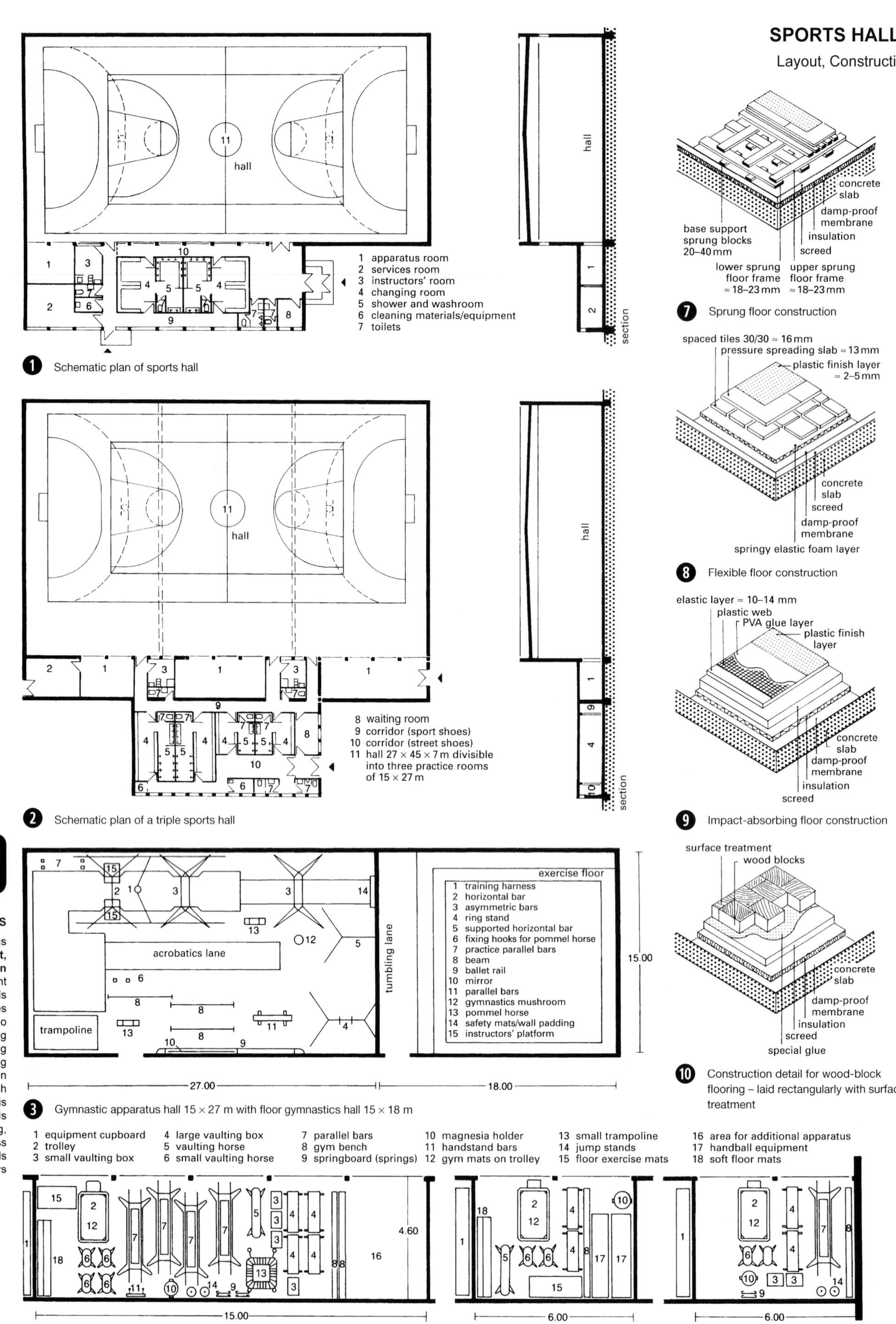

❶ Schematic plan of sports hall

❷ Schematic plan of a triple sports hall

❸ Gymnastic apparatus hall 15 × 27 m with floor gymnastics hall 15 × 18 m

❹ Arrangement plan for large equipment in the apparatus storeroom of a 15 × 27 m sports hall

❺ Equipment room

❻ Equipment room

❼ Sprung floor construction

❽ Flexible floor construction

❾ Impact-absorbing floor construction

❿ Construction detail for wood-block flooring – laid rectangularly with surface treatment

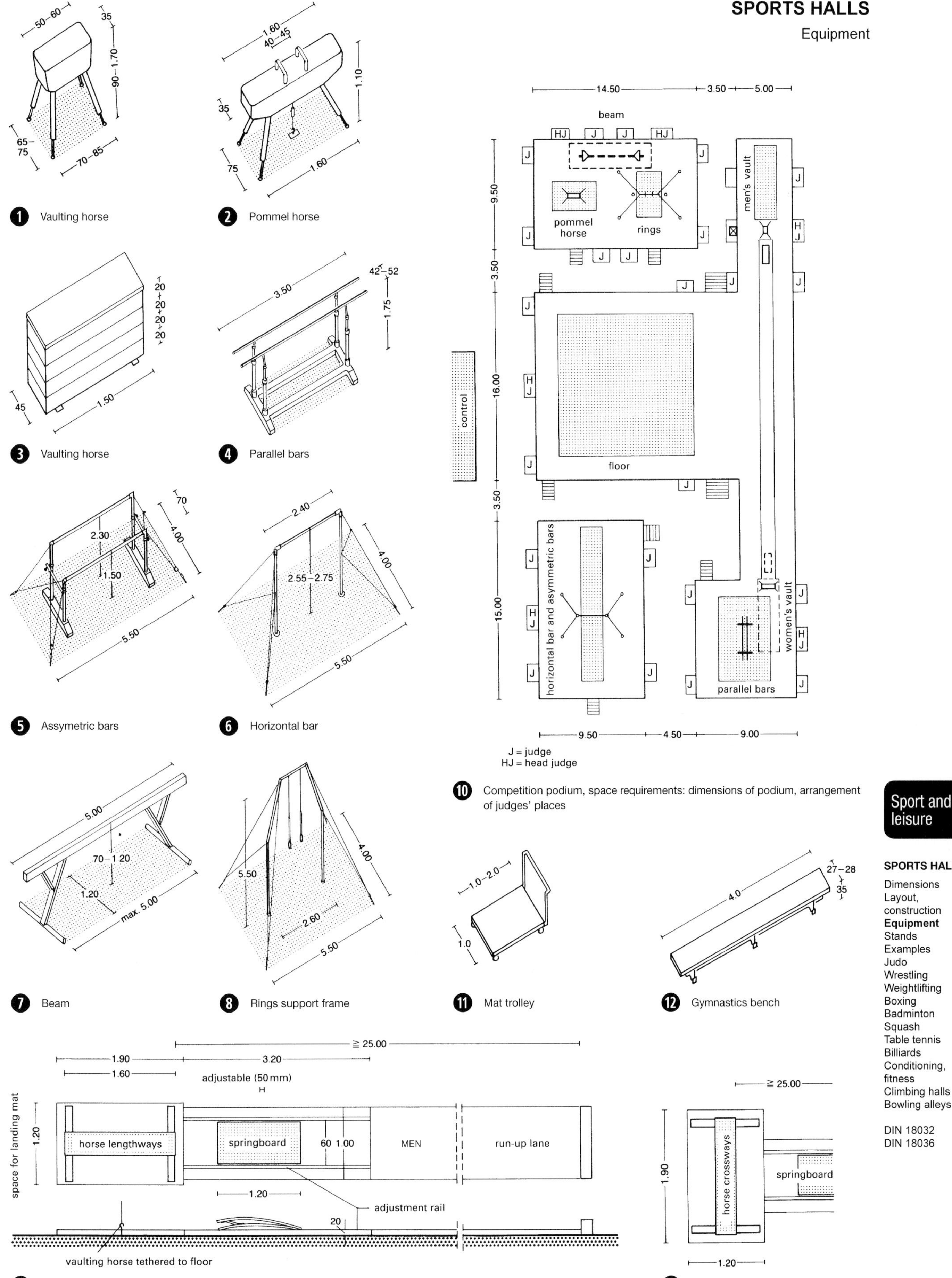

1 Vaulting horse

2 Pommel horse

3 Vaulting horse

4 Parallel bars

5 Assymetric bars

6 Horizontal bar

7 Beam

8 Rings support frame

9 Vaulting layout, men

10 Competition podium, space requirements: dimensions of podium, arrangement of judges' places

11 Mat trolley

12 Gymnastics bench

13 Vaulting layout, women

DIN 18032
DIN 18036

Spectator stands → ❶ – ❹ can be fixed or mobile. For smaller installations with up to 10 rows of seats, a linear rise of the seats (height 0.28–0.32 m) can be assumed. All other installations should have a parabolic rise (height for seats 1.25 m, standing places 1.65 m), sightline rise for seats 0.15 m, standing places 0.12 m. Row spacing for seats 0.80–0.85 m → ❷ – ❸. For standing places, 0.4–0.45 m. Sightline origin point 0.5 m above the boundary marking of the playing area.

Protect spectator places behind goals with mobile catch nets. Seats in upper levels and galleries should be closed off with nets while practice matches are underway. For the group of rooms including entrance hall, changing and sanitary facilities, teachers' room, additional sport room and hall, it is recommended to arrange a separation of the routeing of people wearing street shoes and sports shoes → ❾ – ⓬. Showers must be immediately accessible from changing rooms, with a drying area between the wet area of the shower room and the changing room. Shower rooms divided into two room units must be connected to the two adjacent changing rooms so that one or both of the room units can be used from either of the changing rooms → ❾ – ⓬. Teachers' rooms should be near the changing rooms. The first aid room must be on the same level as the sports area and can be integrated into the teachers' room.

Spectator stands can generally be accessed from below or above; from below leads to lower costs (spending on stairs and access galleries is saved), but this is disadvantageous for the organisation of events because of visitors passing the base of the stand, disturbing competitors and existing spectators → ❸. Free sides should be protected by ≧1 m high barriers, measured from the traffic surface.

The design of the wall and ceiling area next to the partition must ensure that no noise transfer takes place when the partition is down → ❺ – ❽.

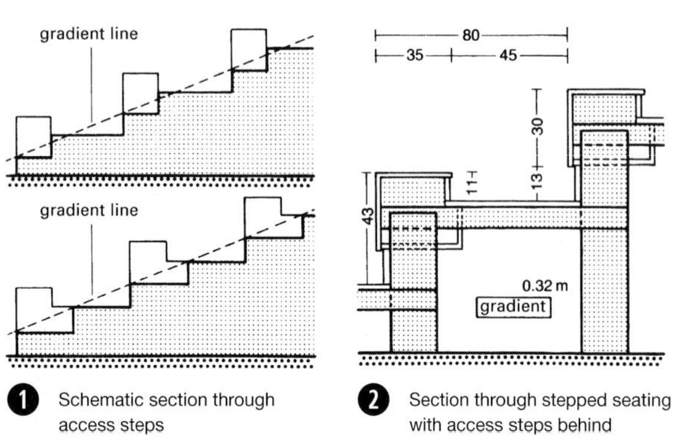

❶ Schematic section through access steps

❷ Section through stepped seating with access steps behind

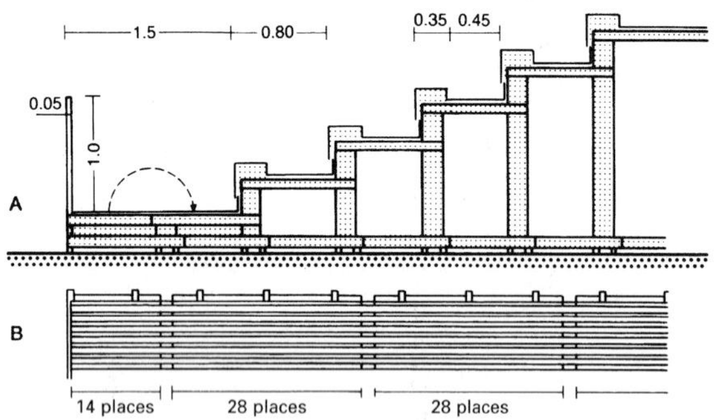

❸ Stand with access from below (A); stand with access from above (B)

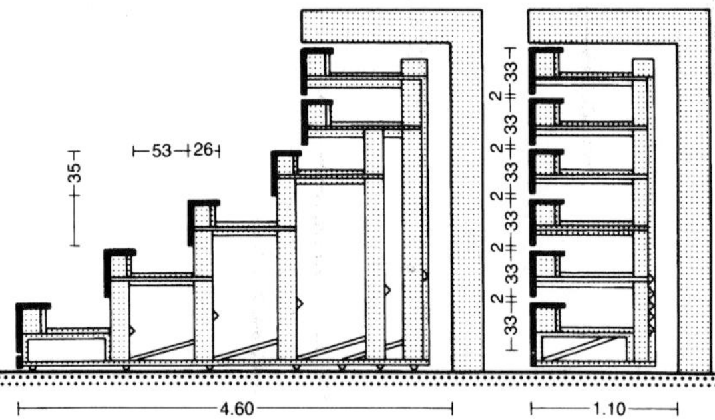

❹ Retractable stand, length ≦6.0 m

❺ Partition curtain between two beams

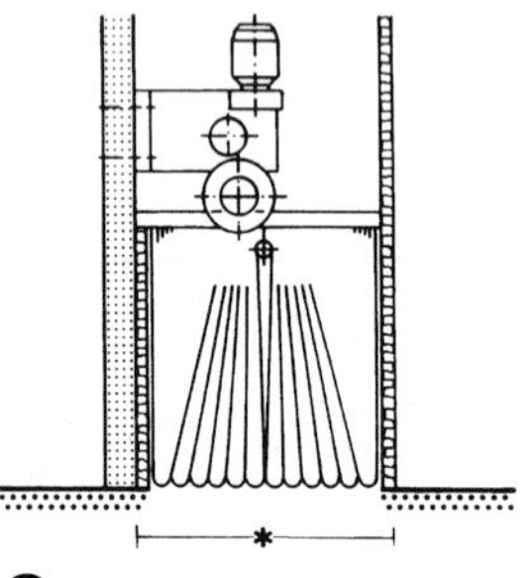
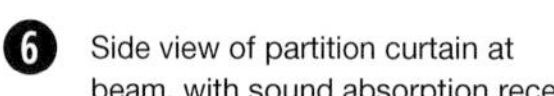

❻ Side view of partition curtain at beam, with sound absorption recess

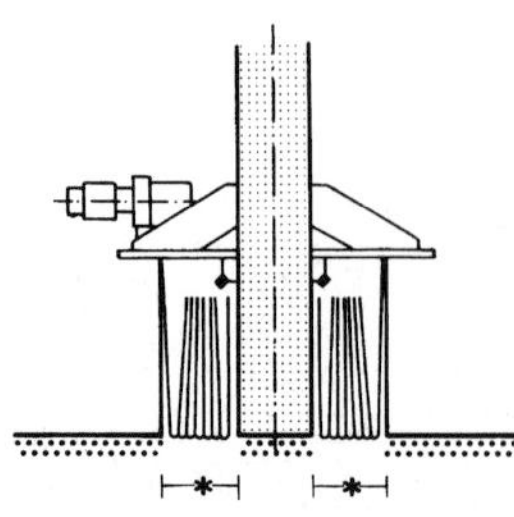
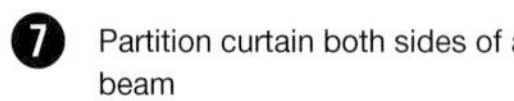

* – width, depending on height of hall and thickness of material

❼ Partition curtain both sides of a beam

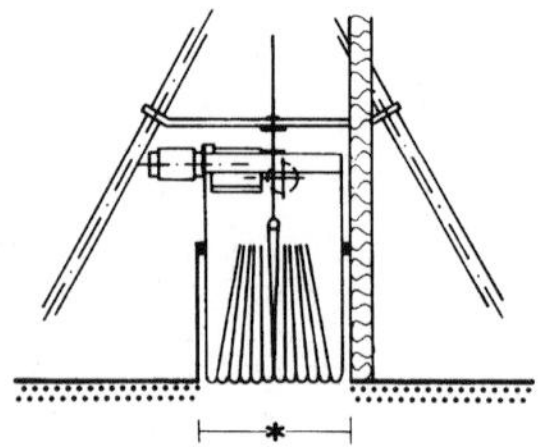

❽ Partition curtain with pulley system mounted in sound-absorbing recess inside a space frame

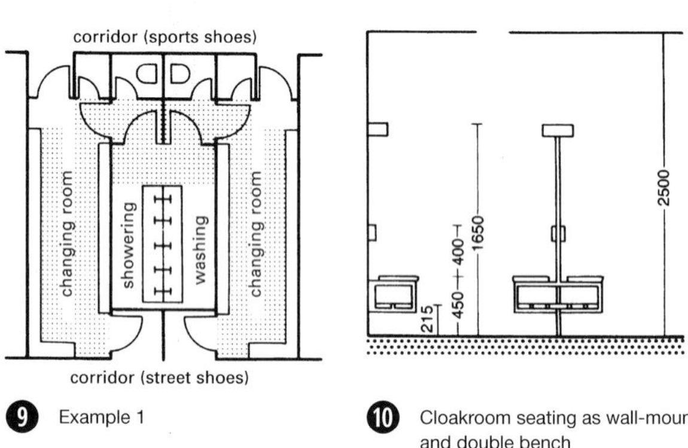

❾ Example 1

❿ Cloakroom seating as wall-mounted and double bench

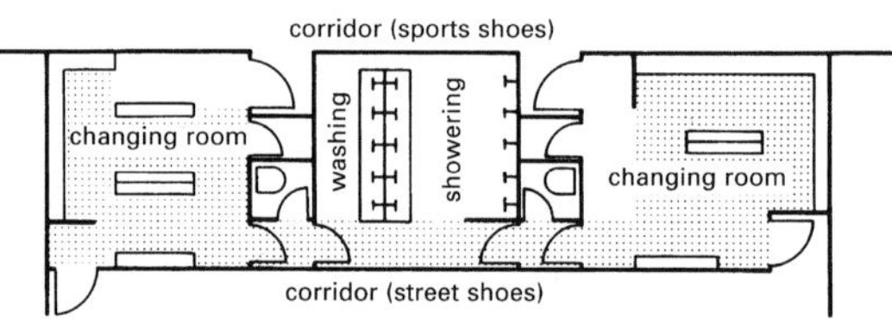

⓫ Example 2

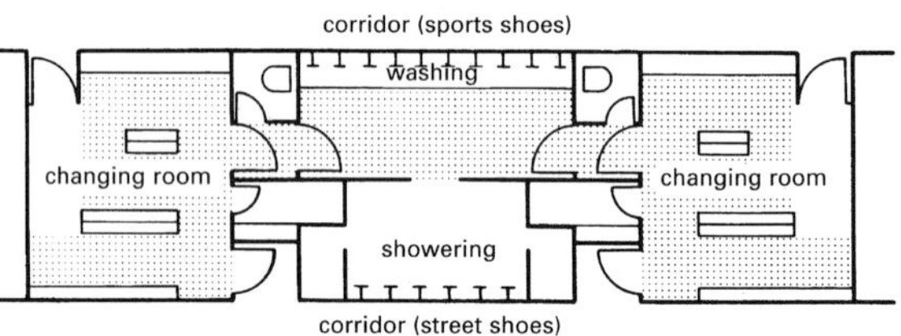

⓬ Example 3 Three proposed solutions for the changing and sanitary facilities (shaded: floor areas laid with PVC grid mats)

❶ Arrangement of spectators

version A: running track — version B: boxing arena

key → ❷

- ► direct entrance
- ▷ alternative emergency exit
- —— principal connection
- -·-·- visual connection
- - - - alternative connection
- ······ additional connection
- • additional rooms with multipurpose halls
- ∘ additional rooms and facilities depending on local situation and need

❷ Room relationship scheme

❸ Europa Hall, Karlsruhe, ground floor plan Arch.: Schmitt, Kasimir, Blanke

section → ❸

key → ❸
plan of entrance floor level
1 competitors' access at perimeter level, 2 entrance and foyer for spectators, 3 administration, 4 cash desks, 5 cloakroom, 6 gents' toilets, 7 ladies' toilets, 8 space above warming-up hall, 9 information, 10 training room and lounge, 11 access to basement,12 drinks bar, 13 stairs to balcony, 14 administration room with display and announcements, 15 permanent stand, 16 changing room area/hall connection, 17 200 m track, 18 sports hall, 19 large display board, 20 mobile stand, 21 score board, 22 hall perimeter route with emergency exits.

Flexible use of hall is possible → ❸

1. Tennis, 2. Handball, 3. Athletics, 4. Boxing, 5. School sport. Ball-catching safety nets at the front separate the interior into four units, each the size of a school sports hall. With warming-up hall in front of the training area 'under' the telescopic stand, the large sports hall offers schools and clubs six practice locations, competition conditions for top-level sport, and practice and training facilities for school and club sport.

Sport-relevant data: → ❹ 200 m circular track (competition), 130 m + 100 m straight sprint (training) track, 60 m straight sprint (training) track, 400 m stadium curve (training) shot put, discus and high jump facilities.

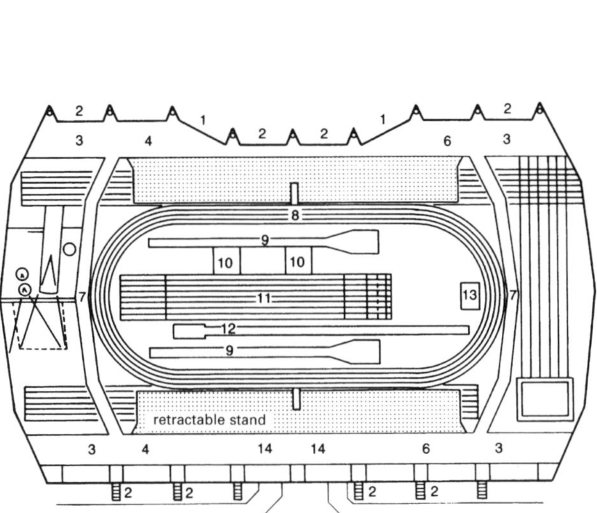

❹ Athletics Hall, Dortmund, ground floor plan Design: Hochbauamt Dortmund

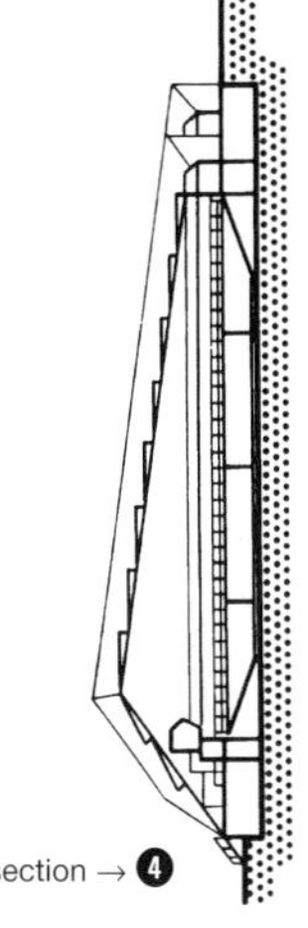

section → ❹

key → ❹
plan of entrance floor level
1 entrance hall with cash desks, 2 exits/emergency exits, 3 foyer, 4 drinks bar, 5 telephone, 6 stairs to spectator toilets, 7 access as bridge over the sports level, 8 200 m circular track, 9 pole vault, 10 high jump, 11 sprint competition track, 12 long jump, 13 shot put, 14 stairs up to administration

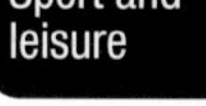

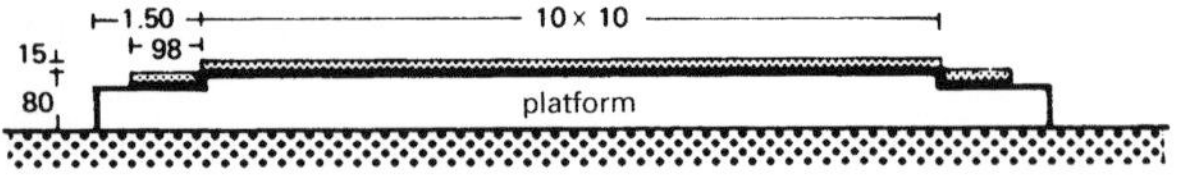

❶ Judo contest area on a platform

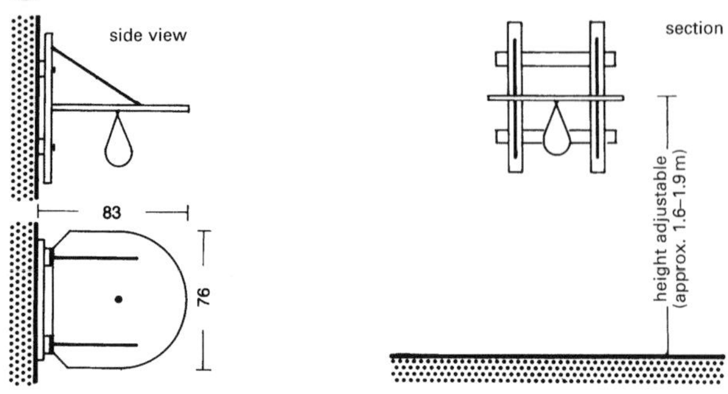

❷ Punch ball front view → ❷

padding
5.50
4.9–6.1
≧50
1.0
40
80
1.30
ropes 30–50 mm diameter wrapped in cloth (also all metal parts)
30–40 mm side canvas strip
91–1.22
steps of robust construction

❸ Boxing ring

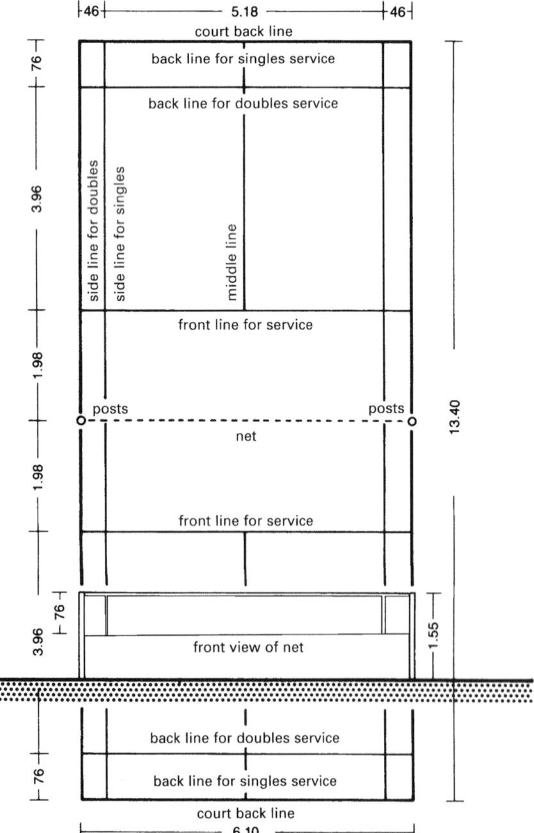

❹ Badminton court

JUDO

Contest area 6 × 6 m to 10 × 10 m or ≧6 × 12 m, covered with soft, springy mats. For German championships and international events, contest area ≧10 × 10 m. Upholstered mats are not allowed. Ideally, the mats should be raised by 15 cm. The separating line between the contest area and the surround should be clearly visible → ❶.

WRESTLING

Mat size for competitions 5 × 5 m; for German championships and international competitions ≧6 × 6 m, possibly 8 × 8 m, for international championships and Olympic games 8 × 8 m. The middle of the mat is marked with a ring of ≧1 m diameter with 10 cm wide edge strip. Mat thickness: 10 cm, soft covering. Surrounding protection strip should if possible be 2 m wide, otherwise boundary tapes at 45° angle. 1.2 m width of the protection strip should be in mat thickness, with colour difference. Protection strip for national competitions 1 m wide. Platform height ≦1.1 m; no corner posts or ropes.

WEIGHTLIFTING

Lifting area 4 × 4 m; ideally with strong timber base, chalk markings, floor should not spring, solid footing for weightlifters.
Largest weight diameter ≧450 mm
Weight for one-handed exercises 15 kg,
Weight for two-handed exercises 20 kg.

BOXING

Dimensions of a boxing ring to international requirements, 4.9 × 4.9 m to 6.10 × 6.10 m. 5.5 × 5.5 m is usual. Raised rings are usual, with a podium 1 m wide on all sides. Entire podium 7.5 × 7.5 m to 8 × 8 m → ❸.

BADMINTON

The standard is a doubles court, singles court only if space is lacking.

spacing between courts at side	≧0.30 m
between court and walls	≧1.50 m
backwards spacing between courts	≧1.30 m
safety strip at each side	1.25 m
safety strip front and back, each	2.50 m

Spectators should be behind the safety strip.

Hall height: 8 m international games, 6 m over rear partition. Net height at posts 1.55 m; in middle 1.525 m, net surface 76 cm high → ❹. Floor covering lightly resilient. Lighting: if possible no windows, but rooflight (glare-free) ≧300 lx.

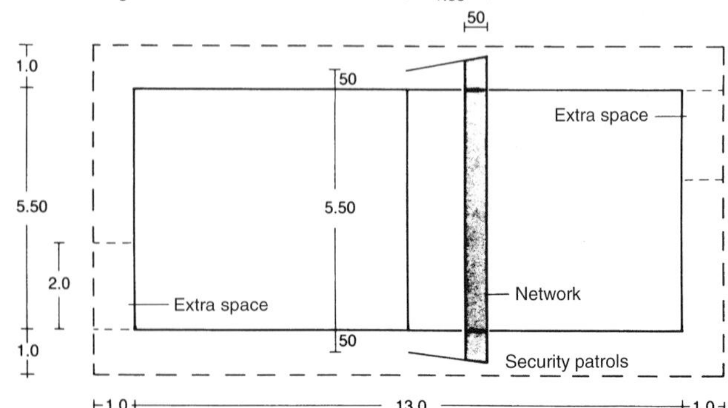

❺ Indiaca playing area (game played using hands and special ball)

Sport and leisure

SPORTS HALLS
Dimensions
Layout, construction
Equipment
Stands
Examples
Judo
Wrestling
Weightlifting
Boxing
Badminton
Squash
Table tennis
Billiards
Conditioning, fitness
Climbing halls
Bowling alleys

❶ Squash court end wall

❷ Squash court side wall

❸ Basic dimensions for squash court

❹ Basic dimensions for table tennis

❺ Basic dimensions and spacings for billiards

❻ Ball cupboard

❼ Cue rack

Normal table size (dimensions in cm)		I	II	III	IV	V	VI
internal (playing area)	A	285×142^5	230 × 115	220 × 110	220 × 100	200 × 100	190 × 95
external	B	310×167^5	255 × 140	245 × 135	225 × 125	225 × 125	215 × 120
room		575×432^5	520 × 405	510 × 400	500 × 395	490 × 390	480 × 385
weight (kg)		800	600	550	500	450	350

❽ Usual billiards table sizes

SQUASH

The normal construction of squash courts involves massive walls with special plastered surfaces, pre-cast concrete elements, prefabricated panelled timber-framed roof, collapsible seating.

Room size: 9.745 × 6.40 m
Room height: 6.00 m
A glass back wall is advantageous for spectators.

Floor: slightly springy, light wood (maple or beech), good surface slip-resistance, floorboards parallel to the side walls. A practical flooring is tongue and groove parquet strips 25 mm thick and a sealing layer, parquet according to DIN 280 parts 3, 4 and 5.

Walls: Special plaster, flat, white. Strip (the 'tin') running across foot of front wall: of sheet metal 2.5 mm or plywood with sheet metal cladding, painted white → ❶ – ❸.

TABLE TENNIS

At championship level takes place only in halls. **Table surface** horizontal, matt green with white border lines.
Table area .... 152.5 × 274 cm
Table height .... 76 cm
Board thickness .... ≧2.5 cm
For tables in the open air, fibre cement board 20 mm thick.

Board hardness: so a normal ball bounces 23 cm when dropped from 30 cm
Net length, centre .... 183 cm
Net height, entire length .... 15.25 cm
Playing box (formed by canvas screens 60–65 cm high) ≧6 × 12 m, international 7 × 14 m, spectators beyond screen → ❹.

BILLIARDS

Location of rooms:
First floor or well-lit basement, seldom ground floor.

Space requirement: for the various table sizes → ❺ – ❽.
Common sizes for private purposes .... IV, V and VI
For cafés and clubs .... IV and V
In billiards halls and academies .... I, II and III
Spacing of table sizes I and II from each other .... ≧1.70 m
Spacing of table sizes III–V from each other .... ≧1.60 m
and, from the wall, a bit more if possible.
At the side where the waiter passes or the spectators stand, correspondingly more space, plus room for chairs, tables, food and drink (→ pp. 174, 175).
Wall mounting for cue rack and rules of the game.
1 cue rack for 12 cues, overall 150 × 75 cm.

Lighting

The smallest possible lights with full and even light distribution onto the playing area. Usual height for light above table: 80 cm

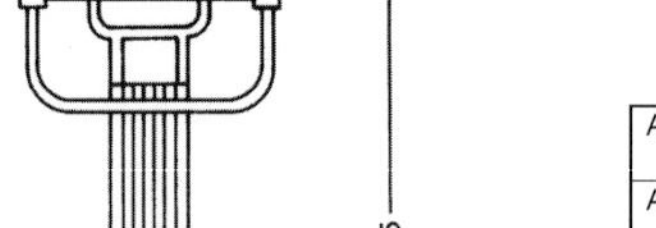
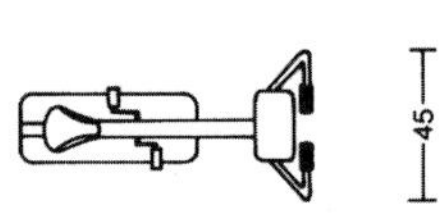

1 Rowing machine and bicycle ergometer

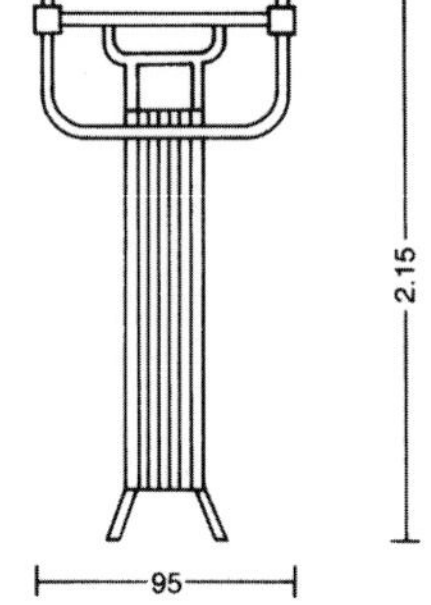

2 Stomach muscle board with push-up bar and wall bars

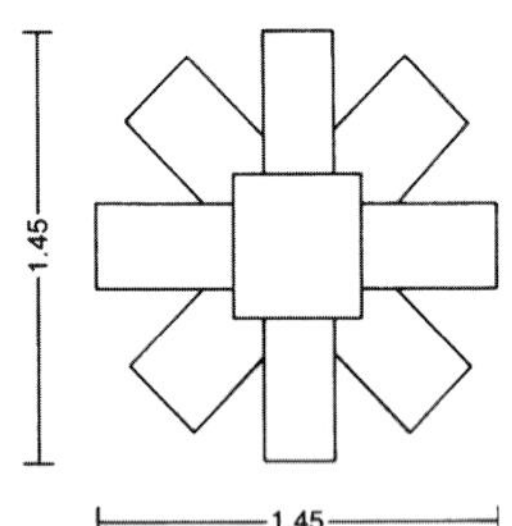

3 Multi-exercise centre

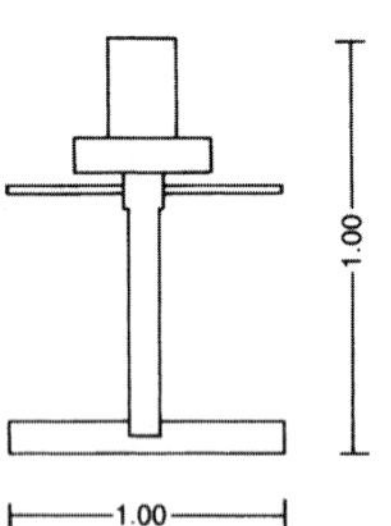

4 Pulling machine

Area	Apparatus or equipment	Exercises	Motor functions	Training intention
A	general training stations	single joint	power flexibility	fitness condition
B	special training stations	many joints	power, speed	fitness condition
C	lifting surface (with multipress or isometric bar)	many joints	power, speed, coordination	condition
D	traditional small apparatus	one and many joints	power flexibility	fitness
E	special training apparatus and open area to warm up (gymnastics etc.)	many joints one and many joints	duration coordination flexibility coordination	fitness condition fitness condition

5 Categories of machine by use

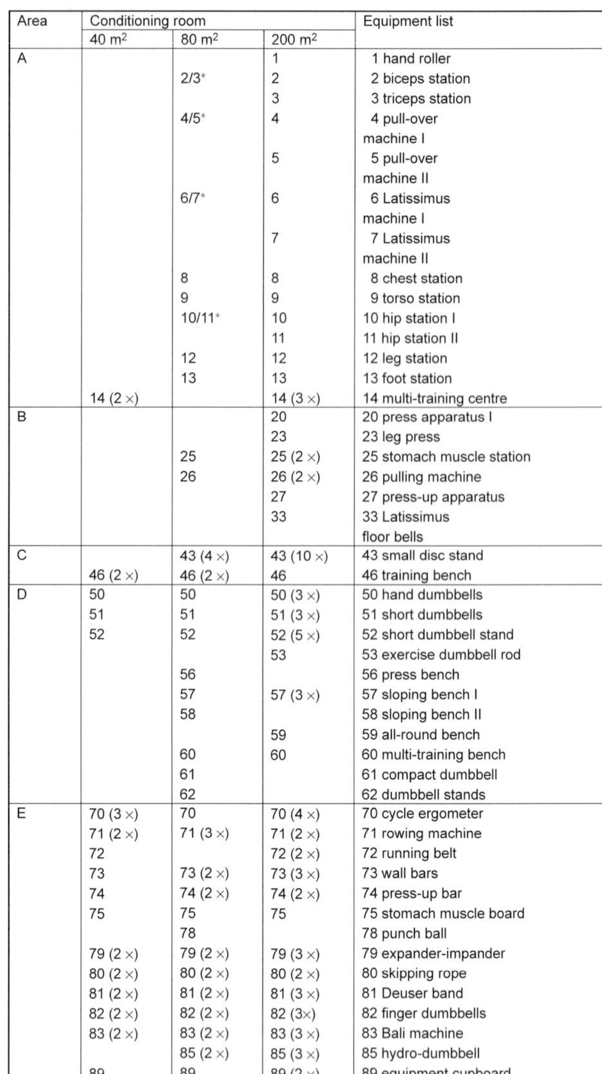

Area	Conditioning room 40 m²	80 m²	200 m²	Equipment list
A			1	1 hand roller
		2/3*	2	2 biceps station
			3	3 triceps station
		4/5*	4	4 pull-over machine I
			5	5 pull-over machine II
		6/7*	6	6 Latissimus machine I
			7	7 Latissimus machine II
		8	8	8 chest station
		9	9	9 torso station
		10/11*	10	10 hip station I
			11	11 hip station II
		12	12	12 leg station
		13	13	13 foot station
	14 (2 ×)		14 (3 ×)	14 multi-training centre
B			20	20 press apparatus I
			23	23 leg press
		25	25 (2 ×)	25 stomach muscle station
		26	26 (2 ×)	26 pulling machine
			27	27 press-up apparatus
			33	33 Latissimus floor bells
C		43 (4 ×)	43 (10 ×)	43 small disc stand
	46 (2 ×)	46 (2 ×)	46	46 training bench
D	50	50	50 (3 ×)	50 hand dumbbells
	51	51	51 (3 ×)	51 short dumbbells
	52	52	52 (5 ×)	52 short dumbbell stand
			53	53 exercise dumbbell rod
		56		56 press bench
		57	57 (3 ×)	57 sloping bench I
		58		58 sloping bench II
			59	59 all-round bench
		60	60	60 multi-training bench
		61		61 compact dumbbell
		62		62 dumbbell stands
E	70 (3 ×)	70	70 (4 ×)	70 cycle ergometer
	71 (2 ×)	71 (3 ×)	71 (2 ×)	71 rowing machine
	72		72 (2 ×)	72 running belt
	73	73 (2 ×)	73 (3 ×)	73 wall bars
	74	74 (2 ×)	74 (2 ×)	74 press-up bar
	75	75	75	75 stomach muscle board
		78		78 punch ball
	79 (2 ×)	79 (2 ×)	79 (3 ×)	79 expander-impander
	80 (2 ×)	80 (2 ×)	80 (2 ×)	80 skipping rope
	81 (2 ×)	81 (2 ×)	81 (3 ×)	81 Deuser band
	82 (2 ×)	82 (2 ×)	82 (3×)	82 finger dumbbells
	83 (2 ×)	83 (2 ×)	83 (3 ×)	83 Bali machine
		85 (2 ×)	85 (3 ×)	85 hydro-dumbbell
	89	89	89 (2 ×)	89 equipment cupboard

* Apparatus 2 and 3, 4 and 5, 6 and 7, 9 and 10 and are available in very different versions and should therefore be provided to suit the number of dumbbells and weights to be chosen: 7 as well as 10 and 11 can be used for two functions from various manufacturers.

7 Equipment suggestions for fitness rooms

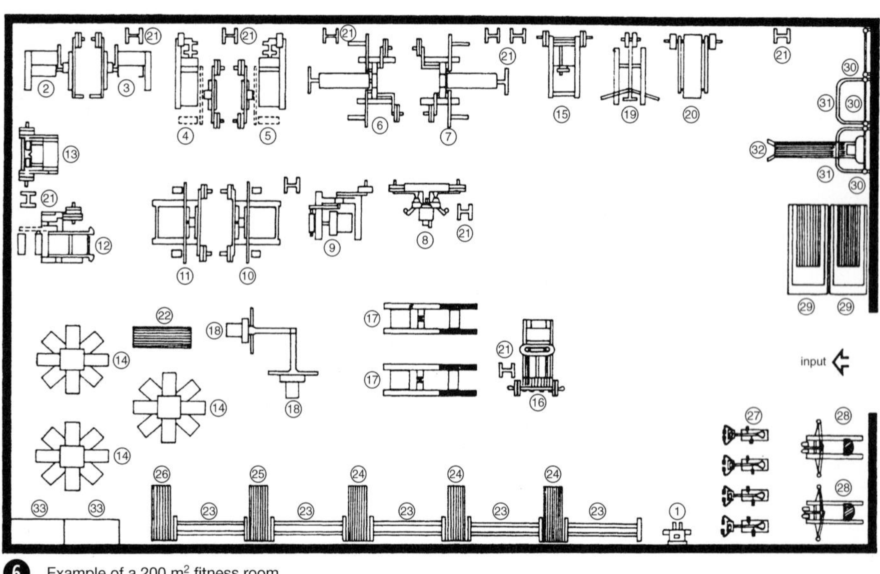
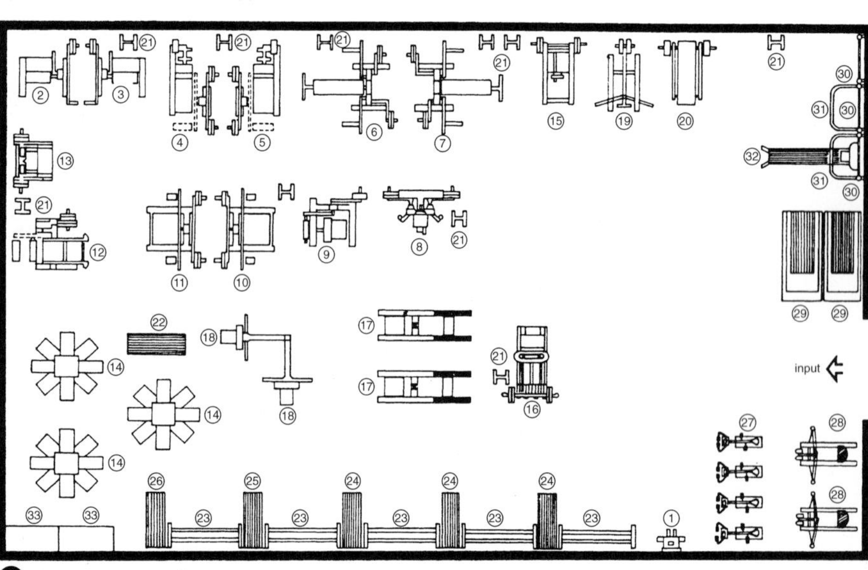

1 hand roller
2 biceps station
3 triceps station
4 pull-over machine I
5 pull-over machine II
6 Latissimus machine I
7 Latissimus machine II
8 chest station
9 torso station
10 hip station I
11 hip station II
12 leg station
13 foot station
14 multi-training centre
15 press apparatus I
16 leg press apparatus I
17 stomach muscle station
18 pulling machine
19 press-up apparatus
20 Latissimus floor bells
21 small disc stand
22 training bench
23 short dumbbell stand
24 sloping bench I
25 all-round bench
26 multi-training bench
27 cycle ergometer
28 rowing machine
29 running belt
30 wall bars
31 press-up bar
32 stomach muscle board
33 equipment cupboard

6 Example of a 200 m² fitness room

Area	Machine no.	Description	Movements	Space (cm)
A	1	hand roller	hand bends, hand stretching	60/30
	2	biceps station	arm bends	135/135
	3	triceps station	arm stretching	135/135
	4	pull-over machine I	arm lifting in front of the body	190/110
	5	pull-over machine II	arm lowering in front of the body	190/110
	6	Latissimus machine I	sideways arm lowering and lifting	200/120
	7	Latissimus machine II	bring arms together and apart in front of the body	200/120
	8	chest station	bring arms angled together in front of the body	165/100
	9	torso station	stretch and bend torso	135/125
	10	hip station I	lift and lower legs	175/125
	11	hip station II	lift and retract legs	175/125
	12	leg station	stretch and bend legs	125/155
	13	foot station (calves apparatus)	stretch and bend feet	140/ 80
	14	multi-exercise centre	various leg and multi-joint movements	various
B	20	push apparatus I	arm stretching, horizontal (standing)	120/140
	21	push apparatus II	arm stretching, vertical and/or calf training (standing)	70/160
	22	Hackenschmidt apparatus	leg stretching on slope	90/140
	23	leg-press apparatus	leg stretching, horizontal (sitting)	120/160
	24	knee-bend apparatus (with weights)	leg stretching, vertical (standing)	200/ 90
	25	stomach muscle station	various exercises for stomach and back muscles	65/200
	26	pulling machine	various single and multi-joint basic movements	100/140
	27	press-up apparatus	arm bends and arm stretching, vertical (hang or push-up)	120/155
	28	press bench I	arm stretching, vertical (lying bench pressing)	200/120
	29	dumbbell apparatus (multipress machine)	bench press, knee bend, standing presses and pull exercises (all with weights)	200/100 185/100
	30	press bench II (sloping bench for long dumbbell)	sloping bench presses (sitting)	150/ 70
	31	curl bench	arm bends	
	32	press bench III	bench press (on back sloping downwards)	160/170
	33	Latissimus floor dumbbell	arm bends, pull in with forward torso	120/130
C	40	lifter bed with rubber inserts	all exercises with free dumbbell (knee bend, press and impact)	300/300
	41	practice dumbbell bar		200
	42	large weight stand		50/100
	43	small weight stand		30/30
	44	magnesia container		0/38
	45	knee-bend stand (in pairs)		35/70 ea.
	46	training bench		40/120
	47	full-rubber mixed weights (10; 15; 20; 25 kg)		
	48	weights with vulcanised rubber edge (15; 2; 25 kg)		
	49	cast weights (1.25; 2.50; 5; 10; 25; 50 kg)		
D	50	hand dumbbell (1; 2; 3; 4; 5; 6; 8; 10 kg)	various single and multi-joint exercises with hand, compact and long dumbbells	
	51	short dumbbells (2.5; 5; 7.5 etc. – 30 kg		
	52	short dumbbell stand		140/130
	53	training dumbbell bar		185
	54	knee-bend bar		200
	55	(upholstered) curl bar		
	56	press bench (adjustable)		140
	57	sloping bench I		40/120
	58	sloping bench II		40/120
	59	all-round bench		40/120
	60	multi-training bench (12-fold adjustable)		40/120
	61	compact dumbbell (2–60 kg)		
	62	dumbbell stand		145/80
E	70	cycle ergometer	endurance, coordination; nos. 70–76	40/ 90
	71	rowing machine	arm bends	120/140
	72	running belt		80/190
	73	wall bars		100/15
	74	press-up bar for wall bars		120/120
	75	hanging stomach-muscle board		100/180
	76	spine relief apparatus	flexibility, coordination, nos. 77–88	70/150
	77	jumping power tester		
	78	punch ball		
	79	expander-impander		
	80	skipping rope		
	81	Deuser band		
	82	finger dumbbell		
	83	Bali machine		
	84	ball dumbbells		
	85	hydro-dumbbells		
	86	weight vests		
	87	weight bags for arms/legs		
	88	mirror		
	89	equipment cupboard		50/110

❶ List of machines and apparatus for conditioning and fitness training

Room size for 40–45 people min. 200 m² → ❷, clear ceiling height for all rooms 3.0 m. Conditioning and fitness rooms should generally be 6 m wide for an optimal arrangement of machines in two rows. Room length ≦ 15 m, otherwise there is no overview while training. The smallest room unit of 40 m² is suitable for 12 users.

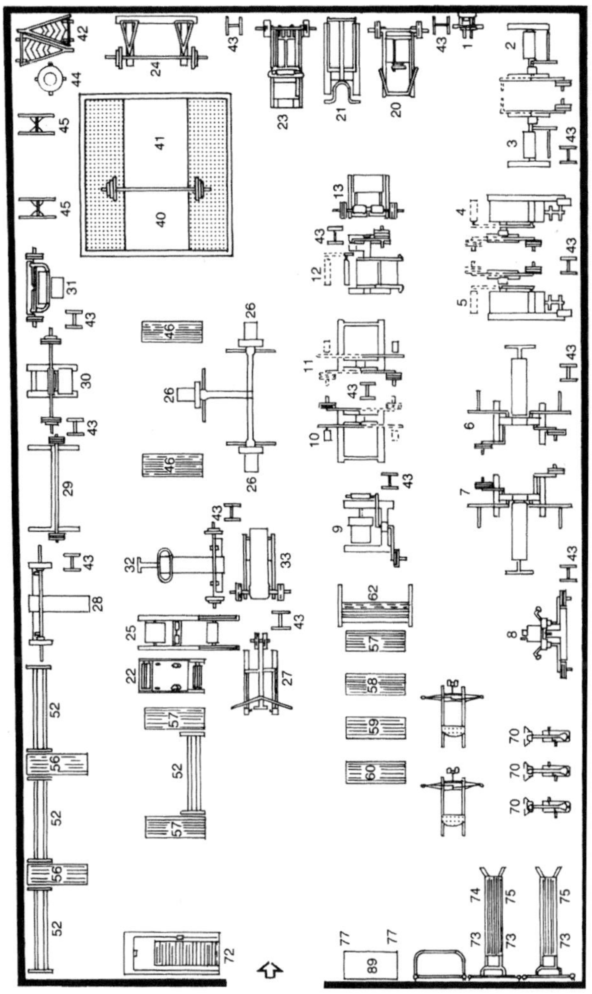

❷ Example of 200 m² conditioning room

Construction	Description	Properties
solid concrete (formwork)	compact standing concrete panels with positive and negative structures	sharp edges, additional grips, variable surface design is possible
shotcrete	mesh of steel wires (reinforcement) sprayed with concrete.	organic shapes can be bolted on subsequently, only for outdoor walls
timber	timber-based boards with or without coating bolted directly to an internal wall or onto a support construction	install numerous drilled holes. Projecting and recessed grips can be installed cheaply
GRP (glass fibre-reinforced plastic)	boards or various shapes made of GRP can be bolted directly to an internal wall or onto a support construction	natural surface, various surface-fixed or recessed grips are possible. Disposal could be a problem

❶ Climbing wall construction types (Deutcher Alpenverein → refs)

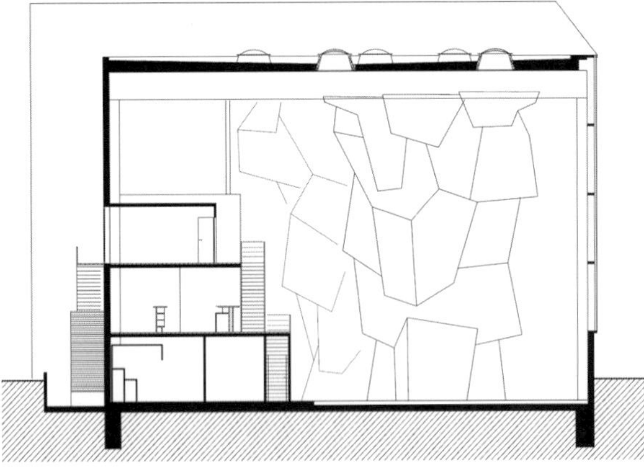

❷ Magic Mountain climbing hall, Berlin, section Arch.: Gantz Weber Architects

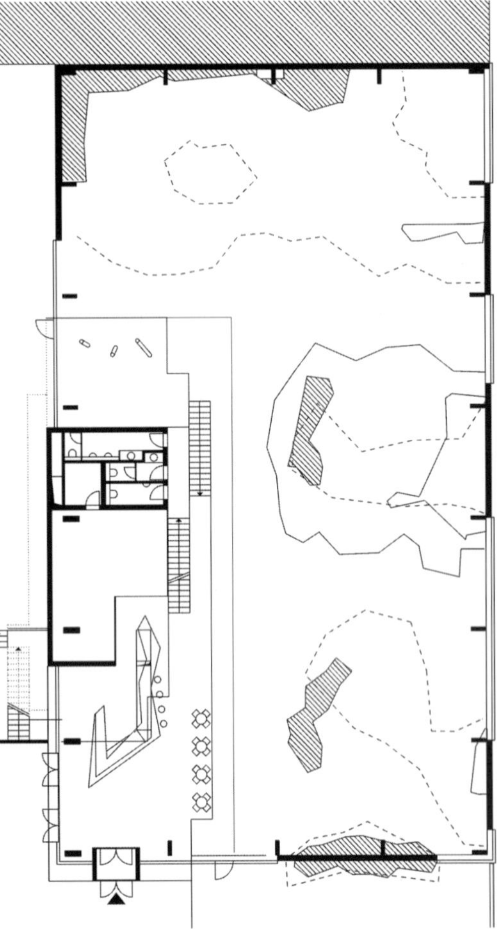

❸ Magic Mountain climbing hall, Berlin, ground floor Arch.: Gantz Weber Architects

Climbing halls make climbing possible all year round, whatever the weather. The size and shape of halls is variable depending on the operator's ideas and space available (up to 2500 m^2 indoor area).

Concentrating the subsidiary functions is practical in order to keep a large part of the area for climbing. The entrance with reception and cash desk can be supplemented by a cafeteria and shop for climbing equipment.

Sanitary facilities are similar to those in a fitness centre. Sensible additions would be a steam bath/sauna with rest zone, possibly also a fitness area.

A high degree of daylight is desirable (smoke extraction domes as daylight sources) and artificial light should only be indirect to avoid dazzling of climbers and safety staff. Climbing walls must be regularly maintained by an expert according to the manufacturer's recommendations.

Types of climbing wall:

Boulder wall: This is climbed at low height without safety ropes. The climbers move horizontally ('traverse') or 'boulder' short stretches upwards. The wall can be climbed without supervision. There must be a jumping-off area of gravel, bark mulch or mats.

Top rope or **lead wall:** Roping is necessary on account of the height. The climbers mainly climb upwards and, at the top of the wall, are let down by a climbing partner or abseil themselves. It is also possible to boulder at the foot of this wall and it must be secured against unsupervised climbing. No grip should be reachable up to a height of 2.5 m. If a top rope or lead wall is in a sports hall, the requirements for sport operation in sports halls still have to be met (e.g. impact protection)

Climbing walls are modelled on natural rock faces in their surface and design. The colour scheme is variable and often in accord with a CI scheme. Dimensions and shape are flexible. The height for sport climbing is up to 18 m, exceptionally to 30 m. Climbing walls are built by specialist firms and are offered as a building-block system or as a free design of the climbing area.

The support construction (steel or wood) must support itself or be extended from the hall construction, with cladding of various materials → ❶. Various grip and step elements can be screwed to these types of climbing wall. The climbing grips are made of a resin mix with quartz sand dusting and are fixed to the wall with M10 Allen bolts. The types range from 3 cm to beer crate size. Grips of various colours can mark different 'colour' routes. The combination of various colours in one route enables a number of routes on the same section of wall. The number of grips per m^2 should be in accordance with the intended user group.

An ideal layout provides differentiated areas for beginners and experts, and separate areas for children.

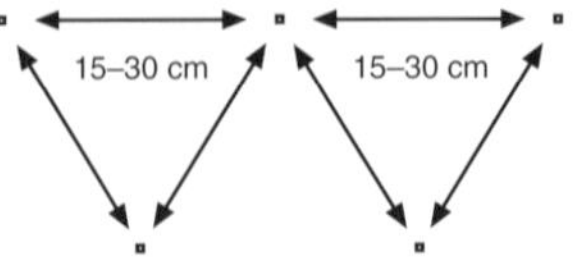

❹ Grip pattern staggered (or square) (Deutcher Alpenverein → refs)

Climbing standard	Children, young people	Adult beginners	Normal	Training
grips/m^2	8–10	4–8	3–5	>10

❺ Number of grips/m^2 according to user group (Deutcher Alpenverein → refs)

❶ Construction of lane with side bands

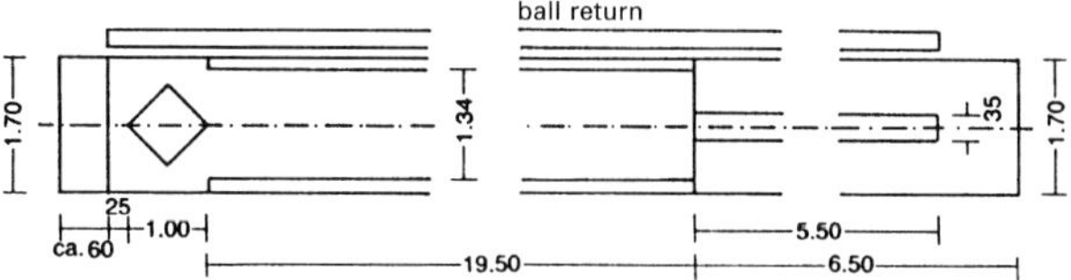

❷ Construction of lane with side channels

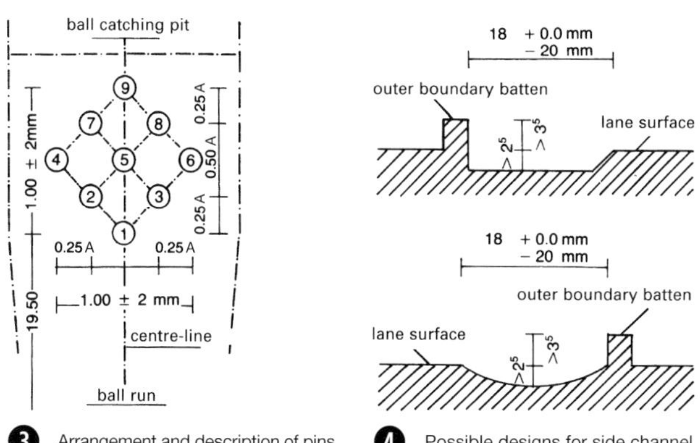

❸ Arrangement and description of pins

❹ Possible designs for side channel

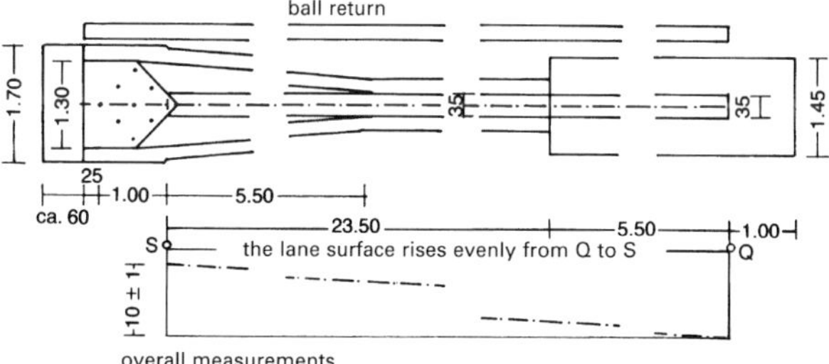

❺ Planked lane

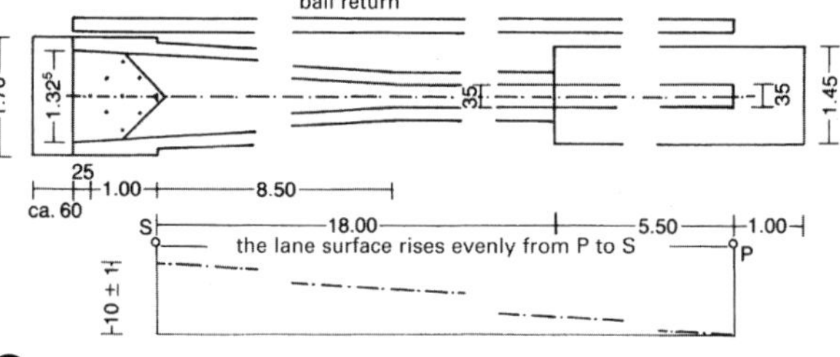

❻ Layout and main dimensions of tapered lane

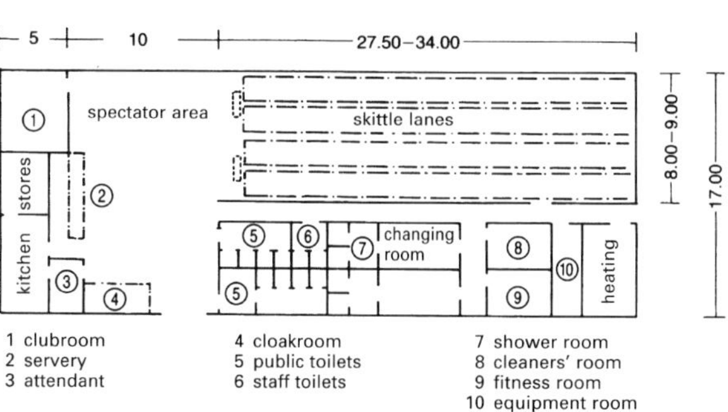

❼ Example of a bowling alley

A bowling alley contains the following areas:

1. Run-up area, where the ball is rolled after a few steps.
2. Lane, the actual rolling area of the ball.
3. Catching area, where the pins stand and where fallen pins and the bowling ball are collected.

Asphalt track is a specific sporting track and places the highest demands on the bowlers because of its particular surfacing. The lane is 19.50 m long and 1.50 wide (with side strips) or 1.34 m (side bordered by gutter) asphalt or plastic lane → ❶ – ❹.

Planked lane was originally a timber bowling lane, but may also be constructed of plastic → ❺. The particular feature is the rise of 10 cm, measured from the bowling position to the first pin. The lane is 23.50 m long and 0.35 m wide with elevated edges.

Tapered (or scissor) lane is also a timber bowling lane (or plastic) → ❻. The lane widens after 9.5 m to 1.25 m at the centre of the pins.

In bowling alleys → ⓬ the run-up area is made of cleanly sanded parquet over the entire width (1.041–1.065 m). The lane is polished or varnished parquet. The bowling balls are 21.8 cm with a maximum weight of 7257 g, with three finger holes.

On asphalt and tapered lanes, balls are of diameter 16.5 cm, weighing ≧2800–2900 g. Planked lane balls are 16.5 cm, ≧3050–3150 g. The balls are made of plastic mixture and the pins of hardwood (beech) or plastic with standardised sizes. Pins are also made of plastic-coated wood or plastic, also standardised.

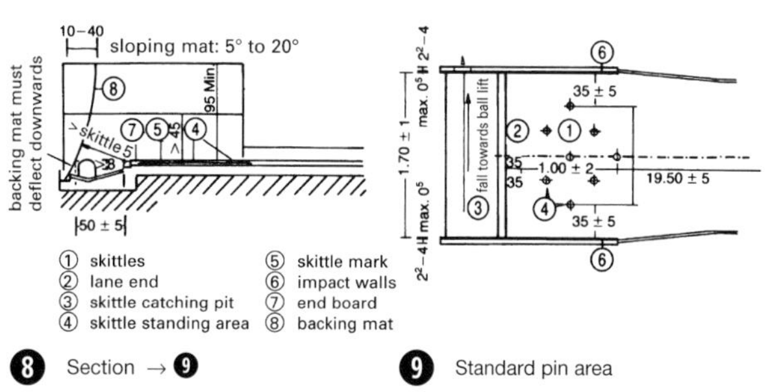

❽ Section → ❾

❾ Standard pin area

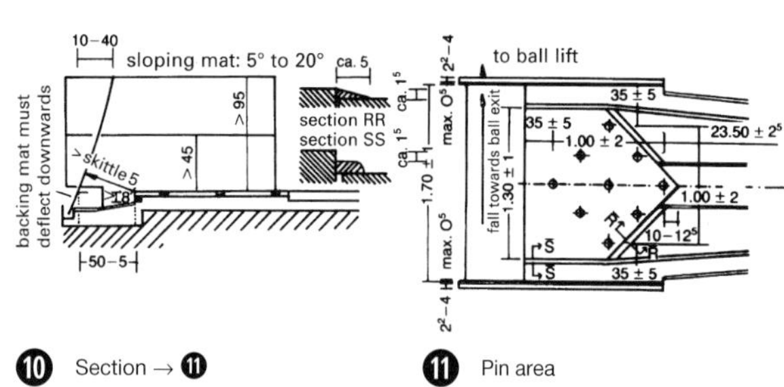

❿ Section → ⓫

⓫ Pin area

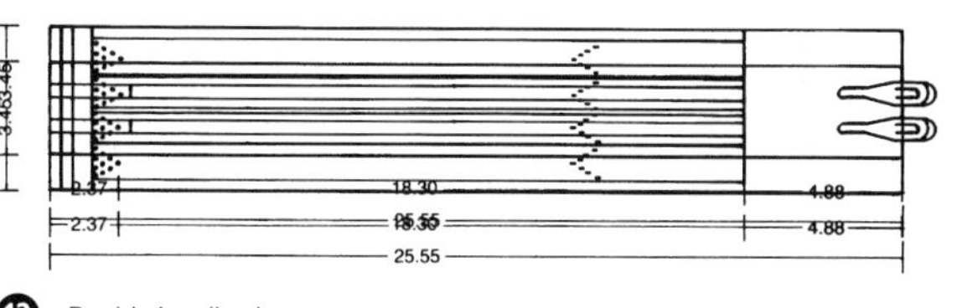

⓬ Double bowling lane

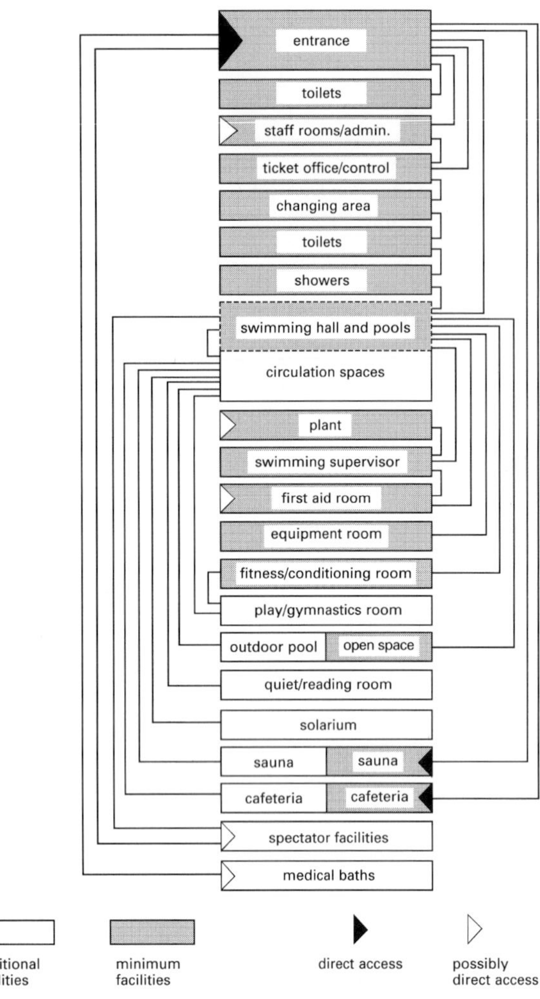

❶ Indoor swimming pool – room relationship scheme

The size of an indoor swimming pool building depends on the size of the pool/water area (or the dimensions of the basin and the diving boards), the surrounding areas, additional facilities and required room heights.

Building plot

For indoor pools (without parking) allow a plot size of 6–8 m² per m² of planned pool area; if the water area is very large, a smaller value will suffice. Additional open-air areas (terraces, sun decks, sunbathing lawns) can add about 10–20% to the total plot size.

A building plot which is flat or with a max. slope of 15° enables the design of a public indoor pool on one level, which is a precondition for an economically and functionally optimised design. A greater slope to the terrain will lead to higher building costs or functional disadvantages.

Parking

1 car parking space per 5–10 clothes lockers for the swimming pool.

1 bicycle space per 5 clothes lockers for the swimming pool.

If there are facilities for spectators: 1 additional parking space for every 10–15 spectators. If catering is included: 1 additional parking space for every 4–8 seats.

Subsidiary spaces

The **total water area** serves as the basic value for determining the subsidiary rooms. With leisure pools this value should be supplemented to take additional functions into consideration.

Area in front of entrance: 0.2 m²/m² of water area.

Entrance hall: floor area 0.15–0.25 m²/m² of water area, depending on the pool size and the leisure orientation. Also 5 m² wind lobby, 5 m² cash desk or automated paying area, 1–2 m² cleaning room and toilets (1 WC each for ladies and gents).

Total water area (WA) (m²)	Pool types[1]	Example 1		Example 2		Example 3		Diving facilities[2]	Plot area without parking (m²)[3]
		Pool size (m or m²)	WA (m²)	Pool size (m or m²)	WA (m²)	Pool size (m)	WA (m²)		
1	2	3		4		5		6	7
up to 300	CP PP	10.00 × 25.00 approx. 15	250	—		—		1 B + 3P	approx. 2500
up to 450	CP NSP PP	10.00 × 25.00 8.00 × 12.50 approx. 20	250 100 20	10.00 × 25.00 8.00 × 12.50 approx. 20	250 125 20	12.50 × 25.00 8.00 × 12.50 approx. 20	313 100 20	1B + 3B	approx. 3000–3500
up to 600	CP NSP DP PP	12.50 × 25.00 8.00 × 12.50 approx. 25	313 100 25	12.50 × 25.00 8.00 × 16.66 approx. 25	313 133 25	12.50 × 25.00 8.00 × 12.50 10.60 ×12.50 approx. 25	313 100 133 25	for CP: 1 B + 3 B or 1 B + 3 B + 1 P + 3 P + 5 P for DP: 1 B + 1 P comb. +3 B + 3 P comb. + 5 P	3500–4000
up to 750	CP NSP DP[4] PP	12.50 × 25.00 8.00 × 12.50 10.60 × 12.50 approx. 30	313 100 133 30	12.50 × 25.00 8.00 × 16.66 10.60 × 12.50 approx. 30	313 133 133 30	16.66 × 25.00 8.00 × 16.66 12.50 × 11.75 approx. 30	417 133 147 30	for CP and DP: 1 B + 1 P comb. + 3 B + 3 P comb. + 5 P or: 1 b + 3 B + 1 P + 3 P + 5P	4000–4500
up to 800	CP NSP DP[4] PP	16.66 × 25 8.00 × 16.66 12.50 × 11.75 approx. 35	417 133 147 35	16.66 × 25 8.00 × 16.66 16.90 × 11.75 approx. 35	417 133 199 35			for CP and DP: 2 × 1 B. 2 × 3 B 1 P + 3 P + 5 P or: 1 B + 3 B + 1 P + 3 P +	approx. 5000

Notes: [1] Abbreviations: PP = paddling pool; NSP = non-swimmer pool; CP = combined pool; DP = diving pool.
In special cases, a swimmers' pool (SP) can be provided instead of a combined pool (CP).
[2] Abbreviations: B = board; P = platform; 1–10 = diving height (m); WA = water area.
[3] Recommended plot sizes
[4] Dimensions under consideration of safety/measurements
Pool size = pool width (diving board side) × pool length in diving direction

❷ Design examples for indoor swimming pools (division of the water area between swimmers and non-swimmers approx. 2:1)

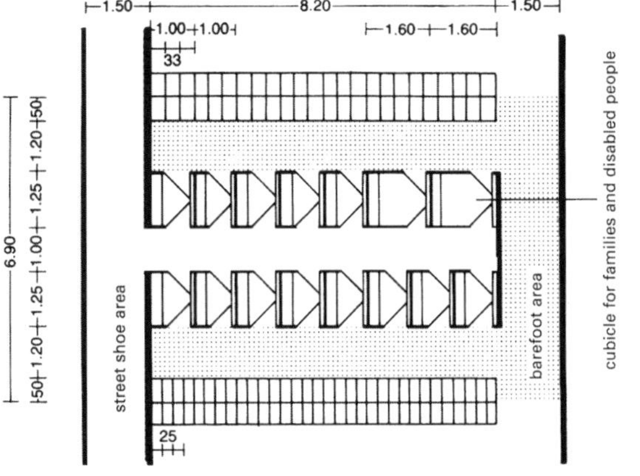

❶ Changing area: cubicles with clothes locker

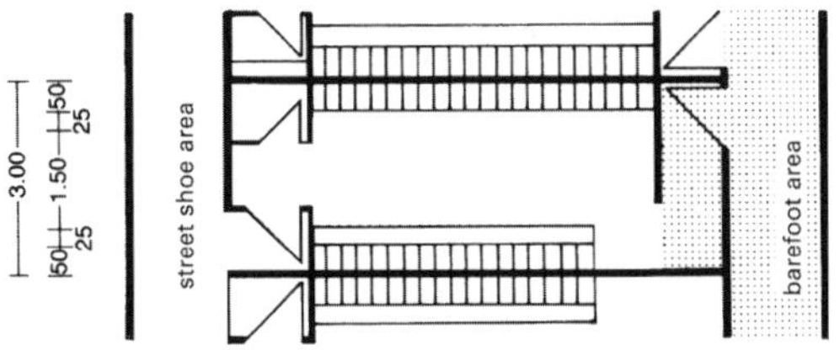

❷ Communal changing room: without shoe-removal bench

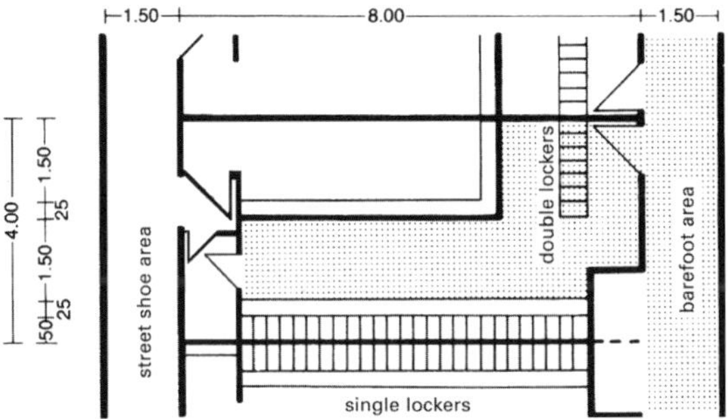

❸ Communal changing room: without shoe-removal bench

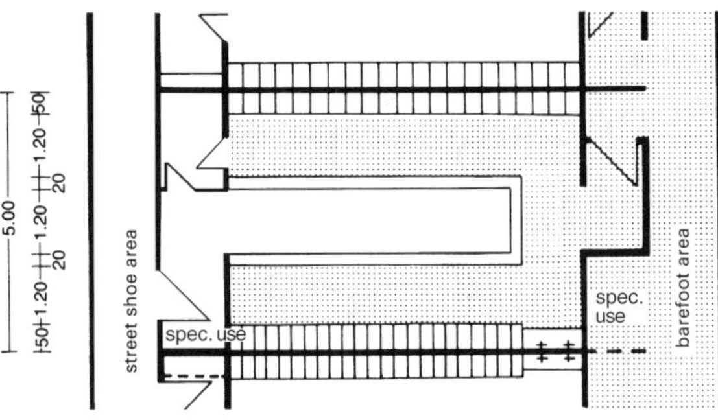

❹ Communal changing room: with shoe-removal bench

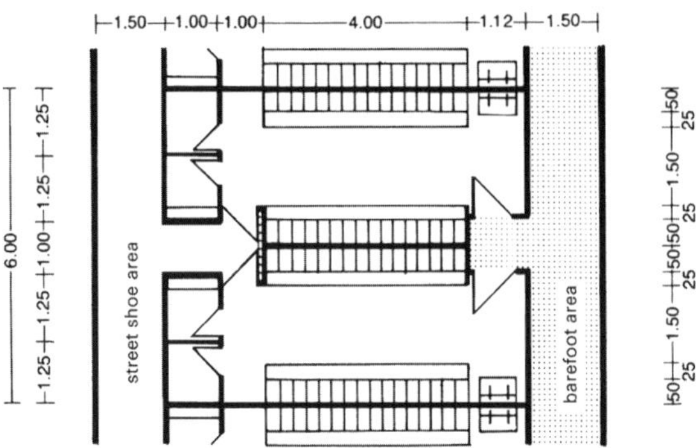

❺ Changing area: mixed type

Changing area

The size of the changing area can be derived from the water area (m^2). Rough estimate for a swimming time of about 1.5 hours: no. cloakroom places = 0.3–0.4 m^2 water area. No. changing places: 0.08–0.1 m^2 water area, of which 40–50% as cubicles, the rest as changing benches in communal rooms. Ratio of changing places to clothes lockers 1:4.

Family or wheelchair cubicles: 10% of the cubicles

No. communal changing places: min. 2; each communal changing place with min. 30 clothes lockers.

Dimensions

Minimum dimensions of installed fittings:

Cubicle: axis dimensions 1.00 m wide, 1.25 m deep, 2.00 m high.

Family changing cubicle: internal dimensions 1.60 m wide, 1.25 m deep, 2.00 m high.

Changing cubicle for wheelchair users: internal dimensions 2.45 m wide, 1.50 m deep, 2.00 m high, clear door width 0.94 m → ❻ – ❼.

Clothes locker → ❽ 0.25 m or 0.33 m wide (axis dimensions), 0.50 m deep (clear), 1.80 m high for full-height lockers or 0.90 m high for stacked lockers. For wheelchair users, the lockers are 0.40 m wide and should be provided only as full-height lockers in order to be able to house walking aids etc.

Changing bench: 0.20–0.25 m seat depth, for wheelchair users 0.40 m seat depth, 0.45 m seat height. Min. 7.50 m bench length in communal changing rooms (for school use min. 10.00 m).

No. **sanitary fittings per guideline unit**: 0.03 hair care places with dryer, 0.015 foot disinfection points, 0.015 bucket sink, cleaning equipment room 1–2 m^2, near changing area. Ceiling height 2.50 m.

Foot disinfection point (traffic area): 0.75 m wide, 0.50 m deep.

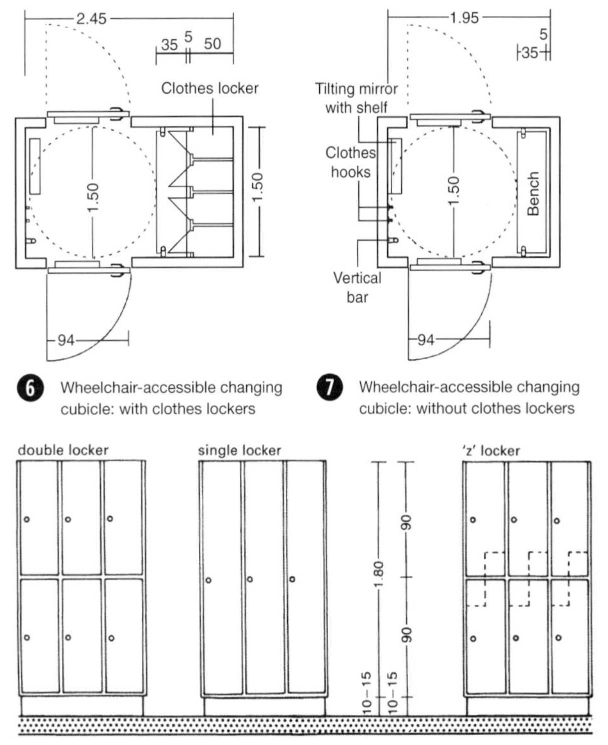

❻ Wheelchair-accessible changing cubicle: with clothes lockers

❼ Wheelchair-accessible changing cubicle: without clothes lockers

❽ Clothes lockers: details (examples)

Scheme of sanitary facilities

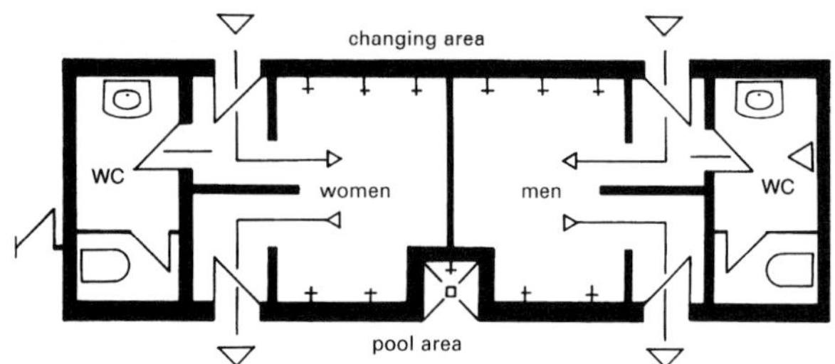

Scheme of sanitary facilities with divided shower room

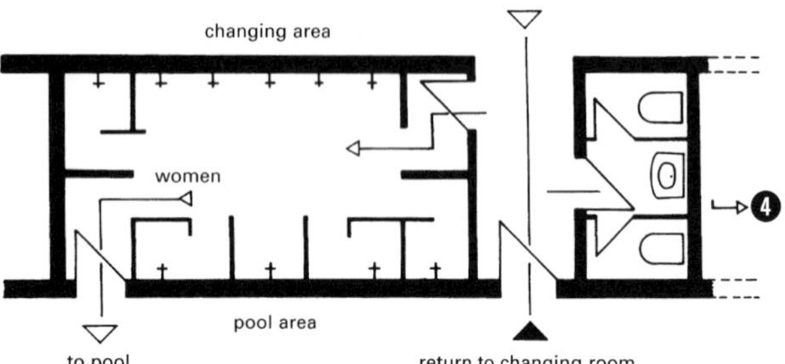

Sanitary facilities (example ladies)

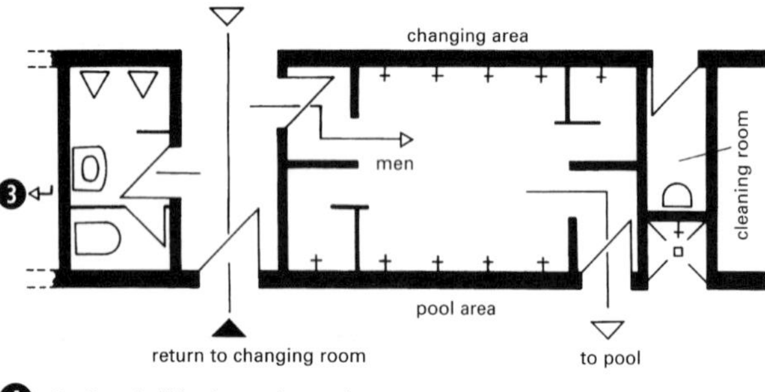

Sanitary facilities (example gents)

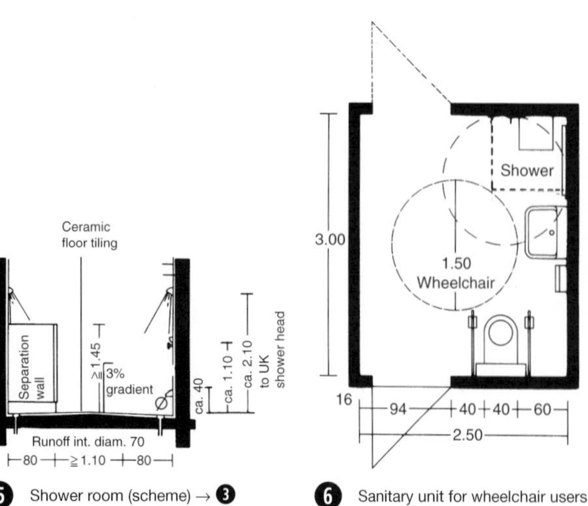

Shower room (scheme) → ❸

Sanitary unit for wheelchair users

The **sanitary facilities** include showers and toilets, ladies' and gents' separated. Location should be between the changing and the pool areas. The toilets should be arranged so that, after use and before entering the pool area, the bather has to cross a shower room → ❶ – ❹. A direct route back from the pool area to the changing area is definitely to be recommended.

Size of the sanitary facilities: basic equipment min. 1 shower room each for ladies and gents with min. 10 showers (applies for water area up to 500 m^2). In addition, a further shower should be provided for every 25–50 m^2 of water area. In indoor swimming pools in schools up to 150 m^2 water area, 1 divisible shower room each for girls and boys with 5 showers is sufficient → ❷.

Toilets: each shower room requires 2 WCs for ladies, 1 WC and 2 urinals for gents → ❶.

Minimum dimensions of movement areas in sanitary facilities:

shower without partition:	0.80 m wide
(open row of showers)	0.80 m deep
shower with partition:	0.95 m or
(row of showers with spray guard)	0.80 m wide
	1.45 m high
shower with double-T partition:	0.80 m or
(with spray and sight partition)	0.95 m wide
	1.40 m deep
	1.45 m high
corridor width between two rows of showers:	1.10 m
toilet with inward opening door	0.90 m wide
	1.40 m deep
	2.00 m high
toilet with outward opening door:	0.90 m wide
	1.20 m deep
	2.00 m high
urinal (axis dimensions):	0.65 m
free standing area:	0.40 m
installation height:	approx. 0.70 m
installation height for children:	approx. 0.50 m
washbasin (axis dimensions):	approx. 0.70 m
free standing area:	approx. 0.60 m
installation height	approx. 0.80 m
minimum clear ceiling height	2.50 m
recommended	2.75 m

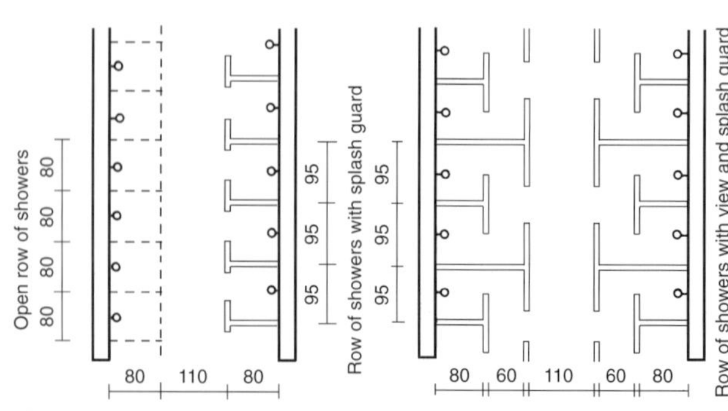

Shower and partition arrangement

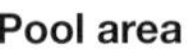

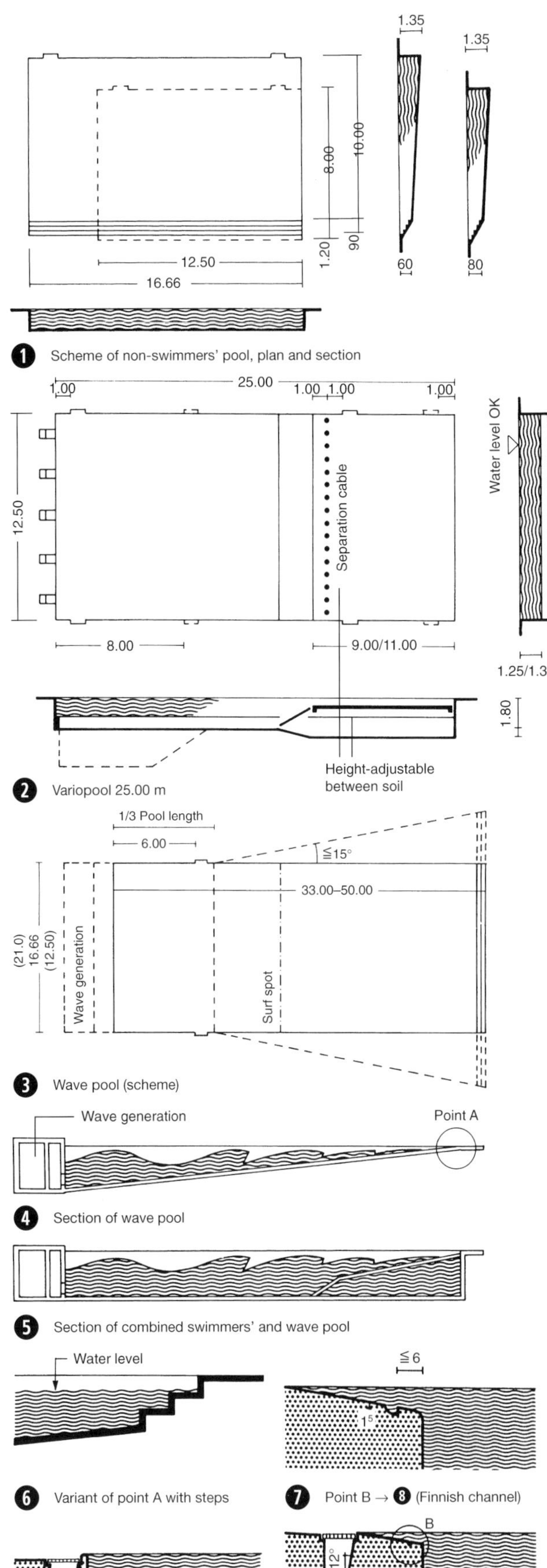

❶ Scheme of non-swimmers' pool, plan and section

❷ Variopool 25.00 m

❸ Wave pool (scheme)

❹ Section of wave pool

❺ Section of combined swimmers' and wave pool

❻ Variant of point A with steps

❼ Point B → ❽ (Finnish channel)

❽ Examples of overflow channels

Pool area

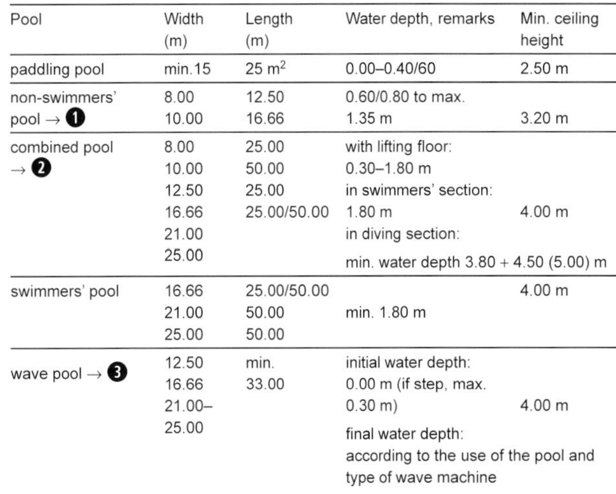

Pool	Width (m)	Length (m)	Water depth, remarks	Min. ceiling height
paddling pool	min.15	25 m²	0.00–0.40/60	2.50 m
non-swimmers' pool → ❶	8.00 10.00	12.50 16.66	0.60/0.80 to max. 1.35 m	3.20 m
combined pool → ❷	8.00 10.00 12.50 16.66 21.00 25.00	25.00 50.00 25.00 25.00/50.00	with lifting floor: 0.30–1.80 m in swimmers' section: 1.80 m in diving section: min. water depth 3.80 + 4.50 (5.00) m	4.00 m
swimmers' pool	16.66 21.00 25.00	25.00/50.00 50.00 50.00	min. 1.80 m	4.00 m
wave pool → ❸	12.50 16.66 21.00– 25.00	min. 33.00	initial water depth: 0.00 m (if step, max. 0.30 m) final water depth: according to the use of the pool and type of wave machine	4.00 m

Pool perimeter; perimeter areas generally at the same level as water	Width (m)
in the main access area to the swimming pool:	3.00
in main entrance area between pool steps and hall wall:	2.50
at the starting blocks:	3.00
at the diving facility:	4.50
(behind the 1 m diving board: free passage min. 1.25 m)	
at the access to the paddling pool	2.00
non-swimmers' pool – steps side:	2.50
non-swimmers' pool – narrow side:	2.00
between diving, swimmers' or combined pool and the non-swimmers' pool or non-swimmer's section of the combined pool:	4.00
between swimmers' pool or swimmers' section of a combined pool and the divers' pool:	3.00
remaining widths for a water area less than 300 m²	min. 1.25
over 300 m²	min. 1.50

ceiling height at pool perimeter:		2.50
lifeguard's room	space requirement: min. 6 m²	2.50
sanitary room	space requirement: min. 8 m²	2.50
equipment room	up to 450 m² water area, min. 15 m²	2.50
	over 450 m² water area, min. 20 m²	2.50
	lounge for competitors:	2.50
	6 swimming lanes = 30 m², 8 = 50 m², 10 = 70 m²	
	teaching and club: 30 up to 60 m²	2.50
spectator facilities	stands: 0.5 seats per 1 m² water area used for sport space required for 1 seat: 0.5 m² including immediate traffic area spectator cloakrooms, space required: 0.025 m² per 1 m² water area used for sport spectator toilets: the toilets in the entrance area (ladies: 1 WC, gents: 1 WC, 1 urinal) are sufficient for 200 spectators. For larger spectator facilities, 1 additional toilet (WC or urinal) for every 100 further spectators plus 1 toilet (WC or urinal), with a ratio of ladies: 2 WCs, gents: 1 WC, 2 urinals.	
workplaces for press and television	Good view of the start and finish (raised position) required: 5–20 places, each place 0.75 × 1.20 m Required: 4–6 places, each place 1.20 m × 1.50 m	
catering (café/restaurant)	Space required per vending machine: 0.5–0.8 m² Seated area: min 50 seats, each seat 1–2 m² supply and subsidiary rooms (additional): for café approx. 60% of seating area, for restaurant approx. 100% of seating area, of which 20–25% for stores and cool room, for empty packaging 15–20%, for kitchen, pantry, office, staff, remaining area. Toilets: min. ladies, 1 WC, gents, 1 WC, 1 urinal.	
services area	Total area for services (without wave water tank, storeroom, sub-station and gas supply room): up to 1 m² per 1 m² planned water area; for larger indoor pools, a reduction of up to 30% is possible.	

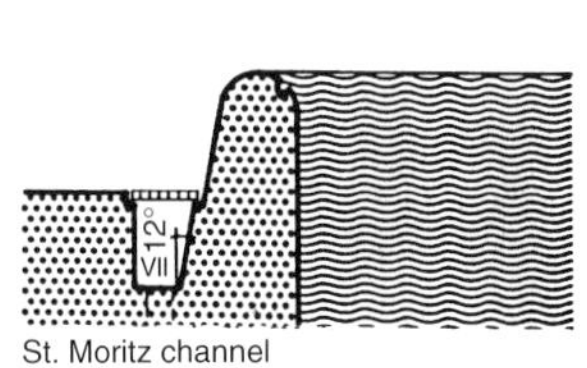

St. Moritz channel

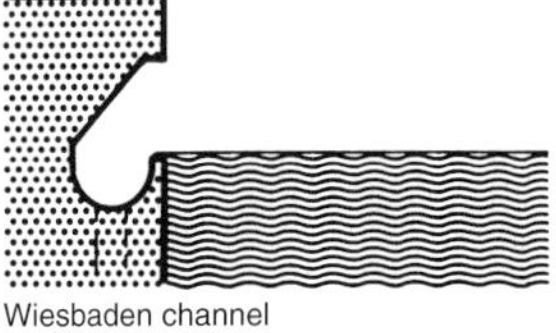
Wiesbaden channel

Diving facilities are used for school and competitive sport. Two diving-off points are used: a rigid platform at heights of 1, 3, 5 and 10 m, and a rebounding springboard, made of aluminium, wood or plastic, at heights of 1 and 3 m. The height of the diving positions is measured from the water surface. The climb up to the board or to the platform is up steep steps. All diving facilities are on one side of the pool → ❶ – ❷. **Water temperature**: 24–28 °C. In order for divers to be able to discern the water surface better, water rippling devices or sprinkler jets can be provided.

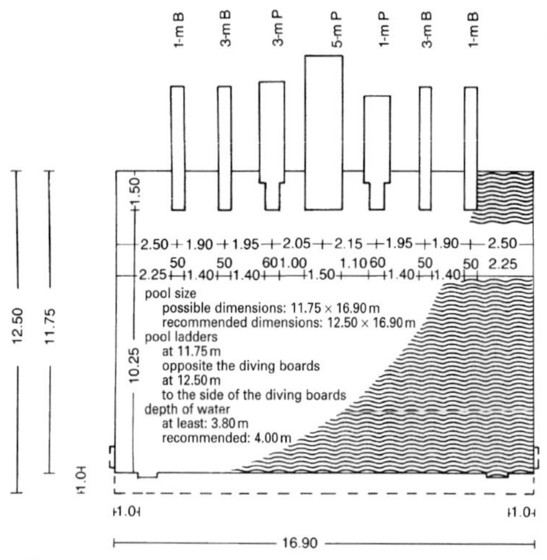

❶ 1–5 m diving facilities (complete). B = board, P = platform

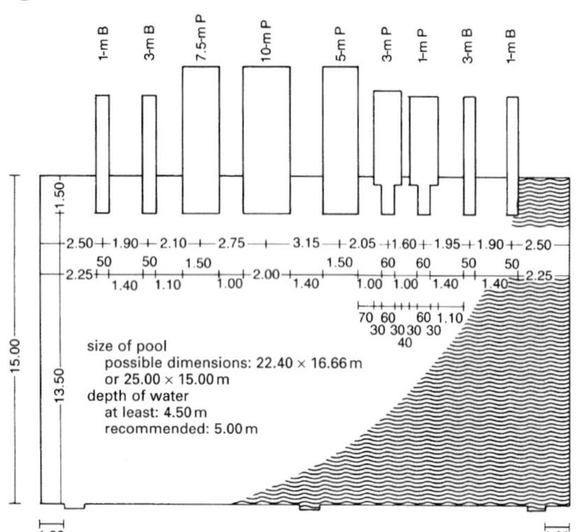

❷ 1–10 m diving facilities (complete). B = board, P = platform

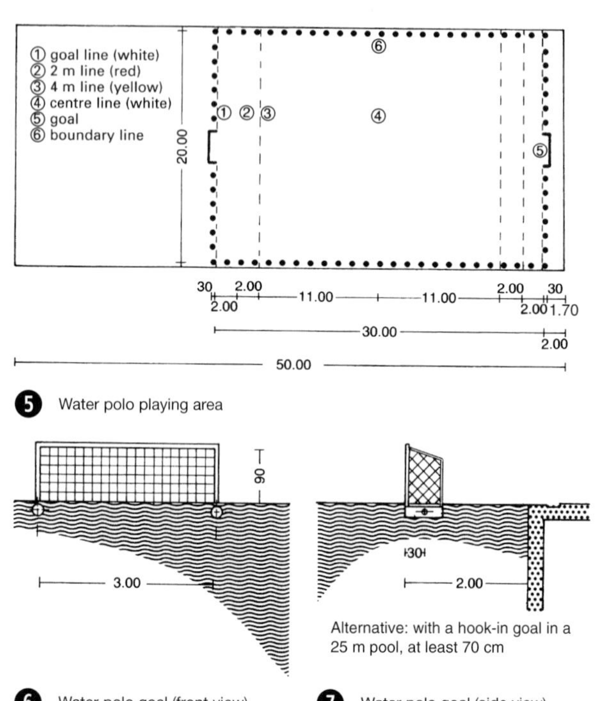

❺ Water polo playing area

❻ Water polo goal (front view)

❼ Water polo goal (side view)

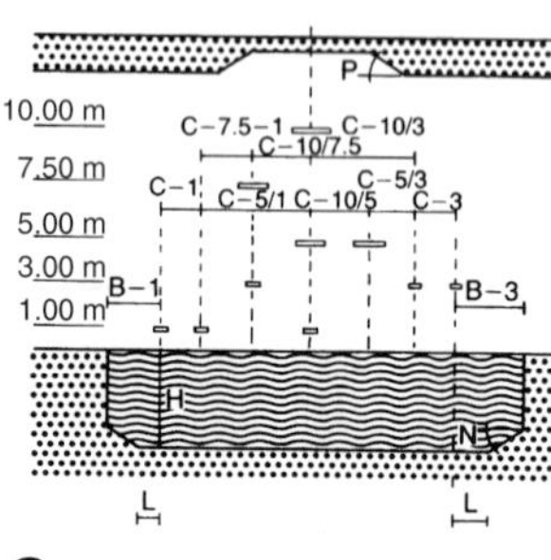

❸ Cross-section

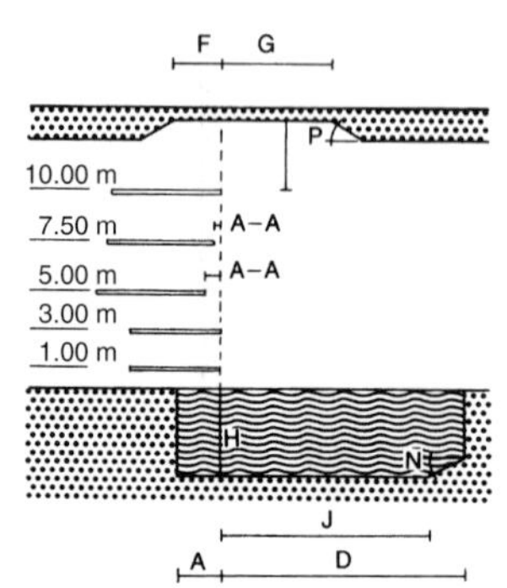

❹ Longitudinal section

	Dimensions of diving facilities	Length/width	1 m board 4.80/0.50	3 m board 4.80/0.50	1 m platform 4.50/0.60	3 m platform 5.00/0.60	5 m platform 6.00/1.50	7.5 m platform 6.00/1.50	10 m platform 6.00/2.00
A	from front edge of board/ platform back to pool side	min. dimension	1.50	1.50	1.50	1.50	1.50	1.50	1.50
A-A	from front edge of uppermost board/platform back to pool sidewall	min. dimension				1.25	1.25	1.25	
B	from centre of board/platform sideways to pool sidewall	min. dimension	2.50	3.50	2.30	2.80	4.25	4.50	5.25
C	from centre to centre	min. dimension	1.90	1.90	—	—	2.10	2.10 or 2.45	3.13 or 2.65
D	from front edge of board/ platform to forward pool sidewall	min. dimension	9.00	10.25	8.00	9.50	10.25	11.00	13.50
E	from top of board/platform to underside of ceiling	min. dimension	5.00	5.00	3.00	3.00	3.00	3.20	3.40
F	space, within which the dimension 'E' is to be complied with backwards and to each side of the centre of the board/platform	min. dimension	2.50	2.50	2.75	2.75	2.75	2.75	2.75
G	space, within which the dimension 'E' is to be complied with from the front edge of the board/platform	min. dimension	5.00	5.00	5.00	5.00	5.00	5.00	6.00
H	water depth under the board/ platform	min. dimension	3.40	3.80	3.40	3.40	3.80	4.10	4.50
J	distance from the front edge of the board/platform forwards	min. dimension	6.00	6.00	5.00	6.00	6.00	8.00	12.00
K	water depth at distance to 'J'	min. dimension	3.30	3.70	3.30	3.30	3.70	4.00	4.25
L	distance sideways of the centre of the board/platform	min. dimension	2.25	3.25	2.05	2.55	3.75	3.75	4.50
M	water depth at a distance from 'L'	min. dimension	3.30	3.70	3.30	3.30	3.70	4.00	4.25

❽ Safety dimensions for diving facilities → ❶ – ❼

catering | catering
covered entrance area (street side)
ticket office
covered entrance area (pool side)
changing area
showers
toilets
mother and child
warm and recreation room
administration
staff
club rooms
swimming supervisors' room
first aid room
plant area
stores and equipment rooms
competition rooms
staff flat
sitting area
sunbathing terrace
play area
leisure/sports facilities
foot rinse pool
children's play area
paddling area
pool area
toilets

▶ direct access
▷ optional direct access

note: the illustration represents only the internal links; do not use this for room planning.

❶ Room and area relationship scheme

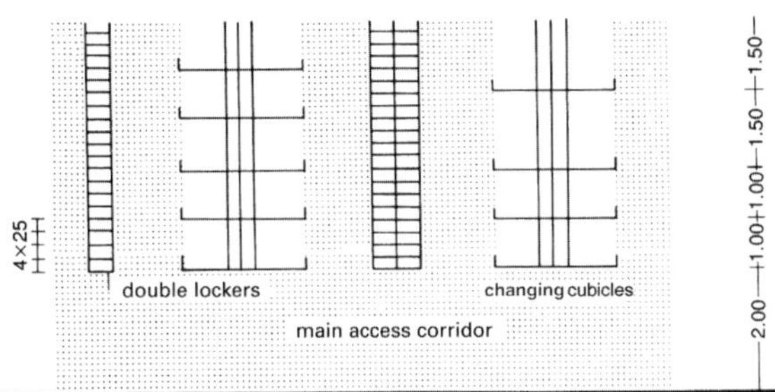

❷ Cloakroom unit (scheme)

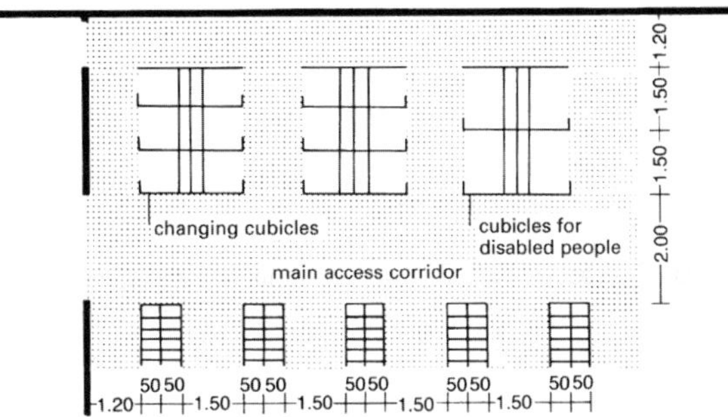

❸ Cloakroom unit (scheme)

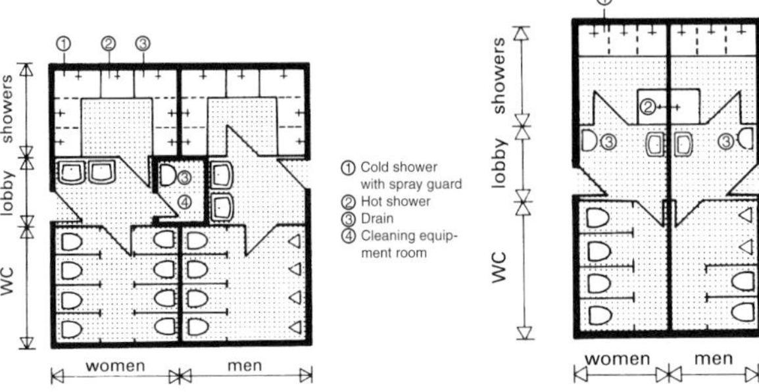

❹ Sanitary facilities for 2000 m² water area (scheme)

❺ Sanitary facilities for 1000 m² water area (scheme)

Building plot size: 10–16 m² of the planned water area.

Parking: 1 car and 2 bicycle spaces per 200–300 m² of building plot area.

Space in front of entrance: 150 m² per 1000 m² water area, 50 m² per 1000 m² water area for roofed entrance zones, including cash desk and access control equipment.

Changing area: changing places as cubicles: 0.01 per m² water area, per 1000m² water area min. 10 changing places, of which: 8 changing places as cubicles including 2 cubicles for families and wheelchair users and 2 privacy-screened changing places on the sunbathing lawn. Communal changing rooms: as required, min. 2 communal changing rooms, each with 10.00 m bench length.

Cloakrooms: cloakroom places and lockers for valuables: 0.1 per m² water area, 20 lockers for valuables per 100 cloakroom places.

Sanitary facilities: child–parent area: 15–25 m².

Showers: per 1000 m² water area 3 warm showers for ladies, 3 warm showers for gents, possibly also 1 cold shower per shower room.

Toilets: per 1000 m² water area: 4 WCs for ladies, 2 WCs and 4 urinals for gents, anteroom with washbasin.

Foot disinfection point: according to local regulations. Foot washing and rinsing point (combined): per 1000 m² water area, 4 taps.

Covered area for weather protection: per 1000 m² water area, 100 m² covered area.

Warm lounge room: per 1000 guideline units 30–70 m², min. 50 m².

Staff rooms: up to 1500 m² water area, up to 10 m²; over 1500 m² water area, up to 30 m².

Lifeguard's room: approx. 10 m².

First aid room: approx. 8 m², if combined with lifeguard's room and sanitary facilities, approx. 14 m².

Store and equipment room: up to 1000 m² water area, min. 30 m² (recommended: 50 m²); over 1000 m² water area, min. 50 m² (recommended 80 m²).

Pool area

Paddling pool: water area: 80–200 m², water depth: 0.00–0.60 m, division into a number of pools of differing depths is ideal.

Non-swimmers' pool: water area: 600–1500 m², water depth: 0.50/0.60–1.35 m, possibly divided into a number of pools of differing depths.

Swimming pool: water area: 313–1050 m², water depth: > 1.80 m, pool size according to number of swimming lanes.

Swimming lanes	Pool width	Pool length
5	12.50 m	25.00 m
6	16.66 m	25.00 m
6	16.66 m	50.00 m
8	21.00 m	50.00 m
10	25.00 m	50.00 m

Wave pool: pool width: 12.50 m, 16.66 m, 21.00 m, 25.00 m, pool length: 50.00 m, min. 33.00 m, initial water depth: 0.00 m, final water depth according to pool use and type of wave machine.

Pool perimeter: min. width 2.50 m. Near the access points and the starting blocks, 3.00 m; near the pool steps to the non-swimmers' pool 3.00 m, near the diving facility 5.00 m.

Open areas: approx. 60% of the building plot area, divided into sunbathing, leisure sport and children's play areas. Ratio sunbathing area: sport area = 2:1 to 3:1.

Children's play area: dry area: sandpit 100–300 m², play area 300–700 m². Wet area: water play area 100–500 m².

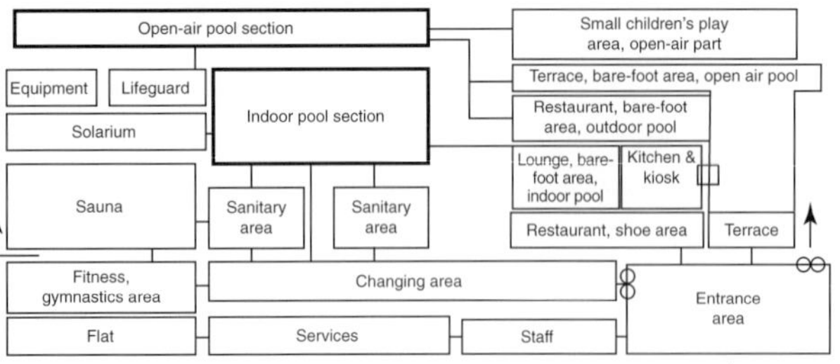

1 Room and functional scheme

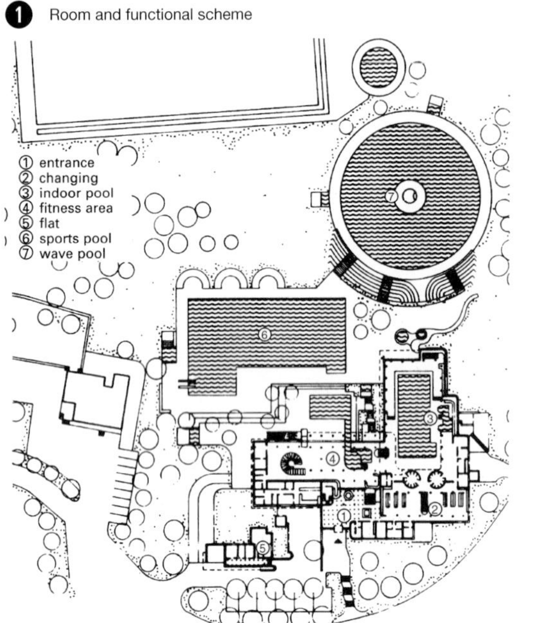

2 The Wellenberg, Oberammergau — Arch.: P. Seifert

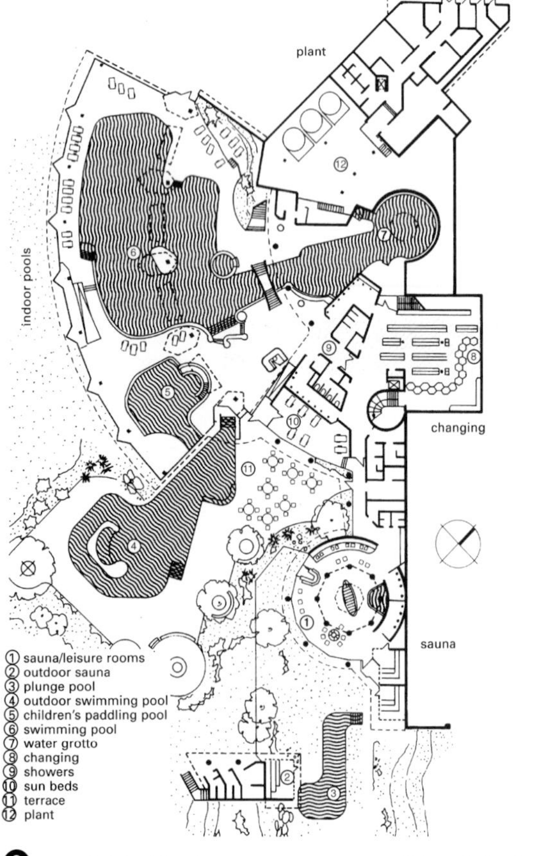

3 Leisure pool, Heveney — Arch.: Aichele; Fiedler; Heller

Combinations of indoor and outdoor swimming pools enable, according to the type of operation, almost complete spatial, functional and operational combination of the individual facilities' components. At the same time, they also offer more flexible opportunities for use and thus possess a higher leisure value than outdoor or indoor pools alone. The differing needs at different times of year require different areas of water indoors and outdoors. Operation can be categorised into summertime, wintertime and in-between (pre-season and after-season).

The following types of operation can be considered: simultaneous use of the inside and outside water areas with common opening times, unlimited bathing time and unitary entrance price; separate use of the indoor and outdoor water areas with different opening times, partially unlimited opening times (outdoors) and different prices; seasonal use of only one part, e.g. by mothballing one part. Combinations of indoor and outdoor swimming pools can sometimes also be achieved by extending the facilities at existing pools, adding an indoor or outdoor section. If the indoor and outdoor parts of a new project are not to be opened in one construction phase, then the design of the entire facility should be undertaken, including technical specialist design work. This can avoid double expenditure. The first construction phase should generally be the indoor swimming pool.

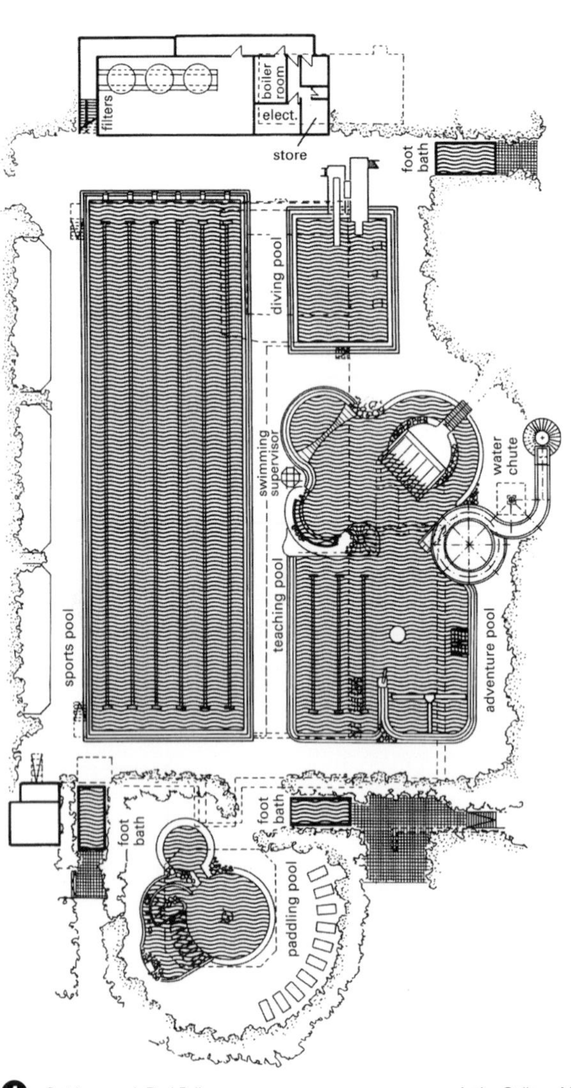

4 Outdoor pool, Bad Driburg — Arch.: Geller + Müller

The building plot size should be in line with the requirements for an outdoor pool. With a plot requirement <10,000 m^2 for the indoor element, a supplement of 5.00 m^2 per m^2 of water area should be added for the outdoor. Otherwise, the design recommendations for indoor or outdoor pools apply.

The pool area of the outdoor pool should ideally be connected to the pool area of the indoor pool. This ensures better utilisation between seasons, central supervision and a favourable technical combination. The lounge area with catering should have a view of both pools if possible.

Access to the outdoor pool is normally through the entrance hall of the indoor pool, but at peak times this can be supplemented by the covered entrance zone. The cash desk and access control area should serve both parts if possible.

A close link between the pool areas in the indoor and the outdoor facilities enables flexible use. The connection between the two, preferably to the non-swimmers' section of the outdoor pool, can be through a swimming channel (with access in the indoor pool) or a closed corridor. The intention is that the bathers can reach an outdoor pool from the indoor pool without contact with cold outside air.

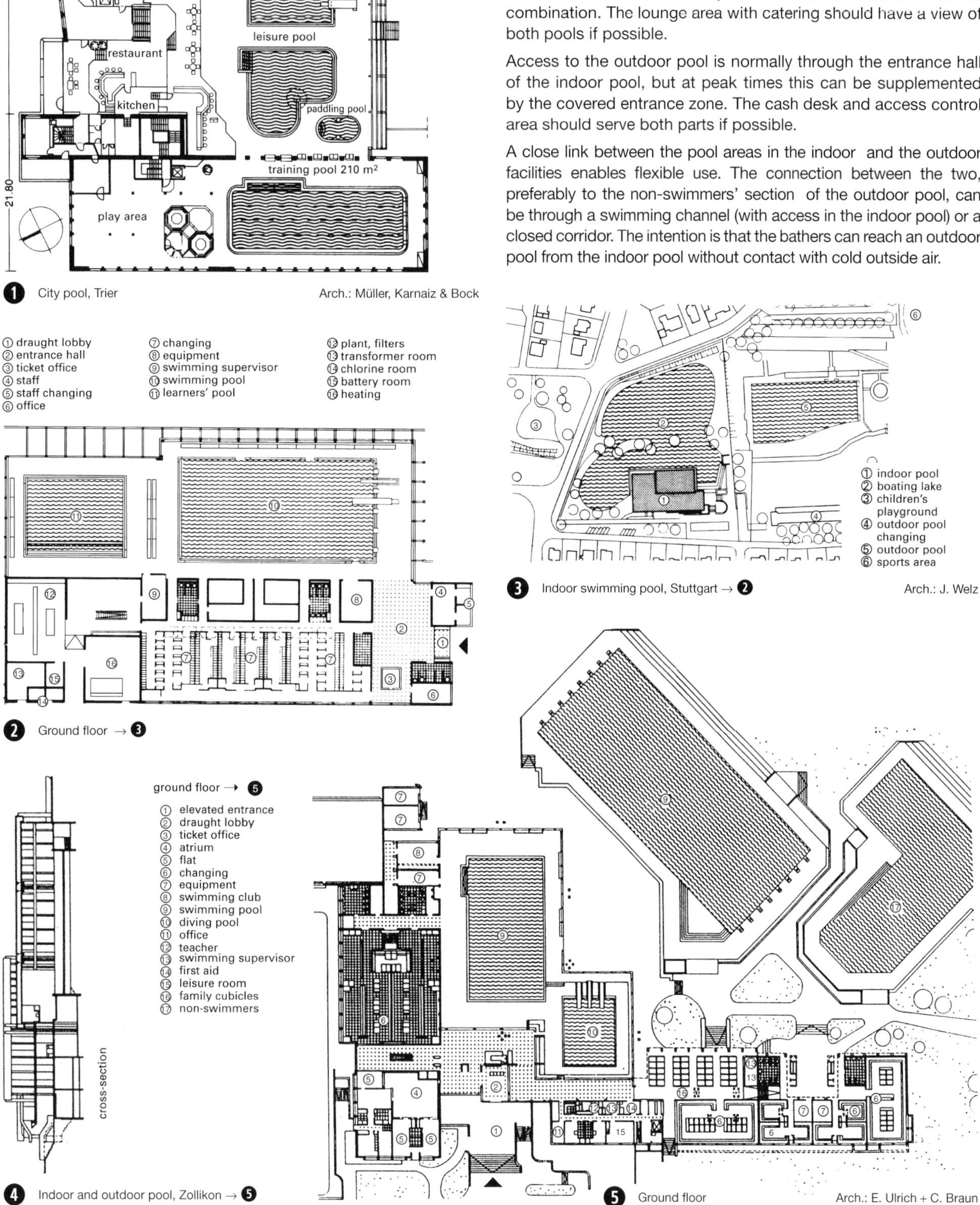

1 City pool, Trier — Arch.: Müller, Karnaiz & Bock

2 Ground floor → 3

3 Indoor swimming pool, Stuttgart → 2 — Arch.: J. Welz

4 Indoor and outdoor pool, Zollikon → 5

5 Ground floor — Arch.: E. Ulrich + C. Braun

Sport and leisure

SWIMMING POOLS
Indoor public pools
Outdoor public pools
Indoor and outdoor pools
Private pools

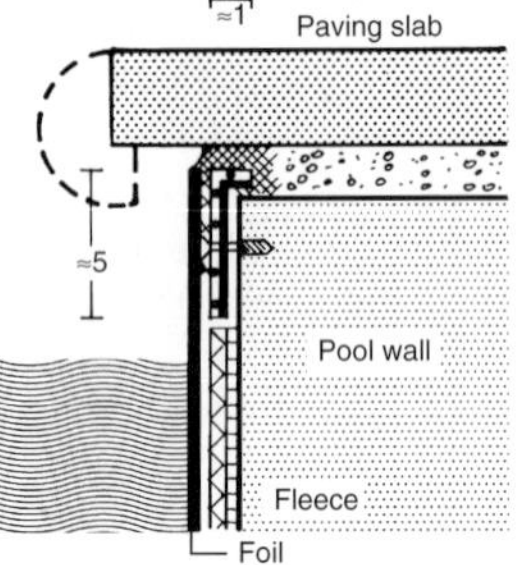

❶ Edge connection/foil lined pool with bonded sheet metal

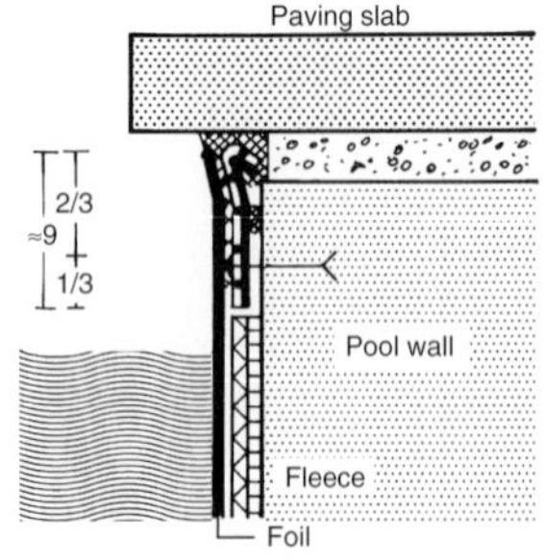

❷ Variant → ❶

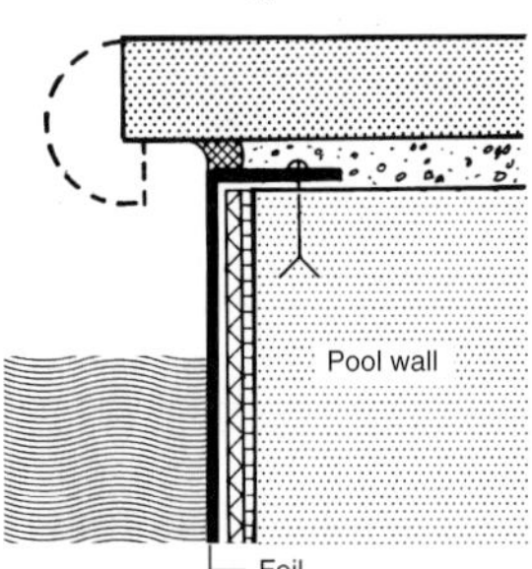

❸ Foil fixed to pool wall

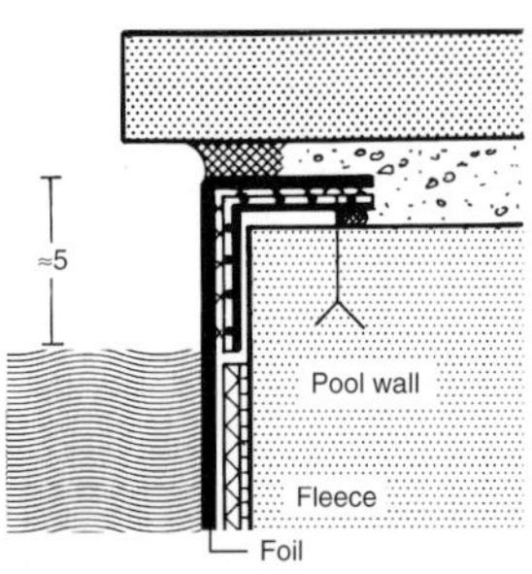

❹ Edge connection with angle of bonded sheet metal

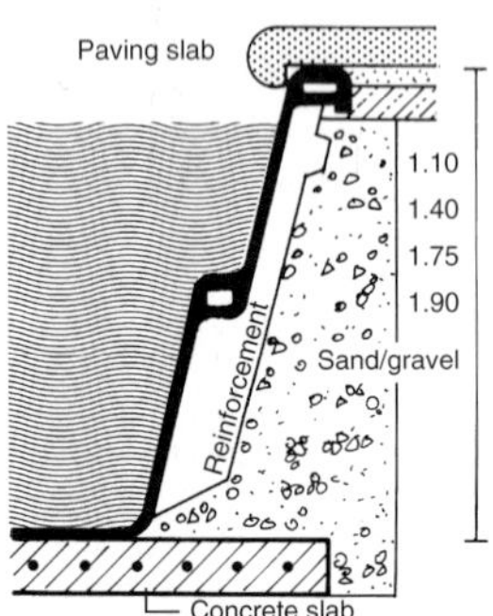

❺ Pre-fabricated pool

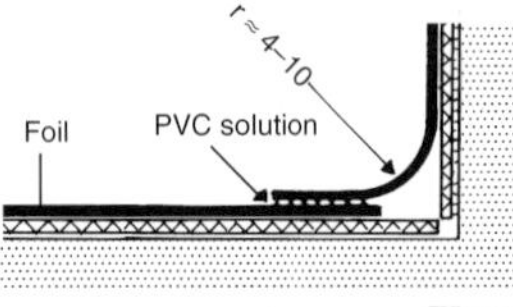

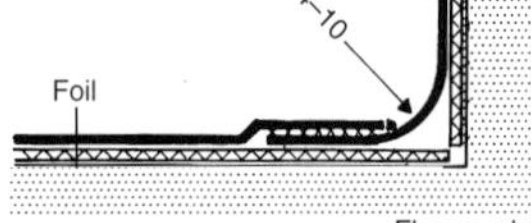

❻ Connections at floor/sidewall with rounded corner

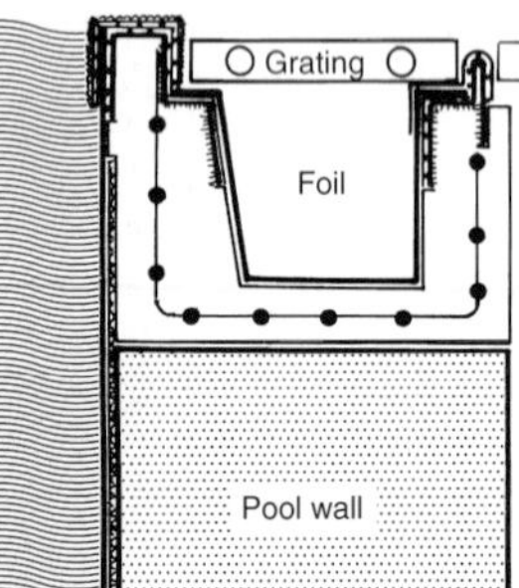

❼ Pre-cast concrete gutter/foil liner

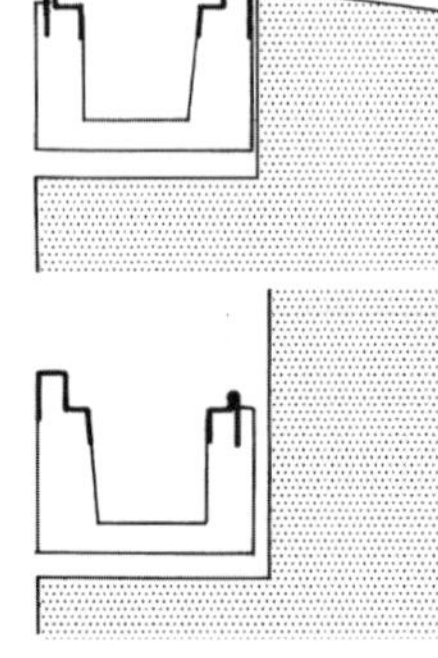

❽ Variant → ❻

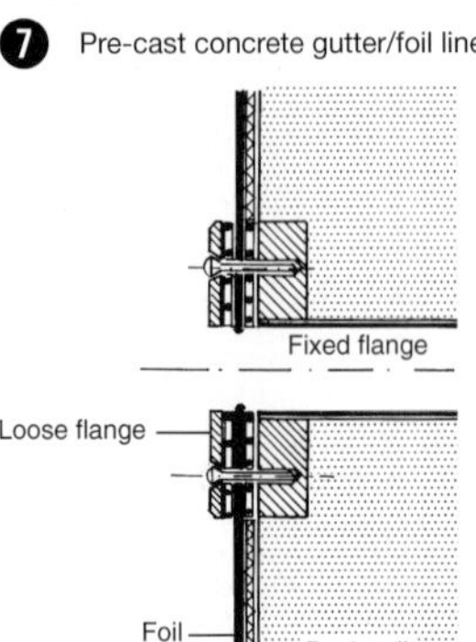

❾ Fixed flange connection

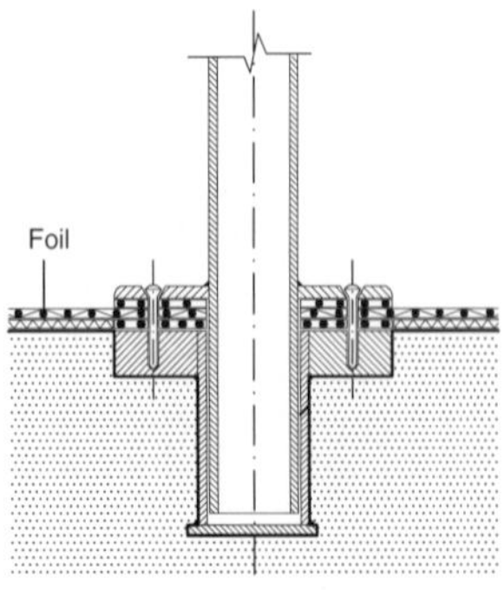

❿ Fixed flange with anchor sleeve

Construction details

The use of foils for the lining of swimming pools saves the normal expense of waterproof sub-structure. The foil in areas around stairs, standing steps and children's paddling pools should have an embossed and structured surface for safety reasons. At penetrations, fixed flange connections are helpful → ❾ – ❿. Possible condensation on the side away from the water should be considered, and secondary drainage or relief drillings should be provided under the waterproofing layer. In order to empty the pool, the floor is constructed with a gradient of 5% or max. 10%. In order to securely connect the foil, use bonded sheet metal profiles → ❶ – ❹. Also possible are prefabricated pools in one piece as a shell structure, or segmental pools.

	Relative air humidity				
	50%	60%			70%
	Air temperature				
	28°C	26°C	28°C	30°C	28°C
24°C R	21	13	0	– [1)]	0
M	219	193	143	– [1)]	67
26°C R	48	53	21	2	0
M	294	269	218	163	143
28°C R	96	104	66	31	36
M	378	353	302	247	227
30°C R	157	145	123	81	89
M	471	446	395	339	320

[1)] temperature difference 4 K water/air cannot be held in the long term

⓫ Specific quantity of evaporation in an indoor pool (g/m³h): out of operation (R) and max. use (M) (Kappler → refs)

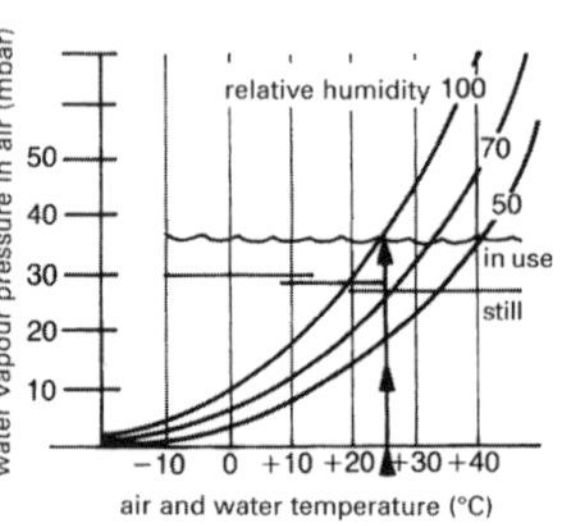

⓬ Evaporation limit for an indoor pool: upper line, in use; lower line, out of operation

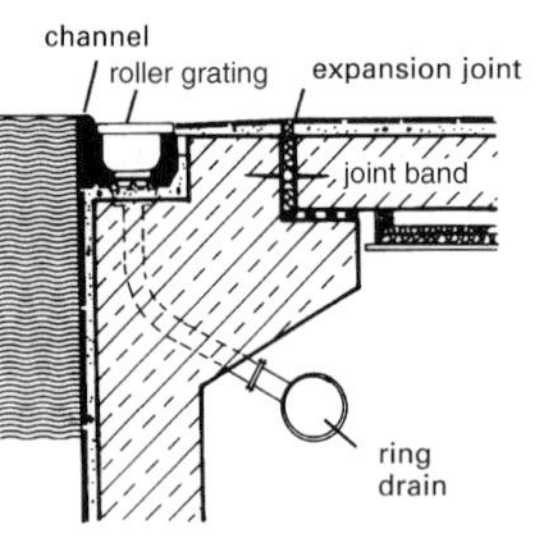

⓭ 'Zürich' pool edge overflow system

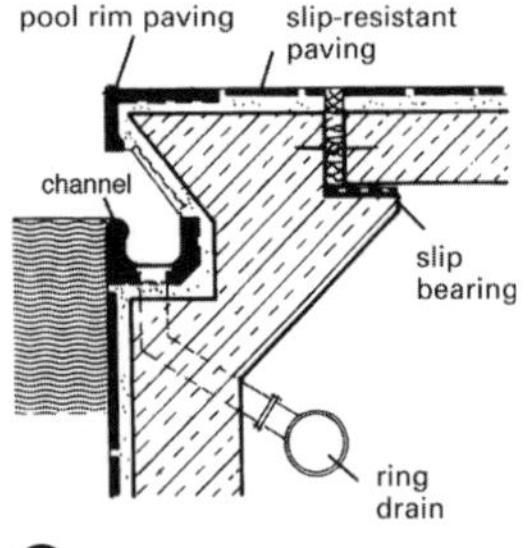

⓮ 'Wiesbaden' overflow channel system

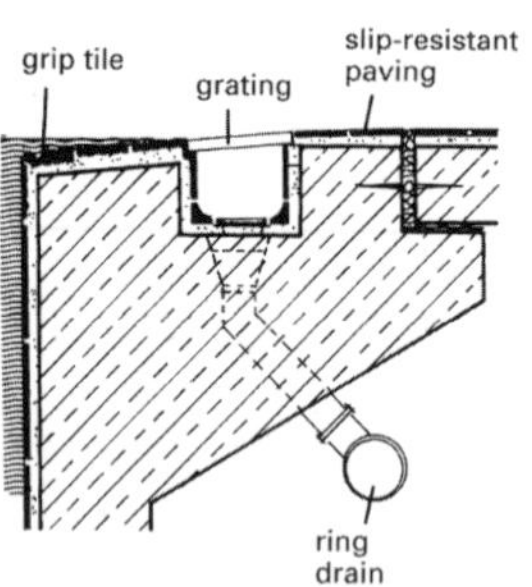

⓯ Finnish channel

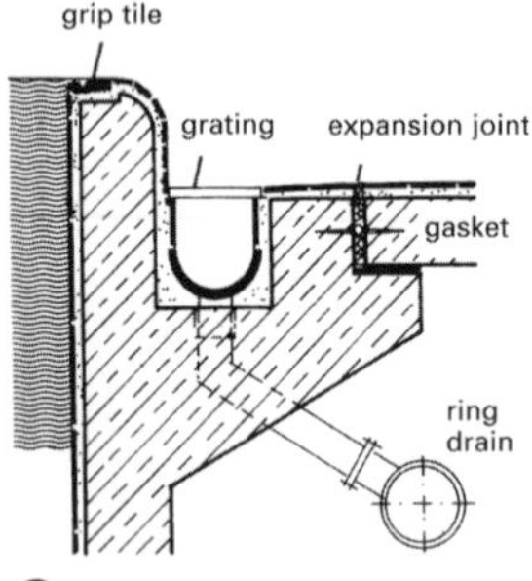

⓰ 'St. Moritz' overflow channel system

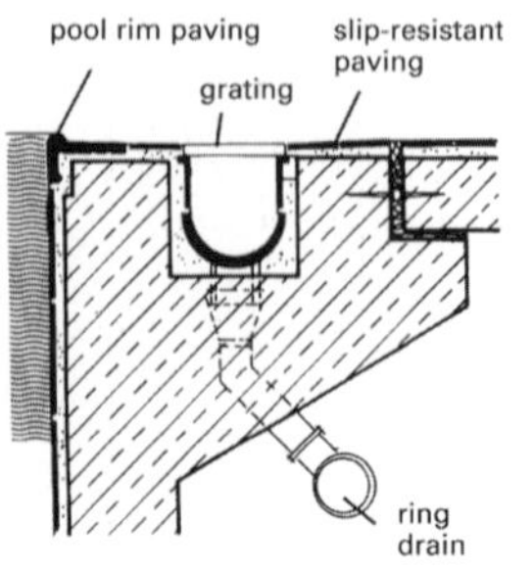

⓱ Overflow channel with pool edge kerbstone and drainage channel

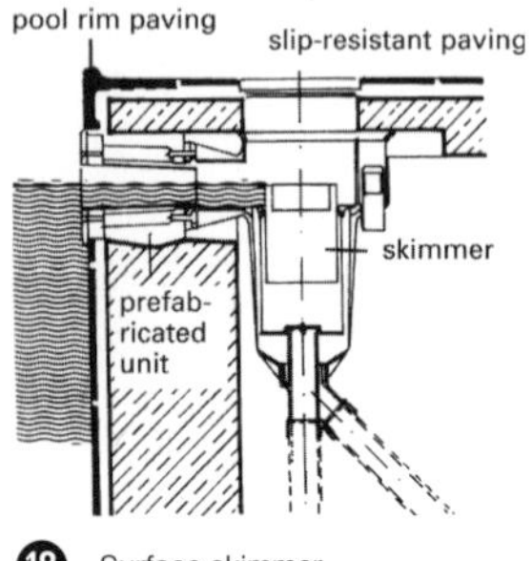

⓲ Surface skimmer

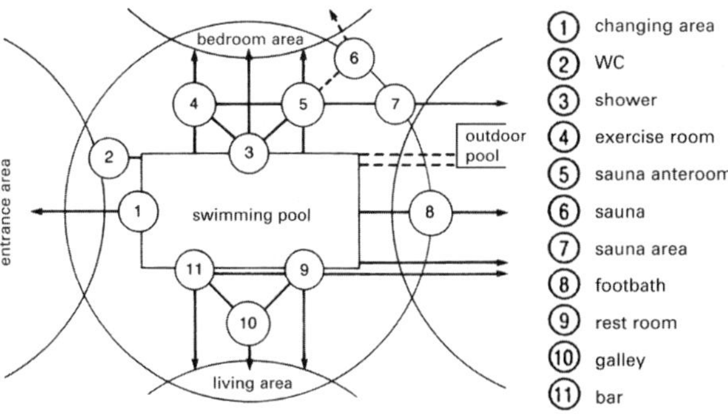

❶ Related elements of the indoor pool of a detached house. A flat part of the swimming hall can also be the living room.

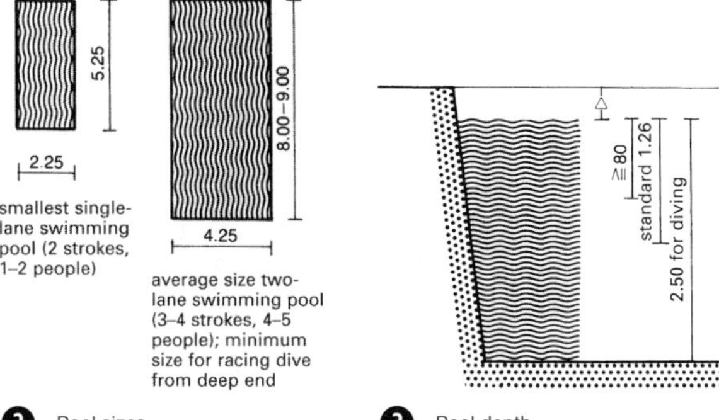

❷ Pool sizes

❸ Pool depth

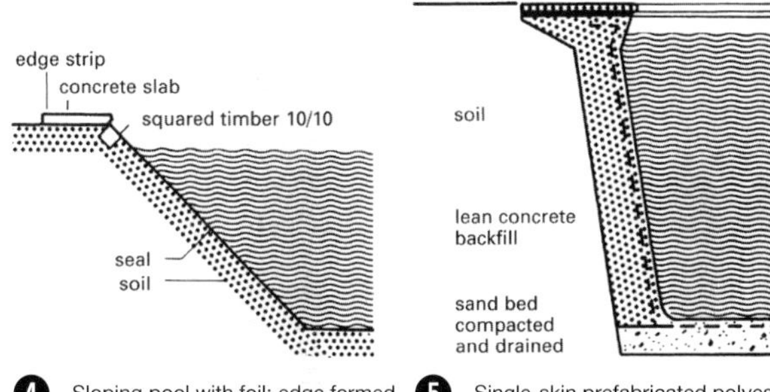

❹ Sloping pool with foil; edge formed by timber beam

❺ Single-skin prefabricated polyester pool

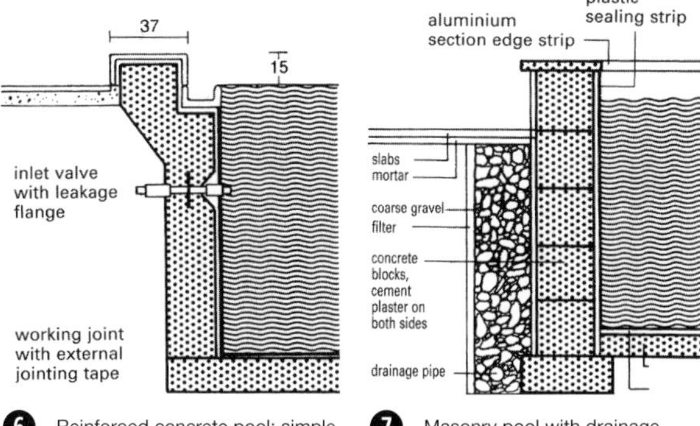

❻ Reinforced concrete pool: simple version with Wiesbaden channel

❼ Masonry pool with drainage

Water	Season			Additional months	
temp.	4 Months	5 Months	6 Months	5th Month	6th Month
22°C	1.25/6.5	1.33/7.2	1.55/7.8	1.65/7.2	2.65/7.8
23°C	1.50/7.2	1.70/7.9	2.00/8.5	2.50/7.9	3.50/8.5
24°C	2.08/7.9	2.26/8.6	2.66/9.2	2.98/8.6	4.66/9.2
25°C	2.60/8.5	2.80/9.3	3.20/9.8	3.60/9.5	5.25/9.8
26°C	3.50/9.2	3.75/10.0	4.00/10.5	4.75/10.0	5.25/10.5

❽ Heat loss of an outdoor pool (average/maximum) in kWh/m^{2}d according to measurements by energy company RWE. Special influences are not considered, e.g. considerable heat loss of public pools (hotel pool etc.) through the use of heated pool water for filter back-flushing (up to 1.5 kW/m^{2}d or 1300 kcal/m^{2}d).

Location

Protected from wind → ❶, near the bedroom (for use on cool days), visible from the kitchen (keep an eye on children) and living room (scenery effect), i.e. in view. No deciduous trees or bushes next to the pool (falling leaves). Prevent grass etc. falling in at the sides, possibly with a raised edge (design question).

Size

Lane width 2.25 m, stroke length approx. 1.50 m, plus body length: 4 strokes = 8 m length. Water depth: chin height for the smallest adult, not the children! Difference between pool depth/ water depth → ❸, depends on the type of extractor system.

Shape

As simple as possible due to cost and water management (see below), rectangular, always with ladder or step recess.

Types of pool

Normal foil pool (foil = waterproof surface) on masonry-bearing construction → ❼, concrete, steel (also above ground) or sunk into ground → ❹.

Polyester pools, seldom locally produced, mostly with pre-fabricated elements, are generally not self-supporting. Lean concrete backfilling is necessary → ❺.

Watertight concrete pool → ❻ (two-sided in situ concrete, shotcrete with formwork for one side, pre-cast concrete elements); surface mostly ceramic or glass mosaic, occasionally paint (chlorine rubber, cement paint).

Water cleaning

A recirculation system is usual today, generally providing flat water flow with the good surface cleaning effect of a skimmer or a channel.

Filter types

Gravel (deep filter, sometimes with cleaning air injection), diatomite (surface filter), plastic foam. Algae is combated with chlorine, chlorine-free algae agent, or copper sulphate.

Heating

With counter-current apparatus or through-flow heater in the heating boiler – mind the regulations! This prolongs the swimming season considerably at relatively low cost →❽ – ❾.

Protection of children

Can be through fencing, covering the pool or self-activating alarm device (reacts to waves).

Frost protection

For rigid pools with inserted edge beam, heating or overflow kept frost-free. A pool should not be emptied in winter (sloping edge of pool).

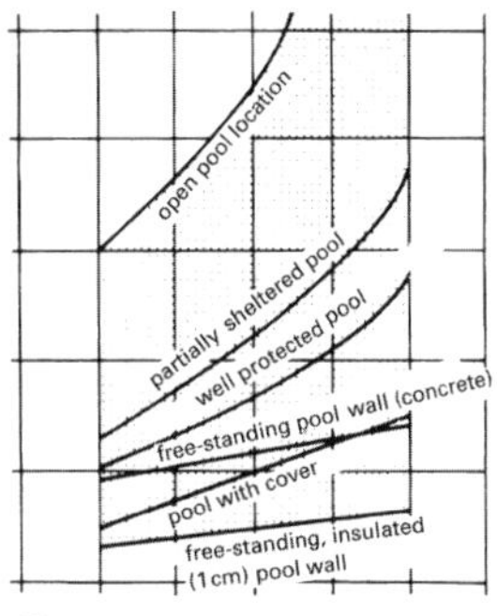

❾ Heat loss from a pool surface or the free-standing poolside wall for a 5-month season (average values)

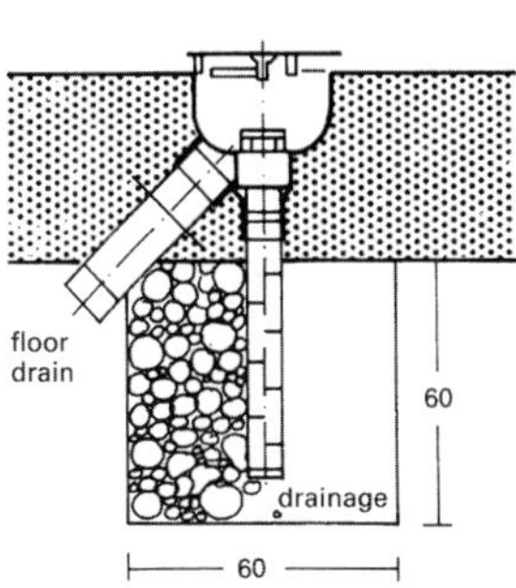

❿ Floor gully with groundwater pressure balance

In contrast to the separated features of a commercially operated sauna → p. 373 f., the functions of a private sauna can all be integrated into one room, e.g. changing and relaxation (can also take place in the house) or pre-cleaning and cooling (can take place in the same room with the same sanitary facilities).

Free-standing **sauna cabins** or facilities (e.g. in the garden) are normally constructed of spruce in log cabin style, and are either self-built or bought pre-fabricated. The log cabins are available in various versions, either as sauna cabins → ❿ or also with shower and changing or relaxation room → ❾. There are also sauna cabins available as prefabricated or kit elements for installation in existing rooms → ⓭ + ⓯.

Sauna stove: Sauna cabins for installation usually have electric stoves (which require a three-phase supply above a certain size), while log cabin types mostly have solid fuel stoves (which require a chimney).

Plunge pool → ❸ – ❹ max. depth 1.20 m.

An important part of a proper sauna, a (warm) **footbath** → ❷ with a seat are required.

Room temperatures: changing room 20–22°C, wash room ≧24–26°C, cooling room ≦18–20°C, rest room 20–22°C, massage room 20–22°C.

Humidity: 100°C: 2–5% rel. humidity, 80°C: 3–10% rel. humidity, 70°C: 5–15% rel. humidity, 60°C: 8–28% rel. humidity.

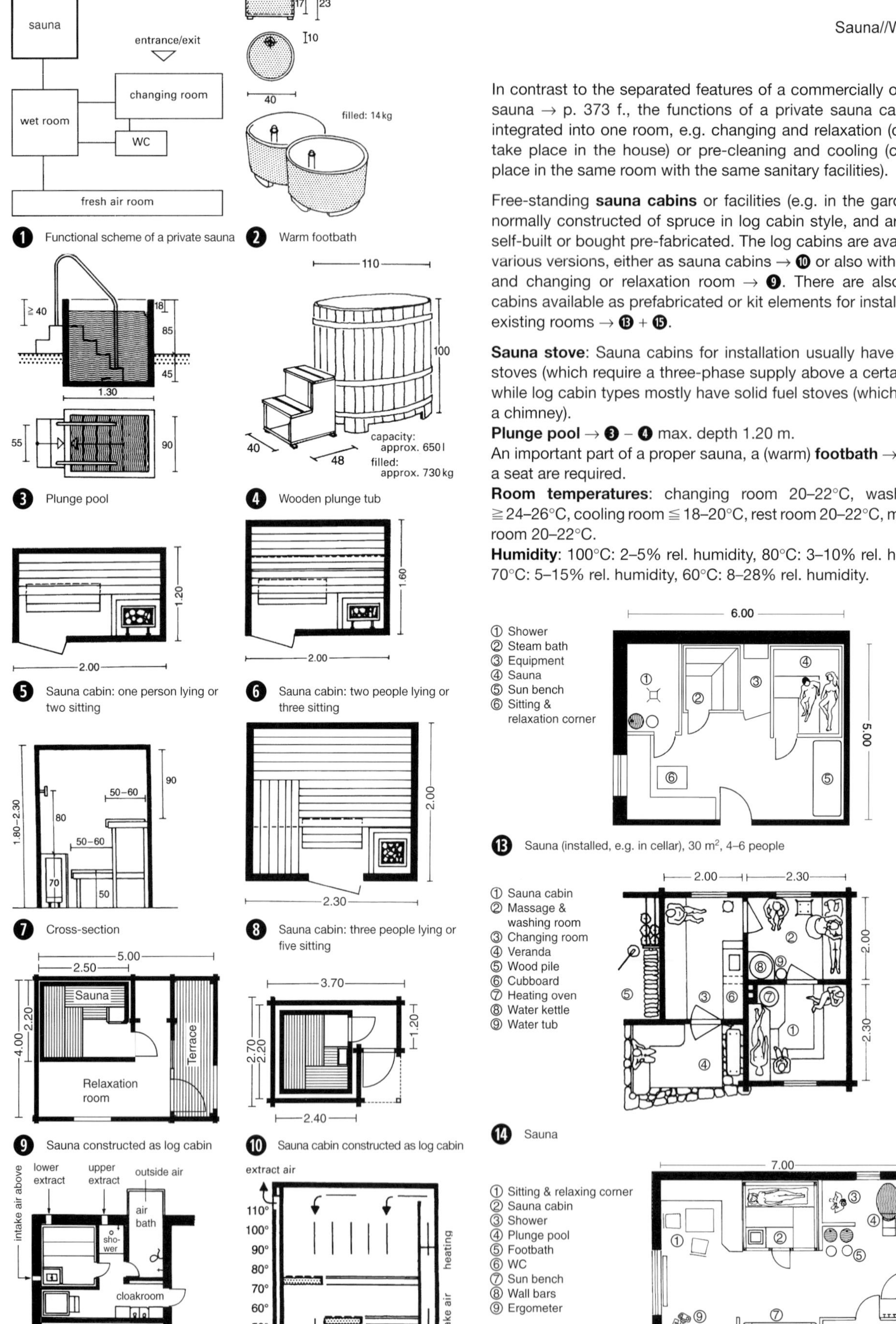

❶ Functional scheme of a private sauna

❷ Warm footbath

❸ Plunge pool

❹ Wooden plunge tub

❺ Sauna cabin: one person lying or two sitting

❻ Sauna cabin: two people lying or three sitting

❼ Cross-section

❽ Sauna cabin: three people lying or five sitting

❾ Sauna constructed as log cabin

❿ Sauna cabin constructed as log cabin

⓫ House sauna

⓬ Cross-section of sauna with indirect heating (Bemberg)

⓭ Sauna (installed, e.g. in cellar), 30 m², 4–6 people

⓮ Sauna

⓯ Sauna, 35 m², 4–6 people, sauna cabin as built-in element

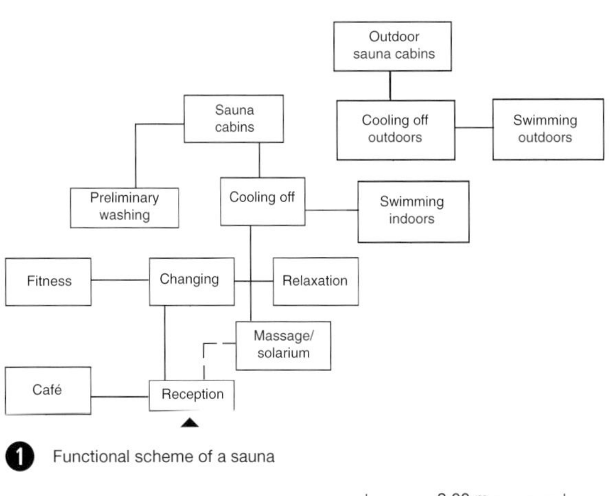

❶ Functional scheme of a sauna

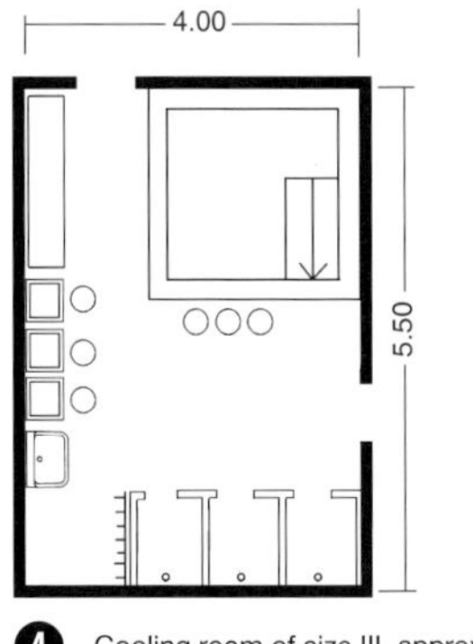

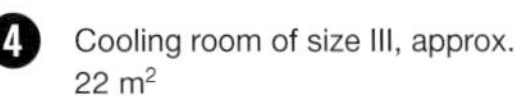

❷ Wash room of size III, approx. 12.00 m²

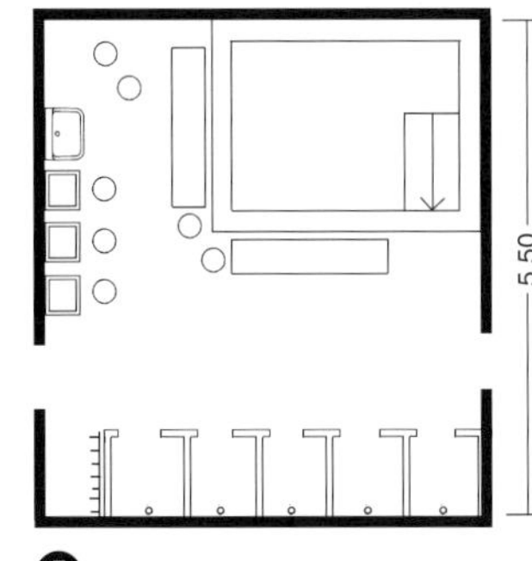

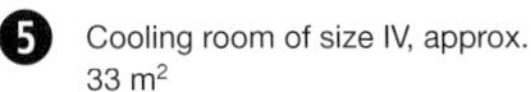

❸ Wash room of size IV, approx. 15.00 m²

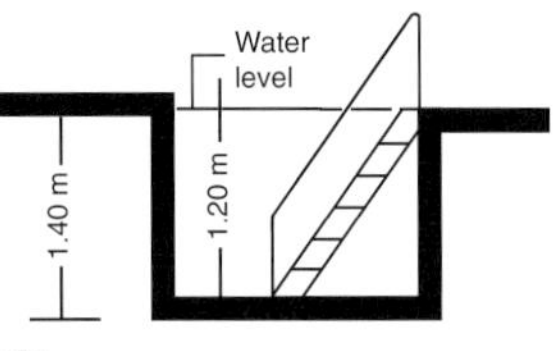

❹ Cooling room of size III, approx. 22 m²

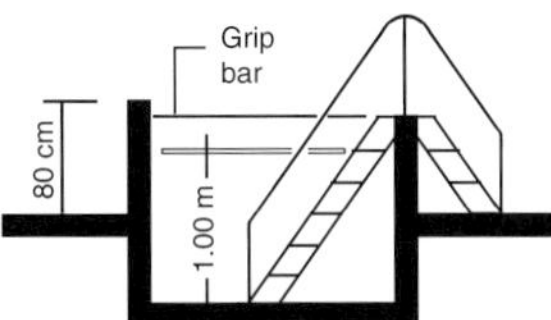

❺ Cooling room of size IV, approx. 33 m²

❻ Plunge pool, sunken

❼ Plunge pool, half-sunken

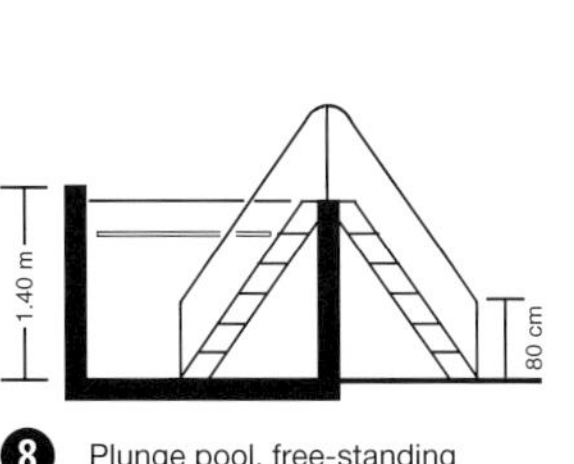

❽ Plunge pool, free-standing

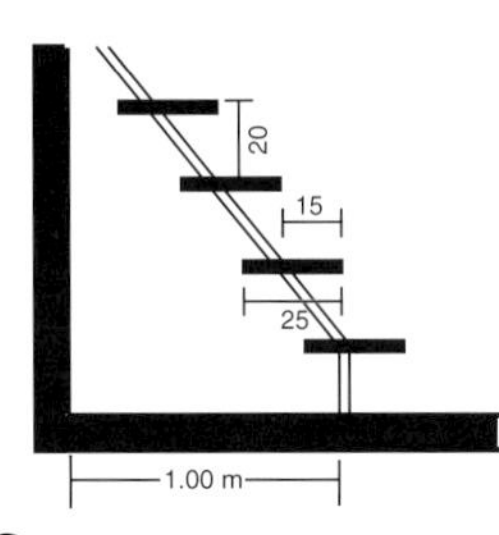

❾ Steps in plunge pool

Spa is the general term for health and wellness establishments, which should generally include: sauna facility, massage and solarium, relaxation, fitness and condition training (including swimming → Indoor and outdoor swimming pools).

A commercially operated **sauna** (size III–IV → ❾) will include:

Changing room, shower room with **washing facilities, sauna cabins, rest/relaxation room** and **subsidiary rooms** (staff room, reception, cash desk, sanitary facilities for visitors and staff). In public saunas, separate rooms are provided for changing, preliminary washing and toilets; for staff and visitors' toilets, the relevant building regulations apply. Access to swimming areas, food/drink providers and fitness areas is increasingly being offered in spa and wellness establishments.

The **wash room** is used for washing with warm water before entering the sauna → ❷ – ❸.

The **cooling room** is used for cooling off between visits to the sauna using cold air or cold water in, for example, plunge pools, pouring water, showers and footbaths → ❹ – ❾.

Size	No. sauna places	Type of use
I	2–4	very small or family sauna
II	4–5	family sauna
III	6–10	commercially operated sauna
IV	11–15	large commercially operated sauna

Room type	Size	Average room size (m²)	Places	Usable area (m²)
sauna	I	1.0–4.0	2–4	
	II	7.0–11.0	4–5	
	III	12.0–17.0	6–10	
	IV	17.5–21.0	11–15	
cooling room	II	16.0	up to 12	16.0
	III	22.0	up to 12	22.0
	IV	30.5	up to 17	30.5
washing room	II	9.0	up to 8	9.00
	III	12.0	up to 12	12.00
	IV	17.0	up to 17	17.00
changing room	II	16.0	up to 20	12.00
	III	24.0	up to 30	18.00
	IV	34.0	up to 45	20.00
rest room	II	13.2	2–3	10.00
	III	18.0	6	20.00
	IV	27.0	8	30.00

Capacity parameter	Size			
	I	II	III	IV
no. sauna places	2–3	4–5	6–10	11–15
usable area (m²)	1.7–2.2	2.4–4.0	5.0–10.0	8–13
cabin size (m/place)	1.7–2.3	1.2–1.6	2.0–2.4	1.8–2.0
ceiling height (m)	2.00	2.10	2.40	2.40
in the smallest sauna with 2 seating levels: ceiling height: 1.90 m, min. 1.80 m; clear height above the upper seat: 1.00–1.10 m				

❿ Approximate room and space requirements for various sizes of sauna (Höckert → refs)

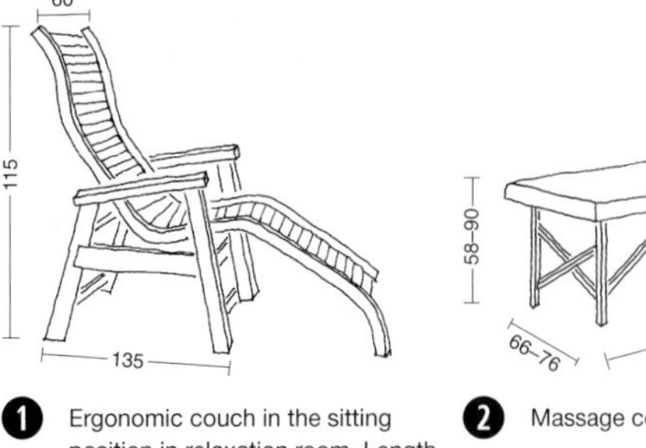

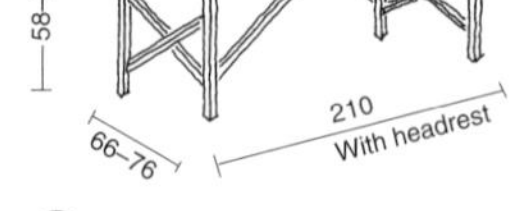

❶ Ergonomic couch in the sitting position in relaxation room. Length in lying position: 1.70–1.90 m

❷ Massage couch with head rest

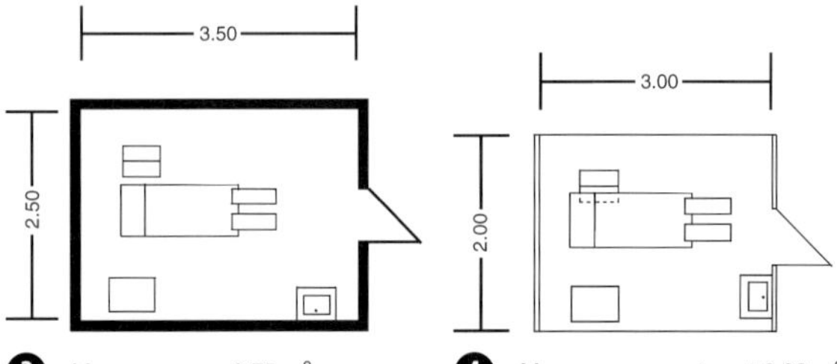

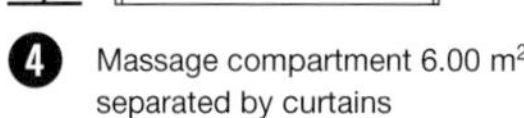

❸ Massage room 8.75 m^2, surrounded by solid walls

❹ Massage compartment 6.00 m^2, separated by curtains

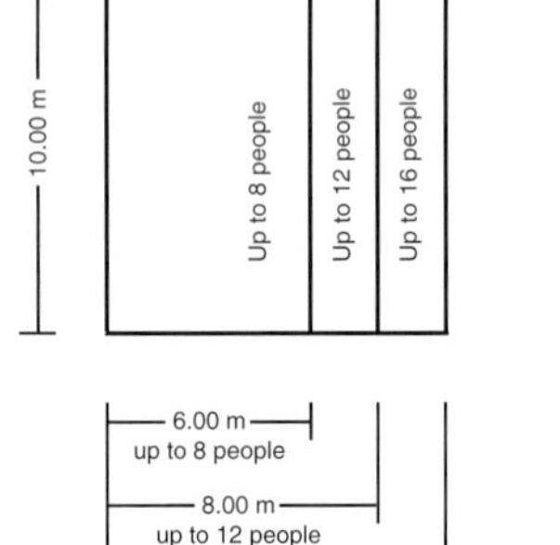

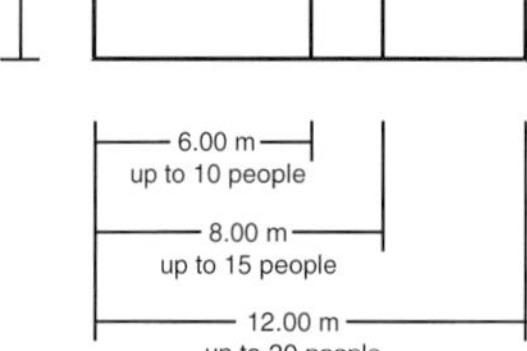

❺ Pool sizes for swimming and exercise pools in sauna area (usable capacity)

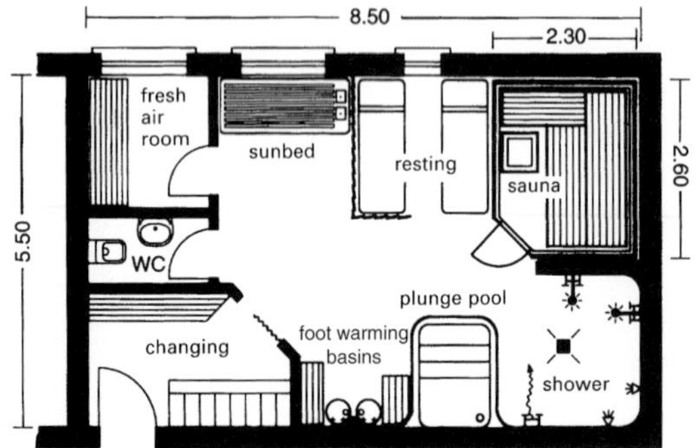

❻ Hotel sauna 5.50 × 8.50 m

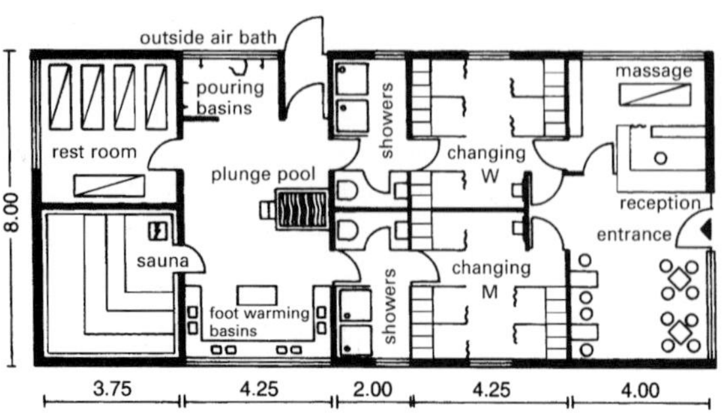

❼ Sauna for approx. 30 people

Rest room

Provides relaxation between or after visits to the sauna. It should be well ventilated and have visual contact with the outside and a low noise level. The design and furnishing should be suitable for rest and relaxation.

Solarium: an area of approx. 0.80 × 2.00 m is required per lying place. The side aisle width is 0.40 m.

Pool types and sizes → ❺:

Whirlpool: for relaxation and recovery. Max. water depth: 1.0 m.

Exercise pool: for relaxation, rehabilitation, water gymnastics and health care, max. water depth: 1.35 m, water area 25–60 m^2:

- **salt-water pool:** water with a salt content of min. 5.5 g sodium and 8.5 g chloride per litre.
- **mineral pool:** water with a mineral content of min. 1 g per litre.
- **thermal pool:** water with a natural temperature >20 °C. Because this pool is not for swimming, it can, according to use, be designed in almost any shape.

Size of sauna cabin (m^2)	Air supply opening (cm^2)	Air extraction opening (cm^2)
5	100	70
10	150	105
15	200	140
20	250	175

❽ Size of ventilation openings in relationship to floor area of sauna cabin (Höckert → refs)

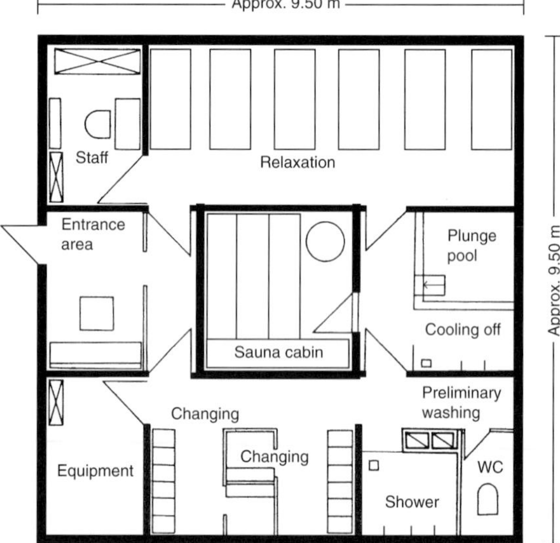

❾ Sauna facility with washing and cooling rooms for about 12 people, approx. 90 m^2

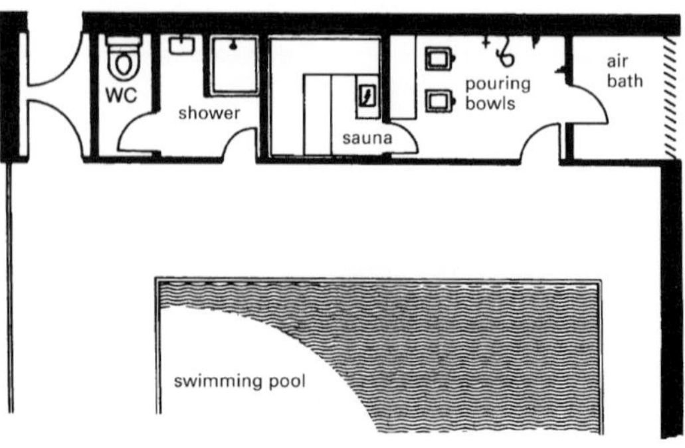

❿ Sauna and indoor swimming pool

Sport and leisure
SPA
Sauna/wellness

AMUSEMENT ARCADES

The provision of gambling machines, often called fruit machines or slot machines, is controlled by gambling regulations. According to these, a gambling machine offering the possibility of winning money or goods may be made available in amusement arcades or similar enterprises.

On a floor area of 15 m^2, only one gambling machine to win money or goods may be positioned. The total number may not exceed 10 machines → ❾. In the calculation of floor area, storerooms, corridors, toilets, anterooms and stairs are not considered.

In addition to building regulations, planning regulations also have to be borne in mind for the building of amusement arcades. Amusement arcades are permissible as places of entertainment in urban planning zones. In exceptional cases, they can be approved in other zones, in which commercial businesses which could cause a nuisance are not allowed. Automated entertainment machines, which offer prizes as goods, can also be made available in amusement arcades, but other games only if their winnings are paid in cash.

Games may not be organised in amusement arcades without permission. Neighbouring amusement arcades can share common toilet facilities → ❾.

The 'Pachinko' amusement arcades usual in Japan → ❿ – ⓫ are not permissible in Germany. Balls won in these games can be exchanged for goods.

In the UK, gaming by means of machines is restricted and is governed by the Gaming Act 1968.

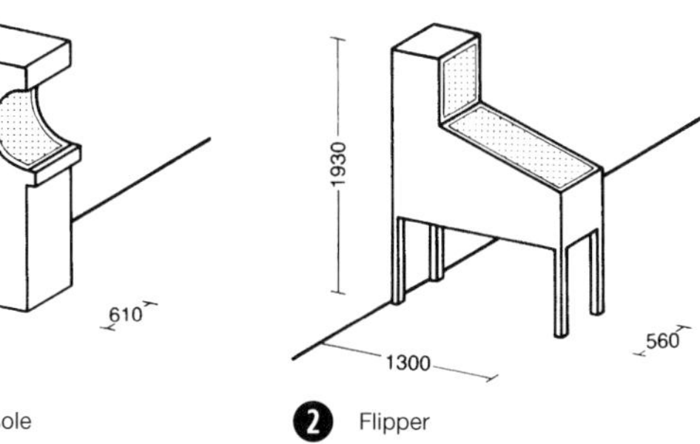

❶ Games console

❷ Flipper

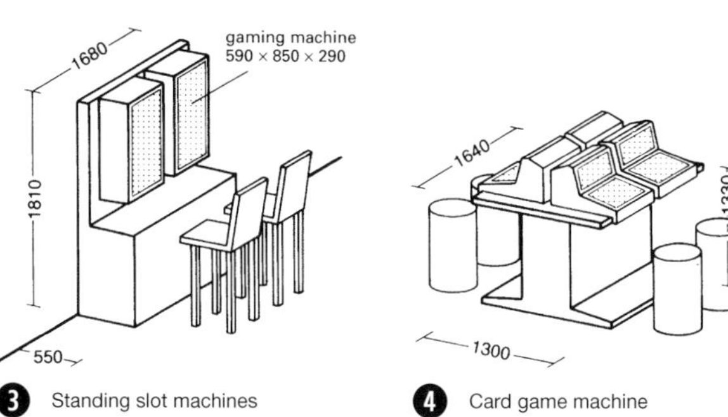

❸ Standing slot machines

❹ Card game machine

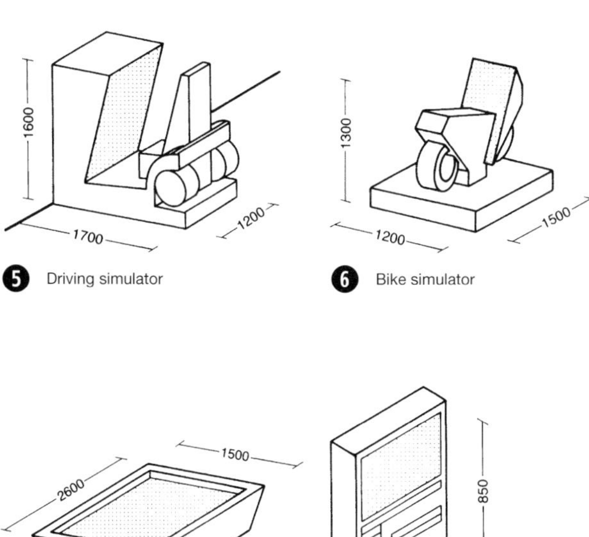

❺ Driving simulator

❻ Bike simulator

❼ Pool table

❽ Slot machine

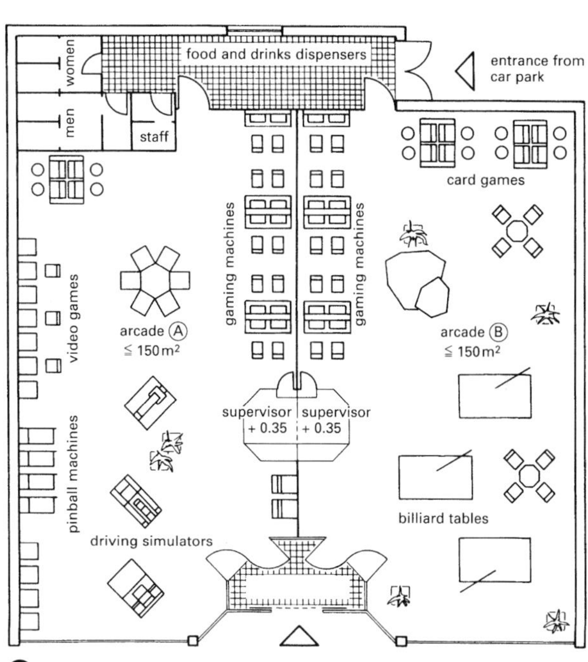

❾ Plan of amusement arcade

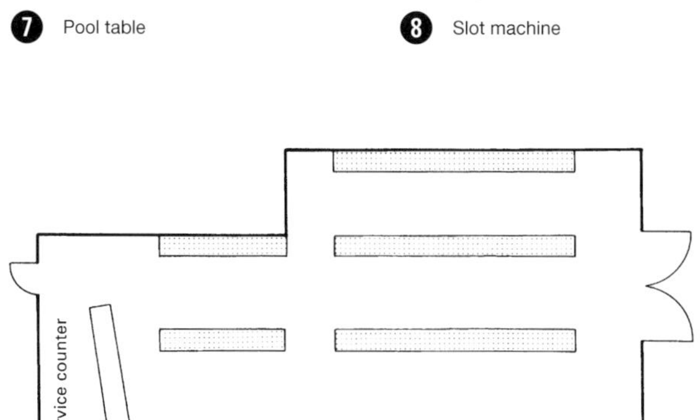

❿ Japanese 'Pachinko' amusement arcade

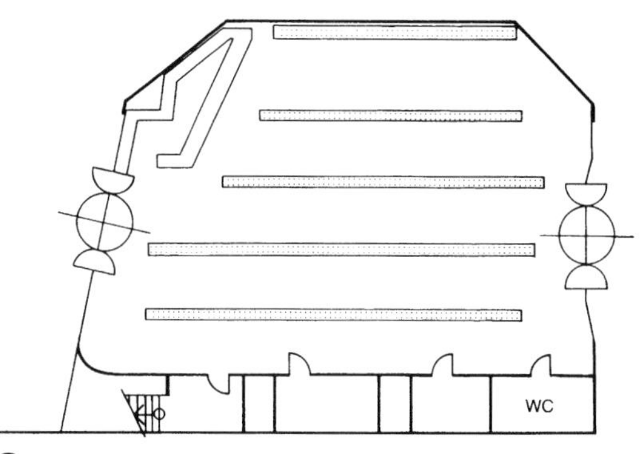

⓫ Japanese 'Pachinko' amusement arcade

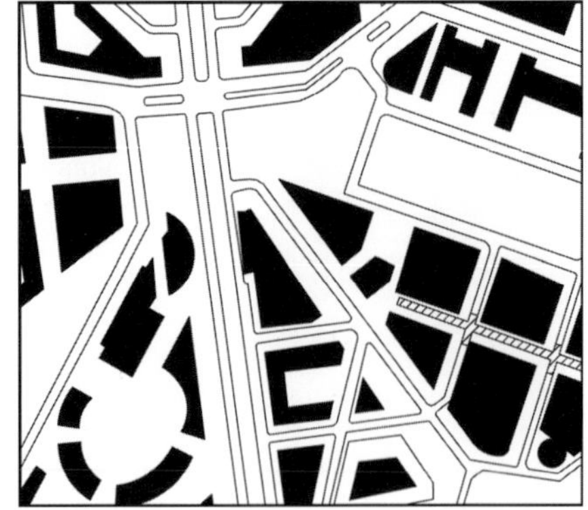

❶ Street spaces in cities become readable when their areas are blacked in, because the eye understands black areas as cohesive and white areas as holes.

The percentage of space boundaries in the field of view determines how open or closed a street space is read as. The perception of architectural details on buildings also depends on the distance from the building → p. 40. The formula on p. 40 can be used to determine the relationship between the distance of an observer from a building and the scale of a drawing of a building. The degree of detailing at a scale can thus be matched to a certain distance of the observer.

The relationship of scale to distance according to the formula is approximately:

1 : 100	120–170 m
1 : 50	50–80 m
1 : 20	10–20 m

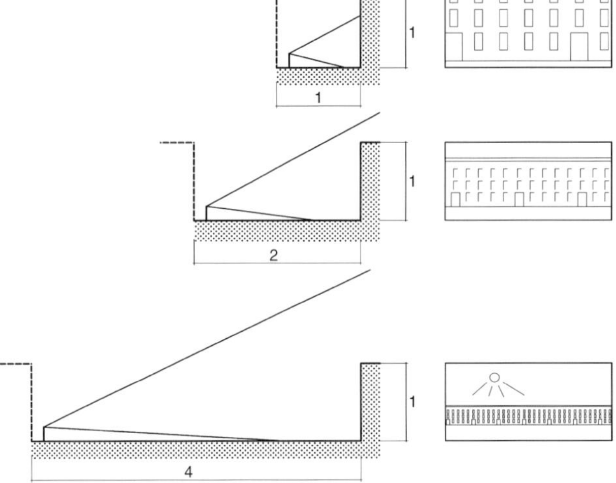

❷ The relationship of width to height determines how a street space is read (FGSV → refs)

Design

Street spaces are formed by roads with surrounding buildings. These can easily be illustrated on black layouts, on which the roads and squares are coloured black and the buildings remain white → ❶. The spacing and height of opposing buildings have an influence on the impression made by a street space. Considering an angle of view of about 45°, the effects of street spaces can range from closed (like a ravine) to open (like a square) → ❷.

The design intentions for street spaces, in addition to the fulfilment of traffic and supply functions, are to create an identity, give orientation and provide residential quality. Identity is the result of emphasising particular local features, and relation to topography and to view axes. Distinctive places provide more ways of orientation and offer means of identification.

Apart from building façades, trees are the strongest space-building factor. They can also bind the street space upwards. Trees can direct the eye, create scale and fill in gaps → ❺.

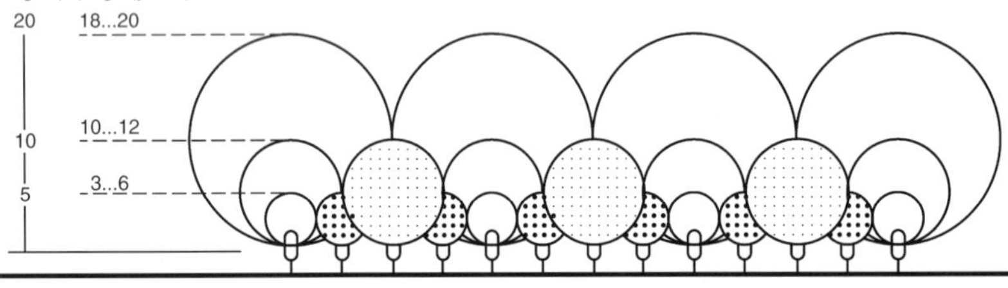

❸ When choosing the positioning of trees for planting, the space that will be required by the fully grown trees should be considered (FGSV → refs)

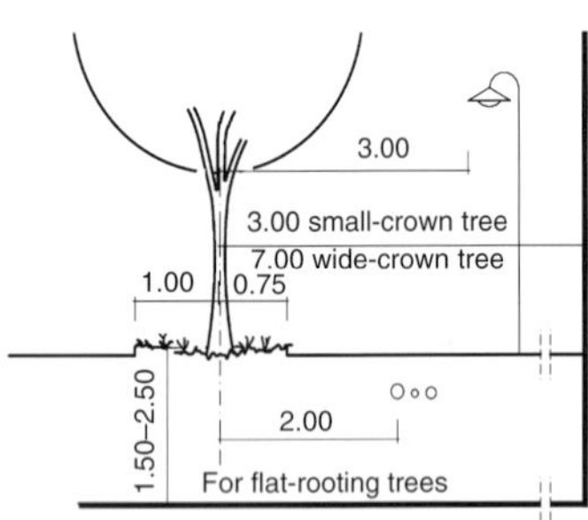

❹ Distances of trees from other street elements

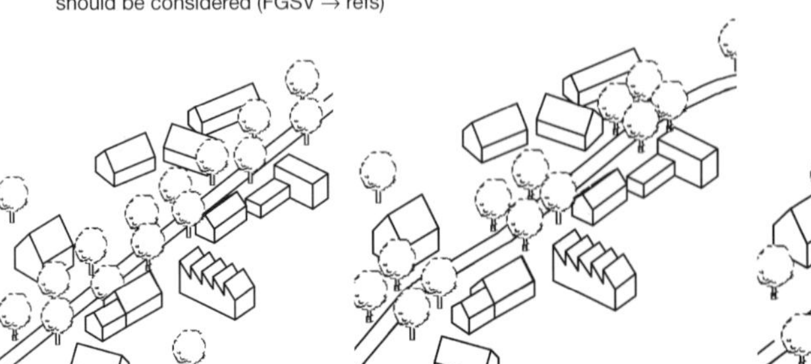

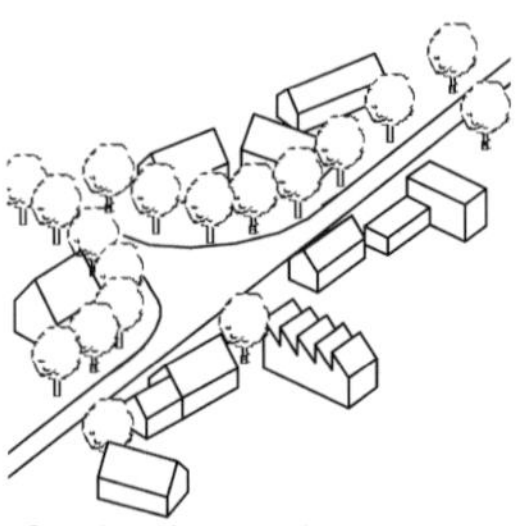

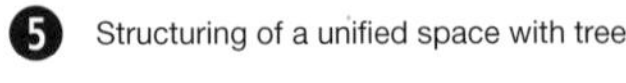

Emphasise linearity Sequence of spaces Developing a square Creation of an island

❺ Structuring of a unified space with trees

Category group / Link function level		Not in built-up area	Inside built-up area			
		No adjacent buildings		Adjacent buildings		
		Link			Access	Stay
		A	B	C	D	E
Large–area road link	I	A I	B I	C I	D I	E I
Extra–regional road link	II	A II	B II	C II	D II	E II
Road link between towns	III	A III	B III	C III	D III	E III
Road link between residential areas	IV	A IV	B IV	C IV	D IV	E IV
Minor road link	V	A V	–	–	D V	E V
Track	VI	A VI	–	–	–	E IV

RAS–Q, RAS–L | EAHV 1993 | EAE 1985/95

❶ Determination of road categories (FGSV → refs). RAS-L: Guidelines for Construction of Roads – Road Layout; RAS-Q: – Cross-section; EAHV: Recommendations for Construction of Main Roads; EAE: ... Access Roads.

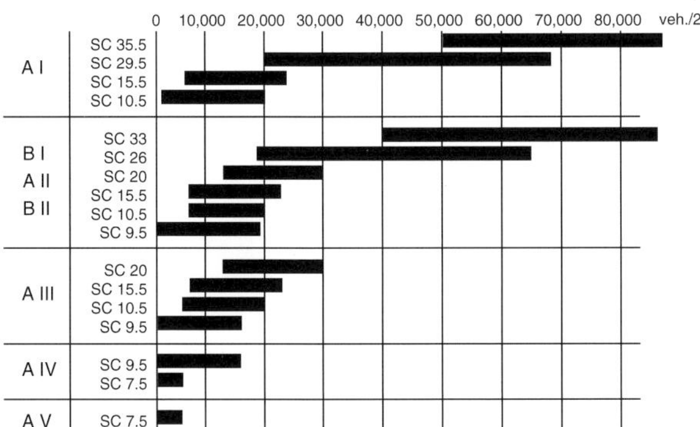

❷ Determination of standard cross-sections for roads without adjacent building (FGSV → refs). SC: standard cross-section.

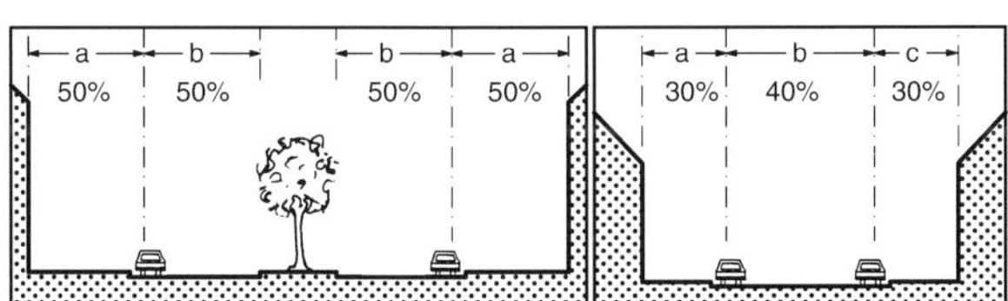

❸ Desirable width relationships between vehicle areas and pedestrian spaces (FGSV: RAS-Q 96 → refs)

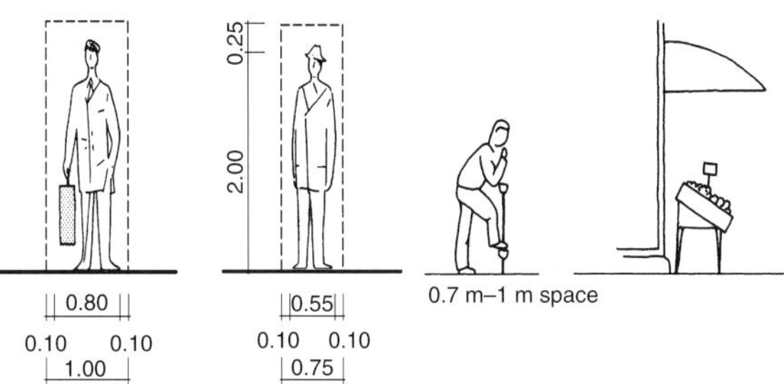

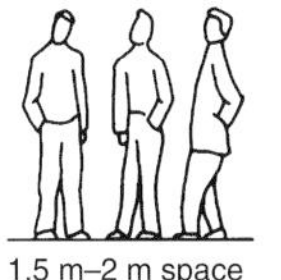

❹ Basic dimensions for various uses of pedestrian areas (FGSV: EAR 05 → refs)

Classification

As part of the transport network, the layout of roads depends on their function in the network's structure. The classification of roads has to differentiate their location inside or outside a built-up area and above all their function as access for properties and buildings next to the road, leading to the important distinction between roads which are built along and those which are not.

Roads without adjacent building

These roads are almost entirely used for vehicle traffic. Their design is based on the planned average speed, the connection function level and the category group. The correct road category can be found in → ❶ and, together with the forecast number of vehicles, the cross-section of the road can be determined → p. 378 ❶.

Roads with adjacent building

These roads are part of the public space and serve a multitude of uses in addition to transport, though the predominance of motorised transport has today led to them being mostly formed by the needs of road traffic. Town and transport planning has the purpose of achieving a balanced relationship between road traffic and the other important functions of the street space. These are, for example:

communication areas	relaxation, strolling, walking, demonstrating...
play areas	cycling, roller skating, ball games, playing hide and seek
commercial use	market stalls, pavement cafés, food stands
green areas	binding dust and pollutants, oxygen production, microclimate improvement

Elements of road cross-section

The publications of the Research Company for Roads and Traffic (FGSV) give basic dimensions for the various uses of street spaces. The traffic space is measured from the width required by the traffic participant plus a margin for movement, dependent on the speed. Together with the safety distance from solid obstacles, which has to be kept free, this gives the clear space required for traffic → p. 379. To determine the profile of the street space, the recommendations in the Appendix for Main Roads and the Recommendations for the Construction of Access Roads state a number of criteria which enable a differentiated adaptation of the available space for various needs. The most important decision criteria are:

1. Zones, divided into town centre zones, areas of old buildings near to the town centre, residential areas, industrial and commercial areas and village areas.
2. Type of connection road: main road, main feeder road, residential street and residential side street.
3. Requirement for park and green areas.
4. Type and frequency of public transport.
5. Type of use of the pedestrian areas. In addition to pedestrian routes, these offer opportunities for the social and communications functions of street spaces.

After these factors have been evaluated, a decision is made as to which size of vehicles will be allowed to travel on the road and at what speed. The required carriageway width is then derived from considering possible encounters → p. 379.

Motorways are roads without adjacent building, designed for high-speed vehicles and express transport. The two carriageways, one in each direction, are separated by a central reservation. Each carriageway consists of two or more lanes and normally a hard shoulder → ❶.

Motorways are linked to each other by grade-separated (→ p. 381) intersections. These can be three-directional → ❽ – ❿ or four-directional intersections → ❹ – ❻ and specialised junctions for joining and leaving the motorway → ❼ + ⓫.

Motorways are the safest roads and have the highest capacity. The most important factor in the design and construction of new motorways is environmental impact.

Route signage → ❷: the location of the sign for junctions is at 1000 m, and for intersections 2000 m before the turn-off.

In order that built infrastructure next to the motorway does not negatively affect traffic (obstruction of view and reduction of concentration), legislators have identified adjacent zones where building is either forbidden or restricted → ❸. Building restriction: the erection or significant alteration of buildings and facilities at a distance 40–100 m from the outer edge of the carriageway of motorways is subject to a special application. Buildings of all types are forbidden up to 40 m from the outer edge of the carriageway of motorways.

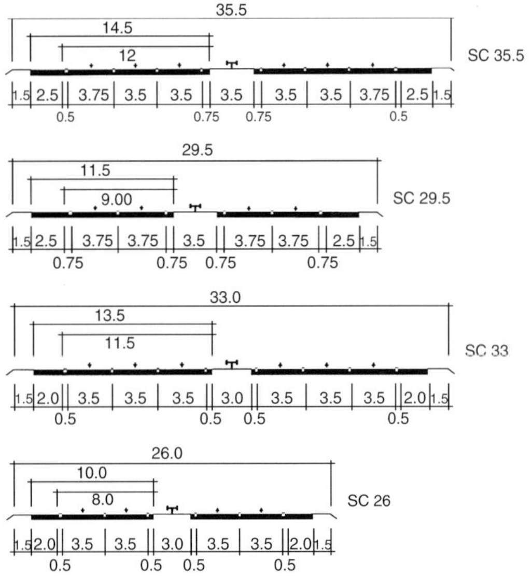

❶ Standard cross-sections (SC) for motorways (FGSV: RAS-Q 96 → refs).

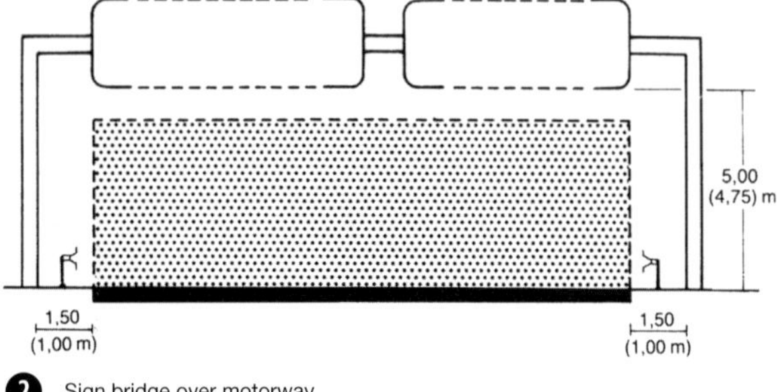

❷ Sign bridge over motorway

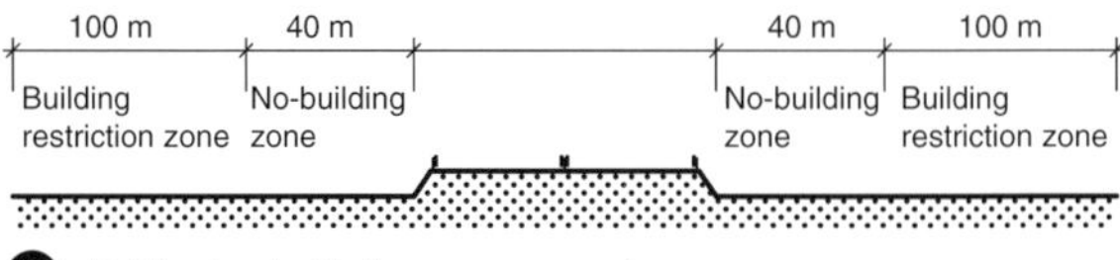

❸ Building ban/restriction zones near motorways

Motorway junctions (four-way)

❹ Clover leaf

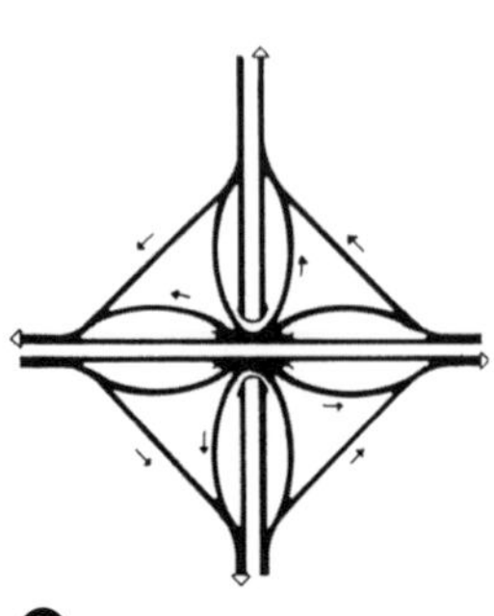

❺ Maltese cross

❻ Windmill

Motorway interchanges (four-way)

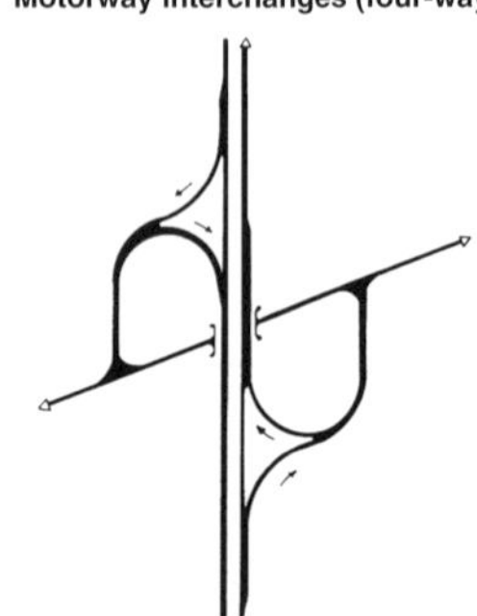

❼ Half clover leaf

Motorway junctions (three-way)

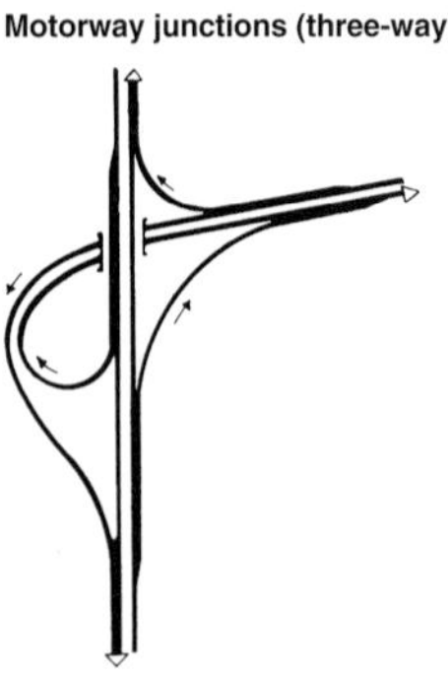

❽ Trumpet

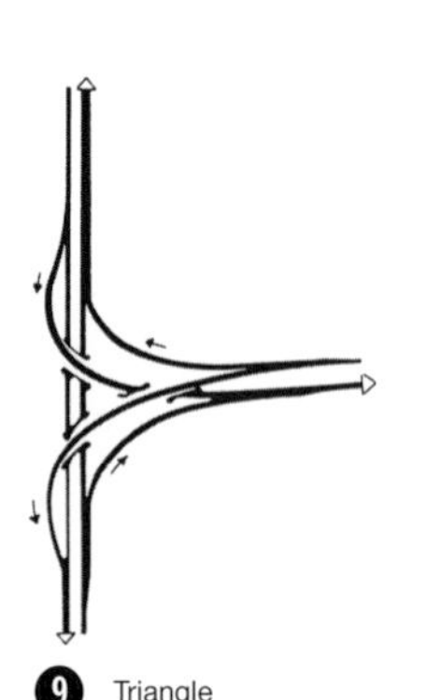

❾ Triangle

❿ Fork

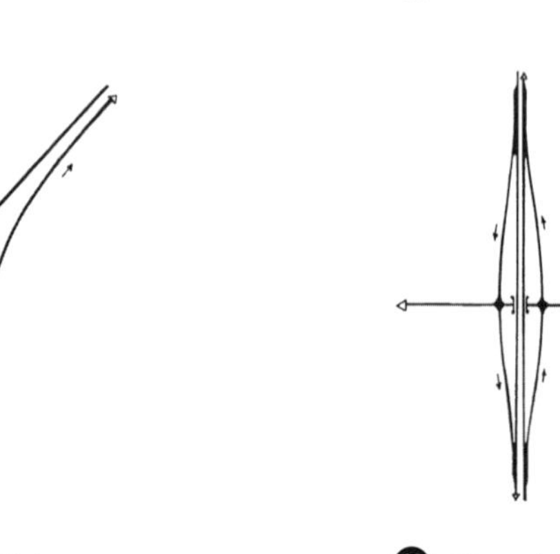

⓫ Diamond

Space required at full speed (≧50 km/h)

General dimensions for traffic spaces and clear spaces for the stated encounter type with full and reduced speed

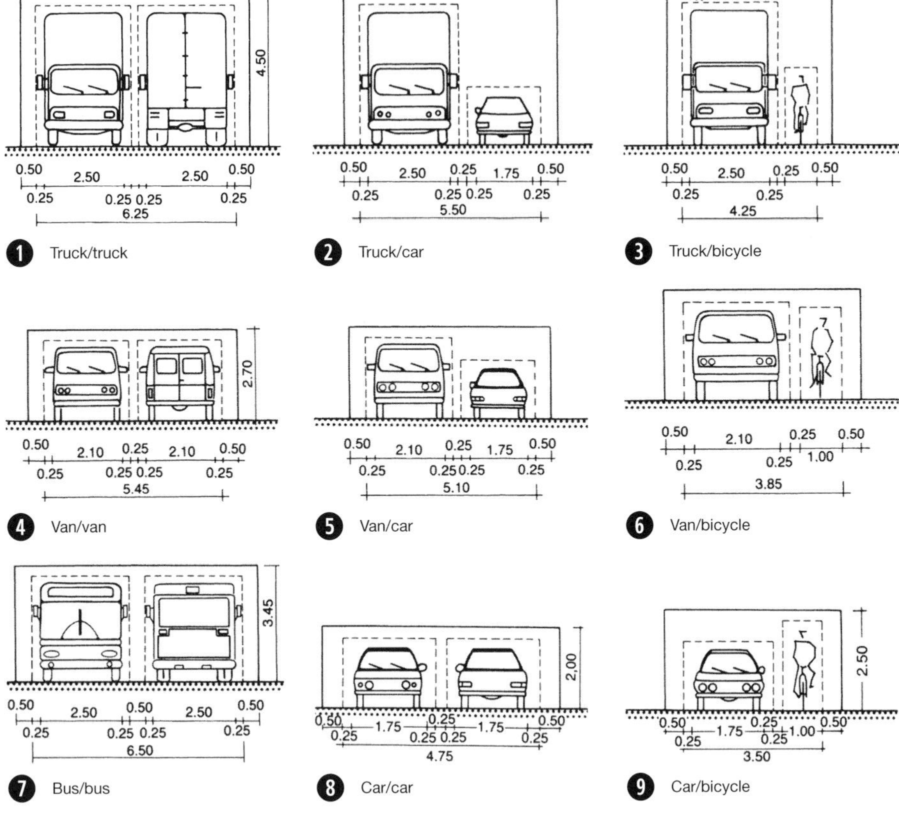

1 Truck/truck
2 Truck/car
3 Truck/bicycle
4 Van/van
5 Van/car
6 Van/bicycle
7 Bus/bus
8 Car/car
9 Car/bicycle

Vehicle traffic space is the sum of the space required by the assessment vehicle, the margin for movement at the sides and above, the addition for two-directional traffic, and the spaces above the drainage channel at the edge of the road and the hard shoulder. The maximum width of the assessment vehicle is, in accordance with European standards, 2.55–2.60 m.

Traffic space for bicycles is one lane each, 1.00 m wide and 2.25 m high → p. 384. Traffic space for pedestrians is a walking strip 0.75 m wide and 2.25 m high. The height of the traffic space for vehicles is 4.20 m, plus a safety margin 4.50 m (or, better, 4.70 m), in order to be able to renew elevated superstructure. For footpaths and cycle tracks, the clear height is 2.50 m.

The width of the safety space at the sides is measured from the edge of the traffic space to the side. The necessary width depends on the permissible maximum speed.

Permissible speed ≧70 km/h, safety space ≧1.25 m (1.00 m)

Permissible speed ≧50 km/h, safety space ≧0.75 m → 18

Space required at reduced speed (≦40 km/h)

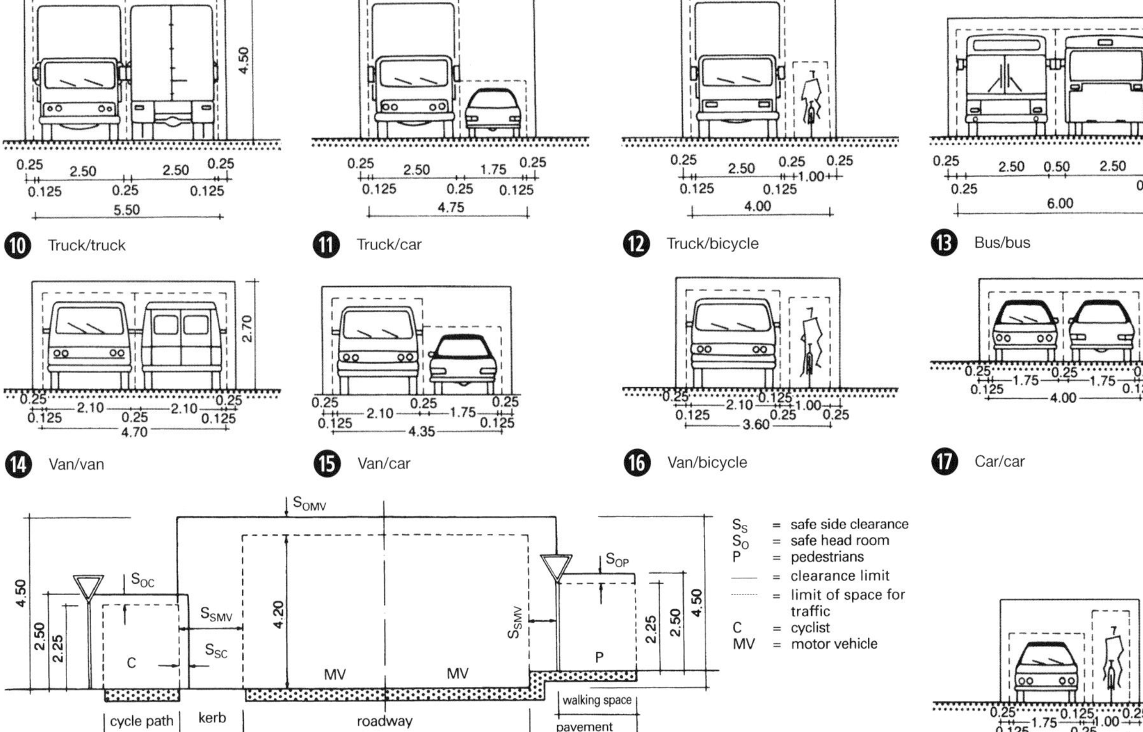

10 Truck/truck
11 Truck/car
12 Truck/bicycle
13 Bus/bus
14 Van/van
15 Van/car
16 Van/bicycle
17 Car/car
18 Dimensions of clear space/traffic space for vehicles
19 Car/bicycle

In order to achieve standardised design in the construction and operation of roads, standard cross-sections are provided for the roads outside built-up areas, which should not be deviated from without reason → ❶. Knowing the number of vehicles forecast and the category of the road, the suitable cross-section can be determined using → ❷ p. 377.

For roads with adjacent building, there are no standard cross-sections. A suitable profile is developed considering the various requirements of users and adjacent property owners for sections of the road. The precondition for this is the decision as to which type of vehicle the road space should be designed for → p. 391. Examples of various built-up road cross-sections are given here → ❷ – ❼.

The intention should be to give the road a distinctive image. This can be achieved through clear, differentiated dimensions, differing arrangement of the various cross-sections, a balanced relationship of the width and height of the street space and diversity of planting. As a result of this, the layout of the street space should enable orientation in the street and also in the town itself.

The cross-sections lying at each side of the carriageway influence the creation of functional and visual structure. For design purposes, the following elements should be discussed in addition to function and effect: the footpaths and cycle tracks associated with the road, stopping and parking areas, screening and protection areas, delivery areas and commercial and sales areas.

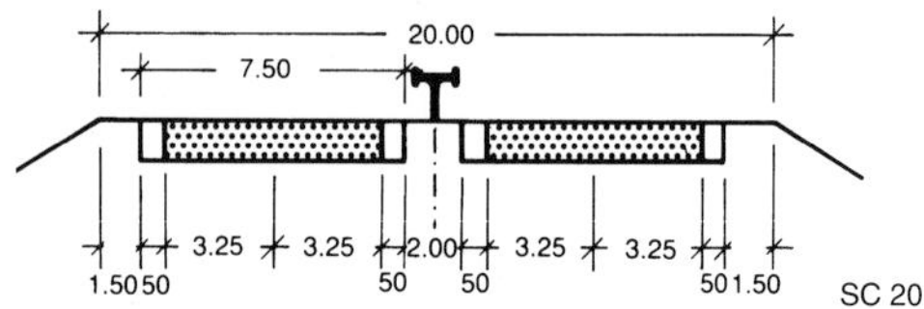

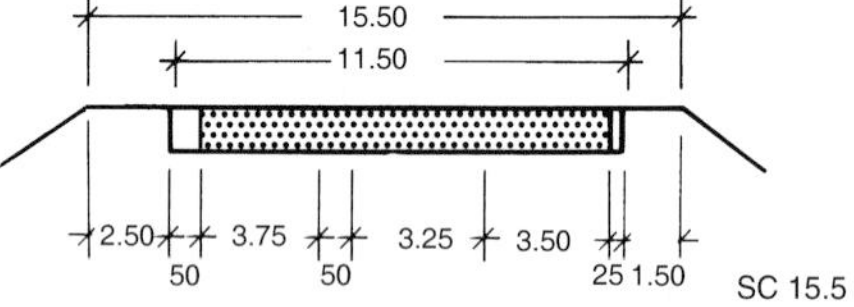

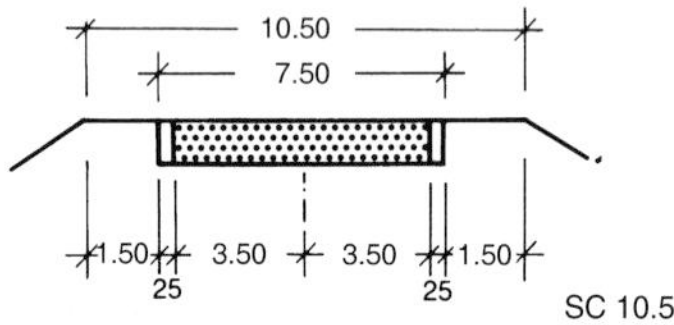

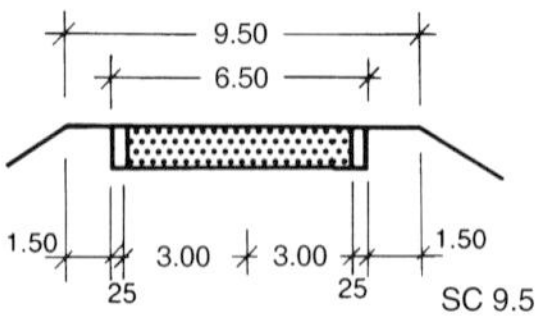

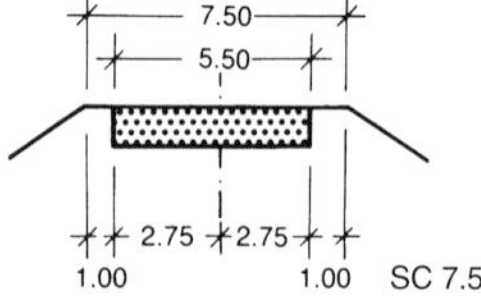

❶ Standard cross-sections (SC) for roads without adjacent buildings

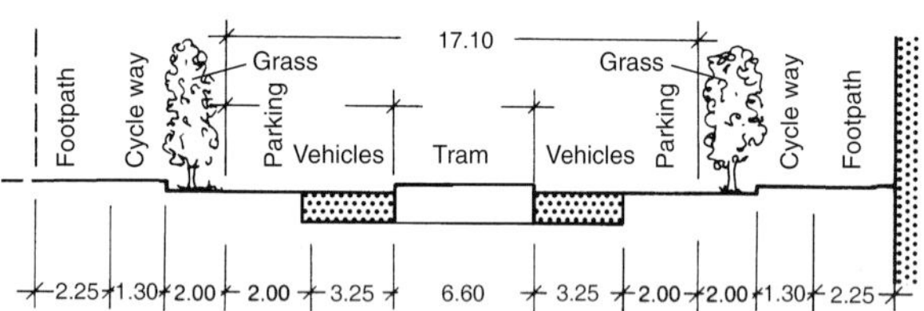

❷ Pedestrian and cyclist area separated from road and parking by grass strips; tram on its own track bed

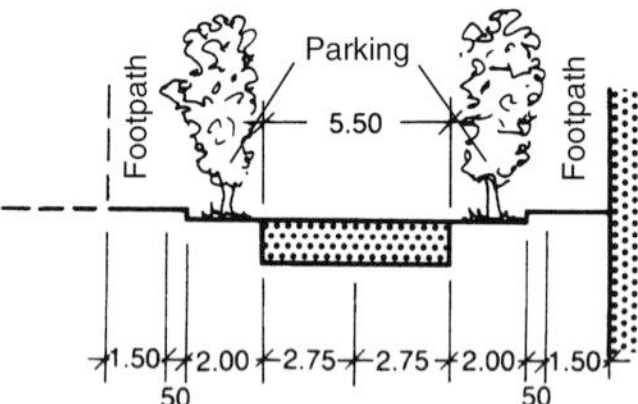

❸ Feeder road, carriageway designed for encounters of trucks with reduced speed; drivable side strip in case larger vehicles meet

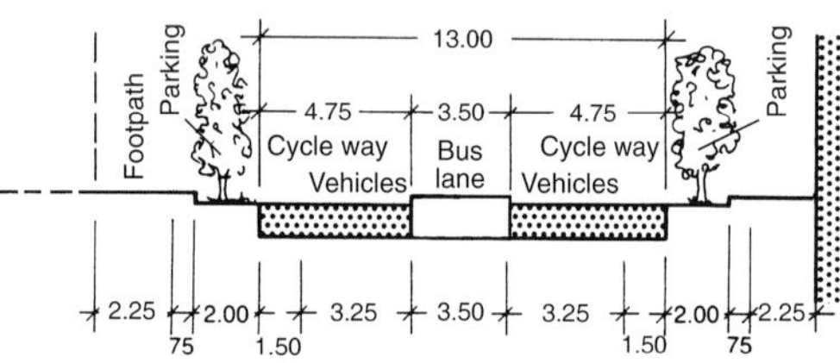

❹ Cycle way near the road has advantage at crossings; bus lane in middle of road

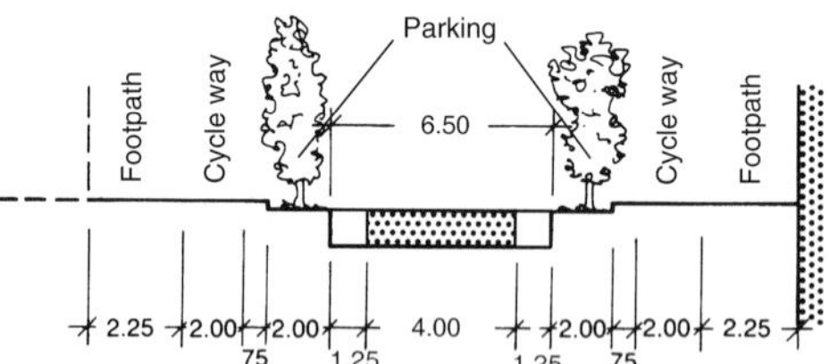

❺ Feeder road, carriageway designed for encounters of cars with reduced speed; drivable side strip in case larger vehicles meet

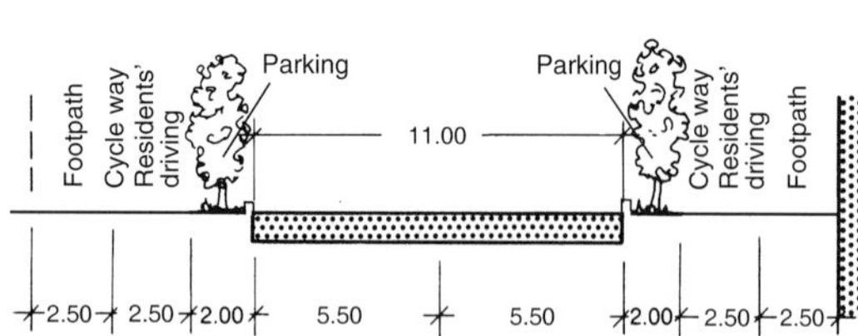

❻ Extra-wide road, which can be driven in four lanes, with the parking strips physically separated from the road. They can be accessed across the lanes for cyclists and adjacent residents.

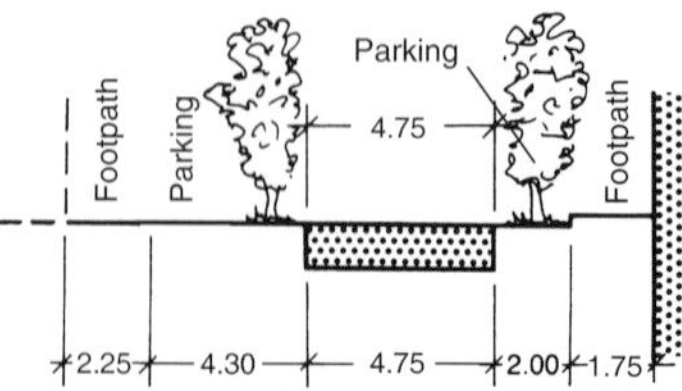

❼ Road for residents, designed for the reduced speed car/truck encounter; parking strips parallel and at right angles to the road

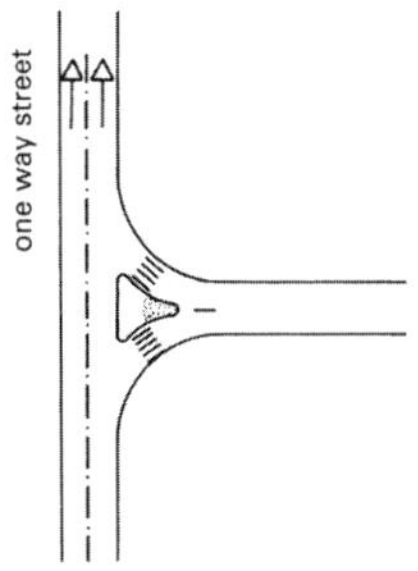

❶ At-grade T-junction

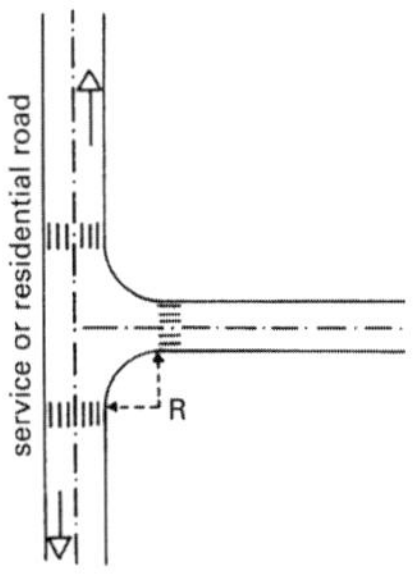

❷ → as ❶

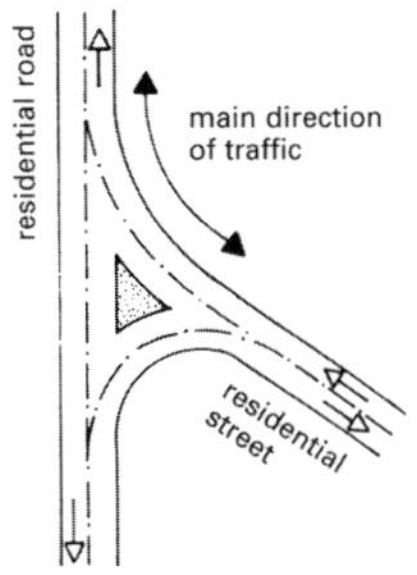

❸ T-junction in a residential feeder road

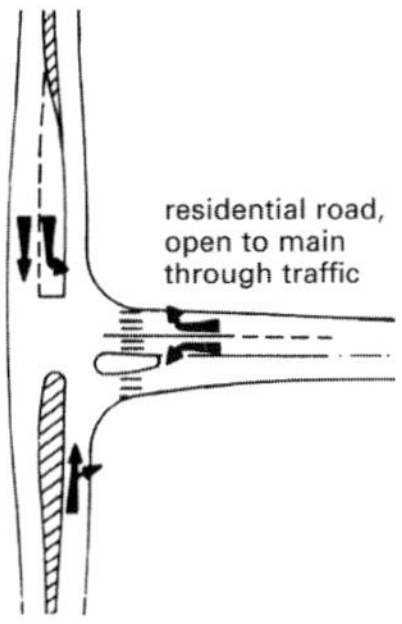

❹ With profile widened for left turning vehicles

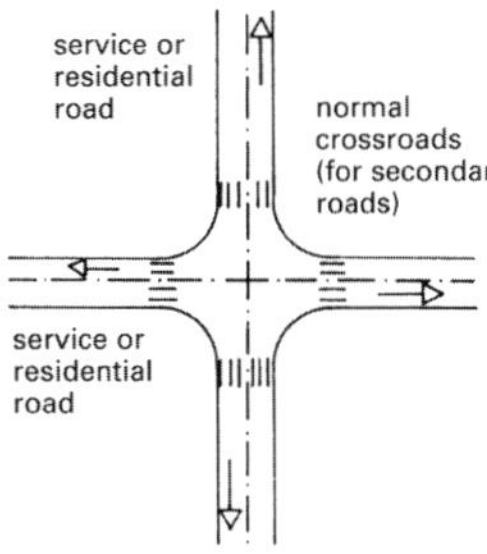

Intersections are categorised into **grade-separated** and **at-grade**. Grade-separated means that the roads cross at different levels (with at least one bridge) and are connected by ramps or slip roads (a motorway-type junction). Intersections on one level are at-grade (with and without traffic lights). These can be T-junctions (one road meets another) → ❶ – ❷ or crossroads (two roads cross) → ❺ – ❽.

The design of crossings as roundabouts → ⓮ – ⓯ has become common in some countries (e.g. UK, Germany). Small roundabouts are defined as diameter = 25–40 m, large roundabouts >40 m. Their advantages are: less danger of serious accidents, traffic light control no longer required, less noise nuisance, energy saving and reduction in speed on urban roads. The diameter of the roundabout depends on the necessary waiting queue length, which depends on the traffic volume.

A staggered traffic crossing allows more space, clearly understandable road section and spatial definition of the road. This is suitable for slow traffic in residential areas → ⓰.

Building is forbidden within 20 m of federal main roads, measured from the outer edge of the carriageway. Building is restricted up to 40 m from the edge of the carriageway. → p. 378 Motorways.

❺ At-grade crossroads

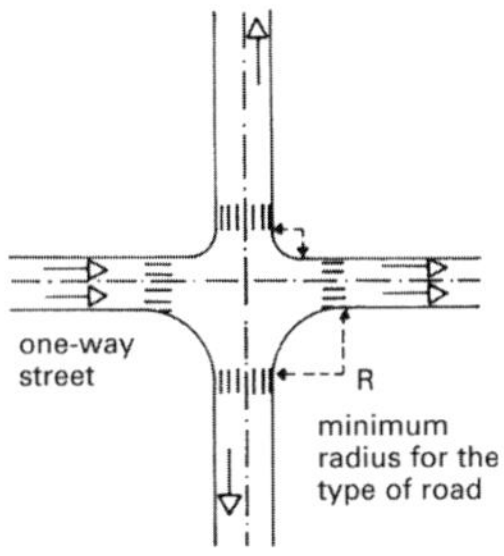

❻ → as ❺

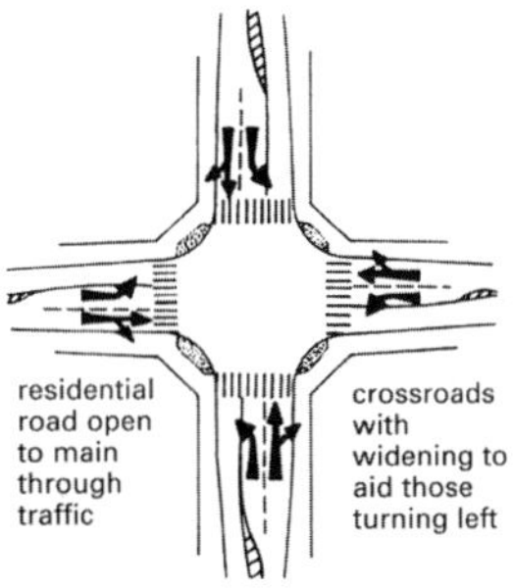

❼ → as ❺

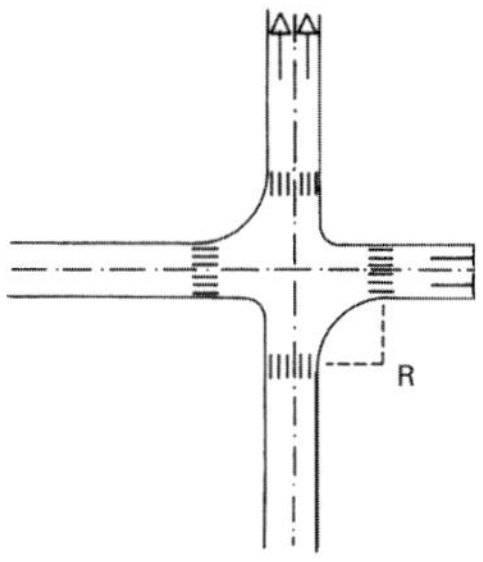

❽ → as ❺

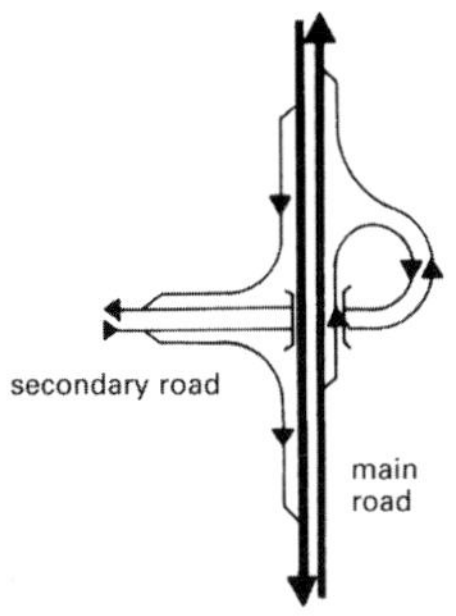

❾ T-junction/crossroads, grade-separated

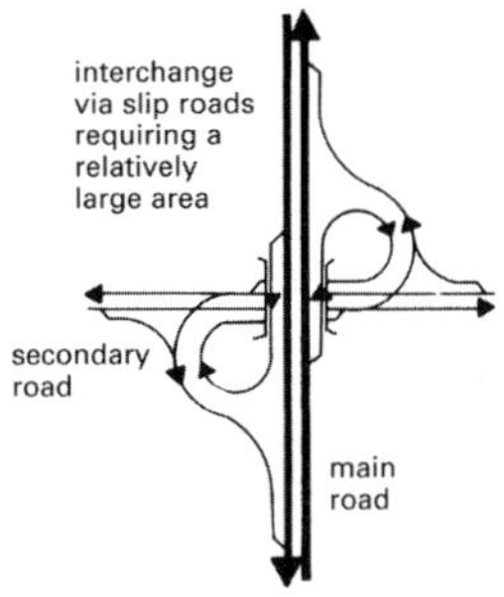

❿ → as ❾

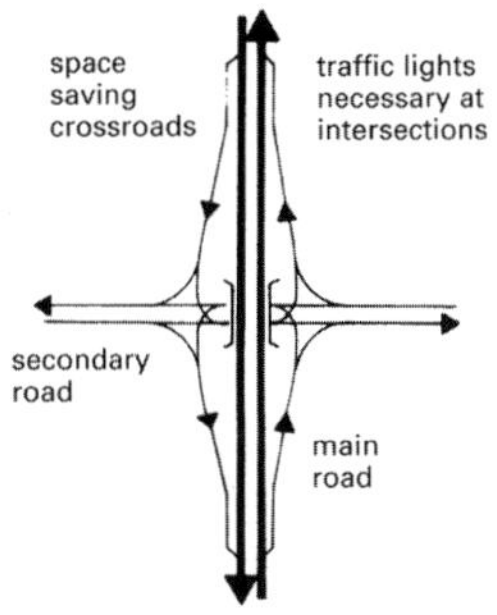

⓫ → as ❾

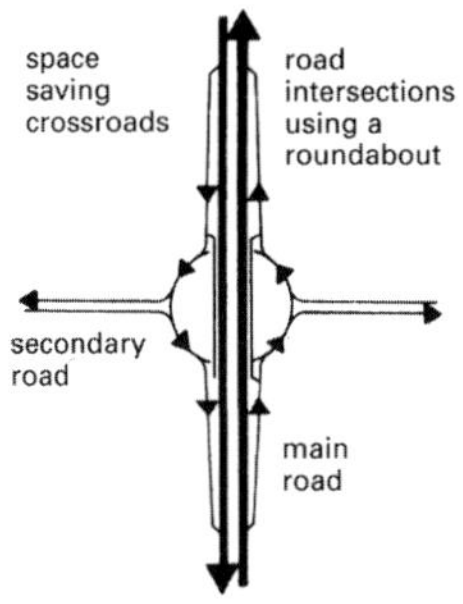

⓬ → as ❾

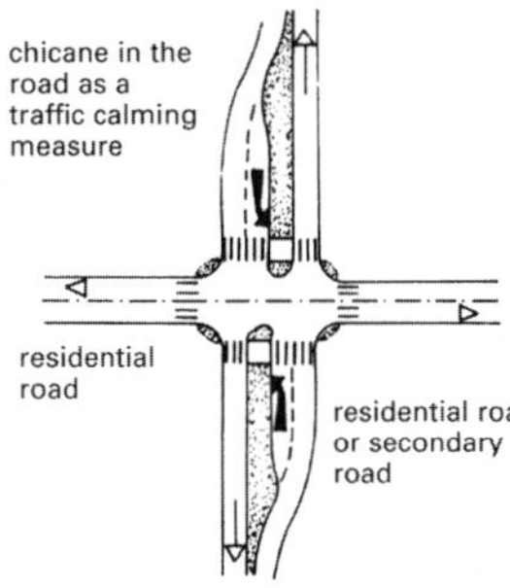

⓭ Narrowing of the carriageway

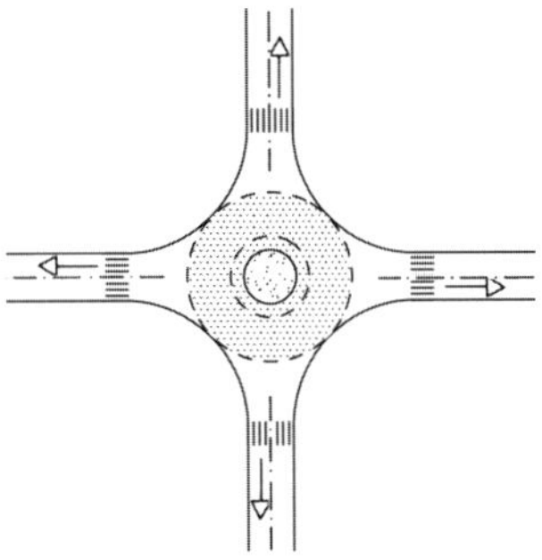

⓮ Small roundabout, D = 25–35 m, inner circle paved

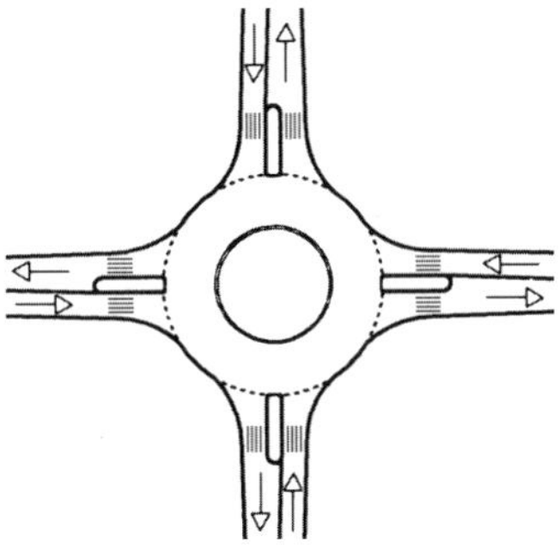

⓯ Larger roundabout, D >40 m, with pedestrian islands

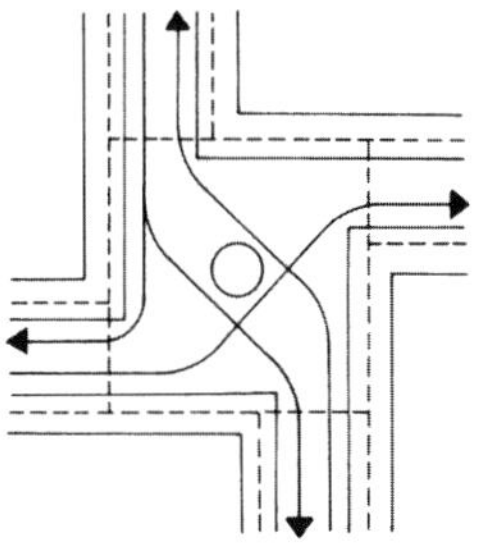

⓰ Staggered road crossing, only for slower traffic

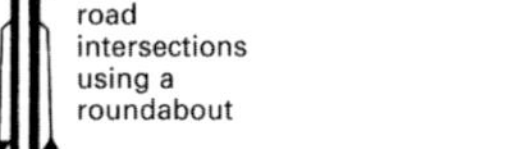

Areas for walking should always be designed to be varied and interesting, also taking into account likely children's usage. Weather protection can be provided by trees, arcades and maybe protecting roofs. Roadside pavements should if possible not be narrower than 2 m (of which 1.50 m min. width and 0.50 m safety distance from the carriageway). A much wider pavement is, however, often appropriate. Near schools, shopping centres, leisure facilities etc., a min. width of 3 m is ideal. → ❶ – ❼ Roadside cycle ways should be min. 1.00 m wide for one-way traffic and 2.00 m (min. 1.60 m) wide for two-way traffic, with safety strips of 0.75 m added to the road. Combined footpaths and cycle ways should be 2.50 m (min. 2.00 m) wide → p. 384.

cross-sections[1] (values in brackets are minimum dimensions in existing built-up area)

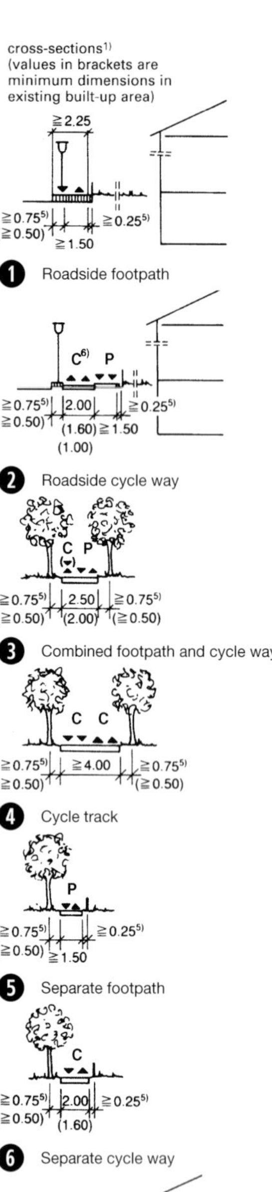

❶ Roadside footpath

❷ Roadside cycle way

❸ Combined footpath and cycle way

❹ Cycle track

❺ Separate footpath

❻ Separate cycle way

❼ Residential access, not for vehicles

Values of design parameters				
R_1 min [m]	S[2] max [%]	R_B min [m]	R_S min [m]	min. clear height [m]
	6(12)[8]			2.50
10 (2)[7]	as for relevant type of road	30	10	2.50
10 (2)[7]	3 (4 in <250 m)[8] (8 in <30 m)[8]	30	10	2.50
10 (2)[7]	3 (4 in <250 m)[8] (8 in <30 m)[8]	30	10	2.50
	6(12)[8]			2.50
10 (2)[7]	3 (4 over <250 m)[8] (8 over <30 m)[8]	30	10	2.50
	6(12)[8]			3.50 (2.50)

Notes

[1] slight deviations from the given dimensions can be necessary to suit the size of paving slabs

[2] S_{min} = 0.5% (drainage)

[3] length of non-vehicle residential access: up to 2 storeys ≦80 m, 3 storeys ≦60 m, 4 and more storeys ≦50 m

[4] with separated drainage system 4.00–4.50 m

[5] additional width suggestions: continuous rows of trees require at least 2.50 m wide planting strip

[6] two-way traffic only in exceptional cases

[7] rounded out radius at intersections

[8] in exceptional cases

Abbreviations: → ❶ – ❼

P = pedestrian
C = cyclist
R_1 = radius of curves
S = longitudinal slope
R_B = rounded out brow radius
R_S = rounded out dip radius

❶ – ❼ Pedestrian and cycle traffic areas

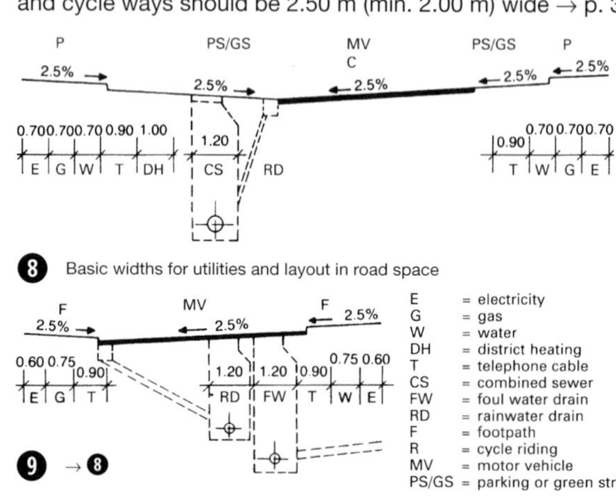

❽ Basic widths for utilities and layout in road space

❾ → ❽

E = electricity
G = gas
W = water
DH = district heating
T = telephone cable
CS = combined sewer
FW = foul water drain
RD = rainwater drain
F = footpath
R = cycle riding
MV = motor vehicle
PS/GS = parking or green strip

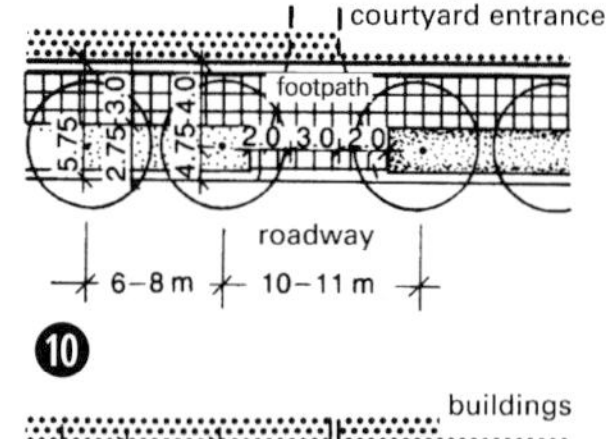

❿

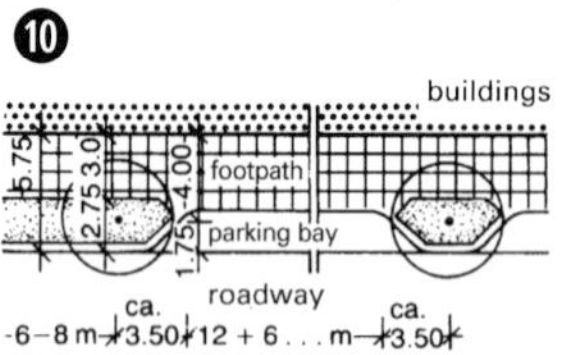

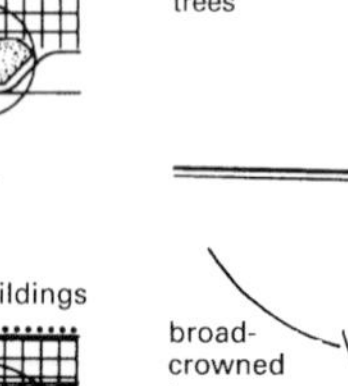

⓫

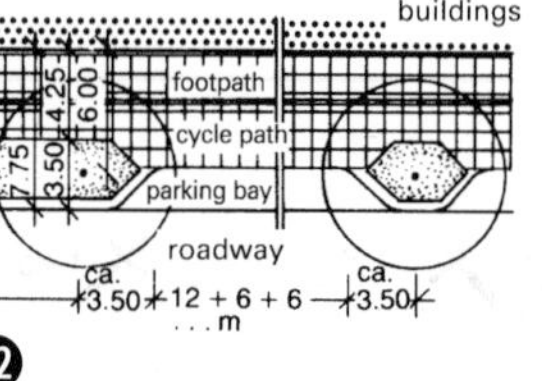

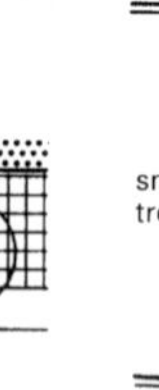

⓬

⓭

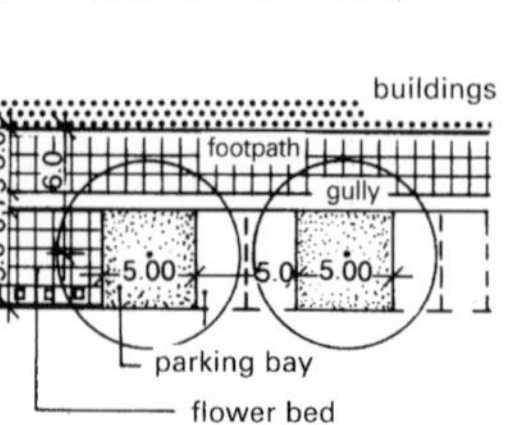

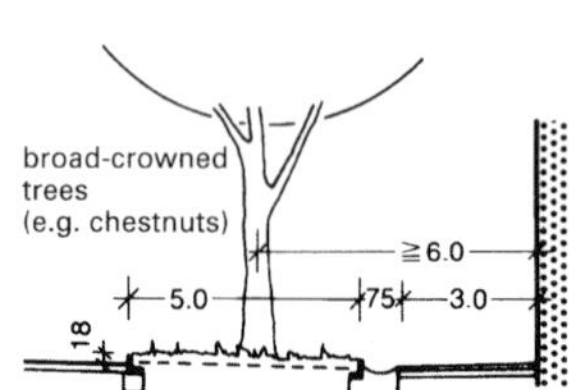

⓮

❿ – ⓮ Examples of the layout of street space in built-up areas

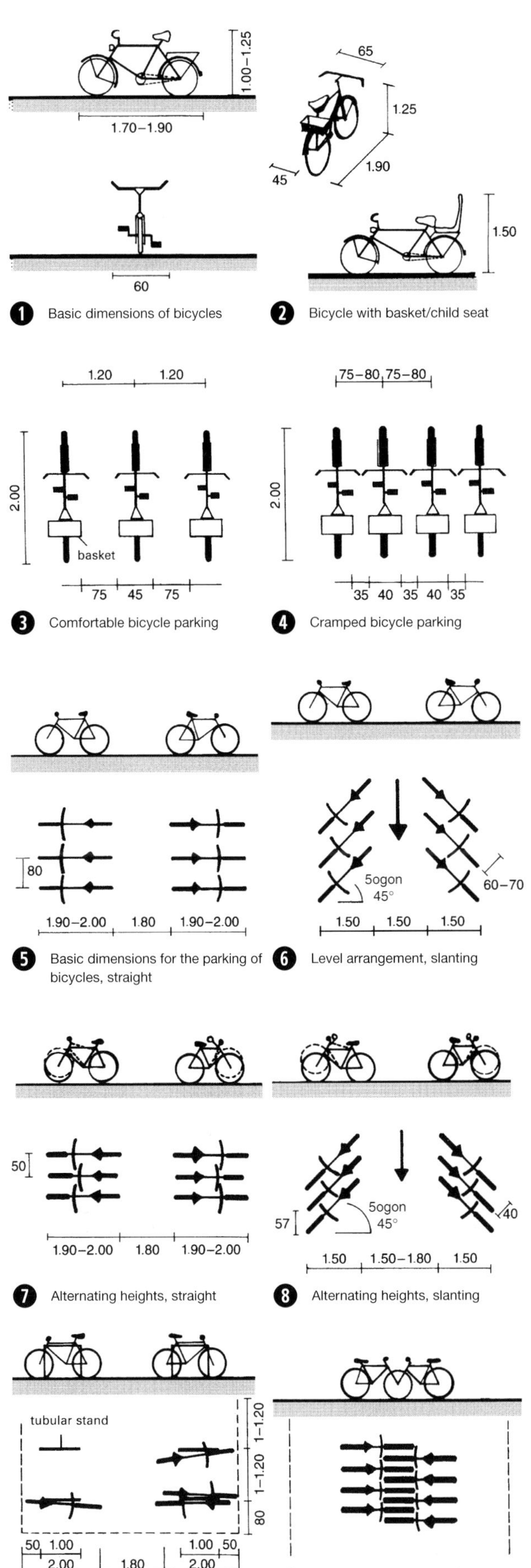

❶ Basic dimensions of bicycles

❷ Bicycle with basket/child seat

❸ Comfortable bicycle parking

❹ Cramped bicycle parking

❺ Basic dimensions for the parking of bicycles, straight

❻ Level arrangement, slanting

❼ Alternating heights, straight

❽ Alternating heights, slanting

❾ Bicycle parking space with stands

❿ Overlapping bicycles

Dimensions of bicycles → ❶ – ❷. Note allowances for baskets and children's seats. Include space for special bicycles: recumbent bicycles are up to 2.35 m long; tandems up to 2.60 m; bicycle trailer (with shaft) approx. 1.60 m long, 1.00 m wide; bicycles adapted for disabled people and for delivering goods.

Offer comfortable parking → ❸ wherever possible; cramped parking can cause injury, soiling and damage when locking, loading or wheeling in and out. Double rows with overlapping front wheels can save space → ⓬. In contrast, stacking vertically is problematic as it can cause damage.

There should be an appropriate number of parking spaces, according to rules of thumb and building regulations → ⓫. Cycle stands offer steady support, even when loading the bicycle. Locking should be possible using only one U-lock, securing the front wheel and the frame to the stand at the same time. Frame stands are therefore suitable → ❾. Bicycle stands which do not provide sensible locking opportunities are only suitable for internal use in areas of restricted access. Provide an intermediate bar for children's bicycles. Bicycle stands are mostly used on both sides, in which case the space required is 1.20 m → ❾.

Bicycle passage width 1.80 m → ❼ – ❾; also provide cross-aisles. The entire layout should be as clear and helpful for orientation as possible. Additional parking areas may be required for bicycle trailers and special bicycles.

Where bicycles are parked for many hours, provide roofing and lighting. The parking location should be placed so it is easy to find and ride into, and where there are social controls. Supervised bicycle parking can be appropriate for major events, stations, open-air swimming pools and shopping centres. Locations for bicycle parking can also be converted from car parking spaces.

Flats	1 per 30 m² total residential area
Visits for private flats	1 per 200 m² total residential area
Student residence	1 per bed
General school	0.7 per pupil
Adult education	0.5 per visitor
Lecture theatre	0.7 per seat
Libraries	1 per 40 m² of main usable area
College refectory	0.3 per seat
Workplace	0.3 per workplace
Stores for daily shopping	1 per 25 m² sales area
Shopping centre	1 per 80 m² sales area
Shop-type services for daily needs	1 per 35 m² sales area
Office services, doctor's surgery	0.2 per simultaneously present customers
Sport grounds, halls, indoor pool	0.5 per cloakroom place
Assembly place with wide usage	1 per 20 visitor places
Other assembly places	1 per 7 visitor places
Urban public house	1 per 7 seats
Beer garden	1 per 2 seats

If more than one use occurs in one building at the same time, then the values should be added together.

⓫ Guideline values for determining the capacity of bicycle parking

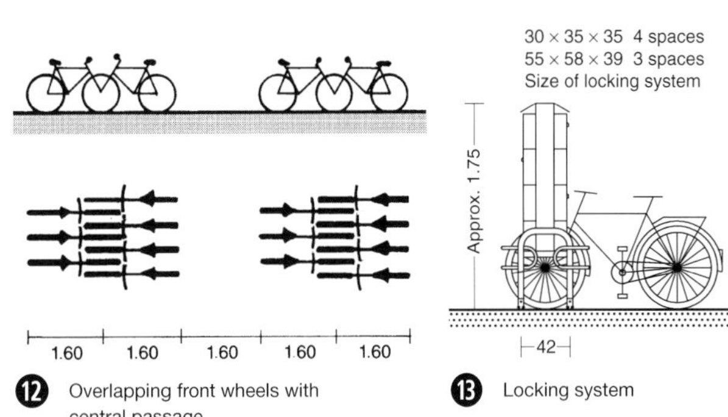

⓬ Overlapping front wheels with central passage

⓭ Locking system

Space required by bicycles: brisk riding in one direction from 1.40 m width, better 1.60 m; overtaking and meeting oncoming bicycles at reduced speed 1.60–2.00 m width; widths of 2.00–2.50 m are better, if bicycles with trailers also use the cycle way.

The basic dimensions for the traffic space of bicycles can be deduced from the basic width of 0.60 m plus the height of the cyclist → ❺ and the required margin of movement in various situations.

Passages between cycle stands should not be made too narrow: passage width min. 1.50 m (preferably 2.00 m) up to a length of 10 m, 1.80 m width up to 15 m, 2.20 m width up to 25 m. Interrupt with a passage every 15 m. Passage width between multi-storey stands min. 2.50 m. The longer the stands, the wider the passage.

Bike-Safe 1–3 storeys, 15–42 bicycles. Ground area 4 × 4 m height above ground level 5 m → ⓮

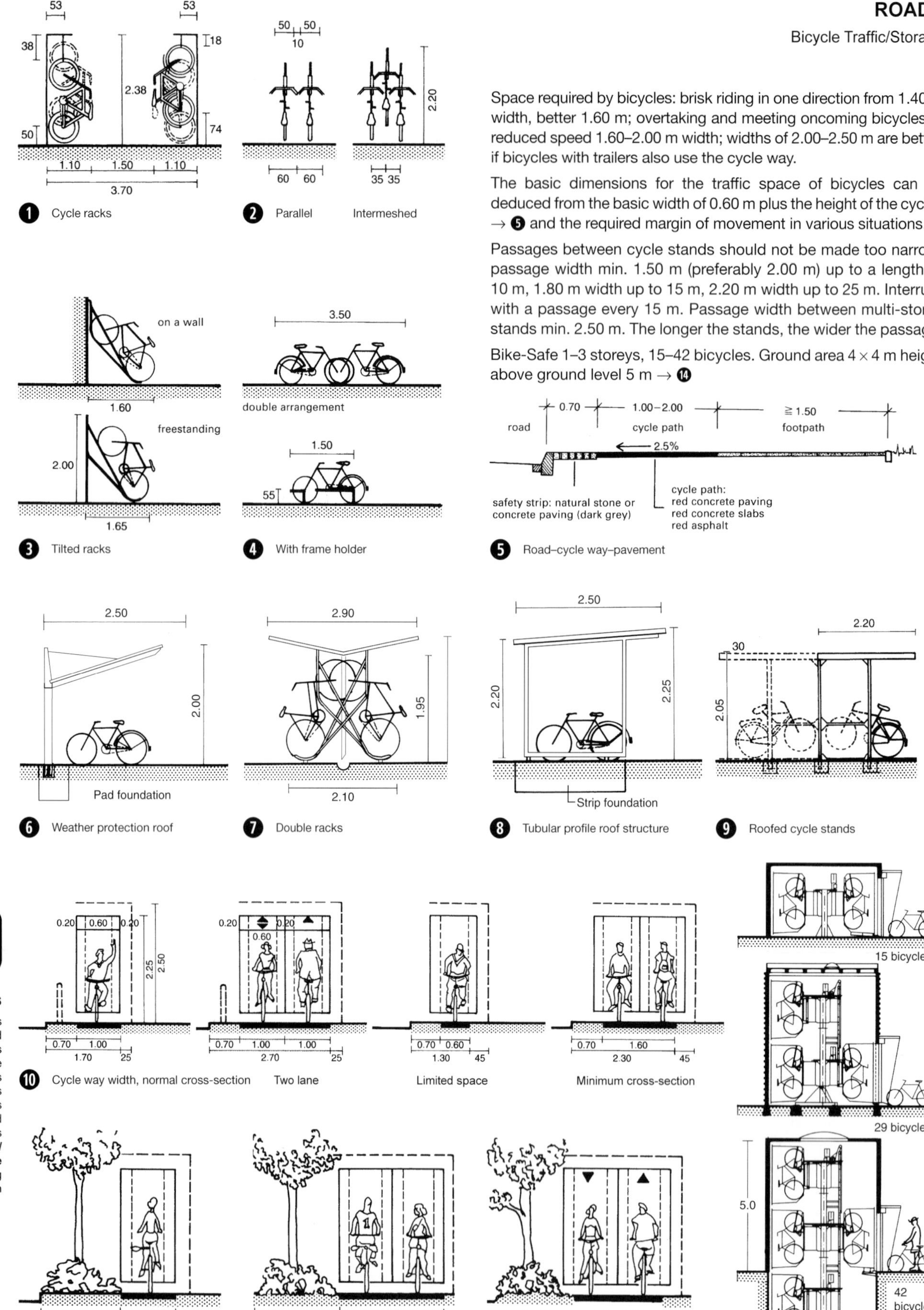

❶ Cycle racks

❷ Parallel Intermeshed

❸ Tilted racks

❹ With frame holder

❺ Road–cycle way–pavement

❻ Weather protection roof

❼ Double racks

❽ Tubular profile roof structure

❾ Roofed cycle stands

❿ Cycle way width, normal cross-section Two lane Limited space Minimum cross-section

⓫ Grass strips between cycle way and road. Good solution

⓬ Optimal solution

⓭ Grass strips are necessary for two-way traffic

⓮ Bike-Safe

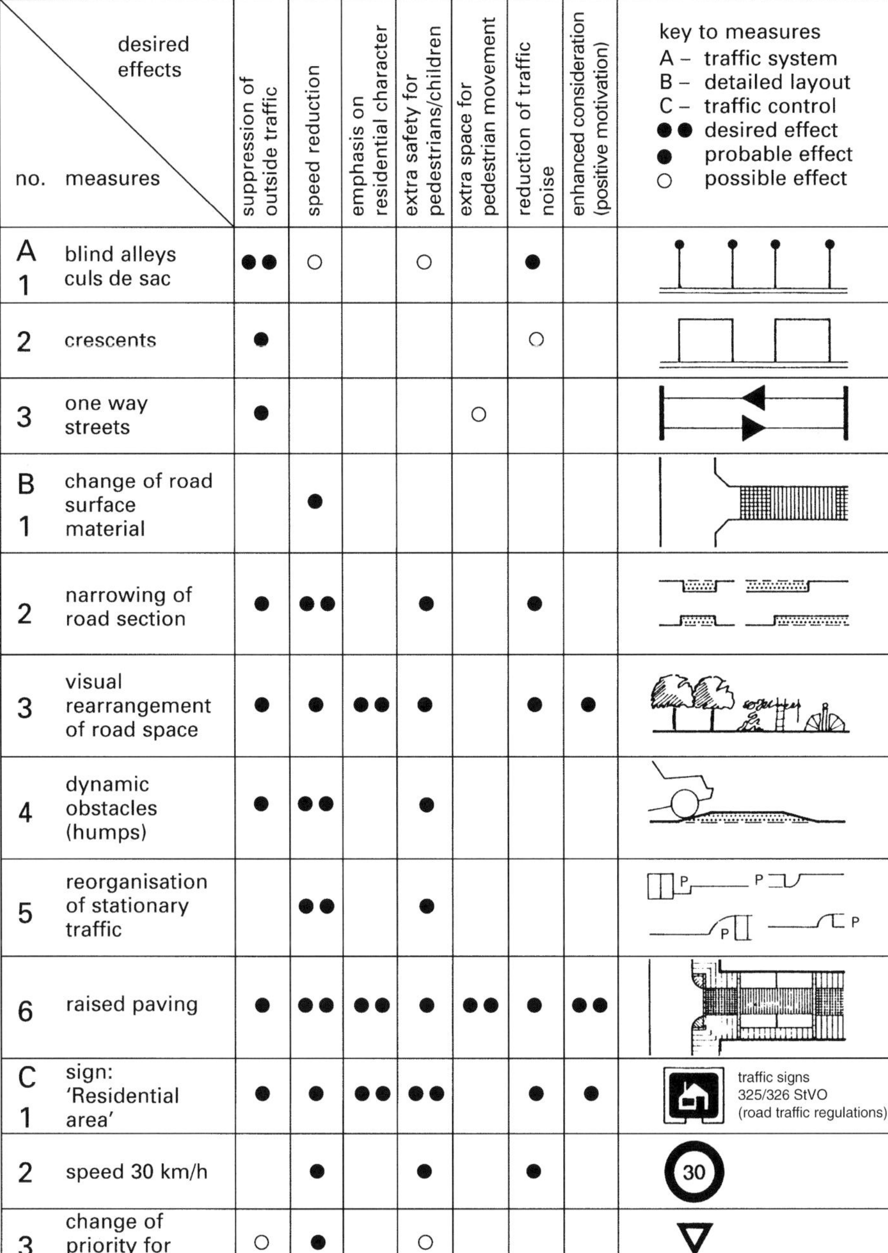

no.	measures (rows) / desired effects (columns)	suppression of outside traffic	speed reduction	emphasis on residential character	extra safety for pedestrians/children	extra space for pedestrian movement	reduction of traffic noise	enhanced consideration (positive motivation)	key to measures: A – traffic system; B – detailed layout; C – traffic control; ●● desired effect; ● probable effect; ○ possible effect
A 1	blind alleys culs de sac	●●	○		○		●		
2	crescents	●					○		
3	one way streets	●				○			
B 1	change of road surface material		●						
2	narrowing of road section	●	●●		●		●		
3	visual rearrangement of road space	●	●	●●	●		●	●	
4	dynamic obstacles (humps)	●	●●		●				
5	reorganisation of stationary traffic		●●		●				P
6	raised paving	●	●●	●●	●	●●	●	●●	
C 1	sign: 'Residential area'	●	●	●●	●●		●	●	traffic signs 325/326 StVO (road traffic regulations)
2	speed 30 km/h		●		●		●		30
3	change of priority for drivers	○	●		○				

❶ Traffic calming of roads in residential areas: overview of measures and effects

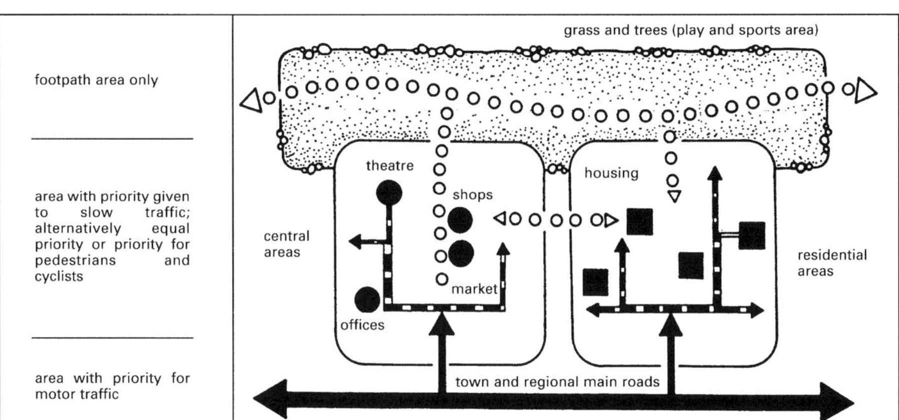

❷ Schematic diagram of the spatial layout of traffic management priorities

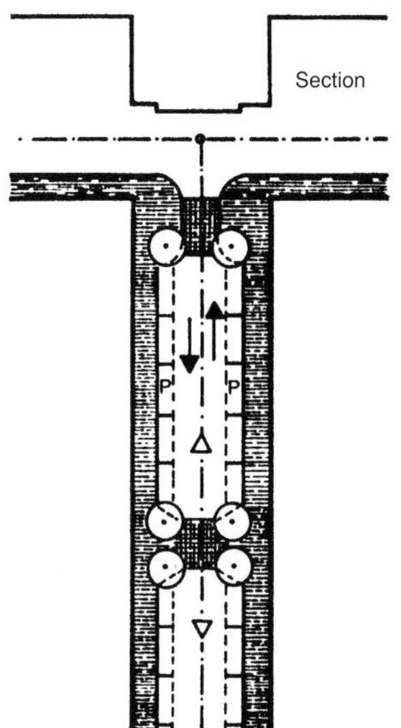

individual measures:
B1 + B2 + B3 +
(where appropriate, B4 + B6) + C1 + C2;
driving and pedestrian areas separated, reduction in road size in favour of wider pavements, speed reduction by narrowing the road and partial use of raised paving;
this gives more space and greater safety for pedestrians – improved layout through space subdivision

❸ Road layout proposal A → ❶

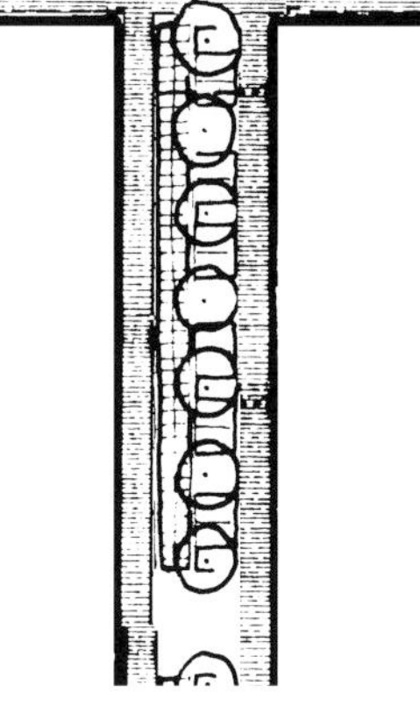

(A3) + B1 + B2 + B3 + B4 + B5 + B6 + C1;
layout for driving, parking and walking in a common (mixed) area so multiple use of the whole road area is possible;
speed is limited to 'walking pace' (or 20 km/h max.);
total reorganisation of the whole layout, taking into consideration the primarily residential needs

❹ Road layout proposal B → ❶

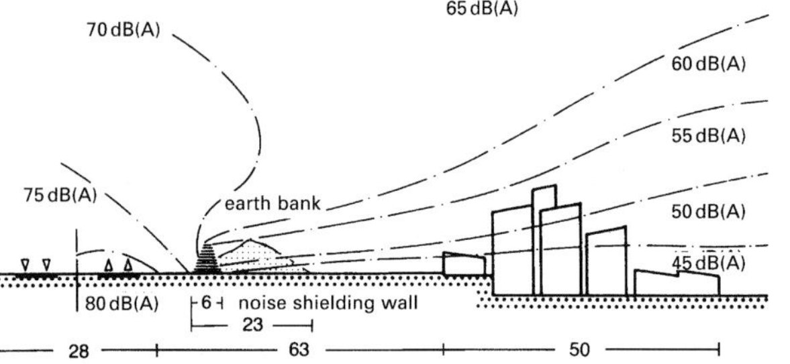

❶ Isophone diagram. The effect on noise level on earth wall or noise mitigation wall

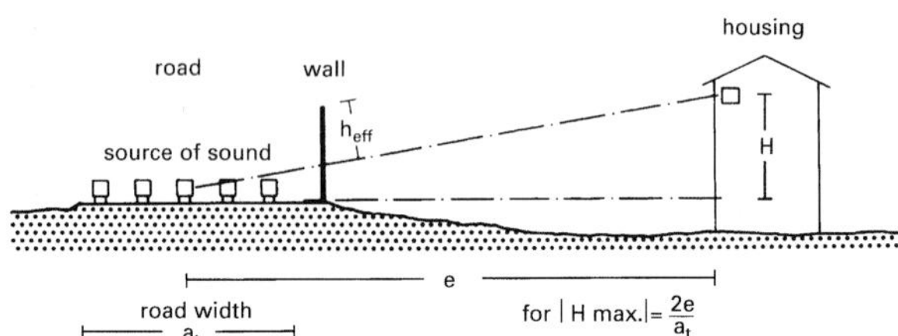

❷ Determining the required height of a noise mitigation wall

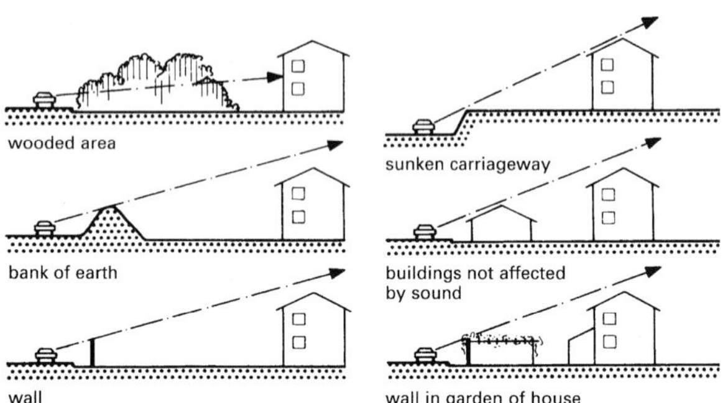

❸ Noise mitigation measures on a main road

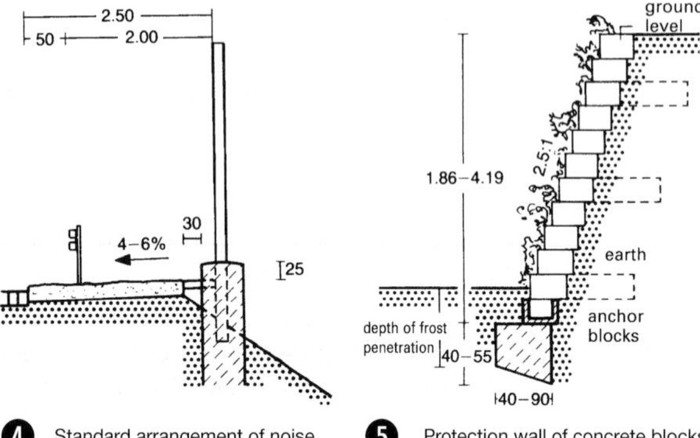

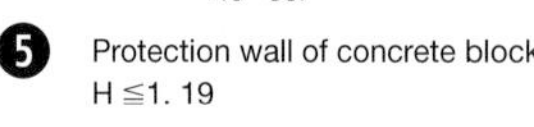

❹ Standard arrangement of noise barriers on roads

❺ Protection wall of concrete blocks H ≦1. 19

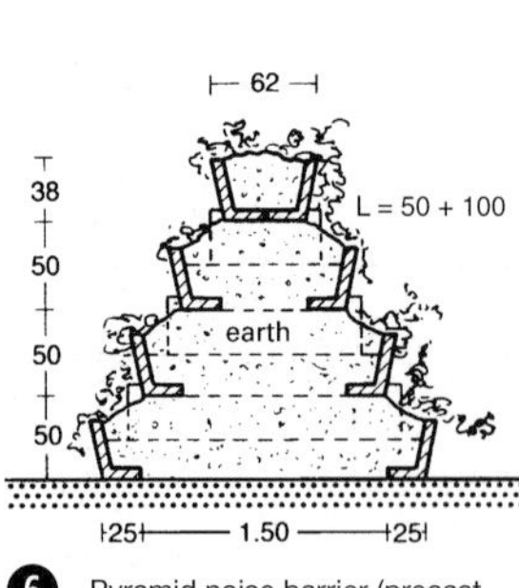

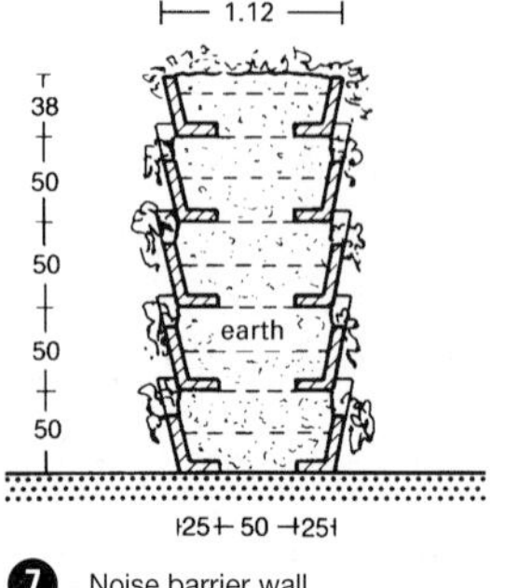

❻ Pyramid noise barrier (precast concrete elements)

❼ Noise barrier wall

Guidelines for road noise protection

Increased environmental awareness has made noise mitigation ever more important, especially in traffic spaces. In particular, the intensity of noise caused by greater traffic load, and denser building, demands effective protection in the form of earth walls, noise reduction walls and noise reduction pyramids → ❶ – ❼. Road traffic noise should be reduced by about ≦25 dB (A) on the other side of the noise reduction wall. This reduction is described as Δ LA, R, STR. and is a modified noise reduction value for road traffic noise. Noise reduction walls can be reflecting Δ LA, a, STR. <4 dB (A), absorbing 4 dB (A) ≦LA a STR. <8 dB (A), highly absorbing 8 dB (A) ≦LA a STR. The relevant standard and the Guidelines for Road Noise Protection (RLS – 81) give detailed calculation methods. The mitigation effect of a wall is not dependent on the construction material, but mostly on the height of the wall. The effect against road traffic noise is based on the creation of a noise shadow, but this, in contrast to a visual shadow, is not fully effective. Bending of the noise allows a part to reach the shadow zone. The proportion is smaller, the higher the wall and the longer the bypass route of the deflected noise. A multitude of pre-cast concrete elements are available from the industry, and also noise reduction walls of glass, timber and steel.

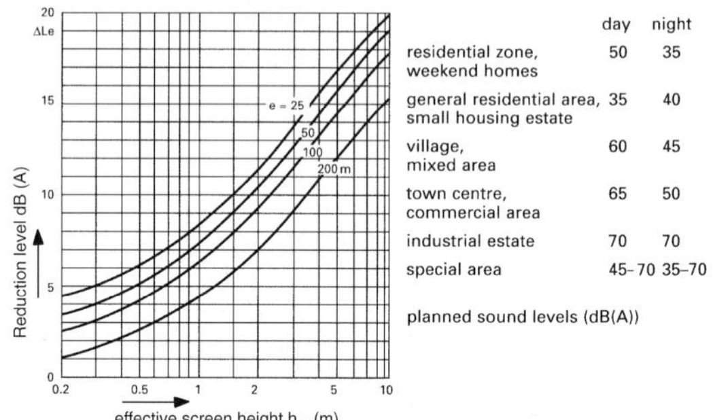

❽ Reduction of noise level

Required reduction		10	15	20	25	30	35
Required distance (m)	Grass area	75–125	125–250	225–400	375–555	—	—
	Woods	50–75	75–100	100–125	125–175	175–225	200–250

❾ Reduction of noise with distance

Barrier or wall, height (m)	1	2	3	4	5	6	7
Reduction in dB (A)	6	10	14	16.5	18.5	20.5	23.5

❿ Reduction of road traffic noise with height of barrier

Traffic loading both directions daytime, vehicles/h	Assignment of road types to traffic loading	Distance of emissions location from centre of road (m)	Noise level range
<10	residential road	—	0
10–50	residential road (2-lane)	>35 26–35 11–25 ≦10	0 I II III
>50–200	residential feeder road (2-lane)	>100 36–100 26–35 11–25 ≦10	0 I II III IV
>200–1000	built-up section of rural road and residential feeder road (2-lane)	101–300 36–100 11–35 ≦10	I II III V
	rural road outside residential area or in industrial zone (2-lane)	101–300 36–100 11–35 ≦10	II III IV V
>1000–3000	urban main traffic road or road in industrial zone (2-lane)	101–300 36–100 <35	IV IV V
>3000–5000	motorway link/main road, motorway (4-lane)	101–300 ≦100	IV V

⓫ Approx. estimation of existing or expected road traffic noise

see also:
Windows pp. 97, 100
Glass pp. 105, 107

PARKING FACILITIES

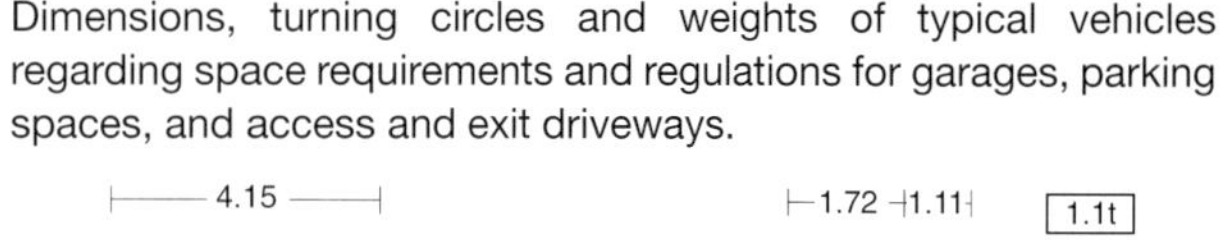

Dimensions, turning circles and weights of typical vehicles regarding space requirements and regulations for garages, parking spaces, and access and exit driveways.

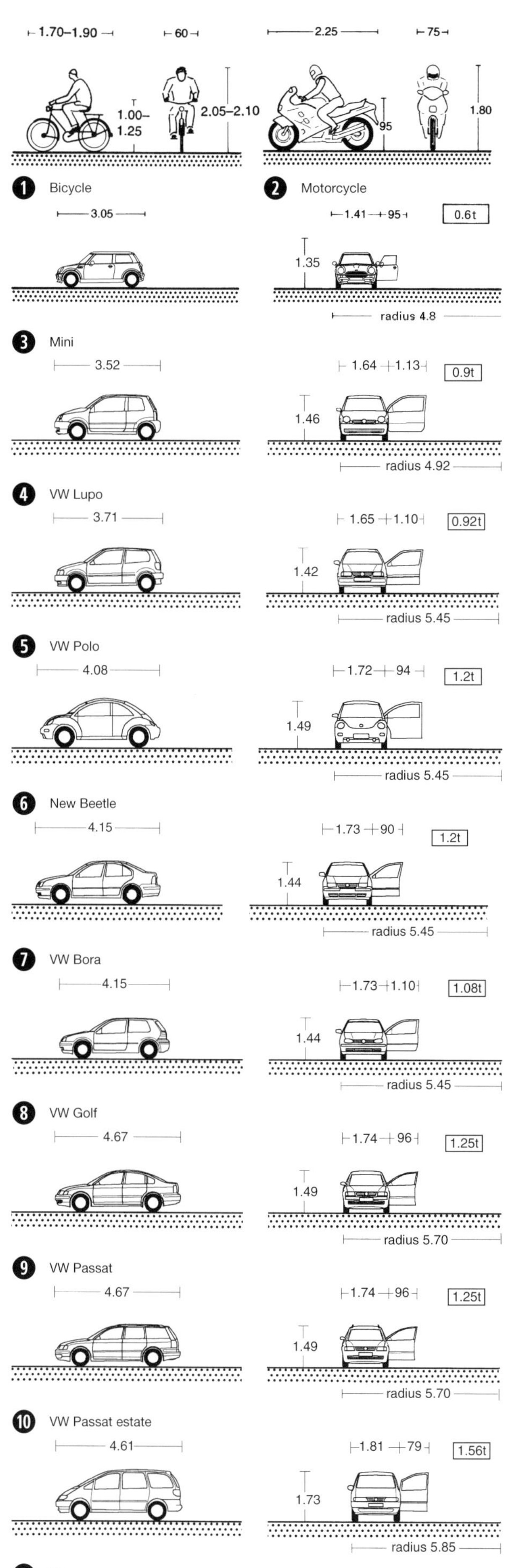

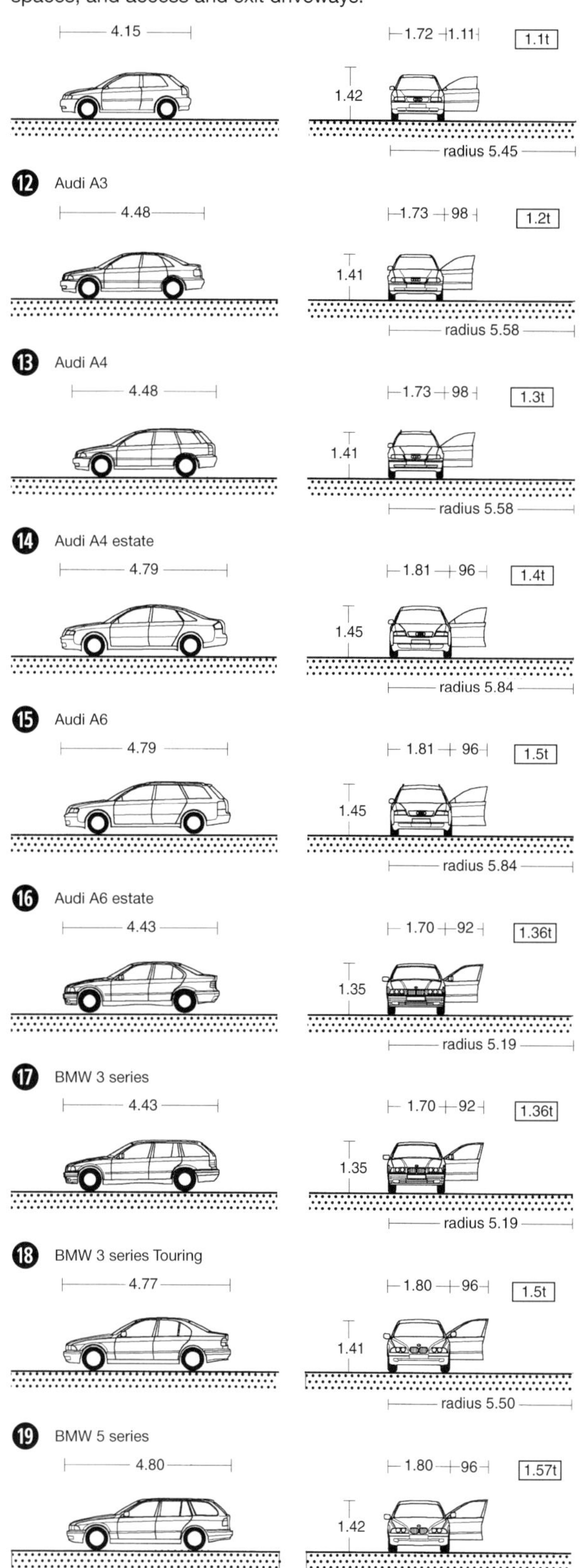

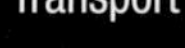

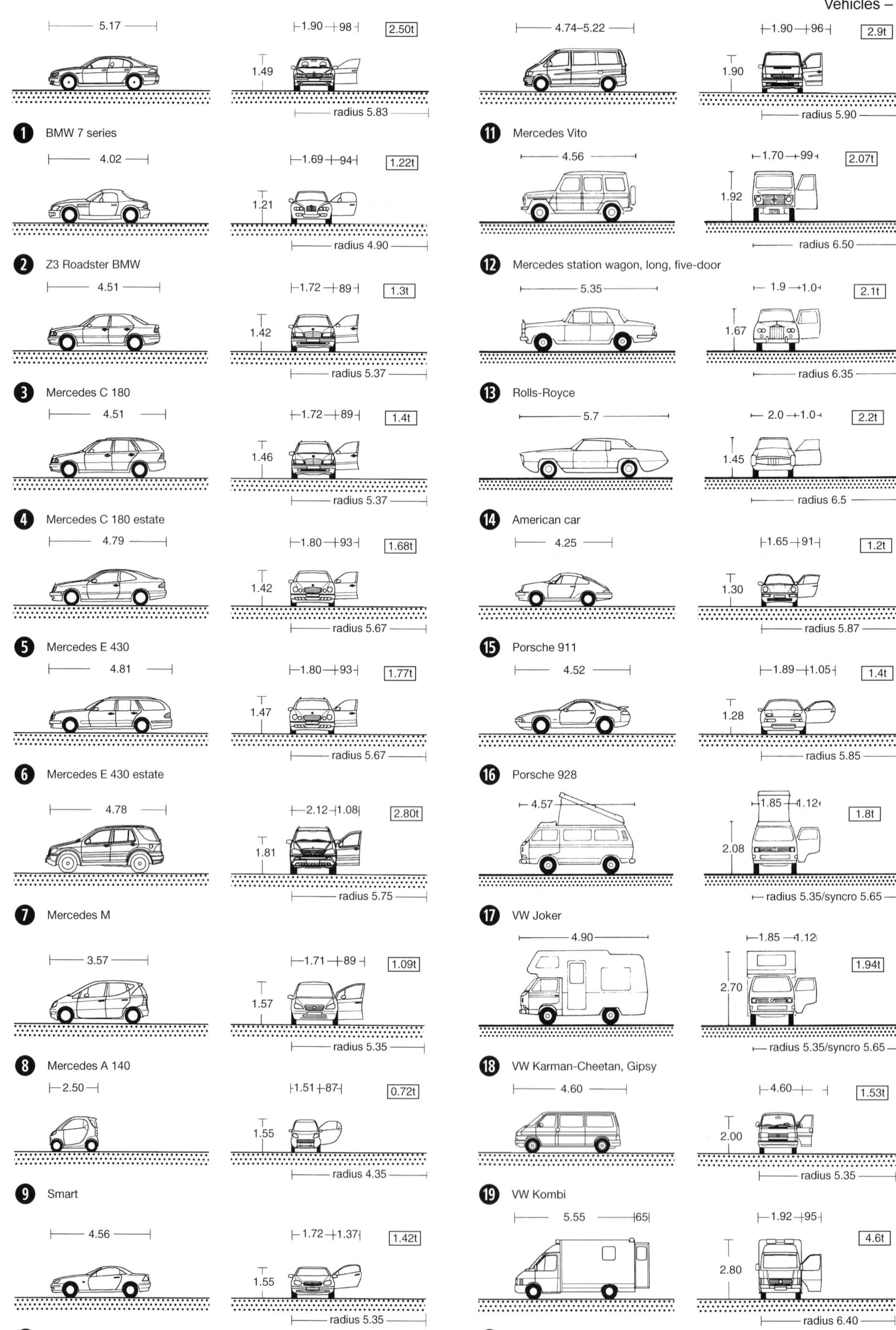
5.17
1.90 98
2.50t
1.49
radius 5.83
1 BMW 7 series
4.02
1.69 94
1.22t
1.21
radius 4.90
2 Z3 Roadster BMW
4.51
1.72 89
1.3t
1.42
radius 5.37
3 Mercedes C 180
4.51
1.72 89
1.4t
1.46
radius 5.37
4 Mercedes C 180 estate
4.79
1.80 93
1.68t
1.42
radius 5.67
5 Mercedes E 430
4.81
1.80 93
1.77t
1.47
radius 5.67
6 Mercedes E 430 estate
4.78
2.12 1.08
2.80t
1.81
radius 5.75
7 Mercedes M
3.57
1.71 89
1.09t
1.57
radius 5.35
8 Mercedes A 140
2.50
1.51 87
0.72t
1.55
radius 4.35
9 Smart
4.56
1.72 1.37
1.42t
1.55
radius 5.35
10 Mercedes CLK
4.74–5.22
1.90 96
2.9t
1.90
radius 5.90
11 Mercedes Vito
4.56
1.70 99
2.07t
1.92
radius 6.50
12 Mercedes station wagon, long, five-door
5.35
1.9 1.0
2.1t
1.67
radius 6.35
13 Rolls-Royce
5.7
2.0 1.0
2.2t
1.45
radius 6.5
14 American car
4.25
1.65 91
1.2t
1.30
radius 5.87
15 Porsche 911
4.52
1.89 1.05
1.4t
1.28
radius 5.85
16 Porsche 928
4.57
1.85 1.12
1.8t
2.08
radius 5.35/syncro 5.65
17 VW Joker
4.90
1.85 1.12
1.94t
2.70
radius 5.35/syncro 5.65
18 VW Karman-Cheetan, Gipsy
4.60
4.60
1.53t
2.00
radius 5.35
19 VW Kombi
5.55 65
1.92 95
4.6t
2.80
radius 6.40
20 Ambulance

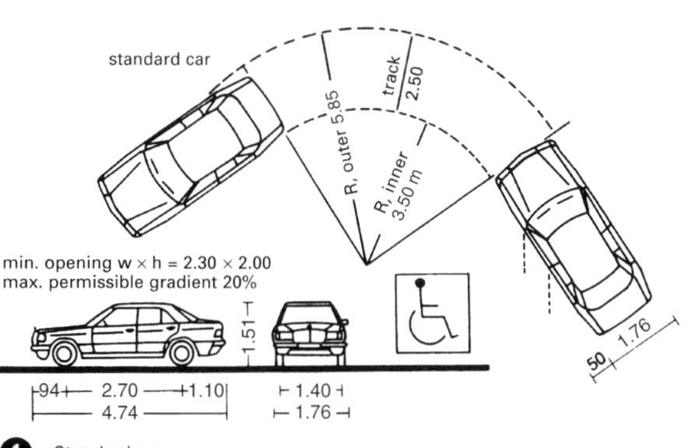

❶ Standard car

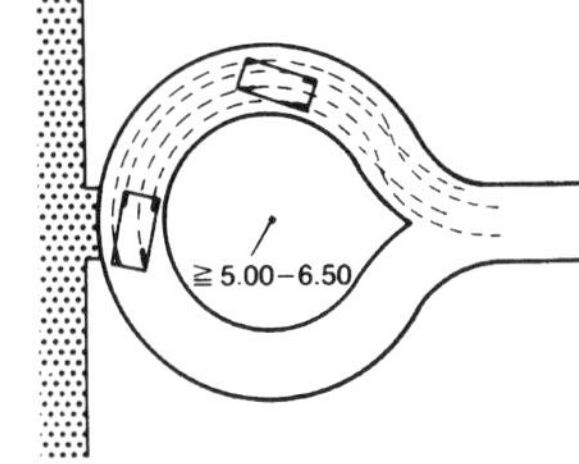

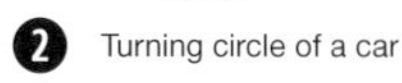

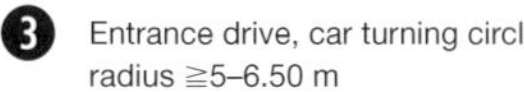

❷ Turning circle of a car

❸ Entrance drive, car turning circle radius ≧5–6.50 m

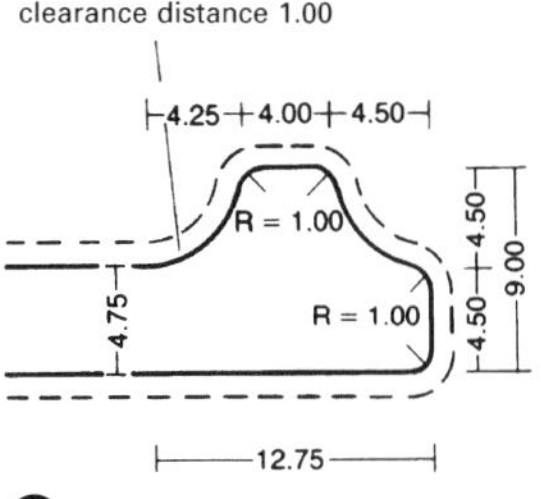

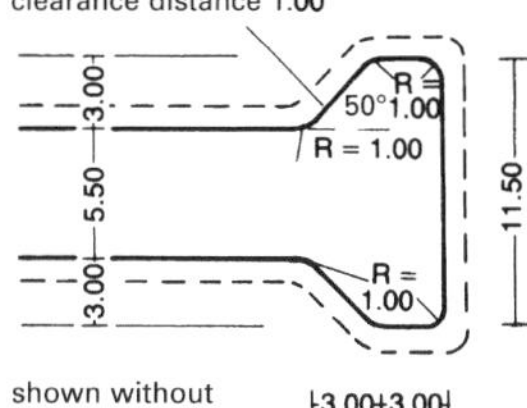

❹ Hammerhead turning place for cars

❺ Hammerhead turning place for cars and HGVs up to 8 m length (refuse collection vehicle, fire engine, HGV 6 t)

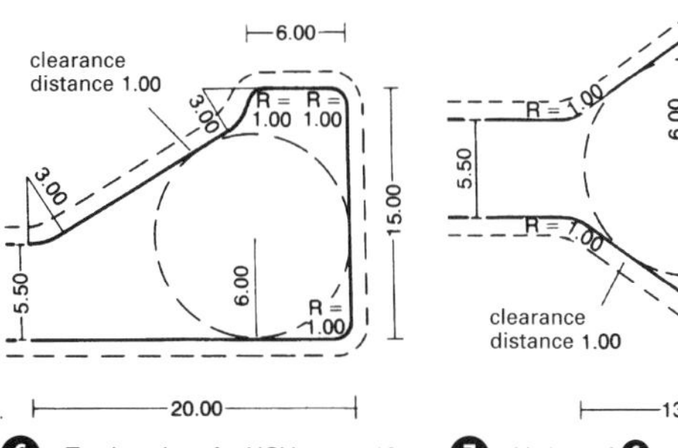

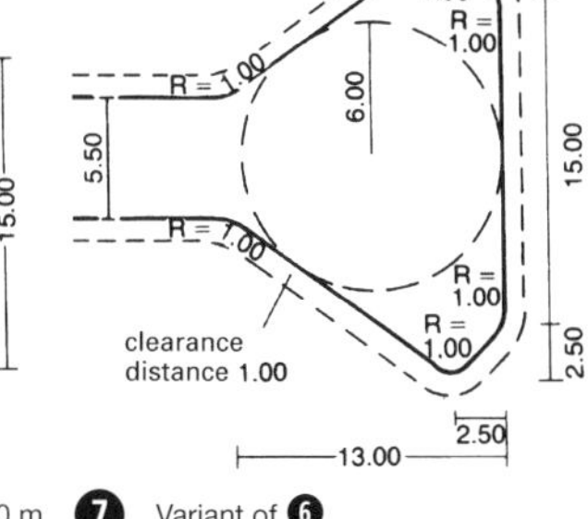

❻ Turning place for HGVs up to 10 m and 22 t (3-axle refuse collection vehicle)

❼ Variant of ❻

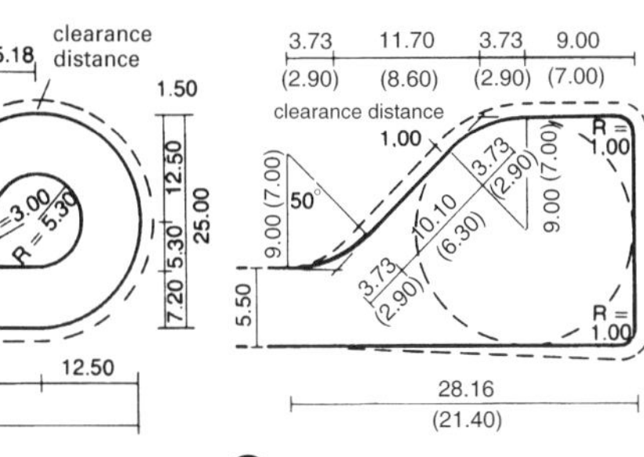

❽ Turning loop for HGVs with trailer and articulated buses

❾ Turning circle for 2-axle refuse collection vehicle (r = 9) or for vans (r = 7), values in brackets

The type, size and design of a place where vehicles can turn depend on the particular use of an area, the vehicles and the urban planning function. It is difficult to make generally valid recommendations for the selection of the correct turning place. The requirements of the fire services and refuse disposal trucks have to be considered in turning place decisions. Some authorities responsible for waste disposal decline to remove rubbish from dead-end streets where refuse disposal trucks can only perform a three-point turn or have to drive backwards for considerable distances.

Turning places can be formed as hammerheads → ❹ – ❺, turning circles or turning loops → ❻ – ❾. Hammerheads demand manoeuvres such as three-point turns, so turning circles and loops are preferable as they allow trucks to turn in one swing.

Turning places should for practical reasons be laid out asymmetrically to the left → ❻ – ❾. The perimeter of turning places should allow sufficient space without fixed objects being endangered by the overhanging parts of vehicles. The centre of turning loops can be planted → ❽. Hammerhead turning places → ❹ are only suitable for cars. They are not necessary where the road is more than 6 m wide, which can also include garage forecourts or footpath crossings.

	External dimensions						
			Overhang length				
Type of vehicle	Length [m]	Wheelbase [m]	Front [m]	Back [m]	Width [m]	Height [m]	External turning circle radius [m]
Bicycle	1.90				0.60	1.00	
Moped	1.80				0.60	1.00	
Motorcycle	2.20				0.70	1.00	
Car	4.74	2.70	0.94	1.10	1.76	1.51	5.85
HGVs:							
Van/campervan	6.89	3.95	0.96	1.98	2.17	2.70	7.35
HGV (2 axles)	9.46	5.20	1.40	2.86	2.29	3.80	9.77
HGV (3 axles)[1)]	10.10	5.30[1)]	1.48	3.32	2.50[4)]	3.80	10.05
HGVs with trailer:	18.71						
Towing vehicle (3 axles)[1)]	9.70	5.28[1)]	1.50	2.92	2.50[4)]	4.00	10.30
Trailer (2 axles)	7.45	4.84	1.35[3)]	1.26	2.50	4.00	10.30
Articulated HGVs:	16.50						
Tractor unit (2 axles)	6.08	3.80	1.43	0.85	2.50[4)]	4.00	7.90
Semi-trailer (3 axles)[1)]	13.61	7.75[1)] 1.61	4.25	2.50	4.00	7.90	
Buses:							
Coach, bus	12.00	5.80	2.85	3.35	2.50[4)]	3.70[6)]	10.50
Coach, bus[2)]	13.70	6.35[2)]	2.87	4.48	2.50[4)]	3.70[6)]	11.25
Coach, bus[2)]	14.95	6.95[2)]	3.10	4.90	2.50[4)]	3.70[6)]	11.95
Articulated bus	18.75	5.98/5.99	2.65	3.37	2.50[4)]	2.95	11.80
Refuse collection vehicles:							
2 axles (2 Mü)	9.03	4.60	1.35	3.08	2.50[4)]	3.55	9.40
3 axles (3 Mü)	9.90	4.77[1)]	1.53	3.60	2.50[4)]	3.55	10.25
3 axles (3 MüN)[2)]	9.95	3.90	1.35	4.70	2.50[4)]	3.55	8.60
Highest values permitted in Germany:							
HGV	12.00						
Trailer	12.00				2.55[4)5)]	4.00[6)]	12.50
HGV with trailer	18.75						
Articulated HGV	16.50						
Articulated bus	18.00						

Notes: 1) for vehicles with 3 axles, the rear tandem axle is integrated to a middle axle
2) for 3-axle vehicles with a trailing axle, the wheelbase corresponds to the distance between the front axle and the forward axle of the rear tandem axle
3) without tow bar length
4) without external mirror
5) additional equipment for air-conditioned HGVs up to 2.60 m
6) as double-decker bus 4.00 m

❿ Basic vehicle data → p. 397–398

Type of road	Use of zone	Design vehicle	R (m)	Notes
access road to houses, residential road with little traffic	residential	car	6	– turning circle for cars – special provision for refuse collection vehicles (e.g. link road connection via lanes with limited traffic access)
residential road	predominantly residential	cars, 2-axle refuse collection vehicle	8	– turning circle for small buses and most refuse collection vehicles – possibility for all permissible vehicles to perform three-point turn
residential road	residential, also considerably commercial	car, waste disposal, 3-axle HGV, standard bus, articulated bus	10 11 12.5	– adequate turning circle for great majority of permissible HGVs – turning circle for newer buses – turning circle for articulated buses
	predominantly commercial	lorry with trailer, articulated bus	12.5	– adequate turning circle for all permissible HGVs

An additional 1.00 m width should be kept free at the outside of turning places for vehicle overhangs.

⓫ Recommendations for determination of external turning circle radius (R)

Transport

PARKING FACILITIES
Vehicles – cars
Vehicles – turning
Parking spaces
Multi-storey car parks
Ramps
Multi-storey car park regulations
Parking systems
Vehicles – trucks
Trucks – parking and turning
Service areas
Petrol stations
Car wash

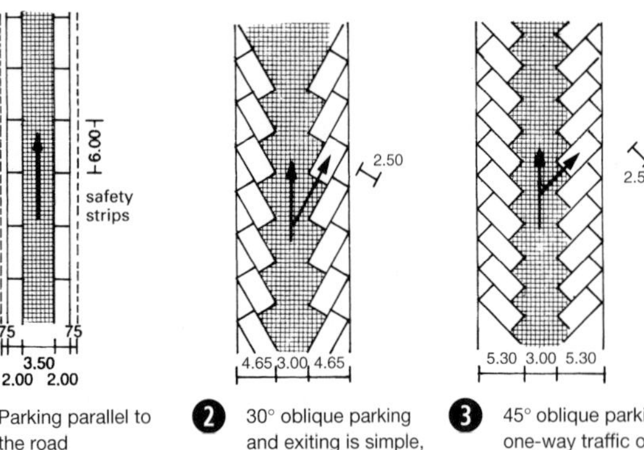

❶ Parking parallel to the road

❷ 30° oblique parking and exiting is simple, but one-way traffic only

❸ 45° oblique parking, one-way traffic only

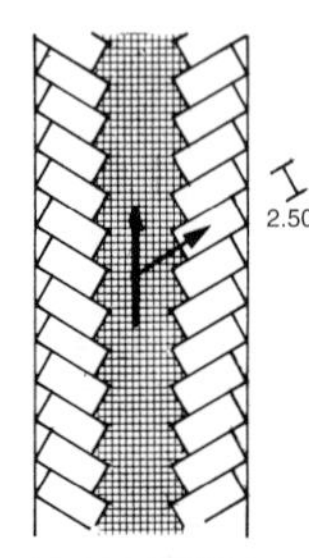

❹ 60° oblique parking, one-way traffic only

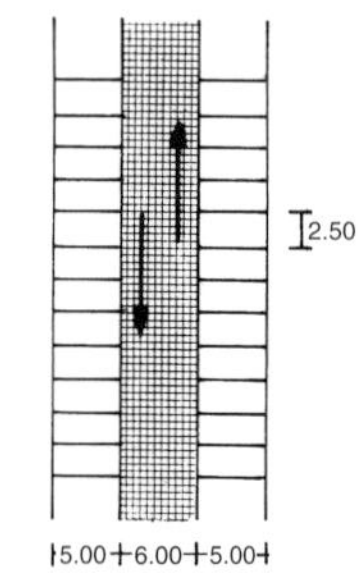

❺ 90° parking and exiting is possible in both directions. Access width 5.50 m for increased manoeuvring

2.30

5.00 6.50 5.00

❻ 90° parking and exiting is possible in both directions. Parking space width 2.30 m

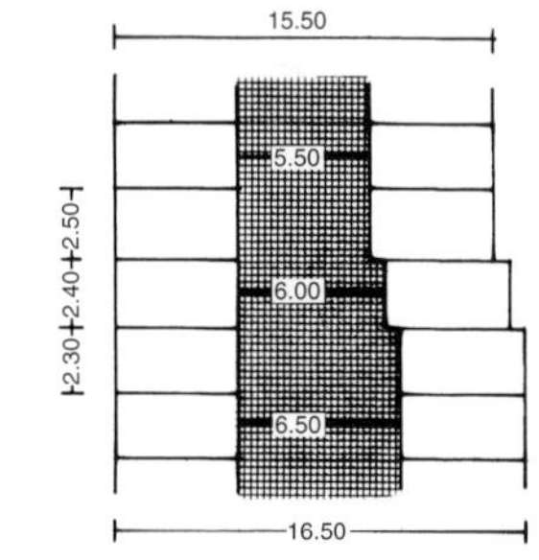

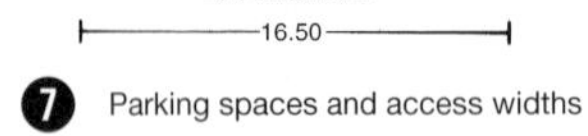

❼ Parking spaces and access widths

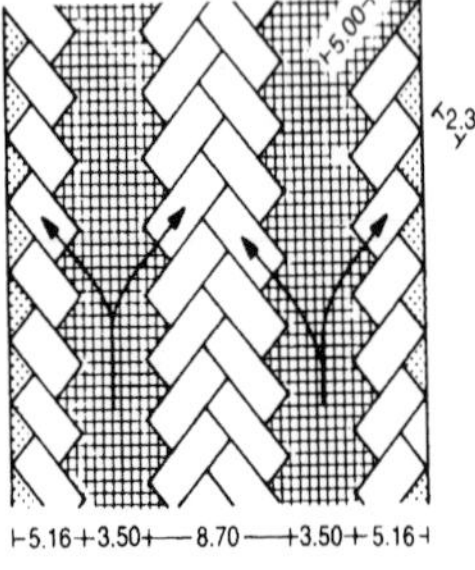

❽ 45° parking, one way traffic only

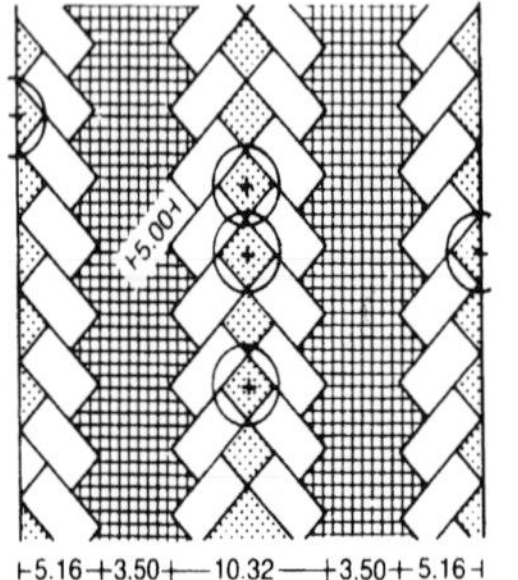

❾ Parking, one way traffic only (leaves space for planting)

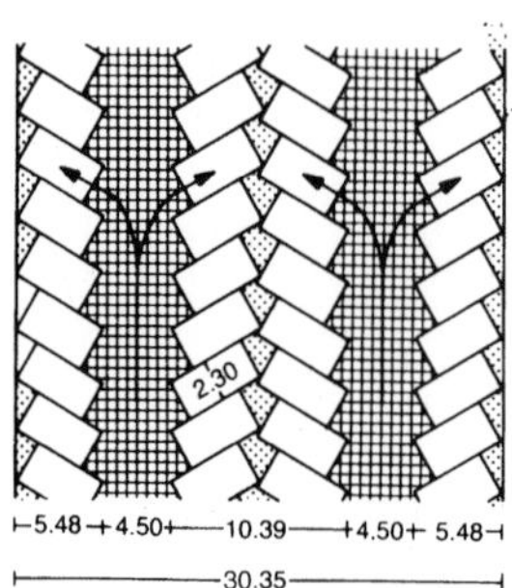

❿ 60° parking, one way traffic only

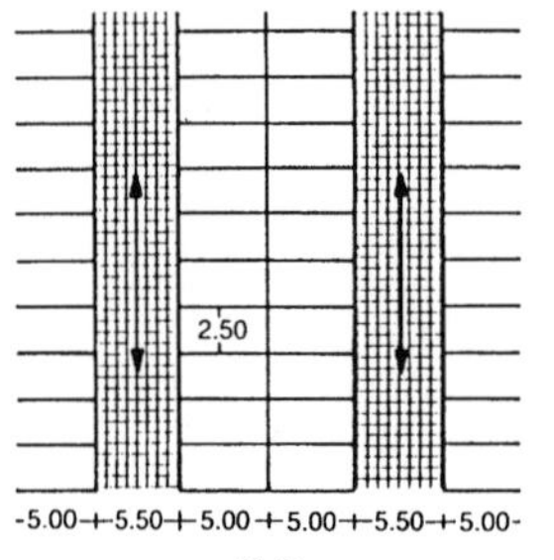

⓫ 90° parking, access 5.50 m wide, parking space 2.50 m wide

Parking spaces are usually outlined by 12–20 mm wide yellow or white painted lines. When parking is facing a wall, these lines are often painted at a height of up to 1 m for better visibility. Guide rails in the floor along the side have also proved popular for demarcation of parking limits, and can be about 50–60 cm long, 20 cm wide and 10 cm high.

Where vehicles are parked in lines facing walls or at the edge of the parking deck in a multi-storey car park, it is common practice to provide buffers, restraining bars or railings up to axle height to prevent cars from going over the edge. Where cars are parked face to face, transverse barriers about 10 cm high can be used to act as stops at the front. Overhang on vehicles must be taken into account → ⓯. For lining up in front of a wall, a stop rail or rubber buffer will be sufficient → ⓯.

Parking arrangement	Space requirement per place incl. access (m²)	No. places in 100 m² area	No. places on 100 m of road (one side only)
→ ❶ 0° parallel to road. Difficult parking and exiting – good for narrow roads	22.5	4.4	17
→ ❷ 30° oblique to road. Simple parking and exiting. Area busy	30.8 (27.6)	3.2 (3.6)	20 (21)
→ ❸ 45° oblique to road. Good parking and exiting. Area per place relatively low. Normal type of layout	24 (21.7)	4.2 (4.6)	29 (31)
→ ❹ 60° oblique to road. Relatively good parking and exiting. Area per place low. Frequently used layout	22.5 (20.5)	4.4 (4.9)	34 (37)
→ ❺ and ❻ 90° right angle to road. Low area per place. Considerable turning of vehicle necessary	20 (19.0)	5 (5.3)	40 (44)

The given values are for a parking space 2.50 m wide.
The values in brackets (parking place width 2.30 m) should be used only in justified and exceptional cases.

⓬ Space requirements

Arrangement of garage parking spaces to the access. At an angle of:	Required access width (in m) for a garage parking space width of:		
	2.30	2.40	2.50
90°	6.50	6.00	5.50
75°	5.50	5.25	5.00
60°	4.50	4.25	4.00
45°	3.50	3.25	3.00
up to 30°	3.00	3.00	3.00

⓭ Access width. (Parking space 2.50 m wide is standard. This value should if possible always be complied with in public areas)

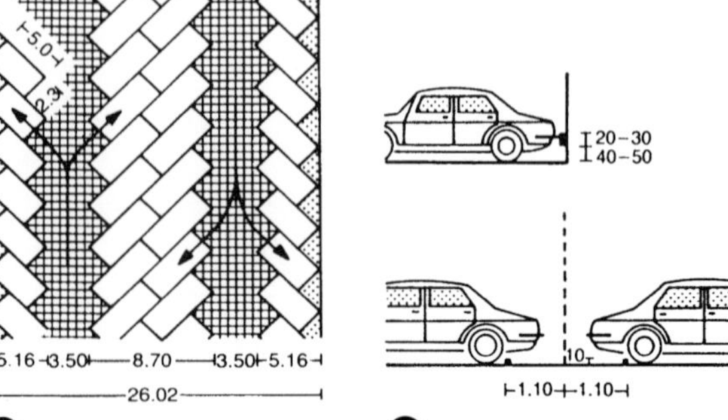

⓮ Oblique parking layout

⓯ Transverse bumpers and impact buffers

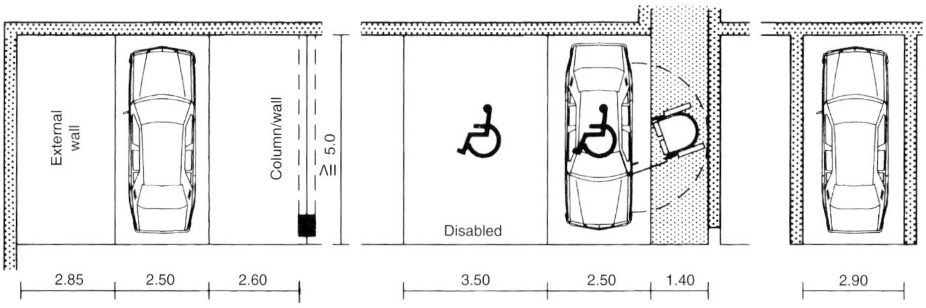

PARKING FACILITIES

Parking Spaces

If individual parking spaces are bordered by pillars, walls or columns, then the width of the parking space on the relevant side is increased by 0.10 m → ❶ – ❸. (This does not, however, apply to mechanical lifting platforms or automatic garages.) If parking spaces are bounded by a footpath, cycle way or separation strip on the facing side via a kerb, then the kerb will be used to estimate the border of the parking space → ❹ + ❽. The examples show how parking spaces can be integrated into their surroundings by design elements without impairing their function → ❺ – ❼.

To increase open areas, parking spaces can be partly or completely lowered or provided with green roofs. The greening not only has design value but also provides shadow and improves the ecological situation (dust absorption) → ❼.

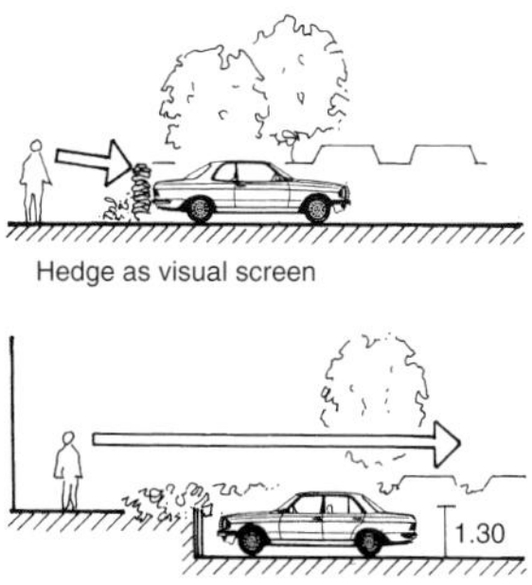

❶ If parking spaces are bordered by pillars or walls, then the width is increased

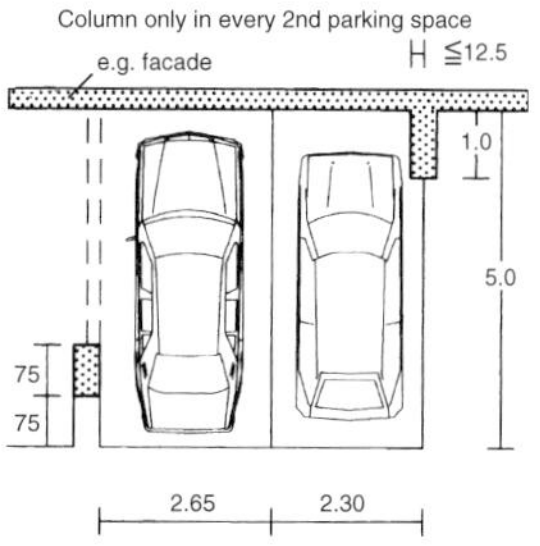

❷ Reductions are possible in private buildings

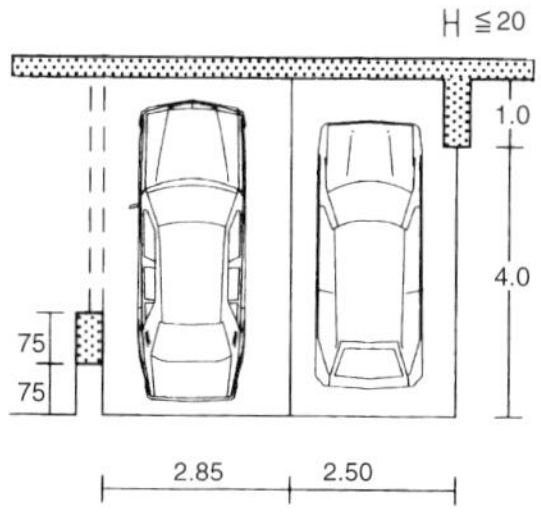

❸ Comfortable parking and exiting

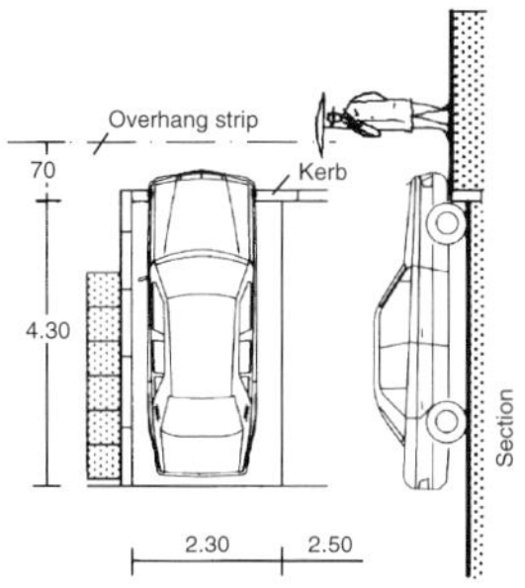

❹ With kerb border

❺ Lowered parking space

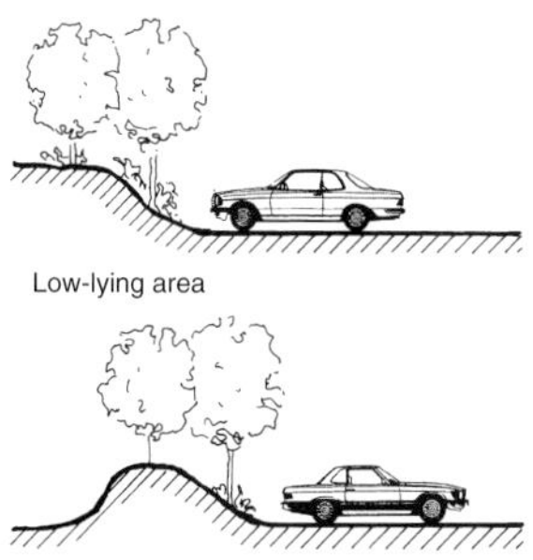

❻ Parking behind an earth wall

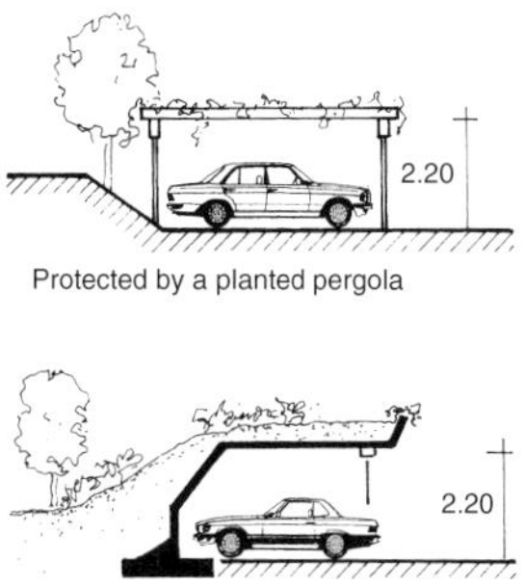

❼ With earth covering

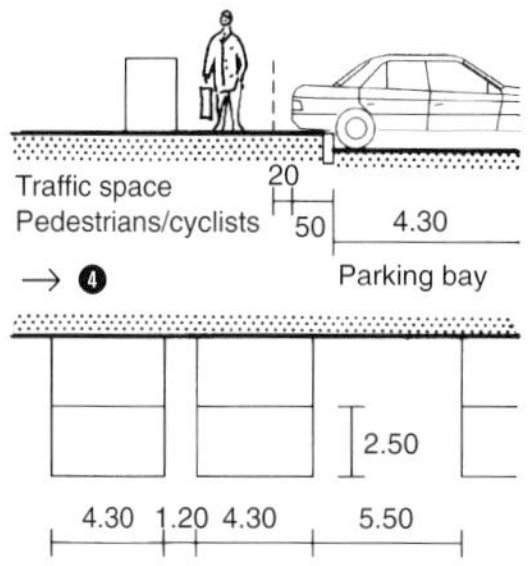

❽ Block layout

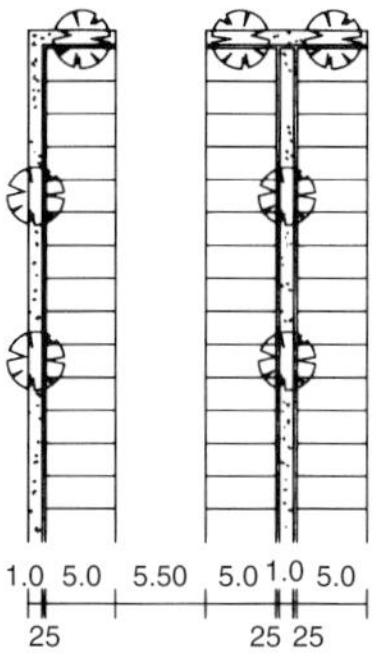

❾ Car park with planting

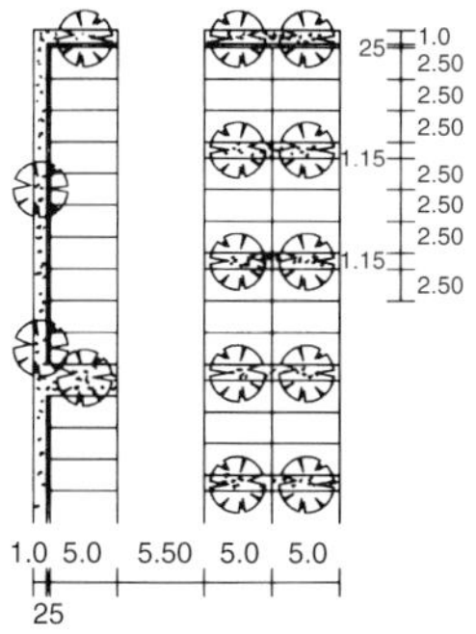

❿ Planting at right angles to the access passage

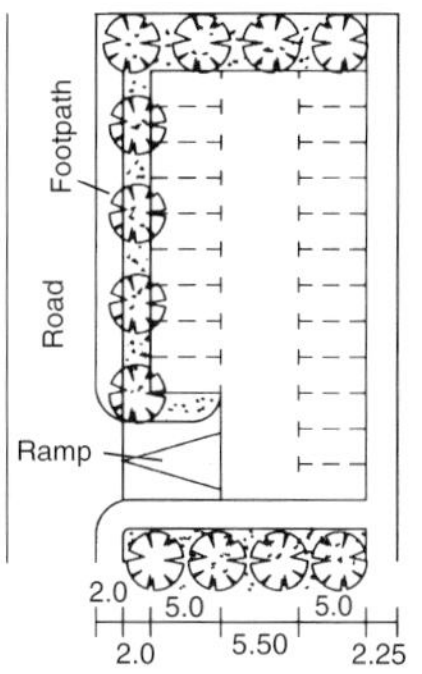

⓫ Lowered parking area → ❺ – ❻

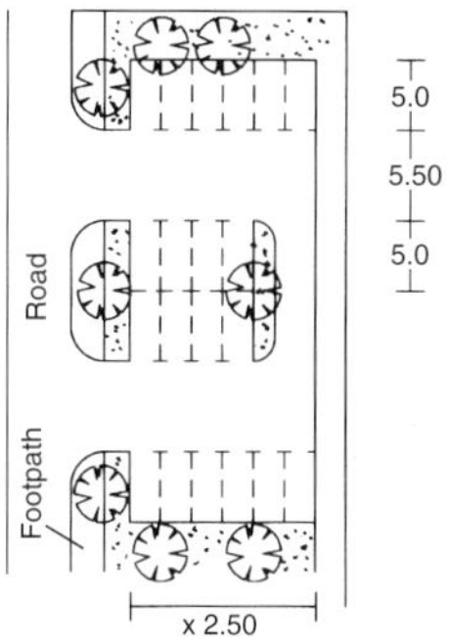

⓬ Parking next to the road

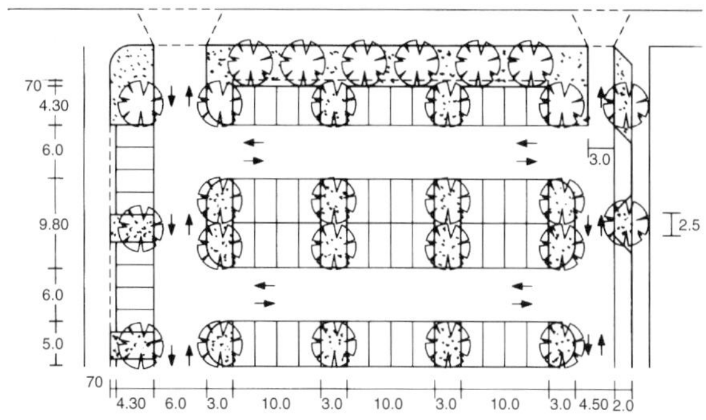

⓭ Example: car park

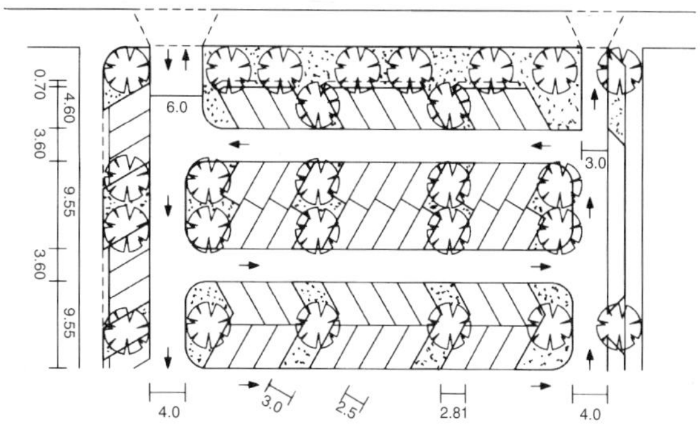

⓮ Variant: oblique layout in car park

Transport

PARKING FACILITIES
Vehicles – cars
Vehicles – turning
Parking spaces
Multi-storey car parks
Ramps
Multi-storey car park regulations
Parking systems
Vehicles – trucks
Trucks – parking and turning
Service areas
Petrol stations
Car wash

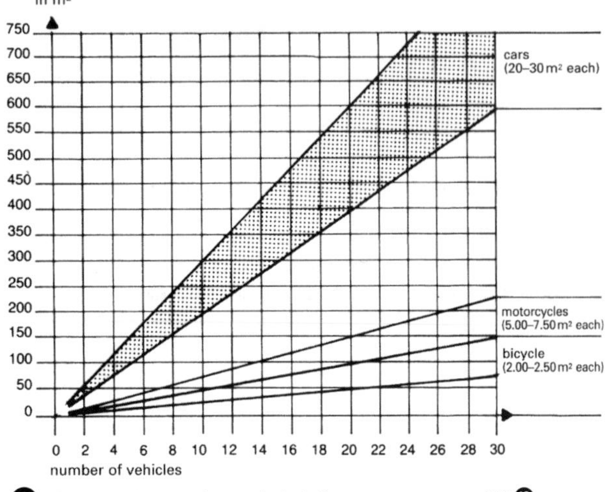

❶ Space requirement of car parks including access areas → p. 390 ⓬

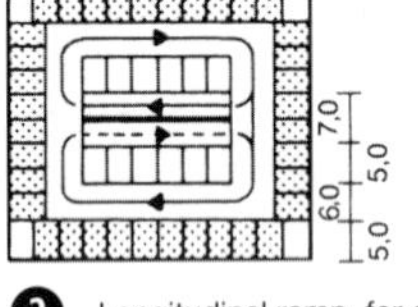

❷ Longitudinal ramp, for exact dimensions see p. 390

❸ Transverse ramp

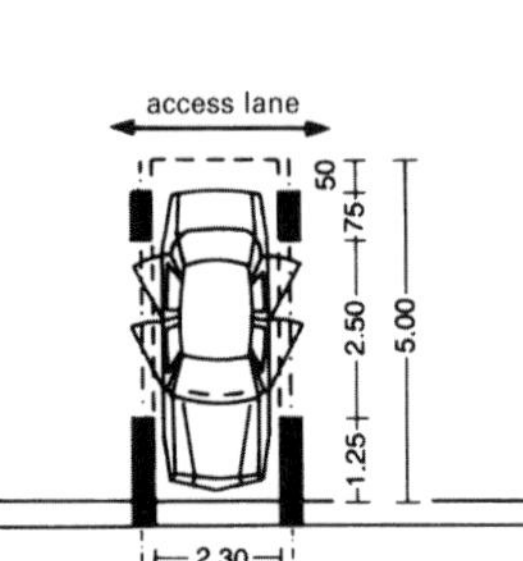

❹ Possible column arrangement for right-angled parking

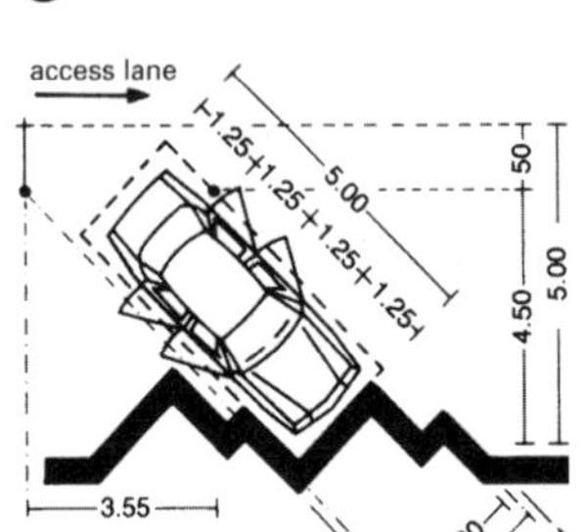

❺ 45° oblique parking

For multi-storey car parks the requirements for the layout of parking spaces and access are in principle the same as for open car parks. The Garage (multi-storey car park) Regulations require a minimum width for parking spaces of 2.30 m. The Research Company for Roads and Traffic (FGSV), however, recommends a minimum width of 2.50 m for all publicly accessible parking spaces on account of the increasing size of cars.

All structural elements (ceilings, walls, columns, reinforcements) of multi-storey car parks must be fire resistant. The recommended clear access height for car parks above and below the ground is 2.20 m. An addition of 25 cm is practical for the direction signage for cars and pedestrians, plus a further 5 cm for later resurfacing. This gives a total height of 2.50 m plus construction over the access ways, thus a storey height of 2.75–3.50 m, depending on the chosen method of construction. A relatively close spacing of columns can reduce building cost without impairing function if the construction height is carefully chosen → ❷ – ❸. Wide-spanning column-free constructions have 7–12% less column area on plan → ❹.

Underground car parks result in considerably higher costs for construction and operation than those above ground.

Uphill sections and ramps must be designed and built in line with the above → ❽. Straight or spiral car park ramps are created by sloping the floor slab → p. 393, or forming spirals → ❻, with vehicles both sides of the access way. The areas, including access areas, on which a certain number of vehicles can be parked can be determined for preliminary design from → ❶. The examples → p. 393 and p. 394 show layouts of multi-storey car parks and ramp arrangements. Reinforced concrete construction (in in-situ concrete, pre-cast elements or a combined form) comply best with the fire-resistance requirements. Steel structures are normally designed as a main beam/secondary beam system and mostly have to be clad with concrete or fire protection boards, or sprayed, for fire resistance reasons. Car parks catering for passenger cars should be designed for a live loading of 3.5 kN/m² and the ramps for 5 kN/m² for design purposes, for greened roofs 10 kN/m².

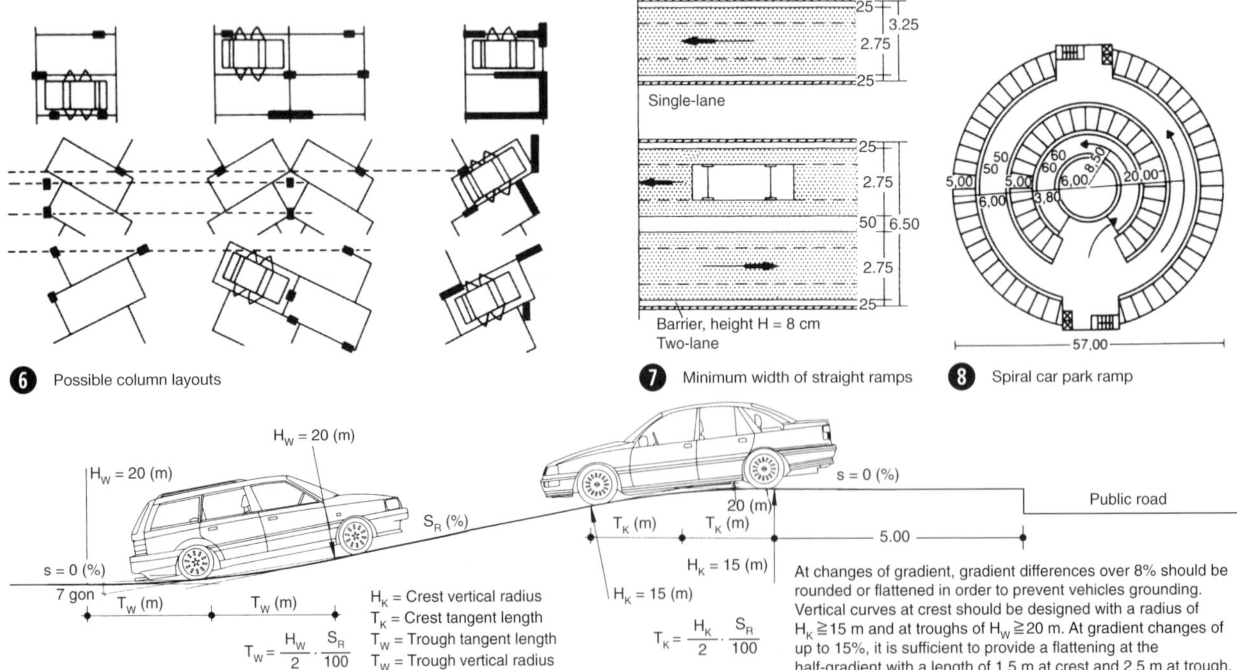

❻ Possible column layouts

❼ Minimum width of straight ramps

❽ Spiral car park ramp

At changes of gradient, gradient differences over 8% should be rounded or flattened in order to prevent vehicles grounding. Vertical curves at crest should be designed with a radius of $H_K \geqq 15$ m and at troughs of $H_W \geqq 20$ m. At gradient changes of up to 15%, it is sufficient to provide a flattening at the half-gradient with a length of 1.5 m at crest and 2.5 m at trough.

❾ Ramps – changes of slope

There are various systems of ramps to overcome height differences and to access the various storeys of multi-storey car parks. The gradient of ramps should not exceed 15%, for small car parks 20%. Between public roads and ramps with more than 5° gradient, there must be a horizontal run of ≧5 m length, or in the case of ramps for cars the run should be ≧3 m long, with ramps at up to 10% gradient. Possible arrangements of ramps can be divided into four groups:

Straight, parallel and continuous multi-storey ramps with intermediate landing, access and exit opposite → ❶.

Sloping floor levels (no-loss full ramp system). The entire area with parking spaces is on a slope, a space-saving system. Slope ≧6%.

Half-storey offset levels (D'Humy ramps). Parking spaces are on half-storeys and the height difference is overcome by short ramps. This is a space-saving system but not very smooth to drive around and therefore only intended for smaller car parks → ❶, ❻ and ❽.

Spiral ramps. This system is relatively expensive yet has poor visibility, and the circular form leads to residual areas, which are hard to exploit → ❶ – ❺. The spiral ramps must have a transverse gradient of ≧3%. The radius of the inner road edge is ≧5 m. In large multi-storey car parks, ramps also used by pedestrians must have a ≧80 cm wide raised pavement, unless routes for pedestrians are provided elsewhere.

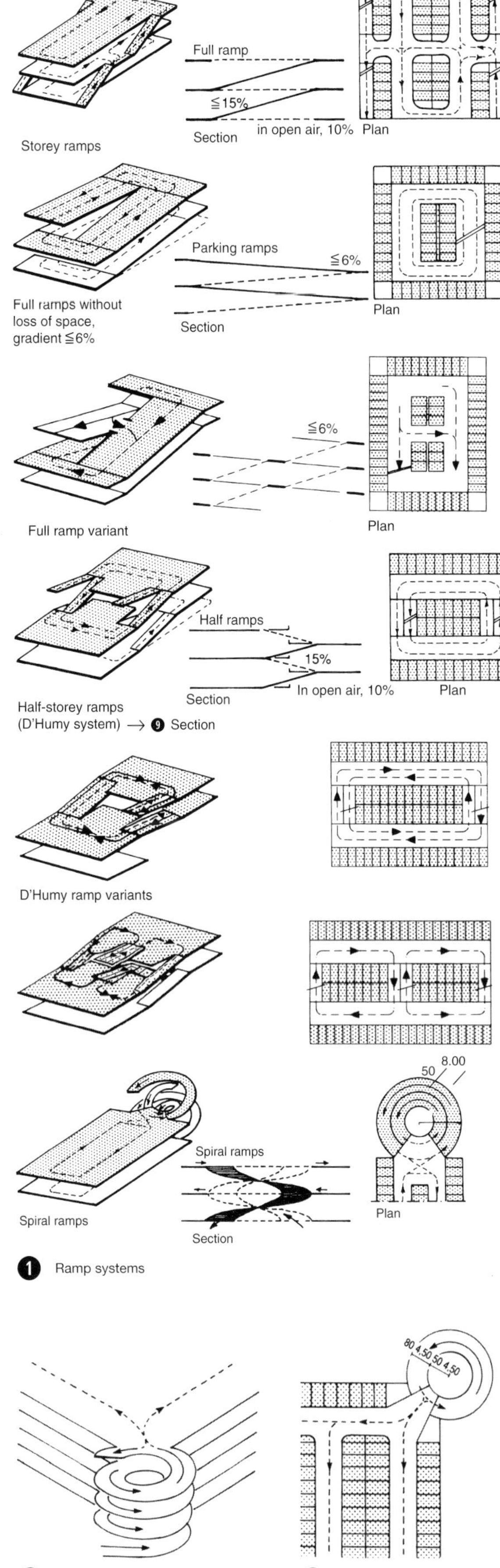

❶ Ramp systems

❷ Separate spiral ramp towers at the corners of the building

❸ Schematic plan → ❷

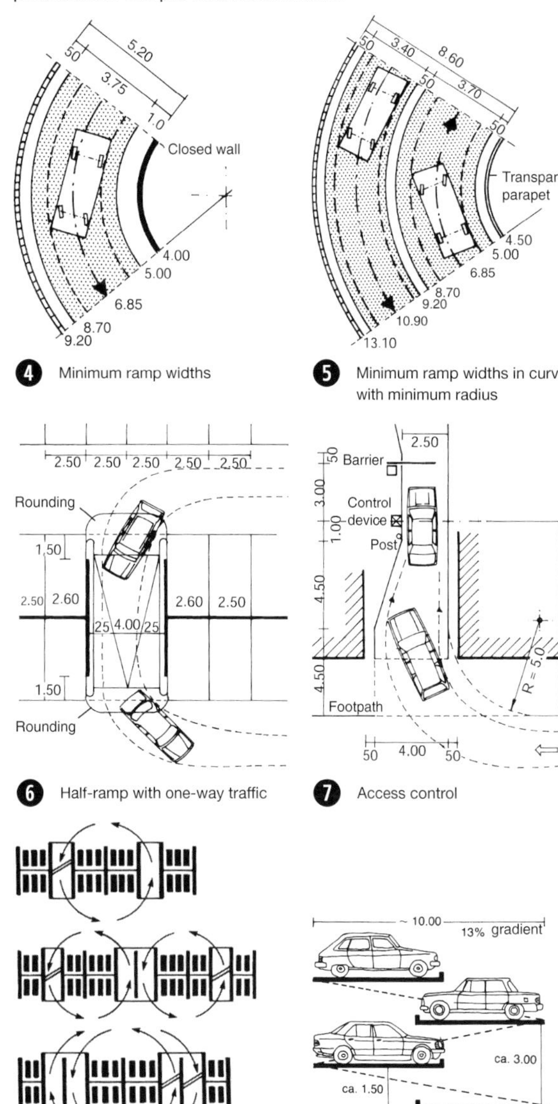

❹ Minimum ramp widths

❺ Minimum ramp widths in curve with minimum radius

❻ Half-ramp with one-way traffic

❼ Access control

❽ Basic forms of D'Humy ramps. Ramps with 13–15% gradient

❾ Dovetailing of half-storeys → ❽

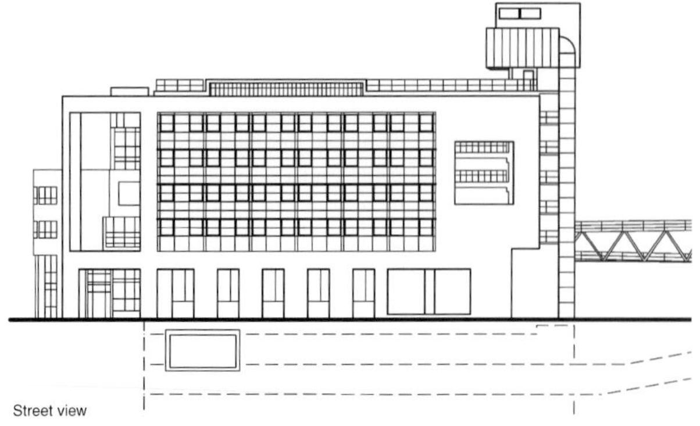

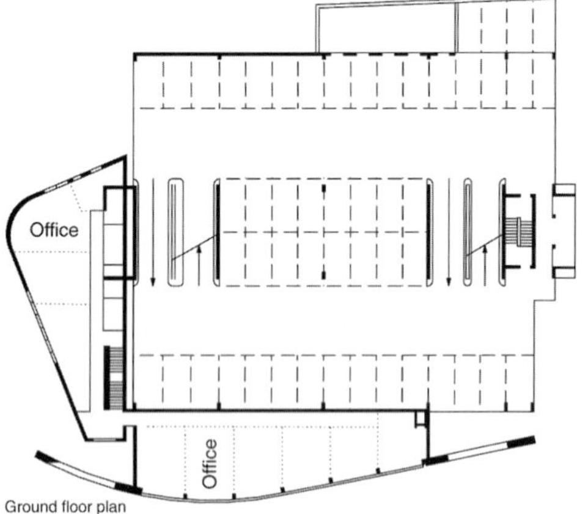

1 Multi-storey car park with additional use: offices incorporated in the façade
Arch.: Kister Scheithauer Gross

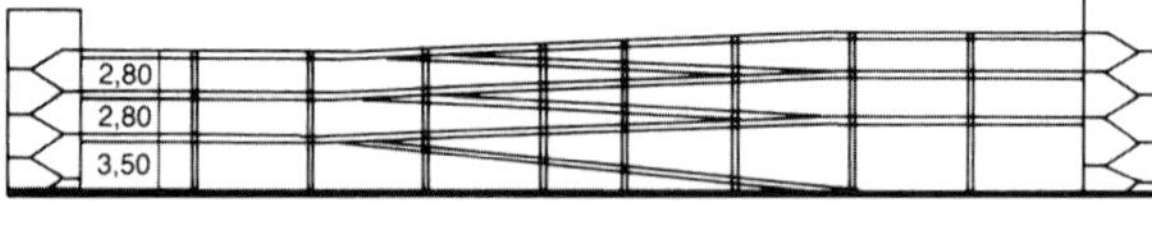

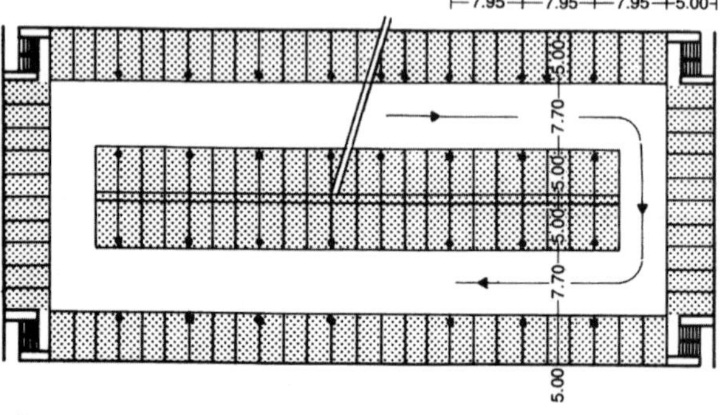

2 Multi-storey car park with access route ramps

According to the Garage (multi-storey car park) Regulations, small car parks are of ≧100 m², medium car parks 100–1000 m² and large car parks ≧1000 m² usable area. Underground car parks are defined as having the floor level ≧1.30 m below ground level. Large multi-storey car parks must have separate access and exits. They are located near large traffic concentrations like those at stations, airports, shopping centres, theatres, cinemas, offices, administrative buildings and large residential buildings. Medium and large multi-storey car parks must be in easily accessible areas.

Such car parks must have a clear height of min. 2.0 m in areas accessible on foot, also under support beams, ventilation ducts and other building elements. The ground floor is generally higher, as it usually has other uses.

Escape routes of max. 30 m are required to the stairs or exits.

For vans the clear height is 2.50 m. Floor loadings according to the relevant standard. Open multi-storey car parks have apertures, which cannot be closed, leading directly into the open air, with a size of one third of the total area of the envelope wall, with the opposite wall at a maximum distance of 70 m. These provide transverse ventilation even with weather protection measures.

Concerning the minimum dimensions for access, exits and internal routes, these must include no space for starting to drive round a curve. Particularly where ramps join to internal routes at right angles, additional room must be provided for the start of driving round the corner and the relevant minimum radii must be complied with. It must also be possible for larger cars to drive in and out without manoeuvring processes → p. 393 **6**. The planned traffic routeing must always be checked against the relevant swept curves.

Criteria for the quality of multi-storey car parks:
The scale of the façades of multi-storey car parks should fit into their surroundings. The façade elevation can also be used for other functions, for example as offices → **1**. Further criteria: integration into urban planning coherence, natural lighting and ventilation, greening, uncomplicated system for charging fees, good access to public transport – Park and Ride.

Safe operation
Video surveillance, glass areas in lobbies (observe fire protection requirements), visual contact with the outside, visibility through the longest possible column spacing, light colours differentiating the storeys, distinctive marking of parking spaces to help visitors find them again.

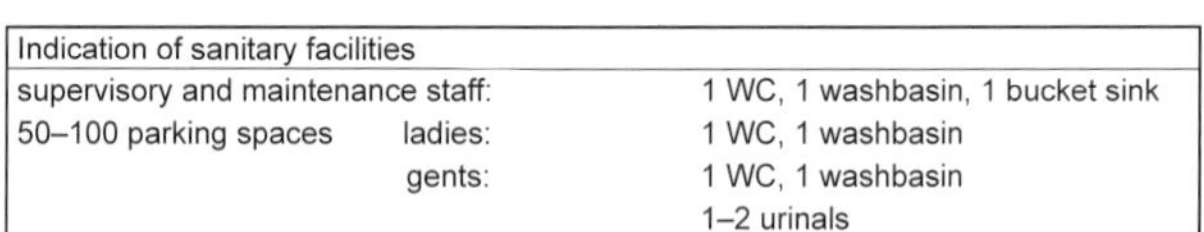

Indication of sanitary facilities		
supervisory and maintenance staff:		1 WC, 1 washbasin, 1 bucket sink
50–100 parking spaces	ladies:	1 WC, 1 washbasin
	gents:	1 WC, 1 washbasin
		1–2 urinals

3 Guidelines for sanitary facilities in large multi-storey car parks

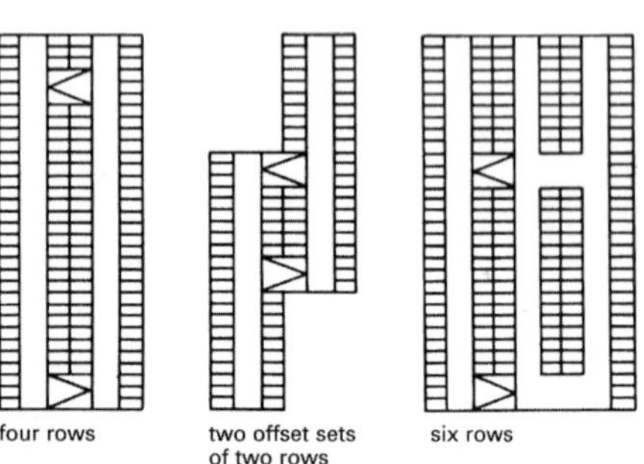

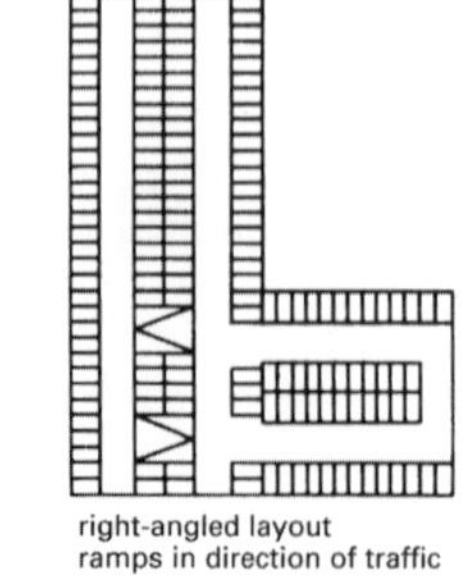

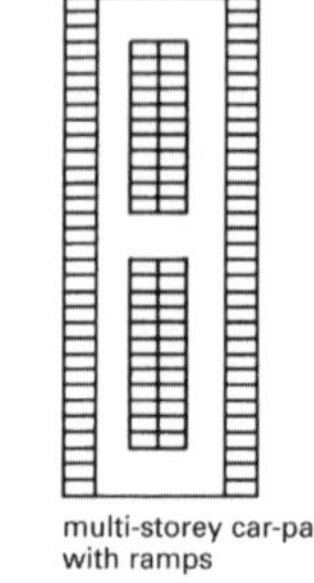

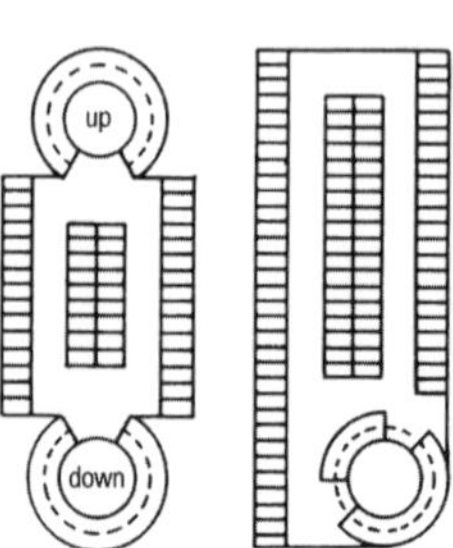

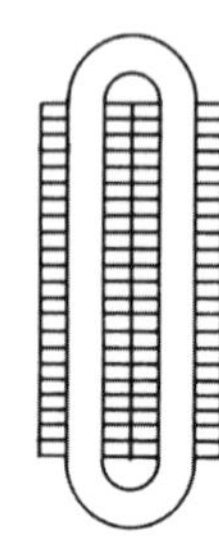

4 Examples of the layout of parking spaces and ramps

5.30–5.40 3.40

❶ Dependent parking of two vehicles

5.50 3.20

❷ Dependent parking, inclined, without a pit

Single Double 2.60–3.00 4.90–5.15–5.35

❸ Plan

5.30–5.40 3.25 1.70

❹ Independent parking of two (four) vehicles above each other

5.30–5.40 2.90 1.70 1.55

❺ Space-saving parking on an incline

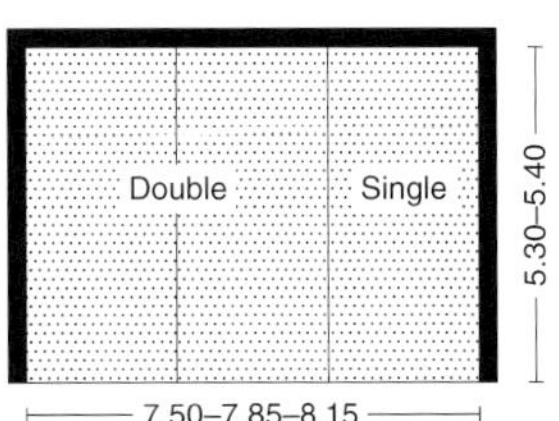

❻ Plan

5.30–5.40 5.00 3.45

❼ Three parking spaces, accessible horizontally

5.30–5.40 4.60 3.45

❽ Accessible on an incline

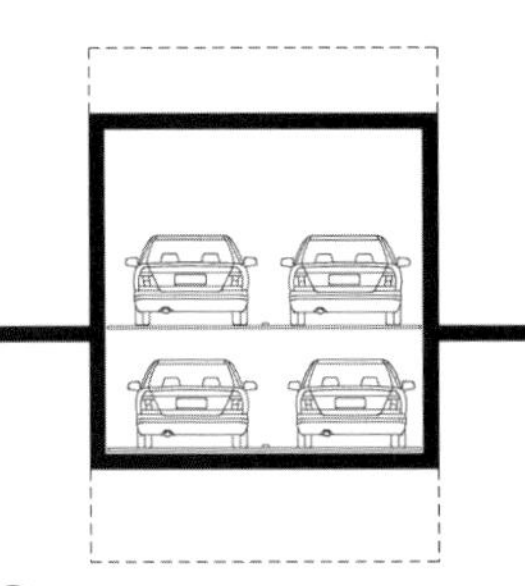

❾ Parking lift double system → ❸ – ❻

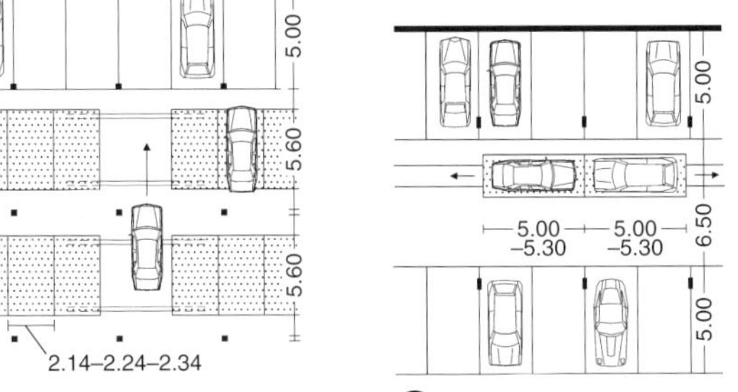

❿ Parking platform – sideways movement

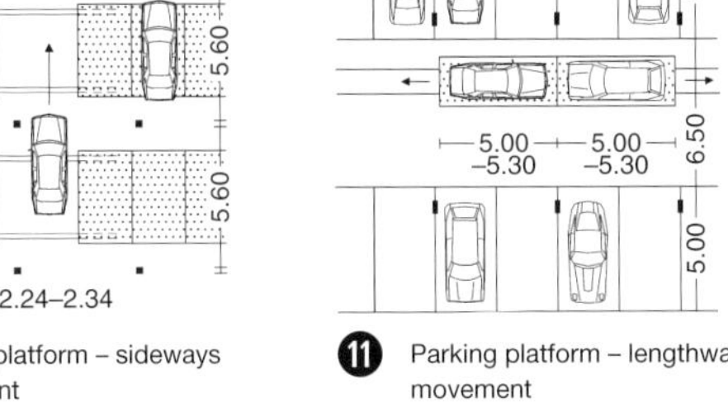

⓫ Parking platform – lengthways movement

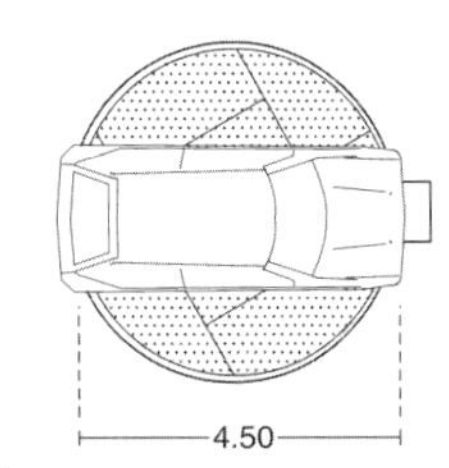

⓬ Turntable rotating 360°

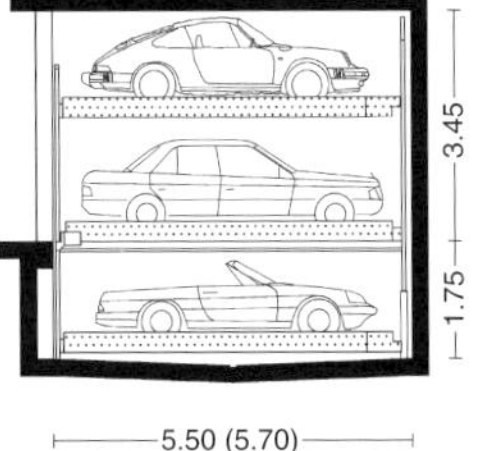

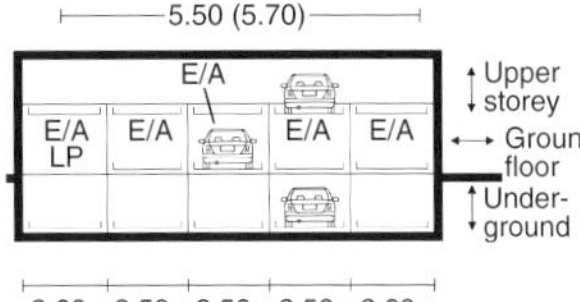

⓭ Combilift with three parking levels and pit

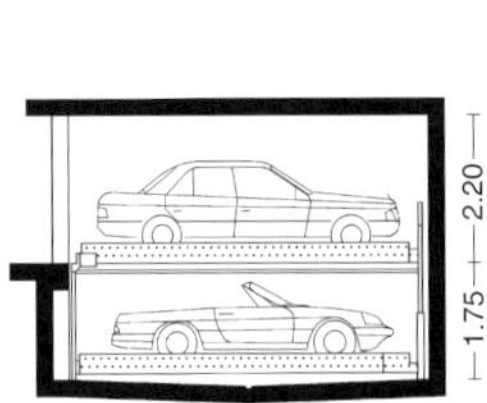

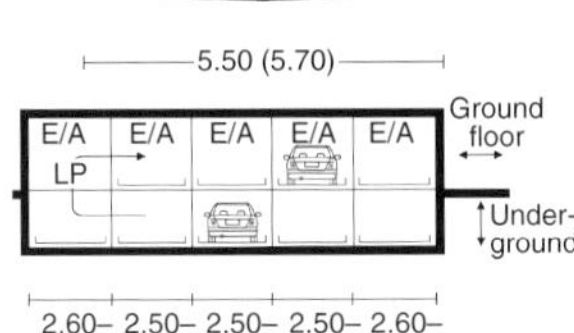

⓮ Combilift with two parking levels and pit

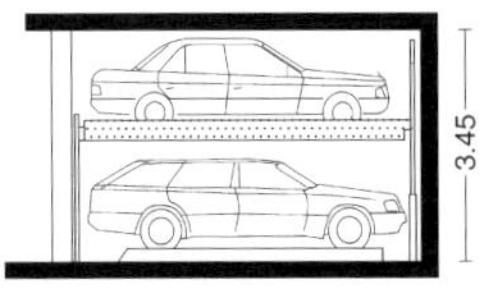

5.40 (5.70)

E/A; E/A LP; E/A; E/A; E/A; Upper storey; Ground floor

2.60– 2.80 2.50– 2.70 2.50– 2.70 2.50– 2.70 2.60– 2.80

LP = empty space E/A = Entry, exit

⓯ Combilift with two parking levels

Parking systems are mostly used for private parking. The selection and specification of the system should also take larger than normal vehicles into account (e.g. off-road vehicles, vans and sports utility vehicles – SUVs).

Two cars can be parked one above the other in single garages on movable platforms → ❶ – ❷. The operation is electric, or in case of power cuts, with a hand pump. A parking lift can handle up to three cars → ❼ – ❽ as a row of garages in a courtyard or parking garages, and operated by the doorman with a control panel. Loading per parking space is 2500 kg. The gradient on driving into and out of the garage ≦14%.

Parking platform systems → ❿ – ⓫ enable space-saving parking for various amounts of room. Cars stand on parking platforms, which are moved via a control desk to clear the access route.

Parking platforms – lengthways movement: parking platforms are moved at the touch of a button → ⓫. Unoccupied parking platforms can be driven over. Sideways movement → ❿ is used where greater available depth could provide two, three or more rows of places but too much area would otherwise be lost for access. Therefore, in front of a stationary row of places, sideways-moving parking platforms are provided, which can be moved so that the places behind can be reached.

Parking platform/parking lift → ❶ – ❾ dependent parking: in the open air parking systems can be built only with horizontal platforms → ❶ see also p. 396.

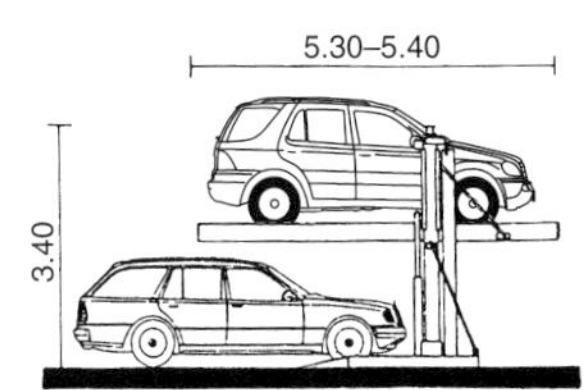

⓰ Parking systems should consider the heights of different cars

Transport

PARKING FACILITIES

Vehicles – cars
Vehicles – turning
Parking spaces
Multi-storey car parks
Ramps
Multi-storey car park regulations
Parking systems
Vehicles – trucks
Trucks – parking and turning
Service areas
Petrol stations
Car wash

PARKING FACILITIES

Parking Systems

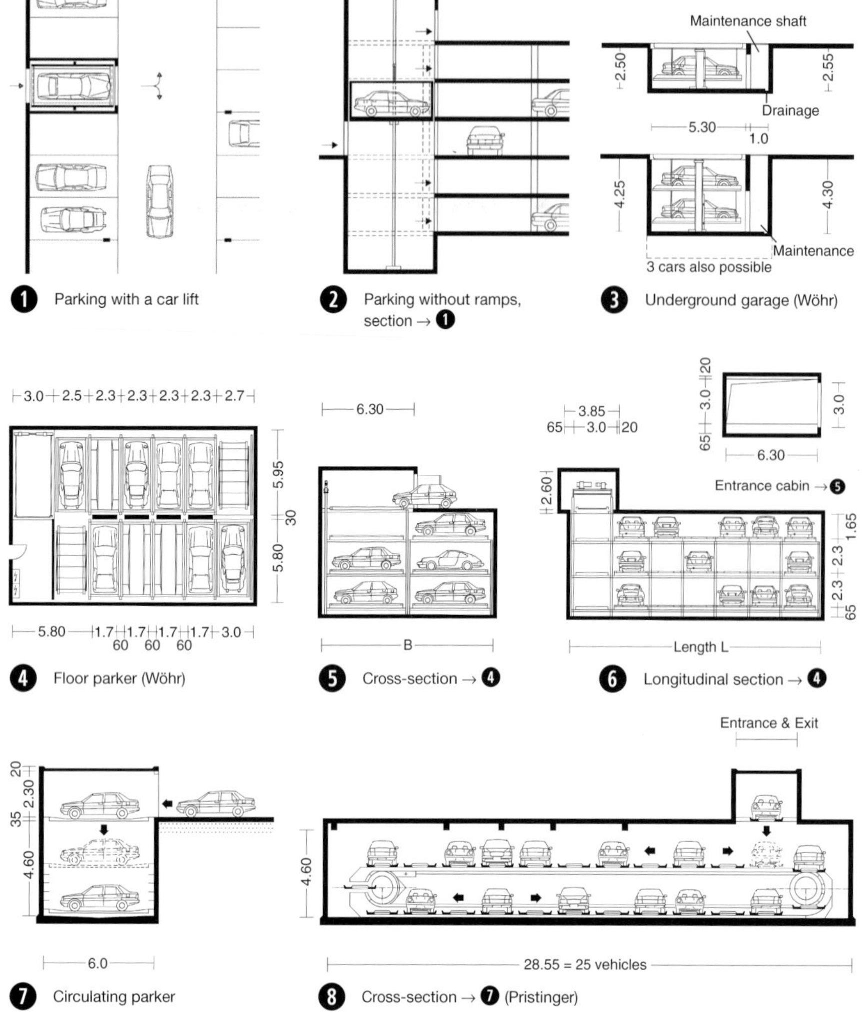

❶ Parking with a car lift

❷ Parking without ramps, section → ❶

❸ Underground garage (Wöhr)

❹ Floor parker (Wöhr)

❺ Cross-section → ❹

❻ Longitudinal section → ❹

❼ Circulating parker

❽ Cross-section → ❼ (Pristinger)

Car lift – parking lift → ❶
A simple mechanical parking mechanism that can be installed in multi-storey car parks to replace the function of ramps, normally because they are impossible due to lack of space. The lift transports the vehicle with driver to the chosen level. Horizontal transport is usually by driving as normal. The average number of parking spaces is 8–30 on one or more levels.

The fully mechanical parking tower → ❾ – ❿ creates additional parking space not horizontally but mainly vertically. Vehicles are no longer moved horizontally; the lift transports the vehicles to levels with a parking bay to the left and right. Parking towers are ideal for providing 10–40 parking spaces in building gaps, and can be underground or overground.

Parking shelves → ❻ provide vertical and horizontal transport of vehicles. This is an expensive system and only suitable for large installations. Theoretically, it can be extended in height and length as required.

The **circulating parker** → ❼ – ❽ can be delivered in vertical and horizontal versions, usually with 20–40 parking platforms. The platforms circulate until a free platform or the requested car arrives at the entrance. The advantage of the vertical circulating parker is its small ground area of approx. 50 m^2 for about 20 cars. Horizontal circulating parkers are more suitable for underground parking.

Parking cylinder → ⓫ – ⓮ Internal parking spaces are arranged in a circle with approx. 10 vehicles per storey. 10–12 levels are usual, mostly underground. The parking spaces are accessed by a rotating lift, or rotating parking spaces are delivered by a vertical lift.

Sliding parker/floor parker → ❹ – ❻. Lengthways and sideways sliding on one or more levels provides 6–24 places per floor. There must be two empty spaces per floor for manoeuvring. A car lift provides vertical transport.

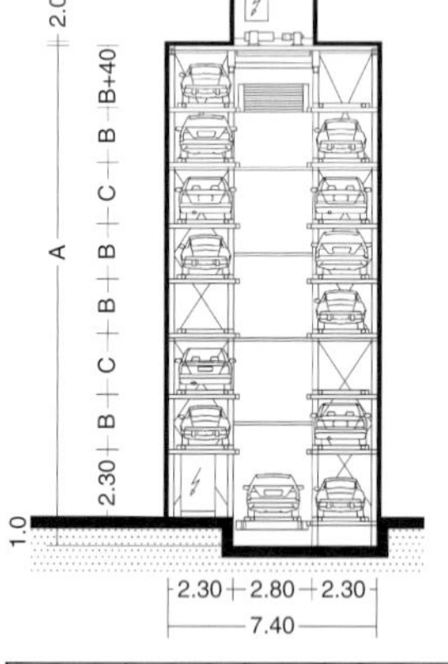

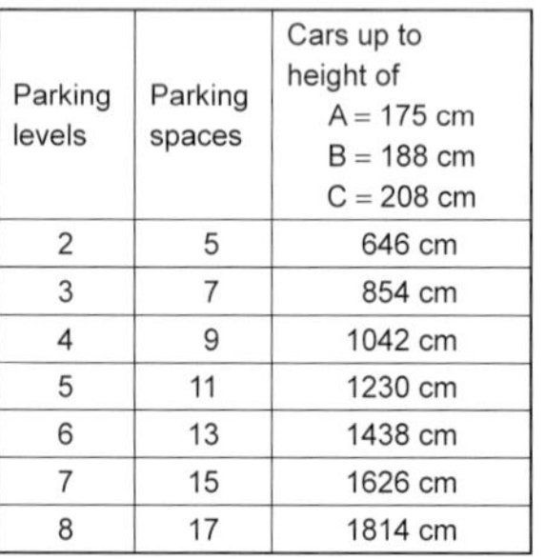

Parking levels	Parking spaces	Cars up to height of A = 175 cm B = 188 cm C = 208 cm
2	5	646 cm
3	7	854 cm
4	9	1042 cm
5	11	1230 cm
6	13	1438 cm
7	15	1626 cm
8	17	1814 cm

❾ Cross-section of Parksaf (Wöhr)

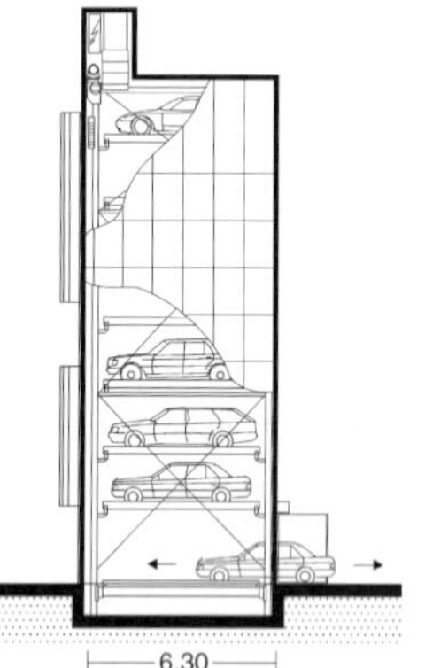

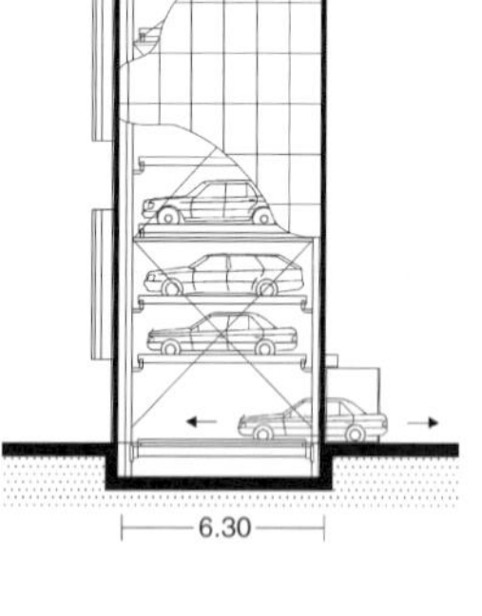

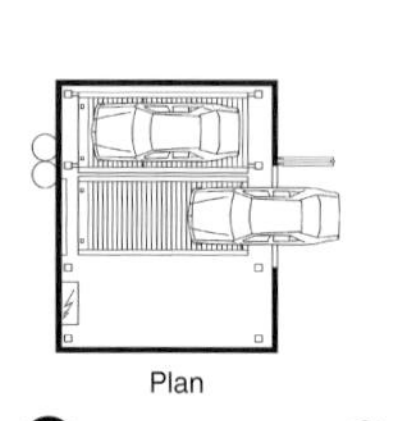

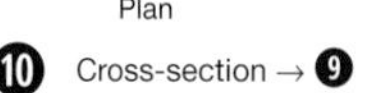

Plan

❿ Cross-section → ❾

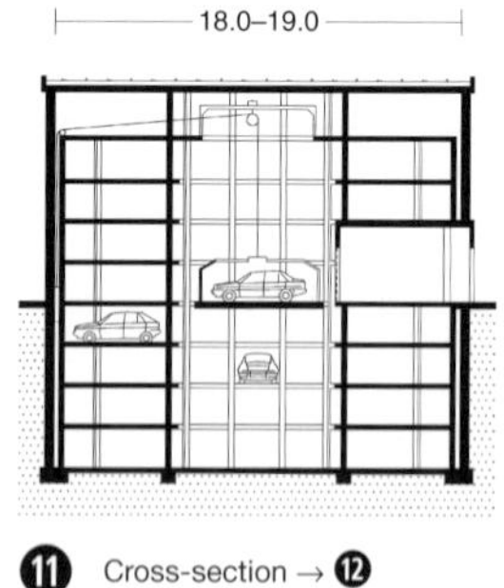

⓫ Cross-section → ⓬

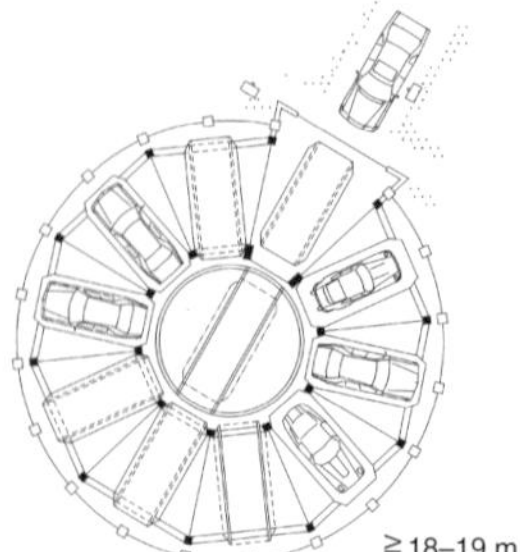

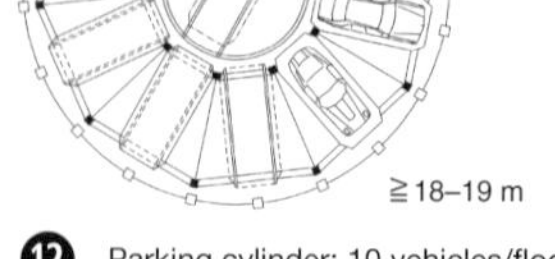

⓬ Parking cylinder: 10 vehicles/floor (Meyer)

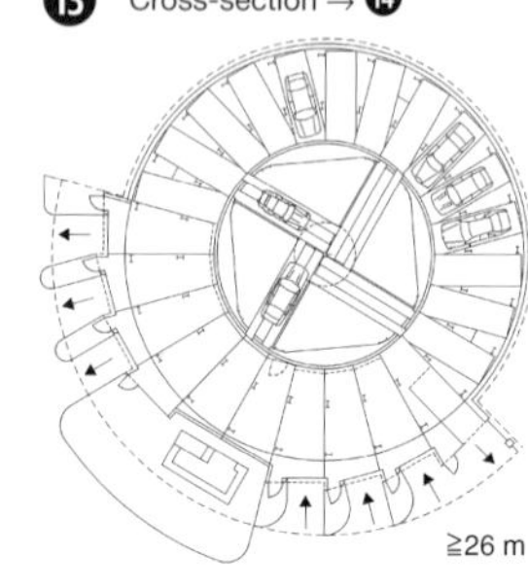

⓭ Cross-section → ⓮

⓮ Parking cylinder: 24 vehicles/floor

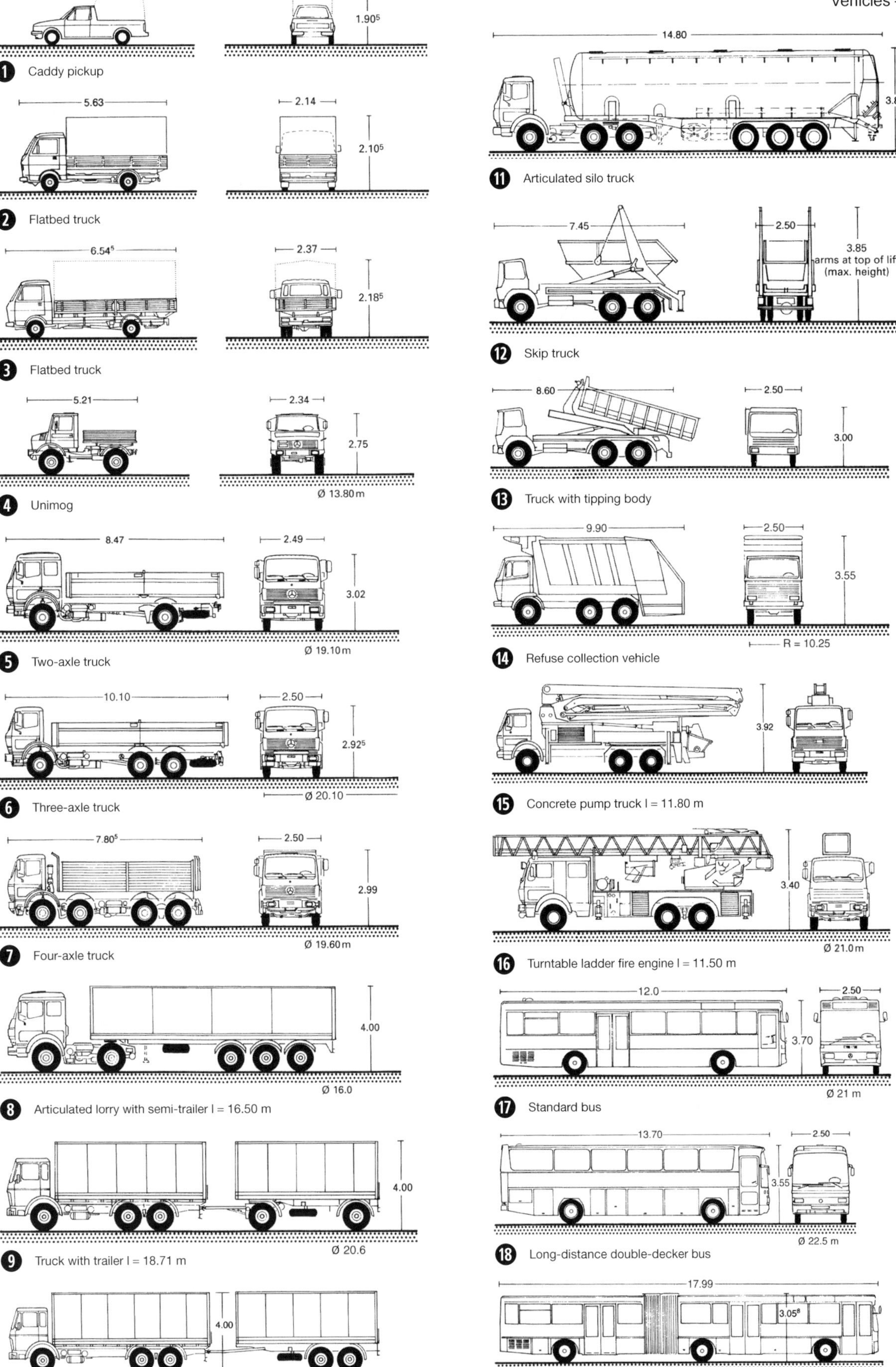

1 Caddy pickup

2 Flatbed truck

3 Flatbed truck

4 Unimog

5 Two-axle truck

6 Three-axle truck

7 Four-axle truck

8 Articulated lorry with semi-trailer l = 16.50 m

9 Truck with trailer l = 18.71 m

10 Truck with tandem trailer l = 18 m, w = 2.50 m

11 Articulated silo truck

12 Skip truck

13 Truck with tipping body

14 Refuse collection vehicle

15 Concrete pump truck l = 11.80 m

16 Turntable ladder fire engine l = 11.50 m

17 Standard bus

18 Long-distance double-decker bus

19 Standard articulated bus, w = 2.50 m

5.75 — 11.25 — 5.75   6.50 — 15.50 — 6.50   3.50   ≤ 18.00

❶ 45° parking, HGVs and buses
45° parking, articulated buses and lorries

5.00 — 13.00 — 5.00   3.50

❷ 30° parking, truck with trailer

12.00 — 12.00   4.00

❸ 90° parking, 12 m bus

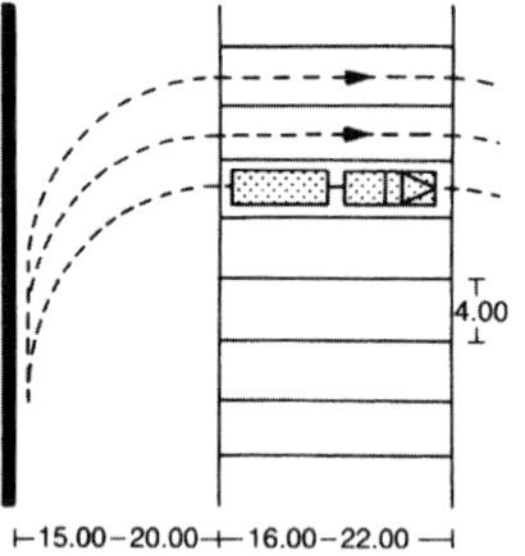

❹ 90° parking, truck with trailer

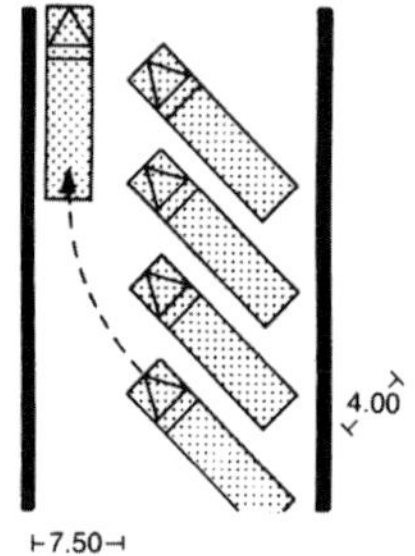

❺ Parking, less than 45°

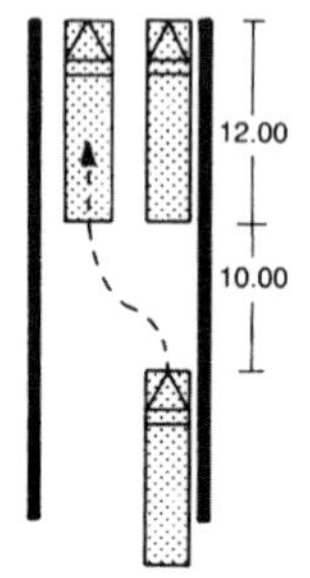

❻ Loss of space, parking parallel to kerb

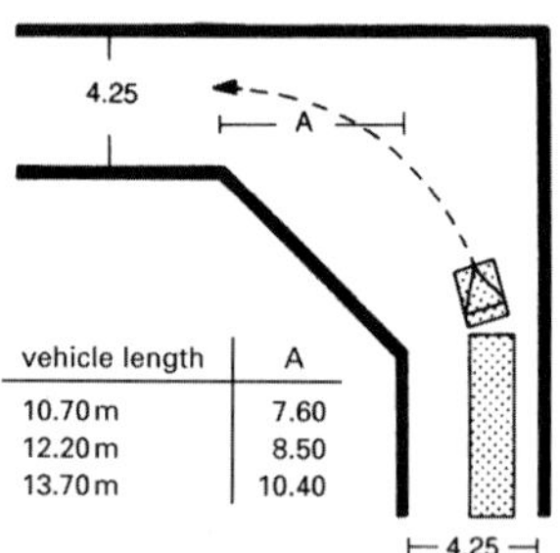

vehicle length	A
10.70 m	7.60
12.20 m	8.50
13.70 m	10.40

❼ Space needed at street corners

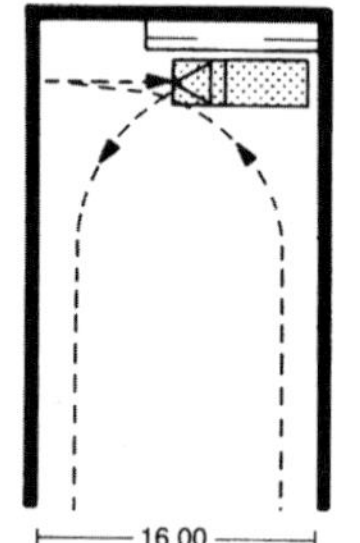

❽ Turning possibilities in restricted locations

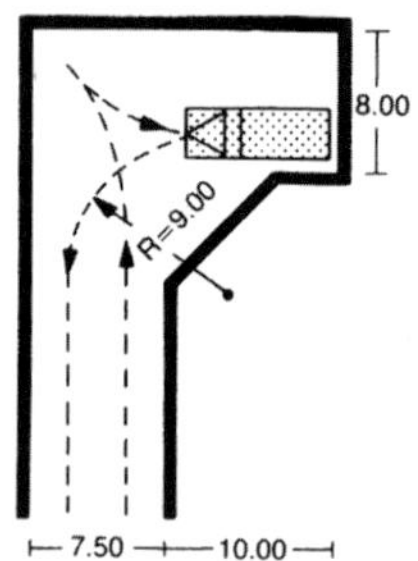

❾ Hammerhead turn in very restricted space

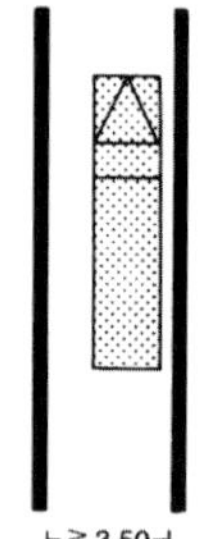

❿ Access

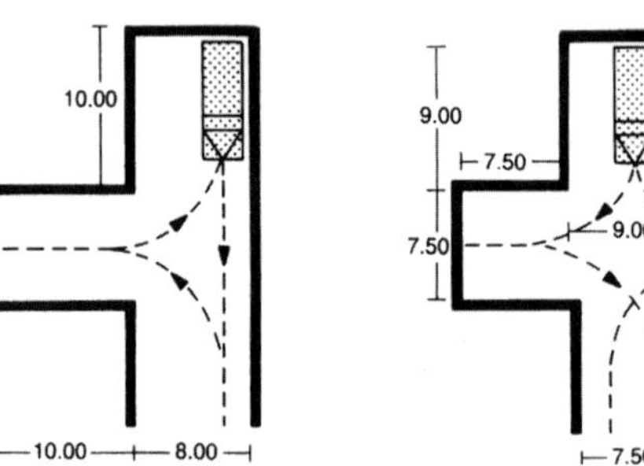

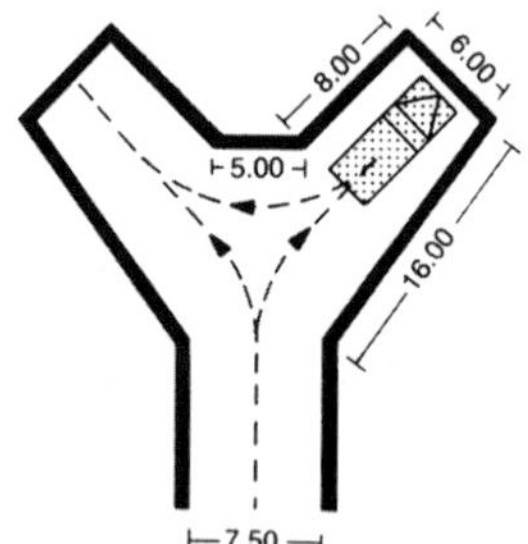

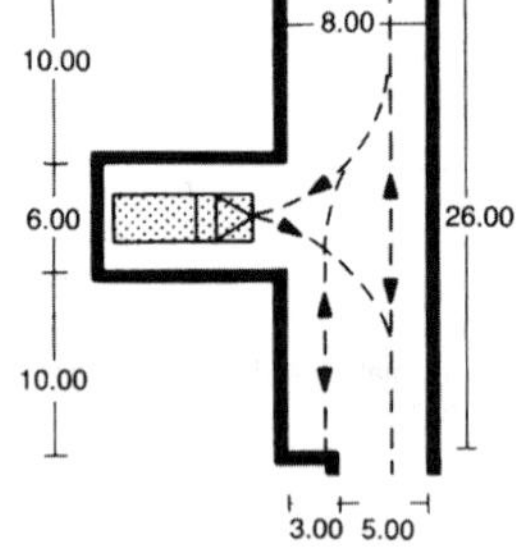

⓫ Further turning places: options for delivery trucks

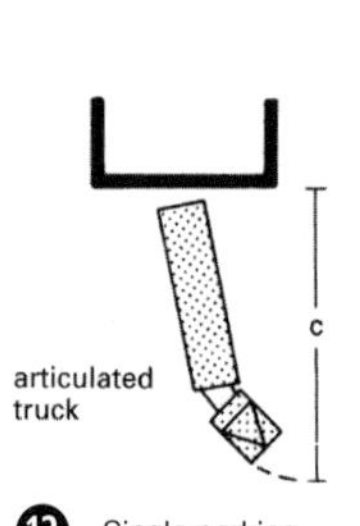

⓬ Single parking

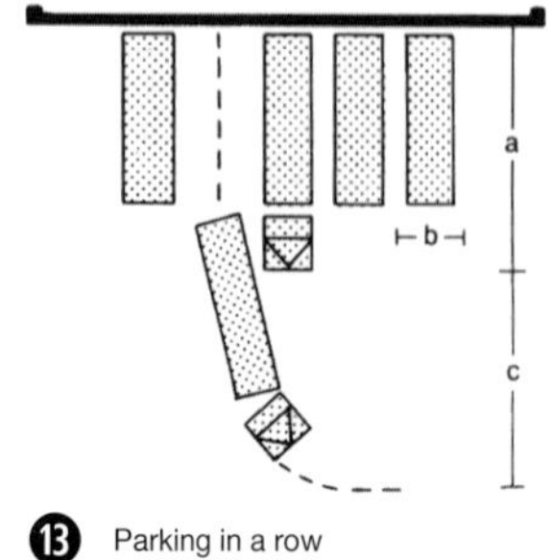

⓭ Parking in a row

Free zone for entry and exit of:	Vehicle length a	Parking space width b	Keep free zone c
HGV 22 t	10.00	3.00	14.00
		3.65	13.10
		4.25	11.90
HGV single vehicle	12.00	3.00	14.65
		3.65	13.50
		4.25	12.80
articulated lorry	15.00	3.00	17.35
		3.65	15.00
		4.25	14.65

⓮ Table for ⓬ and ⓭

Owing to the large variation in the size of trucks, it is not worth marking out permanent lanes or bays on the ground. The basic measurements for space and actual requirements for the manoeuvring and parking of trucks are taken from the vehicle dimensions and whether driving straight, cornering, or entering or driving out of the parking place. Especially while cornering, the swept curve of the trailing inner rear wheels must be taken into account.

The turning circle for the largest vehicles permitted under the road traffic regulations is an outer turning circle radius of 12 m. An outer turning circle radius of 10 m is nevertheless considered sufficient for the vast majority of trucks which come within the scope of the regulations → p. 389.

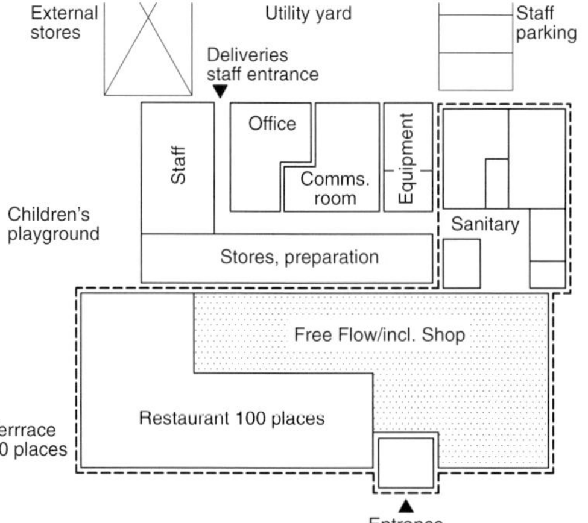

1 Functional scheme for a service area for 100 people

CUSTOMER AREA		approx. m²
Sales rooms		**345.0**
1	Variably assigned	
	according to tenant structure	245.0
	Customer wet rooms	94.8
2	WC corridor	24.8
3	Baby changing room	3.4
4	Truck drivers' showers	8.4
5	Gents WC	22.3
6	Cleaner	6.9
7	Ladies WC	22.5
8	Disabled WC	6.5
BUILDING SERVICES AREA		
9	**Corridor building services area**	**39.5**
	Building services	**25.9**
10	Electricity	7.3
11	Heating	5.3
19	Media	3.3

Stores area		**70.6**
12	Cold store cell	2.7
13	Cool room cell	8.8
14	Cool room cell	8.3
21	Washing up	13.0
23	Preparation	13.7
22/24/25	Stores	26.1
Administration/staff		**57.4**
15	Office	25.6
16/17	Changing rooms Ladies/gents	18.1
18	Staff rest room	6.9
20	Staff WCs Gents/ladies	6.8
Net floor area		**633.2**

The increased capacity of HGV transport and the required rest times for the drivers have resulted in a great demand for service areas featuring parking facilities of generous dimensions and corresponding infrastructure.

Service areas

Service areas (Raststätte) on autobahns in Germany are administered by the company Tank und Rast. The facilities are situated directly on the autobahn with access by slip roads. In addition to the petrol station, further service units are operated by leaseholders. According to the size of the facilities, this can be fast snack bars, restaurants, sales areas or overnight accommodation.

Autohofs are service areas which are next to the autobahn, but also accessible through normal junctions.

Many other countries have arrangements for service areas similar to those described above.

Service stations

In urban areas, mostly in industrial zones, petrol stations are combined with car washes. The care of cars is the main business.

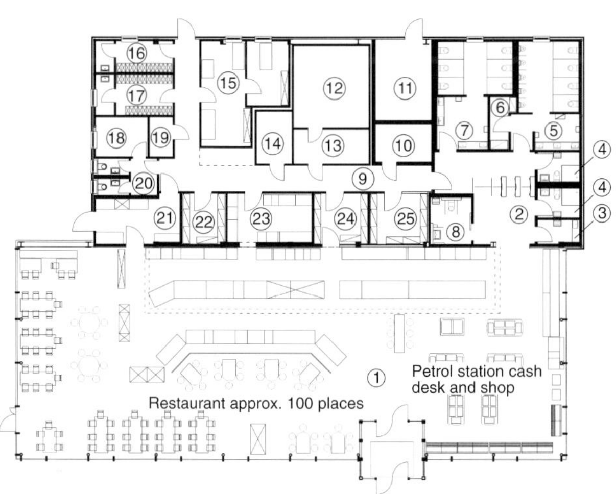

2 In smaller service stations, petrol supply and service areas are combined in one building

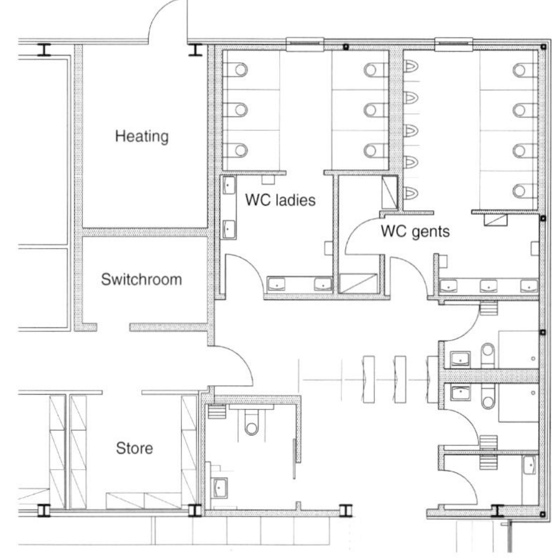

3 Toilet facilities in service areas are leased like the other services. Charging is made possible by a turnstile

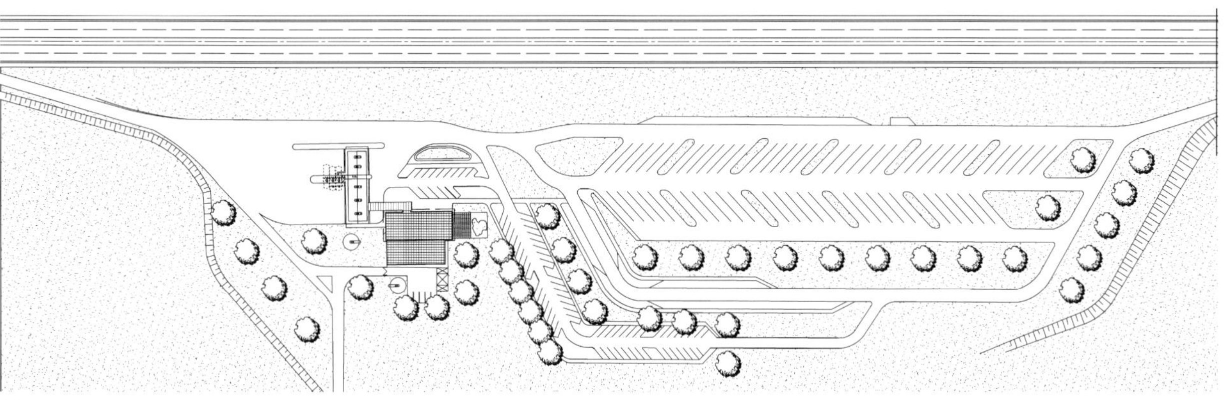

4 Layout of a petrol and service area

Design: Autobahn Tank u. Rast AG

Transport

PARKING FACILITIES
Vehicles – cars
Vehicles – turning
Parking spaces
Multi-storey car parks
Ramps
Multi-storey car park regulations
Parking systems
Vehicles – trucks
Trucks – parking and turning
Service areas
Petrol stations
Car wash

❶ Petrol pump: the multi-product dispenser usual today offers up to five types of fuel at one unit with simultaneous operation from both sides. Single- and double-fuel pumps are now mainly found in company yards.

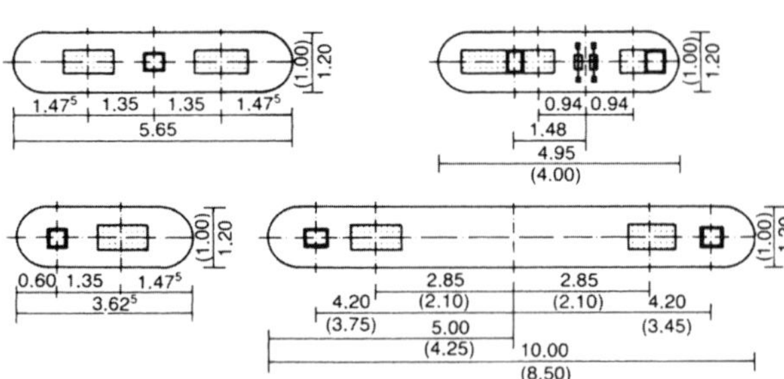

❷ Petrol pump island dimensions (minimum dimensions)

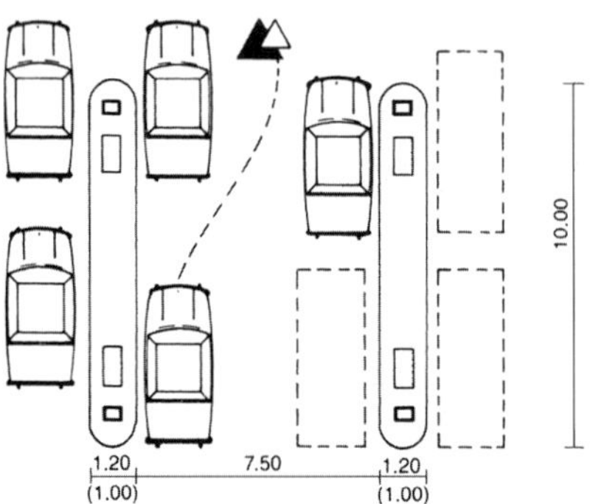

❸ Two long islands parallel to the road, requiring disciplined driving behaviour (minimum dimensions)

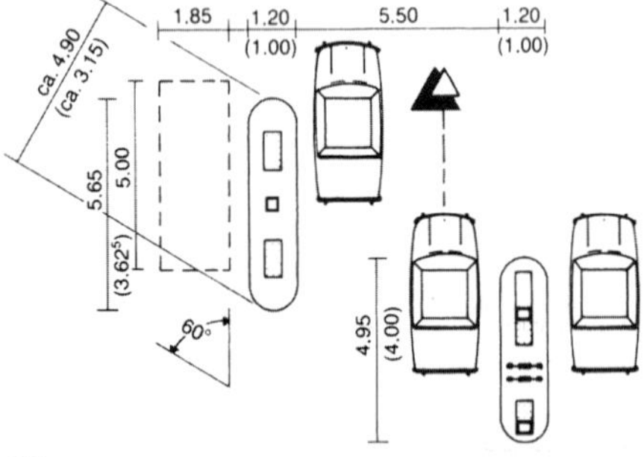

❹ Two short islands at angle less than 60° to the road (minimum dimensions)

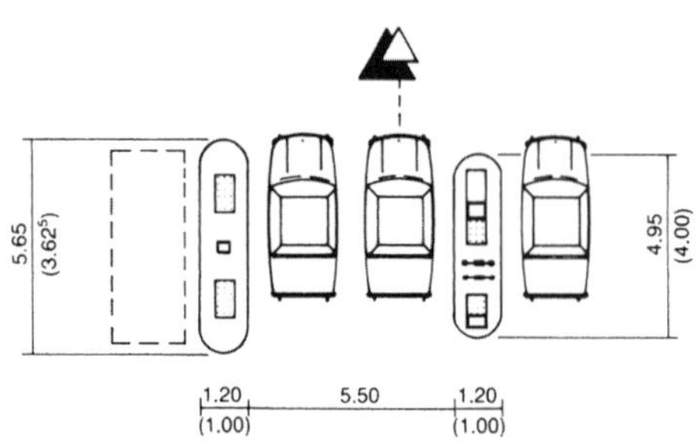

❺ Two short islands parallel to the road (minimum dimensions)

Petrol stations supply fuel and lubricants, mostly in combination with maintenance and care services. Because petrol station shops in Germany are excepted from the shop closing time regulations, the proportion of sales area devoted to car accessories and goods required daily has increased considerably.

Important regulations and technical rules:
In addition to the relevant building regulations:
WHG (water management law) applies, on account of the storage of fuel and associated water, fire and explosion hazards.
VAwS (regulation of requirements for the handling of substances harmful to groundwater) mostly concerns specialist firms and testing duties.
TRwS (technical rules for substances harmful to water)
TRbF (technical rules for flammable liquids)
Petrol stations must be erected by certified specialist firms (WHG).
State regulations control:

1. Parking space size (2.50 × 5.00 m = 12.50 m^2)
2. Required number of parking spaces (e.g. depending on the extent of premises, and the number of petrol pumps and people working at the station).
3. Required queuing space for automatic car wash (e.g. area sufficient for 50% of the hourly washing capacity).

For design purposes, dimensions specific to cars should be considered:

Turning circle:	car 12.50 m	HGV 26.00 m
Vehicle width:	car 1.85 m	HGV 2.50 m
Vehicle length:	car 5.00 m	HGV 18.00 m with trailer

These data can be used to derive the dimensions of pump islands and passage widths → ❸ – ❺.

The paving around the petrol pumps must be impervious to liquids and the run-off channelled into side kerbs and/or a downward slope. These areas (length of the petrol hose + 1 m) must drain through a suitable liquid interceptor or be roofed over. Reduced dimensions for the surfaced area impervious to liquids and the siting of the tanks apply to private petrol stations, categorised as petrol stations for private use with low consumption (the quantities are regulated by the states).

Petrol pumps must have protection against vehicle impact with at least 20 cm spacing and 12 cm height → ❷.

Each petrol pump should if possible dispense all the fuels on offer (multi-dispenser petrol pump). For private petrol stations, there are simple petrol pumps with electronic control systems for personalised control of access and quantity → ❶. Autogas (LPG) filling stations require their own dispensers. There are no requirements concerning surfacing, because autogas is not classed as a liquid hazardous to groundwater. Measures should be taken to ensure rapid distribution of any leaking gas (earth wall or dip into which the gas can be blown by the wind).

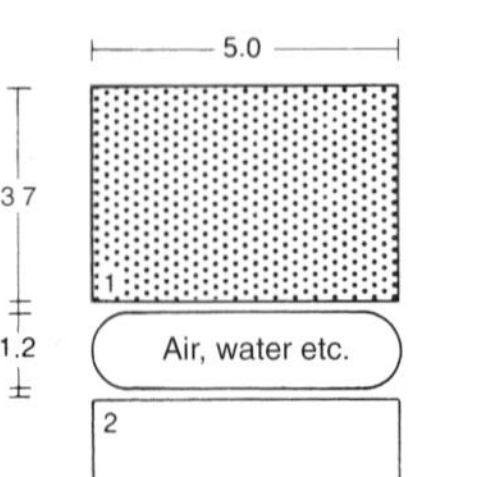

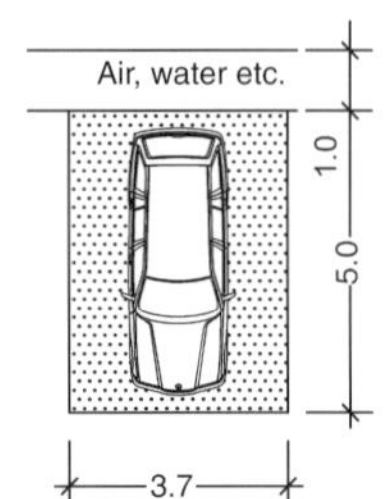

❻ Service points for self-service oil change, air, water etc.

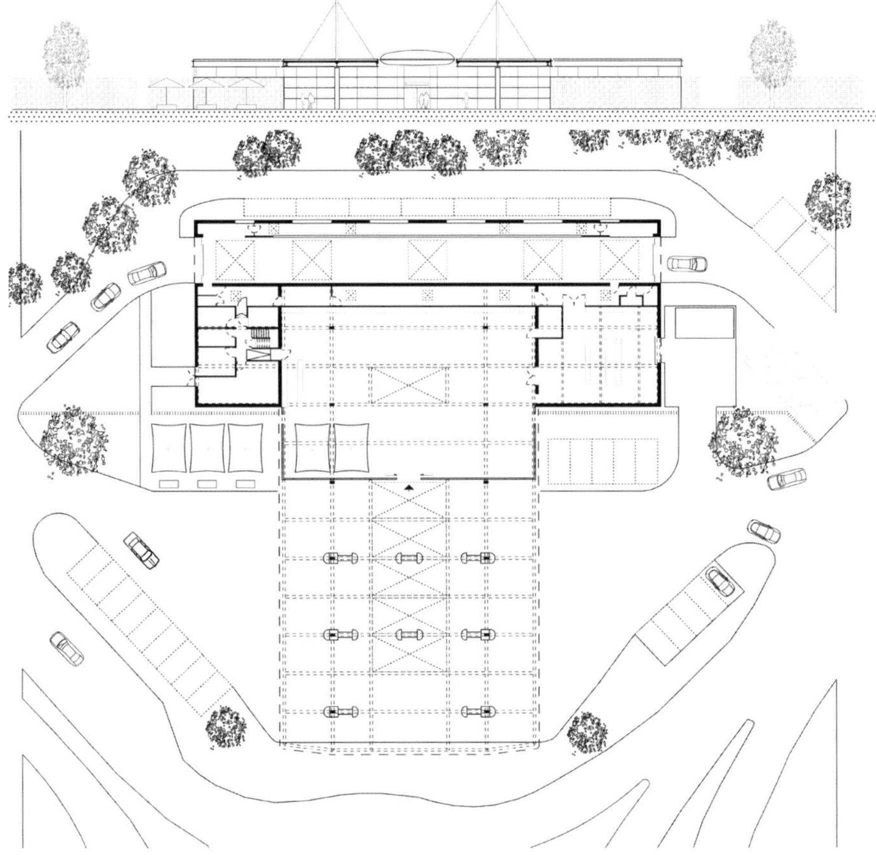

❶ Plan of petrol station with sales, food and car wash. Allguth Station, Unterföhring — Architects: Haack + Höpfner, Munich

Area required

For a simple petrol station, an area of approx. 800 m² is sufficient, with additional services normally approx. 1000 m², and for large service stations 2000 m² and more → ❷.

Services and location

Car drivers should be able to fill up with petrol; check the oil level, radiator water level and tyre pressures (and top them up if necessary) and fill up the windscreen washer water; clean the windscreen, headlight glasses and their hands; buy goods; use the WCs; and carry out various car care tasks (car washing, vacuum cleaner etc.). Petrol stations should be easy to drive into, clearly laid out, easily recognisable from a distance and as near to the road as possible.

The location should be on the left hand side of the road on the way out of town and not in the queuing area in front of traffic lights. Also unfavourable are road crossings, in which case a better solution is a location before the corner with an exit into the side street.

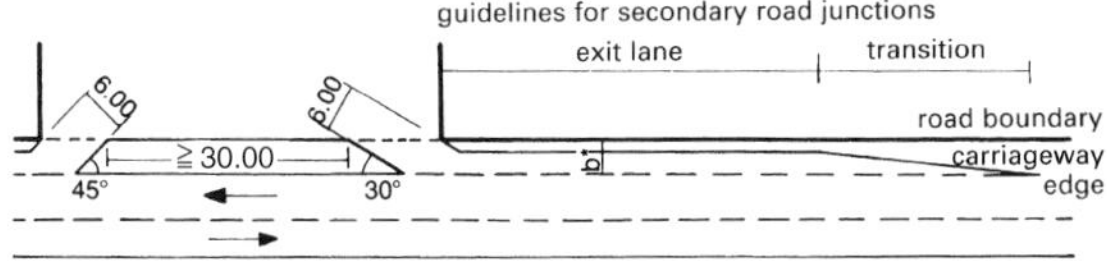

❷ Petrol station access and exit on a clear road

road boundary
carriageway edge
45°
30°
≧30.00
6.00
6.00

❸ Without slowing and accelerating lanes

* for one-way traffic (only needed on access side)
** ≧20 m for 2 pump islands parallel to road. This must be correspondingly greater for additional islands and ≧ 16 m when pump islands are staggered further into the site

sufficient number of parking bays
diesel fuel for trucks
≧25.00*
≧25.00
≧1.20 ≧3.00
≧1.20 ≧3.00
≧1.20
≧10.00*
≧20.00**
road
≧45°
≧45°
6.00
6.00

❹ Petrol station with angled position of the pump islands in an urban area (primarily for traffic in one direction)

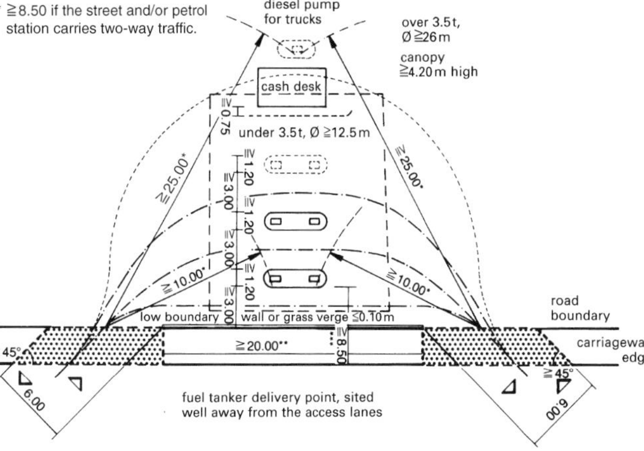

❺ Petrol station for petrol and possibly diesel (HGV ≧3.5 t) in an urban area

❶ Self-service car wash stalls, protected by splash guard walls

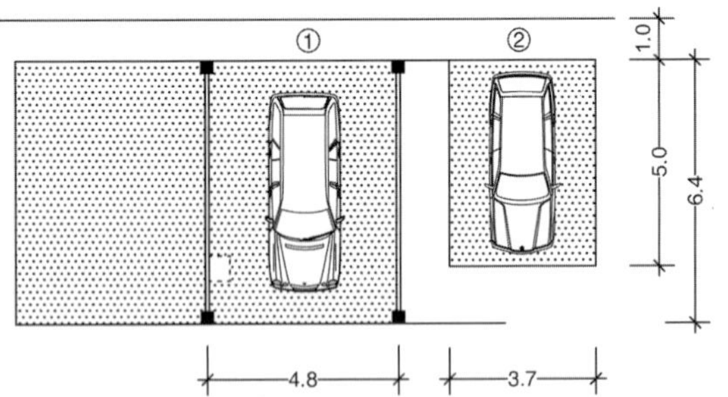

❷ Dimensions for a self-operated car wash ❶ operating with separating walls and a central services room ❷ minimum dimensions for an open-air installation

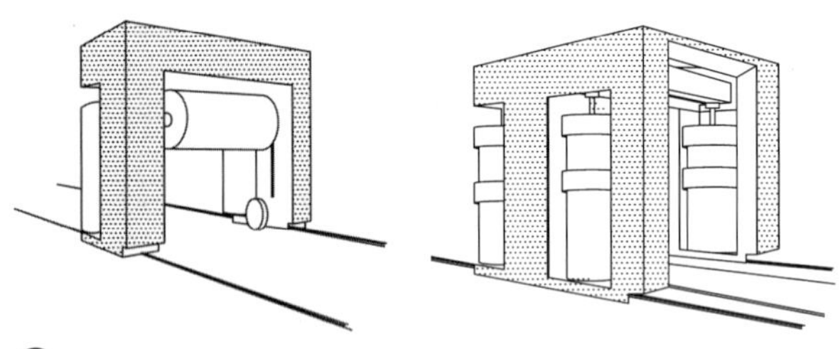

❸ Portal car wash with two sides and a roof brush, and double car wash with four sides and a roof brush

Car wash facilities

These are used for the environmentally friendly washing of cars and are installed as a public service business, also for trucks on the premises of the haulage company. Mobile tyre-washing equipment is available for building sites, tips and landfill sites.

As with petrol stations, the groundwater protection regulations are to be observed. Car washes require, according to system, 100–600 l of water per car. This must be reprocessed and at least 80% recycled. For closed systems (no drainage connection), there is a simplified approval process under groundwater protection regulations. A car wash needs about 40–50 m^3 for settling and silt retention basins (underground tank ∅ 3 m). Fresh water is required to cover evaporation losses, to reduce the salt content in winter, to rinse off and for the application of liquid waxes.

Self-service car wash stalls

These are mostly roofed parking spaces, on which cars can be cleaned by the customer with a high-pressure cleaner and hand washing brushes. Small installations have one or two places, larger installations up to 12 places, which can be served by a central services room → ❶ – ❷.

Portal car wash

This takes up little space. The customer has to get out and the entire washing equipment in the portal then travels over to the parked car. This type of car wash can be installed in the open air, but is better indoors, ideally enabling the customer to drive through. Because the portal stops in front of the car parking space when not in operation, the building is min. 9–10 m long, width min. 4.60 m, height min. 3 m (for portals for cars up to 2.1 m in height). The clear space at the side between portal and building elements is min. 50 cm.

A portal car wash can wash about 5000–50 000 cars per year or 5–18 vehicles per hour → ❸.

Tunnel car wash

The vehicles are carried on a conveyor through fixed washing and after-care portals. This technology enables a high capacity and various washing programmes in the same pass time. The length of the car wash is 20–60 m. A tunnel car wash can process 30–100 vehicles per hour or 20 000–200 000 per year. → ❹.

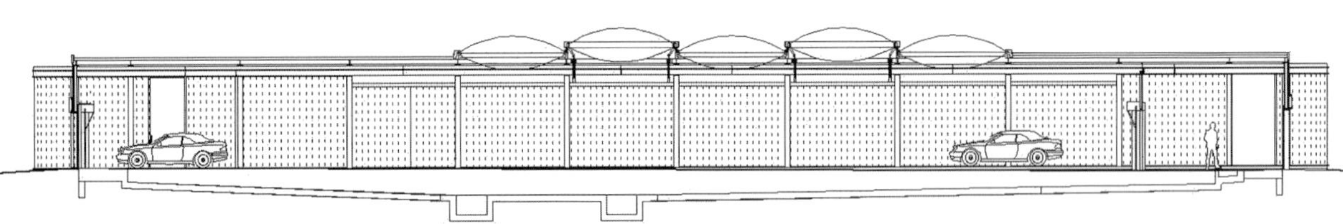

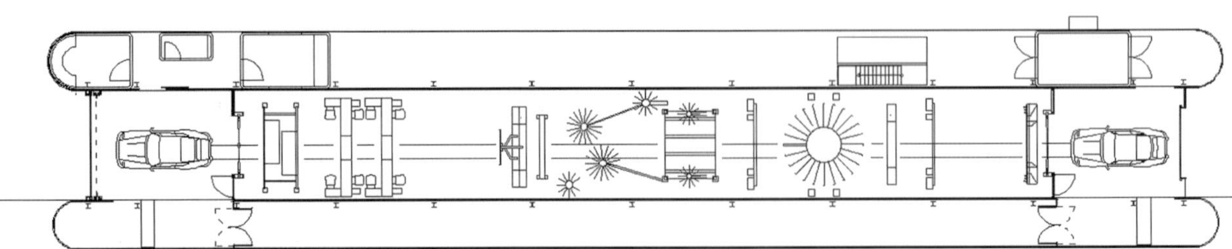

❹ Plan and section of the Allguth car wash, Germering. The surrounding glazing of the side wings (one side for staff and equipment, the other for customers, each approx. 2.8 m wide) permits the functioning of the car wash to be seen. Architects: Haack + Hüpfner, Munich

	Underground/urban rail (m)	Tram/bus (m)
Large urban centre		
core zone	400	300
zone with high-density use	600	400
zone with low-density use	1000	600
Medium-sized urban centre		
central zone	400	300
zone with high-density use	600	400
zone with low-density use	1000	600
Subsidiary urban centre		
central area	600	400
remaining area	1000	600
Community	1000	600
for urban railways, the value for tram or underground applies, depending on transport function		

❶ Distances to public transport stops and stations (VDV → refs)

city bus	150–300
bus, tram	250–600
underground	400–1500
urban railway	600–2500

❷ Average distance to a public transport stop in metres (approx., depends on local conditions) (VDV → refs)

	Bus	Tram	Underground, (e.g. small-profile, Berlin)	Underground (e.g. Munich)	Urban rail
vehicle lengths, trainsets	single bus 8–15 m; articulated bus 18.75 m; double articulated bus 25 m; bus + trailer 25 m	single car 15–45 m; trainsets up to 75 m (according to BOStrab)	25.7 m up to 4 double trainsets	114 m one non-separable train	ET 423: 67.4 m up to 3 trainsets
width	2.55 m	2.20–2.65 m	2.30 m	2.90 m	3.02 m
height	approx. 2.90 up to 4.10 m (double-decker)	approx. 3.40 m*	3.20 m	3.45 m	4.30 m*
platform height	0.12–0.24 m	0.20–1.00 m	0.90 m	1.00 m	0.96 m

* height without pantograph extended to overhead

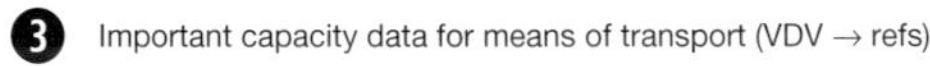

❸ Important capacity data for means of transport (VDV → refs)

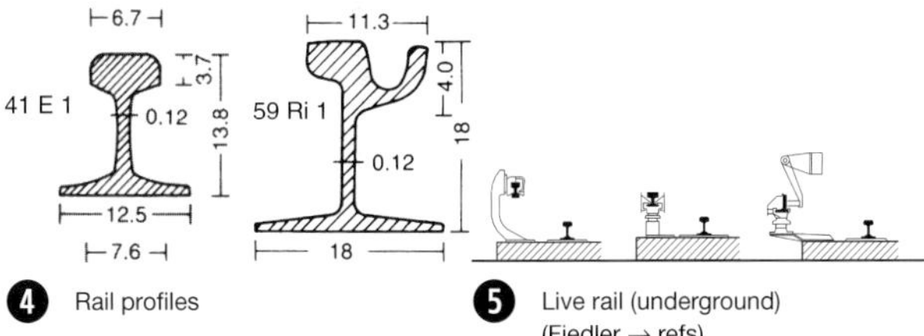

❹ Rail profiles

❺ Live rail (underground) (Fiedler → refs)

Shelters, weather protection

Shelters are required to protect passengers from the weather at transport stops. These are mostly standardised systems made up of basic elements or supplementary modules, often in combination with advertising materials (City Light Posters, for example) as part of the street furniture. Shelters should also attend to customers' safety needs by being transparent.

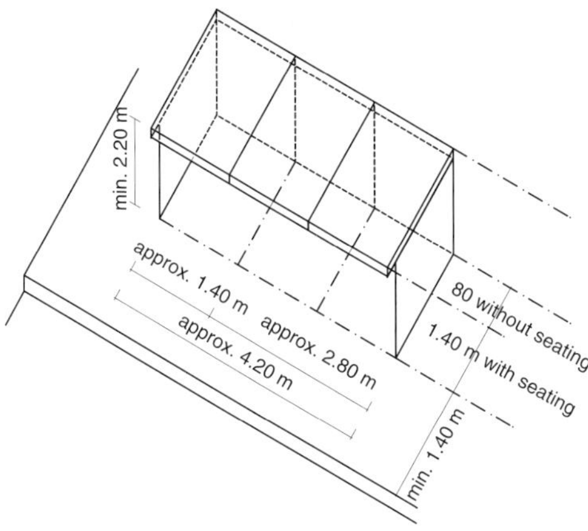

❻ Waiting shelter for public transport

Legal basis: General Railway Law (AEG), Passenger Transport Law (PBefG), Regulations for the Construction and Operation of Trams (BOStrab), state public transport laws.

Each residential, commercial or industrial area should be accessible by public transport. Accessible means that the distance (as the crow flies) to a transport stop complies with the values in ❶.

All areas with contiguous building development and more than 200 inhabitants (or a corresponding number of commuters and/or students), should be accessible, as should comparable establishments in terms of traffic generation (locations with special functions).

In addition to the bus, there are various types of rail vehicle that can make public transport quicker, more convenient and more attractive than individual travel:

– **Rapid urban transit railways:** predominantly electric, independent rail systems within an urban area (overground and underground – subway in USA) or region, sometimes with at-grade crossings but with absolute priority

– **Urban railways:** as underground railways partially independent from road traffic, or above ground on dedicated permanent tracks or with at-grade crossings with road traffic without absolute priority

– **Trams:** on track beds integrated into roads or dedicated; when trams make use of the public street space, they are subject to road traffic regulations (StVO).

Mixed systems are also possible, e.g. urban railways and trams on the same permanent track or trams using rail tracks (e.g. in Karlsruhe). The use of the permanent track by buses is feasible, resulting in better integration of different transportation elements (stops, bus/tram stations) and priority switching at traffic lights. Of great importance is the spatial and scheduling integration of various means of public transport with each other and also with road and cycle traffic (P(ark) + R(ide), B(icycle) + R(ide) etc.) and appropriate design of changing points → ❼.

Overhead line systems

Power supply is normally provided by overhead wire and pantograph on the roof, although underground railways and some urban railways can also use live third rails at the side (approx. 20 cm above the running rails) → ❺.

Rail profiles

Wide-base rails of various dimensions are normally employed (urban rapid transit or urban rail 49 E 1, trams 41 E 1, dimensions → ❹). In street space, grooved rails (59 Ri 1, 60 Ri 1) are used, which can be joint-sealed to the paving at the sides. Open track beds are sometimes greened.

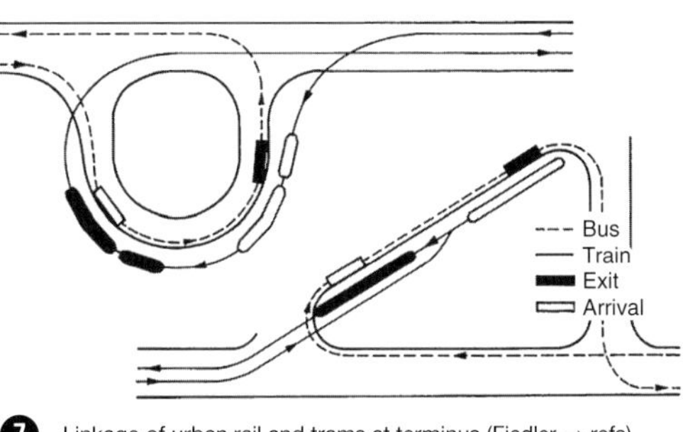

❼ Linkage of urban rail and trams at terminus (Fiedler → refs)

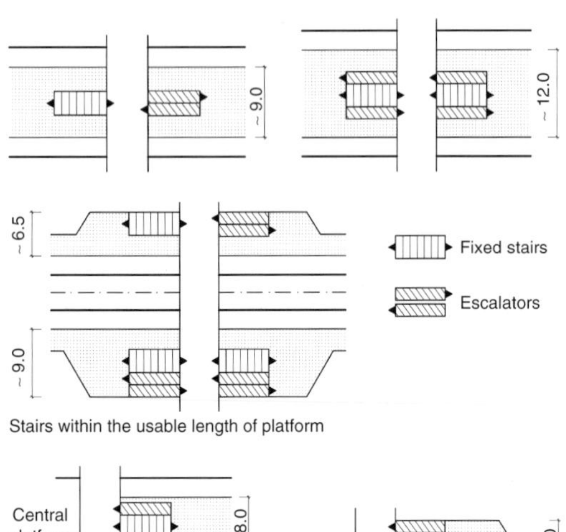

Stairs within the usable length of platform

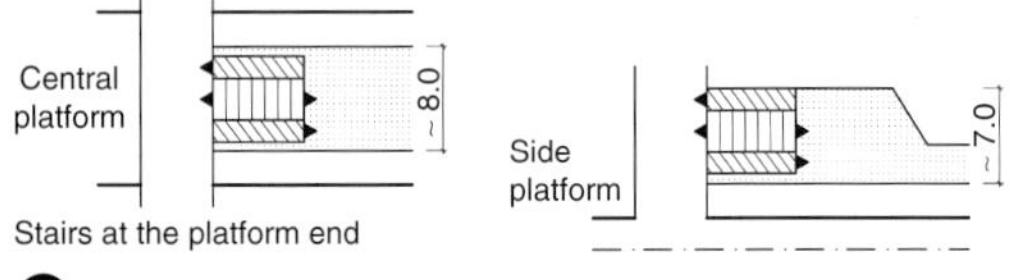

Stairs at the platform end

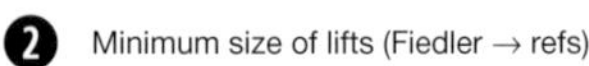

❶ Stair layout for side and central platforms (Fiedler → refs)

No. people/potential hindrance	Width × Depth (m)	Capacity (kg)
8/suitable for disabled	1.10 × 1.40	630
13/suitable for carrying loads	1.10 × 2.10	1000
19/suitable for cycles	1.40 × 2.10	1450

❷ Minimum size of lifts (Fiedler → refs)

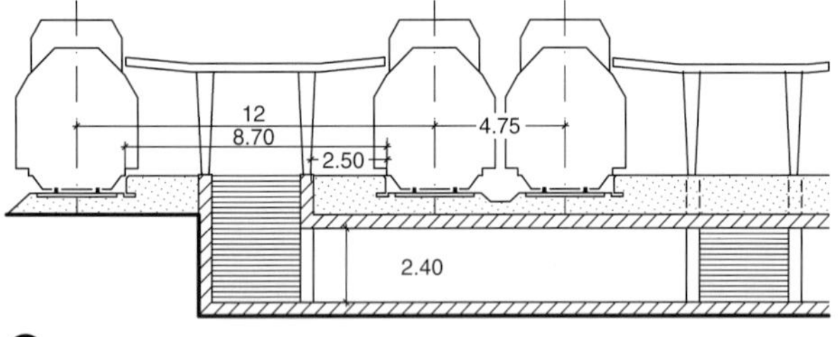

❸ Cross-section through platforms (Fiedler → refs)

Tram stops: platform min. 3.50 m or, to provide space for waiting shelters and two-sided platforms, min. 5.50 m. The permissible minimum width in the road space (according to BOStrab) of 1.50 m should be improved on out of consideration for the passengers (where space is restricted, 2 m is the minimum for a side exit). Safety space: 0.85 m wide from the vehicle gauge on the door side of the rail vehicle, which can also lie on the road pavement.

Dynamic stop: if there is no transport stop island, a traffic light should be placed further back along the road to protect the passengers getting in and out.

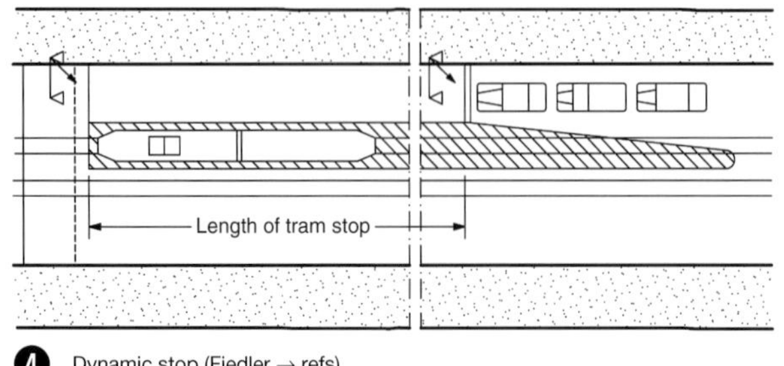

❹ Dynamic stop (Fiedler → refs)

The design of public transport stops is important. Railway systems are normally designed very specifically for the location. Therefore, platform and floor heights in the vehicle have to be matched in order to ensure passenger-friendly and accessible entrances and exits.

Platform layout

The layout of central and side platforms depends on construction, operational and transport considerations, especially for **platforms in tunnels**.

Central platforms are simpler for the passengers to navigate, but two-way carriages are necessary. If stations are lower and an intermediate storey is required, then this can be used as a grade-separated road crossing by general pedestrian traffic. When the platforms are on one side, then twice the number of accesses, stairs and installations (kiosks, timetables etc.) are needed. One-way carriages are possible because doors are required on the right-hand side only. When stops are located on viaducts, side platforms are preferable because platforms can be projected, so no surface is lost apart from the supports. Successive stops should if possible have the same platform layout (for passenger orientation).

Platform length

This depends on the length of the longest train intended to stop at the station. In the case of underground and urban rapid transit, platform length is the train length plus 5 m (to allow for imprecise braking). Double stops are also possible for trams.

Platform width

The platform width depends on the number of passengers and the location, type and width of the access and exit routes. Platform, stairs and exits should be designed so that the platform can be cleared, without queues, before the next train arrives. The minimum widths are, in general:

- side platforms 3 m
- central platforms with stairs at the end of the platform 6 m
- with stairs within the usable platform length 7 m.

Stairs

Staircases can be located at the end of the platform or within the usable platform length. The width of fixed stairs should be a multiple of 0.60 m (at least 2.40 m) plus width for handrail and cleaning channel. Provide a handrail both sides and additionally in the middle of stairs wider than 6.00 m → ❶.

Escalators provide extra comfort for passengers, and accelerate and canalise the traffic flow; they should be used for medium and high passenger numbers. 1–1½-track, or preferably 2-track, escalators should be used (800/1000 mm step width). Construction widths vary between 1.40 and 1.65 m, according to manufacturer.

Lifts

Additional passenger lifts should be installed (possibly as a refit) in above-ground and underground railway stations to aid the journeys of disabled people and others with restricted mobility (due to pushchairs, luggage etc.) → ❷. Lifts should be easily recognisable with waiting areas outside the main traffic flow.

Platform surfacing

To improve drainage, this should have a camber of at least 1% (max. 3–5% in tunnel stops and 2–3% in open-air stops). Platform edges should be slip-resistant and made of profiled and clearly coloured material (if appropriate with a broad white band) to help those with poor eyesight. Contrasting guide strips, which can be felt with a white stick, should also be provided for visually impaired people.

a) in open sections b) at stops and protection islands

❶ Minimum spacing of tracks in the carriageway of a public road

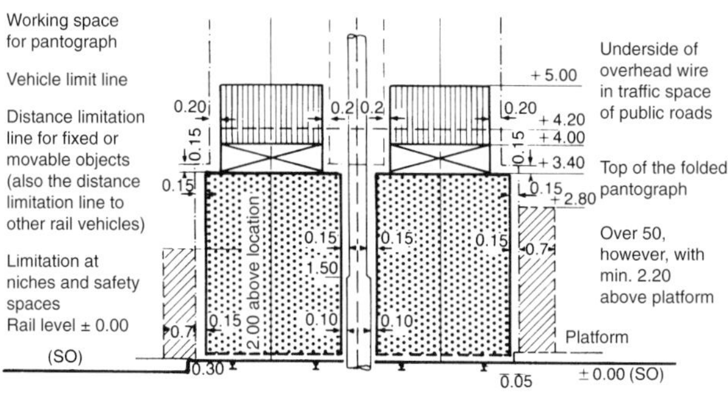

❷ Minimum spacing of tracks on a special track bed within the traffic space of a public road

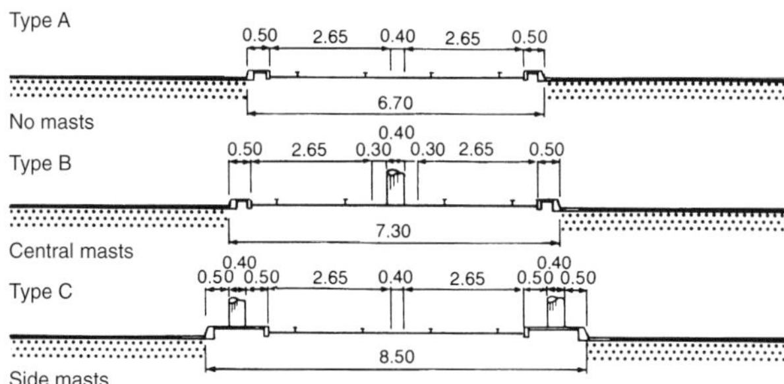

❸ Standard widths for special track beds in m

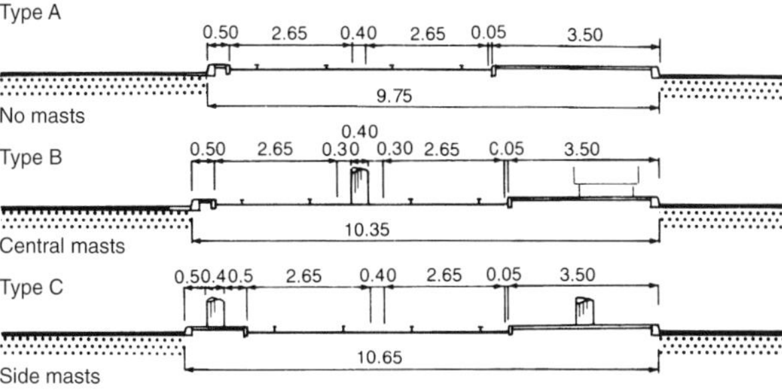

❹ → ❸ One-sided stops

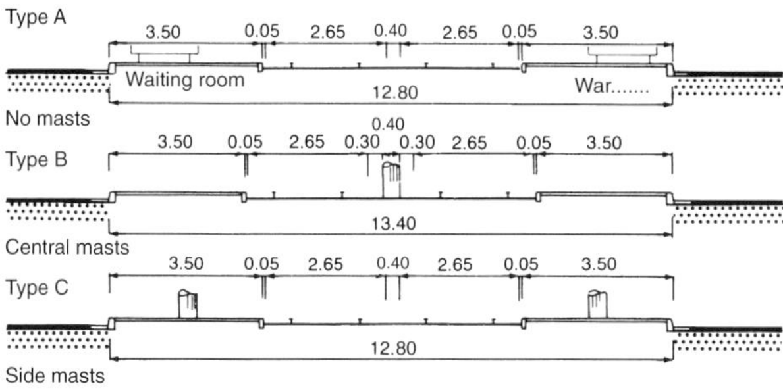

❺ Two-sided stops → ❸

Distance between track centre-lines: depending on the type of transport and its dimensions, min. 2.60 m or 2.95 m, or preferably 3.10 m to compensate for the sideways movement of carriages in medium-sized curve radii. Width of clearance = width of the carriage body, geometrical carriage curvature and extra width for overtaking and oscillation (min. 2 × 0.15 m).

Distance of kerb from carriage body: for special track beds 0.5 m, in exceptional cases also 0.30 m.

Track radii: if possible >180 m, in forks and turning loops min. 25 m.

Gradient: maximum 25‰, exceptionally 40‰.

Camber: max. 1:10, camber max. 165 mm for normal gauge, 1.20 m for metre gauge. If possible, there should be a transition curve before a circular curve, which should coincide with a camber ramp (here greatest slope 1:6 × V).

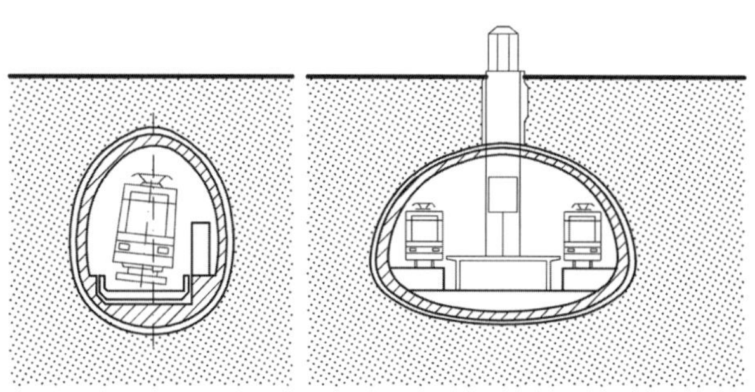

❻ Tunnel cross-section: in a running tunnel and in a station (Stadt Bochum → refs)

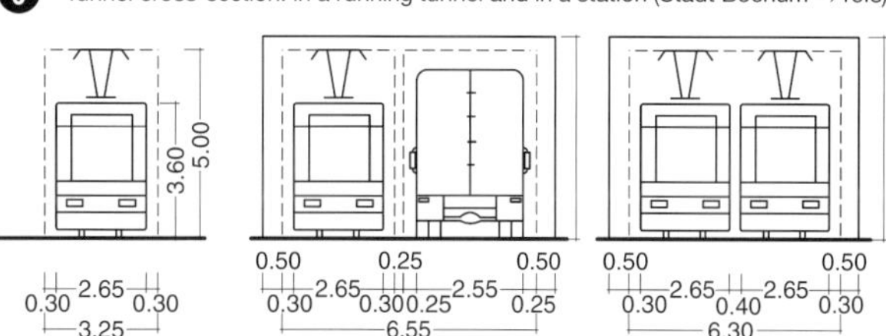

❼ Space requirement for a tram in the road space

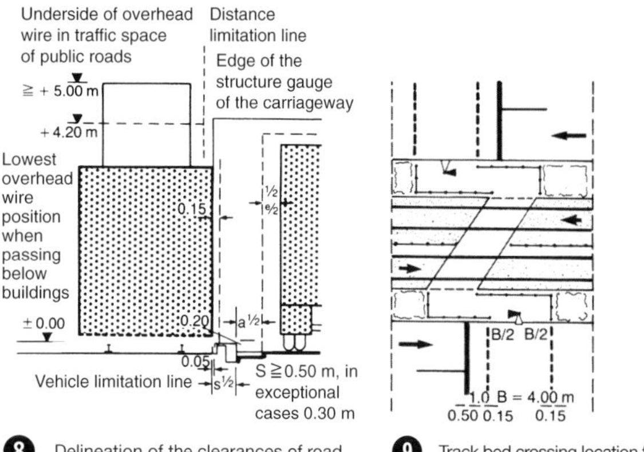

❽ Delineation of the clearances of road vehicle and tram

❾ Track bed crossing location for pedestrians without crossing lights

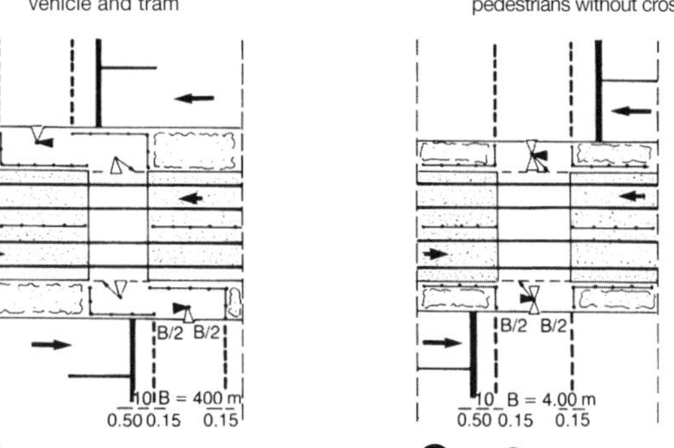

❿ Track crossing controlled by crossing lights

⓫ → ❿

see also: Stairs pp. 120 ff.
Lifts pp. 128 ff.
Railways pp. 408 ff.

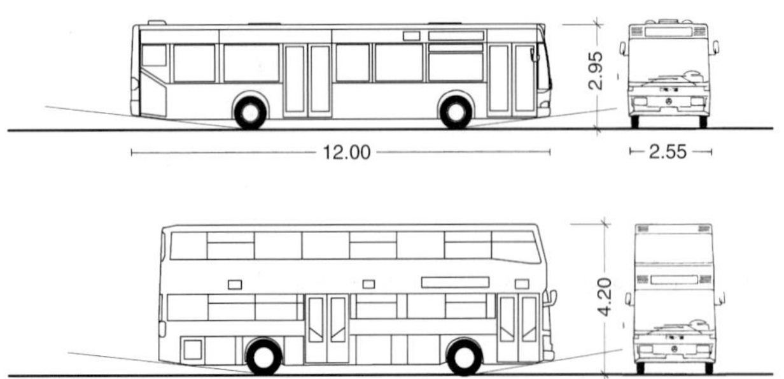

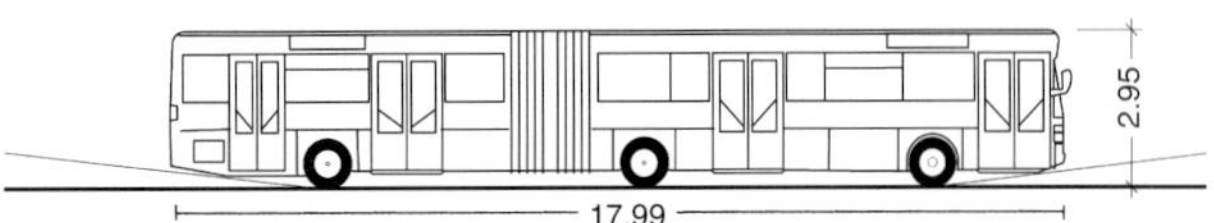

❶ Dimensions of widely used low-floor buses, entry height 30–35 cm, or with kneeling technology approx. 10 cm less

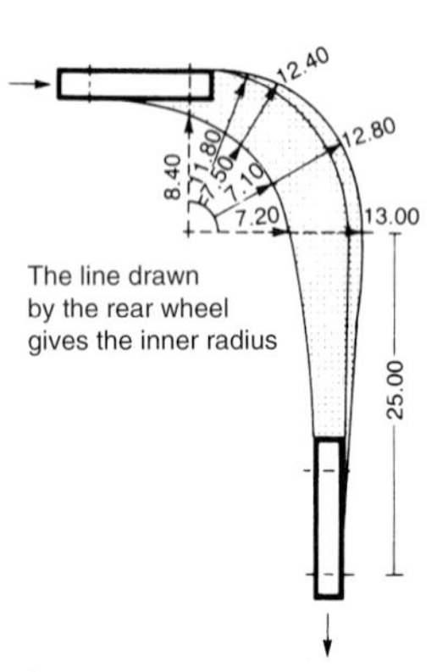

❷ 90° turning circle for rigid, 12 m long vehicles

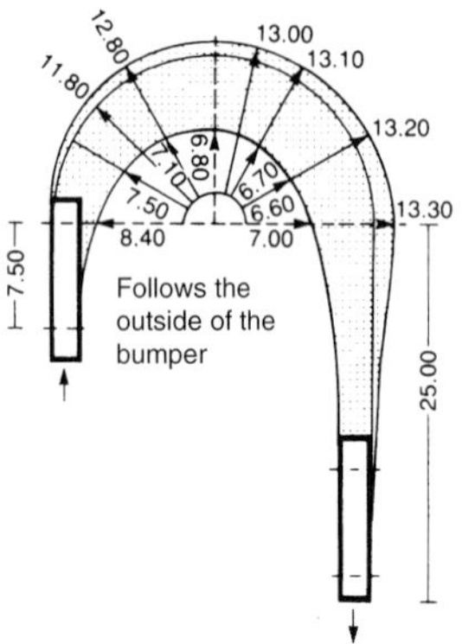

❸ 180° turning circle for rigid, 12 m long vehicles

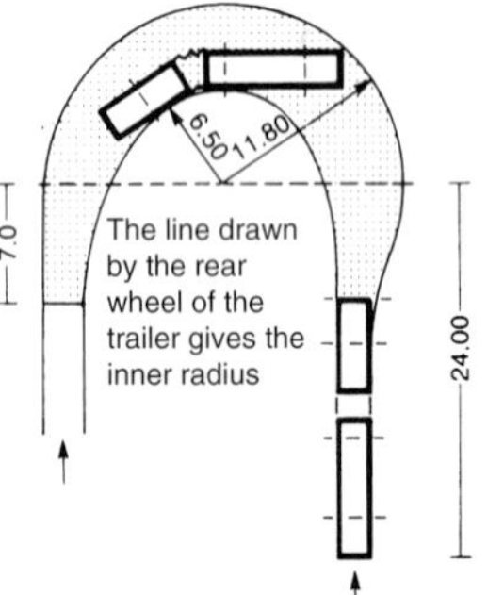

❹ 180° turning circle for articulated, 17 m long vehicles

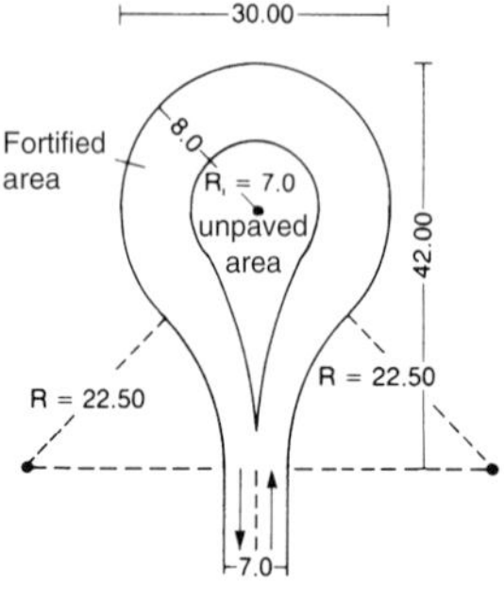

❺ Turning area

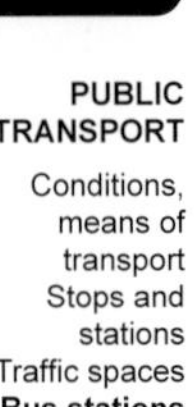

PUBLIC TRANSPORT
Conditions, means of transport
Stops and stations
Traffic spaces
Bus stations

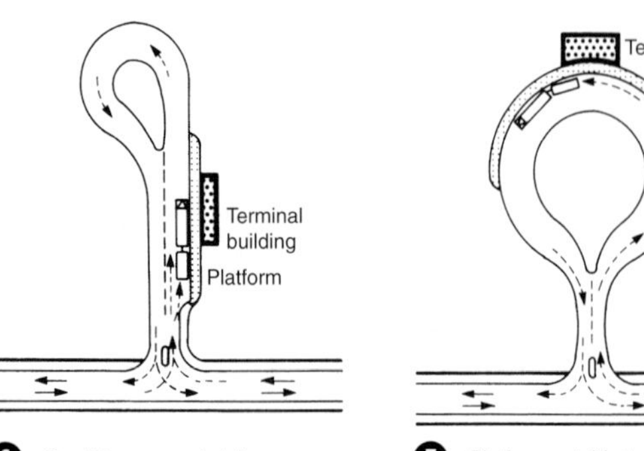

❻ Small turnaround station

❼ Platform outside turning loop

Special widening of curves and turning circles has to be taken into account → ❷ – ⓭. Stops require special dimensions. Bus stop bays are provided only on main feeder roads and roads with heavy traffic loads → ❽. It is desirable for the bus stop to be covered. The many possible platform layouts are shown → ❶ – ❾. Ramps should be provided at the front to allow easy access up a step height of 30 cm → ⓫ – ⓬.
Provide space for temporary parking of cars (Park and Ride).

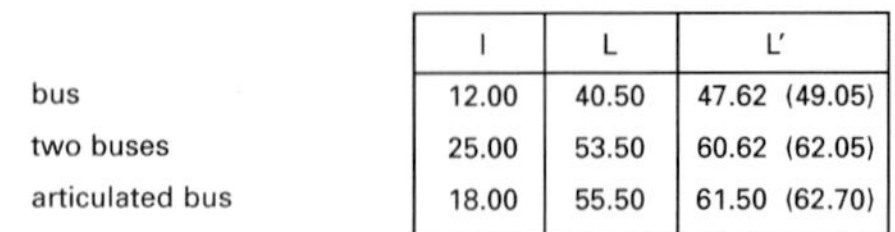

	l	L	L'
bus	12.00	40.50	47.62 (49.05)
two buses	25.00	53.50	60.62 (62.05)
articulated bus	18.00	55.50	61.50 (62.70)

for 3 m wide bus stop bays
*) 25 m for bus stop bays for articulated buses

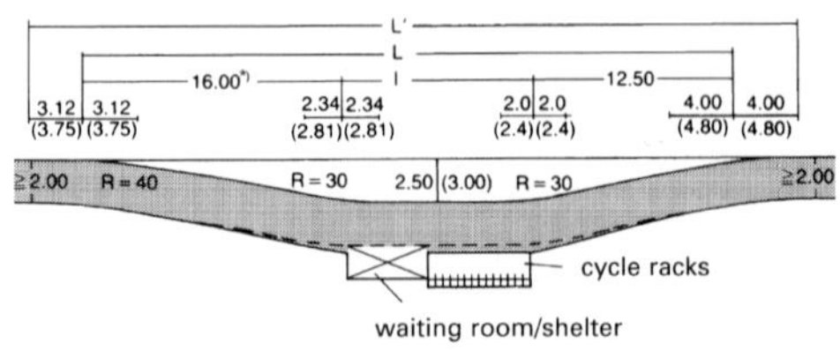

❽ Bus stop

Platform shape	Without passing lane			With passing lane		
	Aa	Ab	Ac	Ba	Bb	Bc
layout of arrival line	parallel	at 45°	at 90°	parallel	at 45°	at 90°
length of platform (m)	24	24	24	36–60	36–60	36–60
width of platform (m)	3	3	3	3.5–4.0	3.5–4.0	3.5–4.0
no. parking places						
a) for buses	2	2	2	2–3	2–3	2–3
b) for artic. buses	1	1	1	1–2	1–2	1–2
area of platform, roadway and arrival lane (m^2) a) per bus	138	176	189	293	296	313
b) per artic. bus	276	340	378	439	444	470

❾ Space required for platforms

Layout of arrival line	Parallel	At 45°		At 90°	
length of parking space (m)	32	12	24	12	24
possible parking for:	1 artic. bus or 2 buses	1 bus	1 artic. bus or 2 buses	1 bus	1 artic. bus or 2 buses
width of one parking space	3.5	3.5	3.5	3.5	3.5
width of arrival lane (m)	4.0	8.0	8.0	14	14
parking area inc. roadway area (m^2) a) per bus	88	135	89	140	91
b) per articulated bus	176		178		182

❿ Space required for parking places

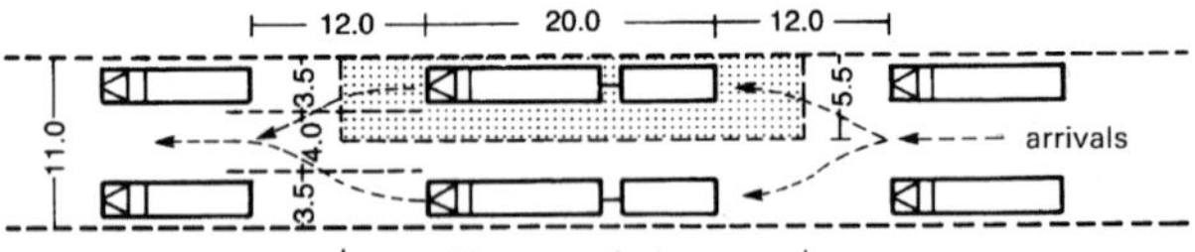

⓫ Layout of parking spaces, parallel to direction of approach

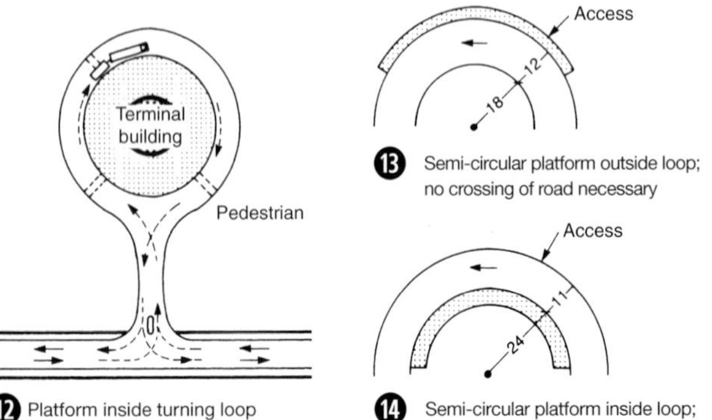

⓬ Platform inside turning loop

⓭ Semi-circular platform outside loop; no crossing of road necessary

⓮ Semi-circular platform inside loop; accessible only by crossing road

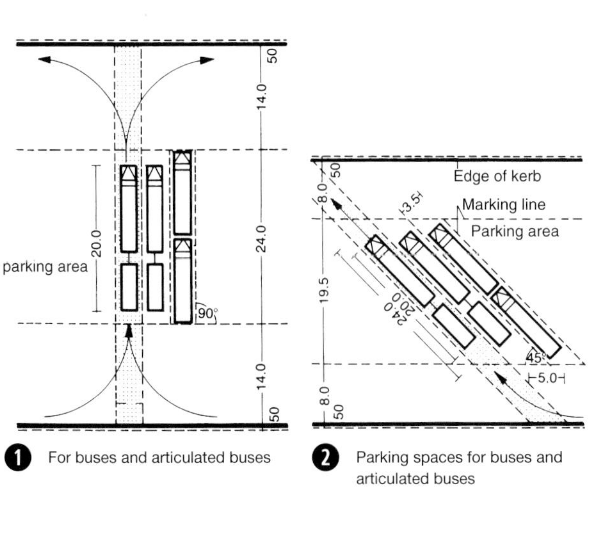

❶ For buses and articulated buses

❷ Parking spaces for buses and articulated buses

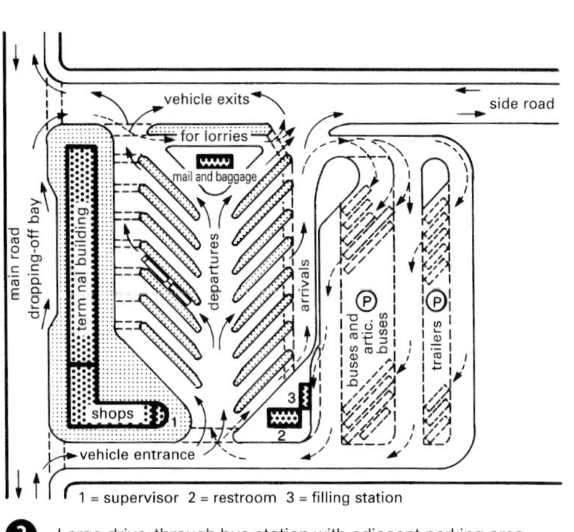

❸ Large drive-through bus station with adjacent parking area

❹ Normal parallel staggering, according to Time-Saver standard

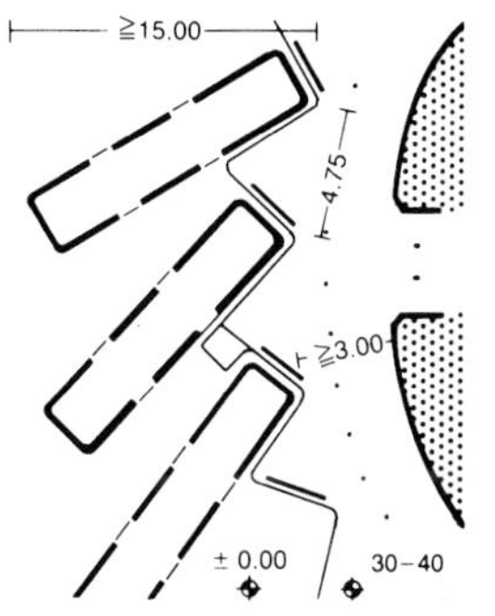

❺ Radial layout extends free space at front

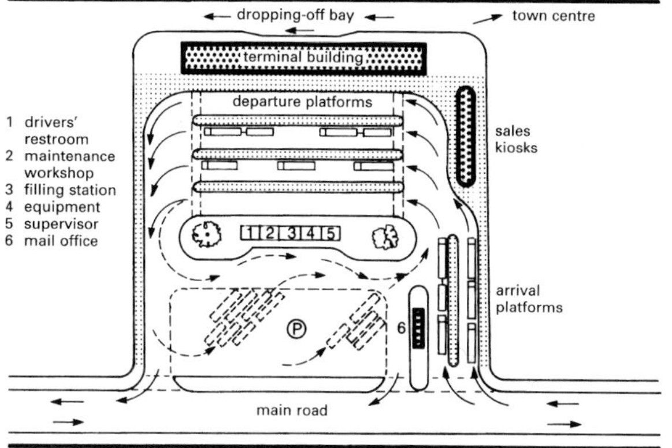

❻ Large drive-through bus station with separate arrival and departure platforms

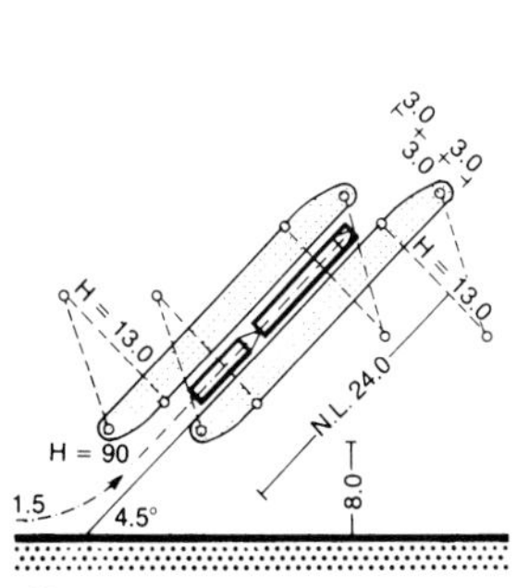

❼ Long platform at angle

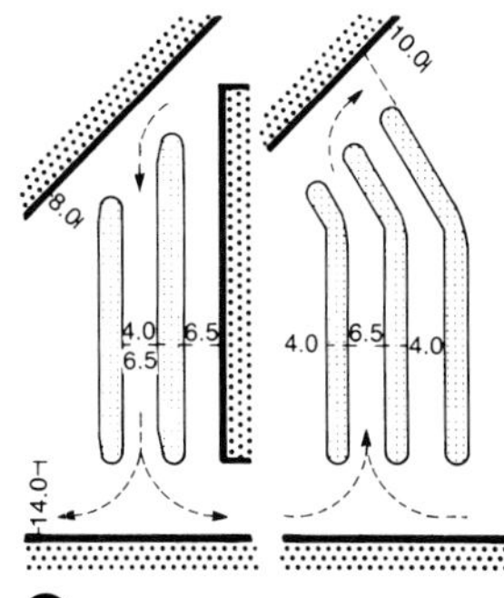

❽ Right-angled departure, oblique arrival, oblique departure

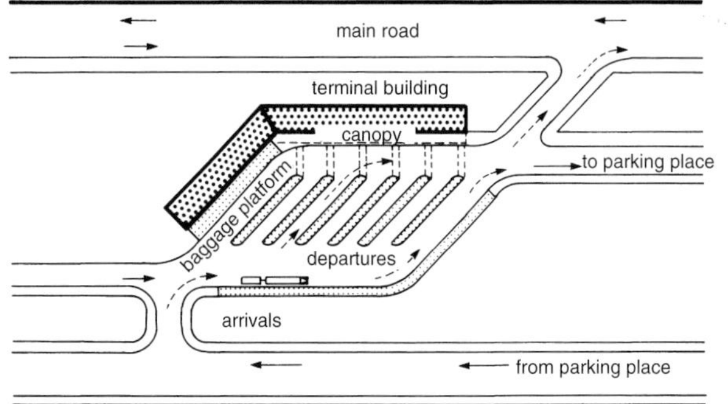

❾ Drive-through bus station with separate arrival and departure platforms, oblique layout and distant parking area

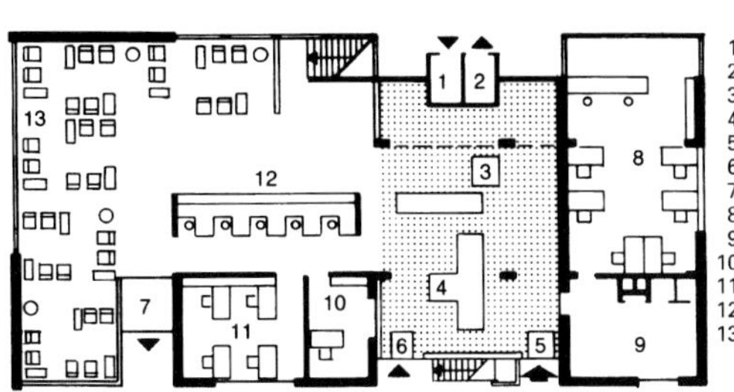

1 entrance for departing passengers
2 exit for arriving passengers
3 concourse
4 baggage despatch
5 entrance for arriving passengers
6 entrance for arriving baggage
7 exit for departing passengers
8 baggage office
9 baggage deposit
10 office manager
11 office
12 information and air tickets
13 waiting room

❿ Ground floor of KLM bus station

1 WC men
2 WC women
3 nursery
4 cloakroom
5 kitchen
6 canteen staff
7 drivers' restroom
8 meter cupboard and storeroom
9 filing room
10 pump room

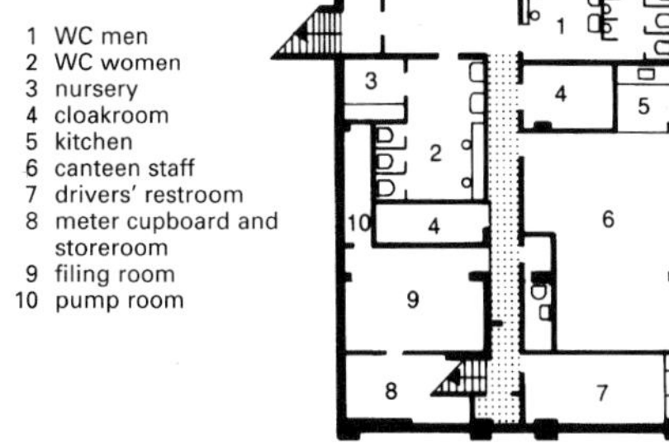

⓫ Basement → ❿

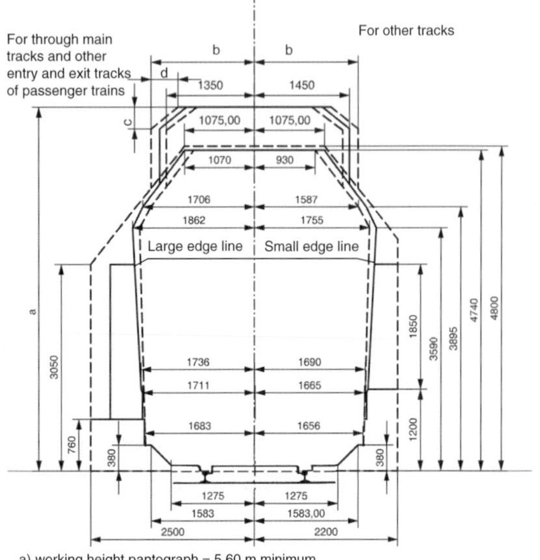

a) working height pantograph = 5.60 m minimum, depending on type of electricity 5.00–5.34 m

b) maximum 1.58 m b, c and d dependent on working height range of pantograph (EBO appendix 1)

1 Standard clearance space, according to the Railway Construction and Operation Regulation (EBO), valid on straight and curved lines with radius ≧250 m

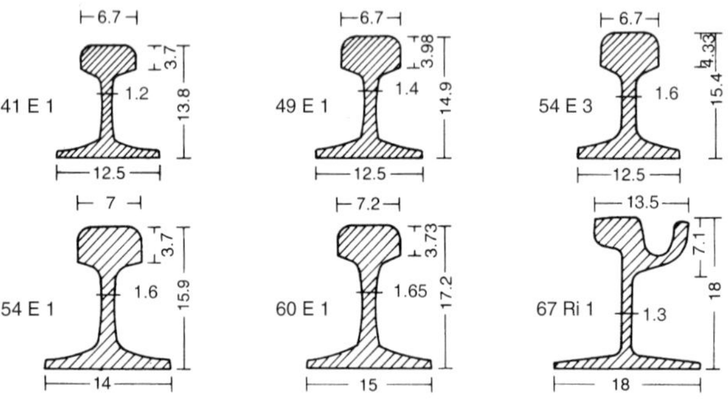

3 Sections of common types of rail (the first number is the rail weight in kg/m)

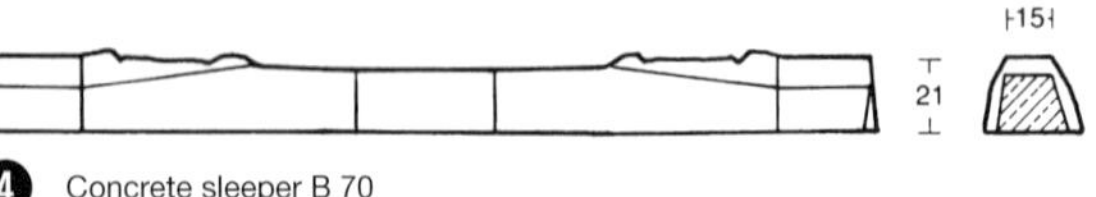

4 Concrete sleeper B 70

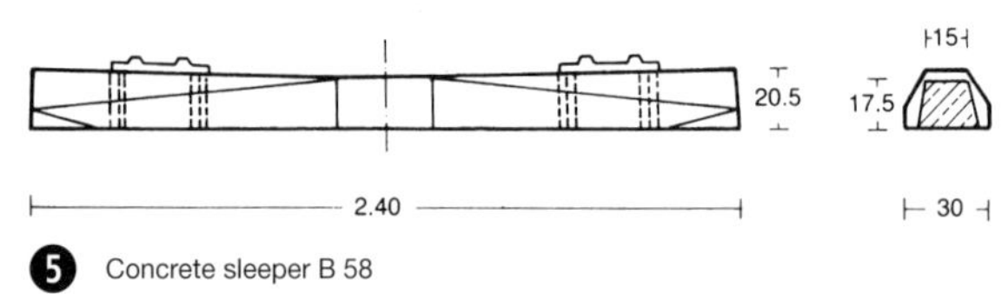

5 Concrete sleeper B 58

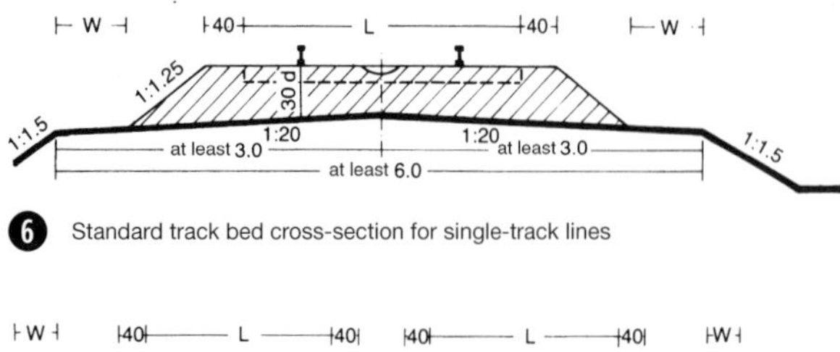

6 Standard track bed cross-section for single-track lines

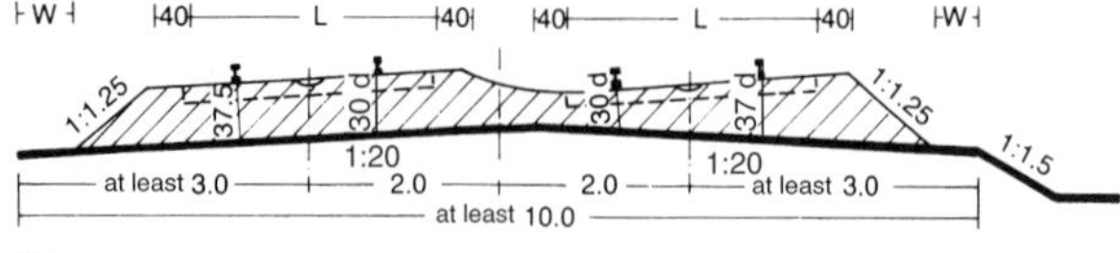

7 Standard track bed cross-section for two-track lines

The key standard distances (d) between track centre-lines are:

- On open stretches of track — 4.00 m (3.50 m on older lines)
  - where signals installed — 4.50 m
  - as safety space after every 2nd track — 5.40 m
  - newly built stretches, V >200 km/h — 4.50 m
- In stations — 4.50 m (4.75 m)
  - main lines, straight through — 4.00 m
  - in sets of 5–6 lines — 6.00 m
  - for brake inspection/test tracks — 5.00 m
  - in sidings for carriage cleaning — 5.00 m

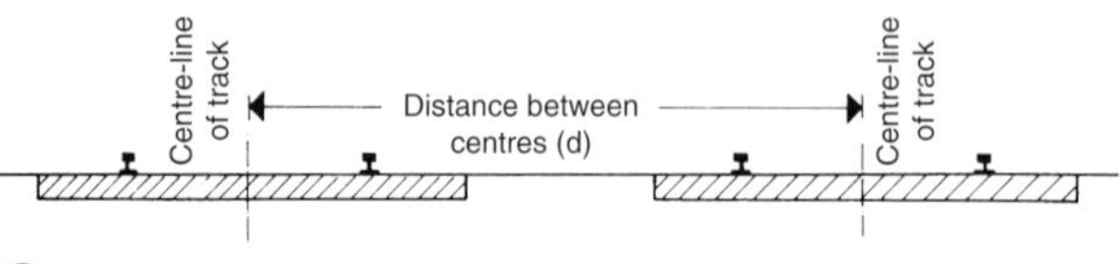

2 Track spacings

Standard gauge of German Railways:
gauge (for 71% of the world's railways) 1.435 m
gauge tolerances:
–3/+30 mm on main lines
–3/+35 mm on branch lines
(other gauges: Russia 1.520 m; Spain and Portugal 1.668 m, South Africa 1.067 m, Chile, Argentina, India 1.673 m)

Lifetime of sleepers:

- timber sleepers impregnated with creosote (Rüping process) — 25–40 years
- timber sleepers, not impregnated — 3–15 years
- steel sleepers — about 45 years
- concrete sleepers, estimated — min. 40 years

Trench depth in cuttings ≧0.4–0.6 m under ground level
Slope of the trench 3–10% according to the type of consolidation of the trench floor. Groundwater at retaining walls is to be drained through pipes or drainage holes.

The longitudinal gradient of open stretches of main line ≦12.5‰, on branch lines and urban railways ≦40‰ and on station tracks ≦2.5‰. Gradients of up to 25‰ are possible on main lines with special approval.

Static wheel load = 9 t. On stretches with sufficiently strong track and supporting structures, higher wheel loads (up to 11.25 t) are possible.

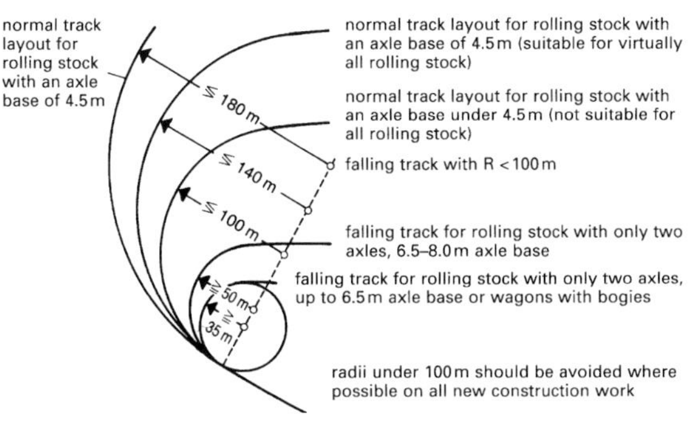

❶ Track radius (turnability) of the connecting tracks

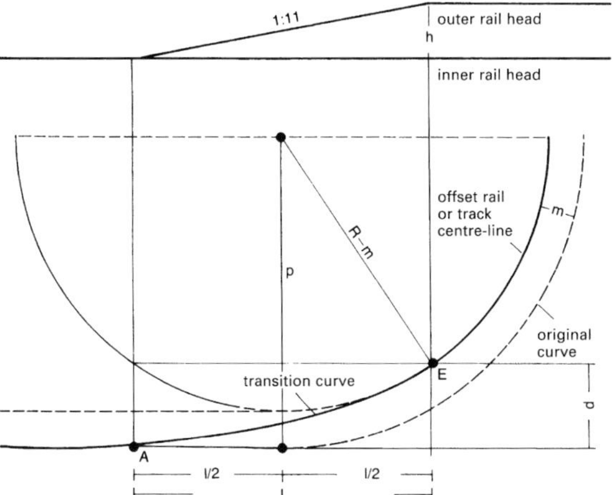

❷ Track cant ramp and transition curve

R	l	m	Ramp gradient
180–200	40	0.370	1: 320
		0.333	1: 320
250–350	30	0.1150	1: 300
		0.107	1: 400
400–2000	20	0.012	1: 310
		0.008	1: 1300

❸ Branch lines and normal sidings (m)

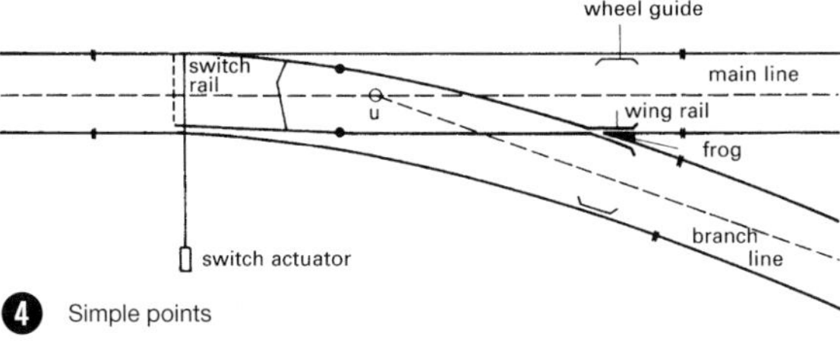

❹ Simple points

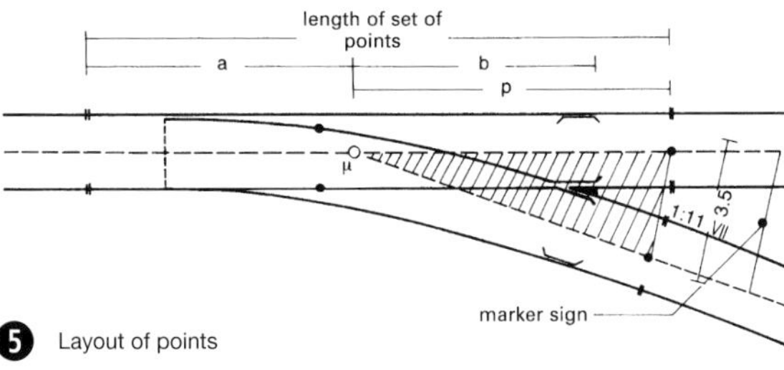

❺ Layout of points

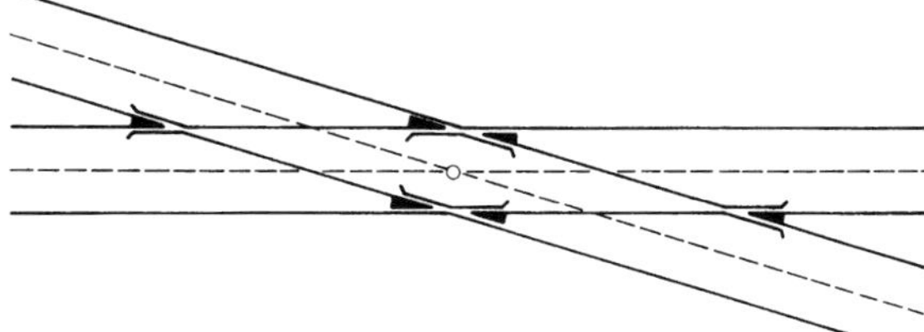

❻ Oblique crossing (wheel guide as example diameter ❹ – ❺)

Curved radii (to track centre-line) = R
main lines, direct main tracks .... ≧300 m
station tracks .... ≧180 m
branch lines with main line rolling stock .... ≧180 m
without main line rolling stock .... ≧100 m
sidings used by main line engines .... ≧140 m
sidings not used by main line engines, preferably .... ≧100 m
minimum .... ≧35 m

If 100 m >R ≧35 m, carriages should if possible only be pulled; with radius >130 m not all carriage types can any longer be driven.

Radii for narrow-gauge railways
for 1.00 m gauge track .... R ≧50 m
for 0.75 m gauge track .... R ≧40 m
for 0.60 m gauge track .... R ≧25 m

For tracks to be used at greater than shunting speed, a transitional section of curve must be installed between the straight section and the circular arc with radius R, with the curvature of the transition curve increasing constantly from 1: ∞ up to 1: R → ❷. Circular curves may have to be canted in order to keep the centrifugal force arising when travelling round the curve within reasonable bounds (≦0.65 m/sec). Canted curves and transition curves should coincide.

For details, see German Railways combined guideline KoRil 820/1.

Points
Sets of points are characterised according to the shape of the rail, the turning track radius and the inclination of the frog, e.g. 49–190–1:9.
only use the points for carriages up to the limit sign → ❺
spacing of the track centreline at the warning sign ≧3.5 m
point length / length of the point blade → ❽
49–190–1:7.5 = 25.222 m/12.611 m
49–190–1:9 = 27.138 m/10.523 m
49–300–1:9 = 33.230 m/16.615 m
normal turntable = D
for axle turntable 2–3 m, for carriage turntable 3.5–10.0 m, for locomotive turntable 12.5–23.0 m

Traversers
Size = minimum axle spacing of the carriage to be pushed + 0.5 m

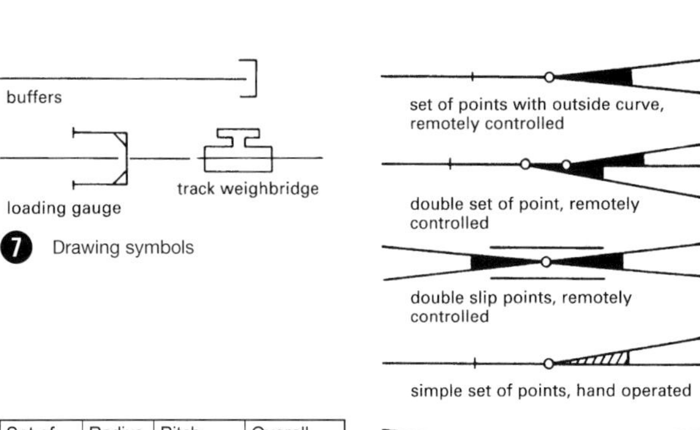

❼ Drawing symbols

Set of points	Radius (m)	Pitch ratio	Overall length (m)
ABW 49	215	1:4.8	22.100
EW 49	190	1:7.5	30.039
EW 49	190	1:9	27.138
DKW 49	190	1:9	33.230
DW 49	190	1:9r/1:9l	37.661

❽ Dimensions for sets of points

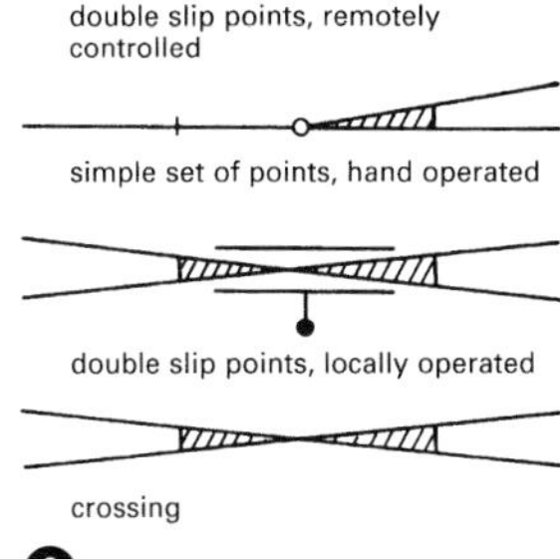

❾ Drawing symbols

Standard gauge railways

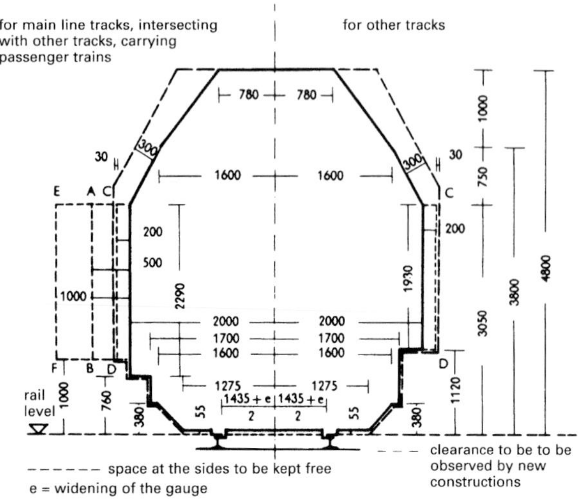

A–B for main lines on open stretches for all objects with the exception of fabricated structures
C–D for station sidings and for open stretches of main lines with special structures and signals between the tracks
E–F for fixed objects on passenger platforms

1 Standard clearance profiles (straight track plus curves with radii ≧250 m)

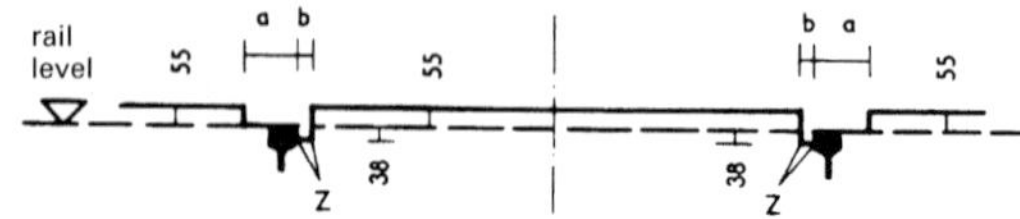

a ≧ 150 mm for immovable objects which are not firmly connected to the rail
a ≧ 135 mm for immovable objects which are firmly connected to the rail
b = 41 mm for devices guiding the wheel on the inside of the front surface
b ≧ 45 mm for level crossings
b ≧ 70 mm for all other cases
Z = corners which have to be radiused

2 Standard structure gauging and clearances at low level

Curve radius (m)	Necessary increase in standard clearance on the	
	Inside of the curve (mm)	Outside of the curve (mm)
250	0	0
225	25	30
200	50	65
190	65	80
180	80	100
150	135	170
120	335	365
100	530	570

3 Necessary increase in the standard clearance for curves with radii <250 m

Narrow gauge railways

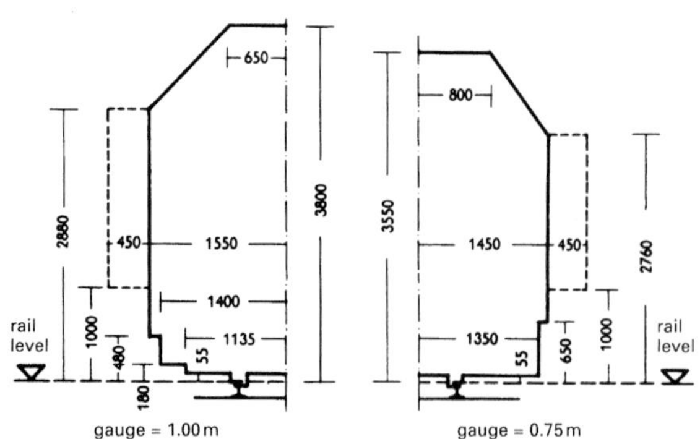

7 Standard clearance profiles, straight line track

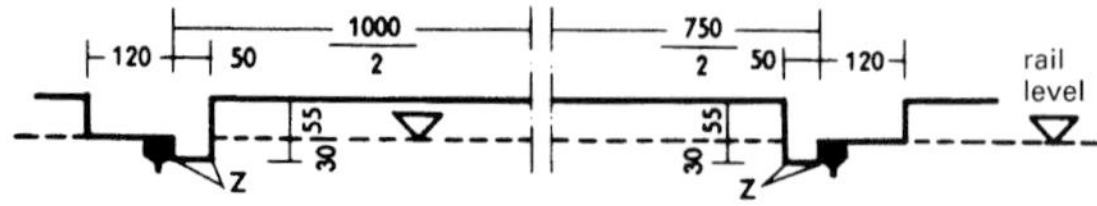

8 Standard structure gauging and clearances at low level

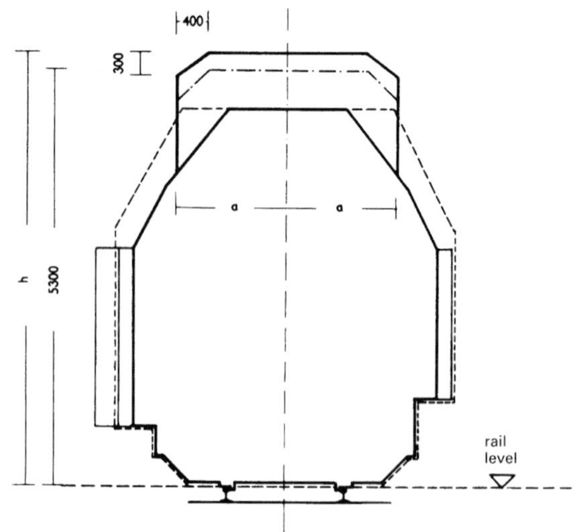

for existing superstructures, tunnels and engine shed doors when electrification takes place

4 Top limit of clearance for stretches with overhead conductor wire (15kV)

Half the radius of the curve (m)	Dimensions of half the width a (mm)
up to 250	1445
225	1455
200	1465
180	1475
150	1495
120	1525
100	1555

5 Dimensions for half the width of the upper limit of the clearance

	h
heavy superstructures up to 15 m wide and in tunnels	5500 mm
heavy superstructures over 15 m wide	6000 mm
light superstructures, such as footbridges, sheds including doors	6000 mm
signal gantries and brackets	6300 mm

6 Minimum clearance under structures

Other dimensions: European standards (Germany)

For entrance doorways the clear width should be ≧3.35m and for new structures ≧4.00 m.

For tunnels, the extra clearance needed beyond the trains' kinematic envelope clearance to the wall for a single-track stretch of line is 0.40 m; for a double-track stretch of line it is 30 cm.

There are minimum distances required between buildings and railway tracks for new structures. These vary according to location. Typical examples are: a fire resistant structure with suitable cladding must be separated by ≧7.50 m from railway land; the corresponding distance for soft covered structures that are not fire resistant is ≧15 m. The latter also applies to structures in which combustible materials are stored.

Platform heights vary from country to country, and can be as small as 0.38 m. However, access to platforms must not involve passengers having to cross the track. This requires tunnels or bridges, which should have a width of 2.5–4.0 m. If there is circulation in both directions, 4.00–8.00 m is desirable. Steps on bridges or in tunnels should be the same width as the bridge or tunnel.

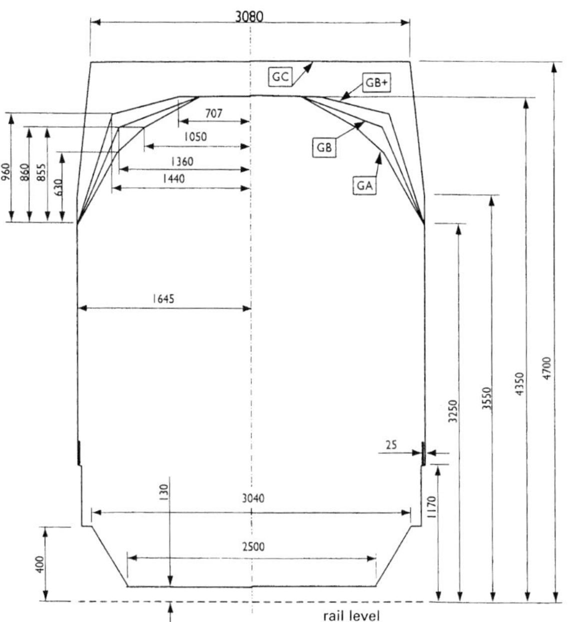

1 All dimensions are in mm.
2 The kinematic envelope is the cross-sectional profile of a vehicle at any position along its length, enlarged to include the effects of dynamic sway and vertical movement caused by speed, (dynamic effects of) track curvature and cant, track positional tolerances, rail wear, rail head/wheel flange clearances, vehicle wear and suspension performance for the particular track location under consideration. The determination of the kinematic envelope is the responsibility of the operator of the proposed vehicle and shall be in accordance with the Railway Group Standard.

1 UIC (International Union of Railways) reference profiles for kinematic gauges (GA, GB, GB+, GC)

Further information: Safety and Standards Board, Network Rail, London

This information is based on the Railway Group Standard which applied to all new design and new route clearances for railway vehicles and loads from 3 February 1996.

The purpose of this Railway Group Standard is to set down the engineering requirements for the safe passage of rail vehicles and their loads by reconciling their physical size and dynamic behaviour with the opportunities offered by the railway infrastructure.

This standard applies to infrastructure owned by Network Rail and any other infrastructure interfacing with it and affecting its physical clearances (e.g. private sidings or works into which, or out of which, trains will work onto Network Rail lines).

It shall be complied with in the design, maintenance and alteration of the railway infrastructure, in the design and modification of traction and rolling stock and in the conveyance of out of gauge loads.

Standards are constantly evolving as faster trains are developed and heavier loads are transported. The national rail administration should, therefore, always be contacted for the latest standards and details.

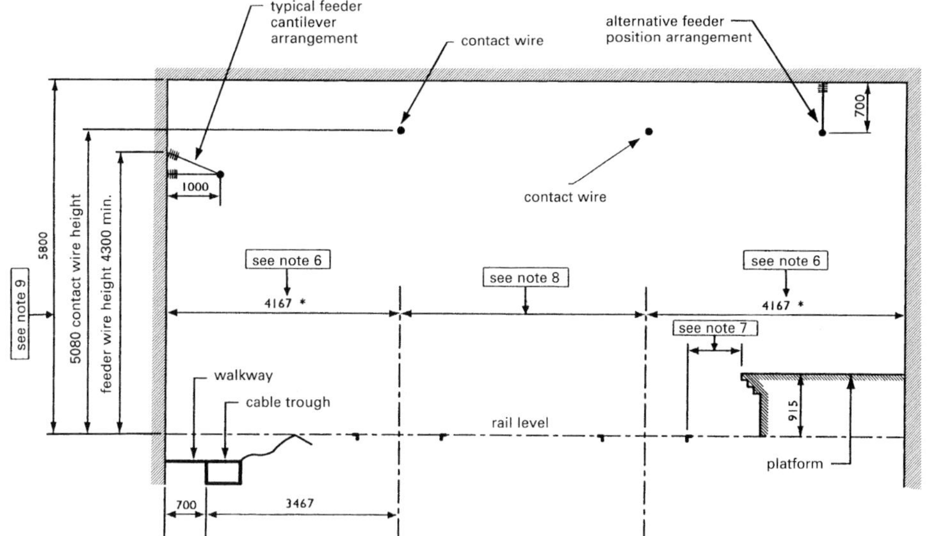

1 This drawing is not applicable to viaducts and tunnels.
2 All dimensions are in mm.
3 Track centres for a mixed traffic railway.
4 Applicable only to straight and level track.
5 Refer to GC/TW496 *Requirements for Constructional Work on or near Railway Operational Land for Non-Railtrack Contracts* for the design of supports for structures built over or close to railway lines.
6 It may be possible in tight situations to reduce the dimension marked with an asterisk, but only where alternative access is available, via a route in a petition of safety, connecting with the walkways each side of the structure or where the railway operates on a 'no person' basis, whereby staff are only allowed on the track when special protection measures are in place.
7 Platform clearances are subject to maintenance of HMRI stepping distances and specific requirement shall be calculated from the chosen kinematic envelope with an allowance made for structural clearance.
8 This dimension shall be calculated from the dimensions associated with the chosen kinematic envelope with an allowance made for passing clearance. At the time of calculating the required dimension an assessment shall be made of traffic proposed for the route such that aerodynamic effects can be taken into account.
9 This dimension accommodates full UIC GC reference profile and assumes train speeds up to 300 km/h. Commercial considerations will dictate whether it is necessary to amend this dimension and contact wire height for the actual type and speed of vehicles proposed for the route.

2 New construction gauge (derived from the UIC GC reference profile)

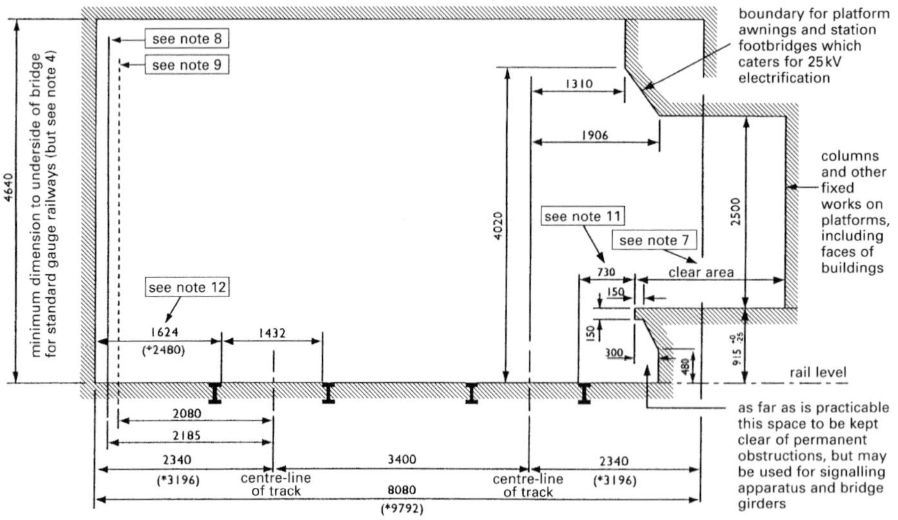

1 This diagram illustrates minimum lateral and overhead clearances to be adopted in construction or reconstruction and for alterations or additions to existing track and structures for line speeds up to 165km/h (100mph).
2 All dimensions are in mm.
3 * The dimension to be used when line speed exceeds 165 km/h (100 mph).
4 The clearance dimensions given are valid for straight and level track only and due allowance must be made for the effects of horizontal and vertical curvature, including super-elevation (cant).
5 The standard structure gauge allows for overhead electrification with voltages up to 25kV. However, to permit some flexibility in the design of overhead equipment, the minimum dimension between rail level and the underside of the structures should be increased, preferably to 4780mm or more if this can be achieved with reasonable economy. The proximity of track features such as level crossings or OHE sectioning may require greater than 4780mm.
6 Permissible infringements in respect of conductor rail equipment, guard and check rails, train stops and structures in the space between adjacent tracks are not shown.
7 The minimum dimensions of a single face platform measured from the edge of the platform to the face of the nearest building structure or platform furniture shall be 2500mm for speeds up to 165km/h and for speeds greater than 165km/h the minimum dimension shall be 3000mm. The minimum distance to the face of any column shall be 2000mm.
8 Nearest face of all other structures including masts carrying overhead line equipment of electrified railways.
9 Nearest face of signal posts and other isolated structures less than 2m in length but excluding masts carrying overhead line equipment on electrified railways.
10 Vertical clearances to the canopy above the platform shall be 2500mm up to 2000mm minimum from the platform edge or up to 3000mm where the line speed exceeds 165km/h. At distances beyond 2000mm or 3000mm from the platform edge, as applicable, the minimum headroom shall be 2300mm.
11 Platform clearances are subject to the maintenance of HMRI stepping distances and specific requirements shall be calculated from the particular kinematic envelope with an allowance made for structural clearance. The minimum lateral dimension is 730mm and is shown for guidance.
12 Where reasonably practicable these dimensions shall be increased by 300mm to facilitate the provision of an access walkway in accordance with CC/RT5203 *Infrastructure Requirements for Personal Safety in Respect of Clearance and Access.*

3 Standard structure gauge

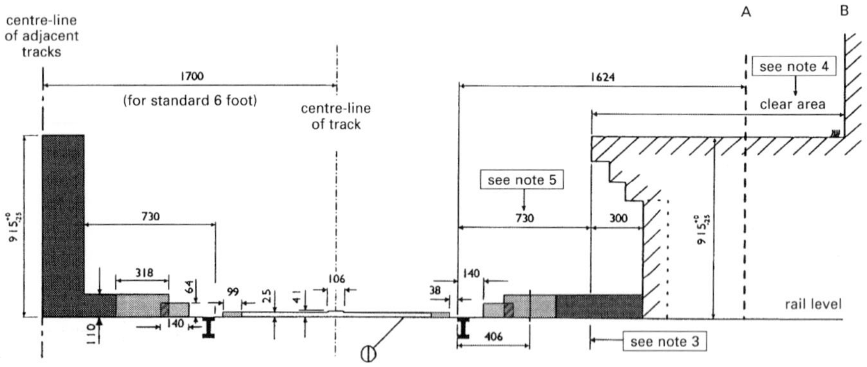

1 All dimensions are in mm.
2 The dimensions shown are for straight alignment and appropriate adjustments must be made for curvature. Except for dispensation which allows station platforms on curves with a radius greater than 360m to be placed at standard dimensions (as shown), the amount of platform set-back for curves with a radius less than 360m shall be determined by Network Rail.
3 Bridge girders, dwarf signals and other lineside equipment up to a height of 915mm ARL may be positioned in the space available for platforms.
4 The minimum dimension of a single face platform shall be 2500mm for speeds up to 165km/h and for speeds greater than 165km/h the minimum distance shall be increased to 3000mm. The minimum distance to the face of any column shall be 2000mm.
5 Platform clearances are subject to the maintenance of HMRI stepping distances and specific requirements shall be calculated from the particular kinematic envelope with an allowance made for structural clearance. The minimum lateral dimension is 730mm and is shown for guidance.

key

A abutments, piers, stanchions etc. (clear of platform)
B columns and other works on platforms
- areas for conductor rails and guard boards
- areas for guard and check rails only
- areas available for dwarf signals, bridge girders and other lineside equipment
- ⦶ unhatched areas so marked are for permanent way, signal fittings and fourth rail electrification

4 Standard structure gauge applicable at and below 1089 mm above rail level (ARL)

Network Rail shall give consideration to passenger safety by limiting the maximum stepping distance from the top edge of the platform to the top edge of the step board or floor of passenger rolling stock.

The following maximum dimensions for stepping distances, calculated from the centre of the bottom of the door opening, shall apply unless dispensation has been sought from HSV/HMRI for site specific cases relating to identified rolling stock. All such cases must be recorded in writing and maintained for future reference.

horizontal	275 mm
vertical	250 mm
diagonal	350 mm

effective length
side platform
ramp gradient 1:12–1:20
effective length
end platform

❶ Plan of a loading ramp with head and side ramps with a slope of 1:12–1:20

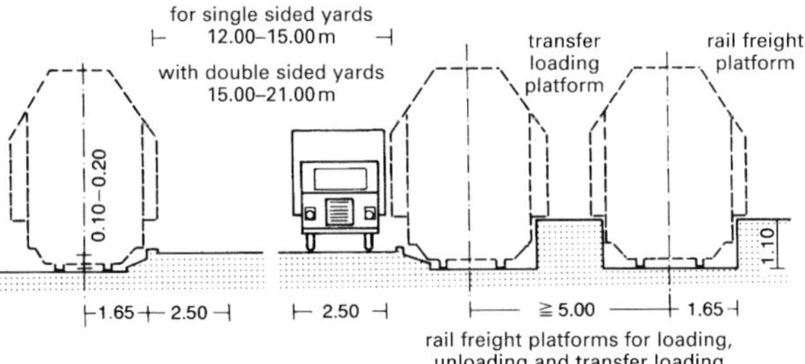

❷ Profile of a loading road (top of rail to road level)

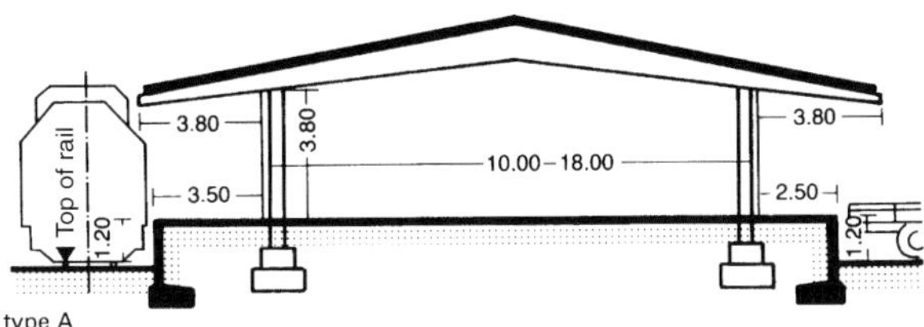

❸ Section through a loading warehouse

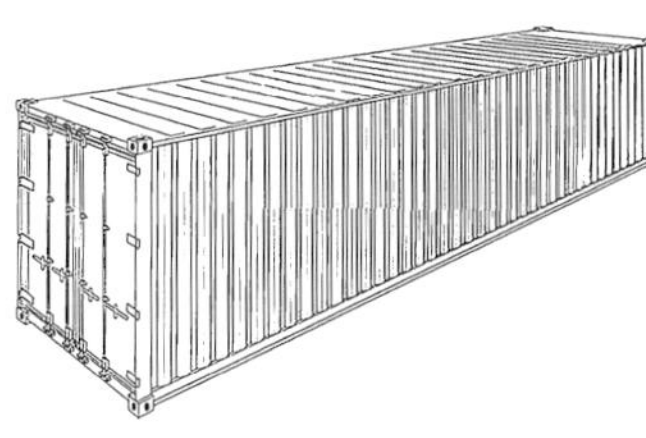

Type 4
Type 1 | Type 3
Type 2 | Type 2
Type 2 | Type 1 | Type 1

❹ Modular system of ISO containers

Code	Container length (mm)	ft' in"
1	2991	10'
2	6058	20'
3	9125	30'
4	12192	40'
A	7150	
B	7315	24'
C	7430	
D	7450	24' 6"
E	7820	
F	8100	
G	12500	41'
H	13106	43'
K	13600	
L	13716	45'
M	14630	48'
N	14935	49'
P	16154	
only USA		53'
only USA*		57'

*only in some states

❺ Codes for container lengths

Container description	External dimensions						Permissible gross mass
	Length		Width		Height		
	mm	ft' in"	mm	ft' in"	mm	ft' in"	kg
1AAA	12192	40'	2438	8'	2896	9'6"	30480
1AA					2591	8'6"	
1A					2438	8'	
1AX					<2438	<8'	
1CC	6058	19' 10.5"	2438	8'	2591	8' 6"	24000
1C					2438	8'	
1CX					<2438	<8'	

❻ External dimensions and weights of common types of 20 and 40 foot containers. The construction size of a 20 foot container is a joint smaller, so that shorter and longer containers can be stacked together.

Today rail-borne freight transport is a part of international goods transport. In order to remain competitive with road transport, rationalised loading and unloading systems (combined transport) have been developed.

Loading ramps

These can be head or side ramps situated in or next to stores or logistics warehouses. The length is approx. 700 m in order to load and unload entire trains. Clear opening width of entry doors ≧3.35 m or for new buildings = 4.00 m. Inside buildings the railway structure gauge (p. 408 → ❶) and the clear profile and swept curves for HGV traffic (p. 461 and p. 398) should be considered. Loading ramps: see also Supply and disposal (pp. 461–462).

Side ramps, at which goods wagons are unloaded and loaded through outward-opening doors, may not be higher than 1.10 m. The height must not exceed 1.00 m if the outward-opening doors of passenger carriages may also have to be opened. Otherwise, side ramps for the loading and unloading of wagons may, except on main lines, be up to 1.20 m above the top of the rail. Details of safety distances (for workplaces) according to GUV-VD 30.1 are also to be complied with. Storage and logistics warehouses should be designed for the goods to be handled. Goods are normally transported on pallets, as these are easier to load. For logistics reasons, Europool pallets (abbreviated to **Europallet**) are mostly used (→ p. 269). They are standardised according to UIC Bulletin 435-2 of the International Union of Railways.

Combined transport

Combined transport denotes the transport of the goods in one and the same transport unit (exchangeable container, container, semi-trailer) or it can be transported in the same road vehicle with one or more transport methods. Starting with shipping, containers have become universal for the transport of unit goods and are also increasingly used for bulk materials. They enable short handling times between the various means of transport on water, road and rail.

The logistics centre is described as a combined or inter-modal transport terminal and is mostly part of a freight centre. Portal cranes stack the containers automatically for intermediate storage and load them onto other vehicles.

Containers

Containers used for international transport are predominantly ISO containers with a width of 8 ft (2.44 m) and a length of either 20 ft (6.06 m) or 40 ft (12.19 m), with the abbreviated descriptions: TEU (Twenty-foot Equivalent Unit) and FEU (Forty-foot Equivalent Unit). Other lengths → ❺. Standard containers are 8 ft 6 in high (2.59 m), and 'High-Cube' (also described as HQ 'High-Quantity') containers are 9 ft 6 in (2.90 m). The dimensions are chosen so that containers can also be transported in most countries by truck or rail. In European land traffic, containers with a width of 2.50 m or 2.55 m are used (inland containers). Containers are so robustly constructed that they can be stacked up nine high (load-bearing capacity min. 4 fully loaded containers).

There are various special types of containers, like refrigerated containers for perishable freight, tank containers for liquid and gas loads, car containers for car transport and living containers for temporary accommodation. Another combined transport possibility is the loading of complete trucks or road trailers onto special wagons. This 'rolling road' or piggyback transport requires only a ramp at the end of the track, because the trucks can drive onto the train under their own power.

Transport
RAILWAYS
Tracks
Freight transport
Stations
Station buildings
Platforms
Platform furniture

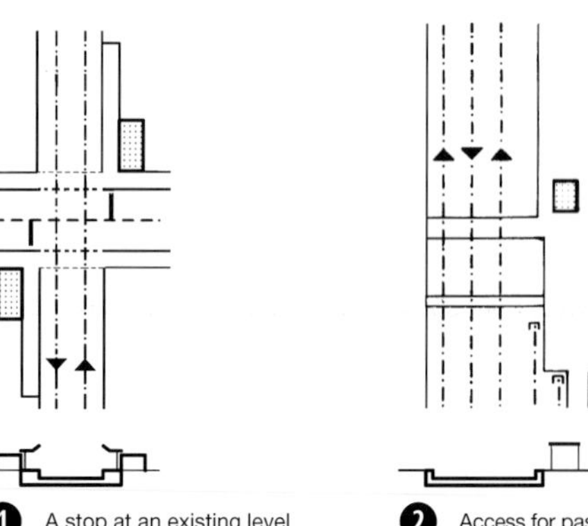
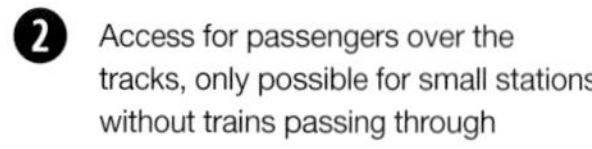

❶ A stop at an existing level crossing to change side of platform

❷ Access for passengers over the tracks, only possible for small stations without trains passing through

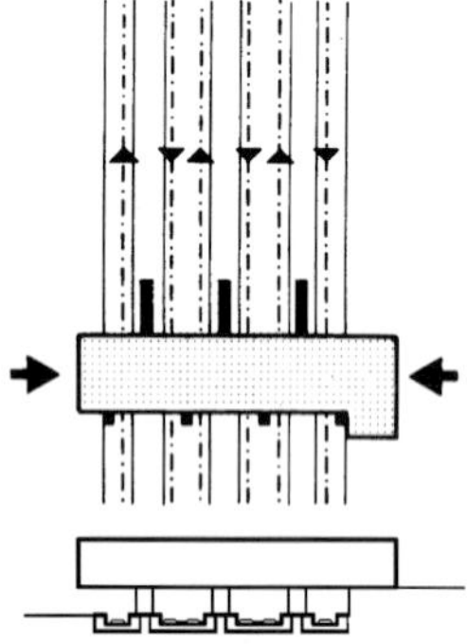

❸ Station building over the tracks. Bridge for passengers and luggage.

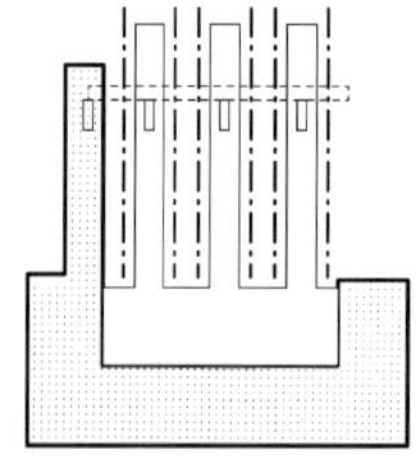

❹ Station building of a terminus, ideally at track level. This is suitable only for stations with no through traffic at all, because otherwise too much track area is needed

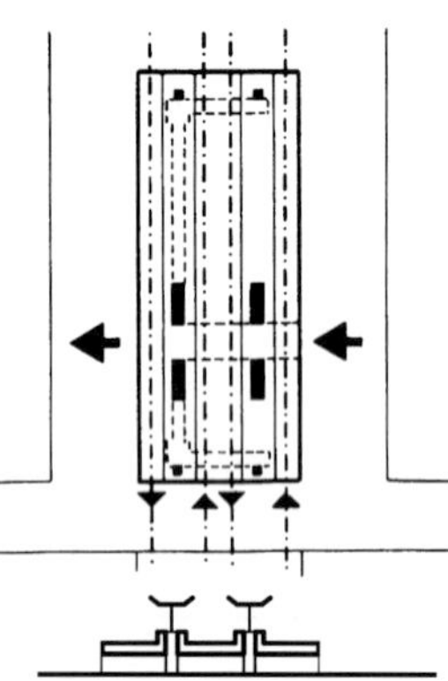

❺ Station building centrally located below the tracks. Short routes, good waiting area lighting, otherwise as before

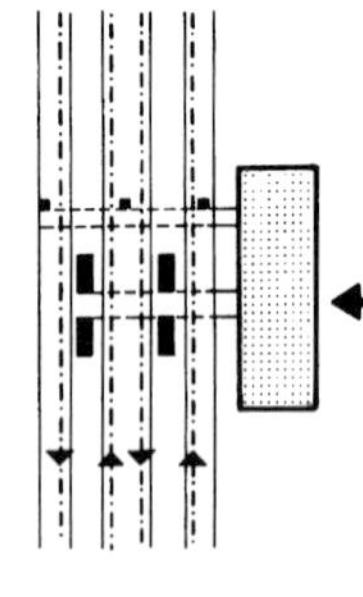
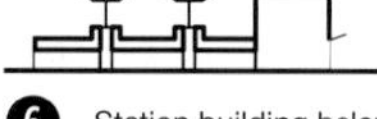

❻ Station building below track level. Tunnel for passengers and luggage. Popular and effective layout with level access

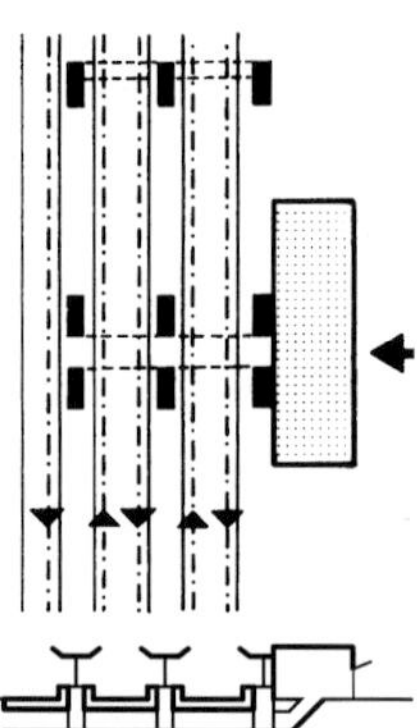

❼ Station building at the side at track level. Tunnel for passengers (with slope)

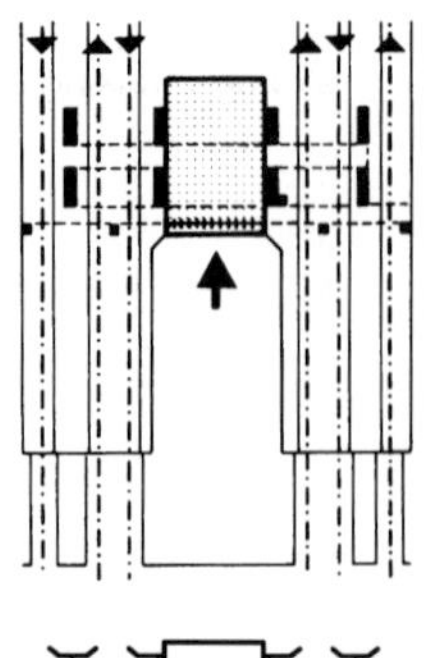
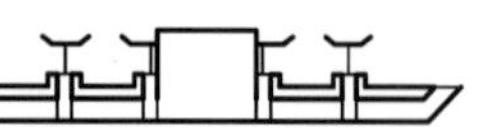

❽ Station building below and between the tracks, generous forecourt, short routes, otherwise as before

Stations can be halts with a platform located next to a line without points, or stations with at least one point so the trains can bypass the station or turn. Stations are described according to the layout of the tracks and the location of the station building (depot).

1. Through station (most frequent layout, e.g. Cologne main station, Hannover main station) → ❻.
2. Terminus (e.g. Leipzig or Munich main stations) → ❹.
3. Multi-level station (e.g. Osnabrück main station, Berlin main station)
4. Island station (station building between the tracks, e.g. Halle/Saale main station) → ❽.

The approach line to the station through the city can be at street level, on banks with roads passing underneath or in cuttings or tunnels with the streets passing over. The route alignment leads to the location of the station → ❶ – ❻, with a low-level arrangement being the most acceptable variant for urban planning (e.g. the design for Stuttgart 21, conversion of the terminus to an underground through station while still using the old station building).

Design basics

The following principles apply to new building and also refurbishment (in order according to importance):

1. Operational safety and accident prevention
2. Feeling of security and well-being
3. Simple orientation
4. Simple building maintenance
5. Brand recognition/formation
6. Attractiveness of form

Stations should be designed to achieve the shortest possible walking distances to other forms of transport. Urban rail and underground stations should be under the station building if possible. Local public transport should be available as near as possible to the platform. It should be possible to park long term and taxis and private cars should be able to draw up.

The station building contains areas leased to external leaseholders (normally shops or services) in addition to the services operated by the railway company, like a TravelCentre, a ServicePoint, waiting areas, a lounge (at large stations) and luggage storage.

Pedestrian underpasses and bridges

The minimum width of underpasses and bridges is 2.50 m. Larger widths should assume a multiple of the walking width of 0.80 m. The clearance height should be at least 2.50 m, but has to be only 2.25 m under supplementary installations.

Accessibility

If more than 1000 passengers per day catch a train, then at least one barrier-free access (i.e. convenient for disabled passengers) should be provided. Ramps are always available and maintenance-free. Lifts should be pass-through (Roll-On Roll-Off principle) with glazed cabins. The minimum size is regulated by the state building regulations. It should also be possible to transport prams, pushchairs, luggage trolleys and cycles without problems. Access to the platform is permissible only along the platform with a 1.5 m × 1.5 m waiting area in front of the lift.

Tactile and colour-contrasted guide strips should be provided on the floor. On the platforms, these mark potentially dangerous areas. At stairs and ramp handrails, the platform numbering should be applied in Braille.

Transport

RAILWAYS
Tracks
Freight transport
Stations
Station buildings
Platforms
Platform furniture

① Main entrance with service point
② Side entrance, access to underground

❶ Station aisle, Hannover

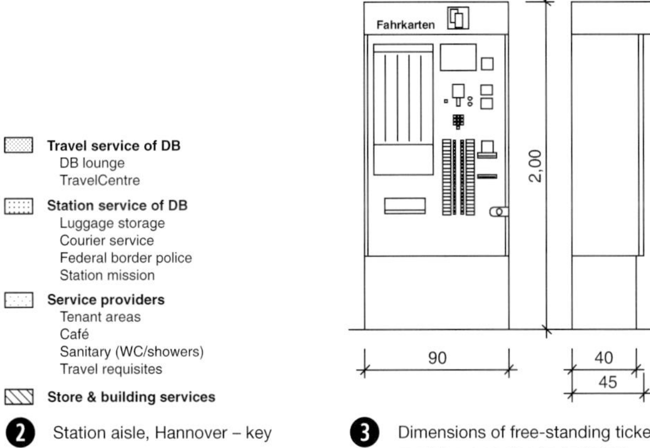

❷ Station aisle, Hannover – key

❸ Dimensions of free-standing ticket machine; can also be installed.

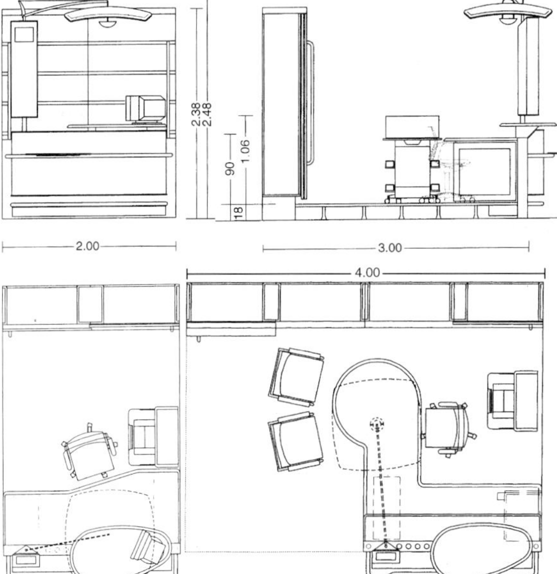

❹ Modular fitting out system for the TravelCentre (DB → refs)

Station buildings (German Railways uses the term reception buildings) serve to connect the railway network to other means of transport. The services offered in-house by the railway company are limited to essentials like sales of tickets and tours, information and taking care of luggage. Other services and shops are operated by leaseholders in the station area → ❶ – ❷.

TravelCentre

The TravelCentre is for personal advice and the sale of tickets. The fitting out is modular on a metre grid, and the smallest unit, a counter, is 2 m × 3 m. The elements are delivered completely pre-installed. The adjustable legs enable adaptation of the installation and compensation for the height difference between the seated staff and the standing passengers. The system can be completed with various supplementary elements → ❹.

A sufficiently large area should be provided for waiting customers with a free space in front of the counter. If there is more than one counter, organise one centralised queue if possible. Ticket machines are also provided to relieve the workload at the counter → ❸.

ServicePoint

The ServicePoint is the central source of information between customer and service staff and is the direct point of contact for travellers. In order to cover the different requirements and local conditions, a product family has been developed with three basic types:

1. Singular type ServicePoint: free-standing in the reception building, various sizes, modular, different layouts for 1–4 employees (for two workplaces LWH: 3.00 m × 5.00 m × 3.50 m).
2. Integrated type ServicePoint: within a façade or inside the station building, adjacent to the TravelCentre, for 1–4 employees (LWH: 2.00 m × 2.60 m × 3.10 m for one workplace, with each further workplace elongating the fixture by 1.70 m.)
3. Mobile type ServicePoint: a rolling stand for flexible use in the station building and also on platforms, for one employee each (LHB: 0.90 m × 0.80 m × 2.30 m). These sizes are at the design stage and could still alter.

Stairs

The usable stair width should be a multiple of 80 cm (walking passage width) but at least 2.40 m clear. The stair width can also be determined from the expected passenger numbers according to the formula:

$$b_{Tn} = \frac{n_p}{v \times d \times t} + w$$

n_p	no. passengers at peak travel time	
v m/s	average walking speed	= 0.65
d people/m²	pedestrian traffic density	= 1.0
t s	time to clear the platform	= 120–180 s
w m	walking width in the other direction	= 0.80 m
	for local and urban traffic	= 0.60 m

Stair dimensions, see → p. 120 ff. The waiting space in front of the stairs should be 1.5 times the stair width. The first and last steps must, and all other steps should, be provided with a 6 cm wide contrasting strip.

Escalators

From a passenger density of more than 3000 people per hour or, with a difference in levels of 8 m, more than 500 people, escalators should be provided. The minimum width should be 1 m in order to be able to transport luggage trolleys → p. 126 ff.

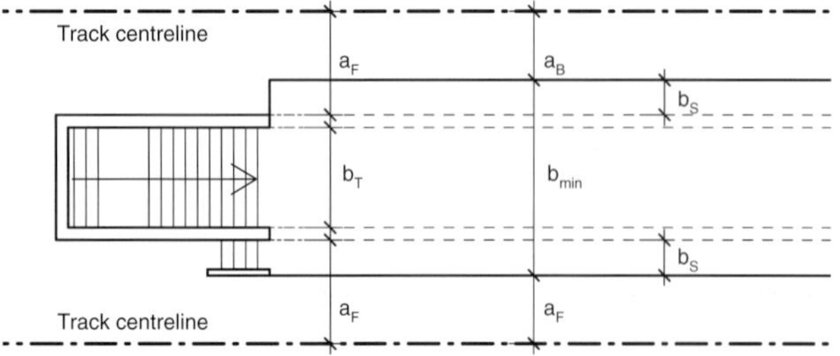

Platform width $b_{min} = b_T + 2_w + 2(a_F - a_F)$

- a_F Minimum distance of fixed objects (e.g. columns) from the track centreline
  - on the platform = 3.00 m
  - at the end of the platform = 2.50 m
- a_A Distance between platform structures and platform edge taking into consideration barrier-free access width and the danger area b_S
  - next to short structures (e.g. columns) min. $a_A = b_S + 0.90$ m
  - next to longer structures with min. 1 entrance min. $a_A = b_S + 1.20$ m
- a_B Distance of the platform edge from the track edge
- b_{min} Minimum width of the platform
- b_S Width of the danger area
  - $V \leqq 160$ km/h $b_S = 2.50$ m – 1.65 m (for straight tracks)
  - $160 > V \leqq 200$ kmh $b_S = 3.00$ m – 1.65 m (for straight tracks)
- b_T Clear width of stairs or ramps between the strings
- w Width of the stair string (including cladding)

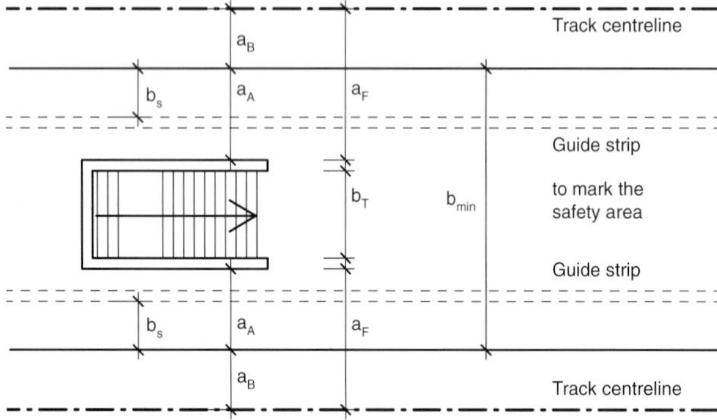

❶ Platform widths and danger zones

Platform classification	A	A1	A2	A3	B	B1	B2	C	D
Platform standard length	405 m	370 m	320 m	280 m	210 m	170 m	140 m	120 m	60 m

❷ Platform lengths (A express, B local, C and D less significant halts). A full Inter-City Express (ICE) high-speed train needs 405 m and a half ICE train 210 m

Widths

Platforms can be described, according to their location, as central platforms (between two tracks) or side platforms (with only one platform edge). The width of a platform is essentially derived from the number of passengers. The decisive factors are the waiting zone, the walking route width of 0.80 m and the width of the safety zone, which is determined from the permissible highest speed of trains passing through → ❶. The details of distances to the track bed always relate to the track centre-line.

The minimum widths are:
Side platforms $= 2.50$ m – 1.65 m $+ 2 \times 0.80$ m $= 2.45$ m
Central platforms $= 2 \times (2.50$ m – 1.65 m$) + 2 \times 0.80$ m $= 3.30$ m

Platform heights and lengths

The heights of platforms are related to the top of rail level. Common values are 76 cm, for local transport also 55 cm, and for urban rapid transit 96 cm. Old platforms may still be 38 cm high. The heights and lengths of platforms depend on the expected operational schedule → ❷. These lengths can be extended to meet local requirements for signalling equipment.

Platform roofing

Three standard types of platform roofing are available for selection according to the status of the station and cost of building. Systems which need only a short construction time in the danger zone and place less stringent requirements on their foundations (frame construction on the table principle) are good, because they disrupt scheduled services only for a short time. These closures have a high cost for safety staff, the securing of the overhead wire system and closing tracks.

Roof construction is based on a multiple of the 30 cm grid (standard 9 m) of the platform paving. The clear height should be min. 3.25 m in order that a free height of 2.50 m remains under the suspended information system. Attention should be paid to the necessary queuing and waiting areas and the specified distances to the track. The design of structures and of elements hanging from the roof construction needs to take into account the additional loading from buffeting by passing trains.

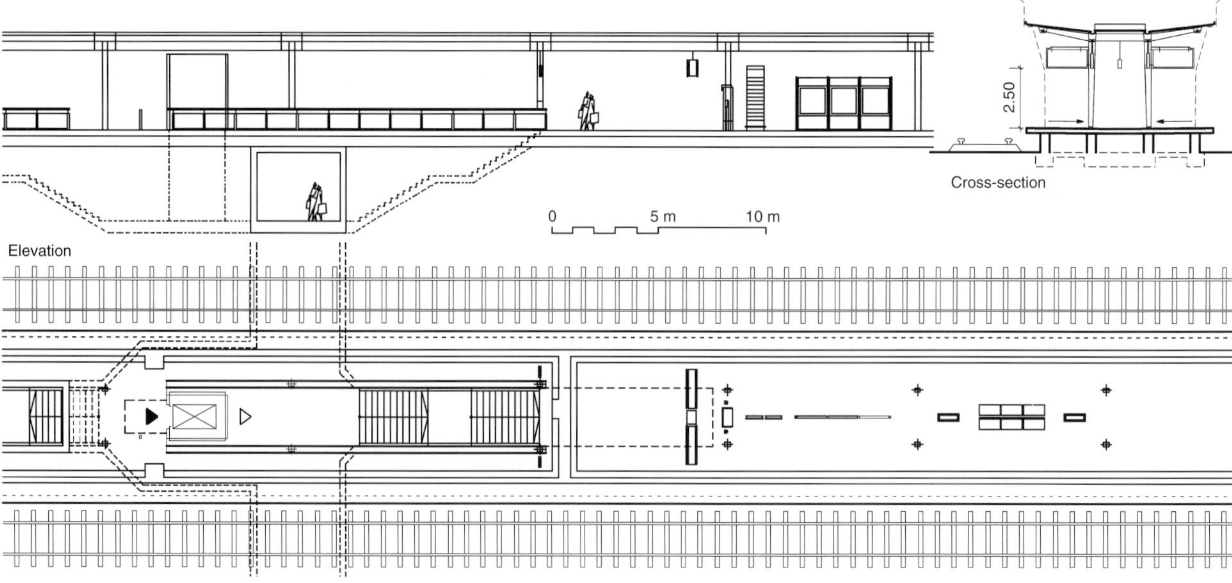

❸ Standard platform with 'Zwiesel' type roof, plan and section

1.75 2.20 45 1.10 60 2.10

❶ Space required by passengers

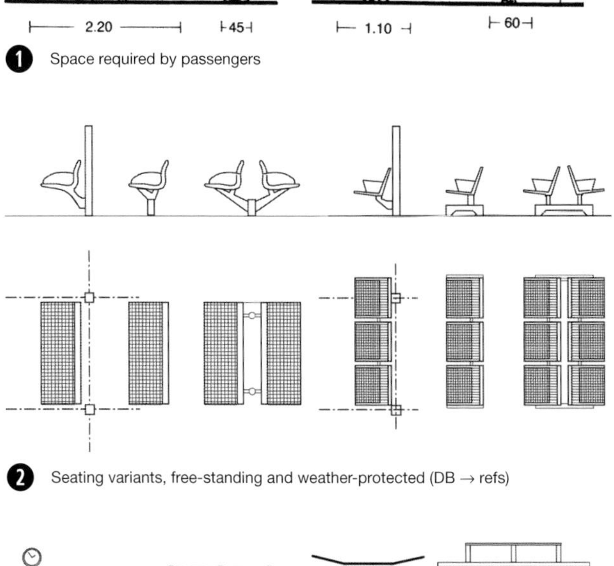

❷ Seating variants, free-standing and weather-protected (DB → refs)

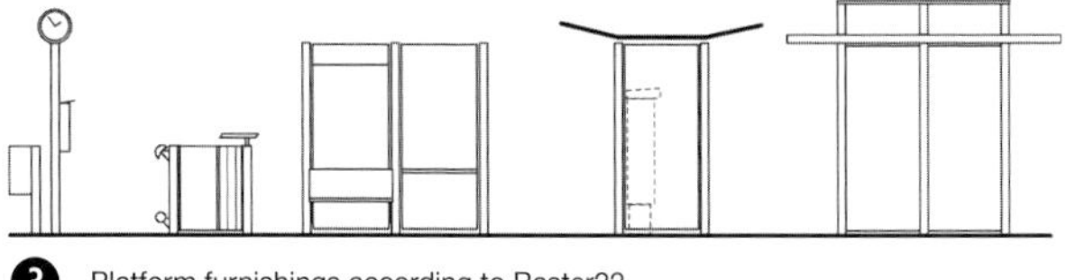

❸ Platform furnishings according to Raster22

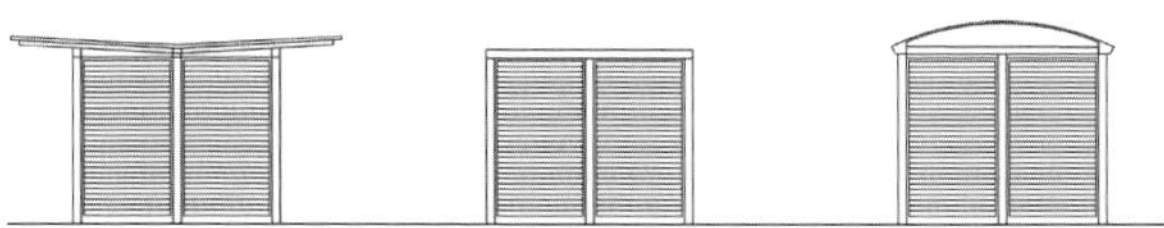

❹ Variants of roofs for weather protection

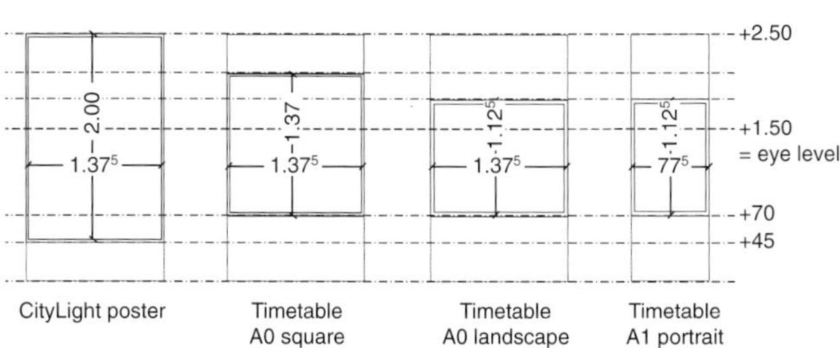

❺ Display cases for various poster and timetable formats. In back-lit display cases, the gap to the paper dimensions is made up with transparent surrounds. The vertical dimensions should enable short people to read the posters (DB → refs)

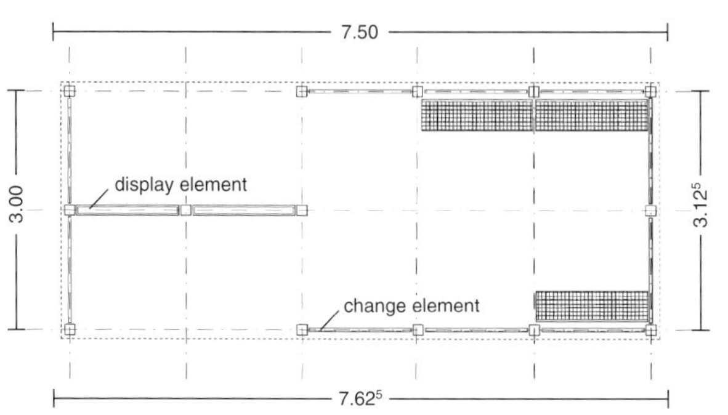

❻ Weather and wind protection type T-in-U for central platforms (DB → refs)

The federal railway authority (EBA) is the approval body for structures built on areas dedicated to the railway. Small buildings under 100 m^2 require no building permission. It is normally obligatory to select structural and fitting out elements from a listed product portfolio, which has been optimised and tested with regard to safety, maintenance expense and corporate design.

Raster22®

DB Station&Service AG has developed the product-independent Raster22 (Grid22) for weather protection systems, wall elements, display cases and seating furniture. This is a dimension and interface system (90 and 150 cm) derived from the paving slab module of 30 cm. 12.5 cm construction space is provided for columns and connection elements, so that the remaining fields of 77.5 or 137.5 cm can be filled with installed elements like wall panels or display cases. The dimensions of the display cases are derived from the maximum size of a CityLight poster of approx. 200 × 136 cm. The vertical dimensions are taken from the grid dimension of the route guidance elements of 12.5 cm. This grid system enables construction elements from various manufacturers to be combined and simplifies the design of connections and foundations. Two product families of seating furniture are available, a bench and an individual seat system. Various types of fixing and seating made of 4 mm wire (weather- and vandalism-resistant), or plywood rails for indoors, offer various possible uses.

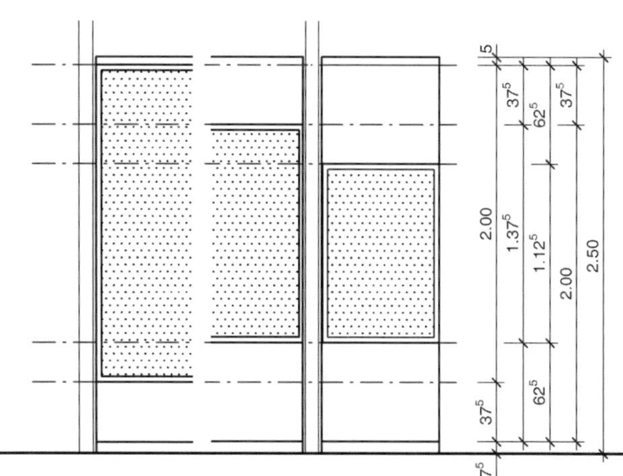

❼ Raster22 vertical module

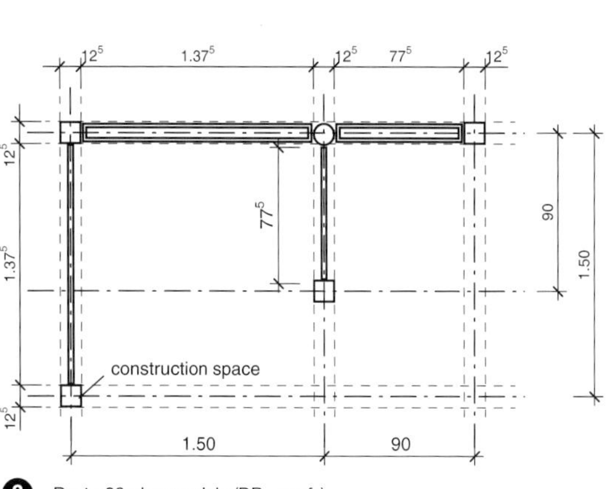

❽ Raster22 plan module (DB → refs)

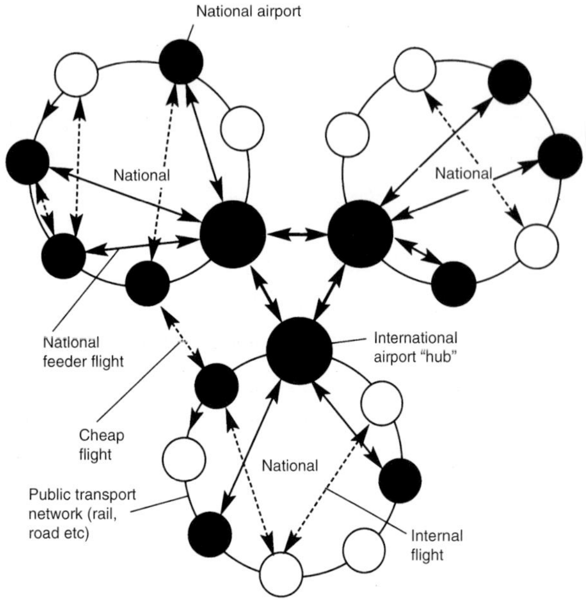

❶ Aviation as part of the inter-modal transport network

❷ Airport density (example: Rhine-Main area)

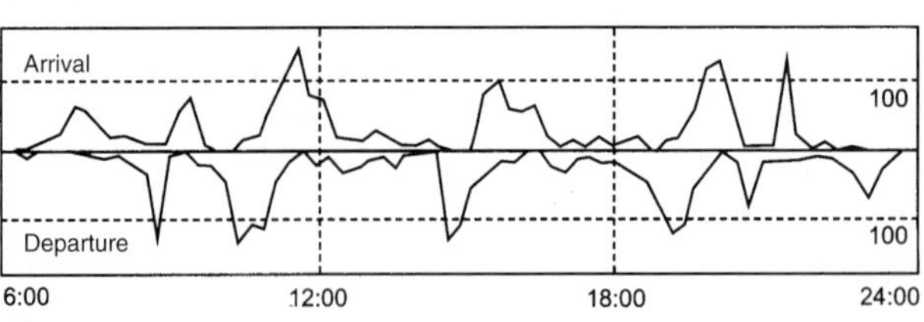

❹ Node system at a major airport (hub): no. flights / time of day

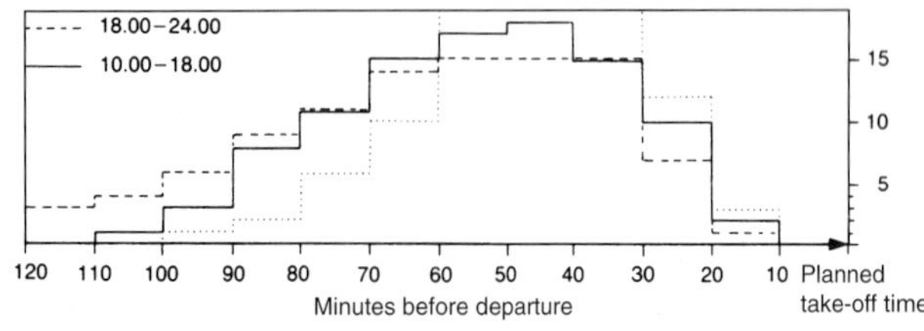

❺ Arrival time of passengers before a scheduled flight

The aviation market

The wave of privatisation in aviation (airlines, airports, etc.) has created a complex market with hard competition. The **passenger transport** segment (business and holiday flights, either scheduled or charter) is differentiated from the **air freight** sector, and each is split into the geographical segments Germany, Europe and outside Europe. Highly varied business strategies are pursued by the airlines with the main differences being **speed** (flight times, flight durations, rapid transfers) and **price** → ❶. For example, the **'Hub-and-Spoke'** model: major 'International' airports (hubs) are connected by large planes and the spokes are represented by the regional connections to national airports. In order to reduce waiting time for transfers, flights are bundled at certain times of day into **'nodes'** → ❹.

The '**cheap flight**' model: these use low-cost airports (few runways) and cheap slots (unfavourable flight times) and are flown with medium-sized planes.

The traditional income source for airports, their take-off and landing fees, are becoming ever less significant in contrast to rent received for commercial and office space at the airport. This development is having a great influence on modern airport design and architecture.

ICAO Convention	The **design basis** for the construction and operation of airports is the provisions of annex 14, volume 1 of the Convention of the **International Civil Aviation Organisation** (ICAO) as the basis for national laws. The International Civil Aviation Organisation (ICAO) is a specialised agency of the United Nations responsible for the planning of civil aviation. Over 180 countries belong to the ICAO. Germany is represented by a permanent delegation from the federal ministry of transport, building and housing. The tasks of the ICAO include the standardisation and safety of aviation, the development of infrastructures and the production of recommendations and guidelines. The ICAO also allots the ICAO codes.
Public planning law	(National) **public planning law** includes **approval conditions** for the construction of airports. This normally affects large-scale projects with regional significance, for which a **regional planning procedure** with additional conditions (e.g. environmental impact assessment, landscape impact and mitigation) is required → p. 56.
Aviation noise law etc.	Because of the environmental nuisance produced by an airport (noise, emissions, etc., see below), the construction and operation are subject to many further **environmental laws**. (e.g. **airport regulations, aviation noise law).**

❸ Planning basics

Environmental aspects

As part of the planning and approval process, the design of an airport has to consider many aspects of environmental protection (environmental impact assessment, landscape impact and mitigation plan, etc.). In addition to the transport connection, the noise nuisance from the airport is a central evaluation criterion, with corresponding thresholds. The area on the ground where the take-off or landing of a plane produces a certain level of noise specific to the plane is called the noise carpet.

In addition, the daily operation of an airport is connected with a range of environmental problems. This particularly concerns **noise reduction** (e.g. through night flying restrictions, noise-related fee structures, construction sound insulation measures), **groundwater protection** (e.g. through rainwater retention basins to control the surface water run-off from airside paving, sparing use of environmentally harmful chemicals (de-icing agents for planes and runways), **energy-** and **environmental management** and **waste management**).

Convention of the International Civil Aviation Organisation (ICAO), annex 14, volume 1
Aviation Law
Building Law (BauGB)
Airport regulations
Aviation Noise Law

Quick taxiway
Transverse taxiway
Parking
Runway
Parallel taxiway
Services administration
Autobahn
Apron
Apron
Autobahn
Urban railway
Urban railway
Air freight
Central handling area
Maintenance, hangar
Parallel taxiway
Runway
Hotel
Terminal
Terminal

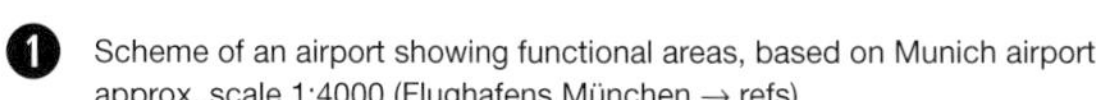

1 Scheme of an airport showing functional areas, based on Munich airport, approx. scale 1:4000 (Flughafens München → refs)

① Terminal
② Tank stores
③ Aircraft maint.
④ Air freight
⑤ Industry
⑥ Residential area
0 1000 2000

2 Frankfurt am Main airport (Riehl → refs) – not for navigational purposes

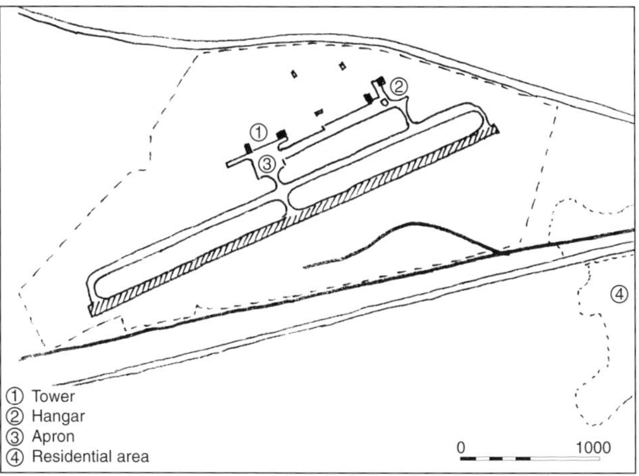

3 Schwerin-Parchim airfield (Riehl → refs) – not for navigational purposes

Categorisation of airfields
The term airport, according to Aviation Law, is a general term for:

- airports (with surrounding area subject to additional building regulations)
- airfields (perhaps with a limited surrounding area subject to additional building regulations)
- glider airfields, heliports

Airports and airfields are divided into transport and special airports and airfields, either accessible for every aviator or serving special purposes (e.g. airfields belonging to companies or flying clubs).

Design parameters for an airport → 1
Runway system: the number and arrangement (spacing) of the take-off and landing runways determines the possible number of movements per unit of time → p. 420.
Terminal: (handling, check-in and customs building) the capacity of the handling system for passengers and baggage or the freight flow per unit of time is determined by the following parameters: connections to ground transport (main line trains, urban rail, car parking, length of approach roads); passenger handling (number of check-in counters); baggage handling (number of counters and capacity of the transport system); and the organisation of passport control, security controls, access controls before boarding (size of waiting rooms, number of gates) → p. 421.
Apron: the term apron includes parking ramps for planes with the associated taxiways, roads and parking areas for handling vehicles. The apron connects the runways and taxiway system with the terminal and is functionally closely related to it. Apron and terminal should be designed together → p. 422.
Additional buildings: various additional functions are essential for the operation of an airport, and have to be included in the overall layout: administration, maintenance, fire service, airfreight, etc.
Service areas: (non-aviation) the strategic assignment of commercial and service areas (hotels, restaurants, parking, shops, etc.) to the actual functional areas of the airport is of increasing significance in the design of an airport → p. 421.
Ground transport network: the comfortable, reliable and punctual connection of an airport to the ground transport network (inter-modality) is of decisive importance for the functioning of an airport.

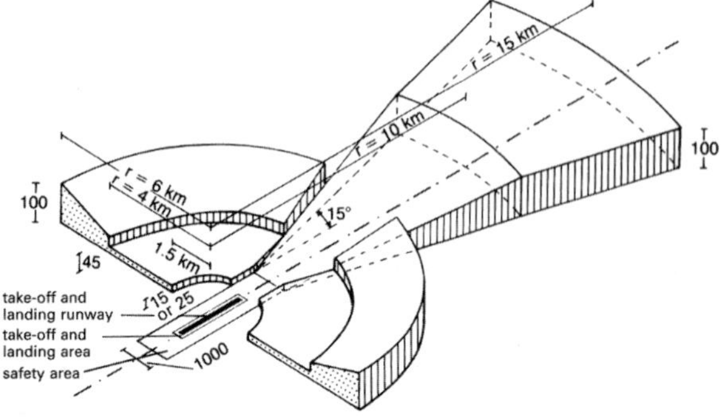

1 Area of additional building regulations for an airport with an instrument landing runway (Aviation Law)

Wind direction	7–24 km/h	26–37 km/h	39–76 km/h	Overall
N	4.3	1.3	0.1	6.2
NNE	3.7	0.8	—	4.5
NE	1.5	0.1	—	1.6
ENE	2.3	0.3	—	2.6
E	2.4	0.4	—	2.8
ESE	5.0	1.1	—	6.1
SE	6.4	3.2	0.1	9.7
SSE	7.3	7.7	0.3	15.3
S	44	2.2	0.1	6.7
SSW	2.6	0.9	—	3.5
SW	1.6	0.1	—	1.7
WSW	3.1	0.4	—	3.5
W	1.9	0.3	—	2.2
WNW	5.8	2.6	0.2	8.6
NW	4.8	2.4	0.2	7.4
NNW	7.8	4.9	0.3	13.0
still	(0–6 km/h)			4.6
total				100.0

Orientation of main take-off runway
orientation of crosswind runway
4.6% calm (0–6 km/h)

2 Layout of a runway according to wind direction (example)

Landing area
l = 15,000 m
w = 300/4800 m
inclination = 1:50

Take-off area
l = 15,000 m
w = 180/1800 m
inclination = 1:50

Runway

Longitudinal section A-A

Upper transition area
inclination 1:20
to h = 100 m

Edge zone
l = 600 m
w = runway length + 2 × 900 m

Horizontal area
r = 3600 m
h = 45 m above airport height

Side transition area
inclination 1:7
to h = 100 m

Runway and safety area (RESA)
l = min. 90 m

"Strips"
w = 300 m
l = runway length + 2 × 60 m

3 Obstruction limitation areas of runways with instrument operation (through the example of precision lanes according to ICAO, annex 14 code 3/4)

Runways (abbreviated RWY) are for the acceleration of planes for take-off and for slowing after landing. The direction, length/width and number are determined by various factors:

The **direction** is determined by the local wind and topographical conditions. The intention should be that the airport can be flown into 95% of the time. A high frequency of strong crosswinds can make necessary a second runway for taking off and landing → **2**.

The **number** depends on the traffic volume; a parallel arrangement with a spacing of more than 1310 m is beneficial to enable simultaneous taking off and landing, thus achieving full capacity → **4**.

The **length/width** depends on the type of the aeroplane's design and the predominant local climatic and topographical conditions, like temperature, air pressure (analogous to elevation), terrain gradient etc. (large airports have a runway of up to 4000 m length and 40–65 m width). At both sides and as an extension of the runways, the Aviation Law prescribes **areas with additional building regulations** → **1**. The aviation authority issues approvals for building projects in these areas. In addition, **obstruction limitation areas** → **3** are specified, within which there are limitations to building structures.

Runways are described according to their compass direction (in tenths of a degree), and if parallel with an additional R (right), L (left) or C (centre). Marking and lights code the individual sections, centre-line, width and load-bearing capacity of the runway. The taxiway systems of an airport are designed so that the runway can be cleared as fast as possible after landing (quick exit taxiway) and the take-off position can be reached as quickly as possible.

take-off/landing runways	hourly capacity VFC (movements/hour)	hourly capacity IFC (movements/hour)	annual traffic volume (movements)
single runway	51–98	50–59	195000–240000
parallel, 215–761 m	94–197	56–60	260000–355000
parallel, 762–1310 m	103–197	62–75	275000–365000
parallel, 1311 m +	103–197	99–119	305000–370000
open V	73–150 (⟶)	56–60	220000–270000
	73–132 (← – –)	56–60	215000–265000
intersecting	72–98	56–60	200000–265000

VFC = visual flight conditions
IFC = instrument flight conditions

4 Possible capacity of various runway systems (according to: ICAO Airport Design Manual)

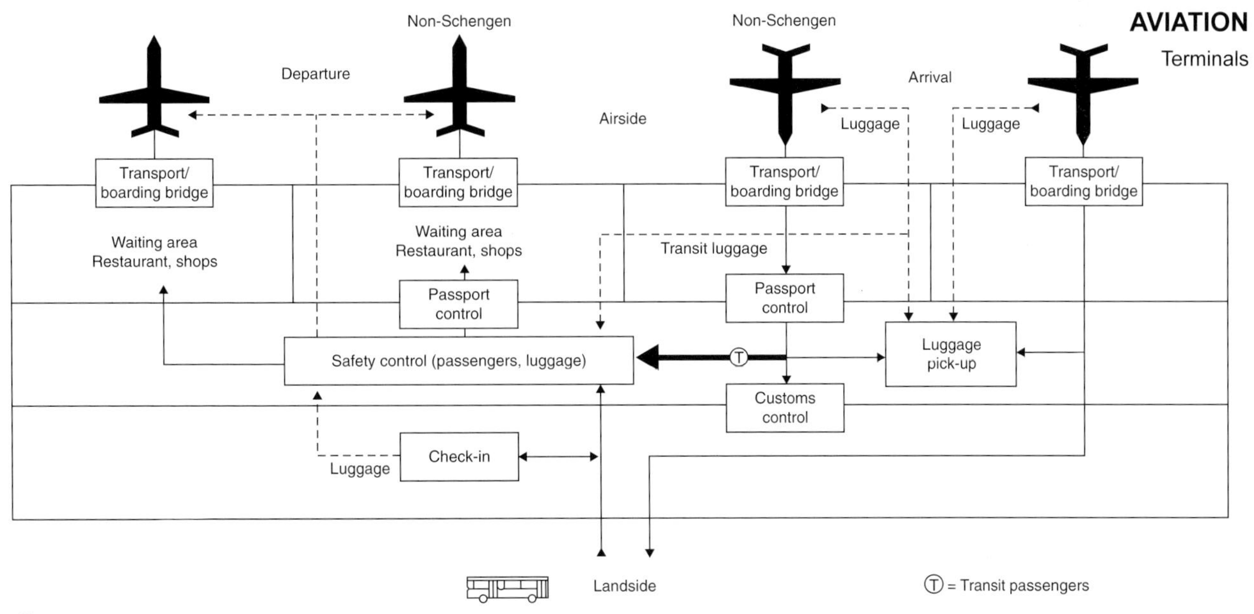

❶ Functional scheme of a terminal (theoretical representation)

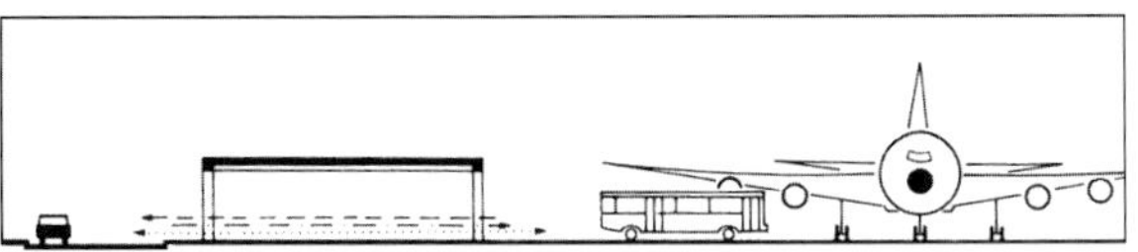

❷ Ground-level road and single-floor terminal on the same level

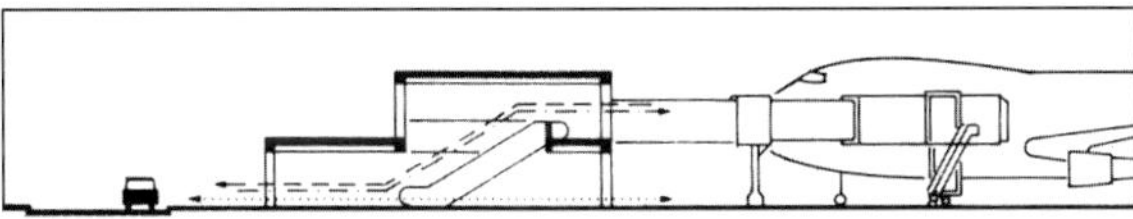

❸ Ground level road / two-storey terminal

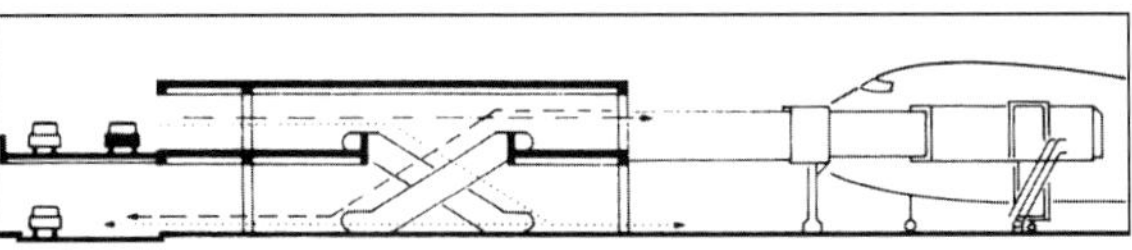

❹ Road on two levels / two-storey terminal

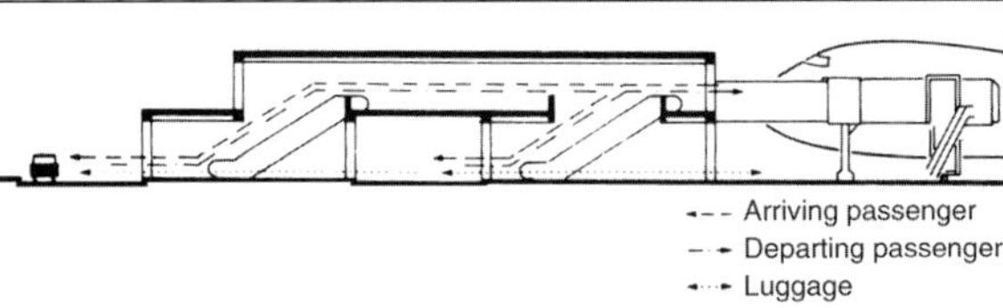

❺ Ground-level road / two-storey terminal

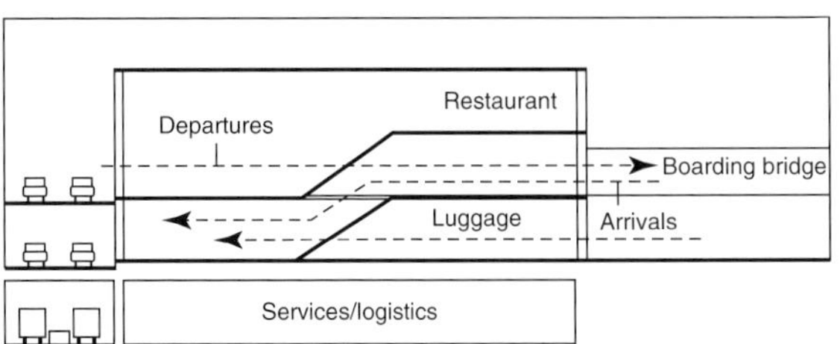

❻ Road on two levels / urban rail link and three-storey terminal with service floor

In the design of a terminal, complex technical and functional interactions → ❶ (separation of the public and the secure areas, organisation and dimensioning of the handling areas, movement and waiting zones, conveyor systems with multi-storey routes) have to be balanced with many other prerequisites. The size and variety of requirements give the design some of the character of town planning.

Handling

Handling of passenger traffic covers all customer contact and services, from checking in through security controls until boarding the plane. Handling is performed in specified stages → ❶ and is undertaken by the airline itself or by an outside company acting as handling agent. The principle of handling is to make sure that **no unchecked passenger or unchecked piece of baggage can gain access to a plane and that there is no contact between checked and unchecked passengers**.

A further important principle is the separation of national and international (or 'Schengen'/'non-Schengen') passengers. The increasing variety of security levels (various source and destination countries and the transit traffic of passengers within an airport) leads to a multitude of parallel routes and security controls with corresponding lobbies (and waiting times). The handling and transit speed is an important factor in the success of an airport in international competition and the routes should therefore be quick and short.

Non-aviation

Non-aviation includes all commercial activities at the airport which are not directly associated with flying (hotels, congress centres, shopping, restaurants, etc.). The turnovers in the non-aviation sector at major airports are larger than charges for taking off and landing. The organisation of a terminal therefore has to balance functional procedures (short routes and transfer times) against strategically positioned service and shopping areas, as well as, to an increasing degree, hotels, congress centres and other secondary facilities.

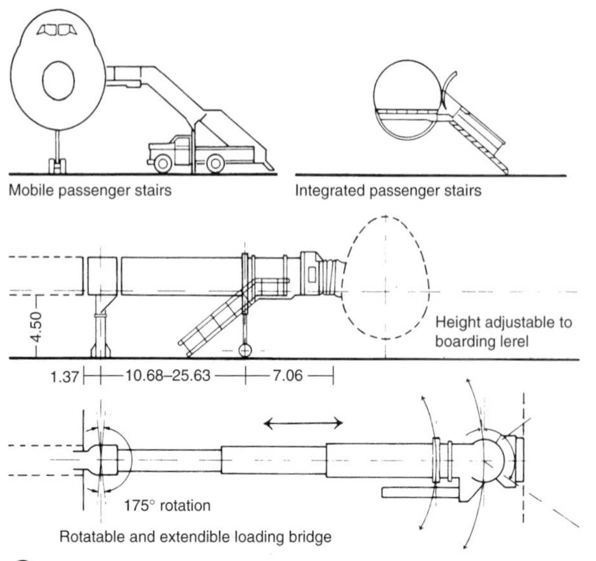

❶ Passenger steps and loading bridges

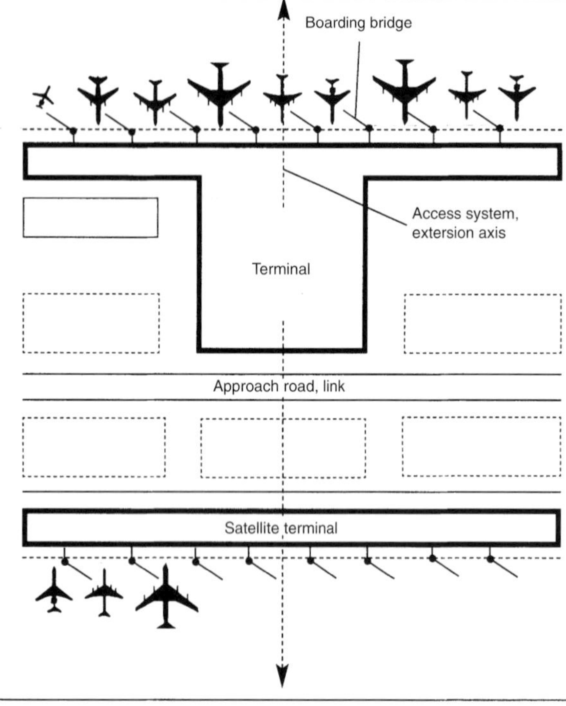

❷ Linear concept with satellites

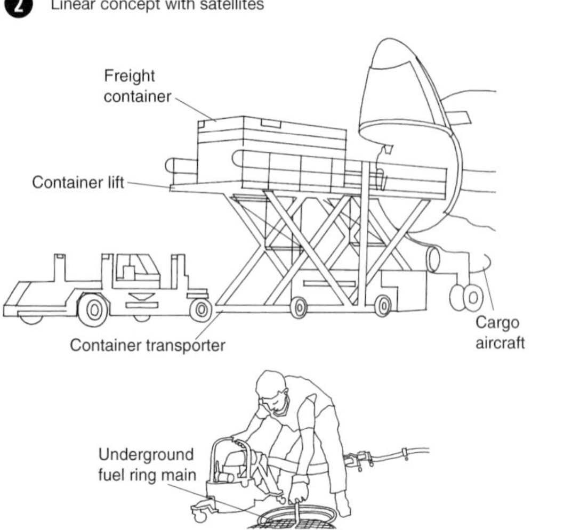

❺ Handling vehicles and machinery on the airport apron

Terminal concepts

Terminals differ according to the arrangement of the gates, their linking to each other and to the building. In addition to the capacity and the areas required, the **possibility of extension** is an important factor in the selection of a terminal concept. **Modular concepts** have become increasingly common in airport design in recent years: **linear concepts** with **satellites** are usual, which means that a linear main terminal building is connected underground or over bridges to satellite units that are also linear → ❷. Access from the building into the planes is normally direct along jet bridges (passenger boarding bridges) → ❶.

A cheaper but lower capacity variant (waiting areas) is offered by **transporter concepts** → ❸, where the passengers are indirectly transported from building to plane on buses. There are also pier concepts with central reception buildings → ❹. When there are two or more piers, however, sufficient room must be provided in-between for at least two planes to taxi in and out, which leads to corresponding distances.

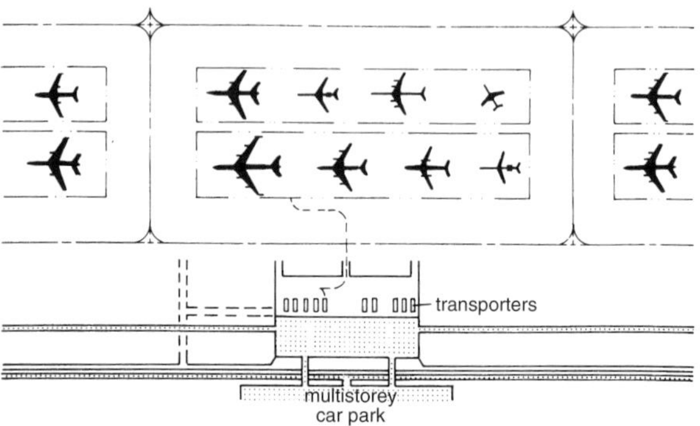

❸ Transporter concept

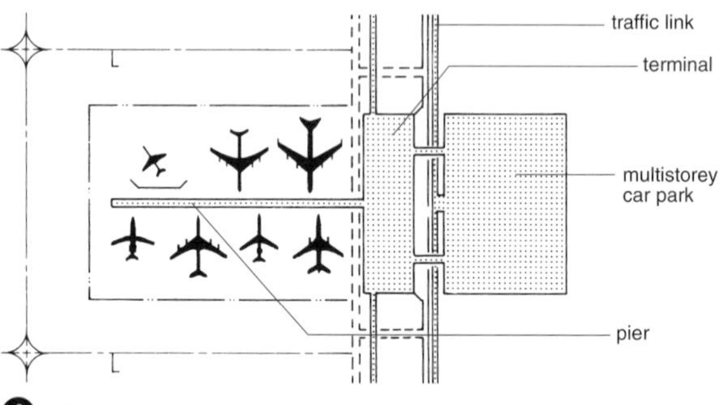

❹ Pier concept

Apron

The apron provides parking spaces for the planes and the associated movement areas (apron taxiways), roads for handling vehicle traffic and parking areas for handling vehicles. The assignment and dimensioning of operational roads on the apron is of great significance for efficient and safer running of the airport. Roads on the apron enable direct and safer connection between the apron and other operating areas of the airport and there should be a minimum of crossings with taxiing planes or other operational functions. Apron roads can be run in front of or behind the planes or next to the ends of the tarmac. If they pass under loading bridges, this imposes a certain clearance profile on all handling vehicles. As a result of the extensive mechanisation and containerisation in aeroplane handling, sufficient space must be provided for handling vehicles and machinery.

Transport

AVIATION
Basics
Airports
Runways
Terminals
Apron
Aeroplanes

The convention of the International Civil Aviation Organisation (ICAO), annex 14, classifies aeroplanes into **categories**, with letters A– F.

Category A	small and leisure planes (Piper, Cessna etc.)
Category B	RJ 100
	Canadair RJ
	ATR 72
	F 50/F 100
Category C	Airbus A 319/ A 320/ A 321
	Boeing B 737
	MD 80
Category D	Airbus A 300/ A 310
	Boeing B 767
	MD 11
Category E	Airbus A 330/ A 340
	Boeing B 747/ B 777
Category F	Airbus A 380

7 Types of planes in categories A–F

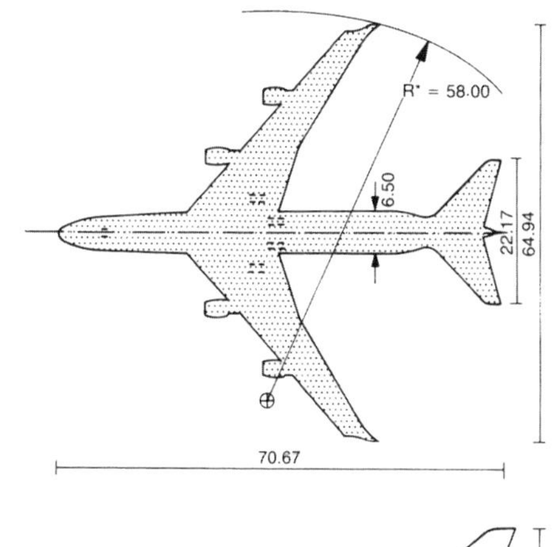

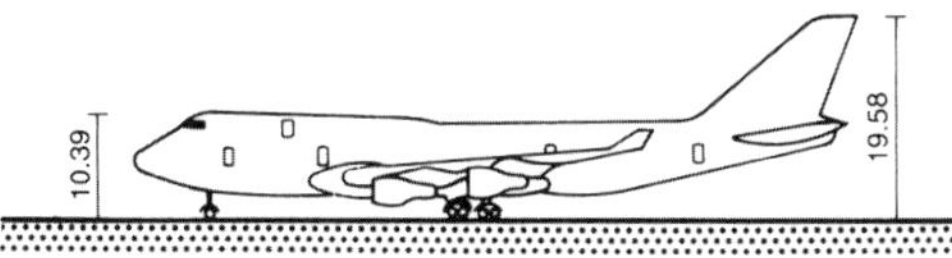

1 B 747-400

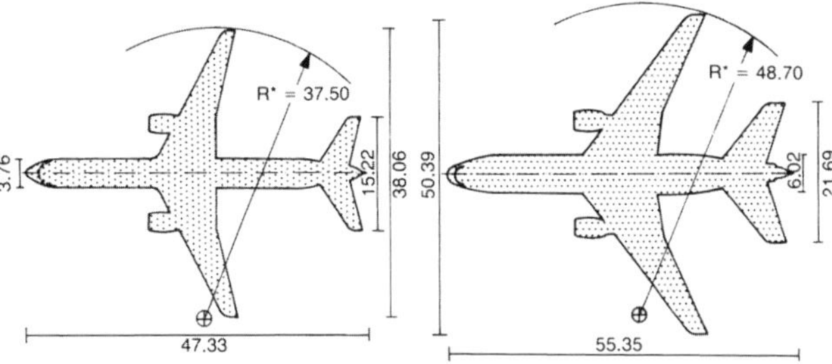

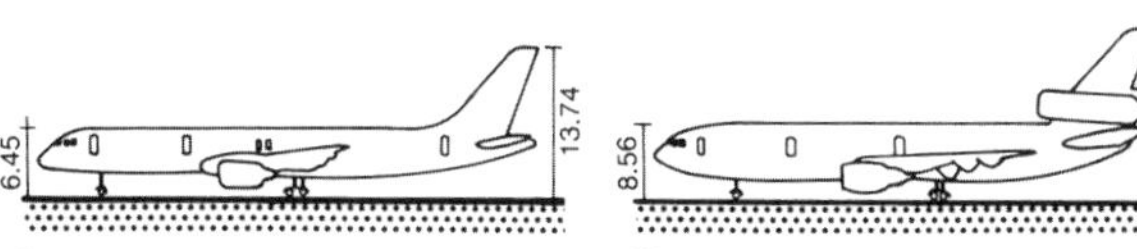

2 B 757-200

3 DC 10-30

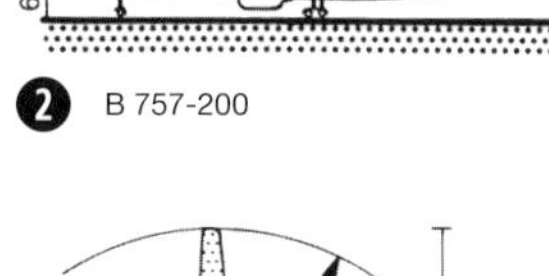

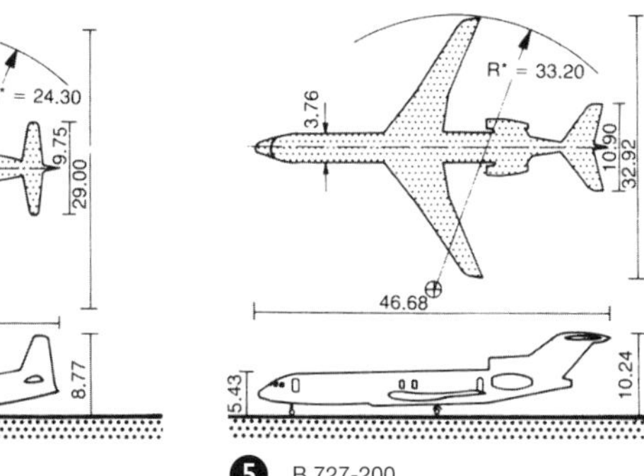

4 F 50

5 B 727-200

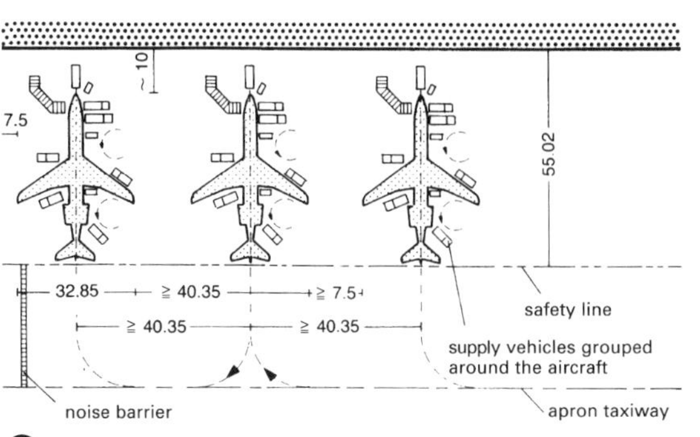

6 Parking position nose-in

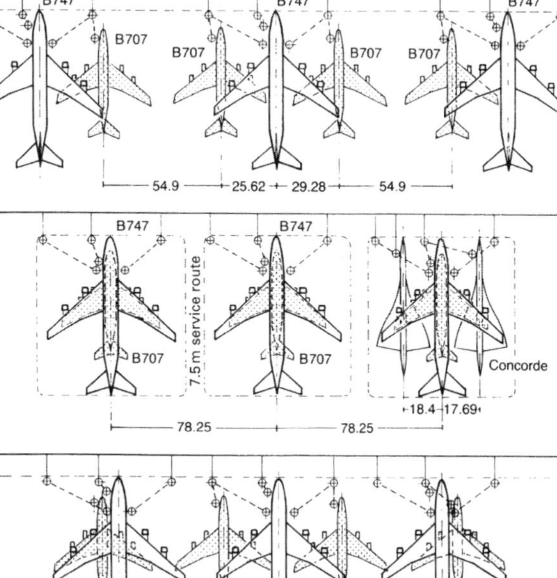

8 Parallel parking layout

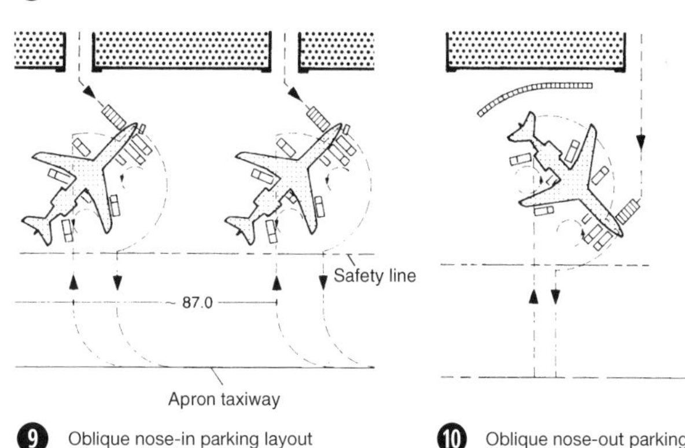

9 Oblique nose-in parking layout

10 Oblique nose-out parking layout

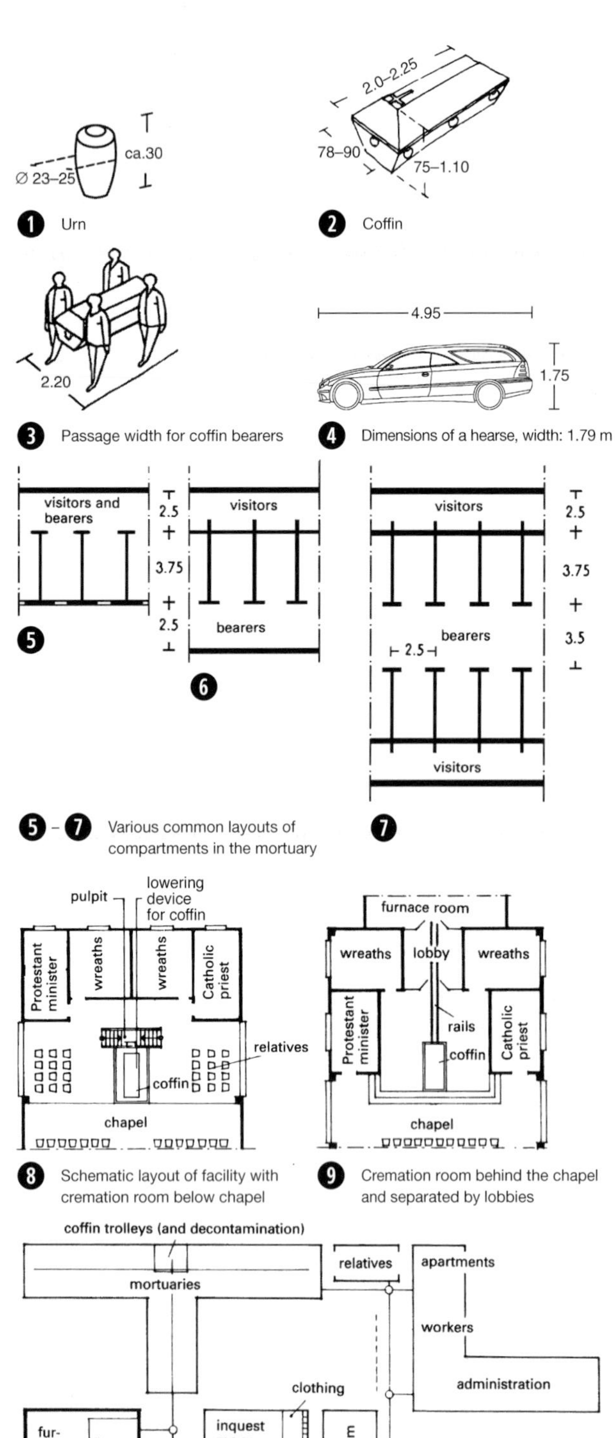

❶ Urn

❷ Coffin

❸ Passage width for coffin bearers

❹ Dimensions of a hearse, width: 1.79 m

❺ – ❼ Various common layouts of compartments in the mortuary

❽ Schematic layout of facility with cremation room below chapel

❾ Cremation room behind the chapel and separated by lobbies

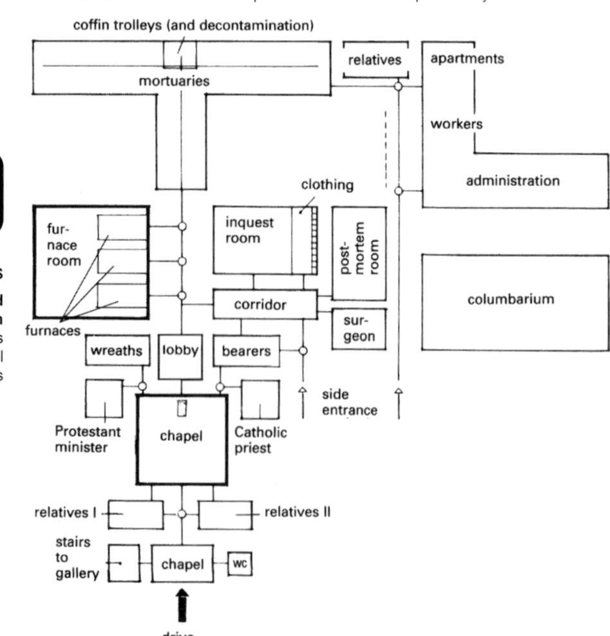

❿ Functional diagram of a mortuary with crematorium and ancillary rooms, for a larger cemetery

Urns are containers for the ashes resulting from the cremation of a body. Their dimensions are normally restricted by cemetery rules → ❶. Wall compartments in urn halls (columbariums) are mostly 38–40 cm wide and 50–60 cm high.

Coffins are sized to suit the deceased person. The laying out of the dead takes place in compartments (or cells) in the **mortuary**, which are separated from each other by lightweight half-height walls (composed of sheet metal or plants) → ❺.

In larger facilities, the **compartment passage** for coffin bearers is separated from the **viewing passage** for mourners → ❻, who can see the body through airtight panes until the burial/cremation ceremony. Projecting pillars between the cells avoid the mourners disturbing each other as far as possible → ❻. Newer facilities, however, often have no special passage for mourners, as shown in → ❺ without side passage. **Compartments**: usual dimensions 2.2 × 3.5; 2.5 × 3.75; 3.0 × 3.5 m.

Mortuary: a room where the deceased person is placed until the funeral, situated either at the entrance or in the middle of the cemetery with a passage (3.5–4.0 m wide) for hearses. The temperature in a **mortuary** should be ≧2°C to ≦12°C. Central heating and cooling must be provided to maintain this temperature, above all in summer, with constant ventilation. The floor of the mortuary must be impervious, smooth and easy to clean, and the simplest wall finish is lime wash, which has to be renewed often. Larger mortuaries also require: one room for attendants and coffin bearers of 15–20 m^2 with toilet and washroom.

A location should be provided for the bier (size 2.20 × 1.08 to 3.0 × 1.1 m).

Crematorium: facility for cremating bodies into ashes; example → p. 426 ❷ In the **incineration room**, the coffin is taken from the transport trolley and placed on the carriage, which carries the coffin onto the fireclay grating in the oven. The **combustion chamber** is either in the basement with the coffin being lowered in → ❽, or behind the assembly room and separated from it by a lobby → ❽ – ❿; and → p. 426 ❶.

Transport on the level is most simply provided by manual winches, but the lift is better hydraulically driven. The doors to the lobby or the floor opening then close slowly as the coffin disappears into the lobby or the basement.

The **cremation** is performed by special ovens fuelled by coke, gas or electricity (consumption about 45 kW for each cremation; height of the two-storey oven 4.3 m) with no production of dust or odour through 900–1000° dry air, so that the flames do not touch the body. The oven is heated 2–3 hours in advance and the cremation itself lasts 1¼–1½ hours. The ashes are collected in a steel box for preservation in the urn. Viewing apertures are provided for monitoring the cremation.

The facilities described above are ideally situated behind the crematorium **chapel**. The size of the chapel varies; typical might be ≦100 seats and 100 standing places, also 1–2 rooms for the mourners (which may be additional to the chapel) and other ancillary rooms → ❿. It serves all denominations (and so requires two rooms for clergymen).

The **administration offices** should be relatively near: one room for the board, 2–3 offices, coffin store, stoker etc. Behind that, a gardener's area with greenhouse, room for the gardener and possibly garden architect, social rooms for employees, equipment room, seed room, WC etc.

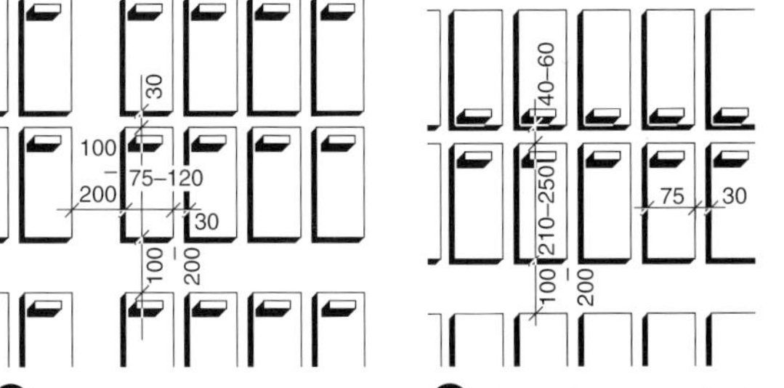

❶ Graves in rows, head to foot

❷ Graves in rows, head to head, possibly separated by a small hedge

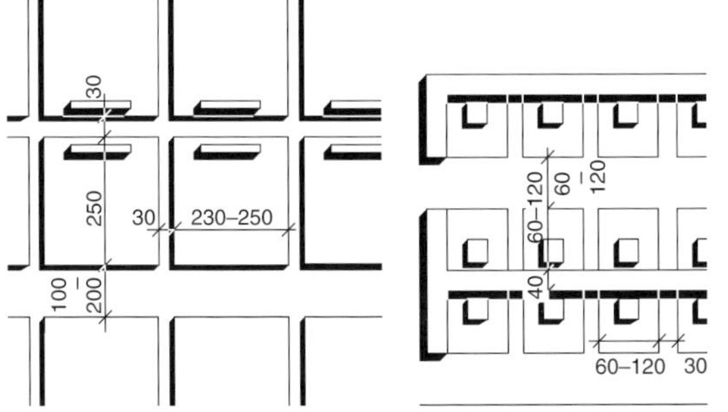

❸ Double graves

❹ Urn burials, separated by a small hedge

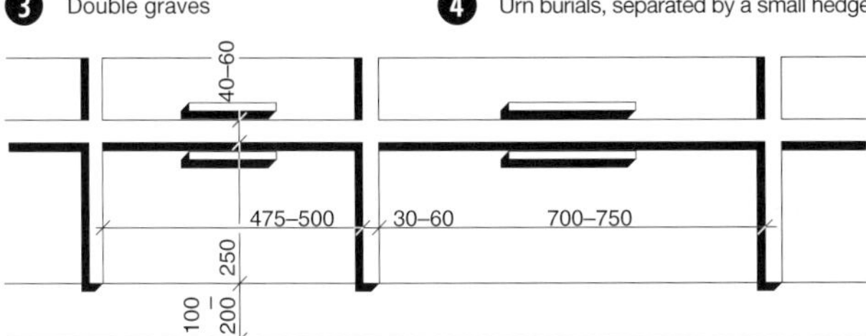

❺ Larger family graves: four- or six-place family grave plot

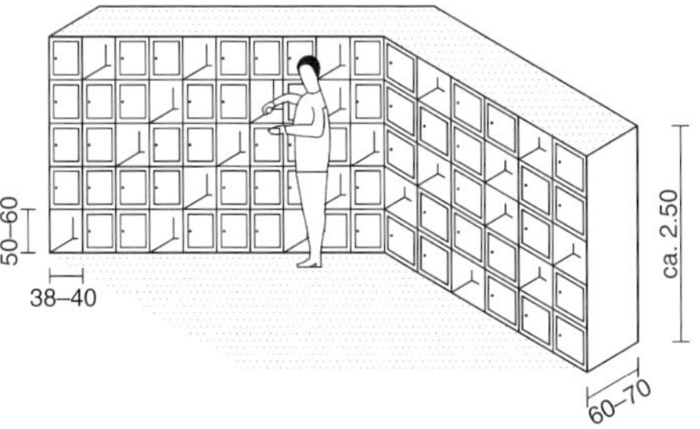

❻ View of a columbarium

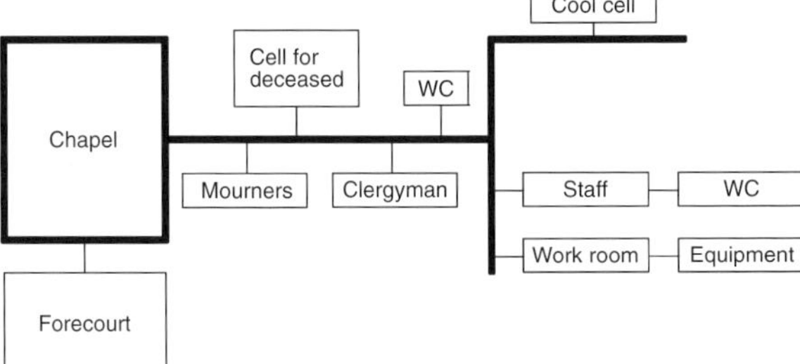

❼ Functional diagram of crematorium chapel and ancillary rooms

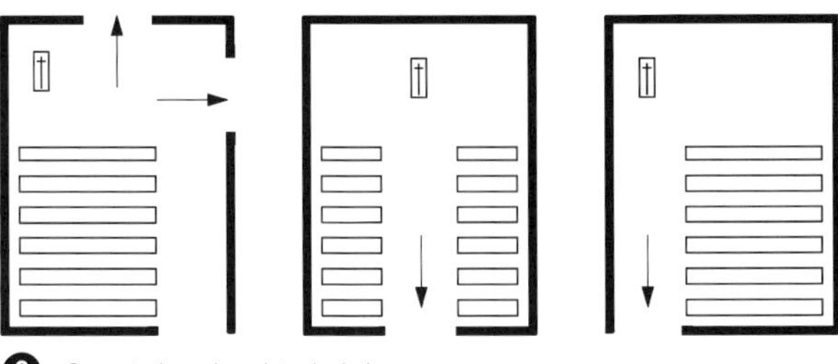

❽ Crematorium chapel: typical plans

Overall cemetery facilities

Assembly area for mourners, stands for sale of wreaths and flowers, WCs. Groundwater table ≧2.50–3.00 m deep, which may require drainage. A large water supply pipe is necessary for watering.

The best exploitation of space is achieved by straight paths and the division of the cemetery into groups with similar grave sizes, like urns, purchased, children's and adults' graves → ❾. Dimensions of the group areas: 30 × 30–40 × 40 m.

Planting with trees and shrubs is often an essential design feature, and some possibilities are tree strips within the cemetery, larger stands of trees as a boundary or outside the plot, high hedges or groups of shrubs to offer orientation.

Graves and gravestones

In an unhedged grave area, there should be only flat or standing gravestones, the size (see following table) and colour mostly uniform.

Grave form	High	Wide	Thick
simple graves	1.0–1.05	40–45	9–10
double graves planted at rear	120–125	50–55	10–12
triple graves at suitable locations	120	150	13–15

Earth burials are located on the main paths, boundary walls and ends of paths. Urn burials are located in the planting belt, urn groves and hedge fences.

Grave depths

Graves for adults in rows: 2.00–2.40 m
Children up to 10 years: 1.50 m
Children up to 3 years: 1.00 m
Grave mounds were formerly 25–30 cm with stone surround; today sloping and 15–20 cm high or quite flat.

The size and period of use of graves in the cemetery regulations are very varied. The following values are a rough guide:

Type of grave	Size [cm]	Space between [cm]	Period of use* [years]
adult graves in rows	210 × 75–250 × 120	30	20–25
graves in rows for children up to 10 years old	150 × 60–150 × 75	30	20
graves in rows for children up to 3 years old	100 × 60	30	15
inherited graves with hedges	300 × 150–350 × 150		40–100
crypts	300 × 120–350 × 150		50–100
urn meadows	100 × 100–150 × 100	60	10–100
prominent places	150 × 150	100	30–100

*depends on the soil

❾ Size and period of use of graves

Columbarium

Urns not intended for burial can be stored in a columbarium. This can be a room (hall) or also just a wall with niches for the urns → ❻.

Crematorium chapel

This serves all denominations. If within a cemetery, it will be an important design element in the overall concept. It is normally situated in the middle of larger cemeteries, but in smaller and medium-sized cemeteries it can be at the entrance, or at the edge or end of a main path.

The focus of the chapel is where the funeral service is held. Its form has a significant effect on the course of the ceremony → ❼ in conjunction with the other rooms.

External works

CEMETERIES
Mortuary and crematorium
Graves
Cemetery chapel
Cemeteries

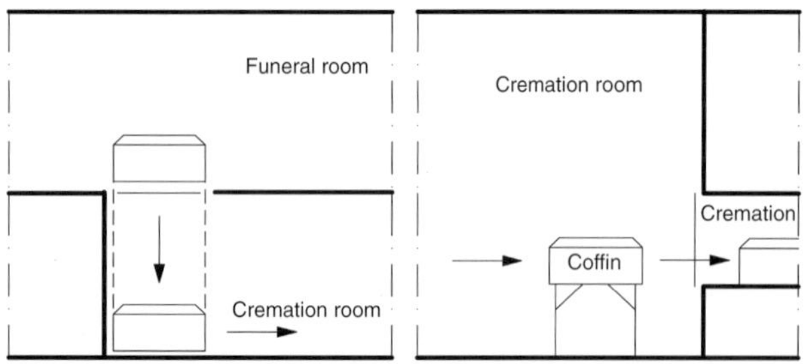

❶ Vertical and horizontal transport of the coffin for cremation

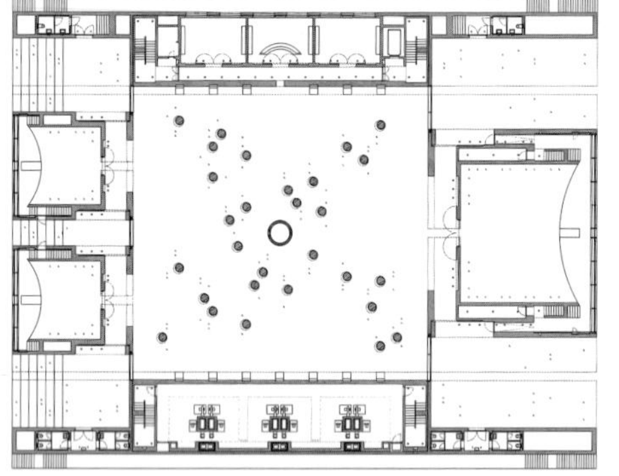

Ground floor with funeral room and enclosed wood area

Basement with crematorium

❷ Baumschulenweg Crematorium, Berlin Arch.: Schultes Frank Architekten

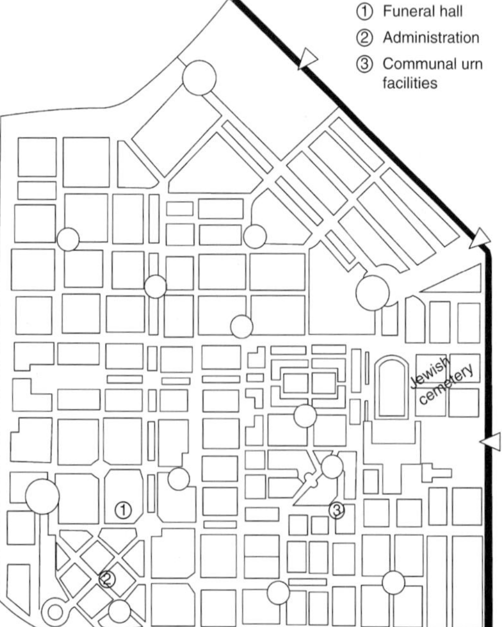

❸ Cemetery as geometrical park layout: Gertrauden Cemetery, Halle (Saale)

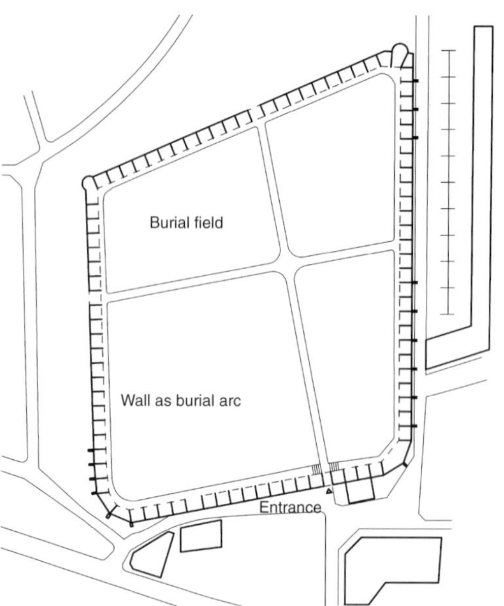

❹ Cemetery as walled 'campus': Stadtgottesacker, Halle (Saale)

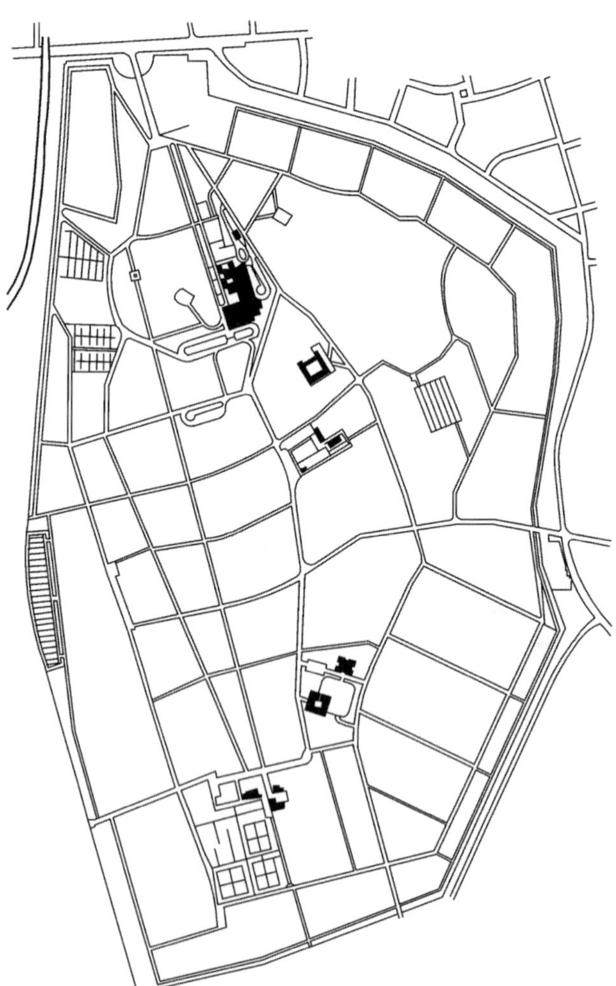

❺ Cemetery as the amalgamation of architecture and man-made landscape: Skogskyrkogarden woodland cemetery, Stockholm
Arch.: Gunnar Aspund, Sigurd Lewerentz

Horizontal aspects

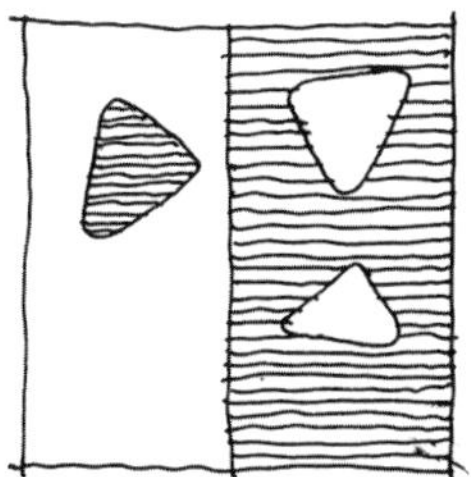

1 Reference and contrast

2 Superimposition

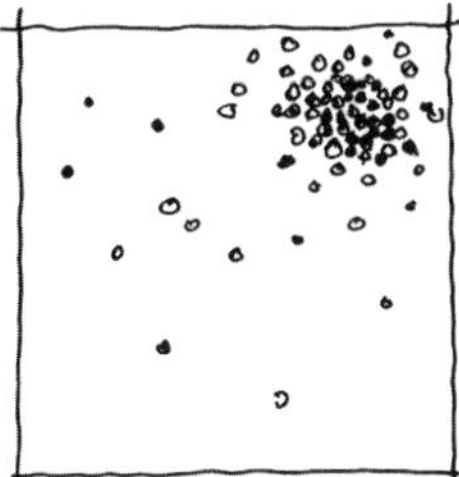

3 Single and heaped

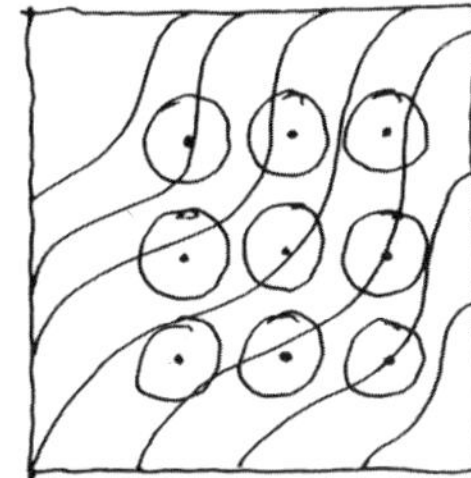

4 Structures

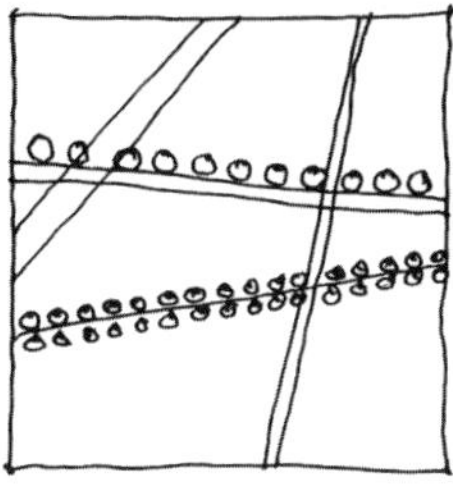

5 Lines and intersections

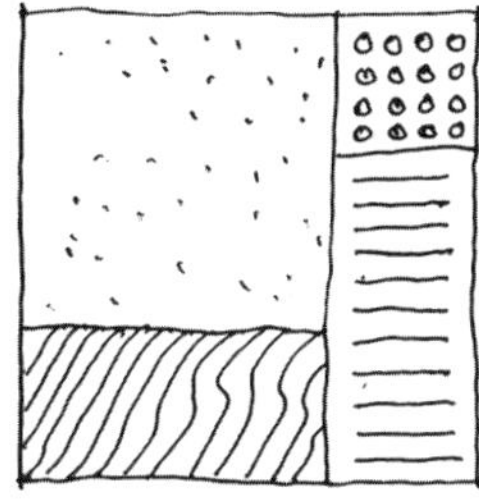

6 Areas of materials

Vertical aspects

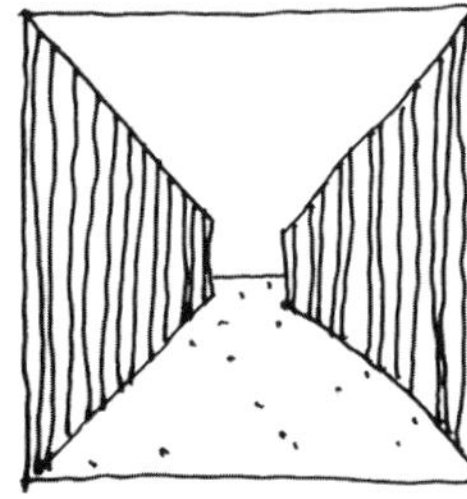

7 Walls

8 Solitary objects

9 Edges

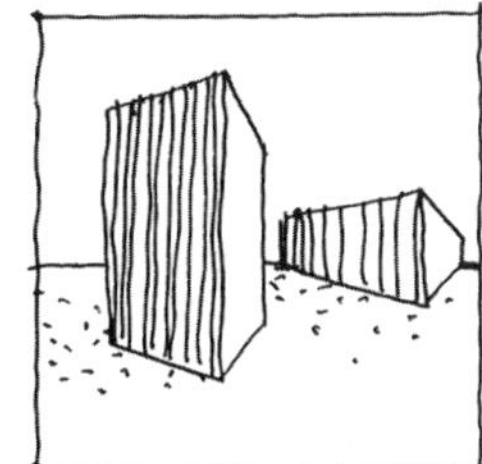

10 Bodies

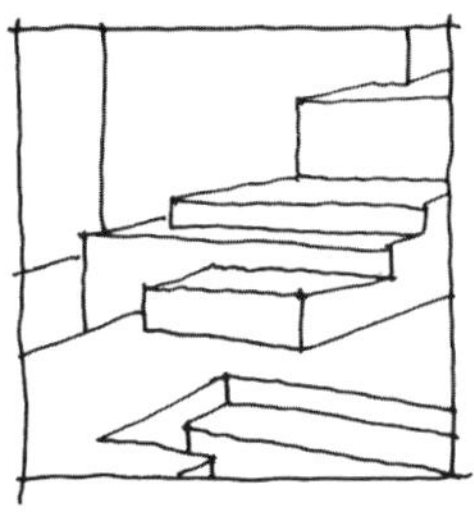

11 Topography

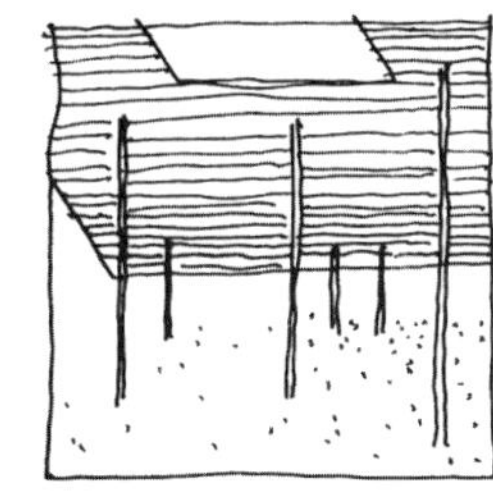

12 Roofs

LANDSCAPE ARCHITECTURE

Design Aspects and Concepts

The term **landscape design** covers two apparently contradictory elements. Landscape is traditionally thought to refer to undisturbed natural landscapes, and design is evidently artificial. But we must recognise that untouched landscapes are almost absent from large parts of the world, or exist only as a temporarily abandoned terrain subject solely to sporadic attacks.

Built and unbuilt land are today strongly related in a dialectic relationship (we refer to urban landscapes). This has also generated a spatial way of thinking in landscape design, comparable with architectural or town planning design processes.

Aesthetic landscape compositions are no longer based on classical garden designs or providing greenery around the building as a decorative accessory – they are congenial solutions for a space, which form an inseparable unit with buildings or town planning. So it is evident that landscape architects are integrated into the project team right from the start, like structural or services engineers.

The foundations are:

Horizontal aspects

The general structuring of outdoor areas in context with the surroundings is regarded as a horizontal aspect. This is a fundamental organisation following considerations like idea, function, design and form. It can produce horizontal results (paving, lawns etc.) and also vertical (buildings, trees, pergolas etc.).

According to concept, items can be related to each other, repeated or contrasted; or a number of items can be superimposed. Open areas can, for example, continue themes or materials from buildings or provide a contrast. The ideal is to produce a central theme without functional limitations and then develop a design to make it readable.

Vertical aspects

Vertical aspects of concepts for outdoor areas derive from the fundamental horizontal aspects and substantiate them. Not only is the selection of materials important but also the spatial contexts of the immediate surroundings. If there is a dip or a rise in the field of view, this lends the space to different interpretations.

On the peak of a rise or in an open area, a roof, object or shelter can offer an impression of spatial definition. In street environments, trees can reduce the proportions of high buildings to a human scale and create small spaces within large. Vertical aspects, whether built or planted, should be to a sensible scale and integrate seamlessly into the overall concept of landscape architecture.

Form of illustration

The decision how to illustrate with plans or drawings depends greatly on the stage of the project work. In the preliminary design and actual design phases, hand sketches and drawings can even today still contribute to a project's presentation. At these stages, forms of illustration have a great significance. Quick 2D or 3D sketches can be a great help in explaining open areas at meetings with the client.

In the phases of detailed design and the production of working drawings, the functional depiction of structures and objects is more important.

The type of illustration will be aligned with the design concept. A minimalist design will not, for example, include playful depictions of trees and vice versa. This enables the consideration of the 'world' in the design with few limitations. Pictures associated with individual components of the design can be selected and presented to supplement the ideas behind it.

water channel
1.20 m
3–4 m

❶ Topsoil pile

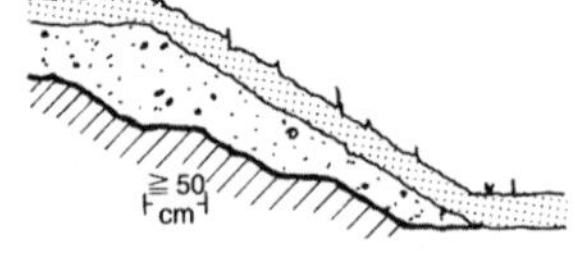

❷ Cohesive material in the core with flat stepping

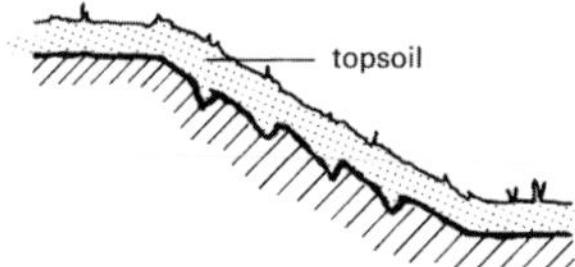

❸ Soil spreading on slightly sloping surfaces

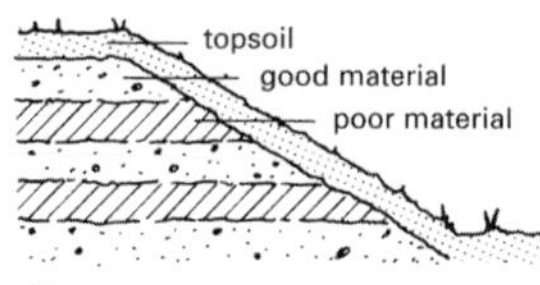

❹ Filling in layers

	Soil class	Description
1	topsoil	upper layer of soil of natural origin or artificially prepared mixture; contains humus and soil life forms in addition to inorganic materials.
2	flowing soil types	soil with consistency of slurry or liquid, of which the high water content can only be reduced with difficulty.
3	easily excavated soil types	non-cohesive soil, soil with d $<$0.06 mm $<$15% and d = 63–300 mm $<$30%; stable organic soil.
4	relatively easily excavated soil types	mixed soils with d $<$0.06 mm ≧15% and d = 63–300 mm $<$30%; cohesive soils with slight to medium plasticity.
5	soil which is hard to excavate	soil classes 3 and 4 with d = 63–300 mm ≧30% or d = 300–600 mm $<$30%; highly plastic clays with I_c ≧0.5.
6	easily excavated rock and comparable types of soil	soil classes 3–5 with d = 300–600 mm ≧30%; jointed, broken, foliated, soft or weathered rock types or correspondingly consolidated soils.
7	hard rock	only slightly weathered, mineral-bound rock types; slag heaps etc., stones (blocks) ≧600 mm.

❺ Soil categorisation

Type		Density (kN/m^3)	Angle of repose (°)
Topsoil	loosened and dry	14.0	35–40
	loosened and naturally moist	16.0	45
	loosened and water-saturated	18.0	27–30
	stamped and dry	17.0	42
	stamped and naturally moist	19.0	37
Loam soil	loosened and dry (average value for light soils)	15.0	40–45
	loosened and naturally moist	15.5	45
	loosened and water-saturated (average value for medium soils)	20.0	20–25
	stamped and dry	18.0	40
	stamped and naturally moist	18.5	70
Gravel	(pebbles), medium-graded and dry	18.0	30–45
	medium-graded and moist	20.0	25–30
	dry	18.0	35–40
Sand	fine and dry	16.0	30–35
	fine and naturally moist	18.0	40
	fine and water-saturated	22.0	25
	coarse and dry	19.0–20.0	35
Coarse gravel, wet		20.0–22.0	30–40
Clay	loosened and dry	16.0	40–50
	loosened and wet through	20.0	20–25
	solid and naturally moist (heavy soil)	25.0	70
Dry sand and rubble		14.0	35

❻ Density and angle of repose of various soil types

Design of earthworks

Modelled areas of ground are generally perceived as pleasant and interesting and can have a strong effect on the perception of a space. The human eye looks for viewpoints and fixed objects in an open area. An example of this is the common hilly landscape with meadows, farmland and isolated trees in open man-made countryside. This impression can be achieved with intentionally designed terrain modelling as an addition to vertical structures or plants.

Homogeneously occupied areas (lawns, ground-cover planting of uniform height, paving), with sunken centres in particular, make spaces seem larger. Wavy or hilly ground modelling can also enlarge the impression of space. According to the situation, this can enable economic synergies to be gained through the management of earth quantities.

Definition of soil

Soil is the outermost layer of the earth's crust and is largely formed by organisms. Soil can be generally categorised into **subsoil** and **topsoil**. While topsoil is often dark-coloured and bustling with life and roots, subsoil is often lighter-coloured and rather less weathered, with few living things and roots. The topsoil extends downwards as far as signs are discernible of living things, weathering or roots, often down to solid rock.

A classification of soil can be found in → ❺. Soil types can be roughly identified by appearance, smell and rolling in the fingers.

Preservation of topsoil

This is ensured on building sites by temporary storage in stockpiles → ❶. If these are not in the shade, the tops should be covered (with turf, straw etc.) to prevent excessive drying out. If the storage is to last longer, green manure plants may be planted. Topsoil piles should be turned over at least once a year with the addition of 0.5 kg of quicklime per m^3.

Filling has to be **compacted**, if garden structure, lawn or planting work is to be carried out (particularly important for the construction of paths and paving).

1. Driving over with construction machinery (bulldozer) will mostly compact filling sufficiently.
2. Sluice only good filling material such as sand and gravel.
3. Cohesive material should be rolled in layers of 30–40 cm, always from outside to inside, i.e. from the slope into the middle of the filling area. Gravel also has to be rolled to construct paths.
4. Stamping or ramming is possible for all stable soil types.
5. Only loose, non-cohesive soils can be vibrated for compaction.

All compaction work should take account of the later use. For paths and paving, the soil has to be compacted fully but lawns require 10 cm, and areas for planting 40 cm, of loose soil at the surface.

Slope protection

To avoid erosion, slips, wind erosion etc. Generally, the most stable slopes for all bulk materials are achieved by filling in layers. Profiling of the layer beneath → ❷ serrates the loose filling material into the subsoil and prevents the formation of slip planes.

In the case of higher banks with steeper slopes, the formation of steps → ❸ provides security against slipping (step width ≧50 cm). If the steps are inclined into the slope, then a longitudinal gradient should be provided to permit the drainage of collecting water.

Feature	Reference guideline		
	ZTVE-StB	ZTV-LW	RLW
deviation from the correct level (according to profile):		no requirement	no requirement
– under unbound surfacing	+ 3 cm		
– under bound surfacing	+ 2 cm		
– formation of soil consolidation	+ 2 cm		
– top of noise barriers	is to be maintained in case of settlement		
flatness of formation (deviation under a 4 m straight edge):			
– for applied bound levels	no requirement	< 2 cm	no requirement
– for applied unbound levels	no requirement	no requirement	no requirement
– formation for soil consolidation	< 2 cm	no requirement	no requirement
cross-slope of formation:			
– non-consolidated, not water-susceptible ground	> 2.5%	at least as good as the layers above	normally, as the layers above
– water-susceptible ground	> 2.5%		

❶ Precise requirements for soil formations for earthworks, according to Additional Technical Contract Terms for Earthworks in Road Construction (ZTVE-StB), . . . for Rural Road Construction (ZTV-LW) and Guideline for Rural Road Construction (RLW) (Lehr → refs)

Scope of application	Soil type	Reference guideline		
		ZTVE-StB		RLW
		Deformation modulus E		
construction classes SV, I to IV acc. RStO	construction classes	120 MN/m^2	100 MN/m^2	
construction classes V to VI acc. RStO	100 MN/m^2	80 MN/m^2		
construction classes SV to VI acc. RStO	construction classes	45 MN/m^2		
rural roads:				
– very low traffic load or insignificant route or reinforced bearing course		—	—	30 MN/m^2
– average traffic load (corresponds to construction class VI acc. RStO)	no statements about soil type	—	—	45 MN/m^2
– high load and main route connection (corresponds to VI acc. RStO)		—	—	80 MN/m^2

❷ Minimum requirements for the load-bearing capacity of the soil formation. Abbrevs → ❶. (Lehr → refs)

Effect		Process	Area of application: Earthworks, road building	Landscape construction	Foundations	Fill material	Formation	Ground for construction	Can influence: Workability, installation process	Load-bearing capacity	Stability, securing slopes	Surface erosion	Suffusion	Contact erosion	Permeability	Capillarity	Frost susceptibility
Physikal	construction	soil exchange	+	+	0	+	+	+	+	+	+	+	+	+	+	+	+
		geotextiles	+	+	0	0	+	–	–	+	0	–	–	+	+	+	–
		reinforced earth	+	+	–	+	–	–	–	+	+	–	–	–	–	–	–
		drainage	+	+	+	+	+	0	+	+	+	+	+	+	–	–	+
		groundwater lowering	+	0	+	–	0	+	–	+	+	–	–	–	–	–	0
	mechanical	compaction, loosening	+	+	0	+	+	0	–	+	+	+	–	–	+	+	+
		alteration of grading	+	+	–	+	0	–	+	+	+	+	+	+	+	+	+
	thermal/ electrical	heating	–	–	+	–	–	+	–	+	0	–	–	–	–	–	–
		freezing	–	–	+	–	–	+	–	+	+	–	–	–	+	+	+
		electro-osmosis	0	–	+	–	–	+	–	+	+	–	–	–	–	–	+
Chemical		injection: liquids,	–	–	+	–	–	+	–	+	+	–	–	–	0	0	0
		gases	–	–	+	–	–	+	–	+	+	–	–	–	0	0	0
		mixing in: chemicals	+	+	–	+	+	–	–	+	+	+	+	0	0	0	0
		hydraul. binders	+	+	–	+	+	–	+	+	+	+	+	+	+	+	+
		bitum. binders	+	+	–	+	+	–	–	+	+	+	0	+	0	0	0
Biobgical	covering stability	sowing	–	+	–	+	–	–	–	–	0	+	0	–	–	–	–
		laying turf	–	+	–	+	–	–	–	–	+	+	+	–	–	–	–
		tree planting	–	+	–	+	–	–	–	–	0	–	–	–	–	–	–
		propagation, cuttings	–	+	–	+	–	–	–	–	+	–	–	–	–	–	–
	intermediate greening	inert materials	+	–	–	+	–	–	–	0	+	0	0	–	–	–	–
		sowing	0	+	–	+	–	–	0	–	+	+	+	–	–	–	–

Explanation: + normal process / good effect
0 sometimes used / may work
– never used / no effect

Processes for soil improvement and consolidation: scope of application and properties which can be influenced (Lehr → refs)

Soil formation

Soil formation is achieved by the excavation of topsoil and removal of obstructions. It should ensure the following:

1. Correct profile (short and long term)
2. Water run-off
3. Degree of compaction
4. Load-bearing capacity and suitability for transporting

With earth structures the soil formation must comply with certain requirements → ❶, which should be checked in each individual case. Soil in these areas also has to comply with various degrees of compaction according to use.

The individual degrees of compaction are, for example, evaluated with the deformation modulus EV 2 → ❷ and differ above all in the existing subsoil conditions and the planned pavement loading. When a formation for earth structures or roads is described, a differentiation is normally made between coarse and fine soil formation for vegetation areas. For sport grass areas, this fine formation can even demand a precision of max. 30 mm on a 4 m straight edge.

Soil loosening

According to the nature of the subsoil, it can often be subjected to unintended further compaction during and after various construction activities on the site. In particular driving on wet soil has a negative influence on the soil structure. In over-compacted soil, roots remain small and flat. The compacted soil is also particularly susceptible to damage from drying and waterlogging.

Soil is loosened in landscape construction by digging over 30–40 cm deep, or through the use of a pick or machines for loosening. Care should be taken not to cause further compaction with the necessary machines.

The best-known machines are the subsoil grubber, reversible share grubber and plough. Rotary tillers, which are often also used, should not be employed too often or too intensively as they destroy the soil's crumbly structure and create a soil that can no longer absorb and store water and has to be replaced.

Soil improvement

Soil improvement denotes processes to improve the properties of the soil for planting as quickly as possible and improve unsuitable sandy or clay soils through the appropriate measures. The risk of damage due to drought (sandy soils) or waterlogging (clay soils) is reduced if soil containing loam or clay is mixed into sandy soils, or sand is mixed into clay soils. Soil improvement using peat or dung is possible but either not readily available or too expensive. At the moment, well-rotted organic compost from organic waste is recommended for the improvement of all growing soils. The normal treatment is about 10 litres per m^2 of organic compost with the RAL (German quality assurance) mark. This means a layer 1.0–2.0 cm thick.

This compost is worked flat into the soil, not deeper than 20 cm. This improves the soil structure significantly and works in enough nutrients to start the growth of all plants, meaning that no additional mineral fertiliser is required at the start of planting.

Soil improvement or soil consolidation is also carried out to improve load-bearing subsoils. This is often done through the addition of binder. Firstly, the deficiency of the soil in the relevant property should be determined in light of the intended improvement (to provide a temporary road etc.). The individual processes are shown in → ❸. The term 'soil treatment' is often used in Germany but internationally this is described as 'soil stabilisation'.

❶ Fence with projecting posts

❷ With horizontal bars

❸ With vertical wooden louvres

❹ Paddock fence with round wooden rail at the top

❺ Of overlapping glued boards

❻ Simple wooden fence

❼ Paddock fence with overlapping posts and rails

❽ Unfinished, sawn boards nailed to posts

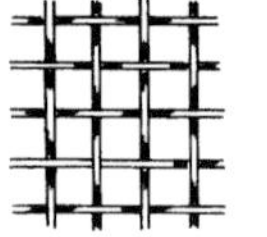

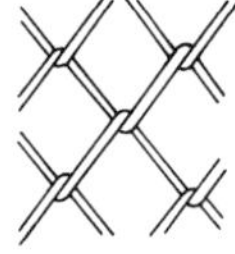
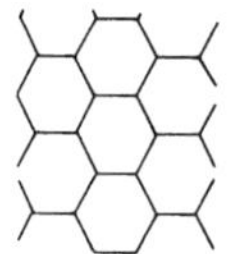

❾ Wire mesh, normal wire spacing 4–5.5 cm

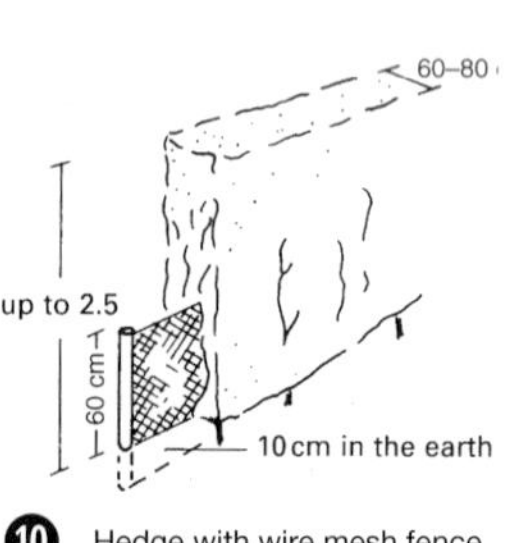

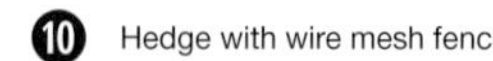

❿ Hedge with wire mesh fence

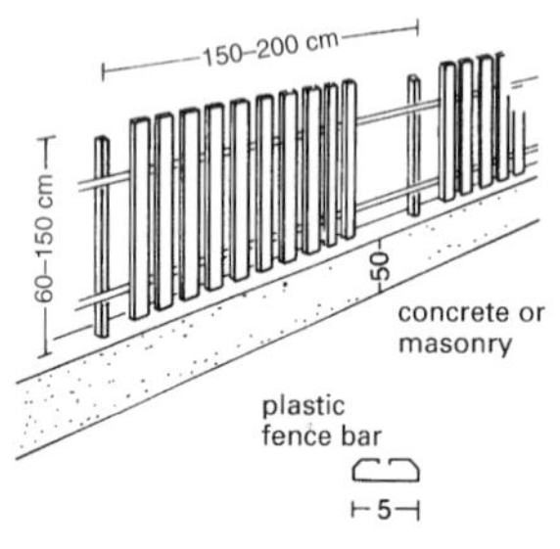

⓫ Fence of galvanised steel profiles with wooden uprights

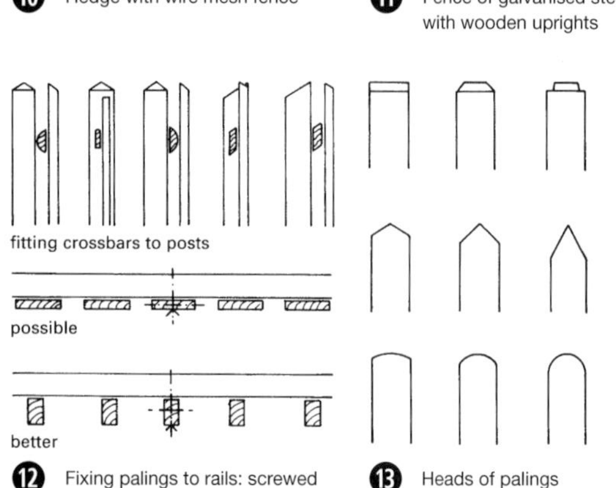

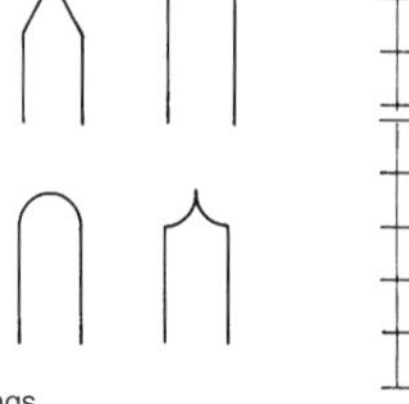

⓬ Fixing palings to rails: screwed from behind, thin palings screwed on the face side

⓭ Heads of palings

Design aspects of walls and fences

During the planning stage it should generally be noted that walls and fences form vertical optical barriers. This should be used intentionally to create spaces or particular views (visual domains). Individual spaces can be created out of large areas either geometrically or also organically. The selection of materials should consider the overall design concept. For example, paving can be of materials (natural stone, brick etc.) that 'grow out of' their original location, and can be continued into walls to create a tranquil and homogeneous effect. Walls and fencing offer a multitude of design forms and types.

Fences are normally made of wood or metal. Wooden fencing is generally cheaper but not so durable.

Wooden fences are normally used in rural areas or for special requirements (animal pounds etc.). Functional enclosures, like fencing to keep out wild animals, can also be integrated into hedges → ❿. Wooden posts should always be well protected against soil moisture if at all possible → ⓯.

Metal fences can offer a high-quality and durable appearance. Industrially manufactured metal fencing with panels of wire mesh or metal rods → ⓮ are a compromise between cost and usefulness and are available in builder's merchants or DIY shops.

Metal mesh or grilles are more stable than wire mesh fences and can be used to meet security requirements. The spacing of the bars is normally varied with height → ⓮.

High-quality metal fences require design work in advance, and are then made up by a smith/metalworker. The design should include criteria like overall appearance, suitability of the various parts for processing (galvanising, coating) and function. Corrosion-protected metal fences can be concreted into the ground without further treatment.

The rights of neighbours/duty to enclose

Regulations about the distance of walls and fences from boundaries are laid down in the Law on the Rights of Neighbours and the individual state building regulations. The normal situation is that every house owner has to fence the right-hand side of their boundary as seen from the road. The joint back is to be fenced communally, i.e. the costs of minimal fencing (wire mesh fence, height = 1.25 m) are to be shared. If a house owner has a sole duty of enclosure, then they must bear the cost of fencing alone and the fencing must stand on their own property. If the enclosure duty is shared, then the barrier must be centred on the boundary. There is a general duty of enclosure when it is usual in the location. Exceptions are regulated in the law mentioned above. Walls and retaining walls (including enclosures) do not require, for example, according to the building regulations in Berlin, building permission unless they exceed 2.0 m in height.

Under English law, ownership of, and responsibility for, walls and fences etc. are specified in the deeds of the property.

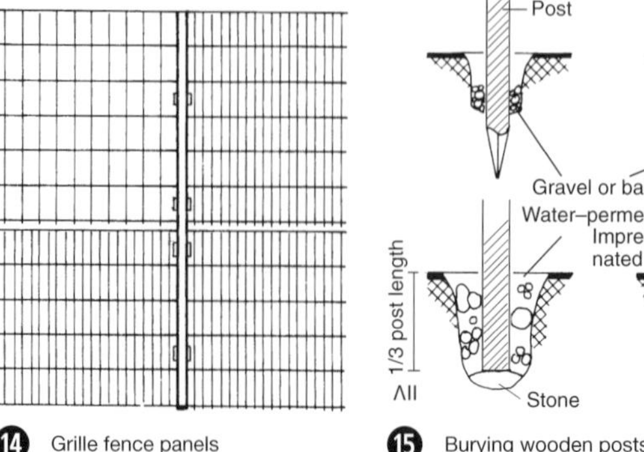
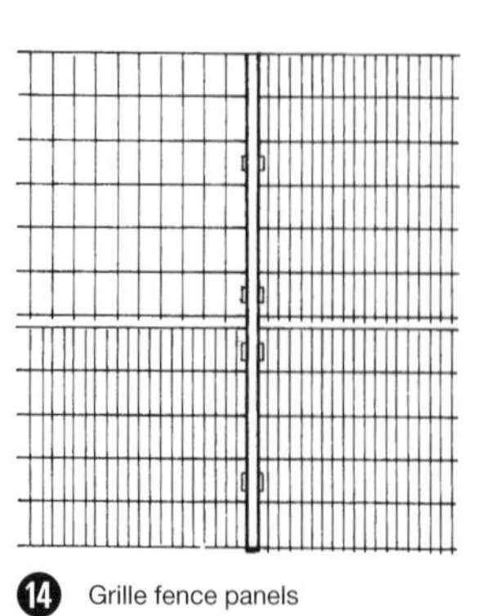

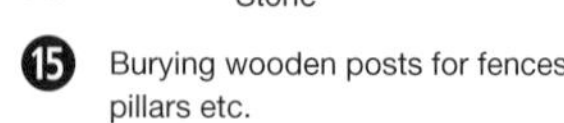

⓮ Grille fence panels

⓯ Burying wooden posts for fences, pillars etc.

Walls are differentiated into retaining walls and freestanding walls. The particular feature of retaining walls is the earth filling to one side → ❾ so the effects of moisture and the longevity of the materials have to be taken into account.
Retaining walls can be self-supporting → ❿, of concrete with facing brick or of dry stone → ❾.
The simplest form of retaining wall is the angled pre-cast concrete wall → ⓫ – ⓬. These walls are structurally reinforced and are available in the trade from a height of 55 cm. They have the advantage of a pre-defined structural design according to loading case. **Freestanding walls** are only subject to damp from the soil through the foundations and are therefore less problematic in the choice of materials. The selection of materials and dimensions of the bricks or blocks is important to enable a face on both sides.
The appearance of the face of walls is very varied according to material → ❶ – ❷ and depends on the possibilities offered by the material (brick, natural stone, broken stone etc.).
Walls over 1 m high should generally be structurally calculated. There are guidelines and standards for each type of masonry (brick, stone etc.). The effect of the pointing on the material should be investigated because otherwise there is a danger of efflorescence.
In order to protect the masonry from damp from above, a coping should be provided → ❺ – ❻.

Copings

The tops of walls must be protected against rain and snow by covering them with large slabs or stones. The coping element should have a cross-fall of at least 0.5%. Longitudinal joints in the coping are not allowed and butt joints must be at right angles to the wall centre-line. A drip mould should be provided min. 3 cm outside the face of the wall → ❺ in order to keep vertically falling water off the face. For natural stone walls, copings of the same material can be used. Nailed zinc or aluminium coverings are also suitable → ❻.

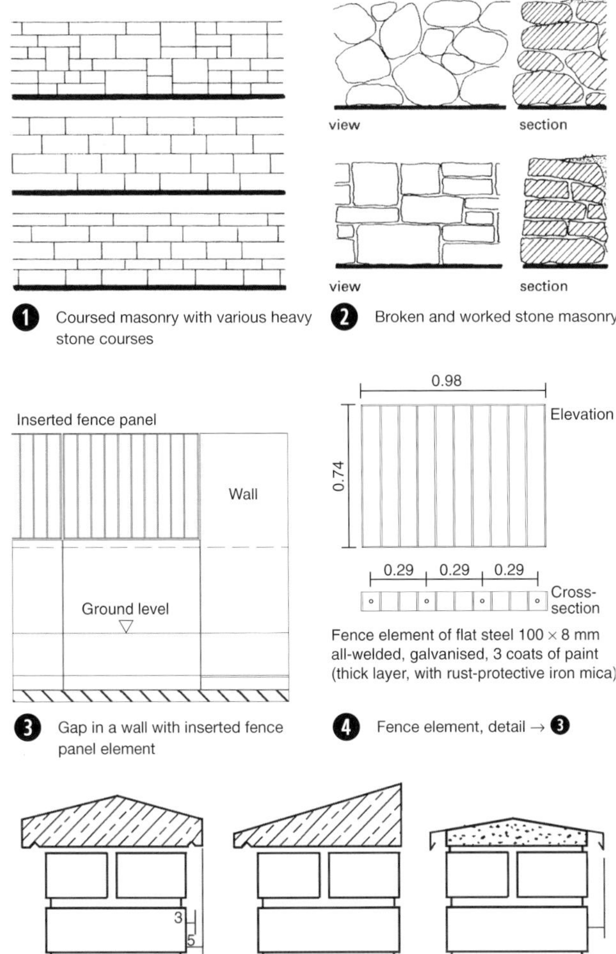

❶ Coursed masonry with various heavy stone courses

❷ Broken and worked stone masonry

❸ Gap in a wall with inserted fence panel element

Fence element of flat steel 100 × 8 mm all-welded, galvanised, 3 coats of paint (thick layer, with rust-protective iron mica)

❹ Fence element, detail → ❸

❺ Pre-cast concrete coping stones

❻ Cladding with zinc sheet (Lehr → refs)

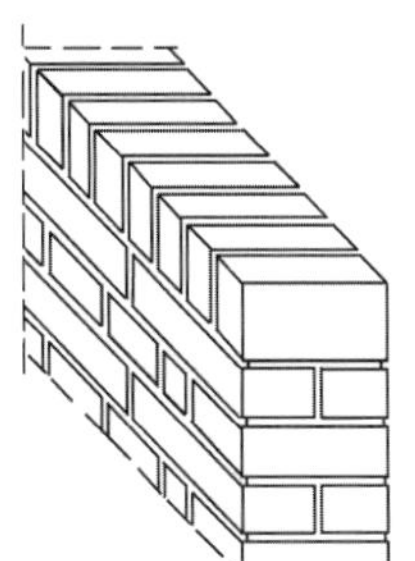
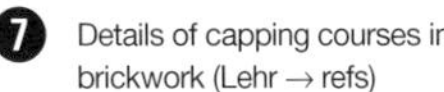

❼ Details of capping courses in brickwork (Lehr → refs)

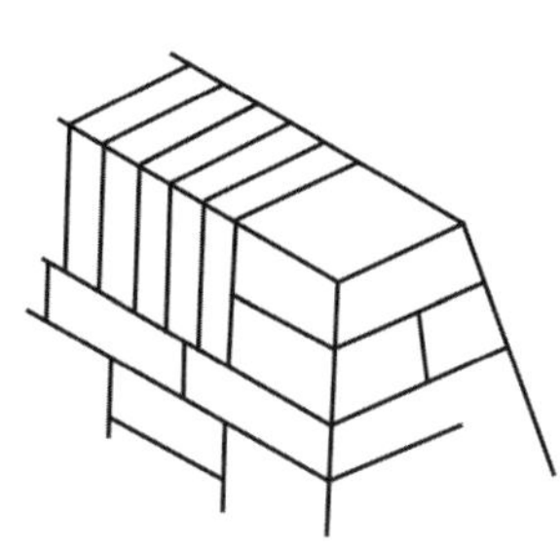

❽ Details of capping courses in natural stonework (Lehr → refs)

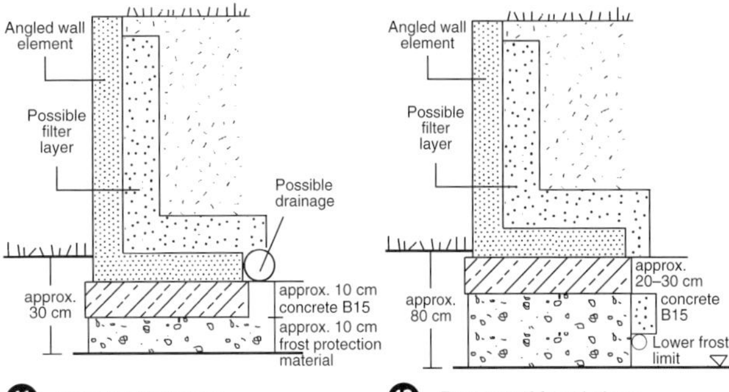

⓫ Simple foundations

⓬ Frost-proof foundations

7–8
Earth (uncultivated)
Separation layer against unpressurised water on slope side
2.00
Bonded layers
Frostproof foundation

❾ Dry stone wall: drainage measures are necessary according to soil type

drainage of filter gravel or solid-body drainage

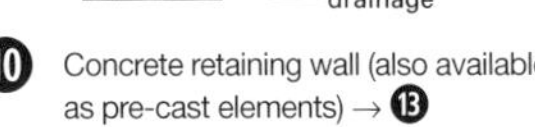

❿ Concrete retaining wall (also available as pre-cast elements) → ⓭

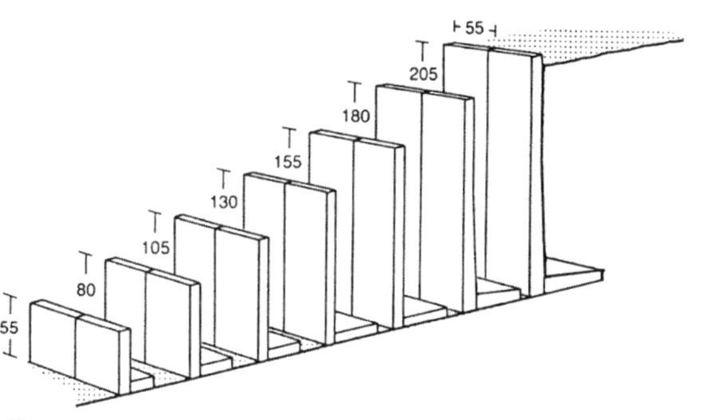

⓭ Retaining wall of pre-cast concrete elements, which are available as standard up to about 4.55 m high

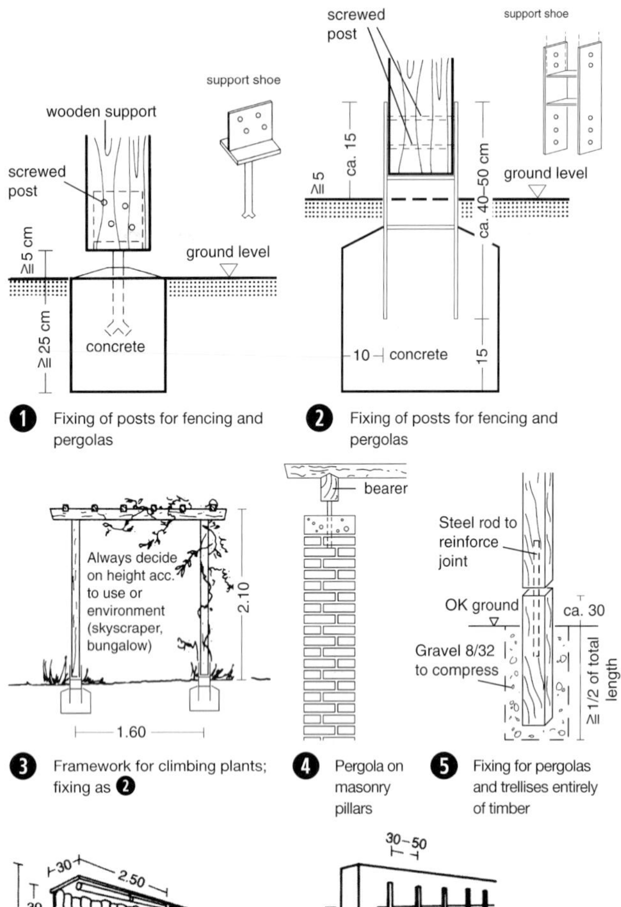

❶ Fixing of posts for fencing and pergolas

❷ Fixing of posts for fencing and pergolas

❸ Framework for climbing plants; fixing as ❷

❹ Pergola on masonry pillars

❺ Fixing for pergolas and trellises entirely of timber

Design aspects of pergolas and trellises

In addition to the selection of a material for the planned **pergola**, its position within the outdoor area needs to be considered carefully. Large pergolas form spaces almost like buildings, and should be justified by their function or particular aesthetic value. Pergolas can lead to special places or viewpoints (linear arrangement), and can be used to divide spaces and/or as a sitting area (point arrangement). Pergolas with climbing plants should be detailed in accordance with the particular characteristics of the intended plant (spacing of supports for climbing or winding plants).

A pergola is a room-forming row of columns or pillars. The verticals can be masonry pillars → ❹ or simple timber → ❷. If timber uprights are used, they should be protected against damp from the ground → ❶ + ❷. The construction generally appears lighter if the overhead construction is thinner or lighter than the verticals. It should be clarified in advance whether climbing plants are to be integrated.

Trellises are supports for climbing plants and can also be used as a visual barrier.

Espalier-trained fruit trees are classically grown against façades. The supports are mostly made of wood → ❻ – ❼, ❿ – ⓮. When designing support systems for climbing plants, attention should be paid to the growth height of the intended climbers, as the uppermost wire may, for example, not be reached by the plants. It is generally advisable to consider the architectural effect of the façade without plants. The basic decision is between linear and full-area growth according to local conditions.

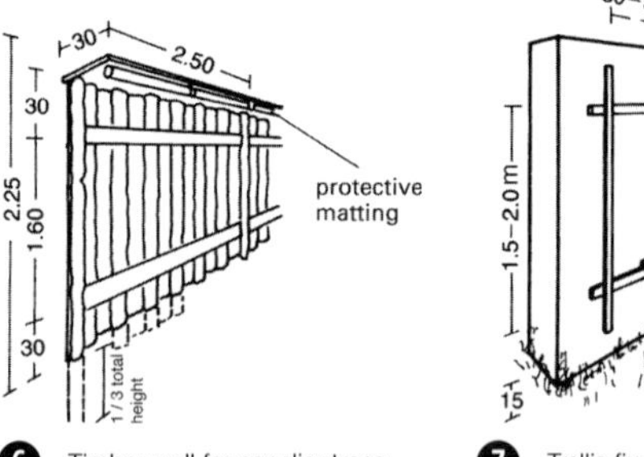

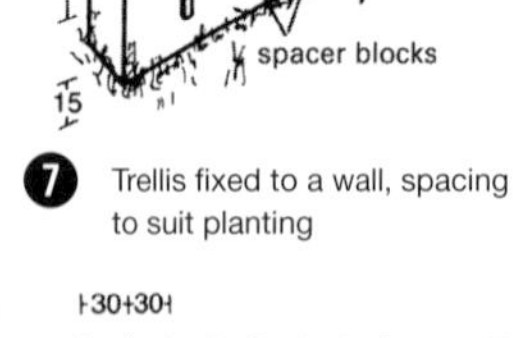

❻ Timber wall for espalier trees, detail in the ground as ❷

❼ Trellis fixed to a wall, spacing to suit planting

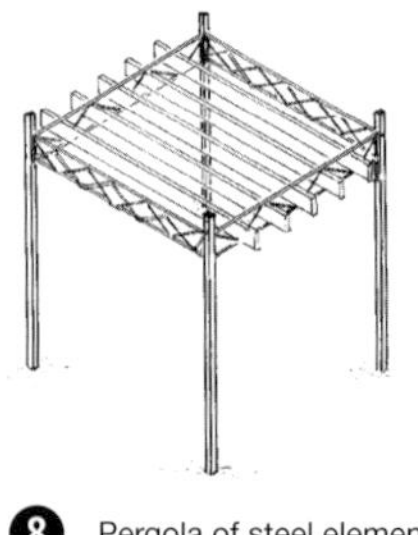

❽ Pergola of steel elements

	Height
cup and saucer vine	4–6 m
ornamental gourd	2–5 m
Japanese hops	3–4 m
morning glory	3–4 m
sweet peas	1–2 m
runner beans	2–4 m
nasturtiums	2–3 m

❾ Climbing plants: annual species

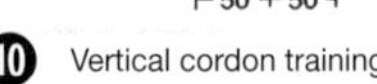

❿ Vertical cordon training

⓫ U-shaped cordon training

⓬ Palmette verrier training (six and eight branches)

⓭ Chandelier palmette training

Perennial species	Height	Growth	Trellis? x = yes	Leaves	Watering	Flowering: month/colour	Location
ivy – *Hedera helix*	up to 25 m	slow	x needed	winter	-	9–10 greenish	○–●
polygonum – *Polygonum aubertii*	up to 15 m	quick	x	summer	+	7–9 white	○–●
wild vine – *P. tricuspidata* 'Veitchii'	up to 15 m	quick	x	summer	(+)	5–6 greenish	○◑
clematis – *Clematis montana*	up to 8 m	quick	x	summer	+	5–6 white	○◑
wisteria – *Wisteria sinensis*	up to 10 m	medium	(x) sensible	summer	(+)	5–6 blue	○◑
old man's beard – *Clematis vitalba*	up to 10 m	quick	x	summer	+	7–9 white	○◑
hydrangea – *Hydrangea petiolaris*	5–8 m	medium	(x) sensible	summer	-	6–7 white	◑
pipe vine – *Aristolocchia macrophylla*	up to 10 m	medium	x	summer	(+)	5–6 brown	◑●
trumpet vine – *Campsis radicans*	up to 8 m	slow	x	summer	+	7–8 orange	○
crimson glory vine – *Vitis coignetiae*	up to 10 m	medium	x	summer	(+)	5–6 greenish	○●
grape vine – *Vitis vinifera*	up to 10 m	medium	x	summer	+	5–6 greenish	○●
honeysuckle golden flame – *Lonicera heckrottii*	3–4 m	medium	x	summer	(+)	6–9 yellow-red	◑
hop – *Humulus lupulus*	4–6 m	quick	x	summer	-	5–6 greenish	◑
Italian woodbine – *Lonicera caprifolium*	up to 5 m	medium	(x) sensible	summer	+	5–6 yellow-red	◑
climbing roses	up to 5 m	medium	x	summer	-	6–8 varied	○◑
winter creeper – *Euonymus fortunei*	2–4 m	slow	x	winter	(+)	6–8 greenish	◑●
clematis – clematis hybrids	2–4 m	medium		summer	+	6–9 varied	○◑
winter jasmine – *Jasminum nudiflorum*	up to 3 m	slow		winter	+	1–4 yellow	○◑

○ = sunny location ◑ = semi-shadow e.g. north wall ● = shadow

⓮ Overview of some climbing and winding plants (see also p. 434)

PERGOLA AND TRELLIS

Trellises

Trellises or other support systems for climbing plants can be used for the decoration of walls or also in the vegetable garden (where it is important to keep the plants within reach for picking). Various methods have proved successful → ❸ – ❼.

Fan and espalier training of fruit trees → ❽ – ❾ is found in farm gardens or, more often, in private fruit and vegetable plots. In commercial fruit plantations, trees are planted in patterns → ❿ – ⓬ to optimise economic success.

Green walls, formed of plants that cannot support themselves, require climbing aids. Such support systems are made of wood for small areas but larger areas, above all at heights, use metal wires → ❶. The spacing of the wires should be suited to the intended plant. In addition to the growth height, the type of plant (with tendrils, winding etc.) should be investigated.

Growth heights of 2–20 m are possible. Some plants, especially twining and winding plants such as Celastrus (staff vine), can squeeze and damage trees or downpipes.

The spacing of the horizontal wires should be between 20 and max. 50 cm according to species. Spanned wires should be plastic-coated to protect the plants from frost damage.

The greening of walls can sometimes have legal significance: for example, fire walls require special permission and should generally not be planted as this could spread a fire. The greening of a wall should generally be agreed with the owner. If, for example, the neighbour's wall is to be greened, this should be agreed in a contract.

Supports for climbing plants are generally excepted from approval procedures. The relevant building regulations should be complied with, and listed building regulations or local regulations concerning the appearance of buildings may also be applicable.

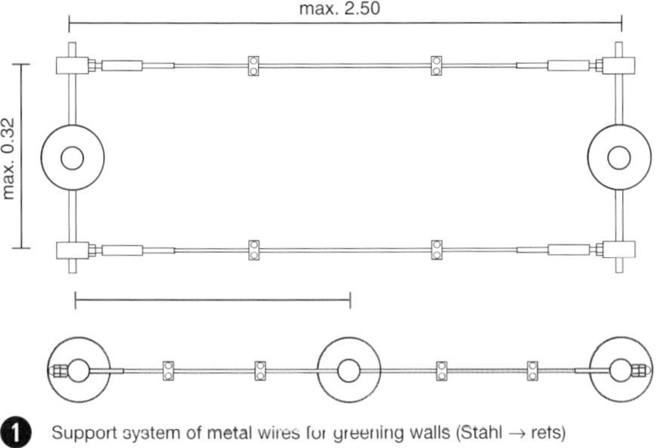

❶ Support system of metal wires for greening walls (Stahl → rets)

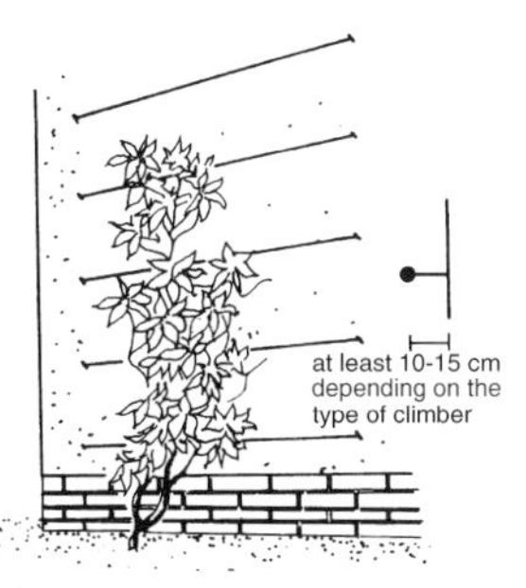

❷ Horizontal supports

❸ Wigwam method for 8–11 plants

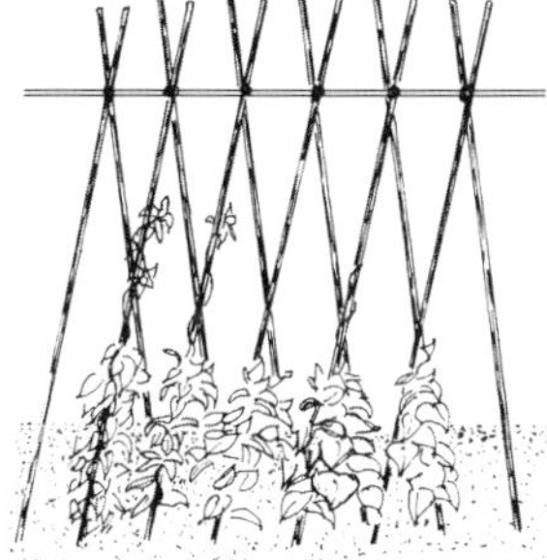

❹ Tent method

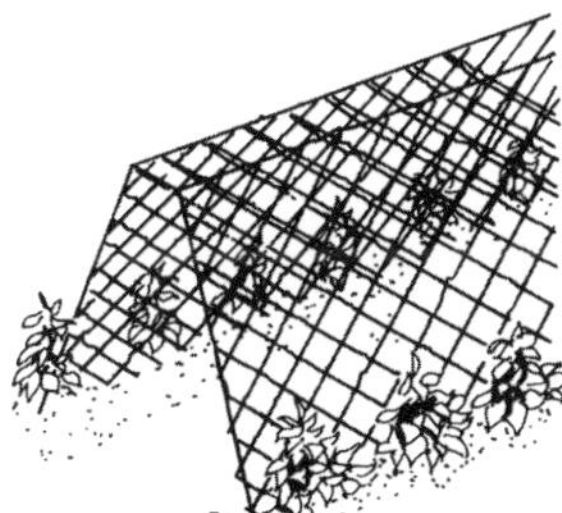
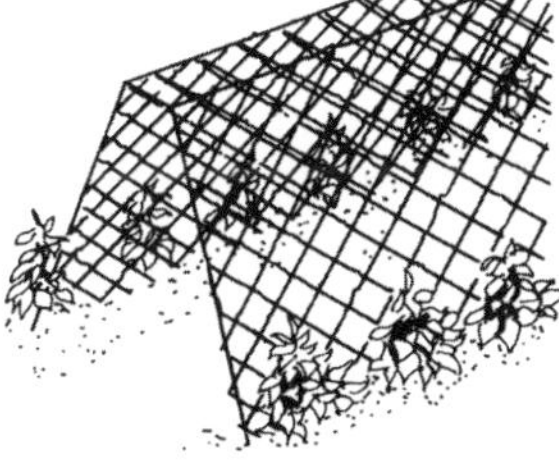

❺ Double grating of wire mesh

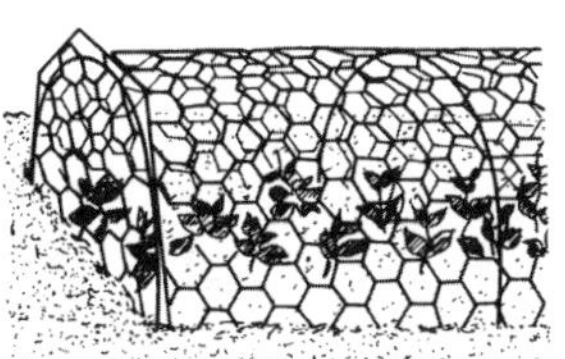

❻ Wire mesh protection against birds

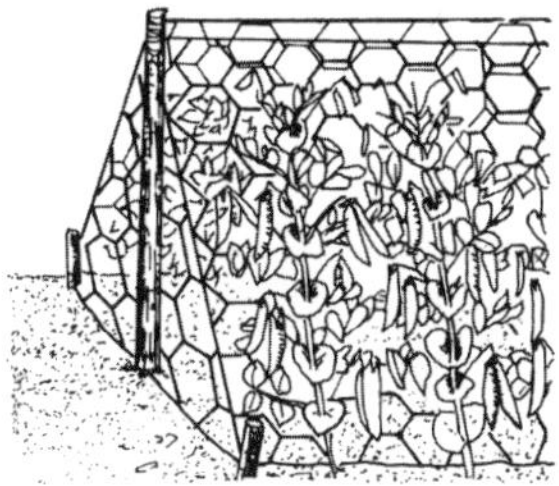

❼ Wire mesh support for peas

❽ Fan: only two branches at an angle of 45° to the ground are allowed to grow and the fan is formed from their shoots in the spring.

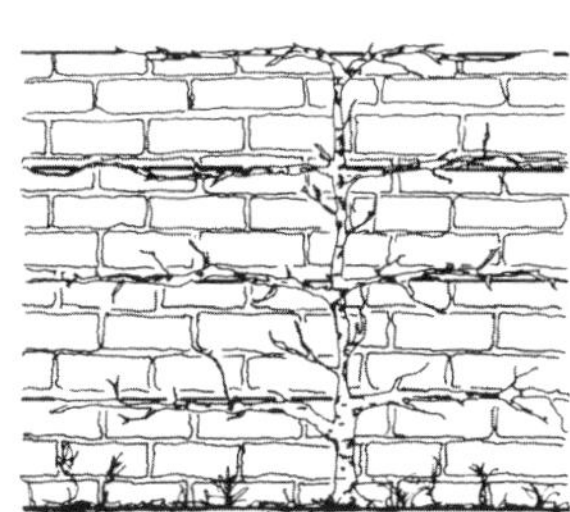

❾ Espalier: the central trunk of an espalier is trained vertically and the side branches at right angles to the left and right.

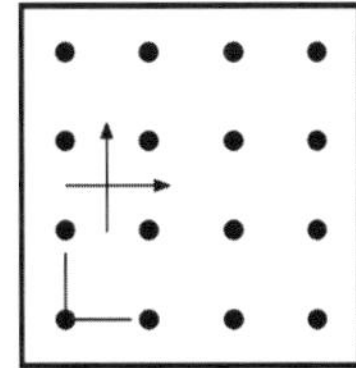

Spacing	Trees per ¼ ha
4×4m	156
6×6m	69
10×10m	25

❿ Square pattern planting

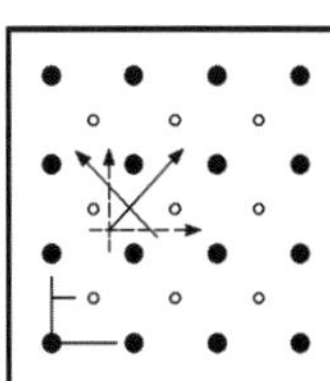

Spacing	Trees per ¼ ha	
	Standing trees	Fillers
4×4×(2)m	156	156
6×6×(3)m	69	69
10×10×(5)m	25	25

⓫ Square pattern planting with fillers

Spacing	Trees per ¼ ha		
	Standing trees	1st filler	2nd filler
6×3×3m	69	69	103
8×4×4m	39	39	58
10×5×5m	25	25	37

⓬ Square pattern planting with double fillers

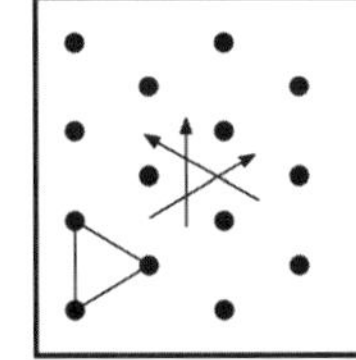

spacing	trees per ¼ ha
3×3×3m	320
4×4×4m	178
6×6×6m	80

⓭ Triangular planting equilateral

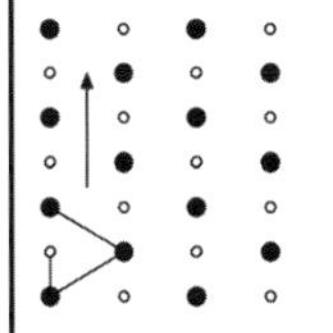

spacing	trees per ¼ ha	
	standing trees	fillers
1.5×3×3m	320	320
2×4×4m	178	178
3×6×6m	80	80

⓮ Triangular planting with fillers

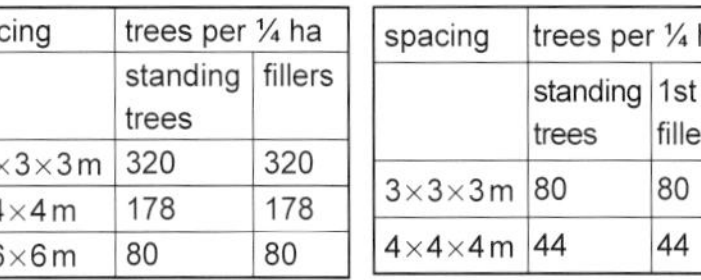

spacing	trees per ¼ ha		
	standing trees	1st filler	2nd filler
3×3×3m	80	80	160
4×4×4m	44	44	88

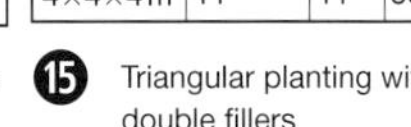

⓯ Triangular planting with double fillers

❿ – ⓯ Planting system according to De Haas; and see p. 437 ❸ – ❺

PERGOLA AND TRELLIS

Examples of Plants

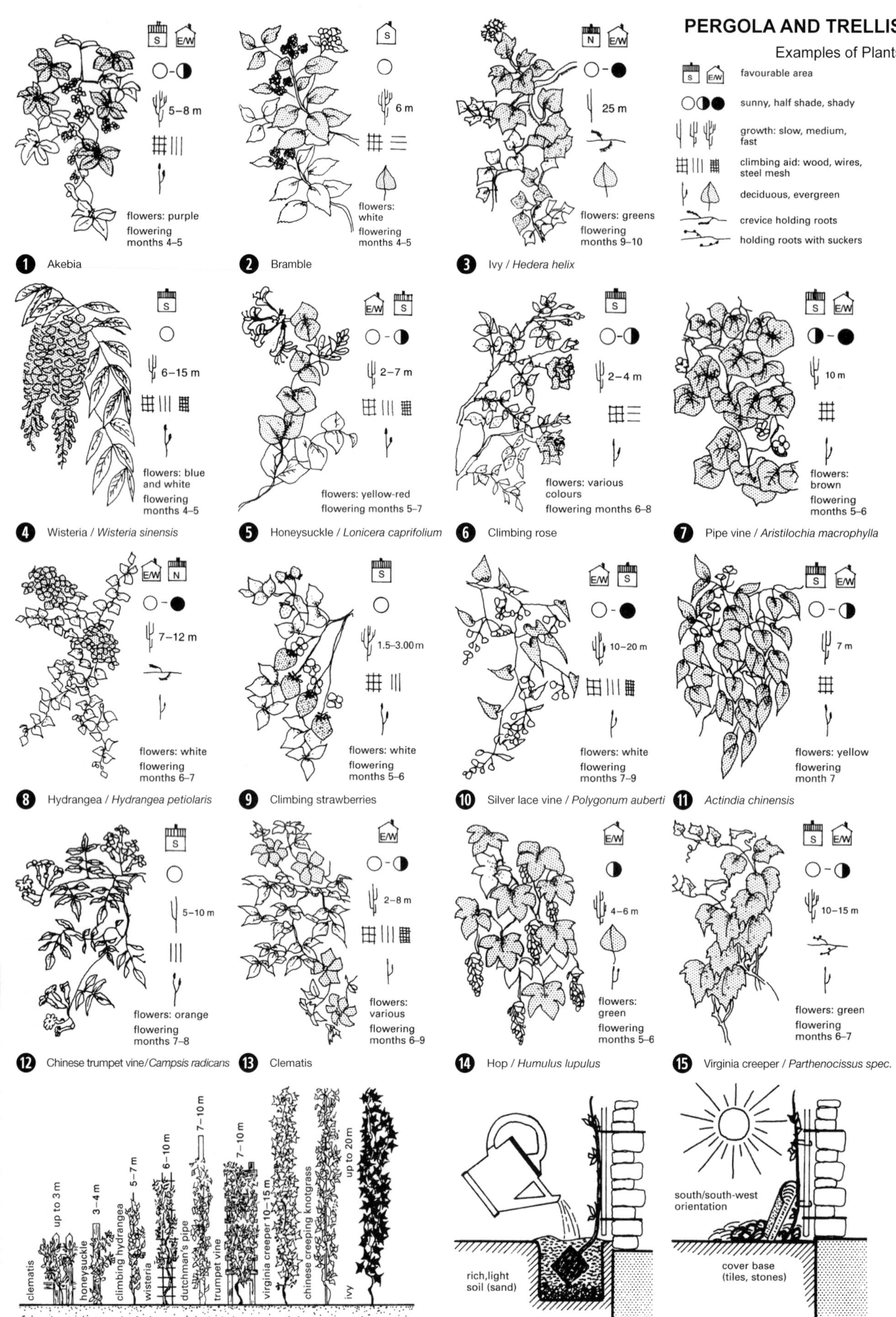

1 Akebia

2 Bramble

3 Ivy / *Hedera helix*

4 Wisteria / *Wisteria sinensis*

5 Honeysuckle / *Lonicera caprifolium*

6 Climbing rose

7 Pipe vine / *Aristilochia macrophylla*

8 Hydrangea / *Hydrangea petiolaris*

9 Climbing strawberries

10 Silver lace vine / *Polygonum auberti*

11 *Actindia chinensis*

12 Chinese trumpet vine/*Campsis radicans*

13 Clematis

14 Hop / *Humulus lupulus*

15 Virginia creeper / *Parthenocissus spec.*

16 Climbing plants and their growth height

17 Watering

18 Clematis need cold feet and a warm head

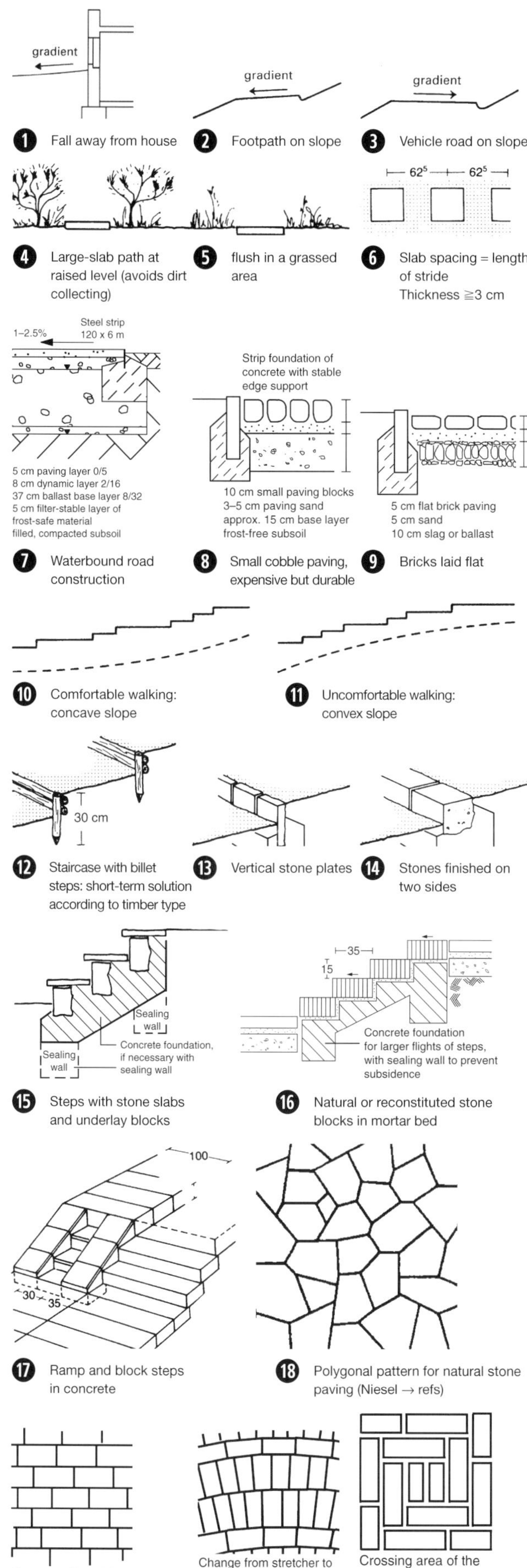

1 Fall away from house
2 Footpath on slope
3 Vehicle road on slope
4 Large-slab path at raised level (avoids dirt collecting)
5 flush in a grassed area
6 Slab spacing = length of stride Thickness ≧3 cm
7 Waterbound road construction
8 Small cobble paving, expensive but durable
9 Bricks laid flat
10 Comfortable walking: concave slope
11 Uncomfortable walking: convex slope
12 Staircase with billet steps: short-term solution according to timber type
13 Vertical stone plates
14 Stones finished on two sides
15 Steps with stone slabs and underlay blocks
16 Natural or reconstituted stone blocks in mortar bed
17 Ramp and block steps in concrete
18 Polygonal pattern for natural stone paving (Niesel → refs)
19 Variants of brick paving (Niesel → refs)

PATHS, PAVING, STEPS

Design Aspects

For the design of paths and paved areas, questions of proportion are important and the selection of materials is decisive. Firstly, the correct dimensions for path width, free paved areas and enclosed spaces need to be determined according to the use and surroundings. The human being should always determine the scale.

Then the colour and type of paving material should be chosen in connection with the overall design, and the surrounding buildings or roads. Light-coloured, large-format paving appears generous. With special edging or structuring, segments can have the effect of rooms. The general rule is to make a function or use easily read from path widening or paved areas.

Paved areas in gardens can be surfaced with the most varied materials. Areas to be driven on are normally paved with asphalt, concrete, or concrete or stone paving. A surface for vehicles (e.g. fire service access) can be created by rolling broken stone and permitting grass to grow on it. For less frequently driven areas, paving slabs, waterbound macadam or timber paving can also be used. Road building is subject to specialist regulations, which define the surfacing in accordance with local ground conditions. In principle, this can be with binder (special construction), without binder or waterbound (standard construction). Waterbound construction → 7 – 9 should be carried out with entirely permeable layers including open joints.

Roads with heavier traffic should be constructed with a hard edge to act as an abutment → 7 – 9. Clear areas where no vehicles can gain access can be covered loosely → 4 – 5 or with concreted back supports. The technical regulations concerning sufficient camber → 1 – 3 should be complied with. There should always be a fall away from buildings: in public areas, a minimum fall of 2.5% is required. The various laying patterns → 18 + 19 should always be suited to the material being used.

For all paving, the surface treatment is important for the function and design. For natural stone, flamed, consolidated, sawn, sandblasted or split surfaces are usual. The slip-resistance of paved surfaces in external works is important.

Design aspects of steps
Steps overcome height differences: they are therefore always significant as a vertical design aspect and require detailed matching to the overall theme. Flat and wide steps with low risers appear softer, more spacious and stronger in design. The steeper and narrower the steps, the more functional the impression.

In addition to the dimensions of the steps, the material and colour should also be selected in harmony with the external works design. The possibilities range from expensive natural stone materials with high-quality processing to simple timber steps in woodland. The other important accessories to steps, like handrails, should also be well matched to the design in order to present the end result as a homogeneous finished product. One good idea is to continue the paving leading to and from the steps like a carpet in the form of similar steps. The cheeks of the steps should always be considered with the proportions and function of the overall work

Steps should always be laid out according to the step length rule ($2 \times h + b \leqq 65$). Steps have a fall to the front → 16 in order to prevent ice formation. According to the size of the steps, additional measures can be necessary to secure the foundations → 15 – 16. Handrails should normally be provided if there are more than three steps (the exact details are given in the state building regulations). It can be sensible to have ramps integrated into the steps, particularly at house entrances and access routes to bicycle storage → 17.

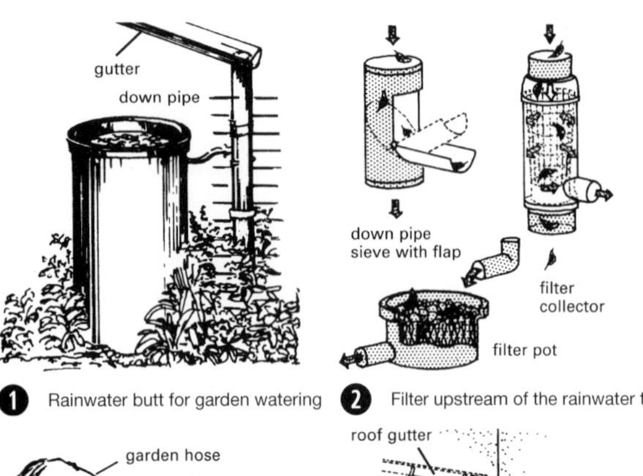

❶ Rainwater butt for garden watering ❷ Filter upstream of the rainwater tank

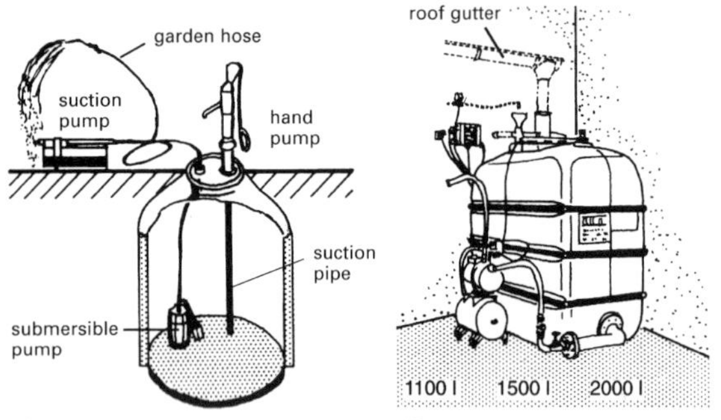

❸ Rainwater tank for garden watering ❹ Rainwater utilisation system

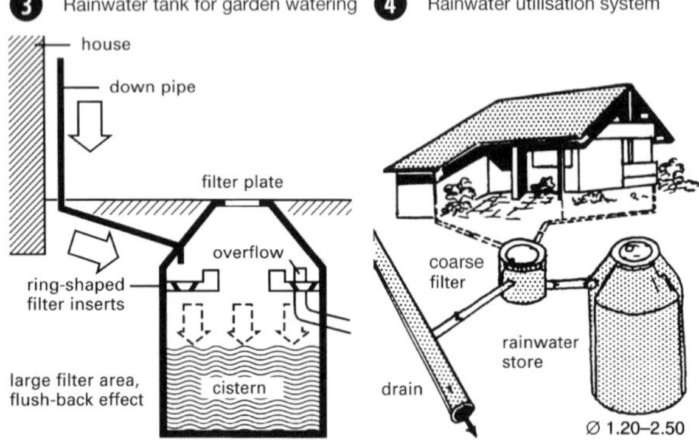

❺ Principle of a cistern ❻ Rainwater tank up to 12 500 litres

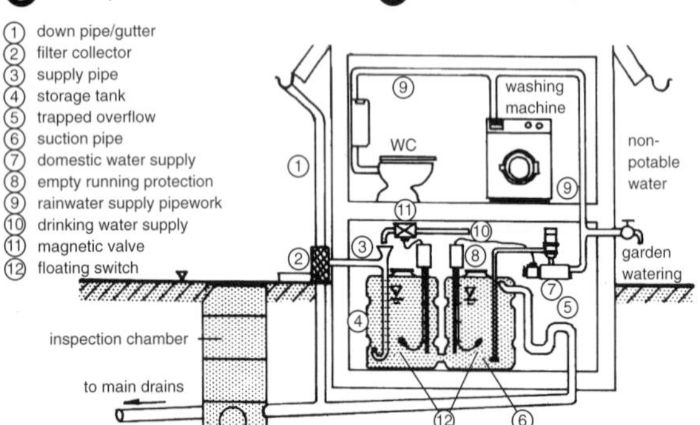

❼ Rainwater system

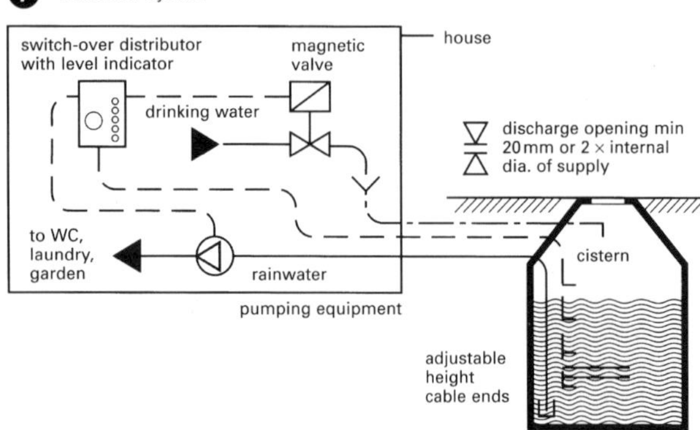

❽ Drinking water refilling system → ❼

Design for drainage

Normal drainage installations like box gutters or floor gullies allow room for design in their material (metal, cast iron) and form (grating, slot gutter etc.), and the effect of these choices should not be underestimated. Above all the positioning should be planned exactly, e.g. fitting into the pattern of slabs.

Complete system solutions (rainwater management) can be implemented as a design idea. Modelled landscape with integrated percolation basins or rain gardens, where water collects in a dip and soaks away, water areas to accept the drainage and ditches with corresponding planting can all enable nature-like or more formal design. The topography of the terrain should be closely considered. Attractive water landscapes can be combined with the necessary provision of drainage functions. Technical facilities like French drains, cisterns etc. should be kept in the background if feasible.

Rainwater management is urgently suggested for ecological and economic reasons in order to preserve the natural rainwater cycle as far as possible. Optimised rainwater management means that no rainwater drains into the sewers. The basic principle of rainwater management is to avoid, reduce or at least greatly delay surface water running off into the drains where it arrives or in the immediate vicinity. The following measures can contribute to this: soakaways, permeable paving, rainwater exploitation (water harvesting) and roof planting

Drainage is generally differentiated into linear or point drainage. Depending on the surfacing, surface falls should be provided to drain surface water appropriately at all times of year. It should be ensured that no surface water is drained to susceptible structures, buildings or onto neighbouring properties. The precipitation is collected in gutters or gullies and then mostly run into gully traps in the underground drainage pipes or to soak away in infiltration facilities. The hydraulic capacity of the inlets and thus the collected area should be calculated according to Guidelines for Street Layout – Drainage (RAS-EW). The approximate rule is:

- for yard gullies: up to approx. 200 m^2 collected area
- for road gullies: up to approx. 400 m^2 collected area
- spacing of the road gullies not less than 40 m.

Infiltration measures (surface infiltration or rain gardens, French drains). In addition to underground drainage, water can also be removed by surface drainage through terrain modelling and infiltration. Either constructional features (French drains, infiltration in dips in the ground, infiltration trenches) or grass areas with topsoil covering (rain gardens) are used. The first step is to determine the soil composition and the infiltration capacity of the ground (kf value) in connection with the local precipitation. The guideline is Association for Water, Wastewater and Waste (ATV) 138.

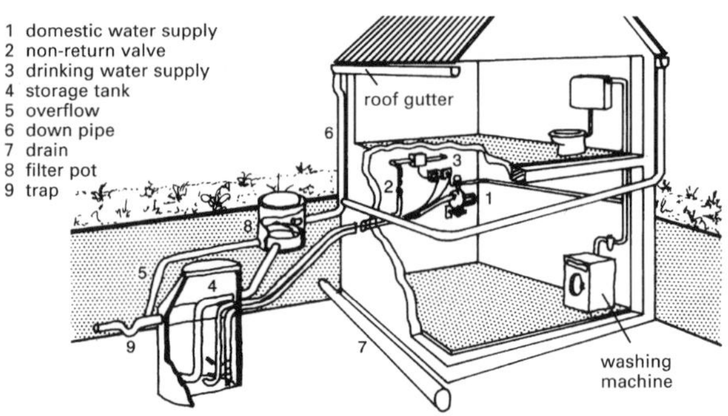

❾ Rainwater collection system with filter pot and external tank

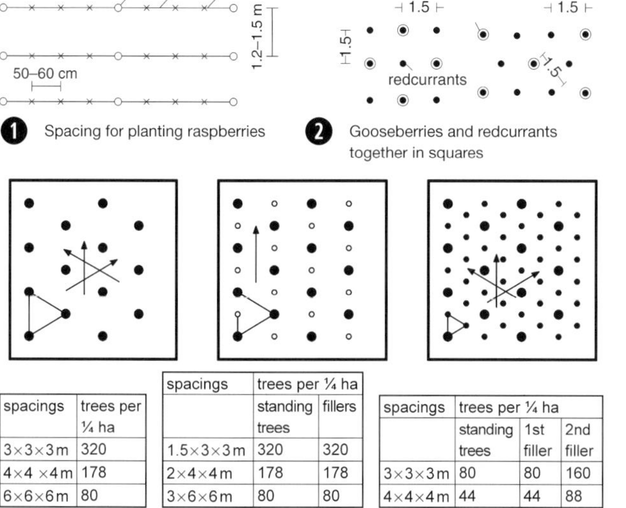

❶ Spacing for planting raspberries

❷ Gooseberries and redcurrants together in squares

spacings	trees per ¼ ha
3×3×3m	320
4×4 ×4m	178
6×6×6m	80

❸ Triangular planting, equilateral

spacings	trees per ¼ ha	
	standing trees	fillers
1.5×3×3m	320	320
2×4×4m	178	178
3×6×6m	80	80

❹ Triangular planting with fillers

spacings	trees per ¼ ha		
	standing trees	1st filler	2nd filler
3×3×3m	80	80	160
4×4×4m	44	44	88

❺ Triangular planting with double fillers

❸ – ❺ Planting system according to De Haas; and see p. 433 ❿ – ⓯

❻ Hedge heights

❼ 'Quick-set' hedge in North Germany

❽ Wire support for brambles

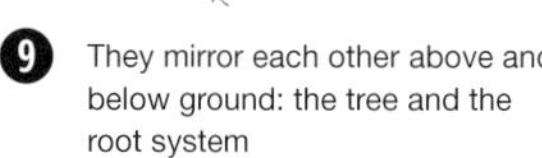

❾ They mirror each other above and below ground: the tree and the root system

❿ The pyramid is the basic 'Christmas tree' shape and is preferred to the goblet shape because the branches are kept very short and thus less likely to break under the weight of fruit or snow. The goblet has an open form with the branches trained outwards to let more light into the crown.

⓫ Large tree while still young. Allow the trunk and two or three branches to grow in order to achieve the desired form

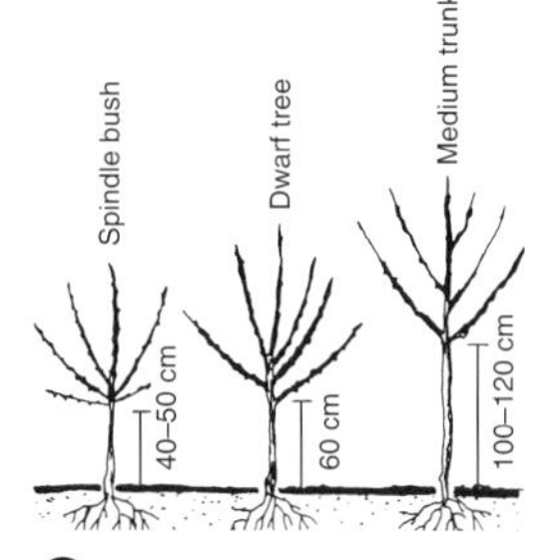

⓬ Tree shapes for small gardens

Design with vegetation

Design with vegetation, which includes plants, trees, bushes, grasses and lawn or meadow plants, is extremely varied. Nonetheless, all landscape design should place the complete concept before the plant selection. Modern landscape architecture understands itself as an open-air architecture, into which the plants have to integrate as an important part of the overall design scheme. Horizontal and vertical spatial characteristics (trees, shrubs etc. in height and form) play an important role before the selection of plant genus, species or type.

Once the spatial units have been decided, the exact choice of plants can be made according to aspects like growth form, leaf form and colour, blossom colour and date, autumn colour and suitability for the location (soil, light). Economic considerations concerning care and maintenance also have to be included. The selection of the correct planting is an elementary part of good landscape design, with the stimulus and challenge that this element always changes with the time of year and with successive years.

Plants

Under the general terms perennial herbs, grasses, ferns, geophytes (bulb plants) and woody plants, there are countless varieties of plants. In general, the botanical names are used to name plants and these are normally derived from Latin and Greek. The botanical name is composed of plant family, genus, species and variety (e.g. family Araliaceae: *Hedera helix* 'Arborescens' – common ivy). Together with the quality grading by the Association of German Tree Nurseries (BdB) of the plants and their abbreviations, the countless varieties can be exactly named and ordered. Particular forms of growth (hanging – pendula or column-shaped – fastigiata) can often be understood from these names.

Plant quantities differ greatly depending on the plant family, genus and species. Different plant spacings apply for productive plants → ❷ – ❺ than for general landscaping. Overall, the objective (fast growth of the plant) should be observed. Perennials and small ground-cover plants are planted at 6–12 plants/m^2, solitary wood plants at 0.5–2 plants/m^2 and a single-row hedge is usually planted with 3–5 plants/running metre.

When **plants are delivered**, attention should be paid to permitting only a short time span between the uprooting at the nursery and planting. Storage should not exceed 48 hours. Delivery includes all ATV requirements and also planting. If intermediate storage is unavoidable, then the plants should be protected against drying out, overheating and frost. Some possible measures are stacking them roots to roots, spraying with water and covering the roots with soil or tarpaulins. A storage place out of the wind and the sun is best. They should be wrapped up only if there is no chance of early planting.

The best **planting time** is generally the autumn and early part of the year; for fruit trees late autumn. In landscapes with early frosts, planting can be as late as October, or in mild regions until November.

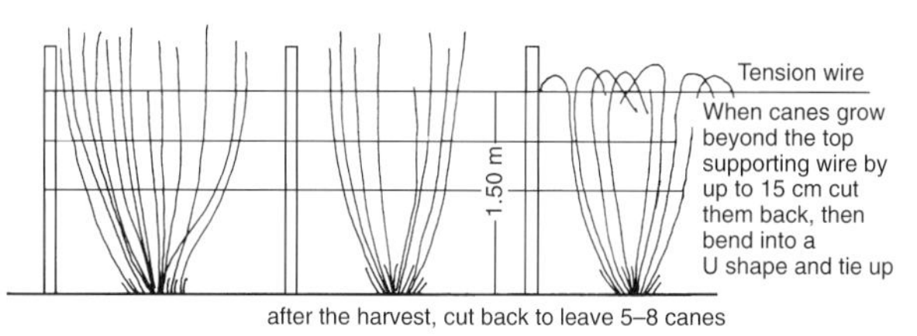

⓭ Raspberries

❶ When planting a conifer, the root ball cloth must be removed. With small trees the support stake is installed at an angle.

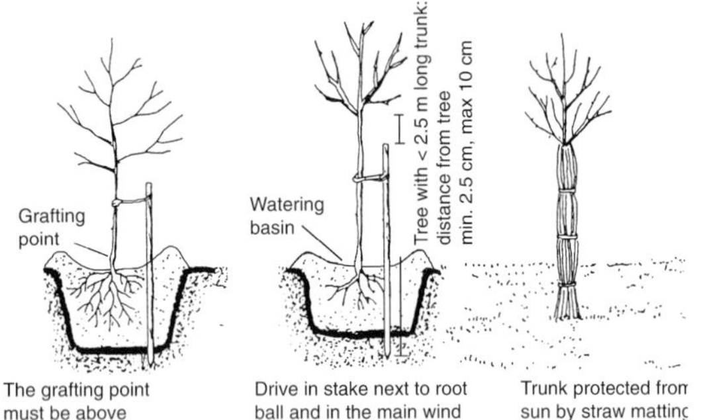

❷ Anchoring trees

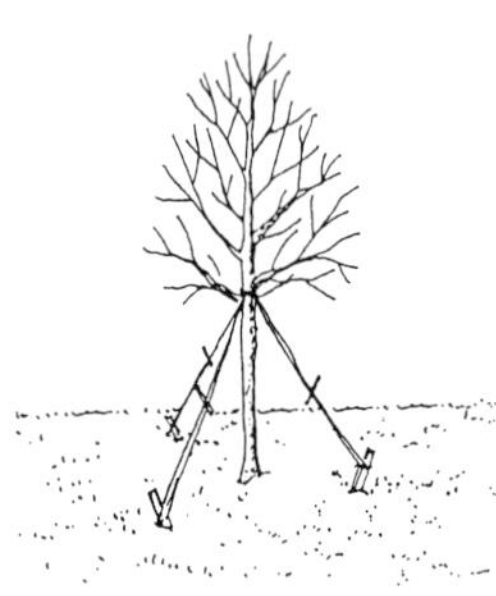

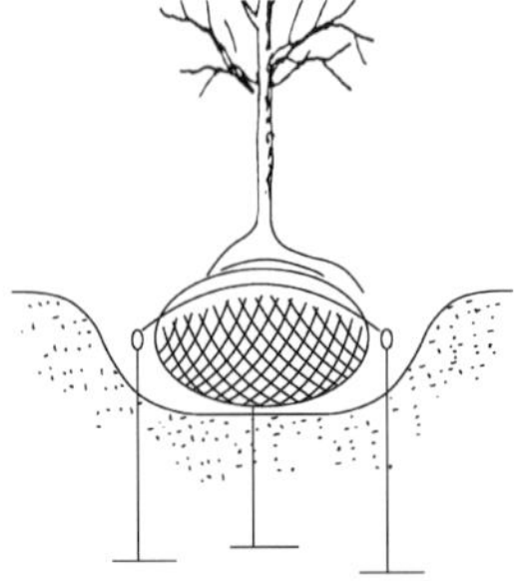

Net or fabric to distribute load; tie-down straps firmly anchored in soil

❸ Anchoring trees

❹ Subsoil anchoring for trees with solid root balls

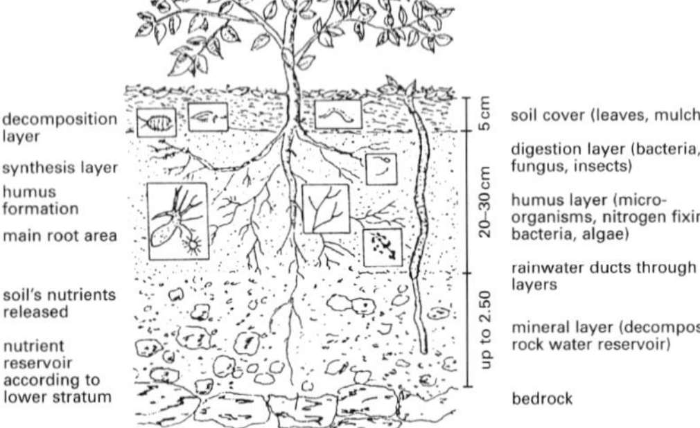

❺ Every layer of humus is full of life. Each spadeful has its occupants

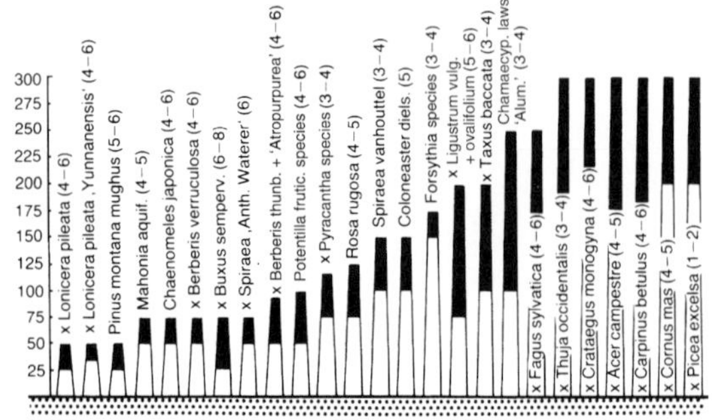

❻ Growth heights of trimmed and free-growing hedges (plants marked x are particularly suitable for trimming) with number of plants required per running m

Planting is regulated in detail in the relevant standard. Planting holes should be dug with a width of 1.5 times the root ball. The topsoil should be separated while digging and replaced at the top again after planting. Trees and larger bushes should be protected against wind damage after planting, for example by **staking** → ❷ – ❹. The stakes should be outside the root ball if possible and always set against the prevailing wind direction. Debarked, round stakes are usual. Plants are removed from pots or small containers (for perennials and ground-cover plants) and put directly into the ground with a planting spade. Planting methods vary according to type of plant.

Distances of plants from boundaries of neighbouring properties, as given by the Law on the Rights of Neighbours, are to be complied with. Hedges up to a height of 2.0 m should be planted at a distance of 0.50 m, or if over 2.0 m in height at 1.0 m, measured from the side surface, small trees at a distance of 1.50 m and large trees at 3.0 m. (measured from the centre of the trunk). There are exceptions and special rules for particular types of neighbouring areas (public roads, woodland etc.).

For gardening professionals, the **care of plants** counts contractually as extra work. Woody plants are normally acceptable when they show signs of new shoots in the last third of June, and for perennials when they have sprouted, budded or produced roots. Area (ground-cover) planting is acceptable when no more than 5% of the plants have died but there is a continuous appearance despite this. Annual and biennial flowers, flower bulbs and tubers, and all other plants are acceptable immediately after planting unless additional care has been agreed.

In addition to the sowing of lawns, expensive turf lawns (thin-cut lawn mats) can also be used. For lawn areas, a fertile soil layer of at least 10 cm should be prepared. Grass generally grows at temperatures above approx. 8°C and stops growing at approx. 30°C. A newly sown lawn can be used after about six weeks. A **selection of sowing types** and sowing quantities (lawn for walking, playing, meadow etc.) is given in RSM (Standardised Seed Mixtures) 2008 from the FLL series.

The **care of lawns** counts contractually as extra work. Sowing work is acceptable when a cover of approx. 75% is reached. Landscape grass areas are acceptable with a projective ground cover of approx. 50%. Turf and rolled lawns are acceptable when the growth of roots into the soil is recognisable.

Standards	Trans-plants	Trunk circumference (cm)	Trunk height (cm)	Crown width (cm)	Standing distance (cm)	Max. standing time (yrs)	Other
light standard	2	8–10 10–12	≧180		wide	4	bundles of 5
standard 3 x v	3	10–12	≧200		extra wide	4	
		12–14					
		14–16					
		16–18					
		18–20					
		20–25					
standard 4 x v and often solitary standard	≧4	16–18	total height 300–400 400–500	60–100	extra wide	4	wire balls or container, number of plantings indicate wire balling
		18–20		100–150			
		20–25		150–200			
		each 5 cm		200–300			
		up to 50 cm		400–500			
		each 10 cm		500–700			
		from 50 cm		700–900			
				900–1200			
				+ 300 cm			
avenue tree			TC up to 25 cm		extra wide	4	
			≧220 cm				
			TC from 25 cm				
			≧250 cm				

❼ Requirements for sorting and bundling of standard trees (Lehr → refs). TC: trunk circumference

Design in the application of biological engineering

Biological measures in engineering are mostly biologically oriented answers to construction requirements, like the support of slopes or riverbanks. They are therefore to be seen as part of the overall planning and to be designed accordingly. It should be clarified whether such measures should be intentionally visible or concealed as far as possible.

Experience of the application of biological measures can enable banks and slopes, which otherwise would have required retaining walls, to be part of the vegetative scene. The overall design idea and the corresponding choice of materials should always influence the implementation of the functional necessities.

The use of biological solutions to support slopes can be divided into the support of slopes and of riverbanks.

Supporting slopes

It is necessary to support steep slopes, but the ideal is to create slopes with rounded transitions to flat terrain and planted with grass, perennials or trees.

When slopes are designed steeper than the natural angle of repose, they should be supported with turf, fascines, paving or masonry. At a slope greater than 1:2, turfs should be nailed with timber pegs. Turfs can also be stacked to hold up steeper slopes with inclinations of 1:1.5 to 1:0.5.

Fascines (bundles of sticks) are suitable for supporting steep slopes where plant cover would become established only with difficulty. They can be living or dead. The latter (willow stakes hammered in) require subsequent planting with deciduous woody plants.

To support large cuttings, as in road building or properties on a slope, elaborate measures are necessary → ❶ – ❻.

Anchored beam grillages are of various types, e.g. consisting of horizontal, pre-anchored beams with standing posts. The panels in-between are sprayed with shotcrete → ❹.

❶ Revetment wall for slope in loose ground with advance support through anchored rail (scheme Badberg II – Badgastein)

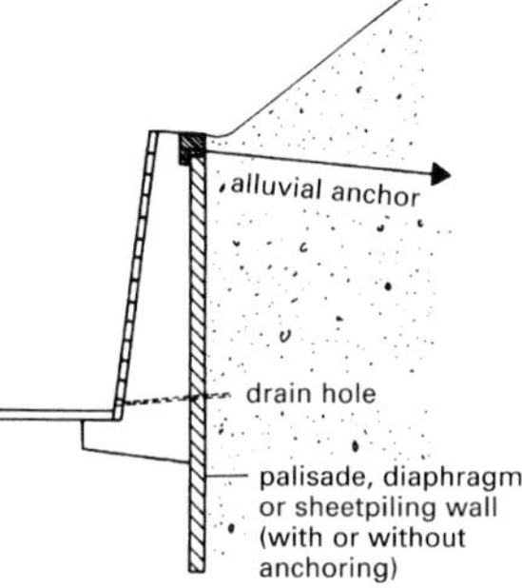

❷ Revetment wall with piled, diaphragm or sheet pile wall (with or without anchoring) in loose ground

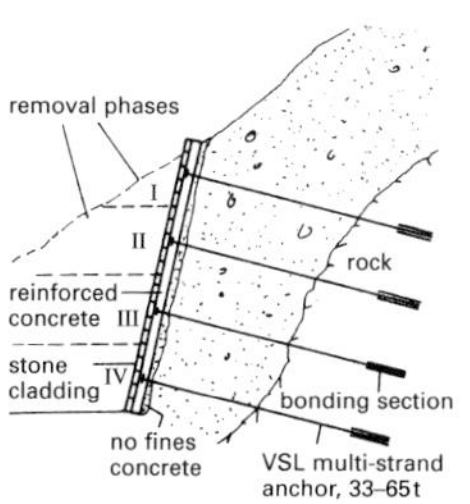

❸ Slope support in loose ground: staged excavation from top to bottom and immediate support with masonry elements and rock bolts (Brenner autobahn)

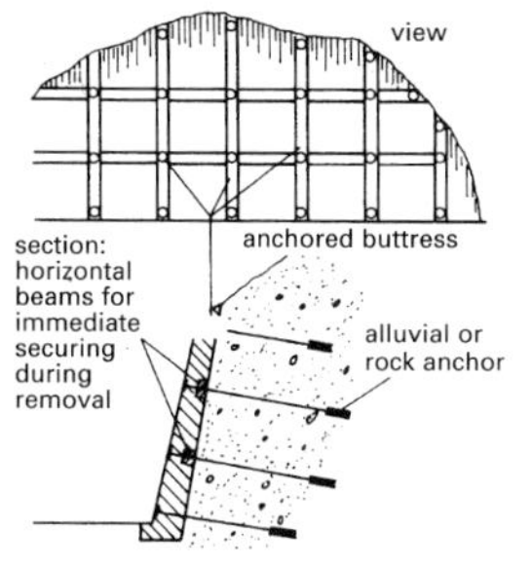

❹ Primary slope support in loam-bound or partially consolidated loose material through anchored beam grillage

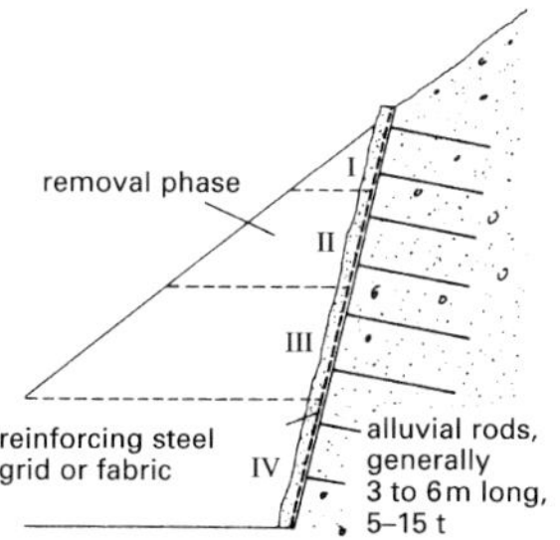

❺ Slope support in loose ground: staged excavation from top to bottom and immediate support with shotcrete with reinforcing mesh and rock bolts

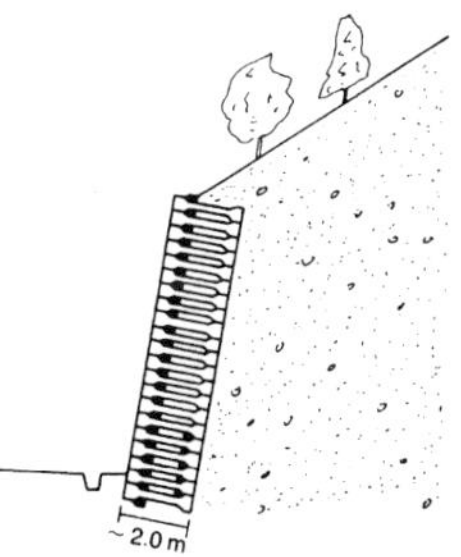

❻ Spatial grid retaining wall (Krainer wall) of concrete (Ebensee system)

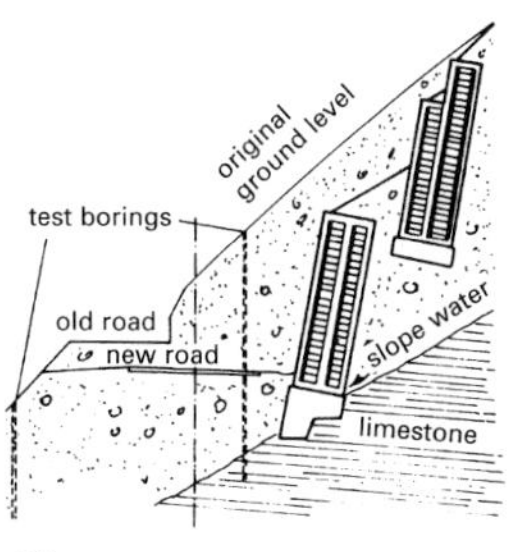

❼ Krainer wall installed in steps provides sufficient room for the new road. The landscape remains green

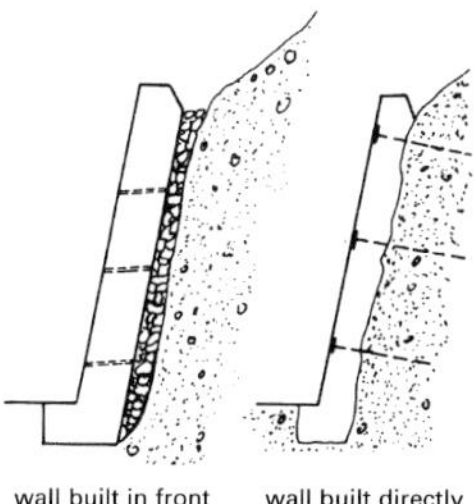

❽ Types of rock cladding as revetment or masonry (after L. Müller 1969)

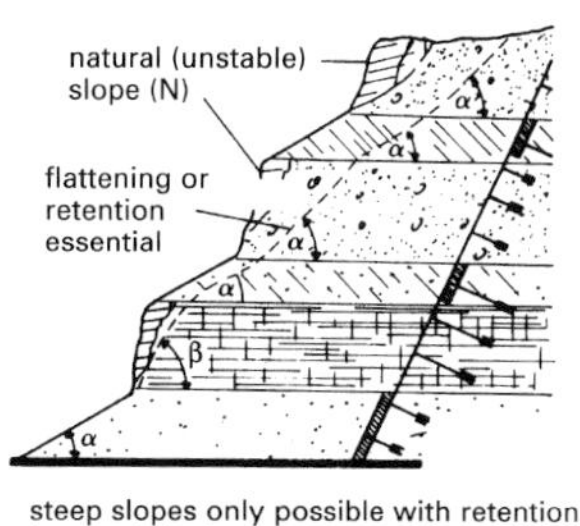

❾ The design of slopes (and support) in strata of variable stability

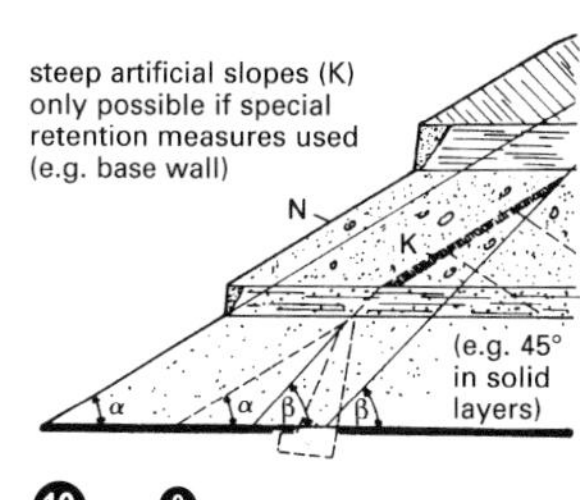

❿ → ❾

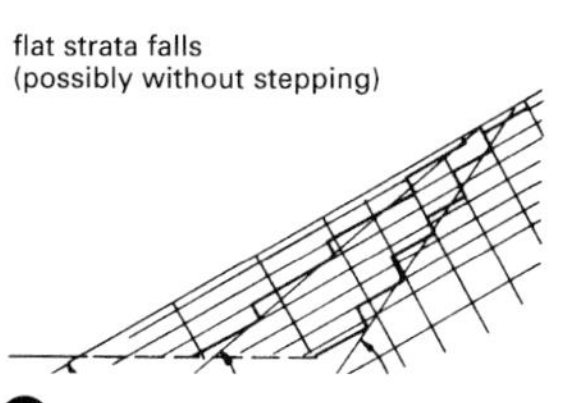

⓫ Rock slopes determined by the geology and jointing

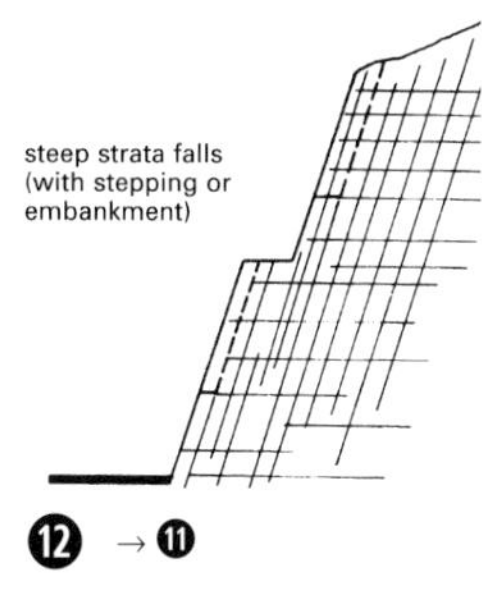

⓬ → ⓫

⓭ Krainer wall

	Length [cm]	Width [cm]	Height [cm]	Weight [kg/unit]
stretcher LE	250	30	10	168
end stretcher ELE	280	30	10	188
half end stretcher EHLE	155	30	10	108
half end stretcher HLE	125	30	10	88
header B 130	90	15	25–32	118
header B 180	130	15	25–32	68
spacer block A	30	15	25–32	20
distance block D	20	10	10	6

⓮ Ebensee Krainer wall → ❻ + ⓭

Planted retaining walls create room for usable properties, roads and paths. Considerable height differences can be overcome. Depending on the system and the slope, high walls can also be built with ground anchors → ❻.

Supporting riverbanks

While, in the design of slope support, earth pressure and gravity are the forces to be considered, the design of riverbank support also has to take into account the effect of water and wave impact. The optimal riverbank protection is a natural vegetation profile next to the flowing water → ❿ and healthy root systems prevent the bank being damaged by wave impact.

There are many methods of protecting against erosion, particularly the area above and below the waterline, which is most subject to wave impact, e.g. bundles of willow fascines, rhizome edgings or brush mattresses are possible.

❶ Living fascines

❷ Dead fascines

❸ Pegged turfs support the slope ≧1:2

❹ Support with stacked turfs

❺ Bush layering, pioneer planting and bitumen straw seeding for the support of woodland slopes and embankments

❻ Support of a slope surface with anchored steel mesh, Weber system

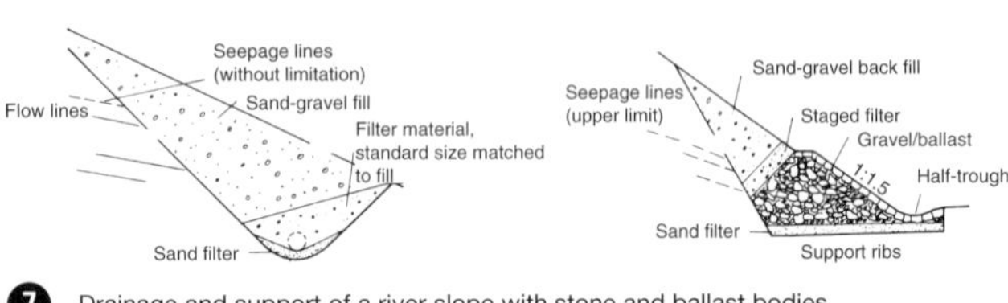

❼ Drainage and support of a river slope with stone and ballast bodies

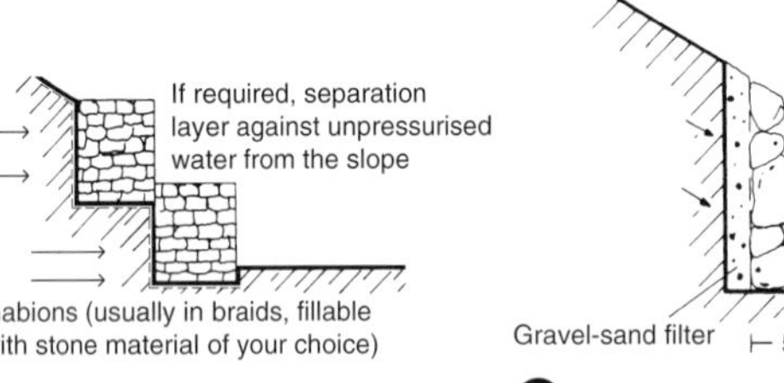

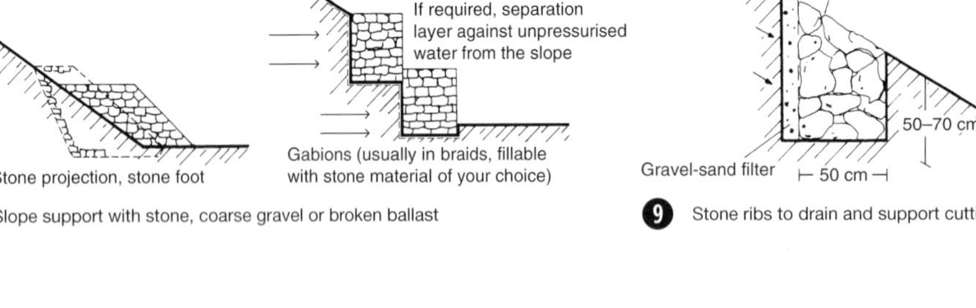

❽ Slope support with stone, coarse gravel or broken ballast

❾ Stone ribs to drain and support cutting slopes

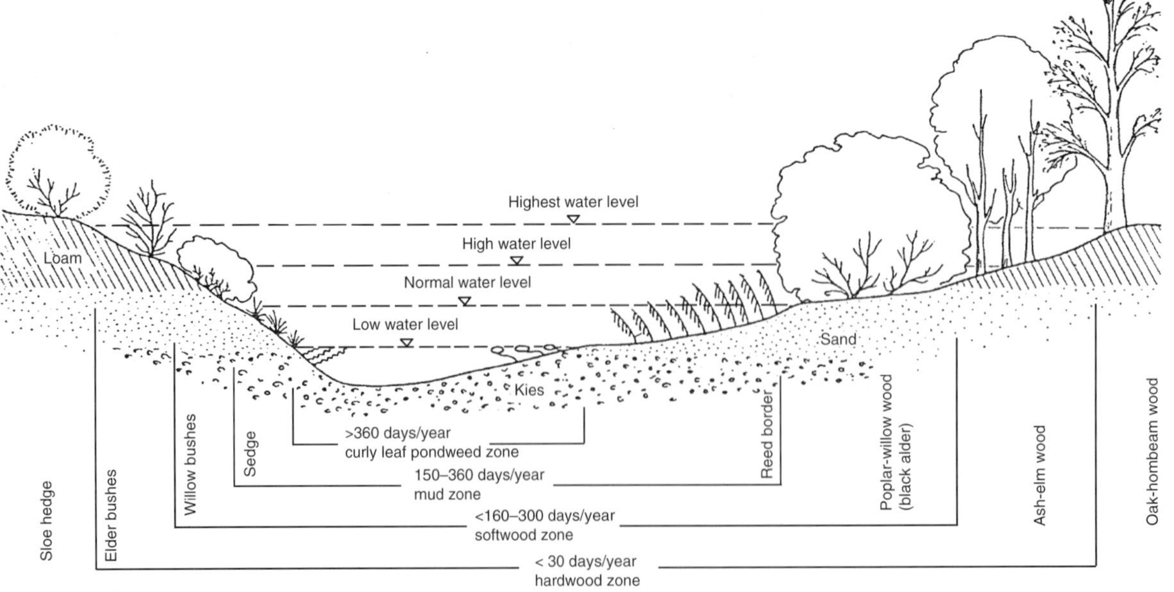

❿ Vegetation profile of a river bank (Bittmann)

GREENHOUSES

The ventilation of a greenhouse should be designed so that, when it is opened, the temperature is almost the same as outside. To achieve this, it is necessary that about 20% of the roof area opens as a ventilation band or a single casement. Sun protection can be necessary if there is insufficient natural shading outside to create a bearable climate under strong sunshine. The sun protection can be mounted inside or outside, but the effect of external sun protection is greater when the distance between it and the glass is large enough → ❶ and ❿ – ⓫.

(1) Roof ventilation
(2) Mechanical window opener
(3) Exterior blinds
(4) Air humidifier
(5) Air circulation fan
(6) Side ventilation window
(7) Double layer plexiglass
(8) Trickle irrigation
(9) Sprinkler system
(10) Water pump
(11) Underground heating cable
(12) Watering tank
(13) Insulation
(14) Heating
(15) Plant table
(16) Propagation bed
(17) Incubation lighting
(18) Automatic mechanical ventilation
(19) Greenhouse lighting
(20) Humidity controller
(21) Air humidity sensor
(22) Thermostat

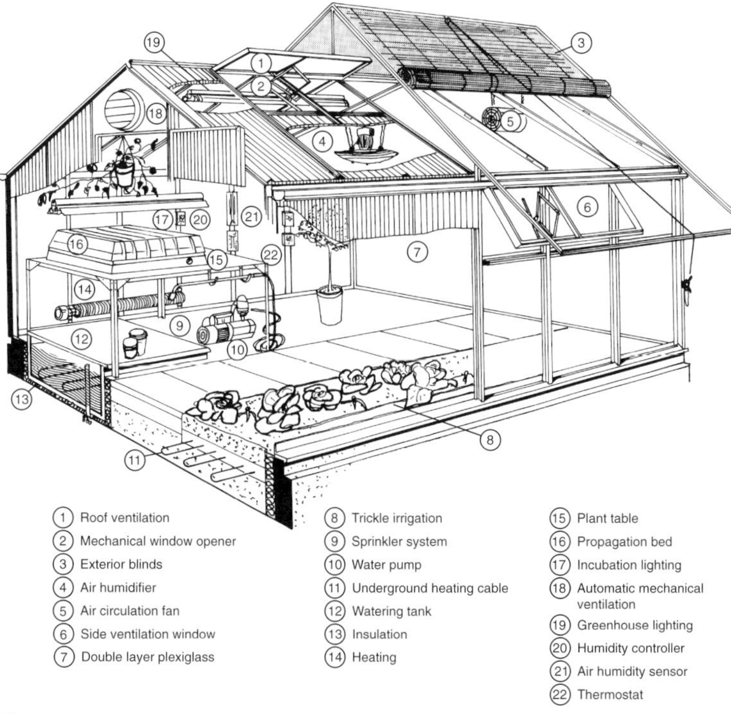

❶ Greenhouse with effective equipment and air-conditioning

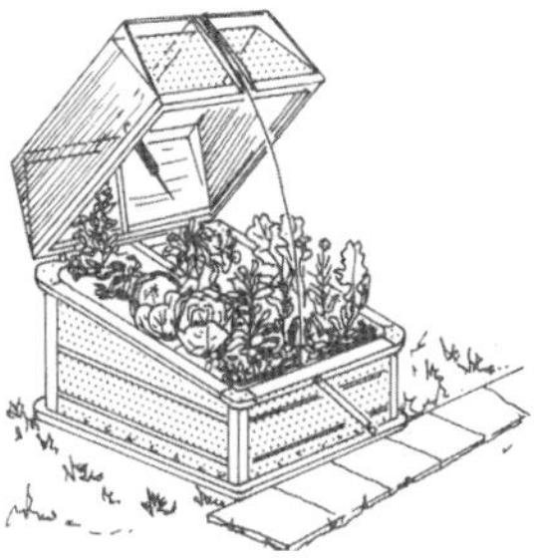

❷ Banked bed with solar hood

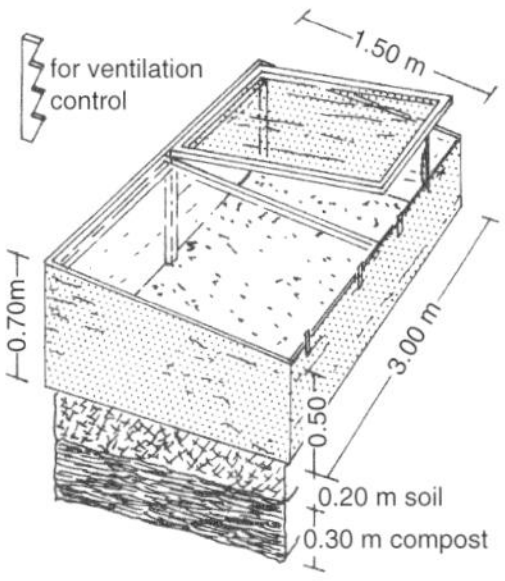

❸ Self-built cold frame

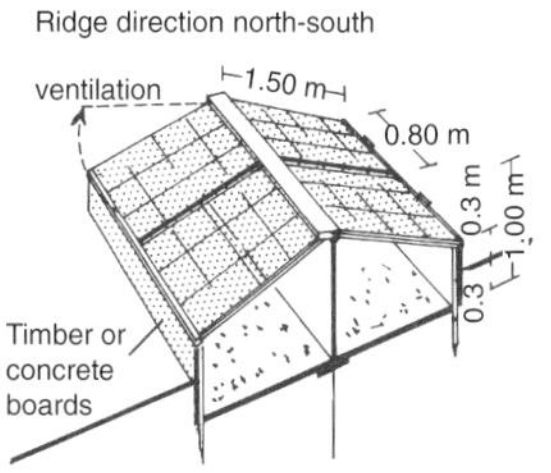

❹ Small greenhouse

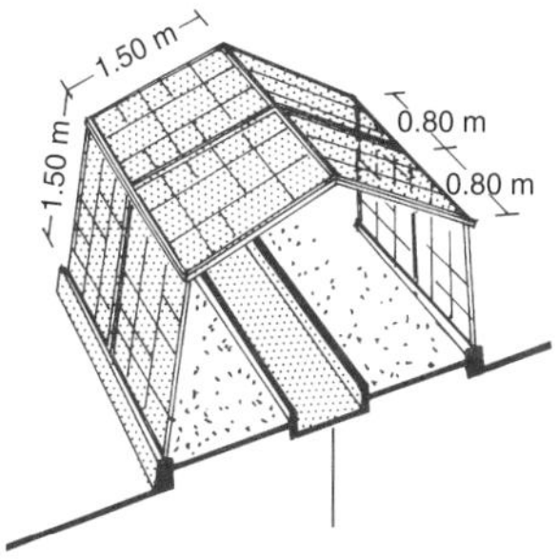

❺ Dutch greenhouse

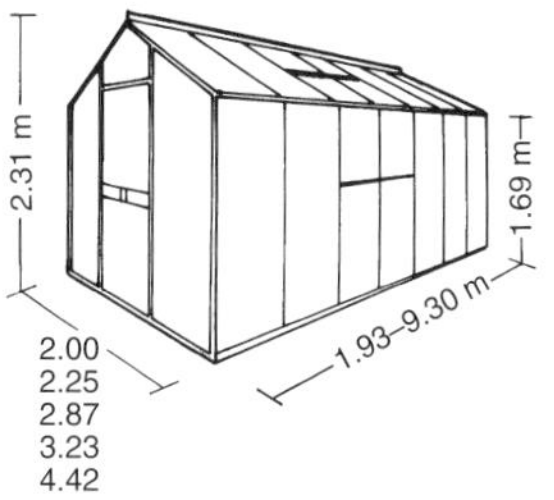

❻ Standard greenhouse

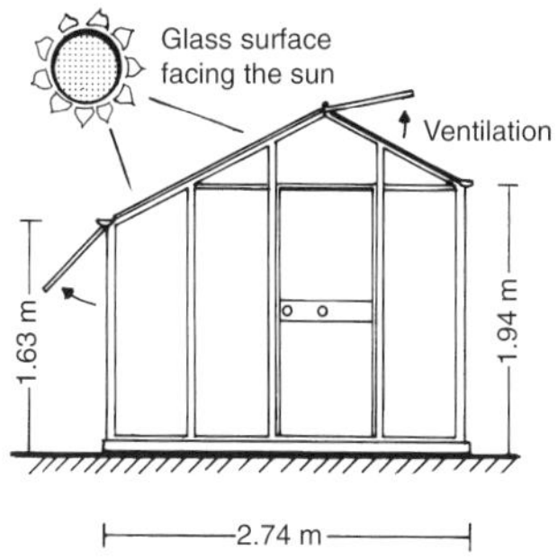

❼ Hothouse

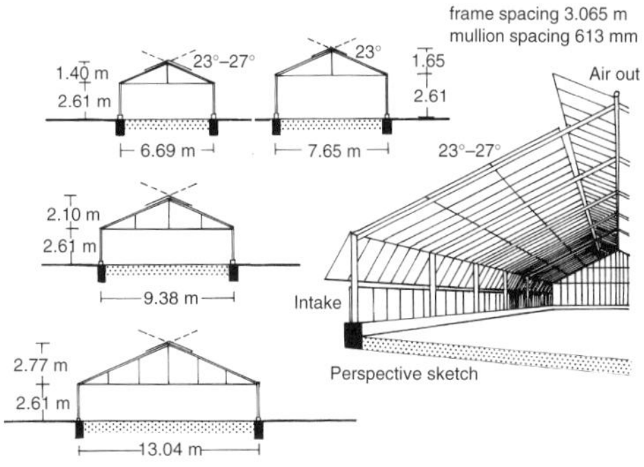

❽ Greenhouses with 23–27° roof pitch

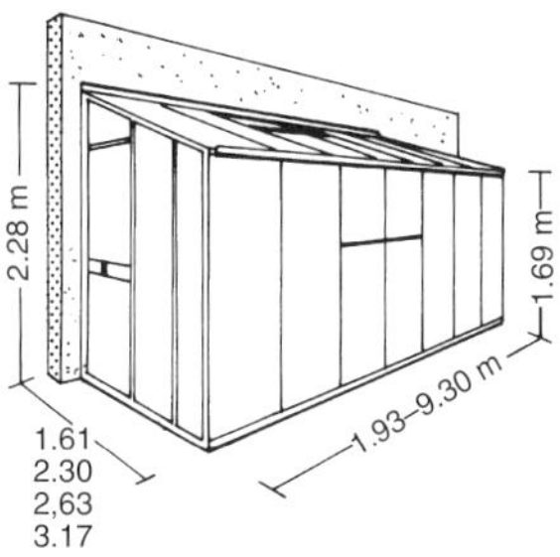

❾ Lean-to greenhouse

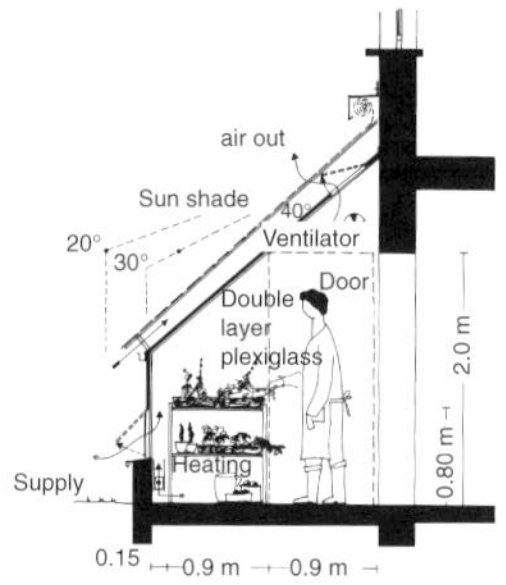

❿ Lean-to greenhouse

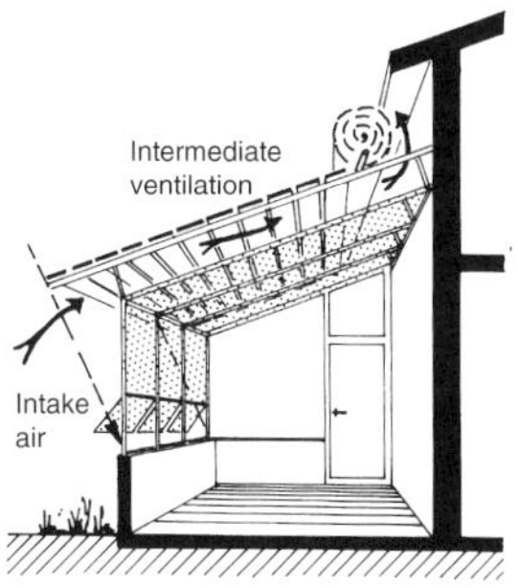

⓫ Exterior blinds with full intermediate ventilation

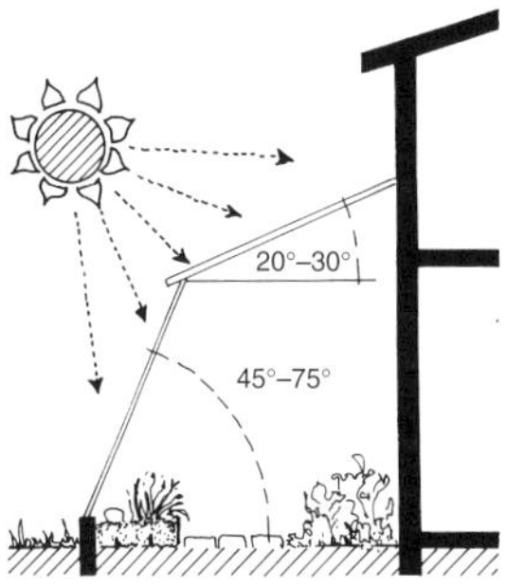

⓬ Optimal angles for glass surfaces

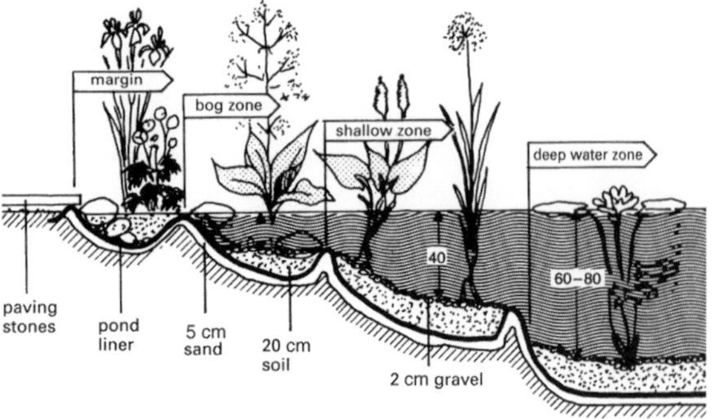

1 Foil pond planting in a stepped arrangement

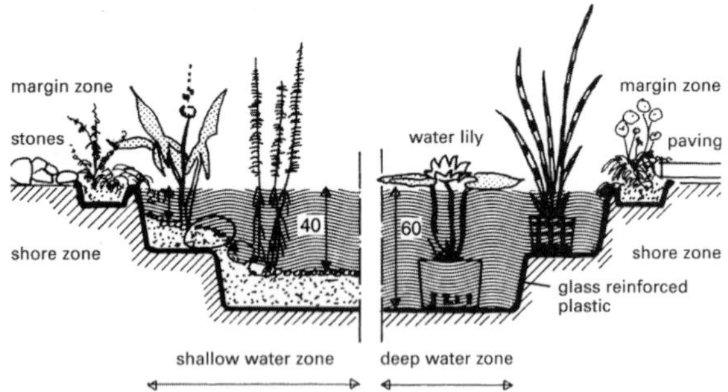

2 Suitably shaped pre-fabricated pond

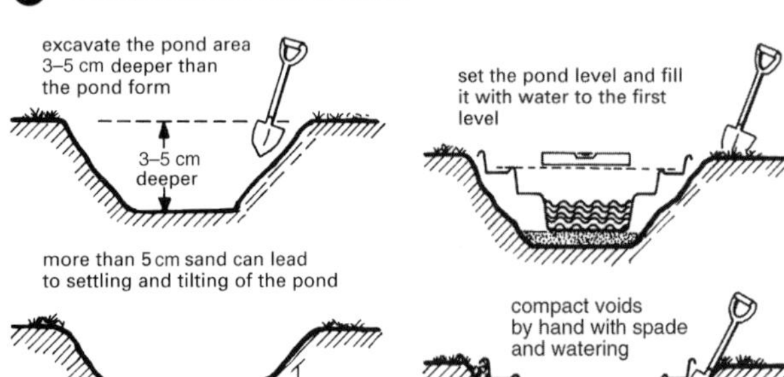

3 Excavation of a garden pond

4 Compacting voids at sides well with excavated earth

Ponds should integrate harmoniously into gardens. The correct location is of decisive significance for the flourishing of plants and life forms. Most bog and water plants require plenty of sunlight, approx. 4–6 hours per day, and the preferred location is near terraces and seating.

If the plants, water and sand have been provided in the appropriate quantities, then a biological equilibrium arises after about 6–8 weeks and the water should become clear. The ratio of water surface area to water quantity must be right (about 400 litres per m^2 of water surface). The garden pond then becomes a habitat for insects and plants.

The planting of the pond is done before topping it up with water, which is added carefully. Planting time: from May to September. In order to achieve a harmonious overall picture, tall plants should be planted individually in the water garden at half-height and with a spacing of 30–40 cm. Low plants at the edge should, in contrast, be set only in groups. Spacing from plant to plant: 20–30 cm.

The first planting with **underwater plants** is sufficient with five plants per m^2. The plants multiply quickly. Plants in containers can be brought to the correct water level by planting higher or lower. They can be planted in baskets, containers or directly into special earth. Pre-fabricated ponds provide planting baskets at the correct depths and prevent the gravel or planting earth slumping or slipping → **2** – **5**.

The pond should be appropriate for the size of the garden. Ideal is a water area of 20–25 m^2, but as little as 3–5 m^2 offers a habitat for many species. Wetland, shallow-water zones → **1** – **2** and waterlogged borders help to expand the pond area and create a more natural balance. Generous water zones 5–20 cm deep and another area at least 80 cm deep are necessary for insect larvae and newts to overwinter. The deep zone serves as an escape zone for the creatures.

The pond should stay full in the winter in order to prevent frost heave. Fish, frogs and amphibians survive the winter only if anti-ice devices and aeration stones are used.

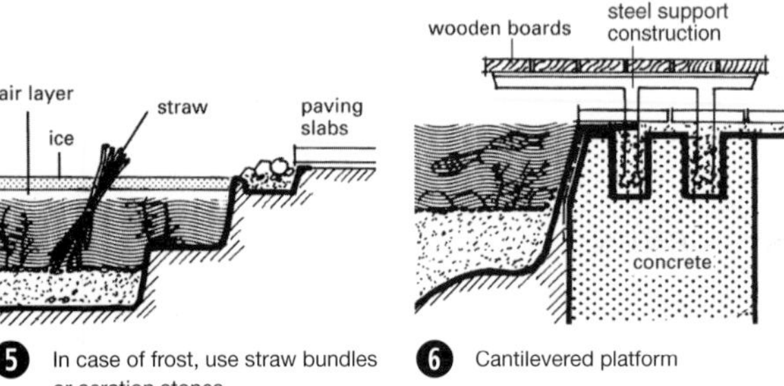

5 In case of frost, use straw bundles or aeration stones

6 Cantilevered platform

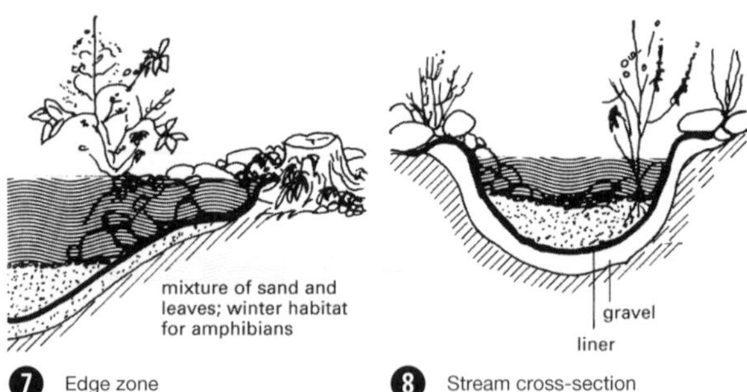

7 Edge zone

8 Stream cross-section

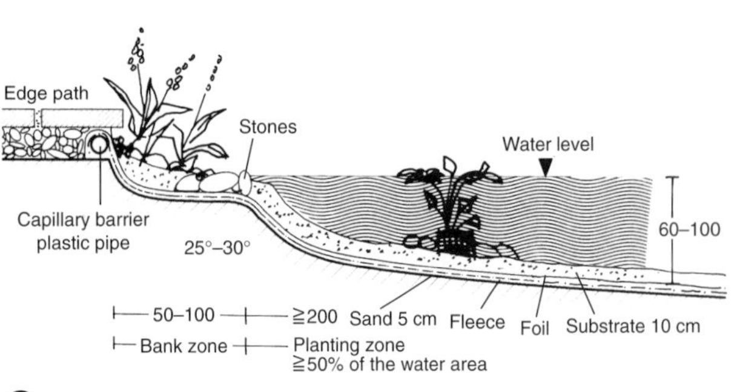
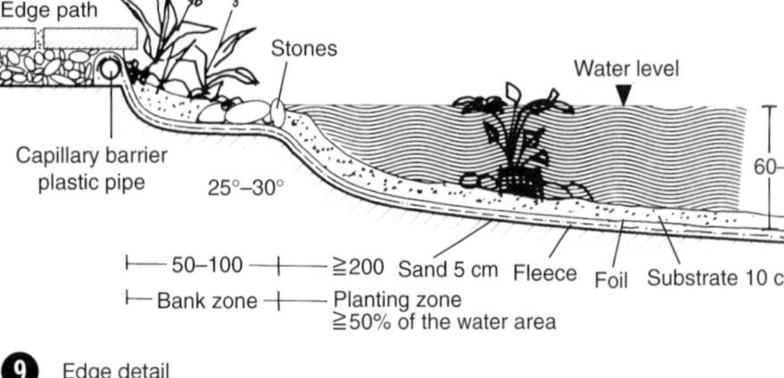

9 Edge detail

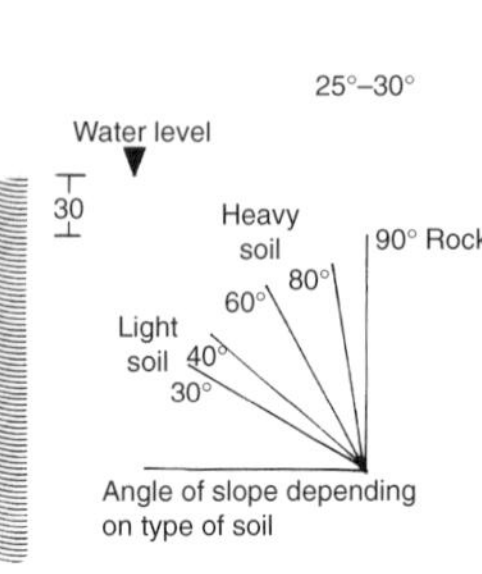

10 In small garden with heavy soil

The edge area should be well thought out with regard to cleaning, capillarity → ❹ – ❺ and required use → ❻ – ❽. The advantage of a natural pool in comparison with conventional pools is low maintenance cost (no cleaning, pump) and its ecological value (biotope effect, allergy-free, as no chlorine is needed). On the other hand, turbidity or temporary formation of algae have to be accepted in some weather conditions. These problems normally disappear fairly quickly without any action. A stream can be part of the pool, 8–10 m being ideal → ❶ – ❷. About 15 m^3 of water runs over the stones and cascades per hour and is oxygenated.

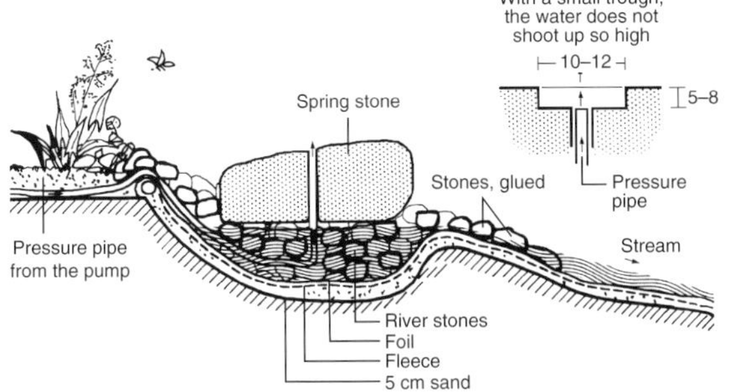

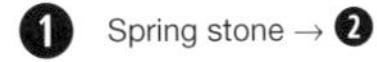
❶ Spring stone → ❷

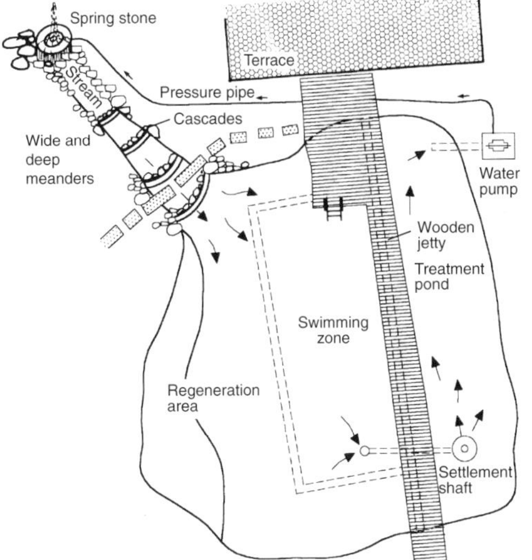

❷ Plan of natural swimming pool → ❸

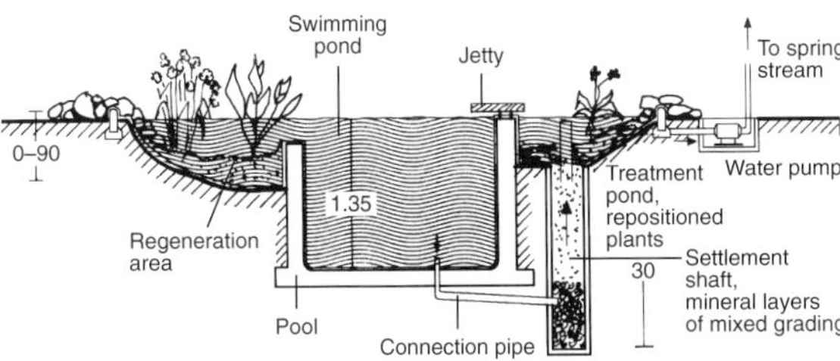

❸ Cross-section of natural swimming pool → ❷

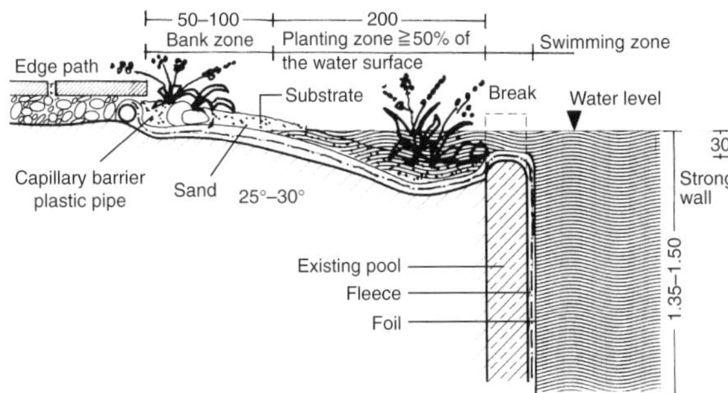

❹ Existing swimming pool converted into a natural pool

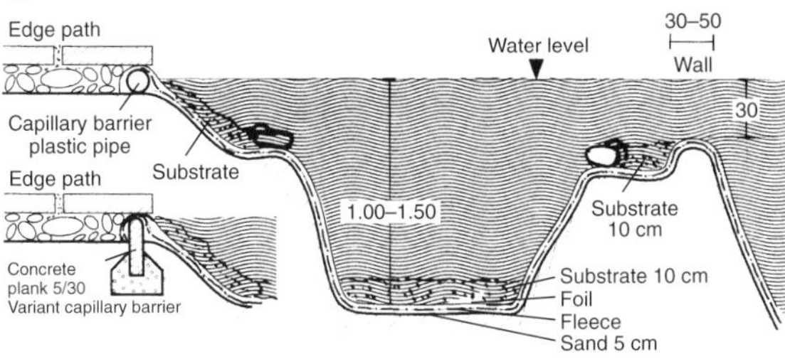

❺ Water treatment zone/hole

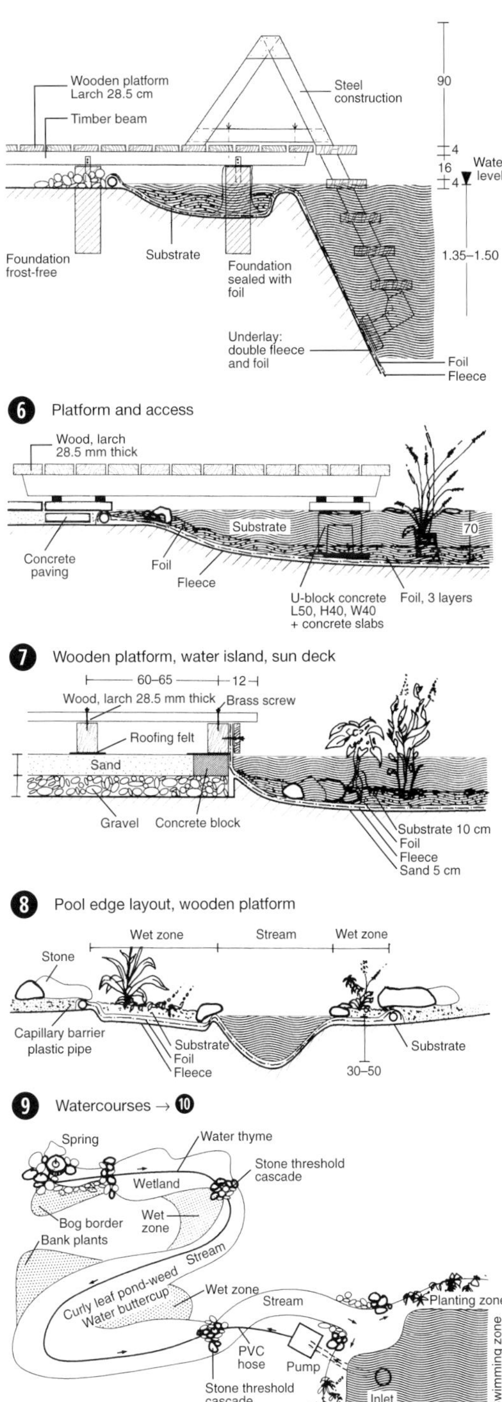

❻ Platform and access

❼ Wooden platform, water island, sun deck

❽ Pool edge layout, wooden platform

❾ Watercourses → ❿

❿ Watercourse with wide and deep meanders and bubbling cascades → ❾.

PONDS AND POOLS

Water Plants for a Natural Swimming Pool

Ecological natural swimming pools require a self-cleaning zone of water plants, which should take up about ⅓ of the total area.

English name	Botanical name	Flowering months	Flower colour
sweet flag	*Acorus calamus*	VI–VII	green-yellow, brown
European water plantain	*Alisma plantago-aquatica*	VI–VII	whitish-pink
lesser water plantain	*Baldellia ranunculoides*	VI–X	brown
flowering rush	*Butomus umbellatus*	VI–VIII	pink, white, red
Cypress sedge	*Carex pseudocyperus*	VI–VII	yellow
reed sweetgrass	*Glyceria maxima 'Variegata'*	V–VII	green
common mare's tail	*Hippuris vulgari*	VII–VIII	insignificant
golden club	*Orontium aquaticum*	V–VI	gold-yellow
water knotweed	*Polygonum amphibium*	VI–VII	pink
pickerel weed	*Pontederia cordata*	VII–VIII	blue
curly-leaf pond-weed	*Potamogeton crispus*	VI–IX	not noticeable
water buttercup	*Ranunculus lingua*	VI–IX	yellow
arrowhead	*Sagittaria sagittifolia*	VI–VIII	white-pink
common tule	*Scirpus lacustris*	VII–VIII	brown
branched bur-reed	*Sparganium erectum*	VII–VIII	green-white
common bulrush	*Typha angustifolia*	VI–VII	black-brown

❶ Shallow-water zone, water depth 10–40 cm → ❺

English name	Botanical name	Flowering months	Flower colour
cape pond-weed	*Aponogeton distachyos*	VII–X	white
frogbit	*Hydrocharis morsus–ranae*	VI–VIII	white
yellow water lily	*Nuphar lutea*	VI–VIII	yolk-yellow
water lily	*Nymphaea hybrids*	VI–IX	acc. type
fringed water lily	*Nymphoides peltata*	VI–VII	gold-yellow
floating pond-weed	*Potamogeton natans*	VI–IX	white
common water crowfoot	*Ranunculus aquatilis*	VI–IX	white
water soldiers	*Stratiotes aloides*	V–VII	white
water chestnut	*Trapa natans*	VI–VII	white, unobtrusive

❷ Water lily zone → ❺

English name	Botanical name	Flowering months	Flower colour
bog arum	*Calla palustris*	VI–VII	white
marsh marigold	*Caltha palustris*	IV–VI	yellow
Gray's sedge	*Carex grayi*	VI–VIII	green heads
variegated horsetail	*Equisetum variegatum*	—	no flowers
common cottongrass	*Eriophorum angustifolium*	V–VI	white
bog spurge	*Euphorbia palustris*	IV–V	yellow
swordleaf rush	*Juncus ensifolius*	VII–IX	brown heads
tufted loosestrife	*Lysimachia thyrsiflora*	V–VI	yellow
American skunk cabbage	*Lysichiton americanus*	IV–V	yellow
water mint	*Mentha aquatica*	VI–VIII	pale violet
bogbean	*Menyanthes trifoliata*	V–VI	white–soft pink
monkey flower	*Mimulus cupreus*	V–X	red
water forget-me-not	*Myosotis palustris*	VI–IX	light blue
watercress	*Nasturtium officinale*	IV–VI	white
sensitive fern	*Onoclea sensibilis*	—	no flowers
European speedwell	*Veronica beccabunga*	V–IX	deep blue

❸ Bog zone → ❺

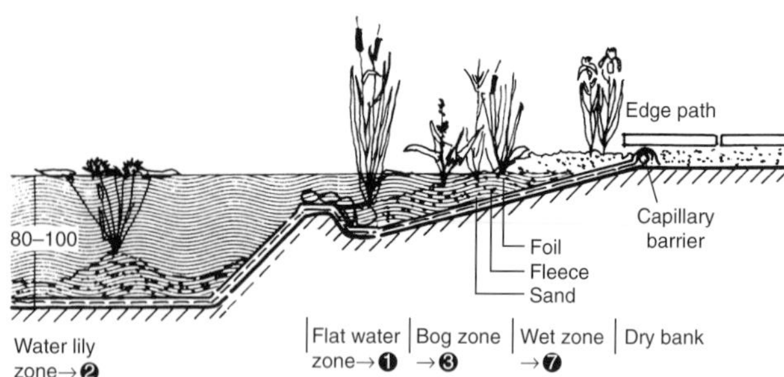

❺ Planting depth

English name	Botanical name	Notes
pondwater starwort	*Callitriche stagnalis*	evergreen, roots into the subsoil
rigid hornwort	*Ceratophyllum demersum*	rootless, overwinters as a bud on the pond floor
Canadian waterweed	*Elodea canadensis*	evergreen, plant in pond floor tends to be invasive
water violet	*Hottonia palustris*	evergreen, roots in bottom mud
water milfoil	*Myriophyllum*	evergreen, roots into pond floor
pond-weed	*Potamogeton species*	plant in a container to control growth
fan-leaved water crowfoot	*Ranunculus circinatus*	evergreen, plant in pond floor
common bladderwort	*Utricularia vulgaris*	rootless, catches small insects with bubbles; overwinters as leaf bud

❻ Oxygenation plants for the pool

English name	Botanical name	Flowering months	Flower colour
sneezewort	*Achillea ptarmica*	VII–VIII	white
blue bugle	*Ajuga reptans*	V–VI	violet
turtle-head	*Chelone obligua*	VIII–IX	pink-red
Indian rhubarb	*Darmera peltata*	IV–V	pink
hemp agrimony	*Eupatorium cannabium*	VII–IX	pink
meadowsweet	*Filipendula ulmaria*	VI–VII	white
leopard plant	*Ligularia przewalskii*	VIII–IX	yellow
creeping jenny	*Lysimachia nummularia*	VI–VII	yellow
purple loosestrife	*Lythrum salicaria*	VII–IX	violet-red
royal fern	*Osmunda regalis*	VI–VII	brown spore frond
Jacob's ladder	*Polemonium caeruleum*	VI–VII	blue to white
bistort	*Polygonum bistorta*	V–VIII	pink
primulas	*Primula*	III–VII	acc.species
meadow buttercup	*Ranunculus acris 'Multiplex'*	V–VI	yellow
globeflower	*Trollius hybrids*	V–VI	yellow tones

❼ Wet zone → ❺

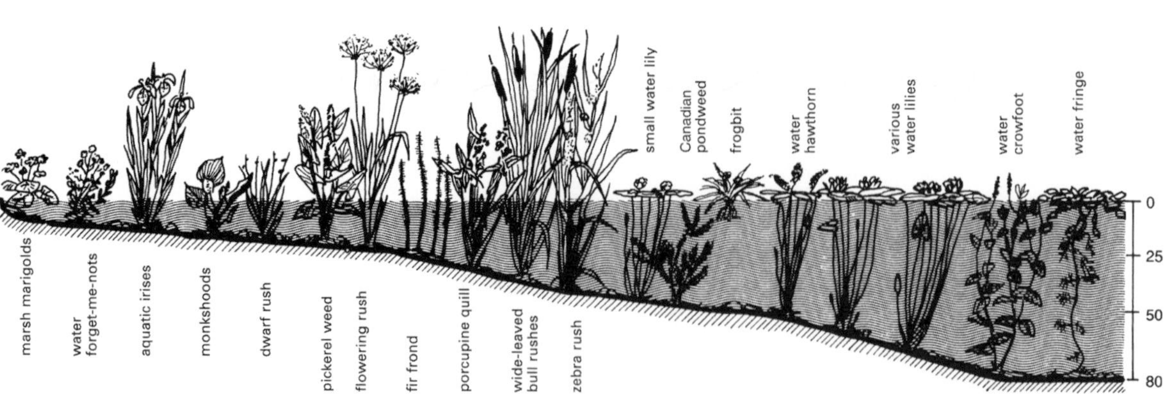

❹ Water plants

EXTERNAL WORKS – EXAMPLE

Federal Environment Agency

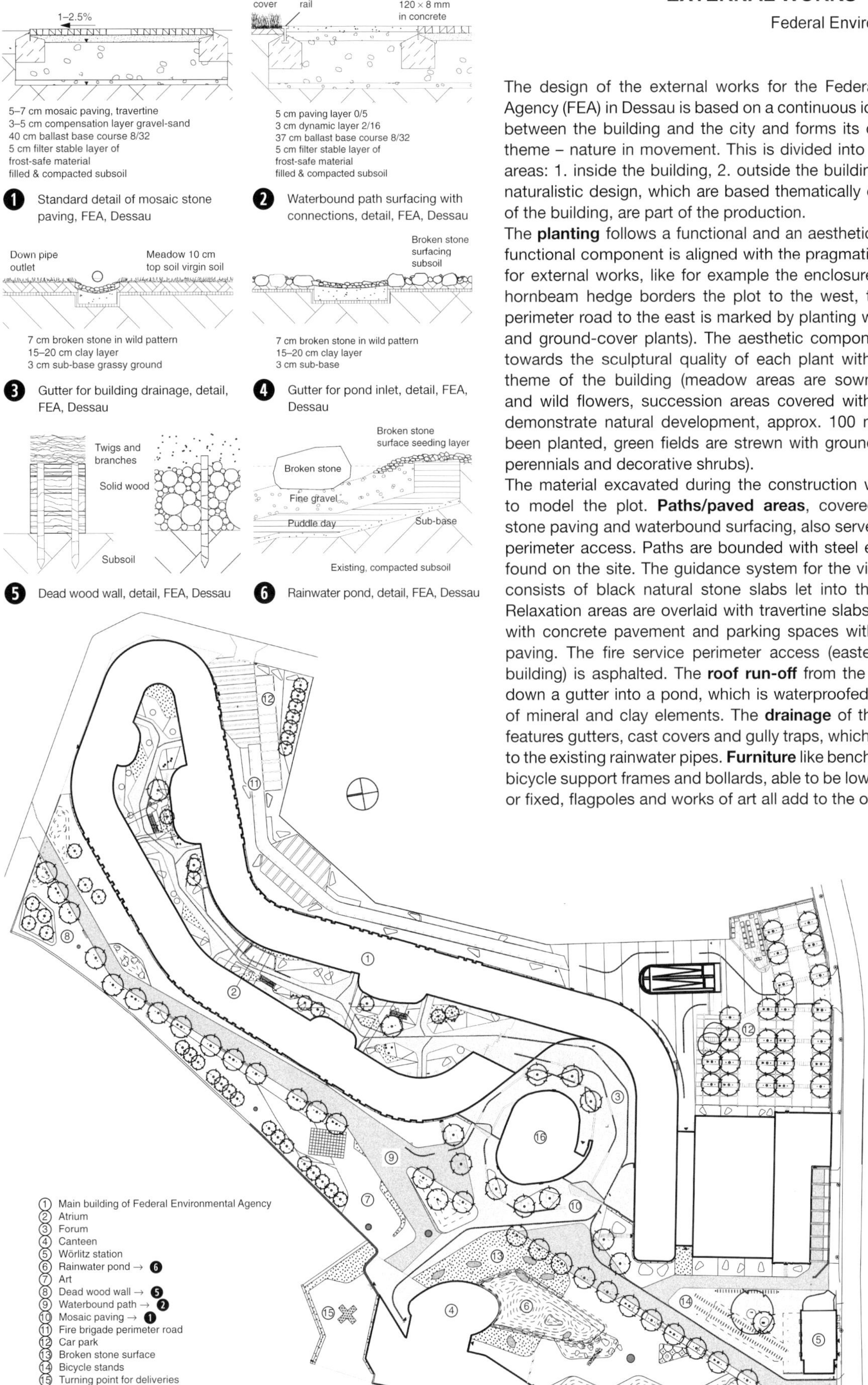

1 Standard detail of mosaic stone paving, FEA, Dessau

2 Waterbound path surfacing with connections, detail, FEA, Dessau

3 Gutter for building drainage, detail, FEA, Dessau

4 Gutter for pond inlet, detail, FEA, Dessau

5 Dead wood wall, detail, FEA, Dessau

6 Rainwater pond, detail, FEA, Dessau

7 External works at the FEA, Dessau

The design of the external works for the Federal Environment Agency (FEA) in Dessau is based on a continuous idea: it mediates between the building and the city and forms its own landscape theme – nature in movement. This is divided into two landscape areas: 1. inside the building, 2. outside the building. Elements of naturalistic design, which are based thematically on the function of the building, are part of the production.

The **planting** follows a functional and an aesthetic principle. The functional component is aligned with the pragmatic requirements for external works, like for example the enclosure of the plot (a hornbeam hedge borders the plot to the west, the fire service perimeter road to the east is marked by planting with red bushes and ground-cover plants). The aesthetic component is oriented towards the sculptural quality of each plant with regard to the theme of the building (meadow areas are sown with grasses and wild flowers, succession areas covered with broken stone demonstrate natural development, approx. 100 new trees have been planted, green fields are strewn with ground-cover plants, perennials and decorative shrubs).

The material excavated during the construction work was used to model the plot. **Paths/paved areas**, covered with mosaic stone paving and waterbound surfacing, also serve as fire service perimeter access. Paths are bounded with steel edges and rails found on the site. The guidance system for the visually impaired consists of black natural stone slabs let into the pale paving. Relaxation areas are overlaid with travertine slabs, access roads with concrete pavement and parking spaces with grass-jointed paving. The fire service perimeter access (eastern side of the building) is asphalted. The **roof run-off** from the canteen pours down a gutter into a pond, which is waterproofed with a mixture of mineral and clay elements. The **drainage** of the paved areas features gutters, cast covers and gully traps, which are connected to the existing rainwater pipes. **Furniture** like benches, waste bins, bicycle support frames and bollards, able to be lowered, taken out or fixed, flagpoles and works of art all add to the overall effect.

The selection of location for a farm has to balance topographical and climatic conditions with business considerations. This should take priority over factors resulting from ownership. Buildings for livestock have almost the same climatic requirements as houses for people. Extremely frosty, misty or very windy regions and particularly exposed locations should be avoided. The relationship of the buildings to each other, the arrangement of the functional areas in relation to nearby residential areas and the prevailing wind direction should all be taken into account. The prevailing wind direction is more important in summer than in winter.

The choice of location should differentiate between the transport connections internally and externally. The quality of external transport connections is determined by the connection of the farm to public roads, leading to customers and marketing organisations (farm shop, dairy etc.). For the quality of internal connections, a good link to the main farm road network in the vicinity is more important than the farm itself being near the fields.

The arrangement of the buildings should observe the following distances: min. 10 m between all buildings, from the farmhouse to the buildings for livestock at least 15 m; from the farmhouse southwards to the plot boundary at least 10 m and west or east min. 6 m → ❶.

Animal husbandry operations with technical facilities normally require areas of 4000–5000 m^2, with plot widths of 35–45 m, and approx. 1000 m^2 for the residential area including garden. (UK farms tend to be larger than those in other European countries, which may be in part the result of differing inheritance practices.) Working and transport routes within and outside the buildings should not exceed the following gradients: for hand trucks = 5%, motor vehicles = 10%, short hills max. 20%.

The residential garden serves as an extension of the house. The location should if possible be to the south or west of the house, min. 100 m^2 lawn, paved and secluded sitting area, borders for flowers, bushes, children's play area and washing line, altogether needing approx. 400–500 m^2. Personal consumption requires a vegetable garden with 50–60 m^2 per person and an orchard approx. 100 m^2 per person.

❶ Schematic layout of the elements of a farmyard (farmhouse, working areas, traffic areas)

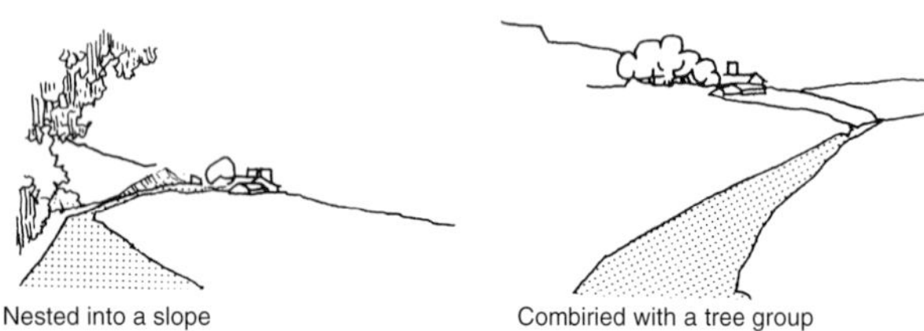

Nested into a slope | Combiried with a tree group

❷ Integration of the farmyard into the landscape

❸ Planning system for a flexible barn area

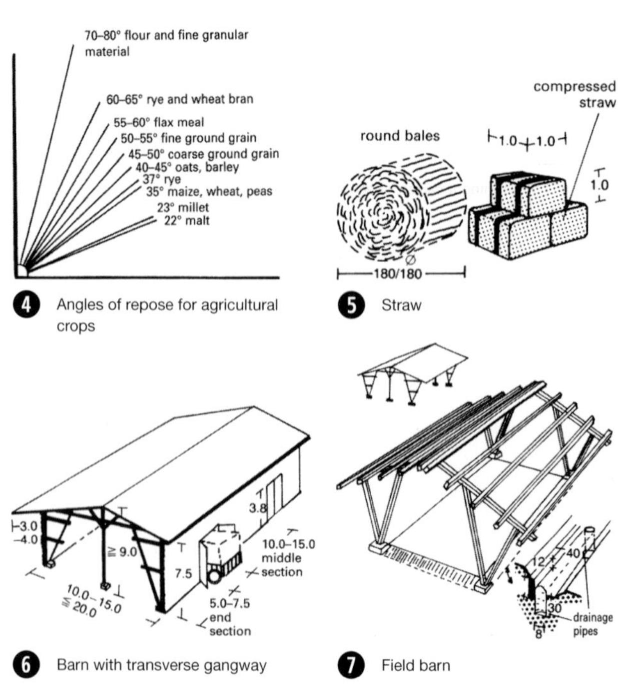

❹ Angles of repose for agricultural crops

❺ Straw

❻ Barn with transverse gangway

❼ Field barn

FARMYARDS

Space Requirements

The following tables show the plot size required according to production capacity and type of operation, based on investigations by Herms and Hillendahl. Various plot areas can be reduced, e.g. through the installation of a tower silo instead of a silage heap, upstairs instead of downstairs feed rooms, slurry storage under the slatted floor instead of in outdoor containers, building up to boundaries etc.

The tables of plot size → ❶ – ❼ do not take into account all the space required for housing machines and workshops or for the residential area, as these do not have to be in the farmyard.

Space required (m^2)	No. pigs 500	1000	1500	2000
pig shed	850	1700	2500	3400
slurry pit	250	400	600	800
transport area	240	400	440	400
yard area	1300	2300	2700	3000
total area required (m^2)	2640	4800	6290	7600
plot width required (m)	35	35	55	55

❶ Pig fattening: space required

Space required (m^2)	No. sows				No. sows: S No. piglets: P		
	80	100	120	150	46 S 400 P	88 S 800 P	142 S 1200 P
pig shed	720	850	1020	1200	880	1760	2640
slurry pit	90	100	110	120	240	400	600
transport area	230	250	270	300	240	400	480
yard area (incl. run-out)	1600	1850	2100	2400	1480	2640	3120
total area required (m^2)	2640	3050	3500	4020	2840	5200	6830
plot width required (m)	45	45	45	50	45	45	50

❷ Pig breeding (with fattening): space required

Space required (m^2)	Calf fattening in single pens No. calves				Bullock fattening, loose, fully slatted floor No. bullocks			
	100	200	300	400	100	200	300	400
cowshed	340	640	930	1200	400	940	1410	1880
green fodder	—	—	—	—	50	100	150	200
silage heap	—	—	—	—	560	1000	1250	1500
slurry pit	50	100	150	200	120	200	300	400
transport area	200	200	200	200	650	560	750	850
yard area	1110	1600	2200	2640	1210	2100	3140	2170
total area required (m^2)	1700	2540	3480	4240	2990	4900	7000	7000
plot width required (m)	45	45	45	45	35	35	50	50

❸ Finishing beef cattle: space required

Space required (m^2)	Stanchions/feeding/ cubicles No. cows			Loose pens No. cows			
	40	60	80	50	80	120	200
cowshed	250	380	500	400	640	960	1600
milk area	10	20	30	50	80	120	200
silage heap	200	300	400	250	400	600	1000
green fodder	80	120	160	100	160	240	400
slurry pit	160	240	320	200	320	480	800
transport area	400	600	720	500	720	960	1400
yard area	800	1050	1200	1250	1760	2400	3000
total area required (m^2)	1900	2710	3330	2750	4080	5760	8400
plot width required (m)	33	33	33	45	45	45	45

❹ Milk cows without calves: space required

Space required (m^2)	Stanchions/feeding/ cubicles No. cows			Loose pens No.cows			
	40	60	80	50	80	120	200
cowshed	320	470	630	440	700	1050	1750
milk area	20	20	30	60	80	80	80
silage heap	250	380	500	310	500	750	1250
green fodder	100	150	200	130	200	300	500
slurry pit	200	300	400	260	400	600	1000
transport area	500	750	900	620	900	1200	1750
yard area	1000	1270	1500	1560	2200	3000	3750
total area required (m^2)	2390	3340	4160	3380	4980	6980	10080
plot width required (m)	33	33	43	45	45	45	45

❺ Milk cows with calves: space required

Space required (m^2)	Laying hens, 3 per cage No. hens			Fattening chickens, battery No. hens		
	10000	50000	100000	10000	50000	100000
hen house	630	3000	6000	400	2000	4000
egg sorting room	—	400	800	—	—	—
dung	110	550	1100	50	250	500
transport area	200	1200	1800	100	500	1000
yard area	1260	5050	8000	1000	4000	7000
total area required (m^2)	2200	10200	17700	1550	6750	12500
plot width required (m)	35	100	100	35	80	80

❻ Chickens: space required

Space required (m^2)	Roots/corn production No. ha			Corn/feed production No. ha		
	60	80	100	80	100	120
machine shed	250	290	320	230	270	300
grain and storage	250	250	250	250	250	250
traffic and machine parking	180	200	220	180	200	220
additional yard area	200	230	250	200	230	250
total area required (m^2)	880	970	1040	860	950	1020
plot width required (m)	33	33	40	33	33	40

❼ Arable farming: space required

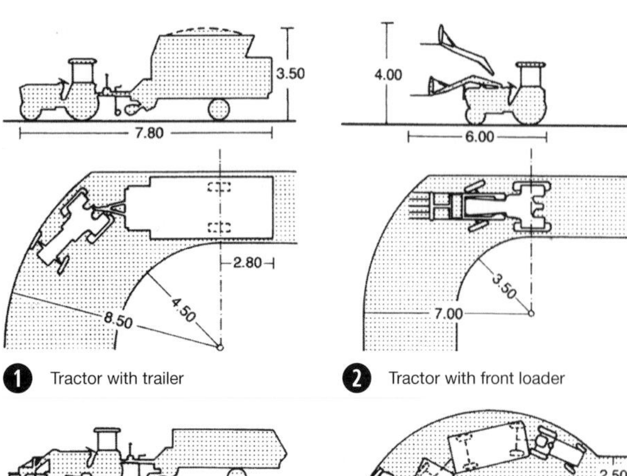

❶ Tractor with trailer

❷ Tractor with front loader

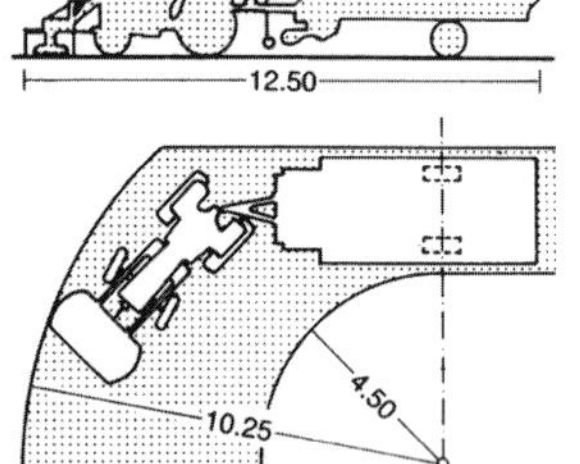

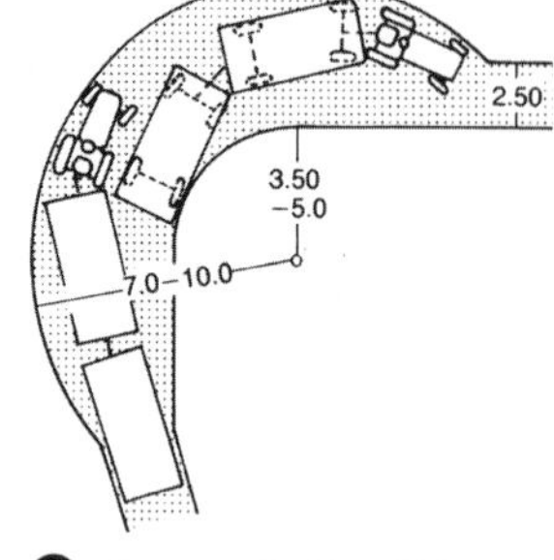
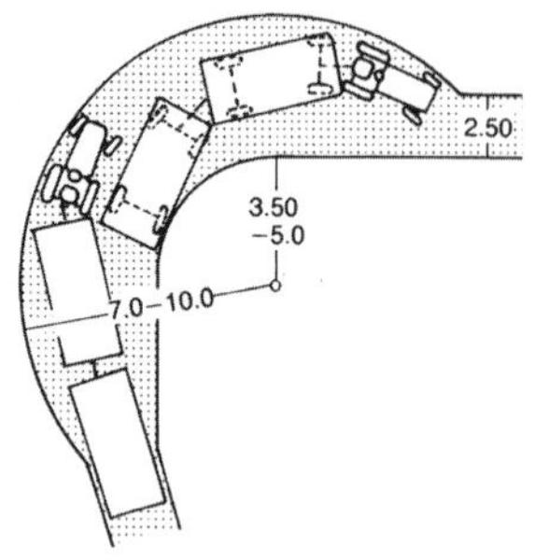
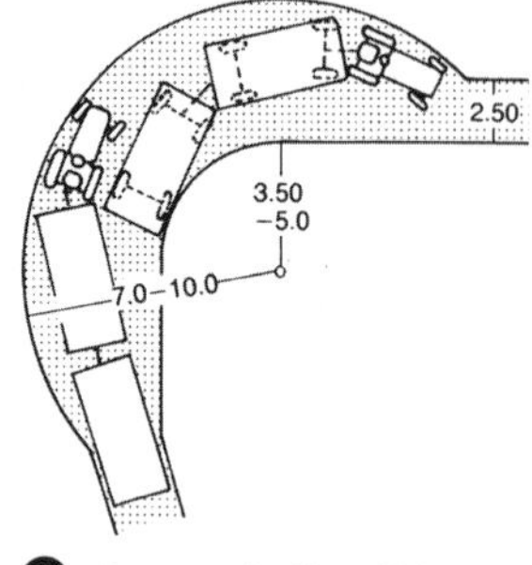

❸ Tractor with front mower and trailer

❹ Space required for vehicles turning

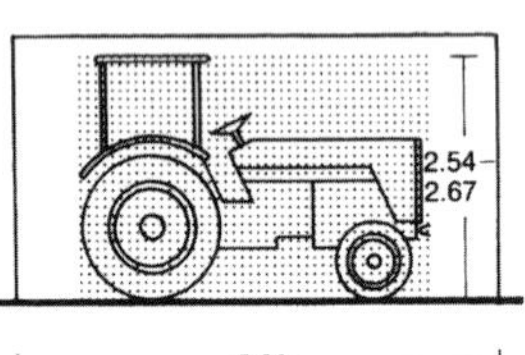

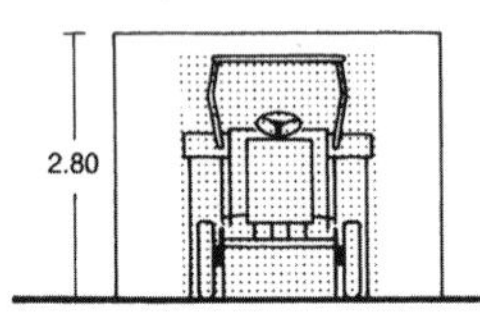

	m²	Length	Width	Height
green fodder	12	6.95	2.35	2.26
dry fodder	19			2.94
green fodder	11	7.80	2.46	2.45
dry fodder	17			3.10
green fodder	12	7.25	2.25	2.30
dry fodder	18			3.25
green fodder	14	8.00	2.35	2.25
dry fodder	20			2.90
guideline for trailer	13–20	7.70	2.40	310
guideline for shed		8.70	3.40	3.40

❺ Space required for a single tractor (rough dimensions of shed)

❻ Small tractor shed with side gangway

❼ Large tractor shed with central gangway; supported structure

Type of building/farm	Reference dimension	Farm size			
		10 ha	15 ha	20 ha	30 ha
Garage for tractors and motor mowers	Floor area	26.0 m²	43.0 m²	44 m²	62 m²
	Depth	5.0 m	5.2 m	5.2 m	5.4 m
	Height	2.7 m	2.8 m	2.8 m	2.9 m
Garage for mountain farm transporter with loader, motor mower and self-propelled belt reaper	Floor area	46.0 m²			
	Depth	7.3 m			
	Height				
	Transporter	2.9 m			
	Motor mower	2.2 m			
Workshop	Floor area	12.0 m²	12.0 m²	14.0 m²	16.0 m²
Shed for fodder-producing farm without own arable	Floor area	160.0 m²	230.0 m²	260.0 m²	350.0 m²
	Depth	7.6 m	8.7 m	8.7 m	9.5 m
	Height	3.3 m	3.4 m	3.4 m	3.5 m
Shed for mixed fodder/ arable farm	Floor area	180.0 m²	310.0 m²	370.0 m²	520.0 m²
	Depth	7.6 m	8.7 m	8.7 m	9.5 m
	Height	3.3 m	3.5 m	3.5 m	3.6 m
Shed for arable farm with no animals	Floor area		240.0 m²	340.0 m²	450.0 m²
	Depth		8.0 m	8.0 m	9.7 m
	Height		3.5 m	3.5 m	5.8 m
Shed for mountain farm	Floor area		120.0 m²		
	Depth		8.3 m		
	Height		3.2 m		

❽ Space required for garages/sheds

Machine	Features	L (m)	W (m)	H (m)
Tractors (with safety harness)				
standard tractor	up to 60 hp	3.30–3.70	1.50–2.00	2.00–2.60
4 × 4 tractor	60–120 hp	4.00–5.00	1.80–1.40	2.50–2.80
(incl. load-carrying tractor)	120–200 hp	5.50–6.00	2.40–2.50	2.50–2.90
equipment carrier with load platform	up to 45 hp	4.50	1.70	2.50
Transporters (with tow bar), twin-axle trailers				
flat-bed trailer	up to 3 t	approx. 6.00	1.80–1.90	approx. 1.50
flat-bed trailer	3–5 t	approx. 6.50	1.90–2.10	approx. 1.60
and tipper	5–8 t	approx. 7.00	2.10–2.20	approx. 1.80
single-axle trailer	up to 3 t	approx. 5.00[1)]	1.90–2.10	approx. 1.60
with scraper floor	3–5 t	5.00–5.50[1)]	2.10	approx. 1.60
or tipper	5–8 t	5.50–6.00	2.20–2.25	approx. 2.00
slurry tank trailer	3–6 m³	5.50–6.50	1.80–2.00	1.80–2.20
Earth-tilling equipment (in transport mode)				
plough (attachment)	2-share	approx. 2.00	approx. 1.20	approx. 1.20
	3-share	2.70–3.30	1.30–1.50	approx. 1.20
	5-share	4.50–5.50	2.00–2.50	approx. 1.20
reversible plough (attachment)	2-share	approx. 2.30	approx. 1.10	1.30–1.70
	3-share	2.90–3.30	1.40–1.60	1.30–1.70
	5-share	4.50–5.50	2.00–2.50	1.30–1.70
grubber		1.50–3.00	2.30–3.00	0.60–1.10
disc harrow		3.20–3.50	1.70–3.50	0.70–1.10
attachment combination		2.70–3.00	1.10–1.30	
rotary hoe		1.10–1.40	2.00–3.00	1.10–1.20
vibrating harrow		0.80	up to 3 m	1.00
rotary harrow		2.00–3.00	up to 3 m	1.00
rollers	3-part	2.50	up to 3 m	0.80
Mineral fertiliser spreaders				
box spreader		0.70–1.20	2.70–3.00	0.70–1.20
centrifugal spreader	attachment	1.00–1.50	1.40–1.50	0.90–1.40
large-capacity spreader	trailer	4.30–5.50	1.80–2.80	1.70–2.00

[1)] muck spreader approx. 0.5 m longer

❾ Dimensions of agricultural machinery

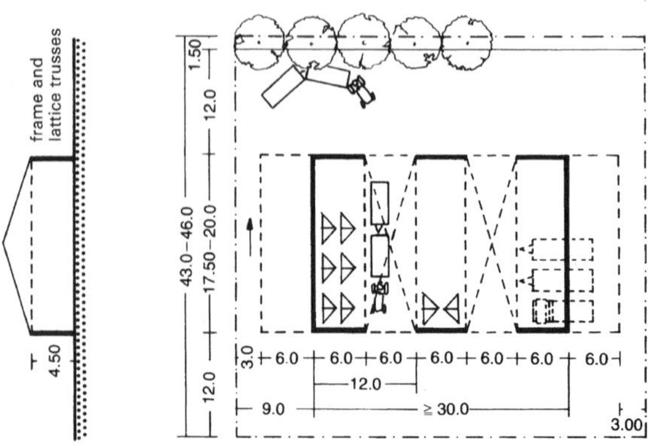

❿ Large machinery and equipment shed with transverse gangway

form of fodder	dimensions (cm)	fresh	wilted (35%)	hay	straw	handling method
long	ca. 25	1.7	1.2–1.5	0.5	0.3	in portions (grab)
cut	4–8	2.0	1.5–1.8	0.8	0.4	bulk material (dosing rollers)
short	4	3.5	2.5–3.0	0.6–1.0	0.5–0.8	bulk material (blower, cutter)
small bales	35 × 50 × 80	–	2.5–3.0	1.0–1.5	0.8–1.3	bulk material (manual)
large bales	Ø 180–150	–	3.0	0.8–1.8	0.6–1.3	bulk material (front loader)
	150 × 150 × 240 (160 × 120 × 70)	–		0.6–0.9	0.7–1.3	

1 Comparison of the various fodder products

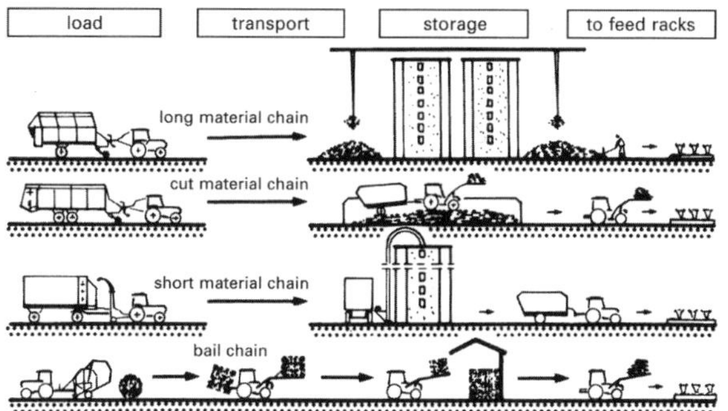

2 Fodder storage and preparation

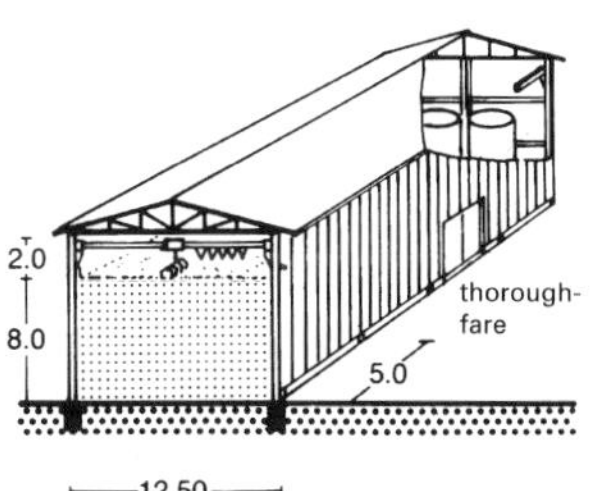

3 Hay storage barn, with grab

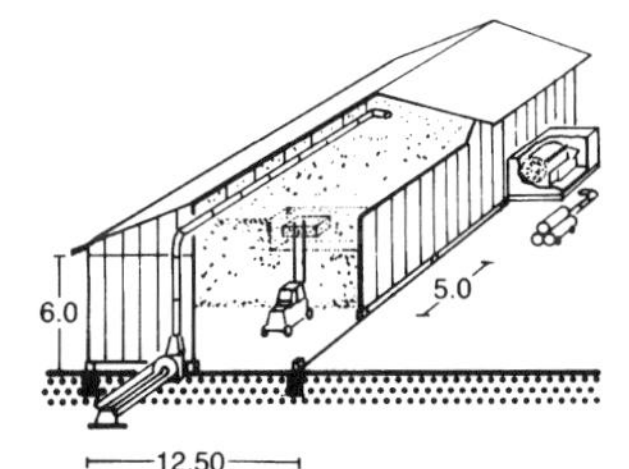

4 Hay storage barn

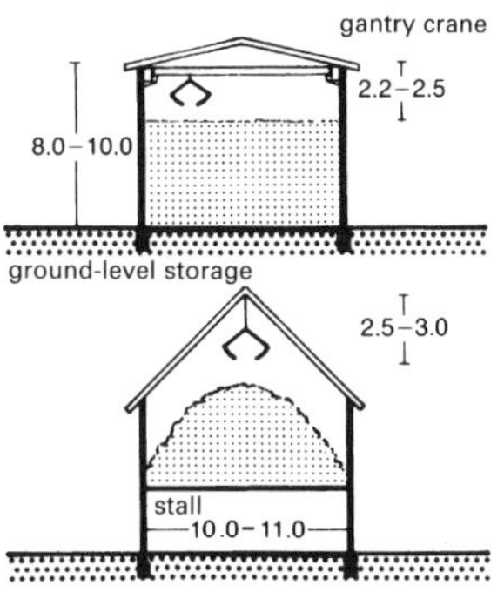

5 Overhead hay store

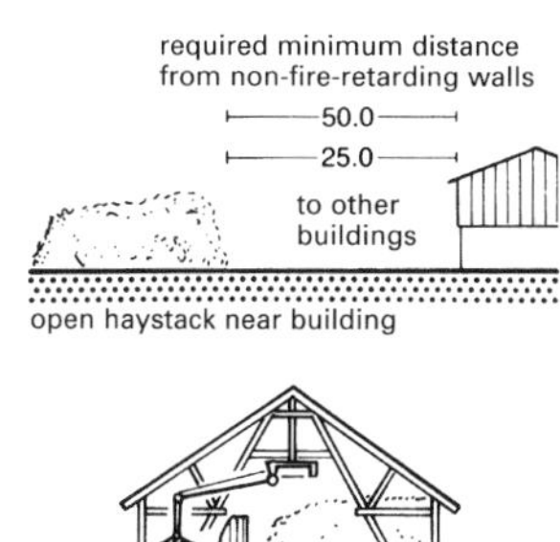

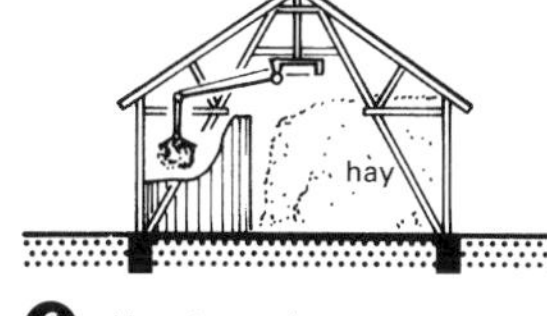

6 Hay storage barn

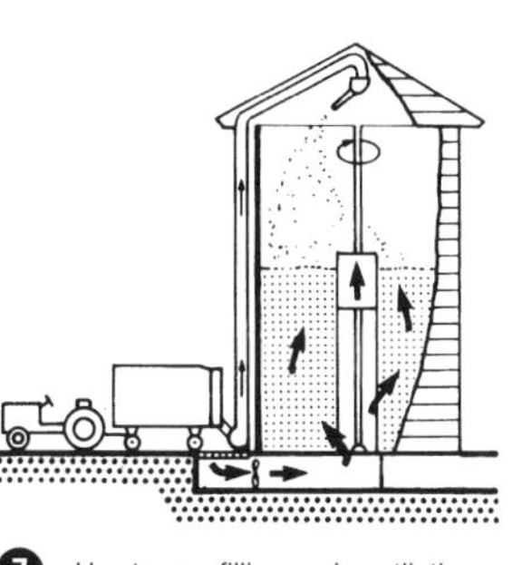

7 Hay tower: filling and ventilation

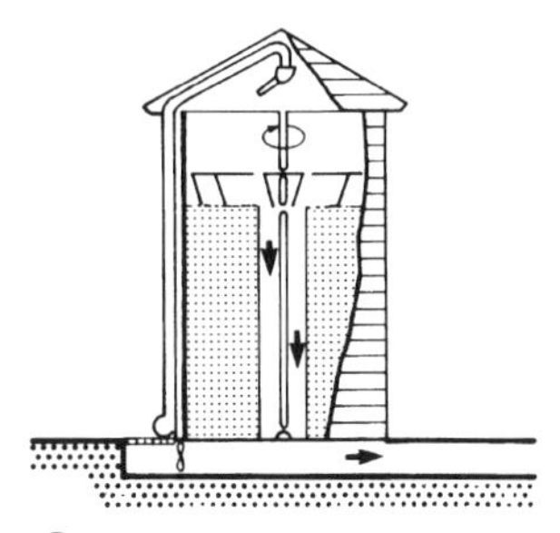

8 Hay tower: emptying

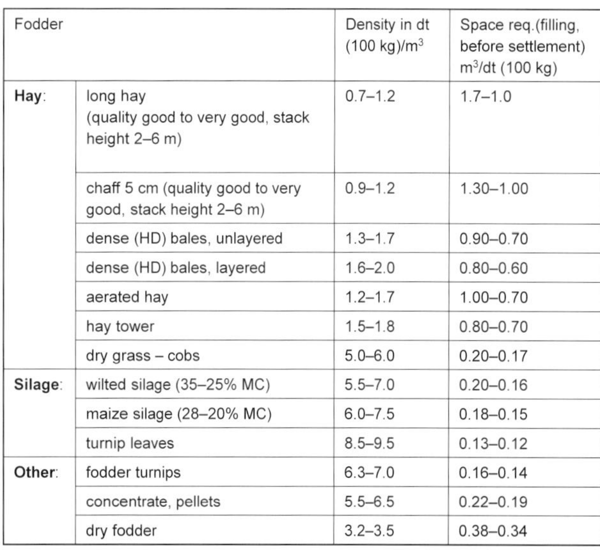

Fodder		Density in dt (100 kg)/m^3	Space req.(filling, before settlement) m^3/dt (100 kg)
Hay:	long hay (quality good to very good, stack height 2–6 m)	0.7–1.2	1.7–1.0
	chaff 5 cm (quality good to very good, stack height 2–6 m)	0.9–1.2	1.30–1.00
	dense (HD) bales, unlayered	1.3–1.7	0.90–0.70
	dense (HD) bales, layered	1.6–2.0	0.80–0.60
	aerated hay	1.2–1.7	1.00–0.70
	hay tower	1.5–1.8	0.80–0.70
	dry grass – cobs	5.0–6.0	0.20–0.17
Silage:	wilted silage (35–25% MC)	5.5–7.0	0.20–0.16
	maize silage (28–20% MC)	6.0–7.5	0.18–0.15
	turnip leaves	8.5–9.5	0.13–0.12
Other:	fodder turnips	6.3–7.0	0.16–0.14
	concentrate, pellets	5.5–6.5	0.22–0.19
	dry fodder	3.2–3.5	0.38–0.34

MC: moisture content. The listed storage space does not include room for loading and unloading technology (e.g. sheds, gangways, space for crane etc.), but does incorporate a filling supplement of 20% for hay and concentrate, and 10% for silage.

9 Storage of fodder

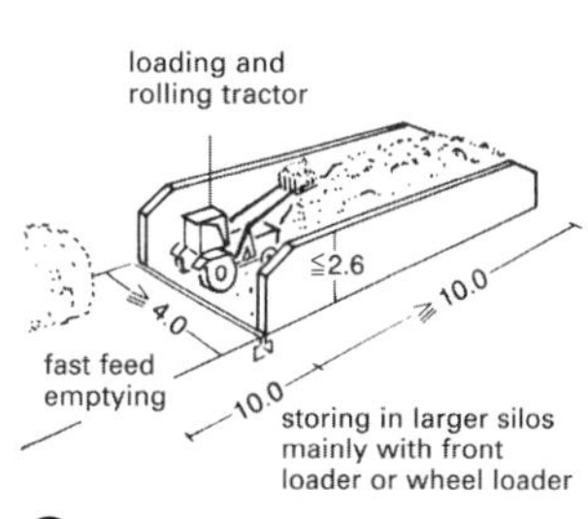

10 Flat silo

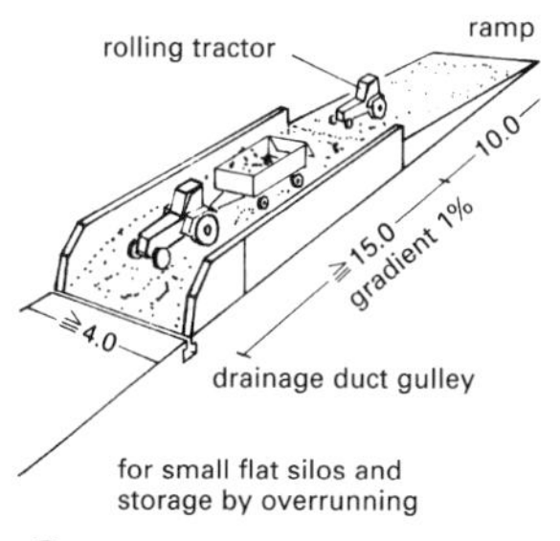

11 Flat silo with ramp

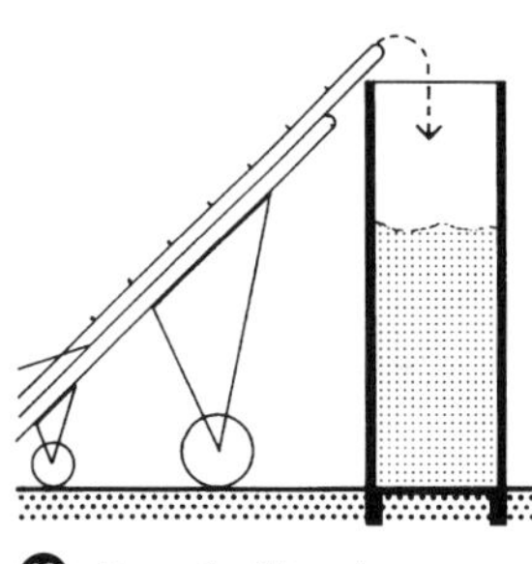

12 Tower silo: filling using conveyor

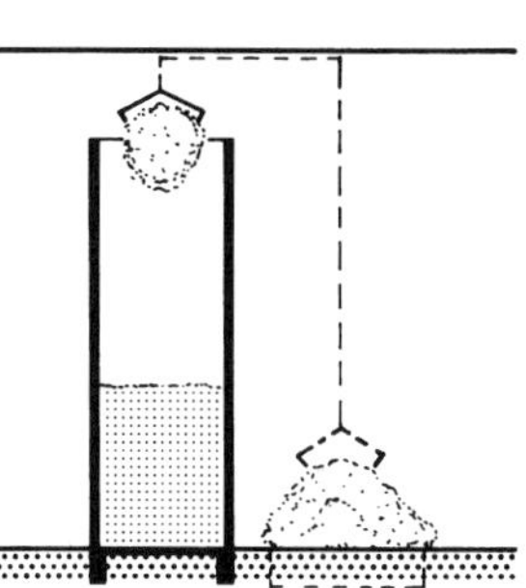

13 Silage tower, filling using grab

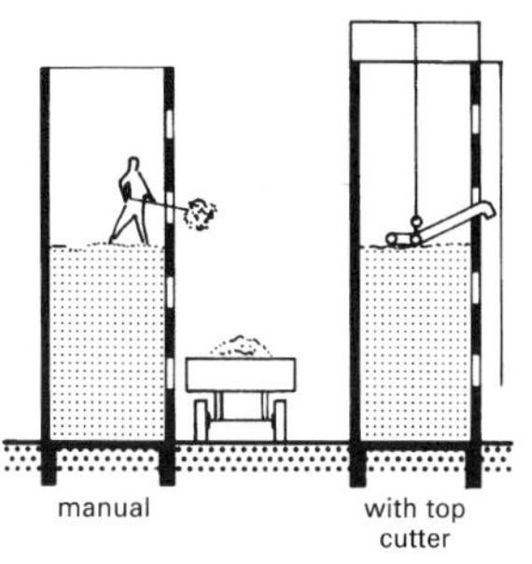

14 Silage tower, removal

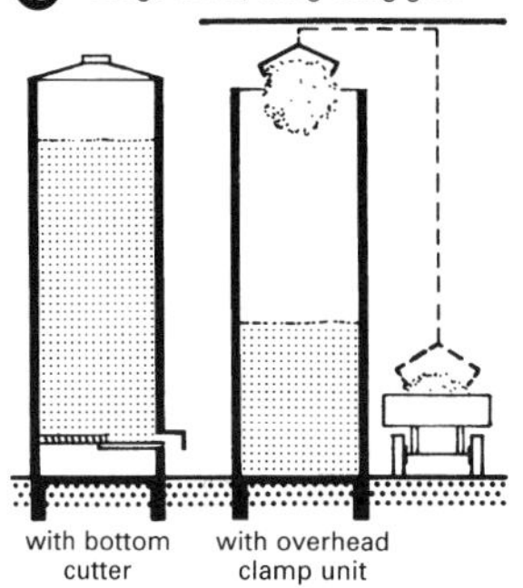

15 Silage tower, removal

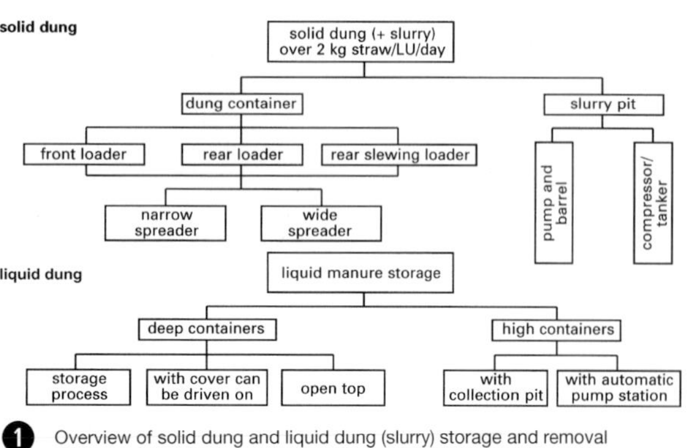

❶ Overview of solid dung and liquid dung (slurry) storage and removal

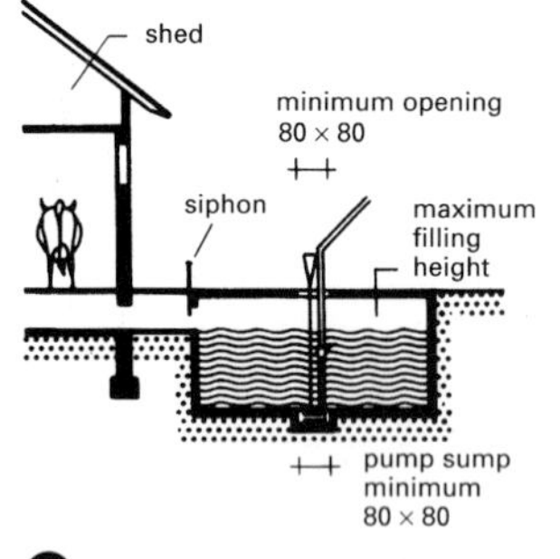

❷ Underground tank (solid)

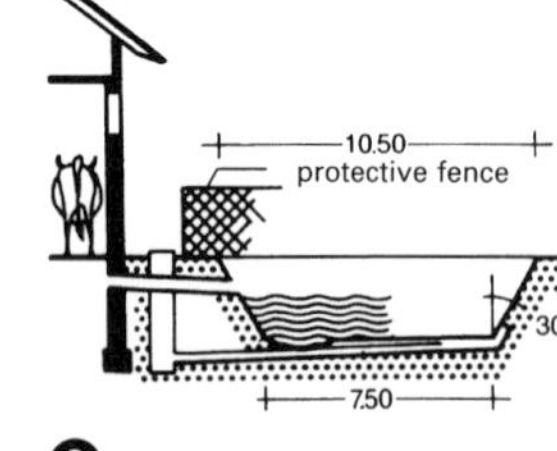

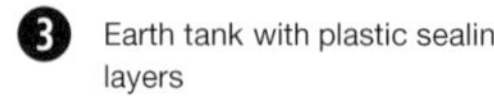

❸ Earth tank with plastic sealing layers

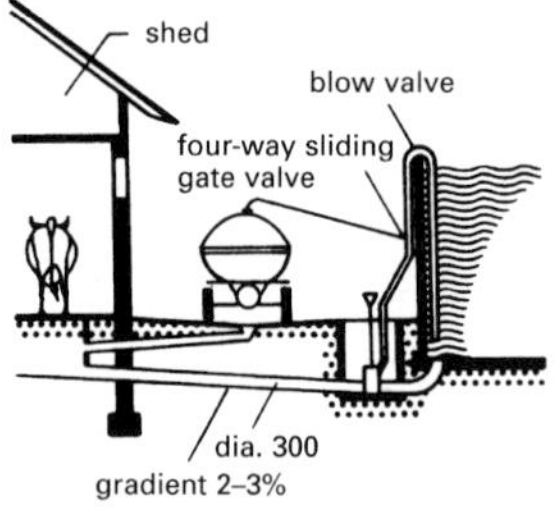

❹ Overground tank with pumping station

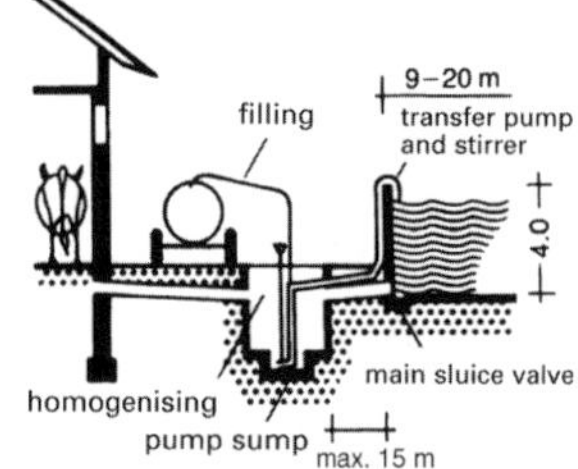

❺ Overground tank with slurry pit

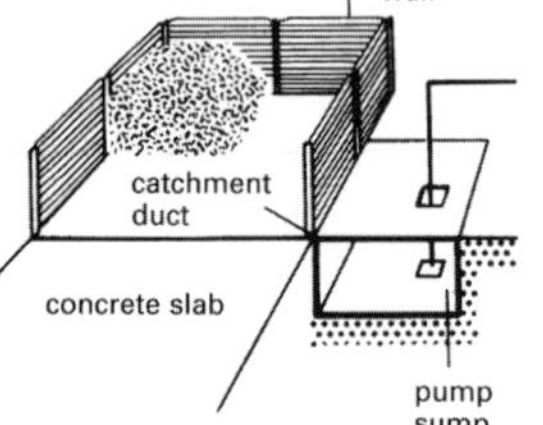

❻ Pit for solid dung including slurry pit

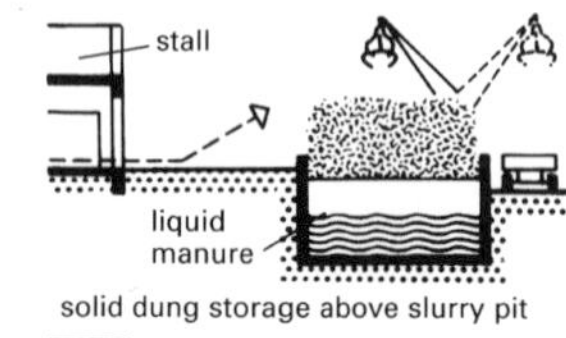

solid dung storage above slurry pit

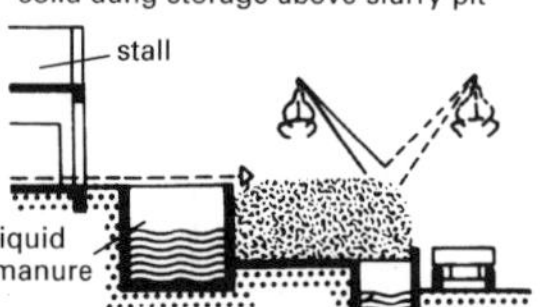

❼ Solid dung store: low-level with slurry pit at side

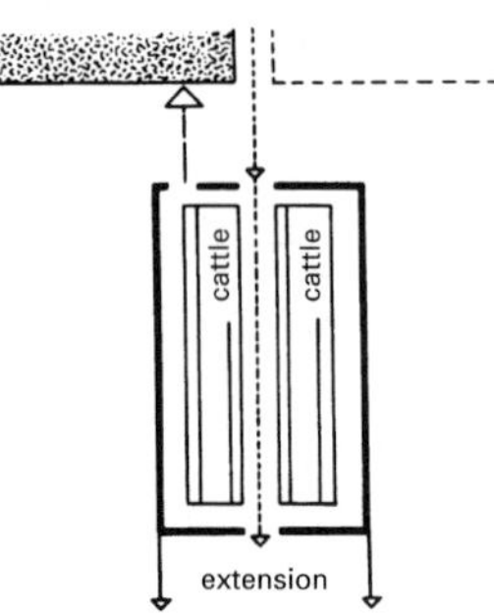

❽ Solid dung store to front, with split dung holders

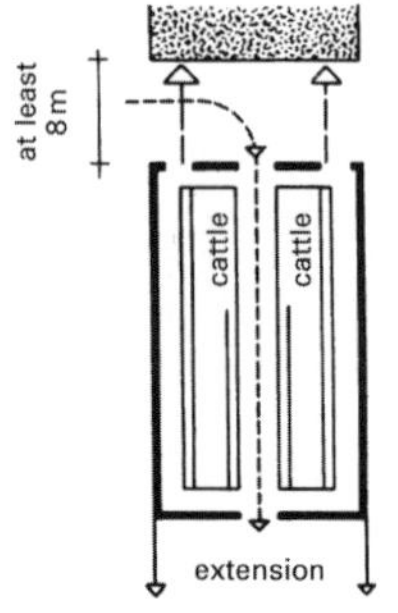

❾ Solid dung store to front, with barn entrance at side

The amount of dung and urine produced by farm animals depends on the type of animal, its live weight (expressed in large animal units, 1 LU = 500 kg live weight) and the type and composition of the fodder and drink. Exact determination of contents is not possible because the composition of fodder normally varies over the farm year, so only average values can be given → ❿ – ⓫.

Solid dung: The normal litter quantity of 1.5–2 kg of straw per LU/day results in a stacking height of solid dung of 2.0–2.5 m, equivalent to a dung slab of 0.5 m^2/LU × month. The slurry pit collects, in addition to urine, cleaning water and a large part of the rain falling through and being polluted by the dung heap. If evaporation of ⅓ of the rain and 3 m^2 dung per LU is assumed (corresponds to 6 months' storage), this gives slurry production of 0.64 m^3/LU × month.

Liquid dung (slurry): Dung, urine and cleaning water are collected. When slurry is stored in closed pits, then no rainwater gets in; for open slurry tanks a free space of 20–30 cm above the highest slurry level should be sufficient to take the rain. Evaporation of the water and part of the slurry liquid makes the free space larger again. Milk cows produce about 1.4 m^3/LU × month of slurry. Intensive fattening of bullocks with maize silage fodder can reduce slurry production to about 1.0 m^3/LU × month.

Regulations: Among the most frequent causes of pollution from farms are structural failure of slurry and effluent stores, mismanagement and lack of maintenance of slurry handling systems and problems with dirty water disposal. National regulations have been tightened in response. In England and Wales the Control of Pollution (Silage, Slurry and Agricultural Fuel Oil) Regulations 1991 set legal minimum standards for installations, including that they may not be located within 10 m of watercourses that might become polluted.

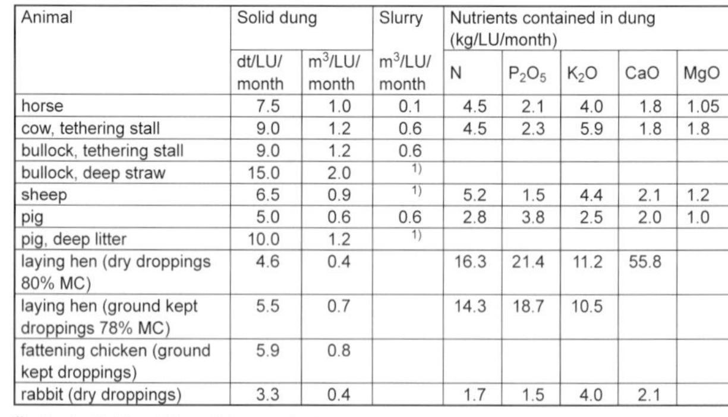

Animal	Solid dung		Slurry	Nutrients contained in dung (kg/LU/month)				
	dt/LU/ month	m^3/LU/ month	m^3/LU/ month	N	P_2O_5	K_2O	CaO	MgO
horse	7.5	1.0	0.1	4.5	2.1	4.0	1.8	1.05
cow, tethering stall	9.0	1.2	0.6	4.5	2.3	5.9	1.8	1.8
bullock, tethering stall	9.0	1.2	0.6					
bullock, deep straw	15.0	2.0	1)					
sheep	6.5	0.9	1)	5.2	1.5	4.4	2.1	1.2
pig	5.0	0.6	0.6	2.8	3.8	2.5	2.0	1.0
pig, deep litter	10.0	1.2	1)					
laying hen (dry droppings 80% MC)	4.6	0.4		16.3	21.4	11.2	55.8	
laying hen (ground kept droppings 78% MC)	5.5	0.7		14.3	18.7	10.5		
fattening chicken (ground kept droppings)	5.9	0.8						
rabbit (dry droppings)	3.3	0.4		1.7	1.5	4.0	2.1	

1) mixed with litter; MC: moisture content.

❿ Solid dung production and composition

Animal	Slurry m^3/LU/ month	MC %	Nutrients									
			N kg/m^3	P_2O_5	K_2O	CaO	MgO	N kg/LU/month	P_2O_5	K_2O	CaO	MgO
cow	1.4	10	4	2	6	2	1	5.6	2.8	8.4	2.8	1.5
pig	1.4	7	6	4	3	3	1	8.4	5.6	4.2	4.2	1.4
laying hen	1.9	15	8	8	5	15	2	15.2	15.2	9.5	28.5	3.8

MC: moisture content

⓫ Slurry production and composition

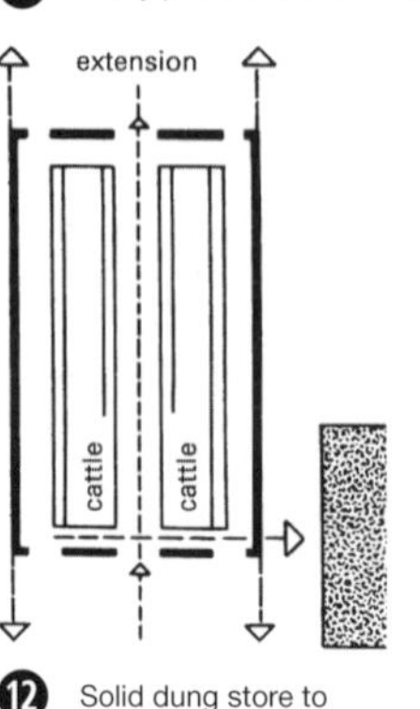

⓬ Solid dung store to side

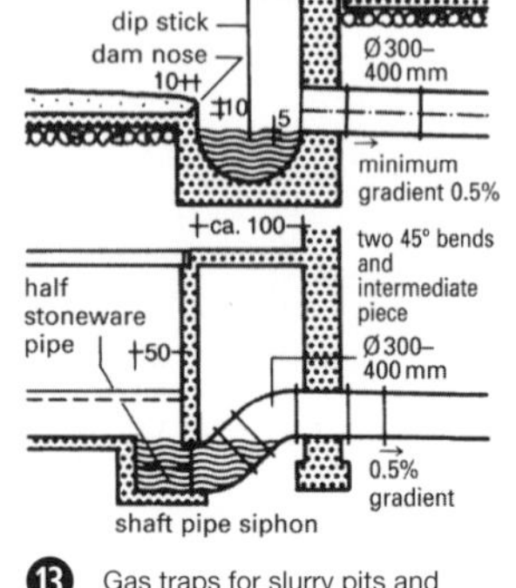

⓭ Gas traps for slurry pits and flowing slurry channels

ventilation systems

convection ventilation: stack ventilation; eaves-ridge ventilation

forced ventilation: pressurised ventilation; extract ventilation; balanced pressure ventilation

❶ Categorisation of ventilation systems

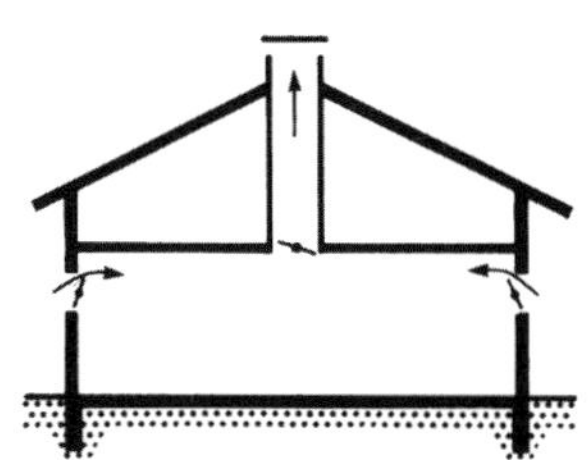

at least 5 m stack height required; works only with low outside temperatures; no energy costs

❷ Shaft ventilation

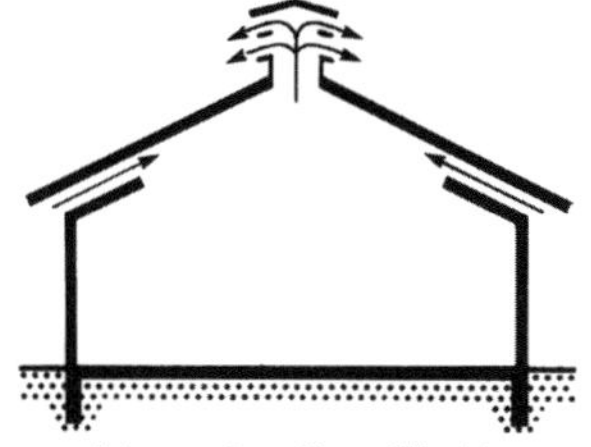

precondition: roof = ceiling; difficulties with inverted weather conditions; the supply air must be regulatable

❸ Eaves–ridge ventilation

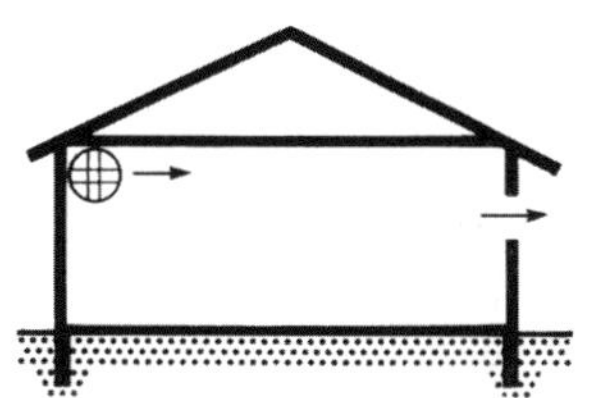

problems with wind direction; no specific outgoing air; good when used in connection with heating; energy requirement: 105–125 kWh/LU/year

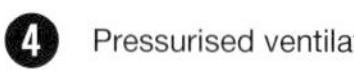

❹ Pressurised ventilation

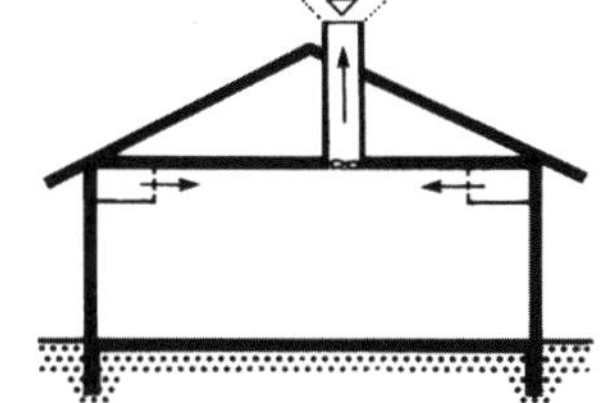

simple system; specific outgoing air (environmental protection); difficult to combine with heating; energy requirements: 98–105 kWh/LU/year

❺ Extract ventilation

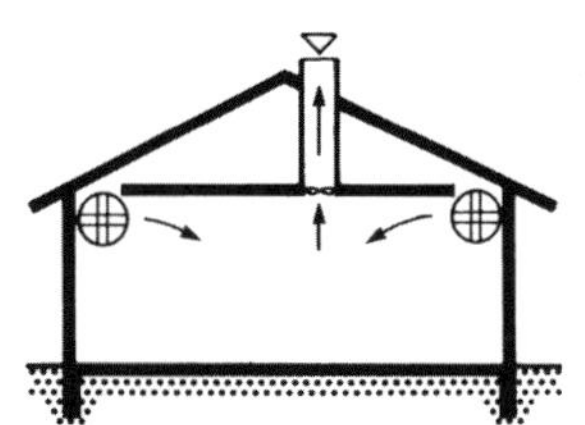

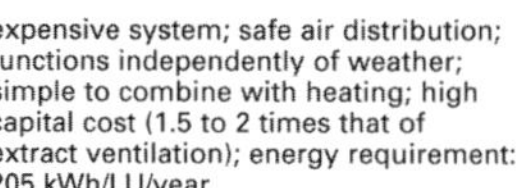

expensive system; safe air distribution; functions independently of weather; simple to combine with heating; high capital cost (1.5 to 2 times that of extract ventilation); energy requirement: 205 kWh/LU/year

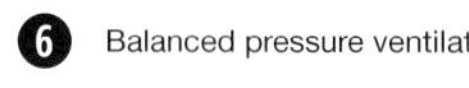

❻ Balanced pressure ventilation

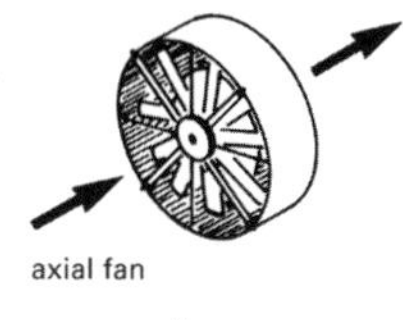

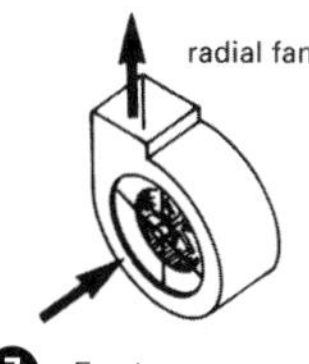

❼ Fan types

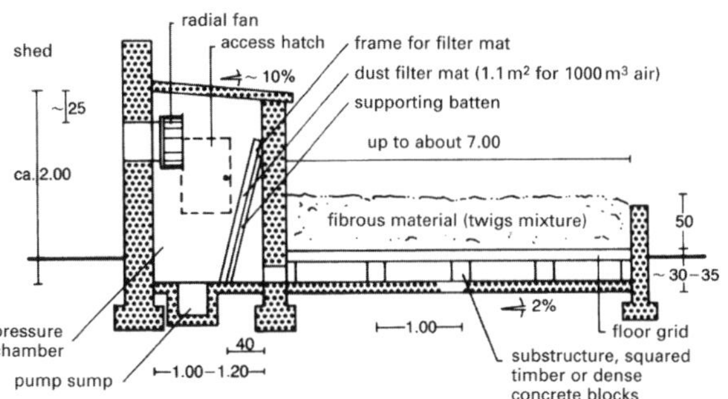

❽ Earth filter system (design by Zeisig)

In addition to their own characteristics, fodder and behaviour, the climate in their housing has the most decisive influence on the performance and health of the animals. 'Climate' includes the factors temperature, humidity, air movement, air composition, light, ventilation, window area, building volume, orientation of building and its thermal insulation. The air intake speed should be between 2.0 and 5.0 m/s according to the width of the building. Ventilation systems are divided into convection ventilation and forced ventilation → ❷ – ❼.

Air temperature (°C)		Recommended air speed (m/s)
under	18	0.15
	20	0.20
over	22	0.24
	24	0.35
	26	0.50

❾ Recommended air speed according to temperature

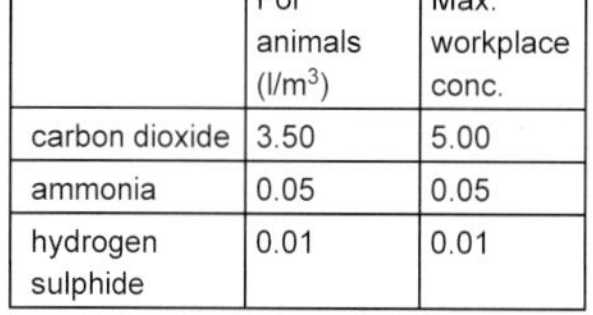

	For animals (l/m^3)	Max. workplace conc.
carbon dioxide	3.50	5.00
ammonia	0.05	0.05
hydrogen sulphide	0.01	0.01

❿ Permissible gas concentration in animal housing

The design should, as with mechanical ventilation, be based on a calculated determination of the size of air inlet and outlet openings. These should be designed according to the summer airflows and in the case of complete wind still according to the following formula:

$$w = \frac{g \cdot H \cdot \Delta t / T_1}{1 + F_1/F_2} \text{ (m/s)} \qquad F_2 = \frac{Vi}{3600 \cdot w} \text{ (m}^2\text{)}$$

w = speed of the outlet air in the ridge opening (m/s)
g = acceleration due to gravity (9.81 m/s^{-2})
H = height from floor to ridge (m)
T_1 = outside temperature in K (subtract 273 for temperature in °C)
Δt = temperature difference between indoor and outdoor air (K)
Vi = summer air renewal rate (m^3/h)
F_1 = inlet air area (m^2)
F_2 = outlet air area (m^2)
(for simplicity, $\frac{F_1}{F_2} = 1$ can be assumed)

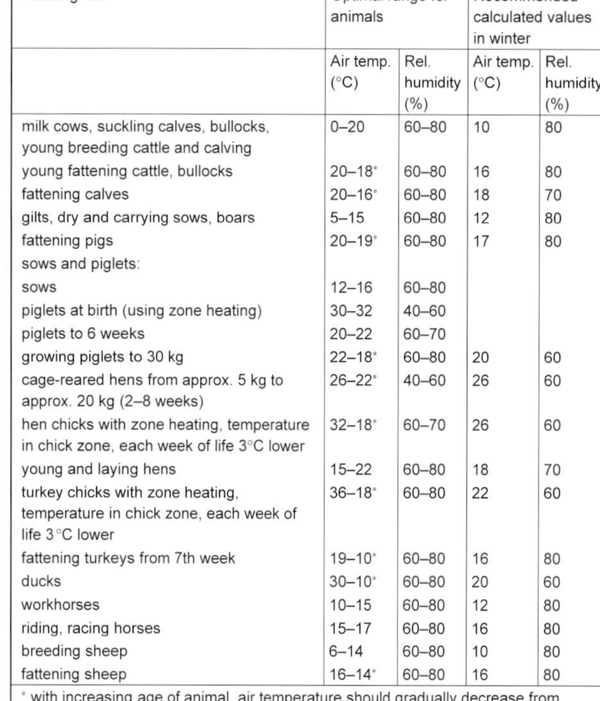

Housing for:	Optimal range for animals		Recommended calculated values in winter	
	Air temp. (°C)	Rel. humidity (%)	Air temp. (°C)	Rel. humidity (%)
milk cows, suckling calves, bullocks, young breeding cattle and calving	0–20	60–80	10	80
young fattening cattle, bullocks	20–18*	60–80	16	80
fattening calves	20–16*	60–80	18	70
gilts, dry and carrying sows, boars	5–15	60–80	12	80
fattening pigs	20–19*	60–80	17	80
sows and piglets:				
sows	12–16	60–80		
piglets at birth (using zone heating)	30–32	40–60		
piglets to 6 weeks	20–22	60–70		
growing piglets to 30 kg	22–18*	60–80	20	60
cage-reared hens from approx. 5 kg to approx. 20 kg (2–8 weeks)	26–22*	40–60	26	60
hen chicks with zone heating, temperature in chick zone, each week of life 3°C lower	32–18*	60–70	26	60
young and laying hens	15–22	60–80	18	70
turkey chicks with zone heating, temperature in chick zone, each week of life 3°C lower	36–18*	60–80	22	60
fattening turkeys from 7th week	19–10*	60–80	16	80
ducks	30–10*	60–80	20	60
workhorses	10–15	60–80	12	80
riding, racing horses	15–17	60–80	16	80
breeding sheep	6–14	60–80	10	80
fattening sheep	16–14*	60–80	16	80

* with increasing age of animal, air temperature should gradually decrease from higher to lower value

⓫ Air temperature and relative humidity in keeping various animals

Housing Poultry

(See also Laying Hens → p. 455.)
Housing for poultry requires careful design and construction in order to keep them successfully. Coops should be clean, airy, free of draughts, dry, thermally insulated and weatherproof. Provision should be made for cleaning out. The window area should be max. 1/10 of the floor area. Timber construction with a thermal insulation layer is best. Adjacent rooms should be provided for feed preparation and storage. The form of the house should be suitable for the direction of the sun, the window side south and the door east. Laying nests will be at the darkest location. A chicken coop is divided into a scratching room with litter and pit for droppings with the perch above → ❾.

The run is ideally of unlimited size and the area should be grassed with a tree for shade → ❿, a compost heap and a sand bath. The number of hens depends on the size of the run and the free floor area of the empty coop. If the run is of unlimited size, 5 hens per m^2 coop floor area. If the run is smaller than 4 times the coop floor area, then 2 hens can be kept per m^2 coop floor area. There should be room for perches, feed bowls etc. in the area.

Loft area per pair . . . . . . 0.15–0.20 m²
(pedigree pigeons correspondingly more)
1 pair of carrier pigeons . . . . 0.5 m³ air space
1 pair of pedigree pigeons . . . 1.0 m³ air space
15–20 pairs of pedigree pigeons in a loft
20–25 pairs of pigeons in a loft

❶ Pigeons

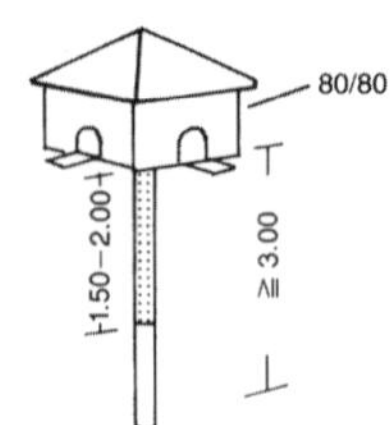

On a 3–4 m high pole, protected from birds of prey with metal sheet, or as dovecote on the east or south side of a house

❷ Dovecote

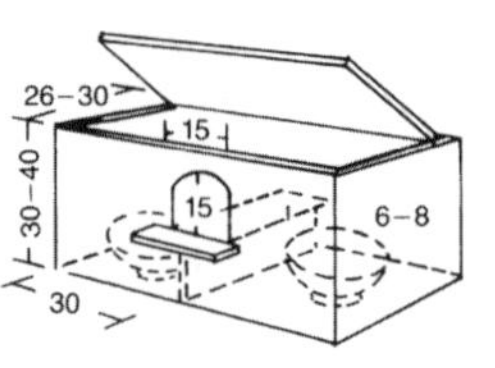

2 nests for each pair of pigeons on the floor of the box or on special frames.
Feeding through wooden box with small openings.
Drinking container with similar openings

❸ Nesting box (Fulton)

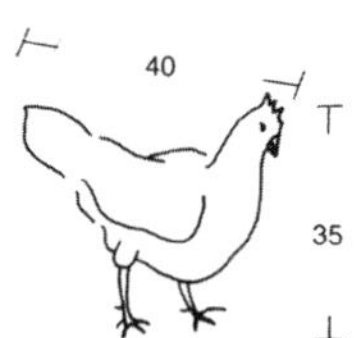

Scratching room for 5 hens	≧3 m²
Scratching room for 10 hens	≧5 m²
Scratching room for 20 hens	≧10 m²

Sleeping room for 5–6 hens or 4–5 heavy hens = 1 running m of perch = 10–12 hens per m²

❹ Hen (Orpington)

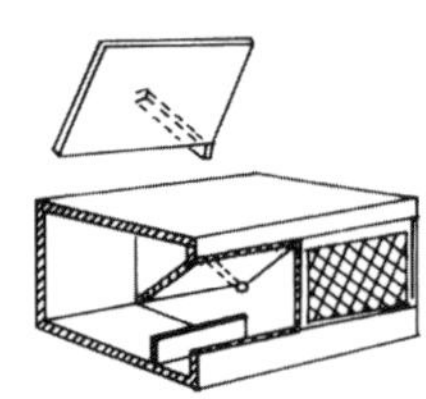

In breeding boxes, the laying nests are built as trap nests, with a trapdoor, which either hangs loose on a hook → ❿ or consists of two linked flaps → ⓫. When the hen goes into the nest, the flap is lifted and falls in.

❺ Laying nest, open

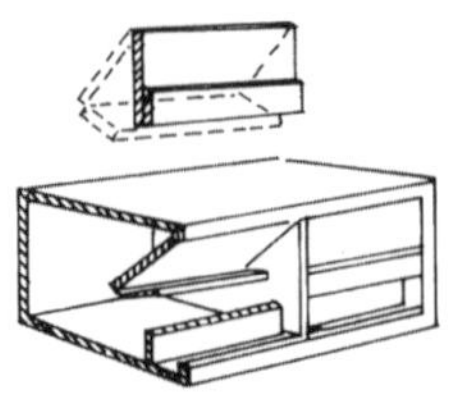

Nests can be on the floor or stacked 3 high, with the upper face sloping.
Nest size 35 × 35 to 40 × 40 cm.
Floor area and 35 cm height, 1 open nest for 5 hens, 1 trap nest for 3–4 hens.

❻ Laying nest with flap

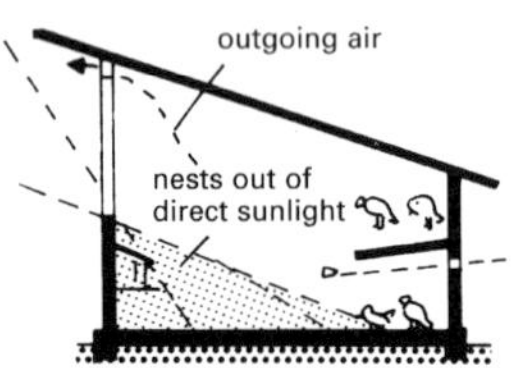

Ventilation without draughts. Laying nests away from window.
Ventilation flaps capable of being closed, if sunny.
Scratching room should adapt to outside heat, but the sleeping room must be warm.
Therefore, sleeping room is often separated with a curtain and built with thermal insulation

❼ Chicken coop (Peseda)

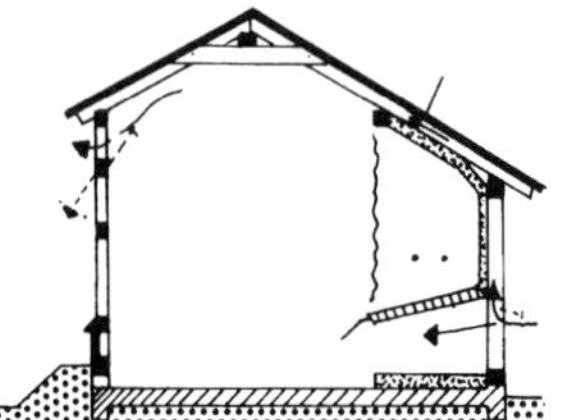

Coop for 20 chickens with separate thermally insulated sleeping niche, with sloping plate for droppings and wall ventilation.
Hatching opening 18 x 20 x 30 cm, protected against draughts with side boards and can be closed with a slider.

❽ Section → ❾

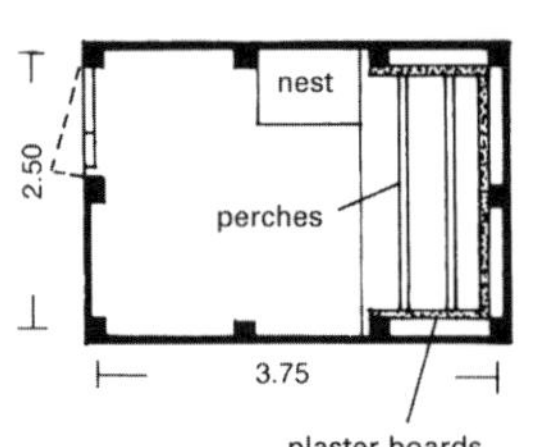

Perches according to the size of the hens 4–7 cm wide, 5–6 cm high, 3.5 m free-spanning, easily removed, 5–6 hens on 1 m perch.

Arch.: W Cords

❾ Plan → ❽

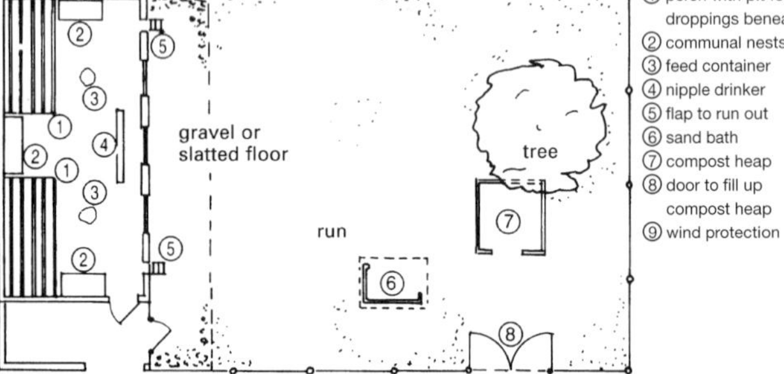

① perch with pit for droppings beneath
② communal nests
③ feed container
④ nipple drinker
⑤ flap to run out
⑥ sand bath
⑦ compost heap
⑧ door to fill up compost heap
⑨ wind protection

❿ Chicken coop and run → ⓫

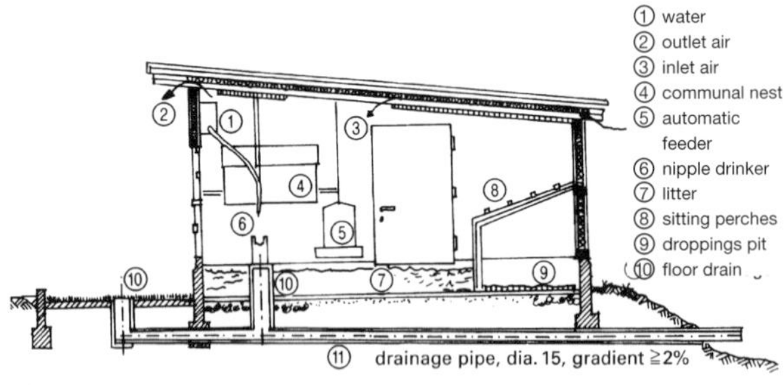

① water
② outlet air
③ inlet air
④ communal nest
⑤ automatic feeder
⑥ nipple drinker
⑦ litter
⑧ sitting perches
⑨ droppings pit
⑩ floor drain

⓫ Section of coop → ❿

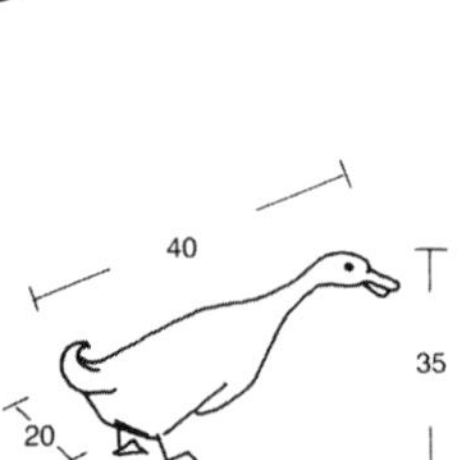

House area (4–5 ducks)	1 m²
House height	1.7–2.0 m

Highest no. for house = 1 drake and 20 ducks.
The floor should be solid, rat-safe, dry and airy.
Run to water, if possible marshy land

⓬ Duck (Peking)

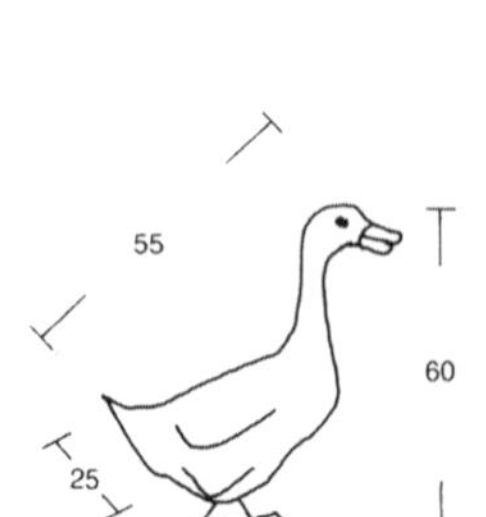

The same applies here as for ducks. For fattening, the birds are kept in small, just sufficient rooms or individual cells, 40 cm long, 30 cm wide, with chute for droppings and feeding tray in front of cell

⓭ Goose (Pomeranian)

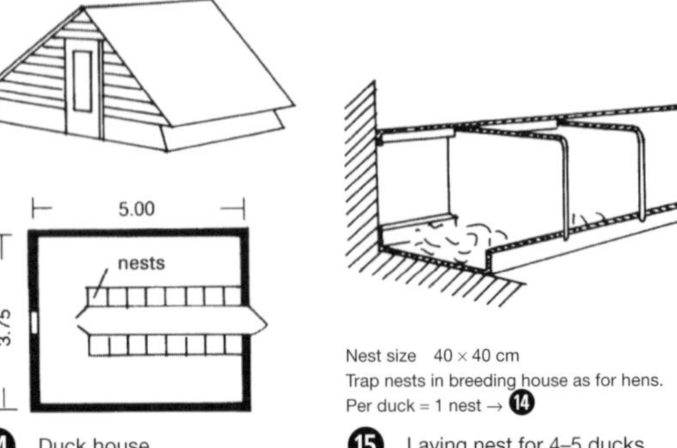

⓮ Duck house

Nest size 40 × 40 cm
Trap nests in breeding house as for hens.
Per duck = 1 nest → ⓮

⓯ Laying nest for 4–5 ducks

Rabbit hutches

These → ❷ – ❹ are often free-standing at wind-protected rear sides of barns and houses. Hutches can be stacked 3 × vertically → ❸. They should be protected against rats and mice, and be easy to clean and with urine drains → ❷. For the breeding of fattening and meat rabbits → ❺ – ❻ in close rooms, there are stringent requirements for the construction of the hutch and the climate. Rabbits react to poor climate much more sensitively than piglets or chicks. Thermally insulated buildings with forced ventilation are required for breeding and fattening. The hutch volume should be 4.5–5.5 m^3 per doe including offspring. The temperature in the breeding hutch should be 10–28 °C, optimally 18 °C, in the fattening hutch 20 °C.

Goat sheds

If possible these should face to the east or south. Dry with good ventilation and lighting, window area = 1/5–1/20 of the floor area. Where goats are tied up in numbers, the standing width should be 75–80 cm, depth 1.50–2.00 m, without including the passages necessary in front and behind the pens. A paddock next door to the south is ideal.

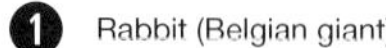

hutch area per animal 0.65–1.0 m^2; should be well ventilated, dry and protected from sun and predators (rats); hutches usually made of wood with drainage → ❷, 5% gradient

❶ Rabbit (Belgian giant)

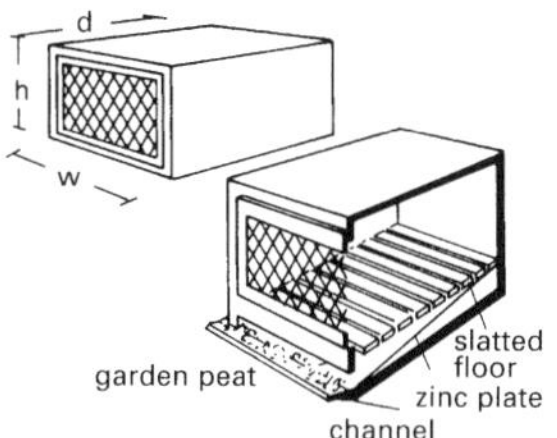

	w	d	h
small purebreds	80	80	55
medium purebreds	100	80	65
large purebreds	120	80	75

(depth is the same to ease subdivision)

❷ Size of rabbit hutches (cm)

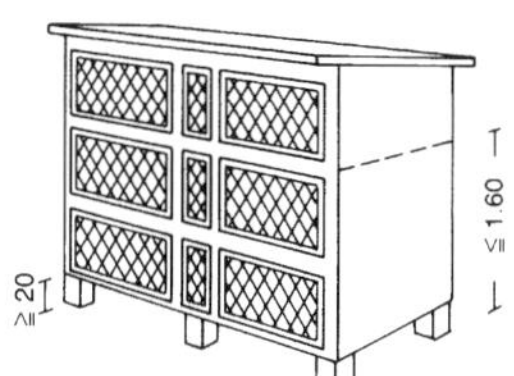

for small purebreds three tiers, for large purebreds two tiers within above limits (length unlimited); slatted floor → ❷ with drainage facilities and common urine collection channel below

❸ Stacked rabbit hutches

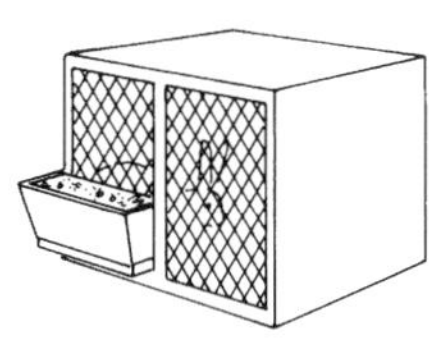

opening front or front section between two hutches → ❸; front wall of galvanised wire netting; hutches for female hares with dark netting and 10cm high bed

❹ Feed rack in hutch

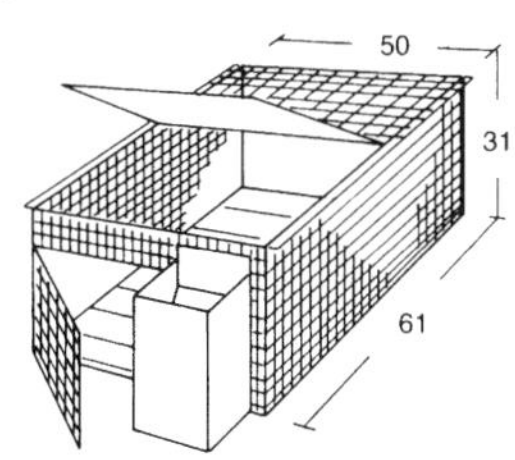

cage is made entirely from galvanised wire netting, mesh size 25 × 25 or 12 × 70 mm

❺ Wire cage with automatic feeder

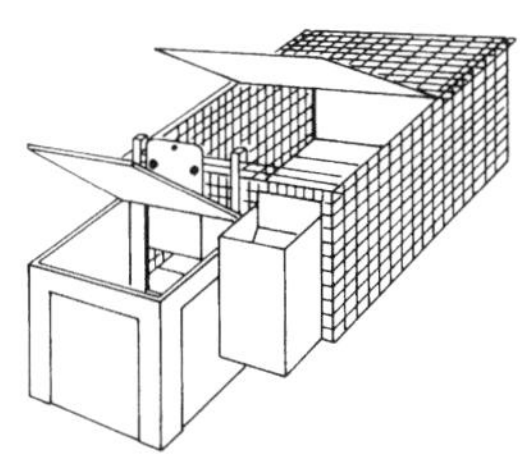

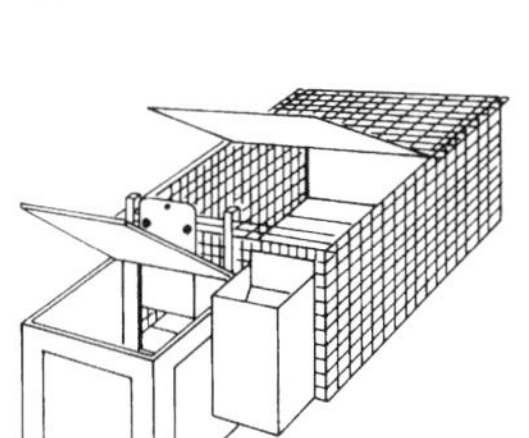

wooden or polyurethane nesting boxes for young animals: floor of nesting boxes at least 70 mm below base of cage

❻ Breeding cage with nesting box and automatic feeder

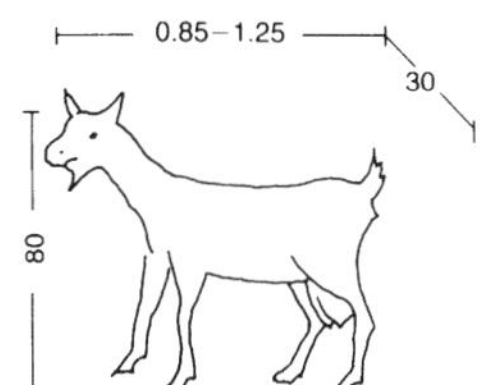

stall area per animal	1.5–2.0 m^2
stall width per animal	0.75–1.00 m
stall depth, tethered	1.8 m
stall depth, free	2.5–2.8 m
stall height	1.7–2.5 m
stall temperature	10–20°C

❼ Goat (German Saanenziege)

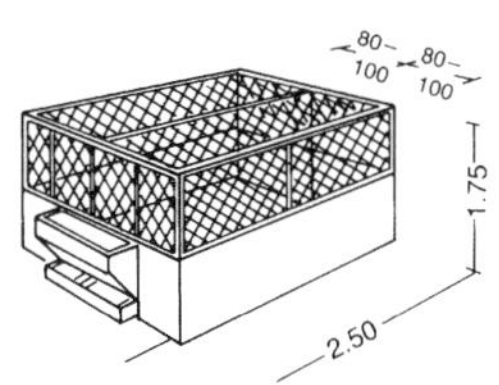

wire mesh above the rack level; tiled flooring at a gradient, with a channel for urine; feed rack and water trough serve both stalls

❽ Modern goat housing with feed rack and trough between two pens

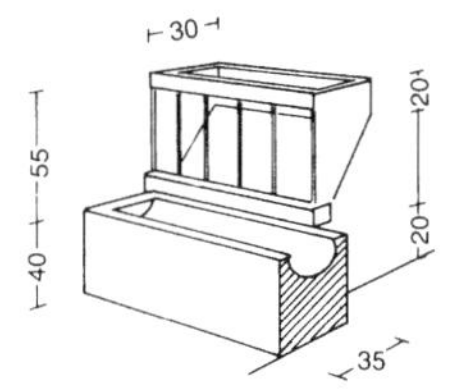

standard dimensions of a feeding rack and drinking trough in the feeding aisle (transverse aisle); daily requirements per goat: 1.2 kg hay, 2.3 kg of root crop, 2–3 l of water

❾ Feed rack and trough for goat pen

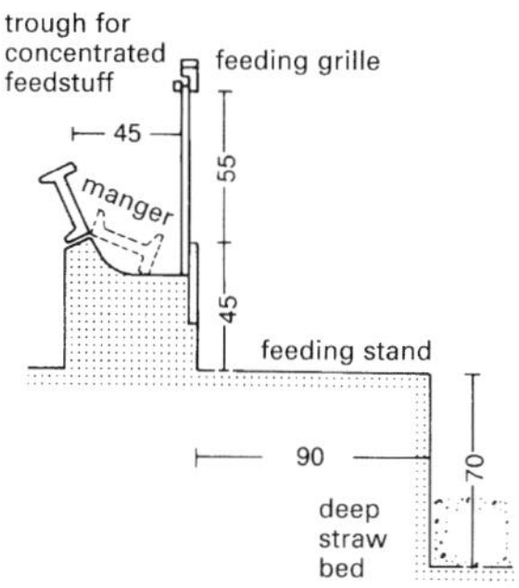

❿ Two-room goat housing with deep litter bed

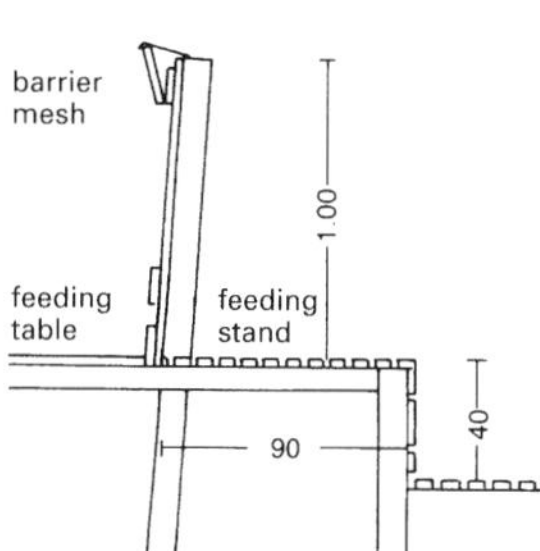

⓫ Loose box with fully slatted floor

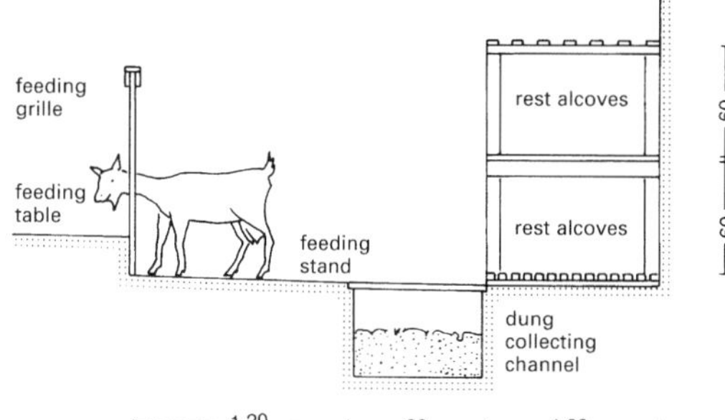

⓬ Multi-space loose housing with wall-mounted bed niches

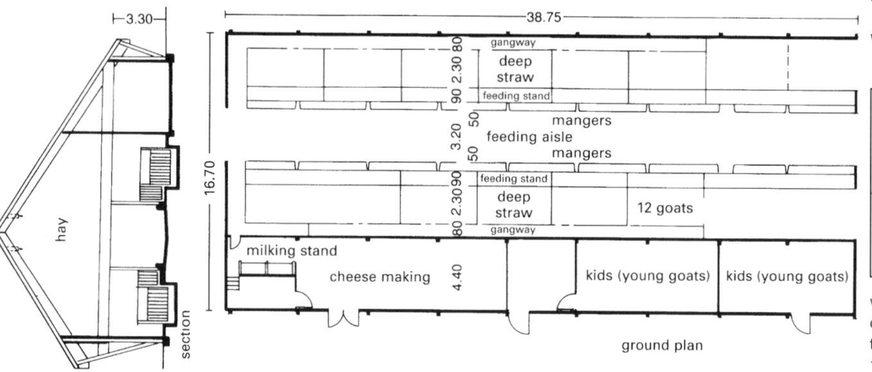

⓭ Two-room housing with deep litter bed

Summer 5 kg grass/day and 0.5 kg hay
6 kg red clover
Winter 1 kg hay/day,
water 2–3 litre/animal/day

Space required	Loose housing	Length of feeding rack	Tethered stall		
	m^2	cm	Standing	Width	Length
kid	0.7	20	—		
young animal	1.2	30–40	50	50	40
goat	1.5	40–50	80	50–70	40
buck	2.2–4.0	80	80	60	50

windows 1/15 –1/20 of the building height
ceiling > 2.50 m
trough: 1 basin for 30 animals; 0.4 kg straw/day, 1.5 dt/year/animal, dung production 7–15 dt/goat

⓮ Goat keeping

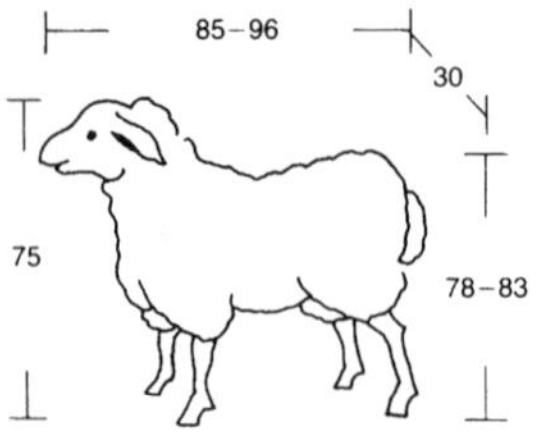

❶ Sheep

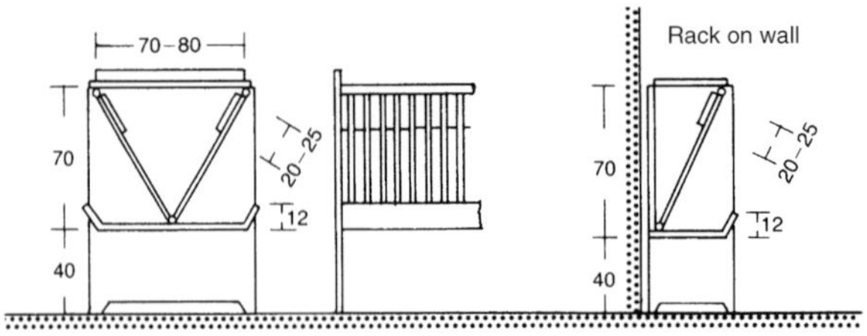

❷ Ladder feed rack with trough

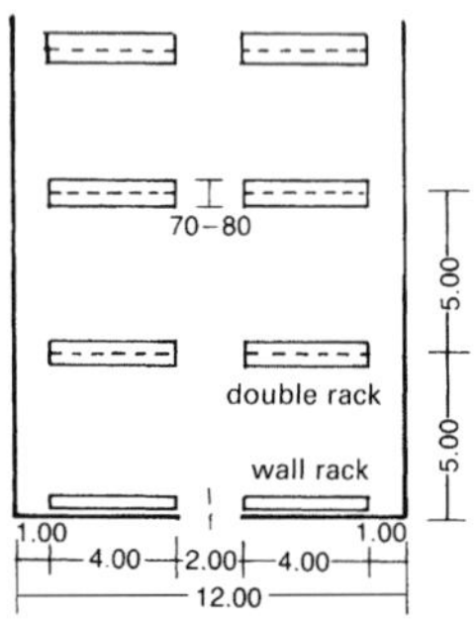

❸ Shed without gangway for feeding

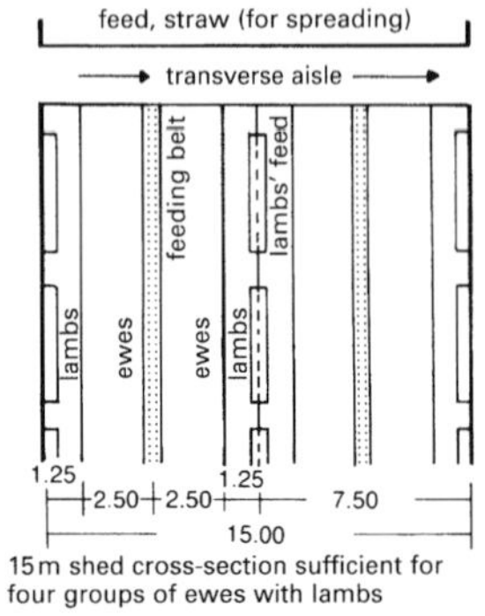

❹ Shed with transverse gangway, 15 m cross-section, adequate for four groups of ewes with lambs

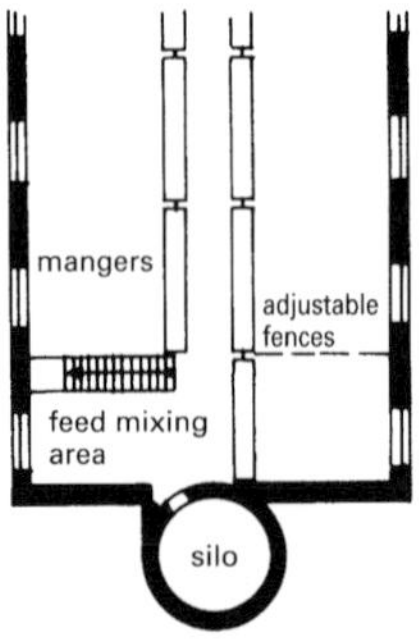

❺ Good arrangement of silo and feed mixing place in sheep shed

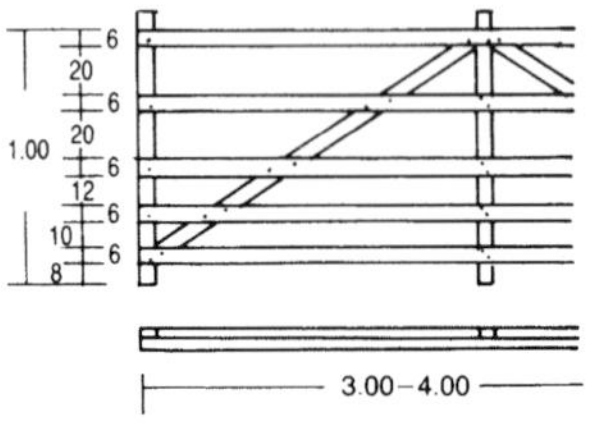

❻ Fence for dividing shed made of 40/60 mm roofing battens

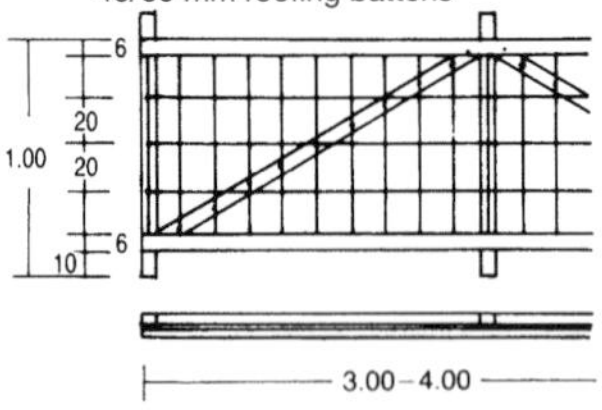

❼ Fence for dividing shed made of roofing battens and wire mesh

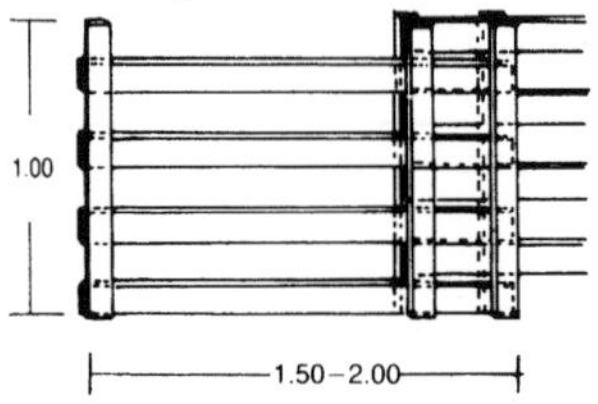

❽ Extendable fence made of battens

Loose, lying and feeding room for sheep

Animal	Loose and lying area (m²/animal)	Necessary feeding width (m²/animal)
mother ewe to 70 kg	0.85	0.4
mother ewe over 70 kg	1.0	0.45
mother ewe with lambs	1.2–1.6	0.6
lambs to 8 weeks	0.3–0.4	0.15
fattening lamb	0.4–0.5	0.2
yearling	0.7–0.8	0.3
breeding ram in single bay	3.0–4.0	0.5
breeding ram in communal bay	1.5–2.0	0.5

Size and weight of the two most important sheep breeds

Merino sheep and black-headed meat sheep	Weight	Wither height	Rump length
ram	120–130 kg	0.83 m	0.96 m
ewe	70–80 kg 65–75 kg	0.78 m	0.85 m

Net space requirement for sheep kept in a herd on fully perforated floor

Animal	m²/animal
ewe	0.8
ewe with lambs	1.2
fattening lamb	0.5
yearling	0.6
ram	1.5

Optimal shed climate values (Burgkart)

Housing for…	Temperature (°C)	Relative humidity (%)
… mothers	8–10	60–75
… lambs and fattening	10–14	60–75
… breeding	14–16	60–70

Fodder storage per ewe (including lambs) in winter indoor period

Stored goods	Space requirement
hay (feeding only hay)	3.3 m³
hay (feeding hay and silage)	1.0 m³
silage	1.0 m³

❾ Sheep sheds

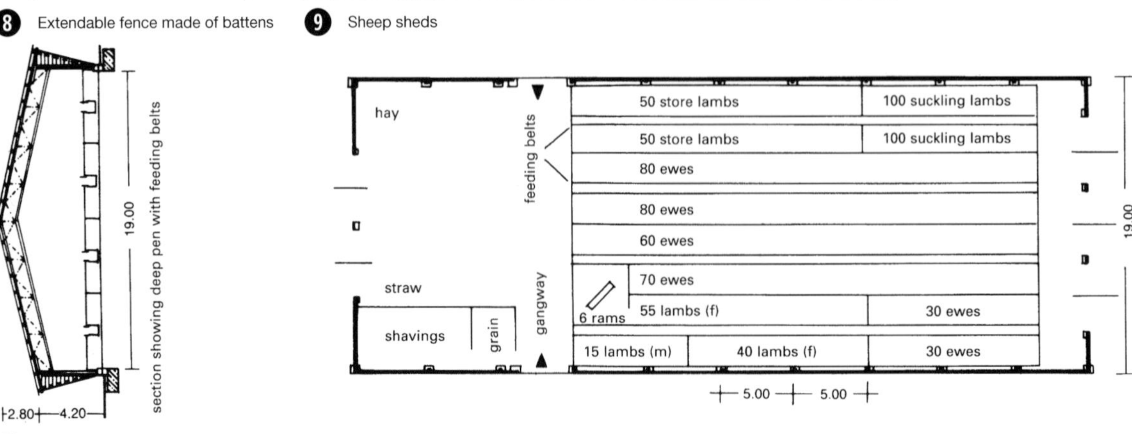

❿ Sheep shed for 350 ewes, 110 young sheep, 200 suckling lambs, 100 fattening lambs

Sheep housing should face to the east or west; single housing is much like goat housing → p. 453. Intensive sheep farming requires large, free-standing sheds with flexible housing according to time of year (winter, early year, lambing time, after lambing), separated by fences according to age and sex.

Floor 50–60 cm below ground level. Door threshold 20 cm above ground level. The height difference of 60–80 cm is filled with dung, which remains for 3–4 months.

Feeding racks should therefore be adjustable, ideally with a manger, either round (diameter 2.20 m) or elongated mangers – 3.40 m is sufficient for 25–30 sheep. Spacing between feed containers 2.30 m, from the wall 1.80 m. Doors to the south, divided at half height. Door width ≧2.50 m, door height ≧2.80 m, to remove the dung.

Building height 3.30–3.50 m, window area 1/20 – 1/25 of the building floor area, high-level tilting window. All building components, timber on plinth 15–20 cm above highest dung level, should be protected against dung salts.

Feed mixing place 1/10–1/15 of the pen area. For small herds ≧m² turnip store should be provided. Storage for hay and straw per sheep 3.00 m³.

❶ Keeping laying hens on floor: on two levels with open area

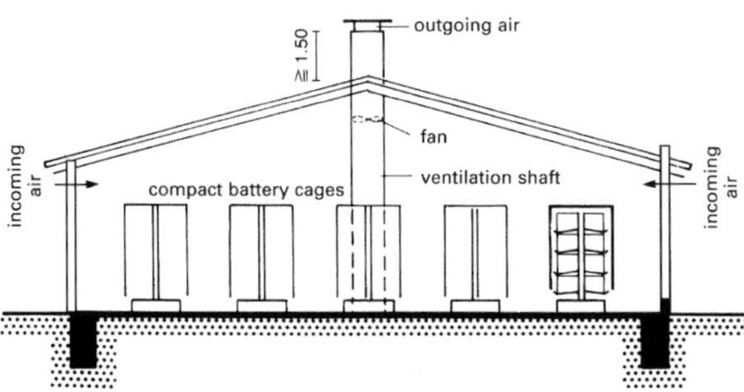

❷ Keeping laying hens in small groups

Minimum area	2.5 m²
Area/bird	min. 800 cm²/bird; for birds weighing more than 2 kg, 900 cm²
Height of the coop	min. 60 cm (trough side), nowhere less than 50 cm
Arrangement of the coops	min. 90 cm gangway width between the rows, floor spacing min. 35 cm
Nest area	min. 900 cm² for groups of up to 10 birds; for groups of 30 birds, the nest is to be enlarged by 90 cm² for every further bird
Feeding trough	min. 12 cm/bird; or 14.5 cm for birds weighing more than 2.5 kg
Roosting perch	min. 15 cm/ bird; min. 2 perches at different heights per holding unit
Light	newbuild: natural lighting min. 3% floor area

❸ Requirements for keeping hens in small groups (Animal Welfare, Animal Husbandry Regulations → refs)

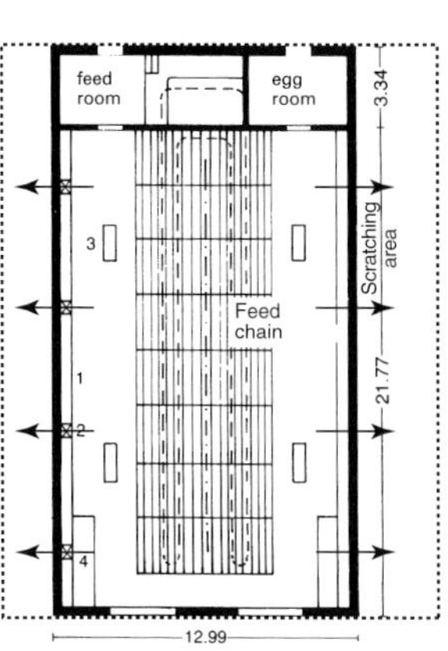

❹ Floor housing for laying hens with open area for 1600 birds

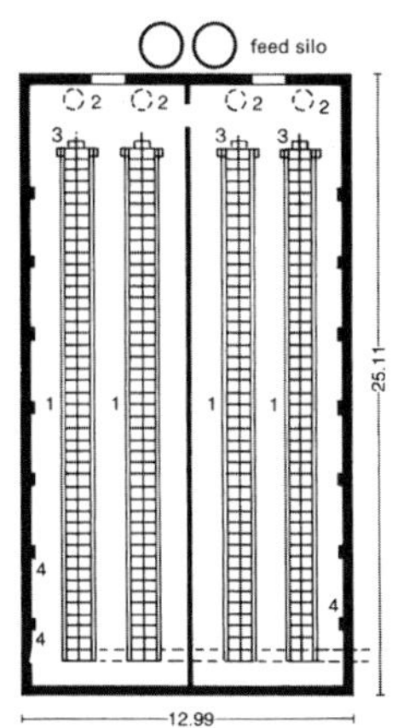

❺ Small group housing with three storeys for approx. 4800 birds

(See also Housing poultry → p. 452.)

The legal requirements for the keeping of laying hens are laid down in the **Animal Welfare Law** and in the **Animal Welfare, Animal Husbandry Regulations**. The regulations contain general provisions about the keeping, feeding and care of farm animals and these apply for all husbandry, with special regulations for the commercial keeping of laying hens:

The keeping of hens is allowed **on the floor** → ❶ on one or more levels with or without free range and in small groups → ❷ in fitted out accommodation with scratching area, nest and perching bars.

A particular requirement for free–range management is the provision of a **cold scratching place** (outside, separated and roofed scratching area with paved surfacing) between the barn and the run.

Occupation density	max. 9 hens/m² usable area, for multi-storey floor keeping, max. 18 birds/m² floor area
Levels	max. 4 levels vertically, with barn floor first level
Group size	without partitions, max. 6000 birds
Feeding	long trough: max. 10 cm edge length/bird round trough: max. 4 cm edge length/bird
Drinking trough	gutter/round trough: 2.5 cm/min. 1 cm edge length/bird nipple/beaker drinker: min. 2 places for up to 10 birds and 1 for every further 10 birds
Nests	group nest: min. 1 m² for max. 120 birds single nest: max. 7 birds/nest (135 × 25 cm)
Perches	min. 15 cm/bird, horizontal spacing of the perches 30 cm, to wall 20 cm
Litter area	at least a third of barn floor area and min. 250 cm²/bird
Cold scratching room	for all poultry farms with access to an open-air run (unless construction or other legal reasons prevent it)
Opening to cold scratching room	min. 35 cm high/40 cm wide, min. 1 m/500 birds, distributed evenly along external wall
Light	newbuild: natural lighting min 3% floor area

❻ Requirements for keeping hens on the floor (Animal Welfare, Animal Husbandry Regulations → refs)

All types of facility must provide a **minimum area of 2.5 m²** and be equipped so that the hens can move to a reasonable extent according to their personal needs: i.e. can move to **feed, drink and rest**. The lighting is to be sufficient for the birds to recognise each other and for the people responsible for care to be able to see them properly. The floor must provide hard standing for the birds and have access to adequately dimensioned and distributed feeding and drinking facilities. The facility should also provide a freely accessible nest during the laying phase with a floor constructed so that the birds do not come into contact with wire mesh. A litter area should also be provided to enable the laying hens to peck, scratch and dust-bath as is their nature. The laying hens in a group must be able to enjoy simultaneous and undisturbed rest on a perch.

Tables and text from: DLG → refs.

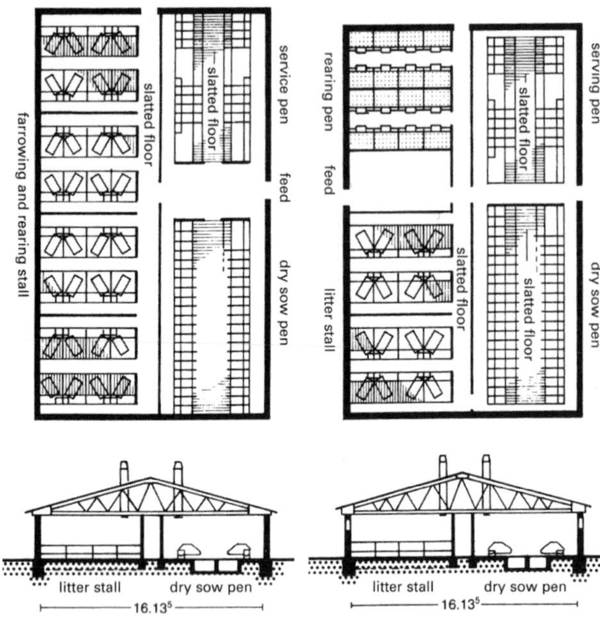

1 Sheds for breeding pigs, with and without feeding gangway (theoretical diagram)

	Shed area m² (net)	**External area** m² (net) open area apart from grazing areas
sows with **piglets** up to 40 days old	7.5	2.5
fattening pigs	0.8 (up to 50 kg live weight) 1.1 (up to 85 kg live weight) 1.3 (up to 110 kg live weight)	0.6 (up to 50 kg live weight) 0.8 (up to 85 kg live weight) 1.0 (up to 110 kg live weight)
piglets over 40 days old and up to 30 kg	0.6	0.4
breeding pigs	2.5 breeding sow 6.0 breeding boar	1.9 breeding sow 8.0 breeding boar

2 Requirements for pig keeping (EU Eco Directive 2092/91, annex VIII → refs)

	Usable floor area m² (net)
young sows	1.85 (group size up to 5 animals) 1.65 (group size 6–39 animals) 1.50 (group size > 40 animals)
sows	2.50 (group size up to 5 animals) 2.25 (group size 6–39 animals) 2.05 (group size > 40 animals)
young breeding pigs and fattening pigs	0.50 (30–50 kg live weight) 0.75 (50–110 kg live weight) 1.00 (> 110 kg live weight)
fattening piglets	0.15 (>5–10 kg average weight) 0.20 (>10–20 kg average weight) 0.35 (>20 kg average weight)

3 Requirements for pig keeping (Animal Welfare, Animal Husbandry Regulations → refs)

ANIMAL HUSBANDRY
Keeping small animals
Sheep housing
Laying hens
Pig keeping
Dairy farming
Finishing beef cattle
Keeping horses

Animal Welfare Law
Animal Welfare, Animal Husbandry Regulations
EU Eco Directive

Agriculture

The animal welfare requirements for the commercial keeping of pigs are laid down in the Animal Welfare Law and in the Animal Welfare, Animal Husbandry Regulations. The regulations contain general provisions for pig-keeping facilities and for the keeping of pigs:

Pig sheds (except for birthing pens) must be constructed so that the pigs have eye contact with the other pigs kept there. The pigs must be able **easily to lie, stand up, lie down and adopt a natural posture**. The pigs must have a dry lying area available. They must not unavoidably come into contact with urine and dung.

There must be adequate equipment for the reduction of heat stress at high shed temperatures. The **floor** of the pig shed must be **slip-resistant** and provide a **firm footing** over the entire area where the pigs live and in the driving gangways. The construction must be appropriate for the size and weight of the pigs and no holes, gaps or cavities are allowed which might lead to risk of injury.

If a **slatted floor** is used, the maximum width of the gaps is 11 cm for suckling piglets, 14 mm for fattening piglets, 18 mm for young pigs for breeding and 20 mm for young sows, sows and boars. The width of the tread surface in areas where the pigs live must correspond to the slatted floor and, if slatted concrete flooring is used, it must be at least 5 cm for suckling and fattening piglets and 8 cm for all other pigs. If **metal grating flooring** is made of wire mesh, the wires must be plastic coated and the external diameter of the coated wire must be at least 9 mm.

In the area where the pigs lie, the floor must be constructed so that the health of the pigs cannot be harmed and heat transmission is not too high or too low. The degree of perforation of the floor may not be more than 15% (except for fattening piglets).

The **lighting** of the sheds must (applies to new building from 04/08/2006) be natural daylight. The window areas must have a total area of at least 3% of the shed floor area and be arranged so that the lighting is as uniform as possible. The window area can be reduced to 1.5% of the shed floor area on account of technology, construction or building regulations as long as artificial lighting as comparable as possible to natural lighting is also provided.

It should be ensured that each pig has access at all times to **activity material** without health risks, which serves their natural inquisitiveness and can be investigated, moved and altered by the pig. Each pig must have constant access to **water** in sufficient quantity and quality, and if the pigs are kept in groups additional drinking troughs are to be provided in sufficient quantity separate from the feeding trough.

In addition to the general requirements, the Animal Welfare, Animal Husbandry Regulations contain further provisions for the keeping of **sucking piglets, young sows, sows and boars** → **3**.

If the farm intends to market products as **organic**, the provisions of the EU Eco Directive will also have to be complied with → **2**.

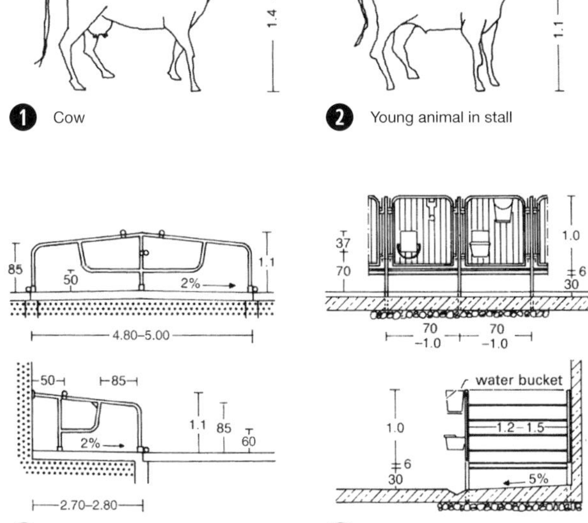

❶ Cow

❷ Young animal in stall

❸ Lying boxes for cows (AFP)

❹ Single stalls for young cattle (14 days to 10 weeks)

The requirements for cow sheds, according to the **Agricultural Investment Support Programme (AFP)**, annex 1, 'Special requirements for particularly welfare-oriented husbandry', represent the current standard for keeping cows in terms of animal welfare and can be considered as minimum requirements (which can be deviated from in exceptional cases according to the farm's situation). The provisions of the EU Eco Directive and Recommendations for horned cows also contain ideas of future developments in conventional livestock farming.

Lying box dimensions and design

The dimensions of the lying boxes have to be based on the average bodily dimensions of the 25% largest animals in a herd. The values below therefore represent lower limits. The dimensions for individual cows can be worked out as follows:

Lying length: (0.92 × diagonal rump length) + 21 cm

Lying box length: lying length + 21 cm + (wither height × 0.56)

Lying box width: wither height × 0.86

Tables and text from Aulendorf → refs.

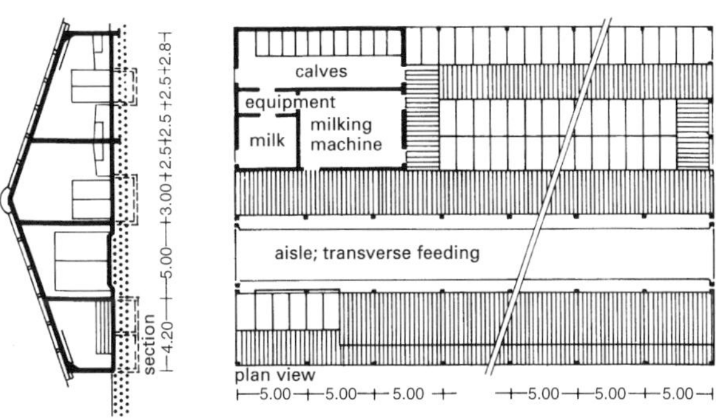

❺ Box pens, 3 rows, for dairy cows with young cattle

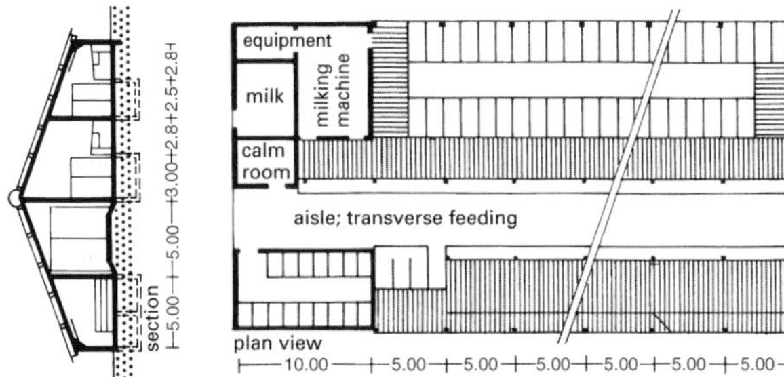

❻ Box pens, 2 rows, for dairy cows with young cattle

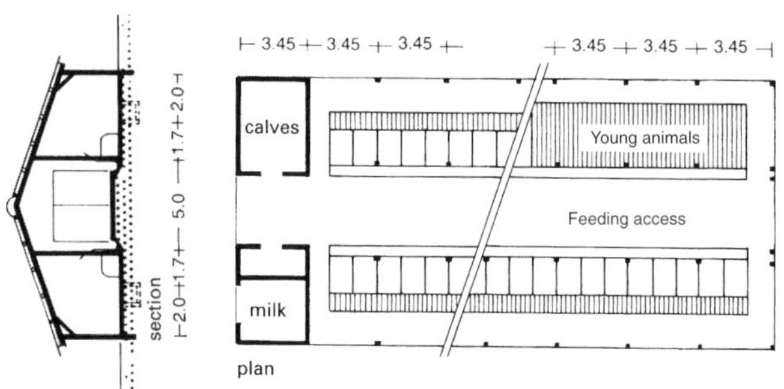

❼ Conventional stalls with stanchions, 2 rows, for dairy cows with young cattle

Criterion	AFP (esp. animal welfare-oriented	EU Eco Directive	Recommendations for horned cows
space available (m²) stall yard	 5.0 per LU[1]	 6.0 per animal 4.5 per animal	 9.0 per LU[1] 12 per animal
lying box width (cm)	120–130		120
lying box length (cm)	240–250/ 270–280[2]		270–300[2]
separating bar distance from floor (cm)	60		
feeding place width (cm)	75		80–90
feeding gangway width (cm)	>350		450
gangway width (cm)	>250		400
animal/feeding place ratio	1:1 (1:2:1)[3]		1:1.1 to 1:1.2
animal/lying box ratio	1:1		1:1.1 to 1:1.2
lighting area: % of cowshed floor area	5		
lying area in deep stall/cow	4.5		8[5]
lying area in deep stall (m)			max. 6
max. gap width (cm)			3
other	gangway between 12–15 cubicles	– max. 50% of the usable cowshed area slatted floor – yard or pasture – straw litter	

[1] lying box, stall and feeding place area
[2] opposite/wall mounted, deep box recommended
[3] when stock of feed, i.e. guideline, mixed fodder in swathes
[4] movement area from age of 1 year (area which is always accessible, 50% lying box area)
[5] of which 3 m² can be reckoned as movement area

❽ Requirements for the keeping of dairy cows (Aulendorf → refs)

The methods used to finish beef cattle are divided into single and group management → ❶. Keeping animals singly requires constant adaptation of the stall on account of the fast growth of a bull. Different stalls are therefore required for different ages. Pay attention to good drainage of urine from the lying area.

The advantage of keeping cattle singly is that herd behaviour is excluded. Group management (6–15 animals of the same age and similar weights is usual) requires that the animals have already got used to each other as calves.

According to the bedding quantity and the system of dung removal, either the animal can walk and lie in the entire area of the pen, which is completely straw-bedded, or the lying and feeding areas are separated. Animals kept singly are tied and short stalls are recommended → ❷. The design of a shed for finishing beef cattle must create the possibility of bringing single animals or groups in or out of the stalls without danger. The best ventilation is provided by convectors or extractor systems. These work reliably with roof pitches of about 20°. Beef cattle are normally fed maize silage.

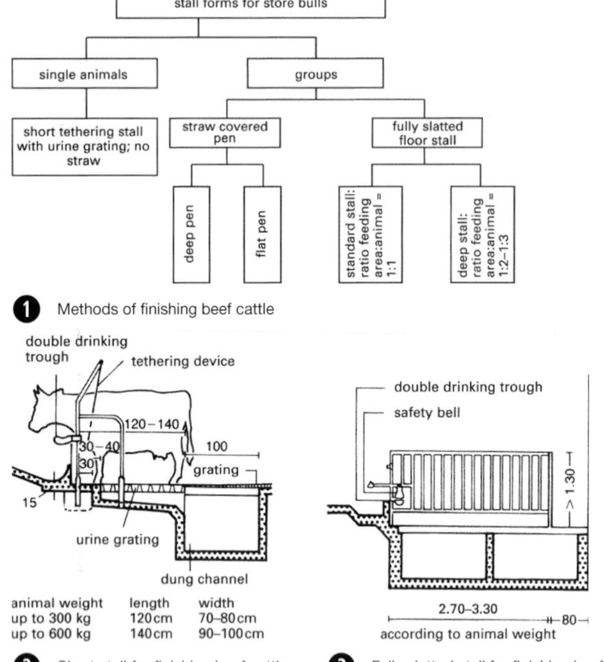

❶ Methods of finishing beef cattle

❷ Short stall for finishing beef cattle without straw

❸ Fully slatted stall for finishing beef cattle with driving gangway

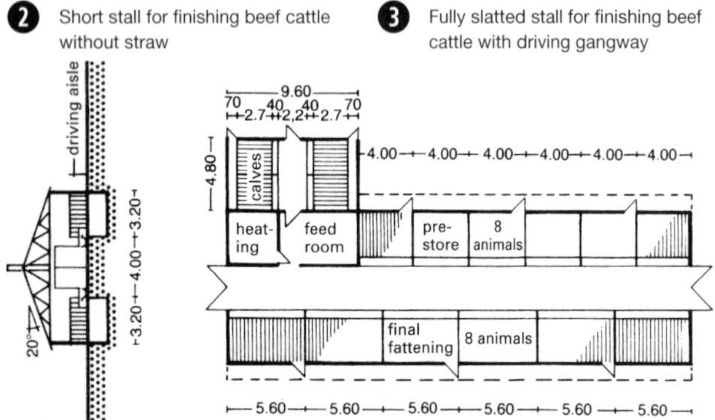

❹ Fully slatted shed for 96 finishing beef cattle with stall changing, external driving gangway

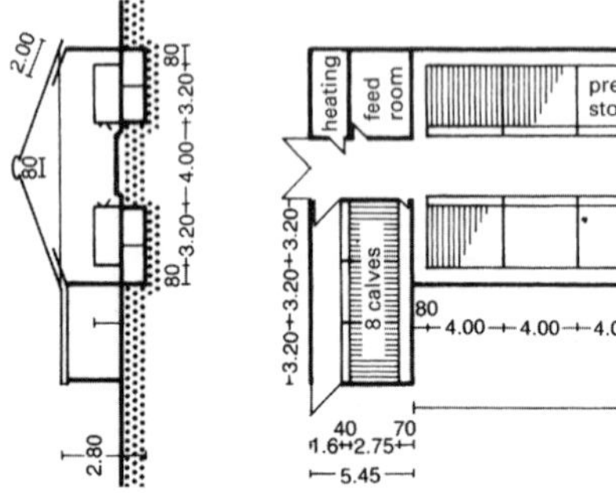
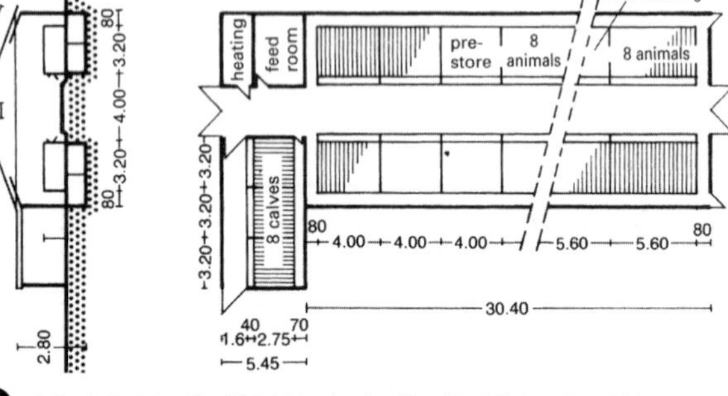

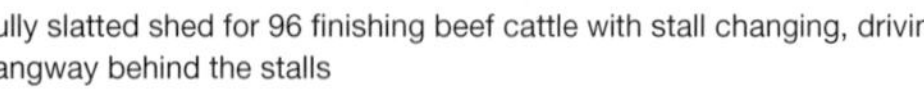

❺ Fully slatted shed for 96 finishing beef cattle with stall changing, driving gangway behind the stalls

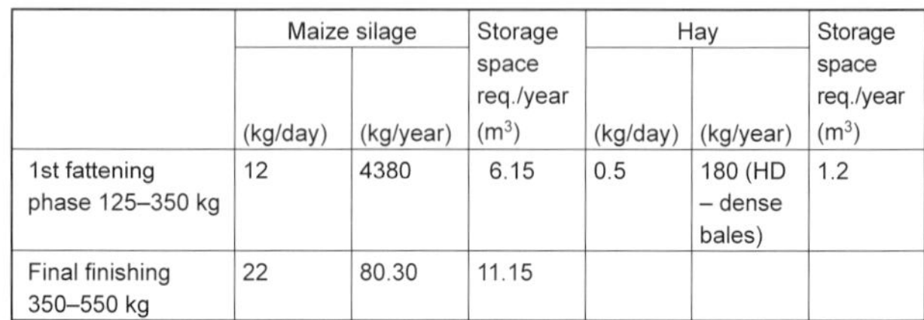

	Maize silage		Storage space req./year	Hay		Storage space req./year
	(kg/day)	(kg/year)	(m³)	(kg/day)	(kg/year)	(m³)
1st fattening phase 125–350 kg	12	4380	6.15	0.5	180 (HD – dense bales)	1.2
Final finishing 350–550 kg	22	80.30	11.15			

❼ Fodder required per animal place in finishing beef cattle stall

Weight range (kg)	Floor area per animal (m²)	Feeding width per animal (cm)	Recommended slatted floor dimensions: Width (mm)	Gap width (mm)
125–150	1.20	40		
150–220	1.40	45		
220–300	1.50	50	1.20	
300–400	1.80	57	to	35
400–500	2.00	63	1.60	
> 500	2.20	70		

❽ Space required and slatted floor size for finishing beef cattle stalls

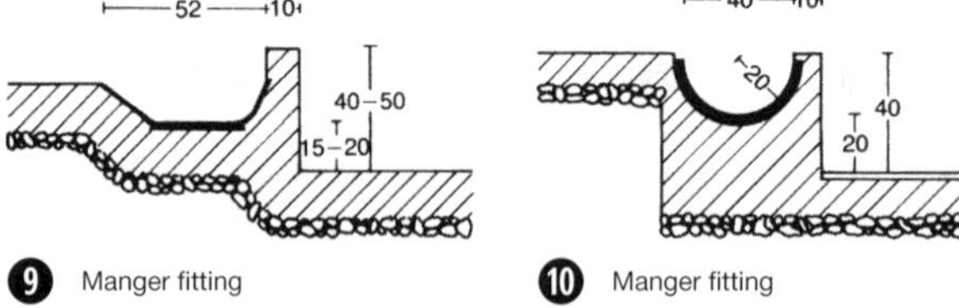
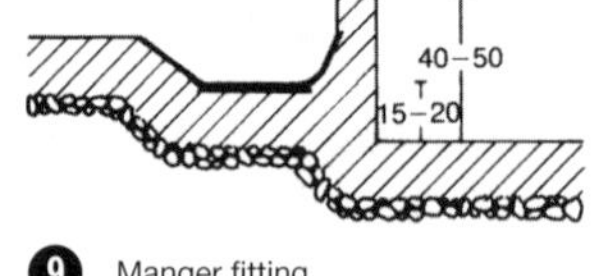

❾ Manger fitting

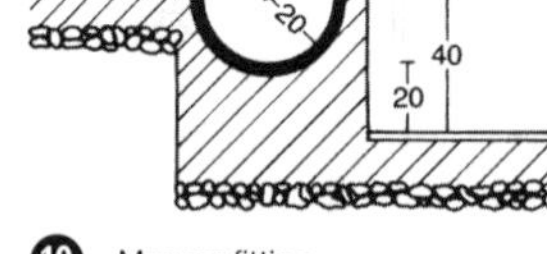

❿ Manger fitting

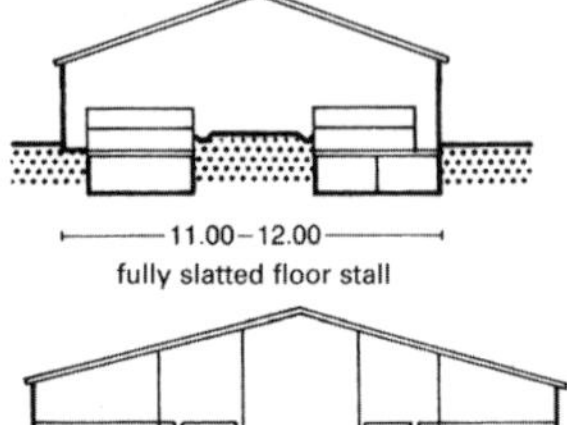

❻ Shed sections for various forms of finishing beef cattle stall

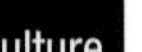

ANIMAL HUSBANDRY

Keeping Horses

The correct care according to the needs of the species is a precondition for the health, performance and long life of the horse, and also for its willingness and mental stability. Today, after 5000 years of domestication, the needs of horses are still similar to those of wild animals on the steppes. Horses are herd animals and social contact is essential. Whether kept in groups or singly, attention should be paid to the social relationships and compatibility of horses. When horses are kept separately, ensure at least sight, sound and smell contact between the animals. Foals and young horses must grow up in groups.

Keeping in groups: This can be in single boxes or group boxes with adjacent paddock.

Single boxes: Tie stalls are not to be recommended in the long term. When horses are kept singly, a movement area at least as large as a single box is better than none at all. Stables for heavy horses should be planned with a ceiling height of at least 1.5 × withers height, i.e. approx. ≧2.70 m.

Pony 1.0–1.45 | Donkey 1.20 | Horse 1.45–1.70

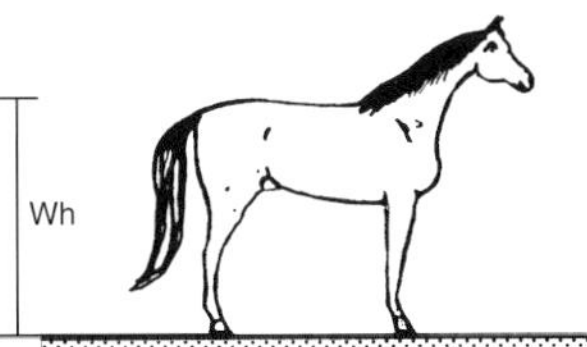

All dimensions are based on withers height (Wh)
= very large horse = 1.80 m
= average large horse = 1.67 m
= pony = 1.45 m

❶ Withers height

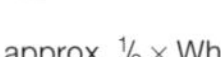

approx. ⅓ × Wh
= very large horse = approx. 60 cm
= average large horse = approx. 55 cm
= pony = approx. 50 cm
= small pony = approx. 30–40 cm

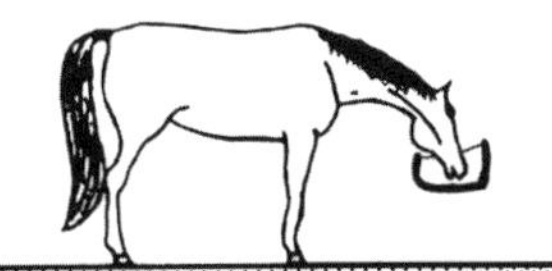

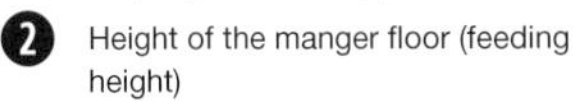

❷ Height of the manger floor (feeding height)

approx. 0.60 × Wh
= very large horse = approx. 1.45 m
= average large horse = approx. 1.35 m
= pony = approx. 1.20 m

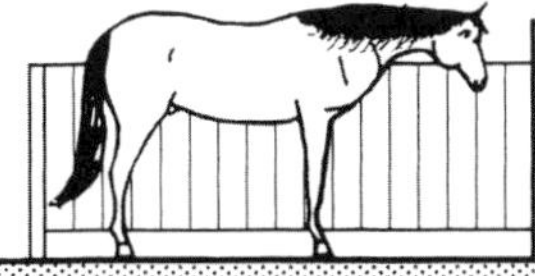

❸ Height of the box partition (breast height)

approx. 1.30 × Wh
= very large horse = approx. 2.35 m
= average large horse = approx. 2.45 m
= pony = approx. 1.95 m

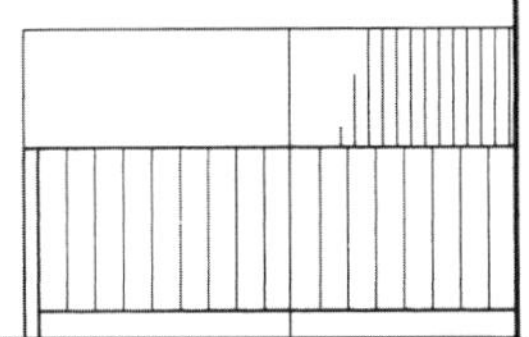

❹ Height of the box partition (upper part lattice, visual contact)

min. 1.45 × Wh
= very large horse = approx. 2.60 m
= average large horse = approx. 2.40 m
= pony = approx. 2.20 m

Separate stallions and mares; do not accommodate in adjacent boxes

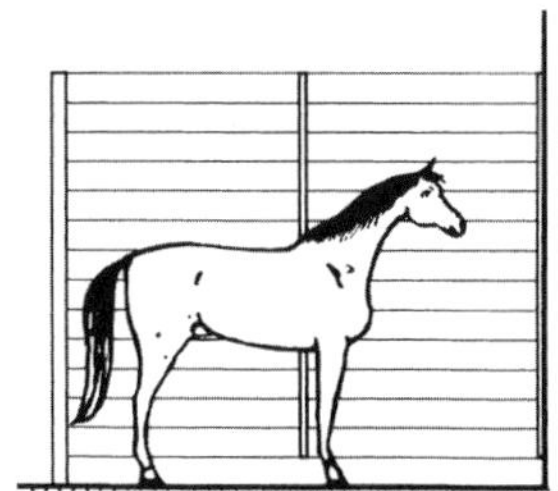

❺ Height of the box partition (upper part provides no visual contact; only recommended in exceptional cases)

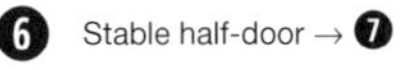

❻ Stable half-door → ❼

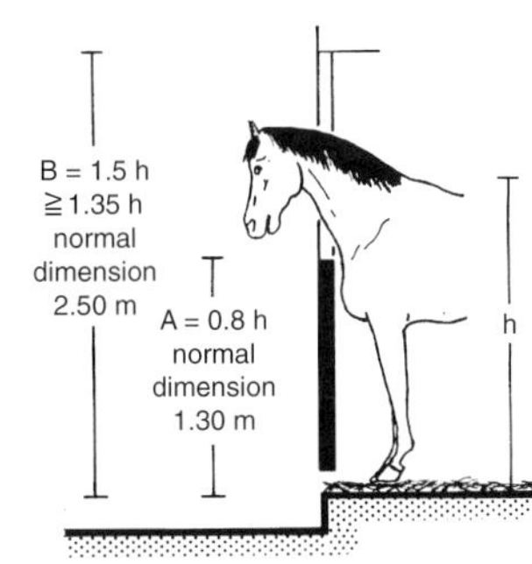
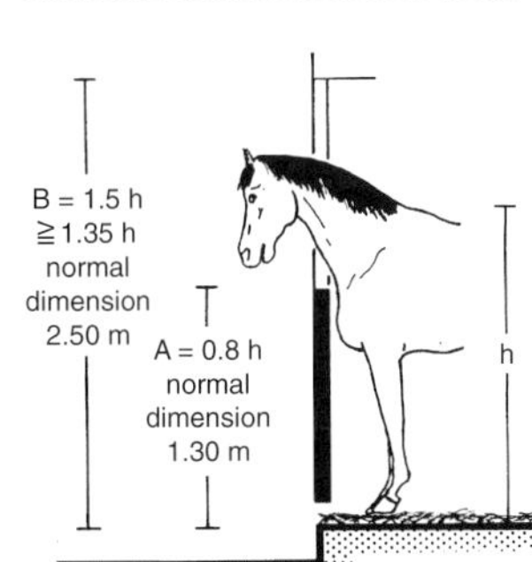

❼ → ❻ Section and dimensions

Width of access passages
= large horse = approx. 1.20 m
= pony = approx. 1.00 m

Width of stable passages should be 3 m if possible; min. 2 × access passage width is necessary to turn horses round.

= average large horse = approx. 2.40 m
= pony = approx. 2.00 m

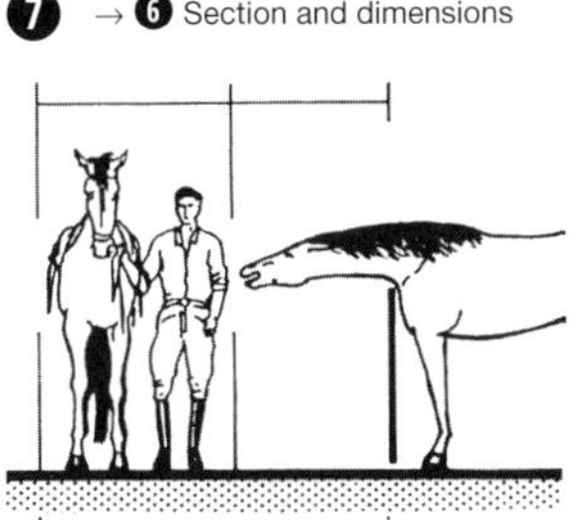

❽ Width of through and box passages

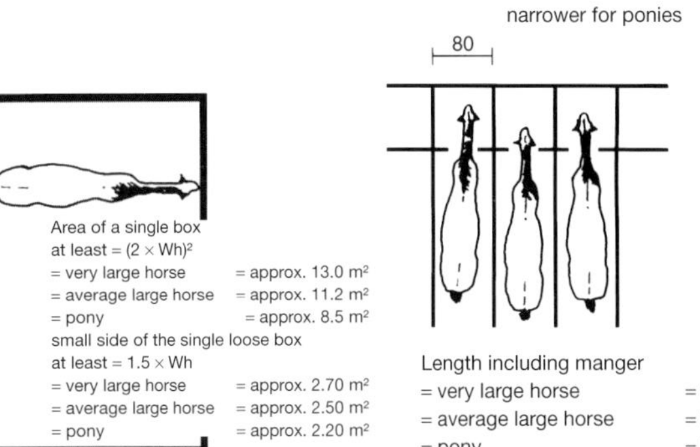

Area of a single box
at least = (2 × Wh)²
= very large horse = approx. 13.0 m²
= average large horse = approx. 11.2 m²
= pony = approx. 8.5 m²
small side of the single loose box
at least = 1.5 × Wh
= very large horse = approx. 2.70 m²
= average large horse = approx. 2.50 m²
= pony = approx. 2.20 m²

❾ Keeping a horse singly

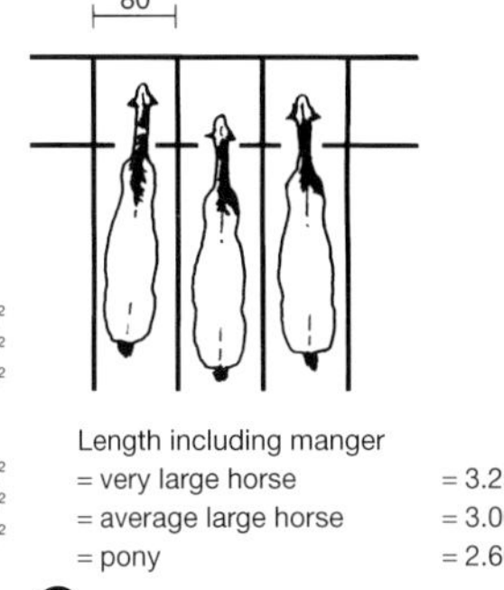

Length including manger
= very large horse = 3.25 m
= average large horse = 3.00 m
= pony = 2.60 m

❿ Feeding stalls

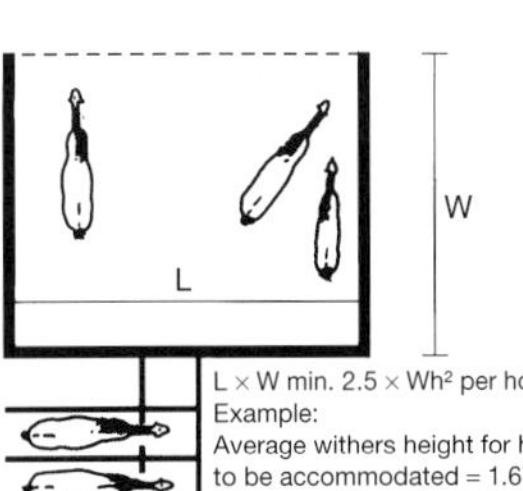

L × W min. 2.5 × Wh² per horse
Example:
Average withers height for horse to be accommodated = 1.67 m
Space requirement = 2.5 × 1.67² per horse = 7.00 m² per horse
If room structure, horses and carers favourable, a reduction of up to 20% is possible

⓫ Open stable for a group with separate feeding stands and constant access to the paddock

L × W =
→ ⓭ **Single box open stable without permanent access to paddock** at least **(2 × Wh)²** per horse (as for single boxes)
Example:
Average withers height for horse to be accommodated = 1.67 m
Space requirement = (2 × 1.67)² per horse = 11.2 m² per horse

L × W =
→ ⓮ **Group open stable with integrated mangers and constant access to paddock** at least **3 × Wh²** per horse (without space for feeding stands)
Example:
Average withers height for horse to be accommodated = 1.67 m
Space requirement = (3 × 1.67²) per horse = 8.4 m² per horse

⓬ Space requirement per horse with two different keeping arrangements

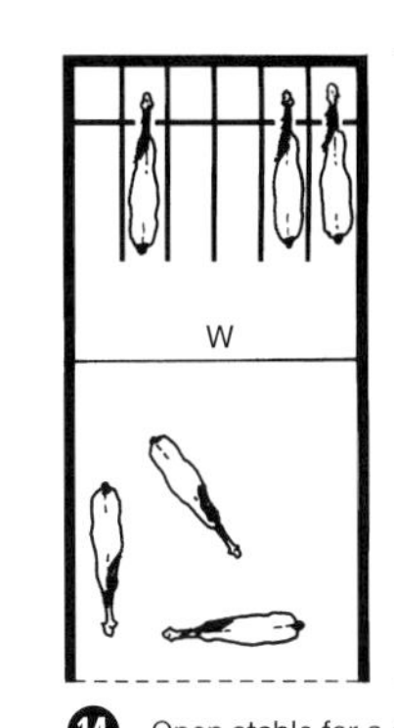

⓭ Single box, open stable → ⓬

⓮ Open stable for a group → ⓬

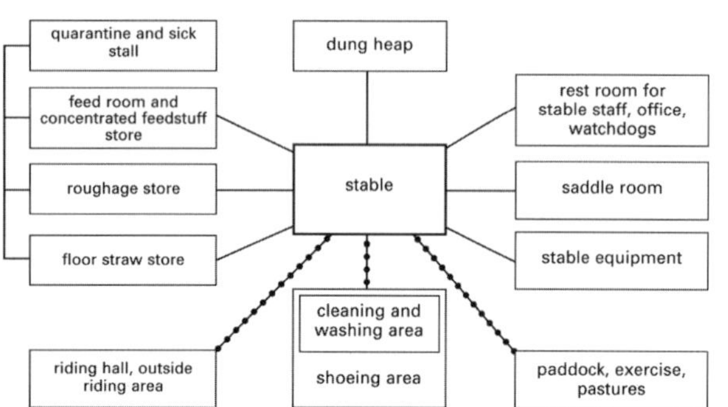

❶ Relationships of ancillary rooms to the stable

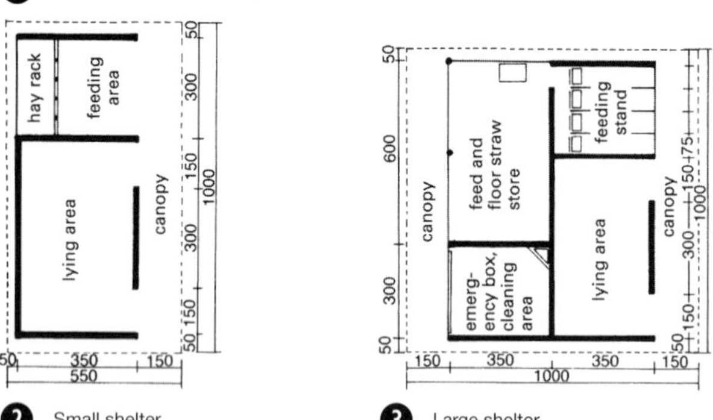

❷ Small shelter

❸ Large shelter

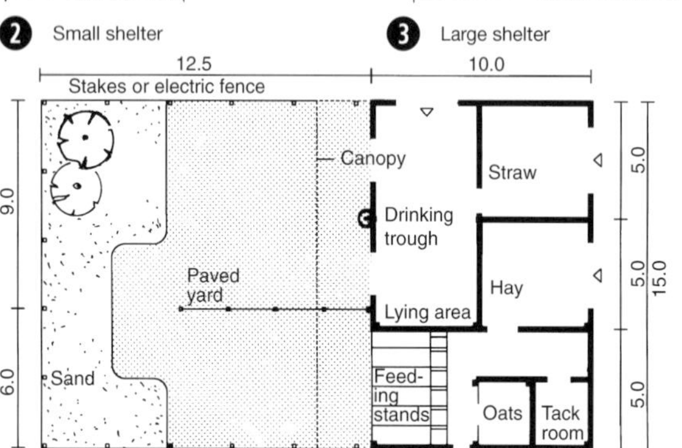

❹ Multi-room open stable for 5–6 horses with feeding stands

❺ Group open stable

Cross-section → ❺

Although the horse is insensitive to wind (and has a physiological need of air movement), draughts should be prevented. This is done with artificial ventilation systems providing constant airflow. There is little point in attempting an 'ideal' stable temperature. With sufficient preparation and appropriate management, any horse can tolerate winter temperatures in the stable, even a few degrees of frost → ❽.

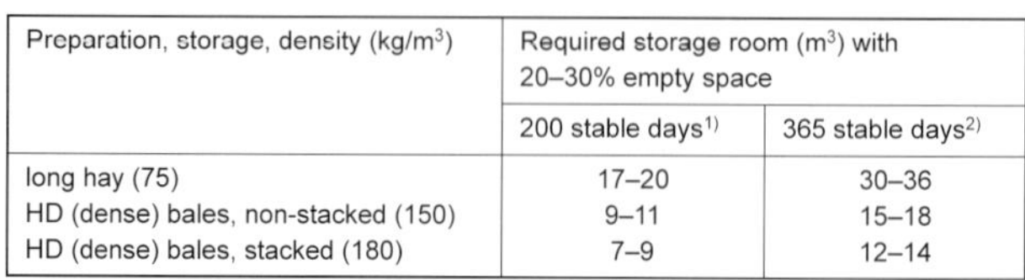

Preparation, storage, density (kg/m³)	Required storage room (m³) with 20–30% empty space	
	200 stable days[1]	365 stable days[2]
long hay (75)	17–20	30–36
HD (dense) bales, non-stacked (150)	9–11	15–18
HD (dense) bales, stacked (180)	7–9	12–14

[1] corresponds to 1000–1200 kg [2] corresponds to 1800–2200 kg

❻ Space required for hay storage for 5–6 kg/horse/day

Preparation, storage, density (kg/m³)	Required storage room (m³) for three months[1] with 20–30% empty space
long straw (50)	22
HD (dense) bales, non-stacked (70)	15
HD (dense) bales, stacked (100)	11

[1] corresponds to 900 kg

❼ Space required for straw storage for 10 kg/horse/day

Air temperature	Stable temperature should roughly follow outside temperature even in winter
humidity	60–80%
airflow speed in animal area	min. 0.1 m/s
CO_2 content in air as harmful gas indicator	< 0.10 vol. %
ammonia content in air	< 10 ppm
hydrogen sulphide	0 ppm

❽ Climatic requirements in stables

ANIMAL HUSBANDRY
Keeping small animals
Sheep housing
Laying hens
Pig keeping
Dairy farming
Finishing beef cattle
Keeping horses

Agriculture

	Sales area (m²)			
	5000–10 000	10 000–15 000	15 000–20 000	20 000–30 000
HGV standing places at the loading ramp	2–3	3–4	4–5	5–6
waiting area for delivery	100	120	180	250
no. and size of trucks with trailers	1: 2.00 × 3.00 1: 2.00 × 4.20	2: 2.00 × 3.00 1: 2.00 × 4.20	3: 2.00 × 3.00 1: 2.00 × 4.20	2: 2.00 × 3.00 2: 2.00 × 4.20
lift lobbies (m²)	20	30	40	40
area for disposal (m²) empty packaging waste paper bales	30 20 15	30 40 25	50 60 35	100 80 35
stationary press with container (m)	3.00 × 9.00 in front of the loading ramp			
channel baling press with container (m)	2.50 × 9.00 in front of the loading ramp			

❶ Loading yards of department stores and shopping centres

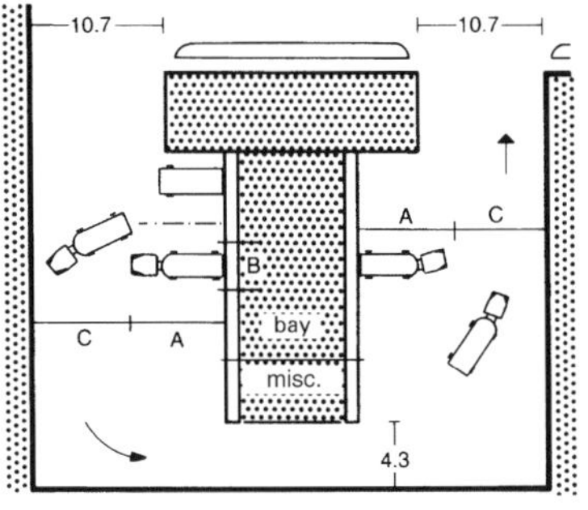

A tractor with trailer	B loading position	C shed forecourt
10.7	3.0	14.0
	3.7	13.1
	4.3	11.9
12.2	3.0	14.6
	3.7	13.4
	4.3	12.8
13.7	3.0	17.4
	3.7	14.9
	4.3	14.6

❷ Loading and unloading in inner yard

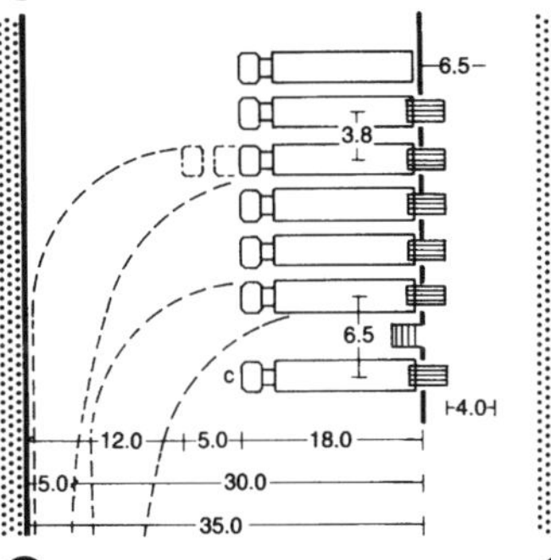

❸ Loading and unloading ramp: very closely parked vehicles must drive forward a little before they can drive out

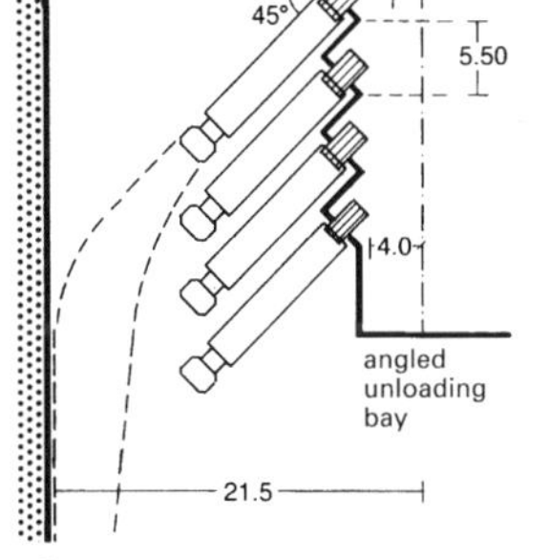

❹ Loading and unloading ramp

❺ Loading and unloading dock with raised ramps and side unloading

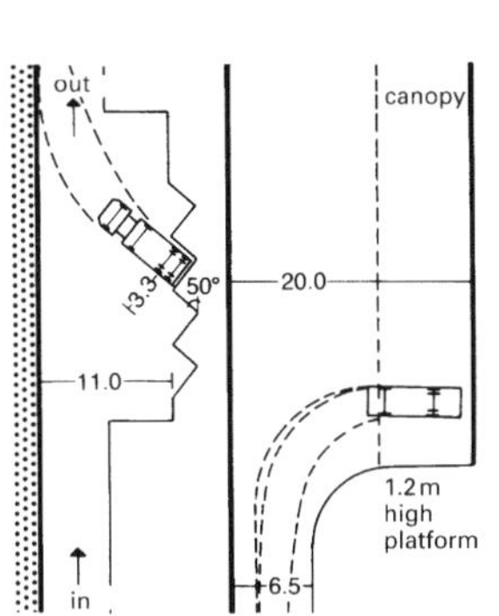

❻ Smallest possible space for loading ramps

For shops up to approx. 200 m², it is safe to assume smaller delivery vehicles, which can stop in normal car parks. Shops over 200 m² should provide a parking area of 3.5 m × 12 m for HGV deliveries. Vehicles should if possible be able to drive in and out forwards.

Average design values for loading yards are given for larger department stores and supermarkets in → ❶. Yards which are built over should have a clear height of at least 4.90 m. The width of single-lane straight ramps should be min. 3.50 m, with two-way traffic min. 6.75 m. Ramps should not have a gradient of more than 10%. Changes of gradient of more than 8% should have a transition curve of radius 50 m. At changes of gradient, height supplements must be considered according to the length of the HGVs. Spiral ramps should be designed in accordance with the swept curves of the FGSV.

Safety distance between two trucks with trailers standing next to each other: on ramps min. 1.50 m, at loading hatches min. 3.00 m.

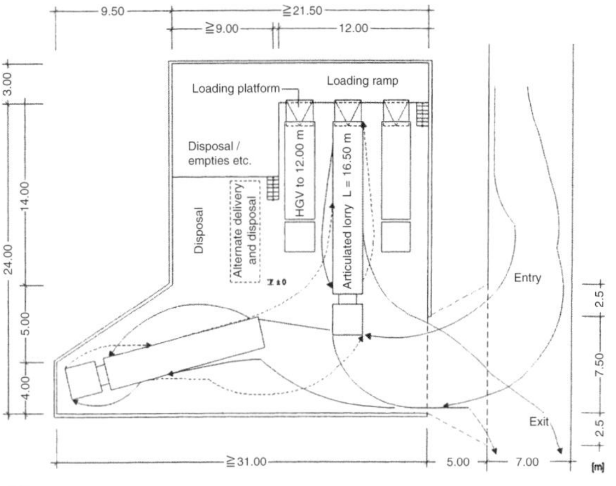

❼ Open loading yard for a department store (FGSV → refs)

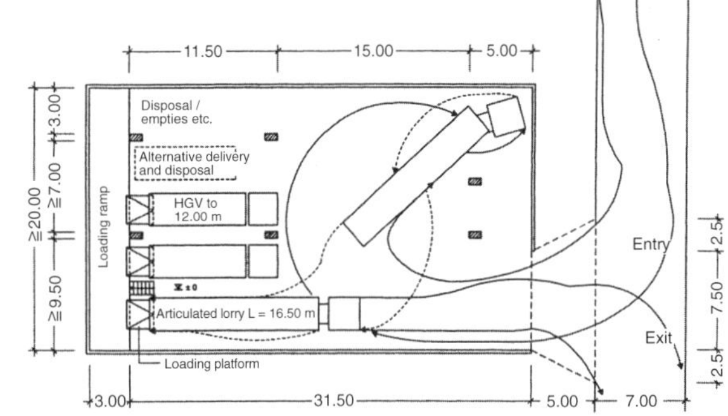

❽ Roofed-over loading yard, space height min. 4.90 m, under lighting when rubbish containers have to be loaded and unloaded. The swept curves of the expected vehicles should be checked for feasibility. Also consider the location of columns (FGSV → refs)

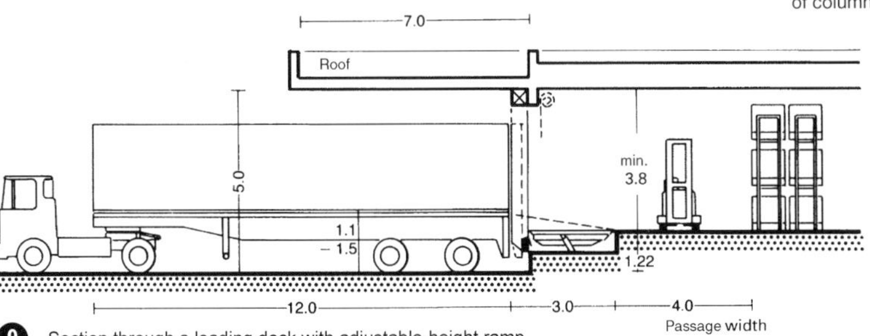

❾ Section through a loading dock with adjustable-height ramp

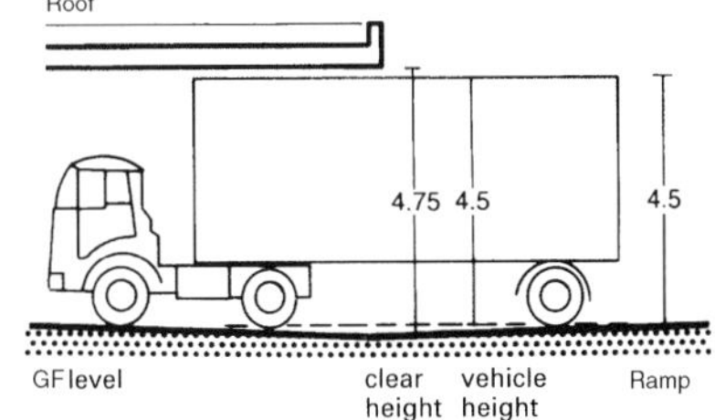

❿ Dimensions of roofed-over loading dock

SUPPLY AND DISPOSAL

Loading yards
Loading ramps
Rubbish chute systems
Rubbish collection rooms
Emergency power rooms

see also: Trucks – parking and turning pp. 387 ff.

Supply and disposal

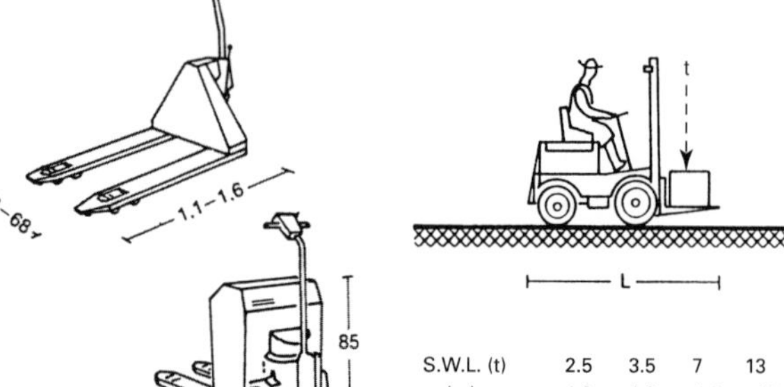

❶ Pallet truck

❷ Forklift truck: dimensions

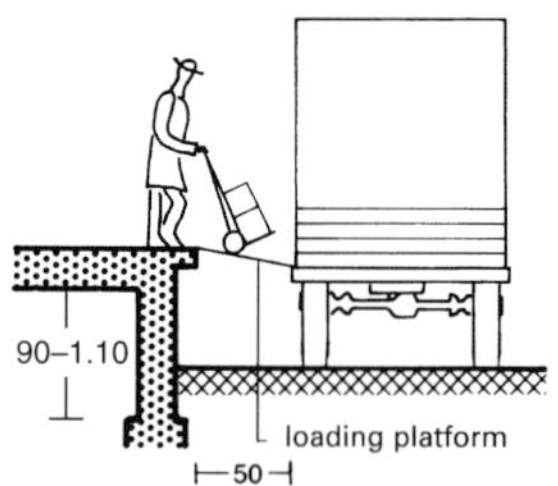

❸ Mobile loading bridge, ramp height normally 1.10 m, larger vehicles 1.25 m

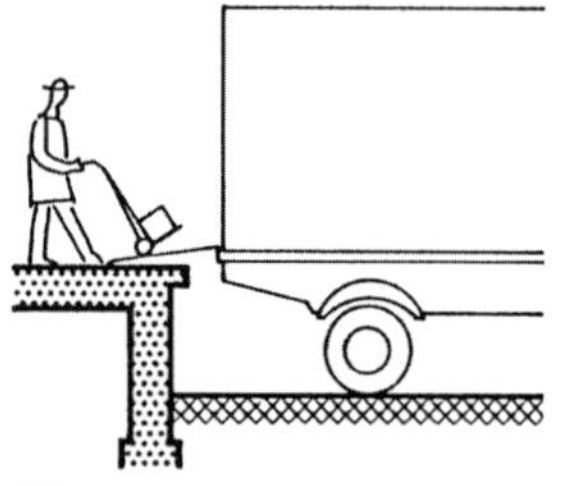

❹ Bridging plate, flexible

❺ Lifting the rear axle

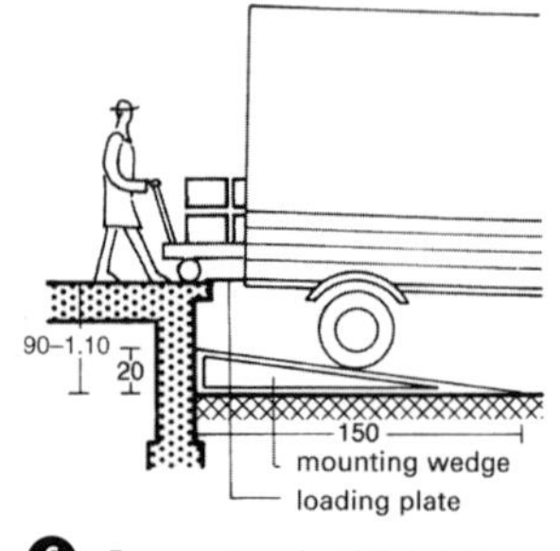

❻ Permanent and mobile height adjustment wedges

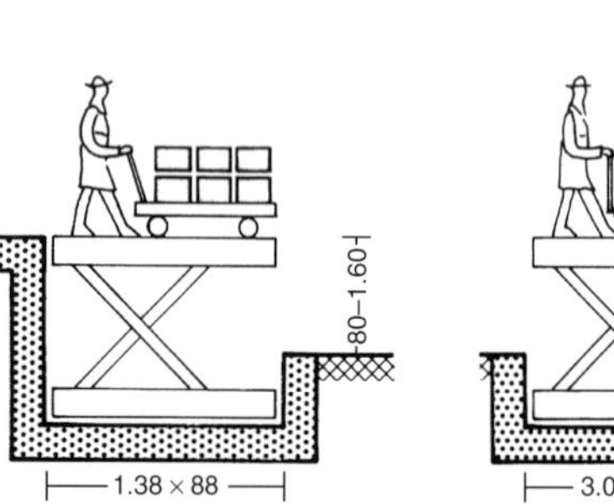

❼ Hydraulic scissorlift to overcome level difference ramp/yard

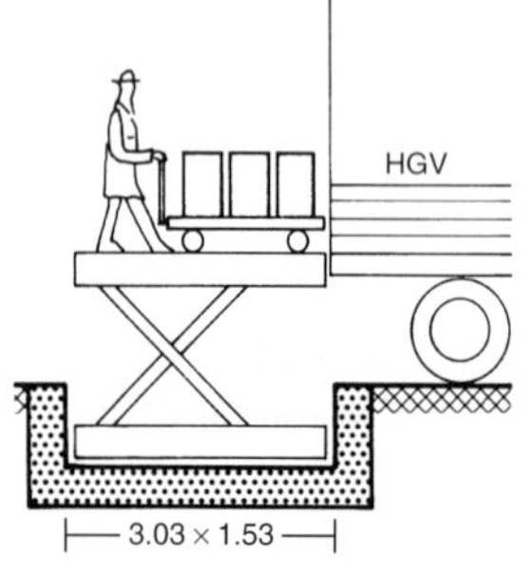

❽ HGV loaded using hydraulic scissorlift

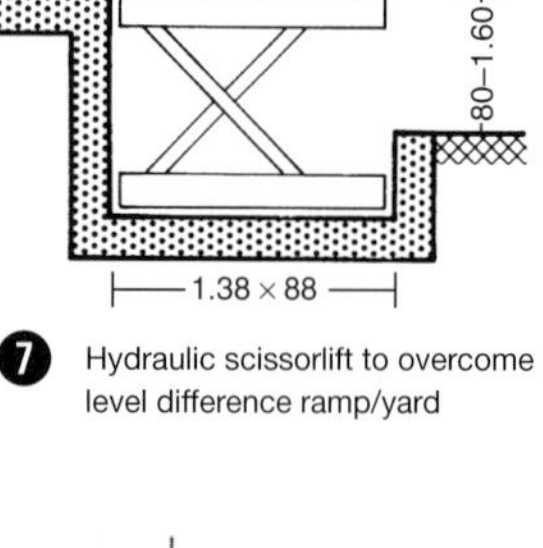

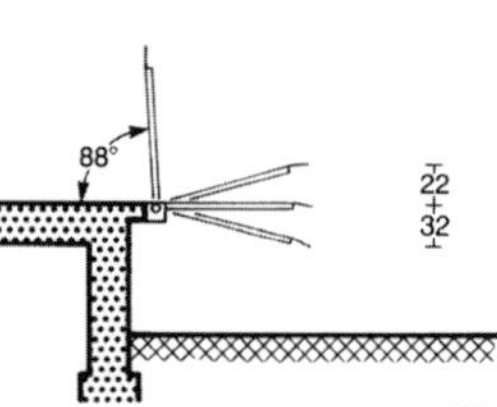

Length (mm)	Width (mm)	Load capacity (kg)
1500	1500	3000
1750	1500	3000
1750	1750	5000

❾ Slewing loading bridge, adjustable sideways

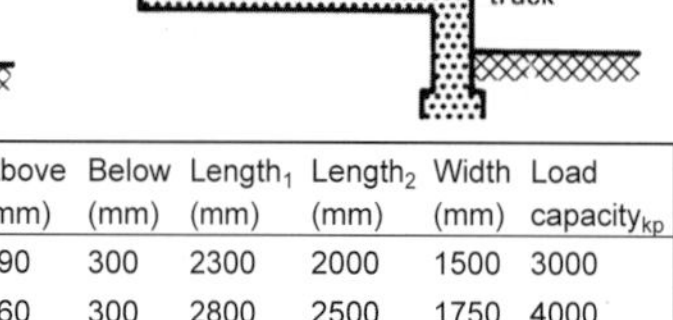

Above (mm)	Below (mm)	$Length_1$ (mm)	$Length_2$ (mm)	Width (mm)	Load $capacity_{kp}$
290	300	2300	2000	1500	3000
360	300	2800	2500	1750	4000
430	300	3300	3000	2000	5000

❿ Loading bridge

In order to load trucks safely, ramps and vehicles must be safely bridged. Loading bridges should connect to any vehicle or trailer in safety, and the loading surface of the vehicle can be higher or lower than the ramp → ❸ – ❹. Aluminium lifting wedges are ideal to lift lower vehicles up to ramp height → ❻. Lifting wedges can be rolled easily to various locations for use. Slewing loading bridges of light metal can be adjusted sideways → ❸ + ❾.
Mobile loading bridges can be rolled or carried and also used for loading railway wagons → ❹. Automatic hydraulic loading bridge with projecting lip → ❿
Hydraulic scissorlift platforms can overcome level differences between yard and vehicle → ❽ or between yard and ramp → ❼. Continuous adaptation to the truck level for loading and unloading → ❿. Forklift trucks are available in electric, diesel, petrol or gas versions → ❷.

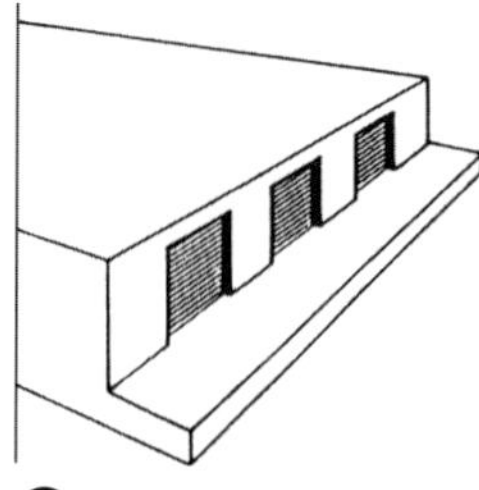

⓫ Simple ramp → ❸ – ❻

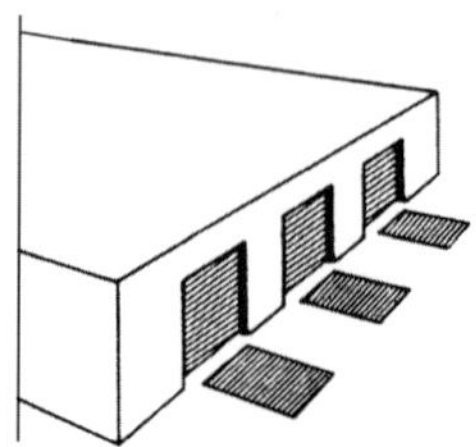

⓬ Yard level, loading with lifting platforms or loading ramps → ❽

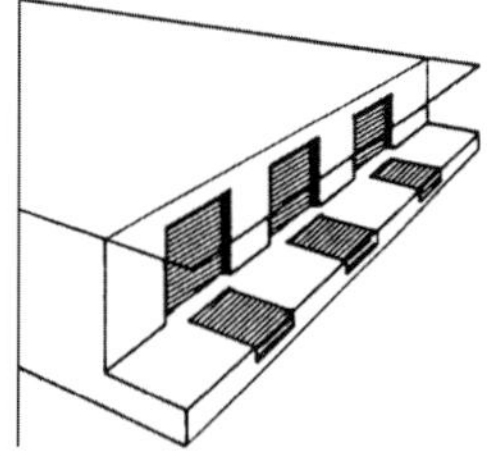

⓭ Roofed-over ramp with electrohydraulic loading ramps → ❿

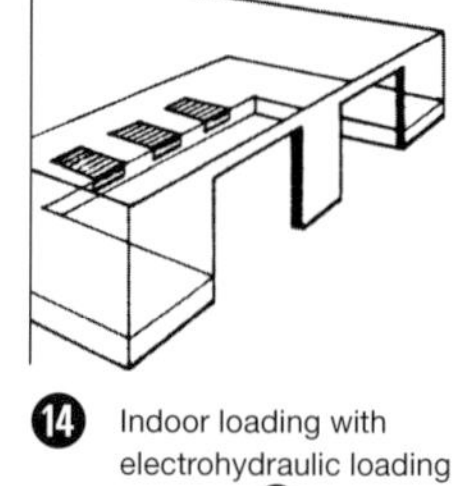

⓮ Indoor loading with electrohydraulic loading ramps → ❿

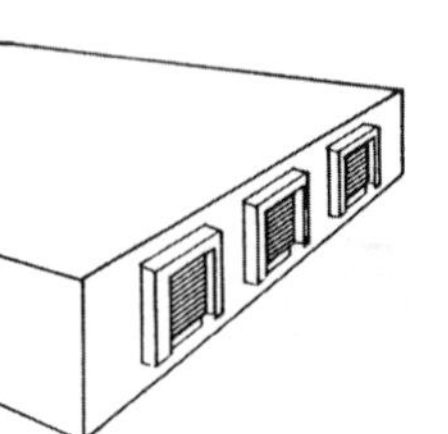

⓯ Integrated loading ramp and ramp weather protection system

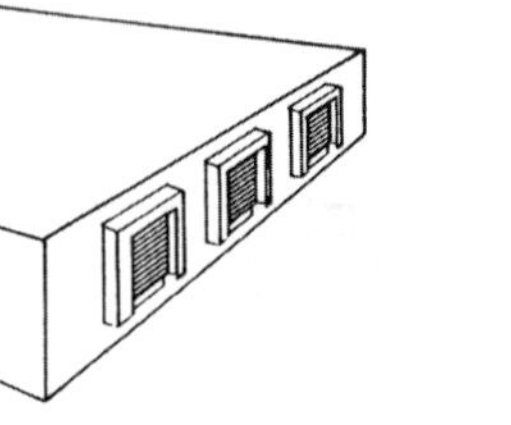

⓰ Saw-tooth ramps where manoeuvring space is limited

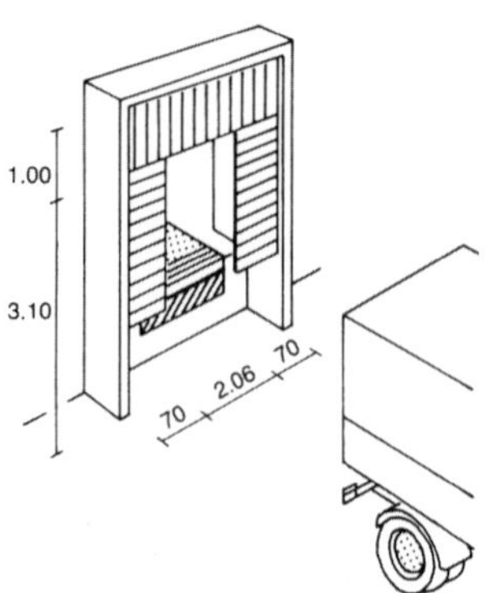

⓱ Rubber segment gate waterproofing

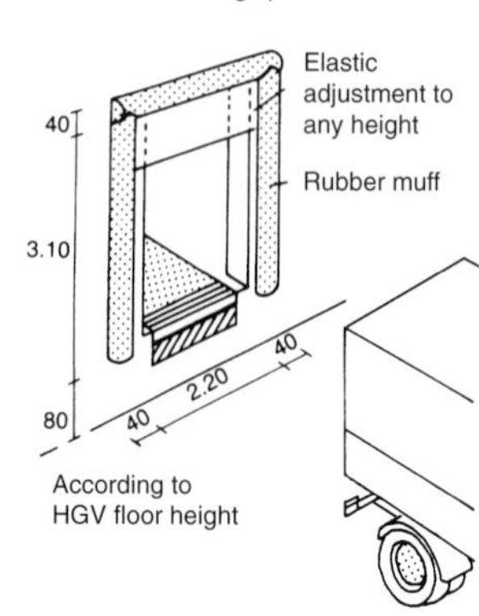

⓲ Rubber bead gate waterproofing

see also: Trucks – parking and turning pp. 387 ff.

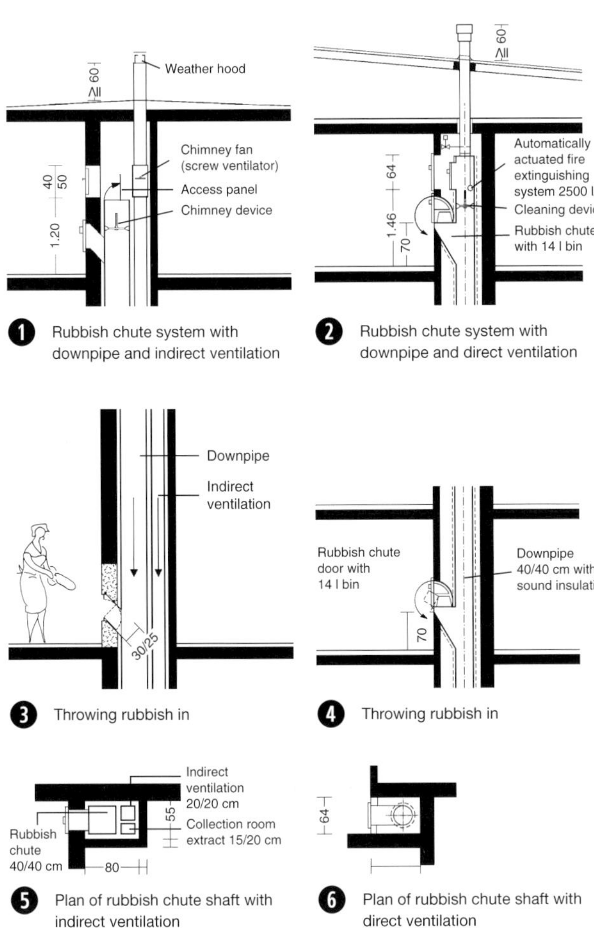

❶ Rubbish chute system with downpipe and indirect ventilation

❷ Rubbish chute system with downpipe and direct ventilation

❸ Throwing rubbish in

❹ Throwing rubbish in

❺ Plan of rubbish chute shaft with indirect ventilation

❻ Plan of rubbish chute shaft with direct ventilation

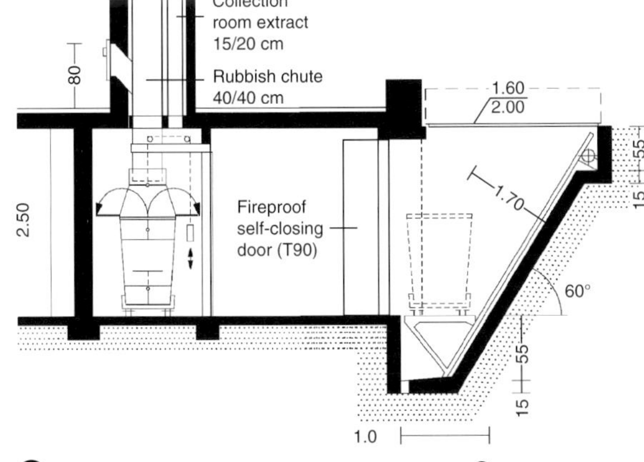

❼ Rubbish collection room with inclined lift, section → ❽

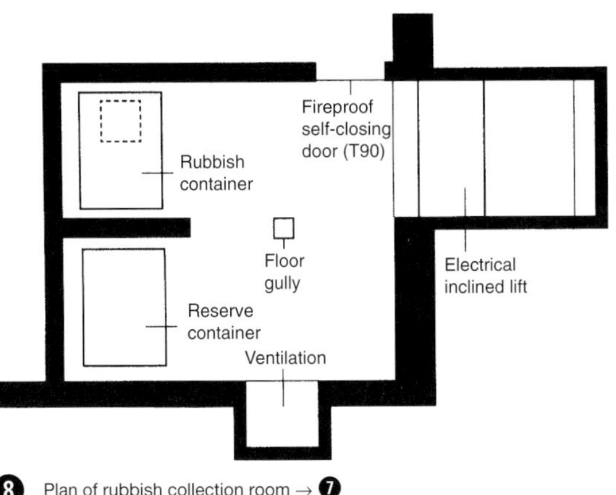

❽ Plan of rubbish collection room → ❼

Rubbish chute systems can be provided in multi-storey buildings to simplify the transport of waste from upper floors to waste collection bins. They were very popular for a time (particularly in high-rise flats) and were even a requirement for buildings of more than five storeys, but because of the maintenance costs and increased construction requirements (rubbish separation, fire protection) they are now provided only in special buildings.

The design is normally undertaken by a specialist firm, and an appropriate maintenance contract should be agreed with them.

Rubbish chutes can easily spread fire from one storey to another and therefore represent a **considerable fire hazard**. They are therefore forbidden in some (more recent) state building regulations, or are associated with appropriate construction requirements.

Construction
Rubbish chute systems consist of the following elements: the drop chute with the rubbish intake location, the rubbish collection room with holding bins, rubbish presses, etc. and the ventilation system.

Type of rubbish	Chute diameter (cm)		
	Rubbish	Ventilation	Fire protection
loose domestic waste	40	25	fire-resistant
rubbish in sacks 110 l	50	30	
paper (office waste)	55	30	
laundry (one-family house)	30	15	
laundry (hotels, hospitals)	40–50	25–30	

❾ Chute dimensions for rubbish chute systems (guideline values)

Details
Rubbish chute systems must have **separate intake doors** for the various categories of rubbish. These must be away from occupied rooms.

Rubbish chutes and collection rooms must be constructed of **fire-resistant materials**. Cladding, insulation materials, internal wall skins and all equipment near the shaft and collection room must also consist of **non-flammable materials**. The installation of a **fire extinguishing system** may be required → ❷.

The **drop shafts** of rubbish chute systems must fall from the uppermost rubbish intake location vertically and with no changes of cross-section. Constantly effective **ventilation** → ❶ – ❷ must be ensured. Rubbish chutes must be constructed so that fire, smoke, odour and dust cannot get into the building, waste is transported safely and the transmission of noise is prevented. The intake doors → ❸ – ❹ must be constructed so that no dust nuisance occurs and no oversize waste can be inserted. There should be a cleaning opening at the top of rubbish chutes. All openings must be fitted with doors made of non-flammable materials.

Rubbish collection rooms → ❼ – ❽ must be of adequate size. Their internal access must be through fire-resistant and self-closing doors. Collection rooms must be accessible from the open air for disposal and should have constant ventilation and a floor gully with odour trap. The waste should be collected in wheeled bins.

RUBBISH COLLECTION ROOMS

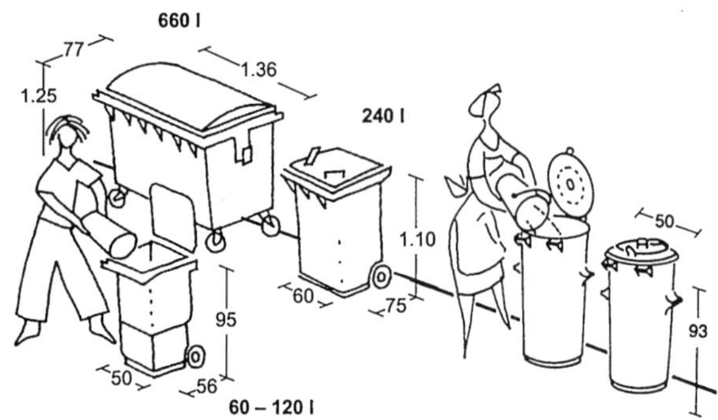

❶ Rubbish bins (selection)

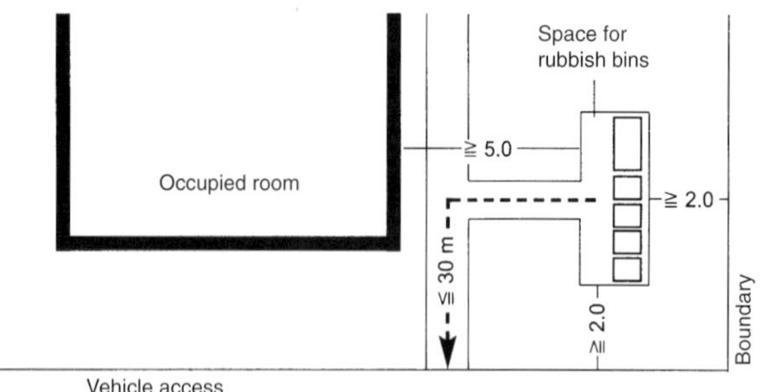

❷ Layout of storage space for rubbish bins (according to building regulations in Berlin)

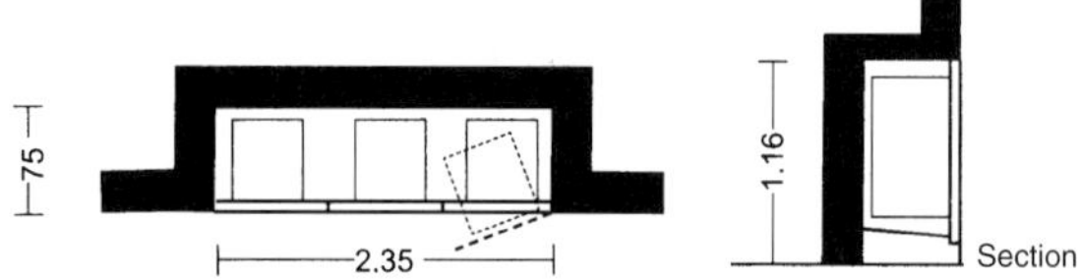

❸ Built-in rubbish box for 360 l of domestic rubbish (diagram)

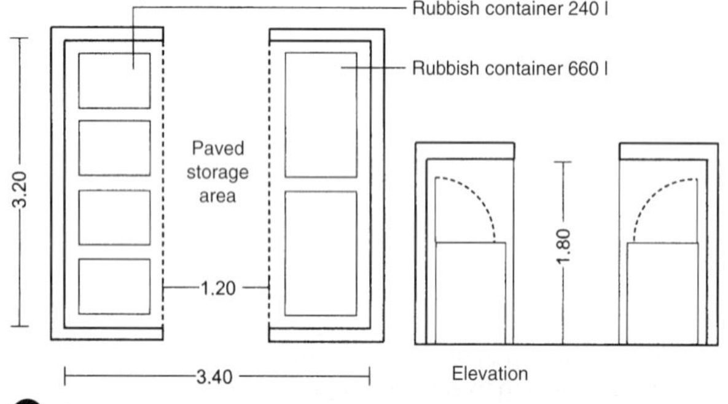

❹ Paved and roofed storage for 1680 l of domestic rubbish (diagram)

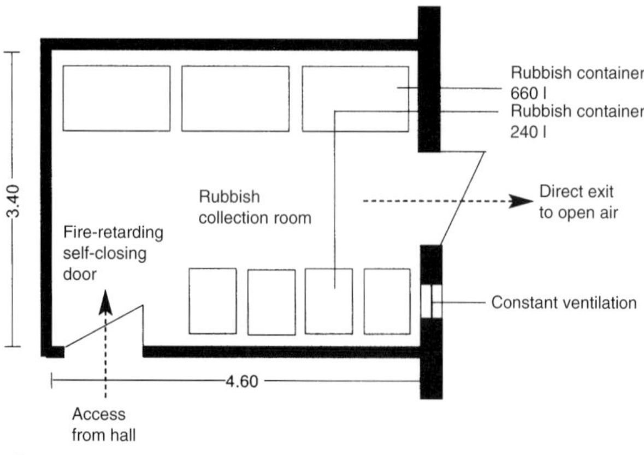

❺ Rubbish collection room for 2940 l of domestic rubbish (diagram) inside a building of class 3–5

Waste must be collected separately in suitable containers and be disposed of appropriately. This objective can be achieved by the provision of rubbish collection rooms, which are easily and safely accessible for the waste disposal provider either within the building or in corresponding areas outside the building, for the temporary storage of waste materials. Either option should be equipped with tightly closed rubbish bins in different sizes for the various categories of waste → ❶.

On account of the high fire load of solid rubbish (and the associated odour nuisance), the **model building regulations** include the following provisions:

Solid waste can be temporarily stored **inside** the building. Waste can be stored temporarily inside buildings with more than two flats or a usable area of 400 m^2 (building classes 3–5) only if the **rubbish collection room** complies with the following requirements:

1. The partition walls and ceilings are constructed as room-forming elements according to building regulations with the fire-resistance of load-bearing walls.
2. Openings from the inside of the building into the collection room should have fire-retarding, self-closing closures.
3. The rubbish collection rooms can be emptied directly from the open air.
4. Constantly effective ventilation is provided.

production of domestic rubbish (kg/resident/day)	**approx. 0.5**
suitable for recycling (%)	**approx. 74**

❻ Production of domestic rubbish (guideline values)

Some **state building regulations** include further provisions regarding the storage of solid waste **outside** the building. Storage spaces for rubbish bins should be at least **5 m** from openings into occupied rooms and flammable building elements, and at least **2 m** from property boundaries. Areas for mobile rubbish bins are to be paved. The distance from accessible roads should not exceed **30 m** → ❷. It is also important that areas for rubbish bins outside buildings can be reached easily in bad weather; they may require lighting and roofing.

Commercial refuse

Collection rooms for the disposal of commercial refuse should be at ground level and near the delivery area. Their size varies according to the size of the business; it would be about **90–200 m²**. If skips are used and collected by truck, a clear ceiling height (under sprinklers or lights) of at least 4.80–4.90 m should be provided.

If the quantity of waste is large, then the use of waste crushers or waste presses is worth considering. Offices and administration buildings will also need a paper shredder. Collection rooms for foodstuff waste (wet rubbish) must be cooled. In large buildings, rubbish collection rooms should be provided on the floors (near the lift) if possible, to avoid the lift lobby being used as a waste collection centre.

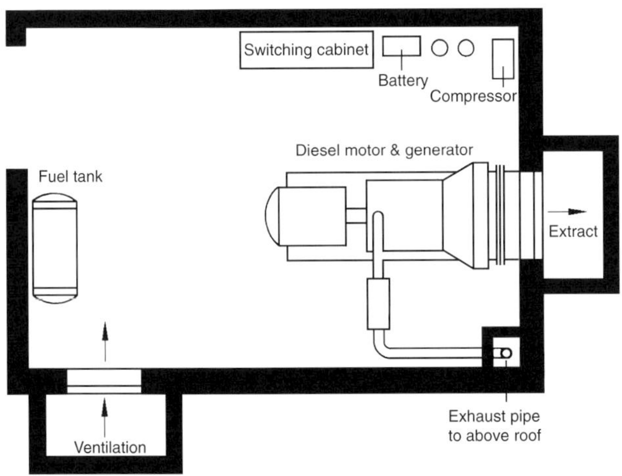

❶ Room for diesel emergency generator set with separate air supply and extraction

Generator capacity (kVa)	20–60	100–200	250–500	650–1500
Room size (m)	5.0–4.0	6.0–4.5	7.5–5.0	10.5–5.5
Room height (m)	3.0	3.5	4.0	4.0
Door width (m)	2.0–1.5	2.0–1.5	2.2–2.0	2.2–2.0

❷ Dimensions of emergency generator rooms

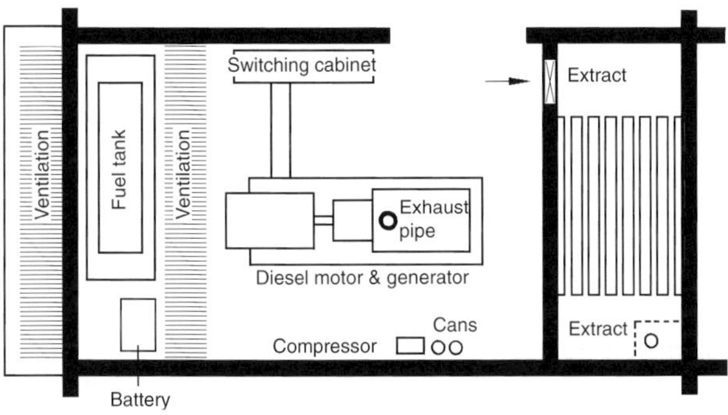

❸ Room for diesel emergency power generator with separate air supply and extraction

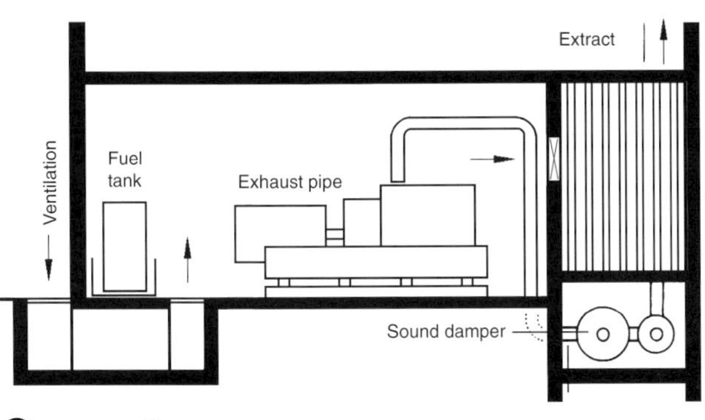

❹ Section → ❸

Emergency power supply systems (diesel generator sets)
Emergency power units are combustion motors (usually diesel) which are coupled to generators to produce electricity. They are used for a limited time in case of a power cut (and are thus not for constant power supply) and supply emergency and safety lighting, lifts and other critical usages (e.g. in operating theatres in hospitals, server rooms and industrial processes etc.). They consist of a diesel motor and a generator mounted on a base frame (e.g. steel) on a foundation with elastic supports between machine set and frame, and a starter and battery → ❶.

There are mobile (container generator sets) and permanently installed diesel generator sets including switching gear. The performance range is between 5 and 2000 kVA (kilovolt amp) according to specification.

The design starts with the determination of:
- motor power
- sound insulation
- exhaust system

Emergency power rooms
The required dimensions, height and openings of the room for a generator set vary according to the power and configuration of the motor → ❸. Air supply and extraction can be through forced ventilation (shaft) → ❶. It is also possible to run the extract air together with the exhaust of the diesel motor up a vertical shaft to exit above the roof → ❸ – ❹. In this case, sufficient sound insulation should be provided with a silencer in the ductwork → ❸ – ❹. The manufacturers of the motors give information about the required quantity of air and thus the size of the supply and extract ducts.

On account of the high noise level involved in running a generator set for testing and maintenance, it is recommended not to place it near inhabited rooms which should be particularly quiet (e.g. the care rooms of a hospital). Measures should also be undertaken to keep the noise level as low as possible. Another measure is to position the frame, on which the generator and motor are mounted, on spring dampers to reduce the sound transmission into the structure.

Uninterruptible power supply (UPS) systems
There is normally a gap of at most 15 seconds between the power cut and the switching to emergency power. UPS systems are used to continue power supply without interruption during this time. Static UPS systems are bridging battery power devices, whose batteries are constantly charged from the mains.

According to equipment and requirements, a UPS system should be able to protect the connected consumer from the following risks: power cuts, voltage fluctuations, voltage peaks, low voltage, excessive voltage, lightning effects/switching peaks, interference voltage and frequency fluctuations.

While UPS systems are designed to cope with a power cut of at most 30–60 minutes, diesel-powered emergency generators can supply power during much longer interruptions.

SUPPLY AND DISPOSAL
Loading yards
Loading ramps
Rubbish chute systems
Rubbish collection rooms
Emergency power rooms

RENEWABLE ENERGY

Overview

Energy source	Primary energy	Natural energy conversion	Technical energy conversion	Secondary energy: heat	Secondary energy: electricity	Secondary energy: fuels
sun	water power	evaporation, precipitation, thawing	hydropower station		x	
	wind power	atmospheric movement (wind)	wind energy converter		x	
		wave movement	wave power station		x	
	solar radiation	ocean currents	ocean current power station		x	
		warming of earth's surface and atmosphere	ocean warmth power station		x	
		solar radiation	collector, solar thermal power station	x		
			solar cell, photovoltaic power station		x	
			photolysis			x
	biomass	biomass production	conversion plant			x
			thermal power station	x	x	
earth	isotopic decay	geothermic	geothermal power station	x	x	
moon	gravitation	tides	tidal power station		x	

1 Renewable energies and their uses

Passive measures	Active measures	Hybrid measures
– town planning ecology – building form and alignment – thermal inertia – thermal insulation – special types of glass – double façades, buffer zones – atriums	– combined heat and power – total energy plants – solar thermal energy – photovoltaic – building element heating and cooling – heat pump technology – geothermal energy – fuel cells – condensing boilers – cooling systems (e.g. cool storage)	– storage of warmth and cold in connection with active systems – air conditioning through building elements/ground

2 Measures in ecological building technology

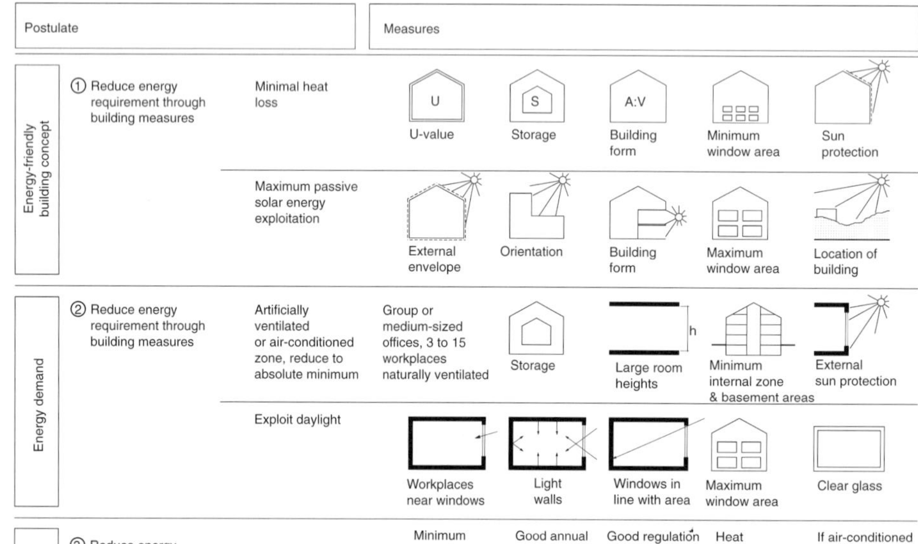

3 Objectives and measures for the design of energy and building technology (Economic Affairs → refs)

Scarcer resources and increasing energy prices are resulting in more interest in renewable energy sources. The limited supply and increasing consumption of energy reserves is leading to the necessity of developing alternatives. The construction and operation of buildings represents a large proportion of overall energy consumption.

In addition to saving energy through ever improved thermal insulation and more effective methods of energy processing with higher efficiencies, the use of renewable energies is becoming increasingly significant. The development and diffusion of new and optimised processes and equipment is supported by grant programmes.

The optimal design of each building project has an essential role to play. The forecast demand for electrical and heat energy for a particular building should be compared with the opportunities available at the location and the most efficient process selected. As new processes and devices are developed or made effective, existing buildings and systems should be checked often for efficiency and may need to be upgraded.

The methods of exploiting renewable energies are multifarious and are being extended constantly. The type and extent of this use depends on the possibilities at the location, the type and size of the building project and the budget.

The application of a particular process can be supported by public grant programmes and the energy industry. What can be grant-aided and to what level varies according to region and is regularly adapted to altered conditions (regulated in the Renewable Energy Law – EEG).

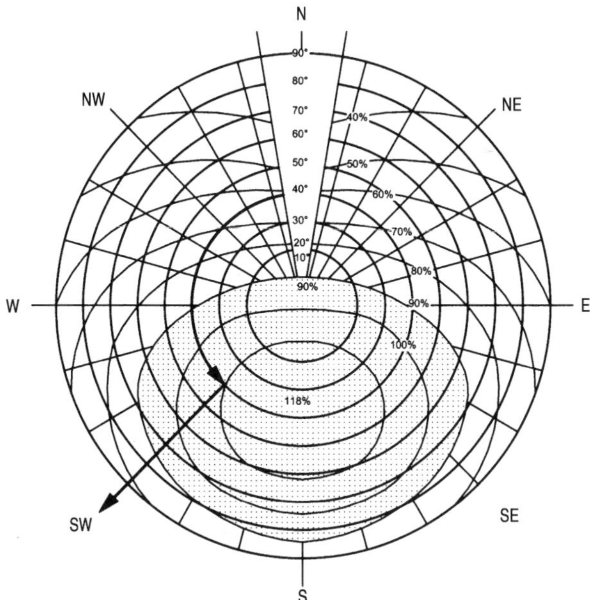

❶ Performance of photovoltaic elements according to tilt and alignment (Shell → refs)

Solar modules

Generator connection box

House supply box (also indoors)

Main distribution

MD

Supply kWh kWh

Feed-in AC Meter Meter Inverter

❷ Principle of a grid-connected photovoltaic system (Bohne → refs)

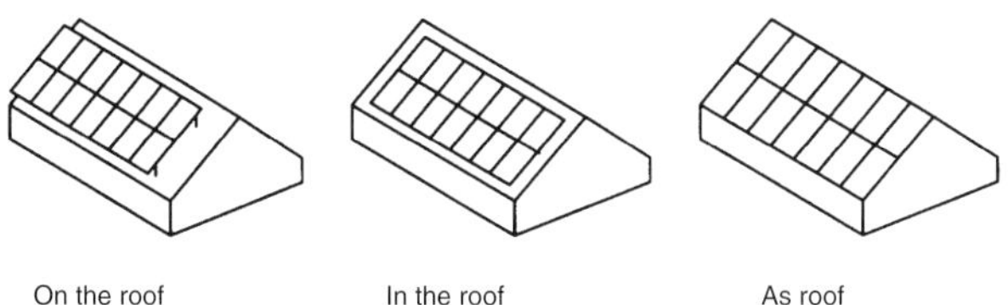

❸ Possible roof-related arrangements of photovoltaic elements

Photovoltaics

Sunlight is converted into electricity in solar cells. This is an important element of the ecological design of buildings, because renewable electrical energy is generated. Solar cells can use direct and diffused solar radiation. Shadowing of their surface is to be avoided, with partial shadows having a more serious effect than temporary shadows (i.e. trees are worse than clouds).

The solar yield depends on the climate and the alignment of the panels → ❶. The optimum alignment in northern latitudes is facing due south, with a tilt angle from the horizontal dependent on latitude. At good locations, in Germany for example, an average annual yield of 800–900 kWh/m^2 can be expected, or under optimum conditions approx. 1100 kWh/m^2. A rule of thumb is to expect to require 7.5 m^2 of panels for each kW of installed capacity.

Solar cells are connected together into larger units called modules. Various types of module (mono-crystalline, multi-crystalline, amorphous) differ in performance, efficiency and appearance. Mono-crystalline cells have uniformly dark grey to black surfaces, multi-crystalline grey to blue and variable; semi-transparent modules are also possible.

The conversion of the direct current coming from the solar cells into alternating current in the inverter causes little conversion loss. Most systems are connected to the grid for more cost-effective operation: the electricity coming from the solar modules is fed into the grid, which requires a separate feed-in meter.

Large photovoltaic installations should be operated with changing tilt and alignment (tracking), with separate solar generators and grid feed-in equipment to achieve the optimum yield. Grid-connected systems work completely automatically without maintenance and have a lifetime of at least 20 years. Solar-generated electricity fed into the public grid is paid for over a guaranteed period as regulated in the Renewable Energy Law (EEG).

Photovoltaic elements can be integrated into the building envelope in various ways or mounted subsequently. They are designed for use in the open air and can be used as an independent part of a façade or roof. Solar cells are UV-resistant and weatherproof.

They can play an important architectural role and also fulfil other functions: sound, visual, sun and weather protection. Solar cells are mostly built on roofs, for which there are various possibilities: mounted on the roof (independently, mostly for later installation), integrated into the roof covering or forming the roof itself. The installation of photovoltaic modules in façades is also possible, in which case they should be back-ventilated in order to avoid reduction of yield → ❸ + ❹.

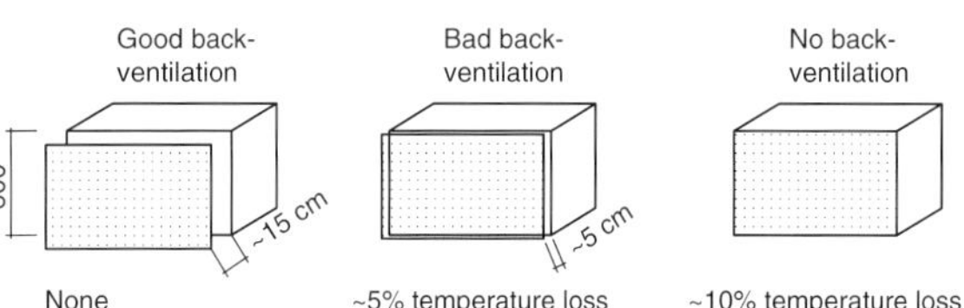

❹ Photovoltaic elements on a façade with possible yield reductions (Bohne → refs)

Wood type	kWh/m³	kWh/kg	Wood type	kWh/m³	kWh/kg
maple	1,900	4.1	spruce	1,700	4.4
birch	1,900	4.3	larch	1,700	4.4
beech	2,100	4.0	poplar	1,200	4.1
oak	2,100	4.2	robinia	2,100	4.1
alder	1,500	4.1	fir	1,400	4.5
ash	2,100	4.2	willow	1,400	4.1

❶ Calorific value of various types of wood (Bohne → refs)

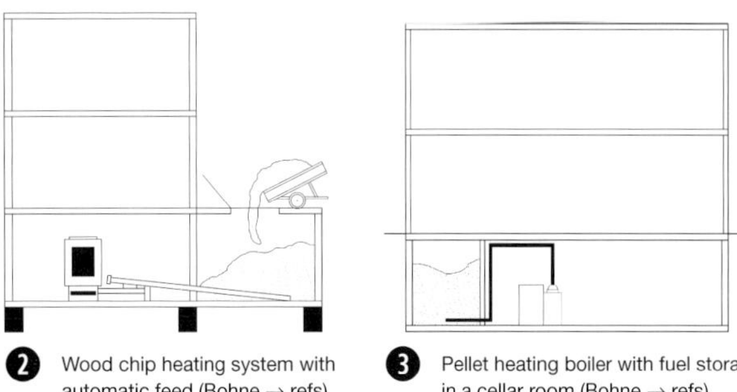

❷ Wood chip heating system with automatic feed (Bohne → refs)

❸ Pellet heating boiler with fuel storage in a cellar room (Bohne → refs)

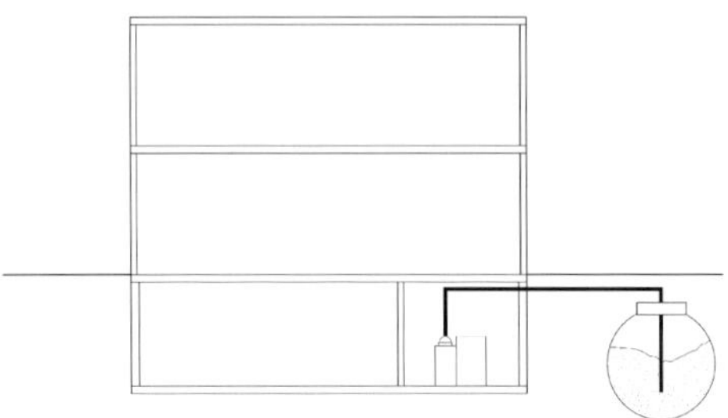

❹ Pellet heating boiler with fuel storage in an underground container (Bohne → refs)

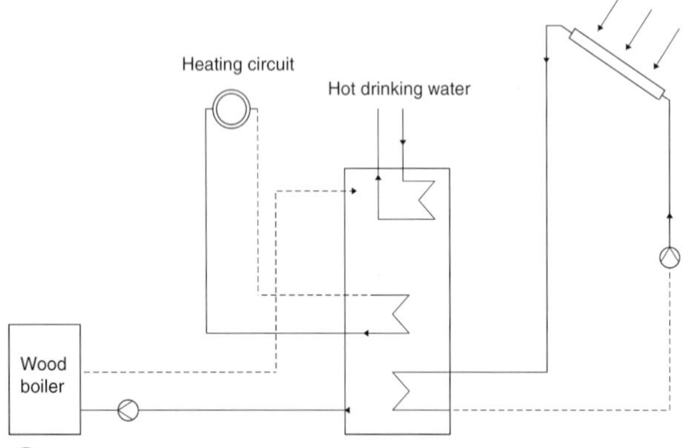

❺ Heating plant with thermal solar system, wood-burning boiler and buffer cylinder for heating water (Bohne → refs)

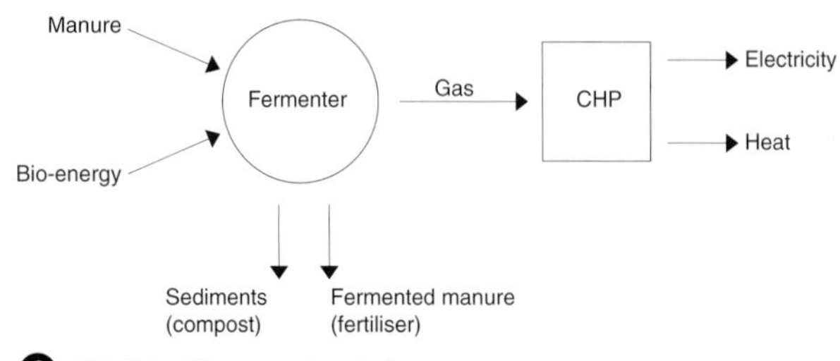

❻ Principle of biogas use in agriculture

Biomass energy

Biomass is exploited for energy through thermo-chemical or biological processes (burning, gasification or liquefaction). The most significant sources are biodiesel, wood and agricultural waste products. Biodiesel is made by liquefying renewable raw materials which contain oil. It can replace heating oil or conventional oil and be used in appropriate boilers or block heating and power plants.

Wood as an energy source

Wood is available in great quantities and can be used in various forms. The water content of newly felled wood is 40–50%. Air-dried wood contains 15–20% water and produces twice the calorific value. There are various types of wood with different moisture contents, density, calorific value and also size, form and processing. Wood for burning is available as logs, wood chips and pellets.

For smaller installations up to 15 kW nominal heat output, natural logs can be used, which can be hardwood or softwood from forestry or waste products from timber processing. Demolition timber should be avoided. In larger installations, it is also possible to use sawdust, straw and further sources.

Centralised boilers are preferable to single stoves on account of better possibilities for controlling emissions. Automatically fed boilers show better emissions values than hand-fed.

In wood chip or pellet systems, the fuel is fed into the combustion chamber from an adjacent room or from a container using a spiral auger conveyor or pressure system. The continuous supply of fuel ensures a good degree of efficiency and enables the output to be adapted according to demand.

Pellets (pressed waste products of wood-processing industries with a very high energy value of 4.3–5.0 kWh/kg, about ⅓ that of heating oil) are delivered in trucks and blown into the storage container. The technology and the space required for the installation is comparable to an oil heating system.

The size of the boiler also corresponds to a boiler for oil or gas. The safety standards are, however, lower than for heating oil. Containers for wood chips are filled by tipping from a truck.

In order to extend the burning time in the boiler, heating water buffer cylinders are a sensible addition to a pellet or wood chip heating system, and are necessary for log heating systems; 40 litres per kW of nominal output should be assumed. Boilers for solid fuel up to 1 MW thermal output do not require a permit.

A further technological possibility is gasification of wood (e.g. of wood chips) for use in a block heating and power plant, for which some heating oil is required to start the motor. The combination of a wood-fired boiler with a thermal solar system is sensible because the water can be pre-warmed by solar energy and heated to feed temperature by the boiler → ❺.

Biogas

The agricultural production of biogas on farms from slurry or harvested materials has great potential and is of increasing importance. The biomass is gasified in a digester, which then feeds a gas engine for combined heat and power. The digested slurry is spread on the fields as fertiliser and the residual sludge can be used as compost. Biomass gasification is a continuous and sensitive process and requires constant monitoring. A biogas plant requires a permit under the Federal Emissions Control Law.

Gas from landfill sites (fermentation of solid matter) can also be employed to produce heat and power using gas probes or gas collecting drains for the operation of heat and power systems or simply as heating gas.

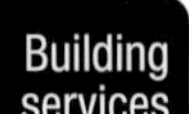

Water	Surface water	river, lake, seawater
	Underground water	groundwater, spring water, well water, deep/thermal water
	Waste heat	cooling water, municipal drain water, domestic drain water, industrial service water outflow, lighting heat
	Circulating water	district heating network, water supply main, process water
Air	outdoor air, escaping air, industrial extract air, lighting heat, heat from people, process heat	
Ground		
Solar energy		

1 Heat sources for the running of a heat pump

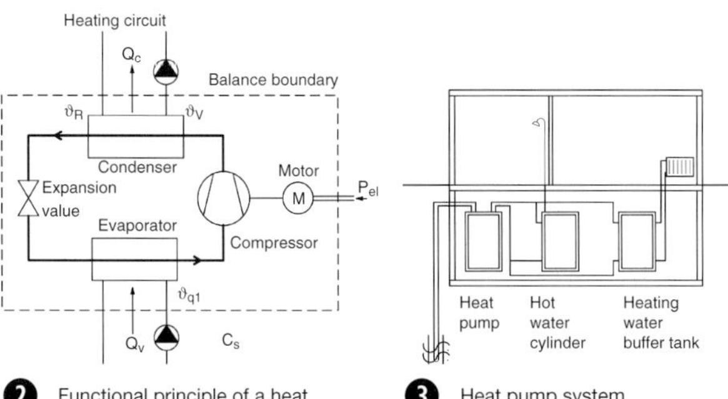

2 Functional principle of a heat pump (Schmid → refs)

3 Heat pump system

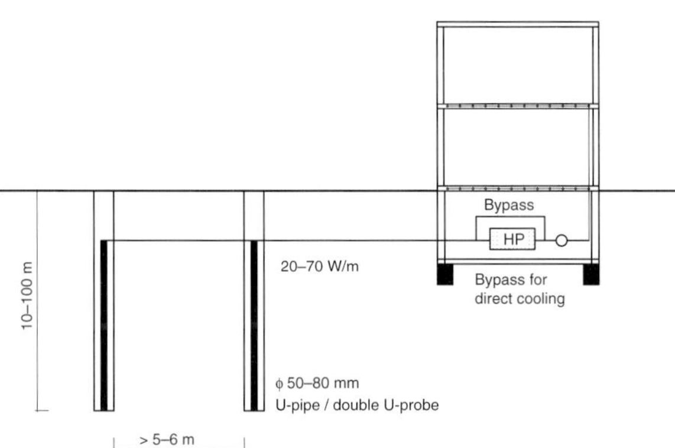

4 Downhole heat exchanger as heat source for a heat pump (in combination with the activation of a building element for air conditioning) (Bohne → refs)

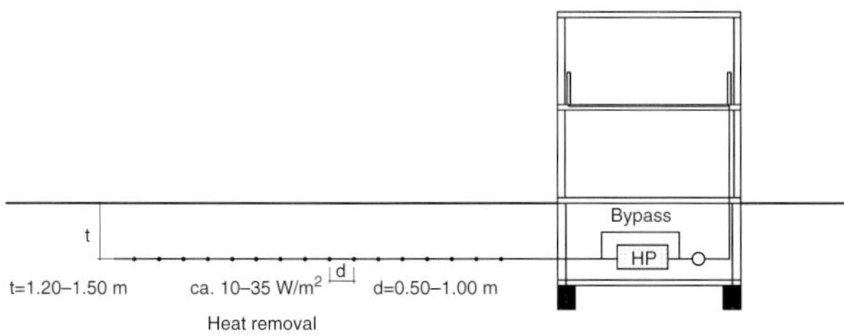

5 Ground source heat collectors as heat source for a heat pump (Bohne → refs)

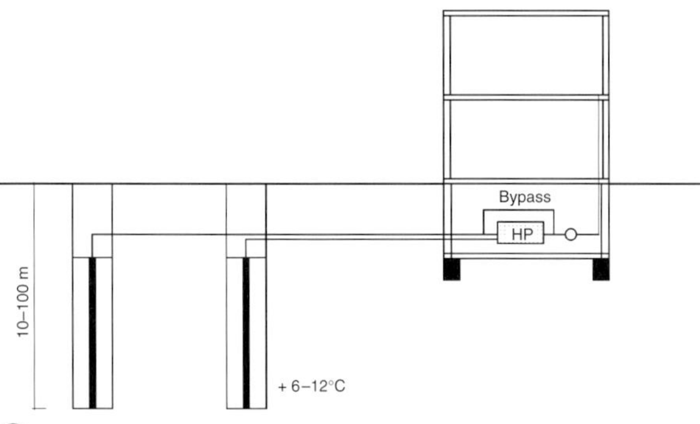

6 Groundwater as heat source for a heat pump (in combination with underfloor heating) (Bohne → refs)

Ground source energy

This describes the exploitation of geothermal energy at a depth to approx. 400 m. The temperature gradient is about 3 K/100 m of depth and temperatures of approx. 7–11°C can be expected at a depth of 10–20 metres; the flow of warmth is influenced only by weather and air temperature near the surface. The relatively constant temperatures can be exploited for heating and cooling. Many processes are available for energy use:

Ground source heat collectors

These are metal or plastic pipes laid horizontally under the ground. The spacing and depth are dependent on the properties of the soil. The heat extraction is 10–40 W/m². Geothermal heat collectors should not be built over and the surface should not be impermeably paved.

Downhole heat exchangers

These require less space and have better thermal performance than ground source heat collectors. They can be installed as indirect or, less often, as direct systems in a closed circuit. An indirect system would, for example, connect a brine circuit with the heat pump through an intermediate heat exchanger. There are various construction types: U-pipe or double-pipe probes and coaxial probes, where the borehole is grouted with a cement-bentonite suspension for better heat transfer. The extraction output is 20–70 W/m.

Groundwater wells as a heat source

Heat can be extracted directly from an aquifer: heat exchangers shaped like an immersion heater are lowered down boreholes into the aquifer and connected to a heat pump with a brine circuit. The usual process is the extraction and refilling of the groundwater with pumping or suction wells. Such systems (and also downhole heat exchangers) generally require a permit, and the required drilling work must always be performed by approved firms. Then extracted energy can be used directly to heat or cool building elements or indirectly with heat pumps.

The suitability of using air or surface water as a heat source should be investigated for each specific project, because the annual variation of temperature is directly opposite to the heating demand.

Heat pump

Environmental or geothermal energy is exploited in a thermodynamic process through the introduction of mechanical energy: ¾ of the energy required for heating is gained from the environment and the remainder is consumed as electricity to power the compressor. Heat pumps are of particular interest for integrated energy supply concepts, because they can be used for heating and also cooling.

A heat pump essentially consists of evaporator, compressor, condenser and expansion valve. These parts are connected with pipes in a closed medium circuit. The effect is to extract heat from the surroundings by evaporation. The now gaseous medium is compressed in an electrically driven compressor, increasing the temperature and pressure. A further heat exchanger then transfers this heat to the heating system, causing the medium to condense again. The control valve serves to reduce the pressure in the medium to the low initial pressure.

Heat pumps can be used with low-temperature heating systems (optimal for relatively low feed temperature such as in underfloor heating) and central water heating. The heat delivered by the compressor of the heat pump must always be dissipated, thus the installation of a buffer cylinder (not necessary for underfloor heating).

The heat pump works independent of the time of day or season and is considered to be an environmentally beneficial heating system. The electricity for the operation of a heat pump is sometimes grant-aided through lower electricity prices and requires a separate meter.

❶ Functional principle of combined heat and power (Schmid → refs)

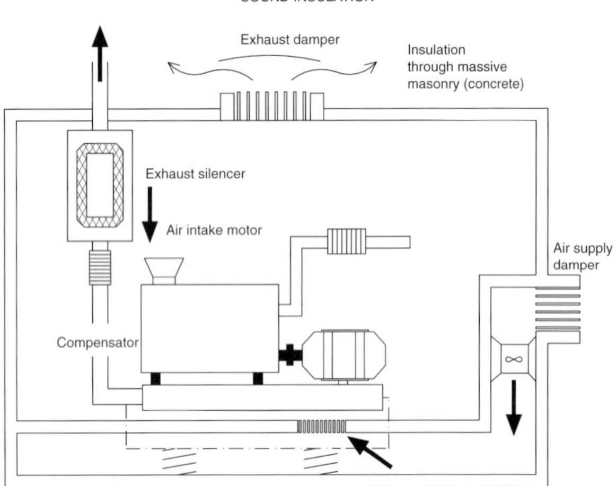

❷ Block heating and power system and constructional ancillaries (Bohne → refs)

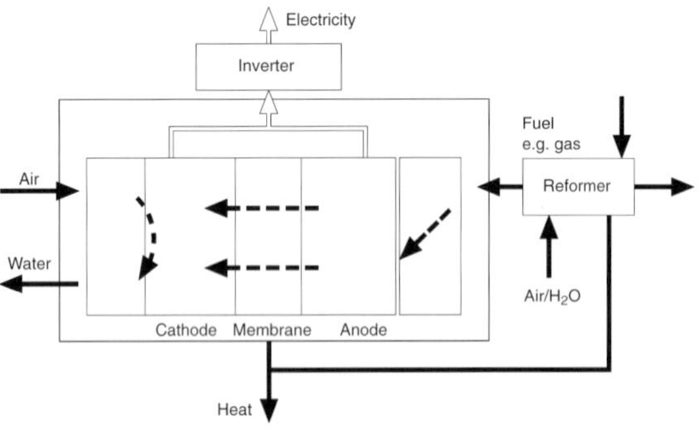

❸ Principle of a fuel cell (Bohne → refs)

Description	Abbreviation	Operating temperature	Electrolyte	Fuel	Oxidant	Application
alkaline FC	AFC	80 °C	caustic potash	hydrogen	oxygen	space
polymer-electrolyte-membrane FC	PEMFC	80 °C	solid polymer	hydrogen, methanol	oxygen/ air	transport, small power station
phosphoric acid FC	PAFC	200 °C	phosphoric acid	natural gas	air	thermal power station
molten carbonate FC	MCFC	650 °C	lithium and potassium carbonate	natural, town and biogas	air	power station, thermal power station
oxide ceramic FC	SOFC	1000 °C	zirconium oxide	natural, town and biogas	air	power station, thermal power station

❹ Overview of fuel cell types

Combined heat and power (CHP) is the combined production of heating and mechanical energy, which is converted into electricity in a generator. The basic idea is the generation of electrical energy and the exploitation of the heat, which is always produced at the same time. Smaller installations (for one or more buildings) use combustion motors or gas turbines instead of the water/steam circuit normally found in a power station.

A **block heating and power system** is a small power station, which produces electricity and space heating at the same time, working as a mini- or micro-CHP system. The size of a block heating and power system has a decisive influence on its cost-effectiveness, because the energy produced by a CHP system consists of about ⅓ electricity and ⅔ heat. The variable energy demand for buildings according to time of day and season necessitates the sizing of the block heating and power system according to electricity or heating demand. If the block heating and power system is designed to meet heating demand, then excess electricity is fed into the grid and electricity is consumed from the grid when the output is insufficient. If the block heating and power system is designed to meet electricity demand, then excess heat is stored in a buffer cylinder and an external boiler is required when the heat produced is insufficient.

Block heating and power systems are mostly designed to meet the heating demand. The precondition is that the curve of heat and electricity demand against time is known for the building or consumer group. For the design of new residential buildings, the demand can be estimated fairly accurately using characteristic curves. A block heating and power system will normally produce enough heat to meet basic requirements and excess electricity is fed into the grid though an additional meter. The heating demand at peak times is then met by an additional source of heating.

Block heating and power systems are available in various sizes: the smallest models for single houses from approx. 2 kW of electrical power and powered by a four-stroke or Stirling motor (micro-CHP), small plants up to 30 kW can be used for blocks of up to six flats (mini-CHP). Compact block heating and power systems cover the range up to 400 kW, above that large systems are needed. The space required for a mini-CHP system from 5.5 kW electricity output is 4 m^2, for 15 kW 6.5 m^2, and any areas for additional heating boilers should be added.

For installation in buildings, sufficient air supply and extract openings should be specified and the exhaust pipe continued to above the roof. The system should either be encapsulated as a module or sufficiently sound insulated between itself and occupied rooms.

Fuel cells produce electricity and heat out of water and hydrogen in a reverse-electrolysis process. They consist of electrodes (anode and cathode) and an electrolyte. This separates the electrodes and the reaction partner supplied. Fuel cells generate DC, which is concerted into AC in an inverter. The waste heat can be used for space heating through a cooling circuit. Hydrogen is produced from natural gas or methane/methanol in a reformer. Like CHP systems, fuel cells produce electricity and heat simultaneously, but without mechanical parts or noise.

As with a CHP system, the selection of the correct fuel cell can be based either on electricity or heating demand, and in the same way design to cover base load with an alternative source for the production for peak loads is sensible. The excess heat in the summer months can be used to drive an absorption refrigeration machine.

Fuel cells are differentiated according to operating temperatures (high-temperature, low-temperature fuel cells) and electrolyte used. Low-temperature fuel cells are already available for smaller building applications like blocks of flats or small commercial use, but high-temperature fuel cells are practical only in large applications because they produce electricity and heat in large quantities and the high temperatures have to be dispersed through multiple use in an energy cascade. Fuel cells are suitable for upgrading and new installations.

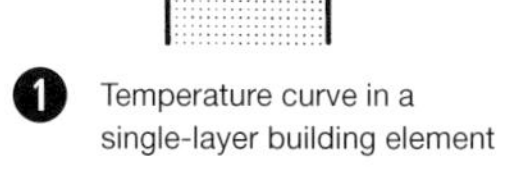

❶ Temperature curve in a single-layer building element

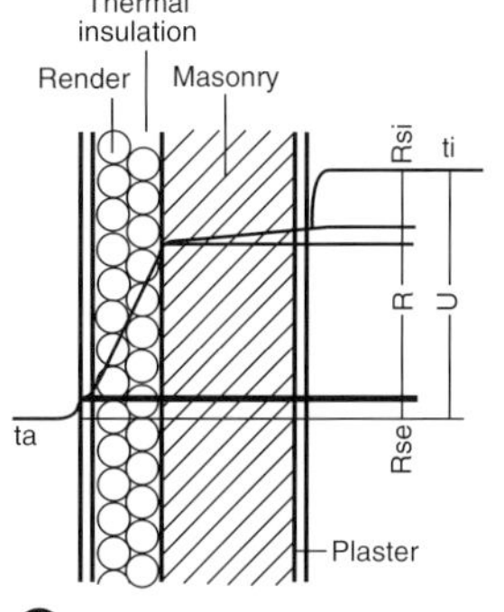

❷ Temperature curve in a multi-layer building element

External wall with external wall insulation system

U req 0.35 W/m²K
R req 1.2 m²K/W

Thermal transmittance
U exstg = 0.29 W/m²K

	Building material layer	Density kg/m³	Thickness d (m)	Weight/area kg/m²	λ W/mK	d/λ m²K/W
	Rsi					0.040
1	Render		0.01			
2	Insulation	30	0.12	32.6	0.040	3.000
3	Sand-lime masonry	1800	0.24	432.0	0.990	0.242
4	Plaster	1400	0.01	14.0	0.700	0.014
	Rsi					0.130
Σ						RT = 3.427

❸ Calculation of thermal transmittance (U-value) for an external wall with an external wall insulation system

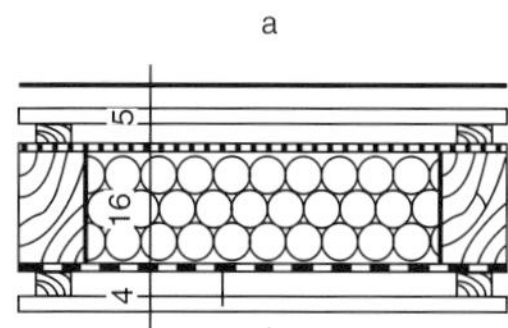

Pitched roof

U req 0.30 W/m²K
R req 1.75 m²K/W
according to DIN 4108-2

Insulation proportion fa 85%
Rafter proportion fb 15%

Thermal transmittance
U exstg = 0.29 W/m²K

	Building material layer	Density kg/m³	Thickness d (m)	Weight/area kg/m²	λ W/mK	d/λ m²K/W
	Rse					0.040
1	Roof covering					
2	Battens					
3	Underlay					
4	Insulation	30	0.16	4.8	0.040	4.000
5	Rafters	600	0.16	96.0	0.130	1.231
6	Battens, enclosed air layer		0.025			0.16
7	Plasterboard	900	0.0125	11.3	0.250	0.050
	Rsi					0.100
Σ	Upper limit value **R**'T = 1/(fa/RT, insulation + fb/RT, rafters) = 3.445					
	Lower limit value **R**"T = Rse + R1 + R2 + R3 + R4 + R5 + R6 + R7 + Rsi = 3.341					
	R'T = (**R**'T + **R**"T)/2 = 3.393					

❹ Calculation of thermal transmittance (U-value) for a pitched roof construction

Thermal insulation measures are necessary in buildings to limit heat loss and to protect against condensation; verifications that these have been carried out are required, as stated in various standards and regulations:

The **Energy Saving Regulation (EnEV 2007)** contains limiting values for the **primary energy demand** and the **transmitted heat demand** of residential and non-residential buildings → p. 474. The determination of the coefficients of thermal conductivity (U-values), the energetic design values (heat transmission resistance, thermal conductivity) and the essential basic terms are described below.

Heat quantity, unit Wh [= 1.16 kcal]; temperature °C; temperature difference K (Kelvin). 1.16 Wh (= 1 kcal) increases the temperature of 1000 g of water by 1 K (= **thermal capacity**)

Heat transfer can be by convection (carrying), conduction, radiation or water vapour diffusion; heat transfer can be slowed by thermal insulation, but never prevented.

Thermal conductivity λ, unit W/mK [kcal/mhK], is a property of a material; the smaller this value, the less the thermal conductivity. The design values include, in contrast to the nominal values, a supplement for practical application (temperature, moisture, ageing).

Thermal resistance R, unit m²K/W [m²hK/kcal] is a property of a layer: **R** = d/λ (d = layer thickness in m). The calculation of the thermal resistance is important for the determination of the heat transfer coefficient U → ❸ – ❹.

Surface resistance is the thermal insulation value of the air film adhering to the building element. The external surface resistance ($\mathbf{R}_{se}$) and the internal surface resistance ($\mathbf{R}_{si}$) are differentiated.

Overall resistance 1/U, unit m²K/W [m²hK/kcal], is the sum of the resistances of a building element to the transmission of heat (thermal resistances and surface resistances): $\mathbf{1/U} = \mathbf{R}_{si} + \mathbf{R} + \mathbf{R}_{se}$

Thermal transmittance U, unit W/m²K [kcal/m²hK], is the reciprocal of the overall resistance 1/U and the most important parameter for the calculation of thermal insulation.

Maximum values are prescribed for various cases.

Energetic values (design values) for individual building products (thermal conductivity λ, thermal resistance **R**) are required for the calculation of the U-values. → ❸ – ❹ show the calculation of thermal transmittance **U** through the example of an external wall with an external wall insulation system and also a pitched roof.

(This building element consists of a rafter component (15%) and an insulated area between the rafters (85%). Thermal resistance **R** in this case is composed of the average of the upper limit value **R**'T and the lower limit value **R**"T. For the determination of **R**'T, the rafter component and the insulation component are added according to area. For the determination of **R**"T, the individual thermal resistances and surface resistances are added.)

BUILDING PHYSICS
Thermal insulation
Sound insulation
Room acoustics
Lightning protection

BS EN ISO 9229
BS EN ISO 13370
BS EN ISO 13790
DIN 4108
DIN EN ISO 6946
DIN EN 12524

EnEV 2007

Air	Dew point temperature at a relative humidity of:										
temperature	35%	40%	45%	50%	55%	**60%**	65%	70%	75%	80%	85%
30°C	12.9	14.9	16.8	18.4	20.0	21.4	22.7	23.9	25.1	26.2	27.2
25°C	8.5	10.5	12.2	13.9	15.3	16.7	18.0	19.1	20.3	21.3	22.3
24°C	7.6	9.6	11.3	12.9	14.4	15.8	17.0	18.2	19.3	20.3	21.3
23°C	6.7	8.7	10.4	12.0	13.5	14.8	16.1	17.2	18.3	19.4	20.3
22°C	5.9	7.8	9.5	11.1	12.5	13.9	15.1	16.3	17.4	18.4	19.4
21°C	5.0	6.9	8.6	10.2	11.6	12.9	14.2	15.3	16.4	17.4	18.4
20°C	4.1	6.0	7.7	9.3	10.7	**12.0**	13.2	14.3	15.4	16.4	17.4
19°C	3.2	5.1	6.8	8.3	9.8	11.1	12.3	13.4	14.5	15.5	16.4
18°C	2.3	4.2	5.9	7.4	8.8	10.1	11.3	12.5	13.5	14.5	15.4
17°C	1.4	3.3	5.0	6.5	7.9	9.2	10.4	11.5	12.5	13.5	14.5
16°C	0.5	2.4	4.1	5.6	7.0	8.2	9.4	10.5	11.6	12.6	13.5
15°C	–0.3	1.5	3.2	4.7	6.1	7.3	8.5	9.6	10.6	11.6	12.5

❶ Dew point temperatures of air, depending on air temperature and relative humidity

Temp. °C	Max. partial vapour pressure of air (kp/m²)
–10	26.9
– 5	40.9
± 0	62.3
+ 5	88.9
+ 10	125.2
+ 15	173.9
+ 20	238.1
+ 25	323.0

❷ Partial vapour pressure of air

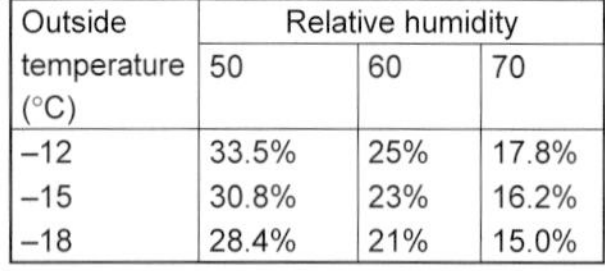

Outside temperature (°C)	Relative humidity 50	60	70
–12	33.5%	25%	17.8%
–15	30.8%	23%	16.2%
–18	28.4%	21%	15.0%

❸ Max. proportion of the surface air film or up to the vapour limit ('X')

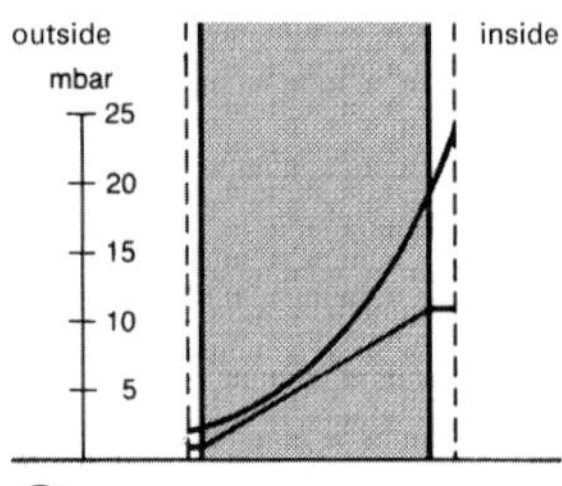

❹ Partial water vapour pressure remains under the maximum possible; no condensation

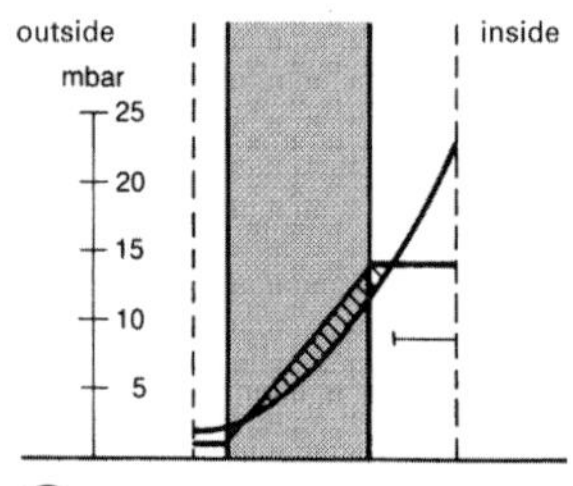

❺ Too great a proportion of surface air film due to too little insulation; condensation at and in building element; X = max. permissible proportion of the surface air film

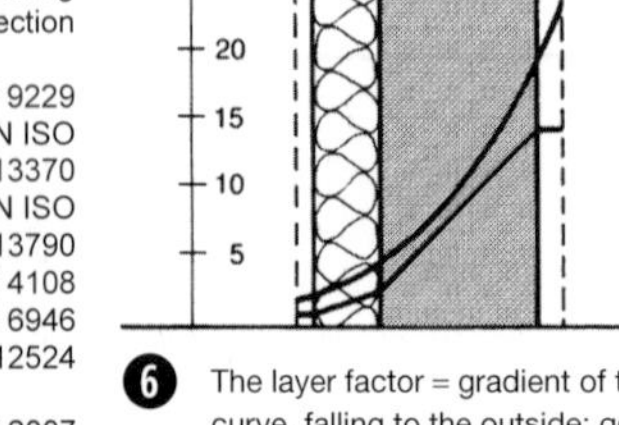

❻ The layer factor = gradient of the curve, falling to the outside: good

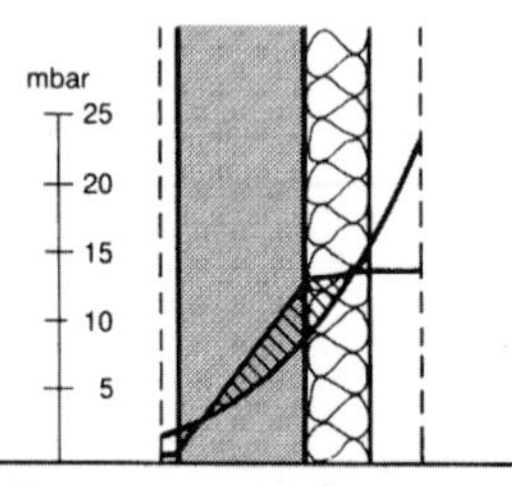

❼ Incorrect sequence of layers: the layer factor = gradient of the curve, uphill to the outside: condensation inside the building element

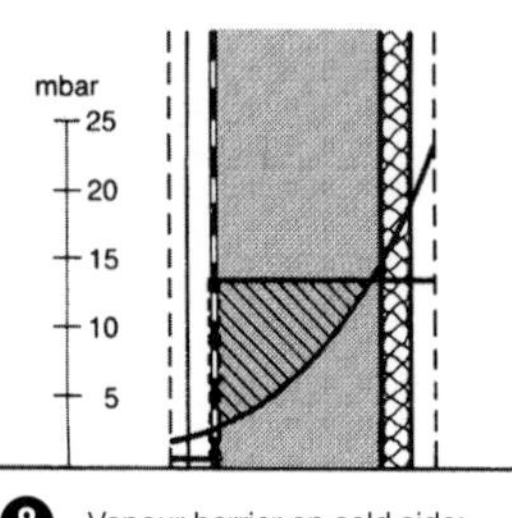

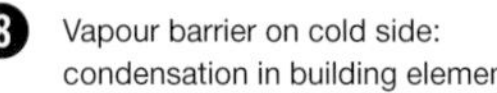

❽ Vapour barrier on cold side: condensation in building element

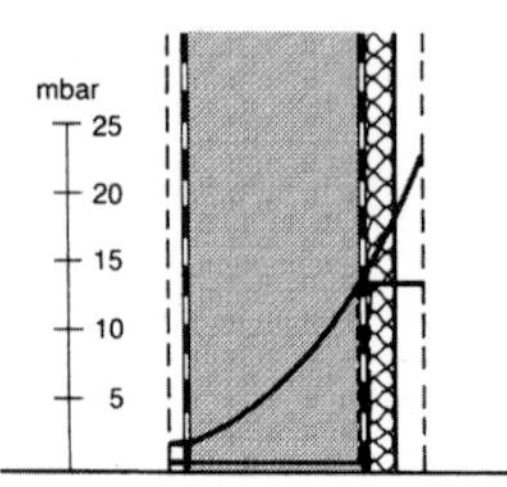

❾ Vapour barrier on warm side prevents formation of condensation

Water vapour diffusion

The air in a room, and also the air in general, contain water in the form of water vapour. The quantity of water in the air, depending on temperature, is called the **relative humidity**. It is important to note that warm air can absorb much more water vapour than cold air. The relative humidity can therefore fluctuate greatly according to the temperature conditions, although the absolute quantity of water remains constant. For the formation of condensation, an important factor is that **the relative air humidity increases with falling temperatures**. In extreme cases, this can be so pronounced that the air is no longer capable of holding the water in the form of vapour and it is then deposited as condensation.

The atmospheric air pressure is 1 bar or 1000 mbar (also called hecto-pascal). In a water vapour–air mixture, part of this pressure (called the **partial water vapour pressure** or partial vapour pressure) is created by water vapour. It is also advantageous to use this value to describe the water vapour content of the air (→ ❷) because this enables considerations about diffusion to be illustrated more clearly (0.6 mbar = 1 g water/kg air). Differences of partial vapour pressure are then only different contents of water vapour molecules at the same overall (air) pressure.
Different partial vapour pressures attempt to equalise through diffusion (by wandering through the building elements and their layers). The layers of the building element oppose this with their **diffusion resistance;** this gives the thickness of the air layer, which would have the same diffusion resistance as the building element; it is calculated as the product of the layer thickness **d** (cm, m) and the material-specific vapour resistivity **m**. Under diffusion, a partial vapour pressure gradient is set up inside the building element; as with the temperature distribution in the building element, this gradient is distributed among the individual layers of the building element according to their proportion of its overall diffusion resistance. The surface air film layers in this case can be neglected on account of their lack of thickness (outside 0.5, inside 2 cm). (Example: inside 20°/50% C = 11.7 mbar, outside –15°/18% = 1.3 mbar, difference 10.4 mbar. **Wall** (24 cm extruded clay block): m × d = 4.5 × 24 = 108 cm. **Internal plaster** (1.0 cm): m × d = 6 × 1.0 = 6 cm. 108 + 6 = 114 cm (100%) (108 cm = 94.7% = 9.8 mbar, 6 cm = 5.3% = 0.6 mbar)

❿ Calculation of partial vapour pressure

Diffusion examples

In order to avoid damage to buildings, condensation in building elements should be avoided.

Condensation occurs where the actual water vapour content threatens to become more than that possible for the temperature. In the examples → ❹ – ❾ the building element including its surface air films is shown to a scale according to its insulation; the curved line is the curve of the maximum possible partial vapour pressure, which is determined by the straight temperature curve.

The following are important to avoid damage:

Sufficient thermal insulation

Example → ❹ shows a single-layer building element without condensation.

But in example → ❺ condensation is formed on the inner face of the building element, because the proportion of the surface air film is too large. The surface air film cannot exceed a certain proportion X of the overall resistance 1/U → ❸.

Correct sequence of layers

The gradient of the diffusion curve should be as steep as possible on the inside and flat on the outside → ❻; otherwise, condensation occurs → ❼. This gradient is given by the layer factor $\mu\lambda$: inside, high water vapour resistance factor, good thermal conductivity = high layer factor $\mu\lambda$: outside, low water vapour resistance factor, low thermal conductivity = low layer factor $\mu\lambda$.

Vapour barrier at the correct location

If there is a vapour barrier on the outside, then the entire vapour pressure gradient occurs there and the result is condensation → ❽; if this is to be avoided, then a vapour barrier must be installed on the warm side with an equivalent diffusion resistance suitable for the location, in which case the layers in front of the vapour barrier must not exceed a certain proportion of the overall thermal resistance **1/U** → ❾.

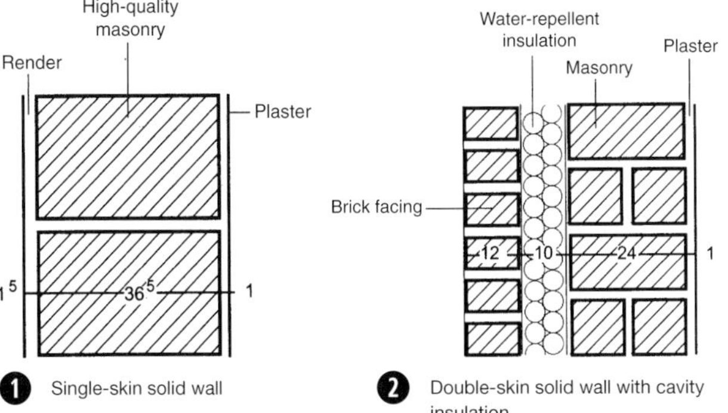

❶ Single-skin solid wall

❷ Double-skin solid wall with cavity insulation

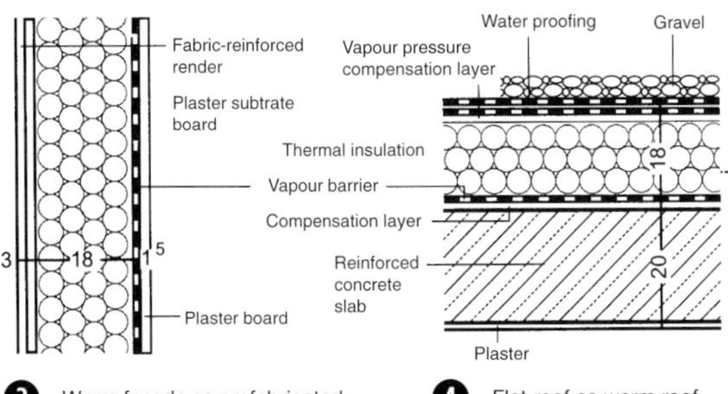

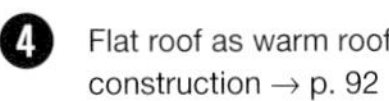

❸ Warm façade as prefabricated construction

❹ Flat roof as warm roof construction → p. 92

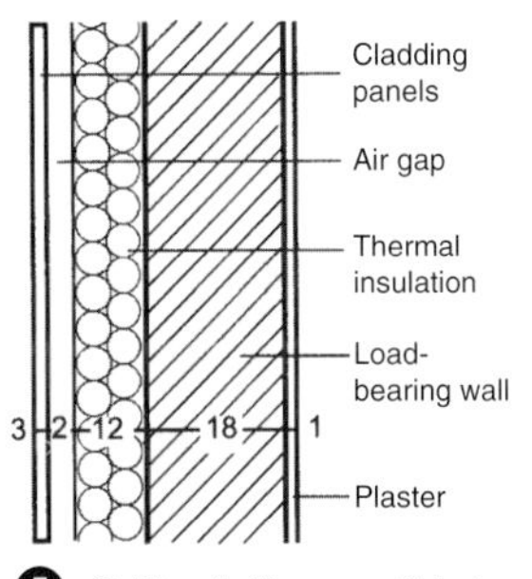

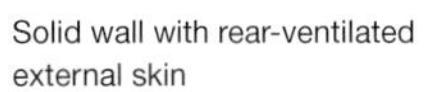

❺ Solid wall with rear-ventilated external skin

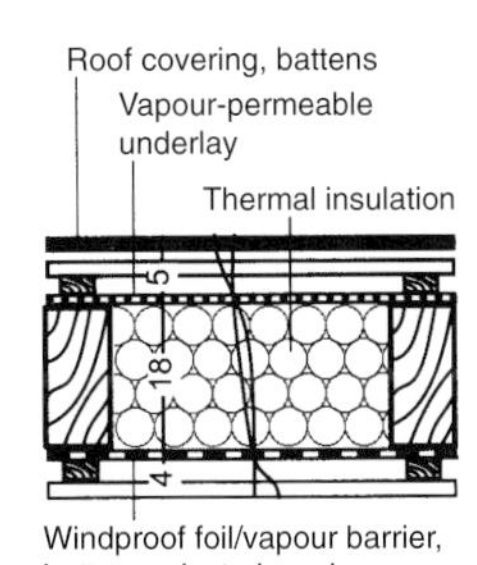

❻ Pitched roof as rear-ventilated construction (cold roof)

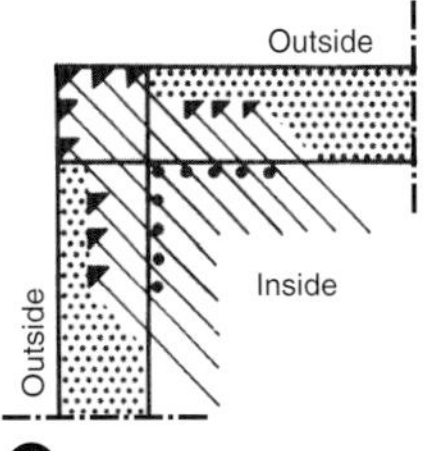

❼ Condensation forms at the internal surface of the external corner

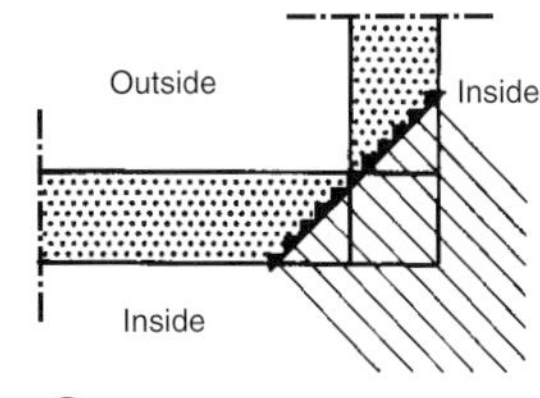

❽ No condensation forms at the internal corner

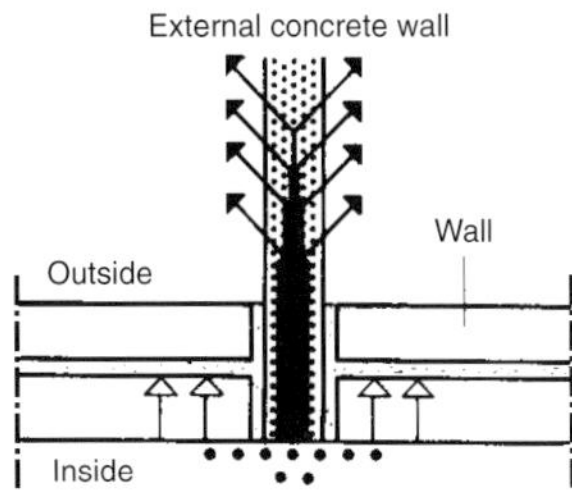

❾ When the external surface area of the thermal bridge is large, condensation is formed (high heat loss per unit of area)

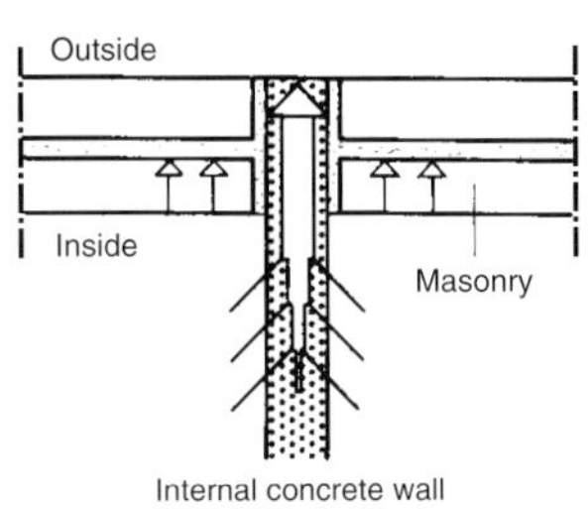

❿ When the internal surface area of the thermal bridge is large, the heat loss per unit area is considerably less

Construction without vapour barrier → ❶ – ❷
The traditional way of building does not use vapour-retarding barriers. The layers are arranged so that no condensation is formed → p. 472. In very damp rooms, the vapour pressure distribution should be checked by calculation. Multi-layered walls are constructed as two layers with cavity insulation or as an external wall insulation system.

On the external side of the insulating layers, there is a risk of cracking due to heat build-up and substrate with poor shear strength, so mineral render reinforced with mesh is used here (or plastic modified render).

Construction with vapour barrier → ❸ – ❹
More recent building ('warm roof', 'warm façade') features an external vapour barrier layer (e.g. waterproofing) and, on account of this, an additional **internal vapour barrier**. In order to prevent condensation on the inside face of the building element, the layers in front of the vapour barrier cannot exceed a certain proportion of the overall thermal resistance → p. 472. Warm façades require careful construction and have therefore mostly become established as prefabricated systems (sandwich construction). In a warm roof, a water vapour pressure equalisation layer is arranged under the waterproofing, and only an **equalisation layer for the damping of stresses** is provided under the vapour barrier.

Construction with rear-ventilated outer skin → ❺ – ❻
The rear ventilation of the skin removes the vapour barrier effect of the relatively vapour-sealed outer layers. The width of the air gap with panel-like external skin amounts to min. 20 mm, or for brickwork outer skin min. 40 mm.

Functional ventilation requires a height difference (minimum fall 10%) between air inlet and outlet.

If there is less fall, then a vapour-retarding/vapour barrier layer is required (arranged as → Construction with vapour barrier, above), because there would otherwise be condensation on the outer skin resulting from excessive vapour transmission. The layers of the inner skin are to be formed as with the construction without vapour barrier and with falling layer factor. The inner skin must nonetheless always be airtight.

Thermal bridge
Thermal bridges are parts of building elements with low thermal insulation compared with surrounding areas. This results in the proportion of the surface air film in the overall resistance increasing so that the surface temperature of the inner side of the thermal bridge sinks and condensation forms.

The **increased heating cost** due to the thermal bridge are often insignificant, as long as it is relatively small, but in order to avoid **condensation** on the inner surface of the building element, with unpleasant results like mould etc., the temperature of the inner surface of the thermal bridge must be improved (e.g. by reducing the cooling effect of the thermal bridge with an insulation layer against the 'external cold', increasing the heat transfer to the thermal bridge by increasing its surface area, high-conducting surroundings for the thermal bridge and/or blowing with warm air).

This means that thermal resistance $\mathbf{R_{si}}$ is reduced in relation to the thermal bridge and thus also the proportion of the surface air film in the overall resistance **1/U** → p. 471.

Typical examples of thermal bridges are shown in → ❾ – ❿. However, even a normal external corner in a building → ❼ forms a thermal bridge, because a smaller internal surface introduces heat opposite a larger external surface, which loses heat. In addition, the surface resistance of the surface air film in the corners is considerably higher than between the corners.

BUILDING PHYSICS
Thermal insulation
Sound insulation
Room acoustics
Lightning protection

BS EN ISO 9229
BS EN ISO 13370
BS EN ISO 13790
DIN 1053
DIN 4108
DIN EN ISO 6946
DIN EN 12524

EnEV 20077

Building services

BUILDING PHYSICS
Thermal insulation
Sound insulation
Room acoustics
Lightning protection

BS EN ISO 9229
BS EN ISO 13370
BS EN ISO 13790
DIN EN 832
DIN 4108
DIN EN 12524
DIN V 18599

EnEV 2007

Building services

Energy Saving Regulation

The Energy Saving Regulation 2007 (**EnEV 2007**) replaces the formerly applicable energy saving regulations 2002/2004. The limit values for residential buildings have not been altered. For non-residential buildings, however, a new verification process is now required. In addition to thermal insulation regulations, subsidiary measures like, for example, those concerning condensing boilers, are required, as already in EnEV 2002/2004.

Under EnEV 2007, a new overall consideration of the energy required for heating, hot water, ventilation, cooling and lighting (only for non-residential buildings) is to be produced.

The energy consumption necessary to heat rooms will no longer be the regulated parameter, but the quantity of primary energy to be used for heating, hot water etc. under standard conditions.

Excerpts from the Energy Saving Regulation, using the example of a new residential building:

Normally heated houses are to be evaluated according to whether they adequately limit the annual primary energy demand and the transmitted heat requirement in accordance with the new EnEV 2007.

Depending on the ratio of **heat-transmitting area A to heated building volumes V_e (A/V_e ratio)**, the maximum permissible annual primary energy demand will be determined according to EnEV 2007, according to the **envelope area process**. The basis for this is the monthly balance procedure (DIN EN 832) with the conditions given in DIN 4108.

For the **thermal insulation design of stairwells,** a temperature of ≧15°C can be assumed in accordance with the design. This temperature may have to be ensured by the provision of radiators in the lower stairwell.

Design values of building products

For the determination of U-values in the verification of thermal insulation, the **energetic characteristics** are required for each building product. These are called the **design values** of the thermal conductivity and the thermal resistance of the materials and components, and also the design values of the thermal transmittance coefficients of glazing, windows and French windows, including frames. The design values can be taken from the tables in DIN EN 12524.

Some important building products, like thermal insulation and masonry components, are, however, not included in this standard. For these items, the design values are to be determined from the **nominal value** in DIN V 4108-4 or from **type approvals** under building regulations or other guidelines.

The nominal value for a product is multiplied by conversion values for temperature, moisture and ageing to give the design values. The nominal values for the thermal conductivity of thermal insulation materials are also to be subjected to a partial safety factor of $\gamma = 1.2$, which has been laid down by the responsible standards committee. According to harmonised European standards, this should apply to all insulation materials, which carry a CE mark. DIN V 4108-4 deals, in tabular form, with the conversion into the design value for all common building products.

In a similar way, the above two standards are to be used for the determination of the required energetic characteristics for the calculation of thermal insulation according to EnEV 2007.

Heating system and drinking water heating

The heating system and drinking water heating are to be constructed in accordance with the requirements of EnEV 2007.

Sun protection

According to EnEV 2007, protection from summer heat is to be verified independent of the proportion of the building's surface taken by the window area following DIN 4102-2. This states that summer heat protection depends on the **climatic region** and **sun input factor S** of the transparent external building elements.

The verification of thermal protection in summer depends on the following factors, among others: Overall degree of energy transmission of the glazing, window inclination and orientation, frame as proportion of the windows, effectiveness of the sun protection apparatus, proportion of window area in the façade (related to rooms), climatic region (building location), light or heavy construction (effective thermal capacity). These factors are collected into a maximum permissible sun input factor S_{max}, which may not be exceeded by the room-related sun input factor S.

Wind and airtightness

EnEV 2007 states that new buildings are to be constructed so that the heat-transmitting surface envelope, including joints, is sealed **permanently airtight** in accord with the state of the technology.

This means that air infiltration at the joints of the external windows, French windows and roof windows must be compliant. As part of the EnEV 2007 stipulations, when using **mechanical ventilation systems** the inclusion in calculations of **heat recovery** or a controlled **reduced rate of air changes** is permissible only if the airtightness of the building is verified. Ventilation systems must also be equipped with means for the user to influence the airflow volume per unit of use. It must be ensured that the heat recovered from the extract air is used before the heat provided by the heating system. In closed condition, there must be compliance with EnEV requirements. A test of airtightness (blower door test) can be taken into account in the calculation of the annual primary energy demand for the verification of thermal insulation.

Thermal bridges

Good thermal insulation includes not only highly insulated building components, but also the appropriate connections between the building elements. There is a danger of additional heat loss at these joints and low surface temperature in the building elements during the heating period. **Additional consumption of energy** for heating and the possibility of condensation and mould formation are the result. Thus it should be borne in mind that this thermal bridging effect can have considerably worse consequences with highly insulated elements than with building elements with less thermal insulation. Thermal bridges can be considered, according to EnEV, for the determination of the annual heating energy demand by increasing the thermal transmission values (U-values) or in a separate verification.

heated volume	Va:	**535.86 m³**						
usable building area	AN = 0.32*Va:	**171 m²**						
Building element	**Description**	**Area**	**Thermal transmittance U**	**Temperature correction factor**			**Heat loss**	**Unit**
		m²			FX			
external wall		147.35	0.24		1.00		35.364	W/K
dormer wall	east/west	0.00	0.17		1.00		0.000	W/K
windows	north	9.41	0.80		1.00		7.528	W/K
	east/west	7.01	0.80		1.00		5.608	W/K
	south	8.50	0.80		1.00		6.800	W/K
	roof	3.28	0.80		1.00		2.624	W/K
front door	north	3.50	1.40		1.00		4.900	W/K
roof pitch	to outside air	159.78	0.13		1.00		20.771	W/K
floors	to insulated roof space	0.00	0.19		0.50		0.000	W/K
floor slab	to ground	154.95	0.19		0.50		14.720	W/K
	sum :	**493.78**		**sum A*U*F**			98.316	W/K
thermal bridge supplement				H_{WB}				W/K
transmission heat loss H_T				sum A*U*F+H_{WB}			98.316	W/K
air volume V	building up to 3 full storeys			0.76 V_e			407.253	m³
	building over 3 full storeys			0.80*V_e				m³
ventilation heat loss Hv		airtightness $n_{50} > 3.0\ h^{-1}$		0.70*0.34*V_e				W/K
		airtightness $n_{50} < 3.0\ h^{-1}$		0.60*0.34*V_e			109.314	W/K
envelope area factor				A/V_e			0.922	m^{-1}
solar heat gain of transparent building elements	element	area	overall degree of energy transmittance g	F_F	F_S	F_C	specific gain A*g*0.9*F_F*F_S*F_C	
	windows north	9.41	0.53	0.70	0.90	1.00	2.83	
	windows east/west	7.01	0.53	0.70	0.90	1.00	2.11	
	windows south	8.50	0.53	0.70	0.90	1.00	2.55	
	front door	3.50	0.80	0.70	0.90	1.00	1.59	
solar gain of opaque building elements			degree of absorption a	form factor F_t				
	external walls		0.50	0.50				
	roof pitch		0.80	1.00				
internal heat gain specific thermal mass Cwirk*Ve	surface-specific solid construction			5 W/m² 50 Wh/m³K*V_e			855.00 26793.00	W Wh
	light construction			15 Wh/m³K*V_e				
annual heating energy demand	absolute			Qh = Q_t+Q_v–Q_g			5597.00	kWh/a
	specific			Q'_h			33.11	kWh/m²a
plant input number eP				e_P			1.29	
primary energy demand Q'P		existing	Q_P exstg. = ep*(Q"h + 12.5)				58.94	kWh/m²a
		permissible	Q"p perm. = 50.94 + 75.29*A/V_e + 2600/(100 + AN)				116.52	kWh/m²a
specific transmission heat loss related to envelope area H'T		existing	H/T exstg. = HT/A				0.24	W/m²K
		permissible	H'T perm. = 0.3 + 0.15/(A/V_e)				0.77	W/m²K
final energy demand		heating	gas/oil/electricity	q WE,E			51.80	kWh/m²a
		operating energy	electricity	q HE,E			2.30	kWh/m²a

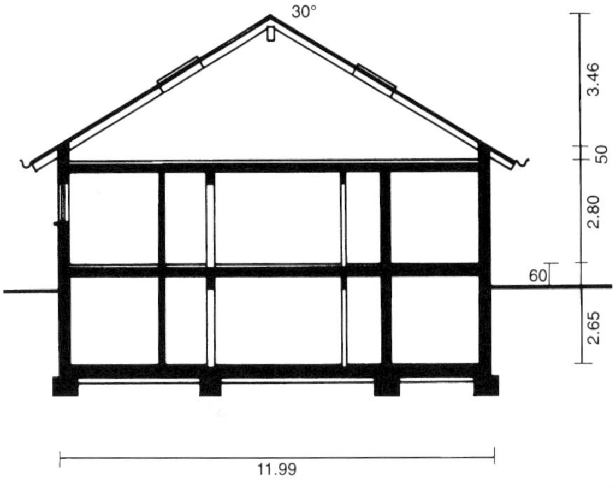

Cross-section a-a

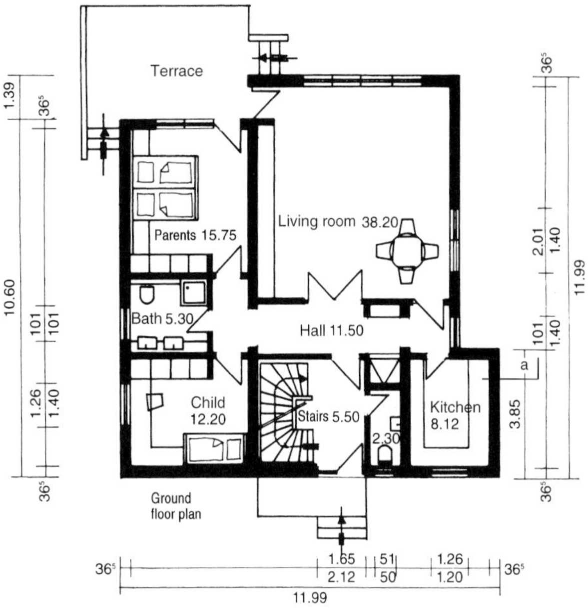

Ground floor plan

❶ Calculation example: determination of the annual primary energy demand of a property, EnEV 2007

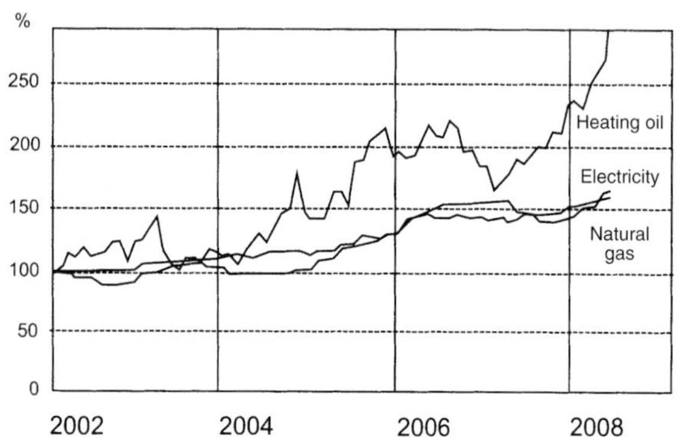

❶ Average development of producer energy prices (Federal Statistics Office → refs)

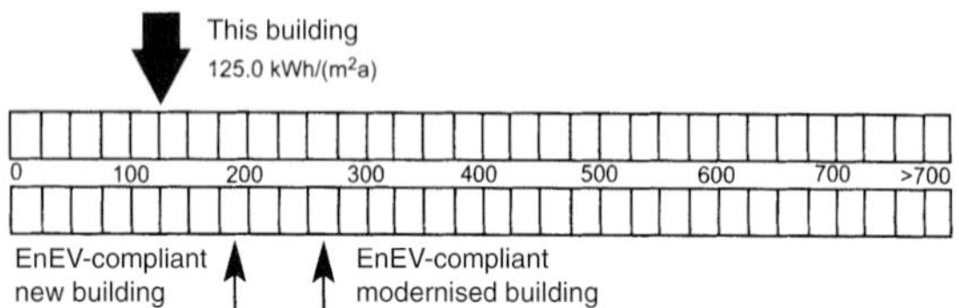

❷ Graphic comparison of annual energy demand of building with average similar building (example)

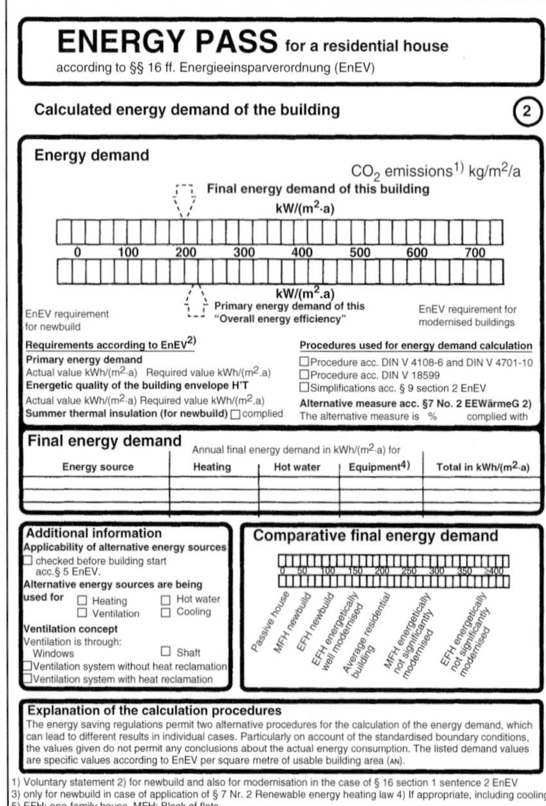

ENERGY PASS for a residential house
according to §§ 16 ff. Energieeinsparverordnung (EnEV)

Calculated energy demand of the building (2)

Energy demand

CO_2 emissions[1)] kg/m²/a

Final energy demand of this building kW/(m²·a)

0 100 200 300 400 500 600 700

kW/(m².a)

Primary energy demand of this "Overall energy efficiency"

EnEV requirement for newbuild

EnEV requirement for modernised buildings

Requirements according to EnEV[2)]
Primary energy demand
Actual value kWh/(m²·a) Required value kWh/(m².a)
Energetic quality of the building envelope H'T
Actual value kWh/(m²·a) Required value kWh/(m².a)
Summer thermal insulation (for newbuild) ☐ complied

Procedures used for energy demand calculation
☐ Procedure acc. DIN V 4108-6 and DIN V 4701-10
☐ Procedure acc. DIN V 18599
☐ Simplifications acc. § 9 section 2 EnEV
Alternative measure acc. §7 No. 2 EEWärmeG 2)
The alternative measure is % complied with

Final energy demand

Energy source	Heating	Hot water	Equipment[4)]	Total in kWh/(m²·a)
	Annual final energy demand in kWh/(m²·a) for			

Additional information
Applicability of alternative energy sources
☐ checked before building start acc.§ 5 EnEV.
Alternative energy sources are being used for ☐ Heating ☐ Hot water ☐ Ventilation ☐ Cooling
Ventilation concept
Ventilation is through:
Windows ☐ Shaft
☐ Ventilation system without heat reclamation
☐ Ventilation system with heat reclamation

Comparative final energy demand

0 50 100 150 200 250 300 350 >400

Passive house
MFH newbuild
EFH newbuild
EFH energetically well modernised
Average residential building
MFH energetically not significantly modernised
EFH energetically not significantly modernised

Explanation of the calculation procedures
The energy saving regulations permit two alternative procedures for the calculation of the energy demand, which can lead to different results in individual cases. Particularly on account of the standardised boundary conditions, the values given do not permit any conclusions about the actual energy consumption. The listed demand values are specific values according to EnEV per square metre of usable building area (AN).

1) Voluntary statement 2) for newbuild and also for modernisation in the case of § 16 section 1 sentence 2 EnEV
3) only for newbuild in case of application of § 7 Nr. 2 Renewable energy heating law 4) If appropriate, including cooling
5) EFH: one-family house, MFH: Block of flats

❸ Sample of an energy pass for residential building with graphic presentation of energy demand and comparative values (excerpt) (EnEV → refs)

BS EN ISO 9229
BS EN ISO 13370
BS EN ISO 13790
DIN EN 832
DIN 4108
DIN EN 12524
DIN V 18599
EnEV 2007

Energy pass
According to the Energy Saving Regulation (**EnEV),** an energy pass must be issued within a specified period (and with certain limitations), for new buildings and for structural alterations, in connection with which energetic calculations are carried out for the entire building. Normally this also applies to existing buildings that are for sale or a new let (there are exceptions, e.g. listed buildings!).

The energy pass documents the energy demand or consumption of a building and, with a graphic evaluation (see → ❷), provides a simple comparison with an average similar building

The procedure for the determination of the energy figures in the energy pass is laid down by EnEV : **energy demand** is presented as annual primary energy demand and final energy demand, and **energy consumption** as the energy consumption value.

Primary energy demand shows the overall energy efficiency of the building. It also takes into account, besides the final energy, the supply chain (e.g. investigation, extraction, distribution, conversion) of the energy source being exploited. Low values point to a low demand and thus to high energy efficiency and energy use which is light on resources and the environment.

Final energy demand is the annual energy requirement for heating, ventilation and hot water (in non-residential buildings also for cooling and lighting) according to the technical rules and is a measure of the energy efficiency of the building and its facilities' technology. Low values signal a low demand and thus high energy efficiency.

These figures are calculated on the basis of construction and other building-related documents and assume standardised conditions (e.g. climatic data, user behaviour, indoor temperature). In this way, the energetic quality of a building should be documented independent of the user behaviour and weather situation, but the calculated values permit no forecast of the actual energy consumption on account of the standardised conditions.

The **energy consumption value** is determined for the building based on the heating and hot water cost invoicing. Climatic factors are applied to the recorded energy consumption for heating to convert this to an average value for Germany. The energy consumption value does give an indication of the energetic quality of the building and its heating system, but there can be clear deviations on account of the differing heating and ventilation behaviours of the users.

EnEV 2007 contains in its annexes samples of energy passes for residential and non-residential buildings → ❸. Energy passes also have to be displayed for public buildings $>$ 1000 m². They are issued by qualified neutral building experts and are valid for 10 years.

If measures are possible for the sensible improvement of a building's energetic properties, these are appended to the energy pass as a modernisation recommendation. The energy pass brings advantages when marketing a building, offers a spur to investment and provides additional certainty for decisions about buying or renting.

❶ Relationship between sound intensity (phon), sound pressure (μb), sound level (dB) and sound intensity (μW/cm²)

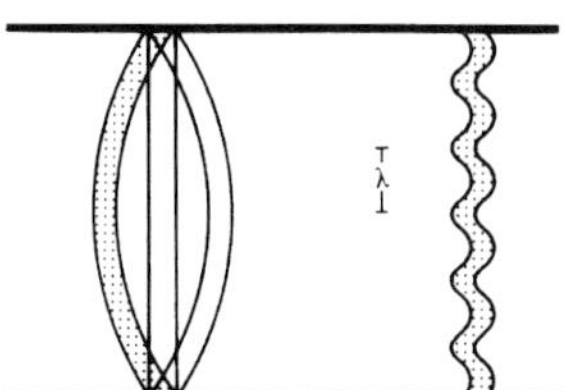

❷ Illustration of a bending wave on a wall at normal frequencies: the wall (left) does not vibrate as a whole, but (right) its parts vibrate against each other

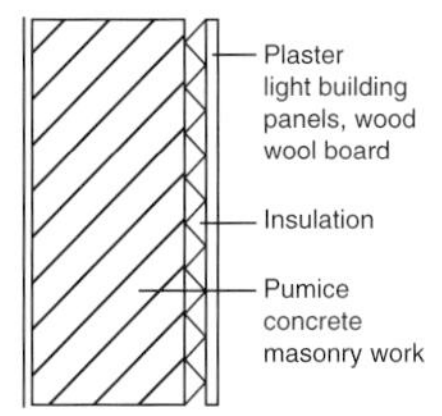

❸ Improvement in sound insulation up to +7 dB with free-standing soft cladding and cavity filling

0–10	start of hearing perception
20	light rustling of leaves
30	lower limit of everyday residential noise
40	medium residential noise, quiet conversation, quiet residential street
50	normal conversation, radio music at room volume in closed rooms, city noise without individual noises
60	noise from a relatively quiet vacuum cleaner, normal street noise in commercial streets
70	single typewriter, telephone ringing at 1 m distance
80	street with heavy traffic, typing pool
90	loud factory interior
100	car horn at 7 m distance, motorcycle
100–130	very noisy industrial works (metalworking etc.)

❹ Scale of sound intensities, values in dB(A)

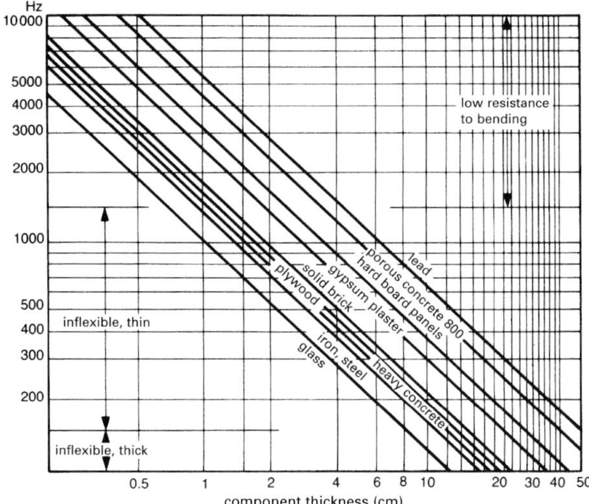

❺ Boundary frequency for panels of various materials

Sound

Sound propagates as mechanical vibrations and pressure waves, which cause very small increases or reductions of pressure, measurable in microbars (μb), compared to atmospheric pressure (= 1.0333 kg/cm²). For example, the pressure variation when speaking with a raised voice is about a millionth of an atmosphere.

Audible sound vibrations lie in a frequency range of **20–20000 Hz (hertz);** 1 Hz = 1 vibration/second (for **sound insulation in building,** the range between **100 and 3200 Hz** is of significance, as this is where the human ear is particularly sensitive). Sound pressures within the range of human hearing vary from the audibility threshold to the pain threshold → ❶. This range is divided into 12 parts = **12 B (bel)** (named after Alexander Graham Bell, inventor of the telephone). As 1/10 bel = **1 decibel (dB)** is just audible to the human ear as a pressure difference at the standard frequency of 1000 Hz, decibels are used as the physical measure of sound intensity related to an area unit → ❶. Sound levels are normally given in dB (A) or, above 60 dB, in dB (B), a measure roughly equivalent to the former phon.

Sound reduction

Sound reduction denotes all measures undertaken to reduce sound transmission from the source to the hearer; it is not possible to entirely prevent transmission. If the sound source and the hearer are in one room, this is done by sound absorption; if they are in different rooms, it is mainly achieved with **sound insulation.** Sound reduction measures are differentiated according to the source of the noise into **airborne sound** (if the sound source agitates the surrounding air), **structure-borne sound** (when the sound source agitates a building element) and **impact sound** (structure-borne sound typically caused by footsteps on a floor or stairs).

The measurement of airborne sound is normally given as the weighted sound reduction R'_{w}, i.e. the difference in sound level between the room containing the source (loud room) and the receiving room (quiet room), taking into account bypass transmission through flanking building elements. For impact sound, the analogous parameter to be determined is the weighted impact sound level $L'_{n,w}$.

The sound is transmitted through air as a longitudinal wave and in solid materials as a bending wave → ❷. The transmission speed of a longitudinal wave is 340 m/s, that of a bending wave varies according to material, layer thickness and frequency.

The **boundary frequency** is that at which the transmission speed of the bending wave in a building element is also 340 m/s; at this frequency, the transfer of sound out of the air into the building element and vice versa is particularly good and thus the sound insulation of the element particularly bad, worse than would be expected for the wall density. For heavy elements, which bend stiffly, the boundary frequency is above, and for thin, soft materials is below, the relevant frequency range → ❺.

Generally **sound insulation is produced by mass**, and works better with heavy, thick building elements where the sound energy first has to transfer from air into the element, then excites the mass of the element and then repeatedly transfers from the material into the air, which all cause a reduction in sound. If, however, the building element is directly excited (impact sound), then the insulation is naturally less effective.

Sound-insulating lightweight construction in the form of cladding layers, which bend flexibly, and with the cavity filled to prevent the internal reflection of the sound, makes use of the repeated transfers air–element–air–element → ❸.

resistant to excitation

sound radiation

main path

secondary path

❶ Airborne sound transmission

dB 70 60 50 40 30

standard impact sound level (dB)

100 200 400 800 1600 3200

frequency (Hz)

❷ Standard curve for airborne sound

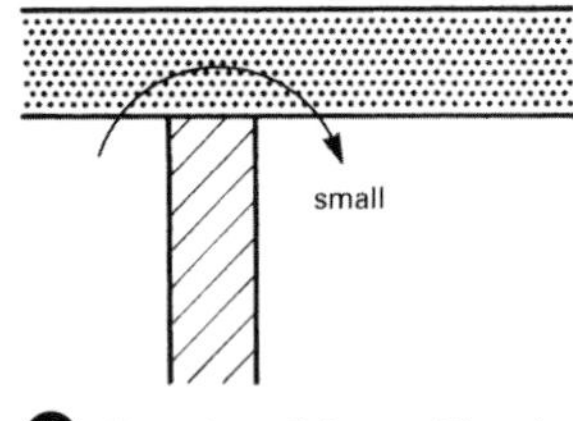

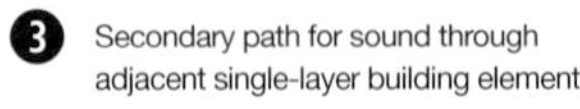

❸ Secondary path for sound through adjacent single-layer building element

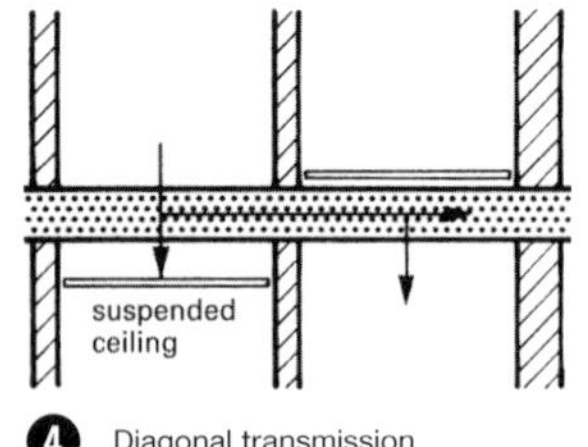

❹ Diagonal transmission

1	simple door with threshold, without special sealing	up to 20 dB
2	heavy door, with threshold and good sealing	up to 30 dB
3	double doors with threshold, without special sealing, opening individually	up to 40 dB
4	heavy double doors, with threshold and good sealing	up to 50 dB
5	door with sound insulation	up to 15 dB
6	simple window, without additional sealing	up to 25 dB
7	simple window, with good sealing	up to 25 dB
8	double window, without special sealing	up to 30 dB
9	double window, with good sealing	up to 32 dB
10	double glazing 4/12–16/4 mm	up to 32 dB

❺ Sound insulation of doors and windows

BUILDING PHYSICS

Thermal insulation

Sound insulation

Room acoustics

Lightning protection

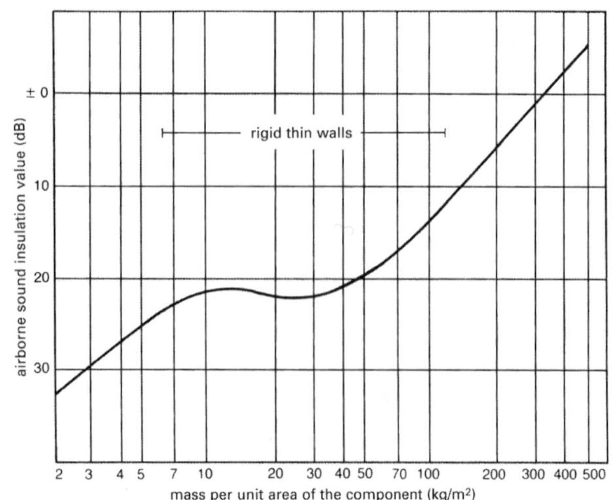

❻ Airborne sound insulation, weight per area and component thickness (Gösele)

With **airborne sound,** the sound wave excites the building element → ❶, so the influence of the boundary frequency on the sound insulation increases → ❻. DIN 4109 lays down values for the sound insulation required to prevent sound transmission from neighbouring homes or workplaces (weighted building sound reduction including 'secondary path' transmission R'_{w}) → ❼.

Secondary path transmission reduces the effectiveness of airborne sound insulation more than that of impact sound insulation. For this reason, test certificates for sound-insulated walls should always include the consideration of secondary paths normal in a building. Particularly effective as secondary paths are panels which bend stiffly and have a density of 10–160 kg/m^2; for this reason, party walls between flats or houses should always weigh at least 400 kg/m^2.

Doors and windows with their low sound insulation values → ❺ have a particularly negative influence on airborne sound insulation. Even if their proportion of the wall area is small, the resulting sound insulation value is mostly less than the arithmetic mean of insulation values of wall and opening, which makes the sound insulation of the door or window always the first priority.

Walls with insufficient sound insulation can be improved with an insulating layer → p. 477 ❸. These have particularly good sound insulation if they bend flexibly and are supported by soft springy insulation (cavity filling).

Soft, flexible cladding layers are relatively insensitive to small sound bridges (in contrast to hard cladding layers).

Only type-tested construction systems should be used for sound insulation cladding.

Layers of plaster on insulating materials of normal hardness (e.g. on normal Styrofoam) reduce the sound insulation considerably.

Building element	Airborne sound insulation R'_{w} [dB]	Impact sound insulation $L'_{n,w}$ [dB]
Multi-storey buildings with residential and working areas		
residential units, party walls	53	
walls between common hallways and stairwells	52	
floor slabs and stairs separating residential units	54	53
floor slabs over cellars, common hallways and stair spaces	52	53
stair flights and landings		58
doors from stairwells into flat corridors	27	
Schools and educational institutions		
walls between classrooms and stairwells	47	
floor slabs between classrooms	55	53
doors from classrooms into corridors	53	
Accommodation, hospitals, sanatoriums		
walls of bedrooms, patient rooms and examination rooms	47	
floor slabs in general	54	53
stair flights and landings		58
doors to examination and consulting rooms	37	

The values given for the **sound insulation** of the partitioning elements count as the **resulting insulation** of all building materials involved in sound transmission and of secondary paths in the installed condition.

The values for doors apply solely to transmission through the door.

❼ Protection of occupied rooms against sound transmission from neighbouring residential and working areas (minimum requirements, excerpt → refs)

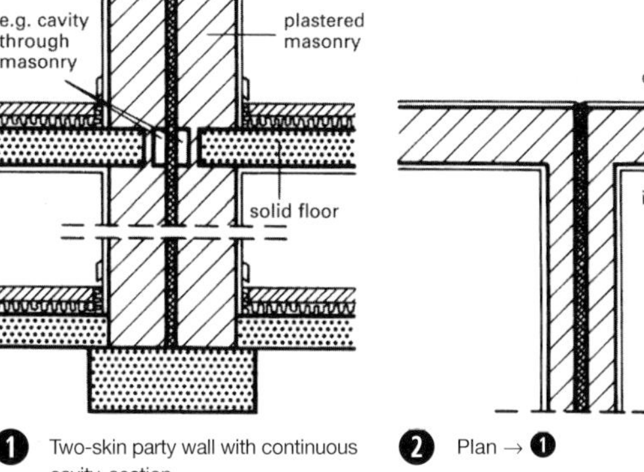

1 Two-skin party wall with continuous cavity, section

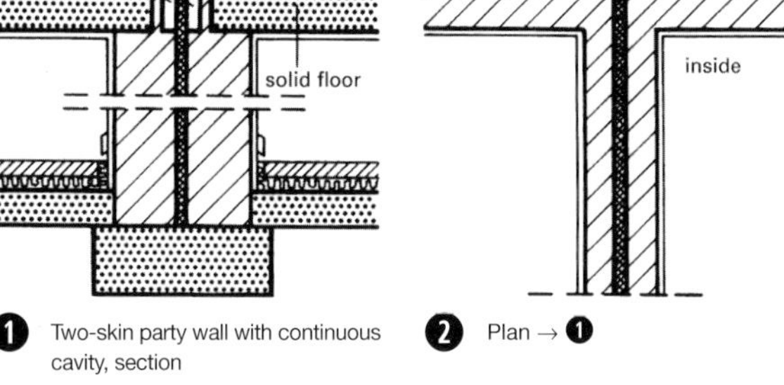

2 Plan → 1

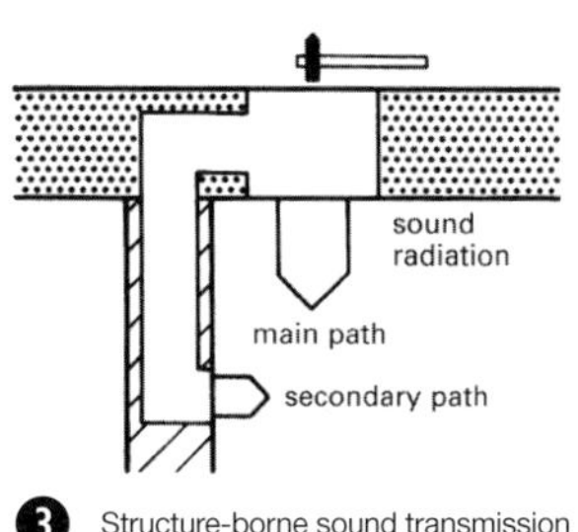

3 Structure-borne sound transmission

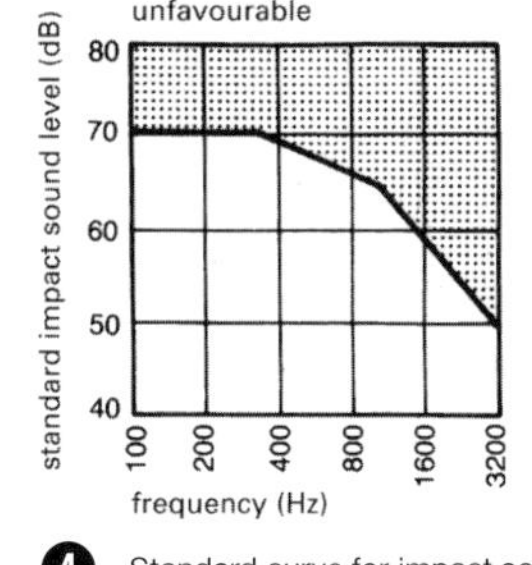

4 Standard curve for impact sound

Party walls

The diagram → 1 shows a two-skin party wall with a separating joint over the entire depth of the houses. The **mass per unit area** of the individual layers with plaster must be **at least 150 kg/m^2**, and the thickness of the separating joint must be at least **30 mm**. With a thickness of the separating joint (layer spacing) of more than 50 mm, the mass of each skin can be 100 kg/m^2. The **joint cavity** is to be filled with gapless full-surface fibre insulating boards, as in DIN 18165 (impact sound insulation boards or separating joint boards approved for this application) without sound bridges.

If the **skins** are constructed of **in situ concrete,** mineral fibre insulating boards with particular suitability for the high loadings during concreting are to be used. If the single skins have a weight per unit area of **more than 200 kg/m^2** and the separating joint has a thickness of **more than 30 mm,** no insulation boards have to be installed as long as suitable construction measures are taken to avoid sound bridges (e.g. through timber guides removed after the wall has been built).

For cavity walls, the **weighted sound reduction $R'_{w,R}$** can be determined from the sum of the weights per unit area of the single skins. The continuous separating joint without sound bridges can then be assumed to be 12 dB better for the two-skin wall construction.

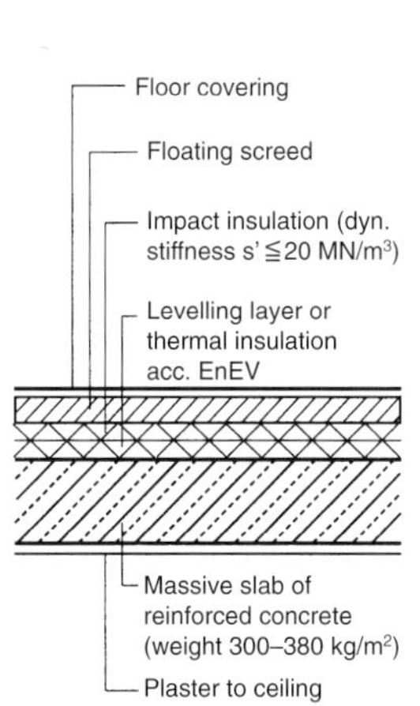

5 Solid slab with floating screed (R'_w 55–57 dB, $L'_{n,w}$ approx. 50 dB) → p. 478 7

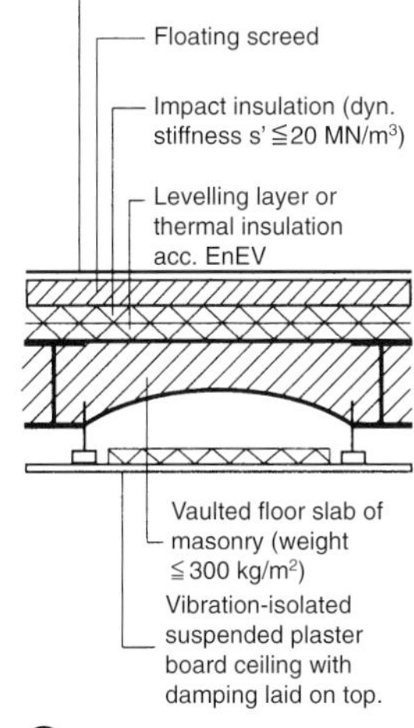

6 Vaulted floor with improved sound insulation (R'_w approx. 58 dB, $L'_{n,w}$ approx. 47 dB) → p. 478 7

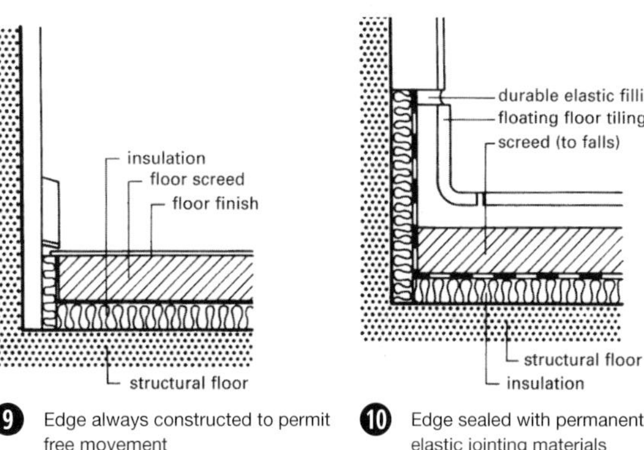

9 Edge always constructed to permit free movement

10 Edge sealed with permanently elastic jointing materials

Impact sound insulation

Impact sound is caused by the floor slab being directly excited to vibration. The standard curve → 4 gives a **standard level of impact sound**, i.e. the maximum level that can be heard in the room below, when a standardised 'stamper' is at work above. The values immediately after completion must be 3 dB, better to allow for the effect of ageing. The normal form of impact sound insulation is a **floating screed** consisting of a gapless soft springy **insulation layer** covered with a **protecting layer**. The actual screed layer can be of cement screed, anhydrite or poured asphalt (thickness laid down in DIN 4109). The floating screed also provides the required protection against airborne sound and is permissible for all types of floor slab (slab groups I and II). The **edge** is always to be constructed to permit free movement → 9 and can only be sealed with permanently elastic jointing materials → 10, because the screed layer is prone to bending and is therefore extremely susceptible to sound bridging. When slabs are used which provide adequate insulation against airborne sound (slab groups I and II), the sound insulation can be provided by a soft springy floor covering. Slabs in slab class I can become class II through a suspended soft ceiling. The measurement unit of the improvement of impact sound insulation through floating screed or soft springy floor covering is called the impact sound reduction (dB).

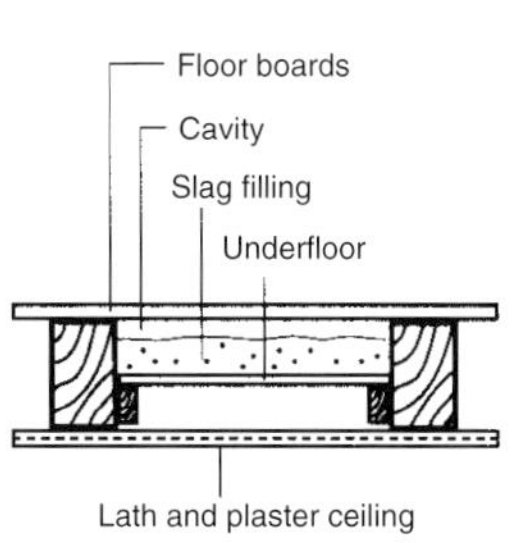

7 Conventional timber joist floor in existing building (R'_w approx. 45 dB, $L'_{n,w}$ approx. 66 dB) → p. 478 7

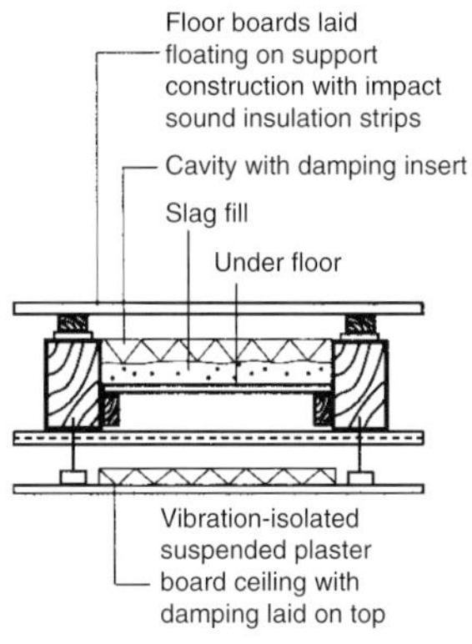

8 Timber joist floor with improved sound insulation (R'_w approx. 54 dB, $L'_{n,w}$ approx. 50 dB) → p. 478 7

BS 8233
BS EN ISO 717
DIN 4109
DIN 18165

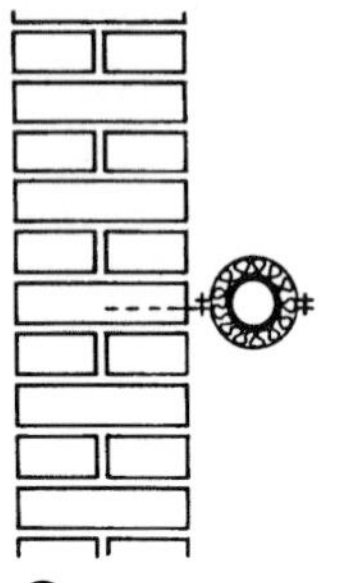

❶ Sound-insulated pipe clip

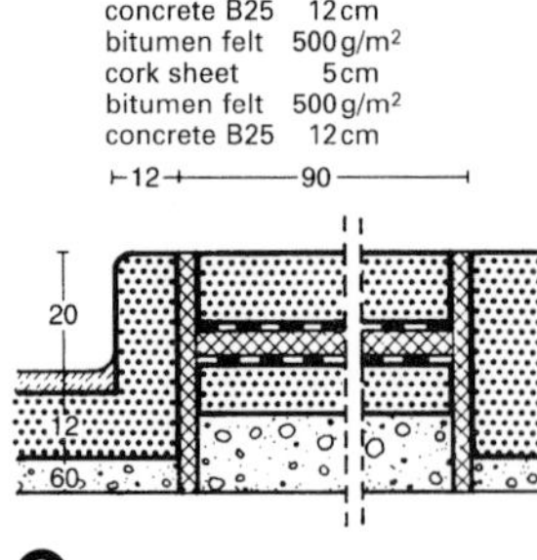

❷ Sound-insulated boiler foundation 90 cm wide

A = sound insulating material, e.g. rubber
B = air space – if necessary, filled with sound insulating material

❸ Metal/rubber element

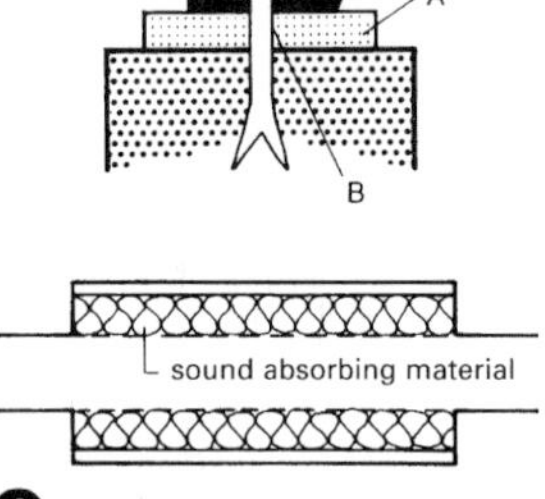

❹ Ventilation duct fitted with sound-absorbing material (silencer)

❺ Sound absorption measures can reduce the level of reflected sound; this makes the echo radius larger, and at the same time the sound level within the previous echo radius drops

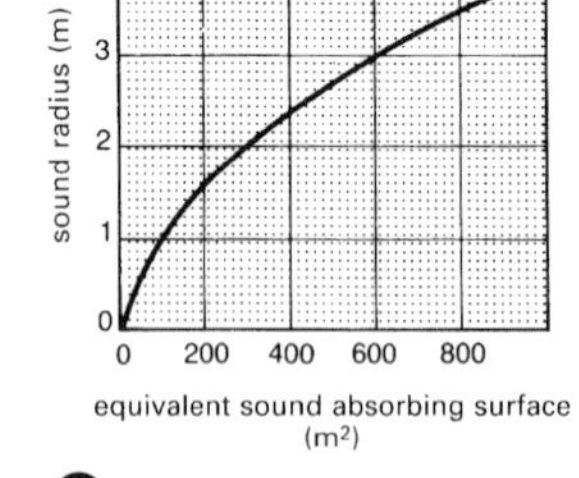

❻ Echo radius and sound absorbing capacity of a room

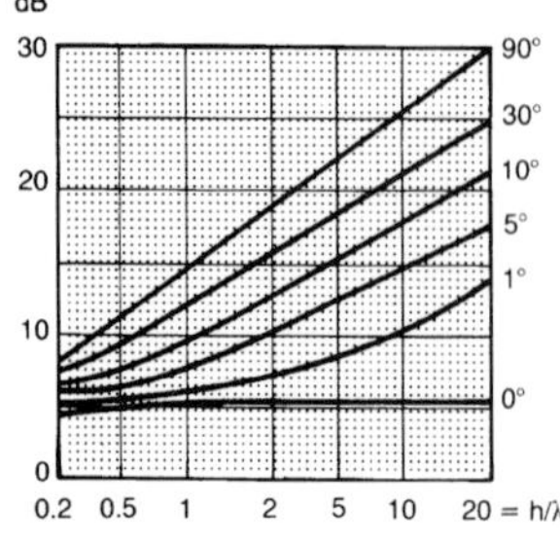

❼ Sound reduction effect of open-air obstructions (A.I. King); the y axis shows the sound reduction according to angle a → ❽; example: a = 30°, h = 2.50 m: at 500 Hz (medium range frequency) wavelength λ = 340/500 = 0.68 h/λ = 2.5/0.68 = 3.68, sound reduction = 17 dB

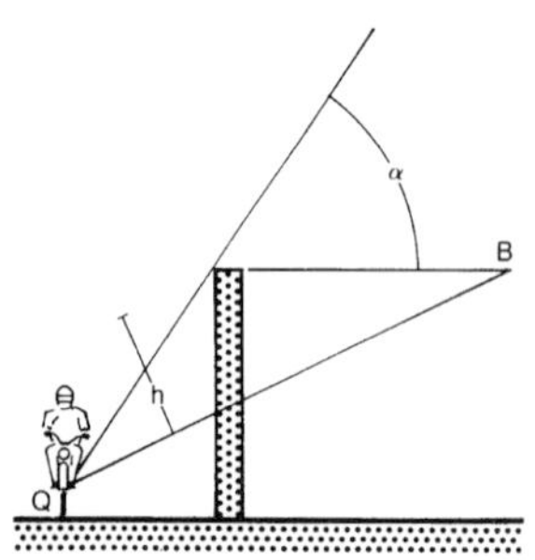

❽ Diagram showing dimensions → ❼
Q = sound source
B = hearer

Sound from services

Sound from services can occur as **plumbing fixture sound, pipework sound** or **filling/emptying sounds**. The **maximum permissible sound level** from services in neighbouring residential units is 35 dB (A). Noisy elements of services (water pipes, waste pipes, gas riser pipes, waste disposal units, lifts) may not be installed in the walls of rooms where quiet is required (living rooms, bedrooms).

Plumbing fixture sounds can be reduced through the specification of sound-insulated valves with test certificate. Test group I with ≦20 dB (A) fixture sound level is approved for anywhere; test group II with ≦30 dB (A) fixture sound level is approved only for internal house walls and for walls adjoining services rooms. Installing sound dampers can achieve additional improvement in all fixtures. **Pipework sounds** are caused by the formation of vortices in the pipework. Remediation is possible through the specification of bends instead of sharp angles, adequate dimensioning and sound-insulated fixtures → ❶.

Filling sounds are caused by water pouring into bathtubs etc.; improvement is possible by muffling the objects, fitting aerators on the taps or sound-insulating the feet of the bath (in which case the edge has to be permanently elastically sealed). **Emptying sounds** (gurgling) can be prevented by proper sizing and ventilation of drainpipes. **Heating boilers** can be sound-insulated by supporting them on insulated supports (isolated foundation → ❷), sound-absorbing boiler base, sound-dampening hood for the burner, connection to the chimney with sound-insulated leading-in tube and to the heating circuit with rubber compensators.

Sound transmission in **air ducts, ventilation and air conditioning systems** can be reduced by the fitting of silencers. These consist of sound-absorbing packing, between which the air flows → ❹. The thicker the packing, the deeper the frequencies which are absorbed. Ventilation ducts should also be sound-insulated → ❹.

Sound absorption

Sound absorption, in contrast to sound insulation, does not normally reduce the transmission of sound through a building component. Neither does it influence the sound, which reaches the ear directly from the source; it **only reduces the reflected sound**. Because the direct sound reduces with distance from the source, the reflected sound is just as loud or louder than the direct sound outside an 'echo' radius around the sound source → ❺. If sound reflection is reduced, then the level of reflected sound sinks outside the previous echo radius. The sound absorption capacity of a room is given in m² of equivalent sound absorption area, the ideal sound-absorbing area, which would have the same absorption capacity as the room itself. (For a reverberation time of 1.5 s, the equivalent sound-absorbing area (A) would have to be 0.1 m^2 per m^3 of room volume (V); for half the reverberation time, it would be twice the size.)

Protection from external noise

The best protection against noise from outside (traffic noise, etc.): appropriate design of the building – occupied rooms positioned on the side away from the noise; sound-insulated construction of the external walls; above all, sound-insulated doors and windows; installation of sound-insulating blinds on the façade side; and sound protection through landscaping (embankments, walls, planting). The sound reduction effect of these measures can be read from → ❼ for various wavelengths (wavelength approx. 340 m/frequency).

❶ Examples of single-spring elements

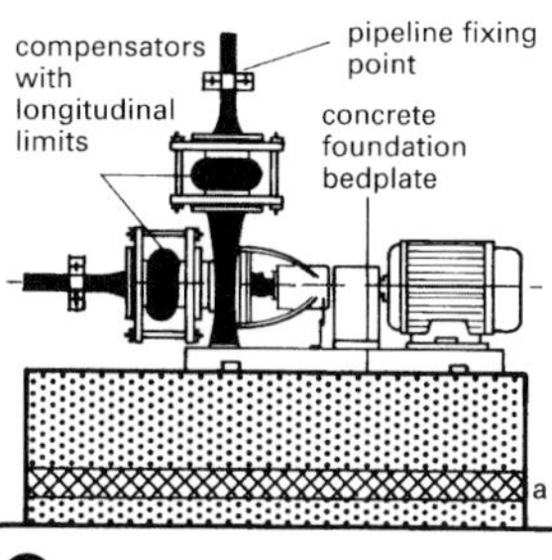

❷ Installing equipment with elastic insert in foundation

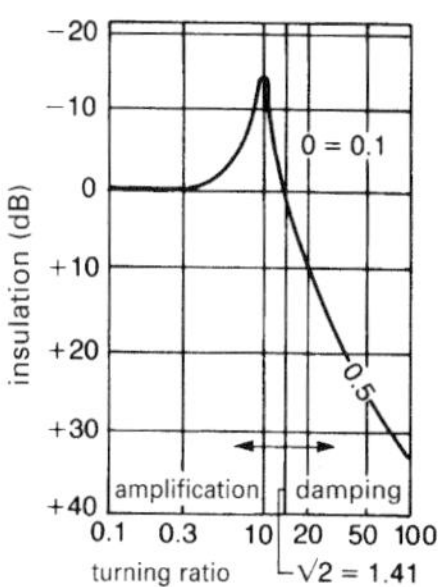

❸ Effect of elastic bearing

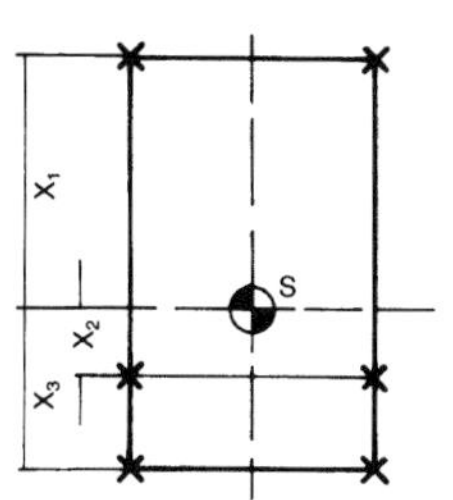

❹ Adaptation of springs to the centre of gravity

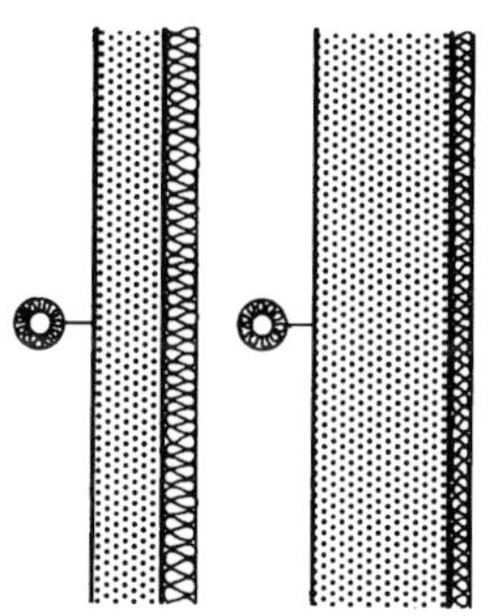

❺ Light wall = great excitation
Heavy wall = little excitation

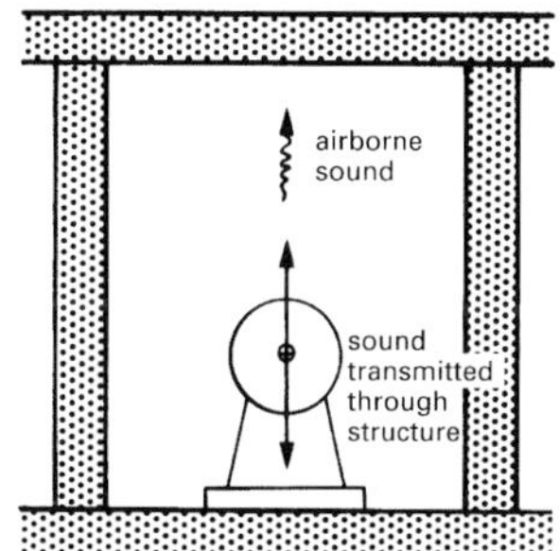

❻ Excitation of structure-borne sound

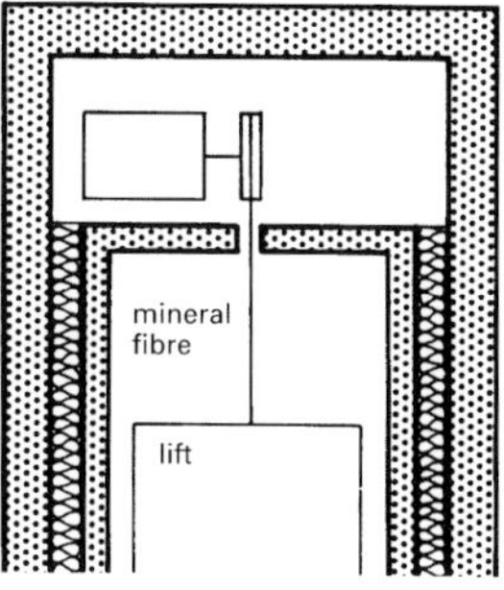

❼ Separate lift shaft with ≧3 cm mineral fibre lining

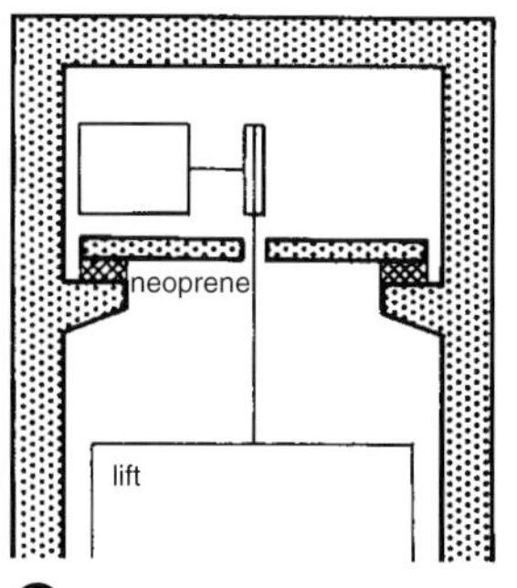

❽ Top of shaft with neoprene support

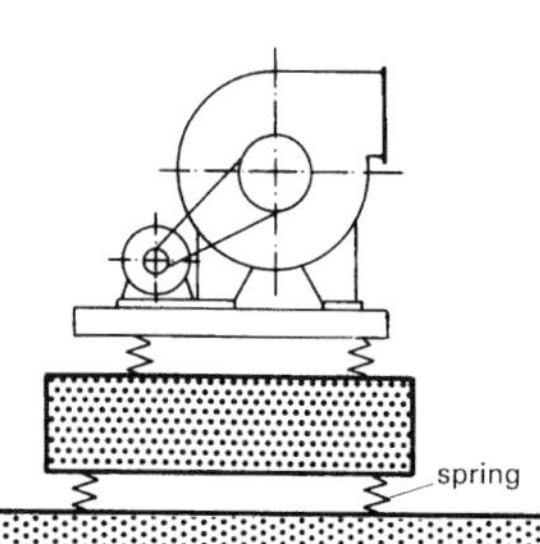

❾ Double elastic suspension for ventilator

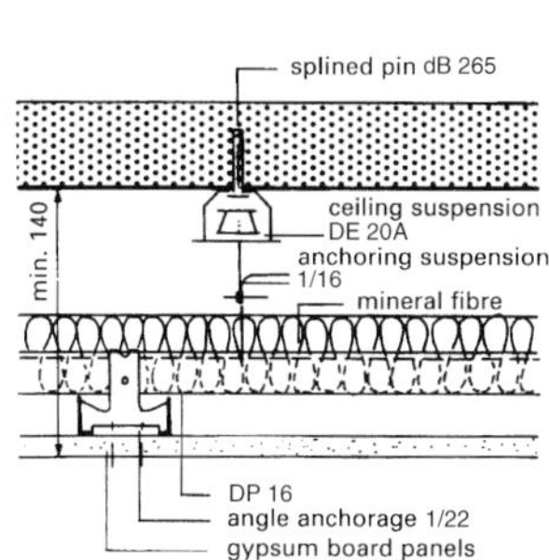

❿ Example of rubber-bonded metal ceiling element

Structure-borne sound

Vibrations in solid bodies are described as structure-borne sound. This is produced either by airborne sound or by direct mechanical excitation → ❻.

Because the alternating mechanical forces are mostly higher than those caused by pressure fluctuations in the air, the audible result of direct excitation is also normally louder. Resonance phenomena often occur, which can lead to louder audible radiation in narrow frequency ranges.

If the radiated airborne sound is monotonic, then the cause is usually direct structural excitation. Protection from structure-borne sound therefore has to aim at stopping the direct excitation or its propagation.

Precautions against structure-borne sound transmission

In **water installations,** only fixtures of testing mark groups I or II should be used; the water pressure should be as low as possible. The water velocity is of less significance.

Baths and shower trays should be supported on floating screed and separated from the wall. They should be installed with joints to the wall. Wall-hanging **WCs** cause direct structural sound excitation, but a rigid fixing is unavoidable. Elastic layers could perhaps be introduced.

Water and drain pipes must be fixed with elastic materials and should have no contact with the building structure. Pipework is to be fixed in accordance with DIN 4109 to walls with surface loading >250 kg/m^2 → ❺.

Lifts should be installed in separate shafts (joints filled with >3 cm mineral fibre) → ❼; otherwise, the top of the shaft should be elastically supported → ❽.

Pumps and equipment must be supported on structure-borne, sound-insulated foundations and elastically connected. Expansion compensators require stress relievers because the internal pressure also acts along the longitudinal axis of the pipe → ❶.

Rubber granulate panels are particularly suitable for insulating foundations because of their high compression strength. Impact sound insulation of mineral fibre or polystyrene foam could also be used in some cases. Cork and solid rubber are unsuitable because they are too stiff. The more the insulation compresses under loading without being overloaded, the better is the effect.

For flat insulation layers, the loading should normally be >0.5 N/mm^2. If this cannot be ensured, then single elements, designed to add to the weight of the equipment, should be used. The insulation effect is also best in this case if the elements are subjected to maximum loading without being overloaded. These single elements can be made of neoprene or steel.

Steel springs have low stiffness, which leads to the best structure-borne sound insulation → ❶. For some special cases, **air springs** are used. The individual springs should be correctly located in relation to the centre of gravity so they are evenly loaded → ❹.

If the excitation is periodic, e.g. vibrating or rotating masses, the excitation frequency must not coincide with the natural frequency of the elastically mounted system. Any resonance could cause large displacements, which could break elements with low damping → ❸.

Particularly good sound insulation is achieved by using double elastic suspension → ❾. Unfavourable interaction, e.g. foundations on floating screed, can lead to a worsening of the situation.

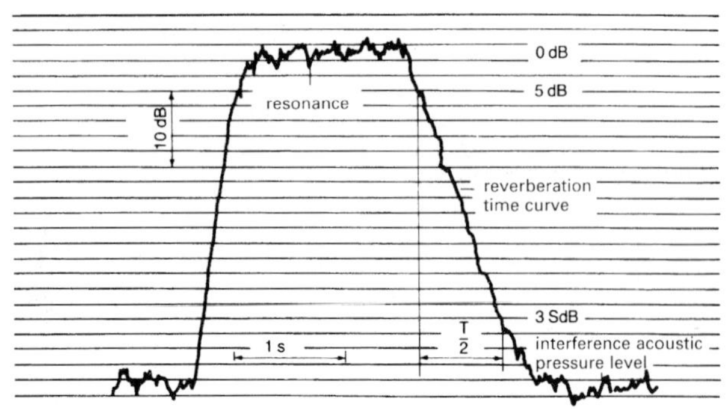

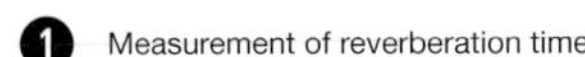

❶ Measurement of reverberation time

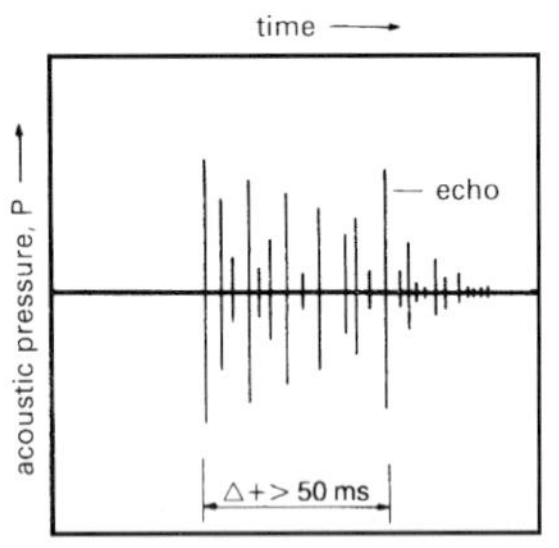

❷ Echo criteria

room function		reverberation time (s)
speech:	cabaret	0.8
	plays lectures	1.0
music:	chamber music	1.0–1.5
	opera	1.3–1.6
	concert	1.7–2.1
	organ music	2.5–3.0

❸ Range of optimal reverberation times

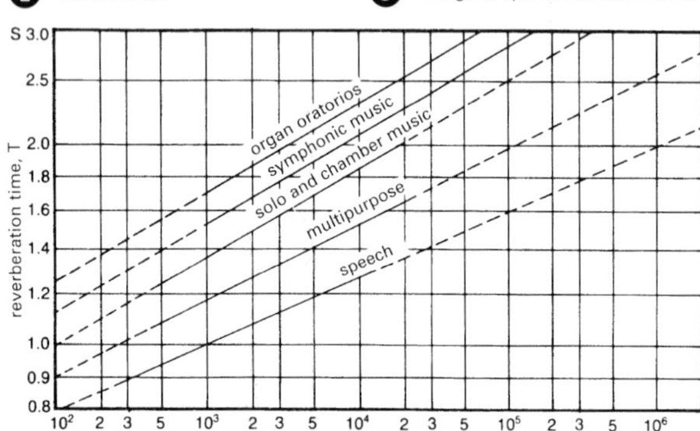

❹ Reverberation time tolerance ± 20%

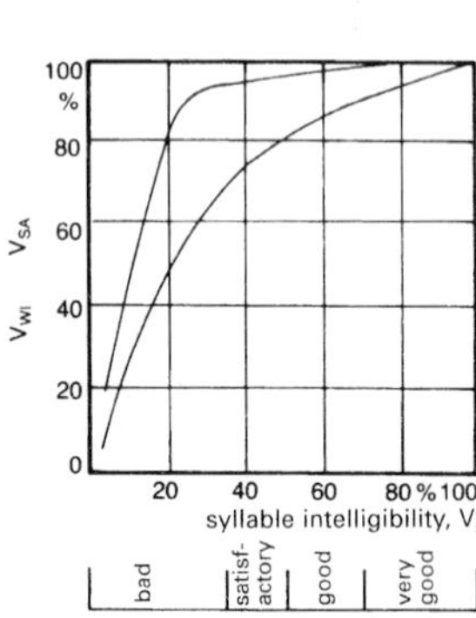

❺ Speech intelligibility

function	volume factor (m^3/seat)	max. volume (m^3)
assembly room, spoken theatre	3–5	5000
multi-purpose, speech/music	4–7	8000
musical theatre (opera, operetta)	5–8	15 000
chamber music room	6–10	10 000
concert halls for symphonic music	8–12	25 000
rooms for oratorios and organ music	10–14	30 000

❻ Table of specific volumes; V = f (type)

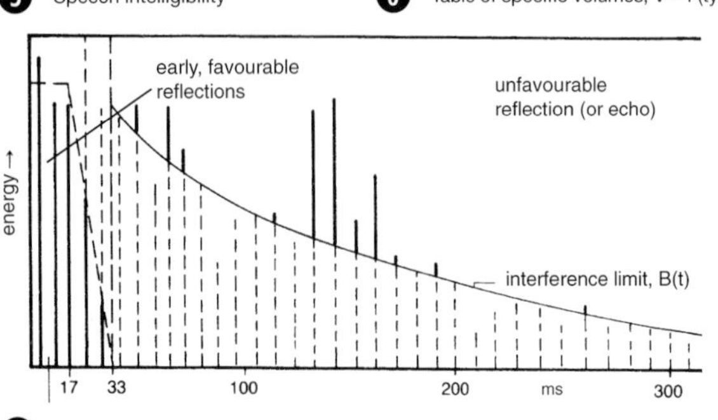

❼ Reflection sequence in a room

The design of room acoustics should produce the optimal conditions for listeners to hear speech or music.

Various factors have to be considered, of which the most important is the **reverberation time**, i.e. the time taken for the sound level to **drop** by 60 dB after the sound source has ceased → ❶. This is evaluated in the range of a drop of –5 to –35 dB.

Another factor is the **absorption surface** of the room, determined by its quantity of absorbing material and the **echo**.

The calculation of the **reverberation time t** of a **room volume V** normally uses the **Sabine formula**:

$$t = \frac{0.163 \cdot V}{\alpha_s \cdot S}$$

The **degree of sound absorption** α_s is material-specific and is determined in echo chambers. The **individual surfaces** S (e.g. people, seating, decoration) of the total sound-absorbing surface in the room are entered into the calculation with their specific values. The reverberation time is calculated for the frequencies f = 125, 250, 500, 1000, 2000, 4000 Hz. References to medium frequency are normally based on 500 Hz.

If a single, subjectively recognisable peak projects from a regularly falling reverberation curve → ❶, this is described as an **echo** → ❷. Different values of time and intensity count as echo criteria for speech and music. Because rooms intended for music should be designed for a longer reverberation time, they are normally regarded as less critical with regard to echoes.

Requirements for rooms

Reverberation time

The optimal reverberation time depends on the intended use (music, speech → ❸) and room volume. The reverberation time is generally dependent on frequency, i.e. it is longer at deeper, and shorter at higher, frequencies. For frequencies of f = 500 Hz, the empirically determined values according to → ❹ can be given as optimal.

Speech intelligibility

This serves to judge the comprehensibility of the spoken word → ❺. This is not standardised, so various concepts – like sentence, and syllable, intelligibility and evaluation with logatomes – are usual.

For the measurement with logatomes, large groups of listeners have to write down individual meaningless syllables, e.g. 'lin', 'ter' (logatomes), and the degree of correctness is used for evaluation. >70% counts as excellent speech intelligibility. Newer, objective processes use modulated rustling signals and lead to reproducible results at less expense.

Impression of space

The impression of space describes the perception of the reflections emanating from the room according to time and direction. For music, diffuse reflections are favourable for sound volume, while early reflections with delays of up to approx. 80 ms (corresponding to 27 m of distance) improve clarity compared with direct sound. Speech requires shorter delays, of up to 50 ms, to protect comprehension.

❶ Berlin Philharmonic: staggering the rows of seating

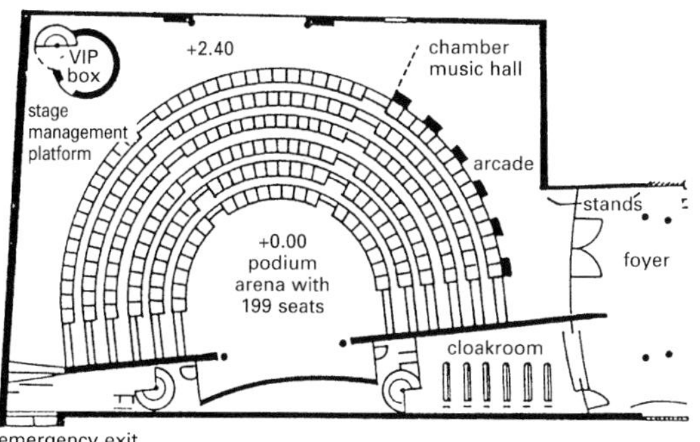

❷ Podium in the small chamber music room, Beethoven Archive, Bonn

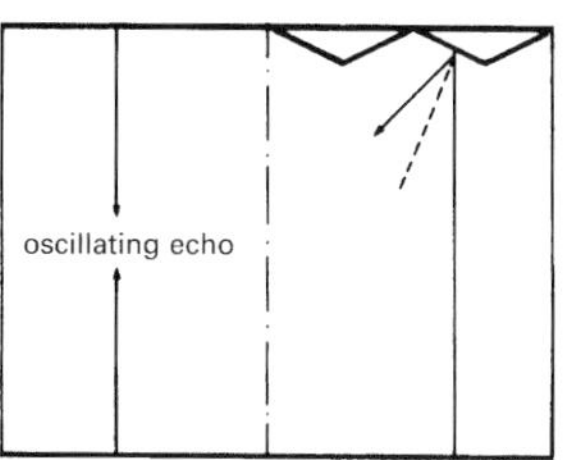

❸ Flutter echo from parallel unstructured walls

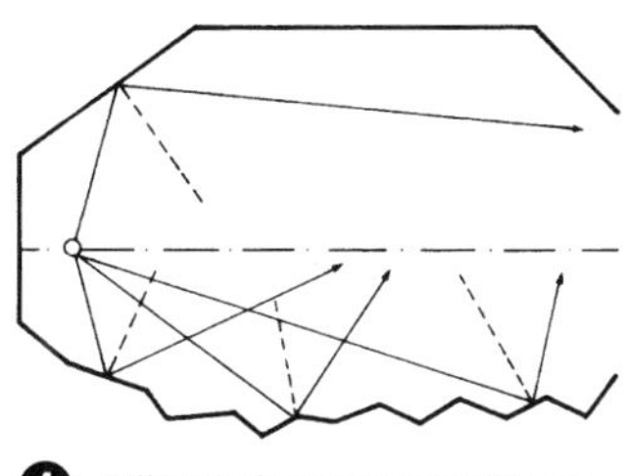

❹ Diffused reflections created through folds in the wall surface

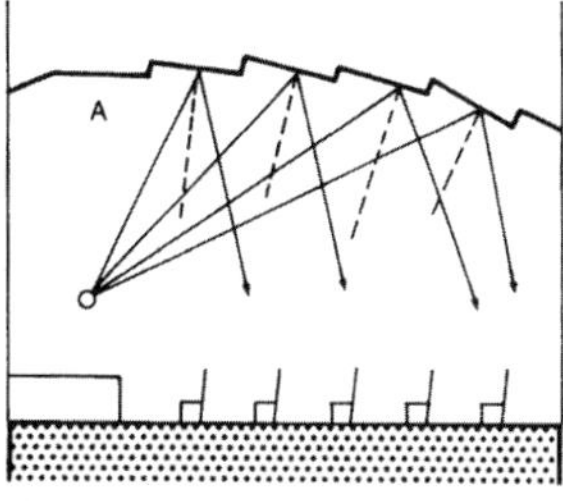

❺ Ceiling shape flat for music, sloping to the back for speech

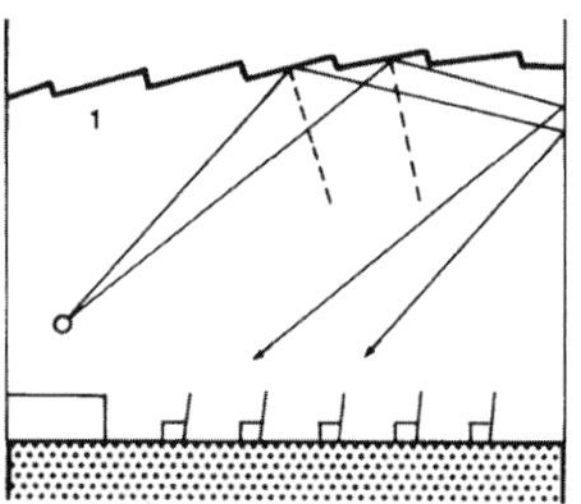

❻ Unfavourable ceiling shapes

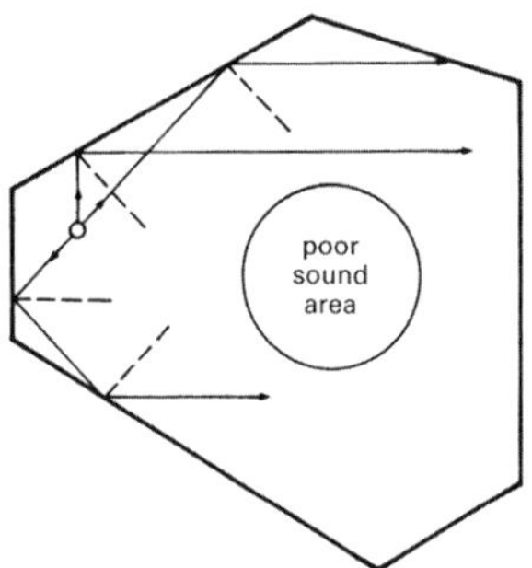

❼ Folding of the wall surface

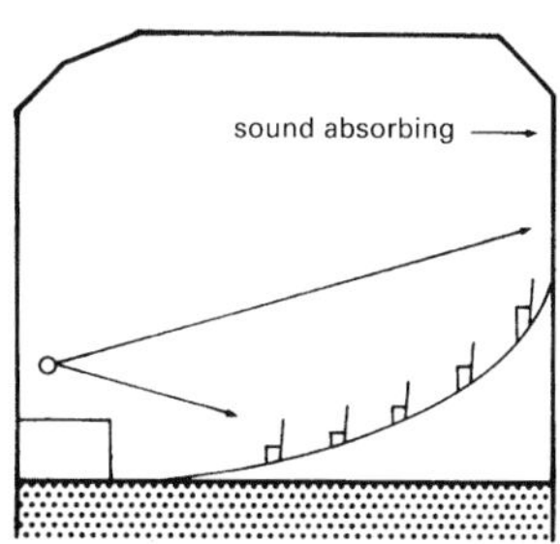

❽ Uniform direct sound to all places through banking the rows of seats. The curve should follow a logarithmic spiral

Primary structure of rooms

The design of the primary structure of a room is the most important acoustic design criterion. Early side reflections are subjectively considered to be better than ceiling reflections, even with very low delay times (because of the asymmetry of the acoustic impression), because the two ears receive different signals. **Narrow, high rooms with structured, geometrically reflecting walls and diffusely reflecting ceilings** are therefore the most simple for room acoustics.

The **volume required for good sound** depends on the purpose of the room (→ p. 482 ❻). Guideline values are 4 m^3/person for speech and 10 m^3/person for (concert) music. If the volume is too small, this allows too little reverberation.

Room shape

For music, narrow, high rooms with structured **walls** (early side reflections) are particularly suitable. Near the podium, reflection surfaces are necessary for early initial reflections and the balance of the orchestra. The **back wall** of the room should not cause any reflections towards the podium, because this could have an echo effect.

Parallel, unstructured surfaces are to be avoided in order to prevent flutter echoes through multiple refection → ❸. Providing folds in the walls with angles of >5° can remove the parallel effect and achieve diffused reflections → ❹.

Ceilings serve to lead the sound into the back of the auditorium and must be shaped accordingly → ❺ – ❻. If the shape of the ceiling is unfavourable, this causes great fluctuations of volume through sound concentrations.

Less favourable are rooms with side walls becoming further apart towards the back, because this could make side reflections too weak → ❼. This disadvantage can be compensated for with **additional reflective surfaces** (Weinberg steps) in the room or a heavy folding of the walls to guide the sound (e.g. Berlin and Cologne Philharmonics → ❶).

Multi-purpose rooms with variable podiums and level floors are often problematic for music. The **location of the podium** should if possible be on the narrow side of the room. For speech or small rooms (chamber music), podiums along the long walls are also possible (Beethoven Archive → ❷). Podiums must be clearly raised above the level of the floor in order to assist direct sound transmission, because otherwise too much volume is quickly lost → ❾.

Banking of the seats is also acoustically advantageous (uniform direct sound to all seats). The rise of the curve should follow a logarithmic spiral → ❼.

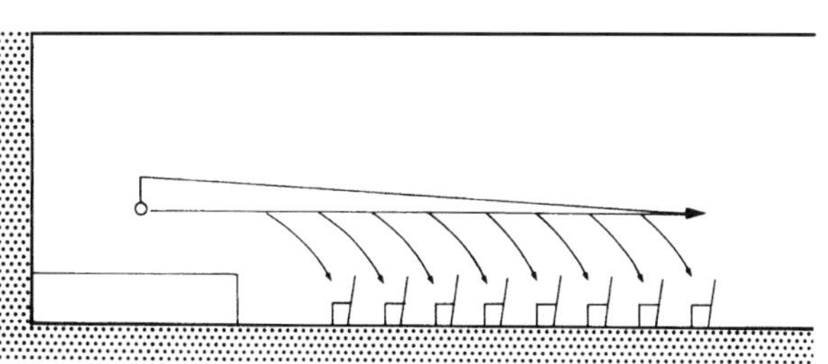

❾ Drop in sound level over absorbing surfaces

Sound-guiding 'sails'

Splitting unfavourable reflection surfaces into elements

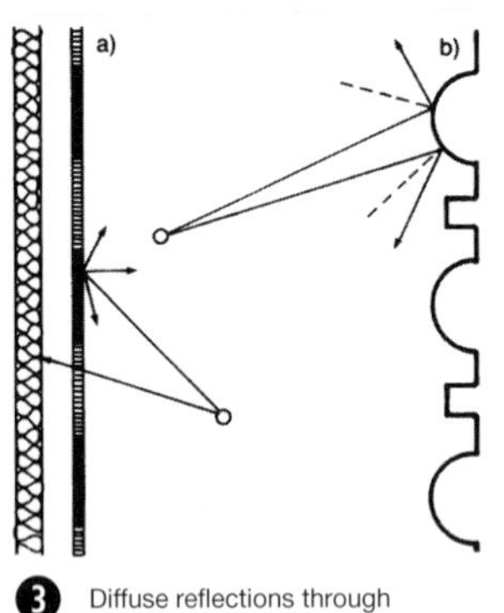

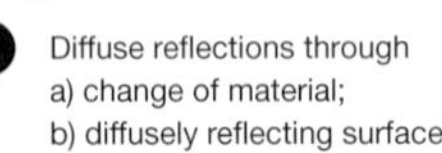

Diffuse reflections through
a) change of material;
b) diffusely reflecting surface

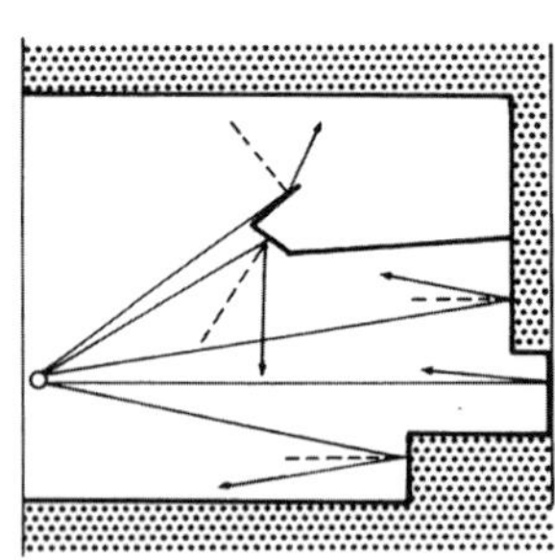

Diffusion through reflections occurring at different times

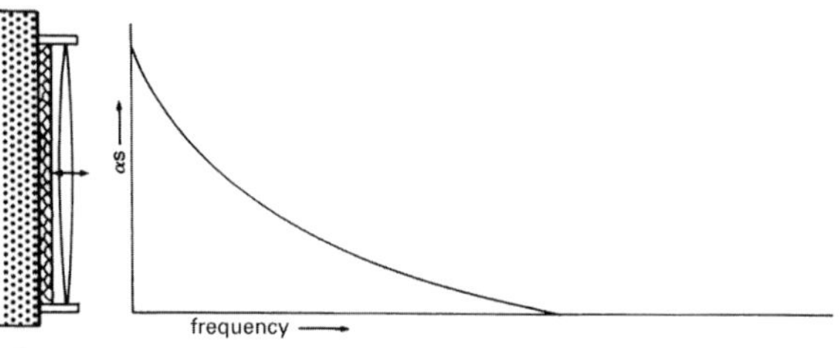

Absorption of lower frequencies due to surface oscillator

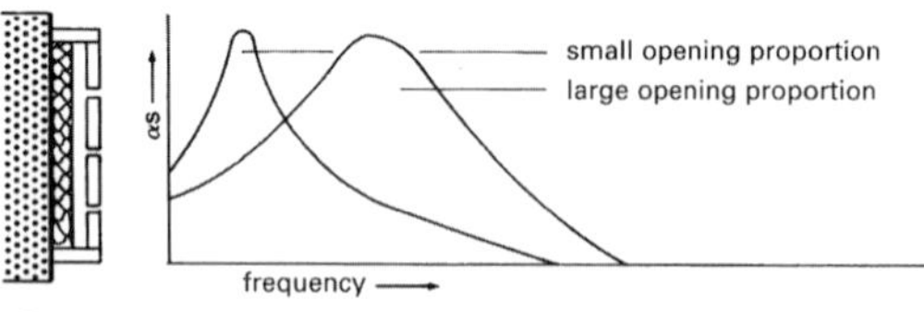

Absorption behaviour of resonators

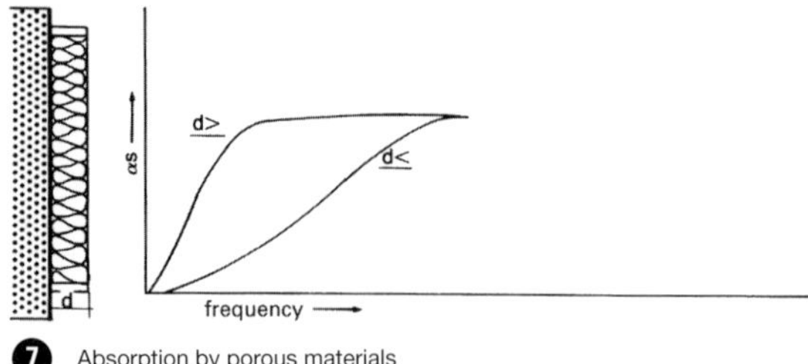

Absorption by porous materials

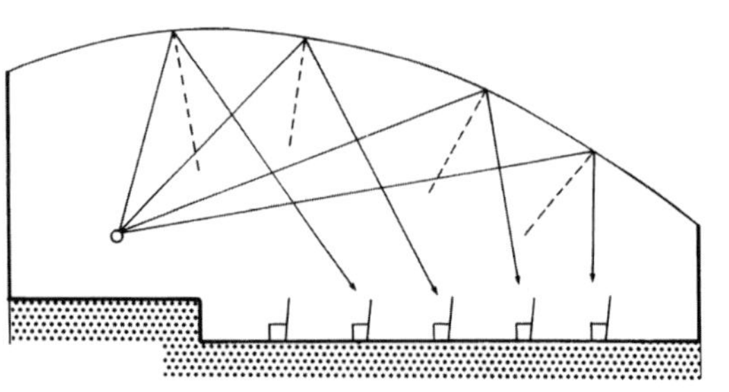

Good sound-guiding through adapted curve

Secondary structures

For the calculation of reverberation time, the entire sound-absorbing surface of the room is taken into consideration, i.e. all individual surfaces in the room (e.g. people, seating, decoration) are taken into account, together with their specific degree of sound absorption (→ Sabine formula p. 482).

The selection, arrangement and material of the **secondary structures** can largely compensate for the disadvantages of an unfavourable primary structure. Flexible (electronically controlled) sound-insulated surfaces can also achieve adjustable reverberation times.

Secondary reflection surfaces

Reflection surfaces can be used to remedy the faults of a primary structure (e.g. walls widening towards the back of the room addressed through folding of wall surface; and an undesirable ceiling shape through suspended sails or splitting surfaces into elements → ❶ – ❷.) An appropriately curved ceiling can achieve very good sound guidance → ❽.

Diffuse reflections: Surfaces from which echoes can be expected must reflect diffusely, i.e. scatter the sound reaching them → ❸. Diffuse reflections lead to flat, uniform reverberation time curves through the uniform distribution of sound.

Structuring of walls by folding surfaces necessitates angles $>5°$. Prominent surface structures (parapets, niches etc.) are also effective, through splitting of the sound waves or delayed reflections → ❹.

Absorbing surfaces

Absorbing surfaces can avoid sound concentrations and adapt the reverberation time to the required values. The desired reverberation time is balanced using a combination of absorbing surfaces with different properties. This is determined by their structure:

- resonant surfaces (which move with vibrations) absorb **low frequencies**. Area, separation and level of cavity filling can be varied for fine adjustment → ❺.
- surfaces with openings in front of cavities mostly absorb **medium frequencies** (Helmholtz resonator); proportion of surface taken by hole, cavity volume and damping of cavity determine frequency, extent and form of maximum absorption → ❻.
- porous materials are used for the absorption of **higher frequencies**. Layer thickness and flow resistance influence the distribution towards lower frequencies → ❼. An appropriate alternation of reflecting and absorbing surfaces has an effect on the reflection like a serious structuring of the surface → ❸.

Seating

The achievable reverberation time is often determined just through absorption by the listeners and the seating. In order to make the reverberation time less dependent on the number in the audience, a type of seat material is needed which provides such great **absorption**, both on the seat and its backrest, that, occupied or not, its absorption is the same. Additional absorption surfaces for high frequencies are then only necessary if the specific volume of the room is significantly exceeded (→ p. 482 ❻). If room volume and seating are correctly matched to each other, then it is mostly necessary to correct the reverberation time only for lower frequencies.

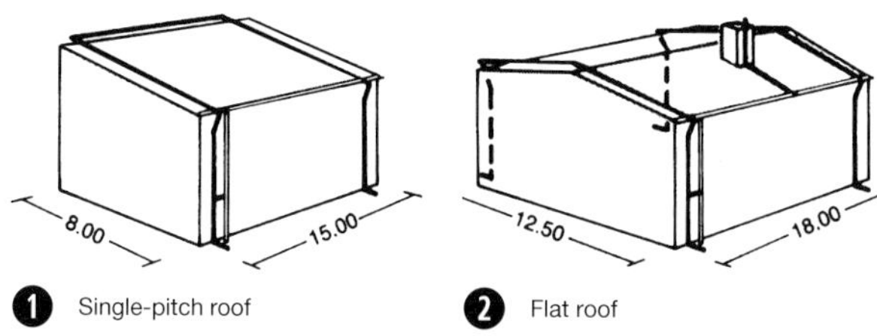

1 Single-pitch roof **2** Flat roof

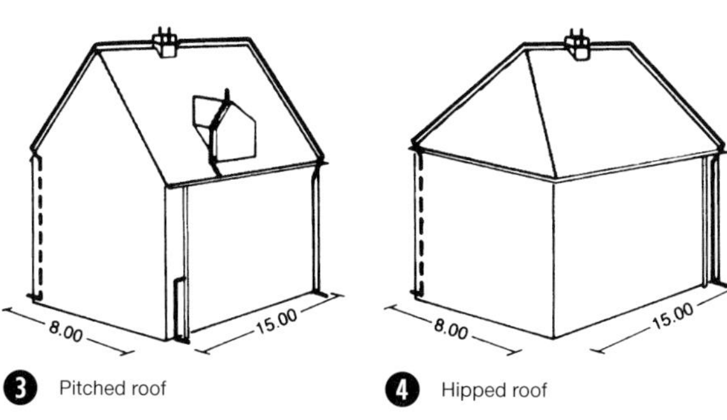

3 Pitched roof **4** Hipped roof

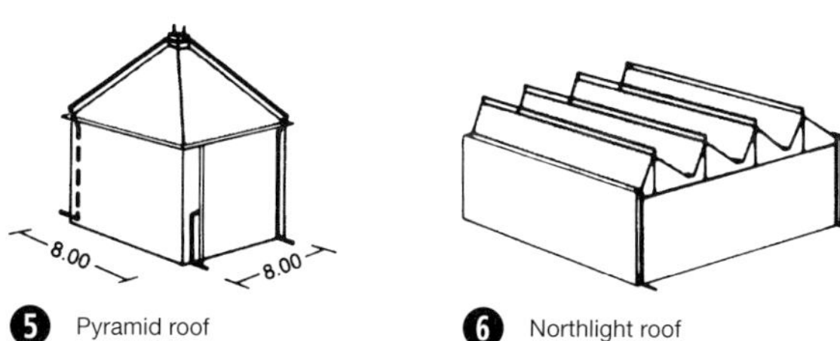

5 Pyramid roof **6** Northlight roof

At a latitude of 50°, each hour of thunderstorm causes about 60 lightning strikes to the ground and 200–250 cloud to cloud discharges.

People in the open air are endangered by step voltages within 30 m of the strike location (trees, masonry etc.) Damage to buildings is mostly the result of the heat produced by ground strikes, which can heat and turn the water content of soil to steam, and of excess pressure, which can cause explosive destruction of walls, masts, trees etc.

Lightning protection systems

A lightning protection system is intended to fix the lightning strike using roof conductors and ensure that the building remains inside a protected zone ('Faraday cage'). A lightning protection system consists of **'roof conductors', conductor lines and earthing rods or electrodes**.

'Roof conductors'

These are metal lightning rods, conductor lines and roof surfaces. No point of the roof should be more than 15 m from the nearest 'roof conductor'. Structures projecting from the roof, bay windows, chimneys and ventilation cowls are of particular significance for the detailing of lightning protection systems and should always be connected.

On account of the danger of ignition from the corona effect, thatched roofs should have metal bands on timber supports 60 cm above the ridge → **8** – **9**.

When a lightning current flows through the earthing resistance, this creates a voltage drop, e.g.: 100 000 A × 5 cm = 500 000 V. The entire lightning protection system and all parts with metal connections to it are subjected to this potential at the moment of a lightning strike. The very effective measure of connecting all large metal parts and cables to the lightning protection system is described as equipotential bonding.

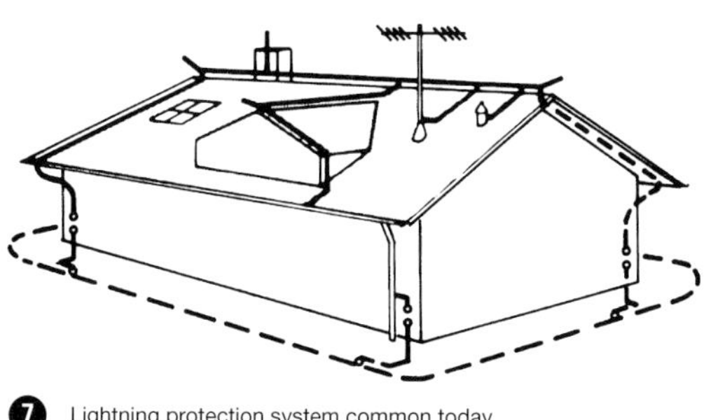

7 Lightning protection system common today

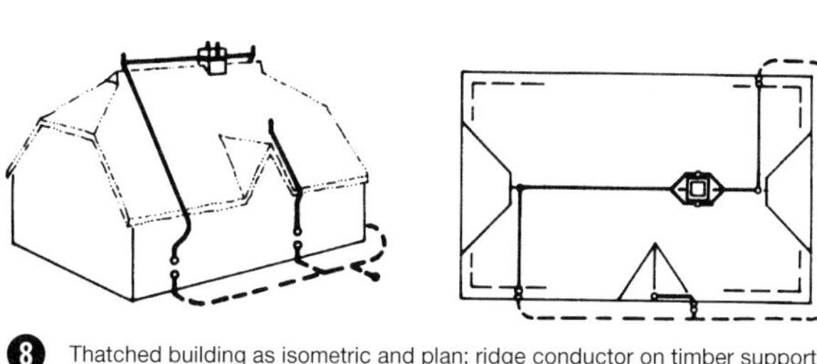

8 Thatched building as isometric and plan; ridge conductor on timber supports 60 cm above ridge; conductor 40 cm from roof surface; earth conductor

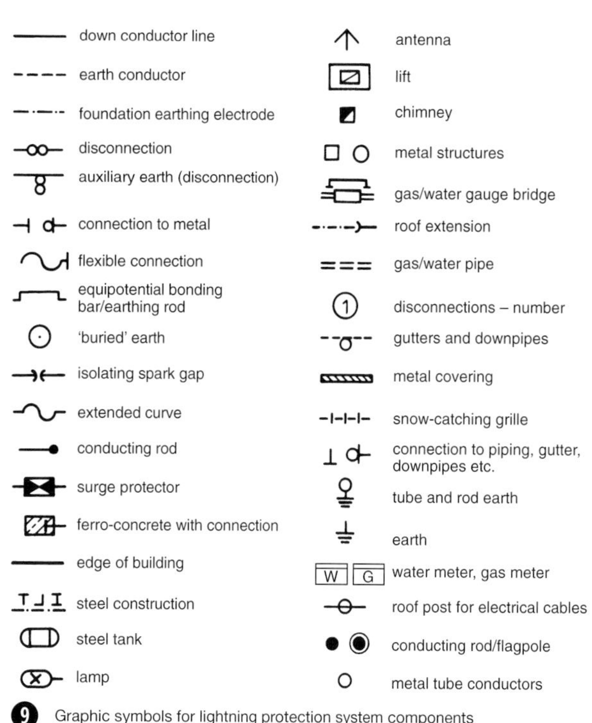

9 Graphic symbols for lightning protection system components

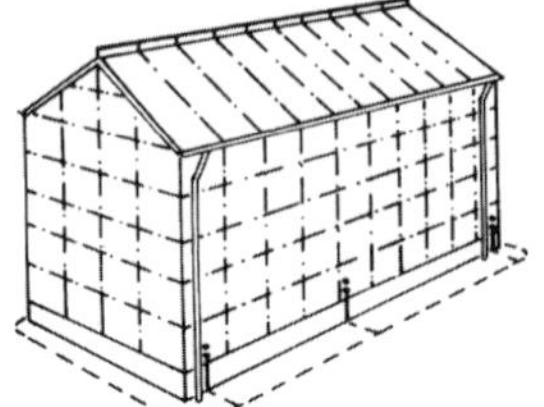

❶ Steel framed building: steel frame connected to the 'air terminal' and also to the conductor to earth

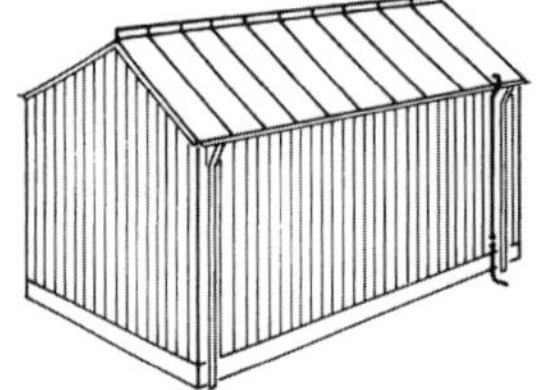

❷ Metal roof with timber-clad walls: roof connected to ridge conductor and conductor to earth

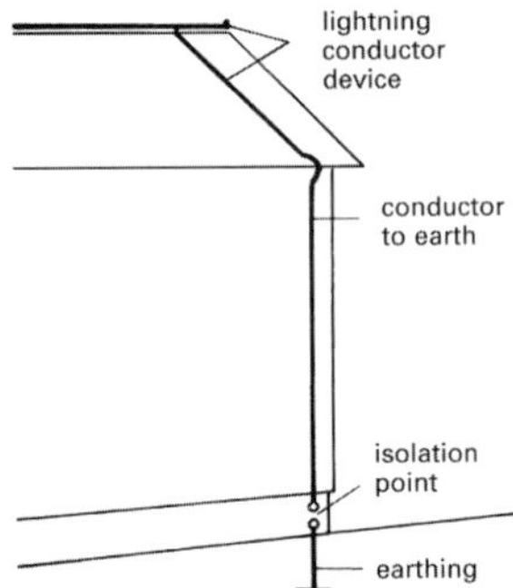

❸ Main components of a lightning protection system

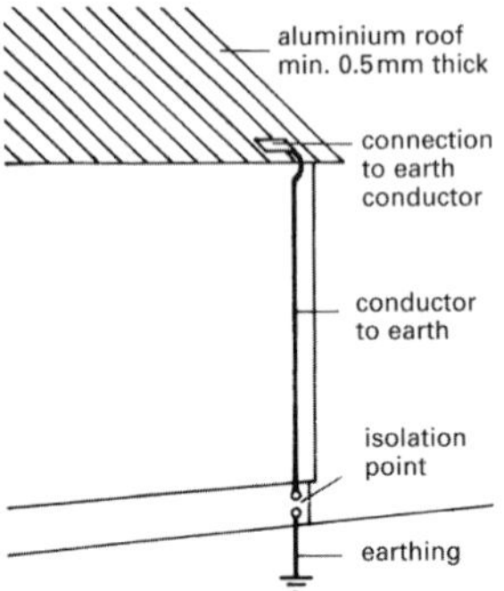

❹ Aluminium roof covering as an 'air terminal'

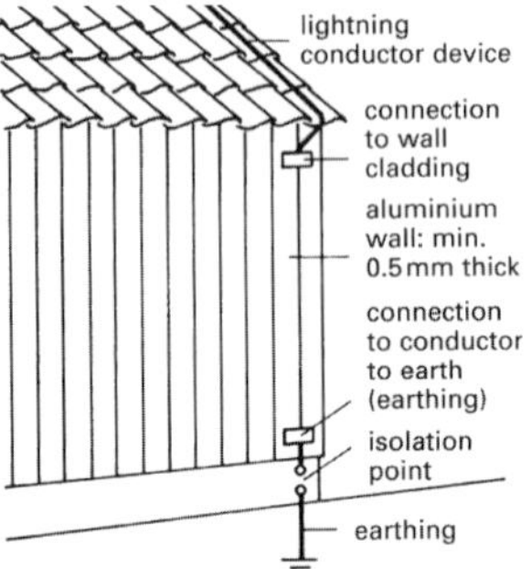

❺ Aluminium wall cladding as conductor to earth

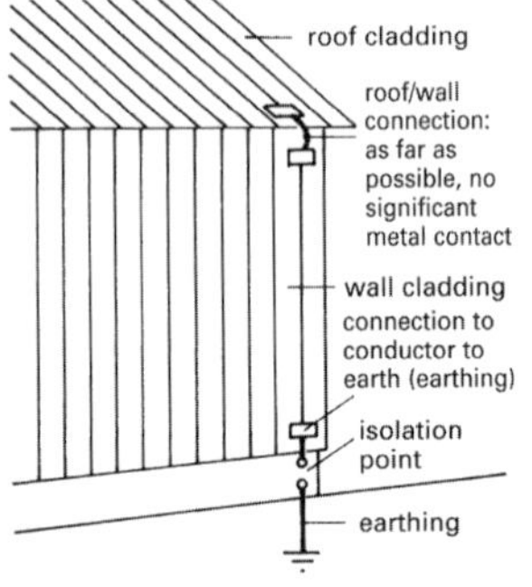

❻ Aluminium roof and wall

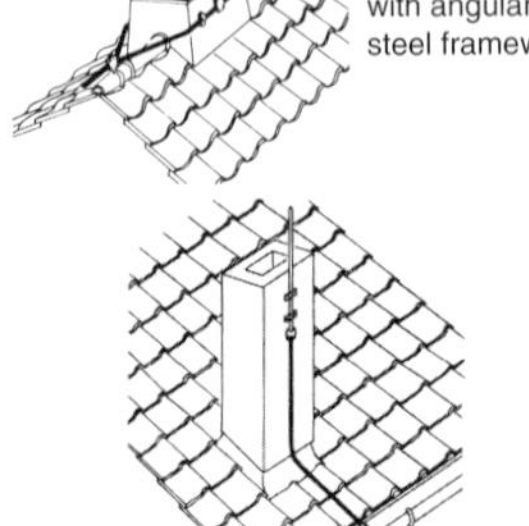

❼ Lightning conductor on chimney close to the eaves and connected to the roof guttering

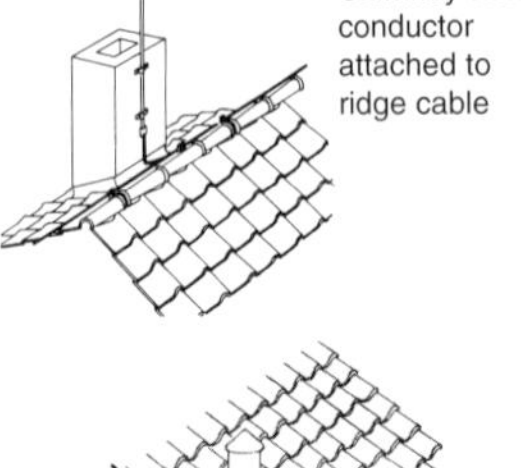

❽ All metal structures and ventilation ducts on the roof are connected to the lightning protection system

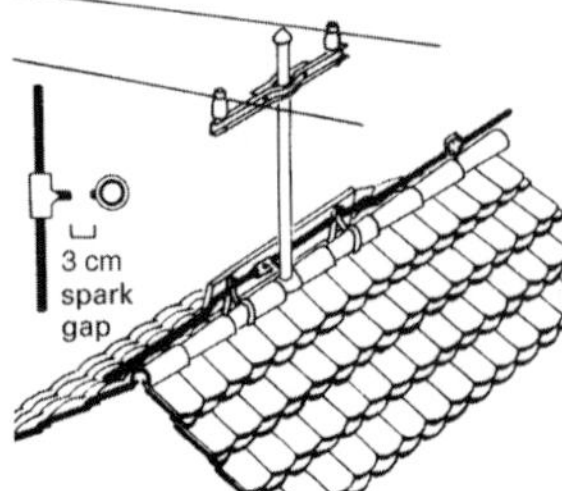

❾ Do not directly connect roof mast for high-voltage cable; the open transmission path has a spark gap of 30 mm

❿ Install voltage surge protection device in steel structures with electrical installations

Earthing electrodes

The earthing system has the task of conducting the lightning current quickly and uniformly into earthing electrodes. These can be tapes (surface) or rods (underground, sometimes called 'buried') earthing electrodes:

Surface earthing electrodes (earthing tapes) are laid as a ring or strip, preferably embedded in the foundation concrete. Earthing tapes consist of galvanised steel strip (30 × 3.5 mm/25 × 4.0 mm) or round steel (diameter = 10 mm) → ⓬ – ⓭.

Underground earthing electrodes (rods). These are round or with an open profile. They are driven, inside tubes, so deep into the ground without insulation that a low ground resistance is achieved → ⓬ – ⓭. The level of the ground resistance varies according to soil type and moisture content → ⓫. If earthing electrode rods are driven more than 6 m into the ground, they are described as 'buried'.

A star-shaped earthing electrode consists of individual tapes projecting outward in a star shape from a conductor.

Type of earthing electrode	Marshy soil	Loam, clay, arable soil	Damp sand	Damp gravel	Dry sand and gravel	Stony ground	Ground resistance (Ω)
tape (length, m)	12	40	80	200	400	1200	
rod (depth, m)	6	20	40	100	200	600	5
tape (length, m)	6	20	40	100	200	600	
rod (depth, m)	3	10	20	50	100	300	10
tape (length, m)	4	13	27	67	133	400	
rod (depth, m)	2	7	14	34	70	200	15
tape (length, m)	2	7	13	33	67	200	
rod (depth, m)	1	3	7	17	33	100	30

⓫ Ground resistance of tape and rod earthing electrodes in various soils

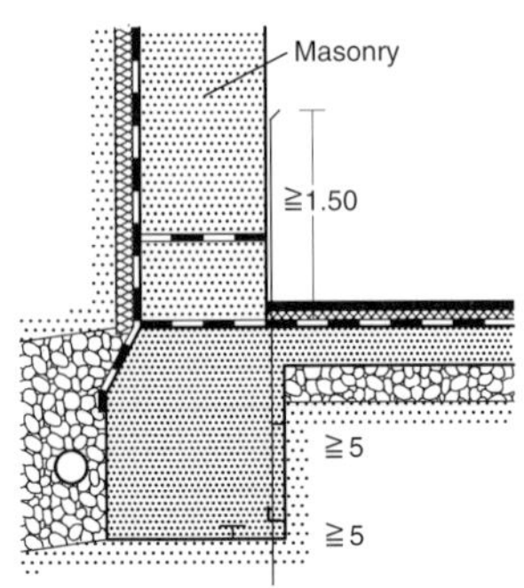

⓬ Earthing electrode in unreinforced concrete foundation

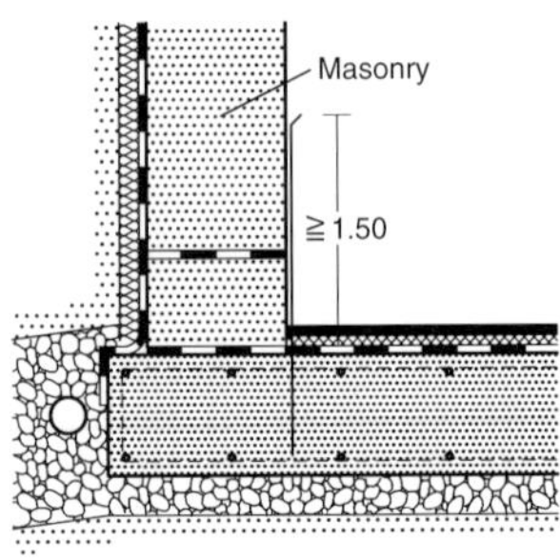

⓭ Earthing electrode in reinforced concrete foundation

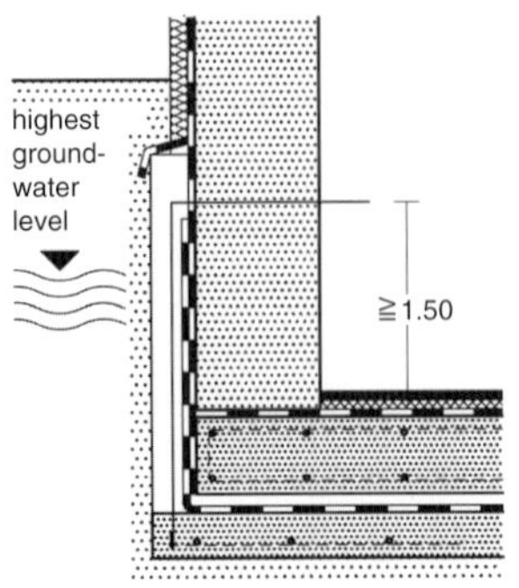

⓮ Layout of a foundation earthing electrode with waterproofing of tanks

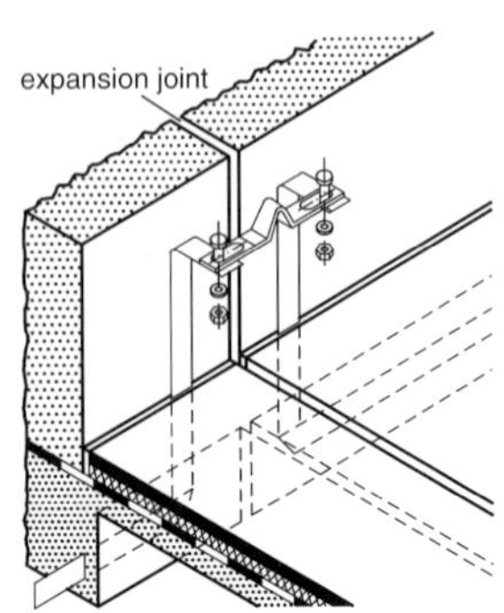

⓯ Bridging of movement joints with expansion joint on inside of building work

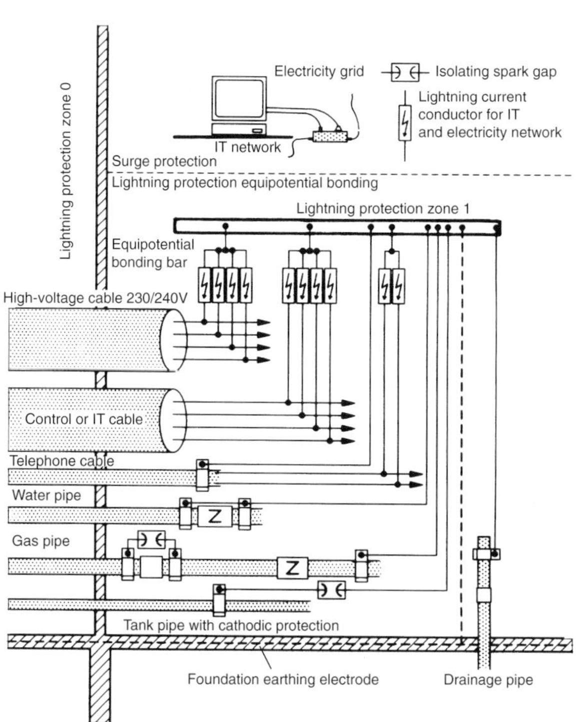

❶ Principle of lightning protection equipotential bonding

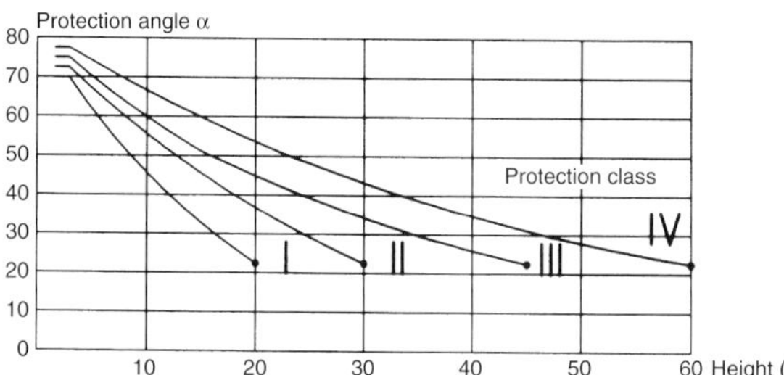

❷ Protection angle depending on the lightning protection class and the height above the area to be protected

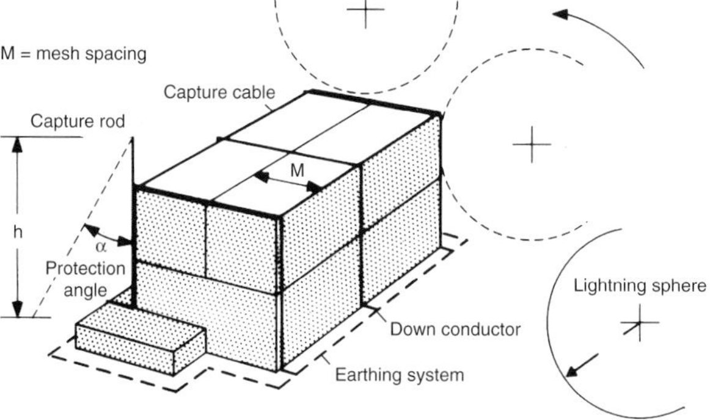

❸ Procedure for designing lightning protection systems: lightning sphere, protection angle and mesh process

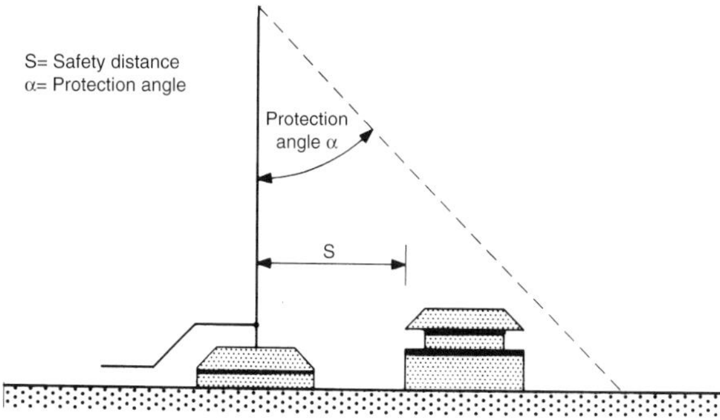

❹ Roofs protected by lightning rod

Lightning protection zones

The property to be protected is categorised into various lightning protection zones (LPZ) → ❻.

Protection zone 0A:

This is outside a building to be protected. Direct lightning strikes are possible in this area, and there is an undamped field of lightning discharge.

Protection zone 0B:

The lightning protection equipment on the building to be protected results in areas in which direct lightning strikes can be ruled out according to the protection class. There is an undamped field of lightning discharge. Such areas outside the building are described as protection zone 0B.

Protection zone 1:

This describes the actual building to be protected The boundary of protection zone 0 is normally the roof, the external walls and the cellar floor of the building to be protected, of which the characteristics (shielding of the external envelope of the building) have to fulfil certain requirements.

Protection zone 2 and higher:

It can be sensible, or requested, to provide further protection zones inside protection zone 1. For example, the central server room as protection zone 2 and individual electronic devices as protection zone 3.

lightning protection class (P)	effectiveness (E)	lightning sphere radius (r)	mesh width (w)	typical down conductor spacing	protection angle (α)	peak lightning current (i)
I	98%	20 m	5 m × 5 m	10 m	→ ❷	200 kA
II	95%	30 m	10m × 10 m	15 m		150 kA
III	90%	45 m	15 m × 15 m	20 m		100 kA
IV	80%	60 m	20 m × 20 m	25 m		

❺ Lightning protection classes

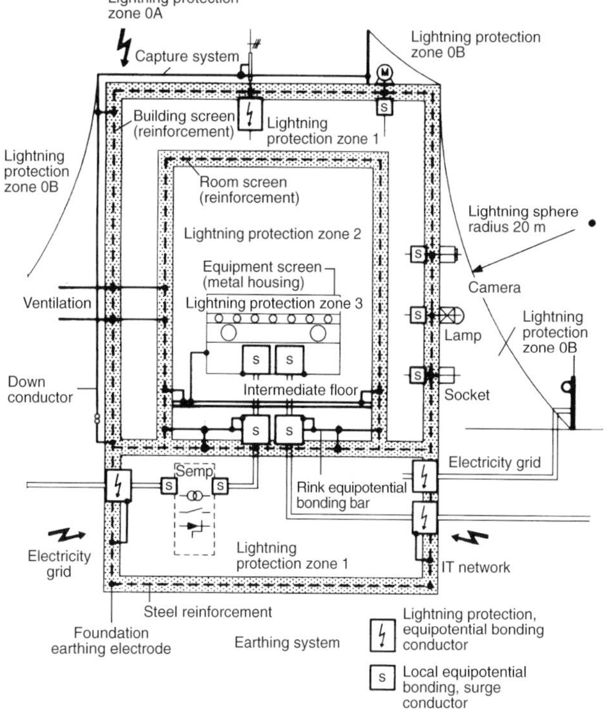

❻ Categorisation of a building into lightning protection zones

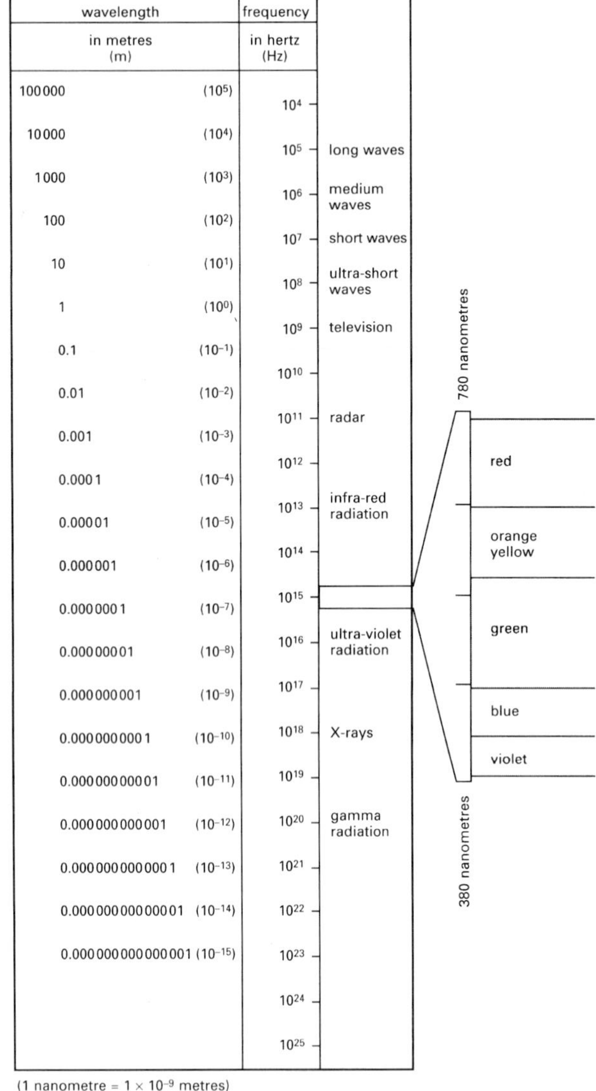

(1 nanometre = 1 × 10^{-9} metres)

❶ Energy spectrum of electromagnetic radiation (1 nanometre = 1 millionth millimetre)

❷ The seasons – in the northern hemisphere

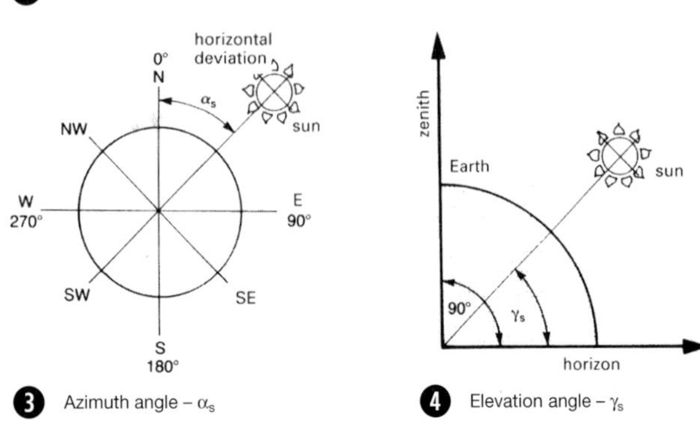

❸ Azimuth angle – α_s

❹ Elevation angle – γ_s

Requirements for daylight in internal rooms

All rooms for permanent human occupation should be lit with sufficient daylight. There should also be a reasonable visual connection with the outside. The corresponding requirements are essentially laid down in DIN 5034, in the Workplace Guidelines and in the state building regulations.

Light, wavelength, colour, unit

Within the range of electromagnetic radiation, visible light is a relatively small part, with wavelengths of approx. 380–780 nm → ❶. Light (daylight and artificial light) is the range of electromagnetic radiation between ultra violet and infra red, which can be processed by the eye. The colours of the spectrum in daylight all have their wavelength, from violet with relatively short wavelength to red with the longest wavelength. Daylight, which is experienced by the human eye as white, contains all wavelengths. The analysis of wavelengths is of significance for architectural design.

The intensity of light or illuminance – particularly for artificial light – is measured in lux (lx), and daylight in internal rooms is given in %.

Astronomical basics: the sun

The sources of radiation and light-producing daylight are not constant. The sun is our 'primary source' for the creation of daylight, independent of the time and various weather situations. The angle of the earth's axis of 23.5°, the daily rotation of the earth around its own axis and the annual rotation of the earth around the sun result in the position of the sun depending on date and time for any particular place on earth → ❷. This is described by two angles:

azimuth α_s and elevation angle γ_s

Azimuth α_s: projection on plan of the position of the sun, measured as the horizontal angle from 0°. 0° = north, 90° = east, 180° = south, 270° = west → ❸, as seen by the observer. Elevation angle γ_s: projection of the position on elevation of the sun above the horizon, as seen by the observer → ❹.

Determination of sun's position

There are various methods of determining the position of the sun for a particular location, e.g. determination of the azimuth and elevation angle.

On account of the declination of the sun in the course of the year → ❷ there are four essential sections of the year (seasons) or sun positions: on the equinox dates of 21 May and 23 September, the day and night are of equal length and the declination of the sun is 0°.

On 21 December is the winter solstice (shortest day) with solar declination –23.5°, and the 21 June is the summer solstice (longest day) with solar declination +23.5°.

The position of the sun results from the latitude. On the 21/3 and the 23/9 at noon (α_s = 180°), the sun has the same zenith angle at each latitude. For example, at latitude 51° north (London), the zenith angle at noon (α_s = 180°) is 51°→ p. 489 ❷. The elevation angle of the sun above the horizon is then 90° – 51° = 39°.

The sun at noon (α_s = 180°) stands about 23.5° higher on the 21/6 than on the 21/3 and the 23/9, that is 39° + 23.5° = 62.5°, and on the 21/12, the sun is about 23.5° lower than at the equinoxes, that is 39° – 23.5° = 15.5°. These differences are the same for all latitudes.

This enables the corresponding elevation angle of the sun to be determined for all latitudes and times of year.

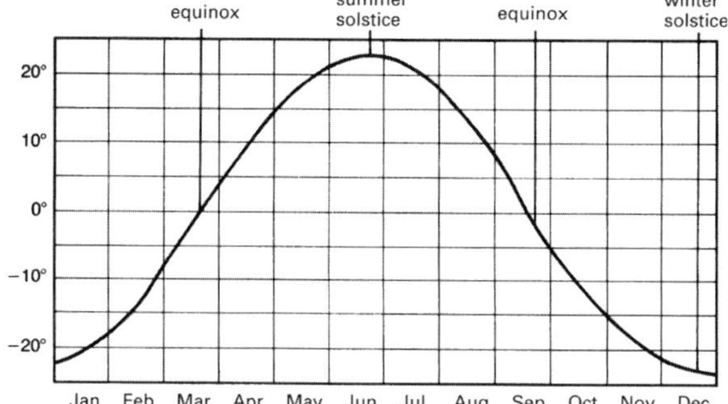

❶ Solar declination δ in the course of the year

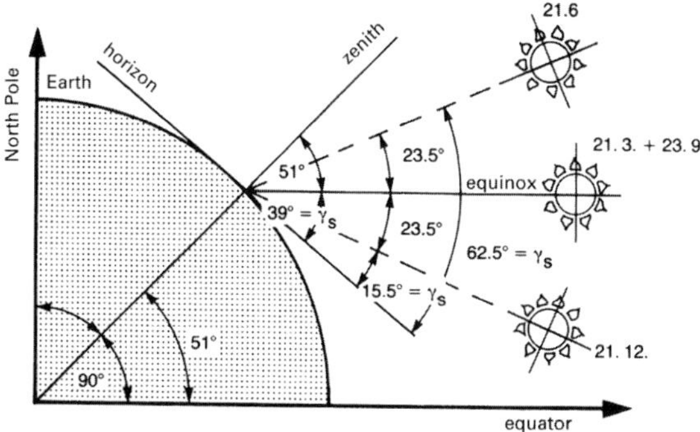

❷ 51° latitude and elevation angle γ_s

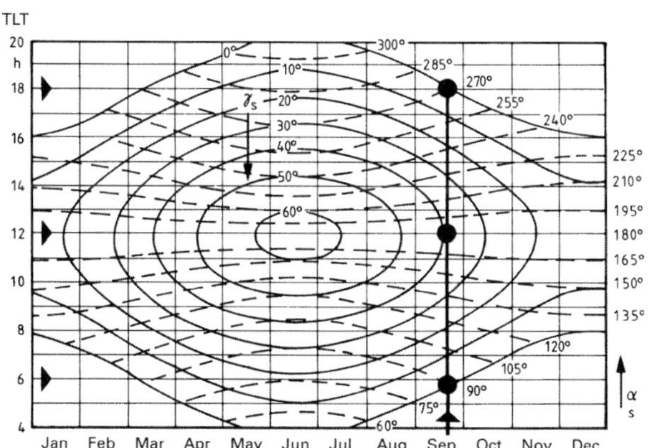

❸ Solar azimuth α_s and solar elevation angle γ_s 51° north (Brighton, UK), according to time of year and day

Sun position diagram

→ ❸ shows the positions of the sun for Brighton, UK, i.e. for 51° north. The diagram shows the projection of the sun's position on plan at real local time, i.e. for Brighton on 23/9, sunrise is at 6:00 at $\alpha_s = 90°$ (east); at 12:00; $\alpha_s = 180°$ (south) and the elevation angle is 39°; and at sunset at 18:00 $\alpha_s = 270°$.

To determine the path of the sun's position for any location, Shell Solar in Hamburg provide a colour sun position diagram → ❹. This contains the plan projection of azimuth α_s and elevation angle γ_s according to day and date for each latitude and with a statement of the reference meridian.

To determine the position of the sun, loop-shaped curves are drawn for each full hour, with the thick line representing the first half of the year and the thin line the second. The loop shape of the hourly curves results from the elliptical orbit of the earth and the inclination results from the ecliptic. The times given refer to the time reference meridian in each case, i.e. the local time at the relevant location (Darmstadt).

The intersection points of the daily curves with the hourly curves with the same line thickness mark the position of the sun to the day and the hour. In the polar diagram, the position of the sun can be read from the right angle of the sun (azimuth) and the vertical angle of the sun (elevation) → ❹.

Projection of the path of the sun

With the stereographic projections → ❺, the discs supplied can be used to determine the path of the sun (in each case on 21st of the month) according to season and time.

Sun position, time and date determination

The position of the sun determines daylight conditions according to time of day and date. For purposes of determining daylight (e.g. for sun position diagrams) solar time is normally given. Each location is part of a time zone with uniform local time: if the local time is of interest, then the solar time has to be converted into local time = solar time + time conversion + time difference, including possible consideration of summer time.

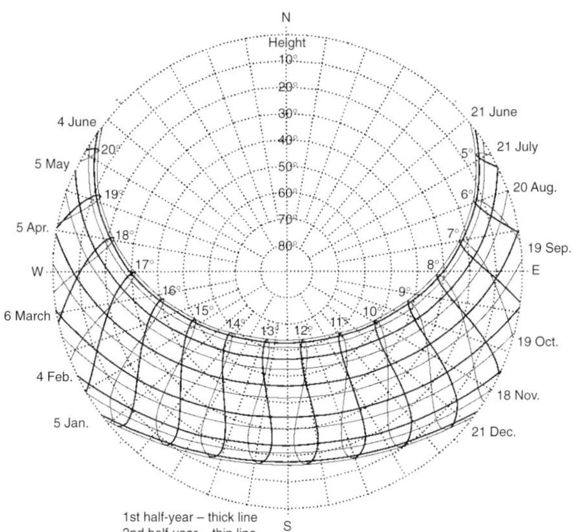

❹ Solar position diagram, Darmstadt, Germany: longitude = 8.65° east, latitude = 49.87° north

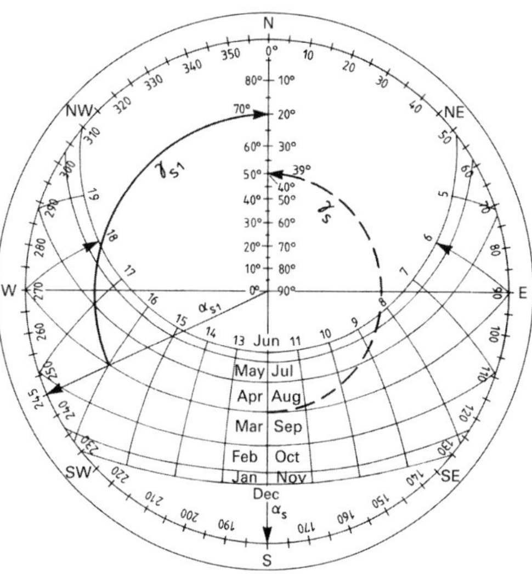

❺ Stereographic projection of the path of the sun, e.g. for latitude 51°. On 21/3 or 23/9: sunrise at 6:00, sunset at 18:00, $\gamma_s = 39°$ at 12:00

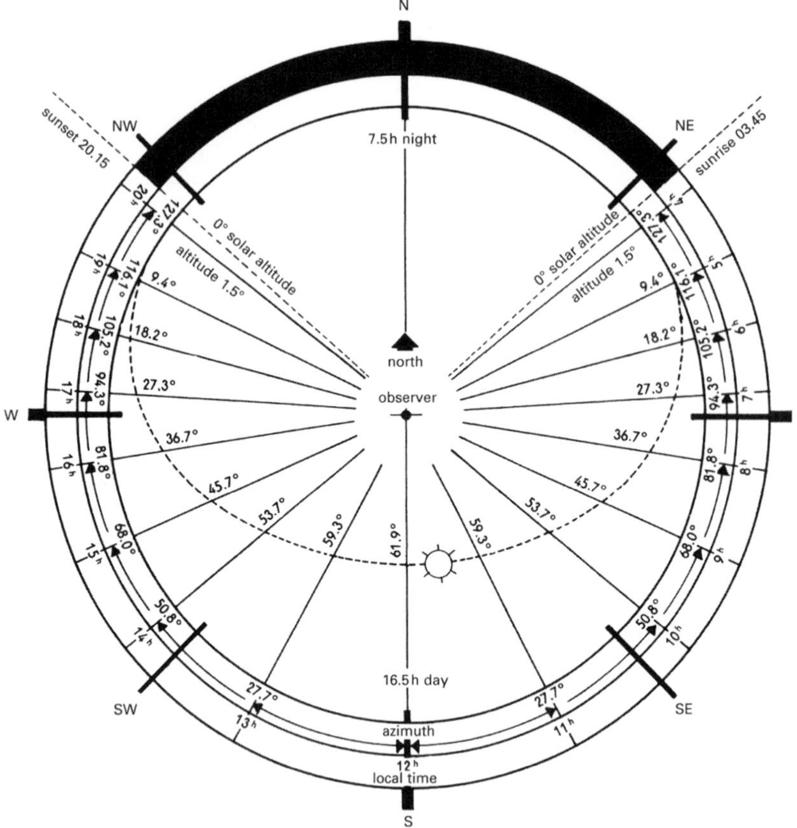

❶ Path of the sun at the **summer solstice** (about 21 June), longest day of the year, at latitude 51.5° north (London – Cardiff – Dortmund)

N
NW
NE
12 h night
north
observer
W
E
0° solar altitude
90° azimuth
90°
sunset 18.00
sunrise 06.00, 21 March and 23 September
altitude 9.3°
18.2°
26.2°
32.7°
37.1°
38.5°
78.3°
65.7°
51.9°
36.5°
19°
12h day
azimuth
12h
local time
SW
SE
S
17h
16h
15h
14h
13h
11h
10h
9h
8h
7h

❷ Path of the sun at the **spring equinox** (about 21 March) and **autumn equinox** (about 23 September)

Determination of insolation on buildings
This process enables the insolation on a planned building to be read immediately by laying a plan drawn on transparent paper according to its actual compass direction over the table of the sun's path or vice versa. The following details of the sun's path refer to the area at latitude 51.5° north (London – Cardiff – Dortmund) → ❶.

For the southern area at latitude 48° north (Freiburg im Breisgau – Munich – Salzburg – Vienna), 3.5° should be added to the calculated solar elevations.

For the northern area at latitude 55° north (Edinburgh – Newcastle – Bornholm – Königsberg), 3.5° should be deducted. The degrees shown in the second outer ring refer to the azimuth, i.e. the angle of the projection of the apparent east–west movement of the sun on the horizontal plane. The standard local times given on the outer ring refer within Germany to locations at longitude 15° east (Görlitz – Stargard – Bornholm = meridian of Central European Time). For locations at longitudes to the east of this, the local time is 4 minutes earlier than the standard time for every degree of longitude; for locations to the west of 15° = 4 minutes later than the standard time per degree. In London, specifically in Greenwich at 0° longitude, the local time is therefore 60 minutes later than the standard time.

Duration of insolation
The possible duration of insolation during the days from 21 May to 21 July = 16–16¾ hours, and from 21 November to 21 January = 8¼–7½ hours. In the months between these ranges, the duration of insolation changes by almost 2 hours per month. The actual amount of insolation is scarcely 40% of the above figures on account of clouds and mist. The actual degree of insolation is highly variable according to location. Berlin has relatively favourable conditions (in July almost 50%, Stuttgart 35%). Exact details can be obtained from the official weather services covering the particular area.

Sun and warmth
The natural warmth in the open air depends on the position of the sun and the release of heat by the ground. The warmth curve is delayed by about 1 month compared to the solar elevation curve, which means that the warmest days are not around 21 June but rather the later days of July, and the coldest days are not around 21 December but in the later part of January. Naturally the conditions at any specific location can vary widely in this respect as well.

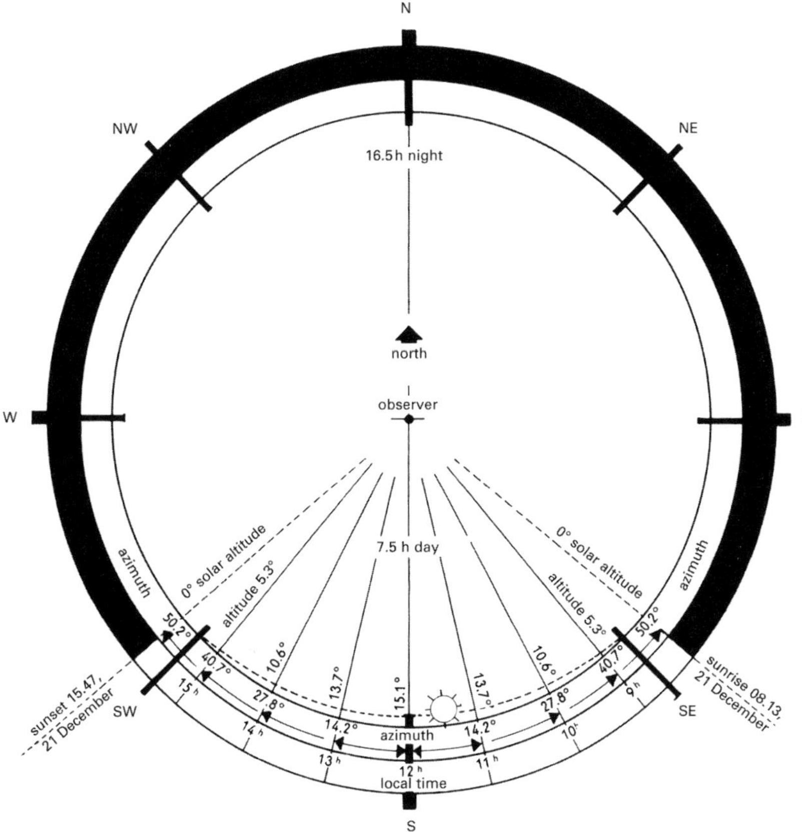

1 **Path of the sun:** winter solstice (about 21 December), shortest day of the year, latitude 51.5° north (London – Dortmund)

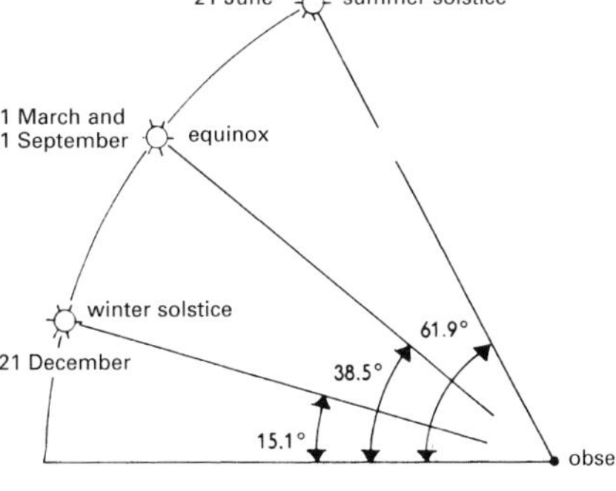

2 **Position of the sun** at midday on significant days of the year. The distance of the sun from the observer corresponds to the inner radius of the sun path diagrams → **1**, p. 490 **1** – **2**, with the dotted sun path on plan, which represents a projection of the relevant sun height on plan.

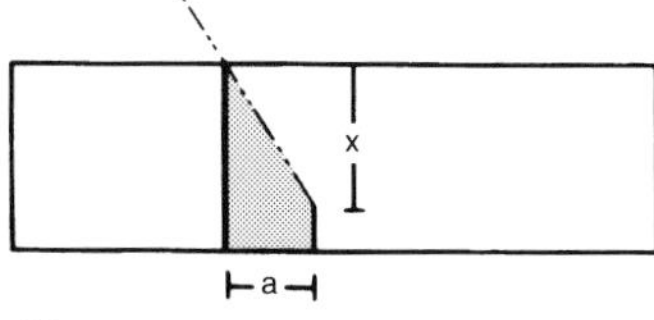

3 Elevation

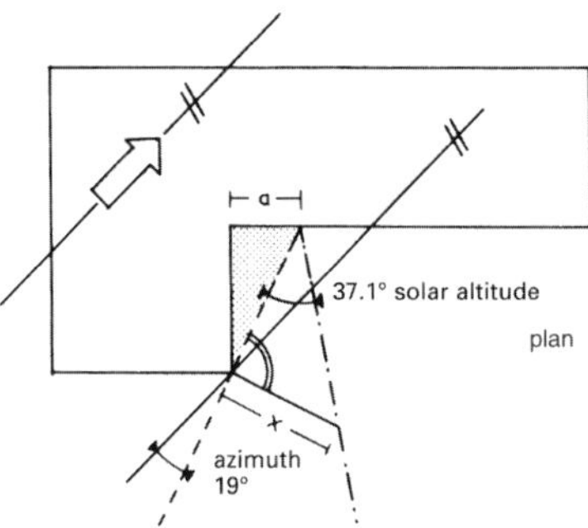

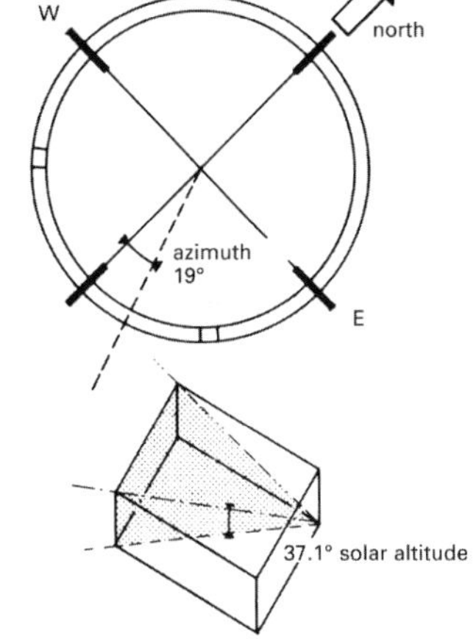

4 **Shadow construction:** to establish sunshine or shadow at any particular time of year and day (e.g. equinox at 11.00), the azimuth angle is drawn on the plan from the relevant corner. This represents the boundary of the shadow on the plan, on which the height of the sun (actual ray of light) is then drawn folded down onto the plan. The length x, measured perpendicularly onto the plan shadow, is entered onto the elevation to give, in connection with the building's upper edge, the boundary of the shadow on the front

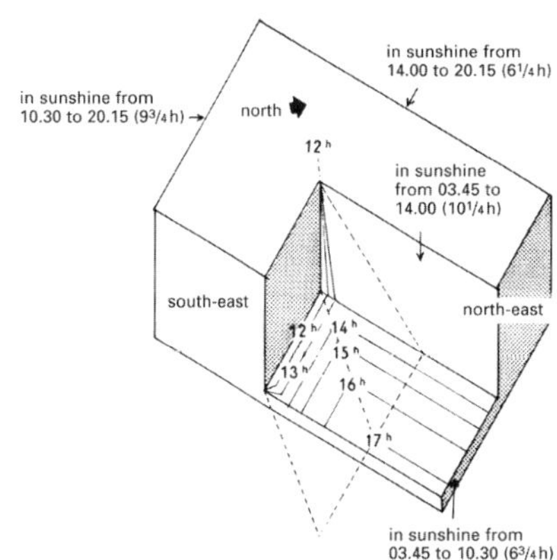

5 **Summer solstice.** Shadowing starts on the north side shortly after 11:00, the south-east side is also in shadow shortly after 13:00, during which times the other sides are in sunshine.

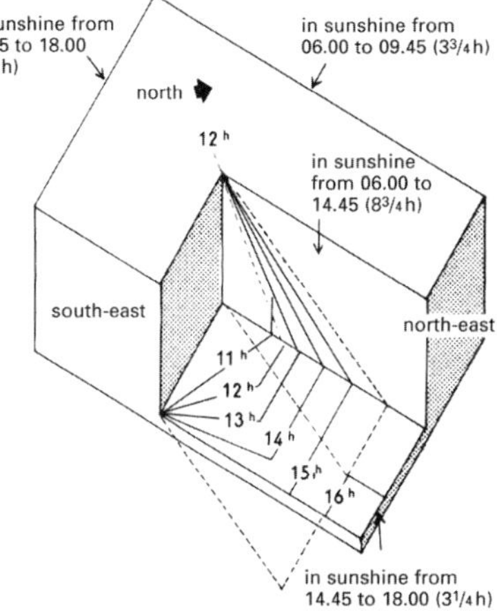

6 **Equinox.** The north-east side is in shadow shortly after 10:00, and the south-east side shortly before 15:00.

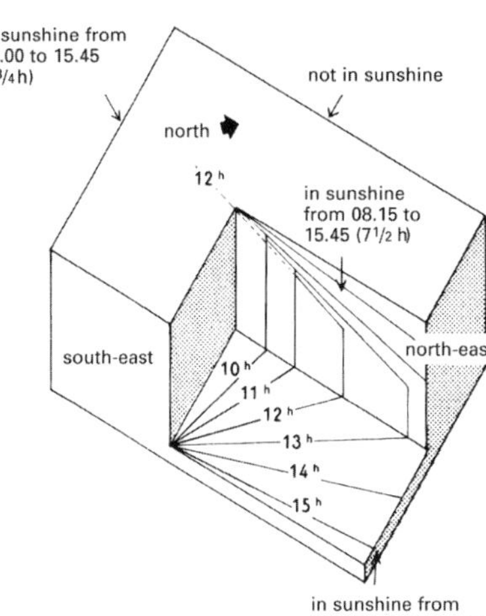

7 **Winter solstice.** The north-east side has scarcely an hour of sun and the south-east side is in shadow shortly after 15:00.

DAYLIGHT
Physical basics
Position of the sun
Insolation
Shadow
Radiation energy
Window lighting
Rooflighting
Quality criteria
Directing sunlight
Shading

BS 82062
DIN 5034

Building services

1 **Path of the sun** at the winter solstice = W, at the equinoxes = T, at the summer solstice = S, as experienced by a house or observer in north European countryside (51.5° latitude)

The correct alignment of a building and its windows to the sun, in order to exploit its beneficial effects or to provide protection against its excessive heat, is decisive for the practicality of a building. Sunshine entering all rooms in the autumn and winter, and in the morning, is desirable. Sunshine at midday and in the afternoon in June to August is not desirable. Correct alignment of the building → **10** – **13** and the appropriate construction measures → **14** – **17** can fulfil these requirements. The form of window reveals and glazing bar profiles should not unduly impair the entry of sunlight. High windows allow the sun to shine deeply into a room → p. 499 Directing sunlight.

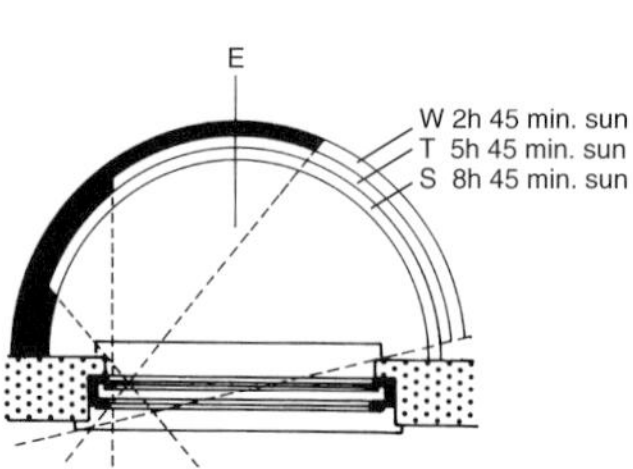

2 **East and west windows,** at the equinoxes, receive horizontal rays of sunlight, which become higher until the summer solstice. W = winter solstice, T = equinoxes, S = summer solstice.

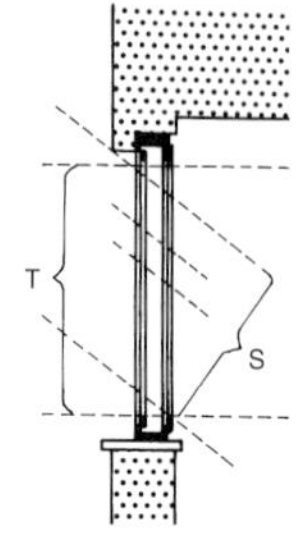

3 **Section of 2**

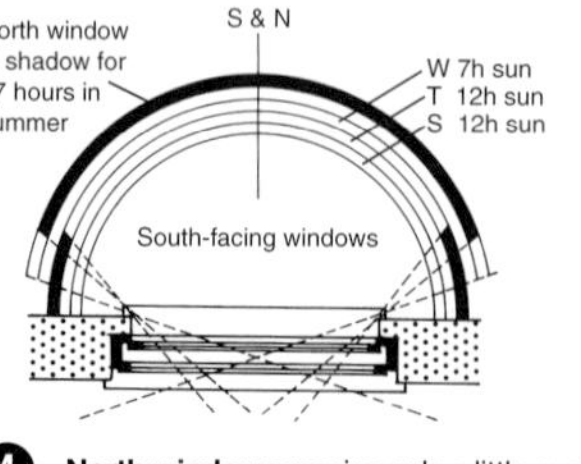

4 **North windows** receive only a little sunlight in the summer, around the summer solstice. South windows have flat rays of sunshine in the winter and steep rays in the summer, making these particularly suitable for rooms which should be sunny in the summer and winter

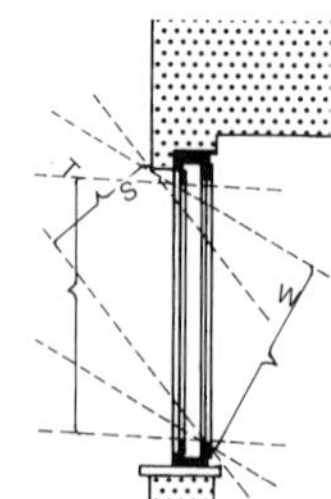

5 **Section of 4**

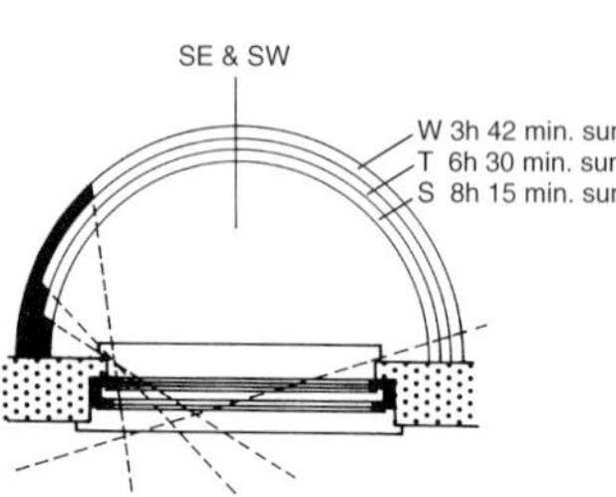

6 **South-east and south-west windows** receive pleasant sunshine in the summer and winter through flat, deeply penetrating rays

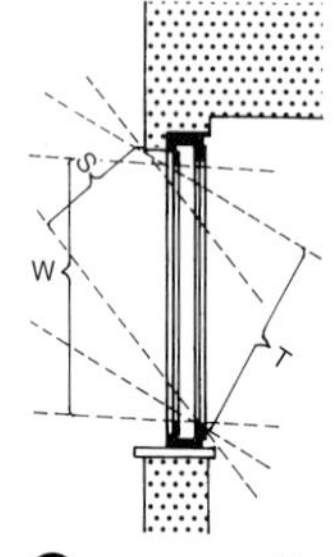

7 **Section of 6**

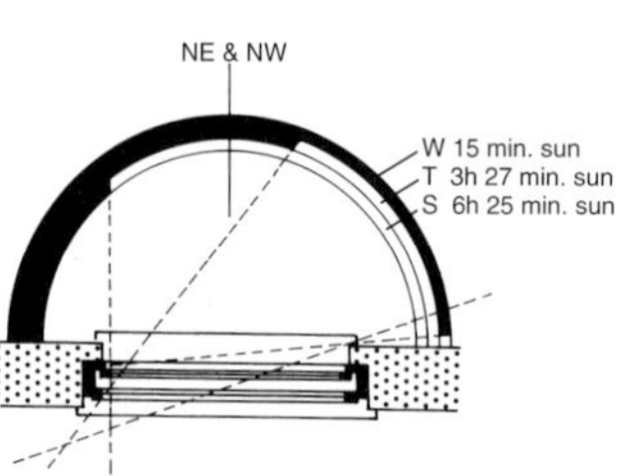

8 **North-east and north-west windows** receive no sun in the winter but effective sunshine in the early year and the autumn; in the summer, the sun comes in horizontally

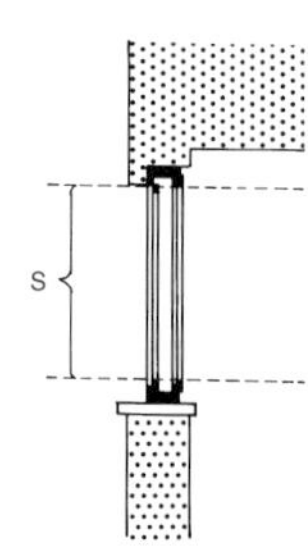

9 **Section of 8**

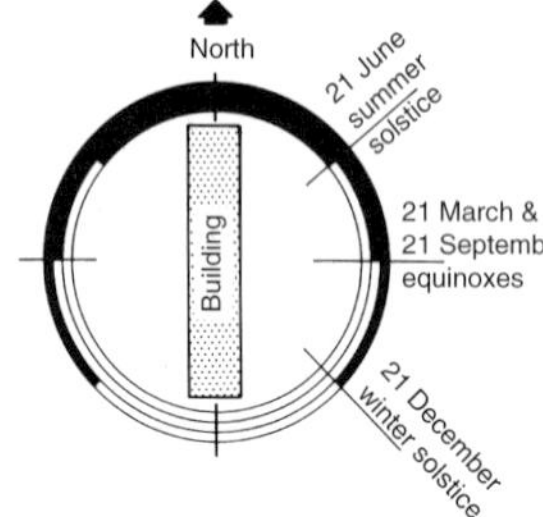

10 **A north–south block** receives sunshine on both sides, but has no windows on the north or south sides and therefore no sun into any rooms in November, December and January

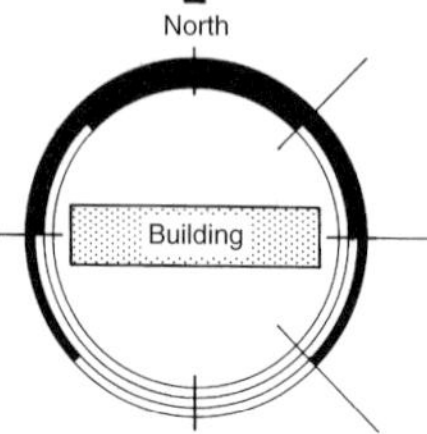
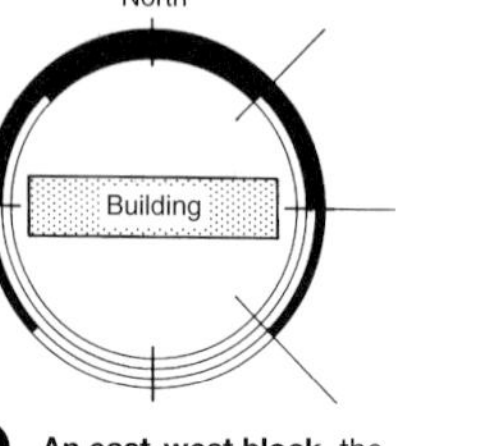

11 **An east-west block,** the best layout for small flats with 1–2 rooms: living rooms and bedrooms to the south (or open plan to the north); stairs, bathroom, lobby, kitchenette etc. to the north.

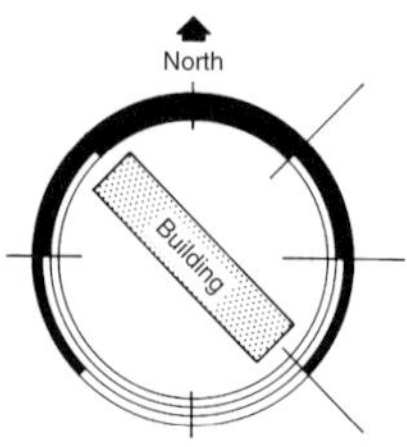

12 **A north-west to south-east block** is favourable for larger flats with bedrooms and utility rooms to the north-east and living rooms and children's rooms to the south-west

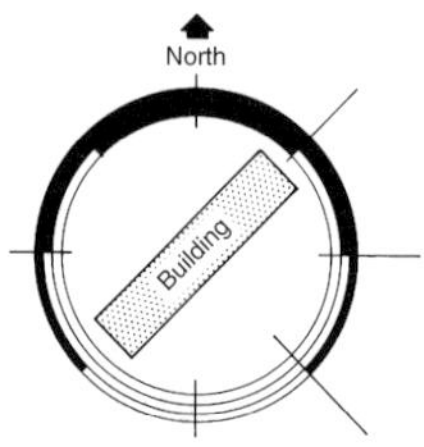

13 **A north-east to south-west block** is the best orientation for three- and four-room flats with living rooms and bedrooms to the south-east and utility and subsidiary rooms to the north-west

14 **South side:** sun and warmth penetrate deep into the house. In summer, sun and heat is kept out by windows and walls

15 **East side:** the flat sun rays from the east permit broad, mostly also wind-protected, terraces without hindering the entry of sunshine into the rooms

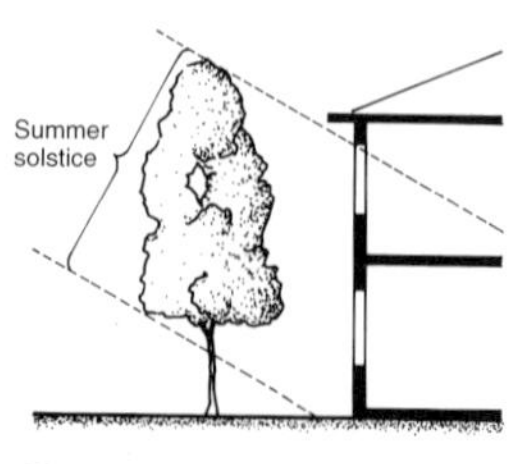

16 **West side:** disagreeable sunshine from the west and summer weather are best shaded by deciduous trees, which in the winter lose their leaves and permit the sun to enter

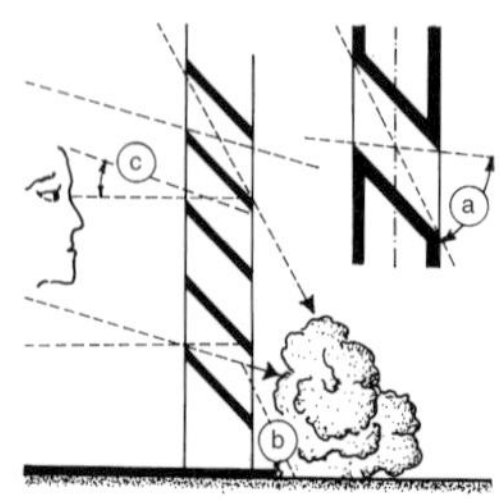

17 **A planked fence or balcony parapet** in this form lets most sunshine through → ⓐ, deflects the remaining rays → ⓑ and protects against overlooking and wind → ⓒ

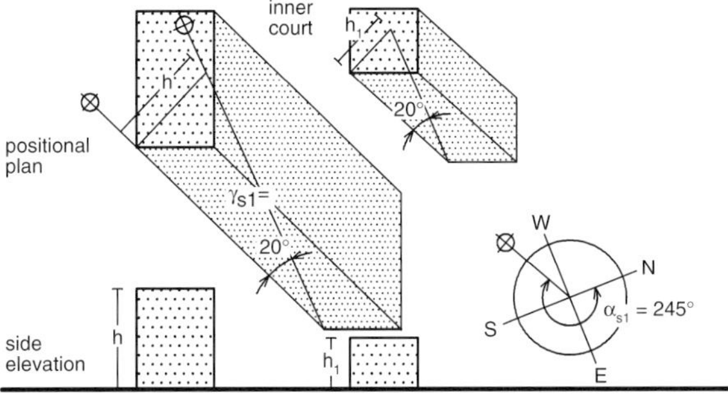

❶ Graphical shadow construction

❷ Panorama mask (curved) in position

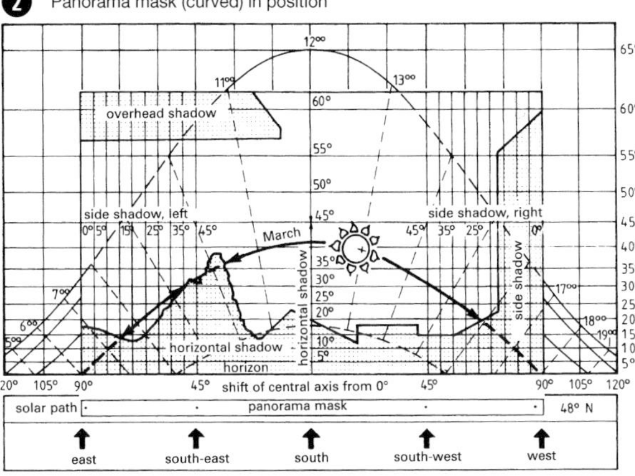

❸ Possible shadow distributions on the film

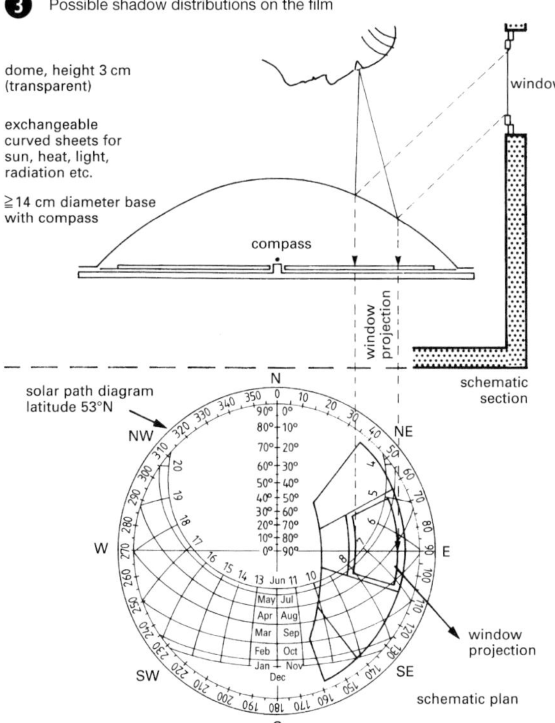

❹ Horizontoscope with projection of a window – east side

Sun position, shadow, aids

The following equipment is available for the determination and checking of the actual sunshine or shadowing inside and outside a building according to geographical location, time of day and year, construction details and local conditions:

Graphical shadow construction

The determination of the shadow thrown by a building can be constructed using the projected path of the sun → p. 489 ❹ + ❺ on plan and in elevation. For example, the shadowing of a courtyard in Brighton, UK, latitude 51° north, is to be constructed for 21 March at 16:00. The sun is shining at this time at an azimuth angle (α_{s1}) of 245° and an elevation (γ_{s1}) of 20° → p. 489 ❺. The layout plan is aligned with north. The shadow direction is determined by the horizontal building edges and a parallel displacement of the sunshine direction (α_{s1} = 245°) through the corners of the building. The length of the shadow is determined by the vertical building edges, so the actual building height (h) is constructed folded down onto the plan and with the elevation angle of 20°. The intersection with the shadow direction gives the shadow length.

Panorama mask

In many countries, a representation of the path of the sun is available for various geographical areas with details of azimuth and elevation, day and time of year. These panorama masks are copied onto transparent film and used at the location under investigation by holding them in the direction the sun will come from → ❷. Looking through the panorama template, any shadowing from the surroundings, including overhead shadows, can be transferred at 1:1 onto the copied path of the sun → ❸. The film can therefore be used to determine shadowing and sunshine on façades or in building recesses to the correct scale.

Horizontoscope

This is a tool to determine the real sun and shadow conditions on the building site, on or in a building. The horizontoscope consists of a transparent dome representing the sky, a compass, a base and exchangeable curve sheets, which can be laid underneath for light, radiation or heat as required.

The principle of the horizontoscope is to construct the prevailing light and shadow conditions, e.g. for a room → ❹. At a particular point in the room, the projection of a window opening on the sky dome, and at the same time the curve sheet beneath it, can be used to show the actual opening section and the incoming light. This makes it possible to determine the sunshine conditions and also the lighting effects for any point in the room, depending on the alignment of the building, for any time of day and year → ❹.

Model and computer simulation

In order to be able to establish the exact annual shadowing or sunshine around, in and on a building, it is recommended to construct a scale model under an artificial sun and also to test the design with a computer simulation. The model gives an immediate idea of the rooms and the effect of the lighting. Because the parallel sunlight is modelled with a 60–100 cm concave mirror, the model cannot be larger. Computer simulations can be used to determine exact daylight quotients, illuminances and distributions of luminance, but normally do not give information about the mood and effect of lighting in the room.

Average global radiation in kWh/m², April to September (1976–1989)

1 Solar radiation map for Germany for the summer half year

2 Mean daily solar radiation (above) and hours of sunshine (below) in the UK

condition of sky, e.g. latitude 51°N			
weather	clear, cloudless blue sky	misty, cloudy; sun visible as white disc	full cloud cover
horizontal radiation strength (W/m²)	600–800	200–400	50–150
horizontal illuminance (lx)	60 000–100 000	19 000–40 000	5000–20 000
proportion of diffused light	10–20%	20–30%	80–100%

3 Annual variation in radiation intensity and changing daylight qualities for various weather conditions

4 Intensity of solar radiation

Meteorological conditions

The heat radiation and the intensity of daylight reaching the earth's surface over the course of a year is determined by the geographical latitude, the weather and various states of the sky (clear, clouded, hazy, partially clouded etc.) → ❸. The following facts are relevant to typical daylight and sunshine duration:

The year has 8760 hours. The duration of 'bright daylight' averages approx. 4300 hours per year.

The number of hours of sunshine in Germany varies between 1300 and 1900 hours per year → ❶, of which at least ¾ are in the summer half of the year → European Sun Atlas.

For most of the year, that is about ⅔ of the daylight hours, only more or less diffuse sunlight reaches the earth on account of the local weather conditions.

Global radiation

Direct and indirect solar radiation on the earth's surface (global radiation) creates a locally variable climate and light environment on the surface → ❶ – ❷. The global radiation creates 'heat and light' simultaneously, i.e. the short-wave solar radiation is converted into long-wave radiation (heat) at the surface – the greenhouse effect. This heat should be exploited passively and actively in architecture, and also the simultaneous daylight.

The locally specific light and heat conditions therefore require a precise analysis in order to exploit them for optimal daylight in and around a building.

Radiation: physical basics

Solar radiation is a very 'fickle' source of light and heat. Only a small part of the sun's energy is transferred to the ground as heat because the earth's atmosphere weakens the solar radiation or makes it seem irregular in intensity. This reduction is essentially due to various diffusion processes like scattering, reflection and absorption of the radiation by dust and mist particles (the cause of diffused daylight) and the water vapour, carbon dioxide and ozone content in the air → ❹.

Distribution of the total energy at the surface: about 6% of ultra violet radiation in the wavelength range 0.2–0.38 μm, about 50% of visible radiation in the wavelength range 0.38–0.78 μm (the maximum lies at 0.5 μm in the visible range) and about 40% infra red radiation in the wavelength range 0.78–3.0 μm.

Solar radiation reaching the ground is shown in → ❹. The solar constant to be applied in the central European region is about 1300 W/m² on a vertically radiated area.

Lighting and radiation strength

The power of the radiation is reduced by very thick cloud cover to about 200 W/m² and with only diffused radiation (cloudy sky with completely covered sun) to about 50–200 W/m² → ❹. This also applies analogously to the strength of the daylight in lux → ❸.

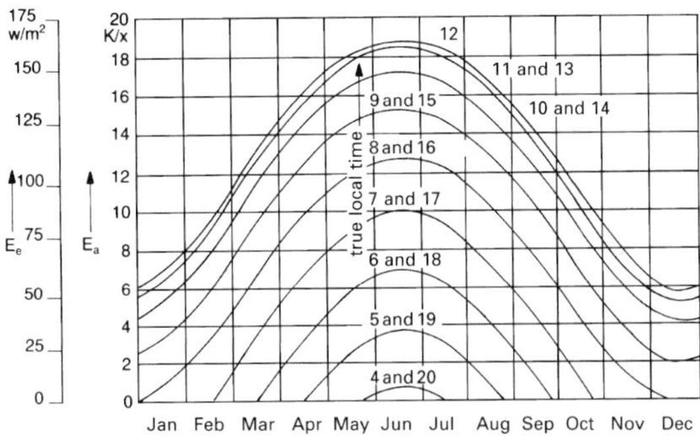

❶ Horizontal illuminance Ea under a clouded sky at 51°N, depending on time of year and day. E_e = horizontal irradiance

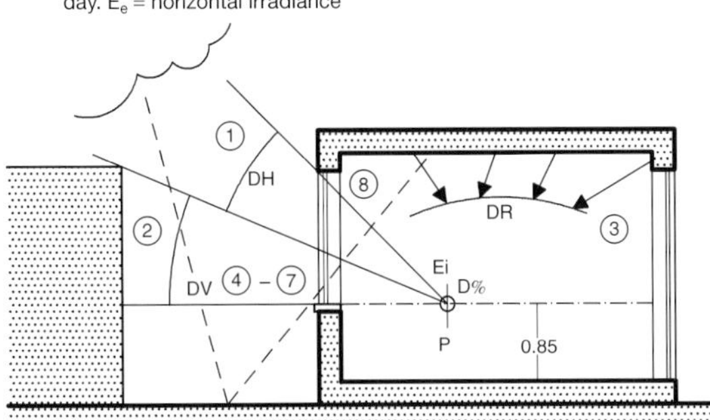

❷ Factors influencing daylight in interiors, e.g. at point P

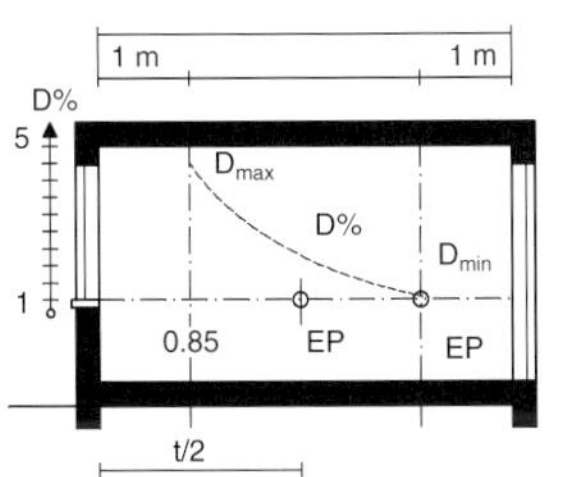

❸ Daylight factor D% with reference plane in section

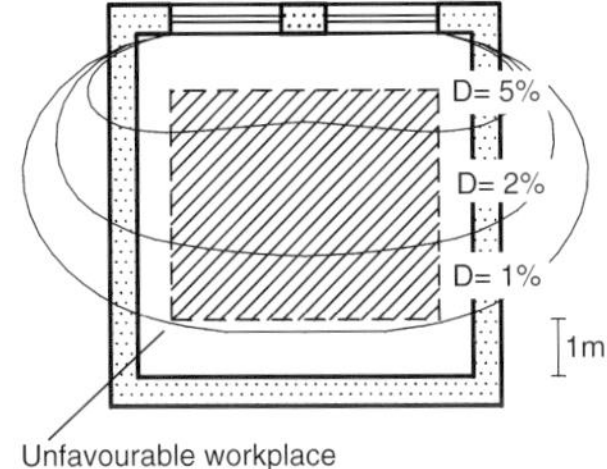

❹ Daylight distribution D% on a plan with two side windows

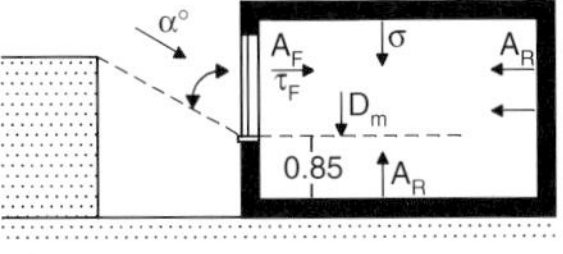

❺ Average daylight factor D_m – influential factors

Determination

$$D_m = \frac{A_F}{A_R} \times \frac{\tau \times \alpha^\circ}{(1 \times \sigma_m)}\%$$

A_F = Window area

A_R = all room areas

τ_F = transmittance of windows

α° = angle of incidence of daylight

σ_m = average reflectivity of room surfaces

σ_m (0.5) = light surfaces

σ_m (0.2) = dark surfaces

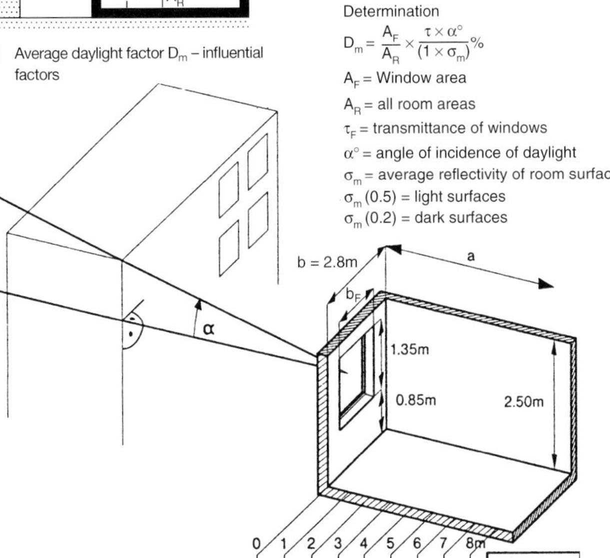

❻ The minimum window width as a percentage, before finishings, should not be less than 65% of the room width. For larger room depths and a wide angle to adjacent buildings, even a window width of 100% may not be sufficient.

Daylight inside buildings with window lighting

The daylight inside buildings can be evaluated according to the following quality criteria and scales: illuminance and brightness; uniformity, D_{min}/D_{max}; reflection; colour rendering; glare; room lines, shadowing; view out.

Basics

The evaluation of the daylight inside buildings is always based on the illuminance of the clouded sky (i.e. diffuse radiation). Daylight entering an interior through a window at the side is measured by the daylight factor D. This describes the ratio of the interior illuminance (Ei) to the illuminance outside at the same time (Ea): $D = E_i : E_a \times 100\%$. The daylight in interiors is always given in per cent, for example outside illuminance 5000 lx and inside illuminance 500 lx gives D = 10%. The daylight factor is always constant, and the interior illuminance alters only in relationship to the outside illuminance at the same time. The outside illuminance of the clouded sky varies according to the time of day and year: 5000 lx in the winter, and up to 20,000 lx in the summer → ❶.

Daylight distribution in interiors

The daylight factor at a point (P) is a combination of many influential factors: $D = (DH + DV + DR) \times \tau \times k_1 \times k_2 \times k_3$ → ❷. where:

1. DH = component of light from sky – daylight incidence $< \alpha^\circ$
2. DV = building component
3. DR = interior reflection component
4. τ = light transmittance of glazing
5. k_1 = glazing bars and window construction component
6. k_2 = glazing bars
7. k_3 = angle of incidence of daylight
8. window position and size → ❷.

The reference plane for the horizontal illuminance of window lighting is provided in DIN 5034 → ❸. The level of the windowsill is assumed at 0.85 m and the distance to the surrounding surfaces of the room is 1 m. On this reference plane, the points (EP) to be named for the horizontal illuminance are determined. The corresponding (to be determined) daylight factors can then be displayed as a curve of daylight factors → ❸ + ❺. The shape of this curve in section and on plan provides information about the horizontal illuminance on the reference plane (at the corresponding points), and can be used to determine D_{min} and D_{max} (uniformity). The daylight factor curve also supplies information about the daily lighting curve in the room.

Required daylight factors D%

The applicable regulations for this are in DIN 5034. While this gives exact details of the minimum requirements for daylight distribution in interiors and workrooms, the distribution of daylight is not precisely defined in the Workplace Guidelines:

- $D_{min} \geqq 1\%$ in residential rooms: reference point – middle of the room, windows in workrooms: reference point = deepest point in room
- $D_{min} \geqq 2\%$ in workrooms – with windows on two sides
- G = uniformity: $D_{min}/D_{max} \geqq 1{:}6$ indirect light
- D_m = average daylight factor. It gives information about the average daylight lighting in the room → ❺.

View out and visual connections

Visual contacts from inside to outside are a necessary part of life. The standard therefore gives tables of minimum window widths depending on room depths, room widths and building angles: window width should be ≧65% of room width → ❻ → DIN 5034, state building regulations.

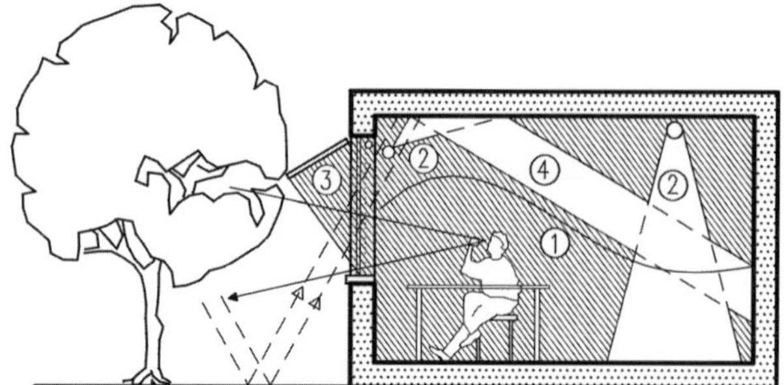

❶ Control of daylight and artificial lighting: 1, daylight pattern D%; 2, daylight-enhancing lighting; 3, prevention of glare; 4, reflecting surface

Aims → ❶ – ❽
- no glare, direct or indirect
- differentiated shadowing
- optimal daylight lighting, control
- view out at all times of year
- balanced lighting environment day and night
- colourful daylight-enhancing but similar lighting, in the depths of the room
- reduced artificial lighting component
- matt, light, pastel-coloured surfaces

Requirements
- DIN 5034
- European Standard for Computer Workplaces
- German state building regulations

In detail:
- $D_{min} \geqq 2\%$
- $G \geqq 1:6$ (uniformity D_{min}/D_{max})
- estimated window sizes for room depths, approx.:
  $\leqq$8 m approx. 16–20%
  $\leqq$8–11 m approx. 25%
  $\leqq$11–14 m approx. 30%
  $\leqq$14 m approx. 35% of the room area

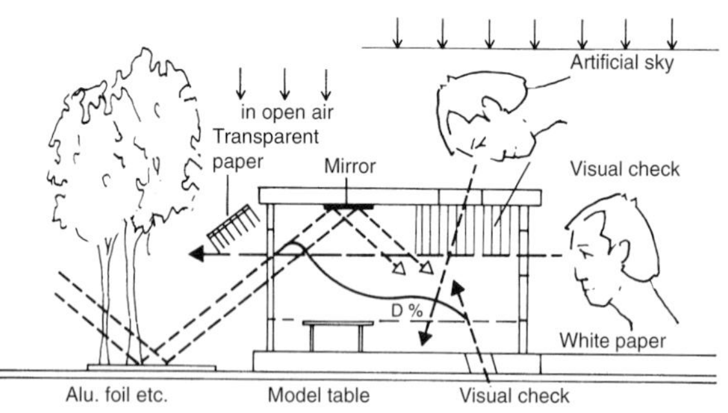

❷ Experimenting with daylight on a model in the open air and under an artificial sky

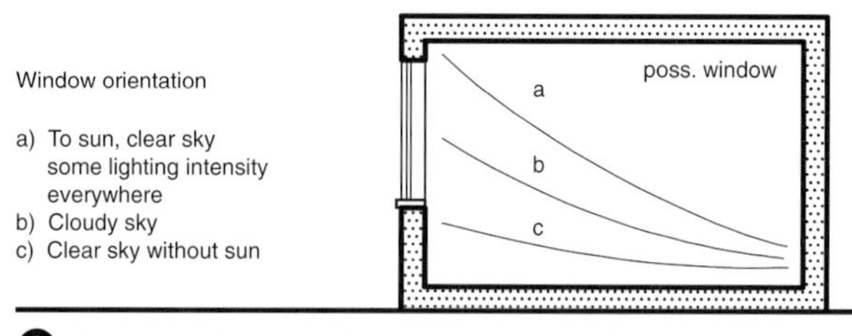

❸ Daylight level in a room with various sky lighting conditions

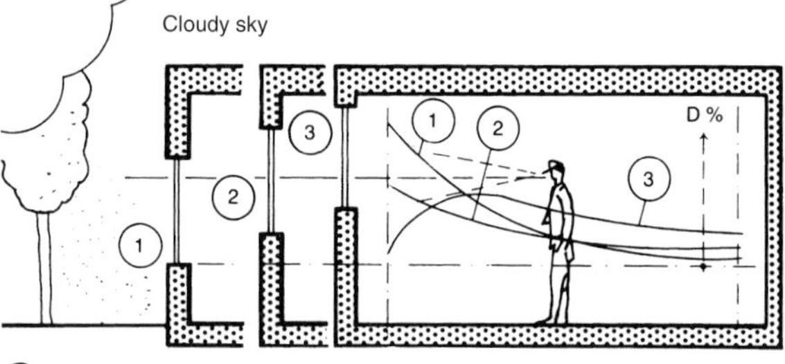

❹ Different distributions of daylight with various positions of window

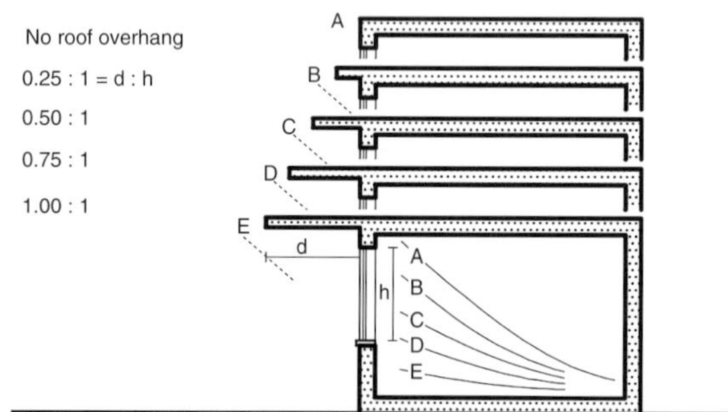

❺ Daylight distributions in a room with various projections under a cloudy sky

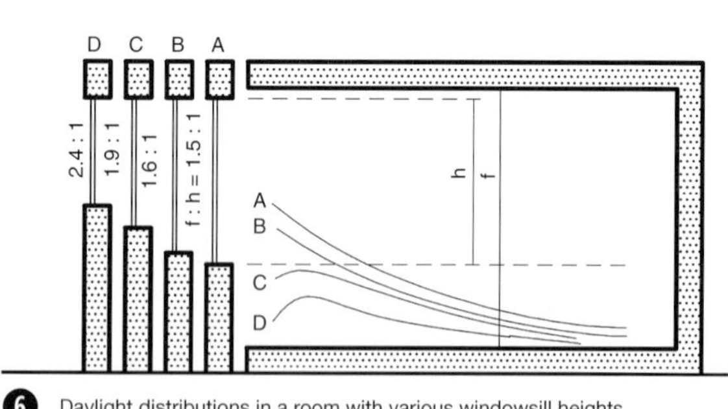

❻ Daylight distributions in a room with various windowsill heights

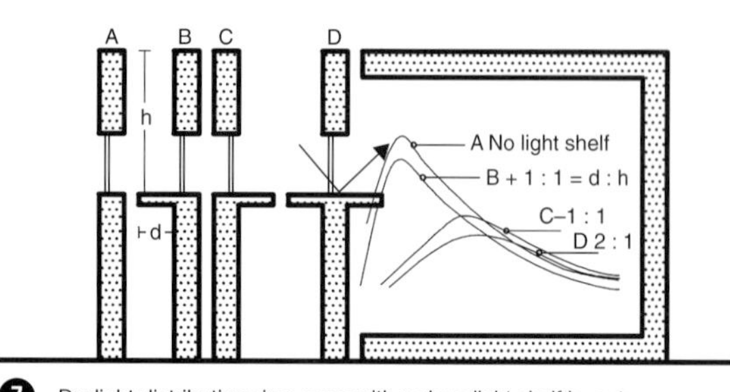

❼ Daylight distributions in a room with various light shelf layouts

❽ Daylight situations from the first to the eighth floor in an atrium, excerpt → ❾

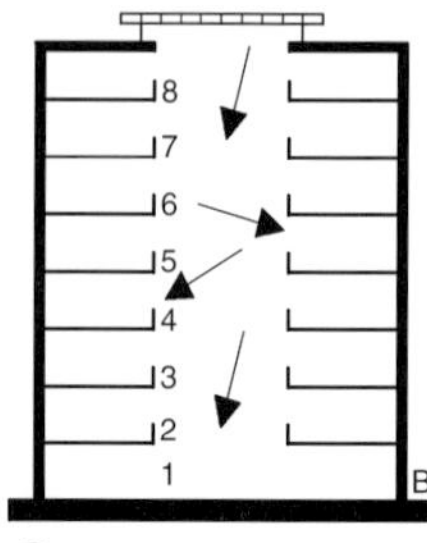

❾ Section of atrium, first to eighth floors, with glass roof

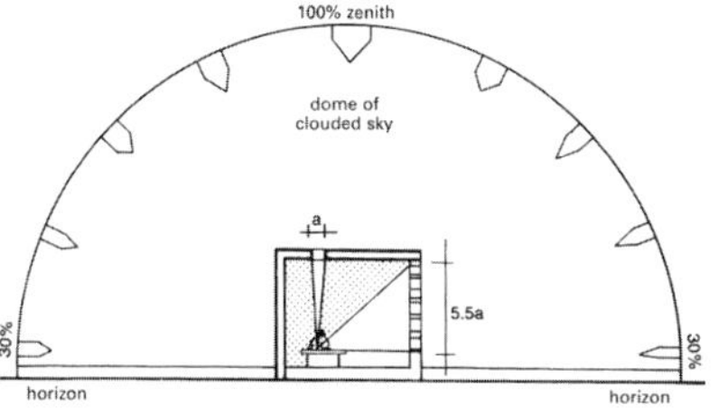

❶ Room with roof opening and side window, according to distribution of light from the zenith

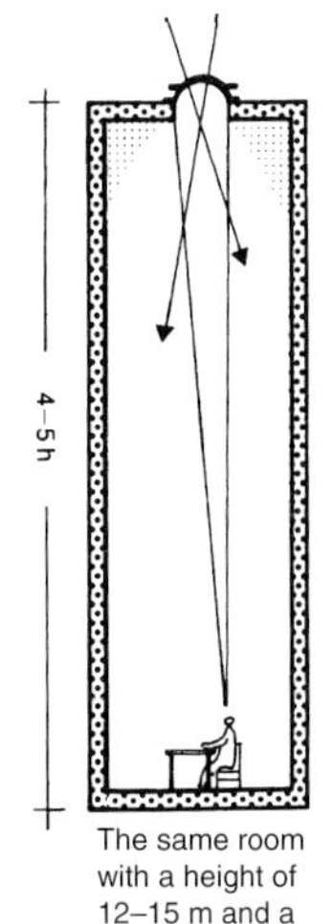

The same room with a height of 12–15 m and a roof opening

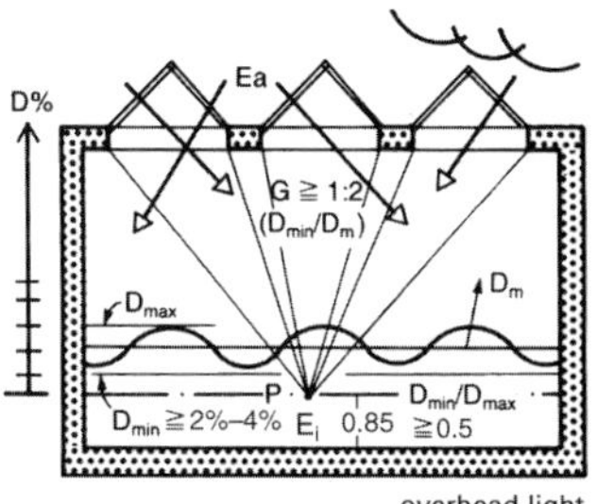

❷ Section through a room with rooflight

❸ Square room with a height of 3 m

Basics

The lighting of interiors with daylight from above is subject to the same basic principles and conditions as for windows at the sides, that is natural lighting under a cloudy sky. Whereas light from the sides creates relatively poor uniformity, this is different with lighting from above. In interiors the quality of daylight coming from rooflights is mainly determined or influenced by the following factors: light density at the zenith, room proportions, room reflection, rooflight opening and reduction factors. The work area → ❶ in a room is placed precisely as far from a window as from the rooflight above. If the same illuminance is to be produced on the reference plane (0.85 m above sill level) through the side window as through the rooflight, then the window area would have to be 5.5 times larger than the roof opening.

Reason: light from above is brighter. The zenith illuminance is three times that at the horizon. So 100% of the light from the sky reaches the rooflight, whereas only 33.3% of the light from the sky reaches the windows at the sides. The lighting of a room 'from above' (light incidence) depends on the room proportions, i.e. the length, width and height. The 'cave effect' should be avoided → ❷.

Required minimum daylight factors

In order to guarantee adequate lighting in a room, the following points have to be noted:

$D_{min}/D_{max} \geqq 0.5$, $D_{min} \geqq 2\%$, in workrooms $\geqq 4\%$

Uniformity G $\geqq$ 1:2, a corresponding opening area of approx. $\geqq$ 16–22% of the plan area → ❸.

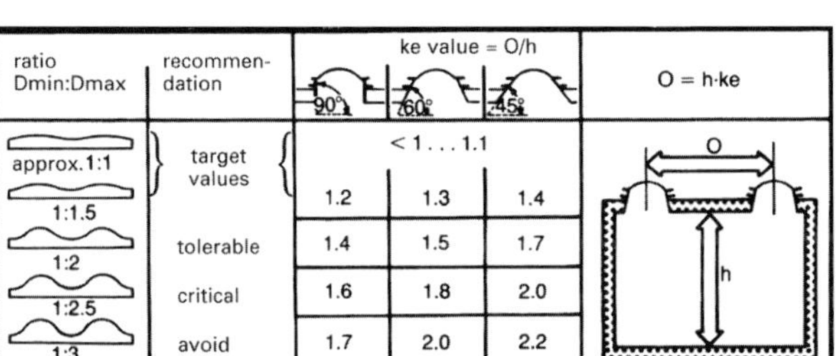

ratio Dmin:Dmax	recommendation	ke value = O/h 90°	60°	45°	O = h·ke
approx. 1:1	target values	< 1 . . . 1.1			
1:1.5		1.2	1.3	1.4	
1:2	tolerable	1.4	1.5	1.7	
1:2.5	critical	1.6	1.8	2.0	
1:3	avoid	1.7	2.0	2.2	

❹ Rooflight spacing, room height and the uniformity of lighting which is sought, including corresponding detailing of the rooflight (ke factor)

Rooflight openings

The advantage of lighting with daylight 'from above' is influenced by the following design factors: room height and clear opening (ke factor). An ideal uniformity is achieved if the spacing of the rooflights (O) corresponds to the room height (h), i.e. a ratio of 1:1. In practice, the following rule applies: the ratio of rooflight spacing to room height should be 1:1.5 to 1:2 → ❹. This table shows these relationships and their effect. The insertion of light shafts is also recommended.

Type and construction of rooflight opening

The pitch of a rooflight determines the percentage of light from the section of the sky framed by it. In → ❺, the amount of light entering through a side window is compared with the amount of light entering through a rooflight at various pitches. The greatest amount of light comes in though a horizontal opening.

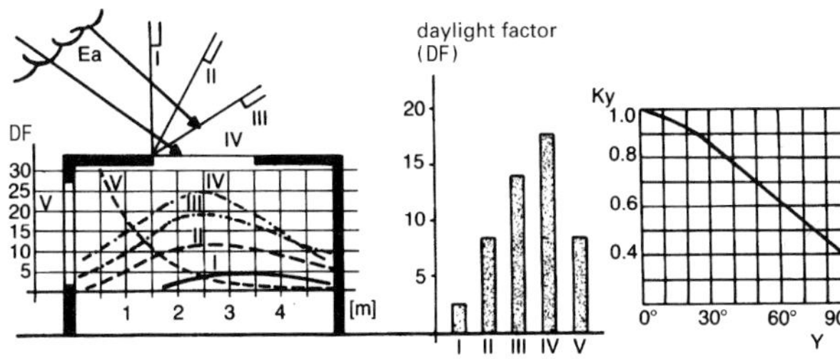

❺ (a) Comparative variations in daylight factor for side windows and rooflights, depending on four differently pitched rooflight openings

(b) Reduction factor ky, depending on pitch y of glazing in shed roofs

The maximum illuminance through a side window, in contrast, is achieved only near the window. With a vertical rooflight, the lowest illuminance is on the reference plane. There is therefore a reduction factor (ky) for the amount of light entering, depending on the different pitches of the roof openings. In → ❺ (b), the corresponding reduction factors (ky) are shown for sheds with various pitches.

The diffused radiation falling on the rooflight is, however, also affected by its construction and installation depth before it supplies the interior with daylight. → ❻ demonstrates the different amounts of light entering through various proportions of the shaft below the rooflight cover. Excessively high and massive shaft construction or installation depths should therefore be avoided. A delicate, highly reflective construction is recommended.

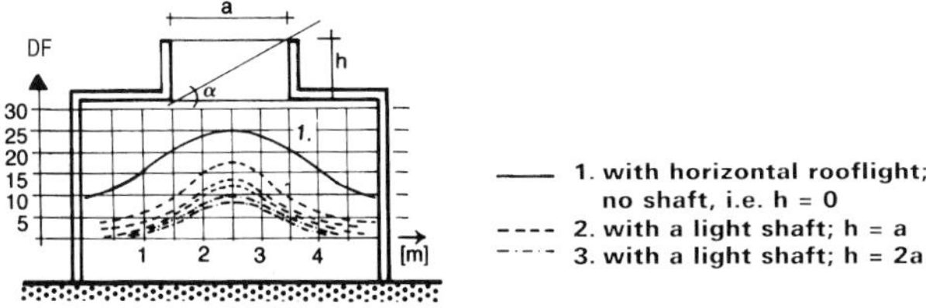

❻ Uniformity of lighting, depending on height of rooflight shaft

DAYLIGHT

Physical basics
Position of the sun
Insolation
Shadow
Radiation energy
Window lighting
Rooflighting
Quality criteria
Directing sunlight
Shading

BS 8206-2
DIN 5034

Building services

Type of work	Daylight D%
coarse	1.33
medium fine	2.66
fine	5.00
very fine	10.00
note: 10% is too much on the south side, but good on the north side	

❶ Illuminances D%

Colour by brightness		Materials without colour treatment		Floor coverings: rolls and tiles	
(dark to bright)		(dark to bright)		(dark to bright)	
red	0.1–0.5	smooth concrete	0.25–0.5	dark	0.1–0.15
yellow	0.25–0.65	facing brick		medium	0.15–0.25
green	0.15–0.55	red brick	0.15–0.3	bright	0.25–0.4
blue	0.1–0.3	yellow brick	0.3–0.45		
brown	0.1–0.4	lime sandstone	0.5–0.6		
white (medium)	0.7–0.75	timber surfaces			
grey	0.15–0.6	dark	0.1–0.2		
black	0.05–0.1	medium	0.2–0.4		
		bright	0.4–0.5		

❷ Degree of reflection (further details and material colours → p. 506)

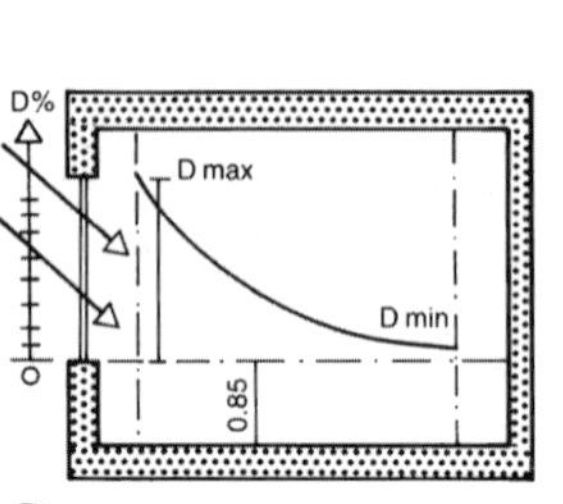

❸ Uniformity of lighting from the side

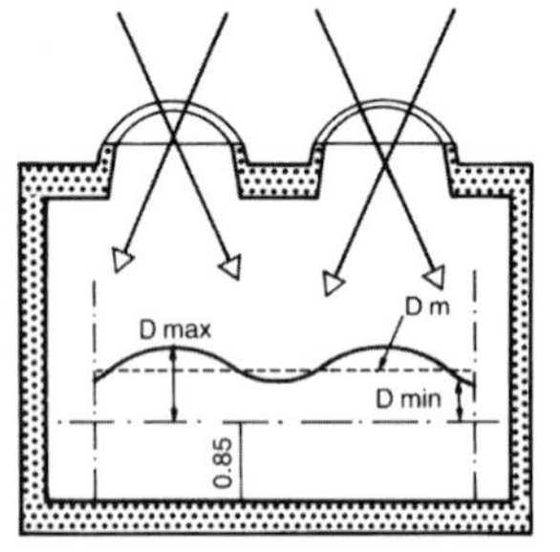

❹ Uniformity of lighting from above

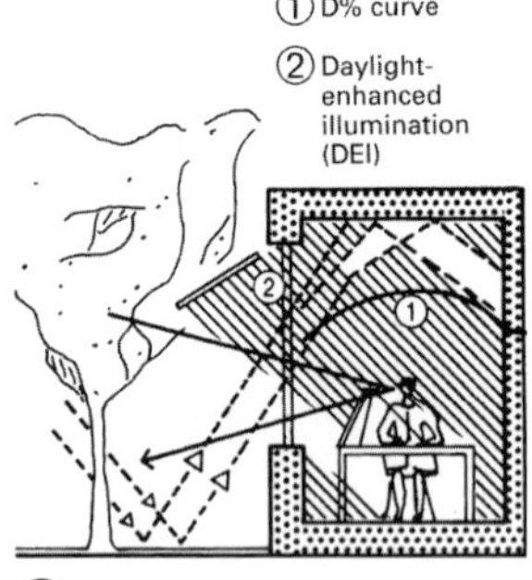

❺ Shadow formation with lighting from the side

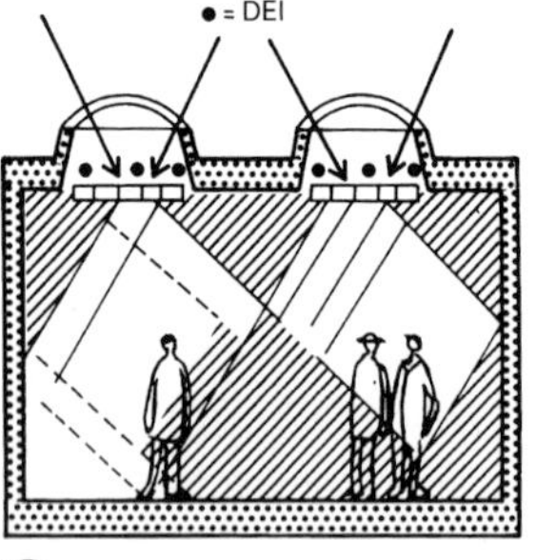

❻ Shadow formation with lighting from above

❼ Influence of daylight openings (for the same main dimensions of the room, k_F = window area/plan area = 1:6) on the variation in daylight factor. D_{min} = 5% of necessary k_F value is also given.

Illuminance, degree of reflection and colour rendering

The interaction of these parameters of daylight has a great influence on the brightness inside a room. In order to fulfil certain visual tasks, various levels of illuminance are required, according to the type of activity → ❶.

So the specification of the degree of reflection for the surrounding surfaces of the interior has to be appropriate for the visual tasks to be carried out. The different structuring of brightness in a room is directly dependent on the degree of reflection of the surfaces and the different arrangements of windows in the façade → ❷ → p. 496 ❹.

The uniformity (G) of the daylight in the interior should be $G \geqq D_{min}/D_{max}$ 1:6 for lighting from windows → ❸, and $G \geqq$ 1:2 → ❹ for lighting from above. This generally determines the characteristics of light distribution in the interior. Rooflight lighting is more uniform because the light density at the zenith is three times greater than at the horizon.

The uniformity can be influenced by variation of the following factors:
- degree of reflection (if very high)
- deflecting the light with shades
- arrangement of the windows.

Glare

Glare is caused by direct and indirect reflection from surfaces and by unfavourable contrasts of light density. Measures to avoid glare are:
- external sun protection (shades)
- glare protection inside and outside in combination with sun protection
- matt surfaces
- correct positioning of daylight-enhancing lighting

Shadow formation

Shadow formation is beneficial to some extent in order to be able to differentiate objects in the room → ❺. Measures to increase three-dimensional shadow formation under side lighting are:
- sun protection
- glare protection (even in the north)
- balanced daylight distribution
- no direct glare
- multi-layered or staggered façade.

Measures for such shadow formation with rooflights:
- → ❻. Filter incoming daylight at the underside of the light opening with translucent materials, light grating or similar.
- daylight-enhancing lighting
- bright, matt surfaces combined with coloured differentiation (e.g. supporting structure).

Summary: quality criteria for daylight from side windows

It is generally best to implement the above daylight quality criteria so as to create spatial identity. The distribution of daylight in interiors and the possibilities of seeing out are mainly determined by the design of the façade at the transition from inside to outside. A staggered, multi-layered and at the same time transparent transition from interior to exterior can cope with the various requirements for daylight during the changing seasons.

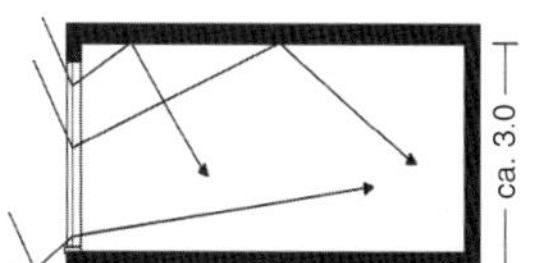

Light direction within the facade with appropriately reflecting room surfaces for large room depths

Light direction in the roof for the lighting or rooms, e.g. in atriums, museums, sport halls. . . pale floor!

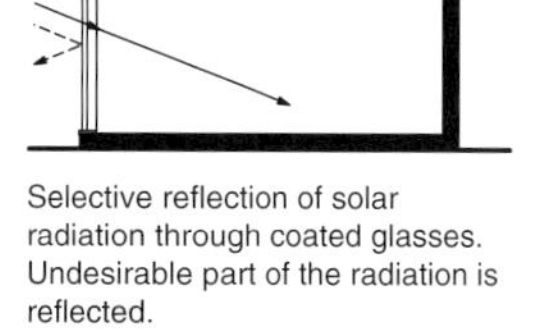

Selective reflection of solar radiation through coated glasses. Undesirable part of the radiation is reflected.

1 Principles of light direction

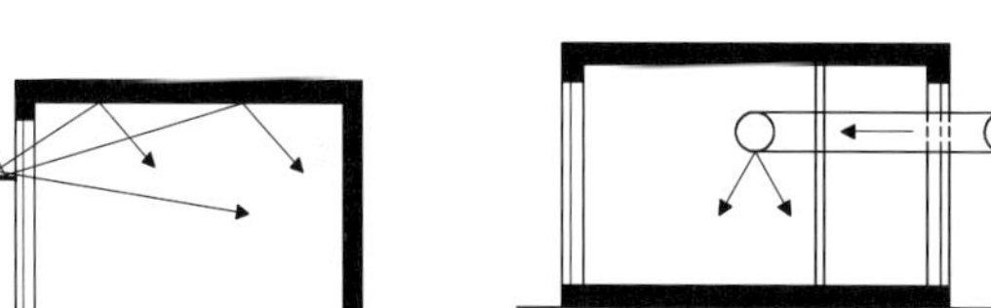

- Redirection
- Curved reflecting surface, projection in transom area

2 Light blade

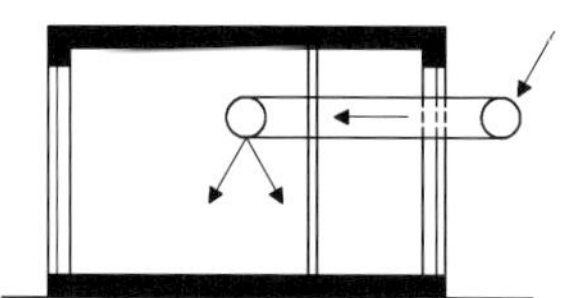

- Light direction in the room depth
- Highly reflecting tubes or glass fibres (e.g. Schott)

3 Light pipe

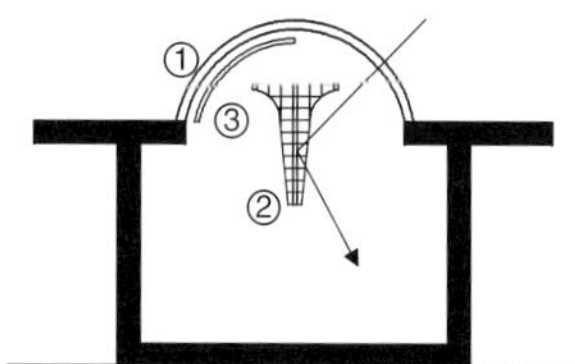

(1) Glass dome (2) Mirror (3) Sun protection

- e.g. Reichstag building, Berlin, Arch. Foster
- Light redirection: direct and indirect light as light reflection

4 Mirror

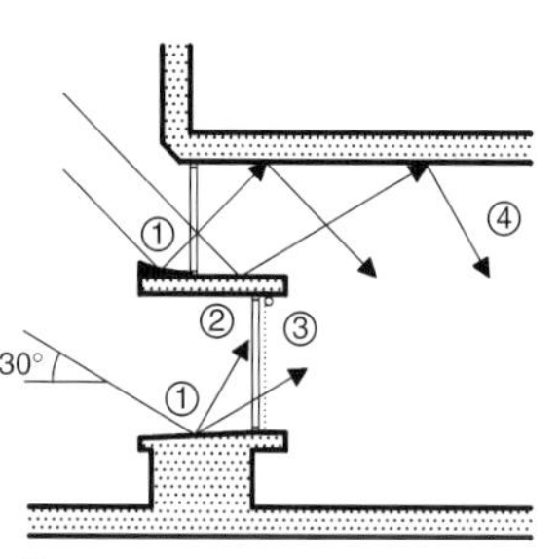

① Light or reflective surfaces
② Light or reflective transoms
③ Glare protection
④ Light, gloss ceiling

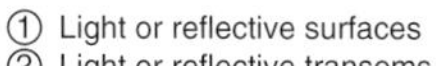

5 Light shelf direction

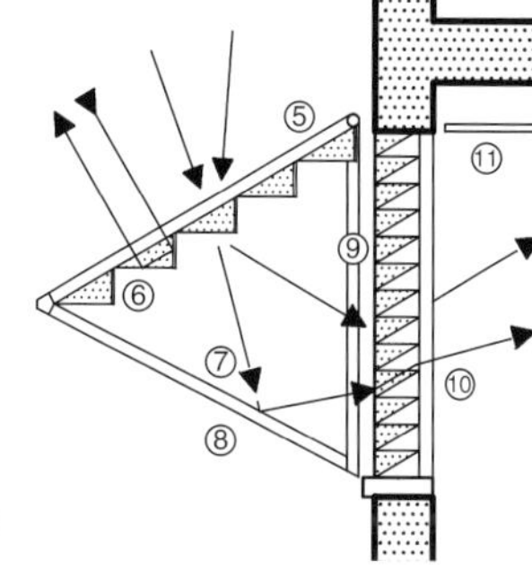

⑤ Glazing
⑥ Glass prism
⑦ Mirroring
⑧ Insulation
⑨ Glass prisms
⑩ Glazing
⑪ Reflective ceiling

6 Prisms: shading and directing according to the time of year

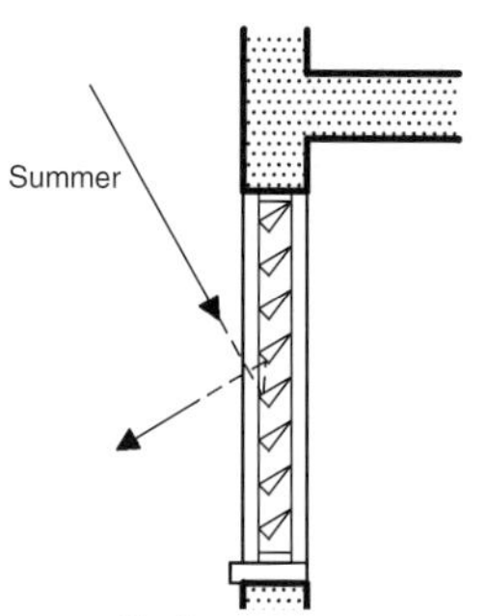

Shading

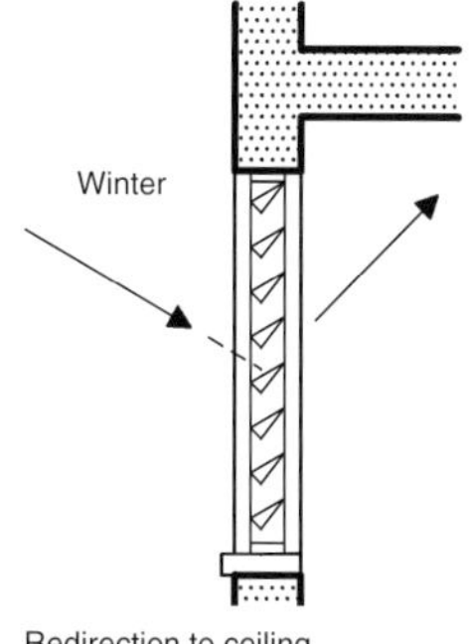

Redirection to ceiling

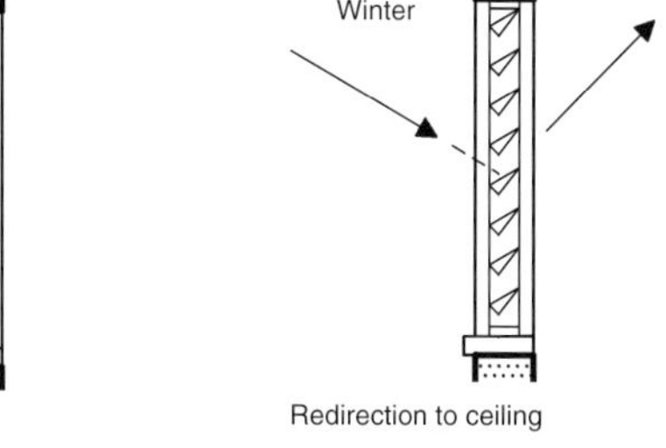

7 Mirror profiles: between insulated glazing, light direction in accordance with the position of the sun in summer and winter

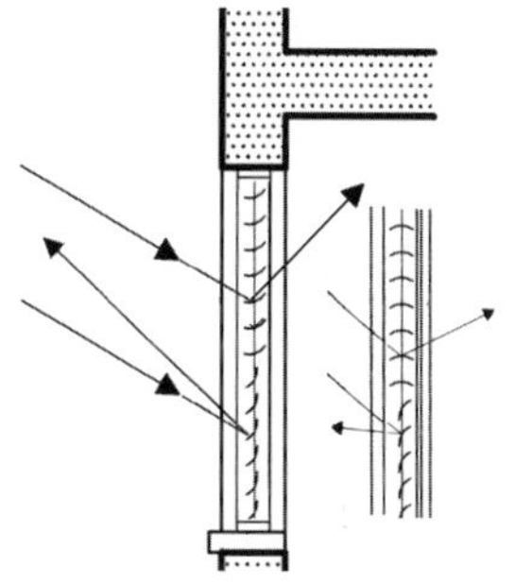

8 Venetian blind: between insulated glazing, with different setting angles for glare protection in lower part and ceiling lighting in upper part

① ② ③
60°
30°

① Float glass
② Profile / acrylic glass
③ Cast / clear glass

Redirection for direct and also for diffused light
Take note of the limitation of transparency

9 Light-directing glass types

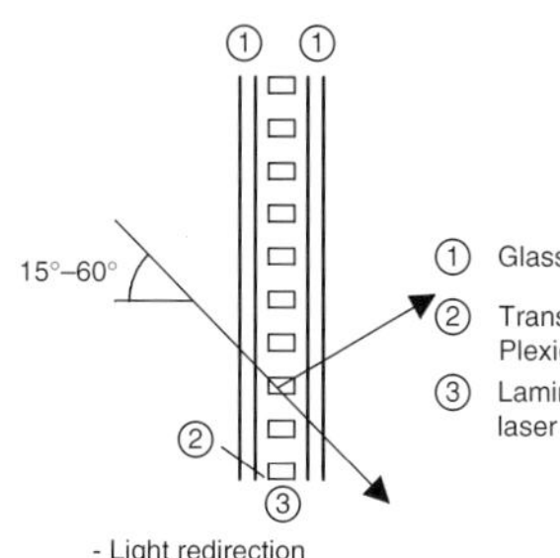

① Glass
② Transparent Plexiglas
③ Laminate with laser cuts

- Light redirection
- Laser cuts: cuts between double glazing
Take note of the limitation of transparency

10 Laser cuts

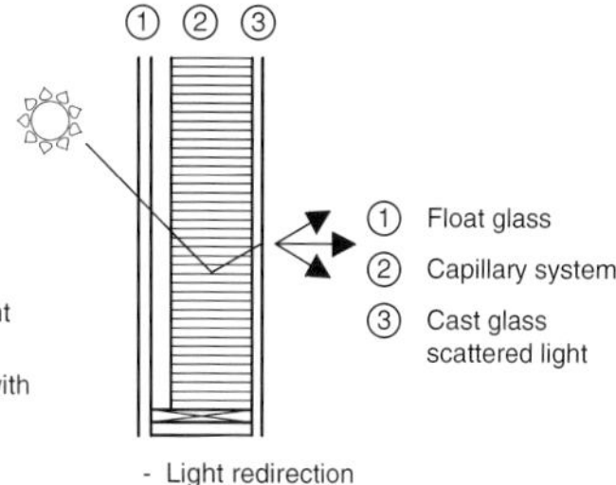

① Float glass
② Capillary system
③ Cast glass scattered light

- Light redirection
- High light transmission
- Flooding with light
Take note of the limitation of transparency

11 Translucent thermal insulation

Integrated light direction and sun protection systems

Aims

- separation and control of incoming light according to angle of incidence
- avoid glare
- increase harvest of light
- enable greater room depths
- lighter environment
- reduce heat build-up
- reduce proportion of artificial lighting

Systems

The following systems are available for light direction:

1. **Reflection** of undesirable heat radiation with special coatings (combi-glass). Different types of coating and sequences of panes can be used to determine the energy transmittance (g-value), the light transmittance (LT-value), the light reflectance (mirror effect) and the colour rendering.
2. **Shading** of direct sunshine and exploitation of diffused zenith light. Mainly rigid systems, which reflect the direct sunshine's light. Mirrors, prisms, or other light-directing components are integrated permanently into the window or glass construction. They must be selected according to their alignment to the sun.
3. **Direction and scattering** of direct sunlight, normally reflection onto the ceiling in order to avoid glare. Movable systems, which can be adapted to the current angle of the sun, are necessary for this purpose.
4. **Collection and forwarding** of direct sunlight. Heliostats collect sunlight and transport it to the intended location by mirroring. The necessary precision of these systems requires expensive production and maintenance. In particular, the wide dimensional tolerances in the building have to be taken into account.

DAYLIGHT

Physical basics
Position of the sun
Insolation
Shadow
Radiation energy
Window lighting
Rooflighting
Quality criteria
Directing sunlight
Shading

see also: Glass pp. 104 and 100

BS 8206-2
DIN 5034

Building services

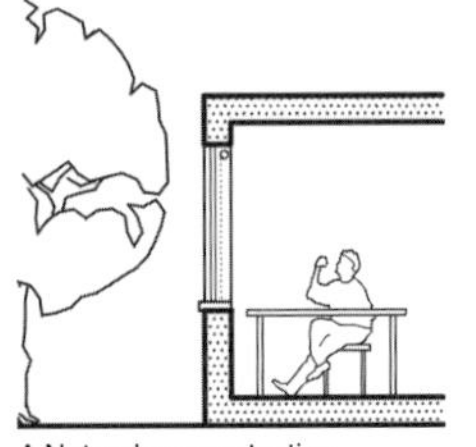

A Natural sun protection

B Facade – sideways light incidence

① Sun protection – outside – summer
② Glare protection – indoors

C Rooflight entry from above

③ Winter sun in room
④ Daylight course
⑤ Possible light-scattering ceiling

❶ Principles of sun protection

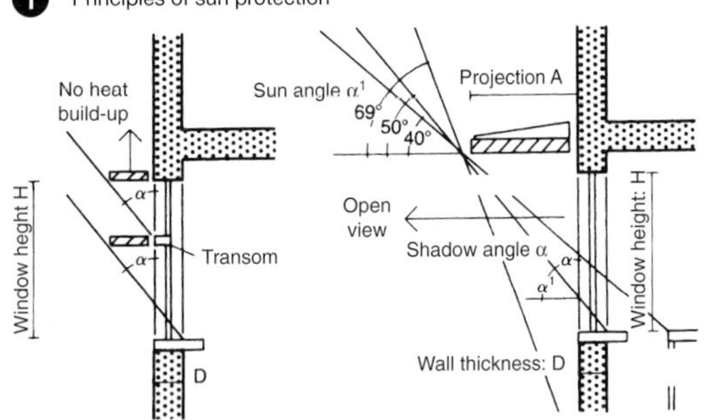

Sun angle α' and shadow angle for a south wall less than 50° northern latitude (London)

21 June (summer solstice), midday α' = 63°, α = 27°; 1 May and 31 July, midday α' = 50°, α = 40°; 21 March and 21 September (equinoxes) midday α' = 40°, α = 50°.
Projection A = tan shadow angle α × window height H;
but min. projection A = (tan shadow angle α × window height H) – wall thickness D

❷ Calculation of necessary projection of sun protection components

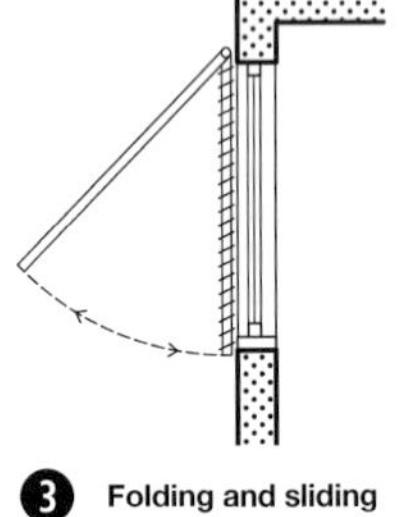

❸ **Folding and sliding shutters** provide very effective and constructionally simple sun protection. Possibly with adjustable slats

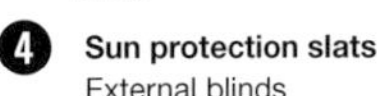

❹ **Sun protection slats** External blinds Most adaptable sun protection, suitable for all directions

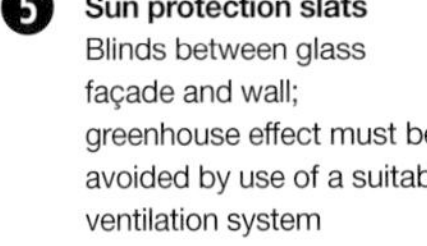

❺ **Sun protection slats** Blinds between glass façade and wall; greenhouse effect must be avoided by use of a suitable ventilation system

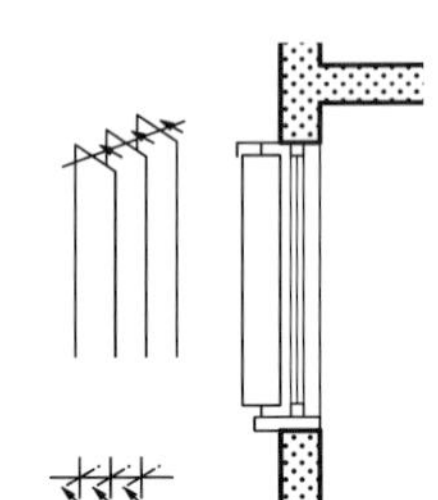

❻ **Sun protection slats** Vertical blades are suitable for all compass points; no heat build-up problems

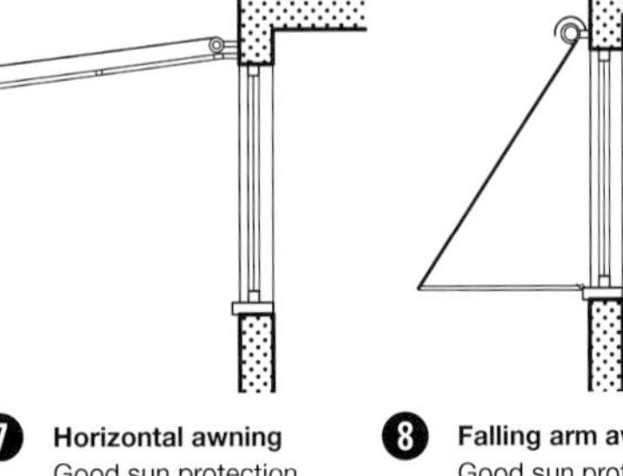

❼ **Horizontal awning** Good sun protection but very susceptible to weather damage, thus if possible automatic operation in connection with a weather station

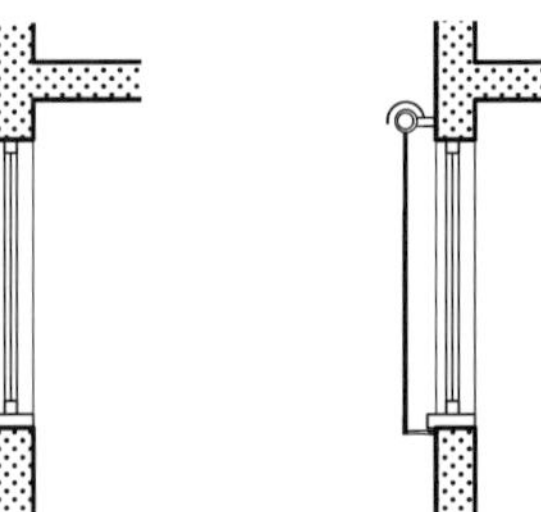

❽ **Falling arm awning** Good sun protection, better weather stability but less view to the outside than ❼

❾ **Falling arm awning** Closeness to window brings danger of overheating and impaired window ventilation

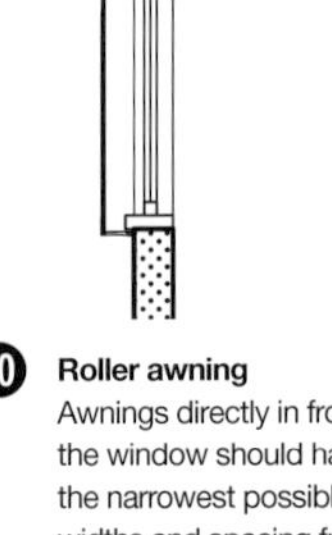

❿ **Roller awning** Awnings directly in front of the window should have the narrowest possible widths and spacing from the wall in order to enable ventilation

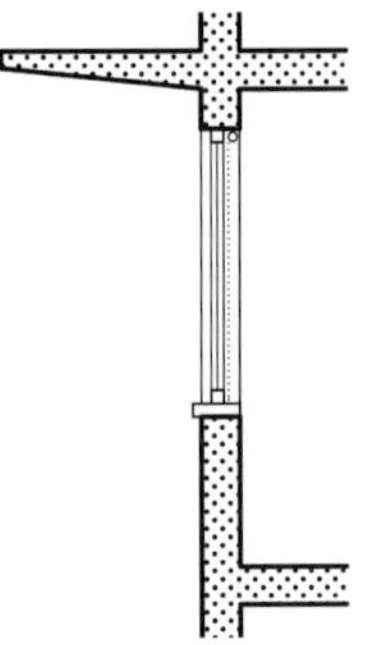
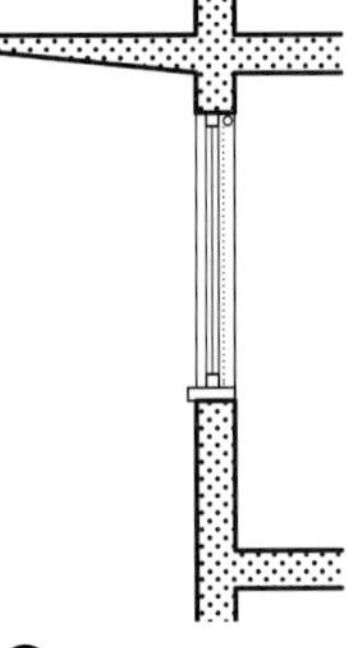

⓫ **Projections** Roof overhangs, balconies etc. Rigid, the projection depends on the direction

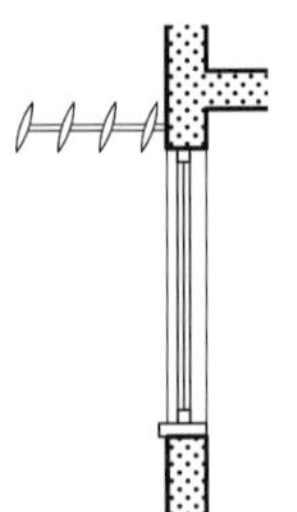

⓬ **External blinds** Rigid sun and glare protection; translucent grating or slats, rigid

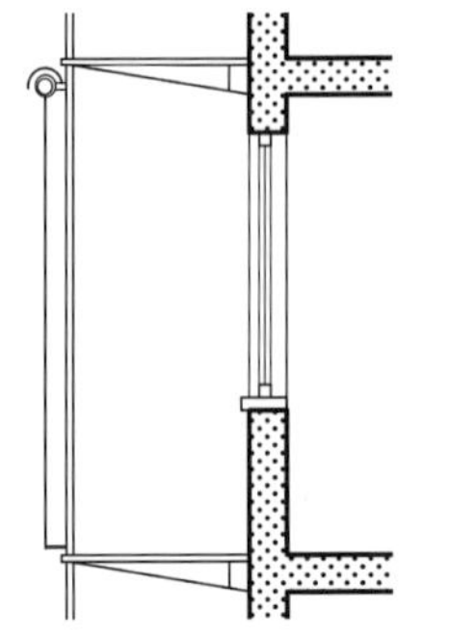

⓭ **Double façade** Sun protection in front of façade, avoids greenhouse effect, susceptible to weather damage

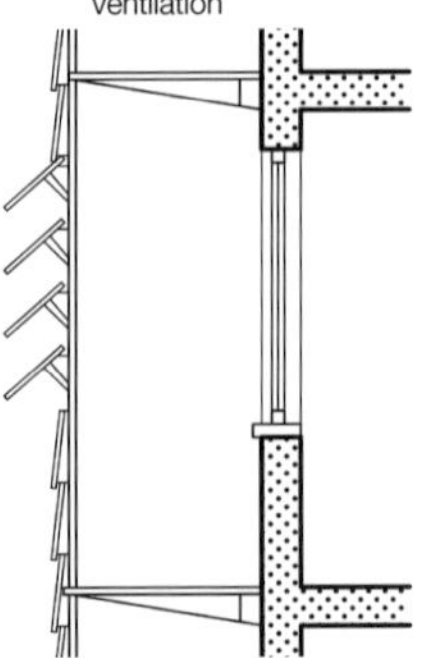

⓮ **Double façade** Glass panes, transparent sun protection and light direction system, controllable

Additive light direction and sun protection systems – aims:

- avoidance of excessive incoming heat radiation and light differences (glare) through windows or façades
- individual control by the user
- no hindrance of individual control of ventilation.

Natural sun protection

Deciduous trees offer natural sun protection in summer. In winter, the leafless trees allow warmth and light into the room.

Systems

System selection depends mainly on the compass direction of the window to be protected. On north sides, direct sunshine can only be expected in the mornings in June and July and simple internal systems are sufficient. If the alignment is largely west or east, movable systems should shade the low sun.

South windows need effective shading above all in the early year and autumn, with low sun. In the high summer, slight roof overhangs are sufficient to avoid direct sunshine.

If external closed shading components (awnings, shutters) are used, it must be possible for the heat build-up behind the component to escape. Such systems are not suitable for rooms with natural ventilation.

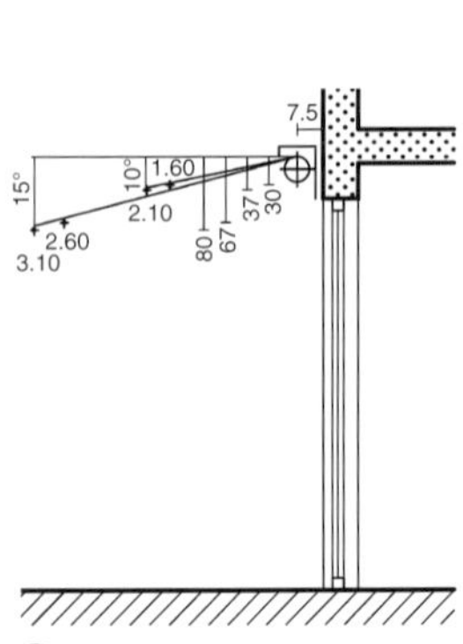

⓯ **Horizontal awning** Dimensions for all large awnings over shop windows and displays

BS 8206-2
DIN 5034

Radiometric quantity	Photometric quantity and symbol	Photometric unit and abbreviation
radiant flux	luminous flux F	lumen (lm)
radiant intensity	luminous intensity I	candela (cd)
irradiance	illuminance E	lux (lx)
radiance	luminance L	cd/m^2
radiant energy	luminous energy Q	(lm × h)
exposure	luminous exposure H	(lx × h)

❶ Physical units in radiometry and photometry

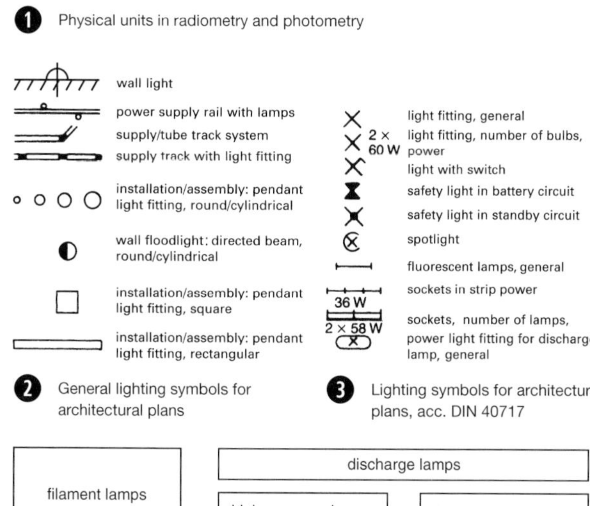

❷ General lighting symbols for architectural plans

❸ Lighting symbols for architectural plans, acc. DIN 40717

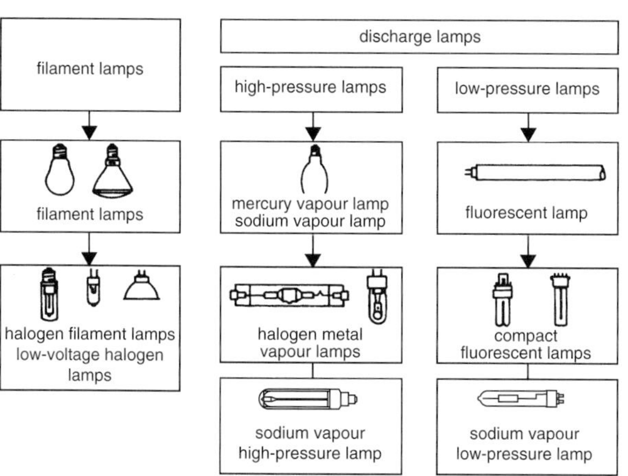

❹ Categorisation of lamps

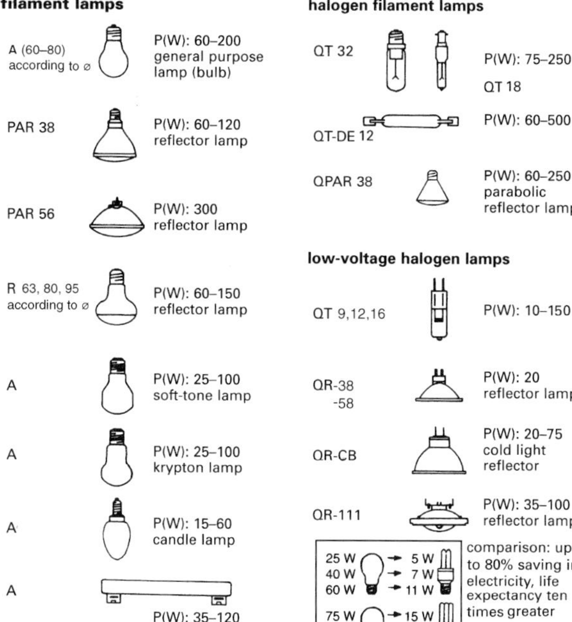

❺ Descriptions of filament lamps according to ZVEI (Central Association of the Electrical and Electronic Industry)

Lighting parameters

The radiated power perceived by the eye is described as luminous flux F. The luminous flux radiated per solid angle in a defined direction is the luminous intensity I. The luminous intensity of a lamp in all directions of radiation gives its distribution, generally displayed as a luminous intensity distribution curve (LIDC) → p. 503 ❷. The LIDC describes the radiation of a lamp as narrow, medium or wide beam and as symmetrical or asymmetrical. The luminous flux reaching a unit of area is the illuminance E. Typical values are:

Global radiation (clear sky)	max. 100,000 lx
Global radiation (cloudy sky)	max. 20,000 lx
Optimal for seeing	2000 lx
Minimum at workplace	200 lx
Orientation lighting	20 lx
Street lighting	10 lx
Moonlight	0.2 lx

Luminance L is a measure of the perceived brightness. The luminance of lamps is relatively high and can lead to glare. This results in the requirement for shading of lamps in interiors. The luminance of surfaces in a room is a function of the illuminance E and the reflectance ($L = E \times r/p$). Lamps convert electrical power (W) into luminous power (lumen, lm). A further measure is luminous efficacy (lm/W).

Lamps

Artificial lighting sources consist of lamp and fitting. The part producing the light is described as the lamp. Fittings serve to hold the lamp and distribute the light (scattering, glare shading). Lamps are differentiated, according to the principle of light production, into filament lamps and discharge lamps → ❹.

1. Filament lamps

Filament lamps are temperature radiators, in which a filament is made to glow to produce light. A large part of the energy produced is therefore heat radiation (infra red) and a relatively small part is visible light (approx. 15–20%). Typical features of filament lamps: light warm white colour, can be dimmed without limitation, very good colour rendering, operation without flickering. Further characteristics: low luminous efficacy (approx. 6–12 lm/W), short lifetime of lamps at about 1000 hours.

Halogen filament lamps achieve high luminance with their compact construction. The bulb contains a halogen gas, which prevents tungsten from the glowing filament being deposited on the inside of the bulb and reducing the luminous efficacy. The small dimensions of the lamps enable compact fittings with very good bundling properties, thus making them very suitable for narrow beam spotlights. Halogen lamps produce brilliant light, further properties: better luminous efficacy (up to 24 lm/W) than simple light bulbs; lamp lifetime approx. 4000–6000 hours (for low-voltage halogen lamps). For lamp power ratings of up to 75 W, low-voltage 12 V lamps are mostly used, which require a transformer for connection to mains power. For power ratings of 75–2000 W, 220 V mains lamps are suitable.

BS EN 60432
BS EN 12665
DIN 5035
DIN EN 12464
DIN 40717

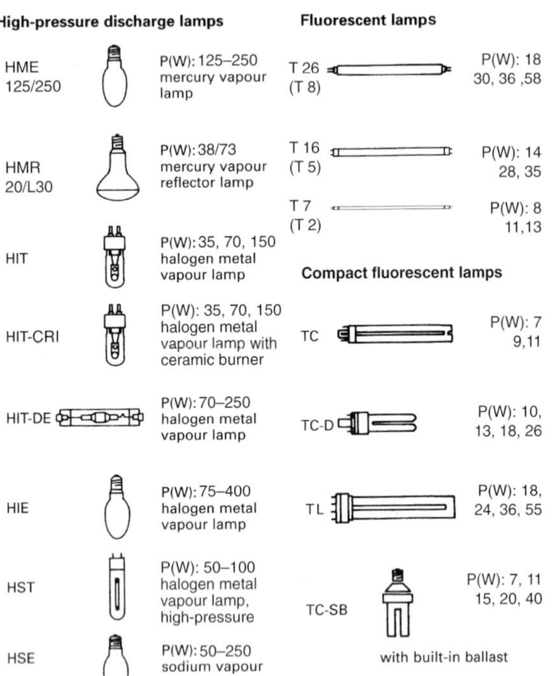

❶ Description of discharge lamps according to ZVEI (Central Association of the Electrical and Electronic Industry)

Type of lamp	Lifetime (h)	Luminous efficacy (lm/W)	Abbreviation (→ ❶ above and → p. 501 ❺)
filament lamp	1000	6–12	A...
parabolic reflector lamp	2000	15	PAR...
halogen filament lamp	1500–2000	12–24	Q...
low-voltage halogen lamp	2000–6000	12–24	Q...
mercury vapour lamp (high-voltage)	6000–8000	70–120	HM...
metal vapour and halogen lamp (high-pressure)	6000–12 000	70–120	HI...
sodium vapour high-pressure lamp	8000–10 000	70–120	HS...
fluorescent tube	20000	80–104	T...
compact fluorescent tube	8000–12000	60–75	TC...

❷ Lamps: lifetime and luminous efficacy

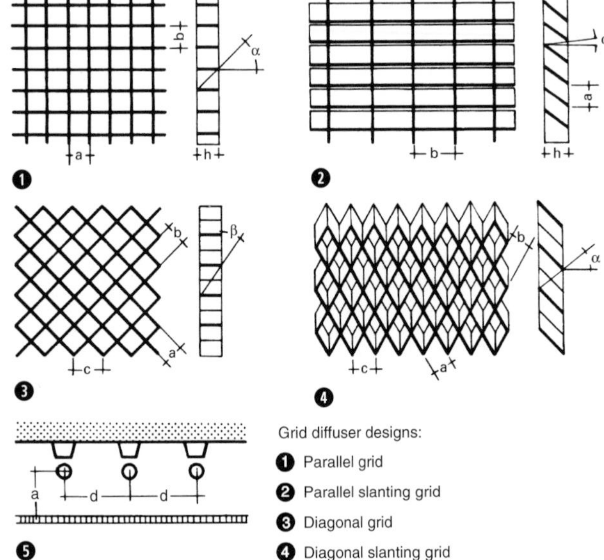

Grid diffuser designs:
❶ Parallel grid
❷ Parallel slanting grid
❸ Diagonal grid
❹ Diagonal slanting grid
❺ Arrangement of lamps a ≧ 2/3 d

❸ Grid patterns for suspended ceiling luminaires

LIGHTING
Artificial lighting
Lamps
Types of lighting
Lighting layout
Quality criteria
Illuminance
Application
Workplace
Guidelines

BS EN 60921
DIN 5035
DIN EN 12464

Building services

2. Discharge lamps:
Light bulbs or tubes contain a gas, which is made to glow by the application of a voltage. Typical characteristics of discharge lamps: operation generally with ballast and in some cases starter device; high luminous efficacy and relatively long lamp lifetime, 5000–20,000 h; little heat production; light colour, according to the type of lamp: warm white, neutral white or daylight white; colour rendering moderate to very good; lamps cannot always be dimmed. Flicker-free operation is only possible with the use of an electronic ballast. Discharge lamps are differentiated according to the type of gas used and the gas pressure in the tube.

Fluorescent lamps
Also known as fluorescent tubes, these are the commonest discharge lamp. The discharge causes mostly UV radiation inside the tube and this is converted into visible radiation by a coating inside the tube. Luminous efficacy 104 lm/W. In the description, the number after the T gives the diameter of the tube in mm (T 16 = 16 mm diameter) or in 1/8 in (T 5 = 5 × 1/8 in ~ 16 mm). Smaller diameters enable more precise direction of light in the lamps. The ballast is nowadays normally controlled electronically.
Fluorescent lamps are used in offices and commercial buildings in **ceiling grids**. The light mostly shines directly downwards → ❸ or in **light bands** and **linear luminaires** (shining directly or indirectly). This enables uniform overall lighting, similar to daylight, with mild shadow formation.

Compact fluorescent lamps
These have been developed as a replacement for filament light bulbs. The ballast is normally integrated into the screw base. Their luminous efficacy is not as good as that of fluorescent tubes.

Fluorescent tubes for advertising displays
Glass tubes filled with inert gas (e.g. neon, thus the common name neon lighting) are subjected to a voltage. The tubes then light up in various colours according to the gas. The tubes can be curved as required before filling with gas, so that writing, ornaments and depictions of figures are possible. They are easily controllable using regulating resistors or transformers and are often used in cinemas, theatres, sales outlets and advertising.

Mercury vapour and sodium vapour high-pressure lamps
In high-pressure lamps, an arc between electrodes creates the light. They have a long lifetime and high luminous efficacy, but poor colour rendering (mercury: blue, sodium: yellow). They are therefore mostly used for the lighting of factories, works sheds, stores and street lighting. Coated mercury high-pressure lamps have improved colour rendering.

Metal vapour and halogen high-pressure lamps
These produce a light with good colour rendering values (the light colours white, warm tone, and daylight are possible) and high luminous efficacy. The compact point light source enables precise direction of the light. The high luminance and a high UV share of the light must be taken into account in the selection of lamps to avoid glare, reflection and the fading of objects susceptible to UV radiation. If fitted with ceramic burners, these lamps are more colour-stable over their lifetime.

Light-emitting diode (LED) lamps
A solid-body crystal is made to glow by the application of direct current (recombination of electrons in a semi-conductor). The colour is determined by the choice of crystal. White light is produced by a combination of coloured LEDs or through luminescent phosphors, which convert the originally coloured light into white. The luminance values today are similar to low-voltage halogen lamps, but will be improved further in the future. Advantages: small size of the light source, little degradation of the lighting performance over the lifetime, no infra red or ultra violet radiation, no impact susceptibility, long lifetime (approx. 25,000–50,000 h)

lighting type			flood lighting	spotlights	uplights	downlights	grid lighting: square grids	grid lighting: rectangular grids
	A	general purpose lamp 60–200W		○		○		
	PAR, R	parabolic reflector lamp reflector lamp 60–300W		○		○		
	QT 32	halogen filament lamp 75–250W	○	○	○	○		
	QT–DE	halogen filament lamp, sockets both sides 100–500W	○		○			
	QT–LV NV	low-voltage halogen lamp 10–150W		○		○		
	QR–LV NV	low-voltage halogen reflector lamp 20–100W		○		○		
	T 16 8 2	fluorescent lamp 8–58W	○		○		○	○
	TC TC–D TC–L	compact fluorescent lamp 7–55W	○	○	○	○	○	○
	HME	mercury vapour lamp 50–400W				○		
	HSE/ HST	sodium vapour lamp 50–250W				○		
	HIT HIT-DE CDM-T	halogen metal vapour lamp 35–250W	○	○	○	○		

1 Suitability of lamps and fittings

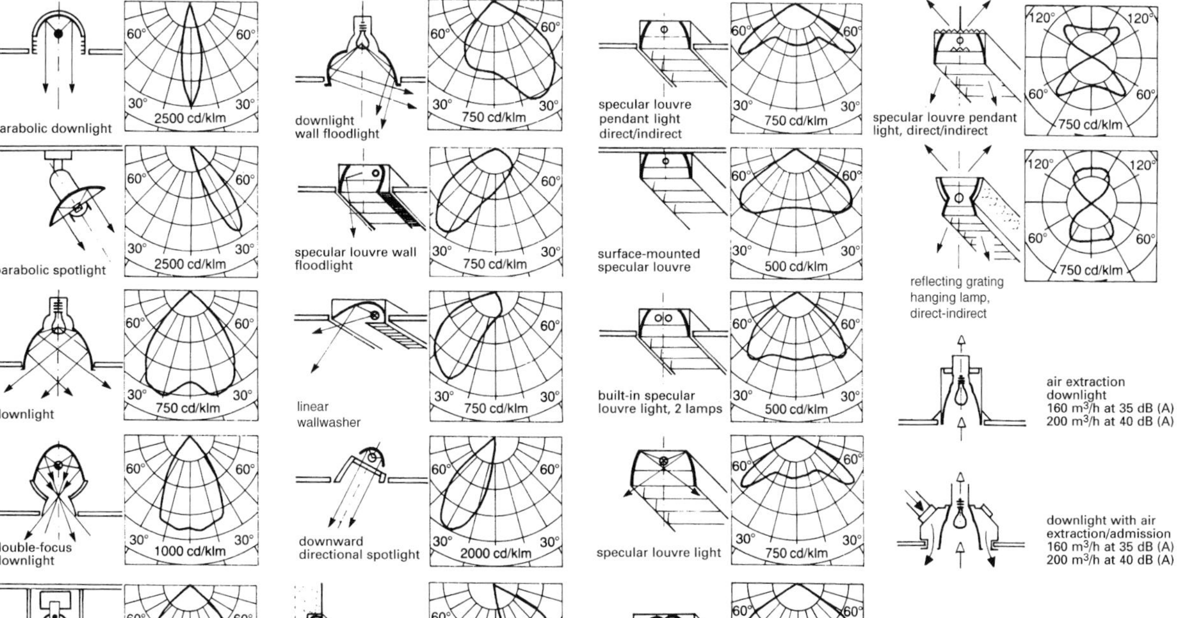

2 Light fittings and light distribution

Room height	Nominal illuminance	Rooms	A ≦ 100 W	A > 100 W	PAR 38	PAR 56	R	QT ≦ 250 W	QT – DE	QT > 250 W	QT – LV	QR – CB – LV	QR – LV	T	TC	TC – D	TC – L	HME ≦ 80 W	HME > 80 W	HSE	HST	HIT – DE ≤ 70 W	HIT – DE > 70 W	HIT ≦ 70 W	HIT > 70 W	HIE
up to 3 m	up to 200 lx	parking garages, packing rooms												●				●		●	●					
		side rooms												●	●	●	●			●	●					
		workshops												●												
		restaurants	●				●				●	●	●													
		foyers	●	●	●						●	●			●	●										
	up to 500 lx	standard offices, teaching rooms, counters and cash desks												●		●	●									
		sitting rooms	●	●							●	●		●	●	●	●									
		workshops												●				●	●							
		libraries						●						●			●									
		sales rooms									●	●		●	●	●	●					●		●		
		exhibition rooms			●						●			●	●	●	●	●				●		●		
		museums, galleries, event rooms	●	●	●	●	●	●		●	●	●	●	●			●									
		entrance halls	●	●				●			●			●	●	●	●									
	up to 750 lx	data processing, standard offices with higher visual requirements												●			●									
		workshops												●					●				●		●	
		department stores												●			●	●								
		supermarkets												●												
		display windows						●	●	●	●	●	●									●	●	●	●	
		hotel kitchens												●			●									
		concert stages				●		●	●																	
		technical drawing, open-plan offices												●												
3–5 m	up to 200 lx	storerooms												●				●	●	●	●					
		workshops												●				●								
		industrial sheds												●				●		●	●	●		●		
		foyers	●	●	●						●				●	●										
		restaurants	●				●				●	●	●		●	●										
		churches	●	●	●			●								●										
		concert halls, theatres	●	●				●																		
	up to 500 lx	workshops												●					●				●		●	
		industrial sheds												●					●				●		●	
		lecture theatres, auditoriums, assembly rooms		●				●						●			●									
		sales rooms												●		●	●	●					●		●	
		exhibition rooms, museums, art galleries		●	●	●	●	●	●	●				●		●	●									
		entrance halls		●	●	●		●						●	●	●	●						●		●	
		pubs														●	●									
		sports halls, multi-purpose and gymnastics halls						●						●					●				●		●	●
	up to 750 lx	workshops												●				●	●				●		●	●
		drawing offices												●			●									
		laboratories												●												
		libraries, reading rooms						●						●			●									
		exhibition rooms												●			●		●				●		●	●
		exhibition halls																	●							●
		department stores												●			●						●		●	●
		supermarkets												●												
		large kitchens												●												
		concert stages			●	●		●	●																	
over 5 m	up to 200 lx	industrial and machine sheds, switchrooms												●					●	●	●					●
		storerooms of high-bay warehouses												●					●							
		churches		●		●		●																		
		concert halls, theatres		●		●		●																		
	up to 500 lx	industrial sheds												●					●				●		●	●
		museums, art galleries				●		●						●			●									
		airports, stations, traffic zones												●			●		●	●	●		●		●	●
		event halls				●		●																		
		sports and multi-purpose halls						●						●									●		●	●
	up to 750 lx	industrial sheds																	●	●	●					●
		auditoriums, lecture theatres						●						●			●									
		exhibition rooms							●					●			●						●		●	●
		exhibition halls																	●				●		●	●
		supermarkets												●					●				●		●	●

A = general purpose lamps
PAR = parabolic reflector lamps
R = reflector lamps
QT = halogen filament lamps
QT – DE = halogen filament lamps, 2 sockets
QT – LV = low-voltage halogen lamps
QR – LV = low-voltage reflector lamps
QR – CB – LV = low-voltage reflector lamps, cold light
T = fluorescent lamps
TC = compact fluorescent lamps
TC – D = compact fluorescent lamps, 4 tubes
TC – L = compact fluorescent lamps, long
HME = mercury vapour lamps
HSE = sodium vapour lamps
HST = sodium vapour lamps, tubular
HIT = halogen metal vapour lamps
HIE = halogen metal vapour lamps, elliptical

1 Usual lamps for interior lighting

Types of interior lighting

Direct, symmetrical lighting → ❶ is preferred for the general lighting of workrooms, meeting rooms, rooms with public access and traffic zones. Relatively little electrical power is required to achieve a specified lighting level. Guideline values for specific mains consumption → p. 508 ❶. The shading angle of the light fittings in work and meeting rooms is 30°, in conditions of very high visual comfort 40° and more. For the design of a lighting system, a radiation angle of between 70° and 90° should be the first assumption.

Downlight wallwasher, ceiling grid wallwasher → ❷. For use near the wall for uniform wall illumination. The effect in the room is of indirect lighting.

Wallwasher on power supply rail → ❸. Uniform illumination of the wall with a part also lighting the room. According to the chosen spacing of the light fittings, illuminance of up to 500 lx (vertical) can be achieved. The use of fluorescent or halogen filament lamps is also possible (see below also and → ⓫).

Wallwasher for ceiling installation → ❹. With no room component, this only illuminates the wall, using halogen filament or fluorescent lamps.

Downlight directional spotlight → ❺. Regular arrangement of light fittings in the ceiling can achieve spatially differentiated lighting. The relatively closely bundled reflectors can be rotated vertically up to 40° and horizontally through 360°. Halogen filament lamps can be used, particularly low-voltage.

Indirect lighting → ❻. This approach to lighting can produce a bright impression in the room, even at a low level of lighting and without reflected glare. Sufficient room height is a precondition. Careful matching of the lighting and the ceiling architecture is necessary. For the lighting of workplaces, an upper limit to ceiling luminance of 1000 cd/m^2 (above the radiation angle of 65°) should be observed. Indirect lighting requires up to three times the energy consumption of direct.

Direct/indirect lighting → ❼. On account of the bright impression in the room and the reasonable energy consumption (70% direct, 30% indirect), direct/indirect lighting is preferred as long as the ceiling height is sufficient (h ≧ 3 m). Fluorescent tubes are mostly used, or in combination with halogen filament and filament lamps (seldom).

Ceiling uplighter, floor downlighter → ❽ – ❾ are used for the area lighting of ceilings or floors. The lamps can be halogen filaments, fluorescent tubes or high-pressure discharge lamps.

Wall light → ❿. Predominantly for decorative wall lighting – also light effects, e.g. colour filters and prisms. There is also some limited lighting of the ceiling and floor.

Wallwasher on power supply rail → ⓫ does not light the room and is used particularly for exhibitions and in museums. Vertical lighting level from 50 lx, 150 lx and 300 lx can be produced for the lighting of displays.

Narrow beam on power supply rail → ⓬. Preferred radiation angles: 10° ('spot'), 30° ('flood'), 90° ('washer'). The light cone from narrow beam lights can be altered with lenses (sculpture lenses and Fresnel lenses); the spectrum can be altered with ultra violet or infra red filters (in museums, exhibitions, shops) or colour filters. Glare protection is through louvres or anti-glare flaps.

❶ Direct lighting, symmetrical

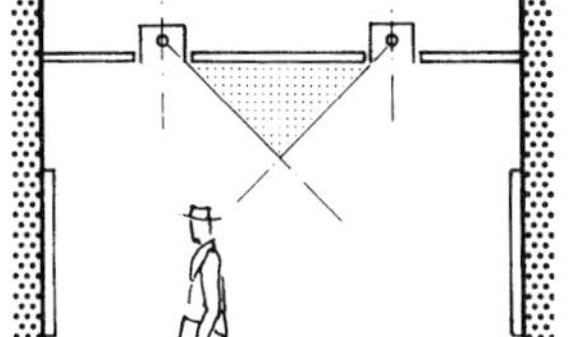

❷ Wallwasher, direct lighting

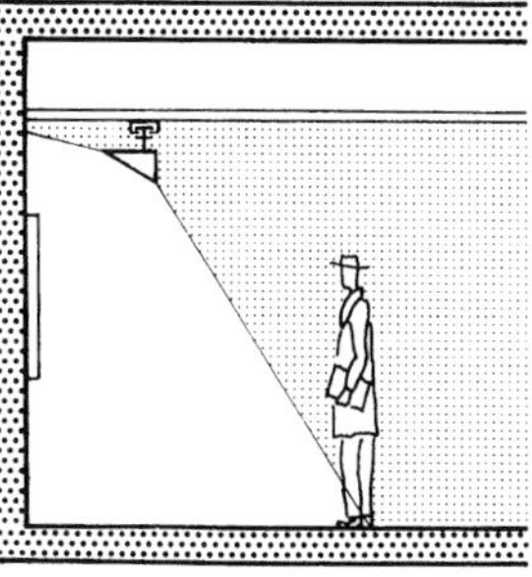

❸ Wallwasher on power supply rail with partial room lighting

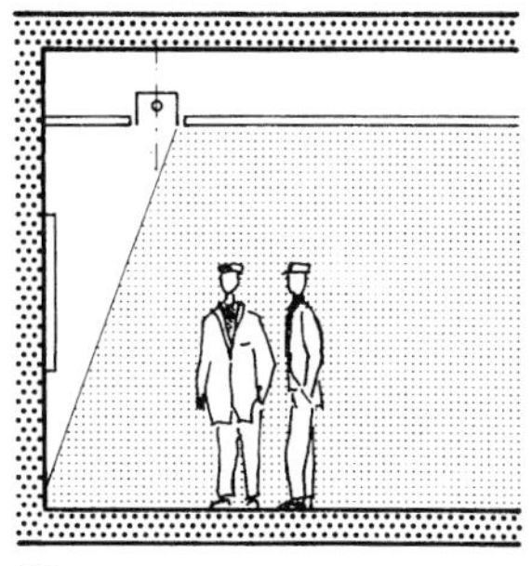

❹ Wallwasher

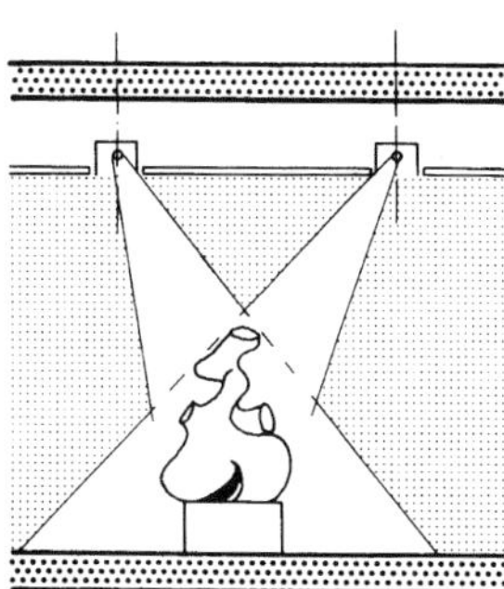

❺ Directional spotlights

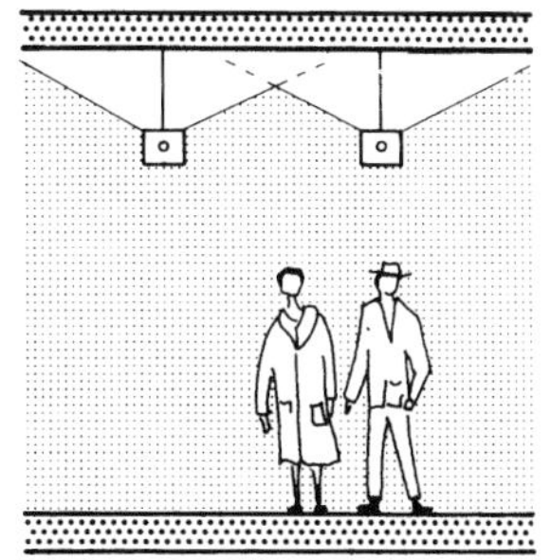

❻ Indirect lighting

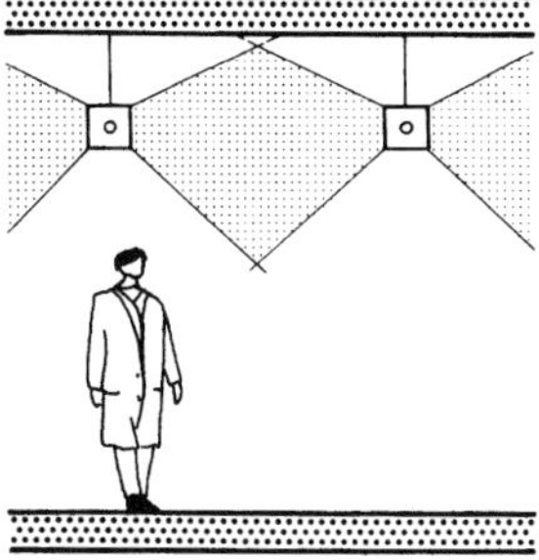

❼ Direct/indirect lighting

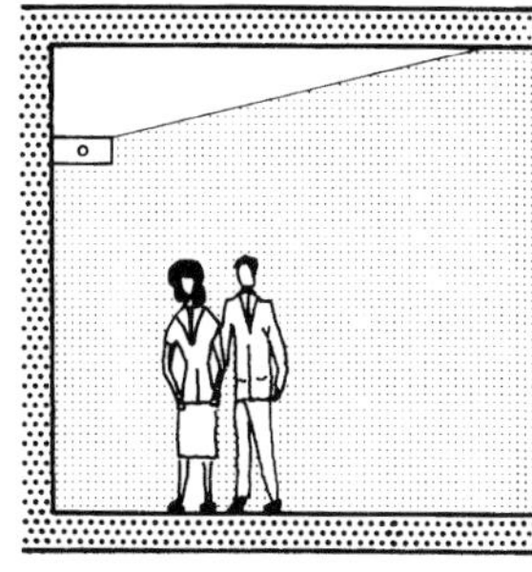

❽ Ceiling uplighter

❾ Floor downlighter

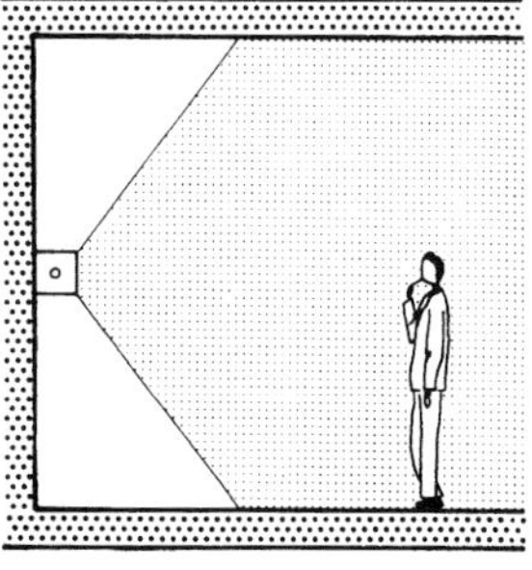

❿ Wall light, direct/indirect lighting

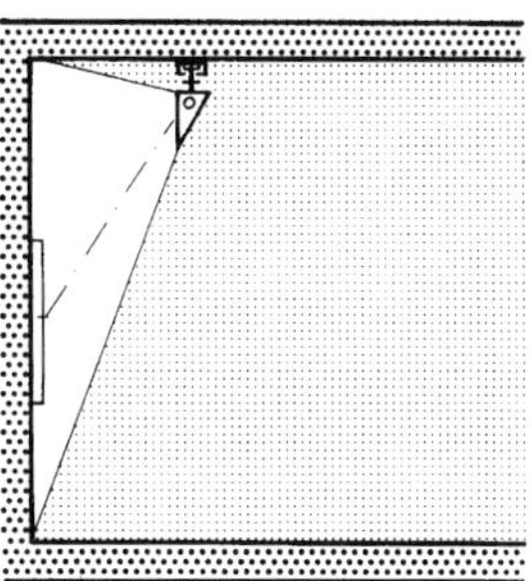

⓫ Wallwasher on power supply rail

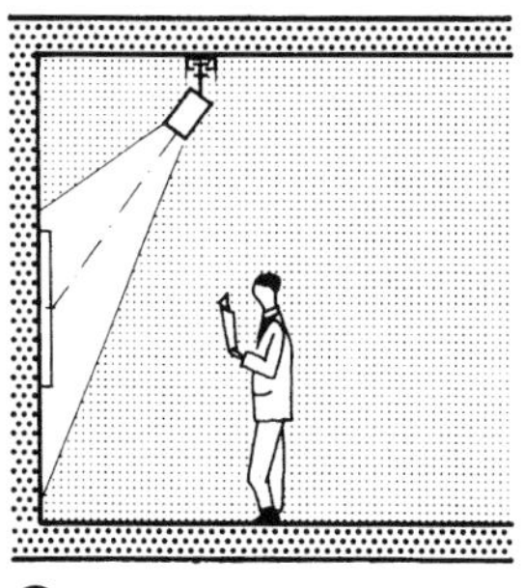

⓬ Spotlight on power supply rail

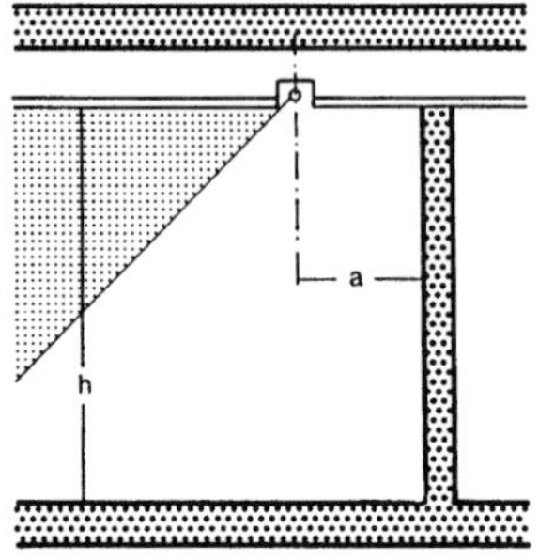

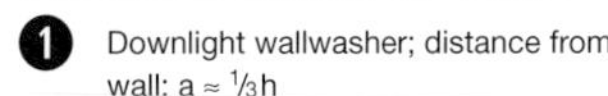

❶ Downlight wallwasher; distance from wall: a ≈ ⅓h

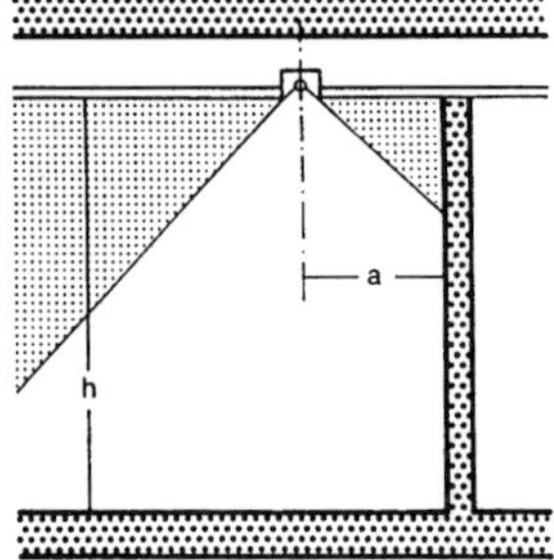

❷ Downlight; distance from wall: a ≈ ⅓h

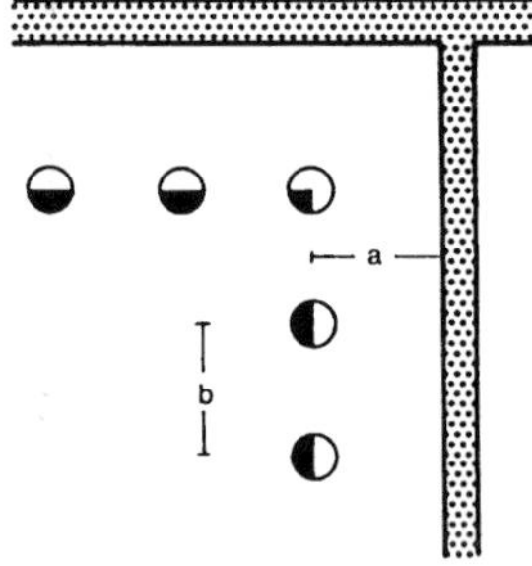

❸ Downlight wall washer; spacing of lights: b = 1–1.5a

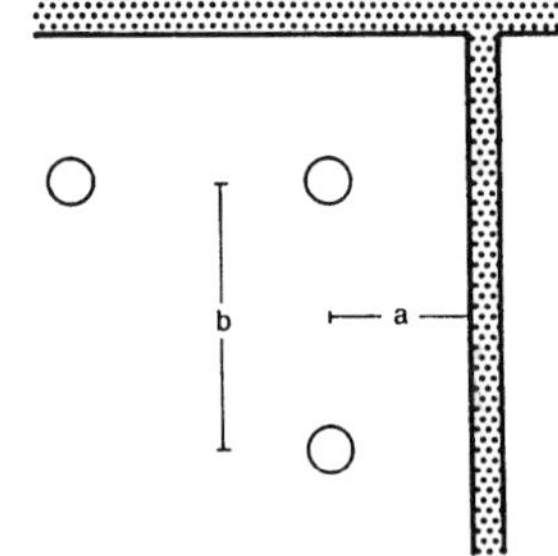

❹ Downlight; spacing of lights: b ≈ 2a

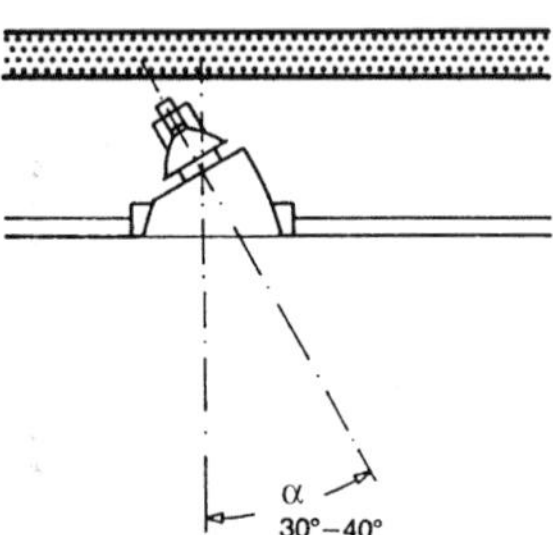

❺ Inclination angle of directional spotlights and downlighters: α = 30–40° (optimal)

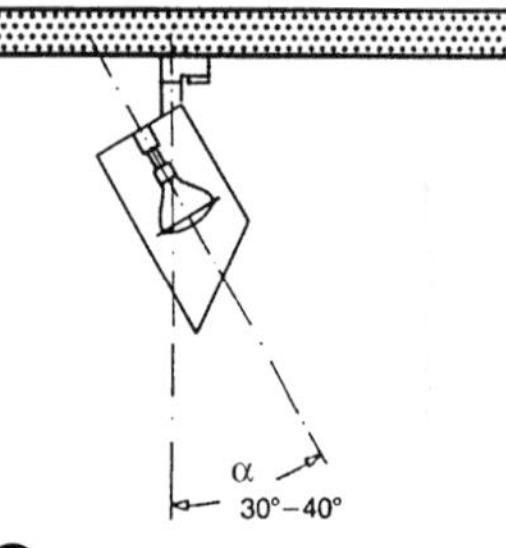

❻ Inclination angle of spotlights for lighting objects and wall: α = 30–40° (optimal)

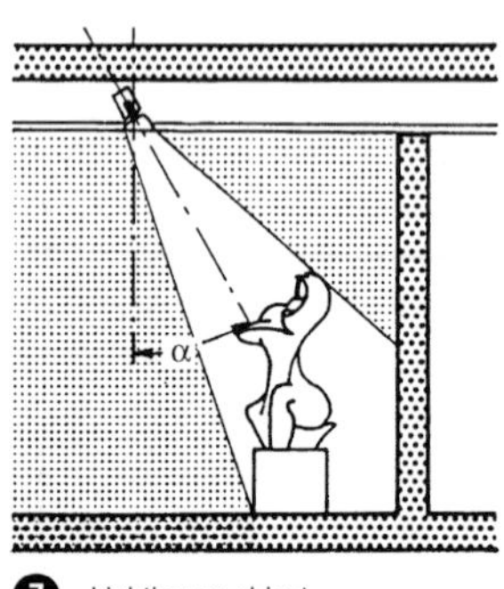

❼ Lighting an object

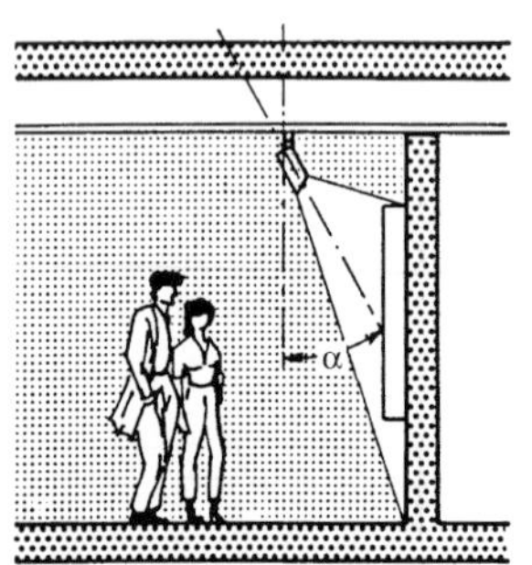

❽ Wall lighting; spotlight

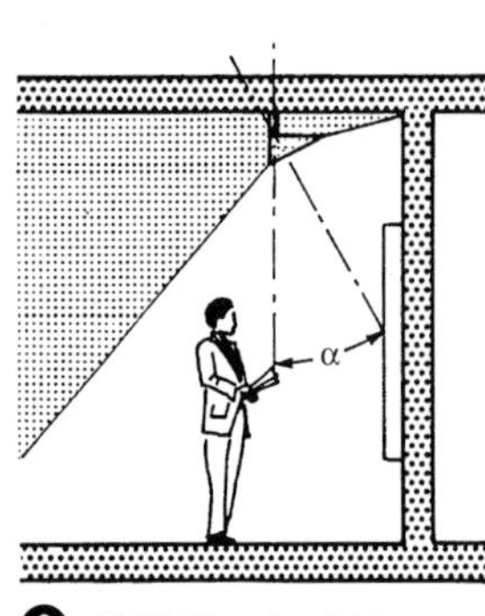

❾ Wall lighting; downlighter

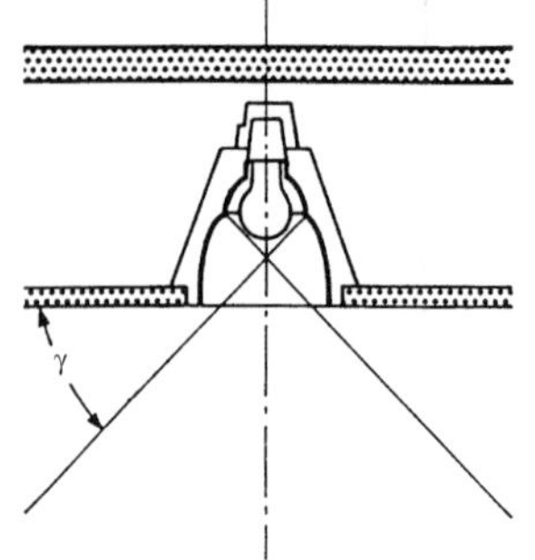

❿ Shading angle (γ = 15°/20°/30°)

Geometry of the lighting layout

The spacing of lights, between each other and from the wall, is related to room height → ❶ – ❹.

The preferred incidence of light onto objects and areas of wall is between 30° (optimal) and 40° → ❺ – ❾. The shading angle for downlights is between 30° (wide light, adequate glare protection) and 50° (deep light, high glare protection) → ❿, for grid lights between 30° and 40°.

Recommended illuminance			Area, activity
20	30	50	paths and working areas outdoors
50	100	150	orientation in rooms with short occupancy
100	150	200	workrooms not used constantly
200	300	500	visual tasks with few demands
300	500	750	visual tasks with medium demands
500	750	1000	visual tasks with high demands, e.g. office work
750	100	1500	visual tasks with high demands, e.g. fine assembly
1000	1500	2000	visual tasks with very high demands, e.g. checking activities
	over	2000	additional lighting for difficult and special visual tasks

⓫ Recommended illuminance values, Commission International de l'Eclairage (CIE)

code: IP	example IP 44
1st number: 0–6	degree of protection against contact and foreign bodies
2nd number: 0–8	degree of protection against water penetration

	1st number, degree of protection against contact/foreign bodies
0	no protection
1	protection against large foreign bodies (>50 mm)
2	against medium foreign bodies (>12 mm)
3	against small foreign bodies (<2.5 mm)
4	against granular foreign bodies (<1 mm)
5	against dust deposits
6	against dust entry

	2nd number, degree of protection against water penetration
0	no protection
1	protection against vertical water drops
2	water drops at incidence up to 15°
3	against splashing water
4	against spraying water
5	against water jets
6	against water penetration from flooding
7	against dipping in water
8	against immersion in water

⓬ Protection classes for light fittings

Stage	Ra colour rendering index	Typical applications
1A	>90	paint sampling, art gallery
1B	90 > Ra > 80	residence, hotel, restaurant, office, school, hospital, printing/textile industry
2A	80 > Ra > 70 70 > Ra > 60	industry
3	60 > Ra > 40	industry and other areas with low requirements for colour rendering
4	40 > Ra > 20	ditto

⓭ Colour rendering of lighting

Reflector type	Property
parabolic	directs light rays in parallel from point light source
spherical	reflects light into focal point of reflector
ellipsoidal	collects light to second focal point

⓮ Reflector forms

Lamp luminance (cd/m^2)	20 000 ≦ 50 000	50 000 ≦ 500 000	<500 000
Minimum shading angle γ	15°	20°	30°

⓯ Shading angle against glare

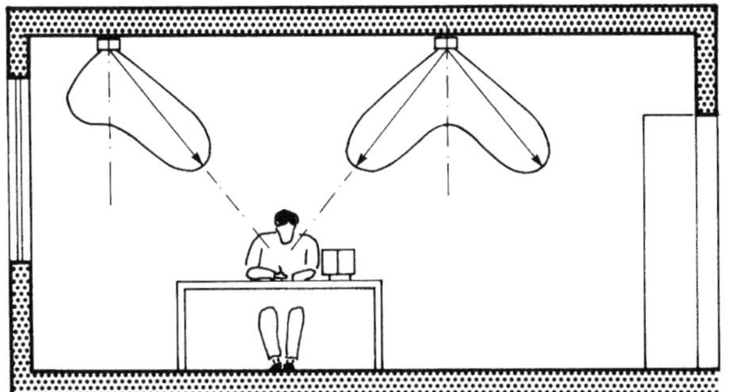

❶ Correct arrangement of lights for a work area, falling from the side

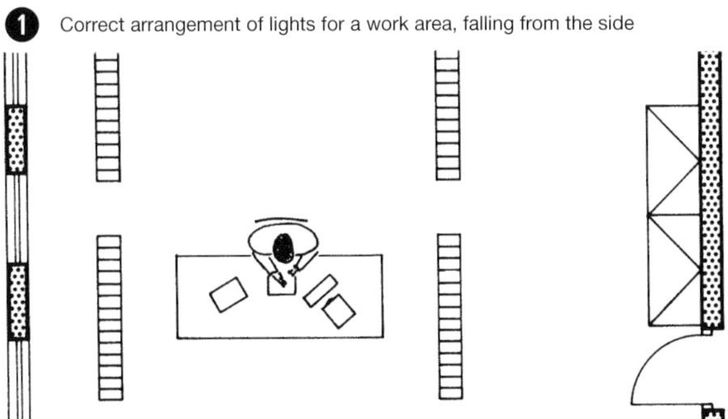

❷ Working surfaces, monitor screens, keyboards and paper should have matt surfaces

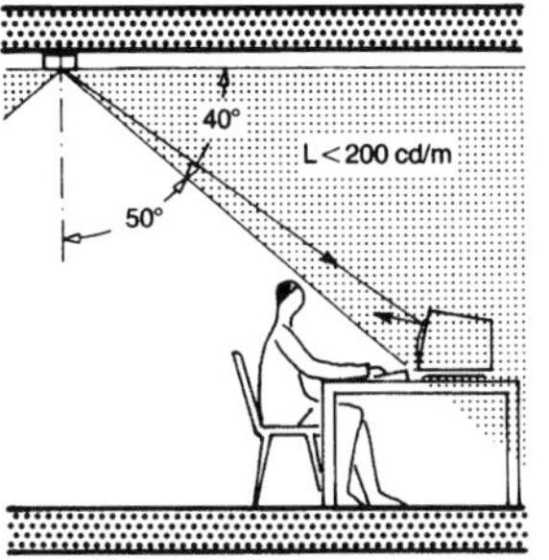

❸ Lights which could cause reflections should have low luminance in the critical lighting area

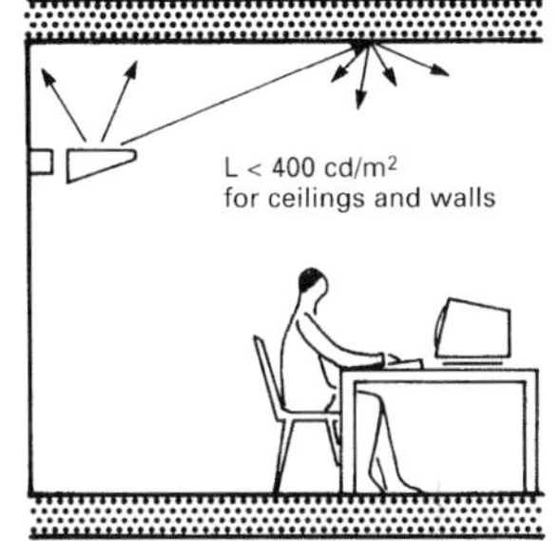

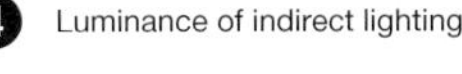

❹ Luminance of indirect lighting

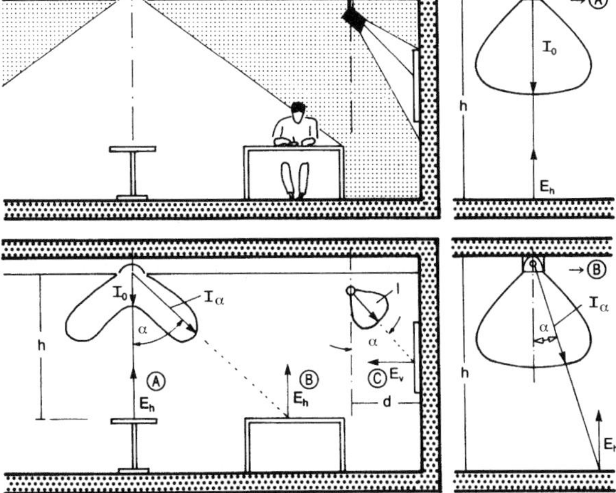

❺ Point illuminances

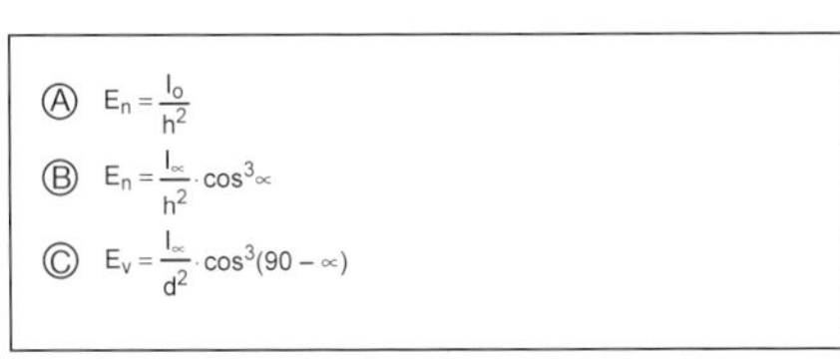

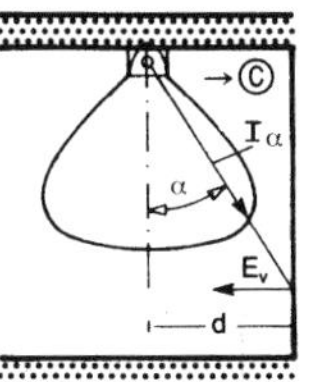

❻ Law of photometric distance

Quality criteria for lighting

A good lighting design must satisfy functional and ergonomic requirements while taking cost-effectiveness into account. In addition to these quantitative demands, qualitative, above all architectural, criteria must be observed.

Quantitative criteria

Lighting level

In contrast to former standards, DIN EN 12464 no longer specifies an average illuminance, but an illuminance at locations where visual work is carried out. In such places, the uniformity must be 0.7, and 0.5 in comparison with the surroundings.

Light direction → ❶

The light should preferably fall sideways onto the work area; the precondition for this is a wing-shaped LIDC → p. 503 ❷.

Glare limitation → ❷ – ❸

The glare to be limited includes direct glare, reflection glare and mirroring on monitor screens. Limitation of direct glare is achieved by the use of luminaires with shading angles of ≧30°.
The formation of reflections is prevented by the light falling sideways onto the work area in connection with using matt surfaces around the working environment → ❷ + ❺. Mirror reflections on screens can be limited through appropriate screen positioning. Lights which could nonetheless cause screen reflections must have a luminance of ≦200 cd/m² (use of high-gloss reflectors).

Distribution of luminance

The harmonic distribution of luminance is the result of a careful matching of all reflectances in the room → ❼. The luminance of indirect lighting should not exceed 400 cd/m².

Colour of light and colour rendering → p. 505 ⓭

The colour of the light is determined by the choice of lamps. There are three light colour groups: warm white light (colour temperature under 3300 K), neutral white light (3300 K–5000 K) and daylight white light (over 5000 K). In offices, lighting is normally chosen to produce warm white and neutral white. The colour rendering, which is determined by the spectral composition of the light, should generally be 1 (very good colour rendering).

Calculation of point illuminance levels → ❺ – ❻

Illuminances (horizontal E_h and vertical E_v) produced by individual lights can be determined from the luminous intensity and the spatial geometry using the law of photometric distance (height h, distance d and lighting angle α).

	Reflectance (%)		Reflectance (%)
Light fittings material			
aluminium, pure gloss	80–90	mortar, light, lime mortar	40–45
aluminium, anodised, matt	80–85	mortar, dark	15–25
aluminium, polished	65–75	sandstone	20–40
aluminium, matt	55–76	plywood, rough	25–40
aluminium coatings, matt	55–65	cement, concrete, rough	15–30
chrome, polished	60–70	brick, red, new	10–15
enamel, white	65–75		
paint, pure white	80–85	**Paints**	
copper, highly polished	60–70	white	70–75
brass, highly polished	70–75	light grey	40–60
nickel, highly polished	50–60	medium grey	25–35
paper, white	70–80	dark grey	15–25
silvered mirror behind glass	80–90	light blue	40–50
silver, highly polished	90–92	dark blue	15–20
		light green	45–55
Building materials		dark green	15–20
oak, light, polished	25–35	pale yellow	50–65
oak, dark, polished	10–15	brown	10–40
granite	20–25	light red	35–50
limestone	35–55	dark red	10–35
marble, polished	30–70		

❼ Reflectances of light fittings materials and building materials

LIGHTING
Artificial lighting
Lamps
Types of lighting
Lighting layout
Quality criteria
Illuminance
Application
Workplace
Guidelines

BS EN 12665
DIN 5035
DIN EN 12464

Specific connected load P* W/m² for 100 lx for height 3 m, area ≧ 100 m² and reflection 0.7/0.5/0.2		
A		12 W/m²
QT		10 W/m²
HME		5 W/m²
TC		5 W/m²
TC-L		4 W/m²
T26		3 W/m²

❶ Specific mains load P* for various types of lamps

Correction factor k				
Height H	Area A (m²)	Light reflectance		
		070502 light	050201 medium	000 dark
Up to 3 m	20	0.75	0.65	0.60
	50	0.90	0.80	0.75
	≧100	1.00	0.90	0.85
3–5 m	20	0.55	0.45	0.40
	50	0.75	0.65	0.60
	≧100	0.90	0.80	0.75
5–7 m	50	0.55	0.45	0.40
	≧100	0.75	0.65	0.60

❷ Correction factor table

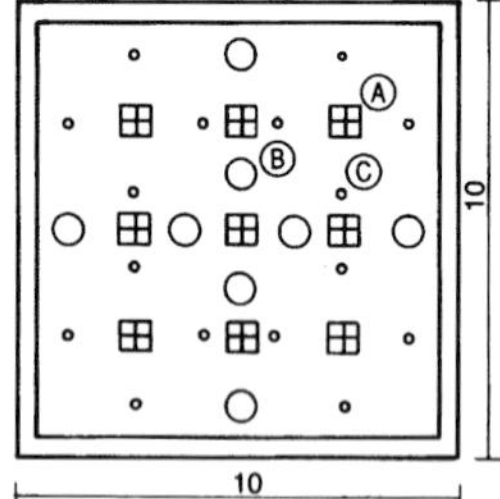

❸ Calculation of illuminance for an interior

example
room area A = 100 m³
room height H = 3 m
reflection factor 0.5/0.2/0.1 (medium)
type of light A
P* = 4 W/m² × (compact fluorescent lamp)
P* = 9 × 45 W = 405 W
type of light B
P* = 12 W/m² × (general purpose lamp)
P* = 8 × 100 W = 800 W
type of light C
P* = 10 W/m² × (halogen filament lamp)
P* = 16 × 20 W = 320 W
formula → ❽

$$E_n\left(\frac{100\times405}{100\times4}+\frac{100\times800}{100\times12}+\frac{100\times320}{100\times10}\right)\times0.9$$

E_n = 180 lx

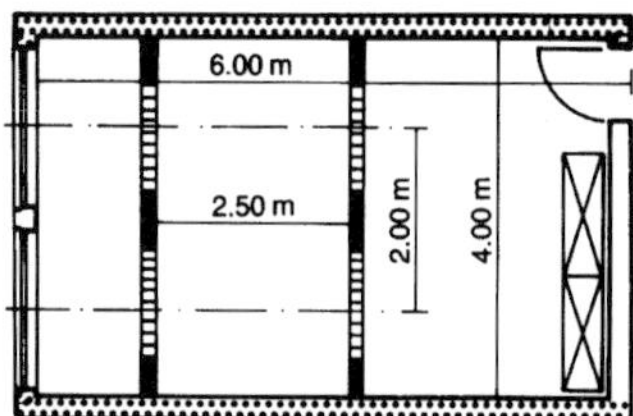

A = 24 m²
k = 0.75 (bright reflection)
P = 4 × 90 W = 360 W

$$E_n = \frac{100\times4\times90}{24.3}\times0.75$$

E_n = 375 lx

❹ Calculation for an office

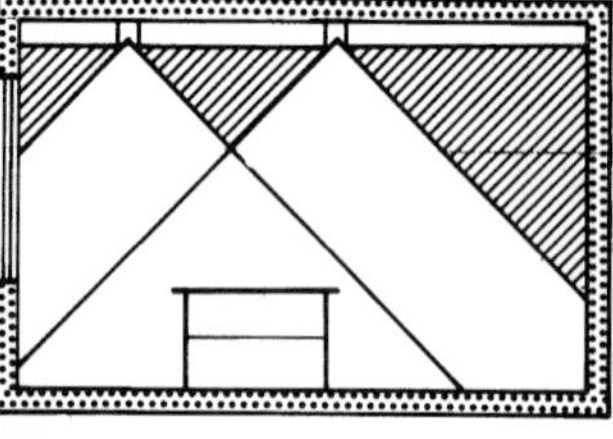

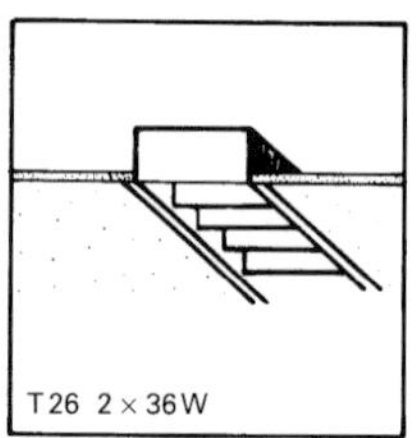

❺ Ceiling grid light fitting (ERCO)

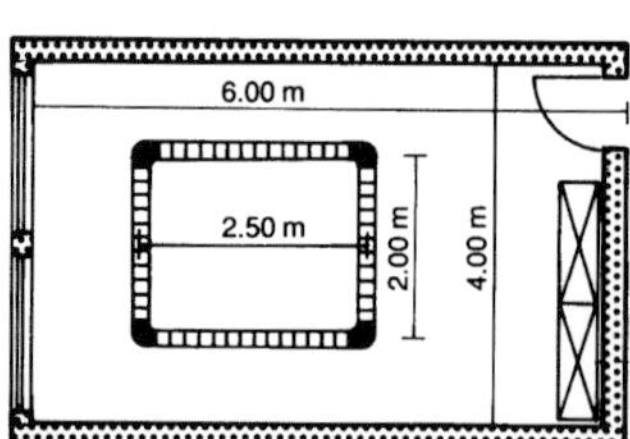

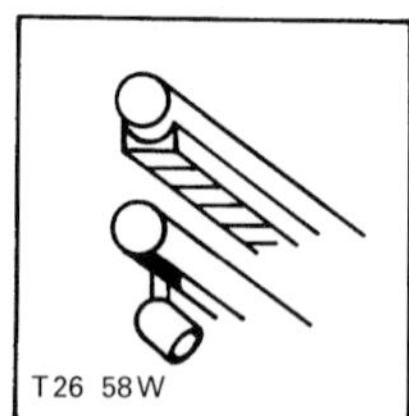

❻ Light structure (ERCO)

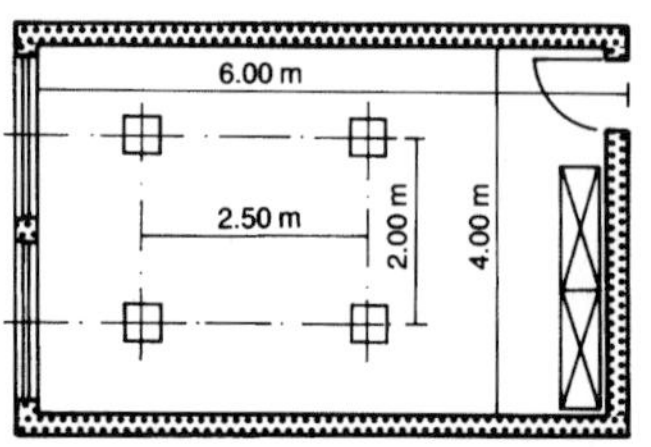

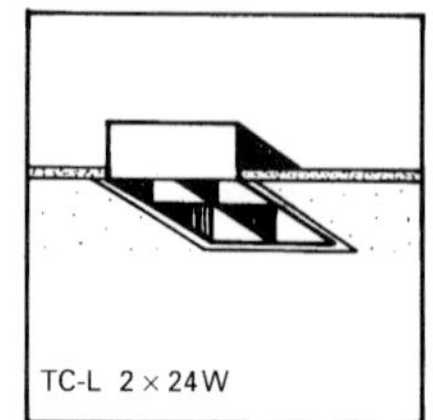

❼ Ceiling grid light fitting (ERCO)

Calculation of mean illuminance

In practice, it is often necessary to make a rough determination of mean illuminance values (E_n) for a given amount of electrical power used by lights, or to determine the use by the lights of electrical power P for a required illuminance level. E_n and P can be approximately determined by using the formula → ❽. The required mains power P* depends on the type of lights used → ❶, referring to direct lighting. The correction factor k depends on the size of the room and the reflectance of the walls, ceiling and floor → ❷. If calculations have to be made for rooms containing various types of lighting then the components are calculated singly and added together → ❸.

The calculation of illuminance using the specific mains power is also applicable to office spaces. A two-axis room with an area of 24 m² is in this example → ❹ fitted with four lights. With an assembly of 2 × 36 W (mains power including ballast 90 W), then according to → ❽ the illuminance is approx. 375 lx.

In offices, in addition to conventional mirrored ceiling grid fittings, square ceiling luminaires with compact fluorescent lamps → ❼ or light structures → ❻ are often installed. Light structures enable the combination with busbars for the mounting of spotlights.

Floodlighting buildings

The luminous flux required for floodlighting can be calculated using the formula → ❾. The luminance levels are between 3 cd/m² (free-standing buildings) and 16 cd/m² (buildings in very bright surroundings).

$E_n = \frac{100\times P}{A\times P}\times k$	E_n nominal illuminance (lx)
	P connected load (W)
$P = \frac{E_n\times A\times P^*}{100}\times\frac{1}{k}$	P* specific connected load (W/m²) → ❶
	A room floor area
	k correction factor → ❷

❽ Formula for mean illuminance E_n and mains load P

formula for calculation of luminous flux of lights

$$\Phi = \frac{\pi\times L\times A}{\eta_B\times\rho}$$

luminance of building to be floodlit	cd/m² L
free-standing	3–6.5
dark surroundings	6.5–10
medium surroundings	10–13
very bright surroundings	13–16

lighting effectiveness, building	η_B
large and small area	0.4
great distance	0.3
towers	0.2

Φ = required luminous flux
L = mean luminance (cd/m²)
A = surface to be floodlit
η_B = lighting effectiveness
ρ = reflectance of building material

reflectance for floodlighting	
building material	ρ
brick, white glazed	0.85
white marble	0.6
light render	0.3–0.5
dark render	0.2–0.3
light sandstone	0.3–0.4
dark sandstone	0.1–0.2
light brick	0.3–0.4
dark brick	0.1–0.2
light timber	0.4–0.5
granite	0.1–0.2

❾ Required luminous flux for floodlights

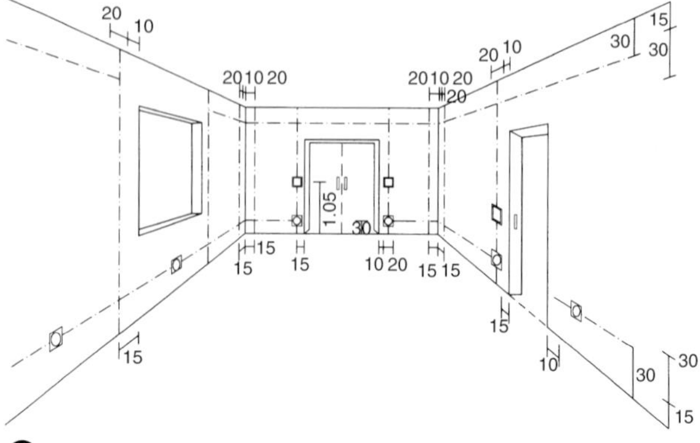

❿ Preferred dimensions for electrical cabling of residential buildings (cm)

Recommendations for application

	Warm white				Neutral white		Daylight white		
light colours	827	927	830	930	840	940	950	865	965
colour rendering value	1B	1A	1B	1A	1B	1A	1A	1B	1A
sales areas									
foodstuffs	●		X						
textile, leather goods		X	●	X	●	X			
furniture, carpets	X	X	●	X					
sport, games, stationery			X		X				
photography, clocks, jewellery			X	●	X	●			
cosmetics, hairdressing	●	X	●	X	●	X			
flowers				X		X			
bakery products	X								
refrigerated counters, chests	X								
cheese, fruit, vegetables	X								
fish	X		X		X				
department stores, supermarkets	X	X	X	X	X	X			
industry, trades									
workshops					X				
electrical, mechanical engineering					X			X	
textile manufacture					●	X	X	●	X
printing, graphic trades					●	X	X	●	X
paint shops							●	X	●
warehousing, despatch					X				
woodworking					X		X	X	
steelworks, rolling mills					X				
laboratories			●	X	●	X	X	X	●
colour testing							X		X
office and administration									
offices, corridors			X		X				
meeting rooms	X		X		X				
education									
lecture theatres, classrooms, kindergartens			X	●	X				
libraries, reading rooms	X	●	X						
social spaces									
restaurants, pubs, hotels	X	X							
theatres, concert halls, hotels	X								
event spaces									
exhibition and trade fair halls	X		X		X				
sports and multi-purpose halls			X		X				
galleries, museums		X		X					
clinics, medical practices									
diagnosis and treatment				X		●			
patients' rooms, waiting rooms		X		X					
residential									
living rooms	X		●						
kitchen, bathroom, hobby room, cellar	X		X		X	X			

1 Light colour recommendations for various application areas

● = recommendation X = possible

Workplace Guidelines 'Artificial Lighting', 7/3; DIN EN 12464-1 (Excerpt)

Indoor workplaces

type of interior or activity	E_n/lx
General rooms:	
traffic zones in storage rooms	50
service point	200
canteens, tea kitchens	200
break rooms	100
gymnastic rooms	300
changing, washing and toilet rooms	200
sanitary rooms	500
service rooms, switchrooms	200
telex and post rooms, telephone switchboards	500
despatch and packing areas	300
pantry and storage areas	100
(High-bay) warehouse	
traffic route with no pedestrians	20
traffic route with pedestrians	150
Vehicle and/or traffic routes:	
– no pedestrians	20
– for pedestrians	100
– for pedestrians and vehicles	150
stairs, escalators, moving walkways	150
loading ramps, loading areas	150
Offices and similar rooms:	
filing, copying	300
traffic zones in workrooms	300
writing, typing	500
reading, data processing	500
technical drawing	750
meeting rooms	500
reception desk	300
rooms for public access	200
CAD workplaces	500
Chemical industry:	
plants with remote control	50
plants with occasional manual inputs	150
constantly manned locations in process plants	300
maintenance	300
laboratories	500
work with increased visual tasks	500
colour testing	1000
Ceramics, tiles, glass, glassware:	
drying	50
mixing, material preparation, working at kilns	200
enamelling, rolling, pressing, forming simple parts, glazing, glass blowing	300
grinding, engraving, polishing glass, forming glass instruments	750
manual grinding and engraving	750
fine work	1000
making/polishing artificial gems	1500
Steelworks, rolling mills, large foundries:	
production plants without input	50
production plants with input	150
constantly manned workplaces in production plants	200
maintenance	300
checking stations	500
Metal preparation and processing:	
free-form cutting	200
drop forging	200
welding	300
coarse and medium machine work	300
fine machine work	500
checking stations	750
cold rolling mills	200
wire drawing plants	300
processing of heavy sheet metal	200
processing of light sheet metal	300
manufacture of hand tools	750
coarse assembly	200
medium-fine assembly	300
fine assembly	500
foundries, cellars etc.	50
scaffolding	100
sanding	200
cleaning cast metal	200
workplaces at mixers	200
foundry halls	200
emptying positions	200
machine moulding shop	200
manual moulding shop	300
core-making shop	300
model making	500
galvanising	300
painting	300
checking stations	750
tool making, fine mechanical work	1000
bodybuilding	500
spraying	750
retouching sprayed paint	1000
upholstery	1000
finished assembly	500
final checking	1000
Power stations:	
fuel supply plants	50
boiler house	100
pressure compensation room	200
machine halls	200
side rooms	200
switching gear in buildings	100
switching gear in the open air	20
switching maintenance	500
repair work	500
Electrical industry:	
cable and conductor manufacture, assembly work, winding coarse wire	300
assembly of telephones	750
winding medium wire	500
assembly of fine devices	750
adjusting, testing	1500
assembly of very fine components, electronic components	1500
Jewellery and clock industry:	
manufacture of jewellery	1000
processing gemstones	1500
optician and watchmaker workshop (manual work)	1500
Timber processing and manufacture:	
wet pits	150
sawmill	300
assembly	300
selection of veneers, varnishing, model joinery	750
work on timber processing machines	500
timber treatment	500
quality control	1000
Paper making, and processing, graphical trades:	
wood grinding	200
paper machines, cardboard manufacture	300
bookbinding, printing wallpaper	500
Printing plant	
cutting, gilding, embossing, etching blocks, working on stones and plates, printing machines, preparation of stencils, hand printing, sorting paper	500
retouching, lithography, hand and machine use, preparing type	1000
expert checking of colour printing	1500
steel and copper etching	2000
Leather industry:	
working at vats	200
processing skins	300
saddler	500
leather dying	750
leather colours, mechanical	500
quality control	1000
colour testing	1000
Textile manufacture and processing:	
workplaces at baths	200
spinning shops	300
dyeing	500
spinning, knitting, weaving	500
sewing	750
millinery	750
cleaning	1000
goods checking, colour checking	1000
invisible mending	1500
printing fabric, automatic	500
Food, drinks and tobacco industry:	
general workplaces	200
mixing, packing	300
abattoirs, dairies, mills	500
cutting and sorting	300
making fine foods and cigarettes	500
product control, decorating, sorting	500
laboratories	500
colour checking	1000
Wholesale and retail:	
sales rooms, permanent workplaces	300
cash desks	500
Trade: (examples for various branches)	
painting of steel components	200
preliminary assembly of heating and ventilation systems	200
metalwork	300
vehicle workshops	300
joinery	300
repair workshops	500
radio and television workshops	500
Service companies:	
reception/cash desk	300
kitchens	500
dining rooms, restaurants	200
buffets	300
self-service restaurants	200
conference rooms	500
washing and chemical cleaning	300
ironing and pressing	300
control and retouching	750
hair care	500
cosmetics	750
Plastic processing:	
injection moulding	500
plastic blowing	300
plastic pressing	300

Outdoor workplaces

type of outdoor workplaces, traffic routes, traffic zones and workshops	E_n/lx
Traffic routes in the works area, works roads	
gate facilities	50
footpaths	5
cycle ways $E_{min} \geqq$	3
works roads with loading and unloading or with heavy crossing traffic and with speed limit $\leqq$30 km/h	10
works roads with loading and unloading or with heavy crossing traffic and with speed limit	20
Car parks	3
Harbours	
container handling areas	
parking areas and traffic zones	20
loading and unloading containers	100
quay facilities	
quay edge	5
loading unit goods	20
loading bulk goods (loose goods, liquids)	10
working areas in storage facilities	
unit goods	20
bulk goods	5
dangerous liquids	5
landing stage for passenger traffic	30
landing stage for mixed traffic	50
docks	50
repair workshops in harbours	50
handling areas, loading areas	30
Working areas in storage and stacking facilities:	
unit goods	30
bulk goods	10
Rail facilities:	
track yards, marshalling yards	
1 public transport	3
2 other traffic	5
platforms	
cargo handling	30
at-grade level crossings	20
Construction sites:	
building	20
civil engineering	20
steelwork, metalwork	30
tunnelling	30
Large chemical works, power stations:	
traffic zone	10
1 traditional power station	10
2 nuclear power station	20
switching gear	20
Open cast mining:	
1 orientation lighting	3
2 extra area lighting	20
Water treatment works:	
routes	5
Petrol stations	100

❶ Nominal guideline illuminance values for workplaces

LIGHTING
Artificial lighting
Lamps
Types of lighting
Lighting layout
Quality criteria
Illuminance
Application
Workplace
Guidelines

BS EN 60921
DIN 5035
DIN EN 12464

Workplace
Guidelines

Building services

Preventative fire protection

Construction measures | Technical measures | Organisational measures

❶ Preventative fire protection measures (in contrast to the fire-fighting measures of the fire brigade)

Regulation	Content
DIN 4102	Fire behaviour of building materials and components
DIN EN 13501	Classification of building products and building types according to fire behaviour
MBO	Model building regulations with the general constructional requirements for preventative fire protection
MIndBauR	Guideline for constructional fire protection in industrial buildings
MVStättV	Regulations for the construction and operation of places of assembly
MSchulBauR	Guidelines for the building supervision requirements for schools
MHHR	Guidelines for the building supervision treatment of high-rise buildings
ArbStättV/ASR	Workplace Regulations/Workplace Guidelines
BGV	Regulations of the accident insurers for trades
VdS/CEA	Regulations and notices of the specialist insurers

❷ Technical rules for fire protection (excerpt)

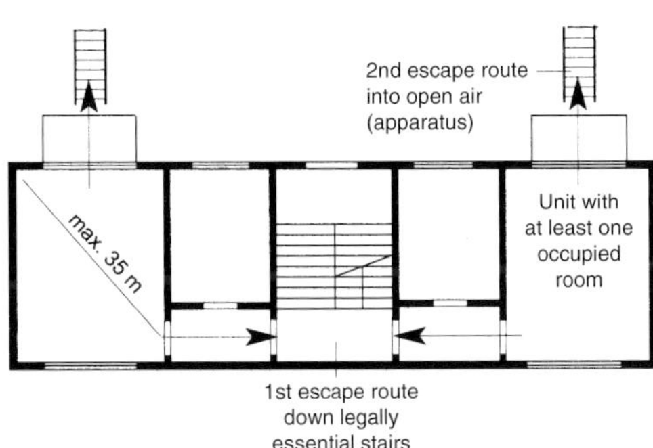

❸ First and second escape routes for occupied units not on the ground floor (theoretical diagram, MBO)

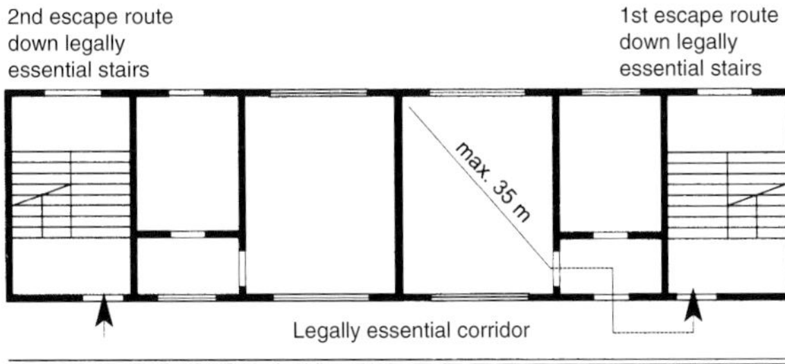

❹ First and second escape routes via two legally essential stairwells and legally essential corridor (theoretical diagram, MBO)

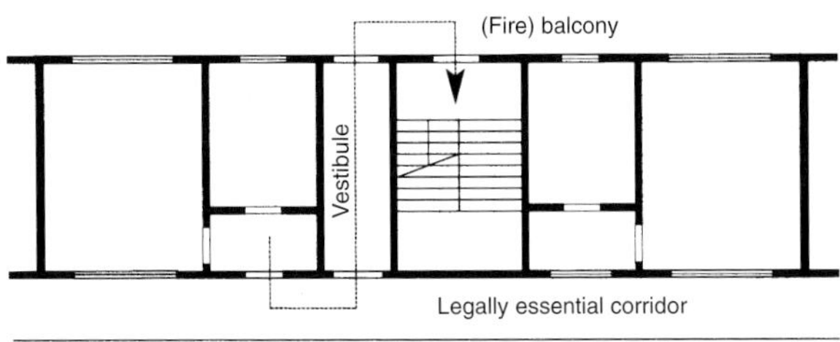

❺ Escape route via safety stairwell (theoretical diagram, MBO) → p. 246 High-rise buildings

Buildings must be constructed so that the **start of fire,** and the **spread of fire and smoke,** are prevented, and **rescue of people** and animals and **effective fire fighting** are possible. Consequently there are requirements concerning flammability of building materials, building components' duration of fire resistance (fire resistance rating), the sealing of closures to openings and the provision of escape routes.

There are basically three categories of preventative fire protection measures → ❶:

Construction measures apply to the design (e.g. escape routes, number and construction of stairwells and the formation of fire compartments). They also apply to all construction solutions for the building and its components (e.g. minimum cross-sections, envelope, claddings and coatings, provision of riser pipes, installation of fire protection doors and glazing etc.). **Technical fire protection measures** include all technical precautions, which activate automatically in case of fire (e.g. smoke and fire detector systems, sprinkler systems, smoke and heat extraction systems). **Organisational fire protection measures** describe the appointment of a fire protection representative and the creation of a fire safety organisation and plans.

The general construction requirements for preventative fire protection are based on the state building regulations (LBO) or the **model building regulations (MBO)** that they are derived from:

For buildings in **building classes 1–5,** the MBO include, in addition to fire protection requirements, the provision of clearance or setback areas → p. 64 and regulations for the detailing of load-bearing walls, columns, external walls, partitions, fire compartment walls, slabs and roofs → p. 514–516 and requirements for the provision of escape routes.

Special buildings are subject to special fire protection requirements, which are laid down in additional regulations and provisions. **At the design phase of such a building, a fire protection expert must be appointed to produce a fire protection plan.**

For a selection of significant technical rules for fire protection → ❷.

Escape routes

Residential or commercial units with at least one occupied room must have at least **two independent escape routes leading to the open air** on each storey. (If the units are not at ground level, the first escape route must be via a **legally essential staircase, if required in its own (legally essential) stairwell**, and the second escape route via a second essential staircase or a single unified location which is accessible with the rescue equipment of the local fire brigade → ❸. From every location in an occupied room, there must be within max. 35 m at least one exit into a legally essential stairwell or into the open air → ❹. A second escape route is not required if escape is via a **safety stairwell** → ❺, into which fire and smoke cannot penetrate due to the provision of 'fire balconies' or safety vestibules with forced ventilation → p. 246 High-rise buildings.

The material and construction of legally essential staircases and the location, construction, surfaces and openings of legally essential stairwells are subject to special fire protection requirements. For **legally essential corridors**, through which the escape routes from occupied rooms or units lead to legally essential stairwells or to the open air, there are also particular fire protection requirements.

FIRE PROTECTION

Basics
Fire compartment walls
Building components
Fire protection glazing
Fire protection door sets
Extinguisher pipelines
Smoke and heat extraction systems
Sprinkler systems
Other extinguisher systems

BS 9999
DIN 4102
DIN EN 13501

MBO
LBO

Building services

FIRE PROTECTION

Classification

The model building regulations (MBO) differentiate requirements for fire resistance into: fire-resistant, highly fire-retarding and fire-retarding **building components** made of completely non-flammable materials or with just the structural parts made of non-flammable materials; special building components (with special fire protection requirements); and associated **building materials,** divided, according to their fire behaviour, into non-combustible, flame-resistant, normally flammable and readily flammable.

Building components and materials are categorised into classes according to their fire behaviour. For purposes of classification, the state building regulations (LBO) differentiate between **regulated, non-regulated** and other building products. Regulated building products essentially comply with the standards and other technical regulations included in the **construction products lists** of the German Institute for Building Technology (DiBt). The permissibility of using non-regulated products must be verified by a national technical test certificate, a national technical approval or a single-case approval.

Classification is according to DIN 4102 or DIN EN 13501. These standards classify building materials according to building material classes → (4) and building components according to fire resistance classes → (1) – (2). **Classifications are applicable according to either DIN 4102 or DIN EN 13501 for the verification of the fire behaviour of building materials.**

Fire resistance duration (min) DIN 4102/ DIN EN 13501-2	30	60	90	120	180
building components	F 30/ *R 30*	F 60/ *R 60*	F 90/ *R 90*	F 120/ *R 120*	F 160/ *R 160*
non-load-bearing external walls	W 30/ *E 30* 1) *EI 30* 2)	W 60/ *E 60* 1) *EI 60* 2)	W 90/ *E 90* 1) *EI 90* 2)	W 120/ *E 120* 1) *EI 120* 2)	W 180/ *E 180* 1) *EI 180* 2)
fire protection boundaries	T 30/ *EI 30 C* 2)	T 60/ *EI 60 C* 1)	T 90/ *EI 90 C* 2)	T 120/ *EI 120 C* 2)	T 180/ *EI 180 C* 2)
F-glazing	F 30/ *EI 30*	F 60/ *EI 60*	F90/ *EI 90*	F 120/ *EI 120*	F 180/ *EI 130*
G-glazing	G 30/ *E 30*	G 60/ *E 60*	G 90/ *E 90*	G 120/ *E 120*	G 180/ *E 180*

1) from inside to outside
2) from outside to inside

(1) Fire resistance classes of building components, DIN EN 13501-2 and DIN 4102-2, -3, -5

Building regulations requirements	Fire compartment boundaries		Smoke protection doors	Cable stopping	Pipe stopping
fire-resisting	*EI 30 C* 2)	F 60/ *R 60*	F 90/ *R 90*	F 120/ *R 120*	F 160/ *R 160*
highly fire-resisting	W 30/ *E 30* 1) *EI 30* 2)	W 60/ *E 60* 1) *EI 60* 2)	W 90/ *E 90* 1) *EI 90* 2)	W 120/ *E 120* 1) *EI 120* 2)	W180/ *E 180* 1) *EI 180* 2)
fireproof	T 30/ *EI 30 C* 2)	T 60/ *EI 60 C* 2)	T 90/ *EI 90 C* 2)	T 120/ *EI 120 C* 2)	T 180/ *E*2 *180 C* 2)
fire resistance 120 min.	F 30/ *EI 30*	F 60/ *EI 60*	F 90/ *EI 90*	F 120/ *EI 120*	F 180/ *EI 180*
smoke-proof and self-closing	G 30/ *E 30*	G 60/ *E 60*	G 90/ *E 90*	G 120/ *E 120*	G 180/ *E 180*

1) from inside to outside
2) from outside to inside

(2) Fire resistance classes of special building components according to DIN EN 13501-2, -3, -4 and their categorisation by building regulations requirements (excerpt)

	1	2	3
	Description in building regulations	Description according to DIN 4102	Short code
1	fire-retarding	fire resistance class F 30	F 30-B[2)]
2	fire-retarding and consisting of structural parts of non-combustible building materials	fire resistance class F 30 and with essential parts[1)] of non-combustible building materials	F 30-AB[2)]
3	fire-resisting and consisting of non-combustible building materials	fire resistance class F 30 and consisting of non-combustible materials	F 30-AB[2)]
4	fire-retarding and consisting of structural parts of non-combustible building materials	fire resistance class F 60 and with essential parts of non-combustible building materials	F 60-AB
5	highly fire-retarding and consisting of non-combustible building materials	fire resistance class F 60 and consisting of non-combustible materials	F 60-A
6	fireproof (e.g. walls); fireproof and consisting of structural parts of non-combustible building materials	fire resistance class F 90 and with essential parts[1)] of non-combustible building materials	F 90-AB[2)]
7	fireproof and consisting of non-combustible building materials (e.g. walls)	fire resistance class F 90 and consisting of non-combustible materials	F 90-A[2)]

[1)] The **essential parts** include:
[a)] all load-bearing or bracing parts, and in the case of non-load-bearing parts also constructions which produce their structural stability (e.g. frame construction of non-load-bearing walls).
[b)] for building components forming the boundary of a room, a continuous layer in the building component, which may not be destroyed during the test according to this standard. For ceilings, this layer must have a total thickness of at least 50 mm; voids within this layer are permissible. In the evaluation of the fire behaviour of building materials, paint or coatings up to a thickness of approx. 0.5 mm are not considered.
[2)] For the complete description of building components according to DIN 4102 the **building materials** class is given after the **fire resistance class**.

(3) Listing of fire resistance designations according to MBO and DIN 4102, according to the model introduction decree to DIN 4102 (→ refs)

Building regulations requirements according to MBO	Additional requirements: no smoke	Additional requirements: no falling burning parts/drops	DIN EN 13501-1	DIN 4102-1
non-combustible	x	x	A1	A1
at least	x	x	A2 s1 dO	A2
flame-resistant	x	x	B,C-s1 d0	B1
		x	A2 -s1 d0 A2,B,C-s3 d0	
	x		A2,B,C-s1 d1 A2,B,C-s1 d2	
at least	x	x	A2,B,C-s3 d2	
normally flammable		x	D-s1 d0 D-s2 d0 D-s3 d0 E	B2
			D-s1 d2 D-s2 d2 D-s3 d2	
at least			E -d2	
readily flammable			F	B3

(4) Classification of the fire behaviour of building materials, MBO, DIN EN 13501-1 and DIN 4102-1 (DiBt → refs)

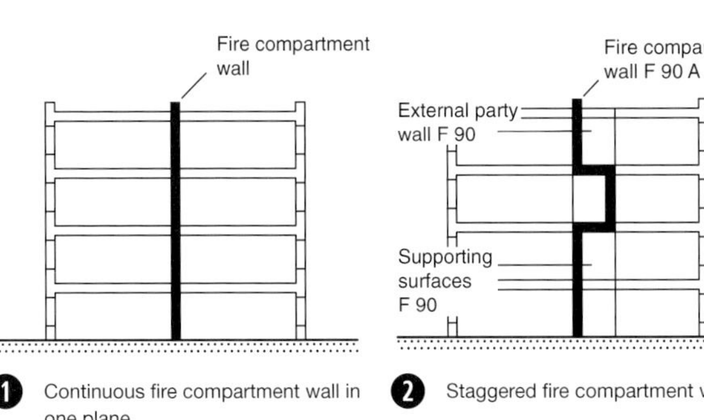

❶ Continuous fire compartment wall in one plane

❷ Staggered fire compartment wall

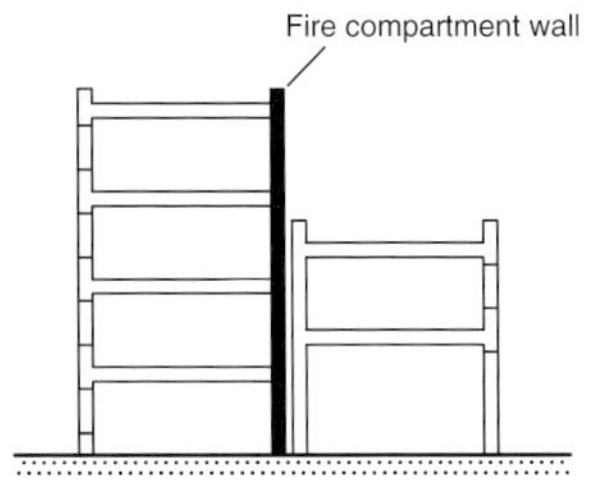

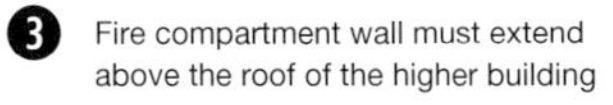

❸ Fire compartment wall must extend above the roof of the higher building

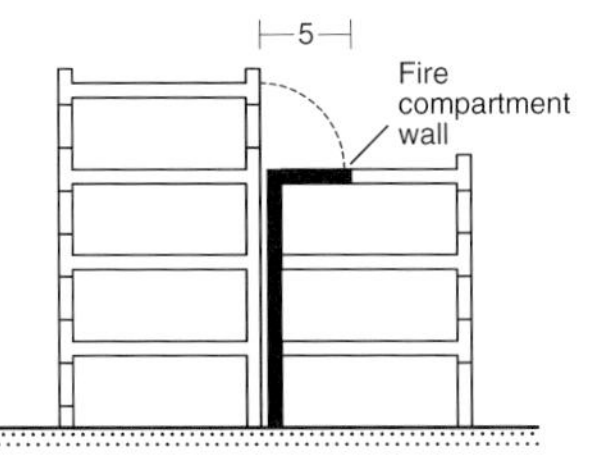

❹ If the fire compartment wall is in the lower building, then the roof slab must be constructed of fire compartment wall quality

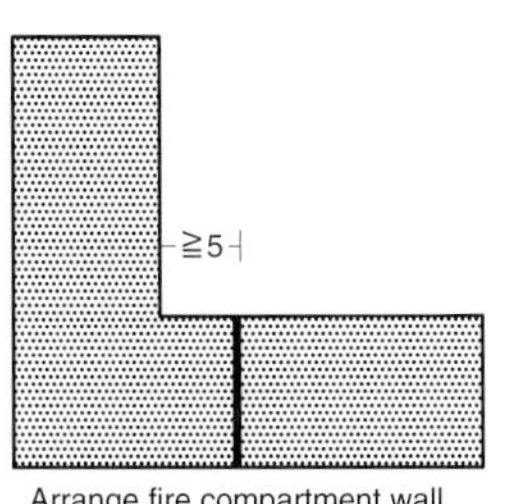

Arrange fire compartment wall ≧5 m from internal corners

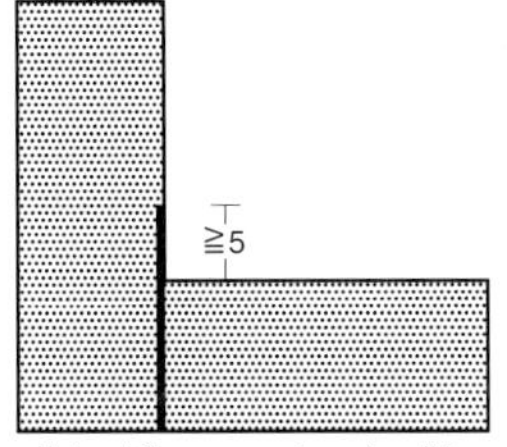

Extend fire compartment wall in an internal corner by ≧5 m to both sides (variant 1)

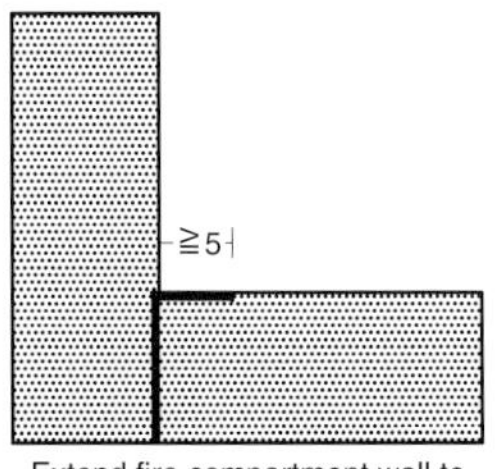

Extend fire compartment wall to one side by ≧5 m (variant 2)

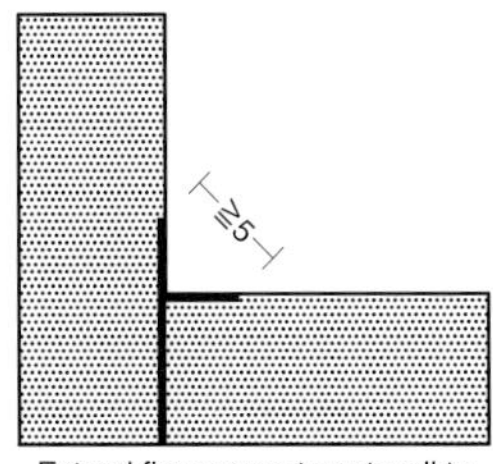

Extend fire compartment wall to both sides

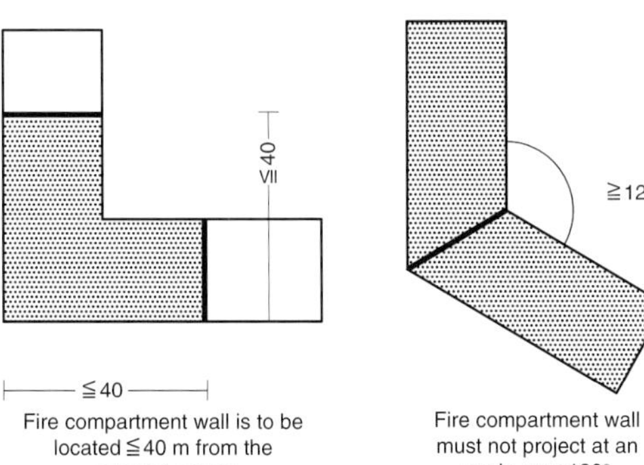

Fire compartment wall is to be located ≦40 m from the external corner

Fire compartment wall must not project at an angle over 120°

❺ Layout of fire compartment walls at building corners

According to the MBO, **fire compartment walls** are to be constructed in the following locations: the **external walls** of buildings, when the wall is less than 2.50 m from the plot boundary; between terraced buildings on the same plot boundary; and to **sub-divide** larger buildings into fire compartments of not more than **40 m**.

Fire compartment walls must be fireproof, structurally stable when exposed to fire and consist of non-combustible materials **(F 90A).** They must normally extend continuously from the foundations to **min. 30 cm above the roof** (min. 50 cm for a soft roof covering and in industrial buildings) or be capped with a projecting slab → ❻. For low buildings, they must continue to immediately under the roof covering. **Cables and pipes** which penetrate fire compartment walls must have a 90 min fire resistance class. **Openings in fire compartment walls** are generally **impermissible.**They can be allowed through fire compartment walls within buildings and then have to be provided with fireproof self-closing doors (**T 90 door or gate**) → p. 512 ❷.

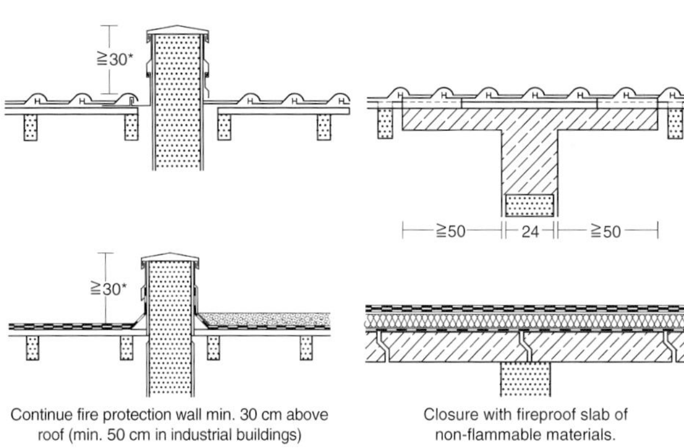

Continue fire protection wall min. 30 cm above roof (min. 50 cm in industrial buildings)

Closure with fireproof slab of non-flammable materials.

❻ Top of fire compartment walls in buildings with hard roof covering

Construction material for fire compartment walls	Min. thickness (mm) Single-skin	Two-skin
Masonry		
according to DIN 1053-1, with mortar group II, IIa, III or IIIa when using bricks according to DIN 105-1 of		
bulk density class ≧1.4	240	2 × 175
bulk density class ≧1.0	300	2 × 175
calcium silicate blocks according to DIN 106-1, 1 A1, 2 of bulk density class ≧1.8	240	2 × 175
Pre-cast brick components		
according to DIN 1053-4 using vertically		
cored brick panels with fully mortared butt joints	165	2 × 165
composite panels with two skins of brick	240	2 × 165
Normal concrete		
unreinforced concrete according to DIN 1045	200	2 × 180
reinforced concrete according to DIN 1045 in the form of non-load-bearing horizontal or vertical wall components	120	2 × 100
load-bearing wall components or in situ concrete	140*)	2 × 120*)
Lightweight concrete		
with porous structure according to DIN 4232 of		
bulk density class ≧1.4	250	2 × 200
bulk density class ≧0.8	300	2 × 200
Aerated concrete		
reinforced min. strength class 4.4 non-load-bearing, vertical or horizontal		
wall components of bulk density class ≧0.7	175	2 × 175
load-bearing vertical components, vertical wall components of bulk density class ≧0.7	200*)	2 × 200*)

*) as long as no higher value is required due to high wall stresses (see DIN 4102-35, table 44).

❼ Minimum thicknesses of building materials for single- and double-skin fire compartment walls (excerpt from DIN 4102-4, table 45 → refs)

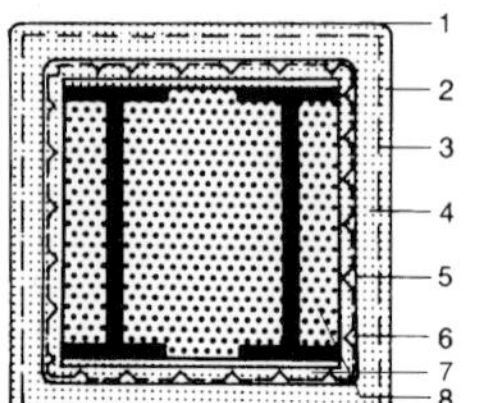

1. Edge protector
2. ≧5 mm ground lime or lime cement plaster, of mortar group I or II acc. DIN 18550
3. Wired fabric
4. ≧35 mm vermiculite-cement plaster
5. Binding wire
6. Ribbed expanded metal
7. Expanded metal and round steel ≧5 mm as spacer
8. Core, min. 1.5 m above the floor, brick/masonry lined or cemented

❶ Steel column with conventional plaster surround F 90

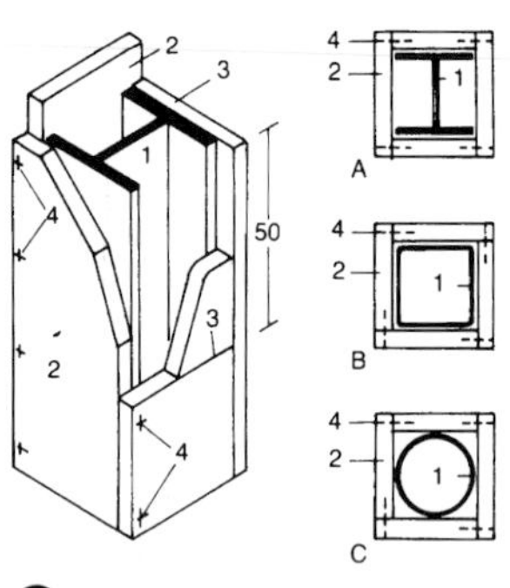

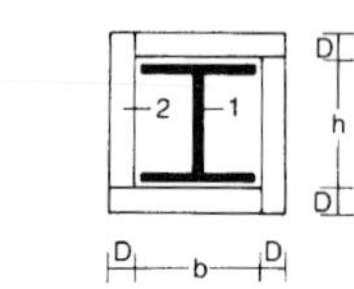

1 Steel column
2 Fire protection board (e.g. PROMATECT®)
3 Staggered joints to boards
4 Wire clamps or drywall screws
h Profile height
b Profile width
D Thickness of the fire-protection cladding

❷ Steel column with fire protection boards F 30 A–F 180 A

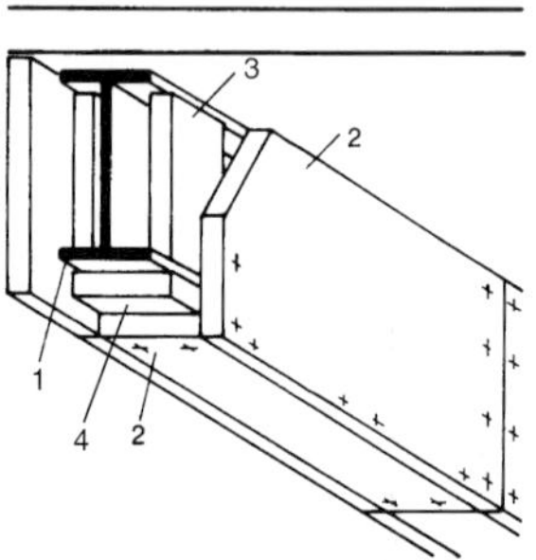

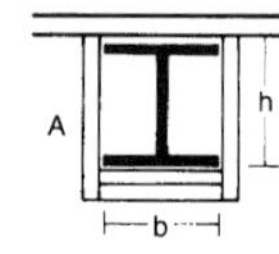

1 Steel support beam
2 Fire protection board (e. g. Promatect®)
3 Fixing piece
4 Extra piece behind joint
5 Profile height
6 Profile width

❸ Fire protection cladding for steel support beams F 30 A–F 180 A

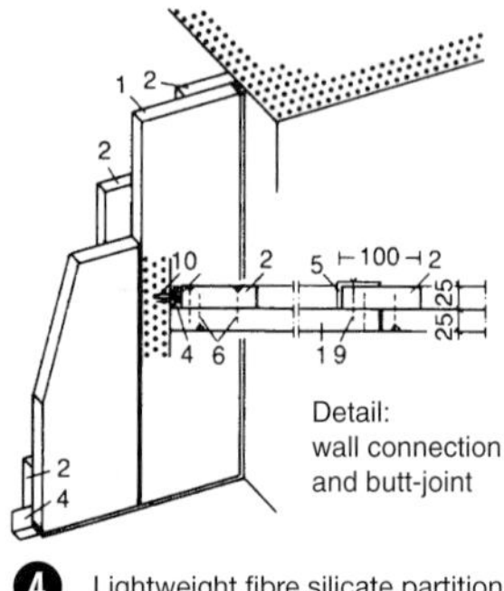

❹ Lightweight fibre silicate partition F 30 A (principle)

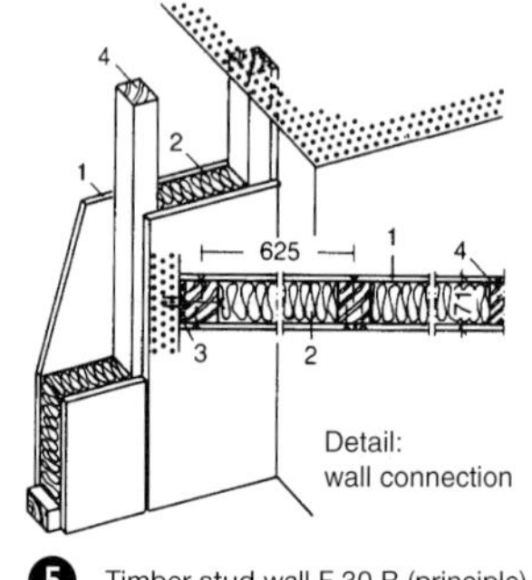

❺ Timber stud wall F 30 B (principle)

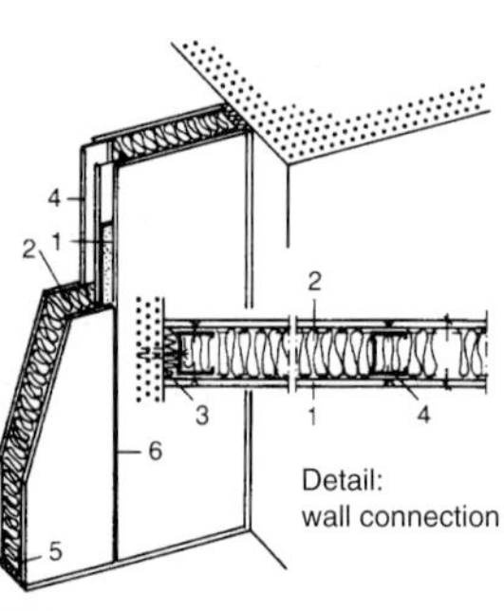

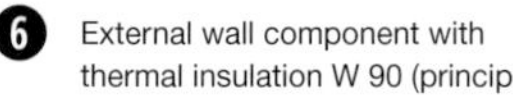

❻ External wall component with thermal insulation W 90 (principle)

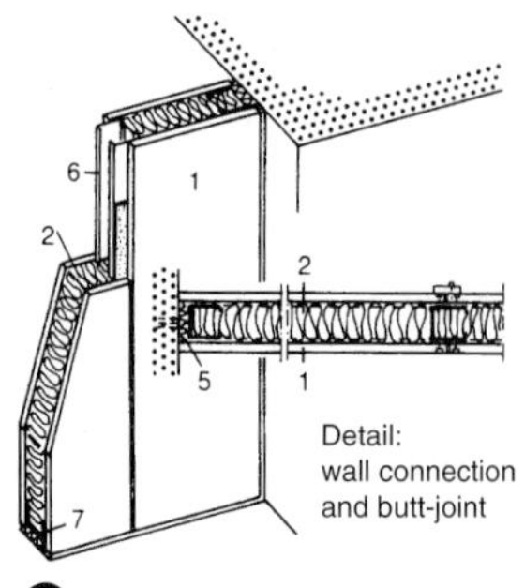

❼ Stable fibre silicate partition with C-profile studs F 90 A

Walls, columns

The **MBO** lay down requirements for walls and columns, of which the essential features are:

Load-bearing and **bracing walls** and **columns** must be constructed **fireproof** in buildings of class 5, **highly fire-retarding** in buildings of class 4 and **fire-retarding** in buildings of classes 1 and 2). This does not apply to the uppermost storeys of roof spaces without occupied rooms above them and balconies. In **cellars,** they have to be constructed **fireproof** and, in buildings of classes 1 and 2, **fire-retarding**.

Non-load-bearing external walls and non-load-bearing parts of load-bearing external walls are (except for buildings of building classes 1–3) to be constructed of non-combustible (at least fire-retarding) materials. **External wall claddings,** including insulation and support construction, have to be made of flame-resistant materials. For buildings of classes 1 and 2, external wall claddings of normally flammable materials are permissible, if the spread of fire to neighbouring buildings is effectively prevented.

Building materials	Class	Certificate	Mark
sand, gravel, loam, clay, natural stone, minerals, earth, lava clinker, natural pumice	A1	cl. B.	no
mineral fibres without organic supplements	A1	cl. B.	no
mineral fibre boards, mats, felt, shells	A½	approval mark	yes
cement, lime, anhydrite, clinker and foamed slag, expanded clay, slate, perlite, vermiculite	A1	cl. B.	no
mortar, concrete, reinforced and pre-stressed concrete, blocks and building boards of mineral composition	A1	cl. B.	no
brick, stoneware, ceramic slabs	A1	cl. B.	no
glass, foam glass	A1	cl. B.	no
glass fibre boards, mats, felt, wadding	A½	approval mark	yes
plexiglass	B1	approval mark	yes
plaster wall and ceiling boards[1]	A1	cl. B.	no
coated and uncoated	A1	approval mark	yes
particle board, veneered boards	B1	approval mark	yes
roofing felt and waterproofing	B2	cl. B.	yes

This table contains:
- classified building materials, according to DIN 4102, which can be included in the given building material class without further verification (cl. B)
- building materials which have to be included in certain building material classes under applicable standards. The verification is normally through a test certificate.
- building materials of classes A and B1, for which approval marks have been issued; these are normally issued to the manufacturer.

❽ Combustibility of construction materials (selection)

Separating walls

The fire resistance duration of separating walls between residential or commercial units (or units and rooms used otherwise) must correspond to the quality of the load-bearing components of the storey. These must extend to the structural slab (in roof spaces up to the roof cladding). Openings are limited to the size and number required for their use and must be closed by components which are at least fire-retarding, sealed and self-closing.

Construction

Classified materials for the construction of conventional massive load-bearing or non-load-bearing walls are shown in → ❽. Steel columns and steel supporting beams are today normally fitted with box-shaped **claddings** of fire protection boards, whose thickness depends on the profile dimensions and the required fire resistance class → ❶ – ❸. There are also **non-foaming coatings** (to F 90) and composite constructions with concrete filling, if necessary with additional reinforcement (F 60). Non-load-bearing separating walls can be constructed as stud partitions of various qualities → ❹ – ❻.

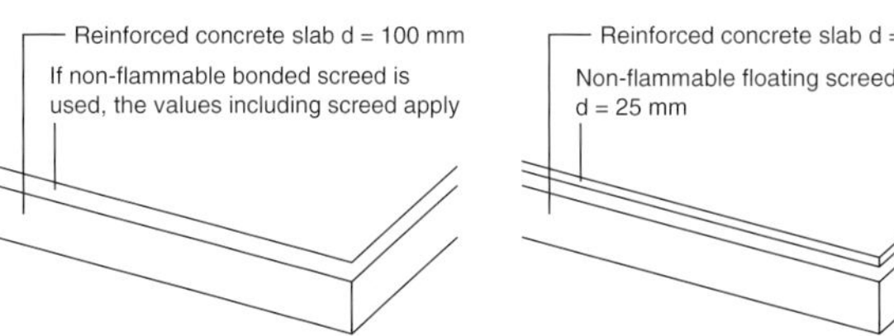

❶ Reinforced concrete slab F 90 A

❷ Reinforced concrete slab F 90 A with floating screed

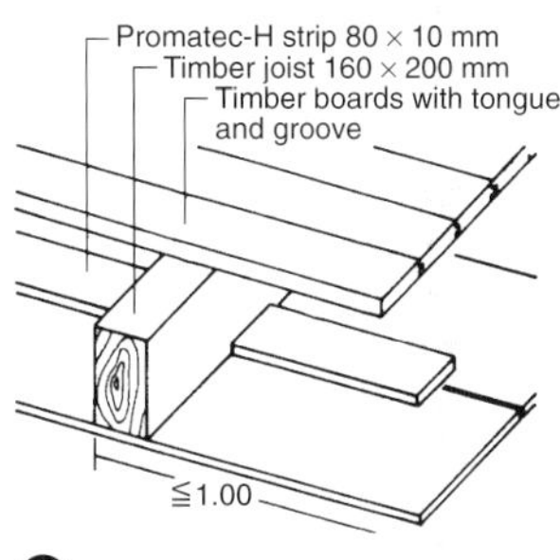

❸ Timber joist floor F 30 B

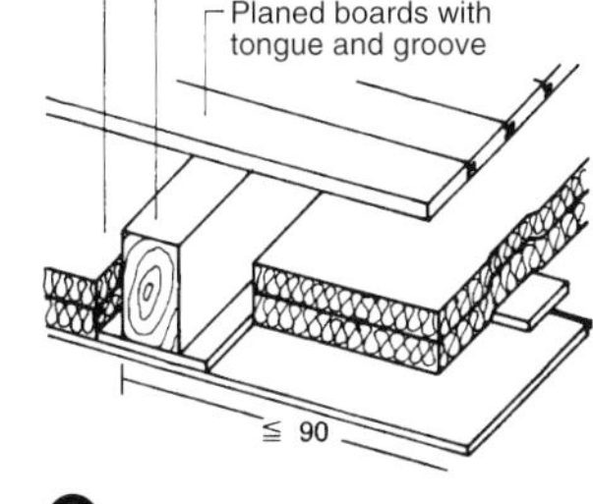

❹ Timber joist floor F 90 B (with thermal insulation)

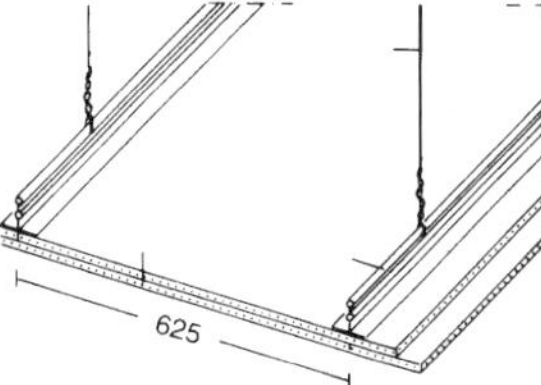

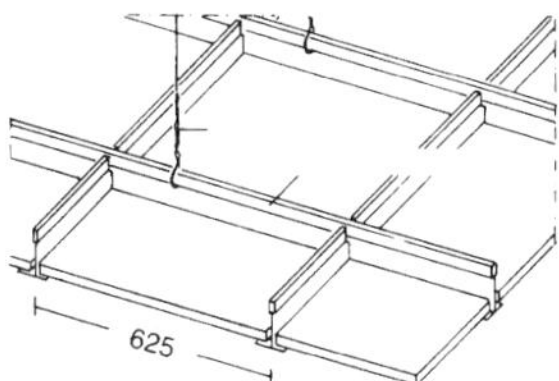

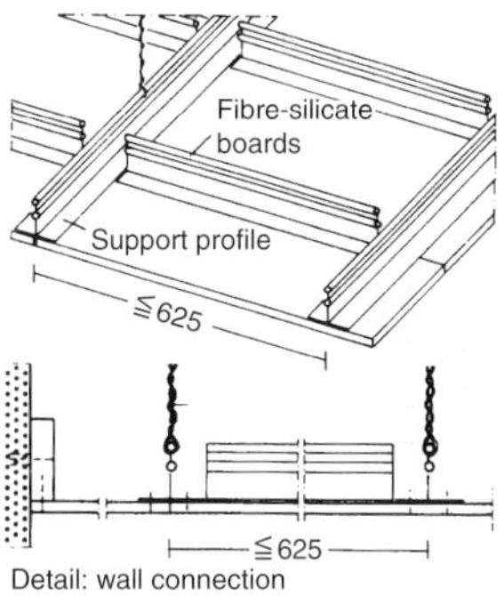

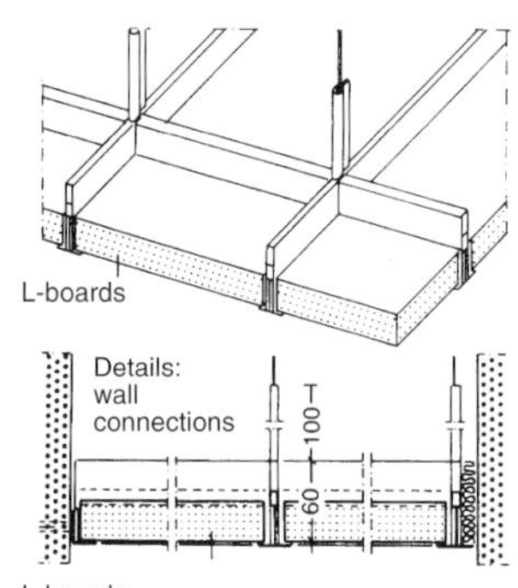

❺ Fibre-silicate suspended ceiling F 90 A (principle)

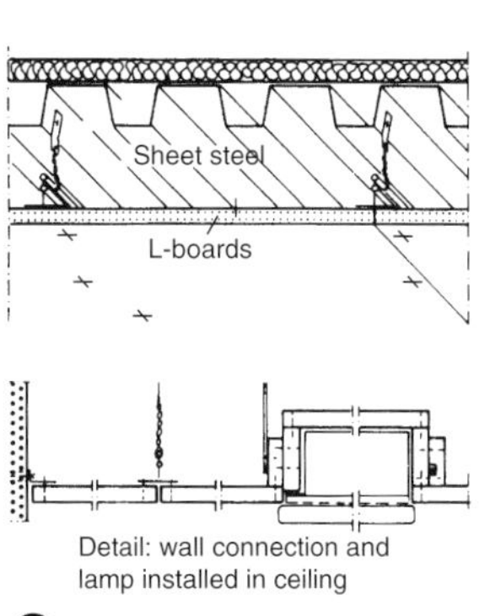

❻ Trapezoid metal sheet roof (fibre silicate suspended ceiling) F 30 AB

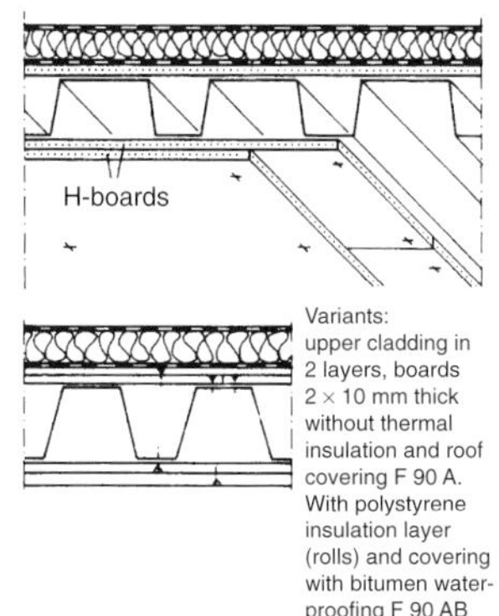

❼ Trapezoid metal sheet roof F 90 A, F 90 AB

Slabs and ceilings

The **MBO** contain fire protection requirements for ceilings, floor slabs acting as ceilings, slabs over cellars and openings through these, of which the most important aspects are described here:

Ceilings must be fireproof, or at least fire-retarding, and **slabs over cellars** must be fireproof. **Openings in ceilings and floor slabs** for which a fire resistance duration is necessary are prohibited. If openings are required, they must be fitted with fire protection closures (doors, etc.) constructed with a fire resistance duration corresponding to that of the slab.

Exceptions apply for buildings of classes 1 and 2, slabs and ceilings above roof spaces, and balconies, slabs and ceilings within residential dwellings.

Construction

The following constructional types of slab and ceiling are differentiated for purposes of fire protection:

Solid slabs (e.g. reinforced concrete slabs → ❶, hollow pot floors) have sufficient fire resistance under certain conditions without additional protection measures. Numerous construction types are classified in DIN 4102 → ❽. Floors consisting of **timber joists, steel joists or concrete slabs on profiled metal decking** must be protected against fire from below (suspended ceiling → ❺) and above (covering, screed), in which case the connections at walls and any inserts in the floor have to be taken into account. The fire resistance achieved is normally verified with a test certificate → p. 512. In this case, the **entire construction** is included in the evaluation. Also usual is the installation of self-supporting suspended ceilings with their own fire resistance class (e.g. to protect the installations in the ceiling void).

Building material and construction	Min. unfinished thickness (mm) for:				
	F 30 A	F 60 A	F 90 A	F 120 A	F 180 A
fully reinforced concrete slabs (exstg.) without cladding beneath	60	80	100	120	150
as above, but with floating screed[1)]	60 (25)[2)]	60 (25)[2)]	60 (25)[2)]	60 (30)[2)]	80 (40)[2)]
hollow pot slabs	115	140	165	240	290
as above, but with screed[1)]	90	90	115	140	165

[1)] non-combustible screed [2)] screed thickness

❽ Classified slab constructions, DIN 4102 (excerpt)

Roofs

The **MBO** also include fire protection requirements for roofs. The essential requirements are:

The roofing must generally consist of 'hard covering' and be resistant against airborne spread of fire and radiated heat. **Roof overhangs, cornices, roof projections, rooflights, transparent roofing,** etc. must have a minimum spacing from fire compartment walls.

There are additional fire protection requirements for buildings in rows (e.g. **terraced houses**) joined at the eaves. The roofs of extensions or components projecting from external walls with openings or without fire resistance must, including any load-bearing and bracing building components within a safety distance (5 m), have the fire resistance of the slabs of the connecting building component.

For buildings in classes 1–3 and partial roof areas, exceptions to these requirements are possible.

BS ISO 10295
BS EN 13501
BS EN 13823
DIN 4102
DIN EN 13501

MBO

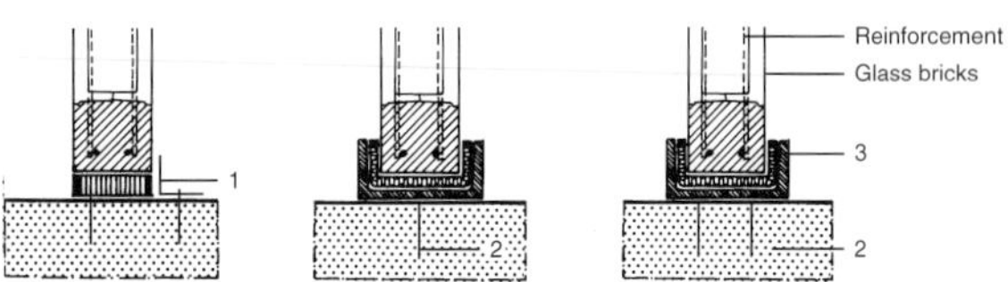

❶ Glazing of fire resistance class G

Reinforcement
Glass bricks

1 Angle steel 50 × 55 mm length ≧100 mm, at least 4 per glass panel
2 Plugs and steel screws M 10 permissible for fire protection
3 Sheet steel for the fixing of the glass brick wall (weld)

❷ Installation details – fire-retarding glazing with glass bricks

Fire resistance duration (min) DIN 4102/ *DIN EN 13501-2*	30	60	90	120	180
F-glazing	F 30/ *EI 30*	F 60/ *EI 60*	F 90/ *EI 90*	F 120/ *EI 120*	F 180/ *EI 180*
G-glazing	G 30/ *E 30*	G 60/ *E 60*	G 90/ *E 90*	G 120/ *E 120*	G 180/ *E 180*

❸ Fire resistance classes of F- and G-glazing, DIN EN 13501-2 and DIN 4102-2, -5

FIRE PROTECTION
Basics
Fire compartment walls
Building components
Fire-resistant glazing
Fire-resistant door sets
Extinguisher pipelines
Smoke and heat extraction systems
Sprinkler systems
Other extinguisher systems

BS ISO 10295
BS EN 13501
BS EN 13823
DIN 4102
DIN EN 13501

MBO

Building services

G-glazing → ❶

Fire-resistant glazing of fire resistance class G (G-glazing) is defined as transparent building components arranged vertically, inclined or horizontally, which, corresponding to their fire resistance duration, can **prevent the spread of fire and smoke, but not the transmission of thermal radiation.**

Construction

The manufacture of G-glazing is possible in the following forms:
- glass bricks, DIN 18175
- wired glass with a spot-welded mesh.
- expensive, special toughened glass combination in a double-glazed unit.
- pre-stressed borosilicate glass, e.g. Pyran.

Scope of application

Under building regulations, G-glazing may be installed only where there are no higher requirements for fire protection reasons. A typical area of application for G-glazing is the openings for lighting installed in corridor walls, which have to be constructed fire-retarding (F 30) as the side walls of escape routes. The lower edge of the glass must in this case be at least 1.80 m above floor level, so that in case of fire the corridor remains usable in the radiation shadow.

G-glazing is also used in the façades of **high-rise buildings**, which are divided into horizontal fire compartments in order to prevent flames leaping from storey to storey → p. 246. For buildings with internal corners, however, the unhindered spread of fire at the window area can be prevented only through the use of F-glazing.

Fire-resistant glazing units are transparent building components consisting of special glass types (single pane size up to approx. 1.20 × 2.40 m) in special thermally separated frame constructions and, when installed in solid building components, can resist fire for 30, 60, 90 or 120 min., corresponding to their classification.

Fire-resistant glazing units are **building components requiring approvals**. The approvals are normally obtained by the manufacturers as part of a general technical approval under building regulations for defined system constructions → p. 512.

Many types of fire-resistant glazing units are not UV-resistant, which should be noted for external applications.

Fire-resistant glazing units are divided into **fire-resistance classes** under DIN EN 13501-2 and DIN 4102-13 → ❸:

F-glazing

Fire-resistant glazing units with fire resistance class F (F-glazing) are defined as transparent building components arranged vertically, inclined or horizontally, which, corresponding to their fire resistance duration, can **prevent the spread of fire and smoke, and also the transmission of thermal radiation.** There must be thermal isolation for the entire duration, which means that the surface of the F-glazing toward the fire may not heat up by more than a certain value (140 K) on average during this time. Additionally, the structural safety must be verified with a strength test under self-load. F-glazing units become opaque in case of fire and behave like walls for purposes of fire protection.

Construction

The manufacture of F-glazing is possible in the following forms:
- pre-stressed glass panes constructed as double-glazed units with the space filled with an organic substance (gel) which contains water
- multi-pane units of three or four float glass panes, between which are placed layers of inorganic composition (e.g. sodium silicate), which produce the fire-retarding effect.

The units are installed, in accordance with the general technical approval, in dry-wall partitions, masonry, reinforced concrete etc.

In the case of a fire, the pane on the fire side bursts and the sodium silicate foams, or the gel resists the heat of the fire by releasing water. (The gel itself consists of a polymer, in which an inorganic salt solution with a high water content is bedded; in the presence of fire, a thermally insulating isolation layer is formed and considerable quantities of energy are consumed. This process repeats itself layer by layer until the gel-type substance has been used up over the entire space between the panes.) The combustion process at the surface of the fire protection layer also colours the glass and makes it impervious to radiation.

Scope of application

F-glazing units are mostly used indoors, but there are also special developments and constructions for outdoor use. Because the panes on the side away from the fire remain at temperatures below the burning through limit for the duration in the fire resistance classification, hardwood can be used for the frame in addition to steel profiles. For fire resistance class T (= doors), the same requirements apply to the glazing as with fire resistance class F.

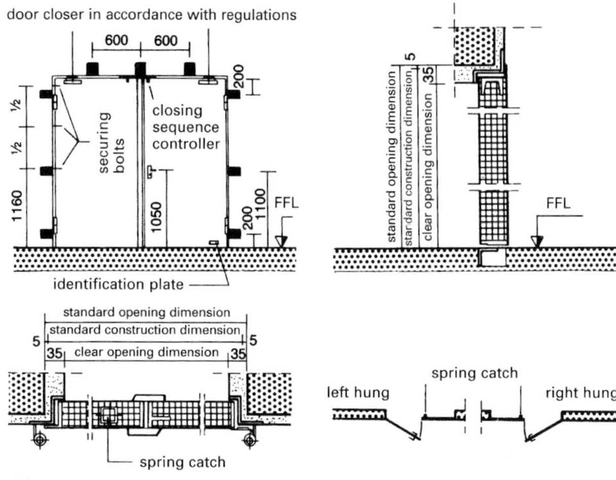

❶ Fire-retarding T 30 double door, DIN 18082

Fire resistance duration (min) DIN 4102/ *DIN EN 13501-2*	30	60	90	120	180
fire-resistant closures	T 30/ *EI 30 C* 1)	T 60/ *EI 60 C* 1)	T 90/ *EI 90 C* 1)	T 120/ *EI 120 C* 1)	T 180/ *EI 180 C* 1)

1) from outside to inside

❷ Fire resistance classes of fire protection closures, DIN EN 13501-2 and DIN 4102-2, -5

Description	Width – modular building size (mm)	Height – modular building size (mm)
T 30-1 hatch	625	625–1750
T 30-1 steel door, DIN 18082	625–1250	1750–2250
T 30-1 hollow section framed door, glazed	625–1250	1750–2250
T 30-2 hollow section framed door, glazed	1250–2500	1750–2250
T 30-1 hollow section framed door with fanlight and fixed glazing of sides	unlimited	≤4000
T 30-1 all-glass door	625–1250	1750–2250
T 30-2 all-glass door	1250–2500	1750–2250
T 60/T 90-1 timber-derived material door, if required with light cut-out	625–1250	1750–2125
T 60/T 90-1 timber-derived material door (see above) with upper part	625–1250	1750–3000
T 90/T 120 roller door	2000–10000	1800–4000
T 30/T 60/ 90 steel sliding door	2000–4500	2000–3500

The dimensions given are in each case the smallest and largest approved sizes (modular building sizes) in mm. Other tested fire-resistant closures:
T 30-1 fire-retarding single-leaf door
T 30-2 fire-retarding double-leaf door
T 60-1 highly fire-retarding single-leaf door
T 60-2 highly fire-retarding double-leaf door
T 90-1 fireproof single-leaf door
T 90-2 fireproof double-leaf door

❸ Size ranges for tested fire-resistant closures (selection)

Fire-resistant door sets (or closures) serve to provide resistance to the spread of fire in walls or slabs which form rooms and are subject to fire resistance requirements, according to their classification → ❸.

Application (selection)
If the provision of openings in **fire compartment walls** inside buildings is permitted under building regulations, then these have to be provided with closures which are self-closing, sealed and fireproof (e.g. T 90 door). Openings in **fireproof separating walls** have to be provided with at least fire-retarding closures (e.g. T 30 door).

Cellars, unoccupied roof spaces, workshops, shops, etc. must have self-closing, smoke-proof and fire-retardant closures (e.g. **T 30 door**) into the stairs.

Closures between **stairways and corridors** legally essential as escape routes and also for the division of legally essential corridors more than 30 m long must be self-closing and smoke-proof → p. 511.

Components
A fire-resistant door set is a **unit** comprising: **door leaf** or leaves, glazing (if present), **metal frame** and fixings for the frame, **heavy-duty steel hinges**, self-closing device in the form of **spring hinges** or **door closer**, selector for double-leaf door sets, specific equipment for sliding, lifting or roller doors, hold-open device with automatic closing for doors which have to be held open for operational reasons and closed in case of fire, and **electrical and other actuators**.

Construction forms
Fire-resistant door sets can be single-leaf **hatches** in the size range up to 62.5 × 175 cm, single- or multi-leaf **hinged or sliding doors** (also as hollow tube frame constructions, sometimes with large-area glazing, timber or timber-derived construction and all-glass doors of special glass) in the size range up to approx. 250 × 250 cm or as **large sliding, lifting or roller doors** in sizes over 250 × 250 cm → ❸.

Certification of suitability
Steel doors which comply with the requirements of DIN 18082-1 or 18082-3 count as T 30 doors without specific certification, according to DIN 4102 → ❶.

For all other fire-resisting closures, certification of suitability is necessary within the framework of a technical approval process under building regulations and classification according to DIN 4102 or DIN EN 13501 → p. 512. Because there is an interaction between wall and door set, fire-resistant door sets are always tested with the type of wall construction for which they are to be approved.

Details of the required certification of suitability are contained in the **construction products list** of the German Institute for Building Technology (DiBt) → p. 512.

Smoke control doors
In certain situations, the authorities demand smoke control doors (DIN 18095), which prevent the penetration of smoke when installed and closed (see above). Smoke control doors also require certification of suitability (see above). Fire-resistant doors are normally also smoke control doors.

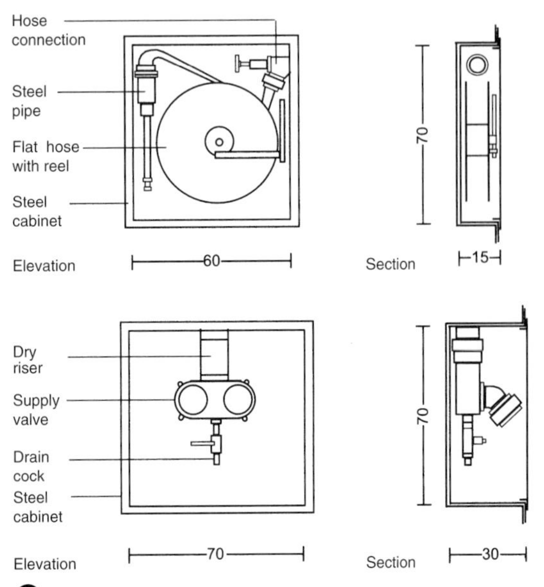

❶ Connection for supply of extinguisher water to a dry riser pipe (below) and wall hydrant (above), DIN 14461-3 etc. (diagram)

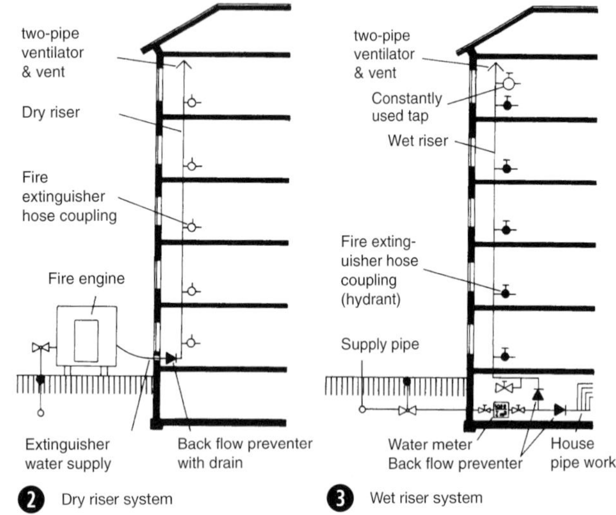

❷ Dry riser system

❸ Wet riser system

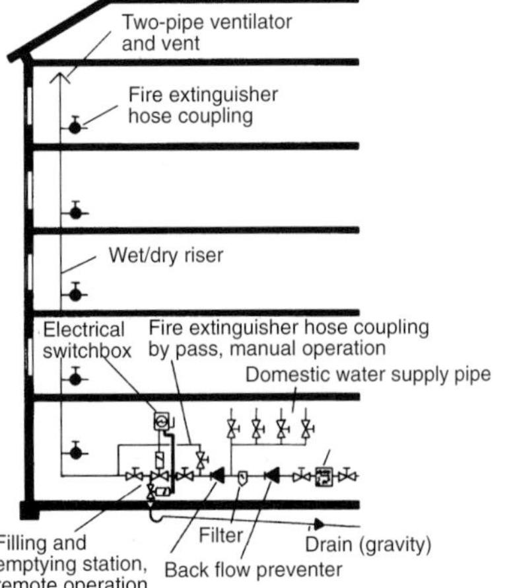

❹ Wet/dry riser system (example for nominal diameter 50–150 mm, nominal pressure PN 16)

Extinguisher water pipelines are those installed in buildings with connections to unlockable fire hoses at water outlet locations. They serve to transport water in sufficient quantities to each storey or fire compartment of a building to extinguish fires. Extinguisher water pipelines are required under building regulations and can be required by the authorities for various types of buildings.

Systems
The following systems are differentiated according to the method of water supply:

Systems with permanently installed **dry riser** vertical pipes → ❷, into which water is pumped by the fire service when required. The water is normally supplied from a hydrant connected to the public water supply network. Dry risers are **not** directly connected to the drinking water network. They must have a nominal diameter of at least 80 mm, be capable of being drained and be fitted with automatic vent valves at their ends.

Systems with permanently installed **wet riser** vertical pipes → ❸ are pipelines for extinguisher water which are constantly under water pressure and therefore immediately available. They are equipped at the outlet locations on each storey with wall hydrants → ❶, with hoses, installed in niches, built-in or in wall cupboards, already coupled and ready for use. Standing water is forbidden in these pipes on account of possible microbial contamination!

Wet risers are therefore normally supplied by a **combined system:** together with the drinking water system of a building through a common supply pipe. This should be sized so that the withdrawal of drinking water can never endanger fire fighting; in larger complexes this may make several water supply connections necessary. In combined systems, **constant renewal of the water** in the riser pipes is necessary in order to guarantee the quality of drinking water at all locations. There must be constant abstraction of water at the upper end of the riser or an (automatic) flushing system.

Systems with permanently installed **wet/dry riser** vertical pipes → ❹ are extinguisher water pipelines which are normally empty of water but when required can be supplied with water from the mains by remote activation of a valve. The water in this case is also available for fire fighting **with little delay**, while the disadvantages of the combined system (standing water in the riser pipe, danger of freezing) are avoided.

All extinguisher water pipework must be laid with downward gradient towards the emptying location. The minimum nominal diameters laid down in the relevant standards must be complied with. The fixed coupling of the supply connection, according to DIN 14461-2, must be 800 + 200 mm above ground level → ❶.

When riser pipes are installed in slots in walls, the minimum thicknesses according to fire safety regulations must be observed.

FIRE PROTECTION
Basics
Fire compartment walls
Building components
Fire-resistant glazing
Fire-resistant door sets
Fire fighting installations
Smoke and heat extraction systems
Sprinkler systems
Other extinguisher systems

BS 5306
DIN 4102
DIN EN 13501

MBO

Building services

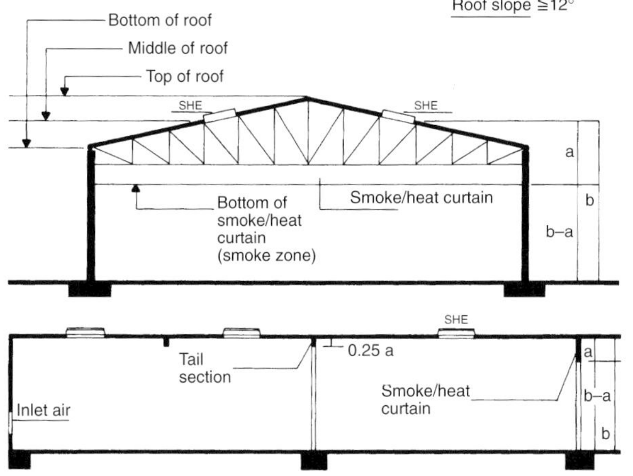

❶ Arrangement of smoke and heat extractors (SHEs) in the roofs of industrial units (example)

	Type of facility	Fire hazard
Low fire hazard	schools (certain areas)	**LH**
Medium fire hazard	cement works photo laboratory dye works paint shops (water-based substances)	**OH1** **OH2** **OH3** **OH4**
High fire hazard	printing works car factory tyre manufacture (for cars / HGVs) firework manufacture	**HHP1** **HHP2** **HHP3** **HHP4**

For the classification of stored products into categories, additional factors must be determined, specifically the packaging (combustible/non-combustible), type of packaging (e.g. wooden pallets, sacks, cardboard boxes, tins) and the proportion of plastics by volume and weight.

fire risk	max. storage height	evaluation group (EG)
LH		1
OH 1		2
OH 2		3
OH 3		
OH 4		
HHP 1	6.8	4
HHP 2	5.0	
HHP 3	3.2	3
HHP 4	2.3	4
HHS 1	6.8	3
HHS 2	5.0	4
HHS 3	3.2	5
HHS 4	2.3	3

Assignment of fire risk to evaluation group (example).

Calculated ceiling height b (m)	Calculated smoke layer a (m)	Percentage α			
		EG 1	EG 2	EG 6	EG 7
4.0	1.00	0.30	0.43	1.29	1.46
4.5	1.50	0.25	0.35	1.05	1.19
	1.25	0.31	0.43	1.30	1.47
5.0	2.00	0.21	0.30	0.91	1.03
	1.75	0.26	0.37	1.10	1.24
	1.50	0.31	0.44	1.33	1.50
	1.25	0.38	0.54	1.61	1.82
5.5	2.50	0.19	0.27	0.82	0.92
	2.25	0.23	0.32	0.97	1.10
	2.00	0.27	0.38	1.15	1.30

Evaluation table for the required smoke extraction area (example) – EG: evaluation group

The basis of the design of a naturally ventilated smoke extraction system is the calculation of the required (aerodynamically effective) opening area of the smoke extractor (smoke extraction area)

First, it is necessary to determine the evaluation group of the relevant use of the room independent of the assumed fire spread speed with the relevant fire hazard, the thickness of the calculated smoke layer (min. 2.50 m), dimensions and installation height (top edge as a distance from the calculated smoke layer) and area of the supply air openings (supply area generally 1.5 times smoke extraction area).

Considering the calculated room height and calculated smoke layer thickness, the required opening area for each smoke compartment can be taken from the table and the appropriate smoke and heat extractor can be selected.

The smoke and heat extractors should be arranged as regularly as possible within the roof compartment.

At least one smoke and heat extractor should be installed per 200m^2.

In addition, the spacing of the extractors between each other and to the edges of the roof areas (5 m $<$ a $<$ 20 m) and to fire compartment walls (5 m) should be observed in order to avoid the danger of fire spreading by flash-over.

In pitched roof surfaces, smoke extractors must be installed as high as possible and must be specially certified in steep roofs (e.g. northlight roofs).

The individual smoke extractors must have minimum dimensions (l = b = 1.0 m) and must not exceed certain maximum dimensions. This makes it practical to specify a larger number of openings, each with a smaller opening area.

❷ Design of a naturally ventilated smoke extraction system, DIN 18232 and VdS CEA 4001 (principle)

Smoke and heat extraction systems consist of the smoke and heat extractor and also activation and control components, opening actuators, power supply wiring, air supply ducts, smoke curtains if required and the appropriate accessories. Smoke and heat extraction systems are intended to **remove smoke and heat** in the event of a fire. They serve to keep escape, rescue and fire fighting routes free of smoke, make fire fighting easier by creating a **low-smoke layer**, delay or avoid flash-over and thus the start of a full fire, protect installations, reduce the damage caused by combustion gases and thermal decomposition products and reduce fire damage to building components.

There are various systems:

Naturally ventilated smoke extraction systems are based on the principle that hot air rises (e.g. via skylight domes). Their function depends on:
– an aerodynamically effective opening area
– the influence of wind
– the size of air supply openings
– timing of their opening
– installation situation (e.g. arrangement and building dimensions).

Mechanically operated smoke extraction systems have **motors** (e.g. with fans) to extract the fumes. **Heat extractors** are openings in wall or roof surfaces which open automatically in case of fire (e.g. through the melting of a thermal link) and allow the heat of the fire to escape.

Scope of application and sizing

The MBO require the general use of smoke extractors for certain areas:

In buildings with internal stairwells and in buildings with more than five storeys above ground, a smoke extraction device (size at least 1 m^2) must be installed at the **top of the stairwell**, which must be capable of being opened from the ground floor and from the top landing of the stairs. Smoke extraction equipment must also be installed in **lift shafts** (size 2.5% of the floor area of the lift shaft but at least 0.10 m^2).

For special buildings (places of assembly, industrial plants, etc.) the applicable regulations can also demand additional installations → ❶ – ❷. Smoke extraction systems must be installed, for example, in:

– (single-storey) sales areas, over-sized production and storage rooms
– buildings with excessively long rescue and escape routes, if these cannot be kept smoke-free for a sufficiently long time by other means
– buildings where special protection of assets is required in a particular case by relevant regulations
– buildings containing materials or equipment which are particularly valuable or susceptible to damage by smoke or facilities where there is a particular reason for increased protection of assets.

Smoke extraction systems are normally designed by the determination of a desired low-smoke layer and the calculation of the aerodynamically effective opening area required to ensure it → ❷ (as percentage ratio of the floor area of where smoke is to be removed from to the effective area of the smoke extraction opening).

The required values differ according to the application and are laid down in the relevant regulations.

BS EN 1210
DIN 18232

MBO
VdS CEA Guidelines 4001

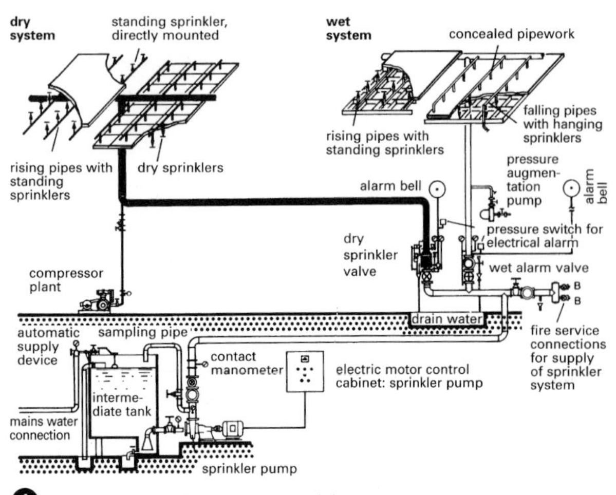

❶ Layout of a sprinkler system: wet and dry systems

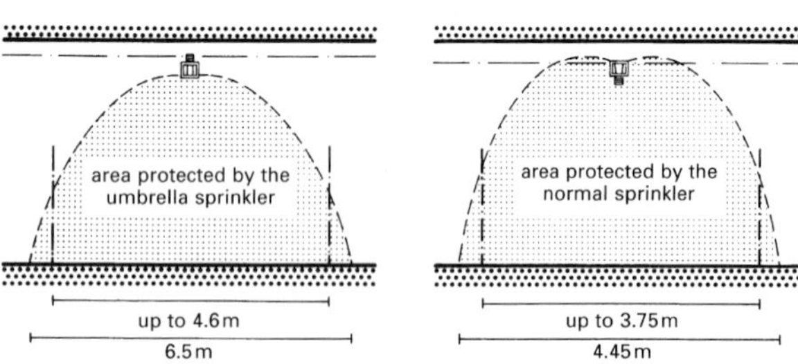

❷ Spray characteristics of umbrella and normal sprinklers (example)

Design of sprinkler systems

The design of a sprinkler system is based on the **fire hazard** in the area to be protected. This is defined in the **VdS CEA Guidelines** → p. 511 and areas to be protected by sprinklers are divided into fire hazard classes (**LH, OH, HHP, HHS**).

Further factors significant for the design of sprinkler systems are: the **effective area**, which according to calculations can be covered by the quantity of water; the maximum **protected area per sprinkler,** depending on sprinkler type and fire hazard; the **water quantity,** i.e. how much is to be sprinkled per minute onto the effective area; and the **operating time**, how long the water quantity must be available

Fire hazard class	(Minimum) water quantity (mm/min)	Effective area (m²)	
		wet / pre-action system	dry / wet dry system
LH	2.25	84	prohibited layout according to OH1
OH1	5.0	72	90
OH2	5.0	144	180
OH3	5.0	216	270
OH4	5.0	360	prohibited layout according to HHP1
HHP1	7.5	260	325
HHP2	10.0	260	325
HHP3	12.5	260	325
HHP4	**special consideration required**		

Water quantity and effective area for LH, OH and HHP fire hazard classes, VdS CEA Guidelines 4001

Sprinkler systems are technical, **automatically actuated fire fighting systems.** They consist of a network of permanently installed pipework under water pressure, to which **closed jets** called sprinklers are connected at a regular spacing. The pipework should be exposed or only concealed by a suspended ceiling to enable repair and maintenance and is normally connected through an intermediate tank to the drinking water mains.

If the air temperature increases as the result of a fire and exceeds the **operating temperature** set for the sprinkler (approx. 30°C above the highest normally expected air temperature), then the sprinkler opens and the pressurised water flows out of the pipe through the sprinkler and is sprayed over the protected area by the **deflector**. Each sprinkler system also has a **mechanical-acoustic alarm.**

Scope of application

The use of sprinkler systems is necessary in many cases when the fire safety requirements or the escape route requirements in the building regulations cannot be complied with.

For many special projects (e.g. stores, hotels, high-rise buildings, hospitals, shopping centres, etc.) the installation of sprinkler systems is generally required. Details for the design are given in the relevant regulations and guidelines.

Systems

Wet sprinkler systems → ❶ are the most common type. The pipework behind the **wet alarm valve** is constantly filled with water. When a sprinkler is activated, water sprays out **without delay**.

In **dry sprinkler systems** → ❶, the pipework behind the **alarm valve** is filled with compressed air, which stops water flowing into the sprinkler pipework. If a sprinkler is opened, this preventative air pressure is released and the water sprays out **after a delay**. Dry sprinklers are mostly installed in areas subject to frost.

Rapid reaction dry sprinkler systems are dry sprinkler systems, which operate with **little delay** because the alarm valve is opened by additional smoke or flame detectors **before** a sprinkler opens.

Tandem systems are dry sprinkler systems (e.g. in areas of a building at risk of frost) which are connected to the pipework of a wet system installed elsewhere in the building.

Pre-action sprinkler systems are dry systems designed so that water is sprayed only when a fire is detected and a sprinkler is opened (in order to avoid accidental activation, e.g. if a sprinkler is damaged).

Sprinklers

The most common types are the **glass bulb sprinkler,** with a glass bulb as temperature-dependent activation component, and the **fusible link sprinkler,** with a soldered link that opens when heated. Different types according to the type of spraying pattern are: **normal sprinkler** → ❷, with a ball-shaped water distribution directed to the floor and the ceiling. They can be used in the upright or pendant position. **Umbrella sprinklers** → ❷ feature a parabolic-shaped distribution of water towards the floor. They can be used in the upright or pendant position. Side wall **sprinklers** and further special versions (e.g. **long-throw sprinklers**) are also available.

Water spray extinguisher systems
Water spray extinguisher systems are water distribution systems **with permanently installed pipework**, on which **open nozzles** are mounted at regular intervals. When the system is on standby, the pipework is not filled with water. When the system is activated, this immediately releases the **peak flow** from the water supply into the pipework.

The water spray pattern is based on the shape and dimensions of the room to be protected, the type of building, type and quantity of goods to be protected, height and type of storage, and wind influence, and must spray at a rate of 5–60 l/m^2/min.

Systems arranged into groups normally protect an area of 100–400 m^2 per group. The total effective area for rooms $\geqq$200 m^2, which are divided into group effective areas, is normally the sum of the two effective areas with the largest water requirement. For the determination of the total effective area, a fire breaking out at the intersection of the group effective areas is assumed. This means that all group effective areas which are within a radius of 7 m of the location at most risk for the outbreak of fire can be supplied with water simultaneously.

Water spray extinguisher systems are used, for example, in aircraft hangars, waste bunkers and incineration plants, stages, transformers, tanks and systems with flammable liquids, cable ducts, chipping silos, chipboard works, power stations, hydraulic rooms, and firework and munitions factories.

Oxygen-reducing extinguisher systems
These fire fighting systems work by **reducing the content of oxygen in the air** to a level at which the combustion process no longer continues.

CO_2 is commonly used as a gaseous fire-fighting agent. CO_2 systems are intended to extinguish fires as they are developing and maintain an effectively high CO_2 concentration for so long that there is no danger of reignition. CO_2 floods the relevant area rapidly and uniformly, to provide protection in whole rooms. A CO_2 system essentially consists of **CO_2 bottles** containing a supply of gas, the necessary valves and **permanently installed pipework** with open nozzles in an appropriate arrangement in the area to be protected and **equipment for fire detection, control, alarm and activation**. For systems intended to protect rooms, one nozzle may supply at most 30 m^2 of floor area. If the room is more than 5 m high, the nozzles are installed not only in the ceiling but also at approx. ⅓ of room height.

CO_2 is a suitable agent against fires affecting the following substances and equipment: combustible liquids and other substances which behave like combustible liquids in a fire; combustible gases, in which case it must be ensured that no combustible gas-air mixture can form after the fire has been extinguished; electrical and electronic equipment, and combustible solid materials like wood, paper and textiles, although fires involving these materials require a higher CO_2 concentration and a longer action time. CO_2 is not suitable for some types of fire, for example: deeply seated fires of wood, paper and textiles, etc.; materials and chemicals containing oxygen; materials and chemicals which react with CO_2, e.g. alkali metals and metal hybrids.

Particular attention must be paid to safety in the design of CO_2 systems, because concentrations of over 5% are lethal and strongly corrosive. Systems should therefore be installed only by officially accredited firms. (VdS Guidelines 2093)

Powder extinguisher systems
Fire extinguisher powders are **homogenous mixtures of chemicals** which are suitable for fighting fires. The main ingredients are sodium/potassium bicarbonate, potassium sulphate, potassium/sodium chloride and ammonium phosphate/sulphate.

Because the extinguisher powder can be used under normal conditions at temperatures from –20 to +60°C, it is employed in buildings, enclosed rooms and also in open-air areas of industrial plants.

Powder is suitable for extinguishing fires involving the following substances and equipment: combustible solid materials like wood, paper and textiles, in which case the appropriate powder must be used; combustible liquids and other substances which behave like combustible liquids in a fire; combustible gases; combustible metals like aluminium, magnesium and their alloys, for which only suitable special powder should be used.

Examples of areas of industry where powder systems are often installed are: chemical and process plants, oil cellars, sumps, filling stations, compressor stations, pumping stations, transfer stations for oil and gas. Powder is not suitable for extinguishing fires involving certain plant, equipment and areas, for example: machinery, plant and equipment susceptible to dust; low-voltage electrical equipment (telephone, IT, measurement and regulation systems, distribution cabinets with trips and relays etc.); areas or installations where there is a danger of chemical reaction with the powder. (VdS Guidelines 3038)

Foam extinguisher
Foam for fire extinguishing is made by **foaming a mixture of water and foaming agent with air**. Foaming agents consist of water-soluble protein detergents and may also contain fluorinated agents. Multi-purpose foaming agents are suitable for the production of heavy, medium and light foam. Protein and fluoro-protein foaming agents are suitable for the production of heavy foam.

Foam extinguisher systems are used to extinguish fires in buildings, rooms and the open air. They can also be used for the precautionary coverage of areas. Particular measures are necessary in the case of liquids which destroy foam, e.g. alcohol, ester, ketone etc. A foam extinguisher system should be designed so that in the case of fire sufficient foam can reach the area to be protected or the area is effectively covered.

The essential parameters of a foam extinguisher system are: water quantity, foaming agent consumption, foam ratio (ratio of foam to water-foaming agent mixture) and minimum operating time. When systems with medium and heavy foam are used, the foam must be able to cover the entire area to be foamed, taking into account the flowing and throwing range, any obstacles, and the distance and type of object to be protected. When systems with light foam are used, the foam must be able to effectively fill the room or building.

If a number of separate objects are to be protected by the same foam extinguisher system, the water supply requirement is designed for the largest single object. The water supply must be designed for operation for at least 120 min for heavy foam and 60 min for medium foam. (VdS Guidelines 2108)

BS 5306
DIN 1988
DIN 14494

VdS Guidelines

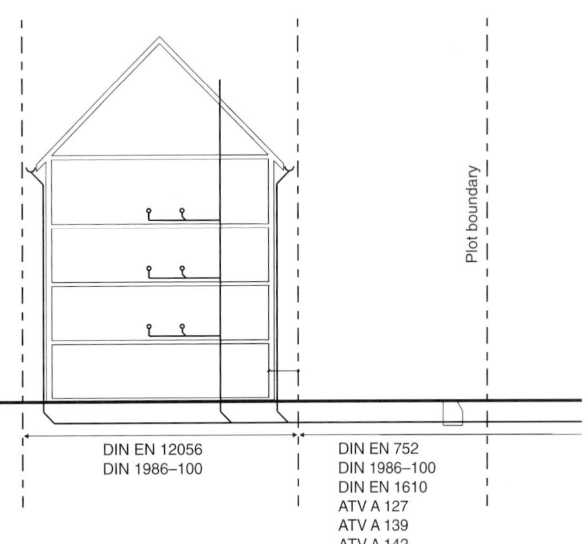

❶ Areas where standards and regulations apply (Wellpott, Bohne → refs)

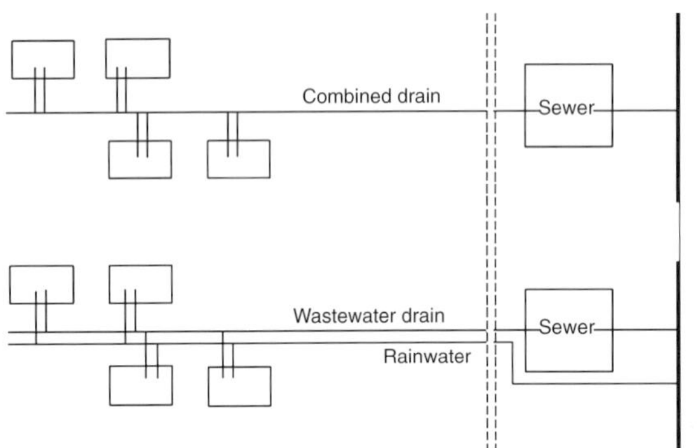

❷ Combined and separate systems (Wellpott → refs)

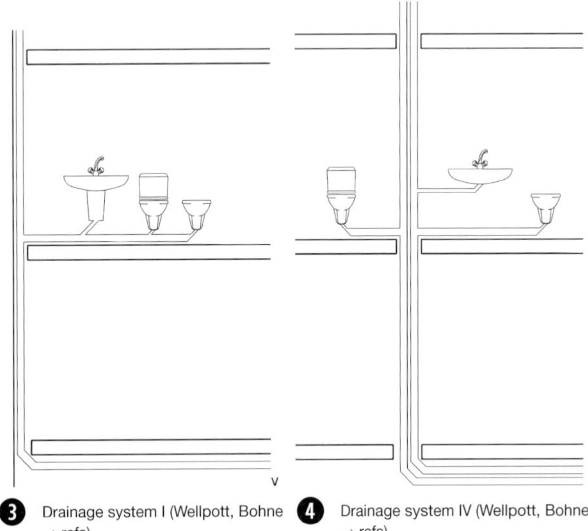

❸ Drainage system I (Wellpott, Bohne → refs)

❹ Drainage system IV (Wellpott, Bohne → refs)

System I	single downpipe, partially filled branch pipe, degree of filling 0.5
System II	single downpipe, system branch pipe, partially filled, degree of filling 0.7
System III	single downpipe with full branch pipe, degree of filling 1.0
System IV	separation into two pipe systems (greywater, wastewater)

❺ Drainage systems: for Germany, systems I and IV are permissible

Drainage systems for buildings and sites

Drainage systems for buildings are constructed to work under gravity wherever possible. The European standard DIN EN 12056 applies to all drainage systems operating under gravity inside residential, business, institutional or industrial buildings. Additional requirements for Germany are given in DIN 1986-100. Outside the building, DIN EN 752 and further regulations apply → ❶.

Calculation

Calculations are based on the assumed flow in the pipework, which depends on the type of use and of drainage. A basic distinction is made between wastewater and rainwater, and it needs to be decided whether collected wastewater and rainwater are drained into a combined system or have to remain separated according to local by-laws → ❷.

Description of drainage pipes

A **downpipe** is the vertical pipe in a building carrying wastewater or rainwater down to a horizontal pipe and is ventilated above the roof.

A **ground pipe** is the inaccessible pipe laid underground or under a floor slab, carrying groundwater from downpipes, branch waste pipes and floor drains.

A **vent pipe** is the downpipe's extension above the roof to provide pressure balance above unpressurised drainage by means of ventilation.

Collector pipes have the same function as ground pipes, but they are suspended below the cellar ceiling or on cellar walls.

Branch waste pipes connect the odour trap in the sanitary appliance to the further pipework. The **sewer connection** is the pipe connecting the last shaft on the plot to the public sewer.

Design of wastewater drainage

The expected flow of wastewater can be calculated as follows:

$\mathbf{Q_{ww}} = \mathbf{K} \times \sqrt{\mathbf{\Sigma(DU)}}$ where:

Q_{ww} wastewater discharge l/s
K discharge factor
DU Design Units l/s

Typical discharge factors are:

Type of building	Discharge factor K
irregular use, e.g. in houses, guest houses, offices	0.5
regular use, e.g. in hospitals, schools, restaurants, hotels	0.7
frequent use, e.g. in public toilets and/or showers	1.0
special use, e.g. laboratories	1.2

The total wastewater discharge is:
$\mathbf{Q_{tot}} = \mathbf{Q_{ww}} + \mathbf{Q_c} + \mathbf{Q_p}$ where:
Q_{tot} total wastewater discharge l/s
Q_{ww} wastewater discharge l/s
Q_c permanent discharge l/s
Q_p pumped flow l/s

The larger value (Q_{ww} or Q_{tot}) or the value of the wastewater discharge of the sanitary appliance with the largest connection value is decisive for design purposes. DIN EN 12056-2 defines four of the various drainage systems in Europe. These differ according to the degree of filling, the branch waste pipes and the separation or not of the pipework → ❺. For Germany, systems I and IV are permissible → .

Sanitary appliance	Design units (DU)	Single branch pipe
washbasin, bidet	0.5	DN 40
shower without plug	0.6	DN 50
shower with plug	0.8	DN 50
single urinal with flush cistern	0.8	DN 50
single urinal with pressure flush	0.5	DN 50
standing urinal	0.2	DN 50
urinal without water flushing	0.1	DN 50
bath tub	0.8	DN 50
kitchen sink and dishwasher*	0.8	DN 50
dishwasher	0.8	DN 50
washing machine up to 6 kg	0.8	DN 50
washing machine up to 12 kg	1.5	DN 56/60
WC with 4.0/4.5 l cistern	1.8	DN 80/DN 90
WC with 6.0 l cistern/pressure flush	2.0	DN 80-DN 100
WC with 7.5 l cistern/pressure flush	2.0	see remark in DIN
WC with 9.0 l cistern/pressure flush	2.5	DN 100
floor gully DN 50	0.8	DN 50
floor gully DN 70	1.5	DN 70
floor gully DN 100	2.0	DN 100
*with common trap		

❶ Design units (DU) to be assumed for various sanitary appliances (Table 4, DIN 1986-100)

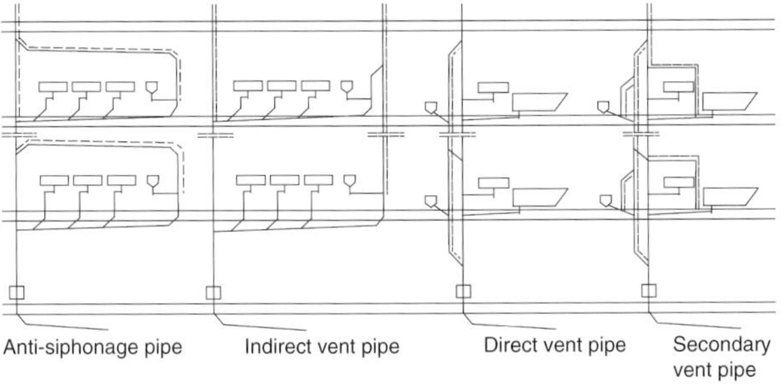

❷ Ventilation systems for wastewater drainage (Wellpott → refs)

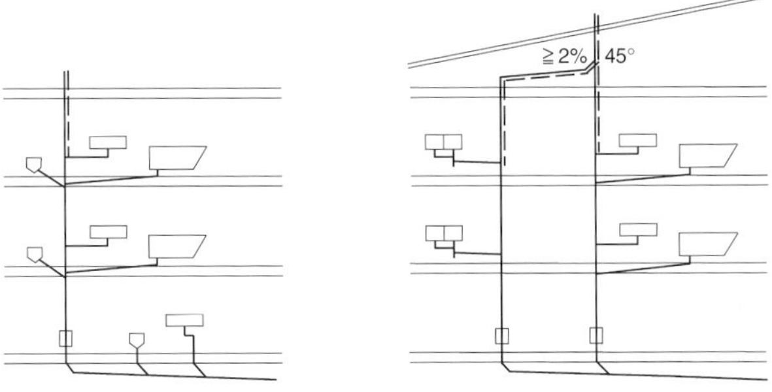

❸ A soil and vent stack can be joined together with one common vent pipe at the uppermost point of the pipework (Wellpott → refs)

Pipe sizing

The determined dimensions, given as nominal diameters (DN) and the associated minimum internal diameters, are given in → ❹.

Nominal diameter (DN)	Min. internal diameter $d_{i\,min}$ (mm)
30	26
40	34
50	44
56	49
60	56
70	68
80	75
90	79
100	96
125	113
150	146
200	184
225	207
250	230
300	290

❹ Nominal diameters (DN) with the relevant minimum internal diameters $d_{i\,min}$ (corresponds to Table 1, DIN EN 12056-2)

Section of pipework	Minimum fall	Standard and section
unvented branch pipe	1.0%	DIN EN 12056-2, Table 5
vented branch pipe	0.5%	DIN 1986-100, section 8.3.2.2 DIN EN 12056-2, Table 8
ground and collector pipes		
a) for wastewater	0.5%	DIN 1986-100, section 8.3.4.
b) for rainwater (degree of filling 0.7)	0.5%	DIN 1986-100, section 9.3.5.2
ground and collector pipes DN 90 (lavatory pan with flush volume 4.5–6 l)	1.5%	DIN 1986-100, Table A.2
ground pipes for rainwater outside the building (degree of filling 0.7)		DIN 1986-100, section 9.3.5.2
up to DN 200	0.5%*	
from DN 250	1 : DN*	
* flow velocity max. 2.5 m/s. Behind a shaft with open flow-through, design can be based on full filling without over-pressure.		

❺ Minimum falls for pipes, unpressurised drainage

Venting of pipework → ❷ + ❸

Drainage systems are still differentiated according to the type of venting. The main types are soil and vent stack (single-pipe system) and soil stack with separate vent pipe. Apart from the soil and vent stack, different systems use anti-siphonage pipes; indirect vent pipe; direct vent pipe; secondary venting; and soil and vent stack with an additional venting valve. The cross-section of a common vent pipe for more than one stack must be at least as big as half the sum of the single cross-sections of the single stack. The nominal size of a common vent pipe must be at least one nominal size larger than the largest size of the relevant stack.

DOMESTIC INSTALLATION

Drainage
Ventilation
Heating
Small sewage treatment plants

BS EN 476
BS 8515
DIN 1986
DIN EN 12056

Application limits	System I	System IV
max. pipe length (l)	4.0 m	10.0 m
max. no. 90° bends	3*	3*
max. drop height (H) (with 45° or more slope)	1.0 m	1.0 m
min. fall	1%	1.5%

* connecting bends not included

❶ Application limits for unvented single branch pipes (corresponds to DIN EN 12056-2, Table 5)

Application limits	System I	System IV
max. pipe length (l)	10.0 m	no limit
max. no. 90° bends	no limit	no limit
max. drop height (H) (with 45° or more slope)	3.0 m	3.0 m
min. fall	0.5%	0.5%

* connecting bends not included

❷ Application limits for vented single and combined branch pipes (corresponds to DIN EN 12056-2, Table 8)

DN	max. pipe length (m)	max. 90° bends	max. height difference (m)	min. fall
50	4.0	3	1.0	1%
56	4.0	3	1.0	1%
70	4.0	3	1.0	1%
80	10.0	3	1.0	1%
90	10.0	3	1.0	1%
100	10.0	3	1.0	1%

❸ Application limits for unvented combined branch pipes (corresponds to DIN 1986-100, section 8.3.2.2)

Soil and vent stack	Q_{max} (l/s)	
DN	Branches	Branches with internal radius
60	0.5	0.7
70	1.5	2.0
80*	2.0	2.6
90	2.7	3.5
100**	4.0	5.2
125	5.8	7.6
150	9.5	12.4
200	16.0	21.0

* min. DN for connection of WCs to system II
** min. DN for connection of WCs to systems I, III, IV

❹ Permissible wastewater discharge Q_{max} and nominal diameter DN for soil and vent stacks (corresponds to DIN EN 12056-2, Table 11)

Application limits for the various vented systems (single and combined branch pipes) are given in → ❶ – ❸.

Design of branch pipes
Single and combined branch pipes are designed in accordance with → ❺ – ❻ (from Geberit). The design of downpipes for wastewater differs according to venting system → ❹ + ❼.

K = 0.5	K = 0.7	K = 1.0	DN	d_i (mm)
Σ DU	Σ DU	Σ DU		
1.0	1.0	0.8	50	44
2.0	2.0	1.0	56/60	49/56
9.0	4.6	2.2	70*	68
13.0**	8.0**	4.0	80	75
13.0**	10.0**	5.0	90	79
16.0	12.0	6.4	100	96

* no WCs
** maximum 2 WCs

❺ Design of unvented combined branch pipes (corresponds to DIN 1986-100, Table 5)

K = 0.5	K = 0.7	K = 1.0	DN	d_i (mm)
Σ DU	Σ DU	Σ DU		
3.0	2.0	1.0	50	44
5.0	4.6	2.2	56/60	49/56
13.0	10.0	5.0	70*	68
16.0	13.0	9.0	80	75
20.0	16.0	11.0	90	79
25.0	20.0	14.0	100	96

* no WCs

❻ Design of vented combined branch pipes (simplified design instead of calculation according to rules for combined pipes, by Prandtl-Colebrook)

Soil and vent stack	Separate vent pipe	Q_{max} (l/s)	
DN	DN	branches	branches with internal radius
60	50	0.7	0.9
70	50	2.0	2.6
80*	50	2.6	3.4
90	50	3.5	4.6
100**	50	5.6	7.3
125	70	12.4***	10.0
150	80	14.1	18.3
200	100	21.0	27.3

* min. DN for connection of WCs to system II
** min. DN for connection of WCs to systems I, III, IV
*** this value may be an error in DIN EN 12045-2. Recommendation: correct to 8.4

❼ Permissible wastewater discharge Q_{max} and nominal diameter DN for soil stack with separate vent pipe (corresponds to DIN EN 12056-2, Table 12)

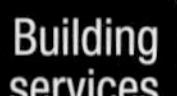

Ground and collector drainage pipes

Inside buildings, collector pipes with a degree of filling of h/D Index i = 0.5 should be installed assuming a minimum fall of 0.5%, and with connection of a drain lift pump, which should be installed with a degree of filling of h/d Index i = 0.7.

Fall	DN 80		DN 90		DN 100		DN 125		DN 150		DN 200		DN 225		DN 250		DN 300	
i	Q_{max}	*v*	Q_{max}	*v*	Q_{max}	*v*	Q_{max}	*v*	Q_{max}	*v*	Q_{max}	*v*	Q_{max}	*v*	Q_{max}	*v*	Q_{max}	*v*
cm/m	l/s	m/s	l/s	m/s	l/s	m/s	l/s	m/s	l/s	m/s	l/s	m/s	l/s	m/s	l/s	m/s	l/s	m/s
0.50	-	-	-	-	1.8	0.5	2.8	0.5	5.4	0.6	10.0	0.8	15.9	0.8	18.9	0.9	34.1	1.0
1.0	1.3	0.6	1.5	0.6	2.5	0.7	4.1	0.8	7.7	0.9	14.2	1.1	22.5	1.2	26.9	1.2	48.3	1.4
1.50	1.5	0.7	1.8	0.7	3.1	0.8	5.0	1.0	9.4	1.1	17.4	1.3	27.6	1.5	32.9	1.5	59.2	1.8
2.00	1.8	0.8	2.1	0.8	3.5	1.0	5.7	1.1	10.9	1.3	20.1	1.5	31.9	1.7	38.1	1.8	68.4	2.0
2.50	2.0	0.9	2.4	1.0	4.0	1.1	6.4	1.2	12.2	1.5	22.5	1.7	35.7	1.9	42.6	2.0	76.6	2.3
3.00	2.2	1.0	2.6	1.1	4.4	1.2	7.1	1.4	13.3	1.6	24.7	1.9	39.2	2.1	46.7	2.2	83.9	2.5
3.50	2.4	1.1	2.9	1.1	4.7	1.3	7.6	1.5	14.4	1.7	26.6	2.0	42.3	2.2	50.4	2.3	90.7	2.7
4.00	2.6	1.2	3.1	1.2	5.0	1.4	8.2	1.6	15.4	1.8	28.5	2.1	45.2	2.4	53.9	2.5	96.9	2.9
4.50	2.8	1.2	3.2	1.3	5.3	1.5	8.7	1.7	16.3	2.0	30.2	2.3	48.0	2.5	57.2	2.7	102.8	3.1
5.00	1.2	2.9	3.4	1.4	5.6	1.6	9.1	1.8	17.2	2.1	31.9	2.4	50.6	2.7	60.3	2.8	108.4	3.2

❶ Permissible wastewater discharge, degree of filling 50% (h/di = 0.5) (corresponds to DIN EN 12056, Table B.1)

Fall	DN 80		DN 90		DN 100		DN 125		DN 150		DN 200		DN 225		DN 250		DN 300	
i	Q_{max}	n	Q_{max}	n	Q_{max}	n	Q_{max}	n	Q_{max}	n	Q_{max}	n	Q_{max}	n	Q_{max}	n	Q_{max}	n
cm/m	l/s	m/s	l/s	m/s	l/s	m/s	l/s	m/s	l/s	m/s	l/s	m/s	l/s	m/s	l/s	m/s	l/s	m/s
0.50	1.5	0.5	-	-	2.9	0.5	4.8	0.6	9.0	0.7	16.7	0.8	26.5	0.9	31.6	1.0	56.8	1.1
1.0	2.2	0.7	2.5	0.6	4.2	0.8	6.8	0.9	12.8	1.0	23.7	1.2	37.6	1.3	44.9	1.4	80.6	1.6
1.50	2.6	0.8	3.0	0.8	5.1	1.0	8.3	1.1	15.7	1.3	29.1	1.5	46.2	1.6	55.0	1.7	98.8	2.0
2.00	3.1	0.9	3.5	0.9	5.9	1.1	9.6	1.2	18.2	1.5	33.6	1.7	53.3	1.9	63.3	2.0	114.2	2.3
2.50	3.4	1.0	4.0	1.1	6.7	1.2	10.8	1.4	20.33	1.6	37.6	1.9	59.7	2.1	71.7	2.2	127.7	2.6
3.00	3.8	1.1	4.3	1.2	7.3	1.3	11.8	1.5	22.3	1.8	41.2	2.1	65.4	2.3	77.9	2.4	140.0	2.8
3.50	4.1	1.2	4.7	1.3	7.9	1.5	12.8	1.6	24.1	1.9	44.5	2.2	70.6	2.5	84.2	2.6	151.2	3.0
4.00	4.4	1.3	5.0	1.3	8.4	1.6	13.7	1.8	25.8	2.1	47.6	2.4	75.5	2.7	90.0	2.8	161.7	3.2
4.50	4.6	1.4	5.3	1.4	8.9	1.7	14.5	1.9	27.3	2.2	50.5	2.5	80.1	2.8	95.5	3.0	171.5	3.4
5.00	4.9	1.5	5.6	1.5	9.4	1.7	15.3	2.0	28.8	2.3	53.3	2.7	84.5	3.0	100.7	3.1	180.8	3.6

❷ Permissible wastewater discharge, degree of filling 70% (h/di = 0.7) (corresponds to DIN EN 12056, Table B.2)

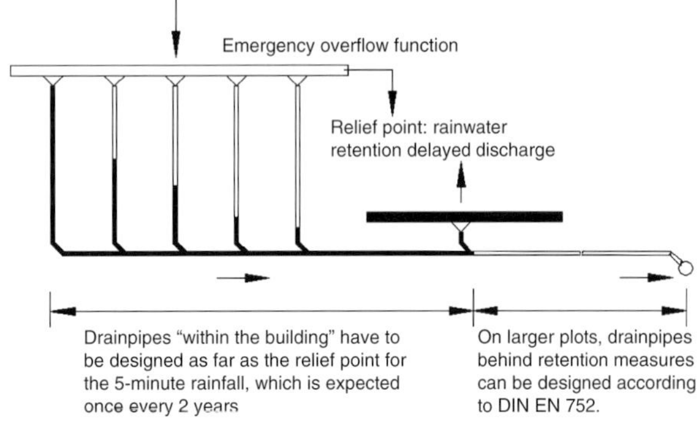
Emergency overflow function
Relief point: rainwater retention delayed discharge
Drainpipes "within the building" have to be designed as far as the relief point for the 5-minute rainfall, which is expected once every 2 years
On larger plots, drainpipes behind retention measures can be designed according to DIN EN 752.

❶ Limits of the scopes of application of DIN EN 12056, DIN 1986-100 and DIN EN 752 (Wellpott, Bohne → refs)

No.	Type of surface	Discharge factor C
1	**impermeable surfaces, e.g.**	
	– roof surfaces	1.0
	– concrete surfaces	1.0
	– ramps	1.0
	– paved areas with pointed joints	1.0
	– blacktop (asphalt)	1.0
	– paving with poured joints	1.0
	– gravel roofs	0.5
	– planted roofs*	
	– for intensive planting	0.3
	– for extensive planting from 10 cm construction depth	0.3
	– for extensive planting under 10 cm construction depth	0.5
2	**partially permeable surfaces or with low run-off, e.g.**	
	– concrete paving laid in sand or clinker, slab paving	0.7
	– paved surfaces with proportion jointed ≧15%, e.g. 10 cm × 10 cm and less	0.6
	– waterbound paving	0.5
	– partially paved children's playgrounds	0.3
	– plastic paving, artificial turf	0.6
	– clay sports surfacing	0.4
	– lawns	0.3
3	**permeable surfaces or with insignificant run-off, e.g.**	0.0
	– parks and areas of vegetation, ballast and clinker surfacing, rolled gravel, also with partial paving, e.g.	0.0
	– garden paths with waterbound surfacing	0.0
	– access roads and parking with grass pavers	0.0

* according to the Guidelines for Design, Construction and Maintenance of Roof Planting – Guidelines for Roof Planting

❷ Discharge factor C for the determination of rainwater run-off (corresponds to DIN 1986-100, Table 6)

Rainwater drainage

Rainwater falling on a roof is drained away via a pipe system. The most important objective is that the rainwater from built-up areas should soak away into suitable percolation systems, on the same plot if possible. If this is not feasible, the rainwater is drained, either separated from the soil drain, or combined. Where the water is drained into a sewer connection, to comply with a discharge limit, rainwater retention may have to be provided in the form of an oversized pipe network or a structure. Each roof surface must have at least one downpipe and one emergency overflow with free discharge. Rainwater must not be fed into soil stacks, even from small roof surfaces. Pipework is designed for average rainfall. Because heavy rainfall has to be expected, however, overloading of the pipework should be countered by suitable measures (emergency overflows, pressure relief for unpressurised pipes) to avoid resulting damage.

Rainwater discharge is calculated according to DIN EN 12056-3 or DIN 1986-100 with the formula:

$$\mathbf{Q} = \mathbf{r_{D(T)}} \cdot \mathbf{C} \cdot \mathbf{A} \cdot \frac{\mathbf{1}}{\mathbf{10{,}000}}$$ where:

$r_{D(T)}$ calculation of rainfall in l/s/ha, determined on the statistical basis of 5 minutes' rainfall, which must be expected once every 2 years
C discharge factor
A precipitation area projected on the plot (m^2)

The duration of rain for design purposes is D = 5 min. Downpipes, collector and ground pipes are to be designed for the local 5 minute rainfall, which is anticipated once in 2 years ($r_{5(2)}$) (applies without planned retention measures).

The limits of the application examples according to DIN EN 12056, DIN 1986-100 and DIN EN 725-4 are as follows: overloading or overflowing is to be limited by the provision of emergency overflows, and pressure relief for unpressurised pipes. Discharge factor C for determination of rainwater discharge is shown in → ❷ (DIN 1986-100, Table 6). The design is to be based on the chosen rain duration of D = 5 minutes. The repeat interval in years (T) is determined by the particular project and must be determined according to the type and use of the building.

Unpressurised drainage

Downpipes must have at least the nominal diameter of the connected roof outlet. The degree of filling can be up to F = 0.33. Collector and ground pipes are to be designed for a degree of filling of 0.7 and a minimum fall of 0.5 cm/m within the building. Outside the building, a maximum velocity of 2.5 m/s should be assumed. The maximum degree of filling here is 0.7.

Downstream of a shaft with open flow-through, complete filling without over-pressure can be assumed. The minimum fall is up to DN 200 0.5 cm/m, and from DN 250 1: DN.

Application area	Approved types of backflow prevention device according to DIN EN 13564-1[a)]
faeces-free water, precipitation water	types 2, 3 and 5
water containing faeces	type 3 with marking 'F'
rainwater utilisation facilities[b)]	types 0, 1, 2

[a)] until the introduction of DIN EN 13564-1, DIN 1997 and DIN 19578 apply
[b)] only permissible for overflows from underground tanks which are connected to a surface water sewer (see DIN 1989-1)

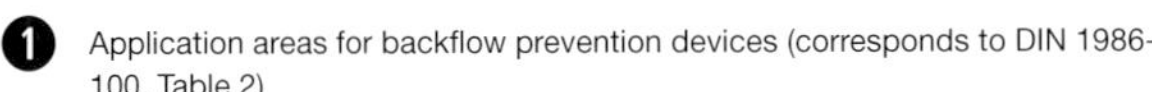

❶ Application areas for backflow prevention devices (corresponds to DIN 1986-100, Table 2)

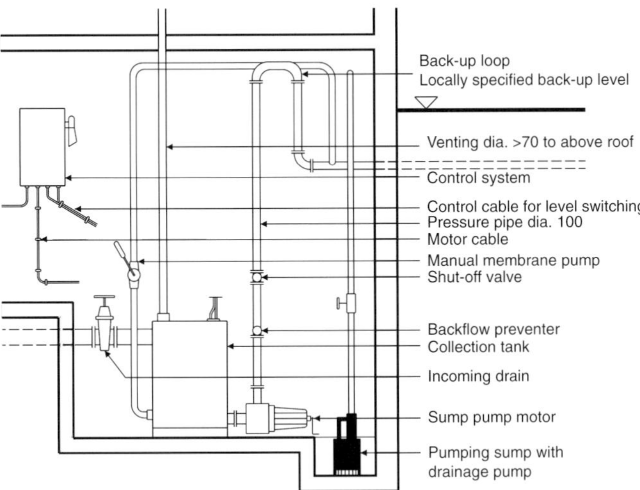

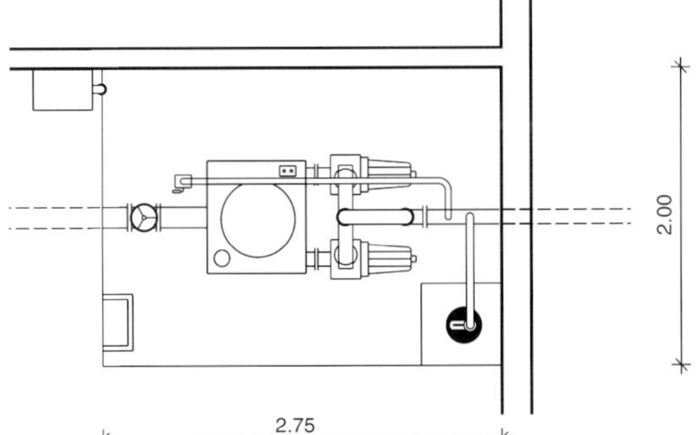

❷ Wastewater lifting pump as double system, DIN 12056-4 (Wellpott, Bohne → refs)

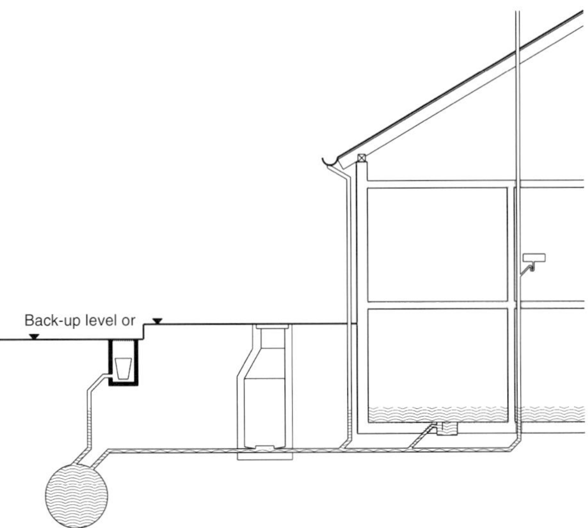

❸ Backing-up in the discharge pipe of a combined drainage system, resulting from overloading of the drains after heavy rainfall. Surface water mixed with wastewater pours out of the lowest gullies, unless they are protected (Wellpott, Bohne → refs)

Roof drainage with pressurised flow

For this system, hydraulic certification should be produced for each individual project. The backing-up at the outlet required for the function does not count as flooding of the roof surface, as long as the requirements of outlets according to DIN 19599 are not exceeded.

Roof surfaces with, for example, regular flooding are to be waterproofed up to the flooding level and appropriately structurally designed. At the most the difference in level between the roof outlet and the backing-up level should be assumed for the rainwater pressure drainage system. If a pressure drainage system is fed into an unpressurised system of pipework, conversion of the high kinetic energy should be ensured by the reduction of the flow velocity to <2.5 m/s.

Backing-up

Discharge locations below the sewer backing-up level are to be protected against backing-up in the sewer by automatic wastewater lifting pumps with backing-up loop or backflow prevention device (DIN EN 12056-4). Backflow prevention devices have a limited scope of application → ❶.

Wastewater lifting pumps, in which the flow of wastewater must not be interrupted, are to be installed as double lifting systems → ❷. These pumps should also be provided for precipitation water, which is to be drained below the sewer backing-up level. These should be designed so that the occurrence of a hundred-year event $r_{5(100)}$ cannot cause damage (to surfaces like house entrances, cellar entrances, garage access drives, internal courtyards).

A flooding certification, required by DIN EN 752-4, assuming rainfall of $r_{15(30)}$, is to be produced for larger areas below the sewer backing-up level, which do not endanger buildings or assets. The wastewater lifting pump should be designed for at least $r_{5(2)}$.

For roof surfaces which can be drained without the provision of an emergency overflow, the planned flooding level must be discussed with and checked by the structural engineer. Furthermore, an overloading certification is to be obtained for internally routed drainage systems as far as a pressure relief point. Flooding and overloading certifications are to be obtained for a 100-year rainstorm $r_{5(100)}$.

Special wastewater

Wastewater of commercial and industrial origin is generally to be treated so that it is permissible to feed it into a public foul sewer. This may require the installation of separation or treatment facilities such as grease separators, separators for volatile liquids, starch separators or emulsion splitting plant. For mineral oil or volatile liquids, separators are to be dimensioned according to DIN 1999. These devices normally consist of a silt trap, separator and chamber for taking samples. In particular, areas on which vehicles are washed, maintained or fuelled should be connected to the drains through a separator for volatile liquids.

BS 6229
BS 8490
BS EN 12056
DIN 752
DIN 1986
DIN 1999
DIN EN 12056
DIN 19599

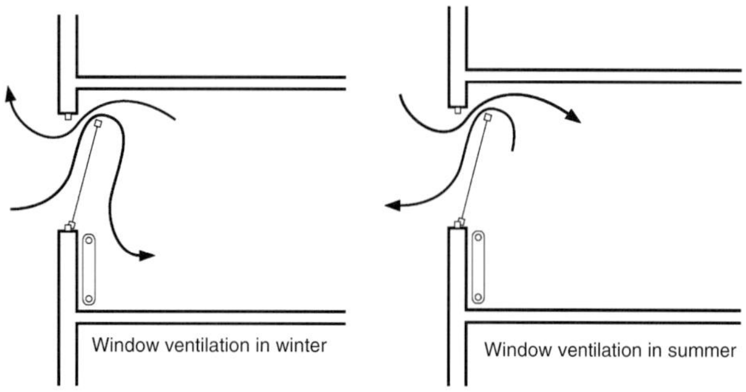

Window ventilation in winter

Window ventilation in summer

❶ Flow patterns for window ventilation: situation in winter and summer (Wellpott, Bohne → refs)

System I	ventilation from one side through an opening in an external wall
System II	cross-ventilation with openings in opposing external walls or in one external wall and the roof surface
System III	cross-ventilation with openings in one external wall and an opposing shaft. The shaft must have a cross-section of min. 80 cm^2 and 4 m height, of which 3 m is inside the building (may need to protect against excessive cooling).
System IV	cross-ventilation with roof ventilators (domes, deflectors, openings) and openings in one wall or in opposing external walls.

❷ Free ventilation systems, Workplace Guidelines 5

Room group A	workrooms with work areas for predominantly sedentary activities
Room group B	workrooms with work areas for predominantly standing activities (sales and comparable rooms)
Room group C	workrooms with work areas for predominantly sitting and standing activities, where there is heavy odour nuisance, or for heavily physical work

❸ Room groups

System	Clear room height (H)	Max. room depth	Air supply and exit openings (cm^2) per m^2 floor area
I	up to 4 m	2.5 × H	200
II	up to 4 m	5.0 × H	120
III	up to 4 m	5.0 × H	80
IV	over 4 m	5.0 × H	80

❹ Ventilation cross-sections for free ventilation in workrooms with work areas for predominantly sitting activities, Workplace Guidelines 5 (room group A)

Air temperature (°C)	Relative humidity (%)
20	80
22	70
24	62
26	55

❺ Recommended relative humidity according to air temperature

Natural ventilation

The air quality in rooms or buildings is one of the significant user pleasure criteria and an essential factor in personal comfort. If a building is operated without mechanical ventilation equipment, this is called natural ventilation. This is the exchange of air through window ventilation, additional shafts in the building or other openings. Natural ventilation is produced by wind pressure on and around the building, which depends on numerous other factors. The air exchange within a building is also influenced by thermal effects around and in the building. The air exchange within each room is significant for the evaluation of natural ventilation.

If a building is to be predominantly naturally ventilated, then its limitations have to be taken into account. These limitations are determined by:

- the location of the building in a town planning context
- the wind speeds occurring at the building's location
- noise nuisance at the building's location
- building structure, room depths, internal rooms, pressure resistances at the building
- thermal effect in the building and in the rooms

The flow conditions for window ventilation differ in summer and winter according to the temperature difference between inside and outside → ❶. For workrooms, Workplace Guidelines 5 (October 1979 edition) require natural (free) ventilation.

A differentiation is also made here between:

- window ventilation
- shaft ventilation
- supplementary roof ventilation
- ventilation through other air openings

Air quality is defined as adequate when sufficient healthy air for breathing is available in the workrooms and when the air quality essentially corresponds to that of outside air, unless the outdoor air does not have the required quality because of exceptional circumstances (CO_2 concentration, nitrous oxide etc.).

There are four systems of free ventilation: → ❷. The systems apply for a reference area of 6 m^2/worker.

Working rooms are categorised into A, B, C → ❸.

The **ventilation cross-sections** for free ventilation can be determined from → ❹ (excerpt from Workplace Guidelines 5).

It must be possible to reduce ventilation cross-sections through adjustment (shutters). The minimum outside air flows required in the Workplace Guideline correspond approximately to the recommended outside air flows for the maintenance of maximum CO_2 concentrations.

The recommendation:
for predominantly sedentary activities: 20–40 m^3 / h × no. people
for predominantly standing activities: 40–60 m^3/h × no. people
for heavy physical work: 65 m^3 / h × no. people

For the first group (predominantly sedentary activities), a more precise consideration in line with holistic concepts is recommended. The necessary volume flow can be determined through the CO_2 impairment of the outside air and the user frequency of the rooms.

❶ Centralised ventilation of a house with heat recovery. The outside air fed in to renew the inside air is filtered, then passed through a cross-flow heat exchanger, where it receives warmth from the extract air. The warmed air normally flows through a number of rooms before being extracted again. Air from kitchens and bathrooms should not be able to flow into other rooms (Wellpott, Bohne → refs)

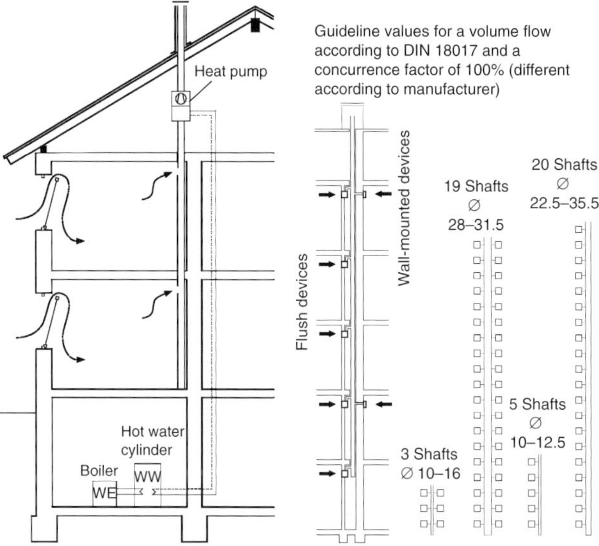

❷ Centralised air extract system with heat recovery by a heat pump and storage in a warm water buffer tank (WW). The remaining energy is supplied by a heating device (WE) (Wellpott, Bohne → refs)]

❸ Single ventilation systems with common extract duct replace large batteries of shafts (Wellpott, Bohne → refs)

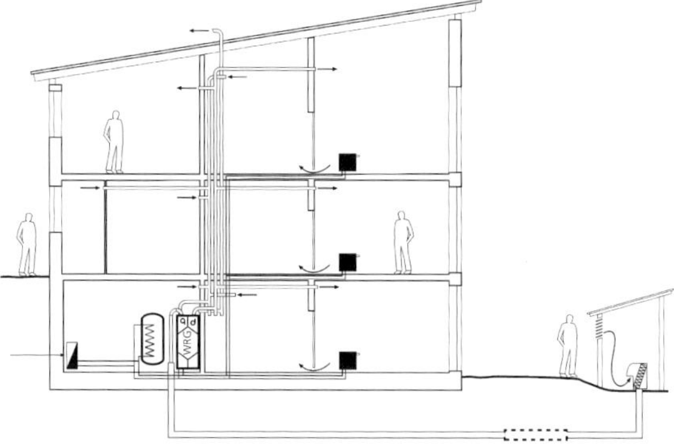

❹ Controlled residential ventilation with ground-source heat exchanger: detached house (Wellpott, Bohne → refs)

	Operation min. 12 h/day[1]	Any duration of operation[2]
cooking niche	40 m^3/h	60 m^3/h
kitchen, background ventilation	40 m^3/h	60 m^3/h
kitchen, intensive ventilation	200 m^3/h	200 m^3/h
bathroom with/without WC	40 m^3/h	60 m^3/h
separate WC	20 m^3/h	30 m^3/h

[1] background operation
[2] demand-controlled operation

❺ Scheduled flow volumes for windowless rooms, DIN 1945-5

Controlled ventilation of homes

For reasons of hygiene and building physics, it is necessary to remove air enriched with odours, water vapour and CO_2 from occupied rooms and replace it with unused oxygen-rich air. There is a difference between background ventilation (for building physics reasons) and demand-controlled ventilation (for hygienic reasons).

Background ventilation: An air exchange at least 0.5–1.0 times per hour can ensure that no damage occurs to a building through normal use. High internal air humidity caused by too little air exchange (airtight joints) can lead to mildew and mould formation. This phenomenon is particularly apparent when new windows with draught seals have been installed without improving the thermal insulation of the external walls of the building.

Demand-controlled ventilation: Bodily odours, cigarette smoke, kitchen and toilet odours pollute the air and make air exchanges necessary.

Air changes recommended for hygienic reasons: 0.5–1.0 times per hour in residential, occupied and bedrooms, 4–5 times per hour in internal sanitary rooms, 0.5–25 times per hour in kitchens (intermittent requirement).

Mechanical ventilation of homes

Mechanical ventilation without heat recovery should have the effect of renewing the inside air sufficiently often and also keeping the heat loss through air extraction within reasonable bounds. Mechanical ventilation with heat recovery → ❶ brings the extract air into thermal contact with the intake air. At least 80% of the waste heat (degree of temperature exchange) can be recovered from the extract air.

Central air extract system with heat recovery

In extract systems, outside air flows through openings and joints into the rooms. The required heat energy must be supplied by the heating system (normally static radiators or surface heating systems). The thermal energy transported out of the building with the extract air is lost without additional measures. The low temperature level (approx. 20–24°) prevents heat recovery in the heating system. One way of recovering the heat is to use the temperature level of the extract air as a heat source for a heat pump. The energy can then, for example, be saved in a domestic hot water cylinder → ❷.

Single ventilation systems with common extract duct (main duct) → ❸

These require only a single vertical extract duct (DIN 18017-3). This can be, according to the manufacturer, up to 20 storeys high with one or two fans connected on each storey (which can also be from two adjacent living areas). The main extract duct is of 10–35 cm diameter and can be located in an installation shaft with sufficient fire resistance. The box-form radial fans are installed on the plaster or flush and have a capacity of 50 or 90 m^3/h. Airtight backflow flaps prevent heat loss or odour nuisance while the fan is not running and provide fire protection (up to fire resistance class L 90) in case of fire.

DIN 18017

PD CEN/TR 14788

Controlled domestic ventilation with ground-source heat exchanger → ❹

The ground-source heat exchanger provides air cooling in summer. Warm outside air can be cooled from +30°C to +20°C by passing it through one. The heat exchanger is used in the winter to pre-warm the outside air (from −10°C to +2°C). Further heating of the air can heat a well-insulated building on mild winter days.

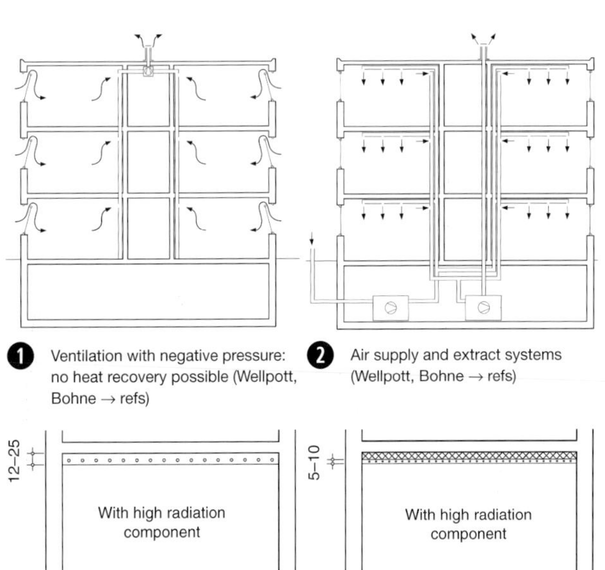

❶ Ventilation with negative pressure: no heat recovery possible (Wellpott, Bohne → refs)

❷ Air supply and extract systems (Wellpott, Bohne → refs)

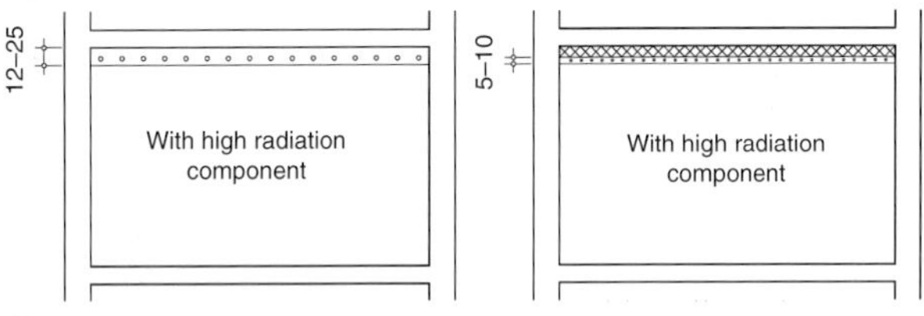

❸ Chilled ceiling system with thin constructional thickness, e.g. metal panel ceiling and capillary pipe ceiling (Wellpott → refs)

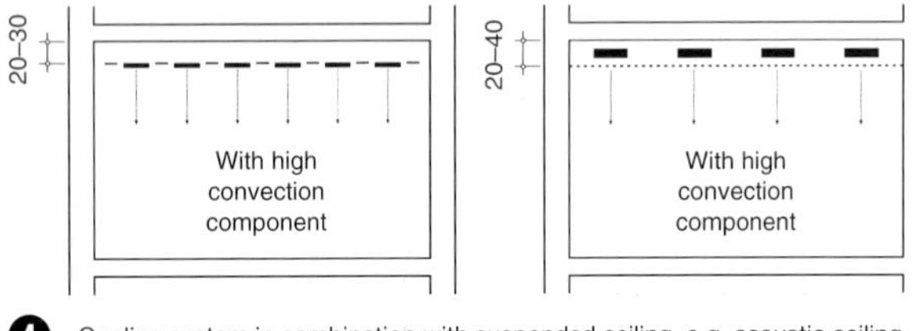

❹ Cooling system in combination with suspended ceiling, e.g. acoustic ceiling. Installation into an existing ceiling is often possible (Wellpott → refs)

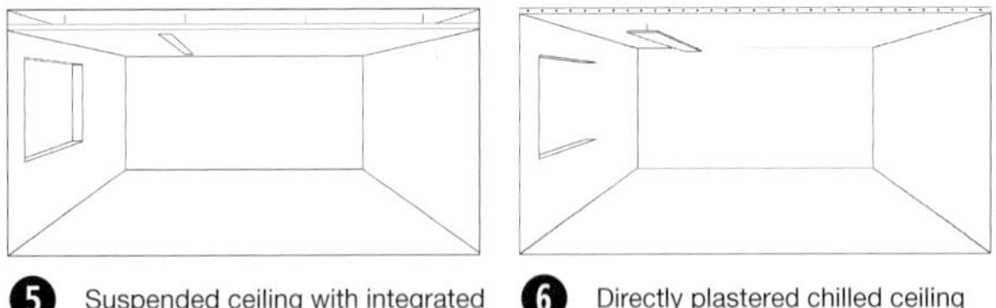

❺ Suspended ceiling with integrated ceiling light (Wellpott, Bohne → refs)

❻ Directly plastered chilled ceiling with hanging light (Wellpott, Bohne → refs)

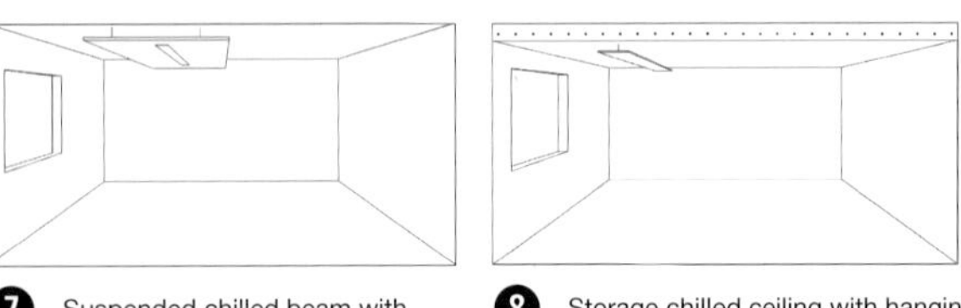

❼ Suspended chilled beam with integrated ceiling light (Wellpott, Bohne → refs)

❽ Storage chilled ceiling with hanging light (Wellpott, Bohne → refs)

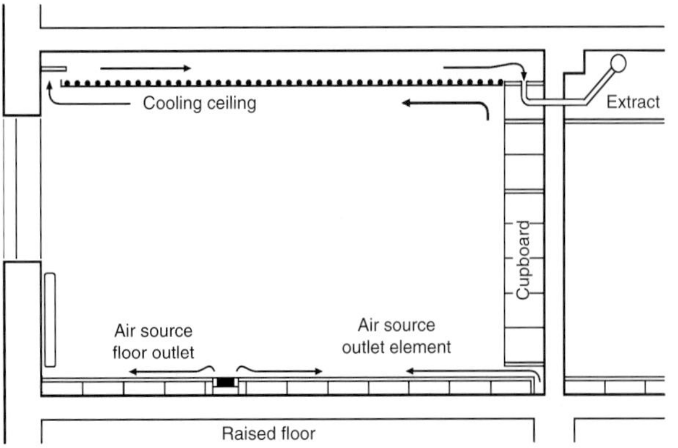

❾ Cooling systems in combination with suspended ceilings, e.g. acoustic ceilings. Installation into an existing ceiling is often possible. (Wellpott, Bohne → refs)

Purposes of ventilation

In occupied rooms, the air should be in a condition to meet our comfort requirements. The following comfort-relevant parameters can be influenced by ventilation systems:

- cleanliness of air/odour level
- room air temperature
- air movement, draughts
- air humidity.

Construction of ventilation systems

A room ventilation system normally consists of an outside air intake with fan, the central processing device, air distribution ductwork and air outlets → ❷. There are various systems, according to the intended purposes. Another consideration is whether the ventilation system can fulfil the intended purpose solely through the transported and processed air, or in combination with a water circulation system.

The first categorisation of air handling systems is whether they have a ventilation function or not. Systems with a ventilation function must be provided with a sufficient supply of outside air. In addition to ventilation, such systems can also perform functions like heating, cooling, humidification or dehumidification. Systems without a ventilation function fulfil the same conditions, but cannot exchange used air from rooms.

A further categorisation of air handling systems is according to the type and method of air processing, fundamentally the thermodynamic processing functions: heating, cooling, humidifying and dehumidifying. A system which only transports air and filters it if required is a **ventilation system**. If no outside air is used, then it is a **closed ventilation system**.

Air-water systems

Air-water systems are air handling systems operated in combination with additional water-circulation heating or cooling. These include, for example:

Chilled ceilings → ❸ – ❾

Chilled ceilings have a passive cooling effect. Instead of mechanical air circulation, there is a radiation exchange between ceiling components with cold water flowing through them and the room. Air exchange can remain at the minimum hygienically required level. In office rooms, the internal cooling load, i.e. the heat produced by people, devices and lighting that has to be removed, is normally greater than the heat loss though the external envelope of the building. In order to deal with this cooling load, normally about 40–80 W/m^2, conventional air conditioning requires high air exchange rates, large ducts and expensive central air handling units. These are increasingly being replaced by chilled ceilings, also referred to as 'silent cooling', because no noise-producing mechanical devices like fans are used. Water is used as transport medium instead of air.

Advantages of chilled ceilings

Little space required for ductwork, shafts and service rooms. Low energy costs, energy saving. High acceptance due to less noise from air movement and less room air velocity. Chilled ceiling systems are available for up to 100 W/m^2 of cooling. A further variant of '**silent cooling'** (cooling system with radiation or free convection) is suspended **chilled beams** → ❼ (which, however, offer less cooling capacity than full-surface systems due to their limited area), plus combinations of ceiling beam with convection component (e.g. convection component increased through perforated plates), storage chilled ceilings and various combinations of the above systems.

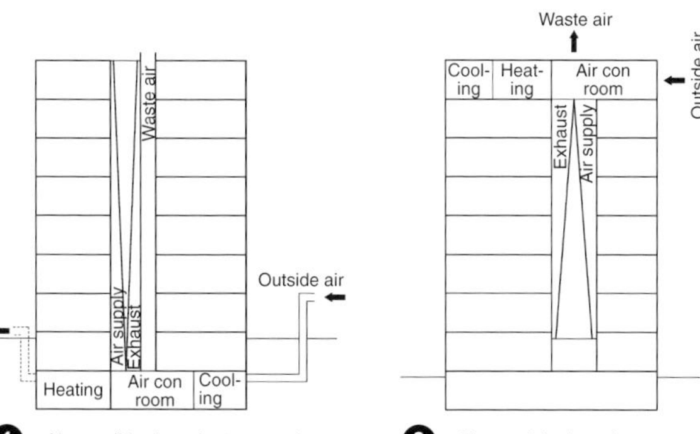

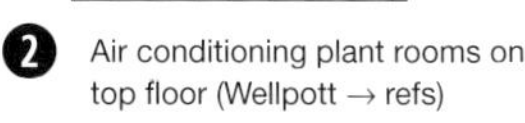

❶ Air conditioning plant rooms in basement (Wellpott → refs)

❷ Air conditioning plant rooms on top floor (Wellpott → refs)

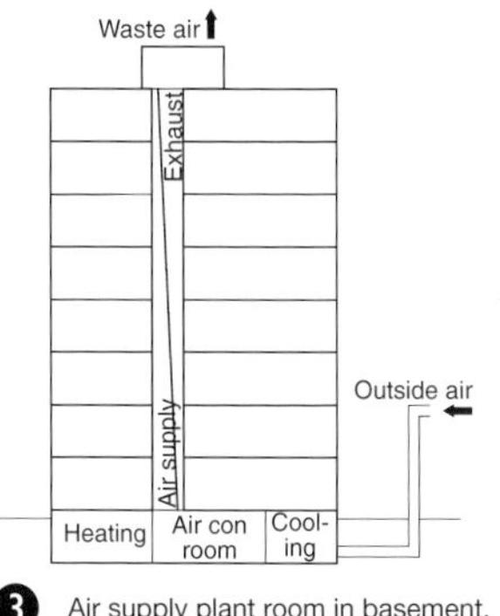

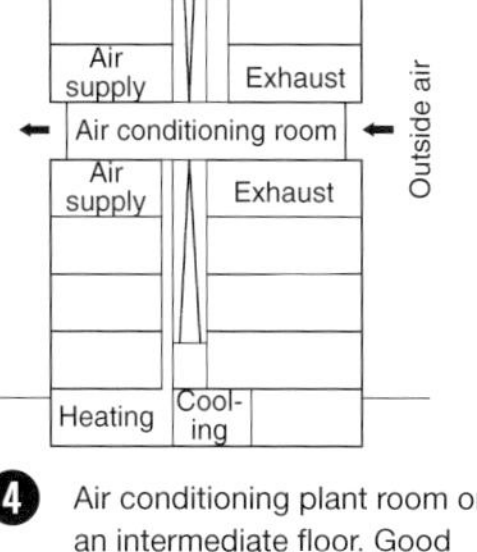

❸ Air supply plant room in basement. Extract air plant room on the roof (induction air conditioning system). No air circulation (Wellpott → refs)

❹ Air conditioning plant room on an intermediate floor. Good solution for high-rise buildings (Wellpott → refs)

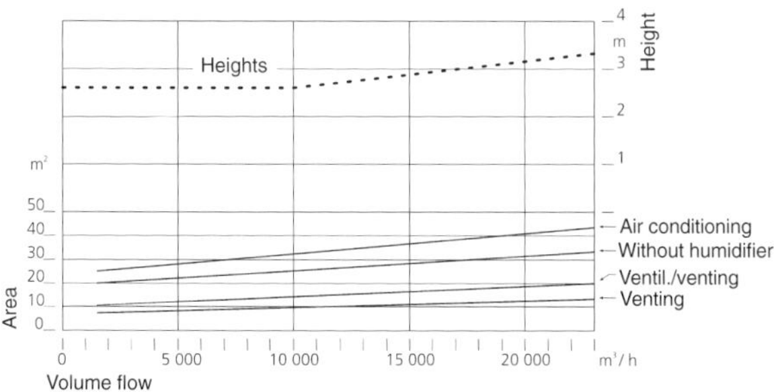

❺ Approximate determination of area and room heights required for air conditioning plant rooms in which to site several units for air flows of up to 50m³/s, according to VdI 3803, for smaller systems (Wellpott → refs)

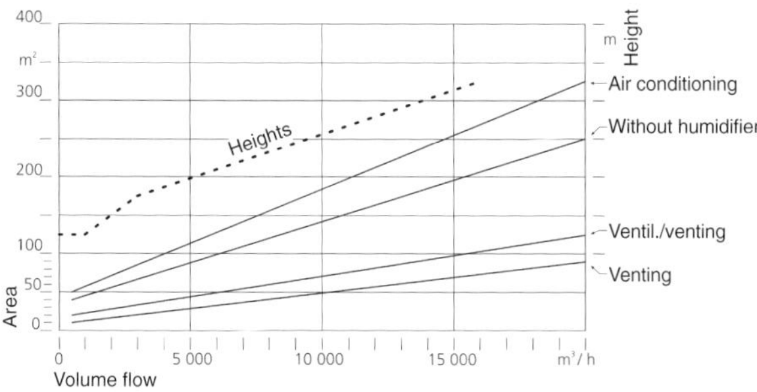

❻ As ❺, but for larger systems (Wellpott → refs)

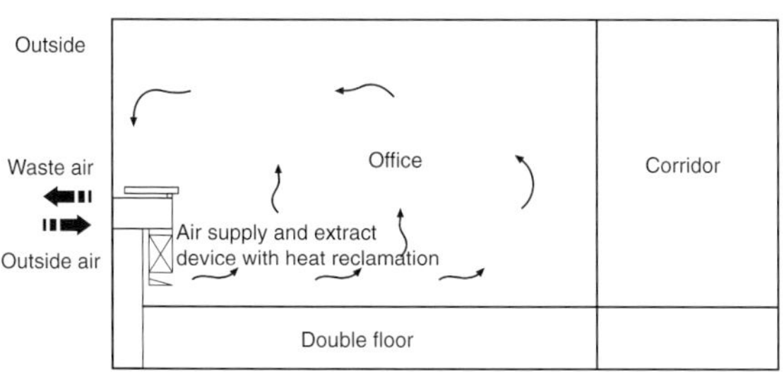

❼ Combined parapet air supply and extract unit (Wellpott, Bohne → refs)

Air conditioning plant rooms → ❶ – ❹

Arrangement for air handling equipment According to a sample design by the expert Building Supervision (RbAL), air handling equipment must have a dedicated service room (air conditioning plant room) in buildings of more than three storeys, if the connecting ductwork leads into more than one storey or fire compartment.

Ventilation and air conditioning systems mostly have their services rooms on a services floor, near the heating plant room (heating room with distribution) and the cooling plant (chiller). The combination of air conditioning plant and heating plant in one room is not allowed (fire protection). Spatial connection of plant rooms to the building cores with their vertical installation shafts is an important design consideration. The horizontal and vertical distances to the main areas of demand (e.g. large kitchens, canteens or server rooms) from the air conditioning plant room should also be considered.

The formal integration of a services floor into the body of a building can considerably influence its appearance. Placed on one of the upper storeys, a dedicated services floor will have almost no windows or none at all (noise emission), but will need intake and extract louvres and will also contrast with other floors with its different storey height.

Room sizes

An approximate estimation of the size of an air conditioning plant room can be undertaken using the VDI Guideline 2052, working from the assumed volume flow and the type of air handling. Example calculations for the size of the plant room in an administration building → ❺ – ❻.

Façade ventilation systems → ❼ – ❾

These are also referred to as **decentralised ventilation systems**. The units are placed near the façades with a direct duct connection. In contrast to fan convectors with recirculation, the flow of outside air is fed directly from the façade to the unit. This means that no more air conditioning installation is required in the building. Façade ventilation units can be designed in various forms such as underfloor air supply units, combined air supply and extract units or with a central extract air plant.

It is important to consider the influence of wind pressure on the volume flow. The temperature boundary layer at the façade can also affect the air supply temperature, depending on the layout and design of the building.

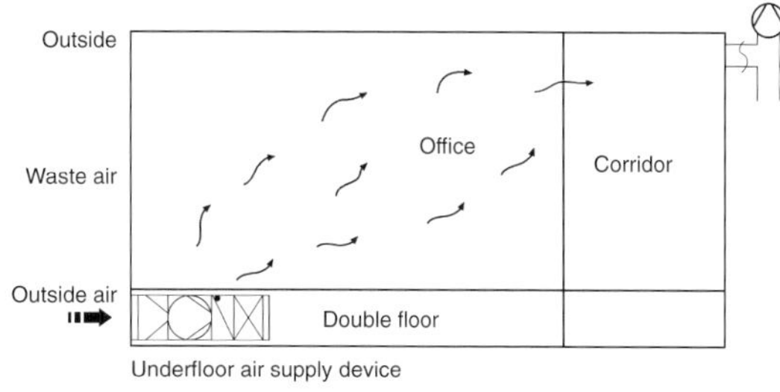

❽ Underfloor air supply unit combined with centralised extract air system (Wellpott, Bohne → refs)

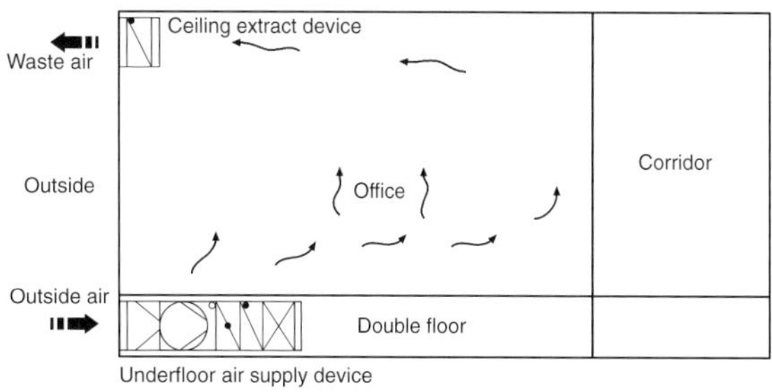

❾ Underfloor air supply unit combined with over-current component (Wellpott, Bohne → refs)

Heating systems

Heating systems for buildings normally use water as the heat distribution medium, less often air (steam is used as a heating medium only for industrial purposes). The necessary temperature of the heat distribution medium (water, air, steam) depends on the temperature chosen and the type of heating surface in the rooms. A heat generator provides the necessary temperature. Most existing heating systems use gas or oil as the primary energy source. The heating gas or oil is normally burnt in boilers with a combustion temperature of about 1000°C and the heat is transferred to the distribution medium in a heat exchanger.

Because a temperature of 70°C is typically sufficient for the heat distribution medium, a holistic design will attempt to avoid the burning of fossil fuels. Methods of exploiting renewable energy are: (ground-source) geothermal energy → p. 469 in connection with a heat pump system; combination of heat and power generation (CHP); or perhaps falling back on a CO_2-neutral energy source like wood. It can also be possible to store seasonal sources of energy from the environment (thermal solar energy) during the summer months and make it available in the winter.

Heat distribution

Much the most common system is **warm water central heating**. This transfers the heat produced in the heat generator into water as distribution medium to the radiators, which emit heat. The cooled water returns to the heat generator to be warmed up again (flow and return). Warm water central heating systems have a max. flow temperature of approx. 100°C, but 45–70°C is normally preferred today, described as the low temperature range. Heating systems with flow temperatures of over 120°C count as hot water heating and are more often used with district heating systems.

The heat distribution is normally circulated as **warm water pumped heating**. There are various pipework layouts → ❷ – ❼.

Heat generation with gas or heating oil

Gas firing: gas has become prevalent in recent years. Advantages: no storage costs, low maintenance costs, payment after use, can be used in groundwater protection zones, easily regulated, high annual efficiency, can be used for the heating of individual flats or rooms (compact gas boilers), little environmental impact. Disadvantages: dependent on public utility network, higher energy costs. A conversion from oil to gas usually makes a new chimney necessary.

Oil firing: is also common today using light heating oil as fuel. Advantages: requires no public utility network, easily controllable. Disadvantages: high cost of storage and tank installation, rent income losses in rented houses due to the oil storage room, only possible under stringent regulations in areas at risk of flooding or groundwater protection zones, payment before use, high environmental impact.

Solid fuel firing

Coal, brown coal and wood are now used less often for heating buildings. Depending on the fuel, large quantities of environmental pollutants can be released, which are subject to stringent controls under the Federal Anti-Emissions Law. Advantages: independent of fuel imports, low fuel costs. Disadvantages: more work for the operator, larger storeroom necessary, high emission of pollutants, poor controllability.

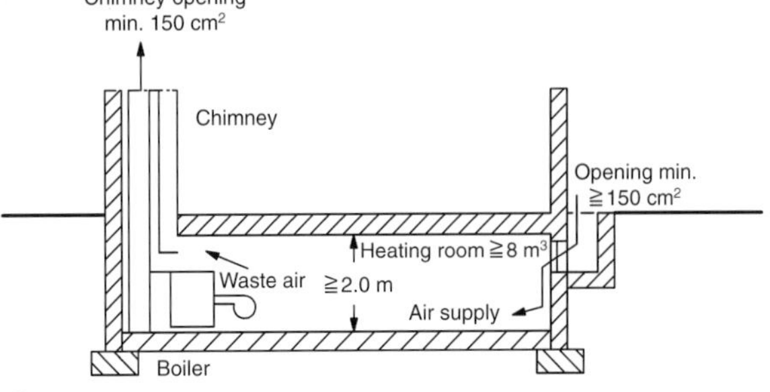

❶ Heating room for solid fuel, min. area 8 m³ necessary for heating capacity ≧50 kW

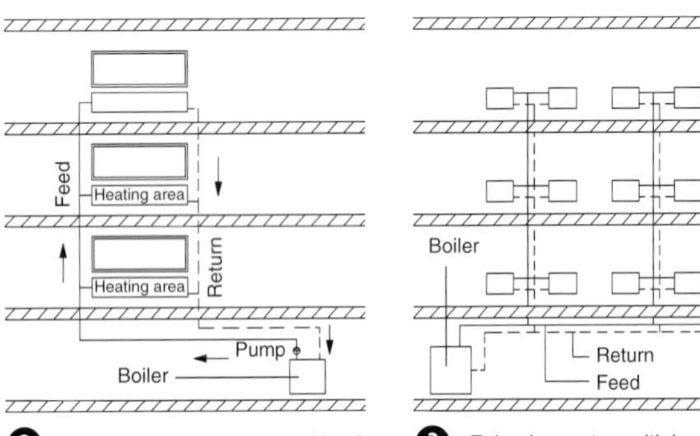

❷ Principle of warm water central heating system: water is heated by the boiler and circulated constantly to radiating surfaces by a pump (Wellpott → refs)

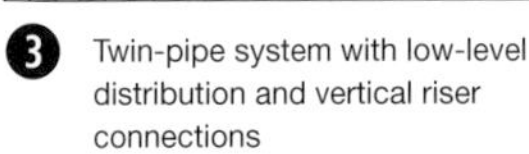

❸ Twin-pipe system with low-level distribution and vertical riser connections

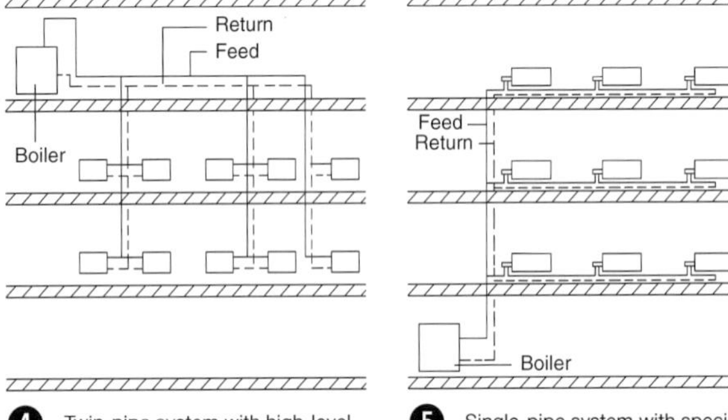

❹ Twin-pipe system with high-level distribution and vertical riser connections

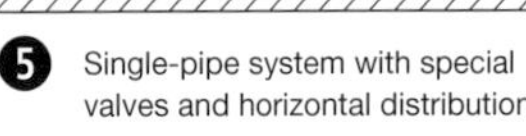

❺ Single-pipe system with special valves and horizontal distribution

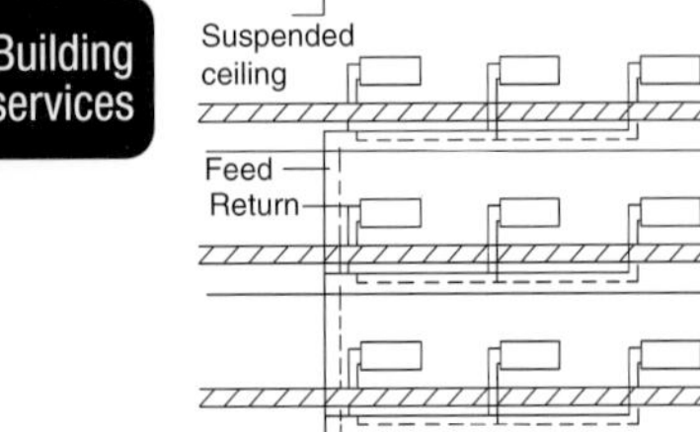

❻ Twin-pipe system with horizontal distribution (standard layout for office buildings)

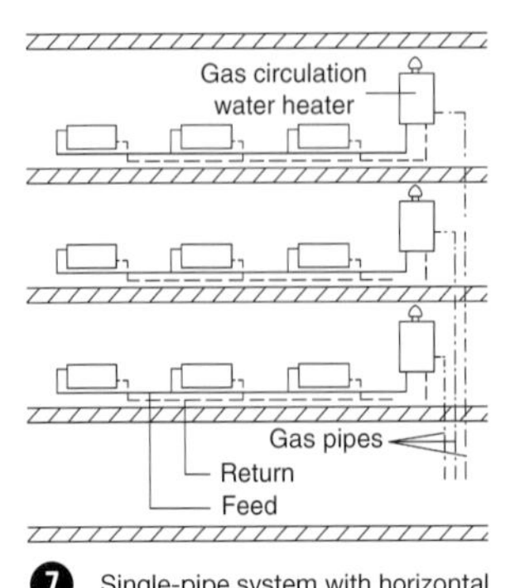

❼ Single-pipe system with horizontal distribution on each floor

BS 5871
BS EN 12828
BS EN 15316
DIN EN 215
DIN EN 442
DIN EN 1264
DIN EN 12170
DIN EN 12171
DIN EN 12828
DIN EN 12831

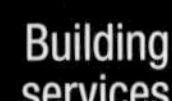

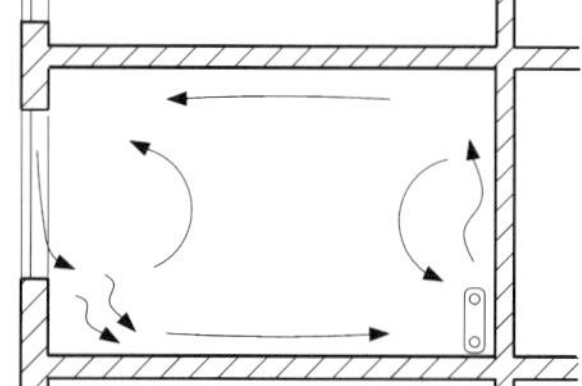

❷ Air movement with sectional radiator at internal wall

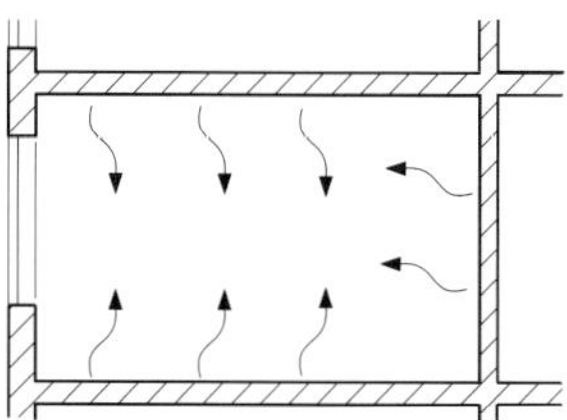

❸ Air movement with surface heating (wall, ceiling or floor)

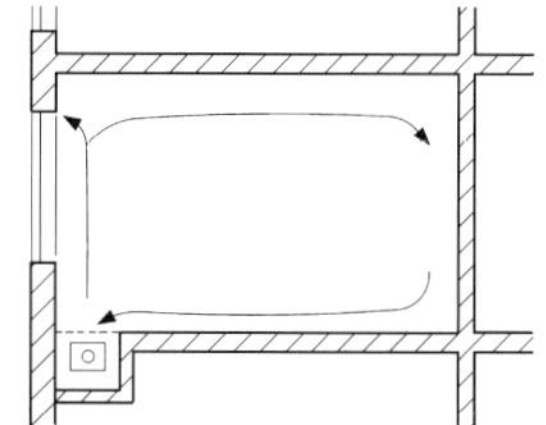

❹ Air movement with underfloor convectors

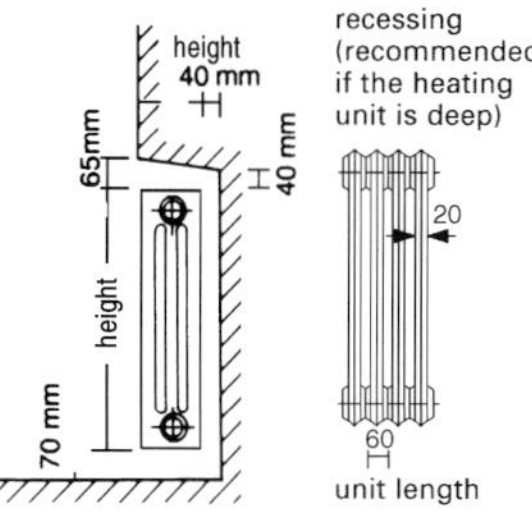

❺ Cast-iron radiators, DIN 4703

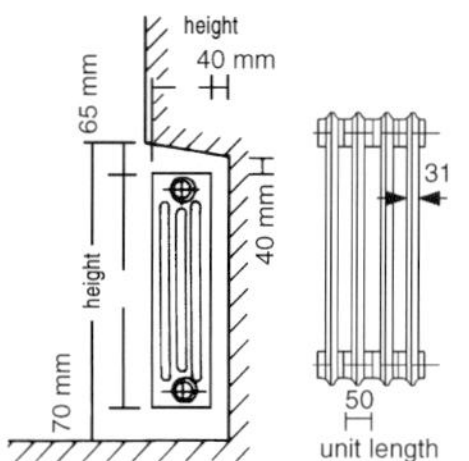

❻ Steel radiators, DIN 4703

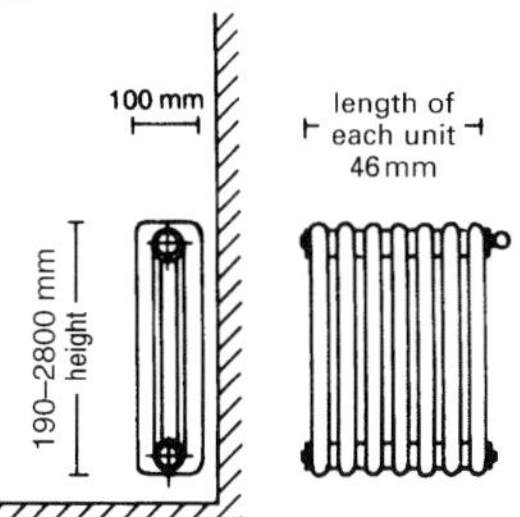

❼ Tubular radiator

Height	Boss spacing	Depth
280	220	250
430	350	70, 110, 160, 220
580	500	70, 110, 160, 220
680	600	160
980	900	70, 160, 220

❽ Dimensions (mm) of standardised cast-iron radiators, DIN 4703-1

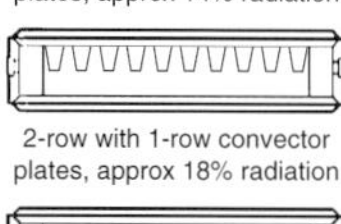

2-row with 2-row convector plates, approx 14% radiation

2-row with 1-row convector plates, approx 18% radiation

2-row without convector plates, approx 21% radiation

❾ Horizontal sections through panel radiators

Height	Boss spacing	Depth
300	200	160, 250
450	350	70, 110, 160, 220
600	600	70, 110, 160, 220
1000	900	70, 110, 160, 220

❿ Dimensions (mm) of standardised steel radiators, DIN 4703-1

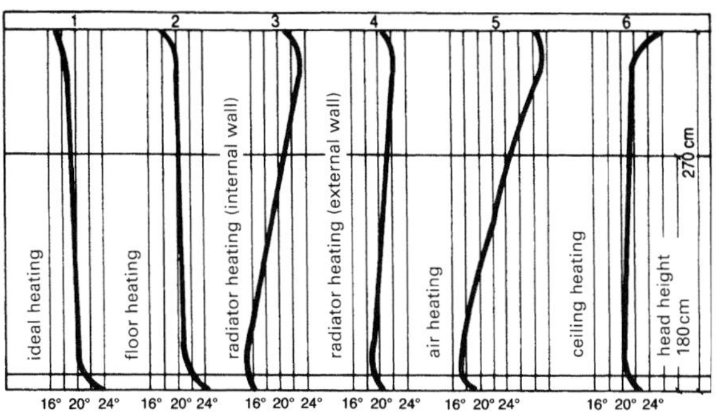

⓫ Room temperature curves: physiological warmth evaluation of a heating system

Heating surfaces in rooms

Arrangement of heating surfaces and resulting air circulation → ❶ – ❹ Radiators placed below windows can prevent draughts near the windows. The air cooled by the glass surface is intercepted by the air rising from the radiator → ❶.

Located on internal walls, radiators can provoke air circulation with the effect of producing cool air near the floor and warm air near the ceiling. Such relatively large temperature differences between floor and ceiling are not comfortable → ❷.

Surface heating (underfloor, ceiling and wall heating) is operated in room perimeter areas with low temperatures. The heat output is uniform and solely through radiation. The low heating demand of buildings built according to the Energy Saving Regulations (EnEV) means that surface heating systems are ideal in this respect, yet provide a comfortable temperature → ❸.

Convectors transfer heat not by radiation, but by direct heat transfer to the air molecules. For this reason, convectors can be clad or built in without reducing their heating capability. The performance of a convector depends on the recess height above the heater → ❹, see also p. 534.

Types of heating surfaces

Sectional radiators include steel tube, cast-iron and steel radiators. They release 40% of their heat as radiation.

Steel tube radiators are available as 2–6-row tubular radiators, have no sharp edges and provide good performance in relationship to their length → ❼.

Steel radiators → ❻ are welded out of a number of components into a block and have connections between the blocks at the ends. Until a few years ago, these were the standard radiators for warm water heating, but panel radiators are now more usual.

Cast-iron radiators have a small market share. They react slowly to control inputs but are very corrosion-resistant → ❺.

Panel radiators consist of flat and profiled steel plate double panels with water flowing through. The front gives out heat mostly as radiation, the back mostly by convection into the air. If a number of panels are arranged in front of each other, then the proportion of convection increases accordingly. In practice, up to three panels are used.

Because of their shallow constructional depth (2–5 cm), panel radiators require only very shallow window niches. They can emit up to 40% of their heat as radiation and can be operated with relatively low flow temperatures (making them suitable for operation with ground-source heat pumps). In order to improve the heating performance, vertical folded fins (convector plates) can be mounted between the panels → ❾.

A duct width = C + 2K
B distance from floor - min. 70 mm (120 mm better)
C heater depth
E distance between connections
H min. overall height
K separation from wall of covering (min. 50 mm)

⓬ Effect on heat output of various radiator covers

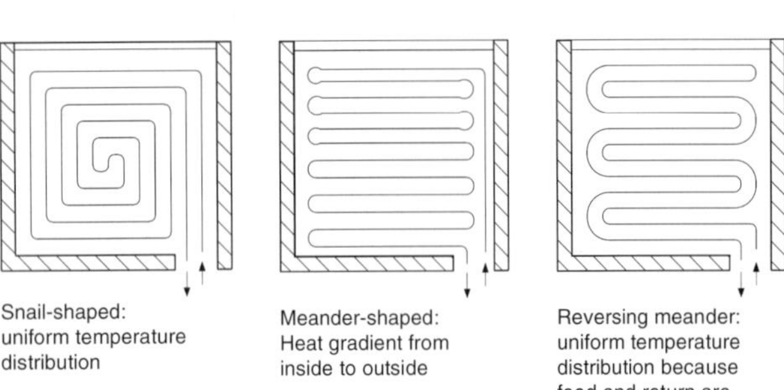

Snail-shaped: uniform temperature distribution

Meander-shaped: Heat gradient from inside to outside

Reversing meander: uniform temperature distribution because feed and return are next to each other

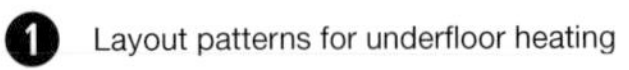

1 Layout patterns for underfloor heating

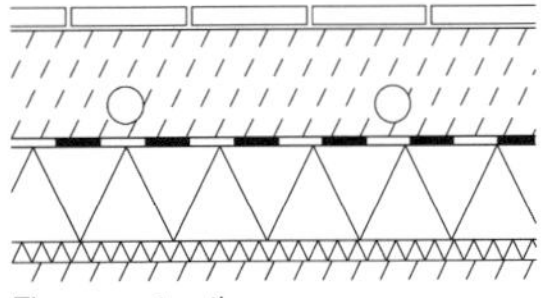

Floor construction:
- Floor covering
- Screed (cover to pipes min. 45 mm)
- PE foil 0.2 mm
- Insulation 40 mm
- Impact sound insulation
- Structural floor slab

2 Underfloor heating (wet laying)

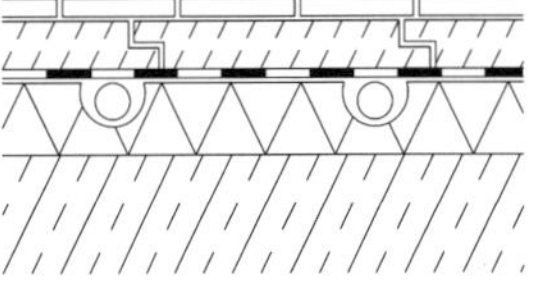

Floor construction:
- Floor covering
- Dry screed 45 mm
- PE foil 0.2 mm
- Laying element/insulation layer 30 mm
- Impact sound insulation
- Structural floor slab

3 Underfloor heating (dry laying)

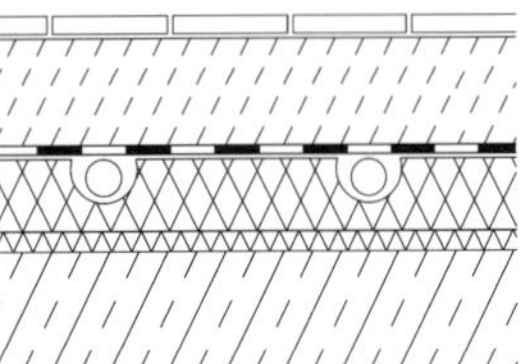

Floor construction:
- Floor covering
- Dry screed 45 mm
- PE foil 0.2 mm
- Laying element/insulation layer 30 mm
- Structural floor slab

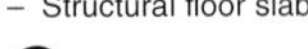

4 Underfloor heating – pipes laid within the insulation layer

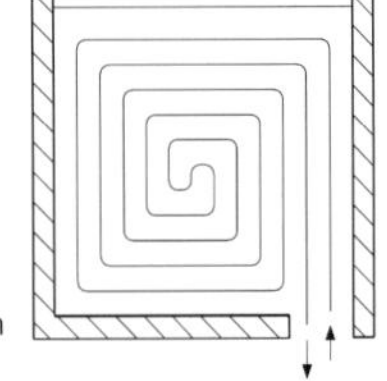

5 Layout pattern of a ceiling heating system

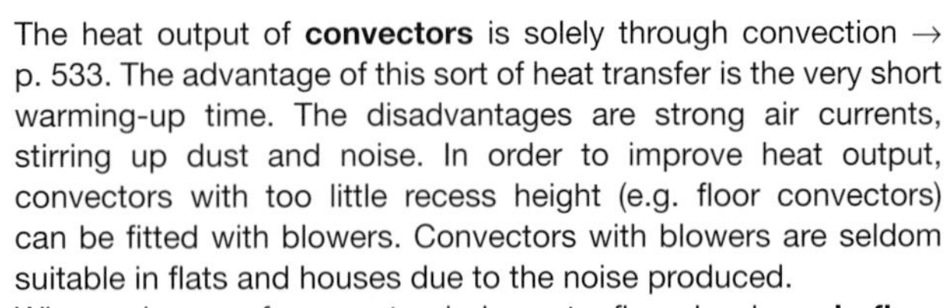

The heat output of **convectors** is solely through convection → p. 533. The advantage of this sort of heat transfer is the very short warming-up time. The disadvantages are strong air currents, stirring up dust and noise. In order to improve heat output, convectors with too little recess height (e.g. floor convectors) can be fitted with blowers. Convectors with blowers are seldom suitable in flats and houses due to the noise produced.

Where glass surfaces extend down to floor level, **underfloor convectors** → **6** can be used. These replace radiators in front of the glass (particularly with sliding glass components).

Mini- or screed convectors → **7**, which are installed flush with screed level, can be combined successfully with surface heating systems like underfloor heating. These are particularly suitable for seasonal transitions, to avoid having to put the rather sluggishly reacting underfloor heating into operation.

Radiator covers: radiators can be covered in various ways, resulting in a loss of efficiency of 10–15%. If the air intake and outlet openings are insufficiently large, this loss can even increase to 30%, which then has to be compensated for with larger radiator areas to cover the heating demand.

Metal coverings transfer the radiation component almost completely to the air in the room, but coverings of other materials with low thermal conductivity considerably reduce the radiation → p. 533 **12**.

Underfloor heating → **1** – **4** transfers the heat from the floor to the air and also to the walls and ceiling. Heat transfer to the air is by convection, i.e. through air movement at the surface of the floor, but heat transfer to the walls and ceiling is by radiation. The heat output, depending on floor construction, can be 70–110 W/m^2. Ceramics, wood or textiles and almost any common floor covering are suitable for the floor construction, but the thermal resistance should not exceed 0.15 m^2 kW. The screed on top of underfloor heating should be in accordance with DIN 18560 or the bulletins of the Central German Building Industry Association. The thickness of the screed depends on its type, method of laying and the assumed load.

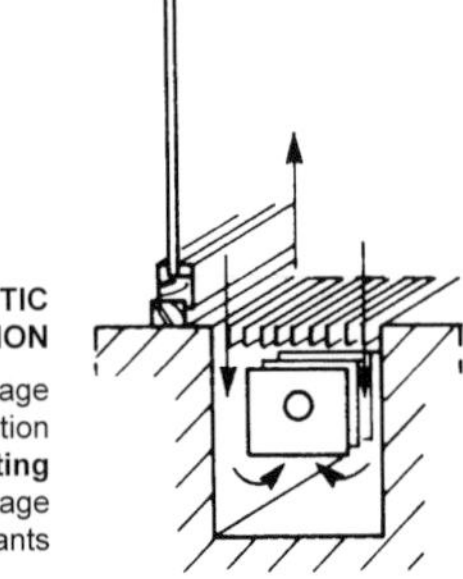

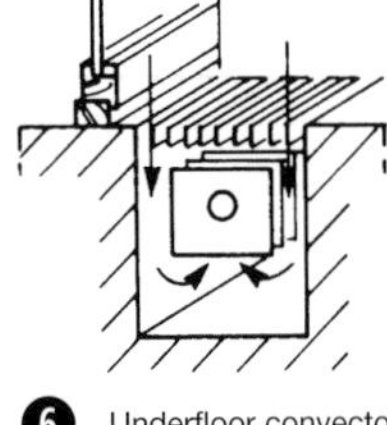

6 Underfloor convector

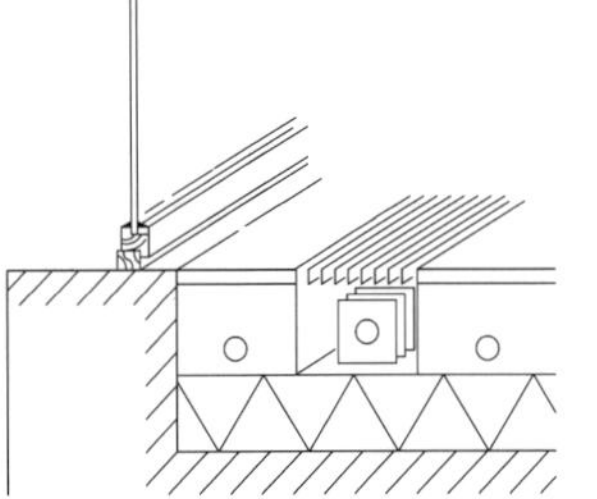

7 Mini-convector (screed convector) in combination with underfloor heating (principle)

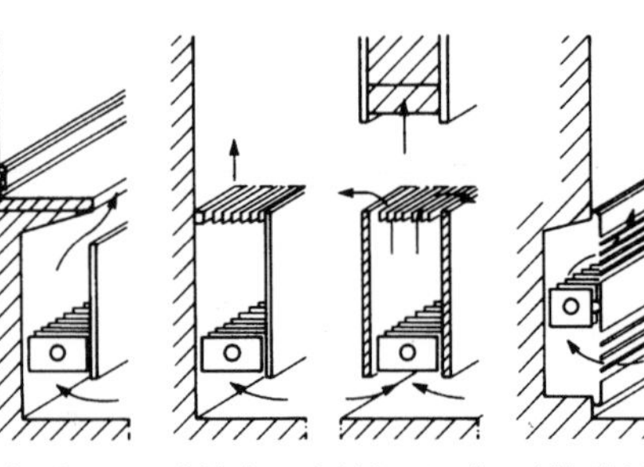

(a) under window
(b) in front of smooth wall
(c) free standing (for heating of 2 rooms)
(d) built into wall
(e) built into wall

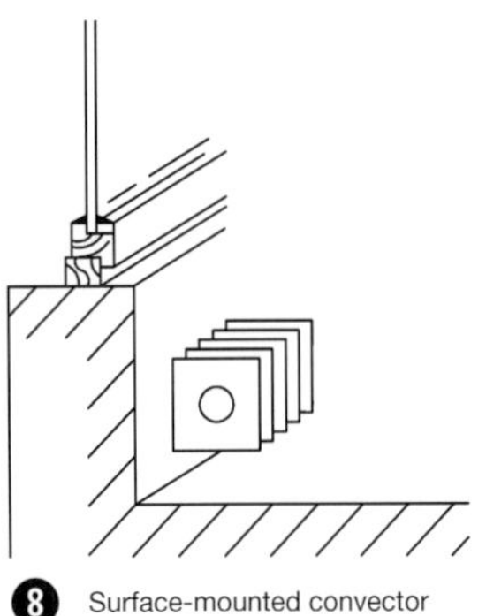

8 Surface-mounted convector

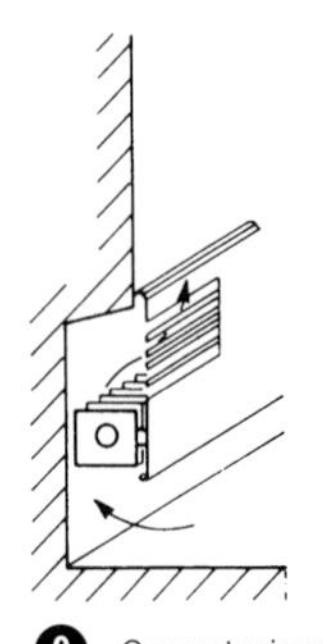

9 Convector in recess

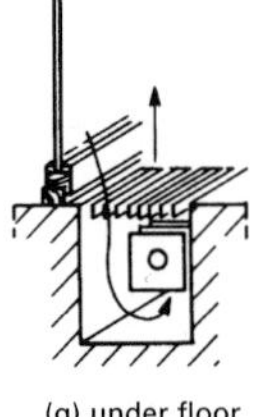

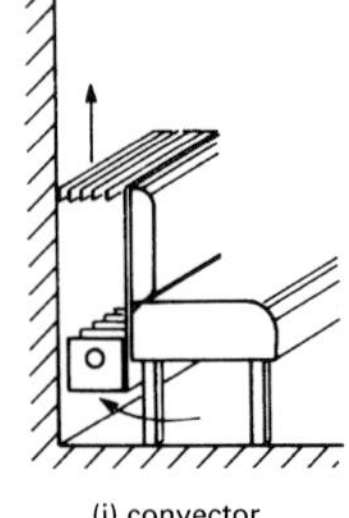

(f) under floor convector with room air intake
(g) under floor convector with cold air intake
(h) under floor convector with intake on both sides
(i) convector behind bench seat

10 Various ways of installing convectors

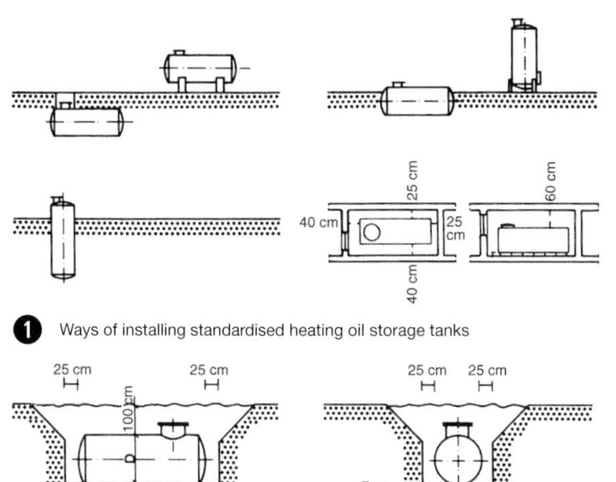

❶ Ways of installing standardised heating oil storage tanks

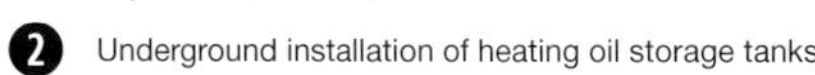

❷ Underground installation of heating oil storage tanks

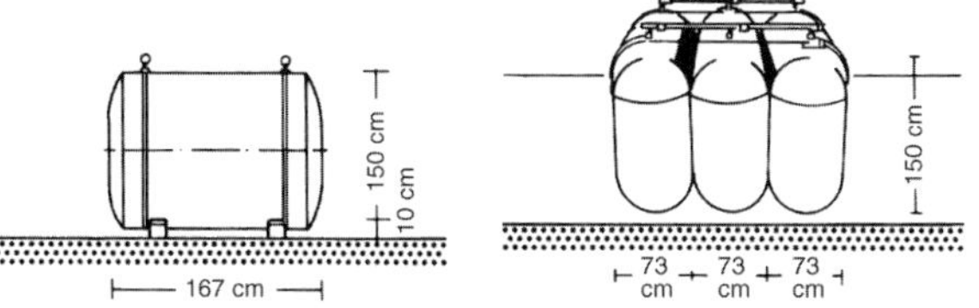

❸ Battery storage tank made of nylon (polyamide)

❹ Battery storage tanks made of nylon (polyamide)

Nominal capacity: vol. in litres (dm³)	Max. dimensions (mm)		Weight incl. accessories (kg)
	Length l	Depth d	
1100 (1100)	1100 (1100)	720	approx. 30–50 kg
1500 (1600)	1650 (1720)	720	approx. 40–60 kg
2000	2150	720	approx. 50–80 kg

❺ Available dimensions of plastic battery tanks

Min. capacity: vol. in (m³)	Min. dimensions (mm)					Weight (kg) of			
	External diameter d_1	Length l	Sheet thickness 1-walled	Sheet thickness 2-walled.	Filler cap diam.	1.1 1-walled		1.2 A/C	B
1	1000	1510	5	3	–	265		–	–
3	1250	2740	5	3	–	325		–	–
5	1600	2820	5	3	500	700		700	790
7	1600	3740	3	3	500	885		930	980
10	1600	5350	5	3	500	1200		1250	1300
16	1600	8570	5	3	500	1800		1850	1900
20	2000	6969	6	3	600	2300		2400	2450
25	2000	8540	6	3	600	2750		2850	2900
30	2000	10120	6	3	600	3300		3400	3450
40	2500	8800	7	4(5)	600	4200		4400	4450
50	2500	10800	7	4	600	5100		5300	5350
60	2500	12800	7	4	600	6100		6300	6350
						Weight (kg) of			
						1.3 A	B	2.1	2.2 B
1.7	1250	1590	5	–	500	–	–	–	390
2.8	1600	1670	5	–	500	–	–	–	390
3.8	1600	2130	5	–	500	–	–	–	600
5	1600	2820	5	3	500	700	745	–	740
6	2000	2220	5	–	500	–	–	–	930
7	1600	3740	5	3	500	885	930	935	–
10	1600	5350	5	3	500	1250	1250	1250	–
16	1600	8570	5	3	500	1800	1950	1850	–
20	2000	6960	6	3	600	2300	2350	2350	–
25	2000	8540	6	3	600	2750	2800	2800	–
30	2000	10120	6	3	600	3300	3350	–	–
	2500	6665	7	–	600	–	–	3350	–
40	2500	8800	7	4	600	4200	4250	4250	–
50	2500	10800	7	4	600	5100	5150	–	–
	2900	8400	9	–	600	–	–	6150	–
60	2500	12800	7	4	600	6100	6150	–	–
	2900	9585	9	–	600	–	–	6900	–

❻ Dimensions of cylindrical oil tanks → ❼

When **cement screed** ZE 20 is laid on heating pipes, which are laid directly on thermal insulation, a minimum cover to the pipes of 45 mm is specified, which results in a total construction thickness of min. 75 mm without floor construction. Screed expands during the operation of the heating, with temperature differences between top and bottom. This differential expansion leads to tension stresses under ceramic flooring, which can only be resisted by an upper reinforcement layer. Reinforcement is not necessary when the floor is covered with carpet or parquet, because the temperature gradient between top and bottom of the screed is less than with ceramic flooring.

DIN 4725 gives the maximum permissible floor surface temperatures: 29°C for permanently occupied areas, and for the edge zone (no wider than 1 m) 35°C. The maximum permissible floor temperature for bathrooms is 9°C above standard room temperature. Underfloor heating is possible under these conditions in normal circumstances,because the heating demand is seldom above 90 W/m².

Storage of heating oil: the quantity of heating oil should last for at least three months and at the most for one heating period (winter). No more than 5000 l may be stored in the heating room. The tanks must be inside a collecting tank with a volume sufficient to take the entire oil quantity (secondary containment). If the tanks are underground, equipment must be installed to protect against leakage, like double-walled tanks or plastic inner lining. In groundwater protection zones, maximum quantities and additional protection measures are prescribed.

Inside buildings: either plastic battery tanks each containing 500–2000 l or steel tanks welded together on site, which can be any size. The tank storage room must be accessible and the tanks must be regularly checked for leaks. An internal tank room must also be able to contain the entire volume of oil in case of a leak. Tank installations must have filling and venting equipment, and also protection against overfilling. According to the type of storage, leak-warning systems may be required (e.g. with underground tanks).

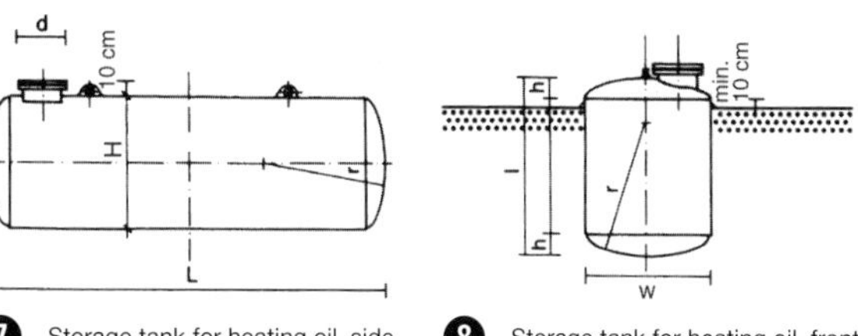

❼ Storage tank for heating oil, side view

❽ Storage tank for heating oil, front view

❾ Tank laid in pre-cast protection component

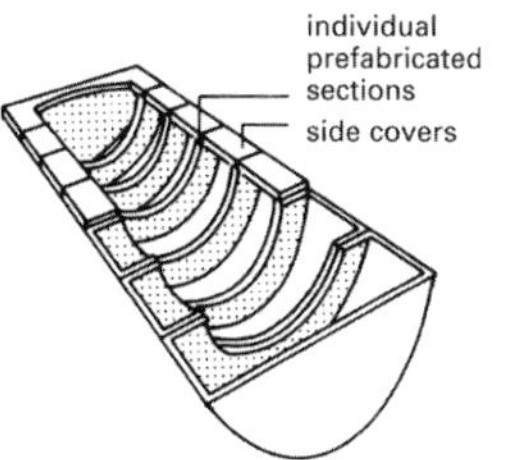

❿ Pre-cast concrete protection trough for oil tanks

➊ Basic layouts of multi-chamber sedimentation tanks

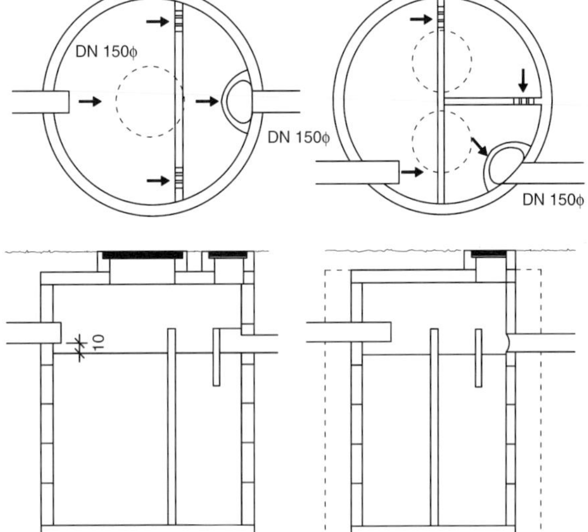

➋ Multi-chamber sedimentation tanks of pre-cast components, with two or three chambers, plans and sections

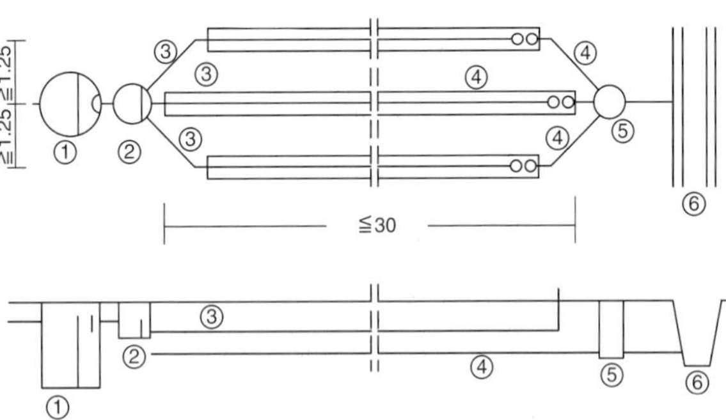

➌ Principle of a filter trench, plan and section
➊ Multi-chamber sedimentation tank, ➋ distribution shaft, ➌ feed pipes, ➍ drainpipes, ➎ collection shaft, ➏ discharge

Small sewage treatment plants are facilities for the cleaning of wastewater, which are used when the disposal of wastewater in municipal treatment works is not possible for technical, regulatory or financial reasons: maybe there is no public sewer network available, or as a temporary measure. They are only permissible for the treatment of wastewater from, for example, kitchens, laundries, bathrooms, toilets and wash rooms.

Principle of a small-scale sewage treatment plant:

1. Mechanical cleaning, i.e. sludge removal from a multi-chamber sedimentation tank → ➊ – ➋.
2. Biological cleaning in a filter trench or trickle filter or through underground filtration.

The construction of a small-scale sewage treatment system consists of: multi-chamber sedimentation tank, distribution shaft, filter trench (trickle filter or underground filtration), collection shaft, discharge into waterway.

Treatment process

The residential wastewater is first fed into a sedimentation tank (mechanical cleaning), where solid matter settles to the bottom. It then flows into a distribution shaft, from where it is fed intermittently into a filter trench (with perforated pipes) or into a trickle filter (biological cleaning). The outflow pipes from the filter trench drain via a collection shaft into a waterway or soakaway.

The mechanical process of wastewater treatment takes place in a **multi-chamber sedimentation tank**. Undissolved solids and solids capable of settling are sedimented (sludge removal) → ➊ – ➋.

Biological cleaning (secondary treatment) of the wastewater takes place in a **filter trench**. The wastewater percolates from a perforated pipe into a layer of fine gravel (2–8 mm), the filter layer, into a deeper perforated pipe (depth min. 1.25 m). This then transports the water for discharge into a waterway → ➌.

Wastewater production

For a residential building, 150 l of water per occupant per day should be assumed. For other buildings, the equivalent inhabitant value is 150 l for every:

- 3 seats in pubs without kitchens
- 1 seat in pubs with kitchens and max. 3 rotations of each seat in 24 hours.
- 10 seats in pubs with gardens but without kitchens
- 2 employees in factories or workshops without kitchens
- 3 employees in administration buildings without kitchens.

	Multi-chamber sedimentation tanks		Multi-chamber septic tanks
no. chambers	2	3–4	3
specific usable capacity	300 l/RU*	300 l/RU*	1500 l/RU*
total usable capacity (min.)	3000 l	3000 l	6000 l
total usable capacity (max.)	4000 l	—	—
capacity of 1st chamber	⅔ of total capacity	½ of total capacity	½ of total capacity
min. water depth	1.20 m	1.20 m	1.20 m
greatest permissible water depth for usable capacity of 3000–4000 l >4000–10 000 >10 000–50 000 l >50 000 l	 1.90 m — — —	 1.90 m 2.20 m 2.50 m 3.00 m	 1.90 m 2.20 m 2.50 m 3.00 m

*RU, each residential unit with 50 m² of residential area is assumed to have 2 inhabitants, over 50 m² min. 4 inhabitants.

➍ Sizing of multi-chamber sedimentation tanks and septic tanks, DIN 4261-1

CHIMNEYS AND VENTILATION SHAFTS

Chimneys

Chimneys are shafts, within or next to buildings, intended to carry flue gases from fireplaces (including ovens and appliances) into the open air above the roof. The following must be connected to their **own chimney**: each fireplace with a nominal heat output of more than 20 kW (for gas fires and appliances, more than 30 kW), each fireplace in buildings of more than five full storeys, each open fireplace, each fireplace with burner and blower. **Shared chimneys** may connect up to three fireplaces for solid or liquid fuel with a nominal heating capacity of up to 20 kW or three gas fireplaces with nominal heating capacity of up to 30 kW.

Cross-sections

Chimneys must have a circular or rectangular clear cross-section. The **minimum cross-sectional area** for chimneys made of shaped bricks is 100 cm^2, the minimum side length 10 cm (for masonry chimneys 140 cm^2, 13.5 cm). The longer side may not be more than 1.5 times the shorter.

The cross-section can be calculated or taken from the approved tables produced by manufacturers of prefabricated chimneys → ❾ – ❿. In order to prevent condensation, a chimney should be fully utilised.

Fire protection

The external surfaces of chimneys must be ≧5 cm from both combustible and flame-resistant building materials. Non-combustible building materials may be in direct contact or be separated by a 2 cm wide insulated gap.

❶ Chimney heights above roofs

❷ Wind and chimney draught

❸ Modular chimney installation

❹ Pre-assembled chimney (storey height)

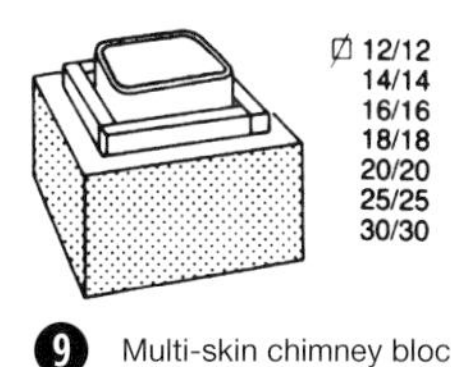

❾ Multi-skin chimney block

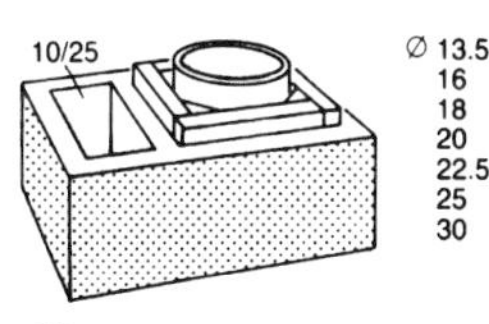

❿ Chimney block with ventilation ducts (to ventilate the heating room)

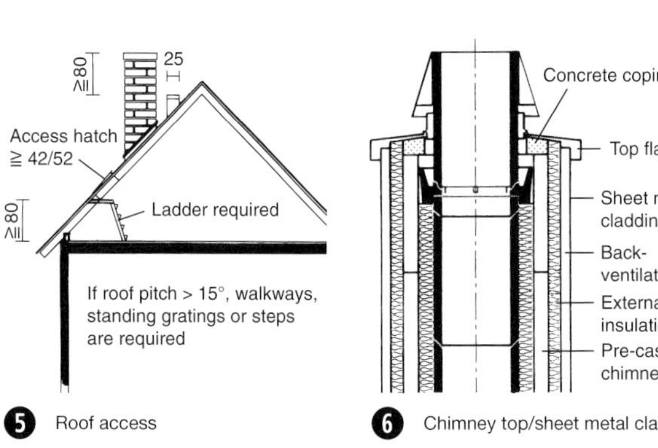

❺ Roof access

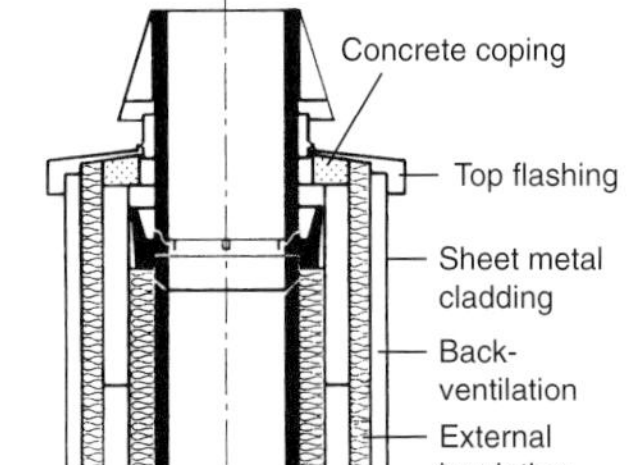

❻ Chimney top/sheet metal cladding

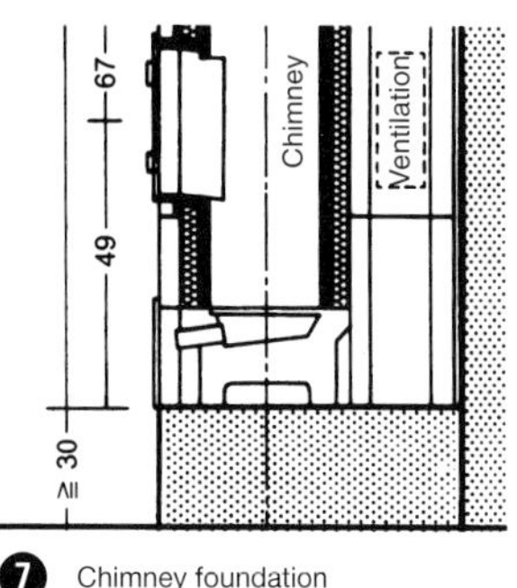

❼ Chimney foundation

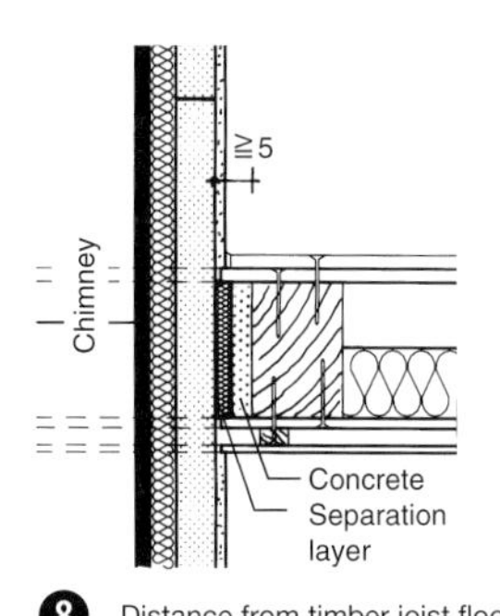

❽ Distance from timber joist floor to chimney

Heights

The **minimum height** (distance from fireplace level to chimney top) is 4 m (for joint chimneys 5 m). Chimney tops must be ≧40 cm above the highest point of roofs with a pitch ≧20° or 1.00 m from other roof surfaces. Chimneys which are nearer to roof structures than 1.5–3 times the height of the structure must clear the structure by ≧1 m. Chimney tops above roofs with a perimeter parapet must be ≧1 m above the parapet → ❶.

Construction

In addition to the traditional single-skin masonry chimney, **multi-skin systems with shaped bricks** are commonly used today, consisting of flue liner, thermal insulation and chimney block (available with integrated ventilation ducts) → ❾ – ❿. **Pre-assembled chimneys** are also available → ❹ with storey-height assembly units, and completely prefabricated steel-pipe chimneys. Chimneys have to be gas-tight and constructed of **fireproof materials**, and the temperature of the external surface may not exceed 100°C. Chimneys must be built on **foundations** and be braced over the height. Each chimney has a **cleaning opening** → ❼ (≧10/18 cm, at least 20 cm below the lowest fireplace connection). Chimneys which cannot be swept from the top must have an additional cleaning opening in the roof space.

BS EN 1449
BS EN 1857
DIN EN 1443
DIN V 18160
MBO

see also: Fire protection pp. 511 ff.

see also: Fire protection pp. 511 ff.

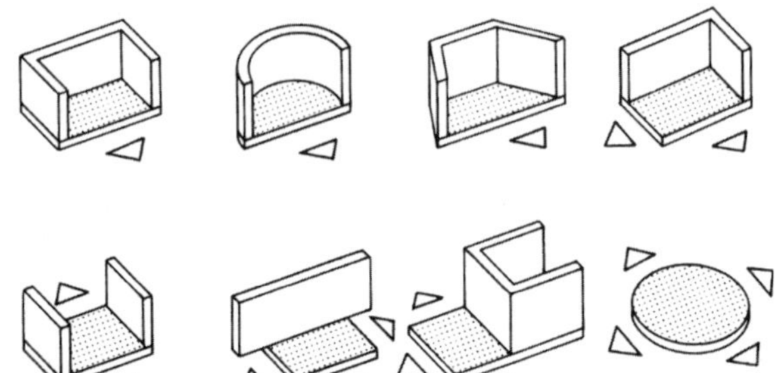

❶ Forms of radiating surfaces

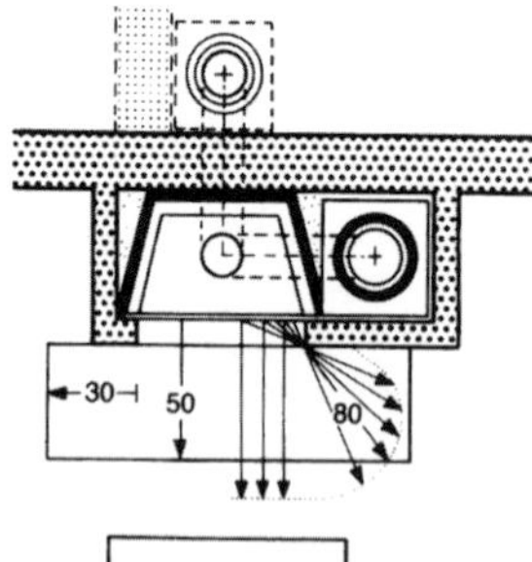

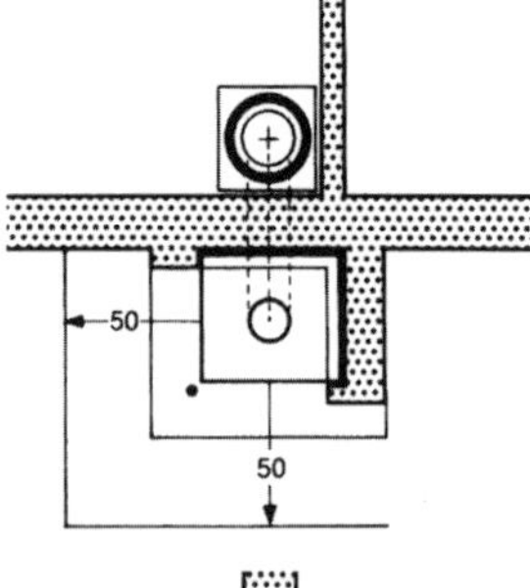

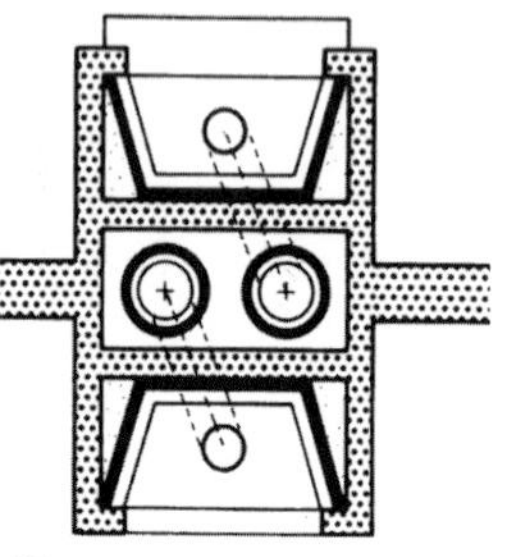

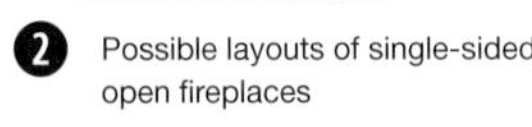

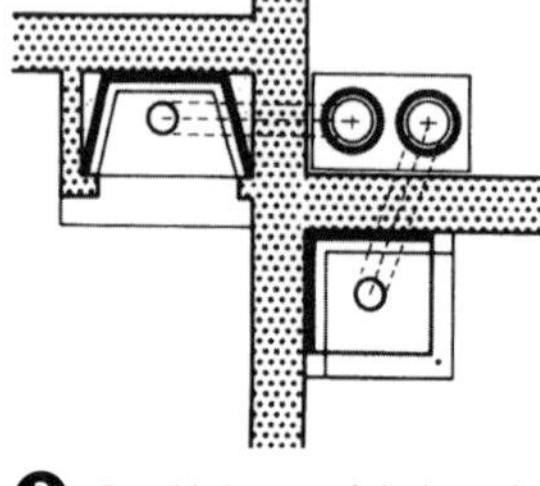

❷ Possible layouts of single-sided open fireplaces

❸ Possible layouts of single- and two-sided open fireplaces

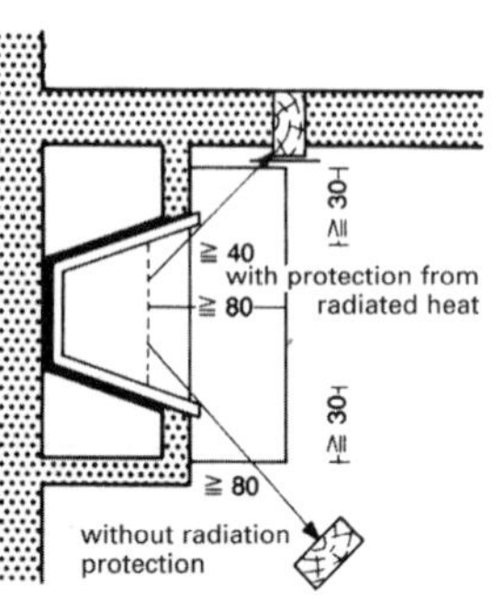

❹ Distance between combustion chamber opening and building components of combustible materials

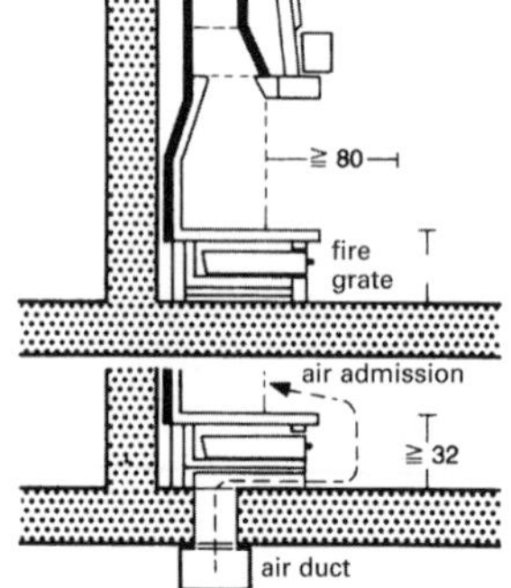

❺ Protection of combustible floor from combustion chamber/air supply

Open fireplaces must be structurally stable and made of **non-combustible building materials**. They can be built of fireclay blocks or slabs, bricks or blocks suitable for chimney construction, fireproof concrete or grey cast iron. Smoke hoods can be made of steel, brass or copper sheet.

Each fireplace must be connected to its **own chimney** with a cross-section suitable for the fire → ❷ – ❸. Fireplace and chimney should be built next to each other. The **effective chimney height** from smoke flue connection to chimney top ≧4.5 m. The flue pipe is connected to the chimney at an angle of 45° → ❻ – ❽.

Open fireplaces must not be installed in rooms of less than 12 m² floor area. Sufficient air supply must be ensured: **air ducts**, which introduce air near to the combustion chamber opening (e.g. installed under the fireplace), are suitable → ❺. There must be at least **80 cm clear space** from the combustion chamber (to the front, sides and upwards) to combustible building components and objects → ❹ – ❺.

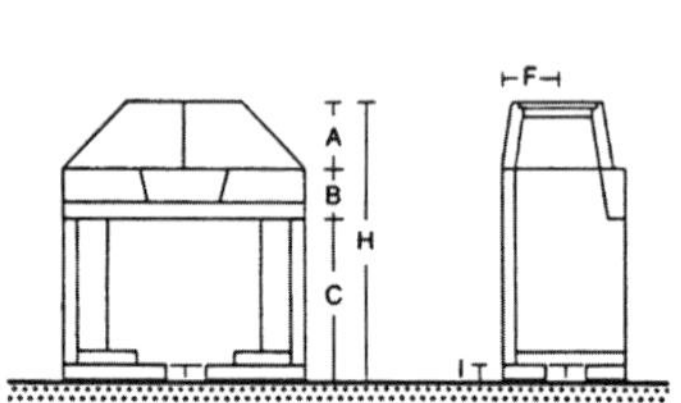

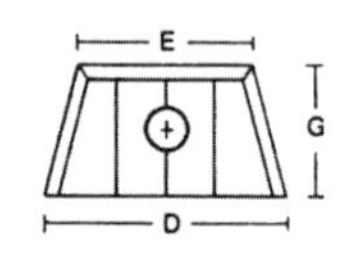

Type		Single-sided open					Two-sided open			Three-sided open		
		1	2	3	4	5	6	7	8	9	10	11
room area approx. (m²)		small rooms	16–22	22–30	30–35	33–40	25–35	35–45	over 48	35–45	45–55	over 55
room volume approx. (m³)		small rooms	40–60	60–90	90–105	105–120	90–105	105–150	over 150	105–150	150–150	over 200
size of fire opening (cm²)		2750	3650	4550	5750	7100	5000	6900	9500	7200	9800	13500
clear dimensions of fire opening (cm)		60/46	70/52	80/58	90/64	100/71						
diameter of flue pipe (cm)		20	22	25	30	30	25	30	35	25	30	35
dimensions (cm)	A	22.5	24	25.5	28	30	30	30	30	30	30	30
	B	13.5	15	15	21	21	—	—	—	—	—	—
	C	52	58	64	71	78	50	58	65	50	58	65
	D	72	84	94	105	115	77	—	108	77	90	114
	E	50	60	65	76	93	77	90	108	77	90	114
	F	19.5	19.5	22.5	26	26	27.5	30	32.5	27.5	30	32.5
	G	42	47	51	55	59	64	71	82	64	71	82
	H	88	97	104.5	120	129	80	88	95	80	88	95
	I	6	6	6	7	7	6.4	6.4	6.4	6.4	6.4	—
weight (kg)		165	80	310	385	470	225	300	405	190	255	360

❽ Open fireplaces: dimensions

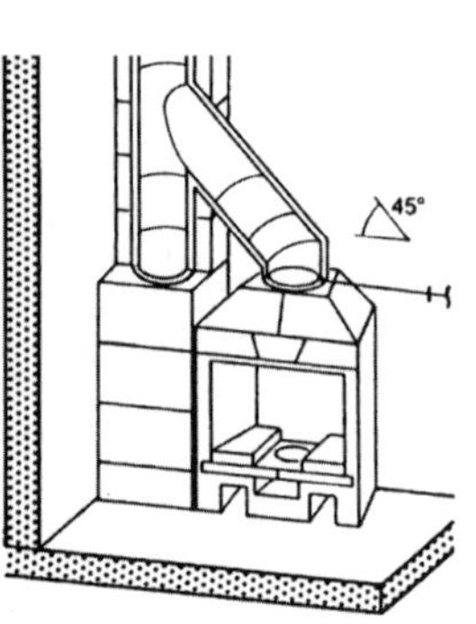

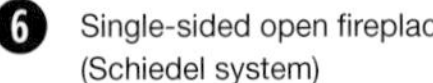

❻ Single-sided open fireplace (Schiedel system)

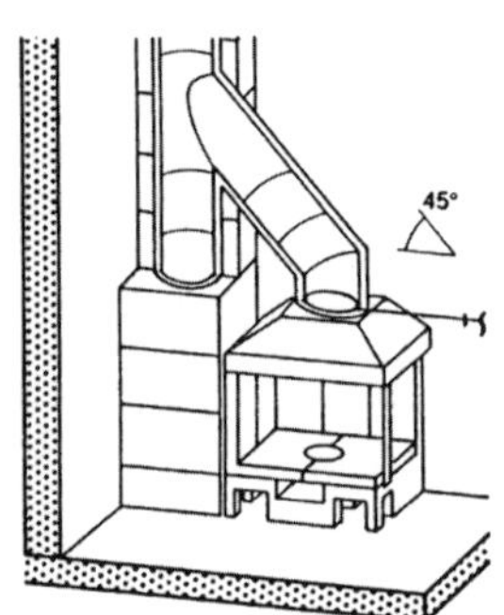

❼ Fireplace open on two sides

❾ Fireplace open on two sides

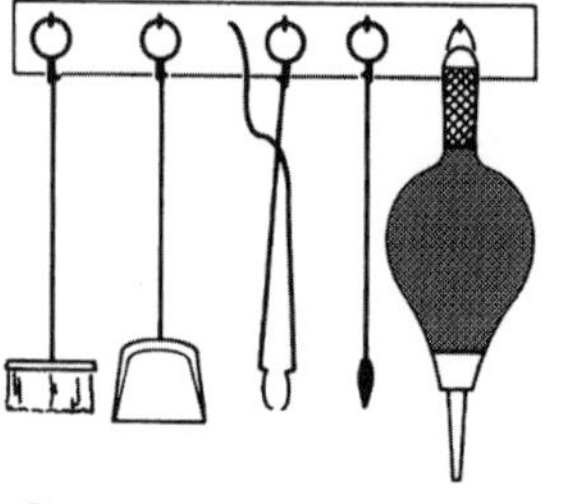

❿ Fireplace tools

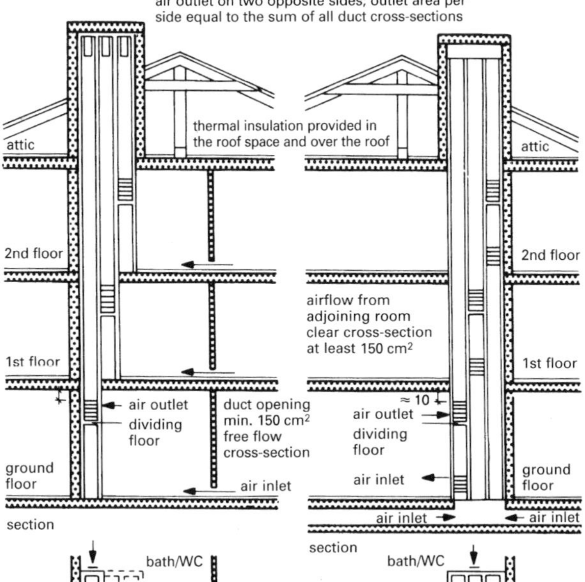

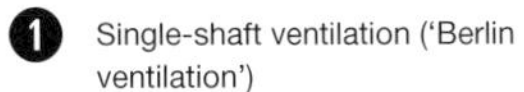

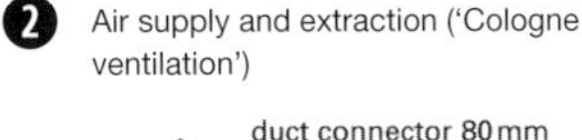

1 Single-shaft ventilation ('Berlin ventilation')

2 Air supply and extraction ('Cologne ventilation')

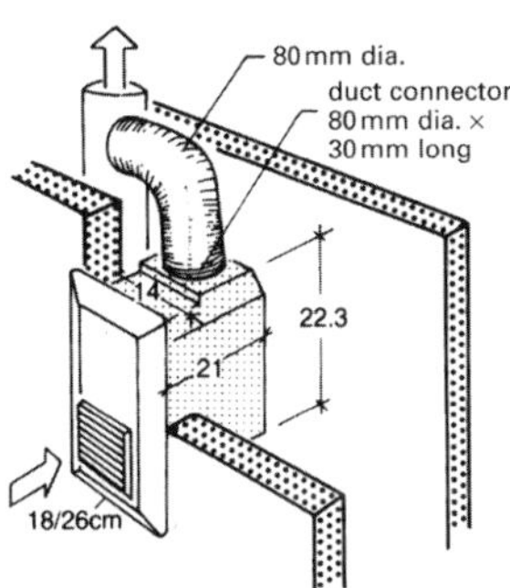

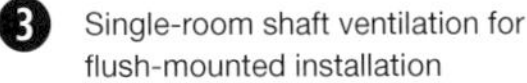

3 Single-room shaft ventilation for flush-mounted installation

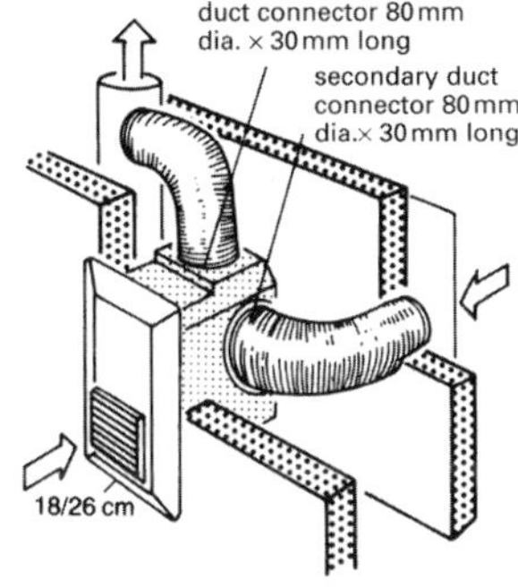

4 Two-room shaft ventilation for flush-mounted installation

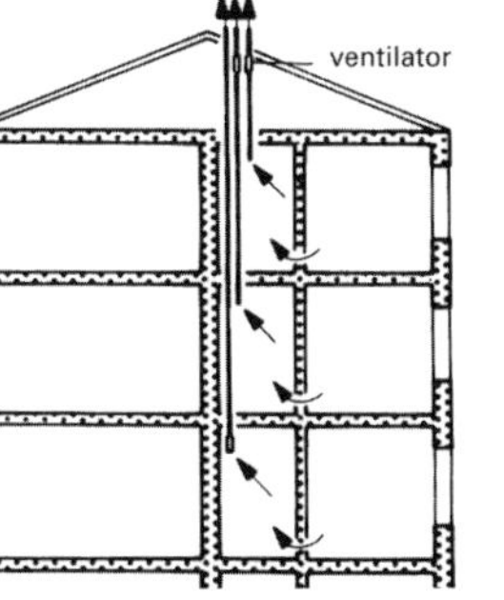

5 Central extraction system with waste air exhaust above roof

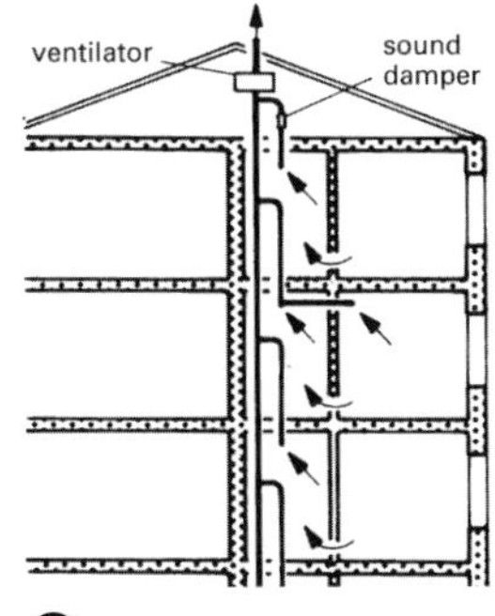

6 Central extraction system with main duct and branch ducts

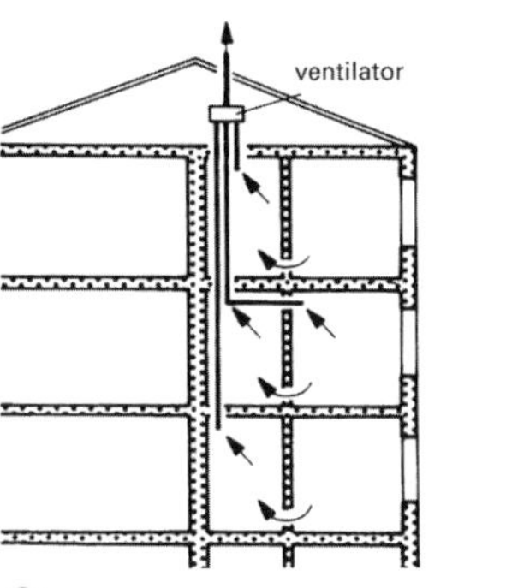

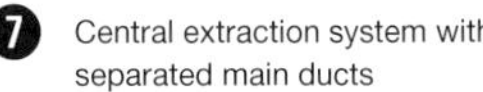

7 Central extraction system with separated main ducts

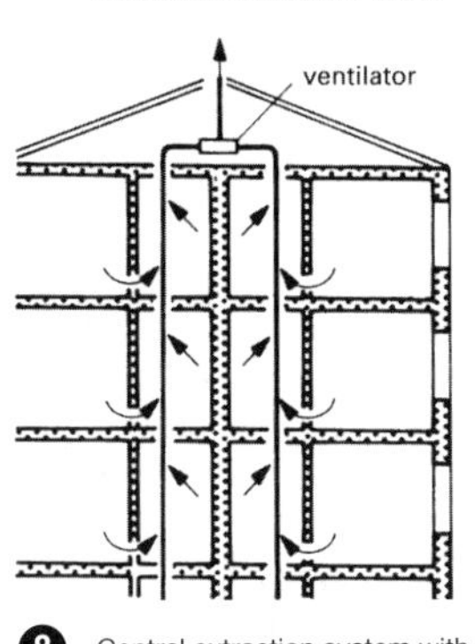

8 Central extraction system with a number of main ducts

Internal bathrooms and toilets must have air supplied and extracted through shafts or ducts. Traditionally, such shafts were built similarly to chimneys, but today they are more often installed in services shafts as part of the services.

Ventilation systems without fans

Masonry ventilation shafts without fans → **1** – **2** are practically maintenance-free but take up a lot of space. Their function (**thermal up-draught**) is highly dependent on the climatic conditions at the time and can often be deficient during high-pressure weather conditions. Because of the sound transfer and heat losses, ventilation systems without fans are now considered out of date and will therefore be found only in older buildings.

A shaft is provided for each room with an extension above the roof, in accordance with the regulations for chimney tops (→ p. 537), and a minimum cross-section of 140 cm². An air supply duct from the open air must be installed at the lower end of the shaft.

Clear cross-section of main shaft (m²)	Permissible no. side shaft connections for effective total height of			Internal dimensions	
	Up to 10 m	10–15 m	Over 15 m	Main shaft (cm)	Side shaft (cm)
340	5	6	7	20 × 17	9 × 17
400	6	7	8	20 × 20	12 × 20
500	8	9	10	25 × 20	12 × 20
340	5	6	7	20 × 17	2 × 9 /17
400	6	7	8	20 × 20	2 × 12/20
500	8	9	10	25 × 20	2 × 12 × 20
340	5	6	7	2 × 20/17	9 × 17
400	6	7	8	2 × 20/20	12 × 20
500	8	9	10	2 × 25/20	12 × 20

9 Dimensions for collector shaft ventilation with thermal up-draught

Ventilation systems with fans

For the on-demand ventilation of sanitary facilities in residential and commercial buildings like schools, hotels, pubs etc., to ventilate one or more rooms with one shaft → **3** – **4**. Extraction systems should be designed for at least 4 air changes per hour in the rooms. A sufficient flow of air for bathrooms, including those with WC, is 60 m³/h and for toilets per WC 30 m³/h. Each internal room to be ventilated must also have an air supply opening, which cannot be closed, with a cross-section of 10 cm² per m³ room volume. The air leakage of the door can be assumed to be 25 cm².

In bathrooms, a minimum temperature of 22°C must be maintained during operation of the fan. Airflow speeds in occupied zone ≧0.2 m/s. The air should be extracted into the open air, or for single extraction systems into permanently well-ventilated roof spaces. Each single extraction system must have its own main riser duct. Central extraction systems have common extract ducts for a number of occupied areas → **6**.

Fire protection

According to building regulations, ventilation ducts including cladding and insulation must be of non-combustible materials. Ventilation systems in buildings of more than two full storeys or more than two residential units or systems, which cross fire compartments, must be constructed so that fire and smoke cannot be carried into other storeys or fire compartments.

Abbr.	Journal title	Published
A+D	= Architecture + Detail	Stuttgart
AF	= Architectural Forum	prev. New York
AIT	= Architektur Innenarchitektur Techn. Ausbau, until 1979 Architektur und Wohnwelt	Leinfelden-Echterdingen
AJ	= Architectural Review	London
AR	= Architectural Record	New York
ArK	= Arkitekten	Helsinki
AW	= Architektur und Wohnform	prev. Stuttgart
AWW	= Architektur und Wohnwelt	prev. Stuttgart
B	= Bau	prev. Saarbrücken
bba	= Bau – Beratung – Architektur	Leinfelden-Echterdingen
Bau	= Baugewerbe	Cologne
BBauBl	= Bundesbaublatt	Gütersloh
Bg	= Baugilde	prev. Berlin
Beton	= Betonfachzeitschrift für Bau + Technik	Erkrath
BIT	= Business × Information × Technology	prev. Leinfelden-Echterdingen
Bm	= Baumeister	Munich
Bw	= Bauwelt	Berlin
Bz	= Das Bauzentrum	Darmstadt
Cu	= Die Küche (L'ambiente Cucina)	Milan
DA	= Der Architekt (BDA)	Berlin
DAB	= Deutsches Architektenblatt	Esslingen
db	= Deutsche Bauzeitung	Leinfelden-Echterdingen
DBZ	= Deutsche Bauzeitschrift	Gütersloh
Detail	= Architektur und Baudetail	Munich
d-extrakt	= Informationsdienst für neuzeitliches Bauen	prev. Bonn
EGH	= Informationsdienst Holz	Bonn
Gf	= Glasform	prev. Schorndorf
GI	= Gesundheitsingenieur	Munich
Häuser	= Magazin für Internationales Wohnen	Hamburg
Il Bagno	= Das Bad	Milan
In	= Interiors	prev. New York
Licht	= Planung-Design-Technik-Handel	Munich
MB	= Moderne Bauformen	prev. Stuttgart
SBF	= Sport + Bäder + Freizeit-Bauten	Düsseldorf
SHE	= Stein – Holz – Eisen	prev. Munich
TAB	= Technik am Bau	Gütersloh
VDI	= V.D.I. Zeitschrift	Düsseldorf
WA	= Wettbewerbe Aktuell	Freiburg/Breisgau
WMB	= Wasmuths Monatshefte für Baukunst und Städtebau	prev. Berlin
ZB	= Zentralblatt der Bauverwaltung	prev. Berlin
ZI	= Zentralblatt für Industriebau	prev. Hannover

REFERENCES

Page	Author(s)	Title	Publisher, place, date
12–13	Schneider, H. J.	Handbuch – Sanitärtechnik	Vogel, Würzburg, 1979
17	Hebgen	Sicheres Haus	Vieweg, Wiesbaden, 1980
18	Dt. Verein des Gas-und Wasserfaches e.V. Eschborn	Techn. Regeln für Gas-Installation	DVGW-TRGI, 1986
	Flotow, P. v., Leiermann, H.	Gas-Installationsdetails	Ruhrgas AG, Essen, 1990
21–22	D.P. Philippen	Bauen für Behinderte	DBZ 6/86, 9/87
	Kuldschun, H.	Bauen für Behinderte	Der Architekt 1/81
27	Dürer, A.	4 Bücher von menschlichen Proportionen	Nuremberg, 1528
	Le Corbusier	Der Modulor	Paris, 1953
	Mössel, E.	Die Proportionen in Antike.	Munich, 1926
	Zeising, A. v.	Pentagramm, Deutsche Vierteljahresschrift	Stuttgart, 1868
		Neue Lehre von den Proportionen des menschlichen Körpers aus einem bisher unbekannt gebliebenen, die Natur und Kunst durchdringenden morphologischen Gesetz	Leipzig, 1854
	Bochenek, J.	Canon aller menschlichen Gestalten und Tiere	Berlin, 1885
	Boesinger, W.	Le Corbusier, oeuvre complète 1938–1946 (Le Modulor)	Zürich, 1946
26–29	Jones, V.	Neufert. Architects' Data	Collins, London, 1980
30–33	Freckmann, K.	Proportionen in der Architektur	Munich, 1965
	Scholefield, P.H.	The theory of proportion in Architecture	Cambridge, 1958
	Thiersch, H.	Als Architekt und Forscher	Munich, 1923
	Wolf, O.	Tempelmaße	Vienna, 1932
	Boesianer, W.	Le Corbusier, oeuvre complète 1938–1946 (Le Modulor, p. 170ff.)	Zürich, 1946
	Portmann, D.	Componentiertes Bauen	DBZ 11/83
34–35	Boemke, K.	Die Anwendung der Modulordnung	DBZ 7/79
	Kerschkamp, Portmann	Erläuterung zu DIN 18000 'Modulordnung im Bauwesen'	Beuth Verlag GmbH, Berlin, 5/84
36–38	RWE	RWE Handbuch, Techn. Ausbau	Energie Vlg., Heidelberg, 1995
	Frank, W.	Raumklima und thermische Behaglichkeit	Ernst + Sohn, Düsseldorf,
		Berichte aus der Bauforschung	Issue 104, 1975
	Grandjean, Etienne	Wohnphysiologie — Kap. 6 Raumklima	Architektur-Vlg., Artemis, Zürich, 1973
	Fuchs, Günther	Kleine Raumklimatologie	Private press, 1970
	Eisenschink, Alfred	Falsch Geheizt ist Halb Gestorben	Resch, 3rd ed., 1989
	Lutz + Jenisch + Klopfe + Freymuth + Krampf	Lehrbuch der Bauphysik	Teubner, Stuttgart, 1985
	Krusche + Althaus + Gabriel	Ökologisches Bauen	Bauverlag, Wiesbaden, 1982
	Arwed, Tomm	Ökologisch Planen und Bauen	Vieweg, Wiesbaden, 1994
	Buss, Harald	Aktuelles Tabellenhandbuch Feuchte, Wärme, Schall	Weka Vlg., Kissing, 1987
	Dürer, A.	Buch der Messungen	Arnheim, 1640
	Ottel, R.	Baubiologische Standortfaktoren	DBZ 4/80
	Beton-Verlag	Wohnen in Betonbauten	Beton-Verlag, Düsseldorf, 1976
	—	Luftelektrische Felder in umbauten Räumen und im Freien	Beton-Verlag, Düsseldorf, 1975
	—	Weitere Untersuchungen über luftelektrische Felder in Gebäuden	Beton-Verlag, Düsseldorf, 1978
	Inform, Zentrum Bonn	Machen Baustoffe krank?	Cologne, 1975
	Reiter, R.	Luftel. Raumklima	Fraunhofer Gesellschaft, Garmisch Partenkirchen
	Lotz, K.E.	Willst du gesund wohnen?	Biberach, 1975
	Palm, H.	Das gesunde Haus	Dettingen, 1975
	Endrös, R.	Das gestörte Strahlungsfeld über Grundwasserströmungen	Eberbach, 1970
38	BfS – Bundesamt für Strahlenschutz	Elektromagnetische Felder	Salzgitter: www.bfs.de/elektro, 2008
	Kleinmachnow, H.	Schutz vor niederfrequenten elektrischen und magnetischen Feldern der Energieversorgung und — anwendung.	SSK Berichte der Strahlenschutz-kommission (SSK), Issue 7, 1997.
40	Neufert, E.	Bauordnungslehre	Hoffmann Fachverlag, Ullstein, Berlin, 1961
	Moessel, E.	Die Proportion in Antike und Mittelalter. Urformen des Raumes als Grundlagen der Formgestaltung	Munich, 1926
	Fischer, Th.	Zwei Vorträge über Proportionen	Berlin, 1934
	Boehm, O.	Von geheimnisvollen Maßen, Zahlen und Zeichen	Leipzig, 1929
	Le Corbusier	Der Modulor	Stuttgart, 1953
	Rösel	Stichwort AVA, Bd. 1, Verfahren	Bauverlag GmbH, Wiesbaden/Berlin, 1986
	Franke, Portz	Handbuch für die Baupraxis	Werner Verlag, Düsseldorf, 1985
	Gaeb	Anwenderhandbuch	Beuth Verlag GmbH, Berlin/Cologne, 1985
	Schwarz	Daten und Informationsverarbeitung in Planung und Steuerung von Bauprojekten	Ernst & Sohn, Berlin, 1988
	Aita, Veit, Schilchegger	Planungs- und Bauablauf – die Steuerung bauwirtschaftlicher und baubetrieblicher Prozesse	Springer Verlag, Vienna, 1976

REFERENCES

Page	Author(s)	Title	Publisher, place, date
	Rösel	Baumanagement, Grundlagen, Technik, Praxis	Springer Verlag, Vienna, 1976
	Neufert, Rösel	Bauzeitplanung	Bauverlag, Wiesbaden, 1974
		Standardleistungsbücher für das Bauwesen	Beuth Verlag GmbH, Berlin, 1989
46	Bundesamt für Bauwesen und Raumordnung (ed.)	Leitfaden Nachhaltiges Bauen.	Bundesamt für Bauwesen und Raumordnung, Berlin, 2001
57	Boisserée, Dominik, Mantscheff, Jack	Baubetriebslehre 1. Neuwied	Werner, 2004
58	—	HOAI. Fee Regulations for Architects and Engineers	DTV, Munich, 2003
65	Neddermann, Rolf:	Die Kosten im Griff	DAB 12(2003)/01(2004)
66–72	Grundbau	Teubner, Stuttgart, 1994	
	Freihart, G.	Einfluß der Baugrundelastizität	DBZ 7/59
	Muhs, H.	Die Lagerungsdichte des Untergrunds als Voraussetzung für die Gründung des Bauwerks	Berlin, 1959
	Wendehorst, Muth	Erd- und Grundbau	Teubner, Stuttgart
	Muth	Dränung erdberührter Bauteile	Eigenverlag Muth, Karlsruhe
	—	DIN 18195-1, Table 1	Beuth Verlag, Berlin
74	—	DIN 1053-1, Table 1	Beuth Verlag, Berlin
77	—	DIN 1053-1, Table 10	Beuth Verlag, Berlin
82	Kind-Barkansas, Friedbert	Beton-Atlas	Birkhäuser, Basel, 2003
	Association of the German Cement Industry. Bayer, Edwin (ed.)	Parkhäuser – aber Richtig, 2nd ed.	Verlag Bau + Technik, Düsseldorf, 2000
83–84	Rau, O., Braune, V.	Der Altbau	A. Koch, Leinfelden, 1985
	Hebel AG	Handbuch Wohnbau	Emmering-Forstenfeldbruck
	Unipor-Ziegel	Ziegeldecken	Munich
	Arbeitsgemeinschaft Holz e.V.	Dielenböden	Düsseldorf 1998
	Arbeitsgemeinschaft Holz e.V.	Neuer Wohnwert mit Holz	Düsseldorf 1996
	Schwerm, D., Laurini, G.	Deckensysteme aus Betonfertigteilen	Bonn 1997
86–87	Fonrobert, F.	Grundzüge des Holzbaues im Hochbau	Berlin, 1948
	Führer, W.	Holzkonstruktion	DBZ 3/78
	Hempel, G.	Freigespannte Holzbinder	Herrenalp
	—	100 Knotenpunkte	Herrenalp, 1949
	Kress, F.	Der praktische Zimmerer	Ravensburg, 1940
	Kullmann, H.	Holz im Bauwesen	DBZ 10/63, 1/64
	Stoy, W.	Der Holzbau	Berlin, 1941
	Willie, F.	Statische. . . Kehlbalkendaches	DBZ 12/54, 3/55
88–92	A.C.D.A	Copper Roofing	London, 1959
	Deutsches Kupfer Institut	Kupfer Dachdeckung	Berlin, 1956
	Fritz Röbbert	Kupfer, Planen, Gestalten, Verarbeiten	KM, Osnabrück, 1999
	Fingerhut, P.	Altdeutsche Schieferdeckung	Bochum, 1959
	—	Dächer, Dachdeckungen	DBZ 12/65
	VDD	Anschlüsse, Abschlüsse, Durchdringungen und Dehnungsfugen bei bituminösen Dachdichtungen	Frankfurt/M., 1979
	Flotow, P. v.	Dachdetails (Metalldächer)	Stuttgart, 1964
	Halsband, G.	Dachdeckung auf verz. Stahlblech	DBZ 12/54
	Langer, A.	Flachdächer	DBZ 3/68
	Liersch, W.	Konstruktive Hinweise zum geneigten Dach	DAB 2/79
93–95	Dt. Dachgärtnerverband e.V.	Grüne Dächer – Gesunde Dächer – Dachgärtnerrichtlinien	Baden-Baden, 1985
	Leca Deutschland GmbH	Company information	Halstenbeck
	re-natur GmbH	Company information	Ruhwinkel-Wankendorf
96–103	Meyer-Bohe,t W.	Sonnenschutz	DBZ 7/87
	Houghton E. L.	Wind Forces on Buildings and Structures	New York, 1976
	Tutt, P. + Adler, D.	Window Cleaning, New Metric Handbook	Butterworth Arch., London, 1979
105	—	EnEV Energiesparverordnung.	Bundesgesetzblatt, Bonn, 2007
113–114	Reitmayer, U.	Holztüren und Holztore	J. Hofmann, Stuttgart, 1979
118–119	Adarma	Gebäude- und Geländesicherung	Munich, 1979
	Hebgen, H.	Sicheres Haus	Vieweg, Braunschweig, 1980
	Bielmeyer, Riehle	Planung von Türen und Toren	DAB 4/86
121	—	Treppenarten	DAB 6/86
126	Meyer-Bohe, W.	Transportsysteme im Hochbau	DBZ 9/84
135–138	Prinz, D.	Städtebau	Kohlhammer, Stuttgart, 1987
	—	UN Studio c: Möbius Haus	Arch + 146 1999
	Bott, Helmut, von Haas, Volker	Verdichteter Wohnungsbau	Kohlhammer, Stuttgart, 1996, p. 44
140	Ludes, M.	Häuser mit Gangerschließung	DBZ 9/78
	Schneider, Friederike (ed.)	Grundrissatlas Wohnungsbau.	Birkhäuser, Basel, 1997
141	—	Terrassenhäuser	DBZ 2/68
146–166	Arbeitsgemeinschaft	Die moderne Küche e.V.	Darmstadt
	RWE Energie	Bauhandbuch technischer Ausbau	Energie Verlag, Heidelberg, 1995
	Neufert, P. + Neff, L.	Gestaltung, Haus Wohnung Garten	Vieweg, Wiesbaden, 1995
	—	Techn. Leitfaden Glas am Bau	Vegla GmbH, Aachen
168	—	Altenwohnungen in Bremen	DBZ 9/88
171–173	Knirsch J.	Hotels planen u. gestalten	A. Koch, Leinfelden-Echterdingen, 1993

Page	Author(s)	Title	Publisher, place, date
175	Hepperle, H. A.	Bauten für die Gastronomie	DAB 9/86, DAB 10/86
178–180	Loeschcke, G., Höfs, J.	Großküchen	Bauverlag, Wiesbaden u. Berlin, 1985
	Fuhrmann, P.	Restaurantküchen	DBZ 9/89
	Neufert	Architects' Data	Blackwell Scientific Publications, London, 1985
188	—	Kindertagesstätte	DBZ 2/76
	Gralle, Horst	Port Christian: Bauten für Kinder: ein Leitfaden zur Kindergartenplanung	Kohlhammer, Stuttgart, 2002
190	Land NRW	Spielen	Düsseldorf, 1985
191–196	Maass, J.	Institut für Schulbau RWTH	Aachen
	Heinze GmbH	Schulen	Celle
	—	Excerpt from Parts B and C of the announcement of Saxony's Ministry of State for Education for school building in Saxony	15 Dec 1993, SMK 18/93 (pp. 437 ff.); amended 1 Aug 1995, SMK 11 (pp. 294 ff.)
198–202	—	Hochschulen	DBZ 1/68, 7/72, 6/76, 5/78
	—	Mensa-Bauten	DBZ 10/80
203–206	—	Laboratorium	DBZ 5/73, 10/76
207–208	Rosenfield, J.	Light in museum planning. — Mit Angaben über die Bostoner Versuche und die von S. H. Seager	
	Stein, C. S.	Making Museums Function	
209–218	—	Bühnentechnische Rundschau, Ztsch. für Technik, Bühnenbau und -gestaltung in Theatern, Film, Fernsehen und Mehrzweckhallen	Orell Füssli + Friedrich, CH-Zürich
	Kranich, Fr.	Bühnentechnik der Gegenwart Bd. 1 und 2	Munich/Berlin, 1929/1933
	Schubert, H.	Moderner Theaterbau	Stuttgart, 1971
	Ruhnau, W.	Versammlungsstätten	Gütersloh, 1969
	Graubner, G.	Theaterbau – Aufgabe und Planung	Munich, 1968
	Semper, M.	Theater, Handbuch der Architektur, Part 4	Stuttgart, 1904
	Institut für Kulturbauten	Rekonstruktion von Theatern	Berlin (E), 1979
	Cremer, L. + Müller, H.	Die wissenschaftlichen Grundlagen der Raumakustik, vol. 1	Stuttgart, 1978
	Unruh, W.	Theatertechnik	Berlin, 1969
	Baumgartner, R.	Versammlungsstätten und Geschäftshäuser	Munich, 1986
	Brauneck, M. + Schneilin, G.	Theaterlexikon	Rowohlt Taschenbuch, Hamburg, 1986
	Izenour, G.	Theater Design	New York, 1977
219	Skoda, Rudolf Huss	Die Leipziger Gewandhausbauten	Medien GmbH, Verlag Bauwesen, Berlin, 2001
221	Kuttruff, Heinrich	Akustik. Eine Einführung	S. Hirzel Verlag, Stuttgart, 2004
	Hall, Donald E.	Musikalische Akustik.	Schott Musik International, Mainz, 1997
222–223	—	Versammlungsstättenverordnung – VStättVO	Bundesländer
228–230	Sansman, Karen	Zoological Park and Aquarium Fundamentals	American Association of Zoological Parks and Aquariums, Weelin (W.Va), 1982
	Schomberg, Geoffrey	General Principles of Zoo Design	Intra Consultants Ldt., London, 1972
231–243	Puell, Richard	Die Dritte Alternative?	Bauwelt 6/91
	Joedicke, Jürgen	Bürobauten	Stuttgart, 1962
	Sieverts, Ernst	Bürohaus- und Verwaltungsbau	Stuttgart, 1980, Baumeister 10/1985
	—	Tendenz heute: Vom Großraum zum Individualraum	Baumeister 10/1985
	Henkel, AG	Seminarbericht vom 21. Apr. 1989, 'Bürosanierung in der Praxis'	1989
	Gottschalk, Ottomar	Verwaltungsbau für die 90er Jahre	DBZ 3/89
	Sieverts, Ernst	Probleme der Reversibilität	Der Architekt 10/1978
	Gottschalk, Ottomar	Neue Kriterien fr Verwaltungsgebäude	DBZ 12/87, 8/85, 3/89
	Fuchs, Wolfram	Das Kombi-Büro	Bauwelt 6/1991
	Puffert, Maren + Steiner, Bernhard	Acht Prüfungen	Bauwelt 6/1991
	Sieverts, Ernst	Büro der Zukunft	DAB 9/90
	Duffy, Eley, Giffone	ORBIT 2-Study on Organizations, Buildings and Information	Ct., 1986
	DEGI, Deutsche Gesellschaft für Immobilienfonds (ed.)	Neue Perspektiven. Marktreport	2004
	Worthington	Technology Northwalk	
	van der Rohe, Ludwig Mies	Zeitschrift G	Berlin, 1923
	Kahl, Eberhard	Gebäudestrukturen des Bürobaues	DBZ 3/85
	Ehrke, Rainer	Natürlich klimatisieren	DBZ 9/90
	Reuter, Fritz	Luft- und Lichttechnik	Industriebau 4/80
	Ahrens, Günther	Das Bürogebäude im Wandel	DBZ 4/89
	Sieverts, Ernst	Aktueller Stand der Planung von Büroarbeitsplätzen	DAB 9/90
	Schulz, Peter:	Schallschutz, Wärmeschutz, Feuchteschutz, Brandschutz im Innenausbau	Deutsche Verlagsanstalt, Stuttgart, 2004
	Volpert, Walter	Psychologie des EDV-Arbeitsplatzes	VFA Profil, 9/1990
	—	Wolkenkratzer in den USA	Baumeister 2/1984
	Hascher, Rainer (ed.).	Entwurfsatlas Bürobau	Birkhäuser, Berlin, 2002
	Fuhrmann, Peter	Aufzugsanlagen	DBZ 9/87
244–246	Palesch, Siegfried	Die Entwicklung des Hochhauses und das John Hancock Center Chicago	Architektur + Wettbewerbe 113/1983
	Grube, Oswald W.	Himmelhoch konstruieren, Werk	Bauen + Wohnen 9/87
	Schirmer, Wolf (ed.)	Egon Eiermann 1904–1970, Bauten und Projekte	DVA, Stuttgart, 1984
	Carl Gerber GmbH (ed.)	Entscheidung zur Form	modulverlag GmbH, 1973
	Beratungsstelle f. Stahlver wendung (ed.)	Stahl und Form — Egon Eiermann	Atelier Kinold, 1974
	J. Knirsch	Büroräume, Bürohäuser	A. Koch, Leinfelden-Echterdingen, 1996

REFERENCES

Page	Author(s)	Title	Publisher, place, date
247–252	Schweigler, P.	Einrichtung und techn. Ausstattung von Bibliotheken	Reichert, Wiesbaden, 1977
	Höfler + Kandel	Hochschulbibliotheken	Sauer, Munich, 1984
	Banghard, A.	Gebäudeanalysen zur Funktionskontrolle	Berlin, 1986
	Arbeitsgruppe Bibliotheksplan Baden-Württemberg	Gesamtplan für das wissenschaftliche Bibliothekswesen	Munich, 1973
	Fuhlrott, R. + Jopp, K.	DIN Fachbericht 13	Beuth Verlag GmbH, Berlin, 1988
	Henning, Wolfram	Bibliotheksbau in Deutschland von 1973–1980	Gütersloh, 1980
		Bilbliotheksbau in der Bundesrepublik Deutschland 1968–1983	Klostermann, Frankfurt/M., 1983
		Bibliotheken '93. Strukturen – Aufgaben – Positionen	Deutsches Bibliotheksinstitut, Berlin, 1994
		Bibliotheksbau: Kompendium zum Planungs- und Bauprozeß	Deutsches Bibliotheksinstitut, Berlin, 1994
	Metcalf, Keyes D.	Planning Academic and Research Library Buildings. 2nd ed.	ALA, Chicago, London, 1985
	Ramcke, R.	Die Präsentation der öffentl. Bibliothek 2 'Die Kinderbibliothek'	Berlin, 1982
	—	Die Präsentation der öffentl. Bibliothek 3 'Architektur und Ausstattung'	Berlin, 1982
	Thompson, G.	Planning and Design of Library Buildings	London/New York, 1977
263–267	Ackermann, Kurt	Industriebau	Stuttgart, 1984
	Aggeteleky, Bèla	Fabrikplanung	Munich, 1970
	Auggeteleky, Bèla	Systemtechnik in der Fabrikplanung	Munich, 1973
	Aggeteleky, Bèla	Fabrikplanung vol. 1	Munich, 1987
	Dolezalek, C. M. + Warnecke, H. J.	Planung von Fabrikanlagen	Berlin, 1981
	Henn, Walter	Industriebau vol. 1	Munich, 1961
	Henn, Walter	Industriebau vol. 3	Munich, 1966
	Henn, Walter	Industriebau vol. 4	Munich, 1962
	Neufert, Ernst	Industriebauten	Bauverlag, Wiesbaden, 1973 Vincentz Verlag, Hannover, 1973
	Schmalor, Rolf	Industriebauplanung	Düsseldorf, 1971
	Schramm, W.	Lager und Speicher	Wiesbaden, 1965
	Sommer + Degenhard	Industriebauten gestalten	Vienna, 1989
	Weller, Konrad	Industrielles Bauen vol. 1	Stuttgart, 1986
	Weller, Konrad	Industrielles Bauen vol. 2	Stuttgart, 1989
	Wildemann, Horst (ed.)	Fabrikplanung	Frankfurt, 1989
268–269	—	Verband für Lagertechnik und Betriebsführung	Hagen
	Führer, Hansjakob, Störmer, Dorothea	Industriebau, Grundlagen 1.	Das Beispiel, Darmstadt,1999, p.161
270–273	Sage, K.	Handbuch der Haustechnik	Gütersloh, 1971
274–280	Landesgewerbeamt Baden-Württemberg	Planungshilfen	Stuttgart, 1981
	VAG	Planungsbeispiele	Wolfsburg
	Rühl, G. + Hantsch, G. + Heitz, F.	Planung und Einrichtung von Karosseriereparaturbetrieben	Karlsruhe, 1982
	Dt. Handwerksinst., Munich	Planung und Einrichtung von Kraftfahrzeugbetrieben	Schorndorf, 1981
281–282	Firma Miele	Wäscherei/Waschanlagen	Gütersloh
283–284	—	Feuerwehrgerätehaus	DBZ 10/74
	Ackermann, K.	Feuerwache 4 Munich	DBZ 10/74
287	Beratungsausschuß für das Dt. Glockenwesen	Ratschläge zur Verbesserung der Schallabstrahlung aus Glockentürmen	1973
	Beratungsausschuß für das Dt. Glockenwesen	Ratschläge für die Gestaltung von Glockentümen	1964
288	Schwarz, H.P.	Die Architektur der Synagoge	Dt. Architekturmuseum, Frankfurt, 1988
289	—	Islamisches Kulturzentrum	AF, p. 600/1932
299–317	—	Krankenhausbau	Baumeister 10/93
	Krankenhausbauverordnung	Verordnung über den Bau und Betrieb von Krankenhäusern – KhBauVo	1978
	—	Krankenhaus	Baumeister 10/93
	—	Krankenhausbau	Medita 4/74
	Suter + Suter	Krankenhaus- und Gesundheitswesen Krankenhaus	Baumeister 10/93
	Roesmer + Labryga + Wischer	Internationales Krankenhaussymposium	1983
	Deilmann, H.	Allgemeinkrankenhaus, Grundlagen	
	—	Krankenhaus	Das Krankenhaus 4/95
	—	Krankenhaus	Wettbewerbe Aktuell 12/93
	Eichhorn + Stahl + Vanessen	Speisenverteilung in Krankenhäusern, Wärmewagensystem und Tablettsystem	1968
318	Idelberger, K.	Tribünen	DBZ 5/78
319–326	Bundesinstitut für Sport-wissenschaften	Sportplätze	Cologne, 1982

Page	Author(s)	Title	Publisher, place, date
327–328	Dt. Tennisbund e.V. — DTB	Tennisanlagen Planung, Bau, Unterhaltug	Hannover, 1981
329–330	Dt. Bahnen-Golf-Verband e.V.	Handbuch	Vienna, 1986
331–332	Bundesinstitut für Sportwissenschaften	Planung, Bau, Unterhaltung von Golfplätzen	Cologne, 1987
333–348	Stange, W.	Sportbauten	Berlin, 1982
	—	Jachthäfen Planungsgrundlagen	DBZ 12/68
	—	Jachthafen	DBZ 12/70
	Schröter, B.	Marinas – Jachthäfen	DBZ 11/73
	Heard, J. + H.	Handbook of Sports and Recreational Building Design	London
	Haass, H.	Wassersportanlagen	DBZ 5/88
	Haass, H.	Planungsgrundlagen für Segel- und Surfsportanlagen	Sportstättenbau + Bäderanlagen 4/1985
	Haass, H.	Der Wassersportentwicklungsplan als Instrument der Kooperation und Sicherung einer umwelt- und menschengerechten Sportausübung	Sport-, Bäder-, Freizeitbauten, 6/1989
	Haass, H.	Grundlagen zur Planung von Wassersportanlagen — Umwelt-, Objekt- und Detailplanung	Das Garten Amt 11/1989
	Haass, H.	Handbuch für den Segelsport	Aachen, 1993
	Haass, H.	Planungsgrundlagen für Sportboothäfen	Hansa 4/94
	Haass, H.	Neue Nutzung städtischer Uferbereiche und -brachen	DBZ 8/96
	Haass, H. (ed.)	Handlungsrahmen zur Standortplanung von Wassersportanlagen im Spannungsfeld von Nutzerattraktivität, Ökologie und Ökonomie	Münster, 1996
	Overschmidt + Gliewe	Sportbootführerschein Binnen	Klasing, Bielefeld, 1992
339–340	Bundesminister für Verkehr	Richtlinien für Wassersportanlagen an Binnenwasserstraßen	Bonn, 1973
341–342	Schnitzler, U.	Untersuchungen zur Planung von Reitanlagen	KTBL-Bauschrift, 6/1970, Darmstadt
	Schnitzler, U.	Der Bau von Reitanlagen, Forschungsauftrag des ehem. Instituts für Sportstättenbau/DSB	Cologne
	Schnitzler, U.	Reitanlagen-Beispielentwürfe	KTBL-Schriften 162, Darmstadt
	Amtl. Forschungs- und Materialprüfungsanstalt für das Bauwesen, Otto-Graf-Institut der TU Stuttgart	Reitbahnbeläge	TU Stuttgart
	Deutsche Reiterliche Vereinigung e.V.	Orientierungshilfen für den Bau und die Planung von Reitanlagen und Reitwegen	Warendorf, 1993
	TVT	Techn. Vorschriften für Tragschichten der Forschungsgesellschaft für Straßen- u. Verkehrswesen	FGSV, Cologne
	—	Außen- und Hallenbeläge von Reithallen	Bundesinst. f. Sportwissenschaft, Cologne, 1974
	—	Jahresberichte der Dt. Reiterlichen Vereinigung e.V.	Warendorf
	—	Datensammlung Pferdehaltung – Dt. Warmblut	KTBL, 2nd ed., Münster-Hiltrup, 1976
	Pirkelmann + Schäfer + Schulz	Pferdeställe und Pferdehaltung	Ulmer, Stuttgart, 1976
	Marten, J.	Auslaufhaltung – Artgerechte Pferdehaltung	KTBL, Darmstadt
	Marten, J.	Betriebswirtschaftslehre für Reitbetriebe	FN-Vlg., Warendorf
	Zeeb, K. + Krautwig, P. + Huskamp, B. +	Pferde für Turnier und Freizeit, Haltung – Markt – Kauf Kranzbühler, W.O.	DLG-Manuskript, 5/1982
	Zeeb, K. + Schnitzer, U.	Pferdeverhalten und Pferdehaltung, Handbuch für Pferde	Kamlage, Osnabrück
344–345	Deyle	Kombinierte Kunsteisbahnen	DBZ 4/79
	Bundesinstitut für Sportwissenschaften	Planung und Bau Rollsportanlagen	Cologne, 1980
346	Skate Park GmbH	Champion Ramps	Munich
347	Hofmeister, G.	BMX-Motocross mit dem Fahrrad	Schul- und Sportstättenbau 3/87
348–349	Dt. Schützenbund	Schießstandanlagen	Wiesbaden, 1984
350	Bundesinstitut für Sportwissenschaften	Planungsgrundlagen Sporthallen	Cologne, 1988
355	—	Leichtathletikhalle Dortmund	Sb 6/80
	Archiv des Badewesens	Freizeitbad Heveney	Issue 4/87
	Archiv des Badewesens	Freibad Bad Driburg	Issue 2/88
357	DLW Bautechnik	Schwimmbecken-Auskleidungen	Bietigheim-Bissingen
357–358	Kappler, H. P.	Das private Schwimmbad	Bauverlag, Wiesbaden, 1986
368–369	Bundesinstitut für Sportwissenschaften	Orientierungshilfen zur Planung u. Ausstattung von Konditionsund Fitneßräumen	Cologne, 1987
359–360	Deutscher Alpenverein (ed.)	Informationen über Bauweisen von künstlichen Kletteranlagen	Internet: http://www.alpenverein.de (2005)
361	DKB	Dt. Keglerbund – Technische Vorschriften	Augsburg, 1983
362–367	Koordinierungskreis Bäder	Dt. Gesellschaft für das Badewesen e.V. Richtlinien für den Bäderbau	Essen, 1982
370	Neufert, P. + Neff, L.	Gestaltung, Haus Wohnung Garten	Vieweg, Wiesbaden, 1997
373–386	Höckert, Manfred	Sauna – Planung Konstruktion. Ausführung	9th ed.: Bauwesen, Berlin, 2000; 10th ed.: Huss-Medien, Bauwesen, 2003
	Forschungsgesellschaft für Strassen- u. Verkehrswesen (ed.)	ESG 96 Empfehlungen zur Straßenraumgestaltung innerhalb bebauter Gebiete	FGSV Verlag, Cologne,1996
	Forschungsgesellschaft für Strassen- u. Verkehrswesen (ed.)	EAE 85/95. Empfehlung for die Anlage von Erschließungsstraßen	FGSV Verlag, Cologne, 1995
	Forschungsgesellschaft für Strassen- u. Verkehrswesen (ed.)	RAS-Q 96 Richtlinien für die Anlage von Straßen.	FGSV Verlag, Cologne, 1996
	Forschungsgesellschaft für Strassen- u. Verkehrswesen (ed.)	EAHV 93 Empfehlung für die Anlage von Hauptverkehrsstraßen	FGSV Verlag, Cologne,1993

REFERENCES

Page	Author(s)	Title	Publisher, place, date
	Prinz, D.	Städtebau, volumes 1 + 2	Kohlhammer, Stuttgart, 1987
389–401	Forschungsgesellschaft für	EAE 85/95 Empfehlung für die Anlage von Erschließungsstraßen	FGSV, Cologne, 1995
	Straßen- u. Verkehrswesen	EAR 91 Empfehlungen für Anlagen des ruhenden Verkehrs (Neuauflage EAR 05 2005)	FGSV, Cologne, 1991
390, 393, 398	—	Anordnung von Stellplätzen in Gruppen	DBZ 5/82
396	Spies, K.	Garagen Grundlagen für das konstruktive Entwerfen	DAB 2/79
	Temme, F. J.	Be- u. Entlüftung von Tiefgaragen	DBZ 4/86
	—	Vergleich von Stellplätzen u. Parkbauten	DBZ 5/82
400	Forschungsgesellschaft für Straßen- u. Verkehrswesen	Richtlinien für die Anlage von Tankstellen an Straßen RAT	FGSV, Cologne, 1985
403–405	Verband Deutscher Verkehrsunternehmer (VDV) (ed.)	Verkehrserschließung und Verkehrsangebot im ÖPNV	VDV-Schrift No. 4, Cologne
	Fiedler, Joachim	Bahnwesen. Planung, Bau und Betrieb von Eisenbahnen, S- U-, Stadt- und Straßenbahnen	4th ed. Werner Verlag, Düsseldorf, 1999
	Stadt Bochum Tiefbauamt (ed.)	Baulos F1 Lohring	Stadt Bochum Tiefbauamt, Bochum, 1995
407	—	Omnibusbahnhöfe	DBZ 5/78
415	DB Station&Service (ed.)	Handbuch zum Einrichtungssystem ReiseZentre.	DB Services Technische Dienste GmbH, Karlsruhe
417	DB Station&Service (ed.)	Produktkatalog. Ausstattung von Bahnhöfen auf einen Blick	DB Services Technische Dienste GmbH, Karlsruhe, 2003
418–423	—	Airport Planning Manual, Part 1, Master Planning	ICAO, DOC 9184-AN/902, 1987
	Viers, J., Bundesanstalt für Flugsicherung, Flugsicherungsschule	Flugplätze	1st ed., April 1987
		after: Gesamtübersicht des Flughafens München	munich-airport.de
	Riehl, Karsten	Flieger Taschenkalender 2005	Luftfahrtverlag, Bergisch Gladbach, 2005. By kind permission of DFS Deutsche Flugsicherung GmbH
	IATA Montreal	Airport Terminals Reference Manual	6th ed., 1978
425	Schwarz, H. P.	Friedhöfe/Friedhofsbauten	
	Lehr, Richard	Taschenbuch für den Garten-, Landschafts- und Gartenbau	4th ed, Blackwell, Wissenschafts-Verlag, Berlin,1994, and 6th ed., Ulmer Verlag, Stuttgart, 2002
430	Henjes, K.	Holz am Bau	DBZ 7/68
433–435,	Brandecker, H.	Gestaltung von Böschungen	Salzburg
437–438, 441	Stahl, Carl	Begrünungslösung des Grundsystems I-sys im Herstellerkatalog der Firma Carl Stahl GmbH, Süßen	
	Niesel, Alfred	Bauen mit Grün. Die Bau- und Vegetationstechnik des Landschafts- und Sportplatzbaus	2nd ed. Blackwell Wissenschafts-Verlag, Berlin, 1995
	Kreuter, M. L.	Der Biogarten	BLV, Munich
	De Haas	Marktobstanbau	Munich
446–451	FAT	Blätter für Landtechnik, Entwurfsgrundlagen für landwirtschaftliche Betriebsgebäude	CH-Tänikon, 1984
	KTBL	Leitsatz: Die Hofanlage KTBL-Arbeitsblatt	Verl. Beckmann KG, Lehrte, 1981
	KTBL	Abgänge und Abwässer aus landwirtschaftlichen Betrieben	Verl. Beckmann KG, Lehrte, 1987
	Heinze	Handbuch Landwirtschaftliche Betriebsgebäude	Celle, 1988
452–458	KTBL	Bauliche Anlagen zur Zucht und Mast von Fleischkaninchen	Verl. Beckmann KG, Lehrte, 1987
	Steiner, T. + Leimbacher, K.	Aufstallungssysteme in der Ziegenhaltung	CH-Tänikon, 1987
	—	Animal Welfare, Animal Husbandry Regulations.Tierschutz – Nutztierhaltungsverordnung	Bundesgesetzblatt, Bonn, 2006
	Marten, J., KTBL	Leitsatz Stallbau für Schafe	Verl. Beckmann KG, Lehrte, 1986
	Bessen, W.	Bäuerliche Hühnerhaltung	Ulmenverlag, 1988
	Heinze GmbH	Geflügelhaltung	Celle
	DLG e.V. (ed.)	Notice 343 Legehennenhaltung.	Frankfurt am Main, 2007
	KTBL	Baukosteninformation Mastschweineställe	Verl. Beckmann KG, Lehrte, 1987
	Marten, J.	Rindviehhaltung KTBL-Arbeitsblatt	Verl. Beckmann KG, Lehrte, 1982
	—	EU Eco Directive. EG-Öko-Verordnung No. 2092/91.	Bundesministerium for Ernährung, Landwirtschaft und Verbraucherschutz, 2008
	—	Viehhaltung, Grünlandwirtschaft, Wald und Fischerei	Bildungs- und Wissenszentrum Aulendorf
	Eilers, Uwe	Planungshilfen für den Rinder-Stallbau.	Aulendorf, 2008
459–460	Deutsche Reiterliche Vereinigung e.V.	Orientierungshilfen für den Bau und die Planung von Reitanlagen und Reitwegen	Warendorf, 1993
	Marten, J.	Pferdehaltung KTBL-Arbeitsblatt	Verl. Beckmann KG, Lehrte, 1982
	Bundesministerium für Ernährung, Landwirtschaft u. Forsten	Leitlinien zur Beurteilung von Pferdehaltung unter Tierschutzgesichtspunkten	BML Bonn, 1995
461	Neufert	Architects' Data	Collins S., London, 1985
	FGSV Forschungsgesellschaft für Strassen- u. Verkehrswesen (ed.)	EAR 05. Empfehlungen for Anlagen des ruhenden Verkehrs	FGSV Verlag, Cologne, 2005
467	Swiss Federal Office for Economic Affairs. Bundesamt für Konjunkturfragen.	Haustechnik in der integralen Planung	Bundesamt for Konjunkturfragen, Bern, 1986
		www.shell-solar.de	
	Bohne, Dirk	Ökologische Gebäudetechnik.	Kohlhammer Verlag, Stuttgart, 2004

REFERENCES

Page	Author(s)	Title	Publisher, place, date
468	Schmid, Christoph	Heizungs- und Lüftungstechnik. Leitfaden für Planung und Praxis. New ed.: Bau und Energie 5. Heizung, Lüftung, Elektrizität. Leitfaden für Planung u. Praxis	Verlag der Fachvereine, Zürich, 1993 New ed.: vdf Hochschulverlag, Zürich, 2004
471–476	—	Energieeinsparverordnung-EnEV	2007
	Federal Statistics Office. Statistisches Bundesamt	Index der Erzeugerpreise gewerblicher Produkte (Inlandsabsatz) – Lange Reihen.	Wiesbaden, 2008
477–484	Trümper, G., Overath, D.	Körperschall, Raumakustik	Odenthal
		DIN 4109, Table 3	Beuth Verlag, Berlin
485–487	Fibier, M.	Innerer und äußerer Blitzschutz	DBZ 8/80
488–500	Eckstein, R.	Vorlesung, Umdrucke-Tageslicht TUD, FB. 15	TU-Darmstadt, FB Architektur
	Fischer, U.	Tageslicht	R. Müller, Cologne, 1982
	Shen Socor (ed.)	Sonnenstandsdiagramme u.a., für Sonne, Verschattung ab Mai 2000	Hamburg 2000
	Energieagentur NRW (ed.)	Solaratlas für NRW	Energieagentur NRW Wuppertal
	Hofmann, H.	Umdruck-Entwerfen u. Beleuchtungstechnik	TU Darmstadt, FB. 15, 1999
	Dt. Norm Normenausschuß Lichttechnik	Tageslicht in Innenräumen	Beuth Verlag GmbH, Berlin, 1985–1994 Internet
	Tonne, F.	Besser Bauen	K. Hofmann, Stuttgart, 1954
	Becker, D., Epsen	Tageslicht + Architektur	C. F. Müller, Karlsruhe, 1986
	Redaktionsteam d. Klaus Esser KG	Wie hell ist hell?	K. Esser KG, Düsseldorf, 1970
	Rhein.-Westfälische Energie AG	RWE Bau-Handbuch 12. Ausgabe	Energie Verlag, Heidelberg
	Lutz, P., Jenisch, R., Klopfer, H., Freymuth, H., Krampf, L. et al.	Lehrbuch der Bauphysik	Teubner, Stuttgart, 1997
	Balkow, Schuler, Sobek, Schittich, Staib	Glasbau-Atlas	Edition Detail Inst. f. intern. Architekturdokumentation GmbH, Munich, 1998
	Palz, W., Kommission der Europäischen Gemeinschaft	Atlas über die Sonneneinstrahlung Europas, vol. I	TüV Rheinland, Cologne, 1990 et seq.
	Recknagel, Sprenger, E. (ed.)	Taschenbuch für Heizung und Klimatechnik, 68th ed.	Munich, 1997
	Wachenberger, H. and M.	Mit der Sonne bauen. Anwendung passiver Sonnenenergie	Callwey, Munich, 1983
	Inform. Erdgasheizung Essen	Faustwerte	K. Krämer, Stuttgart, 1987
	Kürte, W.	Deutsche Darstellung und Umrechnung auf hiesige Verhältnisse der Sonnentafeln von H. Fisher	Bauformen p. 531–540, 1932
501–510	Arbeitsstättenrichtlinien	Künstliche Beleuchtung	ASR 7/3, 1993-11
	Ganslandt, R., Hofmann, H.	Handbuch der Lichtplanung	Vieweg, Wiesbaden 1992
511–513	—	DIN 4102 Mustereinführungserlass	Beuth Verlag, Berlin
	DiBT; Herzog, Irene	Information zur Einführung des Europäischen Klassifizierungssystems für den Brandschutz (im nichtamtlichen Teil der Bauregelliste)	DiBt, Berlin, 2007
		DIN 4102-4, Table 45	Beuth Verlag, Berlin
519–522	Verband der Sachvers. e.V.	Richtl. für Rauch- u. Wärmeabzugsanlagen (RWA) Planung u. Einbau	VDS, Cologne
	H. Schmitt, A. Heene	Brandschutz	Vieweg, Wiesbaden 2001
	Wellpott, Edwin	Technischer Ausbau von Gebäuden	8th ed., Kohlhammer Verlag, Stuttgart, 2000
	Wellpott, Edwin; Bohne, Dirk	Technischer Ausbau von Gebäuden	9th ed., Kohlhammer Verlag, Stuttgart, 2006
537	—	Technik des Schornsteins	DBZ 2/65
	—	Schornsteine	DBZ 8/72
	Göhring, O.	Schornsteine	Vienna, 1950
538	—	Offene Kamine	DBZ 4/64, 2/65
	Dörreberg, H.	Offene Kamine und Bestimmungen	DBZ 5/80
	—	Time Saver Standards	New York, 1950
	Mährlein, K.	Offene Kamine	DAB 10/80
	—	Offener Kamin zieht nicht	DAB 6/80
	Meuth	Der Einfluß des Windes auf den Kaminzug	Sonderdruck aus 'Berufsarbeit und Wissen', 5 + 6/34
	Schrag, E.	Offene Kamine	Bm 3/64
	Sleeper, H. R.	Building standards	New York, 1955
	Sweet's Catalogue file	Jedes Jahr Neu	New York, N.Y.

There are numerous handbooks, indexes, product registers and company catalogues available for almost all building products made in Germany.
The best-known are:

1. The regionally published telephone directories from Deutsche TELEKOM.
2. The indexes of the supervisory authorities and the building industry, Verlag Zippel, Berlin.
3. The 'Bauweltkatalog', Berlin.
4. 'Deutsche Bau-Dokumentation', Verlag Heinze, Celle.
5. Bauteilkataloge der Fachgemeinschaft 'componentiertes Bauen', Verlag FEB, Cologne 1.
6. 'Bauteil-Katalog', Verlag Bau 2000, Munich.
7. Register 'pro-bau', Wiesbaden.
8. Tantzen-Marktführer 'Objecta', Verlag Tantzen, Düsseldorf.

The specialist associations in the industry also distribute pocket books about:
Steel, aluminium, zinc, titanium-zinc, cement, plastics etc., reinforced concrete, concrete, artificial stone, marble, brick, ceramic slabs etc., timber, composite panels, finishing components and electrical and sanitary installation accessories. And of course there are the numerous catalogues from the building materials industry.

Building Standards
These are selected standards from those issued by the British Standards Institute (BSI) and the German Institute for Standardisation (DIN).

BRITISH STANDARDS (BS)

Building basics

PD 6079-4	Project management. Guide to project management in the construction industry
BS ISO 22263	Organization of information about construction works. Framework for management of project information
BS 7000-4	Design management systems. Guide to managing design in construction
BS ISO 15686-5	Buildings and constructed assets. Service life planning. Life cycle costing
ASTM E917-05	Standard Practice for Measuring Life-Cycle Costs of Buildings and Building Systems
BS EN 1991-1-1	Eurocode 1. Actions on structures. General actions. Densities, self-weight, imposed loads for buildings (Other topics in Actions series)
BS EN ISO 8560	Construction drawings. Representation of modular sizes, lines and grids
BS 6750	Specification for modular coordination in building
BS EN ISO 128	Technical drawings. General principles of presentation
BS EN ISO 4157	Construction drawings. Designation systems

Building design

DD 266	Design of accessible housing. Lifetime home. Code of practice
DD CEN/TS 15209	Tactile paving surface indicators produced from concrete, clay and stone
BS ISO 23599	Assistive products for blind and vision impaired persons. Tactile walking surface indicators
BS 9999	Code of practice for fire safety in the design, management and use of buildings
BS EN 54	Fire detection and fire alarm systems
BS 5306	Fire extinguishing installations and equipment on premises
BS EN 50110	Operation of electrical installations
BS EN 62052	Electricity metering equipment (AC). General requirements, tests and test conditions
BS EN 50164	Lightning protection components (LPC)
BS 6100	Building and civil engineering. Vocabulary. Services
BS 8210	Guide to building maintenance management
BS EN 15331	Criteria for design, management and control of maintenance services for buildings
BS 6954	Tolerances for building
BS 6465	Sanitary installations
BS 5925	Code of practice for ventilation principles and designing for natural ventilation
PD CEN/TR 14788	Ventilation for buildings. Design and dimensioning of residential ventilation systems
BS 585	Wood stairs
BS 5578-2	Building construction – stairs. Modular co-ordination: specification for coordinating dimensions for stairs and stair openings
BS 6375	Performance of windows and doors

Building materials and elements

BS 6100	Building and civil engineering. Vocabulary/ Glossary
BS 6037	Code of practice for the planning, design, installation and use of permanently installed access equipment

GERMAN STANDARDS (DIN)

Building basics

DIN 18205	Brief for building design
DIN 107	Building construction; identification of right and left side
DIN 277	Areas and volumes of buildings
DIN 276	Building costs
DIN 18960	User costs of buildings
DIN 1055	Action on structures
DIN 4172	Modular coordination in building construction
DIN 18000	Modular coordination in building
DIN EN ISO 128	Technical drawings

Building design

DIN 18024	Barrier-free built environment
DIN 18025	Accessible dwellings
DIN 32984	Ground surface indicators in public traffic areas
DIN 14096	Fire precaution regulation
DIN 14675	Fire detection and fire alarm systems. Design and operation
DIN 18015	Electrical installations in residential buildings
DIN 18013	Recesses for meter boards (electric meters)
DIN 18014	Foundation earth electrode. General planning criteria
DIN 18012	House service connections facilities. Principles for planning
DIN 31051	Fundamentals of maintenance
DIN 18203	Tolerances in building construction – Structures
DIN 68935	Coordinating dimensions for bathroom furniture, appliances and sanitary equipment
DIN 18017	Ventilation of bathrooms and WCs without outside windows
DIN 18065	Stairs in buildings
DIN 18100/18101	Doors
DIN 58125	Construction of schools
DIN 13080	Division of hospitals into functional areas and functional sections

Building materials and elements

DIN V 20000	Application of construction products in structures
DIN 4426	Equipment for building maintenance
DIN EN 13162	Thermal insulation products for buildings
DIN 18515/6	Cladding for external walls

Building materials and elements *(continued)*

BS EN ISO 9229	Thermal insulation. Vocabulary
BS 8298	Code of practice for the design and installation of natural stone cladding and lining
BS EN 1928	Flexible sheets for waterproofing. Bitumen, plastic and rubber sheets for roof waterproofing. Determination of watertightness
BS EN 12730	Flexible sheets for waterproofing. Reinforced bitumen sheets for roof waterproofing. Definitions and characteristics
BS EN 12697	Bituminous mixtures. Test methods for hot mix asphalt.
BS EN 15820	Polymer modified bituminous thick coatings for waterproofing. Determination of watertightness
BS 8204	Screeds, bases and in situ floorings
BS EN 13813	Screed material and floor screeds. Screed material. Properties and requirements
BS 8000-9	Workmanship on building sites. Cementitious levelling screeds and wearing screeds. Code of practice
BS EN 771-1	Specification for masonry units. Clay masonry units
BS EN 771-2	Specification for masonry units. Calcium silicate masonry units
BS EN 12369-2	Characteristic values for design. Plywood
BS EN 312	Particleboards. Specifications
BS EN 622-1	Fibreboards. Specifications. General requirements
BS EN 520	Gypsum plasterboards. Definitions, requirements and test methods
BS EN 12859	Gypsum blocks. Definitions, requirements and test methods
BS EN 12860	Gypsum based adhesives for gypsum blocks. Definitions, requirements and test methods
ISO 9050	Glass in building – Determination of light transmittance, solar direct transmittance, total solar energy transmittance, ultraviolet transmittance and related glazing factors
BS EN 336/8	Structural timber
BS EN 338	Structural timber. Strength classes
BS EN 14732	Timber structures. Prefabricated wall, floor and roof elements
BS EN 14080	Timber structures. Glued laminated timber. Requirements
BS EN 14220(14221)	Timber and wood-based materials in external (internal) windows, external (internal) door leaves and external (internal) doorframes. Requirements and specifications
BS EN 14761	Wood flooring. Solid wood parquet. Vertical finger and module brick
BS EN 13226	Wood flooring. Solid parquet elements with grooves and/or tongues
BS EN 13488	Wood flooring. Mosaic parquet elements
BS EN 14342	Wood flooring. Characteristics, evaluation of conformity and marking
BS EN 12871	Wood-based panels. Performance specifications and requirements for load bearing boards for use in floors, walls and roofs
BS 13986	Wood-based panels for use in construction
BS EN 14221	Timber and wood-based materials in internal windows, internal door leaves and internal doorframes. Requirements and specifications
BS EN 13168	Thermal insulation products for buildings. Factory made wood wool (WW) products. Specification

Building materials and elements *(continued)*

DIN 18531	Waterproofing of roofs
DIN 52143	Bitumen roofing felt with glass fleece base
DIN 52130/3	Bitumen
DIN 52129	Uncoated bitumen saturated coating
DIN 18560	Floor screeds in building construction
DIN EN 13813	Screed material and floor screeds
DIN 272	Testing of magnesium oxychloride screeds
DIN EN 771	Clay masonry units
DIN V 106	Calcium silicate units
DIN 68705	Plywood
DIN EN 312	Particle boards – specifications
DIN EN 622	Fibreboards
DIN 18180/4	Gypsum plasterboards
DIN EN 12859	Gypsum blocks
DIN EN 12860	Gypsum-based adhesives for gypsum blocks
DIN EN 410/637	Glass in building – Determination of luminous and solar characteristics of glazing
DIN EN 336/338	Structural timber
DIN 4074	Strength grading of wood
DIN 18530	Solid structural decks for roofs; design and construction
ISO 19993	Timber structures – Glued laminated timber
DIN 68121	Timber or windows and window doors
DIN EN 14761	Wood flooring – Solid wood parquet
DIN EN 13226	Wood flooring – Solid parquet elements with grooves and/or tongues
DIN EN 13488	Wood flooring – Mosaic parquet elements
DIN EN 14342	Wood flooring – Characteristics, evaluation of conformity and marking
DIN 68702	Wood paving
DIN EN 13986	Wood-based panels for use in construction
DIN 68706	Internal doors made from wood and wood-based panels
DIN 1101	Wood wool lightweight boards
DIN 66095	Textile floor coverings
DIN EN 14085	Resilient floor coverings
DIN EN 14411	Ceramic tiles – Definitions, classifications, characteristics and marking
DIN 18156/7	Materials for ceramic tiling in thin mortar bed technique
DIN 18158	Clinker floor tiles
DIN 4226	Aggregates for concrete and mortar
DIN EN 197	Cement
DIN EN 413	Masonry cement
DIN EN 459	Building lime
DIN EN 206	Concrete
DIN EN 1520	Application in structures of prefabricated reinforced components of lightweight aggregate concrete with open structure
DIN 18148	Lightweight-concrete hollow-boards
DIN V 18153	Concrete masonry units (normal weight concrete)
DIN V 18152	Lightweight concrete solid bricks and blocks
DIN 18162	Lightweight concrete wallboards – unreinforced
DIN V 4165	Autoclaved aerated concrete masonry units
DIN 4166	Autoclaved aerated concrete slabs and panels
DIN 18551	Shotcrete
DIN 18159	In-situ cellular plastics in building
DIN 18164	Foamed plastics as insulating materials
DIN 18550	Plastering / rendering and plastering / rendering systems
DIN 18558	Synthetic resin plasters
DIN 4121	Hanging wire-plaster ceilings

(continued)

BRITISH STANDARDS (BS)

Building materials and elements *(continued)*

BS ISO 2424	Textile floor coverings. Vocabulary
BS EN 14041	Resilient, textile and laminate floor coverings. Essential characteristics
BS EN 14411	Ceramic tiles. Definitions, classification, characteristics and marking
BS 5385-3	Wall and floor tiling. Design and installation of internal and external ceramic floor tiles and mosaics in normal conditions. Code of practice
BS 5385-5	Wall and floor tiling. Design and installation of terrazzo, natural stone and agglomerated stone tile and slab flooring. Code of practice
BS EN 13055-1	Lightweight aggregates. Lightweight aggregates for concrete, mortar and grout
DIN EN 197	Cement
BS EN 459	Building lime
BS EN 413	Masonry cement
BS EN ISO 15630	Steel for the reinforcement and prestressing of concrete. Test methods.
BS EN 206	Concrete
BS EN 1168	Precast concrete products. Hollow core slabs
BS 6073	Precast concrete masonry units. Guide for specifying precast concrete masonry units
BS EN 771-3	Specification for masonry units. Aggregate concrete masonry units (dense and lightweight aggregates)
BS EN 1520	Prefabricated reinforced components of lightweight aggregate concrete with open structure with structural or non-structural reinforcement
BS EN 771-4	Specification for masonry units. Autoclaved aerated concrete masonry units
BS EN 12602	Prefabricated reinforced components of autoclaved aerated concrete
ASTM C1436	Standard specification for materials for shotcrete
ISO 4898	Rigid cellular plastics. Thermal insulation products for buildings. Specifications
BS EN 13164 (13165)	Thermal insulation products for buildings. Factory made products of extruded polystyrene foam – XPS. (Factory made rigid polyurethane foam – PUR – products) Specification
BS EN 13914	Design, preparation and application of external rendering and internal plastering
BS EN 14246	Gypsum elements for suspended ceilings. Definitions, requirements and test methods
BS EN 13964	Suspended ceilings. Requirements and test methods
BS EN 1993	Eurocode 3. Design of steel structures
BS EN 1090	Execution of steel structures and aluminium structures

Building services

BS EN 60335-2-30	Household and similar electrical appliances. Safety. Particular requirements for room heaters. Thermal storage room heaters
BS 5871	Specification for the installation and maintenance of gas fires, convector heaters, fire/back boilers and decorative fuel effect gas appliances
BS EN 12831	Heating systems in buildings. Method for calculation of the design heat load

GERMAN STANDARDS (DIN)

Building materials and elements *(continued)*

DIN EN 13964	Suspended ceilings – Requirements and test methods
DIN 18800	Steel structures
DIN 18801	Structural steel in building; design and construction
DIN 18807	Trapezoidal sheeting in building; trapezoidal steel sheeting

Building services

DIN 4703	Heating appliances
DIN EN 12831	Heating systems in buildings – Method for calculation of the design heat load
DIN EN 12828	Heating systems in buildings – Design of water-based systems
DIN EN 1264	Floor heating – Systems and components
DIN 4725	Warm water underfloor heating
DIN 4724	Plastic piping systems for warm water floor heating systems and radiator connecting

Building services *(continued)*

BS EN 12828	Heating systems in buildings. Design for water-based heating systems
BS EN 1264	Floor heating. Systems and components
BS EN ISO 22391	Plastics piping systems for hot and cold water installations. Polyethylene of raised temperature resistance (PE-RT)
BS EN 14337	Heating systems in buildings. Design and installation of direct electrical room heating systems
BS EN 15316	Heating systems in buildings. Method for calculation of system energy requirements and system efficiencies
BS EN 15239	Ventilation for buildings. Energy performance of buildings. Guidelines for inspection of ventilation systems
BS EN 13141	Ventilation for buildings. Performance testing of components/products for residential ventilation
BS EN ISO 13790	Energy performance of buildings. Economic evaluation procedure for energy systems in buildings
BS EN ISO 13370	Thermal performance of buildings. Heat transfer via the ground. Calculation methods

Building physics and building protection measures

BS 8000-4	Workmanship on building sites. Code of practice for waterproofing
BS EN 1014	Wood preservatives. Creosote and creosoted timber. Methods of sampling and analysis
BS 8417	Preservation of wood. Code of Practice
BS EN 14188	Joint fillers and sealants
BS EN 13880	Hot applied joint sealants
BS EN 14187	Cold applied joint sealants
BS EN 13022	Glass in building. Structural sealant glazing
BS EN ISO 717	Acoustics. Rating of sound insulation in buildings and of building elements
BS EN 12354	Building acoustics
BS EN ISO 3382	Acoustics. Measurement of room acoustic parameters
BS 8233	Sound insulation and noise reduction for buildings. Code of practice
BS EN 61293	Marking of electrical equipment with ratings related to electrical supply. Safety requirements
BS EN 13823	Reaction to fire tests for building products. Building products excluding floorings exposed to thermal attack by a single burning item
BS EN 13501	Fire classification of construction products and building elements
BS EN 12101	Smoke and heat control systems
BS EN 1147	Portable ladders for fire service use
BS EN 54	Fire detection and fire alarm systems
BS EN 1634	Fire resistance and smoke control tests for door, shutter and **openable** window assemblies and elements of building hardware
BS EN 14600	Doorsets and openable windows with fire resisting and/or smoke control characteristics. Requirements and classification
BS EN ISO 10077	Thermal performance of windows, doors and shutters
BS EN 13187	Thermal performance of buildings – Qualitative detection of thermal irregularities in building envelopes. Infrared method
BS EN ISO 7345	Thermal insulation – Physical quantities and definitions

Building services *(continued)*

DIN 44576	Electrical room heating
DIN V 4701	Energy efficiency of heating and ventilation systems in buildings
DIN EN 12792	Ventilation for buildings – Symbols, terminology and graphical symbols
DIN 4108	Thermal insulation and energy economy in buildings
DIN EN 832	Thermal protection and energy economy in buildings
DIN EN ISO 13370	Thermal performance of buildings – Heat transfer via the ground – Calculation methods

Building physics and building protection measures

DIN 18195	Waterproofing of buildings
DIN 68800	Protection of timber used in buildings — General specifications
DIN 18541	Sealing of joints in concrete with water stops
DIN 18540	Sealing of exterior wall joints in building using joint sealants
DIN 18545	Glazing with sealants
DIN EN ISO 717	Acoustics – Rating of sound insulation in buildings and of building elements
DIN EN 12354	Building acoustics
DIN 18041	Acoustic quality in small to medium-sized rooms
DIN 18005	Noise abatement in town planning
DIN 4844	Safety marking
DIN 4102	Fire behaviour of building materials and building components
DIN EN 13501	Fire classification of construction products and building elements
DIN 18093	Fire barriers
DIN 18232	Smoke and heat control systems
DIN 14094	Fire fighting purposes – Escape ladder installations
DIN 14090	Areas for the fire brigade on premises
DIN 18230	Structural fire protection in industrial buildings
DIN 14095	Ground plans of components of buildings for fire brigade use
DIN EN 14600	Doorsets and openable windows with fire resisting and/or smoke control characteristics. Requirements and classification
DIN EN ISO 10077	Thermal performance of windows, doors and shutters
DIN EN 13187	Thermal performance of buildings – Qualitative detection of thermal irregularities in building envelopes. Infrared method
DIN EN 13829	Thermal performance of buildings – Determination of air permeability of buildings. Fan pressurization method
DIN V 4108	Thermal insulation and energy economy in buildings

(continued)

BRITISH STANDARDS (BS)

Building physics and building protection measures *(continued)*

BS EN 13162–7 2	Thermal insulation products for buildings
BS EN 14064	
BS EN ISO 6946	Building components and building elements – Thermal resistance and thermal transmittance – Calculation method
BS EN ISO 10211	Thermal bridges in building construction. Heat flows and surface temperatures. Detailed calculations
BS EN ISO 13788	Hygrothermal performance of building components and building elements

Finishings

BS EN 1443	Chimneys – General requirements
BS EN 1857	Chimneys. Components. Concrete flue liners
BS EN 1906	Building hardware. Lever handles and knob furniture. Requirements and test methods
BS EN 81	Safety rules for the construction and installation of lifts
BS EN 12665	Light and lighting. Basic terms and criteria for specifying lighting requirements
BS EN 60432	Incandescent lamps. Safety specification
BS EN 60921	Ballasts for tubular fluorescent lamps. Performance requirements
BS EN 60598	Luminaires. Parrticular requirements
BS EN 50285	Energy efficiency of electric lamps for household use
BIP 2081	A Guide to Emergency Lighting
BS 8206-2	Lighting for buildings. Code of practice for daylighting
BS EN 13829	Thermal performance of buildings – Determination of air permeability of buildings. Fan pressurization method
BS ISO 18292	Energy performance of fenestration systems for residential buildings. Calculation procedure
BS EN 13659	Shutters. Performance requirements including safety
BS 6375	Performance of windows and doors
BS 5642	Sills and copings. Specification for window sills of precast concrete, cast stone, clayware, slate and natural stone
BS 8213	Windows, doors and rooflights. Code of practice: safety in use / survey and installation / installation of replacement windows and doorset in dwellings
BS EN 1051	Glass in building. Glass blocks and glass pavers
BS EN 607	Eaves gutters and fittings made of PVC-U. Definitions, requirements and testing
BS 8212	Code of practice for dry lining and partitioning using gypsum plasterboard
BS 8000-8	Workmanship on building sites. Code of practice for plasterboard partitions and dry linings

GERMAN STANDARDS (DIN)

Building physics and building protection measures *(continued)*

DIN EN ISO 7345	Thermal insulation – Physical quantities and definitions
DIN EN 13162–7 2	Thermal insulation products for buildings
DIN EN ISO 6946	Building components and building elements – Thermal resistance and thermal transmittance – Calculation method
DIN EN ISO 10211	Thermal bridges in building construction. Heat flows and surface temperatures. Detailed calculations
DIN EN ISO 13788	Hygrothermal performance of building components and building elements

Finishings

DIN EN 1443	Chimneys – General requirements
DIN V 18160	Chimneys
DIN 18255/18257	Building hardware – Door lever handles, backplates and escutcheons / Security plates
DIN 15306	Lifts – Passenger lifts in residential buildings
DIN 15309	Lifts – Passenger lifts in non-residential buildings and bed lifts
DIN 18090/1	Lifts – Lift landing doors
DIN 5035	Artificial lighting
DIN EN 12464	Light and lighting – Lighting of workplaces
DIN EN 1838	Lighting applications – Emergency lighting
DIN 5034	Daylight in interiors
DIN 18055	Windows
DIN V 18073	Roller shutters, awnings, rolling doors and other blinds and shutters in buildings
DIN EN 12207/08	Windows and doors – Air permeability
DIN 18057	Concrete windows
DIN EN 12210	Windows and doors – Resistance to wind load — Classification
DIN 4242	Glass block walls; construction and dimensioning
DIN EN 612	Eaves gutters with bead-stiffened fronts and rainwater pipes with seamed joints made of metal sheet
DIN 18183	Partitions and wall linings with gypsum boards on metal framing
DIN 4103	Internal non-loadbearing partitions

Sports and play facilities, landscaping

BS EN 13200	Spectator facilities
BS EN 12231	Surfaces for sports areas. Method of test, Determination of ground cover of natural turf
ASTM F2442	Standard Guide for Layout of Ice Arena
BS EN 1176	Playground equipment and surfacing
ASTM F1487	Standard consumer safety performance specification for playground equipment
BS 3882	Specification for topsoil and requirements for use

Sports and play facilities, landscaping

DIN 18032	Halls and rooms for sports and multi-purpose use
DIN 18035	Sports grounds
DIN 18036	Ice-sport facilities with artificial ice
DIN 18034	Playgrounds and outdoor play areas
DIN 33942	Barrier-free accessible playground equipment
DIN 18915/18920	Gardening technology in landscaping – soil working

Construction contract

BS 6100-10	Building and civil engineering. Vocabulary. Contract terms

Construction contract

DIN 1960/1961	German construction contract procedures (VOB)

	Conversion to:		Multiply by:
Measures of length	1 mm		= 0.0394 inch
	1 cm	= 10 mm	= 0.3937 inch
	1 dm	= 10 cm	= 3.9370 inches
	1 m	= 10 dm	= 1.0936 yards
	1 dam	= 10 m	= 10.9361 yards
	1 hm	= 10 dam	= 109.3614 yards
	1 km	= 10 hm	= 0.6214 mile
	cm	inch (″)	0.3937
	m	foot (′)	3.2808
	m	yard (yd)	1.0936
	km	statute mile (st.mi)	0.6214
	inch	cm	2.5400
	foot	m	0.3048
	yard	m	0.9144
	statute mile	km	1.6093
Measures of area	1 mm^2		= 0.00155 square inch
	1 cm^2	= 100 mm^2	= 0.15499 square inch
	1 dm^2	= 100 cm^2	= 15.499 square inches
	1 m^2	= 100 dm^2	= 1.19599 square yards
	1 dam^2	= 100 m^2	= 119.5993 square yards
	1 hm^2	= 100 dam^2	= 2.4711 acres
	1 km^2	= 100 hm^2	= 247.11 acres = 0.3861 square mile
	1 m^2		= 1549.9 square inches
	1 a	= 100 m^2	= 119.5993 square yards
	1 ha	= 100 a	= 2.4711 acres
	1 km^2	= 100 ha	= 247.11 acres = 0.3861 square mile
	cm^2	square inch (sq. in)	0.1550
	m^2	square foot (sq. ft)	10.7639
	m^2	square yard (sq. yd)	1.1960
	1000 m^2	acre	0.2471
	km^2	square mile (sq. mi)	0.3861
	square inch	cm^2	6.4516
	square foot	m^2	0.0929
	square yard	m^2	0.8361
	acre	m^2	4046.8
	square mile	km^2	2.5900
Measures of volume	1 mm^2		= 0.000061 cubic inch
	1 cm^2	= 1000 mm^3	= 0.061023 cubic inch
	1 dm^2	= 1000 cm^3	= 61.024 cubic inches
	1 m^2	= 1000 dm^3	= 35.315 cubic feet
			= 1.3079 cubic yards
Measures of timber	1 mm^2	= 1 stere	= 423.3 board feet
Volumes of liquids	1 ml	= 1 cm^3	= 16.89 minims
	1 cl	= 10 ml	= 0.352 fluid ounce
	1 dl	= 10 cl	= 3.52 fluid ounces
	1 l	= 10 dl	= 1.76 pints
	1 dal	= 10 l	= 2.1998 gallons
	1 hl	= 10 dal	= 2.75 bushels
	1 kl	= 10 hl	= 3.437 quarters

	Conversion to:		Multiply by:
Volumes of dry substances	litre	peck	0.1100
	litre	bushel	0.0275
	litre	kilderkin	0.0122
	m^3	barrel	6.1103
	m^3	quarter	3.4370
	peck	litre	9.0922
	bushel	litre	36.3687
	kilderkin	litre	81.829
	barrel	m^3	0.1637
	quarter	m^3	0.2909
Volumes of liquids	litre	gill (liq)	7.0390
	litre	pint (liq)	1.7598
	litre	quart (liq)	0.8799
	litre	pottle	0.4399
	litre	gallon	0.2200
	gill (liq)	litre	0.1421
	pint (liq)	litre	0.5683
	quart (liq)	litre	1.1365
	pottle	litre	2.2730
	gallon	litre	4.5461
Measures of volume	cm^3	cubic inch (cu.in)	0.06102
	litre	cubic foot (cu. ft)	0.03531
	m^3	cubic yard (cu. yd)	1.308
	m^3	register ton (reg. tn)	0.3531
	cubic inch	cm^3	16.387
	cubic foot	litre	28.317
	cubic yard	m^3	0.7646
	register ton	m^3	2.8317
Measures of weight	1 mg		= 0.0154 grain
	1 cg	= 10 mg	= 0.1543 grain
	1 dg	= 10 cg	= 1.543 grains
	1 g	= 10 dg	= 15.432 grains
	1 dag	= 10 g	= 0.353 ounce = 0.321 ounce
	1 hg	= 10 dag	= 3.527 ounces = 3.215 ounces
	1 kg	= 10 hg	= 2.205 pounds = 2.679 pounds
	1 t	= 1000 kg	= 1.102 short tons
Measures of weight	g	grain	15.4323
	g	dram (av.)	0.5644
	g	ounce (av.)	0.0353
	kg	pound (av.)	2.2046
	t	long ton (Brit.)	0.9842
	grain	g	0.0648
	dram	g	1.7718
	ounce	g	28.3495
	pound	kg	0.4536
Metric carat weights	200 mg	= 1 carat	
	100 mg	= ½ carat	= 0.5 carat
	50 mg	= ¼ carat	= 0.25 carat
	20 mg	= 1/10 carat	= 0.10 carat
	10 mg	= 1/20 carat	= 0.05 carat
	2 mg	= 1/100 carat	= 0.01 carat

Metric weights and measures	
	Instead of the abbreviations sq. m, sq. dm, sq. cm, sq. mm, it is now more usual to use m^2, dm^2, cm^2, mm^2 and, instead of cu. m, cu. dm, cu. cm, cu. mm, now m^3, dm^3, cm^3, mm^3
Measures of length	The unit is the metre (m) = one ten-millionth of the Earth's meridian quadrants (i.e. the direct route from pole to equator) 1 km (kilometre) .... 1000 m 1 m (metre) .... 10 dm 1 dm (decimetre) .... 10 cm 1 cm (centimetre) .... 10 mm (millimetre)
Measures of area	1 km^2 (square kilometre) .... 100 ha 1 ha (hectare) .... 100 a 1 a (are) .... 100 m^2 1 m^2 (square metre) .... 100 dm^2 1 dm^2 (square decimetre) .... 100 cm^2 1 cm^2 (square centimetre) .... 100 mm^2
Measures of volume	1 m^3 (cubic metre) .... 1000 dm^3 1 dm^3 (cubic decimetre or litre) .... 1000 cm^3 1 cm^3 (cubic centimetre) .... 1000 mm^3
Volumes of liquid	1 m^3 (cubic metre) .... 10 hl 1 hl (hectolitre) .... 100 l 1 l (litre) .... 0.001 m^3
Measures of weight	1 t (tonne) .... 10 dz (1000 kg) 1 dz (Doppelzentner) .... 100 kg 1 kg (kilogram) .... 1000 g 1 g (gram .... 1000 mg (milligram)

Non-metric weights and measures	
1 equatorial degree	111.3 km
1 meridian degree	111.12 km
1 new geographical mile (15 = 1 equatorial degree)	7.42 km
1 cable (120 fathoms)	0.22 km
1 fathom	1.829 m
1 geographical square mile	55.0629 km^2

	Imperial weights and measures
Measures of length	1 nautical mile (knot) = 6080 feet = 1.8532 km 1 statute mile = 8 furlongs = 8 × 220 yards = 1760 × 3 feet = 5280 feet = 1.6093 km 1 London mile = 5000 feet = 1.5239 km 1 fathom = 2 yards = 6 feet = 72 inches = 1.8287 m 1 yard = 3 feet = 36 inches = 0.9144 m 1 foot (ft) = 12 inches = 0.3048 m 1 inch = 25.399 mm
Measures of area	1 square mile (sq. mile) = 640 acres = 2.59 km^2 1 acre = 160 square poles = 4840 square yards = 40.4685 m^2 1 square pole = 25.293 m^2 1 square yard = 9 square feet = 0.8361 m^2 1 square foot = 144 square inches = 0.0929 m^2 1 square inch = 6.4516 cm^2
Measures of volume	1 register ton = 100 cubic feet = 2.832 m^3 1 ocean ton = 40 cubic feet = 1.1327 m^3 1 cubic yard (cu. yd.) = 27 cubic feet = 0.7646 m^3 1 cubic foot (cu. ft.) = 1728 cubic inches = 0.0283 m^3 1 cubic inch (cu. in.) = 16.387 cm^3
Measures of liquid	1 Imperial quarter = 8 bushels = 2.90789 hl 1 bushel = 8 gallons = 0.3635 hl 1 Imperial gallon = 4 quarts = 4.5435 l 1 quart = 2 pints = 1.14 l 1 pint = 0.56 litre 1 American gallon = 231 cubic inches = 3.7852 l
Measures of weight	1 ton (long ton) = 20 hundredweight = 20 × 4 quarters = 80 × 28 stone 1 ship's ton (short ton) = 2000 pounds = 907.1853 kg [= 1016.0471 kg] 1 hundredweight (cwt) = 4 quarters = 50.8 kg 1 quarter = 2 stones = 12.701 kg 1 stone = 14 pounds = 6.35 kg 1 pound = 16 ounces = 0.4536 kg 1 ounce = 0.0284 kg

Temperatures:

degree Celsius (°C) = $\frac{5}{9}$(°F -32) = $\frac{5}{4}$°R

degree Réaumur (°R) = $\frac{4}{5}$°C = $\frac{4}{9}$ (°F −32)

degree Fahrenheit (°F) = $\frac{9}{5}$°C + 32 = $\frac{9}{4}$°R

+320°C = 273.15 Kelvin

comparison table:

°C	=	°R	=	°F
− 40		−32		− 40
− 35		−28		− 31
− 30		−24		− 22
− 25		−20		− 13
− 20		−16		− 4
− 17.8		−14.2		0
− 15		−12		+ 5
− 10		− 8		+ 14
− 5		− 4		+ 23
0		0		+ 32
+ 5		+4		+ 41
+ 10		+ 8		+ 50
+ 15		+12		+ 59
+ 20		+16		+ 68
+ 25		+20		+ 77
+ 30		+24		+ 86
+ 35		+28		+ 95
+ 40		+32		+104
+ 45		+36		+113
+ 50		+40		+122
+ 55		+44		+131
+ 60		+48		+140
+ 65		+52		+149
+ 70		+56		+158
+ 75		+60		+167
+ 80		+64		+176
+ 85		+68		+185
+ 90		+72		+194
+ 95		+76		+203
+100		+80		+212

inch(")	1/16	1/12	1/8	1/6	3/16	1/4	5/16	1/3	3/8	5/12	7/16	1/2
mm.............	1.59	2.12	3.18	4.23	4.76	6.35	7.94	8.47	9.52	10.58	11.11	12.70
inch (")	9/16	7/12	5/8	2/3	11/16	3/4	13/16	5/6	7/8	11/12	15/16	1
mm.............	14.29	14.82	15.87	16.93	17.46	19.05	20.64	21.17	22.22	23.28	23.81	25.40

English foot and inch to millimetres
1 ft = 304.79973 mm

ft	in	0"	1"	2"	3"	4"	5"	6"	7"	8"	9"	10"	11"	12"
0	**0**	0	25.4	51	76	102	127	152	178	203	229	254	279	305
1	**12**	305	330	356	381	406	432	457	483	508	533	559	584	610
2	**24**	610	635	660	686	711	737	762	787	813	838	864	889	914
3	**36**	914	940	965	991	1016	1041	1067	1092	1118	1143	1168	1194	1219
4	**48**	1219	1245	1270	1295	1321	1346	1372	1397	1422	1448	1473	1499	1524
5	**60**	1524	1549	1575	1600	1626	1651	1676	1702	1727	1753	1778	1803	1829
6	**72**	1829	1854	1880	1905	1930	1956	1981	2007	2032	2057	2083	2108	2134
7	**84**	2134	2159	2184	2210	2235	2261	2286	2311	2337	2362	2388	2413	2438
8	**96**	2438	2464	2489	2515	2540	2565	2591	2616	2642	2667	2692	2718	2743
9	**108**	2743	2769	2794	2819	2845	2870	2896	2921	2946	2972	2997	3023	3048
10	**120**	3048	3073	3099	3124	3150	3175	3200	3226	3251	3277	3302	3327	3353
11	**132**	3353	3378	3404	3429	3454	3480	3505	3531	3556	3581	3607	3632	3658
12	**144**	3658	3683	3708	3734	3759	3785	3810	3835	3861	3886	3912	3937	3962
13	**156**	3962	3988	4013	4039	4064	4089	4115	4140	4166	4191	4216	4242	4267
14	**168**	4267	4293	4318	4343	4369	4394	4420	4445	4470	4496	4521	4547	4572
15	**180**	4572	4597	4623	4648	4674	4699	4724	4750	4775	4801	4826	4851	4877
16	**192**	4877	4902	4928	4953	4978	5004	5029	5055	5080	5105	5131	5156	5182
17	**204**	5182	5207	5232	5258	5283	5309	5334	5359	5385	5410	5436	5461	5486
18	**216**	5486	5512	5537	5563	5588	5613	5639	5664	5690	5715	5740	5766	5791
19	**228**	5791	5817	5842	5867	5893	5918	5944	5969	5994	6020	6045	6071	6096
20	**240**	6096	6121	6147	6172	6198	6223	6248	6274	6299	6325	6350	6375	6401
21	**252**	6401	6426	6452	6477	6502	6528	6553	6579	6604	6629	6655	6680	6706
22	**264**	6706	6731	6756	6782	6807	6833	6858	6883	6909	6934	6960	6985	7010
23	**276**	7010	7036	7061	7087	7112	7137	7163	7188	7214	7239	7264	7290	7315
24	**288**	7315	7341	7366	7391	7417	7442	7467	7493	7518	7545	7569	7594	7620
25	**300**	7620	7645	7671	7696	7722	7747	7772	7798	7823	7849	7874	7899	7925
26	**312**	7925	7950	7975	8001	8026	8052	8077	8102	8128	8153	8179	8204	8230
27	**324**	8230	8255	8280	8306	8332	8357	8382	8408	8433	8458	8484	8509	8534
28	**336**	8534	8559	8585	8610	8636	8661	8686	8712	8737	8763	8788	8814	8839
29	**348**	8839	8864	8890	8915	8941	8966	8991	9017	9042	9068	9093	9118	9144
30	**360**	9144	9169	9195	9220	9246	9271	9296	9322	9347	9373	9398	9423	9449
31	**372**	9449	9474	9500	9525	9551	9576	9601	9627	9652	9677	9703	9728	9753
32	**384**	9754	9779	9804	9830	9855	9881	9906	9931	9957	9982	10008	10033	10058
33	**396**	10058	10083	10109	10134	10160	10185	10210	10236	10261	10287	10312	10337	10363
34	**408**	10363	10388	10414	10439	10465	10490	10515	10541	10566	10592	10617	10642	10668
35	**420**	10668	10693	10719	10744	10770	10795	10820	10846	10871	10897	10922	10947	10973
36	**432**	10973	10998	11024	11049	11075	11100	11125	11151	11176	11202	11227	11252	11278
37	**444**	11278	11303	11328	11354	11379	11405	11430	11455	11481	11506	11532	11557	11582
38	**456**	11582	11607	11633	11658	11684	11709	11734	11760	11785	11811	11836	11861	11887
39	**468**	11887	11912	11938	11963	11989	12014	12039	12065	12090	12116	12141	12166	12192
40	**480**	12192	12217	12243	12268	12294	12319	12344	12370	12395	12421	12446	12471	12497
41	**492**	12497	12522	12548	12573	12598	12624	12649	12675	12700	12725	12751	12776	12802
42	**504**	12802	12827	12852	12878	12903	12929	12954	12979	13005	13030	13056	13081	13106
43	**516**	13106	13132	13157	13183	13208	13233	13259	13284	13310	13335	13360	13386	13411
44	**528**	13411	13437	13462	13487	13513	13538	13564	13589	13614	13640	13665	13691	13716
45	**540**	13716	13741	13767	13792	13818	13843	13868	13894	13919	13945	13970	13995	14021
46	**552**	14021	14046	14072	14097	14122	14148	14173	14199	14224	14249	14275	14300	14326
47	**564**	14326	14351	14376	14402	14427	14453	14478	14503	14529	14554	14580	14605	14630
48	**576**	14630	14656	14681	14707	14732	14757	14783	14808	14834	14859	14884	14910	14935
49	**588**	14935	14961	14986	15011	15037	15062	15088	15113	15138	15164	15189	15215	15240
50	**600**	15240	15265	15291	15316	15342	15367	15392	15418	15443	15469	15494	15519	15545
51	**612**	15545	15570	15596	15621	15646	15672	15697	15723	15748	15773	15799	15824	15850
52	**624**	15850	15875	15900	15926	15951	15977	16002	16027	16053	16078	16104	16129	16154
53	**636**	16154	16180	16205	16231	16256	16281	16307	16332	16358	16383	16408	16434	16459
54	**648**	16459	16485	16510	16535	16561	16586	16612	16637	16662	16688	16713	16739	16764
	in	0"	1"	2"	3"	4"	5"	6"	7"	8"	9"	10"	11"	12"

CONVERSION OF UNITS

Conversion factors
Conversion tables

metric	'imperial'/US
length	
1.0 mm	0.039 in
25.4 mm (2.54 cm)	1 in
304.8 mm (30.48 cm)	1ft
914.4 mm	1yd
1000.0 mm (1.0 m)	1yd 3.4 in (1.093 yd)
20.117 m	1 chain
1000.00 m (1 km)	0.621 mile
1609.31 m	1 mile
area	
100 mm^2 (1.0 cm^2)	0.155 in^2
645.2 mm^2 (6.452 cm^2)	1 in^2
929.03 cm^2 (0.093 m^2)	1ft$^{2'}$
0.836 m^2	1yd^2
1.0m^2	1.196 yd^2 (10.764 ft^2)
0.405 ha (4046.9 m^2)	1 acre
1.0 ha (10000 m^2)	2.471 acre
1.0 km^2	0.386 mile^2
2.59 km^2 (259 ha)	1 mile^2
volume	
1000 mm^3 (1.0 cm^3; 1.0 ml)	0.061 in^3
16387 mm^3 (16.387 cm^3; 0.01641; 16.387 ml)	1 in^3
1.01(1.0 dm^3; 1000 cm^3)	61.025 in^3 (0.035 ft^3)
0.028 m^3 (28.321)	1ft^3
0.765 m^3	1yd^3
1.0 m^3	1.308 yd^3 (35.314 ft^3)
capacity	
1.0 ml	0.034 fl oz US
1.0 ml	0.035 fl oz imp
28.41 ml	1 fl oz imp
29.57 ml	1 fl oz US
0.473 litre	1 pint (liquid) US
0.568 litre	1 pint imp
1.0 litre	1.76 pint imp
1.0 litre	2.113 pint US
3.785 litre	1 gal US
4.546 litre	1 gal imp
100.0 litre	21.99 gal imp
100.0 litre	26.42 gal US
159.0 litre	1 barrel US
164.0 litre	1 barrel imp
mass	
1.0g	0.035 oz (avoirdupois)
28.35 g	1 oz (avoirdupois)
454.0 g (0.454 kg)	1lb
1000.0 g (1kg)	2.205lb
45.36 kg	1 cwt US
50.8 kg	1 cwt imp
907.2 kg (0.907t)	1 ton US
1000.0 kg (1.0t)	0.984 ton imp
1000.0 kg (1.0t)	1.102 ton US
1016.0 kg (1.016t)	1 ton imp
mass/unit length	
0.496 kg/m	1 lb/yd
0.564 kg/m (0.564 t/km)	1 ton US/mile
0.631 kg/m (0.631 t/km)	1 ton imp/mile
1.0 kg/m	0.056 lb/in (0.896 oz/in)
1.116kg/m	1 oz/in
1.488 kg/m	1 lb/ft
17.86 kg/m	1 lb/in
length/unit mass	
1.0 m/kg	0.496 yd/lb
2.016 m/kg	1 yd/lb

metric	'imperial'/US
mass/unit area	
1.0 g/m^2	0.003 oz/ft^2
33.91 g/m^2	1 oz/yd^2
305.15 g/m^2	1 oz/ft^2
0.011 kg/m^2	1 cwt US/acre
0.013 kg/m^2	1 cwt imp/acre
0.224 kg/m^2	1 ton US/acre
0.251 kg/m^2	1 ton imp/acre
1.0 kg/m^2	29.5 oz/yd^2
4.882 kg/m^2	1 lb/ft^2
703.07 kg/m^2	1 lb/in^2
350.3 kg/km^2 (3.503 kg/ha; 0.35 g/m^2)	1 ton US/mile^2
392.3 kg/km^2 (3.923 kg/ha; 0.392 g/m^2)	1 ton imp/mile^2
density (mass/volume)	
0.593 kg/m^3	1 lb/yd^3
1.0 kg/m^3	0.062 lb/ft^3
16.02 kg/m^3	1 lb/ft
1186.7 kg/m^3 (1.187 t/m^3)	1 ton US/yd^3
1328.9 kg/m^3 (1.329 t/m^3)	1 ton imp/yd^3
27680.0 kg/m^3 (27.68 t/m^3; 27.68 g/cm^3)	1 lb/in^3
specific surface (area/unit mass)	
0.823 m^2/t	1 yd^2/ton
1.0m^2/kg	0.034 yd^2/oz
29.493 m^2/kg	1 yd^2/oz
area/unit capacity	
0.184 m^2/l	1 yd^2/gal
1.0m^2/l	5.437 yd^2/gal
concentration	
0.014 kg/m^3	1 grain/gal imp
0.017 kg/m^3	1 grain/gal US
1.0 kg/m^3 (1.0 g/l)	58.42 grain/gal US
1.0 kg/m^3 (1.0 g/l)	70.16 grain/gal imp
6.236 kg/m^3	1 oz/gal imp
7.489 kg/m^3	1oz/galUS
mass rate of flow	
0.454 kg/s	1 lb/s
1.0 kg/s	2.204 lb/s
volume rate of flow	
0.063 l/s	1 gal US/minute
0.076 l/s	1 gal imp/minute
0.472 l/s	1 ft^3/minute
1.0 l/s (86.4 m^3/day)	13.2gal imp/s
1.0 l/s	0.264 gal US/s
1.01/min	0.22 gal imp/min
1.01/min	0.264 gal US/min
3.785 l/s	1 gal US/s
4.546 l/s	1 gal imp/s
28.32 l/s	1 ft^3/s
0.0038 m^3/min	1 gal US/min
0.0045 m^3/min	1 gal imp/min
1.0 m^3/s	183.162 gal US/s
1.0 m^3/s	219.969 gal imp/s
1.0m^3/h	35.31 ft^3/h
0.0283 m^3/s	1 ft^3/s
velocity	
0.005 m/s	1 ft/minute
0.025 m/s	1 in/s
0.305 m/s	1 ft/s
1.0 m/s	3.28 ft/s
1000.0 m/hr(1 km/hr)	0.621 mile/hr
1609.0 m/hr (0.447 m/s)	1 mile/hr

metric	'imperial'/US
fuel consumption	
1.0 l/km	0.354 gal imp/mile
1.0 l/km	0.425 gal US/mile
2.352 l/km	1 gal US/mile
2.824 l/km	1 gal imp/mile
acceleration	
0.305 m/s^2	1 ft/s^2
1.0 m/s^2	3.28 ft/s^2
9.806 m/s^2 = g (standard acceleration due to gravity)	g = 32.172 ft/s^2
temperature	
X°C	($\frac{9}{5}$ X + 32)°F
$\frac{5}{9}$ ξ(X-32)°C	X°F
temperature interval	
0.5556 K	1°F
1 K = 1°C	1.8°F
energy	
1.0J	0.239 calorie
1.356 J	1 ft lbf
4.187J	1.0 calorie
9.807 J(1 kg fm)	7.233 ft lbf
1 055.06 J	1 Btu
3.6 MJ	1 kilowatt-hr
105.5 MJ	1 therm (100 000 Btu)
power (energy/time)	
0.293 W	1 Btu/hr
1.0 W	0.738 ft lbf/s
1.163 W	1.0 kilocalorie/hr
1.356 W	1 ft lbf/s
4.187 W	1 calorie/s
1 kgf m/s (9.807 W)	7.233 ft lbf/s)
745.7 W	1 horsepower
1 metric horsepower (75 kgf m/s)	0.986 horsepower
intensity of heat flow rate	
1 W/m^2	0.317 Btu/(ft^{2}hr)
3.155 W/m^2	1.0 Btu/(ft^{2}hr)
thermal conductivity	
0.144 W/(m.K)	1 Btu in/(ft^2 hr°F)
1.0 W/(m.K)	6.933 Btu in/(ft^{2}hr°F)
thermal conductance	
1.0 W/(m^2.K)	0.176 Btu/(ft^{2}hr°F)
5.678 W/(m^2.K)	1.0 Btu/(ft^2 hr°F)
thermal registivity	
1.0 m K/W	0.144 ft^2 hr°F/(Btuin)
6.933 m K/W	1.0 ft^2 hr°F/(Btu in)
specific heat capacity	
1.0 kJ/(kg.K)	0.239 Btu/(lb°F)
4.187 kJ/(kg.K)	1.0 Btu/(lb°F)
1.0 kJ/(m^3 K)	0.015 Btu/(ft^3°F)
67.07 kJ/(m^3 K)	1.0 Btu/(ft^3°F)
specific energy	
1.0 kJ/kg	0.43 Btu/lb
2.326 kJ/kg	1.0 Btu/lb
1.0 kJ/m^3 (1 kJ/l)	0.027 Btu/ft^3
1.0 J/l	0.004 Btu/gal
232.1 J/l	1.0 Btu/gal

metric	'imperial'/US
refrigeration	
3.517 kW	12000 Btu/hr = 'ton of refrigeration'
illumination	
1 lx (1 lumen/m^2)	0.093 ft-candle (0.093 lumen/ft^2)
10.764 lx	1.0ft-candle(1 lumen/ft^2)
luminance	
0.3183 cd/m^2	1 apostilb
1.0 cd/m^2	0.000645 cd/ft^2
10.764 cd/m^2	1 cd/ft^2
1550.0 cd/m^2	1.0 cd/in^2
force	
1.0N	0.225 lbf
1.0 kgf (9.807 N; 1.0 kilopond)	2.205 lbf
4.448 kN	1.0 kipf (1000 lbf)
8.897 kN	1.0 tonf US
9.964 kN	1.0 tonf imp
force/unit length	
1.0 N/m	0.067 lbf/ft
14.59 N/m	1.0 lbf/fl
32.69 kN/m	1.0 tonf/ft
175.1 kN/m (175.1 N/mm)	1.0 lbf/in
moment of force (torque)	
0.113 Nm (113.0Nmm)	1.0 lbf in
1.0 Nm	0.738 lbf ft
1.356 Nm	1.0 lbf ft
113.0 Nm	1.0 kipf in
253.1 Nm	1.0 tonf in
1356.0 Nm	1.0 kipf ft
3037.0 Nm	1.0 tonf ft
pressure	
1.0 Pa (1.0 N/m^2)	0.021 lbf/ft^2
1.0 kPa	0.145 lbf/in^2
100.0 Pa	1.0 millibar
2.99 kPa	1 ft water
3.39 kPa	1 in mercury
6.9 kPa	1.0 lbf/in^2
100.0 kPa	1.0 bar
101.33 kPa	1.0 standard atmosphere
107.25 kPa	1.0 tonf/ft^2
15.44 MPa	1.0 tonf/in^2

Length

1 millimetres to inches

mm	0	1	2	3	4	5	6	7	8	9
	in									
0		0.04	0.08	0.11	0.16	0.2	0.24	0.28	0.31	0.35
10	0.39	0.43	0.47	0.51	0.55	0.59	0.63	0.67	0.71	0.75
20	0.79	0.83	0.87	0.91	0.94	0.98	1.02	1.06	1.1	1.14
30	1.18	1.22	1.25	1.3	1.34	1.38	1.41	1.46	1.5	1.57
40	1.57	1.61	1.65	1.69	1.73	1.77	1.81	1.85	1.89	1.93
50	1.97	2.00	2.05	2.09	2.13	2.17	2.21	2.24	2.28	2.32
60	2.36	2.4	2.44	2.48	2.52	2.56	2.6	2.64	2.68	2.72
70	2.76	2.8	2.83	2.87	2.91	2.95	3.0	3.03	3.07	3.11
80	3.15	3.19	3.23	3.27	3.31	3.35	3.39	3.42	3.46	3.5
90	3.54	3.58	3.62	3.66	3.7	3.74	3.78	3.82	3.86	3.9
100	3.94	3.98	4.02	4.06	4.09	4.13	4.17	4.21	4.25	4.29
110	4.33	4.37	4.41	4.45	4.49	4.53	4.57	4.61	4.65	4.69
120	4.72	4.76	4.8	4.84	4.88	4.92	4.96	5.0	5.04	5.08
130	5.12	5.16	5.2	5.24	5.28	5.31	5.35	5.39	5.43	5.47
140	5.51	5.55	5.59	5.63	5.67	5.71	5.75	5.79	5.83	5.87
150	5.91	5.94	5.98	6.02	6.06	6.1	6.14	6.18	6.22	6.26
160	6.3	6.34	6.38	6.42	6.46	6.5	6.54	6.57	6.61	6.65
170	6.69	6.73	6.77	6.81	6.85	6.89	6.93	6.97	7.01	7.05
180	7.09	7.13	7.17	7.21	7.24	7.28	7.32	7.36	7.4	7.44
190	7.48	7.52	7.56	7.6	7.64	7.68	7.72	7.76	7.8	7.83
200	7.87	7.91	7.95	7.99	8.03	8.07	8.11	8.15	8.19	8.23
210	8.27	8.31	8.35	8.39	8.43	8.46	8.5	8.54	8.58	8.62
220	8.66	8.7	8.74	8.78	8.82	8.86	8.9	8.94	8.98	9.02
230	9.06	9.09	9.13	9.17	9.21	9.25	9.29	9.33	9.37	9.41
240	9.45	9.49	9.53	9.57	9.61	9.65	9.69	9.72	9.76	9.8
250	9.84									

2 decimals of inch to millimetres

in	0.000	0.001	0.002	0.003	0.004	0.005	0.006	0.007	0.008	0.009
	mm									
0.0		0.0254	0.0508	0.0762	0.1016	0.127	0.1524	0.1778	0.2032	0.2286
0.01	0.254	0.2794	0.3048	0.3302	0.3556	0.381	0.4064	0.4318	0.4572	0.4826
0.02	0.508	0.5334	0.5588	0.5842	0.6096	0.635	0.6604	0.6858	0.7112	0.7366
0.03	0.762	0.7874	0.8128	0.8382	0.8636	0.889	0.9144	0.9398	0.9652	0.9906
0.04	1.016	1.0414	1.0668	1.0922	1.1176	1.143	1.1684	1.1938	1.2192	1.2446
0.05	1.27	1.2954	1.3208	1.3462	1.3716	1.397	1.4224	1.4478	1.4732	1.4986
0.06	1.524	1.5494	1.5748	1.6002	1.6256	1.651	1.6764	1.7018	1.7272	1.7526
0.07	1.778	1.8034	1.8288	1.8542	1.8796	1.905	1.9304	1.9558	1.9812	2.0066
0.08	2.032	2.0574	2.0828	2.1082	2.1336	2.159	2.1844	2.2098	2.2352	2.2606
0.09	2.286	2.3114	2.3368	2.3622	2.3876	2.413	2.4384	2.4638	2.4892	2.5146
0.1	2.54									

3 inches and fractions of inch to millimetres

in		1/16	1/8	3/16	1/4	5/16	3/8	7/16	1/2	9/16	5/8	11/16	3/4	13/16	7/8	15/16
	mm															
		1.6	3.2	4.8	6.4	7.9	9.5	11.1	12.7	14.3	15.9	17.5	19.1	20.6	22.2	23.8
1	25.4	27.0	28.2	30.2	31.8	33.3	34.9	36.5	38.1	39.7	41.3	42.9	44.5	46.0	47.6	49.2
2	50.8	52.4	54.0	55.6	57.2	58.7	60.3	61.9	63.5	65.1	66.7	68.3	69.9	71.4	73.0	74.6
3	76.2	77.8	79.4	81.0	82.6	84.1	85.7	87.3	88.9	90.5	92.1	93.7	95.3	96.8	98.4	100.0
4	101.6	103.2	104.8	106.4	108.0	109.5	111.1	112.7	114.3	115.9	117.5	119.1	120.7	122.2	123.8	125.4
5	127.0	128.6	130.2	131.8	133.4	134.9	136.5	138.1	139.7	141.3	142.9	144.5	146.1	147.6	149.2	150.8
6	152.4	154.0	155.6	157.2	158.8	160.3	161.9	163.5	165.1	166.7	168.3	169.9	171.5	173.0	174.6	176.2
7	177.8	179.4	181.0	182.6	184.2	185.7	187.3	188.9	190.5	192.1	193.7	195.3	196.9	198.4	200.0	201.6
8	203.2	204.8	206.4	208.0	209.6	211.1	212.7	214.3	215.9	217.5	219.1	220.7	222.3	223.8	225.4	227.0
9	228.6	230.2	231.8	233.4	235.0	236.5	238.1	239.7	241.3	242.9	24.5	246.1	247.7	249.2	250.8	252.4
10	254.0	255.6	257.2	258.8	260.4	261.9	263.5	265.1	266.7	268.3	269.9	271.5	273.1	274.6	276.2	277.8

4 feet and inches to metres

	in											
	0	1	2	3	4	5	6	7	8	9	10	11
	m											
ft												
0		0.0254	0.0508	0.0762	0.1016	0.127	0.1524	0.1778	0.2032	0.2286	0.254	0.2794
1	0.3048	0.3302	0.3556	0.381	0.4064	0.4318	0.4572	0.4826	0.508	0.5334	0.5588	0.5842
2	0.6096	0.635	0.6604	0.6858	0.7112	0.7366	0.762	0.7874	0.8128	0.8382	0.8636	0.889
3	0.9144	0.9398	0.9652	0.9906	1.016	1.0414	1.0668	1.0922	1.1176	1.143	1.1684	1.1938
4	1.2192	1.2446	1.27	1.2954	1.3208	1.3462	1.3716	1.397	1.4224	1.4478	1.4732	1.4986
5	1.524	1.5494	1.5748	1.6002	1.6256	1.651	1.6764	1.7018	1.7272	1.7526	1.778	1.8034
6	1.8288	1.8542	1.8796	1.905	1.9304	1.9558	1.9812	2.0066	2.032	2.0574	2.0828	2.1082
7	2.1336	2.159	2.1844	2.2098	2.2352	2.2606	2.286	2.3114	2.3368	2.3622	2.3876	2.413
8	2.4384	2.4638	2.4892	2.5146	2.54	2.5654	2.5908	2.6162	2.6416	2.667	2.6924	2.7178
9	2.7432	2.7686	2.794	2.8194	2.8448	2.8702	2.8956	2.921	2.9464	2.9718	2.9972	3.0226
10	3.048											

5 metres to feet

m	0	1	2	3	4	5	6	7	8	9
	ft									
0		3.28	6.56	9.84	13.12	16.40	19.69	22.97	26.25	29.53
10	32.8	36.09	39.37	42.65	45.93	49.21	52.49	55.77	59.06	62.34
20	65.62	68.9	72.17	75.45	78.74	82.02	85.3	88.58	91.86	95.14
30	98.43	101.7	104.99	108.27	111.55	114.82	118.11	121.39	124.67	127.95
40	131.23	134.51	137.8	141.08	144.36	147.63	150.91	154.2	157.48	160.76
50	164.04	167.32	170.6	173.89	177.17	180.45	183.73	187.01	190.29	193.57
60	196.85	200.13	203.41	206.69	209.97	213.25	216.54	219.82	223.1	226.38
70	229.66	232.94	236.22	239.5	242.78	246.06	249.34	252.63	255.91	259.19
80	262.46	265.75	269.03	272.31	275.59	278.87	282.15	285.43	288.71	292.0
90	295.28	298.56	301.84	305.12	308.4	311.68	314.96	318.24	321.52	324.8
100	328.08	331.37	334.65	337.93	341.21	344.49	347.77	351.05	354.33	357.61
110	360.89	364.17	367.45	370.74	374.02	377.3	380.58	383.86	387.14	390.42
120	393.7	396.98	400.26	403.54	406.82	410.1	413.39	416.67	419.95	423.23
130	426.51	429.79	433.07	436.35	439.63	442.91	446.19	449.48	452.76	456.04
140	459.32	462.6	465.88	469.16	472.44	475.72	479.0	482.28	485.56	488.85
150	492.13	495.41	498.69	502.0	505.25	508.53	511.81	515.09	518.37	521.65
160	524.93	528.22	531.5	534.78	538.06	541.34	544.62	547.9	551.18	554.46
170	557.74	561.02	564.3	567.59	570.87	574.15	577.43	580.71	583.99	587.27
180	590.55	593.83	597.11	600.39	603.68	606.96	610.24	613.52	616.8	620.08
190	623.36	626.64	629.92	633.2	636.48	639.76	643.05	646.33	649.6	652.89
200	656.17	659.45	662.73	666.01	669.29	672.57	675.85	679.13	682.42	685.7
210	688.98	692.26	695.54	698.82	702.1	705.38	708.66	711.94	715.22	718.5
220	721.79	725.07	728.35	731.63	734.91	738.19	741.47	744.75	748.03	751.31
230	754.59	757.87	761.16	764.44	767.72	771.0	774.28	777.56	780.84	784.12
240	787.4	790.68	793.96	797.24	800.53	803.81	807.09	810.37	813.65	816.93
250	820.21									

7 metres to yards

m	0	1	2	3	4	5	6	7	8	9
	yd									
0		1.09	2.19	3.28	4.37	5.47	6.56	7.66	8.75	9.84
10	10.94	12.03	13.12	14.22	15.31	16.4	17.5	18.59	19.69	20.78
20	21.87	22.97	24.06	25.15	26.25	27.34	28.43	29.53	30.62	31.71
30	32.8	33.9	35.0	36.09	37.18	38.28	39.37	40.46	41.56	42.65
40	43.74	44.84	45.93	47.03	48.12	49.21	50.31	51.4	52.49	53.59
50	54.68	55.77	56.87	57.96	59.06	60.15	61.24	62.34	63.43	64.52
60	65.62	66.71	67.8	68.9	69.99	71.08	72.18	73.27	74.37	75.46
70	76.55	77.65	78.74	79.83	80.93	82.02	83.11	84.21	85.3	86.4
80	87.49	88.58	89.68	90.77	91.86	92.96	94.05	95.14	96.24	97.33
90	98.43	99.52	100.61	101.7.1	102.8	103.89	104.99	106.08	107.17	108.27
100	109.36	110.46	111.55	112.64	113.74	114.83	115.92	117.02	118.11	119.2
110	120.3	121.39	122.49	123.58	124.67	125.74	126.86	127.95	129.05	130.14
120	131.23	132.33	133.42	134.51	135.61	136.7	137.8	138.89	139.99	141.08
130	142.17	143.26	144.36	145.45	146.54	147.64	148.73	149.83	150.92	152.01
140	153.1	154.2	155.29	156.39	157.48	158.57	159.67	160.76	161.86	162.95
150	164.04	165.14	166.23	167.32	168.42	169.51	170.6	171.7	172.79	173.89
160	174.98	176.07	177.17	178.26	179.35	180.45	181.54	182.63	183.73	184.82
170	185.91	187.0	188.1	189.2	190.29	191.38	192.48	193.57	194.66	195.76
180	196.85	197.94	199.04	200.13	201.23	202.32	203.41	204.51	205.6	206.69
190	207.79	208.88	209.97	211.07	212.16	213.26	214.35	215.44	216.53	217.63
200	218.72	219.82	220.91	222.0	223.1	224.19	225.28	226.38	227.47	228.57
210	229.66	230.75	231.85	232.94	234.03	235.13	236.22	237.31	238.41	239.5
220	240.56	241.69	242.78	243.88	244.97	246.06	247.16	248.25	249.34	250.44
230	251.53	252.63	253.72	254.81	255.91	257.0	258.09	259.19	260.28	261.37
240	262.47	263.56	264.65	265.75	266.84	267.94	269.03	270.12	271.22	272.31
250	273.4									

9 kilometres to miles

km	0	1	2	3	4	5	6	7	8	9
	mile									
0		0.62	1.24	1.86	2.49	3.11	3.73	4.35	4.98	5.59
10	6.21	6.84	7.46	8.08	8.7	9.32	9.94	10.56	11.18	11.81
20	12.43	13.05	13.67	14.29	14.91	15.53	16.16	16.78	17.4	18.02
30	18.64	19.29	19.88	20.5	21.13	21.75	22.37	22.99	23.61	24.23
40	24.85	25.47	26.1	26.72	27.34	27.96	28.58	29.2	29.83	30.45
50	31.07	31.69	32.31	32.93	33.55	34.18	34.8	35.42	36.04	36.66
60	37.28	37.9	38.53	39.15	39.77	40.39	41.01	41.63	42.25	42.87
70	43.5	44.12	44.74	45.36	45.98	46.6	47.22	47.85	48.47	49.09
80	49.7	50.33	50.95	51.57	52.2	52.82	53.44	54.06	54.68	55.3
90	55.92	56.54	57.17	57.79	58.41	59.03	59.65	60.27	60.89	61.52
100	62.14									

6 feet to metres

ft	0	1	2	3	4	5	6	7	8	9
	m									
0		0.31	0.6	0.91	1.22	1.52	1.83	2.13	2.44	2.74
10	3.05	3.35	3.66	3.96	4.27	4.57	4.88	5.18	5.49	5.79
20	6.1	6.4	6.71	7.01	7.31	7.62	7.92	8.23	8.53	8.84
30	9.14	9.45	9.75	10.06	10.36	10.67	10.97	11.28	11.58	11.89
40	12.19	12.5	12.80	13.1	13.41	13.72	14.02	14.36	14.63	14.94
50	15.24	15.54	15.85	16.15	16.46	16.76	17.07	17.37	17.68	17.98
60	18.29	18.59	18.9	19.2	19.58	19.81	20.12	20.42	20.73	21.03
70	21.33	21.64	21.95	22.25	22.56	22.86	23.16	23.47	23.77	24.08
80	24.38	24.69	24.99	25.3	25.6	25.91	26.21	26.52	26.82	27.13
90	27.43	27.74	28.04	28.35	28.65	28.96	29.26	29.57	29.87	30.18
100	30.48	30.78	31.09	31.39	31.7	32.0	32.31	32.61	32.92	33.22
110	33.53	33.83	34.14	34.44	34.75	35.05	35.37	35.67	36.0	36.3
120	36.58	36.88	37.19	37.49	37.8	38.1	38.41	38.7	39.01	39.32
130	39.62	39.93	40.23	40.54	40.84	41.15	41.45	41.76	42.06	42.37
140	42.67	42.98	43.28	43.59	43.89	44.2	44.5	44.81	45.11	45.46
150	45.72	46.02	46.33	46.63	46.94	47.24	47.55	47.85	48.16	48.46
160	48.77	49.07	49.38	49.68	49.99	50.29	50.6	50.9	51.21	51.51
170	51.82	52.12	52.43	52.73	53.04	53.34	53.64	53.95	54.25	54.56
180	54.86	55.17	55.47	55.78	56.08	56.39	56.69	57.0	57.3	57.61
190	57.91	58.22	58.52	58.83	59.13	59.44	59.74	60.05	60.35	60.66
200	60.96	61.26	61.57	61.87	62.18	62.48	62.79	63.09	63.4	63.7
210	64.01	64.31	64.62	64.92	65.23	65.53	65.84	66.14	66.45	66.75
220	67.06	67.36	67.67	67.97	68.28	68.58	68.89	69.19	69.49	69.79
230	70.1	70.41	70.71	71.02	71.32	71.63	71.93	72.24	72.54	72.85
240	73.15	73.46	73.76	74.07	74.37	74.68	74.98	75.29	75.59	75.9
250	76.2									

8 yards to metres

yd	0	1	2	3	4	5	6	7	8	9
	m									
0		0.91	1.83	2.74	3.65	4.57	5.49	6.4	7.32	8.23
10	9.14	10.06	10.97	11.89	12.8	13.71	14.63	15.54	16.46	17.37
20	18.29	19.2	20.12	21.03	21.95	22.86	23.77	24.69	25.6	26.52
30	27.43	28.35	29.26	30.18	31.09	32.0	32.92	33.83	34.75	35.66
40	36.58	37.49	38.4	39.32	40.23	41.15	42.06	42.98	43.89	44.81
50	45.72	46.63	47.55	48.46	49.38	50.29	51.21	52.12	53.04	53.95
60	54.86	55.78	56.69	57.61	58.52	59.44	60.35	61.27	62.18	63.09
70	64.0	64.92	65.84	66.75	67.67	68.58	69.49	70.41	71.32	72.24
80	73.15	74.07	74.98	75.9	76.81	77.72	78.64	79.55	80.47	81.38
90	82.3	83.21	84.12	85.04	85.95	86.87	87.78	88.7	89.61	90.53
100	91.44	92.35	93.27	94.18	95.1	96.01	96.93	97.84	98.76	99.67
110	100.58	101.5	102.41	103.33	104.24	105.16	106.07	106.99	107.9	108.81
120	109.73	110.64	111.56	112.47	113.39	114.3	115.21	116.13	117.04	117.96
130	118.87	119.79	120.7	121.61	122.53	123.44	124.36	125.27	126.19	127.1
140	128.02	128.93	129.85	130.76	131.67	132.59	133.5	134.42	135.33	136.25
150	137.16	138.07	138.99	139.9	140.82	141.73	142.65	143.56	144.48	145.39
160	146.3	147.22	148.13	149.05	149.96	150.88	151.79	152.71	153.62	154.53
170	155.45	156.36	157.28	158.19	159.11	160.02	160.93	161.85	162.76	163.68
180	164.59	165.51	166.42	167.34	168.25	169.16	170.08	170.99	171.9	172.82
190	173.74	174.65	175.57	176.48	177.39	178.31	179.22	180.14	181.05	181.97
200	182.88	183.79	184.71	185.62	186.54	187.45	188.37	189.28	190.2	191.11
210	192.02	192.94	193.85	194.77	195.68	196.6	197.51	198.43	199.34	200.25
220	201.17	202.08	203.0	203.91	204.83	205.74	206.65	207.57	208.48	209.4
230	210.31	211.23	212.14	213.06	213.97	214.88	215.8	216.71	217.63	218.54
240	219.46	220.37	221.29	222.0	223.11	224.03	224.94	225.86	226.77	227.69
250	228.6									

10 miles to kilometres

mile	0	1	2	3	4	5	6	7	8	9
	km									
0		1.61	3.22	4.83	6.44	8.05	9.66	11.27	12.87	14.48
10	16.09	17.7	19.31	20.92	22.53	24.14	25.75	27.36	28.97	30.58
20	32.19	33.8	35.41	37.01	38.62	40.23	41.84	43.45	45.06	46.67
30	48.28	49.89	51.5	53.11	54.72	56.33	57.94	59.55	61.16	62.76
40	64.37	65.98	67.59	69.2	70.81	72.42	74.03	75.64	77.25	78.86
50	80.47	82.08	83.69	85.3	86.9	88.51	90.12	91.73	93.34	94.95
60	96.56	98.17	99.78	101.39	103.0	104.61	106.22	107.83	109.44	111.05
70	112.65	114.26	115.87	117.48	119.09	120.7	122.31	123.92	125.53	127.14
80	128.75	130.36	131.97	133.58	135.19	136.79	138.4	140.01	141.62	143.23
90	144.84	146.45	148.06	149.67	151.28	152.89	154.5	156.11	157.72	159.33
100	160.93									

Area

11
square centimetres to square inches

cm²	0	1	2	3	4	5	6	7	8	9
	in²									
0		0.16	0.31	0.47	0.62	0.78	0.93	1.09	1.24	1.4
10	1.6	1.71	1.86	2.02	2.17	2.33	2.48	2.64	2.79	2.95
20	3.1	3.26	3.41	3.57	3.72	3.88	4.03	4.19	4.34	4.5
30	4.65	4.81	4.96	5.12	5.27	5.43	5.58	5.74	5.9	6.05
40	6.2	6.36	6.51	6.67	6.82	6.98	7.13	7.29	7.44	7.6
50	7.75	7.91	8.06	8.22	8.37	8.53	8.68	8.84	9.0	9.15
60	9.3	9.46	9.61	9.77	9.92	10.08	10.23	10.39	10.54	10.7
70	10.85	11.01	11.16	11.32	11.47	11.63	11.78	11.94	12.09	12.25
80	12.4	12.56	12.71	12.87	13.02	13.18	13.33	13.49	13.64	13.8
90	13.95	14.11	14.26	14.42	14.57	14.73	14.88	15.04	15.19	15.35
100	15.5	15.66	15.81	15.97	16.12	16.28	16.43	16.59	16.74	16.9
110	17.05	17.21	17.36	17.52	17.67	17.83	17.98	18.14	18.29	18.45
120	18.6	18.76	18.91	19.07	19.22	19.38	19.53	19.69	19.84	20.0
130	20.15	20.31	20.46	20.62	20.77	20.93	21.08	21.24	21.39	21.55
140	21.7	21.86	22.01	22.17	22.32	22.48	22.63	22.79	22.94	23.1
150	23.25	23.41	23.56	23.72	23.87	24.03	24.18	24.34	24.49	24.65
160	24.8	24.96	25.11	25.27	25.42	25.58	25.73	25.89	26.04	26.2
170	26.35	26.51	26.66	26.82	26.97	27.13	27.28	27.44	27.59	27.75
180	27.9	28.06	28.21	28.37	28.52	28.68	28.83	28.99	29.14	29.3
190	29.45	29.61	29.76	29.92	30.07	30.23	30.38	30.54	30.69	30.85
200	31.0	31.16	31.31	31.47	31.62	31.78	31.93	32.09	32.24	32.4
210	32.55	32.71	32.86	33.02	33.17	33.33	33.48	33.64	33.79	33.95
220	34.1	34.26	34.41	34.57	34.72	34.88	35.03	35.19	35.34	35.5
230	35.65	35.81	35.96	36.12	36.27	36.43	36.58	36.75	36.89	37.05
240	37.20	37.36	37.51	37.67	37.82	37.98	38.13	38.29	38.44	38.6
250	38.75									

13
square metres to square feet

m²	0	1	2	3	4	5	6	7	8	9
	ft²									
0		10.76	21.53	32.29	43.06	53.82	64.58	75.35	86.11	96.88
10	107.64	118.4	129.17	139.93	150.66	161.46	172.22	182.97	193.75	204.51
20	215.29	226.01	236.81	247.57	258.33	269.1	279.86	290.63	301.39	312.15
30	322.92	333.68	344.45	355.21	365.97	376.74	387.5	398.27	409.03	419.79
40	430.56	441.32	452.08	462.85	473.61	484.38	495.14	505.91	516.67	527.43
50	538.2	548.96	559.72	570.49	581.25	592.02	602.78	613.54	624.31	635.07
60	645.84	656.6	667.36	678.13	688.89	699.65	710.42	721.18	731.95	742.71
70	753.47	764.24	775.0	785.77	796.53	807.29	818.06	828.82	839.59	850.35
80	861.11	871.88	882.64	893.41	904.17	914.93	925.7	936.46	947.22	957.99
90	968.75	979.52	990.28	1 001.04	1 011.81	1 022.57	1 033.34	1 044.1	1 054.86	1 065.63
100	1 076.39	1 087.15	1 097.92	1 108.68	1 119.45	1 130.21	1 140.97	1 151.74	1 162.5	1 173.27
110	1 184.03	1 194.79	1 205.56	1 216.32	1 227.09	1 237.85	1 248.61	1 259.38	1 270.14	1 280.91
120	1 291.67	1 302.43	1 313.2	1 323.96	1 334.72	1 345.49	1 356.25	1 367.02	1 377.78	1 388.54
130	1 399.31	1 410.07	1 420.84	1 431.6	1 442.36	1 453.13	1 463.89	1 474.66	1 485.42	1 496.18
140	1 506.95	1 517.71	1 528.48	1 539.24	1 550.0	1 560.77	1 571.53	1 582.29	1 593.06	1 603.82
150	1 614.59	1 625.35	1 636.11	1 646.88	1 657.64	1 668.41	1 679.17	1 689.93	1 700.7	1 711.46
160	1 722.23	1 732.99	1 743.75	1 754.52	1 765.28	1 776.05	1 786.81	1 797.57	1 808.34	1 819.1
170	1 829.86	1 840.63	1 851.39	1 862.16	1 872.92	1 883.68	1 894.45	1 905.21	1 915.98	1 926.74
180	1 937.5	1 948.27	1 959.03	1 969.8	1 980.56	1991.32	2 002.09	2 012.85	2023.62	2 034.38
190	2 045.14	2 055.91	2 066.67	2 077.43	2 088.2	2 098.96	2 109.73	2 120.49	2 131.25	2 142.02
200	2 152.78	2 163.55	2 174.31	2 185.07	2 195.84	2 206.6	2 217.37	2 228.13	2 238.89	2 249.66
210	2 260.42	2 271.19	2 281.95	2 292.71	2 303.48	2 314.24	2 325.0	2 335.77	2 346.53	2 357.3
220	2 368.06	2 378.82	2 389.59	2 400.35	2411.12	2 421.88	2 432.64	2 443.41	2 454.17	2 464.94
230	2 475.7	2 486.46	2 497.23	2 507.99	2 518.76	2 529.52	2 540.28	2 551.05	2 561.81	2 572.57
240	2 583.34	2 594.1	2 604.87	2 615.63	2 626.39	2 637.16	2 647.92	2 658.69	2 669.45	2 680.21
250	2 690.98	2 701.74	2 712.51	2 723.27	2 734.03	2 744.8	2 755.56	2 766.32	2 777.09	2 787.85
260	2 798.62	2 809.38	2 820.14	2 830.91	2 841.67	2 852.44	2 863.2	2 873.96	2 884.73	2 895.49
270	2 906.26	2 917.02	2 927.78	2 938.55	2 949.31	2 960.08	2 970.84	2 981.6	2 992.37	3 003.13
280	3 013.89	3 024.66	3 035.42	3 046.19	3 056.95	3 067.71	3 078.48	3 089.24	3 100.01	3 110.77
290	3121.53	3 132.3	3 143.06	3 153.83	3 164.59	3175.35	3 186.12	3 196.88	3 207.65	3 218.41
300	3 229.17	3 239.94	3 250.7	3 261.46	3 272.23	3 282.99	3 293.76	3 304.52	3 315.28	3 326.05
310	3 336.81	3 347.58	3 358.34	3 369.1	3 379.87	3 390.63	3 401.4	3 412.16	3 422.92	3 433.69
320	3 444.45	3 455.22	3 465.98	3 476.74	3 487.51	3 498.27	3 509.03	3 519.8	3 530.56	3 541.33
330	3 552.09	3 562.85	3 573.62	3 584.38	3 595.15	3 605.91	3 616.67	3 627.44	3 638.2	3 648.97
340	3 659.73	3 670.49	3 681.26	3 692.02	3 702.79	3 713.55	3 724.31	3 735.08	3 745.84	3 756.6
350	3 767.37	3 778.13	3 788.9	3 799.66	3 810.42	3 821.19	3 831.95	3 842.72	3 853.48	3 864.24
360	3 875.01	3 885.77	3 896.54	3 907.3	3 918.06	3 928.83	3 939.59	3 950.36	3 961.12	3 971.88
370	3 982.65	3 993.41	4 004.17	4 014.94	4 025.7	4 036.47	4 047.23	4 057.99	4 068.76	4 079.52
380	4 090.29	4 101.05	4111.81	4 122.58	4 133.34	4 144.11	4 154.87	4 165.63	4 176.4	4 187.16
390	4 197.93	4 208.69	4 219.45	4 230.22	4 240.98	4 251.74	4 262.51	4 273.27	4 284.04	4 294.8
400	4 305.56	4 316.33	4 327.09	4 337.86	4 348.62	4 359.38	4 370.15	4 380.91	4 391.68	4 402.44
410	4 413.2	4 423.97	4 434.73	4 445.49	4 456.26	4 467.02	4 477.79	4 488.55	4 499.31	4 510.08
420	4 520.84	4 531.61	4 542.37	4 553.13	4 563.9	4 574.66	4 585.43	4 596.19	4 606.95	4 617.72
430	4 628.48	4 639.25	4 650.01	4 660.77	4 671.54	4 682.3	4 693.06	4 703.83	4 714.59	4 725.36
440	4 736.12	4 746.88	4 757.65	4 768.41	4 779.18	4 789.94	4 800.7	4 811.47	4 822.23	4 833.0
450	4 843.76	4 854.52	4 865.29	4 876.05	4 886.82	4 897.58	4 908.34	4 919.11	4 929.87	4 940.63
460	4 951.4	4 962.16	4 972.93	4 983.69	4 994.45	5 005.22	5 015.98	5 026.75	5 037.51	5 048.27
470	5 059.04	5 069.8	5 080.57	5 091.33	5 102.09	5112.86	5 123.62	5 134.39	5 145.15	5 155.91
480	5 166.68	5 177.44	5 188.2	5 198.97	5 209.73	5 220.5	5 231.26	5 242.02	5 252.79	5 263.55
490	5 274.32	5 285.08	5 295.84	5 306.61	5 317.37	5 328.14	5 338.9	5 349.66	5 360.43	5 371.19
500	5 381.96									

12 square inches to square centimetres

inf	0	1	2	3	4	5	6	7	8	9
	cm²									
0		6.45	12.9	19.36	25.81	32.26	38.71	45.16	51.61	58.06
10	64.52	70.97	77.41	83.87	90.32	96.77	103.23	109.68	116.13	122.58
20	129.03	135.48	141.94	148.39	154.84	161.29	167.74	174.19	180.65	187.1
30	193.55	200.0	206.45	212.9	219.35	225.8	232.26	238.71	245.16	251.61
40	258.06	264.52	270.97	277.42	283.87	290.32	296.77	303.23	309.68	316.13
50	322.58	329.03	335.48	341.94	348.4	354.84	361.29	367.74	374.19	380.64
60	387.1	393.55	400.0	406.45	412.91	419.35	425.81	432.26	438.71	445.16
70	451.61	458.06	464.52	470.97	477.42	483.87	490.32	496.77	503.23	509.68
80	516.13	522.58	529.03	535.48	541.93	548.39	554.84	561.29	567.74	574.19
90	580.64	587.1	593.55	600.0	606.45	612.91	619.35	625.81	632.26	638.71
100	645.16	651.61	658.06	664.51	670.97	677.42	683.87	690.32	696.77	703.22
110	709.6	716.13	722.58	729.03	735.48	741.93	748.39	754.84	761.29	767.74
120	774.19	780.64	787.1	793.55	800.0	806.45	812.9	819.35	825.81	832.26
130	838.71	845.16	851.61	858.06	864.51	870.97	877.42	883.87	890.32	896.77
140	903.22	909.68	916.13	922.58	929.03	935.48	941.93	948.39	954.84	961.29
150	967.74	974.19	980.64	987.1	993.55	1 000.00	1 006.45	1 012.9	1 019.35	1 025.8
160	1 032.26	1 038.71	1 045.16	1 051.61	1 058.06	1 064.51	1 070.97	1 077.42	1 083.87	1 090.32
170	1 096.77	1 103.22	1 109.68	1 116.13	1 122.58	1 129.03	1 135.48	1 141.93	1 148.38	1 154.84
180	1 161.29	1 167.74	1 174.19	1 180.64	1 187.09	1 193.55	1 200.0	1 206.45	1 212.9	1 219.35
190	1 225.8	1 232.26	1 238.71	1 245.16	1251.61	1 258.06	1 264.51	1 270.97	1 277.42	1 283.87
200	1 290.32	1 296.77	1 303.22	1 309.67	1 316.13	1 322.58	1 329.03	1 335.48	1 341.93	1 348.38
210	1 354.84	1 361.29	1 367.74	1 374.19	1 380.64	1 387.09	1 393.55	1 400.0	1 406.45	1 412.9
220	1 419.35	1 425.8	1 432.26	1 438.71	1 445.16	1 451.61	1 458.06	1 464.51	1 470.96	1 477.42
230	1 483.87	1 490.32	1 496.77	1 503.22	1 509.67	1 516.13	1 522.58	1 529.03	1 535.48	1 541.93
240	1 548.38	1 554.84	1 561.29	1 567.74	1 574.19	1 580.64	1 587.09	1 593.55	1 600.0	1 606.45
250	1 612.9									

14 square feet to square metres

ft²	0	1	2	3	4	5	6	7	8	9
	m²									
0		0.09	0.19	0.28	0.37	0.46	0.56	0.65	0.74	0.84
10	0.93	1.02	1.11	1.21	1.3	1.39	1.49	1.58	1.67	1.77
20	1.86	1.95	2.04	2.14	2.23	2.32	2.42	2.51	2.6	2.69
30	2.79	2.88	2.97	3.07	3.16	3.25	3.34	3.44	3.53	3.62
40	3.72	3.81	3.9	3.99	4.09	4.18	4.27	4.37	4.46	4.55
50	4.65	4.74	4.83	4.92	5.02	5.11	5.2	5.3	5.39	5.48
60	5.57	5.67	5.76	5.85	5.95	6.04	6.13	6.22	6.32	6.41
70	6.5	6.6	6.69	6.78	6.87	6.97	7.06	7.15	7.25	7.34
80	7.43	7.53	7.62	7.71	7.8	7.9	7.99	8.08	8.18	8.27
90	8.36	8.45	8.55	8.64	8.73	8.83	8.92	9.01	9.1	9.2
100	9.29	9.38	9.48	9.57	9.66	9.75	9.85	9.94	10.03	10.13
110	10.22	10.31	10.41	10.5	10.59	10.68	10.78	10.87	10.96	11.06
120	11.15	11.24	11.33	11.43	11.52	11.61	11.71	11.8	11.89	11.98
130	12.08	12.17	12.26	12.36	12.45	12.54	12.63	12.73	12.82	12.91
140	13.01	13.1	13.19	13.29	13.38	13.47	13.56	13.66	13.75	13.84
150	13.94	14.03	14.12	14.21	14.31	14.4	14.49	14.59	14.68	14.77
160	14.86	14.96	15.05	15.14	15.24	15.33	15.42	15.51	15.61	15.7
170	15.79	15.89	15.98	16.07	16.17	16.26	16.35	16.44	16.54	16.63
180	16.72	16.82	16.91	17.0	17.09	17.19	17.28	17.37	17.47	17.56
190	17.65	17.74	17.84	17.93	18.02	18.12	18.21	18.3	18.39	18.49
200	18.58	18.67	18.77	18.86	18.95	19.05	19.14	19.23	19.32	19.42
210	19.51	19.6	19.7	19.79	19.88	19.97	20.07	20.16	20.25	20.35
220	20.44	20.53	20.62	20.72	20.81	20.9	21.0	21.09	21.18	21.27
230	21.37	21.46	21.55	21.65	21.74	21.83	21.93	22.02	22.11	22.2
240	22.3	22.39	22.48	22.58	22.67	22.76	22.85	22.95	23.04	23.13
250	23.23	23.32	23.41	23.5	23.6	23.69	23.78	23.88	23.97	24.06
260	24.15	24.25	24.34	24.43	24.53	24.62	24.71	24.81	24.9	24.99
270	25.08	25.18	25.27	25.36	25.46	25.55	25.64	25.73	25.83	25.92
280	26.01	26.11	26.2	26.29	26.38	26.48	26.57	26.66	26.76	26.85
290	26.94	27.03	27.13	27.22	27.31	27.41	27.5	27.59	27.69	27.78
300	27.87	27.96	28.06	28.15	28.24	28.34	28.43	28.52	28.61	28.71
310	28.8	28.89	28.99	29.08	29.17	29.26	29.36	29.45	29.54	29.64
320	29.73	29.82	29.91	30.01	30.1	30.19	30.29	30.38	30.47	30.57
330	30.66	30.75	30.84	30.94	31.03	31.12	31.22	31.31	31.4	31.49
340	31.59	31.68	31.77	31.87	31.96	32.05	32.14	32.24	32.33	32.42
350	32.52	32.61	32.7	32.79	32.89	32.98	33.07	33.17	33.26	33.35
360	33.45	33.54	33.63	33.72	33.82	33.91	34.0	34.1	34.19	34.28
370	34.37	34.47	34.56	34.65	34.75	34.84	34.93	35.02	35.12	35.21
380	35.3	35.4	35.49	35.58	35.67	35.77	35.86	35.95	36.05	36.14
390	36.23	36.33	36.42	36.51	36.6	36.7	36.79	36.88	36.98	37.07
400	37.16	37.25	37.35	37.44	37.53	37.63	37.72	37.81	37.9	38.0
410	38.09	38.18	38.28	38.37	38.46	38.55	38.65	38.74	38.83	38.93
420	39.02	39.11	39.21	39.3	39.39	39.48	39.58	39.67	39.76	39.86
430	39.95	40.04	40.13	40.23	40.32	40.41	40.51	40.6	40.69	40.78
440	40.88	40.97	41.06	41.16	41.25	41.34	41.43	41.53	41.62	41.71
450	41.81	41.9	41.99	42.09	42.18	42.27	42.36	42.46	42.55	42.64
460	42.74	42.83	42.92	43.01	43.11	43.2	43.29	43.39	43.48	43.57
470	43.66	43.76	43.85	43.94	44.04	44.13	44.22	44.31	44.41	44.5
480	44.59	44.69	44.78	44.87	44.97	45.06	45.15	45.24	45.34	45.43
490	45.52	45.62	45.71	45.8	45.89	45.99	46.08	46.17	46.27	46.36
500	46.45									

15 square metres to square yards

m²	0	1	2	3	4	5	6	7	8	9
	yd²									
0		1.2	2.39	3.58	4.78	5.98	7.18	8.37	9.57	10.76
10	11.96	13.16	14.35	15.55	16.74	17.94	19.14	20.33	21.53	22.72
20	23.92	25.12	26.31	27.51	28.7	29.9	31.1	32.29	33.49	34.68
30	35.88	37.08	38.27	39.47	40.66	41.86	43.06	44.25	45.45	46.64
40	47.84	49.04	50.23	51.43	52.62	53.82	55.02	56.21	57.41	58.6
50	59.8	61.0	62.19	63.39	64.58	65.78	66.98	68.17	69.37	70.56
60	71.76	72.96	74.15	75.35	76.54	77.74	78.94	80.13	81.33	82.52
70	83.72	84.92	86.11	87.31	88.5	89.7	90.9	92.09	93.29	94.48
80	95.68	96.88	98.07	99.27	100.46	101.66	102.86	104.05	105.25	106.44
90	107.64	108.84	110.03	111.23	112.42	113.62	114.82	116.01	117.21	118.4
100	119.6	120.8	121.99	123.19	124.38	125.58	126.78	127.97	129.17	130.36
110	131.56	132.76	133.95	135.15	136.34	137.54	138.74	139.93	141.13	142.32
120	143.52	144.72	145.91	147.11	148.31	149.5	150.7	151.89	153.09	154.28
130	155.48	156.68	157.87	159.07	160.26	161.46	162.66	163.85	165.05	166.24
140	167.44	168.64	169.83	171.03	172.22	173.41	174.62	175.81	177.01	178.2
150	179.34	180.59	181.79	182.99	184.18	185.38	186.57	187.77	188.97	190.16
160	191.36	192.55	193.75	194.95	196.14	197.34	198.53	199.73	200.93	202.12
170	203.32	204.51	205.71	206.91	208.1	209.3	210.49	211.69	212.89	214.08
180	215.28	216.47	217.67	218.87	220.06	221.26	222.45	223.65	224.85	226.04
190	227.24	228.43	229.63	230.83	232.02	233.22	234.41	235.61	236.81	238.0
200	239.2	240.39	241.59	242.79	243.98	245.18	246.37	247.57	248.77	249.96
210	251.16	252.35	253.55	254.75	255.94	257.14	258.33	259.53	260.73	261.92
220	263.12	264.31	265.51	266.71	267.9	269.1	270.29	271.49	272.69	273.88
230	275.08	276.27	277.47	278.67	279.86	281.06	282.25	283.45	284.65	285.84
240	287.04	288.23	289.43	290.63	291.82	293.02	294.21	295.41	296.61	297.8
250	299.0	300.19	301.39	302.59	303.78	304.98	306.17	307.37	308.57	309.76
260	310.96	312.15	313.35	314.55	315.74	316.94	318.13	319.33	320.53	321.72
270	322.92	324.11	325.31	326.51	327.7	328.9	330.09	331.29	332.49	333.68
280	334.88	336.07	337.27	338.47	339.66	340.86	342.05	343.25	344.45	345.64
290	346.84	348.03	349.23	350.43	351.62	352.82	354.02	355.21	356.41	357.6
300	358.78	359.99	361.19	362.39	363.58	364.78	365.97	367.17	368.37	369.56
310	370.76	371.95	373.15	374.35	375.54	376.74	377.94	379.13	380.33	381.52
320	382.72	383.91	385.11	386.31	387.5	388.7	389.89	391.09	392.29	393.48
330	394.68	395.87	397.07	398.27	399.46	400.66	401.85	403.05	404.25	405.44
340	406.64	407.83	409.03	410.23	411.42	412.62	413.81	415.01	416.21	417.4
350	418.6	419.79	420.99	422.18	423.38	424.58	425.77	426.97	428.16	429.36
360	430.56	431.75	432.95	434.14	435.34	436.54	437.73	438.93	440.12	441.32
370	442.52	443.71	444.91	446.11	447.3	448.5	449.69	450.89	452.08	453.28
380	454.48	455.67	456.87	458.06	459.26	460.46	461.65	462.84	464.04	465.24
390	466.44	467.63	468.83	470.02	471.22	472.42	473.61	474.81	476.0	477.2
400	478.4	479.59	480.79	481.98	483.18	484.38	485.57	486.77	487.96	489.16
410	490.36	491.55	492.75	493.94	495.14	496.34	497.53	498.73	499.92	501.12
420	502.32	503.51	504.71	505.9	507.1	508.3	509.49	510.69	511.88	513.08
430	514.28	515.47	516.67	517.86	519.06	520.26	521.45	522.65	523.84	525.04
440	526.24	527.43	528.63	529.82	531.02	532.22	533.41	534.61	535.8	537.0
450	538.2	539.39	540.59	541.78	542.98	544.18	545.37	546.57	547.76	548.96
460	550.16	551.35	552.55	553.74	554.94	556.14	557.33	558.53	559.72	560.92
470	562.12	563.31	564.5	565.71	566.9	568.1	569.29	570.49	571.68	572.88
480	574.08	575.27	576.47	577.66	578.86	580.06	581.25	582.45	583.64	584.84
490	586.04	587.23	588.43	589.62	590.82	592.02	593.21	594.41	595.6	596.8
500	598.0									

17 hectares to acres

ha	0	1	2	3	4	5	6	7	8	9
	acre									
		2.47	4.94	7.41	9.88	12.36	14.83	17.3	19.77	22.24

ha	0	10	20	30	40	50	60	70	80	90
	acre									
0		24.71	49.42	74.13	98.84	123.55	148.26	172.97	197.68	222.4
100	247.11	271.82	296.53	321.24	345.95	370.66	395.37	420.08	444.8	469.5
200	494.21	518.92	543.63	568.34	593.05	617.76	642.47	667.19	691.9	716.61
300	741.32	766.03	790.74	815.45	840.16	864.87	889.58	914.29	939.0	963.71
400	988.42	1 013.13	1 037.84	1 062.55	1 087.26	1 111.97	1 136.68	1 161.4	1 186.11	1 210.82
500	1 235.53	1 260.24	1 284.95	1 309.66	1 334.37	1 359.08	1 383.79	1 408.5	1 433.21	1 457.92
600	1 482.63	1 507.34	1 532.05	1 556.76	1 581.47	1 606.18	1 630.9	1 655.61	1 680.32	705.03
700	1 729.74	1 754.45	1 779.16	1 803.87	1 828.58	1 853.29	1 878.0	1 902.71	1 927.42	1 952.13
800	1 976.84	2 001.55	2 026.26	2 050.97	2 075.69	2 100.4	2 125.11	2 149.82	2 174.53	2 199.24
900	2 223.95	2 248.66	2 273.37	2 298.08	2 322.79	2 347.5	2 372.21	2 396.92	2 421.63	2 446.34
1 000	2 471.05									

16
square yards to square metres

yd²	0	1	2	3	4	5	6	7	8	9
	m²									
0		0.84	1.67	2.51	3.34	4.18	5.02	5.85	6.69	7.53
10	8.36	9.2	10.03	10.87	11.71	12.54	13.38	14.21	15.05	15.89
20	16.72	17.56	18.39	19.23	20.07	20.9	21.74	22.58	23.41	24.25
30	25.08	25.92	26.76	27.59	28.43	29.26	30.1	30.94	31.77	32.61
40	33.45	34.28	35.12	35.95	36.79	37.63	38.46	39.3	40.13	40.97
50	41.81	42.64	43.48	44.31	45.15	45.99	46.82	47.66	48.5	49.33
60	50.17	51.0	51.84	52.68	53.51	54.35	55.18	56.02	56.86	57.69
70	58.53	59.37	60.2	61.04	61.87	62.71	63.55	64.38	65.22	66.05
80	66.89	67.7	68.56	69.3	70.23	71.07	71.9	72.74	73.5	74.4
90	75.25	76.09	76.92	77.76	78.6	79.43	80.27	81.10	81.94	82.78
100	83.61	84.45	85.29	86.12	86.96	87.79	88.62	89.47	90.3	91.14
110	91.97	92.81	93.65	94.48	95.32	96.15	96.99	97.83	98.66	99.5
120	100.34	101.17	102.0	102.84	103.68	104.52	105.35	106.19	107.02	107.86
130	108.7	109.53	110.37	111.21	112.04	112.88	113.71	114.55	115.39	116.22
140	117.06	117.89	118.73	119.57	120.41	121.24	122.08	122.91	123.75	124.58
150	125.42	126.26	127.09	127.93	128.76	129.6	130.44	131.27	132.11	132.94
160	133.78	134.62	135.45	136.29	137.13	137.96	138.8	139.63	140.47	141.31
170	142.14	142.98	143.81	144.65	145.49	146.32	147.16	148.0	148.83	149.67
180	150.5	151.34	152.18	153.01	153.85	154.68	155.52	156.36	157.19	158.03
190	158.86	159.7	160.54	161.37	162.21	163.05	163.88	164.72	165.55	166.39
200	167.23	168.06	168.9	169.73	170.57	171.41	172.24	173.08	173.91	174.75
210	175.59	176.42	177.26	178.1	178.93	179.77	180.61	181.44	182.28	183.11
220	183.95	184.78	185.62	186.46	187.29	188.13	188.97	189.80	190.64	191.47
230	192.31	193.15	193.98	194.82	195.65	196.49	197.33	198.16	199.0	199.83
240	200.67	201.51	202.34	203.18	204.02	204.85	205.69	206.52	207.36	208.2
250	209.03	209.87	210.7	211.54	212.38	213.21	214.1	214.89	215.72	216.56
260	217.39	218.3	219.07	219.9	220.74	221.57	222.41	223.25	224.08	224.92
270	225.75	226.59	227.43	228.26	229.1	229.94	230.77	231.61	232.44	233.28
280	234.12	234.95	235.79	236.62	237.46	238.3	239.13	239.97	240.81	241.64
290	242.48	243.31	244.15	244.99	245.82	246.66	247.49	248.33	249.17	250.0
300	250.84	251.67	252.51	253.35	254.18	255.02	255.86	256.69	257.53	258.36
310	259.2	260.04	260.87	261.71	262.54	263.38	264.22	265.05	265.89	266.73
320	267.56	268.4	269.23	270.07	270.91	271.74	272.58	273.41	274.25	275.09
330	275.92	276.76	277.59	278.43	279.27	280.11	280.94	281.78	282.61	283.45
340	284.28	285.12	285.96	286.79	287.63	288.46	289.3	290.14	290.97	291.81
350	292.65	293.48	294.32	295.15	295.99	296.83	297.66	298.5	299.33	300.17
360	301.0	301.84	302.68	303.51	304.35	305.19	306.02	306.86	307.7	308.53
370	309.37	310.2	311.04	311.88	312.71	313.55	314.38	315.22	316.06	316.89
380	317.73	318.57	319.4	320.24	321.07	321.91	322.75	323.58	324.42	325.25
390	326.09	326.93	327.76	328.6	329.43	330.27	331.11	331.94	332.78	333.62
400	334.45	335.29	336.12	336.96	337.8	338.63	339.47	340.31	341.14	341.98
410	342.81	343.65	344.48	345.32	346.16	346.99	347.83	348.67	349.51	350.34
420	351.17	352.01	352.85	353.68	354.52	355.35	356.19	357.03	357.86	358.7
430	359.54	360.37	361.21	362.04	362.88	363.72	364.55	365.39	366.22	367.06
440	367.9	368.73	369.57	370.41	371.24	372.08	372.91	373.75	374.59	375.42
450	376.26	377.09	377.93	378.77	379.6	380.44	381.27	382.11	382.95	383.78
460	384.62	385.46	386.29	387.13	387.96	388.8	389.64	390.47	391.31	392.14
470	392.98	393.82	394.65	395.49	396.32	397.16	398.0	398.83	399.67	400.51
480	401.34	402.18	403.01	403.85	404.69	405.52	406.36	407.19	408.03	408.87
490	409.7	410.54	411.38	412.21	413.05	413.88	414.72	415.56	416.39	417.23
500	418.0									

18
acres to hectares

acre	0	1	2	3	4	5	6	7	8	9
	ha									
		0.4	0.81	1.21	1.62	2.02	2.42	2.83	3.23	3.64

acre	0	10	20	30	40	50	60	70	80	90
	ha									
0		4.05	8.09	12.14	16.19	20.23	24.28	28.33	32.37	36.42
100	40.47	44.52	48.56	52.6	56.66	60.71	64.75	68.8	72.84	76.89
200	80.94	84.98	89.03	93.08	97.12	101.17	105.22	109.26	113.31	117.36
300	121.41	125.46	129.5	133.55	137.59	141.64	145.69	149.73	153.78	157.83
400	161.87	165.92	169.97	174.02	178.06	182.11	186.16	190.20	194.25	198.3
500	202.34	206.39	210.44	214.48	218.53	222.58	226.62	230.67	234.71	238.77
600	242.81	246.86	250.91	254.95	259.0	263.05	267.09	271.14	275.19	279.23
700	283.28	287.33	291.37	295.42	299.47	303.51	307.56	311.61	315.66	319.7
800	323.75	327.8	331.84	335.84	339.94	343.98	348.03	352.07	356.12	360.17
900	364.22	368.26	372.31	376.36	380.41	384.45	388.5	392.55	396.59	400.64
1 000	404.69									

Volume

19 cubic centimetres to cubic inches

cm^3	0	1	2	3	4	5	6	7	8	9
	in^3									
		0.06	0.12	0.18	0.24	0.31	0.37	0.43	0.49	0.55

cm^3	0	10	20	30	40	50	60	70	80	90
	in^3									
0		0.61	1.22	1.83	2.44	3.05	3.66	4.27	4.88	5.49
100	6.1	6.71	7.32	7.93	8.54	9.15	9.76	10.37	10.98	11.59
200	12.2	12.82	13.43	14.04	14.65	15.26	15.87	16.48	17.09	17.7
300	18.31	18.92	19.53	20.14	20.75	21.36	21.97	22.58	23.19	23.8
400	24.41	25.02	25.63	26.24	26.85	27.46	28.07	28.68	29.29	29.9
500	30.51	31.12	31.73	32.34	32.95	33.56	34.17	34.78	35.39	36.0
600	36.61	37.22	37.83	38.45	39.06	39.67	40.28	40.89	41.5	42.11
700	42.72	43.38	43.94	44.55	45.16	45.77	46.38	46.99	47.6	48.21
800	48.82	49.43	50.04	50.65	51.26	51.87	52.48	53.09	53.7	54.31
900	54.92	55.53	56.14	56.75	57.36	57.97	58.58	59.19	59.8	60.41
1 000	61.02									

21 cubic metres to cubic feet

m^3	0	1	2	3	4	5	6	7	8	9
	ft^3									
0		35.31	70.63	105.94	141.26	176.57	211.89	247.2	282.52	317.83
10	353.15	388.46	423.78	459.09	494.41	592.72	565.04	600.35	635.67	670.98
20	706.29	741.61	776.92	812.24	847.55	882.87	918.18	953.5	988.81	1 024.13
30	1 059.44	1 094.75	1 130.07	1 165.38	1 200.7	1 236.01	1 271.33	1 306.64	1341.96	1 377.27
40	1 412.59	1 447.9	1 483.22	1 518.53	1 553.85	1 589.16	1 624.47	1 659.79	1 695.1	1 730.42
50	1 765.73	1 801.05	1 836.36	1 871.68	1 906.99	1 942.31	1 977.62	2 012.94	2 048.25	2 083.57
60	2 118.88	2 154.19	2 189.51	2 224.82	2 260.14	2 295.45	2 330.77	2 366.08	2 401.4	2 436.71
70	2 472.03	2 507.34	2 542.66	2 577.97	2 613.29	2 648.6	2 683.91	2 719.23	2 754.54	2 789.86
80	2 825.17	2 860.49	2 895.8	2 931.12	2 966.43	3 001.75	3 037.06	3 072.38	3 107.69	3 143.01
90	3178.32	3 213.63	3 248.95	3 284.26	3 319.58	3 354.89	3 390.21	3 425.52	3 460.84	3 496.15
100	3 531.47	3 566.78	3 602.1	3 637.41	3 672.73	3 708.04	3 743.35	3 778.67	3 813.98	3 849.3
110	3 884.61	3 919.93	3 955.24	3 990.56	4 025.87	4 061.19	4 096.5	4 131.82	4 167.13	4 202.45
120	4 237.76	4 273.07	4 308.39	4 343.7	4 379.02	4 414.33	4 449.65	4 484.96	4 520.28	4 555.59
130	4 590.91	4 626.22	4 661.54	4 696.85	4 732.17	4 767.48	4 802.79	4 838.11	4 873.42	4 908.74
140	4 944.05	4 979.37	5 014.68	5 050.0	5 085.31	5 120.63	5 155.94	5 191.26	5 226.57	5 261.89
150	5 297.2	5 332.51	5 367.83	5 403.14	5 438.46	5 473.77	5 509.09	5 544.4	5 579.72	5 615.03
160	5 650.35	5 685.66	5 720.98	5 756.29	5 791.61	5 826.92	5 862.23	5 897.55	5 932.86	5 968.18
170	6 003.49	6 038.81	6 074.12	6109.44	6 144.75	6180.07	6 215.38	6 250.7	6 286.01	6 321.33
180	6 356.64	6 391.95	6 427.27	6 462.58	6 497.9	6 533.21	6 568.53	6 603.84	6 639.16	6 674.47
190	6 709.79	6 745.1	6 780.42	6 815.73	6 851.05	6 886.36	6 921.67	6 956.99	6 992.3	7 027.62
200	7 062.93	7 098.25	7 133.56	7 168.88	7 204.19	7 239.51	7 274.82	7 310.14	7 345.45	7 380.77
210	7 416.08	7 451.39	7 486.71	7 522.02	7 557.34	7 592.65	7 627.97	7 663.28	7 698.6	7 733.91
220	7 769.23	7 804.54	7 839.86	7 875.17	7 910.49	7 945.8	7 981.11	8 016.43	8 051.74	8 087.06
230	8 122.37	8 157.69	8 193.0	8 228.32	8 263.63	8 298.95	8 334.26	8 369.58	8 404.89	8 440.21
240	8 475.52	8 510.83	8 546.15	8 581.46	8 616.78	8 652.09	8 687.41	8 722.72	8 758.04	8 793.35
250	8 828.67									

23 litres to cubic feet

litre	0	1	2	3	4	5	6	7	8	9
	ft^3									
0		0.04	0.07	0.11	0.14	0.18	0.21	0.25	0.28	0.32
10	0.35	0.39	0.42	0.46	0.49	0.53	0.57	0.60	0.64	0.67
20	0.71	0.74	0.78	0.81	0.85	0.88	0.92	0.95	0.99	1.02
30	1.06	1.09	1.13	1.17	1.2	1.24	1.27	1.31	1.34	1.38
40	1.41	1.45	1.48	1.52	1.55	1.59	1.62	1.66	1.7	1.73
50	1.77	1.8	1.84	1.87	1.91	1.94	1.98	2.01	2.05	2.08
60	2.12	2.15	2.19	2.22	2.26	2.3	2.33	2.37	2.4	2.44
70	2.47	2.51	2.54	2.58	2.61	2.65	2.68	2.72	2.75	2.79
80	2.83	2.86	2.9	2.93	2.97	3.0	3.04	3.07	3.11	3.14
90	3.18	3.21	3.25	3.28	3.32	3.35	3.39	3.42	3.46	3.5
100	3.53									

20
cubic inches
to cubic
centimetres

in³	0	1	2	3	4	5	6	7	8	9
	cm³									
		16.39	32.77	49.16	65.55	81.94	98.32	114.71	131.1	147.48

in³	0	10	20	30	40	50	60	70	80	90
	cm³									
0		163.87	327.74	491.61	655.48	819.35	983.22	1 147.09	1 310.97	1 474.84
100	1 638.71	1 802.58	1 966.45	2 130.32	2 294.19	2 458.06	2 621.93	2 785.8	2 949.67	3 113.54
200	3 277.41	3 441.28	3 605.15	3 769.02	3 932.9	4 096.77	4 260.64	4 424.51	4 588.38	4 752.25
300	4 916.12	5 079.99	5 243.86	5 407.73	5 571.6	5 735.47	5 899.34	6 063.21	6 227.08	6 390.95
400	6 554.83	6 718.7	6 882.57	7 046.44	7 210.31	7 374.18	7 538.05	7 701.92	7 865.79	8 029.66
500	8193.53	8 357.4	8 521.27	8 685.14	8 849.01	9 012.89	9 176.76	9 340.63	9 504.5	9 668.37
600	9 832.24	9 996.11	10 160.0	10 323.9	10 487.7	10 651.6	10 815.5	10 979.3	11 143.2	11 307.1
700	11 470.9	11 634.8	11 798.7	11 962.6	12 126.4	12 290.3	12 454.2	12 618.0	12 781.9	12 945.8
800	13109.7	13 273.5	13 437.4	13 601.3	13 765.1	13 929.0	14 092.9	14 256.7	14 420.6	14 584.5
900	14 748.4	14 912.2	15 076.1	15 240.0	15 403.8	15 567.7	15 731.6	15 895.5	16 059.3	16 223.2
1 000	16 387.1									

22
cubic feet to
cubic metres

ft³	0	1	2	3	4	5	6	7	8	9
	m³									
0		0.03	0.06	0.08	0.11	0.14	0.17	0.2	0.23	0.25
10	0.28	0.31	0.34	0.37	0.4	0.42	0.45	0.48	0.51	0.54
20	0.57	0.59	0.62	0.65	0.68	0.71	0.74	0.77	0.79	0.82
30	0.85	0.88	0.91	0.93	0.96	0.99	1.02	1.05	1.08	1.1
40	1.13	1.16	1.19	1.22	1.25	1.27	1.3	1.33	1.36	1.39
50	1.42	1.44	1.47	1.5	1.53	1.56	1.59	1.61	1.64	1.67
60	1.7	1.73	1.76	1.78	1.81	1.84	1.87	1.9	1.93	1.95
70	1.98	2.01	2.04	2.07	2.1	2.12	2.15	2.18	2.21	2.24
80	2.27	2.29	2.32	2.35	2.38	2.41	2.44	2.46	2.49	2.52
90	2.55	2.58	2.61	2.63	2.66	2.69	2.71	2.75	2.78	2.8
100	2.83	2.86	2.89	2.92	2.94	2.97	3.01	3.03	3.06	3.09
110	3.11	3.14	3.17	3.2	3.23	3.26	3.28	3.31	3.34	3.37
120	3.4	3.43	3.46	3.48	3.51	3.54	3.57	3.6	3.62	3.65
130	3.68	3.71	3.74	3.77	3.79	3.82	3.85	3.88	3.91	3.94
140	3.96	4.0	4.02	4.05	4.08	4.11	4.13	4.16	4.19	4.22
150	4.26	4.28	4.3	4.33	4.36	4.39	4.42	4.45	4.47	4.51
160	4.53	4.56	4.59	4.62	4.64	4.67	4.7	4.73	4.76	4.79
170	4.81	4.84	4.87	4.9	4.93	4.96	4.99	5.01	5.04	5.07
180	5.1	5.13	5.15	5.18	5.21	5.24	5.27	5.3	5.32	5.35
190	5.38	5.41	5.44	5.47	5.49	5.52	5.55	5.58	5.61	5.64
200	5.66	5.69	5.72	5.75	5.78	5.8	5.83	5.86	5.89	5.92
210	5.95	5.98	6.0	6.03	6.06	6.09	6.12	6.14	6.17	6.2
220	6.23	6.26	6.29	6.31	6.34	6.37	6.4	6.43	6.46	6.48
230	6.51	6.54	6.57	6.6	6.63	6.65	6.69	6.71	6.74	6.77
240	6.8	6.82	6.85	6.88	6.91	6.94	6.97	6.99	7.02	7.05
250	7.08									

24
cubic feet
to litres

ft³	0	1	2	3	4	5	6	7	8	9
	litre									
0		28.32	56.63	84.95	113.26	141.58	169.9	198.21	226.53	254.84
10	283.16	311.48	339.79	368.11	396.42	424.74	453.06	481.37	509.69	538.01
20	566.32	594.64	622.95	651.27	679.59	707.9	736.22	764.53	792.85	821.17
30	849.48	877.8	906.11	934.43	962.75	991.06	1 019.38	1 047.69	1 076.01	1 104.33
40	1 132.64	1 160.96	1 189.27	1 217.59	1 245.91	1 274.22	1 302.54	1 330.85	1 359.17	1 387.49
50	1 415.8	1 444.12	1 472.43	1 500.75	1 529.07	1 557.38	1 585.7	1 614.02	1 642.33	1 670.65
60	1 698.96	1 727.28	1 755.6	1 783.91	1 812.23	1 840.54	1 868.86	1 897.18	1 925.49	1 953.81
70	1 982.12	2 010.44	2 038.76	2 067.07	2 095.39	2 123.7	2 152.02	2 180.34	2 208.65	2 236.97
80	2 265.28	2 293.6	2 321.92	2 350.23	2 378.55	2 406.86	2 435.18	2 463.5	2 491.81	2 520.13
90	2 548.44	2 576.76	2 605.08	2 633.39	2 661.71	2 690.03	2 718.34	2 746.66	2 774.97	2 803.29
100	2 831.61									

25 litres to imperial gallons

litre	0	1	2	3	4	5	6	7	8	9
	gal imp									
0		0.22	0.44	0.66	0.88	1.1	1.32	1.54	1.76	1.98
10	2.2	2.42	2.64	2.86	3.08	3.3	3.52	3.74	3.96	4.18
20	4.4	4.62	4.84	5.06	5.28	5.5	5.72	5.94	6.16	6.38
30	6.6	6.82	7.04	7.26	7.48	7.7	7.92	8.14	8.36	8.58
40	8.8	9.02	9.24	9.46	9.68	9.9	10.12	10.34	10.56	10.78
50	11.0	11.22	11.44	11.66	11.88	12.1	12.32	12.54	12.76	12.98
60	13.2	13.42	13.64	13.86	14.08	14.3	14.52	14.74	14.96	15.18
70	15.4	15.62	15.84	16.06	16.28	16.5	16.72	16.94	17.16	17.38
80	17.6	17.82	18.04	18.26	18.48	18.7	18.92	19.14	19.36	19.58
90	19.8	20.02	20.24	20.46	20.68	20.9	21.12	21.34	21.56	21.78
100	22.0									

27 litres to US gallons

litre	0	1	2	3	4	5	6	7	8	9
	gal US									
		0.26	0.53	0.79	1.06	1.32	1.59	1.85	2.11	2.38
10	2.64	2.91	3.17	3.43	3.7	3.96	4.23	4.49	4.76	5.02
20	5.28	5.55	5.81	6.08	6.34	6.61	6.87	7.13	7.4	7.66
30	7.93	8.19	8.45	8.72	8.98	9.25	9.51	9.78	10.04	10.3
40	10.57	10.83	11.1	11.36	11.62	11.89	12.15	12.42	12.68	12.95
50	13.21	13.47	13.74	14.0	14.27	14.53	14.8	15.06	15.32	15.59
60	15.85	16.12	16.38	16.64	16.91	17.17	17.44	17.7	17.97	18.23
70	18.49	18.76	19.02	19.29	19.55	19.82	20.08	20.34	20.61	20.87
80	21.14	21.4	21.66	21.93	22.19	22.46	22.72	22.96	23.25	23.51
90	23.78	24.04	24.31	24.57	24.83	25.1	25.36	25.63	25.89	26.16
100	26.42									

Mass

29 kilograms to pounds

kg	0	1	2	3	4	5	6	7	8	9
	lb									
0		2.21	4.41	6.61	8.82	11.02	13.23	15.43	17.64	19.84
10	22.05	24.25	26.46	28.66	30.86	33.07	35.27	37.47	39.68	41.89
20	44.09	46.3	48.5	50.71	52.91	55.12	57.32	59.52	61.73	63.93
30	66.14	68.34	70.55	72.75	74.96	77.16	79.37	81.57	83.78	85.98
40	88.18	90.39	92.59	94.8	97.0	99.2	101.41	103.61	105.82	108.03
50	110.23	112.44	114.64	116.85	119.05	121.25	123.46	125.66	127.87	130.07
60	132.28	134.48	136.69	138.89	141.1	143.3	145.51	147.71	149.91	152.12
70	154.32	156.53	158.73	160.94	163.14	165.35	167.55	169.76	171.96	174.17
80	176.37	178.57	180.78	182.98	185.19	187.39	189.6	191.8	194.01	196.21
90	198.42	200.62	202.83	205.03	207.24	209.44	211.64	213.85	216.05	218.26
100	220.46	222.67	224.87	227.08	229.28	231.49	233.69	235.9	238.1	240.3
110	242.51	244.71	246.92	249.12	251.33	253.53	255.74	257.94	260.15	262.35
120	264.56	266.76	268.96	271.17	273.37	275.58	277.78	279.99	282.19	284.4
130	286.6	288.81	291.01	293.22	295.42	297.62	299.83	302.03	304.24	306.44
140	308.65	310.85	313.06	315.26	317.47	319.67	321.88	324.08	326.28	328.49
150	330.69	332.9	335.1	337.31	339.51	341.72	343.92	346.13	348.33	350.54
160	352.74	354.94	357.15	359.35	361.56	363.76	365.97	368.17	370.38	372.58
170	374.79	377.0	379.2	381.4	383.6	385.81	388.01	390.22	392.42	394.68
180	396.83	399.04	401.24	403.45	405.65	407.86	410.06	412.26	414.47	416.67
190	418.88	421.08	423.29	425.49	427.68	429.9	432.11	434.31	436.52	438.72
200	440.93	443.13	445.33	447.54	449.74	451.95	454.15	456.36	458.56	460.77
210	462.97	465.18	467.38	469.59	471.79	473.99	476.2	478.4	480.61	482.81
220	485.02	487.22	489.43	491.63	493.84	496.04	498.25	500.45	502.65	504.86
230	507.06	509.2	511.47	513.6	515.88	518.0	520.29	522.4	524.7	526.9
240	529.1	531.31	533.5	535.72	537.9	540.13	542.3	544.54	546.7	548.9
250	551.16	553.36	555.57	557.77	559.97	562.18	564.38	566.59	568.79	571.0
260	573.2	575.41	577.61	579.82	582.02	584.23	586.43	588.63	590.84	593.04
270	595.25	597.45	599.66	601.86	604.07	606.27	608.48	610.68	612.89	615.09
280	617.29	619.5	621.7	623.91	626.11	628.32	630.52	632.73	634.93	637.14
290	639.34	641.55	643.75	645.95	648.16	650.36	652.57	654.77	656.98	659.18
300	661.39	663.59	665.8	668.0	670.21	672.41	674.62	676.82	679.02	681.23
310	683.43	685.64	687.84	690.05	692.25	694.46	696.66	698.87	701.07	703.28
320	705.48	707.68	709.89	712.09	714.3	716.5	718.71	720.91	723.12	725.32
330	727.53	729.73	731.93	734.14	736.34	738.55	740.75	742.96	745.16	747.37
340	749.57	751.78	753.98	756.19	758.39	760.6	762.8	765.0	767.21	769.41
350	771.62	773.82	776.03	778.23	780.44	782.64	784.85	787.05	789.26	791.46
360	793.66	795.87	798.07	800.28	802.48	804.69	806.89	809.1	811.31	813.51
370	815.71	817.92	820.12	822.32	824.53	826.73	828.94	831.14	833.35	835.55
380	837.76	839.96	842.17	844.37	846.58	848.78	850.98	853.19	855.39	857.6
390	859.8	862.0	864.21	866.41	868.62	870.8	873.03	875.2	877.44	879.64
400	881.85	884.05	886.26	888.46	890.67	892.87	895.08	897.28	899.49	901.69
410	903.9	906.1	908.31	910.51	912.71	914.92	917.12	919.33	921.53	923.74
420	925.94	928.15	930.35	932.56	934.76	936.97	939.17	941.37	943.58	945.78
430	947.99	950.19	952.4	954.6	956.81	959.01	961.22	963.42	965.63	967.83
440	970.03	972.24	974.44	976.65	978.85	981.06	983.26	985.47	987.67	989.88
450	992.08	994.29	996.49	998.69	1 000.9	1 003.1	1 005.31	1 007.51	1 009.72	1 011.92
460	1 014.13	1 016.33	1 018.54	1 020.74	1 022.94	1 025.15	1 027.35	1 029.56	1 031.76	1 033.97
470	1 036.17	1 038.38	1 040.58	1 042.79	1 044.99	1 047.2	1 049.4	1 051.6	1 053.81	1 056.01
480	1 058.22	1 060.42	1 062.63	1 064.83	1 067.04	1 069.24	1 071.45	1 073.65	1 075.86	1 078.06
490	1 080.27	1 082.47	1 084.67	1 086.88	1 089.08	1 091.29	1 093.49	1 095.7	1 097.9	1 100.11
500	1 102.31									

26 imperial gallons to litres

gal imp	0	1	2	3	4	5	6	7	8	9
	litre									
0		4.55	9.09	13.64	18.18	22.73	27.28	31.82	36.37	40.91
10	45.46	50.0	54.55	59.1	63.64	68.19	72.74	77.28	81.83	86.38
20	90.92	95.47	100.01	104.56	109.1	113.65	118.2	122.74	127.29	131.83
30	136.38	140.93	145.47	150.02	154.56	159.1	163.66	168.21	172.75	177.3
40	181.84	186.38	190.93	195.48	200.02	204.57	209.11	213.66	218.21	222.75
50	227.3	231.84	236.39	240.94	245.48	250.03	254.57	259.12	263.67	268.21
60	272.76	277.3	281.85	286.4	290.94	295.49	300.03	304.58	309.13	313.67
70	318.22	322.76	327.31	331.86	336.4	340.95	345.49	350.04	354.59	359.13
80	363.68	368.22	372.77	377.32	381.86	386.41	390.95	395.5	400.04	404.59
90	409.14	413.68	418.23	422.77	427.32	431.87	436.41	440.96	445.5	450.05
100	454.6									

28 US gallons to litres

gal US	0	1	2	3	4	5	6	7	8	9
	litre									
0		3.79	7.57	11.36	15.14	18.93	22.71	26.5	30.28	34.07
10	37.85	41.64	45.42	49.21	52.99	56.78	60.56	64.35	68.13	71.92
20	75.7	79.49	83.27	87.06	90.84	94.63	98.41	102.2	105.98	109.77
30	113.55	117.34	121.12	124.91	128.69	132.48	136.26	140.05	143.83	147.62
40	151.40	155.19	158.97	162.76	166.54	170.33	174.11	177.9	181.68	185.47
50	189.25	193.04	196.82	200.61	204.39	208.18	211.96	215.75	219.53	223.32
60	227.1	230.89	234.67	238.46	242.24	246.03	249.81	253.6	257.38	261.17
70	264.95	268.74	272.52	276.31	280.09	283.88	287.66	291.45	295.23	299.02
80	302.81	306.59	310.37	314.16	317.94	321.73	325.51	329.3	333.08	336.87
90	340.65	344.44	348.22	352.01	355.79	359.58	363.36	367.14	370.93	374.72
100	378.51									

30 pounds to kilograms

lb	0	1	2	3	4	5	6	7	8	9
	kg									
0		0.45	0.91	1.36	1.81	2.27	2.72	3.18	3.63	4.08
10	4.54	4.99	5.44	5.9	6.35	6.8	7.26	7.71	8.16	8.62
20	9.07	9.53	9.98	10.43	10.89	11.34	11.79	12.25	12.7	13.15
30	13.61	14.06	14.52	14.97	15.42	15.88	16.33	16.78	17.24	17.69
40	18.14	18.6	19.05	19.5	19.96	20.41	20.87	21.32	21.77	22.23
50	22.68	23.13	23.59	24.04	24.49	24.95	25.4	25.85	26.31	26.76
60	27.22	27.67	28.12	28.58	29.03	29.48	29.94	30.39	30.84	31.3
70	31.75	32.21	32.66	33.11	33.57	34.02	34.47	34.93	35.38	35.83
80	36.29	36.74	37.19	37.65	38.1	38.56	39.01	39.46	39.92	40.37
90	40.82	41.28	41.73	42.18	42.64	43.09	43.54	44.0	44.45	44.91
100	45.36	45.81	46.27	46.72	47.17	47.63	48.08	48.53	48.99	49.44
110	49.9	50.35	50.8	51.26	51.71	52.16	52.62	53.07	53.52	53.98
120	54.43	54.88	55.34	55.79	56.25	56.7	57.15	57.61	58.06	58.51
130	58.97	59.42	59.87	60.33	60.78	61.24	61.69	62.14	62.6	63.05
140	63.5	63.96	64.41	64.86	65.32	65.77	66.22	66.68	67.13	67.59
150	68.04	68.49	68.95	69.4	69.85	70.31	70.76	71.21	71.67	72.12
160	72.57	73.03	73.48	73.94	74.39	74.84	75.3	75.75	76.2	76.66
170	77.11	77.56	78.02	78.47	78.93	79.38	79.83	80.29	80.74	81.19
180	81.65	82.1	82.55	83.01	83.46	83.91	84.37	84.82	85.28	85.73
190	86.18	86.64	87.09	87.54	88.0	88.45	88.9	89.36	89.81	90.26
200	90.72	91.17	91.63	92.08	92.53	92.99	93.44	93.89	94.35	94.8
210	95.25	95.71	96.16	96.62	97 07	97.52	97.98	98.43	98.88	99.34
220	99.79	100.24	100.7	101.15	101.61	102.06	102.51	102.97	103.42	103.87
230	104.33	104.78	105.23	105.69	106.14	106.59	107.05	107.5	107.96	108.41
240	108.86	109.32	109.77	110.22	110.68	111.13	111.58	112.04	112.49	112.95
250	113.4	113.85	114.31	114.76	115.21	115.67	116.12	116.57	117.03	117.48
260	117.93	118.39	118.84	119.3	119.75	120.2	120.66	121.11	121.56	122.02
270	122.47	122.92	123.38	123.83	124.28	124.74	125.19	125.65	126.1	126.55
280	127.01	127.46	127.91	128.37	128.82	129.27	129.73	130.18	130.64	131.09
290	131.54	132.0	132.45	132.9	133.36	133.81	134.26	134.72	135.17	135.62
300	136.08	136.53	136.99	137.44	137.89	138.35	138.8	139.25	139.71	140.16
310	140.61	141.07	141.52	141.97	142.43	142.88	143.34	143.79	144.24	144.7
320	145.15	145.6	146.06	146.51	146.96	147.42	147.87	148.33	148.78	149.23
330	149.69	150.14	150.59	151.05	151.5	151.95	152.41	152.86	153.31	153.77
340	154.22	154.68	155.13	155.58	156.04	156.49	156.94	157.4	157.85	158.3
350	158.76	159.21	159.67	160.12	160.57	161.03	161.48	161.93	162.39	162.84
360	163.29	163.75	164.2	164.65	165.11	165.56	166.02	166.47	166.92	167.38
370	167.83	168.28	168.74	169.1	169.64	170.1	170.55	171.0	171.46	171.91
380	172.37	172.82	173.27	173.73	174.18	174.63	175.09	175.54	175.99	176.45
390	176.9	177.36	177.81	178.26	178.72	179.17	179.62	180.08	180.53	180.98
400	181.44	181.89	182.34	182.8	183.25	183.71	184.16	184.61	185.07	185.52
410	185.97	186.43	186.88	187.33	187.79	188.24	188.69	189.15	189.6	190.06
420	190.51	190.96	191.42	191.87	192.32	192.78	193.23	193.68	194.14	194.59
430	195.05	195.5	195.95	196.41	196.86	197.31	197.77	198.22	198.67	199.13
440	199.58	200.03	200.49	200.94	201.4	201.85	202.3	202.76	203.21	203.66
450	204.12	204.57	205.02	205.48	205.93	206.39	206.84	207.29	207.75	208.2
460	208.65	209.11	209.56	210.01	210.47	210.92	211.37	211.83	212.28	212.74
470	213.19	213.64	214.1	214.55	215.0	215.46	215.91	216.36	216.82	217.27
480	217.72	218.18	218.63	219.09	219.54	219.99	220.45	220.9	221.35	221.81
490	222.26	222.71	223.17	223.62	224.08	224.53	224.98	225.44	225.89	226.34
500	226.8									

Density (mass/volume)
31
kilograms per cubic metre to pounds per cubic foot

kg/m^3	0	10	20	30	40	50	60	70	80	90
	lb/ft^3									
0		0.62	1.25	1.87	2.5	3.12	3.75	4.37	5.0	5.62
100	6.24	6.87	7.49	8.12	8.74	9.36	9.99	10.61	11.24	11.86
200	12.49	13.11	13.73	14.36	14.98	15.61	16.23	16.86	17.48	18.11
300	18.73	19.35	19.98	20.61	21.23	21.85	22.47	23.1	23.72	24.35
400	24.97	25.6	26.22	26.84	27.47	28.09	28.72	29.34	29.97	30.59
500	31.21	31.84	32.46	33.09	33.71	34.33	34.96	35.58	36.21	36.83
600	37.46	38.08	38.71	39.33	39.95	40.58	41.2	41.83	42.45	43.08
700	43.7	44.32	44.95	45.57	46.2	46.82	47.45	48.07	48.7	49.32
800	49.94	50.57	51.19	51.82	52.44	53.06	53.69	54.31	54.94	55.56
900	56.19	56.81	57.43	58.06	58.68	59.31	59.93	60.56	61.18	61.81
1000	62.43									

Velocity
33
metres per second to miles per hour

m/s	0	1	2	3	4	5	6	7	8	9
	mile/hr									
0		2.24	4.47	6.71	8.95	11.18	13.42	15.66	17.9	20.13
10	22.37	24.61	26.84	29.08	31.32	33.55	35.79	38.03	40.26	42.51
20	44.74	46.96	49.21	51.45	53.69	55.92	58.16	60.4	62.63	64.87
30	67.11	69.35	71.58	73.82	76.06	78.29	80.53	82.77	85.0	87.24
40	89.48	91.71	93.95	96.19	98.43	100.66	102.9	105.13	107.37	109.61
50	111.85	114.08	116.32	118.56	120.8	123.03	125.27	127.5	129.74	131.98
60	134.22	136.45	138.69	140.93	143.16	145.4	147.64	149.88	152.11	154.34
70	156.59	158.82	161.06	163.3	165.53	167.77	170.0	172.24	174.48	176.72
80	178.96	181.19	183.43	185.67	187.9	190.14	192.38	194.61	196.85	199.09
90	201.32	203.56	205.8	208.04	210.27	212.51	214.75	216.98	219.22	221.46
100	223.69									

Pressure, stress
35
kilograms force per square centimetre to pounds force per square inch

kgf/cm^2	0.0	0.1	0.2	0.3	0.4	0.5	0.6	0.7	0.8	0.9
	lbf/in^2									
0		1.42	2.84	4.27	5.6	7.11	8.53	9.96	11.38	12.8
1	14.22	15.65	17.07	18.49	19.91	21.34	22.76	24.18	25.6	27.02
2	28.45	29.87	31.29	32.71	34.13	35.56	36.98	38.4	39.83	41.25
3	42.67	44.09	45.51	46.94	48.36	49.78	51.2	52.63	54.05	55.47
4	56.9	58.32	59.73	61.16	62.58	64.0	65.43	66.85	68.27	69.69
5	71.12	72.54	73.96	75.38	76.81	78.23	79.65	81.07	82.5	83.92
6	85.34	86.76	88.18	89.61	91.03	92.45	93.87	95.3	96.72	98.14
7	99.56	100.99	102.41	103.83	105.25	106.68	108.1	109.52	110.94	112.36
8	113.79	115.21	116.63	118.05	119.48	120.9	122.32	123.74	125.17	126.59
9	128.01	129.43	130.86	132.28	133.7	135.12	136.54	137.97	139.39	140.81
10	142.23									

37
kilonewtons per square metre to pounds force per square inch

kN/m^2 (kPa)	0	10	20	30	40	50	60	70	80	90
	lbf/in^2									
0		1.45	2.9	4.35	5.8	7.25	8.7	10.15	11.6	13.05
100	14.50	15.95	17.40	18.85	20.30	21.75	23.21	24.66	26.11	27.56
200	29.01	30.46	31.91	33.36	34.81	36.26	37.71	39.16	40.61	42.06
300	43.51	44.96	46.41	47.86	49.31	50.76	52.21	53.66	55.11	56.56
400	58.01	59.46	60.91	62.36	63.81	65.26	66.71	68.17	69.62	71.07
500	72.52	73.97	75.42	76.87	78.32	79.77	81.22	82.67	84.12	85.57
600	87.02	88.47	89.92	91.37	92.82	94.27	95.72	97.17	98.62	100.07
700	101.52	102.97	104.42	105.87	107.32	108.77	110.22	111.68	113.13	114.58
800	116.03	117.48	118.93	120.38	121.83	123.28	124.73	126.18	127.63	129.08
900	130.53	131.98	133.43	134.88	136.33	137.78	139.23	140.68	142.13	143.58
1 000	145.03									

32
pounds per cubic foot to kilograms per cubic metre

lb/ft³	0	1	2	3	4	5	6	7	8	9
	kg/m³									
0		16.02	32.04	48.06	64.07	80.09	96.11	112.13	128.15	144.17
10	160.19	176.2	192.22	208.24	224.26	240.28	256.3	272.31	288.33	304.35
20	320.37	336.39	352.41	368.43	384.44	400.46	416.48	432.5	448.52	464.54
30	480.55	496.57	512.59	528.61	544.63	560.65	576.67	592.68	608.7	624.72
40	640.74	656.76	672.78	688.79	704.81	720.83	736.85	752.87	768.89	784.91
50	800.92	816.94	832.96	848.98	865.0	881.02	897.03	913.05	929.07	945.09
60	961.11	977.13	993.15	1 009.16	1 025.18	1 041.2	1 057.22	1 073.24	1 089.26	1 105.27
70	1 121.29	1 137.31	1 153.33	1 169.35	1 185.37	1 201.38	1 217.4	1 233.42	1 249.44	1 265.46
80	1 281.48	1 297.5	1 313.51	1 329.53	1 345.55	1 361.57	1 377.59	1 393.61	1 409.62	1 425.64
90	1441.66	1 457.68	1 473.7	1 489.72	1 505.74	1521.75	1 537.77	1 553.79	1 569.81	1 585.83
100	1 601.85									

34
miles per hour to metres per second

mile/hr	0	1	2	3	4	5	6	7	8	9
	m/s									
0		0.45	0.89	1.34	1.79	2.24	2.68	3.13	3.58	4.02
10	4.47	4.92	5.36	5.81	6.26	6.71	7.15	7.6	8.05	8.49
20	8.94	9.39	9.83	10.28	10.73	11.18	11.62	12.07	12.52	12.96
30	13.41	13.86	14.31	14.75	15.2	15.65	16.09	16.54	16.99	17.43
40	17.88	18.33	18.78	19.22	19.67	20.12	20.56	21.01	21.46	21.91
50	22.35	22.8	23.25	23.69	24.14	24.59	25.03	25.48	25.93	26.38
60	26.82	27.27	27.72	28.16	28.61	29.06	29.5	29.95	30.4	30.85
70	31.29	31.74	32.19	32.63	33.08	33.53	33.98	34.42	34.87	35.32
80	35.76	36.21	36.66	37.1	37.55	38.0	38.45	38.89	39.34	39.79
90	40.23	40.68	41.13	41.57	42.02	42.47	42.92	43.36	43.81	44.26
100	44.7									

36
pounds force per square inch to kilograms force per square centimetre

lbf/in²	0	1	2	3	4	5	6	7	8	9
	kgf/cm²									
0		0.07	0.14	0.21	0.28	0.35	0.42	0.49	0.56	0.63
10	0.7	0.77	0.84	0.91	0.98	1.05	1.12	1.2	1.27	1.34
20	1.41	1.48	1.55	1.62	1.69	1.76	1.83	1.9	1.97	2.04
30	2.11	2.18	2.25	2.32	2.39	2.46	2.53	2.6	2.67	2.74
40	2.81	2.88	2.95	3.02	3.09	3.16	3.23	3.3	3.37	3.45
50	3.52	3.59	3.66	3.73	3.8	3.87	3.94	4.01	4.08	4.15
60	4.22	4.29	4.36	4.43	4.5	4.57	4.64	4.71	4.78	4.85
70	4.92	4.99	5.06	5.13	5.2	5.27	5.34	5.41	5.48	5.55
80	5.62	5.69	5.77	5.84	5.91	5.98	6.05	6.12	6.19	6.26
90	6.33	6.4	6.47	6.54	6.61	6.68	6.75	6.82	6.89	6.96
100	7.03									

38
pounds force per square inch to kilonewtons per square metre

lbf/in²	0	1	2	3	4	5	6	7	8	9
	kN/m²(kPa)									
0		6.9	13.79	20.68	27.58	34.48	41.37	48.26	55.16	62.06
10	68.95	75.84	82.74	89.64	96.53	103.42	110.32	117.22	124.11	131.0
20	137.9	144.8	151.69	158.58	165.48	172.38	179.27	186.16	193.06	199.96
30	206.85	213.74	220.64	227.54	234.43	241.32	248.22	255.12	262.01	268.9
40	275.8	282.7	289.59	296.48	303.38	310.28	317.17	324.06	330.96	337.86
50	344.75	351.64	358.54	365.44	372.33	379.22	386.12	393.02	399.91	406.8
60	413.7	420.6	427.49	434.38	441.28	448.18	455.07	461.96	468.86	475.76
70	482.65	489.54	496.44	503.34	510.23	517.12	524.02	530.92	537.81	544.7
80	551.6	558.5	565.39	572.28	579.18	586.08	592.97	599.86	606.76	613.66
90	620.55	627.44	634.34	641.24	648.13	655.02	661.92	668.82	675.71	682.6
100	689.5									

Refrigeration
39
watts to British thermal units per hour

w	0	1	2	3	4	5	6	7	8	9
	Btu/hr									
0		3.41	6.82	10.24	13.65	17.06	20.47	23.89	27.3	30.71
10	34.12	37.53	40.95	44.36	47.77	51.18	54.59	58.01	61.42	64.83
20	68.24	71.66	75.07	78.5	81.89	85.3	88.72	92.13	95.54	98.95
30	102.36	105.78	109.12	112.6	116.01	119.43	122.76	126.25	129.66	133.07
40	136.49	139.91	143.31	146.72	150.13	153.55	156.96	160.37	163.78	167.2
50	170.61	174.02	177.43	180.84	184.26	187.67	191.08	194.49	197.9	201.31
60	204.73	208.14	211.55	214.97	218.38	221.79	225.2	228.61	232.03	235.44
70	238.85	242.26	245.68	249.09	252.5	255.91	259.32	262.74	266.15	269.56
80	272.97	276.38	279.8	283.21	286.62	290.03	293.45	296.86	300.27	303.68
90	307.09	310.51	313.92	317.33	320.74	324.15	327.57	330.98	334.39	337.8
100	341.22									

Thermal conductance

41
watts per square metre kelvin to British thermal units per square foot hour degree F

w/ (m^2K)	0.0	0.1	0.2	0.3	0.4	0.5	0.6	0.7	0.8	0.9
	Btu/($ft^2hr°F$)									
0.0		0.018	0.035	0.053	0.074	0.088	0.106	0.123	0.141	0.158
1.0	0.176	0.194	0.211	0.229	0.247	0.264	0.282	0.299	0.317	0.335
2.0	0.352	0.370	0.387	0.405	0.423	0.440	0.458	0.476	0.493	0.511
3.0	0.528	0.546	0.564	0.581	0.599	0.616	0.634	0.652	0.669	0.687
4.0	0.704	0.722	0.740	0.757	0.775	0.793	0.810	0.828	0.845	0.863
5.0	0.881	0.898	0.916	0.933	0.951	0.969	0.986	1.004	1.021	1.039
6.0	1.057	1.074	1.092	1.110	1.127	1.145	1.162	1.180	1.198	1.215
7.0	1.233	1.250	1.268	1.286	1.303	1.321	1.34	1.356	1.374	1.391
8.0	1.409	1.427	1.444	1.462	1.479	1.497	1.515	1.532	1.550	1.567
9.0	1.585	1.603	1.620	1.638	1.656	1.673	1.691	1.708	1.726	1.744
10.0	1.761									

40 British thermal units per hour to watts

Btu/hr	0	1	2	3	4	5	6	7	8	9
	W									
0		0.29	0.59	0.88	1.17	1.47	1.76	2.05	2.34	2.64
10	2.93	3.22	3.52	3.81	4.1	4.4	4.69	4.98	5.28	5.57
20	5.86	6.16	6.45	6.74	7.03	7.33	7.62	7.91	8.21	8.5
30	8.79	9.09	9.38	9.67	9.97	10.26	10.55	10.84	11.14	11.43
40	11.72	12.02	12.31	12.6	12.9	13.19	13.48	13.78	14.07	14.36
50	14.66	14.95	15.24	15.53	15.83	16.12	16.41	16.71	17.0	17.29
60	17.59	17.88	18.17	18.47	18.76	19.05	19.34	19.64	19.93	20.22
70	20.52	20.81	21.1	21.4	21.69	21.98	22.28	22.57	22.86	23.15
80	23.45	23.74	24.03	24.33	24.62	24.91	25.21	25.5	25.79	26.09
90	26.38	26.67	26.97	27.26	27.55	27.84	28.14	28.43	28.72	29.02
100	29.31									

42 British thermal units per square foot hour degree F to watts per square metre kelvin

Btu/ (ft².hr°F)	0.00	0.01	0.02	0.03	0.04	0.05	0.06	0.07	0.08	0.09
	W/(m²K)									
0.0	0.568	0.057	0.114	0.17	0.227	0.284	0.341	0.397	0.454	0.511
0.1	1.136	0.624	0.681	0.738	0.795	0.852	0.908	0.965	1.022	1.079
0.2	1.703	1.192	1.249	1.306	1.363	1.42	1.476	1.533	1.59	1.647
0.3	2.271	1.76	1.817	1.874	1.931	1.987	2.044	2.101	2.158	2.214
0.4		2.328	2.385	2.442	2.498	2.555	2.612	2.669	2.725	2.782
0.5	2.839	2.896	2.953	3.009	3.066	3.123	3.18	3.236	3.293	3.35
0.6	3.407	3.464	3.52	3.577	3.634	3.691	3.747	3.804	3.861	3.918
0.7	3.975	4.031	4.088	4.145	4.202	4.258	4.315	4.372	4.429	4.486
0.8	4.542	4.599	4.656	4.713	4.77	4.826	4.883	4.94	4.997	5.053
0.9	5.11	5.167	5.224	5.281	5.337	5.394	5.451	5.508	5.564	5.621
1.0	5.678									

A

B

INDEX

C

D

E

F

G

H

INDEX

I

M

N

Q

R

T

INDEX

X

Y

Z